J.K. LASSER'S™
YOUR INCOME TAX 2000
EXPANDED EDITION

Prepared by the

J.K. LASSER INSTITUTE™

IDG Books Worldwide, Inc.

Staff for This Book

J.K. Lasser Editorial

Elliott Eiss, Member of the New York Bar, Editorial Director of the J.K. Lasser Institute™
Bernard Greisman, Member of the New York Bar, Senior Consultant to the J.K. Lasser Institute™
Donna LeValley, Member of the New York Bar, Contributing Editor
Priya R. Masilamani and Elizabeth R. Robins, Research Assistants
Angelo C. Jack, Editorial/Layout-Production Manager
F. Mookie Bustamante, Production Specialist
Carolyn Francis, Proofreading and Copyediting
Bill Hamill, Production Assistant
Helen Chin, Indexer

IDG Books Worldwide

Kathy Nebenhaus, Publisher, Lifestyle Publishing Group
Cindy Kitchel, Associate Publisher, Lifestyle Publishing Group
Brice Gosnell, Managing Editor
Michelle Patterson, Marketing Manager
Rebecca Cremonese, Senior Production Manager
George McKeon, Cover Designer

Special thanks to
The staff at Webcrafters, especially Lori Coonen, Tim Imhoff, and Michael Prestigiacomo; and
the staff of Arthur Andersen, especially Stephen Corrick, Philip Groves, and Stacey O'Neill.

IDG Books Worldwide

IDG Books Wordwide, Inc.
An International Data Group Company
919 E. Hillsdale Boulevard
Suite 400
Foster City, CA 94404

ISBN 0-02-863691-0 / 0-13-015864-X *(PHD)*

Manufactured in the United States of America

10 9 8 7 6 5 4 3 2 1

Sixty-third edition

ISBN 0-13-015864-X

9 780130 158642

How to Use *The Professional Edition of J.K. Lasser's Your Income Tax* 2000

Tax alert symbols. Throughout the text of *The Professional Edition of Your Income Tax*, these special symbols alert you to advisory tips about filing your return and tax planning opportunities:

 Filing Tip or Filing Instruction . . . . . .

A **Filing Tip** or **Filing Instruction** helps you prepare your 1999 return.

 Planning Reminder . . . .

A **Planning Reminder** highlights year-end tax strategies for 1999 or planning opportunities for 2000 and later years.

 Caution . . . .

A **Caution** points out potential pitfalls to avoid and areas where IRS opposition may be expected.

 Law Alert . . . .

A **Law Alert** indicates recent changes in the tax law and pending legislation before Congress.

 Court Decision . . . .

A **Court Decision** highlights key rulings from the Tax Court and other federal courts.

The PROFESSIONAL EDITION of *Your Income Tax* is divided into two volumes.

Volume One includes the complete 2000 edition of *Your Income Tax,* which for over 62 years has helped subscribers solve their tax problems and has proven to be a solid reference work for tax professionals.

Volume Two expands the usefulness of *Your Income Tax* for tax professionals by providing citations of tax authorities and sections devoted to practice before the IRS.

VOLUME I: YOUR INCOME TAX

This volume includes the complete 2000 edition of *Your Income Tax* (see the guide to Parts 1-8 on page v) .

VOLUME II: PROFESSIONAL TAX PRACTICE

This volume includes the following technical tax information:

TAX LAW SOURCES (Part 10). Here is an explanation of tax authorities, legislative, administrative, and judicial—and their relative importance in the practice of tax law. Part 10 begins on page 799.

CITATIONS OF AUTHORITY (Part 11). Here are key authorities for the text of *Your Income Tax* that can save you time and effort in researching income tax problems. The authorities cited are the Internal Revenue Code, IRS regulations and rulings, and court decisions. Law review and professional tax journal articles also are cited as an additional aid. Part 11 begins on page 805.

PRACTICE BEFORE THE IRS (Part 12). This section discusses how to handle tax audits and negotiate with the IRS. Part 12 begins on page 889.

PREPARING A FEDERAL ESTATE TAX RETURN (Part 13). This section provides a sample filled-in estate tax return and explanation of how to prepare and file an estate tax return. Part 13 begins on page 921.

INDEX. The index to Volume I (Parts 1-8) begins on page 967.

Contents at a Glance

Diversify Your Retirement Assets With Vanguard

A time-tested way to keep your retirement plan on course is to diversify your assets among stocks, bonds, and cash investments. Spreading your investment among these basic asset classes can help cushion your hard-earned dollars against the ups and downs of the financial markets.

Broad Diversification

To achieve broad diversification, Vanguard offers you more than 50 investment opportunities. So whether you're an aggressive, moderate, or conservative investor, you can tailor a program to *your* financial objectives.

Transfer Today

Whether you're planning to transfer your retirement assets from another institution, make a direct rollover from an employer sponsored plan, or establish your first IRA, our Investment Kit contains all the forms you need to complete the transaction.

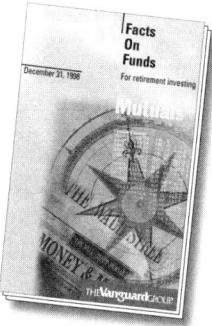

Vanguard IRA Choices

Aggressive Growth Funds
Vanguard Explorer Fund
Vanguard Specialized Funds
Vanguard Small-Cap Index Funds
Vanguard Horizon Funds

Growth Funds
Vanguard Extended Market Index Fund
Vanguard Growth Index Fund
Vanguard International Equity Index Funds
Vanguard International Growth Fund
Vanguard Mid-Cap Index Fund
Vanguard Morgan Growth Fund
Vanguard U.S. Growth Fund

Growth and Income Funds
Vanguard 500 Index Fund
Vanguard Convertible Securities Fund
Vanguard Equity Income Fund

Vanguard Growth and Income Fund
Vanguard International Value Fund
Vanguard Selected Value Fund
Vanguard Total Stock Market Index Fund
Vanguard Value Index Fund
Vanguard Windsor II Fund

Balanced Funds
Vanguard Asset Allocation Fund
Vanguard Balanced Index Fund
Vanguard LifeStrategy Funds
Vanguard STAR Fund
Vanguard Wellington Fund

Income Funds
Vanguard Admiral Funds
Vanguard Bond Index Fund
Vanguard Bond Funds
Vanguard Wellesley Income Fund

Money Market Funds
Vanguard Money Market Funds

For Your Free IRA Kit, Including Our "Facts On Funds For Retirement Investing" Booklet,
Call 1-800-319-3647
www.vanguard.com

THE**Vanguard**GROUP.

Contents Chapter by Chapter

What's New for 1999

Item	Tax Pointer
Tax legislation proposed	A comprehensive tax bill passed by Congress was vetoed by the President. Proposed legislation to extend expired provisions, if enacted, will be detailed in the Supplement.
Tax brackets	Inflation adjustment provides a slight tax reduction by widening the 1999 tax brackets; see 1.2 and page 731.
Standard deduction	Basic standard deduction increased by $50 for singles and married filing separately and $100 for joint returns and heads of households; see 13.1.
Personal exemptions	Personal exemption deduction is $2,750 (up from $2,700), subject to the phase-out rules for high-income taxpayers; see 21. 1 and 21.15.
Filing requirements	Higher income thresholds for filing 1999 returns; see page 2.
Home office	New deduction opportunities for self-employed persons who use a home office for administrative work; see 40.12.
Commuting to temporary work location	Travel expense deductions allowed for assignments of one year or less; see 20.2.
Roth IRA reconversions	Limits set on reconverting back to a Roth IRA from a traditional IRA; see 8.21.
Stop- smoking costs	Unreimbursed costs of prescription medications and programs to stop smoking are now deductible subject to 7.5% floor; see 17.2.
Self-employed health insurance	Deductible percentage for self-employed health insurance premiums increased to 60% from 45%; see 12.2 and 40.6.
Averaging lump sum distributions	1999 is the last year for five- year averaging; see 7.4.
IRS business mileage rates	There are two mileage rates for 1999: 32.5 cents per mile for travel prior to 4/1/99 and 31 cents per mile for travel on or after 4/1/99; see 43.1.
First -year auto depreciation limit	First-year depreciation and expensing limit for automobile placed in business service in 1999 is $3,060, $100 less than the 1998 limit; see 43.1.
Capital gains distributions from mutual funds	Mutual fund shareholders who have no other capital gains or losses generally do not have to file Schedule D; see 32.5.
Student loan interest deduction	Maximum student loan interest deduction is $1,500 (up from $1,000); see 38.6.
FICA and self-employment tax base	The 1999 wage and self-employed earnings base for 6.2% Social Security tax is $72,600 (up from $68,400);see 26.10 and 45.3.

Item	Tax Pointer
Deprecation of furnishings in residential rental property	Recovery period is now five years (down from seven years); see 9.2.
Earned income credit (EIC)	Increased credit and phase-out limits; see 25.12–25.14.
First-year expensing	First-year expensing on business equipment placed in service in 1999 limit is $19,000 (up from $18,500); see 42.3.
Itemized deduction reduction	Itemized deductions such as mortgage interest, taxes, and miscellaneous expenses are reduced by 3% of the amount, of your 1999 adjusted gross income over $126,000 ($63,300 if married filing separately see 13.7.
Traditional IRA deduction phase-out	Phase-out range begins at $31,000 if single; $51,000 if married filing jointly; see 8.4.
Voluntary withholdings	You can ask the government to withhold tax from Social Security and unemployment benefits; see 26.7.
Balkan combat zone	Tax-free pay and tax filing deadlines for Balkan service; see 35.4-35.5.
Child tax credit	Credit for child under 17 is $500 (up from $400); see 25.1.
Attorneys' fees	Cap on attorneys' fees for prevailing taxpayers is $130 per hour; see 48.7.
Estimated tax safe harbor	Prior-year safe harbor test for figuring 1999 estimated tax penalty and estimated payments for 2000; see 27.1.
Group term insurance	New valuation table provides lower tax costs; see 3.3.
Continuing care facility	The loan threshold for taxing imputed interest on entrance fees to qualified facilities is $137,000 (up from $134,800); see 34.11.
Foreign earned income exclusion	Exclusion is $74,000 (up from $72,000); see 36.1.
Charitable split-dollar insurance arrangements	IRS will disallow deductions claimed for split-dollar plans offered by certain organizations; see 14.11.
Auto donations	Auto donation programs subject to IRS warning; see 14.9.
Estate tax exemption	Exemption from estate tax is $650,000 (up from $625,000); see 39.5.

Special Tax Situations

What You May Exclude from Gross Income

Alimony, which does not meet rules of Chapter 37

Annuity payments that repay your cost; *7.22*

Armed Forces benefits and pay; *35.2, 35.4*

Armed Forces disability pensions; *35.2*

Borrowed money returned to you; *2.9*

Casualty insurance and other reimbursement losses not exceeding basis of property; *18.15*

Child support; *37.5*

Clergymen's rental or parsonage allowances; *3.12*

Combat or hazardous duty area pay; *35.4*

Damages for personal injury; *11.7*

Dependent care assistance from qualified employer plan, within limits; *3.7*

Dividends on life insurance policies until net premiums you paid for the contract are recovered; *4.11*

Education assistance under employer plans; *3.6*

Employer contributions to a qualified pension plan for employee's benefit, within limits; *7.25*

Employer contributions to tax-sheltered annuities for employee's benefit, within limits; *7.25*

Employer furnished meals or lodging for the convenience of the employer; *3.11*

Employer paid business subscriptions or reimbursed membership dues in professional associations; *3.8*

Flexible spending arrangement reimbursements, subject to certain limits; *3.14*

Foreign earned income up to $74,000 in 1999; *36.2*

Forgiven debts that meet tax exclusion rules; *11.8*

Free or low-cost company services or products; *3.15*

Gifts; *11.4*

Government disability pensions; *2.13*

Group-term life insurance premiums paid by employer for coverage up to $50,000; *3.3*

Health and accident coverage under employer plans; *3.1*

Home sale profit of up to $250,000 if single, $500,000 if married on joint return; *29.1*

Improvements by lessees; *42.15*

Inherited money or property; *11.4*

Interest credited on frozen deposits; *4.13*

Interest on Series EE bonds issued after 1989 if used for tuition and income tests met; *38.4*

Interest earned on qualified employer retirement plans or IRA's until withdrawal; *7.17, 8.1*

Interest received on tax-exempt government bonds; *4.24*

IRA distributions timely rolled over to another IRA; *8.10*

Job placement assistance, subject to certain limitations; *3.8*

Life insurance received because of the death of the insured; *33.7*

Like-kind exchanges of investment property; *6.1*

Liquidating distributions that are a return of capital; *44.12*

Moving expense reimbursements under accountable plan; *12.8*

Mileage allowance from employer up to IRS limit; *20.33, 43.1*

Overtime meal money and cab fare; *3.9*

Pre-tax salary deferrals to 401(k) or other qualified retirement plans, within limits; *7.18*

Refund of state or local tax for year you claimed standard deduction; *11.5*

Reimbursed business travel and entertainment expenses under accountable plan; *20.30*

Reimbursed medical expenses for permanent physical injury from qualifying employer plan; *3.2*

Rollovers from one qualified employer retirement plan to another, or to an IRA; *7.8, 8.10*

Scholarship awards covering degree candidate's tuition and related fees; *38.1*

Social Security benefits, if under base amount; *34.3*

Stock dividends and stock options; *4.6*

Van pool, transit pass, or employer-provided parking, within limits; *3.5*

Worker's compensation benefits; *2.12*

What You May Deduct

Alimony paid under the rules of Chapter 37

Amortized bond premium; *4.17*

Appraisal costs for donated property; *14.12*

Bad debts subject to limits for nonbusiness loans; *5.33*

Bank deposit loss in insolvent bank; *18.4*

Burglary losses; *18.8*

Business expenses; *40.6 – 40.11*

Business gifts up to $25; *20.25*

Business use or rental of a car; *19.12*

Capital loss within limits; *5.13*

Casualty losses within limits; Chapter 18

Charges for services on rental property, e.g., water, sewer, trash; *9.2*

Charitable contributions; Chapter 14

Christmas presents and other holiday gifts to employees, clients, or customers up to $25 a person; *2.4*

Clothing, uniforms, costumes, laundering, and cleaning; *19.6*

Condominium owner's interest and real estate taxes; *15.9*

Convention (business or professional) expenses; *20.12*

Depletion of oil and gas wells, other natural deposits, and timber; *9.14, 9.15*

Depreciation of home computers or cellular telephones, subject to restrictions; *19.9*

Depreciation of leasehold improvements; *42.15*

Depreciation of rental building; *9.2, 42.13*

Depreciation of rental property furniture and appliances; *9.2*

Disaster losses; *18.2*

Education—cost of tuition, books, if required to keep your job or improve job or professional skills; *19.16*

Embezzlement losses; *18.8*

Employment agency fees; *19.7*

Foreign housing costs if self-employed within limits; *36.3*

Foreign income tax and property taxes; *16.12*

Gambling losses to extent of gambling gains; *11.3*

Half of self-employment tax liability; *46.3*

Health-care insurance premiums; *17.5*

Home mortgage interest; *15.1*

Impairment-related work expenses; *19.4*

Income tax return preparation fees; *19.25*

Individual retirement account (IRA) contributions, within limits; *8.2 – 8.4*

Investment interest within limits; *15.10*

Job-search expenses; *19.7*

Keogh plan contributions within limits; *41.5*

Legal expenses; *19.26*

Long-term care insurance and services; *17.15*

Losses on small business stock; *5.4*

Magazine subscriptions used for business or professional purposes; *19.5*

Malpractice insurance; *40.6, 40.7*

Medical and dental expenses within limits; *17.1*

Medical savings account (MSA) contributions; *17.17*

Moving expenses to new job location; *12.3*

Nurses' wages; *17.12*

Points paid on purchase or improvement of principal residence; *15.8*

Real estate taxes; *16.6*

Rent for business property; *9.1*

Repairs of business or income-producing property; *9.3*

Schooling costs for a mentally or physically handicapped dependent; *17.10*

Simplified Employee Pension (SEP) contributions, within limits; *8.15, 8.16*

Standard deduction; Chapter 13

State and local income taxes; *16.2*

State and local personal property tax; *16.3*

Student loan interest; *38.6*

Taxes that are business expenses; *16.11*

Tools used on your job having a life of less than a year; *19.11*

Travel expenses necessary to maintain property; *9.2*

Travel costs to take education courses; *19.22*

Travel costs to get medical care; *17.9*

Work clothes and uniforms; *19.6*

Worthless securities; *5.32*

Frequently Asked Questions

Q.   How can I check on the status of my refund?

A.   Call the IRS Tele-tax number to get automated refund information. See 46.6 for the number.

Q.   I just completed my return and find that I owe the IRS money that I cannot pay. What should I do?

A.   You should file your return even if you cannot pay all of the amount owed. File by April 17, 2000, and pay as much as possible. By filing on time, you avoid the late filing penalty. By paying as much of the amount as possible, you reduce the amount of interest and late payment penalty you will owe. See 46.3, 47.5.

Q.   Can I ask to make installment payments on the amount I owe on any 1999 return?

A.   Yes. You may request an installment arrangement on Form 9465. However, you will be charged interest and possibly a late payment penalty on the tax not paid by April 17, 2000, even if your request to pay in installments is granted. See 46.3.

Q.   If I am unable to finish my return by April 17, 2000, how can I get an extension?

A.   You can get a four-month extension by filing Form 4868 by April 17, 2000. By filing for the extension, you avoid the late filing penalty. However, Form 4868 does not extend the time to pay your income tax. You will have to pay interest, and possibly late payment penalties. See 46.3.

Q.   What can I do to make sure I will not owe the IRS tax on my 2000 return?

A. You can either increase the amount of income tax withheld from your pay or make estimated tax payments to meet your 2000 tax liability. See 27.1.

Q.   How can I get forms and publications?

A.   Call 1-800-TAX-FORM (1-800-829-3676) or visit your local IRS office. A local library, bank, or post office may have tax forms. Forms may also be obtained by using a computer modem to access Fedworld, an IRS information service. See the IRS site on the world wide web located at http://www.irs.ustreas.gov or direct dial by modem at (703) 321-8020.

Q.   If my father has Social Security benefits over $2,750, can I claim him as my dependent for 1999?

A.   Yes, if the Social Security is not taxable under the rules of 34.3. Dependents other than certain children must have gross income of less than $2,750, but gross income does not include nontaxed items such as gifts, tax-exempt interest, or nontaxable Social Security. See 21.3.

Q.   My aunt was solely dependent on me for years. Last spring she died. Can I claim an exemption for her in 1999?

A. Yes. You get the full exemption of $2,750 for the year even though she lived only a few months in 1999. The same rule applies to dependents born during the year. For example, if your child was born in late December you may claim a full $2,750 exemption for the child. See 21.3.

Q.   My father lived with me for only three months during 1999; my brother took care of him the rest of the time. But I contributed more than 50% of his support. Who may claim the exemption?

A. You do. The test is not the "time" of support but the value of the support. You get the exemption because you furnished more than half of his support during the whole year. See 21.3, 21.7.

Q.   My sister and I have been taking care of our parents. We split the support 50–50. Who may claim the exemption?

A. If you and another support the same person, the one furnishing more than half of the support is entitled to the credit. Here you and your sister furnish equal support. You may decide between yourselves who is to claim the exemption. The one who claims the exemption must attach Form 2120, the Multiple Support Agreement, to his or her return. See 21.7, 21.10.

Q.   I am paid on a percentage of my sales. But I got an advance on my next year's pay. Is that taxed?

A. Yes, if it is an unrestricted advance, one where you can keep the money. If your employer does not have a policy of demanding repayment for unearned commissions, the advance is taxable. However, if it is really a loan which you must repay if you do not earn the amount, it is not taxed. See 2.1, 2.5.

Q.   I bought some stock on the dividend record date. The corporation declared a dividend to holders of record on July 16, 1999, and I bought the stock that same day. Do I pay a tax on this?

A. No. You do not include the dividend on your return. The dividend is paid to the seller of the stock, who must report it as income. See 4.9.

Q.   I hear that some stock dividends are not taxed. How can I tell which I can exclude from my tax return?

A. Keep the dividend statements and other literature accompanying your distributions. They usually tell you exactly how to treat dividends on your return. See 4.8.

Q.   My father died last year and I received $100,000 as the beneficiary under his insurance policy. Do I report the payment?

A. No. Life insurance payments are not subject to income tax. See 33.7.

Q.   I received $10,000 under my uncle's will. Is that taxed?

A. No. Inheritances are exempt from tax. But any income (say, the interest you earn) from this property after you receive it is taxed. See 11.4.

Q.   In October 1999, I sold my house at a profit of $100,000. I have owned and lived in the house for 20 years. Can I avoid tax on the profit, even though I do not intend to buy a new house?

A. Yes. You do not pay tax on the profit even though you do not purchase a new principal residence. See 29.1.

Q. I sold my principal residence at a loss. Can I deduct that loss on my return?

A. No. You cannot. Loss deductions are not allowed for personal-use property. See 29.8.

Q. My son worked in my shop during the summer. I paid him $2,100 and withheld taxes from his wages. This was his only income. May I deduct the wages and still claim an exemption for him as my dependent?

A. If you paid your son reasonable wages you may deduct what you paid him as a business expense. Since your son's wages were under $2,750 you may claim him as your dependent, assuming you provided most of his support. If at the end of the year he was under age 19 or a full-time student under age 24, he could be your dependent even if his income were $2,750 or more. He should also file a separate tax return to get a refund of the taxes withheld from his pay. See 1.12, 21.6.

Q. How can I make certain that a scientific organization to which I am planning to donate some money is qualified to receive deductible donations?

A. Ask organization officials for proof of their qualified status, or check IRS Publication 78, which lists most qualified organizations. See 14.1.

Q. May I deduct my unreimbursed costs for gasoline and oil while doing work for a charitable organization?

A. Yes. The expenses are deductible if you claim itemized deductions on your return. In 1999, you may deduct a flat 14-cents-a-mile if that is greater than actual costs. Do not forget to deduct expenses for uniforms required for your charity work. See 14.1, 14.4.

Q. Do I need to get a receipt from a charity for a cash donation?

A. Yes, if you gave $250 or more. If you gave under $250, your cancelled check is acceptable substantiation; a receipt is optional. For donations of $250 or more, get the receipt by the time you file. The charity should include in the receipt an estimate of the value of any benefits you received. See 14.15.

Q. In 1999, I paid state taxes for two taxable years. I prepaid my 1999 state income tax before the end of 1999, and I previously paid my 1998 state tax in 1999. Can I deduct both?

A. Yes. Your payment of the 1999 income tax before it was due does not affect your right to deduct the amount, provided the state accepts it as a tax payment and it is a reasonable approximation of what you owe. See 16.3.

Q. My personal camera and video equipment were stolen from my apartment. I do not know who did it. Can I deduct the loss?

A. A theft loss may be claimed as an itemized deduction, but as a practical matter the deduction may not be allowed because it does not exceed 10% of your adjusted gross income. Even if it exceeded this and the $100 floor, the IRS could disallow the loss in an audit and argue that there is no proof of a theft. If there were witnesses to a break-in, see if you can get their statements. Reporting a theft to the police or offering a reward does not prove a theft occurred, but having a police record that there was a robbery would help you support the deduction. See 18.8.

Q. Can I get a bad debt loss for a salary which I earned but was not paid?

A. No. If you are on the cash basis (and most individuals are), you cannot get the deduction for unpaid salary, rent, or fees. On the cash basis you do not include salary as income until you are paid. Merely being entitled to payment but not receiving it does not entitle you to a deduction. See 2.2 , 5.33.

Q. I loaned money to my sister-in-law. She has not paid back the loan. Can I claim a bad debt loss?

A. Yes, if there was an enforceable promise to repay at the time the debt was created and you can show that she became financially unable to pay in 1999. The deduction would be claimed as a short-term capital loss. If the advance you made was really a gift and you did not expect to be repaid, you may not take a deduction. See 5.34.

Q. Can I make a deductible contribution to an IRA if I contribute to a 401 (k) plan at work?

A. It depends on your income. For active plan participants, IRA deductions for 1999 are phased out over a modified adjusted gross income range of $31,000–$41,000 for single persons, or $51,000–$61,000 for married persons filing jointly. See 8.4.

Q. Can I take an IRA deduction for the amount I contributed to a 401(k) plan in 1999?

A. No. A 401(k) plan is not an IRA. However, the amount contributed is not included as income in Box 1 of your W-2 Form, so you don't pay tax on it this year. See 7.17.

Q. What is "itemizing"? How can it help me?

A. You should itemize if you have deductible expenses that exceed your standard deductions. You itemize deductions by filing Schedule A with Form 1040. On Schedule A, you list amounts you paid during the year for items such as medical and dental care, state and local income taxes, real estate taxes, home mortgage interest, casualty losses, gifts to charity and miscellaneous job costs, investment expenses and tax preparation fees. See 13.2.

Q. I refinanced my home in 1999 and paid "points." Can I deduct the entire amount as interest on my 1999 return?

A. No. Points paid solely to refinance your home may not be deducted in the year paid. Instead, they must be deducted over the life of the loan. See 15.7–15.8.

Q. What are the deductible mileage rates for 1999?

A. The rate for business travel is 32.5 cents per mile for miles traveled from January 1, 1999, through March 31, 1999, and 31 cents per mile for miles traveled from April 1, 1999, through December 31, 1999. The rate for travel for medical care and moving expenses is 10 cents per mile. The rate for travel for deductible volunteer work is 14 cents per mile. See 12.3, 14.4, 17.9, 20.33, 43.1.

Q. I withheld Social Security taxes from the wages of a person who cared for my child while I worked in 1999. How do I report the withheld taxes?

A. You report the withholdings, as well as your own employer's share of Social Security and Medicare taxes, on Schedule H. You pay the taxes when you file your personal 1999 Form 1040. See 25.10.

30 Checkpoints Before Filing

1. Check that you have filed the correct tax returns. Use Form l040EZ or Form 1040A only if it will save you time and not cause you to give up tax-savings deductions or credits that can only be claimed on Form 1040.

2. Check your arithmetic.

3. Check that you have indicated the correct filing status. If you are married, review whether filing separately would save you more than filing jointly. If you are single and support a dependent, check whether you may claim head of household status.

4. Check that your Social Security number is written correctly, and the number is written on all schedules and statements attached to your return.

5. Check the amount of your itemized deductions against the standard deduction allowed for your filing status. Claim the larger deduction. Check that you have claimed the additional standard deduction allowed if you are age 65 or over, or blind.

6. Check that all tax withholdings are entered on your return so they can be credited against your tax liabilities.

7. Check when using the tax tables that the tax taken is from the line and column applicable to your filing status.

8. Check that a refund amount shown on your return is correct and indicate whether you want the refund in cash or credited to your first estimated tax installment payment for 2000.

9. Check that the amount of tax liability indicated on your return and the amount written on your check or money order is the same. Also, your check or money order should include your Social Security number and note that it is in payment of your 1999 tax liability.

10. Check that all the necessary schedules and statements are attached to your tax return. Make two copies of the return, one for your own records and one for the state income tax authorities.

11. Check that you have signed the return. If you are filing jointly, check that your spouse has also signed.

12. Check that in calculating the amount of taxable Social Security benefits you use the base amounts applicable to your filing status.

13. Check whether you are entitled to a tax credit for excess FICA taxes withheld on your wages if you worked for more than one employer.

14. Check whether you are liable for Alternative Minimum Tax (AMT), especially if you have substantial itemized deductions and dependency exemptions.

15. Check whether you received a refund of state income taxes and correctly determined how much of the refund is taxable as a recovery of a tax benefit.

16. Check passive loss restrictions if you have income or losses from real estate investments.

17. Check that your withdrawals from IRAs and employer retirement accounts meet the minimum distribution requirements if you are age $70^1/_2$ or over.

18. Check the amount you contributed to your IRA against income limits that may reduce or eliminate your deduction if you are covered by an employer retirement plan.

19. Check, if you are self-employed, that you have figured your self-employment tax, claimed a deduction for 50% of the tax, and claimed a deduction for Keogh or SEP plan contributions.

20. Check that you have attached all your withholding tax statements. Also check whether the statements are accurate. If not, ask your employer or other payer for a corrected copy.

21. Check whether you must begin to make estimated tax installments or whether your rate of withholding is in line with your estimated tax for 2000.

22. Check that you have claimed all deductible interest expenses. If you have been claiming amortizable points in prior years, include the amount deductible this year. If the mortgage ended early, deduct the balance of amortizable points this year.

23. Check that you have used the correct cost basis for sales of property bought in prior years.

24. Check that you have not reported tax-exempt interest as taxable interest.

25. Check your deductible auto expenses against the IRS allowance. Claim the larger amount.

26. Check that your Forms 1099 are accurate. If the forms are inaccurate ask the payer to prepare corrected forms.

27. Check if you are entitled to the tax credit for child and dependent care, that you prepare Form 2441 if filing a Form 1040, or Schedule 1, if filing a Form 1040A and attach the additional forms to the return.

28. Check that all documentary evidence including power of attorney or court certificate of legal representative is attached to a return not signed by the taxpayer.

29. Check, if deducting alimony, that the Social Security number of your former spouse is reported on Line 31, Form 1040.

30. Check, if filing for a deceased taxpayer, that the date of death of the deceased is on the return.

Filing Basics

In this part, you will learn these income tax basics:

- Whether you must file a return
- When and where to file your return
- Which tax form to file
- What filing status you qualify for
- When filing separately is an advantage for married persons
- How to qualify as head of household
- How filing rules for resident aliens and nonresident aliens differ
- How to claim personal exemption deductions for yourself, your spouse, and your dependents.

Do You Have To File a 1999 Tax Return?

If you are—	You must file if gross income is at least—
Single	
Under age 65	$7,050
Age 65 or older on or before January 1, 2000	8,100
Married and living together at the end of 1999	
Filing a joint return—both spouses under age 65	12,700
Filing a joint return—one spouse age 65 or older	13,550
Filing a joint return—both spouses age 65 or older	14,400
Filing a separate return (any age)	2,750
Married and living apart at the end of 1999	
Filing a joint or separate return	2,750
Head of a household maintained for a child or other relative (see 1.11)	
Under age 65	9,100
Age 65 or older on or before January 1, 2000	10,150
Widowed in 1998 or 1997 and have a dependent child (see 1.10)	
Under age 65	9,950
Age 65 or older on or before January 1, 2000	10,800

Marital status. For 1999 tax purposes, marital status is generally determined as of December 31, 1999. Thus, if you were divorced or legally separated during 1999, you are not considered married for 1999 tax purposes, and you must use the filing threshold for single persons unless you qualify as a head of household (1.11), or you remarried in 1999 and are filing a joint return with your new spouse.

If your spouse died in 1999 and you were living together on the date of death, use the filing threshold shown for married persons living together at the end of 1999. If you were not living together on the date of death, the $2,750 filing threshold applies, unless you remarried during 1999 and are filing jointly with your new spouse.

Age 65. Whether you are age 65 or older is generally determined as of the end of the year, but if your 65th birthday is on January 1, 2000, you are treated as being age 65 for 1999 tax purposes.

Gross income. Gross income is generally all the income that you received in 1999, except for items specifically exempt from tax.

Include wages, tips, self-employment fees (Chapter 45), taxable scholarships (Chapter 38), taxable interest and dividends (Chapter 4), capital gains (Chapter 5), taxable pensions and annuities (Chapter 7), rents (Chapter 9), and trust distributions (Chapter 11). Home sale proceeds that are tax free (Chapter 29) and tax-free foreign earned income (Chapter 36) *are* considered gross income for purposes of the filing test.

Exclude tax-exempt interest (Chapter 4), Social Security (provided provisional income is below the floor specified at 34.3), tax-free fringe benefits (Chapter 3), qualifying scholarships (Chapter 38), and life insurance (Chapter 33).

Other situations when you must file. Even if you are not required to file under the gross income tests, you must file a 1999 return if:

- You are self-employed and your net self-employment earnings for 1999 are $400 or more (Chapter 45), *or*
- You are entitled to a refund of taxes withheld from your wages or a refund based on the earned income credit for working families (Chapter 25), *or*
- You received any earned income credit payments in advance from your employer (Chapter 25), *or*
- You owe any special tax such as alternative minimum tax (Chapter 23), IRA penalty (Chapter 8), and FICA on tips (Chapter 26), *or*
- You are a nonresident alien with a U.S. business or tax liability not covered by withholding; *see* Form 1040NR.

Filing tests for dependents. If you can be claimed as a dependent by your parent, or by any other taxpayer, see the rules on the next page to determine if you must file a return.

Filing Tests for Dependents

The income threshold for filing a tax return is generally lower for an individual who may be claimed as a dependent than for a nondependent. If your 1999 gross income was $2,750 or more, you may be claimed as a dependent only by your parent, and only if you were either under age 19 or a full-time student under age 24. This income test and the other tests for dependents are explained in Chapter 21.

If, under the tests in Chapter 21, you may be claimed as a dependent by someone else, use the chart on this page to determine if you must file a 1999 return. Include as unearned income taxable interest and dividends, capital gains, pensions, annuities, taxable Social Security benefits *(34.3)*, unemployment compensation, and distributions of unearned income from a trust. Earned income includes wages, tips, self-employment income, and taxable scholarships or fellowships (Chapter 38). Gross income is the total of unearned and earned income.

For married dependents, the filing requirements in the chart assume that the dependent is filing a separate return and not a joint return (Chapter 1). Generally, a married person who files a joint return may not be claimed as a dependent by a third party who provides support.

If you are the parent of a dependent child who was under age 14 on January 1, 2000, and who had only investment income, you may elect to report the child's income on your own return instead of filing a separate return for the child; *see 24.5* for the election rules.

For purposes of the following chart, a person is treated as being age 65 (or older) if his or her 65th birthday is on or before January 1, 2000. Blindness is determined as of December 31, 1999.

File a 1999 Return If You Are—

Single dependent under age 65 and not blind and any of the following apply:
- You had only unearned income and it exceeded $700
- You had only earned income and it exceeded $4,300
- You had both unearned income and earned income and *either*—
  Your unearned income exceeded $250 and gross income exceeded $700, *or*
  Your unearned income was $250 or less and gross income exceeded $4,300.

Single dependent and either age 65 or older or blind and any of the following apply:
- You had only unearned income and it exceeded $1,750 ($2,800 if age 65 or older and also blind); *or*
- You had only earned income and it exceeded $5,350 ($6,400 if age 65 or older and also blind); *or*
- You had both earned income and unearned income and gross income exceeded—
  The larger of (1) $700 and (2) your earned income up to $4,050 plus $250 (total here cannot exceed $4,300) PLUS $1,050 ($2,100 if age 65 or older and also blind)

Married dependent under age 65 and not blind and any of the following apply:
- You had only unearned income and it exceeded $700
- You had only earned income and it exceeded $3,600
- You had both unearned income and earned income and *either*—
  Your unearned income exceeded $250 and gross income exceeded $700, *or*
  Your unearned income was $250 or less and gross income exceeded $3,600.
- Your gross income was at least $5 and your spouse itemizes deductions on a separate return

Married dependent and either age 65 or older or blind and any of the following apply:
- You had only unearned income and it exceeded $1,550 ($2,400 if age 65 or older and also blind)
- You had only earned income and it exceeded $4,450 ($5,300 if age 65 or older and also blind)
- You had both unearned income and earned income and gross income exceeded—
  the larger of (1) $700 and (2) your earned income up to $3,350 plus $250 (total here can not exceed $3,600) PLUS $850 ($1,700 if age 65 or older and also blind)
- Your gross income was at least $5 and your spouse itemizes deductions on a separate return

Where To File

If you are filing—	File with the Internal Revenue Service Center—
A personal return	For your place of legal residence. If you received an IRS packet of forms with a pre-addressed envelope, use it unless you have moved. If you do not have an envelope, mail your return to the Service Center shown below for your residence.
A business return	For the location of your principal place of business.
As a U.S. citizen working abroad	File Form 1040 at Philadelphia, PA 19255-0215.*
As a service member in the Armed Forces	For the place you are stationed. If you have an APO or FPO address, file Form 1040 with the Service Center at Philadelphia, PA 19255-0215.*

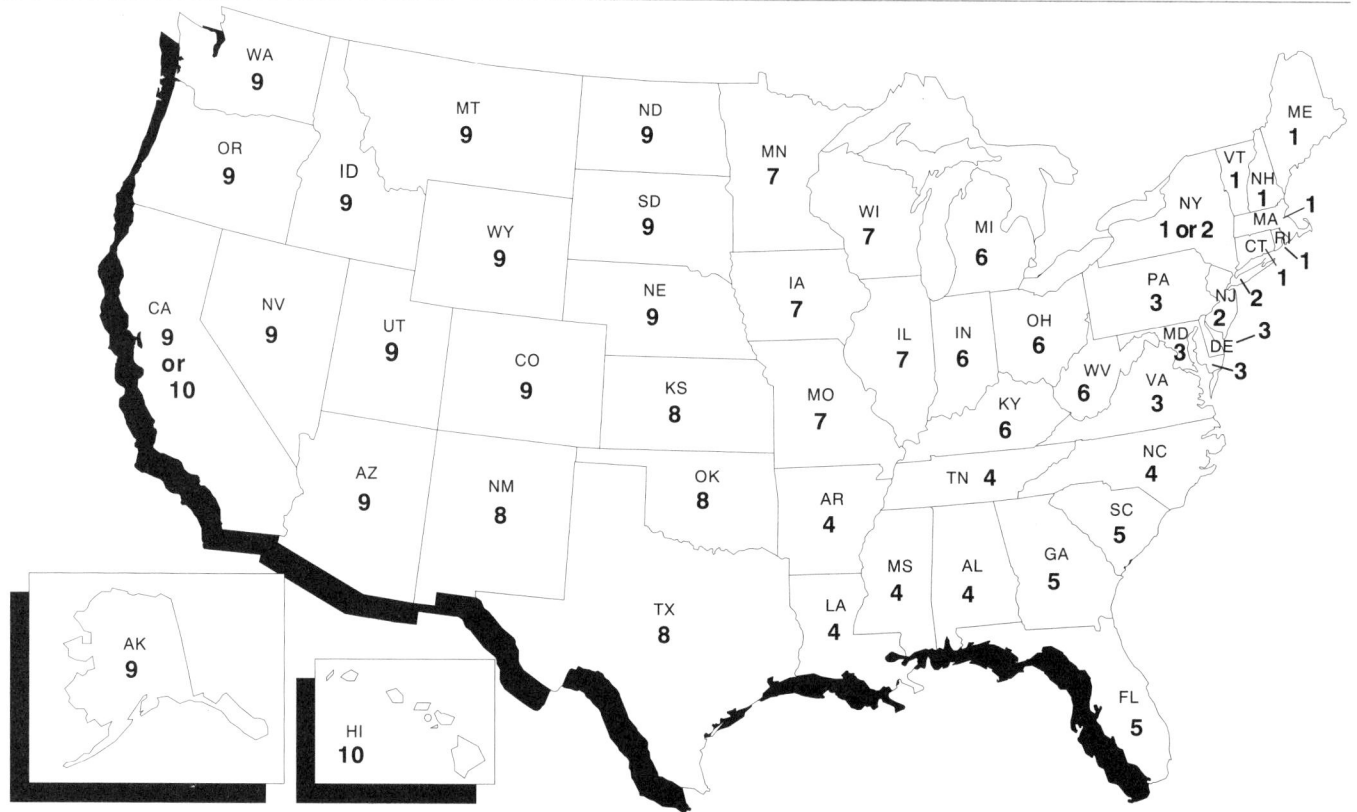

Key To Service Center Map

Key	Form 1040 Mailing Address—
1.	Internal Revenue Service Center, Andover, Massachusetts 05501-0102 if claiming a refund; otherwise 05501-0002. New York residents file here if they reside outside of New York City or counties of Nassau, Rockland, Suffolk, or Westchester.
2.	Internal Revenue Service Center, Holtsville, New York 00501-0102 if claiming a refund; otherwise 00501-0002. New York residents in New York City or counties of Nassau, Rockland, Suffolk, or Westchester file here.
3.	Internal Revenue Service Center, Philadelphia, Pennsylvania 19255-0102 if claiming a refund; otherwise 19255-0002. Residents of the District of Columbia file here.
4.	Internal Revenue Service Center, Memphis, Tennessee 37501-0102 if claiming a refund; otherwise 37501-0002.
5.	Internal Revenue Service Center, Atlanta, Georgia 39901-0102 if claiming a refund; otherwise 39901-0002.
6.	Internal Revenue Service Center, Cincinnati, Ohio 45999-0102 if claiming a refund; otherwise 45999-0002.
7.	Internal Revenue Service Center, Kansas City, Missouri 64999-0102 if claiming a refund; otherwise 64999-0002.
8.	Internal Revenue Service Center, Austin, Texas 73301-0102 if claiming a refund; otherwise 73301-0002.
9.	Internal Revenue Service Center, Ogden, Utah 84201-0102 if claiming a refund; otherwise 84201-0002. California residents file here if living in the counties of: Alpine, Amador, Butte, Calaveras, Colusa, Contra Costa, Del Norte, El Dorado, Glenn, Humboldt, Lake, Lassen, Marin, Mendocino, Modoc, Napa, Nevada, Placer, Plumas, Sacramento, San Joaquin, Shasta, Sierra, Siskiyou, Solano, Sonoma, Sutter, Tehama, Trinity, Yolo, and Yuba.
10.	Internal Revenue Service Center, Fresno, California 93888-0102 if claiming a refund; otherwise 93888-0002. California residents file here if not listed under Key 9 above.

*Filing Form 1040A or 1040EZ: If you are filing Form 1040A, the last four digits of the zip codes for the IRS Service Centers are 0015 (instead of 0102 or 0002); for Form 1040EZ the last four digits are 0014. Check your tax form instructions and the Supplement for any late changes to the addresses or zip codes on this page.

Filing Deadlines (on or Before)

January 18, 2000
Pay the balance of your 1999 estimated tax. If you do not meet this date, you may avoid an estimated tax penalty for the last quarter by filing a final return for 1999 and paying the balance of your 1999 tax by February 1, 2000.

Farmers and fishermen: File your single 1999 estimated tax payment by this date. If you do not, you may still avoid an estimated tax penalty by filing a final tax return and paying the full tax by March 1, 2000.

January 31, 2000
Make sure you have received a Form W-2 from each employer for whom you worked in 1999.

April 17, 2000
File your 1999 tax return and pay the balance of your tax. If you cannot meet the April 17 deadline, you may file Form 4868 to obtain an automatic four-month filing extension. However, interest will still be charged for taxes not paid by this date, and late payment penalties will be imposed unless at least 90% of your tax liability is paid by this date. If you cannot pay the full amount of tax you owe when you file your return, you can file Form 9465 to request an installment payment arrangement.

If on this date you are a U.S. citizen or resident living and working abroad or in military service outside the U.S. or Puerto Rico, you have an automatic two-month filing extension until June 15, 2000.

Pay the first installment of your 2000 estimated tax by this date.

June 15, 2000
Pay the second installment of your 2000 estimated tax. You may amend your estimate at this time.

If on April 17 you were a U.S. citizen or resident living and working abroad or in military service outside the U.S. or Puerto Rico, file your 1999 return and pay the balance due. You may obtain an additional two-month filing extension until August 15, 2000, by filing Form 4868.

If you are a nonresident alien who did not have tax withheld from your wages, file Form 1040NR by this date and pay the balance due.

August 15, 2000
File your 1999 return if you received an automatic four-month filing extension using Form 4868. Also file your 1999 return and pay the balance due if on April 17 you were a U.S. citizen or resident living and working abroad or in military service outside the U.S. or Puerto Rico, and by June 15 you qualified for an additional two-month extension by filing Form 4868.

September 15, 2000
Pay the third installment of your 2000 estimated tax. You may amend your estimate at this time.

December 31, 2000
If self-employed, this is the last day to set up a Keogh plan for 2000.

January 16, 2001
Pay the balance of your 2000 estimated tax.

April 16, 2001
File your 2000 return and pay the balance of your tax. Pay the first installment of your 2001 estimated tax by this date.

15th day of the 4th month after the fiscal year ends
File your fiscal year return and pay the balance of the tax due. If you cannot meet the filing deadline, apply for an automatic four-month filing extension on Form 4868.

2000

JANUARY	MAY	SEPTEMBER

FEBRUARY	JUNE	OCTOBER

MARCH	JULY	NOVEMBER

APRIL	AUGUST	DECEMBER

2001

JANUARY	MAY	SEPTEMBER

FEBRUARY	JUNE	OCTOBER

MARCH	JULY	NOVEMBER

APRIL	AUGUST	DECEMBER

Choosing Which Tax Form To File

There are three individual tax forms: Form 1040, Form 1040A, and Form 1040EZ. Use the simplified Form 1040EZ or Form 1040A only if you find the return will save you time and not cause you to give up tax-saving deductions or credits that are only available if you file Form 1040. To help you make your selections, fill in the following chart.

By checking the box that indicates your tax status, income, expenses, and credit items, you will be guided in choosing which form to use.

Item—	Form 1040EZ—	Form 1040A—	Form 1040—
Single	X[1, 2]	X[1]	X
Head of household		X[1]	X
Married filing jointly	X[1, 2]	X[1]	X
Married filing separately		X[1]	X
Widow and widower		X[1]	X
Exemption for dependents		X	X
Wages, salary	X	X	X
Interest	X[3]	X	X
Ordinary dividends		X	X
Unemployment compensation	X	X	X
Self-employment income			X
Pension-annuity		X	X
IRA distributions		X	X
Rents and royalties			X
Gains and losses from property sales			X
Capital gain distributions from mutual funds			X
Alimony			X
State tax refunds			X
Social Security benefits		X	X
IRA deduction		X	X
Alimony paid			X
Student loan interest		X	X
Moving expenses			X
Self-employed health insurance			X
50% of self-employment tax			X
Medical Savings Account deduction (MSA)			X
Penalty for early withdrawal of savings			X
Deduction for Keogh, SEP, and SIMPLE plans			X
Employee business expenses			X
State and local income taxes			X
Real estate taxes			X
Home mortgage interest, investment and business interest			X
Charitable contributions			X
Medical and dental expenses			X
Casualty and theft losses			X
Miscellaneous deductions (investment expenses, tax preparation)			X
Credit for child and dependent care		X	X
Earned income credit	X[4]	X	X
Credit for elderly and totally disabled		X	X
Child credit		X	X
Education credits		X	X
All other credits			X
Estimated tax payments and estimated tax penalty		X	X
Advance earned income credit (EIC) payments		X	X
Self-employment tax			X
Roth conversion IRAs			X
Penalty tax on an IRA			X
Alternative minimum tax			X
Social Security tax on tips not reported to your employer			X
Uncollected Social Security tax on tips shown on your Form W-2			X
"Kiddie" tax on child's return		X	X
"Kiddie" tax on parent's return			X
Household employee taxes			X
All other taxes or penalties			X

[1] Taxable income less than $50,000.
[2] Under age 65 and not blind on January 1, 2000.
[3] Up to $400.
[4] If you did not receive any advance earned income credit payments.

Filing Status

The filing status you use when you file your return determines the tax rates that will apply to your taxable income; *see 1.2.* Filing status also determines the standard deduction you may claim if you do not itemize deductions *(see 13.1)* and your ability to claim certain other deductions, credits, and exclusions.

This chapter explains the five different filing statuses: single, married filing jointly, married filing separately, head of household, and qualifying widow(er). If you are married, filing a joint return is generally advantageous, but there are exceptions discussed in *1.3.* If you are unmarried and are supporting a child who lives with you, you may qualify as a head of household *(see 1.11)*, which will enable you to use more favorable tax rates than those allowed for single taxpayers. If you were widowed in either 1998 or 1997 and in 1999 a dependent child lived with you, you may be able to file as a qualifying widow(er) for 1999, which allows you to use joint return rates.

Special filing situations, such as for children, nonresident aliens, and deceased individuals, are also discussed in this chapter.

Your personal or family status also determines the number of personal exemptions you may claim on your return. For 1999, each personal exemption you claim is the equivalent of a $2,750 deduction. Exemptions for children, parents, and other dependents are allowed if the tests in Chapter 21 are met.

Importance of Filing Status

Law Alert

No Marriage Penalty Relief Yet

Married persons are subject to a "marriage penalty" when the tax they must pay on a joint return exceeds the combined tax they would pay if they were single and filing individual returns. The marriage penalty generally applies where each spouse earns a substantial share of the combined income. On the other hand, if one spouse has little or no income, there generally is a marriage bonus or "singles penalty" in that the spouse with most of the income pays a lower tax as a married person filing jointly than if he or she were single.

Congress is considering legislation to provide at least partial relief from the marriage penalty. Proposed changes include: (1) raising the standard deduction for married couples filing joint returns to twice that available to single filers and (2) increasing the size of the 15% regular income tax bracket for married couples filing joint returns to twice the size of the corresponding bracket for unmarried individuals.

1.1 Which Filing Status Should You Use?

Your filing status generally depends on whether you are married at the end of the year, and, if unmarried, whether you maintain a household for a qualifying dependent. The five filing statuses are: single, married filing jointly, married filing separately, head of household, and qualifying widow or widower.

If you are *married at the end of the year*, you may file jointly *(1.4)* or separately *(1.3)*. If you lived apart from your spouse for the last half of 1999 and your child lived with you, you may qualify as an "unmarried" head of household *(see 1.11)*, which allows you to apply more favorable tax rates than you could as a married person filing separately.

If you are *unmarried at the end of the year*, your filing status is single unless you meet the tests for a head of household or qualifying widow(er). Generally, you are a head of household if you pay more than 50% of the household costs for a relative who lives with you, or a parent, whether or not he or she lives with you; *see 1.11*. You generally are a qualifying widow(er) if you were widowed in 1997 or 1998 and in 1999 you pay more than 50% of the household costs for you and your dependent child; *see 1.10*. The tax rates for heads of households and for qualifying widow(ers) are more favorable than those for single taxpayers; *see 1.2*.

The filing status you use determines the tax rates that apply to your taxable income, as shown in *1.2*, as well as the standard deduction you may claim *(see 13.1)* if you do not itemize deductions. Certain other deductions, credits, or exclusions are also affected by filing status. For example, if you are married, certain tax benefits are only allowed if you file jointly, but more deductions overall may be allowed in certain cases if you file separately; *see 1.3*. The deduction for personal exemptions is phased out for high income taxpayers at levels based upon filing status; *see 21.15*.

Marital status determined at the end of the year. If you are divorced during the year under a final decree of divorce or separate maintenance, you are treated as unmarried for that whole year, assuming you have not remarried before the end of the year. For the year of the divorce, file as a single person unless you care for a child and qualify as a head of household under the rules at *1.11*.

If at the end of the year you are living apart from your spouse, or you are separated under a provisional decree that has not yet been finalized, you are not considered divorced. If you care for a child and meet the other tests at *1.11*, you may file as an unmarried head of household. Otherwise, you must file a joint return or as a married person filing separately.

If at the end of the year you live together in a common law marriage that is recognized by the law of the state in which you live or the state where the marriage began, you are treated as married.

If your spouse dies during the year, you are treated as married for that entire year and may file a joint return for you and your deceased spouse, assuming you have not remarried before year's end; *see 1.9*.

1.2 Tax Rates Based on Filing Status

The most favorable tax brackets apply to married persons filing jointly and qualifying widow(ers) *(see 1.10)*, who also use the joint return rates. The least favorable brackets are those for married persons filing separately, but filing separately is still advisable for married couples in certain situations, as discussed in *1.3*. The table on the next page compares 1999 tax rate brackets.

If you are unmarried at the end of the year, do not assume that your filing status is single. If your child lives with you in a home you maintain, you generally may file as a head of household *(see 1.11)*, which allows you to use more favorable tax rates than a single person. If you were widowed in either of the two prior years and maintain a household for your dependent child, you generally may file as a qualified widow(er), which allows you to use favorable joint return rates; *see 1.10*.

If you are married at the end of the year but for the second half of the year you lived with your child apart from your spouse, and you and your spouse agree not to file jointly, you may use head of household tax rates, which are more favorable than those for married persons filing separately.

Applying the tax table or tax rate schedule. If your taxable income is less than $100,000, you will look up your tax in the tax tables, which are shown in Part 9 of this book. If your taxable income is $100,000 or more, you figure your tax using the tax rate schedules, also in Part 9. Chapter 22 has examples applying the tax tables or rate schedules to determine regular income tax liability.

Taxable Income Brackets for 1999

	15% bracket ends at—	28% bracket ends at—	31% bracket ends at—	36% bracket ends at—	39.6% bracket applies to—
Married filing separately	$ 21,525	$ 52,025	$ 79,275	$ 141,575	over $ 141,575
Single	25,750	62,450	130,250	283,150	over 283,150
Head of Household	34,550	89,150	144,400	283,150	over 283,150
Married filing jointly or Qualifying widow(er)	43,050	104,050	158,550	283,150	over 283,150

Married Taxpayers

1.3 Filing Separately Instead of Jointly

Filing a joint return saves taxes for a married couple where one spouse earns all, or substantially all, of the taxable income. If both you and your spouse earn taxable income, you should figure your tax on joint and separate returns to determine which method provides the lower tax.

Separate returns may save taxes where filing separately allows you to claim more deductions. On separate returns, larger amounts of medical expenses, casualty losses, or miscellaneous deductions may be deductible because lower adjusted gross income floors apply. Unless one spouse earns substantially more than the other, separate and joint tax rates are likely to be the same, regardless of the type of returns filed. The Example on page 11 illustrates how filing separately can save you taxes.

Suspicious of your spouse's tax reporting? If you suspect that your spouse is evading taxes and may be liable on a joint return, you may want to file a separate return. By filing separately, you avoid liability for unpaid taxes due on a joint return, plus interest and penalties.

If you do file jointly and the IRS tries to collect tax due on the joint return from you personally, you may be able to avoid liability under the innocent spouse rules *(see 1.7)*. If you are no longer married to or are separated from the person with whom you jointly filed, you may be able to elect separate liability treatment *(see 1.8)*.

Standard deduction restriction on separate returns. Keep in mind that if you and your spouse file separately, both must either itemize or claim the standard deduction, which is $3,600 in 1999 for married persons filing separately *(13.3)*. Thus, if one spouse itemizes, the other spouse must also itemize even if he or she would get a larger deduction by taking the $3,600 standard deduction.

Joint return required for certain benefits. Also be aware that certain tax benefits may be claimed by married persons only if they file jointly.

If you want to take advantage of the $25,000 rental loss allowance *(10.2)* or the credit for the elderly (Chapter 34), you must file jointly unless you live apart for the whole year. You must file jointly to claim an IRA deduction for a nonworking spouse *(8.3)*. A joint return is also required to claim the new Hope or Lifetime Learning Credits (Chapter 38). You must file jointly to claim the dependent care credit or the earned income credit (Chapter 25), unless you live apart for the last six months of the year. Furthermore, if you receive Social Security benefits, 85% of your benefits are generally subject to tax on a separate return; *see* Chapter 34.

Filing Tip

AMT Liability

If you are subject to alternative minimum tax (AMT), filing separately may allow a full AMT exemption on one of the separate returns if your spouse's income does not come within the phase-out range for the exemption; *see* Chapter 23.

Filing Status If Married at the End of 1999

Filing Jointly	Filing Separately	Living Apart From Spouse: Filing as Unmarried Head of Household
Married couples may pay less tax by filing jointly. Filing jointly allows the use of joint return rates. You may file a joint return if you are legally married on the last day of 1999. You need not live together provided you are legally married. A couple legally separated under a final decree of divorce or separate maintenance as of the end of 1999 may not file a joint return. You may file jointly if your spouse died during 1999; see 1.9. If one spouse is a nonresident alien, you may file jointly only if you make a special election to be taxed on your worldwide income; see 1.5. You must file jointly to make an IRA deduction on behalf of a nonworking spouse (8.3). To claim the credit for the elderly (Chapter 34), you must file jointly unless you lived apart for the entire year or qualify as head of household. You must file jointly to claim the dependent care credit or the earned income credit (Chapter 25) unless you live apart and qualify as a head of household. On a joint return, each spouse is liable for the entire tax. If one spouse does not pay, the other spouse may be liable even though all of the income was earned by the spouse who failed to pay the tax. An "innocent" spouse who files a joint return may be relieved of penalties and tax liability in certain circumstances; see 1.7. For community property rules, see 1.6.	Filing separately, instead of jointly, may be advisable where you and your spouse each earn taxable income and have separate deductions, as explained at 1.3. You are required to use tax rates for married persons filing separately in these cases: 1. Your spouse files a separate return. If you are experiencing marital discord, you may be forced to file separately unless your spouse consents to a joint return. 2. Someone else claims you or your spouse as a dependent; see 21.13. 3. You and your spouse have different tax reporting years. If you report on the calendar year but your spouse reports on a fiscal year, you must file separately unless you get permission from the IRS to change your reporting year (Form 1128). This bar to joint filing does not apply when your tax years begin on the same day but one or both end because of the death of either or both spouses. A spouse who has never filed a tax return may elect to use the other spouse's tax year as his or her first tax year; then they can file a joint return. A husband and wife can file a joint return even if they had different tax years before their marriage. 4. You or your spouse is a nonresident alien and you do not make an election to be taxed on your worldwide income; see 1.5.	If you lived apart from your spouse during the last half of 1999, and your child lived with you for most of the year, you may qualify for tax purposes as "unmarried" and use head of household tax rates, which are lower than rates for married persons filing separately. The following four tests must be met for you to file separately from your spouse as a head of household: 1. Your spouse was not a member of your household during the last six months of 1999. 2. You maintain your home as the principal place of abode for your child, adopted child, or stepchild for more than half of 1999. However, a foster child must be a member of your household for the entire year. 3. You are entitled to claim the child as a dependent. Ignore this test if the noncustodial spouse claims the exemption for the child under the rules of 21.11. 4. You provide over half of the cost of supporting the household. See 1.11 for further details.

Filing Status If Not Married at the End of 1999

Single	Head of Household	Qualifying Widow(er)
If you are not married at the end of 1999, use the rate for single individuals, unless you qualify as a surviving spouse or a head of household. If you are widowed, you are "unmarried" and use rates for single individuals regardless of the number of years you were married. There is an exception for recent widows or widowers supporting children, as explained in the "qualifying widow(er)" column.	If at the end of the year you are not married, you may use special head of household rates if you meet these tests: 1. You maintain a household for more than half of 1999 for your child or grandchild, or for a dependent relative. The household must be your home and the main residence of your relative except that a dependent parent need not live with you. However, you must maintain a dependent parent's separate household for the entire year to claim head of household status based on that support. 2. You pay more than one-half the cost of supporting the household. 3. You are a U.S. citizen or resident alien during the entire tax year. These rules are explained in detail in 1.11.	If you are a widow or widower and your spouse died in 1997 or 1998, you may use 1999 joint return tax rates if you meet these four tests: 1. You maintain your home as the main home of your child for the entire year and you furnish over half the cost of maintaining the household. 2. You are entitled to claim the child as a dependent; see 21.1. 3. In the year your spouse died, you could have filed a joint return. 4. You did not remarry before January 1, 2000. If you meet these tests, your filing status is qualifying widow or widower; see 1.10.

EXAMPLE

Mike Palmer's 1999 adjusted gross income (AGI) is $65,000 and his wife Fran has AGI of $50,000. Mike has deductible medical expenses of $7,000; Fran's are $1,000. Mike has an $8,000 casualty loss *(18.12)* on property owned in his name. He also has unreimbursed miscellaneous expenses of $2,600 and Fran has $500. Mike has deductible mortgage interest expenses of $5,000 and Fran has $2,000. Mike's deductible state and local taxes are $2,000; Fran's are $1,000. Neither of them claims exemptions for dependents.

As the example worksheet below shows, filing separate returns saves Mike and Fran an overall $1,141, because they can deduct more on separate returns. If they filed jointly they would have received no deduction for medical expenses and casualty losses because the deductions would have been eliminated by the higher adjusted gross income floors. If they file separately, the 3% reduction of itemized deductions *(13.7)* applies to Mike but not Fran because only Mike's AGI exceeds the $63,300 threshold. If they file jointly, the 3% reduction does not apply because their AGI is below the $126,600 threshold for joint returns. The phaseout of personal exemptions *(21.15)* does not apply regardless of how they file.

Item		Mike (Separately)	Fran (Separately)	Joint Return
1.	**AGI**	**$ 65,000**	**$ 50,000**	**$ 115,000**
2.	Medical expenses	7,000	1,000	8,000
	Less 7¹/₂% of AGI	4,875	3,750	8,625
	Allowable medical	2,125	0	0
3.	Taxes	2,000	1,000	3,000
4.	Mortgage interest	5,000	2,000	7,000
5.	Casualty loss	8,000	0	8,000
	Less 10% of AGI	6,500		11,500
	Allowable casualty	1,500		0
6.	Miscellaneous expenses	2,600	500	3,100
	Less 2% of AGI	1,300	1,000	2,300
	Allowable miscellaneous	1,300	0	800
7.	**Total itemized (*Lines 2–6*)**	**11,925**	**3,000**	**10,800**
	Less 3% reduction*	51	0	0
8.	**Net itemized**	**11,874**	**3,000**	**10,800**
9.	Personal exemptions	2,750	2,750	5,500
10.	**Net itemized plus exemptions**	**14,624**	**5,750**	**16,300**
11.	Taxable income *(Line 1 minus Line 10)*	50,376	44,250	98,700
12.	**Tax liability**	**11,307**	**9,599**	**22,047**
	Total tax filing separately			20,906
	Savings from filing separately			***1,141***

* $51 reduction = 3% (65,000 AGI – 63,300 floor)

1.4 Filing a Joint Return

If you are married at the end of the year, you may file a joint return with your spouse. Filing jointly saves taxes for many married couples, but if you and your spouse both earn taxable income, in some cases overall tax liability is reduced by filing separately; *see 1.3*.

You may not file a 1999 joint return if you were divorced under a decree of divorce or separate maintenance that is *final* by the end of the year. You may file jointly if you separated during 1999 under an interlocutory (temporary or provisional) decree or order, so long as a final divorce decree was not entered by the end of the year. If during the period that a divorce decree is interlocutory you are permitted to remarry in another state, the IRS recognizes the new marriage and allows a joint return to be filed with the new spouse. However, courts have refused to allow a joint return where a new marriage took place in Mexico during the interlocutory period in violation of California law.

Planning Reminder

Switching From Separate to Joint Return

If you and your spouse file separate returns, you have three years from the due date (without extensions) to change to a joint return. If a joint return is filed, you may not change to separate returns once the due date has passed. The filing of separate or joint estimated tax installments (Chapter 27) does not commit you to a similar tax return.

Filing Tip

Can Filing Separately Avoid Exemption Phaseout or Itemized Deduction Reduction?

Filing separately will sometimes allow either you or your spouse to avoid part of the personal exemption phaseout *(21.15)* or the 3% reduction to specified itemized deductions *(13.7)*. If you file jointly and have total 1999 adjusted gross income (AGI) exceeding $189,950, the exemption phaseout applies. If you file separately, the phaseout does not apply to the spouse reporting separate AGI of $94,975 or less. On the other hand, where your joint AGI is $189,950 or less, a spouse reporting AGI over $94,975 on a separate return will be subject to the phaseout although no phaseout would apply on a joint return.

If for 1999 you itemize deductions, the deductions for taxes, mortgage interest, charitable donations, and miscellaneous deductions are reduced by 3% of AGI exceeding $126,600 on a joint return, or exceeding $63,300 on a separate return. If you file separately, the reduction does not apply on a separate return showing AGI of $63,300 or less. Where joint AGI is $126,600 or less, a spouse filing separately with separate AGI over $63,300 is subject to the 3% reduction although no reduction would apply on a joint return.

Both spouses generally liable on joint return but there are exceptions. When you and your spouse file jointly, each of you may generally be held individually liable for the entire tax due, plus interest and any penalties. The IRS may try to collect the entire amount due from you even if your spouse earned all of the income reported on the joint return, or even if you have divorced under an agreement that holds your former spouse responsible for the taxes on the joint returns you filed together. However, there are exceptions to this joint liability rule for "innocent" spouses and for divorced or separated persons.

A new law has made it easier to obtain *innocent spouse* relief where tax on the joint return was understated without your knowledge because your spouse omitted income or claimed erroneous deductions or tax credits. In such a case, you may make an innocent spouse election within two years from the time the IRS begins a collection effort from you for taxes due on the return. *See 1.7* for details on the innocent spouse rules.

Furthermore, if you are divorced, legally separated, living apart or the spouse with whom you filed jointly has died, you may be able to avoid tax on the portion of a joint return deficiency that is allocable to your ex-spouse by making an election within two years of the time the IRS begins collection efforts against you. *See 1.8* for details on this separate liability election. You may make the separate liability election even if you apply for innocent spouse relief. In some cases, it may be easier to qualify for relief under the separate liability rules than under the innocent spouse rules because innocent spouse relief may be denied if you had "reason to know" that tax was understated on the joint return, whereas the IRS must show that you had "actual knowledge" of the understatement to deny a separate liability election.

Signing the joint return. Both you and your spouse must sign the joint return. Under the following rules, if your spouse is unable to sign, you may sign for him or her.

If, because of illness, your spouse is physically unable to sign the joint return, you may, with the oral consent of your spouse, sign his or her name on the return followed by the words "By _____, Husband (or Wife)." You then sign the return again in your own right and attach a signed and dated statement with the following information: (1) the type of form being filed, (2) the tax year, (3) the reason for the inability of the sick spouse to sign, and (4) that the sick spouse has consented to your signing.

To sign for your spouse in other situations, you need authorization in the form of a power of attorney, which must be attached to the return. IRS Form 2848 may be used.

If your spouse does not file, you may be able to prove you filed a joint return even if your spouse did not sign and you did not sign as your spouse's agent where:

- You intended it to be a joint return—your spouse's income was included (or the spouse had no income).
- Your spouse agreed to have you handle tax matters and you filed a joint return.
- Your answers to the questions on the tax return indicate you intended to file a joint return.
- Your spouse's failure to sign can be explained.

Filing Tip

Election To File a Joint Return

Where a U.S. citizen or resident is married to a nonresident alien, the couple may file a joint return if both elect to be taxed on their worldwide income. The requirement that one spouse be a U.S. citizen or resident need be met only at the close of the year. Joint returns may be filed in the year of the election and all later years until the election is terminated.

> **EXAMPLE**
>
> The Hills generally filed joint returns. In one year, Mr. Hill claimed joint return filing status and reported his wife's income as well as his own; in place of her signature on the return, he indicated that she was out of town caring for her sick mother. She did not file a separate return. The IRS refused to treat the return as joint. The Tax Court disagreed. Since Mrs. Hill testified that she would have signed had she been available, her failure to do so does not bar joint return status. The couple intended to make a joint return at the time of filing.

1.5 Nonresident Alien Spouse

If either you or your spouse was a nonresident alien *(1.15)* during any part of the year, a joint return may be filed only if both of you make a special election to be taxed on your worldwide income. Thus, if you are a U.S. citizen and your spouse is a nonresident alien at the beginning of the year who becomes a resident during the year, the special election to file jointly must be made.

If the election is not made, you may be able to claim your nonresident alien spouse as an exemption on a return filed as married filing separately, but only if the spouse had no income and could not be claimed as a dependent by another taxpayer; *see 21.2*. If the alien spouse becomes a resident before the beginning of the next tax year, you may file jointly for that year.

A couple who make the election must keep books and records of their worldwide income and give the IRS access to such books and records. If either spouse does not provide the necessary information to the IRS, the election is terminated. Furthermore, the election is terminated if either spouse revokes it or dies; revocation before the due date of the return is effective for that return. The election automatically terminates in the year following the year of the death of either spouse. However, if the survivor is a U.S. citizen or resident and has a qualifying child, he or she may be able to use joint return rates as a qualifying widow or widower in the two years following the year of the spouse's death; *see 1.10*. The election to file jointly also terminates if the couple is legally separated under a decree of divorce or separate maintenance. Termination is effective as of the beginning of the taxable year of the legal separation. If neither spouse is a citizen or resident for any part of the taxable year, an election may not be made and an existing election is suspended. If an election is suspended it may again become effective if either spouse becomes a U.S. citizen or resident. Once the election is terminated, neither spouse may ever again make the election to file jointly.

Electing to file a joint return does not terminate the special withholding on the nonresident alien's income.

1.6 Community Property Rules

If you live in Arizona, California, Idaho, Louisiana, Nevada, New Mexico, Texas, Washington, or Wisconsin, the income and property you and your spouse acquire during the marriage is generally regarded as community property. Community property means that each of you owns half of the community income and community property, even if legal title is held by only one spouse. But note that there are some instances in which community property rules are disregarded for tax purposes; these instances are clearly highlighted in the pertinent sections of this book.

Separate property may still be owned. Property owned before marriage generally remains separate property; it does not become community property when you marry. Property received during the marriage by one spouse as a gift or an inheritance from a third party is generally separate property. In some states, if the nature of ownership cannot be fixed, the property is presumed to be community property.

In some states, income from separate property may be treated as community property income. In other states, income from separate property remains the separate property of the individual owner.

Divorce or separation. If you and your spouse divorce, your community property automatically becomes separate property. A separation agreement or a decree of legal separation or of separate maintenance may or may not end the marital community, depending on state law.

Community income rules may not apply to separated couples. If a husband and wife in a community property state file separate returns, each spouse must generally report one-half of the community income. However, a spouse may be able to avoid reporting income earned by his or her spouse if they live apart during the entire calendar year and do not file a joint return.

To qualify, one or both spouses must have earned income for the year and none of that earned income may be transferred, directly or indirectly, between the spouses during the year. One spouse's payment to the other spouse solely to support the couple's dependent children is not a disqualifying transfer. If the separated couple qualifies under these tests, community income is allocated as follows:

- Earned income (excluding business or partnership income) is taxed to the spouse who performed the personal services.
- Business income (other than partnership income) is treated as the income of the spouse carrying on the business.
- Partnership income is taxed to the spouse entitled to a distributive share of partnership profits.

Innocent spouse rules apply to community property. As discussed above, community property rules may not apply to earned income where spouses live apart for the entire year and file separate returns. In addition, a spouse who files a separate return may be relieved of tax liability on community income that is attributable to the other spouse if he or she does not know (or have reason to know) about the income and if it would be inequitable under the circumstances for him or her to be taxed on such income. Even if you fail to qualify for such relief because you knew (or had reason to know) about the income, a new law allows the IRS to relieve you of liability if it would be inequitable to hold you liable.

Filing Tip

Nonresident Alien Becomes Resident

Where one spouse is a U.S. citizen or resident and the other is a nonresident alien who becomes a resident during the tax year, the couple may make a special election to file a joint return for that year and be taxed on their worldwide income. Thereafter, neither spouse may make the election again even if married to a new spouse. Tests for determining status as a resident or nonresident alien are at *1.17*.

Filing Tip

Claiming Dependents on Separate Returns

Married parents in community property states who plan to file separate returns should be aware that neither parent may be able to claim an exemption for a dependent child. Where all of the couple's income is considered community income, each parent on a separate return is treated as having provided exactly one-half of the child's support, regardless of who actually paid it. Since neither parent has provided more than one-half of the support, neither can claim the child as a dependent.

To avoid this result, parents whose sole income is community income and who want to file separately should consider signing a multiple support agreement, Form 2120, designating which parent may claim the exemption.

The IRS may disregard community property rules and tax income to a spouse who treats such income as if it were solely his or hers and who fails to notify the other spouse of the income before the due date of the return (including extensions).

Relief from liability on joint return. If you file jointly, you may elect to avoid liability under the innocent spouse rules discussed at *1.7* and the separate liability rules at *1.8*. In applying those rules, items that would otherwise be allocable solely to your spouse will not be partly allocated to you merely because of the community property laws.

Death of spouse. The death of a spouse dissolves the community property relationship, but income earned and accrued from community property before death is community income.

Moving from a community property to a common law (separate property) state. Most common law states (those which do not have community property laws) recognize that both spouses have an interest in property accumulated while residing in a community property state. If the property is not sold or reinvested, it may continue to be treated as community property. If you and your spouse sell community property after moving to a common law state and reinvest the proceeds, the reinvested proceeds are generally separate property, which you may hold as joint tenants or in another form of ownership recognized by common law states.

Moving from a common law to a community property state. Separate property brought into a community property state generally retains its character as separately owned property. However, property acquired by a couple after moving to a community property state is generally owned as community property. In at least one state (California), personal property that qualifies as community property is treated as such, even though it was acquired when the couple lived in a common law state.

Supporting a dependent with separate rather than community income. Filing a Form 2120 multiple support agreement is not necessary where either parent can prove that he or she has income that is considered separate income rather than community income; that parent may be able to satisfy the more-than-50% support test. In certain community property states, the law may provide that income of a husband and wife living apart is considered separate income rather than community income.

Avoiding or Limiting Liability on Joint Return

1.7 Innocent Spouse Rules

Whether you are still married to the spouse with whom you filed the joint return or you have since divorced or separated, you are liable as an individual for any tax due.

If you are still married and living with the same spouse, the only way to avoid personal liability on the joint return is to qualify as an innocent spouse under the rules in this section, or to apply for equitable relief from the IRS.

If you are divorced, legally separated, living apart, or your spouse has died, you may either seek relief under the innocent spouse rules or may be able to elect separate liability treatment as discussed at *1.8* or seek equitable relief from the IRS.

Qualifying tests for innocent spouse election. The 1998 Tax Act made it easier to qualify as an innocent spouse for small tax understatements by eliminating thresholds applied under prior law. Also, it is no longer necessary to show that deductions or credits claimed by the other spouse had no basis in fact or law. However, the "knowledge" test (*see* below) that barred many claims for relief under the old rules still applies, although the effect of the test is eased by a new rule allowing partial innocent spouse relief.

You must satisfy all of the following conditions to qualify for innocent spouse relief:

1. The tax on the joint return was understated due to the omission of income by your spouse, or erroneous deductions or credits claimed by your spouse.
2. When signing the joint return, you did not know and had no reason to know that tax on the return was understated.
   This same test applied under prior law. In applying the test, courts held that where relief is based on the omission of income by the other spouse, mere knowledge of the underlying transaction that produced the omitted income (such as knowledge of an investment held by your spouse in his own name) is enough to bar a claim for innocent spouse relief.

Caution

Knowledge May Bar Innocent Spouse Relief

Some spouses or former spouses may be able to rely on recent tax law changes to qualify for innocent spouse relief, but only if there was no knowledge that tax was understated on the joint return.

The Tax Court has held that knowledge of the underlying transaction alone is also enough to bar innocent spouse relief based on the other spouse's claim of improper deductions or credits. However, most appeals courts have held that in erroneous deduction cases, the issue is whether the spouse seeking relief knew or had reason to know that the deduction would result in a tax understatement, and this depends on his or her education level and involvement in the couple's financial affairs.

Although the "knowledge" test will continue to be a significant hurdle in some cases, the new law allows partial relief. If you knew or had reason to know that there was "some" tax understatement on the return but were unaware of the extent of the understatement, innocent spouse relief is available for the liability attributable to the portion of the understatement that you did not know about or have reason to know about.

3. Taking all the circumstances into account, it would be inequitable to hold you liable for the tax. This test also applied under prior law. In deciding the "equity" issue, the IRS and courts consider the extent to which you benefitted from the tax underpayment, beyond receiving normal support. Thus, it is possible to be held liable for a tax understatement that you did not know about or have reason to know about, on the grounds that you benefitted from the underpayment in the form of a high standard of living. The IRS will also consider whether you later divorced or were deserted by your spouse.

4. You file an innocent spouse election with the IRS, as discussed in the next paragraph.

Election must be filed to obtain relief. You must file an election on Form 8857 to claim innocent spouse relief. The election must be made no later than two years from the date that the IRS first begins collections activity against you for tax due on the joint return. If the election is not made by the end of that two-year period, you will not be granted innocent spouse relief even if you meet the above qualification tests.

A special transition rule applies if collection activities against you began before July 22, 1998, the date the new law took effect. In this case, the two-year period for making the election ends two years after the first collection activity occurring after July 22, 1998.

Tax Court appeal. If the IRS denies an election for innocent spouse relief, you have 90 days to petition the Tax Court for review under the rules discussed at *1.8*.

Did your spouse fail to pay the tax due on a correct return? Innocent spouse relief applies to tax understatements; that is, where the amount of tax shown on a joint return is incorrect. This form of relief is not available for tax underpayments, but the IRS can provide equitable relief where innocent spouse relief is unavailable and it would be unfair to hold you liable. *See* below.

Other equitable relief may be possible. The separate liability election and innocent spouse relief are not available where the proper amount of tax was reported on a joint return but your spouse failed to pay the tax owed. For example, you signed a correct return on which tax was owed and, without your knowledge, your spouse used the funds intended for payment of the tax for other purposes. Under the innocent spouse and separate liability election rules, you may not avoid liability for the taxes owed, but the IRS may grant equitable relief in this sort of case.

The IRS's discretion to grant equitable relief is not limited to the above situation, but the Service has indicated that it will consider requests for equitable relief only if:

1. Relief is not available under the innocent spouse or separate liability election rules.

2. The request is made on Form 8857 no later than two years after the IRS began collection proceedings against you, or within two years following the date of the first IRS collection action after July 22, 1998, if collection efforts began before that date.

3. Taxes are unpaid when the request for relief is made; refunds will only be granted in limited situations.

4. You and your spouse did not file the joint return or transfer assets to one another in order to avoid paying taxes or with fraudulent intent.

An ideal candidate for equitable relief is a person who is divorced, separated from, or has been living apart from his or her spouse for 12 months, who expected his or her spouse to pay taxes attributable to the spouse, and will suffer undue hardship if relief is not granted. However, the IRS will also consider other factors, such as that the couple is divorced or separated, that the requesting spouse was abused by the other spouse, that the other spouse is obligated to pay the tax liability under a divorce or separation agreement, or hardship to the requesting spouse. Relief will gener-

 Planning Reminder

Deadline for Innocent Spouse Election
You have until two years from the date that the IRS first attempts to collect tax from you on the joint return to make an innocent spouse election.

ally not be granted if the requesting spouse knew or had reason to know of the unpaid liability, the liability is attributable to the requesting spouse, the requesting spouse has the legal obligation to pay the tax under a divorce or separation agreement, or if the nonpayment of the liability by the other spouse provided the requesting spouse with benefits beyond normal support.

1.8 Separate Liability Election for Former Spouses

If the IRS attempts to collect the taxes due on a joint return from you and you have since divorced or separated, you may be able to avoid or at least limit your liability by filing a separate liability election with the IRS. If you qualify, you will be liable only for the part of the tax liability (plus interest and any penalties) that is allocable to you. If you make the election and a tax deficiency is entirely allocable to your former spouse under the rules discussed below, you will not have to pay any part of it.

Are you eligible for the separate liability election? You may make the separate liability election if at the time of the election:

1. You are divorced or legally separated from the spouse with whom you filed the joint return, *or*
2. You have not lived with your spouse (with whom you filed the return) at any time in the 12-month period ending on the date you file the election, *or*
3. The spouse with whom you filed the joint return has died.

If you qualify under any of the above, you may make the separate liability election. You may make the separate liability election in addition to the innocent spouse election *(1.7)*. Choose the method that provides the larger relief from liability on the joint return.

However, you may not avoid liability for any part of a tax deficiency allocable to the other spouse if you had actual knowledge that an item giving rise to his or her share of the liability was incorrectly reported on the return. *See* below for details of the knowledge test.

Furthermore, you may not avoid liability to the extent that certain disqualified property transfers were made between you and the other spouse. An election may be completely denied for both spouses if transfers were made as part of a fraudulent scheme.

Timing of the election. The separate liability election must be filed with the IRS on Form 8857 no later than two years after the IRS begins collection activities against you. If collections began before July 22,1998 (when the law took effect), the two-year election period ends two years after the date of the first IRS collection action after July 22, 1998.

Allocating tax liability between spouses. If you elect the separate liability limitation, you are liable only for the portion of the tax due on the joint return that is allocable to you. You are not responsible for the part of a tax deficiency allocable to the other spouse unless you had actual knowledge that the other spouse's reporting was incorrect. If you had such knowledge, you and the other spouse are both liable for part or all of a deficiency, in which case the IRS may collect the tax due from either of you individually.

Follow the instructions on Form 8857 for making the allocation. In general, the allocation of a tax deficiency depends on which spouse's "items" gave rise to the deficiency. The items may be omitted income or disallowed deductions or credits. Items are generally allocated to the spouse who would have reported them on a separate return. If a deficiency is based on unreported income, the deficiency is allocated to the spouse who earned the income. Income from a jointly owned business is allocated equally unless you provide evidence that more should be allocated to the other spouse. Similarly, if a deficiency is based on the denial of personal deductions, the deficiency is allocated equally between you unless you show that a different allocation is appropriate. A deficiency based on the denial of business deductions is allocated according to your respective ownership shares in the business. If the IRS can show fraud, it can reallocate joint return items.

> ### EXAMPLES
> 1. After you obtain a divorce, the IRS examines a joint return you filed with your former husband and assesses a tax deficiency attributable to income he failed to report. If you did not know about the omitted income and timely elect separate liability treatment, you are not liable for any part of the tax deficiency, which is entirely allocable to your former husband who earned the income. You are not liable even if the IRS is unable to

Caution

Actual Knowledge Bars Relief
The separate liability election generally allows you to avoid liability for the portion of a tax deficiency that is allocable to the other spouse. Such relief is unavailable, however, to the extent that you had actual knowledge that tax was understated on the return.

collect the tax from your former husband and you have substantial assets from which the tax could be paid.

2. The IRS assesses a joint return deficiency attributable to $35,000 of income that your former spouse failed to report and $15,000 of disallowed deductions that you claimed. Both of you may make the separate liability election and limit your respective liabilities.

If you make the election, your liability will be limited to 30% of the deficiency, as your disallowed deductions of $15,000 are 30% of the $50,000 of items causing the deficiency. If your former husband makes the election, he will be liable for the remaining 70% of the deficiency (his $35,000 of unreported income is 70% of the $50,000 of items causing the deficiency).

If either of you does not make the election, the non-electing person could be held liable for 100% of the deficiency unless innocent spouse relief is available or the IRS grants equitable relief.

Allocation of self-employment tax deficiency or deficiency attributable to disallowed credit. If a deficiency includes additional self-employment liability for one spouse, that liability is allocated first to the spouse before the rest of the deficiency is allocated. The same rule applies to the portion of a deficiency attributable to a disallowed tax credit that is allocable to one spouse.

For example, if the IRS determines a $7,200 income tax deficiency and a $2,800 self-employment tax deficiency, and the additional self-employment tax is due to your former spouse's omission of $20,000 of income from your joint return, the $2,800 self-employment tax deficiency is first allocated to your former spouse. Assume that the $7,200 income tax deficiency is based on the $20,000 of omitted income and also $5,000 of itemized deductions allocable to you. Your former spouse is liable for 80% of the $7,200 deficiency, or $5,760 ($20,000 ÷ $25,000 = 80%) and you are liable for the other 20%, or $1,440.

You may be liable because of income offset limitation. When a deduction or credit attributed to your former spouse is disallowed, you may be liable on part of a deficiency if the deduction or credit provides you with a tax benefit. A Congressional committee report gives the following example.

EXAMPLE

On a joint return, you report wages of $100,000 and your husband reports $15,000 of self-employment income. You divorce the following year. The IRS examines the return and disallows a $20,000 deduction claimed by your former husband, resulting in a $5,600 tax deficiency. As the disallowed $20,000 deduction entirely offsets the $15,000 of his income, and the $5,000 balance offsets part of your income, you received a tax benefit from the deduction. Your former husband will be liable for 75% of the deficiency ($4,200) and you will be liable for the 25% balance ($1,400).

If your former husband had reported income of $30,000 instead of $15,000, you would not be liable for any part of the deficiency under the separate liability election. The deduction is attributed entirely to his income, so that the entire deficiency is his.

Actual knowledge bars relief. If you elect separate liability treatment and the IRS shows that at the time you signed the joint return you had actual knowledge that an item allocable to your spouse was incorrectly reported, you may not avoid liability for the portion of a deficiency attributable to that item. However, if you signed the return under duress, separate liability is not barred despite your knowledge.

The actual knowledge test is intended by Congress to be more favorable to the taxpayer than the "had reason to know" test under the innocent spouse rules *(1.7)*. Congressional committee reports state that the IRS is required to prove that an electing spouse had actual knowledge that an item on the return was incorrect and may not infer such knowledge. If the IRS proves actual knowledge of an erroneous item, that item is treated as allocable to both spouses.

EXAMPLE

You file a joint return on which you report wages of $150,000 and your husband reports $30,000 of self-employment income. The IRS examines your return and determines that your husband failed to report $20,000 of income, resulting in a $9,000 deficiency. You file a separate liability election with the IRS after obtaining a divorce.

 Planning Pointer

Unpaid tax on correct return
The separate liability election is not available where the proper amount of tax was reported on a joint return but your spouse did not pay the tax. However, equitable relief may be available in this type of tax underpayment situation.

Assume that the IRS proves that you had actual knowledge of $5,000 of the unreported income but not the other $15,000. You are liable for 25% of the deficiency, or $2,250, allocable to the $5,000 of income that you knew about ($2,250 = $5,000 ÷ $20,000 × $9,000). Your former spouse is liable for the entire deficiency since the unreported income was his. The IRS can collect the entire deficiency from him, or can collect $2,250 from you and the balance from him.

Transfers intended to avoid tax. You may be held liable for more than your allocable share of a deficiency if a disqualified asset transfer was made to you by your spouse with a principal purpose of avoiding tax. Transfers made to you within the one-year period preceding the date on which the IRS sends the first letter of proposed deficiency are presumed to have a tax avoidance purpose unless they are pursuant to a divorce decree or decree of separate maintenance. You may rebut the presumption by showing that tax avoidance was not the principal purpose of the transfer. If the tax avoidance presumption is not rebutted, the transfer is considered a disqualified transfer and the value of the transferred asset adds to your share of the liability as otherwise determined under the above election rules.

If the IRS proves that you and your former spouse transferred assets between you as part of a fraudulent scheme, neither of you will be allowed to make the separate liability election; both of you will remain individually liable for the entire joint return deficiency.

Appeal to Tax Court. You may petition the Tax Court if the IRS disputes your election or your allocation of liability. The petition must be filed within 90 days of the date on which the IRS mails a determination to you by registered or certified mail if the IRS mailing is within six months of the filing of the election. If an IRS notice is not mailed within the six-month period, a Tax Court petition may be filed without waiting for an IRS response or, if you do wait, you have until 90 days after the date the IRS mails the notice to file the petition.

The IRS may not take any collection action against you during the 90-day period and if the Tax Court petition is filed, the suspension lasts until a final court decision is made.

How Widows and Widowers File

1.9 Death of Your Spouse in 1999

You do not lose the right to file a joint return when your spouse dies during the year. In general, a joint return is filed by you and the executor or administrator. But you alone may file a joint return if you are otherwise entitled to file jointly and:

1. The deceased did not file a separate return, and

2. Someone other than yourself has not been appointed as executor or administrator before the due date for filing the return. An executor or administrator appointed after the joint return is filed may revoke the joint return within the one-year period following the due date.

If you do file jointly, you include on the return all of your income and deductions for the full year and your deceased spouse's income and deductions *up to the date of death (see 1.13)*.

As a surviving spouse, you may not file a joint return for you and your deceased spouse if:

1. You remarry before the end of the year of your spouse's death. In this case you may file jointly with your new spouse. A final return for the deceased spouse must be filed by the executor or administrator using the filing status of married filing separately.

2. You or your deceased spouse has a short year because of a change in annual accounting period.

3. Either of you was a nonresident alien at any time during the tax year; but *see 1.5*.

Executor or administrator may revoke joint return. If an executor or administrator is later appointed, he or she may revoke a joint return that you alone have filed by filing a separate return for the decedent. Even if you have properly filed a joint return for you and the deceased spouse (as just discussed), the executor or administrator is given the right to revoke the joint return. But a state court held that a co-executrix could not refuse to sign a joint return where it would save the estate money.

To revoke the joint return, the executor must file a separate return within one year of the due date (including extensions). The executor's separate return is treated as a late return; interest charges and a late filing penalty apply. The joint return that you filed is deemed to be your separate return. Tax on that return is recalculated by excluding items belonging to your deceased spouse.

 Filing Instruction

Reporting Income of Deceased Spouse

If your spouse died during the year and you are filing a joint return, include his or her income earned through the date of death.

Signing the return. A joint return reporting your deceased spouse's income should list both of your names. Where there is an executor or administrator, the return is signed by you as the surviving spouse and the executor or administrator in his or her official capacity. If you are the executor or administrator, sign once as surviving spouse and again as the executor or administrator. Where there is no executor or administrator, you sign the return, followed by the words, "taxpayer and surviving spouse."

Surviving spouse's liability. If a joint return is filed and the estate cannot pay its share of the joint income tax liability, you, as the surviving spouse, may be liable for the full amount. Once the return is filed and the filing date passes, you can no longer change the joint return election and file a separate return unless an administrator or executor is appointed after the due date of the return.

In that case, as previously discussed, the executor may disaffirm the joint return.

1.10 Qualifying Widow(er) Status If Your Spouse Died in 1998 or 1997

If your spouse died in either 1997 or 1998 and you meet the following three requirements, your 1999 filing status is *qualifying widow or widower*, which allows you to use joint return rates on an individual return.

1. You did not remarry before 2000 (if you did remarry, you may file a 1999 joint return with your new spouse).
2. You may claim as your dependent (*see* Chapter 21) in 1999 a child, stepchild, adopted child, or foster child who lived with you during 1999 (except for temporary absences) and you paid over half the cost of maintaining your home.
3. You were able to file jointly in the year of your spouse's death, even if you did not do so.

If you meet all these tests and do not itemize deductions (Schedule A, Form 1040), use the standard deduction for married couples filing jointly *(13.1)*. Use the 1999 tax table or rate schedule for qualifying widows or widowers, the same schedule used by married couples filing jointly; *see 1.2.*

Spouse's death before 1997. If your spouse died before 1997 and you did not remarry before 2000, you may be able to use head of household rates for 1999 if you qualify under the rules of *1.11.*

Planning Reminder

Possible Estate Insolvency

If you will be appointed executor or administrator and are concerned about estate insolvency, it may be advisable to hedge as follows: (1) File separate returns. If it is later seen that a joint return is preferable, you have three years to change to a joint return. (2) File jointly but postpone being appointed executor or administrator until after the due date of the joint return. In this way, the joint return may be disaffirmed if the estate cannot cover its share of the taxes.

Filing as Head of Household

1.11 Qualifying as Head of Household

If you are unmarried at the end of 1999, maintain a household for a child, parent, or other relative, and are a U.S. citizen or resident *(see 1.17)* the entire year, you can file as "head of household." Tax rates are lower for a head of household than for a person filing as single *(see 1.2)* and the standard deduction is higher *(see* Chapter 13). If you are married but for the last half of 1999 you lived apart from your spouse, you may be treated as unmarried and able to qualify for head of household tax rates and standard deduction, which are more favorable than those for a married person filing separately; *see* Test 1 below.

Test 1. Are you unmarried? You are "unmarried" for 1999 head of household purposes if you are any one of the following:

- *Single as of the end of 1999.*
- *A widow or widower and your spouse died before 1999.* If a dependent child lives with you, *see 1.10* to determine if you may use the even more advantageous filing status of qualifying widow(er). If your spouse died in 1999, you are treated as married and cannot qualify as a 1999 head of household, but a joint return may be filed; *see 1.9.*
- *Legally separated or divorced under a final court decree as of the end of 1999.* A custody and support order does not qualify as a legal separation. A provisional decree (not final), such as a support order *pendente lite* (while action is pending) or a temporary order, has no effect for tax purposes until the decree is made final.
- *Married but living apart from your spouse.* You are considered unmarried for 1999 head of household purposes if your spouse was not a member of your household during the last six months of 1999, you file separate returns, and you maintain a household for more than half the year for a dependent child, stepchild, or adopted child. A foster child qualifies if he or she is a member of your household for the whole year. You must be able to claim the child as a dependent unless your spouse (the non-custodial parent) has the right to the exemption under the rules of *21.11.*

Filing Tip

Advantages of Head of Household Status

Tax rates are lower for a head of household than for those filing as single. The standard deduction is also higher. For a married person who lived apart from his or her spouse during the last half of the year, qualifying as a head of household allows use of tax rates that are more favorable than those for married persons filing separately.

• *Married to an individual who was a nonresident alien during any part of 1999 and you do not elect to file a joint return reporting your joint worldwide income (1.5).*

Test 2: Did you maintain a home for a qualifying relative? You must pay more than half of the costs of maintaining a household for a qualifying relative, and that relative must live with you in that home unless he or she is your parent. Your parent does not have to live with you, but you must pay more than half the costs of your parent's household, whether your parent lives alone, with someone else, or in a senior citizen residence.

Relative generally must be your dependent. The table below shows the relatives who may qualify you to claim head of household status. As the table shows, the relative generally must be your dependent, except for children and grandchildren who are unmarried as of the end of the year. Under another exception, if you are a divorced or separated parent of a *married* child and you meet the other tests, you may claim head of household status even though you waive the exemption for the child in favor of the other parent, or the other parent may claim the exemption under a pre-1985 agreement *(see 21.11).*

If you live apart from your spouse for the last six months of the year and maintain a home for a child, stepchild, adopted child, or foster child, the child, *whether married or unmarried,* must be your dependent unless the dependency exemption is claimed by the other parent because you have waived the exemption or the other parent is entitled to the exemption under a pre-1985 agreement *(21.11).*

QUALIFYING RELATIVES FOR HEAD OF HOUSEHOLD PURPOSES

Relationship	Does the Relative Have To Be Your Dependent?	Does the Relative Have To Live With You?
Unmarried child, stepchild or adopted child	**No***	Yes
Unmarried foster child	Yes	Yes
Unmarried grandchild or great-grand child	**No**	Yes
Married child, stepchild, adopted child, foster child, grandchild, or great-grandchild	Yes*	Yes
Parent	Yes	**No**
Step-parent	Yes	Yes
Grandparent	Yes	Yes
Brother, sister, half brother, half sister, stepbrother, stepsister	Yes	Yes
Father-in-law, mother-in-law	Yes	Yes
Son-in-law, daughter-in-law	Yes	Yes
If related by blood: uncle, aunt, niece, nephew	Yes	Yes

*See the text under "Relative generally must be your dependent," above, for a contrary rule that may apply in the case of divorced or legally separated parents, or parents living apart during the last half of the year.

 Filing Tip

Child May Be Head of Household

You may qualify as a head of household for filing purposes even if you are not head of the family. For example, a son who earns more than his father and contributes more than half of the cost of maintaining the family may qualify as a head of household. That the father, not the son, exercises family control does not matter. The important factor is a dollar test: whether the head of household for tax purposes contributed more than half the cost of maintaining the household that is his or her home and the principal home of the qualifying dependents.

EXAMPLE

Your mother lived with your sister in your sister's apartment, which cost $7,000 to maintain in 1999. Of this amount, you contributed $4,000 and your sister $3,000. Your mother has no income and did not contribute any funds to the household. You qualify as head of household: For 1999, you paid over half the cost of maintaining the home for your mother, who also qualifies as a dependent on your return. A child or dependent relative other than your parent would have to live with you to enable you to file as head of household.

Two-family house. A mother was allowed head of household status by the Tax Court in the following case. She and her unmarried daughter rented one floor of a multilevel home. A married daughter lived on a different floor with her family. Parts of the home were shared. According to the court, the mother was a head of household, based on support of her unmarried daughter. Although she did not pay more than half of the total household expenses, she paid more than half the expenses attributable to her and her unwed daughter.

Do you have to live in the home you maintain? You generally must pay more than half of the cost of a home that is your qualifying relative's principal residence for more than half the year. If your parent is the qualifying relative and he or she does not live with you, the home must be the parent's principal residence for the entire year. If the relative is not your parent, then, according to the IRS, the home you maintain for the relative must also be your principal residence for more than half the year. Some courts have held that the taxpayer must live for a "substantial" period of time in the same house as the dependent. An appeals court in one case allowed a mother to claim head of household status where she maintained a home for a child in one state and had her principal residence in another state. In the Example below, the Tax Court upheld the IRS position.

Costs of maintaining the household. You must pay for *more than half* of the property taxes, mortgage interest, rent, utility charges, upkeep and repairs, domestic help, property insurance, and food eaten in the household. Do not consider the rental value of the lodgings provided the dependent or clothing, education costs, medical expenses, vacation costs, life insurance premiums, transportation costs, and the value of your work around the house. However, these expenses may be considered in figuring your support contribution in determining whether you may claim the child or other relative as a dependent; *see 21.7.*

Caution

Multiple Support Agreement
You are *not* eligible for head of household status if the qualifying relative is your dependent only because you are allowed to claim the exemption under a multiple support agreement (Form 2210).

Household Costs for the Year

1. Property taxes $ _____
2. Mortgage interest _____
3. Rent paid _____
4. Property insurance _____
5. Utilities _____
6. Domestic help _____
7. Repairs and upkeep _____
8. Food eaten in the home _____
9. Total of Lines 1–8 _____
10. 50% of Line 9 $ _____

If you paid more than the amount on Line 10, you "maintain" the household for purposes of Test 2 on page 20.

EXAMPLE
Doctors advised McDonald that her mentally ill son might become self-sufficient if he lived in a separate residence, but one nearby enough for her to provide supervision. She took the advice and kept up a separate home for her son that was about a mile from her own home. She frequently spent nights at his home and he at hers. The Tax Court agreed with the IRS that McDonald could not file as head of household since her principal residence was not the same as her son's.

Temporary absences disregarded. In determining whether you and a dependent relative lived together for more than half the year, temporary absences are ignored if the absence is due to illness, or being away at school, on a business trip, on vacation, serving in the military, or staying with a parent under a child custody agreement. The IRS requires that it be reasonable to expect your qualifying child or dependent to return to your household after such a temporary absence, and that you continue to maintain the household during the temporary absence. Under this rule, you would lose the right to file as head of household if your dependent moved into his or her own permanent residence before the end of the year.

You may claim head of household status when your qualifying relative is confined to a hospital or a sanitarium and his or her absence is temporary and you continue to maintain a household in expectation of his or her return.

In the year a qualifying relative is born or dies, meeting the residence test for the portion of the year the dependent is alive allows you to claim head of household status.

Tax Returns for Children

1.12 Filing for Your Child

The income of your minor child is *not* included on your return unless you make a special election to report a child's investment income under the rules of *24.5*. A minor is considered a taxpayer in his or her own right. If the child is required to file a return but is unable to do so because of age or for any other reason, the parent or guardian is responsible for filing the return.

A tax return must be filed for a dependent child who had more than $700 of investment income and no earned income (for personal services). If your child had only earned income (for personal services) and no investment income, a tax return must be filed if the earned income exceeded $4,300.

If the child is unable to sign the return, the parent or guardian should sign the child's name in the proper place, followed by the words, "by [signature], parent [or guardian] for minor child." A parent is liable for tax due on pay earned by the child for services, but not on investment income.

A child who is not required to file a return should still do so for a refund of taxes withheld.

Social Security numbers. A parent or guardian must obtain a Social Security number for a child before filing the child's first income tax return. The child's Social Security number must also be provided to banks, brokers, and other payers of interest and dividends to avoid penalties and backup withholding; *see 26.12*. To obtain a Social Security number, file Form SS-5 with your local Social Security office. If you have applied for a Social Security number but not yet received it by the filing due date, write "applied for" on the tax return in the space provided for the number.

Whether or not you are filing a return for a child, you must obtain and report on your return a Social Security number for a child whom you are claiming as a dependent; *see 21.14*.

Wages you pay your children. You may deduct wages paid to your children in your business. Keep records showing that their activities are of a business rather than personal nature.

Withholding for children. Children with wages are generally subject to withholding and should file Form W-4 with their employer. An exemption from withholding may be claimed only in limited cases. For example, in 1999, a child with any investment income who expected to be claimed as another taxpayer's dependent could claim an exemption from withholding only if the expected amount of investment income plus wages was $700 or less (this amount may change annually). Furthermore, the child must certify on Form W-4 that he or she had no federal tax liability in the prior year and expects no liability in the current year for which the withholding exemption is sought.

Wages you pay to your own children under age 18 for working in your business are not subject to FICA taxes (Social Security and Medicare); *see 26.10*.

Filing Tip

Kiddie Tax for Children Under Age 14

Children who are under age 14 at the end of 1999 generally must use Form 8615 to figure their 1999 tax if they had more than $1,400 of investment income; see 24.3. On Form 8615, the investment earnings over $1,400 are taxed at the parent's top tax rate. However, in certain cases under the rules of 24.5, parents may elect to report their children's investment income on their own return using Form 8814.

Filing for a Deceased or Incompetent Person

1.13 Return for Deceased

When a person dies, another tax-paying entity is created—the decedent's estate. Until the estate is fully distributed, it will generally earn income for which a return must be filed. For example, Carlos Perez dies on June 30, 1999. The wages and bank interest he earned through June 30 are reported on his final income tax return, Form 1040, which is due by April 17, 2000. Income earned on the bank account from July 1 is attributed to the estate. The income must be reported by the estate on Form 1041, the income tax return for the estate, if the estate has gross income of $600 or more.

What income tax returns must be filed? If the individual died after the close of the taxable year but before the income tax return was filed, the following must be filed:

1. Income tax return for the prior year;
2. Final income tax return, covering earnings in the period from the beginning of the taxable year to the date of death; *and*
3. Estate income tax return, covering earnings in the period after the decedent's death.

If the individual died after filing a return for the prior tax year, then only 2 and 3 are filed.

> **EXAMPLE**
>
> Steven Jones died on March 31, 2000, before he could file his 1999 tax return. The 1999 income tax return must be filed by April 17, 2000. A final income tax return to report earnings from January 1, 2000, through March 31, 2000, will have to be filed on April 16, 2001.

Jones's estate will have to file an income tax return on Form 1041 to report earnings and other income that were not earned by Jones before April 1, 2000, unless the gross income of the estate is under $600.

Who is responsible for filing? The executor, administrator, or other legal representative is responsible for filing all returns. For purposes of determining whether a final income tax return for the decedent is due, the annual gross income test at page 2 is considered in full. You do not prorate it according to the part of the year the decedent lived. A surviving spouse may assume responsibility for filing a joint return for the year of death if no executor or administrator has been appointed and other tests are met *(1.9)*. However, if a legal representative has been appointed, he or she must give the surviving spouse consent to file a joint return for the year of the decedent's death. In one case, a state court held that a co-executrix could not refuse consent and was required to sign a joint return where it would save the estate money.

How do you report the decedent's income and deductions? You follow the method used by the decedent during his or her life to account for the income up to the date of death. The income does not have to be put on an annual basis. Each item is taxed in the same manner as it would have been taxed had the decedent lived for the entire year.

If the decedent owned U.S. Savings Bonds, *see 4.29*.

When one spouse dies in a community property state *(1.6)*, how should the income from the community property be reported during the administration of the estate? The IRS says that half the income is the estate's and the other half belongs to the surviving spouse.

Medical expenses of the decedent. If the estate pays the decedent's medical expenses within one year of the date of death, the expenses can be deducted on the decedent's last return, subject to the regular 7.5% of adjusted gross income floor *(17.8)*. However, the expenses are not deductible for income tax purposes if they are deducted for estate tax purposes. To deduct such medical expenses on the decedent's last return, a statement must be filed affirming that no estate tax deduction has been taken and that the rights to the deduction have been waived.

Partnership income. The final return includes partnership income or loss only from a partnership year that ends within the decedent's tax year. Thus, if a partner dies in July 1999 and the partnership's taxable year ends December 31, 1999, no partnership income or loss is included on the partner's final 1999 return. It is reported by the partner's executor or other successor in interest on the estate's income tax return.

Exemptions allowed on a final return. These are generally the same exemptions the decedent would have had if he or she had not died. You do not reduce the exemptions because of the shorter taxable year. If the deceased had contributed more than one-half of a dependent's annual support, a dependency exemption is claimed on his or her final return.

Estimated taxes. No estimated tax need be paid by the executor after the death of an unmarried individual; the entire tax is paid when filing the final tax return. But where the deceased and a surviving spouse paid estimated tax jointly, the rule is different. The surviving spouse is still liable for the balance of the estimated tax unless an amended estimated tax voucher is filed. Further, if the surviving spouse plans to file a joint return *(1.9)* that includes the decedent's income, estimated tax payments may be required; *see* Chapter 27.

Where the estate has gross income, estimated tax installments are not required on Form 1041-ES for the first two years after the decedent's death.

Signing the return. An executor or administrator of the estate signs the return. If it is a joint return, *see 1.9*.

When a refund is due on a final return. The decedent's final return may also be used as a claim for a refund of an overpayment of withheld or estimated taxes. Form 1310 may be used to get the refund, but the form is not required if you are a surviving spouse filing a joint return for the year your spouse died. If you are an executor or administrator of the estate and you are filing Form 1040, 1040A, or 1040EZ for the decedent, you do not need Form 1310, but you must attach to the return a copy of the court certificate showing your appointment as personal representative.

1.14 Return for an Incompetent Person

A legal guardian of an incompetent person files Form 1040 for an incompetent whose gross income meets the filing tests on page 2. Where a spouse becomes incompetent, the IRS says the other spouse may file a return for the incompetent without a power of attorney, if no legal guardian has

Filing Instruction

Decedent's Final Return

Do not report on the decedent's final return income that is received after his or her death, or accrues after or because of death if the decedent used the accrual method. This income is considered "income in respect of a decedent," and is taxed to the estate or beneficiary receiving the income in the year of the receipt. On the decedent's final return, only deductible expenses paid up to and including the date of death may be claimed. If the decedent reported on the accrual basis, those deductions accruable up to and including the date of death are deductible. If a check for payment of a deductible item was delivered or mailed before the date of the decedent's death, a deduction is allowable on the decedent's last return, even though the check was not cashed or deposited until after the decedent's death. If the check was not honored by the bank, the item is not deductible.

Planning Reminder

Promptly Closing the Estate

To expedite the closing of the decedent's estate, an executor or other personal representative of the decedent may file Form 4810 for a prompt assessment. Once filed, the IRS has 18 months to assess additional taxes. Without making the request, the IRS has three years from the due date of the return to make assessments. Form 4810 must be filed separately from the final return, but should be sent to the District Director for the IRS district in which the return is filed.

been appointed. For example, during the period an individual was in a mental hospital, and before he was adjudged legally incompetent, his wife continued to operate his business. She filed an income tax return for him and signed it for him although she had no power of attorney. The IRS accepted the return as properly filed. Until a legal guardian was appointed, she was charged with the care of her husband and his property.

The IRS has accepted a joint return filed by a wife in her capacity as legal guardian for her missing husband. However, the Tax Court has held that where one spouse is mentally incompetent, a joint return may not be filed because the incompetent spouse was unable to consent to a joint return; an appeals court agreed.

How Resident and Nonresident Aliens File

1.15 How a Nonresident Alien Is Taxed

A *nonresident* alien is generally taxed only on income from U.S. sources. A nonresident alien's income that is *effectively connected* with a U.S. business or capital gains from the sale of U.S. real estate are subject to tax at regular U.S. rates. Other capital gains are not taxed unless a nonresident alien has a U.S. business or is in the U.S. for 183 days during the year. Generally, investment income of a nonresident alien from U.S. sources that is *not effectively connected* with a U.S. business is subject to a 30% tax rate (or lower rate if provided by treaty).

Nonresident aliens who are required to file must do so on Form 1040NR. If you are a nonresident alien, get a copy of IRS Publication 519, U.S. Tax Guide for Aliens. It explains how nonresident aliens pay U.S. tax.

Dual status. In the year a person arrives in or departs from the U.S., both resident and nonresident status may apply.

EXAMPLE

On May 1, 1999, Leon Marchand arrived on a non-immigrant visa and was present in the U.S. for the rest of the year. From January 1 to April 31, 1999, he is a nonresident; from May 1 to the end of the year, he is a resident, under the 183-day test *(1.17)*. Despite "dual status," he does not file two returns. Since he is a U.S. resident on the last day of the year, he files Form 1040 and reports income on the basis of his status for each part of the year. The income for the nonresident portion of the year should be shown on a separate schedule.

Certain restrictions apply to dual status taxpayers. For example, a joint return may not be filed, unless you and your spouse agree to be taxed as U.S. residents for the entire year.

For details on filing a return for a dual status year, *see* IRS Publication 519 and the instructions to Form 1040NR.

1.16 How a Resident Alien Is Taxed

A resident alien is taxed on worldwide income from all sources, just like a U.S. citizen. The exclusion for foreign earned income may be claimed if the foreign physical presence test is satisfied or if the bona fide residence test is met by an individual residing in a treaty country; *see 36.5.* A resident alien may generally claim a foreign tax credit; *see 36.14.* A resident alien's pension from a foreign government is subject to regular U.S. tax. A resident alien working in the United States for a foreign government is not taxed on the wages if the foreign government allows a similar exemption to U.S. citizens.

1.17 Who Is a Resident Alien?

The following tests determine whether an alien is taxed as a U.S. resident. Intent to remain in the U.S. is not considered.

You are treated as a resident alien and taxed as a U.S. resident if you meet either of the following tests for 1999:

1. You have been issued a "green card," which grants you the status of lawful permanent resident. If you were outside the U.S. for part of 1999 and then became a lawful permanent resident, *see* the rules for dual tax status on the next page.
2. You meet a 183-day substantial presence test. Under this test, you are treated as a U.S. resident if you were in the U.S. for at least 31 days during the calendar year and have been in the U.S. for 183 days within the last three years (the current year and the two preceding calendar years). The 183-day test is complicated and there are several exceptions.

Caution

Who Is a Resident?
An alien's mere presence in the U.S. does not make him or her a "resident." An alien is generally treated as a "resident" only if he or she is a lawful permanent resident who has a "green card" or meets a substantial presence test; *see 1.17.*

To determine if you meet the 183-day test for 1999, the following cumulative times are totaled. Each day in the U.S. during 1999 is counted as a full day. Each day in 1998 counts as $\frac{1}{3}$ of a day; each day in 1997 counts as $\frac{1}{6}$ of a day. Note that you must be physically present in the U.S. for at least 31 days in the current year. If you are not, the 183-day test does not apply.

Other exceptions to the substantial presence test are: commuting from Canada or Mexico; keeping a tax home and close contacts or connections in a foreign country; having a diplomat, teacher, trainee, or student status; being a professional athlete temporarily in the U.S. to compete in a charitable sports event; or being confined in the U.S. for certain medical reasons. These exceptions are explained in the following paragraphs.

Commute from Mexico or Canada. If you regularly commute to work in the U.S. from Mexico or Canada, commuting days do not count as days of physical presence for the 183-day test.

Tax home/closer connection exception. If you are in the United States for less than 183 days during 1999, show that you had a closer connection with a foreign country than with the U.S., and keep a tax home there for the year, you generally will not be subject to tax as a U.S. resident under the substantial presence test. Under this exception, it is possible to have a U.S. abode and a tax home in a foreign country. A tax home is usually where a person has his or her principal place of business; if there is no principal place of business, it is the place of regular abode. Proving a tax home alone is not sufficient; the closer connection relationship must also be shown.

To claim the closer connection exception, you must file Form 8840 explaining the basis of your claim. The tax home/closer connection test does not apply to an alien who is present for 183 days or more during a year or who has applied for a "green card." A relative's application is not considered as the alien's application.

Exempt-person exception. Days of presence in the U.S. are not counted under the 183-day test if you are considered an exempt person such as a teacher, trainee, student, foreign government-related person, or professional athlete temporarily in the U.S. to compete in a charitable sports event.

To exclude days of presence as a teacher, trainee, student, or professional athlete, you must file Form 8843 with the IRS.

A foreign government-related person is any individual temporarily present in the U.S. who (1) has diplomatic status or a visa that the Secretary of the Treasury (after consultation with the Secretary of State) determined represents full-time diplomatic or consular status; or (2) is a full-time employee of an international organization; or (3) is a member of the immediate family of a diplomat or international organization employee.

A teacher or trainee is any individual other than a student who is temporarily present in the U.S. under a "J" or "Q" visa and who substantially complies with the requirements for being so present.

A student is any individual who is temporarily present in the U.S. under either an "F," "J," "M," or "Q" visa and who substantially complies with the requirements for being so present.

The exception generally does not apply to a teacher or trainee who has been exempt as a teacher, trainee, or student for any part of two of the six preceding calendar years. However, if during the period you are temporarily present in the U.S. under an "F," "J," "M," or "Q" visa and all of your compensation is received from outside the U.S., you may qualify for the exception if you were exempt as a teacher, trainee, or student for less than four years in the six preceding calendar years. The exception also does not apply to a student who has been exempt as a teacher, trainee, or student for more than five calendar years, unless you show that you do not intend to reside permanently in the U.S. and that you have substantially complied with the requirements of the student visa providing for temporary presence in the U.S.

Medical exception. If you plan to leave but cannot physically leave the U.S. because of a medical condition that arose in the U.S., you may be treated as a nonresident, even if present here for more than 183 days during the year. You must file Form 8843 to claim the medical exception.

Tax treaty exceptions. The lawful permanent residence test and the substantial physical presence test do not override tax treaty definitions of residence. Thus, you may be protected by a tax treaty from being treated as a U.S. resident even if you would be treated as a resident under either test.

Dual tax status in first year of residency. If you first became a lawful permanent resident of the U.S. (received a green card) during 1999 and were not a U.S. resident during 1998, your period of U.S. residency begins with the first day in 1999 that you are present in the U.S. with the status of lawful permanent resident. Before that date, you are a nonresident alien. This means that if you become a lawful permanent resident after January 1, 1999, you have a dual status tax year. On Form 1040, you attach a separate schedule showing the income for the part of the year you are a nonresident.

 Planning Reminder

Is 1999 First Year of Residency?
If you were not a resident during 1998 but in 1999 you satisfy both the lawful resident (green card) test and the 183-day presence test, your residence begins on the earlier of the first day you are in the U.S. while a lawful permanent resident and the first day of physical presence.

To figure tax for a dual status year, *see* IRS Publication 519 and the instructions to Form 1040NR.

You also may have a dual status year if you were not a U.S. resident in 1998, and in 1999 you are a U.S. resident under the 183-day presence test. Your period of U.S. residency starts on the first day in 1999 for which you were physically present; before that date you are treated as a nonresident alien. However, if you meet the 183-day presence test (but not the green card test) and also spent 10 or fewer days in the U.S. during a period in which you had a closer connection to a foreign country than to the U.S., you may disregard the 10-day period. The purpose of this exception is to allow a brief presence in the U.S. for business trips or house hunting before the U.S. residency period starts.

EXAMPLES

1. Manuel Riveras, who has never before been a U.S. resident, lives in Spain until May 15, 1999. He moves to the U.S. and remains in the U.S. through the end of the year, thereby satisfying the physical presence test. On May 15, he is a U.S. resident. However, for the period before May 15, he is taxed as a nonresident.
2. Same facts as in Example 1, but Riveras attends a meeting in the U.S. on February 2 through 8. On May 15, he moves to the U.S.; May 15, not February 2, is the starting date of the residency. During February, he had closer connection to Spain than to the U.S. Thus, his short stay in February is an exempt period.

First-year choice. If you do not meet either the green card test or the 183-day substantial presence test for the year of your arrival in the U.S. or for the immediately preceding year, but you do meet the substantial presence test for the year immediately following the year of your arrival, you may elect to be treated as a U.S. resident for part of the year of your arrival. To do this, you must (1) be present in the U.S. for at least 31 consecutive days in the year of your arrival; and (2) be present in the U.S. for at least 75% of the number of days beginning with the first day of the 31-consecutive-day period and ending with the last day of the year of arrival. For purposes of this 75% requirement, you may treat up to five days of absence from the U.S. as days of presence within the U.S.

Do not count as days of presence in the U.S. days for which you are an *exempt individual* as discussed earlier.

You make the first-year election to be treated as a U.S. resident by attaching a statement to Form 1040 for the year of your arrival. A first-year election, once made, may not be revoked without the consent of the Internal Revenue Service.

If you make the election, your residence starting date for the year of your arrival is the first day of the earliest 31-consecutive-day period of presence that you use to qualify for the choice. You are treated as a U.S. resident for the remainder of the year.

Last year of residence. You are no longer treated as a U.S. resident as of your *residency termination date*. If you do not have a green card but are a U.S. resident for the year under the 183-day presence test, and you leave the U.S. during that year, your residency termination date is the last day you are present in the U.S., provided that: (1) after leaving the U.S. you had a closer connection to a foreign country than to the U.S. and had your tax home in that foreign country for the rest of the year, and (2) you are not treated as a U.S. resident for any part of the next calendar year.

If during the year you give up your green card (lawful permanent resident status) and meet tests (1) and (2), your residency termination date is the first day that you are no longer a lawful permanent resident. If during the year you meet both the green card test and the 183-day presence test and meet tests (1) and (2), your residency termination date is the *later* of the last day of U.S. presence or the first day you are no longer a lawful permanent resident. If tests (1) and (2) are not met, the residency termination date is the last day of the calendar year. In the year of your residency termination date, the filing rules for dual status taxpayers at *1.15* apply.

1.18 When an Alien Leaves the United States

Current law generally requires an alien who leaves the U.S., regardless of how long the trip is, to obtain a "sailing" or "departure" permit, technically known as a "certificate of compliance." The permit states that you have fulfilled your income tax obligations to the U.S. Without it, unless you are excused from obtaining one, you will be required at your point of departure to file a tax return and pay any tax due or post a bond. Diplomats, employees of international organizations or foreign governments, and students are generally exempt from the permit requirement. You should apply for a sailing permit from your local District Director of Internal Revenue about two weeks, but no earlier than 30 days, before your departure. See IRS Form 1040-C and Publication 519 for further details.

Planning Reminder

Departure Permit

An alien planning to leave the U.S. should obtain a copy of Form 1040-C from the IRS to review his or her tax reporting obligations.

1.19 Expatriation Tax

Special tax rules apply to U.S. citizens who renounce their citizenship and long-term residents who end their residency if tax avoidance is one of their principal purposes for leaving. For a 10-year period, such individuals are subject to regular U.S. tax on income and gains from U.S. sources. A long-term resident is someone who was a lawful permanent resident (with a green card) in at least eight of the last 15 years ending with the last year of residency.

The law presumes a tax avoidance purpose in certain cases. For 1999, tax avoidance is presumed if (1) the departing individual's average net income tax for the last five years before losing citizenship or terminating residency was more than $110,000 or (2) net worth when citizenship or residency ended was $552,000 or more. These dollar amounts are subject to annual adjustments for inflation. To rebut the presumption of a tax avoidance purpose, a ruling request may be submitted to the IRS; *see* IRS Notice 98-34 for details of the ruling procedure.

All individuals who lose their citizenship or who end long-term residency must file information statements with the federal government; *see* IRS Publication 519.

Reporting Your Income

In this part, you will learn what income is taxable what income is tax free, and how to report income on your tax return.

Pay special attention to—

- Form W-2, which shows your taxable wages and provides other important information on fringe benefits received (Chapter 2).
- Tax-free fringe benefit plans available from your employer (Chapter 3).
- Reporting rules for interest and dividend income (Chapter 4).
- Reporting gains and losses from sales of property. (Chapter 5).
- Rules for tax-free exchanges of like-kind property (Chapter 6).
- Planning for retirement distributions. Lump-sum distributions from employer plans may qualify for special averaging or tax-free rollover (Chapter 7).
- IRA contributions and distributions. Penalties for distributions before age 59 $\frac{1}{2}$ and after age 70 $\frac{1}{2}$ may be avoided by advance planning (Chapter 8).
- Restrictions on rental losses where a rented residence is used personally by you or by family members during the year (Chapter 9).
- Passive activity restrictions. Losses from rentals or passive business operations are generally not allowed, but certain real estate professionals are exempt from the loss restrictions, and for others, a special rental loss allowance of up to $25,000 may be available (Chapter 10).
- Reporting refunds of state and local taxes. A refund of previously deducted taxes is generally taxable unless you had no benefit from the deduction (Chapter 11).
- Cancellation of debts. When your creditor cancels debts you owe, you generally have taxable income, but there are exceptions for debts discharged while you are bankrupt or insolvent (Chapter 11).
- Damages received in court proceedings. Learn when these are tax free and when taxable (Chapter 11).

Taxable Wages, Salary, and Other Compensation

Except for tax-free fringe benefits (*see* Chapter 3), practically everything you receive for your work or services is taxed, whether paid in cash, property, or services. Your employer will generally report your taxable compensation on Form W-2 and other information returns, such as Form 1099-R for certain retirement payments. Do not reduce the amount you report on your return by withholdings for income taxes, Social Security taxes, union dues, or U.S. Savings Bond purchases. Your Form W-2 does not include in taxable pay your qualifying salary-reduction contributions to a retirement plan, although the amount may be shown on the form.

Attach Copy B of Form W-2 to your return; do not attach Forms 1099 unless there are withholdings.

Unemployment benefits are fully taxable. The benefits are reported to the IRS on Form 1099-G. You do not have to attach your copy of Form 1099-G to your return.

Income and expenses from self-employment are discussed in Chapter 40.

Reporting Compensation

Disability and Workers' Compensation

Pay Plans for Executives

Also refer to:

Key to Your Form W-2

Amount in—	What You Should Know—
Box 1	***Taxable wages and tips.*** Your taxable wages and tips are listed in Box 1. Taxable fringe benefits that may be shown in Box 12 will also be included in Box 1 as other compensation. The value of tax-free fringe benefits is not shown on Form W-2. Mileage or per diem travel allowances will not be reported in Box 1 as taxable wages unless they exceed the IRS rate. *See* the discussion of Box 13, below. Do not decrease the amount shown in Box 1 by the amount your employer withholds for income taxes, Social Security taxes, disability insurance payments, hospitalization insurance premiums, U.S. Savings Bonds, union dues, or payments to a creditor who has attached your salary. Box 1 does not include salary reduction contributions to a retirement plan. Compensation shown in Box 1 must be reported on Line 7 of Form 1040 or 1040A, or Line 1 of Form 1040EZ.
Box 2	***Federal tax withholdings.*** This is the amount of federal income tax withheld from your pay. Enter the amount on Line 57, Form 1040, Line 35, Form 1040A, or on Line 7, Form 1040EZ. If the withheld amount plus your estimated tax installments exceeds your tax liability, you are entitled to a refund for the excess payments.
Boxes 3, 4, and 7	***Social Security withholdings.*** Withholdings for Social Security coverage are at a rate of 6.2% on up to $72,600 of 1999 wages and tips. If your wages were $72,600 or more, Box 4 should show the maximum tax of $4,501.20. If you worked for more than one employer and a total of more than $4,501.20 was withheld for Social Security taxes, you claim the excess as a tax payment on your tax return; *see 26.10.* Wages subject to Social Security withholdings are shown in Box 3. Elective salary deferrals to a 401(k) plan or SIMPLE plan are included; Social Security withholding applies, although the deferrals are not subject to income tax and are not included in Box 1. Similarly, employer payments of qualified adoption expenses (Chapter 3) are included in Box 3 although not included in Box 1 taxable wages. Tips you reported to your employer are shown separately in Box 7. The total of Boxes 3 and 7 should not exceed $72,600.
Boxes 5–6	***Medicare tax withholdings.*** Wages, tips, elective salary deferrals, and employer-paid adoption expenses subject to Social Security tax (Boxes 3 and 7) are also subject to a 1.45% Medicare tax, except that there is no wage base limit for Medicare tax. Thus, the Medicare wages shown in Box 5 are not limited to the $72,600 maximum for Box 3. For example, if your wages were $100,000, the amount shown in Box 3 (Social Security wages) would be $72,600, but in Box 5, the full $100,000 would be reported. In Box 6, total Medicare withholdings are reported. On wages of $100,000, the Medicare tax would be $1,450 (1.45% × $100,000).
Box 8	***Allocated tips.*** If you worked in a restaurant employing at least 10 people, your employer will report in Box 8 your share of 8% of gross receipts unless you reported tips at least equal to that share *(26.8)*. The amount shown here is not included in Box 1 wages, but you must add it to wages on Line 7 of Form 1040; you cannot file Form 1040A or 1040EZ.
Box 9	***Advance earned income payment.*** If you filed a Form W-5 asking for a part of the credit to be added to your wages, the amount of the advance is shown in Box 9. You report the advance as a tax liability when you file Form 1040 or 1040A. *See* Chapter 25 for details on claiming the earned income credit for 1999, and for advance earned income payments.
Box 10	***Dependent care benefits.*** Reimbursements from your employer for dependent care expenses and the value of employer-provided care services under a qualifying plan *(3.4)* are included in Box 10. Amounts in excess of $5,000 are also included as taxable wages in Boxes 1, 3, and 5. Generally, amounts up to $5,000 are tax free, but you must determine the amount of the exclusion on Form 2441 if you file Form 1040, or on Schedule 2 if you file Form 1040A. The tax-free amount reduces expenses eligible for the dependent care credit; *see* Chapter 25.
Box 11	***Nonqualified plan distributions.*** Distributions shown in Box 11 are from a nonqualified deferred compensation plan, or a Section 457 plan *(7.21)*. Do not report these distributions separately since they have already been included as taxable wages in Box 1.
Box 12	***Taxable fringe benefits.*** If you received taxable fringe benefits, your employer has the option to show the amount in Box 12 unless it is reportable in Box 10 or Box 13. The lease value of using a company car *(3.7)* must be included in Box 12 if your employer pays the entire cost of the car. Do not separately report the Box 12 amount as income, since it has already been included in Box 1 as taxable wages.

Box 13	***Elective deferrals to retirement plans.*** If you made elective salary deferrals to an employer retirement plan, Box 15, "deferred compensation," will be checked and your contribution (including any excess over the annual deferral limit) is shown in Box 13. Deferrals to a 401(k) plan *(7.18)* should be labeled with Code D. For example, if you made pre-tax salary deferrals of $4,500 to a 401(k) plan, your employer would enter D 4,500.00 in Box 13. Code E is used for deferrals to a 403(b) tax-sheltered annuity plan *(7.20)*, Code F for deferrals to a simplified employee pension *(8.16)*, Code G for deferrals (including non-elective as well as elective) to a Section 457 plan *(7.21)*, Code H for elective deferrals to a pension plan created before June 25, 1959, and funded only by employee contributions, and Code S for salary-reduction deferrals to a SIMPLE IRA *(8.18)*.

Travel allowance reimbursements. If you received a flat mileage allowance from your employer for business trips *(20.33)*; or a per diem travel allowance to cover meals, lodging, and incidentals *(20.32)*; and the allowance exceeded the IRS rate, the amount up to the IRS rate (the nontaxable portion) is shown in Box 13 using Code L. The excess is included as taxable wages in Box 1.

Group-term life insurance over $50,000. The cost of coverage over $50,000 is taxable. It is shown in Box 13 using Code C. It is also included in Box 1 wages, Box 3 Social Security wages, and Box 5 Medicare wages and tips.

    If you are a retiree or other former employee who received group-term coverage over $50,000, any uncollected Social Security tax is shown using Code M and uncollected Medicare tax using Code N. The uncollected amount must be reported on Line 56 of Form 1040 (total tax); write "uncollected tax" next to it.

Nontaxable sick pay. If you contributed to a sick pay plan, an allocable portion of benefits received is tax free and is shown using Code J.

Uncollected Social Security and Medicare taxes on tips. If your employer could not withhold sufficient Social Security on tips, the uncollected amount is shown using Code A. For uncollected Medicare tax, Code B is used. This amount must be reported on Line 56 of Form 1040 (total tax); write "uncollected tax" next to it.

Excess golden parachute payments. If you received an "excess parachute payment as wages," Code K identifies the 20% penalty tax on the excess payment that was withheld by the employer. This withheld amount is included in Box 2, but you also must add it as an additional tax on Line 56 (total tax) of Form 1040.

Moving expense reimbursements. Tax-free employer reimbursements to you for deductible moving expenses (Chapter 12) are shown with Code P.

Employer contributions to medical savings account (MSA). Total employer contributions to a medical savings account are shown with Code R. Contributions exceeding the excludable limit (Chapter 3) are included as taxable wages in Box 1.

Employer-financed adoption benefits. With Code T, your employer shows qualified adoption expenses paid by the employer *(3.5)* or pre-tax contributions you made to an adoption plan account under a cafeteria plan *(3.13)*. |
| **Box 14** | ***Miscellaneous payments.*** Your employer may use Box 14 to report payments such as union dues, educational assistance, health insurance premiums, or voluntary after-tax contributions to profit-sharing or pension plans. |
| **Box 15** | ***Statutory employee.*** If this box is checked you get a tax break. You report your wage income and deductible job expenses on Schedule C *(see 40.6)*. This treatment allows you to avoid the 2% adjusted gross income (AGI) floor that applies to job expenses reported on Schedule A. *See 40.6.* Your earnings are not subject to income tax withholding, but are subject to Social Security and Medicare taxes.

Pension plan. If the box "pension plan" is checked, this indicates that you were an active participant in an employer plan at some point during the year. As an active participant, you may be unable to make deductible IRA contributions; IRA deductions start to phase out if your AGI exceeds $31,000 (single) or $51,000 (married filing jointly); *see* Chapter 8.

Deferred compensation. The box "deferred compensation" is checked if you made salary deferrals to a 401(k) plan *(7.18)*, tax-sheltered 403(b) annuity *(7.20)*, SIMPLE IRA *(8.18)*, or simplified employee pension plan *(8.16)*. In Box 13, the employer lists the total elective deferrals to these plans. |
| **Boxes 18 and 21** | ***State and local taxes.*** If you itemize, deduct on Schedule A state and local tax withholdings shown in Boxes 18 and 21. |

Sample Form W-2

You should receive your Form W-2 for 1999 from your employer by January 31, 2000.
Note: Box 3 below includes the wages in Box 1 plus $1,000
401(k) elective deferral shown in Box 13 with Code D; *see* the
Key to Your Form W-2 on the preceding pages.

a Control number		OMB No. 1545-0008		
b Employer identification number **08-X1X0X1X**			1 Wages, tips, other compensation **35,000**	2 Federal income tax withheld **5,250**
c Employer's name, address, and ZIP code **Finkle Construction Co. 5532 Glasgow Plaza City, State XX111**			3 Social security wages **36,000**	4 Social security tax withheld **2,232**
			5 Medicare wages and tips **36,000**	6 Medicare tax withheld **522**
			7 Social security tips	8 Allocated tips
d Employee's social security number **0X1-XX-1X00**			9 Advance EIC payment	10 Dependent care benefits
e Employee's name, address, and ZIP code **Mary Moll 176 Garden Road City, State 1XXX1**			11 Nonqualified plans	12 Benefits included in box 1 **1,500**
			13 See instrs. for box 13 **D 1,000**	14 Other

15 Statutory employee ☐	Deceased ☐	Pension plan ☐	Legal rep. ☐	Deferred compensation ☐

16 State	Employer's state I.D. no.	17 State wages, tips, etc.	18 State income tax	19 Locality name	20 Local wages, tips, etc.	21 Local income tax
State	**11-X1X 0X1X**	**35,000**	**1,580**	**City**	**35,000**	**765**

Form **W-2** Wage and Tax Statement **1999**

Copy B To Be Filed With Employee's FEDERAL Tax Return

Department of the Treasury—Internal Revenue Service

This information is being furnished to the Internal Revenue Service.

Reporting Compensation

2.1 Salary and Wage Income

The key to reporting your pay is Form W-2, sent to you by your employer. It lists your taxable wages, which may include not only your regular pay, but also other taxable items, such as taxable fringe benefits. A guide to the important information listed on Form W-2 is on pages 30 and 31.

Your employer reports your taxable pay under a simple rule. Unless the item is specifically exempt from tax, you are taxed on practically everything you receive for your work whether paid in cash, property, or services. Taxed pay includes:

Back pay	Honoraria
Bonuses	Jury fees
Commissions	Royalties
Director's fees	Salaries
Sick pay	Severance pay
Employee prizes or awards	Dismissal pay
Expense allowances or reimbursements under	Tips
non-accountable plans	Vacation pay
	Wages

The items that the law specifically excludes from tax are discussed in Chapter 3. The most common tax-free benefits are employer-paid premiums for health and accident plans and certain group-term life insurance plans for coverage up to $50,000.

Withholdings for retirement plans. Amounts withheld from wages as your contribution to your pension or profit-sharing account are generally taxable unless they are tax-deferred under the limits allowed for Section 401(k) plans *(7.18)*, simplified employee pension plans *(8.16)*, SIMPLE IRAs *(8.18)*, or tax-sheltered annuity plans *(7.20)*. Tax-deferred amounts are reported in Box 13 of Form W-2.

Wages withheld for compulsory forfeitable contributions to a nonqualified pension plan are not taxable if these conditions exist:

1. The contribution is forfeited if employment is terminated prior to death or retirement.
2. The plan does not provide for a refund of employee contributions and, in the administration of the plan, no refund will be made. Where only part of the contribution is subject to forfeiture, the amount of withheld contribution not subject to forfeiture is taxable income.

You should check with your employer to determine the status of your contributions.

Assigning your pay. You may not avoid tax on income you earned by assigning the right to payment to another person. For example, you must report earnings that you donate to charity, even if they are paid directly by your employer to a charity. If you claim itemized deductions, you may claim a contribution deduction for the donation; *see* Chapter 14. Assignments of income-generating intellectual property are held taxable to the assignee. However, if the assignor retained power or control of the property, the assignor could be held liable for the tax according to the 8th Circuit.

The IRS allowed an exception for doctors working in a clinic. The doctors were not taxed on fees for treating patients with limited income (teaching cases) where they were required to assign the fees to a foundation.

Salary advances. Salary paid in advance for services to be rendered in the future is generally taxable in the year received if it is subject to your free and unrestricted use.

Child's wages. A parent is not taxed on wages paid for a child's services even if payment is made to the parent. However, a parent is taxed on income from work contracted for by the parent even if the child assists in the labor. For example, a parent whose children helped her with part-time work at home claimed that the children should be taxed on 70% of the income since they did 70% of the work. The IRS claimed that the parent was taxable on all the income because she, not the children, was the true earner, and the Tax Court agreed. Although the company knew that the children were doing part of the work, it had no agreement with them.

Employee leave-sharing plan. Some companies allow employees to contribute their unused leave into a "leave fund" for use by other employees who have suffered medical emergencies. If you use up your regular leave and benefit from additional leave that has been donated to the plan, the benefit is taxable and will be reported as wages on Form W-2.

 Caution

Severance Pay Taxable

You must pay tax on severance pay received upon losing a job. The severance pay is taxable even if you signed a waiver releasing your former employer from potential future damage claims. The waiver does not change the nature of the payments from taxable pay to tax-free personal injury damages; *see 11.7.*

 Filing Instruction

Tips

Tips you receive are taxable income. You must report tips to your employer so your employer can withhold FICA and income tax from your regular pay to cover the tips; *see 26.8.*

Court Decision

Tax on Assigned Contingent Fee
An attorney who took a medical malpractice case on a contingent fee basis agreed to split the net fee with his ex-wife pursuant to their divorce agreement. After a favorable settlement, the attorney's take was approximately $40,000 after expenses, half of which went to his ex-wife. Each paid tax on his or her share. The attorney argued that his partial assignment of the fee could shift the tax liability because collection was contingent on the outcome of the lawsuit. However, the IRS and the Tax Court held that the attorney was liable for the tax on the entire contingent fee, and an appeals court agreed. The attorney transferred only the right to receive income. Although his fee was contingent upon the successful outcome of the case, once the fee materialized, it was indisputably compensation for his personal services.

"Golden parachute" payments. Golden parachute arrangements are agreements to pay key employees additional compensation upon a change in company control. If you receive such a payment, part of it may be deemed to be an "excess payment" under a complex formula in the law. You must pay a 20% penalty tax on the "excess" amount in addition to regular income tax on the total. The 20% penalty should be identified on Form W-2 with Code K in Box 13; *see* the Key to Your Form W-2 at the beginning of this chapter.

If the golden parachute payment was reported on Form 1099-MISC as non-employee compensation, it will be included in the total compensation shown in Box 7 of Form 1099. If you are self-employed, report the total compensation on Schedule C *(40.6)* and compute self-employment tax on Schedule SE *(45.3)*. Any "excess parachute payment" should be separately labeled in Box 13 of Form 1099-MISC as "EPP." Multiply the "EPP" by 20% and report it on Line 56 (total tax) of Form 1040.

2.2 Year-End Paychecks

As an employee, you use the cash-basis method of accounting. This means that you report all income items in the year they are actually received and deduct expenses in the year you pay them.

You are also subject to the "constructive receipt rule," which requires you to report income not actually received but which has been credited to your account, subject to your control, or put aside for you. Thus, if you received a paycheck on December 31, 1999, you must report the pay on your 1999 return, even though you do not cash or deposit it to your account until 2000. This is true even if you receive the check after banking hours and cannot cash or deposit it until the next year. The Tax Court has also ruled that receipt by an agent (e.g., an attorney) is constructive receipt by the principal. In one case, a woman argued that alimony received by her in 1991 was taxable in 1991. Because the funds were given to her attorney on December 27, 1990, the Tax Court held that she was in constructive receipt of the funds and that they were taxable in 1990.

If your employer does not have funds in the bank and asks you to hold the check before depositing it, you do not have taxable income until the check is cashed. If services rendered in 1999 are paid for by check dated for 2000, the pay is taxable in 2000.

The IRS has ruled that an employee who is not at home on December 31 to take delivery of a check sent by certified mail must still report the check in that year. However, where an employee was not at home to take certified mail delivery of a year-end check that she did not expect to receive until the next year, the Tax Court held that the funds were taxable when received in the following year.

2.3 Pay Received in Property Is Taxed

Your employer may pay you with property instead of cash. You report the fair market value of the property as wages.

EXAMPLE

For consulting services rendered, Kate Chong receives a check for $10,000 and property with a fair market value of $5,000. She reports $15,000 as wages.

If you receive your company's stock as payment for your services, you include the value of the stock as pay in the year you receive it. However, if the stock is nontransferable or subject to substantial risk of forfeiture, you do not have to include its value as pay until the restrictions no longer apply. You must report dividends on the restricted stock in the year you receive the income.

If you receive your employer's note that has a fair market value, you are taxed on the value of the note less what it would cost you to discount it. If the note bears interest, report the full face value. But do not report income if the note has no fair market value. Report income on the note only when payments are made on it.

A debt cancelled by an employer is taxable income.

Salespeople employed by a dealer have taxable income on receipt of "prize points" redeemable for merchandise from a distributor.

2.4 Gifts From Employers

A payment may be called a gift but still be taxable income. Any payment made in recognition of past services or in anticipation of future services or benefits is taxable even if the employer is not obligated to make the payment. Exceptions for employee achievement awards are discussed at *3.10*.

To prove a gift is tax free, you must show that the employer acted with pure and unselfish motives of affection, admiration, or charity. This is difficult to do, given the employer-employee relationship. A gift of stock by majority stockholders to key employees has been held to be taxable.

2.5   When Commissions Are Taxed

Earned commissions are taxable in the year they are credited to your account and subject to your drawing, whether or not you actually draw them.

On your 1999 tax return, you do not report commissions that were earned in 1999 but cannot be computed or collected until a later year.

EXAMPLE

Arno Jeffers earns commissions based on a percentage of the profits from realty sales. In 1999 he draws $10,000 from his account. However, at the end of 1999 the full amount of his commissions is unknown because profits for the year have not been figured. In January 2000, his 1999 commissions are computed to be $15,000, and the $5,000 balance is paid to him. The $5,000 is taxable in 2000 even though earned in 1999.

Advances against unearned commissions. Under standard insurance industry practice, an agent who sells a policy does not earn commissions until premiums are received by the insurance company. However, the company may issue a cash advance on the commissions before the premiums are received. Agents have claimed that they may defer reporting the income until the year the premiums are earned. The IRS, recognizing that in practice companies rarely demand repayment, requires that advances be included in income in the year received if the agent has full control over the advanced funds. A repayment of unearned commissions in a later year is deducted on Schedule A; *see 2.9.*

Salespeople have been taxed on commissions received on property bought for their personal use. In one case, an insurance agent was taxed on commissions paid to him on his purchase of an insurance policy. In another case, a real estate agent was taxed on commissions he received on his purchase of land. A salesman was also taxed for commissions waived on policies he sold to friends, relatives, and employees.

Kickback of commissions. An insurance agent's kickback of his or her commission is taxable where agents may not under local law give rebates or kickbacks of premiums to their clients. The commissions are income and may not be offset with a business expense deduction; illegal kickbacks may not be deducted.

However, in one case, a federal appeals court allowed an insurance broker to avoid tax when he did not charge clients the basic first-year commission. The clients paid the broker the net premium (gross premium less the commission), which he remitted to the insurance company. The IRS and Tax Court held that the commissions were taxable despite the broker's voluntary waiver of his right to them. He could not deduct them because his discount scheme violated state anti-rebate law (Oklahoma). On appeal, the broker won. The Tenth Circuit Court of Appeals held that since the broker never had any right to commissions under the terms of the contracts he structured with his clients, he was not taxed on the commissions. The court cautioned that if the broker had remitted the full premium (including commission) to the insurance company and then reimbursed the client after having received the commission from the company, the commission probably would have been taxable.

2.6   Unemployment Benefits Are Taxable

All unemployment benefits you receive in 1999 from a state agency or the federal government are treated as taxable income. You should receive Form 1099-G, showing the amount of the payments. Report the payments separately from wages on Line 19 of Form 1040, Line 12 of Form 1040A, or Line 3 of Form 1040EZ.

Supplemental unemployment benefits paid from company-financed funds are taxable as wages and not reported as unemployment compensation. Such benefits are usually paid under guaranteed annual wage plans made between unions and employers.

Unemployment benefits from a private or union fund to which you voluntarily contribute dues are taxable as "other" income on Form 1040, but only to the extent the benefits exceed your contributions to the fund. Your contributions to the fund are not deductible.

Worker's compensation payments are not taxable; *see 2.12.*

Taxable unemployment benefits include federal trade readjustment allowances (1974 Trade Act), airline deregulation benefits (1978 Airline Deregulation Act), and disaster unemployment assistance (1974 Disaster Relief Act).

Caution

Earned Commissions Credited to Your Account

You may not postpone tax on earned commissions credited to your account in 1999 by not drawing them until 2000 or a later year. However, where a portion of earned commissions is not withdrawn because your employer is holding it to cover future expenses, you are not taxed on the amount withheld.

Repaid Settlement Benefits. If you had to repay supplemental unemployment benefits to receive trade readjustment allowances (1974 Trade Act), taxable unemployment benefits are reduced by repayments made in the same year. If you repay the benefits in a later year, the benefits are taxed in the year of receipt and a deduction may be claimed in the later year. If the repayment is $3,000 or less, the deduction is added to your other adjustments to income on Line 32 of Form 1040. If the repayment exceeds $3,000, a deduction or a credit may be claimed under the rules at *2.9.*

2.7 Strike Pay Benefits and Penalties

Strike and lockout benefits paid out of regular union dues are taxable as wages unless the payment qualifies as a gift, as discussed below. However, if you have made voluntary contributions to a strike fund, benefits you receive from the fund are tax free up to the amount of your contributions and are taxable to the extent they exceed your contributions.

Strike benefits as tax-free gifts. Here are factors indicating that benefits are gifts: Payments are based on individual need; they are paid to both union and non-union members; and no conditions are imposed on the strikers who receive benefits.

If you receive benefits under conditions by which you are to participate in the strike and the payments are tied to your scale of wages, the benefits are taxable.

> **EXAMPLE**
>
> A striking union pilot claimed that strike benefits were tax-free gifts because they were funded by assessments paid by other union pilots who were not on strike. The IRS and Tax Court held that the benefits were taxable. They were not gifts because they were not motivated by a "detached and disinterested generosity." The union was promoting its own self-interest by giving pilots an incentive to support the strike. The non-striking pilots contributed to the strike fund as an obligation of union membership. The strikers were eligible for benefits only if they agreed to perform any strike activities requested by the union, did not fly for airlines in dispute with the union, and did not take actions that could adversely affect the outcome of the dispute.

Caution

Law Violation Not Deductible

No deduction is allowed for a fine or penalty paid to a government for the violation of a law.

Strike pay penalties. Pay penalties charged to striking teachers are not deductible. State law may prohibit public school teachers from striking and charge a penalty equal to one day's pay for each day spent on strike. For example, when striking teachers returned to work after a one-week strike, a penalty of one week's salary was deducted from their pay. Although they did not actually receive pay for the week they worked after the strike, they earned taxable wages. Furthermore, the penalty is not deductible. No deduction is allowed for a fine or penalty paid to a government for the violation of a law.

Caution

Deferring Your Pay But Assuming Risk

To avoid current tax on pay, you may contract with your employer to defer pay to future years. You are not allowed to have control of the deferred amounts. Remember to consider that tax rates could be higher in the future and you may be subject to a higher tax on the deferred pay.

2.8 Deferring Tax on Pay

If you want to avoid current tax on pay, you may contract with your employer to defer pay to future years. To reduce possible IRS opposition, it is advisable to enter into a deferral compensation arrangement before the year in which the services are to be performed; for example, agree in 2000 to defer pay for 2001 services to 2002 or later years. Furthermore, to defer pay to a future period, you must take some risk. You cannot have any control over your deferred pay account. If you are not confident of your employer's ability to pay in the future, you should not enter into a deferred pay plan.

Before agreeing to a deferral arrangement, consider the possibility that if tax rates are raised further, you may be subject to a higher tax on deferred pay than if you had received and paid tax currently on the income.

If IRS tests are met, a trust arrangement, commonly nicknamed a "rabbi trust," can be used by an employer to hold deferred pay contributions; *see 2.14.*

An employee is not taxed on employer contributions to a qualified cash or deferred arrangement (401(k)) plan even though the employee had the option to take the cash; *see 7.17.* Qualified salary reductions under a simplified employee pension (SEP) plan *(8.15)*, SIMPLE IRA *(8.17)*, or tax-sheltered annuity plan *(7.20)* are also not taxed, even though you could have received cash currently.

2.9 Did You Return Wages Received in a Prior Year?

Did you return income in 1999 such as salary or commissions that you reported in a prior taxable year because it appeared you had an unrestricted right to them in the earlier year? If so, you may deduct the repayment as a miscellaneous itemized deduction. If the repayment of wages exceeds $3,000, the deduction is claimed on Line 27 of Schedule A and is not subject to the 2% adjusted gross income (AGI) floor *(19.1)*. However, the law is not clear on the issue of whether a deduction of $3,000 or less is subject to the 2% floor; the IRS takes the position that the 2% floor applies.

Option of tax credit or deduction for repayments over $3,000. If your repayment of wages exceeded $3,000, you may claim the repayment as an itemized deduction, *or* you may claim a tax credit, based upon a recomputation of the prior year's tax; *see* the Filing Instruction on this page.

Repayment of supplemental unemployment benefits. Where repayment is required to qualify for trade readjustment allowances, you may deduct the repayment from gross income. Claim the deduction on Line 32 of Form 1040, and to the left of the line write "subpay TRA." The deduction is allowed even if you do not itemize. If repayment exceeds $3,000, you have the choice of a deduction or claiming a tax credit based on a recomputation of your tax for the year supplemental unemployment benefits were received, as explained in the Filing Instruction on this page.

Repayment of disallowed travel and entertainment expenses. If a "hedge" agreement between you and your company requires you to repay salary or travel and entertainment ("T & E") expenses if they are disallowed to the company by the IRS, you may claim a deduction in the year of repayment. According to the IRS, you may not recalculate your tax for the prior year and claim a tax credit under the rules of Section 1341. However, an appeals court rejected the position taken by the IRS and allowed a tax recomputation under Section 1341 to an executive who returned part of a disallowed salary under the terms of a corporate by-law.

2.10 Waiver of Executor's and Trustee's Commissions

Commissions received by an executor for services performed are taxable as compensation. An executor may waive commissions without income or gift tax consequences by giving a principal legatee or devisee a formal waiver of the executor's right to commissions within six months after the initial appointment or by not claiming commissions at the time of filing the usual accountings.

The waiver may not be recognized if the executor takes any action that is inconsistent with the waiver. An example of an inconsistent action would be the claiming of an executor's fee as a deduction on an estate, inheritance, or income tax return.

A *bequest* received by an executor from an estate is tax free if it is not compensation for services.

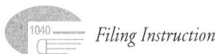

Filing Instruction

Repayments Exceeding $3,000

If a repayment of wages in 1999 exceeds $3,000, a special law (Code Section 1341) gives this alternative: Instead of claiming an itemized deduction from 1999 income, you may recompute your tax for the prior year as if the wages had not been reported. The difference between the actual tax paid in the prior year and the recomputed tax may be claimed as a credit on your 1999 return. The credit is claimed on Line 63 of Form 1040; write next to the line "IRC 1341." If you claim the repayment as a miscellaneous itemized deduction, enter it on Line 27 of Schedule A, where it is not subject to the 2% floor. Choose either the credit or the itemized deduction, whichever gives you the larger tax reduction.

Disability and Workers' Compensation

2.11 Sick Pay Is Taxable

Sick pay is generally taxable as wages unless it qualifies as workers' compensation under the rules at *2.12*. Payments received under accident or health plans are generally tax free *(3.2),* unless they constitute excess reimbursements, as discussed at *17.4*. Payments from your employer's plan for certain serious permanent injuries are tax free; *see 3.2.*

Disability pensions are discussed at *2.13.*

Sick pay received from your employer is subject to income tax withholding as if it were wages. Sick pay from a third party such as an insurance company is not subject to withholdings unless you request it on Form W-4S.

2.12 Workers' Compensation Is Tax Free

You do not pay tax on workers' compensation payments for job-related injuries or illness. However, your employer might continue paying your regular salary but require you to turn over your workers' compensation payments. Then you are taxed on the difference between what was paid to you and what you returned.

EXAMPLE

John Wright was injured while at work and was out of work for two months. His company continues to pay his weekly salary of $475. He also receives workers' compensation of $100 a week from the state, which is tax free. He gives the $100 back to his employer. The balance of $375 a week is considered taxable wages.

Caution

Job-Related Injury or Illness

Not all payments for job-related illness or injury qualify as tax-free workers' compensation. Unless the statute or regulation authorizing your disability payment restricts awards to on-the-job injury or illness, your payment is taxable. Even if your payments are in fact based upon job-related injury or illness, they are taxed if other individuals can receive payments from the plan for disabilities that are not work related; *see* the Kane Example on the next page.

To qualify as tax-free workers' compensation, the payments must be made under the authority of a *law* (or regulation having the force of a law) that provides compensation for on-the-job injury or illness. Payments made under a labor agreement do *not* qualify as tax-free workers' compensation; *see* the Examples below.

EXAMPLE

Kane, a federal district judge, suffered from sleep apnea, a condition characterized by a cessation of breathing during sleep, which was aggravated by the stress of his judicial work. He received a retirement disability payment of $65,135.

A federal appeals court held that the payment was taxable because it was paid under a statute which did not specifically require that the payments be for work-related injuries. Here, the federal law under which the judge received his payments provided benefits for all permanent disabilities, whether or not job related.

Effect of workers' compensation on Social Security. In figuring whether Social Security benefits are taxable *(34.2)*, workers' compensation that reduces Social Security or equivalent Railroad Retirement benefits is treated as a Social Security (or Railroad Retirement) benefit received during the year. Thus, the workers' compensation may be indirectly subject to tax as discussed at *34.2*.

EXAMPLES

1. A teacher, injured while working, received full salary during a two-year sick leave. She argued that the payments, made under board of education regulations, were similar to workers' compensation and thus tax free. The IRS disagreed; the regulations were not the same as a workers' compensation statute. The Tax Court supported the teacher. The payments were made because of job-related injuries and were authorized by regulations having the force of law.

2. A disabled New York City policeman argued that sick leave payments in 1978 under a union labor contract were tax-free workers' compensation because his disability was work related. However, the IRS, Tax Court, and an appeals court disagreed. The payments were made under a labor contract and not a workers' compensation statute or pursuant to government regulations. Furthermore, even if authorized by a statute or regulations, the officer's sick leave would be taxable since under the labor contract, officers received sick pay whether or not their injury or illness was work related.

   A change in New York City law now qualifies sick leave payments to firefighters and police officers for line-of-duty injuries as tax-free workers' compensation.

3. The IRS, relying on the court decision in Example 2, claimed that a police officer in Lynbrook, N.Y., was subject to tax on line-of-duty disability pay because the payment was under a labor agreement with the Police Benevolent Association (PBA). The Tax Court supported the police officer's claim that the payments were authorized by a specific New York State law requiring full salary for job-related police injuries. The PBA agreement did not affect the officer's rights to those state law payments. Lynbrook treated the case as a workers' compensation claim and in fact received reimbursement from the state workers' compensation board for the payments made to the officer.

4. A Los Angeles sheriff injured on the job retired on disability and, under the Los Angeles workers' compensation law, was allowed to elect sick pay in lieu of the regular workers' compensation amount because the sick pay was larger. The IRS argued that the sheriff had merely received taxable sick pay because he would have received the same amount as sick pay if his injuries had been suffered in a personal accident. However, the Tax Court allowed tax-free treatment. The sick leave was paid under a workers' compensation law that applied solely to work-related injuries. The fact that sick leave may also have been available to other employees under other laws does not mean that it may not be included as an option under a workers' compensation statute.

   The IRS announced that it does not agree with the Tax Court's decision allowing full tax-free treatment. According to the IRS, benefits up to the regular workers' compensation amount should be tax free but excess amounts should be taxed.

Court Decision

Is Sick Leave Tax-Free Workers' Compensation?

According to the Tax Court, sick leave may qualify as tax-free workers' compensation if it is paid under a specific workers' compensation statute or similar government regulation that authorizes the sick leave payment for job-related injuries or illness; *see* Examples 1, 3, and 4 on this page.

2.13 Employer and Federal Government Disability Pensions

Disability pensions financed by your employer are reported as wage income unless they are for severe permanent physical injuries that qualify for tax-free treatment under the rules at *3.2* or they are tax-free government payments as discussed in this section.

If you receive little or no Social Security and your other income is below a specified threshold, you may be eligible to claim a tax credit for disability payments received while you are under the age of 65 and permanently and totally disabled; *see 34.7.*

Taxable disability pensions are reported as wages until you reach the minimum retirement age under the employer's plan. After reaching minimum retirement age, payments are reported as a pension under the rules of *7.25.*

Federal government services. Certain disability pensions from the military or federal government agencies are tax free. Military disability benefits from the Veterans Administration are tax free, as are payments for combat and terrorist attack–related injuries. Other disability pensions for personal injuries or sickness resulting from active service in the armed forces are taxable if you joined the service after September 24, 1975.

Military disability payments are tax free if before September 25, 1975, you were entitled to military disability benefits or if on that date you were a member of the armed forces (or reserve unit) of the U.S. or any other country or were under a binding written commitment to become a member. A similar tax-free rule applies to disability pensions from the following government agencies if you were entitled to the payments before September 25, 1975, or were a member of the service (or committed to joining) on that date: The Foreign Service, Public Health Service, or National Oceanic and Atmospheric Administration. The exclusion for pre–September 25, 1975, service applies to disability pensions based upon percentage of disability. However, if a disability pension was based upon years of service, you do not pay tax on the amount that would be received based upon percentage of disability.

Veterans Administration benefits. Disability pensions from the Veterans Administration (now called the Department of Veterans Affairs) are tax free. Military retirees who receive disability benefits from other government sources are not taxed on amounts equal to the benefits they would be entitled to receive from the VA. If you retire from the military and are later given a retroactive award of VA disability benefits, retirement pay during the retroactive period is tax free (other than a lump-sum readjustment payment upon retirement) to the extent of the VA benefit.

Pension based on combat-related injuries. Tax-free treatment applies to payments for combat-related injury or sickness that is incurred as a result of any one of the following activities: (1) as a direct result of armed conflict; (2) while engaged in extra-hazardous service, even if not directly engaged in combat; (3) under conditions simulating war, including maneuvers or training; or (4) that is caused by an instrumentality of war, such as weapons.

Terrorist attacks. Tax-free treatment applies to a disability pension paid to a civilian U.S. employee for injuries incurred as a direct result of a violent attack that the Secretary of State determines to be a terrorist attack and that occurred while the employee was working for the United States in the performance of official duties outside the United States.

 Filing Tip

Military Disability Tax Free
Military disability benefits from the Veterans Administration are tax free.

Pay Plans for Executives

2.14 Deferred Pay Plans

The major objective of a deferred pay plan is to postpone the tax on pay benefits to a year in which you will be in a lower tax bracket than in the year you provide the services. However, a deferred pay plan is generally not advisable where a projection of future income shows that there probably will be no substantial income decline, and/or the tax bracket differentials will not be wide. An after-tax dollar in hand for current use is preferable to an expected tax saving that may not materialize.

As discussed at *2.8,* a deferral arrangement will succeed in postponing tax only if there is an element of risk. An employee with control over the pay account will be treated by the IRS as in "constructive receipt," and thus currently taxable on employer contributions.

Rabbi trusts. If IRS tests are met, employer contributions to a "rabbi trust" are not taxed until distributions from the trust are received or made available. The trust must be irrevocable and the trust assets must be subject to the claims of the employer's creditors in the event of insolvency or bankruptcy. Employees and their beneficiaries have no preferred claim on the trust assets. *See* a model rabbi trust agreement in Revenue Procedure 92-64.

Pension and profit-sharing plans. A company qualified pension or profit-sharing plan offers the following benefits: (1) you do not realize current income on your employer's contributions to the plan on your behalf; (2) funds contributed by both your employer and you compound tax free within the plan; (3) if you receive a lump-sum distribution, tax on employer contributions may in certain cases be reduced by a special averaging rule *(7.4)*; and (4) if you receive a lump-sum distribution in company securities, unrealized appreciation on those securities is not taxed until you finally sell the stock.

In plan years starting in 1999, the maximum amount of compensation that can be taken into account for purposes of determining qualified employer plan contributions and benefits is $160,000. The $160,000 limit may be adjusted annually for inflation.

Where you are allowed to choose the type of payout from a qualified plan, make sure that you compare the tax on receiving a lump-sum distribution with the projected tax cost of deferring payments over a period of years or rolling over the distribution to an IRA account; *see 7.3* and *7.8*. Distributions before age 59 ½ are generally subject to penalties, but *see* exceptions at *7.15*.

401(k) plan. If your company has a profit-sharing or stock bonus plan, it has the opportunity to give you additional tax-sheltered pay; *see 7.17*. The tax law allows the company to add a cash or deferred pay plan, called a "401(k) plan." If your company permits salary-reduction deferrals to a 401(k) plan, you may be able to make contributions on a pre-tax basis up to the annual limit set by law, which for 1999 was $10,000. However, the limit may be reduced for highly compensated employees in order for the company to satisfy nondiscrimination requirements; *see 7.18*.

2.15 Insurance Plans May Be Tax Free

Company-financed insurance gives employees benefits at low or no tax cost.

Group life insurance. Group insurance plans may furnish not only life insurance protection but also accident and health benefits. Premium costs are low and tax deductible to the company while tax free to you unless you have nonforfeitable rights to permanent life insurance, or, in the case of group-term life insurance, your coverage exceeds $50,000; *see 3.3*. Even where your coverage exceeds $50,000, the tax incurred on your employer's premium payment is generally less than what you would have to pay privately for similar insurance.

It may be possible to avoid estate tax on the group policy proceeds if you assign all of your ownership rights in the policy, including the right to convert the policy, and if the beneficiary is other than your estate. Where the policy allows assignment of the conversion right, in addition to all other rights, and state law does not bar the assignment, you are considered to have made a complete assignment of the group insurance for estate tax purposes.

The IRS has ruled that where an employee assigns a group life policy and the value of the employee's interest in the policy cannot be ascertained, there is no taxable gift. This is so where the employer could simply have stopped making payments. However, there is a gift by the employee to the assignee to the extent of premiums paid by the employer. Depending on the assignee, the gift may be a present interest qualifying for the $10,000 annual exclusion discussed at *33.1*.

Split-dollar insurance. Where you want more insurance than is provided by a group plan, your company may be able to help you get additional protection through a split-dollar insurance plan. Under the basic split-dollar plan, your employer purchases permanent life insurance on your life and pays the annual premium to the extent of the yearly increases in the cash surrender value of the policy. You pay only the balance of the premium. At your death, your employer is entitled to part of the proceeds equal to the cash surrender value or any lesser amount equalling the total premiums he or she paid. You have the right to name a beneficiary to receive the remaining proceeds which, under most policies, are substantial compared with the employer's share.

The IRS has ruled that you must report as taxable income an amount equal to the one-year term cost of the declining life insurance protection to which you are entitled, less any portion of the premium provided by you. According to the IRS, there is an additional tax liability to employees under "equity split-dollar plans" that allow the employees to receive the cash surrender value in excess of the premiums paid by the employer. For example, a company paid in a lump sum the premium on a life insurance policy for an executive and it was projected that the cash surrender value would exceed the employer's premium payment in the fourth policy year. The IRS ruled that once the cash surrender value of the policy exceeds the premiums that are returnable to the employer upon the employer's death (or termination of the agreement upon the executive's leaving the company), the employee must report as income the excess cash surrender value. This is in addition to the income realized on the one-year term cost for the declining insurance protection.

2.16 Stock Appreciation Rights (SARs)

SARs are a form of cash bonus tied to an increase in the price of employer stock. Each SAR entitles an employee to receive cash equal to the excess of the fair market value of one share on the date of exercise over the value on the date the SAR was granted.

EXAMPLE

When a stock is worth $30 a share, you get 100 SARs exercisable within five years. Two years later, when the stock price increases to $50 a share, you exercise the SAR and receive $2,000. You are taxed when you receive the cash.

An executive may realize taxable income when he or she becomes entitled to the maximum SAR benefit allowed by the company plan. For example, in 1994, when company stock is worth $30, an executive is granted 100 SARs exercisable within five years. By exercising the SARs, the executive may receive cash equal to the appreciation up to $20 per share. If the stock appreciates to $50 per share in 1999, the executive realizes taxable income of $2,000 ($20 per share × 100) in 1999, even if he or she does not exercise the SARs. The reason is that once the stock value appreciates to $50, the maximum SAR benefit of $20 is realized.

Performance shares. The company promises to make an award of stock in the future, at no cost to you, if the company's earnings reach a set level. You are taxed on the receipt of stock (unless the stock is restricted, as discussed in *2.17*).

2.17 Stock Options and Restricted Stock

Executives receiving qualified statutory stock options generally do not incur tax liability either at the time the option is granted or when the option is exercised, although the option spread may be subject to AMT; *see* Chapter 23. Qualified statutory options include incentive stock options and options under an employee stock purchase plan. Receipt of a nonqualified stock option may result in an immediate tax.

Incentive stock options (ISOs). A corporation may provide its executives with incentive stock options to acquire its stock (or the stock of its parent or subsidiaries). For regular income tax purposes, ISOs meeting tax law tests are not taxed when granted or exercised. Income or loss is not reported until you sell the stock acquired from exercising the ISO. The option must be exercisable within 10 years of the date it is granted and the option price must be at least equal to the fair market value of the stock when the option is granted. If the fair market value of stock for which ISOs may first be exercised in a particular year exceeds $100,000 (valued at date of grant), the excess is not considered a qualifying ISO.

For alternative minimum tax (AMT) consequences, *see* Chapter 23.

Gain or loss on sale of option stock. If the stock acquired by the exercise of the ISO is held for more than one year after acquisition and more than two years after the ISO was granted, you have long-term capital gain or loss on the sale, equal to the difference between the selling price of the stock and the option price you paid when you exercised the ISO. If you sell before meeting the one-year and two-year holding period tests, a gain on the sale is treated as ordinary income to the extent of the option spread—the excess of the value of the stock when you exercised the option over the option price. Any gain in excess of the spread is reported as capital gain.

Employee stock purchase plans. These plans allow employees to buy their company's stock, usually at a discount. The plan must be nondiscriminatory and meet tax law tests on option terms. Options granted under qualified plans are not taxed until the shares acquired are sold. If you sell the shares more than two years after the granting of the option, and more than one year after you acquired the stock, gain on the sale is reported as ordinary wage income to the extent the option price was less than the fair market value of the shares when the option was granted. Any excess gain is capital gain; *see 5.2* for the tax rate on net capital gains. For sales before the end of the two-year/one-year holding period, the amount reportable as ordinary wage income is the excess of the value of the shares when the option was exercised over the option price.

Nonqualified stock options. Where a nonqualified option has no ascertainable fair market value, as is generally the case for options that are not actively traded on a public exchange, no income is realized on the receipt of the option. When the option is exercised, you are taxed on the difference between the fair market value of the stock when you exercise the option and the option

Caution

Watch SAR Expiration Date

If the rights increase in value, keep a close watch on the expiration date. Do not let them expire before exercise. If you do, not only will you lose income but you will be taxed on income you never received. According to the IRS, an employee who does not exercise the SARs is taxed as if they have been exercised immediately before they expire. The IRS claims that an employee has constructive receipt of income immediately before they expire. At that time, the amount of gain realized from the SARs is fixed because the employee can no longer benefit from future appreciation in value.

Caution

Possible AMT Adjustment

When your rights in incentive stock option stock are transferrable and not subject to a substantial risk of forfeiture, you have to treat as an adjustment for alternative minimum tax purposes *(23.2)* the excess of the fair-market value of the stock when the option was exercised over the option price.

price. If a nonqualified stock option has an ascertainable fair market value, the value of the option less any amount you paid is taxable under the restricted property rules as ordinary wage income in the first year that your right to the option is freely transferable or not subject to a substantial risk of forfeiture. For other details and requirements, *see* IRS Regulation Section 1.83-7.

Nonqualified stock options may be granted in addition to or in place of incentive stock options. There are no restrictions on the amount of nonqualified stock options that may be granted.

When sale of stock is treated as grant of option. If company stock is purchased on the basis of the executive's promissory note and he or she is not personally liable, the company can recover only its stock in the event of default on the note. If the stock value drops, he or she may walk away from the deal with no personal risk. According to an IRS regulation, the deal may be viewed as an option arrangement. Application of the IRS regulation would give the executive ordinary taxable income when the stock is purchased if the value of the stock at the time of purchase exceeds the purchase price. For example, on July 1, 1997, a corporation sells 100 shares of its stock to an executive. The stock has a fair market value on that date of $25,000 and the executive executes a nonrecourse note secured by the stock in that amount, plus 8% annual interest. An annual payment of $5,000 of principal, plus interest, is required beginning the following year. In 1998, the executive collects the dividends, votes the stock, and pays the interest on the note but no principal. In 1999, when the stock has appreciated in value to $30,000, the executive pays off the note. Under the IRS regulation, the executive would realize ordinary income upon payment of the nonrecourse note to the extent of the difference between the amount paid ($25,000 in 1999) and the value of the stock ($30,000).

Stock subject to restricted property rules. If in return for performing services you receive company stock or other property subject to restrictions, special tax rules apply. Stock subject to restrictions is taxed as pay in the first year in which it is substantially vested, meaning that it is either transferable or not subject to a substantial risk of forfeiture. A risk of forfeiture exists where your rights are conditioned upon the future performance of substantial services. Generally, taxable income is the difference between the amount, if any, that you pay for the stock and its value at the time the risk of forfeiture is removed. The valuation at the time the forfeiture restrictions lapse is not reduced because of restrictions imposed on the right to sell the property. However, restrictions that will never lapse do affect valuation.

SEC restrictions on insider trading are considered a substantial risk of forfeiture, so that there is no tax on the receipt of stock subject to such restrictions. However, the SEC permits insiders to immediately resell stock acquired through exercise of an option granted at least six months earlier. As the stock acquired through such options is not subject to SEC restrictions, the executive is subject to immediate tax upon exercise of an option held for at least six months.

If the stock is subject to a restriction on transfer to comply with SEC pooling-of-interests accounting rules, the stock is considered to be subject to a substantial restriction.

Note: The tax rules for restricted property are not restricted to employees. They also apply to independent contractors who are compensated for services with restricted stock or other property.

Election to include value of restricted stock in income when received. Although restricted stock is generally not taxable until the year in which it is substantially vested, you may elect to be taxed in the year you receive it on the unrestricted value (as of the date received), less any payment you made. The election must be made by filing a statement with the IRS no later than 30 days after the date the stock is transferred to you. The election may not be revoked without the consent of the IRS.

If you make the election, you are treated as an investor and later appreciation in value is not taxed as pay when your rights to the stock become vested. To figure gain or loss when you sell the stock, your cost basis for the stock is increased by the amount of income you reported as pay under the election. If you forfeit the stock after the election is made, a capital loss is allowed for your cost minus any amount realized on the forfeiture.

2.18 Educational Benefits for Employees' Children

Private foundations. The IRS has published guidelines under which a private foundation established by an employer may make tax-free grants to children of employees. An objective, nondiscriminatory program must be adopted. If the guidelines are satisfied, employees are not taxed on the benefits provided to their children. Advance approval of the grant program must be obtained from the IRS.

Planning Reminder

Electing Immediate Tax on Restricted Stock

If you expect restricted stock to appreciate, consider making an election to be immediately taxed on the value of the restricted stock, minus your cost. If you make the election, any appreciation in value that has accrued since the election was made will not be taxable when the stock becomes substantially vested. Tax on appreciation will not be due until the stock is sold.

IRS guidelines require that:

- Grant recipients must be selected by a scholarship committee that is independent of the employer and the foundation. Former employees of the employer or the foundation are not considered independent.
- Eligibility for the grants may be restricted to children of employees who have been employed for a minimum of up to three years, but eligibility may not be related to the employee's position, services, or duties.
- Once awarded, a grant may not be terminated if the parent leaves his job with the employer, regardless of the reason for the termination of employment. If a one-year grant is awarded or a multi-year grant is awarded subject to renewal, a child who reapplies for a later grant may not be considered ineligible because his parent no longer works for the employer.
- Grant decisions must be based solely upon objective standards unrelated to the employer's business and the parent's employment such as prior academic performance, aptitude tests, recommendations from instructors, financial needs, and conclusions drawn from personal interviews.
- Recipients must be free to use the grants for courses that are not of particular benefit to the employer or the foundation.
- The grant program must not be used by the foundation or employer to recruit employees or induce employees to continue employment.
- There must be no requirement or suggestion that the child or parent is expected to render future employment services.

The grant program must also meet a percentage test. The number of grants awarded in a given year to children of employees must not exceed (1) 25% of the number of employees' children who were eligible, applied for the grants, and were considered by the selection committee in that year; or (2) 10% of the number of employees' children who were eligible during that year, whether or not they applied. Renewals of grants are not considered in determining the number of grants awarded.

Educational benefit trusts and other plans. A medical professional corporation set up an educational benefit plan to pay college costs for the children of "key" employees, those salaried at over $15,000. Children enrolled in a degree program within two years of graduating from high school could participate in the plan. If an eligible employee quit for reasons other than death or permanent disability, his or her children could not longer receive benefits except for expenses actually incurred before termination. The company made annual contributions to a trust administered by a bank. According to the IRS, amounts contributed to the trust were a form of pay to qualified employees, because the contributions were made on the basis of the parents' employment and earnings records, not on the children's need, merit, or motivation. However, the employees could not be taxed when the funds were deposited because the children's right to receive benefits was conditioned upon each employee's future performance of services and was subject to a substantial risk of forfeiture. Tax is not incurred until a person has a vested right to receive benefits; here, vesting did not occur until a child became a degree candidate and incurred educational expenses while his or her parent was employed by the corporation. Once the child's right to receive a distribution from the plan became vested, the parent of the child could be taxed on the amount of the distribution. The company could deduct the same amount.

The Tax Court and appeals court have upheld the IRS position in similar cases.

 Caution

Primary Purpose Determination

If all guidelines other than the percentage test are satisfied, the IRS will determine whether the primary purpose of the program is to educate the children. If it is, the grants will be considered tax-free scholarships or fellowships; if it is not, the grants are taxed to the parent-employees as extra compensation.

Fringe Benefits

Employer-furnished fringe benefits are exempt from tax if the tests discussed in this chapter are met.

The most common tax-free benefits are accident and health plans, group-term life insurance plans, dependent care plans, education assistance plans, tuition reduction plans, adoption benefit plans, cafeteria plans, and plans providing employees with discounts, no-additional-cost services, or employer-subsidized meal facilities.

Employees of qualifying small employers who have medical coverage through a high-deductible plan may be able to set up a medical savings account (MSA) to pay for medical costs not covered by insurance; *see 3.1*.

Highly compensated individuals may be taxed on certain benefits from such plans if nondiscrimination rules are not met.

Key to Fringe Benefits

Fringe Benefit—	*Tax Pointer—*
Adoption benefits	Employer payments to a third party or reimbursements to you for qualified adoption expenses are generally tax free up to a limit of $5,000, or $6,000 for a child with special needs. The exclusion is phased out if modified adjusted gross income is between $75,000 and $115,000; *see 3.5* for further details.
Athletic facilities	The fair market value of athletic facilities, such as gyms, swimming pools, golf courses, and tennis courts, is tax free if the facilities are on property owned or leased by the employer (not necessarily the main business premises) and substantially all of the use of the facilities is by employees, their spouses, and dependent children. Such facilities must be open to all employees on a nondiscriminatory basis in order for the company to deduct related expenses.
Child or dependent care plans	The value of day-care services provided or reimbursed by an employer under a written, nondiscriminatory plan is tax free up to a limit of $5,000, or $2,500 for married persons filing separately. Expenses are excludable if they would qualify for the dependent care credit; *see* Chapter 25. On your tax return, you must report employer-provided benefits to figure the tax-free exclusion. Tax-free employer benefits reduce eligibility for the dependent care tax credit; *see 3.4*.
De minimis *(minor) fringe benefits*	These are small benefits that are administratively impractical to tax, such as occasional supper money and taxi fares for overtime work, company parties or picnics, and occasional theater or sporting event tickets; *see 3.9*.
Discounts on company products and services	Services from your employer that are usually sold to customers are tax free if your employer does not incur additional costs in providing them to you; *see 3.15*. Merchandise discounts and other discounted services are also eligible for a tax-free exclusion; *see 3.16*.
Education plans	An up-to-$5,250 exclusion applies to employer-financed undergraduate courses beginning before June 1, 2000; *see 3.6*.
Employee achievement awards	Achievement awards are taxable unless they qualify under special rules for length of service or safety achievement; *see 3.10*.
Group-term life insurance	Premiums paid by employers are not taxed if policy coverage is $50,000 or less; *see 3.3*.
Health and accident plan benefits	Premiums paid by an employer are tax free. Benefits under an employer plan are also generally tax free; *see 3.1* and *3.2*.
Interest-free or low-interest loans	Interest-free loans received from your employer may be taxed; *see 4.30*.
Transportation benefits	Within limits, employer-provided parking benefits and transit passes are tax free; *see 3.7*.
Tuition reductions	Tuition reductions for courses below the graduate level are generally tax free. Graduate students who are teaching or research assistants are not taxed on tuition reduction unless the reduction is compensation for teaching services; *see 3.6*.
Working condition benefits	Benefits provided by your employer that would be deductible if you paid the expenses yourself are a tax-free working condition fringe benefit. Company cars are discussed at *3.7* and other working condition benefits at *3.8*.

Health, Accident, and Group Insurance and Death Benefits

3.1 Tax-Free Health and Accident Coverage Under Employer Plans

You are not taxed on *contributions* or *insurance premiums* your employer makes to a health, hospitalization, or accident plan to cover you, your spouse, or your dependents. If you are temporarily laid off and continue to receive health coverage, the employer's contributions during this layoff period are tax free. If you are retired, you do not pay tax on insurance paid by your former employer. Medical coverage provided to the family of a deceased employee is tax free since it is treated as a continuation of the employee's fringe-benefit package.

If your employer provides health and accident coverage to your live-in companion, the coverage is taxable to you where the companion is not recognized as a "spouse" under state law or "dependent" status is barred (even if support and household membership tests in Chapter 21 are met) because the relationship violates local law. Furthermore, under the 1996 Defense of Marriage Act, a gay or lesbian companion is not treated as a spouse for federal tax purposes.

If you are age 65 or older, Medicare premiums paid by your employer are not taxed. If you retire and have the option of receiving continued coverage under the medical plan or a lump-sum payment covering unused accumulated sick leave instead of coverage, the lump-sum amount is reported as income at the time you have the option to receive it. If you elect continued coverage, the amount reported as income may be deductible as medical insurance if you itemize deductions; *see 17.5.*

Long-term care coverage. An employee is not taxed on employer-provided long-term care coverage that pays benefits in the event the employee becomes *chronically ill*, as defined at *17.15*. However, the coverage is not tax free if provided through a cafeteria plan *(3.13)* and reimbursements of long-term care expenses may not be made through a flexible spending arrangement *(3.14)*.

Hiring spouse allows self-employed individual to obtain tax breaks. A self-employed person is not considered an "employee" and thus is generally not eligible for tax-free health coverage or reimbursements *(3.2)* of medical expenses. However, the benefit of a 100% deduction plus tax-free coverage and reimbursements can be obtained by a married self-employed person who hires his or her spouse and provides family coverage to the employee-spouse under an accident and health plan purchased in the name of the business. By covering the spouse, the employer-spouse can then obtain coverage under the plan as a member of the employee's family. As long as the employee-spouse is a bona fide employee, and not a self-employed co-owner of the business, the cost of the family's coverage is not taxed to the employee and any reimbursements received by the employee-spouse for his or her medical expenses, or those of the employer-spouse or their dependents, are tax-free under the exclusion rules discussed at *3.2*. The employer-spouse can deduct 100% of the coverage costs, including reimbursements, as a business deduction on Schedule C; *see 40.6.*

Medical Savings Account Contributions for Employees of Small Employers Offering High-Deductible Plans

Self-employed individuals and employees of eligible small employers (*see* below) who have health insurance coverage under a high-deductible plan may set up a medical savings account (MSA) that can be used to pay unreimbursed medical costs. The tax consequences for a self-employed individual are illustrated at *17.17*. If you are an eligible employee, your employer may make contributions to your MSA that are tax free to you, subject to the limits discussed below. If the employer does not contribute, you may make deductible contributions up to the same limits; *see* Chapter 12 for claiming the deduction. An MSA may be set up with an insurance company, bank, or any institution qualified to offer IRAs. Distributions from MSAs are discussed at *3.2*.

The law authorizing MSAs allows only 750,000 MSAs to be set up between 1997 and the end of 2000, and there are separate annual limits for the years before 2000. However, given the relatively low number of MSAs established thus far, it is unlikely that MSA eligibility will be cut off before 2001. If and when the cutoff limit is reached, contributions may continue to be made to MSAs of individuals who remain eligible. Employees who first become eligible to join a high-deductible plan after the cut-off date may qualify in certain cases.

Law Alert

Medicare MSA

If you are enrolled in Medicare, you may elect an MSA option. Contact your local Social Security office for details.

Filing Pointer

Deducting MSA Contributions

If you work for a qualifying small employer who has a high-deductible health plan, you may make deductible contributions to a medical savings account (MSA) only if the employer does not contribute to your account for the year. Report your contributions on Form 8853, and claim the deduction directly from gross income on Line 25 of Form 1040. *See also 17.17.*

MSA eligibility for employees. To be eligible for an MSA, you must be under age 65 and work for a "small" employer, one that had an average of 50 or fewer employees during either of the two preceding years. You must be covered by a high-deductible health plan, which for 1999 must have a deductible of: (1) at least $1,550 and no more than $2,300 for individual coverage or (2) at least $3,050 and no more than $4,600 for family coverage. The deduction ranges for the year 2000 may be increased by an inflation factor.

The IRS has ruled that a high-deductible family plan may not set a lower deductible for individual family members. For example, a plan does not qualify if it sets an overall annual family deductible of $3,050 but allows an individual who incurs expenses exceeding $1,550 to receive benefits.

The plan must limit out-of-pocket costs for covered expenses. For 1999, the out-of-pocket limit is $3,050 for single coverage and $5,600 for family coverage. Premiums are not subject to the limit. An inflation adjustment could increase the limits for the year 2000.

Generally, you are not eligible for an MSA if you have any other health insurance in addition to the high-deductible plan coverage, except for policies covering only disability, vision or dental care, long-term care, or accidental injuries, or plans that pay a flat amount during hospitalization.

If you are a Medicare beneficiary, you are not eligible for an MSA. However, starting in 1999, Medicare beneficiaries may be able to combine a Medicare MSA (savings account) with a high-deductible Medicare MSA health policy as an alternative to traditional Medicare coverage.

Employer contribution limits. Your employer's contributions to your MSA are tax free up to an annual limit of 65% of the plan deductible if you have individual coverage and 75% of the deductible for family coverage. The limit is reduced on a monthly basis if you are not covered for the entire year. For example, if for all of 1999 you were covered by a qualifying family coverage high-deductible plan with a $4,600 annual deductible, the maximum tax-free contribution is $3,450 (75% of $4,600). If you had coverage for only 10 months, the limit would be $2,875 ($^{10}/_{12}$ × $3,450). All employer contributions to your MSA are reported in Box 13 of Form W-2 (Code R). If the contributions exceed the tax-free limit, the excess is reported in Box 1 of Form W-2 as taxable wages.

If your employer makes any contributions to your account, you may not make any contributions for that year. In addition, if you and your spouse have family coverage under a high-deductible plan and your spouse's employer contributes to his or her MSA, you cannot contribute to your MSA. If your employer (or spouse's employer) does not contribute, you may make deductible contributions up to the above employer contribution limits. Your deduction is claimed on Line 25 of Form 1040. Contributions exceeding the annual limit are subject to a 6% penalty.

Self-employed also eligible. A self-employed person may make deductible contributions to an MSA up to the employer contribution limits discussed above; *see* Chapter 17 for deduction details.

Access and Portability Rules for Group Health Plans

Generally, a group health plan may not bar eligibility to an employee and his or her dependents because of health status or medical history. A plan may exclude coverage for specified conditions or procedures, or limit such coverage, but only if there is no discrimination among similarly situated employees based on health-related factors. Employers are subject to daily penalties if they do not comply with the rules, but small employers with an average of no more than 50 employees in the preceding year are exempt.

Pre-existing conditions can bar coverage only in limited circumstances. Coverage may be denied for a condition that was diagnosed or treated within six months before enrollment. However, the exclusion cannot last more than 12 months, or 18 months for those who enroll late, and the 12-or-18-month period must be reduced by creditable coverage the employee had before enrollment in the new plan if there was no break in the prior coverage of more than 62 days. Coverage may not be denied to women pregnant on the enrollment date. Newborn children who are enrolled within 30 days of birth must be covered and if the parent changes jobs and enrolls in a new plan without a break in coverage of more than 62 days, the new plan may not exclude the child. A similar protective rule applies to adopted children under age 18 who are enrolled within 30 days of the adoption.

Continuing coverage for group health plans (COBRA coverage). Employers are subject to daily penalties unless they offer continuing group health and accident coverage to employees who leave the company and to spouses and dependent children who would lose coverage in the case of divorce or the death of the employee. The employer may charge the employee or beneficiary a premium of up to 102% of the regular premium imposed under the plan for the applicable (individual or family) coverage. The employer must wait at least 45 days after continuing coverage is elected to require payment of premiums.

 Court Decision

COBRA Required Despite Other Coverage

The Supreme Court has held that an employer may not deny continuing care coverage to a former employee who on the date of election has coverage under his or her spouse's group health plan.

Continuing coverage rules do not apply to small employers who in the previous calendar year had fewer than 20 employees on a typical day, or government agencies and churches. For other employers, continuing coverage must be offered in these situations:

1. An employee with coverage who voluntarily or involuntarily leaves the company—unless termination is for gross misconduct. Employees who would lose coverage because of a reduction in hours must also be offered continuing coverage. Continuing coverage must also be offered for the employee's spouse and dependent children who were covered before the employee's termination or reduction in hours. If accepted, the coverage must last for at least 18 months. Within this period, an employee who elects continuing coverage is protected against the possibility of a coverage gap if he or she joins a new company that limits group health coverage for pre-existing conditions; the old employer's continuing coverage must remain available.

   Extended coverage may apply to disabled individuals. The coverage period is extended from 18 months to 29 months for individuals who notify the plan administrator within 60 days of a determination under Title II or XVI of the Social Security Act that they are disabled. Before 1997, the disability had to exist when employment terminated or hours were reduced. After 1996, the coverage extension applies if the disability exists at any time during the first 60 days of continuing coverage. During the extended coverage period, the maximum premium that can be charged is increased from 102% to 150% of the applicable premium.

2. On the death of a covered employee, continuing coverage must be offered to the surviving spouse and dependent children who are beneficiaries under the plan on the day before the death. Coverage must be for at least 36 months.

3. If a covered employee obtains a divorce or legal separation, continuing coverage must be offered to the spouse and dependent children for at least 36 months.

4. If a covered employee becomes eligible for Medicare benefits, continuing coverage under the employer's plan must be offered to the employee's spouse and dependent children for at least 36 months.

5. If a dependent child becomes ineligible under the plan upon reaching a certain age, continuing coverage must be offered for at least 36 months.

6. If an employee with health coverage takes unpaid leave under the Family and Medical Leave Act of 1993 (FMLA) upon the birth or adoption of a child or to deal with a serious family illness, and the employee does not return to work following the leave, continuing coverage must be offered as of the last day of the leave. Continuing coverage must also be offered to the employee's spouse and dependent children if they would otherwise lose coverage.

Employers must provide written notice of the continuing coverage option. If one of the previously discussed qualifying events occurs, the eligible employees, spouses, and/or dependent children generally have 60 days to elect continuing coverage.

3.2 Tax-Free Payments From Employer Health and Accident Plans

There are two general categories of tax-free benefits paid from employer-financed health and accident plans: (1) reimbursements of medical expenses, and (2) payments for permanent physical injuries. In addition, payments from a long-term care insurance contract or medical savings account may be tax free. Details on these categories are below.

Tax-free benefits from qualifying long-term care policy. Payments from a qualifying long-term care policy (meeting the tests in *17.15*) are tax free if they reimburse long-term care expenses. If payments are received in 1999 under a per diem plan that provides a flat daily amount, the tax-free limit is $190 per day unless you can show that you had actual expenses for long-term services equal to part or all of the excess over the $190 limit. *See 17.15* for further details.

Tax-free benefits from medical savings account. If you work for a small-business employer and have a qualifying medical savings account (MSA), earnings accumulate in the account tax free. Withdrawals from an MSA are tax free if used to pay deductible medical costs for you, your spouse, or dependents. Withdrawals used for any other purpose are taxable and a taxable distribution before age 65 or becoming disabled is also subject to a 15% penalty. *See* Chapter 17 for further details.

Taxable payments. Benefits that are not tax free under the above rules are *fully taxable* if: (1) your employer paid all the premiums, and (2) you were not required to report the premiums as taxable income. If you and your employer each paid part of the premiums and you were not taxed on your employer's payment, the portion of the benefits allocable to the employer's contribution is taxed to you. You are not taxed on benefits to the extent that you paid the premiums with after-tax contributions. Examples of figuring the taxable portion of the benefits are at *17.4*.

Reimbursed Medical Expenses

Tax-free payments generally include specific reimbursements of medical expenses for yourself, your spouse, or any dependent. Payment does not have to come directly to you to be tax free; it may go directly to your medical care providers.

Tax-free treatment applies only for reimbursed expenses, not amounts you would have received anyway, such as sick leave that is not dependent on actual medical expenses.

Reimbursements for cosmetic surgery do *not* qualify for tax-free treatment, unless the surgery is for disfigurement related to congenital deformity, disease, or accidental injury.

Reimbursements in 1999 for your *dependents'* medical expenses are tax free, even if you may not claim them as personal exemptions because they had more than $2,750 of income or filed a joint return. Furthermore, if you are divorced and your children have health coverage under your plan, reimbursements of their expenses are not taxable to you, even if your ex-spouse claims them as dependents; *see 21.11*.

A qualifying dependent does *not* include a live-in mate where the relationship violates local law.

If the reimbursement is for medical expenses you deducted in a previous year, the reimbursement may be taxable. *See 17.4* for the rules on reimbursements of deducted medical expenses.

If you receive payments from more than one policy in excess of your actual medical expenses, the excess is taxable if your employer paid the entire premium; *see* Examples in *17.4*.

Self-employed health plan for spouse. As discussed in *3.1*, if a self-employed person hires his spouse and provides family coverage under a health plan purchased in the name of the business, the employee-spouse may be reimbursed tax-free for medical expenses incurred by both spouses and their dependent children.

Executives taxed in discriminatory self-insured medical reimbursement plans.
Although reimbursements from an employer plan for medical expenses of an employee and his or her spouse and dependents are generally tax free, this exclusion does not apply to certain highly compensated employees and stockholders if the plan is self-insured and it discriminates on their behalf. A plan is self-insured if reimbursement is not provided by an unrelated insurance company. If coverage is provided by an unrelated insurer, these discrimination rules do not apply. If a self-insured plan is deemed discriminatory, rank-and-file employees are not affected; only highly compensated employees are subject to tax.

Highly compensated participants subject to these rules include employees owning more than 10% of the employer's stock, the highest paid 25% of all employees (other than employees who do not have to be covered under the law), and the five highest paid officers.

If highly compensated employees are entitled to reimbursement for expenses not available to other plan participants, any such reimbursements are taxable to them. For example, if only the five highest paid officers are entitled to dental benefits, any dental reimbursements they receive are taxable. However, routine physical exams may be provided to highly compensated employees (but not their dependents) on a discriminatory basis. This exception does not apply to testing for, or treatment of, a specific complaint.

If highly compensated participants are entitled to a higher reimbursement limit than other participants, any excess reimbursement over the lower limit is taxable to the highly compensated participant. For example, if highly compensated employees are entitled to reimbursements up to $5,000, while all others have a $1,000 limit, a highly compensated employee who receives a $4,000 reimbursement must report $3,000 ($4,000 received minus $1,000 lower limit) as income.

A separate nondiscrimination test applies to plan *eligibility*. The eligibility test requires that the plan benefit: (1) 70% or more of all employees or (2) 80% or more of employees eligible to participate, provided that at least 70% of all employees are eligible. A plan not meeting either test is considered discriminatory unless proven otherwise. In applying these tests, employees may be excluded if they have less than three years of service, are under age 25, do part-time or seasonal work, or are covered by a union collective bargaining agreement. A fraction of the benefits received by a highly compensated individual from a nonqualifying plan is taxable. The fraction equals the total reimbursements to highly compensated participants divided by total plan reimbursements; benefits

 Caution

Reimbursed Cosmetic Surgery
An employer's reimbursement of expenses for cosmetic surgery is taxable unless the employee had surgery to correct disfigurement from an accident, disease, or congenital deformity.

available only to highly compensated employees are disregarded. For example, assume that a plan failing the eligibility tests pays total reimbursements of $50,000, of which $30,000 is to highly compensated participants. A highly compensated executive who is reimbursed $4,500 for medical expenses must include $2,700 in income:

$$\frac{30,000}{50,000} \times 4,500 = 2,700$$

Taxable reimbursements are reported in the year during which the applicable plan year ends. For example, in early 2000 you are reimbursed for a 1999 expense from a calendar-year plan. If under plan provisions the expenses are allocated to the 1999 plan year, the taxable amount should be reported as 1999 income. If the plan does not specify the plan year to which the reimbursement relates, the reimbursement is attributed to the plan year in which payment is made.

Permanent Physical Injuries

Payments from an employer plan are tax free if they are for the permanent loss of part of the body, permanent loss of use of part of the body, or for permanent disfigurement of yourself, your spouse, or a dependent. To be tax free, the payments must be based on the kind of injury and have no relation to the length of time you are out of work or prior years of service. If the employer's plan does not specifically allocate benefits according to the nature of the injury, the benefits are taxable even if an employee is in fact permanently disabled.

EXAMPLE

After he loses a foot in an accident, Marc Jones receives $50,000 as specified in his employer's plan. The payment is tax free as it does not depend on how long Jones is out from work.

An appeals court held that severe hypertension does not involve loss of a bodily part or function and thus does not qualify for the exclusion.

Disability payments from profit-sharing plan. The Tax Court has held that a profit-sharing plan may provide benefits that qualify for the exclusion for permanent disfigurement or permanent loss of bodily function. The plan must clearly state that its purpose is to provide qualifying tax-free benefits, and a specific payment schedule must be provided for different types of injuries. Without such provisions, payments from the plan are treated as taxable retirement distributions.

3.3 Group-Term Life Insurance Premiums

You are not taxed on your employer's payments of premiums on a policy of up to $50,000 on your life. You are taxed only on the cost of premiums for coverage of over $50,000 as determined by the IRS rates shown in the table on the next page. On Form W-2 your employer should include the taxable amount as wages in Box 1 and separately label the amount in Box 13. You may not avoid tax by assigning the policy to another person.

If two or more employers provide you with group-term insurance coverage, you get only one $50,000 exclusion. You must figure the taxable cost for coverage over $50,000 by using the IRS rates on the next page.

Regardless of the amount of the policy, you are not taxed if, for your entire tax year, the beneficiary of the policy is a tax-exempt charitable organization or your employer.

Your payments reduce taxable amount. If you pay part of the cost of the insurance, your payment reduces dollar for dollar the amount includible as pay on Form W-2.

Retirees. If you retired before 1984 at normal retirement age or on disability and are still covered by a company group-term life insurance policy, you are not taxed on premium payments made by your employer even if coverage is over $50,000. If you retired after 1983 because of disability and remain covered by your company's plan, you are not taxed even if coverage exceeds $50,000. Furthermore, if you retired after 1983 and are not disabled, you may qualify for tax-free coverage over $50,000 if the following tests are met:

1. The insurance is provided under a plan existing on January 1, 1984, or under a comparable successor plan;
2. You were employed during 1983 by the company having the plan, or a predecessor employer; and
3. You were age 55 or over on January 1, 1984.

However, even if the three tests are met, you may be taxed under the rule below for discriminatory plans if you retired after 1986 and were a key employee.

Filing Tip

Permanent Physical Injuries

An employer's payment for permanent disfigurement or permanent loss of bodily function is tax free if the payment is based solely on the nature of the injury. Whether or not you qualify for this exclusion, you may deduct as an itemized deduction any unreimbursed medical expense you have in connection with these injuries subject to the 7.5% adjusted gross income floor; *see 17.1* for details.

Filing Instruction

Uncollected Social Security and Medicare

You must pay with Form 1040 (Line 56) your share of Social Security and Medicare taxes on group-term life insurance over $50,000. The taxable amounts are shown in Box 13 of Form W-2, with Codes M and N.

Key employees taxed under discriminatory plans. The $50,000 exclusion is not available to key employees unless the group plan meets nondiscrimination tests for eligibility and benefits. Key employees include those who during the year or during any of the four preceding years were: (1) more than 5% owners; (2) more than 1% owners earning over $150,000; (3) one of the 10 largest owners with compensation over an annual limit; and (4) officers with compensation over an annual limit. The 1999 compensation limit is $30,000 for the 10 largest owners and $65,000 for officers. If the plan discriminates, a key employee's taxable benefit is based on the larger of (1) the actual cost of coverage, and (2) the amount for coverage using the IRS rate table below.

The nondiscrimination rules also apply to former employees who were key employees when they separated from service. The discrimination tests are applied separately with respect to active and former employees.

Group-term life insurance for dependents. Employer-paid coverage for your spouse or dependents is a tax-free *de minimis* fringe benefit *(3.9)* if the policy is $2,000 or less. For coverage over $2,000, you are taxed on the excess of the cost (determined under the IRS table below) over your after-tax payments for the insurance, if any.

Permanent life insurance. If your employer pays premiums on your behalf for permanent nonforfeitable life insurance, you report as taxable wages the cost of the benefit, less any amount you paid. A permanent benefit is an economic value that extends beyond one year and includes paid-up insurance or cash surrender value, but does not include, for example, the right to convert or continue life insurance coverage after group coverage is terminated. Where permanent benefits are combined with term insurance, the permanent benefits are taxed under formulas found in IRS regulations.

 Law Alert

Change in Coverage Valuation Rates

New IRS rates for valuing employer-provided group-term life insurance coverage took effect on July 1, 1999. The new rates reflect longer life expectancies and provide lower taxable amounts than the prior rates. The table on the left reflects both the old and new rates for purposes of valuing 1999 coverage exceeding $50,000.

Taxable Monthly Premiums for Each $1,000 of Coverage Over $50,000

Age—*	Coverage before July 1, 1999—	Coverage on or after July 1, 1999—
Under 25	$0.08	$0.05**
25–29	0.08	0.06
30–34	0.09	0.08
35–39	0.11	0.09
40–44	0.17	0.10
45–49	0.29	0.15
50–54	0.48	0.23
55–59	0.75	0.43
60–64	1.17	0.66
65–69	2.10	1.27
70 and over	3.76	2.06

* Age is determined at end of year.
** For coverage between July 1, 1999 and the end of 1999, an employer may treat employees under age 25 as if they were in the 25–29 category for purposes of calculating the taxable amount to be reported on Form W-2.

EXAMPLE

Lynda Jackson, a 52-year-old executive, is provided $200,000 of group-term life insurance in 1999. The taxable value of the coverage is based on $150,000 of excess coverage ($200,000 – $50,000). As shown in the rate table above, the premium used to determine the taxable portion of the coverage between January 1,1999, and June 30,1999, is $0.48 for every $1,000 of coverage over $50,000. For the excess coverage of $150,000, the taxable amount for that period is $432 ($0.48 (premium) x 6 months x 150). The premium for the coverage after June 30,1999, as shown in the table, is $0.23 for every $1,000 of coverage over $50,000. The taxable amount for the second six-month period is $207 ($0.23 x 6 months x 150). For the year, the taxable amount is $639 ($432 + $207).

If Lynda had paid $120 towards the coverage, the taxable amount would be reduced to $519 ($639 – $120).

Dependent Care, Adoption Benefits, and Educational Assistance

3.4   Dependent Care Assistance

The value of qualifying day-care services provided by your employer under a written, nondiscriminatory plan is generally not taxable up to a limit of $5,000, or $2,500 if you are filing separately. The same tax-free limits apply if you make pre-tax salary deferrals to a flexible spending account for reimbursing dependent care expenses *(3.14)*. However, you may not exclude from income more than your earned income. If you are married and your spouse earns less than you do, your tax-free benefit is limited to his or her earned income. If your spouse does not work, all of your benefits are taxable unless he or she is a full-time student or is disabled. If a full-time student or disabled, your spouse is treated as earning $200 a month if your dependent care expenses are for one dependent, or $400 a month if the expenses are for two or more dependents.

Expenses are excludable from income only if they would qualify for the dependent care credit; *see* Chapter 25. If you are being reimbursed by your employer, the exclusion is not allowed if dependent care is provided by a relative who is your dependent (or your spouse's dependent) or by your child under the age of 19. You must give your employer a record of the care provider's name, address, and tax identification number. The identifying information also must be listed on your return.

Reporting employer benefits on your return. Your employer will show the total amount of your dependent care benefits in Box 10 of your Form W-2. Any benefits over $5,000 will also be included as taxable wages in Box 1 of Form W-2 and as Social Security wages (Box 3) and Medicare wages (Box 5).

If you file Form 1040, you must report the benefits on Part III of Form 2441. If you file Form 1040A, you report the employer benefits on Schedule 2. On these forms, you determine both the tax-free and taxable (if any) portions of the employer-provided benefits. If any part is taxable, that amount must be included on Line 7 of your return as wages and labeled "DCB."

Follow IRS instructions for identifying the care provider (employer, babysitter, etc.) on Form 2441 or on Schedule 2 of Form 1040A.

The tax-free portion of employer benefits reduces eligibility for the dependent care credit; see *Chapter 25.*

3.5   Adoption Benefits

If your employer pays or reimburses you for qualifying adoption expenses under a written, nondiscriminatory plan, up to $5,000 may be tax free (*see* below); the excludable limit increases to $6,000 for the adoption of a child with special needs. If you have other qualifying adoption expenses, you may also be able to claim a tax credit up to a separate $5,000 or $6,000 limit; both the exclusion and the credit may be claimed for the same adoption if they are not for the same expenses. The exclusion and the credit are subject to similar limitations, including a phaseout based on income. *See* Chapter 25 for a full discussion of the credit.

Employer-provided adoption assistance may be for any child under age 18, or a person physically or mentally incapable of self-care. A "special needs" designation may be made for a child who is a U.S. citizen or resident where special factors (such as physical condition) indicate that adoption assistance is required.

Reporting employer benefits and claiming the exclusion on your return. You must file Form 8839 to report your employer's payments and to figure the tax-free and taxable portions of the benefits. The employer's payments will be included in Box 13 of Form W-2 (Code T). This total includes pre-tax salary reduction contributions that you made to a cafeteria plan *(3.13)* to cover such expenses.

If you are married, you generally must file a joint return to exclude the benefits as income. However, if you are legally separated or if you lived apart from your spouse for the last six months of the year, the exclusion may be available on a separate return; see Form 8839 for details.

The $5,000 exclusion limit ($6,000 for a special needs child) is not an annual limit; it applies to each effort to adopt an eligible child even if the effort lasts longer than one year. The exclusion applies to adoption fees, attorney fees, court costs, travel expenses, and other expenses directly related to a legal adoption. Expenses for adopting your spouse's child and the costs of a surrogate-parenting arrangement do *not* qualify.

Caution

Figuring Tax-Free Exclusion for Employer-Provided Dependent Care

You cannot assume that your employer-provided dependent care benefit is completely tax free merely because your employer has not included any part of it in Box 1 of Form W-2 as taxable wages. Although up to $5,000 of benefits are generally tax free, the tax-free amount is reduced where you or your spouse earn less than $5,000 or where you file separately from your spouse. You must show the amount of your qualifying dependent care expenses and figure the tax-free exclusion on Form 2441 if you file Form 1040, or on Schedule 2 of Form 1040A.

Filing Tip

Claiming Credit and Exclusion

If you paid adoption expenses in 1999 that were not reimbursed by your employer, and the adoption was final in 1999, you may be able to claim the adoption credit; *see* Chapter 25.

The exclusion applies in the year your employer pays the qualifying expenses *unless* you are adopting a foreign child. If the child is not a U.S. citizen or resident when the adoption effort begins, the exclusion is available only in the year the adoption becomes final. For example, if in 1998 your employer pays for expenses of adopting a foreign child but the adoption has not become final by the end of the year, you must report the employer's payment as 1998 income. You will claim the exclusion on Form 8839 in the year the adoption is final.

The allowable exclusion is phased out if your modified adjusted gross income is between $75,000 and $115,000 (including the employer's adoption assistance and adding back certain tax-free income from foreign sources). Figure the tax-free amount on Form 8839. If your modified adjusted income is $115,000 or more, employer-paid adoption expenses are fully taxable.

3.6 Education Assistance Plans

If your employer pays for job-related courses, the payment is tax free to you provided that the courses do not satisfy the employer's minimum education standards and do not qualify you for a new profession. If these tests are met, the employer's education assistance is a tax-free working condition fringe benefit *(3.8)*.

Even if not job related, your employer's payment for *undergraduate* courses beginning before January 1, 2002, is tax free up to $5,250, provided the assistance is under a qualifying Section 127 plan meeting nondiscriminatory tests. This exclusion does not apply to graduate-level courses.

Tuition reductions. Employees and retired employees of educational institutions, their spouses, and their dependent children are not taxed on tuition reductions for *undergraduate* courses provided the reduction is not payment for teaching or other services. Widows or widowers of deceased employees or of former employees also qualify. Officers and highly paid employees may claim the exclusion only if the employer plan does not discriminate on their behalf. The exclusion applies to tuition for undergraduate education at any educational institution, not only the employer's school.

Graduate students who are teaching or research assistants at an educational institution are not taxed on tuition reductions for courses at that school if the tuition reduction is in addition to regular pay for the teaching or research services.

The graduate student exclusion for tuition reductions applies only to teaching and research assistants, and not to faculty or other staff members (or their spouses and dependents) who take graduate courses and also do research for or teach at the school. However, if the graduate courses are work related, a tuition reduction for faculty and staff may qualify as a tax-free working condition fringe benefit *(3.8)*.

Planning Reminder

Graduate Courses
Your employer's payment of graduate school expenses does not qualify for the $5,250 exclusion. However, if the courses are job related, the employer's payment may be a tax-free working condition fringe benefit; *see 3.8*.

Company Cars, Working Conditions and *De Minimis* Benefits, and Employee Achievement Awards

3.7 Company Cars, Parking, and Transit Passes

The costs of commuting to a regular job site are not deductible *(20.2)*, but employees who receive transit passes or travel to work on an employer-financed van get a tax break by not having to pay tax on some or all of such benefits. Where a company car is provided, the value of personal use is generally taxable, as discussed below.

Company cars. The use of a company car is tax free under the working condition fringe benefit rule *(3.8)*, provided you use the car for business. If you use the car for personal driving, you may be taxed on the value of such personal use. Your company has the responsibility of calculating taxable income based on IRS tables that specify the value of various priced cars. For certain cars, a flat mileage allowance may be used to measure personal use. You are also required to keep for your employer a mileage log or similar record to substantiate your business use. Your employer should tell you what type of records are required.

Regardless of personal use, you are not subject to tax for a company vehicle that the IRS considers to be of limited personal value. These are ambulances or hearses; flatbed trucks; dump, garbage, or refrigerated trucks; one-passenger delivery trucks (including trucks with folding jump seats); tractors, combines, and other farm equipment; or forklifts. Also not taxable is personal use of school buses, passenger buses (seating at least 20), and moving vans where such personal use is restricted; and police or fire vehicles, or an unmarked law enforcement vehicle, where personal use is authorized by a government agency.

Planning Reminder

Year-End Benefits
Your employer may decide to treat fringe benefits provided during the last two months of the calendar year as if they were paid during the following year. If this election is made for a company car in 1999, only the value of personal use from January through October is taxable in 1999; personal use in November and December is taxable in 2000. If your employer elects this special year-end rule, you should be notified near the end of the year or when you receive Form W-2.

Demonstration cars. The value of a demonstration car used by a full-time auto salesperson is tax free as a working condition fringe benefit if the use of the car facilitates job performance and if there are substantial personal-use restrictions, including a prohibition on use by family members and for vacation trips. Furthermore, mileage outside of normal working hours must be limited and personal driving must generally be restricted to a 75-mile radius around the dealer's sales office.

Chauffeur services. If chauffeur services are provided for both business and personal purposes, you must report as income the value of the personal services. For example, if the full value of the chauffeur services is $30,000 and 30% of the chauffeur's workday is spent driving on personal trips, then $9,000 is taxable (30% of $30,000) and $21,000 is tax free.

If an employer provides a bodyguard-chauffeur for business security reasons, the entire value of the chauffeur services is considered a tax-free working condition fringe benefit if: (1) the automobile is specially equipped for security and (2) the bodyguard is trained in evasive driving techniques and is provided as part of an overall 24-hour-a-day security program. If the value of the bodyguard-chauffeur services is tax free, the employee is still taxable on the value of using the vehicle for commuting or other personal travel.

How your employer reports taxable automobile benefits. Social Security and Medicare tax must be withheld. Income tax withholding is not required, but your employer may choose to withhold income tax. If income tax is *not* withheld, you must be notified of this fact so that you may consider the taxable benefits when determining whether to make estimated tax installments; *see* Chapter 27. Whether or not withholdings are taken, the taxable value of the benefits is entered on your Form W-2 in Box 12 or on a separate Form W-2 for fringe benefits.

A special IRS rule allows your employer to include 100% of the lease value of using the car on Form W-2, even if you used the car primarily for business. Your employer must specifically indicate on Form W-2 (Box 12) or on a separate statement if 100% of the lease value has been included as income on your Form W-2. If it has, you should compute a deduction on Form 2106 for the business-use value of the car. However, this deduction, plus any unreimbursed car operating expenses, may be claimed only as a miscellaneous itemized deduction on Schedule A subject to the 2% AGI floor; *see 19.1.*

Company planes. Under rules similar to those for company cars, employees who use a company airplane for personal trips are taxable on the value of the flights, as determined by the employer using IRS tables.

Employer-provided transit passes and van pooling. For regular employees, up to $65 a month is tax free in 1999 for the combined value of employer-provided transit passes plus commuting on an employer's van or bus. For example, if in 1999 the monthly value of a transit pass was $70, $5 per month was treated as taxable wages. If the value of benefits was less than $65 in any month, the unused exclusion cannot be carried over to later months. For years after 1999, the $65 monthly exclusion may be adjusted for inflation.

Qualifying transit passes include tokens, fare cards, or vouchers for mass transit or private transportation businesses using highway vehicles seating at least six passengers.

Qualifying van or bus pool vehicles must seat at least six passengers and be used at least 80% of the time for employee commuting; on average, the number of employees must be at least half the seating capacity.

The up-to-$65 monthly exclusion generally applies to cash reimbursements from the employer under a bona fide reimbursement arrangement. However, cash advances are taxable. If an employer has access to vouchers readily exchangeable for transit passes, the vouchers must be used; in that case, cash reimbursements would be taxable.

The $65 exclusion applies only to regular employees. For partners, more than 2% S corporation shareholders, and independent contractors who are provided transit passes, the IRS allows up to $21 per month as a tax-free *de minimis* benefit. If the monthly value exceeds $21, the full value is taxable and not just the excess over $21.

Parking provided by employer. For regular employees, the value of employer-provided parking spots or subsidized parking is tax free in 1999 up to a limit of $175 per month. Parking must be on or near the employer's premises, at a mass transit facility such as a train station or car pooling center. The value of parking benefits exceeding $175 per month is taxable in 1999. For years after 1999, the $175 monthly cap may be adjusted for inflation.

The tax will generally apply to employees working in major urban business districts where parking is costly, or in suburban areas where commercial lots are available.

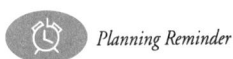
Planning Reminder

Transportation Benefits
If your employer offers you the choice of receiving parking, transit pass, or van pooling benefits instead of cash salary as part of a "cafeteria" plan *(3.13)* and you elect the benefits rather than the cash, you are not taxed, provided the value does not exceed the monthly tax-free limit.

Commuter parking benefits for self-employed partners or more than 2% S corporation share-holders do not qualify for an exclusion and are fully taxable. However, parking benefits provided by the employer while the employee is away from the regular office, such as on one-day business trips to other company locations, are generally treated as tax-free working condition fringe benefits *(3.8)* or *de minimis* benefits *(3.9)*. Parking benefits provided to independent contractors are also generally tax free *de minimis* benefits.

According to the IRS, parking benefits are to be valued according to the regular commercial price for parking at the same or nearby locations. For example, if an employer in a rural or suburban location provides free parking for employees and there are no commercial parking lots in the area, the employee parking is tax free. Where free parking is available to both business customers and employees, the employee parking is considered to have "zero" value unless the employee has a *reserved* parking space that is closer to the business entrance than the spaces allotted to customers.

If the value of the right of access to a parking space exceeds $175 in a month, an employee will be taxed on the excess even if he or she actually uses the space for only a few days during the month.

If the employee pays a reduced monthly price for parking in 1999, there is a taxable benefit for that month only if the price paid plus the $175 exclusion is less than the value of the parking.

3.8 Working Condition Fringe Benefits

An employer-provided benefit that would be deductible by you if you paid for it yourself *(19.3)* is a tax-free working condition fringe benefit. Under IRS regulations, such benefits include:

Company car or plane. The value of a company car or plane is tax free to the extent that you use it for business; *see 3.7* for more on company cars.

Employer-paid business subscriptions or reimbursed membership dues in professional associations.

Product testing. This is a limited exclusion for employees who test and evaluate company manufactured goods away from company premises.

Employer-provided education assistance. Employer-paid undergraduate and graduate courses may be a tax-free working condition fringe benefit if the courses maintain or improve job skills but are not needed to meet your employer's minimum educational requirements and do not prepare you for a new profession.

Job-placement assistance. According to the IRS, job placement services are tax free so long as they are geared to helping the employees find jobs in the same line of work and the employees do not have an option to take cash instead of the benefits. The employer must also have a business purpose for providing such assistance, such as maintaining employee morale.

For tax-free treatment, there is no nondiscrimination requirement; different types of job placement assistance may be offered, or no assistance at all, in the case of discharged employees with readily transferable skills. Tax-free benefits include the value of counseling on interviewing skills and resume preparation. Executives may be given secretarial support and the use of a private office during the job search.

Job placement benefits received as part of a severance pay arrangement are taxable to the extent that cash could have been elected. An offsetting deduction can be claimed only as a miscellaneous itemized deduction subject to the 2% adjusted gross income floor *(19.3)*.

3.9 *De Minimis* Fringe Benefits

Small benefits that would be administratively impractical to tax are considered tax-free *de minimis* (minor) fringe benefits. Examples are personal use of company copying machines, company parties, or tickets for the theater or sporting events. Other *de minimis* benefits include:

Company eating facility. The value of meals received by employees on workdays at a subsidized eating facility is a tax-free *de minimis* fringe benefit if the facility is located on or near the business premises and the annual revenue from meal charges equals or exceeds the facility's direct operating costs. Revenue is treated as equal to operating costs for meals that are tax-free to employees under the employer convenience test discussed at *3.11*.

Highly compensated employees or owners with special access to executive dining rooms may not exclude the value of their meals as a *de minimis* fringe benefit; however, the meals may be tax free under the rules in *3.11* if meals must be taken on company premises for business reasons.

Planning Reminder

Occasional overtime meal money or cab fare

If you work overtime and occasionally receive meal money or cab fare home, the amount is tax free. The IRS has not provided a numerical standard for determining when payments are "occasional."

Caution

Underpriced Award Items

If the value of an achievement award item is disproportionately high compared to the employer's cost, the IRS may conclude that the award is disguised compensation, in which case the entire value would be taxable to you.

Commuting under unsafe circumstances. If you are asked to work outside your normal working hours and due to unsafe conditions your employer provides transportation such as taxi fare, the first $1.50 per one-way commute is taxable but the excess over $1.50 is tax free. This exclusion is not available to certain highly compensated employees and officers, corporate directors, or owners of 1% or more of the company.

Even when working their regular shift, hourly employees who are not considered highly compensated are taxed on only $1.50 per one-way commute if their employer pays for car service or taxi fare because walking or taking public transportation to or from work would be unsafe. The excess value of the transportation over $1.50 is tax free. These rules can apply to day-shift employees who work overtime as well as night-shift employees working regular hours so long as transportation is provided because of unsafe conditions.

3.10 Employee Achievement Awards

Achievement awards are taxable unless they meet special rules for awards of tangible personal property (such as a watch, television, or golf clubs) given to you in recognition of length of service or safety achievement. Cash awards, gift certificates, and similar items are taxable.

As a general rule, if your employer is allowed to deduct the cost of a tangible personal property award, you are not taxed. The employer's deduction limit, and therefore the excludable limit for you, is $400 for awards from nonqualified plans and $1,600 for awards from qualified plans or from a combination of qualified and nonqualified plans. If your employer's deduction is less than the item's cost, you are taxed on the greater of: (1) the difference between the cost and your employer's deduction, but no more than the award's fair market value; and (2) the excess of the item's fair market value over your employer's deduction. Deduction tests for achievement awards are discussed at 20.25. Your employer must tell you if the award qualifies for full or partial tax-free treatment.

An award will not be treated as a tax-free safety achievement award if employee safety achievement awards (other than those of *de minimis* value) were granted during the year to more than 10% of employees (not counting managers, administrators, clerical employees, or other professional employees). An award made to a manager, administrator, clerical employee, or other professional employee for safety achievement does not qualify for tax-free treatment.

Tax-free treatment also does not apply when you receive an award for length of service during the first five years of employment or when you previously received such awards during the last five years, unless the prior award qualified as a *de minimis* fringe benefit.

Meals and Lodging

Law Alert

Meal Exclusion Liberalized

Under the 1998 Tax Act, you may be able to avoid tax on meals that you receive on your employer's premises even if your meals do not satisfy the employer convenience test. If more than half of the employees to whom meals are furnished on the employer's business premises are furnished the meals for the employer's convenience, *all* of the on-premises meals are treated as being furnished for the employer's convenience.

The new law applies retroactively. Thus, a refund claim may be filed on a timely filed amended return *(see 49.1)* for taxes paid on employer-provided meals now tax free under the new law.

3.11 Employer-Furnished Meals or Lodging

The value of employer-furnished *meals* is not taxable if furnished on your employer's business premises for the employer's convenience. The value of *lodging* is not taxable if, as a condition of your employment, you must accept the lodging on the employer's business premises for the employer's convenience. The condition of employment test applies to lodging but not meals.

Business premises test. The IRS generally defines business premises as the place of employment, such as a company cafeteria in a factory for a cook or an employer's home for a household employee. The Tax Court has a more liberal view, extending the area of business premises beyond the actual place of business in such cases as these:

- A house provided a hotel manager, although located across the street from the hotel. The IRS has agreed to the decision.
- A house provided a motel manager, two blocks from the motel. However, a court of appeals reversed the decision and held in the IRS's favor.
- A rented hotel suite that is used daily by executives for a luncheon conference.

Convenience of employer test. The employer convenience test requires proof that an employer provides the free meals or lodging for a business purpose other than providing extra pay. In the case of meals, the employer convenience test is deemed to be satisfied for *all* meals provided on employer premises if a qualifying business purpose is shown for more than 50% of the meals. *See* the Law Alert on this page. If meals and lodging are described in a contract or state statute as extra pay, this does not bar tax-free treatment provided they are *also* furnished for other substantial, noncompensatory business reasons; for example, you are required to be on call 24 hours a day, or there are inadequate eating facilities near the business premises.

EXAMPLES

1. A Las Vegas casino operator provided free cafeteria meals to employees, who were required to remain on casino premises during their entire shift. A federal appeals court (Ninth Circuit) held that the casino's "stay-on-premises" requirement constituted a legitimate business reason for the meals and thus all of the employee meals were tax free under the employer convenience test. The court refused to second guess the casino's business decision that a "stay-on-premises" policy was necessary for security and logistics reasons. Once that policy was adopted, the casino employees had no choice but to eat on the premises. The IRS responded to the decision by announcing that it would not challenge "employer convenience" treatment in similar cases where employees are precluded from obtaining a meal off-premises within a normal meal period.

2. A waitress who works from 7 a.m. to 4 p.m. is furnished two meals a day without charge. Her employer encourages her to have her breakfast at the restaurant before working, but she is required to have her lunch there. The value of her breakfast and lunch is not taxable under IRS regulations because it is furnished during her work period or immediately before or after the period. But say she is also allowed to have free meals on her days off and a free supper on the days she works. The value of these meals is taxable; they are not furnished during or immediately before or after her work period.

3. A hospital maintains a cafeteria on its premises where all of its employees may eat during their working hours. No charge is made for these meals. The hospital furnishes meals to have the employees available for emergencies. The employees are not required to eat there. Since the hospital furnishes the meals in order to have employees available for emergency call during meal periods, the meals are not income to any of the hospital employees who obtain their meals at the hospital cafeteria.

4. To assure bank teller service during the busy lunch period, a bank limits tellers to 30 minutes for lunch and provides them with free meals in a cafeteria on the premises so they can eat within this time period. The value of the meals is tax free.

Meal charges. Your company may charge for meals on company premises and give you an option to accept or decline the meals. However, by law, the IRS must disregard the charge and option factors in determining whether meals that you buy are furnished for noncompensatory business reasons. If such business reasons exist, the convenience-of-employer test is satisfied. If such reasons do not exist, the value of the meals may be tax free as a *de minimis* benefit *(3.9)*; otherwise, the value of the meal subsidy provided by the employer is taxable.

Where your employer provides meals on business premises at a fixed charge that is subtracted from your pay whether you accept the meals or not, the amount of the charge is excluded from your taxable pay. If the meal is provided for the employer's convenience, as in the previous Examples, the value of the meals received is also tax free. If it is not provided for the employer's convenience, the value is taxable whether it exceeds or is less than the amount charged.

Lodging must be condition of employment. This test requires evidence that the lodging is necessary for you to perform your job properly, as where you are required to be available for duty at all times. The IRS may question the claim that you are required to be on 24-hour duty. For example, at one college, rent-free lodgings were provided to teaching and administrative staff members, maintenance workers, dormitory parents who supervised and resided with students, and an evening nurse. The IRS ruled that only the lodgings provided to the dorm parents and the nurse met the tax-free lodging tests because for the convenience of the college, they had to be available after regular school hours to respond to emergencies.

If you are given the choice of free lodging at your place of employment or a cash allowance, the lodging is not considered to be a condition of employment, and its value is taxable.

If the lodging qualifies as tax free, so does the value of employer-paid utilities such as heat, electricity, gas, water, sewerage, and other utilities. Where these services are furnished by the employer and their value is deducted from your salary, the amount deducted is excluded from taxable wages on Form W-2. But if you pay for the utilities yourself, you may not exclude their cost from your income.

EXAMPLE

Tyrone Jones is employed at a construction project at a remote job site. His pay is $800 a week. Because there are no accessible places near the site for food and lodging, the employer furnishes meals and lodging for which it charges $240 a week, which is taken out of Jones's pay. Jones reports only the net amount he receives—$560 a week. The value of the meals and lodging is a tax-free benefit.

Court Decision

House One Block Away

Two federal courts held that a school superintendent received tax-free lodging where the home was one block away from the school and separated by a row of other houses. This met the business premises test. The IRS disagrees with the result and says that it will continue to litigate similar cases arising outside the Eighth Circuit in which the case arose. The Eighth Circuit includes the states of Arkansas, Iowa, Minnesota, Missouri, Nebraska, and North and South Dakota.

Caution

Housing as Job Requirement

If housing is provided to some employees with a certain job and not others, the IRS may hold that the lodging is not a condition of employment. For example, the IRS taxed medical residents on the value of hospital lodging where other residents lived in their own apartments.

Caution

Partners Are Not Employees
The IRS does not consider partners or self-employed persons as employees and so does not allow them to exclude the value of partnership-provided meals and lodging.

Are Your Board and Lodging Tax Free?

Yes—	No—
Hotel executives, managers, housekeepers, and auditors who are required to live at the hotel.	Your employer gives you a cash allowance for your meals or lodgings.
Domestics, farm laborers, fishermen, canners, seamen, servicemen, building superintendents, and hospital and sanitarium employees who are required to have meals and lodging on employer premises.	You have a choice of accepting cash or getting the meals or lodging. For example, under a union contract you get meals, but you may refuse to take them and get an automatic pay increase.
Restaurant and other food service employees who have meals furnished during or immediately before or after working hours.	A state hospital employee is given a choice. He or she may live at the institution rent free or live elsewhere and get extra pay each month. Whether he or she stays at the institution or lives outside, the extra pay is included in his or her income.
Employees who must be available during meal periods for emergencies.	A waitress, on her days off, is allowed to eat free meals at the restaurant where she works.
Employees who, because of the nature of the business, must be given short meal periods.	
Workers who must use company-supplied facilities in remote areas.	
Park employees who voluntarily live in rent-free apartments provided by a park department in order to protect the park from vandalism.	

Groceries. An employer may furnish unprepared food, such as groceries, rather than prepared meals. Courts are divided on whether the value of the groceries is excludable from income. One court allowed an exclusion for the value of nonfood items, such as napkins and soap—as well as for groceries—furnished to a doctor who ate at his home on the hospital grounds so that he would be available for emergencies.

Cash allowances. A cash allowance for meals and lodging is taxable.

Faculty lodging. Teachers and other employees (and their spouses and dependents) of an educational institution, including a state university system or academic health center, do not have to pay tax on the value of school-provided lodging if they pay a minimal rent. The lodging must be on or near the campus. The minimal required rent is the smaller of: (1) 5% of the appraised value of the lodging; and (2) the average rental paid for comparable school housing by persons who are neither employees nor students. Appraised value must be determined by an independent appraiser and the appraisal must be reviewed annually.

For purposes of the 5% minimum rent rule, academic health centers include medical teaching hospitals and medical research organizations with regular faculties and curricula in basic and clinical medical science and research.

EXAMPLE

Carol Eng, a professor, pays annual rent of $6,000 for university housing appraised at $100,000. The average rent for comparable university housing paid by non-employees and non-students is $7,000. She does not have to pay any tax on the housing since her rental payments exceed 5% of the appraised housing value (5% of $100,000, or $5,000). If her rent was $4,000, she would have to report income of $1,000 ($5,000 minimum required rent – $4,000).

Peace Corps and VISTA volunteers. Peace Corps volunteers working overseas may exclude subsistence allowances from income under a specific code provision. The law does not provide a similar exclusion for the small living expense allowances received by VISTA volunteers.

3.12 Minister's Rental Allowance

A duly ordained minister pays no tax on the rental value of a home provided as part of his or her pay. If a minister is provided with a rental allowance rather than a home itself, the allowance is tax free if the entire amount is used to pay rent (including the rent of a furnished or unfurnished apartment or house, garage, and utilities).

A housing allowance is also tax free if used as a down payment to buy a house, or used to pay mortgage installments, or for utilities, interest, tax, and repair expenses of the house. Any part of the allowance not used for these housing purposes is taxed. For example, that part of an allowance used to pay rent on business or farm property or for food or the services of a maid is taxed.

A minister who rents his or her home while abroad on church business may exclude his or her rental allowance only up to amounts used for capital improvements. These amounts are treated as expenses of keeping up his or her regular home. The balance of the rental allowance is taxable compensation even though he or she had expenses for maintenance, interest, taxes, repairs, and utilities during the rental period. The expenses may be deducted from rental income.

Who qualifies for tax-free allowance? Tax-free treatment is allowed to ordained ministers, rabbis, and cantors who receive housing allowances as part of their compensation for ministerial duties. Retired ministers qualify if their allowance is furnished in recognition of past services.

The IRS has allowed the tax-free exclusion to ministers working as teachers or administrators for a parochial school, college, or theological seminary which is an integral part of a church organization. A traveling evangelist was allowed to exclude rental allowances from out-of-town churches to maintain his permanent home. Church officers who are not ordained, such as a "minister" of music (music director) or "minister" of education (Sunday School director), do not qualify.

The IRS has generally barred an exclusion to ordained ministers working as executives of nonreligious organizations even where services or religious functions are performed as part of the job. The Tax Court has focused on the duties performed. A minister employed as a chaplain by a municipal police department under church supervision was allowed a housing exclusion, but the exclusion was denied to a minister-administrator of an old-age home that was not under the authority of a church and a rabbi who worked for a religious organization as director of inter-religious affairs.

Allowance subject to self-employment tax. Although parsonage allowances are not taxable income, they are reported as self-employment income for Social Security purposes; *see* Chapter 45. If you do not receive a cash allowance, report the rental value of the parsonage as self-employment income. Rental value is usually equal to what you would pay for similar quarters in your locality. Also include as self-employment income the value of house furnishings, utilities, appurtenances supplied—such as a garage—and the value of meals furnished that meet the rules at *3.11*.

 Planning Reminder

Allowance Must Be Authorized
The church or local congregation must officially designate the part of the minister's compensation that is a rental allowance. To qualify for tax-free treatment, the designation must be made in advance of the payments. Official action may be shown by an employment contract, minutes, a resolution, or a budget allowance.

Cafeteria Plans and Flexible Spending Arrangements

3.13 Cafeteria Plans Provide Choice of Benefits

"Cafeteria plans" is a nickname for plans that give an employee a choice of selecting either cash or at least one qualifying nontaxable benefit. You are not taxed when you elect qualifying nontaxable benefits, although cash could have been chosen instead. A cafeteria plan may offer tax-free benefits such as group health insurance or life insurance coverage, long-term disability coverage, dependent care or adoption assistance, medical expense reimbursements, or parking benefits. Long-term care insurance may *not* be offered through a cafeteria plan under current law, but Congress was considering a proposal to eliminate this restriction when this book went to press; *see* the Supplement for an update.

Employees may be offered a premium-only plan (POP), which allows them to purchase group health insurance coverage or life insurance on a pre-tax basis using salary-reduction contributions.

Under a flexible spending arrangement (FSA), employees may be allowed to make tax-free salary-reduction contributions to a medical or dependent care reimbursement plan; *see 3.14*.

A qualified cafeteria plan must be written and not discriminate in favor of highly compensated employees and stockholders. If the plan provides for health benefits, a special rule applies to determine whether the plan is discriminatory. If a plan is held to be discriminatory, the highly compensated participants are taxed to the extent they could have elected cash. Furthermore, if key employees *(3.3)* receive more than 25% of the "tax-free" benefits under the plan, they are taxed on the benefits.

Caution

Estimating FSA Contributions

Because of the "use-it-or-lose-it" rule for FSA contributions, make a conservative estimate of your expenses when you make your election. This is particularly true for medical expenses which are generally difficult to project in advance.

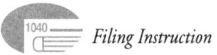

Filing Instruction

Tax-Free Dependent Care Reimbursements

Whether all or only part of your dependent care FSA reimbursements are tax free is figured on Part III of Form 2441 if you file Form 1040. If you file Form 1040A, the calculation is made on Part III of Schedule 2.

3.14 Flexible Spending Arrangements

A flexible spending arrangement (FSA) allows employees to get reimbursed for medical or dependent care expenses from an account they set up with pre-tax dollars. Under a typical FSA, you agree to a salary reduction which is deducted from each paycheck and deposited in a separate account. The salary-reduction contributions are not included in your taxable wages reported on Form W-2. As expenses are incurred, you are reimbursed from the account.

Funds from a *health* FSA may be used to reimburse you for the annual deductible under your employer's regular health plan, co-payments you must make to physicians, and any other expenses that your health plan does not cover. These may include eye examinations, eyeglasses, routine physicals, and orthodontia work for you and your dependents. However, a health FSA may *not* be used to pay for health insurance premiums, including premiums for coverage under a plan of your spouse or dependent. Also, expenses for long-term care services *cannot* be reimbursed under a health FSA, although Congress was considering eliminating this rule when this book went to press.

The tax advantage of an FSA is that your salary reduction contributions are not subject to federal income tax or Social Security taxes, allowing your medical or dependent care expenses to be paid with pre-tax rather than after-tax income. The salary deferrals are also exempt from state and local taxes except in New Jersey and Pennsylvania; check with the administrator of your employer's plan.

In the case of a health FSA, paying medical expenses with pre-tax dollars allows you to avoid the 7.5% adjusted gross income (AGI) floor *(17.1)* that limits itemized deductions for medical costs.

However, to get these tax advantages, you must assume some risk. Under a "use-it-or-lose-it rule," if your out-of-pocket expenses for the year are less than your contributions, the balance is forfeited, as discussed below.

FSA election to contribute generally irrevocable. The IRS has imposed restrictions on FSAs that make them unattractive for many employees. An election to set up an FSA for a given year must be made before the start of that year. You elect how much you want to contribute during the coming year and that amount will be withheld from your pay in monthly installments.

Once the election for a particular year takes effect, you may not discontinue contributions to your account or increase or decrease a coverage election unless there is a change in family or work status that qualifies under IRS regulations.

Use-it-or-lose-it rule. Only expenses incurred during the plan year may be reimbursed, and a "use-it-or-lose-it" rule applies: any unused account balance at the end of the plan year is forfeited. Unused amounts may not be refunded to you or carried over to the next year. There is a grace period, generally until April 15 of the following year, to submit reimbursement claims for expenses incurred during the previous year.

Although there are some differences in the reimbursement rules for health-care and dependent care FSAs, as discussed below, the "use-it-or-lose-it" feature applies to both.

EXAMPLE

At the end of 1998 you elected to make 1999 salary reduction contributions of $1,200 to a health-care FSA. If you incurred only $1,000 of reimbursable medical expenses during 1999, the $200 balance is forfeited; you are not allowed to carry it forward to 2000.

Health-care FSA. At all times during the year, you may receive reimbursements up to your designated limit, even if your payments to the FSA are less. For example, if you elect to make salary-reduction contributions of $100 per month to a health-care FSA, and you incur $500 of qualifying medical expenses in January, you may get the full $500 reimbursement even though you have paid only $100 into the plan. Your employer may not require you to accelerate contributions to match reimbursement claims.

You may *not* receive tax-free reimbursements for cosmetic surgery expenses unless the surgery is necessary to correct a deformity existing since birth or resulting from a disease or from injury caused by an accident. Nonqualifying reimbursements are taxable.

Employees on medical or family leave. Employees who take unpaid leave under the Family and Medical Leave Act (FMLA) to deal with medical emergencies or care for a newborn child may either continue or revoke their coverage during FMLA leave. If the coverage continues, the maximum reimbursement selected by that employee must be available at all times during the leave period. If the coverage is terminated, the employee must be reinstated under the FSA after returning from the leave, but no reimbursement claims may be made for expenses incurred during the leave.

Dependent care FSA. You may contribute to a dependent care FSA if you expect to have expenses qualifying for the dependent care tax credit discussed in Chapter 25, but if you contribute to a dependent care FSA, *any tax-free reimbursement from the account reduces the expenses eligible for the credit; see 25.7.* If you are married, both you and your spouse must work in order for you to receive tax-free reimbursements from an FSA, unless your spouse is disabled or a full-time student; *see 3.4.*

The maximum tax-free reimbursement under the FSA is $5,000, but if either you or your spouse earns less than $5,000, the tax-free limit is the lesser earnings. If your spouse's employer offers a dependent care FSA, total tax-free reimbursements for both of you are limited to $5,000. Furthermore, if you are considered a highly compensated employee, your employer may have to lower your contribution ceiling below $5,000 to comply with nondiscrimination rules.

Unlike health FSAs, an employer may limit reimbursements from a dependent care FSA to your account balance. For example, if you contribute $400 a month to the FSA, and in January you pay $1,500 to a day care center for your child, your employer may reimburse you $400 a month as contributions are made to your account.

 Filing Instruction

Dependent Care Reimbursements Affect Credit
Reimbursements received tax free from your dependent care FSA reduce the $2,400 or $4,800 expense base for figuring the dependent care credit; *see* Chapter 25.

Free or Low-Cost Company Products or Services

3.15 Company Services Provided at No Additional Cost

Employees are not taxed on the receipt of services usually sold by their employer to customers where the employer does not incur additional costs in providing them to the employees. Examples are free or low-cost flights provided by an airline to its employees; free or discount lodging for employees of a hotel; and telephone service provided to employees of telephone companies. These tax-free fringes also may be provided to the employee's spouse and dependent children; retired employees, including employees retired on disability; and widows or widowers of deceased or retired employees. Tax-free treatment also applies to free or discount flights provided to parents of airline employees. Benefits provided by another company under a reciprocal arrangement, such as standby tickets on another airline, may also qualify as tax free.

The employer must have excess service capacity to provide the service and not forego potential revenue from regular customers. For example, airline employees who receive free reserved seating on company planes must pay tax on the benefit because the airline is foregoing potential revenue by reserving seating that could otherwise be sold.

Line of business limitations. If a company has two lines of business, such as an airline and a hotel, an employee of the airline may not receive tax-free benefits provided by the hotel. However, there are exceptions. An employee who provides services to both business lines may receive benefits from both business lines. Benefits from more than one line in existence before 1984 may also be available under a special election made by the company for 1985 and later years. Your employer should notify you of this tax benefit.

3.16 Discounts on Company Products or Services

The value of discounts on company products is a tax-free benefit if the discount does not exceed the employer's gross profit percentage. For example, if a company's profit percentage is 40%, the maximum tax-free employee discount for merchandise is 40% of the regular selling price. If you received a 50% discount, then 10% of the price charged customers would be taxable income. The employer has a choice of methods for figuring profit percentage.

Discounts on services that are not tax free under *3.15* for no-additional-cost services qualify for an exclusion, limited to 20% of the selling price charged customers. Discounts above 20% are taxable. An insurance policy is treated as a service. Thus, insurance company employees are not taxed on a discount of up to 20% of the policy's price.

Some company products do not qualify for the exclusion. Discounts on real estate and investment property such as securities, commodities, currency, or bullion are taxable. Interest-free or low-interest loans given by banks or other financial institutions to employees are not excludable. The loan is subject to tax under the rules of *4.31.*

Highly compensated employees are subject to the nondiscrimination rules discussed at *3.15* for no-additional-cost services.

EXAMPLE

The airline that you work for gives you a free round-trip ticket with a confirmed seat to California. The benefit is not tax free under the rule for no-additional-cost services *(3.15),* but a 20% tax-free discount is allowed. If customers are charged $600 for comparable tickets, $120 is a tax-free benefit (20% of $600) and $480 is taxable.

 Caution

Highly Compensated Employees
Highly compensated employees can receive tax-free company services only if the same benefits are available to other employees on a nondiscriminatory basis. For 1999, highly compensated employees include employees owning more than a 5% interest in 1999 or 1998, and employees who in 1998 had compensation over $80,000. Employers have the option of including only the top-paid 20% in the over $80,000 category.

 Caution

Line of Business Rule
The line of business limitation discussed at *3.15* for no-additional-cost services also applies to qualified employee discounts. Thus, if a company operates an airline and a hotel, employees who work for the airline may generally not receive tax-free hotel room discounts. However, if a special election was made by the company, employees may receive tax-free benefits from any line of business in existence before 1984.

Dividend and Interest Income

Dividends and interest that are paid to you in 1999 are reported by the payer to the IRS on Forms 1099.

You will receive copies of:

- Forms 1099-DIV, for dividends
- Forms 1099-INT, for interest
- Forms 1099-OID, for original issue discount

Report the amounts shown on the Forms 1099 on your tax return. The IRS uses the Forms 1099 to check the income you report. If you fail to report income reported on Forms 1099, you will receive a statement asking for an explanation and a bill for the tax deficiency. If you receive a Form 1099 that you believe is incorrect, contact the payer for a corrected form.

Do not attach your copies of Forms 1099 to your return. Keep them with a copy of your tax return.

Name(s) shown on Form 1040. Do not enter name and social security number if shown on other side.	Your social security number

Schedule B—Interest and Ordinary Dividends

Attachment Sequence No. **08**

Part I Interest

(See pages 20 and B-1.)

Note: If you received a Form 1099-INT, Form 1099-OID, or substitute statement from a brokerage firm, list the firm's name as the payer and enter the total interest shown on that form.

Note: If you had over $400 in taxable interest income, you must also complete Part III.

1 List name of payer. If any interest is from a seller-financed mortgage and the buyer used the property as a personal residence, see page B-1 and list this interest first. Also, show that buyer's social security number and address ▶

Payer		Amount
National Savings Bank		925
Chase Manhattan Bank		515
Municipal Bonds	1	350
Total		1,790
less: tax exempt interest		(350)

2 Add the amounts on line 1	**2**	**1,440**
3 Excludable interest on series EE or I U.S. savings bonds issued after 1989 from Form 8815, line 14. You MUST attach Form 8815 to Form 1040 . . . . . ▶	**3**	**- 0 -**
4 Subtract line 3 from line 2. Enter the result here and on Form 1040, line 8a ▶	**4**	**1,440**

Note: If you had over $400 in ordinary dividends, you must also complete Part III.

Part II Ordinary Dividends

(See pages 21 and B-1.)

Note: If you received a Form 1099-DIV or substitute statement from a brokerage firm, list the firm's name as the payer and enter the ordinary dividends shown on that form.

5 List name of payer. Include only ordinary dividends. If you received any capital gain distributions, see the instructions for Form 1040, line 13. ▶

Payer		Amount
Auto Company		126
Bio-Chem Corp.		217
Utility Corp.	5	155
Mutual Fund XYZ		500

6 Add the amounts on line 5. Enter the total here and on Form 1040, line 9 . ▶	**6**	**998**

Part III Foreign Accounts and Trusts

(See page B-2.)

You must complete this part if you **(a)** had over $400 of interest or ordinary dividends; **(b)** had a foreign account; or **(c)** received a distribution from, or were a grantor of, or a transferor to, a foreign trust.

	Yes	No
7a At any time during 1999, did you have an interest in or a signature or other authority over a financial account in a foreign country, such as a bank account, securities account, or other financial account? See page B-2 for exceptions and filing requirements for Form TD F 90-22.1		√
b If "Yes," enter the name of the foreign country ▶		
8 During 1999, did you receive a distribution from, or were you the grantor of, or transferor to, a foreign trust? If "Yes," you may have to file Form 3520. See page B-2		√

For Paperwork Reduction Act Notice, see Form 1040 instructions.   Schedule B (Form 1040) 1999

Key to Dividend Reporting

Type of Dividend Payment—	How and Where To Report—
Cash dividends	Dividends paid out of a corporation's earnings and profits are taxable. The corporation will report taxable dividends to you on Form 1099-DIV (or an equivalent statement).
	On Form 1040, report ordinary dividends on Line 9; Schedule B must be filed where the total exceeds $400. If you file Form 1040A, report ordinary dividends on Line 9, and if the total exceeds $400, complete Part II of Schedule 1. Dividends may not be reported on Form 1040EZ.
Dividends on accounts in credit unions, cooperative banks, savings and loan associations, mutual savings banks, and building and loan associations	Distributions from these financial institutions are called "dividends" but are actually interest and are reported to you on Form 1099-INT.
Life insurance policy dividends	Dividends on individual life insurance policies are actually a refund of your premiums and are not taxed unless they exceed the total premiums paid.
Money-market mutual-fund dividends	Dividends paid by a money-market mutual fund are reported on Form 1099-DIV. Report ordinary dividends on Line 9 of Form 1040, and include them on Schedule B if the total exceeds $400. On Form 1040A, report ordinary dividends on Line 9, and fill out Part II of Schedule 1 if the total exceeds $400.
	Do not confuse money-market funds managed by mutual funds with bank money-market accounts. Bank money-market accounts pay interest reported on Form 1099-INT, not dividends.
Mutual-fund distributions	Mutual funds may pay several kinds of distributions. On Form 1099-DIV, the fund will report ordinary dividends in Box 1, including net short-term capital gains distributions. Long-term capital gain distributions are reported in Box 2a of Form 1099-DIV. Nontaxable distributions are listed in Box 3. Form 1099-DIV for 1999 will include dividends declared in October, November, or December of 1999, even if not actually paid to you until January 2000. How to report these dividends on your return is detailed in *4.3* and *32.5.*
Nominee distribution—joint accounts	If you receive dividends on stock held as a nominee for someone else, or you receive a Form 1099-DIV that includes dividends belonging to another person, such as a joint owner of the account, you are considered to be a "nominee recipient." If the other owner is someone other than your spouse, you should file a separate Form 1099-DIV showing you as the payer and the other owner as the recipient of the allocable income. Give the owner a copy of Form 1099-DIV by January 31, 2000, so the dividends can be reported on his or her 1999 return. File the Form 1099-DIV, together with a Form 1096 ("Transmittal of Information Return"), with the IRS by February 28, 2000.
	On your Schedule B, you list on Line 5 the ordinary dividends reported to you on Form 1099-DIV. Several lines above Line 6, subtract the nominee distribution (the amount allocable to the other owner) from the total dividends. Thus, the nominee distribution is not included in the taxable dividends shown on Line 6, Schedule B.
Return of capital distributions	A distribution that is not paid out of earnings is a nontaxable return of capital, that is, a partial payback of your investment. The company will report the distribution on Form 1099-DIV as a nontaxable distribution. You must reduce the cost basis of your stock by the nontaxable distribution. If your basis is reduced to zero by a return of capital distributions, any further distributions are taxable as capital gains, which you report on Schedule D.
	You must use Form 1040 if you received any return of capital distributions; Form 1040A or Form 1040EZ may not be used. If your total dividends, including nontaxable returns of capital, are $400 or less, you do not report the nontaxable distribution on your return unless your basis has been reduced to zero. In that case, further distributions are taxable and are reported on Schedule D.
Stock dividends and stock splits	If you own common stock and receive additional shares of the same company as a dividend, the dividend is generally not taxed. A dividend is taxed where you had the option to receive cash instead of stock, or if the stock is of another corporation. Preferred shareholders are generally taxed on stock dividends. Taxable stock dividends are discussed at *4.7* and *4.8.* Your corporation will determine whether stock dividends are taxable and report the taxable amount on Form 1099-DIV.
	If you receive additional shares as part of a stock split, the receipt of new shares is not taxable; although you own more shares, your ownership percentage has not changed.

Reporting Dividends

4.1 Reporting Corporate Dividends

Dividends paid out of current or accumulated earnings of a corporation are subject to tax. Most dividends fall into this class, except for stock dividends and stock rights on common stock, which are generally not taxed; *see 4.6.*

Dividends that are paid to you during 1999 are reported to the IRS by the company on Form 1099-DIV. The IRS uses this information as a check on your reporting of dividends. You receive a copy of Form 1099-DIV. You do not have to attach it to your tax return.

Publicly held corporations generally inform stockholders of the tax consequences of stock dividends and other distributions. Keep such letters with your tax records. You may also want to consult investment publications such as Moody's or Standard & Poor's annual dividend record books for details of dividend distributions and their tax treatment.

4.2 Dividends From a Partnership, S Corporation, Estate, or Trust

You report dividend income you receive as a member of a partnership, stockholder in an S corporation, or as a beneficiary of an estate or trust. The fiduciary of the estate or trust should advise you of the dividend income to be reported on your return.

A distribution from a partnership or S corporation is reported as a dividend only if it is portfolio income derived from nonbusiness activities. Your allowable share of the dividend will be shown on the Schedule K-1 you receive from the partnership or S corporation.

4.3 How Mutual-Fund Distributions Are Taxed

Mutual funds (open-ended, regulated investment companies) pay their shareholders several kinds of dividends and other distributions. Whether the distribution is received by you or reinvested by the fund, you must report it on your return.

The fund will send you Form 1099-DIV (or a similar written form), giving you a breakdown of the type of dividends and distributions paid during the taxable year. In Box 1, the fund reports ordinary dividends, including short-term capital gains. Total capital gain distributions (long term) are reported in Box 2a. Boxes 1 and 2a include dividends and distributions that you reinvested instead of receiving in cash. Nontaxable distributions are reported in Box 3. In the case of a non-publicly offered fund, your share of fund expenses is included as an ordinary dividend in Box 1, and separately shown in Box 5 for itemized deduction purposes *(see 19.24)*.

Dividends from a fund's foreign investments are included in the appropriate boxes of Form 1099-DIV, and the fund will indicate in Boxes 6 and 7 any foreign tax paid, which you may claim as a tax credit or deduction; *see 36.14.*

Form 1099-DIV for 1999 will include a dividend received in January 2000 so long as it was declared and was payable in October, November, or December of 1999.

See *Chapter 32 for a closer look at the types of distributions reported on Form 1099-DIV, as well as the rules for figuring gain or loss when you sell mutual-fund shares.*

4.4 Real Estate Investment Trust (REIT) Dividends

Dividends from a real estate investment trust (REIT) are shown on Form 1099-DIV. Ordinary dividends reported in Box 1 are fully taxable. Dividends designated by the trust as capital gain distributions in Box 2a are reported by you as long-term capital gains regardless of how long you have held your trust shares. A loss on the sale of REIT shares held for six months or less is treated as a long-term capital loss to the extent of any capital gain distribution received before the sale plus any undistributed capital gains. However, this long-term loss rule does not apply to sales under periodic redemption plans.

4.5 Taxable Dividends of Earnings and Profits

You pay tax on dividends only when the corporation distributing the dividends has earnings and profits. Publicly held corporations will tell you whether their distributions are taxable. If you hold stock in a close corporation, you may have to determine the tax status of its distribution. You need to know earnings and profits at two different periods:

Filing Tip

"Dividends" on Stock Used for Short Sale

If a broker used and transferred your securities for a short sale made by a third party and received substitute dividend payments on your behalf while the short sale was open, the broker must report the payments on Form 1099-DIV or 1099-MISC, depending on what the payment covers. Report substitute payments shown on Form 1099-MISC as "Other income" on Line 21 of Form 1040, and not as dividends.

Filing Instruction

Mutual-Fund Gross Distributions

Gross dividends and distributions are no longer reported in one box on Form 1099-DIV. You do not have to enter the gross amount on your tax return. Taxable amounts shown on Form 1099-DIV, such as for ordinary dividends or capital gains, are reported on the appropriate lines of your tax return. See Chapter 32 for reporting details.

1. Current earnings and profits as of the *end of the current taxable year*. A dividend is considered to have been made from earnings most recently accumulated.
2. Accumulated earnings and profits as of the *beginning of the current year*. However, when current earnings and profits are large enough to meet the dividend, you do not have to make this computation. It is only when the dividends exceed current earnings (or there are no current earnings) that you match accumulated earnings against the dividend.

The tax term "accumulated earnings and profits" is similar in meaning to the accounting term "retained earnings." Both stand for the net profits of the company after deducting distributions to stockholders. However, "tax" earnings may differ from "retained earnings" for the following reason: Reserve accounts, the additions to which are not deductible for income tax purposes, are ordinarily included as tax earnings.

EXAMPLES
1. During 1999, Corporation A paid dividends of $25,000. At the beginning of 1999 it had accumulated earnings of $50,000. It lost $25,000 during 1999. You are fully taxed on your dividend income in 1999 because the corporation's net accumulated earnings and profits exceed its dividends.
2. At the end of 1998, Corporation B had a deficit of $200,000. Earnings for 1999 were $100,000. In 1999, it paid stockholders $25,000. The dividends are taxed; earnings exceeded the dividends.

4.6   Stock Dividends on Common Stock

If you own common stock in a company and receive additional shares of the same company as a dividend, the dividend is generally not taxable; *see 30.4* and *30.5* for the method of computing cost basis of stock dividends and rights and sales of such stock.

Exceptions to tax-free rule. A stock dividend on common stock is taxable when (1) you may elect to take either stock or cash; (2) there are different classes of common stock, one class receiving cash dividends and another class receiving stock; or (3) the dividend is of convertible preferred stock; *see 4.8* for further details on taxable stock dividends.

Fractional shares. If a stock dividend is declared and you are only entitled to a fractional share, you may be given cash instead. To save the trouble and expense of issuing fractional shares, many companies directly issue cash in lieu of fractional shares or they set up a plan, with shareholder approval, for the fractional shares to be sold and the cash proceeds distributed to the shareholders. Your company should tell you how to report the cash payment. According to the IRS, you are generally treated as receiving a tax-free dividend of fractional shares, followed by a taxable redemption of the shares by the company. You report on Schedule D capital gain or loss equal to the excess of the cash over the basis of the fractional share; long- or short-term treatment depends on the holding period of the original stock. In certain cases, a cash distribution may be taxed as an ordinary dividend and not as a sale reported on Schedule D; your company should tell you if this is the case.

Stock rights. The rules that apply to stock dividends also apply to distributions of stock rights. If you, as a common stockholder, receive rights to subscribe to additional common stock, the receipt of the rights is not taxable provided the terms of the distribution do not fall within the taxable distribution rules of *4.8*.

4.7   Dividends Paid in Property

A dividend may be paid in property such as securities of another corporation or merchandise. You report as income the fair market value of the property. A dividend paid in property is sometimes called a *dividend in kind*.

EXAMPLE
You receive one share of X corporation stock as a dividend from the G company of which you are a stockholder. You received the X stock when it had a market value of $25; you report $25, the value of the property received.

Corporate benefits. On an audit, the IRS may charge that a benefit given to a shareholder-employee is a taxable dividend.

Filing Tip

Stock Splits Are Not Taxed
The receipt of stock under a stock split is not taxable. Stock splits resemble the receipt of stock dividends, but they are not dividends. They do not represent a distribution of surplus as in the case of stock dividends. The purpose of a stock split is generally to reduce the price of individual shares in order to increase their marketability. The basis of the old holding is divided among all the shares in order to find the basis for the new shares; *see 30.4*.

☐ CORRECTED (if checked)			
PAYER'S name, street address, city, state, ZIP code, and telephone no. Mutual Fund XYZ 155 East 38th Street City, State 010X0	**1** Ordinary dividends $ 500 **2a** Total capital gain distr. $ 310	OMB No. 1545-0110 **19**99 Form **1099-DIV**	**Dividends and Distributions**
PAYER'S Federal identification number X1 - 01X0110	RECIPIENT'S identification number	**2b** 28% rate gain $	**2c** Unrecap. sec. 1250 gain $	**Copy B** **For Recipient**

RECIPIENT'S name Noelle Ballesteros — 2d Section 1202 gain $ — 3 Nontaxable distributions $

This is important tax information and is being furnished to the Internal Revenue Service. If you are required to file a return, a negligence penalty or other sanction may be imposed on you if this income is taxable and the IRS determines that it has not been reported.

Street address (including apt. no.) 21 Chauncy Street — 4 Federal income tax withheld $ — 5 Investment expenses $

City, state, and ZIP code City, State 111X0 — 6 Foreign tax paid $ — 7 Foreign country or U.S. possession

Account number (optional) — 8 Cash liquidation distr. $ — 9 Noncash liquidation distr. $

Form **1099-DIV**   (Keep for your records.)   Department of the Treasury - Internal Revenue Service

4.8 Taxable Stock Dividends

The most frequent type of stock dividend is not taxable: the receipt by a common stockholder of a common stock dividend; *see 4.6.*

Taxable stock dividends. The following stock dividends are taxable:

- Stock dividends paid to holders of preferred stock. However, no taxable income is realized where the conversion ratio of convertible preferred stock is increased only to take account of a stock dividend or split involving the stock into which the convertible stock is convertible.
- Stock dividends elected by a shareholder of common stock who had the choice of taking stock, property, or cash. A distribution of stock that was immediately redeemable for cash at the stockholder's option was treated as a taxable dividend.
- Stock dividends paid in a distribution where some shareholders receive property or cash and other shareholders' proportionate interests in the assets or earnings and profits of the corporation are increased.
- Distributions of preferred stock to some common shareholders and common stock to other common shareholders.
- Distributions of convertible preferred stock to holders of common stock, unless it can be shown that the distribution will not result in the creation of disproportionate stock interests.

Constructive stock dividends. You may not actually receive a stock dividend, but under certain circumstances, the IRS may treat you as having received a taxable distribution. This may happen when a company increases the ratio of convertible preferred stock.

4.9 Who Reports the Dividends

Stock held by broker in street name. If your broker holds stock for you in a street name, dividends earned on this stock are received by the broker and credited to your account. You report all dividends credited to your account in 1999. The broker is required to file an information return on Form 1099 (or similar form) showing all such dividends.

If your statement shows only a gross amount of dividends, check with your broker if any of the dividends represented nontaxable returns of capital.

Dividends on stock sold or bought between ex-dividend date and record date. Record date is the date set by a company on which you must be listed as a stockholder on its records to receive the dividend. However, in the case of publicly traded stock, an ex-dividend date, which usually precedes the record date by several business days, is fixed by the exchange to determine who is entitled to the dividend.

Planning Reminder

Dividend Reinvestment in Company Stock

Your company may allow you either to take cash dividends or automatically reinvest the dividends in company stock. If you elect the stock plan, and pay fair market value for the stock, the full cash dividend is taxable.

If the plan lets you buy the stock at a discount, the amount of the taxable dividend is the fair market value of the stock on the dividend payment date plus any service fee charged for the acquisition. The basis of the stock is also the fair market value at the dividend payment date. The service charge may be claimed as an itemized deduction subject to the 2% adjusted gross income floor; *see 19.24.* If at the same time you also have the option to buy additional stock at a discount and you exercise the option, you have additional dividend income for the difference between the fair market value of the optional shares and the discounted amount you paid for the shares.

If you buy stock before the ex-dividend date, the dividend belongs to you and is reported by you. If you buy on or after the ex-dividend date, the dividend belongs to the seller.

If you sell stock before the ex-dividend date, you do not have a right to the dividend. If you sell on or after the ex-dividend date, you receive the dividend and report it as income.

The dividend declaration date and date of payment do not determine who receives the dividend.

Nominees or joint owners. If you receive ordinary dividends on stock held as a nominee for another person, other than your spouse, give that owner a Form 1099-DIV and file a copy of that return with the IRS, along with a Form 1096 ("Transmittal of U.S. Information Return"). The actual owner then reports the income. List the nominee dividends on Schedule B of Form 1040 (or Schedule 1, Form 1040A) along with your other dividends, and then subtract the nominee dividends from the total.

Follow the same procedure if you receive a Form 1099-DIV for an account owned jointly with someone other than your spouse. Give the other owner a Form 1099-DIV, and file a copy with the IRS, along with a Form 1096. The other owner then reports his or her share of the joint income. On your return, you list the total dividends shown on Forms 1099-DIV and avoid tax by subtracting from the total the nominee dividends reported to the other owner.

EXAMPLE

You receive Form 1099-DIV showing dividends of $960 including a $200 nominee distribution. You prepare a Form 1099-DIV for the actual owner showing the $200 distribution, and file a copy of the form with the IRS, plus Form 1096. On your own Schedule B, report the nominee distribution along with other ordinary dividends and then subtract it from the total.

Dividend Income	Amount
Mutual Fund	$ 310
Computer Inc.	450
Utility Inc.	200
Subtotal	$ 960
Less: Nominee distribution	(200)
Net dividends	$ 760

 Caution

Year-End Dividend From Mutual Fund

A dividend declared and made payable in October through December by a mutual fund or REIT is taxable in the year it is declared, even if it is not paid until January of the following year.

4.10 Year Dividends Are Reported

Dividends are generally reported on the tax return for the year in which the dividend is credited to your account or when you receive the dividend check.

Dividends received from a corporation in a year after the one in which they were declared, when you held the stock on the record date, are taxed in the year they are received; *see* Example 4 below.

EXAMPLES

1. A corporation declares a dividend payable on December 31, 1999. It follows a practice of paying dividends by checks that are mailed so that stockholders do not receive them until January 2000. You report this dividend on your 2000 return.

2. On December 31, 1999, a dividend is declared by a mutual fund. You receive it in January 2000. The dividend is taxable in 1999, when declared, and not 2000, when received.

3. On December 31, 1999, a dividend is credited by a corporation to a stockholder's account and made immediately available. The dividend is taxable in 1999, as the crediting is considered constructive receipt in 1999, even though the dividend is not received until 2000 or a later year.

4. You own stock in a corporation. In April 1998, the corporation declared a dividend, but it provided that the dividend will be paid when it gets the cash. It finally pays the dividend in September 1999; the dividend is taxable in 1999.

4.11 Distribution Not Out of Earnings: Return of Capital

A return of capital or "nontaxable distribution" reduces the cost basis of the stock. If your shares were purchased at different times, reduce the basis of the oldest shares first. When the cost basis is reduced to zero, further returns of capital are taxed as capital gains on Schedule D. Whether the gain is short term or long term depends on the length of time you have held the stock. The company paying the dividend will usually inform you of the tax treatment of the payment.

Life insurance dividends. Dividends on insurance policies are not true dividends. They are returns of premiums you previously paid. They reduce the cost of the policy and are not subject to tax until they exceed the net premiums paid for the contract. Interest paid or credited on dividends left with the insurance company is taxable. Dividends on VA insurance are tax free, as is interest on dividends left with the VA.

Where insurance premiums were deducted as a business expense in prior years, receipts of insurance dividends are either included in income or taken as a reduction of the insurance expense deduction of the current year. Dividends on capital stock of an insurance company are taxable.

Filing Tip

Insurance Premium Refund

Dividends on insurance policies are actually returns of premiums you previously paid. They are not subject to tax until they exceed the net premiums paid for the contract.

Reporting Interest Income

4.12 Reporting Interest on Your Tax Return

You must report all taxable interest. If you earn over $400 of taxable interest, you list the payers of interest on Schedule B if you file Form 1040, or on Part I of Schedule 1 if you file Form 1040A. Form 1040EZ may not be used if your taxable interest exceeds $400. You must also list tax-exempt interest on your return even though it is not taxable.

You must also list interest that has been shown on Forms 1099 in your name although it may not be taxable to you. For example, you may have received interest as a nominee or as accrued interest on bonds bought between interest dates. In these cases, list the amounts reported on Form 1099 along with your other interest income on Schedule B if you file Form 1040, or Schedule 1 if you file Form 1040A. On a separate line, label the amount as "Nominee distribution," or "Accrued interest," and subtract it from the total interest shown. Accrued interest is discussed at *4.15* and in the "Who Reports Interest Income" chart on page 73. Nominee distributions are discussed further in the chart on page 73.

If you received interest on a frozen account *(4.13)*, include the interest from Form 1099 on Schedule B if you file Form 1040, or on Schedule 1 if you use Form 1040A. On a separate line, write "frozen deposits" and subtract the amount from the total interest reported.

You do not have to list the payers of interest if your interest receipts are $400 or less, unless you have to reduce the interest shown on Form 1099 by nontaxable amounts such as accrued interest, nominee distributions, or frozen deposit interest.

Joint accounts. If you receive a Form 1099-INT for interest on an account you own with someone other than your spouse, you should file a nominee Form 1099-INT with the IRS to indicate that person's share of the interest, together with Form 1096 ("Transmittal of Information Return"). Give a copy of the Form 1099-INT to the other person. When you file your own return, you report the total interest shown on Form 1099-INT and then subtract the other person's share so you are taxed only on your portion of the interest; *see* the Example below.

Do not follow this procedure if you contributed all of the funds and set up the joint account merely as a "convenience" account to allow the other person to automatically inherit the account when you die. In this case, you report all of the interest income.

Filing Instruction

Tax-Exempt Interest

Tax-exempt interest, such as from municipal bonds, must be reported on your return although it is not taxable. Report it on Line 8b of Form 1040 or Form 1040A. On Schedule B of Form 1040 or Schedule 1 of Form 1040A, report the tax-exempt interest on Line 1 but then subtract it from a subtotal of the total interest so that it is not included in the amount shown on Line 2 of the schedule.

EXAMPLE

Your Social Security number is listed on a bank account owned jointly with your sister. You each invested 50% of the account principal and have agreed to share the interest income. You receive a Form 1099-INT for 1999 reporting total interest of $1,500 on the account. By January 31, 2000, prepare and give to your sister another Form 1099-INT that identifies you as the payer and her as the recipient of her share, or $750 interest. Send a copy of the Form 1099-INT and a Form 1096 to the IRS no later than February 28, 2000. Your sister will report the $750 interest on her return. On your Form 1040, report the full $1,500 interest on Line 1 of Schedule B, along with your other interest income. Above Line 2, subtract the $750 belonging to your sister to avoid being taxed on that amount; label the subtraction "Nominee distribution."

4.13 Interest on Frozen Accounts Not Taxed

If you have funds in a bankrupt or insolvent financial institution that freezes your account by limiting withdrawals, you do not pay tax on interest allocable to the frozen deposits. The interest is taxable when withdrawals are permitted. Officers and owners of at least a 1% interest in the financial institution, or their relatives, may not take advantage of this rule and must still report interest on frozen deposits.

On Schedule B of Form 1040 or on Schedule 1 of Form 1040A, report the full amount shown on Form 1099-INT, even if the interest is on a "frozen" deposit. Then, on a separate line, subtract the amount allocable to the frozen deposit from the total interest shown on the Schedule; label the subtraction "frozen deposits." Thus, the interest on the frozen deposit is not included on the line of your return showing taxable interest.

Refund opportunity. If you reported interest on a frozen deposit on a tax return for 1996–1998, you may file a refund claim for the tax paid on the interest; *see* Chapter 49.

4.14 Interest Income on Debts Owed to You

You report interest earned on money that you loan to another person. If you are on the cash basis, you report interest in the year you actually receive it or when it is considered received under the "constructive receipt rule." If you are on the accrual basis, you report interest when it is earned, whether or not you have received it.

See 4.31 for minimum interest rates required for loans and *4.18* when OID rules apply.

Where partial payment is being made on a debt, or when a debt is being compromised, the parties may agree in advance which part of the payment covers interest and which covers principal. If a payment is not identified as either principal or interest, the payment is first applied against interest due and reported as interest income to the extent of the interest due.

Interest income is not realized when a debtor gives you a new note for an old note where the new note includes the interest due on the old note.

If you give away a debtor's note, you report as income the collectible interest due at the date of the gift. To avoid tax on the interest, the note must be transferred before interest becomes due.

4.15 Reporting Interest on Bonds Bought or Sold

Where you buy or sell bonds between interest dates, interest is included in the price of the bonds. The purchaser does not report as income the interest that accrued before he or she owned the bond. The seller reports the accrued interest. The purchaser reduces the basis of the bond by the accrued interest reported by the seller. The following Examples illustrate these rules.

EXAMPLES

1. *Purchase.* On April 30, you buy for $5,250 a $5,000 corporate bond bearing interest at 8% per year, payable January 1 and July 1. The purchase price of the bond included accrued interest of $133 for the period January 1–April 30.

Interest received on 7/1	$200
Less: Accrued interest	133
Taxable interest	$ 67

Form 1099 sent to you includes the $133 of accrued interest. On Schedule B of Form 1040, you report the total interest of $200 received on July 1 and then on a separate line subtract the accrued interest of $133. Write "Accrued Interest" on the line where you show the subtraction.

Your basis for the bond is $5,117 ($5,250 – $133) for purposes of figuring gain or loss on a later sale of the bond.

2. *Sale.* On April 30, you sell for $5,250 a $5,000 8% bond with interest payable January 1 and July 1. The sales price included interest of $133 accrued from January 1–April 30. Your cost for the bond was $5,000. On your return, you report interest of $133 and capital gain of $117.

You receive	$ 5,250
Less: Accrued interest	133
Sales proceeds	$ 5,117
Less: Your cost	5,000
Capital gain	$ 117

Filing Tip

Lost Deposits

If you lose funds because of a financial institution's bankruptcy or insolvency, and you can reasonably estimate such a loss, you may deduct the loss as a nonbusiness bad debt, as a casualty loss, or as a miscellaneous itemized deduction; *see 18.4.*

Filing Tip

Accrued Interest

When you buy bonds between interest payment dates and pay accrued interest to the seller, this interest is taxable to the seller. The accrued interest is included on the Form 1099-INT you receive, but you should subtract it from your taxable interest; *see* Example 1 on this page.

Who Reports Interest Income

If interest is—	It is reported by—
Joint account interest	The person whose Social Security number is reported to the bank (or other payer) on Form W-9 when the account is opened. If the other owner is not your spouse and you receive a Form 1099-INT for the interest, you should report all the income on your return and also file a nominee Form 1099-INT with the other owner to indicate the other owner's share of the interest. These rules are discussed in the next item. Do not file a nominee form if you contributed all the funds and named a joint owner so that he or she may automatically inherit the account. You report all the interest.
Nominee distribution	If you receive a Form 1099-INT that includes interest belonging to someone other than you or your spouse, file a nominee Form 1099-INT with the IRS to indicate that person's income, and give a copy to that person. Complete a Form 1099-INT on which you are listed as the payer and the other person is listed as the recipient. Give the Form 1099-INT to the other owner by January 31, 2000. File Form 1099-INT plus Form 1096 ("Transmittal of Information Return") with the IRS by February 28, 2000. On your own Form 1040 or Form 1040A, you list the nominee interest, along with the other interest reported to you on Forms 1099-INT. Then subtract the nominee interest from the total. *See 4.12* for an example of nominee reporting.
Accrued interest on a bond bought between interest payment dates	Interest accrued between interest payment dates is part of the purchase price of the bond. This amount is taxable to the seller as explained at *4.15*. If you purchased a bond and received a Form 1099-INT that includes accrued interest on a bond, include the interest on Line 1 of Schedule B, and then on a separate line above Line 2 subtract the accrued interest from the Line 1 total.
Custodian account of a minor (Uniform Transfers to Minors Act)	The interest is taxable to the child. For a child under age 14, net investment income exceeding $1,400 is subject to tax at the parent's top tax rate; *see* Chapter 24.

□ CORRECTED (if checked)

PAYER'S name, street address, city, state, ZIP code, and telephone no. National Savings Bank 45 Sunnyside Drive City, State 010XX	Payer's RTN (optional)	OMB No. 1545-0112 **1999** Form **1099-INT**	**Interest Income**
PAYER'S Federal identification number 0X - XX100X1 **RECIPIENT'S identification number** 0X1 - 00 - XX11	**1** Interest income not included in box 3 $ 925		**Copy B** **For Recipient**
RECIPIENT'S name Enrique Ballesteros	**2** Early withdrawal penalty $	**3** Interest on U.S. Savings Bonds and Treas. obligations $	This is important tax information and is being furnished to the Internal Revenue
Street address (including apt. no.) 21 Chauncy Street	**4** Federal income tax withheld $	**5** Investment expenses $	Service. If you are required to file a return, a negligence penalty or
City, state, and ZIP code City, State 111X0	**6** Foreign tax paid	**7** Foreign country or U.S. possession	other sanction may be imposed on you if this income is taxable and
Account number (optional)	$		the IRS determines that it has not been reported.

Form **1099-INT**   (Keep for your records.)   Department of the Treasury - Internal Revenue Service

Key to Interest Income Rules

Item—	Pointer—
Forms 1099-INT	Forms 1099-INT, sent by payers of interest income, simplify the reporting of interest income. The forms give you the amount of interest to enter on your tax return. Although they are generally correct, you should check for mistakes, notify payers of any error, and request a new form marked "corrected." If tax was withheld (26.12), claim this tax as a payment on your tax return. The IRS will check interest reported on your return against the Forms 1099-INT sent by banks and other payers.
Deposits in a savings account	Interest credited to your account in 1999 is taxable for 1999. This is true for a "passbook" savings account even though you do not present your passbook to have the interest entered. Dividends on deposits or accounts in the following institutions are reported as interest income: mutual savings banks; cooperative banks; domestic building and loan associations; and domestic and federal savings and loan associations.
Savings certificates, deferred interest	The interest element on certificates of deposit and similar plans of more than one year is treated as original issue discount (OID) and is taxable on an annual basis. The bank notifies you of the taxable OID amount on Form 1099-OID. If you discontinue a savings plan before maturity, you may have a loss deduction for forfeited interest, which is listed on Form 1099-INT or Form 1099-OID; see 4.16. Tax on interest can be deferred on a savings certificate with a term of one year or less. Interest is taxable in the year it is available for withdrawal without substantial penalty. Where you invest in a six-month certificate before July 1, the entire amount of interest is paid six months later and is taxable in the year of payment. However, when you invest in a six-month certificate after June 30, only interest actually paid or made available for withdrawal without substantial penalty is taxable in the year of issuance. The balance is taxable in the year of maturity. You can defer interest to the following year by investing in a six-month certificate after June 30, provided the payment of interest is specifically deferred to the year of maturity by the terms of the certificate. Similarly, interest may be deferred to the following year by investing in longer term certificates of up to one year, provided that the crediting of interest is specifically deferred until the year of maturity.
U.S. Savings Bonds— Series E, EE	The increase in redemption value of these Savings Bonds is interest income, but if you choose to defer the interest, you do not have to report the annual increase in value until the year in which you cash the bond or the year in which the bond finally matures, whichever is earlier; see 4.28.
U.S. Savings Bonds— Series H, HH	Semiannual interest on these bonds is taxable when received.
U.S. Treasury bills	If your T-bill matured in 1999, report as interest the difference between the amount received at redemption and your cost. If in 1999 you sold a bill before maturity, you may have a capital loss, or a gain that is partly interest income and partly capital gain; see 4.27.
Zero Coupon Bonds	The interest element is treated as original issue discount (OID) and is taxable annually. You receive a Form 1099-OID reporting the taxable amount.
Interest on funds invested abroad	Interest must be reported in U.S. dollars. If foreign tax has been paid, you may be entitled to a deduction or credit; see 36.14. See also 36.12 for blocked currency reporting rules.
Bearer or coupon bonds	Interest coupons due and payable in 1999 are taxable on your 1999 return regardless of when they were presented for collection. For example, a coupon due January 1999 and presented for payment in 1998 is taxable in 1999. Similarly, a December 1999 coupon presented for payment in 2000 is taxable in 1999.
Corporate obligations in registered form	You report interest when it is received or made available to you. See 4.15 on how to treat interest when you buy or sell bonds between interest dates.
Interest on state and local government obligations	Although you may receive a Form 1099-INT for interest on state or municipal bonds, you do not pay federal tax on the interest. You are required to list the tax-exempt interest on your tax return, although it is not taxable. The interest may be subject to state income tax.
Borrowing to meet minimum deposit requirements for savings certificates	Interest expenses may be deductible as itemized investment interest deductions (15.10). Report the full amount of interest income listed on Form 1099-INT, even if you do not take interest deductions.
Insurance proceeds	You report interest paid on insurance proceeds left with an insurance company or included in installment payments (under optional modes of payment). Exception: A surviving spouse of an insured who died before October 23, 1986, is not taxed on up to $1,000 a year of interest included in installment payments.
Interest on prepaid premium	Taxable interest is reported by insurance company on Form 1099-INT.
Interest on tax refunds	Interest on tax refunds is fully taxable.
Bank gifts	To attract new deposits, banks and thrifts may offer cash, televisions, toasters, and the like as inducements. The gifts are taxable as interest and reported on Form 1099-INT.
Interest on withdrawn life insurance dividends	If you can withdraw the interest annually, you report the interest in the year it is credited to your account. However, if, under the terms of the insurance policy, the interest can be withdrawn only on the anniversary date of the policy (or some other specified date), then you report the interest in the year in which the anniversary date of the policy (or some other specified date) falls. Interest on GI insurance dividends on deposit with the Department of Veterans Affairs (VA) is not taxable.

Redemptions, bankruptcy, reorganizations. On a redemption, interest received in excess of the amount due at that time is not treated as interest income but as capital gain.

EXAMPLE

You hold a $5,000 9% bond with interest payable January 1 and July 1. The company can call the bonds for redemption on any interest date. In May, the company announces it will redeem the bonds on July 1. But you may present the bond for redemption beginning with June 1 and it will be redeemed with interest to July 1. On June 1 you present the bond and receive $5,225 – $5,000 principal, $187.50 interest to June 1, and $37.50 extra interest to July 1. The $37.50 is treated as a capital gain; the $187.50 is interest.

Taxable interest may continue on bonds after the issuer becomes bankrupt, if a guarantor continues to pay the interest when due. The loss on the bonds will occur only when they mature and are not redeemed or when they are sold below your cost. In the meantime, the interest received from the guarantor is taxed.

Bondholders exchanging their bonds for stock, securities, or other property in a tax-free reorganization, including a reorganization in bankruptcy, have interest income to the extent the property received is attributable to accrued but unpaid interest; *see* Internal Revenue Code Section 354.

Bonds selling at a flat price. When you buy bonds with defaulted interest at a "flat" price, a later payment of the defaulted interest is not taxed. It is a tax-free return of capital that reduces your cost of the bond. This rule applies only to interest in default at the time the bond is purchased. Interest that accrues after the date of your purchase is taxed as ordinary income.

4.16 Forfeiture of Interest on Premature Withdrawals

Banks usually impose an interest penalty if you withdraw funds from a savings certificate before the specified maturity date. You may lose interest if you prematurely withdraw funds in order to switch to higher paying investments, or if you need the funds for personal use. In some cases, the penalty may exceed the interest earned so that principal is also forfeited to make up the difference.

If you are penalized, you must still report the full amount of interest credited to your account. However, on Form 1040, you may deduct the full amount of the penalty-forfeited principal as well as interest. The deductible penalty-forfeited amount is shown in Box 2 of Form 1099-INT sent to you. You may claim the deduction even if you do not itemize deductions. On Form 1040, enter the deduction on Line 30, marked "Penalty on early withdrawal of savings."

Loss on redemption before maturity of a savings certificate. If you redeem a long-term (more than one year) savings certificate for a price less than the stated redemption price at maturity, you are allowed a loss deduction for the amount of original issue discount (OID) reported as income but not received. The deductible amount is shown in Box 3 of Form 1099-OID. Claim the deduction on Line 30 of Form 1040. The basis of the obligation is reduced by the amount of the deductible loss.

Do not include in the computation any amount based on a fixed rate of simple or compound interest that is actually payable or is treated as constructively received at fixed periodic intervals of one year or less.

Caution

CD Early Withdrawal

If you are penalized for making an early withdrawal from a certificate of deposit, you may lose part of your interest or principal. You must report the full amount of interest credited to your account, but you may deduct the full amount of the penalty-forfeited principal as well as interest on Line 30 of Form 1040.

Premiums and Discounts on Bonds

4.17 Amortization of Bond Premium

Bond premium is the extra amount paid for a bond in excess of its principal or face amount when the value of the bond has increased due to falling interest rates. Investors may elect to amortize the premium on a taxable bond by deducting it over the life of the bond. Amortizing the premium annually is usually advantageous because it gives an annual deduction to offset the interest income from the bond. Basis of the bond is reduced by the amortized premium. If you claim amortization deductions and hold the bond to maturity, basis is reduced by the entire amortized premium and you have neither gain nor loss at redemption.

You may not claim a deduction for a premium paid on a *tax-exempt* bond; however, you must still decrease your basis by the premium.

Dealers in bonds may not deduct amortization but must include the premium as part of cost.

Filing Tip

How To Deduct Amortized Premium

If you paid a premium on a taxable bond during 1999, you offset interest income on the bond by the amortized premium. You must file Form 1040 and show the reduction on Schedule B. Report the full interest from the bond on Line 1 of Schedule B, along with the rest of your interest income. On a separate line, subtract the amortized premium from a subtotal of the other interest. Label the subtraction "ABP Adjustment."

This interest offset rule applies to all taxable bonds acquired at a premium after 1987; *see 4.17* for bonds acquired before 1988.

Planning Reminder

Amortized Premium Reduces Basis

You reduce the cost basis of the bond by the amount of the premium taken as a deduction.

If you hold the bond to maturity, the entire premium is amortized and you have neither gain nor loss on redemption of the bond. If before maturity you sell the bond at a gain (selling price exceeds your basis for the bond), you realize long-term capital gain if you held the bond long term. A sale of the bond for less than its adjusted basis gives a capital loss.

Capital loss alternative to amortizing premium. If you do not elect to amortize the premium on a taxable bond, you will realize a capital loss when the bond is redeemed at par or you sell it for less than you paid for it. For example, you bought a $1,000 corporate bond for $1,300 and did not amortize the $300 premium; you will realize a $300 capital loss when the bond is redeemed at par: $1,000 proceeds less $1,300 cost basis ($1,000 face value plus $300 premium). You could realize a capital gain if you sell the bond for more than the premium price you paid.

Determining the amortizable amount for the year. The annual amortizable premium is based on the yield-to-maturity method (also called the constant yield method) if the bond was issued after September 27, 1985. This method is the same as the optional constant yield method for reporting market discount discussed at *4.20*. *See* IRS Publication 1212 or consult a tax professional for making the complex computations.

For bonds issued before September 28, 1985, a monthly straight-line method or a yield method based upon IRS Revenue Ruling 82-10 could be used.

For taxable bonds subject to a call before maturity, the amortization computation is based on the earlier call date if that results in a smaller amortization deduction.

Amortization election made after the year you acquire a bond. An election to amortize premium on a taxable bond does not have to be made in the year you acquire the bond. Attach a statement to the tax return for the first year to which you want the election to apply. If the election is made after the year of acquisition, the premium allocable to the years prior to the year of election is not amortizable; the unamortized amount is included in your cost basis for the bond and will result in a capital loss when the bond is redeemed at par or sold prior to maturity for less than basis.

How to deduct amortized premium on taxable bonds acquired after 1987. The premium amortization for such bonds offsets your interest income from the bonds; *see* the Filing Tip on this page. For bonds acquired on or after March 2,1998, the excess of the allocable premium over interest income may be fully deducted as a miscellaneous deduction on Line 27 of Schedule A (Form 1040). However, the miscellaneous deduction is limited to the excess of total interest inclusions on the bonds in prior years over total bond premium deductions in the prior years.

How to deduct premium amortization on taxable bonds acquired after October 22, 1986, but before 1988. The method of claiming amortized premium on taxable bonds acquired after October 22,1986, but before 1988 depends on whether you made an election to amortize premium for any taxable bond before 1998. If the election was first made for 1998 or 1999, the allocable premium amortization for the bonds offsets interest income on your return. If a pre-1998 election to amortize was made, the allocable premium is treated as investment interest subject to the deduction limits at *15.10*.

How to deduct premium amortization on taxable bonds acquired before October 23, 1986. For bonds acquired before October 23, 1986, the allocable premium is fully deductible on Line 27 of Schedule A (Form 1040) as a miscellaneous deduction not subject to the 2% floor *(19.1)*.

Effect of amortization election on other taxable bonds you acquire. If you elect to amortize the premium for one bond, you must also amortize the premium on all similar bonds owned by you at the beginning of the tax year, and also to all similar bonds acquired thereafter. An election to amortize may not be revoked without IRS permission. If you file your return without claiming the deduction, you may not change your mind and make the election for that year by filing an amended return or refund claim.

Callable bonds. On taxable bonds, amortization is based either on the maturity or earlier call date, depending on which date gives a smaller yearly deduction. This rule applies regardless of the issue date of the bond. If the bond is called before maturity, you may deduct as an ordinary loss the unamortized bond premium in the year the bond is redeemed.

Convertible bonds. A premium paid for a convertible bond that is allocated to the conversion feature may not be amortized; the value of the conversion option reduces basis in the bond.

Premium on tax-exempt bonds. You may not take a deduction for the amortization of a premium paid on a tax-exempt bond. When you dispose of the bond, you amortize the premium for the period you held the bond and reduce the basis of the bond by the amortized amount. If the bond has call dates, the IRS may require the premium to be amortized to the earliest call date.

4.18 Discount on Bonds

There are two types of bond discounts: original issue discount and market discount.

Market discount. Market discount arises when the price of a bond declines because its interest rate is less than the current interest rate. For example, a bond originally issued at its face amount of $1,000 declines in value to $900 because the interest payable on the bond is less than the current interest rate. The difference of $100 is called market discount. The tax treatment of market discount is explained in *4.20*.

Original issue discount (OID). OID arises when a bond is issued for a price less than its face or principal amount. OID is the difference between the principal amount (redemption price at maturity) and the issue price. For publicly offered obligations, the issue price is the initial offering price to the public at which a substantial amount of such obligations were sold. All obligations that pay no interest before maturity, such as zero coupon bonds, are considered to be issued at a discount. For example, a bond with a face amount of $1,000 is issued at an offering price of $900. The $100 difference is OID.

Generally, part of the OID must be reported as interest income each year you hold the bond, whether or not you receive any payment from the bond issuer. This is also true for certificates of deposit (CDs), time deposits, and similar savings arrangements with a term of more than one year, provided payment of interest is deferred until maturity. OID is reported to you by the issuer (or by your broker if you bought the obligation on a secondary market) on Form 1099-OID; *see 4.19* for reporting OID.

Exceptions to OID. OID rules do *not* apply to: (1) obligations with a term of one year or less held by *cash-basis taxpayers*; *see 4.21*; (2) tax-exempt obligations, except for certain stripped tax-exempts; *see 4.26*; (3) U.S. Savings Bonds; (4) an obligation issued by an individual before March 2, 1984; and (5) loans of $10,000 or less from individuals after March 1, 1984.

 Filing Tip

When OID May Be Ignored
You may disregard OID that is less than one-fourth of one percent (.0025) of the principal amount multiplied by the number of full years from the date of original issue to maturity. On most long-term bonds, the OID will exceed this amount and must be reported.

EXAMPLES
1. A 10-year bond with a face amount of $1,000 is issued at $980. One-fourth of one percent (.0025) of $1,000 times 10 is $25. As the $20 OID is less than $25, it may be ignored for tax purposes.
2. Same facts as in Example 1, except that the bond is issued at $950. As OID of $50 is more than the $25, OID must be reported under the rules explained at *4.19*.

Bond bought at premium or acquisition premium. You do not report OID as ordinary income if you buy a bond at a premium. You buy at a premium where you pay more than the total amount payable on the bond after your purchase, not including qualified stated interest. When you dispose of a bond bought at a premium, the difference between the sale or redemption price and your basis is a capital gain or loss; *see 4.17*.

If you do not pay more than the total due at maturity, you do not have a premium, but there is "acquisition premium" if you pay more than the adjusted issue price. This is the issue price plus previously accrued OID but minus previous payments on the bond other than qualified stated interest. The acquisition premium reduces the amount of OID you must report as income. The rules for computing the reduction to OID depend on when the bond was purchased. For bonds purchased after July 18, 1984, OID is reduced by a fraction, the numerator of which is the acquisition premium; the denominator is the OID remaining after your purchase date to the maturity date. *See* IRS Publication 1212 for further details on how to make the computation.

4.19 How To Report Original Issue Discount (OID) on Your Return

The issuer of the bond (or your broker) will make the OID computation and report in Box 1 of Form 1099-OID the OID for the actual dates of your ownership during the calendar year. However, the amount shown in Box 1 of Form 1099-OID must be adjusted if you bought the obligation at a premium or acquisition premium, if the obligation is a stripped bond or stripped coupon, or if you received Form 1099-OID as a nominee for someone else.

If you did not receive a Form 1099-OID, contact the issuer or check IRS Publication 1212 for OID amounts.

Filing Tip

Reporting OID and Recomputed OID

If you are reporting the full amount of OID from Box 1 of Form 1099-OID include the amount as interest on your Form 1040, 1040A, or 1040EZ. However, if, as discussed in *4.19*, you are reporting less OID than the amount shown in Box 1 of Form 1099-OID, you must file Form 1040 and fill out Schedule B. Include the full amount shown in Box 1 of Form 1099-OID on Line 1 of Schedule B, along with other interest income. Make a subtotal of the Line 1 amounts and subtract from it the OID you are not required to report. Write "OID Adjustment" on the line where you show the subtraction, or "Nominee distribution," if that is the reason for the reduction. If you are reporting more OID than the amount shown in Box 1 of Form 1099-OID, add the additional amount to the subtotal of the interest on Line 1 of Schedule B, and label it "OID Adjustment."

Your basis for the obligation is increased by the taxable OID for purposes of figuring gain on a sale or redemption; *see 4.23.*

Filing Tip

Older Tax-Exempts

Tax-exempt bonds bought before May 1, 1993, are *not* subject to the market discount interest income rule; all the gain at disposition is capital gain.

Premium. If you paid a premium *(see 4.18)* for a bond originally issued at discount, you do not have to report any OID as income. Report the amount shown on Form 1099-OID and then subtract it as discussed in the Filing Tip on this page.

Acquisition premium. The amount that is shown in Box 1 of Form 1099-OID is not correct if you pay an acquisition premium *(see 4.18)* because such premium reduces the amount of OID you must report as income. *See* IRS Publication 1212 to recompute OID. On your return, report the amount shown on Form 1099-OID and then reduce it, as discussed in the Filing Tip on this page.

Stripped bonds or coupons. The amount that is shown in Box 1 of Form 1099-OID may not be correct for a stripped bond or coupon; *see 4.22.* If it is incorrect, adjust it following the rules in Publication 1212 and report the proper amount, as discussed in the Filing Tip on this page.

Nominee. If you receive a Form 1099-OID for an obligation owned by someone else, other than your spouse, you must file another Form 1099-OID for that owner. The OID computation rules shown in IRS Publication 1212 should be used to compute the other owner's share of OID. You file the other owner's Form 1099-OID and a transmittal Form 1096 with the IRS, and give the other owner a copy of the Form 1099-OID. On your own tax return, report the amount shown on the Form 1099-OID you received and then reduce it, as discussed in the Filing Tip on this page.

Periodic interest reported on Form 1099-OID. If in addition to OID there is regular interest payable on the bond, such interest will be reported in Box 2 of Form 1099-OID. Report the full amount as interest income if you held the bond for the entire year. If you acquired the bond or disposed of it during the year, *see 4.15* for figuring the interest allocable to your ownership period.

REMICS. If you are a regular interest holder in a REMIC (real estate mortgage investment conduit), Box 1 of Form 1099-OID shows the amount of OID you must report on your return and Box 2 includes periodic interest other than OID. If you bought the regular interest at a premium or acquisition, the OID shown on Form 1099-OID must be adjusted as discussed above. If you are a regular interest holder in a single-class REMIC, Box 2 also includes your share of the REMIC's investment expenses. These expenses should be listed in a separate statement and are deductible on Schedule A as a miscellaneous itemized deduction subject to the 2% adjusted gross income floor; *see 19.24.*

4.20 Reporting Income on Market Discount Bonds

Market discount arises where the price of a bond declines below its face amount because it carries an interest rate that is below the current rate of interest.

When you realize a profit on a market discount bond, the portion of the profit equal to the accrued discount must be reported as ordinary interest income rather than as capital gain. Alternatively, an election may be made to report the accrued market discount annually instead of in the year of disposition.

These rules apply to taxable as well as tax-exempt *bonds bought after April 30, 1993.* However, there are these exceptions: (1) bonds with a maturity date of up to one year from date of issuance; (2) certain installment obligations; and (3) U.S. Savings Bonds. Furthermore, you may treat as zero any market discount that is less than one-fourth of one percent (.0025) of the redemption price multiplied by the number of full years after you acquire the bond to maturity. Such minimal discount will not affect capital gain on a sale.

Bonds bought before May 1, 1993. A *tax-exempt* bond bought before May 1, 1993, is not subject to the market discount rules; *see* the Filing Tip on this page. For *taxable* bonds bought before May 1, 1993, application of the market discount rules depends on the issue date.

If you bought a *taxable* bond before May 1, 1993, the market discount interest income rule applies if the bond was issued *after* July 18, 1984. If the bond was issued before July 19, 1984, the market discount interest income rule does *not* apply; however, a portion of the gain on disposition can still be treated as interest income if you borrowed money to purchase or carry a market discount bond acquired after July 18, 1984. As discussed in the next paragraph, interest deductions for such loans are restricted and in the year you sell the bond, gain is treated as interest income to the extent of the deferred interest that is deductible in the year of disposition.

Deferral of interest deduction and ordinary income at disposition if you borrow to buy market discount bonds after July 18, 1984. If you took such a loan, and your interest expense exceeds the income earned on the bond (including OID income, if any), the excess may not be currently deducted to the extent of the market discount allocated to the days you held the bond during the year. The limitation on the interest deduction applies to bonds you acquire after July 18, 1984, regardless of the issue date of the bond. The allocation of market discount is based on either the ratable accrual method or constant yield method; *see* below.

You can avoid this interest deduction limitation if you elect to report the market discount annually as interest income; *see* below for "How to figure accrued market discount."

In the year you dispose of the bond, you may deduct the interest expenses that were disallowed in prior years because of the above limitations. *Gain* on the disposition is interest income to the extent of the deferred interest you may deduct in the year of disposition; the balance is capital gain.

You may choose to deduct disallowed interest in a year before the year of disposition if you have net interest income from the bond. Net interest income is interest income for the year (including OID) less the interest expense incurred during the year to purchase or carry the bond. This election lets you deduct any disallowed interest expense to the extent it does not exceed the net interest income of that year. The balance of the disallowed interest expense is deductible in the year of disposition.

EXAMPLE

In 1999, you borrowed to buy a market discount bond. During 1999, your interest expense is $1,000. Income from the bond is $900 and ratable market discount allocated to the annual holding period is $75. On Form 4952 (Investment Interest Expense Deduction), $925 of interest ($1,000 – $75) is reported as investment interest; *see 15.10.*

A similar interest deduction limitation will apply every year you hold the bond, assuming you do not elect to report the market discount annually.

In the year you dispose of the bond, interest deferred under the limitation will be deductible, subject to the investment interest limits of *15.10.* Gain on the disposition will be treated as interest income to the extent of this deferred interest deduction.

How to figure accrued market discount. Where the market discount rules apply, gain is taxed as ordinary interest income to the extent of the market discount accrued to the date of sale. There are two methods for figuring the accrued market discount. The basic method, called the *ratable accrual method*, is figured by dividing market discount by the number of days in the period from the date you bought the bond until the date of maturity. This daily amount is then multiplied by the number of days you held the bond to determine your accrued market discount; *see* Example 1 below.

Instead of using the ratable accrual method to compute accrual of market discount you may elect to figure the accrued discount for any bond under an optional *constant yield* (economic accrual) method. If you make the election, you may not change it. The constant yield method initially provides a smaller accrual of market discount than the ratable method, but it is more complicated to figure. It is generally the same as the constant yield method used in IRS Publication 1212 to compute taxable OID *(4.19).* For accruing market discount, treat your acquisition date as the original issue date and your basis for the market discount bond (immediately after you acquire it) as the issue price when applying the formula in Publication 1212.

Reporting discount annually. Rather than report market discount in the year you sell the bond, you may elect, in the year you acquire the bond, to report market discount currently as interest income. You may use either the ratable accrual method, as in Example 3 below, or the elective constant yield method discussed earlier. Your election to report annually applies to all market discount bonds subject to the interest income rule that you later acquire. You may not revoke the election without IRS consent. If the election is made, the interest deduction deferral rule discussed earlier does not apply. Furthermore, the election could provide a tax advantage if you sell the bond at a profit and you can benefit from lower tax rates applied to net long-term capital gains.

 Filing Instruction

Discount Bonds Held to Maturity

If you do not report the discount annually and hold a bond until maturity, the discount is reported as interest income in the year of redemption; *see* Example 2 on the following page. However, you have the option of reporting the market discount annually instead of at sale.

EXAMPLES

1. You buy a taxable bond at a market discount of $200. There are 1,000 days between the date of your purchase and the maturity date. The daily accrual rate is 20 cents. You hold the bond for 600 days before selling it for a price exceeding what you paid for the bond. Under the ratable accrual method, up to $120 of your profit is market discount taxable as interest income (600 × $0.20).

2. You paid $9,100 for a $10,000 bond maturing in 2000. If you hold the bond to maturity, you will receive $10,000, giving you a gain of $900, equal to the market discount. The entire $900 market discount will be taxable as interest income in 2000 when the bond is redeemed.

3. In 1999, you buy at a $200 discount a bond that was issued after July 18, 1984. There are 1,000 days between the date of your purchase and the maturity date, so that daily accrual is 20 cents. You elect to report the market discount currently using the ratable accrual method. If you held the bond for 112 days in 1999, on your 1999 return you report $22 as interest income (112 × $0.20).

Partial principal payments on bonds acquired after October 22, 1986. If the issuer of a bond (acquired by you after October 22, 1986) makes a partial payment of the principal (face amount), you must include the payment as ordinary interest income to the extent it does not exceed the accrued market discount on the bond. *See* IRS Publication 550 for options on determining accrued market discount. A taxable partial principal payment reduces the amount of remaining accrued market discount when figuring your tax on a later sale or receipt of another partial principal payment.

Market discount on a bond originally issued at a discount. A bond issued at original issue discount may later be acquired at a market discount because of an increase in interest rates. If you acquire at market discount an OID bond issued after July 18, 1984, the market discount is the excess of: (1) the issue price of the bond plus the total original issue discount includible in the gross income of all prior holders of the bond over (2) what you paid for the bond.

Exchanging a market discount bond in corporate mergers or reorganizations. If you hold a market discount bond and exchange it for another bond as part of a merger or other reorganization, the new bond is subject to the market discount rules when you sell it. However, under an exception, market discount rules will not apply to the new bond if the old market discount bond was issued before July 19, 1984, and the terms of interest rates of both bonds are identical.

4.21 Discount on Short-Term Obligations

Short-term obligations (maturity of a year or less from date of issue) may be purchased at a discount from face value. If you are on the cash basis, you report the discount as interest income in the year the obligation is paid. The interest is reported on Form 1099-INT.

EXAMPLE

In May 1998, you paid $920 for a short-term note with a face amount of $1,000. In January 1999, you receive payment of $1,000 on the note. On your 1999 tax return, you report $80 as interest.

Discount must be currently reported by dealers and accrual-basis taxpayers. Discount allocable to the current year must be reported as income by accrual-basis taxpayers, dealers who sell short-term obligations in the course of business, banks, regulated investment companies, common trust funds, certain pass-through entities, and for obligations identified as part of a hedging transaction. Current reporting also applies to persons who separate or strip interest coupons from a bond and then retain the stripped bond or stripped coupon; the accrual rule applies to the retained obligation.

For short-term nongovernmental obligations, OID is generally taken into account instead of acquisition discount, but an election may be made to report the accrued acquisition discount. *See* IRS Publication 550 for details.

Basis in the obligation is increased by the amount of acquisition discount (or OID for nongovernmental obligations) that is currently reported as income.

Filing Tip

Discount on Short-Term Government Obligations

For short-term governmental obligations (other than tax-exempts), the acquisition discount is accrued in daily installments under the ratable method, unless an election is made to use the constant yield method.

Interest deduction limitation for cash-basis investors. A cash-basis investor who borrows funds to buy a short-term discount obligation may not fully deduct interest on the loan unless an election is made to report the accrued acquisition discount as income. If the election is not made, a complicated formula limits deductible interest to the excess of the interest expense for the year over the taxable interest from the bond during the year less (1) the portion of the discount allocated to the days you held the bond during the year, and (2) the portion of interest not taxable for the year under your method of accounting. Any interest expense disallowed under this limitation is deductible in the year in which the obligation is disposed.

The interest deduction limitation does *not* apply if you elect to include in income the accruable discount under the ratable accrual method or constant yield method discussed in *4.20*. The election applies to all short-term obligations acquired during the year and also in all later years.

Gain or loss on disposition of short-term obligations for cash-basis investors. If you have a gain on the sale or exchange of a discounted short-term *governmental* obligation (other than tax-exempt local obligations), the gain is ordinary income to the extent of the ratable share of the acquisition discount received when you bought the obligation. Follow the computation shown in *4.27* for Treasury bills to figure this ordinary income portion. Any gain over this ordinary income portion is short-term capital gain; a loss would be a short-term capital loss.

Gain on short-term *nongovernmental* obligations is treated as ordinary income up to the ratable share of OID. The formula for figuring this ordinary income portion is similar to that shown in *4.27* for short-term governmental obligations, except that the denominator of the fraction is days from original issue to maturity, rather than days from acquisition. A constant yield method may also be elected to figure the ordinary income portion. Gain above the computed ordinary income amount is short-term capital gain (*see* Chapter 5). For more information, *see* IRS Publication 550.

4.22 Stripped Coupon Bonds and Stock

Brokers holding coupon bonds may separate or strip the coupons from the bonds and sell the bonds or coupons to investors. Examples include zero-coupon instruments sold by brokerage houses that are backed by U.S. Treasury bonds (such as CATS and TIGRS).

The U.S. Treasury also offers its version of zero coupon instruments, with the name STRIPS, which are available from brokers and banks.

Brokers holding preferred stock may strip the dividend rights from the stock and sell the stripped stock to investors.

If you buy a stripped bond or coupon, the spread between the cost of the bond or coupon and its higher face amount is treated as original issue discount (OID). This means that you annually report a part of the spread as interest income. For a stripped bond, the amount of the original issue discount is the difference between the stated redemption price of the bond at maturity and the cost of the bond. For a stripped coupon, the amount of the discount is the difference between the amount payable on the due date of the coupon and the cost of the coupon. The rules for figuring the amount of OID to be reported annually are in IRS Publication 1212. *See 4.19* for reporting OID.

If you strip a coupon bond, interest accrual and allocation rules prevent you from creating a tax loss on a sale of the bond or coupons. You are required to report interest accrued up to the date of the sale and also add the amount to the basis of the bond. If you acquired the obligation after October 22, 1986, you must also include in income any market discount that accrued before the date you sold the stripped bond or coupons. The method of accrual depends on the date you bought the obligation; *see* IRS Publication 1212. The accrued market discount is also added to the basis of the bond. You then allocate this basis between the bond and the coupons. The allocation is based on the relative fair market values of the bond and coupons at the date of sale. Gain or loss on the sale is the difference between the sales price of the stripped item (bond or coupons) and its allocated basis. Furthermore, the original issue discount rules apply to the stripped item which you keep (bond or coupon). Original issue discount for this purpose is the difference between the basis allocated to the retained item and the redemption price of the bond (if retained) or the amount payable on the coupons (if retained). You must annually report a ratable portion of the discount.

4.23 Sale or Retirement of Bonds and Notes

Gain or loss on the sale, redemption, or retirement of debt obligations issued by a government or corporation is generally capital gain or loss. If the bond was issued before 1955, there is capital gain or loss only if the obligation was issued with interest coupons or in registered form on or before March 1, 1954.

Caution

Recomputing Form 1099-OID Amount

Do not report the amount shown in Box 1 of Form 1099-OID for a stripped bond or coupon; that amount must be recomputed under complicated rules described in IRS Publication 1212. *See 4.19* for reporting the recomputed OID on your return.

A redemption or retirement of a bond at maturity must be reported as a sale on Schedule D of Form 1040 *(5.6)* although there may be no gain or loss realized.

Corporate bonds with OID issued after 1954 and before May 28, 1969, and government bonds with OID issued before July 2, 1982. If the bonds were originally issued at a discount (OID), you report your ratable monthly share of the OID element as ordinary income when the bonds are sold or redeemed; any gain exceeding OID is reported as capital gain. However, if there was an intention to call before maturity, gain is ordinary income to the full extent of the OID. A loss is a capital loss. IRS Publication 1212 has examples for figuring the amount taxable as ordinary income.

Corporate bonds with OID issued after May 27, 1969, and government bonds with OID issued after July 1, 1982. The accrued amount of OID is reported annually as interest income *(see 4.19)* and added to basis; this includes the accrued OID for the year the bond is sold. If the bonds are sold or redeemed before maturity, you realize capital gain for the proceeds over the adjusted basis (as increased by accrued OID) of the bond, provided there was no intention to call the bond before maturity. If at the time of original issue there was an intention to call the obligation before maturity, the entire OID that has not yet been included in your income is taxable as ordinary income; the balance is capital gain.

Market discount on bonds is taxable under the rules at *4.20.*

Tax-exempts. *See 4.26* for discount on tax-exempt bonds.

Obligations issued by individuals. If you hold an individual's note issued after March 1, 1984, for over $10,000, accrued OID must be reported annually *(4.19)* and added to basis. Gain on your sale of the note is subject to the rules discussed above for corporate and government OID bonds.

If the note is $10,000 or less (when combined with other prior outstanding loans from the same individual), OID is not reported annually provided you are not a professional lender and tax avoidance was not a principal purpose of the loan. On a sale of the note at a gain, your ratable share of the OID is taxed as ordinary income; any balance is capital gain. A loss is a capital loss.

Tax-Free Interest on State and Local Government Obligations

 Filing Tip

Reporting on Schedule B or Schedule 1

On your 1999 return, you must list the amount of tax-exempt interest received during the year although it is not taxable. On Form 1040, you list the tax-exempt interest on Line 8b. On Form 1040A, you list the amount on Line 8b. On Form 1040EZ, you write "TEI" and then the amount of tax-exempt interest to the right of the last word on Line 2, but do not include it in the taxable interest shown on Line 2.

4.24 State and City Interest Generally Tax Exempt

Generally, you pay no tax on interest on bonds or notes of states, cities, counties, the District of Columbia, or a possession of the United States. This includes bonds or notes of port authorities, toll road commissions, utility services activities, community redevelopment agencies, and similar bodies created for public purposes. Bonds issued after June 30, 1983, must be in registered form for the interest to be tax exempt. Interest on federally guaranteed obligations is generally taxable, but *see* exceptions at *4.25.*

Check with the issuer of the bond to verify the tax-exempt status of the interest.

Private activity bonds. Interest on so-called private activity bonds is generally taxable *(see 4.25)*, but there are certain exceptions. For example, interest on the following bonds is tax exempt even if the bond may technically be in the category of private activity bonds: qualified student loan bonds; exempt facility bonds; qualified small issue bonds; qualified mortgage bonds and qualified veterans' mortgage bonds; qualified redevelopment bonds; and qualified 501(c)(3) bonds issued by charitable organizations and hospitals.

However, while interest on such bonds is not subject to regular tax, interest that you receive on such bonds issued after August 7, 1986, is considered a tax preference item that may be subject to alternative minimum tax; *see* Chapter 23.

Check with the issuer for the tax status of a private activity bond.

4.25 Taxable State and City Interest

Interest on certain state and city obligations is taxable. These taxable obligations include federally guaranteed obligations, mortgage subsidy bonds, private activity bonds, and arbitrage bonds.

Federally guaranteed obligations. Interest on state and local obligations issued after April 14, 1983, is generally taxable if the obligation is federally guaranteed, but there are exceptions allowing tax exemptions for obligations guaranteed by the Federal Housing Administration, Department of Veterans Affairs, Bonneville Power Authority, Federal Home Loan Mortgage Corporation, Federal National Mortgage Association, Government National Mortgage Corporation, Resolution Funding Corporation, and Student Loan Marketing Association.

Mortgage subsidy bonds. Interest on bonds issued by a state or local government after April 24, 1979, may not be tax exempt if funds raised by the bonds are used for home mortgages. There are exceptions for certain qualified mortgage bonds and veterans' bonds. Check on the tax-exempt status of mortgage bonds with the issuing authority.

Private activity bonds. Generally, a private activity bond is any bond where more than 10% of the issue's proceeds are used by a private business whose property secures the issue, or if at least 5% of the proceeds (or $5 million if less) are used for loans to parties other than governmental units. Interest on such bonds is generally taxable, but there are exceptions as discussed in *4.24*. Check on the tax status of the bonds with the issuing authority.

4.26 Tax-Exempt Bonds Bought at a Discount

Original issue discount (OID) on tax-exempt obligations is not taxable, and on a sale or redemption, gain attributed to OID is tax exempt. Gain attributed to market discount is capital gain or ordinary income depending on whether the bond was purchased before May 1, 1993, or on or after that date; *see 4.20*.

Original issue discount tax-exempt bond. This arises when a bond is issued for a price less than the face amount of the bond. The discount is considered tax-exempt interest. Thus, if you are the original buyer and hold the bond to maturity, the entire amount of the discount is tax free. If before maturity you sell a bond that was issued before September 4, 1982, and acquired before March 2, 1984, your part of the OID is tax free. On a disposition of a tax-exempt bond issued after September 3, 1982, and acquired after March 1, 1984, you must add to basis accrued OID before determining gain or loss. OID must generally be accrued using a constant yield method; *see* IRS Publication 1212.

When bonds issued after June 8, 1980, are redeemed before maturity, the portion of the original issue discount earned to the date of redemption is tax-free interest; the balance is capital gain. Bonds issued with an intention to redeem before maturity are not subject to this rule; all interest is tax exempt.

Amortization of premiums is discussed at *4.17*.

Market discount tax-exempts. A market discount arises when a bond originally issued at not less than par is bought at below par because its market value has declined. If *before* May 1, 1993, you bought at a market discount a tax-exempt bond which you sell for a price exceeding your purchase price, the excess is capital gain. If the bond was held long term, the gain is long term. A redemption of the bond at a price exceeding your purchase price is similarly treated.

However, for market discount tax-exempt bonds purchased *after* April 30, 1993, the ordinary income rules discussed at *4.20* apply.

Stripped tax-exempt obligations. OID is not currently taxed on a stripped tax-exempt bond or stripped coupon from the bond if you bought it before June 11, 1987. However, for any stripped bond or coupon you bought or sold after October 22, 1986, OID must be accrued and added to basis for purposes of figuring gain or loss on a disposition. Furthermore, if you bought the stripped bond or coupon after June 10, 1987, part of the OID may be taxable; *see* Publication 1212 for figuring the tax-free portion.

Caution

Arbitrage Bonds

These are state and local bonds issued after October 9, 1969, used to provide funds for reinvestment in higher yielding instruments except where the bond proceeds are part of a required reserve or replacement fund or are being invested temporarily before the purposes of a bond issue can be fulfilled. Interest on arbitrage bonds is taxable.

Planning Reminder

Tax Deferral: T-Bill Maturing Next Year

If you are a cash-basis taxpayer, you may postpone the tax on Treasury bill interest by selecting a Treasury bill maturing next year. Income is not recognized until the date on which the Treasury bill is paid at maturity, unless it has been sold or otherwise disposed of earlier.

Interest on Treasury Securities and U.S. Savings Bonds

4.27 Treasury Bills, Notes, and Bonds

Interest on securities issued by the federal government is fully taxable on your federal return. However, interest on federal obligations is not subject to state or local income taxes. Interest on Treasury bills, notes, and bonds is reported on Form 1099-INT. *See 30.14* and *30.17* for investment information on Treasury securities.

Treasury bonds and notes. Treasury notes have maturities of two to 10 years. Treasury bonds have maturities of over 10 years. You report the fixed or coupon interest as interest income in the year the coupon becomes due and payable. Treasury bonds and notes are capital assets; gain or loss on their sale, exchange, or redemption is reported as capital gain or loss on Schedule D; *see* Chapter 5. If you purchased a federal obligation below par (at a discount) after July 1, 1982, *see 4.18* for the rules on reporting original issue discount. If you purchased a Treasury bond or note above par (at a premium), you may elect to amortize the premium; *see 4.17*. If you do not elect to amortize and you hold the bond or note to maturity, you have a capital loss.

Treasury bills. These are short-term U.S. obligations issued at a discount with maturities of three, six, or 12 months. On a bill held to maturity, you report as interest the difference between the discounted price and the amount you receive on a redemption of the bills at maturity.

Treasury bills are capital assets and a loss on a disposition before maturity is taxed as a capital loss. If you are a cash-basis taxpayer and have a gain on a sale or exchange, ordinary income is realized up to the amount of the ratable share of the discount received when you bought the obligation. This amount is treated as interest income and is figured as follows:

$$\frac{\text{Days T-bill was held}}{\text{Days from acquisition to maturity}} \times \frac{\text{T-bill's value at}}{\text{maturity } minus \text{ your cost}}$$

Any gain over this amount is capital gain; *see* the Example below. Instead of using the above fractional computation for figuring the ordinary income portion of the gain, an election may be made to apply the constant yield method. This method follows the OID computation rules shown in IRS Publication 1212 for obligations issued after 1984, except that the acquisition cost of the Treasury bill would be treated as the issue price in applying the Publication 1212 formula.

Accrual-basis taxpayers and dealers who are required to currently report the acquisition discount element of Treasury bills using either the ratable accrual method or the constant yield method *(4.20)* do not apply the above formula on a sale before maturity. In figuring gain or loss, the discount included as income is added to basis.

EXAMPLE

In May 1999, you buy at original issue a six-month $10,000 Treasury bill (180-day maturity) for $9,650. You sell it 90 days later for $9,800. Your entire gain of $150 ($9,800 – $9,650) is taxed as interest income on your 1999 return. Under the ratable daily formula, gain up to $175 would be treated as interest income:

$$\frac{\text{90 days held}}{\substack{\text{180 days from}\\\text{acquisition to maturity}}} \times \text{\$350 discount} = \text{\$175}$$

Interest deduction limitation. Interest incurred on loans used to buy Treasury bills is deductible by a cash-basis investor only to the extent that interest expenses exceed the following: (1) the portion of the acquisition discount allocated to the days you held the bond during the year; and (2) the portion of interest not taxable for the year under your method of accounting. The deferred interest expense is deductible in the year the bill is disposed of. If an election is made to report the acquisition discount as current income under the rules in *4.21* for governmental obligations, the interest expense may also be deducted currently. The election applies to all future acquisitions.

Filing Tip

Savings Bond in Child's Name
You may make an election on behalf of your child to report the savings bond interest annually if your child is unable to file his or her own return. The interest may be offset by the child's standard deduction. To make the election, report the accumulated bond interest and add a statement that the interest will be reported each year. In a later year, the child may change from annual reporting to the deferral method under the rules discussed in *4.29*.

4.28 Interest on U.S. Savings Bonds

Savings Bond Tables: The Supplement will contain redemption tables showing the 1999 year-end values of Series E and EE U.S. Savings Bonds.

Series E and EE Bonds. Series EE bonds have been available since 1980; before 1980, Series E bonds were issued. Both Series E and Series EE bonds may be cashed for what you paid for them plus an increase in their value over stated periods of time. See *30.21* for investment information on U.S. Savings Bonds.

The increase in redemption value is taxable as interest, but you do not have to report the increase in value each year on your federal return. You may defer *(4.29)* the interest income until the year in which you cash the bond or the year in which the bond finally matures, whichever is earlier. But if you want, you may report the annual increase by merely including it on your tax return. If you use the accrual method of reporting, you must include the interest each year as it accrues. Savings bond interest is not subject to state or local taxes.

If you initially choose to defer the reporting of interest and later want to switch to annual reporting, you may do so. You may also change from the annual reporting method to the deferral method. See *4.29* for rules on changing reporting methods.

Series I Bonds. "I Bonds," first offered in 1998, are inflation-indexed bonds issued at face amount *(see 30.22)*. As with EE bonds, you may defer the interest income (the increase in redemption value each year is interest) until the year in which the bond is redeemed or matures, whichever is earlier; *see 4.29.*

Education funding. If you buy EE bonds to pay for educational expenses and you defer the reporting of interest *(4.29)*, you may be able to exclude the accumulated interest from income when you redeem the bonds. *See* Chapter 38.

Bonds for child. Interest on savings bonds bought in the name of a child will be taxed to the child, even if the parent paid for the bonds and is named as beneficiary. Unless an election is made to report the increases in redemption value annually, the accumulated interest will be taxable to the child in the year he or she redeems the bond, or if earlier, when the bond finally matures. However, if the interest is reported annually by a child under age 14, or the child is under age 14 in the year bonds are redeemed, the interest may be subject to tax at the parent's top rate under the "kiddie tax"; *see* Chapter 24. For example, if a child under age 14 has 1999 investment income over $1,400, the excess is taxed at the parent's top tax rate on the child's 1999 return; *see 24.3.* To avoid kiddie tax, savings bond interest may be deferred, as discussed in *4.29.*

Bonds must be reissued to make gift. Assume you have bought E or EE bonds and had them registered in joint names of yourself and your daughter. The law of your state provides that jointly owned property may be transferred to a co-owner by delivery or possession. You deliver the bonds to your daughter and tell her they now belong to her alone. According to Treasury regulations, this is not a valid gift of the bonds. The bonds must be surrendered and reissued in your daughter's name.

If you do not have the bonds reissued and you die, the bonds are taxable to your estate. Ownership of the bonds is a matter of contract between the United States and the bond purchaser. The bonds are nontransferable. A valid gift cannot be accomplished by manual delivery to a donee unless the bonds also are surrendered and registered in the donee's name in accordance with Treasury regulations.

Series HH. These bonds are issued only in exchange for E or EE bonds, or for Freedom Shares. They are issued at face value and pay semiannual interest that is taxable when received.

To be exchanged for HH bonds, the E or EE bonds must have a redemption value of at least $500. If the total value is not a multiple of $500, you will receive cash for the difference. You report the cash received as interest income to the extent of the unreported interest earned on the EE bonds exchanged.

For example, if you trade EE bonds with a redemption value of $3,723.35 for HH bonds, you get $3,500 in HH bonds and cash of $223.35. Report the cash as interest income to the extent it is unreported interest on the EE bonds exchanged.

Series H. These bonds were available before 1980. They were bought at face value and pay semiannual interest that is taxable when received. If you obtained Series H bonds in an exchange for Series E bonds, and you did not report the E bond interest annually, you do not have to report the interest due on the old E bonds until the H bonds are redeemed or mature, whichever occurs first. H bonds issued after January 1957 cease earning interest when they mature in 30 years. At maturity, or on a disposal before maturity, you must report as interest the accumulated interest from any exchanged E bonds.

Freedom Shares. These savings notes were available between 1967 and 1970. They have maturities of 30 years. As with E bonds, owners may defer the reporting of interest until the notes mature.

4.29 Deferring U.S. Savings Bond Interest

You do not have to make a special election on your tax return in order to defer the interest on Series E, EE, or I savings bonds. You may simply postpone reporting the interest until the year you redeem the bond or the year in which it reaches final maturity, whichever is earlier. If you choose to defer the interest, you may decide in a later year to begin annual reporting of the increase in value. You may also switch from annual reporting to the deferral method. These options are discussed on the next page.

Planning Reminder

Election for Children Under 14
Where the kiddie tax for children under age 14 *(24.3)* does not apply, making the election to report the interest annually may be advisable, such as where the child has little or no other income and the bond interest can be offset by personal deductions. For example, a dependent child is not allowed to claim a personal exemption, but he or she may claim a 1999 standard deduction of at least $700; *see 13.5.* If the election to report the savings bond interest currently was made for 1999, up to $700 of the interest would be offset by the standard deduction, assuming the child had no other income.

Filing Tip

Form 1099-INT When Savings Bond Is Cashed

When you cash in an E or EE bond, you receive Form 1099-INT that lists as interest the difference between the amount received and the amount paid for the bond. The form may show more taxable interest than you are required to report because you have regularly reported the interest or a prior owner reported the interest. Report the full amount shown on Form 1099-INT on Schedule B if you file Form 1040, or on Part I of Schedule 1 if you file Form 1040A, along with your other interest income. Enter a subtotal of the total interest and then, on a separate line, reduce the subtotal by the savings bond interest that was previously reported and identify the reduction as "Previously Reported U.S. Savings Bond Interest." The interest is exempt from state and local taxes.

Caution

When Accumulated Interest Becomes Taxable

You may not indefinitely defer the tax on E bond interest. E bonds cease earning interest once the bonds reach their final maturity date. For example, bonds issued during 1959 cease earning interest in 1999, 40 years from the date of issuance. On your 1999 return, you must pay tax on all the accumulated interest on 1959 bonds—unless the bonds are traded for new HH bonds in multiples of $500. E bonds issued in 1969 also reach final maturity in 1999, 30 years from the date of issuance. Exchanging E bonds for HH bonds will continue the tax deferral on E bond interest. *See 30.21* for a listing of final maturity dates.

Changing from deferral to annual reporting. If you have deferred reporting of annual increases in value and want to elect to report annual increases on your 1999 return, make sure you report as 1999 interest income the total of all prior and 1999 increases in value. But next year, report only the increases accruing then, plus increases accruing on bonds newly purchased. Suppose you do not include the annual increase on your 1999 return and later change your mind. If the due date of the return has passed, it is too late to make the election. You may not file an amended return reporting the increase in value for 1999. You have to wait until next year's return to make the election.

Changing from annual reporting to deferral. If you have been reporting annual increases in value, you may change your method and elect to defer interest reporting until the bonds mature or are redeemed. You make the election by attaching to your federal income tax return for the year of the change a statement that meets the conditions of IRS Revenue Procedure 97-37; *see* IRS Publication 550 for details.

Extended maturity periods. E bonds may be held for additional periods of maturity after their initial maturity dates. Bonds held for additional periods increase in value and may be cashed in at any time. If you chose to postpone paying tax on accumulated interest, you may continue to postpone the tax during the extended period. You would then report the entire accumulated interest at the final maturity date or in the year you redeem the bond, whichever occurs earlier.

Co-Owners of E and EE Bonds. How to report interest on the bond depends on how it was bought or issued:

1. You paid for the entire bond: Either you or the co-owner may redeem it. You are taxed on all the interest, even though the co-owner cashes the bond and you receive no proceeds. If the other co-owner does cash in the bond, he or she will receive a Form 1099-INT reporting the accumulated interest. However, since that interest is taxable to you, the co-owner should give you a nominee Form 1099-INT, as explained in the rules for nominee distributions on page 73 in the chart "Who Reports Interest Income."
2. You paid for only part of the bond: Either of you may redeem it. You are taxed on that part of the interest which is in proportion to your share of the purchase price. This is so even though you do not receive the proceeds.
3. You paid for part of the bond, and then had it reissued in another's name. You pay tax only on the interest accrued while you held the bond. The new co-owner picks up his or her share of the interest accruing afterwards.
4. You and another person were named co-owners on a bond bought as a gift by a third party. You are taxed on 50% of the interest income; your co-owner is taxed on the remaining half.

Changing the form of registration. Changing the form of registration of an E or EE bond may result in tax. Assume you use your own funds to purchase a bond issued in your name, payable on your death to your son. Later, at your request, a new bond is issued in your son's name only. The increased value of the original bond up to the date it was redeemed and reissued in your son's name is taxed to you as interest income.

The Examples below show changes in registration that do not result in an immediate tax.

EXAMPLES

1. Jones buys an E bond and has it registered in his name and in the name of his son as co-owner. Jones has the bonds reissued solely in his own name; he is not required to report the accumulated interest at that time.
2. You and your spouse each contributed an equal amount toward the purchase of a $1,000 E bond, which was issued to you as co-owners. You later have the bond reissued as two $500 bonds, one in your name and one in your spouse's name. Neither of you has to report the interest earned to the date of reissue. But if you bought the $1,000 bond entirely with your own funds, you report half the interest earned to the date of reissue.
3. You add another person's name as co-owner to facilitate a transfer of the bond on death. The change in registration does not result in a tax.

Transfer to a spouse. Interest on U.S. Savings Bonds transferred to a spouse in a divorce or settlement may result in tax to the transferor; *see 6.6.*

Transfer to a trust. If you transfer U.S. Savings Bonds to a trust giving up all rights of ownership, you are taxed on the accumulated interest to date of transfer. If, however, you are considered to be the owner of the trust and the interest earned before and after the transfer is taxable to you, you may continue to defer reporting the interest.

Transfer to a charity. Tax on the accumulated E or EE bond interest is not avoided by having the bonds reissued to a philanthropy. Further, tax may not be deferred by first converting E bonds to HH bonds and then reissuing the HH bonds in the philanthropy's name. The IRS held that by having the bonds reissued in the philanthropy's name, the owner realized taxable income on the accumulated bond interest.

Transfer of an E or EE bond at death. If an owner does not report E or EE bond interest annually and dies before redeeming the bond, the income tax liability on the interest accumulated during the deceased's lifetime becomes the liability of the person who acquires the bond, unless an election is made to report the accrued interest in the decedent's final income tax return; *see 1.12*. If the election is not made on the decedent's final return, the new owner may choose to report the accumulated interest annually, or defer reporting it until the bond is redeemed or reaches final maturity, whichever is earlier. If the election is made on the decedent's final return, the new owner is taxable only on interest earned after the date of death.

Filing Tip

Deduction for Estate Tax Paid on Interest

Where an estate tax has been paid on bond interest accrued during the owner's lifetime, the new bondholder may claim the estate tax as a miscellaneous itemized deduction in the year that he or she pays tax on the accumulated interest. The deduction is not subject to the 2% adjusted gross income floor *(19.1)*.

Minimum Interest for Loans and Seller-Financed Debt

4.30 Minimum Interest Rules

The law requires a minimum rate of interest to be charged on loan transactions unless a specific exception covers the transaction. Where minimum interest is not charged, the law imputes interest as if the parties agreed to the charge.

The rules are complicated and have been subject to several revisions. There are different minimum interest rates and reporting rules depending on the nature of the transaction. The following discussion provides the important details for understanding the rules. For specific cases and computations, we suggest that you consult IRS regulations for details not covered in this book.

There are two broad classes of transactions:

Loans. These are generally covered by Internal Revenue Code Section 7872. Below-market or low-rate interest loans are discussed at *4.31*.

Seller-financed sales of property. These are covered by either Internal Revenue Code Section 1274 or Section 483. Seller-financed sales are discussed at *4.32*. If parties fail to charge the minimum required interest rate, the same minimum rate is imputed by law.

4.31 Interest-Free or Below-Market-Interest Loans

For many years, the IRS tried to tax interest-free or below-market interest loans. However, court decisions supported taxpayers who argued that such loans did not result in taxable income or gifts. To reverse these decisions, the IRS convinced Congress to pass a law imposing tax on interest-free or low-interest loans made by individuals and businesses. You may not make interest-free or low-interest loans to a relative who uses the loan for personal or investment purposes without adverse income tax consequences, unless the exception discussed in this section for $10,000 or $100,000 loans applies.

How the imputed interest rules work. If interest at least equal to the applicable federal rate set by the IRS is not charged, the law generally treats a below-market interest loan as two transactions:

1. The law assumes that the lender has transferred to the borrower an amount equal to the "foregone" interest element of the loan. In the case of a loan between individuals, such as a parent and child, the lender is subject to gift tax on this element; in the case of a stockholder borrowing from a company, the element is a taxable dividend; in the case of a loan made to an employee, it is taxable pay.
   Note: For *gift tax* purposes *(33.1)*, a term loan is treated as if the lender gave the borrower the excess of the amount of the loan over the present value of payments due during the loan term. Demand loans are treated as if the lender gave the borrower annually the amount of the foregone interest.

2. The law assumes that imputed interest equal to the applicable federal rate is paid by the borrower to the lender. The borrower may be able to claim a deduction for the interest if the funds are used to buy investment property; *see 15.10*.

In applying the imputed interest rules, all loans to or from a husband are combined with all loans to or from his wife; they are treated as one person.

Caution

Get Professional Advice To Draft Loan Agreement

Given the complexity of the imputed interest rules and exceptions, you and your tax advisor should carefully review regulations to the Internal Revenue Code Section 7872 when drafting a loan agreement.

Charging the applicable federal rate avoids the imputed interest rules. Gift loans qualifying for the $10,000 and $100,000 exceptions are not subject to imputed interest rules. For other loans, the rules imputing income to you as the lender may be avoided by charging interest at least equal to the applicable federal rate. Applicable federal rates are set by the IRS monthly and published in the Internal Revenue Bulletin; you can also get the rates from your local IRS office. For a term loan, the applicable rate is the one in effect as of the day on which the loan is made, computed semiannually. The short-term rate applies to loans of three years or less; the mid-term rate to loans over three and up to nine years; the long-term rate applies to loans over nine years. For a demand loan, the applicable federal rate is the short-term rate in effect at the start of each semi-annual period (January and July).

Different computations for different types of loans. There are two general classes of loans: (1) Gift loans, whether term or demand, and nongift demand loans, and (2) nongift term loans.

The distinction is important for figuring and reporting imputed interest. For example, in the case of nongift term loans, the imputed interest element is treated as original issue discount; *see 4.19.*

Gift loans and nongift loans payable on demand. As a lender, you are taxable on the "foregone interest," that is, the interest that you would have received had you charged interest at the applicable federal rate over any interest actually charged. The borrower may be able to claim an interest deduction if the funds are used to buy investment property; *see 15.10.*

Nongift term loans. A term loan is any loan not payable on demand. As a lender of a nongift term loan, you are taxable on any excess of the loan principal over the present value of all payments due under the loan. The excess is treated as original issue (OID) which you report annually as interest income; *see 4.19.*

Gift loans may be exempt from imputed interest rules

In certain cases, gift loans of up to $10,000 may avoid the imputed interest rules. Under another exception, for gift loans of up to $100,000 imputed interest may be completely avoided or limited, depending on the borrower's net investment income.

With gift loans between individuals, interest computed during the borrower's taxable year is treated for both the lender and the borrower as earned on the last day of the borrower's taxable year. Treasury regulations to Section 7872 provide rules for figuring "foregone" interest. Where a demand loan is in effect for the entire calendar year, a "blended annual rate" issued by the IRS to simplify reporting may be used to compute the imputed interest. The blended annual rate is announced by the IRS each July. For 1999, the blended rate is 4.94%. The blended rate is not available if the loan was not outstanding for the entire year or if the loan balance fluctuated; computations provided by Treasury regulations must be used.

The $10,000 gift loan exception. In the case of a gift loan to an individual, no interest is imputed to any day on which the aggregate outstanding amount of all loans between the parties is not over $10,000, provided the loan is not attributed to the purchase or carrying of income-producing assets.

The $100,000 gift loan exception. An exception in the law may allow you to give another person an interest-free or low-interest loan of up to $100,000 without having interest income imputed to you; *see* the Planning Reminder on this page.

EXAMPLES

1. At the beginning of 1999, you make a $45,000 interest-free loan to your son, payable on demand, which he uses for a down payment on a home. This is the only outstanding loan between you and your son. In 1999, your son's net investment income is $650. Since the loan does not exceed $100,000, and your son's net investment income does not exceed $1,000, the imputed interest rules do not apply; you do not have to report the "foregone interest" as interest income.

   For gift tax purposes, the foregone interest is a taxable gift. Using the IRS blended annual rate for 1999 of 4.94%, the taxable gift would be the foregone interest of $2,223 ($45,000 × 4.94%), but *see 33.1* for the annual gift tax exclusion of $10,000 per donee and other gift tax reporting details.

Planning Reminder

Gift Loans up to $100,000

If you give a child or other relative an interest-free loan to buy a home or start a business, the imputed interest rules will not apply provided (1) the total outstanding loan balance owed to you by the borrower at all times during the year does not exceed $100,000, and (2) the borrower's net investment income (15.10) is $1,000 or less.

If the borrower's net investment income for the year exceeds $1,000, the imputed interest rules apply, but the imputed interest is limited to his or her net investment income. If on any day during the year the outstanding loan balance owed to you by the borrower exceeds $100,000, interest will be imputed for that day under the regular rules. If a principal purpose of a loan is the avoidance of federal taxes, imputed interest is not limited to the borrower's net investment income.

2. Same facts as in Example 1 above except that your son's net investment income is $1,500. Since net investment income exceeds $1,000, the imputed interest income rules apply, but the imputed interest is limited to the $1,500 of net investment income. Thus, although the foregone interest using the blended annual rate is $2,700, you report only $1,500 of imputed interest income.

Exceptions for compensation-related loans. A $10,000 exception applies for compensation-related and corporate-shareholder loans, provided the principal purpose of the loan is not tax avoidance. Certain low-interest loans given to employees by employers to buy a new residence in a new job location are exempt from the imputed interest requirements.

Loans to continuing care facilities. Senior citizens moving into a community with a continuing care facility are required to pay a fee to the facility. The fee may be treated as a "loan" subject to the imputed interest rules to the extent the fee is refundable and it exceeds specified limits. These rules are discussed in Chapter 34.

Reporting imputed interest. Imputed interest is generally treated as transferred by the lender to the borrower and retransferred by the borrower to the lender on December 31 in the calendar year of imputation and is reported under the regular accounting method of the borrower and lender.

EXAMPLE

On January 1, 1999, Jones Company makes a $200,000 interest-free demand loan to Frank, an executive. The loan remains outstanding for the entire 1999 calendar year. Jones Company has a taxable year ending September 30. Frank is a calendar year taxpayer. For 1999, the imputed compensation payment and the imputed interest payment are treated as made on December 31, 1999.

4.32 Minimum Interest on Seller-Financed Sales

The law requires minimum interest charges for seller-financed sales. If the minimum rate is not charged, the IRS imputes interest at the minimum applicable rate requiring both buyer and seller to treat part of the purchase price as interest even though it is not called interest in the sales contract. Generally, interest at the applicable federal rate (AFR) must be charged; see the chart at the end of this section for minimum required rates. For example, investment property is sold on the installment basis for $100,000 and the parties fail to charge adequate interest. Assume the IRS imputes interest of $5,000. For tax purposes, $95,000 is allocated to the sale of the property and the principal amount of the debt; the balance is imputed interest of $5,000, taxable to the seller and deductible by the buyer if allowed under the rules of Chapter 15.

Two statute classes. The minimum or imputed interest rules are covered by two Internal Revenue Code statutes: Sections 1274 and 483. Under both, the same minimum interest rates apply but the timing of interest reporting is different, as discussed below.

Section 483 applies to any payment due more than six months after the date of sale under a contract which calls for some or all payments more than one year after the date of sale. If the sales price cannot exceed $3,000, Section 483 does not apply. Transactions within Section 483 are sales or exchanges of: (1) principal residences; (2) any property if total payments, including interest and any other consideration to be received by the seller, cannot exceed $250,000; (3) farms if the total price is $1 million or less; and (4) sales of land between family members to the extent the aggregate sales price of all sales between the same parties in the same year is $500,000 or less.

If the selling price exceeds the respective $250,000, $1 million, or $500,000 amount listed in (2) through (4) above, the sale is subject to Section 1274 reporting rules provided some or all payments are due more than six months after the date of sale. Section 1274 also applies to all other transactions where neither the debt instrument nor the property being sold is publicly traded as long as some payments are deferred more than six months.

Timing of interest reporting. One important practical difference between the two statutes covering minimum interest involves the timing of the reporting and deducting of interest.

Under Section 483, a seller and lender use their regular reporting method for imputed interest. For a cash-basis seller, interest is taxed when received; a cash-basis buyer deducts interest when paid if a deduction is allowable. However, if too much interest is allocated to a payment period, the

Filing Instruction

Tax Return Statement Requirements.

A lender reporting imputed interest income or a borrower claiming an interest deduction must attach statements to their income tax returns reporting the interest, how it was calculated, and the names of the parties and their tax identification numbers.

Caution

Buyer's Personal-Use Property

If adequate interest is not charged on an installment sale of personal-use property, such as a residence to be used by the buyer, imputed interest rules do not apply to the buyer. Thus, the buyer may not deduct the imputed interest. The buyer's deduction is limited to the payment of interest stated in the contract if a deduction is allowed under the home mortgage interest rules in Chapter 15.

excess interest is treated as prepaid interest, and the deduction is postponed to the year or years interest is earned. Section 483 also describes imputed interest as unstated interest.

Under Section 1274, the interest element is generally reported by both buyer and seller according to the OID accrual rules, even if they otherwise report on the cash basis. Where the seller financing is below an annual threshold ($2,775,400 for 1999 sales), the parties can elect the cash method to report the interest regardless of the OID and accrual rules if: (1) the seller-lender is on a cash-basis method and is not a dealer of the property sold; and (2) the seller and buyer jointly elect to use the cash method. The cash-basis election binds any cash-basis successor of the buyer or seller. If the lender transfers his interest to an accrual-basis taxpayer, the election no longer applies; interest is thereafter taxed under the accrual-method rules. The OID rules also do not apply to a cash-basis buyer of personal-use property; here, the cash-basis debtor deducts only payments of interest required by the contract, assuming a deduction is allowed under the home mortgage rules discussed in Chapter 15.

Figuring Applicable Federal Rate (AFR). There is no imputed interest if the sales contract provides for interest that is at least equal to the AFR. *See* the chart on the next page for determining the AFR.

Assumptions of loans. The imputed interest rules of Sections 1274 and 483 do not generally apply to debt instruments assumed as part of a sale or exchange, or if the property is taken subject to the debt, provided that neither the terms of the debt instrument nor the nature of the transactions are changed.

Important: In planning deferred or installment sales, review Treasury regulations to the Internal Revenue Code Sections 483 and 1274 for further examples and details.

Minimum Interest Rate for Seller Financing

Type—	Description—
Applicable federal rates	The IRS determines the AFR rates which are published at the beginning of each month in the Internal Revenue Bulletin. There are three AFR rates depending on the length of the contract: *Short-term AFR*—A term of three years or less. *Mid-term AFR*—A term of over three years but not over nine years. *Long-term AFR*—A term of over nine years. The parties may choose the lowest AFR for the three-month period ending with the month in which a binding written sales contract is entered into. Thus, if the AFR for either of the prior two months is lower than the AFR for the month of contract, the lowest of the three AFRs applies. If insufficient interest is charged, the total unstated interest is allocated to payments under an OID computation.
9% safe harbor rate	If seller financing in 1999 is $3,885,500 or less, the minimum required interest is the lower of 9% compounded semiannually and the applicable federal rate (AFR). The amount of seller financing is the stated principal amount under the contract. If the seller-financed amount exceeds $3,885,500, the minimum interest rate is 100% of the AFR. For sales after 1998, the threshold for the 9% safe harbor will be indexed for inflation. The 9% safe harbor provides a benefit only if it is less than the AFR, but in recent years the AFR has been lower than 9%. Thus, until prevailing interest rates increase, charging interest at the AFR will allow a lower rate than the 9% safe harbor. IRS regulations allow the parties to use an interest rate lower than the AFR if it is shown that the borrower could obtain a loan on an arm's-length basis at lower interest.
Seller-financed sale-leaseback transactions	Interest equal to 110% of AFR must be charged.
Sales of land between family members	To the extent that the sales price does not exceed $500,000 during a calendar year, the minimum interest rate is 6%, compounded semiannually. To prevent multiple sales from being used to avoid the $500,000 limit, the $500,000 ceiling applies to all land sales between family members during the same year. To the extent that the $500,000 sales price limit is exceeded, the general 9% or 100% of AFR rules apply.

Reporting Property Sales

Long-term capital gains are generally taxed at lower rates than those imposed on ordinary income. You receive the benefit of these low rates by preparing Schedule D, on which you report property sales and compute tax on long-term capital gains.

If in 1999 you sold property and will be receiving payments in a later year, you may report the sale as an installment sale on Form 6252 and spread the tax on your gain over the installment period; *see 5.21*.

Sales of business assets are reported on Form 4797. As discussed in *44.8*, most assets used in a business are considered Section 1231 assets, and capital gain or ordinary loss treatment may apply depending upon the result of a netting computation made on Form 4797 for all such assets sold during the year.

Special types of sale situations are detailed in other chapters.

See Chapter 29 for the exclusion of gain on the sale of a principal residence.

See Chapter 32 for figuring gain or loss on the sale of mutual-fund shares.

See Chapter 6 for tax-free exchanges of property.

See Chapter 30 for sales of stock dividends, stock rights, wash sales, and short sales.

Figuring Capital Gains and Losses

5.1   Tax Pattern of Property Sales

1. Property is classified according to its nature and your purpose for holding it; *see 5.2*, the table on the next page, and holding period rules at *5.3, 5.9*, and *5.11*.

2. Different tax rates are applied to gains depending on the classification of the property and, in the case of capital assets, according to the period you held the property before sale. Short-term capital gains are subject to regular income tax rates. Rates lower than the regular rates apply only to long-term capital gains. Capital gain rates are applied in Part IV, page 2 of Schedule D, the tax computation section. A capital gain rate is applied if it is less than the top regular income tax rate applied to your taxable income. If your top tax bracket is 15%, the capital gains tax rate of 10% is applied to gains realized from the sale of long-term capital assets held for more than a year. If your top regular income tax bracket is 28% or more, the 20% tax rate applies to gains realized on sales of property held for more than a year and a 25% tax rate applies to certain sales of depreciable property; *see 5.3*. If your top bracket exceeds 15%, a 28% rate will apply to sales of collectibles; *see 5.3*.

3. Loss deductions are determined by the classification of the property sold; *see* the table on the next page. *See also 5.4* for capital loss deductions.

5.2   How Property Sales Are Classified and Taxed

The tax treatment of gains and losses is not the same for all types of property sales. Tax reporting generally depends on your purpose in holding the property, as shown in the table on the next page.

When capital gain or loss treatment does not apply. Certain sales do not qualify for capital gain or loss treatment. Business inventory and property held for sale to customers are not capital assets. Depreciable business and rental property are not capital assets, but you may still realize capital gain after following a netting computation for Section 1231 assets discussed at *44.8*.

Although assets held for *personal* use, such as a car or home, are technically capital assets, you may not deduct a capital loss on their sale.

Certain other assets held for investment or personal use are excluded by law from the capital asset category. These include copyrights, literary or musical compositions, letters, memoranda, or similar property that: (1) you created by your personal efforts or (2) you acquired as a gift from the person who created the property or for whom the property was prepared or produced. Also excluded are letters, memoranda, or similar property prepared or produced for you by someone else. Finally, U.S. government publications obtained from the government for free or for less than the normal sales price do not qualify as capital assets.

Stock is generally treated as a capital asset, but losses on *Section 1244 stock* of qualifying small businesses may be claimed as ordinary losses on Form 4797, rather than on Schedule D as capital losses subject to the $3,000 annual deduction limit ($1,500 if married filing separately) for losses in excess of capital gains. The ordinary loss rules for Section 1244 stock are discussed in Chapter 30.

Small business stock deferral or exclusion. As discussed in *5.7*, taxable gains from the sale of publicly traded securities may be postponed if you roll over the proceeds to stock or a partnership interest in an SSBIC (specialized small business investment company). Furthermore, gains from the sale of qualifying small business stock may be deferred by making a tax-free rollover to other small business stock.

Gains on the sale of qualifying small business stock issued after August 10, 1993, and held for more than five years qualify for a 50% exclusion; *see 5.7*.

Like-kind exchanges of business or investment property. Exchanges of *like-kind* business or investment property are subject to special rules that allow gain to be deferred, generally until you sell the property received in the exchange; *see 6.1*. When property received in a tax-free exchange is held until death, the unrecognized gain escapes income tax forever because the basis of property in the hands of an heir is generally the fair market value of the property at the date of death; *see 5.17*. A loss on a like-kind exchange is not deductible.

Filing Instruction

Organize Sales by Holding Period
The way you report 1999 sales depends on the holding periods of the sold property, as explained in *5.3*.

Caution

Loss on Personal-Use Assets
You may not deduct a capital loss on the sale of property held for personal use, such as a car or vacation home. The loss is not deductible.

Capital or Ordinary Gains and Losses From Sales and Exchanges of Property

If you sell—	Your gain is—	Your loss is—	Reported on—
Stocks, mutual-fund shares, bonds, land, art objects, gems, stamps, and coins held for investment are capital assets.	*Capital gain.* Holding period determines short-term or long-term gain treatment; *see 5.3.*	*Capital loss.* Capital losses are deductible from capital gains with only $3,000 of any excess deductible from ordinary income, $1,500 if married filing separately; *see 5.4.*	Schedule D. However, if the only amounts you have to report on Schedule D are mutual-fund capital gain distributions, then you do not have to file a Schedule D; *see 32.5.*
Business inventory held for sale to customers. Also, accounts or notes receivable acquired in the ordinary course of business or from the sale of inventory or property held for sale to customers, or acquired for services as an employee.	*Ordinary income.* Such property is excluded by law from the definition of capital assets.	*Ordinary loss.* Ordinary loss is not subject to the $3,000 deduction limit imposed on capital losses. However, passive loss restrictions, discussed in Chapter 10, may defer the time when certain ordinary losses are deductible.	Schedule C if self-employed; Schedule F if a farmer; Form 1065 for a business operated as a partnership; Form 1120 or 1120-S for an incorporated business.
Depreciable residential rental property or trucks, autos, computers, machinery, fixtures, or equipment used in your business.	*Capital gain or ordinary income.* Section 1231 as explained in *44.8* determines whether gain is taxable as ordinary income or capital gain. Where an asset such as an auto or residence is used partly for personal purposes and partly for business or rental purposes, the asset is treated as two separate assets for purposes of figuring gain or loss; *see 44.9.*	*Ordinary loss if there is a net Section 1231 loss; see 44.8.* However, if you are considered to be an investor in a passive activity, see *10.12* and *10.13*.	Form 4797
Personal residence, car, jewelry, furniture, art objects, and coin or stamp collection held for personal use.	*Capital gain.* See *5.3* for the holding period rules that determine short-term or long-term gain treatment. Where an asset such as an auto or residence is used partly for personal purposes and partly for business or rental purposes, the asset is treated as two separate assets for purposes of figuring gain or loss; *see 44.9.* Tax on all or part of a profit from a sale of a principal residence may be avoided; *see* Chapter 29.	*Not deductible.* Losses on assets held for personal use are not deductible although profits are taxable.	Schedule D

5.3 Capital Gains Rates and Holding Periods

Organize your sales of capital gain assets according to the following time periods and enter the sales in Schedule D in the lines designated for such sales. By following the order of Schedule D, you will properly net losses and gains and get the benefits of lower capital gain rates if you realize net long-term capital gain. *See* the sample Schedule D at *5.8.*

Held for a year or less. Gains and losses realized on sales of capital assets held for a year or less are short term and reported in Part I of Schedule D. Short-term gains and losses are netted in this part; a net gain is subject to regular tax rates; a net loss, if you have long-term gains in Part II, will be applied against such gains.

Held for more than a year. Gains and losses of sales of capital assets held for more than a year are long term and reported in Part II of Schedule D. Gains on sales of capital assets held for more than a year are generally subject to a 20% tax rate (10% if you are in the 15% regular tax bracket).

Gain from sales of collectibles. Long-term gains on the sale of collectibles such as art, antiques, stamps, and coins are taxable at 28% if your top regular tax bracket exceeds 15%. Such gains are listed in column (g) of Part II of Schedule D.

Unrecaptured Section 1250 gain. Gain attributable to depreciation that is not recaptured as ordinary income on Form 4797 *(see 44.2)* is subject to a 25% tax rate if your top regular tax bracket exceeds 15%. Use the worksheet in the Schedule D instructions to figure the unrecaptured Section 1250 gain to be entered on Line 25, Part IV of Schedule D.

Capital gain distributions from mutual funds. Your fund will report long-term capital gain distributions on Form 1099-DIV. *See* Chapter 32 for details.

Capital gain from Schedule K-1. Net capital gain or loss from a pass-through entity such as a partnership, S corporation, estate, or trust is reported to you on a Schedule K-1. Report net short-term gain or loss in Part I of Schedule D and net long-term gain or loss in Part II of Schedule D.

Gain from sale of small business stock subject 50% gain exclusion. If you claim the 50% exclusion on the sale of small business stock *(see 5.7)*, the remaining long-term gain is not eligible for the 10% or 20% rate but is subject to the 28% rate if your top regular tax bracket exceeds 15%. Such gain is identified in column (g) of Part II of Schedule D.

Schedule D tax computation section. In Part IV of Schedule D, you figure your tax liability for 1999, taking into account the applicable 10%, 20%, 25%, or 28% capital gain rates.

If you elect to treat part or all of your net capital gain as investment income in order to increase your itemized deduction for investment interest on Form 4952 *(see 15.10)*, the elected amount is not eligible for preferential capital gain rates. When making the tax computation in Part IV of Schedule D, the net capital gain that you include on Form 4952 must be subtracted from the net capital gain figured in Parts II and III of Schedule D; the subtraction is made on Line 22 of Schedule D.

5.4 Capital Losses and Carryovers

Capital losses are fully deductible against capital gains on Schedule D, and if losses exceed gains, you may deduct the excess from up to $3,000 of other income on Form 1040. Net losses over $3,000 are carried over to future years. The $3,000 limit is reduced to $1,500 for married persons filing separately. In preparing your 1999 Schedule D, remember to include any capital loss carryovers from your 1998 return. Short-term carryover losses are entered on Line 6 of Part I and long-term carryover losses are entered on Line 14, Part II.

Death of taxpayer cuts off carryover. If an individual dies and on his or her final income tax return net capital losses, including prior year carryovers, exceed the $3,000 or $1,500 limit, the excess may not be deducted by the individual's estate. If the deceased individual was married, his or her unused individual losses may not be carried over by the surviving spouse; *see 5.5*.

Carryover if you have "negative" taxable income. A special computation may increase your carryover deduction where you have "negative" taxable income. If without considering personal exemptions you have a "negative taxable income," a net capital loss may not provide a tax benefit because other deductions have reduced taxable income to zero. In this case, you may be allowed a capital loss carryover for all or part of your net capital loss.

To determine the amount of the carryover, follow the steps of the worksheet in the Schedule D instructions. You first will figure how much of your net loss is treated as "used up" in the current year. The balance of the loss, if any, is carried over to the next year.

5.5 Capital Losses of Married Couples

On a joint return, the capital asset transactions of both spouses are combined and reported on one Schedule D. A carryover loss of one spouse may offset capital gains of the other spouse on a joint return. Where you and your spouse separately incur net capital losses, $3,000 is the maximum capital loss deduction that may be claimed for the combined losses on your joint return. This limi-

Filing Tip

Holding Periods

The time you own an asset determines short-term or long-term treatment. The short-term holding period is a year or less, the long-term period more than one year; *see 5.9–5.12*.

Filing Tip

Keep Records of Loss Carryovers

Prior year capital losses that are not deductible may be claimed this year or in later years when you have capital gains to offset.

tation may not be avoided by filing separate returns. If you file separately, the deduction limit for each return is $1,500. Neither of you may deduct any of the other's losses on a separate return.

EXAMPLE

In 1999, you individually incurred net long-term capital losses of $5,000 and your spouse incurred net long-term losses of $4,000. If you file separate returns, the maximum amount deductible from ordinary income on each return is $1,500. The balance must be carried forward to 2000.

If you had net losses below the $1,500 limit, you could not claim any part of your spouse's losses on your separate return.

Death of a spouse. The IRS holds that if a capital loss is incurred by a spouse on his or her own property and that spouse dies, the surviving spouse may not claim any unused loss carryover on a separate return.

EXAMPLE

In 1996, Alex Smith realized a substantial net long-term capital loss on separately owned property, which was reported on a 1996 joint return filed with his wife, Anne. Part of the excess loss was carried over to the couple's 1997 joint return, and in 1998, before the carryover loss was used up, Alex died. Anne could claim the unused carryover, up to the $3,000 limit, on a joint return filed for 1998, the year of Alex's death. However, any remaining loss carryover to 1999 or later years is lost. Although the loss was originally reported on a joint return, Anne may claim only her allocable share of the loss on her individual returns for years after 1998. However, since the loss property was owned solely by Alex, no part of the loss is allocable to Anne.

 Filing Tip

Carryovers From Joint or Separate Returns

If you or your spouse has a capital loss carryover from a year in which separate returns were filed, and you are now filing a joint return, the carryovers from the separate returns may be combined on the joint return. If you previously filed jointly and are now filing separately, any loss carryover from the joint return may be claimed only on the separate return of the spouse who originally incurred the loss; *see 5.5.*

5.6 Losses May Be Disallowed on Sales to Related Persons

A loss on a sale to certain related taxpayers may not be deductible, even though you make the sale at an arm's-length price, the sale is involuntary (for example, a member of your family forecloses a mortgage on your property), or you sell through a public stock exchange and related persons buy the equivalent property; *see* Examples 1 and 2 below.

Related parties. Losses are not allowed on sales between you and your brothers or sisters (whether by the whole or half blood), parents, grandparents, children, or grandchildren. Furthermore, no loss may be claimed on a sale to your spouse; the tax-free exchange rules discussed at 6.6 apply.

A loss is disallowed where the sale is made to your sister-in-law, as nominee of your brother. This sale is deemed to be between you and your brother. But you may deduct the loss on sales to your spouse's relative (for example, your brother-in-law or spouse's step-parent) even if you and your spouse file a joint return.

The Tax Court has allowed a loss on a direct sale to a son-in-law. In a private ruling, the IRS allowed a loss on a sale of a business to a son-in-law where it was shown that his wife (the seller's daughter) did not own an interest in the company. Losses have been disallowed upon withdrawal from a joint venture and from a partnership conducted by members of a family. Family members have argued that losses should be allowed where the sales were motivated by family hostility. The Tax Court ruled that family hostility may not be considered; losses between proscribed family members are disallowed in all cases.

Losses are barred on sales between an individual and a controlled partnership or controlled corporation (where that individual owns more than 50% in value of the outstanding stock or capital interests). In calculating the stock owned, not only must the stock held in your own name be taken into account, but also that owned by your family. You also add (1) the proportionate share of any stock held by a corporation, estate, trust, or partnership in which you have an interest as a shareholder, beneficiary, or partner; and (2) any other stock owned individually by your partner.

Losses may also be disallowed in sales between controlled companies, a trust and its creator, a trust and a beneficiary, a partnership and a corporation controlled by the same person (more than 50% ownership), or a tax-exempt organization and its founder. An estate and a beneficiary of that estate are also treated as related parties, except where a sale is in satisfaction of a pecuniary bequest.

Check with your tax counselor whenever you plan to sell property at a loss to a buyer who may fit one of these descriptions.

Related buyer's resale at profit. Sometimes, the disallowed loss may be saved. When you sell to a related party who resells the property at a profit, he or she gets the benefit of your disallowed loss. Your purchaser's gain up to the amount of your disallowed loss is not taxed; *see* Example 4 below.

EXAMPLES

1. You sell 100 shares of A Co. stock to your brother for $1,000. They cost you $5,000. You may not deduct your $4,000 loss.
2. The stock investments of a mother and son were managed by the same investment counselor. But neither the son nor mother had any right or control over the other's securities. The counselor followed separate and independent policies for each. Without the son's or his mother's prior approval, the counselor carried out the following transactions: (1) on the same day, he sold at a loss the son's stock in four companies and bought the same stock for the mother's account; and (2) he sold at a loss the son's stock in a copper company, and 28 days later bought the same stock for his mother. The losses of the first sale were disallowed, but not the losses of the copper stock sale because of the time break of 28 days. However, the court did not say how much of a minimum time break is needed to remove a sale-purchase transaction from the rule disallowing losses between related parties.
3. You own 30% of the stock of a company. A trust in which you have a one-half beneficial interest owns 30%. Your partner owns 10% of the stock of the same company. You are deemed the owner of 55% of the stock of that company (30%, plus one-half of 30%, plus 10%) and may not deduct a loss on the sale of property to that company since your deemed ownership exceeds 50%.
4. Smith bought securities in 1990 that cost $10,000. In 1993, he sold them to his sister for $8,000. The $2,000 loss was not deductible by Smith. His sister's basis for the securities is $8,000. In 1999, she sells them for $9,000. The $1,000 gain is not taxed because it is washed out by part of the brother's disallowed loss. If she sold the securities for $11,000, then only $1,000 of the $3,000 gain would be taxed.

5.7 Deferring or Excluding Gain on Small Business Stock Investment

To encourage investments in certain "small" businesses, the tax law provides special tax benefits.

Rollover from small business stock to small business stock. Gain on the sale of qualifying small business stock held for more than six months may be rolled over tax free to other small business stock. The rollover must be made within 60 days of the sale. To qualify as a small business, the gross assets of the corporation must be no more than $50 million when the stock is issued. An active business requirement must also be met.   If the reinvestment in a qualifying small business is for less than the sale proceeds, your gain is taxed to the extent of the difference. Your basis in the small business stock acquired during the 60-day period is reduced by the amount of the deferred gain.

To elect deferral, follow the the instructions to Schedule D.

Exclusion of 50% of gain on small business stock. You only have to pay tax on 50% of a gain from the sale of qualified small business stock issued after August 10, 1993, *provided* you hold the stock for more than five years before the sale. If you qualify for the exclusion, the 50% of the gain that is taxable is subject to the 28% capital gain rate (unless your top regular tax bracket is 15%) on Schedule D, not the 20% or 10% rate; *see 5.3* and Schedule D instructions.

The amount of gain from any one issuer that is eligible for the 50% exclusion is limited to the greater of (1) 10 times your basis in the qualified stock that you disposed of during the year, or (2) $10 million ($5million if married filing separately) minus any gain on stock from the same issuer that you excluded in prior years.

Rollover from publicly traded securities to SSBIC. You may be able to defer taxable gain on the sale of publicly traded securities provided the sale proceeds are rolled over within 60 days into common stock or a partnership interest in a "specialized small business investment company," or SSBIC. The entire gain is deferrable if the cost of your SSBIC stock or partnership interest is at least equal to the sale proceeds. If the SSBIC investment is less than the sale proceeds, your gain is taxed to the extent of the difference.

Planning Reminder

50% Exclusion

You generally may claim a 50% exclusion on a profitable sale of qualifying small business stock issued after August 10, 1993, provided you held the stock for more than five years before the sale. The balance of the gain is subject to the 28% capital gain rate unless your top regular tax bracket is 15%; *see 5.3.* A qualifying small business is one eligible for rollover treatment; 42% of the excluded gain must be added back to income as a preference item for purposes of the alternative minimum tax (Chapter 23).

To elect deferral, you must report the sale on Schedule D and attach an explanation of your SSBIC investment; follow the Schedule D instructions. The deferred gain reduces the basis of your SSBIC stock or partnership interest.

An SSBIC is a small business (partnership or corporation) licensed by the Small Business Administration to invest in small businesses which are owned by socially or economically disadvantaged individuals.

Limit on deferrable amount. The amount of gain you may annually elect to roll over to an SSBIC is limited to $50,000, or $25,000 if you are married filing separately. There is a lifetime limit of $500,000, or $250,000 if married filing separately.

5.8   Sample Entries of Capital Asset Sales

You report many different types of transactions on Schedule D: sales of securities, mutual-fund shares, worthless personal loans, sales of stock rights and warrants, sales of land held for investment, and in some cases sales of personal residences.

Different types of Schedule D entries are illustrated in the sample Schedule beginning on page 98. The entries correspond to the transactions below. For each transaction, assume that broker's commissions and state and local transfer taxes, if any, are added to the cost of the stock.

As shown on the sample Schedule D, the result of these transactions is a net short-term capital loss of $40 and a net long-term capital gain of $3,100. Combining them gives a net capital gain of $3,060 (see Line 17). In showing how tax liability is computed in Part IV of Schedule D, we have assumed that the taxpayer is married filing jointly and has taxable income (Line 39 of Form 1040) of $75,000. Under this set of facts, the 20% rate applies to the $3,060 net capital gain, and the total tax liability of $15,155 that is shown on Line 54 of the sample Schedule D is $256 lower than it would be if the gain were subject to ordinary income rates.

The following transactions are entered on the sample Schedule on page 97:

1. *Sale of stock (short-term gain)*—You bought 200 shares of Buma Rubber stock on July 22, 1999, for $400. On October 7, 1999, you sell the 200 shares for $600.

2. *Sale of stock received as a gift (short-term loss)*—Your father gave you a gift of 100 shares of Ajax Auto stock on March 12, 1999, which he had bought on February 15, 1990, for $4,000. The value of the stock at the time of the gift was $3,000. You sell the stock on March 25, 1999, for $2,500. Since the value of the stock at the time of the gift was less than your father's basis, your basis for loss purposes is the date-of-gift value *(5.17)* and the holding period begins on the day after the date of the gift *(5.12)*.

3. *Worthless personal loan (short-term loss)*—You loaned $500 to your friend, Dan Debtor, on May 1, 1997. He was adjudged bankrupt on March 15, 1999. A worthless personal debt is deducted as a short-term capital loss; *see 5.33.* The IRS requires that you explain the deduction in a statement attached to your return. The statement should show: (1) the nature of the debt; (2) the name of the debtor and his or her relationship, if any, to you; (3) when the debt was due; (4) how you tried to collect it; and (5) how you determined it was worthless.

4. *Sale of mutual-fund shares (short-term gain)*—You bought 160 shares of the XYZ Mutual Fund on February 4, 1999, for $4,000. On August 5, you bought another 240 shares for $6,480. You sell 200 of the shares on September 23, 1999, for $6,000. You decide to use the average basis method (single category) to figure the basis of the sold shares. Your average basis is $26.20 per share, the total cost basis of $10,480 divided by 400 shares. Thus, your basis for the 200 sold shares is $5,240 (200 × $26.20). *See* Chapter 32 for further details on basis of mutual-fund shares.

5. *Sale of stock (long-term gain)*—You bought 100 shares of Acme Steel stock on October 1, 1991, for $5,000. On December 10, 1999, you sell the 100 shares for $6,000.

6. *Sale of stock (long term)*—You bought 200 shares of Zero Computer Co. stock for $2,000 on July 10, 1997. On August 4, 1999, you sell it for $5,000.

7. *Worthless bond*—On August 10, 1981, you bought a $1,000 bond of Rail Co. at par. The bond became completely worthless during 1999; *see 5.32.*

8. *Capital gain distributions*—You received capital gain distributions of $1,050 in 1999 from mutual funds.

9. *Long-term capital loss carryover*—You had a 1998 long-term capital loss carryover of $950. Note that the carryover would be first applied against long-term gains subject to the 28% rate *(see 5.3)*, if there were any.

 Caution

IRS Review of Schedule D
The IRS compares the proceeds that are reported on Schedule D with the selling prices reported on Form 1099-B and Form 1099-S. If you receive an incorrect Form 1099-B or 1099-S, report the proper amount and attach a statement explaining the difference between the amount you entered on Schedule D and the amount shown on the Form 1099.

SCHEDULE D
(Form 1040)

Department of the Treasury
Internal Revenue Service (99)

Capital Gains and Losses

▶ Attach to Form 1040.　▶ See Instructions for Schedule D (Form 1040).

▶ Use Schedule D-1 for more space to list transactions for lines 1 and 8.

OMB No. 1545-0074

1999

Attachment
Sequence No. **12**

Name(s) shown on Form 1040　　　　　　　　　　　　Your social security number

Part I　Short-Term Capital Gains and Losses—Assets Held One Year or Less

(a) Description of property (Example: 100 sh. XYZ Co.)	(b) Date acquired (Mo., day, yr.)	(c) Date sold (Mo., day, yr.)	(d) Sales price (see page D-5)	(e) Cost or other basis (see page D-5)	(f) GAIN or (LOSS) Subtract (e) from (d)	
1 (1) **200 Shares Buma Rubber**	7-22-99	10-7-99	600	400	200	
(2) **100 Shares Ajax Auto**	3-12-99	3-25-99	2,500	3,000	(500)	
(3) **Dan Debtor**	Worthless	loan	Statement Attached	500	(500)	
(4) **200 Shares XYZ Mutual Fund**	"Various"	9-23-99	6,000	5,240	760	

2 Enter your short-term totals, if any, from Schedule D-1, line 2 . . . . | **2** | | |

3 Total short-term sales price amounts. Add column (d) of lines 1 and 2 . . . . . | **3** | 9,100 | |

4 Short-term gain from Form 6252 and short-term gain or (loss) from Forms 4684, 6781, and 8824 . . . . | **4** | |

5 Net short-term gain or (loss) from partnerships, S corporations, estates, and trusts from Schedule(s) K-1 . . . . . | **5** | |

6 Short-term capital loss carryover. Enter the amount, if any, from line 8 of your 1998 Capital Loss Carryover Worksheet | **6** ( ) |

7 Net short-term capital gain or (loss). Combine lines 1 through 6 in column (f) ▶ | **7** | (40) |

Part II　Long-Term Capital Gains and Losses—Assets Held More Than One Year

(a) Description of property (Example: 100 sh. XYZ Co.)	(b) Date acquired (Mo., day, yr.)	(c) Date sold (Mo., day, yr.)	(d) Sales price (see page D-5)	(e) Cost or other basis (see page D-5)	(f) GAIN or (LOSS) Subtract (e) from (d)	(g) 28% RATE GAIN or (LOSS) * (see instr. below)
8 (5) **100 Shares Acme Steel**	10-1-91	12-10-99	6,000	5,000	1,000	
(6) **200 Shares Zero Computer**	7-10-97	8-4-99	5,000	2,000	3,000	
(7) **Bond, Rail Co.**	8-10-81	Worthless	—	1,000	(1,000)	

9 Enter your long-term totals, if any, from Schedule D-1, line 9 . . . . | **9** | | |

10 Total long-term sales price amounts. Add column (d) of lines 8 and 9 . . . . . | **10** | 11,000 | |

11 Gain from Form 4797, Part I; long-term gain from Forms 2439 and 6252; and long-term gain or (loss) from Forms 4684, 6781, and 8824 . . . . | **11** | |

12 Net long-term gain or (loss) from partnerships, S corporations, estates, and trusts from Schedule(s) K-1 . . . . . | **12** | |

(8) **13** Capital gain distributions. See page D-1 . . . . | **13** | 1,050 |

(9) **14** Long-term capital loss carryover. Enter in both columns (f) and (g) the amount, if any, from line 13 of your 1998 Capital Loss Carryover Worksheet . . . . . | **14** (950) | (950) |

15 Combine lines 8 through 14 in column (g) . . . . | **15** | (950) |

16 Net long-term capital gain or (loss). Combine lines 8 through 14 in column (f) ▶
Next: Go to Part III on the back. | **16** | 3,100 | |

*28% Rate Gain or Loss includes all "collectibles gains and losses" (as defined on page D-6) and up to 50% of the eligible gain on qualified small business stock (see page D-4).

For Paperwork Reduction Act Notice, see Form 1040 instructions.　　Cat. No. 11338H　　Schedule D (Form 1040) 1999

Schedule D (Form 1040) 1999   Page **2**

Part III	**Summary of Parts I and II**			

17 Combine lines 7 and 16. If a loss, go to line 18. If a gain, enter the gain on Form 1040, line 13 | **17** | **3,060** |

    Next: Complete Form 1040 through line 39. Then, go to **Part IV** to figure your tax if:
        • Both lines 16 and 17 are gains, **and**
        • Form 1040, line 39, is more than zero.

18 If line 17 is a loss, enter here and as a (loss) on Form 1040, line 13, the **smaller** of these losses:
    • The loss on line 17, **or**
    • ($3,000) or, if married filing separately, ($1,500) . . . . | **18** (|) |

    Next: Skip **Part IV** below. Instead, complete Form 1040 through line 37. Then, complete the **Capital Loss Carryover Worksheet** on page D-6 if:
        • The loss on line 17 exceeds the loss on line 18, **or**
        • Form 1040, line 37, is a loss.

Part IV	**Tax Computation Using Maximum Capital Gains Rates**			

#	Description	inner	outer
19	Enter your taxable income from Form 1040, line 39		**19** **75,000**
20	Enter the **smaller** of line 16 or line 17 of Schedule D	**20** **3,060**	
21	If you are filing Form 4952, enter the amount from Form 4952, line 4e	**21** **- O -**	
22	Subtract line 21 from line 20. If zero or less, enter -0-	**22** **3,060**	
23	Combine lines 7 and 15. If zero or less, enter -0-	**23** **- O -**	
24	Enter the **smaller** of line 15 or line 23, but not less than zero . . .	**24** **- O -**	
25	Enter your unrecaptured section 1250 gain, if any, from line 14 of the worksheet on page D-7	**25** **- O -**	
26	Add lines 24 and 25	**26** **- O -**	
27	Subtract line 26 from line 22. If zero or less, enter -0-		**27** **3,060**
28	Subtract line 27 from line 19. If zero or less, enter -0-		**28** **71,940**
29	Enter the **smaller** of:		
	• The amount on line 19, **or**		
	• $25,750 if single; $43,050 if married filing jointly or qualifying widow(er); $21,525 if married filing separately; or $34,550 if head of household		**29** **43,050**
30	Enter the **smaller** of line 28 or line 29	**30** **43,050**	
31	Subtract line 22 from line 19. If zero or less, enter -0-	**31** **71,940**	
32	Enter the **larger** of line 30 or line 31 . . . . ▶	**32** **71,940**	
33	Figure the tax on the amount on line 32. Use the Tax Table or Tax Rate Schedules, whichever applies		**33** **14,543**
	Note: *If line 28 is greater than or equal to line 29, go to line 38.*		
34	Enter the amount from line 29	**34**	
35	Enter the amount from line 28	**35**	
36	Subtract line 35 from line 34. If zero or less, enter -0- . . . . ▶	**36**	
37	Multiply line 36 by 10% (.10)		**37**
	Note: *If line 27 is greater than zero and equal to line 36, go to line 52.*		
38	Enter the **smaller** of line 19 or line 27	**38** **3,060**	
39	Enter the amount from line 36	**39** **- O -**	
40	Subtract line 39 from line 38 . . . . ▶	**40** **3,060**	
41	Multiply line 40 by 20% (.20)		**41** **612**
	Note: *If line 25 is zero or blank, skip lines 42 through 47 and read the Note before line 48.*		
42	Enter the **smaller** of line 22 or line 25	**42**	
43	Add lines 22 and 32	**43**	
44	Enter the amount from line 19	**44**	
45	Subtract line 44 from line 43. If zero or less, enter -0-	**45**	
46	Subtract line 45 from line 42. If zero or less, enter -0- . . . . ▶	**46**	
47	Multiply line 46 by 25% (.25)		**47**
	Note: *If line 24 is zero or blank, go to line 52.*		
48	Enter the amount from line 19	**48**	
49	Add lines 32, 36, 40, and 46	**49**	
50	Subtract line 49 from line 48	**50**	
51	Multiply line 50 by 28% (.28)		**51**
52	Add lines 33, 37, 41, 47, and 51		**52** **15,155**
53	Figure the tax on the amount on line 19. Use the Tax Table or Tax Rate Schedules, whichever applies		**53** **15,411**
54	**Tax on all taxable income (including capital gains).** Enter the **smaller** of line 52 or line 53 here and on Form 1040, line 40.		**54** **15,155**

Holding Period for Capital Assets

5.9 Counting the Months in Your Holding Period

The period of time you own a capital asset before its sale or exchange determines whether capital gain or loss is short term or long term.

These are the rules for counting the holding period:

1. A holding period is figured in months and fractions of months.
2. The beginning date of a holding month is generally the day after the asset was acquired. The same numerical date of each following month starts a new holding month regardless of the number of days in the preceding month.
3. The last day of the holding period is the day on which the asset is sold.

As a rule of thumb, use the numerical date on which you acquired the asset as the numerical date ending a holding month in each following month. However, if you acquire an asset on the last day of a month, a holding month ends on the last day of a following calendar month, regardless of the number of days in each month.

> **EXAMPLES**
>
> 1. On September 10, 1999, you buy stock. The holding months begin on September 11, October 11, November 11, and December 11, and end on October 10, November 10, December 10, etc.
> 2. You buy stock on November 30. A holding month ends on December 31, January 31, February 28 (or 29 in a leap year), etc.

5.10 Holding Period for Securities

Rules for counting your holding period for various securities transactions are as follows:

Stock sold on a public exchange. The holding period starts on the day after your purchase order is executed (trading date). The day your sale order is executed (trading date) is the last day of the holding period, even if delivery and payment are not made until several days after the actual sale (settlement date).

Planning Reminder

Long-Term Holding Period of More Than a Year

To obtain the benefit of the 20% or 10% (if in the 15% bracket) capital gains rate, you must hold an asset more than a year before selling it.

> **EXAMPLES**
>
> 1. On June 3, you sell a stock at a profit. Your holding period ends on June 3, although proceeds are not received until June 6.
> 2. You sell stock at a gain on a public exchange on December 31, 1999. The gain must be reported in 1999 even though the proceeds are received in 2000. The installment sale rule does not apply; *see 5.21.*

Stock subscriptions. If you are bound by your subscription but the corporation is not, the holding period begins the day after the date on which the stock is issued. If both you and the company are bound, the acceptance of the subscription by the corporation is the date of acquisition, and your holding period begins the day after.

Tax-free stock rights. When you exercise rights to acquire corporate stock from the issuing corporation, your holding period for the stock begins on the day of exercise, not on the day after. You are deemed to exercise stock rights when you assent to the terms of the rights in the manner requested or authorized by the corporation. An option to acquire stock is not a stock right.

Stock sold from different lots. If you purchased shares of the same stock on different dates and cannot determine which shares you are selling, the shares purchased at the earliest time are considered the stock sold first; this is called the FIFO (first-in, first-out) method; *see 30.2.*

> **EXAMPLE**
>
> You purchased 10 shares of ABC stock on May 3, 1985, 10 shares of ABC stock on May 1, 1987, and 10 shares of ABC stock on September 2, 1988. In 1999, you sell 25 shares of ABC stock, and are unable to determine when those particular shares were bought. Using the "first-in, first-out" method, 10 shares are from May 3, 1985, 10 shares from May 1, 1987, and five shares are from September 2, 1988. *See also 30.2.*

Commodities. If you acquired a commodity futures contract, the holding period of a commodity accepted in satisfaction of the contract includes your holding period of the contract, unless you are a dealer in commodities.

Employee stock options. When an employee exercises a stock option, the holding period of the acquired stock begins on the day after the option is exercised. If an employee option plan allows the exercise of an option by giving notes, the terms of the plan should be reviewed to determine when ownership rights to the stock are transferred. The terms may affect the start of the holding period for the stock.

Wash sales. After a wash sale, the holding period of the new stock includes the holding period of the old stock for which a loss has been disallowed; *see 30.6*.

Other references. For the holding period of stock dividends, *see 30.3*; for short sales, *see 30.5*; and for convertible securities, *see 30.7*.

5.11 Holding Period for Real Estate

The holding period starts the day after the date of acquisition, which is the earlier of: (1) the date title passes to you and (2) the date you take possession and you assume the burdens and privileges of ownership. In disputes involving the starting and closing dates of a holding period, you may refer to the state law that applies to your sale or purchase agreement. State law determines when title to property passes.

If you convert a residence to rental property and later sell the house, the holding period includes the time you held the house for personal purposes.

Year-end sale. The date of sale is the last day of your holding period even if you do not receive the sale proceeds until the following year. For example, you sell land at a gain on December 31, 1999, receiving payment in January 2000. The holding period ends on December 31, although the sale is reported in 2000 when the proceeds are received. Note that the December 31 gain transaction can be reported in 1999 by making an election to "elect out" of installment reporting; *see 5.23*. A sale at a loss is reported in 1999.

5.12 Holding Period for Gifts, Inheritances, and Other Property

Gift property. If, in figuring a gain or loss, your basis for the property under *5.17* is the same as the donor's basis, you add the donor's holding period to the period you held the property. If you sell the property at a loss using as your basis the fair market value at the date of the gift *(5.17)*, your holding period begins on the day after the date of the gift.

Inherited property. The law gives an automatic holding period of more than one year for inherited property. Follow the Schedule D instructions for reporting the sale of inherited property.

Where property is purchased by the executor or trustee and distributed to you, your holding period begins the day after the date on which the property was purchased.

Partnership property. When you receive property as a distribution in kind from your partnership, the period your partnership held the property is added to your holding period. But there is no adding on of holding periods if the partnership property distributed was inventory and was sold by you within five years of distribution.

Involuntary conversions. When you have an involuntary conversion and elect to defer tax on gain, the holding period for the qualified replacement property generally includes the period you held the converted property. A new holding period begins for new property if you do not make an election to defer tax.

Planning Reminder

Year-End Sales

Tax reporting for year-end sales of real estate is different from that for publicly traded securities. Gain on a 1999 year-end sale of realty may be deferred under the installment sale rules *(5.22)* if payments will be received in 2000 or later years. Gain on a 1999 year-end sale of publicly traded securities must be reported on your 1999 return although you receive payment in 2000.

Filing Tip

Selling Inherited Property

When you sell property that you inherited, report the sale as long-term gain or loss on Schedule D even if you actually held the property for less than one year. The law automatically treats inherited property as if it were held for more than one year.

Figuring Your Profit or Loss

5.13 Calculating Gain or Loss

In most cases, you know if you have realized an *economic* profit or loss on the sale or exchange of property. You know your cost and selling price. The difference between the two is your profit or loss. The computation of gain or loss for tax purposes is similarly figured, except that the basis adjustment rules may require you to increase or decrease your cost or selling price and the amount-realized rules may require you to increase the selling price. As a result, your gain or loss for tax purposes may differ from your initial calculation.

Records for Rental Property Improvements

Keep records of permanent improvements and legal fees for rental property. These increase your basis and lower any potential gain when you sell the property.

Figuring Gain or Loss on Schedule D

1. Amount realized or total selling price *(5.14)*. $_____
2. Cost or other unadjusted basis *(5.16)*. $_____
3. *Plus:* Improvements; certain legal fees *(5.20)*. $_____
4. *Minus:* Depreciation, casualty losses *(5.20)*. $_____
5. Adjusted basis: 2 *plus* 3 *minus* 4 *(5.20)*. $_____
6. Add selling expenses to 5. This is the total cost shown on Schedule D. $_____ $_____
7. Gain or loss: Subtract 6 from 1. $_____

EXAMPLE

You sell rental property to a buyer who pays you cash of $50,000 and assumes your $35,000 mortgage. You bought the property for $55,000 and made $12,000 of permanent improvements. You deducted depreciation of $7,250. Selling expenses were $2,000. Your gain on the sale is $23,250, figured as follows:

1. Amount realized *(5.14)*
   Cash $50,000
   Mortgage assumed by buyer   35,000
       $85,000
2. Original cost   55,000
3. *Plus* improvements   12,000
       $67,000
4. *Minus* depreciation   7,250
5. Adjusted basis   59,750
6. *Plus* selling expenses*   2,000
7. Total cost: Combined result of Lines 2–6   61,750
8. Gain: Subtract Line 7 from Line 1 $23,250

***Selling expenses on Schedule D.** When reporting a sale on Schedule D, IRS instructions require you to include *selling expenses* (Step 6) in the column for *cost*, rather than as a reduction to the sales price. The only exception is where a broker has reported *net* sale proceeds (gross proceeds *less* selling expenses) on Form 1099-B; you would then report the net amount as the sales price. Where a broker has reported the *gross* sales price on Form 1099-B, the IRS wants you to treat sales commissions as an addition to cost (rather than a reduction to selling price) so that it can compare the gross amount shown on Form 1099-B with the sales price reported on your return.

Using the facts in the previous Example, you report the gross selling price of $85,000 in column (d) of Schedule D. In column (e), enter the adjusted basis of $59,750 *plus* the selling expenses of $2,000 for a total of $61,750. The final result, a gain of $23,250 ($85,000 – $61,750), is the same as if the selling price were reduced by the selling expenses.

5.14   Amount Realized Is the Total Selling Price

Amount realized is the tax term for the total selling price. It includes cash, the fair market value of additional property received, and any of your liabilities that the buyer agrees to pay. The buyer's note is included in the selling price at fair market value. This is generally the discounted amount that a bank or other party will pay for the note.

Sale of mortgaged property. The selling price includes the amount of the unpaid mortgage. This is true whether or not you are personally liable on the debt, and whether or not the buyer assumes the mortgage or merely takes the property subject to the mortgage. The full amount of the unpaid mortgage is included, even where the value of the property is less than the unpaid mortgage. *See also 31.10* for computing amount realized on foreclosure sales.

If, at the time of the sale, the buyer pays off the existing mortgage or your other liabilities, you include the payment as part of the sales proceeds.

EXAMPLES

1. You sell property subject to a mortgage of $60,000. The seller pays you cash of $30,000 and takes the property subject to the mortgage. The sales price or "amount realized" is $90,000.

2. A partnership receives a nonrecourse mortgage of $1,851,500 from a bank to build an apartment project. Several years later, the partnership sells the project for the buyer's agree-

Caution

Mortgaged Property

When you sell mortgaged property, you must include the unpaid balance of the mortgage as part of the sales price received, in addition to any cash.

ment to assume the unpaid mortgage. At the time, the value of the project is $1,400,000 and the partnership basis in the project is $1,455,740. The partnership figures a loss of $55,740, the difference between basis and the value of the project. The IRS figures a gain of $395,760, the difference between the unpaid mortgage and basis. The partnership claims the selling price is limited to the lower fair market value and is supported by an appeals court. The Supreme Court reverses, supporting the IRS position. That the value of property is less than the amount of the mortgage has no effect on the rule requiring the unpaid mortgage to be part of the selling price. A mortgagor realizes value to the extent that his or her obligation to repay is relieved by a third party's assumption of the mortgage debt.

5.15 Finding Your Cost

In figuring gain or loss, you need to know the "unadjusted basis" of the property sold. This term refers to the original cost of your property if you purchased it. The general rules for determining your unadjusted basis are in *5.16*. Basis for property received by gift or inheritance is in *5.17*; rules for surviving joint tenants are in *5.18*. Keep in mind that you have to adjust this figure for improvements to the property, depreciation, or losses; *see 5.20*.

5.16 Unadjusted Basis of Your Property

To determine your tax cost for property, first find in the following section the unadjusted basis of the property, and then increase or decrease that basis as explained at *5.20*.

Property you bought. Unadjusted basis is your cash cost plus the value of any property you gave to the seller. If you assumed a mortgage or bought property subject to a mortgage, the amount of the mortgage is part of your unadjusted basis.

Purchase expenses are included in your cost, such as commissions, title insurance, recording fees, survey costs, and transfer taxes.

When you buy real estate, you usually reimburse the seller for property taxes he or she paid that cover the period after you took title. If you bought the property before 1954, you add such payments to basis. If you bought the property after 1953, taxes paid are not added to basis because they are immediately deductible in the year paid; *see 16.6*. However, if at the closing you also paid property taxes attributable to the time the seller held the property, you add such taxes to basis.

Filing Tip

Basis of Mutual-Fund Shares
To figure gain or loss on the sale of mutual-fund shares where purchases are made at various times, you may use an averaging method to determine the cost basis of the shares sold; *see 32.10*.

> EXAMPLE
>
> You bought a building for $120,000 in cash and a purchase money mortgage of $60,000. The unadjusted basis of the building is $180,000.

Property obtained for services. If you paid for the property by providing services, the value of the property, which is taxable compensation, is also your adjusted basis.

Property received in taxable exchange. Technically, your unadjusted basis for the new property is the fair market value of the surrendered property at the time of exchange. In practice, however, the basis usually is equal to the fair market value of the property received. *See* below for "tax-free" exchanges.

> EXAMPLE
>
> You acquire real estate for $35,000. When the property has a fair market value of $40,000, you exchange it for machinery also worth $40,000. You have a gain of $5,000 and the basis of the machinery is $40,000.

Property received in a "tax-free" exchange. The computation of basis is made on Form 8824. If the exchange is completely tax free *(6.1)*, your basis for the new property will be your basis for the property you gave up in the exchange, plus any additional cash and exchange expenses you paid. If the exchange is partly nontaxable and partly taxable because you received "boot" *(6.3)*, your basis for the new property will be your basis for the property given up in the exchange, decreased by any cash received and by any liabilities on the property you gave up, and increased by any cash and exchange expenses you paid, liabilities on the property you received, and gain taxed to you on the exchange. Gain is taxed to the extent you receive "boot," in the form of cash or a transfer of liabilities that exceeds the liabilities assumed in the exchange; *see 6.3* for a discussion on taxable boot. *The Example at 6.3 illustrates the basis computation.*

Carryover Basis From Spouse or Ex-Spouse

If you receive a gift of property from your spouse or you receive property from a former spouse in a divorce settlement, your basis for the property is generally the same as the spouse's basis; *see 6.6*.

EXAMPLES

1. You exchange investment real estate, which cost you $20,000, for other investment real estate. Both properties have a fair market value of $35,000 and neither property is mortgaged. You pay no tax on the exchange. The unadjusted basis of the new property received in the exchange is $20,000.

2. Same facts as in Example 1, but you receive real estate worth $30,000 and cash of $5,000. On this transaction, you realize gain of $15,000 (amount realized of $35,000 less your basis of $20,000), but only $5,000 of the gain is taxable, equal to the cash "boot" received. Your basis for the new property is $20,000, figured this way:

Basis of old property	$20,000
Less: Cash received	5,000
	15,000
Plus: Gain recognized	5,000
Basis of new property	$20,000

Property received from a spouse or former spouse. As explained at *6.6*, tax-free exchange rules apply to property transfers after July 18, 1984, to a spouse, or to a former spouse where the transfer is incident to a divorce. The spouse receiving the property takes a basis equal to that of the transferor. Certain adjustments may be required where a transfer of mortgaged property is made in trust.

If you received property before July 19, 1984, under a prenuptial agreement in exchange for your release of your dower and marital rights, your basis is the fair market value at the time you received it.

New residence purchased under tax deferral rule of prior law. If you sold your old principal residence and bought a qualifying replacement under the prior law deferral rules, your basis for the new house is what you paid for it, less any gain that was not taxed on the sale of the old residence.

Property received as a trust beneficiary. Generally, you take the same basis the trust had for the property. But if the distribution is made to settle a claim you had against the trust, your basis for the property is the amount of the settled claim.

If you received a distribution in kind for your share of trust income before June 2, 1984, the basis of the distribution is generally the value of the property to the extent allocated to distributable net income. For distributions in kind after June 1, 1984, in taxable years ending after June 1, 1984, your basis is the basis of the property in the hands of the trust. If the trust elects to treat the distribution as a taxable sale, your basis is generally fair market value.

Property acquired with involuntary conversion proceeds. If you acquire replacement property with insurance proceeds from destroyed property, or a government payment for condemned property, basis is the cost of the new property decreased by deferred gain; *see 18.23* for figuring the deferred gain. If the replacement property consists of more than one piece of property, basis is allocated to each piece in proportion to its respective cost.

EXAMPLE

A building with an adjusted basis of $100,000 is destroyed by fire. The owner receives an insurance award of $200,000, realizing a gain of $100,000. He buys a building as a replacement for $150,000. Of the $100,000 gain, $50,000 is taxable, while the remaining $50,000 is deferred. Taxable gain is limited to the portion of the insurance award not used to buy replacement property ($200,000 − $150,000). The basis of the new building is $100,000:

Cost of the new building	$150,000
Less: deferred gain	50,000
Basis	$100,000

5.17 Basis of Property You Inherited or Received as a Gift

Special basis rules apply to property you received as a gift or that you inherited. Gifts from a spouse are subject to the rules discussed in *6.6*. If you are a surviving joint tenant who received full title to property upon the death of the other joint tenant, *see 5.18*.

Basis of Property Received as Gift

If the fair market value of the property *equalled or exceeded* the donor's adjusted basis *(5.20)* at the time you received the gift, your basis for figuring gain or loss when you sell it is the donor's adjusted basis plus all or part of any gift tax paid; *see* the gift tax rule below.

If on the date of the gift the fair market value was less than the donor's adjusted basis, your basis for purposes of figuring gain is the donor's adjusted basis, and your basis for figuring loss is the fair market value on the date of the gift.

EXAMPLE

Assume that in 1986 you received a gift of stock from your father that you sold in 1999. His adjusted basis was $1,000.

The basis you use to determine gain or loss depends on whether the fair market value of the stock on the date of the gift equalled or exceeded your father's $1,000 adjusted basis. If it did, your basis is your father's $1,000 basis and you will realize a gain if your selling price exceeds $1,000, as on Line 1 below, or a loss if the selling price is below $1,000, as on Line 4.

If the value of the stock on the date of the gift was less than $1,000 (father's basis) then you have: a gain if you sell for more than $1,000, as on Line 5; a loss if you sell for less than the date-of-gift value, as on Line 2; or neither gain nor loss if you sell for more than the date-of-gift value but no more than $1,000 (father's basis), as on Line 3.

If value of the gift at receipt was—	And you sold it for—	Your basis is—	Your gain is—	Your loss is—
1. $3,000	$2,000	$1,000	$1,000	none
2. 700	500	700	none	$200
3. 300	500	*	none	none
4. 1,500	500	1,000	none	500
5. 500	1,200	1,000	200	none

*On Line 3 of the Example, where you sell for more than the date-of-gift value but for no more than the donor's basis, there is neither gain nor loss. To see if you have a gain, you use the donor's $1,000 basis as your basis, but on a sale for $500, you have a loss ($500) and not a gain. To see if you have a loss, you use the $300 date-of-gift value of the stock as your basis, but on a sale for $500, you have a gain ($200) and not a loss. Thus, you have neither gain nor loss under the basis rules, which require you to use the donor's basis for determining if you have a gain and the date-of-gift value for determining if you have a loss.

Did the donor pay gift tax? If the donor paid a gift tax *(33.1)* on the gift to you, your basis for the property is increased under these rules:

1. For property received after December 31, 1976, the basis is increased for the gift tax paid by an amount that bears the same ratio to the amount of tax paid as the net appreciation in the value of the gift bears to the amount of the gift after taking into account the $10,000 annual gift tax exclusion *(33.1)*. The increase may not exceed the tax paid. Net appreciation in the value of any gift is the amount by which the fair market value of the gift exceeds the donor's adjusted basis immediately before the gift. *See* Example 2 below.

2. For property received after September 1, 1958, but before 1977, basis is increased by the gift tax paid on the property but not above the fair market value of the property at the time of the gift.

3. For property received before September 2, 1958, the gift tax paid increases the basis. But this increase may not be more than the excess of the fair market value of the property at the time of the gift over the basis of the property in the donor's hands. Ask the donor or his or her advisor for these amounts.

EXAMPLES

1. In 1975, your father gave you rental property with a fair market value of $78,000. The basis of the property in his hands was $60,000. He paid a gift tax of $15,000 on the gift. The basis of the property in your hands is $75,000 ($60,000 + $15,000).

2. In 1999, your father gave you rental property with a fair market value of $178,000. His basis in the property was $160,000. He paid a gift tax of $44,560 on a taxable gift of

$168,000, after claiming the $10,000 annual exclusion. The basis of the property in your hands is your father's basis increased by the gift tax attributable to the appreciation. Gift tax attributable to the appreciation is:

$\dfrac{\text{Appreciation}}{\text{Gift } minus \text{ annual exclusion}}$	×	Gift tax paid
$\dfrac{\$18,000}{\$168,000}$	×	$44,560 = $ 4,774

Your basis for figuring gain or loss or depreciation is $164,774 ($4,774 + $160,000 father's basis).

Gift you received before 1921. Your basis is the fair market value of the property at the time of the gift.

Depreciation on property received as a gift. If the property is depreciable (*see* Chapter 42), your basis for computing depreciation deductions is the donor's adjusted basis *(5.20)*, plus all or part of the gift tax paid by the donors as previously discussed.

When you sell the property, you must adjust basis *(5.20)* for depreciation claimed. If accelerated depreciation is claimed and you sell at a gain, you are subject to the ordinary income recapture rules discussed at *44.1*.

Basis of Inherited Property

Your basis for inherited property is generally the fair market value of the property on the date of the decedent's death, regardless of when you acquire the property. If the decedent died after October 21, 1942, and the executor elected to use an *alternate valuation date* after the death, your basis is the alternate value at that date.

If you owned the property jointly with the deceased, *see 5.18*.

If you inherit appreciated property that you (or your spouse) gave to the deceased person within one year of his or her death, your basis is the decedent's basis immediately before death, not its fair market value.

If the inherited property is subject to a mortgage, your basis is the value of the property, and not its equity at the date of death. If the property is subject to a lease under which no income is to be received for years, the basis is the value of the property—not the equity.

You might be given the right to buy the deceased person's property under his or her will. This is not the same as inheriting that property. Your basis is what you pay—not what the property is worth on the date of the deceased's death.

If property was inherited from an individual who died after 1976 and before November 7, 1978, and the executor elected to apply a carryover basis to all estate property, your basis is figured with reference to the decedent's basis. The executor must inform you of the basis of such property.

Community property. Upon the death of a spouse in a community property state, one-half of the fair market value of the community property is generally included in the deceased spouse's estate for estate tax purposes. The surviving spouse's basis for his or her half of the property is 50% of the total fair market value. For the other half, the heirs of the deceased spouse also have a basis equal to 50% of the fair market value.

5.18 Joint Tenancy Basis Rules for Surviving Tenants

If you are a surviving joint tenant, your basis for the property depends on how much of the value was includible in the deceased tenant's gross estate, and this depends on whether the joint tenant was your spouse or someone other than your spouse.

Qualified joint interest rule for survivor of spouse who died after 1981. A "qualified joint interest" rule applies to a joint tenancy with right of survivorship where the spouses are the only joint tenants, and to a tenancy by the entirety between a husband and wife. Where the surviving spouse is a U.S. citizen, the general rule for deaths occurring *after 1981* is as follows: One-half of the fair market value of the property is includible in the decedent's gross estate. This is true regardless of how much each spouse contributed to the purchase price. Fair market value is fixed at the date of death, or six months later if an estate tax return is filed and the optional alternate valuation date is elected.

The surviving spouse's basis equals the one-half estate tax share plus one-half of the original cost basis for the property; *see* Example 1 below. If no estate tax return was due because the value of the

Filing Tip

Advantage of Leaving Appreciated Property to an Heir

Since your basis for inherited property is the value at the decedent's death or alternate valuation date, income tax is completely avoided on the appreciation in value that occurred while the decedent owned the property.

estate was below the filing threshold, the surviving spouse's basis is one-half of the fair market value of the property at the date of death (alternate valuation is not available) plus one-half of the original cost basis. If depreciation deductions for the property were claimed before the date of death, the surviving spouse must reduce basis by his or her share (under local law) of the depreciation; *see* Example 2 below.

If the surviving spouse is *not* a U.S. citizen on the due date of the estate tax return, the basis rule is generally the same as the rule discussed below for unmarried joint tenants.

EXAMPLES

1. John and Jennifer Jones jointly own a house that cost them $50,000 in 1979. John paid $45,000 of the purchase price and Jennifer $5,000. In 1999, John dies when the house is worth $200,000. One-half, or $100,000, is included in his estate although he contributed 90% of the purchase price. For income tax purposes, Jennifer's basis for the house is $125,000.

One-half of cost basis	$25,000
Inherited portion	100,000
Jennifer's basis	$125,000

2. Same facts as in Example 1 except that the home was rental property for which $20,000 of depreciation deductions had been allowed before John's death. Under local law, Jennifer had a right to 50% of the income from the property and, thus, a right to 50% of the depreciation. Her basis for the property is $115,000: $125,000 as shown in Example 1, reduced by $10,000, her share of the depreciation.

3. The Gallensteins purchased farm property in 1955 as joint tenants; Mr. Gallenstein provided all the funds. When he died in 1987, Mrs. Gallenstein claimed that 100% of the property was includible in her husband's gross estate and she had a stepped-up basis for that full amount. The IRS argued that under the rules for estates of spouses dying after 1981, she received a stepped-up basis for only 50% of the date-of-death value. The federal appeals court for the Sixth Circuit (Kentucky, Michigan, Ohio, and Tennessee) agreed with Mrs. Gallenstein. The appeals court held that pre-1977 spousal joint tenancies were not affected when the law was changed to provide a 50% estate tax inclusion and 50% stepped-up basis for spousal deaths after 1981. For pre-1977 spousal joint tenancies, the prior law rule continues to apply: 100% of the date-of-death value of jointly held property is included in the estate of the first spouse to die unless it is shown that the survivor contributed towards the purchase. In this case, where Mrs. Gallenstein's deceased husband had paid the entire purchase price, her basis was 100% of the value of the property and she realized no taxable gain when she sold the property at a price equal to that stepped-up basis.

   The Tax Court and the Fourth Circuit Appeals Court (Maryland, North Carolina, South Carolina, Virginia, West Virginia) have agreed with the Sixth Circuit's *Gallenstein* approach of allowing a 100% stepped-up basis for a pre-1977 spousal joint interest where the deceased spouse had paid the entire purchase price.

   If the statute of limitations has not expired, a surviving spouse who reported gain on a sale of property using the 50% basis rule should consult with his or her tax adviser about filing a refund claim based upon the 100% basis rule in the *Gallenstein* case. However, the IRS may reject such refund claims outside the Sixth and Fourth Circuits.

Unmarried joint tenants. If you are a surviving joint tenant who owned property with someone other than your spouse, your basis for the entire property is your basis for your share before the joint owner died plus the fair market value of the decedent's share at death (or on the alternate valuation date if the estate uses the alternate date). Even if the estate is too small to require the filing of an estate tax return, you may still include the decedent's share of the date-of-death value in your basis. However, if no estate tax return is required, you may not use the alternate valuation date basis.

EXAMPLE

You and your sister bought a home in 1950 for $20,000. She paid $12,000, and you paid $8,000. Title to the house was held by both of you as joint tenants. In 1999, when she died, the house was worth $150,000. Since she paid 60% of the cost of the house, 60% of the value at her death, $90,000, is included in her estate tax return (or would be included if an estate tax return was due). Your basis for the house is now $98,000—the $8,000 you originally paid plus the $90,000 fair market value of your sister's 60% share at her death.

 Caution

Spousal Joint Tenancies Created Before 1977

The IRS claims that if spouses jointly own property and one spouse dies, the surviving spouse receives a stepped-up basis for 50% of the date-of-death value, regardless of when the joint tenancy was created. However, the Tax Court and two federal appeals courts have allowed the surviving spouse a 100% stepped-up basis if the spousal joint tenancy was created before 1977; *see* Example 3 in the left column.

 Planning Reminder

Joint Property Held With Non-Spouse

If you own property with someone other than your spouse, then at the other owner's death your basis for the property equals your original contribution to the purchase plus the portion of the property's value that was includible in the gross estate of the deceased owner.

Exception for pre-1954 deaths. Where property was held in joint tenancy and one of the tenants died before January 1, 1954, no part of the interest of the surviving tenant is treated, for purposes of determining the basis of the property, as property transmitted at death. The survivor's basis is the original cost of the property.

Survivor of spouse who died before 1982. The basis rule for a surviving spouse who held property jointly (or as tenancy by the entirety) with a spouse who died before 1982 is generally the same as the above rule for unmarried joint tenants. However, special rules applied to qualified joint interests and eligible joint interests are discussed below.

EXAMPLE

A husband and wife owned rental property as tenants by the entirety that they purchased for $30,000. The husband furnished two-thirds of the purchase price ($20,000) and the wife furnished one-third ($10,000). Depreciation deductions taken before the husband's death were $12,000. On the date of his death in 1979, the property had a fair market value of $60,000. Under the law of the state in which the property is located, as tenants by the entirety, each had a half interest in the property. The wife's basis in the property at the date of her husband's death is $44,000, computed as follows:

Interest acquired with her own funds	$10,000
Interest acquired from husband ($^2/_3$ of $60,000)	40,000
	$50,000
Less: Depreciation of $^1/_2$ interest not acquired by reason of death ($^1/_2$ of $12,000)	6,000
Wife's basis at date of husband's death	$44,000

If she had not contributed any part of the purchase price, her basis at the date of her husband's death would be $54,000 ($60,000 fair market value less $6,000 depreciation).

Qualified joint interest and eligible joint interest where spouse died before 1982. Where, after 1976, a spouse dying before 1982 elected to treat realty as a "qualified joint interest" subject to gift tax, such joint property was treated as owned 50–50 by each spouse, and 50% of the value was included in the decedent's estate. Thus, for income tax purposes, the survivor's basis for the inherited 50% half of the property is the estate tax value; the basis for the other half is determined under the gift rules detailed in *5.17*. Personal property is treated as a "qualified joint interest" only if it was created or deemed to have been created after 1976 by a husband and wife and was subject to gift tax.

Where death occurred before 1982 and a surviving spouse materially participated in the operation of a farm or other business, an estate may elect to treat the farm or business property as an "eligible joint interest," which means that part of the investment in the property may be attributed to the surviving spouse's services and that part is not included in the deceased spouse's estate. Where such an election was made, the survivor's basis for income tax purposes includes the estate tax value of property included in the decedent's estate.

5.19 Allocating Cost Among Several Assets

Allocation of basis is generally required in these cases: when the property includes land and building; the land is to be divided into lots; securities or mutual-fund shares are purchased at different times; stock splits; and in the purchase of a business.

Purchase of land and building. To figure depreciation on the building, part of the purchase price must be allocated to the building. The allocation is made according to the fair market values of the building and land. The amount allocated to land is not depreciated.

Purchase of land to be divided into lots. The purchase price of the tract is allocated to each lot, so that the gain or loss from the sale of each lot may be reported in the year of its sale. Allocation is not made ratably, that is, with an equal share to each lot or parcel. It is based on the relative value of each piece of property. Comparable sales, competent appraisals, or assessed values may be used as guides.

Securities. *See 30.2* for details on methods of identifying securities bought at different dates. *See 30.3* for allocating basis of stock dividends and stock splits and *30.4* for allocating the basis of stock rights.

Mutual-fund shares. *See 32.10* for determining the basis of mutual-fund shares where purchases were made at different times.

Purchase price of a business. *See 44.9* for allocation rule.

5.20 How To Find Adjusted Basis

After determining the *unadjusted* cost basis for property under the rules at *5.16–5.19*, you may have to increase it or decrease it to find your *adjusted basis*, which is the amount used to figure your gain or loss on a sale, as shown at *5.13*.

1. Additions to basis. You add to unadjusted basis the cost of these items:

- **All permanent improvements and additions to the property and other capital costs.** Increase basis for capital improvements such as adding a room or a fence, putting in new plumbing or wiring, and paving a driveway. Also include capital costs such as the cost of extending utility service lines, assessments for local improvements such as streets, sidewalks, or water connections, and repairing your property after a casualty (for example, repair costs after a fire or storm).
- **Legal fees,** including fees incurred for defending or perfecting title, or for obtaining a reduction of an assessment levied against property to pay for local benefits.
- **Sale of unharvested land.** If you sell land with unharvested crops, add the cost of producing the crops to the basis of the property sold.

2. Decreases to basis. You reduce cost basis for these items:

- **Return of capital,** such as dividends on stock paid out of capital or out of a depletion reserve when the company has no available earnings or surplus; *see 4.11*.
- **Losses from casualties,** including insurance awards and payments in settlement of damages to your property.

EXAMPLE

Your vacation home, which cost $75,000, is damaged by fire. You deducted the uninsured loss of $10,000 and spent $11,000 to repair the property. Several years later, you sell the house for $90,000. To figure your profit, increase the original cost of the house by the $11,000 of repairs and then reduce basis by the $10,000 casualty loss to get an adjusted basis of $76,000 ($75,000 + $11,000 – $10,000). Your gain on the sale is $14,000 ($90,000 – $76,000).

- **Depletion allowances;** *see 9.15*.
- **Depreciation, first-year expensing deduction, ACRS deductions, amortization, and obsolescence on property used in business or for the production of income.** In some years, you may have taken more or less depreciation than was allowable.

  If you claim less than what was allowable, you must deduct from basis the allowable amount rather than what was actually claimed. You may file an amended return to claim the full allowable depreciation for a year. If the amended return deadline has passed, you may still get a deduction for the unclaimed depreciation by filing for an accounting method change under IRS Revenue Procedure 97-37. A deduction is generally claimed over a four-year period, but if the adjustment is less than $25,000, a one-year adjustment is allowed; *see* Revenue Procedure 97-37 for details.

  If you took more depreciation than was allowable, you may have to make the following adjustments: If you have deducted more than what was allowable and you received a tax benefit from the deduction, you deduct from basis the full amount of the depreciation. But if the excess depreciation did not give you a tax benefit, because income was eliminated by other deductions, the excess is not deducted from basis. These rules affect all tax years after 1951.
- **Amortized bond premium;** *see 4.17*.
- **Cancelled debt excluded from income.** If you did not pay tax on certain cancellations of debt because of bankruptcy or insolvency, or on qualifying farm debt or business real property, you reduce basis of your property for the amount forgiven under the rules at *11.7* and *11.8*.
- **Investment credit.** Where the full investment credit was claimed in 1983 or later years, basis is reduced by one-half the credit.

 Court Decision

Improvements Covered by Note

In an unusual case, the owner of office condominiums financed substantial improvements to the units by giving promissory notes to a contracting company that he controlled. Before paying off the notes he sold the units. He included the cost of the improvements in basis to figure his gain on the sale, but the IRS, with the approval of a federal district court, held that this was improper. The court held that as a cash-basis taxpayer, he could not include the face amount of the notes in the basis of the condominiums until the notes were paid.

Reporting an Installment Sale

5.21 Tax Advantage of Installment Sales

If you sell property at a *gain* in 1999 and you will receive one or more payments in a later year or years, you may use the installment method to defer tax unless the property is publicly traded securities or you are a dealer of the property sold. If you report the sale as an installment sale on Form 6252, your profit is taxed as installments are received. You may elect not to use the installment method if you want to report the entire profit in the year of sale; *see* Example 1 below and *5.23*.

Losses may not be deferred under the installment method.

How the installment method works. For each year you receive installment payments, report your gain on Form 6252. Installment income from the sale of a capital asset is then transferred to Schedule D. If your gain in the year of sale is long-term capital gain, gain in later years is also long term; short-term treatment in the year of sale applies also to later years. Interest payments you receive on the deferred sale installments are reported with your other interest income on Schedule B of Form 1040, not on Form 6252.

Installment income from the sale of business or rental property is figured on Form 6252 and then entered on Form 4797. If you make an installment sale of depreciable property, any *depreciation recapture (44.1)* is reported as income in the year of disposition. The recaptured amount is first figured on Form 4797 and then entered on Form 6252. On Form 6252, recaptured income is added to basis of the property for purposes of figuring the gross profit ratio for the balance of gain to be reported, if any, over the installment period; *see also 44.7*.

Installment sales of business or rental property for over $150,000 may be subject to a special tax if deferred payments exceed $5 million; *see 5.31*.

EXAMPLES

1. In 1999, you sell real estate for $100,000 that you bought in 1985 for $44,000. Selling expenses were $6,000. You are to receive $20,000 in 1999, 2000, and 2001; and $40,000 in 2002, plus interest of 7% compounded semiannually. Your gross profit is $50,000 ($100,000 contract price less $44,000 cost and $6,000 selling expenses). For installment sale purposes, your gross profit percentage, which is the percentage of each payment that you must report, is 50% ($50,000 profit ÷ $100,000 contract price). When the buyer makes the installment note payments, you report the following:

| | You report | |
In	Payment of:	Income of:
1999	$20,000	$10,000
2000	20,000	10,000
2001	20,000	10,000
2002	40,000	20,000
Total	$100,000	$50,000

   In 1999, you file Form 6252 to figure your gross profit and gross profit percentage. You report only $10,000 as profit on Schedule D (or Form 4797, if applicable). If you do not want to use the installment method, you make an election by reporting the entire gain of $50,000 on Schedule D or Form 4797.

   The buyer's interest payments are separately reported as interest income on Form 1040.

2. On December 21, 1999, you sell a building for $150,000, realizing a profit of $25,000. You take a note payable in January 2000. You report the gain in 2000. Receiving a lump-sum payment in a taxable year after the year of sale is considered an installment sale.

Year-end sales of publicly traded stock or securities. You have no choice about when to report the gain from a sale of publicly traded stock or securities made at the end of 1999. Any gain must be reported in 1999, even if the proceeds are not received until early 2000. The sale is not considered an installment sale.

Farm property. A farmer may use the installment method to report gain from the sale of property that does not have to be inventoried under his method of accounting. This is true even though such property is held for regular sale.

Dealer sales. Generally, dealers must report gain in the year of sale for personal property regularly sold on an installment plan or real estate held for resale to customers. However, the installment method may be used by dealers of certain time shares (generally time shares of up to six weeks per year) and residential lots, but only if an election is made to pay interest on the tax deferred by using the installment method. For further details, *see* the instructions to Schedule C of Form 1040.

Filing Tip

Deferring Income With Installment Sale

Using the installment sale method on Form 6252 gives you the chance to defer tax on profits realized on property sales where payments will be received in one or more later years.

Law Alert

Accrual-Basis Taxpayers

A new law generally bars accrual-basis taxpayers from using the installment method. Exceptions apply to sales of farm property and certain dealer sales of time shares and residential lots. At the time this book went to press in December 1999, the legislation repealing the installment method for accrual-basis taxpayers had not yet been signed into law by the President. The repeal applies to sales on or after the enactment date; *see* the Supplement for the exact date.

Caution

Year-End Sales of Securities

You cannot defer to 2000 reporting of gain on a 1999 year-end sale of publicly traded securities, even if you do not receive payment until early January 2000.

5.22 Figuring the Taxable Part of Installment Payments

On the installment method, a portion of each payment other than interest represents part of your gain and is taxable. This taxable gain amount is based on the gross profit percentage or ratio, which is figured by dividing gross profit by the selling price or the contract price. The contract price is the same as the selling price unless an adjustment is made for an existing mortgage assumed or "taken subject to" by the buyer. The term *contract price* is used in the computation to describe only payments that the seller receives or is considered to have received. Thus, it does not include the buyer's assumption of an existing mortgage; *see* below for the mortgage adjustment to contract price. By following the line-by-line instructions to Form 6252, you get the gross profit percentage. Selling price, gross profit, and contract price are explained in the following paragraphs.

Interest equal to the *lesser* of 100% of the applicable federal rate and 9% compounded semiannually must generally be charged on a deferred payment sale. Otherwise, the IRS treats part of the sale price as interest; *see 4.32*.

EXAMPLE

On December 7, 1999, you sell real estate for $100,000. The property had an adjusted basis of $56,000. Selling expenses are $4,000. You are to receive installment payments of $25,000 in 1999, 2000, 2001, and 2002, plus interest at 7%, compounded semiannually. The gross profit percentage of 40% is figured as follows:

Selling price (contract price)	$100,000
Less: Adjusted basis and selling expenses	60,000
Gross profit	$ 40,000

$$\frac{\text{Gross profit}}{\text{Contract price}} = \frac{\$40,000}{\$100,000} = 40\% \text{ (gross profit percentage)}$$

In 1999, you report a profit of $10,000 (40% of $25,000) on Form 6252. Interest received is separately reported as income on your Form 1040. Similarly, in each of the following three years, a profit of $10,000 is reported so that by the end of four years, the entire $40,000 profit will have been reported.

Selling price. Include cash, fair market value of property received from the buyer, the buyer's notes (at face value), and any outstanding mortgage on the property that the buyer assumes or takes subject to. If, under the contract of sale, the buyer pays off an existing mortgage or assumes liability for any other liens on the property, such as taxes you owe, or pays the sales commissions, such payments are also included in the selling price.

Interest, including interest imputed under the rules of *4.32*, is not included in the selling price. Notes of a third party given to you by the buyer are valued at fair market value.

Gross profit and gross profit percentage. Gross profit is the selling price less what the IRS calls installment sale basis, which is the total of adjusted basis of the property *(5.20)*, selling expenses, such as brokers' commissions and legal fees, and recaptured depreciation income, if any *(44.1)*.

Divide the gross profit by the contract price to get the gross profit percentage. Each year, you multiply this percentage by your payments to determine the taxable amount under the installment method.

Contract price where the buyer takes subject to or assumes an existing mortgage. To figure the gross profit percentage first reduce the selling price by the amount of your existing mortgages that the buyer assumes or takes the property subject to. The reduced amount is the *contract price*. You then divide your gross profit by the contract price to get the gross profit percentage.

If the mortgage exceeds your installment sale basis (total of adjusted basis of the property, selling expenses, and depreciation recapture), you are required to report the excess as a payment received in the year of sale and also increase the *contract price* by that excess amount. Where the mortgage equals or exceeds your installment sale basis, the gross profit percentage will be 100%; *see* Example 3 on the next page.

In a wraparound mortgage transaction, the buyer does not assume the seller's mortgage or take the property subject to it, but instead makes payments that cover the seller's outstanding mortgage liability. At one time, the IRS treated a wraparound mortgage transaction as an assumption of a mortgage by the buyer and required a reduction of the selling price by the mortgage. The Tax Court

 Caution

Foreclosures
If your property is foreclosed, the amount of the mortgage is treated as sales proceeds even if you do not receive anything on the sale.

rejected the IRS position, and the IRS acquiesced in the decision. However, a temporary regulation requiring the reduction has not been withdrawn. Currently, the IRS does not require a reduction of selling price for a wraparound mortgage in the Form 6252 instructions or in Publication 537; *see* Example 4 below.

EXAMPLES

1. You sell a building for $300,000. The building was secured by an existing mortgage of $50,000 that you pay off at the sale closing from the buyer's initial payment. The contract price is $300,000.

2. Same facts as in Example 1, but the buyer assumes the mortgage of $50,000. The contract price is $250,000 ($300,000 – $50,000).

3. You sell a building for $90,000. The buyer will pay you $10,000 annually for three years and assume an existing mortgage of $60,000. The adjusted basis of the property is $45,000. Selling expenses are $5,000. The total installment sale basis is $50,000 ($45,000 plus $5,000). The mortgage exceeds this basis by $10,000 ($60,000 – $50,000). This $10,000 excess is included in the contract price and treated as a payment made in the year of sale. The contract price is $40,000:

Selling price	$90,000
Less: Mortgage	60,000
	$30,000
Add: Excess of mortgage ($60,000) over installment sale basis ($50,000)	10,000
Contract price	$40,000
Selling price	$90,000
Less: Installment sale basis	50,000
Gross Profit	$40,000
Gross profit percentage ($40,000 gross profit ÷ $40,000 contract price)	100%

4. Abel sells real property worth $2 million, encumbered by a mortgage of $900,000. Installment sale basis (adjusted basis plus selling costs) is $700,000. The buyer pays $200,000 cash and gives an interest-bearing wraparound mortgage note for $1.8 million. Abel remains obligated to pay off the $900,000 mortgage. The gross profit ratio is 65% ($1,300,000 gross profit ÷ $2,000,000 contract price). In the year of sale, Abel reports the $200,000 cash of which 65% of $200,000, or $130,000, is taxable income.

Caution

Recapture of Depreciation or First-Year Expensing Deduction

The entire recaptured amount, discussed in 44.1–44.3, is reported in the year of sale, even though you report the sale on the installment basis. An installment sale does not defer the reporting of the recaptured deduction. You also add the recaptured amount to the basis of the sold asset to compute the amount of the remaining gain to be reported on each installment. *See* the instructions to Form 6252.

Change of selling price. If the selling price is changed during the period payments are outstanding, the gross profit percentage is refigured on the new selling price. The adjusted profit ratio is then applied to payments received after the adjustment.

EXAMPLE

Jones sold real estate in 1996 for $100,000. His basis, including selling expenses, was $40,000, so his gross profit was $60,000. The buyer agreed to pay, starting in 1997, five annual installments of $20,000 plus 10% interest. As the gross profit percentage was 60% ($60,000 ÷ $100,000), Jones reported profit of $12,000 (60% of $20,000) on the installments received in 1997 and 1998.

In 1999, the parties renegotiated the sales price, reducing it from $100,000 to $85,000, and reducing payments for 1999, 2000, and 2001 to $15,000. Jones's original profit of $60,000 is reduced to $45,000 ($85,000 revised sales price less $40,000 basis). Of the $45,000 profit, $12,000 was reported in 1997 and an additional $12,000 in 1998. To get the revised profit percentage, Jones must divide the $21,000 of profit not yet received by the remaining sales price of $45,000 ($85,000 *less* $40,000 installments in 1997 and 1998). The revised profit percentage is 46.67% ($21,000 ÷ $45,000). In 1999, 2000, and 2001, Jones reports profit of $7,000 on each $15,000 installment (46.67% of $15,000).

Payments received. Payments include cash, the fair market value of property, and payments on the buyer's notes. Payments do not include receipt of the buyer's notes or other evidence of indebtedness, unless payable on demand or readily tradable. "Readily tradable" means registered bonds, bonds with coupons attached, debentures, and other evidences of indebtedness of the buyer that are readily tradable in an established securities market. This rule is directed mainly at corporate acquisitions. A third-party guarantee (including a standby letter of credit) is not treated as a payment received on an installment obligation.

If the buyer has assumed or taken property subject to a mortgage that exceeds your installment sale basis (adjusted basis plus selling expenses plus depreciation recapture, if any), you include as a payment in the year of the sale the excess of the mortgage over the installment basis; *see* the Johnson Example below.

EXAMPLE

Johnson sells a building for $160,000, subject to a mortgage of $60,000. Installments plus interest are to be paid over five years. His adjusted basis in the building was $30,000 and his selling expenses were $10,000, so his installment sale basis is $40,000 and his gross profit is $120,000 ($160,000 – $40,000). The contract price is also $120,000, the selling price of $160,000 less $40,000, the part of the mortgage that did not exceed the installment sale basis.

The $20,000 difference between the $60,000 mortgage and the installment sale basis of $40,000 is part of the contract price and is also treated as a payment received in the year of sale. Since the mortgage exceeds Johnson's installment sale basis, he is treated as having recovered his entire basis in the year of sale, and all installment payments will be taxable, as his gross profit ratio is 100%: gross profit of $120,000 ÷ contract price of $120,000. In the year of sale, Johnson must report as taxable gain 100% of the installment payment received, plus the $20,000 difference between the mortgage and his installment sale basis.

Pledging installment obligation as security. If, as security for a loan, you pledge an installment obligation from a sale of property of more than $150,000 (excluding farm or personal-use property), the net loan proceeds must be treated as a payment on the installment obligation. The net loan proceeds are treated as received on the later of the date the loan is secured and the date you receive the loan proceeds. These pledging rules do not apply if the debt refinances a debt that was outstanding on December 17, 1987, and secured by the installment obligation until the refinancing. If the refinancing exceeds the loan principal owed immediately before the refinancing, the excess is treated as a payment on the installment obligation. *See* the Form 6252 instructions.

5.23 Electing Not To Report on the Installment Method

If any sale proceeds are to be received after the year of sale, you must file Form 6252 and use the installment method unless you "elect out" by making a timely election to report the entire gain in the year of sale. If you want to report the entire gain in the year of sale, include it on Schedule D or Form 4797 by the due date for filing your return (plus extensions) for the year of sale. Do not use Form 6252. After the due date (plus extensions), a change from the installment method to full reporting in the year of sale may be made only with IRS consent. The IRS will give consent only in rare cases where it finds "good cause." The IRS may give consent if your tax preparer erroneously reported on the installment method and you promptly ask IRS permission to change to reporting of the entire gain. A change in the tax law is not considered "good cause" by the IRS.

Switching from full reporting to installment method. If you do report the entire gain in the year of sale, you may change to the installment method on an amended return only with the consent of the IRS. In a private ruling, the IRS refused to allow a seller to use the installment method after inadvertently including the entire gain from the sale on his return. Although reporting of the entire gain was a mistake, this was treated as an election not to use the installment method. The IRS refused permission to revoke the election on the grounds that a second chance to apply the installment method would be tax avoidance. However, in other private rulings, permission to revoke was granted where the seller's accountant erroneously reported the entire gain.

In one case, a seller "elected out" in a year in which he planned to deduct a net operating loss carryforward from an installment sale gain. In a later year, the IRS substantially reduced the loss. The seller then asked the IRS to allow him to revoke the "election out" so he could use the installment method. The IRS refused in a private ruling, claiming that the seller asked for the revocation to avoid tax. The installment sale would defer gain to a later year, which is a tax avoidance purpose.

5.24 Restriction on Installment Sales to Relatives

The installment sale method is not allowed where you sell depreciable property to a controlled business, or to a trust in which you or your spouse is a beneficiary. All payments to be received over the installment period are considered received in the year of sale.

Further, if you sell property to a relative on the installment basis, and the relative later resells the property, you could lose the benefit of installment reporting. If the family member's resale is within two years of the original sale, the original seller is taxed on that sale under the two-year rule discussed on the next page.

 Filing Tip

"Electing Out" of Installment Reporting

When you have losses to offset your gain in the year of sale, installment sale reporting may not be advantageous. In such a case, you may want to report the full gain in the year of sale so the gain may be offset by the losses. However, there is a risk. If the losses are later disallowed by an IRS audit, you may not be given a second chance to use the installment method to spread the gain over the payment period. The IRS *may* not allow you to revoke your "election out" on the grounds that to do so would result in tax avoidance.

EXAMPLE

In 1999, Jones sells land to his son for $250,000, realizing a profit of $100,000. The son agrees to pay in five annual installments of $50,000 starting in 2000. Later in 1999, the son sells the land to a third party for $260,000. Jones Sr. reports his profit of $100,000 in 1999, even though he received no payment that year. Payments other than interest received by Jones Sr. after 1999 are tax free because he reported the entire profit in 1999.

Two-year rule for property other than marketable securities. If you make an installment sale to a related party of property other than marketable securities, you are taxed on a second sale by the related party only if it occurs within two years of the initial installment sale and before all payments from the first installment sale are made. Related parties include a spouse, child, grandchild, parent, grandparent, brother or sister, controlled corporation (50% or more direct or indirect ownership), any S corporation in which you own stock or partnership in which you are a partner, a trust in which you are a beneficiary, or a grantor trust of which you are treated as the owner. You are treated as owning stock held by your spouse, brothers, sisters, children, grandchildren, parents, and grandparents.

You must report as additional installment sale income: (1) the proceeds from the related party's sale or the contract price from the initial installment sale, whichever is less, *minus* (2) installment payments received from the related party as of the end of the year. The computation is made in Part III of Form 6252.

The two-year period is extended during any period in which the buyer's risk is lessened by a put on the property, an option by another person to acquire the property, or a short sale or other transaction lessening the risk of loss.

Marketable securities. The two-year cutoff does not apply to the sale of marketable securities. For such marketable securities, you can be taxed on any related party's sale occurring before you receive all the payments under the initial installment sale.

Marketable securities are:

1. Securities listed on the New York Stock Exchange, the American Stock Exchange, or any city or regional exchange in which quotations appear on a daily basis, including foreign securities listed on a recognized foreign, national, or regional exchange;

2. Securities regularly traded in the national or regional over-the-counter market, for which published quotations are available;

3. Securities locally traded for which quotations can readily be obtained from established brokerage firms;

4. Units in a common trust fund; and

5. Mutual-fund shares for which redemption prices are published.

Exceptions to two-year rule. There are exceptions to this related-party rule. Second dispositions resulting from an involuntary conversion of the property will not be subject to the related-party rule so long as the first disposition occurred before the threat or imminence of conversion. Similarly, transfers after the death of the person making the first disposition or the death of the person acquiring the property in the first disposition are not treated as second dispositions. Also, a sale or exchange of stock to the issuing corporation is not treated as a first disposition. Finally, you may avoid tax on a related party's second sale by satisfying the IRS that neither the initial nor the second sale was made for tax avoidance purposes.

Sales of depreciable property to related party. Installment reporting is not allowed for sales of depreciable property made to a controlled corporation or partnership (50% control by seller) and between such controlled corporations and partnerships. In figuring control of a corporation, you are considered to own stock held by your spouse, children, grandchildren, brothers or sisters, parents, and grandparents. Installment reporting is also disallowed on a sale to a trust in which you or a spouse is a beneficiary unless your interest is considered a remote contingent interest whose actuarial value is 5% or less of the trust property's value. On these related-party sales, the entire gain is reported in the year of sale, unless the seller convinces the IRS that the transfer was not motivated by tax avoidance purposes.

On a sale of depreciable property to a related party, if the amounts of payments are contingent (for example, payments are tied to profits), the seller must make a special calculation. He or she must treat as received in the year of sale all noncontingent payments plus the fair market value of the contingent payments if such value may be reasonably ascertained. If the fair market value of the contingent payments may not be reasonably calculated, the seller recovers basis ratably. The purchaser's basis for the acquired property includes only amounts that the seller has included in income under the basis recovery rule. Thus, the purchaser's basis is increased annually as the seller recovers basis.

5.25 Contingent Payment Sales

Where the final selling price or payment period of an installment sale is not fixed at the end of the taxable year of sale, you are considered to have transacted a "contingent payment sale." Special rules apply where a maximum selling price may be figured under the terms of the agreement or there is no fixed price but there is a fixed payment period, or there is neither a fixed price nor a fixed payment period.

Stated maximum selling price. Under IRS regulations, a stated maximum selling price may be determined by assuming that all of the contingencies contemplated under the agreement are met. When the maximum amount is later reduced, the gross profit ratio is recomputed.

EXAMPLE

Smith sells stock in Acme Co. for a down payment of $100,000 plus an amount equal to 5% of the net profits of Acme for the next nine years. The contract provides that the maximum amount payable, including the $100,000 down payment but exclusive of interest, is $2,000,000. Smith's basis for the stock is $200,000; $2,000,000 is the selling price and contract price. Gross profit is $1,800,000. The gross profit ratio is 90% ($1,800,000 ÷ $2,000,000). Thus, $90,000 of the first payment is reportable as gain and $10,000 as a recovery of basis.

Fixed period. When a stated maximum selling price is not determinable but the maximum payment period is fixed, basis—including selling expenses—is allocated equally to the taxable years in which payment may be received under the agreement. If, in any year, no payment is received or the amount of payment received is less than the basis allocated to that taxable year, no loss is allowed unless the taxable year is the final payment year or the agreement has become worthless. When no loss is allowed in a year, the basis allocated to the taxable year is carried forward to the next succeeding taxable year.

EXAMPLE

Brown sells property for 10% of the property's gross rents over a five-year period. Brown's basis is $5,000,000. The sales price is indefinite and the maximum selling price is not fixed under the terms of the contract; basis is recovered ratably over the five-year period.

Year	Payment	Basis recovered	Gain
First	$ 1,300,000	$ 1,000,000	$ 300,000
Second	1,500,000	1,000,000	500,000
Third	1,400,000	1,000,000	400,000
Fourth	1,800,000	1,000,000	800,000
Fifth	2,100,000	1,000,000	1,100,000

No stated maximum selling price or fixed period. If the agreement fails to specify a maximum selling price and payment period, the IRS may view the agreement as a rent or royalty income agreement. However, if the arrangement qualifies as a sale, basis (including selling expenses) is recovered in equal annual increments over a 15-year period commencing with the date of sale. If in any taxable year no payment is received or the amount of payment received (exclusive of interest) is less than basis allocated to the year, no loss is allowed unless the agreement has become worthless. Excess basis not recovered in one year is reallocated in level amounts over the balance of the 15-year term. Any basis not recovered at the end of the 15th year is carried forward to the next succeeding year, and to the extent unrecovered, carried forward from year to year until basis has been recovered or the agreement is determined to be worthless. The rule requiring initial level allocation of basis over 15 years may not apply if you prove to the IRS that a 15-year general rule will substantially and inappropriately defer recovery of basis.

 Caution

Contingent Sales

An example of a contingent sale in which the selling price cannot be determined by the end of the year of the sale is a sale of your business where the selling price includes a pecentage of future profits. You and your tax advisor should consult the technical rules in IRS regulation 15A.453-1(c) for details on reporting such sales.

In some cases, basis recovery under an income forecast type of method may also be allowed.

Foreign currency. An installment sale with payments to be made in foreign currency or tangible payment units (such as bushels of wheat) is a contingent payment sale, but basis is allocated as if payment were fixed in U.S. dollars.

EXAMPLE

In 1998, Jones sells property for 10,000 English pounds. In 1999, 2,500 pounds are payable. In 2000, the balance of 7,500 pounds is payable. Basis in the property is $2,000. In 1999, 25% of the basis, or $500 (25% of $2,000), is allocated to the first payment. In 2000, $1,500 (75% of $2,000) is allocated to the second payment.

5.26 Using Escrow and Other Security Arrangements

You sell property and the sales proceeds are placed in escrow pending the possible occurrence of an event such as the approval of title or your performance of certain contractual conditions. The IRS may argue that installment reporting is not allowed unless there are escrow restrictions preventing immediate payment.

If the terms of the escrow involve no genuine conditions that prevent you from demanding immediate payment, there will be immediate tax. Substitution of an escrow account for unpaid notes or deeds of trust disqualifies installment reporting.

EXAMPLES

1. Anderson sold stock and mining property for almost $5 million. He agreed to place $500,000 in escrow to protect the buyer against his possible breaches of warranty and to provide security for certain liabilities. The escrow agreement called for Anderson to direct the investments of the escrow fund and receive income from the fund in excess of $500,000.

   The IRS claimed that in the year of sale Anderson was taxable on the $500,000 held in escrow on the ground that Anderson's control of the fund rendered the fund taxable immediately. Anderson argued he was only taxable as the funds were released to him, and the Tax Court agreed. The fund was not under his unqualified control. He might never get the fund if the liabilities materialized. Although Anderson had a free hand with investment of the money, he still lacked ultimate ownership.

2. Rhodes sold a tract to a buyer who was willing to pay at once the entire purchase price of $157,000. But Rhodes wanted to report the sale on the installment basis over a period of years. The buyer refused to execute a purchase money mortgage on the property to allow the installment sale election (required under prior law) because he wanted clear and unencumbered title to the tract. As a solution, Rhodes asked the buyer to turn over the purchase price to a bank, as escrow agent, which would pay the sum over a five-year period.

   The escrow arrangement failed to support an installment sale. Rhodes was fully taxable on the entire price in the year of the sale. The buyer's payment was unconditional and irrevocable. The escrow arrangement involved no genuine conditions that could defeat Rhodes's right to payment, as the buyer could not revoke, alter, or end the arrangement.

3. In January, an investor sold real estate for $100,000. He received $10,000 as a down payment and six notes, each for $15,000, secured by a deed of trust on the property. The notes, together with interest, were due annually over the next six years. In July, the buyer deposited the remainder of the purchase price with an escrow agent and got the seller to cancel the deed of trust.

   The agreement provides that the escrow agent will pay off the buyer's notes as they fall due. The buyer remains liable for the installment payments. The escrow deposit is irrevocable, and the payment schedule may not be accelerated by any party under any circumstances. According to the IRS, the sale, which initially qualified as an installment sale, is disqualified by the escrow account.

5.27 Minimum Interest on Deferred Payment Sales

The tax law requires a minimum amount of interest to be charged on deferred payment sales. The rules for imputing interest are discussed at *4.32*. Imputed interest is included in the taxable income of the seller. Imputed interest is deductible by the buyer if the property is business or investment property, but not if it is used substantially all the time for personal purposes.

Filing Tip

Installment Reporting on Escrow Allowable

If an escrow arrangement imposes a substantial restriction, the IRS may allow installment reporting. An example of a substantial restriction: Payment of the escrow is tied to the condition that the seller refrain from entering a competing business for a period of five years. If, at any time during the escrow period, he or she engages in a competing business, all rights to the amount then held in escrow would be forfeited.

Caution

Charging Minimum Interest

If you do not charge a minimum interest rate, the IRS may do so. This would require you and the buyer to treat part of the purchase price as interest.

5.28 Dispositions of Installment Notes

A sale, a gift, an exchange or other transfer or cancellation of mortgage notes or other obligations received in an installment sale has tax consequences. If you sell or exchange the notes or if you accept less than face value in satisfaction of the obligation, gain or loss results to the extent of the difference between the basis of the notes and the amount realized. For example, if in satisfaction of an installment note, the buyer gives you other property worth less than the face value of the note, you have gain (or loss) to the extent your amount realized exceeds (or is less than) your *basis* in the installment note. The basis of an installment note or obligation is the face value of the note less the income that would be reported if the obligation were paid in full; *see* Example 2 below.

Gain or loss is long term if the original sale was entitled to long-term capital gain treatment. This is true even if the notes were held short term. If the original sale resulted in short-term gain or ordinary income, the sale of the notes gives short-term gain or ordinary income, regardless of the holding period of the notes.

Suppose you make an installment sale of your real estate, taking back a land contract. Later a mortgage is substituted for the unpaid balance of the land contract. The IRS has ruled that the substitution is not the same as a disposition of the unpaid installment obligations. There is no tax on the substitution.

EXAMPLES

1. You sell a lot for $20,000 that cost you $10,000. In the year of the sale, you received $5,000 in cash and the purchaser's notes for the remainder of the selling price, or $15,000. A year later, before the buyer makes a payment on the notes, you sell them for $13,000 cash:

Selling price of property	$20,000
Cost of property	10,000
Total profit	$10,000
Profit percentage, or proportion of each payment returnable as income, is 50% ($10,000 total profit ÷ $20,000 contract price)	
Unpaid balance of notes	$15,000
Amount of income reportable if notes were paid in full (50% of $15,000)	7,500
Adjusted basis of the notes	$7,500

   Your profit on the sale is $5,500 ($13,000 – $7,500). It is capital gain if the sale of the lot was taxable as capital gain.

2. You sell a lot on the installment basis for $200,000 that cost you $120,000. In the year of sale, you received $20,000 in cash and the buyer's note for $180,000. Your gross profit percentage is 40% ($80,000 total profit ÷ $200,000 contract price).

   Two years later, the buyer is facing financial difficulties and is unable to make payments on the $180,000 note. In satisfaction of the installment note, the buyer agrees to give you two other parcels of real estate, each worth $50,000. By accepting less than the $180,000 face value of the note in satisfaction of the obligation, you realize an $8,000 capital loss; the difference between the amount you realize and your basis in the installment obligation is figured as follows:

Amount realized	$100,000
($50,000 for each parcel)	
Face value of note	180,000
Less: Amount of income reportable if note was paid in full given 40% profit percentage (40% of $180,000 = $72,000)	72,000
Basis in installment note	$108,000

   The difference between the $100,000 amount realized and $108,000 basis gives you an $8,000 loss. Assuming your profit on the original sale was long-term capital gain, the loss would be deducted as a long-term capital loss.

Gift of installment obligation. If the installment obligations are disposed of other than by sale or exchange, such as when you make a gift of the installment obligations to someone else, gain or loss is the difference between the basis of the obligations and their fair market value at the time of the disposition. If an installment obligation is *cancelled* or otherwise becomes unenforceable, the same rule for determining gain or loss applies.

 Filing Tip

Installment Notes in Marital Transfer

A transfer of installment obligations to your spouse or a transfer to a former spouse that is incident to a divorce is treated as a tax-free exchange under the rules discussed in *6.6* unless the transfer is in trust.

A gift of installment obligations to a person or charitable organization is treated as a taxable disposition. Gain or loss is the difference between the basis of the obligations and their fair market value at the time of the gift. If the notes are donated to a qualified charity, you may claim a contribution deduction for the fair market value of the obligations at the time of the gift.

Transfer at death. A transfer of installment obligations at the death of the holder of the obligation is not taxed as a disposition. As the notes are paid, the estate or beneficiaries report income in the same proportion as the decedent would have, had he or she lived. A transfer of installment obligations to a revocable trust is also not taxed. However, the estate is subject to tax if the obligation is cancelled, becomes unenforceable, or is transferred to the buyer because of the death of the obligation holder.

5.29 Repossession of Personal Property Sold on Installment

When a buyer defaults and you repossess personal property, either by a voluntary surrender or a foreclosure, you may realize gain or loss. The method of calculating gain or loss is similar to the method used for disposition of installment notes; see 5.28. Gain or loss is the difference between the fair market value of the repossessed property and your basis for the installment obligations satisfied by the repossession. This rule is followed whether or not title has been kept by you or transferred to the buyer. The amount realized is reduced by costs incurred during the repossession. The basis of the obligation is face value less unreported profit.

If the property repossessed is bid in at a lawful public auction or judicial sale, the fair market value of the property is presumed to be the purchase or bid price, in the absence of proof to the contrary.

Gain or loss in the repossession is reported in the year of the repossession.

EXAMPLE

In December 1998, you sell furniture for $1,500—$300 down and $100 a month plus 9% interest beginning January 1998. You reported the installment sale on your 1998 tax return. The buyer defaulted after making three monthly payments. You foreclosed and repossessed the property; the fair market value was $1,400. The legal costs of foreclosure were $100. The gain on the repossession in 1998 is computed as follows:

Fair market value of property repossessed		$ 1,400
Basis of the buyer's notes at time of repossession:		
Selling price	$ 1,500	
Less: Payments made	600	
Face value of notes at repossession	$ 900	
Less: Unrealized profit (assume gross profit percentage of 33⅓ × $900)	$ 300	
		600
Gain on repossession		$ 800
Less: Repossession costs		100
Taxable gain on repossession		$ 700

Repossession gain or loss keeps the same character as the gain or loss realized on the original sale. If the sale originally resulted in a capital gain, the repossession gain is also a capital gain.

Your basis in the repossessed property is its fair market value at the time of repossession.

Real property. Repossessions of real property are at *31.13*.

5.30 Boot in Like-Kind Exchange Payable in Installments

An exchange of like-kind property is tax free unless boot is received. "Boot" may be cash or notes. If you transfer property subject to a mortgage and the amount of the mortgage you give up exceeds the mortgage you assume on the property received, that excess is boot; see 6.3. Boot is taxable, and if payable in installments, the following rules apply. Contract price is reduced by the fair market value of like-kind property received. Gross profit is reduced by gain not recognized. "Payment" does not include like-kind property.

The same treatment applies to certain tax-free reorganizations that are not treated as dividends, to exchanges of certain insurance policies, exchanges of the stock of the same corporation, and exchanges of United States obligations.

In 1999, property with an installment sale basis (basis plus selling expenses) of $400,000 is exchanged for like-kind property worth $200,000, plus installment obligations of $800,000, of which $100,000 is payable in 2000, plus interest. The balance of $700,000 plus interest will be paid in 2001. The contract price is $800,000 ($1 million selling price less $200,000 like-kind property received). The gross profit is $600,000 ($1 million less $400,000 installment sale basis). The gross profit ratio is 75% (gross profit of $600,000 ÷ contract price of $800,000). Like-kind property is not treated as a payment received in the year of sale, so no gain is reported in 1999. In 2000, gain of $75,000 will have to be reported (75% gross profit ratio × $100,000 payment), and in 2001 there will be a gain of $525,000 (75% of $700,000 payment).

5.31 "Interest" Tax on Sales Over $150,000 plus $5 Million Debt

If deferred payments from installment sales of over $150,000 exceed $5 million, an interest charge is imposed on the tax-deferred amount. The special tax applies to sales of business or rental personal property as well as real estate for over $150,000.

Farm property and personal-use property, such as a residence, are exempt from the tax.

How to report interest tax. The interest charge is an additional tax. The method of computing the interest tax is complicated; the rules are in Internal Revenue Code Section 453A. In general, you compute the ratio of the face amount of outstanding installment obligations in excess of $5 million to the face amount of all outstanding installment obligations. This ratio is multiplied by the year-end unrecognized gain on the obligation, the top tax rate (currently 39.6%), and also by the IRS interest rate for the last month of the year.

The interest tax is reported on Line 56 of Form 1040, the line for total tax. The tax is considered personal interest, and is not deductible; *see* Chapter 15.

Pledge rule for property sales over $150,000. If as security for a debt you pledge an installment obligation received on a sale of property exceeding $150,000 (other than farm property or personal-use property), the net proceeds of the secured debt are treated as a payment on the installment obligations, as discussed at *5.22*.

Dealer sale of time shares and residential lots. The above interest tax and pledging rules do not apply to installment obligations from the sale of certain time-share rights (generally time shares of up to six weeks per year) or residential lots. However, under a separate rule, the seller must pay interest on tax deferred under the installment method; *see* the instructions to Schedule C of Form 1040 for reporting the interest charge as an additional tax.

Worthless Securities and Bad Debt Deductions

5.32 Worthless Securities

You may deduct as a capital loss on Schedule D the cost basis of securities that have become worthless in 1999. Capital loss treatment applies unless ordinary loss treatment is available for worthless Section 1244 stock; *see* Chapter 30.

A loss of worthless securities is deductible only in the year the securities become completely worthless. The loss may not be deducted in any other year. Because it is sometimes difficult to determine the year in which a security becomes completely worthless, the law allows you to file a refund claim within seven years from the due date of the return for the proper year (the year the security actually became completely worthless), or if later, within two years from the date you paid the tax for that year.

You may not claim a loss for partially worthless stock. However, if there is a market for it, sell the stock and deduct the loss.

To support a deduction for 1999, you must show:

1. The stock had some value in 1998. That is, you must be ready to show that the stock did not become worthless in a year prior to 1999. If you learn that the stock did become worthless in a prior year, file an amended return for that year; *see* the Filing Tip on refunds on the right.
2. The stock became totally worthless in 1999. You must be able to present facts fixing the time of loss during this year. For example, the company went bankrupt, stopped doing business, and is insolvent. Despite evidence of worthlessness, such as insolvency, the stock may be considered to have some value if the company continues to do business, or there are plans to reorganize the company. No deduction may be claimed for a partially worthless corporate bond.

Planning Reminder

Taxable Boot Received in Exchange

If you make an exchange of like-kind property and also receive cash or other property that is payable in one or more future years, you may report the gain using the installment method.

Filing Tip

Refund Deadline for Worthless Stock

You have seven years from the due date of your return to claim a refund based on a deduction of a bad debt or worthless security.

For example, if you have held securities that you learn became worthless in 1992, you still have until April 17, 2000, to file for a refund of 1992 taxes by claiming a deduction for the worthless securities on an amended return (Form 1040X) for 1992.

Selling Before the Security Becomes Worthless

To claim a deduction for worthless stock or bonds, you must be able to prove that the stock became completely worthless in the year for which you are claiming the deduction. Sometimes you can avoid the problem of proving worthlessness by selling while there is still a market for the security. For example, a company is on the verge of bankruptcy, but in 2000 there is some doubt about the complete worthlessness of its securities. You might sell the securities for whatever you can get for them and claim the loss on the sale. However, if the security became worthless in a prior year, say in 1999, a sale for a nominal sum in 2000 will not give you a deduction in 2000.

Accounts and Notes Receivable

You may claim a bad debt deduction for accounts and notes receivable on unpaid goods or services only if you have included the amount due as gross income. Thus, if a client or customer fails to pay a bill for services rendered, you do not have a deductible bad debt where you have not reported the amount as income; *see 40.6.*

If you are making payments on a negotiable note you used to buy the stock that became worthless and you are on the cash-basis method, your payments are deductible losses in the years the payments are made, rather than in the year the stock became worthless.

If the security is a bond, note, certificate, or other evidence of a debt incurred by a corporation, the loss is deducted as a capital loss, provided the obligation is in registered form or has attached interest coupons. A loss on a worthless corporate obligation is always deemed to have been sustained on the last day of the year, regardless of when the company failed during the year.

If the obligation is not issued with interest coupons or in registered form, or if it is issued by an individual, the loss is treated as a bad debt. If you received the obligation in a business transaction, the loss is fully deductible. You may also make a claim for a partially worthless business bad debt. If it is a nonbusiness debt, the loss is a capital loss and no claim may be made for partial worthlessness; *see 5.33.*

When to deduct worthless stock. If at the end of 1999 a company is in financial trouble but you are not sure whether its condition is hopeless, it is advisable to claim the deduction for 1999 to protect your claim. This advice was given by a court: "The taxpayer is at times in a very difficult position in determining in what year to claim a loss. The only safe practice, we think, is to claim a loss for the earliest year when it may possibly be allowed and to renew the claim in subsequent years if there is a reasonable chance of its being applicable for those years."

If you claim the deduction for 1999 and it turns out that complete worthlessness did not occur until a later year, claim the deduction for the proper year and then file an amended return for 1999 to eliminate the deduction.

Long-term or short-term loss. A sale is presumed to have occurred at the end of the year, regardless of when worthlessness actually occurred during the year.

EXAMPLE

You bought 100 shares of Z Co. stock on July 1, 1980. On March 16, 1999, the stock is considered wholly worthless. The loss is deemed to have been incurred on December 31, 1999. The loss is deducted as a long-term capital loss; the holding period is from July 2, 1980, to December 31, 1999.

Ordinary loss on Small Business Investment Company (SBIC) stock. On Form 4797, investors may take ordinary loss deductions for losses on the worthlessness or sale of SBIC stock. The loss may also be treated as a business loss for net operating loss purposes. However, a loss realized on a short sale of SBIC stock is deductible as a capital loss. A Small Business Investment Company is a company authorized to provide small businesses with equity capital. Do not confuse investments in these companies with investments in small business stock (Section 1244 stock) discussed at Chapter 30.

S corporation stock. If an S corporation's stock becomes worthless during the taxable year, the basis in the stock is adjusted for the stockholder's share of corporate items of income, loss, and deductions before a deduction for worthlessness is claimed.

Bank deposit loss. If you lose funds in a bank that becomes insolvent, you may claim the loss as a nonbusiness bad debt *(5.33)*, a casualty loss *(18.4)*, or in some cases, an investment expense *(19.24)*.

5.33 Tax Consequences of Bad Debts

When you lend money or sell on credit and your debtor does not repay, you may deduct your loss. The type of deduction depends on whether the debt was incurred in a business or personal transaction. This distinction is important because business bad debts receive favored tax treatment.

Business bad debt. A business bad debt is fully deductible from gross income on Schedule C if you are self-employed, or on Schedule F if your business is farming. In addition, you may deduct partially worthless business debts; *see 40.6* for details.

Nonbusiness bad debt. A nonbusiness bad debt is deducted as a short-term capital loss on Schedule D. This is a limited deduction. In 1999, you deduct it from capital gains, if any, and $3,000 of other income. Any excess is deductible as a capital loss carryover in 2000 and later years; *see 5.4.* You may not deduct partially worthless nonbusiness bad debts. The debt must be totally worthless.

Examples of nonbusiness bad debts:

- You enter into a deal for profit that is not connected with your business; for example, debts arising from investments are nonbusiness bad debts.

- You make a personal loan to a family member or friend with a reasonable hope of recovery and are not in the business of making loans.
- You are assigned a debt that arose in the assignor's business. The fact that he or she could have deducted it as a business bad debt does not make it your business debt. A business debt must arise in your business.
- You pay liens filed against your property by mechanics or suppliers who have not been paid by your builder or contractor. Your payment is considered a deductible bad debt when there is no possibility of recovering reimbursement from the contractor and a judgment obtained against him or her is uncollectible.
- You lose a deposit on a house when the contractor becomes insolvent.
- You loan money to a corporation in which you are a shareholder, and your primary motivation is to protect your investment rather than your job; *see 5.35.*
- You had an uninsured savings account in a savings association that went into default; *see 18.4.*
- You are held secondarily liable on a mortgage debt assumed but not paid by a buyer of your home. Your payment to the bank or other holder of the mortgage is deductible as a bad debt if you cannot collect it from the buyer of the home.

5.34 Four Rules To Prove a Bad Debt Deduction

To determine whether you have a bad debt deduction in 1999, read the four rules explained below. Pay close attention to the fourth rule, which requires proof that the debt became worthless in the year the deduction is claimed. Your belief that your debt is bad, or the mere refusal of the debtor to pay, is not sufficient evidence. There must be an event, such as the debtor's bankruptcy, to fix the debt as worthless.

Rule 1. You must have a valid debt. You have no loss if your right to repayment is not fixed or depends upon some event that may not happen. Thus, advances to a corporation already insolvent are not valid debts. Nor are advances that are to be repaid only if the corporation has a profit. Voluntary payment of another's debt is also nondeductible. If usurious interest was charged on a worthless debt, and under state law the debt was void or voidable, the debt is not deductible as a bad debt. However, where the lender was in the business of lending money, a court allowed him to deduct the unpaid amounts as business losses.

If advances are made to a company that has lost outside borrowing sources and is thinly capitalized, with heavy debt-to-equity ratio, this indicates that the advances are actually capital contributions and not loans.

Rule 2. A debtor-creditor relationship must exist at the time the debt arose. You have a loss if there was a promise to repay at the time the debt was created and you had the right to enforce it. If the advance was a gift and you did not expect to be repaid, you may not take a deduction. Loans to members of your family, to a controlled corporation, or to a trust may be treated as gifts or contributions to capital.

Rule 3. The funds providing the loan or credit were previously reported as income or part of your capital. If you are on the cash basis, you may not deduct unpaid salary, rent, or fees. On the cash basis, you do not include these items in income until you are paid.

Rule 4. You must show that the debt became worthless during 1999. To prove the debt became worthless in 1999, you must show:

First, that the debt had some value at the end of the previous year (1998), and that there was a reasonable hope and expectation of recovering something on the debt. Your personal belief unsupported by other facts is not enough.

Second, that an identifiable event occurred in 1999—such as a bankruptcy proceeding—that caused you to conclude the debt was worthless. In the case of a business debt that has become partially worthless, you need evidence that the debt has declined in value. Additionally, reasonable collection steps must have been undertaken. That you cancel a debt does not make it worthless. You must still show that the debt was worthless when you cancelled it. You do not have to go to court to try to collect the debt if you can show that a court judgment would be uncollectible.

Third, that there is no reasonable hope the debt may have some value in a later year. You are not required to prove that there is no possibility of ever receiving some payment on your debt.

Effect of statute of limitations. A debt is not deductible merely because a statute of limitations has run against the debt. Although the debtor has a legal defense against your demand for payment, he or she may still recognize the obligation to pay. A debt is deductible only in the year it becomes worthless. This event—for example, the debtor's insolvency—may have occurred even before the statute became effective. What if your debtor recognized his or her moral obligation to

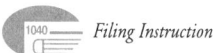
Filing Instruction

Nonbusiness Bad Debt
If a nonbusiness bad debt became totally worthless in 1999, claim it as a short-term capital loss in Part I of Schedule D. Attach a statement describing the loan, your relationship to the debtor, how you tried to collect it, and why you decided it was worthless.

Planning Reminder

Debt Worthless Before Due
You do not have to wait until the debt is due in order to deduct a bad debt. Claim the deduction for the year that you can prove worthlessness occurred.

pay in spite of the expiration of the statute of limitations, but dies before paying? Your claim would be defeated if the executor raises the statute of limitations. You have a bad debt deduction in the year you made the claim against the estate.

Guarantor or endorsement losses as bad debts. If you guarantee a loan and must pay it off after the principal debtor defaults, your payment is deductible as a business bad debt if you had a business reason for the guarantee. For example, to protect a business relationship with a major client, you guarantee the client's loan. Your payment on the guarantee qualifies as a business bad debt. If as a result of your payment, you have a legal right to recover the amount from the client (right of subrogation or similar right), you may not claim a bad debt deduction unless that right is partially or totally worthless.

A loss on a guarantee may be a nonbusiness bad debt if you made the guarantee to protect an investment, such as where you are a main shareholder of a corporation and guarantee a bank loan to the company. No deduction is allowed if you guaranteed the loan as a favor to a relative or friend. *Bank deposit losses are discussed at* 18.4.

5.35 Loans by Stockholders

Court Decision

Loan To Protect Job

A Supreme Court test requires a shareholder-employee claiming a business bad debt deduction to show that the primary and dominant motive of the loan was to protect his or her job, rather than investment in the company; *see* the Examples at *5.35.*

It is a common practice for stockholders to make loans to their corporations or to guarantee loans made by banks or other lenders. If the corporation fails and the stockholder is not repaid or has to make good on the guarantee, the stockholder is generally left with a nonbusiness bad debt (nonbusiness bad debts are deductible only as a short-term capital loss on Schedule D; *see* 5.33) unless he or she can prove that a business loan was made. To prove a business loan, the stockholder usually has to show one of these facts:

1. He or she is in the business of making loans and the loan was made in that capacity; or he or she is in the business of promoting corporations for a fee or for profits on their sale.
2. He or she wanted to protect his or her job with the company.

Self-employed individuals deduct business bad debts on Schedule C; *see 40.6.* Employee-stockholders who loan money to their corporations to keep their jobs may claim bad debt deductions for unpaid amounts only as miscellaneous itemized deductions subject to the 2% floor; *see 19.1.*

EXAMPLES

1. To determine an executive's motive for making a loan, the Supreme Court reviewed his salary, outside income, investment in the company, and the size of his loan. His pay was $12,000 ($7,000 after tax); his outside income was $30,000. He had a $38,900 investment in the company and loaned it $165,000. On the basis of these figures, the Court concluded he could not have advanced $165,000 to protect an after-tax salary of $7,000. He was protecting his investment, not his job, and only a nonbusiness bad debt could be claimed.

2. Litwin founded several energy start-up companies after he retired in 1974 from the Litwin Corporation. In 1980, he founded AFS, to which he made loans of $150,000 and guaranteed another $350,000 of loans. AFS went bankrupt in 1984.

   A federal appeals court followed the Supreme Court's approach (Example 1) to determine that Litwin had an employment-related motive for the loans. His primary reason for setting up the company was to stay employed and remain "useful" to society. Given his background and advanced age, his best chance for ongoing employment was to start his own company. The majority of his time and energy was spent on AFS, even after he sold his controlling interest in the corporation and had only limited opportunities to capitalize on his remaining investment. True, Litwin deferred his salary for three years, but evidence showed that he intended to draw a salary in the future. Most importantly, Litwin took a sizeable risk when he personally guaranteed loans that exceeded his investment in AFS. The court noted that a taxpayer is probably not attempting to protect an investment in a company when guaranteed loans far exceed the value of the investment.

Loan to key employees. A loan by a stockholder to key employees was held to be a business bad debt in the following case.

EXAMPLE

Carter, the president and majority owner of two corporations, loaned money to two key employees to buy stock in the corporations. He wanted to guarantee the employees' future participation in the company. Both corporations went bankrupt, and the employees defaulted on the loans. Carter deducted both loans as business bad debts, contending he was protecting his job.

The IRS argued he had a nonbusiness bad debt; he was merely protecting his investment as a stockholder. The Tax Court disagreed. He made the loans to encourage the future of a business that would provide him salary income rather than dividends or appreciation on his stock.

5.36 Family Bad Debts

The IRS views loans to relatives, especially to children and parents, as gifts, so that it is rather difficult to deduct family bad debts.

To overcome the presumption of a gift when you advance money to a relative, take the same steps you would in making a business loan. Take a note, set a definite payment date, and require interest and collateral. If the relative fails to pay, make an attempt to collect. Failure to enforce collection of a family debt is viewed by the courts as evidence of a gift, despite the taking of notes and the receipt of interest.

Husband's default on child support—a basis for wife's deductible bad debt? A wife who supports her children when her husband defaults on court-ordered support payments may consider claiming her expenses as a nonbusiness bad debt deduction, arguing that her position is similar to a guarantor who pays a creditor when the principal debtor defaults. The IRS does not agree with the grounds of such a claim and will disallow the deduction; its position is supported by the Tax Court.

The federal appeals court for the Ninth Circuit left open the possibility that such a claim may have merit if a wife can show: (1) what she spent on the children; and (2) that her husband's obligation to support was worthless in the year the deduction is claimed.

The Tax Court has subsequently reiterated its position that defaulted child support payments are not a basis for a bad debt deduction. Following these Tax Court decisions, the IRS also announced its continuing opposition to the Ninth Circuit's suggestion that a deduction may be possible. The IRS holds that since the support obligation of the defaulting spouse is imposed directly by the divorce court, the other parent who pays support to make up for the arrearage has no "basis" to support a bad debt deduction.

 Caution

Formalize Loan With Relative
To protect against a possible IRS claim that your loan was a gift and not a loan, put the loan in writing with repayment terms as if the debtor were a third party.

Chapter 6

Tax-Free Exchanges of Property

You may exchange property without incurring a tax in the year of exchange if you meet the rules of this chapter. Gain may be taxed upon a later disposition of the property because the basis of the property received in the exchange is usually the same as the basis of the property surrendered in the exchange. Thus, if you exchange property with a tax basis of $10,000 for property worth $50,000, the basis of the property received in exchange is fixed at $10,000, even though its fair market value is $50,000. The gain of $40,000 ($50,000 – $10,000), which is not taxed, is technically called "unrecognized gain." If you later sell the property for $50,000, you will realize a taxable gain of $40,000 ($50,000 – $10,000).

Where property received in a tax-free exchange is held until death, the unrecognized gain escapes income tax forever because basis of the property in the hands of an heir is generally the value of the property at the date of death. If the exchange involves the transfer of boot, such as cash or other property, gain on the exchange is taxable to the extent of the value of boot.

You may not exchange U.S. real estate for foreign real estate tax-free.

Tax-free exchanges between related parties may become taxable if either party disposes of the exchanged property within a two-year period.

6.1 Trades of Like-Kind Property

You may not have to pay tax on gain realized on the "like-kind" exchange of business or investment property. By making a qualifying exchange, you can defer the gain. For tax-free treatment, you must trade property held for business use or investment for like-kind business or investment property. If the properties are not simultaneously exchanged, the time limits discussed in *6.4* must be satisfied. Gain is *completely* tax free only if you do not receive any "boot"; as discussed in *6.3*, gain is taxed to the extent of boot received. Where gain on a qualifying exchange is deferred and not immediately taxed, it may be taxable in a later year when you sell the property because your basis for the new property is generally the same as the basis for the property you traded; basis is discussed at *5.16 – 5.20*.

If you make a qualifying like-kind exchange with certain related parties, tax-free treatment may be lost unless both of you keep the exchanged properties for at least two years; *see 6.5*.

The term *like-kind* refers to the nature or character of the property, that is, whether real estate is traded for real estate. It does not refer to grade or quality, that is, whether the properties traded are new or used, improved or unimproved. In the case of real estate, land may be traded for a building, farm land for city lots, or a leasehold interest of 30 years or more for an outright ownership in realty. Trades of personal property are discussed at *6.2*.

EXAMPLES

1. Jones, a real estate investor, purchased a parcel for investment in 1986 for $5,000. In 1997, he exchanged it for another parcel, Parcel B, which had a fair market value of $50,000. The gain of $45,000 was not taxed in 1997.
2. Same facts as above, except that in 1999 Jones sells Parcel B for $50,000. His taxable gain is $45,000. The "tax-free" rules have the effect of deferring tax on appreciation. Tax is finally imposed when the exchanged item is sold.
3. Same facts as in 1 above, but the value of Parcel B was $3,000 in 1997. Jones could not deduct the loss in 1997. The basis of the parcel is $5,000. If Jones sells Parcel B in 1999 for $3,000, he may deduct a loss of $2,000.

Losses. If a loss is incurred on a like-kind exchange, the loss is not deductible, whether you receive only like-kind property or "unlike" property together with like-kind property. However, a deductible loss may be incurred if you give up unlike property as part of the exchange; the loss equals any excess of the adjusted basis of the unlike property over its fair market value.

Reporting an exchange. You must file Form 8824 to report an exchange of like-kind property. If you figure a recognized gain or loss on Form 8824, you also must report the exchange on Schedule D (investment property) or Form 4797 (business property).

See 6.5 for reporting an exchange with a related party.

Property not within the tax-free trade rules:

Property used for personal purposes (except for exchanges of personal residences; *see* Chapter 29)
Foreign real estate
Property held for sale
Inventory or stock-in-trade
Securities
Notes
Partnership interest; *see* below

See also 31.3 for tax-free exchanges of realty and *6.11* for tax-free exchanges of insurance policies.

Exchange of partnership interests.
Exchanges of partnership interests in different partnerships are not within the tax-free exchange rules. Under IRS regulations, tax-free exchange treatment is denied regardless of whether the interests are in the same or different partnerships.

If you made an election to exclude a partnership interest from the application of partnership rules, your interest is treated as interest in each partnership asset, not as an interest in the partnership.

Real estate in foreign countries.
You may not make a tax-free exchange of U.S. real estate for foreign real estate. However, in the case of an involuntary conversion *(18.22)*, a tax-free reinvestment may be made in foreign real estate.

Law Alert

Personal Property Used Predominantly in U.S.

You may not make tax-free exchanges of personal property used predominantly in the U.S. for personal property used predominantly outside the U.S. This law applies to transfers after June 8, 1997, but an exception applies for transfers made under contracts binding as of June 8, 1997.

Caution

Exchanging Depreciable Realty Subject to Depreciation Recapture

Recapture provisions override tax-free exchange rules. Thus, if you exchange a depreciable building placed in service before 1987, check the consequences of any "recapture" element. For example, if you exchange the building for land, the recapture amount is fully taxable as ordinary income; *see 44.2*.

6.2 Personal Property Held for Business or Investment

An exchange of depreciable tangible personal property held for productive business or investment use may qualify for tax-free treatment if it meets either the general like-kind test of *6.1* or a more specific "like-class" test created by IRS regulations. The assumption of liabilities is treated as "boot"; *see 6.3*. Where each party assumes a liability of the other party, the respective liabilities are offset against each other to figure boot, if any.

Under the like-class test, there are two types of "like" classes: (1) General Asset Classes; and (2) Product Classes. The like-class test is satisfied if the exchanged properties are both within the same General Asset Class or the same Product Class. A specific asset may be classified within only one class. Thus, if an asset is within an Asset Class, it is not within a Product Class. The Asset Class or Product Class is determined as of the date of the exchange. This limitation may disqualify an exchange when exchanged assets do not fit within the same Asset Class and are not allowed to qualify within the Product Class; *see* the Brown Example below.

General Asset Classes. There are 13 classes of depreciable tangible business property. Here are some of the asset classifications: office furniture, fixtures, and equipment (class 00.11); information systems: computers and peripheral equipment (class 00.12); data handling equipment, except computers (class 00.13); airplanes and helicopters, except for airplanes used to carry passengers or freight (class 00.21); automobiles and taxis (class 00.22); light trucks (class 00.241); heavy trucks (class 00.242); and over-the-road tractor units (class 00.26). For example, trades of trucks in class 00.241 would be of like class.

Product Classes. Under a coding system of the Standard Industrial Classification (SIC) Manual, tangible depreciable assets are assigned a four-digit product-class number. For example, a grader is exchanged for a scraper. Neither item is within a General Asset Class, but both are in the same Product Class, SIC Code 3533. They are, therefore, of a like class.

EXAMPLES

1. Baker exchanges a personal computer used in his business for a printer. Both assets are productively used in business and are in the same General Asset Class of 00.12; the exchange meets the like-class test.

2. Brown exchanges an airplane (asset class 00.21) used in her business for a heavy truck (asset class 00.242). The exchanged properties are not of a like class. Furthermore, since each property is within a specific General Asset Class, the Product Class test may not be applied to qualify the exchange. Brown must report any gain realized on the exchange because the properties also do not meet the general like-kind test.

Intangible personal property and goodwill. Exchanges of intangible personal property (such as a patent or copyright) or nondepreciable personal property must meet the general like-kind test to qualify for tax-free treatment; the like-class tests do not apply. However, regulations close the door for qualifying exchanges of goodwill in an exchange of going businesses. According to the regulations, goodwill or going concern value of one business can never be of a like kind to goodwill or going concern value of another business.

Exchanges of multiple properties. Generally, exchanges of assets are considered on a one-to-one basis. Regulations provide an exception for exchanges of multiple properties, such as on an exchange of businesses. Transferred assets are separated into exchange groups. An exchange group consists of all properties transferred and received in the exchange that are of a like kind or like class. All properties within the same General Asset Class or same Product Class are in the same exchange group. For example, automobiles and computers are exchanged for other automobiles and computers; two exchange groups are set up—one for the automobiles and the other for the computers. If the aggregate fair market values of the properties transferred and received in each exchange group are not equal, the regulations provide calculations for setting up a residual group for purposes of calculating taxable gain, if any.

All liabilities of which a taxpayer is relieved in the exchange are offset against all liabilities assumed by the taxpayer in the exchange, regardless of whether the liabilities are recourse, nonrecourse, or are secured by the specific property transferred or received. If excess liabilities are assumed by the taxpayer as part of the exchange, regulations provide rules for allocating the excess among the properties.

Planning Reminder

The "Like-Class" Test

To qualify for tax-free treatment, depreciable tangible property held for productive business or investment use does not need to satisfy the "like-kind" test. The exchanged properties only need to be like in "class." This test is satisfied if the exchanged properties are both within the same General Asset Class or the same Product Class; *see 6.2*. The Asset Class or Product Class is determined at the time of transfer.

6.3   Receipt of Cash and Other Property—"Boot"

If, in addition to like-kind *(6.1)* property, you receive cash or other property (unlike kind), gain is taxable up to the amount of the cash or other property received. The additional cash or other property is called "boot." If a loss was incurred on the exchange, the receipt of boot does not permit you to deduct the loss unless it is attributable to *unlike*-kind property you gave up in the exchange.

If you transfer mortgaged property, the amount of the mortgage is part of your boot. If both you and the other party transfer and receive mortgaged property, the party giving up the larger debt treats the excess as taxable boot. The party giving up the smaller debt does not have boot; *see also 31.3*. If you pay cash to the other party, add this to the mortgage you receive in figuring which party has given up the larger debt.

Form 8824. The computation of boot, gain (or loss), and basis of the property received is made on Form 8824.

Caution

Deducting a Loss

You may deduct a loss incurred on an exchange if it is attributable to unlike property *transferred* in the exchange. The loss is recognized to the extent that the basis of the unlike property (other than cash) transferred exceeds its fair market value. However, a loss is not recognized if the unlike property is *received* together with the like-kind property in the exchange. Such a loss is *not* deductible.

EXAMPLE

Jones owns an apartment house with a fair market value of $220,000, subject to an $80,000 mortgage. His adjusted basis is $100,000. Jones exchanges his building for Smith's apartment building, which has a value of $250,000, subject to a $150,000 mortgage. Jones also receives $40,000 in cash. Smith's adjusted basis for the building he trades is $175,000. Smith and Jones each pay $5,000 in exchange expenses.

The sample Forms 8824 for Jones and Smith on the next page show how they report the exchange. On Line 15, they show the boot received; their taxable gain is limited to this boot. For Jones, boot is the $40,000 in cash received. The $80,000 in liabilities transferred to Smith is not included because it does not exceed the $150,000 of liabilities Jones assumed. For Smith, the Line 15 boot is $30,000:

Mortgage transferred	$150,000
Less: Mortgage assumed	(80,000)
Less: Cash paid	(40,000)
	$30,000

On Line 18, Jones and Smith increase their basis for the buildings they traded by exchange expenses and the net amounts paid to the other party. For Jones, the Line 18 total of $175,000 includes:

Adjusted basis of building traded		$100,000
Plus: Exchange expenses		5,000
Plus: Net mortgage assumed:		
Mortgage assumed	$150,000	
Less: Mortgage transferred	80,000	70,000
	70,000	$175,000

For Smith, the Line 18 total of $180,000 includes:

Adjusted basis of building traded		$175,000
Plus: Exchange expenses		5,000
Plus: Net amount paid:		
Mortgage assumed	$80,000	
Plus: Cash paid	40,000	
Less: Mortgage transferred	(150,000)	0
	(30,000)	$180,000

The liabilities Smith assumed and the cash he paid are not included on Line 18 because their total does not exceed the $150,000 of liabilities he transferred to Jones.

Line 25 shows the basis of the buildings Jones and Smith received in the exchange.

6.4   Time Limits for Deferred Exchanges

Assume you own property that has appreciated in value. You want to sell it and reinvest the proceeds in other property, but you would like to avoid having to pay tax on the appreciation. You can avoid the tax if you are able to arrange an exchange for similar property.

The problem is that it may be difficult to find a buyer who has property you want in exchange, and the time for closing the exchange is restricted. If IRS tests are met, intermediaries and security arrangements may be used without running afoul of constructive receipt rules that could trigger an immediate tax.

Sample Form 8824 for Jones (see Example on previous page)

Part III	**Realized Gain or (Loss), Recognized Gain, and Basis of Like-Kind Property Received**

Caution: *If you transferred and received (a) more than one group of like-kind properties, or (b) cash or other (not like-kind) property, see Reporting of multi-asset exchanges in the instructions.*

Note: *Complete lines 12 through 14 ONLY if you gave up property that was not like-kind. Otherwise, go to line 15.*

12	Fair market value (FMV) of other property given up	**12**	
13	Adjusted basis of other property given up	**13**	
14	Gain or (loss) recognized on other property given up. Subtract line 13 from line 12. Report the gain or (loss) in the same manner as if the exchange had been a sale	**14**	
15	Cash received, FMV of other property received, plus net liabilities assumed by other party, reduced (but not below zero) by any exchange expenses you incurred. See instructions	**15**	**40,000**
16	FMV of like-kind property you received	**16**	**250,000**
17	Add lines 15 and 16	**17**	**290,000**
18	Adjusted basis of like-kind property you gave up, net amounts paid to other party, plus any exchange expenses **not** used on line 15. See instructions	**18**	**175,000**
19	**Realized gain or (loss).** Subtract line 18 from line 17	**19**	**115,000**
20	Enter the smaller of line 15 or line 19, but not less than zero	**20**	**40,000**
21	Ordinary income under recapture rules. Enter here and on Form 4797, line 16. See instructions .	**21**	**- 0 -**
22	Subtract line 21 from line 20. If zero or less, enter -0-. If more than zero, enter here and on Schedule D or Form 4797, unless the installment method applies. See instructions	**22**	**40,000**
23	**Recognized gain.** Add lines 21 and 22	**23**	**40,000**
24	Deferred gain or (loss). Subtract line 23 from line 19. If a related party exchange, see instructions .	**24**	**75,000**
25	**Basis of like-kind property received.** Subtract line 15 from the sum of lines 18 and 23 . .	**25**	**175,000**

For Paperwork Reduction Act Notice, see back of form.   Cat. No. 12311A   Form **8824** (1999)

Sample Form 8824 for Smith (see Example on previous page)

Part III	**Realized Gain or (Loss), Recognized Gain, and Basis of Like-Kind Property Received**

Caution: *If you transferred and received (a) more than one group of like-kind properties, or (b) cash or other (not like-kind) property, see Reporting of multi-asset exchanges in the instructions.*

Note: *Complete lines 12 through 14 ONLY if you gave up property that was not like-kind. Otherwise, go to line 15.*

12	Fair market value (FMV) of other property given up	**12**	
13	Adjusted basis of other property given up	**13**	
14	Gain or (loss) recognized on other property given up. Subtract line 13 from line 12. Report the gain or (loss) in the same manner as if the exchange had been a sale	**14**	
15	Cash received, FMV of other property received, plus net liabilities assumed by other party, reduced (but not below zero) by any exchange expenses you incurred. See instructions	**15**	**30,000**
16	FMV of like-kind property you received	**16**	**220,000**
17	Add lines 15 and 16	**17**	**250,000**
18	Adjusted basis of like-kind property you gave up, net amounts paid to other party, plus any exchange expenses **not** used on line 15. See instructions	**18**	**180,000**
19	**Realized gain or (loss).** Subtract line 18 from line 17	**19**	**70,000**
20	Enter the smaller of line 15 or line 19, but not less than zero	**20**	**30,000**
21	Ordinary income under recapture rules. Enter here and on Form 4797, line 16. See instructions .	**21**	**- 0 -**
22	Subtract line 21 from line 20. If zero or less, enter -0-. If more than zero, enter here and on Schedule D or Form 4797, unless the installment method applies. See instructions	**22**	**30,000**
23	**Recognized gain.** Add lines 21 and 22	**23**	**30,000**
24	Deferred gain or (loss). Subtract line 23 from line 19. If a related party exchange, see instructions .	**24**	**40,000**
25	**Basis of like-kind property received.** Subtract line 15 from the sum of lines 18 and 23 . .	**25**	**180,000**

For Paperwork Reduction Act Notice, see back of form.   Cat. No. 12311A   Form **8824** (1999)

Time limits for completing exchanges. You generally have up to 180 days to complete an exchange, but the period may be shorter. Specifically, property will not be treated as like-kind property if received (1) more than 180 days after the date you transferred the property you are relinquishing or (2) after the due date of your return (including extensions) for the year in which you made the transfer, whichever is earlier. Furthermore, the property to be received must be identified within 45 days after the date on which you transferred property.

If the transaction involves more than one property, the 45-day identification period and the 180-day exchange period are determined by the earliest date on which any property is transferred. When the identification or exchange period ends on a Saturday, Sunday, or legal holiday, the deadline is not advanced to the next business day (as it is when the deadline for filing a tax return is on a weekend or holiday).

How to identify property. You must identify replacement property in a written document signed by you and either hand delivered, mailed, telecopied, or otherwise sent before the end of the 45-day identification period to a person involved in the exchange other than yourself or a related party. The identification may also be made in a written agreement. The property must be unambiguously described by a legal description or street address.

You may identify more than one property as replacement property. However, the maximum number of replacement properties that you may identify without regard to the fair market value is three properties. You may identify any number of properties provided the aggregate fair market value at the end of the 45-day identification period does not exceed 200% of the aggregate fair market value of all the relinquished properties as of the date you transferred them. If, as of the end of the identification period, you have identified more than the allowable number of properties, you are generally treated as if no replacement property has been identified.

Receipt of security. In a deferred exchange, you want financial security for the buyer's performance and compensation for delay in receiving property. To avoid immediate tax, you must not make a security arrangement that gives you an unrestricted right to funds before the deal is closed.

 Caution

Strict Time Limits

No extensions of time are allowed if the 45-day or 180-day statutory deadlines cannot be met. If extra time is needed for finding suitable replacement property, it is advisable to delay the date of your property transfer because the transfer date starts the 45-day identification period.

EXAMPLE

You and Jones agree to enter a deferred exchange under the following terms and conditions. On May 17, 1999, you transfer to Jones real estate that has been held for investment; it is unencumbered and has a fair market value of $100,000. On or before July 1, 1999 (the end of the 45-day identification period), you must identify like-kind replacement property. On or before November 13, 1999 (the end of the 180-day exchange period), Jones is required to buy the property and transfer it to you. At any time after May 17, 1999, and before Jones has purchased the replacement property, you have the right, upon notice, to demand that he pay you $100,000 instead of acquiring and transferring the replacement property. However, you identify replacement property, and Jones purchases and transfers it to you. According to the regulations, you have an unrestricted right to demand the payment of $100,000 as of May 17, 1999. You are therefore in constructive receipt of $100,000 on that date. Thus, the transaction is treated as a taxable sale, and the transfer of the real property does not qualify as a tax-free exchange. You are treated as if you received the $100,000 for the sale of your property and then purchased replacement property.

Safe harbor tests for security arrangements. If one of the following safe harbors applies to your security arrangement, you are not taxed as if a sale were made.

The first two "safe harbors" cover transfers dealing directly with the buyer. The third allows the use of professional intermediaries who, for a fee, arrange the details of the exchange. The fourth allows you to earn interest on an escrow account. The safe harbors generally prohibit you from receiving money or other non–like-kind property before replacement property is received. The terms of the agreement govern whether your right to receive the funds is limited as required by the safe harbor rules; possible state law complications are disregarded.

1. The transferee may give you a mortgage, deed of trust, or other security interest in property (other than cash or a cash equivalent), or a third-party guarantee. A standby letter of credit may be given if you are not allowed to draw on such standby letter except upon a default of the transferee's obligation to transfer like-kind replacement property.
2. The transferee may put cash or a cash equivalent in a qualified escrow account or a qualified trust. The escrow holder or trustee must not be related to you. Your rights to receive, pledge, borrow, or otherwise obtain the cash must be limited. For example, you may obtain the cash after all of the replacement property to which you are entitled is received. After you identify replacement property, you may obtain the cash after the later of (1) the end of the identification period and (2) the occurrence of a contingency beyond your control that you have specified in writing. You may receive the

funds after the end of the identification period if within that period you do not identify replacement property. In other cases, there can be no right to the funds until the exchange period ends.

3. You may use a *qualified intermediary* if your right to receive money or other property is limited (as discussed in safe harbor rule 2, above). A qualified intermediary is an unrelated party who, for a fee, acts to facilitate a deferred exchange by entering into an agreement with you for the exchange of properties pursuant to which the intermediary acquires your property from you, acquires the replacement property, and transfers the replacement property to you. The acquisitions may be on the intermediary's own behalf or as the agent of any party to the transaction.

   The transfer of property that is facilitated by the use of a qualified intermediary may occur through a "direct deed" of legal title by the current owner of the property to you. The transferee of your property does *not* have to receive title to the property you want and then transfer it to you.

   There are restrictions on who may act as an intermediary. You may not employ any person as an intermediary who is your employee or is related to you or has generally acted as your professional adviser, such as an attorney, accountant, investment broker, real estate agent, or banker, in a two-year period preceding the exchange. Related parties include family members and controlled businesses or trusts *(see 5.6)*, except that for purposes of control, a 10% interest is sufficient under the intermediary rule. The performance of routine financial, escrow, trust, or title insurance services by a financial institution or title company within the two-year period is not taken into account. State laws that may be interpreted as fixing an agency relationship between the transferor and transferee or fixing the transferor's right to security funds are ignored.

   In a simultaneous exchange, the intermediary is not considered the transferor's agent.

4. You are permitted to receive interest or a "growth factor" on escrowed funds if your right to receive the amount is limited as discussed under safe harbor rule 2.

Payment of acquisition and closing costs. The use of funds from a security account to pay specific acquisition and closing costs such as commissions, prorated taxes, and recording and transfer fees will not result in constructive receipt of the remaining funds.

6.5 Exchanges Between Related Parties

Tax-free treatment of like-kind exchanges between related persons may be lost if either party disposes of property received in the exchange within two years after the date of the last transfer that was part of the exchange. Any gain not recognized on the original exchange is taxable as of the date of the later disposition of the original like-kind property by either party within the two-year period. If a loss was not recognized, the loss becomes deductible if allowed under the rules in *5.6*. This two-year rule does not apply to transfers made under a written binding contract that was in effect on and after July 10, 1989, or to the exceptions listed below.

Indirect dispositions of the property within the two-year period, such as transfer of stock of a corporation or interests in a partnership that owns the property, may also be treated as taxable dispositions.

Related parties. Related persons falling within the two-year rule include your children, grandchildren, parent, brother, or sister, controlled corporations or partnerships (more than 50% ownership), and a trust in which you are a beneficiary. A transfer to a spouse is not subject to the two-year rule unless he or she is a nonresident alien.

Plan to avoid two-year rule. If you set up a prearranged plan under which you first transfer property to an unrelated party who within two years makes an exchange with a party related to you, the related party will not qualify for tax-free treatment on that exchange.

Exceptions. No tax will be incurred on a disposition made because of death; in an involuntary conversion provided the original exchange occurred before the threat of the conversion; or if you can prove that neither the exchange nor the later disposition was for a tax avoidance purpose.

6.6 Property Transfers Between Spouses and Ex-Spouses

All transfers between spouses are tax-free, *other* than transfers to a nonresident alien spouse, certain trust transfers of mortgaged property, and transfers of U.S. Savings Bonds; these exceptions are discussed below. The tax-free exchange rules apply to transfers during marriage as well as to property settlements incident to a divorce. A transfer is "incident to a divorce" if it occurs either within one year after the date the marriage ceases or, if later, is related to the cessation of the marriage, such as a transfer authorized by a divorce decree. Under temporary regulations, any transfer pursuant to a divorce or separation agreement occurring within six years of the end of the marriage is considered "incident to a divorce." Later transfers qualify only if a transfer within the six-year period was hampered by legal or business disputes such as a fight over the property value.

Nonresident alien. The tax-free exchange rule does not apply to transfers to a nonresident alien spouse or former spouse. A transfer before June 22, 1988, to a former spouse who was a nonresident alien was subject to the tax-free exchange rule if the transfer was "incident to a divorce."

EXAMPLES

1. In a property settlement accompanying a divorce, a husband plans to transfer to his wife stock worth $250,000 that cost him $50,000. In deciding whether to agree to the transfer, the wife should be aware that her basis for the stock will be $50,000; if she sells the stock, she will have to pay tax on the $200,000 gain. This tax cost should be accounted for in arriving at the settlement.

2. Basis of the property in the hands of the transferee-spouse is not increased even if cash is paid as part of the transfer. For example, a husband received a house originally owned by the wife as part of a marital settlement. Her basis for the house was $32,200. He paid her $18,000 cash as part of the settlement and when he later sold the house for $64,000, he argued that his basis for purposes of computing profit was $50,200—the wife's $32,200 basis plus his $18,000 cash payment. The IRS refused to consider the cash payment as part of basis, and the Tax Court agreed that the carryover basis rule applies.

Is a divorce-related redemption of stock in a closely held corporation subject to the tax-free exchange rules?

The IRS has consistently disputed tax-free treatment for a spouse whose closely held corporation's stock is redeemed as part of an overall divorce settlement. The IRS argues that a stock redemption between one spouse and a closely held corporation results in a taxable sale and does not fall within the exception for transfers to third parties, discussed in the Planning Reminder on the right. To hedge against the possibility that a court may rule against the position that the redeeming spouse should be taxed on the proceeds, the IRS will maintain a fallback position: If the redeeming spouse is not taxable, the nonredeeming shareholder should be treated as having received a taxable constructive dividend as a result of the redemption.

EXAMPLES

1. The IRS position that a closely held corporation's redemption of one spouse's stock is taxable was rejected by a federal district court and the Ninth Circuit Court of Appeals, which held that a wife was not taxable on the redemption of her stock by the couple's closely held corporation where the redemption was pursuant to their divorce agreement and incorporated into the divorce decree. The Ninth Circuit viewed the transfer as if the husband had received the stock directly from the wife and then transferred it to the company.

   After the Ninth Circuit held that the redemption was not taxable to the wife, the IRS argued in a separate case against the nonredeeming husband that he received a taxable constructive dividend. However, the Tax Court disagreed, holding that there was no dividend to the husband because under state law he was merely a guarantor; he was not primarily and unconditionally obligated to buy the stock. The IRS did not appeal the Tax Court decision.

   In this unusual case, the IRS is in the position of being unable to collect tax on the redemption proceeds from either the transferor or transferee spouse.

2. The Tax Court refused to follow the Ninth Circuit decision referred to in Example 1 and denied tax-free treatment to a redeeming spouse although the redemption was required by the divorce decree. The Tax Court held that the redemption did not satisfy an obligation of the nonredeeming spouse, and thus it was not paid on his behalf.

   Relevant differences between this case and the one in Example 1 include the facts that in the first case, the corporation was a franchise that the parent required to have only one owner, that the nonredeeming spouse personally guaranteed the corporation's obligation, and that the matter arose in a community property state.

3. A federal district court allowed tax-free treatment of a wife's stock redemption, following the Ninth Circuit decision referred to in Example 1. The husband personally guaranteed the notes paying for the redemption, which was sufficient proof that the redemption satisfied his obligation to divide the marital property under state law, considering that the corporation was closely held, that he was the dominant shareholder and officer, and that he guaranteed the note due to his wife's attempt to force the sale and division of the corporate assets pursuant to the divorce.

   However, interest on the corporation's note to the wife was imputed under original issue discount rules, which applied because the corporation was paying for stock over several years without paying any stated interest. The court held that this interest was taxable to the wife. Although the underlying obligation did not give rise to a tax, this did not preclude taxation of the interest imputed to the redemption agreement.

Planning Reminder

Recipient Spouse Bears Tax Consequences

Under the tax-free exchange rules, there is no taxable gain or deductible loss on the transfer of property, even if cash is received for the property or the other spouse (or former spouse) assumes liabilities or gives up marital rights as part of a property settlement. The spouse who receives property may incur tax on a later sale because his or her basis in the property is the same as the transferor-spouse's basis; *see* the Examples on the left. Because the transferee bears the tax consequences of a later sale, he or she should consider the potential tax on the appreciation in negotiating a marital settlement. In a marital settlement, the transferee spouse can lessen the tax burden by negotiating for assets that have little or no unrealized appreciation.

Planning Reminder

Transfers to Third Parties

A transfer to a third party on behalf of a spouse or former spouse qualifies for tax-free exchange treatment where the transfer is required by a divorce or separation instrument, or if you have your spouse's or former spouse's written request or consent for the transfer. The transfer is treated as if made to your spouse or former spouse, who then retransfers the property to the third party. A written request or consent must specifically state that the tax-free exchange rules of Code Section 1041 are intended, and you must receive it before filing the tax return for the year of the transfer; *but see* divorce-related stock redemption on this page.

Transfers of U.S. Savings Bonds. The IRS has ruled that the tax-free exchange rules do not apply to transfers of U.S. Savings Bonds. For example, if a husband has deferred the reporting of interest on E or EE bonds and transfers the bonds to his ex-wife as part of a divorce settlement, the deferred interest is taxed to him on the transfer. The wife's basis for the bonds is the husband's basis plus the income he realizes on the transfer. When she redeems the bonds, she will be taxed on the interest accrued from the date of the transfer to the redemption date.

Payment for release of community property interest in retirement pay. The Tax Court allowed tax-free treatment for a payment made to a wife for releasing her community property claim to her husband's military retirement pay. The IRS had argued that the tax-free exchange rules discussed in this section did not apply to the release of rights to retirement pay that would otherwise be subject to ordinary income tax. The Tax Court disagreed, holding that the tax-free exchange rule applies whether the transfer is for relinquishment of marital rights, cash, or other property.

Transfers in trust. The tax-free exchange rules generally apply to transfers in trust for the benefit of a spouse or a former spouse if incident to a divorce. However, if the trust property is mortgaged, the transferor spouse must report a taxable gain to the extent that the liabilities assumed by the transferee spouse plus the liabilities to which the property is subject (even if not assumed) exceed the transferor's adjusted basis for the property. If the transferor realizes a taxable gain under this rule, the transferee's basis for the property is increased by the gain.

Sole proprietorship sale to spouse. Tax-free exchange rules may apply to a sale of business property by a sole proprietor to a spouse. The buyer spouse assumes a carryover basis even if fair market value is paid. The transferor is not required to recapture previously claimed depreciation deductions or investment credits. However, the transferee is subject to the recapture rules on premature dispositions or if the property ceases to be used for business purposes.

Agreements existing on July 18, 1984. The tax-free exchange rules generally apply to transfers made after July 18, 1984. Transfers made under agreements in effect before July 19, 1984, are subject to the tax-free rule only if both spouses make an election to have the tax-free rule apply. The election must be made on a signed statement attached to the first tax return filed by the transferor-spouse for the year in which the first transfer occurs. The transferor must also attach the statement to returns for later years in which a transfer is made under the election.

6.7 Tax-Free Exchanges of Stock

Gain on the exchange of common stock for other common stock (or preferred for other preferred of the same company) is not taxable. Similarly, loss realized on such an exchange is not deductible. The exchange may take place between the stockholder and the company or between two stockholders.

An exchange of preferred stock for common, or common for preferred, in the same company is generally not tax free, unless the exchange is part of a tax-free recapitalization. In such exchanges, the company should inform you of the tax consequences.

Convertible securities. Conversion of securities under a conversion privilege is tax free under the rules discussed at *30.7*.

6.8 Joint Ownership Interests

The change to a tenancy in common from a joint tenancy is tax free. You may convert a joint tenancy in corporate stock to a tenancy in common without income-tax consequences. The transfer is tax free even though survivorship rights are eliminated. Similarly, a partition and issuance of separate certificates in the names of each joint tenant is also tax free.

A joint tenancy and a tenancy in common differ in this respect. On the death of a joint tenant, ownership passes to the surviving joint tenant or tenants. But on the death of a tenant holding property in common, ownership passes to his or her heirs, not to the other tenant or tenants with whom the property was held.

A tenancy by the entirety is a form of joint ownership recognized in some states and can be only between a husband and wife.

Dividing properties held in common. A division of properties held as tenants in common may qualify as tax-free exchanges.

For example, three men owned three pieces of real estate as tenants in common. Each man wanted to be the sole owner of one of the pieces of property. They disentangled themselves by exchanging

Caution

Trust Transfer of Leveraged Property
You will not be able to avoid gain on heavily mortgaged property transferred to a trust for your spouse or to a former spouse under a divorce decree. The excess of the liabilities on the property over your adjusted basis is taxable gain.

interests in a three-way exchange. No money or property other than the three pieces of real estate changed hands, and none of the men assumed the others' liability. The transactions qualified as tax-free exchanges and no gain or loss was recognized.

Receipt of boot. Exchanges of jointly owned property are tax free as long as no "boot," such as cash or other property, passes between the parties; *see 6.3.*

6.9 Setting up Closely Held Corporations

Tax-free exchange rules facilitate the organization of a corporation. When you transfer property to a corporation that you control solely in exchange for corporate stock, no gain or loss is recognized on the transfer. For control, you alone or together with other transferors (such as partners, where a partnership is being incorporated) must own at least 80% of the combined voting power of the corporation and 80% of all other classes of stock immediately after the transfer to the corporation. If you receive securities in addition to stock, the securities are treated as taxable "boot." The corporation takes your basis in the property, and your basis in the stock received in the exchange is the same as your basis in the property. Gain not recognized on the organization of the corporation may be taxed when you sell your stock, or the corporation disposes of the property.

EXAMPLE

You transfer a building worth $100,000, which cost you $20,000, to your newly organized corporation in exchange for all of its outstanding stock. You realize an $80,000 gain ($100,000 – $20,000) that is not recognized. Your basis in the stock is $20,000; the corporation's basis in the building is $20,000. The following year, you sell all your stock to a third party for $100,000. The $80,000 gain is now recognized.

Transfer of liabilities. When assets subject to liabilities are transferred to the corporation, the liability assumed by the corporation is not treated as taxable "boot," but your stock basis is reduced by the amount of liability. The transfer of liabilities may be taxable when the transfer is part of a tax avoidance scheme, or the liabilities exceed the basis of the property transferred to the corporation.

6.10 Exchanges of Coins and Bullion

An exchange of "gold for gold" coins or "silver for silver" coins may qualify as a tax-free exchange of like-kind investment property. An exchange is tax free if both coins represent the same type of underlying investment. An exchange of bullion-type coins for bullion-type coins is a tax-free like-kind exchange. For example, the exchange of Mexican pesos for Austrian coronas has been held to be a tax-free exchange as both are bullion-type coins.

However, an exchange of silver bullion for gold bullion is not tax free. Silver and gold bullion represent different types of property. Silver is an industrial commodity, whereas gold is primarily an investment in itself. Similarly, an exchange of U.S. gold collector's coins for South African Krugerrands is taxable. Krugerrands are bullion-type coins whose value is determined solely by metal content, whereas the U.S. gold coins are numismatic coins whose value depends on age, condition, number minted, and artistic merit, as well as metal content. Although both coins appear to be similar in gold content, each represents a different type of investment.

6.11 Tax-Free Exchanges of Insurance Policies

These exchanges of insurance policies are considered tax free:

Life insurance policy for another life insurance policy, endowment policy, or an annuity contract.
Endowment policy for another endowment policy that provides for regular payments beginning no later than the date payments would have started under the old policy, or in exchange for an annuity contract.
Annuity contract for another annuity contract with identical annuitants.

These exchanges are not tax free:

Endowment policy for a life insurance policy, or for another endowment policy that provides for payments beginning at a date later than payments would have started under the old policy.
Annuity contract for a life insurance or endowment policy.
Transfers of life insurance contracts where the insured is not the same person in both contracts. The IRS held that a company could not make a tax-free exchange of a key executive policy where the company could change insured executives as they leave or join the firm.

 Caution

Consider Taxable Transfer
Before making a property transfer to a closely held corporation, consult an accountant or an attorney on the tax consequences. It may not be to your advantage to fall within the tax-free exchange rules. This is so when you have property with potential losses or you wish the corporation to take a stepped-up basis for property.

 Planning Reminder

Financially Troubled Insurer
If your annuity contract or insurance policy is with an insurance company that is in a rehabilitation, conservatorship, insolvency, or a similar state proceeding, you may surrender the policy and make a tax-free reinvestment of the proceeds in a new policy with a different insurance company. The transfer must be completed within 60 days. If a government agency does not allow you to withdraw your entire balance from the troubled insurance company, you must assign all rights to any future distributions to the issuer of the new contract or policy. Full details are in IRS Revenue Procedure 92-44.

Chapter 7

Retirement and Annuity Income

Retirement planning may be the final frontier for achieving substantial tax shelter benefits. For employees, coverage in a qualified employer retirement plan is a valuable fringe benefit, as employer contributions are tax free within specified limits. Certain salary-reduction plans allow you to make elective deferrals of salary that are not subject to income tax. An advantage of all qualified retirement plans is that earnings accumulate tax free until withdrawal.

Along with tax savings opportunities come technical restrictions and pitfalls. For example, retirement plan distributions eligible for rollover are subject to a mandatory 20% withholding tax if you do not instruct your employer to make a direct trustee-to-trustee transfer of the distribution to an IRA or another qualified employer plan.

This chapter discusses tax treatment of annuities and employer plan distributions, including how to avoid tax penalties, such as for distributions before age 59 $\frac{1}{2}$. IRAs are discussed in Chapter 8. Retirement plans for self-employed individuals are discussed further in Chapter 41.

Key to Tax-Favored Retirement Plans

Type—	General Tax Considerations—	Tax Treatment of 1999 Distributions—
Company qualified plan	A company qualified pension or profit-sharing plan offers these benefits: (1) You do not realize current income on your employer's contributions to the plan on your behalf. (2) Income earned on funds contributed to your account compounds tax free. (3) Your employer may allow you to make voluntary contributions. Although these contributions may not be deducted, income earned on the voluntary contributions is not taxed until withdrawn.	If you receive a lump sum after age 59 $\frac{1}{2}$, tax on employer contributions may be reduced by a special averaging rule; *see 7.4.* If you receive a lump-sum distribution including company securities, unrealized appreciation on those securities is not taxed until you finally sell the stock; *see 7.10.* Distributions before age 59 $\frac{1}{2}$ are generally subject to penalties, but there are exceptions; *see 7.15.* Rather than pay an immediate tax, you may elect to roll over a lump-sum payment to an IRA account; *see 7.8.* If you collect your retirement benefits as an annuity over a period of years, *see 7.25.*
Keogh or self-employed plans	You may set up a self-employed retirement plan called a Keogh plan if you earn self-employment income through your performance of personal services. You may deduct contributions up to limits discussed in Chapter 41; income earned on assets held by the plan is not taxed. You must include employees in your Keogh under rules explained in Chapter 41. Other retirement plan options, such as an SEP or SIMPLE plan, are also discussed in Chapter 41.	As a self-employed person, you generally may not withdraw funds until age 59 $\frac{1}{2}$ unless you are disabled. Premature withdrawals are subject to a 10% penalty. Qualified distributions to self-employed persons or to beneficiaries at death may qualify for favored lump-sum treatment under the rules discussed in 7.2.
IRA and Roth IRA	Anyone who has earned income may contribute to an IRA, but the contribution is deductible only if certain requirements are met. Your status as a participant in an employer retirement plan and your income determine whether you may claim a full $2,000 IRA deduction, a partial deduction, or no deduction at all. *See* Chapter 8 for these deduction limitations. Where deductible contributions are allowed, IRAs offer these benefits: (1) deductions of up to $2,000 for single persons, $4,000 for married couples filing jointly, and (2) income earned on IRA accounts is not taxed until the funds are withdrawn. This tax-free buildup of earnings also applies where you make nondeductible contributions to a Roth IRA under the rules in Chapter 8.	An IRA withdrawal in 1999 before age 59 $\frac{1}{2}$ is subject to a 10% penalty, but there are exceptions if you are disabled, have substantial medical expenses, pay medical premiums while unemployed, or receive payments in a series of substantially equal installments; *see 8.12* for exception details. Starting at age 70 $\frac{1}{2}$, you must receive minimum annual distributions to avoid a 50% penalty; *see 8.13.* IRA distributions are fully taxable unless you have previously made nondeductible contributions; *see 8.9.* Distributions from a Roth IRA of contributions are tax free and distributions of earnings are taxable unless you are over age 59 $\frac{1}{2}$ and have held the account for at least five years; *see 8.22.*
SEP	A simplified employee pension plan set up by your employer allows the employer to contribute to an IRA more than you can under regular IRA rules. You do not have to include in 1999 income any employer contributions to your account. If your employer qualifies, you may be allowed to make elective deferrals of salary to the plan, up to $10,000 in 1999; *see also 8.16.*	Withdrawals are taxable under the rules explained above for IRAs.
Deferred salary or 401(k) plans	If your company has a profit-sharing or stock bonus plan, the tax law allows the company to add a cash or deferred pay plan that can operate in one of two ways: (1) Your employer contributes an amount for your benefit to your trust account. You are not taxed on your employer's contribution. (2) You agree to take a salary reduction or to forego a salary increase. The reduction is placed in a trust account for your benefit. The reduction is treated as your employer's contribution. In 1999, the maximum salary reduction is $10,000. Income earned on the trust account accumulates tax free until it is withdrawn.	Withdrawals are penalized unless you have reached age 59 $\frac{1}{2}$, become disabled, or meet other exceptions listed at 7.15. If you receive a qualifying lump sum after age 59 $\frac{1}{2}$, tax on the lump sum may be computed according to the rules in 7.2.

Distributions From Qualified Retirement Plans

7.1 Retirement Distributions on Form 1099-R

On Form 1099-R, payments from pensions, annuities, IRAs, Roth IRAs, SIMPLE IRAs, insurance contracts, profit-sharing, and other employer plans are reported to you and the IRS. Social Security benefits are reported on Form SSA-1099; *see* Chapter 34 for the special rules to apply in determining the taxable portion of Social Security benefits.

Here is a guide to the information reported on Form 1099-R. A sample form is on the next page.

Box 1. The total amount received from the payer is shown here without taking any withholdings into account. If you file Form 1040, report the Box 1 total on Line 15a if the payment is from an IRA, or on Line 16a if from a pension or an annuity. However, if the amount is a qualifying lump-sum distribution for which you are claiming averaging, use Form 4972; *see 7.4.*

If you file Form 1040A, report the Box 1 total on Line 10a if from an IRA or on Line 11a if from a pension or an annuity.

If you are receiving the distribution as a beneficiary of an employee who died before August 21, 1996, you may be entitled to a $5,000 death benefit exclusion; *see 7.27.*

If an exchange of insurance contracts was made, the value of the contract will be shown in Box 1, but if the exchange qualified as tax free, a zero taxable amount will be shown in Box 2a and Code 6 will be entered in Box 7.

Boxes 2a and 2b. The taxable portion of distributions from employer plans and insurance contracts may be shown in Box 2a. The taxable portion does not include your after-tax contributions to an employer plan or insurance premium payments.

If the payer cannot figure the taxable portion, the first box in 2b should be checked; Box 2a should be blank. You will then have to figure the taxable amount yourself. A payment from a pension or an annuity is only partially taxed if you contributed to the cost and you did not recover your entire cost investment before 1999. See *7.22* (commercial annuity) or *7.25* (employee annuity) for details on computing the taxable portion if you have an unrecovered investment.

The payer of an IRA distribution will probably not compute the taxable portion, and in this case, the total distribution from Box 1 will be entered as the taxable portion in Box 2a. This amount is fully taxable unless you have made nondeductible contributions; *see 8.9.*

If the payment is from an employer plan and the "total distribution" box has been checked in 2b, *see 7.2* for possible rollover and special averaging options. The taxable amount in Box 2a should not include net unrealized appreciation in any employer securities included in the lump sum or the value of an annuity contract included in the distribution.

Box 3. If the payment is a lump-sum distribution, and you participated in the plan before 1974, the amount shown here may be treated as capital gain; *see 7.5.*

Box 4. Any federal income tax withheld is shown here. Do not forget to include it on Line 57 of Form 1040 or Line 35 of Form 1040A. If Box 4 shows any withholdings, attach Copy B of Form 1099-R to your return.

Box 5. If you made after-tax contributions to your employer's plan, or paid premiums for a commercial annuity or insurance contract, your contribution is shown here, less any such contributions previously distributed. IRA or SEP contributions (*see* Chapter 8) are not shown here.

Box 6. If you received a qualifying lump-sum distribution that includes securities of your employer's company, the net unrealized appreciation is shown here. Unless you elect to pay tax on it currently *(7.10)*, this amount is not taxed until you sell the securities. If you did not receive a qualifying lump sum, the amount shown here is the net unrealized appreciation attributable to your after-tax employee contributions, which are also not taxed until you sell the securities; *see 7.10.*

Box 7. In Box 7, the payer will indicate if the distribution is from an IRA, SEP, or SIMPLE and enter codes that are used by the IRS to check whether you have reported the distribution correctly, including the 10% penalty for distributions before age 59 $\frac{1}{2}$.

If you are under age 59 $\frac{1}{2}$ and the employer knows that you qualify for an exception to the 10% early distribution penalty *(7.15)*, such as the exception for separation of service after age 55, your employer will enter Code 2 in Box 7. Code 3 will be used if the disability exception applies. Code 4 is the exception for distributions paid to beneficiaries. If Code 1 is entered, this indicates that you were under age $59^1/_2$ at the time of the distribution and as far as the payer knows, no pen-

---

Filing Instruction

Conversion of Traditional IRA to Roth IRA

If in 1999 you converted a traditional IRA to a Roth IRA, the conversion amount is included in Box 1 and in Box 2a of Form 1099-R as a taxable distribution. The entire conversion amount is taxable on your 1999 return; *see 8.21.*

alty exception applies. However, although Code 1 is entered, you may not be subject to a penalty. For example, you may qualify for the medical expense exception *(7.15)* or you may have made a tax-free rollover instead of having your employer make a direct rollover under the rules at *7.8*. If the employer did make a direct rollover, Code G will be entered if the direct rollover was to an IRA and Code H if to another employer's qualified plan or tax-sheltered annuity.

If you are at least age 59¹/₂, Code 7 should be entered.

If you are the beneficiary of a deceased employee, Code 4 should be entered. The 10% early distribution penalty does not apply.

If you contribute to a 401(k) plan and are a highly compensated employee, your employer may have to make a corrective distribution to you of contributions (and allocable income) that exceed allowable nondiscrimination ceilings. In this case, the employer will enter Code 8 if the corrective distribution is taxable in 1999, Code P if taxable in 1998, or Code D if taxable in 1997.

If you receive a lump-sum distribution that qualifies for special averaging, Code A will be entered; *see 7.4* for averaging rules.

Box 8. If the value of an annuity contract was included as part of a lump sum you received, the value of the contract is shown here. It is not taxable when you receive it and should not be included in Boxes 1 and 2a. For purposes of computing averaging on Form 4972, this amount is added to the ordinary income portion of the distribution; *see 7.4*.

Box 9. If several beneficiaries are receiving payment from an employer plan total distribution, the amount shown in Box 9a is your share of the distribution.

Boxes 10–15. The payer may make entries in these boxes to show state or local income tax withholdings.

7.2   Lump-Sum Distributions

If you are entitled to a lump-sum distribution from a company retirement plan or self-employed Keogh plan, you may avoid current tax by asking your employer to make a direct rollover of your account to an IRA or another qualified employer plan. If the distribution is made to you, 20% will be withheld, but it is still possible to make a tax-free rollover within 60 days; *see 7.8* for rollover details.

If you receive a lump sum and do not make a rollover, the taxable part of the distribution must

 Filing Tip

Lump-Sum Distribution
If you are paid a distribution that qualifies for lump-sum averaging, Code A will be entered in Box 7 of Form 1099-R. *See 7.4* for averaging rules.

☐ CORRECTED (if checked)

PAYER'S name, street address, city, state, and ZIP code	1 Gross distribution $ 174,384	OMB No. 1545-0119
Starshine Systems, Inc. 1220 Silver Lake Drive City, State 1X001	2a Taxable amount $ 174,384	1999 Form 1099-R

| 2b Taxable amount not determined ☐ | Total distribution ☒ | Copy B |

| PAYER'S Federal identification number X0-1101X01 | RECIPIENT'S identification number 010-XX-10XX | 3 Capital gain (included in box 2a) $ 7,241 | 4 Federal income tax withheld $ |

RECIPIENT'S name Andrew Kellogg

| 5 Employee contributions or insurance premiums $ | 6 Net unrealized appreciation in employer's securities $ |

Street address (including apt. no.) 44 Hampton Lane

| 7 Distribution code 7A | IRA/SEP/SIMPLE ☐ | 8 Other $ % |

City, state, and ZIP code City, State 1X011

| 9a Your percentage of total distribution % | 9b Total employee contributions $ |

Account number (optional)

| 10 State tax withheld $ 8,719.20 $ | 11 State/Payer's state no. State | 12 State distribution $ $ |
| 13 Local tax withheld $ $ | 14 Name of locality City | 15 Local distribution $ $ |

Form **1099-R**   Department of the Treasury - Internal Revenue Service be reported as ordinary pension income unless you qualify for special averaging as discussed below. A taxable distribution before age $59^1/_2$ is also subject to a 10% penalty unless you qualify for an exception; *see 7.15.*

Averaging method for 1999 lump-sum distributions. If a lump-sum distribution received in 1999 was not rolled over *(7.8)*, tax may be computed using special averaging if you have not previously elected averaging after 1986 *(see 7.4)* and all of the following tests are met:

(1) you were at least age $59^1/_2$ when the distribution was made, or you were self-employed and the distribution was made after you became totally disabled before age $59^1/_2$,

(2) you participated in the plan for at least five years before the year of the distribution,

(3) the plan was a "qualified" plan meeting tax law tests, *and*

(4) you received all that is due from the plan within one of your taxable years.

Under test (4), a series of payments may qualify as a lump-sum distribution provided you receive them within the same tax year. Lump-sum treatment is not lost if you receive in one year a qualifying lump-sum distribution after separation from service and, in the next year, you receive a payment that is attributable to your last year of work; the later payment is not part of the "balance" that must be received within one of your tax years. If your employer has more than one plan of the same kind (more than one profit-sharing plan or several stock bonus plans), you must receive your entire balance from all of such plans within the same tax year to use special averaging. For averaging purposes, the account balance does not include deductible voluntary contributions you made after 1981 and before 1987; these are not eligible for averaging.

If you meet these rules and were born before 1936, you may figure tax on the lump sum using either 10-year or five-year averaging; *see 7.4.* If you participated in the plan before 1974, you may elect to apply a 20% rate to the pre-1974 part of the distribution if 20% is lower than the averaging rate.

If you were born after 1935, five-year averaging, but not 10-year, may be elected for a qualifying lump sum received before 2000. Five-year averaging will not be allowed for years after 1999. A rollover *(7.8)* will be the only alternative to paying regular tax on the full distribution for the year it is made.

See 7.4 for further details on electing averaging.

Important: If you are married, you must generally obtain your spouse's consent to elect a lump-sum distribution; *see 7.11.*

Withholding tax. An employer must withhold a 20% tax from a lump-sum distribution that is paid to you and not rolled over directly by the employer; *see 7.8* for further details.

Beneficiaries. A surviving spouse who receives a lump-sum distribution upon the death of an employee may avoid tax by making a tax-free rollover to his or her own IRA. Beneficiaries other than surviving spouses may not make a tax-free rollover; *see 7.8.*

If the deceased employee was born before 1936, any beneficiary (not just a surviving spouse) may elect special averaging or capital gain treatment for a lump-sum distribution of the account; *see 7.7.* If the deceased employee was born after 1935 and was at least age $59^1/_2$ when he or she died, the beneficiary of a lump-sum distribution account received before 2000 may elect five-year averaging.

Court ordered lump-sum distribution to a spouse or former spouse. A distribution received by a spouse or former spouse of an employee under a qualified domestic relations order (QDRO) may be eligible for tax-free rollover or, in some cases, special averaging treatment; *see 7.12.*

7.3 Lump-Sum Options If You Were Born Before 1936

If you were born before 1936 but are not eligible for averaging under the other tests at *7.2*, you may avoid current tax by rolling over the distribution. To avoid withholding tax on the distribution, you must have your employer directly transfer the distribution to an IRA or qualified plan of another employer. The IRS allows the plan of a new employer to accept a rollover from your old employer even though you are not yet able to contribute to the new plan because of a minimum length of service or age requirement.

If you receive the distribution, a 20% tax will be withheld. If you later decide to make a rollover, you have 60 days from the time of receiving the distribution to do so; *see 7.8.* However, to avoid tax on the entire distribution, you will have to include in the rollover an amount equal to the withheld tax. Withholding is discussed further at *7.8* and *26.11.*

Caution

Prior Rollover Bars Averaging
Even if you received a 1999 distribution that meets the lump-sum tests, you may not claim averaging if you previously received a distribution from the same plan that was rolled over tax free *(7.8)* to an IRA or to another qualified employer plan.

If you can average, you should determine whether paying tax currently using the averaging method *(7.4)* will be more favorable to you than making a tax-free rollover. If you receive more than one lump sum during the year, you must make the same choice for all of them; you may not roll over one distribution and claim averaging for another.

If you need the lump-sum payout immediately or may need it within a few years, pay tax now using special averaging.

If you qualify for special averaging but do not plan to use the funds until retirement, estimate whether you will build a larger retirement fund by rolling over the distribution and letting earnings accumulate tax free, or by using special averaging and investing the funds to give you the greatest after-tax return. This is not an easy projection. You must consider the number of years to retirement, your expected tax bracket at retirement, and the estimated yield you can earn on your funds. Generally speaking, a person who is not planning to retire for many years may get a greater after-tax return by making a rollover and then taking withdrawals over his or her life expectancy at retirement.

You must consider the one-time-only rule for averaging; *see* the sidebar on the right. If in 1999 you received a qualifying lump sum upon separation from service but you plan to continue working for someone else, electing averaging for the 1999 distribution will bar you from applying averaging to any lump-sum distribution you receive from another employer plan.

If you have not previously elected averaging and expect to receive a qualifying lump sum in 2000, but you will continue to work and would like to preserve the option of electing averaging for a future lump sum, you may ask your former employer to make a direct rollover of the 2000 distribution to the plan of your new employer or to an IRA that could serve as a "conduit" to another employer's plan. If you later join a plan that accepts rollovers from the "conduit IRA," the transfer could be made and 10-year averaging could apply to a qualifying distribution from the new plan.

An IRA rollover cannot be revoked to claim averaging. If you make a rollover to an IRA, you cannot change your mind and cancel the IRA account in order to apply special averaging. The rollover election is irrevocable, according to an IRS regulation that has been upheld by the Tax Court. If an IRA rollover account is revoked, the entire distribution is taxable as ordinary income, and a 10% penalty may be imposed if the recipient is under age $59^1/_2$ *(7.15)*.

Disqualification of retirement plan. If you receive a lump-sum distribution from a plan that loses its exempt status, the IRS may argue that the distribution does not qualify for lump-sum treatment. Under the IRS position, you may not roll over the distribution to an IRA or elect special averaging. The Tax Court previously took the position that if the plan qualified when contributions were made, an allocable portion of the distribution was a qualified lump sum. However, the majority of appeals courts that reviewed Tax Court decisions on this issue supported the IRS position. In response, the Tax Court reversed its position and adopted the harsher IRS approach: no part of the distribution qualifies for rollover or averaging if the plan loses its exempt status.

7.4 Averaging on Form 4972

If you meet the age test and the other lump-sum qualifying tests discussed at *7.2*, you may elect averaging on Form 4972 for a 1999 lump-sum distribution.

Age test. There are two age tests for averaging a lump-sum distribution received in 1999 and your averaging options depend on which test you meet:

Were you born before 1936? If you were born before 1936, you may elect on Form 4972 either a 10-year averaging method based on 1986 tax rates for single persons, or a five-year averaging method based on single person rates for 1999.

Were you born after 1935? If you were born after 1935, you may elect five-year averaging for a qualifying distribution made in 1999 after you reached age $59^1/_2$. Ten-year averaging is not allowed.

A distribution received after 1999 will *not* be eligible for averaging.

Averaging on 1999 returns. If you meet the age test and were a participant in the plan for five or more years before 1999, follow IRS instructions to Form 4972 for applying averaging to a qualifying lump-sum distribution received during 1999. If you received more than one qualified lump sum, you may elect averaging for one of the distributions only if you elect averaging for all.

The amount eligible for averaging is the taxable portion of the distribution shown in Box 2a of Form 1099-R. You may also elect to add to the Box 2a amount any net unrealized appreciation in

Planning Reminder

Once in a Lifetime Election
You are allowed to elect averaging only once after 1986. If before 1987 you elected 10-year averaging and were under age $59^1/_2$, you may elect averaging for a 1999 distribution. However, if you were over age $59^1/_2$ when you made the pre-1987 election, you are barred from electing averaging again.

If you were born before 1936 and elect averaging for a 1999 distribution, you will not be able to claim averaging again if you join another company and receive a lump-sum distribution from the new employer.

If you were born after 1935, 1999 is the last year for which averaging may be claimed, regardless of whether a previous election has been made.

Caution

1999 Is Last Year for Averaging for Those Born After 1935
If you were born after 1935, a lump-sum distribution received after 1999 will not be eligible for averaging.

4972—Worksheet

Part II	**Complete this part to choose the 20% capital gain election** (See instructions.) Do not complete this part unless the participant was born **before** 1936.		

6	Capital gain part from box 3 of Form 1099-R	**6**		**7,241**
7	Multiply line 6 by 20% (.20)	**7**		**1,448**
	If you also choose to use Part III, go to line 8. Otherwise, include the amount from line 7 in the total on Form 1040, line 40, or Form 1041, Schedule G, line 1b, whichever applies.			

Part III	**Complete this part to choose the 5- or 10-year tax option** (See instructions.)	

8	Ordinary income from Form 1099-R, box 2a minus box 3. If you did not complete Part II, enter the taxable amount from box 2a of Form 1099-R	**8**	**167,143**
9	Death benefit exclusion for a beneficiary of a plan participant who died before August 21, 1996	**9**	**- 0 -**
10	Total taxable amount. Subtract line 9 from line 8	**10**	**167,143**
11	Current actuarial value of annuity (from Form 1099-R, box 8)	**11**	**- 0 -**
12	Adjusted total taxable amount. Add lines 10 and 11. If this amount is $70,000 or more, **skip** lines 13 through 16, and enter this amount on line 17	**12**	**167,143**
13	Multiply line 12 by 50% (.50), but **do not** enter more than $10,000 **13**		
14	Subtract $20,000 from line 12. If the result is less than zero, enter -0- **14**		
15	Multiply line 14 by 20% (.20) **15**		
16	Minimum distribution allowance. Subtract line 15 from line 13	**16**	
17	Subtract line 16 from line 12	**17**	**167,143**
18	Federal estate tax attributable to lump-sum distribution	**18**	**- 0 -**
19	Subtract line 18 from line 17	**19**	**167,143**
	If line 11 is blank, skip lines 20 through 22 and go to line 23.		
20	Divide line 11 by line 12 and enter the result as a decimal (rounded to at least four places) . .	**20**	**.**
21	Multiply line 16 by the decimal on line 20	**21**	
22	Subtract line 21 from line 11	**22**	

5-year tax option

23	Multiply line 19 by 20% (.20)	**23**	**33,429**
24	Tax on amount on line 23. Use the Tax Rate Schedule for the 5-Year Tax Option in the instructions	**24**	**6,013**
25	Multiply line 24 by five (5). If line 11 is blank, skip lines 26 through 28, and enter this amount on line 29	**25**	**30,065**
26	Multiply line 22 by 20% (.20) **26**		
27	Tax on amount on line 26. Use the Tax Rate Schedule for the 5-Year Tax Option in the instructions **27**		
28	Multiply line 27 by five (5)	**28**	
29	Subtract line 28 from line 25. (Multiple recipients, see page 2 of the instructions.) . . .	**29**	**30,065**

	Note: *Complete lines 30 through 36 ONLY if the participant was born before 1936. Otherwise, enter the amount from line 29 on line 37.*		

10-year tax option

30	Multiply line 19 by 10% (.10)	**30**	**16,714**
31	Tax on amount on line 30. Use the Tax Rate Schedule for the 10-Year Tax Option in the instructions	**31**	**2,851**
32	Multiply line 31 by ten (10). If line 11 is blank, skip lines 33 through 35, and enter this amount on line 36	**32**	**28,510**
33	Multiply line 22 by 10% (.10) **33**		
34	Tax on amount on line 33. Use the Tax Rate Schedule for the 10-Year Tax Option in the instructions **34**		
35	Multiply line 34 by ten (10)	**35**	
36	Subtract line 35 from line 32. (Multiple recipients, see page 2 of the instructions.) . . .	**36**	**28,510**

37	Compare lines 29 and 36. Generally, you should enter the **smaller** amount here (see instructions) . . . . ▶	**37**	**28,510**
38	Tax on lump-sum distribution. Add lines 7 and 37. Also, include this amount in the total on Form 1040, line 40, or Form 1041, Schedule G, line 1b, whichever applies . . . . . ▶	**38**	**29,958**

employer securities (shown in Box 6) included in the lump sum. If you are receiving the distribution as a beneficiary of a plan participant who died before August 21, 1996, follow the instructions to Form 4972 for claiming a death benefit exclusion that reduces the Box 2a taxable portion.

If you were born before 1936 and the distribution includes capital gain (Box 3 of Form 1099-R) and you want to apply the special 20% capital gain rate *(7.5)*, you should subtract the capital gain in Box 3 from the taxable amount in Box 2a and apply averaging to the balance of ordinary income.

Tables for applying the 10-year and 5-year averaging methods are included in the 1999 instructions to Form 4972. In most cases, except where extremely large distributions (over $318,833) are received, 10-year averaging will provide the lower tax.

Whichever averaging method you use, the tax computed on Form 4972 is reported on Form 1040, Line 40, as an additional tax. It is completely separate from the tax computed on your other income reported on Form 1040.

Planning Reminder

Five-Year Averaging Repealed After 1999

If you were born after 1935, the opportunity to claim five-year averaging for a lump-sum distribution after age 59$^1/_2$ ends in 1999. Starting in 2000, five-year averaging is repealed. If you were born before 1936, the right to use 10-year averaging will not be affected after 1999 but the five-year averaging option will not be available.

EXAMPLE

Andrew Kellogg retired from StarShine Systems, Inc., in 1999 at age 65. He received a lump-sum distribution of $174,384 at the end of 1999. The Form 1099-R provided by the company shows in Box 3 a capital gain portion of $7,241, attributable to pre-1974 participation.

On Form 4972, Andrew applies the special 20% rate to the capital gain portion for a tax of $1,448. He then figures the tax on the $167,143 ordinary income part of the distribution under the five-year and 10-year averaging methods. As shown on the Form 4972 worksheet on page 140, the tax using 10-year averaging is lower than the five-year averaging tax. Andrew's total tax on the distribution is $29,958, the sum of the $28,510 tax under 10-year averaging and the $1,448 tax on the capital gain portion. In Andrew's case, the special 20% capital gains rate is advantageous because it results in a lower tax than if the capital gain were treated as ordinary income subject to the averaging computation.

Community property. Only the spouse who has earned the lump sum may use averaging. Community property laws are disregarded for this purpose. If a couple files separate returns and one spouse elects averaging, the other spouse is not taxed on the amount subject to the computation.

EXAMPLE

A husband in a community property state receives a lump-sum distribution of which the ordinary income portion is $10,000. He and his wife file separate returns. If averaging is not elected, $5,000, or one-half, is taxable on the husband's return and the other $5,000 on his wife's return. However, if he elects the averaging method, only he reports the $10,000 on Form 4972.

Pre-1974 capital gain portion of distribution. If you were born before 1936 and a portion of your 1997 lump-sum distribution is attributable to plan participation before 1974 *(7.5)*, you may treat it as ordinary income eligible for averaging, or you may elect to treat it as capital gain part taxed at a flat 20% rate; *see also 7.5.*

7.5 Capital Gain Treatment for Pre-1974 Participation

The portion of a qualifying lump-sum distribution attributable to pre-1974 participation is eligible for a 20% capital gain rate if you were born before 1936.

On Form 1099-R, the company paying the lump-sum distribution shows the capital gain portion in Box 3. The ordinary income portion is Box 2a (taxable amount) *minus* Box 3.

Born before 1936. You may elect to treat the pre-1974 portion as capital gain subject to a flat rate of 20% on Form 4972. The tax on the balance of the distribution may be figured under the averaging method. The 20% rate for the capital gain portion is fixed by law, and applies regardless of the tax rate imposed on your other capital gains. Alternatively, you may elect to treat the capital gain portion as ordinary income eligible for averaging. You may not elect to report any portion of the pre-1974 portion of the lump-sum distribution as long-term capital gain on Schedule D.

Caution

Cash Out of Benefits

When you leave your job, you generally have the option of leaving your account balance in the plan of your old employer. However, if the present value of your benefits is $5,000 or less, the plan may without your consent "cash out" your interest by distributing it to you in a lump sum. A cash-out distribution is subject to the rollover rules at *7.8*.

Filing Tip

Lump Sums to Multiple Beneficiaries

A lump-sum distribution to two or more individuals may qualify for averaging and capital gain treatment. Each beneficiary may separately elect the averaging method for the ordinary income portion, even though other beneficiaries do not so elect. Follow the Form 4972 instructions for multiple recipients.

Under the one-time election rule, if you elect to apply the averaging and/or 20% capital gain rule for a 1999 distribution, you may not elect averaging or capital gain treatment for any later distribution.

Capital gain treatment not allowed for individuals born after 1935. If you were born after 1935, you may *not* treat any portion of a lump-sum distribution as capital gain. You may not apply the flat 20% rate to the pre-1974 portion of the lump-sum distribution, or include any part of it as capital gain on your 1999 Schedule D. An election to claim capital gain treatment on Schedule D was phased out between 1987 and 1991. If you made such an election, you will not be allowed to claim five-year averaging for a lump-sum distribution received after age $59^1/_2$.

7.6 Lump-Sum Distribution Upon Separation From Service

You may receive a lump-sum distribution from a qualified employer retirement plan when you separate from service, that is, when you resign, retire, or are fired from your job. Your age, not the fact that you have separated from service, determines your right to claim special averaging:

If you were born before 1936, you may elect either special averaging *(see 7.4)* or tax-free rollover treatment for a lump-sum distribution *(see 7.8)*.

If you were born after 1935, tax-free rollover is allowed but not special averaging for a lump-sum distribution received after 1999. If a rollover is not made under the rules at *7.8*, the distribution is fully taxable and it will also be subject to the 10% penalty for early withdrawals, unless one of the exceptions at *7.15* applies. For years before 2000, the rule was different. An individual who received a pre-2000 lump-sum distribution after attaining age $59^1/_2$ could claim five-year averaging or make a tax-free rollover.

7.7 Lump-Sum Payments Received by Beneficiary

A beneficiary of a deceased employee may elect special averaging on Form 4972 for a qualifying lump-sum distribution *(7.2)* received in 1999 because of the employee's death, provided the employee was at least age $59^1/_2$. The age of the beneficiary is irrelevant. A beneficiary may elect averaging even though the deceased employee was in the plan for less than five years.

Either 10-year or five-year averaging may be claimed if the employee was born before 1936. If the employee was born before 1936 and had participated in the plan before 1974, a 20% capital gain election may be made for that portion of the distribution *(7.5)*, and the averaging method applied to the balance.

If the employee was born after 1935 and was at least age $59^1/_2$, five-year averaging may be used for a 1999 lump-sum distribution. In 2000 and later years, a beneficiary of an employee who was born after 1935 will *not* be able to claim special averaging.

Form 4972 is used to compute tax under the averaging method or to make the 20% capital gain election *(7.5)*. Follow the Form 4972 instructions to claim the up-to-$5,000 death benefit exclusion for a 1999 distribution *(7.27)* where the plan participant died before August 21, 1996. Any federal estate tax attributable to the distribution reduces the taxable amount on Form 4972. Any election made as a beneficiary does not affect your right to elect lump-sum treatment for a distribution from your own plan.

A lump sum paid because of an employee's death may qualify for capital gain and averaging treatment, although the employee received annuity payments before death.

An election may be made on Form 4972 only once as the beneficiary of a particular employee. A beneficiary who receives more than one lump-sum distribution for the same beneficiary in the same year must treat them all the same way. Averaging must be elected for all of the distributions on a single Form 4972 or for none of them.

Payment received by a second beneficiary (after the death of the first beneficiary) is not entitled to lump-sum treatment or the death benefit exclusion.

Beneficiaries of self-employed individuals who receive a qualifying lump-sum distribution from a Keogh plan apply the same rules as beneficiaries of deceased employees, as just discussed.

Distribution to trust or estate. If a qualifying lump sum is paid to a trust or an estate, the employee, or, if deceased, his or her personal representative, may elect averaging.

EXAMPLE

Gunnison's father was covered by a company benefit plan. The father died, as did Gunnison's mother, before benefits were fully paid out. Gunnison received a substantial lump sum. He argued that he collected on account of his father's death. The IRS disagreed.

The Tax Court and an appeals court sided with the IRS. Gunnison was entitled to the payment following his mother's death, not his father's death. For special lump-sum treatment, the payout must arise solely on account of the death of the covered employee.

7.8 Tax-Free Rollovers

A rollover allows you to make a tax-free transfer of a distribution from a qualified employer retirement plan to another qualified plan or to an IRA. If a rollover is made to an IRA, later distributions are subject to the IRA rules *(8.8)* and will not qualify for special averaging *(7.4)*.

Eligible rollover distributions. Almost all taxable distributions received from a qualified corporate or self-employed pension, profit-sharing, stock bonus, or annuity plan, or from a 403(b) tax-sheltered annuity, are eligible for tax-free rollover. The major exceptions are your *after-tax* contributions, substantially equal periodic payments over your lifetime or over a period of at least 10 years, hardship distributions and minimum distributions *(7.13)* required after age $70^1/_2$; *see* below for other ineligible distributions.

Caution: If the distribution is for part of your account balance and you roll it over, a later lump-sum distribution from the plan will not qualify for averaging; *see 7.4.*

Rollover options. If you want to make a tax-free rollover of an eligible rollover distribution, you should instruct your employer to directly roll over the funds to an IRA you designate or to the plan of your new employer. You could also choose to have the distribution paid to you, and within 60 days you could make a tax-free rollover yourself. *However, to avoid the 20% mandatory withholding tax, you must elect to have the plan make a direct rollover. If an eligible rollover distribution is paid to you, the 20% withholding tax applies. Your employer must provide you with written notice concerning the rollover options and the withholding tax rules.*

Rollover from employer plan to IRA after age $70^1/_2$. Starting with the year you reach age $70^1/_2$, you may no longer make IRA contributions. However, if you are over age $70^1/_2$ and you receive an eligible rollover distribution from your employer's plan, you may instruct your employer to make a direct rollover of the distribution to an IRA, as discussed below. If you receive the distribution from the employer, a 20% tax will be withheld; you may make a tax-free rollover within 60 days of the distribution; *see* the following page for the discussion of "personal rollovers." In the year of the rollover, you must receive a minimum distribution from the IRA; *see 8.13.*

Beneficiaries. The only beneficiary who may make a tax-free rollover is a surviving spouse, as discussed later in this section.

Distributions that may not be rolled over. Any lump-sum or partial distribution from your account is eligible for rollover *except for the following:*

- Hardship distributions made after 1999 from a 401(k) plan or 403(b) plan *(7.19)*.
- Payments that are part of a series of substantially equal payments made at least annually over a period of 10 years or more or over your life or life expectancy (or the joint lives or joint life and last survivor expectancies of you and your designated beneficiary).
- Minimum required distributions after attaining age $70^1/_2$ or retiring *(7.13)*.
- Distributions of your voluntary after-tax contributions to the plan. These are nontaxable when distributed to you and thus are not eligible for rollover or subject to withholding.
- Corrective distributions of excess 401(k) plan contributions and deferrals.
- Dividends on employer stock.
- Life insurance coverage costs.
- Loans that are deemed to be taxable distributions because they exceed the limits discussed in *7.16*.

For all of the above taxable distributions that are *ineligible* for rollover, you may elect to completely avoid withholding on Form W-4P.

Direct Rollover to IRA or Another Employer Plan

If you choose to have your employer make a direct rollover of an eligible rollover distribution to an IRA or another qualified plan, you avoid tax on the payment and no tax will be withheld. If you are changing jobs and want a direct rollover to the plan of the new employer, make sure that the plan accepts rollovers; if it does not, choose a direct rollover to an IRA.

Planning Reminder

Transfer to Roth IRA
You may *not* roll over an employer plan distribution to a Roth IRA. You may make a tax-free rollover to a traditional IRA and then make a taxable conversion to a Roth IRA if you qualify under the rules at *8.21.*

Planning Reminder

IRA Conduit Between Employer Plans
If you roll over an employer plan distribution to an IRA, the IRA may be used as a conduit to another company plan. If you join a company with a plan that accepts rollovers, the funds in the IRA may be transferred to the new plan. A qualifying lump-sum distribution from the new employer plan may be eligible for special averaging; *see 7.4.* The IRA must consist of only the assets (or proceeds from the sale of such assets) distributed from the first qualified plan and income earned on the account. You may not contribute to the account set up as a conduit. If you want to make IRA contributions, set up another IRA.

When you select the direct rollover option, your employer may transfer the funds directly by check or wire to the new plan, or you may be given a check payable to the new plan that you deliver.

In choosing a direct rollover to an IRA, the terms of the payer-employer's plan will determine whether you may divide the distribution among several IRAs or whether you will be restricted to one IRA. For example, you may want to split up your distribution into several IRAs, but the employer may force you to select only one. After the direct rollover is made, you may then diversify your holdings by making tax-free trustee-to-trustee transfers to other IRAs.

You may elect to make a direct rollover of part of your distribution and to receive the balance. The portion paid to you will be subject to 20% withholding and is not eligible for special averaging. The IRS allows plan administrators to bar a partial direct rollover if the rollover amount is less than $500.

A direct rollover will be reported by the payer plan to the IRS and to you on Form 1099-R, although the transfer is not taxable. The direct rollover will be reported in Box 1 of Form 1099-R, but zero will be entered as the taxable amount in Box 2a. In Box 7, Code G should be entered if the direct rollover was to an IRA and Code H if to another qualified employer plan or to a tax-sheltered annuity.

Personal Rollover After Receiving a Distribution

If you do not tell your employer to make a direct rollover of an eligible rollover distribution, and you instead receive the distribution yourself, you will receive only 80%; 20% will be withheld. Withholding does not apply to the portion of the distribution consisting of net unrealized appreciation from employer securities that is tax-free under the rules at 7.10.

Although you receive only 80% of the eligible rollover distribution, the full amount is required as a taxable distribution on Form 1099-R. To avoid tax you must roll it over within 60 days to an IRA or another employer plan. However, to roll over 100% of the distribution you will have to use other funds to replace the 20% withheld. If you roll over only the 80% received, the 20% balance will be taxable; see the John Anderson Example below. For the taxable part that is not rolled over, you may not use special averaging or capital gain treatment even if you meet the age test of 7.4. In addition, if the distribution was made to you before you reached age $59\frac{1}{2}$, the taxable amount will be subject to a 10% penalty unless you are disabled, separating from service after reaching age 55, or have substantial medical expenses (7.15).

The rollover amount may not include your voluntary after-tax contributions to the qualified plan; they are tax free to you when you receive them. The rollover *may* include salary deferral contributions that were excludable from income when made, such as qualifying deferrals to a 401(k) plan. The rollover may also include accumulated deductible employee contributions (and allocable income) made after 1981 and before 1987. Your employer's retirement plan may invest in a limited amount of life insurance which is then distributed to you as part of a lump-sum retirement distribution. You may be able to roll over the life insurance contract to the qualified plan of your new employer but not to an IRA. The law bars investment of IRA funds in life insurance contracts.

You may not claim a deduction for your rollover to an IRA.

EXAMPLE

In January 2000, John Anderson retires. He is due a lump-sum distribution of $100,000 from a qualified plan of his company. If he instructs his employer to make a direct rollover of the amount to an IRA, there is no tax withholding and the $100,000 is transferred to the IRA tax free.

Now assume that John decides not to choose a direct rollover because he is planning to use the funds to invest in a business. The plan will pay him $80,000 and withhold a tax of $20,000 that John will apply to his tax liability for 2000. But, say, a month later John changes his mind about the investment and now wants to roll over his benefits to an IRA. He must make the rollover within 30 days because 30 days of the 60-day rollover period have already passed. Furthermore, to avoid tax on the entire distribution, he must deposit $100,000 in the IRA, even though $20,000 tax has been withheld. If he does not have the $20,000, he must borrow the $20,000 and deposit it in the IRA. If he rolls over only $80,000, he must report $20,000 as a taxable distribution on his 2000 return and if John is under age 59 $\frac{1}{2}$, the 10% penalty for early withdrawals would apply; based on these facts, John does not qualify for a penalty exception (7.15).

Reporting a personal rollover on your return. When you receive a distribution that could have been rolled over, the payer will report as the taxable amount on Form 1099-R the full amount before withholding, although 20% has been withheld. However, if you make a rollover yourself within the 60-day period, the rollover reduces the taxable amount on your tax return. For example, if in 1999 you were entitled to a $100,000 lump-sum distribution and received $80,000 after mandatory 20% withholding and then you rolled over the full $100,000 into an IRA, report $100,000 on Line 16a of Form 1040 or Line 11a of Form 1040A, but enter zero as the taxable amount on Line 16b or Line 11b. If you roll over only part of the distribution, the amount of the lump sum *not* rolled over is entered as the taxable amount. Remember to include the 20% withholding on the line for federal income tax withheld.

Figuring the 60-day period for personal rollovers. A rollover must be completed by the 60th day following the day on which you receive the distribution.

The IRS has strictly applied the 60-day requirement for personal rollovers even where failure to meet the deadline is not the taxpayer's fault. For example, an investor wanted to transfer a lump-sum distribution from a terminated company plan to an IRA. The company plan had been invested in five different funds maintained by a mutual-fund "family," and the investor merely wanted to reregister his account as an IRA while keeping the same fund investments. However, his written instructions were followed for only four of the funds because of a clerk's error. The failure to reregister the fifth account was not discovered and corrected until six months later. An unsympathetic IRS held that the amount from the fifth fund, $15,100, was a taxable distribution because it was not rolled over within the 60-day period.

In a similar case, the Tax Court allowed tax-free rollover treatment where Merrill Lynch made a bookkeeping error by failing to properly record a rollover of a lump-sum distribution of cash and stock from a company plan. The cash was deposited into the IRA within the 60-day period but the stock was not. The court held that the date of the rollover was fixed when the taxpayer signed the necessary documentation and transferred the funds to establish the IRA within the 60-day period.

Extension of 60-day rollover period for frozen deposits. If you receive a qualifying distribution from a retirement plan and deposit the funds in a financial institution that becomes bankrupt or insolvent, you may be prevented from withdrawing the funds in time to complete a rollover within 60 days. If this happens, the 60-day period is extended while your account is "frozen." The 60-day rollover period does not include days on which your account is frozen. Further, you have a minimum of 10 days after the release of the funds to complete the rollover.

Multiple rollover accounts allowed. You may wish to diversify a distribution in different investments. There is no limit on the number of rollover accounts you may have. A lump-sum distribution may be rolled over to several IRAs or retirement annuities.

Rollover by Surviving Spouse

A surviving spouse is the only beneficiary who may make a tax-free rollover. If you are your deceased spouse's beneficiary, you may roll over your interest in his or her qualified plan account. You may choose to have the plan make a direct rollover to your IRA; you cannot make the rollover to your employer's qualified plan. The advantage of choosing the direct rollover is to avoid a 20% withholding. If the distribution is paid to you, 20% will be withheld. You may make a rollover within 60 days, but to completely avoid tax, you must include in the rollover the withheld amount, as illustrated in the John Anderson Example on page 144. If you receive the distribution but do not make the rollover, you will be taxed on the distribution, but if your spouse was age 59$\frac{1}{2}$ or older, you may be able to use special averaging (7.4) to compute the tax. As a surviving spouse, you are not subject to the 10% penalty for premature distributions (7.15) even if you are under age 59$\frac{1}{2}$.

Rollover of distribution received under a divorce or support proceeding. In a qualified domestic relations order (QDRO) meeting special tax law tests, a state court may give you the right to receive all or part of your spouse's or former spouse's retirement benefits. You can choose to have the payment made to you or you can instruct the plan to make a direct rollover to an IRA or to your employer's qualified plan if it accepts rollovers. Alternatively, if the distribution is paid to you, 20% withholding will apply. You may complete a rollover within 60 days under the rules for personal rollovers discussed earlier. If you do not make the rollover, the payments you receive are taxable, but you may be able to elect special averaging; *see 7.12.* If only part of the distribution is rolled over, the balance is taxed in the year of receipt. In figuring your tax, you are al-

 Caution

IRA Rollover Election Is Irrevocable

A rollover from an employer plan to an IRA is irrevocable, according to the IRS. At the time of the rollover, you must elect in writing to irrevocably treat the contribution as a rollover. If a qualifying lump-sum distribution is made to you after you are age 59$\frac{1}{2}$, and you roll it over, you may not later change your mind in order to claim averaging. Before making a rollover, figure what the current tax would be on the lump-sum distribution under the special averaging method. Compare it with an estimate of the regular tax that will be payable on a later distribution of the rolled-over account from the IRA.

Other points to consider in deciding whether to roll over a lump sum are discussed at 7.3.

lowed a prorated share of your former spouse's cost investment, if any. You may not elect averaging or capital gain treatment for the portion not rolled over. You are not subject to the 10% penalty for premature distributions even if under age $59^{1}/_{2}$.

Nonspouse beneficiaries. If you are a beneficiary other than a spouse, you cannot choose to have the plan make a direct rollover and you cannot make a rollover yourself if payment is made to you. Distributions must begin under the payment rules for beneficiaries discussed at *7.14*, unless special averaging is available for a lump-sum distribution of the account; *see 7.4*.

7.9 Rollover of Proceeds From Sale of Property

A lump-sum distribution from a qualified plan may include property, such as non-employer stock; *see 7.10* for employer securities. If you plan to roll over the distribution, you may find that a bank or other plan trustee does not want to take the property. You cannot get tax-free rollover treatment by keeping the property and rolling over cash to the new plan. If you sell the property, you may roll over the sale proceeds to an IRA as long as the sale and rollover occur within 60 days of receipt of the distribution. If you roll over all of the proceeds, you do not recognize a gain or loss from the sale; the proceeds are treated as part of the distribution. If you make a partial rollover of sale proceeds, you must report as capital gain the portion of the gain that is allocable to the retained sale proceeds.

If you receive cash and property, and you sell the property but only make a partial rollover, you must designate how much of the rolled-over cash is from the employer distribution and how much from the sale proceeds. The designation must be made by the time for filing your return (plus any extensions) and is irrevocable. If you do not make a timely designation, the IRS will allocate the rollover between cash and sales proceeds on a ratable basis; the allocation will determine tax on the retained amount.

If you made after-tax contributions to the plan, you may not roll over the portion of the distribution equal to your contributions.

7.10 Distribution of Employer Securities

When a plan distributes securities of your company, the value of the securities may or may not be subject to tax at the time of the distribution. The amount reported as income depends on the value of the securities, the amount contributed by the company toward their purchase, and whether or not the distribution qualifies as a total lump-sum payment.

Lump-sum payments. If you receive appreciated securities as part of a lump-sum distribution, net unrealized appreciation (increase in value since purchase of securities) is not subject to tax at the time of distribution unless you elect to treat it as taxable. This exclusion for net unrealized appreciation applies to distributions meeting the lump-sum tests at *7.2*, except that the five-year participation test does not have to be met.

Assuming the election to treat the unrealized appreciation as current income is not made, only the amount of the employer's contribution is subject to tax. Tax on the appreciation is delayed until the shares are later sold by you at a price exceeding cost basis. If, when distributed, the shares are valued at below the cost contribution of the employer, the fair market value of the shares is subject to tax. If you contributed to the purchase of the shares and their value is less than your contribution, you do not realize a loss deduction on the distribution. You realize a loss only when the stock is sold or becomes worthless *(5.8)* at a later date. If a plan distributes worthless stock, you may deduct your contributions to the stock as a miscellaneous itemized deduction subject to the 2% of adjusted gross income floor.

The net unrealized appreciation in employer's securities is shown in Box 6 of the Form 1099-R received from the payer. It is not included in the taxable amount in Box 2a.

Election to waive tax-free treatment. You may elect to include the unrealized appreciation in employer securities as income. You might consider making this election when you want to accelerate income to the current year by taking into account the entire lump-sum distribution. If you are claiming averaging or capital gain treatment on Form 4972 *(7.4)*, follow the form instructions for adding the unrealized appreciation to the taxable distribution. If you are not filing Form 4972, the election to include the unrealized appreciation as income is made by reporting it on Line 16a (pensions and annuities) of Form 1040.

Court Decision

Stock Purchased With Cash Withdrawal Cannot Be Rolled Over

A taxpayer withdrew cash from his Keogh accounts and used most of the net distribution (after withholdings) to buy stock, which was then transferred to an IRA within 60 days of the withdrawal. He treated the entire distribution as a tax-free rollover but the IRS and Tax Court held it was taxable. The transfer of stock to the IRA was not a tax-free rollover; only the cash distribution itself could be rolled over. A negligence penalty was also imposed.

A direct rollover from the Keogh accounts to an IRA would have been tax free; the stock could then have been purchased through the new IRA.

EXAMPLES

1. *Shares valued below your cost contribution.* You contributed $500 and your employer contributed $300 to buy 10 shares of company stock having at the time a fair market value of $80 per share. When you retire, the fair market value of the stock is $40 per share, or a total of $400. You do not realize income on the distribution, and you do not have a deductible loss for the difference between your cost contribution and the lower fair market value. Your contribution to the stock is its basis. This is $50 per share. If you sell the stock for $40 per share, you have a capital loss of $10 per share. However, if you sell the stock for $60 per share, you have gain of $10 per share.

2. *Appreciated shares.* You receive 10 shares of company stock that was purchased entirely with the employer's funds. Your employer's cost was $50 a share. At the time of a lump-sum distribution, the shares are valued at $80 a share. Your employer's contribution of $50 a share, or $500, is included as part of your taxable distribution. The appreciation of $300 is not included, assuming you do not elect to be taxed currently on the appreciation. The cost basis of the shares in your hands is $500 (the amount currently taxable to you). The holding period of the stock starts from the date of distribution. However, if you sell the shares for any amount exceeding $500 and up to $800, your profit is long-term gain regardless of how long you held the shares. If you sell for more than $800, the gain exceeding the original unrealized appreciation of $300 is subject to long-term capital gain treatment only if the sale is long term from the date of distribution. Thus, if within a month of the distribution you sold the shares for $900, $300 would be long-term gain; $100 would be short-term gain.

Other than lump-sum payments. If you receive appreciated employer securities in a distribution that does not meet the lump-sum tests of *7.2* (disregarding the five-year participation requirement), you report as ordinary income the amount of the employer's contribution to the purchase of the shares and the appreciation allocated to the employer's cost contribution. You do not report the amount of appreciation allocated to your own after-tax contribution to the purchase.

EXAMPLE

A qualified plan distributes 10 shares of company stock with an average cost of $100, of which the employee contributed $60 and the employer, $40. At the date of distribution, the stock had a fair market value of $180. The portion of the unrealized appreciation attributable to the employee's contribution is $48 (60% of $80); the employer's is $32 (40% of $80). The employee reports $72 as income: the employer's cost of $40 and the employer's share of appreciation, which is $32. The basis of each share is $132, which includes an employee contribution of $60 and the $72 reported as taxable income. Net unrealized appreciation and cost contributions must be supplied by the company distributing the stock.

7.11 Survivor Annuity for Spouse

If you have been married for at least a year, the law generally requires that payments of vested benefits be in a specific annuity form to protect your surviving spouse. All defined benefit and money purchase plans must provide benefits in the form of a *qualified joint and survivor annuity (QJSA)* unless you, with the written consent of your spouse, elect a different form of benefit. A qualified joint and survivor annuity must also be provided by profit-sharing or stock bonus plans, unless you do not elect a life annuity payment and the plan provides that your nonforfeitable benefit is payable in full upon your death to your surviving spouse, or to another beneficiary if the spouse consents or there is no surviving spouse.

Under a QJSA, you receive an annuity for your life and your surviving spouse receives an annuity for his or her life that is no less than 50% of the amount payable during your joint lives. You may waive the QJSA only with your spouse's consent. Without the consent, you may not take a lump-sum distribution or a single-life annuity ending when you die. A single-life annuity pays higher monthly benefits during your lifetime than the qualified joint and survivor annuity.

The law also requires that a *qualified pre-retirement survivor annuity (QPSA)* be paid to your surviving spouse if you die before the date vested benefits first become payable or if you die after the earliest payment date but before retiring. The QPSA is automatic unless you, with your spouse's consent, agree to a different benefit.

 Planning Reminder

Spouse Must Consent in Writing to Your Waiver

Your spouse must consent in writing to your waiver of a required annuity and the selection of a different type of distribution. A spouse's consent must be witnessed by a plan representative or notary public. An election to waive the qualified joint and survivor annuity may be made during the 90-day period ending on the annuity starting date. An election to waive the qualified pre-retirement survivor annuity may be made any time after the first day of the plan year in which you reach age 35. A waiver is revocable during the time permitted to make the election.

Your plan should provide you with a written explanation of these annuity rules within a reasonable period before the annuity starting date, as well as the rules for electing to waive the joint and survivor annuity benefit and the pre-retirement survivor annuity.

Plan may provide exception for marriages of less than one year. The terms of a plan may provide that a QJSA or QPSA will not be provided to a spouse of the plan participant if the couple has been married for less than one year as of the participant's annuity starting date (QJSA) or, if earlier, the date of the participant's death (QPSA).

Cash out of annuity. If the present value of the QJSA is $5,000 or less, your employer may "cash out" your interest without your consent or your spouse's consent by making a lump-sum distribution of the present value of the annuity before the annuity starting date. After the annuity starting date, you and your spouse must consent to a cash-out. Written consent is required for a cash-out if the present value of the annuity exceeds $5,000. Similar cash-out rules apply to a QPSA.

7.12 Court Distributions to Former Spouse

As a part of a divorce-related property settlement, or to cover alimony or support obligations, a state domestic relations court can require that all or part of a plan participant's retirement benefits be paid to a spouse, former spouse, child, or other dependent. Administrators of pension, profit-sharing, or stock bonus plans are required to honor a qualified domestic relations order (QDRO) that meets specific tax law tests. For example, the QDRO generally may not alter the amount or form of benefits provided by the plan, but it may authorize payments after the participant reaches the earliest retirement age, even if he or she continues working. A QDRO may provide that the recipient spouse is entitled to all, some, or none of the spousal survivor benefits payable under the plan.

QDRO distributions to spouse or former spouse. If you are the spouse or former spouse of an employee and you receive a distribution pursuant to a QDRO, the distribution is generally taxable to you. However, you may make a tax-free rollover to an IRA or to a qualified plan, as discussed at 7.8. Furthermore, if your spouse or former spouse (the plan participant) was born before 1936 or was over age $59^1/_2$, a distribution of your entire share of the benefits may be eligible for special averaging, provided the distribution, if received by your spouse (or former spouse), would satisfy the lump-sum distribution tests at 7.2. If your spouse (or former spouse) was born before 1936, you may use Form 4972 to claim either 10-year or five-year averaging, and possibly the 20% capital gain election; *see 7.4.* If your spouse (or former spouse) was born after 1935 but was at least age $59^1/_2$ when the distribution was made, five-year averaging is available on Form 4972 for a lump-sum distribution made before 2000. Transfers from a governmental or church plan pursuant to a qualifying domestic relations order are also eligible for special averaging or rollover treatment.

For these tax rules to apply, the court order must contain specific language required to create a QDRO. The recipient spouse (or former spouse) must be assigned rights to the plan participant's retirement benefits plan, and must be referred to as an "alternate payee" in the court decree. The decree must identify the retirement plan and indicate the amount and number of payments subject to the QDRO. Both spouses must be identified by name and address.

If the above information is not clearly provided in the decree, QDRO treatment may be denied and the plan participant taxed on the retirement plan distributions, rather than the spouse who actually receives payments.

Distributions to a child or other dependent. Payments from a QDRO are taxed to the plan participant, not to the dependent who actually receives them, where the recipient is not a spouse or former spouse.

7.13 When Retirement Benefits Must Begin

The longer you can defer taking retirement distributions from your company plan or self-employed Keogh plan, the greater will be the tax-free buildup of your retirement fund. To cut off this tax deferral, the law requires minimum distributions to begin by a specified date.

Unless you are a more-than-5% owner, the required beginning date is the later of (1) April 1 following the year in which you reach age $70^1/_2$ and (2) April 1 following the year in which you retire. For example, if you reach age $70^1/_2$ in 2000 and do not retire until 2002, the first required minimum distribution from the plan does not have to be made to you until April 1, 2003, the year after the year of retirement.

Planning Reminder

Drafting a QDRO

Drafting a QDRO involves technical details that legal counsel must carefully review. To ease the drafting burdens and reduce litigation over the effect of QDRO provisions, Congress passed a law requiring the IRS to provide sample language for inclusion in a QDRO that meets tax law requirements. The IRS sample language and a discussion of QDRO requirements is in IRS Notice 97-11.

Caution

Effect of Waiting Until April Deadline

You have until April 1 of the year after the year in which you reach age $70^1/_2$, or if later, until April 1 of the year following the year of retirement, to take your first required minimum distribution from your employer's plan; *see 7.13.* However, if no distribution is taken during your $70^1/_2$ year or retirement year (whichever is later), you will have to take two distributions during the following year. For example, if you retire and reach age $70^1/_2$ in 2000, and delay receipt of your first distribution until between January 1 and April 1, 2001, you must also receive a distribution for 2001 by December 31, 2001. This could substantially increase your 2001 taxable income, and possibly subject more of your Social Security benefits to tax (*see* Chapter 34).

If you own a business interest of more than 5%, your required beginning date is April 1 of the year following the year in which you reach age $70^1/_2$, even if you are still working.

The above rules took effect in 1997. Under prior law, all employees (except those in governmental and church plans) were required to begin minimum required distributions by April 1 following the year in which they reached age $70^1/_2$.

Transition from prior law. When the law was changed to generally delay the required beginning date until after retirement, it was not clear how the new law applied to employees who had already begun receiving minimum required distributions after age $70^1/_2$ under the prior law, or to employees who were nearing age $70^1/_2$ when the new law took effect. In response, the IRS released transition rules.

If you reached age $70^1/_2$ before 1997 and started to receive minimum required distributions while still working, your plan may give you the option of discontinuing the distributions until you retire, provided the cessation does not interfere with the terms of a qualified domestic relations order *(7.12)*.

If you reached age $70^1/_2$ in 1997 or 1998 and continued working, you may be given a choice between receiving distributions currently or deferring the distributions until after retirement. Alternatively, the plan may be amended to allow current distributions of benefits that had accrued as of the amendment date; distributions of future accruals would be barred until after retirement. Your plan may not completely cut off the option of receiving benefits before retirement.

For employees who reach age $70^1/_2$ after 1998, IRS regulations allow (but do not require) an employer plan to eliminate pre-retirement distributions. If this plan amendment is made, required minimum distributions would start after retirement but no later than April 1 of the year following the year of retirement.

How Much Must You Receive After the Required Beginning Date?

The required beginning date rules apply to distributions from all qualified corporate and self-employed Keogh plans, qualified annuity plans, and Section 457 plans of tax-exempt organizations. The rules also apply to distributions from tax-sheltered annuities *(7.20)* but only for benefits accrued after 1986; there is no mandatory beginning date for tax-sheltered annuity benefits accrued before 1987. When you begin distributions under the required beginning date rule, you may spread payments over your life, over the joint lives of yourself and any designated beneficiary, or over a specific period that does not exceed your life expectancy or the joint life expectancies of yourself and any designated beneficiary. To determine your life expectancy, use Table V shown at *7.23*. For joint life expectancies, *see* the sample table at the end of Chapter 8.

Once you choose your beneficiary and a payment period, the plan administrator should figure the minimum required distributions you must receive annually.

Required minimum distributions based on life expectancy. In figuring the payout schedule, the terms of the plan may require that your life expectancy, and the life expectancy of a spousal beneficiary, be recalculated annually. Alternatively, the plan may allow you to choose between the recalculation method and a term-certain method. The initial joint life expectancy under both methods is your single life expectancy or the joint life expectancy of you and your designated beneficiary as of the year in which you reach age $70^1/_2$ or in which you retire, whichever is later. Under the term-certain method, the initial life expectancy is reduced by one in each later year. Under the recalculation method, the initial life expectancy is reduced more slowly because the recalculated life expectancy is based on your age on your birthday in each year. Although the recalculation method generally allows you to spread out distributions over a longer period than the term-certain method, the term-certain method generally has advantages after the death of you or your beneficiary by requiring smaller minimum distributions for the survivor.

Basing payments on the joint life expectancies of yourself and a younger beneficiary will extend the withdrawal period, but the law imposes a limit if the beneficiary is someone other than your spouse. For example, a beneficiary more than 10 years younger than you will be treated as being only 10 years younger, regardless of actual age. This requirement does not affect payments required for spouses under the qualified joint and survivor annuity rule of *7.11*. As discussed at *7.11*, your plan must automatically provide annuity benefits in the form of a qualified joint and survivor annuity if you are married, unless you and your spouse elect otherwise.

Minimum distributions that you are required to take under these rules may not be rolled over tax free.

Planning Reminder

Plan in Advance for Minimum Distributions

The rules for determining minimum required distributions are complicated. Contact your employer's plan administrator well in advance to determine your options in selecting beneficiaries and figuring a payment schedule. Also, consult with your tax adviser about the choice between the term-certain method and the recalculation method if your plan allows you to make an election.

Caution

Penalty for Insufficient Distributions

Before you reach your required beginning date, set up a payment schedule with your employer's plan administrator. You will be subject to a 50% penalty if you fail to take a distribution from the plan by the required beginning date or you receive a distribution that is insufficient under the required distribution methods. Unless waived by the IRS, the 50% penalty will apply to the difference between the amount you should have received and the amount you did receive. The IRS may waive the penalty if you show that the shortfall was due to reasonable error and that you are taking steps to correct it. To apply for a waiver, compute the penalty on Form 5329 and attach a letter of explanation. Individuals who made a special election before 1984 to receive distributions under pre-1984 rules will not be subject to the penalty.

7.14 Payouts to Beneficiaries

The distribution rules for beneficiaries depend on whether the employee or self-employed plan participant had started to receive required minimum distributions under the rules at 7.13.

If an employee dies after the start of required minimum distributions. In this case, beneficiaries must continue to take distributions at least as rapidly as under the method being used by the plan participant during his or her lifetime. For example, if an employee had elected under the term-certain method (see 7.13) to receive benefits over the 24-year joint life expectancy for himself and his beneficiary, but died after 10 years, the beneficiary would have to receive installments over the remaining 14 years but could elect to accelerate payments over a shorter period. Where the employee's life expectancy had been recalculated annually (see 7.13), the minimum required distributions to the beneficiary are based on his or her remaining single life expectancy; that is, the single life expectancy in the first distribution year reduced by one for each elapsed year.

A beneficiary who chooses a lump-sum distribution instead of installment payments may claim special averaging if the employee met the age test; see 7.7. A surviving spouse may also elect a tax-free rollover; see 7.8.

A surviving spouse receiving an annuity under the survivor benefit rules at 7.11 receives payments over his or her lifetime, starting at the participant's death.

If an employee dies before required minimum distributions have begun. In this case, distribution rules depend on who the beneficiary is and the terms of the plan. The plan may give the beneficiary the option of (1) taking distributions annually over his or her life expectancy or (2) completing all distributions by December 31 of the fifth year following the year of the employee's death. On the other hand, the plan may specify which method must be used or place restrictions on use of the life expectancy method, such as limiting it to a specific term of years. If the plan does not specify the method and the beneficiary does not make an election by December 31 of the year following the year of death, the life expectancy method discussed below must be used by a surviving spouse; a beneficiary other than a surviving spouse must use the five-year method. For a lump-sum distribution, a beneficiary may use special averaging if the employee would have qualified; see 7.7. A surviving spouse may make a tax-free rollover of a lump sum; see 7.8.

Life expectancy method. If the plan gives the beneficiary the option of taking distributions over his or her life expectancy, the distribution starting date depends on who the beneficiary is:

A *surviving spouse* who is not receiving annuity payments under the rules at 7.11 may delay the start of distributions until the later of: (1) December 31 of the year in which the deceased spouse would have reached age $70^1/_2$, and (2) December 31 of the year after the year of the employee's death. By that later date, the surviving spouse must take the first distribution based upon his or her life expectancy.

A *nonspouse beneficiary* has until December 31 of the year following the year of the employee's death to take the first distribution under his or her life expectancy. If he or she has the option to elect this life expectancy method but fails to do so by December 31 of the year following the year of the employee's death, the five-year method must be used.

Five-year method. Under this method, all distributions must be completed by December 31 of the fifth year following the year of the employee's death. For example, if an employee dies on January 6, 1999, the entire account must be distributed to the beneficiary by December 31, 2004, under the five-year method.

7.15 Penalty for Distributions Before Age $59^1/_2$

A 10% penalty generally applies to taxable distributions made to you before you reach age $59^1/_2$ from a qualified corporate or Keogh plan, qualified annuity plan, and tax-sheltered annuity plan, but there are several exceptions. For example, the penalty does not apply to distributions made to you after separation from service if the separation occurs during or after the year in which you reach age 55. A full list of exceptions is shown below.

If no exception applies, the penalty is 10% of the taxable distribution. If you make a tax-free rollover (7.8), the distribution is not taxable and not subject to the penalty. If a partial rollover is made, the part not rolled over is taxable and subject to the penalty.

A similar 10% penalty applies to IRA distributions before age $59^1/_2$; see 8.12 for IRA penalty rules. The penalty is 25% if a distribution before age $59^1/_2$ is made from a SIMPLE IRA in the first two years of plan participation; see 8.19. The penalty for pre–age $59^1/_2$ distributions from deferred annuities is at 7.22. The penalty does *not* apply to Section 457 plans of tax-exempt employers or state or local governments.

 Caution

Penalty Exception for Substantially Equal Payments

The substantially equal payments exception to the 10% early distribution penalty is revoked if qualifying payments are not received for at least five years. For example, you separate from service when you are age 57 and you begin to receive a series of qualifying substantially equal payments. When you are age 61, you stop the payments or modify the payment schedule so that it no longer qualifies. A recapture penalty applies. The 10% penalty applies to the payments received before age $59^1/_2$ because the five-year test was not met.

Exceptions to the penalty. The following distributions are exempt from the 10% penalty, even if made to you before age $59^1/_2$. If your employer "knows" that an exception applies, a code for the exception will be entered in Box 7 of Form 1099-R on which the distribution is reported.

- Distributions that you roll over tax free under the "direct rollover" or "personal rollover" rules of *7.8*.
- Distributions made on account of your total disability.
- Distributions after separation from service if you are age 55 or over in the year you retire or leave the company.
- Distributions used to pay deductible medical expenses exceeding 7.5% of adjusted gross income (whether or not an itemized deduction for medical expenses is claimed).
- Distributions received after separation from service that are part of a series of substantially equal payments (at least annually) over your life expectancy, or over the joint life expectancy of yourself and your designated beneficiary. If you claim the exception and begin to receive such a series of payments but then before age $59^1/_2$ you receive a lump sum or change the distribution method and you are not totally disabled, a recapture penalty tax will apply. The recapture tax applies the 10% penalty to all amounts received before age $59^1/_2$, as if the exception had never been allowed, plus interest for that period. The recapture tax also applies to payments received before age $59^1/_2$ if substantially equal payments are not received for at least five years.
- Distributions paid to an alternate payee pursuant to a qualified domestic relations court order (QDRO).
- Distributions made pursuant to a designation under the 1982 Tax Act (TEFRA).
- Distributions to an employee who separated from service by March 1, 1986, provided that accrued benefits were in pay status as of that date under a written election specifying the payout schedule.

Hardship distributions for college or home-buying costs. The 10% penalty applies to a hardship distribution that you receive before age $59^1/_2$ from a 401(k) plan *(7.19)* or 403(b) tax-sheltered annuity plan *(7.20)* where it is used to pay tuition costs or to buy a principal residence. Such hardship distributions do not qualify for a penalty exception, although a penalty exception generally applies for IRA distributions used for such purposes (*see 8.12* for limitations).

Corrective distributions from 401(k) plans. If you are considered a highly compensated employee and excess elective deferrals or excess contributions are made on your behalf, a distribution of the excess to you is not subject to the penalty.

Beneficiaries exempt from the penalty. If you are the beneficiary of a deceased plan participant, you are not subject to the 10% penalty, regardless of your age or the participant's age.

Filing Form 5329 for exceptions. If your employer correctly entered a penalty exception code in Box 7 of Form 1099-R, you do not have to file Form 5329 to claim the exception. You also do not have to file Form 5329 if you made a tax-free rollover of the entire taxable distribution. You must file Form 5329 if you qualify for an exception, other than the rollover exception, that is not indicated in Box 7 of Form 1099-R.

7.16 Restrictions on Loans From Company Plans

Within limits, you may receive a loan from a qualified company plan, annuity plan, 403(b) plan, or government plan without triggering tax consequences. The maximum loan you can receive without tax is the lesser of 50% of your vested account balance and $50,000, but the $50,000 limit is subject to reductions where there are other loans outstanding; *see* below. Loans must be repayable within five years, unless they are used for buying your principal residence. Loans that do not meet these guidelines are treated as taxable distributions from the plan.

These rules generally apply only to employees. For a self-employed person, a retirement plan loan is a prohibited transaction that usually results in penalties; *see 41.9*.

If your vested accrued benefit is $20,000 or less, you are not taxed if the loan, when added to other outstanding loans from all plans of the employer, is $10,000 or less. However, as a practical matter, your maximum loan may not exceed 50% of your vested account balance because of a Labor Department rule that allows only up to 50% of the vested balance to be used as loan security. Loans in excess of the 50% cap are allowed only if additional collateral is provided.

If your vested accrued benefit exceeds $20,000, then the maximum tax-free loan depends on whether you borrowed from any employer plan within the one-year period ending on the day before the date of the new loan. If you did not borrow within the year, you are not taxed on a loan that does not exceed the lesser of $50,000 and 50% of the vested benefit.

Filing Instruction

Reporting the Early Distribution Penalty

If you received a distribution before age $59^1/_2$, do not qualify for a penalty exception, and Code 1 is shown in Box 7 of your Form 1099-R, multiply the taxable distribution by 10% and enter that amount as the penalty on Line 53 of Form 1040; write "no" next to Line 53 to indicate that Form 5329 does not have to be filed. If you are subject to the penalty and Code 1 is not entered in Box 7 of Form 1099-R, you must file Form 5329.

You may also have to file Form 5329 to claim a penalty exception. However, filing the form is not required if you qualify for the rollover exception or you qualify for another exception that is correctly coded in Box 7 of Form 1099-R.

Planning Reminder

Borrowing From Your Company Retirement Account

You generally may obtain a tax-free loan from your employer's retirement plan up to the lesser of 50% of your vested account balance and $50,000. See *7.16* for lower tax-free loan limits where you have other outstanding loans, and for repayment requirements.

If there were loans within the one-year period, the $50,000 limit must be further reduced. The loan, when added to the outstanding loan balance, may not exceed $50,000 less the excess of (1) the highest outstanding loan balance during the one-year period (ending the day before the new loan) over (2) the outstanding balance on the date of the new loan. This reduced $50,000 limit applies where it is less than 50% of the vested benefit; if 50% of the vested benefit was the smaller amount, that would be the maximum tax-free loan.

> **EXAMPLE**
>
> Your vested plan benefit is $200,000. Assume that in December 1999 you borrow $30,000 from the plan. On November 1, 2000, when the outstanding balance on the first loan is $20,000, you want to take another loan without incurring tax.
>
> You may borrow an additional $20,000 without incurring tax: The $50,000 limit is first reduced by the outstanding loan balance of $20,000—leaving $30,000. The reduced $30,000 limit is in turn reduced by $10,000, the excess of $30,000 (the highest loan balance within one year of the new loan) over $20,000 (the loan balance as of November 1).

Repayment period. Generally, loans within the previously discussed limits must be repayable within five years to avoid being treated as a taxable distribution. However, if you use the loan to purchase a principal residence for yourself, the repayment period may be longer than five years; any reasonable period is allowed. This exception does not apply if the plan loan is used to improve your existing principal residence, to buy a second home, or to finance the purchase of a home or home improvements for other family members; such loans are subject to the five-year repayment rule.

Level loan amortization required. To avoid tax consequences on a plan loan, you must be required to repay using a level amortization schedule, with payments at least quarterly. According to Congressional committee reports, you may accelerate repayment, and the employer may use a variable interest rate and require full repayment if you leave the company.

Giving a demand note does not satisfy the repayment requirements. The IRS and Tax Court held the entire amount of an employee's loan to be a taxable distribution since his demand loan did not require level amortization of principal and interest with at least quarterly payments. It did not matter that the employee had paid interest quarterly and actually repaid the loan within five years.

If required installments are not made, the entire loan balance must be treated as a "deemed distribution" from the plan under IRS proposed regulations. However, the IRS allows the plan administrator to permit a grace period of up to one calendar quarter. If the missed installment is not paid by the end of the grace period, there is at that time a deemed distribution in the amount of the outstanding loan balance.

Under IRS proposed regulations, loan repayments may be suspended for up to one year if the borrower takes a leave of absence during which he or she is paid less than the installments due. However, the installments after the leave must at least equal the original required amount and the loan must be repaid by the end of the allowable repayment period (five years if not used to buy a principal residence). For example, when his vested account balance is $80,000, Joe Smith takes out a $40,000 non–principal residence loan on July 1, 1999, to be repaid with interest in level monthly installments of $825 over five years. He makes nine payments and then takes a year of unpaid leave. When he returns to work he can either increase his monthly payment to $1,130 or resume paying $825 a month and on June 30, 2004, repay the entire balance owed in a lump sum.

Spousal consent generally required to get a loan. All plans subject to the joint and survivor rules of *7.11* must require spousal consent in order to be able to use your account balance as security for the loan in case you default. Check with your plan administrator for consent requirements.

Interest deduction limitations. If you want to borrow from your account to buy a first or second residence and you are not a "key" employee *(3.3)*, you can obtain a full interest deduction by using the residence as collateral for the loan. Your account balance may not be used to secure the loan. Key employees are not allowed any interest deduction for plan loans.

If you use a plan loan for investment purposes and are not a key employee, and the loan is not secured by your elective deferrals (or allocable income) to a 401(k) plan or tax-sheltered annuity, the loan account interest is deductible up to investment income; *see 15.10*. Interest on loans used for personal purposes is not deductible, unless your residence is the security for the loan.

 Caution

Unpaid Loan Taxable If You Leave Job

If you leave your company before your loan is paid off, the company will reduce your vested account balance by the outstanding debt. For example, if your vested account balance is $100,000, and the outstanding loan is $20,000, your account balance is reduced to $80,000. If you elect to receive the balance, rather than choosing a direct rollover, $20,000 will be withheld (20% of the full $100,000) and you will receive only $60,000; *see 7.8*. However, the full $100,000 is treated as a taxable distribution. If you do not roll over *(7.8)* the entire $100,000 within 60 days, you will be taxed on the portion not rolled over, and possibly be subject to a 10% penalty if you were under age $59\frac{1}{2}$ at the time of the distribution (*see 7.15*).

401(k), 403(b), and Government Tax-Deferred Savings Plans

7.17 Tax Benefits of 401(k) Plans

If your company has a profit-sharing or stock bonus plan, it has the opportunity of giving you additional tax-sheltered pay. The tax law allows the company to add a cash or deferred pay plan, called a 401(k) plan.

Your company may offer to contribute to a 401(k) plan trust account on your behalf if you forego a salary increase, but in most plans, contributions take the form of salary-reduction deferrals. Under a salary-reduction agreement, you elect to contribute a specified percentage of your wages to the 401(k) plan instead of receiving it as regular salary. In addition, your company may match a portion of your contribution. A salary-reduction deferral is treated as a contribution by your employer that is not taxable to you if the annual contribution limits are not exceeded.

Salary-reduction deferrals. Making elective salary deferrals allows you to defer tax on salary and get a tax-free buildup of earnings within your 401(k) plan account until withdrawals are made.

An annual limit applies to salary-reduction deferrals; for 1999, the limit was $10,000. The maximum deferral is lower for employees of "small" employers who adopt a SIMPLE 401(k); for 1999, the maximum SIMPLE elective salary deferral was $6,000. The deferral limits may be increased for 2000 by an inflation factor. *See 7.18* for further details on the deferral limits.

Elective deferrals within the annual limit are *pre-tax* contributions so they are not subject to income tax withholding. However, the contributions are subject to Social Security and Medicare withholdings.

Your employer may not require you to make elective deferrals in order to obtain any other benefits, apart from matching contributions. For example, benefits provided under health plans or other compensation plans may not be conditioned on your making salary deferrals to a 401(k) plan.

Distributions. Withdrawals from a 401(k) plan before age $59^1/_2$ are restricted, as explained at *7.19*. A lump-sum distribution after age $59^1/_2$ may be eligible for averaging under the rules of *7.4*. Mandatory 20% withholding applies to a lump sum as well as other distributions that are eligible for averaging; exceptions are at *7.8*.

Nondiscrimination rules. The law imposes strict contribution percentage tests to prevent discrimination in favor of employees who are highly compensated. If these tests are violated, the employer is subject to penalties and the plan could be disqualified unless the excess contributions (plus allocable income) are distributed back to the highly compensated employees within specified time limits.

SIMPLE 401(k). Nondiscrimination tests are eased for employers who adopt a 401(k) plan with SIMPLE contribution provisions. A SIMPLE 401(k) may be set up only by employers who in the preceding year had no more than 100 employees with compensation of at least $5,000. An employer who contributes to a SIMPLE 401(k) must report on a calendar-year basis and may not maintain another qualified plan for employees eligible to participate in the SIMPLE plan.

If the SIMPLE contribution requirements are met, the plan is considered to meet 401(k) nondiscrimination requirements. Employee elective deferrals may not exceed $6,000. The employer must either match the employee deferral, up to 3% of compensation, or contribute 2% of compensation for all eligible employees, whether or not they make elective deferrals. All contributions are nonforfeitable. No other type of contribution is allowed. In figuring the 3% or 2% employer contributions, compensation is subject to an annual compensation ceiling; for 1999 it was $160,000.

Partnership plans. Partnership plans that allow partners to vary annual contributions are treated as 401(k) plans by the IRS. Thus, elective deferrals are subject to the annual limit *(7.18)* and the special 401(k) plan nondiscrimination rules apply.

7.18 Limit on Salary-Reduction Deferrals

The law limits the maximum tax-free salary reduction contribution you can make. For 1999, the limit is $10,000. The $10,000 limit may be increased for 2000 by an inflation factor. Employer plans must limit elective deferrals to the annual tax-free ceiling; otherwise, the plan could be disqualified. Certain highly compensated employees may be unable to take advantage of the maximum tax-free ceiling ($10,000 in 1999) because of restrictions imposed by nondiscrimination tests.

To avoid the strict nondiscrimination tests for employee elective deferrals and employer matching contributions, an employer may make contributions to a SIMPLE 401(k); *see 7.17*.

 Law Alert

SIMPLE 401(k) Plans

An employer that does not maintain another qualified plan is deemed to satisfy 401(k) plan nondiscrimination requirements if employee elective deferrals are limited to $6,000 (this amount may increase for 2000) and the employer either matches the first 3% of compensation deferred to the plan or contributes 2% of compensation for all eligible employees with at least $5,000 in compensation. All contributions must be 100% vested.

 Planning Reminder

Automatic 401(k) Plan Coverage

The IRS has given approval to 401(k) plans in which newly hired employees who do not elect to opt out are enrolled automatically, with a specified percentage of their pay contributed to the plan. Even though the employees do not make affirmative elections to contribute, such plans are qualified provided that the employees are given advance notice of their right either to receive cash or have the designated amount contributed by the employer to the plan.

 Law Alert

Proposed Increase to Deferral Limit for Those Age 50 or Older

At the time this book went to press, Congress was considering legislation that would increase the maximum limit on salary-reduction deferrals to 401(k) plans, SIMPLE IRAs, and Section 457 plans for employees age 50 or older. From 2001 to 2005, the deferral limit would be increased 10% each year so that by 2005, an additional 50% of the regular dollar limit could be deferred; *see* the Supplement for legislative developments.

Caution

Reduced Deferral Limit for Highly Compensated Employees

To avoid discrimination problems an employer may set a lower limit for elective salary deferrals by highly compensated employees than the ceiling generally allowed ($10,000 for 1999).

If, after contributions are made, the plan fails to meet the nondiscrimination tests, the excess contributions will either be returned to the highly compensated employees or kept in the plan but recharacterized as after-tax contributions. In either case, the excess contribution is taxable. Form 1099-R will indicate the excess contribution.

Employers may avoid the nondiscrimination tests by meeting the SIMPLE plan contribution rules; *see 7.17.*

Law Alert

No Rollover of Hardship Distribution After 1999

A hardship distribution from a 401(k) plan made after 1999 is not eligible for rollover *(7.8)* to an IRA or a qualified employer plan. Your employer will not apply 20% withholding to the distribution, as mandatory withholding applies only to rollover-eligible distributions *(7.8).*

The restrictions on rollovers had been scheduled to take effect in 1999, but to give employers time to adapt to the new law the IRS gave them an option to allow a direct rollover of a 1999 hardship distribution to another plan as under prior law. Even if the employer did not allow direct rollover treatment, the IRS allowed employees who received a 1999 hardship distribution to make a personal rollover within 60 days; *see 7.8.*

The annual salary-reduction limit ($10,000 for 1999) applies to total salary reduction deferrals made to 401(k) plans as well as to 403(b) tax-sheltered annuity plans *(7.20)* and simplified employee pension plans established before 1997 *(8.15)*. If you participate in more than one such plan, the limit applies to the total salary reductions for all the plans.

An employer may make matching or other contributions, provided the total contribution for the year, including the employee's pre-tax salary deferral and any employee after-tax contributions, does not exceed the *lesser* of 25% of compensation and the annual limit for defined contribution plans, which for 1999 was $30,000.

Correcting excess deferrals. A single plan must apply the annual limit on salary deferrals ($10,000 for 1999) in order to maintain qualified status. However, if you participate in more than one plan, and the total salary deferrals for the year exceed the annual limit, the IRS requires you to report the excess as wages on Line 7 of Form 1040. Furthermore, by April 15 of the year following the year of the excess, you should allocate the excess among the plans and withdraw it, plus income allocable to the excess. If you do, the corrective distribution is not taxable; the distribution of the excess income is taxable in the year it is distributed. If an excess deferral allocated to a 401(k) plan or 403(b) tax-sheltered annuity is not withdrawn by the April 15 deadline, it will be taxed again when distributed from the plan. If an excess deferral to a salary-reduction SEP set up before 1997 *(see 8.16)* is *not* withdrawn by the April 15 deadline, it is treated as a regular IRA contribution that could be subject to the penalty for excess IRA contributions *(see 8.7)*. Excess deferrals (and earnings) distributed by the April 15 deadline are not subject to the 10% penalty for premature distributions *(7.15)* even if you are under age $59^1/_2$.

7.19 Withdrawals From 401(k) Plans Restricted

By law, you may not withdraw funds attributable to elective salary reduction contributions until you reach age $59^1/_2$, are separated from service, become totally disabled, or show financial hardship. Under IRS rules, it is difficult to qualify for hardship withdrawals; *see* below. If you do qualify, the withdrawal is taxable, and if you are under age $59^1/_2$, it is subject to the 10% early distribution penalty unless you are disabled or meet the medical expense exception to the penalty *(7.15)*. Lump-sum withdrawals are also allowed if the plan terminates, or the corporation sells its assets or its interest in a subsidiary and you continue to work for the buyer or the subsidiary. However, the hardship provision and age $59^1/_2$ withdrawal allowance do not apply to certain "pre-ERISA" money purchase pension plans (in existence June 27, 1974).

Withdrawals before age $59^1/_2$. Withdrawals for medical disability, financial hardship, or separation from service are subject to the 10% penalty for premature withdrawals unless you meet one of the exceptions listed at *7.15*.

Loans. If you are allowed to borrow from the plan, the loan restrictions at *7.16* apply.

Qualifying for hardship withdrawals. IRS regulations restrict hardship withdrawals of pre-tax salary deferrals. If you qualify under the following restrictive rules you may withdraw your elective deferrals. However, income allocable to elective deferrals may be withdrawn only if it was credited to your account as of the end of the last plan year ending before July 1, 1989; the plan may provide an even earlier cutoff date for income.

The IRS requires you to show an immediate and heavy financial need that cannot be met with other resources.

Financial need includes the following expenses (this list may be expanded by the IRS in rulings):

- Purchase of a principal residence for yourself (but not mortgage payments);
- Tuition, related fees and room and board for the next 12 months of post-secondary education for yourself, your spouse, children, or other dependents;
- Medical expenses previously incurred for yourself, your spouse, or dependents or expenses incurred to obtain medical care for such persons;
- Preventing your eviction or mortgage foreclosure; and
- Paying funeral expenses for a family member.

Even if you can show financial need, you may not make a hardship withdrawal if you have other resources to pay the expenses. You do not have to provide your employer with a detailed financial statement, but you must state to your employer that you cannot pay the expenses with: compensation, insurance, or reimbursements; liquidation of your assets without causing yourself hardship by virtue of the liquidation; stopping your contributions, including salary deferrals, to the plan; other distributions or nontaxable loans from plans of any employer; or borrowing from a commercial lender. Your spouse's assets, as well as those of your minor children, are considered to be yours unless you show that they are not available to you. For example, property held in trust for a child or under the Uniform Transfers (or Gifts) to Minors Act is not treated as your property.

Under a special rule, you are considered to lack other resources if you have taken all available distributions from all plans of the employer, including nontaxable loans, and you suspend making any contributions to any of the employer's qualified and nonqualified deferred compensation plans for at least 12 months after receipt of the hardship distribution. Furthermore, all of the employer's plans must provide that for the year after the year of the hardship distribution, elective contributions must be limited to the excess of the annual salary deferral limitation over the elective contributions made for the year of the hardship distribution.

7.20 Annuities for Employees of Tax-Exempts and Schools (403(b) Plans)

If you are employed by a state or local government public school, or by a tax-exempt religious, charitable, scientific, or educational organization, or are on the civilian staff or faculty of the Uniformed Services University of the Health Sciences (Department of Defense), you may be able to arrange for the purchase of a nonforfeitable tax-sheltered annuity. Tax-sheltered annuities may also be purchased by self-employed ministers and by non–tax-exempt employers of ordained or licensed ministers or chaplains. Another name for a tax-sheltered annuity is a 403(b) plan. A 403(b) plan may invest funds for employees in mutual-fund shares as well as in annuity contracts.

The purchase of the annuity or mutual-fund shares is generally made through a reduction of salary that is used to pay for the contract. The amount of the salary reduction used to buy the contract is not taxable if it comes within specified limits. The tax rules for computing the exclusion are complicated, as there are several limitations and exceptions.

Note: As the following contribution rules for tax-sheltered annuities have been stated in general terms and are subject to Treasury regulations, we suggest that you also consult your employer or the issuer of the contract. IRS Publication 571 has detailed examples.

Tax-free exclusion allowance. Salary-reduction contributions are treated as employer contributions. The salary reduction plus any non-elective contributions made by the employer for the year are generally tax free up to an amount called the *exclusion allowance*. The exclusion allowance is generally 20% of your pay multiplied by the number of years of service with your employer, *less* tax-free contributions made in prior years by your employer (including your tax-free salary reductions) to a tax-sheltered annuity or to any qualified plan maintained by your employer.

Contributions that are within the exclusion allowance are tax free only if they do not exceed the annual limit on employer contributions, which for 1999 is the lesser of 25% of pay and $30,000.

Furthermore, tax-free salary reductions are limited to the annual ceiling for elective deferrals, which for 1999 is $10,000. However, employees with at least 15 years of experience may be able to defer an additional $3,000.

 Caution

$10,000 Salary Deferral Limit for 1999

Even if allowed by the general exclusion allowance rule, the maximum tax-free salary reduction from a tax-sheltered annuity plan cannot exceed the *lower* of 25% of pay and an annual limit, which for 1999 was $10,000. If you work for more than one employer, the $10,000 limit applies to your total elective deferrals made for the year to all plans, even if they are maintained by different employers. An increased limit for certain employees with 15 years of service is discussed at *7.20.*

The $10,000 salary-reduction limit may be increased after 1999 by an inflation factor.

EXAMPLE

Carol Grossinger, a public school teacher earning $32,000, agreed to a $3,600 salary reduction for 1999 to be used to purchase an annuity contract. The employer also contributed $1,800 to a pension trust for the teacher's account. For 1999, the entire salary reduction contribution is tax free as it is within the $6,400 exclusion allowance (20% of $32,000 salary × one year service). Pay is not reduced by elective salary-reduction contributions when figuring the 20% exclusion allowance. In later years, Carol's exclusion allowance will be reduced by tax-free employer contributions including salary-reduction contributions made in the prior years.

Alternative contribution ceilings. Subject to the maximum salary-reduction limit ($10,000 for 1999), employees of schools, hospitals, churches, health and welfare service agencies, and home health service agencies may be able to elect tax-free contributions that exceed 25% of pay, or that exceed the exclusion allowance. There are three alternative methods, but only one may be elected and an election is irrevocable.

One alternative allows such employees to irrevocably elect a limitation equal to the *lower* of (1) the general 20% of pay exclusion allowance, (2) 25% of pay plus $4,000, and (3) $15,000. Another alternative election allows such employees to make an irrevocable election to disregard the general 20% exclusion allowance. If the election is made, the tax-free contribution equals the contribution limit for defined contribution plans, the *lesser* of 25% of pay and $30,000 (this amount may be increased after 1999).

The third alternative allows such employees in the year of separation from service to elect a tax-free contribution limit equal to the *lower* of (1) $30,000 (this amount may be increased after 1999), (2) the exclusion allowance, taking into account only the last 10 years of service, and (3) the annual limit on salary-reduction deferrals, which is $10,000 for 1999. This limit may be used only once.

Church employees. A church employee whose adjusted gross income is $17,000 or less is allowed a minimum exclusion allowance equal to the *lesser* of $3,000 and his or her includible compensation. In addition, an election may be made permitting contributions exceeding the 25% of pay test, up to $10,000 per year; however, there is a lifetime contribution limit of $40,000.

If, in addition to a tax-sheltered annuity, you make salary deferrals to a 401(k) plan or simplified employee pension plan, the annual salary reduction limit applies to the total deferrals; *see 7.18*. If you defer more than the annual limit, the excess is taxable. Further, if a salary reduction deferral in excess of the annual limit is made and the excess is not distributed to you by April 15 of the following year, the excess will be taxed twice—not only in the year of deferral but again in the year it is actually distributed. To avoid the double tax, any excess deferral plus the income attributable to such excess should be distributed no later than April 15 of the year following the year in which the excess deferral is made; *see 7.18*.

If your employer makes separate contributions in addition to your salary-reduction deferrals, the total of elective salary reductions (not to exceed the annual limit) plus the employer contributions may be up to the contribution limit for defined contribution plans, which is generally the lower of 25% of pay and $30,000; the $30,000 ceiling may be increased after 1999.

Special catch-up election for certain employees with 15 years of service. If allowed under the general 20% of *pay/years* of service exclusion formula, and by the 25% of pay limit, the annual salary reduction ceiling ($10,000 for 1999) is increased by $3,000 for employees of educational organizations, hospitals, churches, home health service agencies, and health and welfare service agencies who have completed 15 years of service. However, the extra $3,000 annual deferral may not be claimed indefinitely. There is a lifetime limit of $15,000 on the amount of extra deferrals allowed. Furthermore, the extra deferrals may not be claimed after lifetime elective deferrals to the plan exceed $5,000 multiplied by your years of service.

Distributions from tax-sheltered annuities. Distributions attributable to salary-reduction contributions to a 403(b) tax-sheltered annuity are allowed only when an employee reaches age 59$^{1}/_{2}$, separates from service, becomes disabled, suffers financial hardship, or dies. The hardship distribution rules are the same as for 401(k) plans; *see 7.19*. Annuity payments are taxed under the general rules for employees, discussed at *7.25*. Payments are fully taxable if the only contributions to the plan were salary-reduction contributions excluded from income (pre-tax contributions) under the annual limits discussed earlier in this section.

Non-annuity distributions from a tax-sheltered annuity do not qualify for special averaging *(7.4)*, but a tax-free rollover of a distribution may be made to another tax-sheltered annuity or IRA unless the distribution is not eligible for rollover under the rules at *7.8*. If you do not choose to have the payer of the distribution make a direct rollover, mandatory 20% withholding will be applied. You may then personally make a rollover within 60 days, but you would have to include the withheld amount in the rolled-over amount to avoid tax on the entire distribution. *See 7.8* for further rollover and withholding details.

Benefits accruing after 1986 are subject to the required beginning date rules discussed at *7.13* and a penalty may be imposed for failure to take minimum required distributions. Benefits accrued before 1987 are not subject to the required minimum distribution rules until the year you reach age 75.

7.21 Government and Exempt Organization Deferred Pay Plans

Federal government employees may make tax-free salary-reduction contributions to the Federal Thrift Savings Fund. Employees of state and local governments and of tax-exempt organizations may be able to make tax-free salary-reduction contributions to a Section 457 deferred compensation plan.

Federal employees. Federal employees may elect to defer up to 10% of their basic pay to the Federal Thrift Savings Fund, but no more than the limit on elective deferrals. The deferral limit for 1999 is $10,000, the same as for 401(k) plans; *see 7.18*. The limit is subject to increases for inflation. Deferrals are not taxed until distributed from the plan. The deferred amount is counted as wages for purposes of computing Social Security taxes and benefits.

 Planning Reminder

Switching Annuity Investments

To change tax-sheltered annuity investments, you may direct the issuer of your current annuity contract to make a direct transfer of your account to a different issuer. The transfer is tax free, provided that distributions with respect to salary reduction contributions are allowed under both contracts only when the employee reaches age 59$^{1}/_{2}$, separates from service, becomes disabled, suffers financial hardship, or dies.

Distributions from the Thrift Savings Fund are generally fully taxable. However, lump-sum distributions are eligible for special averaging under the rules of *7.4*, or tax-free rollover treatment; *see 7.8*. If you separate from service before the year in which you reach age 55, you are subject to the 10% penalty for premature distributions unless you are disabled or qualify for the medical exception discussed at *7.15*.

Section 457 plans. State and local governments and tax-exempt organizations other than churches may set up deferred compensation plans that allow employees to defer annually up to the *lesser* of $33^1/_3$% of includible compensation (not including the deferrals) *and* an annual limit that for 1999 was $8,000. The $8,000 limit may be increased for 2000 by an inflation adjustment.

A limited "catch-up" provision allows employees in the last three years before reaching normal retirement age to defer larger amounts, provided that the full $8,000 or $33^1/_3$% limit has not been used in prior years. The catch-up deferral, figured under IRS regulations, may not exceed $15,000. Deferred pay and income allocable to the deferrals is not taxed until the year it is distributed or made available to the employee. Distributions are fully taxable; averaging and rollover treatment may not be claimed.

The annual deferral limit does not apply to vacation leave, sick leave, disability pay, compensatory time, severance pay, or death benefits plans.

If an employee participates in more than one Section 457 plan, the annual limit applies to total deferrals under all the plans. Furthermore, if an employee also participates in a tax-sheltered annuity plan, simplified employee pension (SEP), 401(k) plan, or Section 501(c)(18) plan (created before June 25, 1959, and funded solely by employee contributions), the annual Section 457 plan limit is reduced by tax-free deferrals to the other plan.

Distributions to employees or beneficiaries generally may not be made before the year the employee turns age $70^1/_2$, the employee separates from service, or faces an "unforeseeable" emergency, assuming the plan allows payment in cases of emergency. Under IRS regulations, an unforeseeable emergency generally means severe financial hardship resulting from a sudden illness or accident of the employee or a dependent, or loss of property due to a casualty. If the employee can obtain funds by ceasing deferrals to the plan or by liquidating assets without causing himself or herself severe financial hardship, payment from the plan is not allowed. The regulations specifically prohibit payments from the plan to purchase a home or pay for a child's college tuition.

A one-time in-service distribution may be made if the account balance is $5,000 or less and there have been no plan deferrals in the prior two-year period.

See 7.13 for required distribution starting dates after age $70^1/_2$ and minimum payout rules. Where an employee dies before receiving distributions, the account balance must be paid to non-spouse beneficiaries over a period of 15 years or less. Payments to a surviving spouse may be made over the spouse's life expectancy.

Note: Check with your employer for other details on Section 457 contributions and distribution rules.

Caution

Unforeseen Emergency Distributions

If you can show severe financial hardship arising from a sudden illness or accident, or loss of property due to events beyond your control, and you are unable to obtain funds elsewhere, you may make a withdrawal from your employer's Section 457 plan. However, the need to buy a home or pay college expenses does not qualify as an unforeseeable emergency.

Reporting Commercial Annuities

7.22 Figuring the Taxable Part of Your Annuity

Tax treatment of a distribution depends on whether you receive it before or after the annuity starting date, and on the amount of your investment. A cash withdrawal before age $59^1/_2$ from an annuity contract is generally subject to a 10% penalty, but there are exceptions; the penalty is discussed at the end of this section. If your annuity is from an employer plan and it started after July 1, 1986, *see 7.25*.

The *annuity starting date* is either the first day of the first period for which you receive a payment or the date on which the obligation under the contract becomes fixed, whichever is later. If your monthly payments start on August 1 for the period starting July 1, July 1 is your annuity starting date.

Payments before the annuity starting date. If your commercial annuity contract was purchased *after* August 13, 1982, withdrawals before the annuity starting date are taxable to the extent that the cash value of the contract, immediately before the distribution, exceeds your investment in the contract. This rule also applies to withdrawals that are attributed to investments made after August 13, 1982, where the contract was purchased before August 14, 1982. Loans under the contract or pledges are treated as cash withdrawals. Withdrawals from contracts bought by a qualified retirement plan are discussed at *7.25*.

Filing Tip

Surrender of Contract

Payments on a complete surrender of the annuity contract or at maturity are taxable only to the extent they exceed your investment.

If the contract was purchased before August 14, 1982, withdrawals *before* the annuity starting date are taxable only if they exceed your investment. Loans are tax free and are not treated as withdrawals subject to this rule. Where additional investments were made after August 13, 1982, cash withdrawals are first considered to be tax-free distributions of the investment before August 14, 1982. If the withdrawal exceeds this investment, the balance is fully taxable to the extent of earnings on the contract, with any excess withdrawals treated as a tax-free recovery of the investment made after August 14, 1982.

Payments on or after the annuity starting date. If the withdrawal is a regular annuity payment, that part of the annuity payment allocated to your cost investment is treated as a nontaxable return of the cost; the balance is taxable income earned on the investment. You may find the taxable part of your annuity payment by following the six steps listed below under "Taxable Portion of Annuity Payments." If you have a variable annuity, the computation of the tax-free portion is discussed following Step 6.

Payments on or after the annuity starting date that are not part of the annuity, such as dividends, are generally taxable, but there are exceptions. If the contract is a life insurance or endowment contract, withdrawals of earnings are tax free to the extent of your investment, unless the contract is a modified endowment contract.

Taxable Portion of Annuity Payments

If the payer of the contract does not provide the taxable amount in Box 2a of Form 1099-R, you can compute the taxable amount of your commercial annuity using the following steps.

If you have an employee annuity *(7.25)* that started before July 2, 1986, you also can use the following six steps to figure your taxable payment. If your employee annuity started after July 1, 1986, you may use a simplified method discussed at *7.26*.

Step 1: Figure your investment in the annuity contract. If you have no investment in the contract, annuity income is fully taxable; therefore, ignore Steps 2 through 6.

If your annuity is—	Your cost is—
Single premium annuity contract	The single premium paid.
Deferred annuity contract	The total premiums paid.
A gift	Your donor's cost.
An employee annuity	The total of your after-tax contributions to the plan plus your employer's contributions that you were required to report as income; see 7.25.
With a refund feature	The value of the refund feature.

From cost, you subtract the following items:

- Any premiums refunded, and rebates or dividends received on or before the annuity starting date.
- Additional premiums for double indemnity or disability benefits.
- Amounts received under the contract before the annuity starting date to the extent these amounts were not taxed; *see* above.
- Value of a refund feature; *see* below.

Value of refund feature. Your investment in the contract is reduced by the value, if any, of the refund feature.

Your annuity has a refund feature when these three requirements are present: (1) the refund under the contract depends, even in part, on the life expectancy of at least one person; (2) the contract provides for payments to a beneficiary or the annuitant's estate after the annuitant's death; and (3) the payments to the estate or beneficiary are a refund of the amount paid for the annuity.

The value of the refund feature is figured by using a life expectancy multiple that may be found in Treasury Table III or Table VII, depending on the date of your investment; the tables are in IRS Publication 939.

Where an employer paid part of the cost, the refund is figured on only the part paid by the employee.

The refund feature is considered to be zero if (1) for a joint and survivor annuity, both annuitants are age 74 or younger, the payments are guaranteed for less than $2\frac{1}{2}$ years, and the survivor's

Planning Reminder

Lifetime Exclusion Limit

For an annuity starting after 1996, payments become taxable once they exceed your investment minus the value of any refund feature.

annuity is at least 50% of the first annuitant's (retiree's) annuity or (2) for a single-life annuity without survivor benefits, the payments are guaranteed for less than $2^1/_2$ years and you are age 57 or younger if using the new (unisex) annuity tables, age 42 or younger if male and using the old annuity tables, or age 47 or younger if female and using the old annuity tables.

Also subtract from cost any tax-free recovery of your investment received *before* the annuity starting date, as previously discussed.

Step 2: Find your expected return. This is the total of all the payments you are to receive. If the payments are to be made to you for life, your expected return is figured by multiplying the amount of the annual payment by your life expectancy as of the nearest birthday to the annuity starting date. The annuity starting date is the first day of the first period for which an annuity payment is received. For example, on January 1 you complete payment under an annuity contract providing for monthly payments starting on July 1 for the period beginning June 1. The annuity starting date is June 1. Use that date in computing your investment in the contract under Step 1 and your expected return.

If payments are for life, you find your life expectancy in IRS tables included in IRS Publication 939. The table for single life annuities is in *7.23*. When using the table, your age is the age at the birthday nearest the annuity starting date. If you have a joint and survivor annuity and after your death the same payments are to be made to a second annuitant, the expected return is based on your joint life expectancy. Use Treasury Table II in IRS Publication 939 to get joint life expectancy if the entire investment was before July 1, 1986. Use Treasury Table VI if any investment was made after June 30, 1986. If your joint and survivor annuity provides for a different payment amount to the survivor, you must separately compute the expected return for each annuitant; this method is explained in Publication 939. Adjustments to the life expectancy multiple are required when your annuity is payable quarterly, semiannually, or annually. The required adjustment is discussed in *7.23*.

If the payments are for a fixed number of years or for life, whichever is shorter, find your expected return by multiplying your annual payments by a life expectancy multiple found in Treasury Table IV if your entire investment was before July 1, 1986, or Table VIII if any investment was made after June 30, 1986.

If payments are for a fixed number of years (as in an endowment contract) without regard to your life expectancy, find your expected return by multiplying your annual payment by the number of years.

Note: See *7.23* for more information on the life expectancy tables.

Step 3: Divide the investment in the contract (Step 1) by the expected return (Step 2). This will give you the tax-free percentage of your yearly annuity payments. The tax-free percentage remains the same for the remaining years of the annuity, even if payments increase due to a cost-of-living adjustment. A different computation of the tax-free percentage applies to variable annuities; *see* below.

If your annuity started before 1987, and you live longer than your projected life expectancy (shown in the IRS table), you may continue to apply the same tax-free percentage to each payment you receive. Thus, you may exclude from income more than you paid. However, if your annuity starting date is after 1986, your lifetime exclusion may not exceed your cost investment, less the value of any refund feature. Once you have recovered your cost, further payments are fully taxable.

If your annuity starting date is after July 1, 1986, and you die before recovering your investment, a deduction is allowed on your final tax return for the unrecovered cost. If a refund of the investment is made under the contract to a beneficiary, the beneficiary is allowed the deduction. The deduction is claimed as a miscellaneous itemized deduction that is not subject to the 2% adjusted gross income floor; *see* Chapter 19.

Step 4: Find your total annuity payments for the year. For example, you received 10 monthly payments of $100 as your annuity began in March. Your total payments are $1,000, the monthly payment multiplied by 10.

Step 5: Multiply the percentage in Step 3 by the total in Step 4. The result is the nontaxable portion (or excludable amount) of your annuity payments.

Step 6. Subtract the amount in Step 5 from the amount in Step 4. This is the part of your annuity for the year that is subject to tax.

Note: An example of figuring the taxable and nontaxable portions for a single life annuity is in *7.23*.

Planning Reminder

Life Expectancy Tables
The life expectancy tables for figuring your expected return are in IRS Publication 939.

Variable annuities. If you have a variable annuity that pays different benefits depending on cost-of-living indexes, profits earned by the annuity fund, or similar fluctuating standards, the tax-free portion of each payment is computed by dividing your investment in the contract (Step 1 above) by the total number of payments you expect to receive. If the annuity is for a definite period, the total number of payments equals the number of payments to be made each year multiplied by the number of years you will receive payments. If the annuity is for life, you divide the amount you invested in the contract by a multiple obtained from the appropriate life expectancy table; *see* Step 2. The result is the tax-free amount of annual annuity income.

If you receive a payment that is *less* than the nontaxable amount, you may elect when you receive the next payment to recalculate the nontaxable portion. The amount by which the prior nontaxable portion exceeded the payment you received is divided by the number of payments you expect as of the time of the next payment. The result is added to the previously calculated nontaxable portion, and the sum is the amount of each future payment to be excluded from tax. A statement must be attached to your return explaining the recomputation.

EXAMPLES

1. Andrew Taylor's total investment of $12,000 for a variable annuity was made after June 30, 1986. The annuity starting date is January 1, 1999. The annuity will be paid starting July 1, 1999, in varying annual installments for life. Andrew's age (nearest birthday) at the January 1 starting date is 65. He uses a life expectancy multiple of 20.0, the amount shown in Table V on page 162 for a person age 65. The amount of each payment excluded from tax is:

Investment in the contract	$12,000
Multiple (from Table V)	20.0
Amount of each payment excluded from tax ($12,000 ÷ 20)	$600

   If the first payment is $920, then 320 ($920 – $600) will be included in Andrew's 1999 income.

2. Assume that, after receiving the 1999 payment of $920 in Example 1, Andrew receives $500 in 2000 and $1,200 in 2001. None of the 2000 payment is taxed, as $600 is excludable from each annual payment. Andrew may also elect to recompute his annual exclusion starting with the 2001 payment. The exclusion is recomputed as follows:

Amount excludable in 2000	$600
Amount received in 2000	500
Difference	$100
Multiple as of 1/1/2000 (*see* Table V on page 162 for age 67)	18.4
Amount added to previously determined annual exclusion ($100 ÷ 18.4)	$5.43
Revised annual exclusion for 2000 and later years ($600 + $5.43)	$605.43
Amount taxable in 2000 ($1,200 – $605.43)	$594.57

Penalty on Premature Withdrawals From Deferred Annuities

As discussed above, withdrawals before the annuity starting date may be taxable or tax free, depending on whether investments were made after August 13, 1982.

Withdrawals before age $59\frac{1}{2}$ are also generally subject to a penalty of 10% of the amount includable in income. A withdrawal in 1999 from an annuity contract is penalized unless:

1. You have reached age $59\frac{1}{2}$ or have become totally disabled.
2. The distribution is part of a series of substantially equal payments, made at least annually over your life expectancy or over the joint life expectancies of you and a beneficiary. If you can avoid the penalty under this exception and you change to a nonqualifying distribution method within five years or before age $59\frac{1}{2}$, such as where you receive a lump sum, a recapture tax will apply to the payments received before age $59\frac{1}{2}$.
3. The payment is received by a beneficiary or estate after the policyholder's death.
4. Payment is from a qualified retirement plan, tax-sheltered annuity, or IRA; in this case the penalty rules of *7.15* (qualified plans) or *8.8* (IRAs) apply.
5. Payment is allocable to investments made before August 14, 1982.
6. Payment is from an annuity contract under a qualified personal injury settlement.
7. Payment is from a single-premium annuity where the starting date is no more than one year from the date of purchase.
8. Payment is from an annuity purchased by an employer upon the termination of a qualified retirement plan and held until you separated from service.

 Filing Tip

Form 5329

If no exception to the early withdrawal penalty applies, you compute the 10% penalty on Form 5329. The penalty is 5% instead of 10% if as of March 1, 1986, you were receiving payments under a specific schedule pursuant to your written election. Attach an explanation to Form 5329 if you are applying the 5% rate.

7.23 Life Expectancy Tables

IRS unisex actuarial tables must be used if you made any investment in the annuity contract after June 30, 1986. Generally, life expectancies are longer under the unisex tables than under the prior male-female tables. The unisex life expectancy table for single life annuities is IRS Table V, shown on page 162. A sample of the unisex table for ordinary joint life and last survivor annuities is at the end of Chapter 8. The full table is Table VI, in IRS Publication 939.

If your entire investment was before July 1, 1986, you use the older male/female tables. The tables, IRS Tables I through IV, are in Publication 939. Table I, shown on page 162, is for single life expectancies. Table II, for ordinary joint life and last survivor annuities, is in Publication 939.

You may make an irrevocable election to use the unisex tables for all payments received under the contract, even if you did not make an investment after June 30, 1986.

If you invested in the contract both before July 1, 1986, and after June 30, 1986, and you are the first person to receive annuity payments under the contract, you may make a special election to use the prior tables for the pre–July 1986 investment and the unisex tables for the post–June 1986 investment. *See* IRS Publication 939 for further information. Treasury Regulation 1.72-6(d) has examples showing how to figure the post–June 1986 and pre–July 1986 investments.

Birthday nearest annuity starting date. In looking up single life or joint life expectancy in the applicable table, use your age (and the age of a joint annuitant) at the birthday nearest to the annuity starting date. The number in the table next to this age is the life expectancy multiple used to figure the tax-free and taxable portions of a monthly annuity; see the following Examples.

Adjustments for nonmonthly payments. An adjustment is required when your annuity payments are received quarterly, semiannually, or annually; *see* Example 3 below.

 Planning Reminder

IRS Tables

See IRS Publication 939 for the life expectancy tables to use if you invested in an annuity contract both before July 1, 1986, and after June 30, 1986.

EXAMPLES

1. Bill Jones was 66 years old on March 14, 1999. On April 1, 1999, he received his first monthly annuity check of $1,000. This covered his annuity payment for March. Bill's annuity starting date was March 1, 1999, and his entire investment was before July 1, 1986.

    Looking at Table I on page 162 under "Male" at age 66 (age on birthday nearest January starting date), Bill finds the multiple 14.4. (He does not have to adjust that multiple because the payments are monthly.) Bill multiplies the 14.4 by $12,000 ($1,000 a month for a year) to find his expected return of $172,800. Say the annuity cost Bill $129,600. He divides his expected return into the investment in the contract (the cost) and gets his exclusion percentage of 75%. In every year for the rest of his life, Bill receives tax free 75% of his annuity payments and is taxable on 25%. In 1999, Bill receives $9,000 ($1,000 in April through December) and reports $2,250 as the taxable amount:

Amount received	$9,000
Amount excludable (75%)	6,750
Taxable portion	$2,250

    For 2000 and later years, Bill will receive annuity payments for the full year. The amount received will be $12,000; amount excludable, $9,000; and taxable portion, $3,000.

2. Same facts as in Example 1 except there was an investment after June 30, 1986, and Table V is used. Looking at Table V under age 66, Bill finds the multiple 19.2. The same multiple applies to males and females. Multiplying the 19.2 by $12,000 gives an expected return of $230,400. Using a cost of $129,600, the exclusion percentage is 56.25% ($129,600 ÷ $230,400). For 1998, Bill reports annuity income as follows:

Amount received	$9,000.00
Amount excludable (56.25%)	5,062.50
Taxable portion	$3,937.50

    For 1999 and later years in which annual payments of $12,000 are received, the amount excludable will be $6,750, and the taxable portion, $5,250.

3. You receive quarterly annuity payments. Your first payment comes on January 15, covering the first quarter of the year. Since the period between the starting date of January 1 and the payment date of January 15 is less than one month, you adjust the life expectancy multiple according to the table at the bottom of page 162, by adding 0.1. If the life expectancy multiple from the IRS table was 14.4, the adjusted multiple is 14.5.

TABLE I: Investments Before July 1, 1986

Male	Female	Multiples	Male	Female	Multiples	Male	Female	Multiples
6	11	65.0	41	46	33.0	76	81	9.1
7	12	64.1	42	47	32.1	77	82	8.7
8	13	63.2	43	48	31.2	78	83	8.3
9	14	62.3	44	49	30.4	79	84	7.8
10	15	61.4	45	50	29.6	80	85	7.5
11	16	60.4	46	51	28.7	81	86	7.1
12	17	59.5	47	52	27.9	82	87	6.7
13	18	58.6	48	53	27.1	83	88	6.3
14	19	57.7	49	54	26.3	84	89	6.0
15	20	56.7	50	55	25.5	85	90	5.7
16	21	55.8	51	56	24.7	86	91	5.4
17	22	54.9	52	57	24.0	87	92	5.1
18	23	53.9	53	58	23.2	88	93	4.8
19	24	53.0	54	59	22.4	89	94	4.5
20	25	52.1	55	60	21.7	90	95	4.2
21	26	51.1	56	61	21.0	91	96	4.0
22	27	50.2	57	62	20.3	92	97	3.7
23	28	49.3	58	63	19.6	93	98	3.5
24	29	48.3	59	64	18.9	94	99	3.3
25	30	47.4	60	65	18.2	95	100	3.1
26	31	46.5	61	66	17.5	96	101	2.9
27	32	45.6	62	67	16.9	97	102	2.7
28	33	44.6	63	68	16.2	98	103	2.5
29	34	43.7	64	69	15.6	99	104	2.3
30	35	42.8	65	70	15.0	100	105	2.1
31	36	41.9	66	71	14.4	101	106	1.9
32	37	41.0	67	72	13.8	102	107	1.7
33	38	40.0	68	73	13.2	103	108	1.5
34	39	39.1	69	74	12.6	104	109	1.3
35	40	38.2	70	75	12.1	105	110	1.2
36	41	37.3	71	76	11.6	106	111	1.0
37	42	36.5	72	77	11.0	107	112	0.8
38	43	35.6	73	78	10.5	108	113	0.7
39	44	34.7	74	79	10.1	109	114	0.6
40	45	33.8	75	80	9.6	110	115	0.5
						111	116	0.0

TABLE V: Investments After June 30, 1986

Age	Multiple	Age	Multiple	Age	Multiple
5	76.6	42	40.6	79	10.0
6	75.6	43	39.6	80	9.5
7	74.7	44	38.7	81	8.9
8	73.7	45	37.7	82	8.4
9	72.7	46	36.8	83	7.9
10	71.7	47	35.9	84	7.4
11	70.7	48	34.9	85	6.9
12	69.7	49	34.0	86	6.5
13	68.8	50	33.1	87	6.1
14	67.8	51	32.2	88	5.7
15	66.8	52	31.3	89	5.3
16	65.8	53	30.4	90	5.0
17	64.8	54	29.5	91	4.7
18	63.9	55	28.6	92	4.4
19	62.9	56	27.7	93	4.1
20	61.9	57	26.8	94	3.9
21	60.9	58	25.9	95	3.7
22	59.9	59	25.0	96	3.4
23	59.0	60	24.2	97	3.2
24	58.0	61	23.3	98	3.0
25	57.0	62	22.5	99	2.8
26	56.0	63	21.6	100	2.7
27	55.1	64	20.8	101	2.5
28	54.1	65	20.0	102	2.3
29	53.1	66	19.2	103	2.1
30	52.2	67	18.4	104	1.9
31	51.2	68	17.6	105	1.8
32	50.2	69	16.8	106	1.6
33	49.3	70	16.0	107	1.4
34	48.3	71	15.3	108	1.3
35	47.3	72	14.6	109	1.1
36	46.4	73	13.9	110	1.0
37	45.4	74	13.2	111	0.9
38	44.4	75	12.5	112	0.8
39	43.5	76	11.9	113	0.7
40	42.5	77	11.2	114	0.6
41	41.5	78	10.6	115	0.5

Multiple Adjustment Table

If the number of whole months from the annuity starting date to the first payment date is—	0–1	2	3	4	5	6	7	8	9	10	11	12
And payments under the contract are to be made:												
Annually	+0.5	+0.4	+0.3	+0.2	+0.1	0.0	0.0	−0.1	−0.2	−0.3	−0.4	−0.5
Semiannually	+0.2	+0.1	0.0	0.0	−0.1	−0.2						
Quarterly	+0.1	0.0	−0.1									

7.24 When You Convert Your Endowment Policy

When an endowment policy matures, you may elect to receive a lump sum, an annuity, an interest option, or a paid-up life insurance policy. If you elect—

A lump sum. You report the difference between your cost (premium payments less dividends) and what you receive.

An annuity before the policy matures or within 60 days after maturity. You report income in the years you receive your annuity. *See 7.22* for how to report annuity income. Use as your investment in the annuity contract the cost of the endowment policy less premiums paid for other benefits such as double indemnity or disability income. If you elect the annuity option more than 60 days after maturity, you report income on the matured policy as if you received the lump sum; *see* above rule. The lump sum is treated as the cost investment in the annuity contract.

An interest option before the policy matures. You report only the interest as it is received, provided you do not have the right to withdraw the policy proceeds. If you have the right to withdraw the proceeds, you are treated as in constructive receipt; the difference between your cost and what you receive would be taxed as if you had received a lump sum.

Paid-up insurance. You report the difference between the present value of the paid-up life insurance policy and the premium paid for the endowment policy. In figuring the value of the insurance policy, you do not use its cash surrender value, but the amount you would have to pay for a similar policy with the company at the date of exchange. Your insurance company can give you this figure. The difference is taxed at ordinary income tax rates.

Tax-free exchange rules apply to the policy exchanges listed at *6.11*.

Sales of endowment, annuity, or life insurance policies are taxable as ordinary income, not as capital gains.

The proceeds of a veteran's endowment policy paid before the veteran's death are not taxable.

7.25 Reporting Employee Annuities

Tax treatment of employee annuity payments from a qualified employee plan, qualified employee annuity, or tax-sheltered annuity *(7.20)* depends on the amount of your contributions and your annuity starting date. These rules are discussed in *7.25–7.28*. If payments are from a nonqualified employee plan, you must use the rules at *7.22* for commercial annuities.

Fully taxable payments if you have no investment in the plan. If you did not contribute to the cost of a pension or employee annuity, and you did not report as income your employer's contributions, you are fully taxed on payments after the annuity starting date. On your 1999 return, you report fully taxable payments on Line 16b of Form 1040 or Line 11b of Form 1040A.

An employee is taxed on the full value of a nonforfeitable annuity contract that the employer buys him or her if the employer does not have a qualified pension plan. Tax is imposed in the year the policy is purchased. A qualified plan is one approved by the IRS for special tax benefits.

Disability pension before minimum retirement age. Disability payments received before you reach the minimum retirement age (at which you would be entitled to a regular retirement annuity) are fully taxable as wages. After minimum retirement age, payments are treated as an annuity subject to the cost recovery rules of *7.22* or the simplified rules of *7.26*.

Partially taxable payments if you have an investment in the plan. If you and your employer both contributed to the cost of your annuity, the part of each payment allocable to your investment is tax free and the balance is taxable.

Cost and cost adjustments are explained in *7.27*.

Changing cost-recovery methods. If your annuity starting date was before November 19, 1996, you can switch from the regular six-step method discussed at *7.22* to the simplified method *(7.26)* or from the simplified to the regular method within the period for filing an amended return *(49.1)* for the first year. For example, if your annuity started in April 1996 and on your 1996 return you used the six-step method, and later realize within the amendment period that you could get a larger tax-free return with the simplified method, you may file amended returns for 1996 and later years using the simplified method to recompute your tax-free exclusion for all the years. The amended returns must be filed within three years from the due date of your return for the year in which the first annuity payment was received, or if later, within two years after you paid the tax for that year. After recomputing the tax-free percentage of each payment under the new method, use that same percentage every year until your investment has been completely recovered.

Employee Annuities

 Filing Tip

Form 1099-R
On Form 1099-R, the payer of a pension or annuity may tell you how much is taxable. If not, you may make the tax-free calculation (1) using the "simplified" method explained at *7.26* or (2) for a fee, ask the IRS to calculate the taxable amount.

If your annuity starting date is after March 18, 1996, you must use the simplified method *(7.26)* if you are eligible and the six-step method *(7.22)* if you are not eligible for the simplified method. You may not change the method.

7.26 Simplified Rule for Calculating Taxable Employee Annuity

Filing Instruction

Simplified Method Mandatory

If your annuity starting date is after November 18, 1996, you must use the simplified rule at *7.26* unless you are age 75 and have payments guaranteed for five or more years.

If you have an investment in the plan and your annuity starting date is *after November 18, 1996,* you must use the simplified method explained below to figure the tax-free portion of your annuity payments from a qualified employer plan, qualified employee annuity, or 403(b) tax-sheltered annuity. The only exception is for annuitants who are age 75 or older at the time payments begin and who have payments guaranteed for at least five years; they must use the six-step method discussed at *7.22* for commercial annuities rather than the simplified rule.

A beneficiary receiving a survivor annuity may use the simplified method.

Figuring taxable and tax-free payments under the simplified method. Under the simplified method, a level tax-free portion is determined for each monthly payment with the following steps:

Step 1. Figure your investment in the contract as of the annuity starting date. Include premiums you paid and any after-tax contributions you made to the employer's pension plan; *see 7.27*. Beneficiaries may increase the investment by any allowable death benefit exclusion, up to $5,000, but only if the employee died before August 21, 1996.

Step 2. Divide the investment from Step 1 by the number of expected monthly payments shown in Table I or Table II below, using your age at the birthday preceding the annuity starting date. The result is the tax-free recovery portion of each monthly payment. However, multiply this amount by three (3 months) to get the tax-free portion if payments are made quarterly rather than monthly. The tax-free portion remains the same if a spouse or other beneficiary receives payments under a joint and survivor annuity after the employee's death.

Use either Table I or Table II, described below. Table II is used for annuities based on more than one life if the annuity starting date is after December 31, 1997.

Table I: Use this table if the annuity starting date was after November 18, 1996, and before January 1, 1998, whether the annuity is based on your life only or is a joint and survivor annuity.

Also use Table I if the annuity starting date was after December 31, 1997, and the annuity is based on your life only.

Table II: Use this table if the annuity starting date is after December 31, 1997, and benefits are based on the life of *more than* one annuitant. For example, use this table if you started to receive payments in 1999 under a joint and survivor annuity. If there is more than one survivor annuitant, the primary annuitant's age plus the youngest survivor annuitant's age is the combined age used for Table II. If there is no primary annuitant and the annuity is payable to several survivor annuitants, the ages of the oldest and youngest are combined. Disregard a survivor annuitant whose entitlement to payment is contingent on something other than the primary annuitant's death.

Table I

Age of primary annuitant at starting date	Number of expected monthly payments
55 and under	360
56–60	310
61–65	260
66–70	210
71 and over	160

Table II

Combined ages of annuitants at starting date	Number of expected monthly payments
110 and under	410
111–120	360
121–130	310
131–140	260
141 and over	210

Step 3. Multiply the Step 2 result by the number of monthly payments received during the year; this is the total tax-free payment for the current year. However, if any part of your cost was previously recovered tax free in years after 1986, the tax-free amount is limited to the excess of your investment from Step 1 over the prior year recoveries.

Step 4. Subtract the Step 3 tax-free payment from the total pension received this year; this is the taxable pension you must report on Form 1040 or Form 1040A. If the payer of the annuity shows a higher taxable amount on Form 1099-R, use the amount figured here.

EXAMPLE

Fred Smith, age 57, retires and beginning July 1, 1999, he receives payments under a joint and 50% survivor annuity with his wife Betty, also age 57. Fred receives an annuity of $1,500 per month and Betty will receive a survivor annuity of $750 per month after Fred's death. Fred's investment in the plan was $29,000. To figure the tax-free portion of each payment, Fred divides his $29,000 investment by 360, the number of expected monthly payments shown in Table II for two annuitants with a combined age of 114 years. The result, or $80.56, is the tax-free portion of each $1,500 payment. The balance of each payment, or $1,419.44 ($1,500 – $80.56), is taxable. On his 1999 return, Fred reports $8,516.64 (6 payments × $1,419.44) as taxable annuity payments.

If Fred dies before the receipt of 360 payments, Betty will also exclude $80.56 from each of her payments of $750 until a total of 360 payments (hers and Fred's) have been recovered. After 360 payments are received, all subsequent payments will be fully taxable. If Betty dies before the 360th payment, a deduction for the unrecovered investment is allowed on her final income tax return; the deduction is a miscellaneous itemized deduction not subject to the 2% AGI floor.

7.27 Employee's Cost in Annuity

For purposes of figuring the tax-free recovery of your investment under the general rules of *7.22* or the simplified rule of *7.26*, include the following items paid as of the annuity starting date as your cost in an employee annuity:

- Premiums paid by you or by after-tax withholdings from your pay.
- Payments made by your employer and reported as additional pay.
- Premiums paid by an employer in a non-approved plan for your benefit give you immediate income if you have nonforfeitable rights to the policy.
- Premiums paid by your employer which, if the amounts had been paid to you directly, would have been tax free to you because you were working abroad; see Chapter 36.
- Pre-1939 contributions by a city or state to its employees' pension fund. (Before 1939, salaries to state and city employees were tax free for federal income tax purposes.)

If you are a beneficiary of a deceased employee who died before August 21, 1996, you may be able to claim a death benefit exclusion of up to $5,000 to reduce the tax on 1999 payments received on behalf of the employee. You may be entitled to all or part of the up-to-$5,000 exclusion. If the employee had more than one beneficiary, the total exclusion for that employee is $5,000, and it must be divided among you and the other beneficiaries in proportion to the benefits received.

 Filing Instruction

Annuity Starting Date Before November 19, 1996

If you have reported annuity payments using the prior law simplified method for annuities starting before November 19, 1996, continue using that method for figuring the tax-free part of your 1999 payments.

 Filing Instruction

Separate Death Benefit Payment

If as a beneficiary you receive a one-time death benefit payment that is *not* made from a qualified employer retirement plan, report the payment as "Other income" on Form 1040. Report the excess of the payment over the allowable death benefit exclusion if the employee died before August 21, 1996.

If you are receiving a survivor annuity, the allowable exclusion is added to the employee's cost investment in the annuity to figure the tax-free and taxable portion of the payments under the simplified method *(7.26)* or general method *(7.22)*. If you are the survivor under a joint and survivor annuity, you may *not* claim the death benefit exclusion if the deceased had received any payment under the joint and survivor contract after reaching minimum retirement age.

7.28 Withdrawals Before Annuity Starting Date

You generally may not make tax-free withdrawals from your employer's plan before the annuity starting date, even if your withdrawals are less than your investment. On a withdrawal before the annuity starting date, you must pay tax on a portion of the withdrawal unless the exceptions below apply. The portion of the withdrawal allocable to your investment is recovered tax free; the portion allocable to employer contributions and income earned on the contract is taxed. To compute the tax-free recovery, multiply the withdrawal by this fraction:

$$\frac{\text{Your total investment}}{\text{Your vested account balance or accrued benefit}}$$

Your investment and vested benefit are determined as of the date of distribution.

Exceptions. More favorable investment recovery rules are allowed in the following cases:

Caution

Favorable Recovery Rules

Both of the favorable cost recovery rules discussed in *7.28* under "Exceptions" are complicated and you should consult your plan administrator to determine if the exceptions apply and how to make the required calculations.

1. *Employer plans in effect on May 5, 1986.* If on May 5, 1986, your employer's plan allowed distributions of employee contributions before separation from service, the above pro-rata recovery rule applies only to the extent that the withdrawal exceeds the total investment in the contract on December 31, 1986.

   For example, assume that as of December 31, 1986, you had an account balance of $9,750, which included $4,000 of your own contributions. If the plan on May 5, 1986, allowed pre-retirement distributions of employee contributions, you may receive withdrawals up to your $4,000 investment without incurring tax. Thus, if you have not made previous withdrawals and receive a $3,000 distribution in 1994, it is not subject to tax.

2. *Separate accounts for employee contributions.* A defined contribution plan (such as a profit-sharing plan) is allowed to account for employee contributions (and earnings on the contributions) separately from employer contributions. If separate accounting is maintained, withdrawals of employee contributions from the separate account may be made tax free. A defined benefit pension plan may also maintain employee contributions (and earnings) in a separate account to which actual earnings and losses are allocated.

7.29 Civil Service Retirement

As discussed at *7.26*, the simplified method must be used to compute the tax-free and taxable portions of each withdrawal if your annuity starting date is after November 18, 1996.

If you leave federal government service before retirement or transfer to a job not under the federal retirement system and you are not entitled to an immediate annuity, you may receive a refund of your contributions (plus any interest). If the refund exceeds your contributions, the excess is taxable.

Retirees with a life-threatening illness may be able to elect a reduced annuity in order to receive a lump-sum credit for their total contributions to the plan; *see* IRS Publication 721 for figuring the taxable portion of the lump sum if the election was made.

Cost of civil service annuity. For purposes of figuring the tax-free portion of each annuity payment your *cost* equals the withholdings from your federal government pay that were contributed to the Civil Service retirement fund. Also, if you repaid to the retirement fund amounts that you previously had withdrawn, or paid into the fund to receive full credit for certain uncovered service, the entire amount you paid, including that designated as interest, is part of your cost. You may not claim an interest deduction for any amount designated as interest.

The annuity statement you received when your annuity was approved shows your "total contributions" to the retirement fund (your cost) and the "monthly rate" of your annuity benefit. The monthly rate is the rate before adjustment for health benefits coverage and life insurance, if any.

A future increase in your civil service pension or your survivor's benefit is not treated as annuity income but is reported in full as miscellaneous income and is not reduced by the exclusion ratio. However, an increase effective on or before a survivor's civil service annuity commences must be taken into account in computing the expected return or in determining the aggregate amount receivable under the annuity.

If you made voluntary contributions to the retirement fund that you use to fund an additional monthly benefit, you report the portion of your annuity attributable to the voluntary contributions as a separate annuity, taxable under the rules at *7.26*. If you made voluntary contributions, an information return which you receive each year will state the portion of your monthly payments attributable to your voluntary contributions. If instead of increasing your monthly benefit you receive a refund of your voluntary contributions plus accrued interest, the interest is taxable in the year you receive it.

7.30 Retired Military Personnel Allowed Annuity Election

If, when you retire from the military, your pay is reduced to provide an annuity for your spouse or certain child beneficiaries, you do not report that part of your retirement pay used to fund the annuity.

For example, you are eligible to receive retirement pay of $500 a month. You elect to receive $400 a month to obtain an annuity of $200 a month for your spouse on your death. You report $400 a month for tax purposes during your lifetime, rather than the $500. On your death, your spouse generally will report the full $200 a month received as income.

Veteran's benefit deposits. If you elected to receive veteran's benefits instead of some or all of your retirement pay, you may have been required to deposit with the U.S. Treasury an amount equal to the reduction for the annuity. If so, you do not report retirement pay until it equals the amount deposited.

Beneficiaries. If all of the retired person's consideration for the contract (previously taxed reductions) has not been offset against retirement income at the time of death, the beneficiary excludes all payments under the contract until the exclusions equal the remaining consideration for the contract not previously excluded by the deceased. As soon as this amount is excluded, the beneficiary reports all later payments as income.

Planning Reminder

Accrued Leave

A lump-sum payment for accrued annual leave received upon retirement is not part of your annuity. It is treated as a salary payment and is taxable as ordinary income.

IRAs

There are several types of IRAs: Traditional IRAs, Roth IRAs, SIMPLE IRAs, and SEPs. You may personally set up a traditional or Roth IRA with your bank or broker. SIMPLE IRAs and SEPs are available only if your employer offers such plans.

Traditional IRA contributions of up to $2,000 a year are deductible if you and your spouse do not have retirement plan coverage where you work. If you have coverage, you may claim a deduction if your adjusted gross income is below a specified phase-out range; *see 8.4.*

Traditional IRA distributions received in 1999 are fully taxable, except to the extent of nondeductible contributions. You must file Form 8606 to figure the tax-free portion of distributions allocable to nondeductible contributions; *see 8.9.*

Traditional IRA distributions received before age 59 $\frac{1}{2}$ are generally subject to a penalty (*see 8.12* for exceptions). Minimum distributions from an IRA must begin after you reach age 70 $\frac{1}{2}$; *see 8.13.*

SIMPLE IRAs of qualifying small employers allow employees to defer up to $6,000 of pay to the plan; *see 8.18.* Under a special type of IRA, a simplified employee pension (SEP) set up by an employer, an employee may make larger tax-sheltered contributions than to a regular IRA; *see 8.16.*

Roth IRAs are an alternative to traditional IRAs. Although contributions are not deductible, the major tax advantage of the Roth IRA is that tax-free withdrawals of earnings may be made after a five-year waiting period if you are over age 59 $\frac{1}{2}$; *see 8.22.* Tax-free withdrawals of contributions may be made at any time. A traditional IRA may also be converted to a Roth IRA. Contributions and conversions are subject to an income-based phaseout; *see 8.20* for annual contributions and *8.21* for conversions. A conversion is treated as a taxable distribution from the traditional IRA; *see 8.21.*

Starting and Contributing to a Traditional IRA

8.1 Starting a Traditional IRA

You may set up a traditional (non-Roth) IRA by making annual contributions that may be deductible *(see 8.4 for deduction rules)* or nondeductible *(see 8.6)*, or by rolling over a distribution received from a qualified employer plan or from another IRA. If your employer allows it, you may contribute to a traditional IRA (or Roth IRA; *see 8.19*) by direct deposit through a payroll deduction plan. IRA accounts provide tax-free accumulation of earnings until withdrawals are made. The rollover option also allows you to avoid immediate tax when you receive a lump-sum payment upon retirement, changing jobs, or disability; *see 7.8*.

	With interest compounded daily		
Invest $2,000 in an IRA on January 1, every year for—	*6%*	*8%* gives you—	*10%*
5 years	$12,015	$12,794	$13,633
10 years	28,233	31,879	36,109
15 years	50,125	60,349	73,164
20 years	79,676	102,820	134,252
25 years	119,563	166,176	234,962
30 years	173,405	260,688	400,993

 Filing Tip

Trustee's fees and brokerage commissions.

Trustee's fees paid to set up or manage an IRA are not considered IRA contributions provided they are separately billed. They are investment expenses which may be deducted as a miscellaneous itemized deduction subject to the 2% adjusted gross income floor; *see 19.1*. However, broker's commissions that are paid when you make investments for your IRA are not separately deductible, according to the IRS. They are considered IRA contributions subject to the $2,000 contribution limit.

Roth IRAs. Annual contributions to a Roth IRA and conversions of traditional IRAs to Roth IRAs are discussed at *8.19–8.21*.

Restrictions on traditional IRAs. You may not freely withdraw IRA funds until the year you reach age 59 ½ or become disabled. If you take money out before that time, you are subject to a penalty; *see 8.8*. Pledging the account as collateral is treated as a taxable distribution from the account; *see 8.8*. In the year you reach age 70 ½, you may no longer make traditional IRA contributions, and you must start to withdraw *(8.13)* from the account. All IRA withdrawals are fully taxable except for amounts allocable to nondeductible contributions; *see 8.8* and *8.9*. Special averaging for lump-sum distributions does not apply. Excess contributions *(8.7)* are penalized.

If your IRA loses value because of poor investments, you may not deduct the loss. A loss is allowed only if you make nondeductible contributions that you have not recovered when the account is depleted; *see 8.9*.

Types of traditional IRAs. You may set up an IRA as:

1. *An individual retirement account* with a bank, savings and loan association, federally insured credit union, or other qualified person as trustee or custodian. An individual retirement account is technically a trust or custodial account. Your contribution may be invested in vehicles such as certificates of deposit, mutual funds, and certain limited partnerships.

2. *An individual retirement annuity* by purchasing an annuity contract (including a joint and survivor contract for the benefit of you and your spouse) issued by an insurance company; no trustee or custodian is required. The contract, endorsed to meet the terms of an IRA, is all that is required. Contracts issued after November 6, 1978, must provide for flexible premiums up to $2,000 a year, so that if your compensation changes, your payment may also change. As borrowing or pledging of the contract is not allowed under an IRA, the contracts will not contain loan provisions. Endowment contracts issued after November 6, 1978, that provide life insurance protection may not be used as individual retirement annuities.

 Caution

Investment Restrictions for Self-Directed IRA

If you have a self-directed IRA, you may not invest in collectibles, such as art works, gems, stamps, antiques, rugs, metals, or guns. Coins are not allowed except for state-issued coins or certain U.S. minted gold and silver coins. Investments are allowed in certain platinum coins, as well as certain gold, silver, platinum, or palladium bullion held by the trustee. Assets used to acquire a prohibited collectible are treated as distributions and are taxed.

You may set up one type of IRA one year and choose another form the next year. You also may split your contribution between two or more investment vehicles. For example, you are eligible to contribute $2,000. You may choose to put $1,000 into an investment retirement annuity and $1,000 into an individual retirement account with your local bank.

You do not have to file any forms with your tax return when you set up or make contributions to a deductible IRA. Form 8606 must be attached to Form 1040 or Form 1040A if you make nondeductible IRA contributions; *see 8.6*. The bank or company where you set up your IRA will report your contribution to the IRS on Form 5498, and you should receive a copy.

Self-Directed IRA. If you wish to take a more active role in managing your IRA investments, you may set up a "self-directed" IRA using an IRS model form. The model trust (Form 5305) and the model custodial account agreement (Form 5305-A) meet the requirements of an exempt individual retirement account and so do not require a ruling or determination letter approving the exemption of the account and the deductibility of contributions made to the account. If you use this method, you still have to find a bank or other institution or trustee to handle your account or investment. Investments in a self-directed IRA are subject to restrictions; *see* the Caution on this page.

SIMPLE IRA. If you work for a company with 100 or less workers, your employer may set up a SIMPLE IRA to which you may make salary-reduction contributions; *see 8.18.*

Contributions after the end of the taxable year. You have until April 17, 2000 (the regular filing due date for your 1999 return), to make deductible or nondeductible IRA contributions for 1999. You must make your contribution by April 17, 2000, even if you get an extension to file your return. If you are short of cash, you may borrow the funds to make the contribution without jeopardizing the deduction. If an IRA deduction entitles you to a refund, you can file your return early, claim the IRA deduction, and if you receive the refund in time, apply it towards an IRA contribution before the due date.

8.2 Contributions Must Be Based on Earnings

You may make contributions to a traditional IRA for 1999 of up to $2,000, provided you have wage, salary, or net self-employment earnings and that you have not reached age 70 ½ by the end of the year. If your earned income is less than $2,000, the contribution limit is 100% of your pay or net earned income if self-employed. Contributions for 1999 may be made up to the filing deadline of April 17, 2000; this is the deadline even if you obtain a filing extension.

If you are married filing jointly, you may each contribute up to $2,000 to an IRA, as long as your combined compensation covers the contributions; *see 8.3.*

Contributions up to these limits are *fully deductible* on your 1999 return if *neither you nor your spouse* is an active participant in an employer or self-employed retirement plan. Deductions for active plan participants are phased out for single persons with 1999 adjusted gross income over $31,000; *see 8.4.* If you are married and only one of you is an active participant, you are both considered active participants, but a much more favorable phase-out test applies to the nonparticipant spouse than to the participant spouse if you file jointly; these rules are discussed at *8.3.*

IRA contributions must be based on payments received for rendering personal services, such as salary, wages, commissions, tips, fees, bonuses, jury fees, or net earnings from self-employment (less Keogh plan contributions on behalf of the self-employed). Compensation does *not* include:

1. Investment income such as interest, dividends, or profits from sales of property;
2. Deferred compensation, pensions, or annuities; *or*
3. Income earned abroad for which the foreign earned income exclusion is claimed.

EXAMPLE

A trader whose sole income was derived from stock dividends and gains in buying and selling stocks contributed to an IRA. The IRS disallowed the deduction on the grounds that his income was not earned income.

If you live in a community property state, the fact that one-half of your spouse's income is considered your income does not entitle you to make contributions to an IRA. The contributions must be based on pay earned through your services.

Only cash contributions are deductible; contributions paid by check are considered cash for this purpose.

Working for spouse. If you work for your spouse, you may make an IRA contribution provided you actually perform services and receive an actual payment of wages. A wife who worked as a receptionist and assistant to her husband, a veterinarian, failed to meet the second test. Her husband did not pay her a salary. Instead, he deposited all income from his business into a joint bank account held with his wife. In addition, no federal income tax was withheld from her wages. In a ruling, the IRS held that the wife could not set up her own IRA, even though she performed services; she failed to receive actual payment. Depositing business income into a joint account is neither actual nor constructive payment of the wife's salary. Furthermore, any deduction claimed for the wife's wages was disallowed.

Caution

Broker's Restriction on IRA Transfers

Before you invest in an IRA, carefully review the terms of the agreement for restrictions. One investor who put his IRA in a brokerage account was not allowed by the trustee to transfer from one account to another. Furthermore, the trustee reserved some of the IRA funds to cover broker fees and other transfer costs. The investor asked the IRS if these restrictions violated the tax law. The IRS, in a private letter ruling, said there was no violation. An IRA is a contractual agreement between the IRA trustee and the participant. Although the tax laws do not place limitations on direct IRA-to-IRA transfers, the trustees of a particular account may restrict such transfers.

Law Alert

Proposed Increase in Contribution Amount

When this book went to press, Congress was considering legislation that would increase the maximum $2,000 contribution limit for traditional and Roth IRAs to $3,000 for 2001–2003, $4,000 for 2004–2005, and $5,000 for 2006–2008. After 2008, the $5,000 limit would be subject to inflation indexing. Another proposal would further increase the contribution limit for individuals age 50 or older starting in 2001. *See* the Supplement for a legislation update.

Filing Tip

Self-Employed Earnings.

If you have a net profit from a sideline business and make a deductible contribution to a Keogh plan or SEP (*see* Chapter 41), the deductible contribution reduces modified adjusted gross income for IRA deduction purposes (and for Roth IRA contribution purposes; *see 8.19*).

Planning Reminder

Roth IRA Contributions after 70 ½

Contributions to a traditional IRA may not be made after age 70 ½, but contributions to a Roth IRA may be made even if you are over age 70 ½, provided you have compensation (8.2) to support the contribution and your income is within the limit allowed under the Roth IRA contribution rules; *see 8.20*.

Self-employed may make IRA contributions. IRA contributions may be based on net self-employment earnings *(45.1)*, after taking into account deductible Keogh or SEP retirement plan contributions *(41.5)* and the deduction for one-half of self-employment tax liability *(45.3)*. If you have a net loss for the year, you may not make an IRA contribution unless you also have wages.

If you have more than one self-employed activity, you must aggregate profits and losses from all of your self-employed businesses to determine if you have net income on which to base an IRA contribution. For example, if one self-employed business produces a net profit of $15,000 but another a net loss of $20,000, you may not make an IRA contribution based on the net profit of $15,000 since you have an overall loss. This netting rule does not apply to salary or wage income. If you are an employee who also has an unprofitable business, you may make an IRA contribution based on your salary.

If you have a self-employed retirement plan from your business, you are considered an active participant in a retirement plan for purposes of the adjusted gross income phase-out rules discussed at *8.4*.

Taxable alimony treated as compensation. A divorced spouse with little or no earnings in 1999 may treat taxable alimony as compensation, giving a basis for deductible IRA contributions. If you are divorced, you make an IRA contribution equal to 100% of taxable alimony up to $2,000. However, the deduction may be reduced or eliminated if you are an active participant in an employer plan and your adjusted gross income exceeds the $31,000 threshold for unmarried individuals; *see 8.4*. Taxable alimony is alimony paid under a decree of divorce or legal separation, or a written agreement incident to such a decree; *see* Chapter 37. It does not include alimony payments made under a written agreement that is not incident to such a decree.

No deductible contributions allowed for those age 70 ½. Even if you still have earnings, you may not make deductible contributions to a traditional IRA for the year in which you reach age 70 ½, or any later year. For example, if you were born in the last six months of 1928 or the first six months of 1929, you will reach age 70 ½ in 1999 and may not make any deductible IRA contributions for 1999 or later years.

If you have a nonworking spouse under age 70 ½, you may contribute up to $2,000 to his or her IRA, even though no contribution may be made to your own deductible IRA because you have reached age 70 ½; *see 8.3*.

8.3 Contributions to a Traditional IRA If You Are Married

If both you and your spouse earned compensation in 1999 of at least $2,000 and are under age 70 ½ at the end of the year, each of you may make a contribution of up to $2,000 to a traditional IRA for 1999 by April 17, 2000. Under the spousal IRA rule, the $2,000 per spouse contribution limit applies even if only one of you works, provided you file jointly and your combined compensation is at least $4,000.

Contributions for 1999 are fully deductible up to the $2,000 limit if neither you nor your spouse was covered by an employer retirement plan during the year. If either of you was an active plan participant, you are both considered active participants, and a deduction may be limited or disallowed depending on your modified adjusted gross income (MAGI). However, if you file jointly and only one of you was an active plan participant, a more favorable MAGI phase-out rule applies to the nonparticipant spouse, so that the spouse without coverage may be able to claim a deduction even if the participant spouse may not. The deduction phase-out rules are discussed below.

Spousal IRA contribution on joint return for nonworking or low-earning spouse. On a joint return, the contribution limit is $2,000 for each spouse as long as the combined compensation of both spouses is at least $4,000. This spousal IRA rule allows a spouse who earns less than $2,000 to "borrow" compensation from his or her spouse in order to reach the maximum $2,000 contribution limit. In figuring their combined compensation for purposes of the "borrowing" rule, the higher earning spouse's compensation is reduced by his or her deductible IRA contribution and by any regular contributions made by the higher earning spouse to a Roth IRA for the year.

> **EXAMPLE**
>
> Lynn and Ted Baker file a joint return for 1999. Lynn had salary income of $42,000 in 1999. Ted was a full-time student and had no compensation. Lynn may contribute up to $2,000 to an IRA for 1999. Even though Ted did not work, he also may contribute up to $2,000 to an IRA. Since Lynn's earnings exceeded $4,000, $2,000 of the earnings may be credited to Ted for contribution purposes.

If Lynn and Ted's modified adjusted gross income (MAGI; *see 8.4*) for 1999 does not exceed $51,000, contributions up to the $2,000 limit are fully deductible. If MAGI on their joint return exceeds $51,000 and if Lynn was an active participant in her employer's retirement plan during 1999, her deduction would be phased out over a MAGI range of $ 51,000–$61,000. Ted would be allowed a full $2,000 deduction so long as the joint return MAGI was less than $150,000. *See* the phase-out rule below.

Deduction phase-out rule for spouses filing jointly for 1999. If either you or your spouse was an active participant in an employer retirement plan during 1999, the phase-out rule may limit or completely disallow an IRA deduction. However, even if one or both of you were active participants in an employer plan, the phase-out rule does not apply and you may each deduct contributions up to the $2,000 limit if your 1999 joint return modified adjusted gross income (MAGI, *see 8.4*) is $51,000 or less.

If both of you were active plan participants for 1999, the deduction limit is phased out if your joint return MAGI is $ 51,001–$60,999. No deduction is allowed for either of you if joint return MAGI is $61,000 or more.

If you were not an active plan participant in 1999 but your spouse was, a different phase-out rule applies to each of you. Your spouse, as an active plan participant, is subject to the deduction phaseout if MAGI on the joint return is $51,001–$60,999; no deduction is allowed if MAGI is $61,000 or more. However, as the nonparticipant spouse, your deduction limit is not subject to phaseout unless MAGI on the joint return is over $150,000. Your deduction is phased out if joint MAGI is $150,001–$159,999, and no deduction is allowed if MAGI is $160,000 or more.

See 8.4 *for an example of how the reduced deduction limit is figured if MAGI is within the above phase-out ranges.*

Deduction phase-out rule for married persons filing separately for 1999. If you are married, live together at any time during 1999, file separately, and either of you is an active participant in an employer plan, the other spouse is also considered an active participant. Both of you are subject to the $0 to $10,000 AGI deduction phaseout; *see 8.4.*

If you live apart for all of 1999, you each figure IRA deductions as if single. Thus, the more favorable deduction phase-out range of $31,000 to $39,999 applies if you are covered by an employer retirement plan; *see 8.4.* If you are not covered, you may claim a full deduction on your separate return.

Contributions for spouses under age 70 $\frac{1}{2}$. If you are over age 70 $\frac{1}{2}$ and still working, you may contribute to a spousal IRA if your spouse is nonworking and is under age 70 $\frac{1}{2}$ at the end of the year. The entire contribution of up to $2,000 must be allocated to the nonworking spouse. No contribution may be made to your own account for the year in which you reach age 70 $\frac{1}{2}$, or any later year. However, you may contribute to a Roth IRA even if you are over age 70 $\frac{1}{2}$, provided your compensation is within the Roth IRA limits; see 8.20.

8.4 Deduction Restrictions for Active Participants in Employer Plan

If you are covered by an employer retirement plan, including a self-employed plan, you may be unable to make deductible IRA contributions. When you have coverage, your right to claim a full $2,000 deduction, a limited deduction, or no deduction at all depends on your modified adjusted gross income (MAGI). If you are married, and your spouse has employer plan coverage for 1999, you are also considered to have coverage in most cases. However, if you file jointly and do not individually have employer plan coverage, a special MAGI phase-out rule may allow you to deduct IRA contributions even if a deduction for your spouse is limited or barred.

If you are unmarried and do *not* have employer plan coverage, or if you are married and neither of you has coverage (*see* the rule for spouses on page 174), an IRA deduction of up to $2,000 is allowed as long as you have compensation of $2,000 or more. The deduction phase-out rules do not apply, regardless of your income.

Generally, you are considered to be "covered" by a retirement plan if you are an *active participant* in the plan for any part of the plan year ending within your taxable year; see the Sara Wartes Example on the next page. If you are an employee, your 1999 Form W-2 should indicate whether you are covered for the year; if you are, the "pension plan" box within Box 15 of Form W-2 should be checked. Active participation in a self-employed Keogh plan or SEP (Chapter 41) is treated as employer plan coverage for purposes of the IRA deduction phase-out rules. Active participation is explained further at *8.5.*

Filing Tip

Deduction on Joint Return

If you and your spouse have combined earnings of at least $4,000 and modified adjusted gross income of $51,000 or less, each of you may claim an IRA deduction for contributions of up to $2,000 on your joint return.

Planning Reminder

Phase-Out Rule for Nonparticipant Spouses

If you are not covered by an employer retirement plan but your spouse is, and you file a joint return, your individual $2,000 deduction limit is not subject to phase-out rules unless modified adjusted gross income (MAGI) on the joint return is between $150,000 and $160,000. Your spouse, who is covered by an employer plan, is subject to the deduction phaseout for 1999 if modified adjusted gross income on the joint return is between $51,000 and $61,000.

EXAMPLE

Sara Wartes, a college teacher, quit her job in 1988 and withdrew all of the contributions she had made to her employee pension plan. The Tax Court held that Sara could not claim an IRA deduction in that year. Sara was an active participant in the college plan during 1988 and under the phase-out rules based upon adjusted gross income, no IRA deduction was allowed. The court noted that the active participation test is not made at the end of the year. Participation in a company plan at any time during the year triggers the deduction phase-out rules. This is true even where a person has forfeitable benefits.

You are not an active plan participant but your spouse is. Even if you were not an active participant in an employer retirement plan at any time in 1999, your IRA deduction limit for 1999 may be phased out because of your spouse's coverage. However, if you file jointly, your own deduction is not limited unless modified adjusted gross income (MAGI) on the joint return exceeds $150,000. For your spouse who has employer plan coverage, the rule is different: the phase-out threshold for his or her deduction is joint MAGI of $51,000.

The deduction is phased out over the next $10,000 of MAGI exceeding the phase-out threshold. Thus, you as a nonparticipant are not allowed any deduction if MAGI on your joint return is $160,000 or more. A deduction for your spouse as an active participant is completely phased out if joint return MAGI is $61,000 or more.

Stricter phase-out rules apply to married persons filing separately if they live together at any time during the year. If you lived with your spouse at any time during 1999 and either of you was an active plan participant, neither of you may claim an IRA deduction if you file separately and your MAGI is $10,000 or more.

If you are married filing separately and you lived apart for all of 1999, your spouse's plan participation does not affect your IRA deduction. Take into account only your own participation, if any, and if you are an active participant, your IRA deduction under the phase-out rules is figured as if you were single. If you are not an active participant, you may claim the full $2,000 deduction.

Modified adjusted gross income (MAGI) determines your deduction limit if you or your spouse is an active plan participant. If either you or your spouse is an active plan participant, you still may be allowed a full or limited deduction, but this will depend on whether your 1999 modified adjusted gross income (MAGI) is within the phase-out range that applies to you as shown below.

MAGI is generally equal to the total income shown on your return *minus* adjustments to income other than for IRA deductions. However, if you are claiming a deduction for student loan interest (38.6), the deduction must be *added back* to adjusted gross income to get MAGI. If you are claiming an exclusion for employer-provided adoption assistance (3.5) or an exclusion for interest on U.S. EE Savings Bonds used for tuition (38.4), you must *add back* that excluded amount to adjusted gross income to get MAGI. If you worked abroad and are claiming the foreign earned income exclusion (36.1), or a foreign housing exclusion or deduction (36.3), these amounts also must be added back to adjusted gross income to get MAGI.

Figuring Your 1999 IRA Deduction Under The Phase-Out Rules

If you are an active plan participant for 1999, or you are considered to be a participant because of your spouse's participation, the $2,000 IRA deduction limit is phased out where your 1999 modified adjusted gross income (MAGI) exceeds a phase-out threshold.

Phase-out threshold for 1999 returns. On 1999 returns, the $2,000 deduction limit is not subject to phaseout unless modified adjusted gross income exceeds:

- $31,000 if you are single, head of household, or married filing separately and treated as single because you lived apart from your spouse for all of 1999;
- $51,000 if you are married filing jointly and both you and your spouse were active plan participants during 1999, *or* you are a qualifying widow or widower;
- $51,000 if you are married filing jointly and you are an active plan participant during 1999 but your spouse was not. You use the $51,000 threshold; your spouse uses the $150,000 threshold;
- $150,000 if you are married filing jointly and you were not an active plan participant at any time during 1999 but your spouse was. You use the $150,000 threshold; your spouse uses the $51,000 threshold; *and*
- $0 if you are married filing separately and lived with your spouse at any time in 1999.

The phase-out applies to the first $9,999 of MAGI exceeding the $31,000, $51,000, $150,000, or zero phase-out threshold. If your MAGI exceeds the threshold by $10,000 or more, you are not allowed any IRA deduction.

Phase-out Range for $2,000 Deduction Limit on 1999 Returns

If your phase-out threshold (see above) is—	Deduction limit is phased out if MAGI is—	No deduction if MAGI is—
$31,000	$31,001–$40,999	$41,000 or more
$51,000	$51,001–$60,999	$61,000 or more
$150,000	$150,001–$159,999	$160,000 or more
$0	$0–$9,999	$10,000 or more

Figure the excess MAGI and use the Deduction Limit Table. If your MAGI is within the $9,999 phase-out range, you can refer to the Deduction Limit Table on page 177 to look up your maximum IRA deduction limit for 1999. To use the Table, figure your *excess MAGI* by subtracting the phase-out threshold from your MAGI. If the excess MAGI is less than $10,000, refer to the Table. Keep in mind that you may make deductible contributions up to the phase-out limit from the Table only if your compensation is at least that much or your contribution is based on your spouse's compensation under the spousal IRA rules at 8.3. If the excess MAGI is $10,000 or more, you are not allowed any IRA deduction.

Using the Table saves you the trouble of figuring the deduction limit yourself. The Table reflects the following phase-out formula in the law: Deduction limit equals $2,000 minus 20% of the MAGI exceeding the phase-out threshold. A result that is not a multiple of $10 is rounded up to the next highest multiple of $10. If the rounded up amount is less than $200, it is increased to $200. The law allows the $200 deduction to taxpayers with MAGI in the final $1,000 of the phase-out range, such as single persons with MAGI over $40,000 but less than $41,000, whose deduction limit would otherwise be below $200. Example 1 below illustrates how the deduction limit works.

Nondeductible contributions. Any contributions exceeding the amount allowed under the above rules are treated as nondeductible IRA contributions. *See 8.6* for further details. Alternatively, the excess may be contributed to a Roth IRA if allowed under the rules at *8.20*.

Figuring your IRA deduction if you receive Social Security benefits. If you or your spouse *(8.3)* is an active participant in an employer plan and either of you receives Social Security benefits, you need to make an extra computation before you can figure whether an IRA deduction is allowed. Follow the rules discussed at *34.3* to determine if part of your Social Security benefits would be subject to tax, assuming no IRA deduction were claimed. If none of your benefits would be taxable, you follow the regular rules above for determining IRA deductions. If part of your Social Security benefits would be taxable, MAGI for IRA purposes is increased by the taxable benefits. The allowable IRA deduction is then taken into account to determine the actual amount of taxable Social Security.

 Law Alert

Income Phase-out Limits
From 2000 through 2002, the deduction phase-out ranges will expand each year by an additional $1,000 at each end. Starting in 2003, bigger jumps will apply, until the phase-out range reaches $50,000–$60,000 in 2005 for single persons and $80,000–$100,000 in 2007 for married persons filing jointly.

EXAMPLES

1. Rob Porter is single and for 1999 has a salary of $30,000 and a MAGI of $32,343. His MAGI exceeds the $31,000 phase-out floor for single persons by $1,343. As the table on page 177 shows, the maximum IRA deduction limit is $1,740 for someone with excess MAGI of $1,343. Using the table saves Rob the trouble of computing the $1,740 deduction limit under the phase-out formula:

    1. Excess of MAGI over phase-out threshold
       for single persons ($32,343 – $31,000) $1,343.00
    2. 20% of step 1   268.60
    3. $2,000 minus step 2 $1,731.40
    4. Round step 3 to the next highest multiple of $10.
    This is the deductible limit.   1,740.00

2. Ted and Lynn Baker file a joint return for 1999. They report wages of $25,000 for Ted and $27,000 for Lynn. Their modified adjusted gross income (MAGI) is $54,025. Ted and Lynn were both active participants in employer retirement plans in 1999.

   Their excess MAGI is $3,025 ($54,025 – $51,000 phase-out threshold). As the Deduction Limit Table on page 177 shows, the IRA deduction limit is $1,400 where excess MAGI is $3,025. This is the limit for each of them. Ted may deduct contributions up to $1,400 and so may Lynn.

3. Assume the same facts as in Example 2 except that only Lynn was an active participant in an employer plan. Ted and Lynn must figure their deduction limitations separately using different phase-out thresholds.

   For Lynn, the same $1,400 deduction limit applies as in Example 2. The $51,000 phase-out threshold applies, her excess MAGI is $ 3,025 ($54,025 MAGI on joint return – $51,000 threshold), and the deduction limit from the table is $1,400.

   For Ted, the special $150,000 threshold for nonparticipant spouses applies. Since joint return MAGI is well below the $150,000 threshold, he is not affected by the phase-out rules and may deduct IRA contributions up to the $2,000 ceiling.

8.5 Active Participation in Employer Plan

Active participants in an employer retirement plan are subject to the adjusted gross income tests for deducting contributions as discussed at 8.4. Married individuals are generally treated as active participants if either spouse has plan coverage; see 8.3. An employer retirement plan means:

1. A qualified pension, profit-sharing, or stock bonus plan, including a qualified self-employed Keogh plan, SIMPLE IRA, or simplified employee pension (SEP) plan;

2. A qualified annuity plan;

3. A tax-sheltered annuity; and

4. A plan established for its employees by the United States, by a state or political subdivision, or by any agency or instrumentality of the United States or a state or political subdivision, but not eligible state Section 457 plans.

Form W-2. If your employer checks the "Pension plan" box within Box 15 of your 1999 Form W-2, this indicates that you were an active participant in your employer's retirement plan during the year. If you want to make a contribution before you receive your Form W-2, check the following guidelines and consult your plan administrator for your status.

Type of plan. Under any type of plan, if you are considered an active participant for any part of the plan year ending with or within your taxable year, you are treated as an active participant for the entire taxable year. Because of this plan year rule, you may be treated as an active participant even if you worked for the employer only part of the year. Under IRS guidelines, it is possible to be treated as an active participant in the year of retirement and even in the year after retirement if your employer maintains a fiscal year plan.

The plan year rule works differently for defined benefit pension plans than for defined contribution plans such as profit-sharing plans, 401(k) plans, money purchase pension plans, and stock bonus plans. These rules are discussed below.

If you are married, and either you or your spouse is treated as an active participant for 1999, see 8.3 for the effect on the other spouse.

Defined benefit pension plans. You are treated as an active participant in a defined benefit pension plan if, for the plan year ending with or within your taxable year, you are eligible to participate in the plan. Under this rule, as long as you are eligible, you are treated as an active participant, even if you decline participation in the plan or you fail to make a mandatory contribution specified in the plan. Furthermore, you are treated as an active participant even if your rights to benefits are not vested.

Defined contribution plan. For a defined contribution plan, you are generally considered an active participant if "with respect to" the plan year ending with or within your taxable year (1) you make elective deferrals to the plan; (2) your employer contributes to your account; or (3) forfeitures are allocated to your account. If any of these events occur, you are treated as an active participant for that taxable year, even if you do not have a vested right to receive benefits from your account.

 Caution

Active Participant Status

You are treated as an active participant in a 401(k) plan, profit-sharing plan, stock bonus plan, or money-purchase pension plan if contributions are made or allocated to your account for the plan year that ends within your tax year. Under this rule, you may be considered an active participant for a year during which no contributions by you or your employer are made to your account; see the Examples on page 178.

IRA Deduction Limit Table for 1999—*See* page 175 for figuring excess MAGI.

If Excess MAGI Is		
From—	Up to—	Your Maximum Deduction Is—
$0.00	$49.00	$2,000.00
$50.00	$99.00	$1,990.00
$100.00	$149.00	$1,980.00
$150.00	$199.00	$1,970.00
$200.00	$249.00	$1,960.00
$250.00	$299.00	$1,950.00
$300.00	$349.00	$1,940.00
$350.00	$399.00	$1,930.00
$400.00	$449.00	$1,920.00
$450.00	$499.00	$1,910.00
$500.00	$549.00	$1,900.00
$550.00	$599.00	$1,890.00
$600.00	$649.00	$1,880.00
$650.00	$699.00	$1,870.00
$700.00	$749.00	$1,860.00
$750.00	$799.00	$1,850.00
$800.00	$849.00	$1,840.00
$850.00	$899.00	$1,830.00
$900.00	$949.00	$1,820.00
$950.00	$999.00	$1,810.00
$1,000.00	$1,049.00	$1,800.00
$1,050.00	$1,099.00	$1,790.00
$1,100.00	$1,149.00	$1,780.00
$1,150.00	$1,199.00	$1,770.00
$1,200.00	$1,249.00	$1,760.00
$1,250.00	$1,299.00	$1,750.00
$1,300.00	$1,349.00	$1,740.00
$1,350.00	$1,399.00	$1,730.00
$1,400.00	$1,449.00	$1,720.00
$1,450.00	$1,499.00	$1,710.00
$1,500.00	$1,549.00	$1,700.00
$1,550.00	$1,599.00	$1,690.00
$1,600.00	$1,649.00	$1,680.00
$1,650.00	$1,699.00	$1,670.00
$1,700.00	$1,749.00	$1,660.00
$1,750.00	$1,799.00	$1,650.00
$1,800.00	$1,849.00	$1,640.00
$1,850.00	$1,899.00	$1,630.00
$1,900.00	$1,949.00	$1,620.00
$1,950.00	$1,999.00	$1,610.00
$2,000.00	$2,049.00	$1,600.00
$2,050.00	$2,099.00	$1,590.00
$2,100.00	$2,149.00	$1,580.00
$2,150.00	$2,199.00	$1,570.00
$2,200.00	$2,249.00	$1,560.00
$2,250.00	$2,299.00	$1,550.00
$2,300.00	$2,349.00	$1,540.00
$2,350.00	$2,399.00	$1,530.00
$2,400.00	$2,449.00	$1,520.00
$2,450.00	$2,499.00	$1,510.00
$2,500.00	$2,549.00	$1,500.00
$2,550.00	$2,599.00	$1,490.00
$2,600.00	$2,649.00	$1,480.00
$2,650.00	$2,699.00	$1,470.00
$2,700.00	$2,749.00	$1,460.00
$2,750.00	$2,799.00	$1,450.00
$2,800.00	$2,849.00	$1,440.00
$2,850.00	$2,899.00	$1,430.00
$2,900.00	$2,949.00	$1,420.00
$2,950.00	$2,999.00	$1,410.00
$3,000.00	$3,049.00	$1,400.00

If Excess MAGI Is		
From—	Up to—	Your Maximum Deduction Is—
$3,050.00	$3,099.00	$1,390.00
$3,100.00	$3,149.00	$1,380.00
$3,150.00	$3,199.00	$1,370.00
$3,200.00	$3,249.00	$1,360.00
$3,250.00	$3,299.00	$1,350.00
$3,300.00	$3,349.00	$1,340.00
$3,350.00	$3,399.00	$1,330.00
$3,400.00	$3,449.00	$1,320.00
$3,450.00	$3,499.00	$1,310.00
$3,500.00	$3,549.00	$1,300.00
$3,550.00	$3,599.00	$1,290.00
$3,600.00	$3,649.00	$1,280.00
$3,650.00	$3,699.00	$1,270.00
$3,700.00	$3,749.00	$1,260.00
$3,750.00	$3,799.00	$1,250.00
$3,800.00	$3,849.00	$1,240.00
$3,850.00	$3,899.00	$1,230.00
$3,900.00	$3,949.00	$1,220.00
$3,950.00	$3,999.00	$1,210.00
$4,000.00	$4,049.00	$1,200.00
$4,050.00	$4,099.00	$1,190.00
$4,100.00	$4,149.00	$1,180.00
$4,150.00	$4,199.00	$1,170.00
$4,200.00	$4,249.00	$1,160.00
$4,250.00	$4,299.00	$1,150.00
$4,300.00	$4,349.00	$1,140.00
$4,350.00	$4,399.00	$1,130.00
$4,400.00	$4,449.00	$1,120.00
$4,450.00	$4,499.00	$1,110.00
$4,500.00	$4,549.00	$1,100.00
$4,550.00	$4,599.00	$1,090.00
$4,600.00	$4,649.00	$1,080.00
$4,650.00	$4,699.00	$1,070.00
$4,700.00	$4,749.00	$1,060.00
$4,750.00	$4,799.00	$1,050.00
$4,800.00	$4,849.00	$1,040.00
$4,850.00	$4,899.00	$1,030.00
$4,900.00	$4,949.00	$1,020.00
$4,950.00	$4,999.00	$1,010.00
$5,000.00	$5,049.00	$1,000.00
$5,050.00	$5,099.00	$990.00
$5,100.00	$5,149.00	$980.00
$5,150.00	$5,199.00	$970.00
$5,200.00	$5,249.00	$960.00
$5,250.00	$5,299.00	$950.00
$5,300.00	$5,349.00	$940.00
$5,350.00	$5,399.00	$930.00
$5,400.00	$5,449.00	$920.00
$5,450.00	$5,499.00	$910.00
$5,500.00	$5,549.00	$900.00
$5,550.00	$5,599.00	$890.00
$5,600.00	$5,649.00	$880.00
$5,650.00	$5,699.00	$870.00
$5,700.00	$5,749.00	$860.00
$5,750.00	$5,799.00	$850.00
$5,800.00	$5,849.00	$840.00
$5,850.00	$5,899.00	$830.00
$5,900.00	$5,949.00	$820.00
$5,950.00	$5,999.00	$810.00
$6,000.00	$6,049.00	$800.00
$6,050.00	$6,099.00	$790.00

If Excess MAGI Is		
From—	Up to—	Your Maximum Deduction Is—
$6,100.00	$6,149.00	$780.00
$6,150.00	$6,199.00	$770.00
$6,200.00	$6,249.00	$760.00
$6,250.00	$6,299.00	$750.00
$6,300.00	$6,349.00	$740.00
$6,350.00	$6,399.00	$730.00
$6,400.00	$6,449.00	$720.00
$6,450.00	$6,499.00	$710.00
$6,500.00	$6,549.00	$700.00
$6,550.00	$6,599.00	$690.00
$6,600.00	$6,649.00	$680.00
$6,650.00	$6,699.00	$670.00
$6,700.00	$6,749.00	$660.00
$6,750.00	$6,799.00	$650.00
$6,800.00	$6,849.00	$640.00
$6,850.00	$6,899.00	$630.00
$6,900.00	$6,949.00	$620.00
$6,950.00	$6,999.00	$610.00
$7,000.00	$7,049.00	$600.00
$7,050.00	$7,099.00	$590.00
$7,100.00	$7,149.00	$580.00
$7,150.00	$7,199.00	$570.00
$7,200.00	$7,249.00	$560.00
$7,250.00	$7,299.00	$550.00
$7,300.00	$7,349.00	$540.00
$7,350.00	$7,399.00	$530.00
$7,400.00	$7,449.00	$520.00
$7,450.00	$7,499.00	$510.00
$7,500.00	$7,549.00	$500.00
$7,550.00	$7,599.00	$490.00
$7,600.00	$7,649.00	$480.00
$7,650.00	$7,699.00	$470.00
$7,700.00	$7,749.00	$460.00
$7,750.00	$7,799.00	$450.00
$7,800.00	$7,849.00	$440.00
$7,850.00	$7,899.00	$430.00
$7,900.00	$7,949.00	$420.00
$7,950.00	$7,999.00	$410.00
$8,000.00	$8,049.00	$400.00
$8,050.00	$8,099.00	$390.00
$8,100.00	$8,149.00	$380.00
$8,150.00	$8,199.00	$370.00
$8,200.00	$8,249.00	$360.00
$8,250.00	$8,299.00	$350.00
$8,300.00	$8,349.00	$340.00
$8,350.00	$8,399.00	$330.00
$8,400.00	$8,449.00	$320.00
$8,450.00	$8,499.00	$310.00
$8,500.00	$8,549.00	$300.00
$8,550.00	$8,599.00	$290.00
$8,600.00	$8,649.00	$280.00
$8,650.00	$8,699.00	$270.00
$8,700.00	$8,749.00	$260.00
$8,750.00	$8,799.00	$250.00
$8,800.00	$8,849.00	$240.00
$8,850.00	$8,899.00	$230.00
$8,900.00	$8,949.00	$220.00
$8,950.00	$8,999.00	$210.00
$9,000.00	$9,999.00	$200.00
$10,000.00	or more	$0.00

EXAMPLES

1. Pat O'Neil joins a company that has a 401(k) plan (a type of defined contribution plan) with a plan year starting July 1 and ending the following June 30. He is not eligible to participate in the plan year ending June 30, 1999. He elects to defer 6% of his 1999 salary to the 401(k) plan for the plan year ending June 30, 2000. Although he makes elective deferrals to the plan during 1999, he is *not* considered an active participant for 1999 because his contributions were made for the plan year ending in 2000. He *will* be considered an active participant in 2000, even if he decides not to defer any part of his 2000 salary for the plan year ending June 30, 2001.

2. Clarise Jones's employer has a defined benefit pension plan with a plan year starting July 1 and ending the following June 30. She is not excluded from participating. If she retired during September 1999, she is considered an active participant for 1999 because she was eligible to participate during the plan year ending during 1999. She will also be considered an active participant for 2000. Although she will retire before the end of the plan year starting July 1, 1999, and ending June 30, 2000, she will still be eligible to participate during part of that plan year (July 1, 1999, until retirement in September 1999), and since the 1999–2000 plan year ends within her 2000 tax year, she will be considered an active participant for 2000.

8.6 Nondeductible IRA Contributions

If you are not allowed to deduct any IRA contributions for 1999 because of the phase-out rule *(8.4)*, you may make *nondeductible* contributions of up to $2,000, or $4,000 if married filing jointly, where you have compensation of at least that much. If a deduction of less than $2,000 is allowed under the phase-out rules, you may make a nondeductible contribution to the extent the maximum contribution limit of $2,000 exceeds the deductible limit figured under *8.4*.

However, if you are not barred from making Roth IRA contributions *(see 8.20)* because of your income level, the Roth IRA has advantages over the nondeductible traditional IRA. Although both types of plans allow earnings to accumulate tax free until withdrawal, the Roth IRA has advantages at withdrawal. After a five-year period, completely tax-free withdrawals of earnings as well as contributions may be made from a Roth IRA if you are age 59 $\frac{1}{2}$ or older, you are disabled, or you withdraw no more than $10,000 for first-time home-buyer expenses. Even within the first five-year period, contributions may be withdrawn tax free from a Roth IRA. On the other hand, withdrawals from a nondeductible traditional IRA are partially taxed if any deductible contributions to any traditional IRA were previously made. Even if only nondeductible contributions had been made, earnings from traditional IRAs are taxed at withdrawal. Furthermore, contributions after age 70 $\frac{1}{2}$ may be made only to a Roth IRA, and mandatory required minimum distributions are not required from a Roth IRA, as they are from a traditional IRA. *See 8.20–8.22* for Roth IRA details.

Form 8606. You must file Form 8606 to report nondeductible IRA contributions to a traditional IRA unless you withdraw the contribution as discussed below. You must list on Form 8606 the value of all of your IRAs as of the end of the year, including amounts based on deductible contributions. If you are married and you and your spouse both make nondeductible contributions, you must each file a separate Form 8606. A $50 penalty may be imposed for not filing Form 8606 unless there is reasonable cause. Furthermore, if you overstate the amount of designated nondeductible contributions made for any taxable year, you are subject to a $100 penalty for each such overstatement unless you can demonstrate that the overstatement was due to reasonable cause. You may file an amended return for a taxable year and change the designation of IRA contributions from deductible to nondeductible or nondeductible to deductible.

If you make contributions to a traditional IRA during the year, you may not know whether you will be allowed to claim a deduction under the phase-out rules of *8.4*. You can make your contribution without knowing whether it is deductible or not and figure your deduction when you file your return. Any nondeductible amount would be reported on Form 8606. However, if you do not want to make nondeductible contributions, you may wait until after the end of the year when you can determine your MAGI and active participant status; you have until the April filing due date (without extensions) to make a deductible contribution; for 1999 returns, the filing due date is April 17, 2000.

Law Alert

Nondeductible Roth IRA

A Roth IRA is a nondeductible IRA that offers significant tax and retirement planning advantages. Nondeductible contributions of up to $2,000 may be made if modified adjusted gross income is below $95,000 if you are single and $150,000 if married filing jointly. In general, after the five-year period beginning with the first taxable year for which a Roth IRA contribution was made, tax-free withdrawals may be made if you are age 59 $\frac{1}{2}$ or older, you are disabled or you have qualifying first-time home-buyer expenses. Existing IRAs may be rolled over to Roth IRAs if your modified adjusted gross income is $100,000 or less. *See 8.21* for further details.

Withdrawing nondeductible contributions. If you make an IRA contribution for 1999 and later realize it is not deductible, you may make a tax-free withdrawal of the contribution by the filing due date (plus extensions), instead of designating the contribution as nondeductible on Form 8606. To do this, you must also withdraw the earnings allocable to the withdrawn contribution and include the earnings as income on your 1999 return. You might want to make the withdrawal if you incorrectly determined that a contribution would be deductible and you do not want to leave nondeductible contributions in your account. However, making the withdrawal could subject you to bank penalties for premature withdrawals, or other withdrawal penalties imposed by the IRA trustee. Furthermore, if you are under age 59 $\frac{1}{2}$, the 10% premature withdrawal penalty applies to the withdrawn earnings unless one of the exceptions at *8.12* is available.

8.7 Penalty for Excess Contributions to Traditional IRAs

If you contribute more than the allowable amount to a traditional IRA, whether deductible or nondeductible, the excess contribution may be subject to a penalty tax of 6%. The penalty tax is cumulative. That is, unless you correct the excess, you will be subject to another penalty on the excess contribution in the following year. The penalty tax is not deductible. The penalty is figured in Part II of Form 5329, which must be attached to Form 1040.

The 6% penalty may be avoided by withdrawing the excess contribution by the due date for your return, including extensions, plus any income earned on it. The withdrawn excess is not taxable provided no deduction was allowed for it. The withdrawn income must be reported as income on your return for the year in which the excess contribution was made. If you are under age 59 $\frac{1}{2}$ (and not disabled) when you receive the income, the 10% premature withdrawal penalty applies to the income. Similar rules apply to withdrawals of excess employer contributions to a simplified employee pension plan *(8.15)* made by the due date for your return.

You may also avoid a penalty for 1999 by reducing your allowable 1999 IRA contribution by the 1998 excess and then including the 1998 excess amount in your 1999 IRA deduction. *See* IRS Publication 590 and Form 5329 for details.

If an excess contribution for 1999 is not withdrawn by the due date for your 1999 return, the 6% penalty will apply to your 1999 return but it may be avoided for 2000 by withdrawing the excess by the end of 2000.

If you deducted an excess contribution in an earlier year for which total contributions were $2,000 or less, you may make a tax-free withdrawal of the excess by filing an amended return to correct the excess deduction. However, the 6% penalty tax applies for each year that the excess was still in the account at the end of the year.

After the due date of your return, you may make a tax-free withdrawal of excess employer contributions to a simplified employee pension plan *(8.15)* if they are $30,000 or less. However, the 6% penalty tax applies for each year that the excess was still in the account at the end of the year.

See IRS Publication 590 for further information on correcting excess contributions made in a prior year.

Roth IRAs. A similar 6% penalty applies on Form 5329 to excess contributions to a Roth IRA; *see* Form 5329 and IRS Publication 590 for further details.

Planning Reminder

Form 8606 for Traditional IRA Distributions

Keep a copy of each Form 8606 filed showing nondeductible contributions and keep a separate record of deductible contributions. When you make IRA withdrawals, the portion of each withdrawal allocable to nondeductible contributions is not taxed. You may not completely avoid tax even if you withdraw an amount equal to your nondeductible contributions. The tax-free portion of the withdrawal is figured on Form 8606. The rules for figuring tax on withdrawals are at *8.9*.

Taking Money Out of a Traditional IRA

8.8 Taxable Distributions From Traditional IRAs

If all of your IRA contributions were deductible, any traditional IRA distribution you receive that you do not roll over or redeposit within 60 days *(8.10)* will be taxable. Not only are distributions taxable, but the timing and amount of IRA payments is subject to these restrictions:

- Distributions in 1999 before age 59 $\frac{1}{2}$ are subject to a 10% tax penalty, unless you are totally disabled, meet exceptions for paying medical costs, or you receive annual payments under an annuity-type schedule. The penalty and the exceptions are discussed at *8.12*.
- After you reach age 70 $\frac{1}{2}$, you must start to receive annual distributions under a life-expectancy calculation. The required starting date is the April 1 of the year after the year in which you reach age 70 $\frac{1}{2}$. For example, if you reach age 70 $\frac{1}{2}$ during 1999 you must start taking IRA distributions by April 1, 2000. Failure to take the minimum required annual distribution can result in penalties. These rules are discussed in *8.13*.

Law Alert

Proposed Tax-Free Distributions for Charitable Purpose

When this book went to press, Congress was considering legislation that would allow IRA owners over age 70 ½ to withdraw IRA funds without tax starting in 2003 if the distribution is made directly to a qualified charitable organization. No charitable deduction would be allowed for IRA transfers excluded from income. *See* the Supplement for a legislation update.

Court Decision

Penalty on Garnished IRA

The Tax Court held that an IRA owner received a taxable distribution when a bank enforced a court's garnishment award for past-due child support by transferring his IRA to his ex-wife. The Tax Court found that the distribution to the owner's former wife was a discharge of indebtedness to her and was constructively received by him. Whether the transfer of funds was voluntary or in settlement of a legal obligation was held to be of no consequence. The 10% tax penalty for distributions before age 59 ½ also applied.

How to report IRA distributions on your 1999 return. All IRA distributions are reported to you and to the IRS on Form 1099-R; *see* the guide to Form 1099-R on page 136. Form 1099-R must be attached to your return only if federal tax has been withheld. You can avoid withholding by instructing the payer not to withhold using Form W-4P (or a substitute form); *see* 26.11.

If you have never made nondeductible contributions, your IRA withdrawals are fully taxable and should be reported on Line 15b of Form 1040 or Line 10b of Form 1040A. If you have made deductible and nondeductible contributions, complete Form 8606 to figure the nontaxable and taxable portions as discussed in 8.9. Then you report the total IRA withdrawal on Line 15a of Form 1040 or Line 10a of Form 1040A and enter only the taxable portion on Line 15b or Line 10b, respectively.

If you have an individual retirement annuity, your investment in the contract is treated as zero so all payments are fully taxable. Distributions from an endowment policy due to death are taxed as ordinary income to the extent allocable to retirement savings; to the extent allocable to life insurance, they are considered insurance proceeds.

Proceeds from U.S. retirement bonds (which were issued by the Treasury before May 1982) are taxable in the year the bonds are redeemed. However, you must report the full proceeds in the year you reach age 70 ½ even if you do not redeem the bonds.

Loan treated as distribution. If you borrow from your IRA account or use it as security for a loan, you generally are considered to have received your entire interest. Borrowing will subject the account or the fair market value of the contract to tax at ordinary income rates as of the first day of the taxable year of the borrowing. Your IRA account loses its tax-exempt status. If you use the account or part of it as security for a loan, the portion that is pledged is treated as a distribution. However, under the rollover rules, a short-term loan may be made by withdrawing IRA funds and redepositing them in an IRA within 60 days, subject to the once-a-year rollover rule at 8.10.

IRS seizure of IRA treated as distribution. The Tax Court has held that an IRS levy of an IRA to cover back taxes is a taxable distribution to the account owner, even though the funds are transferred directly from the account to the IRS and not actually received by the owner. Where the owner is under age 59 ½, the Tax Court has held that the 10% penalty for early withdrawals does not apply to involuntary distributions attributable to an IRS levy. A new law adopts the Tax Court position barring the penalty, effective for IRS levies made after 1999.

8.9 Partially Tax-Free Traditional IRA Distributions Allocable to Nondeductible Contributions

If you ever made a nondeductible contribution to a traditional IRA, you must file Form 8606 to report a 1999 distribution from any of your traditional IRAs, even if the distribution is from an IRA to which only nondeductible contributions were made. All of your IRAs are treated as one contract. If you receive distributions from more than one IRA in the same year, they are combined for reporting purposes on Form 8606. When you withdraw an amount from any IRA during a taxable year and you previously made both deductible and nondeductible IRA contributions, the part of your withdrawal that is allocable to your nondeductible contributions is tax-free; any balance is taxable. You may not claim that you are withdrawing only your tax-free contributions, even if your withdrawal is less than your nondeductible contributions. If you withdraw amounts from your nondeductible account, you will incur tax. You make the computations on Form 8606. The six steps below reflect the IRS method used on Form 8606 to figure the nontaxable and taxable portions of the IRA distributions.

The rule requiring you to combine nondeductible and deductible IRAs when making IRA withdrawals does not apply to withdrawals from a Roth IRA. A Roth IRA is treated separately. After a five-year period, withdrawals after age 59 ½ are completely tax-free; *see* 8.22.

A bank or other payer of a distribution from a traditional IRA will not indicate on Form 1099-R whether any part of a distribution is a tax-free return of basis allocable to nondeductible contributions. It is up to you to keep records that show the nondeductible contributions you have made. IRS instructions require you to keep copies of all Forms 8606 on which nondeductible contributions have been designated, as well as copies of (1) your tax returns for years you made nondeductible contributions to traditional IRAs; (2) Forms 5498 showing all IRA contributions and showing the value of your IRAs for each year you received a distribution; and (3) Form 1099-R and Form W-2P showing IRA distributions. According to the IRS, you should keep such records until you have withdrawn all IRA funds.

Figuring the taxable portion of a traditional IRA distribution. If you received a distribution from a traditional IRA in 1999 and have ever made nondeductible contributions to any of your traditional IRAs, follow Steps 1–6 to determine the tax-free and taxable portions of the 1999 distributions. These steps assume that you did not convert a traditional IRA to a Roth IRA during 1999. If you did convert a traditional IRA to a Roth IRA, follow the instructions to Form 8606.

Step 1. Total IRA withdrawals during 1999.

Step 2. Total nondeductible contributions to all IRAs made by the end of 1999. Tax-free withdrawals of nondeductible contributions in prior years reduce the total. If you made any contributions to traditional IRAs for 1999 (including a contribution made between January 1 and April 17, 2000) that may be partly nondeductible because your modified adjusted gross income is within the deduction phase-out range shown in *8.4* for active plan participants, you should include the contributions in the Step 2 total.

Step 3. Add Step 1 to the value of all your IRAs (include SIMPLE IRAs and SEP IRAs) as of the end of 1999. If you received an IRA distribution within the last 60 days of 1999 that was rolled over to another IRA within the 60-day rollover period *(8.10) but* not until 2000, add the 2000 rollover to the year-end balance.

Step 4. Divide Step 2 by Step 3. This is the tax-free percentage of your IRA withdrawal.

Step 5. Multiply the Step 4 percentage by Step 1. This amount is tax free.

Step 6. Subtract Step 5 from Step 1. This amount is fully taxable.

EXAMPLE

In 1999, Nick James withdraws $5,000 from his IRA, having made deductible IRA contributions of $8,000 and nondeductible contributions of $6,000 as follows:

Year	Deductible	Nondeductible
1991	$2,000	0
1992	2,000	0
1993	2,000	0
1994	1,000	$1,000
1995	1,000	1,000
1996	0	2,000
1997	0	2,000
	$8,000	$6,000

Assume that at the end of 1999, Nick's total IRA account balance, including earnings, is $17,500, and that this is his first IRA withdrawal. On Form 8606 for 1999, Nick figures that $1,350 of the $5,000 IRA withdrawal is tax free and $3,650 is taxable.

Step 1.	IRA withdrawal	$5,000
Step 2.	Nondeductible contributions	6,000
Step 3.	IRA balance at end of the year ($17,500) *plus* Step 1	22,500
Step 4.	Tax-free percentage: $6,000 ÷ $22,500	27%
Step 5.	Tax-free withdrawal: 27% × $5,000	1,350
Step 6.	Taxable withdrawal: $5,000 – $1,350	$3,650

The total $5,000 withdrawal should be reported on Line 15a of Form 1040 or on Line 10a of Form 1040A, and the taxable $3,650 portion should be entered on Line 15b (Form 1040) or on Line 10b (Form 1040A).

Deductible IRA loss based on unrecovered nondeductible contributions. According to the IRS, a loss may be allowed if all IRA funds have been distributed and you have not recovered your basis in nondeductible contributions.

EXAMPLE

Paula Brown makes nondeductible IRA contributions of $10,000 from 1994–1998. At the end of 1999, she withdraws $6,000. The year-end balance is $8,000. The tax-free portion of the withdrawal is $4,286 ($10,000 nondeductible contributions ÷ $14,000 total of withdrawal plus year-end balance × $6,000 withdrawal).

After the withdrawal, her account balance is $8,000; her basis is $5,714 ($10,000 – $4,286). If because of poor investments the value of the IRA fell to $3,000 by the end of 2000 and she withdrew the entire $3,000 balance, she could claim a $2,714 loss ($5,714 basis – $3,000 distribution), but only as a miscellaneous itemized deduction subject to the 2% floor *(19.1)* on Schedule A of Form 1040.

Planning Reminder

Deducting Loss

A loss on an IRA investment is deductible only if your basis in nondeductible contributions has not been received after the entire account has been distributed.

Planning Reminder

60-Day Loan From IRA

You can take advantage of the rollover rule to borrow funds from your IRA if you need a short-term loan to pay your taxes or other expenses. As long as you redeposit the amount in an IRA within 60 days you are not taxed on the withdrawal; the redeposit is considered a tax-free rollover. You may roll over the funds to a different IRA from the one from which the withdrawal was made. A second withdrawal from the same IRA within one year would be taxable as discussed in the right column of this page.

Filing Tip

Reporting a Rollover on Your 1999 Return

If you rolled over a qualifying distribution from an employer plan to an IRA *(7.8)*, report the total distribution on Line 16a of Form 1040 or Line 11a of Form 1040A. Enter zero as the taxable amount on Line 16b or Line 11b if the entire amount was rolled over. If only part of the distribution was rolled over, enter the portion not rolled over on Line 16b or Line 11b. Write "Rollover" next to the line.

If you rolled over funds from one IRA to another, the total distribution should be reported on Line 15a of Form 1040 or Line 10a of Form 1040A. If the entire distribution was rolled over, enter zero as the taxable amount on Line 15b or Line 10b. Otherwise, enter the amount not rolled over on Line 15b or Line 10b. Write "Rollover" next to the line.

If you made a tax-free direct transfer from one IRA to another, you do not have to report it on your return.

8.10 Tax-Free Rollovers and Direct Transfers to Traditional IRAs

There are two types of tax-free rollovers that you can make to an IRA. You may roll over funds to an IRA from a qualified company or self-employed retirement plan, as discussed at *7.8*. You may also use a rollover to switch funds from one IRA to another, although another option, a direct transfer, may be a more advantageous way of changing IRA investments.

Direct transfer. A *direct transfer* is made by instructing the trustee of an IRA to transfer all or part of your account to another IRA trustee. Direct transfers are tax free because you do not receive the funds. The tax law does not require a waiting period between direct transfers, whereas rollovers are subject to a once-a-year limitation, as discussed below.

For example, assume you have an IRA at Bank "A" and decide to switch your account to Mutual Fund "ABC." The mutual fund will provide you with transfer request forms that you complete and return to the fund, which will then forward the forms to the bank to complete the direct transfer. The transfer from the bank to the mutual fund is tax free. Because the IRA funds were not paid to you, the transfer is not considered a rollover subject to the once-a-year rollover limitation. This means that if within one year you become unhappy with the performance of Mutual Fund "ABC," you may make another tax-free direct transfer of your IRA to Fund "XYZ" or to Bank "B."

Rollover. With a *rollover* you withdraw funds from an IRA and have 60 days to invest in another IRA. To avoid tax on a rollover from one IRA to another, these tests must be met: (1) the amount you receive from your old IRA must be transferred to the new plan within 60 days of your receiving it and (2) a tax-free rollover may occur only once in a one-year period starting on the date you receive the first distribution. If within that one-year period you receive a distribution from the previously rolled over IRA, the distribution is taxable and if you are under age 59 ½, could be subject to the 10% penalty for premature distributions; *see 8.12.* A *direct transfer* may be used as discussed above if you want to invest in another IRA within the one-year period.

The once-a-year rollover rule applies separately to each of your IRAs. For example, you have one IRA invested in a bank and another IRA invested in a mutual fund. Within the same one-year period, you may roll over the bank IRA to a different IRA and you may also roll over the mutual-fund IRA to a different IRA. However, neither of the new IRAs may be rolled over again within the one-year period starting on the date that you received the distribution from the original IRA plan.

There is an exception to the one-year waiting period between rollovers if the second distribution is made from an insolvent financial institution by the FDIC (Federal Deposit Insurance Corporation) acting as receiver. The exception applies only if the receiver makes the distribution to you because it is unable to find a buyer for the insolvent institution.

Deposits in insolvent financial institutions. The 60-day limit for completing a rollover is extended if the funds are "frozen" and may not be withdrawn from a bankrupt or insolvent financial institution. The 60-day period is extended while the account is frozen and you have a minimum of 10 days after the release of the funds to complete the rollover.

If a government agency takes control of an insolvent bank, you might receive an "involuntary" distribution of your IRA account from the agency. According to the IRS and Tax Court, such a payment is subject to the regular IRA distribution rules. For example, a couple received payment for their $11,000 IRA balance from the Maryland Deposit Insurance Fund after the bank in which the funds were invested became insolvent. The Tax Court held that the payment was taxable, even though the distribution was from a state insurance fund and not from the bank itself. Furthermore, since they were under age 59 ½, the 10% penalty for early distributions *(8.12)* was imposed, even though the distribution was involuntary. The tax and penalty could have been avoided by making a rollover of the distribution within 60 days, but this was not done.

8.11 Transfer of Traditional IRA to Spouse at Divorce or Death

If you receive your former spouse's IRA pursuant to a divorce decree or written instrument incident to the decree, the transfer is not taxable to either of you. From the date of transfer the account is treated as your IRA. If you are legally separated, a transfer of your spouse's IRA to you is tax free if made under a decree of separate maintenance or written instrument incident to the decree. The transferred account is then treated as your IRA.

QDRO transfer to IRA. If you receive your share of your spouse's or former spouse's benefits from an employer plan under a qualified domestic relations order (QDRO), the distribution is taxable to you unless you roll it over to an IRA. Special averaging may be available; *see 7.12.* If you roll over only part of a qualifying QDRO distribution, you figure the tax on the retained portion by taking into account a prorated share of your former spouse's cost investment.

Surviving spouse. If you inherit your spouse's IRA when he or she dies, you may elect to treat the IRA as your own, or you may receive distributions from the account as a beneficiary. *See 8.14* for a discussion of these options.

8.12 Penalty for IRA Withdrawals Before Age 59$^{1/}_{2}$

You have to pay a 10% penalty if you receive a distribution from a traditional IRA before you are age 59 $\frac{1}{2}$, *unless* (1) you make a qualifying rollover to another IRA *(8.10),* (2) you are totally disabled, (3) you pay medical expenses exceeding 7.5% of adjusted gross income, (4) you receive unemployment compensation for at least 12 consecutive weeks and pay medical insurance premiums, (5) you pay qualified higher education expenses, (6) the distribution is $10,000 or less and used for qualified first-time homebuyer expenses, (7) the distribution is one of a series of payments being made under one of several annuity-type methods, or (8) you are a beneficiary receiving IRA distributions following the death of the owner.

The penalty is 10% of the taxable IRA distribution. For example, if before age 59 $\frac{1}{2}$ you withdraw $3,000 from your IRA, you must include the $3,000 as part of your taxable income and, in addition, pay a $300 penalty tax. If part of a premature distribution is tax free because it is allocable to nondeductible contributions *(see 8.9)* or rolled over to another IRA *(8.10),* the 10% penalty applies only to the taxable portion of the distribution.

If you are subject to the 10% early distribution penalty but not to the penalties discussed at *8.7* and *8.13,* the penalty is entered directly on Form 1040, Line 53.

If you do not owe the penalty because you qualify for an exception, you may have to file Form 5329 with Form 1040, depending on whether the payer of the distribution correctly marked the exception in Box 7 of Form 1099-R. If you qualify for the annuity-method exception and the payer correctly indicated that exception by marking Code 2 in Box 7, you do not have to file Form 5329. Similarly, if you are the beneficiary of a deceased IRA owner and the payer has correctly noted that with Code 4 in Box 7, you do not have to file Form 5329 to claim the exception.

If you qualify for the disability exception *(see* below), it is unlikely that the payer will know of that fact and thus Code 3 (for the disability exception) will probably not be marked in Box 7 of Form 1099-R. In that case, you must file Form 5329 to claim the exception. You also must file Form 5329 if the annuity method or beneficiary exception applies but it is not coded in Box 7 of Form 1099-R.

If you rolled over your entire distribution within 60 days to another IRA *(8.10),* the penalty does not apply and Form 5329 does not have to be filed.

Spousal beneficiaries. Beneficiaries are exempt from the pre–59 $\frac{1}{2}$ penalty. If you inherit an IRA from your deceased spouse and elect to treat it as your *own* IRA as discussed at *8.14,* you are not eligible for the beneficiary exception; distributions from the account before you reach age 59 $\frac{1}{2}$ will be subject to the penalty. The beneficiary exception applies if the account is maintained in the name of your deceased spouse and you are receiving the distribution as a spousal beneficiary under the rules at *8.14.*

Disability exception. To qualify for the disability exception, you must be able to show that you have a physical or mental condition that can be expected to last indefinitely or result in death and that prevents you from engaging in "substantial gainful activity" similar to the type of work you were doing before the condition arose.

In one case, a 53-year-old stockbroker claimed that his IRA withdrawal of over $200,000 should be exempt from the 10% penalty because he suffered from mental depression. However, the Tax Court upheld the IRS imposition of the penalty because he continued to work as a stockbroker.

Medical expense exception. If you withdraw IRA funds in a year in which you pay substantial medical costs, part of the distribution may avoid the pre–age 59 $\frac{1}{2}$ penalty. If your unreimbursed medical expenses in the year of the distribution exceed 7.5% of your adjusted gross income, the distribution, to the extent of the excess, is not subject to the penalty. The medical costs must be eligible for the itemized medical deduction *(see* Chapter 17), but the IRA penalty exception applies whether you itemize or claim the standard deduction.

 Law Alert

Medical Expense Penalty Exceptions

Two medical-related exceptions apply to the pre–age 59 $\frac{1}{2}$ penalty. If in the year of the IRA distribution you pay deductible medical expenses that exceed 7.5% of your adjusted gross income, the penalty does not apply to distributions that exceed the 7.5% threshold.

The other exception applies to IRA owners who receive unemployment benefits for at least 12 consecutive weeks. If medical insurance premiums are paid in the year of the IRA distribution, the penalty does not apply to the extent of the premiums.

Unemployed person's medical insurance exceptions. If you are unemployed and received unemployment benefits under Federal or state law for at least 12 consecutive weeks, you may make penalty-free IRA withdrawals to the extent of medical insurance premiums paid during the year for you, your spouse, and your dependents. The withdrawals may be made in the year the 12-week unemployment test is met, or in the following year. However, the penalty exception does not apply to distributions made more than 60 days after you return to the work force.

Self-employed persons who are ineligible by law for unemployment benefits may be treated as meeting the 12-week test, and thus eligible for the exception, under regulations to be issued by the IRS.

Higher education expenses exception. A penalty exception is allowed for IRA distributions that do not exceed higher education expenses, including graduate school costs, for you, your spouse, your or your spouse's children, or your or your spouse's grandchildren that you paid during the year of the IRA distribution. Eligible expenses include tuition, room and board for a person who is at least a half-time student, fees, books, supplies, and equipment.

First-time home-buyer expense exception. A penalty exception is allowed for up to $10,000 of qualifying "first-time" home-buyer expenses. The penalty does not apply to IRA distributions that are used within 120 days to buy, construct, or reconstruct a principal residence for you, your spouse, child, grandchild, or ancestor of you or your spouse. A qualifying first-time home-buyer is someone who did not have a present ownership interest in a principal residence in the two-year period before the acquisition of the new house. The exception applies only for $10,000 of home-buyer expenses. This is a lifetime cap per IRA owner and not an annual limit.

Annuity Schedule Payments Avoid 10% Penalty

You may avoid the penalty if you are willing to receive annual distributions under one of the annuity-type methods discussed in this section. Before arranging an annuity-type schedule, consider these points: all of the payments will be taxable (unless allocable to nondeductible contributions under 8.8), and if you do not continue the payments for a minimum number of years, the IRS will impose the 10% penalty for all taxable payments received before age 59 $\frac{1}{2}$, plus interest charges.

The payments must continue for five years, or until you reach age 59 $\frac{1}{2}$, whichever period is *longer*. Thus, if you are in your 40s, you would have to continue the scheduled payments until you are age 59 $\frac{1}{2}$. If you are in your mid-50s, the minimum payout period is not as serious a burden, as you only need to continue the scheduled payments for a five-year period, starting with the date of the first distribution, provided that the period ends after you reach age 59 $\frac{1}{2}$. During this minimum period, the arranged annuity-type schedule may not be changed. For example, taking a lump-sum distribution of your account balance before reaching age 59 $\frac{1}{2}$ would trigger the retroactive penalty, plus interest charges. After the minimum payout period, you can discontinue the payments or change the method without penalty.

The minimum payout period rules do not apply to totally disabled individuals or to beneficiaries of deceased IRA owners.

If you would like to take advantage of this penalty exception, you may apply one of the following three payout methods that have been approved by the IRS in private rulings:

1. *Life expectancy method.* This is the easiest method to figure but provides smaller annual payments than the other methods. Figure the annual withdrawal by dividing your account balance by your life expectancy or by the joint life and last survivor expectancy of you and your beneficiary. This is the same method discussed at 8.13 for figuring minimum required distributions after age 70 $\frac{1}{2}$.

For example, you are age 50 in 2000 and have an IRA of $100,000 at the beginning of the year. You may take a penalty-free payment of $3,021 in 2000 ($100,000 account balance ÷ 33.1 life expectancy). Individual life expectancies are shown in Table V at 7.23. The annual penalty-free amount will generally increase in later years, with the exact amount depending on your account balance and whether you recalculate your life expectancy under the table each year (based on your age) or you simply reduce your life expectancy by one for each year that has elapsed since the year that you received the first payment.

If instead of using your single life expectancy you used the joint life and last survivor expectancy of you and your beneficiary (*see* sample table on page 201) the annual penalty-free amount would be smaller given the longer joint life expectancy. For example, if your beneficiary was age 45, your joint life and last survivor life expectancy would be 42 years (using ages 50 and 45), and

Planning Reminder

Annuity-Schedule Penalty Exceptions

If you are planning a series of payments to avoid the 10% early-distribution penalty, keep in mind that payments under this exception must continue for at least five years, or until you reach age 59 $\frac{1}{2}$, whichever is the longer period.

the penalty-free withdrawal $2,381 ($100,000 account balance ÷ 42). *See* page 201 for the sample section of the IRS joint life and last survivor life expectancy table. The full IRS Table VI showing joint life and last survivor life expectancy is in IRS Publication 939 and can also be obtained from your IRA trustee.

    2. ***Amortization method.*** Under this method, you amortize your IRA account balance like a mortgage, using the same life expectancy as under Method 1 (your single life expectancy or the joint life and last survivor expectancy of you and your beneficiary) and a long-term interest rate that is reasonable when the payments commence. In private rulings, the IRS approved the use of interest rates based on federal rates, such as the applicable federal rate used for figuring minimum interest on seller-financed sales *(4.32)*, or the rate of interest under Pension Benefit Guaranty Corporation regulations.

    Under the amortization method, the annual penalty-free withdrawal will be larger than under Method 1. For example, using an interest rate of 8% (assuming that is a reasonable rate), a 50-year-old with a $100,000 account balance may withdraw $8,679 without penalty in the first year, as opposed to $3,021 under Method 1. The payment in future years will depend on how life expectancy is adjusted.

    3. ***Annuity factor method.*** This method is similar to the amortization method but it allows you to use insurance mortality tables (such as the UP-1984 Mortality Table) that project shorter life expectancy tables than the IRS life expectancy tables used under Methods 1 and 2. If an interest rate of 8% and the UP-1984 mortality table were used for a 50-year-old with a $100,000 account balance, the penalty-free withdrawal in the first year would be $9,002, as opposed to $3,021 under Method 1 or $8,679 under Method 2.

8.13   Mandatory Distributions From a Traditional IRA After Age 70$\frac{1}{2}$

By April 1 of the year following the year in which you reach age 70 $\frac{1}{2}$, you have to start receiving annual IRA distributions under a schedule that meets tax law tests. If you do not receive the minimum amount required by the tax law, a penalty tax of 50% applies to the difference between the minimum amount you should have received and the amount you did receive. The penalty is reported on Form 5329, which must be attached to Form 1040. These minimum distribution rules apply only to traditional IRAs, not Roth IRAs *(8.19)*.

EXAMPLE

During 1999, Chris Calano reaches age 70 $\frac{1}{2}$ and receives $500 from his traditional IRA. The minimum amount required to be paid to him was $700. He must pay a penalty tax of $100 (50% of $200), unless it is waived by the IRS.

When must your first required minimum distribution be received? Your required beginning date is April 1 of the year following the year in which you reach age 70 $\frac{1}{2}$. For example, if you reached age 70 $\frac{1}{2}$ during 1999, you must receive a minimum distribution for 1999 no later than April 1, 2000. You will also have to receive a minimum distribution for 2000 by December 31, 2000. Thus, if you do not take your first distribution during 1999, and wait until between January 1 and April 1, 2000, you will have to make two distributions in 2000, one by April 1 and another by December 31. This could increase your 2000 taxable income substantially. Distributions for later years must be made by December 31 of each year.

    If you reach age 70 $\frac{1}{2}$ during 2000, your first distribution must be no later than April 1, 2001. If you have an individual retirement annuity, your insurance company should gear your payments to meet minimum distribution requirements.

Key decisions to make by your required beginning date. By your required beginning date (April 1 of the year after the year you reach age 70 $\frac{1}{2}$), you should designate a beneficiary and elect either the term-certain or recalculation method of adjusting life expectancy. Your choices will determine the minimum amount you must receive from your IRA each year, and, in some cases, also determine the payout options for your beneficiaries after your death.

    For example, the age of your designated beneficiary affects the calculation of the minimum distributions you must receive, as discussed below under Step 2. If you select a charitable organization as your beneficiary, or your estate as the beneficiary, you will have to use your single life expectancy in figuring your required minimum distributions.

Caution

Professional Advice Required

For Methods 2 and 3, you should get the assistance of a tax professional and an actuary to help plan a series of payments that will qualify for the penalty exception.

Filing Tip

Penalty Waiver for Reasonable Mistakes

If you do not receive a sufficient required minimum distribution from your traditional IRA, the IRS may waive the penalty for insufficient withdrawals if they are due to reasonable error and if steps have been taken in order to remedy the situation. You must submit evidence to account for shortfalls in withdrawals and how you are rectifying the situation. The IRS has indicated that examples of acceptable reasons for insufficient withdrawals include erroneous advice from the sponsoring organization or other pension advisors or that your own good faith efforts to apply the required withdrawal formula produced a miscalculation or misunderstanding of the formula. You should attach your letter of explanation to Form 5329. You must pay the penalty; if the IRS grants a waiver, it will refund the penalty.

Figuring Minimum IRA Distributions

Your IRA trustee should help you figure how much you must withdraw to avoid an IRS penalty. If that does not happen and you must figure the required minimum distribution yourself, follow the five steps below. In general, the required minimum distribution for each year equals the applicable life expectancy divided into the account balance at the end of the prior year. If you have more than one IRA, you must figure the required annual minimum distribution for each IRA separately, although once you have done so, the total required minimum distribution for the year may be withdrawn from any of the accounts in any combination you choose. Figure the required minimum distribution for *each* of your IRAs by following these steps:

Step 1: Find the account balance of your IRA as of the previous December 31. If you reach age 70 $\frac{1}{2}$ during 1999, the account balance to be used for figuring your first required minimum distribution is the account balance for December 31, 1998, even if the actual distribution for 1999 is not made until the first quarter of 2000 (January 1–April 1). For purposes of figuring your required minimum distribution for 2000, use the 1999 year-end balance, reduced by the first-year distribution if you took it in the first quarter of 2000.

Step 2: Find your life expectancy. For the year you reach age 70 $\frac{1}{2}$, use the joint life and last survivor life expectancy of you and the beneficiary that was designated by the required beginning date (April 1 of the year after the year you reach age 70 $\frac{1}{2}$). If you name more than one beneficiary, the age of the oldest beneficiary (the shortest life expectancy) is taken into account. Joint life and last survivor life expectancy is found in IRS unisex Table VI, a sample section of which is shown on page 201. The rest of the table is in IRS Publication 939 and can also be obtained from your IRA trustee.

Use only your single life expectancy from Table V at *7.23* if your beneficiary as of the required beginning date is your estate or a charitable organization; the charity or estate has no life expectancy. Your single life expectancy is also used if no beneficiary has been designated by the required beginning date.

The initial joint life and last survivor life expectancy of you and your beneficiary is determined by your ages on your respective birthdays in the year in which you reach age 70 $\frac{1}{2}$. For example, if you were born in October 1928, you reached age 70 $\frac{1}{2}$ in April 1999 and age 71 on your birthday in October 1999. Assume your beneficiary is age 67 on his or her birthday in 1999. For purposes of figuring your first required IRA distribution for the year 1999 (due by April 1, 2000), your joint life and last survivor expectancy from the table on page 201 is 21.7 years (using ages 71 and 67). For 2000 and later years, the required minimum distributions will depend on whether you choose to recalculate your life expectancies annually or to use the term-certain method; *see* Step 3 below.

Is your nonspouse beneficiary more than 10 years younger than you are? You are not allowed to use the actual joint life expectancy of you and a beneficiary who is more than 10 years younger than you are, unless the beneficiary is your spouse. If your beneficiary is not your spouse, you must treat the beneficiary as being only 10 years younger than yourself, although he or she may be much younger. This 10-year age rule is called the MDIB (minimum distribution incidental benefit) requirement.

For example, if you are age 71 on your birthday in the year you reach age 70 $\frac{1}{2}$, and your beneficiary is your 20-year-old grandchild, the grandchild is considered to be age 61 for purposes of figuring your initial joint life and last survivor expectancy. In subsequent years, you are each considered to be one year older, so your joint life and last survivor expectancy for the second distribution year is based on ages 72 and 62, for the third year it is based on ages 73 and 63, and so on.

The MDIB requirement applies each year while you are alive, regardless of whether you filed an election with the IRA plan to use the term-certain method or recalculation method of adjusting life expectancy as discussed under Step 3 below. However, the MDIB requirement no longer applies in years after your death. The payout rules to your beneficiary *will* depend on whether you elected the term-certain or recalculation method; *see* Step 3 and the rules for nonspouse beneficiaries at *8.14*.

Step 3: How to adjust life expectancy each year. The initial joint life and last survivor life expectancy for you and your beneficiary has to be adjusted every year to figure the minimum required IRA withdrawal. There are four methods for adjusting life expectancy—the *recalculation* method, the *term-certain* method, the *MDIB* method, and the *hybrid* method.

Planning Reminder

Using Life Expectancy of Revocable Trust Beneficiary

If a revocable trust is named beneficiary of your IRA, IRS proposed regulations allow the life expectancy of the trust beneficiary to be taken into account in figuring your minimum required distributions, provided the trust becomes irrevocable at your death. If there is more than one trust beneficiary, the life expectancy of the oldest beneficiary is used.

This IRS rule applies to qualified employer plans *(7.13)*, as well as to IRAs.

You must use the MDIB rule to figure each of your annual required minimum distributions if your designated beneficiary as of the required beginning date is more than 10 years younger than you are and is not your spouse. This is true regardless of whether you have elected in the IRA plan to use the term-certain or the recalculation method; *see* Step 2 above.

If you do not have to use the MDIB rule for a nonspouse designated beneficiary, a *hybrid* method (*see* the Planning Reminder on page 188) applies where you do not elect the term-certain method.

If your spouse is your designated beneficiary as of the required beginning date, the recalculation method may apply automatically under the terms of your IRA plan unless an election to use the term-certain method is specifically made by the required beginning date (April 1 of the year after the year you reach age 70 $\frac{1}{2}$). Check your plan to determine whether a specific election is necessary to apply the method you want. The method that takes effect as of the required beginning date cannot be changed.

Recalculation method. Under the recalculation method, your life expectancy may be recalculated annually and so may the life expectancy of a spouse who was designated as your beneficiary as of the required beginning date. If your beneficiary is not your spouse, you may recalculate your own life expectancy under the hybrid method discussed below.

If your spouse is your beneficiary and you both recalculate life expectancy, this means that each year your joint life expectancy from the IRS table is based on your ages at your birthdays in that year. For example, assume that your spouse is your beneficiary and that in 1999, the year you reached age 70 $\frac{1}{2}$, you were age 71 on your birthday and your spouse was age 67 on his or her birthday. Based on ages 71 and 67, your initial joint life and last survivor life expectancy from the IRS table (page 201) is 21.7 years, for purposes of figuring your required distribution for 1999. If you and your spouse recalculate life expectancies, your adjusted joint life expectancy for 2000, based on ages 72 and 68 (your ages on your birthdays in 2000), would be 20.8 years from the IRS table. For 2001, based on ages 73 and 69, the adjusted joint life expectancy from the IRS table would be 20.0 years, and for 2002 it would be 19.1 years (ages 74 and 70). As you can see, the joint life expectancy is reduced by *less than one* with each annual recalculation; as you grow older, the annual reduction in joint life expectancy becomes even smaller.

Term-certain method. Under the *term-certain* method, you do not have to use IRS life expectancy tables once you determine your initial joint life and last survivor expectancy for you and your beneficiary. You simply reduce that initial life expectancy by one in each later year. This method may be used with a spouse or non-spouse beneficiary unless you must use the MDIB rule for a non-spouse beneficiary as discussed in Step 2. Thus, if your initial joint life and last survivor expectancy for 1999 based on ages 71 and 67 is 21.7 years, it would be reduced to 20.7 years for 2000, 19.7 years for 2001, 18.7 years for 2002, and so on under the term-certain method.

Should you use the recalculation or term-certain method? Each method has advantages and disadvantages. The recalculation method generally allows you to conserve principal longer than the term-certain method by requiring you to take slightly smaller annual distributions; life expectancy is reduced each year by less than one under the recalculation method, while under the term-certain method life expectancy is reduced by a full year.

However, there is a disadvantage to the recalculation method if your spouse is your beneficiary and your spouse dies first. After the death of a recalculating owner or recalculating spousal beneficiary, that person's life expectancy is reduced to zero starting in the year after the year of death. Thus, if your recalculating spouse is your designated beneficiary and he or she dies first, you must use your single life expectancy to figure your minimum required distributions starting in the year after the year of your spouse's death; the joint life expectancy rules may no longer be used. Then, when you die, your secondary beneficiary will have to receive the entire account by the end of the year following the year of your death and pay tax on the entire amount. Similar rules would apply to your surviving spouse and your secondary beneficiary if you die before your spouse and your spouse receives distributions from your account as a *beneficiary*. The payout period can be extended where a surviving spouse elects to be treated as the *owner* of the IRA instead of receiving distributions as a beneficiary. The options for surviving spouses are detailed in *8.14*.

If your estate is the beneficiary, these recalculation rules may be particularly costly. Since your life expectancy is reduced to zero as of the year following the year of your death, and the estate has no life expectancy on which distributions may be based, the entire account must be distributed to the estate by the end of the year after the year of your death.

 Planning Reminder

Choose Life Expectancy Method

If you have not chosen a life expectancy method by your required beginning date, the terms of the plan may apply the recalculation method as the default method, which could be disadvantageous following your death or the death of your spouse if he or she is your designated beneficiary; *see* the discussion of life expectancy methods under Step 3, beginning on page 186.

On the other hand, when you elect the term-certain method to figure your minimum required distributions, the balance of the initial joint life expectancy period remains available following the death of you or your beneficiary. This allows the survivor to spread out the distributions, and the tax on the distributions, over the rest of the term-certain period.

Step 4: Divide the account balance from Step 1 by the Step 2 life expectancy. This is the minimum amount you must receive. If you have more than one IRA, divide Step 1 by Step 2 for each account and *see* Step 5.

Step 5: If you have more than one IRA, total the Step 4 amounts for all the accounts. This is the minimum you must receive for the year; you are of course free to withdraw more than that. Although you must calculate the minimum required distribution separately for each account, you do not have to make withdrawals from each of them. The total minimum required distribution from all accounts may be taken from any one account, or more than one account if you prefer. For example, if you have five bank IRAs you may take the entire required distribution from the bank where you have the largest balance, or from any other combination of banks. *See* Example 2 below. The entire distribution is taxable unless part is allocable to nondeductible IRA contributions, as explained in *8.9*.

Note: For further information on calculating minimum required distributions, *see* IRS proposed regulations Sections 1.408-8 and 1.401(a)(9)-1. Also *see* IRS Publication 590.

EXAMPLES

1. Joe Blake reached age 70 ½ in March 1999. A minimum distribution for 1999 must be received from his traditional IRA by April 1, 2000. As of December 31, 1998, Joe's IRA balance was $26,300. The 1998 year-end balance is used in the computation even if the distribution for 1999 is made in the first quarter of 2000 (by the April 1 deadline). Joe's beneficiary is his wife, who is age 63 on her birthday in 1999. On his 1999 birthday, Joe is age 71.
    - Step 1. Account balance of $26,300.
    - Step 2. Joint life and last survivor expectancy from the table on page 201 is 24 years, using ages 71 and 63.
    - Step 3. Divide Step 1 by Step 2.
      $26,300 ÷ 24 = $1,096. Joe must receive the $1,096 by April 1, 2000.

   The second minimum distribution, due by December 31, 2000, is based upon the 1999 year-end account balance, but if the 1999 distribution was not made until early 2000 (by April 1), the account balance is reduced by that distribution. Thus, assume that Joe took the $1,096 distribution for 1999 in March 2000 and that the 1999 year-end balance is $27,500. For purposes of figuring the required distribution for 2000, an account balance of $26,404 ($27,500 – $1,096) is used.

   Assuming Joe and his wife recalculate their life expectancies, their joint expectancy from the table on page 201 would be 23.1 (using ages 72 and 64). Thus, the minimum required distribution for 2000, due by December 31, 2000, would be $1,143 ($26,404 ÷ 23.1).

   However, if Joe had elected not to recalculate life expectancy but to use the term-certain method, the first-year joint life expectancy of 24 years would be reduced to 23 years. The minimum 2000 distribution would be $1,148 ($26,404 ÷ 23).

2. Cynthia Lowell has two IRAs. She reached age 70 ½ on January 15, 1999, and thus must receive her first distribution by April 1, 2000. The beneficiary of IRA-1 is her brother, who is age 61 on his birthday in 1999; the account balance of IRA-1 as of December 31, 1998, was $100,000. The beneficiary of IRA-2 is her husband, who was age 74 on his birthday in 1999; the account balance at the end of 1998 was $10,000.
    - IRA-1: The first minimum required distribution is $3,952.57. This is the account balance of $100,000 divided by 25.3, the joint life and last survivor expectancy using ages 71 and 61 from the table.
    - IRA-2: The first minimum required distribution is $537.63, the account balance of $10,000 divided by 18.6, the joint life and last survivor expectancy using ages 71 and 74.

   The total required distribution of $4,490.20 from both IRAs must be received by April 1, 2000. Cynthia may withdraw the money from either one or both of the IRAs.

   If the withdrawal is delayed until the first quarter of 2000, the 1999 year-end balance is reduced by the withdrawal when she figures her minimum required distribution for 2000. The distribution for 2000 must be received by December 31, 2000.

3. Assume that in Example 1, Joe Blake's beneficiary was not his wife but his brother

Frank, who was 63 on his birthday in 1999. Also assume that Joe did not elect to use the term-certain method. For 1999, the first distribution year, the required distribution is $1,096 (the same as under Step 3 of Example 1). Assume Joe received the $1,096 distribution in March 2000. To figure the required minimum distribution for 2000, the second distribution year, Joe's recalculated age is 72 (his age on his birthday in 2000). To determine Frank's revised age, and then their joint life and last survivor life expectancy, the following hybrid method computation is made:

Step 1.	Frank's life expectancy in first distribution year of 1999, using age 63. Life expectancy is shown in Table V at *7.23.*	21.6
Step 2.	Number of years that have passed since the first distribution year of 1999 (nearest whole number).	1.0
Step 3.	Remaining life expectancy (Step 1 *minus* Step 2)	20.6
Step 4.	To determine Frank's revised age for 2000, find the age corresponding to the life expectancy in Table V *(7.23),* that is closest to, but less than, the Step 3 life expectancy of 20.6. In Table V, 20.6 falls between an expectancy of 20.8 years for age 64 and 20.0 years for age 65; thus, the higher age of 65 is used.	65
Step 5.	Joe's revised age for 2000.	72
Step 6.	Joint life and last survivor expectancy using ages 72 and 65 (Steps 4 and 5) from the table on page 201.	22.5

To figure his required minimum distribution for 2000, Joe divides the revised life expectancy of 22.5 years (Step 6) by the account balance at the end of 1999. Since under the facts of Example 1 Joe took his $1,096 minimum required distribution for 1999 in March 2000, an account balance of $26,404 is used ($27,500 year-end 1999 balance minus $1,096 distribution taken in March 2000). Thus, Joe's minimum required distribution for 2000 is $1,174 ($26,404 ÷ 22.5 revised joint life expectancy). The $1,174 minimum required distribution for 2000 must be received by December 31, 2000.

For 2001, Joe's age in Step 5 will be 73, and the computation for Frank will be similar, except that Step 3 remaining life expectancy will be 19.6.

8.14 Inherited IRAs

Although inheritances are generally tax free *(11.4),* distributions that you receive as a beneficiary of a traditional IRA are taxable. However, if nondeductible contributions had been made to the account, distributions allocable to those contributions on Form 8606 are tax free under the rules at *8.6.*

Different rules apply to inherited Roth IRAs. In general, a beneficiary is taxed only if the owner dies within the first five years after establishing the Roth IRA account and distributions of account earnings are received by the beneficiary within the five-year period; *see 8.23.*

Distribution options if you inherit traditional IRA. When an IRA owner dies, the rules for handling the account depend on who the beneficiary is. A surviving spouse beneficiary has certain advantages not available to other beneficiaries because only a surviving spouse may treat the inherited IRA as his or her own IRA.

The options for spousal and nonspousal beneficiaries are discussed below.

Surviving Spouse Is Beneficiary of Traditional IRA

Surviving spouse may treat inherited IRA as his or her own. If you are the beneficiary of your deceased spouse's traditional IRA, you may elect to treat it as your own IRA by rolling it over to an IRA in your name, by making IRA contributions to the account, or by making rollover contributions into the account from other IRAs or from a qualifying employer-plan distribution; *see 8.10.*

An advantage of treating the amount *as your own* is that if you are under age 70 ½, you may delay the start of your distributions until your required beginning date (April 1 of the year after the year in which you reach 70 ½), at which time your minimum required distributions may be based on the joint life and last survivor life expectancy of yourself and the beneficiary you have designated; *see 8.13.* Even if you are over age 70 ½ when your spouse dies, treating the IRA as your own and naming your own beneficiary generally allows you to take smaller distributions from the account than if you did not treat the IRA as your own but instead took distributions from the account as a beneficiary; *see* below. Distributions from the account are taxable (unless allocable to nondeductible contributions) and, if received before age 59 ½, may be subject to the 10% penalty for early withdrawals; *see 8.12.*

 Planning Reminder

Surviving Spouse Under Age 70 ½

If you inherit your spouse's traditional IRA and you are under age 70 ½, you may delay the start of minimum required distributions by treating the IRA as your own.

Surviving spouse may receive distributions as a beneficiary. If you inherit a traditional IRA from your spouse and do not want to treat the account as your own IRA, you may receive payments from the account as a beneficiary; the account stays in the name of your deceased spouse. As a beneficiary, distributions you receive are taxable (unless allocable to nondeductible contributions) but if you are under age 59 $\frac{1}{2}$, you are not subject to the 10% penalty for early withdrawals *(8.12)*. Avoiding the 10% penalty if you are under age 59 $\frac{1}{2}$ is the advantage of receiving distributions as a beneficiary; if you treated the IRA as your own *(see* above), the 10% penalty for pre–age 59 $\frac{1}{2}$ distributions would apply.

The payout period for withdrawing funds from the account as a beneficiary depends on when your spouse died:

- If your spouse died *after* starting to receive required minimum distributions under the rules at *8.13* for individuals age 70 $\frac{1}{2}$ and older, and you do not elect to treat the IRA as your own, you generally must receive distributions from the IRA at least as rapidly as your spouse was receiving them.

  This means that if your spouse had elected the *term-certain* method *(8.13)* for figuring distributions, you must receive minimum distributions over the balance of the term-certain period. That is, for each year, you divide the account balance at the end of the prior year *(see* Step 1 at *8.13)* by the joint life and last survivor expectancy for both of you in the year your spouse reached age 70 *minus* one year for each year that has passed. For example, if in the year your spouse reached age 70 $\frac{1}{2}$ your joint life and last survivor life expectancy (Step 2 at *8.13)* was 21.7 years and your spouse died after receiving three annual required minimum distributions under the term-certain method, you use the balance of the term-certain period, or 18.7 years, to figure your first required minimum distribution.

  However, if your spouse was *recalculating* life expectancy annually *(8.13)*, his or her life expectancy is treated as zero starting in the year following the year of death. For the years after the year of your spouse's death, your minimum distributions are based on your single life expectancy, which is either your recalculated expectancy, or, if you were not recalculating, your life expectancy in the first distribution year (shown in Table V at *7.23*), reduced by one for each elapsed year.

- If your spouse died *before* starting to receive required minimum distributions under the rules at *8.13* for individuals age 70 $\frac{1}{2}$ and older, the IRA plan will probably allow you either to (1) withdraw funds from the IRA over your life expectancy or (2) withdraw the entire account balance by the end of the fifth year following the year of your spouse's death. Some plans allow the account owner to elect the method to be used by the beneficiary, and some plans do not allow a choice but specify the method.

  If the life expectancy method is elected or specified for you, you do not have to begin the distributions until the later of (1) December 31 of the year in which your spouse would have reached age 70 $\frac{1}{2}$ and (2) December 31 of the year following the year of your spouse's death.

IRA Beneficiaries Other Than Surviving Spouses

If you inherit a traditional IRA from someone who was not your spouse, you may not treat it as your own IRA account. Thus, you may not make contributions to the account or roll it over to an IRA in your name. You must begin receiving withdrawals from the plan. Distributions you receive as a beneficiary are taxable (unless allocable to nondeductible contributions), but if you are under age 59 $\frac{1}{2}$ you are *not* subject to the 10% early withdrawal penalty *(8.12)*. The payout period for withdrawing funds from the account as a beneficiary depends on when the account owner died:

- If the owner died *after* starting to receive required minimum distributions under the rules at *8.13* for individuals age 70 $\frac{1}{2}$ and older, you generally must receive distributions at least as rapidly as the owner was receiving them. If the owner was using the *term-certain method (8.13)*, you must receive minimum distributions over the balance of the term-certain period.

  A similar rule applies if the owner had filed a term-certain election with the IRA plan but was nevertheless required to use the MDIB method because you were more than 10 years younger than the owner *(see* Step 2 at *8.13)*. The life expectancy you use to figure your minimum required distributions is the balance of the initial term-certain period. This is your joint life and last survivor expectancy for the year in which the owner reached age 70 $\frac{1}{2}$ minus one year for each year that has passed.

  However, if the owner used the hybrid method *(see* Step 3 at *8.13)*, your minimum distributions starting in the year after the year of death are based on your single life expectancy as of the first distribution year (Table V at *7.23*), reduced by one for each elapsed year.

- If the owner died *before* starting to receive required minimum distributions under the rules at *8.13* for individuals age 70 $\frac{1}{2}$ and older, the inherited plan may give you the option of receiving funds from the account over your life expectancy or over the five-year period following the owner's death. Some plans specify which method must be used or permit the owner to designate the method.

Planning Reminder

Beneficiary Options

If you inherit an IRA, check the terms of the plan. The plan may give you flexibility in choosing the period over which you may receive distributions from the IRA.

If the IRA plan gives you the choice of taking withdrawals from the account over your life expectancy, you may choose this option by beginning distributions no later than December 31 of the year following the year of the IRA owner's death. If the plan does not allow the life expectancy option, or if you choose the five-year method, you must withdraw the entire account by December 31 of the fifth year following the year of the owner's death.

Simplified Employee Pension Plans (SEPs)

8.15 SEP Basics

A simplified employee pension plan (SEP) set up by an employer allows the employer to contribute to an employee's IRA account more money than is allowed under regular IRA rules. For 1999, your employer may contribute and deduct up to 15% of your compensation or $24,000, whichever is less ($24,000 is 15% of $160,000, the maximum amount of compensation that may be taken into account for 1999). Your employer's SEP contributions are excluded from your pay and are not included on Form W-2 unless they exceed the limit. If contributions exceed the limit, the excess is included in your gross income and a 6% penalty tax may be imposed unless the excess (plus allocable income) is withdrawn by the due date of the return, plus extensions; *see 8.7*. If you are under age 59 ½, the 10% early distribution penalty may apply to the withdrawal of income earned on the excess contributions; *see 8.12*.

Self-employed plans. Self-employed individuals may set up a SEP as an alternative to a Keogh plan; *see* Chapter 41.

Eligibility. A SEP must cover all employees who are at least age 21, earn over $400 (this amount may be adjusted after 1999 for inflation), and who have worked for the employer at any time during at least three of the past five years. Union employees covered by union agreements may generally be excluded.

SEP salary-reduction arrangements. If a qualifying small employer set up a salary reduction SEP before 1997, employees may contribute a portion of their pay to the plan instead of receiving it in cash; *see 8.16*.

SEP distributions. Distributions from a SEP are subject to the regular distribution rules for traditional IRAs discussed at *8.8*.

8.16 Salary-Reduction SEP Set up Before 1997

Qualifying small employers may offer employees the option of deferring a portion of their salary to an IRA. There are two types of salary reduction IRAs, with different eligibility and contribution rules: (1) salary reduction SEPs established before 1997 and (2) "SIMPLE" IRA accounts established after 1996.

After 1996, an employer may establish a SIMPLE plan but not a salary reduction SEP. Rules for SIMPLE IRAs established after 1996 are at *8.17*. A salary reduction SEP that was established before 1997 may continue to receive contributions under the prior law rules discussed below, and employees hired after 1996 may participate in the plan, subject to those rules.

Salary-reduction SEPs established before 1997. Salary reductions are allowed for a year only if the employer had no more than 25 employees eligible to participate in the SEP at any time during the prior taxable year. Furthermore, at least 50% of the eligible employees must elect the salary-reduction option, and the deferral percentage for highly compensated employees may not exceed 125% of the average contribution of regular employees. State or local government agencies and tax-exempt organizations may not set up salary reduction SEPs.

If salary reductions are allowed, the maximum salary reduction contribution for 1999 is $10,000; the limit is subject to future inflation adjustments. Deferrals over $10,000 are taxable, and if not timely distributed to the employee, can be taxed again when distributed from the plan.

If an employee contributes to both a SEP and a 401(k) plan, the annual limit ($10,000 for 1999) applies to the total salary reductions from both plans. If an employee makes salary reduction contributions to a SEP and also to a tax-sheltered annuity plan *(7.20)*, the annual limit generally applies to the total salary reductions to both plans. In some cases, employees with at least 15 years of service may be able to defer an additional $3,000 to the tax-sheltered annuity plan as discussed at *7.20*.

 Caution

Employees over Age 70 ½

An employee over age 70 ½ may still participate in an employer SEP plan. Minimum distributions from the plan must begin as discussed in *7.13*.

Salary-reduction deferrals are treated as employer contributions. For 1999, total employer contributions including salary reductions may not exceed the lesser of 15% of pay and $24,000. $24,000 is 15% of $160,000, the maximum amount of compensation that the plan may take into account for 1999; this amount may be increased for 2000 by an inflation adjustment.

SIMPLE IRAs

8.17 Who Is Eligible for a SIMPLE IRA?

A SIMPLE IRA is a salary-reduction retirement plan that qualifying small employers may offer their employees. Salary-reduction contributions of up to $6,000 per year may be made by eligible employees, and employers are required to make matching contributions or a flat contribution, as discussed in 8.18. The SIMPLE IRA replaces the salary-reduction SEP, which after 1996 may be used only by an employer that had established the plan before 1997; see 8.16.

Qualifying employers. A SIMPLE IRA may be maintained only by an employer that (1) in the previous calendar year had no more than 100 employees who earned compensation of $5,000 or more and (2) does not maintain any other retirement plan (unless the other plan is for collective bargaining employees). A self-employed individual who meets these tests may set up a SIMPLE IRA, as discussed in Chapter 41.

In determining whether the 100-employee test is met for the prior year, all employees under the common control of the employer must be counted. For example, Joe Smith owned two businesses in 1999—a computer rental company with 80 employees and a computer repair company with 60 employees. If they all earned at least $5,000, they all count towards the 100 limit, so if Joe decides in 2000 to set up a retirement plan for his businesses, a different type of plan must be used. He may not establish a SIMPLE IRA for either business under the 100-employee limit.

If a SIMPLE IRA is established but the employer in a later year grows beyond the 100-employee limit, the employer generally has a two-year "grace period" during which contributions may continue to be made.

Eligible employees. In general, an employee must be allowed to contribute to a SIMPLE IRA for a year in which he or she is reasonably expected to earn $5,000 or more, provided at least $5,000 of compensation was received in *any two* prior years, whether or not consecutive. If the employer owns more than one business (under common control rules) and sets up a SIMPLE IRA for one of them, employees of the other business must also be allowed to participate if they meet the $5,000 compensation tests. Employees who are covered by a collective bargaining agreement may be excluded if retirement benefits were the subject of good-faith negotiations.

The employer may lower or eliminate the $5,000 compensation requirement in order to broaden participation in the plan. No other conditions on eligibility, such as age or hours of work, are permitted.

Deadline for setting up a SIMPLE IRA. An employer generally may establish a SIMPLE IRA effective on any date between January 1 and October 1 of a year. If the employer (or a predecessor employer) previously maintained a SIMPLE IRA, a new SIMPLE IRA may be effective only on January 1 of a year. A new employer that comes into existence after October 1 of a year may establish a SIMPLE IRA for that year if the plan is established as soon as administratively feasible after the start of the business.

The employer may use a model SIMPLE IRA approved by the IRS to set up a SIMPLE IRA. Form 5304-SIMPLE allows employees to select a financial insitution to which the contributions will be made. With Form 5305-SIMPLE, the employer selects the financial institution to which contributions are initially deposited, but employees have the right to subsequently transfer their account balances without cost or penalty to another SIMPLE-IRA at a financial institution of their own choosing. Use of the IRS model forms is optional; other documents satisfying the statutory requirements for a SIMPLE IRA may be used.

SIMPLE IRA contributions and distributions. Contribution and distribution rules for SIMPLE IRAs are discussed in 8.18.

8.18 SIMPLE IRA Contributions and Distributions

The only contributions that may be made to a SIMPLE IRA are elective salary-reduction contributions by employees and matching or non-elective contributions by employers. All contributions are fully vested and nonforfeitable when made.

Planning Reminder

401(k) SIMPLE Plans

An employer with a 401(k) plan that reports on the calendar year may avoid the regular 401(k) nondiscrimination tests by following the contribution rules for SIMPLE IRAs; see 7.17.

Eligible employees *(see 8.17)* may elect each year to make salary-reduction contributions to the plan of up to $6,000 per year. The $6,000 limit may be increased by an inflation adjustment. Salary-reduction contributions are excluded from the employee's taxable pay on Form W-2 and not subject to federal tax withholding. They are subject to FICA withholding for Social Security and Medicare tax.

Eligible employees must be given notice by the employer of their right to elect salary reduction contributions and at least 60 days to make the election. After the first year of eligibility, the election to defer for the upcoming year is made during the last 60 days (at minimum) of the prior calendar year. If the employer uses model IRS Form 5304-SIMPLE or 5305-SIMPLE, a notification document is included.

If an employee contributes to a SIMPLE-IRA and also to a 401(k) plan of another employer for the same year, the annual limit on tax-free salary reduction deferrals ($10,000 for 1999) applies. Deferrals over the annual limit are taxable and must be removed to avoid being taxed again when distributed from the plan; *see 7.18.*

Employer contributions. Each year, the employer must make either a matching contribution or a fixed "non-elective" contribution. If the employer chooses matching contributions, the employee's elective salary-reduction contribution (no more than $6,000 for 1999) generally must be matched, up to a limit of 3% of the employee's compensation. For up to two years in any five-year period, the 3% matching limit may be reduced to as low as 1% for each eligible employee.

Instead of making either the 3% or reduced limit matching contribution, the employer may make a "non-elective" contribution equal to 2% of each eligible employee's compensation. If this option is chosen, the 2% contribution must be made for eligible employees whether or not they elect to make salary reduction contributions for the year. The 2% contribution is subject to an annual compensation limit, which for 1999 was $160,000. Thus, for 1999, the maximum 2% non-elective contribution was $3,200 (2% of $160,000) even if an employee earned more than $160,000. The 3% matching contribution is not subject to the annual compensation limit, but only to the $6,000 salary-reduction limit.

The employer must notify eligible employees of the type of contribution it will be making for the upcoming year prior to the employees' 60-day election period for making elective salary-reduction contributions.

The employer must make the matching or non-elective contributions by the due date for filing the employer's tax return (plus extensions) for the year.

EXAMPLE

Martin's 2000 salary is $60,000. He elects to make a $6,000 salary-reduction contribution to his employer's SIMPLE IRA plan. If his employer elects the 3% matching rule, the matching contribution is limited to $1,800, 3% of Martin's compensation.

If Martin's salary was $260,000, he could make the $6,000 salary-reduction contribution and the employer's matching contribution would also be $6,000; the 3% match (3% of $260,000 is $7,800) cannot exceed the $6,000 contribution made by Martin.

Distributions from a SIMPLE IRA. A distribution from a SIMPLE IRA is generally subject to the regular IRA distribution rules; *see 8.8.* However, for the first two years, a higher penalty for distributions before age 59 $\frac{1}{2}$ *(see 8.12)* applies. The pre-59 $\frac{1}{2}$ penalty is increased to 25% from 10%, assuming no penalty exception applies, if the distribution is received during the two-year period starting with the employee's initial participation in the plan. After the first two years, the regular 10% penalty applies.

In the initial two-year period, a tax-free rollover or direct trustee-to-trustee transfer *(see 8.10)* of a SIMPLE IRA may be made to another SIMPLE IRA. After the first two years, a tax-free rollover or direct transfer may be made to a regular IRA as well as to a SIMPLE IRA.

The mandatory distribution rules that apply to regular IRAs after age 70 $\frac{1}{2}$ also apply to SIMPLE IRAs *(see 8.13).*

Planning Reminder

Employer's Intended Contributions

The IRS model notification included with Form 5304-SIMPLE or 5305-SIMPLE requires the employer to tell employees how much the employer will be contributing for the upcoming year; required employer contributions are discussed in this section.

Caution

Increased Pre-59 $\frac{1}{2}$ Penalty

In the first two years of SIMPLE IRA participation, the penalty for distributions before age 59 $\frac{1}{2}$ is increased from 10% to 25%.

Roth IRAs

8.19   Roth IRA Advantages

The Roth IRA became available in 1998. As with traditional IRAs, earnings accumulate within a Roth IRA tax free until distributions are made. The key benefit of the Roth IRA is that tax-free distributions of earnings may be received after a five-year holding period by an individual who is age 59 $\frac{1}{2}$ or older, is disabled, or who pays qualifying first-time home-buyer expenses.

Contributions after age 70 $\frac{1}{2}$ may be made to a Roth IRA, but not to a traditional IRA, and the minimum required distribution rules that apply to traditional IRAs after age 70 $\frac{1}{2}$ (8.13) do not apply to Roth IRAs. Thus, a Roth IRA can remain intact after age 70 $\frac{1}{2}$ and continue to grow tax free. The balance of the account not withdrawn during the owner's lifetime may be paid out to the beneficiaries tax free over their life expectancies, thereby providing a substantial tax-deferred buildup within the plan over an extended period.

The opportunity to obtain such benefits makes the Roth IRA an attractive retirement planning and estate planning option. However, certain high-income taxpayers are not eligible to make Roth IRA contributions.

There are two ways in which you may establish a Roth IRA: (1) by making annual contributions or (2) by converting a traditional IRA to a Roth IRA. Each alternative is subject to an income limitation. Individuals with modified adjusted gross income up to $100,000 may convert a traditional IRA to a Roth IRA by paying a current tax, as discussed in 8.21. Nondeductible annual contributions of up to $2,000 may be made to a Roth IRA subject to the income limitation discussed at 8.20. Individuals who qualify for deductible IRA contributions as well as the Roth IRA should consider whether the tax value of deductible contributions outweighs the advantage of future tax-free distributions from the Roth IRA; distributions from deductible IRAs are taxable.

Roth IRA contributions are discussed at 8.20 and distribution rules at 8.22.

8.20 Annual Contributions to a Roth IRA

Nondeductible contributions up to $2,000 may be made annually to a Roth IRA if you have compensation of at least that much, provided that your modified adjusted gross income (MAGI) is less than $95,000 if you are unmarried, or less than $150,000 if married filing jointly. The contribution limit is phased out for unmarried taxpayers with MAGI between $95,000 and $110,000, and for joint filers with MAGI between $150,000 and $160,000. For a married person filing separately who lived with his or her spouse at any time during the year, the contribution limit is phased out for MAGI between $0 and $10,000. A married person filing separately who lived apart from his or her spouse for the entire year is treated as unmarried.

The Roth IRA does not replace the regular nondeductible contribution rules (8.6). For an individual who is unable to contribute to a Roth IRA because of the income limits, and is unable to make deductible IRA contributions because of the phase-out rules for active plan participants, nondeductible contributions may still be made to a regular IRA under the rules at 8.6.

Spousal contribution on joint return for nonworking or low-earning spouse. If you are married filing jointly, you generally may contribute up to $2,000 for each spouse to a Roth IRA so long as the total compensation of both spouses is at least $4,000. This is the same spousal contribution rule as for traditional IRAs (8.3); the lower-earning spouse is allowed to "borrow" compensation of the higher-earning spouse for contribution purposes. However, the contribution limit of $2,000 per spouse (or total compensation if under $4,000) may be reduced because of the MAGI phase-out rules discussed below.

MAGI phase-out of Roth IRA contribution limit. In general, the maximum Roth IRA contribution is the same as for traditional IRAs: $2,000 or your compensation for the year, if that is less. However, if your modified adjusted gross income (MAGI) is within the phase-out range, the $2,000 limit (or compensation, if less) is ratably reduced.

The contribution limit for Roth IRAs is phased out between MAGI of:

- $150,000 and $160,000, if you are married filing jointly;
- $95,000 and $110,000, if you are single, head of household, qualified widow(er), or married filing separately and you lived apart for the entire year;
- $0 and $10,000, if you are married filing separately and you lived with your spouse at any time during the year.

For purposes of the phase-out rule, MAGI is figured in the same way as under the traditional IRA deduction phase-out rules (8.4), except that a taxable conversion (8.21) from a traditional IRA to a Roth IRA is disregarded and any deductible traditional IRA contribution is also disregarded. The MAGI phase-out rule applies to Roth IRA contributions regardless of whether you are covered by an employer retirement plan, unlike the deductible traditional IRA phase-out rules (8.4), which apply only to active plan participants.

The MAGI formula reduces the $2,000 limit (or compensation, if less) by an amount that bears the same ratio to $2,000 (or lesser compensation) as your "excess MAGI" (MAGI over phase-out threshold) bears to the phase-out range (which is either $10,000 or $15,000, depending on your filing status as shown above). *See* the Example below for the way the phase-out limit is computed. If the phase-out formula results in a reduced contribution limit that is not a multiple of $10, round it up to the next highest $10. If the reduced limit is between $0 and $200, you are allowed a $200 contribution limit.

Contributing to Roth IRA and traditional IRA for the same year. If you contribute to both a traditional IRA and Roth IRA for the same year, total contributions for the year to all the accounts are limited to $2,000, or your compensation if that is less. The $2,000 (or compensation, if less) limit is applied first to the traditional IRA contributions and then to the Roth IRA contributions. Thus, the maximum contribution limit for the Roth IRA is $2,000 (or compensation, if that is less) minus deductible *(8.4)* or nondeductible *(8.6)* contributions to traditional IRAs.

However, if you are subject to the MAGI phaseout for Roth IRA contributions, as discussed above, the maximum Roth IRA contribution limit is the lesser of: (1) $2,000 (or, if less, compensation) minus contributions for the year to traditional IRAs and (2) the contribution limit figured under the MAGI phase-out rule.

Excess contributions. If Roth IRA contributions exceed the allowable limit, the excess contribution is subject to a 6% penalty tax unless you withdraw the excess, plus any earnings on the excess contribution, by the filing due date including extensions. The earnings must be reported as income for the year the contribution was made.

Contribution deadline. Contributions to a Roth IRA for a year may be made by the filing due date, without extensions. For 1999 contributions, the deadline is April 17, 2000 (April 15 is a Saturday).

EXAMPLE

Mark is single and for 1999 has salary of $90,000 and modified adjusted gross income (MAGI) of $98,000, $3,000 more than the $95,000 phase-out threshold for Roth IRA contributions. Under the MAGI phase-out rule, the $2,000 contribution ceiling is reduced by $400 ($2,000 × $3,000 ($98,000 MAGI – $95,000 phase-out threshold) / $15,000 phase-out range). Mark's maximum Roth IRA contribution for 1999 is $1,600 under the phase-out rule.

If traditional IRA contributions are also made for 1999, the Roth IRA contribution may not exceed the excess of $2,000 over the traditional IRA contributions. Assume that for 1999 Mark was not an active participant in an employer plan and makes a deductible IRA contribution *(see 8.4)* of $1,000. The Roth IRA contribution may not exceed $1,000 ($2,000 combined limit – $1,000 deductible IRA contribution) although the MAGI phase-out formula would allow a $1,600 Roth IRA contribution.

If Mark was an active plan participant and therefore barred from making a deductible IRA contribution (under the phase-out rules at *8.4*), he could make the $1,600 Roth IRA contribution and also a $400 nondeductible contribution to a traditional IRA *(8.6)*.

8.21 Converting a Traditional IRA to a Roth IRA

If your modified adjusted gross income (MAGI) is $100,000 or less, and you are not married filing separately, you may make a taxable conversion of a traditional IRA to a Roth IRA. A conversion may be made by directing the trustee of your traditional IRA to make a trustee-to-trustee transfer of your IRA to a new Roth IRA trustee, or by keeping the account with the same trustee but instructing the trustee to change the registration of the account from a traditional IRA to a Roth IRA. You may also make a conversion by receiving a distribution from your traditional IRA and rolling it over to a Roth IRA; the rollover must be completed within 60 days from the time you receive the distribution.

You may also convert a SEP *(8.15)* to a Roth IRA. A SIMPLE IRA *(8.18)* may be converted to a Roth IRA if more than two years have passed since you began participation in the SIMPLE IRA.

$100,000 MAGI limit. The transfer to a Roth IRA is allowed only if your modified adjusted gross income (MAGI) for the year of the rollover or conversion is $100,000 or less. A married person filing separately who lives with his or her spouse at any time during the year may *not* convert a non-Roth IRA to a Roth IRA, regardless of income.

The amount of the rollover or conversion is not taken into account in determining if the $100,000 MAGI limit is exceeded. However, the transferred amount is included in income for regular tax purposes; *see* below.

If a conversion to a Roth IRA is made towards the end of the year by taking a withdrawal from a traditional IRA and then rolling it over to the Roth IRA within 60 days, the income for the year of the withdrawal, rather than the income for the year the rollover is completed, is used when determining if the $100,000 MAGI conversion ceiling is exceeded. The conversion contribution is considered made for the year in which the withdrawal from the traditional IRA is made.

For a taxpayer who is eligible to make deductible contributions to a traditional IRA, MAGI is not reduced by the deductible contribution when applying the $100,000 MAGI limit.

Married IRA owners. If you are married, a conversion to a Roth IRA is generally allowed only if you file a joint return. The $100,000 MAGI ceiling applies to the combined MAGI of both spouses on the joint return. If you file a separate return and lived with your spouse at any time during the year, a conversion to a Roth IRA is not allowed. If you lived apart from your spouse for the entire year, you may make a conversion to a Roth IRA; the $100,000 MAGI ceiling applies to the MAGI reported on your separate return.

Minimum required IRA distributions. If you are considering a rollover or conversion of a traditional IRA to a Roth IRA, and are age 70 $\frac{1}{2}$ or older, minimum required distributions from the traditional IRA before 2005 are counted by the IRS towards the $100,000 income ceiling for rollovers and conversions. For example, if your modified adjusted gross income (MAGI) for 2000 without considering your minimum required distribution is $92,000, and the required distribution for 2000 from your traditional IRA is $10,000, your MAGI for Roth IRA purposes is $102,000 according to the IRS and you are not eligible to make a conversion or rollover to a Roth IRA. Starting in the year 2005, minimum required distributions will be disregarded for purposes of the $100,000 MAGI test.

Required minimum distributions may not be converted. If you are age 70 $\frac{1}{2}$ or older, you may not convert to a Roth IRA amounts that represent required minimum distributions *(8.13)* from a traditional IRA. The required minimum distribution is not eligible for conversion and if you make a conversion to a Roth IRA before receiving your required minimum distribution for the year of conversion, an amount equal to the required minimum distribution is treated as a taxable distribution from the traditional IRA, followed by a regular annual contribution to a Roth IRA subject to the $2,000 contribution limit *(8.20)*. Amounts over the $2,000 limit would be an excess contribution subject to a 6% penalty tax unless the excess is withdrawn.

How a conversion is taxed. You must report the conversion of a traditional IRA to a Roth IRA on Form 8606 as a taxable distribution, except to the extent that the account was allocable to nondeductible contributions (under the rules at *8.6*). The conversion is taxable in the year it is made. If you make a transfer by withdrawing funds from a traditional IRA towards the end of 1999 and in 2000 you complete a rollover to a Roth IRA within 60 days of the withdrawal, this is treated as a 1999 conversion that is taxable on your 1999 return, except for any part allocable to nondeductible traditional IRA contributions.

The increase in your regular adjusted gross income from the conversion could reduce the itemized deductions *(13.7)*, personal exemptions *(21.15)*, or rental losses *(10.2)* you may claim. The increase could also trigger tax on Social Security benefits *(34.3)* or subject more of the benefits to tax.

The special four-year spread (*see* below) that was allowed for 1998 conversions does not apply to conversions in 1999 or later years.

A rollover or conversion from a traditional IRA to a Roth IRA is exempt from the 10% penalty on taxable distributions received before age 59 $\frac{1}{2}$.

Four-year spread for 1998 conversions. If a conversion was made during 1998, there is this tax break: the taxable rollover or conversion amount is spread ratably over four years (1998, 1999, 2000, and 2001) unless you elected on Form 8606 to report the entire amount on your 1998 return by the due date (with extensions) for your 1998 return.

Under the ratable inclusion rule, one-fourth of the taxable rollover or conversion was reported as income on your 1998 return and one-fourth will be reported on your returns for 1999–2001.

If you are using the four-year spread for a 1998 conversion and during the years 1998 through 2000 you withdraw from the Roth IRA any amount allocable to the taxable part of the conversion, income that would otherwise be deferred to a later year within the four-year period may be accelerated into the year of the withdrawal; *see 8.22.*

If you are using the four-year reporting rule for a 1998 conversion to a Roth IRA and die during the four-year period, any amount remaining to be included in income must generally be reported on your final federal income tax return. However, a surviving spouse who is the sole beneficiary may elect to continue the deferral over the remainder of the four-year period. The election is made by the surviving spouse on Form 8606 for the year of the death.

Caution

Consider the Tax Cost of a Conversion

If your modified adjusted gross income is $100,000 or less, you may roll over or convert an existing IRA to a Roth IRA. If you do so, the rollover or conversion is taxable, unless the transferred amount is allocable to nondeductible contributions.

If you plan to convert a traditional IRA to a Roth IRA, figure the tax due on the conversion and then weigh (1) whether you have sufficient funds outside the plan to pay the tax and (2), where there is a substantial tax due on the conversion, whether you want to give up the future income that would be earned on the funds used to pay the tax.

Undoing a Roth IRA conversion by recharacterizing the contribution. If you convert a traditional IRA to a Roth IRA and it turns out that your modified adjusted gross income exceeds the $100,000 ceiling, you avoid tax penalties by recharacterizing the contribution, in effect "undoing" the invalid conversion. This is done by making a direct trustee-to-trustee transfer of the Roth IRA contribution, plus the allocable earnings, to a traditional IRA, or by transferring the Roth IRA to a traditional IRA within the same financial institution (same trustee). The effect of the recharacterization is to disregard the conversion to the Roth IRA and to treat the original transfer from the traditional IRA as having been originally contributed to the transferee IRA.

There are also other types of recharacterizations. A recharacterization to undo a conversion to a Roth IRA may be made by a married person who is filing separately; separate filers are ineligible for a conversion to a Roth IRA unless they live apart for the entire year. You may want to recharacterize your Roth IRA contribution as part of a plan to reconvert back to a Roth IRA when the taxable conversion value is lower; *see* the discussion of reconversions below. You also may recharacterize a regular Roth IRA contribution as a traditional IRA contribution, or a traditional IRA contribution as a regular Roth IRA contribution.

To make an election to recharacterize, notify the trustee of the account being recharacterized and the transferee trustee (if different) of your intent to recharacterize, specifically identify the amounts subject to the election, and direct the transferor trustee to make the transfer.

IRS regulations require that a recharacterization election and the actual transfer be made on or before the due date, including extensions, for filing the tax return for the year of the conversion. However, there were complaints that this rule gave an advantage to taxpayers who had obtained a four-month filing extension for their 1998 return by allowing them more time to recharacterize a 1998 conversion than taxpayers who had filed by April 15, 1999. In response, the IRS allowed recharacterizations to be made until October 15,1999, under a regulation that allows timely filers an automatic six-month extension—from April 15 to October 15—to make an election otherwise required to be made by the filing due date plus extensions. The IRS later extended the deadline from October 15 to December 31, 1999. Taxpayers who took advantage of the extension must file an amended return for 1998 to report the recharacterization on Form 8606. The amended return may be filed within the regular amendment period, generally three years; *see 49.1.*

The October 15 recharacterization deadline is likely to apply for 1999 contributions. Assuming it does, you would have until October 16, 2000 (October 15 is on Sunday), to recharacterize a 1999 conversion, provided that you file your 1999 return by April 17, 2000 (April 15 is on Saturday), or you file Form 4868 by April 17 for a four-month extension and then file by the extended due date. *See* the Supplement for any update.

Reconverting to a Roth IRA after a recharacterization. As discussed above, a traditional IRA that has been converted to a Roth IRA may be transferred back to a traditional IRA in a recharacterization. That amount may subsequently be reconverted back to a Roth IRA. This recharacterization/reconversion rule may allow an IRA owner to lower the tax due on a conversion to a Roth IRA. For example, if you convert a traditional IRA to a Roth IRA and the value of the account drops as a result of a stock market decline, you may be able to reduce the taxable conversion amount value by recharacterizing the account as a traditional IRA and then reconverting to a Roth IRA at a time when the value of the account is lower. The amount that you must include in income from the conversion is based on the value of the account as of the date of the reconversion.

However, the IRS has placed limitations on the number and timing of reconversions. The IRS allowed an IRA owner who made a conversion to a Roth IRA during 1998 to recharacterize his or her contribution back to a traditional IRA and reconvert that amount once after October 31, 1998, and before January 1, 1999; reconversions completed before November 1, 1998, were not counted. That amount may also be recharacterized and reconverted one time during 1999.

An IRA owner who in 1999 converts a traditional IRA to a Roth IRA that has not been previously converted may recharacterize that amount back to a traditional IRA and then reconvert it once (but only once) on or before December 31, 1999.

If more than the one allowable reconversion for 1998 or 1999 is made, the Roth IRA established in the "excess" reconversion will be treated as a valid Roth IRA but it will not change the taxable conversion amount. Unless the excess reconversion is transferred back to a traditional IRA in a recharacterization, the taxable conversion amount will be based on the last reconversion that was not an excess reconversion,

Planning Reminder

Recharacterizations of IRA Contributions

The recharacterization rule is not limited to reversing an invalid conversion to a Roth IRA. A regular Roth IRA contribution (up to the $2,000 limit) may be recharacterized as a contribution to a traditional IRA if, for example, doing so would allow you to claim an IRA deduction under the rules discussed at 8.4. Similarly, if you contribute to a traditional IRA and decide that you would like to switch to a Roth IRA, you may recharacterize the contribution by transferring the contribution plus allocable income to a Roth IRA. A recharacterization generally must be made by the filing due date, but an extension may be allowed as discussed in 8.21.

Caution

Limits on Reconversions to Roth IRA

After converting a traditional IRA to a Roth IRA, you may undo the conversion by recharacterizing the account as a traditional IRA. If you want to reconvert to a Roth IRA, you must stay within the IRS guidelines. Only one reconversion is allowed during 1999. Starting in 2000, a reconversion may not be made until the year following the year of the original conversion. *See 8.21* for further details.

Waiting period for reconversions after 1999. Effective January 1, 2000, the IRS has imposed a waiting period before a reconversion may be made. If a traditional IRA is converted to a Roth IRA and later in the same calendar year the conversion is recharacterized back to a traditional IRA, the IRA owner must wait at least until January 1 of the next year before a reconversion to a Roth IRA may be made. If a recharacterization is made within the last 30 days of the year of the conversion or the recharacterization occurs in the year following the year of the conversion, the owner may not reconvert that amount to a Roth IRA before the end of the 30-day period beginning with the date of the recharacterization. The effect of the waiting period is to make it impossible to take immediate advantage of a stock market decline that lowers the value of a Roth IRA. If you want to recharacterize back to a traditional IRA and then reconvert to a Roth IRA in order to lower the taxable conversion amount, you will have to wait a minimum of 30 days before reconverting. By that time, the value of the reconverted account may be as high, or higher, than it was at the time of the recharacterization.

If a reconversion is attempted before the end of the waiting period, the attempt will be treated as a "failed" conversion. A failed conversion is treated as a taxable distribution from the traditional IRA followed by a regular contribution to a Roth IRA. The pre–age 59 $\frac{1}{2}$ early distribution penalty could apply to the taxable distribution *(8.12)* and the deemed regular contribution to the Roth IRA would be subject to the 6% excess contribution penalty *(8.7)*. A failed conversion may be remedied by making a timely recharacterization to a traditional IRA.

EXAMPLE

Joe Smith converts a traditional IRA to a Roth IRA during 2000. In early 2001, he realizes that his modified adjusted gross income (MAGI) for 2000 exceeds the $100,000 ceiling, making him ineligible for a conversion. He recharacterizes the Roth IRA as a traditional IRA on January 18, 2001. Joe may not reconvert that amount to a Roth IRA until February 17, 2001. This is the first day after the end of the 30-day period that began on January 18, 2001, the date of the recharacterization.

If Joe attempts to reconvert before February 17, 2001, the transfer will be treated as a "failed" conversion. Unless the failed conversion amount is recharacterized back to a traditional IRA, it will be treated as a taxable distribution from the traditional IRA; the 10% penalty for pre–age 59 $\frac{1}{2}$ distributions could also apply. It will also be treated as a regular contribution to a Roth IRA and the amount over the $2,000 limit *(8.20)* would be subject to the 6% excess contribution penalty tax. To avoid these tax consequences, Joe may recharacterize the failed conversion and reconvert it to a Roth IRA at any time on or after February 17, 2001. Of course, a conversion for 2001 will be valid only if Joe's MAGI for that year does not exceed the $100,000 ceiling. If a reconversion is made after February 17, 2001, Joe must wait until 2002 before he may reconvert that amount again.

8.22 Distributions From a Roth IRA

A distribution from a Roth IRA is tax free if it is a *qualified* distribution, as discussed below. Even if a distribution is not a qualified distribution, it is tax free to the extent of your regular Roth IRA contributions *(8.20)* and conversion contributions *(8.21)*. The part of a non-qualified distribution allocable to earnings is taxable, but distributions are considered to be from contributions first and then from earnings; *see* the ordering rule below for the allocation between contributions and earnings.

You may make a tax-free direct transfer from one Roth IRA to another. A tax-free rollover of a Roth IRA distribution may be made to another Roth IRA if you complete the rollover within 60 days.

You do not have to receive minimum required distributions from a Roth IRA after you reach age 70 $\frac{1}{2}$ as you would from a traditional IRA *(see 8.13)*. No Roth IRA distributions at all are required during your lifetime. After your death, your beneficiaries will be subject to a minimum distribution requirement; *see 8.23.*

Qualified Roth IRA distributions are tax free. Two tests must be met for a Roth IRA distribution to be "qualified," and thus completely tax free: (1) the distribution must be made after the end of the five-year period beginning with the first day of the first taxable year for which any Roth IRA contribution was made *and* (2) one of the following conditions must be met:

- you are age 59 $\frac{1}{2}$ or older when the distribution is made,
- you are disabled,
- you use the distribution to pay up to $10,000 of qualifying first-time home-buyer expenses as discussed below, *or*
- you are a beneficiary receiving distributions following the death of the account owner.

Filing Instruction

Form 8606

IRS Form 8606 must be filed to report Roth IRA distributions. It is also used to report a conversion to a Roth IRA or a recharacterization of a Roth IRA contribution.

Five-year holding period. Even if you are age 59 ½ or older or meet one of the other tests for qualified distributions, you must also satisfy the five-year holding period test in order to make tax-free withdrawals of earnings from a Roth IRA. The five-year holding period begins with January 1 (assuming you are a calendar-year taxpayer) of the first year for which any Roth IRA contribution is made. You have only one five-year period regardless of the number of Roth IRAs you have. For example, if you made a regular Roth IRA contribution for 1998 at any time between January 1, 1998, and April 15, 1999, your five-year holding period begins January 1, 1998. If in a later year you convert *(8.21)* a traditional IRA to a Roth IRA, or make a regular Roth IRA contribution *(8.20)*, you do not begin a new five-year holding period for that Roth IRA. In this case, the five-year period for all your Roth IRAs begins January 1, 1998, and ends December 31, 2002.

If you receive a Roth IRA distribution after the end of your five-year holding period, and you also meet one of the other qualified distribution requirements such as being age 59 ½ or older, the distribution is completely tax free. If you receive a distribution before satisfying both the five-year holding period requirement and one of the other qualified distribution requirements, and the withdrawal exceeds your contributions, the excess is taxable and possibly subject to the 10% penalty for pre–age 59 ½ distributions *(see 8.12)*. Under the ordering rules discussed below, Roth IRA distributions are treated as being made first from contributions and then from earnings.

Ordering rules for distributions. Even if a distribution is not fully tax free as a qualified distribution, it is not taxable to the extent of your Roth IRA contributions. All of your Roth IRAs are treated as one account for purposes of determining if contributions or earnings have been withdrawn. If a distribution does not exceed total contributions to all of your Roth IRAs, it is not taxable.

Where you have made both regular annual contributions and conversion contributions to a Roth IRA, the regular contributions are considered to be withdrawn first. Then, conversion contributions are considered to be withdrawn in the order in which they were made. If part of a conversion contribution was not treated as a taxable distribution (because it was allocable to nondeductible contributions in the converted traditional IRA), the taxable part of the conversion is deemed withdrawn before the nontaxable part. Taking into account the taxable part of a conversion contribution before the nontaxable part (if any) of the conversion contribution is important for purposes of determining whether the acceleration rule for 1998 conversions applies *(see* below), or whether the 10% early distribution penalty applies to the withdrawal of a conversion contribution within five years of the conversion *(see* below).

Earnings on Roth IRA contributions are considered to be withdrawn last, after all contributions are taken into account. If the distribution is not a qualified distribution, the withdrawn earnings are subject to tax and if you are under age 59 ½, to the 10% early distribution penalty *(see 8.12* for penalty exceptions).

Acceleration of income from 1998 conversion. If you elected the four-year spread for a 1998 conversion and before 2001 receive a Roth IRA distribution that is allocable (under the above ordering rule) to the taxable portion of the conversion (without considering the four-year spread), you must report in the year of withdrawal income that would otherwise be deferred to the balance of the four-year period. Under the ordering rule *(see* above), the withdrawal is allocable to the taxable 1998 conversion after any regular Roth IRA contributions are taken into account. The allocable amount is reported in the year of withdrawal in addition to 25% of the 1998 conversion that is subject to tax under the four-year spread. *See* IRS Publication 590 for further details.

Withdrawals within five years of conversion to Roth IRAs. The regular 10% early withdrawal penalty applies if withdrawals from a conversion Roth IRA are made by taxpayers under age 59 ½ before January 1 of the fifth year after the year of the conversion. Unless a penalty exception is available, the 10% penalty applies to the extent that a withdrawal within the five-year period is allocable under the ordering rule *(see* above) to the taxable part of the conversion. Under the ordering rule for Roth IRA distributions, the entire withdrawal may be tax free, but the 10% penalty still applies if a taxable conversion amount is deemed to be withdrawn before the end of the five-year period. The five-year period for purposes of this penalty rule is figured separately for each conversion contribution.

Distribution used for up to $10,000 of first-time home-buyer expenses. Tax-free treatment will apply to a Roth IRA distribution received after the first five-year period and used for up to $10,000 of qualifying "first-time" home-buyer expenses. The $10,000 limit is a lifetime cap per IRA owner, not an annual limitation. Expenses qualify if they are used within 120 days of the distribution to pay the acquisition costs of a principal residence for you, your spouse, your child, or your grandchild, or an ancestor of you or your spouse. The residence does not have to be the homeowner's "first" home. A qualifying first-time home-buyer is considered to be someone who

Planning Reminder

Five-Year Holding Requirement

For a withdrawal of earnings from a Roth IRA to be tax free, the five-year holding period test must be met as well as one of the other conditions for a qualified distribution. Since 1998 was the first year for which Roth IRA contributions could be made, it will be impossible for anyone to receive a qualified distribution before January 1, 2003, at the earliest.

Caution

Early Withdrawal From Conversion IRA

The 10% penalty *(8.12)* for pre–age 59 ½ distributions may apply if within five years of making a conversion to a Roth IRA, a distribution from that Roth IRA is received. The penalty applies to the portion of the withdrawal allocable to the conversion amount that was taxable in the year of the conversion. This is so even if the withdrawal is tax free under the ordering rule for Roth IRA distributions.

did not have a present ownership interest in a principal residence in the two-year period before the acquisition of the new home. If the home-buyer is married, both spouses must satisfy the two-year test. Eligible acquisition costs include buying, constructing, or reconstructing the principal residence, including reasonable settlement, financing, and closing costs.

8.23 Distributions to Beneficiaries After the Death of a Roth IRA Owner

If you inherit a Roth IRA, you are generally subject to the same minimum distribution rules *(8.14)* that apply when a traditional IRA owner dies before his or her required beginning date.

When distributions must begin. If you are the surviving spouse of the Roth IRA owner and you are the owner's sole Roth IRA beneficiary, you may elect to treat the inherited account as your own Roth IRA. If you treat the account as your own, you do not have to take distributions from the account at any time, since a Roth IRA owner is not subject to minimum distribution requirements. If you take some distributions from the account, you are not locked into a specific distribution schedule unless you agree to that schedule.

If you are not a surviving spouse beneficiary, or you are a surviving spouse beneficiary who does not elect to treat the inherited Roth IRA as your own, you must receive distributions over your life expectancy or the entire account by December 31 of the fifth year following the year of the owner's death. The owner or the plan document may designate which payout period applies or you may be given the option of choosing between the five-year rule or the life expectancy rule.

Electing distributions over your life expectancy. If you are not a surviving spouse beneficiary and the plan gives you the option of choosing to receive distributions over your life expectancy, this method must be selected and the first minimum distribution must be made by December 31 of the year following the year of the owner's death. If you are a surviving spouse and are the owner's only Roth IRA beneficiary, you may delay the start of distributions over your life expectancy until the owner would have reached age 70 $\frac{1}{2}$, if that is later than December 31 of the year following the year of the owner's death.

Five-year holding period for tax-free treatment. The same five-year holding period for receiving fully tax-free distributions that applied to the account owner *(8.22)* also applies to you as the beneficiary, whether your distributions are made under the five-year pay-out period or over your life expectancy. The five-year holding period began on January 1 of the year for which the owner's first Roth IRA contribution was made. If you receive distributions before the end of the five-year holding period, the distributions will be tax free to the extent that they are a recovery of the owner's Roth IRA contributions. Under the ordering rule discussed earlier, contributions are deemed to be withdrawn before earnings. Distributions you receive after the end of the five-year holding period are completely tax free.

For example, if the owner dies before the end of the five-year holding period and you elect to receive distributions as a beneficiary over your life expectancy or the plan requires the life expectancy method, your first minimum required annual distribution under the life expectancy distribution method must be taken by December 31 of the year following the year of the owner's death. Since required distributions under the life expectancy method are a small percentage of the account, it is likely that any distributions before the end of the five-year holding period will be tax-free withdrawals of contributions unless you withdraw more than the minimum required distribution.

If you choose to receive a payout of the owner's Roth IRA under the five-year rule, or the terms of the plan require that method, you must receive the entire account balance by December 31 of the fifth year following the year of the owner's death. If you do not take withdrawals from the account until after the end of the owner's five-year holding period (which began January 1 of the year of his or her first Roth IRA distribution), everything you receive from the account will be tax free. If you need or want to take withdrawals before the end of the owner's five-year holding period, you may withdraw the owner's contributions tax free; any excess will be treated as a taxable withdrawal of earnings under the ordering rule.

There is no 10% early distribution penalty for amounts you receive as a beneficiary of a Roth IRA, even if you are under age 59 $\frac{1}{2}$.

Joint Life and Last Survivor Life Expectancy

Ages	45	46	47	48	49	50	51	52	53	54	55	56	57	58	59
40	46.9	46.5	46.2	45.9	45.6	45.3	45.1	44.8	44.6	44.4	44.2	44.1	43.9	43.8	43.7
41	46.3	45.9	45.5	45.2	44.9	44.6	44.3	44.1	43.9	43.6	43.4	43.3	43.1	43.0	42.8
42	45.7	45.3	44.9	44.5	44.2	43.9	43.6	43.3	43.1	42.9	42.7	42.5	42.3	42.1	42.0
43	45.1	44.7	44.3	43.9	43.6	43.2	42.9	42.6	42.4	42.1	41.9	41.7	41.5	41.3	41.2
44	44.6	44.1	43.7	43.3	42.9	42.6	42.2	41.9	41.7	41.4	41.2	40.9	40.7	40.5	40.4
45	44.1	43.6	43.2	42.7	42.3	42.0	41.6	41.3	41.0	40.7	40.4	40.2	40.0	39.7	39.6
46	43.6	43.1	42.6	42.2	41.8	41.4	41.0	40.6	40.3	40.0	39.7	39.5	39.2	39.0	38.8
47	43.2	42.6	42.1	41.7	41.2	40.8	40.4	40.0	39.7	39.3	39.0	38.7	38.5	38.2	38.0
48	42.7	42.2	41.7	41.2	40.7	40.2	39.8	39.4	39.0	38.7	38.4	38.1	37.8	37.5	37.3
49	42.3	41.8	41.2	40.7	40.2	39.7	39.3	38.8	38.4	38.1	37.7	37.4	37.1	36.8	36.6
50	42.0	41.4	40.8	40.2	39.7	39.2	38.7	38.3	37.9	37.5	37.1	36.8	36.4	36.1	35.9
51	41.6	41.0	40.4	39.8	39.3	38.7	38.2	37.8	37.3	36.9	36.5	36.1	35.8	35.5	35.2
52	41.3	40.6	40.0	39.4	38.8	38.3	37.8	37.3	36.8	36.4	35.9	35.6	35.2	34.8	34.5
53	41.0	40.3	39.7	39.0	38.4	37.9	37.3	36.8	36.3	35.8	35.4	35.0	34.6	34.2	33.9
54	40.7	40.0	39.3	38.7	38.1	37.5	36.9	36.4	35.8	35.3	34.9	34.4	34.0	33.6	33.3
55	40.4	39.7	39.0	38.4	37.7	37.1	36.5	35.9	35.4	34.9	34.4	33.9	33.5	33.1	32.7
56	40.2	39.5	38.7	38.1	37.4	36.8	36.1	35.6	35.0	34.4	33.9	33.4	33.0	32.5	32.1
57	40.0	39.2	38.5	37.8	37.1	36.4	35.8	35.2	34.6	34.0	33.5	33.0	32.5	32.0	31.6
58	39.7	39.0	38.2	37.5	36.8	36.1	35.5	34.8	34.2	33.6	33.1	32.5	32.0	31.5	31.1
59	39.6	38.8	38.0	37.3	36.6	35.9	35.2	34.5	33.9	33.3	32.7	32.1	31.6	31.1	30.6

Joint Life and Last Survivor Life Expectancy

Ages	60	61	62	63	64	65	66	67	68	69	70	71	72	73	74	75	76	77	78	79	80
70	26.2	25.6	24.9	24.3	23.7	23.1	22.5	22.0	21.5	21.1	20.6	20.2	19.8	19.4	19.1	18.8	18.5	18.3	18.0	17.8	17.6
71	26.0	25.3	24.7	24.0	23.4	22.8	22.2	21.7	21.2	20.7	20.2	19.8	19.4	19.0	18.6	18.3	18.0	17.7	17.5	17.2	17.0
72	25.8	25.1	24.4	23.8	23.1	22.5	21.9	21.3	20.8	20.3	19.8	19.4	18.9	18.5	18.2	17.8	17.5	17.2	16.9	16.7	16.4
73	25.6	24.9	24.2	23.5	22.9	22.2	21.6	21.0	20.5	20.0	19.4	19.0	18.5	18.1	17.7	17.3	17.0	16.7	16.4	16.1	15.9
74	25.5	24.7	24.0	23.3	22.7	22.0	21.4	20.8	20.2	19.6	19.1	18.6	18.2	17.7	17.3	16.9	16.5	16.2	15.9	15.6	15.4
75	25.3	24.6	23.8	23.1	22.4	21.8	21.1	20.5	19.9	19.3	18.8	18.3	17.8	17.3	16.9	16.5	16.1	15.8	15.4	15.1	14.9
76	25.2	24.4	23.7	23.0	22.3	21.6	20.9	20.3	19.7	19.1	18.5	18.0	17.5	17.0	16.5	16.1	15.7	15.4	15.0	14.7	14.4
77	25.1	24.3	23.6	22.8	22.1	21.4	20.7	20.1	19.4	18.8	18.3	17.7	17.2	16.7	16.2	15.8	15.4	15.0	14.6	14.3	14.0
78	25.0	24.2	23.4	22.7	21.9	21.2	20.5	19.9	19.2	18.6	18.0	17.5	16.9	16.4	15.9	15.4	15.0	14.6	14.2	13.9	13.5
79	24.9	24.1	23.3	22.6	21.8	21.1	20.4	19.7	19.0	18.4	17.8	17.2	16.7	16.1	15.6	15.1	14.7	14.3	13.9	13.5	13.2
80	24.8	24.0	23.2	22.4	21.7	21.0	20.2	19.5	18.9	18.2	17.6	17.0	16.4	15.9	15.4	14.9	14.4	14.0	13.5	13.2	12.8
81	24.7	23.9	23.1	22.3	21.6	20.8	20.1	19.4	18.7	18.1	17.4	16.8	16.2	15.7	15.1	14.6	14.1	13.7	13.2	12.8	12.5
82	24.6	23.8	23.0	22.3	21.5	20.7	20.0	19.3	18.6	17.9	17.3	16.6	16.0	15.5	14.9	14.4	13.9	13.4	13.0	12.5	12.2
83	24.6	23.8	23.0	22.2	21.4	20.6	19.9	19.2	18.5	17.8	17.1	16.5	15.9	15.3	14.7	14.2	13.7	13.2	12.7	12.3	11.9
84	24.5	23.7	22.9	22.1	21.3	20.5	19.8	19.1	18.4	17.7	17.0	16.3	15.7	15.1	14.5	14.0	13.5	13.0	12.5	12.0	11.6
85	24.5	23.7	22.8	22.0	21.3	20.5	19.7	19.0	18.3	17.6	16.9	16.2	15.6	15.0	14.4	13.8	13.3	12.8	12.3	11.8	11.4

Income From Rents and Royalties

Use Schedule E of Form 1040 to report real estate rental income and expenses. You must also file Form 4562 to claim depreciation deductions for buildings you acquired in 1999.

Use Schedule C instead of Schedule E if you provide additional services for the convenience of the tenants, such as maid service. That is, Schedule C is used to report payments received for the use and occupancy of rooms or other areas in a hotel, motel, boarding house, apartment, tourist home, or trailer court where services are provided primarily for the occupant.

If you rent out an apartment or room in the same building in which you live, you report the rent income less expenses allocated to the rental property; *see 9.4.*

The law prevents most homeowners from deducting losses (expenses in excess of income) on the rental of a personal vacation home or personal residence if the owner or close relatives personally use the premises during the year. Tests based on days of personal and rental use determine whether you may deduct losses, as explained in *9.7.*

Rental losses may also be limited by the passive activity rules discussed in Chapter 10. Real estate professionals may avoid passive restrictions on rental income, and an investor who actively manages property may deduct rental losses of up to $25,000.

Use Schedule E to report royalties, but if you are a self-employed author, artist, or inventor, report royalty income and expenses on Schedule C.

Business rentals of equipment, vehicles, or similar personal property are reported on Schedule C, not Schedule E.

Rental Income and Deductions

9.1   Reporting Rental Income and Expenses

On the cash basis, you report rent income on your tax return for the year in which you receive payment or in which you "constructively" receive it, such as where payment is credited to your bank account.

On the accrual basis, you report income on your tax return for the year in which you are entitled to receive payment, even if it is not actually paid. However, you do not report accrued income if the financial condition of the tenant makes collection doubtful. If you sue for payment, you do not report income until you win a collectible judgment.

Advance rentals. Advance rentals or bonuses are reported in the year received, whether you are on the cash or accrual basis.

Tenant's payment of landlord's expenses. The tenant's payment of your taxes, interest, insurance, mortgage amortization (even if you are not personally liable on the mortgage), repairs, or other expenses is considered additional rental income to you. If your tenant pays your utility bills or your emergency repairs and deducts the amount from the rent payment, you must include as rental income the full rental amount, not the actual net payment. However, you can claim an offsetting deduction for expenses, such as repairs, that would have been deductible had you paid them.

Tenant's payment to cancel lease. A tenant's payment for cancelling a lease or modifying its terms is considered rental income in the year you receive it regardless of your method of accounting. You may deduct expenses incurred because of the cancellation or modification and any unamortized balance of expenses paid in negotiating the lease.

Insurance. Insurance proceeds for loss of rental income because of fire or other casualty are rental income.

Improvements by tenants. You do not realize taxable income when your tenant improves the leased premises, provided the improvements are not substitute rent payments. Furthermore, when you take possession of the improvements at the time the lease ends, you do not realize income. However, you may not depreciate the value of the improvements as the basis to you is considered zero.

Property or services. If you receive property or services instead of money, include the fair market value of such property or services as rental income.

If you agree upon a specified price for services rendered, that price is generally treated as the fair market value.

Rental losses. Rental income may be offset by deductions claimed for depreciation, mortgage interest, and repair and maintenance costs. However, if these expenses exceed rental income, the resulting loss is subject to deduction limitations. If you do not qualify as a real estate professional *(10.3)*, you generally may not deduct rental losses from other income (such as salary, interest, and dividends). Rental losses may offset only other rental and passive activity income. However, if you perform some management role, you may deduct from other income *real estate* rental losses of up to $25,000, provided your adjusted gross income does not exceed $100,000 *(see 10.2)*. The passive activity restrictions have the positive effect of making rental income attractive. Consider purchasing rental property if you have passive tax losses that may be used to offset the rental income.

Passive loss restrictions, which also affect tax credits, are discussed in Chapter 10.

9.2   Checklist of Rental Deductions

The expenses in this section are deductible from rental income on Schedule E of Form 1040 in determining your profit.

Real estate taxes. However, special assessments for paving, sewer systems, or other local improvements are not deductible; they are added to the cost of the land. *See 16.6 through 16.9 for* real estate tax deductions.

Construction period interest and taxes. These expenses generally have to be capitalized and depreciated; *see 16.4.*

 Caution

Security Deposits
Distinguish advance rentals, which are income, from security deposits, which are not. Security deposits are amounts deposited with you solely as security for the tenant's performance of the terms of the lease, and as such are usually not taxed, particularly where local law treats security deposits as trust funds. If the tenant breaches the lease, you are entitled to apply the sum as rent, at which time you report it as income. If both you and your tenant agree that a security deposit is to be used as a final rent payment, it is advance rent. Include it in your income when you receive it.

Depreciation Period Change
The IRS had set a seven-year MACRS recovery period for depreciating furniture, appliances, and carpeting used in residential rental property. In a policy change, the IRS has decreased the recovery period to five years. You may use the five-year period for property placed in service before 1999; *see* IRS Announcement 99-82.

Court Decision

Co-Tenant's Deduction for Real Estate Taxes
The Tax Court allowed a co-tenant to deduct more than her proportionate share of real estate taxes. According to the court, the deduction test for real estate taxes is whether the payment satisfies a personal liability or protects a beneficial interest in the property. In the case of co-tenants, nonpayment of taxes by the other co-tenants could result in the property being lost or foreclosed. To prevent this, a co-tenant who pays the tax is protecting his or her beneficial interest and, therefore, is entitled to deduct the payment of the full tax.

Depreciation of a rental building. You may start claiming depreciation in the month the building is ready for tenants. For example, you bought a house in May 1999 and spent June and July making repairs. The house is ready to rent in August and you advertise for tenants. You begin depreciation as of August, even if a tenant does not move in until September or some later month. The month the building is ready for tenants is the month that determines the first-year depreciation write-off under the mid-month convention. *See 9.5* for the monthly depreciation rates.

Depreciation for furniture and appliances. Furniture, carpeting, and appliances such as stoves and refrigerators used in residential rental property are considered five-year property for MACRS depreciation purposes; *see* the *Law Alert* on this page. A seven-year recovery period applies to office furniture and equipment such as desks and files.

Management expenses, such as a fee paid to a company for collecting the rent.

Maintenance expenses, such as heating, repairs, lighting, water, electricity, gas, telephone, coal, and other service costs; *see 9.3.*

Salaries and wages paid to superintendents, janitors, elevator operators, and service and maintenance personnel.

Traveling expenses to look after the properties. If you travel "away from home" to inspect or repair rental property, be prepared to show that this was the primary purpose of your trip, rather than vacationing or other personal purposes. Otherwise, the IRS may disallow deductions for round-trip travel costs.

Legal expenses for dispossessing tenants. But expenses of long-term leases are capital expenditures deductible over the term of the lease.

Interest on mortgages and other indebtedness. But expenses and fees for securing loans are nondeductible capital expenditures.

Commissions paid to collect rentals. But commissions paid to secure long-term rentals must be deducted over the life of the lease. Commissions paid to acquire the property are capitalized.

Premiums for fire, liability, and plate glass insurance. If payment is made in one year for insurance covering a period longer than one year, you amortize and deduct the premium over the life of the policy, even though you are on a cash basis.

Also deductible is a premium paid to secure a release from a mortgage in order to get a new loan.

Tax return preparation. You may deduct as a rental expense the part of a tax preparation fee allocable to Part 1 of Schedule E (income or loss from rentals or royalties). You may also deduct, as a rental expense, a fee paid to a tax consultant to resolve a tax underpayment related to your rental activities.

Charging below fair market rent. If you rent your property to a friend or relative for less than the fair rental value, you may deduct expenses and depreciation only to the extent of the rental income; *see 9.8.*

Co-tenants. One of two tenants-in-common may deduct only half of the maintenance expenses even if he or she pays the entire bill. A tenant-in-common who pays all of the expenses of the common property is entitled to reimbursement from the other co-tenant, so one-half of the bill is not his or her ordinary and necessary expense. Each co-tenant owns a separate property interest in the common property that produces separate income for each. Each tenant's deductible expense is that portion of the entire expense that each separate interest bears to the whole, and no more.

Costs of cancelling lease. A landlord may pay a tenant to cancel an unfavorable lease. The way the landlord treats the payment depends on the reason for the cancellation. If the purpose of the cancellation is to enable the landlord to construct a new building in place of the old, the cancellation payment is added to the basis of the new building. If the purpose is to sell the property, the payment is added to the cost of the property. If the landlord wants the premises for his or her own use, the payment is deducted over the remaining term of the old lease. If the landlord gets a new tenant to replace the old one, the cancellation payment is also generally deductible over the remaining term of the old lease.

EXAMPLE

Handlery Hotels, Inc., had to pay its lessee $85,000 to terminate a lease on a building three years before the lease term expired. Handlery entered into a new 20-year lease at more favorable terms with another lessee. Handlery amortized the $85,000 cancellation payment over the three-year unexpired term of the old lease. The IRS claimed that the payment had to be amortized over the 20-year term of the new lease because it was part of the cost of obtaining the new lease. A federal district court agreed with the IRS, but an appeals court sided with Handlery. Since the unexpired lease term is the major factor in determining the amount of the cancellation payment, the cost of cancellation should be amortized over that unexpired term.

9.3 Distinguishing Between a Repair and an Improvement

Maintenance and repair expenses are not treated in the same way as expenses for improvements and replacements. Only maintenance and incidental repair costs are deductible against rental income. Improvements that add to the value or prolong the life of the property or adapt it to new uses are capital improvements. Capital improvements may not be deducted currently but may be depreciated under the rules at *42.13*. If you make improvements to property before renting it out, add the cost of the improvements to your basis in the property.

A repair keeps your property in good operating condition. For example, repairs include painting, fixing gutters or floors, fixing leaks, plastering, and replacing broken windows. However, putting a recreation room in an unfinished basement, paneling a den, putting up a fence, putting in new plumbing or wiring, putting on a new roof, and paving a driveway are all examples of capital improvements depreciable under *42.13*.

Repairs may not be separated from capital expenditures when both are part of an improvement program; *see* Example 2 below.

EXAMPLES

1. The cost of painting the outside of a building used for business purposes and the cost of papering and painting the inside are repair costs and may be deducted. The replacement of a roof or a change in the plumbing system is a capital expenditure that must be depreciated under MACRS; *see 42.13*.

2. Amanda Jones buys a dilapidated business building and has it renovated and repaired. The total cost comes to about $130,000, of which $17,800 is allocable to the repairs. The cost of the repairs is not deductible because the entire project is a capital expenditure. When a general improvement program is undertaken, you may not separate repairs from improvements. Both become an integral part of the overall betterment and are a capital investment, although a portion could be characterized as repairs when viewed independently.

Normal maintenance or major improvement? Normal maintenance expenses were distinguished from major improvement costs in a case involving a major hotel where improvements and maintenance were generally done at the same time. The operators of the hotel capitalized the cost of the improvements but claimed expense deductions for the cost of painting and repapering rooms. The IRS disallowed the deductions, claiming they were part of the improvement program. The operators claimed that the papering and painting were normal and usual maintenance work required to keep the hotel in first-class condition. The Tax Court disagreed and sided with the IRS. However, on appeal, the appeals court allowed the deduction. The "rehabilitation doctrine" does not apply where it can be shown that repairs are part of a normal range of ongoing maintenance. Here, the painting and papering only served to maintain the first-class status of the hotel. The fact that the work was done under a general improvement plan did not defeat the deduction. Any commercial enterprise, such as a hotel, that annually spends large sums of money on replacements and repairs must do so under a detailed plan and budget.

 Planning Reminder

Repairs and Improvments

What if repairs and improvements are unconnected and not part of an overall improvement program? Assume you repair the floors of one story and improve another story by cutting new windows. You probably may deduct the cost of repairing the floors provided you have separate bills for the jobs. To safeguard the deduction, schedule the work at separate times so that the two jobs are not lumped together as an overall improvement program.

How To Report Rentals of Residential and Vacation Homes

Court Decision

Rented Rooms That Are Not Separate Dwelling Units

A rental loss was denied to an owner of a two-story, four-bedroom house when he rented out two bedrooms to separate tenants after he lost his job. Although individual locks were placed on the doors of the rented bedrooms, the tenants and the owner shared access to the kitchen, bathroom, and other parts of the house. The Tax Court held that the rented rooms were not separate and distinct from the rest of the house that the owner used. The house was a single dwelling unit shared by the owner and tenants and under the personal-use rules at *9.7,* the owner could not claim a rental loss.

9.4 Reporting Rents From a Multi-Unit Residence

If you rent out an apartment or room in a multi-unit residence in which you also live, you report rent receipts and deduct expenses allocated to the rented part of the property on Schedule E of Form 1040. Expenses allocated to rental are deductible, whether or not you itemize deductions. You deduct interest and taxes on your personal share of the property as itemized deductions on Schedule A of Form 1040 if you itemize deductions.

If expenses exceed rental income on Schedule E, your loss deduction is subject to the passive loss rules of Chapter 10. The loss, if it comes within the $25,000 allowance *(10.2)* or the exception for real estate professionals *(10.3),* may be deducted from any type of income. If you cannot claim the allowance, the loss may be deducted only from passive activity income.

If your only passive activity losses are rental losses of $25,000 or less from actively managed rental real estate and your modified adjusted gross income is $100,000 or less, you do not have to use Form 8582 to deduct losses under the $25,000 allowance; *see 10.12.*

EXAMPLE

You bought a three-family house in 1974. You occupy one apartment as a personal residence. The house cost you $30,000 ($27,000 for the building and $3,000 for the land). It had a useful life of 30 years. Two-thirds of the basis of the building has been subject to depreciation, or $18,000 (2/3 of $27,000). Assuming straight-line depreciation of $600 ($18,000 cost ÷ 30 years), this is how you deduct expenses in a taxable year:

	Total	Deduct itemized deductions	Deduct on Schedule E	Not deductible
Taxes	$600	$200	$400	
Interest	390	130	260	
Repairs	300		200	$100
Depreciation	600		600	
	$1,890	$330	$1,460	$100

The taxes and interest allocated to personal use are deductible on Schedule A if you itemize deductions. Repairs allocated to your apartment are nondeductible personal expenses.

If you or close relatives personally use the rented portion during the year and expenses exceed income, loss deductions may be barred under the rules in *9.7.*

9.5 Depreciation on Converting a Home to Rental Property

When you convert your residence to rental property, you may depreciate the building. You figure depreciation on the *lower* of:

- Fair market value of the building at the time you convert it to rental property; *and*
- Adjusted basis. This is your original cost for the building, exclusive of land, plus permanent improvements minus casualty or theft loss deductions claimed on prior tax returns.

You claim MACRS depreciation based on a $27\frac{1}{2}$-year recovery period. The specific rate for the year of conversion is the rate for the month in which the property is ready for tenants. For example, you move out of your home in May and make some minor repairs. You advertise the house for rent in June. Depreciation starts in June because that is when the home is ready for rental, even if you do not actually obtain a tenant until a later month. Under a mid-month convention, the house is treated as placed in service during the middle of the month. This means that one-half of a full month's depreciation is allowed for that month. In the table on the next page, the monthly depreciation rates for the year the property is placed in service and the next 12 years are shown. The table incorporates the mid-month convention.

In 1987, you bought a house for $125,000, of which $100,000 is allocated to the house; the $25,000 balance is allocated to the land. In June 1999, you move out of the house and rent it. At that time, the fair market value of the house exclusive of the land is $150,000. The depreciable basis of the house is the lower adjusted basis of $100,000. The depreciation rate for placing the house in service in June is 1.970%, as shown in the table below. Thus, your 1999 depreciation deduction is $1,970 ($100,000 × 1.970%). Your 2000 depreciation deduction is $3,636 ($100,000 × 3.636%).

Depreciating a rented cooperative apartment. If you rent out a co-op apartment, you may deduct your share of the total depreciation claimed by the cooperative corporation. The method for computing your share depends on whether you bought your co-op shares as part of the first offering. If you did, follow these steps: (1) Ask the co-op corporation officials for the total real estate depreciation deduction of the corporation, not counting depreciation for office space that cannot be lived in by tenant-shareholders. (2) Multiply Step 1 by the following fraction: number of your co-op shares divided by total shares outstanding. The result is your share of the co-op's depreciation, but you may not deduct more than your adjusted basis.

The computation is more complicated if you bought your co-op shares after the first offering. You must compute your depreciable basis as follows: Increase your cost for the co-op shares by your share of the co-op's total mortgage. Reduce this amount by your share of the value of the co-op's land and your share of the commercial space not available for occupancy by tenant-stockholders. Your "share" of the co-op's mortgage, land value, or commercial space is the co-op's total amount for such items multiplied by the fraction in Step 2 above, that is, the number of your shares divided by the total shares outstanding. After computing your depreciable basis, multiply that basis by the depreciation percentage for the month your apartment is ready for rental.

Basis to use when you sell a rented residence. For purposes of figuring gain, you use adjusted basis at the time of the conversion, plus subsequent capital improvements, and minus depreciation and casualty loss deductions. For purposes of figuring loss, you use the *lower* of adjusted basis and fair market value at the time of the conversion, plus subsequent improvements and minus depreciation and casualty losses. You may have neither gain nor loss to report; this would happen if you figure a loss when using the above basis rule for gains and you figure a gain when using the basis rule for losses.

Depreciation on a vacant residence. If you move from your house before it is sold, you generally may not deduct depreciation on the vacant residence while it is held for sale. The IRS will not allow the deduction, and, according to a Tax Court case, a deduction is possible only if you can show that you held the house expecting to make a profit on an increase in value over and above the value of the house when you moved from it. That is, you held the house for sale on the expectation of profiting on a future increase in value after abandoning the house as a residence.

 Planning Reminder

Obtain Appraisal
Have an appraiser estimate the fair market value of the house when it is rented. The appraisal will help support your basis for depreciation or a loss deduction on a sale if your return is examined.

Depreciation: Use the Row for the Month the Residence Is Ready for Rental in the First Rental Year

Month—	1	2	3	4	5	6	7	8	9	10	11	12
Year												
1	3.485%	3.182%	2.879%	2.576%	2.273%	1.970%	1.667%	1.364%	1.061%	0.758%	0.455%	0.152%
2–9	3.636	3.636	3.636	3.636	3.636	3.636	3.636	3.636	3.636	3.636	3.636	3.636
10	3.637	3.637	3.637	3.637	3.637	3.637	3.636	3.636	3.636	3.636	3.636	3.636
11	3.636	3.636	3.636	3.636	3.636	3.636	3.637	3.637	3.637	3.637	3.637	3.637
12	3.637	3.637	3.637	3.637	3.637	3.637	3.636	3.636	3.636	3.636	3.636	3.636
13	3.636	3.636	3.636	3.636	3.636	3.636	3.637	3.637	3.637	3.637	3.637	3.637

9.6 Renting to a Relative

The tax law distinguishes between a rental of a unit used by a close relative as a principal residence and a rental of a unit that is not the relative's principal residence, such as a second home or vacation home. It is easier to deduct a rental loss on the principal residence rental.

On a fair market rental of a unit used by the close relative as a principal residence, your relative's use is *not* considered personal use by you that could bar a loss under the personal-use test in *9.7.* A relative's use of the unit as a second or vacation home *is* attributed to you in applying the personal-use test at *9.7,* even if you receive a fair market value rent.

Close relatives who come within these rules are: brothers and sisters, half-brothers and half-sisters, spouses, parents, grandparents, children, and grandchildren.

Fair market rental is the amount a person who is not related to you would be willing to pay. The most direct way to determine fair market rental is to ask a real estate agent in your neighborhood for comparative rentals.

9.7 Personal Use and Rental of a Residential Unit During the Year

The number of days of personal and rental use determines how you must report income and expenses of a residential unit in which you live part of a taxable year and rent or offer for rent for the days you do not live there.

Before reading the daily-use tests, list your days of use in 1999:

Fair market rental days:_____

Personal-use days:_____

Personal-use days may also include rental days to family members listed at *9.6* and use days under co-ownership agreements. *See 9.8* for details on personal-use days.

The daily-use tests apply to any "dwelling unit" you rent out that is also used as a residence during the year by yourself or other family members. A dwelling unit may be a house, apartment, condominium, cooperative, house trailer, mini motor home, boat, or similar property with basic living accommodations, including any appurtenant structure such as a garage. A dwelling unit does not include property used exclusively as a hotel, motel, inn, or similar establishment.

EXAMPLE

Barranti inherited a residence from her grandmother. The house was in a state of disrepair. A real estate agent estimated the fair market rental rate for the house to be between $700 and $750 per month. Barranti rented the house to her brother for $500 a month while he repaired the structure. After a year, he moved out and Barranti sold the house and claimed a rental loss and a loss on the sale. The Tax Court disallowed both losses. The below-market rental to Barranti's brother was treated as her own personal use of the house, preventing the rental loss deduction. The below-market rental was also treated as evidence that Barranti held the property for personal purposes and therefore she could not deduct the loss on the sale either.

Rental of less than 15 days during the taxable year. If you rent the unit for fewer than 15 days in the taxable year, you do not report the rental income and the only deductions allowed are those you would be allowed anyway as a homeowner. That is, if you itemize deductions on Schedule A, you deduct mortgage interest, real estate taxes, and casualty losses, if any. No other rental expenses such as depreciation and maintenance expenses are deductible. Interest is generally fully deductible if the home qualifies as a first or second home under the mortgage interest rules discussed in Chapter 15.

Rental of 15 days or more in the taxable year. A daily-use test determines whether your use of the unit during the taxable year is treated as residential use that requires you to figure your deductions under the allocation rules in *9.9* that limit your deductions to the rental income. You are considered to have used the unit as a residence if personal-use days exceed the *larger* of 14 days and 10% of fair market rental days. When the unit is treated as a residence, rental expenses are deductible on Schedule E only to the extent of rental income, following the rules in *9.9.* Expenses not deductible in the current year under this limitation may be carried forward and will be deductible up to rental income in the following year. The deduction limit is irrelevant if your rental income exceeds expenses. You report the rental income and claim the deductible expenses on Schedule E.

Law Alert

15 Day Exception

Congress has considered several proposals requiring property owners to report rental income even if they rent out units for fewer than 15 days per taxable year, but no such proposal had been enacted as of the time this book went to press.

If your personal-use days do not exceed the larger of 14 days and 10% of the fair market rental days, your rental deductions are not limited by the personal-use test. However, a loss deduction is subject to the passive activity loss restrictions discussed at *10.1*.

EXAMPLES

1. In 1999, you rented out a condominium unit in Florida at a fair market rental for 260 days. If you used the unit personally for 27 or more days, the condominium is considered a residence subject to the allocation rules at *9.9* because your personal use exceeds 26 days, 10% of the fair market rental days. If you used the unit for 26 days or less, you may treat the unit for the taxable year as rental property and you may deduct a loss, if any, subject to the passive activity rules at *10.1*.

    Where rental days exceed 140 days, as a rule of thumb, you can figure that for every 10 days of fair-rent use, you may use the unit personally for one day.   Thus, if you rented a vacation unit for 11 months, you could personally use it for a month or so without jeopardizing a deduction of a rental loss (rental of 330 days would permit 33 days of personal use).

2. Assume the same unit as in Example 1 but you rented the unit for 130 days. If you used the unit personally for 14 days or less, you may treat the unit as a rental property. To be treated as a residence, your personal use would have to exceed 14 days, since 14 days is greater than 10% of the rental days.

9.8 Counting Personal-Use and Rental Days

In applying the personal-use test in *9.7*, personal-use days are:

- Days you used the residence for personal purposes other than days primarily spent making repairs or getting the property ready for tenants.
- Days on which the residence is used by your spouse, children, grandchildren, parents, brothers, sisters, or grandparents. However, if such a relative pays you a fair rental value to use the home as a principal residence, the relative's use is not considered personal use by you. If you rent a vacation home to such relatives, their use is considered personal use by you even if they pay a fair rental value amount.

    The same rules apply to days of use by a relative of a co-owner of the property.
- Days on which the residence is used by any person under a reciprocal arrangement that allows you to use some other dwelling during the year.
- Days on which you rent the residence to any person for less than fair market value.
- Days that a co-owner of the property uses the residence, unless the co-owner's use is under a shared-equity financing agreement discussed later in this section.

An owner is not considered to have personally used a home that is used by an employee if the value of such use is tax-free lodging required as a condition of employment; *see 3.11*.

Shared-equity financing agreements for co-owners. Use by a co-owner is not considered personal use by you if you have a shared-equity financing agreement under which: (1) the co-owner pays you a fair rent for using the home as his or her principal residence; and (2) you and your co-owner each have undivided interests for more than 50 years in the entire home and in any appurtenant land acquired with the residence.

Any use by a co-owner that does not meet these two tests is considered personal use by you if, for any part of the day, the home is used by a co-owner or a holder of any interest in the home (other than a security interest or an interest under a lease for fair rental) for personal purposes. For this purpose, any other ownership interest existing at the time you have an interest in the home is counted, even if there are no immediate rights to possession and enjoyment of the home under such other interest. For example, you have a life estate in the home and your friend owns the remainder interest. Use by either of you is personal use.

EXAMPLES

1. A son rented a condominium in Florida to his parents, who split their time between the Florida apartment and the home they owned in Illinois. Although the parents paid a fair amount for the Florida condo, the son's rental deductions were limited by the IRS and the Tax Court to interest and real estate taxes that did not exceed the rental income. The parents' rental days were attributed to the son under the 14 day/10% rental day limit since the home in Illinois, and not the Florida apartment, was their principal residence.

Planning Reminder

Shared-Equity Financing Agreements

As an investor, you can help finance the purchase of a principal residence for a family member or other individual. The rental income you receive for your ownership share in the property may be offset by deductions for your share of the mortgage interest, taxes, and operating expenses you pay under the terms of the agreement, as well as depreciation deductions for your percentage share. Rental losses are subject to the passive loss restrictions in Chapter 10.

The other co-owner living in the house may claim itemized deductions for payment of his or her share of the mortgage interest and taxes.

2. You and your neighbor Joe are co-owners of a vacation condominium. You rent the unit out whenever possible; Joe uses the unit for two weeks every year. As Joe owns an interest in the unit, both of you are considered to have used the unit for personal purposes during those weeks.

3. You and your neighbor Tom are co-owners of a house under a shared-equity financing agreement. Tom lives in the house and pays you a fair rental price. Even though Tom has an interest in the house, the days he lives there are not counted as days of personal-use by you because Tom rents the house as a main home under a shared-equity financing agreement.

4. You rent a beach house to Jane. Jane rents her house in the mountains to you. You each pay a fair rental price. You are using your house for personal purposes on the days that Jane uses it because your house is used by Jane under an arrangement that allows you to use her house.

Rental of principal residence prior to sale. You are not considered to have made any personal use of a principal residence that you rent or try to rent at a fair rental for (1) a consecutive period of 12 months or more *or* (2) a period of less than 12 months that ends with the sale or exchange of the residence. For example, you move out of your principal residence on May 31, 1999, offering it for rental as of June 1. You rent it from June 15 until mid-November, when you sell the house. Under the special rental period rule, your use of the house from January 1 until May 31, 1999, is *not* counted as personal use. This means that deductions for the rental period are not subject to the allocation rules and restrictions discussed in *9.9*.

Rental pool arrangements. In proposed regulations, the IRS holds that a rental pool is not a basis for counting fair rental days. However, the proposed regulations permit rental pool participants to elect to average the actual rental of their units. Unanimous consent is required to elect the averaging rule. If the election is made, the number of rental days for a unit is determined by multiplying the aggregate number of days that all units in the rental pool were rented at fair rental during the pool season by a fraction. The numerator of the fraction is the number of participation days of a particular unit; the denominator is the aggregate number of participation days of all the units.

The IRS may apply the rental pool rule to a rental guarantee option. The Tax Court supported the IRS position, but an appeals court did not, in the following Example.

Caution

Rental Pool Arrangements
Pool arrangements have been devised to avoid the loss restriction by attempting to increase the days the home is held for a fair rental value. They have not been successful. Courts have ruled that only days on which a home is actually rented count as fair rental days, not days of availability through the rental pool.

EXAMPLE

Razavi owned a condo in Florida and elected to take a rental guarantee option from the resort operator over a three-year period. The annual guaranteed rent was $21,000 plus 40% of rentals over $52,500. In 1987, the resort actually received gross rentals of $48,300 for the unit, but Razavi received $21,000 under the guarantee and claimed a rental loss deduction. The IRS disallowed the loss because it claimed that Razavi personally used the unit for 27 days, exceeding 10% of the 200 days the unit had actually been rented.

Razavi claimed that the 27 days were less than 10% of the 338 days covered by a rental guarantee. That is, the guarantee covered 365 days less 27 days of personal use. The Tax Court disagreed on the grounds that the guarantee was based on a rental period of between 142 days and 179 days and this was far below the 270 rental days needed to support his 27 personal-use days.

The Sixth Circuit allowed the loss. The $21,000 guarantee was a fair rental for the entire year based on rentals of comparable units. Although Razavi probably could have earned more than $21,000 with daily or weekly rentals, such short-term rentals also would have carried added risks and responsibilities that he was able to avoid by choosing the rent guarantee.

9.9   Allocating Expenses to Rental Days

When you rent out your home for part of the year at fair market value and also use it personally on some days during the taxable year, expenses are allocated between personal and rental use. By law, deductible expenses of renting are limited by this fraction:

$$\frac{\text{Days of fair market rental}}{\text{Total days of rental and personal use}}$$

The days a vacation home is held out for rent but not actually rented are not counted as rental days.

There is a conflict of opinion between the IRS and the courts over the issue of whether this formula applies also to interest and taxes. According to the courts, interest and taxes are allocated on a daily basis. Thus, if a house is rented for 61 days in the year, one-sixth of the deductible interest and taxes ($^{61}/_{365}$) is deducted first from the rental income. This rule allows a larger amount of other expenses to be deducted from rental income than is allowed under the IRS application of the formula; *see* Example 2 on the next page.

Claiming expenses if personal use bars a loss deduction. If your personal use of a residence exceeds the 14-day /10% test in *9.7*, the residence was rented for at least 15 days during the year, and the expenses allocated to rental use exceed rental income, the allocable rental expenses are deducted from rental income in a specific order:

1. The rental portion of the following expenses is fully deductible on Schedule E of Form 1040, even if the total exceeds rental income: deductible home mortgage interest *(15.1)*, real estate taxes, deductible casualty and theft losses (Chapter 18), and directly related rental expenses. Directly related rental expenses are rental expenses not related to the use or maintenance of the residence itself, such as office supplies, rental agency fees, advertising, and depreciation on office equipment used in the rental activity.

2. If there is any rental income remaining after the income is reduced by the expenses in Step 1, the balance is next offset by the rental portion of operating expenses for the residence itself, such as utilities, repairs, and insurance. Do not include depreciation on the rental part of the home in this group.

3. If any rental income remains after Step 2, depreciation on the rental portion of the residence may be deducted from the balance.

Step 1 expenses, as well as the expenses from Steps 2 and 3 that offset rental income, are deducted on the applicable lines of Schedule E. Operating expenses from Step 2 and depreciation from Step 3 that exceed the balance of rental income are carried forward to the next year as rental expenses for the same property. In the next year, the carried-over expenses are deductible only to the extent of rental income from the property for that year, even if your personal use of the residence does *not* exceed the 14-day/10% test in *9.7* for that year.

If you itemize deductions, you claim the *personal-use* portion of deductible mortgage interest, real estate taxes, and casualty and theft losses on Schedule A of Form 1040.

Interest expenses. If you personally use a rental vacation home for more than the greater of 14 days and 10% of the fair market rental days *(9.7)*, the residence may be treated as a qualifying second residence under the mortgage interest rules; *see 15.1*. The interest on a qualifying second home is generally fully deductible and is not subject to disallowance under the passive activity restrictions in Chapter 10. As shown above, the portion of the deductible mortgage interest allocable to the rental portion is deducted from rental income (along with taxes) before other expenses.

EXAMPLES

1. You rent out your vacation home for 61 days in 1999, receiving rent of $2,000. You use the home yourself for 61 days. You may deduct expenses only up to the amount of this income because your personal use exceeds the 14-day/10% rental test. Your expenses are mortgage interest of $1,600, real estate taxes of $800, and maintenance and utility costs of $1,200. Depreciation (based on 100% rental use) is $1,500. Assume the vacation home is a qualifying second home *(15.1)*, so that all the interest is deductible under the mortgage interest rules. Under the IRS method, one-half of all the expenses (61 rental days divided by 122 total days of use), including the interest and taxes, are deducted in this order:

Rent income		$2,000
Less: Interest	$ 800	
Taxes	400	1,200
		$ 800
Less: Maintenance		600
		$ 200
Less: Depreciation		$ 200

Under the Tax Court's method of allocating interest and taxes, one-sixth of the interest and taxes (61/365) would be deducted from rental income, rather than one-half as under the IRS method.

The balance of the depreciation is not deductible. It may be carried forward to the following year.

The balance of interest and taxes is deductible as itemized deductions provided you claim itemized deductions on Schedule A of Form 1040.

If the vacation home were not a qualifying second residence under *15.1,* the interest would not be deducted with taxes from the $2,000 of rental income, but would be treated as an operating expense and deducted along with the maintenance expenses.

2. The Boltons paid interest and property taxes totaling $3,475 on their vacation home. Maintenance expenses (not including depreciation) totaled $2,693. The Boltons stayed at the home 30 days and rented it for 91 days, receiving rents of $2,700. Because the personal use for 30 days exceeded the 14-day limit, the Boltons could deduct rental expenses only up to the gross rental income of $2,700, reduced by interest and taxes allocable to rental. In figuring the amount of interest and taxes deductible from rents, they divided the number of rental days, or 91, by 365, the number of days in the year. This gave them an allocation of 25%. After subtracting $868 for interest and taxes (25% of $3,475) from rental income, they deducted $1,832 ($2,700 – $868) of maintenance expenses from rental income.

The IRS argued that 75% of the Boltons' interest and tax payments had to be allocated to the rental income. The IRS used an allocation base of 121 days of personal and rental use. Thus, the IRS allocated 75% ($91/_{121}$) of the interest and taxes, or $2,606, to gross rental income of $2,700. This allocation allowed only $94 maintenance expenses to be deducted ($2,700 – $2,606).

The Tax Court sided with the Boltons and an appeals court (the Ninth Circuit) agreed. The IRS method of allocating interest and taxes to rental use is bizarre. Interest and taxes are expenses that accrue ratably over the year and are deductible even if a vacation home is not rented for a single day. Thus, the allocation to rental use should be based on a ratable portion of the annual expense by dividing the number of rental days by the number of days in a year.

The Tenth Circuit appeals court also supports the Tax Court allocation method.

Planning Reminder

Profit Motive

A profit motive is presumed if you can show a profit for at least three of the last five years you engaged in rental activities. The IRS, however, may *rebut* this presumption. For a way to fight this rebuttal, consult *40.10.*

9.10 Rentals Lacking Profit Motive

If you rent a residential unit for 15 days or more and a loss is not barred under the personal-use limitation of *9.7,* the IRS may attempt to disallow a loss by claiming that you had no profit motive in placing the unit up for rent. If the IRS makes such an argument, you must try to prove a profit motive, as discussed in *40.10.* Any loss disallowed on these grounds may not be carried over to a later year.

EXAMPLES

1. *(Loss allowed.)* In 1973, Clancy purchased a house and land in a coastal resort area of California. Prior to the purchase, Clancy was told by a renting agent that he could expect reasonable income and considerable appreciation from the property. Previously, he had sold similar property in the same development at a profit. After the purchase, Clancy spent $5,000 to prepare the house for rental, and gave a rental agency the exclusive right to offer the property for rent. The house was available for rent 95% of the time in 1973, and 100% of the time in 1974. However, rentals proved disappointing, totaling only $280 in 1973 and $1,244 in 1974, despite the active efforts of the agency to rent the property. However, the house did appreciate in value and was eventually sold at a profit of $14,000. In 1973 and 1974, Clancy deducted rental expenses of approximately $21,000, which the IRS disallowed. The IRS claimed that the house was not rental property used in a business. Furthermore, as Clancy knew that he could not make a profit from the rentals, he could not be considered to hold the property for the production of income.

The Tax Court agreed that the expenses were not deductible business expenses. But this did not mean they were not deductible as expenses of income production. Although the rental income from the property was minimal, Clancy acquired and held the property expecting to make a profit on a sale. He had previously sold similar property at a profit and was told to expect considerable rental income as well as appreciation from the new house. Where an owner holds property, as Clancy did here, because he or she believes that it may appreciate in value, such property is held for the production of income. Further evidence that Clancy held the property to make a profit: He rarely used it for personal purposes and an agent actively sought to rent it.

2. *(Loss allowed.)* Nelson bought a condominium, hired a rental agent, and even advertised in the *Wall Street Journal* and *Indianapolis Star.* He also listed the unit for sale. During 1974, he was unable to rent the apartment but deducted expenses and depreciation of over $6,100, which the IRS disallowed. The IRS argued that he did not buy the unit to make a profit but to shelter substantial income from tax. The Tax Court disagreed. Although his efforts to rent were not successful in 1974, he was successful in later years in renting the unit. He rarely visited the apartment other than to initially furnish it. When he went on vacation, he went abroad or to other vacation spots.

3. *(Loss disallowed.)* The Lindows purchased a condominium that they rented out during the prime winter rental season. However, over an eight-year period their expenses consistently exceeded rental income. The Tax Court agreed with the IRS that expenses in excess of rental income were not deductible. Substantial, repeated losses, even after the initial years of operation, indicated that the operation was not primarily profit-oriented. The rental return during the prime rental season could not return a profit. Even if the condominium were fully rented for the entire prime rental season, annual claimed expenses would exceed rent income. The couple also used the unit for several months and intended to live there on retirement. They did not consider putting the unit up for sale with an agent. Finally, that they had detailed records of income and expenses did not prove a business venture. Records, regardless of how detailed, are insufficient to permit the deduction of what are essentially personal expenses.

IRS may challenge losses claimed on temporary rental before sale. If you are unable to sell your home and must move, it may be advisable to put it up for rent. This way you may be able to deduct maintenance expenses and depreciation on the unit even if it remains vacant. However, the IRS has disallowed loss deductions for rentals preceding a sale on the ground that there was no "profit motive" for the rental under the rules discussed at *40.10*. Courts have allowed loss deductions in certain cases.

EXAMPLES

1. The IRS and Tax Court disallowed a loss deduction for rental expenses under the "profit-motive rules" *(40.10)* where a principal residence was rented for 10 months until it could be sold. According to the Tax Court, the temporary rental did not convert the residence to rental property. Since the sales effort was primary, there was no profit motive for the rental. Thus, no loss could be claimed; rental expenses were deductible only to the extent of rental income. The favorable side of the Tax Court position: Since the residence was not converted to rental property, the owners could defer tax on the gain from the sale by buying a new home. An appeals court reversed the Tax Court and allowed both tax deferral and a loss deduction. The rental loss was allowed since the old home was actually rented for a fair rental price. Furthermore, the owners had moved and could not return to the old home, which was rented almost continuously until sold.

2. In 1976, a couple bought a condo apartment in Pompano Beach, Florida. In 1983, they decided to move and listed the unit for either sale or rent with a local real estate broker. Sale of the unit was difficult because of the saturation of the Florida real estate market. Rental of the unit was also difficult because the condominium association's rules barred the rental of condominium units on a seasonal basis. The unit remained unrented until it was sold in 1986 for a substantial gain. In 1984, the couple deducted a $9,576 rental loss ($7,596 for maintenance expenses and $1,980 for depreciation). The IRS disallowed the deduction as not incurred in a bona fide rental activity. The Tax Court allowed the deduction. The couple made an honest and reasonable effort to rent the condominium. Lack of rental income was caused by a slack rental market and the condominium association rules prohibiting short-term rentals.

Royalty Income and Deductions

Planning Reminder

Passive Income Exception

Certain working oil and gas interests are exempt from the passive activity loss restrictions; *see 10.10.*

9.11 Reporting Royalty Income

Royalties are payment for use of patents or copyrights or for the use and exhaustion of mineral properties. Royalties are taxable as ordinary income and are reported on Schedule E (Form 1040). Depletion deductions relating to the royalties are also reported on Schedule E. If you own an operating oil, gas, or mineral interest, or are a self-employed writer, investor, or artist, you report royalty income, expenses, and depletion on Schedule C.

Examples of Royalty Income

License fees received for use, manufacture, or sale of a patented article.

Renting fees received from patents, copyrights, and depletable assets (such as oil wells).

Authors' royalties including advance royalties if not a loan.

Royalties for musical compositions, works of art, etc.

Proceeds of sale of part of your rights in an artistic composition or book, for example, sale of motion picture or television rights.

Royalties from oil, gas, or other similar interests; *see 9.16.* To have a royalty, you must retain an economic interest in the minerals deposited in the land you have leased to the producer. You usually have a royalty when payments are based on the amount of minerals produced. However, if you are paid regardless of the minerals produced, you have a sale that is taxed as capital gain if the proceeds exceed the basis of the transferred property interest. Bonuses and advance royalties that are paid to you before the production of minerals are taxable as royalty income and are entitled to an allowance for depletion. However, bonuses and advanced royalties for gas and oil wells and geothermal deposits are not treated as gross income for purposes of calculating percentage depletion. If the lease is terminated without production and you received a bonus or advanced royalty, you report as income previously claimed depletion deductions. You increase the basis of your property by the restored depletion deductions.

9.12 Production Costs of Books and Creative Properties

Freelance authors, artists, and photographers may deduct their costs of producing original works in the years that the expenses are paid or incurred. The uniform capitalization rules that generally apply to property that you produce *(see 40.3)* do not apply.

You qualify for current expense deductions if you are self-employed and you *personally create* literary manuscripts, musical or dance scores, paintings, pictures, sculptures, drawings, cartoons, graphic designs, original print editions, photographs, or photographic negatives or transparencies. However, the exception to the uniform capitalization rules does not apply to, and thus current deductions are not allowed for, expenses relating to motion picture films, videotapes, printing, photographic plates, or similar items.

If you conduct business as an owner-employee of a personal service corporation, and you are a qualifying author, artist, or photographer, the corporation may claim current deductions related to your expenses in producing books or other eligible creative works. Substantially all of the corporation's stock must be owned by you and your relatives.

Caution

Hobby loss restrictions

Authors and artists with expenses exceeding income may be barred by the IRS from claiming loss deductions; *see 40.10.*

9.13 Deducting the Cost of Patents or Copyrights

If you create an artistic work or invention for which you get a government patent or copyright, you may depreciate your costs over the life of the patent or copyright. Basis for depreciation includes all expenses that you are required to capitalize in connection with creating the work, such as the cost of drawings, experimental models, stationery, and supplies; travel expenses to obtain material for a book; fees to counsel; government charges for patent or copyright; and litigation costs in protecting or perfecting title.

If you purchased the patent or artistic creation, depreciate your cost over the remaining life of the patent or copyright. If your cost for a patent is payable annually as a fixed percentage of the revenue derived from use of the patent, the depreciation deduction equals the royalty paid or incurred for that year. However, if a copyright or patent is acquired in connection with the acquisition of a business, the cost is amortizable over a 15-year period as a Section 197 intangible; *see 42.18.*

If you inherited the patent or rights to an artistic creation, your cost is the fair market value either at the time of death of the person from whom you inherited it *(5.17)* or the alternate valuation date if elected by the executor. You get this cost basis even if the decedent paid nothing for it. Figure your depreciation by dividing the fair market value by the number of years of remaining life.

If your patent or copyright becomes valueless, you may deduct your unrecovered cost or other basis in the year it became worthless.

9.14 Intangible Drilling Costs

Intangible drilling and development costs include wages, fuel, repairs, hauling, and supplies incident to and necessary for the preparation and drilling of wells for the production of oil or gas, and geothermal wells. For wells you are developing in the United States, you can elect to deduct the costs currently as business expenses or treat them as capital expenses subject to depreciation or depletion.

Electing current deductions. The election applies only to costs of drilling and developing items that do not have a salvage value. You must make this election by deducting the expenses on your income tax return for the first tax year in which you pay or incur the costs.

Tax-shelter investors may deduct prepayments of drilling expenses only if the well is "spudded" within 90 days after the close of the taxable year in which the prepayment is made. The prepayment must also have a business purpose, not be a deposit, and not materially distort income. The investor's deduction is limited to his or her cash investment in the tax shelter. For purposes of this limitation, an investor's cash investment includes loans that are not secured by his or her shelter interest or the shelter's assets and loans that are not arranged by the organizer or promoter. If the above tests are not met, a deduction may be claimed only as actual drilling services are provided.

Recapture of intangible drilling costs for oil, gas, geothermal, or mineral property. Upon the disposition of oil, gas, geothermal, or other mineral property placed in service after 1986, ordinary income treatment applies to previously claimed deductions for intangible drilling and development costs for oil, gas, and geothermal wells, and to mineral development and exploration costs. Depletion deductions, discussed in *9.15*, are also generally subject to this ordinary income treatment upon disposition of the property.

For oil, gas, or geothermal property placed in service before 1987, ordinary income treatment applies on the disposition of a working or operating interest to the extent that intangible drilling and development cost deductions exceeded what would have been allowed if the costs had been deducted through cost depletion. Recapture for geothermal property applies only to wells commenced after September 30, 1978.

AMT and intangible drilling costs. If you are an independent oil or gas producer or royalty owner, intangible drilling costs for oil and gas production are not treated as tax preference items for purposes of alternative minimum tax (AMT). However, the reduction in your AMT income from not treating intangible drilling costs as a tax preference is limited. The reduction may not exceed 40% of your AMT income, figured as if excess intangible drilling costs were still a tax preference item and without regard to any AMT net operating loss deduction; *see* the instructions to Form 6251.

9.15 Depletion Deduction

Properties subject to depletion deductions are mines, oil and gas wells, timber, and exhaustible natural deposits.

Two methods of computing depletion are: (1) cost depletion and (2) percentage depletion. If you are allowed to compute under either method, you must use the one that produces the *larger* deduction. In most cases, this will be percentage depletion. For timber, you must use cost depletion.

Cost depletion. The cost depletion of minerals is computed as follows: (1) divide the total number of units (tons, barrels) remaining in the deposit to be mined into the adjusted basis of the property; (2) multiply the unit rate found in Step 1 by the number of units for which payment is received during the taxable year if you are on the cash basis, or the units sold if you are on the accrual basis.

Adjusted basis is the original cost of the property, less depletion allowed, whether computed on the percentage or cost depletion method. It does not include nonmineral property such as mining equipment. Adjusted basis may not be less than zero.

Timber depletion is based on the cost of timber (or other basis in the owner's hands) and does not include any part of the cost of land. Depletion takes place when standing timber is cut. Depletion must be computed by the cost method, not by the percentage method. However, instead of claiming the cost depletion method, you may elect to treat the cutting of timber as a sale subject to capital gain or loss treatment. For further details, *see* IRS Publication 535.

Caution

Drilling Expense Prepayments

Prepayments of drilling expenses are only deductible if the well is "spudded" within 90 days after the close of the taxable year in which the prepayment was made, and the deduction is limited to the original amount of the investment.

Law Alert

Geological and Geophysical Investigation Costs

When this book went to press, Congress was considering allowing a current deduction for geological and geophysical costs incurred while exploring for oil and gas properties. Present law defines these costs as capital in nature. *See* the Supplement for further legislative developments.

Percentage depletion. Percentage depletion is based on a certain percentage rate applied to annual gross income derived from the resource. In determining gross income for percentage depletion, do not include any lease bonuses, advance royalties, or any other amount payable without regard to production. A deduction for percentage depletion is allowed even if the basis of the property is already fully recovered by prior depletion deductions. The percentage to be applied depends upon the mineral involved; the range is from 5% up to 22%. For example, the maximum 22% depletion deduction applies to sulphur, uranium, and U.S. deposits of lead, zinc, nickel, mica, and asbestos. A 15% depletion percentage applies to U.S. deposits of gold, silver, copper, iron ore, and shale.

Taxable income limit. For properties other than oil and gas, the percentage depletion deduction *may not exceed* 50% of taxable income from the property computed without the depletion deduction. In computing the 50% limitation, a net operating loss deduction is not deducted from gross income. A 100% taxable income limit applies to oil and gas properties; *see 9.16.*

Oil and gas property. Percentage depletion for oil and gas wells was repealed as of January 1, 1975, except for the following exemptions: (1) small independent producers and royalty owners and (2) for gas well production. *See 9.16* for these oil and gas percentage depletion exemptions.

9.16 Oil and Gas Percentage Depletion

Small independent producers and royalty owners generally are allowed to deduct percentage depletion at a 15% rate for domestic oil and gas production. However, a higher rate may be allowed for qualifying "marginal" production, as discussed on the next page. The deduction is subject to a taxable income limit.

The 15% rate applies to a small producer exemption that equals the gross income from a maximum daily average of 1,000 barrels of oil or 6 million cubic feet of natural gas, or a combination of both. Gross income from the property does not include advanced royalties or lease bonuses that are payable without regard to the actual production.

The depletable natural gas quantity depends on an election made annually by independent producers or royalty owners to apply part of their 1,000-barrel-per-day oil limitation to natural gas. The depletable quantity of natural gas is 6,000 cubic feet times the barrels of depletable oil for which an election has been made. The election is made on an original or amended return or on a claim for credit or refund. For example, if your average daily production is 1,200 barrels of oil and 6.2 million cubic feet of natural gas, your maximum depletable limit is 1,000 barrels of oil, which you may split between the oil and gas. You could claim depletion for 500 barrels of oil per day and for 3 million cubic feet of gas per day: 3 million cubic feet of gas is the equivalent of the remaining 500 barrels of oil limit (500 barrels × 6,000 cubic feet depletable gas quantity equals 3 million cubic feet of gas).

Transferees who received their interest in a "proven" oil or gas property after October 11, 1990, are allowed percentage depletion under the regular rules.

Transferees receiving "proven" properties after 1974 and before October 12, 1990, are not allowed percentage depletion unless the transfer was made because of the death of the prior owner, a tax-free transfer to a controlled corporation, a transfer between commonly controlled corporations, or changes in beneficiaries of a trust where the changes are due to births, adoptions, or deaths within a single family.

Ineligible retailers and refiners. The small producer exemption is not allowed to any producer who owns or controls a retail outlet for the sale of oil, natural gas, or petroleum products. It is also not allowed to a refiner who refines more than 50,000 barrels of oil on any one day of the taxable year; the limit is based on inputs of crude oil into the refinery process, rather than outputs. A taxpayer is not treated as a retailer where gross sales of oil and gas products are less than $5 million in any one year or if all sales of oil or natural gas products occur outside the United States, and none of the taxpayer's domestic production is exported. Bulk sales of oil or natural gas to industrial or utility customers are not to be treated as retail sales.

Figuring average daily domestic production. Average daily production is figured by dividing your aggregate production during the taxable year by the number of days in the taxable year. If you hold a partial interest in the production (including a partnership interest), production rate is found by multiplying total production of such property by your income percentage participation in such property.

The production over the entire year is averaged regardless of when production actually occurred. If average daily production for the year exceeds the 1,000-barrel or 6-million-cubic-feet limit, the exemption must be allocated among all the properties in which you have an interest.

Taxable income limits on percentage depletion. The percentage depletion deduction for a small producer or royalty owner may not exceed the *lesser* of (1) 100% of the taxable income from the property before the depletion allowance and (2) 65% of your taxable income from all sources computed without regard to the depletion deduction allowed under the small producer's exemption, any net operating loss carry-back, and any capital loss carry-back.

The above 100% limit is suspended for production from marginal production properties (*see* below) during taxable years starting after 1997 and before 2000. When this book went to press, Congress was considering extending suspension of the 100% of net income limit through 2004. Congress was also considering a proposal to suspend the 65% of taxable income limit during the years 1999 through 2004. *See* the Supplement for developments with respect to these legislative proposals.

Limitations where family members or related businesses own interests. The daily exemption rate is allocated among members of the same family in proportion to their respective production of oil. Similar allocation is required where business entities are under common control. This affects interests owned by you, your spouse, and minor children; by corporations, estates, and trusts in which 50% of the beneficial interest is owned by the same or related persons; and by a corporation that is a member of the same controlled group.

Higher depletion for marginal production. Independent producers and royalty owners are allowed a higher depletion rate for *marginal production,* defined as oil or natural gas from "stripper well property" or property producing substantially all "heavy" oil. A stripper well property is one from which average daily production, divided by the number of all producing wells on the property, is 15 or fewer "barrel equivalents." A barrel equivalent is a barrel of oil or 6,000 cubic feet of natural gas.

The 15% rate is increased by 1% for each whole dollar that the "reference price" (the average annual wellhead price as estimated by the IRS) of domestic crude oil for the previous year was below $20 per barrel. The depletion rate for qualifying production in 1999 is 24%.

The higher rate applies only up to the maximum depletable limit, which is the average daily production of up to 1,000 barrels a day of oil, or 6 million cubic feet of gas. If the taxpayer has production from "marginal properties" eligible for the higher depletion rate, as well as production from other properties subject to the 15% rate, the marginal production is taken into account first in applying the 1,000-barrel or 6-million-cubic-feet overall limit. However, a special election may be made to prorate the overall limit among all production, whether marginal or nonmarginal.

 Planning Reminder

Marginal Production

The regular 15% depletion rate for domestic oil and gas production is increased for qualifying marginal production; *see* the left column on this page.

Loss Restrictions: Passive Activities and At-Risk Limits

The passive activity law was legislated to discourage tax-shelter investments, but its reach went beyond tax shelters to cover all real estate investors and persons who invest in businesses as "silent partners" or who are not involved full time in the business. The passive activity law prevents an investor from deducting what the law defines as a passive loss from salary, self-employment income, interest, dividends, or retirement income. Such losses are deductible only from income from other passive activities. Losses disallowed by the passive activity rules are suspended and carried forward to later taxable years and become deductible only when passive income is realized or substantially all of the activity is sold.

Casualty and theft losses are not passive losses unless they are of the type usually occurring in a business, such as shoplifting theft losses.

On your tax return, passive income items and allowable deductible items are reported as regular income and deductions. For example, rental income and allowable deductions are reported on Schedule E. However, before you make these entries, you may have to prepare Form 8582, which identifies your passive income and losses and helps you to determine whether passive loss items are deductible.

At-risk rules generally limit losses for an activity to your cash investment and loans for which you are personally liable, as well as certain nonrecourse financing for real estate investments. *See 10.17*.

10.1 Rental Activities

Rental income and losses are automatically treated as passive unless earned or incurred by a real estate professional *(10.3)* or the rentals are considered by law to be business activity as discussed below. Even where rental income or loss is earned by a professional or is considered to be business income, the passive loss restrictions may still apply if the material participation activity rules at *10.6* are not met.

If you are not a real estate professional and have real estate rental losses, you may be able to deduct without restriction a loss of up to $25,000 under the rules at *10.2*.

The passive activity rules apply to rental income and losses from rentals of tangible property (real estate or personal property) used by customers or held for use by customers. Such activities include rentals of apartments and commercial office space (whether long- or short-term); long-term rentals of office equipment, automobiles, and/or a vessel under a bareboat charter or a plane under a dry lease (no pilot or captain and no fuel); and net-leased property. A property is under a net lease if the deductions (other than rents and reimbursed amounts) are less than 15% of rental income or where the lessor is guaranteed a specific return or is guaranteed against loss of income.

Rentals treated as business activity. Although rental activities are generally treated as "passive," the following six activities are excluded from the category of rental activity and thus the $25,000 rental real estate loss allowance *(10.2)* is not available. However, income or loss from these activities may still be treated as passive income or loss if you fail to meet one of the business material participation tests at *10.6*.

1. **Incidental rental of investment property, property used in a business, or property rented to an employee for the convenience of an employer.** The rental of investment property is treated as a business activity if the principal purpose for holding the property during the tax year is to realize gain from its appreciation, and the gross rental income from the property for the tax year is less than 2% of the lower of the unadjusted basis of the property and fair market value of the property. The rental of business property is treated as incidental if the property was (1) predominantly used in a business during the tax year or during at least two of the five tax years that immediately precede the tax year and (2) gross rental income from the property for the tax year is less than 2% of the lesser of the unadjusted basis of the property and the fair market value of the property.

EXAMPLE

Kyle Gail owns unimproved land with a fair market value of $400,000 and an unadjusted basis of $300,000. He holds it for the principal purpose of realizing gain from its appreciation. To help reduce the cost of holding the land, he leases it to a rancher for grazing purposes at an annual rental of $3,500. The gross rental income of $3,500 is less than 2% of the lower of the fair market value and the unadjusted basis of the land. The rental of the land is not a rental activity.

2. **The average period of customer use of the property is seven days or less.** You figure the average period of customer use for the year by dividing the aggregate number of days in all rental periods that end during the tax year by the number of rentals. Each period during which a customer has a continuous or recurring right to use the property is treated as a separate rental.

This exception covers short-term rentals of vacation units, autos, video cassettes, tuxedos, and hotel and motel rooms.

EXAMPLE

The Toups purchased a cottage in Callaway Gardens, a vacation resort south of Atlanta, Georgia. The unit was rented for short-term periods of seven days or less during the year to resort guests. The resort's operator was the sole managing and rental agent. Over a three-year period, they deducted net losses of $46,848. Under the seven-days-or-less rule, the activity was not a rental activity, but the IRS disallowed the losses as passive activity losses. The Toups argued that they were not passive investors but material participants in the operation. They claimed they spent more than 300 hours each year preparing an annual budget and cash flow analysis and meeting with other owners to set rental fees and inspect the grounds.

 Planning Reminder

Vacation Home Rentals

If you rent out a vacation unit for an average rental period of seven days or less at a loss, the loss is treated as a business loss deductible from nonpassive income if you meet the material participation tests at *10.6*. If you do not materially participate, the loss is treated as a passive loss, deductible only from passive income. The loss does not qualify for the up-to-$25,000 rental loss allowance discussed in *10.2* because the property is not treated as rental property.

The Tax Court sided with the IRS. The losses were passive because the Toups did not materially participate in the resort operation. They had nothing to do with running the resort on a day-to-day basis. Their activity was merely that of investors.

3. **The average period of customer use of the property is more than seven days but is 30 days or less, and you provide significant personal services.** Personal services include only services performed by individuals and do not include (a) services necessary to permit the lawful use of the property; (b) construction or repair services that extend the useful life of the property for a period substantially longer than the average period of customer use; and (c) services that are provided with long-term rentals of high-grade commercial or residential real property such as cleaning and maintenance of common areas, routine repairs, trash collection, elevator service, and security guards.

   Note: For purposes of Exceptions 2 and 3, if more than one class of property is rented as part of the same activity, average period of customer use is figured separately for each class. The average period of customer use (as explained in Exception 2) is multiplied by the ratio of gross rental income from that class to the total rental income from the activity; *see* the Form 8582 instructions.

4. **Regardless of the average period of customer use, extraordinary personal services are provided so that rental is incidental.** This applies to institutions providing hospital patients room and board.

5. **Providing property to a partnership or S corporation that is not engaged in rentals.** If you own an interest in a partnership or S corporation and you contributed property to it as an owner, the contributed property is not considered a rental activity. For example, if as a partner you contribute property to a partnership, your distributive share of partnership income will not be considered as income from a rental activity. However, this exception will not apply if the partnership is engaged in a rental activity.

6. **The property is generally allowed for the non-exclusive use of customers during fixed business hours, such as operating a golf course.** The customers are treated as licensees, not lessees.

Grouping rental and nonrental business activities. Where you conduct rental as well as nonrental business activities, you may not group a rental activity with a nonrental activity, unless they form an appropriate economic unit and one of the activities is considered insubstantial in relation to the other. No guidelines are provided for determining what is "substantial" or "insubstantial."

Under an exception, a rental of property to a business may be grouped together with the business, although one activity is not insubstantial to the other, provided each business owner has the same proportionate ownership in the rental activity and the activities are an appropriate economic unit.

Real property rentals and personal property rentals. An activity involving the rental of realty and one involving the rental of personal property may not be treated as a single activity, unless the personal property is provided in connection with the real property or the realty is provided in connection with the personal property.

10.2 Rental Real Estate Loss Allowance of up to $25,000

If you are not a real estate professional *(10.3)* but you actively participate by performing some management role in a real estate rental venture, you may deduct up to $25,000 of a real estate rental loss against your regular, nonpassive income such as wages. The allowance is phased out if your modified adjusted gross income (MAGI) is between $100,000 and $150,000. You generally take the allowance into account on Schedule E but Form 8582 is sometimes required; *see 10.12*.

The allowance applies only to real estate rentals not excluded from the rental category by the rules at *10.1*. For example, short-term vacation home rentals averaging seven days or less do not qualify for the allowance. The allowance also does not apply to any rentals of equipment or other personal property.

A trust may not qualify for the $25,000 allowance. Thus, you may not circumvent the $25,000 ceiling or multiply the number of $25,000 allowances by transferring rental real properties to one or more trusts. However, an estate may qualify for the allowance if the decedent actively participated in the operation. The estate is treated as an active participant for two years following the death of the owner.

Married filing separately. If you file separately and at any time during the taxable year live with your spouse, you may not claim the allowance. If you are married but live apart from your spouse for the entire year and file a separate return, the $25,000 allowance and the adjusted gross income phase-out range are reduced by 50%. Thus, the maximum allowance on your separate return is $12,500 and this amount is phased out by 50% of MAGI over $50,000. Therefore, if your MAGI exceeds $75,000, no allowance is allowed.

Planning Reminder

Rental of Personal Residence

Renting a personal residence is not treated as a passive rental activity if you personally use the home for more than the greater of (1) 14 days and (2) 10% of the days the home is rented for a fair market rental amount. On Schedule E, you may claim a full deduction for the rental portion of real estate taxes and mortgage interest, assuming the home is a principal residence or qualifying second home under the mortgage interest rules *(15.1)*.

See 9.9 for limitations on deductions of other rental expenses.

Active participation test must be met. To qualify for the allowance, you must meet an *active participation test.* Having an agent manage your property does not prevent you from meeting the test, but you must show that you or your spouse participates in management decisions, such as selecting tenants, setting rental terms, and reviewing expenses. The IRS may not recognize your activity as meeting the test if you merely ratify your manager's decisions. You (together with your spouse) must also have at least a 10% interest in the property. Limited partners are not considered active participants and do not qualify for the allowance.

If a decedent actively participated in property held by an estate, the estate is deemed to actively participate for the two years following the death of the taxpayer.

EXAMPLES

1. You live in New York and own a condominium in Florida that you rent through an agent. You set the rental terms and give final approval to any rental arrangement. You also have final approval over any repairs ordered by the agent. You are an active participant and may claim the $25,000 rental allowance.

2. A married couple who owned a time-share interest in an ocean-front condominium rented the condo during their allotted period to vacationers. They claimed a rental loss that the IRS held did not qualify for the up-to-$25,000 allowance. Since the average rental period for their unit was seven days or less, the rentals were excluded from the category of rental activity; *see 10.1.*

Figuring the $25,000 allowance. First match income and loss from all of your rental real estate activities in which you actively participate. A net loss from these activities is then applied to net passive income (if any) from other activities to determine the $25,000 allowance. Gains from pre-1987 installment sales are passive income if the sold property was from an activity that would have been considered passive had the passive activity rules been in effect before 1987. If you rent out a personal residence, rental income or loss may be exempt from the passive activity rules; *see* the Planning Reminder on page 219. The allowance may not be used against carryover losses from prior taxable years when you were not an active participant.

EXAMPLE

David Chung has a $90,000 salary, $15,000 income from a limited partnership, and a $26,000 loss from rental real estate in which he actively participated. The $26,000 loss is first reduced by the $15,000 of passive income. The remaining balance of the $11,000 rental loss is deducted from the salary income.

Phaseout of the $25,000 allowance. For purposes of the allowance phaseout, *modified adjusted gross income (MAGI)* is adjusted gross income shown on your return, but you should disregard:

- Any passive activity income or loss.
- Any loss allowed under *10.3* for real estate professionals.
- Taxable Social Security and railroad retirement payments (Chapter 34). For example, if your adjusted gross income on Form 1040 is $90,000, and that includes $5,000 of taxable Social Security benefits, your modified adjusted gross income is $85,000.
- Deductible IRA contributions (Chapter 8).
- The deduction on Form 1040 for one-half of self-employment tax liability (Chapter 45).
- Deductible student loan interest (Chapter 38).
- Overall loss from a publicly traded partnership (*see* instructions to Form 8582).
- Excluded interest on U.S. Savings Bonds used for paying tuition in the year the bonds are redeemed. If you are allowed to exclude the interest from income for regular tax purposes (Chapter 33), the interest must still be included for purposes of the allowance phaseout.
- Employer-provided adoption assistance that is a tax-free fringe benefit (Chapter 3). The assistance must be included in MAGI for purposes of applying the allowance phase-out rule.

A rental loss that is carried over because it exceeds the allowance may be deductible in a later year if you continue to meet the active participation rule.

 Filing Tip

Rental Allowance Based on Income

The rental loss allowance is phased out when your modified adjusted gross income is over $100,000. For every dollar of income over $100,000, the loss allowance is reduced by 50 cents. When your modified adjusted gross income reaches $150,000, the allowance is completely phased out. An explanation of modified adjusted gross income and an example of how the phaseout works is under the heading "Phaseout of the $25,000 allowance" on this page.

If modified AGI is–	Loss allowance is–
Up to $100,000	$25,000
110,000	20,000
120,000	15,000
130,000	10,000
140,000	5,000
150,000 or more	0

EXAMPLES

1. In 1999, Liz Blake had $120,000 in salary, $5,000 of partnership income from a limited partnership, and a $31,000 loss from a rental building in which she actively participates. She may deduct only $15,000 of the rental loss. The remaining $11,000 must be carried over to 2000. Her deduction and carryover are computed as follows:

Modified adjusted gross income	$120,000
Less: amount not subject to phaseout	$100,000
Amount subject to phaseout	$ 20,000
Phase-out percentage	50%
Portion of allowance phased out	$ 10,000
Maximum rental allowance offset	$ 25,000
Less: Amount phased out	$ 10,000
Deductible rental loss allowance offset in 1999	$ 15,000
Passive loss from rental real estate	$ 31,000
Less: Passive income from partnership	$ 5,000
Passive activity loss	$ 26,000
Less: Deductible rental loss allowance in 1999	$ 15,000
Carryover loss to 2000	$ 11,000

2. In 2000, Liz's modified adjusted gross income is below the phase-out range and she continues to actively participate in the rental building, which incurred a loss of $5,000. Under the allowance, she may deduct a rental loss of $16,000 (the current loss plus the carryover loss).

Planning Reminder

Proving Management Activities
To take advantage of the $25,000 loan allowance, make sure you have proof of active management, such as approving leases and repairs.

Real estate allowance for tax credits. On Form 8582-CR, a deduction equivalent of up to $25,000 may allow a credit that otherwise would be disallowed. You must meet the active participation test in the year the credit arose. The $25,000 allowance is generally subject to the regular MAGI phase-out rule.

To claim low-income housing and rehabilitation credits, you need not meet the active participation test. Furthermore, for rehabilitation credits and credits for low-income housing property placed in service before 1990, the phaseout for the $25,000 allowance starts at MAGI of $200,000 ($100,000 if married filing separately and living apart the entire year); thus, the deduction equivalent is completely disallowed when MAGI reaches $250,000. The phaseout is figured on Form 8582-CR. There is no MAGI phaseout for low-income housing property placed in service after 1989, unless you have a pass-through interest in a partnership or S corporation that you acquired before 1990.

The *deduction equivalent* of a credit is the amount which, if allowed as a deduction, would reduce your tax by an amount equal to the credit. For example, a tax credit of $1,000 for a taxpayer in the 28% bracket equals a deduction of $3,571 and would come within the $25,000 allowance provided you actively participated. In the 28% bracket, the equivalent of a $25,000 deduction is a tax credit of $7,000 ($25,000 × 28%). Thus, if you have a rehabilitation credit of $8,000 and you are in the 28% bracket, the $25,000 allowance may allow you to claim $7,000 of the credit, while $1,000 of the credit would be carried forward to the following year.

If in one year you have both losses and tax credits, the $25,000 allowance applies first to the losses, then to tax credits from rental real estate with active participation, then to tax credits for rehabilitation or low-income housing placed in service before 1990, and finally to tax credits for low-income housing placed in service after 1989.

The allowance and net operating losses. If losses are allowed by the $25,000 allowance but your nonpassive income and other income are less than the loss, the balance of the loss may be treated as a net operating loss and may be carried back and forward; *see 40.18* for further details.

10.3 Real Estate Professionals

You may be able to treat rental real estate income and loss as nonpassive income and loss by meeting the following two tests for real estate professionals:

Test 1. Your personal services in real estate businesses meet the 50% and 750 hours tests explained below.

Test 2. You materially participate in the rental real estate activity. Here, you consider only services in the rental activity. You may not combine hours of participation in nonrental activities with rental real estate activities to meet this test. To meet the material participation requirement, you may make an election to aggregate all of your rental real estate activities. The material participation tests applied to real estate businesses and real estate rental activities are the same as applied to non–real estate businesses as explained at *10.6.*

Qualifying as a real estate professional (Test 1). You must meet the following two activity tests:

1. More than 50% of your personal services in all of your businesses must be performed in real property businesses in which you materially participate *(10.6)*. For this purpose, a real property business means any real property development, redevelopment, construction, reconstruction, acquisition, conversion, rental operation, management, leasing, or brokerage trade or business. Real estate financing is not included; and

2. More than 750 hours of your services are in real property businesses in which you materially participate *(10.6)*.

For a married couple filing jointly, both the "50% of services test" and the "750 hours test" must be met by one of the spouses individually, without regard to the other spouse's services, although the other spouse's participation counts in determining whether you materially participate in the real property businesses under Test 2.

Personal services performed as an employee are not treated as performed in a real estate business unless you are considered a "more than 5% owner" in the employer. That is, you must own more than 5% of the outstanding stock or more than 5% of total combined voting powers of all stock issued by the corporation. In a noncorporate employer such as a partnership, you must own more than a 5% capital or profit interest.

A closely held C corporation qualifies under the real estate professional rules if in a taxable year more than 50% of the gross receipts of the corporation are from a real property business in which the corporation materially participates under the rules at *10.15*.

Rental real estate activity material participation (Test 2). For purposes of applying the material participation tests *(10.6)*, each interest in rental real estate property is generally treated as a separate activity. However, you may elect to treat all of your interests as one rental activity as discussed below. If, under the rules of *10.1*, you group a rental real estate activity with a business activity, that rental activity is not treated as rental real estate for purposes of the real estate professional rules.

Attorneys who specialize in real estate practice while participating in a rental business may not treat the legal practice as material participation for purposes of qualifying as real estate professionals.

Election to aggregate rental real estate activities. If in a prior year rental real estate activities were treated separately, you may elect to aggregate activities for any year you qualify as a real estate professional by attaching a statement to your original tax return for that year. The statement must contain a declaration that you are a qualifying real estate professional and are treating all of your rental real estate activities as a single activity under Internal Revenue Code Section 469(c)(7)(A). The election is binding for all future years in which you qualify as a real estate professional, even if there are intervening years in which you do not qualify. In the nonqualifying years, the election has no effect. You may not revoke the election in a later year unless there has been a material change in circumstances that you explain in a statement attached to your original return for the year of revocation. That the election no longer gives you a tax advantage is not a basis for a revocation.

If the election to aggregate is made, prior-year suspended losses from any of the aggregated rental real estate activities may be used to offset net income in the current year from the aggregated activity, regardless of which of the rental activities produced the income.

Rental loss allowance may apply to nonqualifying rental activity. A real estate professional may also claim the $25,000 rental loss allowance. For example, you are a real estate professional and meet the material participation test for one rental real estate activity but not for another and do not elect to aggregate. Losses from the nonqualifying activity qualify for the rental allowance. Furthermore, suspended prior year losses from the qualifying activity may also be deductible under the rental loss allowance, as illustrated in the following Example.

 Planning Reminder

Tax Break for Real Estate Professionals

Proving professional status allows you to avoid passive loss limitations. You may improve your ability to meet the material participation tests in *10.6* by aggregating your rental real estate activities. However, you may not want to aggregate activities if you have passive losses from non–real estate activities and have rental income from an operation that, if treated as passive income, could be offset by the losses.

Also be aware that if you elect to group all of your rental real estate activities as one activity and later sell one of the rental properties, you will probably be unable to deduct suspended losses from that property because of the rule that requires "substantially all" of your interest in an activity (here, the combined activity) to be disposed of in order to deduct suspended losses; *see 10.13*.

EXAMPLE

Jane Morton owns a rental building in Manhattan and a rental building in Newark. In 1999, she qualifies as a real estate professional. She does not elect to treat the two buildings as one activity. She materially participates in the operations of the Manhattan building, which has $100,000 of disallowed passive losses from prior years and a $20,000 loss for 1999. She does not materially participate in the operation of the Newark building, which has $40,000 of rental income for 1999. Jane also has $50,000 of income from other nonpassive sources.

The $20,000 loss from the Manhattan building is treated as nonpassive and offsets $20,000 of the $50,000 nonpassive income from other sources.

Jane can also use $40,000 of the $100,000 prior year suspended losses from the Manhattan building to offset the $40,000 of passive income from the Newark building in 1999. Of the $60,000 remaining suspended loss, $25,000 may be deducted under the rental loss allowance.

The rental loss allowance is deducted from the $30,000 of remaining nonpassive income, leaving Jane with $5,000 of nonpassive income for 1999. The balance of suspended losses of $35,000 ($60,000 – $25,000 rental allowance) may be used in 2000 to offset income from the Newark building or passive income from other sources.

Interests in S corporations and partnerships. Your interest in rental real estate held by a partnership or an S corporation is treated as a single interest in rental real estate if the entity grouped its rental real estate as one rental activity. If not, each rental real estate activity of the entity is treated as a separate interest in rental real estate. However, you may elect to treat all interests in rental real estate, including the rental real estate interests held by an S corporation or partnership, as a single rental real estate activity.

If you hold a 50% or greater interest in the capital, income, gain, loss, deduction, or credit in a partnership or S corporation for the taxable year, each interest in rental real estate held by the entity is treated as a separate interest in rental real estate, regardless of the entity's grouping of activities. However, you may elect to treat all interests in rental real estate, including your share of the rental real estate interests held by the entities, as a single rental real estate activity.

Limited partners. Generally, a person who has a limited partnership interest in rental real estate must establish material participation by participating for more than 500 hours during the year or meeting Test 5 or Test 6 at *10.6*. This material participation rule also generally applies if an election is made to aggregate limited partnership interests in rental real estate with other rental real estate interests. However, these more stringent rules may be avoided if less than 10% of the gross rental income for the taxable year from all rental real estate activities is attributed to limited partnership interests. In such a case, you may make the election to aggregate all rental real estate activities and determine material participation under any of the seven tests at *10.6*.

10.4 Participation May Avoid Passive Loss Restrictions

To avoid passive activity treatment of income and loss from a business investment, you must show material participation in that activity. The word "activity" does not necessarily relate to one specific business. If you invest in several businesses, you may be able to treat all or some of those activities as one activity or treat each separately.

Determining aggregate or separate treatment for your activities is discussed at *10.5* and material participation tests are discussed at *10.6*.

For a rental activity, material participation tests apply only if you are trying to qualify for the passive activity exception for real estate professionals at *10.3*. For other rental real estate operators or investors, an "active" participation test that requires only certain management duties may allow you to deduct rental losses of up to $25,000; see *10.2*.

10.5 Classifying Business Activities as One or Several

If you are in more than one activity, determining aggregate or separate treatment is important for:

Deducting suspended losses when you dispose of an activity. If the activity is considered separate from the others, you may deduct a suspended loss incurred from that activity when you dispose of it. If it is not separate from the others, the suspended loss is deductible only if you dispose of substantially all of your investment; *see 10.13*.

Applying the material participation rules of *10.6*. If activities are separate and apart from each other, the material participation tests are applied to each activity separately. If the activities are aggregated as one activity, material participation in one activity applies to all.

Determining if you meet the 10% interest requirement for active participation under the rules discussed at *10.2*.

Earmarking a business activity. You may use any reasonable method under the facts and circumstances of your situation to determine if several business activities should be grouped together or treated separately. To be grouped together, the IRS says that the activities should be "an appropriate economic unit" for measuring gain or loss. For making this determination, the IRS

Caution

Consistent treatment required
Once you treat activities separately or group them together as a single activity, the IRS generally requires you to continue the same treatment in later taxable years. You can regroup activities only if the original treatment was "clearly inappropriate" or has become clearly inappropriate because of a material change in circumstances.

sets these general guidelines: (1) similarities and differences in types of business; (2) the extent of common control; (3) geographic location; (4) the extent of common ownership; and (5) interdependencies among the activities. Interdependency is measured by the extent to which several business activities buy or sell among themselves, use the same products or services, have the same customers and employees, or use a single set of books and records.

The IRS will not require that all five factors be present for grouping for multiple activities.

Rental activities. Rental activities may not be grouped with business activities unless one of the exceptions discussed at *10.1* applies.

EXAMPLE

Lance Jones has a significant interest in a bakery and a movie theater at a shopping mall in Baltimore and in a bakery and a movie theater in Philadelphia. The IRS does not explain what constitutes a significant interest. In grouping his activities into appropriate economic units based on the relevant facts and circumstances, Jones could: (1) group the theaters and bakeries into a single activity; (2) place the two theaters into one group and the bakeries into a second group; (3) put his Baltimore businesses into one group and his Philadelphia businesses in another group; or (4) treat the two bakeries and two movie theaters as four separate activities.

Once he chooses a grouping, he must consistently use that grouping for all future years unless a material change makes the grouping inappropriate. His decision is also subject to IRS review and, if questioned, he must show the factual basis for his grouping.

IRS may regroup activities. The IRS may regroup your activities if your grouping does not reflect one or more appropriate economic units and a primary purpose of the grouping is to circumvent the passive loss rules.

EXAMPLE

Five doctors operate separate medical practices and also invest in tax shelters that generate passive losses. They form a partnership to operate X-ray equipment. In exchange for the equipment contributed to the partnership, each doctor receives limited partnership interests. The partnership is managed by a general partner selected by the doctors. Partnership services are provided to the doctors in proportion to their interests in the partnership and service fees are set at a level to offset the income generated by the partnership against individual passive losses. Under these facts, the IRS will not allow the medical practices and the partnership to be treated as separate activities as this would circumvent the passive loss limitations by generating passive income from the partnership to offset the tax-shelter losses. The IRS will require each doctor to treat his or her medical practice and interests in the partnership as a single activity.

Partnerships and S corporations. A partnership or S corporation must group its activities under the facts and circumstances test. Once a partnership or S corporation determines its activities, the partners or shareholders are bound by that decision and may not regroup them. The partners and shareholders then apply the facts and circumstances test to combine the partnership or S corporation activities with, or separate them from, their other activities.

Special rule for certain limited partners and limited entrepreneurs. A limited entrepreneur is a person with an ownership interest who does not actively participate in management. A limited entrepreneur or limited partner in films, videotapes, farming, oil and gas, or the renting of depreciable property generally may combine each such activity only with another of such activities in the same type of business, and only if he or she is a limited entrepreneur or partner in both. Grouping of such activities with other activities in the same type of business in which he or she is not a limited partner or entrepreneur is allowed if the grouping is appropriate under the general facts and circumstances test.

Planning Reminder

Proof of Material Participation

Material participation must be determined on an annual basis. Show proof of your participation by keeping an appointment book, calendar, or log of the days and time spent in the operation. If you want to treat contacts by phone as material activity, keep a log of phone calls showing the time and purpose of the calls.

Caution

Overcoming Investor Status

The IRS will not recognize time spent as an investor as "participation" unless you can show you are involved in daily operations or management of the activity. According to the IRS, this requires you to be at the business site on a regular basis. Even if you do appear daily, the IRS may ignore such evidence if there is an on-site manager or you have full-time business obligations at another site. Activity of an investor includes the studying and reviewing of financial reports for your own use that are considered unrelated to management decisions. If you invest in a business that is out of state or a distance from your home, you may also find it difficult to prove material participation.

10.6 Material Participation Tests for Business

The IRS has seven tests for determining material participation in a business. Some tests require only a minimum amount of work, such as 500 hours a year, and others only 100 hours. You need to meet only one of the seven tests to qualify as a material participant. If you do, then the income and loss from that business is treated as *nonpassive*.

The tests apply whether you do business as a sole proprietor or in an S corporation or partnership. Losses and credits passed through S corporations and partnerships are subject to passive activity rules.

If you are a limited partner, you are by law not a material participant unless you satisfy certain conditions discussed at *10.11*.

Your tax position towards the IRS participation rules will depend on whether the particular activity produces income or loss. If you have passive activity losses from other activities, you may prefer to have a profitable business activity treated as a passive activity in order to offset the income by the losses from passive activities. On the other hand, if the business activity operates at a loss and you do not have passive income from other sources, you may want to meet the material participation test for that business activity in order to claim current loss deductions. IRS strategy in reviewing your activities would be the opposite. If your return were under audit, an agent would attempt to prevent you from treating income from a business activity as passive. For example, the IRS, by applying Tests 5 and 6, can prevent a retired person from treating post-retirement income from a prior business or profession as passive income to offset passive losses from another activity. If you realize a loss in one passive activity, Test 4 may prevent you from generating passive income by merely reducing your participation in another activity.

Material participation results in nonpassive treatment. There are two key terms: material participation and significant participation. If you materially participate by meeting one of the seven IRS tests, your activity is not a passive activity. For example, under Test 1, work for more than 500 hours in an activity is considered material participation. Under Test 4, significant participation is work for more than 100 hours but less than 500 hours at an activity in which you do not otherwise materially participate. The IRS applies a significant participation rule to convert passive activity income into nonpassive income and to convert several significant participation activities into material participation if the total participation in those activities exceeds 500 hours; *see* Test 4.

Work by you or your spouse that counts as participation. Any work you do in a business in which you have an ownership interest is treated as "participation." If you are married, work by your spouse in the activity during the tax year is treated, for purposes of the following tests, as participation by you. This is true even if your spouse does not own an interest in the business or if you file separately. However, the following type of work is not treated as participation:

1. Work that is not of a type customarily done by an owner of an activity, if one of the principal reasons for the performance of the work is to avoid the passive loss rules (*see* the Example below).
2. An investor's review of financial statements or analysis that is unrelated to day-to-day management or operation of the activity.

EXAMPLE

An attorney owns an interest in a professional football team for which he performs no services. He anticipates a net loss from the football activity and to qualify as a material participant, he hires his wife to work 15 hours a week as an office receptionist for the team. Although a spouse's participation in an activity generally qualifies as participation by both spouses, the receptionist work here does not qualify as participation because (1) it is not the type of work customarily done by an owner of a football team and (2) the attorney hired his spouse to avoid disallowance of a passive loss.

IRS Tests for Material Participation

If you meet one of the following tests for the year in question, you are considered to have materially participated in that activity, and therefore the activity is considered *nonpassive* for that year. Tests 5 and 6 prevent retired individuals from treating post-retirement income as passive income.

Test 1. You participate in the activity for more than 500 hours during the tax year.

Test 2. Your participation in the activity for the tax year constitutes substantially all of the participation in the activity of all individuals including non-owners for the year.

Test 3. You participate in the activity for more than 100 hours during the tax year, and your participation is at least as great as that of any other person including non-owners for that year.

EXAMPLE

Joan Brown and Pat Collins are partners in a moving van business that they conduct entirely on weekends. They both work for eight hours each weekend. Although neither partner participates for more than 500 hours (Test 1), they are both treated as material participants under Test 3 because they each participate for more than 100 hours and no one else participates more.

Test 4. You are active in several enterprises but each activity does not in itself qualify as material participation. However, if you spend more than 100 hours in each activity and the total hours of these more-than-100-hours activities exceeds 500, you are treated as a material participant in each of these activities. This test is described as the *significant participation test.*

EXAMPLES

1. Mike Smith is a full-time accountant with ownership interests in a restaurant and shoe store. He works 150 hours in the shoe store and 360 hours in the restaurant. Under the significant participation test (Test 4), Smith is considered a material participant in both activities, as the total hours of both exceed 500.
2. Carl Young invests in five businesses. In activity (a) he works 110 hours; in activity (b), 100 hours; in activity (c), 125 hours; in activity (d), 120 hours; and in activity (e), 140 hours. He does not qualify under the significant participation test (Test 4). Although his total hours in the five activities exceed 500, activity (b) is ignored in the total count because the hours did not exceed 100. The total of the four other activities is 495.
3. Assume that Young worked one hour more for activity (b). It and all of the other activities would be considered as meeting the significant material participation test. The total hours are 596. Assuming that activity (a) totaled 125 hours and activity (b) remained at 100 hours or less, he would meet the test for all of the activities except for activity (b), which did not exceed 100 hours. The total of the four qualified activities is 510 hours.

Test 5. You materially participated in the activity for any five tax years during the 10 tax years preceding the tax year in question. The five tax years do not have to be consecutive. Use only Test 1 for determining material participation in years before 1987. Thus, if you are retired but meet the five-out-of-10-year participation test, you are currently considered a material participant, with the result that net income is treated as nonpassive, rather than passive. If you retired from a personal service profession, an even stricter rule applies; *see* Test 6.

Test 6. In a personal service activity, you materially participated for any three tax years preceding the tax year in question. The three years do not have to be consecutive. Use only Test 1 for determining material participation in years before 1987. Examples of personal services within this test are the professions of health, law, engineering, architecture, accounting, actuarial science, the performing arts, consulting, or any other trade or business in which capital is not a material income-producing factor.

Test 7. Under the facts and circumstances test, you participate in the activity on a regular, continuous, and substantial basis. *According to the IRS, you do not come within this test if you participate less than 100 hours in the activity.*

For limited partner rules, *see 10.11.* For participation rules for personal service and closely held corporations, *see 10.15.*

 Caution

Retired Farmers
Retired or disabled farmers are treated as materially participating in a farming activity if they materially participated for five of the eight years preceding their retirement or disability. A surviving spouse is also treated as materially participating in a farming activity if the real property used in the activity meets the estate tax rules for special valuation of farm property passed from a qualified decedent and the surviving spouse actively manages the farm.

10.7 Tax Credits of Passive Activities Limited

You may generally not claim a tax credit from a passive activity unless you report and pay taxes on income from a passive activity. Furthermore, the tax allocated to that income must be at least as much as the credit. If the tax credit exceeds your tax liability on income allocable to passive activities, the excess credit is not allowed. Use Form 8582-CR to figure the allowable credit. Suspended credits are not allowed when property is disposed of. The credits may be used only when passive income is earned.

Ben Wall has a $1,000 credit from a passive activity. He does not report income from any passive activity. He may not claim the credit because no part of his tax is attributed to passive activity income. The credit is suspended until he has income from a passive activity and he incurs tax on that income. All or part of the credit may then be claimed to offset the tax. If he disposed of his interest before using a suspended credit, the credit may no longer be claimed but the election to reduce basis, discussed below, could be made.

Credits for real estate activities. As discussed at *10.2*, more favorable tax credit rules apply to real estate activities.

Basis adjustment for suspended credits. If the basis of property was reduced by tax credits, you may elect on Form 8582-CR to add back a suspended credit to the basis when your entire interest in an activity is disposed of. If the property is disposed of in a transaction that is not treated as a fully taxable disposition as discussed at *10.13*, then no basis adjustment is allowed.

Mark places in service rehabilitation credit property and claims an allowable credit of $50, which also reduces basis by $50. However, under the passive loss rule, he is prevented from claiming the credit. In a later year, he disposes of his entire interest in the activity, including the property whose basis was reduced. He may elect to increase basis of the property by the amount of the original basis adjustment.

10.8 Nonpassive Income and Losses

The purpose of the passive loss rules is to prevent you from deducting passive losses from nonpassive income. Passive losses are generally losses from business activities in which you do not materially participate or from rental activities that generate losses that are not deductible under the $25,000 allowance or do not qualify you as a real estate professional. In some cases, as explained in *10.9*, passive income may be treated as nonpassive income.

Where you do not materially participate in a business activity, passive income or loss is determined by matching income and expenses of that activity. Portfolio income earned by the activity or any pay that you earn is not included to determine passive income or loss.

Portfolio income is nonpassive income and broadly defined as income that is not derived in the ordinary course of business of the activity. Portfolio income includes interest, dividends, annuities, and royalties from property held for investment. However, interest income on loans and investments made in the business of lending money or received on business accounts receivable is generally not treated as portfolio income; *see 10.9* for special recharacterization rules. Similarly, royalties derived from a business of licensing property are not portfolio income to the person who created the property or performed substantial services or incurred substantial costs.

Portfolio income also includes gains from the sale of properties that produce portfolio income or are held for investment.

Expenses allocable to portfolio income, including interest expenses, do not enter into the computation of passive income or loss.

Sale of property used in activity. Gain realized on the sale of property used in the activity is treated as passive activity income if at the time of disposition the activity was passive; *see* the exception at *10.16*. Under this rule, if you transact an installment sale, the treatment of installment payments depends on your status at the time of the initial sale. If you were not a material participant, installment payments in a later year are treated as passive income, even if you become a material participant in the later year.

Installment payments from a pre-1987 installment sale are treated as passive income if the activity would have been considered passive had the passive activity rules been in effect before 1987.

Although gain on the sale of property is generally passive income if the activity is passive at the time of sale, there is an exception that could recharacterize the gain as nonpassive income if the property was formerly used in a nonpassive activity; *see 10.16* for details.

Compensation for personal services is not passive activity income. The term "compensation for personal services" includes only (1) earned income, including certain payments made by a partnership to a partner and representing compensation for the services of the partner; (2)

Filing Tip

Portfolio Income Accounting
You cannot deduct passive losses from portfolio income. The tax law broadly defines "portfolio income" to include nonbusiness types of income including interest, dividends, and profits on the sale of investment property.

amounts included in gross income involving the transfer of property in exchange for the performance of services; (3) amounts distributed under qualified plans; (4) amounts distributed under retirement, pension, and other arrangements for deferred compensation of services; and (5) Social Security benefits includible in gross income.

Passive activity gross income also does not include (1) income from patent, copyright, or literary, musical, or artistic compositions, if your personal efforts significantly contributed to the creation of the property; (2) income from a qualified low-income housing project; (3) income tax refunds; and (4) payments on a covenant not to compete.

Passive activity deductions. Deductible expenses that offset passive income of an activity must be related to the passive activity, such as real property taxes. The following are not considered passive activity deductions:

Casualty and theft losses if similar losses do not recur regularly in the activity.
Charitable deductions.
Miscellaneous itemized deductions subject to the 2% AGI floor.
State, local, and foreign income taxes.
Carryovers of net operating losses or capital losses.
Expenses clearly and directly allocable to portfolio income.
Loss on the sale of property producing portfolio income.
Loss on the sale of your entire interest in a passive activity to an unrelated party. The loss is allowed in full; *see 10.13.*

Interest deductions. Interest expenses attributable to passive activities are treated as passive activity deductions and are not subject to the investment interest limitations. For example, in 1999, if you have net passive loss of $100, $40 of which is of interest expense, the entire $100 is a passive loss. $40 of the loss is not subject to the investment interest limitation discussed in *15.10*. Similarly, income and loss from passive activities generally are not treated as investment income or loss in figuring the investment interest limitation.

If you rent out a vacation home that you personally use for more than the greater of 14 days and 10% of the fair market rental days *(9.7)*, you may treat the residence as a qualified second residence under the mortgage interest rules; *see 15.1*. Interest on such a qualifying second home is generally fully deductible, and the deductible interest *(15.1)* is not treated as a passive activity deduction. The rental portion of the interest is deducted on Schedule E of Form 1040 and the personal-use portion on Schedule A if itemized deductions are claimed; *see 9.9*.

10.9 Passive Income Converted Into Nonpassive Income

There is an advantage in treating income as passive income when you have passive losses that may offset the income. However, the law may prevent you from treating certain income as passive income. The conversion of passive income to nonpassive income is technically called "recharacterization." This may occur when you do not materially participate in the business activity, but are sufficiently active for the IRS to consider your participation as significant. Recharacterization may also occur when you rent nondepreciable property or sell development rental property.

Significant participation. The IRS compares income and losses from all of your activities in which you work more than 100 hours but less than 500 and that are not considered material participation under the law. If you show a net aggregate gain, part of your gain is treated as nonpassive income according to the computation illustrated in the following Example.

 Caution

"Recharacterization" of Passive Income

As discussed at *10.16*, gain on the sale of property used in a passive activity may be recharacterized as nonpassive income if the property was formerly used in a nonpassive activity.

EXAMPLE

Carol Warren invests in three business activities—A, B, and C. She does not materially participate in any of the activities during 1999 but participates in Activity A for 105 hours, in Activity B for 160 hours, and in Activity C for 125 hours. Her net passive income or loss from the three activities is:

	A	B	C	Total
Passive activity gross income	$600	$700	$900	$2,200
Passive activity deductions	(200)	(1,000)	(300)	(1,500)
Net passive activity income	$400	($ 300)	$600	$700

Carol's passive activity gross income from significant participation passive activities of $2,200 exceeds passive activity deductions of $1,500. A ratable portion of her gross income from significant participation activities with net passive income for the tax year (Activities A and C) is treated as gross income that is not from a passive activity. The ratable portion is figured by dividing:

1. The excess of her passive activity gross income from significant participation over passive activity deductions from such activities (here $700) by
2. The net passive income of only the significant participation passive activities having net passive income (here $1,000). The ratable portion is 70%.

Thus, $280 of gross income from Activity A ($400 × 70%) and $420 of gross income from Activity C ($600 × 70%) is treated as nonpassive gross income. This adjustment prevents $700 from being offset by passive losses from another activity.

Net interest income from passive equity-financed lending. Gross income from "equity-financed lending activity" is treated as nonpassive income to the extent of the lesser of the equity-financed interest income and net passive income. An activity is an "equity-financed lending activity" for a tax year if (1) the activity involves a trade or business of lending money and (2) the average outstanding balance of the liabilities incurred in the activity for the tax year does not exceed 80% of the average outstanding balance of the interest-bearing assets held in the activity.

Incidental rental of property by development activity. Where gains on the sale of rental property are attributable to recent development, passive income treatment may be lost if the sale comes within the following tests: (1) the rental started less than 12 months before the date of disposition; and (2) you materially participated or significantly participated in the performance of services enhancing the value of the property. The 12-month period starts at the completion of the development services that increased the property's value.

Rental of property with an insubstantial depreciable basis. This rule prevents you from generating passive rental income with vacant land or land on which a unit is constructed that has a value substantially less than the land. If less than 30% of the basis of rental property is depreciable, and you have net passive income from rentals (taking into account carried-over passive losses from prior years), the net passive income is treated as nonpassive income. Basis here is generally adjusted basis without any adjustments.

EXAMPLES

1. A limited partnership buys vacant land for $300,000, constructs improvements on the land at a cost of $100,000, and leases the entire property. After the rental period, the partnership sells the property for $600,000, realizing a gain. The unadjusted basis of the depreciable improvements of $100,000 is only 25% of the basis of the property of $400,000. The rent and the gain allocated to the improvements are treated as nonpassive income.

2. Shirley offset a passive rental loss from an investment in a limited partnership, LP, which was a substantial owner of a general partnership, GP, against rental income from an investment in a joint venture, JV. JV had leased to GP land on which GP constructed a shopping center. The IRS held that the rental income from JV was nonpassive rental income within the 30% test and could not be offset by the passive rental loss. The Tax Court agreed and also rejected Shirley's attempt to aggregate her investment activities in JV and LP as one activity. The operations of each group, JV, LP, and GP, were separate and not owned by the same person. She was not the direct owner of any of the units. Further, the aggregation rule does not apply to property falling within the 30% test.

Property rented to nonpassive activity (self-rental property). You may not generate passive income by renting property to a business in which you materially participate.

Licensing of intangible property. Your share of royalty income in a partnership, S corporation, estate, or trust is treated as nonpassive income if you invested after the organization created the intangible property, performed substantial services, or incurred substantial costs in the development or marketing of it. *See* Publication 925 for further details.

10.10 Working Interests in Oil and Gas Wells

Working interests are generally not treated as passive activities. This is true whether you hold your interest directly or through an entity, provided your liability is not limited. As long as you have unlimited liability, you need not materially participate in the activity. A working interest is one burdened with the financial risk of developing and operating the property, such as a share in tort liability (for example, uninsured losses from a fire); some responsibility to share in additional costs; responsibility for authorizing expenses; receiving periodic reports about drilling, completion, and expected production; and the possession of voting rights and rights to continue operations if the present operator steps out.

Limited liability. If you hold a working interest through any of the following entities, the entity is considered to limit your liability and you are subject to the passive loss rules: (1) a limited partnership interest in a partnership in which you are not a general partner; (2) stock in a corporation; or (3) an interest in any entity other than a limited partnership or corporation that, under applicable state law, limits the liability of a holder of such interest for all obligations of the entity to a determinable fixed amount.

Working interests are considered on a well-by-well basis. Rights to overriding royalties or production payments, and contract rights to extract or share in oil and gas profits without liability for a share of production costs, are not working interests.

10.11 Partnership Rules

If you are a partner, your level of personal participation in partnership activity during the partnership year determines whether your share of income or loss is passive or nonpassive. Generally, limited partners are subject to passive activity treatment, but there are some exceptions. On Schedule K-1 of Form 1065, the partnership will identify each activity it conducts and specify the income, loss, deductions, and credits from each activity.

EXAMPLE

Don Bailey is a general partner of a fiscal year partnership that ends on March 31, 1999. During that fiscal year he was inactive. Since he did not materially participate, his share of partnership income or loss reported in 1999 is passive activity income or loss, even if he becomes active from April 1, 1999, to the end of 1999.

Not treated as passive income are payments for services and certain guaranteed payments made in liquidation of a retiring or deceased partner's interest unless attributed to unrealized receivables and goodwill at a time the partner was passive.

Gain or loss on the disposition of a partnership interest may be attributed to different trade, investment, or rental activities of the partnership. The allocation is made according to a complicated formula included in IRS regulations.

Payments to a retired partner. Gain or loss is treated as passive only to the extent that it would be treated as such at the start of the liquidation of the partner's interest.

Limited partners. A limited partner is generally not considered to be a material participant in a partnership activity, and, thus, treats income or loss as passive, except in these cases:

1. The limited partner participates for more than 500 hours during the tax year; *see* Test 1 in *10.6.*
2. The limited partner materially participated in the partnership during prior years under either Test 5 or Test 6 at *10.6.*
3. The limited partner is also a general partner at all times during the partnership tax year that ends with or within the partner's taxable year and any of the material participation tests *(10.6)* are met.

To determine material participation in rental real estate activities under the special rules for real estate professionals, Test 1 or Test 5 of *10.6* must generally be met, but *see* the exception at *10.3.*

A limited partner is not considered to be an "active participant" and thus does not qualify for the $25,000 rental loss allowance under *10.2.*

10.12 Form 8582

The purpose of Form 8582 is to assemble in one place items of income and expenses from passive activities in order to determine the effect of the passive loss rules on these items. After this determination, income and allowable deductions are reported as regular income and deductions in appro-

Planning Reminder

Limited Liability for Oil or Gas Well

A working interest in an oil or gas well is exempt from the passive activity restrictions if your liability is not limited. The following forms of loss protection are disregarded and, thus, are not treated as limiting your liability: protection against loss by an indemnification agreement; a stop-loss agreement; insurance; or any similar arrangement or combination of agreements.

Planning Reminder

Publicly Traded Partnerships (PTPs)

A PTP is a partnership whose interests are traded on established securities exchanges or are readily tradable in secondary markets. PTPs that are not treated as corporations for tax purposes are subject to special rules that allow losses to be used only to offset income from the same PTP. *See* the instructions to Form 8582.

priate schedules attached to your tax return. For example, net profits of a self-employed person who is not active in the business are reported on Schedule C, sales of capital assets of a passive activity are reported on Schedule D, your share of partnership income and allowable deductions is reported on Schedule E, and rental income and allowable deductions are reported on Schedule E.

Schedule D or Form 4797. Gains or losses from the sale of assets from a passive activity or from the sale of a partial interest which is less than "substantially all" of your entire interest in a passive activity are reported on Schedule D or on Form 4797 (sale of business property, *see* Chapter 44). The gain is also entered on Form 8582. Losses must first be entered on Form 8582 to see how much, if any, is allowable under the passive loss restrictions before an amount can be entered as a loss on Schedule D or Form 4797.

A disposition of an insubstantial part of your interest in the activity does not allow a deduction of suspended passive losses from prior years. When you dispose of your *entire* interest in a passive activity to a nonrelated party in a fully taxable transaction, your losses for the year plus prior year suspended losses from the activity are fully deductible. The same rule applies to a partial disposition only if you are disposing of *substantially all* of the activity and you have proof of the current year and prior year suspended losses allocable to the disposed-of portion. You net the gain or loss from the disposition with the net income or loss from current year operations and any prior year suspended passive losses. If the netting gives you an overall gain, you need to file Form 8582 only if you have other passive activities. If you have an overall loss after the netting, you do not file Form 8582.

Schedule E. If you have a net profit from rental property or other passive activity reported on Schedule E and you also have losses from other passive activities, the income reported on Schedule E is also entered on Form 8582. A net loss from rental activities generally must be entered on Form 8582 but Form 8582 is not needed if you qualify for the full $25,000 allowance *(10.2)* for rental real estate losses and meet these tests:

Your only passive activities are rental real estate activities and you have no suspended prior year passive losses from such activities;

You have no credits related to passive activities;

You actively participated in the rental real estate operations;

Your total losses from the rental real estate activities are $25,000 or less ($12,500 or less if married filing separately and you lived apart from your spouse all year);

Your modified adjusted gross income is $100,000 or less ($50,000 or less if married filing separately and you lived apart from your spouse all year); and

You do not own any interest in a rental real estate activity as a limited partner or beneficiary of a trust or estate.

If you have a loss from a passive interest in a partnership, trust, estate, or S corporation, you first determine on Form 8582 whether the loss is deductible on Schedule E.

Schedule F. A passive activity farm loss is entered on Form 8582 to determine the deductible loss. If only part of the loss is allowed, only that portion is claimed on Schedule F. A net profit from passive farm activities is also entered on Form 8582 to offset losses from other passive activities.

Other tax forms. Other forms tied to Form 8582 are Form 4797 (sale of business assets or equipment), Form 4835 (farm rental income), and Form 4952 (investment interest deductions). For further details see Form 8582; also *see* IRS Publication 925 for filled-in sample forms.

Caution

Partial Disposition
To deduct suspended passive losses on a disposition of part of an activity, the part disposed of must constitute substantially all of the activity; *see 10.13.*

10.13 Suspended Losses Allowed on Disposition of Your Interest

Losses and credits that may not be claimed in one year because of the passive activity limitations are suspended and carried forward to later years. The carryover lasts indefinitely, until you have passive income against which to claim the losses and credits. No carryback is allowed. What if you have suspended losses and later materially participate in the business in which the loss was realized? The losses remain as passive losses but may offset nonpassive income of that activity.

EXAMPLE

In 1998, Nick Milo was not a material participant in a business activity and his share of losses was $10,000, which was suspended because he had no passive income. In 1999, he becomes a material participant in the business and his share of income is $1,000. The $1,000 is treated as nonpassive income, and he may apply $1,000 of the suspended loss to offset that income.

Allocation of suspended loss. If your suspended loss is incurred from several activities, you allocate the loss among the activities using the worksheets accompanying Form 8582. The loss is allocated among the activities in proportion to the total loss. If you have net income from significant participation activities (Test 4 at *10.6*), such activities may be treated as one single activity in making the allocation; *see* instructions to Form 8582.

Disposition of a passive interest. A fully taxable sale of your interest to a nonrelated person will allow you to claim suspended deductions from the activity. Worthlessness of a security in a passive activity is treated as a disposition. An abandonment also releases suspended losses.

On a disposition, the suspended losses plus any current year income or loss from the activity are combined with the gain or loss from the disposition; *see* the Examples below and follow the instructions to Form 8582 for reporting the net gain or loss.

Partial disposition. You may for the taxable year in which there is a disposition of *substantially all* of an activity treat the part disposed of as a separate activity. You must show: (1) the amount of prior year suspended deductions and credits allocable to that part of the activity for the taxable year, and (2) the amount of gross income and any other deductions and credits allocable to that part of the activity for the taxable year.

Caution

$3,000 Capital Loss Limit
Capital losses incurred on a disposition of a passive interest are also subject to the general $3,000 loss limitation ($1,500 if married filing separately) discussed at *5.4.*

EXAMPLES

1. Jill Stein has a 5% interest in a limited partnership with an adjusted basis of $42,000. In 1999, she sells her interest in the partnership to an unrelated person for $50,000. For 1999, she has a current year loss from the partnership (shown on Schedule K-1) of $3,000. She also has $2,000 of suspended passive losses from prior years that have been carried forward to 1999. Jill's $8,000 gain from the sale of her interest is combined on Form 8582 with the current year loss and suspended losses giving her an overall gain of $3,000, figured as follows:

Sales price	$50,000	
Less: Adjusted basis	$42,000	
Gain	$8,000	
Less: Current year loss	$3,000	
Suspended losses	$2,000	$5,000
Overall gain		$3,000

   If Jill has *other* passive activities, the $8,000 gain would be reported as current year income on Form 8582. The $3,000 current year loss and $2,000 suspended losses would also be entered on Form 8582.

   If this was Jill's *only* passive activity, she does not have to file Form 8582. The gain from the sale is reported on Schedule D and the current year and suspended losses are reported as nonpassive losses on Schedule E.

2. Assume that Jill's suspended losses from prior years were $10,000 instead of $2,000. She has an overall loss of $5,000 after combining the gain from the sale of $8,000, the current year loss of $3,000, and the suspended losses of $10,000.

   Since there is an overall loss after combining the gain and losses, Jill does not file Form 8582. The current year loss plus the suspended losses are reported as nonpassive losses on Schedule E and the gain from the disposition on Schedule D.

3. Assume in Example 1 that Jill sold her interest for $30,000 instead of $50,000. She would have a $12,000 loss on the sale ($42,000 adjusted basis less $30,000 sales price). Combining the loss with the current year loss of $3,000 and the $2,000 of suspended losses, she has an overall loss of $17,000.

   Since there is an overall loss, Jill does not file Form 8582. The current year loss plus the suspended losses are reported as nonpassive losses on Schedule E. The $12,000 loss on the sale is reported on Schedule D as a capital loss. Under the regular rules for capital losses, the loss will offset capital gains for 1999 and any excess will be deductible only up to $3,000 *(5.4)*. Assuming the $3,000 limit applies, Jill has a $9,000 capital loss carryover to 2000.

Gifts. When a passive activity interest is given away, you may not deduct suspended passive losses. The donee's basis in the property is increased by the suspended loss if he or she sells the property at a gain. If a loss is realized by the donee on a sale of the interest, the donee's basis may not exceed fair market value of the gift at the time of the donation.

Death. On the death of an investor in a passive interest, suspended losses are deductible on the decedent's final tax return, to the extent the suspended loss exceeds the amount by which the basis of the interest in the hands of the heir is increased.

EXAMPLE

An owner dies holding an interest in a passive activity with a suspended loss of $8,000. After the owner's death, the heir's stepped-up basis for the property (equal to fair market value) is $6,000 greater than the decedent's basis. On the decedent's final return, $2,000 of the loss is deductible ($8,000 – $6,000).

Installment sales. If the passive activity interest is sold at a profit on the installment basis, suspended losses are deducted over the installment period in the same ratio as the gain recognized each year bears to the gain remaining to be recognized as of the start of the year. For example, if you realize a gain of $10,000 and report $2,000 of gain each year for five years, in the year of sale you report 20% of your total gain under the installment method, and 20% of your suspended losses are also allowed. In the second year, you report $2,000 of the remaining $8,000 gain and 25% of the remaining losses ($2,000 ÷ $8,000) are allowed.

10.14 Suspended Tax Credits

If you have tax credits that were barred under the passive activity rules, they may be claimed only in future years when you have tax liability attributable to passive income. However, in the year you dispose of your interest, a special election may be available to decrease your gain by the amount of your suspended credit; *see* below.

Basis election for suspended credits. If you qualify for an investment credit (under transition rules) or a rehabilitation credit, you are required to reduce the basis of the property even if you are unable to claim the credit because of the passive activity rules. If this occurs and you later dispose of your entire interest in the passive activity, including the property whose basis was reduced, your gain will be increased by virtue of the basis reduction although you never benefited from the credit. To prevent this, you may reduce the taxable gain by electing to increase the pretransfer basis of the property by the amount of the unused credit.

EXAMPLE

Dan Brown places in service rehabilitated credit property qualifying for a $50 credit, but the credit is not allowed under the passive loss rules. However, his basis is still reduced by $50. In a later year, Brown makes a taxable disposition of his entire interest in the activity and in the rehabilitation property. Assuming that no part of the suspended $50 credit has been used, Brown may elect to increase his basis in the property by the unused $50 credit.

10.15 Personal Service and Closely Held Corporations

To prevent avoidance of the passive activity rules through use of corporations, the law imposes restrictions on income and loss offsets in closely held C corporations and personal service corporations.

Unless the material participation tests discussed in this section are met, the activities of a personal service corporation or a closely held corporation are considered passive activities, subject to the restrictions on loss deductions and tax credits. For purposes of these passive activity rules, a closely held C corporation is a corporation in which more than 50% in value of the stock is owned by five or fewer persons during the last half of the tax year.

A personal service corporation is a C corporation the principal activity of which is the performance of personal services by the employee-owners. Personal services are services in the fields of health, law, engineering, architecture, accounting, actuarial sciences, performing arts, or consulting. An employee-owner is any employee who on any day in the tax year owns any stock in the corporation. If an individual owns any stock in a corporation which in turn owns stock in another corporation, the individual is deemed to own a proportionate part of the stock in the other corporation. Further, more than 10% of the corporation's stock by value must be owned by owner-employees for the corporation to be a personal service corporation.

Filing Tip

Installment Sale of Your Interest

If you sell your passive activity interest at a profit and have suspended losses, you may deduct a percentage of the losses each year during the installment period; *see 10.13.*

Material participation. A personal service corporation or closely held corporation is treated as materially participating in an activity during a tax year *only if* either:

1. One or more stockholders are treated as materially participating in the activity and they directly or indirectly hold in the aggregate more than 50% of the value of the corporation's outstanding shares; *or*
2. The corporation is a closely held corporation and in the 12-month period ending on the last day of the tax year, the corporation had at least one full-time manager, three full-time employees, none of whom own more than 5% of the stock, and business deductions exceeded 15% of gross income from the activity.

A stockholder is treated as materially participating or significantly participating in the activity of a corporation if he or she satisfies one of the seven tests in *10.6* for material participation. For purposes of applying the significant participation test (Test 4 at *10.6*), an activity of a personal service or closely held corporation will be treated as a significant participation activity for a tax year *only if*:

1. The corporation is not treated as materially participating in the activity for the tax year; and
2. One or more individuals, each of whom is treated as significantly participating in the activity directly or indirectly, hold in the aggregate more than 50% of the value of the outstanding stock of the corporation. Furthermore, in applying the seven participation tests, all activities of the corporation are treated as activities in which the individual holds an interest in determining whether the individual participates in an activity of the corporation; and the individual's participation in all activities other than activities of the corporation is disregarded in determining whether his or her participation in an activity of the corporation is treated as material participation under the significant participation test (Test 4 at *10.6*).

Closely held corporation's computation of passive loss. Even if a closely held corporation does not meet the material participation tests above, it still qualifies for a slight break from the passive loss restrictions. A closely held corporation may use passive activity deductions to offset not only passive activity gross income but also *net active income.* Generally, net active income is taxable income from business operations, disregarding passive activity income and expenses, and also disregarding portfolio income and expenses; *see 10.8.* Passive activity losses cannot offset portfolio income.

If a corporation stops being closely held, its passive losses and credits from prior years are not allowable against portfolio income but continue to be allowable only against passive income and net active income.

Tax liability on net active income may be offset by passive activity credits.

 Filing Tip

Stockholder Activity
A stockholder may be treated as materially participating in his company's business; *see* tests on this page.

10.16 Sales of Property and of Passive Activity Interests

Generally, gain on the sale or disposition of property is passive or nonpassive, depending on whether your activity is passive or nonpassive in the year of sale or disposition. Thus, gain on the sale of property used in a rental activity is treated as passive income, and gain on property used in a nonrental business is passive if you did not materially participate in the business in the year of sale. However, exceptions may prevent you from generating passive income by arranging certain sales described in this section. For example, gain on the sale of substantially appreciated property formerly used in a nonpassive activity may be treated as nonpassive income, even if sold by a passive activity.

Where you transact an installment sale, treatment of gain in later years depends on your status in the year of sale. For example, if you were considered a material participant in a business, all gain is treated as nonpassive income, including gain for later installments. If you were in a rental activity or were not a material participant in a nonrental business, the gain is treated as passive income, unless the exceptions in this section apply.

Current gain from a pre-1987 installment sale is passive income if the activity would have been passive, assuming the passive activity rules were in effect at the time of the sale.

Gain on appreciated property formerly used in nonpassive activity. Gain from a disposition of substantially appreciated property is treated as passive activity income if the property was used in a passive activity for either 20% of its holding period or the entire 24-month period ending on the date of the disposition. Property is substantially appreciated if fair market value exceeds 120% of its adjusted basis.

EXAMPLE

In 1990, Andy Jones buys a building for use in a business in which he materially participates until March 31, 2000. On April 1, 2001, he rents the building. On December 31, 2002, he sells the building. Gain from the sale is treated as not from a passive activity. The building was used in a passive rental activity for 21 months before disposition (April 1, 2001, through December 31, 2002). Thus, it was not used in a passive activity for the entire 24-month period ending on the date of the sale. Further, the 21-month period during which the building was used in a passive activity is less than 20% of Jones's holding period of 12 years.

Property used in more than one activity in a 12-month period preceding disposition. You are required to allocate the amount realized on the disposition and the adjusted basis of the property among the activities in which the property was used during a 12-month period preceding the disposition. For purposes of this rule, the term "activity" includes personal use and holding for investment. The allocation may be based on the period for which the property is used in each activity during the 12-month period. However, if during the 12-month period the value of the property does not exceed the lesser of $10,000 and 10% of the value of all property used in the activity at the time of disposition, gain may be allocated to the predominant use.

EXAMPLE

Joe Smith sells a personal computer for $8,000. During the 12-month period that ended on the date of the sale, 70% of Smith's use of the computer was in a passive activity. Immediately before the sale, the fair market value of all property used in the passive activity, including the personal computer, was $200,000. The computer was predominantly used in the passive activity during the 12-month period ending on the date of the sale. The value of the computer, $8,000, did not exceed the lesser of $10,000 and 10% of the $200,000 value of all property used in the activity immediately before the sale. Thus, the amount realized and the adjusted basis are allocated to the passive activity.

Disposition of partnership and S corporation interests. Gain or loss from the disposition of an interest in a partnership and S corporation is generally allocated among the entity's activities in proportion to the amount that the entity would have allocated to the partner or shareholder for each of its activities if the entity had sold its interest in the activities on an "applicable valuation date."

Gain is allocated only to appreciated activities. Loss is allocated only to depreciated activities. The entity may select either the beginning of its tax year in which the holder's disposition occurs or the date of the disposition as the applicable valuation date.

Claiming suspended loss on disposition of interest in passive activity. A fully taxable sale of your entire interest or of substantially all of your interest to a nonrelated person will allow you to claim suspended loss deductions from the activity. These rules are fully discussed in *10.13.*

Dealer's sale of property similar to property sold in the ordinary course of business. IRS regulations set down complex tests which determine whether the result of the sale is treated as passive or nonpassive income or loss.

At-Risk Rules

 Caution

At-Risk Rules Limit Loss Deductions

The purpose of at-risk rules is to keep you from deducting losses from investments in which you have little cash invested and no personal liability for debts.

10.17 At-Risk Limits

The at-risk rules prevent investors from claiming losses in excess of their actual tax investment by barring them from including nonrecourse liabilities as part of the tax basis for their interest. Almost all ventures are subject to the at-risk limits. Real estate placed in service after 1986 is subject to the at-risk rules as well, but most real estate nonrecourse financing can qualify for an exception; *see 10.18.*

EXAMPLE

Crystal Parker invests cash of $1,000 in a venture and signs a nonrecourse note for $8,000. In 1999, her share of the venture's loss is $1,200. The at-risk rules limit her deduction to $1,000, the amount of her cash investment; as she is not personally liable on the note, the amount of the liability is not included as part of her basis for loss purposes.

Losses disallowed under the at-risk rules are carried over to the following year; *see 10.21.*

Form 6198. If you have amounts that are not at risk, you must file Form 6198 to figure your deductible loss. A separate form must be filed for each activity. However, if you have an interest in a partnership or S corporation that has more than one investment in any of the following four categories, the IRS currently allows you to aggregate all of the partnership or S corporation activities within each category. For example, all partnership or S corporation films and videotapes may be treated as one activity in determining amounts at risk. The aggregation rules may be changed by the IRS; *see* the instructions to Form 6198.

1. Holding, producing, or distributing motion picture films or videotapes;
2. Exploring for or exploiting oil or gas properties;
3. Exploring for, or exploiting, geothermal deposits (for wells commenced on or after October 1, 1978); *and*
4. Farming. For this purpose, farming is defined as the cultivation of land and the raising or harvesting of any agricultural or horticultural commodity—including raising, shearing, breeding, caring for, or management of animals. Forestry and timber activities are not included, but orchards bearing fruits and nuts are within the definition of farming. Certain activities carried on within the physical boundaries of the farm may not necessarily be treated as farming.

In addition to the previous categories, the law treats as a single activity all leased depreciable business equipment (Section 1245 property) that is placed in service during any year by a partnership or S corporation.

Exempt from the at-risk rules are C corporations which meet active business tests and are not in the equipment leasing business or any business involving master sound recording, films, videotapes, or other artistic, literary, or musical property. For details on the active business tests, as well as a special at-risk exception for equipment leasing activities of closely held corporations, *see* IRS Publication 925.

The at-risk limitation applies only to tax losses produced by expense deductions which are not disallowed by reason of another provision of the law. For example, if a prepaid interest expense is deferred under the prepaid interest limitation *(15.14)*, the interest will not be included in the loss subject to the risk limitation. When the interest accrues and becomes deductible, the expense may be considered within the at-risk provision. Similarly, if a deduction is deferred because of farming syndicate rules, that deduction will enter into the computation of the tax loss subject to the risk limitation only when it becomes deductible under the farming syndicate rules.

Effect of passive loss rules. Where a loss is also subject to the at-risk rules, you apply the at-risk rules first. If the loss is deductible under the at-risk rules, the passive activity rules then apply. On Form 6198 (at risk), you figure the deductible loss allowed as at risk and then carry the loss over to Form 8582 to determine the passive activity loss.

10.18   What Is At Risk?

The following amounts are considered at risk in determining your tax position in a business or investment:

Cash;
Adjusted basis of property that you contribute; and
Borrowed funds for which you are personally liable to pay.

At-risk basis is figured as of the end of the year. Any loss allowed for a year reduces the at-risk amount as of the start of the next year. Therefore, if a loss exceeds your at-risk investment, the excess loss will not be deductible in later years unless you increase your at-risk investment; *see* the Example below and *10.21.*

Personal liability alone does not assure that the borrowed funds are considered at risk. The lender must have no interest in the venture other than as creditor.

 Filing Tip

Form 6198

If you have invested an amount for which you are not at risk, such as a nonrecourse loan, you generally must file Form 6198 to figure a deductible loss. However, nonrecouse financing for real estate that secures the loan is treated as an at-risk investment in most cases; *see 10.18.*

EXAMPLE

Julie Kahn, an investor, pays a promoter of a book purchase plan $45,000 for a limited partnership interest. The promoter is the general partner. Kahn pays $30,000 cash and gives a note for $15,000 on which she is personally liable. Her amount at risk is $30,000; the $15,000 personal liability note is not counted because it is owed to the general partner.

Law Alert

Possible Modification of Real Estate Financing Tests

At the time this book went to press, Congress was considering a modification of rules for real estate financing using qualified publicly traded debt. *See* the Supplement for an update.

Special at-risk rule for real estate financing. For real property placed in service after 1986, you may treat nonrecourse financing from unrelated commercial lenders or from government agencies as amounts at risk if the financing is secured by the real estate. Loans from the seller or promoter do not qualify. Third-party nonrecourse debt from a related lender, other than the seller or promoter, may also be treated as at risk, providing the terms of the loan are commercially reasonable and on substantially the same terms as loans involving unrelated persons.

If you acquired an interest after 1986 in a partnership or S corporation, the above at-risk rules apply to your share of real estate losses, regardless of when the partnership or S corporation placed the property in service.

Pledges of other property. If you pledge personally owned real estate used outside the activity to secure a nonrecourse debt and invest the proceeds in an at-risk activity, the proceeds may be considered part of your at-risk investment. The proceeds included in basis are limited by the fair market value of the property used as collateral (determined as of the date the property is pledged as security) less any prior (or superior) claims to which the collateral is subject.

Partners. A partner is treated as at-risk to the extent that basis in the partnership is increased by the share of partnership income. That partnership income is then used to reduce the partnership's nonrecourse indebtedness will have no effect on a partner's amount at risk. If the partnership makes actual distributions of the income in the taxable year, the amount distributed reduces the partner's amount at risk. A buy-sell agreement, effective at a partner's death or retirement, is not considered for at-risk purposes.

Activities begun before 1976. A special rule determines the amount at risk as of the first day of the first tax year after 1975. Again, you start with the amounts considered at risk. Losses incurred and deducted in taxable years before 1976 first reduce the basis allocated to amounts considered not at risk, such as nonrecourse loans. If the losses exceed the amount not at risk, the excess reduces the at-risk investment. Distributions reduce at-risk amounts. *See* the instructions to Form 6198.

10.19 Amounts Not At Risk

The following may not be treated as part of basis for at-risk purposes in determining your tax position in a business or investment:

Liabilities for which you have no personal liability, except in the case of certain real estate financing; *see 10.18.*

Liabilities for which you have personal liability, but the lender also has a capital or profit-sharing interest in the venture.

Recourse liabilities convertible to a nonrecourse basis.

Money borrowed from a relative listed at *5.6* who has an interest in the venture, other than as a creditor, or from a partnership in which you own more than a 10% interest.

Funds borrowed from a person whose recourse is solely your interest in the activity or property used in the activity.

Amounts for which your economic loss is limited by a nonrecourse financing guarantee, stop-loss agreement, or other similar arrangement.

Investments protected by insurance or loss reimbursement agreement between you and another person. If you are personally liable on a mortgage but you separately obtain insurance to compensate you for any mortgage payments, you are at risk only to the extent of the uninsured portion of the personal liability. You may, however, include as at risk any amount of premium paid from your personal assets. Taking out casualty insurance or insurance protecting you against tort liability is not considered within the at-risk provisions, and such insurance does not affect your investment basis.

Caution

Lender Has Interest

Even if you are personally liable for a debt, you are not considered at risk if the lender has an interest in the activity other than as a creditor.

EXAMPLES

1. Some commercial feedlots in livestock feeding operations may reimburse investors against any loss sustained on sales of the livestock above a stated dollar amount per head. Under such "stop-loss" orders, an investor is at risk only to the extent of the portion of his or her capital against which he or she is not entitled to reimbursement. Where a limited partnership makes an agreement with a limited partner that, at the partner's election, his or her partnership interest will be bought at a stated minimum dollar amount (usually less than the investor's original capital contribution), the partner is considered at risk only to the extent of his or her investment exceeding the guaranteed repurchase price.

2. A TV film promoter sold half-hour TV series programs to individual investors. Each investor gave a cash down payment and a note for which he or she was personally liable for the balance. Each investor's note, which was identical in face amount, terms, and maturity date, was payable out of the distribution proceeds from the film. Each investor also bought from the promoter the right to the unpaid balance on another investor's note. The promoter arranged the distribution of the films as a unit and was to apportion the sales proceeds equally among the investors.

   The IRS held that each investor is not at risk on the investment evidenced by the note. Upon maturity, each may receive a payment from another investor equal to the one that he or she owes.

3. A gold mine investment offered tax write-offs of four times the cash invested. For $10,000 cash, an investor buys from a foreign mining company a seven-year mineral claim lease to a gold reserve. Under the lease, he or she can develop and extract all of the gold in the reserve. At the same time, he or she agrees to spend $40,000 to develop the lease before the end of the year. To fund this commitment, the investor authorizes the promoter to sell an option for $30,000 to a third party who is to buy all the gold to be extracted. The $30,000 along with the $10,000 down payment is to be used to develop the reserve. The promoter advises the investor that he or she may claim a $40,000 deduction for certain development costs.

   The IRS ruled that $30,000 is not deductible because the amount is not "risk capital." The investor gets $30,000 by selling an option that can be exercised only if gold is found. If no gold is found, he or she is under no obligation to the option holder. His or her risk position for the $30,000 is substantially the same as if he or she had borrowed from the option holder on a nonrecourse basis repayable only from his or her interest in the activity.

   The Tax Court struck down a similar plan on different grounds. Without deciding the question of what was at risk, the court held that the option was only a right of first refusal. Thus, $30,000 was taxable income to the investor in the year of the arranged sale.

4. David Krepp, an investor, purchases cattle from a rancher for $10,000 cash and a $30,000 note payable to the rancher. Krepp is personally liable on the note. In a separate agreement, the rancher agrees to care for the cattle for 6% of Krepp's net profits from the cattle activity. Krepp is considered at risk for $10,000; he may not increase the amount at risk by the $30,000 borrowed from the rancher.

Limited partner's potential cash call. Under the terms of a partnership agreement, limited partners may be required to make additional capital contributions under specified circumstances. Whether such a potential cash call increases the limited partner's at-risk amount has been a matter of dispute.

In one case, the IRS and Tax Court held that a limited partner was not at risk with respect to a partnership note where, under the terms of the partnership agreement, he could be required to make additional capital contributions if the general partners did not pay off the note at maturity. The possibility of such a potential cash call was too uncertain; the partnership might earn profits to pay off the note and even if there were losses, the general partners might not demand additional contributions from the limited partners.

However, a federal appeals court reversed, holding that the limited partner was at risk because his obligation was mandatory and "economic reality" insured that the general partners would insure their rights by requiring the additional capital contribution.

In another case, limited partners relied upon the earlier favorable federal appeals court decision to argue that they were at risk where they could be required by the general partners to make additional cash contributions, but only in order to cover liabilities or expenses that could not be paid out of partnership assets. So long as the partnership was solvent, the limited partners could "elect out" of the call provision. Because of this election, the Tax Court held that the limited partners' obligation was contingent, rather than unavoidable as in the earlier federal appeals court case. Thus, the cash call provision did not increase their at-risk amount.

10.20 At-Risk Investment in Several Activities

If you invest in several activities, each is generally treated separately when applying the at-risk limitation on Form 6198. You generally may not aggregate basis, gains, and losses from the activities for purposes of at-risk limitations. Thus, income from one activity may not be offset by losses from another; the income from one must be reported while the losses from the other may be nondeductible because of at-risk limitations.

However, you may aggregate activities that are part of a business you actively manage. Activities of a business carried on by a partnership or S corporation qualify if 65% or more of losses for the year are allocable to persons who actively participate in management.

The law allows partnerships and S corporations to treat as a single activity all depreciable equipment (Section 1245 property) that is leased or held for lease and placed in service in any tax year. Furthermore, you may aggregate all partnership or S corporation activities within the four categories of films and videotapes, oil and gas properties, geothermal properties, and farms; *see 10.17.*

10.21 Carryover of Disallowed Losses

A loss disallowed in a current year by the at-risk limitation may be carried over and deducted in the next taxable year, provided it does not fall within the at-risk limits or the passive loss limits in that year. The loss is subject to an unlimited carryover period until there is an at-risk basis to support the deduction. This may occur when additional contributions are made to the business or when the activity has income which has not been distributed.

Gain from the disposition of property used in an at-risk activity is treated as income from the activity. In general, the reporting of gain will allow a deduction for losses disallowed in previous years to be claimed in the year of disposition.

10.22 Recapture of Losses Where At Risk Is Less Than Zero

To prevent manipulation of at-risk basis after a loss is claimed, there is a special recapture rule. If the amount at risk in an activity is reduced to below zero because of a distribution or a change in the status of an indebtedness from recourse to nonrecourse, income may be realized to the extent of the negative at-risk amount. The taxable amount may not exceed the amount of losses previously deducted.

The recaptured amount is not treated as income from the activity for purposes of determining whether current or suspended losses are allowable.

The recaptured amount is treated as a deduction allowable to that activity in the following year. *See* IRS Publication 925 for futher details.

 Filing Tip

Carryover Losses

Losses disallowed by at-risk rules are carried over and may be deductible in a later year.

Other Income

Income items discussed in this chapter are reported on Line 10 or 21 of Form 1040 or on a Schedule E and then transferred to Line 17 of Form 1040.

- Taxable state tax refunds are reported on Line 10 of Form 1040.

- Prizes, gambling winnings, and awards are reported on Line 21 of Form 1040.

- Your share of partnership, S corporation, trust, or estate income or loss is reported in Schedule E according to Schedule K-1 statements provided you by the entity.

- Income from farming is reported on Schedule F.

Further reporting details are discussed in this chapter.

Prizes; Lottery and Gambling Winnings

11.1 Prizes and Awards

Prizes and awards are taxable income except for an award or prize that meets *all* these four tests:

1. It is primarily in recognition of religious, charitable, scientific, educational, artistic, literary, or civic achievement.
2. You were selected without any action on your part.
3. You do not have to perform services.
4. You assign the prize or award to a government unit or tax-exempt charitable organization. You must make the assignment before you use or benefit from the award. You may not claim a charitable deduction for the assignment.

Prize taxed at fair market value. A prize of merchandise is taxable at fair market value. For example, where a prize of first-class steamship tickets was exchanged for tourist-class tickets for a winner's family, the taxable value of the prize was the price of the tourist tickets. What is the taxable fair market value of an automobile won as a prize? In one case, the Tax Court held that the taxable value was what the recipient could realize on an immediate resale of the car.

Employee achievement awards. The above restrictions on tax-free treatment do not apply to awards from employers for length of service or safety achievement. The rules for such employee awards are at *3.10* and *20.25*.

11.2 Lottery and Sweepstake Winnings

Sweepstake, lottery, and raffle winnings are taxable as "other income" on Line 21 of Form 1040. The cost of tickets is deductible only to the extent you report winnings, and only if you itemize deductions. The deduction is claimed on Schedule A as a miscellaneous deduction that is *not* subject to the 2% adjusted gross income (AGI) floor (Chapter 19). For example, if you buy state lottery tickets and win a 1999 drawing, you may deduct the cost of your losing tickets in 1999 up to the amount of your winnings.

When a minor wins a state lottery and the prize is held by his or her parents as custodians under the Uniform Gifts to Minors Act, the prize is taxed to the minor in the year the prize is won.

Installment payments. If winnings are payable in installments, you pay tax only as installments are received. If within 60 days of winning a prize you have an option to choose a discounted lump-sum payment instead of an annuity, and you elect the annuity, you are taxed as the annuity payments are received. Merely having the cash option does not make the present value of the annuity taxable in the year the prize is won. This law generally applies to prizes won after October 21, 1998. The law applies to casino jackpots as well as lottery or sweepstake winnings.

11.3 Gambling Winnings and Losses

Gambling winnings are taxable. Losses from gambling are deductible only up to the gains from gambling. You may not deduct a net gambling loss even though a particular state says gambling is legal. Nor does it matter that your business is gambling. You may not deduct the loss even if you are a professional gambler.

If you are not a professional gambler, gambling income is included on Form 1040 as "other income" on Line 21. Gambling losses (not exceeding the amount of the gains) are deductible as "miscellaneous deductions" on Schedule A. The losses are *not* subject to the 2% AGI floor (Chapter 19). According to the IRS, professional gamblers who bet only for their own account are not in a business and must deduct losses (up to gains) as itemized deductions. However, the Supreme Court has held that full-time gamblers may deduct losses as business expenses even if they place wagers only for themselves. According to the Supreme Court, in order to be considered engaged in a business, a gambler must prove that he or she gambles full time to earn a livelihood and not merely as a hobby.

To prove your losses in the event your return is questioned, you must retain evidence of loss.

EXAMPLES

1. To appear on *Wheel of Fortune*, Whitten traveled from Chicago to Los Angeles, spending $1,820 for transportation, meals, and lodging. When he won cash prizes of $14,850 plus an automobile, he tried to offset his winnings by the travel costs, claiming they were gambling losses on Schedule A not subject to the 2% AGI floor. The IRS and Tax Court disagreed; travel costs are not like wager or bet losses.

 Filing Tip

Winnings Paid in Installments

Gambling losses are deductible as miscellaneous deductions up to the amount of your gambling winnings. Lottery winnings paid in installments qualify as such gambling winnings. If you receive lottery winnings in 1999, for instance, you may deduct any gambling losses incurred in 1999 up to the amount of that installment. Lottery winnings paid in installments do not lose their characteristic as gambling winnings.

 Caution

Splitting Lottery Winnings

To split income, potential lottery winnings may be divided among family members or others before the prize is won. You might buy the lottery ticket in your name and the names of others. The prize is shared and each portion separately taxed. However, the IRS has not allowed income splitting after the prize is won. In one case, a couple who bought a winning lottery ticket that under state law was payable to only one person proved they shared the ticket before the drawing by having their attorneys draw up a joint ownership agreement.

2. Trump Casino in Atlantic City gave Libutti, a high roller at its gaming tables, over $2.5 million in "comps" during a three-year period in which he lost over $8 million. The comps included 10 expensive automobiles, jewelry, European vacations, and tickets to sporting events. Libutti reported the comps as income and then claimed a matching miscellaneous deduction for gambling losses not subject to the 2% floor. The IRS disallowed the deduction, claiming that the comps were not gambling income because they were perks given to stimulate his desire to gamble at Trump's, and not winnings from the success of his wagers.

   The Tax Court disagreed. Libutti would not have received the comps unless he gambled at high stakes in Trump's casino. Although the comps did not directly hinge on the success or failure of his wagers, the comps were sufficiently related to his gambling losses to allow the deduction.

11.4 Gifts and Inheritances

Gifts and inheritances you *receive* are not taxable. However, distributions taken from an inherited IRA *(8.14)* are taxable as are distributions from inherited qualified plan accounts such as 401(k) and profit-sharing plan accounts.

Income earned from gift or inherited property after you receive it is taxable.

Describing a payment as a gift or inheritance will not necessarily shield it from tax if it is, in fact, a payment for your services. Treatment of gifts to employees is covered at *2.4.*

A sale of an expected inheritance from a living person is taxable as ordinary income.

EXAMPLES

1. An employee is promised by his employer that he will be remembered in his will if he continues to work for him. The employer dies but fails to mention the employee in his will. The employee sues the estate, which settles his claim. The settlement is taxable.
2. A nephew left his uncle a bequest of $200,000. In another clause of the will, the uncle was appointed executor, and the bequest of the $200,000 was described as being made in lieu of all commissions to which he would otherwise be entitled as executor. The bequest is considered tax-free income. It was not conditioned upon the uncle performing as executor. If the will had made the bequest contingent upon the uncle's acting as executor, the $200,000 would have been taxed.
3. An attorney performed services for a friend without expectation of pay. The friend died and in his will left the attorney a bequest in appreciation for his services. The payment was considered a tax-free bequest. The amount was not bargained for.
4. A lawyer agreed to handle a client's legal affairs without charge; she promised to leave him securities. Twenty years later, under her will, the lawyer inherited the securities. The IRS taxed the bequest as pay. Both he and the client expected that he would be paid for legal services. If the client meant to make a bequest from their agreement, she should have said so in her will.

 Court Decision

Gambler Not Taxed on Cancelled Gambling Debt

The federal appeals court for the Third Circuit (New Jersey, Pennsylvania, and Delaware) held that the settlement by an Atlantic City casino of a gambler's $3.4 million debt for $500,000 was not taxable. The debt was not enforceable under New Jersey law because the casino did not comply with state regulations on issuance of credit. Furthermore, the gambling chips were not "property" securing the debt; they had no economic value outside the casino.

 Planning Reminder

Gifts You Make

You may have to file a gift tax return if your gifts to an individual within the year exceed $10,000; *see 33.1.*

State Tax Refunds and Other Recovered Deductions

11.5 Refunds of State and Local Income Tax Deductions

A refund of state or local income tax is not taxable if you did not previously claim the tax as an itemized deduction in a prior year. For example, if you claimed the standard deduction on your 1998 return and in 1999 you received a refund for state tax withheld from your 1998 wages, the refund is not taxable on your 1999 return.

If you did claim the refunded tax as an itemized deduction, the refund is taxable only to the extent that your itemized deductions exceeded the standard deduction you could have claimed in the prior year. If, in addition to the tax refund, you received recoveries of other itemized deductions, the same computation applies to determine the taxable portion of the total recovery; *see 11.6.*

The computation of the taxable refund is different if, in the year the refunded item was claimed, you were subject to the 3% reduction of itemized deductions. In this case, the IRS provides a special method explained in Publication 525.

Refund of State and Local Tax

A state and local tax refund received in 1999 is taxable only if you claimed the tax as an itemized deduction, and only to the extent that your itemized deductions in that year exceeded the standard deduction you could have claimed.

To help you figure the taxable portion of 1998 itemized deductions recovered in 1999, 1998 standard deduction amounts are shown on the next page.

EXAMPLE

On your 1998 return, you filed as a single taxpayer. You claimed itemized deductions of $4,550, of which $2,300 was for state and local taxes, $1,650 was for mortgage interest, and $600 was for charitable contributions. Your deductions exceeded by $300 the $4,250 standard deduction you could have claimed. The deductions were not subject to the 3% reduction discussed at *13.7*.

In 1999, you received from the state a $750 refund for 1998 state taxes. You must report $300 of the refund as income on your 1999 Form 1040. The taxable recovery is limited to the $300 difference between the itemized deductions claimed and the $4,250 standard deduction for 1998.

If you had a negative taxable income in 1998, the taxable recovery figured under the above rule is reduced by the negative amount. If you had a negative taxable income of $100 in 1998, only $200 of the refund would be taxable instead of $400.

Allocating a refund recovery. If in 1999 you received a refund of state or local taxes and also a recovery of other deductions, and only part of the total recovery is taxable, you allocate the taxable amount of the recovery according to the ratio between the state tax refund and the other recovery. You do this by first dividing the state refund by the total of all itemized deductions recovered. The resulting percentage is then applied to the taxable recovery to find the amount to report as the tax refund on Line 10 of Form 1040; other taxable recoveries are reported on Line 21.

EXAMPLE

In 1999, you received a refund of state income taxes of $500 and a recovery of other itemized expenses of $2,000 deducted in 1998. You figure that only $1,500 of the recovery is taxable because your total 1998 itemized deductions were $1,500 more than the standard deduction you could have claimed. As a state tax refund is reported separately from other recoveries, you must find how much of the taxable recovery is attributed to the refund. By dividing the state tax refund by the amount of the total recovery, you find that 20% is attributed to the refund ($500/$2,500). Thus, 20% of the taxable recovery, or $300 (20% of $1,500), is reported as a state refund on Line 10, Form 1040, and the balance of $1,200 on Line 21, Form 1040. Also attach a statement showing that the allocation of recoveries required the reporting on Line 10, Form 1040, of an amount less than the actual state refund shown on Form 1099-G.

Refund of state tax paid in installments over two tax years. If you pay estimated state or local income taxes, your last tax installment may be in the year you receive a refund. In this case, you allocate the refund between the two years; *see* the following Example.

EXAMPLE

Your estimated state income tax for 1998 was $4,000, which you paid in four equal installments. You made your fourth payment in January 1999. No state income tax was withheld during 1998. In 1999, you received a tax refund of $400. You claimed itemized deductions each year on your federal return. You allocate the $400 refund between 1998 and 1999. As you paid 75% ($3,000 ÷ $4,000) of the estimated tax in 1998, 75% of the $400 refund, or $300, is allocated to 1998. On your 1999 return, you include $300 as income on Line 10, Form 1040. You also attach a statement explaining that the amount on Line 10 is less than the $400 refund shown on the Form 1099-G received from the state because of the allocation required by the estimated tax payment in 1999.

When you figure your 1999 deduction for state income taxes, you reduce the $1,000 paid in January by $100. Your 1999 deduction for state income taxes will include the January net amount of $900 plus any estimated taxes paid in 1999 for 1999, any state income tax withheld during 1999, and any 1998 tax paid with your state income tax return filed in 1999.

Note: If the $300 refund allocated to 1998 in the previous Example was more than the excess of your 1998 itemized deductions over the 1998 standard deduction you could have claimed, you report only that excess as 1999 income. If in 1998 you were subject to the 3% reduction to itemized deductions, *see* IRS Publication 525 for figuring the taxable portion of the refund. Also *see* 11.6 for reducing the taxable amount if you had a negative taxable income, or if you recovered a bad debt or other non-itemized deduction.

1998 Standard Deduction for Figuring Recoveries of 1998 Itemized Deductions

If you were—	1998 standard deduction was—
Married filing jointly	$7,100
Single	4,250
Head of household	6,250
Married filing separately	3,550
Qualifying widow or widower	7,100
Single age 65 or over	5,300
Single and blind	5,300
Single age 65 or over and also blind	6,350
Married filing jointly with:	
One spouse age 65 or over	7,950
Both spouses age 65 or over	8,800
One spouse blind under age 65	7,950
Both spouses blind under age 65	8,800
One spouse age 65 or over and also blind	8,800
One spouse age 65 or over and other spouse blind and under age 65	8,800
One spouse age 65 or over and also blind; other spouse blind and under age 65	9,650
Both spouses age 65 or over and also blind	10,500
Qualifying widow or widower age 65 or over	7,950
Qualifying widow or widower and blind	7,950
Qualifying widow or widower age 65 or over and also blind	8,800
Head of household age 65 or over	7,300
Head of household and blind	7,300
Head of household age 65 or over and also blind	8,350
Married filing separately age 65 or over*	4,400
Married filing separately and blind*	4,400
Married filing separately age 65 or over and also blind*	5,250

*If in 1998 you claimed your spouse as an exemption (21.2), add $850 if he or she was either blind or age 65 or older; add $1,700 if he or she was both blind and age 65 or older.

11.6 Other Recovered Deductions

The income rule applied to refunds of state income tax in *11.5* applies also to the recovery of other items for which you claimed a tax deduction, such as a refund of adjustable rate mortgage interest *(15.1)*, reimbursement of a deducted medical expense *(17.4)*, a reimbursed casualty loss *(18.1)*, a return of donated property that was claimed as a charitable deduction *(14.1)*, and a payment of debt previously claimed as a bad debt *(5.9)*.

 Filing Pointer

Negative Taxable Income

If your taxable income was a negative amount in the year in which the recovered item was deducted, you reduce the recovery includible in income by the negative amount. For example, if the taxable recovery would be $1,700 but you had a negative taxable income of $500 for the year the deduction was claimed, only $1,200 is taxable.

In 1998, you filed a joint return and claimed itemized deductions of $8,200, which exceeded your standard deduction of $7,100. You were not subject to the 3% reduction to itemized deductions. In 1999, you received the following recoveries for amounts deducted in 1998:

Medical expenses	$ 200
State income tax refund	400
Interest expense	325
Total	$ 925

The total recovery of $925 is taxable. It is less than $1,100, the excess of your itemized deductions over the allowable standard deduction ($8,200 – 7,100). You report the state and local income tax refund of $400 on Line 10, Form 1040, and the balance of $525 on Line 21, Form 1040.

If the total recovery had been $2,500 instead of $925, $1,100 would be taxable (the excess of $8,200 over $7,100). The $1,400 balance would be tax free.

Tax credit in prior year. If you recover an item deducted in a prior year in which tax credits exceeded your tax, you refigure the prior year tax to determine if the recovery is taxable. Add the amount of the recovery to taxable income of the prior year and figure the tax on the increased taxable income. If your tax credit exceeds the recomputed tax, do not include the recovery in income. If the tax credit is less than the recomputed tax, include the recovery in income to the extent the recovery reduced your tax in the prior year. The recovery may reduce an available credit carryforward to a later year.

Alternative minimum tax in the prior year. If you were subject to the alternative minimum tax (AMT) in the year the recovered deduction was claimed, recompute your regular and AMT tax for the prior year based on the taxable income you reported plus the recovered amount. If inclusion of the recovery does not change your total tax, you do not include the recovery in income. If your total tax increases by any amount, you include the recovery in income to the extent the deduction reduced your tax in the prior year. The recovery may reduce a carryforward of a tax credit based on prior year AMT.

Recovery of previously deducted items used to figure carryover. A deductible expense may not reduce your tax because you have an overall loss. If in a later year the expense is repaid or the obligation giving rise to the expense is cancelled, the deduction of that expense will be treated as having produced a tax reduction if it increased a carryover that has not expired by the beginning of the taxable year in which the forgiveness occurs. For example, you are on the accrual basis and deducted, but did not pay, rent in 1998. The rent obligation is forgiven in 1999. The 1998 rent deduction is treated as having produced a reduction in tax, even if it resulted in no tax savings in 1998 if it figured in the calculation of a net operating loss that has not expired or been used by the beginning of 1999, the year of forgiveness. The same rule applies to other carryovers such as the investment credit carryover.

Damages and Debt Cancellation

11.7 How Legal Damages Are Taxed

Awards recovered through legal action, whether fixed by a court or a settlement between the parties, are generally taxable, unless they qualify as compensation for a personal injury, such as damages awarded for a physical injury in an auto accident. Interest paid on a tax-free damage award is taxable.

When damages compensate for the loss of property, you have taxable gain if the damages exceed adjusted basis of the property. A deductible loss will generally be allowed when the recovery is less than adjusted basis. The nature of the gain or loss takes on the same character (that is, capital gain or loss or ordinary income gain or loss) as the property lost.

When your attorney receives payment of taxable damages and then turns over the money after deducting his or her fee, you are taxed in the year you receive your share.

Discrimination and other nonphysical injury awards are taxed. Damages received after August 20, 1996, are tax free only if on account of a physical injury or physical sickness. Awards for emotional distress attributable to a physical injury or physical sickness are tax free.

Damages received in discrimination or other nonphysical injury cases are taxable with one exception: Damages up to the amount of actual medical care expenses attributable to emotional distress are tax free. Apart from the medical care exception, emotional distress, including physical symptoms such as insomnia, headaches, and stomach disorders, is not by itself considered a physical injury or sickness.

 Planning Reminder

Legal Fees

If the damages are tax free, you may not deduct your litigation costs. If your damages are fully taxed, you deduct all of your litigation costs. If your damages are only partially taxed, then you deduct only that portion of your litigation costs attributed to the taxed damages.

Legal fees that are deductible as miscellaneous expenses are subject to the 2% adjusted gross income floor; *see* Chapter 19.

Punitive damages. Punitive damages are taxable, even if they relate to a physical injury or sickness. This law specifically applies to damages received after August 20, 1996, but a 1996 Supreme Court decision held that punitive damages were taxable even under the prior law because punitive damages do not provide compensation for injuries, but are intended to punish wrongdoing by the defendant who was sued. However, under an exception, punitive damages awarded in a wrongful death suit are excluded from income if they are the only damages that may be awarded under state law. The state law must have been in effect on September 13, 1995, or a court decision holding that punitive damages were the only remedy must have been issued on or before that date.

11.8 Cancellation of Debts You Owe

If a debt is cancelled or forgiven other than as a gift or a bequest the debtor generally must include the cancelled amount in gross income for tax purposes. Exclusions are allowed for discharges of farm or business real estate debt and debts of insolvent and bankrupt persons, as explained below.

Form 1099-C. You should receive Form 1099-C from a federal government agency, credit union, or bank that cancels or forgives a debt you owe of $600 or more. The IRS receives a copy of the form. Generally, the amount of canceled debt shown in Box 2 of Form 1099-C must be reported as "other income" on Line 21 of Form 1040, unless one of the exclusions discussed below applies.

Discounted mortgage repayment. A prepayment of a home mortgage at a discount is taxable. The income is reported on Line 21, Form 1040. The tax treatment of a foreclosure sale or voluntary conveyance to a creditor is discussed at *31.9*.

EXAMPLE

A bank allows a homeowner to prepay a low-interest mortgage of $20,000 for $18,000. The discount of $2,000 is taxable as ordinary income.

Cancellation of student loans. A cancelled student loan is taxable income with this exception: If a loan by a government agency, by a government-funded loan program of an education organization, or by a qualified hospital organization is cancelled because you worked for a period of time in certain geographical areas for certain types of employers, such as practicing medicine in rural areas or teaching in inner-city schools, then the cancelled amount is not taxable. The Tax Court held that a student loan cancelled by the State of Alaska was taxable. The Alaska law conditioned forgiveness only on working in Alaska and there was no requirement that work be in a special area for specified employers.

Debts cancelled in bankruptcy. Debt cancelled in a bankruptcy case is not included in your gross income. Instead, certain losses, credits, and basis of property must be reduced by the amount excluded from income. These losses, credits, and basis of property are called "tax attributes." The amount of cancelled debt is used to reduce the tax attributes in the order listed below:

1. Net operating losses and carryovers—dollar for dollar of debt discharge;
2. Carryovers of the general business credit—$33^1/_3$ cents for each dollar of debt discharge;
3. AMT minimum tax credit as of the beginning of the year immediately after the taxable year of the discharge—$33^1/_3$ cents for each dollar of debt discharge;
4. Net capital losses and carryovers—dollar for dollar of debt discharge;
5. Basis of depreciable and nondepreciable assets—dollar for dollar of debt discharge (but not below the amount of your total undischarged liabilities);
6. Passive activity loss and credit carryovers—dollar for dollar of debt discharge for passive losses; $33^1/_3$ cents for each dollar of debt discharge in the case of passive credits; and
7. Foreign tax credit carryovers—$33^1/_3$ cents for each dollar of debt discharge.

After these reductions, any remaining balance of the debt discharge is disregarded. On Form 982, you may make a special election to first reduce the basis of any depreciable assets before reducing other tax attributes in the order above. Realty held for sale to customers may be treated as depreciable assets for purposes of the election. The election allows you to preserve your current deductions, such as a net operating loss carryover or capital loss carryover, for use in the following year. The election also will have the effect of reducing your depreciation deductions for years following the year of debt cancellation. If you later sell the depreciable property at a gain, the gain attributable to the basis reduction will be taxable as ordinary income under the depreciation recapture rules discussed at *44.1*.

 Law Alert

Loans Cancelled by Foundations
Student loans cancelled by educational organizations may be tax free if the loan was made under a program that encourages students to provide public service by working in occupations or areas with unmet needs. The services must be under the direction of a governmental unit or tax-exempt charity. Services to the lender organization do not qualify.

Separate bankruptcy estate. If you are an individual debtor who files for bankruptcy under Chapter 7 or 11 of the Bankruptcy Code, a separate "estate" is created consisting of property that belonged to you before the filing date. This bankruptcy estate is a new taxable entity, completely separate from you as a taxpayer. The estate is represented by a trustee who manages the estate for the benefit of any creditors. The estate earns its own income and incurs expenses. The trustee reports the estate's income or loss on a separate return (Form 1041). The creation of a separate bankruptcy estate also gives you a "fresh start"; with certain exceptions, wages you earn and property you acquire after the bankruptcy case has begun belong to you and do not become part of the bankruptcy estate.

A separate estate is not created for an individual who files for bankruptcy under Chapter 12 or 13.

In a Chapter 7 or 11 case, the tax attribute reductions are made to the attributes in the bankruptcy estate. Reductions are not made to attributes of an individual debtor that come into existence after the bankruptcy case begins or that are treated as exempt property under bankruptcy rules. Basis reduction does apply to property transferred by the bankruptcy estate to the individual.

Debts discharged while you are insolvent. If your debt is cancelled outside of bankruptcy while you are insolvent, the cancellation does not result in taxable income to the extent of the insolvency. Insolvency means that liabilities exceed the fair market value of your assets immediately before the discharge of the debt. The discharged debt is not taxed to the extent of your insolvency and is applied to the reduction of tax attributes on Form 982 in the same manner as to a bankrupt individual. If the cancelled debt exceeds the insolvency, any remaining balance is treated as if it were a debt cancellation of a solvent person and, thus, it is taxable unless it is a qualifying farming debt or business real estate debt as discussed later in this section.

See the Example below for the IRS approach to figuring insolvency upon a debt cancellation.

EXAMPLE

In 1993, Jones borrowed $1,000,000 from Chester and signed a note payable for that amount. Jones was not personally liable on the note, which was secured by an office building valued at $1,000,000 that he bought from Baker with the proceeds of Chester's loan. In 1999, when the value of the building declined to $800,000, Chester agreed to reduce the principal of the loan to $825,000. At the time, Jones held other assets valued at $100,000 and owed another person $50,000.

To determine the extent of Jones's insolvency, the IRS compares the value of Jones's assets and liabilities immediately before the discharge. According to the IRS, his assets total $900,000: the building valued at $800,000 plus other assets of $100,000. His liabilities total $1,025,000: the other debt of $50,000 plus the liability on the note, which the IRS considered to be $975,000, equal to the $800,000 value of the building and the discharged debt of $175,000. Jones is insolvent by $125,000 ($1,025,000 in liabilities less $900,000 in assets). As $175,000 was the amount of the discharged debt and Jones was insolvent to the extent of $125,000, only $50,000 is treated as taxable income.

Partnership debts. When a partnership's debt is discharged because of bankruptcy, insolvency, or if it is qualified farm debt or business real estate debt that is cancelled, the discharged amount is allocated among the partners. Bankruptcy or insolvency is tested not at the partnership level, but separately for each partner. Thus, a bankrupt or insolvent partner applies the allocated amount to reduce the specified tax attributes as previously discussed. A solvent partner may not take advantage of the rules applied to insolvent or bankrupt partners, even if the partnership is insolvent or bankrupt.

Purchase price adjustment for solvent debtors. If you buy property on credit and the seller reduces or cancels the debt arising out of the purchase, the reduction is generally treated as a purchase price adjustment (reducing your basis in the property). Since the reduction is not treated as a debt cancellation, you do not realize taxable income on the price adjustment. This favorable price adjustment rule applies only if you are solvent and not in bankruptcy, you have not transferred the property to a third party, and the seller has not transferred the debt to a third party, such as with the sale of your installment contract to a collection company.

Qualified farm debt. A solvent farmer may avoid tax from a discharge of indebtedness by an unrelated lender, including any federal, state, or local government agency, if the debt was incurred in farming or is a farm business debt secured by farmland or farm equipment used in the farming business. You are eligible for this relief only if 50% or more of your total gross receipts for the pre-

Filing Tip

Bankrupt Persons

Special rules apply to debt cancellations under bankruptcy law. A debt cancelled in a bankruptcy case is not included in your income, but certain losses, credits, and basis of property must be reduced by the amount of excluded income.

ceding three taxable years was derived from farming. The excluded amount first reduces tax attributes such as net operating loss carryovers and business tax credits. The excluded amount then reduces the farmer's basis in all property other than farmland, and then the basis in land used in the farming business.

Business real estate debt. A solvent taxpayer may elect to avoid tax on a discharge of qualifying real property business debt. Such a discharge may occur where the fair market value of the property securing the debt has fallen in value. This relief applies to debt discharges after 1992. The debt must have been incurred or assumed in connection with business real property and must be secured by such property. A debt incurred or assumed after 1992 must be incurred or assumed to buy, construct, or substantially improve real property used in a business, or to refinance such acquisition debt (up to the refinanced amount). Debt incurred after 1992 to refinance a pre-1993 business real property debt (up to the refinanced amount) also qualifies. The debt must be secured by the property. Discharges of farm indebtedness do not qualify but may be tax free under the separate rules discussed earlier.

The maximum amount that can be excluded from income is the excess of the outstanding loan principal (immediately before the discharge) over the fair market value (immediately before the discharge) of the real property securing the debt, less any other outstanding qualifying real property business debts secured by the property. The excludable amount also may not exceed the taxpayer's adjusted basis for all depreciable real property held before the discharge. The excluded amount reduces basis in all depreciable real property.

Effect of basis reduction on later disposition of property. A reduction of basis is treated as a depreciation deduction so that a profitable sale of the property at a later date may be subject to the rules of recapture of depreciation; *see 44.1.*

 Filing Pointer

Price Adjustments Not Taxed

If you bought property on credit and the seller cancels or reduces your purchase-related debt, this is a price adjustment, not a taxable cancellation of debt; *see 11.8* for details.

Partners, S Corporation Shareholders, and Trust and Estate Beneficiaries

11.9 Schedule K-1

Although partnerships, S corporations, trusts, and estates are different types of tax entities, they share a common tax-reporting characteristic. The entity itself generally does not pay income taxes. As a partner, shareholder, or beneficiary, you report your share of the entity's income or loss. The entity files a Schedule K-1 with the IRS that indicates your share of the income, deductions, and credits passed through from the entity. You will receive a copy of the Schedule K-1, which you should keep for your records; it does not have to be attached to your tax return.

11.10 How Partners Report Partnership Profit and Loss

A partnership files Form 1065, which informs the IRS of partnership profit or loss and each partner's share on Schedule K-1. The partnership pays no tax on partnership income; each partner reports his or her share of partnership net profit or loss and special deductions and credits, whether or not distributions are received from the partnership, as shown on Schedule K-1. Income that is not distributed or withdrawn increases the basis of a partner's partnership interest.

Your share reported to you on Schedule K-1 (Form 1065) is generally based on your proportionate capital interest in the partnership, unless the partnership agreement provides for another allocation.

Your partnership must give you a copy of Schedule K-1 (Form 1065), which lists your share of income, loss, deduction, and credit items, and where to report them on your return. For example, your share of income or loss from a business or real estate activity is reported on Schedule E and is subject to passive activity adjustments, if any. Interest and dividends are reported on Schedule B, royalties on Schedule E, and capital gains and losses on Schedule D. Your share of charitable donations is claimed on Schedule A if you itemize deductions. Tax preference items for alternative minimum tax purposes are also listed.

Health insurance premiums. A partnership that pays 1999 premiums for health insurance for partners has a choice. It may treat the premium as a reduction in distributions to the partners. Alternatively, it may deduct the premium as an expense and charge each partner's share as a guaranteed salary payment taxable to the partner. The partner reports the guaranteed payment shown on Schedule K-1 as nonpassive income on Schedule E and may deduct 60% of the premium on Line 28, Form 1040. *See 12.1* and adjoining tax alert for upcoming and proposed increases to the medical insurance deduction for self-employed individuals.

 Filing Tip

Schedule K-1

You need a copy of Schedule K to properly report your share of partnership, S corporation, trust, and estate income or loss.

Filing Instruction

Partnership Elections

The partnership, not the individual partners, makes elections affecting the computation of partnership income such as the election to defer involuntary conversion gains, to amortize organization and start-up costs, and to choose depreciation methods, including first-year expensing. An election to claim a foreign tax credit is made by the partners.

Guaranteed salary and interest. A guaranteed salary that is fixed without regard to partnership income is reported as ordinary income. If you receive a percentage of the partnership income with a stipulated minimum payment, the guaranteed payment is the amount by which the minimum guarantee exceeds your share of the partnership income before taking into account the minimum guarantee.

Interest on capital is reported as interest income.

Self-employment tax. As a partner, you pay 1999 self-employment tax on your partnership profits, including a guaranteed salary and other guaranteed payments. The self-employment tax is explained in Chapter 45. Limited partners do not pay self-employment tax, unless guaranteed payments are received; *see 45.2.*

Special allocations. Partners may agree to special allocations of gain, income, loss, deductions, or credits disproportionate to their capital contributions. The allocation should have a substantial economic effect to avoid an IRS disallowance. The IRS will not issue an advance ruling on whether an allocation has a substantial economic effect. If the allocation is rejected, a partner's share is determined by his or her partnership interest.

To have substantial economic effect, a special allocation must be reflected by adjustments to the partners' capital accounts; liquidation proceeds must be distributed in accordance with the partners' capital accounts, and following a liquidating distribution, the partners must be liable to the partnership to restore any deficit in their capital.

If there is a change of partnership interests during the year, items are allocated to a partner for that part of the year he or she is a member of the partnership. Thus, a partner who acquires an interest late in the year is barred from deducting partnership expenses incurred prior to his entry into the partnership. If the partners agree to give an incoming partner a disproportionate share of partnership losses for the period after he or she becomes a member, the allocation must meet the substantial economic effect test to avoid IRS disallowance.

See IRS regulations to Code Section 704, IRS Publication 541, and Form 1065 instructions for further details.

Reporting transfers of interest to IRS. If you transfer a partnership interest that includes an interest in partnership receivables and appreciated inventory, you must report the disposition to the partnership within 30 days, or, if earlier, by January 15 of the calendar year after the year of the transfer. The partnership in turn files a report with the IRS on Form 8308. You must also attach a statement to your income tax return describing the transaction and allocating basis to the receivables and inventory items. The IRS wants to keep track of such dispositions because partners have to pay ordinary income tax on the portion of profit attributable to the receivables and inventory.

For transfers before August 6, 1997, the ordinary income rule for appreciated inventory applies to inventory with a fair market value exceeding 120% of adjusted basis. For transfers after August 5, 1997, the profit attributable to *all* inventory is ordinary income unless the transfer is pursuant to a contract binding on and after June 8, 1997.

Within 30 days of your transfer, provide the partnership with a statement that includes the date of the exchange and identifies the transferee (include Social Security number if known). You can be penalized for failure to notify the partnership. You and your transferee should receive a copy of the Form 8308 that the partnership will send to the IRS along with its Form 1065.

Generally, the partnership must file a separate Form 8308 for each transfer but the IRS may allow a composite Form 8308 for the calendar year if there were at least 25 reportable transfers.

Recognition of gain by partner on distribution of contributed property. Under a restrictive law (Code Section 737), a partner who contributes appreciated property to a partnership may incur tax on the pre-contribution gain if within seven years *other* property is received from the partnership that is valued at more than the partner's basis in the partnership. Under another law (Code Section 704(c)(1)(B)), if appreciated property contributed by a partner is distributed to a *different* partner within seven years of the contribution, the contributing partner is taxed on the pre-contribution gain as if the property had been sold at fair market value on the date of distribution.

Caution

Partner May Be Taxed on Pre-Contribution Gain

The rules subjecting partners to tax on pre-contribution gain when they contribute property and the partnership makes a later distribution are complicated and hedged with restrictions. Consult a tax advisor before making transfers of appreciated property to, or taking distributions from, a partnership.

11.11 When a Partner Reports Income or Loss

You report your share of the partnership gain or loss for the partnership year that ends in your tax reporting year. If you and the partnership are on a calendar-year basis, you report your share of the 1999 partnership income on your 1999 income tax return. If the partnership is on a fiscal year ending March 31, for example, and you report on a calendar year, you report on your 1999 return your share of the partnership income for the whole fiscal year ending March 31, 1999—that is, partnership income for the fiscal year April 1, 1998, through March 31, 1999.

If a Section 444 election of a fiscal year is made on Form 8716, a special tax payment must be computed for each fiscal year and if the computed payment exceeds $500, it must be paid to the IRS. The tax payment is figured and reported on Form 8752. The tax does not apply to the first tax year of a partnership's existence but Form 8752 must still be filed. In later years, a refund of prior payments is available to the extent the prior payments exceed the payment required for the current fiscal year. For example, if the required payment was $12,000 for the fiscal year July 1, 1999–June 30, 2000, and the required payment for the fiscal year starting July 1, 2000, is $10,000, a $2,000 refund may be claimed on Form 8752. Refunds of prior year payments also are available if the fiscal-year election is terminated and a calendar year adopted or if the partnership liquidates.

See *IRS Publication 541 for further information on partnership reporting.*

11.12 Partnership Loss Limitations

Your share of partnership losses may not exceed the adjusted basis of your partnership interest. If the loss exceeds basis, the excess loss may not be deducted until you have partnership earnings to cover the loss or contribute capital to cover the loss. The basis of your partnership interest is generally the amount paid for the interest (either through contribution or purchase) less withdrawals plus accumulated taxed earnings that have not been withdrawn. You also have a basis in loans to the partnership for which you are personally liable.

A partner's basis is not increased by accrued but unpaid expenses such as interest costs and accounts payable unless the partnership uses the accrual accounting method. However, basis is increased by capitalized items allocable to future periods such as organization and construction period expenses.

Partners are subject to the "at-risk" loss limitation rules. These rules limit the amount of loss that may be deducted to the amount each partner personally has at stake in the partnership, such as contributions of property and loans for which the partner is personally liable. *See 10.17* for a discussion of the "at-risk" rules.

Furthermore, if the IRS determines that a tax-shelter partnership is not operated to make a profit, deductions may be disallowed even where there is an "at-risk" investment.

Finally, any loss not barred by these limitations may be disallowed under the passive activity rules discussed in Chapter 10.

11.13 Unified Tax Audits of Partnerships

Tax audits of both a partnership of more than 10 partners and its partners must be at the partnership level. To challenge the partnership treatment of an item, the IRS must generally audit the partnership, not the individual partner. To avoid a personal audit of a partnership item, a partner should report partnership items as shown on the partnership return or identify any inconsistent treatment on his or her return. Otherwise, the IRS may assess a deficiency without auditing the partnership.

For a partnership-level audit, the partnership names a "tax matters partner" (TMP) to receive notice of the audit. If one is not named, the IRS will treat as a TMP the general partner having the largest interest in partnership profits at the end of the taxable year involved in the audit. Notice of the audit must also be given to the other partners. All partners may participate in the partnership audit. If the IRS settles with some partners, it is not required to offer consistent settlement terms. However, the IRS is required to apply the tax law consistently.

Within 90 days after the IRS mails its final determination, the TMP may appeal to the Tax Court; individual partners have an additional 60 days to file a court petition if the TMP does not do so. An appeal may also be filed in a federal district court or the claims court if the petitioning partner first deposits with the IRS an amount equal to the tax that would be owed if the IRS determination were sustained. A Tax Court petition takes precedence over petitions filed in other courts. The first Tax Court petition filed is heard; if other partners have also filed petitions, their cases will be dismissed. If no Tax Court petitions are filed, the first petition filed in federal district court or the claims court takes precedence. Regardless of which petition takes precedence, all partners who hold an interest during the taxable year involved will be bound by the decision (unless the statute of limitations with respect to that partner has run out).

Exception for 10 or fewer partners. The unified audit rules do not apply if there are 10 or fewer partners. The exception applies if all the partners are individuals (but not nonresident aliens), estates of deceased partners, or C corporations. C corporations are allowed under this exception under a law effective for taxable years ending after August 5, 1997. A husband and wife (and their estates) are treated as one partner.

 Court Decision

Settlements Need Not Be Consistent

Neither the IRS nor the Department of Justice is required to offer consistent settlements to audited partners so long as they do not discriminate for arbitrary reasons. After a partner sued for a refund, the Court of Federal Claims refused to compel the government to settle his case on the same favorable terms offered to other partners.

11.14 Stockholder Reporting of S Corporation Income and Loss

S corporations are subject to tax reporting rules similar to those applied to partnerships. However, shareholders who work for the corporation are treated as employees for payroll tax purposes. They do not pay self-employment tax on their salary income or other receipts from the corporation.

Your company must give you a copy of Schedule K-1 (Form 1120-S), which lists your share of income or loss, deductions, and credits that must be reported on your return. For example, your share of business income or loss is reported on Schedule E and is subject to passive activity adjustments, if any. Interest and dividends from other corporations are reported on Schedule B, capital gains and losses on Schedule D, Section 1231 gains or losses on Form 4797, and charitable donations on Schedule A. Tax preference items for alternative minimum tax purposes are also listed.

Health insurance premmiums paid by an S corporation for more than 2% stockholders are treated as wages, deductible on Form 1120-S by the corporation and reported to the stockholder on Form W-2. A more-than-2% shareholder who reports premiums as wages for 1999 may deduct 60% of the premium on Line 28 of Form 1040 as an adjustment to income.

Allocation to shareholders. The following items are allocated to and pass through to the shareholders based on the proportion of stock held in the corporation:

- Gains and losses from the sale and exchange of capital assets and Section 1231 property, as well as interest and dividends on corporate investments and losses. Investment interest expenses subject to the rules discussed at *15.10* also pass through.
- Tax-exempt interest. Tax-exempt interest remains tax free in the hands of the stockholders but increases the basis of their stock. Dividends from other companies may qualify for the exclusion.
- First-year expense deduction (Section 179 deduction).
- Charitable contributions made by the corporation.
- Foreign income or loss.
- Foreign taxes paid by the corporation. Each stockholder elects whether to claim these as a credit or deduction.
- Tax preference items.
- Recovery of bad debts and prior taxes.

If your interest changed during the year, your pro rata share must reflect the time you held the stock.

The Tax Court and several federal appeals courts have held that an S corporation shareholder's basis is not increased by guaranteeing a loan to the corporation where there is no actual economic outlay. The Tax Court disagrees with the approach of another federal appeals court that allowed an increased basis where the lender looked to the guarantor-shareholder as the primary obligor on the guaranteed loan.

Passive activity rules limit loss deductions. Losses allocated to you may be disallowed under the passive activity rules discussed in Chapter 10.

Basis adjustments. Because of the nature of S corporation reporting, the basis of each shareholder's stock is subject to change. Basis is increased by the pass-through of income items and by loans to the S corporation for which the shareholder is personally liable, and basis is reduced by the pass-through of loss items and the receipt of certain distributions. Because income and loss items pass through to stockholders, an S corporation has no current earnings and profits. An income item will not increase basis, unless you actually report the amount on your tax return. The specific details and order of basis adjustments are listed in IRS Publication 589.

EXAMPLES

1. A calendar-year corporation incurs a loss of $10,000. Smith and Jones each own 50% of the stock. On May 1, Smith sells all of his stock to Harris. For the year, Smith was a shareholder for 120 days, Jones for 365 days, and Harris for 245 days. The loss is allocated on a daily basis; the daily basis of the loss is $27.3973 ($10,000 divided by 365 days). The allocation is as follows:

Smith:	$1,644 ($27.3973 × 120 days × 50% interest)
Jones:	$5,000 ($27.3973 × 365 days × 50% interest)
Harris:	$3,356 ($27.3973 × 245 days × 50% interest)

Caution

Family S Corporations

The IRS has the authority to change the amounts of items passed through to stockholders to properly reflect the value of services rendered or capital contributed by family members of one or more S corporation shareholders. If you are the member of a family of an S corporation shareholder and perform services or furnish capital to the corporation without receiving reasonable compensation, the IRS may reallocate salary or interest income to you from the other shareholders to reflect the value of your services or capital. The term "family" includes only a spouse, parents, ancestors, children, and any trusts for the benefit of such relatives.

2. Same facts as in Example 1, except that on May 1, Smith sells only 50% of his stock to Harris. The allocation for Smith accounts for his 50% interest for 120 days and his 25% interest for the remainder of the year.

> Smith: $3,322 ($27.3973 × 120 days × 50% plus $27.3973 × 245 days × 25%)
>
> Jones: $5,000 (as above)
>
> Harris: $1,678 ($27.3973 × 245 days × 25%)

11.15 How Beneficiaries Report Estate or Trust Income

Trust or estate income is treated as if you had received the income directly from the original source instead of from the estate or trust. This means capital gain remains capital gain, ordinary income is fully taxed, and tax-exempt income remains tax free. Tax preference items of a trust or estate are apportioned between the estate or trust and beneficiaries, according to allocation of income.

You report your share of trust or estate income on Schedule B as shown on the Schedule K-1 (Form 1041) sent to you by the trustee. Dividends and interest from the trust are reported on Schedule B of Form 1040 and capital gains on Schedule D. Income or loss from real estate or business activities shown on Schedule K-1 is reported by you on Schedule E, subject to the passive activity restrictions discussed in Chapter 10.

Reporting rule for revocable grantor trusts. A grantor who sets up a revocable trust or keeps certain powers over trust income or corpus must report all of the trust income, deductions, and credits. This rule applies if a grantor retains a reversionary interest in the trust that is valued at more than 5% of the trust (valued at the time the trust is set up); *see* Chapter 33. If a grantor is also a trustee of a revocable trust and all the trust assets are in the United States, filing Form 1041 is not necessary. The grantor simply reports the trust income, deductions, and credits on Form 1040. This reporting rule is optional for revocable trusts created before 1981. Grantors of such trusts who want to report trust income on their own returns without having to file Form 1041 must first file a final Form 1041 for the current tax year with a notation on the form alerting the IRS that in later years they will report trust income on their own returns; *see* the instructions to Form 1041.

11.16 Repeal of Throwback Rule for Distributions of Accumulated Trust Income

Where you are the beneficiary of an accumulation trust, the trust accumulates income on which it pays tax. When the trust distributes income to you, the trustee tells you what part of the distribution is attributable to current income reported under the general rules at *11.15* and how much is attributable to accumulations of prior income. If you receive a distribution of accumulated income from a trust, contact the trustee or an experienced tax practitioner for advice in computing your tax on the accumulation.

For distributions made in trust taxable years beginning before August 6, 1997, tax on the accumulation distribution was figured on Form 4970, subject to a throwback rule. However, the throwback rule has been repealed for distributions made by most domestic trusts in trust taxable years beginning after August 5, 1997. The throwback rule continues to apply to distributions from domestic trusts that were formerly foreign trusts, or which were created before March 1, 1984, and subject to the rules for multiple trusts with a tax avoidance purpose. The throwback rules continue to apply to foreign trusts.

Throwback rule for distributions not affected by new law repeal. Distributions of accumulated income are subject to tax, provided the accumulation exceeds the distributable net income of the trust for the year. However, under the throwback rule, only that portion of the accumulation distribution that would have been included in the beneficiary's income had it been distributed when earned is currently taxed. Thus, tax-exempt interest is never taxed. Income accumulated prior to the beneficiary's reaching the age of 21 and the years before a beneficiary was born is not subject to the throwback rule unless distributions are made under a multiple trust rule explained in the instructions to Form 4970.

Although a beneficiary pays a tax in the year of receiving the accumulation distribution, tax is computed as if the accumulated income were actually distributed in the years in which it was earned. For the year of the accumulation distribution, the beneficiary pays tax on the sum of: (1) a tax on taxable income exclusive of the accumulation distribution; (2) a tax on the accumulation distribution computed using a short-cut method that takes into account taxable income in three of the five years preceding the year of distribution; and (3) an interest charge in the case of a foreign trust.

Planning Reminder

Basis Limits Loss Deductions

Deductible losses may not exceed your basis in S corporation stock and loans to the corporation. If losses exceed basis, the excess loss is carried over and becomes deductible when you invest or lend an equivalent amount of money to the corporation. This rule may allow for timing a loss deduction. In a year in which you want to deduct the loss, you may contribute capital to the corporation. If a carryover loss exists when an S election terminates, a limited loss deduction may be allowed.

Law Alert

Consistent Reporting by Beneficiaries

Beneficiaries of trusts and estates must report items consistently with the Schedule K-1 provided by the trust or estate. If an item is treated inconsistently and a statement identifying the inconsistency is not attached to the return, the IRS may make a summary assessment for additional tax without issuing a deficiency notice.

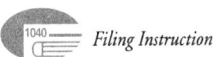

Lump-Sum Distributions From Qualified Retirement Plans

When a beneficiary receiving a lump-sum distribution because of an employee's death reports the distribution using the special averaging method (Chapter 7), the taxable amount of the distribution must be reduced by the estate taxes attributable to the distribution. *See* the Form 4972 instructions when calculating the tax under averaging.

In preparing your return, the tax on your regular taxable income is computed on Form 1040; the tax on the distribution is computed on Form 4970 and added to the tax on Form 1040.

Where a trust has already been subject to estate tax or the generation-skipping transfer tax, the partial tax on a distribution is reduced by the estate or generation-skipping tax attributable to the accumulated income. The reduction is limited by a special statutory formula for determining the pre-death portions.

Where the beneficiary receives an accumulation distribution from more than two trusts for the same year, tax for the distributions from the third trust is computed under the method described above, except that no credit is given for any taxes previously paid by the trust with respect to the accumulation distribution. A *de minimis* rule provides that accumulation distributions are not subject to the multiple trust rule unless the distribution equals or exceeds $1,000.

Trust for the benefit of a spouse. Where a spouse creates a trust for the benefit of the other spouse, income of the trust is taxed to the spouse who created the trust as income is earned. Trust transfers before October 10, 1969, are not subject to this rule.

11.17 Deductions for Income Subject to Estate Tax

If you receive income that was earned by, but not paid to, a decedent before death, you are said to have "income in respect of a decedent." You report the income, and if an estate has paid a federal estate tax on the income, you may deduct part of the estate tax allocated to the income. No deduction is allowed for state death taxes. Ask the executor of the estate for data in computing the deduction.

EXAMPLE

When Jim Bennett's uncle died, he was owed a fee of $1,000. He also had not collected accrued bond interest of $500. Bennett, as the sole heir, will collect both items and pay income tax on them. These items are called income in respect of a decedent. Assume that an estate tax of $390 was paid on the $1,500. Bennett collects the $1,000, which he reports on his income tax return. If he itemizes deductions, he may deduct $260, computed as follows:

$$\frac{\$1,000}{\$1,500} \times \$390 = \$260$$

When he collects the $500, he will deduct the balance, or $130 ($390 – $260).

Schedule A deduction. The deduction is generally claimed on Line 27 of Schedule A as a miscellaneous itemized deduction that is not subject to the 2% AGI floor. However, if you receive long-term capital gain income, such as an installment payment on a sale transacted before a decedent's death, the estate tax attributed to the capital gain item is not claimed as a miscellaneous deduction. The deduction is treated as if it were an expense of sale and, thus, reduces the amount of gain.

Farm Income or Loss

Gentleman Farming

To be treated as farmers, individuals must be engaged in farming for gain or profit. Farm losses of a part-time "gentleman" farmer may be disallowed on the grounds that the farm is not operated to make a profit but is a hobby. The hobby rules explained at *40.10* apply in determining the existence of a profit motive in farming operations. Favorable evidence of an intention to make a profit are: you do not use your farm for recreation. You have tried to cut losses by switching from unsuccessful products to other types of farming. Losses are decreasing. Losses were caused by unexpected events. You have a bookkeeping system. You consult experts. You devote personal attention to the farm.

11.18 Who is a Farmer?

The term "farmer" includes all individuals, partnerships, syndicates, and corporations that cultivate, operate, or manage a farm for profit or gain, either as owners or tenants. Thus, partners in a partnership that operates a farm are considered farmers.

The term "farm" includes stock, dairy, poultry, fruit and truck farms, plantations, ranches, and all land used for farming operations. A fish farm where fish are specially fed and raised, and not just caught, is a farm. Animal breeding farms, such as mink, fox, and chinchilla farms, are also considered farms.

Farm loss deductions may also be restricted by the at-risk rules and passive activity rules described in Chapter 10.

If your farm losses exceed your other income, *see 40.18.*

Important: A guide to reporting farm income and loss may be obtained at your local Internal Revenue Service Center or from your County Farm Agent. It is called *Farmer's Tax Guide* (IRS Publication 225).

11.19 Forms Farmers File

Use Schedule F to report income from a farm you operate as an individual. The profit or loss computed on Schedule F is then included on Line 18 of Form 1040. Schedule F is also used as a basis for figuring self-employment tax on Schedule SE, which must also be filed with Form 1040. Sales of farm equipment and dairy or breeding livestock are reported on Form 4797.

If you operate through a partnership, the details of your farm operation are shown on Schedule F and Form 1065. Your share of the partnership net income or loss is included in Form 1040.

Individual farmers who are on a calendar-year basis (ending December 31) may pay their entire 1999 estimated tax on Form 1040-ES by January 18, 2000, if at least two-thirds of 1999 estimated gross income is from farming, or if at least two-thirds of 1998 total gross income was from farming. A final return is required by April 17, 2000. However, you may file your final return by March 1, 2000, instead of making an estimated tax payment for 1999 in January, 2000.

11.20 Income Averaging for Farmers

A farmer may elect to average 1999 farm income over three years on Schedule J of Form 1040. On Schedule J, you allocate one-third of elected farm income to each of the prior tax years of 1996, 1997, and 1998. The 1999 tax equals 1999 tax liability figured without elected farm income plus increases in tax liability for the three prior years by including allocated elected farm income.

Elected farm income is taxable income attributable to a farming business. Gain from the sale of property, other than land, regularly used by the farmer for a substantial period in a farming business is treated as attributable to a "farming business." A farming business is the trade or business of farming, including operating a nursery or sod farm, or the raising or harvesting of trees bearing fruit, nuts, or other crops, or ornamental trees.

The election to average farming income is irrevocable unless Treasury regulations allow an exception.

Income averaging is available for all tax years beginning after December 31, 1997.

Income averaging may not be elected by estates or trusts.

 Law Alert

Farm Income Averaging

When this book went to press, Congress was considering a proposal that would extend income averaging to fishermen as well as farmers. Additionally, income averaging would be coordinated with the alternative minimum tax (AMT) so that taxpayers who elect to average income would owe AMT only to the extent it would be owed if the taxpayer had not elected to average income. If the proposal is adopted, it will go into effect in 2000. *See* the Supplement for legislative developments.

Claiming Deductions

In this part, you will learn how to reduce your tax liability by claiming deductions from gross income, and either the standard deduction or itemized deductions. Pay special attention to—

- Deductions you may claim directly from gross income in arriving at adjusted gross income. These are allowed even if you claim the standard deduction. *See* Chapter 12.

- The standard deduction. Although the standard deduction (*see* Chapter 13) may provide an automatic tax reduction, read the chapters on itemized deductions to see that you have not overlooked itemized deductions for charitable donations, interest expenses, state and local taxes, medical expenses, casualty and theft losses, miscellaneous expenses for job costs, and investment expenses.

- The 3% reduction of certain itemized deductions discussed in Chapter 13 if your 1999 adjusted gross income, or AGI (Line 33 of Form 1040), exceeds $126,600 (or $63,300 if you are married and file separate returns).

- Personal exemptions. Each personal exemption claimed on your 1999 return—for yourself, your spouse, your children, and other dependents, is the equivalent of a $2,750 deduction. *See* Chapter 21 for exemptions rules, including the phaseout of exemptions for certain high-income taxpayers.

- Other deductions that are discussed in the following chapters:

Deductions Allowed in Figuring Adjusted Gross Income

Adjusted gross income (AGI) is the amount used in figuring the 7.5% floor for medical expense deductions *(17.1)*, the 10% floor for personal casualty and theft losses *(18.11)*, the 2% floor for miscellaneous itemized deductions *(19.1)*, the charitable contribution percentage limitations *(14.17)*, and the 3% reduction of itemized deductions *(13.7)*.

If you follow the instructions and order of the tax return, you will arrive at adjusted gross income automatically. But if you are planning the tax consequences of a transaction in advance of preparing your return, *12.1* will explain how to figure adjusted gross income (AGI).

There is an advantage in being able to claim deductions directly from gross income in arriving at adjusted gross income, since such deductions are allowed even if you claim the standard deduction and do not itemize deductions on Schedule A of Form 1040. Another advantage of such deductions is that they also reduce state income tax for taxpayers residing in states that compute tax based on federal adjusted gross income. This chapter will explain the deductions that qualify for the direct deduction from gross income.

Expenses Deductible Directly From Gross Income

12.1 Figuring Adjusted Gross Income (AGI)

Adjusted gross income is the difference between gross income in Step 1 and the deductions listed in Step 2.

Step 1. Figure gross income. This is all income received by you from any source, such as wages, salary, tips, gross business income, income from sales and exchanges of property, interest and dividends, rents, royalties, annuities, pensions, etc. But gross income does not include such items as tax-free interest from state or local bonds *(4.24)*, tax-free parsonage allowance *(3.12)*, tax-free insurance proceeds (Chapter 33), gifts and inheritances *(11.4)*, Social Security benefits that are not subject to tax under the rules at *34.3*, tax-free scholarship grants *(38.1)*, tax-free board and lodging *(3.11)*, and other tax-free fringe benefits (Chapter 3).

Step 2. Deduct from gross income only the following items:

Repayment of supplemental unemployment benefits required because of receipt of trade readjustment allowances *(2.9)*

Forfeiture-of-interest penalties because of premature withdrawals *(4.16)*

Capital loss deduction up to $3,000 *(5.4)*

IRA contributions *(8.4)*

Rent and royalty expenses (Chapter 9)

50% of self-employed tax liability *(12.2)*

Health insurance deduction if self-employed *(12.2)*

Student loan interest *(38.6)*

Jury duty pay turned over to your employer *(12.2)*

Performing artists qualifying expenses *(12.2)*

Reforestation expenses *(12.2)*

Moving expenses *(12.3)*

Medical savings account contributions (Chapter 17)

Alimony payments *(37.1)*

Business expenses (Chapter 40)

Net operating losses *(40.19)*

Keogh or SEP retirement plan contributions for yourself (Chapter 41)

Step 3. The difference between Steps 1 and 2 is adjusted gross income.

12.2 Claiming Deductions From Gross Income

Many deductions taken directly from gross income in arriving at adjusted gross income are deducted on Form 1040 schedules devoted to a specific activity, such as business deductions claimed on Schedule C (Chapter 40), capital losses claimed on Schedule D (Chapter 5), and real estate rental expenses claimed on Schedule E (Chapter 9). Where an expense is not claimed on a specific schedule, it is deducted on Lines 23–31 of Form 1040. Deductions that are claimed directly from gross income on Form 1040 are referred to as "above-the-line" deductions, as they are allowed in figuring adjusted gross income and do not have to be claimed as itemized deductions. IRA deductions and student loan deductions on Form 1040A are claimed on Lines 15 and 16.

Here is a list of the deductions claimed on Lines 23–31 of Form 1040. Many of them are discussed in detail elsewhere in this book. Moving expenses are discussed at *12.3–12.8*. The others are discussed below.

IRA deduction—Line 23 of Form 1040; Line 15 of Form 1040A. Enter your deductible IRA contribution here, including a contribution for your spouse if you file jointly. The deductible limits, including the phase-out rules for individuals covered by employer retirement plans, are explained in Chapter 8.

Student loan interest deduction—Line 24 of Form 1040; Line 16 of Form 1040A. Within limits, you may deduct interest you pay on a qualified student loan. *See 38.6* for details.

 Law Alert

Self-Employed Health Insurance
The deductible percentages of health insurance expenses are: 60% in 1999, 2000, and 2001; 70% in 2002; and 100% in 2003 and later years.

Medical savings account (MSA) deduction—Line 25 of Form 1040. If you are self-employed or employed by a qualifying small business and have high-deductible health coverage, a deduction for contributions to an MSA may be allowed. *See 17.17* for the MSA rules.

Moving expenses—Line 26 of Form 1040. Deductible moving expenses are discussed in this chapter at *12.3–12.8.*

50% of self-employment tax—Line 27 of Form 1040. After you figure your self-employment tax liability on Schedule SE, you deduct 50% of it here as an income tax deduction. *See* Chapter 45 for the calculation of self-employment tax.

Self-employed health insurance deduction—Line 28. If you were self-employed in 1999, you may claim 60% of health insurance premiums paid in 1999 for yourself, your spouse, and your dependents. The deduction is also allowed if you are a general partner in a partnership, a limited partner receiving guaranteed payments, or you received wages from an S corporation in which you were more than a 2% shareholder.

If you have a qualified long-term care policy, the deductible portion of the premiums under the rules at *17.15* is included in the 60% deduction.

The 60% deduction may not exceed your net profit from the business under which the health premiums are paid, less deductions claimed on Line 27 (50% of self-employment tax) and Line 29 (Keogh, SEP, or SIMPLE retirement plan contributions).

Any balance of premiums not deductible under the special 60% rule may be claimed as an itemized medical expense subject to the 7.5% income floor *(17.4).*

Keogh plan contributions and self-employed SEP or SIMPLE deductions—Line 29. *See* Chapter 41 for further details.

Penalty on early savings withdrawals—Line 30, *see 4.16.*

Alimony paid—Line 31a, *see* Chapter 37.

Jury duty pay turned over to employer—Line 32. If you receive your regular pay while on jury duty and turn over your jury duty fees to your employer, report the fees as other income on Line 21, Form 1040, claim an offsetting deduction on Line 32. Write "Jury pay" next to Line 32.

Expenses of performing artists—Line 32. As a performing artist, you may deduct job expenses from gross income, whether or not itemized deductions are claimed, if you have:

1. Two or more employers in the performing arts during 1999 with at least $200 of earnings from at least two of them.

2. Expenses from acting or other services in the performing arts that exceed 10% of gross income from such work; and

3. Adjusted gross income (before deducting these expenses) that does not exceed $16,000.

If you are married, a joint return must be filed to claim the deduction, unless you lived apart from your spouse during the whole year. The $16,000 adjusted gross income limitation applies to your combined incomes. If both spouses are performing artists, the $16,000 adjusted income limit applies to the combined incomes, but each spouse must separately meet the two-employer test and 10% expense test for his or her job expenses to be deductible on the joint return.

You report the performing artist expenses on Form 2106 (or Form 2106-EZ where eligible) and enter the total as a "write-in amount" on Line 32 of Form 1040, instead of on Schedule A. Write "QPA" next to Line 32. If you do not meet the tests, the expenses are deducted on Schedule A subject to the 2% AGI floor.

State and local officials—Line 32. State and local officials paid on a fee basis may deduct from gross income unreimbursed business expenses. Next to Line 32 identify the expenses.

Repayment of supplemental unemployment benefits—Line 32. As explained at *2.9,* you may claim a deduction from gross income for the repayment or in some cases a tax credit. If the deduction is claimed, label it "subpay TRA" (trade readjustment allowances) on Line 32.

Reforestation amortization—Line 32. If you do not have to file Schedule C or F to report income from a timber activity, an amortization deduction for qualifying reforestation expenses may be claimed on Line 32. Amortization is allowed over an 84-month period; *see* Code Section 194 for details. On Line 32, the amortization deduction should be labeled "RFST."

Caution

Reduction of 60% Deduction
The 60% health insurance deduction may not be claimed for any month during 1999 that you were eligible to participate in an employer's subsidized health plan, including a plan of your spouse's employer. If the deduction would be barred for any month because of such eligibility, and you have long-term care coverage that is not employer subsidized, you may claim the 60% deduction for the allowable portion of the long-term care premiums *(17.15).*

Moving Costs to New Job Location

12.3 What Moving Costs Are Deductible?

You may deduct unreimbursed expenses of moving your household goods and traveling to a new job location, provided you meet
- A 50-mile distance test, and
- A time test for remaining in the new location.

You claim the moving expense deduction as an adjustment to gross income on Form 1040, Line 26, whether you claim the standard deduction or itemized deductions.

If your expenses are reimbursed, you do not have to report the reimbursement, provided your employer reimburses you under an accountable plan; *see 20.31* and *12.8*.

If the distance test *(12.4)* and time test *(12.5–12.6)* are met, you may deduct on your 1999 return the following unreimbursed moving expenses incurred during 1999:

1. ***Traveling costs of yourself and members of your household en route from your old to the new locality.*** Here, you include the costs of transportation and lodging for yourself and household members while traveling to your new residence. Lodging before departure for one day after the old residence is unusable and lodging for the day of arrival at the new locality are included. If you use your own car, you may either deduct your actual costs of gas, oil, and repairs (but not depreciation) during the trip or take a deduction based on the rate of 10¢ a mile. Also add parking fees and tolls. Meal expenses are not a deductible moving expense.

2. ***The actual cost of moving your personal effects and household goods.*** This includes the cost of packing, crating, and transporting furniture and household belongings, in-transit storage up to 30 consecutive days, insurance costs for the goods, and the cost of moving a pet or shipping an automobile to your new residence. You may also deduct expenses of moving your effects from a place other than your former home, but only up to the estimated cost of such a move from your former home. Also deduct the cost of connecting or disconnecting utilities when moving household appliances. The cost of connecting a telephone in your new home is not deductible.

In one case, a moving expense deduction was allowed for the cost of shipping a sailboat. The IRS had disallowed the deduction, claiming the sailboat was not a "personal effect." The Tax Court, however, allowed the deduction based on these facts: the couple were active sailors and frequently used the boat; they lived on the sailboat for two weeks immediately before they moved and also for nine weeks after they arrived in the new location; and they kept on board personal effects such as a refrigerator, kitchen utensils, and chairs. According to the court, the boat was so "intimately related" to their lifestyle that it should be considered a deductible personal effect.

Delay in moving to new job location. You may delay moving to the area of a new job location. A delay of less than one year does not jeopardize a deduction for moving expenses. Furthermore, if you move to the new job area within one year, your family may stay in the old residence for a longer period. Their later moving expenses will generally be deductible, even though incurred after one year. For example, the IRS allowed a moving expense deduction to a husband who immediately moved to a new job location, although his wife and children did not join him until 30 months after he began the new job. They delayed so that the children could complete their education. The IRS held that since part of the moving expenses were incurred within one year, the moving expenses incurred later were also deductible.

Nondeductible expenses. You may not deduct the cost of travel incurred for a maid, nurse, chauffeur, or similar domestic help (unless the person is also your dependent), expenses of refitting rugs and drapes, forfeited tuition, car tags or driver's license for the state you move to, losses on disposing of memberships in clubs, mortgage penalties, expenses for trips to sell your old house, or loss on the sale of the house. Furthermore, when your employer reimburses you for such costs, you realize taxable income equal to the amount of the reimbursement.

You may not deduct the cost of transporting furniture that you purchased en route from your old home.

You may not deduct the cost of pre-move house-hunting trips, temporary living expenses, or expenses of selling, purchasing, or leasing the old or new residence, such as attorneys' fees, real estate fees, or costs of settling an unexpired lease. Meal expenses while traveling to your new residence are not deductible.

 Filing Tip

Family Move

It is not necessary for you and members of your household to travel together, or at the same time, to claim a deduction for the expenses incurred by each family member.

12.4   The Distance Test

The distance between your new job location and your former home must be at least 50 miles more than the distance between your old job location and your former home. For this purpose, your home may be a house, apartment, trailer, or even a houseboat, but not a seasonal residence such as a summer cottage. If you had no previous job or you return to full-time work after a long period of unemployment or part-time work, the new job location must be at least 50 miles from your former home. Self-employed individuals are also subject to the mileage test.

The location of your new residence is not considered in applying the mileage test. However, if the distance between your new residence and the new job location is more than the distance between your old residence and new job location, your moving expenses may be disallowed unless you can show (1) you are required to live there as a condition of employment or (2) an actual decrease in commuting time or expense results.

If you worked for more than one employer, you find the shortest of the most commonly traveled routes from your old residence to your former principal place of employment.

Your job location is where you spend most of your working time. If you work at various locations, the job location is where you report to work. If you work for several employers on a short-term basis and get jobs through a union hall system, the union hall is considered your job location.

Moving overseas. A member of the Armed Forces may deduct the cost of moving his or her family to an overseas post.

If you take a new job overseas, and qualify for the foreign earned income exclusion, moving expenses allocable to the excluded income are not deductible; *see 36.6.*

Alien moving to the U.S. The deduction is not limited to U.S. citizens and residents. An alien may deduct the cost of travel here to work at a full-time position.

 Filing Tip

Meeting the Mileage Test

Use the following worksheet to see if your move satisfies the 50-mile test. Find the shortest of the most commonly traveled routes in measuring the distances.

Distance between	In miles
1. Old residence and new job location	_____
2. Old residence and old job location	_____
3. Difference (must be at least 50 miles)	_____

EXAMPLES

1. Your company's office is in the center of a metropolitan area. You live 18 miles from your office. You are transferred to a new office and buy a new house. To deduct moving costs, you must show that the location of the new office is at least 50 miles from your previous residence.

2. Your old job was four miles from your former residence and your new job is 55 miles from your former residence. You move to a house that is less than 50 miles from your old house. Nevertheless, you have met the 50-mile test since your new job is 51 miles further from your former home than your old job was.

12.5   The 39-Week Test for Employees

In addition to meeting the distance test *(12.4)*, you must work in the locality of the new job as a full-time employee for at least 39 weeks during the 12-month period immediately following your arrival at the new job location. You do not need to have a job prior to your arrival at the new location. Your family does not have to arrive with you. The 39 weeks of work need not be consecutive or with the same employer. You may change jobs provided you remain in the same general commuting area for 39 weeks. The 39-week test does not apply to employees who become disabled and lose their jobs, or who die.

If you are temporarily absent from work through no fault of your own, due to illness, strikes, shutouts, layoffs, or natural disasters, your temporary absence is counted in the 39 weeks.

EXAMPLE

You accept a position with a company 600 miles from your former position. You move to the new location. After you have worked in the new position 14 weeks, you resign and take another job with a nearby company. You may add the 14 weeks of work with the first company to 25 weeks with the second company to meet the 39-week requirement.

Job transfers. The 39-week period is also waived if you are transferred from your new job for your employer's benefit. However, it must be shown that you could have satisfied the 39-week test except for the transfer.

 Planning Reminder

Loss of Job

If you lose your job for reasons other than your willful misconduct, the 39-week requirement is waived. Should you resign or lose your job for willful misconduct, a part-time job will not satisfy the 39-week test. The time test is not waived because you reach mandatory retirement age first where this retirement was anticipated.

What if *you* initiate the transfer? The IRS held in a ruling that the 39-week test is not waived if an employee initiates the transfer, even if the employer approves. An individual was not allowed to deduct the costs of moving across the country to take a government position when, within 39 weeks of taking the position, he applied for and took another government job in another area. The IRS disallowed the deduction, although the government reimbursed part of the employee's moving expenses to the new job post, thereby indicating that it considered the transfer to be in the government's interest. According to the IRS, the waiver of the 39-week test applies to transfers initiated by employers, not by employees.

Joint returns. On a joint return, either spouse may meet the time test. But the work time of one spouse may not be added to the time of the other spouse.

EXAMPLE

Smith moves from New York to a new job in Denver. After working full time for 30 weeks, he resigns from his job and cannot find another position during the rest of the 12-month period. He may not deduct his moving expenses. But assume that Mrs. Smith also finds a job in Denver at the same time as her husband and continues to work for at least 39 weeks. Since she has met the 39-week test, the moving expenses from New York to Denver paid by her husband are deductible, provided they file a joint return. However, if Mrs. Smith had worked for only nine weeks, her work period could not be added to her husband's to meet the 39-week test.

 Filing Tip

Job Status

For purposes of the 39-week test, full-time status is determined by the customary practices of your occupation in the area. If work is seasonal, off-season weeks count as work weeks if the off-season period is less than six months and you have an employment agreement covering the off-season.

12.6   The 78-Week Test for the Self-Employed and Partners

In addition to meeting the distance test *(12.4)*, you must work full time in the area of the new business for at least 78 weeks during the 24 months immediately following your arrival, of which at least 39 weeks occur in the first 12 months. The full-time work requirement may prevent semi-retired hobbyists, students, or others who work only a few hours a week in self-employed trades or occupations from claiming the deduction.

You are considered to have obtained employment at a new principal place of work when you have made substantial arrangements to begin such work.

The time test is waived if disability or death prevents compliance.

Change of employee or self-employed status. If you start work at a new location as an employee and then become self-employed before meeting the 39-week employee time test, you must meet the 78-week test. Time spent as an employee is counted along with the time spent self-employed in meeting the test.

If, during the first 12 months, you change from working as a self-employed person to working as an employee, you may qualify under the 39-week employee time test, provided you have 39 weeks of work as an *employee*. If you do not have 39 weeks as an employee in the first 12 months, you must meet the 78-week test.

Joint returns. Where you file a joint return, you deduct moving expenses if either you or your spouse can satisfy the time test based on individual work records.

12.7   Claiming Deductible Moving Expenses

Qualifying unreimbursed moving expenses *(12.3)* incurred during 1999 are deductible on your 1999 return whether you claim the standard deduction or itemize deductions. Report your expenses and nontaxable employer reimbursements on Form 3903. Qualifying unreimbursed moving expenses from Form 3903 are then deducted on Form 1040, Line 26, as an adjustment to gross income.

Claiming the deduction before meeting the time test. If the due date for filing your tax return arrives before you can satisfy the applicable time test, you may, nevertheless, deduct unreimbursed moving expenses. If you file your return without taking the deduction, you may file an amended return after meeting the time test to claim the deduction.

EXAMPLE

You move to a new location on November 1, 1999. At the end of the year, you have worked in your new position only nine weeks. You deduct your moving expenses on your 1999 tax return even though you did not complete the 39- or 78-week period of work. But if, after you file the 1999 return, you move from the location before completing the applicable 39-week or 78-week work period, you must report as income the amount of moving expenses deducted in 1999 on the return for the year you move from the location. Alternatively, you may file an amended 1999 return on which you eliminate the deduction.

12.8 Reimbursements of Moving Expenses

If your employer reimburses you for deductible moving expenses *(12.3)* under an accountable plan, the reimbursement should not be reported as salary or wage income on Form W-2. The requirements for an accountable plan are similar to those discussed for business travel expenses at *20.31*.

Qualified moving expenses an employer pays to a third party, such as to a moving company, are not reported on Form W-2.

A reimbursement for expenses that do *not* qualify for a deduction, such as pre-move house-hunting costs, temporary living expenses, meal costs, or real estate expenses, is reported as compensation on your Form W-2.

On Form 3903, you report your deductible expenses in excess of nontaxable reimbursements, and enter the deductible amount on Form 1040, Line 26, as an adjustment to gross income.

If in 1999 you had deductible moving expenses that you claim on your 1999 return and you receive a reimbursement for the expenses in 2000, you report your employer's reimbursement as compensation in 2000.

 Caution

Reimbursement for Loss on Sale of a Home

To encourage or facilitate an employee's move, an employer may reimburse the employee for a loss incurred on the sale of his or her home. The IRS taxes such reimbursements as pay.

Chapter 13

Claiming the Standard Deduction or Itemized Deductions

Claim the standard deduction only if it exceeds your allowable itemized deductions for mortgage interest, property taxes, medical costs, charitable donations, casualty losses, and miscellaneous deductions for job costs and investment expenses. Generally, a single person may claim a 1999 standard deduction of $4,300; a head of household, $6,350; a married couple filing jointly or a qualifying widow(er), $7,200; and a married person filing separately, $3,600. Larger standard deductions are allowed to those who are age 65 or over or blind, and lower standard deductions are allowed to dependents with only investment income.

Before deciding whether to itemize or claim the standard deduction, read Chapters 14 through 20 to see that you have not overlooked any itemized deductions. To itemize, you must file Form 1040 and report your deductions on Schedule A.

Key to Itemized Deductions and the Standard Deduction for 1999

Item—	Explanation—	Limitations and Examples—

Standard deduction	The standard deduction is fixed by law according to your filing status and age. The standard deduction in 1999 is:
	    $7,200 if you are married filing jointly or a qualifying widow or widower.
	    $4,300 if you are single.
	    $6,350 if you are a head of household.
	    $3,600 if you are married filing separately.
	    If you are age 65 or over or blind, your standard deduction is substantially larger; *see 13.4.*
		A married person filing separately may not use the standard deduction if his or her spouse itemizes deductions.
		
		The standard deduction may not be claimed by a nonresident or dual-status alien or on a return filed for a short taxable year caused by a change in accounting period.
		
		A lower standard deduction of $700 is allowed to dependents with only unearned income; *see 13.5.*

Itemized deductions	You should itemize deductions on Schedule A if your deductions exceed the standard deduction for your filing status. Itemized deductions include charitable contributions, interest expenses, local and state taxes, medical and dental costs, casualty and theft losses, job and investment expenses, and educational costs.	There is no dollar limit on the amount of itemized deductions. But individual itemized deductions are subject to limitations and some taxpayers are subject to a 3% reduction, as explained below. **EXAMPLE** You are single and may claim the standard deduction of $4,300 for 1999. However, your itemized deductions are $5,000. You claim $5,000 on Schedule A of Form 1040.
3% reduction	If your 1999 adjusted gross income (AGI) exceeds $126,600, itemized deductions other than medical expenses, casualty and theft losses, gambling losses, and investment interest expenses are reduced by 3% of the excess AGI over $126,600. If you are married filing separately, the reduction applies if your AGI exceeds $63,300; *see 13.7.*	The total reduction may not exceed 80% of your deductions. **EXAMPLE** Your joint return adjusted gross income (AGI) for 1999 is $162,000. Your itemized deductions for mortgage interest, state income taxes, and charitable donations are $20,000. The AGI excess over $126,600 is $35,400. Therefore, itemized deductions are reduced by $1,062 (3% of $35,400). On Schedule A you may deduct $18,938 ($20,000 – $1,062).
Charitable contributions	You may deduct donations to religious, charitable, educational, and other philanthropic organizations that have been approved to receive deductible contributions; *see 14.1.*	The contribution deduction is generally limited to 50% of adjusted gross income. Lower ceilings apply to property donations and contributions to foundations. The deductible amount is included in the 3% reduction explained above.
Interest expenses	You may deduct interest on qualified home mortgages, points, home equity loans, and interest on loans to carry investments.	Interest on investment loans is deductible only to the extent of net investment income. Interest on personal and consumer loans is not deductible. Interest on home mortgages that do not meet the tests at *15.1* is not deductible. Interest and points on home mortgages are included in the 3% reduction explained above.
Taxes	You may deduct payments of state, local, and foreign real property and income taxes, as well as state and local personal property taxes. You claim your deduction on the tax return of the year in which you paid the taxes, unless you report on the accrual basis; *see 16.6.*	No dollar limitation. The deductible amount is included in the 3% reduction explained above.

Item—	Explanation—	Limitations and Examples—
Medical expenses	You may deduct payments of medical expenses for yourself and dependents. A checklist of over 100 deductible medical items is at *17.2*. Deductible drug costs are limited to drugs prescribed by a physician.	Only expenses in excess of 7.5% of adjusted gross income are deductible.
Casualty and theft losses	You may deduct personal property losses caused by storms, fires, and other natural events and as the result of theft.	Each individual casualty loss must exceed $100 and the total of all losses during the year must exceed 10% of adjusted gross income; *see 18.11.*
Job expenses	You may deduct unreimbursed costs of union dues, job educational courses, work clothes, entertainment, travel, and looking for a new job.	Included as miscellaneous expenses of which only the excess over 2% of adjusted gross income is deductible; *see 19.1.* The 2% floor does not apply to performing artists *(12.2)*, handicapped employees, or job-related moving expenses *(12.3)*. The deductible amount is included in the 3% reduction explained above.
Investment expenses and tax preparation costs	You may deduct investment expenses and other expenses of producing and collecting income, expenses of maintaining income-producing property, expenses of preparing your tax return or refund claims, and IRS audits.	Included as miscellaneous expenses of which only the excess over 2% of adjusted gross income is deductible; *see 19.1.*

13.1 Claiming the Standard Deduction

On your 1999 return, you are allowed a standard deduction, which is an "automatic" deduction you may claim regardless of your actual expenses. The standard deduction is not integrated into the tax rate schedules or tax tables. On your return, you deduct the standard deduction from adjusted gross income (AGI), assuming you do not claim itemized deductions on Schedule A of Form 1040; *see* the Example below.

The ***basic standard deduction*** is allowed if you are under age 65 and not blind. The amount is adjusted each year to reflect inflation. For 1999, the basic standard deduction is:

$7,200 if married filing jointly or a qualifying widow(er);

$6,350 if filing as a head of household;

$4,300 if single; *and*

$3,600 if married filing separately.

A married person filing separately must itemize deductions and may not claim any standard deduction if the other spouse itemizes on a separate return; *see 13.3.*

Age 65 or older or blind. For taxpayers age 65 or over, or taxpayers of any age who are blind, the basic standard deduction is increased by an additional amount; *see 13.4.*

Dependents. Individuals who may be claimed as dependents by other taxpayers are generally limited to a $700 standard deduction, unless they have earned income; *see 13.5.*

Dual-status alien. You are generally not entitled to any standard deduction if for part of the year you are a nonresident and part of the year a resident alien. However, a standard deduction may be claimed on a joint return if your spouse is a U.S. citizen or resident and you elect to be taxed on your worldwide income; *see 1.5.*

EXAMPLE

Ben Green is age 25 and single. In 1999, he has salary income of $35,050 and interest income of $2,000. He is not covered by a company retirement plan and contributed $2,000 to an IRA. Green claims the standard deduction because his itemized deductions are less than $4,300.

Gross income:
Salary $35,050

Gross income:		
Salary	$35,050	
Interest income	2,000	$37,050
Deduction from gross income:		
IRA *(8.3)*		2,000
Adjusted gross income		$35,050
Less: Standard deduction		4,300
		$30,750
Less: Exemption *(21.1)*		2,750
Taxable income		$28,000

13.2 When To Itemize

Claim the standard deduction only if it exceeds your allowable itemized deductions for charitable donations, certain local taxes, interest, allowable casualty losses, miscellaneous expenses, and medical expenses. If your deductions exceed your standard deduction, you elect to itemize by claiming the deductions on Schedule A of Form 1040. However, if you are married filing separately and your spouse itemizes deductions, you also must itemize, even if the standard deduction exceeds your itemized deductions; *see 13.3.*

EXAMPLE

Ellen Bates is single and her 1999 adjusted gross income is $35,000. Her itemized deductions total $5,200. As the $4,300 standard deduction is less than her itemized deductions, she claims itemized deductions of $5,200 on Schedule A.

13.3 Husbands and Wives Filing Separate Returns

If you file separate returns for 1999, you and your spouse must first decide whether you will claim itemized deductions or limit yourselves to a standard deduction of $3,600 each. You must make the same election. That is, if one spouse has itemized deductions exceeding $3,600 and elects to itemize, the other spouse must also itemize, even if his or her itemized deductions are less than $3,600.

On a separate return, each spouse may deduct only those itemized expenses for which he or she is liable. This is true even if one spouse pays expenses for the other. For example, if a wife owns property, then the interest and taxes imposed on the property are her deductions, not her husband's. If he pays them, neither one may deduct them on separate returns. The husband may not because they were not his liability. The wife may not because she did not pay them. This is true also of casualty or theft losses.

Claiming itemized deductions when you are living apart from your spouse. When a husband and wife are divorced or legally separated under a decree of divorce or separate maintenance, they are free to compute their tax as they see fit, without reference to the way the other files. They are treated as single. If one has itemized deductions, he or she may elect to claim them, and the other is not required to itemize. The standard deduction is not limited to $3,600. Head of household tax rates may be available under the rules at *1.11.*

If a husband and wife are separated but do not have a decree of divorce or separate maintenance, both must either itemize or claim the 1999 standard deduction of $3,600. There is an exception if you are married and live apart from your spouse and meet the following conditions:

• Your spouse was not a member of your household during the last six months of 1999.
• You maintained as your home a household which was, for more than half of 1999, the principal place of abode for your child, adopted child, foster child, or stepchild.
• You are entitled to claim the child as a dependent *(21.1)* or the child's other parent has the right to the exemption under the rules discussed at *21.11.*
• You provide over half the cost of supporting the household.

If you satisfy these conditions and file a separate return, you generally may file your return as a head of household; however, a foster child must live with you for the entire year (except for temporary absences) to qualify you for head of household status. You may elect to itemize without regard to whether your spouse itemizes or not. If you elect not to itemize, your 1999 standard deduction as a head of household is $6,350 if you are under age 65 and not blind. If you are age 65 or over or blind, your standard deduction is substantially larger; *see 13.4.*

Filing Instruction

Changing an Election

If you filed your return using the standard deduction and want to change to itemized deductions, or you itemized and want to change to the standard deduction, you may do so within the three-year period allowed for amending your return. If you are married and filing separately, each of you must consent to and make the same change; you both must either itemize or claim the standard deduction.

13.4 Standard Deduction If 65 or Older or Blind

A larger standard deduction is provided for persons who are age 65 or over or who are blind. The larger deduction for blindness is allowed regardless of age.

Age and blindness are determined as of December 31, 1999. However, if your 65th birthday is January 1, 2000, you may claim the standard deduction for those age 65 or over on your 1999 return.

Your total standard deduction consists of two parts: (1) The basic standard deduction shown in *13.1* for your filing status plus (2) an extra standard deduction for being age 65 or older, or blind. The amount of the extra deduction is $1,050 if you are filing as single or head of household; and $850 if you are married, whether filing jointly or separately, or your filing status is qualifying widow(er). The chart below lists the total standard deduction, including the extra amount.

If you are married filing separately, you may claim the standard deduction only if your spouse also claims the standard deduction on his or her return.

Check applicable boxes

	65 or older	**Blind**
Yourself	☐	☐
Your spouse if claiming spouse as exemption *(21.2)*	☐	☐
Total checks_____		

If you are—	Number of checks are—	Standard deduction is—
Single	1	$5,350
	2	6,400
Married filing jointly or qualified widow or widower *(1.4)*	1	8,050
	2	8,900
	3	9,750
	4	10,600
Married filing separately	1	4,450
	2	5,300
	3	6,150
	4	7,000
Head of household *(1.11)*	1	7,400
	2	8,450

Filing Instruction

Total or Partial Blindness

An additional standard deduction is allowed to a person who is completely blind as of December 31, 1999. You also qualify if you are partially blind and attach a letter certified by your doctor stating that you cannot see better than 20/200 in your better eye with lenses or that your field of vision is 20 degrees or less. Keep a copy of this letter. If the certification states that your vision will never improve beyond these limits, you will not have to file a new certification in later years; you will only have to attach a statement referring to the earlier certification.

13.5 Standard Deduction for Dependents

The following restrictive rules apply to you only if you may be claimed as a dependent. If you earn gross income of $2,750 or more in 1999, you may *not* be claimed as a dependent by anyone other than your parent, and you may be claimed by your parent only if you are under age 19 or a full-time student under age 24; *see 21.6*. If you are *not* a dependent because of the $2,750 income test, your standard deduction is shown in *13.1* or in *13.4*. If you *may* be claimed as a dependent, your standard deduction is figured under the rules below. You *may* elect to itemize deductions if these exceed the allowable standard deduction. If you are married and your spouse itemizes on a separate return, you *must* itemize; *see 13.3*.

Dependent under age 65 and not blind. If you can be claimed as another taxpayer's dependent for 1999, your standard deduction is the greater of $700 and *earned income* plus $250, but no more than the basic standard deduction shown in *13.1* for your filing status.

EXAMPLE

1. Susan, age 17, is claimed as a dependent by her parents. For 1999, she has earned income of $350 and interest income of $500. Her standard deduction is $700, the greater of $700 and $600, the total of her earned income ($350) and $250.
2. Assume that Susan's earned income is $2,000 rather than $350. Her 1999 standard deduction is $2,250, the greater of $700 and $2,250, the total of her earned income ($2,000) and $250.

Dependents age 65 or older or blind. Your standard deduction is the total of these two steps:

Step 1. The greater of $700 and *earned income* plus $250; *plus*

Step 2. $850 if you are married or a qualifying widow or widower, or $1,050 if single or head of household. If you are age 65 or older *and* you are also blind, multiply the applicable figure, $850 or $1,050, by two.

The worksheets below incorporate these steps for computing your 1999 standard deduction.

Standard Deduction for Dependents in 1999 With Earned Income of $450 or Less

If your filing status is—	Standard deduction is—
Single or head of household	
Under age 65 and not blind	$ 700
Age 65 or older or blind	1,750
Age 65 or older and blind	2,800
Married, or qualifying widow(er)	
Under age 65 and not blind	$ 700
Age 65 or older or blind	1,550
Age 65 or older and blind	2,400

Standard Deduction for Dependents in 1999 Who Are Under Age 65 and Not Blind With Earned Income Exceeding $450

1. Enter your earned income *plus* $250.* — $ _____
2. Enter:

    $4,300 if you are single,
    $6,350 if head of household,
    $7,200 if qualifying widow(er) or married filing jointly, or
    $3,600 if married filing separately.

3. Enter the smaller of Lines 1 and 2. This is your standard deduction. _____

Standard Deduction for Dependents in 1999 Who Are Age 65 or Older or Blind With Earned Income Exceeding $450

1. Enter your earned income *plus* $250.* — $ _____
2. Enter:

    $4,300 if you are single,
    $6,350 if head of household,
    $7,200 if qualifying widow(er) or married filing jointly, or
    $3,600 if married filing separately.

3. Enter the smaller of Lines 1 and 2. _____
4. Enter:

    $1,050 if you are single or head of household and are either age 65 or older or blind.
    $850 if you are married filing jointly or separately, or a qualifying widow(er) and are either age 65 or older or blind.
    If both age 65 or older and blind, the $1,050 or $850 amounts are doubled to $2,100 and $1,700.

5. Add Lines 3 and 4. This is your standard deduction. _____

Include pay for services and taxable scholarships (Chapter 38). However, if your gross income (earned and unearned) is $2,750 or more, you may be claimed as a dependent only by your parent, and only if you are under age 19 or a full-time student under age 24; see 21.6.

Caution

Determine Dependency Status First

The reduced standard deduction rules apply to you if you *may* be claimed as a dependent on another tax return, such as by your parents. If you can be claimed as a dependent under the rules at *21.1*, it does not matter if you are actually claimed as a dependent.

Filing Tip

Higher Standard Deduction for Dependents With Earned Income

For 1999, an individual who may be claimed as a dependent may add $250 to earned income in figuring the allowable standard deduction; *see* the worksheets on this page.

EXAMPLES

1. Jane Dell claims her widowed mother, Beth, who is age 67, as her dependent for 1999. Beth has interest income of $400, wages of $2,000, and Social Security benefits of $10,000 that are exempt from tax under the rules discussed at *34.3*. Beth's standard deduction is $3,300: $2,250 (the greater of $700 and her wage income of $2,000 plus $250) plus $1,050, the additional deduction for a single person over age 65. Beth's taxable income is zero. Although her gross income of $2,400 is below the filing threshold (*see* filing tests for dependents on page 3), she should file a tax return to obtain a refund of income tax withheld from her wages.

2. Same facts as in Example 1 except Beth's wages are $400 and interest income is $2,000. Her standard deduction is $1,750: $700 (the greater of $700 and her earned income of $400 plus $250) plus the additional standard deduction of $1,050. Beth must file a tax return. Her taxable income is $650 ($2,400 – $1,750 standard deduction). She cannot claim a personal exemption for herself since she is Jane's dependent *(21.1)*.

13.6 Prepaying or Postponing Itemized Expenses

Before the end of the year, check your records for payments of deductible itemized expenses. If you find that your payments up to that time are slightly less than the allowable standard deduction for that year, accelerating payment of an expense that you would otherwise pay in the following year could allow you to itemize. For example, at the end of 1999, you may make an additional charitable contribution, or pay a state or local tax bill not due until 2000, or extend by one year professional association dues or job-related subscriptions. You cannot deduct prepayments of interest, insurance premiums, or rent on investment property.

On the other hand, making the year-end payment might still not increase your deductions enough to itemize. In that case, you would get no tax benefit from the payment. By postponing the payment until the next year, you may make it easier to itemize on that year's return.

If your year-to-year payments of itemized expenses have consistently been below the standard deduction, a prepayment or postponement strategy may allow you to itemize in at least one of two consecutive years, enabling you to reduce your taxes over the two-year period without increasing your overall expenditures; *see* the following Example.

Planning Reminder

Prepaying Deductible Expenses May Allow You To Itemize

As the end of the year approaches, check your records for payments of deductible expenses. If these payments are slightly less than the allowable standard deduction for the year, making a year-end payment of a deductible expense that you would otherwise pay in the following year could allow you to itemize.

EXAMPLE

With only a few days remaining in 1999, you determine that your itemized deductions will be $4,000. You are single and expect to have the same amount of expenses in 2000. Instead of taking the $4,300 standard deduction, you could prepay a state income tax of $1,050 to raise your itemized deductions to $5,050. You would then itemize your deductions for 1999 and this would result in a $750 increase in deductions ($5,050 – $4,300). If you cannot itemize in 2000, you will claim the standard deduction. *See* the Supplement for the amount of the 2000 standard deduction.

13.7 3% Itemized Deduction Reduction

If your 1999 adjusted gross income (AGI) exceeds $126,600 ($63,300 if married filing separately) some of your itemized deductions are disallowed. First figure your itemized deductions under the regular rules; *see* Chapters 14 through 20 for details and limitations on specific types of expenses. Then reduce the total of otherwise allowable itemized deductions by the following, which are *not* subject to reduction:

- Medical and dental expenses
- Investment interest
- Casualty losses
- Theft losses
- Gambling losses

The balance of your itemized deductions are generally reduced by 3% of the excess of your AGI over the $126,600 (or $63,300) threshold. Use the worksheet on the next page to figure the reduction. The 3% reduction creates an added tax cost to earning additional income; *see 28.2*.

Worksheet for 3% Reduction

1. Enter your 1999 adjusted gross income. $_____
2. Enter $126,600 ($63,300 if married filing separately).   _____
3. Subtract Line 2 from Line 1.   _____
4. Multiply the amount on Line 3 by 3% (.03).   _____
5. Enter total allowable itemized deductions from Schedule A before the 3% reduction.   _____
6. Enter the amount included on Line 5 for allowable medical and dental expenses, investment interest, casualty or theft losses, and gambling losses. These deductions are not subject to the reduction.   _____
7. Subtract Line 6 from Line 5.*   _____
8. Multiply the amount on Line 7 by 80% (.80).   _____
9. Enter the smaller of Line 4 and Line 8. This is the disallowed amount.   _____
10. Subtract Line 9 from Line 5. This is the net amount of itemized deductions you may claim on your 1999 return. $_____

If the amount on Line 7 is zero, the reduction does not apply.

 Caution

Itemized Deductions May Be Reduced

If your 1999 adjusted gross income exceeds $126,600, or $63,300 if married filing separately, some or all of your itemized deductions are subject to a reduction. In general, your total deduction is reduced by 3% of the excess of your adjusted gross income over the $126,600 or $63,300 floor.

EXAMPLE

Dan Sommer is single and his 1999 adjusted gross income on Form 1040 is $195,700. On Schedule A, Dan reports $31,000 of itemized expenses, after applying the 7.5% floor for itemized medical costs and the 2% floor for miscellaneous itemized deductions. Since his AGI exceeds $126,600, part of his itemized deduction will be disallowed.

Medical expense deduction (after 7.5% floor)	$ 1,000
State and local income taxes	16,000
Real estate taxes	2,000
Home mortgage interest	5,000
Charitable donation	6,000
Miscellaneous expenses (after 2% floor)	1,000
Total	$31,000

All of the deductions except medical expenses are subject to the 3% reduction.

Following the steps of the worksheet shown above, Dan figures that $2,073 of his deductions are disallowed, leaving a net deduction of $28,927:

1.	Adjusted gross income	$195,700
2.	*Less:* threshold	126,600
3.	Excess	69,100
4.	3% of Line 3	2,073
5.	Itemized deductions	31,000
6.	*Less:* medical deductions (not subject to the 3% reduction)	1,000
7.	Itemized deductions subject to the 3% reduction	30,000
8.	80% of Line 7	24,000
9.	Smaller of (4) and (8) is disallowed	2,073
10.	Net itemized deductions allowable on Schedule A (Line 5 *less* Line 9)	$28,927

The Sample Schedule A on the next page shows the reduced deduction on Line 28 ($31,000 − $2,073 disallowed = $28,927).

SCHEDULES A&B (Form 1040) Department of the Treasury Internal Revenue Service (99)	Schedule A—Itemized Deductions (Schedule B is on back) ► **Attach to Form 1040.** ► **See Instructions for Schedules A and B (Form 1040).**	OMB No. 1545-0074 19**99** Attachment Sequence No. **07**

Name(s) shown on Form 1040

Dan Sommer

Your social security number

Medical and Dental Expenses		**Caution:** *Do not include expenses reimbursed or paid by others.*			
	1	Medical and dental expenses (see page A-1)	**1**	15,678	
	2	Enter amount from Form 1040, line 34. ⌊ **2** ⌋ 195,700			
	3	Multiply line 2 above by 7.5% (.075)	**3**	14,678	
	4	Subtract line 3 from line 1. If line 3 is more than line 1, enter -0-		**4**	1,000
Taxes You Paid (See page A-2.)	5	State and local income taxes	**5**	16,000	
	6	Real estate taxes (see page A-2)	**6**	2,000	
	7	Personal property taxes	**7**	- 0 -	
	8	Other taxes. List type and amount ►	**8**		
	9	Add lines 5 through 8		**9**	18,000
Interest You Paid (See page A-3.) **Note:** Personal interest is not deductible.	10	Home mortgage interest and points reported to you on Form 1098	**10**	5,000	
	11	Home mortgage interest not reported to you on Form 1098. If paid to the person from whom you bought the home, see page A-3 and show that person's name, identifying no., and address ►	**11**		
	12	Points not reported to you on Form 1098. See page A-3 for special rules	**12**		
	13	Investment interest. Attach Form 4952 if required. (See page A-3.)	**13**		
	14	Add lines 10 through 13		**14**	5,000
Gifts to Charity If you made a gift and got a benefit for it, see page A-4.	15	Gifts by cash or check. If you made any gift of $250 or more, see page A-4	**15**	6,000	
	16	Other than by cash or check. If any gift of $250 or more, see page A-4. You **MUST** attach Form 8283 if over $500	**16**		
	17	Carryover from prior year	**17**		
	18	Add lines 15 through 17		**18**	6,000
Casualty and Theft Losses	19	Casualty or theft loss(es). Attach Form 4684. (See page A-5.)		**19**	
Job Expenses and Most Other Miscellaneous Deductions (See page A-6 for expenses to deduct here.)	20	Unreimbursed employee expenses—job travel, union dues, job education, etc. You **MUST** attach Form 2106 or 2106-EZ if required. (See page A-5.) ►	**20**		
	21	Tax preparation fees	**21**	300	
	22	Other expenses—investment, safe deposit box, etc. List type and amount ► Tax Court legal fees $4,614	**22**	4,614	
	23	Add lines 20 through 22	**23**	4,914	
	24	Enter amount from Form 1040, line 34. ⌊ **24** ⌋ 195,700			
	25	Multiply line 24 above by 2% (.02)	**25**	3,914	
	26	Subtract line 25 from line 23. If line 25 is more than line 23, enter -0-		**26**	1,000
Other Miscellaneous Deductions	27	Other—from list on page A-6. List type and amount ►		**27**	
Total Itemized Deductions	28	Is Form 1040, line 34, over $126,600 (over $63,300 if married filing separately)?			
		☐ **No.** Your deduction is not limited. Add the amounts in the far right column for lines 4 through 27. Also, enter on Form 1040, line 36, the **larger** of this amount or your standard deduction.	⎫ ⎬ ► ⎭	**28**	28,927
		☒ **Yes.** Your deduction may be limited. See page A-6 for the amount to enter.			

For Paperwork Reduction Act Notice, see Form 1040 instructions.   Cat. No. 11330X   **Schedule A (Form 1040) 1999**

Charitable Contribution Deductions

By making deductible donations, you help your favorite philanthropy and at the same time receive a tax benefit. Donations to organizations qualified to receive deductible contributions give you a tax reduction if you itemize deductions. For example, if you are in the 28% tax bracket, a donation of $1,000 reduces your taxes by $280. By donating appreciated securities and real estate held long term, you can increase the amount of your tax savings by avoiding the tax that would have been owed if you had sold the property and donated the proceeds. If you do volunteer work for a qualified charity, you may deduct your unreimbursed expenses.

If you contributed at least $250 to a charity in 1999, you must get a written receipt from the organization to substantiate the donation. A cancelled check is not sufficient evidence for a cash donation of $250 or more; *see 14.15.*

Also be aware that if you claim deductions for property valued at more than $500, you must attach Form 8283 to Form 1040. If the value you claimed exceeds $5,000, you also may have to obtain a written appraisal.

There are deduction ceilings depending on the type of donation and the nature of the charity. The ceiling for cash donations made to public philanthropies is 50% of adjusted gross income, and for gifts of capital gain property, 30% of adjusted gross income. For other ceilings, *see 14.17.*

If your adjusted gross income exceeds $126,600 ($63,300 if married filing separately), your charitable contribution deduction is subject to the 3% reduction of itemized deductions explained in *13.7.*

Qualifying Charitable Donations

Donations of Property

Reporting Charitable Contributions

Qualifying Charitable Donations

14.1 Deductible Contributions

Charitable contributions are deductible only as itemized deductions on Schedule A of Form 1040. The deduction is subject to the 3% reduction of total itemized deductions explained at *13.7* if your adjusted gross income exceeds $126,600 ($63,300 if married filing separately).

You may deduct donations to religious, charitable, educational, and other philanthropic organizations approved by the IRS to receive deductible contributions; *see* the listing later in this section. If you are unsure of the tax status of a philanthropy, ask the organization about its status, or check the IRS list of tax-exempt organizations (IRS Publication 78). Donations to the federal, state, and local government are also deductible.

Substantiating your donations. Keep a cancelled check or receipt from the charity as proof of donations under $250. For donations of $250 or more, you need to obtain a written acknowledgment that notes any benefits or goods that you received in exchange. *See 14.15* for details on the substantiation requirements.

Year-end donations. You deduct donations on the tax return filed for the year in which you paid them in cash or property. A contribution by check is deductible in the year you give the check, even if it is cashed in the following year. A check mailed and dated on the last day of 1999 is deductible in 1999. A postdated check with a 2000 date is not deductible until 2000. For checks of $250 or more, get a written receipt by the filing due date of your return (the cancelled check is not sufficient substantiation; *see 14.15*). A pledge or a note is not deductible until paid. Donations made through a credit card are deductible in the year the charge is made. Donations made through a pay-by-phone bank account are not deductible until the payment date shown on the bank statement.

Delivering securities. If you are planning to donate appreciated securities near the end of the year, make sure that you consider these delivery rules in timing the donation. If you unconditionally deliver or mail a properly endorsed stock certificate to the donee or its agent, the gift is considered completed on the date of delivery or mailing, provided it is received in the ordinary course of the mails. If you deliver the certificate to your bank or broker as your agent, or to the issuing corporation or its agent, your gift is not complete until the stock is transferred to the donee's name on the corporation's books. This transfer may take several weeks, so, if possible, make the delivery at least three weeks before the end of the year to assure a current deduction.

Debts. You may assign to a charity a debt payable to you. A deductible contribution may be claimed in the year your debtor pays the charity.

Limits on deduction. Depending on the nature of the organization and the donated property, a deduction ceiling of 50%, 30%, or 20% of adjusted gross income applies. In general, the deduction ceiling is 50% for cash contributions and 30% for contributions of appreciated property held long term. *See 14.17* for details on the deduction ceilings. Where donations in one year exceed the percentage limits, a five-year carryover of the excess may be allowed; *see 14.18*.

A deduction may also be limited under the 3% reduction rule discussed at *13.7*.

Organizations Qualifying for Deductible Donations

The following types of organizations may qualify to receive deductible contributions:

A domestic nonprofit organization, trust, community chest, fund, or foundation that is operated exclusively for one of the following purposes:

Religious. Payments for pew rents, assessments, and dues to churches and synagogues are deductible.
Charitable. In this class are organizations such as Boy Scouts, Girl Scouts, American Red Cross, Community Funds, Cancer Societies, CARE, Salvation Army, Y.M.C.A., and Y.W.C.A.
Scientific, literary, and educational. Included in this group are hospitals, research organizations, colleges, universities, and other schools that do not maintain racially discriminatory policies; and leagues or associations set up for education or to combat crime, improve public morals, and aid public welfare.
Prevention of cruelty to children or animals.
Fostering amateur sports competition. However, the organization's activities may not provide athletic facilities or equipment.

Domestic nonprofit veterans' organizations or auxiliary units.

A domestic fraternal group operating under the lodge system. The contributions must be used exclusively for religious, charitable, scientific, literary, or educational purposes; or for the prevention of cruelty to children or animals.

 Filing Tip

Donating Appreciated Securities
You get a tax deduction for the full market value when you donate appreciated securities traded on an established securities market that you have held more than one year. In addition, you also avoid paying capital gains tax on the securities' appreciation.

Nonprofit cemetery and burial companies, where the voluntary contribution benefits the whole cemetery, not only your plot.

Legal services corporations established under the Legal Services Corporation Act. Such corporations provide legal assistance to financially needy people in noncriminal proceedings.

The United States, a U.S. possession, a state, city, or town or Indian tribal government. The gift must be for public purposes. The gift may be directed to a government unit, or it may be to a government agency such as a state university, a fire department, a civil defense group, or a committee to raise funds to develop land into a public park. Donations may be made to the Social Security system (Federal Old Age and Survivors Insurance Trust Fund). Donations may be made to the federal government to help reduce the national debt; checks should be made payable to "Bureau of the Public Debt."

14.2 Nondeductible Contributions

The following types of contributions are not deductible:

1. Payments to political campaign committees or political action committees.

2. Payments to an organization that devotes a substantial part of its activities to lobbying, trying to influence legislation, or carrying on propaganda or whose lobbying activities exceed certain limits set by the law, causing the organization to lose its tax-exempt status. The IRS has disallowed contributions to a civic group opposing saloons, nightclubs, and gambling places, although the group also aided libraries, churches, and other public programs.

3. Donations to or on behalf of specific individuals, even if needy or worthy. Generally, scholarships for specific students, or gifts to organizations to benefit only certain groups. However, the IRS in private rulings has allowed deductions for scholarship funds that are limited to members of a particular religion, so long as that religion is open to all on a racially nondiscriminatory basis, and to scholarship funds open only to male students.

4. Gifts to organizations such as:
   Fraternal groups—except when they set up special organizations exclusively devoted to charitable, educational, or other approved purposes.
   Professional groups such as those organized by accountants, lawyers, and physicians—except when they are specially created for exclusive charitable, educational, or other philanthropic purposes. The IRS will disallow unrestricted gifts made to state bar associations, although such organizations may have some public purposes. Some courts have allowed deductions for donations to bar associations on the ground that their activities benefit the general public. However, an appeals court disallowed deductible donations to a bar association that rates candidates for judicial office.
   Clubs for social purposes—fraternities and sororities are generally in this class. Unless an organization is exclusively operated for a charitable, religious, or other approved purpose, you may not deduct your contribution, even though your funds are used for a charitable or religious purpose.

5. Donations to civic leagues, communist or communist-front organizations, chambers of commerce, business leagues, or labor unions.

6. Contributions to a hospital or school operated for profit.

7. Purchase price of church building bond. To claim a deduction, you must donate the bond to the church. The amount of the deduction is the fair market value of the bond when you make the donation. Interest on the bond is income each year, under the original issue discount rules of *4.19*, where no interest will be paid until the bond matures.

8. Donations of blood to the Red Cross or other blood banks.

9. Contributions to foreign charitable organizations or directly to foreign governments. Thus, a contribution to the State of Israel was disallowed. Similarly, contributions to international charitable organizations are nondeductible; but *see 14.1*.

Donation of services. You may not deduct the value of volunteer work you perform for charities. But you can deduct unreimbursed expenses incurred during such work; *see 14.4*.

Free use of property. You may not deduct the rental value of property you allow a charity to use without charge. That is, if you allow a charity rent-free use of an office in your building, you may not deduct the fair rental value. You also have no deduction when you lend money to a charity without charging interest.

To raise money for a charity, supporters of the organization may donate rental time for their vacation home, to be auctioned off to the public. No deduction is allowed for donating the rental time; *see 14.10*.

 Caution

Foreign Charities

You may deduct donations to domestic organizations that distribute funds to charities in foreign countries, as long as the U.S. organization controls the distribution of the funds overseas. An outright contribution to a foreign charitable organization is not deductible. Some exceptions to this ban are provided by international treaties. A limited exception applies to contributions to certain Canadian or Mexican organizations if you have income from Canadian or Mexican sources. For details, write IRS, Assistant Commissioner (International), Attention CP: IN: D: CS, 950 L'Enfant Plaza, S.W., Washington, D.C. 20024.

Parents' support payments of children serving as Mormon missionaries. According to the Supreme Court, support payments made by parents directly to their children who serve as missionaries are not deductible because the church does not control the funds.

14.3 Contributions That Provide You With Benefits

A contribution to a qualifying organization *(14.1)* is generally deductible only to the extent that you intend to give more than the value of benefits you receive and actually do so.

If you contribute $75 or less and receive benefits, the organization may tell you the value of the benefits. If your contribution exceeds $75, the organization by law *must* give you a written statement that estimates the value of the benefits provided to you and instructs you to deduct only the portion of your contribution that *exceeds* the benefits. However, the disclosure statement does not have to be provided to you if you receive only token benefits, or if you receive from a religious organization only "intangible religious benefits."

EXAMPLES

1. You contribute $200 to a philanthropy and receive a book that you have seen on sale for prices ranging between $18 and $25. The charity estimates the value at $20. As the estimate is between the typical retail prices, it is acceptable to the IRS. Although the book sold at a price as high as $25, you may treat the $20 estimate as fair market value and claim a deduction of $180.

2. A charitable organization sponsors an art auction and provides a catalogue that lists the items being auctioned and estimates of fair market value. The catalogue lists the value of a vase at $100. At the auction, you bid and pay $500 for the vase. As you were aware of the estimate before the auction and paid more for the vase, you may deduct $400 as a contribution.

Dues. Dues paid to a qualified tax-exempt organization are deductible to the extent they exceed the value of benefits or privileges from the organization for the dues, such as monthly bulletins or journals, use of a library, or the right to attend luncheons and lectures. As discussed above, you generally must be provided with an estimate of any benefits you received if your donation exceeds $75.

If dues are paid to a social club with the understanding that a specified part goes to a qualifying charity *(14.1)*, you may claim a charitable deduction for dues earmarked for the charity. If the treasurer of your club is actually the agent of the charity, you take the deduction in the year you give him or her the money. If the treasurer is merely your agent, you may take the deduction only in the year the money is turned over to the charity.

Benefit tickets. Tickets to theater events, tours, concerts, and other entertainments are often sold by charitable organizations at prices higher than the regular admission charge. The difference between the regular admission and the higher amount you pay is deductible as a charitable contribution. If you decline to accept the ticket or return it to the charity for resale, your deduction is the price you paid.

The charity should explain to you how much is deductible. The charity must provide an explanation where you paid more than $75; *see* the discussion above.

If the benefit ticket price is the same or less than the regular admission price, you have no deduction unless you refuse to accept the ticket or you return the ticket to the charity for resale.

If you purchase season tickets to a charity-sponsored series of programs and your average cost per program equals or is less than the cost for individual performances, your deduction for a returned ticket depends upon how long you held the tickets. Generally, you may deduct only your cost. However, if you have held the ticket for more than a year, you may deduct the fair market value, the price the charity will charge on resale of the ticket.

EXAMPLE

A couple claimed a full deduction for regular-price tickets to a high-school fund-raising event that they did not attend. They argued that they were entitled to the deduction because they received no benefit from their ticket purchase. The IRS disallowed the deduction and the Tax Court agreed, holding that a donor receives a benefit by merely having the right to attend the event. To claim a deduction for the price of the tickets the couple should have returned them to the charity.

Caution

Donations That Provide You With Goods or Services

Except for certain token benefits and memberships that are disregarded for tax purposes, you may not deduct a contribution to a qualified charity to the extent that you receive goods, services, or financial benefits in exchange; *see 14.3.*

You may not deduct tuition payments to a parochial or other church-sponsored school for the education of your children if secular courses that lead to a recognized degree are provided. Payments exceeding the usual tuition charge are deductible. Similarly, fees paid to a tax-exempt rest home in which you live, or to a hospital for the care of a particular patient, are not deductible if any benefit is received from the contribution. A gift to a retirement home, over and above monthly fees, is not deductible if the size or type of your quarters depends on the gift.

Donation for the right to buy athletic stadium tickets. If you contribute to a public or nonprofit college or university scholarship program and receive the right to buy preferential seating at the school's football stadium or other sports arena, you may deduct 80% of the contribution to the scholarship program. The 80% deduction also applies where your contribution gives you the right to seating in stadium skyboxes, suites, or special viewing areas. The cost of any tickets you buy is not deductible. The deduction is allowed only if you receive the right to buy tickets rather than tickets themselves. For example, if in exchange for a substantial donation you receive a lifetime season ticket, no deduction is allowed.

Token Items and Membership Benefits That Do Not Reduce Your Deduction

Token items. Popular fund-raising campaigns, such as those for museums, zoos, and public TV, offer token items such as calendars, tote bags, tee shirts, and other items carrying the organization's logo. You are allowed a full deduction for your contribution if the item is considered to be of insubstantial value under IRS guidelines.

The charity must tell you how much of your contribution is deductible in the solicitation that offers the token item. If the items are insubstantial in value, the charity should tell you that your payment is fully deductible. For example, if in 1999 you contributed at least $36, and the offered items cost the charity no more than $7.20, the value of the benefits is ignored and a full 1999 deduction is allowed. A full deduction for 1999 is also allowed if the items were worth no more than 2% of the contribution, or $72, whichever is less. The $36, $7.20, and $72 amounts change annually for inflation.

Newsletters or program guides that are not of commercial quality are treated as token items having no fair market value or cost if their primary purpose is to inform members about the organization's activities, and they are not available to nonmembers by paid subscription or through newsstand sales.

Publications with articles written for compensation and advertising are treated as commercial-quality publications for which the organization must figure value to determine if a full deduction is allowed under the "insubstantial value" test. Professional journals, whether or not they have such articles and advertising, will generally be treated as commercial-quality publications that must be valued.

Membership benefits. If you contribute $75 or less for an annual membership in a qualified charity *(see 14.1)* you may deduct your entire payment under IRS guidelines provided either of the following is true:

1. You receive membership privileges that can be exercised frequently, such as free or discounted parking or admission, or discounts on gift shop or mail order merchandise, *or*
2. Your membership entitles you to admission to events that are open only to members and the organization's reasonably projected cost per person for each event excluding overhead (as of the time the membership package is offered) is no more than the annual limit for "low cost articles." For 1999, the "low cost article" limit is $7.20.

If you pay more than $75 for a membership package, the IRS allows you and the organization to disregard the benefits available under a $75-or-less package.

14.4 Unreimbursed Expenses of Volunteer Workers

If you work without pay for an organization listed at *14.1*, you may deduct as charitable contributions your unreimbursed expenses in providing the services. This includes commuting expenses to and from its place of operations, and meals and lodging on a trip away from home for the organization.

To qualify for the deduction, the expenses must be incurred for a domestic organization that authorizes you to travel. You may not deduct the value of your donated services.

Keep records, such as cancelled checks, to substantiate the amount of your out-of-pocket expenses. To deduct an unreimbursed expense of $250 or more, such as for a plane ticket or a luncheon you hosted on behalf of the organization, IRS regulations require that for each such expense, a statement be obtained from the charitable organization that acknowledges the services you provide. The acknowledgment must describe the services, and state whether you were provided any goods or services by the charity. If so, an estimate of their value must be given unless the benefits are "intangible religious benefits." The acknowledgment must be obtained by the date you file your return, but if you file after the due date (or extended due date if you get an extension), the acknowledgment must be obtained by the due date of your return, including extensions. For 1999 returns, the due date is April 17, 2000, unless you get an extension.

 Caution

Bingo and Lotteries

You may not deduct the cost of raffle tickets, bingo games, or tickets for other types of lotteries organized by charities.

 Filing Tip

Estimated Value of Benefits

You may rely on a written estimate from the organization of the value of any benefits given to you unless it appears to be unreasonable. Although the value of benefits received generally reduces your deductible contribution, certain token items and membership benefits do not reduce the amount of your deduction.

 Law Alert

Volunteer's Auto Allowance

If you use your car to do volunteer work for a charity, you may deduct a flat mileage allowance of 14¢ a mile.

Deductible expenses. If in 1999 you used your car in providing volunteer services for a charity, you may deduct either the actual operating costs of your car or a flat mileage rate of 14¢ a mile allowed by the IRS. Parking fees and tolls are deductible under both methods.

EXAMPLE

Jill Patton is a volunteer worker for a philanthropy. In the course of her volunteer work during 1998, she drove her car 1,000 miles. She may claim a contribution deduction of $140, plus tolls and parking.

Also deductible as charitable contributions are:

Uniform costs required in serving the organization

Cost of telephone calls, and cost of materials and supplies you furnished such as stamps or stationery

Travel expenses, including meals and lodging on overnight trips away from home as an official delegate to a convention of a church, charitable, veteran, or other similar organization. If you are a member but not a delegate, you may not deduct travel costs, but you may deduct expenses paid for the benefit of your organization at the convention.

All related expenses in hosting a fund-raiser are deductible, from the invitations to the food and drink.

The IRS does not allow a deduction for "babysitting" expenses of charity volunteer workers. Although incurred to make the volunteer work possible, babysitting costs are a nondeductible personal expense. Furthermore, the expense is not a dependent care cost; it is not related to a paying job.

Recreational purposes may bar travel expense deduction. To claim a charitable deduction for travel expenses of a research project for a charitable organization, you must show the trip had no significant element of personal pleasure, recreation, or vacation.

EXAMPLES

1. Al Jones sails from one Caribbean island to another and spends eight hours a day counting whales and other forms of marine life as part of a project sponsored by a charitable organization. According to the IRS, he may not claim a charitable deduction for the cost of the trip.

2. Sara Smith works on an archaeological excavation sponsored by a charitable organization for several hours each morning, with the rest of the day free for recreation and sightseeing. According to the IRS, she may not deduct the cost of the trip.

3. Myra Scott, a member of a chapter of a local charitable organization, travels to New York City and spends the entire day at the required regional meeting. According to the IRS, she may deduct her travel expenses as a charitable donation, even if she attends a theater in the evening.

14.5 Support of a Student in Your Home

A limited charitable deduction is allowed for support of an elementary or high school student in your home under an educational program arranged by a charitable organization. If the student is not a relative or your dependent, you may deduct as a charitable contribution your support payments up to $50 for each month the student stays in your home. For this purpose, 15 days or more of a calendar month is considered a full month. You may not deduct any payments received from the charitable organization if any reimbursements are received for the student's maintenance. The only exception is that if you prepay a "one-time" expense such as a hospital bill or vacation for the child at the request of the child's parents or the sponsoring charity, and you are later reimbursed, you may deduct your unreimbursed expenses.

To support the deduction, be prepared to show a written agreement between you and the organization relating to the support arrangement. Keep records of amounts spent for such items as food, clothing, medical and dental care, tuition, books, and recreation in order to substantiate your deduction. No deduction is allowed for depreciation on your house.

Filing Tip

Proposed Tax-Free Reimbursement

When this book went to press, Congress was considering legislation that starting in 2000 would allow tax-free treatment for reimbursements of out-of-pocket automobile costs incurred by volunteer workers. Reimbursements would be tax-free up to the business mileage allowance, which is currently 31cents a mile. *See* the Supplement for a legislation update.

Planning Reminder

Foster Parent Expenses

If you receive payments from a state agency to reimburse you for the costs of caring for a foster child in your home, and you can show that your support costs exceed the reimbursements, the excess is deductible as a charitable contribution. Keep detailed records to substantiate your support payments.

Donations of Property

14.6 What Kind of Property Are You Donating?

Generally, a deduction for the fair market value of donated property may be claimed, but the tax law does not treat all donations of appreciated property in the same way. Whether the full amount of the fair market value of the property is deductible depends on the type of property donated, your holding period, the nature of the philanthropy, and the use to which the property is put by the philanthropy.

Save records to support the market value and cost of donated property. Get a receipt or letter from the charitable organization acknowledging and describing the gift. You *must* get a receipt for donations of property valued at $250 or more; *see 14.15*. Lack of substantiation may disqualify an otherwise valid deduction. Furthermore, if the total claimed value of your 1999 property donations exceeds $500, you must report the donation on Form 8283, which you attach to Schedule A, Form 1040. *See also 14.12* for when you need an appraisal of the value of the property.

Figuring value. When donating securities listed on a public exchange, fair market value is readily ascertainable from newspaper listings of stock prices. It is the average of the high and low sales price on the date of the donation.

To value other property, such as real estate or works of art, you will need the services of an experienced appraiser. Fees paid to an appraiser are not deductible as a charitable contribution, but rather as a miscellaneous itemized deduction *(19.25)* subject to the 2% adjusted gross income floor.

Fair market value deductible for intangible personal property (such as securities) and real estate held long term. Fair market value is deductible where you have held such property long term (longer than one year) and you give it to a publicly supported charity or to a private foundation that qualifies as a 50% limit organization, but you may not deduct more than 30% of adjusted gross income, as discussed at *14.17*. A five-year carryover for the excess is allowed; *see 14.18*. If the donation exceeds the 30% ceiling, you may consider a special election that allows you to apply the 50% ceiling; *see 14.19*.

A contribution of appreciated securities or real estate held long term has two tax advantages that reduce the real cost of making the contribution:

1. Your taxes are reduced by the deduction of the fair market value of the property. For example, you donate appreciated stock that is selling at $1,000. You are in the 28% tax bracket. The deduction for the donation reduces your taxes by $280.

2. You avoid the tax you would have paid on a sale of the stock. Assume that your cost for the stock was $400. On a sale at $1,000, you would pay tax of $120 (20% capital gain rate on $600 profit). By donating the stock, you save that $120 plus $280 from the $1,000 deduction, for a total tax savings of $400. Your "cost" for donating the $1,000 asset is $600 ($1,000 – $400).

The IRS ruled that you may not claim a deduction on donated stock if you retain the voting rights, even though the charity has the right to receive dividends and sell the stock. The right to vote is considered a substantial interest and is crucial in protecting a stockholder's investment.

If planning a year-end donation of securities, keep in mind that the gift is generally not considered complete until the properly endorsed securities are mailed or delivered to the charity or its agent; *see 14.1*.

Deduction limited to cost for property not held long term and ordinary income property. This is property which, if sold by you at its fair market value, would not result in long-term capital gain. The deduction for donations of this kind is restricted to your cost for the property. Examples include: stock and other capital assets held by you for one year or less, inventory items donated by business, farm crops, depreciable business property to the extent that depreciation recapture (Chapter 44) rules would apply on a sale, Section 306 stock (preferred stock received as a tax-free stock dividend, usually in a closely held corporation), and works of art, books, letters, and memoranda donated by the person who prepared or created them. *See 14.9* for art objects. For example, a former Congressman claimed a charitable deduction for the donation of his papers. His deduction was disallowed. His papers were ordinary income property, and since his cost basis in the papers was zero, he could claim no deduction.

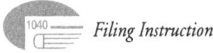

Filing Instruction

Long-Term Holding Period

In this chapter, references to property held long term are to property held more than one year by the donor.

Caution

Appraisal Fees

A fee paid for an appraisal of donated real estate or art is not deductible as a charitable contribution. It may be claimed only as a miscellaneous itemized deduction subject to the 2% floor *(see 19.25)*.

Caution

Tangible Personal Property

When you donate collectibles and artwork, you get a full deduction for the fair market value of the property if the items are used in connection with the charity's main activity or tax-exempt purpose.

If the charity sells your property, your deduction is limited to your basis in the property (what you paid for it, rather than its appreciated value). Protect a deduction for fair market value by obtaining a letter from the charity stating that it intends to use your gift in connection with its tax-exempt purposes.

Bob James holds stock that cost him $1,000. It is now worth $1,500. If he holds it for one year or less and donates it to a philanthropy, his deduction would be limited to $1,000. He would get no tax benefit for the appreciation of $500. On the other hand, if the stock were held long term, he could claim a deduction for the full market value of the stock on its donation.

Tangible personal property held long term. Items such as furniture, books, equipment, fixtures (severed from realty), jewelry, and art objects are tangible personal property. When held long term, deductions for donations of this type of asset may be subject to restrictions that will limit your deduction to cost basis. If the philanthropy to which you donate the property does not put it to a use that is related to its tax-exempt charitable function, the deduction must be reduced by the amount of long-term capital gain that would have been realized if the property had been sold at fair market value. If the charity must sell your gift to obtain cash for its exempt purposes, your donation is treated as being put to a nonrelated use by the charity, and your deduction must be reduced by the long-term gain element.

If the donation of tangible personal property is to a 50% deduction limit organization such as a church or college, and you must reduce the deduction as a *nonrelated* gift, the reduced gift is then subject to the 50% annual deduction ceiling discussed at *14.17*. If the organization's use of the property is *related* to its tax-exempt charitable purposes, and it is a 50% limit organization, you may deduct the property's fair market value subject to the 30% of adjusted gross income deduction ceiling; *see 14.17*. Alternatively, you may elect to deduct up to 50% of adjusted gross income by reducing the deduction by the long-term gain; *see 14.19*.

EXAMPLE

You contribute a painting held long term to a college that displays it in a library where art students may study it. The college's use of the painting is related to its tax-exempt educational purposes and you may deduct fair market value. However, if the college sold the painting and used the proceeds for educational purposes, its use would be treated as nonrelated, and you would have to reduce your deduction by the long-term capital gain element. However, if on the date of the donation you could reasonably anticipate that the painting would not be sold (or put to another nonrelated use), you may deduct fair market value, even if it is in fact sold at a later date.

Donating mortgaged property. A donation of mortgaged property may be taxable. Before you give mortgaged property to a charity, have an attorney review the transaction. You may deduct the excess of fair market value over the amount of the outstanding mortgage. However, you may realize a taxable gain. The IRS and Tax Court treat the transferred mortgage debt as cash received in a part-gift, part-sale subject to the bargain-sale rules discussed at *14.8*. You will realize a taxable gain if the transferred mortgage exceeds the portion of basis allocated to the sale part of the transaction. This is true even if the charity does not assume the mortgage.

EXAMPLE

Bob Hill donates to a college land held long term that is worth $250,000 and subject to a $100,000 mortgage. His basis is $150,000. Hill's charitable contribution deduction is $150,000 ($250,000 – $100,000). He also is considered to have made a bargain sale for $100,000 (transferred mortgage debt) on which he realized $40,000 long-term capital gain. 40% of the transaction is treated as a bargain sale:

$$\frac{\$100,000 \text{ (amount of mortgage)}}{\$250,000 \text{ (fair market value)}} = 40\%$$

Basis allocated to sale: 40% of $150,000, or $60,000

Amount realized	$100,000
Allocated basis	60,000
Gain	$ 40,000

Donating capital gain property to private non-operating foundations. You generally may not deduct the full fair market value of gifts of capital gain property to private non-operating foundations that are subject to the 20% deduction ceiling for non–50% limit organizations discussed at *14.17*. (Capital gain property is property that, if sold by you at fair market value, would result in long-term capital gain.) The deduction must be reduced by the long-term gain that would have been realized if the property had been sold at fair market value. In other words, your deduction is limited to your cost basis.

An exception is available for certain contributions of stock to a private non-operating foundation; *see* the Planning Reminder on this page.

U.S. Saving Bonds. You may not donate U.S. Saving Bonds, such as EE bonds, because you may not transfer them. They are nonnegotiable. You must first cash the bonds and then give the proceeds to the charity, or surrender the bonds and have new ones registered in the donee's name. When you do this, you have to report the accrued interest on your tax return. Of course, you will get a charitable deduction for the cash gift.

Gift of installment obligations. You may deduct your donation of installment notes to a qualified philanthropy. However, if you received them on your sale of property that you reported on the installment basis, you may realize gain or loss on the gift of the notes; *see 5.28*. The amount of the contribution is the fair market value of the obligation, not the face amount of the notes.

14.7 Property That Has Declined Below Cost

Unless the charity needs the property for its own use, you should not donate property whose value has declined below your cost. Your deduction is limited to the fair market value. You may not claim a deductible loss when you make a gift. When the property is held for investment or business purposes, you may get the loss deduction by first selling the property and then a charitable deduction by donating the cash proceeds of the sale.

EXAMPLE

Betty Dunn owns securities that cost $20,000 several years ago but have declined in value to $5,000. A donation of these securities gives a charitable contribution deduction of $5,000. But selling the securities for $5,000 to make a cash donation provides a long-term capital loss of $15,000.

If the property is a personal asset such as clothing, appliances, furniture, or an automobile, you may not deduct a loss on the sale. It makes no difference whether you sell the property and donate the sales proceeds or donate the property. Your deductible donation is the value of the property.

14.8 Bargain Sales of Appreciated Property

A sale of appreciated property to a philanthropy for less than fair market value allows you to claim a charitable deduction while receiving proceeds from the sale. However, you must pay a tax on part of the gain attributed to the sale. That is, the transaction is broken down into two parts: the sale and the gift.

To compute gain on the sale, you allocate the adjusted basis of the property between the sale and the gift following these steps:

Step 1. Divide the sales proceeds by the fair market value of the property. If the property is mortgaged, include the outstanding debt as sale proceeds.

Step 2. Apply the Step 1 percentage to the adjusted basis of the property. This is the portion of basis allocated to the sale.

Step 3. Deduct the resulting basis of Step 2 from the sales proceeds to find the gain.

You may deduct the donated appreciation if full market value would be deductible on a straight donation (no sale) under the rules at *14.6*. Thus, the donated appreciation is deductible if the property is securities or real estate held long term or long-term tangible personal property related to the charity's exempt function; *see* Example 1 below. However, if a deduction for the property (assuming no sale) would be reduced to cost basis under *14.6*, your charitable deduction on the sale is also reduced; *see* Example 2 below. This reduction affects sales of capital gain property held short term; ordinary income property; tangible personal property not related to the charity's exempt function; depreciable personal property subject to recapture; and sales of capital gain property to private non-operating foundations.

Stock Donation to Private Foundation

A deduction for fair market value is allowed on a donation to a non-operating private foundation of appreciated publicly traded stock held long term. If you or family members donated more than 10% of a corporation's stock, the fair market value deduction is allowed only for the first 10%.

Filing Instruction

Donating Used Clothing or Furniture

If you donate used clothing, furniture, or household appliances, deduct their fair market value, which is usually much less than your original cost. For your records, get a statement from the donee organization acknowledging the gift and describing the property. Also keep a record of your original cost. If the claimed value of your 1999 donation exceeds $500, you must complete Form 8283; *see 14.12*. For each individual contribution with a claimed value of $250 or more, you must get a receipt as explained in *14.15*.

Caution

IRS Warning on Auto Donations

The IRS issued a warning to donors and promoters of automobile donation programs promising a charitable donation equal to the current blue book value regardless of the condition of a donated auto. The IRS warned of tax penalties. The charity would jeopardize its tax-exempt status, and the donor could face tax penalties and interest stemming from the disallowance of the charitable deduction.

Not all car donation programs were threatened, such as where a charity holds its own auction or uses the donated car. To substantiate an auto donation deduction, keep photographs, service records, and written appraisals to prove the condition of the donated car.

Caution

Donations of Personal Creative Works

If you are the artist, your deduction is limited to cost regardless of how long you held the art work or to what use the charity puts it. In the case of a painting, the deduction would be the lower of the cost for canvas and paints and the fair market value.

EXAMPLES

1. Lana Briggs sells to a university for $12,000 stock held long term. The adjusted basis of the stock is $12,000, and the fair market value is $20,000. On the sale, she recouped her investment and donated the appreciation of $8,000, but, at the same time, she realized taxable gain of $4,800 computed as follows: The percentage of basis applied to the sale is 60% ($12,000 sale proceeds ÷ $20,000 fair market value). Thus, 60% of the $12,000 basis, or $7,200, is allocated to the sale. Gain on the sale equals the $12,000 sale proceeds less the $7,200 allocated basis, or $4,800.

2. Joel Marx sells to his church stock held short term for his basis of $4,000. The stock is worth $10,000. Using the allocation method in Example 1, 40% ($4,000 sale proceeds ÷ $10,000 fair market value) of his $4,000 basis, or $1,600, is allocated to the sale. Thus, he has a short-term capital gain of $2,400 ($4,000 sale proceeds – $1,600 allocated basis). Furthermore, his deductible charitable contribution is also $2,400, equal to the 60% of basis allocated to the gift (60% of $4,000 = $2,400).

Basis allocation applies even if a deduction is barred by the annual ceiling. The basis allocation rules for determining gain on a bargain sale apply even if the annual deduction ceilings *(14.17)* bar a deduction in the year of the donation and in the five-year carryover period.

EXAMPLE

The Hodgdons contributed real estate valued at $3.9 million but subject to mortgage debt of $2.6 million. The IRS treated the mortgage debt as sales proceeds and figured gain based on the difference between the debt and the portion of basis allocated to the sale element. The Hodgdons claimed that the basis allocation rule, which increased the amount of their gain, should not apply. Earlier in the year, they had made another donation that used up their charitable deduction ceiling for that year as well as for the following five-year carryover period. The Tax Court held that the basis allocation rule applied because a charitable deduction was "allowable," even if the contribution did not actually result in a deduction in the carryover period.

14.9 Art Objects

You may claim a charitable deduction for a painting or other art object donated to a charity. The amount of the deduction depends on (1) whether you are the artist; (2) if you are not the artist, how long you owned it; and (3) the type of organization receiving the gift.

If you owned the art work short term, your deduction is limited to cost, under the rules applying to donations of ordinary income property at *14.6.*

If you owned the art work long term (see 14.6), your deduction depends on how the charity uses the property. If the charity uses it for its exempt purposes, you may deduct the fair market value. However, if the charity uses it for unrelated purposes, your deduction is reduced by 100% of the appreciation. A donation of art work to a general fund-raising agency would be reduced because the agency would have no direct use for it. It would have to sell the art work and use the cash for its exempt purposes.

Appraisals. Be prepared to support your deduction with detailed proof of cost, the date of acquisition, and how value was appraised. The appraisal fee is treated as a "miscellaneous" itemized deduction subject to the 2% adjusted gross income floor; *see 19.25. See also 14.12* for appraisal requirements.

The IRS has its own art advisory panel to assess whether the fair market value claimed for donated art works is reasonable.

Requesting advance valuation of art from IRS. To avoid a later dispute, you may ask the IRS for an advance valuation of art that you have had appraised at $50,000 or more. A request for an IRS Statement of Value (SOV) may be submitted for income tax, gift tax, or estate tax purposes. The IRS has the discretion to value items appraised at less than $50,000 if the SOV request includes at least one item appraised at $50,000 or more, and the IRS determines that the valuation is in the best interest of efficient tax administration.

A request for an SOV must be submitted to the IRS before filing the tax return reporting the donation. The request must include a copy of an appraisal for the item of art and a $2,500 fee, which pays for an SOV for up to three items of art. There is an additional charge of $250 for each item of art over three. It takes the IRS between six and 12 months to issue an SOV.

If the IRS agrees with the value reported on the appraisal, the IRS will issue an SOV approving the appraisal. If not, the IRS will issue a different SOV listing the reason it disagrees with the appraised amount. Regardless of whether you agree with the IRS appraisal, the SOV must be attached to and filed with the return reporting the donation. If you file the return before the SOV is issued, a copy of the SOV must be attached to your return and on receipt of the SOV, an amended return must be filed with the SOV attached. For further SOV details, *see* IRS Revenue Procedure 96-15.

Filing Instruction

Appraisal Required

If you claim a deduction for art of $20,000 or more, you must attach a copy of a signed qualifying appraisal to Form 8283 and file it with your return; *see 14.12* for further details.

EXAMPLES

1. You give your college a painting that you have owned for many years. Its cost was $100 but it is now worth $1,000. The school displays the painting in its library for study by students. This use is related to the school's educational purposes. Your donation is deductible at fair market value. If, however, the school proposed to sell the painting and use the proceeds for general education purposes, its use would not be considered related. Your deduction would be reduced by the $900 appreciation to $100. That the school sells the painting does not necessarily reduce the donation if you show that, when you made the gift, it was reasonable to anticipate that your gift would not be put to such unrelated use.
2. You donate to the Community Fund a collection of first edition books held for many years and worth $5,000. Your cost is $1,000. Since the charity is a general fund-raising organization, its use of your gift is not related. Your deduction would be $1,000 ($5,000 less $4,000).
3. You contribute to a charity antique furnishings you owned for years. The antiques cost you $500 and are now worth $5,000. The charity uses the furnishings in its office in the course of carrying on its functions. This is a related use. Your contribution deduction is $5,000.

Donating a partial interest in an art collection. You may deduct the value of a donated partial interest in an art collection, such as where you give a museum the right to exhibit the works for a specific period during the year. The deduction is allowed even if the museum does not take possession of the art works, provided it has the right to take possession.

Keeping a reversionary interest. The IRS may question a charitable deduction where you do not completely relinquish control over the donated property. However, if the possibility of the property reverting back to you is considered to be remote, a deduction may be allowed. For example, a taxpayer who donated her art collection to a museum was allowed to claim a charitable deduction even though she retained the right to decide where and how the art would be displayed. Disputes concerning art displays would be settled by a mutually acceptable museum curator. If the museum breached a condition, it had a period of time to cure the violation. If the violation was not cured, the ownership would revert back to the donor. The IRS allowed the deduction; the retained rights were fiduciary in nature and the possibility of the art reverting to the donor was so remote as to be negligible.

14.10 Interests in Real Estate

No deduction is allowable for the fair rental value of property you allow a charity to use without charge even in direct furtherance of its charitable functions as, for example, a thrift shop.

If you donate an undivided fractional part of your entire interest, a deduction will be allowed for the fair market value of the proportionate interest donated.

A donation of an option is not deductible until the year the option to buy the property is exercised.

Remainder interest in a home or farm. You may claim a charitable deduction for a gift of the remainder value of a residence or farm donated to a charity, even though you reserve the use of the property for yourself and your spouse for a term of years or life. Remainder gifts generally must be made in trust. However, where a residence or farm is donated, the remainder interest must be conveyed outright, not in trust. A remainder interest in a vacation home or in a "hobby" farm is also deductible. There is no requirement that the home be your principal residence or that the farm be profit-making.

Contribution of real property for conservation purposes. A deduction may be claimed for the contribution of certain partial interests in real property to government agencies or publicly supported charities for exclusively conservational purposes. Deductible contributions include: (1) your entire interest in real property other than retained rights to subsurface oil, gas, or other minerals; (2) a remainder interest; or (3) an easement, restrictive covenant, or similar property restriction granted in perpetuity. The contribution must be in perpetuity and further at least one of the following "conservation purposes"—preservation of land areas for outdoor recreation, education, or scenic enjoyment; preservation of historically important land areas or structures; or the protection of plant, fish, and wildlife habitats or similar natural ecosystems.

To obtain the deduction, there must be legally enforceable restrictions that prevent you from using your retained interest in the property in a way contrary to the intended conservation purpose. The donee organization must be prohibited from transferring the contributed interest except to other organizations that will hold the property for exclusively conservational purposes. If you retain an interest in subsurface oil, gas, or minerals, surface mining must generally be specifically prohibited. However, there is a limited exception where the mineral rights and surface interests have been separately owned since June 12, 1976. A deduction will be allowed if the probability of surface mining is so remote as to be considered negligible. The exception does not apply if you are related to the owner of the surface interest or if you received the mineral interest (directly or indirectly) from the surface owner.

EXAMPLE

To help a charity raise money, one owner allowed the charity to auction off a week's stay in his vacation home, and the highest bidder paid the charity a fair rental. The IRS ruled that not only was the owner's donation not deductible, but the one week stay by the bidder was considered personal use by the owner for purposes of figuring deductions for rental expenses. True, if the owner had directly rented the property to the bidder, the bidder's payment of a fair rental value would have been counted as a rental day and not a personal use day. However, the donation for charitable use is not a business rental, and the bidder's rental payment to the charity is not considered a payment to the owner.

Furthermore, the bidder's use of the home pushed the owner over the personal use ceiling, which in turn prevented him from deducting a rental loss. A rental loss may not be claimed if personal use of a home exceeds the greater of 14 days and 10% of the number of days the home is rented at fair rental value *(9.7)*. Here, the owner personally used the home for 14 days and rented the home for 80 days. The rental expenses exceeded rental income. If the bidder's use of the home was not considered his personal use, the owner could have deducted the loss because his personal use did not exceed the 14-day limit (which was more than 10% of the 80 rental days). However, by adding the bidder's seven days of use to the owner's 14 days, the resulting 21 days of personal use exceeded the 14-day ceiling.

14.11 Life Insurance

You may deduct the value of a life insurance policy if the charity is irrevocably named as beneficiary and you make both a legal assignment and a complete delivery of the policy. A deduction may be disallowed where you reserve the right to change the beneficiary.

The amount of your deduction generally depends on the type of policy donated. Your insurance company can furnish you with the information necessary to calculate your deduction. In addition, you may deduct premiums you pay after you assign the policy.

Deducting premium payments on donated policy. If you assign a life insurance policy to a charity and continue to pay the premiums, you generally may deduct the premiums. However, in states where charities do not have an "insurable interest" in the donor's life, the IRS may challenge income tax and gift tax deductions for the premium payments. The IRS took this position in a private ruling interpreting New York law. In response, New York amended its insurance code to allow individuals to buy a life insurance policy and immediately transfer it to a charity. The IRS then revoked the earlier ruling but it did not announce a change in its position. Thus, the IRS may challenge premium deductions of donors in other states where a charity's insurable interest is not clearly provided by state law.

Caution

Donating Vacation Home Use Not Advisable

To raise funds, a charitable organization may ask contributors who own vacation homes to donate use of the property, which the charity then auctions off to the public. Be warned that if you offer your home in this way you will not only be denied a charitable deduction for your generosity, but you may jeopardize your deduction for rental expenses. A deduction is not allowed for giving a charity the free use of your property. *See* the Example on the right.

Caution

Congress Targets Split-Dollar Insurance Donation Plans

Promoters have encouraged wealthy persons to buy insurance through certain charitable organizations. An individual gives the organization money with the understanding that the funds will be used to buy insurance on the donor's life. The charity splits the proceeds of the policy with the donor's relatives. The IRS warned it would disallow charitable deductions claimed for funds transferred to an organization to buy such insurance. In addition, when this book went to press, Congress passed legislation that supported the IRS policy. *See* the Supplement for further details.

Sample—Form 8283

Form **8283** (Rev. October 1998) Department of the Treasury Internal Revenue Service	**Noncash Charitable Contributions** ▶ **Attach to your tax return if you claimed a total deduction** **of over $500 for all contributed property.** ▶ **See separate instructions.**	OMB No. 1545-0908 Attachment Sequence No. **55**
Name(s) shown on your income tax return David Diaz		Identifying number 01X-X1-01X1

Note: *Figure the amount of your contribution deduction before completing this form. See your tax return instructions.*

Section A—List in this section **only** items (or groups of similar items) for which you claimed a deduction of $5,000 or less. Also, list certain publicly traded securities even if the deduction is over $5,000 (see instructions).

Part I   **Information on Donated Property**—If you need more space, attach a statement.

1	**(a)** Name and address of the donee organization	**(b)** Description of donated property
A	Red Cross City, State 11XXX	Blankets and used clothing items
B	Community Food Center City, State 11X1X	Station Wagon - 1989 (8 Cylinders / 100,000 miles)
C		
D		
E		

Note: *If the amount you claimed as a deduction for an item is $500 or less, you do not have to complete columns (d), (e), and (f).*

	(c) Date of the contribution	**(d)** Date acquired by donor (mo., yr.)	**(e)** How acquired by donor	**(f)** Donor's cost or adjusted basis	**(g)** Fair market value	**(h)** Method used to determine the fair market value
A	7-20-99				200	Thrift Shop Value
B	11-18-99	4-6-89	purchase		2,500	Blue Book Value
C						
D						
E						

14.12   Form 8283 and Written Appraisal Requirements

Attach Form 8283 to your Form 1040 if the total deduction claimed for all of your donations of property in 1999 exceeds $500. The IRS may disallow your deduction if you fail to attach Form 8283.

If you are claiming a deduction exceeding $5,000 for an item, or for a group of similar items (such as coins, stamps, books, paintings, or buildings), you need a written appraisal, which must be summarized in Part I, Section B of Form 8283. The appraiser must complete Part III in Section B of Form 8283. However, you do not need a written appraisal for publicly traded securities and nonpublicly traded stock of $10,000 or less. Keep the appraisal for your records unless you donate art valued at $20,000 or more. In that case, you must attach a complete copy of the appraisal to Form 8283. Furthermore, you may be asked by the IRS to submit a color photograph (8" × 10") or a slide of the art (4" × 5").

If you need an appraisal, get one from an unrelated professional no earlier than 60 days before your gift, and you must receive it by the due date (including extensions) of your return on which you claim the deduction.

For property donations exceeding $5,000, the donee organization must acknowledge the receipt of the property on Part IV, Section B of Form 8283.

Penalty for overvaluation. You may be penalized for a substantial overvaluation of donated property; *see 14.16.*

Appraisal fees. A fee paid to an appraiser is not considered a charitable deduction but is deductible as a "miscellaneous" expense subject to the 2% adjusted gross income floor; *see 19.25.*

14.13   Business Inventory

Self-employed business owners generally may not deduct more than cost for donations of inventory. If a charitable deduction is claimed, costs incurred in a year prior to the year of donation must be removed from opening inventory and excluded from the cost of goods sold when figuring business gross profit for the year of the contribution.

 Caution

Charity Reports Transfer Within Two Years

If the charity sells or otherwise disposes of appraised property within two years after your gift, it must notify the IRS on Form 8282 and send you a copy. The IRS could compare the selling price received by the charity with the value you claimed on Form 8283. Reporting on Form 8282 is not required by the charity if in Part II, Section B of Form 8283 you indicated that the appraised value of the item was not more than $500. Similar items such as a collection of books by the same author, stereo components, or place settings of silverware may be treated as one item. Reporting is also not required for donated property that the organization uses or distributes without consideration, if this use furthers the organization's exempt function or purpose.

No contribution deduction is allowed for a gift of merchandise that was produced or acquired in the year donated. Instead, the cost is added to the cost of goods sold to figure gross profit for the year of the contribution. Business deductions are not subject to the percentage limitation applied to donations.

14.14 Donations Through Trusts

Outright gifts are not the only way to make deductible gifts to charities. You may transfer property to a charitable lead trust or a charitable remainder trust to provide funds for charity.

A charitable lead trust involves your transfer of property to a trust directed to pay income to a charity you name, for the term of the trust, and then to return the property to you or to someone else. A charitable remainder trust is one that provides income for you or another beneficiary for life, after which the property passes to a charity.

Trust arrangements require the services of an experienced attorney who will draft the trust in appropriate form and advise you of the tax consequences.

Deductions for gifts of income interests in trust. Current law is designed to prevent a donor from claiming an immediate deduction for the present value of trust income payable to a charity for a term of years. In limited situations, you may claim a deduction if either: (1) You give away all of your interests in the property to qualifying *(14.1)* organizations. For example, you put your property in trust, giving an income interest for 20 years to a church and the remainder to a college. A deduction is allowed for the value of the property. Or (2) you create a unitrust or annuity trust, and are taxed on the income. A unitrust for this purpose provides that a fixed percentage of trust assets is payable to the charitable income beneficiary each year. An annuity trust provides for payment of a guaranteed dollar amount to the charitable income beneficiary each year. A deduction is allowed for the present value of the unitrust or annuity trust interest.

Because income remains taxable to the grantor, alternative (2) will probably not be chosen, unless the income of the trust is from tax-exempt securities. If such a trust is created, a tax may be due if the donor dies before the trust ends or is no longer the taxable owner of trust income. The law provides for recapture of part of the tax deduction, even where the income was tax exempt.

Charitable remainder trusts. A charitable deduction is allowable for transfers of property to charitable remainder trusts only if the trust meets these requirements: The income payable for a noncharitable income beneficiary's life or a term of up to 20 years must be guaranteed under a unitrust or annuity trust. If a donor gives all of his or her interests in the property to the charities, the annuity or unitrust requirements need not be satisfied. The value of the charitable deduction allowable for a gift in trust is determined by IRS tables.

Reporting Charitable Contributions

14.15 Records Needed To Substantiate Your Contributions

The type of records you must keep to substantiate your donations generally depends on their amount and whether you are contributing cash or property. The requirements are stricter for contributions of $250 or more than for smaller contributions.

Contributions under $250. A cancelled check or a dated receipt is proof of a donation under $250. For a property donation, your receipt should contain a description of the property. You should keep records showing the fair market value of the property and your cost basis.

You need a receipt and explanation from the charity for contributions of $250 or more. A written receipt or acknowledgment is necessary to prove charitable contributions of $250 or more. You may not rely on a cancelled check to document a cash contribution of $250 or more. The receipt requirement does not apply if the donation is less than $250, but if the contribution exceeds $75, you must be given a disclosure statement from the charity estimating the value of any benefits you received in return for the donation.

The IRS exempts from the receipt requirement grantors of a charitable lead trust, charitable remainder annuity trust, or charitable remainder unitrust. Since a specific charity does not have to be designated as beneficiary at the time the trust transfer is made, there may be no organization available to provide a receipt.

Content of receipt. A receipt for a donation of $250 or more may be a letter, form, or post-card. If you gave cash, the amount of the donation must be shown. If you gave property, the property must be described in the receipt or acknowledgment, but the charity does not have to value it.

Planning Reminder

Life Income Plans

A philanthropy may offer a life income plan (pooled income fund) to which you transfer property or money in return for a guaranteed income for life. After your death, the philanthropy has full control over the property. If you enter such a plan, ask the philanthropy for the amount of the deduction that you may claim for the value of your gift.

Caution

Contributions of $250 or More

A cancelled check is not sufficient proof of a donation of $250 or more. You must get a written acknowledgment or receipt from the charitable organization.

The receipt must state whether or not you have received any goods or services from the charity in exchange for the contribution. If you have, the receipt must include a statement describing such benefits and estimating their value. However, "token" items and certain membership benefits, as described in *14.3*, do not have to be described or valued. There is also an exception if the only benefits received are "intangible" religious benefits, such as admission to religious ceremonies; these do not have to be described or valued, but the statement must indicate that they are the sole benefits provided.

Payments throughout the year. For purposes of the $250 receipt threshold, each payment is generally considered separate. Thus, for small donations made during the year, you do not have to obtain a receipt even if they total $250 or more.

If contributions are made by payroll deductions from your wages, the amount withheld from each paycheck is treated separately. A receipt is not required unless withholding on a single paycheck is at least $250. A pay stub or Form W-2 from the employer indicating the amount of a single withholding over $249 is considered a valid "receipt"; a pledge card or other document from the charity must state that you have not received benefits in exchange for the payroll deduction contribution.

Deadline for 1999 donation receipts. For a 1999 contribution, the deadline for obtaining a receipt is the date you file your 1999 return. If you file after the filing due date or extended due date, get the receipt by the due date or extended due date.

A charity must provide a disclosure statement if you contribute more than $75 and receive benefits. If you contribute more than $75 but less than $250 to a charity, you do not have to get a written receipt but the charity is required to give you a "disclosure" statement that estimates the value of any benefits you received, such as concert tickets or books. The statement will tell you to deduct only the excess of your contribution over the value of the benefits. If a required disclosure statement is not provided when contributions are solicited, it must be provided when you make a contribution exceeding $75.

 Filing Tip

Right To Buy Athletic Stadium Tickets

The IRS considers 20% of the amount paid for the right to buy college or university athletic seating to be the fair market value of the right. You may deduct 80% *(see 14.3)*. When your payment is $312.50 or more, you are considered to have made a contribution of at least $250 ($250 = 80% of $312.50), requiring a written acknowledgment from the charity.

Proving Your Donations

If you contribute—	You need—
$75 or less	A cancelled check or receipt from the charity
More than $75 but less than $250	A cancelled check or receipt from the charity. If you received benefits, the charity is required to give you a "disclosure" statement that estimates the value of any benefits you received, such as concert tickets or books. The statement will tell you to deduct only the excess of your contribution over the value of the benefits. If a required disclosure statement is not provided when contributions are solicited, it must be provided when you make a contribution exceeding $75. The disclosure statement is not required if the only benefits you receive are "token items" as discussed in *14.3*. Nor is it required where you contribute to a religious organization and the only benefits you receive are "intangible religious benefits." An example of an intangible religious benefit would be admission to religious ceremonies. A Congressional committee report also suggests that tuition for wholly religious education that does not lead to a recognized degree would qualify.
$250 or more	A receipt or acknowledgment from the charity. You may not rely on a cancelled check to document a cash contribution of $250 or more. A receipt is also required for a donation of property if you are claiming a deduction of $250 or more. If you received any goods or services from the charity in exchange for the contribution, the receipt generally must estimate their value. The deadline for obtaining receipts is the date you file your return. If you file after the filing due date or extended due date, get the receipt by the due date or extended due date. Where the contribution is $250 or more, and both the receipt requirement and the disclosure requirement apply, the charity may satisfy both requirements with the same document. If your total deduction for all property donations exceeds $500, you must report the contributions on Form 8283. If you are not allowed to deduct fair market value for a property donation under the rules at *14.6*, you must attach a statement to Form 8283 explaining the reduction for the appreciation. For property deductions exceeding $5,000, you need a written appraisal, as discussed in *14.12*.

14.16 Penalty for Substantial Overvaluation of Property

If the IRS disallows a portion of your claimed deduction for appreciated property on the grounds that you have overvalued it, you may be subject to a penalty as well as additional tax. The penalty applies only for substantial overvaluations that result in a tax underpayment exceeding $5,000. There are two levels of penalty, depending on the extent of overvaluation:

20% penalty. If the value claimed is 200% or more of the correct amount and results in a tax underpayment exceeding $5,000, the penalty is 20% of the resulting tax underpayment.

40% penalty. If the value claimed is 400% or more of the correct amount and results in a tax underpayment exceeding $5,000, the penalty is 40% of the resulting underpayment.

In determining whether the 200% or 400% overvaluation threshold is met, each property claimed on your return is considered separately. Thus, if on the same return you overvalue Property A by 180% and Property B by 250%, the penalty may be imposed only against Property B, even though on an aggregate basis the overvaluation for both properties is at least 200%.

If there is an overvaluation of at least 200% for more than one property, the resulting tax underpayments are combined to determine if the $5,000 underpayment threshold has been met. For example, Property C is overvalued by 300%, resulting in a $1,000 tax underpayment, and Property D is overvalued by 400%, for a tax underpayment of $4,500. As the total underpayment exceeds $5,000, both overvaluations are subject to the penalty.

Reliance on appraisal may avoid penalty. Even though you have an overvaluation subject to the penalty, you may avoid it under a reasonable cause exception if you relied on an appraisal, but only if the appraisal and the appraiser who prepared it were qualified under IRS regulations and, in addition, you made a good faith, independent investigation of the value of the property.

A professional appraiser who knowingly overvalues charitable deduction property is subject to a $1,000 penalty.

14.17 Ceiling on Charitable Contributions

Unless you make donations that are very substantial in relation to your adjusted gross income (Line 33, Form 1040), you do not have to be concerned with the deduction ceilings discussed in this section. For cash contributions, the deduction ceiling is generally 50% of adjusted gross income, but in some cases a 30% limit applies. For property donations, the deduction limit is generally 30% of adjusted gross income, although it sometimes is 50% or even 20%. As detailed below, the specific limit for each donation depends on whether it is made to a "50% limit organization" and whether it is capital gain property. Where you have made contributions subject to different ceilings, the ceilings are applied in a specific order and are subject to an overall ceiling of 50% of adjusted gross income. If your deduction is limited by any of the ceilings, a five-year carryover is allowed for the excess; *see 14.18.*

Even if none of your charitable contributions are subject to the ceilings, your overall charitable deduction is subject to the 3% reduction to itemized deductions if your 1999 adjusted gross income exceeds $126,600 ($63,300 if married filing separately); *see 13.7.*

Volunteer expenses. The deduction ceiling for unreimbursed expenses you incur doing volunteer work for a charity *(14.4)* is 50% of adjusted gross income if your services were for a 50% limit organization such as a church or college *(see* the list on the following page), or 30% of adjusted gross income if the services were on behalf of an organization other than a 50% limit organization.

30% limit for contributions for the use of an organization. If a donation is treated as for the use of, rather than directly to, any organization, it is deductible under the 30% ceiling described below for contributions to organizations that are not 50% limit organizations.

This 30% ceiling applies to a charitable unitrust or annuity trust income interest that is deductible under the rules discussed at *14.14.* A charitable remainder trust transfer is also subject to the 30% limit if the trust provides that after the death of the income beneficiary, the property is to be held in the trust for the benefit of the charity, rather than distributed to the charity.

Deductible expenses for supporting a student in your home *(see 14.5)* are considered to be for the use of a charitable organization and thus subject to the 30% ceiling for contributions to organizations that are *not* 50% limit organizations.

Contributions to 50% Limit Organizations

Organizations in the 50% limit category include churches, schools, publicly supported charities, and private foundations in the list below. Cash contributions to such organizations are deductible up to 50% of adjusted gross income and contributions of capital gain property held long term generally are deductible up to 30% of adjusted gross income.

The 50% deduction ceiling also applies to donations to the United States, Puerto Rico, a U.S. possession, a state, a political subdivision of a state or U.S. possession, or an Indian tribal government.

50% ceiling. Contributions of cash, ordinary income property, and capital gain property held short term are deductible up to 50% of adjusted gross income if made to the following types of charitable organizations:

- Churches, synagogues, mosques, and other religious organizations.
- Schools, colleges, and other educational organizations that normally have regular faculties and student bodies in attendance on site.
- Hospitals and medical research organizations associated with hospitals.
- Government-supported or publicly supported foundations for state and municipal universities and colleges.
- Religious, charitable, educational, scientific, or literary organizations that receive a substantial part of their financial support from the general public or a government unit. Libraries, museums, drama, opera, ballet and orchestral societies, community funds, the American Red Cross, the Heart Fund, and the United Way are in this category. Also included are organizations to prevent cruelty to children or animals, or to foster amateur sports (provided they do not provide athletic facilities or equipment).
- Private operating foundations.
- Private non-operating foundations that distribute their contributions annually to qualified charities within 2 ½ months after the end of their taxable year.
- Private non-operating foundations that pool donations and allow donors to designate the charities to receive their gifts, if the foundation pays out all income within 2 ½ months after the end of the tax year.
- Organizations that normally receive more than one-third of their support from the general public or governmental units.

30% ceiling for capital gain property held long term. The deduction ceiling is generally 30% (not 50%) of adjusted gross income where you donate to a 50% limit organization property that would have resulted in long-term capital gain had you sold it at fair market value.

The 30% ceiling applies where the fair market value of the property is deductible under the rules of *14.6*. This includes donations of appreciated securities and real estate held long term. It also includes donations of appreciated tangible personal property (such as furniture or art) held long term where the organization's use of your gift is directly related to its tax-exempt charitable purposes.

However, you may elect to apply the 50% ceiling instead of the 30% ceiling to such property donations if you reduce the fair market value of the property by the appreciation; *see 14.19*.

If you donate tangible personal property held long term that is *not* used by the organization for its tax-exempt charitable purposes, so that your deduction must be reduced for the appreciation *(14.6)*, the reduced amount is deductible under the 50% ceiling.

Contributions to Non–50% Limit Organizations

If a contribution is made to a qualifying organization that is *not* in the above list of 50% limit organizations, a 30% or 20% deduction ceiling applies. Organizations in this category include veterans' organizations, fraternal societies, nonprofit cemeteries and private non-operating foundations that do not meet the payout requirements for 50% limit status.

The 30% limit applies to contributions of cash, ordinary income property, and capital gain property held short term. The 20% limit applies to contributions of capital gain property held long term (more than one year). However, the actual ceiling may be less than 30% or 20% of adjusted gross income where in the same year you have made contributions to 50% limit organizations. In that case, follow Steps 2 and 4 of the following section on applying the deduction ceilings.

Filing Instruction

Appreciated Securities and Real Estate

When you contribute appreciated securities or real estate that you have held for more than a year to a church, college, or other organization treated as a 50% limit organization, your deduction for the property donation is limited to 30% of your adjusted gross income unless you elect the 50% ceiling as discussed at *14.19*.

Filing Instruction

Carryover for Excess Contributions

If you contribute cash and property in the same year, your deductions may be subject to different limits, such as 50% of adjusted gross income for the cash and 30% for the property. Follow the steps and Examples at the end of this section for applying the ceilings.

If your donation exceeds the limits, you may carry over the excess for five years.

Applying the Deduction Ceilings

The various deduction ceilings are applied in a specific order, with the total deduction for the year limited to 50% of adjusted gross income. Check above for the ceilings that apply to your donations and then apply the ceilings in the following order. *See 14.19* for carryover rules if a portion of your deduction is barred by the deduction ceilings.

1. 50% deduction ceiling for contributions to 50% limit organizations.
2. 30% of adjusted gross income ceiling for contributions to organizations that are *not* 50% limit organizations, except for contributions of capital gain property subject to the 20% ceiling under Step 4 below.

    If any contributions to 50% limit organizations were made, including donations of capital gain property that are subject to the 30% ceiling under Step 3 below, this Step 2 ceiling is the lesser of (1) 30% of adjusted gross income and (2) 50% of adjusted gross income minus the contributions to the 50% limit organizations.
3. 30% of adjusted gross income ceiling for contributions of capital gain property to 50% limit organizations.

    If contributions qualifying for the 50% ceiling (Step 1) were made, your deduction for these 30% limit contributions is the lesser of (1) 30% of adjusted gross income and (2) 50% of adjusted gross income minus the contributions qualifying for the 50% ceiling.
4. 20% of adjusted gross income ceiling for contributions of capital gain property to organizations that are not 50% limit organizations.

    If contributions are deductible under any of the other ceilings (Steps 1–3), you may deduct contributions subject to the 20% ceiling only to the extent that there is any adjusted gross income remaining under the overall 50% adjusted gross limit.

Filing Instruction

Different Ceilings

If you made charitable contributions subject to several deduction ceilings, the deductions are applied against adjusted gross income in the specific order shown at the right.

EXAMPLES

1. Linda Jones in 1999 contributes to a church $22,000 in cash and land held long term valued at $35,000. Her adjusted gross income is $100,000, so the total deduction for the year may not exceed $50,000 under the 50% overall limit. Since the $22,000 cash contribution subject to the 50% ceiling is considered first, the deduction for the land (subject to the 30% ceiling under Step 3 above) is limited to $28,000, the difference between the $50,000 overall limit and the $22,000 cash gift. Jones may carry over the unused $7,000 donation attributable to the land.

2. Earl Smith in 1999 has an adjusted gross income of $100,000. He contributes land worth $40,000 to a college, deductible under the 30% ceiling of Step 3 above. He also contributes $30,000 in cash to a non-operating private foundation subject to the 30% ceiling discussed in Step 2 above. The 30% limitation for cash gifts to non-operating private foundations is applied before the 30% limitation applicable to gifts of capital gain property to public charities. The deduction for the cash gift is reduced to $10,000 (50% of $100,000 adjusted gross income, or $50,000, minus $40,000 gift to college). The deduction for the land is limited to $30,000 (30% of $100,000). Accordingly, Smith's charitable contribution deduction for 1999 is $40,000 ($10,000 + $30,000).

    Smith is allowed to carry over *(14.18)* the amounts disallowed by the ceilings: $20,000 ($30,000 – $10,000) for the cash gift and $10,000 ($40,000 – $30,000) for the land.

14.18 Five-Year Carryover for Excess Donations

If you make donations that are not deductible because they exceed the 50%, 30%, or 20% of adjusted gross income ceilings discussed in *14.17*, you may carry the excess over the next five years. In each carryover year, the original percentage ceiling applies. For example, where contributions of appreciated long-term intangible personal property or real estate (or tangible personal property put to a related use by the charity) exceed the 30% ceiling for capital gain property *(14.17)*, the excess remains subject to the 30% ceiling in the carryover years.

In any carryover year, you must first figure your deduction for contributions in the current year under the applicable 50%, 30%, or 20% ceilings. For each category of property carried over, the carryover contributions are deductible only after the deduction for current year donations is figured. The total deduction in the carryover year, for both current year and carryover contributions, cannot exceed 50% of adjusted gross income for the carryover year.

EXAMPLE

In 1999, you contribute to a university stock held long term with a fair market value of $19,000. The contribution is subject to the 30% ceiling for capital gain property *(14.17)*. You also have a $2,000 carryover from 1997 for a cash gift to your church which in 1998 remains subject to the 50% ceiling. Your 1998 adjusted gross income is $40,000. Under the 30% ceiling, the deduction for the contribution of stock is limited to $12,000 (30% of $40,000 adjusted gross income). Since the overall deduction limit is $20,000 (50% of $40,000 adjusted gross income), the $2,000 carryover from 1997 is fully deductible. The total deduction on your 1998 return is $14,000 ($12,000 plus $2,000 carryover). You carry over to 1999 the $7,000 balance from the gift of stock that could not be deducted in 1998 because of the 30% ceiling.

14.19 Election To Reduce Property Gift Appreciation

Although the 30% ceiling generally applies to long-term intangible property (such as securities) and real estate contributed to 50% limit organizations *(see 14.17)*, you may elect the 50% ceiling, provided you reduce the fair market value of the property by 100% of the appreciation on all such donations during the year. The reduction also applies to donations of tangible personal property related in use to the organization's charitable function. In most cases, this election should be made only where the amount of appreciation is negligible. Where there is substantial appreciation, the increase in the deduction may not make up or exceed the required 100% reduction, which allows you to claim a deduction only for your cost basis in the property. If the election is made in a year in which there are carryovers of capital gain property subject to the 30% ceiling, the carryovers are subject to reduction; *see* IRS Publication 526.

The election of the 50% ceiling is made by attaching a statement to your original return or amended return filed by the original due date. Even where no formal electing statement is made, claiming a deduction without the appreciation in order to come within the 50% ceiling is treated as an election. A formal or "informal" election is not revocable unless a material mistake is shown. A revocation based on a reconsideration of tax consequences is not considered sufficient grounds.

 Planning Reminder

Project Your Income

When planning substantial donations that may exceed the annual ceiling, make a projection of your income for at least five years. Although the carryover period of five years will probably absorb most excess donations, it is possible that the excess may be so large that it will not be completely absorbed during the year of the contribution and the five-year carryover period. It is also possible that your income may drop in the future so that you cannot adequately take advantage of the excess.

Chapter 15

Itemized Deduction for Interest Expenses

On Schedule A of Form 1040, you may deduct three types of interest charges:

- Home mortgage interest
- Points
- Investment interest

These deductions are also subject to limitations:

- Home mortgage interest and points are subject to the 3% reduction of itemized deductions if your adjusted gross income (AGI) exceeds $126,600 ($63,300 for married persons filing separate returns).
- Investment interest is deductible only up to the amount of net investment income *(15.10)* but is not included in the 3% reduction computation. The 3% reduction rule is discussed at *13.7*.

Interest on personal loans (such as loans to buy autos and other personal items and credit card finance charges) is not deductible with the exception of qualifying student loan interest; *see* Chapter 38.

Interest on loans for business purposes is fully deductible on Schedule C. Interest on loans related to rental property is fully deductible from rental income on Schedule E. Whether interest is a business, investment, or a personal expense generally depends upon the use made of the money borrowed, not on the kind of property used to secure the loan. However, interest on a loan secured by a first or second home may be deductible as home equity mortgage interest regardless of the way you use the loan.

Interest on a loan used to finance an investment in a passive activity is subject to the limitations discussed in Chapter 10. However, if you rent out a second home that qualifies as a second residence, the portion of mortgage interest allocable to rental use is deductible as qualified mortgage interest and is not treated as a passive activity expense.

Home Mortgage Loans

15.1 Home Mortgage Interest

You generally may deduct on Schedule A (Form 1040) qualifying mortgage interest on up to two residences (*see* two-residence limit, below). However, if your 1999 adjusted gross income exceeds $126,600 ($63,300 if married filing separately), your mortgage interest deduction is subject to the 3% reduction of itemized deductions; *see 13.7*.

Mortgage loan obtained after October 13, 1987. Whether you can take a full mortgage interest deduction for a loan taken out after October 13, 1987, depends on the amount of the mortgage debt and how you use the proceeds. Loans used to buy, construct, or improve a first or second home are called *home acquisition loans*, and up to $1 million of such debt qualifies for a mortgage interest deduction, $500,000 if married filing separately. Loans used for any other purpose are called *home equity loans* by the tax law, and up to $100,000 of such debt qualifies for an interest deduction; the home equity limit is $50,000 for married persons filing separately.

Loan must be secured by residence. To deduct interest on a home acquisition or home equity loan, the loan must be secured by your main home or a second home. For the loan to be "secured," it must be recorded or satisfy similar requirements under state law. For example, if a relative gives you a loan to help you purchase a home, the relative must take the legal steps required to record the loan with local authorities; otherwise, you may not deduct interest on the loan.

Home acquisition loans are further discussed at *15.2. Home equity loans* are discussed at *15.3*. If you *refinance your mortgage, see 15.7*.

Mortgage loan obtained before October 14, 1987. You may deduct all of the interest on a loan secured by a first or second home if the loan was obtained before October 14, 1987. Technically, such loans are considered home acquisition debt, but they are treated as "grandfathered debt," exempt from the $1 million loan limit ($500,000 for married persons filing separately).

However, the amount of your pre-October 14, 1987, loan reduces the $1 million limit (or $500,000) on home acquisition debt after October 13, 1987; *see 15.2*. It also reduces the fair market value limit for home equity debt; *see 15.3*. If you refinance your loan, *see 15.7*.

Two-residence limit for qualifying mortgage debt. The rules for deducting qualifying acquisition debt or home equity debt apply to loans secured by your principal residence and one other residence. A residence may be a condominium or cooperative unit, houseboat, mobile home, or house trailer that has sleeping, cooking, and toilet facilities. If you own more than two houses, you decide which residence will be considered your second residence. Interest debt secured by the second residence is deductible under the rules for acquisition debt (15.2) or home equity debt (15.3).

A residence that you rent out for any part of the year may be treated as a second residence only if you use it for personal nonrental purposes for more than the greater of 14 days and 10% of the rental days. In counting rental days, include days that the home is held out for rental or listed for resale. In counting days of personal use, use by close relatives generally qualifies as your personal use; *see 9.6*.

Interest on debt secured by a residence other than your principal or second home may still be deductible, if you use the proceeds for investment or business purposes; *see 15.12*.

Interest on mortgage credit certificates. Under special state and local programs, you may obtain a "mortgage credit certificate" to finance the purchase of a principal residence or to borrow funds for certain home improvements. Generally, a qualifying principal residence may not cost more than 90% of the average area purchase price, 110% in certain targeted areas. A tax credit for interest paid on the mortgage may be claimed. The credit is computed on Form 8396 and claimed on Line 47 of Form 1040. The credit equals the interest paid multiplied by the certificate rate set by the governmental authority, but the maximum annual credit is $2,000. Interest not qualifying for the credit is deductible as home mortgage interest.

Planning Reminder

Home Acquisition Loan Limits

Interest is deductible on up to $1 million of home acquisition loans taken out after October 13, 1987 ($500,000 limit if married filing separately). Mortgage loans taken out before October 14, 1987, are not subject to the $1,000,000 (or $500,000) limit. However, outstanding loans from before October 14, 1987, reduce the $1 million (or $500,000) ceiling for post–October 13, 1987, loans.

Planning Reminder

Mortgage Interest on a Third Home

Interest on debt secured by a residence *other than* your principal or second home may still be deductible, if you use the proceeds for investment or business purposes; *see 15.12*.

EXAMPLE

You pay $5,000 interest for a mortgage issued under a qualifying mortgage credit certificate. Under its terms, you are allowed a tax credit of $750. You may claim the balance of your mortgage interest, or $4,250 ($5,000 – $750), as an itemized deduction. If the allowable credit exceeds tax liability, a three-year carryover is allowed.

If you buy a home using a qualifying mortgage credit certificate and sell that home within nine years, you must recapture part of the tax credit on Form 8828.

15.2 Home Acquisition Loans

Under the mortgage interest rules, a qualifying "home acquisition loan" is a loan used to buy, build, or substantially improve your principal residence or second home, provided the debt is secured by that same residence.

Interest paid on such home acquisition loans is fully deductible if the total debt does not exceed $1,000,000, or $500,000 if you are married filing separately. The $1,000,000 (or $500,000) limit applies to acquisition loans taken out after October 13, 1987.

If your mortgages taken after October 13, 1987, exceed the $1,000,000 (or $500,000) limit, you must use IRS worksheets included in Publication 936 to figure the amount of your deductible interest. Furthermore, if you incurred substantial loans before October 14, 1987, and later purchase a new home, your deduction for the mortgage for the new home may be limited. The $1 million limit for acquisition debt after October 13, 1987, is reduced by the amount of outstanding pre–October 14, 1987, debt.

Although interest on a pre–October 14, 1987, debt is generally fully deductible regardless of the size of the loan, refinancing a pre–October 14, 1987, debt for more than the existing balance subjects the excess to the $1 million ceiling; *see 15.7.*

Generally, a debt qualifies as being incurred in buying, constructing, or improving a residence if you satisfy IRS tracing rules *(15.12)* that prove the use of the loan proceeds for such residential purposes. Even if you cannot prove under the tracing rules that a loan was used to buy a residence, a loan will be treated by the IRS as incurred for buying a house to the extent you can show acquisition expenses within 90 days before or 90 days after incurring the loan. Special construction loan and improvement loan rules are discussed in *15.4* and *15.5.*

Interest on a mortgage to buy or build a home other than your principal residence or qualifying second home is treated as nondeductible personal interest. If a nonqualifying home is rented out, the part of the mortgage interest that is allocable to the rental activity is treated as passive activity interest subject to the limitations discussed in Chapter 10; the interest allocable to your personal use is nondeductible personal interest.

A married couple filing jointly may designate as a second residence a home owned or used by either spouse.

If a married couple files separately, each spouse may generally deduct interest on debt secured by one residence. However, both spouses may agree in writing to allow one of them to deduct the interest on a principal residence plus a designated second residence.

Cooperatives. In the case of housing cooperatives, debt secured by stock as a tenant-stockholder is treated as secured by a residence. The cooperative should provide you with the proper amount of your deductible interest. If the stock cannot be used to secure the debt because of restrictions under local law or the cooperative agreement, the debt is still considered to be secured by the stock if the loan was used to buy the stock. For further details on allocation rules, *see* IRS Publication 936.

Line-of-credit mortgages. If you had a line-of-credit mortgage on your home on October 13, 1987, and you borrowed additional amounts on this line of credit after that date, the additional borrowed amounts are treated as a mortgage taken out after October 13, 1987. If the newly borrowed amounts are used to buy, build, or improve your first or second home, they are treated as home acquisition debt subject to the $1 million or $500,000 limit. If used for any other purpose, the amounts are subject to the home equity debt rules at *15.3.*

Mortgage interest paid after house destroyed. If your principal residence or second home *(15.1)* is destroyed and the land is sold within a reasonable period of time following the destruction, the IRS treats the property as a residence for purposes of deducting interest payments on the mortgage during the period between the destruction of the residence and the sale of the land. In one case, the IRS allowed the interest deduction where a sale of land took place 26 months after the destruction of a home by a tornado.

If the destroyed residence is reconstructed and reoccupied within a reasonable period of time following the destruction, the property will continue to be treated as a residence during that period, and the interest payments on the mortgage on the property will be deductible. The IRS allowed an interest deduction where reconstruction began 18 months after, and was completed 34 months after, destruction of the home.

Court Decision

Family Financing of Residence

The Tax Court allowed a taxpayer to deduct mortgage interest payments on a loan that his brother obtained when the taxpayer's poor credit rating prevented him from obtaining a mortgage loan. The brother bought the house but allowed the taxpayer and his wife to live there on the condition that they make the mortgage payments directly to the bank.

The IRS disallowed the taxpayer's deduction for the mortgage interest on the grounds that he was not liable for the mortgage debt; his brother was. However, the Tax Court allowed the deduction, holding that the taxpayer was the equitable owner of the home and that he was legally obligated to his brother to pay off the mortgage.

15.3 Home Equity Loans

For interest deduction purposes, qualifying home equity debt is the *lesser* of:

1. $100,000, or $50,000 if married filing separately, *and*
2. The fair market value of your principal residence and second home, reduced by the amount of acquisition debt *(15.2)* and by any "grandfathered" pre–October 14, 1987, mortgages *(15.1)*. According to the IRS, fair market value, acquisition debt, and grandfathered debt are determined on the date that the last debt was secured by the home.

The debt must be secured by your first or second home to qualify. If you have a second home as well as a principal residence, the above limitation under (1) and (2) applies to the total debt for both houses. Interest on a qualifying home equity loan is deductible regardless of the way you spend the proceeds, unless it is used to buy tax-exempts *(15.11)*.

On loans exceeding the home equity debt limit, interest may be deductible if the proceeds are used for investment or business purposes. Otherwise, interest on the excess is nondeductible personal interest.

EXAMPLES

1. You bought your house in 1986 for $200,000 subject to a mortgage of $150,000. When the mortgage principal is $120,000 and the fair market value of the house is $210,000, you take out a home equity loan. Interest on a home equity loan of up to $90,000 is fully deductible. Qualifying home equity debt may not exceed the difference between the fair market value of the house ($210,000) and the current acquisition debt ($120,000). If the value of the house exceeded $220,000, you could have borrowed up to the $100,000 limit as a qualifying home equity loan.
2. The fair market value of your house is $200,000 and the current mortgage is $160,000. You may deduct interest on a home equity loan of up to $40,000 ($200,000 – $160,000).

A loan may qualify partially as acquisition debt and partially as home equity debt where part of it is used to refinance an existing acquisition debt. The refinanced amount is still considered acquisition debt. Debt in excess of the refinanced amount is either home equity debt subject to the $100,000 ceiling or home acquisition debt subject to the $1 million ceiling, depending on how the proceeds are used; *see 15.7*.

15.4 Home Construction Loans

Interest on a home construction loan may be fully deductible from the time construction begins for a period of up to 24 months while construction takes place. Within the 24-month period, the loan is considered acquisition debt subject to the $1 million ceiling *(15.2)*, provided that the home is a principal residence or second home when it is actually ready for occupancy. Furthermore, the loan proceeds must be directly traceable to home construction expenses, including the purchase of a lot, and the loan must be secured by the lot to be treated as acquisition debt. According to the IRS, if construction begins before a loan is incurred, the loan is treated as acquisition debt to the extent of construction expenses within the 24-month period *before* the loan. In determining when a loan is "incurred" for purposes of this 24-month rule, you can treat the date of a written loan application as the date the loan was "incurred," provided you receive the loan within 30 days after loan approval.

Interest incurred on the loan before construction begins is treated as nondeductible personal interest (*see* Example 1 on the next page). If construction lasts more than 24 months, interest after the 24-month period also is treated as nondeductible personal interest.

Interest on loans taken out within 90 days *after* construction is completed may qualify for a full deduction. The loan is treated as acquisition debt to the extent of construction expenses within the last 24 months before the residence was completed, plus expenses through the date of the loan (*see* Example 2 on the next page). For purposes of the 90-day rule, the loan proceeds generally are treated as received on the loan closing date. However, a debt may be considered "incurred" on the date a written loan application is made, provided the loan proceeds are actually received within 30 days after loan approval. If a loan application is made within the 90-day period and it is rejected, and a new application with another lender is made within a reasonable time after the rejection, a loan from the second lender will be considered timely even if more than 90 days have passed since the end of construction.

Planning Reminder

Home Equity Loan To Pay Consumer Debts

Interest on consumer loans is not deductible, but you can use a home equity line-of-credit mortgage to pay off existing consumer debts and finance future consumer expenses. However, although interest on a home equity loan is fully deductible for regular tax purposes if within the $100,000 limit, the interest is not allowed for purposes of alternative minimum tax, unless the loan proceeds were used to improve your first or second home; *see 23.2*.

Filing Tip

Mortgage Fees Not Deductible

You may not deduct expenses incurred in obtaining a mortgage loan, such as loan assumption fees or costs of an appraisal or credit report.

EXAMPLES

1. On January 12, 1999, you borrow $100,000 to buy a residential lot. The loan is secured by the lot. You begin construction of a principal residence on January 1, 2000, and use $250,000 of your own funds for construction expenses. The residence is completed December 31, 2001.

    The interest paid in 1999 is nondeductible personal interest. It was paid before the 24-month qualifying construction period that started January 1, 2000, and ended December 31, 2001.

    Interest paid in 2000 and 2001 is fully deductible as the $100,000 loan is treated as acquisition debt for the 24-month construction period.

2. Same facts as in Example 1, but on March 17, 2002, you take out a $300,000 mortgage on the completed house to raise funds. You use $100,000 of the loan proceeds to pay off the $100,000 loan on the lot and keep the balance.

    All of the interest on the $300,000 loan is fully deductible because the loan qualifies as acquisition debt; $100,000 of the debt is treated as acquisition debt used for construction, since it was used to refinance the original 1999 debt to purchase the lot. The $200,000 balance is also treated as a construction loan under the 90-day rule. It was borrowed within 90 days after the residence was completed, and it reimbursed construction expenses of at least $200,000 incurred within 24 months before the completion date.

3. On January 12, 1999, you purchased a residential lot and began building a home on the lot using $45,000 of your personal funds. The home was completed on October 31, 1999. On November 24, 1999, you received a loan of $36,000 that was secured by the home. The debt may be treated as taken out to build the home as it was taken out no later than 90 days after the home was completed, and expenditures of at least $36,000 were made within the period of 24 months before the home was completed.

15.5 Home Improvement Loans

Loans used for substantial home improvements are treated as acquisition debt subject to the $1 million ceiling for loans after October 13, 1987; *see 15.2.* Include only the cost of home improvements that must be added to the basis of the property because they add to the value of the home or prolong useful life. Repair costs are not considered.

EXAMPLE

Your current acquisition mortgage is $100,000. You borrow $20,000 to build a new room. Your qualifying acquisition debt is now $120,000.

If substantial improvements to a home are begun but not completed before a loan is incurred, the loan will be treated as acquisition debt (assuming the debt is secured by the home) to the extent of improvement expenses made within 24 months before the loan. If the loan is incurred within 90 days after an improvement is completed, the loan is treated as acquisition debt (assuming the debt is secured by the home) to the extent of improvement expenses made within the period starting 24 months before completion of the improvement and ending on the date of the loan.

15.6 Mortgage Payment Rules

Payments to the bank or lending institution holding your mortgage may include interest, principal payments, taxes, and fire insurance premiums. Deduct only interest and tax payments. You may not deduct the payments of mortgage principal and insurance premiums.

In the year you sell your home, check your settlement papers for interest charged up to the date of sale; this amount is deductible.

Mortgage credit. If you qualify for the special tax credit for interest on qualified home mortgage certificates, you only deduct interest in excess of the allowable credit; *see 15.1.*

Jointly owned property. When mortgaged property is jointly owned, a joint owner who pays the entire interest charge may deduct the amount of the entire payment.

Prepayment penalty. A penalty for prepayment of a mortgage is deductible as interest.

 Caution

Mortgage Interest Reported on Form 1098

Banks and other lending institutions report mortgage interest payments of $600 or more to the IRS on Form 1098. You should receive a copy of Form 1098 or a similar statement by January 31, 2000, showing your mortgage payments in 1999. Deductible points *(15.8)* paid on the purchase of a principal home are included on Form 1098.

Mortgage assistance payments. You may not deduct interest paid on your behalf under Section 235 of the National Housing Act.

Delinquency charges for late payment. According to the IRS, a late payment charge is deductible as mortgage interest if it was not for a specific service provided by the mortgage holder. In one case, the Tax Court agreed with the IRS that delinquency charges imposed by a bank were not interest where they were a flat percentage of the installment due, regardless of how late payment was. The late charges were primarily imposed by the bank to recoup costs related to collection efforts, such as telephone calls, letters, and supervisory reviews. They were also intended to discourage untimely payments by imposing a penalty.

Graduated payment mortgages. Monthly payments are initially smaller than under the standard mortgage on the same amount of principal, but payments increase each year over the first five- or 10-year period and continue at the increased monthly amount for the balance of the mortgage term. As a cash-basis taxpayer, you deduct the amount of interest actually paid even though, during the early years of the mortgage, payments are less than the interest owed on the loan. The unpaid interest is added to the loan principal, and future interest is figured on the increased unpaid mortgage loan balance. The bank, in a year-end statement, will identify the amount of interest actually paid. (An accrual-basis taxpayer may deduct the accrued interest each year.)

Reverse mortgage loan. Homeowners who own their homes outright may in certain states cash in on their equity by taking a "reverse mortgage loan." Typically, 80% of the value of the house is paid by a bank to a homeowner in a lump sum or in installments. Principal is due when the home is sold or when the homeowner dies; interest is added to the loan and is payable when the principal is paid. The IRS has ruled that an interest deduction may be claimed by a cash-basis homeowner only when the interest is paid, not when the interest is added to the outstanding loan balance.

Shared appreciation mortgage. Under a shared appreciation mortgage (SAM) for a personal residence, the lender agrees to charge a fixed rate of interest that is lower than the prevailing market rate. In return, the homeowner promises to pay a percentage of the appreciation on the property at a later date to make up the difference. The fixed-rate interest is deductible when paid and the percentage of appreciation is also treated as interest that you can deduct in the year of payment, subject to the limits discussed at *15.2*. For example, you agree to pay interest of 9% plus 40% of the appreciation in the value of the property within 10 years or earlier if you sell the house or pay off the mortgage. If, at the end of 10 years, the residence is not sold or the loan repaid, you may refinance at the prevailing rate the outstanding balance plus the interest based on the appreciation. If you refinance with the same lender, you may not claim an immediate deduction for the extra interest. The execution of a note is not considered payment. The amount covering the extra interest is deducted ratably over the period of the new loan. If you refinance with another lender and use the funds to pay off the old loan plus the extra interest, the extra interest is deductible in the year of payment, subject to the limits of *15.2*.

Redeemable ground rents. In a ground rent arrangement, you lease rather than buy the land on which your home is located. Ground rent is deductible as mortgage interest if: (1) the land you lease is for a term exceeding 15 years (including renewal periods) and is freely assignable; (2) you have a present or future right to end the lease and buy the entire interest; and (3) the lessor's interest in the land is primarily a security interest. Payments to end the lease and buy the lessor's interest are not deductible ground rents.

 Filing Tip

Joint Liability on Mortgage

If you do not personally receive a Form 1098 but a person (other than your spouse with whom you file a joint return) who is also liable for and paid interest on the mortgage received a Form 1098, you deduct your share of the interest and attach a statement to your Schedule A showing the name and address of the person who received the form. If you are the payer of record on a mortgage on which there are other borrowers entitled to a deduction for the interest shown on the Form 1098 you received, provide them with information on their share of the deductible amount.

15.7 Interest on Refinanced Loans

When you refinance a mortgage on a first or second home *(15.1)* for the same amount as the remaining principal balance on the old loan, there is no change in the tax treatment of interest. In other words, if interest was fully deductible on the old loan, then it is fully deductible on the new loan.

If you refinance a home mortgage for more than the existing balance, the deductibility of interest on the excess amount depends upon how you use the funds and the amount of refinancing. If the excess amount is used to buy, build, or substantially improve your first or second home, then it is considered home acquisition debt; *see 15.2*. If the excess plus all other home acquisition loans does not exceed $1 million ($500,000 if married filing separately), the interest is fully deductible. If the excess is used for any other purpose, such as to pay off credit card debt or to finance a child's education, the excess is considered home equity debt; *see 15.3*. If the excess plus all other home equity loans does not exceed $100,000 ($50,000 if married filing separately), the interest is fully deductible. If the refinanced loan is partly home acquisition debt and partly home equity debt, the overall limit of $1.1 million applies ($1 million home acquisition debt and $100,000 home equity debt) or, if married filing separately, $550,000 ($500,000 home acquisition debt and $50,000 home equity debt).

Interest paid on loans in excess of home acquisition and home equity debt ceilings is generally treated as nondeductible personal interest unless the proceeds are used for business or investment purposes; *see 15.12*.

EXAMPLE

In 1994, Robert and Michelle Stein purchased a home for $250,000. They put $50,000 down and obtained a $200,000, 30-year mortgage secured by the home. In 1999, when their house is worth $300,000 and there is a $175,000 principal balance on the mortgage, they refinance to take advantage of lower interest rates. The refinanced mortgage is for $225,000, payable over 20 years. The Steins use $175,000 to pay off the old mortgage, $30,000 to purchase a car and to pay off credit card debt, and the remaining $20,000 to build a new deck on their home.

The interest on up to $175,000 of the debt incurred to pay off the old mortgage is fully deductible; the amount equals the outstanding balance before refinancing and also falls within the $1 million home acquisition debt ceiling. The $20,000 used to remodel the house is also treated as home acquisition debt. Interest on this amount is fully deductible; the amount falls within the $1 million ceiling when added to the $175,000.

The $30,000 used to buy a car and pay off credit cards is treated as home equity debt. Interest on this amount is fully deductible; the amount falls within the $100,000 ceiling.

Pre–October 14, 1987, loans. Refinanced pre–October 14, 1987, loans are not subject to the $1 million home acquisition and $100,000 home equity debt ceilings during the period of the original loan term. However, after the end of the original loan term, the ceilings apply to the refinanced amount as explained above. Furthermore, where a refinanced pre–October 14, 1987, debt exceeds the remaining principal balance, the excess is also subject to the $1 million home acquisition and $100,000 home equity debt ceilings.

EXAMPLE

In 1983, Anton and Julia Johnson purchase a home for $400,000. They put $80,000 down and obtain a $320,000, 30-year mortgage secured by their home. In 1999, the house is worth $500,000 and $250,000 is the principal balance remaining on the loan. In 1999, to take advantage of lower interest rates the Johnsons refinance and obtain a $360,000, 20-year mortgage. They use $250,000 to pay off the old mortgage, $90,000 as a down payment on a summer home, and the remaining $20,000 to pay for their daughter's college tuition. They file a joint return.

The interest on up to $250,000 of the debt incurred to pay off the old mortgage is fully deductible; the amount equals the outstanding balance immediately before refinancing. The $90,000 used as a down payment on a summer home is treated as home acquisition debt. Interest paid on this amount is fully deductible; the amount was used to buy a second home and it does not exceed the $1 million ceiling when added to the $250,000 mortgage on the first home. The $20,000 used towards their daughter's college tuition is treated as home equity debt. The interest on this amount is fully deductible; the amount is less than the $100,000 home equity debt ceiling.

Had the Johnsons used $110,000 for college tuition, to buy a new car, and to pay off credit card debt, only the interest paid on up to $100,000 of debt would be deductible home equity interest; interest on the $10,000 excess debt would have been treated as nondeductible personal interest except to the extent a deduction was available under the student loan interest rules (*see* Chapter 38).

Court Decision

Current Deduction for Points on Refinancing

Huntsman replaced a three-year loan used to purchase his principal residence with a 30-year mortgage. He deducted $4,400 of points paid on the new mortgage. The IRS and the Tax Court held that the points had to be deducted over the 30-year loan term.

The Federal Appeals Court for the Eighth Circuit disagreed and allowed a full deduction in the year the points were paid. The first loan was temporary and merely a step in obtaining permanent financing for the purchase of the principal residence.

The IRS has announced that in areas outside of the Eighth Circuit, it will continue to disallow full deductions in the year of payment for points paid on refinancings. The Eighth Circuit includes only these states: Minnesota, Iowa, North and South Dakota, Nebraska, Missouri, and Arkansas. In these states, the IRS will not challenge deductions for points on refinancing agreements similar to Huntsman's that replace short-term financing with long-term permanent financing.

In a later case, the Tax Court held that the *Huntsman* exception does not apply where a borrower refinances a long-term mortgage to take advantage of lower interest rates; the points must be deducted over the term of the new mortgage.

Points Paid on Refinancing

The IRS does not allow a current deduction for points on a refinanced mortgage. According to the IRS, the points must be deducted ratably over the loan period, unless part of the new loan is used for home improvements. Thus, if you pay points of $2,400 when refinancing a 20-year loan on your principal residence, the IRS allows you to deduct only $10 a month, or $120 each full year.

A federal appeals court rejected the IRS allocation rule where points are paid on a long-term mortgage that replaces a short-term loan; *see* the Court Decision on the preceding page.

If part of a refinancing is used for home improvements to a principal residence, the IRS allows a deduction for a portion of the points allocable to the home improvements.

EXAMPLE

In June 1999, Craig Smith refinances his home mortgage, which has a principal of $80,000 outstanding. The new loan is for $100,000, payable over 15 years starting in July 1999. He uses $80,000 to pay off the old $80,000 balance and the remaining $20,000 is used for home improvements. Assume that at the closing of the new loan, Smith pays points of $2,000 from his separate funds. In the year of payment he may deduct $400 allocable to the 20% of the loan used for home improvements. He may also deduct the ratable portion of the $1,600 balance of the points, which must be deducted over the period of the new loan. The ratable portion is $53 ($1,600 ÷ 180-month loan term × 6 months in 1999). Thus, Craig's total deduction for points in 1999 is $453 ($400 + $53).

Mortgage ends early. If you are ratably deducting points on a refinanced loan and you refinance again, or the mortgage ends early because you prepay it or the lender forecloses, you can deduct the remaining points in the year the mortgage ends.

15.8 "Points"

Lenders sometimes charge "points" in addition to the stated interest rate. The points increase the lender's upfront fees, but in return borrowers generally are charged a lower interest rate over the loan term. Points are either treated as a type of prepaid interest *(15.14)* or as a nondeductible service fee, depending on what the charge covers. If the points qualify as interest, they are deductible over the term of the loan unless they are paid on the purchase or improvement of your principal residence as discussed in this section.

Points are treated as interest if your payment is solely for your use of the money and is not for specific services performed by the lender that are separately charged. Whether a payment is called "points" or a "loan origination fee" does not affect its deductibility if it is actually a charge for the use of money. The purpose of the charge—that is, for the use of the money or the services rendered—will be controlling. For example, you may not deduct points that are fees for services, such as appraisal fees, preparation of a mortgage note or deed of trust, settlement fees, notary fees, abstract fees, commissions, and recording fees.

If you are *selling* property and you assume the buyer's liability for points, do not deduct the payment as interest but include it as a selling expense that reduces the amount realized on the sale.

Deduction for Points on Purchase or Improvement of Principal Residence

Points are generally treated as prepaid interest *(15.14)* that must be deducted over the period of the loan. However, there is an exception for points you pay on a loan to buy, build, or improve your principal residence. The points on such loans are deductible in the year paid if these tests are met: (1) the loan is secured by your principal residence; (2) the charging of points is an established business practice in the geographic area in which the loan is made; (3) the points charged do not exceed the points generally charged in the area; (4) the amount of points is computed as a percentage of the loan and specifically earmarked on the loan closing statement as "points," "loan origination fees," or "loan discount"; and (5) you pay the points directly to the lender; *see* "Points withheld from the principal," below.

 Caution

Service Fees Are Not Deductible Points

You may not deduct as points amounts that are for specific lender services. To be deductible, points on the purchase of a principal residence must be prepaid interest for the use of the loan money.

 Filing Tip

Amortize Points Starting in Second Year

A married couple purchased a principal residence and paid points late in the year. For the year of the purchase, their standard deduction exceeded their itemized deductions. The IRS ruled that claiming the standard deduction for the year the points are paid would not forfeit the deduction for points. The points may be amortized starting in the second year. Assuming that they itemize deductions starting in the second year, the allocable portion of the points may be deducted each year over the remaining loan term.

Planning Reminder

Points on Second Home

If you pay points on a loan to purchase or improve a second home, you must deduct the points ratably over the term of the loan.

Caution

Points Reported to the IRS

Points you paid in 1999 on the purchase of your principal residence will be reported to the IRS by the lender on Form 1098 if they meet the five tests explained earlier. Seller-paid points are also included on Form 1098. Form 1098 is used by the IRS to check on the deduction you claim for points on Line 10 of Schedule A. Points paid on an improvement loan for your principal residence are deductible on Line 12 of Schedule A if they meet the tests; they are not shown on Form 1098.

Points paid by seller are deductible by buyer. The seller's payment is treated as an adjustment to the purchase price that the seller gives to you as the buyer and that you then turn over to the lender to pay off the points. You must reduce your cost basis for the home by the seller-paid points.

Points withheld from the principal. Points withheld from the principal of a loan used to buy your principal residence are treated as if you paid them directly to the lender if, at or before closing, you have made a down payment, escrow deposit, or earnest money payment that is at least equal to the amount of points withheld. These payments must have been from your own funds and not from funds that have been borrowed from the lender as part of the overall transaction.

If the loan is used to *improve* your principal residence, the points are not immediately deductible if withheld from the loan principal. You must pay the points with funds that have not been obtained from the lender to claim the full deduction in the year of payment. Otherwise, the deduction must be spread over the loan term.

Points on second home. If you pay points on a mortgage secured by a second home or a vacation home, the points are not fully deductible in the year of payment; you must claim the deduction ratably over the loan term.

Points paid on refinancing. The IRS does not allow a current deduction for points on a refinanced mortgage (*see 15.7* for further information).

Deduct balance of points if mortgage ends early. If you are deducting points over the term of the loan because a full first-year deduction is not allowed, you are allowed to deduct the balance in the year the mortgage ends, such as when you refinance or prepay the loan, or the lender forecloses. For example, if you refinanced your mortgage in 1995 and paid points, those points had to be amortized over the loan term *(15.7)*. If in 1999 you refinance again and pay points again, the balance of the points from the 1995 loan are deductible on your 1999 return, and the points on the new loan must be amortized over the loan term.

15.9 Cooperative and Condominium Apartments

Cooperative apartments. If you are a tenant-stockholder of a cooperative apartment, you may deduct your portion of:

- Interest paid by the cooperative on its debts, provided you do not pay interest on more than two residences; *see 15.1*. This includes your pro rata share of the permanent financing expenses (points) of the cooperative on its mortgage covering the housing project.
- Taxes paid by the cooperative *(16.6)*. However, if the cooperative does not own the land and building but merely leases them and is required to pay real estate taxes under the terms of the lease, you may not deduct your share of the tax payment.

In some localities, such as New York City, rent control rules allow tenants of a building converted to a cooperative to remain in their apartments even if they do not buy into the co-op. A holdover tenant may prevent some co-op purchasers from occupying an apartment. The IRS ruled that the fact that a holdover tenant stays in the apartment will not bar the owner from deducting his or her share of the co-op's interest and taxes.

Condominiums. If you own an apartment in a condominium, you have a direct ownership interest in the property and are treated, for tax purposes, just as any other property owner. You may deduct your payments of real estate taxes and mortgage interest. You may also deduct taxes and interest paid on the mortgage debt of the project allocable to your share of the property. The deduction of interest from condominium ownership is also subject to the two-residence limit discussed at *15.1*. If your condominium is used part of the time for rental purposes, you may deduct expenses of maintenance and repairs and claim depreciation deductions subject to the rules in *9.7*.

Investment Loans

15.10 Investment Interest Limitations

Interest paid on margin accounts and debts to buy or carry other investments is deductible up to the amount of net investment income on Schedule A. If you do not have investment income such as interest, you may not deduct investment interest. Investment interest in excess of net investment income may be carried forward and deducted from next year's net investment income.

You compute the deduction for investment interest on Form 4952, which must be attached to Form 1040. The deduction is *not* subject to the 3% reduction of itemized deductions if your adjusted gross income exceeds $126,600 ($63,300 if married filing separately); *see 13.7*.

What is investment interest? It is all interest paid or accrued on debts incurred or continued to buy or carry investment property such as interest on securities in a margin account. However, interest on loans to buy tax-exempt securities is not deductible; *see 15.11.*

Investment interest does not include any qualified residence interest *(15.1),* production period interest that is capitalized *(16.4),* or interest related to a passive activity.

Investment property includes property producing portfolio income (interest, dividends, or royalties not realized in the ordinary course of business) under the passive activity rules discussed in Chapter 10, and property in activities that are not treated as passive activities, even if you do not materially participate, such as working interests in oil and gas wells.

Passive activity interest is not investment interest. Interest expenses incurred in a passive activity such as rental real estate *(10.1),* or a limited partnership or S corporation in which you do not materially participate *(10.6),* are taken into account on Form 8582 when figuring net passive income or loss. This includes interest incurred on loans used to finance your investment in a passive activity. Do not treat passive activity interest as investment interest on Form 4952.

However, interest expenses allocable to *portfolio* income (non–business activity interest, dividends, or royalties) from a limited partnership or S corporation are investment interest and not passive interest. The investment interest will be listed separately on Schedule K-1 received from the partnership or corporation.

Computing the Deduction

Deductible investment interest is limited to net investment income. Net investment income is the excess of investment income over investment expenses. The key terms *investment income* and *investment expenses* are defined below.

Investment income. Investment income is generally gross income from property held for investment, such as interest, dividends, annuities, and royalties. Income or expenses considered in figuring profit or loss of a passive activity (Chapter 10) is not considered investment income or expenses. Property subject to a net lease is not treated as investment property, as it is within the passive activity rules.

If you have net capital gains (net long-term capital gains exceeding net short-term losses) from the sale of investment property such as stocks or mutual-fund shares, such gains are not treated as investment income unless you specifically elect to include them in investment income on Form 4952. If you make this election, you may not apply preferential capital gain rates *(5.3)* to the amount of the net capital gains treated as investment interest on Form 4952. If you make the election on Form 4952, the elected amount is subtracted from net capital gains when applying the capital gain tax rates on Part IV of Schedule D. *See* the IRS instructions to Form 4952.

Investment expenses. There are expenses, other than interest, directly connected with the production of investment income. However, for purposes of determining net investment income, only those investment expenses (other than interest) allowable after figuring the 2% floor for miscellaneous itemized deductions *(19.24)* are taken into account. The 2% floor will bar a deduction for some of the miscellaneous itemized deductions. For purposes of this net investment income computation, assume that miscellaneous itemized deductions other than investment expenses are disallowed first.

Net investment income. Reducing investment income by investment expenses gives you net investment income. Your deduction for investment interest expenses is limited to this amount; any excess interest expense for 1999 may be carried over to 2000, as discussed below.

Where to enter the deduction on your return. The deduction figured on Form 4952 is generally entered on Line 13 of Schedule A as investment interest. However, if the interest is attributable to royalties, you may have to enter the interest on Schedule E; follow the Form 4952 instructions. Furthermore, there is an additional complication if you have investment interest for an activity for which you are not "at risk" (Chapter 10). After figuring the investment interest deduction on Form 4952, you must enter the portion of the interest that is attributable to the at-risk activity on Form 6198. The amount carried over to Form 6198 is subtracted from the investment interest deduction claimed on Form 4952.

Carryover to 2000 and future years. Investment interest in excess of net investment income for 1999 may be carried forward to 2000 and is deductible in 2000 to the extent that when added to 2000 investment interest expenses it does not exceed net investment income. If not used in 2000, the carryforward extends indefinitely to 2001 and future years.

Caution

Interest on Loans To Buy Market Discount Bonds and Treasury Bills

Limits apply to the deduction for interest on loans used to buy or carry market discount bonds *(4.20)* and Treasury bills *(4.27)* acquired after July 18, 1984.

Caution

Electing To Treat Long-Term Gains as Investment Income

If you elect on Form 4952 to treat net capital gains as investment income in order to increase your 1999 investment interest deduction, that amount of gain is not taken into account when applying capital gain rates in Part IV of Schedule D.

EXAMPLE

For 1999, Larry Jones has $10,000 of investment income from interest and dividends. He has investment expenses, other than interest, of $3,200, after taking into account the 2% floor on miscellaneous itemized deductions. His investment interest expense from securities margin account loans is $8,000. Jones also has income of $2,000 from a passive partnership investment.

Jones's net investment income is $6,800: $10,000 of investment income less $3,200 of non-interest investment expenses. The passive activity income from the partnership is not included in investment income.

Jones's investment interest deduction for 1999 is limited to the $6,800 of net investment income. The $1,200 of investment interest in excess of net investment income ($8,000 − $6,800) is carried forward to 2000.

15.11 Debts To Carry Tax-Exempt Obligations

When you borrow money in order to buy or carry tax-exempt bonds, you may not deduct any interest paid on your loan. Application of this disallowance rule is clear where there is actual evidence that loan proceeds were used to buy tax-exempts or that tax-exempts were used as collateral. But sometimes the relationship between a loan and the purchase of tax-exempts is less obvious, as where you hold tax-exempts and borrow to carry other securities or investments. IRS guidelines explain when a direct relationship between the debt and an investment in tax-exempts will be inferred so that no interest deduction is allowed. The IRS will *not* infer a direct relationship between a debt and an investment in tax-exempts in these cases:

1. The investment in tax-exempts is not substantial. That is, it is not more than 2% of the adjusted basis of the investment portfolio and any assets held in an actively conducted business.

2. The debt is incurred for a personal purpose. For example, an investor may take out a home mortgage instead of selling his tax-exempts and using the proceeds to finance the home purchase. Interest on the mortgage is deductible under the rules at *15.1*.

3. The debt is incurred in connection with the active conduct of a business and does not exceed business needs. But if a person reasonably could have foreseen when the tax-exempts were purchased that he or she would have to borrow funds to meet ordinary and recurrent business needs, the interest expenses are not deductible.

The guidelines infer a direct relationship between the debt and an investment in tax-exempts in this type of case: An investor in tax-exempts has outstanding debts not directly related to personal expenses or to his or her business. The interest will be disallowed even if the debt appears to have been incurred to purchase other portfolio investments. Portfolio investments include transactions entered into for profit, including investments in real estate, that are not connected with the active conduct of a business; *see* the Example below.

EXAMPLE

An investor owning $360,000 in tax-exempt bonds purchased real estate in a joint venture, giving a purchase money mortgage and cash for the price. He deducted interest on the mortgage. The IRS disallowed the deduction, claiming the debt was incurred to carry tax-exempts. A court allowed the deduction. A mortgage is the customary manner of financing such a purchase. Furthermore, since the purchase was part of a joint venture, the other parties' desires in the manner of financing had to be considered.

15.12 Earmarking Use of Loan Proceeds

The IRS has set down complex record keeping and allocation rules for claiming interest deductions on loans used for business or investment purposes, or for passive activities. The rules deal primarily with the use of loan proceeds for more than one purpose and the commingling of loan proceeds in an account with unborrowed funds. The thrust of the rules is to base deductibility of interest on the *use* of the borrowed funds. The allocation rules do not affect mortgage interest deductions on loans secured by a qualifying first or second home; *see 15.1*.

Caution

Tax-Exempt Income From Mutual Fund

You may not deduct interest on loans used to buy or carry tax-exempt securities. If you receive exempt-interest dividends from a mutual fund during the year, you may deduct interest on a loan used to buy or carry the mutual-fund shares only to the extent that the proceeds can be allocated to taxable dividends you also receive.

Keep separate accounts for business, personal, and investment borrowing. For example, if you borrow for investment purposes, keep the proceeds of the loan in a separate account and use the proceeds only for investment purposes. Do not use the funds to pay for personal expenses; interest is not deductible on personal loans other than qualifying student loans (Chapter 38). Furthermore, do not deposit loan proceeds in an account funded with unborrowed money, unless you intend to use the proceeds within 30 days of the deposit. By following these directions, you can identify your use of the proceeds with a specific expenditure, such as for investment, personal, or business purposes, and the interest on the loan may be treated as incurred for that purpose. The 30-day rule is discussed below.

The IRS treats undisbursed loan proceeds deposited in an account as investment property, even though the account does not bear interest. When proceeds are disbursed from the account, the use of the proceeds determines how interest is treated; *see* Examples 1 and 2 later in this section.

30-day disbursement rule. If you deposit borrowed funds in an account with unborrowed funds, a special 30-day rule allows you to treat payments from the account as made from the loan proceeds. Where you make more than one disbursement from such an account, you may treat any expenses paid within 30 days before or after deposit of the loan proceeds as if made from the loan proceeds. Thus, you may allocate interest on the loan to that disbursement, even if earlier payments from the account have been made; *see* Example 3 on the next page. If you make the disbursement after 30 days, the IRS requires you to allocate interest on the loan to the first disbursement; *see* Example 4 on the next page. Furthermore, if an account includes only loan proceeds and interest earned on the proceeds, disbursements may be allocated first to the interest income and then to the loan proceeds.

Allocation period. Interest is allocated to an expenditure for the period *beginning* on the date the loan proceeds are used or treated as used and *ending* on the earlier of either the date the debt is repaid or the date it is reallocated.

Accrued interest is treated as a debt until it is paid, and any interest accruing on unpaid interest is allocated in the same manner as the unpaid interest is allocated. Compound interest accruing on such debt, other than compound interest accruing on interest that accrued before the beginning of the year, may be allocated between the original expenditure and any new expenditure from the same account on a straight-line basis. That is done by allocating an equal amount of such interest expense to each day during the taxable year. In addition, you may treat a year as *twelve 30-day months* for purposes of allocating interest on a straight-line basis.

Payments from checking account. A disbursement from a checking account is treated as made at the time the check is written on the account, provided the check is delivered or mailed to the payee within a reasonable period after the writing of the check. You may treat checks written on the same day as written in any order. A check is presumed to be written on the date appearing on the check and to be delivered or mailed to the payee within a reasonable period thereafter. However, the presumption may not apply if the check does not clear within a reasonable period after the date appearing on the check.

Change in use of property. You must reallocate interest if you convert debt-financed property to a different use; for example, when you buy a business auto with an installment loan, interest paid on the auto is business interest, but if during the year you convert the auto to personal use, interest paid after the conversion is personal interest.

Order of repayment. If you used loan proceeds to repay several different kinds of debt, the debts being repaid are assumed to be repaid in the following order: (1) personal debt; (2) investment debt and passive activity debt other than active real estate debt; (3) debt from a real estate activity in which you actively participate; (4) former passive activity debt; and (5) business debt. *See* Example 5 on the following page. Payments made on the same day may be treated as made in any order.

Planning Reminder

Keep Loans Separate

To safeguard your investment and business interest deductions, you must earmark and keep a record of your loans. You should avoid using loan proceeds to fund different types of expenditures.

EXAMPLES

1. On January 1, you borrow $10,000 and deposit the proceeds in a non-interest-bearing checking account. No other amounts are deposited in the account during the year and no part of the loan is repaid during the year. On April 1, you invest $2,000 of the proceeds in a real estate venture. On September 1, you use $4,000 to buy furniture.

    From January 1 through March 31, interest on the entire undisbursed $10,000 is treated as investment interest. From April 1 through August 31, interest on $2,000 of the debt is

Planning Reminder

Using Borrowed Funds To Pay Interest

To get an interest deduction you must pay the interest; you may not claim a deduction by having the creditor add the interest to the debt. If you do not have funds to pay the interest, you may borrow money to pay the interest. The borrowed funds must be from a different creditor. The IRS disallows deductions where a debtor borrows from the same creditor to make interest payments on an earlier loan. The second loan is considered a device for getting an interest expense deduction without actually making payments. The Tax Court and several federal appeals courts have sided with the IRS.

treated as passive activity interest and interest on $8,000 of the debt is treated as investment interest. From September 1 through December 31, interest on $4,000 of the debt is treated as personal interest; interest on $2,000 is treated as passive activity interest; and interest on $4,000 is treated as investment interest.

2. On September 1, you borrow money for business purposes and deposit it in a checking account. On October 15, you disburse the proceeds for business purposes. Interest incurred on the loan before the disbursement of the funds is treated as investment interest expense. Interest starting on October 15 is treated as business interest. However, you may elect to treat the starting date for business interest as of the first of the month in which the disbursement was made—that is, October 1—provided all other disbursements from the account during the same month are similarly treated.

3. On September 1, you borrow $5,000 to invest in stock and deposit the proceeds in your regular checking account. On September 10, you buy a TV and stereo for $2,500 and on September 11 invest $5,000 in stock, using funds from the account. As the stock investment was made within 30 days of depositing the loan proceeds in the account, interest on the entire loan is treated as incurred for investment purposes.

4. Same facts as in Example 1, but the TV and stereo were bought on October 1 and the stock on October 31. As the stock investment was not made within 30 days, the IRS requires you to treat the purchase of the TV and the stereo for $2,500 as the first purchase made with the loan proceeds of $5,000. Thus, the 50% of loan interest that is allocated to the stereo purchase is nondeductible.

5. On July 12, Smith borrows $100,000 and immediately deposits the proceeds in an account. He uses the proceeds as follows:

August 31	$40,000 for passive activity
October 5	$20,000 for rental activity
December 24	$40,000 for personal use

On January 19 of the following year, Smith repays $90,000. Of the repayment, $40,000 is allocated as a repayment of the personal expenditure, $40,000 of the passive activity, and $10,000 of the rental activity. The outstanding $10,000 is treated as debt incurred in a rental activity.

Timing of Interest Deductions

15.13 Year To Claim an Interest Deduction

As a cash-basis taxpayer, you deduct interest in the year of payment except for prepayments of interest; *see 15.14*. Giving a promissory note is not considered payment. Increasing the amount of a loan by interest owed, as with insurance loans, is also not considered payment and will not support a deduction. If a person pays your interest obligation with the understanding you will repay him or her, you take the deduction in the year the interest is paid, not when you repay him or her. However, an accrual-basis taxpayer generally deducts interest in the year the interest accrues; *see 40.3*.

Here is how a cash-basis taxpayer treats interest in the following situations:

On a life insurance loan, where proceeds are used for a deductible (nonpersonal) purpose, you claim a deduction in the year in which the interest is paid. You may not claim a deduction when the insurance company adds the interest to your debt. You may not deduct your payment of interest on an insurance loan after you assign the policy.

On a margin account with a broker, interest is deductible in the year in which it is paid or your account is credited after the interest has been charged. But an interest charge to your account is not payment if you do not pay it in cash or the broker has not collected dividends, interest, or security sales proceeds that may be applied against the interest due. Note that the interest deduction on margin accounts is subject to investment interest limitations; *see 15.10*.

For partial payment of a loan used for a deductible (nonpersonal) purpose, interest is deductible in the year the payment is credited against interest due. When a loan has no provision for allocating payments between principal and income, the law presumes that a partial payment is applied first to interest and then to principal, unless you agree otherwise. Where the payment is in full settlement of the debt, the payment is applied first to principal, unless you agree otherwise. Where there is an involuntary payment, such as that following a foreclosure sale of collateral, sales proceeds are applied first to principal, unless you agree to the contrary. *See also 15.12* for the effect of payments on the allocation of debt proceeds.

Note renewed. You may not deduct interest by merely giving a new note. You claim a deduction in the year the renewed note is paid. The giving of a new note or increasing the amount due is not payment. The same is true when past due interest is deducted from the proceeds of a new loan; this is not a payment of the interest.

15.14 Prepaid Interest

If you prepay interest on a loan used for *investment* or *business* purposes you may not deduct interest allocable to any period falling in a later taxable year. The prepaid interest must be deducted over the period of the loan, whether you are a cash-basis or accrual-basis taxpayer.

Points paid on the purchase of a *principal residence* are generally fully deductible in the year paid; *see 15.8*. Points paid on refinancing generally are not deductible; *see 15.7*.

Treatment of interest included in a level payment schedule. Where payments of principal and interest are equal, a large amount of interest allocated to the payments made in early years of a loan will generally not be considered prepaid interest. However, if the loan calls for a variable interest rate, the IRS may treat interest payments as consisting partly of interest, computed under an average level effective rate, and partly of prepaid interest allocable to later years of the loan. An interest rate that varies with the "prime rate" does not necessarily indicate a prepaid interest element.

When you borrow money for a deductible purpose and give a note to the lender, the amount of your loan proceeds may be less than the face value of the note. The difference between the proceeds and the face amount is interest discount. For loans that do not fall within the OID rules of *4.18*, such as loans of a year or less, interest is deductible in the year of payment if you are on the cash basis. If you use the accrual basis, the interest is deductible as it accrues.

EXAMPLE

In February 1998, you borrow $1,000 for an investment and receive $900 in return for your $1,000 note. You repay the full loan in January 1999. You are on the cash basis. You do not deduct the interest of $100 when the note is given. The $100 interest is treated as investment interest *(15.10)* when the loan is paid in 1999.

For loans that fall within OID rules, your lender should provide a statement showing the interest element and the tax treatment of the interest.

 Planning Reminder

Business Investment Loans
If you prepay business or investment loan interest, you must spread the interest deduction over the period of the loan. In the year of payment, you may deduct only the interest allocable to that year.

Deductions for Taxes

If you itemize deductions on Schedule A, you may deduct your 1999 payments of state, local, and foreign income taxes and real property taxes, as well as state and local personal property taxes. State and local sales taxes are not deductible.

To increase your deduction for state and local taxes, consider making a year-end prepayment of estimated tax liability. You also may be able to increase withholdings from your pay to increase your deduction.

If you pay transfer taxes on the sale of securities or investment real estate, the taxes are not deductible. However, they increase your cost basis when figuring your profit or loss.

Taxes paid in operating a business are generally deductible, except for sales taxes, which are added to the cost of the property.

Taxes claimed as itemized deductions are subject to the 3% reduction of itemized deductions if your adjusted gross income exceeds $126,600, or $63,300 if married filing separately; *see 13.7.*

16.1 Deductible Taxes

You may deduct as itemized deductions on Schedule A your 1999 payments of:

- State, local, and foreign income taxes
- State, local, and foreign real property taxes
- State and local personal property taxes

In figuring deductible state or local income taxes, include the amount of state or local income tax withheld from your 1999 pay, any state or local estimated tax you paid in 1999, and any part of a prior year refund that you credited to your 1999 state or local tax. Also, do not forget to include tax that you paid in 1999 when you filed your 1998 state and local tax returns.

Taxes incurred in your business are generally deductible on Schedule C; *see 16.11.*

If your 1999 adjusted gross income exceeds $126,600, or $63,300 if married filing separately, your deduction for taxes is subject to the 3% reduction computation explained at *13.7.*

Claim the deduction for deductible taxes on the tax return for the year in which you paid the taxes, unless you report on the accrual basis; *see 16.8.*

 Filing Tip

State Tax Paid in 1999
In figuring your 1999 itemized deduction for state and local income taxes paid, remember to include tax that you paid in 1999 when you filed your 1998 state and local tax returns.

Checklist of Taxes

Type of tax—	Deductible as itemized deduction—
Admission	No
Alcoholic beverage	No
Assessments for local benefits	No
Automobile license fees not qualifying as personal property tax	No
Cigarette	No
Customs duties	No
Driver's license	No
Estate—federal or state	No*
Excise—federal or state, for example, on telephone service	No
Gasoline—federal	No
Gasoline and other motor fuel—state and local	No
Gift taxes—federal and state	No
Income—federal (including alternative minimum tax)	No
Income—state, local, or foreign	Yes
Inheritance tax	No
Mortgage tax	No
Personal property—state or local	Yes
Poll	No
Real estate (state, local, or foreign)	Yes
Regulatory license fees (dog licenses, parking meter fees, hunting and fishing licenses)	No
Sales and use tax on personal property	No
Social Security	No
Tolls	No
Transfer taxes on securities and real estate	No

* But *see 11.17* for miscellaneous itemized deduction for estate tax paid on "income in respect of a decedent"

16.2 Nondeductible Taxes

Sales taxes on personal property are not deductible as itemized deductions. Transfer taxes paid on the sale of securities or investment real estate are not separately deductible, but you may increase your cost basis by the transfer tax in figuring profit or loss on Schedule D.

Gasoline taxes. State and local taxes on gasoline used for personal purposes are not deductible. If you travel for business, the taxes are deductible as part of your gasoline expenses.

16.3 Deducting State Income Taxes

You may deduct on your 1999 return state and local income taxes withheld from your pay and estimated state and local taxes paid in 1999. Also deduct the balance of your 1998 state and local taxes you paid during 1999. If in 2000 you pay additional state income tax on your 1999 income, you deduct the payment on your 2000 tax return.

State income taxes may be claimed only as itemized deductions, even if attributed solely to business income. That is, state income taxes may not be deducted as business expenses from gross income.

To increase your itemized deductions on your 1999 return, consider prepaying state income taxes before the end of 1999. The prepayment is deductible provided the state tax authority accepts prepayments and state law recognizes them as tax payments. The IRS has ruled, however, that prepayments are not deductible if you do not reasonably believe that you owe additional state tax. Do not make prepayments if you may be subject to alternative minimum tax; *see* Chapter 23.

If you report on the accrual basis and you contest a tax liability, claim the deduction in the year of payment.

You may deduct on your federal return state and local income taxes allocable to interest income that is exempt from federal tax but not state and local income tax. However, state and local taxes that are allocated to other federal exempt income are not deductible. For example, state income tax allocated to a cost-of-living allowance exempt from federal income tax is not deductible as a state tax.

Mandatory employee contributions to the following state disability or unemployment insurance funds are deductible as state income taxes: California, New Jersey, New York Nonoccupational Disability Benefit Fund, Rhode Island Temporary Disability Benefit Fund, and Washington State Supplemental Workmen's Compensation Fund.

However, employee contributions to a private or voluntary disability plan in California, New Jersey, or New York have been held by the IRS to be nondeductible.

Mandatory employee contributions to a state unemployment fund are deductible.

Note: A refund of state income taxes claimed as an itemized deduction may have to be reported as income; *see 11.5.*

16.4 When Taxes and Interest Are Capitalized

Uniform capitalization rules (Code Section 263A) may prevent you from deducting taxes and interest incurred on business and investment real estate during a construction or development period; *see 40.3.* According to a Tax Court decision, the development period for land started when a development plan was submitted to zoning authorities. The developer was required to capitalize real estate taxes on the raw land, even though no actual development had occurred.

Election to capitalize. Where property such as nonproductive and undeveloped land is not subject to the uniform capitalization rules of Code Section 263A, you may elect to capitalize taxes and interest instead of deducting them. You capitalize the expenses by adding these amounts to the basis of the property. Capitalization may be to your advantage if you do not need the immediate deduction because you have little or no income to offset, or because you do not have itemized deductions or expect a greater tax benefit by adding the taxes to the basis.

To make the election, attach to your return a statement of expenses you elect to capitalize; IRS permission is not required. The election must apply to all similar expenses for the same project. An election for unimproved and unproductive real property applies only for the year for which it is made.

16.5 Assessments

Assessments by homeowner's association not deductible as taxes. Assessments paid to a local homeowner's association for the purpose of maintaining the common areas of the residential project and for promoting the recreation, health, and safety of the residents are not deductible as real property taxes.

Assessments for government services. If property is used solely as your residence, you may not deduct charges for municipal water bills (even if described as a "tax"), sewer assessments, assessments for sanitation service, or title registration fees. A permit fee to build or improve a personal residence is added to the cost basis of the house.

Filing Tip

Refund Credited to State Estimated Tax

If you were entitled to a refund on your 1998 state tax return and you credited the overpayment towards your 1999 estimated state tax, do not forget to include the credited amount with other 1999 payments of state and local income tax on your 1999 Schedule A.

Assessments for local benefits are deductible if they cover maintenance or repairs of streets, sidewalks, or water or sewer systems, or interest costs on such maintenance. However, assessments for construction of streets, sidewalks, or other local improvements that tend to increase the value of your property are not deductible as real estate taxes. You add such assessments to your cost basis for the property.

If you are billed a single amount, you may deduct the portion allocable to assessments for maintenance or repairs. The burden is on you to support the allocation.

16.6   Deducting Real Estate Taxes

You may deduct payments of real estate tax on your property if you claim itemized deductions on Schedule A. The monthly mortgage payment to a bank or other mortgage holder generally includes amounts allocated to real estate taxes, which are paid to the taxing authority on their due date. Mortgage payments allocated to real estate taxes are deductible in the year you make the payments only if the mortgage holder actually pays the taxes to the tax authority by the end of that year. Typically, banks will furnish you with a year-end statement of disbursements to taxing authorities, indicating dates of payment.

16.7   Tenants' Payment of Taxes

You generally may not deduct a portion of your rent as property taxes. This is so even where state or local law identifies a portion of the rent as being tied to tax increases.

Tenants have been allowed a deduction for property taxes in the following areas: In Hawaii tenants with leases of 15 years or more may deduct the portion of the rent representing taxes. In California, tenants who have their names placed on the tax rolls and who pay the taxes directly to the taxing authority may claim a deduction.

In New York, liability for tax is placed directly on the tenant and the landlord is a collecting agent for paying over the tax to the taxing authorities; the landlord also remains liable for the tax. The IRS ruled that it will not permit tenants to deduct a portion of rent as a payment of taxes.

EXAMPLE

A municipal rent control ordinance allowed landlords to charge real property tax increases to the tenants as a monthly "tax surcharge." The ordinance stated that the surcharge was not to be considered rent for purposes of computing cost-of-living rental increases. The IRS ruled that the tenant may not deduct the "tax surcharge" as a property tax. The tax is imposed on the landlord, not on the tenant. The city ordinance, which permitted the landlord to pass on the tax increases to a tenant, did not shift liability for the property taxes from the landlord to the tenant. For federal tax purposes, the surcharge is merely an additional rental payment by the tenant. Similarly, "rates tax" or "renters' tax" imposed on tenants was ruled to be nondeductible because the tax is imposed on the person using the property rather than the property itself.

16.8   Allocating Taxes When You Sell or Buy Realty

When property is sold, the buyer and seller apportion the real estate taxes imposed on the property during the "real property year." A "real property year" is the period that a real estate tax covers. This allocation is provided for you in a settlement statement at the time of closing. If you want to figure your own allocations, your local tax authority can give you the "real property year" of the taxes you plan to apportion. With this information, you then make the following allocation. If *you* are the:

Seller, you deduct that portion of the tax covering the beginning of the real property year through the day before the sale.

Buyer, you deduct the part of the tax covering the date of the sale through the end of the real property year.

EXAMPLE

The real property year in East County starts April 1 and ends March 31. On July 2, 1999, you sell realty located in East County to Jones. Assume the real estate tax for the real property year ending March 31, 2000, is $1,000. You deduct $252 ($^{92}/_{365}$ of $1,000, since there are 92 days in the period beginning April 1 and ending July 1, 1999). Jones deducts $748 ($^{273}/_{365}$ of $1,000, since there are 273 days in the period beginning July 2, 1999, and ending March 31, 2000).

 Filing Tip

Cooperative Apartments
Tenant-stockholders of a cooperative housing corporation may deduct their share of the real estate taxes paid by the corporation. However, no deduction is allowed if the corporation does not own the land and building but merely leases them and pays taxes under the lease agreement. *See also 15.9.*

The allocation of taxes between the buyer and seller is mandatory whether or not your contract provides for an allocation. However, you do not allocate taxes of a real property year when property is sold before the real property year. This rule prevents the seller from deducting any part of the tax for that year, even though it became a personal liability or lien while he or she owned the property. The buyer gets the deduction because he or she owns the property for the entire real property year. You also do not allocate taxes when property is sold after the real property year. This rule prevents the buyer from deducting the tax for that year even though it becomes a personal liability or lien after he or she takes possession of the property. The seller gets the deduction because the tax covers the property year in which the seller owns the property. The allocation is limited to a tax covering a property year during which both the seller and the buyer own the property.

Form 1099-S. The IRS requires real estate agents to report in Box 5 of Form 1099-S the buyer's share of real estate taxes on a residence. For example, Smith sells her house in Green County, where the real estate tax is paid annually in advance. In the year of sale she paid $1,200 in real estate taxes. Assuming that the home is sold at the end of the ninth month of the real property tax year, the amount of the real estate tax allocable to the buyer is $300 ($100 per month × 3 months). This amount, which is shown as paid by the seller in advance on an HUD-1 (Uniform Settlement Statement) form provided at the closing, must be reported by the real estate agent as the buyer's share of the real estate tax in Box 5 of Form 1099-S.

When to deduct allocated taxes. After you have made the allocation based on the "real property year," you then must fix the year in which you deduct your share of the allocated tax. Here you consider your method of reporting your income—cash or accrual basis—and the date on which either you or the other party became liable for the tax or paid the tax. If neither you nor the other party is liable for the tax under local law, then the party who holds the property at the time the tax became a lien on the property is considered liable. Check the following rules to determine when you deduct the apportioned tax:

Seller on the cash basis—If the buyer is liable for the tax under local law, the seller may deduct his or her share of the allocated tax either in the year of the sale or a later year when the tax is actually paid. If the seller is liable for the tax under local law, and the tax is not payable until after the sale date, the seller may deduct the tax either in the year of sale or in the year he or she pays the tax.

Buyer on the cash basis—If the seller is liable for the tax under local law, the buyer may deduct the tax either in the year of sale or when the tax is actually paid. If the buyer is liable for the tax, he or she deducts the tax in the year the tax is paid.

Seller on the accrual basis—The seller accrues his or her share of the tax on the date of the sale, unless taxes have been accrued ratably over the years. If this is so, the last accrual is the sale date.

Buyer on the accrual basis—If the seller is liable for the tax, the buyer accrues his or her share of the tax on the date of the sale, unless taxes are accrued ratably. If taxes are accrued ratably, the accrual begins with the date of sale. If the buyer is liable for the tax, he or she deducts the tax in the return for the year the tax accrues unless an election is made to accrue ratably from the date of sale.

Seller's deduction in excess of the allocated amount is taxed. If, in the year before the sale, the seller deducts an amount for taxes in excess of the allocated amount, the excess must be reported as income in the year of the sale. This may happen when the seller is on the cash basis and pays the tax in the year before the sale.

EXAMPLE

A real property tax of $1,000 is due and payable on November 30 for the following calendar year. On November 30, 1998, Keith Jones, who uses the cash basis and reports on a calendar year, pays the 1999 tax. On June 30, 1999, he sells the real property. Under the apportionment rule, Jones is allowed to deduct only $493 ($\frac{180}{365}$ of $1,000, since there are 180 days in the period from January 1 to June 29, 1999) of the tax for the 1999 real property tax year. But Jones has already deducted the full amount in the 1998 return. Therefore, he reports as income that part of the tax deduction that he was not entitled to under the apportionment.

Filing Instruction

Buyer's Share of Real Estate Tax

If you sold a house in 1999 and received Form 1099-S, check Box 5 for the amount of real estate tax that you paid in advance and that is allocable to the buyer. The buyer may deduct this amount. You subtract it from the amount you paid when claiming your 1999 itemized deduction for real estate taxes.

Buyer may not deduct payment of seller's back taxes. The back taxes paid are added to the cost of the newly purchased property. The amount realized by the seller is increased by the buyer's payment of back taxes.

Seller's payment upon buyer's failure to pay. If a buyer is obligated to pay taxes under a land contract but fails to pay, the owner who pays the tax may deduct the payment if the tax is assessed to him or her.

Buyer of foreclosed property. If you buy realty at a tax sale and you do not receive immediate title to the property under state law until after a redemption period, you may not be able to deduct payment of realty taxes for several years.

16.9 Who May Deduct Real Property Taxes

A person who pays a property tax must have an ownership interest in the property to deduct the payment. The following table summarizes who may deduct payments of real property taxes.

If the tax is paid by—	Then it is deductible by—
You, for your spouse	Neither, if your spouse has title to the property, and you each file a separate return. This is true even if the mortgage requires you to pay the taxes. The tax is deductible on a joint return.
You, as owner of a condominium	You deduct real estate tax paid on your separate unit. You also deduct your share of the tax paid on the common property.
Your cooperative apartment or corporation	You deduct your share of real estate tax paid on the property; see 15.9. But if the organization leases the land and building and pays the tax under the terms of the lease, you may not deduct your share.
A life tenant	A court allowed the deduction to a widow required to pay the taxes under a will for the privilege of occupying the house during her life.
A tenant	The tenant of a business lease may deduct the payment of tax as additional rent, not tax. The tenant of a personal residence may not deduct the payment as either a tax or rent expense, unless placed on the real estate assessment rolls so that the tax is assessed directly against him or her; see 16.7.
You, as a local benefit tax to maintain, repair, or meet interest costs arising from local benefits	You deduct only that part of the tax that you can show is for maintenance, repair, or interest. If you cannot make the allocation, no deduction is allowed. If the benefit increases the value of the property, you add the non-deductible assessment to the basis of the property.
One whose property was foreclosed for failure to pay taxes	You may not deduct the taxes paid out of the proceeds of the foreclosure sale if your interest in the property ended with the foreclosure.
Tenant by the entirety or joint tenant	The tenant who is jointly and severally liable and who pays the tax. If real property is owned by husband and wife as tenants by the entirety or joint tenants, either spouse may deduct the taxes paid on a separate return or a joint return.
Tenant in common	When property is owned as a tenancy in common, under an IRS rule, a tenant may deduct only his or her share of the tax, even if the entire tax was paid. However, in one case the Tax Court allowed a deduction for the full amount where a co-tenant's payment protected her against the possibility of foreclosure in the event the other co-tenants failed to pay their share of the taxes; see 9.2.
A mortgagee	No deduction. If tax is paid before the foreclosure, it is added to the loan. If paid after the foreclosure, it is added to the cost of property.

 Law Alert

Form 1099-S for Sale of Principal Residence

A sale of a principal residence generally does not have to be reported on Form 1099-S if the seller gives the real estate agent responsible for the closing written assurance that the home was the seller's principal residence and that the full gain on the sale is excludable from income (*see* Chapter 29).

16.10 Automobile License Fees

You may not deduct an auto license fee based on weight, model, year, or horsepower. But you may deduct a fee based on the value of the car as a state personal property tax if these three tests are met: (1) the fee is an *ad valorem* tax, based on a percentage of value of the property; (2) it is imposed on an annual basis, even though it is collected more or less frequently; and (3) it is imposed on personal property. This third test is met even though the tax is imposed on the exercise of a privilege of registering a car or for using a car on the road.

The majority of state motor vehicle registration fees are not *ad valorem* taxes and do not qualify for the deduction. Various states and localities impose *ad valorem* or personal property taxes on motor vehicles that may qualify for the deduction. If you pay fees or taxes on your auto in these states, we suggest you contact a state or local authority to verify the amount of tax qualifying: Arizona, California, Colorado, Connecticut, Georgia, Indiana, Iowa, Maine, Massachusetts, Minnesota, Mississippi, Montana, Nebraska, Nevada, New Hampshire, Oklahoma, Washington, and Wyoming.

16.11 Taxes Deductible as Business Expenses

That a tax is not deductible as an itemized deduction does not mean you may not deduct it elsewhere on your return. For example, you may generally deduct property taxes incurred as a cost of doing business on Schedule C. Here are some other examples:

If you pay excise taxes on merchandise you sell in your business, you deduct the tax as a business expense.

If you pay Social Security taxes (FICA) on your employees' wages, you deduct the tax as a business expense on Schedule C.

If you pay sales tax on business property, you add the tax to the cost of the property for depreciation purposes. If the tax is paid on nondepreciable property, the tax is included in the currently deductible cost.

If you pay sales tax on a deductible business meal, the tax is deductible as part of the meal costs, subject to the cost limit discussed at *20.24*.

50% self-employment tax deduction. One-half of the self-employment tax figured on Schedule SE is deductible from gross income on Line 27 of Form 1040, rather than on Schedule C; *see 45.3*.

Note: If you are not a material participant in the business, your Schedule C expenses are subject to passive activity limitations; *see* Chapter 10.

16.12 Foreign Taxes

You may deduct your payment of foreign real property taxes and income and excess profits taxes as itemized deductions. Where you pay foreign income or excess profits tax, you have an election of either claiming the tax as a deduction or a credit. Claiming the credit may provide a larger tax savings; *see 36.14*.

Filing Tip

Value Portion of Auto License Fee

If an automobile license fee is based partly on value and partly on weight or other tests, the tax attributed to the value is deductible. For example, assume a registration fee based on 1% of value, plus 40¢ per hundred-weight. The part of the tax equal to 1% of value qualifies as an *ad valorem* tax and is deductible as a personal property tax on Schedule A.

Medical and Dental Expense Deductions

Tax relief for the high cost of medical care is limited. Medical expenses are deductible only if you itemize and only if you have expenses exceeding 7.5% of your adjusted gross income. Expenses up to 7.5% of AGI are not deductible.

Carefully review the list of deductible expenses in this chapter so that you do not overlook any deductible expenses. Include payments of doctors' fees, health-care premiums, prescription medicines, travel costs for obtaining medical care, and eligible home improvements.

If you are married, both you and your spouse work, and one of you has substantial medical expenses, filing separate returns may result in a lower overall tax.

Deductible medical expenses are *not* subject to the 3% reduction of itemized deductions that applies on 1999 returns if adjusted gross income exceeds $126,600 ($63,300 if married filing separately).

Qualifying long-term care expenses may be treated as medical expenses subject to the 7.5% of AGI floor, including a specified deductible amount of premiums paid for a qualifying long-term care contract; *see 17.15*.

Deductible contributions to medical savings accounts (MSAs) may be made by self-employed individuals and employees of certain small businesses; *see 17.17*.

17.1 Medical Expenses Must Exceed 7.5% of AGI

The tax law provides only a limited opportunity to deduct medical costs for you, your spouse, and your dependents. A wide range of expenses, such as those listed on page 318, qualify as deductible medical expenses. However, you may not be able to claim the deduction because of a percentage floor. You may deduct only expenses exceeding 7.5% of your adjusted gross income (AGI). Adjusted gross income is explained at *12.1*. For 1999, adjusted gross income is shown on Line 33 of Form 1040.

Married persons filing joint returns apply the 7.5% floor to their combined adjusted gross income.

On your 1999 return, you may deduct expenses paid in 1999 by cash or check (unless the check is postdated to 2000) for yourself, your spouse *(17.6)*, or dependents *(17.7)*. If you borrow to pay medical or dental expenses, you claim the deduction in the year you use the loan proceeds to pay the bill, not in the later year when you repay the loan. If you paid medical or dental expenses by credit card in 1999, the deduction is allowed in 1999, although you do not pay the charge bill until 2000.

EXAMPLES

1. Frank Ryan's adjusted gross income (AGI; *see 12.1*) is $20,000 for 1999. His unreimbursed medical expenses were $1,000 for doctor and dentist visits, $210 for prescribed drugs and medicines, and $625 for medical insurance premiums. If he itemizes deductions on Schedule A, he may deduct medical expenses of $335, figured this way:

Unreimbursed expenses	$1,000
Premiums	625
Drugs	210
Total	$1,835
Less: 7.5% of adjusted gross income (7.5% of $20,000)	1,500
Medical expense deduction	$335

2. Same as facts as in Example 1 except that Frank's AGI is $30,000, not $20,000. Here, Frank may not claim any medical deduction because his expenses of $1,835 do not exceed $2,250, 7.5% of his AGI.

17.2 Allowable Medical Care Costs

In determining whether you have paid deductible medical expenses exceeding the 7.5% AGI floor *(17.1)*, include the cost of diagnosis, cure, mitigation, treatment, or prevention of disease or any treatment that affects a part or function of your body. Also include qualifying costs you paid for your spouse *(17.6)* and your dependents *(17.7)*. *See* the checklist on page 318.

Expenses that are *solely* for cosmetic reasons are not deductible. Also, expenses incurred to benefit your general health are not deductible even if recommended by a physician; *see 17.3*.

Medicine and drugs. To be deductible, medicines and drugs other than insulin must be obtainable solely through a prescription by a doctor. Insulin is deductible even though a prescription may not be required. Marijuana is not deductible even if prescribed by a doctor in a state allowing the prescription. You may not deduct the cost of over-the-counter medicines and drugs, such as aspirin and other cold remedies, even if you have a doctor's prescription.

Special foods. The cost of special foods or beverages is not a deductible medical expense if the food or beverages substitute for those normally consumed.

EXAMPLE

To alleviate an ulcer, your doctor puts you on a special diet. According to the IRS, the cost of your food and beverages is not deductible. The special diet replaces the food you normally eat.

The Tax Court has set its own standard for deducting the extra cost of special foods as medical costs. The test is to show a medical need for taking the special food and the extra cost of the health food over ordinary food. Only the extra cost is deductible.

Caution

Only Unreimbursed Expenses Are Deductible

You may not deduct medical expenses for which you have been reimbursed by insurance or other awards *(17.4)*. Furthermore, reimbursement of medical expenses deducted in prior tax years may be taxable income *(11.6)*.

Caution

Prescription Drugs

With the exception of insulin, you may not deduct the cost of drugs that may be obtained without a prescription by a doctor.

Law Alert

Deduction for Smoking Cessation Programs

The IRS has reversed a prior position and now allows the cost of smoking cessation programs and drugs prescribed to alleviate nicotine withdrawal symptoms as deductible medical expenses, subject to the 7.5% floor. However, the cost of over-the-counter nicotine patches and gums is not deductible. The IRS position applies retroactively to pre-1999 years. If in a prior year you paid for a smoking cessation program or prescription nicotine-withdrawal medication that is deductible under the 7.5% floor, you may claim a refund provided the time limit for amending your return has not expired; *see 49.1*.

EXAMPLES

1. Anna Von Kalb suffered from hypoglycemia and her physician prescribed a special high protein diet, which required her to consume twice as much protein as an average person and exclude all processed foods and carbohydrates. She spent $3,483 for food, and deducted 30%, or $1,045, as the extra cost of her high protein diet. The IRS disallowed the deduction, claiming that the protein supplements were a substitute for foods normally consumed. The Tax Court disagreed. The high protein food did not substitute for her usual diet but helped alleviate her hypoglycemia. Thus, she may deduct its additional expense.

2. The Bechers suffered from allergies and were advised by a physician to eat organically grown food to avoid the chemicals in commercial food. The Bechers claimed a medical expense deduction of $2,255, the extra cost of buying organic food.

   The IRS disallowed the deduction and the Tax Court agreed. They did not present evidence that their allergies could be cured by limiting their diet to organic food. That the food was beneficial to their general health and was prescribed by a doctor is not sufficient for a deduction.

Filing Tip

Childbirth Classes

A mother-to-be may deduct the cost of classes instructing her in Lamaze breathing and relaxation techniques, stages of labor, and delivery procedures. If her husband or other childbirth "coach" also attends the classes, the portion of the fee allocable to the coach is not deductible. Costs of classes on early pregnancy, fetal development, or caring for newborns also are not deductible.

17.3 Nondeductible Medical Expenses

The most common nondeductible medical expense is the cost of over-the-counter medicines and drugs, such as aspirin and other cold remedies. A deduction for over-the-counter medicines is disallowed even if you have a doctor's prescription. Also *see* the checklist on page 319.

Cosmetic surgery. A medical expense deduction is allowed for cosmetic surgery if it is necessary to improve a disfigurement related to a congenital abnormality, disfiguring disease, or an accidental injury.

You may not deduct the cost of cosmetic surgery or other procedures that do not have a medical purpose. Thus, face lifts, hair transplants, electrolysis, and liposuction intended to improve appearance are generally not deductible. However, in one case, the Tax Court allowed an exotic dancer to claim a depreciation deduction for breast implants essential for her business; *see 19.8.*

Exercise and weight-reduction programs. If you incur costs for such programs to improve your *general* health, the costs are not deductible even if your doctor has recommended them. However, if your doctor has recommended a program as treatment for a *specific* condition, the IRS has indicated that the cost would be deductible.

Caution

Deducting Costs of Health Improvement Programs

Exercise and weight-reduction programs are deductible only as treatments for specific conditions, not as ways to improve your general health, even if your doctor has recommended them.

17.4 Reimbursements Reduce Deductible Expenses

Insurance or other reimbursements of your medical costs reduce your potential medical deduction. Reimbursements for loss of earnings or damages for personal injuries and mental suffering do not have to be taken into account. A reimbursement first reduces the medical expense for which it is paid. The excess is then applied to your other deductible medical costs.

EXAMPLE

Gail Hurz paid $800 in medical insurance premiums. She paid doctor and hospital bills totaling $700 and purchased prescription drugs costing $150. Group hospitalization insurance reimbursed $300 for doctors and hospital bills and $25 for medicines and drugs. Her adjusted gross income is $15,000. Her deduction is computed as follows:

Prescription drugs	$150
Medical care expenses	700
Premiums	800
Total	$1,650
Less reimbursement	325
	$1,325
Less: 7.5% of $15,000	1,125
Medical expense deduction	$200

Deductible Medical Expenses

Professional Services

Chiropodist
Chiropractor
Christian Science practitioner
Dermatologist
Dentist
Gynecologist
Neurologist
Obstetrician
Ophthalmologist
Optician
Optometrist
Orthopedist
Osteopath
Pediatrician
Physician
Physiotherapist
Plastic surgeon; but *see 17.3.*
Podiatrist
Practical or other nonprofessional nurse for medical services only, not for care of a healthy person or a small child who is not ill. Costs for medical care of elderly person unable to get about or person subject to spells are deductible; *see 17.12.*
Psychiatrist
Psychoanalyst
Psychologist
Registered nurse
Surgeon
Unlicensed practitioner services are deductible if the type and quality of the services are not illegal.

Dental Services

Artificial teeth
Cleaning teeth
Dental X-rays
Extracting teeth
Filling teeth
Gum treatment
Oral surgery
Straightening teeth

Equipment and Supplies

Abdominal supports
Air conditioner where necessary for relief from an allergy or for relieving difficulty in breathing; *see 17.13.*
Ambulance hire
Arches
Artificial eyes, limbs

Autoette (auto device for handicapped person)
Back supports
Braces
Contact lenses and solutions
Cost of installing stair-seat elevator for person with heart condition; *see 17.13.*
Crutches
Elastic hosiery
Eyeglasses
Fluoridation unit in home
Hearing aids
Heating devices
Invalid chair
Iron lung
Orthopedic shoes—excess cost over cost of regular shoes
Oxygen or oxygen equipment to relieve breathing problems caused by a medical condition
Reclining chair if prescribed by doctor
Repair of special telephone equipment for the deaf
Sacroiliac belt
Special mattress and plywood bed boards for relief of arthritis or spine
Splints
Truss
Wheelchair
Wig advised by doctor as essential to mental health of person who lost all hair from disease

Medical Treatments

Abortion
Acupuncture
Blood transfusion
Childbirth delivery
Diathermy
Electric shock treatments
Hearing services
Hydrotherapy (water treatments)
Injections
Insulin treatments
Navajo healing ceremonies ("sings")
Nursing
Organ transplant
Prenatal and postnatal treatments
Psychotherapy
Sterilization
Radial keratotomy
Radium therapy
Ultraviolet ray treatments

Vasectomy
Whirlpool baths
X-ray treatments

Medicines and Drugs

Cost of prescriptions only; over-the-counter medicine is not deductible.

Laboratory Examinations and Tests

Blood tests
Cardiographs
Metabolism tests
Spinal fluid tests
Sputum tests
Stool examinations
Urine analyses
X-ray examinations

Hospital Services

Anesthetist
Hospital bills
Oxygen mask, tent
Use of operating room
Vaccines
X-ray technician

Premiums for Medical Care Policies

See 17.5 for how to deduct:
Blue Cross and Blue Shield
Contact lens replacement insurance
Federal Voluntary Medicare (Part B) and Federal Medicare (Part A) by persons not covered by Social Security
Health insurance covering hospital, surgical, and other medical expenses
Membership in medical service cooperative

Miscellaneous

Alcoholic inpatient care costs
Asylum; *see 17.11.*
Birth control pills or other birth control items prescribed by your doctor
Braille books—excess cost of Braille works over cost of regular editions
Childbirth classes for expectant mother
Clarinet lessons advised by dentist for treatment of tooth defects
Convalescent home—for medical treatment only; *see 17.11.*
Drug treatment center—inpatient care costs
Fees paid to health institute where the exercises, rubdowns, etc., taken there are prescribed by a physician as treatments necessary to alleviate a physical or mental defect or illness
Kidney donor's or possible kidney donor's expenses
Lead-based paint removal to prevent a child who has had lead poisoning from eating the paint. The cost of repainting the scraped area is not deductible.
Legal fees for guardianship of mentally ill spouse where commitment was necessary for medical treatment
Lifetime care—advance payments made either monthly or as a lump sum under an agreement with a retirement home; *see 17.11.*
Long-term care costs for chronically ill; *see 17.15.*
Nurse's board and wages, including Social Security taxes paid on wages
Remedial reading for child suffering from dyslexia
Sanitarium and similar institutions; *see 17.11.*
School—payments to a special school for a mentally or physically impaired person if the main reason for using the school is its resources for relieving the disability; *see 17.10.*
"Seeing-eye" dog and its maintenance
Smoking cessation programs
Special school costs for physically and mentally handicapped children; *see 17.10.*
Telephone-teletype costs and television adapter for closed caption service for deaf person
Travel transportation for and essential to medical care; *see 17.9.*
Wages of guide for a blind person

Nondeductible Medical Expenses

Antiseptic diaper service

Athletic club expenses

Babysitting fees to enable you to make doctor's visits

Boarding school fees paid for healthy child while parent is recuperating from illness

Bottled water bought to avoid drinking fluoridated city water

Cost of divorce recommended by a psychiatrist

Cost of hotel room suggested for sex therapy

Cost of moving away from airport noise by person suffering a nervous breakdown

Cost of trips prescribed by a doctor for a "change of environment" to boost an ailing person's morale

Dance lessons advised by a doctor as general physical and mental therapy

Divorced spouse's medical bills

Domestic help; but see 17.12 if nursing duties are performed

Ear piercing

Funeral, cremation, burial, cemetery plot, monument, or mausoleum

Health programs offered by resort hotels, health clubs, and gyms

Illegal operations and drugs

Marijuana, even if prescribed by a physician in a state permitting the prescription

Marriage counseling fees

Massages recommended by physician for general stress

reduction

Maternity clothes

Premiums on policies guaranteeing you a specified amount of money each week in the event hospitalization

Scientology fees

Special food or beverage substitutes; but see 17.2

Tattooing

Toothpaste

Transportation costs of a disabled person to and from work

Travel costs to favorable climate when you can live there permanently

Travel costs to look for a new place to live—on a doctor's advice

Tuition and travel expenses to

send a problem child to a particular school for a beneficial change in environment; see 17.10

Weight-loss program to improve general health

How Your Medical Expense Deduction Is Reduced by the 7.5% Floor

Your medical expenses are

If your adjusted gross income is	$1,000	$1,500	$2,000	$2,500	$3,000	$3,500	$4,000	$4,500	$5,000	$5,500	$6,000	$6,500	$7,000	$7,500
						You may deduct								
$ 15,000	0	375	875	1,375	1,875	2,375	2,875	3,375	3,875	4,375	4,875	5,375	5,875	6,375
$ 20,000	0	0	500	1,000	1,500	2,000	2,500	3,000	3,500	4,000	4,500	5,000	5,500	6,000
$ 25,000	0	0	125	625	1,125	1,625	2,125	2,625	3,125	3,625	4,125	4,625	5,125	5,625
$ 30,000	0	0	0	250	750	1,250	1,750	2,250	2,750	3,250	3,750	4,250	4,750	5,250
$ 35,000	0	0	0	0	375	875	1,375	1,875	2,375	2,875	3,375	3,875	4,375	4,875
$ 40,000	0	0	0	0	0	500	1,000	1,500	2,000	2,500	3,000	3,500	4,000	4,500
$ 45,000	0	0	0	0	0	125	625	1,125	1,625	2,125	2,625	3,125	3,625	4,125
$ 50,000	0	0	0	0	0	0	250	750	1,250	1,750	2,250	2,750	3,250	3,750
$ 55,000	0	0	0	0	0	0	0	375	875	1,375	1,875	2,375	2,875	3,375
$ 60,000	0	0	0	0	0	0	0	0	500	1,000	1,500	2,000	2,500	3,000
$ 65,000	0	0	0	0	0	0	0	0	125	625	1,125	1,625	2,125	2,625
$ 70,000	0	0	0	0	0	0	0	0	0	250	750	1,250	1,750	2,250
$ 75,000	0	0	0	0	0	0	0	0	0	0	375	875	1,375	1,875
$ 80,000	0	0	0	0	0	0	0	0	0	0	0	500	1,000	1,500
$ 85,000	0	0	0	0	0	0	0	0	0	0	0	125	625	1,125
$ 90,000	0	0	0	0	0	0	0	0	0	0	0	0	250	750
$ 95,000	0	0	0	0	0	0	0	0	0	0	0	0	0	375
$ 100,000	0	0	0	0	0	0	0	0	0	0	0	0	0	0

Personal injury settlements or awards. Generally, a cash settlement recovered in a personal injury suit does not reduce your medical expense deduction. The settlement is not treated as reimbursement of your medical bills. But when part of the settlement is specifically earmarked by a court or by law for payment of hospital bills, the medical expense deduction is reduced.

If you receive a settlement for a personal injury that is partly allocable to future medical expenses, you reduce medical expenses for these injuries by the allocated amount until it is used up.

Fake claims. Medical reimbursements for fake injury claims are treated as taxable income; *see* the following Example.

EXAMPLE

Dodge, with the aid of a "friendly" doctor, arranged to be hospitalized for alleged back injuries and realized over $200,000 from HIP policies. The IRS charged that the insurance proceeds were taxable income. Dodge argued they were tax-free reimbursements of medical costs.

The Tax Court sided with the IRS. The tax-free rules cover the payment of legitimate medical costs. Here there were no legitimate medical costs of actual injuries. Dodge took out the policies in a scam arrangement with the doctor.

Reimbursements in excess of your medical expenses. If you paid the entire premium of the policy, the excess payment is not taxed. If you and your employer each contributed to the policy, you generally have to include in income that part of the excess reimbursement that is attributable to employer premium contributions not included in your gross income.

However, you do not have to report any excess reimbursements that are tax-free payments for permanent disfigurement or loss of bodily functions, as discussed in 3.2.

If your employer paid the total cost of the policy and the contributions were not taxed to you, you report as income all of your excess reimbursement, unless it covers payment for permanent injury or disfigurement.

For the treatment of insurance reimbursements of long-term care costs, *see 17.15.*

EXAMPLES

1. Henry Knight pays premiums of $240 and $120 for two personal health insurance policies. His total medical expenses are $900. He receives $700 from one insurance company and $500 from the other. The excess reimbursement of $300 ($1,200 – $900) is not taxable because he paid the entire premium on the policy.

2. Lionel Guest's employer paid premiums of $1,800 for two employee health insurance policies covering medical expenses. Guest's medical expenses in one year are $900. He receives $1,200 from the two companies. The entire $300 excess is taxable because Guest's employer paid the total cost of the policy and the contributions were not taxed to him.

3. Kay Brown's employer paid a premium of $1,000 for a group health policy covering Brown, and Brown herself paid $300 for a personal health policy. Her medical expenses are $900. She receives reimbursements of $1,200, $700 under her employer's policy and $500 under her own policy. Brown's reimbursements exceed expenses by $300, but the taxable portion attributed to her employer's premium contribution is $175, computed this way:

Reimbursement allocated to Brown's policy ($500 ÷ $1,200) × $900	$375
Reimbursement allocated to employer's policy ($700 ÷ $1,200) × $900	$525
Taxable excess allocated to employer's policy ($700 – $525)	$175

4. Mike Green's employer paid $1,200 for a health insurance policy but contributed only $450 and deducted $750 from Green's wages. Green also paid $300 for a personal health insurance policy. His medical expenses are $900. He recovered $700 from the employer's policy and $500 from his personal policy. The excess attributable to the employer's policy is $175 (computed as in Example 3 above). However, the taxable portion is only $65.63. Both Green and his employer contributed to the cost of the employer's policy and a further allocation is necessary:

Green's contribution	$750
Employer's contribution	450
Total cost of policy	$1,200
Ratio of employer's contribution to annual cost of policy (450 ÷ 1,200, or 37.50%)	
Taxable portion: 37.50% of excess reimbursement of $175	$65.63

Reimbursement in a later year may be taxed. If you took a medical expense deduction in one year and are reimbursed for all or part of the expense in a later year, the reimbursement may be taxed in the year received. The reimbursement is generally taxable income to the extent the deduction reduced your tax in the prior year. For further details for figuring taxable income on a recovery of a prior deduction, *see 11.6*.

EXAMPLES

1. In 1998, Anna Gurchani had adjusted gross income of $12,000. She claimed itemized deductions that exceeded her allowable standard deduction by $1,000; on her Schedule A, Gurchani listed medical expenses of $1,300. She deducted $400, computed as follows:

Medical expenses	$1,300
Less: 7.5% of $12,000	900
Allowable deduction	$400

   In 1999 she collects $300 from insurance, reimbursing part of her 1998 medical expenses. If she had collected that amount in 1998, her medical expense deduction would have been $100. The entire reimbursement of $300 is subject to tax in 1999. It is the amount by which the 1998 deduction of $400 exceeds the deduction of $100 that would have been allowed if the reimbursement had been received in 1998.
2. Same facts as in Example 1 above, but Anna did not deduct medical expenses in 1998 because she did not itemize deductions. The reimbursement in 1999 is not taxable.

17.5 Premiums of Medical Care Policies

You may deduct as medical expenses premiums paid for medical care policies covering yourself, your spouse (17.6), or dependents (17.7). There is no separate deduction for health insurance premiums. All qualifying premiums are treated as medical expenses subject to the overall 7.5% limit. Included as deductible medical expenses are premiums you paid for health insurance that covers hospital, surgical, drug costs, and other medical expenses. Also deductible are premiums paid for contact lens replacement insurance and premiums on policies providing solely for indemnity for hospital and surgical expenses. Include premiums for Medicare Part B supplemental insurance. Payment for coverage under Medicare (Part A) is deductible by those over age 65 who are not covered by Social Security. Deductions may be claimed for membership payments in associations furnishing cooperative or free-choice medical services, group hospitalization, or clinical care policies, including HMOs (health maintenance organizations) and medical care premiums paid to colleges as part of a tuition bill, if the amount is separately stated in the bill.

Premiums paid before you reach age 65 for medical care insurance for protection after you reach age 65 are deductible in the year paid if they are payable on a level payment basis under the contract (1) for a period of 10 years or more or (2) until the year you reach age 65 (but in no case for a period of less than five years).

Premiums for qualifying long-term care policies are deductible subject to the limits explained in *17.15*.

Nondeductible premiums. You may *not* deduct premiums for a policy guaranteeing you a specified amount each week (not to exceed a specified number of weeks) in the event you are hospitalized. Also, no deduction may be claimed for premiums paid for a policy that compensates you for loss of earnings while ill or injured, or for loss of life, limb, or sight. If your policy covers both medical care and loss of income or loss of life, limb, or sight, no part of the premium is deductible unless (1) the contract or separate statement from the insurance company states what part of the premium is allocated to medical care and (2) the premium allocated to medical care is reasonable.

You may not deduct part of the car insurance premiums for medical insurance coverage for persons injured by or in your car where the premium covering you, your spouse (17.6), or your dependents (17.7) is not stated separately from the premium covering medical care for others.

Law Alert

Self-Employed Deduction

A 60% deduction for health insurance premiums you paid as a self-employed person in 1999 is generally allowed directly from gross income on Line 28 of Form 1040; *see 12.2.* Premiums not deductible under the 60% limitation are included with other premiums for itemized deduction purposes. However, self-employed persons can get a 100% deduction for their own coverage by covering a spouse who is a bona fide employee of the business *(see 3.2).*

The 60% deduction for self-employed taxpayers' medical insurance premiums is scheduled to increase to 70% in 2002 and 100% in 2003 and thereafter. Congress is considering making a 100% deduction available in 2000 and thereafter.

Filing Tip

Should Spouses File Separately?

If you are married and both you and your spouse have separate incomes, and one of you has substantial medical expenses, consider filing separate returns. This way the 7.5% floor will apply separately to your individual incomes, not to the higher joint income. To make sure which option to take—filing jointly or separately—you compute your tax on both types of returns and choose the one giving the lower overall tax; *see 1.2.*

Self-employed deduction of 60%. If you were self-employed in 1999, you may claim a special deduction on Form 1040, Line 28, for 60% of health insurance premiums paid in 1999 for yourself, your spouse, and your dependents. The deduction is also allowed if you received wages from an S corporation in which you were more than a 2% shareholder, you were a general partner, or were a limited partner who received guaranteed payments.

The 60% deduction may not be claimed for any month during 1999 that you were eligible for coverage under an employer's subsidized health plan, including a plan of your spouse's employer. Also, the deduction may not exceed your net earnings from the business under which the health premiums are paid. *See 12.2* for further details on the 60% deduction.

Any balance of premiums not deductible under the 60% rule may be claimed as an itemized medical expense subject to the 7.5% income floor *(17.1).*

17.6 Expenses of Your Spouse

You may deduct as medical expenses your payments of medical bills for your spouse if you were married either at the time the expenses were incurred or at the time the bills were paid. That is, you may deduct your payment of your spouse's medical bills even though you are divorced or widowed, if, at the time the expenses were incurred, you were married. Furthermore, if your spouse incurred medical expenses before you married and you pay the bills after you marry, you may deduct the expense.

EXAMPLES
1. Your spouse has doctor bills covering an operation performed in 1998, before you were married. You married in 1999. You pay those bills in 1999. You may claim a 1999 medical expense deduction for your payment.
2. In October 1998, your spouse had dental work done. In February 1999, you are divorced; in April 1999, you pay your former spouse's dental bills. You may deduct the payment on your 1999 tax return.
3. In 1999, you pay medical expenses for your spouse who died in 1998. You remarry in 1999. On a 1999 joint return filed with your new spouse, you may deduct your payment of your deceased spouse's medical expenses.

Filing separately in community property states. If you and your spouse file separately and live in a community property state, any medical expenses paid out of community funds are treated as paid 50% by each of you. Medical expenses paid out of separate funds of one spouse can be deducted only by that spouse.

17.7 Expenses of Your Dependents

You may deduct your payment of medical bills for your children or other dependents, subject to the 7.5% floor at *17.1.* You may deduct the expenses of a person who was your dependent either at the time the medical services were provided or at the time you paid the expenses. In determining dependent status for medical expense purposes, you may disregard two of the regular tests listed at *21.1* for claiming an exemption for a dependent. You may deduct the medical costs of a person who qualifies as your dependent under the relationship test, the support test, and the citizen or resident test. The gross income test and the joint return test do not have to be met. *See* Examples 1–3 below.

A child may not deduct medical expenses paid with his or her parent's welfare payments; *see* Example 4 on the next page.

EXAMPLES
1. You contribute more than half of your married son's support, including a payment of a medical expense of $800. Because he filed a joint return with his wife, you may not claim him as a dependent *(21.13).* But you still may include your payment of the $800 medical expense with your other qualifying medical expenses since you contributed more than half of his support.
2. Your mother, a U.S. citizen, underwent an operation in November 1998. You paid for the operation in February 1999. You may deduct the cost of the operation in 1999 if you furnished more than one-half of your mother's support in either 1998 or 1999.

3. Same facts as Example 2, except your mother is a citizen and resident of Italy. You may not deduct the cost of the operation. She is not a U.S. citizen or a resident of the United States, Canada, or Mexico and thus does not qualify as a dependent for exemption purposes *(21.12)* or for medical deduction purposes.
4. A son is the legal guardian of his mother who is mentally incompetent. As guardian, he received his mother's state welfare and Social Security benefits, which he deposited in his personal bank account and used to pay part of his mother's medical expenses. On his tax return, he claimed a deduction for the total medical expenses paid on behalf of his mother. The court held that he could deduct only medical expenses in excess of the amounts received as welfare and Social Security payments. The benefits, to the extent used to pay medical expenses, represented the mother's payments in her own behalf.

Divorced and separated parents. You may be able to deduct your payment of your child's medical costs, even though your ex-spouse is entitled to claim the child as a dependent. For purposes of the medical deduction, the child is considered to be the dependent of *both* parents if (1) they are divorced or legally separated under a court agreement, separated under a written agreement, or married but living apart during the last six months of 1999; (2) the child was in the custody of one or both parents for more than half of 1999; and (3) more than half of the child's 1999 support was provided by both parents.

Adopted children. You may deduct medical expenses of an adopted child if you may claim the child as a dependent either when the medical services are rendered or when you pay the expenses. An adopted child may be claimed as a dependent when a court has approved the adoption. In the absence of a court decree, the child is your dependent if he or she was placed in your home by an authorized agency and was a member of your household the rest of the year; *see 21.3*. If he or she has not been placed in your custody by an authorized agency, you have to show that the child lived in your home for the entire year.

If you reimburse an adoption agency for medical expenses it paid under an agreement with you, you are considered to have paid the expenses. But reimbursement of expenses incurred and paid before adoption negotiations does not qualify them as your medical expenses and you may not deduct them.

You may not deduct medical expenses for services rendered to the natural mother of the child you adopt.

Multiple support agreements. If you may claim a person as your dependent under a multiple support agreement *(21.10)*, your unreimbursed payments of that person's medical expenses are deductible. Even if you may not claim the dependent exception for 1999 because the person has a gross income of $2,750 or more, you may still deduct your payment of medical expenses provided the other multiple support agreement tests are met.

 Filing Instruction

Multiple Support Agreement
If you may claim a person as your dependent under a multiple support agreement, include with your medical expenses only the amount you actually pay for the dependent's medical expenses. If you are reimbursed by others who signed the multiple support agreement, you must reduce your deduction by the amount of reimbursement.

EXAMPLE

Ingrid Fromm and her brother and sister share equally in the support of their mother. Part of their mother's support includes medical expenses. Should the three of them share in the payment of the bills or should only one of them pay the bills? The answer: Payment should be made by the person who may claim the mother as a dependent under a multiple support agreement. Only that person may deduct the payment. If Ingrid is going to claim her as an exemption, she should pay the bill. She may deduct the payment although she did not contribute more than half of her mother's support. If her brother and sister reimburse her for part of the bill, she must reduce her medical deduction by the amount of the reimbursement. Neither Ingrid's brother nor her sister may deduct this share. Thus, a deduction is lost for these amounts.

17.8 Decedent's Medical Expenses

If you pay the medical expenses of your deceased spouse or dependent *(17.7)*, you may claim the payment as a medical expense in the year you pay the expenses, whether that is before or after the person's death.

If the executor or administrator of the estate pays the decedent's medical expenses within one year after the date of death, an election may be made to treat the expenses as if the deceased had paid them in the year the medical services were provided. The executor or administrator may file an amended return for the year the services were provided and claim them as a medical deduction for that year, assuming the period for filing the amended return *(49.1)* has not passed.

If the election is made by the executor to claim the expenses as an income tax deduction, they may not be claimed as a deduction on the estate tax return. The executor must file a statement with the decedent's income tax return that the expenses have not been deducted on the estate tax return and the estate waives its right to deduct them for estate tax purposes.

If medical expenses are claimed as an income tax deduction, the portion of the expenses that are below the 7.5% floor, and, therefore, not deductible, may not be deducted on the estate tax return. Although the expenses were not actually deducted, the IRS considers them to be part of the overall income tax deduction.

EXAMPLE

Oscar Reyes incurred medical expenses of $500 in 1998 and $300 in 1999. He died June 1, 1999, without having paid these expenses. He had already filed his 1998 return before the due date. In August 1999, his executor pays the $800 in medical expenses. The executor may file an amended return for 1998, claim a medical expense deduction for the $500, and get a refund for the increased deductions. The executor may claim the remaining $300 as a medical expense deduction on Reyes's final return for 1999.

17.9 Travel Costs May Be Medical Deductions

You may deduct the cost of travel to a place where you receive medical treatment or which is prescribed as a place that will help relieve a specific chronic ailment. Trips to and from a doctor's office are the most common type of deductible travel expense.

The amount of the deduction is limited to the cost of transportation, such as the cost of operating a car or fares for public transportation. If you use your automobile, you may deduct a flat rate of 10¢ a mile and, in addition, you may deduct parking fees and tolls. If, however, auto expenses exceed this standard mileage rate, you may deduct your actual out-of-pocket costs for gas, oil, repairs, tolls, and parking fees. Do not include depreciation, general maintenance, or car insurance.

 Filing Tip

Deductible Travel Costs

The cost of trips to and from a place where you receive medical treatment is deductible. This includes trips to and from a doctor's office.

EXAMPLE

You drive your car to a doctor's office for treatment. You made 40 such round trips of 25 miles each. As the total mileage is 1,000, you claim $100 (1,000 × 10¢) as medical expenses. If you incurred tolls or parking fees during the trips, add these expenses to the mileage costs.

Lodging expenses. Your lodging expenses while away from home are not deductible as medical expenses unless the trip is primarily to receive treatment from a doctor in a licensed hospital, hospital-related outpatient facility, or a facility equivalent to a hospital. Food expenses are not deductible.

EXAMPLE

Polyak spent the winter in Florida on the advice of her doctor to alleviate a chronic heart and lung condition. While in Florida, she stayed in a rented trailer that cost $1,426. She saw a physician for treatment of an infection and to renew medications. She deducted the trailer costs as a medical deduction, which the IRS and Tax Court disallowed. Although her Florida trip was primarily for mitigating her condition, she did not travel to receive medical care from a physician in a licensed hospital or related outpatient facility. The medical care was routine and incidental to her travel to Florida. Her deduction for transportation costs to Florida was not contested by the IRS, which conceded that the trip was primarily for and essential to her health.

The deduction for lodging while receiving treatment at a licensed hospital, outpatient clinic, or hospital-equivalent facility is limited to $50 per night per person. For example, the limit is $100 if a parent travels with a sick child. The IRS ruled that the $50 allowance could be claimed by a parent for a six-week hotel stay while her eight-year-old daughter was treated in a nearby hospital for serious injuries received in an automobile accident. The mother's presence was necessary so that she could sign release forms.

Deductible Transportation Costs

Examples of travel costs that have been allowed as medical deductions by rulings or court decisions are:

- Nurse's fare if nurse is required on trip
- Parent's fare if parent is needed to accompany child who requires medical care
- Parent's fare to visit his child at an institution where the visits are prescribed by a doctor
- Trip to visit specialist in another city
- Airplane fare to a distant city in which a patient used to live to have a checkup by a family doctor living there. That he could have received the same examination in the city in which he presently lived did not bar his deduction.
- Trip to escape a climate that is bad for a specific condition. For example, the cost of a trip from a northern state to Florida during the winter on the advice of a doctor to relieve a chronic heart condition is deductible. The cost of a trip made solely to improve post-operative condition by a person recovering from a throat operation was ruled deductible.
- Travel to an Alcoholics Anonymous club meeting if membership in the group has been advised by a doctor
- Disabled veteran's commuting expenses where a doctor prescribed work and driving as therapy
- Wife's trip to provide nursing care for an ailing husband in a distant city. The trip was ordered by her husband's doctor as a necessity.
- Driving prescribed as therapy
- Travel costs of kidney transplant donor or prospective donor

Nondeductible Transportation Costs

- Trip for the general improvement of your health
- Traveling to areas of favorable climates during the year for general health reasons, rather than living permanently in a locality suitable for your health
- Meals while on a trip for medical treatment—even if cost of transportation is a valid medical cost. However, a court has allowed the deduction of the extra cost of specially prepared food.
- Trip to get "spiritual" rather than medical aid. For example, cost of a trip to the Shrine of Our Lady of Lourdes is not deductible.
- Moving a family to a climate more suitable to an ill mother's condition. Only the mother's travel costs are deductible.
- Moving household furnishings to area advised by physician
- Operating an auto or special vehicle to go to work because of a disability. The cost of wheelchair, autoette, or special auto devices for handicapped persons is deductible.
- Convalescence cruise advised by a doctor for a patient recovering from pneumonia
- Loss on sale of car bought for medical travel
- Medical seminar cruise taken by patient whose condition was reviewed by physicians taking the cruise

17.10 Schooling for the Mentally or Physically Handicapped

You may deduct as medical expenses the costs of sending a mentally or physically handicapped person to a special school or institution to overcome or alleviate his or her handicap. Such costs may cover:

- Teaching of Braille or lip reading
- Training, caring for, supervising, and treating a mentally retarded person
- Cost of meals and lodgings, if boarding is required at the school
- Costs of regular education courses also taught at the school, provided they are incidental to the special courses and services furnished by the school

The fact that a particular school or camp is recommended for an emotionally disturbed child by a psychiatrist will not qualify the tuition as a deduction if the school or camp has no special program geared to the child's specific personal problem. However, you may deduct the costs of maintaining a mentally retarded person in a home specially selected to meet the standards set by a psychiatrist to aid in an adjustment from life in a mental hospital to community living.

 Caution

Meal Costs of Medical Trip

While transportation to receive medical care is a deductible medical expense subject to the 7.5% AGI floor, meals while on a trip for medical treatment are not deductible. They simply replace the meals you normally would eat.

Caution

Counseling at a Private School

The parent of a child with psychological problems may deduct only that part of a private school fee directly related to psychological aid given to the child.

Payment for future medical care expenses is deductible if immediate payment is required by contract.

EXAMPLES

1. An emotionally disturbed child was sent to a private school maintaining a staff of three psychologists. His father deducted the school fee of $6,270 as a medical expense. The IRS disallowed the amount, claiming that the child, who was neither mentally retarded nor handicapped, was sent to school primarily for an education. The Tax Court allowed the father to deduct $3,000 covering the psychological treatment.

2. A retarded boy had been excluded from several schools for the mentally handicapped because he needed close attention. The director of a military academy had extensive experience in training young boys. Although it was not the usual practice of the academy to enroll mentally handicapped children, the director accepted the boy on a day-to-day basis as a personal challenge. The Tax Court held that the cost of both tuition and transportation to bring the boy to and from the school were deductible medical expenses. The primary purpose of the training given the boy was not ordinary education but remedial training designed to overcome his handicap. But note that, in other cases, a deduction for tuition of a military school to which a child was sent in order to remove him from a tense family environment, and the cost of a blind boy's attendance at a regular private school that made a special effort to accommodate his Braille equipment, were disallowed.

17.11 Senior Citizen Care Facilities

A payment for meals and lodging to a nursing home, convalescent home, home for the aged, or sanitarium is a deductible medical expense if the patient is confined for medical treatment.

If you cannot prove that the patient entered the home for medical care (which would permit a deduction for meals and lodging in addition to medical costs), you may nevertheless deduct that part of the cost covering actual medical and nursing care.

In an unusual case, a court allowed a medical expense deduction for apartment rent of an aged parent.

EXAMPLE

A doctor recommended to Ungar that his 90-year-old mother, convalescing from a brain hemorrhage, could receive better care at less expense in accommodations away from a hospital. A two-room apartment was rented, hospital equipment installed, and nurses engaged for seven months. The rent totaled $1,400. Ungar's sister, who worked in her husband's shoe store, nursed her mother for six weeks. Ungar paid the wages of a clerk who was hired to substitute for his sister in the store. Ungar deducted both the rent and wages as medical expenses. The IRS disallowed them; a Tax Court reversed the IRS's decision. The apartment rent was no less a medical expense than the cost of a hospital room. As for the clerk's wages, they too were deductible medical costs. The clerk was hired specifically to allow the daughter to nurse her mother, thereby avoiding the larger, though more direct, medical expense of hiring a nurse.

Establishing medical purpose. The following facts are helpful in establishing the full deductibility of payments to a nursing home, convalescent home, home for the aged, or sanitarium:

* The patient entered the institution on the direction or suggestion of a doctor.
* Attendance or treatment at the institution had a direct therapeutic effect on the condition suffered by the patient.
* The attendance at the institution was for a specific ailment rather than for a "general" health condition. Simply showing that the patient suffers from an ailment is not sufficient proof that he or she is in the home for treatment.

Payment for future lifetime care. Generally, no deduction is allowed for prepayment of medical expenses for services to be performed in a later taxable year. However, in the Examples below, the IRS allowed a deduction where there was a current obligation to pay.

Filing Tip

Meal Costs at a Nursing Home

If the patient entered a nursing home to receive medical care, a deduction may be taken for meals and lodging while there, in addition to medical care costs.

EXAMPLES

1. A 78-year-old man entered into an agreement with a retirement home. For a lump-sum payment, the home agreed to provide lifetime care, including medical care, medicine, and hospitalization. The lifetime care fee was calculated without regard to fees received from other patients and was not insurance. The home allocated 30% of the lump-sum payment to medical expenses based on its prior experience. The IRS holds that this part of the payment is deductible in the year paid. It holds that the legal obligation to pay the medical expenses was incurred at the time the lump-sum payment was made, even though medical services would not be performed until a future time, if at all. Should any portion of the lump-sum payment be refunded, that part attributable to the deducted amount must be reported as income; *see 12.8.*

2. Parents contracted with an institution to care for their handicapped child after their death. The contract provided for payments as follows: 20% on signing, 10% within 12 months, 10% within 24 months, and the balance when the child enters. Payment of specified amounts at specified intervals was a condition imposed by the institution for its agreement to accept the child for lifetime care. Since the obligation to pay was incurred at the time payments were made, they are deductible as medical expenses, although the medical services were not to be performed until a future time, if at all.

3. A couple entered a retirement home that would provide them with accommodations, meals, and medical care for life. They paid a founder's fee of $40,000 and a monthly fee of $800. If they leave the home, they may get a refund of a portion of the founder's fee. Fifteen percent of the monthly fee and 10% of the founder's fee will be used for medical care and 5% of the founder's fee will be used for construction of a health facility. On the basis of these figures, the couple may deduct as medical costs 10% of the founder's fee and 15% of the monthly fee. However, the portion of the founder's fee for the possible health facility does not qualify as a medical expense. Finally, any refund of the founder's fee received in a later year may be income to the extent medical deductions were previously claimed for the fees.

17.12   Nurses' Wages

The costs of a nurse attending an ill person are deductible. Costs include any Social Security or Medicare (FICA) tax paid by you. You may deduct the expenses of a nurse who is not registered or licensed so long as he or she provides you with medical services. Medical services include giving medications, changing dressings, and bathing and grooming the patient. If the nurse also performs domestic services, deduct only that part of the pay attributable to medical services for the patient.

The cost of an attendant's meals is included in your medical expenses. Divide total food costs among the household members to determine the attendant's share.

Costs eligible for tax credit. If, in order to work, you pay a nurse to look after a physically or mentally disabled dependent, you may be able to claim a credit for all or part of the nurse's wages as a dependent care expense. You may not, however, claim both a credit and a medical expense deduction. First, you claim the nurse's wages as a dependent care cost. If not all of the wages are allowed as care costs because of the expense limits (Chapter 25), the remaining balance is deductible as a medical expense.

The salary of a clerk hired specifically to relieve a wife from working in her husband's store in order to care for her ill mother was allowed as a medical expense; *see* the Ungar Example in *17.11.*

EXAMPLES

1. Dodge's wife was arthritic. He was advised by her doctor to have someone take care of her to prevent her from falling. He moved her to his daughter's home and paid the daughter to care for her mother. He deducted the payments to his daughter. The IRS disallowed the deduction, claiming that the daughter was not a trained nurse. The Tax Court allowed that part of the deduction specifically attributed to nursing aid. Whether a medical service has been rendered depends on the nature of the services rendered, not on the qualifications or title of the person who renders them. Here, the daughter's services, following the doctor's advice, qualify as medical care.

2. An attendant hired by a quadriplegic performs household duties, in addition to caring for his medical and personal needs. The quadriplegic pays him wages and also provides food and lodging. According to the IRS, a medical expense deduction is allowable only for that portion of the wages attributable to medical and personal care. The wages

Caution

Nurse's Services

The cost of a nurse's services is a deductible medical expense, even if the nurse is not licensed or registered, so long as he or she provides the patient with medical services. If household services are also provided, only the portion of the nurse's pay attributable to the provision of medical services qualifies.

are apportioned on the basis of time spent performing nursing-type services and time spent performing household duties. The same allocation is used to determine the portion of the cost of the attendant's meals that are deductible as a medical expense. However, the attendant's lodging is not deductible as a medical expense, unless the quadriplegic shows additional expenditures directly attributable to lodging the attendant, such as paying increased rent for an apartment with another bedroom for the attendant.

17.13 Home Improvements as Medical Expenses

A disease or ailment may require the construction of special equipment or facilities in a home: A heart patient may need an elevator to carry him or her upstairs; a polio patient, a pool; and an asthmatic patient, an air cleaning system.

You may deduct the full cost of minor equipment installed for a medical reason if it does not increase the value of your property, as, for example, the cost of a detachable window air conditioner. Where equipment increases the value of your property, you may generally take a medical deduction only to the extent that the cost of the equipment exceeds the increase in the value of the property. This increased-value test does not apply to certain structural changes to a residence made by a handicapped person, as discussed at the end of this section. If the equipment does not increase the value of the property, its entire cost is deductible, even though it is permanently fixed to the property.

EXAMPLE

Mike Gerard's daughter suffered from cystic fibrosis. While there is no known cure for the disease, doctors attempt to prolong life by preventing pulmonary infection. One approach is to maintain a constant temperature and high humidity. A doctor recommended that Gerard install a central air-conditioning unit in his home for his daughter. It cost $1,300 and increased the value of his home by $800. The $500 balance was a deductible medical expense.

Deducting cost of swimming pool. If swimming is prescribed as physical therapy, the cost of constructing a home swimming pool may be partly deductible as a medical expense but only to the extent the cost exceeds the increase in value to the house. However, the IRS is likely to question any deduction because of the possibility that the pool may be used for recreation. If you can show that the pool is specially equipped to alleviate your condition and is not generally suited for recreation, the IRS will allow the deduction unless the expense is considered to be "lavish or extravagant." For example, the IRS allowed a deduction for a pool constructed by an osteoarthritis patient. His physician prescribed swimming several times a day as treatment. He built an indoor lap pool with specially designed stairs and a hydrotherapy device. Given these features, the IRS concluded that the pool was specially designed to provide medical treatment.

In one case the IRS tried to limit the cost of a luxury indoor pool built for therapeutic reasons to the least expensive construction. The Tax Court rejected the IRS position, holding that a medical expense is not to be limited to the cheapest form of treatment; on appeal, the IRS position was adopted.

If, instead of building a pool, you buy a home with a pool, can you deduct the part of the purchase price allocated to the pool? The Tax Court said no. The purchase price of the house includes the fair market value of the pool. Therefore, there is no extra cost above the increase in the home's value that would support a medical expense deduction.

The operating costs of an indoor pool were allowed by the Tax Court as a deduction to an emphysema sufferer.

A deduction is barred where the primary purpose of the improvement is for personal convenience rather than medical necessity.

EXAMPLES

1. Ken Cherry was advised by his doctor to swim to relieve his severe emphysema and bronchitis. He could not swim at local health spas; they did not open early enough or stay open late enough to allow him to swim before or after work. His home was too small for a pool. He bought a lot and built a new house with an indoor pool. He used the

Caution

Does Equipment Increase Value of Home?

When special equipment is installed in your home to alleviate a disease or ailment, you must determine if it increases the value of your home. You generally may claim a medical deduction only to the extent that the cost of the equipment exceeds the increase in value. However, if you install a ramp or railing, widen doorways or hallways, or add similar improvements to cope with a disability, these are usually treated by the IRS as not adding to the value of the home.

pool several times a day, and swimming improved his condition; if he did not swim, his symptoms returned. Cherry deducted pool operating costs of $4,000 for fuel, electricity, insurance, and repairs. The IRS disallowed the deductions, claiming that the pool was used for personal recreation. Besides, it did not have special medical equipment. The Tax Court allowed the deduction. Cherry built the pool to swim in order to exercise his lungs. That there was no special equipment is irrelevant; Cherry did not need special ramps, railings, a shallow floor, or whirlpool. Finally, his family rarely used the pool.

2. Doug Haines broke his leg in a skiing accident and underwent various forms of physical therapy, including swimming. To aid his recovery, his physician recommended that he install a swimming pool at his home. The Tax Court agreed with the IRS that the cost of the pool was not deductible. Although swimming was beneficial to his condition, he needed special therapy only for a limited period of time, and he could have gotten it at less cost at a nearby public pool. Finally, because of weather conditions, the pool could not be used for about half of the year.

Cost of maintaining and operating improvement. The expense of maintaining and operating equipment installed for medical reasons may be claimed as a medical expense, even if the cost of the equipment and its installation is not deductible under the rules in this section.

Handicapped persons. The increased-value test does not apply to a handicapped person who makes structural changes to a residence such as adding ramps, modifying doorways and stairways, installing railings and support bars, and altering cabinets, outlets, fixtures, and warning systems. Such improvements are treated for medical deduction purposes as not increasing the value of the house. Lifts, but not elevators, also are in this category. The full cost of such improvements is added to other deductible expenses and the total is deductible to the extent that it exceeds the 7.5% AGI floor.

17.14 Costs Deductible as Business Expenses

The following Examples illustrate cases in which expenses are deductible as business expenses rather than as medical expenses. Claiming a business deduction is preferable because the deduction is not subject to the 7.5% adjusted gross income floor.

The cost of a checkup required by your employer is a business expense and is not subject to the 7.5% AGI floor.

EXAMPLE

An airline pilot is required by his company to take a semi-annual physical exam at his own expense. If he fails to produce a resultant certificate of good health, he is subject to discharge. The cost of such checkups certifying physical fitness for a job is an ordinary and necessary business expense. If the doctor prescribes a treatment or further examinations to maintain the pilot's physical condition, the cost of these subsequent treatments or examinations may be deducted only as medical expenses, even though they are needed to maintain the physical standards required by the job. Thus, a professional singer who consults a throat specialist may not deduct the fee as a business expense. The fee is a medical expense subject to the 7.5% AGI floor.

 Filing Tip

Disability-Related Job Costs

If you are disabled and incur costs to enable you to work, the payments may be treated as a deductible business expense rather than as a medical expense.

The Tax Court allowed a licensed social worker working as a therapist to deduct psychoanalysis costs as an education expense.

Handicapped persons. Some expenses incurred by a physically handicapped person due to his or her handicap may be deductible as business expenses rather than as medical expenses. A business expense deduction may be allowed if the expense is necessary for you to satisfactorily perform your job and is not required or used, except incidentally, for personal purposes.

If you are self-employed, claim the deduction on Schedule C.

If you are an employee, the expenses are listed on Form 2106 and if not reimbursed, entered on Schedule A. The expenses are a fully deductible miscellaneous itemized deduction; the 2% AGI floor does *not* apply.

EXAMPLES

1. A professor is paralyzed from the waist down and confined to a wheelchair. When he attends out-of-town business meetings, he has his wife, a friend, or a colleague accompany him to help him with baggage, stairs, narrow doors, and to sit with him on airplanes when airlines will not allow wheelchair passengers without an attendant. While he does not pay them a salary, he does pay their travel costs. He may deduct these costs as business expenses. They are incurred solely because of his occupation.

2. An attorney uses prostheses due to bilateral amputation of his legs and takes medication several times a day for other ailments. On both personal and business trips, his wife or a neighbor accompanies him to help him travel and receive medication. He may deduct the out-of-town expenses paid for his neighbor only as a medical expense. The neighbor's services are not business expenses because assistance in personal activities is regularly provided. When his wife accompanies him, he may deduct her transportation costs as a medical expense; her food and lodging are nondeductible ordinary living expenses.

17.15 Long-Term Care Costs of Chronically ill

 Law Alert

Long-Term Care Insurance
Unreimbursed expenses for long-term care services to care for a chronically ill patient are deductible medical expenses subject to the 7.5% AGI floor. Depending on your age, all or part of premiums paid for a qualifying policy are includible in your medical expenses.

You may deduct as medical expenses (subject to the 7.5% adjusted gross income floor) your unreimbursed expenses for qualifying long-term care services that you require because you are "chronically ill" or because your spouse or dependent is chronically ill.

Qualifying long-term care services for a chronically ill individual. A chronically ill person is someone who has been certified by a licensed health-care practitioner within the preceding 12 months as being unable to perform for a period of at least 90 days at least two of the following activities without substantial assistance: eating, toileting, dressing, bathing, continence, or transferring. Also qualifying as chronically ill is someone who requires substantial supervision because of severe cognitive impairment, such as from Alzheimer's disease.

Qualifying long-term care services for a chronically ill individual are broadly defined as necessary diagnostic, preventive, therapeutic, curing, treating, mitigation, and rehabilitative services, and also maintenance or personal care services. The services must be provided under a plan of care prescribed by a licensed health-care practitioner, who may be a physician, a registered nurse, a licensed social worker, or other individual meeting Treasury requirements. Services provided by a spouse or relative are deductible only if that person is a licensed professional; services provided by a related corporation or partnership do not qualify.

Deductible premium costs of long-term care policies. Depending on your age, all or part of your premium payments for a qualified long-term care policy may be included as deductible medical expenses, subject to the 7.5% adjusted gross income floor. To qualify, the policy must provide for long-term care services for the chronically ill (*see* above). The amount of the deductible premium depends on your age at the end of the year. For 1999, the maximum deductible premium amounts are: $210 if you are age 40 or younger at the end of 1999; $400 for those age 41 through 50; $800 for those age 51 through 60; $2,120 for those age 61 through 70; and $2,660 for those over age 70. These limits may be increased after 1999 by an inflation factor.

If you are considering purchase of a long-term care insurance policy, make sure that it qualifies for the tax treatment explained in this section. A qualified contract must provide only for coverage of qualified long-term care services and be guaranteed renewable; it may not provide for a cash surrender value or money that can be assigned, pledged, or borrowed; it may not reimburse expenses covered by Medicare except where Medicare is a secondary payer or the contract makes *per diem* payments without regard to expenses.

Benefits paid by qualified long-term care policies. Benefits for an indemnity-type contract are tax free to the extent they pay or reimburse long-term care expenses. Benefits paid from a *per diem* type contract are tax free up to $190 a day in 1999. (The $190 limit may be adjusted in 2000 for inflation.) If *per diem* payments are received for the full year, the 1999 exclusion is $69,350. If *per diem* payments exceed $190, the excess over $190 is tax free to the extent of unreimbursed long-term care costs. Any balance of the excess is taxable.

In 1999, you receive per diem long-term care benefits of $225 under a qualifying long-term care policy. Your actual daily costs are above $225. No part of the benefit payments is taxable provided you have proof of actual costs.

17.16 Life Insurance Used To Pay Medical Costs of Terminally ill

A person who is terminally ill may be forced to cash in a life insurance policy to pay medical bills and other living expenses. Insurance companies have developed life insurance policies with accelerated death benefit clauses to help terminally ill patients meet the high cost of medical care. Where a policy lacks an accelerated payment clause, it is also possible to sell a life insurance policy to a viatical settlement company that specializes in buying policies from ill persons who require funds to pay expenses.

Accelerated death benefits and viatical settlement proceeds received by terminally ill individuals are *not taxed*.

Life insurance used by chronically ill. A chronically ill individual may sell a life insurance policy to a viatical settlement company to pay for long-term care costs. However, tax-free treatment is determined under the tax rules applied to long-term care policies in *17.15*. Thus, if the proceeds exceed the $190 *per diem* limit for 1999 and also exceed actual long-term care costs, the excess is taxable. Accelerated life insurance proceeds paid under a long-term care rider are also subject to the rules in *17.15*.

17.17 Medical Savings Accounts (MSAs)

Medical Savings Accounts (MSAs) are designed to lower the costs of providing medical expense reimbursement plans for employees of certain small businesses and self-employed persons. To do this, a medical plan combines a high-deductible health insurance policy to cover catastrophic costs and a tax-sheltered savings account that you use to pay routine medical expenses that fall below the policy deductible. More specifically, an MSA plan combines:

1. A high-deductible health insurance policy with premiums fixed by law. For single persons, the deductible in 1999 must be between $1,550 and $2,300. For family coverage, the deductible in 1999 must be between $3,050 and $4,600. Annual out-of-pocket costs excluding premiums must be limited to $3,050 for single coverage and $5,600 for family coverage. The deductible and out-of-pocket limits may be increased for 2000 by an inflation factor.
2. A medical savings account, or MSA, to which annual contributions may be made based on the amount of the deductible set by the health insurance policy. For single persons, the maximum contribution is 65% of the policy deductible charged for single person coverage. For family coverage, the maximum contribution is 75% of the policy deductible for family coverage. To contribute the maximum amount, you must have the policy for the entire year. If you obtained high-deductible health plan coverage during the year, one-twelfth of the limit may be contributed for each full month of coverage.

An MSA account is like an IRA. Income earned on MSA funds accumulates tax free. An MSA can be with an insurance company, bank, or other financial institution that has been approved by the IRS for this purpose. MSA contributions are reported to the IRS on Form 5498-MSA.

Contributions by self-employed. Here are the tax consequences of making an MSA contribution if you are self-employed:

1. You may deduct the health insurance premium element. For 1999, you may deduct 60% of the health insurance premium payments made in 1999 directly from gross income on Line 28 of Form 1040; *see 12.2* for restrictions. The balance of premiums not deductible on Line 28 may be treated as a medical expense deductible on Schedule A if your total medical expenses exceed 7.5% of your adjusted gross income.
2. You report your contribution to the MSA on Form 8853 and deduct the contribution directly from gross income on Line 25 of Form 1040. The contribution may not exceed the net self-employment income from the business through which you have the high-deductible health insurance.

Filing Instruction

Form 8853

If you received payments in 1999 from a qualified long-term care policy, you must figure the amount of taxable payments, if any, on Form 8853.

Planning Reminder

MSA Contribution Deadline

You have until April 17, 2000, to make a deductible MSA contribution for 1999.

Filing Instruction

Report MSA Contribution on Form 8853

Report your MSA contribution on Form 8853 and follow the instructions to figure any limitations on the amount you may deduct and for the rules on handling excess contributions. Form 8853 must be attached to your Form 1040.

Caution

Employer Contribution to Spouse's MSA

If you and your spouse are covered under a high-deductible health plan with family coverage, employer contributions to either of your MSAs bar both of you from making MSA contributions for that year. If you each have MSAs and are separately covered under an individual (self-only coverage) high-deductible health plan, employer contributions to one of your MSAs do not prevent the other from making MSA contributions.

EXAMPLE

Jones, who is self-employed, buys an MSA contract in 1999 that has a monthly charge of $515. Of this amount, $265 is for family health insurance coverage with a $4,000 deductible. The balance of $250 is deposited monthly in an MSA. The $250 monthly MSA contribution is $1/12$ of $3,000, the maximum annual MSA contribution based on 75% of the $4,000 deductible. Jones makes 10 monthly payments during the year. On Line 28 of Form 1040, Jones can deduct $1,590 (60% of $2,650 in premiums) and he can include the balance of the premiums as part of medical expenses subject to the 7.5% adjusted gross income floor on Schedule A.

He reports the $2,500 MSA contribution on Form 8853 and as long as his net earnings from self-employment are at least $2,500, he deducts the $2,500 contribution on Line 25 of Form 1040. Without counting any deduction of premiums on Schedule A, Jones is able to deduct $4,090 of the payments of $5,150 made in 1999.

Contributions by or for employees of qualifying small businesses. Small business employers having an average of 50 or fewer employees in either of the two prior calendar years may choose to offer MSA plans for their employees. The employer may fully finance the contracts or pay for the insurance element while allowing the employee to contribute to the MSA account. If the employer finances the full costs of the plan, the payments are not taxed under the rules at *3.1.* If the employer contributes anything to an employee's MSA, the employee is not allowed to make any MSA contribution for that year; *see 3.1.* If no employer contributions to the MSA are made and the employee contributes to the MSA, the employee reports the contribution on Form 8853 and may deduct the contribution up to the allowable limit from gross income on Line 25 of Form 1040. Any health insurance premiums paid by the employee are combined with other medical expenses paid during the year with the total being deductible only to the extent it exceeds 7.5% of adjusted gross income.

MSA distributions. You can take a distribution from your MSA to pay for medical expenses that are not reimbursable under your high-deductible plan. A distribution is tax free if it is used for qualifying medical expenses of you, your spouse, or your dependents. Generally, these are costs that could be claimed as an itemized deduction if you paid them directly. Premiums for long-term care insurance, for health coverage while you are receiving unemployment benefits, or for continuing coverage (COBRA) from a former employer qualify; other insurance premiums do not. Tax may be imposed on a distribution used to pay medical expenses of someone who was not covered by a high-deductible plan when the expenses were incurred; *see* Form 8853 for details.

MSA distributions are reported on Form 8853, which must be attached to Form 1040. A taxable distribution from Form 8853 is reported on Line 21 of Form 1040 as "other income." A taxable distribution is also subject to a 15% penalty unless you are age 65 or older, or disabled.

Casualty and Theft Losses and Involuntary Conversions

All casualty and theft losses are claimed on Form 4684. The tax treatment of an unreimbursed casualty or theft loss depends on the purpose for which you held the damaged, destroyed, or stolen property. A loss of property held for:

• *Personal purposes* is subject to the sudden events test *(18.5)* and the deduction is reduced by $100 and an additional 10% of your adjusted gross income *(18.11)* on Form 4684.

The itemized deduction claimed for personal-use property is not subject to the 3% reduction computation; *see 13.7.*

• *Income-producing purposes,* such as negotiable securities, should be claimed on Form 4684 and then entered on Line 27 of Schedule A. The loss deduction is not subject to the 2% AGI floor *(19.1)* or the 3% reduction *(13.7)* that applies to a loss deduction for income-producing property.

• *Business or rental purposes* is claimed on Form 4684 and then as a loss on Form 4797. It is not subject to any floor or the sudden event test. Follow the instructions to Form 4684.

If you have realized a gain, you may defer tax by replacing or repairing the property; *see 18.18.*

Appraisal fees and other incidental costs, such as taking photos to establish the amount of the loss, are claimed as a miscellaneous itemized deduction on Line 22 of Schedule A, Form 1040.

Deductible Casualty Losses

18.1 When To Deduct a Casualty or Theft Loss

Generally, you deduct a casualty loss in the year the casualty occurs, regardless of when you repair or replace damaged or destroyed property. If a casualty occurs in one year and you do not discover the damage until a later year, or you know damage has been inflicted, but you do not know the full extent of the loss because you expect reimbursement in a later year, here is what to do:

If you reasonably expect reimbursement in a later year. You should deduct in the year the casualty occurred only that part of your loss (after applying the personal property floors of *18.11*) for which you do not expect reimbursement. For example, if you expect a full insurance recovery in 2000 for a 1999 loss, you would take no deduction on your 1999 return.

If you do not expect any reimbursement and deduct a loss in 1999, but you receive insurance or other reimbursement in 2000, the reimbursement is taxable in 2000 to the extent that the 1999 deduction gave you a tax benefit by reducing your 1999 taxable income; *see 11.6.* You may not amend your 1999 tax return.

EXAMPLE

In 1969, Hurricane Camille destroyed oceanfront real estate owned jointly by two brothers. The buildings were insured under two policies that included wind damage but not losses resulting from floods, tidal waves, or water. The insurers, claiming the tidal wave had caused the destruction, denied their claim. The brothers consulted an attorney about the possibility of suit against the insurance companies, but there seemed to be little likelihood of recovery, so the brothers deducted their shares of the casualty loss in 1969. However, in January 1970, the adjusters of both companies changed their decisions, reimbursing the brothers for more than two-thirds of their loss. One of the brothers filed an amended 1969 tax return, reducing the previously reported casualty loss.

The IRS claimed that the insurance recovery was taxable in the year of receipt, 1970, to the extent that the prior deduction reduced 1969 income. The brother claimed that he made an error in claiming the deduction in 1969 because he had a reasonable prospect of reimbursement. Thus it was proper to reduce the deduction by the reimbursement on an amended return.

The Tax Court disagreed. Tax liability is based on facts as they exist at the end of each year. A recovery in a later tax year does not prove that a reasonable prospect of recovery existed in the earlier year. Amendments to previously filed tax returns may be made only to correct mathematical errors or miscalculations, not to rearrange facts and readjust income for two years.

If your reimbursement is less than you expected. Assume you took no loss deduction in 1998 because you expected to recover your entire loss in 1999—but the insurance company refuses to pay your claim. When do you deduct your loss? You deduct your loss in the year you find that you have no reasonable prospect of recovery. For example, you sue the company in 1999, with a reasonable prospect of winning your claim. However, in 2000, a court rules against you. You deduct your loss in 2000, subject to the personal property floors of *18.11*.

If you, as lessee, are liable to the lessor for damage to property, you may deduct the loss in the year you pay the lessor.

If you do not discover the loss until a later year. In this case, IRS regulations do not specifically allow a deduction for the loss in the year it is discovered, but court decisions have. In one case, an unseasonable blizzard damaged a windbreak planted to protect a house, buildings, and livestock. The damage to the evergreens did not become apparent until the next year, when about half of the trees died and the others were of little value. The court held that the loss occurred in the later year. In another case, hurricane damage did not become apparent for two years. The Tax Court allowed the deduction in the later year. Where drought damage occurs, *see 18.5.*

If your loss is in a federal disaster area. If your property is damaged in an area eligible for federal disaster assistance, you have a choice of years for which the loss may be claimed; *see 18.2.*

If reimbursements exceed your adjusted basis for the property. Receiving reimbursements in excess of adjusted basis results in a gain that you must report on your return unless you acquire qualifying replacement property and elect to defer the gain; *see 18.18.*

If a loss deduction was claimed in a prior year, you must report the reimbursement as income to the extent the prior deduction reduced your taxable income in the year claimed; *see 11.6.*

18.2 Disaster Losses

If you suffer a loss from a disaster in an area declared by the President as warranting federal assistance, you may deduct the loss either on the return for the year of the loss or on the return of the prior tax year. *See 18.12* for figuring the deductible loss.

You may elect to claim the deduction on a tax return for the previous year any time on or before the *later* of (1) the due date (without extensions) of the return for the year of the disaster and (2) the due date considering any extension for filing the return for the prior tax year. For a 1999 disaster loss, you generally have until April 17, 2000, to amend a 1998 tax return to claim the 1999 loss for 1998. In the case of a 2000 disaster loss, you generally have until April 16, 2001, to amend a 1999 tax return to claim the 2000 loss for 1999.

Revoking your decision. After making your election of which year to claim the disaster loss, you have 90 days in which to revoke it. After the 90-day period, the election becomes irrevocable. However, where an early election is made, you have until the due date for filing your return for the year of the disaster to change your election. Your revocation of an election is not effective unless you repay any credit or refund resulting from the election within the revocation period. A revocation made before you receive a refund will not be effective unless you repay the refund within 30 days after you receive it.

Homeowners forced to relocate. If you were forced to relocate or demolish your home in a disaster area, you may be able to claim a loss even though the damage, such as from erosion, does not meet the sudden event test of *18.5.* For example, after a severe storm, there is danger to a group of homes from nearby mudslides. State officials order homeowners to evacuate and relocate their homes. Disaster loss treatment is allowed provided: (1) the President has determined that the area warrants federal disaster relief; (2) within 120 days of the President's order, you are ordered by the state or local government to demolish or relocate your residence; and (3) the home was rendered unsafe by the erosion or other disaster. The law applies to vacation homes and rental properties, as well as to principal residences.

If these tests are met, the loss in value to your home is treated as a disaster loss so that you may elect to deduct the loss either in the year the demolition or relocation order is made or in the prior taxable year.

Fiscal year. If you are on a fiscal year, an election may be made for disaster losses occurring after the close of a fiscal year on the return for that year. For example, if your fiscal year ends June 30, and you suffer a disaster loss at any time between July 1, 1999, and June 30, 2000, you may elect to deduct it on your return for the fiscal year ending June 30, 1999.

Disaster relief grants and loans. Cancellation of part of a disaster loan under the Disaster Relief Act is treated as a reimbursement that reduces your loss; *see 18.12.* Grants to disaster victims under the Disaster Relief Act are not taxable, but the grant is considered a reimbursement reducing your deductible loss.

IRS interest abatement. For declared disasters, the IRS will abate interest on taxes due for the period covered by an extension to file tax returns and pay taxes.

Insurance Proceeds for Damaged Principal Residence

Generally, you have a taxable gain if you receive insurance proceeds in excess of your adjusted basis for your home or its contents. However, under a special rule, if your principal residence (whether owned or rented) is damaged by a Presidentially declared disaster, you pay no tax on gain from insurance proceeds received for *unscheduled* personal property damaged or destroyed in the home. Personal property is *unscheduled* if it is not separately listed on a schedule or rider to the basic policy.

EXAMPLE

You rent an apartment as your principal residence. Your apartment and its contents were completely destroyed by a hurricane in 1999; the county in which your apartment was located was declared a disaster area. You received insurance proceeds of $17,000 for unscheduled personal property in your apartment. The proceeds are not taxable.

 Filing Tip

Accelerating a Tax Refund

Disaster loss rules give you a chance to deduct a loss earlier than under general rules. This may result in a tax refund for the prior year. You may make an election to claim the loss for the prior year in a signed statement attached to an amended return for that year if the original return has already been filed. List the date of the disaster and where the property was located (city, town, county, and state). To amend a filed return for the prior year, use Form 1040X. Consider making the election if the deduction on the return of the prior year gives a greater tax reduction than if claimed on the return for the year in which the loss occurred, or if you need the refund for the prior year tax and do not want to wait until you file your return for the year of the disaster to claim the loss.

Destruction of residence. If your principal residence is destroyed and you realize gain on the receipt of insurance proceeds, you may avoid tax on gain of up to $250,000 if single ($500,000 if married filing jointly) by meeting the use and ownership tests discussed in Chapter 29. If you do not meet these tests, you may defer tax on the gain under the involuntary conversion replacement rules at *18.20.* Here, insurance proceeds received for the home itself or for *scheduled* property are treated as received for a single item of property. Gain on this combined insurance pool may be deferred by re-investing in replacement property that is similar or related in service or use to either the damaged residence or its contents. If the cost of a new principal residence and/or contents equals or exceeds the combined insurance pool, you may elect to defer any gain attributable to the insurance recovery; *see 18.20* for making the election. The deferred gain reduces your basis in the replacement property. The period for purchasing replacement property ends four years after the end of the first tax year in which any part of your gain is realized. If the cost of the replacement property is less than the combined insurance pool, your gain is taxed to the extent of the unspent reimbursement.

Sale of land underlying residence following disaster. If your principal residence is destroyed in a Presidentially declared disaster, and you decide to relocate elsewhere and sell the underlying land, the IRS treats the sale and the destruction as a single involuntary conversion. The land sale proceeds are combined with your insurance recovery for purposes of figuring deferrable gain under the involuntary conversion replacement rules. All of the gain resulting from the insurance recovery may be deferred if a new principal residence is purchased within the four-year replacement period and it costs at least as much as the combined insurance and sales proceeds. A two-year replacement period applies where the damage is to a principal residence but a Presidential disaster declaration is not made.

The same gain deferral rule applies if a second residence such as a vacation home that qualifies for a mortgage interest deduction *(15.1)* is destroyed, but in that case the replacement period is two years *(18.21)* instead of four years. The deferral rule applies whether or not a Presidential disaster declaration is made.

18.3 Who May Claim the Loss Deduction

The casualty and theft loss deduction may be claimed only by the owner of the property. For example, a husband filing a separate return may not deduct the loss of jewelry belonging to his wife; only she may deduct it on her separate return.

On jointly owned property, the loss is divided among the owners. If you and your spouse own the property jointly, you deduct the entire loss on a joint return. If you file separately, each owner deducts his or her share of the loss on each separate return.

If you have a legal life estate in the property, the loss is apportioned between yourself and those who will get the property after your death. The apportionment may be based on actuarial tables that consider your life expectancy.

You may claim a casualty loss for property lost or destroyed by your dependent if you own the property. You may not claim a loss deduction for destroyed property that belongs to your child who has reached majority, even though he or she is still your dependent.

Lessee. A person leasing property may be allowed to deduct payments to a lessor that compensate for a casualty loss. A tenant was allowed to deduct as a casualty loss payment of a judgment obtained by the landlord for fire damage to the rented premises that had to be returned in the same condition as at the start of the lease. However, the Tax Court does not allow a deduction for the cost of repairing a rented car, as the lessee has no basis in the car.

Caution

Damage to Nearby Property
The casualty must have caused damage to your property. Damage to a nearby area that lowered the value of your property does not give you a loss deduction.

EXAMPLE

You buy or lease a lot on which to build a cottage. Along with your purchase or lease, you have the privilege of using a nearby lake. The lake is later destroyed by a storm and the value of your property drops. You may not deduct the loss. The lake is not your property. You only had a privilege to use it, and this is not an ownership right that supports a casualty loss deduction.

18.4 Bank Deposit Losses

If a bank in which you deposit funds fails and your loss is not covered by insurance, generally you may claim your loss either as a bad debt deduction or casualty loss. Furthermore, if none of the deposits were federally insured, an investment loss may be claimed. A casualty loss deduction may not be claimed for lost deposits in foreign financial institutions that are not organized and supervised under federal or state law.

Bad debt. You may claim a bad debt deduction for a loss of a bank deposit in the year there is no reasonable prospect of recovery from the insolvent or bankrupt bank. You claim the loss as a short-term capital loss on Schedule D (Form 1040) unless the deposit was made in your business. A non-business bad debt deduction is deductible from capital gains. If you do not have capital gains or the bad debt loss exceeds capital gains, only $3,000 of the loss may offset other income. The remaining loss is carried over. A lost deposit of business funds is claimed as a business bad debt; *see 5.33.*

Casualty loss. You may elect to take a casualty loss deduction for the year in which the loss can be reasonably estimated. The loss is subject to the 10% AGI floor for casualty losses. Once the casualty loss election is made, it is irrevocable and will apply to all other losses on deposits in the same financial institution.

The casualty loss election may allow you to claim the loss in an earlier year because you do not have to wait until the year there is no prospect of recovery as required in the case of bad debts. The casualty loss election may also be advisable if other casualty losses may absorb all or part of the 10% AGI floor. The casualty loss election is not allowed to stockholders of the bank with more than a 1% interest, officers of the bank, or relatives of shareholders or officers.

Investment loss. If *none* of your deposits were federally insured and you reasonably estimate that you will not recover the funds, up to $20,000 ($10,000 if married filing separately) may be claimed on Schedule A (Form 1040) as an investment loss subject to the 2% adjusted gross income floor for miscellaneous itemized deductions. The $20,000 limit (or $10,000) applies to total losses from any one financial institution, regardless of how many accounts you have. A separate $20,000 deduction limit applies to each financial institution. The $20,000 (or $10,000) limit is reduced by any insurance proceeds authorized by *state* law that you reasonably expect to receive. If you claimed a bad debt deduction for a lost deposit in a prior year and you qualify for the investment loss, you may file an amended return to claim the investment loss if the statute of limitations has not passed.

Reasonable estimate of casualty or investment loss. Generally, the trustees of the troubled bank will provide depositors with an estimate of the expected recovery and loss. In the year of that determination, you may claim the estimated loss deduction. If you deduct an estimated loss that is less than you are entitled to, you may claim the additional loss in the year of the final determination as a bad debt. If you deduct more than the actual loss, the excess loss must be reported as income in the year of the final determination. Failure to claim the loss in the year in which the loss can first be reasonably estimated does not bar a deduction in a later year.

For any particular year, only one election may be made for losses in the same bank. If you elect the up-to-$20,000 investment loss for losses in one bank and your loss exceeds the limit, the balance may not be claimed as a casualty deduction. Similarly, if you elect casualty loss treatment, the amount that is not deductible because of the $100 and 10% of the adjusted gross income floors is not deductible under the $20,000 investment loss rule.

18.5 Sudden Event Test for Personal Property Losses

A loss of personal-use property must result from a sudden, unexpected, or unusual event. A sudden event is one that is swift, not gradual or progressive. An unexpected event is one that is ordinarily unanticipated and unintended. An unusual event is one that is not a day-to-day occurrence and that is not typical of the activity in which you were engaged. Chance or a natural phenomenon must be present. Examples include earthquakes, hurricanes, tornadoes, floods, severe storms, landslides, and fires. Loss due to vandalism during riots or civil disorders also is treated as a casualty loss. Damage to your car from an accident is generally deductible; *see 18.7.* Courts have allowed deductions for other types of accidents; *see* Example 2 below. The requirement of suddenness is designed to bar deductions for damage caused by a natural action such as erosion, corrosion, and termite infestation occurring over a period of time.

Foreseeable events and preventable accidents. The IRS may try to disallow a deduction by claiming that the loss was foreseeable and therefore not a deductible casualty loss; *see* the Examples at the end of this section.

EXAMPLES

1. A homeowner claimed a loss for water damage to wallpaper and plaster. The water entered through the window frame. The loss was disallowed. He gave no evidence that the damage came from a sudden or destructive force, such as a storm. The damage may have been caused by progressive deterioration.

 Filing Tip

Lost Bank Deposit

If you have other miscellaneous deductions that exceed 2% of adjusted gross income, claiming investment loss treatment may be preferable to treating the loss as a casualty subject to the 10% floor or a bad debt subject to the $3,000 limit.

2. Mr. White accidentally slammed the car door on his wife's hand. In pain, she shook her hand vigorously. A diamond flew out of her ring's setting, which was loosened by the impact. The diamond was never found. The IRS disallowed the deduction, contending that a casualty loss requires a cataclysmic event. The Tax Court disagreed. A deductible casualty loss occurs whenever an accidental force is exerted against property, and its owner is powerless to prevent the damage because of the suddenness. The IRS has accepted the decision.

3. A boat, which was in a poor state of repair, was equipped with a pump that automatically began operating when the water in the hull rose above a certain level. One day, the dockside power source failed, and the boat sank at its mooring within four hours. The IRS claimed that no deductible casualty occurred because the leakage was a chronic problem. The Tax Court allowed the deduction. The sinking was not a direct result of the boat's leaking hull, but of the failure of the on-board water pump.

4. A Brentwood couple, whose home was near the O.J. Simpson house, filed for a refund in federal district court to claim a $400,000 casualty loss deduction. The couple claimed that the double murder and the media frenzy surrounding the Simpson trial caused permanent buyer resistance in their neighborhood, lowering the value of their home by at least $400,000. The district court denied the refund. The couple relied on a 1986 case in which the Eleventh Circuit appeals court allowed Finkbohner a casualty loss deduction based on permanent buyer resistance when 12 nearby homes were razed by local authorities following severe floods. However, the Brentwood couple's case was appealable to the Ninth Circuit, and the Ninth Circuit requires that a casualty loss be based on actual physical damage caused by a fire, storm, or other sudden unusual event and not merely buyer resistance. Therefore, the claim for a casualty loss deduction for the Brentwood home was denied.

Is drought damage deductible? The IRS does not generally allow deductions for drought damage. An agent may argue that the loss resulted from progressive deterioration, which does not fit the legal definition of a personal casualty loss. Courts have allowed deductions for severe drought where the damages occur in the same year as the drought.

If the damage becomes noticeable a year later, a court will view this as evidence of progressive deterioration that does not qualify as a deductible casualty. Where there are drought conditions, inspect your property for damage before the end of the year and claim a deduction for the damage in that year to negate an IRS argument that damage was caused by progressive deterioration.

Damage to surrounding property. Loss due to buyer resistance because of damage to surrounding property is generally not deductible. However, the Eleventh Circuit allowed a deduction. *See* Example 4 above.

Damage to trees. The destruction of trees by southern pine beetles over a period of 5 to 10 days was held by the IRS to be a casualty. One court decided similarly where the destruction occurred over a 30-day period. For figuring the casualty deduction for tree and shrub damage, *see 18.6.*

Deduction despite faulty construction. A plumber stepped on a pipe that was improperly installed. Resulting underground flooding caused damage of over $20,000. The IRS argued that this was caused by a construction fault and thus was not a casualty loss. The Tax Court disagreed. The plumber caused the damage. Improper construction was only an element in the causative chain.

EXAMPLES

1. Heyn owned a hillside lot on which he contracted for the building of a home. A soil test showed a high proportion of fine-grain dense sandstone, which is unstable. His construction contract called for appropriate shoring up and support. But, because of the contractor's negligence, a landslide occurred. The IRS disallowed the loss on the ground that it was not a "casualty" because the danger was known before Heyn undertook the project and because of the negligence involved. The court disagreed. The contractor's negligence is not a factor in determining whether there was a casualty. For example, an automobile collision is considered a casualty, even if caused by negligent driving. Foreseeability is not a factor. A weather report may warn property owners to take protective steps against an approaching hurricane, but losses caused by the hurricane are deductible. The IRS has agreed to accept the decision.

 Caution

Loss Prevention Measures
The cost of preventive measures, such as burglar alarms or smoke detectors, or the cost of boarding up property against a storm, is not deductible.

2. Mrs. Kane placed her dirty ring in a glass of ammonia. Not knowing the contents of the glass, her husband emptied it into the sink and started the automatic garbage disposal, crushing the ring. The court allowed a full deduction for the loss, which it said resulted from a destructive force. That Mr. Kane was negligent has no bearing on whether the event was a casualty.

3. At Christmas time in 1982, Hananel left his 1974 Plymouth Valiant in Chicago in an area in which the city was towing away cars to make room for construction work. When he returned a week later, he found that his car was missing and reported it stolen. A month later, he learned that the city pound had towed the car away and then crushed it because its ownership could not be determined. He claimed a casualty loss for the car. The IRS disallowed the deduction, claiming that the towing and crushing was not an unforeseeable event, and thus did not qualify as a casualty.

   The Tax Court agreed that Hananel could have foreseen that leaving the car on the street subjected it to being towed. He was negligent. However, the penalty for this is a towing charge. He could not have foreseen its destruction. Therefore, the destruction occurred from an unusual and unexpected event, and he was allowed to claim a casualty loss deduction.

4. Destruction of a lawn through the careless use of weed killer has been held to be a casualty.

18.6 Damage to Trees and Shrubs

Not all damage to trees and shrubs qualifies as a casualty loss. The damage must be occasioned by a sudden event; *see 18.5*. Destruction of trees over a period of 5–10 days by southern pine beetles is deductible. One court allowed a deduction for similar destruction over a 30-day period. However, damage by Dutch Elm disease or lethal yellowing disease has been held to be gradual destruction not qualifying as a casualty loss. The Tax Court has allowed a deduction for the cost of removing infested trees, but denied a deduction for the loss of trees after a horse ate the bark.

If shrubbery and trees on *personal-use property* are damaged by a sudden casualty, you figure the loss on the value of the entire property before and after the casualty. You treat the buildings, land, and shrubs as one complete unit; *see Example 2 below*.

In fixing the loss on *business* or *income-producing property*, however, shrubs and trees are valued separately from the building; *see Example 1 below*.

 Caution

Loss From Termites

Termite damage is generally nondeductible since it often results from long periods of termite infestation. Proving a sudden action in the sense of fixing the approximate moment of the termite invasion is difficult. Some courts have allowed a deduction, but the IRS will bar deductions for termite damage under any conditions based on a study that found that serious termite damage results only after an infestation of three to eight years. Examples of other nondeductible casualty losses are at *18.9*.

EXAMPLES

1. Wayne Smith bought an office building for $90,000. The purchase price was allocated between the land ($18,000) and the building ($72,000). Smith planted trees and ornamental shrubs on the grounds surrounding the building at a cost of $1,200. When the basis of the building had been depreciated to $66,000, a hurricane caused extensive property damage. The fair market value of the land and building immediately before the hurricane was $18,000 and $80,000; immediately afterwards it was $18,000 and $52,000. The fair market value of the trees and shrubs immediately before the casualty was $2,000 and immediately afterwards, $400. Insurance of $15,000 is received to cover damage to the building. Deductible losses are figured separately for the building and the trees and shrubs. The deduction for the building is $13,000, computed as follows:

Value of building immediately before casualty	$80,000
Less: Value immediately after casualty	52,000
Loss in value	$28,000
Less: Insurance received	15,000
Deduction allowed	$13,000

The deduction for the trees and shrubs is $1,200:

Value immediately before casualty	$2,000
Less: Value of trees immediately after casualty	400
Loss in value	$1,600*

*However, the deductible loss cannot exceed the adjusted basis of the property, $1,200.

Filing Tip

Auto Damage

Unreimbursed accident damage may be a deductible casualty loss.

2. Same facts as in Example 1, except that Smith purchases a personal residence instead of an office building. Smith's adjusted gross income is $25,000, and this is his only loss. No allocation of the purchase price is necessary for the land and house because the property is not depreciable. Likewise, no individual evaluation of the fair market values of the land, house, trees, and shrubs is necessary. The amount of the deduction for the land, house, trees, and shrubs is $12,000, computed as follows:

Value of property immediately before casualty		$100,000
Less: Value of property immediately after casualty		70,400
Loss in value		$29,600
Less: Insurance received	$15,000	
10% floor ($2,500) and $100 floors	2,600	17,600
Deduction allowed		$12,000

18.7 Deducting Damage to Your Car

Damage to your car in an accident may be a deductible casualty loss unless caused by your willful conduct, such as drunken driving.

You may not deduct legal fees and costs of a court action for damages or money paid for damages to another's property because of your negligence while driving for commuting or other personal purposes. But if at the time of the accident you were using your car on business, you may deduct as a business loss a payment of damages to the other party's car. For purposes of a business loss deduction, driving between two locations of the same business is considered business driving but driving between locations of two separate businesses is considered personal driving. Therefore, the payment of damages arising from an accident while driving between two separate businesses is not deductible.

A court has allowed deductions for damage resulting from a child pressing the starter button of a car and from flying stones while driving over a temporary road. In a private letter ruling, the IRS disallowed a loss for damage to a race car by an amateur racer on the ground that in races, crashes are not an unusual event and so do not constitute a casualty.

If the deduction is questioned, be prepared to show the amount, if any, of your insurance recovery. A deduction is allowed only for uninsured losses. Not only must the loss be proved, but also that it was not compensated by insurance.

Towing costs are not included as part of the casualty loss.

A parent may not claim a casualty loss deduction for damage to a car registered in a child's name, although the parent provided funds for the purchase of the car.

Expenses of personal injuries arising from a car accident are not a deductible casualty loss.

Court Decision

Failure To Winterize Car

The Tax Court held that the loss of an engine because of a failure to use anti-freeze is not deductible as a casualty loss since the damage is not the result of a destructive force or accident but of personal neglect.

Automobile used partly for business. When you use an automobile partly for personal use and partly for business, your loss is computed as though two separate pieces of property were damaged—one business and the other personal. The $100 and 10% floors reduce only the loss on the part used for personal purposes.

18.8 Theft Losses

The taking of property must be illegal under state law to support a theft loss deduction. That property is missing is not sufficient evidence to sustain a theft deduction. It may have been lost or misplaced. So if all you can prove is that an article is missing or lost, your deduction may be disallowed. Sometimes, of course, the facts surrounding the disappearance of an article indicate that it is reasonable to assume that a theft took place. A deduction has been allowed for the theft of trees.

You deduct a theft loss in the year you discover the property was stolen. If you have a reasonable chance of being reimbursed for your loss, you may not take a deduction until the year in which you learn there is no reasonable prospect of recovery.

A legal fee paid to recover stolen property has been held to be deductible as part of the theft loss.

To figure the amount of a theft loss deduction, *see 18.12.*

Fraud by building contractors. A deduction was allowed when a building contractor ran away with a payment he received to build a residence. The would-be homeowner was allowed a theft loss deduction for the difference between the money he advanced to the contractor and the value of the partially completed house. In another case, a theft deduction was allowed for payments to subcontractors. The main contractor had fraudulently claimed that he had paid them before he went bankrupt.

Embezzlement losses are deductible as theft losses in the year the theft is discovered. However, if you report on a cash basis, you may not take a deduction for the embezzlement of income you have not reported. For example, an agent embezzled royalties of $46,000 due an author. The author's theft deduction was disallowed. The author had not previously reported the royalties as income; therefore, she could not get the deduction.

Fraudulent sales offers. Worthless stock purchases made on the representation of false and fraudulent sales offers are deductible as theft losses in the year there is no reasonable prospect of recovery. However, the illegal sale of unregistered stock does not support a theft loss deduction. In addition, buying stock from a bad tip and losing money is not deductible.

Kidnapping ransom. Payment of ransom to a kidnapper is generally a deductible theft loss. However, the expense of trying to find an abducted child is not a theft loss.

Fortune tellers. The Tax Court allowed a theft loss deduction in New York, where fortune telling is by law a theft-related offense. The law assumes that telling fortunes or promising to control occult forces is a form of fraud. An exception is made for fortune telling at shows for the purpose of entertaining or amusement. That a person voluntarily asks for advice does not bar the deduction. According to the court, a gullible person who gives money to fortune tellers in the belief that he or she will be helped is still defrauded or swindled. Theft is a broad term and includes theft by swindling, false pretenses, and any other form of guile. In this case, the taxpayer, who was suffering from mental depression, had become attached to two fortune tellers whom he claimed took him for over $19,000.

Riot losses. Losses caused by fire, theft, and vandalism occurring during riots and civil disorders are deductible. To support your claim of a riot loss, keep evidence of the damage suffered and the cost of repairs. Photographs taken prior to repairs or replacement, lists of damaged or missing property, and police reports would help to establish and uphold your loss deduction.

Foreign government confiscations. The IRS and courts have disallowed casualty deductions for confiscations of personal property by foreign governments. This includes deposits in foreign banks; the loss is limited to a short-term capital loss.

Swindled by friend. A theft loss deduction was allowed to a widow who gave her old beau over $2 million to acquire stock for her in his bank. He used the money to pay his personal debts. The IRS barred the theft loss, arguing that the widow failed to prove fraud. A district court disagreed and allowed the deduction. Under Oklahoma state law, a person who makes a promise in return for cash has committed larceny by fraud if he never intended to return the funds or make good on the promise. Here, that the widow gave him the money voluntarily does not bar a theft loss deduction. She parted with the funds based upon his false claim that he would invest the money for her when he had no intention of doing so, but planned all along to pay off his debts with the funds.

18.9 Nondeductible Losses

Certain losses, though "casualties" for you, may not be deducted if they are not due to theft, fire, or from some other sudden natural phenomenon. The following have been held to be nondeductible losses:

- Termite damage; *see 18.5*
- Carpet beetle damage
- Dry rot damage
- Damages for personal injuries or property damage to others caused by your negligence
- Legal expenses in defending a suit for your negligent operation of your personal automobile
- Legal expenses to recover personal property wrongfully seized by the police
- Expenses of moving to and rental of temporary quarters
- Loss of personal property while in storage or in transit
- Loss of passenger's luggage put aboard a ship. The passenger missed the boat and the luggage could not be traced.
- Accidental loss of a ring from your finger
- Injuries resulting from tripping over a wire
- Loss by husband of joint property taken by his wife when she left him
- Loss of a valuable dog (or family pet) that strayed and was not found
- Steady weakening of a building due to normal wind and weather conditions

 Planning Reminder

Proving a Theft
Get statements from witnesses who saw the theft or police records documenting a break-in to your house or car. A newspaper account of the crime might also help.

When you suspect a theft, make a report to the police. Even though your reporting does not prove that a theft was committed, it may be inferred from your failure to report that you were not sure that your property was stolen. But a theft loss was allowed where the loss of a ring was not reported to the police or an attempt made to demand its return from the suspect, a domestic employee. The owner feared being charged with false arrest.

 Filing Instruction

If Stolen Property Is Recovered
If you claim a theft loss and in a later year the property is returned to you, you must refigure your loss deduction. If the refigured deduction is lower than the amount you claimed, the difference must be reported as income in the year of the recovery. To recalculate the loss, follow the steps in *18.12* for figuring deductible losses, but in Step 1, compute the loss in fair market value from the time the property was stolen until you recovered it. The lower of this loss in value, if any, and your adjusted basis for the property is then reduced by insurance reimbursements and the personal-use floors *(18.11)* to get the recalculated loss.

- Damage to a crop caused by plant diseases, insects, or fungi
- Damage to property from drought in an area where a dry spell is normal and usual
- Damage to property caused by excavations on adjoining property
- Damage from rust or corroding of understructure of house
- Moth damage
- Dry well
- Losses occasioned by water pockets, erosion, inundation at still water levels, and other natural phenomena (There was no sudden destruction.)
- Death of a saddle horse after eating a silk hat
- A watch or spectacles dropped on the ground
- Sudden drop in the value of securities
- Loss of contingent interest in property due to the unexpected death of a child
- Improper police seizure of private liquor stock
- Chinaware broken by a family pet
- Temporary fluctuation in value
- Damage to property from local government construction project
- Fire purposely set by owner
- Engine damage due to failure to use antifreeze

Note: Some of the above items may be allowed as business expenses.

Key To Proving a Casualty Loss

To prove—	You need this information—
That a casualty actually occurred	With a well-known casualty, like regional floods, you will have no difficulty proving the casualty occurred, but you must prove it affected your property. Photographs of the area, before and after, and newspaper stories placing the damage in your neighborhood are helpful. If only your property is damaged, there may be a newspaper item on it. Some papers list all the fire alarms answered the previous day. Police, fire, and other municipal departments may have reports on the casualty.
The cost of repairing the property	Cost of repairs is allowed as a measure of loss of repairing the value if it is not excessive and the repair merely restored your property to its condition immediately before the casualty. Save cancelled checks, bills, receipts, and vouchers for expenses of clearing debris and restoring the property to its condition before the casualty.
The value immediately before and after the casualty	Appraisals by a competent expert are important. Get them in writing—in the form of an affidavit, deposition, estimate, appraisal, etc. The expert—an appraiser, engineer, or architect—should be qualified to judge local values. Any records of offers to buy your property, either before or after the casualty, are helpful. Automobile "blue books" may be used as guides in fixing the value of a car. But an amount offered for your car as a trade-in on a new car is not usually an acceptable measure of value.
Cost or other basis of your property—the deductible loss cannot be more than that	A deed, contract, bill of sale, or other document probably shows your original cost. Bills, receipts, and cancelled checks probably show the cost of improvements. One court refused to allow a deduction because an owner failed to prove the original cost of a destroyed house and its value before the fire. In another case, estimates were allowed where a fire destroyed records of cost. A court held that the homeowner could not be expected to prove cost by documents lost in the fire that destroyed her property. She made inventories after the fire and again at a later date. Her reliance on memory to establish cost, even though inflated, was no bar to the deduction. The court estimated the market value based on her inventories. If you acquired the property by gift or inheritance, you must establish an adjusted basis in the property from records of the donor or the executor of the estate; *see 5.17 and 5.18.*

18.10 Proving a Casualty Loss

If your return is audited, you will have to prove that the casualty occurred and the amount of the loss. The time to collect your evidence is as soon after the casualty as possible. The Key To Proving a Casualty Loss, above, indicates the information that you will need when computing your loss under the steps explained in *18.12*.

18.11 Floors for Personal-Use Property Losses

Casualty and theft losses to personal-use property are subject to "floors" that will reduce, and in some cases eliminate, your deduction. For each casualty or theft, a $100 reduction applies after the loss is computed under the steps at *18.12*. In addition, personal casualty and theft losses (after the $100 reduction) are deductible only to the extent they exceed 10% of your adjusted gross income.

The $100 floor. The $100 floor reduces casualty and theft losses of property used for personal purposes; *see* Step 4 in *18.12*. The $100 floor does not apply to losses of business property or property held for the production of income such as securities. If property used both in business and personal activities is damaged, the $100 offset applies only to the loss allocated to personal use.

For each casualty or theft during the year, a separate $100 reduction applies. For example, if you are involved in five different casualties during the year, there will be a $100 offset applied to each of the five losses. But when two or more items of property are destroyed in one event, only one $100 offset is applied to the total loss. For example, a storm damages your residence and also your car parked in the driveway. You figure the loss on the residence and car separately, but only one $100 offset applies to the total loss.

The $100 floor is applied after taking into account insurance proceeds received and insurance you expect to receive in a later year.

The $100 floor applies separately to the loss of each individual whose property has been damaged by a single casualty, even where the damaged property is owned by two or more individuals. The only exception is for a married couple filing jointly who apply only one $100 floor to their losses from a single casualty.

EXAMPLES

1. Two sisters own and occupy a house that is damaged in a storm. Each sister applies the $100 floor to figure her separate deduction.
2. Your house is partially damaged by a fire that also damages the personal property of a houseguest. You are subject to one $100 floor and the houseguest is subject to a separate $100 floor.

10% AGI floor. The 10% adjusted gross income (AGI) floor applies to the total of all losses occurring during the taxable year to personal-use property. You must deduct 10% of your AGI from the total loss to determine your deduction. The Example below illustrates the application of the $100 floor to each separate casualty event and the 10% AGI floor to the total losses.

EXAMPLE

In January 1999, you have an uninsured jewelry theft loss of $1,000, and in July 1999 uninsured damage of $3,000 to your personal car. Your adjusted gross income is $25,000. Your deduction is $1,300 figured as follows:

Theft loss	$1,000	
Less	100	$ 900
Car damage	3,000	
Less	100	2,900
Total loss		3,800
Less 10% of $25,000		2,500
Deductible loss		$1,300

 Filing Tip

$100 Floor for Married Couples

Where a husband and wife file a joint return, only one $100 floor applies to a casualty loss suffered by either spouse, whether the property is owned jointly or separately. If separate returns are filed, each spouse must reduce his or her half of the loss on jointly owned property by $100. If the property is owned by one spouse, only that spouse can claim a casualty loss on a separate return.

Sample—Form 4684

Form **4684**	**Casualties and Thefts**	OMB No. 1545-0177
Department of the Treasury Internal Revenue Service	► See separate instructions. ► Attach to your tax return. ► Use a separate Form 4684 for each different casualty or theft.	**1999** Attachment Sequence No. **26**
Name(s) shown on tax return		Identifying number

SECTION A—Personal Use Property (Use this section to report casualties and thefts of property **not** used in a trade or business or for income-producing purposes.)

1 Description of properties (show type, location, and date acquired for each):

Property **A** .... Residence 2-8-88

Property **B** .... Furniture 3-15-89

Property **C** ....

Property **D** ....

		Properties (Use a separate column for each property lost or damaged from one casualty or theft.)			
		A	**B**	**C**	**D**
2 Cost or other basis of each property	**2**	76,000	5,000		
3 Insurance or other reimbursement (whether or not you filed a claim). See instructions. **Note:** *If line 2 is more than line 3, skip line 4.*	**3**	2,000	500		
4 Gain from casualty or theft. If line 3 is **more than** line 2, enter the difference here and skip lines 5 through 9 for that column. See instructions if line 3 includes insurance or other reimbursement you did not claim, or you received payment for your loss in a later tax year	**4**				
5 Fair market value **before** casualty or theft	**5**	167,500	2,000		
6 Fair market value **after** casualty or theft	**6**	162,500	-0-		
7 Subtract line 6 from line 5	**7**	5,000	2,000		
8 Enter the **smaller** of line 2 or line 7	**8**	5,000	2,000		
9 Subtract line 3 from line 8. If zero or less, enter -0-	**9**	3,000	1,500		

10 Casualty or theft loss. Add the amounts on line 9. Enter the total	**10**	4,500
11 Enter the amount from line 10 or $100, whichever is **smaller**	**11**	100
12 Subtract line 11 from line 10	**12**	4,400
Caution: Use only one Form 4684 for lines 13 through 18.		
13 Add the amounts on line 12 of all Forms 4684	**13**	4,400
14 Combine the amounts from line 4 of all Forms 4684	**14**	- 0 -
15 • If line 14 is **more than** line 13, enter the difference here and on Schedule D. Do not complete the rest of this section (see instructions). • If line 14 is **less than** line 13, enter -0- here and continue with the form. • If line 14 is **equal to** line 13, enter -0- here. Do not complete the rest of this section.	**15**	
16 If line 14 is **less than** line 13, enter the difference	**16**	4,400
17 Enter 10% of your adjusted gross income (Form 1040, line 34). Estates and trusts, see instructions	**17**	2,800
18 Subtract line 17 from line 16. If zero or less, enter -0-. Also enter result on Schedule A (Form 1040), line 19. Estates and trusts, enter on the "Other deductions" line of your tax return	**18**	1,600

For Paperwork Reduction Act Notice, see page 4 of separate instructions.   Cat. No. 129970   Form **4684** (1999)

18.12 Figuring Your Loss on Form 4684

Form 4684 is used to report casualties or thefts of personal-use property, business property, or income-producing property. The deductible loss is usually the difference between the fair market value of the property before and after the casualty or theft *less* (1) reimbursements received for the loss and (2) $100 if the property was used for personal purposes. However, the loss may not exceed your adjusted basis *(5.20)* for the property, which for many items will be your cost. If your adjusted basis is less than the loss in value, your deduction is limited to basis, less reimbursements and the $100 floor for personal-use assets. After figuring all allowable casualty and theft losses for personal-use property, the total is deductible only to the extent it exceeds the 10% adjusted gross income floor *(18.11)*. Use the following five-step method for figuring the deductible amount.

Steps for calculating your deductible loss. The following five steps reflect the procedure on Form 4684 for computing a casualty or theft loss. If your loss is to business inventory, you do not have to use Form 4684, but may take the loss into account when figuring the cost of goods sold; *see* "Inventory losses" later in this section.

To figure your deductible loss, follow these five steps:

Step 1. Compute the loss in fair market value of the property. This is the difference between the fair market value immediately before and immediately after the casualty. You will need written appraisals to support your claim for loss of value. You may not claim sentimental or aesthetic values or a fluctuation in property values caused by a casualty; you must deal with cost or market values of what has been lost. If the value of your property has been lowered because of damage to a nearby area, you do not have a deductible loss since your own property has not been damaged. No deduction may be claimed for estimated decline in value based on buyer resistance in an area subject to landslides.

For household items, the Tax Court has allowed losses based on cost less depreciation, rather than on the decrease in fair market value.

Step 2. Compute your adjusted basis for the property. This is usually the cost of the property plus the cost of improvements, less previous casualty loss deductions and depreciation if the property is used in business or for income-producing purposes. Unadjusted basis of property acquired other than by purchase is explained at *5.16*. Adjusted basis is explained at *5.20*.

Step 3. Take the lower amount of Step 1 and 2. The lower amount, reduced by the adjustments in Step 4, is your casualty loss, with one exception: Where property used for business or income-producing purposes is totally destroyed, and before the casualty its market value is less than its adjusted basis, the measure of the loss is the adjusted basis, less any salvage value.

Step 4. Reduce the loss in Step 3 by the insurance proceeds or other compensation for the loss; *see 18.15*. If the property was used for personal purposes, also reduce the loss by $100; *see 18.11*.

Step 5. If the property was used for personal purposes, the loss is allowed only if it exceeds 10% of your adjusted gross income. If you have more than one personal casualty or theft, reduce the total combined loss by 10% of adjusted gross income; only the excess is deductible; *see 18.11*.

EXAMPLES

1. Your home, which cost $76,000 in 1987, was damaged by a fire. The value of the house before the disaster was $167,500, but afterwards $162,500. The furniture cost $5,000 in 1988. Its value before the fire was set at $2,000. It was totally destroyed. The insurance company reimbursed you $2,000 for your house damage and $500 for your furnishings. This was the only casualty for the year. Your adjusted gross income is $28,000. You figure your loss for the furniture separately from the loss on the house but apply only one $100 reduction *(18.11)* because the damage was from a single casualty.

    1. Decrease in home's fair market value:

Value of house before fire	$167,500
Value of house after fire	162,500
Decrease in value	$ 5,000

    2. Adjusted basis: $ 76,000

    3. Loss sustained (lower of 1 and 2) $5,000

Less: Insurance	2,000
Loss on house	$3,000

    4. Loss on furnishings (decreased value)* $2,000

Less: Insurance	500
Loss on furnishings	$1,500

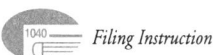

Filing Instruction

Reporting on Form 4684

If you are claiming a loss for personal-use property, use Section A on page 1 of Form 4684. If you suffered more than one casualty or theft during the year, use a separate Form 4684 for each one. The total deductible casualty or theft loss from Section A of Form 4684 is then entered on Line 19, Schedule A of Form 1040.

Filing Tip

Business or Income Producing Property

If you are claiming a loss for property used in your business or income-producing activity, use Section B on page 2 of Form 4684 (not shown here). Losses from income-producing property are entered on Line 27 of Schedule A as "other miscellaneous deductions" and are not subject to the 2% adjusted gross income floor.

Caution

Incidental Expenses

Expenses that are incidental to a casualty or theft, such as medical treatment for personal injury, temporary housing, fuel, moving, or rentals for temporary living quarters, are not deductible as casualty losses.

5. Total loss ($3,000 and $1,500) $4,500
    Less: $100 floor   100
    Casualty loss (subject to 10% floor) $4,400
6. 10% AGI floor (10% of $28,000 AGI) $2,800
7. Casualty loss ($4,400 – $2,800) $1,600

See the sample Form 4684 on page 344 for how this loss is reported.

*The loss for the furnishings on Line 4 is $2,000, the decrease in fair market value, as this is lower than the $5,000 basis.

2. Depreciable business property with a fair market value of $1,500 and an adjusted basis of $2,000 is totally destroyed. Because property used in your business was totally destroyed (*see* Step 3 above), your loss is measured by your adjusted basis of $2,000, which is larger than the $1,500 loss in fair market value. Salvage value, if any, reduces your deduction, but you disregard the $100 floor applied to casualty losses on personal property. If the property was used for personal purposes, the loss would have been limited to the $1,500 loss in market value less $100, leaving a loss of $1,400 subject to the 10% adjusted gross income floor.

Law Alert

Appraisals for Disaster Relief

The IRS may accept an appraisal that is used to obtain federal loans or loan guarantees following a Presidentially declared disaster as proof of the amount of a casualty loss. Check IRS guidelines if available.

Business losses. Losses from business property are generally netted against gains from casualties or thefts on Form 4684 and the net gain or loss is entered on Form 4797. Follow the instructions to Form 4684 .

Inventory losses. A casualty or theft loss of inventory is automatically reflected on Schedule C in the cost of goods sold, which includes the lost items as part of your opening inventory. Any insurance or other reimbursement received for the loss must be included as sales income.

You may separately claim the inventory loss as a casualty or theft loss on Form 4684 instead of automatically claiming it as part of the cost of goods sold. If you do this, you must eliminate the items from inventory by lowering either opening inventory or purchases when figuring the cost of goods sold.

Cost less depreciation method for household items. The Tax Court has allowed casualty loss deductions based on cost less depreciation, rather than on the difference in fair market value immediately before and after the casualty. *See* the following Example.

EXAMPLE

Basing a deduction on the difference between the value of furnishings immediately before and immediately after a casualty may limit your deduction to the going price for second-hand furnishings. A homeowner whose furniture was destroyed by fire claimed that the fair market value immediately before the fire should be original cost less depreciation. He based his figures on an inventory prepared by certified public adjusters describing each item, its cost and age. The deduction figured this way came to approximately $27,500 ($55,000 cost, less $13,000 depreciation, a $14,400 insurance recovery, and the $100 floor).

The IRS estimated that the furniture was worth $15,304 before the fire and limited the deduction to $804 after accounting for the insurance and the $100 floor. The Tax Court disagreed. The householder's method of valuing his furniture is consistent with methods used by insurance adjusters who have an interest in keeping values low. He is not limited to the amount his property would bring if "hawked off by a secondhand dealer or at a forced sale." However, in another case, the court refused to allow the cost less depreciation formula where the homeowner's inventory list was based on memory.

18.13 Personal and Business Use of Property

For property held partly for personal use and partly for business or income-producing purposes, a casualty or theft loss deduction is computed as if two separate pieces of property were damaged, destroyed, or stolen. Follow the steps in *18.12* for figuring the allowable loss, but apply the $100 and 10% of adjusted gross income floors only to the personal part of the loss.

EXAMPLE

A building with two apartments, one used by the owner as his home and the other rented to a tenant, is damaged by a fire. The fair market value of the building before the fire was $169,000 and after the fire, $136,000. Its cost basis was $120,000. Depreciation taken before the fire was $14,000. The insurance company paid $20,000. The owner has adjusted gross income of $40,000. This is his only loss this year. He has a business casualty loss of $6,500 and a deductible personal casualty loss of $2,400 figured as follows:

	Business	Personal
1. Decrease in value of building:		
Value before fire ($169,000)	$84,500	$84,500
Value after fire ($136,000)	(68,000)	(68,000)
Decrease in value	$16,500	$16,500
2. Adjusted basis of building:	$60,000	$60,000
Less: Depreciation	(14,000)	
Adjusted basis	$46,000	$60,000
3. Loss sustained (lower of 1 and 2)	$16,500	$16,500
Less: Insurance (total $20,000)	($10,000)	($10,000)
4. Loss	$6,500	$6,500
Less: $100 floor and 10% of adjusted gross income	—	(4,100)
Deductible casualty loss	$6,500	$2,400

18.14 Repairs May Be a "Measure of Loss"

The cost of repairs may be treated as evidence of the loss of value (Step 1 in *18.12*), if the amount is not excessive and the repairs do nothing more than restore the property to its condition before the casualty. An estimate for repairs will not suffice; only actual repairs may be used as a measure of loss. However, where you measure your loss by comparing appraisals of value for before and after the casualty, repairs may be considered in arriving at a post-casualty value even though no actual repairs are made.

Deduction not limited to repairs. A casualty loss deduction is not limited to repair expenses where the decline in market value is greater, according to a federal appeals court; *see* the following Example.

EXAMPLE

Connor claimed that the market value of his house dropped $93,000 after it was damaged by fire. His $52,000 cash outlay in repairing the house was reimbursed by insurance. He claimed a casualty loss of approximately $40,000, the uncompensated drop in market value. The IRS barred the deduction. The house was restored to pre-casualty condition. The cost of the repairs is a realistic measure of the loss, and, as the expense was fully compensated by insurance, Connor suffered no loss. A federal appeals court disagreed. The house dropped $70,000 in market value, of which $20,000 was uncompensated by insurance. The deduction is measured by the uncompensated difference in value before and after the casualty. It is not limited to the cost of repairs, even where the repair expense is less than the difference in fair market values. Had the repairs cost more than this difference, the IRS would not have allowed a larger deduction.

18.15 Insurance Reimbursements

You reduce the amount of your loss *(18.12)* by insurance proceeds, voluntary payments received from your employer for damage to your property, and cash or property received from the Red Cross. Also reduce your loss by reimbursements you expect to receive in a later year; *see 18.1*. However, cash gifts from friends and relatives to help defray the cost of repairs do not reduce the loss where there are no conditions on the use of the gift. Also, gifts of food, clothing, medical supplies, and other forms of subsistence do not reduce the loss deduction nor are they taxable income.

Cancellation of part of a disaster loan under the Disaster Relief Act is treated as a partial reimbursement of the loss and reduces the amount of the loss. Payments from an urban renewal agency to acquire your damaged property under the Federal Relocation Act of 1970 are considered reimbursements reducing the loss.

Insurance payments for the cost of added living expenses because of damage to a home do not reduce a casualty loss. The payments are treated separate and apart from payments for property damage. Payments for excess living costs are generally not taxable; *see 18.16*.

Filing Tip

Help During Disasters and Emergencies

If you have damaged or lost property in a location declared by the President as a major disaster area, you may find additional assistance from the IRS at their website: www.irs.ustreas.gov/prod/hot/fema.html.

Planning Reminder

Keep Records of Deductible Losses

If your property is damaged, you must reduce the basis of the damaged property by the casualty loss deduction and compensation received for the loss; *see 5.20*. When you later sell the property, gain or loss is the difference between the selling price and the reduced basis.

Passive activity property loss reimbursements. A reimbursement of a casualty or theft loss deduction is not considered passive activity income if the original loss was not treated as a passive deduction; *see 10.1*. The reimbursement may be taxed under the rule discussed at *11.6*.

Realizing a gain from insurance. If you receive insurance proceeds in excess of your adjusted basis for the property, you generally realize a gain, which you may be able to defer by buying replacement property; *see 18.18*.

18.16 Excess Living Costs Paid by Insurance Are Not Taxable

Your insurance contract may reimburse you for excess living costs when a casualty or a threat of casualty forces you to vacate your house. The payment is tax free if these tests are met:

1. Your principal residence is damaged or destroyed by fire, storm, or other casualty or you are denied use of it by a governmental order because of the occurrence or threat of the casualty.
2. You are paid under an insurance contract for living expenses resulting from the loss of occupancy or use of the residence.

Whether you have a taxable or tax-free reimbursement is figured at the end of the period you were unable to use your residence. Thus, if the dislocation covers more than one taxable year, the taxable income, if any, will be reported in the taxable year in which the dislocation ended.

The tax-free amount includes only excess living costs paid by the insurance company. The excess is the difference between (1) the actual living expenses incurred during the time you could not use or occupy your house and (2) the normal living expenses that you would have incurred for yourself and members of your household during the period. Living expenses during the period may include the cost of renting suitable housing and extraordinary expenses for transportation, food, utilities, and miscellaneous services. The expenses must be incurred for items and services (such as laundry) needed to maintain your standard of living that you enjoyed before the loss and must be covered by the policy.

Where a lump-sum settlement does not identify the amount covering living expenses, an allocation is required to determine the tax-free portion. In the case of uncontested claims, the tax-free portion is that part of the settlement that bears the same ratio to total recovery as increased living expense bears to total loss and expense. If your claim is contested, you must show the amount reasonably allocable to increased living expenses consistent with the terms of the insurance contract, but not in excess of coverage limitations specified in the contract.

The exclusion from income does not cover insurance reimbursements for loss of rental income or for loss of or damage to real or personal property; such reimbursements for property damage reduce your casualty loss; *see 18.15*.

If your home is used for both residential and business purposes, the exclusion does not apply to insurance proceeds and expenses attributable to the nonresidential portion of the house. There is no exclusion for insurance recovered for expenses resulting from governmental condemnation or order unrelated to a casualty or threat of casualty.

The insurance reimbursement may cover part of your normal living expenses as well as the excess expenses due to the casualty. The part covering normal expenses is income; it does not reduce your casualty loss.

EXAMPLES

1. On March 1, your home was damaged by fire. While it was being repaired, you and your spouse lived at a motel and ate meals at restaurants. Costs are $1,200 at the motel, $1,000 for meals, and $75 for laundry services. You make the required March payment of $790 on your home mortgage. Your customary $40 commuting expense is $20 less for the month because the motel is closer to your work. Your usual commuting expense is therefore treated as not being incurred to the extent of the $20 decrease. Furthermore, you do not incur your customary $700 food expense for meals at home, $75 for utilities, and $60 for laundry at home. Your insurance company pays you $1,700 for expenses. The tax-free exclusion for insurance payments is limited to $1,420, computed in the third column below. You must report as income $280 ($1,700 – $1,420).

 Caution

Failure To Make an Insurance Claim

If you are insured for your full loss and do not file a claim because you do not want to risk cancellation of liability coverage, you may not claim a deduction. If you do not file an insurance claim but your loss exceeds the coverage, the noncovered loss is deductible. For example, if you have a $500 deductible on your automobile insurance policy, a loss of up to $500 for car damage would be allowed, subject to the $100 and 10% of adjusted gross income floors.

	Expenses from casualty	Expenses not incurred	Increase (Decrease)
Housing	$1,200		$1,200
Utilities		$75	(75)
Meals	1,000	700	300
Transportation		20	(20)
Laundry	75	60	15
Total	$2,275	$855	$1,420

2. Same facts as in Example 1 except that you rented the residence for $400 per month and the risk of loss was to the landlord. You did not pay the March rent. The excludable amount is $1,020 ($1,420 less $400 normal rent not incurred). You would have to report as income the excess of the insurance received over the $1,020 exclusion.

18.17 Do Your Casualty Losses Exceed Your Income?

If your 1999 casualty or theft losses exceed your income, you pay no tax in 1999. You may also carry the excess loss back to 1996 and file a refund claim for that year. Any remaining loss may be carried back to 1997 and 1998 and carried forward to 2000 through 2019, or you may just carry your loss forward 20 years until it is used up. The excess casualty loss is carried back or forward as a net operating loss. *See 40.18* for net operating loss rules.

Note: The $100 and 10% of adjusted gross income floors for personal casualty losses apply only in the year of loss; you do not again reduce your loss in the carryback or carryover years.

Taxable Gain From Involuntary Conversions

18.18 Defer Gain by Replacing Property

If your property is destroyed, damaged, stolen, or taken by a government authority, this is considered to be an *involuntary conversion* for tax purposes. If upon an involuntary conversion you receive insurance or other compensation that exceeds the adjusted basis of the property, you realize a gain that is taxable unless you may defer tax under the rules in *18.19–18.23* or, in the case of a principal residence, avoid tax under the rules in Chapter 29.

You may elect to postpone tax on the full gain provided you invest the proceeds in replacement property the cost of which is equal to or exceeds the net proceeds from the conversion. Reinvestment requirements are discussed at *18.21–18.23.* The replacement period for personal-use property is two years; for business and investment property it is two or three years depending on the type of involuntary conversion; for a residence and its contents involuntarily converted due to a Presidentially declared disaster *(see 18.2)* it is four years; *see 18.21* for replacement periods.

Your basis in the replacement property is its replacement cost, minus any postponed gain. If you find that you cannot buy a replacement by the end of the period, ask the IRS for an extension of time *(see 18.21).*

Buying a replacement from a related party generally qualifies only if your gains from involuntary conversions are $100,000 or less *(see 18.22).*

18.19 Involuntary Conversions Qualifying for Tax Deferral

For purposes of an election to defer tax on gains, "involuntary conversion" is more broadly defined than "casualty loss." You have an involuntary conversion when your property is:

Damaged or destroyed by some outside force.

Stolen, seized, requisitioned, or condemned by a governmental authority. If you voluntarily sell land made useless to you by the condemnation of your adjacent land, the sale may also qualify as a conversion. Condemnation of property as unfit for human habitation does not qualify. Condemnation, as used by the tax law, refers to the taking of private property for public use, not to the condemnation of property for noncompliance with housing and health regulations. Similarly, a tax sale to pay delinquent taxes is not an involuntary conversion.

Sold under a threat of seizure, condemnation, or requisition. The threat must be made by an authority qualified to take property for public use. A sale following a threat of condemnation made by a government employee is a conversion if you reasonably believe he or she speaks with authority and could and would carry out the threat to have your property condemned. If you learn of the plan of an imminent condemnation from a newspaper or other news media, the IRS requires you to confirm the report from a government official before you act on the news.

 Filing Tip

Involuntary Conversion of Personal Residence

Gain on the conversion may escape tax under the rules discussed in Chapter 29. If not, tax may be deferred under the involuntary conversion replacement rules.

Planning Reminder

Basis Reduction

Consider whether postponement of gain at the expense of a reduced basis for property is advisable, compared to the tax consequences of reporting the gain in the year it is realized.

Farmers. Farmers also have involuntary conversions when:

Land is sold within an irrigation project to meet the acreage limitations of the federal reclamation laws; Cattle are destroyed by disease or sold because of disease; *or*

Draft, breeding, or dairy livestock is sold because of drought. The election to treat the sale as a conversion is limited to livestock sold over the number that would have been sold but for the drought. In some cases, livestock may be replaced with other farm property where there has been soil or other environmental contamination.

Should you elect to postpone gain? An election gives an immediate advantage: tax on gain is postponed and the funds that would have been spent to pay the tax may be used for other investments.

However, as a condition of deferring tax, the basis of the replacement property is generally fixed at the same adjusted basis as the converted property. If your reinvestment exceeds the insurance proceeds, the excess increases the basis of the replacement property. As long as the value of the replacement property does not decline, tax on the original gain is finally incurred when the property is sold.

Special rules for federally declared disaster areas are discussed at *18.2*.

EXAMPLE

Assume a rental building is destroyed by fire and a proper replacement is made. Assume that gain on the receipt of the insurance proceeds is taxable as capital gain. An election is generally not advisable if you have capital losses to offset the gain. However, even if you have no capital losses, you may still decide not to make the election and pay tax in order to fix, for purposes of depreciation, the basis of the new property at its purchase price, if the future depreciation deductions will offset income taxable at a higher rate than the current tax. If there is little or no difference between the two rates so that a net after-tax benefit from the depreciation would not arise, an election might be made solely to postpone the payment of tax.

18.20 How To Elect To Defer Tax

To defer tax on your gain, do not report the gain as income for the year it is realized. Attach to your return a statement giving details of the transaction, including computation of the gain and your intention to buy a replacement if you have not yet done so. *See 18.21* for replacement periods and IRS notification requirements.

If your property is condemned and you are given similar property, no election is necessary. Postponement of tax on the gain is required. For example, the city condemns a store building and gives you another store building the value of which exceeds the cost basis of the old one; gain is not taxed.

Partnerships. The election to defer gain must be made at the partnership level. Individual partners may not make separate elections unless the partnership has terminated, with all partnership affairs wound up. Dissolution under state law is not a termination for tax purposes.

18.21 Time Period for Buying Replacement Property

To defer tax, you generally must buy property similar or related in use *(18.22)* to the converted property within a fixed time period. The replacement period is either two, three, or four years:

1. A two-year replacement period applies for destroyed, damaged, or stolen property, whether used for business, investment, or personal purposes, but *see 18.2* for the four-year period for principal residences in Presidentially declared disaster areas.

   A two-year period also applies to condemned property other than business or investment real estate eligible for the three-year replacement period.

2. A three-year replacement period applies for condemned business or investment real estate, excluding inventory. However, the two-year and not the three-year period applies if the condemned business or investment real estate is replaced by your acquiring control of a corporation that owns the replacement property.

3. A four-year replacement period applies for a principal residence damaged in a Presidentially declared disaster; *see 18.2.*

The two-year period for damaged, destroyed, and stolen property *starts* on the date the property was destroyed, damaged, or stolen, and *ends* two years after the end of the year in which you realize a gain.

For condemnations, the two-year or three-year (investment or non-inventory business real estate) replacement period *starts* on the earlier of (1) the date you receive notification of the condemnation threat and (2) the date you dispose of the condemned property. The period *ends* two or three years after the end of the year in which gain on the condemnation is realized.

The four-year replacement period *starts* on the date the residence is involuntarily converted and *ends* four years after the end of the first taxable year in which any part of the gain is realized.

EXAMPLES

1. On January 10, 1999, a parcel of investment real estate is condemned; the parcel cost $15,000. On February 27, 1999, you received a check for $23,500 from the state. You may defer the tax on the gain of $8,500 if you invest at least $23,500 in other real estate not later than December 31, 2002, the end of the three-year replacement period.

2. Business property was contaminated by dangerous chemicals, and after the Environmental Protection Agency ordered businesses and residents to relocate, the property was sold to the local government under a threat of condemnation. The owner was paid the full pre-contamination fair market value for the property. The owner wanted to defer gain under the three-year replacement rule for condemnations. However, the IRS said that part of the gain was deferrable under the two-year rule and part under the three-year rule. There were two conversions: (1) the contamination, subject to the two-year replacement rule; and (2) the later condemnation, subject to the three-year rule.

   To determine the amount eligible for deferral for each period, an allocation must be made between the proceeds allocable to the destruction of the property and the proceeds allocable to the condemnation.

   According to the IRS, the burden for making the allocation between the two conversions rests with the owner. The government's payments are allocable to the condemnation and, therefore, eligible for the three-year replacement rule, only to the extent of the post-contamination value. Practically speaking, it may be advisable to make the replacement within the two-year period, as it may be difficult to show the contaminated land had any value after the contamination.

Advance payment of award. Gain is realized in the year compensation for the converted property exceeds the basis of the converted property. An advance payment of an award that exceeds the adjusted basis of the property starts the running of the replacement period.

An award is treated as received in the year that it is made available to you without restrictions, even if you contest the amount.

Replacement before actual condemnation. You may make a replacement after a threat of condemnation. If you buy property before the actual threat, it will not qualify as a replacement even though you still own it at the time of the actual condemnation.

Replacement by an estate. A person whose property was involuntarily converted may die before he or she makes a replacement. According to the IRS, his or her estate may not reinvest the proceeds within the allowed time and postpone tax on the gain. The Tax Court rejects the IRS position and has allowed tax deferral where the replacement was made by the deceased owner's estate. However, the Tax Court agreed with the IRS that a surviving spouse's investment in land did not defer tax on gain realized by her deceased husband on an involuntary conversion of his land. She had received his property as survivor of joint tenancy and could not, in making the investment, be considered as acting for his estate.

Giving IRS notice of replacement. If you have not bought replacement property by the time you file your return for the year of the involuntary conversion but you intend to do so, attach a statement to your return describing the conversion and the computation of gain, and state that you intend to make a timely replacement. Then, on the return for the year of replacement, attach a statement giving the details of your replacement property. This notice starts the running of the period of limitations for any tax on the gain. Failure to give notice keeps the period open. Similarly, a failure to give notice of an intention not to replace also keeps the period open. When you do not buy replacement property after making an election to postpone tax on the gain, file an amended return for the year in which gain was realized and pay the tax (if any) on the gain.

Assume you have a gain from an involuntary conversion and do not expect to reinvest the proceeds. You report the gain and pay the tax. In a later year, but within the prescribed time limits, you buy similar property. You may make an election to defer tax on the gain and file a claim for tax refund.

 Caution

Nullifying Deferral Election on Amended Return

If you elect to defer tax on a gain, intending to buy replacement property, but you fail to make a replacement within the time limit, you must file an amended return for the year of the gain and pay the tax that you had elected to defer. You also must file an amended return and report the gain not eligible for deferral if you invest in property that does not qualify as a replacement, or which costs less than the amount realized from the involuntary conversion.

However, if you elect to defer and make a timely qualifying replacement, you may not change your mind and pay tax on the gain in order to obtain a higher basis *(18.19)* for the replacement property. The Tax Court has agreed with the IRS that the election to defer is irrevocable once a qualified replacement is made within the time limits. Similarly, once you report to the IRS *(18.21)* that a qualified replacement has been made, you may not substitute other replacement property, even if the replacement period has not yet expired.

Planning Reminder

Extension of Time To Replace

Within the time limits, you must buy replacement property rather than merely contracting to do so. If you cannot replace property within the time required, ask your local District Director for additional time. Apply for an extension before the end of the period. If you apply for an extension within a reasonable time after the statutory period has run out, you must have a reasonable cause for the delay in asking for the extension.

18.22 Types of Qualifying Replacement Property

Although exact duplication is not required, the replacement generally must be *similar* or *related in use* to the property that was involuntarily converted in order to defer tax. Where *real property* held for productive use in a business or for investment is converted through a *condemnation* or threat of condemnation, the replacement test is more liberal. A replacement merely has to be of a *like kind* to the converted property. Under the *like-kind* test, the replacement of improved property by unimproved property qualifies; *see 6.1*.

Under the *related-use* test, the replacement of unimproved land for improved land does not qualify. Under the related-use test, a replacement generally must be closely related in function to the destroyed property. For example, a condemned personal residence must be replaced with another personal residence. The replacement of a house rented to a tenant with a house used as a personal residence does not qualify for tax deferral; the new house is not being used for the same purpose as the condemned one. This functional test, however, is not strictly applied to conversions of rental property. Here, the role of the owner toward the properties, rather than the functional use of the buildings, is reviewed. If an owner held both properties as investments and offered similar services and took similar business risks in both, the replacement may qualify.

You may own several parcels of property, one of which is condemned. You may want to use the condemnation award to make improvements on the other land such as drainage and grading. The IRS generally will not accept the improvements as a qualified replacement. However, an appeals court has rejected the IRS approach in one case.

If it is not feasible to reinvest the proceeds from the conversion of livestock because of soil contamination or other environmental contamination, then other property (including real property) used for farming purposes is treated as similar or related and qualifies as replacement property.

Deferral may be barred when buying a replacement from a relative. The gain deferral rules do not apply if you buy a replacement from a close relative or a related business organization unless the total gain you realized for the year on all involuntary conversions on which there are realized gains is $100,000 or less. In determining whether gains exceed $100,000, gains are not offset by losses. This rule applies to involuntary conversions occurring after June 8, 1997. Affected related parties are the same as defined for loss transactions discussed at *5.6*.

Buying controlling interest in a corporation. The replacement test may be satisfied by purchasing a controlling interest (80%) in a corporation owning property that is similar or related in service to the converted property.

Business and investment property in a disaster area. The similar or related-use tests do not have to be met when replacing business or investment property damaged or destroyed in a Presidentially declared disaster area. You may make a qualified replacement by buying any tangible property held for business use.

18.23 Cost of Replacement Property Determines Postponed Gain

To fully defer tax, the cost of the replacement property must be equal to or exceed the net proceeds from the conversion. If replacement cost is less than the adjusted basis of the converted property, you report the entire gain. If replacement cost is less than the amount realized on the conversion but more than the basis of the converted property, the difference between the amount realized and the cost of the replacement is reported as gain; you may elect to postpone tax on the balance of the gain. *See* Examples 1–3 below.

Condemnation award. The award received from a state authority may be reduced by expenses of getting the award such as legal, engineering, and appraisal fees. The treatment of special assessments and severance damages received when part of your property is condemned is explained at *18.24*. Payments made directly by the authority to your mortgagee may not be deducted from the gross award.

Do not include as part of the award interest paid on the award for delay in its payment; you report the interest as interest income. The IRS may treat as interest part of an award paid late, even though the award does not make any allocation for interest.

Relocation payments are not considered part of the condemnation award and are not treated as taxable income to the extent that they are spent for purposes of relocation; they increase basis of the newly acquired property.

Distinguish between insurance proceeds compensating you for loss of profits because of business interruption and those compensating you for the loss of property. Business interruption proceeds are fully taxed as ordinary income and may not be treated as proceeds of an involuntary conversion.

A single standard fire insurance policy may cover several assets. Assume a fire occurs, and in a settlement the proceeds are allocated to each destroyed item according to its fair market value before the fire. In comparing the allocated proceeds to the tax basis of each item, you find that on some items, you have realized a gain; that is, the proceeds exceed basis. On the other items, you have a loss; the proceeds are less than basis. According to the IRS, you may elect to defer tax on the gain items by buying replacement property. You do not treat the proceeds paid under the single policy as a unit, but as separate payments made for each covered item.

EXAMPLES

1. The cost basis of your four-family apartment house is $175,000. It is condemned to make way for a thruway. The net award from the state is $200,000. Your gain is $25,000. If you buy a similar apartment house for $175,000 or less, you report the entire $25,000 gain.
2. Using the same figures as in Example 1, except that you buy an apartment house for $185,000. Of the gain of $25,000, you report $15,000 as taxable gain ($200,000 – $185,000). You may elect to postpone the tax on the balance of the gain, or $10,000.
3. Using the same figures as in Example 1, but you buy an apartment house for $200,000. You may elect to postpone tax on the entire gain because you have invested all of the award in replacement property.

 Caution

Buying Replacement From Relative

Buying a replacement from a relative or related business organization will not defer gain unless total gains from involuntary conversions for the year are $100,000 or less.

18.24 Special Assessments and Severance Damages

When only part of a property parcel is *condemned* for a public improvement, the condemning authority may:

1. Levy a special assessment against the remaining property, claiming that it is benefited by the improvement. The authority usually deducts the assessment from the condemnation award.
2. Grant an award for severance damages if the condemnation of part of your property causes a loss in value or damage to the remaining property which you keep.

Special assessments reduce the amount of the gross condemnation award. If they exceed the award, the excess is added to the basis of the property. An assessment levied after the award is made may not be deducted from the award.

EXAMPLE

Two acres of a 10-acre tract are condemned for a new highway. The adjusted basis of the land is $30,000, or $3,000 per acre. The condemnation award is $10,000; the special assessment against the remaining eight acres is $2,500. The net gain on the condemnation is $1,500:

Condemnation award		$10,000
Less:		
Basis of two condemned acres	$6,000	
Special assessment	2,500	8,500
Net gain		$1,500

When both the condemnation award and severance damages are received, the condemnation is treated as two separate involuntary conversions: (1) A conversion of the condemned land. Here, the condemnation award is applied against the basis of the condemned land to determine gain or loss on its conversion; and (2) a conversion of part of the remaining land in the sense that its utility has been reduced by condemnation, for which severance damages are paid.

Net severance damages reduce the basis of the retained property. Net severance damages are the total severance damages, reduced by expenses in obtaining the damages and by any special assessment withheld from the condemnation award. If the damages exceed basis, gain is realized. Tax may be deferred on the gain through the purchase of replacement property under the "similar or related in use test" at *18.22*, such as adjacent land or restoration of the property to its original condition.

Allocating the proceeds between the condemnation award and severance damages will either reduce the gain or increase the loss realized on the condemned land. The IRS will allow such a division only when the condemnation authority specifically identifies part of the award as severance damage in the contract or in an itemized statement or closing sheet. The Tax Court, however, has allowed an allocation in the absence of earmarking where the state considered severance damages, and the value of the condemned land was small in comparison to the damages suffered by the remaining property. To avoid a dispute with the IRS, make sure the authority makes this breakdown. Without such identification, the IRS will treat the entire proceeds as consideration for the condemned property.

18.25 Reporting Gains From Casualties

If an involuntary conversion was the result of a *theft* or *casualty,* you have to prepare Form 4684. To report net gains, Form 4684 will direct you to Form 1040, Schedule D, or Form 4797, depending on the type of property involved. Generally, use of Form 4797 reflects the netting requirements for involuntary conversions of business, rental, or royalty property under Section 1231; *see 44.8.*

If the conversion occurred because of a *condemnation,* you use Form 4797 for business or investment property and Schedule D for personal-use property.

Filing Instruction

Business and Income-Producing Property

Follow the instructions to Form 4684 for reporting gains or losses from casualties and thefts of property used in a business or held for the production of income.

Deducting Job Costs and Other Miscellaneous Expenses

Deductible miscellaneous expenses cover a wide and varied range of items, such as employee travel and entertainment expenses, work clothes expenses, union and employee professional dues, investment expenses, legal expenses, tax preparation expenses, and educational expenses. They also share a common limitation: the 2% adjusted gross income (AGI) floor. If your expenses do not exceed this floor, you may not deduct them. If the expenses exceed the floor, only the excess is deductible on Schedule A, as explained in *19.1*. Some job-related deductions, such as moving expenses and impairment-related work expenses, are not subject to the 2% AGI floor.

In addition to the 2% AGI floor, employees who incur unreimbursed meal and entertainment costs face this further restriction: Only 50% of meal and entertainment costs are deductible.

Miscellaneous deductions, except for gambling losses, are subject to the 3% reduction to itemized deductions *(13.7)* if your adjusted gross income exceeds $126,600 ($63,300 if you are married and file separate returns).

Miscellaneous Expenses on Schedule A

19.1 2% AGI Floor Reduces Miscellaneous Deductions

A floor of 2% of adjusted gross income (AGI) applies to the total of most miscellaneous deductions that are claimed on Schedule A of Form 1040. AGI is the amount on Line 33 of Form 1040. The purpose of the floor is to reduce or eliminate such deductions. Only expenses above the floor are deductible.

If your 1999 AGI exceeds $126,600, or $63,300 if married filing separately, deductible miscellaneous expenses (after applying the 2% AGI floor) are then subject to a further reduction under the 3% reduction computation discussed at *13.7*.

Miscellaneous expenses subject to the 2% AGI floor include:

- Unreimbursed travel, meals, and entertainment expenses of employees, *20.1* and *20.31*
- Reimbursed job expenses or expense allowances under non-accountable plans, *20.34*
- Union dues, *19.5*
- Professional and business association dues, *19.5*
- Work clothes expenses, *19.6*
- Cost of looking for a new job, *19.7*
- Job agency fees, *19.7*
- Tax advice and preparation fees, *19.25*
- Appraisal fees related to casualty losses and charitable property contributions, *19.25*
- Investment expenses, such as IRA custodial fees, safe-deposit rentals, and fees to investment counselors, *19.24*
- Employee home office expenses, *19.13*
- Legal fees, *19.26*
- Education costs, *19.15*
- Business bad debt on a loan made to your employer to protect your job, *5.35*

Miscellaneous expenses not subject to the 2% AGI floor include:

- Casualty and theft losses from income-producing property
- Impairment-related work expenses for handicapped employees, *19.4*
- Gambling losses up to gambling income, *11.3*
- Estate tax attributable to income in respect of a decedent, *11.17*
- The deduction for repayment of amounts held under a claim of right, *2.9*
- Amortizable bond premium on bonds purchased before October 23, 1986, *4.17*
- Unrecovered investments in pension on deceased retiree's final return, *7.22*
- Jury duty fees turned over to employer, *12.2*

EXAMPLES

1. You pay union dues of $280, work clothes costs of $300, and $150 for the preparation of your tax return. Your adjusted gross income (AGI) is $25,000. Your miscellaneous deduction on Schedule A after applying the 2% floor is $230:

Union dues	$280
Work clothes	300
Tax preparation	150
	$730
Less: 2% of $25,000	500
Deductible amount	$230

2. Your adjusted gross income (AGI) is $90,000. You pay the following deductible miscellaneous expenses:

Professional dues	$100
Investment counsel fee	300
Safe-deposit box	50
Tax preparation fee	500
Unreimbursed travel expenses	800
	$1,750

Since the 2% floor of $1,800 (2% × $90,000) exceeds your miscellaneous expenses, none of the expenses are deductible.

2% AGI Floor

Most miscellaneous deductions are subject to a floor of 2% of your adjusted gross income (AGI), which may limit or bar a deduction. Your AGI is the amount on Line 33 of Form 1040.

19.2 Effect of 2% AGI Floor on Deductions

The table below shows the effect of the 2% AGI floor on miscellaneous deductible expenses. A higher bracket taxpayer may also be subject to the 3% reduction to itemized deductions discussed at *13.7*.

If your adjusted gross income (AGI) is—	Miscellaneous expenses must exceed this amount for a deduction—
$10,000	$200
20,000	400
30,000	600
40,000	800
50,000	1,000
60,000	1,200
70,000	1,400
80,000	1,600
90,000	1,800
100,000	2,000
200,000	4,000

19.3 Checklist of Job Expenses Subject to the 2% AGI Floor

The following expenses that are job related—ranging from professional dues and subscriptions to employment agency fees—are subject to the 2% AGI floor and so you may be unable to deduct them; *see 19.2*. Generally, you must file Form 2106 to claim job-related expenses that were not reimbursed by your employer. You enter your expenses and any reimbursements on Form 2106, and the allowable amount is then transferred to Line 20 of Schedule A (unreimbursed employee expenses), where it is subject to the 2% AGI floor along with other miscellaneous deductions; *see 19.1*. If you are using the standard mileage rate *(43.1)* for 1999 vehicle expenses, and you were not reimbursed by your employer for any job expenses, you may file Form 2106-EZ to report your auto and other job expenses.

You may enter your unreimbursed expenses directly on Line 20 of Schedule A without having to complete Form 2106 or Form 2106-EZ if you are not claiming any job-related travel, local transportation, meal, or entertainment expenses and you received no employer reimbursement at all for any of your other job costs (such as education expenses, union dues, or uniforms).

 Filing Instruction

Form 2106 or 2106-EZ

You generally must report your job-related expenses, and any employer reimbursements, on Form 2106. Form 2106-EZ is a shorter form that you may use if none of your job expenses are reimbursed and you deduct car expenses, if any, using the IRS flat mileage allowance.

Agency fees for job, *19.7*
Airfares, *20.5*
Auto club membership, *43.2*
Auto expenses, *43.1*
Books used on the job, *19.5*
Bond costs, *19.24*
Business bad debt for loan to employer, *5.33* and *5.35*
Car insurance premiums, *43.2*
Cleaning costs, *19.6*
Commerce association dues, *19.5*
Commuting costs, *20.2*
Computers, *19.9*
Convention trips, *20.12* and *20.14*
Correspondence course, *19.16*
Depreciation, *42.1*
Dues, *19.5*
Educational expenses, *19.15–19.23*
Employment agency fees, *19.7*
Entertainment expenses, *20.15–20.29*
Equipment, *19.9–19.11*
Foreign travel costs, *20.11* and *20.14*

Furniture, *19.13*
Garage rent, *43.2*
Gasoline, *43.2*
Gasoline taxes, *43.2*
Gifts, *20.25*
Home office expenses, *19.13*
Hotel costs, *20.5*
House-hunting costs, *12.7*
Instruments, *19.11*
Labor union dues, *19.5*
Laundry, *19.6*
Legal expenses, *19.26*
Local transportation, *20.1*
Lodging, *20.5*
Magazines, *19.5*
Malpractice liability premiums, *40.6*
Meals, *20.3* and *20.4*
Medical examinations, *17.2*
Membership dues and fees, *19.5*
Motel charges, *20.5*
Moving expenses, *12.7*
Parking fees, *43.2*

Passport fees for business travel, *20.11*
Pay turned over to employer, *2.9*
Periodicals, *19.5*
Protective clothing, *19.6*
Rail fares, *20.5*
Reimbursed expenses, *20.30–20.34*
Safety helmets, *19.6*
Safety shoes, *19.6*
Secretarial convention, *20.12*
Subscriptions, *19.5*
Taxi fares, *20.5*
Telephone calls, *19.14*
Toll charges, *43.2*
Tools, *19.11*
Trade association dues, *19.5*
Transportation and travel expenses, *20.1*
Tuition, *19.15–19.23*
Typewriter, *19.10*
Uniforms, *19.6*
Union dues, *19.5*
Work clothes, *19.6*

19.4 Job Expenses Not Subject to the 2% AGI Floor

Impairment-related work expenses. Unreimbursed impairment-related work expenses are reported on Form 2106 (or Form 2106-EZ where eligible) and then the unreimbursed portion is entered on Line 27 of Schedule A as a miscellaneous itemized deduction that is *not* subject to the 2% AGI floor. You have to show:

1. You are handicapped. A handicapped person must have a physical or mental disability which results in a functional limitation to employment or which substantially limits one or more major life activities. Generally, showing blindness or deafness will meet this test, but other disabilities that impair your ability to walk, speak, breathe, or perform manual tasks also may qualify if they limit the ability to work.

2. You incur the expenses in order to work. The expenses must be ordinary and necessary to allow you to work. Attendant care services at a place of employment that are necessary for you to work are also deductible.

Expenses of performing artists. As a performing artist, you may deduct job expenses from gross income, whether or not itemized deductions are claimed, *see 12.2.*

You report the performing artist expenses on Form 2106 (or Form 2106-EZ where eligible) and enter the total as a "write-in amount" on Line 32 of Form 1040, instead of on Schedule A. Write "QPA" next to Line 32. If you do not meet the tests, the expenses are deducted on Schedule A subject to the 2% AGI floor.

Moving expenses. Moving expenses to a new job location are not subject to the 2% AGI floor; see *12.3.*

19.5 Dues and Subscriptions

You may deduct as miscellaneous itemized deductions, subject to the 2% AGI floor on Schedule A, dues paid to a:

- Professional society if you are a salaried lawyer, accountant, teacher, physician, or other professional
- Trade association if it is conducted for the purpose of furthering the business interests of its members
- Stock exchange if you are a securities dealer
- Community "booster" club conducted to attract tourists and settlers to the locality where the members do business
- Chamber of Commerce if it is conducted to advance the business interests of its members

Union costs. Union members may deduct as "miscellaneous" itemized deductions union dues, and initiation fees. Similarly, non-union employees may deduct monthly service charges to a union. An assessment paid for unemployment benefits is deductible if payment is required as a condition of remaining in the union and holding a union job. Voluntary payments to a union unemployment benefit or strike fund are not deductible.

No deduction is allowed for mandatory contributions to a union pension fund applied toward the purchase of a retirement annuity; the contributions are treated as the cost of the annuity. Furthermore, to the extent that an assessment covers sick, accident, or death benefits payable to you or your family, it is not deductible. Similarly, an assessment for a construction fund to build union recreation centers was disallowed by the Tax Court, even though the payment was required for keeping the job.

Campaign costs for running for union office are not deductible.

Subscriptions. Subject to the 2% AGI floor, you may claim as miscellaneous itemized deductions unreimbursed payments for job-related subscriptions to professional journals and trade magazines.

19.6 Uniforms and Work Clothes

The cost of uniforms and other apparel, including their cleaning, laundering, and repair, is deductible *only* if the clothes are:

1. Required to keep your job; *and*
2. Not suitable for wear when not working.

The deduction is subject to the 2% AGI floor.

Planning Reminder

Exceptions to the 2% Floor

Impairment-related expenses and job expenses of performing artists are not subject to the 2% AGI floor.

Filing Tip

Life Insurance Agents and Food Deliverers

Statutory employees, such as full-time life insurance salespersons, may deduct expenses on Schedule C and so avoid the 2% AGI floor; *see 40.6* for further details.

Special work clothes. Courts have held that the cost of special work clothes that protect you from injury is deductible even if you are not required to wear them to keep your job. However, you may not deduct the cost of special clothing, such as aprons and overalls, which protect your regular street clothing. Nor may you deduct the cost of ordinary clothes used as work clothes on the grounds that: (1) they get harder use than customary garments receive; (2) they are soiled after a day's work and cannot be worn socially; or (3) they were purchased for your convenience to save wear and tear on your better clothes. For example, a sanitation inspector, a machinist's helper, a carpenter, and a telephone repairman were not allowed to deduct the cost of their work clothes.

Employer allowance. An allowance paid by your employer for work clothes or a uniform is not reported as income, unless you do not substantiate the expenses to your employer. If you do substantiate the expenses, those exceeding the reimbursement are reported on Form 2106, and the deduction is subject to the 2% AGI floor; *see 20.30.*

High-fashion work clothes. That your job requires you to wear expensive clothing is not a basis for deducting the cost of the clothes if the clothing is suitable for wear off the job.

Deductions allowed. Deductions for costs of uniforms and work clothes have been allowed to:

Airline pilot
Bakery salesperson—for a uniform with a company label
Baseball player
Bus driver
Cement finisher for gloves, overshoes, and rubber boots
Civilian faculty members of a military school
Commercial fisherman for protective clothing, such as oil cloths, gloves, and boots
Dairy worker for rubber boots, white shirts, trousers, and cap worn only while inside the dairy
Entertainer for theatrical clothing used solely for performances
Exotic dancer for breast implants used as a "stage prop" essential to her business; *see* Example 8 in *19.8*

Factory foreman for white coat bearing the word "foreman" and the name of the company
Factory worker for safety shoes
Firefighter
Hospital attendant for work clothes; he came in contact with patients having contagious diseases
Jockey
Letter carrier
Meat cutter for special white shoes
Musician for formal wear
Paint machine operator for high top shoes and long leather gloves
Plumber for special shoes and gloves
Police officer
Railroad conductor
Railroad firefighter for boots, leather gloves, raincoat, caps, and work gloves

Filing Tip

Uniform Required

Your claim of a work clothes deduction is helped if your employer requires you to wear a uniform. Uniform costs of reservists and service persons are discussed at *35.8.*

EXAMPLES

1. A painter may not deduct the cost of work clothing consisting of a white cap, a white shirt, white bib overalls, and standard work shoes. The clothing is not distinctive in character as a uniform would be. That his union requires him to wear such clothing does not make it a deductible expense.

2. A tennis pro who taught at private clubs was not allowed to deduct the cost of tennis outfits or shoes required for his job. He did not wear them outside of work and argued that he replaced the shoes every few weeks to reduce the chances of injury. However, the Tax Court upheld the IRS's disallowance of his deductions because the clothes and shoes are suitable for everyday wear; warm-up suits and tennis clothes are fashionable and frequently worn as casual wear. Furthermore, there was no evidence that his tennis shoes reduced chances of injury.

19.7 Expenses of Looking for a New Job

You may deduct expenses of looking for a new job in the *same line of work,* whether or not a new job is found. The deduction is subject to the 2% AGI floor. If you are unemployed when seeking a new job, and the period of unemployment has been substantial, the IRS may disallow the deduction.

Filing Tip

Cleaning and Laundering

If you are allowed to deduct the cost of work clothes and uniforms, you also may deduct the cost of cleaning and laundering them. Also, courts have allowed the cost of cleaning and laundering to be deducted in situations where:

- The clothes could only be worn one day at a time because they became too dirty.
- Dirty clothes were a hazard; they became baggy and might have gotten caught in machinery.
- Clothes were worn only at work and a place for changing clothes was provided by the employer.
- A meat cutter had to wear clean work clothes at all times.

EXAMPLE

The IRS disallowed the driving expenses of an unemployed secretary on the ground that she was not currently employed. The Tax Court disagreed and held that for purposes of deducting job-hunting expenses, she could still be considered in the business of being a secretary. She had worked as an administrative secretary with Toyota in San Francisco. The firm relocated, resulting in a 100-mile-per-day commute. She quit her job at the end of January 1984. From February to November 1984, she drove her Cadillac El Dorado over 4,600 miles looking for a new job. The Tax Court allowed her a depreciation deduction of $2,880 and $981 for car operating costs.

Expenses of seeking your *first job* are not deductible, even if a job is obtained. Also, expenses of looking for a job in a different line of work are not deductible, even if you get the job.

The IRS may also dispute the deduction of search expenses of a previously employed professional who forms a partnership.

EXAMPLE

A CPA working for a firm decided to go out on his own. After a period of investigation, he formed a partnership with another CPA. The IRS disallowed his deduction of search expenses, claiming his expenses were incurred in a new business. As an employee he was in a different business from that of a self-employed practitioner. Thus, the expenses should be capitalized as a cost of setting up or organizing the partnership. The Tax Court disagreed, allowing the deduction. The travel expenses were incurred to seek work as a CPA, whether as a self-employed or employed CPA.

Travel expenses. If you travel to find a new job in the same line of work, such as an interview in a distant city, you may deduct travel expenses, including living costs. If, during the trip, you also do personal visiting, you may deduct the transportation expenses if the trip was primarily related to your job search. Time spent on personal activity is compared with time spent looking for a job to determine the primary purpose of the trip. If the transportation expenses to and from the destination are not deductible, you may still deduct the expenses of seeking a new job while you are away.

Are you between jobs? If you are between jobs and you continue to see and entertain your former customers, the IRS holds that you may not deduct the cost of entertainment and other business expenses during this period on the ground that you are not in business and earning income. However, the Tax Court in the following case allowed the deduction.

EXAMPLE

Haft was a successful jewelry salesman earning as much as $60,000 a year. In the fall of one year, he left his employer and started to look for a new connection. During the following year, he continued to maintain contacts with his former customers by entertaining buyers and their representatives. He deducted the expenses of entertaining and other business costs. The IRS disallowed the deduction, claiming he was not in business. The court disagreed. His lack of business income was temporary and resulted from a period of transition which lasted a reasonable time.

19.8 Unusual Job Expenses

The following are not typical deductible expenses. However, deductions in the following cases have been allowed.

EXAMPLES

1. *Shoeshine expense of a pilot.* Company rules required a commercial airline pilot to look neat, keep his hair cut, and wear conservative black shoes, properly shined. The pilot deducted as a business expense $100 for his haircuts and $25 for his shoe shines. The IRS disallowed the deductions, but the Tax Court allowed the cost of the shoe shines. The shoes were of a military type which he wore only with his pilot's uniform. The cost of keeping up a uniform is deductible. The haircuts were merely nondeductible personal expenses.

Caution

First Job

You may not deduct the expenses of seeking your first job.

Filing Tip

Employment Agency Fee

If your new employer pays the fee under an agreement with an agency, you may disregard the payment for tax purposes. However, if you pay the fee and deduct it as a job search expense and in a later year you are reimbursed by your employer, you must report the reimbursement as taxable income to the extent you received a tax benefit from the earlier deduction; *see 11.6.*

A company interested in your services may invite you to a job interview and agree to pay all of the trip expenses to its office, even if you are not hired. The company payment is tax free up to your actual expenses.

2. *Depreciation on furnishings bought by executive for his company office.* Following a quarrel with an interior decorator, a sales manager bought his own office furniture when his firm moved to new quarters. Rather than complain or ask for reimbursement, he footed the bill and deducted depreciation. The IRS disallowed the deduction, claiming the expense was that of his company. The Tax Court allowed the deduction. The manager's action was unusual, but prudent. He did not want to cause difficulties, and at the same time had to maintain his image as a successful manager. His expenses for furniture were appropriate and helpful.

3. *Salesman's cost of operating a private plane.* Sherman flew his own plane to visit clients in six southern states and deducted $18,000 as operating costs of the plane. The IRS disallowed the deduction, claiming there was no business reason for the plane. He could have taken commercial flights or used a company car to reach his clients. Furthermore, his company did not reimburse him for the private airplane costs, although it would cover costs of his car and commercial air travel. Finally, the amount of airplane expenses was unreasonable compared to his salary of $25,000. Sherman convinced the Tax Court that use of a private airplane was the only reasonable way he could cover his six-state sales area. He showed that most of his clients were not near commercial airports. Although the airplane costs were large in relation to his salary, they were still reasonable and, therefore, deductible.

4. *Executive's purchase of blazers for sales force.* Jetty, the president of an oil equipment manufacturing firm, thought that he could generate goodwill for the company if employees who attended industrial trade shows wore a blazer and vest set in the company colors. He personally paid and deducted $6,725 for 27 blazers and vests. The IRS disallowed the deduction on the grounds that it was a company expense and that Jetty should have sought reimbursement from the company.

    The Tax Court allowed the deduction. Paying for the clothes was a legitimate business expense for Jetty since he depended on bonuses for a large portion of his pay, and, as company president, he had responsibility for seeing to it that there were profits to share in. Furthermore, the outlay was not the type of expense covered by the company's manual on expense reimbursements.

5. *Repayment of layoff benefits to restore pension credit.* When he was laid off, an employee received a lump-sum payment from his company based on his salary and years of service. When he was rehired a year later, he repaid the lump sum in order to restore his pension credits and other benefit rights. The IRS ruled that he may deduct the repayment as a condition of being rehired; the repayment was required to restore employee benefits.

6. *Teaching supplies.* The IRS does not allow teachers a deduction for school supplies. Some courts have been lenient and have allowed teachers to deduct out-of-pocket expenses. In one case, however, a teacher could not convince a court that his deduction for the cost of paper, pens, glue, and other supplies was a business expense. He could not support his claim that the school did not supply enough equipment.

7. *Politician's expenses.* Elected officials may incur out-of-pocket expenses in excess of the allowances received from the government. They may deduct as miscellaneous deductions their payment of office expenses such as salaries, office rent, and supplies. Part-time officials may claim the deduction. The expenses are deductible even if they exceed the official's income.

8. *Depreciation for exotic dancer's breast implants.* Hess, an exotic dancer, enlarged her breasts to the abnormal size of 56N and claimed a $2,088 depreciation deduction for their cost. The IRS disallowed the deduction, claiming that cosmetic surgery is a personal expense. The Tax Court disagreed. Hess's expenses were incurred solely in furtherance of her business and not for her own personal benefit. The breast implants were not of the kind that women usually get to enhance their appearance. Rather, Hess enlarged her breasts to a "freakish" size to substantially increase her annual income, which she did. The court also compared the implants to special work clothes *(19.6)*, required for a job and not for personal wear. As an exotic dancer, Hess's large breasts are like a "costume" needed to keep her job. Although she could not remove them daily, she would have, if possible, because they caused her serious medical problems.

Computers, Phones, and Home Office Costs of Employees

19.9 Computers and Cellular Phones

Computers (and peripherals) and cellular phones are treated as "listed property" subject to deduction restrictions: To get a first-year expensing deduction *(42.3)* or to claim any type of depreciation, the computer or cellular phone must be used for the convenience of your employer and also be required as a condition of your job. The IRS strictly interprets these requirements.

Computer. A letter from your employer stating that a computer is needed for your position does not by itself satisfy the deduction tests. Even where your employer encourages use of a personal computer that is used for basic job requirements, the IRS requires proof that you need your own computer to do your job because your employer does not provide one, or because the computer supplied by your employer is not adequate for your job. In the following Examples, the IRS disallowed depreciation writeoffs.

Court Decision

Tax Court Allows Computer Deduction

The Tax Court allowed a first-year expensing deduction to a working couple who used the same home computer given these facts: The husband, a professor, used it to store historical data; the wife, a state transportation planner, used it to do extensive number crunching. What apparently won the decision for the couple was evidence that (1) the husband did not have access to a computer at the university, and (2) the state office in which the wife worked did not have funds to buy a computer. The court held that the use of the computer was necessary for them to properly do their jobs, and as the purchase of a computer spared their employers from having to provide them with computers, the purchase was for the employers' convenience.

In a later case, a telemarketing sales manager was allowed a first-year expensing deduction for a home computer and printer used to prepare reports. The key to winning the deduction was her supervisor's testimony that as a mid-level manager, she could not enter the office after regular hours to use a company computer, and that she was able to keep up with the volume of sales reports she was required to submit by using her home computer and accessing information via modem.

EXAMPLES

1. An electric company offered to help pay for its engineers' personal computers where this would improve productivity. Qualifying engineers received extra pay and had to buy a computer meeting company specifications, take approved computer courses, and agree to restrictions on resale of the computer. An engineer bought a computer and used it 95% of the time for writing business memos and reports, and studying business flow charts. He does not use the computer for entertainment.

   The IRS held that although the engineer's computer was work related and benefitted his employer, buying a computer was not required for his job; it was not "inextricably related" to proper job performance. Further, his participation in the employer's computer program was optional, not mandatory.

2. A professor of nursing, trying to keep her temporary position, bought a personal computer, needing a word processor for independent research papers and to document her qualifications for research grants. The research and external grant support were implied university requirements for faculty appointments. She did not have access to university word-processing equipment during regular work hours; and because of her classroom responsibilities, her research and grant development work had to be done on her own time. To help her pursue outside grants, the university bought her a "modem" that allowed a phone hook-up with its computer at night. Her computer was used 100% for research and grant work.

   As in Example 1, the IRS held that use of the computer was not "inextricably related" to proper job performance and did not qualify for a depreciation writeoff. Furthermore, there was no evidence that employees who did not use computers were professionally disadvantaged.

3. The IRS held that an insurance agent could not deduct depreciation for a laptop computer he used to help develop insurance plans for clients. The insurance company encouraged its agents to buy the computer because office computers were not generally accessible. According to the IRS, it is not enough that the agent's productivity increased or that he used the computer solely for business. Purchasing the computer was optional, not a mandatory job requirement. Employees who did not purchase computers were not professionally disadvantaged.

4. The IRS barred a third-grade teacher from deducting the cost of a Macintosh computer because it was not required for her job. She bought the computer using an interest-free loan from the school after the school decided that report cards and student evaluations would have to be prepared on a Macintosh instead of being written. The Tax Court and an appeals court sided with the IRS. It may have been convenient for the teacher to use a home computer but it was not required. Other teachers were able to timely complete their duties using school computers.

Cellular phones. The IRS has not released specific guidelines or rulings covering deduction requirements for cellular phones. In general, the "convenience of the employer" and "job condition" tests apply.

Claiming a deduction. If you can meet the "convenience of the employer" and "job condition" tests for a computer or cellular phone purchased in 1999, and you have records to prove that the unit is used more than 50% of the time for your job, you may write off up to $19,000 of the cost under the first-year expensing rules; *see 42.3* or regular five-year MACRS depreciation rates may be used; *see 42.10*. If business use of the unit is 50% or less, you may not use first-year expensing or regular MACRS but you may claim straight-line depreciation.

First-year expensing or depreciation is claimed on Form 4562 and then entered on Form 2106 or Form 2106-EZ along with other job-related costs. The deduction from Form 2106 or Form 2106-EZ is subject to the 2% AGI floor for miscellaneous deductions on Schedule A; *see 19.1*. If business use in a later year is 50% or less, *see 42.10* for recapture rules.

You need to keep records documenting your percentage of business use for a computer or cellular phone.

19.10 Calculators, Copiers, Fax Machines, and Typewriters

The listed property requirements applied to computers and cellular phones *(19.9)* do not apply to calculators, copiers, fax machines, adding machines, and typewriters. This means that the restrictive convenience of the employer and job condition rules do not apply. However, to depreciate the cost of such equipment, you should be ready to prove that you need the equipment for your job, and keep a record of the time it is used for business. To claim first-year expensing *(42.3)*, rather than regular depreciation, you must use the equipment *more* than 50% of the time for business.

19.11 Small Tools

If you furnished your own small tools used on your job, you may deduct their cost if they are not expected to last beyond a year. The deduction is subject to the 2% AGI floor. The cost of tools with a useful life of more than a year must be recovered through depreciation or first-year expensing; *see 42.3*. Be prepared to substantiate your deduction with receipts showing the cost and type of tools purchased, and the business necessity for them.

19.12 Automobile Used for Work

If you buy a car that you use for work, you generally may claim the IRS mileage allowance or deduct actual unreimbursed expenses on Form 2106. Commuting costs are generally not deductible unless you are driving to a temporary work location; *see 20.2*. If you claim actual expenses, you are allowed to deduct depreciation only if use of the car is required for the job and for the convenience of the employer. For a car bought in 1999, the maximum depreciation deduction is $3,060, reduced by the percentage of personal use.

The IRS standard mileage allowance is discussed at *43.1*.
Depreciation rules, including annual deduction limits, are at *43.3*.

19.13 Employee Home Office Deductions

The tax law has been drafted to prevent employees from deducting the expenses of an office at a home. The tests for deducting home office expenses are discussed at *40.12*. Even if an employee should meet one of the rules, such as doing administrative work at home, the employee must also show that the home office was required for the "convenience of his or her employer" in order to claim the deduction.

EXAMPLE

Charlie, a teacher, has a small office at school where he can grade papers and tests, work on lesson plans, and meet with parents and students. The school does not require him to work at home, but he prefers to use the office he has set up in his home, and does not use the office the school provides. Although Charlie's home office is used for the administrative duties of teaching, Charlie may not deduct his home office expenses because he does not meet the convenience of the employer test. His employer provides him with an office at school and does not require him to work at home.

 Caution

Deducting Cellular Phone Costs
Cellular phone equipment must be used for the convenience of the employer and be a condition of your employment for you to be able to claim a depreciation deduction for the cost.

 Filing Instruction

Office for Sideline Business
If you are an employee and also have a sideline business for which you use a home office, the office expenses are deductible if the office is used regularly and exclusively as your principal place of business or a meeting place with clients, customers, or patients. If the tests are met, you claim your home office expenses as a self-employed person on Form 8829, which you attach to Schedule C. The deduction may not exceed your income from the sideline business. *See* Chapter 40 for a sample Form 8829 and other deduction details.

Deducting Telephone Costs

To support your deduction, keep a record of business calls made at home or anywhere outside your employer's office.

19.14 Telephone Costs

For business calls made outside of your employer's office or at home, keep a record or diary of business calls to support your deduction. To avoid the problem of allocating the costs of a single home phone for both business and personal use, consider installing a separate home phone for business use only. For long-distance business calls, you might ask the phone company to transfer the charges to your office phone.

Deduction barred for basic charge of first phone line. You may not claim as a deductible home office expense any part of the standard monthly charge for the first telephone line into your home. This disallowance rule only applies to the first telephone line. If you have more than one telephone line and use additional lines in a home office, costs for these lines remain deductible, subject to the restrictions at *19.13*. The restriction does not affect deductibility of long-distance calls, phone rentals, or optional services such as call waiting, call forwarding, three-way calling, or extra directory listings.

Deductible Education Costs

19.15 Types of Deductible Education Costs

If you improve your job or professional skills by attending continuing education or refresher classes, advanced academic courses, or vocational training, you may be able to deduct your expenses. As a self-employed business owner or professional, allowable expenses are deductible on Schedule C. However, as an employee, the tax benefit of an educational expense deduction is limited because the expenses are miscellaneous itemized deductions, which, together with any other miscellaneous expenses, are deductible on Schedule A only to the extent that the total exceeds 2% of your adjusted gross income; *see 19.1*.

To deduct education costs, you must show that the following conditions are met:

1. You are employed or self-employed;

2. You already meet the minimum requirements of your job, business, or profession;

3. The course maintains or improves your job or professional skills, or you are required by your employer or by law to take the course to keep your present salary or position; *and*

4. The course does *not* lead to qualification for a new profession or business. The cost of courses preparing you for a new profession is not deductible, even if you take them to improve your skills or to meet your employer's requirements. This rule prevents the deduction of law school costs; *see 19.17*. Furthermore, the cost of a bar review course or CPA review course is not deductible because it leads to a new profession as an attorney or CPA. If courses lead to qualification for a new business or profession, no deduction is allowed even if you keep your current position.

Qualifying for New Business

Courses that qualify you for a new business or profession are not deductible even if you have no intention of entering that business or profession.

If your courses meet the above requirements you may deduct the following education costs on Schedule C if self-employed or on Schedule A subject to the 2% AGI floor if the courses are related to your job:

1. Tuition, textbooks, fees, equipment, and other aids required by the courses.

2. Local transportation costs as discussed at *19.22*.

3. Travel to and from a school away from home, and lodging and 50% of meals while at school away from home; *see 19.22*. The IRS will not disallow traveling expenses to attend a school away from home or in a foreign country merely because you could have taken the course in a local school. But it may disallow your board and lodging and expenses at the school if your stay lasts longer than a year.

Further details of the deduction requirements are explained at 19.16.

Nondeductible courses. The cost of courses preparing you for a new profession or for meeting the minimum requirements for your job is not deductible, even if you take them to improve your skills or to meet your employer's requirements *(see 19.16)*.

19.16 Work-Related Tests for Education Costs

You must meet an employment test to deduct educational expenses. Educational costs are not deductible if you are unemployed or inactive in a business or profession. The cost of "brush-up" courses taken in anticipation of resuming work is also not deductible. However, in one case, a court allowed an unemployed teacher to deduct the cost of tuition, fees, and books where the IRS conceded that the teacher, although unemployed, remained in the teaching profession while attending college classes.

You are not considered unemployed when you take courses during a vacation or temporary leave of absence; *see 19.21*.

Course does not meet minimum standards. You may not deduct the cost of courses taken to meet the minimum requirements of your job. The minimum requirements of a position are based on a review of your employer's standards, the laws and regulations of the state you live in, and the standards of your profession or business. That you are presently employed does not in itself prove that you have met the minimum standards for your job.

If minimum standards change after you enter a job or profession, courses you take to meet the new standards are deductible.

The minimum standards for teachers are discussed at *19.19*.

Course must maintain or improve job skills. To be deductible, the education must maintain or improve your current job skills. That you are established in your position and that persons in similar positions usually pursue such education indicates that the courses are taken to maintain and improve job skills. However, the IRS may not allow a deduction for a general education course that is a prerequisite for a job-related course.

If the courses lead to a change of position or promotion within the same occupation, a deduction for their cost will usually be allowed if your new duties involve the same general type of work. If, as a consequence of taking a job-related course, you receive a substantial advancement and the IRS questions the deduction of the course costs, be prepared to prove that you took the course primarily to maintain or improve skills of your existing job. However, if the course leads to qualification for a new profession, the IRS will disallow a deduction even if the course also improves current job skills.

Courses must not lead to qualification for a new profession. If a course improves your current job skills but leads to qualification for a new profession, the course is not deductible. For example, a deduction is not allowed for the cost of law school or medical school courses since they prepare you for a new profession. This is true even if you do not intend to practice medicine or law; *see 19.17* and *19.18*. The IRS with Tax Court approval has also held that a deduction is not allowed for the cost of college courses that are part of a degree program, such as a bachelor of arts or science degree.

If you are practicing your profession, the cost of courses leading to a specialty within that profession is deductible.

EXAMPLE

A practicing dentist returned to school full time to study orthodontics while continuing his practice on a part-time basis. When he finished his training, he limited his work to orthodontics. The IRS ruled he could deduct the cost of his studies. His post-graduate schooling improved his professional skills as a dentist. It did not qualify him for a new profession.

Further education required by employer or law. If, to retain your present job or rate of pay, your employer requires you to obtain further education, you may deduct the cost of the courses. The fact that you also qualified for a raise in pay or a substantial advancement in your position after completing the courses should not bar the deduction.

The employer's requirement must be for a bona fide business reason, not merely to benefit you. Only the minimum courses necessary for the retention of your job or rate of pay are considered by the IRS as taken to meet your employer's requirement. You must show any courses beyond your employer's minimum requirements were taken to maintain or improve your job skills.

 Filing Tip

Are MBA Courses Deductible?

The cost of MBA courses is deductible if the courses enhance the skills required in your current position, are not a minimum job requirement, and do not qualify you for a new business. The IRS may question in a particular case whether there has been a change of business, particularly where taking the courses leads to a promotion. For a deduction, the courses must be related to your existing job responsibilities. The Tax Court has allowed deductions for MBA expenses where individuals with some managerial or administrative experience took the courses to improve job skills.

If your employer requires a master's degree as a minimum entrance requirement for your position, the cost of the courses is not deductible.

In one case, a college graduate who took a summer job before starting MBA courses was not allowed a deduction because he had not yet established himself in a business or employment; the summer position was just a temporary stage between schooling.

If your employer reimburses you for MBA courses that qualify for a deduction, the reimbursement is a tax-free working condition fringe benefit; *see 3.6*.

Caution

Law School Costs

Law school costs are not deductible, because a law degree qualifies you for a new profession; *see 19.17*. Costs of obtaining a Master of Laws degree (LL.M.), however, are deductible if you have practiced as an attorney before incurring the expense.

19.17 Law School Costs

The IRS does not allow deductions for law school courses, because they qualify you for a new profession. Courts support the IRS position. A deduction is not allowed even if you do not intend to practice law. For example, teachers who took law school courses have been disallowed deductions although they intended to continue teaching.

Bar review courses. The costs of bar review courses and the bar exam are not deductible, even where you are seeking admission to the bar of a second state. However, fees paid to state bar admission authorities have been held to be amortizable over an attorney's life expectancy.

Additional legal education. An attorney may deduct the cost of a master's degree program (LL.M.). You must practice as an attorney before the expenses of further legal education are deductible.

EXAMPLE

The Tax Court allowed a lawyer to deduct educational expenses to obtain an LL.M. degree where he worked for a law firm as a beginning lawyer during the summer between graduating from law school and starting work on the LL.M. degree. He was admitted to the state bar before he graduated from law school, and the work he did during the summer was normally assigned to beginning lawyers rather than to law students.

In another case, the IRS and Tax Court did not allow a deduction to a law school graduate who took LL.M. courses before passing the state bar or working as an attorney.

19.18 Courses Taken by Doctors and Nurses

The IRS allows general practitioners to deduct the cost of short refresher courses, even though the courses relate to specialized fields. These courses maintain or improve skills and do not qualify the doctor for a new profession.

A practicing psychiatrist may deduct the cost of attending an accredited psychoanalytic institute to qualify to practice psychoanalysis. A social worker has also been allowed a deduction for the cost of learning psychoanalysis. In one case, the Tax Court allowed a psychiatrist to deduct the cost of personal therapy sessions conducted through telephone conversations and tape cassettes. The court was convinced that the therapy improved his job skills by eliminating psychological blind spots that prevented him from understanding his patients' problems.

A licensed practical nurse may not deduct the costs of a college program that qualifies him or her as a "physician's assistant," which is a new business. Physicians' assistants and practical nurses are subject to different registration and certification requirements under state law, and, more importantly, the physician's assistant may perform duties, such as physical examinations and minor surgery, which go beyond practical nursing duties.

19.19 Courses Taken by Teachers

You must meet the minimum level of education for your present position as set down by law or regulations before you may deduct the cost of courses. The educational requirements are those that existed when you were hired. If your employer set no tests fixing a minimum educational level, you meet the minimum requirements when you become a member of the faculty. Whether you are a faculty member depends on the custom of your employer. You are ordinarily considered a faculty member if: (1) you have tenure, or your service is counted toward tenure; (2) the institution is contributing toward a retirement plan based on your employment (other than Social Security or a similar program); or (3) you have a vote in faculty affairs.

Employed teacher taking courses for teaching certificate. That you are already employed as a teacher, with all the responsibilities of a teacher, may not establish that you have met the minimum educational requirements. A school system that requires a bachelor's degree before granting a permanent teaching certificate may grant temporary or provisional certificates after a person has completed a number of college credits. Renewal of the provisional certificate may be conditioned on the teacher's continuing education for a bachelor's degree. In this case, the IRS will disallow a deduction for the educational costs. The minimum requirements are not met until the teacher has the degree. Current Tax Court decisions follow the IRS position, although in the past the court took a contrary view.

19.20 Professor's Research Expenses

Research costs incurred by a college professor are deductible under this condition: He or she is appointed to lecture and teach with the understanding that research in the field will be carried on with the goal of incorporating the findings in teaching and writing. If this test is met, the IRS is satisfied that the research is an express requirement of the teaching position and that research expenses are deductible job expenses.

Deductible research costs include traveling expenses and stenographic and other costs of preparing a manuscript. If income is later realized from the research in the form of lecture or royalty fees, the previously deducted research costs may not again be deducted in determining the income realized from the research.

Expenses of a research project undertaken for a scholarly publication are not deductible if the research is not linked to an income-producing activity or job requirement.

19.21 Leave of Absence To Take Courses

If you are a teacher, the IRS will allow a deduction for full-time graduate courses you take during a leave of absence if these conditions are met: (1) the absence must not be for more than one year and (2) upon completion of the education courses, the same type of employment must be resumed, although you may take a job with a new employer. You may also have to show that you had more than a vague intention to go back to your employment—for example, that you were actually negotiating for a new teaching position and that, in fact, you did obtain a position soon after finishing the graduate courses.

19.22 Local Transportation and Travel Away From Home To Take Courses

If your courses meet the requirements at *19.15* and *19.16*, costs of local transportation and travel away from home are deductible.

Local transportation expenses. If your courses qualify for a deduction under *19.16*, you may deduct transportation costs of going from your job directly to school. According to the IRS, the return trip from school is also deductible if you are going to school on a *temporary* basis. According to the IRS, you are going to school on a temporary basis if your courses are realistically expected to last for one year or less and actually do last no more than one year. This is the same one-year test for determining whether you can deduct the cost of commuting to a "temporary" work location *(20.2)* or living costs while away from home on a "temporary" assignment *(20.9)*. The IRS position is illustrated in the following Examples.

EXAMPLES

1. You regularly work in Camden, New Jersey, and every night for three weeks you drive from home to attend a refresher course. The course is considered temporary. You may deduct the round-trip transportation costs between home and school. The deduction is allowed regardless of how far you travel.

   If you went directly from your job to the school, you may deduct transportation from work to school, and from school to home.

2. On six consecutive Saturdays, which are nonworkdays for you, you drive from home to attend a qualifying course. This is considered a temporary course. You are allowed a deduction for round-trip transportation between home and school, even though you are traveling on a nonworkday.

3. You regularly work in Camden, New Jersey, and after work you drive from home to take classes twice a week for 15 months. The IRS does not consider the course to be temporary. You may deduct the cost of going directly from work to school, but the costs of going between home and school are nondeductible.

Travel and living expenses away from home. "Away from home" as explained at *20.6* has a special tax meaning. You are not away from home unless you are away overnight. If you are away from home to attend a qualifying course, you may deduct the cost of travel to and from the site of the course, plus lodging and 50% of meals while you are there.

 Planning Reminder

Teacher's Job Change

Elementary and secondary school teachers may deduct the cost of courses taken to make any of the following job changes: (1) elementary to secondary school classroom teacher; (2) classroom teacher in one subject (such as mathematics) to classroom teacher in another subject (such as English or history); (3) classroom teacher to guidance counselor; or (4) classroom teacher to principal.

The IRS held that a "discussion leader" in a college adult education program could not deduct the costs of a master's degree program that led to certification as a high school guidance counselor because this was a new business. The Tax Court disagreed, holding that the responsibilities of discussion leader are similar to the responsibilities of a school counselor. The court distinguished an earlier decision in which a classroom paraprofessional assistant was not allowed to deduct education costs that qualified her as a classroom teacher. The court considered this as a change in professions. A paraprofessional does not have the same control and responsibilities for classroom work as a classroom teacher.

Expenses of sightseeing, social visiting, and entertaining while taking the courses are not deductible. If personal reasons are your main purpose in going to the vicinity of the school, such as to take a vacation, you may deduct only the cost of the courses and your living expenses while attending school. You may not deduct the rest of your travel costs.

To determine the purpose of your trip, an IRS agent will pay close attention to the amount of time devoted to personal activities relative to the time devoted to the courses.

Is travel itself a form of education? The law says no. No deduction is allowed for costs of travel claimed as a form of education. For example, no deduction will be allowed to a French teacher traveling to France to maintain general familiarity with the French language and culture, or to a social studies teacher traveling to learn about or photograph people and customs.

A deduction may still be allowed for travel that qualifies as a business expense, as, for example, if a teacher must travel abroad to do research that cannot be done elsewhere.

19.23 How To Deduct Education Costs on Your Return

The way you deduct educational expenses on your return depends on your occupational status. If you are:

An employee. If you have education costs that are deductible under *19.16* but that have not been reimbursed by your employer, you generally report the expenses on Form 2106 or Form 2106-EZ. However, you do not need Form 2106 or Form 2106-EZ and may report your educational expenses directly on Schedule A as unreimbursed employee expenses if: (1) you are not claiming job expenses for travel, transportation, meals, or entertainment; and (2) you received no reimbursements for education expenses or any other job-related costs. If your expenses were partially reimbursed, you must use Form 2106; Form 2106-EZ may not be used. On Schedule A, the 2% of adjusted gross income (AGI) floor applies.

As discussed at *19.4*, deductions for impairment-related work expenses are *not* subject to the 2% floor on Schedule A, and expenses of performing artists are not claimed as itemized deductions but are figured on Form 2106 (or 2106-EZ) and deducted directly from gross income on Line 32 of Form 1040.

Employer reimbursements, including advances of deductible expenses, are not reported as income on your Form W-2 if you substantiate the expenses to your employer and return amounts in excess of the substantiated expenses. If these substantiation tests are not met, the expenses are reported as income on your Form W-2, and you must claim them on Form 2106 (or Schedule A if Form 2106 is not needed) as if they were unreimbursed. If your employer pays the tuition directly to the educational institution, you are not required to report the payment in any way on your return.

Teacher on sabbatical. Where a school system has a policy of paying teachers full salary during sabbatical leaves, a teacher on sabbatical may be required to pay a fixed percentage of salary into a fund to pay substitute teachers. A teacher reports the full amount of the salary paid during the sabbatical but may claim payments to the fund as miscellaneous itemized deductions subject to the 2% AGI floor.

A self-employed business owner or professional. If your education costs qualify under *19.16,* you deduct all of your education costs on Schedule C. You also attach a statement to your return explaining your deduction and the relationship of the education to your position.

A veteran receiving educational benefits from the VA. Educational assistance from the Department of Veterans Affairs (VA) is tax free, whether it covers educational or living expenses. The portion of the payment covering educational costs reduces your deductible educational expenses. If you use only part of the VA payment for qualifying courses, reduce your deduction by the part of the VA reimbursement covering the qualifying courses. The portion of the reimbursement, if any, that covers living expenses does not affect your deduction.

Filing Tip

Deducting Employee Educational Costs

Unreimbursed education costs, such as for travel, tuition, books, fees, and meals, are deductible only if you claim itemized deductions. You generally must report your expenses on Form 2106 or in some cases Form 2106-EZ *(see 19.3)* before entering the deductible amount on Line 20 of Schedule A, where they and other miscellaneous itemized deductions are subject to the 2% AGI floor.

Investment, Legal, and Tax Advice Expenses

19.24 Checklist of Deductible Investment Expenses

The following investment expenses are deductible as miscellaneous expenses on Schedule A subject to the 2% adjusted gross income (AGI) floor. In addition, the 3% reduction for total itemized deductions applies if your adjusted gross income exceeds $126,600, or $63,300 if married filing separately; *see 13.7.*

- Accounting fees for keeping records of investment income.

- Bank deposit loss if not federally insured; *see 18.4.*

- Casualty or theft losses of income-producing property such as stock certificates, but not rental or royalty property; the deduction is figured on Form 4684 and entered on Schedule A.

- Fees for collecting interest and dividends. Also deductible are fees paid to a bank that acts as dividend agent in an automatic dividend reinvestment plan of a publicly owned corporation. Costs of collecting tax-exempt interest are not deductible; expenses deducted on an estate tax return are also not deductible. Fees paid to a broker to acquire securities are not deductible but are added to the cost of the securities. Commissions and fees paid by an investor on the sale of securities reduce the selling price; a dealer, however, may deduct selling commissions as business expenses.

- Fees to set up or administer an IRA. The fees must be billed and paid separately from the regular IRA contribution.

- Guardian fees or fees of committee for a ward or minor incurred in producing or collecting income belonging to the ward or minor or in managing income-producing property of the ward or minor.

- Investment management or investment planner's fees. However, fees allocated to advice dealing with tax-exempt obligations are not deductible.

- Investment fees from non–publicly offered mutual fund, shown in Box 5 of Form 1099-DIV.

- Legal costs; *see 19.26.*

- Premiums and expenses on indemnity bonds for the replacement of missing securities. If part of the expenses are refunded in the year the expenses are paid, only the excess expense is deductible. A refund in a later year is taxable income to the extent the expenses were deducted and reduced your tax; *see 11.6.*

- Proxy fight expenses where the dispute involves legitimate corporate policy issues, not a frivolous desire to gain membership on the board.

- Safe-deposit box rental fee or home safe to hold your securities, unless used to hold personal effects or tax-exempt securities.

- Salary of a secretary, bookkeeper, or other employee hired to keep track of your investment income.

- Subscriptions to investment services.

Computer used to manage investments. Subject to the 2% floor, depreciation may be claimed; *see 42.10.*

Managing investment property. Expenses incurred in managing property held for income are deductible, even if the property does not currently produce income. Similarly, expenses incurred to avoid further losses or to reduce anticipated losses on such property are deductible.

Rental or royalty expenses. Expenses of earning royalty or rental income are deducted directly from the income, rather than as itemized deductions subject to the 2% AGI floor.

 Planning Reminder

Travel to Check Investments
Travel costs of a trip away from home *(20.6)* to look after investments, or to confer with your attorney, accountant, trustee, or investment counsel about the production of income, may be deducted as miscellaneous itemized deductions subject to the 2% of adjusted gross income floor. If you have investment property in a resort area, keep proof that the trip was taken primarily to check your investment property, not to vacation.

EXAMPLE

You pay deductible investment management fees of $1,500 a tax preparation fee of $500, and a safe-deposit box fee of $40. Your other miscellaneous expense deductions subject to the 2% floor are $500 for unreimbursed job expenses. Your adjusted gross income is $80,000. Your deduction after applying the 2% AGI floor is $940, figured as follows:

Investment management fees	$1,500
Tax preparation fee	500
Safe-deposit box fee	40
Other miscellaneous expenses	500
	$2,540
Less: 2% of $80,000	1,600
Total deductible	$ 940

Caution

Investment Seminars
You may not deduct the cost of an investment or financial planning seminar or similar meeting.

Filing Tip

Tax Advice and Tax Return Preparation
You may deduct legal fees paid in 1999 for preparing your tax return or refund claim, or for representing you in a trial, examination, or hearing involving any tax; *see 19.25.* Legal fees incurred in defending against a tax imposed by a foreign country are also deductible. However, legal fees incurred in reducing an assessment on property to pay for local benefits are not deductible; the fees are capital expenses which are added to basis.

Nondeductible travel costs. Investors may not deduct the costs of these types of trips:

- Trips to investigate prospective rental property.
- Trips to attend a convention, seminar, or similar meeting that deals with investment, financial planning, or the production or collection of income. Convention costs are deductible only in the case of a business activity; *see 20.12.*
- Trips to attend stockholder meetings. However, in a private letter ruling, one stockholder was allowed a deduction. He owned substantial stockholdings that had lost value because his corporation had been issuing stock to the public at prices below book value. He went to the annual shareholders' meeting to present a resolution requesting management to stop the practice; the resolution passed. Under such circumstances, the IRS held that the trip was directly related to his stockholdings and allowed him the deduction. The IRS distinguished his case from a ruling that bars most stockholders from deducting the cost of travel to an annual meeting. Here the stockholder's purpose in getting the resolution passed was more closely related to his investment activities than if he had attended the meeting, as most stockholders do, to pick up data for future investment moves.

Hobby expenses. For the limitations on deducting hobby expenses, *see 40.10.*

Home office of an investor. An investor may not deduct the costs of an office at home unless investing constitutes a business. For example, you get no deduction for use of a home office in your residence where you read financial periodicals and reports, and clip bond coupons. These activities are not considered a business.

EXAMPLE

In his home office, Moller spent 40 hours a week managing four stock portfolios worth over $13 million. However, an appeals court held he could not deduct home office expenses despite the time spent there managing his investment. To deduct home office expenses, Moller had to show he was a trader. A trader is in a business; an investor is not. A trader buys and sells frequently to catch daily market swings. An investor buys securities for capital appreciation and income without regard to daily market developments. Here, Moller was an investor. He was primarily interested in the long-term growth potential of stock. He did not earn his income from the short-term stock turnovers. He had no significant trading profits.

19.25 Costs of Tax Return Preparation and Audits

You may deduct your payment of fees charged for the services listed below, subject to the 2% AGI floor and the 3% reduction if AGI exceeds $126,600 ($63,300 if married filing separately); *see 13.7.*

- Preparing your tax return or refund claim involving any tax;
- Preparing and obtaining a private IRS ruling, including IRS filing fees; *and*
- Representing you before any examination, trial, or other type of hearing involving any tax.

The term "any tax" covers not only income taxes but also gift, property, estate, or any other tax, whether the taxing authority be federal, state, or municipal.

Tax practitioner's fees. Deductible fees for services of tax practitioners are claimed on Schedule A as miscellaneous itemized deductions on the tax return for the year in which the fee was paid. For example, if in March 1999 you pay an accountant to prepare your 1998 return, the fee is deductible on your 1999 return.

You deduct fees related to preparing Schedule C or F (and related business Schedules) on the Schedule C or F, thereby avoiding the 2% AGI floor on Schedule A. In one case, the Tax Court allowed a Schedule C deduction for a $55 tax preparation fee claimed by a self-employed lumberjack, although nonbusiness income was also reported on his return. Any allocation to the nonbusiness income would have been minimal. The Court noted that the IRS's position in disallowing the deduction reflected misguided zeal and was not only petty but impractical.

If you report rental or royalty income or loss on Schedule E, you deduct the allocated tax preparation fee on Schedule E.

An accountant's fee for arranging the purchase of real estate was deductible where the purchase was part of a plan to cut taxes; *see* the Collins Example at the end of this section.

Personal checking account fees. These are nondeductible, even though the checks are used for tax records. Similarly, the per-check fee on an interest-bearing NOW account is nondeductible. However, fees charged on a bank money-market account may be deductible if check writing is severely limited and writing excess checks forfeits the status of the account as a money-market account.

Appraisal fees. Appraisals for determining a casualty loss or charitable donation are miscellaneous expenses.

EXAMPLES

1. Stockholders of a closely held corporation negotiated with a publicly held company for a tax-free exchange of their stock. An accounting firm asked the IRS for a ruling to determine whether the exchange would be taxable or tax free. The accounting fee was $8,602. Of this, $7,602 was for the ruling and $1,000 was for fixing the basis of the new stock. The stockholders deducted the full fee, which the IRS disallowed because the fee was not charged for the preparation of a tax return nor for representation at a contest of a tax liability.

   The Tax Court disagreed in part. The fee paid for the ruling was deductible; it was connected with determining the extent of the stockholders' liability, if any, in the proposed exchange. But a deduction could not be allowed for the $1,000 charged to determine the basis of the new stock. This was computed for the stockholders' information, not for determining tax liability. The disallowed fee could be added to the cost basis of the stock.

2. Collins paid an accountant $4,511 for tax advice to reduce his tax on a sweepstakes winning. He was advised to buy an apartment house under a contract obligation to make a large prepayment of interest (which was deductible under prior law). The accountant helped prepare contracts, escrow agreements, and other documents to implement the plan. Collins's deduction of his accountant's fee was disallowed. The IRS held that the fee was a capital expense in acquiring the property. The Tax Court disagreed. The accountant was hired to minimize Collins's income tax through the purchase of the building and the terms of the purchase. Therefore, his fee was deductible.

19.26 Deducting Legal Costs

A legal expense is generally deductible if the dispute or issue arose in the course of your business or employment or involves income-producing property. Legal expenses for personal matters are generally not deductible. If you are self-employed, your deduction for legal fees arising from a business-related dispute is claimed on Schedule C.

Legal expenses related to your job as an employee or to investment activities are claimed as miscellaneous itemized deductions subject to the 2% AGI floor. The IRS may disallow the deduction on the ground that the legal dispute does not directly arise from the business or income activity. Thus, for example, the cost of contesting the suspension of a driver's license for drunken driving is not deductible despite a business need for the license; the suspension arose out of a personal rather than a business-related activity. A deduction may also be disallowed where the dispute involves title to property. Legal fees incurred in obtaining an award of tax-free damages are not deductible.

The legal costs of defending against disbarment are deductible.

For the deductibility of legal fees in organizing a new business, *see 40.11.*

Employment suits. The following Examples illustrate when legal costs for job-related matters may be deductible.

EXAMPLES

1. An Army officer was allowed to deduct the cost of successfully contesting a court martial based on charges of misrepresentations in official statements and reports. He would have lost his position had he been convicted.
2. Tellier, a securities dealer, was convicted of mail fraud and securities fraud. He was allowed to deduct legal fees as business expenses related to his securities business. That he was found guilty of the criminal charge does not affect the deductibility of the expense. The deduction of legal expenses is not disallowed on public policy grounds since a defendant has a constitutional right to an attorney.

 Filing Tip

Deducting the Cost of This Book
The purchase of *Your Income Tax* in 1999 may be claimed as a miscellaneous expense deduction on your 1999 return. The cost, when included with other miscellaneous expenses, is subject to the 2% AGI floor. If you purchase the book in 2000, include the cost with your other miscellaneous expenses on your 2000 return.

 Planning Reminder

Allocate Fees for Tax Advice
There have been disputes over the deductibility of fees charged for general tax advice unconnected to the preparation of a return or a tax controversy. A deduction for fees charged for general tax advice not within these areas may be disallowed, unless the fee can be related to the production of business or investment income or the management of income-producing property. *See* the Examples in *19.25.*

3. In an alimony action, Gilmore was successful in preventing his wife from securing stock and taking control of corporations from which he earned practically all his income. He was not allowed to deduct his legal costs. The dispute did not arise from an income-producing activity; the fact that an adverse determination of the dispute might affect his income did not make the legal expenses deductible.

4. A doctor who attempted to bribe a judge to suspend his sentence for tax evasion was convicted of the bribe attempt and lost his license to practice medicine. He could not deduct his defense costs. His practice of medicine did not give rise to his need for an attorney. The fact that the conviction affected his ability to earn income was merely a consequence of personal litigation.

5. Siket, a police officer, was not allowed to deduct expenses of successfully defending a criminal charge of assault while off duty. The origin of the claim was personal, even though a conviction might have been detrimental to his position as a police officer. The arrest did not occur within the performance of his duties; he was off duty and in a different municipality at the time of the arrest.

6. A resort company instructed its staff to stop serving drinks to intoxicated patrons and to encourage the patrons to either take a taxi home or to stay on the premises at a reduced rate. One of the company's executives attempted to deduct legal defense fees when he was charged with criminal sexual assault, arguing that the assault allegation arose from his business duty to procure a room for three intoxicated guests. The IRS and the Tax Court denied the deduction on the grounds that the allegation arose from the executive's second visit to the guests' room, not from the time he placed them in the room. Even if the alleged assault had occurred during the first visit, the executive personally violated company policy by not stopping the guests from drinking when they were already drunk.

Planning Reminder

Lawyer's Bill Should Be Itemized
Your lawyer should bill you separately or itemize fees for services connected with deductible items (collection of taxable alimony or separate maintenance payments; or preparation of tax returns, tax audits, and tax litigation) and nondeductible capital items (expenses incurred in purchase of property or dispute over title).

Will contests and wrongful death actions. Legal costs of a will contest are generally not deductible because an inheritance is not taxable income. Similarly, legal fees incurred to collect a wrongful death award (which is tax-free income) are not deductible.

EXAMPLE

Parker, an heir who was left out of his grandmother's estate, sued to recover his inheritance. In a settlement, he received his share of his grandmother's property plus income earned on that property. The allocable portion of legal fees attributed to the income, which was taxable, was deductible; the balance of the fees was not deductible.

Title issues or disputes. Legal costs related to the acquisition of property or to the determination of title to property, whether such property is business or personal, are nondeductible capital expenditures. They are added to the basis of the property. For example, litigation costs to fix the value of shares of dissident shareholders are not deductible because they are related to the purchase of the stock and are part of the cost of acquisition.

Legal fees incurred to acquire title to stock are also nondeductible.

Where a dispute over property does not involve title, such as in a recovery of income-producing securities loaned as collateral, the Tax Court holds that legal fees are deductible.

Personal injury or marital actions. Where you recover taxable damages, you may deduct the legal fees. If the damages are not taxable, legal fees are not deductible; *see 11.7.* For legal expenses incurred in marital actions, *see 37.8.*

Collecting Social Security. If you hire an attorney to press a claim for disputed benefits, such as disability benefits, you may deduct the legal fees only to the extent that your benefits are taxable under the rules of *34.3.* For example, if 50% of your Social Security benefits are taxable, 50% of your legal fees are treated as miscellaneous expenses subject to the 2% AGI floor.

Estate tax planning fee. All or part of an attorney's fee for estate tax planning services may be deductible. Estate tax planning usually involves tax and non-tax matters. To the extent that the services do not cover tax advice or income-producing property, the fee is not deductible. A bill allocating a fee between deductible and nondeductible services may help support a deduction claimed for the deductible portion of the fee.

Recovery of attorneys' fees from government. *See* Chapter 47.

Travel and Entertainment Expense Deductions

Unreimbursed employee travel expenses are deductible but are subject to the 2% adjusted gross income (AGI) floor on Schedule A. If you are self-employed, the 2% floor does not apply to travel expenses claimed on Schedule C. The types of deductible travel expenses are highlighted in the key to deductible travel and entertainment expenses at the beginning of this chapter. Generally, you must be away from home to deduct travel expenses on business trips. On one-day business trips within the general area of your employment, only transportation costs may be deducted; meals may not.

To support your travel expense deductions, keep records that comply with IRS rules as explained at *20.26*. To avoid the 2% AGI floor, consider an "accountable" reimbursement arrangement of your travel expenses with your employer; *see 20.31*.

You report unreimbursed employee transportation and travel expenses on Form 2106 or on new short form 2106-EZ if you are not reimbursed by your company and you do not claim depreciation on a car used for business.

Unreimbursed expenses from Form 2106 or 2106-EZ are entered on Schedule A where they are subject to the 2% AGI floor.

An expense allowance for travel costs is not reported as income on Form W-2 if you substantiated the expenses to your employer and returned any unsubstantiated portion of the allowance; *see 20.31* for details.

If you are self-employed, you deduct travel costs on Schedule C. The 2% AGI floor does not apply, but meal and entertainment expenses are subject to the 50% limitation.

Commuting and Meal Expenses

20.1 Deduction Guide for Travel and Transportation Expenses

The following chart summarizes the rules for deducting travel expenses while "away from home" on business trips, and other deductible travel and transportation expenses; *see 20.6* for when you are away from home. Generally, commuting expenses from your home to your place of business are not deductible; *see 20.2*. However, you may be able to claim a deduction for daily transportation expenses incurred in commuting to a temporary job location; *see* the chart below and *20.2*.

Key to Deductible Travel and Transportation Expenses

Your Travel Status—	Tax Rule—
Trips to see customers and clients	You may deduct your transportation expenses but not the cost of personal meals on one-day business trips within the general area of your tax home.
Two job locations for one employer in the same area **EXAMPLE:** Your employer has two business locations in the city in which you live. You work about half of the time in each place—at one location in the morning and at the other in the afternoon.	You deduct transportation expenses from one location to the other. However, if, for personal reasons, such as the choice of a place for eating lunch, you do not go directly from one location to the other, you may deduct your transportation expenses only to the extent that they do not exceed the cost of going directly from the first location to the second. But say your employer has several locations in the same city, but you do not move from one location to another in the same day. You spend the entire day at one place. You may not deduct transportation expenses between your home and the various locations, even if you report to a different location each day.
Two different jobs in the same area **EXAMPLE:** You work for two different employers in the city in which you live. Most of the time you work a full work shift at your principal place of employment. Then you work a part-time shift for your second employer some distance away.	You may deduct the transportation expenses from one job to another within the same working day. But you may not claim the deduction if you return home after the first job and then, after supper, go to your second job.
Permanent job in an area other than where you have your residence **EXAMPLE:** You live with your family in Chicago, but work in Milwaukee. During the week, you stay in a hotel in Milwaukee and eat meals in a restaurant. You return to your family in Chicago every weekend.	Milwaukee is your "home" for tax purposes; *see 20.6*. Thus, your expenses for traveling to Milwaukee and your meals and lodging there are personal, nondeductible expenses.
Temporary assignment in an area other than where you have your residence **EXAMPLE:** You live in Kansas City, where you work. You have been assigned to duty in Omaha for 60 days. Occasionally, you return to Kansas City on your days off, but most of the time you stay in Omaha.	You may deduct the necessary expenses for traveling from Kansas City to Omaha and returning to Kansas City after your temporary assignment is completed. You may also deduct expenses for meals and lodging (even for your days off) while you are in Omaha. As discussed at *20.9*, deductions are not allowed on temporary assignments that are *expected* to last more than one year.
Weekend trip home from temporary assignment **EXAMPLE:** Same facts as in the Example above except that you return home to Kansas City during the weekend.	You are not "away from home" while you are in Kansas City on your days off and your meals and lodging while you are there are not deductible. However, you may deduct your traveling expenses (including meals and lodging, if any) from Omaha to Kansas City and back if they are no more than the amount it would have cost you for your meals and lodging if you had stayed in Omaha. If they are more, your deduction is limited to the amount you would have spent in Omaha. If you retain your room in Omaha while in Kansas City, your expenses of returning to Kansas City on days off are deductible only to the extent of the amount you would have spent for your meals had you stayed in Omaha.

Key to Deductible Travel and Transportation Expenses

Your Travel Status—	*Tax Rule—*
Temporary job location away from home where there are no living accommodations EXAMPLE: You live and work in Chicago. You have been assigned for three months to a construction job located 20 miles outside Nashville. There are no living facilities near the job site and you have to stay at a hotel in Nashville.	Under these circumstances, your necessary expenses in getting to and from your temporary job are business expenses and not commuting expenses. If you were employed at the site for an indefinite period *(20.9),* then the costs of commuting would be nondeductible, regardless of the distance; *see 20.2.*
Taxi trips between customers' locations	The cab fares are deductible; *see 20.2.*
Seasonal jobs in different areas EXAMPLE: You live in Cincinnati, where you work for eight months each year. You earn the greater share of your annual income from that job. For the remaining four months of the year, you work in Miami. When in Miami, you eat and sleep in a hotel. You have been working on both of these jobs for several years and expect to continue to do so.	You have two recurring seasonal places of employment. Cincinnati is your principal place of employment. You may deduct the costs of your traveling expenses while away from Cincinnati working at your minor place of employment in Miami, including meals and lodging in Miami.
Trailer home moved to different job sites EXAMPLE: You are a construction welder. You live in a trailer that you move from city to city, where you work on construction projects. You have no other established home.	You may not deduct your expenses for meals and lodging. Each place where you locate becomes your principal place of business and, therefore, you are not "away from home."
Travel to school after work to take job-related courses	You may deduct travel costs if you meet the rules discussed at *19.23.*
Finding a new job in the same line of work EXAMPLE: You live in New York. You travel to Chicago for an interview for a new position.	You may deduct the cost of the trip and living expenses in Chicago; *see 19.7.*
Convention trip	You may deduct costs of travel to a business convention under the rules in *20.12.* If you are a delegate to a charitable or veterans' convention, you may claim a charitable deduction for the travel costs; *see 14.4.*
Trip to out-of-town college for educational courses	You deduct the cost of the trip if you meet the rules at *19.23.*
Trip for health reasons	You may deduct the cost of the trip as a medical expense if you meet the rules at *17.9.*

20.2 Commuting Expenses

The cost of travel between your home and place of work is generally not deductible, even if the work location is in a remote area not serviced by public transportation. Nor can you justify the deduction by showing you need a car for faster trips to work or for emergency trips. Travel from a union hall to an assigned job is also considered commuting. If you join a car pool, you may not deduct expenses of gasoline, repairs, or other costs of driving you and your passengers to work.

According to the IRS, if you install a telephone in your car and make calls to clients or business associates while driving to your office, you are still commuting and your expenses are not deductible. Similarly, the deduction is not allowed if you drive passengers to work and discuss business.

Deductible commuting expenses. The IRS allows these exceptions to its blanket ban on commuting expense deductions.

If you are on a business trip out of town, you may deduct taxi fares or other transportation costs from your hotel to the first business call of the day and all other transportation costs between business calls.

If you use your car to carry tools to work, you may deduct transportation costs where you can prove that they were incurred in addition to the ordinary, nondeductible commuting expenses. The deduction will be allowed even if you would use a car in any event to commute; *see* the Examples below.

EXAMPLES

1. Jones commuted to and from work by public transportation before he had to carry tools. Public transportation cost $2 per day to commute to and from work. When he had to use the car to carry the tools, the cost of driving was $3 a day and $5 a day to rent a trailer to carry the tools. Jones may deduct only the cost of renting the trailer. The IRS does not allow a deduction for the additional $1 a day cost of operating the car. It is not considered related to the carrying of the tools. It is treated as part of the cost of commuting which is not deductible.

2. Same facts as above, but Jones does not rent a trailer. He uses the car trunk to store his tools. He may not claim a deduction because he incurs no additional cost for carrying the tools.

3. Smith uses his car regardless of the need to transport tools. He rents a trailer for $5 a day to carry tools. He may deduct $5 a day under the "additional-cost" rule.

Commuting to a temporary place of work. Whether you can deduct commuting expenses to a temporary place of work may depend on the location of the temporary assignment and whether you have a regular place of business or a home office that is your principal place of business. According to the IRS, if the temporary location is within the metropolitan area where you live and usually work, you may deduct the cost of commuting between your home and the temporary location only if you have a regular place of business outside your home, or your principal place of business *(40.12)* is your office in your home. If the temporary location is outside the metropolitan area, you may deduct commuting expenses to the temporary location without having to meet either the regular outside place of business test or home office test.

What is a temporary place of work? A temporary work location is one at which your employment is realistically expected to last, and actually does last, for one year or less. If at first you realistically expect an assignment to last for no more than one year but that expectation changes, the IRS will generally treat the employment as temporary until the date that it became realistic to expect that the work would exceed one year.

Accountants, architects, engineers, and other professionals often have to travel to job sites of their clients. If such work at the site is temporary and they can show they also have a regular work office, they may deduct commuting expenses from their homes to their work sites.

EXAMPLE

The IRS ruled that a professional who spent 25–27% of his time at his employer's field office satisfied the regular place of business test. His remaining time was spent at client locations. These were considered temporary because he went to each client location only once every two years for two to three weeks at a time. He was allowed to deduct his unreimbursed costs of driving between his home and the client locations.

20.3 Overnight-Sleep Test Limits Deduction of Meal Costs

The overnight-sleep rule prevents the deduction of meal costs on one-day business trips. To be deductible, meal costs must be incurred on a business trip that lasts longer than a regular working day (but not necessarily 24 hours) and requires time off to sleep (not just to eat or rest) before returning home. Taking a nap in a parked car off the road does not meet the overnight-sleep test.

EXAMPLES

1. A New Yorker flies to Washington, D.C., which is about 250 miles away, to see a client. He arrives at noon, eats lunch, and then visits the client. He flies back to New York. He may deduct the cost of the plane fare, but not the cost of the lunch. He was not away overnight nor was he required to take time out to sleep before returning home.
2. Same facts as above except he sleeps overnight in a Washington hotel. He eats breakfast there, and then sees another client and returns home to New York in the afternoon. He may deduct not only the cost of the plane fare but also the cost of the meals while on the trip and the cost of the hotel, since he was away overnight.
3. A trucker's run is from Seattle to Portland and back. He leaves at about 2:00 A.M. and returns to Seattle the same day, getting in at about 6:00 P.M. While in Portland, he is released from duty for about four hours layover time to get necessary sleep before returning to Seattle. He may deduct the cost of meals because he is released at a layover location to obtain necessary sleep. Official release from duty, however, is not a prerequisite for satisfying the sleep or rest test.

Several courts held that the IRS rule was unreasonable and outdated in the world of supersonic travel, and they would have allowed the New Yorker on the one-day trip to Washington, D.C., to deduct the cost of his lunch. The Supreme Court disagreed and upheld the IRS rule as a fair administrative approach.

Meal costs during overtime. Such costs are not deductible if you are not away from your place of business. Thus, for example, a resident physician could not deduct the cost of meals and sleeping quarters at the hospital during overnight or weekend duty.

20.4 IRS Meal Allowance

If you find it difficult to keep records of meal costs while away from home on business trips, you may prefer to claim an IRS meal allowance. The allowance covers, in addition to meals, incidental expenses, such as laundry and tips for services. Self-employed individuals may claim the allowance as well as employees who are not reimbursed for meals under an "accountable" plan; *see 20.31.* However, the meal allowance may not be used if your employer is your brother, sister, spouse, parent, child, grandparent, or grandchild, or if you own more than 10% of the employer's outstanding stock.

1999 meal allowance. For travel within the continental U.S., the daily allowance for 1999 is usually $30 per day except that in certain high-cost areas designated by the government, the allowance may be $34, $38, $42, or $46 per day. The high-cost areas are generally major metropolitan cities or resort areas. *See* the tables on pages 378–391 for a list of the areas within the continental U.S. that qualify for meal allowance rates over $30 per day for 1999. Any changes to these tables will be in IRS Publication 463.

For travel in Alaska, Hawaii, or other areas outside the continental U.S., an allowance for each location is shown in government tables.

You must keep a record of the time, place, and business purpose of the trips. As long as you have this proof, you may claim the allowance even if your actual costs are less than the allowance.

Transportation industry workers. Employees or self-employed persons in the *transportation industry* may elect to claim a meal allowance of $38 per day for all 1999 travel within the continental U.S. instead of applying the $30, $34, $38, $42, or $46 rate on a trip-by-trip basis. Also, an allowance of $42 per day may be elected for all travel outside the continental U.S.

Claiming the allowance. The allowance is prorated for the first and last day of a trip. You may claim 75% of the allowance for the days you depart and return.

If you are an employee and claim a deduction based on the allowance, you must reduce the deduction by 50% on Form 2106 or Form 2106-EZ. Furthermore, if you are an employee, the balance, when added to your other miscellaneous deductions, is subject to the 2% AGI floor on Schedule A. If you are self-employed, the deduction for meals is claimed on Schedule C, where it is subject only to the 50% reduction; *see 40.6.*

Filing Tip

IRS Meal Allowance
The basic meal allowance rate for 1999 business trips within the continental United States is $30 per day, but a rate of $34, $38, $42, or $46 is available for certain high-cost areas; *see* the table on the following pages.

Filing Tip

Reimbursement Plans.
If your employer has an "accountable" reimbursement plan *(20.31),* and you are reimbursed for meals up to the allowable meal allowance rate, the reimbursement will not be reported as income on your Form W-2.

Locations Eligible for $34, $38, $42, or $46 a Day Meal Allowance for Travel on or After January 1, 1999

KEY CITY	COUNTY/LOCATION	AMOUNT(S)
ALABAMA		
Birmingham	Jefferson	38
Gulf Shores	Baldwin	34
Huntsville	Madison	38
Mobile	Mobile	34
Montgomery	Montgomery	38
ARIZONA		
Casa Grande	Pinal	34
Chinle	Apache	34
Flagstaff	Coconino	34
	(other than the Grand Canyon area)	
Grand Canyon Nat'l Park and Kaibab Nat'l Forest	Coconino	42
Phoenix	Maricopa (other than Scottsdale)	38
Prescott	Yavapai	38
Scottsdale	Scottsdale city limits	42
Tucson	Pima; Davis-Monthan AFB	38
Yuma	Yuma	34
ARKANSAS		
Little Rock	Pulaski	34
CALIFORNIA		
Barstow	Barstow city limits	34
Bridgeport	Mono (other than Mammoth Lakes)	42
Clearlake	Lake	38
Contra Costa County	Contra Costa County	42
Death Valley	Inyo	46
Eureka	Humboldt	38
Fresno	Fresno	38
Gualala	Gualala city limits	38
Kern County	Kern County	38
Los Angeles	Los Angeles; Edwards AFB; Naval Weapons Center and Ordnance Test Station, China Lake	46
Madera	Madera (other than Oakhurst)	34
Mammoth Lakes	Mammoth Lakes city limits	46
Marin County	Marin County	42
Merced	Merced	38
Modesto	Stanislaus	34
Monterey	Monterey	42
Napa	Napa	42
Oakhurst	Oakhurst city limits (other than Madera)	38
Oakland	Alameda	38
Ontario	San Bernardino (other than Barstow)	38
Orange County	Orange County	46
Palm Springs	Riverside	42
Palo Alto	Palo Alto city limits	42
Point Arena	Mendocino (other than Gualala)	38
Redding	Shasta	38
Redwood City	Redwood City limits	42
Sacramento	Sacramento	42
San Diego	San Diego	46
San Francisco	San Francisco	46
San Jose	Santa Clara (other than Palo Alto and Sunnyvale)	46
San Luis Obispo	San Luis Obispo	38
San Mateo	San Mateo (other than Redwood City)	42
Santa Barbara	Santa Barbara	38
Santa Cruz	Santa Cruz	42
Santa Rosa	Sonoma	42
South Lake Tahoe	El Dorado	42
Stockton	San Joaquin	38
Sunnyvale	Sunnyvale city limits	42
Tahoe City	Placer	42
Ventura County	Ventura County	38
Victorville	Victorville city limits	34
Visalia	Tulare	38
Yosemite Nat'l Park	Mariposa	46
COLORADO		
Adams County	Adams County	38
Arapahoe County	Arapahoe County	38
Aspen	Pitkin	46
Boulder	Boulder	42
Colorado Springs	El Paso	38

KEY CITY	COUNTY/LOCATION	AMOUNT(S)
COLORADO (continued)		
Cortez	Montezuma	34
Denver	Denver	42
Durango	La Plata	38
Fort Collins	Larimer (other than Loveland)	34
Glenwood Springs	Garfield	38
Gunnison	Gunnison	34
Jefferson County	Jefferson County	34
Keystone/Silverthorne	Summit	38
Montrose	Montrose	34
Pueblo	Pueblo	34
Steamboat Springs	Routt	38
Telluride	San Miguel	46
Vail	Eagle	46
CONNECTICUT		
Bridgeport	Bridgeport city limits	34
Danbury	Fairfield (other than Bridgeport)	38
Hartford	Hartford	42
Lakeville	Litchfield (other than Salisbury)	38
Middlesex County	Middlesex County	34
New Haven	New Haven	38
New London	New London city limits	34
Salisbury	Salisbury city limits	46
Vernon	Tolland	34
DELAWARE		
Dover	Kent	34
Lewes	Sussex	42
Wilmington	New Castle	34
DISTRICT OF COLUMBIA		
Washington, DC	District of Columbia	46
FLORIDA		
Altamonte Springs	Seminole	38
Boca Raton	Boca Raton city limits	38
Bradenton	Manatee	34
Cocoa Beach	Brevard	34
Daytona Beach	Volusia	38
Delray Beach	Delray Beach city limits	42
Fort Lauderdale	Broward	42
Fort Myers	Lee	42
Fort Walton Beach	Okaloosa	38
Gainesville	Alachua	34
Gulf Breeze	Santa Rosa	38
Jacksonville	Duval County and Naval Station Mayport	34
Jupiter	Jupiter city limits	34
Key West	Monroe	46
Kissimmee	Osceola	34
Lakeland	Polk	34
Miami	Dade	42
Naples	Collier	38
Orlando	Orange	42
Palm Beach	Palm Beach city limits	46
Palm Beach Gardens	Palm Beach city limits	38
Palm Beach Shores	Palm Beach (other than Jupiter, Palm Beach, Delray Beach, West Palm Beach, Boca Raton, and Singer Island)	38
Panama City	Bay	38
Pensacola	Escambia	34
Punta Gorda	Charlotte	38
St. Augustine	St. Johns	38
St. Petersburg	Pinellas	38
Sarasota	Sarasota	38
Singer Island	Singer Island city limits	38
Stuart	Martin	38
Tallahassee	Leon	34
Tampa	Hillsborough	38
Vero Beach	Indian River	38
West Palm Beach	West Palm Beach city limits	38
GEORGIA		
Albany	Dougherty	34
Athens	Clarke	34
Atlanta	Fulton	38
Augusta	Richmond	38
Cobb County	Cobb County	34

Locations Eligible for $34, $38, $42 or $46 a Day Meal Allowance for Travel on or After January 1, 1999

KEY CITY	COUNTY/LOCATION	AMOUNT(S)	KEY CITY	COUNTY/LOCATION	AMOUNT(S)
GEORGIA (continued)			**MARYLAND** (continued)		
Columbus	Muscogee	34	Lexington Park/	St. Marys	34
Conyers	Rockdale	34	Leonardtown/Lusby		
DeKalb County	DeKalb County	34	Montgomery County	Montgomery County	38
Macon	Bibb	34	Ocean City	Worcester	46
Savannah	Chatham	38	Prince Georges County	Prince Georges County	38
Warner Robbins	Houston	34	Salisbury	Wicomico	34
IDAHO			St. Michaels	St. Michaels city limits	42
Boise	Ada	38	**MASSACHUSETTS**		
Coeur d'Alene	Kootenai	34	Andover	Essex	38
Ketchum	Blaine (other than Sun Valley)	42	Boston	Suffolk	46
McCall	Valley	38	Cambridge	Cambridge city limits	46
Stanley	Custer	38	Falmouth	Falmouth	38
Sun Valley	Sun Valley city limits	42	Hyannis	Barnstable	38
ILLINOIS			Lowell	Middlesex (other than Cambridge)	34
Champaign/Urbana	Champaign	34	Martha's Vineyard	Dukes	46
Chicago	Cook	46	Nantucket	Nantucket	46
Decatur	Macon	34	New Bedford	New Bedford city limits	34
Du Page County	Du Page County	38	Northampton	Hampshire	34
Lake County	Lake County	42	Pittsfield	Berkshire	38
Peoria	Peoria	38	Plymouth	Plymouth	34
Rockford	Winnebago	34	Quincy	Norfolk	38
Springfield	Sangamon	38	Springfield	Hampden	34
INDIANA			Worcester	Worcester	34
Bloomington/Crane	Monroe	34	**MICHIGAN**		
Carmel	Hamilton	38	Ann Arbor	Washtenaw	38
Fort Wayne	Allen	34	Auburn Hills	Oakland (other than Pontiac and Troy)	38
Indianapolis	Marion County;	42	Charlevoix	Charlevoix	38
	Fort Benjamin Harrison		Detroit	Wayne	46
Michigan City	La Porte	34	East Lansing	East Lansing city limits	38
Muncie	Delaware	34	Flint	Genesee	34
Nashville	Brown	38	Frankfort	Benzie	34
South Bend	St. Joseph	34	Gaylord	Otsego	38
Valparaiso/	Porter	34	Grand Rapids	Kent	34
Burlington Beach			Grayling	Crawford	34
IOWA			Holland	Ottawa	34
Cedar Rapids	Linn	34	Lansing	Ingham (other than East Lansing)	34
Davenport/Bettendorf	Scott	34	Leland	Leelanau	34
Des Moines	Polk	34	Mackinac Island	Mackinac	46
KANSAS			Midland	Midland	34
Overland Park	Johnson	38	Mount Pleasant	Isabella	34
Wichita	Sedgwick	38	Petoskey	Emmet	38
KENTUCKY			Pontiac	Pontiac city limits	34
Covington	Kenton	38	Sault Ste. Marie	Chippewa	34
Florence	Boone	34	South Haven	Van Buren	34
Lexington	Fayette	34	Traverse City	Grand Traverse	42
Louisville	Jefferson	38	Troy	Troy city limits	38
LOUISIANA			Warren	Macomb	34
Baton Rouge	East Baton Rouge Parish	38	**MINNESOTA**		
Bossier City	Bossier Parish	34	Anoka County	Anoka County	34
Gonzales	Ascension Parish	34	Dakota County	Dakota County	34
Lake Charles	Calcasieu Parish	34	Duluth	St. Louis	42
New Orleans	New Orleans city limits	42	Minneapolis	Hennepin, Fort Snelling	46
Slidell	St. Tammany	34		Military Reservation,	
St. Francisville	West Feliciana	38		Navy Astronautics Group	
MAINE				(Detachment BRAVO)	
Bar Harbor	Hancock	38		and Rosemount	
Bath	Sagadahoc	34	Rochester	Olmstead	34
Kennebunk	York	38	St. Paul	Ramsey	38
Kittery	Portsmouth Naval Shipyard	34	**MISSISSIPPI**		
Portland	Cumberland	38	Bay St. Louis	Hancock	38
Rockport	Knox	42	Biloxi	Biloxi city limits	38
Wiscasset	Lincoln	38	Gulfport	Harrison (other than Biloxi)	34
MARYLAND			Jackson	Hinds	34
Annapolis	Anne Arundel	42	Pascagoula	Jackson	34
Baltimore	Baltimore	42	Ridgeland	Madison	38
Columbia	Howard	42	Robinsonville	Tunica	34
Easton	Talbot	34	Vicksburg	Warren	34
Frederick	Frederick	38	**MISSOURI**		
Grasonville	Queen Annes	38	Branson	Taney	34
Hagerstown	Washington	34	Cape Girardeau	Cape Girardeau	34
Harford County	Harford County	38	Jefferson City	Cole	34
			Kansas City	Jackson	42
			Lake Ozark	Camden	34

Locations Eligible for $34, $38, $42 or $46 a Day Meal Allowance for Travel on or After January 1, 1999

KEY CITY	COUNTY/LOCATION	AMOUNT(S)	KEY CITY	COUNTY/LOCATION	AMOUNT(S)
MISSOURI (continued)			**NEW YORK** (continued)		
Osage Beach	Osage Beach city limits	34	Poughkeepsie	Dutchess	38
Platte County	Platte County	34	Queens	Queens	46
St. Charles County	St. Charles County	34	Rochester	Monroe	42
St. Louis	St. Louis	46	Saratoga Springs	Saratoga	38
MONTANA			Schenectady	Schenectady	34
Polson/Kalispell	Lake/Flathead	34	Staten Island	Richmond	42
West Yellowstone Park	Gallatin	34	Suffolk County	Suffolk	38
NEBRASKA			Tarrytown	Westchester (other than White Plains)	42
Lincoln	Lancaster	34	Utica	Oneida	34
Omaha	Douglas	38	Waterloo/Romulus	Seneca	34
NEVADA			Watkins Glen	Schuyler	34
Incline Village	Northern Lake Tahoe Area within Washoe County	38	West Point	Orange	34
			White Plains	White Plains city limits	42
Las Vegas	Clark County; Nellis AFB	38	**NORTH CAROLINA**		
Reno	Washoe County (other than Incline Village)	38	Asheville	Buncombe	34
			Chapel Hill	Orange	38
Stateline	Douglas	42	Charlotte	Mecklenburg	38
Winnemucca	Humboldt	34	Durham	Durham	42
NEW HAMPSHIRE			Fayetteville	Cumberland	34
Concord	Merrimack	34	Greensboro	Guilford	38
Conway	Carroll	38	Kill Devil	Dare	38
Hanover	Grafton	42	New Bern	Craven	34
Laconia	Belknap	34	Raleigh	Wake	38
Manchester	Hillsborough	34	Research Triangle Park	Research Triangle Park city limits	38
Portsmouth/Newington	Rockingham County; Pease AFB	42	Wilmington	New Hanover	34
Sullivan County	Sullivan County	34	Winston-Salem	Forsyth	38
NEW JERSEY			**OHIO**		
Atlantic City	Atlantic	42	Akron	Summit	38
Bergen County	Bergen County	38	Cambridge	Guernsey	34
Cape May	Cape May (other than Ocean City)	42	Canton	Stark	34
Cherry Hill/ Camden/Moorestown	Camden/Burlington	42	Cincinnati	Hamilton	46
			Cleveland	Cuyahoga	42
Eatontown	Monmouth County; Fort Monmouth	38	Columbus	Franklin	38
Edison	Middlesex (other than Piscataway)	34	Dayton	Montgomery and Wright-Patterson AFB	38
Flemington	Hunterdon	34	Elyria	Lorain	34
Freehold	Freehold city limits	34	Fairborn	Greene	34
Hudson County	Hudson County	38	Geneva/Hamilton	Ashtabula/Butler	34
Millville	Cumberland	38	Lancaster	Fairfield	34
Newark	Essex	42	Port Clinton/Oakharbor	Ottawa	34
Ocean City	Ocean City city limits	38	Portsmouth	Scioto	34
Parsippany/Dover	Morris County; Picatinny Arsenal	38	Sandusky	Erie	38
Passaic County	Passaic County	38	Springfield	Clark	34
Piscataway/Belle Mead	Piscataway city limits	38	Toledo	Lucas	38
Princeton	Princeton city limits	42	**OKLAHOMA**		
Trenton	Mercer (other than Princeton)	38	Oklahoma City	Oklahoma	38
Union County	Union County	38	Tulsa	Tulsa	38
NEW MEXICO			**OREGON**		
Albuquerque	Bernalillo	38	Ashland	Jackson	42
Los Alamos	Los Alamos	34	Beaverton	Washington	38
Sante Fe	Sante Fe	46	Bend	Deschutes	38
Taos	Taos	34	Clackamas	Clackamas	34
NEW YORK			Coos Bay	Coos	34
Albany	Albany	42	Crater Lake	Crater Lake city limits	38
Batavia	Genesee	34	Eugene	Lane (other than Florence)	38
Binghamton	Broome	38	Florence	Florence city limits	34
The Bronx	The Bronx	46	Gold Beach	Curry	34
Brooklyn	Brooklyn	46	Lincoln City/Newport	Lincoln	34
Buffalo	Erie	42	Portland	Multnomah	38
Corning	Steuben	38	Salem	Marion	34
Elmira	Chemung	34	Seaside	Clatsop	34
Glen Falls	Warren	34	**PENNSYLVANIA**		
Great Neck	Nassau County's North Shore, up to and including Great Neck to the west and Oyster Bay to the east	42	Allentown	Lehigh	38
			Chester/Radnor/Essington	Delaware	34
Ithaca	Thompkins	34	Easton	Northampton	34
Kingston	Ulster	38	Gettysburg	Adams	34
Lake Placid	Essex	38	Harrisburg	Dauphin (other than Hershey)	42
Manhattan	Manhattan	46	Hershey	Hershey city limits	42
Nassau County	Nassau County	38	King of Prussia/ Ft. Washington	Montgomery County (other than Bala Cynwyd)	42
Niagara Falls	Niagara	34			
Nyack/Palisades	Rockland	38			
Plattsburgh	Clinton	34	Lancaster	Lancaster	38

Locations Eligible for $34, $38, $42 or $46 a Day Meal Allowance for Travel on or After January 1, 1999

KEY CITY	COUNTY/LOCATION	AMOUNT(S)	KEY CITY	COUNTY/LOCATION	AMOUNT(S)
PENNSYLVANIA (continued)			VIRGINIA		
Malvern/ Downington/Valley Forge	Chester	38	Alexandria	Independent city	42
			Arlington	Arlington	42
Mechanicsburg	Cumberland	34	Blacksburg	Montgomery	34
Philadelphia	Philadelphia County and Bala Cynwyd city limits	46	Charlottesville	Independent city	42
			Chesterfield County	Chesterfield County	38
Pittsburgh	Allegheny	46	Fairfax/Falls Church	Fairfax County	42
Reading	Berks	38	Loudoun County	Loudoun	38
Warminster	Bucks County; Naval Air Development Center	42	Lynchburg	Independent city	38
			Manassas	Prince William County (other than Woodbridge)	34
Wayne	Wayne city limits	42			
RHODE ISLAND			Richmond	Independent city	38
Block Island	Block Island city limits	42	Roanoke	Independent city	34
East Greenwich	Kent County, Naval Construction Battalion Center in Davisville	38	Shenandoah County	Shenandoah County	34
			Virginia Beach	Virginia Beach (also Norfolk, Portsmouth and Chesapeake)	38
Newport	Newport	42			
Providence	Providence	42			
SOUTH CAROLINA			Wallops Island	Accomack	34
Charleston	Charleston	42	Williamsburg	Williamsburg (also Hampton, Newport News, York County, Naval Weapons Station, and Yorktown)	38
Columbia	Richland	38			
Greenville	Greenville	38			
Hilton Head	Beaufort	42			
Myrtle Beach	Horry County; Myrtle Beach AFB	42	Wintergreen	Nelson	46
Spartanburg	Spartanburg	34	Woodbridge	Woodbridge city limits	38
SOUTH DAKOTA			WASHINGTON		
Custer	Custer	34	Anacortes	Skagit	38
Rapid City	Pennington	34	Bellingham	Whatcom	34
TENNESSEE			Bremerton	Kitsap	34
Chattanooga	Hamilton	34	Everett	Snohomish (other than Lynnwood)	38
Gatlinburg	Sevier	38	Friday Harbor	San Juan	42
Knoxville	Knox	38	Island County	Island County	34
Memphis	Shelby	38	Lynnwood	Lynnwood city limits	34
Nashville	Davidson	42	Ocean Shores	Grays Harbor	38
Townsend	Blount	34	Olympia/Turnwater	Thurston	38
TEXAS			Port Angeles	Port Angeles city limits	38
Arlington	Tarrant	34	Port Townsend	Jefferson	34
Austin	Travis	38	Seattle	King	46
Brownsville	Cameron	34	Sequim	Clallam (other than Port Angeles)	34
College Station	Brazos	34	Spokane	Spokane	38
Corpus Christi	Nueces	38	Tacoma	Pierce	38
Dallas	Dallas	46	Vancouver	Clark	38
El Paso	El Paso	38	WEST VIRGINIA		
Fort Worth	Fort Worth city limits	38	Berkeley Springs	Morgan	34
Galveston	Galveston	42	Charleston	Kanawha	38
Houston	Harris County; LBJ Space Center and Ellington AFB	42	Harpers Ferry	Jefferson	34
			Morgantown	Monogalia	34
Laredo	Webb	34	Parkersburg	Wood	34
Lubbock	Lubbock	34	Wheeling	Ohio	34
McAllen	Hidalgo	34	WISCONSIN		
Odessa	Ector	34	Brookfield	Waukesha	38
Plano	Collin	34	Eau Claire	Eau Claire	34
San Antonio	Bexar	42	Green Bay	Brown	34
South Padre Island	Cameron	38	Lake Geneva	Walworth	38
Tyler	Smith	34	Madison	Dane	38
UTAH			Milwaukee	Milwaukee	42
Cedar City	Iron	34	Minocqua/Rhinelander	Oneida	38
Davis County	Davis County	34	Oshkosh	Winnebago	34
Moab	Grand	34	Sturgeon Bay	Door	34
Ogden	Weber	34	Wisconsin Dells	Columbia	38
Park City	Summit	46	WYOMING		
Provo	Utah	38	Jackson	Teton	42
Salt Lake City	Salt Lake, Dugway Proving Ground and Tooele Army Depot	42			
VERMONT					
Burlington/St. Albans	Chittendon; Franklin	38			
Manchester	Bennington	42			
Middlebury	Addison	38			
Rutland	Rutland	34			
White River Junction	Windsor	34			

Deducting Travel Expenses Away From Home

20.5 Business Trip Deductions

The following expenses of a business trip *away from home (20.6)* are deductible if not reimbursed by your employer:

- Plane, railroad, taxi, and other transportation fares
- Hotel and lodging expenses
- Meal costs. Only 50% of the cost of the meal is deductible. The business discussion test in *20.16* does not apply to meal costs on business trips provided you eat alone or with your family or personal acquaintances.
- Tips, telephone, and telegraph costs
- Laundry and cleaning expenses
- Baggage charges (including insurance)
- Cab fares or other costs of transportation to and from the airport or station and your hotel. Also deductible are cab fares or other transportation costs, beginning with your first business call of the day, of getting from one customer to another, or from one place of business to another.
- Travel costs to find a new job are deductible; *see 19.7.*
- Entertainment expenses incurred while traveling away from home are deductible under the rules at *20.6.*

Cruise ship. If you travel by cruise ship on a business trip, your deductible cruise costs are limited to twice the highest federal *per diem* rate for travel in the United States on that date multiplied by the number of days in transit.

EXAMPLE

You sail to Europe on business. While you are away, the highest per diem federal rate is $241 and the trip lasts five days. The maximum deduction for the cost of the trip is $2,410 (2 × $241 × 5). The double *per diem* rule applies without regard to the 50% limit on meal costs if meals are not separately stated in your bill. If a separate amount for meals or entertainment is included, such amount must be reduced by 50%.

The double *per diem* rule does not apply to cruise ship convention costs that are deductible up to $2,000 a year, if all the ports of call are in the U.S. or U.S. possessions and if the ship is registered in the United States; *see 20.14.*

Important: Record-keeping requirements. See the section beginning at *20.26* for record-keeping rules to support a deduction for unreimbursed travel expenses or to avoid being taxed on employer reimbursements.

20.6 When Are You Away From Home?

You have to meet the "away from home" test to deduct the cost of meals (only 50% deductible) and lodging while traveling.

EXAMPLES

1. Your residence is in a suburb within commuting distance of New York City where you work full time. Your personal home and tax home are the same, that is, within the metropolitan area of New York City. You are away from home when you leave this area, say for Philadelphia. Meals and lodging are deductible only if you meet the overnight-sleep test; see 20.3.

2. Your residence is in New York City, but you work in Baltimore. Your tax home is Baltimore; you may not deduct living expenses there. But you may deduct travel expenses on a temporary assignment to New York City even while living at your home there.

3. A construction worker works for a utility company on construction sites in a 12-state area. Assignments are sent from his employer's regional office; he is not required to report to the office. The IRS ruled that his residence, which is in a city in the 12-state area, is his tax home.

Law Alert

Tax Home Defined

For travel expense purposes, your home is your place of business, employment, or post of duty, regardless of where you maintain your family residence. This tax home includes the entire city or general area of your business premises or place of employment. The area of your residence may be your tax home if your job requires you to work at widely scattered locations, you have no fixed place of work, and your residence is in a location economically suited to your work.

Are you constantly on the road? If you move from job to job and do not work within any particular locality, an IRS agent may disallow your travel deductions on the grounds that your tax home is wherever you work; thus, you are never "away from home." You are considered a transient worker.

If your deduction is questioned because you have no regular or main place of business, you may be able to show that your tax home is the area of your residence. If you meet the following three tests, the IRS will treat your residence as your tax home: (1) you do some work in the vicinity of your residence, house, apartment, or room and live there while performing services in the area; (2) you have mortgage expenses or pay rent for the residence while away on the road; and (3) the residence is in an area where you were raised or lived for a long time, or a member of your immediate family such as your parent or child lives in the residence, or you frequently return there.

According to the IRS, if you meet only two of these three tests, it will decide on a case-by-case basis if your residence is your tax home. If you meet less than two of the tests, the IRS will not allow a deduction; each of your work locations is treated as your tax home.

If you live in a trailer at each job assignment and have no other home, each job location is your principal place of business and you are not "away from home."

Permanent duty station of service members. The Supreme Court held that a member of the Armed Forces is not away from home when he or she is at a permanent duty station. This is true even if the service member has to maintain a separate home for family members who are not permitted to live at the duty station.

20.7 Fixing a Tax Home If You Work in Different Locations

If you regularly work in two or more separate areas, your tax home is the area of your principal place of business or employment. You are away from home when you are away from the area of your principal place of business or employment. Therefore, you may deduct your transportation costs to and from your minor place of business and your living costs there.

Professional sports players, coaches, and managers. When the only business of such persons is the professional sport, their home is the "club town." But if they are in another business in addition to their professional playing, how much time is spent and how much is earned at each place determines whether their club's hometown or the place of their off-season business is their tax home. If it is the club's hometown, they deduct travel and living expenses while away from that town—including the time they are where the second business is. (If the second place is where their families also live, they may not deduct the families' expenses there.) If the town where the other business is located is the tax home, then expenses in the club's hometown may be deducted.

Airline pilots. It is important for airline pilots who fly in and out of various locations to determine a tax home for income and deduction purposes. Generally, the IRS considers an airline pilot's tax home to be the airport at which the pilot is regularly based. For example, in one case the IRS barred a pilot from claiming the foreign earned income exclusion *(36.1)* because his tax home was deemed to be his base in New York, rather than in London, where he and his wife actually lived.

EXAMPLES

1. Sherman lived in Worcester, Mass., where he managed a factory. He opened his own sales agency in New York. He continued to manage the factory and spent considerable time in Worcester. The larger part of his income came from the New York business. However, he was allowed to treat New York as his minor place of business and to deduct his travel expenses to New York and his living expenses there because he spent most of his time in Worcester and his income there was substantial.

2. Benson, a consulting engineer, maintained a combination residence-business office in a home he owned in New York. He also taught four days a week at a Technological Institute in West Virginia under a temporary nine-month appointment. He spent three-day weekends, holidays, and part of the summer at his New York address. At the Institute, he rented a room in the student union building. The IRS disallowed transportation expenses between New York and West Virginia and meals and lodging there as not incurred while away from home. The Tax Court disagreed. A taxpayer may have more than one occupation in more than one city. When his occupations require him to spend a substantial amount of time in each place, he may deduct his travel expenses, including meals and lodging, at the place away from his permanent residence. That Benson's teaching salary happened to exceed his income from his private practice does not change the result.

Planning Reminder

Determining Your Principal Place of Business

If you have more than one regular place of business, your tax home is your principal place of business. Your principal place of business or employment is determined by comparing: (1) the time ordinarily spent working in each area; (2) the degree of your business activity in each area; (3) the amount of your income from each area; (4) the taxpayer's permanent residence; and (5) whether employment at one location is temporary or indefinite.

No single factor is determinative. The relative importance of each fact will vary depending on the facts of a particular case. For example, where there are no substantial differences between incomes earned in two places of employment, your tax home is probably the area in which you spend more of your time. Where there are substantial income differences, your tax home is probably the area in which you earn more of your income.

20.8 Tax Home of Married Couple Working in Different Cities

When a husband and wife work and live in different cities during the week, one of them may seek to deduct travel expenses away from home. Such deductions have generally been disallowed, but courts have allowed some exceptions. Although for common law purposes the domicile of the husband may be the domicile of the wife, for tax purposes when each spouse works in a different city, each may have a separate tax home.

EXAMPLES
1. Robert worked in Wilmington, Delaware; his wife, Margaret, worked in New York City. During the weekend, she traveled to Wilmington and deducted, as travel expenses away from home, her living costs in New York and weekend travel expenses to Wilmington. She argued that because she and her husband filed a joint return, they were a single taxable unit, and the tax home of this unit was Wilmington where her husband lived. The deduction was disallowed. That a couple can file a joint return does not give them deductions that are not otherwise available to them as individuals. Margaret's tax home was New York, where she worked. Therefore, her expenses there are not deductible. And, as the weekend trips to Wilmington had no relationship to her job, they, too, were not deductible.
2. Hundt and his wife lived in Arlington, Va., but he wrote and directed films in various parts of the country. He wrote screenplays either at his Arlington home or on location, but most of his business came from New York City, where he lived in hotels. One year, he spent 175 days in New York City on business and rented an apartment for $1,200 because it was cheaper than a hotel. He deducted half the annual rent for the New York apartment, the costs of traveling between Arlington and New York, and the cost of meals in New York. The IRS disallowed the expenses, finding New York to be his tax home. The Tax Court disagreed. Arlington was Hundt's tax home because (1) part of his income came from his creative writing in Arlington; and (2) his travel to other parts of the country was temporary. The fact that most of his income came from New York did not make New York his tax home.

20.9 Deducting Living Costs on Temporary Assignment

A business trip or job assignment away from home *(20.6)* at a single location may last a few days, weeks, or months. If your assignment is considered *temporary*, you may deduct travel costs (*see* below) while there because your tax home has not changed. An assignment is considered temporary by the IRS if you realistically expect it to last for one year or less and it actually does last no more than one year. If an assignment is realistically expected to last more than a year it is considered *indefinite*, and you cannot deduct your living costs at the area of the assignment because that location becomes your tax home. You can be away for a year or less and still be barred from claiming a deduction if at the time you started the assignment you realistically expected it to last for more than a year. Likewise, employment that is initially temporary may become indefinite due to changed circumstances; *see* the Examples below.

EXAMPLES
1. You are on a job assignment away from home in a single location that is expected to last (and it does in fact last) for one year or less. The IRS will treat the employment as temporary, unless facts and circumstances indicate otherwise. Expenses are deductible.
2. You are sent on a job assignment away from home at a *single* location. You expected that the job would last 18 months. However, due to financial difficulties you were transferred home after 11 months. Even though your assignment actually lasted for less than one year the IRS treats the employment as indefinite because you realistically expected it to last more than one year. Thus, your travel and living expenses while away from home are not deductible.
3. You are sent on a job assignment away from home at a *single* location. You expected that the job would last only nine months. However, due to changed circumstances occurring after eight months, you were asked to remain on the assignment for six more months. The IRS treats the assignment as temporary for eight months, and indefinite for the remaining time you are away from home. Thus, travel and living expenses you paid or incurred during the first eight months are deductible; expenses paid or incurred thereafter are not.

 Law Alert

Federal Crime Investigations

Federal employees such as FBI agents and prosecutors who are certified by the Attorney General as traveling on behalf of the federal government in a temporary duty status to investigate, prosecute, or provide support services for the investigation or prosecution of a federal crime are not subject to the one-year limitation on deductibility of expenses while away from home on temporary assignments.

Deductible travel costs on temporary trip. While on a temporary job assignment expected to last a year or less, you may deduct the cost of meals and lodging there, even for your days off. If you return home, say for weekends, your living expenses at home are not deductible. You may deduct travel expenses, meals, and lodging en route between your home and your job assignment provided they do not exceed your living expenses had you stayed at the temporary job location. If you keep a hotel room at the temporary location while you return home, you may deduct your round-trip expenses for the trip home only up to the amount you would have spent for meals had you stayed at the temporary workplace.

EXAMPLE

Michaels, a cost analyst for Boeing, lived in Seattle. He traveled for Boeing, but was generally not away from home for more than five weeks. Michaels agreed to go to Los Angeles for a year to service Boeing's suppliers in that area. He rented his Seattle house and brought his family with him to Los Angeles. Ten months later, Boeing opened a permanent office in Los Angeles and asked Michaels to remain there permanently. Michaels argued that his expenses for food and lodging during the 10-month period were deductible as "away from home" expenses. The IRS contended that the Los Angeles assignment was for an indefinite period.

The Tax Court sided with Michaels. He was told that the stay was for a year only. He leased his Seattle house to a tenant for one year, planning to return to it. He regarded his work in Los Angeles as temporary until Boeing changed its plans. The one-year period justified his taking the family but did not alter the temporary nature of the assignment.

No regular job where you live. That you do not have regular employment where you live may prevent a deduction of living costs at a temporary job in another city. The IRS may disallow the deduction on the grounds that the expenses are not incurred while away from home; the temporary job site is the tax home.

 Caution

Taking Your Family With You
If you take your family with you to a temporary job site, an IRS agent may argue that this is evidence that you considered the assignment to be indefinite. In the Michaels Example on this page, however, such a move was not considered detrimental to a deduction of living expenses at the job location.

Deducting Expenses of a Business-Vacation Trip

20.10 Business-Vacation Trips Within the United States

On a business trip to a resort area, you may also spend time vacationing. If the *primary purpose* of the trip is to transact business and the area is within the United States (50 states and District of Columbia) you may deduct all of the costs of your transportation to and from the area, lodging, and 50% of meal expenses, even if you do spend time vacationing. If the main purpose of the trip was personal, you may not deduct any part of your travel costs to and from the area. The amount of time spent on business as opposed to sightseeing or personal visits is the most important issue in determining your primary purpose. Regardless of the primary purpose of your trip, you are allowed to deduct expenses related to the business you transacted while in the area.

No deductions will be allowed if you attend a convention or seminar where you are given videotapes to view at your own convenience and no other business-related activities or lectures occur during the convention. The trip is considered a vacation.

If your trip is primarily for business, and while at the business destination you extend your stay for a few days for nonbusiness reasons, such as to visit relatives, you deduct travel expenses to and from the business destination.

 Caution

Primary Business Purpose
If your return is examined, proving the business purpose of your trip depends on presenting evidence to convince an examining agent that the trip, despite your vacationing, was planned primarily to transact business. Keep a log or diary to substantiate business activities.

EXAMPLE

You work in Atlanta and make a business trip to New Orleans. You stay in New Orleans for six days and your total costs, including round-trip transportation to and from New Orleans, meals, and lodging, is $600, which you may deduct subject to the 50% limit for meals. If, on your way home, you spend three days in Mobile visiting relatives and incur an additional $200 in travel costs, your deduction is limited to the $600 (less 50% of meals) you would have spent had you gone home directly from New Orleans.

Reimbursement for weekend travel. If your employer extends your business trip over a weekend to take advantage of discount airfares that require a Saturday night stayover, you may deduct the cost of meals, lodging, and other incidental expenses incurred for the additional night. The reason for the stayover has a business purpose: to cut travel costs. If your employer pays for the expenses directly or if you are reimbursed under an accountable plan *(20.31)*, the payment is not taxable to you.

20.11 Business-Vacation Trips Outside the United States

On a business trip abroad, you may deduct your travel expenses (50% of meals), even though you take time out to vacation, provided you can prove: (1) the primary purpose of the trip was business and (2) you did not have control over the assignment of the trip.

Fixing the date of the trip does not mean that you had control over the assignment. IRS regulations assume that when you travel for your company under a reimbursement or allowance arrangement, you do not control the trip arrangements, provided also that you are not: (1) a managing executive of the company; (2) related to your employer; or (3) have more than a 10% stock interest in the company. You are considered a managing executive if you are authorized without effective veto procedures to decide on the necessity of the trip. You are related to your employer if the employer is your spouse, parent, child, brother, sister, grandparent, or grandchild.

Rule for managing executives and self-employed persons. If you are a managing executive, self-employed, related to your employer, or have a more-than-10% stock interest, you may deduct all transportation costs if:

1. The trip outside the United States took a week or less, not counting the day you left the U.S. but counting the day you returned,
2. If the trip abroad lasted more than a week, you spent less than 25% of your time, counting the days your trip began and ended, on vacation or other personal activities, *or*
3. In planning the trip you did not place a major emphasis on taking a vacation.

If the vacationing and other personal activities took up 25% or more of your time on a trip lasting more than one week, and you cannot prove that the vacation was a minor consideration in planning the trip, you must allocate travel expenses between the time spent on business and that spent on personal affairs. The part allocated to business is deductible; the balance is not. To allocate, count the number of days spent on the trip outside the United States, including the day you leave the U.S. and the day you return. Then divide this total into the number of days on which you had business activities; include days of travel to and from a business destination.

If you vacation at, near or beyond the city in which you do business, the expense subject to allocation is the cost of travel from the place of departure to the business destination and back. For example, you travel from New York to London on business and then vacation in Paris before returning to New York. The expense subject to allocation is the cost of traveling from New York to London and back; *see* Example 2. However, if from London you vacationed in Dublin before returning to New York, you would allocate the round-trip fare between New York and Dublin and also deduct the difference between that round-trip fare and the fare between New York and London; *see* Example 3 on the next page.

EXAMPLES

1. You fly from New York to Paris to attend a business meeting for one day. You spend the next two days sightseeing and then fly back to New York. The entire trip, including two days for travel en route, took five days. The plane fare is deductible. The trip did not exceed one week.

2. You fly from Chicago to New York, where you spend six days on business. You then fly to London, where you conduct business for two days. You then fly to Paris for a five-day vacation after which you fly back to Chicago. You would not have made the trip except for the business that you had to transact in London. The nine days of travel outside the United States away from home, including two days for travel en route, exceeded a week, and the five days devoted to vacationing were not less than 25% of the total travel time outside the U.S. The two days spent traveling between Chicago and New York, and the six days spent in New York, are not counted in determining whether the travel outside the United States exceeded a week and whether the time devoted to personal activities was less than 25%.

Caution

Vacation Areas

If the IRS determines that you were primarily on vacation, it will disallow all travel costs except for costs directly related to your business in the area such as registration fees at a foreign business convention; *see 20.14.*

Assume you are unable to prove either that you did not have substantial control over the arrangements of the trip or that an opportunity for taking a personal vacation was not a major consideration in your decision to take the trip. Thus, $\frac{5}{9}$ (five nonbusiness days out of nine days outside the U.S.) of the plane fare from New York to London and from London to New York is not deductible. You may deduct $\frac{4}{9}$ of the New York-to-London round-trip fare, plus lodging, 50% of meals, and other allowable travel costs while in London. No deduction is allowed for any part of the costs of the trip from London to Paris.

3. Same facts as in Example 2, except that the vacation is in Dublin, which is closer to the U.S. than London. The allocation is based on the round-trip fare between New York and Dublin. Thus, $\frac{4}{9}$ of the New York to Dublin fare is deductible and $\frac{5}{9}$ is not deductible. Further, the IRS allows a deduction for the excess of the New York-to-London fare over the New York-to-Dublin fare.

Weekends, holidays, and business standby days. If you have business meetings scheduled before and after a weekend or holiday, the days in between the meetings are treated as days spent on business for purposes of the 25% business test just discussed. This is true although you spend the days for sightseeing or other personal travel. A similar rule applies if you have business meetings on Friday and the next scheduled meeting is the following Tuesday; Saturday through Monday are treated as business days. If your trip is extended over a weekend to take advantage of reduced airfares, the additional expense of meals, lodging, and other incidental expenses is deductible; *see 20.10.*

20.12 Deducting Expenses of Business Conventions

Conventions and seminars at resort areas usually combine business with pleasure. Therefore, the IRS scrutinizes deductions claimed for attending a business convention where opportunities exist for vacationing. Especially questioned are trips where you are accompanied by your spouse and other members of your family. Foreign conventions are discussed at *20.14.*

Generally, you may not deduct expenses of attending investment conventions and seminars; *see 19.24.* You also may not deduct the costs of business conventions or seminars where you merely receive a videotape of business lectures to be viewed at your convenience and no other business-related activities occur during the event.

In claiming a deduction for convention expenses, be prepared to show that the convention was connected with your business. Cases and IRS rulings have upheld deductions for doctors, lawyers, and dentists attending professional conventions. One case allowed a deduction to a legal secretary for her costs at a secretaries' convention. If you are a delegate to a business convention, make sure you prove you attended to serve primarily your own business interests, not those of the association. However, it is not necessary for you to show that the convention dealt specifically with your job. It is sufficient that attendance at the convention may advance or benefit your position. If you fail to prove business purpose, the IRS will allocate your expenses between the time spent on your business and the time spent as a delegate. You then deduct only the expenses attributed to your business activities.

EXAMPLES

1. An attorney with a general law practice was interested in international law and relations. He was appointed a delegate to represent the American branch of the International Law Association at a convention in Paris. The attorney deducted the cost of the trip and convention as business expenses which the IRS and a court disallowed. He failed to prove that attending the conference on international law helped his general practice. He did not get any business referrals as a result of his attendance at the convention. Nor did he prove the chance of getting any potential business from the conference.

2. An insurance agent doing business in Texas attended his company's convention in New York. One morning of the six-day convention was devoted to a business meeting and luncheon; the rest of the time was spent in sightseeing and entertainment. The company paid for the cost of the trip. The IRS added the reimbursement to the agent's pay and would not let him deduct the amount. The convention in New York served no business purpose. It was merely a method of entertaining company personnel. If there was any valid business to be transacted, the company could have called a meeting in Texas, the area of his home office.

 Filing Tip

Weekend Expenses

If your business trip is extended over a weekend to take advantage of reduced airfares, the additional cost of meals, lodging, and other incidental expenses is deductible.

3. A plywood company could not deduct the costs of entertaining 116 customers and employees at a New Orleans hotel during a Superbowl weekend. The company did not reserve conference rooms or make any other arrangements for organized business meetings. The IRS and two federal courts held that although business discussions may have occurred on a random basis, these were secondary to entertainment.

What expenses are deductible? If the convention trip is primarily for business, you may deduct travel costs both to and from the convention, food costs, tips, display expenses (such as sample room costs), and hotel bills. If you entertain business clients or customers, you may deduct these amounts too.

Food and beverage costs are subject to the 50% cost limitation rule as explained in *20.24*.

EXAMPLE

You attend a business convention held in a coastal resort city primarily for business reasons. During the convention period, you do some local sightseeing, social entertaining, and visiting—all unrelated to your business. You may deduct your traveling expenses to and from the resort, your living expenses at the resort, and other expenses such as business entertaining, sample displays, etc. But you may not deduct the cost of sightseeing, personal entertaining, and social visiting.

Keep records of your payments identifying expenses directly connected with your business dealings at the convention and those that are part of your personal activity, such as sightseeing, social visiting, and entertaining. Recreation costs are not deductible even though a part of your overall convention costs.

Fraternal organizations. You may not deduct expenses at conventions held by fraternal organizations, such as the American Legion, Shriners, etc., even though incidental business was carried on. However, delegates to fraternal conventions may in some instances deduct expenses as charitable contributions; *see 14.4.*

20.13 Travel Expenses of a Spouse or Dependents

Travel costs of a spouse, dependent, or any other individual who is not a business associate and who accompanies you on a business trip are not deductible unless that person is also your employee and has a bona fide business reason for taking the trip that would justify claiming a deduction if the person took the trip on his or her own.

Even though the travel costs of a non-employee spouse or other person are not deductible, you may deduct the cost of such person's participation in the entertainment of business clients at conventions or business trips if the trip or entertainment meets the tests at *20.21*. Generally, you may deduct the cost of goodwill entertaining of associates immediately before or after convention business meetings. A convention meeting qualifies as a bona fide business meeting.

EXAMPLES

1. You and your spouse travel by car to a convention. You pay $120 a day for a double room. A single room would have cost $100 a day. Your spouse's presence at the convention was for social reasons. You may deduct the total cost of operating your car to and from the convention city. You may deduct $100 a day for your room. If you traveled by plane or railroad, you would deduct only your own fare.
2. Connie worked with her husband operating a home improvement contracting business. With him, she attended trade shows and conventions, where they ran a display booth. There, she talked about their company's services and solicited new business. The IRS disallowed the company's deduction of her travel expenses as having no business purpose. The Tax Court disagreed. Both Connie and her husband were officers and employees of the company. They attended the conferences together. As the IRS allowed her husband's expenses, it should have also allowed expenses attributed to her participation, especially as they were incurred together as employees.

 Caution

Substantiate Convention Business

Keep a copy of the convention program and a record of the business sessions you attend. If the convention provides a sign-in book, sign it. In addition, keep a record of all of your business expenses as explained in *20.26*.

 Filing Tip

How Much To Deduct for Spouse

If your spouse accompanied you on a business trip, your bills will probably show costs for both of you. These usually are less than twice the cost for a single person. To find what you may deduct where your spouse's presence is for personal and not qualifying business reasons, do not divide the bill in half. Figure what accommodations and transportation would have cost you alone. Only the excess over the single person's costs is not deductible.

20.14 Restrictions on Foreign Conventions and Cruises

You may not deduct expenses at a foreign convention outside the North American area unless you satisfy the rules at *20.11* and also can show the convention is directly related to your business and it was as reasonable for the meeting to be held outside the North American area as within it.

Apart from the United States, the North American area includes Mexico, Canada, Puerto Rico, U.S. Virgin Islands, American Samoa, Northern Mariana Islands, Guam, Marshall Islands, Micronesia, Palau and U.S. island possessions.

Conventions may also be held in eligible Caribbean countries that agree to exchange certain data with the U.S. and do not discriminate against conventions held in the United States. Barbados, Bermuda, Costa Rica, Dominica, Dominican Republic, Grenada, Guyana, Honduras, Jamaica, Saint Lucia, and Trinidad and Tobago have qualified and are considered to be within the North American area.

Check with the convention operator about whether the country in which your convention is being held has qualified.

Limited cruise ship deduction. Up to $2,000 a year is allowed for attending cruise ship conventions if all the ports of call are in the U.S. or U.S. possessions and if the ship is registered in the United States. A deduction is allowed only if you attach to your return statements signed by you and by an officer of the convention sponsor that detail the daily schedule of business activities, the number of hours you attended these activities, and the total days of the trip. Do not confuse the $2,000 limitation with the *per diem* limitation for cruise ship costs discussed at *20.5*. The *per diem* limitation does not apply to cruises that meet the tests for the up-to-$2,000 deduction.

Meals and Entertainment Expenses

20.15 50% Deduction Limit

You may not deduct the full cost of entertainment for customers or clients at restaurants, country clubs, at home, theaters, and sporting events, even if the expenses qualify under the restrictive tests discussed at *20.16*. Only 50% of unreimbursed expenses is deductible and this 50% balance is reduced by the 2% AGI floor if you are an employee. Furthermore, all entertainment costs, including meals, must be backed up with records. If you do not keep adequate records, your deductions will be disallowed. The 50% deduction limit for meals and entertainment is discussed at *20.24*.

20.16 The Restrictive Tests for Meals and Entertainment

You must be prepared to show that meal and entertainment costs are ordinary and necessary to your business, and also:

1. Directly related to the active conduct of your business *(20.17)*, *or*

2. Directly preceding or following a substantial and bona fide business discussion on a subject associated with the active conduct of your business. This test applies to dining and entertainment in which you seek new business or to goodwill entertainment to encourage the continuation of an existing business relationship. Under this test, you may entertain business associates in nonbusiness settings such as restaurants, theaters, sports arenas, and nightclubs, provided the entertainment directly precedes or follows the business discussion. Business associates are: established or prospective customers, clients, suppliers, employees, agents, partners, or professional advisers, whether established or prospective; *see 20.18*.

20.17 Directly Related Dining and Entertainment

The directly related test limits the deduction of dining and entertainment costs at restaurants, nightclubs, on yachts, at sporting events, on hunting trips, and during social events. If such dining or entertainment fails to meet the directly related tests, it may qualify under the rules discussed in *20.18*, which require the holding of a business discussion before or after the entertainment.

The directly related test may be met in one of three ways: (1) under the generally related test; (2) as expenses incurred in a clear business setting; or (3) as expenses incurred for services performed.

Generally related test. Under this test, you must show a business motive for the dining or entertainment and business activity during the entertainment. You must show that you had more than a general expectation of getting future income or other specific business benefit (other than goodwill). Although you do not have to prove that income or other business benefit actually re-

Planning Reminder

Scheduling Entertainment and Business Discussions
A business discussion generally must take place the same day as the dining or entertainment. If not, and your deduction is questioned, you must give an acceptable reason for the interval between the discussion and the dining or entertainment. IRS regulations recognize that a day may separate a business meeting and the entertainment of an out-of-town customer. He or she may come to your office to discuss business one day and you provide entertainment the next day, or you provide the entertainment on the first day and discuss business the day after.

The IRS does not estimate how long a business discussion should last. But it does warn that a meeting must involve a discussion or negotiation to obtain income or business benefits. It does not require that more time be devoted to the meeting than to the entertainment.

Caution

Hunting or Fishing Trips

The IRS presumes entertainment during a hunting or fishing trip or on a yacht is not conducive to business discussion or activity. You must prove otherwise.

sulted from the expense, such evidence will help support your claim. What type of business activity will an IRS agent look for? The agent will seek proof that a business meeting, negotiation, or discussion took place during the period of dining or entertainment. It is not necessary that more time be devoted to business than to entertainment. What if you did not talk business? You must prove that you would have done so except for reasons beyond your control.

Clear business setting test. Expenses incurred in a clear business setting meet the directly related test provided also that you had no significant motive for incurring the expenses other than to further your business. Entertainment of people with whom you have no personal or social relationship is usually considered to have occurred in a clear business setting. For example, entertainment of business representatives and civic leaders at the opening of a new hotel or theatrical production to obtain business publicity rather than goodwill is considered to be entertainment in a clear business setting. Also, entertainment that involves a price rebate is considered to have occurred in a clear business setting, as, for example, when a hotel owner provides occasional free dinners at the hotel for a customer who patronizes the hotel.

Costs of a hospitality room displaying company products at a convention are also a directly related expense.

Entertainment occurring under the following circumstances or in the following places is generally not considered as directly related:

- You are not present during the entertainment.
- The distractions are substantial, as at nightclubs, sporting events, or during a social gathering such as a cocktail party.
- You meet with a group that includes persons other than business associates at cocktail lounges, country clubs, golf and athletic clubs, or at vacation resorts.

Services performed test. An expense is directly related if it was directly or indirectly made for the benefit of an individual (other than an employee) either as taxable compensation for services he or she rendered or as a taxable prize or award. The amount of the expense must be reported on an information Form 1099 (unless the amount is less than $600).

EXAMPLE

A manufacturer provides a vacation trip for retailers whose sales of his products exceed quotas. The value of the vacation is a taxable prize to the retailers. The vacation cost is a directly related entertainment expense for the manufacturer.

20.18 Goodwill Entertainment

Goodwill entertaining may qualify as deductible entertainment. Dining and entertainment costs may be deductible if a substantial and *bona fide* business discussion directly preceded or followed the dining or entertainment.

An officially scheduled meeting at a convention is generally considered a bona fide business discussion.

EXAMPLES

1. During the day, you negotiate with a group of business associates. In the evening, you entertain the group and their spouses at a theater and nightclub. The cost of the entertainment is deductible, even though arranged to promote goodwill.

2. In the evening after a business meeting at a convention, you entertain associates or prospective customers and their spouses. You may deduct the entertainment costs.

20.19 Home Entertaining

The cost of entertaining business customers or clients at home is deductible provided a business discussion occurs before, during, or after the meal. When you claim such a deduction, be ready to prove that your motive for dining with them was business rather than social. Have a record of the entertainment costs, names of the guests, and their business affiliations.

20.20 Your Personal Share

If the entertaining occurred while on a business trip away from home, you deduct your own meal cost as travel expenses away from home. If the entertaining occurred within the locality of your regular place of business, whether you will be allowed a deduction for your share will depend on the agent examining your return. The IRS said in a ruling that an agent will not disallow your deduction of your own part of the meal cost unless he or she finds that you are claiming a substantial amount that includes personal living expenses. In such a case, which generally is limited to situations where personal meals are regularly claimed as part of an "abusive" pattern, the agent will follow the stricter Tax Court rule (sometimes referred to as the "Sutter" rule) and allow only that part of the meal cost that exceeds what you would usually spend on yourself when alone.

20.21 Entertainment Costs of Spouses

A deduction is allowed for the spouses' share of the entertainment costs if they were present during entertainment that qualified as directly related entertainment under the general rule discussed in *20.17*. For goodwill entertainment, the cost of entertainment of the spouses is deductible if your share and the business associate's share of the entertainment is deductible. The IRS recognizes that when an out-of-town customer is accompanied by his or her spouse, it may be impracticable to entertain the customer without the spouse. Under such circumstances, the cost of the spouse's entertainment is deductible if the customer's entertainment costs are also deductible. Furthermore, if your spouse joined the party because the customer's spouse was present, the expenses of your spouse are also deductible.

20.22 Entertainment Facilities and Club Dues

You may not deduct the expenses of maintaining and operating facilities used to entertain. By law, entertainment facilities are not considered business assets. Examples of entertainment facilities are yachts, hunting lodges, fishing camps, swimming pools, tennis courts, automobiles, airplanes, apartments, hotel suites, or homes in a vacation area. A season box seat or pass at a sporting event or theater is not considered an entertainment facility.

The disallowance rule applies to operating expenses such as rent, utilities, and security, and also to depreciation, but not to such expenses as interest, taxes, and casualty losses that are deductible without having to show business purpose.

A deduction may be allowed for expenses such as the cost of food and drinks incurred at an entertainment facility, if they meet the rules of *20.16* through *20.21*.

Club dues. You may not deduct dues for country clubs, golf and athletic clubs, airline clubs, hotel clubs, business luncheon clubs, and other clubs organized for business, pleasure, recreation, or other social purposes. However, IRS regulations generally allow a deduction for dues paid to (1) civic or public service organizations such as Kiwanis, Lions, and Rotary clubs; (2) professional organizations such as medical or bar associations; and (3) chambers of commerce, trade associations, business leagues, real estate boards and boards of trade. The deduction for dues is allowed provided that the organization in (1)–(3) does not have a principal purpose of providing entertainment for members or their guests.

20.23 Restrictive Test Exception for Reimbursements

As an employer, you can deduct expense allowances or other reimbursements of employee expenses that you treat as compensation and from which you withhold federal tax. You are not subject to the 50% deduction limit for meals and entertainment; the employee is, when claiming the meals on Form 2106.

A similar rule applies to meal allowances or reimbursements that you give to an independent contractor and that you report as compensation on Form 1099-MISC where the contractor does not adequately account for the expenses.

The restrictive tests of *20.16* do not apply to such reimbursements. They are deductible if they are "ordinary and necessary" business expenses, and you have records to back up the deduction.

20.24 50% Cost Limitation on Meals and Entertainment

You may not deduct the full amount of your deductible expenses for business meals and entertainment expenses, such as tickets to sports events. Only 50% of the otherwise allowable amount for food, beverages, and entertainment is deductible.

 Filing Tip

Allocating Payment Covering Lodging and Meals

A hotel may include meals in a room charge. In such cases, the room charge must be allocated between the meals, and entertainment and lodging. The amount allocated to meals and entertainment is subject to the 50% cost limitation. If you receive a *per diem* allowance from your employer covering both lodging and meals under an accountable reimbursement plan, you may have to allocate part of the reimbursement to meals in order to deduct expenses in excess of the reimbursement; *see 20.31*.

 Law Alert

Proposed Increase to 50% Meal Limit

When this book went to press, Congress was considering legislation that would increase the deductible percentage for business meals, but not until 2006. The deductible limit would be 55% in 2006 and 60% in 2007 and later years. *See* the Supplement for an update.

Law Alert

Transportation Industry Workers

Individuals subject to Department of Transportation limitations on hours of service, such as interstate truck drivers, may claim a higher deductible percentage of food and beverages when working away from home. The deductible amount is 55% for 1999. The deductible percentage will increase in 2000 and 2001 to 60%, and further increases are scheduled until the deductible amount reaches 80% for 2008 and later years. Proposed legislation would move up the 80% deduction to 2007.

Taxes and tips are considered part of the cost subject to the 50% limit. If your employer reimburses your expenses, the 50% limit applies to the employer.

The 50% limit applies to both employees and the self-employed. It applies to the $30, $34, $38, $42, or $46 IRS meal allowance deduction; see 20.4. For employee expenses the limit is taken into account on Form 2106 or 2106-EZ (if you are not reimbursed by your employer and do not claim depreciation for a business car), and on Schedule C for self-employment expenses.

EXAMPLES

1. You pay meal and entertainment costs of $5,000. Only $2,500 ($5,000 × 50%) is considered deductible.
2. Same facts as above, but your employer reimburses your costs after you account for the expenses. The employer's deduction is limited to $2,500. You have no deduction.

The deductible amount for a ticket treated as an entertainment expense is restricted to the face value of the ticket. Amounts in excess of face value paid to ticket agencies or scalpers are not deductible. The deductible cost of tickets is also subject to the 50% limitation.

EXAMPLE

You buy from a ticket broker five tickets to entertain clients. The face value of the tickets is $250. You paid $300 for them. The deductible amount is $125 (50% × $250).

Exceptions to 50% cost limitation. In the following cases, you may claim a full deduction for meals and entertainment; the 50% limitation does not apply:

1. As an employer, you pay for an employee's meals and entertainment that is treated as taxable compensation to the employee and as wages for purposes of withholding of income tax.

2. You reimburse an independent contractor for meal and entertainment expenses he or she incurs on your behalf and the contractor does not adequately account for the expenses. You deduct the reimbursements as compensation if they are ordinary and necessary business expenses.

3. As an employer, you incur expenses for recreational, social, or similar activities (including facilities) primarily for the benefit of employees who are not highly compensated employees. For example, the expenses of food, beverages, and entertainment for a company-wide summer party are not subject to the 50% limit.

4. Expenses for meals and entertainment, including the use of facilities made available to the general public, such as a free concert, for advertising or goodwill purposes. For example, the IRS allowed a real-estate broker to fully deduct the cost of free dinners it provided to potential investors who attended its sales presentations. The 50% deduction limitation for meals does not apply to promotional activities that are made available to the general public. The IRS relied on the following example in a 1986 Congressional committee report for purposes of allowing a 100% deduction: A wine merchant provides customers with wine and food to demonstrate the suitability of the wine with certain types of meals. The committee report indicated that the cost of the wine, food, and other costs associated with the wine-tasting function would be fully deductible.

5. Expenses for meals and entertainment sold to the public in your business, such as meal expenses if you run a restaurant, or the cost of providing entertainment if you run a nightclub. These expenses are fully deductible.

6. Food or beverage provided to your employees as a tax-free *de minimis* fringe benefit (3.9). This would include expenses of a cafeteria on your premises for employees where meal charges cover the direct operating cost of the cafeteria. The *de minimis* benefit exception allows a full deduction for all meals provided to employees on employer premises if more than half of the employees who are provided meals are furnished them for the employer's convenience (substantial noncompensatory business purpose). If the more-than-half test is met, the meals are tax free to all the employees; see 3.11.

7. The price of tickets to charitable sports events (including amounts in excess of face value) provided the ticket package includes admission to the event. To qualify, a charitable sports event must: (1) be organized for the primary purpose of benefitting a tax-exempt organization; (2) contribute 100% of its net proceeds to such organization; and (3) use volunteers for substantially all work performed in carrying out the event. According to Congressional committee reports, a golf tournament that donates all its proceeds to charity is eligible to qualify under

Filing Tip

Meals Provided to Employees

An employer who provides meals to employees on employer premises is allowed a full deduction for all the meals provided that more than half of the employees who are provided meals are furnished them for substantial noncompensatory business reasons.

this exception, even if it offers prize money to the golfers who participate or uses paid concessionaires or security personnel. However, tickets to a college football game or similar scholastic events generally do not qualify because they do not satisfy the requirement that substantially all work be performed by volunteers.

Skybox rental costs. A skybox is a private luxury seating area at a sports arena. Skybox seats are generally rented for the season or for a series of games such as the World Series. The deductible amount for a rental covering more than one game or performance may not exceed the sum of the face values of non-luxury box seat tickets for the number of seats in the box. The allowable amount is also subject to the 50% cost limitation. Separately stated charges for food or beverage charges at the box are deductible as entertainment expenses and are subject to the 50% cost rule. For example, assume that for two games, you paid $1,480 for a skybox containing 10 seats—$740 per game. The cost of 10 non-luxury box seat tickets for each game was $200, or $400 total. You may deduct 50% of $400 non-luxury face value, or $200. If you had rented the skybox for one game, you could deduct $370 (50% of $740) for that skybox because the special limitation applies only where the rental is for more than one game or other performance.

20.25 Business Gift Deductions Are Limited

Deductions for gifts to business customers and clients are restricted. Your deduction for gifts is limited to $25 a person. You and your spouse are treated as one person in figuring this limitation even if you do not file a joint return and even if you have separate business connections with the recipient. The $25 limitation also applies to partnerships; thus a gift by the partnership to one person may not exceed $25, regardless of the number of partners.

In figuring the $25 limitation to each business associate, do not include the following items:

1. A gift of a specialty advertising item that costs $4 or less on which your name is clearly and permanently imprinted. This exception saves you the trouble of having to keep records of such items as pens, desk sets, plastic bags, and cases on which you have your name imprinted for business promotion.
2. Signs, displays, racks, or other promotional material that is used on business premises by the person to whom you gave the material.
3. Incidental costs of wrapping, insuring, mailing, or delivering the gift. However, the cost of an ornamental basket or container must be included if it has a substantial value in relation to the goods it contains.

If you made a gift to the spouse of a business associate, it is considered as made to the associate. If the spouse has an independent bona fide business connection with you, the gift is not considered as made to the associate unless it is intended for the associate's eventual use.

If you made a gift to a corporation or other business group intended for the personal use of an employee, stockholder, or other owner of the corporation, the gift generally is considered as made to that individual.

Theater or sporting event tickets given to business associates are entertainment, not gift, expenses if you accompany them. If you do not accompany them, you may elect to treat the tickets either as gifts, which are subject to the $25 limitation, or as entertainment expenses subject to the entertainment expense rules, such as the requirement to show a business conference before or after the entertainment and the 50% cost limitation.

Packaged food or drink given to a business associate is a gift if it is to be consumed at a later time.

Gifts not coming within the $25 limit are: (1) scholarships that are tax free under the rules in Chapter 38; (2) prizes and awards that are tax free under the rule of *11.1*; and (3) awards to employees, discussed below.

Awards to employees. There is an exception to the $25 gift deduction limitation for achievement awards of tangible personal property given to your employees in recognition of length of service or safety achievement. Special deduction limits apply to such achievement awards provided they are given as part of a presentation under circumstances indicating that they are not a form of disguised compensation. For example, awards will not qualify if given at the time of annual salary adjustments, or as a substitute for a prior program of cash bonuses, or if awards discriminate on behalf of highly compensated employees.

The amount of your deduction depends on whether the achievement award is considered a qualified plan award. You may deduct up to $1,600 for all qualified plan awards (safety and length of service) given to the same employee during the taxable year. If the award is not a qualified plan award,

 Caution

Employee Bonuses
Employee bonuses should not be labeled as gifts. An IRS agent examining your records may, with this description, limit the deduction to $25 unless you can prove the excess over $25 was compensation. By describing the payment as a gift, you are inviting an IRS disallowance of the excess over $25. This was the experience of an attorney who gave his secretary $200 at Christmas. The IRS disallowed $175 of his deduction. The Tax Court refused to reverse the IRS. The attorney could not prove that the payment was for services.

the annual deduction ceiling for each employee is $400. The $1,600 overall limit applies if the same employee receives some qualified plan awards and some non-qualified awards during the same year.

To be a qualified plan award, the award for length of service or safety achievement must be given under an established written plan or program that does not discriminate in favor of highly compensated employees. The average cost of all awards under the plan for the year (to all employees) must not exceed $400. In determining this $400 average cost, awards of nominal value are not to be taken into account. In case of a partnership, the deduction limitation applies to the partnership as well as to each partner.

Safety and length of service. A length of service award does not qualify as an employee achievement award if it is given during the employee's first five years. Furthermore, only one length of service award every five years is considered an employee achievement award.

Safety awards granted to managers, administrators, clerical employees, or professional employees are not considered employee achievement awards. Furthermore, if during the year more than 10% of other employees (not counting managers, administrators, clerical employees, or professional employees) previously received safety awards, none of the later awards are subject to the employee achievement award rules.

Employee's tax. The employer's deductible amount for an employee achievement award is tax free to the employee; *see 3.10.* For example, you give a qualified plan award costing $1,800 to an employee. You may deduct only $1,600. The employee is not taxed on the award up to $1,600; the $200 balance is taxable.

Travel and Entertainment Records

20.26 Record-keeping Requirements

Your testimony—even if accepted by an IRS agent or a judge as truthful—is not sufficient to support a deduction of travel and entertainment expenses. By law, your personal claim must be supported by other evidence such as records or witnesses. The most direct and acceptable way is to have records that meet IRS rules discussed in the following pages. Failure to have adequate records will generally result in an examination of your return and in a disallowance of your travel and entertainment expense deductions. Only in unusual circumstances will evidence other than records provide all of the required details of proof.

If your expenses are reimbursed by your company, you must keep records to support the reimbursement arrangement with your company; *see 20.30.*

20.27 Substantiating Deductions for Travel and Entertainment

To satisfy the IRS requirements and to substantiate your expense deductions in the event of an audit, you need two types of records:

1. A diary, account book, or similar record to list the time, place, and business purpose of your travel and entertainment expenses; and
2. Receipts, itemized paid bills, or similar statements for lodging regardless of the amount, and for other expenses of $75 or more. But note these exceptions:

- A receipt for transportation expenses of $75 or more is required only when it is readily obtainable. For example, for air travel a receipt or a boarding pass is usually provided.
- A cancelled check by itself is not an acceptable voucher. If you cannot produce a bill or voucher, you may have to present other evidence such as a statement in writing from witnesses to prove business purpose of the expense.

Record-keeping rules for attorneys and other independent contractors who are reimbursed are discussed at *20.23.*

A receipted bill or voucher must show (1) the amount of the expense; (2) the date the expense was incurred; (3) where the expense was incurred; and (4) the nature of the expense.

A hotel bill must show the name, location, date, and separate amounts for charges such as lodgings, meals, and telephone calls. A receipt for lodging is not needed if its cost is covered by a *per diem* allowance; *see 20.32.* The IRS will not allow a credit card statement to substitute for a lodging receipt. The IRS wants detailed receipts to catch personal items such as personal phone calls or the purchase of gifts.

Planning Reminder

Credit Cards

Credit card charge statements for traveling and entertainment expenses meet the IRS tests, provided the business purpose of the expense is also shown. Credit card statements provide space for inserting the names of people entertained, their business relationship, the business purpose of the expense, and the portion of the expense to be allocated to business and personal purposes. These statements generally meet the IRS requirements of accounting to your employer for reimbursed expenses *(20.31)*, provided a responsible company official reviews them. The IRS will not accept a credit card statement as substantiation of a lodging expense.

A restaurant bill must show the restaurant's name and location, the date and amount of the expense, and, when a charge is made for items other than meals or beverages, a description of the charge.

Diary entries. Your diary does not have to duplicate data recorded on a receipt, provided that a notation in the diary is connected to the receipt. You are also not required to record amounts your company pays directly for any ticket or fare. Credit card charges should be recorded.

Your records for entertainment costs must also show (1) the names of those you entertained; (2) the business purpose served by the entertainment; (3) the business relationship between you and your guests; and (4) the place of entertainment. Inattention to these details of substantiation can cost you the deduction. For example, an executive's company treasurer verified that the executive was required to incur entertainment expenses beyond reimbursed amounts. He also kept a cash diary in which he made contemporaneous notes of the amounts he spent. But he failed to note place, purpose, and business relationship. Consequently, there was no record that tied the expenses to his employment and the deduction was disallowed.

Excuses for Inadequate Records

Substantial compliance. If you have made a "good faith" effort to comply with the IRS rules, you will not be penalized if your records do not satisfy every requirement. For example, you would not automatically be denied a deduction merely because you did not keep a receipt.

Accidental destruction of records. If receipts or records are lost through circumstances beyond your control, you may substantiate deductions by reasonable reconstruction of your expenditures.

Exceptional circumstances. If, by reason of the "inherent nature of the situation," you are unable to keep adequate records, you may substantially comply by presenting the next best evidence. A supporting memorandum from your files and a statement from the persons entertained may be an adequate substitute. IRS regulations do not explain the meaning of "inherent nature of the situation."

Planning Reminder

How Long To Keep Records
You should keep your diary and supporting records for at least three years after the due date for the return which the records support. However, you may not have to keep these records if the information from them is submitted to your company under the rules applied to reimbursed expenses and allowances described at *20.30*.

EXAMPLES

1. Bryan's 1966 records were lost by a moving company. He claimed a T&E deduction of $15,301.87. The IRS estimated his T&E and other business expenses as $8,669 on the basis of his 1971 expense records. The Tax Court affirmed the IRS's approach. True, Bryan's loss of records made his burden of proof difficult, but he had to provide a reasonable reconstruction of his records to support his claimed deduction. His testimony of what he incurred in 1966 was not sufficient. A more accurate method was the IRS's use of his 1971 records and receipts.

2. Jackson claimed the IRS lost his records. He left his records with the IRS when he was audited, and the records were never returned. The Tax Court held that to be a good excuse for not producing his records and allowed a deduction on the basis of reconstructed records. Evidence that the IRS lost them: The IRS turned up Jackson's worksheet a year after the audit interview.

3. Murray claimed he lost his records when he was evicted from his apartment for failure to pay rent for a month. The Tax Court accepted his excuse on proof that he had kept records before they were lost. The eviction was beyond his control. However, if the records had been lost during a voluntary move, the loss would not have been excused, as in Example 1.

20.28 Reporting T&E Expenses as Self-Employed Person

You must keep travel and entertainment (T&E) records following the rules in *20.27*. You may claim the meal allowance at *20.4* on overnight business trips. The reimbursement rules discussed in *20.30* do not apply to you.

In preparing your tax return, you report your expenses on the appropriate lines of Schedule C or Schedule C-EZ (if you qualify). You do not use Form 2106. An advantage of reporting on Schedule C (or C-EZ) is that your travel and entertainment expenses (T&E) are not subject to the 2% adjusted gross income (AGI) floor. Only 50% of meals and entertainment costs are deductible.

20.29 Reporting Unreimbursed T&E Expenses

If you are paid a salary with the understanding that you will pay your own expenses and you pay all of your travel and entertainment (T&E) expenses *without* reimbursement, you report all of your salary or commission income as shown on Form W-2. You report your expenses on Form 2106 or Form 2106-EZ (if other tests are met). Meals and entertainment are only 50% deductible. You must also keep records as required by *20.27* to support your deduction. The deductible amount from Form 2106 or Form 2106-EZ is entered on Schedule A as a miscellaneous expense subject to the 2% AGI floor. Therefore, if your total miscellaneous expenses, including the unreimbursed T&E costs, do not exceed 2% of adjusted gross income, none of the miscellaneous expenses will be deductible.

Employer Reimbursement Plans

20.30 Tax Treatment of Reimbursements

Compliance rules are imposed on employees and employers for reporting reimbursed travel and entertainment expenses in order to prevent reimbursement arrangements from being used to avoid the 2% of adjusted gross income (AGI) floor for employee miscellaneous expenses. Plans that allow reimbursements that *do not* comply with the IRS rules are called *nonaccountable plans*. All reimbursements under a nonaccountable plan are reported as salary or wage income on Form W-2. You then deduct your expenses as miscellaneous deductions subject to the 2% AGI floor; *see 20.34*.

Court Decision

Ask for Reimbursement

If you are entitled to reimbursement from your employer, make sure you ask for reimbursement. Failure to be reimbursed may prevent you from deducting your out-of-pocket expenses. A supervisor whose responsibility was to maintain good relations with his district and store managers entertained them and their families and also distributed gifts among them. His cost was $2,500 for which he could have been reimbursed by his company, but he made no claim. Consequently, the Tax Court disallowed it as a deduction on his return. The expense was the company's; any goodwill he created benefitted it. But because he failed to seek reimbursement, he was not allowed to convert company expenses into his own.

If a plan meets the IRS rules, the plan is called an *accountable plan* and reimbursements made by the plan are not reported on Form W-2 as taxable wages. You also do not have to deduct expenses, assuming the reimbursement equals your expenses. In other words, there is a bookkeeping "wash" in which the full amount of expenses offsets the reimbursement without being reduced by the 2% AGI floor and in the case of meal and entertainment costs, by the 50% reduction. Even though the employer may only deduct 50% of qualifying meal and entertainment expenses, you are not taxed on any part of a reimbursement of such costs if the accountable plan rules are met.

To qualify a plan as accountable, your employer must see to it that you submit adequate proof of your expenditures, and that you return any excess advances; *see 20.31*. To reduce record-keeping for actual costs, the company may reimburse you according to certain fixed *per diem* allowance rates; *see 20.32*. Your company must also determine how much of the advance or reimbursement, if any, is to be reported on your Form W-2.

EXAMPLE

Your adjusted gross income is $85,000, and you incur T&E expenses of $1,600 which are reimbursed by your company. If the reimbursement arrangement does not meet the IRS rules, the $1,600 reimbursement is reported as wage income on your Form W-2. You may report the expenses on Form 2106 and after reducing meal and entertainment costs by 50%, enter the balance as a deduction on Schedule A as a miscellaneous expense subject to the 2% AGI floor. However, if these are your only miscellaneous expenses, you will not get the benefit of a deduction because they do not exceed 2% of $86,600 ($85,000 + $1,600) or $1,732. The $1,600 is fully taxable although spent for T&E.

If your reimbursement arrangement qualified as an accountable plan, and you made an adequate reporting to your employer, the $1,600 would not be reported as income on your Form W-2, and you would not have to be concerned with the 2% floor for miscellaneous itemized deductions. There is a bookkeeping "wash." In other words, you receive a full deduction by substantiating the expenses to your employer.

Reimbursements of club dues or spousal travel costs. If you are reimbursed for nondeductible club dues *(20.22)* or nondeductible travel costs of a spouse or other person *(20.13)*, the reimbursement may be treated by your employer as taxable wages. If it is, you are not allowed an offsetting deduction. If the reimbursement is not treated as taxable wages by your employer, and you substantiate a business purpose for the club dues or for a travel companion's presence, the reimbursement is considered to be a tax-free working condition fringe benefit *(3.8)*.

EXAMPLE

A company pays for the country club dues of an executive. In 1999, it reimbursed dues of $20,000, and the executive used the club for business purposes 40% of the time. If the company does not treat the reimbursement as taxable wages but as a fringe benefit, $8,000 of the reimbursement is not taxable to the executive; $12,000 allocated to personal use is taxable.

20.31 What Is an Accountable Plan?

A reimbursement or allowance arrangement is an accountable plan if it requires you to:

- Adequately account to your employer for your expenses; *and*
- Return to your employer any excess reimbursement or allowance which you do not show was spent for ordinary and necessary business expenses.

If these terms are met and your expenses are fully reimbursed, you do not report the expenses or the reimbursement on your return. If the reimbursement is less than your payment of expenses, you use Form 2106 and Schedule A to claim a deduction for the unreimbursed expenses. The unreimbursed expenses are subject to the 2% AGI floor on Schedule A.

What is an adequate accounting? You adequately account to your employer by submitting bills and an account book, diary, or similar record in which you entered each expense at or near the time you had it. You must account to your employer for all amounts received as advances, reimbursements, or allowances, including amounts charged on a company credit card. Your records and supporting information must meet the rules discussed in *20.27*. You must also pay back any reimbursements or allowances for which you do not adequately account or the nonreturned accounts will be taxable under the rules at *20.34* for non-accountable plans.

The accounting requirements are eased if you are reimbursed under a *per diem* arrangement covering meals, lodging, and incidental expenses *(20.32)* or you receive a flat mileage allowance *(20.33)*.

Time limits for receiving advances, substantiating expenses, and returning excess payments. The general rule is that these events must occur within a reasonable time. Under an IRS "safe harbor," the following payments are considered to be within a reasonable time:

- Advance payments—if given to you within 30 days before you reasonably anticipate to pay or incur expenses;
- Substantiation of expenses—if provided to your employer within 60 days after the expense is paid or incurred; and
- Return of excess—if done within 120 days after you pay or incur expense.

An employer may set up a "periodic statement method" to meet IRS rules. Here, an employer gives each employee periodic statements (at least quarterly) that list the amounts paid in excess of expenses substantiated by the employee and request substantiation of the additional amounts paid, or a return of the excess, within 120 days of the date of the statement. Substantiation or return within the 120-day period satisfies the reasonable time test.

Allocating reimbursements to meals and entertainment. Only 50% of meals and entertainment expenses are deductible. Therefore, if you adequately account for your expenses, and receive a flat reimbursement that is partly for meals and entertainment, and partly for other expenses, you must allocate part of the reimbursement to meals and entertainment if the employer has not provided an item-by-item breakdown. You must make this allocation if you want to deduct expenses exceeding reimbursements because on Form 2106, you must separately list meals and entertainment costs and reimbursements for meals and entertainment. The allocation is based on the percentage which your meal costs bear to the total T&E expenses.

EXAMPLE

You receive an allowance of $1,000 for travel expenses and have total expenses of $1,500, including $300 for meals. The percentage of your meals to total expenses is 20% (300 ÷ 1,500). On Form 2106, you show 20% of the allowance or $200 as the allocable reimbursement for meals. The unreimbursed $100 balance for meals ($300 – $200) must be reduced to $50 by the 50% reduction for meals. You may deduct $400 of the $1,200 in expenses that were not for meals; 80% of the $1,000 travel allowance is allocated to such costs. The total deductible amount of $450 ($50 for meals and $400 for other expenses) is transferred from Form 2106 to Schedule A, where it is deductible as a miscellaneous itemized expense subject to the 2% AGI floor.

 Filing Tip

Failure To Timely Return Excess

If you fail to return excess payments within a reasonable time but you meet all of the other tests applied to an accountable plan, such as providing proof of the expenses, only the retained excess is taxed to you as if paid outside of an accountable plan.

20.32 *Per Diem* Travel Allowance Under Accountable Plans

Instead of providing a straight reimbursement for substantiated out-of-pocket travel expenses, an employer may use a *per diem* allowance to cover meals, lodging, and incidental expenses on business trips away from home. Incidental expenses covered by a *per diem* arrangement may include tips, laundry, and cleaning fees, or similar expenses, but, under IRS rules, may not include cab fares, telephone, or telegram costs.

If you are not related to the employer, you do not have to give your employer proof of your actual expenses if you receive a *per diem* allowance or reimbursement that is equal to or less than the federal travel rate for the particular area. You do have to account for the time, place, and business purpose of your travel. If you do not provide such an accounting for some travel days, you must be required to return the *per diem* allowance received for such days in order for the employer's plan to qualify.

For allowances in 1999 covering lodging plus meals and incidental expenses for travel *within* the continental U.S., an employer may use an IRS high-low rate of $115 per day for most areas or $185 per day for "high-cost" areas, instead of the federal travel rate.

Tables published by the government show the federal travel rate for areas within the continental U.S. (called CONUS locations) and for areas outside the continental U.S., including Hawaii and Alaska (called OCONUS locations). The CONUS federal travel rates and IRS high-low rates are in IRS Publication 1542.

Employees related to the employer. The IRS *per diem* rules that allow you to avoid accounting for actual expenses do not apply if you work for a brother, sister, spouse, parent, child, grandparent, or grandchild. They also do not apply if you are an employee-stockholder who owns more than 10% of the company's stock.

Reporting a *per diem* allowance. If the allowance does not exceed the federal travel rate or IRS high-low rate, the reimbursement is not reported on Form W-2. If your expenses do not exceed the reimbursement, you do not have to report the expenses or the reimbursement on your tax return; *see* Example 1 below. If your expenses exceed the allowance, you may deduct the excess by reporting the expenses and reimbursement on Form 2106. The net amount from Form 2106, after applying the 50% reduction for meals, is claimed on Schedule A as a miscellaneous expense subject to the 2% AGI floor; *see* Example 2 below.

Meal allowance only. If your employer gives you a *per diem* allowance covering only meals and incidental expenses, it is not taxable to you if you are not related to the employer and the allowance does not exceed the IRS meal allowance rates discussed at *20.4*.

For meals *outside* the continental U.S., the meal allowance rates in *20.4* do not apply. The allowable meal allowance rates are listed in the government's CONUS tables.

EXAMPLES

1. You take a three-day business trip to a locality at a time when the federal travel rate for the area is $106 per day. You account for the date, place, and business purpose of the trip. Your employer reimburses you $106 a day for lodging, meals, and incidental expenses, for a total of $318. Your actual expenses do not exceed this amount. Your employer does not report the reimbursement on your Form W-2. You do not have to report the reimbursement or deduct any expenses on your return.

2. Same facts as in Example 1, except that the reimbursement is less than your actual expenses of $450 for which you have records. On Form 2106, you report the $318 reimbursement and your $450 of expenses and also must allocate part of the allowance to meals to apply the 50% limit. The net amount from Form 2106 is deductible on Schedule A as a miscellaneous expense subject to the 2% AGI limit.

3. Same facts as in Example 1, except that you receive a *per diem* allowance of $114 per day—$8 per day more than the federal travel rate. If you do not return the excess of $24 ($8 × 3 days) within a reasonable time *(20.31)*, your employer must report the $24 as income in Box 1 of your Form W-2. The amount up to the federal travel rate, or $318, will be reported in Box 13 of Form W-2, but not included as income.

Caution

Excess *Per Diem* Allowances

If a per diem allowance exceeds the federal travel rate or the IRS high-low rate, the excess will be reported as income on your Form W-2, unless you return the excess; *see* Example 3 on this page. The excess reportable on Form W-2 is also subject to income tax and FICA tax withholding.

Planning Reminder

Importance of Adequate Accounting

If you adequately report expenses to your employer and return excess reimbursements, you are treated as being reimbursed under an accountable plan and generally do not have to report any reimbursement on your return; *see* *20.31*.

20.33 Automobile Mileage Allowance

If in 1999 your employer paid you a fixed mileage allowance of up to 32.5 cents per mile from January 1st until March 31st and 31 cents per mile for the remainder of 1999, the amount of your automobile expenses is treated as substantiated, provided you show the time, place, and business purpose of your travel. If the allowance is in the form of an advance, it must be given within a reasonable period before the anticipated travel and you must also be required to return within a reasonable period (20.31) any portion of the allowance that covers mileage that you have not substantiated.

If these tests are met, the allowance will not be reported as income on Form W-2, and you will not have to report the allowance or expenses on your return; see Example 1 in this section. If you do not prove to your employer the time, place, and purpose of your travel the entire reimbursement is treated as paid from a nonaccountable plan and will be reported as income on Form W-2.

If you were given a 1999 mileage allowance in excess of 32.5/31 cents per mile, the excess will be included as wages on your Form W-2; see Example 2. If your allowance was less than 32.5/31 cents per mile, you may deduct the difference as a miscellaneous itemized deduction subject to the 2% AGI floor; see Example 3.

Your employer may reimburse you for parking fees and tolls in addition to the mileage allowance.

EXAMPLES

1. You drove 12,000 miles for business in 1999, 3000 miles from January to March and 9,000 miles from April to December, and account to your employer for the time, place, and business purpose of each trip. Your employer reimbursed you at the IRS rate of 32.5 cents per mile for miles traveled from January through March and 31 cents per mile for miles traveled from April through December. None of the reimbursements will be reported as income on your Form W-2, and you do not have to report the reimbursements or any expenses on your return if your expenses do not exceed 32.5/31 cents per mile.
2. Same facts as in Example 1, except that you were reimbursed at 33 cents per mile. The amount using the IRS rate, or $3,765 (32.5¢ × 3,000 miles plus 31¢ × 9,000 miles), is $195 less than the reimbursement of $3,960 (33¢ × 12,000). The $195 excess over the IRS rate will be reported as wages on your Form W-2.

    If you had records substantiating expenses over 32.5/31 cents per mile, you could claim them on Form 2106. The excess of your expenses over the IRS rate is shown on Form 2106, and that excess is claimed on Schedule A as a miscellaneous itemized deduction subject to the 2% AGI floor.
3. Same facts as in Example 1, except that you were reimbursed only 20 cents per mile. The reimbursements will not be reported as income on your Form W-2. You may deduct expenses up to the IRS rate by reporting the expense reimbursements on Form 2106. The amount using the IRS rate, or $3,765 (32.5¢ × 3,000 miles plus 31¢ × 9,000 miles), is $1,365 more than the reimbursement of $2,400 (20¢ × 12,000). The $1,365 excess of the IRS allowance over your reimbursements is shown on Form 2106 and then may be claimed as a miscellaneous itemized deduction on Schedule A subject to the 2% AGI floor.

    If you had records showing actual expenses of more than $3,765, you would claim those expenses on Form 2106 and not use the IRS fixed mileage allowance rate to figure your deduction.

 Caution

Two Mileage Rates for 1999 Automobile Allowance

There are two rates in effect for the 1999 automobile mileage allowance: 32.5 cents per mile is the rate from January 1 until March 31, and 31 cents per mile is the rate from April 1 until December 31.

Fixed and variable rate allowance (FAVR). In lieu of setting the allowance at the IRS standard mileage rate (32.5/31 cents per mile in 1999), an employer may use a fixed or variable rate allowance, called a FAVR, that gives employees a cents-per-mile rate to cover gas and other operating costs, plus a flat amount to cover fixed costs such as depreciation, insurance and registration. A FAVR allowance must reflect local driving costs and allows employers to set reimbursements at a rate that more closely approximates employee expenses. If your employer sets up a qualifying FAVR under IRS guidelines, you will be required to provide records substantiating your mileage and certain car ownership information. Expenses up to the FAVR limits are deemed substantiated and will not be reported as wages on your Form W-2.

20.34 Reimbursements Under Non-Accountable Plans

A non-accountable plan is one that either does not require you to adequately account for your expenses, or allows you to keep any excess reimbursement or allowances over the expenses for which you did adequately account.

Your employer reports allowances or reimbursements for a nonaccountable plan as part of your salary income in Box 1 of your Form W-2. The allowance is also subject to income tax and FICA tax (Social Security) withholding. To claim deductions, you must use Form 2106 and itemize your deductions on Schedule A. Your expenses are subject to the 2% AGI floor.

Chapter 21

Personal Exemptions

Each personal exemption you claim on your 1999 return is the equivalent of a $2,750 deduction. Exemptions for children, parents, and other dependents are allowed if the tests of this chapter are met.

If you have a high adjusted gross income, you may lose the benefit of your deduction under the phase-out rule discussed in *21.15*.

Number of Exemptions	Deduction Allowed
1	$ 2,750
2	5,500
3	8,250
4	11,000
5	13,750
6	16,500
7	19,250
8	22,000
9	24,750
10	27,500

21.1 How Many Exemptions May You Claim?

On your 1999 return, you may claim a $2,750 exemption for each of the following, provided you are not subject to the phaseout of exemptions for high income taxpayers *(see 21.15)*:

- *Yourself.* You claim an exemption for yourself unless you are the dependent of another taxpayer. If someone else can claim you as a dependent for 1999, you may not claim a personal exemption for yourself on your own return; this is true even if the other person does not actually claim you as a dependent. This rule prevents your child or other dependent from claiming an exemption on his or her return if you may claim an exemption for the child or other dependent.

- *Your spouse.* You claim your spouse as an exemption when you file a joint return. If you file a separate return, you claim your spouse as an exemption if he or she has no income and is not a dependent of another person; *see 21.2.*

- *Children, parents, and other dependents.* An individual qualifies as your dependent if the following tests are met for each person claimed:

  1. The relationship test discussed at *21.3* or the member of household test at *21.4*.

  2. The gross income test for dependents, which does not apply to your children who are under age 19 or full-time students under age 24 as of the end of the year; *see 21.5–21.6.*

  3. The 50% support test at *21.7*, or the 10% multiple support test at *21.10*.

  4. The citizenship or residence test for dependents; *see 21.12.*

  5. For dependents who are married, the joint return test; *see 21.13.*

 Caution

Proposed Exemption for Caretakers
When this book went to press, Congress was considering legislation that would allow an additional personal exemption to taxpayers who maintain a household that includes a parent, step-parent, grandparent, or great-grandparent with long-term care needs that have been certified by a physician. Ancestors of the taxpayer's spouse and spouses of such ancestors also qualify. The exemption would be available only in instances where the parent or other ancestor has the same residence as the taxpayer and the taxpayer pays more than 50% of the household costs. If the provision is adopted, the new exemption will be available in 2000. *See the Supplement for legislative developments.*

Tests for Claiming Dependents

TEST 1. RELATIONSHIP OR MEMBER OF HOUSEHOLD TEST

The person must be either:

Your relative—child, stepchild, adopted child, grandchild, great-grandchild, son- or daughter-in-law, father- or mother-in-law, brother- or sister-in-law, parent, brother, sister, grandparent, step-parent, stepbrother or sister, half-brother or sister, and, if related by blood, an uncle, aunt, niece, or nephew. These relatives do not have to live with you. However, a foster child qualifies only if he or she is a member of your household for the entire year, apart from temporary absences; *see 21.3.*

Or—any person, whether related or not, who is a member of your household for the entire year, except for temporary absences. The exemption is not allowed if the person was your spouse at any time during the year, or if your relationship with such person is in violation of state law; *see 21.4.*

TEST 2. GROSS INCOME TEST

Your child—If at the end of 1999 your child was under age 19, or was a full-time student under age 24 *(21.6)*, his or her income does not matter. You can claim the child as your dependent if Tests 3, 4, and 5 are met. However, a child who was age 19–23 and not a full-time student at the end of the year, *or* who was age 24 or older, may be claimed as your dependent only if his or her gross income was less than $2,750 in 1999.

Other relatives or household members—must have gross income of less than $2,750 in 1999.

For 2000, the $2,750 income limit will be adjusted for inflation.

TEST 3. SUPPORT TEST

You either contribute more than half the dependent's support, or contribute more than 10% and together with others contribute more than half; *see 21.7 and 21.10.*

Total the dollar amount of support spent on a dependent by you, by others, and by the dependent. If your contribution is:

- *More than 50% of the total spent*—you claim the exemption.

- *More than 10% of the total spent and together with what you and the other contributors gave is more than 50% of the total spent*—you or one of the others who also contributed more than 10% may claim the exemption. You and the others must decide who is to claim the exemption. If you take it, you must attach to your return a Form 2120, "Multiple Support Declaration," signed by each person who contributed more than 10%.

- *Less than 50%, either alone or with the contribution of others*—neither you nor the other contributors may claim the exemption for the dependent.

Special support rules apply to divorced or separated parents; *see 21.11.*

TEST 4. CITIZENSHIP OR RESIDENT TEST

Your dependent is a United States citizen or national, or a resident of the United States, Canada, or Mexico; *see 21.12.*

TEST 5. JOINT RETURN TEST

Your married dependent does not file a joint return with his or her spouse; *see 21.13* for an exception.

21.2 Your Spouse as an Exemption

Your spouse is not your dependent for tax purposes. An exemption for a spouse is based on the marital relationship, not support. On a joint return, each spouse receives an exemption as a taxpayer.

On a separate return, you may claim your spouse as an exemption if he or she has no gross income and is not the dependent of another taxpayer. You may not claim an exemption for your spouse who has income, *unless you file a joint return that includes that income.* For example, if a wife files a separate return, her husband may not claim her as an exemption, even if she filed the return merely for a refund of taxes withheld on her wages.

If your spouse is a nonresident alien, has no income from U.S. sources, and is not a dependent of another person, you may claim an exemption for your spouse on a separate return.

If divorced or legally separated during the year. You may not claim your former spouse as an exemption if you are divorced or legally separated under a *final* decree of divorce or separate maintenance, even if you provided his or her entire support. However, an interlocutory (not final) decree does not bar you from claiming your spouse as an exemption.

EXAMPLE

An interlocutory (not final) decree of divorce is entered in 1999, and a final decree in 2000. For 1999, the couple may file a joint return on which exemptions for both are claimed. A marriage is not dissolved until a final decree is entered, which in this case is in 2000.

Your spouse died during the year. If you did not remarry and your deceased spouse had gross income, you may claim an exemption for your spouse only if you file a joint return that includes his or her income. You may claim the exemption on a separate return only if your spouse had no gross income and was not a dependent of another taxpayer.

EXAMPLE

Sylvia Smith dies on June 27. Her husband, Steve Smith, may file a joint return and claim Sylvia as an exemption. They were married as of the date of Sylvia's death. The joint return includes all of Steve's income for the year, but only that part of Sylvia's income earned up to June 27; *see 1.9.*

If you remarry before the end of the year in which your spouse died, you may not claim an exemption for your deceased spouse. If you file a joint return with your new spouse, you may be claimed as an exemption on that return. If you had *no* income for the year, you may be claimed as an exemption on both your deceased spouse's separate return and on a separate return filed by your new spouse, provided no one else may claim you as a dependent.

21.3 Test 1. Relationship Test

If the other tests are met (Tests 2–5 in *21.1*), you may claim an exemption for a dependent relative listed in this section, even if he or she is an adult, healthy, and capable of self-support. An unrelated person or distantly related person not listed may still qualify as an exemption under the tests at *21.4*.

Your children. If your child was born at the end of 1999, you may claim a full $2,750 exemption for that child.

A stillborn child may not be claimed as an exemption. The exemption is allowed for a child who was born alive even if the infant lived for only a moment.

Stepchildren. Your stepchild is considered your child.

Adopted children. A *legally adopted* child is treated as your child. A child is considered legally adopted when a court decree is entered. In states allowing interlocutory (not final) adoption decrees, you may claim the exemption in the year the interlocutory decree is entered.

If a court decree has not been entered, a child may be your dependent provided he or she was placed with you for adoption by an authorized adoption agency and was a member of your household for the rest of the year. If the child has not been placed with you for adoption by an agency, you may claim the child as a dependent *only* if he or she was a member of your household for the entire tax year; *see 21.4.*

Foster child. A foster child is considered to be your child if he or she is a member of your household for the entire year except for temporary absences.

Planning Reminder

You Must Report I.D. Numbers for Dependents

You must obtain and report on your return the Social Security number of each dependent claimed. Nonresident and resident aliens not eligible for Social Security numbers must have an individual taxpayer identification number; *see 21.14.*

Other qualifying relatives. The following individuals also meet the relationship test: your parent, grandparent, great-grandparent, step-parent, grandchild, great-grandchild, brother, sister, half-brother, half-sister, stepbrother, stepsister, son- or daughter-in-law, father- or mother-in-law, and brother- or sister-in-law. If related by blood, aunts, uncles, nieces, and nephews also qualify.

Stepchild's husband or wife or child. Your stepchild's spouse does not meet the relationship test. Nor may you claim an exemption for a step-grandchild if you file a separate return. They are not on the list of relatives qualifying. But you may claim them as exemptions on a joint return. On a joint return, it is not necessary that the close relationship exist between the dependent and the spouse who furnishes the chief support. It is sufficient that the relationship exists with either spouse.

 Filing Tip

Nephew, Niece, Uncle, and Aunt

Nephews, nieces, uncles, and aunts must be your blood relatives to qualify under the relationship test. For example, the brother or sister of your father or mother qualifies as your relative; their spouses do not. You may not claim your spouse's nephews, nieces, uncles, or aunts unless you file a joint return.

EXAMPLE

You contribute more than half of the support of the sister of your wife's mother (your wife's aunt). If you and your wife file a joint return, her aunt is allowed as an exemption on your joint return. But your wife's aunt's husband is not related by blood to you or your wife. You cannot claim an exemption for him, even on a joint return, unless he is a member of your household under the rules in *21.4*.

In-laws. Brother-in-law, sister-in-law, father-in-law, mother-in-law, son-in-law, and daughter-in-law are relatives by marriage. You may claim them as exemptions if you meet the other tests in this chapter.

You may claim an exemption for an in-law who was related to you by marriage and whom you continue to support after divorce or the death of your spouse.

EXAMPLE

Allen has contributed all the support of his father-in-law since he was married. Allen's wife died in 1998. He continued sole support of his wife's father in 1999. Allen may claim him as an exemption in 1999.

Death during the year. If a relative died during 1999 but was supported by you while alive, and you meet the other tests listed in this chapter, you may claim an exemption.

EXAMPLE

On January 21, 1999, your father died. Until that date, you contributed all of his support. You may claim him as an exemption for 1999. The full deduction is taken. Exemptions are not prorated.

21.4 Unrelated or Distantly Related Dependents Living With You

A friend or a relative not listed in *21.3*—such as a cousin who lives with you—can be your dependent. You may claim an unrelated or distantly related person as a dependent if the other dependent tests are met *and:*

1. The person is a member of your household; *and*
2. Your home is his or her principal home for the entire year, except for absences when attending school, vacationing, or being confined to a hospital. You may not claim a friend as an exemption when you live in his or her house even though you provide support. You are living in his or her household—not your own. Also, you cannot claim an exemption for a friend who lives in your house and renders you services in return for your care.

EXAMPLES

1. Carol Barnes supports her cousin Phyllis, who lives in Carol's house all year. Carol can claim Phyllis as a dependent member of her household if Phyllis meets the citizenship test *(21.12)* and has gross income under $2,750 in 1999 *(21.5)*.
2. Roger Johnson provides a home for an orphan for seven months. He cannot claim the child as a dependent; the child did not live in his home for the entire year. However, if the child had been placed in his home for adoption by an authorized adoption agency, he or she may be claimed as Johnson's dependent although not a member of his household for the entire year; *see* the adopted children rule at *21.3*.

3. Mike Pilla supports a cousin, Janet, who lives in a house owned by him. Mike lives elsewhere and may not claim his cousin as a dependent because they do not live in the same house.

Your spouse or former spouse. Under the tax law, one spouse is not considered a dependent of the other; *see 21.2*. If you are divorced or legally separated during the year, your former spouse cannot qualify as your dependent even if he or she is a member of your household for the whole year.

EXAMPLE

Ensminger lived in North Carolina with a woman whom he supported. When he claimed an exemption for her, the IRS disallowed the exemption, claiming that under North Carolina law it is a misdemeanor for an unmarried man and woman to live together. When the Tax Court supported the IRS position, Ensminger appealed, arguing that the North Carolina law was an unconstitutional invasion of his right to privacy. The appeals court held that constitutionality was not an issue for the IRS and Tax Court to decide. The states are responsible for regulating domestic affairs. Federal tax law merely follows the direction of state law. If Ensminger lived in a state that did not hold his relationship illegal, he could claim the exemption.

In a similar case, a dependency exemption was allowed where the court ruled cohabitation did not violate Missouri law.

Caution

Exemption for Unmarried Mate
An exemption for an unmarried mate depends on local law. Where the relationship violates local law, no exemption may be claimed.

21.5 Test 2. Gross Income Limit for Dependents

A gross income limit applies to:

- Dependents who are not your children—such as parents, in-laws, sisters, brothers, uncles, aunts, and members of your household; *and*
- Your children who at the end of the year are age 19 or over and not full-time students, or children who are full-time students age 24 or older at the end of the year; *see 21.6*.

For 1999, the gross income test requires your dependent to have a gross income of less than $2,750. If a dependent has gross income in 1999 of $2,750 or more, he or she may not be claimed as an exemption, even if all of the support is provided by you. The only exception is for your children who are under age 19 or who are full-time students under age 24; *see 21.6*.

Gross income here means taxable income items includible in the dependent's tax return. It does not include nontaxable items such as gifts and tax-exempt bond interest. Gross income for a service-type business is gross receipts without deductions of expenses and for a manufacturing or merchandising business is total sales less cost of goods sold. A partner's share of partnership gross income, not the share of net income, is treated as gross income.

Gross income does not include income earned by a totally and permanently disabled individual at a school operated by a government agency or tax-exempt organization, if the school provides special instruction for alleviating the disability and the income is incidental to medical care received.

Social Security benefits are treated as gross income only to the extent they are taxable under the rules discussed at *34.3*.

EXAMPLES

1. Larry Jones gives $4,000 a year for his father's support. The father owns a two-family house. He lives in one apartment and rents out the other for $250 a month, giving him a gross annual income of $3,000. After deducting interest and taxes, his net income is $1,800. Larry may not claim his father as a dependent as his 1999 gross income is not under $2,750.
2. Lisa Burr's son, age 21 and not a full-time student *(21.6)* in 1999, received $10,000 in damages for personal injuries suffered in an accident. His only other income was bank interest of $450. Since the damages are excluded from gross income *(11.7)*, the gross income test is satisfied. However, if Lisa's son used part of the damages to support himself, she may claim him as a dependent for 1999 only if her support contributions were larger; see the checklist of support items in *21.7*.

3. Kent Dolin's widowed father received $5,000 in Social Security benefits and $1,200 in bank interest that he used to support himself *(21.7)*. Under *34.3*, the benefits are not subject to tax and therefore not treated as gross income. His gross income of $1,200 is below the $2,750 limit. If Kent contributed more than $6,200 to his father's support, he meets the support test *(21.7)* and may claim his father as a dependent.

21.6 Children Under Age 19 or Full-Time Students Under Age 24

The tax law provides you with a break for dependent children. There is no gross income limit *(21.5)* for—

1. Your children who are under age 24 as of the end of the year if they are full-time students; *and*
2. Your children under age 19 as of the end of the year, whether or not they are students.

Such children may earn *any* amount and still be claimed as your dependents, provided you meet the support test *(21.7)* and the other exemption tests discussed in this chapter.

This rule applies to your child, stepchild, and adopted child. It also applies to a foster child who, for the entire year, is a member of your household. It does not apply to a grandchild, a son- or daughter-in-law, or a brother or sister who is a full-time student; they must have gross income of less than $2,750 in 1999 to qualify as your dependents.

Qualifying as a full-time student. A full-time student is one who attends school full time during at least five calendar months in the tax year. For example: attendance from February through some part of June—or from February through May and then at least one month from September through December—qualifies. The five months do not have to run consecutively. Attendance at a vocational, trade, or technical school for the five-month period qualifies, but not correspondence schools or on-the-job training courses.

Caution

Students Age 24 or Older
The favorable rule that disregards income of full-time students applies only to students who are under age 24 as of the end of the year. If your child was age 24 or older at the end of 1999 and had gross income of $2,750 or more, you may not claim him or her as a dependent.

EXAMPLES

1. Benita Rosa's unmarried daughter, who is age 22, attended college full time until she graduated in June 1999. The gross income test does not apply to her earnings in 1999 because she was a full-time student for at least five months during the year. However, Benita must meet the support test *(21.7)* to claim her daughter as her dependent.
2. Peter Block's son John, who is age 19, worked during the first half of the year and then started college in September. Peter may not claim John as an exemption if John earned $2,750 or more. Although John is a full-time student as of the end of the year, he did not attend school for at least five months during the year.

Night school. Your child who attends night school is considered a full-time student *only if* he or she is enrolled for the number of hours or classes that is considered full-time attendance at a similar daytime school.

21.7 Test 3. 50% Support Test

If your dependent has no financial means and you are the only person contributing to his or her support during the year, you can skip the following discussion on support. You meet the support test. You contribute 100% of the dependent's support. If, however, the dependent or other persons or organizations contribute to his or her support, you have to determine whether your contribution exceeds 50% of the dependent's total support.

Meeting the support test. Follow these steps to figure support: (1) Total the value of the support contributed by you, by the dependent, and by others for the dependent. Use the checklists later in this section for determining what to include in total support and what to exclude. (2) Determine your share of the total. If your share is more than 50% of the dependent's total support, you meet the support test. It does not matter how many months or days you provided the support; only the total cost of the support is considered. If the dependent or some other person or organization contributed 50% or more of the dependent's support, you may not take the exemption. If the dependent or someone else did not contribute 50% or more of the support, and you contributed more than 10% of the total support, you may be able to claim the exemption under a multiple support agreement; *see 21.10*.

Divorced or separated parents contributing to support of their children should follow the special support rules at *21.11.*

Checklist of Support Items

- Food and lodging; *see 21.8*
- Clothing
- Medical and dental expenses, including premiums paid for health insurance policies and supplementary Medicare
- Education expenses such as tuition, books, and supplies. If your child receives a student loan and is the primary obligor, the loan proceeds are considered his or her own support contribution. This is true even if you are a guarantor of the loan. Scholarships received by full-time students are not treated as support; *see* the following checklist of nonsupport items.
- Cars and transportation expenses. Include the cost of a car bought for a dependent as support. If you buy a car but register it in your own name, the cost of the car is *not* support provided by you, but any out-of-pocket expenses you have for operating the car are part of your support contribution.
- Recreation and entertainment. A computer or TV set bought for your child or other dependent is support. Also include costs of summer camp, singing and dancing lessons, and musical instruments, as well as wedding expenses.

Personal savings, Social Security, and tax-exempt income may be support. In figuring a person's total support, include his or her tax-exempt income, personal savings, and Social Security benefits if actually used for support items such as food, lodging, or clothing. Also include support items that are financed by loans. Income that is invested and not actually spent for support is not included in the earner's total support.

Where husband and wife are paid Social Security benefits in one check made out in their joint names, 50% is considered to be used by each spouse unless shown otherwise.

Government benefits. In figuring whether you have provided more than 50% of the dependent's support, you have to consider certain government benefits as support provided by a third party. For example, welfare, food stamps, or housing payments based on need are state support payments if they are used for support items. G.I. Bill education assistance is support provided by the government.

Foster care payments by a child placement agency to parents are support provided by the agency and not by the parents. The value of board, lodging, and education provided to a child in a state juvenile home is treated as support provided by the state.

When a person joins the Armed Forces, the value of board, lodging, and clothing he or she receives is treated as the government's support contribution. However, if *you* are in the Armed Forces, dependency allotments withheld from your pay and used to support your dependents are included in *your* support contributions for them. Also included in your support contribution is a military quarters allowance covering a dependent.

Checklist of Items Not Counted as Support

- Federal, state, and local income taxes and Social Security taxes paid by the dependent from his or her own income
- Funeral expenses
- Life insurance premiums
- Medicare Part A (basic Medicare) and Part B (Supplementary Medicare benefits). In one case the IRS argued that Medicaid benefits were includible in total support but the Tax Court disagreed, holding that Medicaid is similar to excludable Medicare benefits.
- Medical insurance benefits received by the dependent
- Scholarships received by your child, stepchild, or legally adopted child who is a full-time student for at least five calendar months during the year. Scholarship aid is counted as support contributed by the child if he or she is not a full-time student for at least five months. Naval R.O.T.C. payments and payments made under the War Orphans Educational Assistance Act are scholarships that are not counted as support. State aid to a handicapped child for education or training, including room and board, is a scholarship.

Caution

Support of Children Earning Income

Although there is no gross income test for your children who are under age 19 or who are full-time students under age 24, you must still meet the support test in *21.7* to claim them as your dependents. If your child has income, be prepared to show either that the income was not used for his or her support, or that your support contributions were larger. Use the checklists at *21.7* for determining what must be treated as "support."

Planning Reminder

Savings and Investments as Support

Income that is invested is not treated as support. However, personal savings are treated as support if they are used for food, clothing, lodging, or other support items.

EXAMPLES

1. Anna Chung's son invests half of his earnings from a part-time job and spends the other half on recreation. The invested earnings are not treated as support. If Anna's support payments exceed the amount her son spent for recreation, and no one else contributes to his support, Anna meets the support test.

2. Eric Hill receives Social Security benefits of $6,000 and also $300 in bank interest. He spends $4,400 on food, clothes, transportation, and recreation. The $4,400 spent is his contribution to his own support. Eric's rent, utilities, medical expenses, and other necessities are paid by his son, Mike. If Mike's payments exceed $4,400, and no one else contributes to Eric's support, Mike may claim Eric as a dependent.

3. Social Security benefits paid to children of deceased workers that are used for their support are treated as the children's contribution to their own support. Follow this rule even though benefits are paid to you as the child's parent or custodian. If the Social Security benefits used for a child's support are more than half of the child's total support, no one may claim the child as a dependent.

Planning Reminder

Dependents in the Armed Forces

If your dependent joins the military, the value of food, lodging, clothing, and educational assistance provided by the government constitutes government support.

21.8 Lodging and Food as Support

You count as support the *fair rental value* of a room, apartment, or house in which the dependent lives. In your estimate, you include a reasonable allowance for the rental value of furnishings and appliances, and for heat and other utilities. You do *not* add payments of rent, taxes, interest, depreciation, paint, insurance, and utilities. These are presumed to be accounted for in the fair rental estimate. The fair rental value of lodging you furnish a dependent is the amount you could reasonably expect to receive from a stranger for the lodging.

Does dependent live in own home? If the dependent lives in his or her own home, treat the total fair rental value as his or her own contribution to support. However, if you help maintain his or her home by giving cash, or you directly pay such expenses as the mortgage, real estate taxes, fire insurance premiums, and repairs, you reduce the total fair rental value of the home by the amount you contributed when figuring his or her own support contributions; *see* Example 1 below.

If you lived with your dependent rent-free in his or her home, the fair rental value of lodging furnished to you must be offset against the amounts you spent for your dependent in determining the net amount of your contribution to his or her support.

Food and other similar household expenses. If the dependent lives with you, you divide your total food expenses equally among all the members of your household, unless you have records showing the exact amount spent on the dependent; *see* the Examples in *21.9*. If he or she does not live with you, you count the actual amount of food expenses spent by or for that dependent.

Do you pay for a relative's care in a health facility? If you pay part of a relative's expenses for care in a state-supported hospital or nursing home, your payment is a support contribution. If you make a lump-sum contribution covering a relative's stay in an old-age home or other care facility, you prorate your payment over the relative's life expectancy to determine the current support contribution; *see* Examples 2 and 3 on the following page.

Planning Reminder

Lump-Sum Payment to Care Facilities

A lump-sum contribution covering a relative's stay in a long-term care facility is prorated over the relatives life expectancy to determine your current support contribution.

EXAMPLES

1. You contribute $7,000 as support to your father who lives in his own home, which has a fair rental value of $8,000 a year. He uses $4,600 of the money you give him to pay real estate taxes and $2,400 for food. He spends $3,000 of his Social Security for recreation and invests the rest. He has no gross income *(21.5)* and receives no other support. Your father's contribution to his own support is $6,400:

Fair rental value of house ($8,000 *less* $4,600 you gave for taxes)	3,400
Social Security spent	3,000
Father's contribution to his own support	$6,400

You may claim your father as a dependent because your contribution of $7,000 exceeds half of his total support of $13,400 (your $7,000 contribution and his $6,400 contribution).

2. A son secures his father's placement in a religious home for a lump-sum payment of $89,600. The payment was determined on the basis of $11,200 a year over the father's life expectancy of eight years. If the father dies within eight years no refund is due. The son counts $11,200 as an annual contribution to his father's support. If this is more than half of his father's yearly support costs, the son may claim the exemption. If the father fails to reach his life expectancy, the son may not deduct any unused part of the $89,600 as a charitable deduction.

3. In 1999, your father was a patient in a state hospital. The state required you to pay part of his expenses and you paid the state $15,000. In the state budget report for 1999, the average cost of maintaining an individual in the hospital was listed as $25,000. As you contributed over half of your father's support, you may claim him as a dependent. If he required special care, such as private nursing or a major operation, the actual cost to the state agency for maintaining him during the year, rather than the average cost, would be used to measure your father's total support.

21.9 Examples of Allocating Support

The Examples in this section illustrate how you should allocate various support items when your contributions benefit more than one person or when your dependent provides part of his or her own support.

Earmarking support to one dependent. If you are contributing funds to a household consisting of several persons and the amount you contribute does not exceed 50% of the total household support, you may be able to claim an exemption for at least one dependent by earmarking your support to his or her use. Your earmarked contributions must exceed 50% of this dependent's support costs. Mark your checks for the benefit of the dependent, or provide the dependents with a written statement of your support arrangement at the time you start your payments. The IRS says its agents will generally accept such evidence of your arrangement. If you do not designate for whom you are providing support, your contribution is allocated equally among all members of a household (*see* Example 3 on the next page).

EXAMPLES

1. Your father lives in your home with you, your spouse, and your three children. He receives Social Security benefits of $9,800, which are not subject to tax *(34.3)* and half of which ($4,900) he spends for his own clothing, travel, and recreation. You spend $6,600 for food during the year. You also paid his dental bill of $500. You estimate the annual fair rental value of the room furnished him is $3,600. Your father's total support is:

Social Security used for support	$4,900
Share of food costs ($^1/_6$ of $6,600)	1,100
Dental bill paid by you	500
Rental value of room	3,600
	$10,100

You can claim him as a dependent. You contributed more than half his total support, or $5,200 ($3,600 for lodging, $500 for dental, and $1,100 for food).

2. Your parents live with you, your spouse, and your two children in a house you rent. The fair rental value of their room is $3,000. Your father receives a tax-free government pension of $5,200, all of which he spent equally for your mother and himself for clothing and recreation. Your parents' only other income was $3,000 of tax-exempt interest. They did not make any other contributions towards their own support. Your total expense in providing food for the household is $6,000. You pay heat and utility bills of $1,200. You paid your mother's medical expenses of $600. Your father's total support from all sources is $5,100; your mother's is $5,700, figured as follows:

	Father	Mother
Fair rental value of room	$1,500	$1,500
Pension used for their support	2,600	2,600
Share of food costs ($^1/_6$ of $6,000)	1,000	1000
Medical expenses for mother		600
	$5,100	$5,700

Filing Tip

Households with Several Dependents

If your contribution does not exceed 50% of total household support, earmark contributions to at least one of the dependents. This will allow you to claim at least one exemption. Without proper records, however, the IRS treats your contributions as made to the entire household.

In figuring your parents' total support, you do not include the cost of heat and utilities, because these are presumed to be included in the fair rental value of the room ($3,000). The support you furnish your father, $2,500 (lodging, $1,500; food, $1,000), is not over half of his total support of $5,100. The support you furnish your mother, $3,100 (lodging, $1,500; food, $1,000; medical, $600), is over half of her total support of $5,700. You can claim your mother as a dependent but not your father. Since she did not have taxable income, the gross income test *(21.5)* is satisfied.

3. A husband who lives apart from his family without a divorce or legal separation sends his wife $3,240 to meet household expenses. A son and daughter live with her. The wife contributes from her own funds $6,480; an uncle sends her $1,080. The total amount going to meet household expenses from all sources is $10,800. On a separate return, the husband may not claim any exemptions for his children; his contributions are less than 50% of their total support. As he has not earmarked who is to get his contributions, his payments are allocated equally among the three members of the household. Each is considered to have received $1,080 from him. His contribution of $1,080 is less than half of the total support of $3,600 allocated to each child.

Contributed by:	Allocated to:			
	Wife	*Son*	*Daughter*	*Total*
Wife	$2,160	$2,160	$2,160	$6,480
Husband	1,080	1,080	1,080	3,240
Uncle	360	360	360	1,080
Total	$3,600	$3,600	$3,600	$10,800

4. Same facts as in Example 3 except that the husband notes on his monthly checks of $270 that $180 is for his son and $90 for his daughter. He may claim his son as an exemption on a separate return; he has contributed more than half of the son's support. As total household costs of $10,800 are allocated equally among the three household members, the wife's contribution is reallocated to make up for the difference created by the husband's increased support to the son. Here, the wife is considered to have contributed $3,240 to her own support.

Contributed by:	Allocated to:			
	Wife	*Son*	*Daughter*	*Total*
Wife	$3,240	$1,080	$2,160	$6,480
Husband		2,160	1,080	3,240
Uncle	360	360	360	1,080
Total	$3,600	$3,600	$3,600	$10,800

5. Assume that in Example 4 the mother contributed only $6,240 and her son contributed $240. There would be no change in tax consequences; however, the allocation of support contributions would differ. The son's contribution is added to the total household costs, which are allocated equally among the family members to find how much applies to each person's support. However, in determining support contributions, the son is treated as contributing $240 to his own support.

Contributed by:	Allocated to:			
	Wife	*Son*	*Daughter*	*Total*
Wife	$3,240	$ 840	$2,160	$6,240
Son		240		240
Husband		2,160	1,080	3,240
Uncle	360	360	360	1,080
Total	$3,600	$3,600	$3,600	$10,800

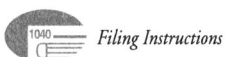

Filing Instructions

Multiple Support Agreement

If you contribute more than 10% of a person's support and all other more-than-10% contributors agree to let you claim the exemption, each of them should sign a consent on separate Forms 2120 that you attach to your return.

21.10 Multiple Support Agreements

Are you and others sharing the support of one person, but with no one individual providing more than 50% *(21.7)* of his or her total support? You may claim the dependent as an exemption if:

1. You gave more than 10% of the support;
2. The amount contributed by you and others to the dependent's support equals more than half the support;
3. Each contributor could have claimed the exemption—except that he or she gave less than half the support; *and*
4. Each contributor who gave more than 10% agrees to let you take the exemption. Each signs a Form 2120, "Multiple Support Agreement." You then attach the forms to your return.

EXAMPLES

1. You and your two brothers contribute $2,000 each toward the support of your mother. She contributes $1,000 of her own to support herself. Your two sisters contribute $500 each. Thus, the total support comes to $8,000. Of this, each brother gave 25% ($2,000 ÷ $8,000), for a total of 75%. Each sister gave $6\frac{1}{4}$% ($500 ÷ $8,000). You or one of your brothers may claim the exemption. The total of your contributions is more than half of your mother's support. Each of you contributed more than 10%. Among yourselves, you must decide which brother is to claim the exemption. If you claim the exemption, your brothers must sign Forms 2120, which you attach to your return. If one of your brothers claims the exemption, you sign a Form 2120, which is attached to the return of the brother who claims the exemption. Since neither of your sisters furnished more than 10%, neither can claim the exemption; they need not sign Forms 2120.

2. Your mother's support totals $6,000; you contribute $1,800; your brother, $1,200; your father, $600; and your mother from her savings contributes $2,400. Assume your father does not file a tax return claiming your mother as an exemption. You and your brother cannot use your father's contribution to meet the more than 50% test required by Rule 2 above. Your father may not join in a multiple support agreement because your mother is not his dependent for tax purposes, although an exemption may be claimed for a wife on the basis of the marital relationship; see 21.2.

Filing Instruction

Waiving Child's Exemption

The custodial parent may waive the exemption for a child for one or more years by signing a Form 8332. The other parent must then attach the form to his or her return for the first year of the waiver and a copy of the form for all future years the exemption is waived.

21.11 Special Support Test for Divorced or Separated Parents

A special rule favoring the "custodial parent" applies where divorced or separated parents together provide more than half of their child's total support and one or both of them have custody of the child for more than half the year. The "custodial parent" is the parent who had custody of the child for the greater portion of the year; *see* the custody rules below. Under the special rule, the custodial parent is treated as meeting the support test *(21.7)* for the child even if the noncustodial parent actually paid most of the child's support. Although the custodial parent is considered to have met the support test, and, thus, is generally able to claim an exemption for the child, the parents may arrange for the noncustodial parent to claim an exemption for a child in a divorce decree or separation agreement, or the custodial parent may waive his or her right to the exemption in favor of the noncustodial parent.

You must answer yes to the following three tests for the special parental-support rule to apply; otherwise, the general support rules discussed at 21.7 *or* 21.10 *apply for determining who may claim the child as a dependent.*

Are you either divorced or legally separated? For the special rules of this section to apply for 1999, you must be divorced or legally separated under a decree of divorce or separate maintenance, or separated under a written agreement, or live apart at all times during the last six months of 1999.

Did either you or the other parent provide over 50% of the child's support? Neither parent may claim the exemption unless the parents together gave more than 50% of the child's support for 1999. If you remarried, support contributions made during 1999 by your new spouse for the child are treated as your own contributions.

These special rules for parents do *not* apply if several people contributing more than 10% of the support enter into a multiple support agreement *(21.10)* authorizing one of them to claim the exemption.

Was the child either in your custody or the custody of both you and the other parent for more than half the year? If the child was not in the custody of either or both parents for more than half of 1999, the exemption is claimed by the person who contributed more than 50% of the child's support (*see 21.7*), or, if there is no such person, by the person designated in a multiple support agreement under the rules at *21.10*.

Custodial parent. If the previously discussed three tests are met and you had custody (defined below) for a greater portion of the year than the other parent, you are treated as meeting the support test regardless of your actual support contribution. Thus, you may claim the exemption unless barred under the other exemption tests. However, you may allow the noncustodial parent to claim the exemption by waiving your right to it. The noncustodial parent may also be able to claim it under the terms of a divorce decree or separation agreement.

Custody is determined by the terms of a decree of divorce or separate maintenance or a written separation agreement. If a decree or agreement does not determine custody, the parent with physical custody for most of the year is the custodial parent. This physical custody rule also applies if parents have joint custody under a decree or agreement, or if the issue of custody is the subject of legal proceedings as of the end of the year.

If you were divorced or separated during 1999, and before that time you had joint custody of the child, the parent who has custody for the greater period of time after the separation is considered the custodial parent.

Custodial parent's waiver on Form 8332 allows noncustodial parent to claim exemption for child. As the custodial parent, you may waive the exemption by signing a written declaration on Form 8332. When you use the form for the first time, you indicate whether you are waiving the exemption for that year only or for future years as well. The noncustodial parent attaches Form 8332 to his or her return and claims the exemption for the child. If the exemption has been waived for future years as well, a copy of Form 8332 must be attached to the noncustodial parent's returns for the later years.

Noncustodial parent granted exemption under divorce agreement after 1984. If you are the noncustodial parent and have been given the unconditional right to the exemption by a divorce decree or separation agreement that went into effect after 1984, you may attach to your return instead of Form 8332 copies of: the page of the agreement allowing you the exemption; the cover page, on which you should write the custodial parent's Social Security number; and the signature page showing the date of the agreement.

Noncustodial parent's exemption under pre-1985 agreement. If a pre-1985 agreement gives you, as noncustodial parent, the exemption, you must provide at least $600 for the support of the child in 1999. The exemption must be specifically allocated to you in a decree of divorce or separate maintenance or a written agreement executed before January 1, 1985.

21.12 Test 4. The Dependent Must Meet a Citizen or Resident Test

To claim a 1999 exemption for a dependent, the dependent must have at some time during 1999 qualified as a:

- Citizen or resident of the United States;
- United States national (one who owes permanent allegiance to the U.S.; principally, a person born in American Samoa who has not become a naturalized American citizen); *or*
- Resident of Canada or Mexico.

Child born abroad. A child born in a foreign country, one of whose parents is a nonresident alien and whose other parent is a U.S. citizen, qualifies as a U.S. citizen and thus as a dependent if the other tests are met.

If you are a U.S. citizen living abroad, you may claim as a dependent a legally adopted child who is not a U.S. citizen or resident if for the entire year your home was the child's principal residence and he or she is a member of your household.

21.13 Test 5. The Dependent Does Not File a Joint Return

You may not claim an exemption for a dependent who files a joint return with another. For example, if you meet the other four tests entitling you to an exemption for your married daughter as your dependent, but she files a joint return with her husband, you may not claim her as your dependent on your tax return.

 Filing Tip

Which Parent Should Claim Exemption?

Generally, if the noncustodial parent is in a higher tax bracket than the custodial parent, and both agree to maximize the tax savings from the exemption, the custodial parent should waive the exemption for the child in favor of the noncustodial parent. However, if a high-income noncustodial parent would be subject to the exemption phaseout (*21.15*), it would be advisable for the lower-earning custodial parent to claim the exemption.

 Caution

Should Married Dependents File Separately?

A parent's loss of an exemption for a dependent child who is married and files jointly may cost the parent more than the joint return saves the couple.

Exception. Even if your dependent files a joint return, you may claim the exemption where the income of each spouse is under the income limit required for filing a return and the couple files a joint return merely to obtain a refund of withheld taxes. Under these circumstances, their return is considered a refund claim, and a dependency exemption may be claimed.

Should dependents file separately? When a married dependent files a joint return, the parent cannot claim an exemption. The loss of the exemption may cost a parent more than the joint return saves the couple. In such a case, it may be advisable for the couple to file separate returns so that the parent may benefit from the larger tax saving.

If the couple decides to revoke their election to file jointly and then file separately in order to preserve the exemption for a parent, they must do so before the filing date for the return. Once a joint return is filed, the couple may not, after the filing deadline, file separate returns for the same year.

21.14 Reporting Social Security Numbers of Dependents

On your 1999 return, you must list the Social Security number (SSN) of each dependent you claim. Include the SSNs of parents or other adults you claim as dependents, as well as those of children.

An SSN may be obtained from the Social Security Administration for U.S. citizens and aliens who have been lawfully admitted for permanent residence or employment. If a dependent is a resident or nonresident alien ineligible to obtain an SSN, an individual taxpayer identification number (ITIN) must be obtained from the IRS by filing Form W-7.

If you fail to include a correct SSN or ITIN for a dependent claimed on your return, the IRS may disallow the exemption, although it may first contact you and give you an opportunity to provide the number. If an exemption is disallowed, the IRS may assess the extra tax using a summary assessment procedure if you fail to request abatement of the assessment within 60 days of receiving notice; this procedure does not require issuance of a deficiency notice, so there is no appeal to the Tax Court.

To obtain a Social Security number for a dependent child, file Form SS-5 with your local Social Security Administration office. Parents of newborn children may request a number when filling out hospital birth-registration records.

21.15 Phaseout of Personal Exemptions for Higher Income Taxpayers

You will lose part or all of the $2,750 deduction for each 1999 personal exemption if your adjusted gross income (AGI) exceeds the threshold amount for your filing status. *Adjusted gross income* is explained at *12.1*. On your 1999 Form 1040, adjusted gross income is the amount shown on Line 33.

If your 1999 status is—	Phaseout applies if AGI exceeds*—	Exemptions completely phased out if AGI exceeds—
Married filing jointly or qualified widow(er)	$189,950	$312,450
Head of household	158,300	280,800
Single	126,600	249,100
Married filing separately	94,975	156,225

These thresholds are adjusted annually for inflation.

How the phaseout increases your marginal tax rate. The phaseout *increases* 1999 marginal rates according to the number of exemptions claimed. For earnings within the $122,500 phase-out range ($61,250 for married filing separately), the effective marginal tax rate increases for each exemption. Thus, taxpayers who support many dependents are hurt more by the phaseout than taxpayers who support few dependents.

Planning Reminder

Filing for SSN or ITIN

If you are planning to claim an exemption for a dependent who as of the end of 1999 does not have the required Social Security number or individual taxpayer identification number, either you or that person should file Form SS-5 with the Social Security Administration or Form W-7 with the IRS (for an ITIN) as soon as possible in 2000 so the number may be obtained before the April 17, 2000, filing deadline.

Caution

Phaseout of Exemptions

On a 1999 return, you are not allowed to claim any deduction for personal exemptions if your adjusted gross income exceeds $249,100 if you are single, $312,450 if you are married filing jointly, $280,800 if you file as head of household, and $156,225 if you are married filing separately.

Exemption Reduction Worksheet

1. Multiply $2,750 by the number of exemptions claimed on
   Form 1040, Line 6d.   1_____
2. Enter adjusted gross income (Line 33, Form 1040).   2_____
3. Enter base amount for your filing status:

Joint return:	$189,950
Single:	$126,600
Head of household:	$158,300
Married filing separately:	$94,975

   3_____
4. Subtract Line 3 from Line 2.*   4_____
5. Divide Line 4 by $2,500 ($1,250 if married filing separately).
   Round up to next higher whole number if result is not a whole
   number (for example, round .005 to 1).   5_____
6. Multiply Line 5 by 2% and enter the number as a decimal.   6_____
7. Multiply Line 1 by Line 6.   7_____
8. Subtract Line 7 from Line 1. **This is the amount that
   you deduct for exemptions on Line 38, Form 1040.**   8_____

*If Line 4 is zero or less, your exemptions are not reduced. Enter the amount from Line 1 on Form 1040, Line 38. If Line 4 is over $122,500 ($61,250 if married filing separately), you may not claim any deductions for exemptions. If Line 4 is more than zero but no more than $122,500 ($61,250 if married filing separately), proceed to Line 5.

EXAMPLE

Howard and Jessica are married. For 1999, they filed a joint return and claimed four exemptions. They reported adjusted gross income of $193,750 on Line 33 of Form 1040. Their exemptions are reduced by $440 to $10,560, figured as follows:

1. $2,750 × 4	$11,000
2. Adjusted gross income	$193,750
3. Base for joint return	189,950
4. Difference	3,800
5. $3,800 (Line 4) ÷ 2,500 (1.52 rounded up to 2)	2
6. 2 (Line 5) × 2%	.04 (4%)
7. $11,000 (Line 1) × 4% (Line 6)	440
8. Exemption deduction allowed (Line 1 less Line 7)	$10,560

Personal Tax Computations

In this part, you will learn how to:

• *Figure your regular tax.* After claiming the standard deduction or itemized deductions *(13.1)* and deducting your allowable personal exemptions *(21.1)*, you figure your regular tax either by looking up the tax in the tax tables or by figuring the tax using the tax rate schedules; *see* Chapter 22.

• *Apply the alternative minimum tax.* If you have reduced your taxable income by certain deductions and tax benefits, you may be subject to the alternative minimum tax (AMT); for further details, *see* Chapter 23.

• *Figure estimated tax payments.* If you have investment and self-employment income, you generally have to pay quarterly estimated tax; *see* 27.1.

• *Compute the "Kiddie Tax."* If your child under age 14 has investment income exceeding $1,400, you must compute tax on that income as if it were your own. "Kiddie Tax" rules are discussed in Chapter 24.

Figuring Your Regular Income Tax Liability

There are two types of income tax rates: (1) regular rates, which apply to all taxpayers, and (2) alternative minimum tax (AMT) rates, which apply only if certain tax benefits, when added back to your income, result in an AMT tax that exceeds your regular tax.

Most taxpayers do not have to compute the regular tax. They find the tax for their income and filing status in IRS tax tables if their taxable income is less than $100,000. Tax rate schedules must be used to figure your regular income tax if taxable income is $100,000 or more. The tables and rate schedules are printed in Part 8 of this book.

Computation of the alternative minimum tax is more complicated and requires the preparation of Form 6251. AMT is discussed in Chapter 23.

22.1 Taxable Income

Your income tax liability is based on your taxable income. If your taxable income is less than $100,000, you must use the IRS tables to look up your tax; *see 22.2*. If your taxable income is $100,000 or more, you use the tax rate schedules to compute the tax; *see 22.3*. However, if you have net capital gains, you use the tax computation worksheet on Schedule D to figure your tax; *see 22.4*. Tax is figured on Form 8615 if the "kiddie tax" computation *(24.4)* must be made.

Taxable income is your adjusted gross income *(12.1)* minus the following: (1) your standard deduction or itemized deductions, whichever you claim (*see* Chapter 13) and (2) deductions for personal exemptions allowed under the rules discussed in Chapter 21. On Form 1040 for 1999, taxable income is entered on Line 39.

On Form 1040A and Form 1040EZ, the computation of taxable income generally takes fewer steps because only limited types of income and deductions may be reported. Itemized deductions may not be claimed. Personal exemptions for dependents may be claimed on Form 1040A but not on Form 1040EZ. *See* the table on page 6 for the types of income and deductions that may not be reported on these forms.

On Form 1040A for 1999, taxable income is entered on Line 24; on Form 1040EZ, it is on Line 6.

22.2 Using the Tax Tables

If you file Form 1040EZ or Form 1040A, you use the tax tables in Part 8 of this book to look up your regular income tax liability. If you file Form 1040, you also use the tax tables if your taxable income is *less* than $100,000; if your taxable income is $100,000 or more, you use the tax rate schedules shown in Part 8.

If you use the tax tables, you do not have to compute your tax mathematically. To use the tables you first figure your taxable income *(see 22.1)*, then turn to your income bracket and look for the tax liability listed in the column for your filing status. Filing status (single, married filing jointly, head of household, married filing separately, and qualifying widow(er)) is discussed in Chapter 1.

You may *not* use the tax tables and *must* use the schedules if you file for a short period (less than 12 months) due to a change of accounting period.

Estates and trusts may not use the tax tables.

Filing Instruction

Taxable Income Under $100,000

If you do not have net capital gains on Schedule D *(see 22.4)*, and are not using Form 8615 to compute the "kiddie tax" for a child under age 14 *(24.4)*, the IRS requires you to use the tax tables to determine the regular tax on your taxable income if it is less than $100,000. The tables are used even though in some cases the tax computed under the tax rate schedules is slightly lower.

EXAMPLES

1. You are single and have an adjusted gross income of $26,095 for 1999. You claim one personal exemption and the standard deduction.

Adjusted gross income		$26,095
Less: Standard deduction	$4,300	
Exemption	2,750	7,050
Taxable income		$19,045

Your tax liability from the tax table is $2,854. The tax is shown in the column for single persons with taxable income of at least $19,000 but less than $19,050.

2. You are married filing jointly and have 1999 adjusted gross income of $35,500, itemized deductions of $7,500, and three exemptions.

Adjusted gross income		$35,500
Less: Itemized deductions	$7,500	
Exemptions (3 × $2,750)	8,250	15,750
Taxable income		$19,750

Your tax liability from the tax table is $2,966.

22.3 Tax Rate Schedules

There are five tax brackets: 15%, 28%, 31%, 36%, and 39.6%. *See* the tax rate schedules in Part 8 of this book. You compute your 1999 regular income tax using the tax rate schedules if either of the following is true:

- Your taxable income is $100,000 or more; *or*
- You file for a short period due to a change of accounting period.

See 22.4 if you have net capital gains.

EXAMPLES

1. You file as a head of household with taxable income of $103,000 for 1999. You use Schedule Z to figure your tax.

Tax on first $89,150 (from Schedule Z)	$20,470.50
Tax on excess $13,850 at 31%	4,293.50
Total tax	$24,764.00

2. You are married and file a joint return with taxable income of $130,000 for 1999. You use Schedule Y-1 to figure your tax.

Tax on first $104,050 (from Schedule Y-1)	$23,537.50
Tax on excess $25,950 at 31%	8,044.50
Total tax	$31,582.00

22.4 Tax Calculation If You Have Long-Term Capital Gains

If a portion of your taxable income *(see 22.1)* consists of net capital gains (net long-term capital gains in excess of net short-term capital losses), you generally may take advantage of a favorable capital gains tax rate of 10% (if your regular top bracket is 15%) or 20% (if your regular top bracket exceeds 15%). Long-term gains on the sale of collectibles and the taxable part of gains on qualifying small business stock *(5.7)* are subject to a maximum rate of 28% (15% if that is your regular top bracket). You apply the capital gains rates and compute your regular income tax liability for the year by completing Schedule D (Form 1040) and attaching it to Form 1040. Part IV of Schedule D will lead you through the full calculations; *see 5.3* and *5.7*.

You may not have to compute your liability on Part IV of Schedule D if the only amounts you must report on Schedule D are capital gain distributions reported on Form 1099-DIV from mutual funds and real estate investment trusts (REITs). If the requirements discussed in Chapter 32 *(see* the "Key to Reporting Mutual-Fund Distributions") are met, your capital gain distributions may be entered on Line 13 of Form 1040 and the Capital Gain Tax Worksheet included in the Form 1040 instructions (Line 40) may be used to apply the capital gain rates and compute your regular income tax liability for 1999.

22.5 Tax Credits

After applying the tax tables or rate schedules to get your regular tax liability, you may be able to reduce that liability by claiming tax credits. The child credit, the dependent care credit, earned income credit, and adoption credit are discussed in Chapter 25. The education tax credits are discussed in Chapter 38. The credit for the elderly is discussed in Chapter 34 and the foreign tax credit in Chapter 36. The business tax credits are discussed in Chapter 40.

Alternative Minimum Tax (AMT)

The purpose of AMT is to increase your tax if certain tax benefits result in a regular income tax that is lower than the tax that would apply if the benefits were added back to taxable income. You may owe AMT if you claimed:

- Itemized deductions, such as taxes, interest on home equity loans used for nonresidential purposes, medical expenses, and miscellaneous job and investment expenses.

- Certain tax-exempt interest, accelerated depreciation, and incentive stock option benefits.

- A substantial number of exemptions for dependents.

There are no specific tests to determine whether or not you are liable for AMT. You must first figure your regular income tax and then see whether tax benefit items must be added back to taxable income to figure alternative minimum taxable income, on which the AMT is figured. If after claiming the AMT exemption and applying the AMT rates of 26% and 28% the tentative alternative minimum tax exceeds your regular income tax, the excess is your AMT liability, which is added to the regular tax on your return.

AMT liability is figured on Form 6251 and is attached to Form 1040. If you file Form 1040A and report tax-exempt interest from private activity bonds subject to AMT, AMT liability, if any, is figured on a worksheet and the AMT is entered on the line for total tax on Form 1040A.

Key to AMT Rules

Item—	AMT Rule—
Tax rate	A 26% rate applies to AMT taxable income of $175,000 or less (after the AMT exemption), $87,500 or less if married filing separately. A 28% rate applies to AMT income exceeding the $175,000 or $87,500 threshold.
AMT taxable income	Regular taxable income without personal exemptions, increased or decreased by adjustments and increased by preferences.
AMT exemption	$45,000 if married filing a joint return (or a qualifying widow(er)); $33,750 if single or head of household; *or* $22,500 if married filing a separate return. Under a phase-out rule, these exemption amounts are reduced by 25¢ for each $1 that AMT taxable income exceeds $150,000 for joint filers or a qualifying widow(er), $112,500 if you file as a single person or head of household, and $75,000 for a married person filing separately. The exemption is completely phased out at $330,000 on a joint return and $247,500 on a single or head of household return. On a married person's separate return, the exemption is eliminated if AMT taxable income is $165,000 or more. There is also a penalty if, as a married person, you file a separate return and have AMT taxable income exceeding $165,000. You must increase AMT taxable income by 25% of the excess over $165,000, but the maximum increase is $22,500.
AMT adjustments	Itemized deductions for taxes, certain interest, and most miscellaneous deductions are not allowed. Personal exemptions and the standard deduction are not allowed. MACRS depreciation is figured under the alternative MACRS system for real estate using 40-year straight-line recovery, and, for personal property, the 150% declining balance method. Incentive stock options; *see 23.2.* Mining exploration and development costs are allowable costs amortized over 10 years. For long-term contracts entered into after February 28, 1986, income is figured under the percentage-of-completion method. Pollution control facilities amortization is figured under alternate MACRS. Alternative tax net operating loss is allowed with adjustments. Circulation expenditures must be amortized ratably over three years. Research and experimental expenditures must be amortized ratably over 10 years. Passive activity losses are recomputed; certain tax-shelter farm losses may not be allowed.
AMT preference items	Tax-exempt interest from private activity bonds issued after August 7,1986, *except* for qualifying 501(c)(3) bonds. Accelerated depreciation on real property and leased personal property placed in service before 1987—excess depreciation or amortization taken over straight-line deduction. If you sell qualified small business stock that qualifies for the 50% exclusion *(5.7),* 42% of the excluded amount is an AMT preference item.
Adjusted gross income	In making AMT computations involving adjusted gross income limitations, use adjusted gross income as computed for regular tax purposes.
Partnership AMT	If you are a partner, include for AMT your distributive share of the partnership's adjustments and tax preference items. These are reported on Schedule K-1 (Form 1065). The partnership itself does not pay alternative minimum tax.
Trust or estate AMT	If you are a beneficiary of an estate or trust, consider for AMT your share of distributable net alternative minimum taxable income shown on Schedule K-1 (Form 1041). The estate or trust must pay tax on any remaining alternative minimum taxable income.
S corporation stockholder	If you are a shareholder, consider for AMT your share of the adjustments and tax preference items reported on Schedule K-1 (Form 1120-S).
Children subject to "kiddie tax"	Children under age 14 who are subject to the "kiddie tax" *(24.3)* may have to compute AMT liability on Form 6251. The 1999 AMT exemption for a child subject to the "kiddie tax" equals the child's earned income plus $5,100, but no more than the regular AMT $33,750 exemption for single persons.

Caution

Tax Breaks May Be Lost Because of AMT

If tax deductions reduce your regular income tax liability below the amount you would have to pay under the AMT, you must pay the difference in the form of AMT liability.

Caution

AMT Exemption Not Adjusted for Inflation

The AMT exemption amounts are not adjusted for inflation, while annual adjustments made to the regular income tax brackets, personal exemption and standard deduction amounts, and the thresholds for the personal exemption phaseout and 3% itemized deduction reduction tend to reduce the regular tax. As a result, the non-adjusted AMT exemption has become less effective in exempting taxpayers from the AMT.

23.1 Form 6251

You use Form 6251 to compute AMT liability, if any. The checklist below gives an indication as to when you may have to use Form 6251. The checklist items are discussed at *23.2* and *23.3*.

If you check any of the items on the list, you should complete Form 6251 to determine if you are liable for AMT. These items are AMT adjustments and preferences and generally are added back to regular taxable income to calculate alternative minimum taxable income (AMT income). After reducing AMT income by the allowable exemption, the AMT rates are applied. The AMT exemption based on filing status and the phase-out rule for the exemption are discussed in the "Key to AMT Rules" on the preceding page.

After reducing AMT income by the allowable exemption, a 26% AMT rate generally applies to the first $175,000 of AMT income ($87,500 if married filing separately), and a 28% rate applies to any balance of the AMT income. However, a special calculation is made on Form 6251 if you had net capital gains that qualify for reduced capital gains rates; *see 5.3*. The effect of the calculation is to apply the same capital gains rate for AMT purposes as for regular income tax purposes.

You report the AMT liability, less any AMT foreign credit, as an additional tax on Line 51 of Form 1040 only to the extent it exceeds your regular income tax without taking into account the special averaging tax on a lump-sum distribution or any regular foreign tax credit.

Follow the line-by-line instructions to Form 6251 to figure your AMT liability, if any.

Items subject to AMT:	Check: ✓
1. Personal exemptions	❏
2. Standard deduction	❏
3. Itemized deductions for taxes, miscellaneous expenses, and medical expenses	❏
4. Interest on home equity debt used for nonresidential purposes	❏
5. Accelerated depreciation in excess of straight line	❏
6. Income from the exercise of incentive stock options	❏
7. Tax-exempt interest from private activity bonds	❏
8. Intangible drilling costs	❏
9. Depletion	❏
10. Circulation expenses	❏
11. Mining exploration and development costs	❏
12. Research and experimental costs	❏
13. Pollution control facility amortization	❏
14. Tax-shelter farm income or loss	❏
15. Passive income or loss	❏
16. Certain installment sale income	❏
17. Income from long-term contracts computed under percentage-of-income method	❏
18. Net operating loss deduction	❏
19. Foreign tax credit	❏
20. Investment expenses	❏
21. Gain on small business stock qualifying for 50% exclusion	❏

EXAMPLE

You are married filing jointly and for 1999 you have adjusted gross income of $130,000. You claim five personal exemptions. The starting point for figuring AMT on Form 6251 is the amount shown on Line 37 of Form 1040. This is $89,556, your AGI of $130,000 minus $40,444 of itemized deductions. Your personal exemptions are ignored for AMT. On Schedule A of Form 1040, you claim itemized deductions of $40,546, which are reduced by $102 under the 3% reduction rule explained at *13.7*, so that your actual allowable itemized deductions are

$40,444. The itemized deductions include $30,000 for state and local taxes and interest of $6,000 on a home equity mortgage loan used for nonresidential purposes *(23.2)*. These deductions are adjustments for AMT purposes. You also have an MACRS depreciation adjustment of $1,000. Before figuring AMT on Form 6251, you complete Form 1040 and compute tax liability of $15,635 on taxable income of $75,806 ($130,000 AGI – $40,444 itemized deductions – $13,750 for five exemptions). You prepare Form 6251 (*see* below) and figure an AMT of $5,543. You must pay the $5,543 in addition to your regular income tax. Enter the $5,543 AMT on Line 51 of Form 1040.

Sample Form 6251

Part I — Adjustments and Preferences

1	If you itemized deductions on Schedule A (Form 1040), go to line 2. Otherwise, enter your standard deduction from Form 1040, line 36, here and go to line 6	1	
2	Medical and dental. Enter the smaller of Schedule A (Form 1040), line 4 **or** 2½% of Form 1040, line 34	2	
3	Taxes. Enter the amount from Schedule A (Form 1040), line 9	3	30,000
4	Certain interest on a home mortgage **not** used to buy, build, or improve your home	4	6,000
5	Miscellaneous itemized deductions. Enter the amount from Schedule A (Form 1040), line 26 . .	5	
6	Refund of taxes. Enter any tax refund from Form 1040, line 10 or line 21	6 (	)
7	Investment interest. Enter difference between regular tax and AMT deduction	7	
8	Post-1986 depreciation. Enter difference between regular tax and AMT depreciation	8	1,000
9	Adjusted gain or loss. Enter difference between AMT and regular tax gain or loss	9	
10	Incentive stock options. Enter excess of AMT income over regular tax income	10	
11	Passive activities. Enter difference between AMT and regular tax income or loss	11	
12	Beneficiaries of estates and trusts. Enter the amount from Schedule K-1 (Form 1041), line 9	12	
13	Tax-exempt interest from private activity bonds issued after 8/7/86	13	
14	Other. Enter the amount, if any, for each item below and enter the total on line 14.		

a	Circulation expenditures .	h	Loss limitations . . . .
b	Depletion	i	Mining costs . . . .
c	Depreciation (pre-1987) .	j	Patron's adjustment . .
d	Installment sales . . .	k	Pollution control facilities .
e	Intangible drilling costs .	l	Research and experimental
f	Large partnerships . . .	m	Section 1202 exclusion . .
g	Long-term contracts . .	n	Tax shelter farm activities .
		o	Related adjustments . .	14	

15	**Total Adjustments and Preferences.** Combine lines 1 through 14 . . . . ▶	15	37,000

Part II — Alternative Minimum Taxable Income

16	Enter the amount from **Form 1040, line 37.** If less than zero, enter as a (loss) . . . . . ▶	16	89,556
17	Net operating loss deduction, if any, from Form 1040, line 21. Enter as a positive amount	17	
18	If Form 1040, line 34, is over $126,600 (over $63,300 if married filing separately), and you itemized deductions, enter the amount, if any, from line 9 of the worksheet for Schedule A (Form 1040), line 28	18 (	102)
19	Combine lines 15 through 18 . . . . ▶	19	126,454
20	Alternative tax net operating loss deduction. See page 7 of the instructions	20	
21	**Alternative Minimum Taxable Income.** Subtract line 20 from line 19. (If married filing separately and line 21 is more than $165,000, see page 7 of the instructions.) . . . . ▶	21	126,454

Part III — Exemption Amount and Alternative Minimum Tax

22	**Exemption Amount.** (If this form is for a child under age 14, see page 7 of the instructions.)		

IF your filing status is . . .	AND line 21 is not over . . .	THEN enter on line 22 . . .		
Single or head of household	$112,500	$33,750		
Married filing jointly or qualifying widow(er) .	150,000	45,000	22	45,000
Married filing separately	75,000	22,500		

If line 21 is **over** the amount shown above for your filing status, see page 7 of the instructions.

#	Description		Amount
23	Subtract line 22 from line 21. If zero or less, enter -0- here and on lines 26 and 28 . . . . . ▶	23	81,454
24	If you reported capital gain distributions directly on Form 1040, line 13, **or** you completed Schedule D (Form 1040) and have an amount on line 25 or 27 (or would have had an amount on either line if you had completed Part IV) (as refigured for the AMT, if necessary), go to Part IV of Form 6251 to figure line 24. **All others:** If line 23 is $175,000 or less ($87,500 or less if married filing separately), multiply line 23 by 26% (.26). Otherwise, multiply line 23 by 28% (.28) and subtract $3,500 ($1,750 if married filing separately) from the result . . . . ▶	24	21,178
25	Alternative minimum tax foreign tax credit. See page 8 of the instructions	25	
26	Tentative minimum tax. Subtract line 25 from line 24 . . . . ▶	26	21,178
27	Enter your tax from Form 1040, line 40 (minus any tax from Form 4972 and any foreign tax credit from Form 1040, line 46)	27	15,635
28	**Alternative Minimum Tax.** Subtract line 27 from line 26. If zero or less, enter -0-. Enter here and on Form 1040, line 51 . . . . ▶	28	5,543

For Paperwork Reduction Act Notice, see separate instructions.   Cat. No. 13600G   Form **6251** (1999)

23.2 Adjustments for AMT

The starting point for figuring AMT is your regular taxable income from Form 1040 *before* personal exemptions. This amount will generally be increased by adjustments on Form 6251.

Standard deduction or itemized deductions. If you did not itemize deductions, you must add back the standard deduction to income when figuring AMT liability.

If you claimed itemized deductions for state and local taxes or miscellaneous deductions subject to the 2% AGI floor, you must add back all of such deductions to your regular taxable income (prior to personal exemptions) in order to figure alternative minimum taxable income.

If medical expenses in excess of the 7.5% AGI floor are deducted for regular tax purposes, you must add back to income on Form 6251 the smaller of the allowable medical deduction from Schedule A and 2.5% of adjusted gross income. The effect of this adjustment is to allow medical expenses as an AMT deduction only to the extent that they exceed 10% of AGI.

Taxes directly deductible from gross income for business or rental purposes remain deductible for AMT purposes.

If claimed for regular income tax purposes, the following itemized deductions are also allowed for AMT; they are not added back to regular taxable income when figuring alternative minimum taxable income.

- Charitable contributions.
- Casualty and theft losses exceeding 10% of AGI
- Wagering losses
- Claim of right deduction; *see 2.9.*
- Estate-tax deductions for income in respect of a decedent
- Impairment-related work expenses
- Home mortgage interest, *except* for interest on home equity debt, taken out after June 30, 1982, where the loan was not used to buy, build, or substantially improve your first or second home (*see* below)
- Investment interest to the extent of net investment income

The 3% reduction for itemized deductions at *13.7* does not apply for AMT purposes.

Mortgage interest. Less interest may be deductible for AMT purposes than for regular tax purposes. No AMT adjustment is required for home mortgage interest paid on a debt incurred to buy, construct, or substantially rehabilitate your principal residence or qualifying second residence. The residence may be a house, apartment, cooperative apartment, condominium, or mobile home not used on a transient basis.

Interest on a mortgage taken out after June 30, 1982, is not deductible for AMT purposes if the proceeds are used for any purpose other than to buy, build, or substantially improve your principal or second residence. Furthermore, in the case of a mortgage refinanced after June 30, 1982, interest is deductible for AMT purposes only to the extent the new debt does not exceed the amount of the old debt immediately before the refinancing. Interest on the excess is not deductible for AMT purposes.

Interest on a mortgage debt incurred before July 1, 1982, for any purpose qualifies for an AMT deduction if the mortgage was secured by your principal residence or any other home used by you or a family member at the time the mortgage was taken out.

If an interest deduction is claimed on Schedule A for debt that does not qualify under these AMT rules, that interest is added back as an adjustment on Form 6251.

State and local taxes. State and local taxes deducted on Schedule A must be added back to taxable income in figuring AMT. If you received in 1999 a refund of state taxes deducted in a prior year, you enter the refund on Form 6251 as a negative adjustment that reduces taxable income in arriving at AMT taxable income.

MACRS depreciation. Depreciation allowed for AMT may differ from that allowed for regular tax purposes. For tangible personal property (such as cars or furniture) placed in service after 1986 and before 1999, the AMT depreciation rate is the 150% declining balance method over the alternative depreciation system recovery periods (ADS; *see 42.9*). For tangible personal property placed in service after 1998, the general depreciation system (GDS) recovery periods of three, five, seven, or 10 years (*42.4*) apply. Real property acquired after 1986 is depreciated for AMT over a

40-year period using the straight-line method. Depreciation deductions for films, videotapes, and sound recordings under the unit-of-production method or other method not based on a term of years are not adjusted under AMT.

If, for regular tax purposes, you use the regular 200% declining balance method to depreciate business equipment with a recovery period of three, five, seven, or 10 years, the difference between the higher regular depreciation and the 150% rate for AMT is an adjustment. You may avoid this adjustment by using the 150% rate for regular tax purposes. For real estate, the adjustment is the difference between the straight-line depreciation claimed for regular tax purposes using the recovery period discussed at *42.13* and the straight-line recovery over the AMT 40-year recovery period.

The adjustment for MACRS may result in providing more depreciation for AMT purposes where the AMT depreciation computation towards the latter part of the useful life of the property provides larger deductions than the regular MACRS deduction.

EXAMPLE

In one taxable year when AMT applies, Jones has two assets acquired after 1986. The regular MACRS depreciation for Asset A is $500 and for Asset B, $400. When applying the AMT rules, the depreciation for Asset A is $400 and for Asset B is $450. AMT taxable income is increased by $50. The adjustment accounts for post-1987 MACRS property held in the current year.

Asset A		
Regular depreciation	$500	
AMT depreciation	400	$100
Asset B		
Regular depreciation	$400	
AMT depreciation	450	(50)
Net adjustment to AMT		
Taxable income		$50

Property placed in service before 1987, unless it qualifies under the MACRS transitional rules, is subject to prior law tax preference rules. Prior law creates tax preference items when the ACRS deduction exceeds regular straight-line depreciation; *see 23.3*. A tax preference item always increases AMT taxable income.

Basis adjustment affects AMT gain or loss. When post-1986 depreciable assets are sold, gain for AMT purposes is figured on the basis of the property as adjusted by depreciation claimed for AMT purposes. This gain or loss will be different from the gain or loss figured for regular tax purposes where regular MACRS depreciation was used. (This AMT basis rule does not apply to property placed in service before 1987 except for transitional property within the post-1986 rules).

Similarly, recalculations of basis and gain are made for prior AMT adjustments taken for circulation expenditures, research and experimental expenditures, pollution control facilities, and mining exploration and development costs.

Incentive stock option (ISO). If you exercised ISO options in 1999 or in an earlier year and the shares first became freely transferable or no longer subject to substantial risk of forfeiture in 1999, the excess of the fair market value of the shares at the time of exercise over the option price is treated as an adjustment increasing 1999 AMT taxable income. When you sell the stock in a later year, and you are subject to AMT in that year, you may increase the basis of the stock for AMT purposes by the amount of the AMT adjustment reported in 1999.

If you exercise an incentive stock option and you sell the acquired stock in the same year, no AMT adjustment is necessary.

Mining exploration and development costs. The deduction allowed for regular tax purposes for mining exploration and development costs is amortized ratably over a 10-year period for AMT purposes.

If a mine is abandoned as worthless, all mining exploration and development costs that have not been written off are deductible in the year of abandonment.

Long-term contracts. The use of the completed contract method of accounting or certain other methods of accounting for long-term contracts is generally not allowable. For AMT, the percentage of completion method must be used. However, there is an exception for home construction contracts.

 Planning Reminder

Incentive Stock Options

The basis of stock acquired through the exercise of an ISO is increased by the amount of the required AMT adjustment. Keep basis records for both AMT and regular tax purposes, since in the year the stock is sold, the gain reportable for AMT purposes should reflect the basis adjustment.

Amortization of certified pollution control facilities. For purposes of the alternative minimum tax, the amortization deduction for a certified pollution control facility placed in service after 1986 is determined under alternative MACRS; *see 42.9.*

Research and experimental expenditures. Costs are amortized over 10 years if incurred in a business in which you are not a material participant.

Passive losses. The law for AMT distinguishes between farm and nonfarm activities. Generally, no loss is deductible for any tax-shelter farm activity. A tax-shelter farm activity is any farming syndicate or any farming activity in which you do not materially participate. You may be treated as a material participant if a member of your family materially participates or you meet certain retirement or disability tests discussed at *10.7.*

Gains and losses reported for regular tax purposes from tax-shelter farm activities must be refigured by taking into account any AMT adjustments and preferences. However, a refigured loss is not allowed for AMT purposes except to the extent that you are insolvent at the end of the year. The amount of the disallowed loss for AMT purposes may be reduced by the amount of insolvency at the end of the taxable year. This means that you can deduct the loss to the extent of your insolvency. Insolvency is the excess of liabilities over fair market value of assets. Any AMT-disallowed loss is carried forward to later years in which there is gain from that same activity, or until you dispose of the activity.

Passive losses from nonfarming activities are adjusted for preference or adjustment items not allowed for AMT purposes. For example, an adjustment for MACRS depreciation is made directly against the passive loss and is not treated as a separate AMT adjustment item. The loss allowed for AMT purposes is increased by the amount by which you are insolvent at the end of the year. *See* the instructions to Form 6251, which suggest that the AMT adjustment of passive losses be figured on a separate Form 8582 that you do not file.

23.3 Tax Preference Items

The following are tax preference items that increase the amount of 1999 AMT taxable income.

Tax-exempt interest on nonessential private activity bonds. For AMT purposes, you must include as a tax preference item the tax-exempt interest on qualified private activity bonds issued after August 7, 1986, except for qualified 501(c)(3) bonds used to benefit tax-exempt groups. Generally, private activity bonds issued after August 7, 1986, are subject to AMT, but for certain bonds meeting specific tests, the AMT rule applies to bonds issued on or after September 1, 1986. Interest paid on buying or carrying such bonds is deductible for AMT purposes.

EXAMPLE
You received $5,000 interest income from a private activity bond issued in 1992. You also had $100 of investment expense related to this bond. You enter $4,900 on Form 6251.

Exclusion on qualifying small business stock. If you sell small business stock qualifying for the 50% exclusion *(5.7)*, 42% of the excluded amount, or 21% of the total gain (21% = 42% of 50% exclusion), is treated as an AMT preference item.

Accelerated depreciation of property acquired before 1987. For real property placed in service before 1987, the difference between the depreciation that would have been allowable if the straight-line method had been used and accelerated depreciation claimed on real property during the taxable year is a tax preference item. The excess is computed separately for each asset depreciated through an accelerated method. For example, if you use ACRS 15-year, 18-year, or 19-year accelerated rates for regular tax purposes, figure the deduction for each such property under the straight-line method and report the excess of your regular tax deduction over the straight-line amount as a preference item.

For personal property leased to others before 1987, the preference item is the excess of the regular tax deduction over the depreciation that would have been allowed under the straight-line method, without regard to salvage value. The excess is computed separately for each asset. For 10-year property, a 15-year recovery period is used.

Note: See 23.2 for the MACRS adjustment rules for post-1986 assets.

 Law Alert

Farmers May Use Installment Method for AMT

Farmers who make deferred crop sales may use the installment sales method for AMT purposes. The IRS had required farmers who used the installment sales method for regular tax purposes to make an adjustment on Form 6251 to compute AMT liability.

Oil and gas preference items. Independent oil and gas producers and royalty owners do not have to compute preference items for excess percentage depletion deductions. Excess intangible drilling costs (IDC) may not be tainted as preference items under a 40% reduction of income computation explained in the instructions to Form 6251.

23.4 Net Operating Losses

A net operating loss (NOL) claimed for regular tax purposes must be recomputed for AMT after all other AMT adjustments and preference items are taken into account. An NOL deductible for AMT purposes is generally the amount of the regular net operating loss except that in figuring the nonbusiness deduction adjustment *(40.19)* only AMT itemized deductions are taken into account. Thus, for AMT purposes, state and local taxes and certain interest that are not allowable AMT deductions do not reduce nonbusiness income in figuring the NOL adjustment.

In some cases, a net operating loss will eliminate your regular tax but not the AMT. The amount of the NOL deduction that may be deducted from AMT taxable income may not exceed 90% of AMT taxable income before the NOL deduction. Net operating losses that are disallowed because of the 90% AMT limit may be carried back under regular NOL rules *(40.18)* but the deduction in the carryback or carryover year is subject to the 90% limit. Carryovers from years beginning after 1982 and before 1987 are figured under prior law rules, subject to the 90% AMT limit.

23.5 AMT Foreign Tax Credit

For 1999, the foreign tax credit is the only credit that may reduce tentative AMT tax liability. The credit is figured in the same way as the regular foreign tax credit *(36.15)* after substituting AMT taxable income for regular taxable income.

The AMT foreign tax credit may not offset more than 90% of AMT tax determined without regard to the foreign tax credit and net operating loss deduction. Any foreign tax credit not allowed by the limit may be carried back and forward; *see 36.16* and instructions to Form 6251 for further details.

23.6 AMT Tax Credit From Regular Tax

You may be able to reduce your regular 1999 tax by a tax credit based on prior year AMT taxes. The credit, which is computed on Form 8801, may be applied against your 1999 regular tax after deducting any credits for dependent care, the elderly or disabled, mortgage interest, foreign taxes, and general business credits. However, the tax credit is allowed only if your regular 1999 tax liability exceeds 1999 tentative alternative minimum tax liability computed on Form 6251. Follow the instructions to Form 8801.

23.7 Avoiding AMT Tax

If you are within the range of the AMT tax, review periodically your income and expenses to determine whether to make certain tax elections, accelerate income, and/or defer the payment of expenses.

There are elections, such as the election of alternative straight-line MACRS depreciation, that may avoid AMT adjustments. However, such elections will increase your regular tax. Similarly, adjustment treatment for mining exploration and development costs, circulation expenses, and research expenses can be avoided by elections to amortize; *see 23.2.*

The following steps may also avoid or soften the impact of the AMT tax:

• Defer deductible expense items to a later year in which your income will be subject to regular tax rates exceeding your AMT tax rate (either 26% or 28% depending on your AMT income). Consider deferring payment of home mortgage interest and medical expenses. You will get a larger tax benefit from the deductions in the later year. In the case of unimproved real estate, consider an election to capitalize taxes and carry charges. Also, do not elect first-year expensing of business equipment.

 Law Alert

Nonrefundable Tax Credits
Certain nonrefundable business credits may be limited by tentative AMT; follow the instructions to Form 3800.

Under a new law, nonrefundable personal credits such as the child tax credit *(25.1)*, the education credits *(38.7)*, and the dependent care credit *(25.3)* are allowed to offset 1999 regular income tax liability in full. If this legislation had not been enacted, the credits would have been allowed only to the extent that the regular income tax liability exceeded the tentative AMT.

In 2000 and 2001, these nonrefundable personal credits will offset AMT liability as well as regular income tax. The foreign tax credit, if any, will be taken into account before the personal credits in computing the regular tax for those years.

Planning Reminder

Accelerating Income

If you decide to accelerate income to a year in which you are subject to AMT, and you hold tax-deferred savings certificates with a maturity of one year or less, you might consider an early redemption to the current year. But here weigh the penalty cost of an early forfeiture. Similarly, you might make an early sale of U.S. Treasury bills to the current year.

• Defer if possible the exercise of an incentive stock option to a later year when you are not subject to AMT. The bargain element of an incentive stock option is an adjustment item subject to AMT. This is the difference between the option price and the fair market price of the stock on the date of exercise. If you exercise the option and it is subject to AMT, you may find yourself with an unexpected liability and short of liquid funds to meet your tax liability.

Accelerating income. If you find that you will be subject to AMT in a current year, you may want to subject additional income in that year to the 26% or 28% AMT tax rate. In such a case, consider accelerating the receipt of income to that year. If you are in business, you might ask for earlier payments from customers or clients. If you control a small corporation, you might prepay salary or pay larger bonuses. But here be careful not to run afoul of reasonable compensation rules. You might also consider paying dividends.

Computing the "Kiddie Tax" for Children Under Age 14

Investment income over $1,400 earned by a child under age 14 is taxed at the child's parent's top tax rate. The child's parent or legal representative generally makes this tax computation, which is nicknamed the "kiddie tax."

The kiddie tax applies only to investment income, such as interest, dividends, rents, royalties, and profits on the sale of property. Income from wages and self-employment is not subject to the kiddie tax.

As the child's parent, you generally must use Form 8615 to report the child's income and compute the tax, which is reported on the child's personal income tax return; *see 24.4*. The Form 8615 computation has no effect on the treatment of items on your own return or on your tax computation. You may instead elect on Form 8814 to report the child's investment income on your own return, provided the child received only interest and dividend income. This election is generally not advisable. If you elect on Form 8814 to report the child's investment income on your own return, your adjusted gross income will increase and this could adversely affect your right to claim various deductions; *see 24.5*.

If you are married but file separately, the parent with the larger amount of taxable income is responsible for the kiddie tax computation. If parents are divorced, separated, unmarried, or living apart for the last six months of the year, the parent who has custody of the child for the greater part of 1999 computes the tax. If a child cannot get tax information directly from a parent, the legal representative of the child may ask the IRS for the necessary information.

24.1 Filing Your Child's Return

To discourage substantial income splitting of investment income between parents and minor children, the tax law has complicated income reporting for parents and children by—

1. Imposing a "kiddie tax" that taxes a child's investment income over $1,400 at the parent's top bracket if the child is under 14 years of age at the end of the taxable year; *see 24.3*.
2. Barring a dependent child from claiming a personal exemption on his or her own tax return.
3. Limiting the standard deduction to $700 for a dependent child who has only investment income; *see 13.5*.

Does your child have to file? For a child who can be claimed as a dependent, the income filing threshold is generally $700. If your dependent child has gross income (earned and investment income) of $700 or less for 1999, he or she is not subject to tax and does not have to file a tax return.

A 1999 return must be filed for a dependent child with investment income exceeding $250 and gross income of more than $700. If a dependent child has salary or other earned income but no investment income, a return does not have to be filed unless such earned income exceeds $4,300 in 1999. If your child's only income is from interest and dividends, you may be able to make an election to report the income on your own return; *see 24.5*.

Although a dependent child may not claim a personal exemption on his or her 1999 tax return, the child is allowed to claim at least a $700 standard deduction. A dependent child with earned income over $700 may claim a standard deduction up to those earnings plus an additional $250, but no more than the basic standard deduction, which is generally $4,300; *see 13.1*.

How to file for your child. If your child was under age 14 as of January 1, 2000, and had investment income of $1,400 or less, follow the regular filing rules and use Form 1040EZ, 1040A, or Form 1040 to report the child's income and deductions. The "kiddie tax" computation does not apply, so all of the child's income will be taxed at his or her own tax rate. If your child is unable to sign his or her tax return, you must do so; *see 1.11*.

If your child's investment income exceeded $1,400, the kiddie tax computation applies; *see 24.3*. Form 8615 must be filed to compute the kiddie tax unless your child's only income is interest and dividends and you elect to report your child's investment earnings on your own return as discussed at *24.5*. On Form 8615 you must provide your tax identification number and taxable income. Form 8615 is attached to the child's tax return; *see 24.4*.

If your child was age 14 or older as of January 1, 2000, your child should file Form 1040EZ, 1040A, or 1040, depending on the type of income and deductions he or she has. The special kiddie tax rules do not apply.

Child's AMT liability. A child who has substantial tax-exempt interest, tax preferences, or tax adjustments subject to the alternative minimum tax must compute tentative AMT liability on Form 6251; *see* Chapter 23.

24.2 Children Not Subject to the "Kiddie Tax"

For 1999 returns, the "kiddie tax" computation does *not* apply to—

- A child who was 14 years old or over on January 1, 2000.
- A child who on January 1, 2000, was under age 14 and who had 1999 gross investment income of $1,400 or less. The kiddie tax computation applies only to investment income exceeding $1,400. Furthermore, children who itemize deductions may in some cases exempt more than $1,400 from the computation; *see 24.3*.
- A child under age 14 if neither parent was alive at the end of 1999.

Filing Instruction

Child 14 or Over

The kiddie tax does not apply to a child who was 14 years old or older on January 1, 2000.

EXAMPLES

1. At the end of 1999, your son, whom you claim as your dependent, is age 14. He has interest income of $1,400 and salary income of $950 from his part-time job. His standard deduction is $1,200, the greater of earned income plus $250 *(see 13.5)* and $700. No personal exemption may be claimed. Assuming he has no itemized deductions, taxable income is $1,150 ($2,350 gross income – $1,200 standard deduction). The kiddie tax computation based on your top rate does not apply because your son is at least age 14 at the end of the year.

2. In 1999, your five-year-old daughter has interest income of $800. Taxable income of $100 is subject to tax at her own tax rate.

Interest income	$800
Less: standard deduction	700
Taxable income	$100

The kiddie tax computation does not apply because investment income does not exceed $1,400.

24.3 Children Under Age 14 Subject to the "Kiddie Tax"

The "kiddie tax" is a tax on a child's investment income at the parent's top marginal tax rate. It applies for 1999 returns to a child who—

- Was under age 14 on January 1, 2000;
- Had either parent alive at the end of 1999; *and*
- Had investment income for 1999 exceeding $1,400. For a child who has itemized deductions of more than $700 that are directly connected to the production of investment income, the $1,400 exemption is increased, as explained below.

Figuring kiddie tax on child's or parent's return. The kiddie tax computation is generally made on Form 8615, which must be attached to your child's return. A sample Form 8615 is at the end of this chapter. However, if the only income of your child who is under age 14 is interest and dividends and other tests are met, you may elect on Form 8814 to include your child's investment income on your own tax return, instead of computing the kiddie tax on Form 8615; *see 24.5.*

Kiddie tax on Form 8615 applies to investment income exceeding $1,400 floor. If your child files his or her own return and the "kiddie tax" is computed on Form 8615, your top rate applies to *net investment income*. For purposes of this rule, *net investment income* equals gross investment income minus $1,400 if your child does not itemize deductions on Schedule A. Thus, if your child does not itemize, the first $1,400 of investment income is exempt from the special computation. Investment income exceeding $1,400 is considered net investment income subject to the special computation; *see* Example 3 on the following page.

Include as gross investment income all taxable income that is not compensation for personal services. Include interest income, unless it is tax-exempt interest, dividends, royalties, rents, and profits on the sale of property. Payments from a trust are also included to the extent of distributable net income. Income in custodial accounts is treated as the child's income and is subject to the kiddie tax computation.

Investment earnings on all of your child's property must be considered, even if the property was a gift from you or someone else, or if the property was produced from your child's wages, such as a bank account into which the wages were deposited. The wages themselves, or self-employment earnings, are not considered.

If your child does itemize deductions, and has more than $700 of deductions that are directly connected to the production of investment income, the $1,400 floor is increased. The floor is $700 plus the directly connected deductions. If the directly connected deductions are $700 or less, the regular $1,400 kiddie tax exemption applies, as in Example 4 on the following page. Directly connected itemized deductions are expenses paid to produce or collect income or to manage, conserve, or maintain income-producing property. Only the part of the total expenses exceeding the 2% AGI floor may be deducted. These expenses include custodian fees and service charges, service fees to collect interest and dividends, and investment counsel fees. If, after you subtract the itemized deductions, your child's net investment income exceeds his or her taxable income, you apply the tax to the lower taxable income, rather than to the net investment income.

EXAMPLES

(In all the following Examples, assume the child is your dependent for 1999 and under age 14 on January 1, 2000.)

1. Child has interest income of $480 and no other income for 1999. The child has no income tax liability and does not have to file a return.

Interest income	$480
Less: standard deduction	480
	0

Filing Tip

Investment Income Exceeding $1,400

You do not have to concern yourself with the kiddie tax computation if your child under age 14 had investment income of $1,400 or less for 1999. If investment income exceeded $1,400, the excess is subject to your top marginal tax rate, rather than your child's tax rate, under the computation on Form 8615.

Filing Tip

Floor Increase

If your child itemizes deductions and has more than $700 of deductions connected to the production of investment income, the $1,400 floor is increased to $700 plus the directly connected deductions.

2. Child has interest and dividend income of $900 and no other income for 1999. A standard deduction of $700 may be claimed. The balance of $200 is taxed at the child's regular tax bracket. Form 8615 does not have to be filed and the kiddie tax computation does not apply since investment income does not exceed $1,400.

3. For 1999, child has dividend income of $1,800. After taking into account a standard deduction of $700, taxable income is $1,100, of which $400 is subject to the kiddie tax computation based on the parent's top tax bracket on Form 8615.

Figuring taxable income:

Dividend income	$1,800
Less: standard deduction	700
	$1,100

Income subject to tax at parent's rate:

Investment income	$1,800
Less: $1,400	1,400
	$400

An example of the actual Form 8615 computation is at *24.4*. As an alternative to computing kiddie tax on $400 on Form 8615, the parent may elect to report the child's dividend income on his or her own return; *see 24.5*.

4. Child has $300 of wages and $1,750 of dividends and interest income for 1999. On Schedule A, the child claims itemized deductions of $400 related to investment income after the 2% AGI floor. The child also has $400 of other itemized deductions. Itemized deductions of $800 are claimed; they exceed the $700 standard deduction.

Figuring taxable income:

Total income	$2,050
Less: itemized deductions	800
Taxable income	$1,250

Income subject to tax at parent's rate:

Investment income	$1,750
Less: greater of (1) $1,400 and (2) the sum of $700 and directly related expenses of $400	1,400
Net investment income subject to tax at parent's rate on Form 8615 *(24.4)*; *see 24.5* for parent's alternative election	$350

24.4 Computing "Kiddie Tax" on Child's Return

If your child is subject to the "kiddie tax" under *24.3*, the tax is computed on Form 8615, which is attached to his or her return, unless you make the parent's election at *24.5*. Before your child's Form 8615 can be completed, your own taxable income must be determined. The amount to be entered on Form 8615 as the parent's taxable income depends on the parent's marital and filing status.

If the parents file a *joint return,* their joint taxable income is entered on Form 8615, along with the net investment income *(24.3)* of all their children under age 14. If the parents file *separate returns,* the larger of the parents' separate taxable incomes is used on the child's Form 8615.

Where parents are legally separated or divorced and custody of the child is shared, Form 8615 should be completed using the taxable income of the parent who has custody for the greater part of the year. If parents are married but living apart, and the custodial parent qualifies as unmarried under Test 1 at *1.11*, that parent's taxable income is used on Form 8615. If the custodial parent is not considered unmarried, the income of the parent with the larger taxable income is used. If the custodial parent has remarried and files a joint return with a new spouse, their joint return taxable income is used on the child's Form 8615. If the parents were never married but they live together with the child, the income of the parent with the larger taxable income is used; if the parents live apart, the income of the parent with custody for most of the year is used on Form 8615.

More than one child subject to kiddie tax. You file a separate Form 8615 for each child and on each form net investment income of all the children subject to the tax is included. The computed tax is allocated to each of your children, according to his or her share of their combined net investment income. This computation is incorporated in the steps of Form 8615 and by following the order of the form, you will make the proper allocation.

Planning Reminder

Prepare Your Return First

Before your child can complete Form 8615, or you prepare it for the child, your own taxable income must be determined.

As parents, the kiddie tax computation on Form 8615 does not affect your tax liability or how you compute any limitation on deductions or credits. For example, the addition of the child's net investment income to your taxable income on Form 8615 does *not* affect the adjusted gross income floors for purposes of figuring your deduction for IRA contributions, medical expenses, or miscellaneous expenses.

EXAMPLE

For 1999, Bill and Betty Brown each file Form 1040A. Bill, age 12, has dividend income of $2,100; Betty, age 10, has $1,500. They each claim a standard deduction of $700. Neither may claim a personal exemption because they are claimed as dependents by their parents, Tom and Lilli Brown. Bill's taxable income after claiming the standard deduction is $1,400. Betty's is $800.

Tom and Lilli Brown do not make the election *(24.5)* to report Bill's and Betty's dividends on their joint return. Forms 8615 are prepared and attached to the children's Forms 1040A, because each child is under age 14 and has more than $1,400 of investment income.

Tom and Lilli report taxable income of $52,000 on their 1999 joint return. They use the IRS tax tables to look up their tax (the tables are in Part 8 at the back of this book). The tax on $52,000 is $8,971. The special computation on Form 8615 does not increase their joint return tax; it determines only the amount of Bill's and Betty's tax.

As shown at the end of this chapter on sample Forms 8615, Bill's 1999 tax is $303 and Betty's 1999 tax is $135. If the special computation did not apply, Bill's 1999 tax would be $212 and Betty's tax would be $122. Thus, as a result of the special computation, the total tax bill for the children is increased by $104 ($438 – $334).

Estimating the kiddie tax in case of filing delay. If you are unable to file your return by April 17, 2000, the child's tax on Form 8615 may be based on an estimate. You may make a reasonable estimate of your taxable income on Form 8615 or may estimate the net investment income of children under age 14 if that information is not yet available. When you have the complete income details, file an amended return.

A reasonable estimate may be based on your 1998 taxable income and the 1998 investment income of the child. If a refund is due, the IRS will pay interest from April 17, 2000, or, if the return was filed late, from the filing date. If additional tax is due on the amended return, interest will be charged from April 17, but no penalty will be imposed.

Planning Reminder

Estimating Tax on Form 8615

If you are unable to file your 1999 return by April 17, 2000, but your child's return is filed by the April 17 deadline, the child's Form 8615 may be based on an estimate of your tax liability. When you have the completed income information, file an amended return.

24.5 Parent's Election To Report Child's Dividends and Interest

Instead of filing a separate return for your child *(24.4)* whose income is subject to the "kiddie tax," you may elect on Form 8814 to compute the kiddie tax on your return if all of the following tests are met:

- The child's income is only from interest and dividends (including mutual-fund capital gain distributions and Alaska Permanent Fund dividends);
- The total interest and dividends are over $700 but less than $7,000;
- Estimated tax payments were not made in the child's name and Social Security number for 1999, and there was no overpayment from the child's 1998 return applied to his or her 1999 estimated tax; *and*
- The child was not subject to 1999 backup withholding.

By making this election, and following the steps of Form 8814, you include in your income the child's interest and dividends to the extent they exceed $1,400. You also figure an additional tax equal to the smaller of $105 and 15% of your child's income over $700.

If parents are divorced, separated, unmarried, or living apart for the last six months of the year, the parent whose taxable income would be taken into account on Form 8615 *(24.4)* is the parent who may elect to report the income on his or her own return.

In figuring whether you owe alternative minimum tax (AMT), you must include as a tax preference item interest income your child receives from specified private activity bonds; *see 23.3* and Form 6251 instructions.

Should you make the election? There is no advantage in making the election, except to skip the paperwork involved in preparing a return in the child's name or returns in your children's names. If you consider this an advantage, you may want to make the election. It may be preferable to take the time to prepare the child's return to keep the child's tax accounting separate from yours. Including the child's income as your own increases your AGI, which may create these disadvantages:

- Subject you to the exemption phaseout *(21.15)* and 3% reduction computation *(13.7)* for itemized deductions.
- Make it more difficult to deduct job expenses and other miscellaneous itemized deductions, which are subject to a 2% AGI floor *(19.1)*, and medical deductions, subject to a 7.5% AGI floor *(17.1)*.
- Limit a deduction for IRA contributions under the phase-out rules *(8.4)*.
- Limit your ability to claim the special $25,000 rental loss allowance under the passive activity rules *(10.2)*.
- Increase local and state tax liability.

Finally, if you elect to report the child's income on your own return, you may not claim any deductions that your child would have been able to claim on his or her return such as investment expenses or a penalty on premature withdrawals from a savings account. On the other hand, reporting your child's interest or dividends increases your net investment income, which may allow you to claim a larger deduction for investment interest; *see 15.10*. Also, your ceiling for charitable donations may be increased. If you plan to report your child's income on your 2000 return, provide for the tax in your estimated tax payments or withholdings during 2000.

Caution

Reporting Child's Income on Your Return

Although reporting your child's income on your own return may be more convenient in terms of saving paperwork, including the extra income on your return could be disadvantageous.

EXAMPLE

Woodrow, age 10, received $2,000 of interest income in 1999. He has no other income and is not subject to backup withholding. No estimated tax payments were made in his name. His parents elect on Form 8814 to include his interest income on their 1999 tax return instead of filing a return for him. They include $600 of the interest ($2,000 – $1,400 floor) on Line 21 (other income) of their Form 1040. They also add $105 to their tax on Line 40 of Form 1040 and indicate that the amount is from Form 8814.

Sample Form 8814

A Child's name (first, initial, and last) **Woodrow Jones**	**B** Child's social security number **001 ⋮ X1 ⋮ 11X1**	

| **C** | If more than one Form 8814 is attached, check here . . . . ▶ | ☐ |

Part I   Child's Interest and Dividends To Report on Your Return

1a	Enter your child's **taxable** interest. If this amount is different from the amounts shown on the child's Forms 1099-INT and 1099-OID, see the instructions	**1a**	2,000
b	Enter your child's **tax-exempt** interest. **DO NOT** include this amount on line 1a . . . . [**1b**]		
2	Enter your child's ordinary dividends, including any Alaska Permanent Fund dividends. If your child received any ordinary dividends as a nominee, see the instructions	**2**	- 0 -
3	Enter your child's capital gain distributions. If your child received any capital gain distributions as a nominee, see the instructions	**3**	- 0 -
4	Add lines 1a, 2, and 3. If the total is $1,400 or less, skip lines 5 and 6 and go to line 7. If the total is $7,000 or more, **do not** file this form. Your child **must** file his or her own return to report the income	**4**	2,000
5	Base amount	**5**	1,400 00
6	Subtract line 5 from line 4. If you checked the box on line C above or if you entered an amount on line 3, see the instructions. Also, include this amount in the total on Form 1040, line 21, or Form 1040NR, line 21. In the space next to line 21, enter "Form 8814" and show the amount. Go to line 7 below. . . . . ▶	**6**	600

Part II   Tax on the First $1,400 of Child's Interest and Dividends

7	Amount not taxed	**7**	700 00
8	Subtract line 7 from line 4. If the result is zero or less, enter -0-	**8**	1,300
9	**Tax.** Is the amount on line 8 less than $700? ☒ **No.** Enter $105 here and see the **Note** below. ☐ **Yes.** Multiply line 8 by 15% (.15). Enter the result here and see the **Note** below.	**9**	105

Note: *If you checked the box on line C above, see the instructions. Otherwise, include the amount from line 9 in the tax you enter on Form 1040, line 40, or Form 1040NR, line 39. Be sure to check box **a** on Form 1040, line 40, or Form 1040NR, line 39.*

Sample Forms 8615—

Child's name shown on return	Child's social security number
Betty Brown	X10 ⋮ 00 ⋮ 1111

A Parent's name (first, initial, and last). **Caution:** *See instructions on back before completing.*

	B Parent's social security number
Tom Brown	XXX ⋮ 11 ⋮ 0X11

C Parent's filing status (check one):

☐ Single ☒ Married filing jointly ☐ Married filing separately ☐ Head of household ☐ Qualifying widow(er)

Part I   Child's Net Investment Income

1	Enter the child's investment income, such as taxable interest and dividends. See instructions. If this amount is $1,400 or less, **stop**; do not file this form	1	1,500
2	If the child **did not** itemize deductions on **Schedule A** (Form 1040 or Form 1040NR), enter $1,400. If the child **did** itemize deductions, see instructions	2	1,400
3	Subtract line 2 from line 1. If the result is zero or less, **stop**; do not complete the rest of this form but **do** attach it to the child's return	3	100
4	Enter the child's **taxable income** from Form 1040, line 39; Form 1040A, line 24; or Form 1040NR, line 38	4	800
5	Enter the **smaller** of line 3 or line 4	5	100

Part II   Tentative Tax Based on the Tax Rate of the Parent Listed on Line A

6	Enter the parent's **taxable income** from Form 1040, line 39; Form 1040A, line 24; Form 1040EZ, line 6; TeleFile Tax Record, line K; Form 1040NR, line 38; or Form 1040NR-EZ, line 14. If less than zero, enter -0-	6	52,000
7	Enter the total net investment income, if any, from Forms 8615, line 5, of **all other** children of the parent identified above. **Do not** include the amount from line 5 above	7	700
8	Add lines 5, 6, and 7	8	52,800
9	Enter the tax on line 8 based on the **parent's** filing status. See instructions. If the **Capital Gain Tax Worksheet** or **Schedule D** or **J** (Form 1040) is used to figure the tax, check here ▶ ☐	9	9,195
10	Enter the parent's tax from Form 1040, line 40; Form 1040A, line 25; Form 1040EZ, line 10; TeleFile Tax Record, line K; Form 1040NR, line 39; or Form 1040NR-EZ, line 15. If any tax is from **Form 4972** or **8814,** see instructions. If the **Capital Gain Tax Worksheet** or **Schedule D** or **J** (Form 1040) was used to figure the tax, check here ▶ ☐	10	8,971
11	Subtract line 10 from line 9 and enter the result. If line 7 is blank, also enter this amount on line 13 and go to **Part III**	11	224
12a	Add lines 5 and 7 ... **12a** 800		
b	Divide line 5 by line 12a. Enter the result as a decimal (rounded to at least three places)	12b	× .125
13	Multiply line 11 by line 12b	13	28

Part III   Child's Tax—If lines 4 and 5 above are the same, enter -0- on line 15 and go to line 16.

14	Subtract line 5 from line 4 ... **14** 700		
15	Enter the tax on line 14 based on the **child's** filing status. See instructions. If the **Capital Gain Tax Worksheet** or **Schedule D** or **J** (Form 1040) is used to figure the tax, check here ▶ ☐	15	107
16	Add lines 13 and 15	16	135
17	Enter the tax on line 4 based on the **child's** filing status. See instructions. If the **Capital Gain Tax Worksheet** or **Schedule D** or **J** (Form 1040) is used to figure the tax, check here ▶ ☐	17	122
18	Enter the **larger** of line 16 or line 17 here and on Form 1040, line 40; Form 1040A, line 25; or Form 1040NR, line 39	18	135

Child's name shown on return	Child's social security number
Bill Brown	0XX ⋮ 11 ⋮ 111X

A Parent's name (first, initial, and last). **Caution:** *See instructions on back before completing.*

	B Parent's social security number
Tom Brown	XXX ⋮ 11 ⋮ 0X11

C Parent's filing status (check one):

☐ Single ☒ Married filing jointly ☐ Married filing separately ☐ Head of household ☐ Qualifying widow(er)

Part I   Child's Net Investment Income

1	Enter the child's investment income, such as taxable interest and dividends. See instructions. If this amount is $1,400 or less, **stop**; do not file this form	1	2,100
2	If the child **did not** itemize deductions on **Schedule A** (Form 1040 or Form 1040NR), enter $1,400. If the child **did** itemize deductions, see instructions	2	1,400
3	Subtract line 2 from line 1. If the result is zero or less, **stop**; do not complete the rest of this form but **do** attach it to the child's return	3	700
4	Enter the child's **taxable income** from Form 1040, line 39; Form 1040A, line 24; or Form 1040NR, line 38	4	1,400
5	Enter the **smaller** of line 3 or line 4	5	700

Part II   Tentative Tax Based on the Tax Rate of the Parent Listed on Line A

6	Enter the parent's **taxable income** from Form 1040, line 39; Form 1040A, line 24; Form 1040EZ, line 6; TeleFile Tax Record, line K; Form 1040NR, line 38; or Form 1040NR-EZ, line 14. If less than zero, enter -0-	6	52,000
7	Enter the total net investment income, if any, from Forms 8615, line 5, of **all other** children of the parent identified above. **Do not** include the amount from line 5 above	7	100
8	Add lines 5, 6, and 7	8	52,800
9	Enter the tax on line 8 based on the **parent's** filing status. See instructions. If the **Capital Gain Tax Worksheet** or **Schedule D** or **J** (Form 1040) is used to figure the tax, check here ▶ ☐	9	9,195
10	Enter the parent's tax from Form 1040, line 40; Form 1040A, line 25; Form 1040EZ, line 10; TeleFile Tax Record, line K; Form 1040NR, line 39; or Form 1040NR-EZ, line 15. If any tax is from **Form 4972** or **8814,** see instructions. If the **Capital Gain Tax Worksheet** or **Schedule D** or **J** (Form 1040) was used to figure the tax, check here ▶ ☐	10	8,971
11	Subtract line 10 from line 9 and enter the result. If line 7 is blank, also enter this amount on line 13 and go to **Part III**	11	224
12a	Add lines 5 and 7 ... **12a** 800		
b	Divide line 5 by line 12a. Enter the result as a decimal (rounded to at least three places)	12b	× .875
13	Multiply line 11 by line 12b	13	196

Part III   Child's Tax—If lines 4 and 5 above are the same, enter -0- on line 15 and go to line 16.

14	Subtract line 5 from line 4 ... **14** 700		
15	Enter the tax on line 14 based on the **child's** filing status. See instructions. If the **Capital Gain Tax Worksheet** or **Schedule D** or **J** (Form 1040) is used to figure the tax, check here ▶ ☐	15	107
16	Add lines 13 and 15	16	303
17	Enter the tax on line 4 based on the **child's** filing status. See instructions. If the **Capital Gain Tax Worksheet** or **Schedule D** or **J** (Form 1040) is used to figure the tax, check here ▶ ☐	17	212
18	Enter the **larger** of line 16 or line 17 here and on Form 1040, line 40; Form 1040A, line 25; or Form 1040NR, line 39	18	303

Child Tax Credit and Dependent Care, Earned Income (EIC) and Adoption Credits

The following family tax credits are discussed in this chapter: child tax credit, dependent care credit, earned income credit (EIC), and the adoption credit. Education tax credits are discussed in Chapter 38.

The child tax credit is $500 for each qualifying dependent child under age 17. To claim the credit, you must follow the steps of the "Child Tax Credit Worksheet." There is a phaseout of the credit, as explained in 25.1. The child tax credit cannot generate a tax refund. However, if the credit does exceed your tax liability, you may be entitled to a refundable credit called the "additional child credit" if you have three or more qualifying children and have paid FICA taxes. To claim this "additional" credit, you must file Form 8812.

The dependent care credit is for working people who pay care costs that allow them the freedom to work. Depending on your income, the credit is 20% to 30% of up to $2,400 of care expenses for one dependent and up to $4,800 of expenses for two or more dependents. If your adjusted gross income exceeds $28,000, the maximum credit is $480 for one dependent and $960 for two or more dependents.

The earned income credit (EIC) is provided to low-income workers who support children, and a limited credit is allowed to certain workers without qualifying children; *see 25.12.* For 1999, the EIC can be as much as $2,312 if you have one qualifying child *(25.12)*, $3,816 if you have more than one qualifying child, and $347 if you do not have a qualifying child. There is a phaseout of the credit; *see 25.13.* You look up the credit amount in IRS tables included in the tax form instructions. The EIC is "refundable"; you will receive a refund from the IRS if the credit exceeds your tax liability.

The adoption credit of up to $5,000 ($6,000 for a special needs child) may be claimed for costs of adopting a child under the age of 18 or a disabled person incapable of self-care.

Child Tax Credit

25.1 Child Tax Credit for Children Under Age 17

For 1999, you generally may claim a tax credit of $500 for each qualifying child who is under age 17 at the end of 1999. To figure the exact amount of your credit, however, you must complete the "Child Tax Credit Worksheet" in the IRS instructions to determine if your credit is limited. The credit may be limited under a phase-out rule based on modified adjusted gross income (*see* below) and the credit may not exceed your regular income tax liability; also *see* the Law Alert in the right column.

If you have three or more qualifying children, you may be able to qualify for an additional child tax credit by filing Form 8812. This credit may provide you a tax refund based on Social Security and Medicare taxes withheld from your pay or the employee share of self-employment taxes that you report.

Qualifying child. The credit may be claimed for a child under age 17 at the end of 1999 whom you claim as a dependent. The child must be your child, stepchild, grandchild, or great-grandchild. An adopted child qualifies if placed with you by an authorized agency for legal adoption, even if the adoption is not final by the end of 1999. A foster child qualifies if he or she lived with you for all of 1999, or was born in 1999 and lived with you the rest of the year, or lived with you in 1999 but died during the year.

Phaseout of credit. The credit is limited or eliminated if your modified adjusted gross income is above a threshold amount for your filing status. Modified AGI is generally the same as AGI. AGI is shown on Line 18 of Form 1040A and on Line 33 on Form 1040. If you excluded income earned abroad or income from Puerto Rico, Guam, American Samoa, or the Northern Mariana Islands, modified AGI is figured by adding the excluded amounts to the AGI shown. The phase-out threshold for each filing status is as follows.

Filing Status	*Phaseout Applies if MAGI exceeds*
Married filing jointly	$110,000
Head of household	75,000
Single	75,000
Qualifying widow(er)	75,000
Married filing separately	55,000

Changing your withholding. If you can claim the child tax credit, you may have too much tax withheld from your wages during the year. If so, you can claim more withholding allowances. File the new Form W-4 with your employer so that less income tax will be withheld.

25.2 Figuring the Child Tax Credit

You use the Child Tax Credit Worksheet supplied by the IRS in the instruction booklet accompanying your tax return to figure the credit. The worksheet will also be in the Supplement to *Your Income Tax*. You do not attach the worksheet to your return.

The credit is $500 times the number of your qualifying children. On the worksheet, it is reduced by $50 for each $1,000 (or fraction of $1,000) that your modified AGI exceeds the phase-out threshold for your filing status, as shown in *25.1*.

 Law Alert

Child Tax Credit Not Limited by AMT

A last-minute law change allowed the child tax credit to be claimed in full against regular income tax liability on 1999 tax returns without regard to alternative minimum tax (AMT).

For 2000 and 2001, the child tax credit and other nonrefundable personal credits (such as the dependent care credit and education credits) will be allowed against regular tax liability (after reduction by the foreign tax credit, if any) and *also* against AMT.

 Filing Tip

Additional Child Credit

The "additional child credit" is not actually a credit in addition to the child tax credit. It is an exception to the rule that you may not use the child tax credit to receive a refund of taxes. If the child tax credit figured for three or more children exceeds your tax liability, you may claim the additional child credit to generate a refund from Social Security and Medicare taxes that were withheld from your pay. By following the "Child Tax Credit Worksheet" and Form 8812, you may determine your eligibility for this credit.

EXAMPLES

1. In 1999, Carl and Abby have two dependent daughters under age 17. They have modified AGI of $34,000. They file a joint return. Their child tax credit is $1,000 ($500 × 2). Their modified AGI is less than the phase-out amount for their filing status ($110,000). Thus, they claim the full credit of $1,000, assuming it is not limited to regular tax liability in the Child Tax Credit Worksheet.

2. Jane is single and has two dependent children under 17. Jane's modified AGI for 1999 is $77,500. She files her tax return as head of household. Because her modified AGI exceeds $75,000 (the phase-out amount for her filing status), her child tax credit is reduced from $1,000 to $850. Her AGI exceeds $75,000 by $2,500. For each $1,000 of excess modified AGI, or fraction of $1,000, $50 of the credit is phased out. The excess income of $2,500, divided by $1,000, equals 2.5, which is rounded up to 3, resulting in a credit reduction of $150 ($50 × 3). The reduction computation is made on the Child Tax Credit Worksheet.

Dependent Care Credit

25.3 Qualifying for Child and Dependent Care Credit

Did you hire someone to care for your children or other dependents while you work? If so, you may qualify for a tax credit for the expenses. You may claim the credit even if you work part time. The credit is generally available to the extent you have earnings from employment. Your employer may have a plan qualifying for tax-free child care and, if you are covered, you may be unable to claim a tax credit; *see 25.7.*

Where to claim the credit. The credit is claimed on Form 2441 if you file Form 1040, or on Form 1040A, Schedule 2. The size of the credit depends on the amount of care expenses and income. Depending on your income, the credit is 20% to 30% of up to $2,400 of care expenses for one dependent and up to $4,800 of expenses for two or more dependents. If your adjusted gross income exceeds $28,000, the maximum credit is $480 for one dependent and $960 for two or more dependents. *See* the chart in *25.4.*

Credit requirements. To qualify for the credit, you must:

1. Incur the care expenses in order to earn income. In the case of a married couple, this requires both spouses to work either at full- or part-time positions. An exception to the earned income rule is made for a spouse who is a full-time student or incapacitated *(25.5)*. Qualifying care expenses are discussed at *25.7.* Limits on the amount of qualifying costs are discussed at *25.4.*
2. Pay over 50% of the household maintenance costs for a qualifying dependent; *see 25.6.* You must report the dependent's name and Social Security number on Form 2441 or Schedule 2 of Form 1040A.
3. File jointly if you are married, unless you are separated under the rules discussed at *25.8.*
4. Hire someone *other than* your child who is under age 19 at the end of the year, your spouse, or a person you can claim as a dependent; *see 25.7.*
5. Have qualifying expenses in excess of tax-free reimbursements received from your employer; *see 25.7.*
6. Report on your tax return the name, address, and taxpayer identification number (Social Security number for individuals) of the child-care provider; *see* below.

Identifying care provider on your return. You must list the name, address, and taxpayer identification number of the person you paid to care for your dependent on Form 2441 if you file Form 1040, or on Form 1040A, Schedule 2. You do not need the taxpayer identification number if a tax-exempt charity provides the dependent care services. Failure to list the correct name, address, and number may result in a disallowance of the credit. To avoid this possibility, ask the provider to fill out Form W-10 or get the identifying information from a Social Security card, driver's license, or business letterhead or invoice. If a household employee has filled out Form W-4 for you, this may act as a backup record.

Withholding tax for housekeeper. Where you employ help to care for your dependent in your home, you may be liable for FICA (Social Security) and FUTA (unemployment) taxes; *see 25.9.*

 Caution

Nonrefundable Credit

Unlike the Earned Income Credit, the dependent care credit is limited to your tax liability. In other words, if the credit amount exceeds the regular income tax that you owe, you will not be given a refund of the difference.

25.4 Limits on the Dependent Care Credit

The credit is a percentage of expenses paid for the care of a dependent to allow you to work and earn income. Qualifying expenses are discussed at 25.7. The credit percentage depends on your income.

Limit on expenses. In figuring the credit, you may only take into account qualifying expenses (25.7) up to a limit of $2,400 for one dependent, or $4,800 for two or more dependents. The $2,400 or $4,800 limit applies even if your actual expenses are much greater. Further, the $2,400 or $4,800 limit must be reduced by tax-free benefits received from an employer's dependent care plan. Finally, if your earned income is less than the $2,400 or $4,800 limit, your credit is figured on the lower income amount.

Take into account only 1999 payments for 1999 services. Your credit for 1999 must be based on payments made in 1999 for care services provided in 1999. If you paid for 1998 services in 1999, you may be able to claim an additional credit on your 1999 return, but only in limited circumstances, as discussed at the end of this section. If in 1999 you prepay for 2000 services, you must allocate your payment. Only payments for 1999 services should be counted towards the $2,400 or $4,800 limit when figuring your 1999 credit.

Credit percentage. Depending on your income, a credit percentage of 20% to 30% applies to your expenses up to the $2,400 (one dependent) or $4,800 (two or more dependents) limit. The maximum credit is 30% for families with adjusted gross income of $10,000 or less. For adjusted gross income over $10,000, the 30% credit is reduced by 1% for each $2,000 of adjusted gross income or fraction of $2,000 over $10,000, but not below 20%. The 20% credit applies to adjusted gross incomes exceeding $28,000.

The dependent care credit is nonrefundable; it is limited to your regular income tax liability; follow the IRS instructions.

Allowable Credit

Adjusted gross income		Your maximum credit	
	Credit percentage	One dependent	Two or more dependents
$10,000 or less	30%	$720	$1,440
10,001–12,000	29	696	1,392
12,001–14,000	28	672	1,344
14,001–16,000	27	648	1,296
16,001–18,000	26	624	1,248
18,001–20,000	25	600	1,200
20,001–22,000	24	576	1,152
22,001–24,000	23	552	1,104
24,001–26,000	22	528	1,056
26,001–28,000	21	504	1,008
28,001–and over	20	480	960

EXAMPLES

1. You pay $6,000 to a neighbor to care for your two children while you work. Your adjusted gross income is $31,000. The minimum credit percentage of 20% is applied to the maximum expense limit of $4,800, giving you a credit of $960.

2. Same as above except you receive a tax-free reimbursement of $2,500 from your employer's plan. The reimbursement reduces the $4,800 expense limit to $2,300 ($4,800 – $2,500); see 25.7. Your credit is $460 (20% of $2,300). If the tax-free reimbursement were $4,800 or more (it cannot exceed $5,000), no credit would be allowed.

 Filing Tip

Employer Reimbursements Reduce Credit

Expenses qualifying for the dependent care credit are reduced by any tax-free reimbursements under a qualified employer dependent care program. That is, the reimbursements reduce the $2,400 expense limit for one dependent, or the $4,800 expense limit for two or more qualifying dependents; see 25.7. Your employer will report reimbursements in Box 10 of your Form W-2. You figure the tax-free portion of the reimbursement, and any reduction to the credit expense base, on Form 2441 if you file Form 1040 or on Schedule 2 if you file Form 1040A.

Additional credit for 1999 payment of 1998 dependent care expenses. Payments made in 1999 for 1998 services may be eligible for an additional credit but only if you did not use up the $2,400 or $4,800 expense limit when claiming your 1998 credit.

For example, the cost of day-care services for your child in 1998 was $3,000, half of which you paid in 1998 and half in early 1999. On your 1998 return, a credit was based on the $1,500 of expenses paid in 1998. Since you used only $1,500 of the $2,400 expense limit in 1998, the $900 of "unused" expenses is carried over to 1999. On your 1998 Form 2441 or Schedule 2 of Form 1040A, you multiply $900 by a credit percentage based on your 1998 adjusted gross income. If your 1998 adjusted gross income was $30,000, the credit percentage is 20%. Thus, your additional 1999 credit is $180 (20% of $900). The $180 credit is claimed on Line 9 of Form 2441 or Schedule 2 (Form 1040A), and is in addition to the regular credit for 1999 care services. You must attach a statement explaining the carryover to 1999 and the computation of the additional credit.

25.5 Earned Income Test for Dependent Care Credit

To claim the credit, you must earn wage, salary, or self-employment income figured without regard to community property laws. Expenses for dependent care incurred while looking for a job may be included. However, you must have earnings during the year to claim the credit.

Earned income rule for married couples. Generally, both spouses must work at least part time, unless one is incapable of self-care or is a full-time student. If either you or your spouse earns less than the maximum $2,400 or $4,800 credit base *(25.4)*, the base is limited to the smaller income.

EXAMPLE

John and Mary are married. John earns $4,000. Mary earns $23,500. They incur care costs of $5,000 for their two children, ages 5 and 7. Their adjusted gross income including interest earnings is $27,742; their credit percentage is 21%. The maximum $4,800 credit base (for two or more dependents) is limited to John's lower income of $4,000. They may claim a credit of $840 ($4,000 × 21%).

Spouses who are students or disabled. An incapacitated spouse or a spouse who is a full-time student is considered to have earned income of $200 a month if expenses are incurred for one dependent, or $400 a month for two or more such dependents.

A full-time student is one who attends school full time during each of five calendar months during the year.

EXAMPLE

Same facts as in the Example above, except John was a full-time student for nine months and earned no income for the year. The credit base is limited to $3,600 ($400 × 9).

25.6 Household and Dependent Tests for Dependent Care Credit

To claim the credit you must maintain as your principal home a household for at least one of the following qualifying persons who lives with you:

1. A child *under the age of 13* whom you may claim as your dependent. If you are divorced or separated, and you had custody of the child for a longer time during the year than the other parent, you may be able to claim the credit even if the other parent is entitled to claim the child as a dependent; *see 25.8.*
2. Your spouse, if physically or mentally incapable of caring for himself or herself.
3. A person, regardless of age, who is physically or mentally incapable of caring for himself or herself. For example, he or she needs help to dress or to take care of personal hygiene or nutritional needs, or requires constant attention to avoid hurting himself or herself or others. Relatives who qualify, if disabled, are listed at *21.3.* A nonrelative may also qualify if he or she is a member of your household for the entire year, except for temporary absences. Generally, the qualifying person must be your dependent, but if he or she has gross income of $2,750 or more, so that you may not claim an exemption *(21.5)* for that person, you may still claim a credit for his or her care costs.

 Filing Tip

No Credit if Neither Spouse Works

If both husband and wife are full-time students and neither works, they may not claim the credit for dependent care costs. While one student-spouse may be considered to have earned income of $200 (or $400) each month, the other spouse's earned income is zero. Care costs eligible for the credit are limited to the lesser amount of earned income, which in this case is zero.

EXAMPLE

You live with your mother, who is physically incapable of caring for herself. You hire a practical nurse to care for her in the home while you are at work. Payments to the nurse qualify as care costs. However, if you placed her in a nursing home, the cost of the nursing home would not qualify as dependent care costs; but *see 17.11* for a possible medical expense deduction.

If your child becomes age 13 during the year. Take into account expenses incurred for his or her care prior to the 13th birthday. However, you do not prorate the $2,400 limitation. For example, if your child becomes age 13 on May 1 and you incurred $2,400 in care expenses between January 1 and April 30, the entire $2,400 qualifies for the credit.

You must pay more than half of household costs. You are considered to have maintained a household if you (or you and your spouse) provided more than half the maintenance costs in 1999. You also qualify if you paid more than half the costs during a lesser period in which you had care cost expenses. Rent, mortgage interest, property tax and insurance, utility bills, upkeep, repairs, and groceries are considered maintenance costs. Do not count costs of clothing, education, medical expenses, vacations, life insurance, mortgage principal, and capital improvements, such as replacing a boiler.

In determining costs of maintaining a household for a care period of less than a year, the annual household costs are prorated over the number of calendar months within the period care costs were incurred. A period of less than a calendar month is treated as a calendar month.

Household of two or more families. If two or more families share living quarters, each family is treated as a separate household.

EXAMPLES

1. The annual cost of maintaining a household is $6,600, and the period during which child care costs qualified for the deduction is from June 20 to December 31. To meet the household test, you must furnish more than $1,925 in maintaining the household from June 1 to December 31. The allocation covers seven months (June 1 to December 31).

   Cost of maintaining home: $^7/_{12}$ of $6,600 = $3,850
   Amount you must pay: 50% of $3,850 = $1,925

2. Two women, each with children, share a house. If each pays more than one-half of the household costs for her own family, each is treated as maintaining her separate household for purposes of the credit.

25.7 Expenses Qualifying for the Dependent Care Credit

If you do not receive tax-free dependent care benefits from an employer's plan, you may take into account up to $2,400 of the following types of expenses when figuring the credit for one dependent, or up to $4,800 for two or more dependents. If you receive employer-financed dependent care, tax-free reimbursements reduce the $2,400 or $4,800 base.

1. Costs of caring for your child under age 13, incapacitated spouse, or incapacitated dependent in your home. If you pay FICA or FUTA taxes on your housekeeper's wages *(25.9)*, you may include your share of the tax (employer) as part of the wages when entering your qualifying expenses. Also include your housekeeper's share of FICA tax if you pay it. Note that these taxes may more than offset your allowable credit.

   The manner of care need not be the least expensive alternative. For example, where a grandparent resides with you and may provide adequate care for your child to enable you to work, the cost of hiring someone to care for the child is still eligible for the credit.

2. Ordinary domestic services in your home, such as laundry, cleaning, and cooking (but not payments to a gardener or chauffeur) that are partly for the care of the qualifying person. Expenses for the dependent's food, clothing, or entertainment do not qualify. Food costs for a housekeeper who eats in your home may be added to qualifying expenses. Extra expenses for a housekeeper's lodging (extra rent or utilities) also qualify.

3. Outside-the-home care costs for a child under age 13, as in a day-care center, day camp, nursery school, or in the home of a babysitter. Outside-the-home care costs also qualify if incurred for a

Filing Tip

Day-Care Center or Nursery School

The amount you pay to a day-care center or nursery school for a dependent child under age 13 is eligible for the credit, even if it covers such incidental benefits as lunch. However, tuition for a child in first grade or higher is not taken into account. If the dependent is not your child, costs for care outside the home qualify only if the dependent regularly spends at least eight hours per day in your home. Up to $2,400 a year of outside-the-home care expenses may be taken into account in figuring the credit for one dependent, and up to $4,800 for two or more.

handicapped dependent, regardless of age, provided he or she regularly spends at least eight hours per day in your home. However, the cost of schooling in the first grade or higher does not qualify for the credit. Costs for sleep-away camp also do not qualify for the credit.

The cost of driving a dependent to or from a day-care center or similar transportation does not qualify for a child-care credit. However, the Tax Court allowed a child-care credit for supervised bus transportation; the transportation was part of the actual child care.

Payments to relatives. No credit may be claimed for payments made to relatives for whom a dependency exemption is allowable *(21.3)*. Thus, if you pay your mother to care for your child and you cannot claim your mother as a dependent, such payments qualify for the credit. The same rule applies for payments to unrelated persons who live with you and qualify as your dependents; *see 21.4.*

No credit may be claimed for payments to your child who is under 19 years of age at the close of the tax year, whether or not you may claim the child as a dependent.

Allocating expenses when employed less than entire year. When an expense covers a period, part of which you were gainfully employed or in active search of gainful employment and part of which you were not employed or seeking employment, you must allocate expenses on a daily basis.

EXAMPLE

You are employed for only two months and 10 days. Monthly care expenses are $300. Eligible care expenses amount to $700 ($300 × 2 months, plus $1/_3$ of $300).

Employer-financed dependent care reduces credit base. Tax-free reimbursements under an employer's dependent care program reduce the $2,400 or $4,800 credit base. For example, if you have one child and you receive a $1,500 reimbursement of child-care costs from your company's plan, the amount eligible for the tax credit is reduced to $900 ($2,400 – $1,500). A reimbursement of $2,400 or more would bar any credit. The $4,800 credit expense limit for two or more dependents is similarly reduced. On your Form W-2, your employer will report the amount of tax-free reimbursement; *see 3.4.*

If your employer's plan allows you to fund a reimbursement account with salary-reduction contributions that are excluded from taxable pay *(3.14)*, reimbursements from the account are considered employer-financed payments that reduce the $2,400 or $4,800 credit base. In deciding whether to make salary-reduction contributions, you should determine whether the tax-free reduction will provide a larger tax savings than that provided by the credit. If your tax bracket is higher than 15%, taking the salary reduction is advantageous. Even if you expect to be in the 15% bracket, you should compare the estimated tax savings from the credit with the estimated savings from a salary reduction. You may find that the salary reduction provides the larger tax savings, taking into consideration not only the decrease in federal income tax, but also the Social Security tax and state and local taxes avoided by using the salary reduction. Further, by lowering your adjusted gross income, a salary reduction may enable you to claim a larger IRA deduction if you are subject to the deduction phase-out rule *(8.4)*, or a larger deduction for miscellaneous itemized deductions subject to the 2% floor *(19.1)*.

Allocation if expenses cover noncare services. If a portion of expenses is for other than dependent care or household services, only the portion allocable to dependent care or household services qualifies. No allocation is required if the nondependent care services are minimal.

EXAMPLES

1. A person accepts a full-time position and sends his 12-year-old child to boarding school. The expenses paid to the school must be allocated. The part representing care of the child qualifies; the part representing tuition does not.

2. A full-time housekeeper is hired to care for two children, ages 9 and 12. The housekeeper also drives the mother to and from work each day. The driving takes no longer than 30 minutes. No allocation is required because the nondependent care services of chauffeuring are minimal.

3. You pay $6,000 for care of your child in your home. The expenses also qualify as medical expenses. Assume your adjusted gross income is $17,000. Your dependent care costs are limited to $2,400 and you may claim a credit of $624 ($2,400 × 26%). The balance of $3,600 is deductible as medical expenses if you itemize deductions on Sched-

Filing Tip

Care Costs Qualifying as Medical Expenses

Care costs, such as a nurse's wages, may also qualify as medical expenses, but you may not claim both the dependent care credit and the medical expenses deduction. If you use the expenses to figure the credit and your care costs exceed the amount allowed as dependent care costs, the excess, to the extent it qualifies as a medical expense, may be added to other deductible medical costs.

ule A. If you had no other medical costs, your medical deduction would be $2,325 after deducting the 7.5% limitation on medical costs ($3,600 – $1,275, or 7.5% of $17,000).

25.8 Dependent Care Credit Rules for Separated Couples

A married person generally must file a joint return to claim the dependent care credit *(25.3)*, but if you are living apart from your spouse you may claim the credit on a separate return if you meet the following tests:

1. You maintain as your home a household that is the principal place of abode of a qualifying person *(25.6)* for more than half the year;

2. You furnish over half the cost of maintaining the household for the entire year; *and*

3. Your spouse was not a member of the household during the *last six months* of the year.

If you satisfy these tests, you are treated as unmarried and may claim the credit on a separate return. You do not have to take your spouse's income into account or show that he or she is employed in order to claim a credit.

Your child may be a qualifying person for purposes of the credit even if you cannot claim the child as your dependent. This favorable rule applies if: you are legally divorced or separated, separated under a written agreement, or you lived apart from your spouse during the last six months of 1999; you or you and the other parent had custody of the child for more than half the year and provided more than half of the child's support; and you are the *custodial parent* (have custody longer than the other parent). If these tests are met, you may claim the credit for care of a dependent child who is under age 13 or physically or mentally incapable of caring for himself or herself even though you waive the dependency exemption on Form 8332 or are unable to claim the exemption under a pre-1985 divorce or separation agreement. The noncustodial parent may not claim the credit even if he or she is allowed the exemption.

Employment Taxes for Household Employees

25.9 Paying and Withholding Taxes for Household Employees

If you employ someone to care for your children or disabled dependents in your home, clean your residence, cook, or provide other personal services in or around your home, you may be obligated to pay and withhold Social Security and Medicare taxes (FICA) and also pay federal unemployment taxes (FUTA). FICA or FUTA taxes do not apply if the household worker is the employee of an agency that assigns the position, sets the fee, and requires reports from the worker.

The reporting requirements for FICA are at *25.10*, and the FUTA requirements at *25.11*.

Income taxes. Income tax withholding is not required for a household employee, but if the employee requests it and you agree, you pay the withheld tax under one of the reporting options discussed in *25.10*. Withholdings are based on a Form W-4 (Withholding Allowance Certificate) filed by the employee.

An employee who qualifies for the earned income credit may receive advance payments by giving you Form W-5; *see 25.15*.

25.10 Social Security and Medicare Taxes (FICA) for Household Employees

You generally must pay and withhold Social Security and Medicare taxes (FICA) if you pay cash wages of $1,100 or more to a household employee in 1999. Wages paid to your spouse, child under age 21, or parent for household services are generally exempt from this tax, as discussed at the end of this section. Also exempt are wages of any amount paid to a household employee who is under the age of 18 at any time during the year, so long as he or she does not work full time as a household worker. For example, if you hire a student under age 18 as a babysitter, Social Security and Medicare taxes do not apply regardless of the amount of wages you pay. However, if wages of $1,100 or more are paid to a person under 18 years of age who works full time as a household employee, Social Security and Medicare taxes apply.

Once payments to non-exempt employees equal or exceed $1,100, the entire amount, including the first $1,100, is subject to FICA taxes.

The $1,100 threshold may be increased for 2000 by an inflation adjustment.

Planning Reminder

FICA Threshold for Each Household Worker

If you employ more than one household worker, a babysitter and a gardener for instance, the $1,100 FICA threshold applies separately to each worker. For example, if in 1999 one worker earns $950 and the other earns $1,099, you do not have to pay Social Security or Medicare taxes for either worker.

Caution

Undocumented Workers

Household employees who work for you on a regular basis must verify their U.S. citizenship or their eligibility to work in the U.S. on Form I-9 from the Immigration and Naturalization Service. It is unlawful to knowingly hire an individual who is not legally entitled to work in the U.S.

Tax rates. As an employer, you pay FICA at the rate of 7.65% of wages: 6.2% for Social Security and 1.45% for Medicare. For example, you pay a housekeeper $125 a week ($6,500 for the year). You must pay $497.25 in FICA and either withhold the same amount from the housekeeper's wages or pay the housekeeper's share yourself. In the unlikely case that wages exceed the wage limit for Social Security taxes (for example, $72,600 in 1999), there is an extra Medicare tax of 2.9%: 1.45% tax owed by you as the employer and 1.45% owed by the housekeeper. There is no wage limit on the additional 2.9% Medicare tax. You and the employee are each liable for the combined FICA rate of 7.65% (6.2% Social Security plus 1.45% Medicare) where 1999 wages are $72,600 or less. If wages exceed $72,600, the 7.65% rate applies to the first $72,600 and the 1.45% rate applies to the excess.

If you do not withhold the employee's share of FICA taxes, you are liable for the full amount. If you pay the employee's share of FICA taxes instead of deducting it from wages, you must treat your payment as additional wages when you report the employee's wages on Form W-2, but the payment is not considered wages for Social Security and Medicare tax purposes.

How to report and pay federal employment taxes. You compute 1999 FICA tax (Social Security and Medicare) on wages paid to household employees on Schedule H, which you attach to your 1999 Form 1040; Schedule H may not be used by Form 1040A filers.

You must include your employer identification number (EIN) on Schedule H. An EIN is a nine-digit number, separate from your Social Security number, that is obtained from the IRS by filing Form SS-4. If you previously obtained an EIN when paying taxes for other employees, use that number on Schedule H.

Form W-2. File a 1999 Form W-2 for each household employee to whom you paid Social Security and Medicare wages, or wages from which you withheld federal income tax. Give copies B, C, and 2 of Form W-2 to your household employee by January 31, 2000, and give copy A to the Social Security Administration by February 29, 2000.

Estimated Tax. In planning whether to make estimated tax installments during 2000 *(27.1)*, you should include an estimate of employment taxes for household employees as part of your estimate of 2000 income tax liability. Failure to consider the employment taxes could trigger an estimated tax penalty for 2000.

Reporting rules for self-employed persons who have regular business employees. Self-employed persons who have employees other than household employees may follow one of these two options:

1. Report FICA and FUTA taxes and any income tax withholding for household employees annually on Schedule H, and report FICA taxes and any income tax withholding for other employees quarterly on Form 941 and FUTA taxes annually on Form 940 (or 940-EZ); *or*

2. Report FICA taxes and any income tax withholding for *all* employees (household employees and other employees) quarterly on Form 941 and report FUTA taxes annually for all employees on Form 940 or Form 940-EZ.

Employers of household employees must also give copies of Form W-2 (Wage and Tax Statement) to each employee and to the Social Security Administration, as discussed above.

Reporting rules for an estate. If a person who hired household help dies during the year and the estate continues to employ the employee for domestic work, the estate includes both the wages paid by the decedent and the estate to determine whether taxes are due under the $1,100 test. Thus, if in 1999 a person before dying paid $500 to a domestic and her estate continued to employ the domestic and paid wages of $800, the estate is required to pay FICA taxes on wages of $1,300.

Payments to your parent, child, or spouse. FICA tax does not apply to wages paid to your spouse for domestic services in your home. A similar exception applies to wages paid to your son or daughter under age 21, but note the rule that bars you from basing a dependent care credit on payments made to a child under age 19 *(25.7)*. Further, FICA generally does not apply to wages paid to your father or mother for domestic work in your home unless (1) you are divorced or widowed, or your spouse is disabled; and (2) you have a child living at home who is under age 18 or is disabled.

Caution

Estimated Tax Penalty

As a household employer, you are subject to an estimated tax penalty *(see 27.5)* if your federal income tax withholdings or estimated tax payments *(see 27.1)* are insufficient to cover your household employment tax (Social Security, Medicare, and federal unemployment) liability.

25.11 Federal Unemployment Taxes (FUTA) for Household Employees

As an employer, you are also liable for FUTA (federal unemployment taxes) if you pay cash wages of $1,000 or more for household services during any calendar quarter, or if you did so in any quarter in the preceding year. You do not pay FUTA on wages paid to your spouse, your parents, or your children under age 21. Your employee is not liable for FUTA.

The FUTA rate for 1999 is 6.2% on the first $7,000 of cash wages. However, there is a credit for payments to a state unemployment fund that reduces FUTA liability.

For wages paid to a household employee in 1999, you will generally report FUTA on Schedule H, which you attach to your Form 1040. If you have regular business employees, *see 25.10* for reporting options.

Earned Income Credit (EIC)

25.12 Qualifying Tests for EIC

The earned income credit (EIC) may be claimed not only by workers with qualifying children who meet the tests below, but also, in limited cases, by childless workers.

Claiming the EIC with Qualifying Children

You may claim the EIC on a 1999 return if you:

- Have earned income, such as wages and self-employment earnings, and also modified adjusted gross income of under $26,928 if you have one qualifying child or under $30,580 if you have two or more qualifying children. *See 25.13* for the credit phase-out rules.
- Have a qualifying child who lived with you in your main home in the U.S. for more than six months in 1999; *see* below.
- File a joint return if married. If you lived apart from your spouse for the last half of the year, you may be able to claim the credit as a head of household.
- File Schedule EIC with your Form 1040 or Form 1040A. On Schedule EIC, you identify and provide information about a qualifying child. Your child's Social Security number must be entered on Schedule EIC.
- Are not a qualifying child of another person.
- Include on your return your Social Security number and, if married, that of your spouse.

A qualifying child. A qualifying child is your son, daughter, adopted child, grandchild, stepchild, or foster child who at the end of 1999 was under age 19, or under age 24 and a full-time student, or any age if permanently and totally disabled. To be a full-time student, a child must be enrolled during any five months for classes treated as full time by the school.

Household requirement. The qualifying child must have lived with you in your main home in the U.S. for more than six months. A foster child must have lived with you for all of 1999. Temporary absences for school or vacation count as time lived in your home.

A person in the U.S. armed forces who is stationed outside the U.S. on extended active duty is treated as maintaining a main residence within the U.S.

If you are married, you must file a joint return with your spouse to claim the credit. However, if your spouse did not live in your household for the last six months of the year, and you maintained a home for a child who lived with you for more than half of the year, you may claim the credit as a head of household; *see 1.11.*

Permanently and totally disabled. A person is permanently and totally disabled if: (1) he or she cannot engage in any substantial gainful activity because of a physical or mental condition and (2) a physician determines that the condition has lasted or is expected to last for at least a year or lead to death.

Married child or qualifying child of another person. You may not take the earned income credit if your child is also a qualifying child of another person who has a higher adjusted gross income in 1999 than you do.

If your child was married at the end of 1999, he or she is your qualifying child only if you claim the child as a dependent on Form 1040 or Form 1040A, Line 6, or you waive the exemption in favor of the child's other parent, or the other parent may claim the exemption under a pre-1985 agreement.

Caution

Denial of Future Credits for Recklessness or Fraud

A taxpayer who negligently or fraudulently claims the EIC is prohibited from claiming future credits over a period of several years. The credit is disallowed for two years from the tax year for which it is determined that the EIC claim was claimed recklessly or in disregard of the rules. The period increases to 10 years from the most recent tax year for which it is found that the EIC was claimed fraudulently.

If *you* are a qualifying child of another person, you may not claim the EIC even if you have a qualifying child and would otherwise qualify for the credit.

Nonresident aliens. An individual who is a nonresident alien for any part of the year is not eligible for the credit unless he or she is married and an election is made by the couple to have all of their worldwide income subject to U.S. tax.

Claiming the Credit Without Qualifying Children

If you do not have a qualifying child, you may claim the EIC on a 1999 return if you:

- Have earned income, such as wages and self-employment earnings, of under $10,200, and also modified adjusted gross income under $10,200. *See 25.13* for the credit phase-out rule.
- Have your main home in the U.S. for more than six months in 1999.
- Are at least 25 but under age 65 at the end of 1999. If filing a joint return, either you or your spouse must satisfy this age test.
- File a joint return if married, unless you lived apart for the last six months and qualify to file as a head of household.
- Are not a dependent of another taxpayer.
- Are not a qualifying child of another taxpayer.
- Include your Social Security number on your return, and, if married, that of your spouse.

The rules discussed earlier for armed forces personnel and nonresident aliens with qualifying children also apply to individuals without children.

25.13   Income Tests for EIC

For purposes of the credit, earned income includes wages, salary, tips, commissions, jury duty pay, union strike benefits, certain disability pensions, tax-free meals and lodging from your employer, the rental value of a parsonage, U.S. military basic quarters and subsistence allowances, combat pay, voluntary salary deferrals, and self-employment earnings.

Disqualifying income. For 1999, an individual is not eligible for the earned income credit if he or she has "disqualified income" exceeding $2,350. Disqualified income includes interest (taxable and tax-exempt), dividends, net rent and royalty income, net capital gain income, and net passive income that is not self-employment income.

Credit phases out with income. If you have one qualifying child *(25.12)*, the 1999 credit begins to phase out in the IRS table *(25.14)* if either earned income or modified adjusted gross income (MAGI) is at least $12,500, and no credit is allowed if either earned income or MAGI is $26,928 or more.

If you have two or more qualifying children, the phaseout of the 1999 credit also begins when either earned income or MAGI is at least $12,500 and the credit is completely phased out if either earned income or MAGI is 30,580 or more.

If you do not have any qualifying children, the phaseout of the credit begins when either earned income or MAGI is at least $5,700, and the credit is completely phased out if either amount is $10,200 or more.

Modified adjusted gross income. For purposes of the EIC phase-out rules, modified adjusted gross income (MAGI) is generally equal to your adjusted gross income but certain losses are disregarded for EIC purposes. These include: net capital losses; net losses from trusts and estates; net losses relating to nonbusiness rents and royalties; and 75% of the net losses from businesses, computed separately with respect to sole proprietorships (other than in farming), sole proprietorships in farming, and other businesses. Furthermore, the following items must be added back to MAGI: tax-exempt interest, nontaxable pension annuity payments, and nontaxable IRA distributions that are allocable to nondeductible contributions.

Self-employed. If you were self-employed in 1999, your earned income for credit purposes is the net earnings shown on Schedule SE, *less* the income tax deduction for 50% of self-employment tax claimed on Line 27 of Form 1040. If your net earnings were less than $400, the net amount is your earned income for purposes of the credit. If you had a net loss, the loss is subtracted from any wages or other employee earned income. If you are a statutory employee, the income reported on Schedule C qualifies for the credit.

Foreign earned income. If you work abroad and claim the foreign income exclusion, you may *not* take the credit.

Law Alert

Workfare Payments

Workfare payments under state-subsidized programs are not included in earned income for EIC purposes.

25.14 Look up EIC in Government Tables

After completing a worksheet in the IRS instructions that determines whether your earned income credit is based on your earned income or modified adjusted gross income *(25.13)*, you then look up the amount of your credit in an IRS table.

If you have children, the table provides a phaseout of the credit once 1999 earnings are at least $12,500. If you have only one qualifying child *(25.12)*, your credit is completely phased out if either earned income or modified adjusted gross income is $26,928 or more. If you have more than one qualifying child, the 1999 credit is completely phased out if either earned income or modified adjusted gross income is $30,580 or more. *See 25.13* for modified adjusted gross income rules.

If you do not have a qualifying child, the phaseout of the credit starts when earned income or modified adjusted gross income is $5,700 or more and no credit is allowed if either amount is $10,200 or more.

EXAMPLE

Jane is divorced. Her only income in 1999 is wages of $10,500. She supports her eight-year-old daughter, who lives with her for the entire year.

To find her credit, Jane turns to the IRS Table in the instruction book accompanying her return. In the table, the credit shown for her income bracket is $2,312.

25.15 Advance Payment of Earned Income Credit

If you believe you are entitled to an earned income credit, you may file a certificate, Form W-5, with your employer to have a portion of the credit added to your paycheck throughout the year. To get advanced earned income payments you must have a qualifying child *(25.12)*.

If you receive any advance payments, you must report them on Form 1040 or Form 1040A; your employer will include the amount in Box 9 of your Form W-2. If you receive advance payments in excess of the credit you are entitled to, the excess is treated as a tax you owe when you file your return. If the credit you are entitled to exceeds the advance payments, the excess credit reduces any other tax you owe. If the credit exceeds your liability, the difference is refunded to you.

Law Alert

Recertification Required if EIC Denied

If the IRS denies an EIC by issuing a deficiency notice, the credit may not be claimed in a future tax year unless you show on Form 8862 that you are eligible to take the credit. If the IRS recertifies eligibility, Form 8862 does not have to be filed again in subsequent tax years unless the IRS again denies the EIC in a deficiency proceeding.

Adoption Credit

25.16 Qualifying for the Adoption Credit

A tax credit of up to $5,000 may be available for the qualifying costs of adopting a child under age 18, or a person who is physically and mentally incapable of self-care. If a child is a U.S. citizen or resident and a state determination has been made that a child is a "special needs" child, the maximum credit is $6,000. The credit is phased out ratably for those with adjusted gross income (after certain adjustments) between $75,000 and $115,000.

The credit is claimed on Form 8839. If you paid qualifying adoption costs in 1999 but the adoption was not final at the end of the year, the credit may *not* be claimed on your 1999 return; *see 25.17* for the credit timing rules.

After 2001, the adoption credit will apply only to qualified expenses for adopting an eligible child with special needs.

Employer plans. As discussed at *3.5*, an exclusion from income is also available to employees if adoption expenses are paid through a qualifying employer program, subject to rules similar to that of the credit. If you receive employer adoption benefits that are less than your adoption expenses, you may be able to claim the credit.

25.17 Claiming the Adoption Credit on Form 8839

The adoption credit is claimed on Form 8839, which you attach to your Form 1040 or 1040A. On Form 8839, you provide the child's name, age, and taxpayer identification number (generally a Social Security number). On Form 8839, you take into account the $5,000 (or $6,000) per child limitation, and reduce the maximum allowable credit if your modified adjusted gross income is over $75,000 and under $115,000. No credit is allowed if modified adjusted gross income is $115,000 or more.

If you are married, you generally must file a joint return to take the adoption credit or exclusion. You may take the credit or exclusion on a separate return if you are legally separated under a decree of divorce or separate maintenance, or if you lived apart from your spouse for the last six

Caution

Adopting a Foreign Child

If an eligible child is not a U.S. citizen or resident, a credit for adoption costs may not be claimed until the year the adoption is final.

Filing Tip

Unused Credit Carryforward
The amount of your allowable adoption credit for a year cannot be more than your tax liability for that year; follow the Form 8839 instructions. If your credit is more than this limit, you can carry forward any unused credit for the next five years, or until used, whichever comes first.

months of the tax year and (1) your home is the eligible child's home for more than half the year and (2) you pay more than half the cost of keeping up your home for the year.

Qualifying Expenses. Qualifying adoption expenses are reasonable and necessary adoption fees, court costs, attorney fees, and other expenses directly related to, and whose principal purpose is for, the legal adoption of an eligible child *(25.16)*. Qualifying expenses do not include expenses paid before January 1, 1997. You may not claim a credit for the costs of a surrogate parenting arrangement or for adopting your spouse's child.

When to claim the adoption credit for a child who is a U.S. citizen or resident. If you pay qualifying expenses in any year before the year the adoption becomes final, the credit may be claimed in the year after the year of the payment, whether or not the adoption is final in that year. If you pay qualifying expenses in the year the adoption becomes final, the credit for those expenses is claimed in that year. If qualifying expenses are paid in any year after the year in which the adoption becomes final, the credit is claimed in the year of payment.

Foreign child. If you adopt a child who is not a U.S. citizen or resident at the time the adoption effort begins, a credit may not be claimed until the year the adoption becomes final. If adoption expenses are paid after the tax year in which the adoption became finalized, a credit for such expenses is allowed for the tax year of payment.

EXAMPLE

Virginia and Chuck Murphy begin adoption proceedings in 1999. During 1999, they incur qualifying adoption expenses of $4,000. During 2000, the year in which the adoption is finalized, they incur additional expenses of $2,000. The Murphys may not claim any credit for 1999. A credit may be claimed for 2000, taking into account the expenses of both years, subject to the $5,000 limit ($6,000 if the child is a special needs child) and the income phase-out for 2000. If the child is a U.S. citizen or resident, a credit would be allowed for the 1999 expenses in 2000 (the year after the year of payment) even if the adoption was not final at the end of 2000. For a child who is not a U.S. citizen or resident when the adoption proceedings begin, a credit is not allowed until the year the adoption is finalized.

Tax Withholdings

Withholding taxes gives the Government part of your income before you have a chance to use it. Withholding tax is imposed on salary and wage income, tip income, certain gambling winnings, pensions, and retirement distributions, but you may avoid withholding on retirement payments; *see 26.11*. Withholding is also imposed on interest and dividends if you do not give your taxpayer identification number to a payer of interest or dividend income.

You may increase or decrease withholdings on your wages by submitting a new Form W-4 to your employer. Withholdings may be reduced by claiming allowances based on tax deductions and credits.

Make sure that tax withholdings meet or help you meet the estimated tax rules that require withholdings plus estimated tax payments to equal 90% of your current year liability or the required percentage of the prior year's liability; *see* Chapter 27.

A 20% withholding rate applies to nonperiodic distributions from an employer retirement plan. You may avoid the withholding by instructing your employer to directly transfer the funds to an IRA or the plan of your new employer; *see 26.11*.

Also see:

26.1 Withholdings Should Cover Estimated Tax

In fixing the rate of withholding on your wages, pay attention to the tests for determining whether sufficient taxes have been withheld from your pay. A penalty will apply if your wage withholdings plus estimated tax payments (including prior year overpayments credited to current estimated tax) do not equal the lesser of 90% of your current tax liability and the required percentage of the prior year's tax; *see 27.1.*

Taxes are withheld from payments made to you for services that you perform as an employee; *see 26.2* for exceptions. By filing Form W-4, you claim exemptions for yourself, your spouse, and dependents. The number of exemptions claimed will either decrease or increase the amount of withholding. You also may claim withholding allowances for itemized deductions and credits such as the child tax credit, child and dependent care credit, education tax credits, adoption credit, credit for the elderly and totally disabled, the foreign tax credit, credit for home mortgages, the general business credit, and earned income credit (if you have not filed for an advance payment of the credit on Form W-5).

26.2 When Income Taxes Are Withheld on Wages

The amount of income tax withheld for your wage bracket depends on your marital status and the number of exemptions you claim. Exemptions for withholding correspond to the exemptions allowed on your tax return; *see 21.1.* You file a withholding certificate, Form W-4, with your employer, indicating your status and exemptions. Without the certificate, your employer must withhold tax as if you are a single person with no exemptions.

Cash payments or the cash value of benefits paid to an employee by an employer are subject to withholding, unless the payments are specifically excluded.

Income Taxes Are Withheld on:

- Payments to employees as salaries, wages, fees, commissions, pensions, retirement pay, vacation allowances, dismissal pay, etc. (whether paid in cash or goods). On separately paid bonuses, commissions and overtime pay, an employer may withhold at a flat rate of 28% if regular wage withholding rates are not used. *See 26.11* for withholding on pensions and annuities.
- Sick pay paid by your employer. If a third party pays you sick pay on a plan funded by your employer, you may request withholding by filing Form W-4S.
- Taxable group insurance coverage over $50,000.
- Reimbursements of expenses that do not meet qualifying rules of accountable plans discussed at *20.31.* Also, reimbursements from accountable plans that exceed federal rates if the employee does not return the reimbursement or show that it is substantiated by proof of expenses.
- Pay to members of the U.S. armed forces.
- Prize awarded to a salesman in a contest run by his employer.
- Retroactive pay and overtime under Fair Labor Standards Act.
- Taxable supplemental unemployment compensation benefits.

Income Taxes Are Not Withheld on:

- Payments to household workers. However, although income tax withholding is not required, the worker and the employer may make a voluntary withholding agreement; *see 25.9.*
- Payments to agricultural workers, college domestics, ministers of the gospel (except chaplains in the armed forces), casual workers, nonresident aliens, public officials who receive fees directly from the public, notaries, jurors, witnesses, precinct workers, etc.; but *see* voluntary withholding agreements, *26.3.*
- Pay for newspaper home delivery by children under age 18.
- Advances for traveling expenses if the employee substantiates expenses to the employer and if the employee returns any unsubstantiated amount; *see 20.31.*
- Value of tax-free board and lodging furnished by an employer.
- Fringe benefits not subject to tax.
- Substantiated reimbursements for deductible moving expenses or medical care benefits under a self-insured medical reimbursement plan.
- Death benefit payments to beneficiary of employee; wages due but unpaid at employee's death and paid to estate or beneficiary.
- Pay for U.S. citizen working abroad or in U.S. possessions to the extent that the pay is tax free; *see* Chapter 36 for rules.
- Earnings of self-employed persons; they may make estimated tax installments throughout the year.

Filing Instruction

Adjust Withholdings

If you do not expect withholdings to meet your final tax liability, ask your employer to withhold a greater amount of tax; *see 26.3.* On the other hand, if the withholding rate applied to your wages results in overwithholding, you may claim extra withholding allowances to reduce withholding during the year; *see 26.5* and *26.6.*

Form W-2. By January 31, 2000, your employer must give you duplicate copies of your 1999 Form W-2, which is a record of your pay and the withheld income and Social Security taxes. If you leave your job during the year, you may ask your employer for a Form W-2 by making a written request within 30 days of leaving the job.

26.3 Increasing Withholding

For withholding tax purposes, you do not have to claim all your exemptions. This will increase the amount withheld and help reduce the final tax payment on filing your tax return. It may also relieve you of having to make quarterly estimated tax payments, provided the withholdings are sufficient to meet your estimated tax liability; *see 27.1*. A waiver of exemptions for withholding taxes does not prevent you from claiming the "waived" exemptions on your final tax return. The waiver is merely a bookkeeping aid to your company's payroll department. If you find that even a waiver of exemptions does not cover all of the tax you want withheld, you may ask your employer on Form W-4 to withhold additional amounts from each paycheck.

26.4 Avoiding Withholding

If you had no income tax liability in 1999 and expect none for 2000, you may be exempt from income tax withholdings on your 2000 wages. If eligible, students working for the summer, retired persons, and other part-time workers do not have to wait for a refund of withheld taxes they do not owe. The exemption applies only to income tax withholding, not to withholdings for Social Security and Medicare *(26.10)*. However, if you can be claimed as a dependent on another person's tax return, and you have any investment income, you may claim this special exemption only if you expect total income (wages plus investments) to be no more than $700 *(13.5)*. If the $700 amount is increased due to an inflation factor, the higher amount will be on the 2000 version of Form W-4.

If you cannot be claimed as a dependent by another person, you can claim the exemption from withholding if your total income is no more than the sum of your personal exemption and the standard deduction for your filing status.

To claim an exemption for 2000, you must file a withholding exemption certificate, Form W-4, with your employer. The form may be obtained from an IRS district office or from your employer. If you will file a joint return for 2000, do not claim an exemption on Form W-4 if the joint return will show a tax. An exemption claimed during 2000 will expire February 15, 2001.

26.5 Withholding Allowances

Too much may be withheld from your pay if you have tax reduction items. The overpayment will be refunded when you file your return, but you lose the use of your money during the year. By filing Form W-4 with your employer, you may avoid this and reduce withholding taxes by claiming additional withholding allowances based on the following: (1) estimated itemized deductions; (2) IRA contribution deductions; (3) alimony deductions; (4) net losses from Schedule C, D, E, or F of Form 1040; and (5) tax credits such as the child tax credit, education credits, dependent care credit, credit for the elderly, earned-income credit (if you did not request advance payment on Form W-5), and general business credit.

Working couples filing jointly figure withholding allowances on their combined wage income, deductions, adjustments, and credits, but can divide the total number of allowances between them in any way they wish. On separate returns, the allowances must be figured separately.

If you work for only one employer and are unmarried, you may claim an additional withholding allowance. If you are married, you may claim the additional allowance if you work for only one employer and your spouse does not work, or your wages from a second job or your spouse's wages are $1,000 or less. This special allowance is only for withholding purposes. You may not claim it on your tax return.

If you work for two or more employers at the same time, you figure your withholding allowances based on the total income, and then split the allowances between the two jobs in any way you wish. Do not claim the same allowances with more than one employer at the same time.

File a new Form W-4 each year for withholding allowances based on itemized deductions and credits. Furthermore, you may have to file a new form to increase your withholding if withholding allowances you had been claiming are no longer allowed; *see 26.6*.

Planning Reminder

When To Change Withholdings
Adjust withholding if there will be a significant change in the tax you owe for 2000. Credits such as the child tax credit, Hope scholarship credit, and lifetime learning credit may reduce your 2000 tax. By decreasing your withholding now, you can get the benefit of the lower taxes throughout the year. On the other hand, a withholding increase may be advisable if previously claimed deductions or credits will not be available to you, or if you expect an increase in nonwage income such as capital gains.

Planning Reminder

Part-Year Employees May Avoid Overwithholding
Starting a new job in the middle of a year presents a withholding problem. The amount of tax withheld from your paycheck is figured by taking your weekly pay and multiplying this by a 52-week pay period. For example, if as a recent graduate you start a job on July 1 and your weekly pay is $1,000 for 26 weeks (July 1–December 31), your withholding will be based on an annual income of $52,000 ($1,000 × 52 weeks) and not the $26,000 you will actually earn that year. This will result in overwithholding. To alleviate this problem, you may ask your employer to calculate withholdings on what is known as the "part year" method if your work days during the year are expected to be 245 or fewer. This formula calculates withholding based on actual earnings rather than expected earnings over a full year of employment. As an alternative, you may elect to claim extra exemptions on Form W-4, which has the same effect of reducing the amount withheld each week from your paycheck.

A civil penalty of $500 may be imposed if, for purposes of claiming tax withholding allowances, you overstate your itemized deductions and credits or understate your wages without a reasonable basis. There is also a criminal penalty of up to $1,000 plus a jail sentence for willfully supplying false information.

26.6 When To File a New Form W-4

You should file a new Form W-4 any time the number of your exemptions or withholding allowances increases or decreases, such as when a child is born or adopted, you marry, you get a divorce, or your deductible expenses change.

Your employer may make the new Form W-4 effective with the next payment of wages. However, an employer may postpone the new withholding rate until the start of the first payroll period ending on or after the 30th day from the day you submit the revised form.

You must file a new Form W-4 within 10 days if the number of allowances previously claimed by you decreases because: you divorce or legally separate; you stop supporting a dependent; or a dependent for whom you claimed a withholding allowance will receive more than the exemption amount for the year ($2,750 in 1999), but this income restriction does not apply to your child who is under 19 years of age or a student under age 24 as of the end of the year.

The death of a spouse or a dependent in a current year does not affect your withholding until the next year but requires the filing of a new certificate, if possible, by the first business day in December, or within 10 days if the death is in December. However, a widow or widower entitled to joint return rates in the next two years as a qualifying widow or widower with a dependent child *(1.10)* need not file a new withholding certificate.

When you file on or before December 1, your employer must reduce your withholding as of January 1 of the next year.

26.7 Voluntary Withholding on Certain Government Payments

You can choose to have income tax withheld from Social Security benefits (and equivalent tier 1 Railroad Retirement benefits), unemployment compensation, crop damage payments, and Commodity Credit Corporation loans. The withholding request is made on Form W-4V. Electing to have tax withheld may eliminate the need to make estimated tax installments; *see 27.1.*

For unemployment compensation you may choose a withholding rate of 15%. For the other government payments, you may select a withholding rate of 7%, 15%, 28%, or 31%.

26.8 When Tips Are Subject to Withholding

Tips are subject to income tax and FICA (Social Security and Medicare) withholdings. If you receive cash tips amounting to $20 or more in a month, you must report the total amount of tips received during the month to your employer on Form 4070 (or a similar written report). You make the report on or before the 10th day after the end of the month in which the tips are received. (If the 10th day is a Saturday, Sunday, or legal holiday, you must submit the report by the next business day.) For example, tips amounting to $20 or more that are received during January 2000 are reported by February 10, 2000. Your employer may require more frequent reporting.

You include cash tips paid to you in your own behalf. If you "split" or share tips with others, you include in your report only your share. You do not include tips received in the form of merchandise or your share of service charges turned over to you by your employer.

You are considered to have income from tips when you make your report to your employer. However, if you do not report your tips to your employer, you are considered to have tip income when you receive the tips. For example, if you received tips of $200 during December 1999 and reported the tips to your employer on January 8, 2000, the tips are considered paid to you in January 2000, and the $200 is included on your 2000 income tax return. On the other hand, if your tips during December 1999 totaled only $18, you are not required to report the amount to your employer. The tips are considered paid to you in 1999 and must be included on your 1999 income tax return.

Your employer withholds the Social Security, Medicare, and income tax due on the tips from your wages or from funds you give him or her for withholding purposes. If the taxes due cannot be collected on the tips, either from your wages or from voluntary contributions, by the 10th day after the end of the month in which tips are reported, you have to pay the tax when you file your income tax return.

 Filing Instruction

Tip Reporting

If you have not reported tips of $20 or more in any month, or tips are allocated to you under the special tip allocation rules, you must compute Social Security and Medicare tax on that amount on Form 4137 and enter it as a tax due on Line 52 of Form 1040; attach Form 4137 to Form 1040. The unreported tips must be included as wages on Line 7 of Form 1040.

Where wages are insufficient to meet all of the withholding liability, the wages are applied first to Social Security and Medicare tax.

Penalty for failure to report tips. Failure to report tip income of $20 or more during the month to your employer may subject you to a penalty of 50% of the Social Security and Medicare tax due on the unreported tips, unless your failure was due to reasonable cause rather than to willful neglect.

Tips of less than $20 per month are taxable but not subject to withholding.

Tip allocation reporting by large restaurants. To help the IRS audit the reporting of tip income, restaurants employing at least 10 people must make a special report of income and allocate tips based on gross receipts. For purposes of the allocation, the law assumes tip income of at least 8%. If you voluntarily report tips equal to your allocable share of 8% of the restaurant's gross receipts, no allocation will be made to you. However, if the total tips reported by all employees is less than 8% of gross receipts and you do not report your share of the 8%, your employer must make an allocation based on the difference between the amount you reported and your share of the 8% amount. The allocated amount is shown on Form W-2. However, taxes are not withheld on the allocated amount. Taxes are withheld only on amounts actually reported by employees. An employer or majority of employees may ask the IRS to apply a tip percentage of less than 8%, but no lower than 2%.

Reporting allocated tips. Your employer will show allocated tips in Box 8 of your Form W-2. However, this amount will not be included in Box 1 wages and you must add it to income yourself by reporting it on Line 7 of Form 1040. You also must compute Social Security and Medicare tax on the allocated tips on Form 4137 and enter the tax from Form 4137 on Line 52 of Form 1040. You may not use Form 1040A or Form 1040EZ.

26.9 Withholding on Gambling Winnings

Gambling winnings are generally reported by the payer to the IRS and to the winner on Form W-2G if the amount paid is $600 or more and at least 300 times the amount of the wager; the payer has the option of taking into account the wager in applying the $600 test. Different reporting rules apply to winnings from keno, bingo, and slot machines. Keno winnings are reported on Form W-2G if they are $1,500 or more, *reduced* by the wager. Winnings from bingo or slot machines of $1,200 or more, *not* reduced by the wager, are reported on Form W-2G.

Your winnings from gambling may be subject to 28% withholding. Withholding applies if your winnings exceed:

1. $5,000 from lotteries, sweepstakes, and wagering pools (whether or not state-conducted) including church raffles, *pari-mutuel* betting pools and on- and off-track racing pools; or
2. $5,000 from other wagering transactions, if the proceeds are at least 300 times as large as the amount wagered, such as from wagers on horse races, dog races, or jai alai.

If your winnings exceed the $5,000 threshold the 28% withholding rate applies to your gross winnings less your wagers, and not just the amounts over $5,000. Any withholdings will be shown on Form W-2G.

The IRS requires you to tell the payers of gambling winnings if you are also receiving winnings from identical wagers; winnings from identical wagers must be added together to determine if withholding is required.

If you have agreed to share your winnings with another person, give the payer a Form 5754. The payer will then prepare separate Forms W-2G for each of you.

26.10 FICA Withholdings

FICA withholdings are employee contributions for Social Security and Medicare coverage. Your employer is liable for the tax if he or she fails to make proper withholdings. The amount withheld is figured on your wages and is not affected by your marital status, number of exemptions, or the fact that you may be over age 65 and are collecting Social Security. On Form W-2, Social Security withholdings are shown in Box 4 and Medicare withholdings in Box 6.

Subject to FICA tax are your regular salary, commissions, bonuses, vacation pay, cash tips, group-term insurance coverage over $50,000, the first six months of sick pay, and contributions to cash or deferred (401(k)) pay plans or salary-reduction contributions to a simplified employee pension (SEP), SIMPLE IRA, or tax-sheltered annuity. Not subject to tax are the value of tax-free meals and lodgings, as discussed in *3.11,* and reimbursements for substantiated travel or entertainment expenses or for moving expenses.

Filing Instruction

Uncollected Social Security and Medicare Taxes

If your employer is unable to collect enough money from your wages during the year to cover the Social Security or Medicare tax on the tips you reported, the uncollected amount is shown on your Form W-2 in Box 13 with Code A next to it for Social Security or Code B for Medicare. You must report the uncollected amount on Line 56 of Form 1040 (Total Tax) as an additional tax due; write "Uncollected Tax on Tips" and show the amount next to Line 56.

Caution

Backup Gambling Withholding

Winnings from bingo, keno, and slot machines are not subject to 28% income tax withholding. However, if you do not provide a taxpayer identification number, the payer will withhold tax at the 31% backup withholding rate *(26.12).*

Excess Social Security and Railroad Retirement withholding. If you have worked for more than one employer during 1999, attach all Copies B of Form W-2 to your return. Check to see that the total withheld in 1999 by your employers does not exceed your liability for Social Security taxes. The maximum 1999 liability for Social Security is $4,501.20, 6.2% on the first $72,600 of salary income. If too much was withheld, claim the excess as a payment on Line 62 of your 1999 Form 1040. On Form 1040A, the excess is added to your total tax payments; you cannot claim the excess on Form 1040-EZ.

Medicare tax is withheld at a rate of 1.45% on *all* salary and wage income.

Employees covered by the Railroad Retirement Tax Act (RRTA) receive Form W-2, which lists total wages paid and withholdings of income and Railroad Retirement taxes. Follow tax form instructions for claiming a credit for excess Railroad Retirement withholding.

If any one employer withheld too much Social Security or Railroad Retirement tax, you cannot claim the excess on your income tax return. You must ask that employer for a refund of the excess.

Wages you pay to your spouse or child. Wages you pay to your spouse for working in your business are subject to FICA tax and income tax withholding. Wages you pay to your child for working in your business are subject to income tax withholding but exempt from FICA if the child is under age 18. Wages you pay to your child under age 21 or to your spouse for domestic work or child care in your own home are exempt from FICA.

Student employees exempt from FICA. A statutory exemption from FICA taxes covers students who work for schools, colleges, and universities. The exemption benefits students whose work is incidental to their studies, as opposed to "career" employees who take courses while working for a school.

IRS guidelines provide a safe harbor for students enrolled at least half-time (half of whatever is considered full time) in undergraduate, graduate, or professional programs. Generally, such half-time students will not be subject to FICA taxes regardless of the number of hours they work for their school, college, or university, or an affiliated organization, or the amount of compensation received. Additionally, students who are in the last marking period of their chosen course of study and enrolled in the number of credit hours needed to complete the requirements for certification will also qualify for the exemption even though they are enrolled with less than half-time status. However, the safe harbor does not apply to services performed while the student is not enrolled during school breaks of more than five weeks. Employment that continues over school breaks of five weeks or less while the student is not enrolled in classes will qualify for the exception so long as the student was enrolled on at least a half-time basis on the last day before the break and is eligible to enroll for the next academic period.

Although the exception generally applies to graduate and professional students, it does not apply to post-doctoral students and fellows, medical residents, and medical interns, who are treated as career employees. However, although the safe harbor exemption does not apply, an exemption may still be available for a particular career employee based on all the facts and circumstances.

26.11 Withholding on Retirement Distributions

Retirement distributions are subject to withholding taxes, but you may avoid withholdings. The method of avoiding withholding varies with the type of payment.

Periodic payments. If you receive periodic payments, such as an annuity, withholding is required unless you elect to avoid withholding on Form W-4P, or on a substitute form furnished by the payer. If you are a U.S. citizen or resident alien, withholding may not be avoided on pensions or other distributions paid outside the U.S. or U.S. possessions. Payment must be to your home address within the U.S. (or in a U.S. possession) to avoid withholding.

Unless you tell the payer otherwise, wage withholding tables are used to figure withholdings on periodic payments as if you were married and claiming three withholding exemptions. Withholding allowances may be claimed on Form W-4P for estimated itemized deductions, alimony payments, student loan interest, and deductible IRA contributions.

You may also request that the payer withhold a specific amount of additional tax for each payment.

Nonperiodic payments from IRAs and commercial annuities. Nonperiodic payments are subject to withholding at a flat 10% rate unless you elect to avoid withholding on Form W-4P (or substitute form). IRA distributions that are payable upon demand are considered nonperiodic and, thus, subject to the 10% withholding rule. Proposed legislation would increase the withholding rate to 15% for distributions after 2000; *see* the Supplement for an update.

Planning Reminder

Wages Paid to Household Employees

See 25.10 for FICA withholding on wages paid to household employees.

Caution

Employer Plan Distributions

Your employer must withhold 20% from a distribution paid to you if the distribution was eligible for tax-free rollover; *see 7.8.*

Nonperiodic payments from qualified employer plans. Employers must withhold 20% from nonperiodic payments, such as lump-sum distributions that are eligible for tax-free rollover but which are paid directly to you. To avoid withholding you must direct your employer to make a direct rollover *(7.8)* of the funds to an IRA or to a defined contribution plan *(8.4)* of your new employer. If you do not instruct your employer to make the direct transfer and elect to personally receive the distribution, 20% will be withheld before payment is made to you.

See 7.8 for a further explanation and an Example showing the effects of the withholding rule where you receive the distribution and then decide to make a rollover yourself.

26.12 Backup Withholding

Backup withholding is designed to pressure taxpayers to report interest and dividend income. You may be subject to backup withholding if you do not give your taxpayer identification number to parties paying you interest or dividend income, you give an incorrect number, or you ignore IRS notices stating that you have underreported interest or dividends. Your taxpayer identification number generally is your Social Security number or your employer identification number. The backup withholding rate is 31%.

Similarly, backup withholding of 31% can apply to fees of $600 or more (Form 1099-MISC) for work you do as an independent contractor, payments from brokers (Form 1099-B), royalty payments (Form 1099-MISC) and certain gambling winnings *(see 26.9)* if you do not give the payer your taxpayer identification number.

Civil and criminal penalties can be imposed if you provide false information to avoid backup withholding.

Planning Reminder

Rollover From Employer Plan
20% withholding does not apply to a distribution eligible for rollover *(7.8)* if you have the employer make a direct rollover to a qualified plan or IRA.

Chapter 27

Estimated Tax Payments

Income taxes are collected on a pay-as-you-go basis through withholding on wages and pensions, as well as quarterly estimated tax payments on other income. Where all or most of your income is from wages, pensions, and annuities, you will generally not have to pay estimated tax, because your estimated tax liability has been satisfied by withholding. But do not assume you are not required to pay simply because taxes have been withheld from your wages. Always check your estimated tax liability. Withholding may not cover your tax; the withholding tax rate may be below your actual tax rate when considering other income such as interest, dividends, business income, and capital gains.

Your estimated tax must also include liability for self-employment tax, alternative minimum tax (AMT), and FICA withholding tax for household employees.

You have to make quarterly estimated tax payments during 2000 if your estimated tax liability, after accounting for withholding taxes, is $1,000 or more and the withholding taxes will not be at least 90% of your 2000 tax liability or 100% of your 1999 tax liability if your 1999 adjusted gross income (AGI) is $150,000 or less ($75,000 or less if you are married filing separately in 2000). If your 1999 AGI exceeds this threshold, the percentage test for 1999 tax liability is 108.6%, rather than 100%.

Failure to pay a required estimated tax installment is subject to a penalty based on the prevailing IRS interest rate applied to tax deficiences.

Estimated tax payments may be made with vouchers included with Form 1040-ES or by charging payments on certain credit cards. Residents of Puerto Rico during the entire taxable year also use Form 1040-ES. Nonresident aliens should use Form 1040-ES (NR).

27.1 Estimating Your Tax

There are three stages of reviewing your estimated tax liability:

1. **When you have computed the exact amount of your 1999 tax liability on your 1999 return.** If you owe less than $1,000 on your 1999 return after taking into account withheld taxes, you are not subject to a penalty. If the tax owed after withholdings is $1,000 or more, you can now determine whether your 1999 withholdings plus estimated tax installments were at least 90% ($66^2/_3$% for farmers and fishermen) of your 1999 total tax. If you met the 90% test, you are not subject to an estimated tax penalty for 1999. For purposes of the 90% test, the total tax shown on your return is *reduced* by any earned income credit, additional child credit, uncollected Social Security and Medicare taxes on tips or group-term insurance, recaptured mortgage subsidy, federal fuels tax credit and any taxes from Form 5329 on retirement plans and medical savings accounts (except for the early distribution penalty that is included in total tax).

   If the 90% test was not met, you are subject to an estimated tax penalty unless your withholdings and estimated tax installments for 1999 were at least 100% of the total tax on your 1998 return. This exception requires that the 1998 return covered all 12 months. If your 1998 adjusted gross income exceeded $150,000 ($75,000 if you are filing separately for 1999), your withholdings plus estimated tax installments for 1999 had to be at least 105% of your 1998 total tax (not 100%) to qualify for this prior-year liability exception.

   To completely avoid a penalty for 1999 under either the 90% current-year exception or the 100%/105% prior-year exception, you must have paid at least 25% of the amount required under the applicable exception by each of the four payment dates. The penalty is figured separately for each payment period; *see 27.5.*

   Even if you owe $1,000 or more (after withholdings) on your 1999 return and you do not qualify for either the 90% current-year exception or 100%/105% prior-year exception, you are not subject to an estimated tax penalty for 1999 if you did not have to file a 1998 return or your 1998 total tax was zero. This exception applies only if you were a U.S. citizen or resident for all of 1998 and your 1998 tax year included 12 full months.

   If you underestimated your 1999 liability because of an unexpected increase in income during 1999, or if you did not earn income evenly throughout 1999, such as where you operated a seasonal business, you may be able to lower or eliminate the penalty by using the *annualized income installment method*. Under this exception, you may avoid a penalty for an estimated tax installment by figuring the installment that would be due if the income (and deductions) earned before the date for the installment were *annualized*. Form 2210 and IRS Publication 505 have worksheets for applying the annualized income exception. The computation is complicated and its use may be discouraged by the complexity, despite the potential benefits.

2. **When you make an estimate for 2000.** You will generally do this after completing your 1999 return. In planning your 2000 payments, you do not want to pay more than necessary to avoid a penalty. If you expect your 2000 income and deductions to be about the same as in 1999, apply 2000 tax rates (which will be in the Supplement and in the 2000 instructions to Form 1040-ES) to your 1999 taxable income and base your 2000 withholdings and quarterly estimated tax installments on 90% of that tax. If you were subject to self-employment tax or alternative minimum tax in 1999, add 90% of such taxes to your 2000 estimate.

   Safe harbor for 2000 based on 1999 tax. If you are uncertain of the amount of your 2000 income and deductions, you can play it safe and avoid a possible penalty in 2000 by having withholdings and quarterly estimated tax installments equal 100% of your 1999 tax liability if your 1999 adjusted gross income is $150,000 or less ($75,000 or less if married filing separately for 2000), provided you filed a 1999 return covering a full 12 months. If your 1999 AGI exceeds the $150,000 (or $75,000) threshold, your payments for 2000 must be at least 108.6% of your 1999 tax.

   If an accurate estimate for 2000 is possible, it is generally advantageous to base your estimated payments on the 90% test rather than the 100%/108.6% prior year test, as using this prior year test will probably result in an overestimation of your liability unless the 2000 tax turns out to be substantially larger than the 1999 tax.

   You may use the worksheet and the tax rate schedule included in the 2000 Form 1040-ES to figure your estimated tax liability and the required annual payment to avoid a penalty under either the 90% current year or prior year liability tests just discussed.

   Reduce your 2000 estimated tax liability by expected withholdings from wages, pensions, and annuities. If after withholdings your estimated tax is $1,000 or more, you must make estimated tax payments unless the withholdings will cover at least 90% of your estimated 2000 liability or 100%/108.6% of your 1999 liability. If withholdings will not cover the amount required under the 90% or 100%/108.6% tests, you may pay the balance of the estimated tax with Form 1040-ES vouchers or by credit card (*see* the Planning Reminder on this page). The first installment is due April 17, 2000.

Planning Reminder

Credit Card Payments

Effective March 1, 2000, you may use an IRS pay-by-phone system to charge estimated tax payments using a MasterCard, American Express, or Discover Card. The number is 1-888-272-9829. If you charge estimated tax payments, you do not have to file Form 1040-ES vouchers.

Law Alert

Estimated Tax Safe Harbor for 2000

In planning withholdings and estimated tax installments for 2000, you can avoid a 2000 estimated tax penalty if your payments are at least the lesser of 90% of your 2000 tax liability and 100% of your total 1999 tax liability if your 1999 adjusted gross income (AGI) is $150,000 or less ($75,000 or less if married filing separately for 2000). If your 1999 AGI exceeded the $150,000 or $75,000 threshold, your payments for 2000 must be at least 108.6% of your 1999 tax to qualify under the prior year exception.

If you are due a refund when you file your 1999 return, it may be credited to your 2000 estimated tax by making an election on your 1999 return. The IRS will credit the refund to the April installment of 2000 estimated tax unless you attach a statement to your return instructing the IRS to apply the refund to later installments.

Members of a partnership declare their estimated taxes in their individual capacities. Each partner's estimate must include his or her share of the partnership income, whether actually paid or not. Similar rules apply to S corporation shareholders.

Farmers or fishermen. In figuring the required annual payment to avoid a penalty for 2000, a farmer or fisherman has to pay only $66^2/_3\%$ of the 2000 estimated liability, rather than 90%. A penalty may also be avoided by paying 100% of the 1999 tax, provided a tax return covering a 12-month period was filed for 1999; the 108.6% test for higher-income taxpayers does not apply to a farmer or fisherman. To qualify as a farmer or fisherman under these rules, at least two-thirds of gross income for 1999 or 2000 must be from farming or fishing.

3. **When preparing your second, third, or fourth estimated tax installment.** If, during the year, your income, expenses, or exemptions change, refigure your estimated tax liability and adjust your payment schedule as shown in the following Examples. Increasing an installment payment cannot make up for an underpayment in a prior quarter; *see* Example 2. Further, withholdings from pay, pensions and IRA withdrawals can be allocated equally over all four quarters and, thus, withholding increased at the end of the year may be applied to earlier quarters.

If taxes paid in the previous installments total more than your revised estimate, you cannot obtain a refund at that time. You must wait until you file your final return showing that a refund is due.

EXAMPLES

1. Smith, who is self-employed, figures that to avoid a penalty for 2000 under the estimated tax rules discussed above, he must make estimated tax installments of $6,000. By April 17, he pays an installment of $1,500. In June, he amends his estimate, showing a tax of $3,000 instead of $6,000. He refigures the installment schedule by dividing $3,000 by 4, which gives a payment rate of $750 for each period. As he paid $1,500 in April, the $750 overpayment covers his June obligation. By September 15, he pays $750; by January 16, 2001, he pays $750.

2. In September 2000, Jones finds that his estimated 2000 tax liability should be $25,000 rather than his original estimate of $20,000. He paid $5,000 as his April and June installments ($10,000 total). Under the amended schedule, he should have paid $6,250 per period ($25,000 ÷ 4); $6,250 by April 17 and $6,250 by June 15. Thus, there is a $2,500 underpayment ($12,500 – 10,000) for the first two periods.

   To cover the underpayment of $2,500, which carries over to the third payment period (June 1 through August 31), Jones's installment by September 15 must be at least $8,750 ($6,250 + $2,500). If less than $8,750 is paid, there will be an underpayment for the third payment period, as payments in that period are applied first to the carried-over underpayment of $2,500. If at least $8,750 is paid by September 15, there is no third period underpayment to be carried over, so the required installment for the fourth period (September 1 through December 31), due by January 16, 2001, will be $6,250. Unless an exception *(27.1)* applies, the underpayments for the first two periods will be subject to a penalty.

27.2 Dates for Paying Estimated Taxes

The four installment dates for 2000 estimated tax are: April 17, 2000; June 15, 2000; September 15, 2000; and January 16, 2001. Later installments may be used to amend earlier ones; *see* the Examples at the end of *27.1*. You do not have to file the January 16, 2001, voucher if you file your 2000 tax return and pay the balance of tax due by January 31, 2001.

If you use a fiscal year. A fiscal year is any year other than the calendar year. If you file using a fiscal year, your first estimated installment is due on or before the 15th day of the fourth month of your fiscal year. The second and third installments are due on or before the 15th day of the sixth and ninth months of your fiscal year with the final installment due by the 15th day of the first month of your next fiscal year.

27.3 Estimates by Husband and Wife

A married couple may pay joint or separate estimated taxes. The nature of the estimated tax does not control the kind of final return you file.

Where a joint estimated tax is paid but separate tax returns are filed, you and your spouse can decide on how to divide the estimated payments between you. Either one of you can claim the whole amount, or you can agree to divide it in any proportion. If you cannot agree, the IRS will allocate the estimated taxes proportionally according to the percentage of total tax each spouse owes.

If separate estimated taxes are paid, overpayment by one spouse is not applied against an underpayment by the other when separate final returns are filed.

A joint estimated tax may be made by a husband and wife only if they are both citizens or residents of the United States. Both must have the same taxable year. A joint estimate may not be made by a couple who are divorced or legally separated under a decree. If a joint estimate is made and the spouses are divorced or legally separated later in that year, they may divide the joint payments between them under the above rule for spouses who file separately.

Responsibility for paying estimated tax rests upon each spouse individually. Each must pay if individually required by the rules.

If a joint estimated tax is made and one spouse dies, the estate does not continue to make installment payments. The surviving spouse is required to pay the remaining installments unless he or she amends. Amounts paid on the joint estimate may be divided as agreed upon by the spouse and the estate of the deceased. If they do not agree, the IRS will apportion the payments according to the percentage of the total tax owed by each spouse.

27.4 Final Payment for 1999

That you paid an estimated tax for 1999 does not excuse you from filing a tax return on or before April 17, 2000. You must file a final return and pay the difference between the total of your withholding plus your estimated tax payments and your final tax. If your 1999 tax is less than your withholdings and payments, you get a refund from the IRS *or* you can apply the overpayment towards your 2000 estimated tax. You may also split up the amount due you. You may take part of the overpayment as a refund. The other part may be credited to your estimate of 2000 taxes.

Check your mathematics before you apply an overpayment as a credit on your next year's estimate. If you apply too much, the amount credited may not be used to offset any additional tax due that the IRS determines you owe. For example, your 1999 return shows a $500 refund due, and you apply it towards your 2000 estimated tax. However, the IRS determines that you overpaid $200, not $500. You will be billed for the additional $300 tax, plus interest due; you may not offset the extra tax with the credited amount.

27.5 Penalty for Underestimating Your 1999 Tax

Penalties are figured separately for each payment period as of the installment due date (April 15, June 15, and September 15 in 1999, and January 18, 2000). This means that if, after taking into account withholdings from your pay, you underpaid an installment, you may owe a penalty for that period even though you overpaid later installments to make up the difference. The penalty for each period, which is based on prevailing interest rates, runs from the installment due date until the amount is paid or until the regular filing date for the final tax return, whichever is earlier.

Withholding payments are treated as if they were payments of estimated tax. In applying them, the total withholdings of the year are divided equally between each installment period unless you want to show the actual payment dates; then they are applied in the period they are actually withheld.

Figure the 1999 penalty for yourself on Form 2210 or let the IRS do it. You can use Form 2210 to determine any 1999 penalty, but the IRS encourages taxpayers to let the IRS compute any penalty. The IRS will figure the amount of any penalty and bill you for the amount if you do not complete Form 2210.

There is no penalty and you do not have to file Form 2210 if the tax liability shown on your 1999 return is less than $1,000, after taking into account withholdings. There also is no penalty if you had no tax liability for 1998, you were a U.S. citizen or resident for all of 1998, and your 1998 taxable year included 12 full months.

You *must* attach Form 2210 to your return if: (1) you use the annualized income exception; (2) you do not allocate wage withholdings in four equal amounts; (3) your required estimated tax payment for 1999 is based on the applicable percentage of the 1998 tax and a joint return is filed for either the prior year or the current year but not both, or (4) you claim a penalty waiver; *see* below for waiver rules.

 Planning Reminder

Withholdings Cover Prior Underpayment

You have a choice in allocating withholdings from pay or other income that is subject to withholding: (1) You may treat your entire year's withholdings as having been withheld in equal amounts for each of the four payment periods or (2) you may allocate to each payment period the actual withholdings paid for that period. Also, if toward the end of the year, you find that you have underestimated for an earlier period, ask your employer to withhold an extra amount that may be allocated equally over the four periods. This way, you may eliminate the underestimate for the earlier periods.

 Planning Reminder

Farmers and Fishermen

Farmers only have to make one installment payment, generally by January 15 of the following year. The payment for 1999 must be made by January 18, 2000, or farmers may file their 1999 returns by March 1, 2000, instead of making an estimated tax payment. To qualify under these rules, a farmer must receive two-thirds of his or her 1998 or 1999 gross income from farming.

Fishermen who expect to receive at least two-thirds of their gross income from fishing pay estimated taxes as farmers do.

If you *underpaid* for any payment period, the amount of the underpayment reduces the payment made in the following period. That is, an underpayment of one period is carried over to succeeding periods on Form 2210. If you underpay for a period, any payment you make after that installment date will be applied first to the earlier underpayment. Thus, even if you make the required payment for a period, you could still be subject to a penalty for that period because your payment is applied to a prior underpayment.

If you *overpaid* for any period, the excess carries over to the next period. The excess cannot be used to make up an underpayment of the prior period. However, these rules apply only to installment payments made with Form 1040-ES vouchers. They do not apply to withholdings, which are allocated equally over the year so that withholdings late in the year can reduce an underpayment for an earlier payment period.

Waiver of penalty for hardship, retirement, or disability. The IRS may waive the penalty if you can show you failed to pay the estimated tax because of casualty, disaster, or other unusual circumstances.

The IRS may also waive a penalty for a 1999 underpayment if in 1999 or 1998 you retired after reaching age 62 or became disabled, and you failed to make a payment due to reasonable cause and not due to willful neglect. This rule would apply to a 2000 underpayment if you became disabled or retired (after age 62) in 1999 or 2000. To apply for the waiver, attach an explanation on Form 2210 that documents the circumstances supporting your waiver request.

Personal Tax Savings Plans

The chapters in this part will alert you to special tax-saving opportunities and tell you how to take advantage of tax-saving ideas and planning strategies.

Tax Planning

Tax planning is a year-round activity. By planning income and deduction strategies, you may be able to reduce your tax. You may realize capital gain income subject to lower capital gain rates, defer certain income to a later year in which you expect to pay a lower tax, and accelerate deductions to a higher tax year. Tax-free investments are available and, within limits, income splitting with family members may be possible.

This chapter illustrates basic tax-planning strategies. In subsequent chapters, tax-savings plans for homeowners, families, investors, and executives are discussed.

28.1 When To Defer Income and Accelerate Deductions

When you expect to pay less tax in a future year than in a current year, consider deferring income and accelerating deductions. There are two strategies: (1) to postpone receipt of income to a year of lower tax rates and/or (2) to claim deductions for losses and expenses in the year you are subject to the higher tax rates. In planning to defer income and accelerate deductions, however, watch these tax-rule limitations.

Postponing income. You may not defer salary income by not cashing a paycheck or not taking salary that you have earned and that you can receive without restrictions. Under certain conditions, you may contract with your employer to defer the taxable receipt of current compensation to future years. To defer pay to a future period you must take some risk. You cannot have any control over your deferred pay account. If you are not confident of your employer's ability to pay in the future, you should not defer pay.

Accelerating deductions. In accelerating deductions, there are these limitations: You may not deduct prepaid interest and rent. Prepaid interest must be deducted over the period of the loan. Rentals must also be deducted over the rental period. However, you can generally deduct prepayments of state income tax and accelerate your payments of charitable contributions. Annual subscriptions to professional journals and business magazines can be renewed before the end of the year. If the subscription is for more than a year, you may deduct only the first-year prepayment. The cost of the later subscription must be deducted in the later year. Contributions, purchases, and business expenses charged to credit card accounts are deductible in the year of charge, even though you do not pay your charge account bill until the next year. You can also realize losses by selling business or investment property that has lost value in the year you want to incur the loss.

Making an extra donation at the end of the year also may provide an added deduction that may lower your tax. You may deduct a charitable gift made by check on the last day of the year, even if the check is not cashed until the new year begins. Charitable donations may be timed to give you the largest possible tax savings. If, toward the end of the year, you find that you need an extra deduction, you may make a deductible donation in late December. Doing so would be especially beneficial if you know that your tax bracket will be lower the following year; *see* Chapter 14 for further planning details.

Also *see* Chapter 13 for claiming the standard deduction and itemizing deductions in alternate years, and Chapter 23 for planning steps when you may be subject to alternative minimum tax.

Deferring interest income to next year. Buying six-month certificates after June 30 can defer interest reporting to the next year. As a general rule, you have to report interest credited to your savings account for 1999, even if the account is a passbook account and you did not present the passbook to have the amount entered. Similarly, interest coupons due and payable in 1999 are taxable on your 1999 return, regardless of when they were presented for collection. For example, a coupon due in December 1999, but presented for payment in 2000, is taxable in 1999. However, there are opportunities to defer interest in the following ways:

1. Buy a savings certificate after June 30 with a maturity of one year or less. Interest is taxable in the next year when the certificate matures, provided that interest is specifically deferred until the following year by the terms of the certificate.

2. Buy Treasury bills that come due next year. Six-month bills bought after June 30 will mature in the next year.

3. Buy Series EE bonds. These bonds may be cashed for their purchase price, plus an increase in their value over stated periods of time. The increase in redemption value is taxed as interest. You may defer the interest income until the year you cash the bond or the year the bond finally matures, whichever is earlier. Income deferral is also available for investments in U.S. "I-Bonds"; *see 30.22.*

Timing sales of property. A sale is generally taxable in the year title to the property passes to the buyer. Since you can control the year title passes, you can usually defer income realized on the sale to the year in which you will pay less tax. Year-end sales of securities are discussed at *30.1.*

Planning Reminder

Deferring Business Income

If you are self-employed and are on the cash basis, you can defer income by delaying your billing at the end of the year or extending the time of collection. If you own a closely held corporation, you can time the payment of dividends and bonuses.

28.2 Tax Cost of Earning Over the Thresholds for the Exemption Phaseout and Itemized Deduction Reduction

In figuring the tax cost of earning additional income, consider the phaseout of personal exemptions *(21.15)* or the 3% reduction to itemized deductions *(13.7)*. When extra income, such as from a bonus, a freelance assignment, or a year-end sale of stock, pushes you over the *threshold* for the exemption phaseout or the 3% reduction, or if you already are over the threshold, your taxable income is increased not only by the earnings but also by the amounts disallowed by the phaseout or the 3% reduction.

For the 3% itemized deduction reduction on 1999 returns, the adjusted gross income (AGI) threshold is $126,600, except for married persons filing separately, who are subject to a $63,300 threshold.

For the exemption phaseout, the AGI threshold is $126,600 for single persons, $158,300 for heads of household, $189,950 for married persons filing jointly and qualifying widow(er)s, and $94,975 for married persons filing separately.

You can estimate the amount of the increase in the effective rate on the additional income due to the exemption phaseout or 3% itemized deduction reduction by this equation:

$$\text{Increase in effective rate} = \frac{\text{Top bracket} \times \text{disallowed amount}}{\text{Excess income over threshold}}$$

Objective—	Explanation—
Realizing long-term capital gains	Long-term capital gains are taxed at rates lower than regular income taxes. *See* Chapter 5 for basic capital gain rules and Chapters 30 and 31 for discussions of special investment situations.
Earning tax-free income	You can earn tax-free income by— 1. Investing in tax-exempt securities. However, before you invest, determine whether the tax-free return will exceed the after-tax return of taxed income; *see 30.13.* 2. Taking a position in a company that pays tax-free fringe benefits, such as health and life insurance protection. For a complete discussion of tax-free fringe benefits, *see* Chapter 3. 3. Seeking tax-free education benefits with scholarship arrangements and educational IRAs; *see* Chapter 38. 4. Taking a position overseas to earn up to $76,000 tax free in 2000 and $78,000 in 2001; *see* Chapter 36. 5. Investing in Roth IRAs; *see* Chapter 8.
Deferring income	You can defer income to years when you will pay less tax through— 1. Deferred pay plans, which are discussed in Chapter 2. 2. Qualified retirement plans such as Keogh plans and traditional IRA investments; *see* Chapter 41 and Chapter 8. 3. The year-end planning techniques explained in *28.1.* 4. Transacting installment sales when you sell property; *see 5.21.* 5. Investing in U.S. Savings EE bonds or I-Bonds; *see 4.28* and *4.29, 30.21,* and *30.22.*
Income splitting	Through income splitting you divide your income among several persons or taxpaying entities that will pay an aggregate tax lower than the tax that you would pay if you reported all of the income. Although the tax law limits income-splitting opportunities, certain business and family income planning through the use of trusts and custodian accounts can provide tax savings. Family income planning is discussed in Chapter 33.
Tax-free exchanges	You can defer tax on appreciated property by transacting tax-free exchanges as discussed at *6.1* and *31.3.*
Buying a personal residence rather than renting	Homeowners are favored by the tax law. 1. Rather than paying rent, buy a home, condominium, or cooperative apartment. You may deduct interest and taxes. When you sell your home, you may avoid tax on gains of up to $250,000 if single and up to $500,000 if married filing jointly; *see* Chapter 29. 2. Homeowners can borrow on their home equity and deduct interest expenses; *see 15.3.*
Taking advantage of special tax benefits	The tax law favors persons seeking education; *see* Chapter 38, which discusses scholarships, grants, tuition plans, bond tuition plans, education credits and IRAs, and student loan interest deduction. *See* Chapter 25 for child tax credits.

Chapter 29

Tax Savings for Residence Sales

You may avoid tax on gain on the sale of a principal residence if you used it for at least two years during a five-year ownership period. If you are single, you may avoid tax on up to $250,000 of gain, $500,000 if you are married and file jointly.

If you used the residence for less than two years, you may avoid tax if you sold because of a change of job location or poor health; *see 29.4.*

You may not deduct a loss on the sale of a personal residence. Losses on the sale of property devoted to personal use are nondeductible. However, *see 29.9* and *29.10,* which explain under what conditions you may claim a loss deduction on the sale of a residence.

If you rent out a residential property and you or family members also use the residence during the year, rental expenses are subject to the special restrictions discussed at *9.7.*

Federal subsidy recapture. If after 1990 your home was financed with the proceeds of a tax-exempt bond or a qualified mortgage credit certificate *(15.1)* and you sell or dispose of the home within nine years of the financing, you may have to recapture the federal subsidy received. Use Form 8828 to figure the amount of the recapture tax, which is reported on Line 56 of Form 1040 as a separate tax.

29.1 Avoiding Tax on Sale of Principal Residence

$250,000/$500,000 Exclusion

You may exclude from income up to $250,000 of gain realized on a sale or exchange of a residence in 1999, if you owned and occupied it as a principal residence for an aggregate of at least two years out of five years before the sale or exchange; *see 29.2*. If you are married filing jointly, you may be able to exclude up to $500,000 of gain; *see 29.3*.

Frequency of exclusion. The exclusion is not a once-in-a-lifetime benefit. If you meet the ownership and use tests for a principal residence, you may claim the exclusion when you sell it although you previously claimed the exclusion for another residence, provided that the sales are more than two years apart. If you claim the exclusion on a sale and within two years of the first sale you sell another principal residence, an exclusion may not be claimed on the second sale even if you meet the ownership and use tests for that residence. There is an exception if the second sale was due to a change in employment, health reasons, or unforeseen circumstances. In that case, a prorated exclusion is allowed; *see* the Reduced Exclusion Worksheet on page 470. Sales before May 7, 1997, are not taken into account in determining the number of sales within a two-year period.

Principal residence. A principal residence is not restricted to one-family houses but includes a mobile home, trailer, houseboat, and condominium apartment used as a principal residence. An investment in a retirement community does not qualify as a principal residence unless you receive equity in the property. In the case of a tenant-stockholder of a cooperative housing corporation, the residence ownership requirement applies to the ownership of the stock and the use requirement applies to the house or apartment that the stockholder occupies. If you sold stock in a cooperative housing corporation during the five-year period ending on the date of sale, you must have:

1. Owned stock for at least two years, *and*
2. Used the house or apartment that the stock entitles you to occupy as your principal residence for at least two years.

Business or rental use. If part of your home was rented out or used for business, *see 29.2* and *29.7*.

Home destroyed or condemned. If your home is destroyed or condemned, any gain realized on the conversion may qualify for the exclusion. Any part of the gain that may not be excluded (because it exceeds the limit) may be postponed under the rules explained in *18.18*.

Sale of remainder interest. You may choose to exclude gain from the sale of a remainder interest in your home. If you do, you may not choose to exclude gain from your sale of any other interest in the home that you sell separately. Also, you may not exclude gain from the sale of a remainder interest to a related party. Related parties include your brothers and sisters, half-brothers and half-sisters, spouse, ancestors (parents, grandparents, etc.), and lineal descendents (children, grandchildren, etc.). Related parties also include certain corporations, partnerships, trusts, and exempt organizations.

Expatriates. You may not claim the exclusion if Section 877(a)(1) of the Internal Revenue Code applies to you. That section applies to U.S. citizens who have renounced their citizenship (and long-term residents who have ended their residency) if one of their principal purposes was to avoid U.S. taxes.

Prior law election. You may take advantage of the prior rollover rules for sale of a principal residence made on or after August 5, 1997, under a contract binding on August 5, 1997. A similar rule applies to a sale transacted under a binding contract in effect as of August 5, 1997, where a replacement residence was acquired before August 6, 1997. *See* IRS Publication 523 for prior rules.

The exclusion is not mandatory. You do not have to apply the exclusion to a particular qualifying sale. For example, you are unable to sell a residence when you acquire a new residence. When you finally are able to find a buyer for the first home, you also decide to sell the second residence. Assume both sales may qualify for the exclusion, but the potential gain on the first house will be less than the potential gain on the sale of the second home. You will not want to apply the exclusion to the sale of the first home if doing so will prevent you from applying the exclusion to the second sale because of the rule allowing an exclusion for only one sale every two years.

29.2 Figuring Ownership and Use Periods

In figuring whether you have owned and occupied a home as your principal residence for at least two years during the five-year period ending on the date of sale, the periods of ownership and use do not have to be continuous. The ownership and use tests may be met in different two-year periods, provided both tests are met during the five-year period ending on the date of sale.

 Caution

Multiple Use of a Residence

If during the entire five-year period ending on the date of sale you used part of a sold residence for business or rental to tenants, you apportion the sales price and basis of the house between the rental portion and the residential portion. The exclusion applies only to the residential portion. *See* the Examples at *29.7*.

 Planning Reminder

Form 1099-S

Sales and exchanges of residences are usually reported to the IRS on Form 1099-S by the attorney or other party responsible for closing the transaction. However, a sale of a principal residence is not reported on Form 1099-S if the seller gives a written certification that the full amount of the gain qualifies for the exclusion. IRS Revenue Procedure 98-20 has a sample certification form.

In counting the period of ownership and use of a residence that you bought as a replacement residence under the prior law rollover rules, you may include the ownership and use of all the prior residences bought under the rollover rules.

EXAMPLES

1. From 1992 through August 1999, Janet lived with her parents in a house that her parents owned. In September 1999, she bought this house from her parents. She continued to live there until December 15, 1999, when she sold it at a gain. Although Janet lived in the home for more than two years, she did not own it for at least two years. She may not exclude any part of her gain on the sale, unless she sold because of a change in health or place of employment; *see 29.4*.

2. John bought and moved into a house in January 1997. He lived in it as his principal residence continuously until October 1, 1998, when he went abroad for a one-year sabbatical leave. On October 1, 1999, he sold the house. He does not meet the two-year use test. Because his leave was not a short, temporary absence, he may not include the period of leave to meet the two-year use test. He may avoid tax on gain if he sold because of a changed job location or poor health; *see 29.4*.

3. Jonah lived in an apartment building that was changed to a condominium. He bought the apartment on December 1, 1995. In 1997, he became ill and on April 14 of that year he moved to his son's home. On July 10, 1999, while still living there, he sold the apartment.
   He may exclude gain on the sale because he met the ownership and use tests. The five-year period is from July 11, 1994, to July 10, 1999, the date of the sale of the apartment. He owned the apartment from December 1, 1995, to July 10, 1999 (over two years). He lived in the apartment from July 11, 1994 (the beginning of the five-year period) to April 14, 1997, a period of use of over two years.

4. On May 30, 1993, Amy moved into a home she bought and lived in it until May 31, 1995, when she moved and put it up for rent. The house was rented from June 1, 1995 to March 31, 1997. Amy moved back into the house on April 1, 1997, and lived there until she sold it on January 31, 1999. During the five-year period ending on the date of the sale (February 1, 1994–January 31, 1999), Amy owned and lived in the house for more than two years.

Five-year period—	Home use (months)—	Rental use (months)—
2/1/94–5/31/95	16	
6/1/95–3/31/97		22
4/1/97–1/31/99	22	
Total	38	22

Amy may exclude gain up to $250,000.

5. In 1990, Carol bought a house and lived in it until January 31, 1997, when she moved and put it up for rent. The house was rented from March 1, 1997, until May 31, 2000. Carol moves back into the house on June 1, 2000, and lives there until she sells it on September 30, 2000. During the five-year period ending on the date of the sale (October 1, 1995 – September 30, 2000), Carol lived in the house for less than two years.

Five-year period—	Home use (months)—	Rental use (months)—
10/1/95–1/31/97	16	
2/1/97–5/31/00		40
6/1/00–9/30/00	4	
Total	20	40

Carol may not exclude any of the gain on the sale, unless she sold the house for health or employment reasons; *see 29.4*.

Incapacitated homeowner. A homeowner who becomes physically or mentally incapable of self-care is deemed to use a residence as a principal residence during the time in which the individual owns the residence and resides in a licensed care facility. For this rule to apply, the homeowner must have owned and used the residence as a principal residence for an aggregate period of at least one year during the five years preceding the sale.

Filing Tip

Short Absences

Short temporary absences for vacations count as time you used the residence. This is true even if you rent out your residence during the vacation period.

If you meet this disability exception, you still have to meet the two-out-of-five-year ownership test to claim the exclusion.

Previous home destroyed or condemned. For the ownership and use tests, you may add time you owned and lived in a previous home that was destroyed or condemned if any part of the basis of the current home sold depended on the basis of the destroyed or condemned home.

29.3 Home Sales by Married Persons

Where a married couple owned and lived in their principal residence for at least two years during the five-year period ending on the date of sale, they may claim an exclusion of up to $500,000 of gain on a joint return.

Under the law, the up-to-$500,000 exclusion may be claimed on a joint return provided that during the five-year period ending on the date of sale: (1) *either* spouse owned the residence for at least two years, (2) *both* spouses lived in the house as their principal residence for at least two years, and (3) *neither* spouse is ineligible to claim the exclusion because an exclusion was previously claimed on a sale of a principal residence within the two-year period ending on the date of this sale.

EXAMPLES

1. You and your wife owned and occupied your principal residence for 10 years. In December 1999, you sell the house for a gain of $450,000. The gain is not taxable if you file jointly.

2. As a widower, you used and owned your principal residence from June 1995 through the end of 1998. In January 1999, you remarried and you and your wife lived in the house for nine months. In October 1999, you sold the house and realized a gain of $350,000. You may claim an exclusion of $250,000 on your joint return; the balance of $100,000 is taxable. You meet the exclusion tests, but your wife does not. Thus, the exclusion is limited to $250,000.

Death of spouse before sale. If your spouse died before the date of sale, you are considered to have owned and used the property during any period of time when your spouse owned and used it as a principal home.

Divorce. If a residence is transferred to a taxpayer incident to divorce, the time during which the taxpayer's spouse or former spouse owned the residence is added to the taxpayer's period of ownership. A taxpayer who owns a residence is deemed to use the residence while the taxpayer's spouse or former spouse uses the residence under the terms of a divorce or separation.

Separate residences. Where a husband and wife own and live in separate residences, each spouse is entitled to a separate exclusion limit of $250,000 on the sale of his or her residence. If both residences are sold in the same year and each spouse met the ownership and use test for his or her separate residence, two exclusions may be claimed (up to $250,000 each), either on a joint return or on separate returns.

29.4 Ownership and Use of Less Than Two Years

If you are forced to sell your principal residence before meeting the two-out-of-five-year ownership and use tests because of a change in the place of employment or health or unforeseen circumstances, the exclusion is prorated. The IRS will define *unforeseen circumstances* in regulations. The exclusion is generally prorated for the time spent in the residence over the two-year period. The IRS allocates the exclusion on a daily basis. You count the number of days of use and divide the sum by 730 days (365 × 2). Use the worksheet on the following page to figure the reduced exclusion.

EXAMPLE

You bought and moved into your residence on April 1, 1998. In 1999, you move to a new job location in another state and sell your house at a gain of $50,000 on March 31, 1999. Since you owned and used your home for 365 days, your exclusion limit is reduced by 50%. You are single. Your reduced exclusion is $125,000 (50% of $250,000) and the gain of $50,000 is totally covered by the exclusion and is not taxable.

Filing Instruction

Schedule D Reporting
You report the sale of a principal residence only if you realize gain because you are not entitled to all or part of the exclusion or decide not to claim the exclusion; *see 29.1.* You report a taxable sale on Schedule D.

Worksheet for Reduced Exclusion

	(a) You	(b)* Your spouse
1. Maximum exclusion.	$250,000	$250,000
2a. Enter the number of days you used the home during the five-year period ending on the date of sale.	_____	_____
2b. Enter the number of days you owned the home during the five-year period ending on the date of sale.**	_____	_____
2c. Enter the smaller of Line 2a and Line 2b.	_____	_____
3. Have you (or your spouse, if filing jointly) excluded gain from the sale of another home after May 6, 1997, and within the two-year period ending on the date of this sale? If no, skip Line 3 and enter the number of days from Line 2c on Line 4. If yes, enter the number of days between the date of sale of the other home and the date of sale of this home.	_____	_____
4. Enter the smaller of Line 2c and Line 3.	_____	_____
5. Divide the amount on Line 4 by 730 days. Enter the result as a decimal.	_____	_____
6. Multiply the amount on Line 1 by the decimal amount on Line 5.	_____	_____
7. Add the amounts in columns (a) and (b) of Line 6. This is your reduced exclusion.	_____	_____

* *Use (b) only if you are married and filing a joint return.*
** *If married filing jointly and one spouse owned the property longer than the other spouse, both spouses are treated as owning the property for the longer period.*

Filing Tip

Sales Within Two Years of August 5, 1997

A prorated exclusion may be claimed even if you do not satisfy the two-year ownership and use tests and a sale is *not* due to a change in employment or unforeseen circumstances, provided the following two tests are met: (1) you owned the residence on August 5, 1997, *and* (2) the sale or exchange occurs during the two-year period beginning August 5, 1997.

29.5 Figuring Gain or Loss

To figure the gain or loss on the sale of your principal residence, you must determine the *selling price*, the *amount realized*, and the *adjusted basis*.

Gain or loss. The difference between the amount realized and adjusted basis is your gain or loss. If the amount realized exceeds the adjusted basis, the difference is a gain that may be excluded under the rules at *29.1*. If amount realized is less than adjusted basis, the difference is a loss. A loss on the sale of your main home may not be deducted, *see 29.8*.

Jointly owned home. If you and your spouse sell your jointly owned home and file a joint return, you figure your gain or loss as one taxpayer. If you file separate returns, each of you must figure your own gain or loss according to your ownership interest in the home. Your ownership interest is determined by state law.

Unmarried joint owners. If you and a joint owner other than your spouse sell your jointly owned home, each of you must figure your own gain or loss according to your ownership interest in the home.

Foreclosure or repossession. If your home was foreclosed on or repossessed, you have a sale. *See* Chapter 31.

Selling price. This is the total amount received for your home. It includes money, all notes, mortgages, or other debts assumed by the buyer as part of the sale, and the fair market value of any other property or any services received. The selling price does not include receipts for personal property sold with your home. Personal property is property that is not a permanent part of the home, such as furniture, draperies, and lawn equipment.

If your employer pays you for a loss on the sale or for your selling expenses, do not include the payment as part of the selling price. Include the payment as wages on Line 7 of Form 1040. (Your employer includes the payment with the rest of your wages in Box 1 of your Form W-2.)

If you grant an option to buy your home and the option is exercised, add the amount received for the option to the selling price of your home. If the option is not exercised, you report the amount as ordinary income in the year the option expires. Report the amount on Line 21 of Form 1040.

Amount realized. This is the selling price minus selling expenses. Selling expenses include commissions, advertising fees, legal fees, and loan charges paid by the seller, such as loan placement fees or "points."

Adjusted basis. This is the cost basis of your home increased by the cost of improvements and decreased by deducted casualty losses, if any, as explained in *29.6*. Cost basis is generally what you paid for the residence. If you obtained possession through other means, such as a gift or inheritance, *see 5.17*.

Seller-paid points. If the person who sold you your residence paid points on your loan, you may have to reduce your basis in the home by the amount of the points. If you bought your residence after 1990 but before April 4, 1994, you reduce basis by the points only if you chose to deduct them as home mortgage interest in the year paid. If you bought the residence after April 3, 1994, you reduce basis by the points, even if you did not deduct the points.

Settlement fees or closing costs. When buying your home, you may have to pay settlement fees or closing costs in addition to the contract price of the property. You may include in basis fees and closing costs that are for buying the home. You may not include in your basis the fees and costs of getting a mortgage loan. Settlement fees also do not include amounts placed in escrow for the future payment of items such as taxes and insurance.

Examples of the settlement fees or closing costs that you may include in the basis of your property are: (1) abstract fees (sometimes called abstract of title fees), (2) charges for installing utility services, (3) legal fees (including fees for the title search and preparing the sales contract and deed), (4) recording fees, (5) survey fees, (6) transfer taxes, (7) owner's title insurance, and (8) any amounts the seller owes that you agree to pay, such as certain real estate taxes, back interest, recording or mortgage fees, charges for improvements or repairs, and sales commissions.

Examples of settlement fees and closing costs *not* included in your basis are: (1) fire insurance premiums, (2) rent for occupancy of the home before closing, (3) charges for utilities or other services relating to occupancy of the home before closing, (4) any fee or cost that you deducted as a moving expense before 1994, (5) charges connected with getting a mortgage loan, such as mortgage insurance premiums (including VA funding fees), loan assumption fees, cost of a credit report, and fee for an appraisal required by a lender, and (6) fees for refinancing a mortgage.

Construction. If you contracted to have your residence built on land you own, your basis is the cost of the land plus the cost of building the home, including the cost of labor and materials, payments to a contractor, architect's fees, building permit charges, utility meter and connection charges, and legal fees directly connected with building the home.

Cooperative apartment. Your basis in the apartment is usually the cost of your stock in the co-op housing corporation, which may include your share of a mortgage on the apartment building.

29.6 Figuring Adjusted Basis

Adjusted basis in your home is cost basis adjusted for items discussed below.

Cost basis is increased by improvements with a useful life of more than one year, special assessments for local improvements, and amounts spent after a casualty to restore damaged property.

Decreases to cost basis include: gain you postponed from the sale of a previous home before May 7, 1997, deductible casualty losses not covered by insurance, insurance payments you received or expect to receive for casualty losses, payments you received for granting an easement or right-of-way, depreciation allowed or allowable if you used your home for business or rental purposes, residential energy credit (generally allowed from 1977 through 1987) claimed for the cost of energy improvements added to the basis of your home, adoption credit you claimed for improvements added to the basis of your home, nontaxable payments from an adoption assistance program of your employer that you used for improvements added to the basis of your home, first-time homebuyers credit (allowed to certain first-time buyers of a home in the District of Columbia) claimed for 1997 or 1998, and energy conservation subsidy excluded from your gross income because you received it (directly or indirectly) from a public utility after 1992 to buy or install any energy conservation measure. An energy conservation measure is an installation or modification that is primarily designed either to reduce consumption of electricity or natural gas or to improve the management of energy demand for a home.

Improvements. Improvements add to the value of your home, prolong its useful life, or adapt it to new uses. You add the cost of improvements to the basis of your property.

Examples of improvements include: bedroom, bathroom, deck, garage, porch, and patio additions, landscaping, paving driveway, walkway, fencing, retaining wall, sprinkler system, swimming pool, storm windows and doors, new roof, wiring upgrades, satellite dish, security system, heating system, central air conditioning, furnace, duct work, central humidifier, filtration system, septic system, water heater, soft water system, built-in appliances, kitchen modernization, flooring, wall-to-wall carpeting, attic, walls, and pipes.

Adjusted basis does not include the cost of any improvements that are no longer part of the home.

Filing Tip

Form 1099-S

If you received Form 1099-S, Box 2 should show the total amount you received for your home. However, Box 2 does not include the fair market value of any property other than cash or notes, or any services you received or will receive. For these, Box 4 will be checked. If you can exclude the entire gain from a sale in 1999, the person responsible for closing the sale generally will not have to report it on Form 1099-S.

Caution

Repairs

These maintain your home in good condition but do not add to its value or prolong its life. You do not add their cost to the basis of your property. Examples of repairs include repainting your house inside or outside, fixing gutters or floors, repairing leaks or plastering, and replacing broken window panes. *See 9.3* when repairs tied to an improvement project may be capital improvements.

Planning Reminder

Gains Postponed Under Prior Law Rules

Gain on a previous home sale that you postponed under the prior law rollover rules reduces the basis of your current home if your current home was a qualifying replacement residence for the previous home. Postponed gains on several earlier sales may have to be taken into account under the basis reduction rule. The basis reduction will increase the gain on the sale of your current home.

EXAMPLE

You installed wall-to-wall carpeting in your home 15 years ago. In 1999, you replace that carpeting with new wall-to-wall carpeting. The cost of the old carpeting is no longer part of adjusted basis.

Record-keeping. You should keep records to prove adjusted basis. Ordinarily, you must keep records for three years after the due date for filing your return for the tax year in which you sold your home. But you should keep home records as long as they are needed for tax purposes. These include: (1) proof of the home's purchase price and purchase expenses, (2) receipts and other records for all improvements, additions, and other items that affect the home's adjusted basis, (3) any worksheets you used to figure the adjusted basis of the home you sold, the gain or loss on the sale, the exclusion, and the taxable gain, and (4) any Form 2119 that you filed to postpone gain from the sale of a previous home before May 7, 1997.

29.7 Personal and Business Use of a Home

You may have used part of your property as your home and part for business or to produce income. If you sell the entire property and part of it was used for business or rental purposes for the entire five-year period ending on the date of sale, consider the transaction as the sale of two properties. You exclude gain only on the part used as your home, assuming you meet the two-out-of-five-year ownership and use tests for that part; *see* Example 1.

EXAMPLES

1. You owned a four-unit apartment house for 10 years. For that entire period, you lived in one unit and rented out three units. You sold the apartment house in July of 1999. Your records show:

Cost	$80,000
Capital improvements	20,000
Depreciation (on 3 rented units only)	40,000
Selling price	120,000
Selling expenses	8,000

   One-fourth of the apartment building was your home; you figure your excluded gain as follows:

	Personal (1/4)	Rental (3/4)
Selling price	$30,000	$90,000
Minus: Selling expenses	2,000	6,000
Amount realized	$28,000	$84,000
Basis (cost *plus* improvements)	$25,000	$75,000
Minus: Depreciation	–0–	40,000
Adjusted basis	$25,000	$35,000
Gain (amount realized *minus* adjusted basis)	$3,000	$49,000
Taxable gain		$49,000
Gain excluded	$3,000	

   The rental portion gain of $49,000 is reported on Form 4797.

2. In 1994, Abel bought a house. He used $\frac{3}{4}$ of the house as his principal residence and $\frac{1}{4}$ for business purposes. On October 29, 1999, Abel retired and started using all of the house as his principal residence. On November 1, 2000, he sells the house at a gain.

   During the five-year period ending on the date of sale, Abel met the two-year use test only for $\frac{3}{4}$ of the house. Only gain from that part of the house qualifies for the exclusion, unless the sale is due to a change in health (or place of employment); *see 29.4.*

Depreciation after May 6, 1997. You may not exclude that part of your gain that is equal to any depreciation allowed or allowable for the business or rental use of your home after May 6, 1997. If you were entitled to take depreciation deductions because you used your home for business purposes or as rental property, you may not exclude the part of your gain equal to any depreciation allowed or allowable as a deduction for periods after May 6, 1997. If you can show by adequate records that the depreciation deduction allowed was less than the amount allowable, the gain up to the allowed depreciation deduction is the amount ineligible for the exclusion.

John sold his home in 1999, realizing a $30,000 gain. He meets the use and ownership tests to exclude the gain on the entire home, including a part of the home he used for business from July through December 1998. For those months of business use, he claimed $500 depreciation. He may exclude $29,500 ($30,000 – $500). He has a taxable gain of $500 equal to the depreciation deduction.

29.8 No Loss Allowed on Personal Residence

Selling Your Home at a Loss

A loss on the sale of your principal residence is not deductible. If part of your principal residence was used for business in the year of sale, treat the sale as if two pieces of property were sold. Report the business part on Form 4797. A loss is deductible only on the business part.

Second home or vacation home. If you sell at a loss a second home or vacation home (not your principal residence) that was used entirely for personal purposes, you report the loss transaction on Schedule D, even though the loss is not deductible. Instead of entering the loss amount in column (f) of Schedule D, write "Personal Loss." If in the year of sale part of the home was rented out or used for business, allocate the sale between the personal part and the rental or business part; report the personal part on Schedule D and the rental or business part on Form 4797.

29.9 Loss on Residence Converted to Rental Property

You are not allowed to deduct a loss on the sale of your personal residence. If you convert the house from personal use to rental use you may claim a loss on a sale if the value has declined below the basis fixed for the residence as rental property.

To figure basis for loss purposes, you first need to know the *lower* of (1) your adjusted basis for the house at the time of conversion and (2) the fair market value at the time of conversion. *Add* to the lower amount the cost of capital improvements made after the conversion, and *subtract* depreciation and casualty loss deductions claimed after the conversion. To deduct a loss, you have to be able to show that this basis exceeds the sales price. For example, if you paid $200,000 for your home and convert it to rental property when the value has declined to $150,000, your conversion date basis for the rental property is $150,000. If the property continues to decline in value, and you sell for $125,000 after having deducted $10,000 for depreciation, you may claim a loss of $15,000 ($140,000 – $125,000). Your loss deduction will not reflect the $50,000 loss occurring before the conversion.

 Filing Tip

Loss Allowed

A loss may be claimed if you sell a house that has been converted from personal to rental use; *see 29.9.*

In 1987, Adams bought a house in Fort Worth, Texas. He paid $124,000, put in capital improvements, and lived there until he was forced to put it on the market when he lost his job. In 1988, he listed the house with a broker for $145,000. After receiving no offers, he decided to lease the house through 1990. By October of 1989 Adams owed $4,551 in property taxes and was three months behind on his mortgage payments. Fearing foreclosure, he sold the house for $130,000.

For purposes of figuring a loss, Adams assumed that the fair market value at the time of conversion was equal to the $145,000 list price. The adjusted basis of the house was $141,026. As this was less than the estimated fair market value of $145,000, he used the $141,026 adjusted basis to figure a loss of $11,026 ($130,000 – $141,026). The IRS claimed the fair market value at the time of conversion was equal to the actual sale price of $130,000. Since basis for the converted property is the lesser of fair market value ($130,000) and adjusted basis ($141,026), Adams had no loss on the sale.

However, the Tax Court allowed a $5,000 loss by fixing the fair market value at the time of conversion at $135,000. It held that Adams sold at a lower price because of his weak financial position of which the buyer took advantage. The court figured the $135,000 as follows: $129,000 fair market value in 1987 (based on an appraisal report, which both parties agree was correct), plus $6,000 of appreciation attributable to the capital improvements made to the property after it was converted.

Profit-making purposes. Renting a residence is a changeover from personal to profit-making purposes. If the house is merely put up for rent or is rented for several months, the IRS may not recognize the house as rental property and may disallow the loss deduction. However, the Tax Court has approved a loss deduction where a house was rented on a 90-day lease with an option to buy. The court set down the following two tests for determining when a house is converted to rental property: (1) the rental charge

Caution

Temporary Rental Before Sale

A rental loss may be barred on a temporary rental before sale. The IRS and Tax Court held that where a principal residence was rented for several months while being offered for sale, the rental did not convert the home to rental property. Deductions for rental expenses were limited to rental income; no loss could be claimed. A federal appeals court disagreed and allowed a rental loss deduction; also *see 9.7.*

returns a profit and (2) the lease prevents you from using or reoccupying the house during the lease period. Under the Tax Court approach, you have a conversion to rental property if you have a lease that gives possession of the house to the tenant during the lease period and if the rent, after deducting taxes, interest, insurance, repairs, depreciation, and other charges, returns you a profit.

Loss allowed on house bought for resale. A loss deduction is also allowed where you acquired the house as an investment with the intention of selling it at a profit, even though you occupied it incidentally as a residence prior to sale. For example, an owner bought a house with the intention of selling it. He lived in it for six years, but during that period it was for sale. He was allowed to deduct the loss on its sale by proving he lived in it to protect it from vandalism and to keep it in good condition so that it would attract possible buyers.

In another case, an architect and builder built a house and offered it for sale through an agent and advertisements. He had a home and no intention to occupy the new house. On a realtor's advice, he moved into the house to make it more saleable. Ten months later, he sold the house at a loss of $4,065 and promptly moved out. The loss was allowed on proof that his main purpose in building and occupying the house was to realize a profit by a sale; the residential use was incidental.

Gain on rented residence. You have a gain on the sale of rental property if you sell for more than your adjusted basis at the time of conversion, plus subsequent capital improvements, and minus depreciation and casualty loss deductions. The sale is subject to the rules in Chapter 44 for depreciable property.

Stock in cooperative apartment. Normally, you get no deduction for a loss on the sale of your stock in a cooperative housing corporation. It makes no difference that you occasionally sublet your apartment. It is still not considered property used in a business. But you may get a loss deduction when there were non-stockholder tenants in the cooperative housing corporation when you bought your stock. Then, you get a partial capital loss deduction if you sell your stock or if it becomes worthless. To figure capital loss:

1. First find the difference between your cost and your selling price. This would ordinarily be your capital loss.
2. Then find the percentage of non-stockholding tenants (based on rental values) in the housing corporation when you bought your stock.
3. Apply this percentage to the loss you figured above. This is the capital loss you are allowed.

See 9.5 for when depreciation may be taken on the basis of the cooperative stock ownership.

Partially rented home. You may deduct a loss on a home sale if you rented part and occupied part for your own purposes. A loss on a sale is allowable on the rented portion, which is reported on Form 4797.

29.10 Loss on Residence Acquired by Gift or Inheritance

You may deduct a loss on the sale of a house received as an inheritance or gift if you personally did not use it and offered it for sale or rental immediately or within a few weeks after acquisition.

Planning Reminder

Inherited Residence

If you inherit a residence in which you do not intend to live, it may be advisable to put it up for rent to allow for an ordinary loss deduction on a later sale. If you merely try to sell, and you finally do so at a loss, you are limited to a capital loss.

EXAMPLES

1. A couple owned a winter vacation home in Florida. When the husband died, his wife immediately put the house up for sale and never lived in it. It was sold at a loss. The IRS disallowed her capital loss deduction, claiming it was personal and nondeductible. The wife argued that her case was no different from the case of an heir inheriting and selling a home, since at the death of her husband her interest in the property was increased. The Tax Court agreed with her reasoning and allowed the capital loss deduction.

2. A widow inherited a house owned by her late husband and rented out by his estate. Shortly after getting title to the house, she sold it at a loss that she deducted as an ordinary loss. The IRS limited her to a capital loss deduction. The Tax Court agreed. She could not show any business activity. She did not negotiate the lease with the tenant who was in the house when she received title. She never arranged any maintenance or repairs for the building. Moreover, she sold the property shortly after receiving title, which indicates she viewed the house as investment, not rental, property.

3. An inherited residence was rented out by the owner to her brother for $500 a month when the fair market rental value was $700 to $750 per month. When she sold the residence at a loss, the IRS disallowed the loss, and the Tax Court agreed. The below-market rental was treated as evidence that she held the property for personal purposes, not as rental property or as investment property held for appreciation in value.

Worksheet 1. **Adjusted Basis of Home Sold**

1. Enter the cost basis of your old home. If you filed Form 2119 when you originally acquired your old home to postpone gain on the sale of a previous home, enter the adjusted basis of the new home from that Form 2119 . . . . _____

2. Seller-paid points, for home bought after 1990. (For *seller-paid points, see 15.8.*) Do not include any seller-paid points you previously subtracted to arrive at the amount entered on line 1, above . . _____

3. Subtract line 2 from line 1 . . . . _____

4. Settlement fees or closing costs. Do not include amounts previously deducted as moving expenses. If line 1 includes the adjusted basis of the new home from Form 2119, go to line 6.

   a. Abstract and recording fees . . . . _____
   b. Legal fees (including title search and preparing document) . . . . _____
   c. Surveys . . . . _____
   d. Title insurance . . . . _____
   e. Transfer or stamp taxes . . . . _____
   f. Amounts the seller owed that you agreed to pay (back taxes or interest, recording or mortgage fees, and sales commissions) . . . . _____
   g. Other . . . . _____

5. Add lines 4a through 4g . . . . _____

6. Cost of capital improvements. Do not include any capital improvements included on line 1 above _____

7. Special tax assessments paid on your old home for local improvements, such as streets and sidewalks _____

8. Other increases to basis . . . . _____

9. Add lines 3, 5, 6, 7, and 8 . . . . _____

10. Depreciation, related to the business use or rental of your old home, claimed (or allowable) . . . . _____

11. Residential energy credit (generally allowed from 1977 through 1987) and adoption credit claimed for any capital improvements included on line 6 and, if applicable, line 1 above. _____

12. Payments received for any easement or right-of-way granted . . . . _____

13. Other decreases to basis . . . . _____

14. Add lines 10 through 13 . . . . _____

15. **ADJUSTED BASIS OF HOME SOLD.** Subtract line 14 from line 9. Enter here and on Worksheet 2, line 4 . . . . _____

Worksheet 2. **Gain (or Loss), Exclusion, and Taxable Gain**

Part 1–Gain (or Loss) on Sale

1. Selling price of home . . . . _____
2. Selling expenses. . . . . _____
3. Subtract line 2 from line 1 . . . . _____
4. Adjusted basis of home sold. (From Worksheet 1, line 15.) . . . . _____
5. Subtract line 4 from line 3. This is the gain (or loss) on the sale. If this is a loss, stop here . . _____

Part 2–Exclusion and Taxable Gain

6. Enter any depreciation claimed on the property for periods after May 6, 1997. If none, enter zero _____
7. Subtract line 6 from line 5. (If the result is less than zero, enter zero.) . . . . _____
8. Maximum exclusion. *See 29.1–29.4.* . . . . _____
9. Enter the smaller of line 7 and line 8. This is your exclusion. If you are reporting the sale on the installment method, enter this amount on line 15 of Form 6252 . . . . _____
10. Subtract line 9 from line 5. This is your taxable gain. If the amount on line 6 of this worksheet is zero, report this taxable gain on Schedule D (Form 1040) on line 1 or 8 depending on how long you owned the residence. (Do not complete lines 11 and 12 of this worksheet.)
    If the amount on line 10 is zero, do not report the sale on your tax return.
    If the amount on line 6 is more than zero, complete lines 11 and 12 . . . . _____
11. Enter the smaller of line 6 and line 10. Enter this amount on line 11 of the *Unrecaptured Section 1250 Gain Worksheet* in the instructions for Schedule D (Form 1040) . . . . _____
12. Subtract line 11 from line 10. If the result is more than zero, report it on Schedule D on line 1 or 8 depending on how long you owned the residence. . . . . _____

Tax Savings for Investors in Securities

You have the opportunity to control the taxable year in which to realize gains and losses. Gains and losses are realized when you sell, and if there are no market pressures, you can time sales to your advantage. To profit from the low 10% or 20% tax rate on long-term capital gains, pay attention to the more-than-one-year holding period for realizing long-term capital gains on the sale of securities. Realizing long-term capital gains will give you tax savings. However, do not overlook the fact that realizing substantial capital gains may subject you to the exemption phaseout and/or 3% reduction of itemized deductions. The 3% reduction increases the effective capital gain rate and, depending on the number of exemptions phased out, the effective rate will be still higher. Thus, it may be advisable to avoid realizing substantial capital gain income in a year you are subject to the exemption phaseout if that income can be deferred to a year in which you will have lower income and not be subject to the phaseout.

The $3,000 limitation ($1,500 for married filing separately) on deducting capital losses from other types of income is a substantial restriction. If you have capital losses exceeding the $3,000 (or $1,500) limit, it is advisable to realize capital gains income that can be offset by the losses.

Security Transactions

Investment Opportunities

Security Transactions

30.1 Planning Year-End Securities Transactions

First establish your current gain and loss position for the year. List gains and losses already realized from completed transactions. Then review the records of earlier years to find any carryover capital losses. Include nonbusiness bad debts as short-term capital losses. Then review your paper gains and losses and determine what losses might now be realized to offset realized gains or what gains might be realized to absorb your realized losses.

If you have already realized net capital losses exceeding $3,000 ($1,500 if married filing separately), you may want to realize capital gains that will be absorbed by the excess loss. Remember, only up to $3,000 (or $1,500) of capital losses exceeding net capital gain may be deducted from other income such as salary, interest, and dividends. Also, project your tax-bracket ranges in the current and next tax year. For example, assume that you are close to the threshold for the phaseout of exemptions and that realizing substantial gains will place you in the exemption phase-out range *(21.15)*. You may want to defer gain transactions to a year in which you will be in a lower bracket or not subject to the phaseout.

Planning for losses. Realizing losses may pose a problem if you believe the security is due to increase in value sometime in the near future. Although the wash-sale rule *(30.6)* prevents you from taking the loss if you buy 30 days before or after the sale, the following possibilities are open to you.

- If you believe the security will go up, but not immediately, you can sell now, realize your loss, wait 31 days, and then recover your position by repurchasing before the expected rise.
- You can hedge by repurchasing similar securities immediately after the sale provided they are not substantially identical. They can be in the same industry and of the same quality without being considered substantially identical. Check with your broker to see if you can use a loss and still maintain your position. Some brokerage firms maintain recommended "switch" lists and suggest a practice of "doubling up"—that is, buying the stock of the same company and then 31 days later selling the original shares. Doubling up has disadvantages: It requires additional funds for the purchase of the second lot, exposes you to additional risks should the stock price fall, and the new shares take a new holding period.

EXAMPLE

You own 100 shares of Steel Co. stock that cost you $10,000. In November 1999, the stock is selling at $6,000 ($60 a share × 100 shares). You would like to realize the $4,000 loss but, at the same time, you want to hold on to the investment. You buy 100 shares at a market price of $60 a share (total investment $6,000) and 31 days later sell your original 100 shares, realizing the loss of $4,000. You retain your investment in the new lot. In 1999, November 30 is the last day to buy new shares to allow a loss sale on December 31.

30.2 Earmarking Stock Lots

Keep a record of all your stock transactions, especially when you buy the stock of one company at varying prices. By keeping a record of each stock lot, you may control the amount of gain or loss on a sale of a part of your holdings.

If your stock is held by your broker, the IRS considers that an adequate identification is made if you give instructions to your broker about which particular shares are to be sold, and you receive a written confirmation from the broker or transfer agent within a reasonable time.

EXAMPLE

Over a three-year period, you bought the following shares of Acme Steel stock: In 1996, 100 shares at $77 per share; in 1997, 200 shares at $84 per share; and in 1998, 100 shares at $105 per share. When the stock is selling at $90, you plan to sell 100 shares. You may use the cost of your 1998 lot and get a $1,500 loss if, for example, you want to offset some gains or other income you have already earned this year. Or you may get capital gains of varying amounts by either selling the 1996 lot or part of the 1997 lot.

You must clearly identify the lot you want to sell. Say you want a loss and sell the 1998 lot. Unless you identify it as the lot sold, the IRS will hold that you sold the 1996 lot under the "first-in, first-out" rule. This rule assumes that, when you have a number of identical items that you bought at different times, your sale of any of them is automatically the sale of the

Planning Reminder

December 31 Deadline for 1999 Gains and Losses

If you want to realize gains on publicly traded securities, you have until December 31, 1999, to transact the sale. Gain is reported in 1999, although cash is not received until the settlement date in 2000. If you do not want to realize the gain in 1999, delay the trade date until 2000.

Losses are also realized as of the trade date; a loss on a sale made by December 31, 1999, is reported on your 1999 return.

first you bought. So the cost of your first purchase is what you match against your selling price to find your gain or loss. Here is what to do to counteract the first-in, first-out rule: If you have stock certificates registered in your name, show that you delivered the 1998 stock certificates. If the broker is holding the stock, specifically identify the 1998 lot in your selling instructions and get a written confirmation. *See* the chart in *32.10* for averaging cost on the sale of mutual-fund shares.

How To Identify Securities

If your securities are—	Identify them by—
Registered in your own name	The number, your name, and any other identification that they bear.
In a margin account registered in a "street" name	A specified block or security bought on a designated day at a particular price. A mere intention to sell a particular share without informing the broker is without significance.
New certificates received for old in a recapitalization	Record the new certificate with the lowest number as being in exchange for the old certificate with the lowest number. Do this until all the new certificates are matched with all the old.
Shares exchanged for shares in a reorganization	Allocate each of the new certificates to each of the old in your records. Where the exchange involves several blocks of stock and there is no specific identification, the IRS says you must average your costs.
Shares received in a stock split	Match the new certificates with the old ones surrendered. Identification of your selling securities as the "highest cost" or "lowest cost" stock is insufficient. You have to match at the time of the split-up.
Stock dividends	The lot of stock on which you received the dividend. The new stock is part of the old lot. But if you receive one certificate for more than one lot, you may have to apply the first-in, first-out rule when you sell.
Acquired by exercise of nontaxed stock rights	The number, or other identification, of the lot you receive by exercising the rights. Each lot you so acquire is considered a separate lot received on the date of subscription.

30.3 Sale of Stock Dividends

A sale of stock originally received as a dividend is treated as any other sale of stock. The holding period of a *taxable* stock dividend *(4.8)* begins on the day after the date of distribution. The holding period of a *tax-free* stock dividend or stock received in a split *(4.6)* starts from the time you acquired the original stock.

EXAMPLE

You bought 100 shares of X Co. stock on December 3, 1996. On August 12, 1999, you receive 10 shares of X Co. stock as a tax-free stock dividend. On December 9, 1999, you sell the 10 shares at a profit. You report the sale as long-term capital gain because the holding period of the 10 shares goes back to your original purchase date of December 3, 1996, not August 12, 1999.

Basis of tax-free dividend in the same class of stock. Assume you receive a common stock dividend on common stock. You divide the original cost by the total number of old shares and new shares to find the new basis per share.

EXAMPLE

You bought 100 shares of common stock for $1,000, so that each share has a basis of $10. You receive 100 shares of common stock as a tax-free stock dividend. The basis of your 200 shares remains $1,000. The new cost basis of each share is now $5 ($1,000 ÷ 200 shares). You sell 50 shares for $560. Your profit is $310 ($560 – $250).

Basis of tax-free dividend in a different class of stock. Assume you receive preferred stock dividends on common stock. You divide the basis of the old shares over the two classes in the ratio of their values at the time the stock dividend was distributed.

EXAMPLE

You bought 100 shares of common stock for $1,000. You receive a tax-free dividend of 10 shares of preferred stock. On the date of distribution, the market value of the common stock is $9 a share and that of the preferred stock is $30. That makes the market value of your common stock $900 and your preferred stock $300. So you allocate 75% ($900 ÷ $1,200) of your $1,000 original cost, or $750, to your common stock and 25% ($300 ÷ $1,200) of your cost to the preferred stock.

Basis of taxable stock dividend. The basis of a taxable stock dividend is its fair market value at the time of the distribution. Its holding period begins on the date of distribution. The basis of the old stock remains unchanged.

EXAMPLE

You bought 1,000 shares of stock for $10,000. The company gives you a choice of a cash dividend or stock (one share for every hundred held). You elect the stock. On the date of the distribution, its market value was $15 a share. The basis of the new stock is $150 (10 × $15). The basis of the old stock remains $10,000.

The tax treatment of the receipt of stock as a dividend and in a split is discussed at *4.6*.

30.4 Stock Rights

The tax consequences of the receipt of stock rights are discussed at *4.6*. The following is an explanation of how to treat the sale, exercise, or expiration of nontaxable stock rights. The basis of taxable rights is their fair market value at the time of distribution.

Expiration of nontaxable distributed stock rights. When you allow nontaxable rights to expire, you do not have a deductible loss; you have no basis in the rights.

Sale of nontaxable distributed stock rights. If you sell stock rights distributed on your stock, you treat the sale as the sale of a capital asset. The holding period begins from the date you acquired the original stock on which the rights were distributed.

Purchased rights. If you buy stock rights, your holding period starts the day after the date of the purchase. Your basis for the rights is the price paid; this basis is used in computing your capital gain or loss on the sale.

If you allow purchased rights to expire without sale or exercise, you realize a capital loss. The rights are treated as having been sold on the day of expiration. When purchased rights become worthless during the year prior to the year they lapse, you have a capital loss that is treated as having occurred on the last day of the year in which they became worthless.

Figuring the basis of nontaxable stock rights. Whether rights received by you as a stockholder have a basis depends on their fair market value when distributed. If the market value of rights is less than 15% of the market value of your old stock, the basis of your rights is zero, unless you elect to allocate the basis between the rights and your original stock. You make the election on your tax return for the year the rights are received by attaching to your return a statement that you are electing to divide basis. Keep a copy of the election and the return.

If the market value of the rights is 15% or more of the market value of your old stock, you must divide the basis of the stock between the old stock and the rights, according to their respective values on the date of distribution.

Planning Reminder

Basis of Public Utility Stock Received Under Dividend Reinvestment Plan

For several years before 1986, an exclusion was allowed for stock dividends received from public utility companies if the dividends were reinvested in stock. If you claimed the exclusion, the stock takes a zero basis. If you sell the stock, the entire sales proceeds of the stock are reported as long-term capital gain.

Planning Reminder

Exercise of Stock Rights

You realize no taxable income on the exercise of stock rights. Capital gain or loss on the new stock is recognized when you later sell the stock. The holding period of the new stock begins on the date you exercised the rights. Your basis for the new stock is the subscription price you paid plus your basis for the rights exercised.

No basis adjustment is required for stock rights that become worthless during the year of issue.

EXAMPLE

You own 100 shares of M Co. that cost $10 a share. On September 15, there is a distribution of stock rights allowing for the purchase of one additional share of common for each 10 rights held at a price of $13 a share. The common stock is now worth $15 (ex-rights). The rights have a market value of 20¢ each. This is less than 15% of the market value of the stock. You can either: (1) choose not to spread the tax cost of the stock between the old stock and the rights or (2) elect to spread the tax cost as follows:

Cost of your old stock, 100 shares at $10, or $1,000.

Fair market value of old stock, 100 shares at $15, or $1,500.

Market value of 100 rights at 20¢, or $20.

Market value of both old stock and rights, $1,520.

Apportionment of old stock:

$$\frac{1,500}{1,520} \times 1,000 = 986.84$$

Your new basis of old stock is $986.84 for 100 shares, or $9.87 a share. The tax cost of the rights is then calculated:

$$\frac{20}{1,520} \times 1,000 = \$13.16$$

Basis of the rights is $13.16 for 100 rights.

When you exercise your rights and 10 shares are bought, your basis for the new stock is $130 plus the cost of the rights of $13.16, or $143.16.

If the option of allocation is not exercised, the rights have a basis of zero and the basis of the new stock is $130. The basis of the old stock remains $1,000.

30.5 Short Sales

A short sale is a sale of stock that you do not own but borrow for purposes of the sale from a broker. The short sale is closed when you later buy stock or deliver stock you already own to replace the borrowed stock. One objective of a short sale is to profit from an anticipated drop in the market price of the stock; another objective may be to use the short sale as a hedge.

Tax rules applied to short sales are designed to prevent you from:

- Postponing gain to a later year when you sell short while holding an appreciated position in the same stock. This type of short sale is called "a sale against the box."
- Converting short-term gains to long-term gains.
- Converting long-term losses to short-term losses.

Generally, you report a short sale in the year in which you close the short sale by delivery of replacement stock. However, this rule does not apply when you execute a short sale while holding an appreciated position in the same stock (short sale against the box). You report the transaction in the year of the short sale, even though delivery of replacement stock is made in a later year. However, there is this exception. The short sale is reported in the year of delivery of the replacement stock if you close the short sale before the end of the 30th day of the next year and continue to hold a similar position in the stock for at least 60 days after the closing of the short sale.

If the stock sold short becomes worthless before you close the short sale, you recognize taxable gain in the year the shares became worthless.

EXAMPLES

1. In February 1999, you expect the stock of Oil Co., which is currently selling at $110, to fall within several months. You sell short 500 shares for $55,000 (500 × $110). Two months later when the price falls to $90, you close the short sale (500 × $90 = $45,000). Your profit of $10,000 ($55,000 – $45,000) is treated as short-term capital gain.

2. In January 1999, you buy 100 shares of Steel Co. stock for $1,000 (100 × $10). In November 1999 when the stock is selling at $50, you execute a short sale of 100 shares (100 × $50 = $5,000). In February 2000, you deliver your shares to close the short sale. The tax law treats the short sale as a constructive sale of an appreciated financial position. You report the gain of $4,000 ($5,000 – $1,000) in 1999, the year of the short sale, not in 2000 when you close the sale. To shift tax reporting to 2000, you would have had to close the short sale by the 30th of January and obtain similar stock, which you would have had to hold for at least 60 days after the closing of the short sale. For further details on constructive sales, *see 30.8.*

When analyzing short-sale transactions, ask yourself these questions:

1. When you sold short, did you or your spouse hold for one year or less securities substantially identical to the securities sold short? (Substantially identical securities are described at *30.6.*)

2. After the short sale, did you or your spouse acquire substantially identical securities on or before the date of the closing of the short sale?

If you answered "yes" to either or both of these questions, apply the following two rules:

Rule 1. Gain realized on the closing of the short sale is short term. The gain is short term regardless of the period of time you have held the securities as of the closing date of the short sale.

Rule 2. The beginning date of the holding period of substantially identical stock is suspended. The holding period of substantially identical securities owned or bought under the facts of question (1) or (2) does not begin until the date of the closing of the short sale (or the date of the sale, gift, or other disposition of the securities, whichever date occurs first). But note that this rule applies only to the number of securities that do not exceed the quantity sold short.

A loss on a short sale is not deductible until shares closing the short sale are delivered to the broker. You may not realize a short-term loss on the closing of a short sale if you held substantially identical securities long term (that is, for more than a year) on the date of the short sale. The loss is long term. This rule prevents you from creating short-term losses when you held the covering stock long term. Loss deductions on short sales may be disallowed under the wash-sale rules of *30.6.*

Expenses of short sales. Before you buy stock to close out a short sale, you pay the broker for dividends paid on stock you have sold short. If you itemize deductions, you may treat your payment as investment interest *(15.10)*, provided the short sale is held open at least 46 days, or more than a year in the case of extraordinary dividends. If the 46-day (or one-year) test is not met, the payment is generally not deductible and is added to basis; in counting the short-sale period, do not count any period during which you have an option to buy or are obligated to buy substantially identical securities, or are protected from the risk of loss from the short sale by a substantially similar position.

Under an exception to the 46-day test, if you receive compensation from the lender of the stock for the use of collateral and you report the compensation as ordinary income, your payment for dividends is deductible to the extent of the compensation; only the excess of your payment over the compensation is disallowed. This exception does not apply to payments with respect to extraordinary dividends.

An extraordinary dividend is generally a dividend that equals or exceeds the amount realized on the short sale by 10% for any common stock or by 5% for any preferred stock dividends. For purposes of this test, dividends on stock received within an 85-day period are aggregated; a one-year aggregation period applies if dividends exceed 20% of the adjusted basis in the stock.

Arbitrage transactions. Special holding-period rules apply to short sales involved in identified arbitrage transactions in convertible securities and stock into which the securities are convertible. These rules can be found in Treasury regulations to Internal Revenue Code Section 1233.

30.6 Wash Sales

The objective of the wash-sale rule is to disallow a loss deduction where you recover your market position in a security within a short period of time after the sale. Under the wash-sale rule, your loss deduction is barred if within 30 days of the sale you buy *substantially identical* stock or securities, or a "put" or "call" option on such securities. The wash-sale period is 61 days—running from 30 days before to 30 days after the date of sale. The end of a taxable year during this 61-day period does not affect the wash-sale rule. The loss is still denied. If you sell at a loss and your spouse buys substantially identical stock within this period, the loss is also barred.

The wash-sale rule does not apply to gains. It also does not apply to acquisitions by gift, inheritance, or tax-free exchange.

The wash-sale rule applies to investors and traders. It does not apply to dealers.

 Planning Reminder

Puts

The acquisition of a *put* (an option to sell) is treated as a short sale if you hold substantially identical securities short term at the time you buy the put. If you have held the underlying stock for one year or less at the time you buy the put, any gain on the exercise, sale, or expiration of the put is a short-term capital gain. The same is true if you buy the underlying stock after you buy the put but before its exercise, sale, or expiration. Your holding period for the underlying stock begins on the earliest of: (1) the date you dispose of the stock; (2) the date you exercise the put; (3) the date you sell the put; or (4) the date the put expires. However, the short-sale rules do not apply if on the same day you buy a put and stock that is identified as covered by the put. If you do not exercise the put that is identified with the stock, add its cost to the basis of the stock.

Loss on the sale of part of a stock lot bought less than 30 days ago. If you buy stock and then, within 30 days, sell some of those shares, a loss on the sale is deductible; the wash-sale disallowance rule does not apply.

EXAMPLE

You buy 200 shares of stock. Within 30 days, you sell 100 shares at a loss. The loss is not disallowed by the wash-sale rule. The wash-sale rule does not apply to a loss sustained in a bona fide sale made to reduce your market position. It does apply when you sustain a loss for tax purposes with the intent of recovering your position in the security within a few days. Thus if, after selling the 100 shares, you repurchase 100 shares of the same stock within 30 days after the sale, the loss is disallowed.

Oral sale-repurchase agreement. The wash-sale rule applies to an oral sale-repurchase agreement between business associates.

Defining "substantially identical." What is substantially identical stock or securities? Buying and selling General Motors stock is dealing in an identical security. Selling General Motors and buying Chrysler stock is not dealing in substantially identical securities.

Bonds of the same obligor are substantially identical if they carry the same rate of interest; that they have different issue dates and interest payment dates will not remove them from the wash-sale provisions. Different maturity dates will have no effect, unless the difference is economically significant. Where there is a long time span between the purchase date and the maturity date, a difference of several years between maturity dates may be considered insignificant. A difference of three years between maturity dates was held to be insignificant where the maturity dates of the bonds, measured from the time of purchase, were 45 and 48 years away. There was no significant difference where the maturity dates differed by less than one year, and the remaining life, measured from the time of purchase, was more than 15 years.

The wash-sale rules do not apply if you buy bonds of the same company with substantially different interest rates, buy bonds of a different company, or buy substantially identical bonds outside of the wash-sale period.

Warrants. A warrant falls within the wash-sale rule if it is an option to buy substantially identical stock. Consequently, a loss on the sale of common stocks of a corporation is disallowed when warrants for the common stock of the same corporation are bought within the period 30 days before or after the sale. But if the timing is reversed—that is, you sell warrants at a loss and simultaneously buy common stock of the same corporation—the wash-sale rules may or may not apply depending on whether the warrants are substantially identical to the purchased stock. This is determined by comparing the relative values of the stock and warrants. The wash-sale rule will apply only if the relative values and price changes are so similar that the warrants become fully convertible securities.

EXAMPLES

1. You bought common stock of Appliance Co. for $10,000 in 1982. On June 25, 1999, you sold the stock for $8,000, incurring a $2,000 loss. A week later, you repurchased the same number of shares of Appliance stock for $9,000. Your loss of $2,000 on the sale is disallowed because of the wash-sale rule. The basis of the new lot becomes $11,000. The basis of the old shares ($10,000) is increased by $1,000, which is the excess of the purchase price of the new shares ($9,000) over the selling price of the old shares ($8,000).

2. Assume the same facts as in Example 1, except that you repurchase the stock for $7,000. The basis of the new lot is $9,000. The basis of the old shares ($10,000) is decreased by $1,000, which is the excess of the selling price of the old shares ($8,000) over the purchase price of the new shares ($7,000).

3. Assume that in February 2000 you sell the new lot of stock acquired in Example 1 above for $9,000 and do not run afoul of the wash-sale rule. On the sale, you realize a loss of $2,000 ($11,000 – $9,000).

Repurchasing fewer shares. If the number of shares of stock reacquired in a wash sale is less than the amount sold, only a proportionate part of the loss is disallowed.

Planning Reminder

Basis Adjusted for New Stock

Although the loss deduction is barred if the wash-sale rule applies, the economic loss is not forfeited for tax purposes. The loss might be realized at a later date when the repurchased stock is sold, because after the disallowance of the loss, the cost basis of the new lot is fixed as the basis of the old lot and adjusted (up or down) for the difference between the selling price of the old stock and purchase price of the new stock; *see* the Examples on this page.

EXAMPLE

You bought 100 shares of Stock A for $10,000. On December 10, 1999, you sell the lot for $8,000, incurring a loss of $2,000. On January 4, 2000, you repurchase 75 shares of Stock A for $6,000. Three-quarters ($^{75}/_{100}$) of your loss is disallowed, or $1,500 ($^{3}/_{4}$ of $2,000). You deduct the remaining loss of $500 on your return for 1999. The basis of the new shares is $7,500 ($6,000 cost *plus* $1,500 disallowed loss).

Holding period of new stock. After a wash sale, the holding period of the new stock includes the holding period of the old lots. If you sold more than one old lot in wash sales, you add the holding periods of all the old lots to the holding period of the new lot. You do this even if your holding periods overlapped as you purchased another lot before you sold the first. You do not count the periods between the sale and purchase when you have no stock.

Losses on short sales. Losses incurred on short sales are subject to the wash-sale rules. A loss on the closing of a short sale is denied if you sell the stock or enter into a second short sale within the period beginning 30 days before and ending 30 days after the closing of the short sale.

30.7 Convertible Stocks and Bonds

You realize no gain or loss when you convert a bond into stock, or preferred stock into common stock of the same corporation, provided the conversion privilege was allowed by the bond or preferred stock certificate.

Holding period. Stock acquired through the conversion of bonds or preferred stock takes the same holding period as the securities exchanged. However, where the new stock is acquired partly for cash and partly by tax-free exchange, each new share of stock has a split holding period. The portion of each new share allocable to the ownership of the converted bonds (or preferred stock) includes the holding period of the bonds (or preferred stock). The portion of the new stock allocable to the cash purchase takes a holding period beginning with the day after acquisition of the stock.

Basis. Securities acquired through the conversion of bonds or preferred stock into common take the same basis as the securities exchanged. Where there is a partial cash payment, the basis of the portion of the stock attributable to the cash is the amount of cash paid; *see* Examples 1 and 2 below.

If you paid a premium for a convertible bond, you may not amortize the amount of the premium that is attributable to the conversion feature.

EXAMPLES

1. On January 5, 1999, you paid $100 for a debenture of A Co. Your holding period for the debenture begins on January 6; *see 5.9*. The debenture provides that the holder may receive one share of A Co. common stock upon surrender of one debenture and the payment of $50. On October 19, you convert the debenture to stock on payment of $50. For tax purposes, you realize no gain or loss upon the conversion regardless of whether the fair market value of the stock is more or less than $150 on the date of the conversion. The basis and holding period for the stock is as follows: $100 basis for the portion attributed to the ownership of the debenture with the holding period beginning January 6; and $50 basis attributed to the cash payment with the holding period for this portion beginning October 20.

2. Same facts as in the above Example, but you acquired the debenture on January 5 through the exercise of rights on that date. Since the holding period for the debenture includes the date of exercise of the rights, *see 30.4*, the portion of the stock allocable to the debenture takes a holding period beginning on January 6.

30.8 Constructive Sales of Appreciated Financial Positions

One aspect of a constructive sale of an appreciated financial position was discussed in *30.5*, dealing with a short sale against the box that was not closed at the end of the taxable year. The constructive sale rules apply not only to short sales of stock but also to other transactions such as an appreciated financial position in a partnership interest or certain debt obligations.

 Planning Reminder

Tax Advantage of Wash-Sale Rule

Sometimes the wash-sale rule can work to your advantage. Assume that during December you are negotiating a sale of real estate that will bring you a large capital gain. You want to offset a part of that gain by selling certain securities at a loss. You are unsure just when the gain transaction will go through. It may be on the last day of the year, at which point it may be too late to sell the loss securities before the end of the same year.

You can do this: Sell the loss securities during the last week of December. If the profitable deal goes through before the end of the year, you need not do anything further. If it does not, buy back the loss securities early in January. The December sale will be a wash sale and the loss disallowed. When the profitable real estate sale occurs next year, you can sell the loss securities again. This time the loss will be allowed and will offset the gain.

You have made a constructive sale of an appreciated financial position if you:

1. Enter into a short sale of the same or substantially identical property,
2. Enter into an offsetting notional principal contract relating to the same or substantially identical property,
3. Enter into a futures or forward contract to deliver the same or substantially identical property, *or*
4. Acquire the same or substantially identical property (if the appreciated financial position is a short sale, an offsetting notional principal contract, or a futures or forward contract).

You are also treated as having made a constructive sale of an appreciated financial position if a person related to you enters into any of the above transactions.

A contract for sale of any stock, debt instrument, or partnership interest that is not a marketable security is not a constructive sale if it settles within one year of the date you enter into it.

Tax treatment. If you are considered to have transacted a constructive sale, you report as taxable income gain on the financial position as if the position was sold at its fair market value on the date of the constructive sale. The property held by you receives a new holding period starting on the date of the constructive sale and its basis is the fair market value at that date. Thus, under the constructive sale rule you are also treated as immediately repurchasing the position as of the date of the constructive sale.

Closing a short sale to avoid a constructive sale. You may avoid the constructive sale rule if:

1. You close the transaction before the end of the 30th day after the end of your tax year,
2. You hold the appreciated financial position throughout the 60-day period beginning on the date you close the transaction,
3. Your risk of loss is not reduced at any time during that 60-day period by holding certain other positions.

If a closed transaction is reestablished in a substantially similar position during the 60-day period beginning on the date the first transaction was closed, this exception still applies if the reestablished position is closed before the end of the 30th day after the end of your tax year in which the first transaction was closed and, after that closing, tests (2) and (3) apply.

EXAMPLE

On October 1, 1999, you buy 100 shares of Oil Co. for $60 a share. On December 2, 1999, you sell short 100 shares of Oil Co. for $80 a share. On January 6, 2000, you buy for $75 a share 100 shares of Oil Co. to close the short sale. You hold the October lot for over 60 days in 2000. The December 1999 short sale is not treated as a constructive sale in 1999. You realized a loss of $5 per share when you closed the short position.

An appreciated financial position. You have an appreciated financial position interest in stock, a partnership interest, or a debt instrument (including a futures or forward contract, a short sale, or an option) if disposing of the interest would result in a gain.

An appreciated financial position does not include any position that is marked to market, including Section 1256 contracts. It also does not include any position in a debt instrument if:

1. The debt unconditionally entitles the holder to receive a specified principal amount,
2. The interest payments on the debt (or other similar amounts) are payable at a fixed rate or a variable rate described in Section 1.860G-1(a)(3) of the Regulations, *and*
3. The debt is not convertible, either directly or indirectly, into stock of the issuer (or any related person).

For the constructive sale rules, an interest in an actively traded trust is treated as stock unless substantially all of the value of the property held by the trust is debt that qualifies for the debt exception above.

A transaction treated as a constructive sale of an appreciated financial position is not treated as a constructive sale of any other appreciated financial position, as long as you continue to hold the original position. However, if you hold another appreciated financial position and dispose of the original position before closing the transaction that resulted in the constructive sale, you are treated as if, at the same time, you constructively sold the other appreciated financial position.

Caution

Constructive Sales of Appreciated Position

If you are subject to the constructive sale rules, you will have to report income as if you had made a sale although you still hold the position.

30.9 Straddle Losses

Tax accounting rules generally match losses against unrealized gains in offsetting straddle positions. Straddle rules apply to commodities and actively traded stock and to stock options used in straddle positions. Straddle positions include any stock that is part of a straddle in which at least one of the offsetting positions is: (1) an option tied to the stock or to substantially identical stock or securities; or (2) a position in substantially similar or related property other than stock. For example, there is a straddle of stock and substantially similar or related property if offsetting positions of stock and convertible debentures of the same corporation are held and price movements of the two positions are related.

Straddle rules apply also to stock of a corporation formed or used to take positions in personal property that offset positions taken by any shareholder. True *hedging* transactions are not subject to the straddle tax rules.

A call option is not treated as part of a straddle position if it is considered a qualified covered call option. A *qualified covered call option* is an option that a stockholder who is not a dealer grants on stock traded on a national securities exchange. Furthermore, the option must be granted more than 30 days before its expiration date and must not be "deep-in-the-money." A covered call option will not qualify if gain on the sale of the stock to be purchased by the option is reported in a year after the year in which the option is closed, and the stock is not held for 30 days or more after the date on which the option is closed. In such a case, the option is subject to the straddle loss deferral rules. The same loss deferment rule applies where the stock is sold at a loss, and gain on the related option held less than 30 days is reported in the next year.

Loss on a qualified covered call option with a strike price less than its applicable stock price is treated as long-term capital loss if loss realized on the sale of the stock would be long term. The holding period for stock subject to the option does not include any period during which the taxpayer is the grantor of the option.

A "deep-in-the-money" option is an option with a strike or exercise price that is below the lowest qualified benchmark. The technical rules for determining these values are not discussed in this book.

Tax rules for straddles. The following is an overview of the subject, and if you have transacted straddles, we suggest that you consult with an experienced tax practitioner.

Realized straddle losses are deductible at the close of a taxable year only if they exceed unrealized gains in an offsetting position. Thus, an investor may not deduct losses incurred in 1999 to the extent that he or she has an unrealized gain position in the open end of the straddle.

Straddle positions of related persons (such as a spouse or child) or controlled flow-through entities (such as a partnership or an S corporation) are considered in determining whether offsetting positions are held.

Realized losses that are not deductible at the end of the year are carried forward and become deductible when there is no unrealized appreciation in an offsetting position bought before the disposition of the loss position. This loss deferral rule may be avoided by identifying straddles before the close of the day of acquisition or at an earlier time that the IRS may set. Gain or loss in identified positions is generally netted; that is, a loss is recognized when the offsetting gain position has been closed.

You must disclose all straddle positions of unrealized gains at the close of a tax year or you may be subject to a negligence penalty unless failure to disclose is due to a reasonable cause.

The loss deferral rule does *not* apply to positions in a regulated futures contract or other Section 1256 contract subject to the marked-to-market system explained later in this section.

The loss deferral rule also does not apply to businesses that must hedge in order to protect their supplies of inventory or financial capital. Hedging transactions are subject to ordinary income or loss treatment. Hedging transactions entered into by syndicates do not qualify for the exception and are subject to the loss deferral rule if more than 35% of losses for a taxable year are allocable to limited partners or entrepreneurs. Furthermore, hedging losses of limited partners or limited entrepreneurs are generally limited to their taxable income from the business to which the hedging transaction relates.

Conversion transactions. On certain so-called "conversion transactions," discussed at *30.10*, gain realized on the disposition of certain positions is treated as ordinary income instead of capital gain.

Marked-to-market rules for gain or loss on regulated futures contracts and other Section 1256 contracts. Gain or loss on regulated futures contracts is reported annually under the marked-to-market accounting system of regulated commodity exchanges. To settle margin

Filing Instruction

Form 6781

You use Form 6781 for reporting gains and losses on straddle positions and on Section 1256 contracts that are open at the end of the year but treated as sold under the marked-to-market rules discussed in this section.

Filing Tip

Carryback Election

If for 1999 you have a net loss on Section 1256 contracts, the loss may be carried back for three years under special rules. To carry back the net loss, you must make the election on Form 6781, file an amended return (Form 1040X) and attach an amended Form 6781 for the applicable year. Follow the instructions to Form 6781.

requirements, regulated exchanges determine a party's account for futures contracts on a daily basis. Each regulated futures contract is treated as if sold at fair market value on the last day of the taxable year. Any capital gain or loss is arbitrarily allocated: 40% is short term and 60% is long term. Use Form 6781 to figure gains and losses on Section 1256 contracts that are open at the end of the year or that were closed out during the year. These amounts are then transferred from Form 6781 to Schedule D.

Under the law, a regulated futures contract is considered a Section 1256 contract. Other Section 1256 contracts subject to the marked-to-market rules are foreign currency contracts, dealer equity options, and non-equity options.

The marked-to-market rules do not apply to true hedging transactions executed in the normal course of business to reduce risks and that result in ordinary income or loss. Syndicates may generally not take advantage of this hedging exception if more than 35% of their losses during a taxable year are allocable to limited partners or entrepreneurs. Further, the ability of entrepreneurs or limited partners to deduct losses from hedging transactions is generally limited to taxable income from the business to which the hedging transaction relates.

Mixed straddle contracts. If you have a mixed straddle in which at least one but not all of the positions is a Section 1256 contract, the marked-to-market rules generally apply but you may elect to avoid this treatment and apply the regular straddle tax rules. The election, made on Form 6781, is irrevocable unless the IRS allows a revocation. Furthermore, the IRS allows an election to offset gains and losses from positions that are part of mixed straddles if you separately identify each mixed straddle or establish mixed straddle accounts for a class of activities for which gain and loss will be recognized and offset on a periodic basis.

Wash sales. Rules similar to wash sale rules apply to losses arising from sales of shares that make up a straddle if within a 30-day period you acquire substantially identical shares; *see* IRS Publication 550 for further details.

Contract cancellations. Investors buying forward contracts for currency or securities may not realize ordinary loss by cancelling the unprofitable contract of the hedge transaction. Loss realized on a cancellation of the contract is treated as a capital loss.

Cash-and-carry transactions. You may not deduct carrying costs for any period during which the commodity or stock or option is part of a balanced position. The costs must be capitalized and added to basis. The rule does not apply to hedging straddles. Capitalized items are reduced by dividends on stock included in a straddle, market discounts, and acquisition discounts. These reductions, however, are limited to so much of the dividends and discounts as is included in income.

30.10 Capital Gain Restricted on Conversion Transactions

A "conversion transaction" is a transaction generally involving two or more positions taken with regard to the same or similar property. The investor is in the economic position of a lender who expects to receive income while undertaking no significant risks other than those of a lender. Where substantially all of your expected return is in the nature of interest on a loan from the following types of transactions, some or all of the income earned on the transaction is treated as ordinary income rather than capital gain:

- You acquire property and also agree to sell the property or substantially identical property for a determined price;
- You take offsetting positions on a straddle transaction; *or*
- You invest in a transaction marketed or sold as producing capital gain but your expected return is in the nature of interest on a loan.

Option dealers and commodity dealers are generally exempt from the new limitations.

Amount treated as ordinary income. In a conversion transaction, the amount of ordinary income is limited to an "applicable imputed income amount." This is generally the amount of interest that would have accrued on the net investment in the conversion transaction for the period ending on the date of disposition. To figure the interest element, 120% of the applicable federal rate, compounded semiannually, is used. The applicable rate is the federal short-term, mid-term, or long-term rate, depending on the term of the transaction. If the term is indefinite, the federal short-term rate is used. The federal rates are determined monthly and published in the Internal Revenue Bulletin.

Filing Tip

Reporting Conversion Transactions

You report conversion transactions on Form 6781. The ordinary income element is not reported as interest income, but as an ordinary gain on Form 4797.

EXAMPLE

On January 3, 1997, Jones buys stock for $100 and on the same day agrees to sell it to Brown for $115 on January 5, 1999. Assume the applicable federal interest rate is 5%. On January 5, 1999, Jones delivers the stock to Brown for $115. If the conversion transaction rule did not apply, Jones would recognize a capital gain of $15 ($115 sale price less $100 purchase price). However, under the conversion transaction rules, $12.36 of the gain is ordinary income ($12.36 is $100 times 6% compounded for two years; 6% is 120% of the 5% federal rate). The balance of the gain, or $2.64, is long-term capital gain ($15 *less* $12.36).

Where a loan finances a conversion transaction and interest is capitalized (under a provision applied to straddles), the amount of ordinary income reported is reduced.

If the conversion transaction involves a "built-in" loss, the loss is recognized without regard to the conversion rules. For example, if the loss is a capital loss, it remains a capital loss although the conversion rules apply to the transaction.

30.11 Puts and Calls and Index Options

You may buy options to buy and sell stock. On the stock exchange, these options are named *calls* and *puts*. A call gives you the right to require the seller of the option to sell you stock during the option period at a fixed price, called the exercise or strike price. A put gives you the right to require the seller of the option to buy stock you own at a fixed price during the option period. *See* the chart on the following page for an explanation of different option terms.

The option price depends on the value of the stock, the length of the option period, the volatility of the stock, and the demand and supply for options for the particular stock.

Puts may be treated as short sales. Be careful in using puts when you own stock covered by the put. If you have held the stock short term, the purchase of the put is a short sale. The exercise or expiration of the put will then be treated as the closing of the short sale. Short-sale rules, however, do not apply (1) when you hold stock long term, and (2) when you buy a put and the related stock on the same day and identify the stock with the put; *see 30.5.*

Buyers of options. If you buy an option, the tax treatment of your investment in the option depends on what you do with it.

1. If you sell it, you realize short-term or long-term capital gain or loss, depending upon how long you held the option.

2. If you allow the option to expire without exercise, you incur a short-term or long-term capital loss, depending on the holding period of the option. The expiration date is treated as the date the option is disposed of.

3. If you exercise a call and buy the stock, you add the cost of the call to the basis of the stock. If you exercise a put, the cost of the put reduces your amount realized when figuring gain or loss on the sale of the underlying stock.

Grantors of options. If you write an option through the exchange, you do not treat the premium received for writing the option as income at the time of receipt. You do not realize profit or loss until the option transaction is closed. This may occur when the option expires or is exercised or when you "buy in" on the exchange an option similar to the one you gave to end your obligation to deliver the stock. Here are the rules for these events:

1. If the option is not exercised, you report the premium as short-term capital gain in the year the option expires.

2. If the option is exercised, you add the premium to the sales proceeds of the stock to determine gain or loss on the sale of the stock. Gain or loss is short term or long term depending upon the holding period of the stock.

3. If you "buy in" an equivalent option in a closing transaction, you realize profit or loss for the difference between the premium of the option you sold and the cost of the closing option. The profit or loss is treated as short-term capital gain or loss. However, a loss on a covered call that has a stated price below the stock price may be long-term capital loss if, at the time of the loss, long-term gain would be realized on the sale of the stock. Furthermore, the holding period of such stock is suspended during the period in which the option is open. Finally, year-end losses from covered call options are not deductible, unless the stock is held uncovered for more than 30 days following the date on which the option is closed.

 Planning Reminder

Speculate With Puts and Calls

Puts and calls allow you to speculate at the expense of a small investment—a call, for expected price rises, and a put, for expected price declines. They may also be used to protect paper profits or fix the amount of your losses on securities you own.

You do not have to exercise a put or call to realize your profit. You may sell the option to realize your profit. If you exercise a call, the cost of the call is added to the cost of the stock purchased. If you exercise a put, you reduce the selling price of stock sold by the cost of the put. If you do not exercise a call or put, you realize a capital loss.

Using a call as leverage. You expect a stock to appreciate in value but you do not have sufficient capital for a further investment. Instead of investing your limited amount of capital in an outright purchase, you might buy a call covering such stock. With a call, the same amount of capital allows you to speculate in many more shares than you could if you purchased stock outright. If the stock rises in value, your call also increases in value.

Key to Option Terms

Item—	Explanation—
Call option	An option contract that gives the holder the right to buy a specified number of shares of the underlying stock at the given exercise price on or before the option expiration date.
Put option	An option contract that gives the holder the right to sell a specified number of shares of the underlying stock at the given exercise price on or before the option expiration date.
Strike price/exercise price	The stated price per share for which the underlying stock may be bought (in the case of a call) or sold (in the case of a put) by the option holder upon exercise of the option contract.
At-the-money	An option is at-the-money if the exercise price of the option is equal to the market price of the underlying security.
In-the-money	A call option is in-the-money if the exercise price is less than the market price of the underlying security. A put option is in-the-money if the exercise price is greater than the market price of the underlying security.
Out-of-the-money	A call option is out-of-the-money if the exercise price is greater than the market price of the underlying security. A put option is out-of-the-money if the strike price is less than the market price of the underlying security.
Premium	The price of the option contract determined in the competitive marketplace, which the buyer of the option pays to the option writer.
Intrinsic value	The amount by which the option is in-the-money.
Time value (premium-intrinsic value)	The portion of the premium that is attributable to the amount of time remaining until the option's expiration date and to the fact that the underlying components that determine the value of the option may change during that time.
Secondary market	A market that provides for the purchase or sale of previously sold or bought options through closing transactions.
Expiration date	The expiration date is the last day on which an option may be exercised.
Writer	The seller of an option contract.

Filing Instruction

Marked-to-Market Rules

Non-equity options and dealer equity options, which include options based on regulated stock indexes and interest rate futures, are taxed like regulated futures contracts. This means that they are reported annually under the marked-to-market accounting system. You treat all such options held at the end of the year as if they were disposed of at year-end for a price equal to fair market value. Any gain or loss is arbitrarily taxed as if it were 60% long term and 40% short term. It is advisable to ask your broker whether the specific options you hold come within this special rule.

You use Form 6781 to report 60/40% gains, which are then transferred to Schedule D.

30.12 Exchange Option Trading

Option market exchanges such as the Chicago Board Options Exchange (CBOE) provide market conditions for trading in puts and call options. Financial sections of the daily newspapers provide data on the market prices and volume of the options.

Trading in options is highly speculative, attracting those who hope to make profits on minimum investments. At the same time, the market has provided investors and institutions holding large portfolios with an opportunity to earn income through the sale of options based on their holdings. Thus, it takes two to play the option game: (1) the owner of shares who sells an option on his or her stock and (2) the option buyer who generally speculates that, by buying an option for a smaller price than he or she would have to pay for the stock, a profit can be made if the price of the stock goes up. The odds generally favor the option seller.

If you are inexperienced in the use of options, read several technical explanations of the use of options before investing. Master the technical use of options such as straddles and hedges used by professional traders, as the outright purchase of straight calls is generally too speculative. Finally, do not overlook commission costs which can cut into your profits or increase your losses.

Stock index options. Index options give you a chance to speculate on the general movement of stock prices. The success of the index option has tended to reduce interest in regular stock options given on individual stocks. On the other hand, index options are pegged to the price movement of the stocks that comprise the index option. Thus, with index options, you do not have to be concerned about the market fate of a particular stock. The stock group of the index option follows the general stock market movement. For example, assume that 100 stocks make up the index. The option contract represents an index multiplier of $100 times the index value of the group or basket of 100 stocks. Therefore, when a newspaper reports an index value of 170, which is also called the "strike price," the contract is worth $17,000. However, as the option is only a right to buy or sell this particular contract, you pay an option price that is only a percentage of the contract value. The particular option price is set by the market in an open auction.

Your role is to weigh how the market will fare within the option period. Should you anticipate lower interest rates within the option period, which can be from approximately a week up to three months, you might buy an index option, betting that the stock market will advance. For example, when the index is at 165, you buy an option for $1,200 with a strike price of 170. If the stock market advances during the option period, pushing the strike price to 177, you have won your bet. At 177, you might sell your option for $7,000, thereby making a $5,800 profit.

Do not let this example encourage you to enter the index option market precipitously. If you guess wrong, you have lost your money. In the example just cited, had the index not moved above 170, you would have lost $1,200. However, unlike other investments where the risk may be unlimited, options offer buyers a known risk in that the buyer cannot lose more than the premium paid for the option or, in other words, the price paid for the option.

If you are interested in playing the index option market, track the market for several months until you get used to the movement of the option. Plot hypothetical purchases and see how you would have fared. You might make a bundle—but, as at roulette, you might lose your shirt in a very short time.

Investment Opportunities

30.13 Reducing the Tax on Dividend Income

The tax on dividend income may be reduced by the following types of transactions:

- ***Selling stock on which a dividend has been declared but not yet paid.*** During the period a dividend is declared but not paid, the price of the stock includes the value of the dividend. If you plan to sell stock in this position and figure that the tax on the dividend reflected in the selling price will be less than the tax on the dividend received, transact the sale before the stock goes ex-dividend; *see 4.9.*
- ***Investing in companies paying tax-free dividends.*** Some companies pay tax-free dividends. A list of companies that do may be provided by your broker. When you receive a tax-free dividend, you do not report the dividend as income as long as the dividend does not exceed your stock basis. A tax-free dividend reduces the tax cost of your stock. Dividends in excess of basis produce capital gain; *see 4.11.*
- ***Investing in companies paying stock dividends.*** On receipt of a stock dividend, you generally do not have taxable income.

30.14 Treasury Bills and CDs

Short-term paper (maturity of one year or less) provides an opportunity for earning income on funds during periods of uncertainty in the stock and other investment markets. Funds that you do not wish to tie up long term and do not want to remain unproductive may be invested in Treasury bills, notes, or certificates of deposit. These investments offer safety and negotiability, earning current interest rates from the day of purchase to the day of redemption, either on maturity or sale.

Treasury bills. These are direct obligations of the U.S. Treasury issued to finance budgetary needs. Bills are offered for three-month, six-month, and 12-month maturities in minimum amounts of $10,000 and multiples of $1,000 above the minimum. Bills are sold at a discount at Treasury auctions held at the Federal Reserve Banks, which serve as agents for the Treasury. They are redeemed at face value. Your return on a Treasury bill is the difference between the discount price you pay for the bill and its face value, if you hold it to maturity, or the amount you receive for it on a sale before maturity. The selling price of a Treasury bill before maturity will vary with changes of current interest rates.

You may buy Treasury bills directly without charge from any Federal Reserve Bank, which gives you a receipt indicating that a book entry of your purchase has been recorded. You also may buy or sell Treasury bills through your bank or stockbroker, who will charge you for handling the transaction.

 Planning Reminder

Buying T-Bills
Most investors submit *noncompetitive tenders* (bids) for the Treasury bills they wish to buy. To submit a *competitive* tender, you must specify the price you are willing to pay for your bill, and you run the risk of bidding too low and not getting the bills you want. Noncompetitive tenders do not have to specify a price. They are filled at a price that is the average of the accepted competitive tenders for that specific auction. Check the Federal Reserve Bank or branch in your area for auction dates on Treasury bills. You may also buy or sell Treasury bills through your bank or your stockbroker, who will charge you for handling the transaction.

Figuring Treasury bill yield. On the day of the auction, the Treasury will figure the average price bid by those who submitted acceptable competitive tenders. The difference between this average price and the full value of the Treasury bill is the *discount* at which the bill is sold. All noncompetitive tenders are filled at this price. The Treasury pays you the difference between the purchase price and the face value.

EXAMPLE

Assume the accepted average bid on three-month bills is $9,850. You gave the government $10,000. To reflect the actual purchase price of $9,850, a "discount" of $150 is paid to you.

The equivalent annual yield on your Treasury bill is figured this way:

1. Find the yield on your investment by dividing discount by purchase price.
2. Convert this yield to the annual rate by multiplying the yield by 4.0110 (365 ÷ 91 days to maturity) if the bill is for three months and by 2.0055 (365 ÷ 182 days to maturity) if the bill is for six months. For example, on a three-month bill your discount is $100 (cost $9,900); the equivalent annual yield is 0.04051:

$$\frac{\$100}{\$9,900} = 0.0101 \text{ and } 0.0101 \times 4.0110 = 0.04051, \text{ or } 4.051\% \text{ per year}$$

Financial pages of the newspapers report the previous day's auction, including the discount rate and what this amounts to as an annual percentage yield.

At maturity. Redemption is automatic at maturity, unless you notify the Federal Reserve Bank that you wish to roll over matured bills into new bills. The Treasury will electronically deposit the face amount of the bill into a savings or checking account you have previously designated. If you bought your bill through a bank, the bank will credit your account on the date the bill matures. To roll over your maturing bill, you follow the same procedures as in buying a new bill and use your matured bill as payment. If you purchase bills directly from the Treasury, a payment for the difference between the price of the new bills and the face value of your matured bills will be transferred electronically to your designated account.

Certificates of deposit. Certificates of deposit (CDs) are another form of short-term investment that offers a high degree of safety and negotiability.

Certificates of deposit represent money lent by investors to a bank for a specified short period of time, generally 30, 60, or 90 days, although certificates of deposit for six months to several years are also available.

Purchasing CDs. Certificates of deposit are generally purchased through your bank or broker. The rate of interest that banks will pay depends on supply and demand in the money market. The interest rate may vary with the size of your investment. For deposits of $100,000 or more, you may be able to get a jumbo CD at a higher rate than offered on smaller deposits.

Before investing, check with the bank for minimum investment requirements, charges, and restrictions on withdrawals, including penalties for withdrawals before maturity.

If you have an account with a broker, you may prefer to invest in CDs through your broker. Brokers offer CDs from various banks throughout the U.S. and can provide at times a higher current rate offered by a bank in an area that is not directly accessible to you.

Repurchase agreements (repos). This investment offered by banks and thrifts allows you to earn high interest rates by sharing in a portion of the bank's portfolio of government securities. The bank is required to repurchase your investment from you at your request. The minimum investment is $1,000; maturities vary, on average, three months. Repos are not FDIC or FSLIC insured, and there is no interest penalty for early repurchase, as long as you hold them for a minimum of a week or more. There may be a small service charge for early repurchase.

Commercial paper. Periodically during the year, many corporations requiring large sums of money to finance short-term customer receivables offer short-term promissory notes at high rates of interest. These notes are generally referred to as commercial paper. Although much of this paper is sold in units of $100,000 or more, commercial paper in denominations of $25,000 and even less is sometimes available.

Finance companies, automobile manufacturers, and large retail stores are types of businesses that typically issue commercial paper for periods ranging from one week to 270 days.

Planning Reminder

Cashing Treasury Bills Before Maturity

If you decide you need funds before the maturity date of your bill, you can sell it through a commercial bank or a securities broker. The Federal Reserve Bank and the Treasury do not handle bills that have not matured.

For bills sold before maturity, current interest rates will determine the amount you receive. The market value of Treasury bills is listed daily in the financial section of newspapers.

Investments in commercial paper may not be as liquid as other short-term paper and are subject to greater risks.

Tax-exempt notes are discussed at *30.18*.

30.15 Investing in Savings Institutions

Bank money-market accounts compete with money-market mutual funds. Bank money-market funds generally guarantee for one-week or one-month periods interest rates tied to the Treasury bill rate or the average money-market rate. Bank funds also offer this added attraction: They are federally insured. Bank money-market accounts require certain average monthly balances and if the account falls below the minimum, the interest rate is reduced.

Investments in money-market accounts allow you to take advantage of rising interest rates, but if market rates decline, so will your return. Investments in CDs allow you to lock into the highest available interest rate for a fixed period of time if you are concerned with a decline of rates during that period.

Withdrawals generally may be made from money-market accounts without penalty, subject to minimum account requirements. Premature withdrawals from CDs are penalized.

CD investments in savings institutions allow you to lock into high interest rates only for the short term, generally up to five years. If you are concerned that rates will substantially decline in the future, you may want to invest in a currently available investment that fixes a high rate over longer periods, such as bonds with long-term maturities. Bond investments are discussed in *30.16*.

As indicated in *30.14*, stockbrokers may offer to their customers issues of CDs from various banks and may allow you to invest at a slightly higher rate than that offered by a local bank.

Investment options vary from bank to bank. Not all banks offer the maximum rates or compound interest in the same manner. Whether interest is compounded daily or annually will affect your rate of return. Each bank also has its own policy on procedures concerning maturity of certificates. Some banks automatically renew the CD for another term at the current rate unless notified to the contrary; some banks will not renew a matured CD without express authority from you. If you fail to act, you may find your funds switched to a day-of-deposit account on maturity. Banking institutions can also change their rules after you have opened an account.

Savings certificates versus Treasury bills. Treasury bills require a minimum $10,000 investment, while certificates keyed to the Treasury bill rate usually require much lower minimums. Treasury bill investments over the minimum must be made in multiples of $1,000; for certificates, additional investments may be made in smaller increments. There is no fee charged for the purchase of certificates, while a fee may be charged to purchase Treasury bills unless purchased directly from the Treasury or a Federal Reserve Bank. Where you do not have the minimum to invest, some institutions may lend the difference at a lower interest rate, typically 1% to 2% over the rate earned on the certificate. Treasury bills have a tax advantage over certificates: interest on savings certificates is subject to state and local income taxes; interest on Treasury bills is exempt from state and local income taxes. Furthermore, there are penalties for redeeming certificates before maturity. *See 4.16* for taxation of interest and for forfeiture of interest on premature withdrawals.

30.16 Investing in Corporate Bonds

When you buy a corporate bond, you are lending money to the issuer of the bonds. You become a creditor of the issuing company. The corporation pledges to pay you interest on specified dates, generally twice a year, and to repay the principal on the date of maturity stated on the bond.

For investment purposes, a bond may be described according to the length of the period of maturity. Short-term bonds usually mature within one to five years, medium-term bonds in five to 20 years, and long-term bonds in 20 or more years.

Where the interest is paid out on a regular schedule, the bond is called a "current income" bond. An accrual or discount bond is a bond on which interest is accumulated and paid as part of the specified maturity value (the bond having been issued at a price lower than the specified maturity value).

Figuring the yield of a bond. The investment value of bonds is generally expressed in rates of yield. There are four types of yield: the nominal or coupon yield; the actual yield; the current market yield; and the net yield to maturity.

The nominal or coupon yield is the fixed or contractual rate of interest stated on the bond. A bond paying 6% has a 6% nominal yield.

The actual yield is the rate of return based on the price at which the bond was purchased. If bought below par, the actual yield will exceed the nominal or coupon yield. If bought at a pre-

 Planning Reminder

Deferring Interest Income

Defer interest income by buying a six-month tax-deferred certificate after June 30. Interest is taxable in the next year when the certificate matures if the terms of the certificate specifically defer the interest to maturity. If your bank offers you the choice of when to receive the interest, deferral is not allowed. You may also defer interest by buying Treasury bills that come due next year.

mium (above par), the actual yield will be less than the coupon or nominal yield. For example, if you paid $850 for a $1,000 bond paying 5% interest, the actual yield is 5.88% ($50 ÷ $850).

The current market yield is the rate of return on the bond if bought at the prevailing market price. It is figured in the same manner as actual yield.

Net yield to maturity represents the rate of return on the bond if it is held to maturity, plus appreciation allocated to a discount purchase or less reductions for any premium paid on a bond selling above par. If you buy a bond below par at a market discount, your annual return is proportionately increased by a part of the discount allocated to the number of years before maturity. If the discount was $50 on a bond with a five-year maturity, then your annual income return on the bond is increased by $10 ($50 ÷ 5). On the other hand, if you bought at a premium, the extra cost is a reduction against your income because you paid more than can be recovered at maturity. This cost is allocated over the remaining life of the bond. Thus, if you bought a five-year bond at $50 over par, your average annual return is reduced by $10 ($50 ÷ 5).

Call privileges may reduce the investment value of the bond. A call privilege gives the issuer a chance to redeem the obligation before maturity if interest rates have declined below the rate fixed by the obligation. A call privilege is a disadvantage to an investor; a favorable investment may be lost at a time the investor may not be able to replace it with another. To take some of the "sting" out of a call provision, the issuer may provide for the payment of a "premium" on the exercise of the call and a minimum period during which the bonds will not be called. The call premium is usually expressed as a percentage of the maturity value, for example, 105%. The amount of the premium varies with the length of the period in which the bond may be called. As the maturity date approaches, the call premium will decrease. Some bonds now carry a guarantee that they will not be called for a specified number of years, such as five or 10 years.

A call privilege generally will not be exercised if the going interest rate remains about the same as, or is higher than, the interest rate of the bond. If interest rates decline below the interest rate of the bond, the bond will probably be called because the issuer can obtain the borrowed money at lower cost elsewhere.

Interest on bearer bonds issued with coupons attached is paid when a bondholder clips the coupon and deposits it for payment. A registered bond carries the name of the owner, who receives his or her interest by mail from the issuing corporation.

Whether a bond is registered or in bearer form has no effect on its investment quality or yield. A coupon-type or bearer bond may be preferred by institutional investors because it can be transferred by hand without registration. However, this advantage must be weighed against the risks of loss through fire, theft, or casualty.

Issuing and trading bonds. New bond issues are generally placed through investment bankers who usually assist in the preparation of the issue. Often an issue may be sold directly by the issuing organization to an institutional investor. Many newly issued bonds are purchased directly from issuers or from their investment bankers by institutional investors before the bonds are offered to individual investors. Issuers prefer this type of placement as it involves less expense than a public offering. Normally, only the new issues (or part of new issues) that cannot be marketed this way are offered to private investors.

Bonds are also traded on the open market where individuals, as well as institutional buyers, may buy or sell them at competitive, market determined prices, through dealers or brokers.

Bond prices fluctuate in response to changes in interest rates and business conditions. In setting the daily price of a bond, the market weighs the current status, performance, and future prospects of the issuing corporation, as well as the interest rate and maturity period of the bond.

Quotations are based on 100 as equal to par, even though the basic unit for an actual bond may be in denominations of $1,000. A quote of 90 ½ simply means a bond with a face value of $1,000 will cost $905 at market.

Calls under sinking fund redemption. A bond may be called in at par under the terms of a sinking fund arrangement. Not all bonds are called and those that are selected are picked by lot. Redemptions for sinking fund purposes account for only a small percentage of a single bond issue. But some issues may retain the right to use a blanket sinking fund under which they may redeem bonds paying interest at their highest rate.

Put privileges. A put privilege is the flipside of a call privilege. It permits the buyer to sell the bonds at par to the issuer after a stated number of years. This feature is valuable to investors in long-term bonds. If interest rates rise, investors are not locked into low yields.

Planning Reminder

Weighing Long-Term Investment

To lock in interest rates, you may invest in a long-term bond. However, you may not want to tie up your capital long term. There is the possibility that a future increase in interest rates may reduce the value of your investment if you should need the principal before maturity.

Current interest rates affect the selling price of bonds so that you may gain or lose on your investment:

1. *If current interest rates increase over the interest rate of your bond, the market value of your bond will decline.* The decline in value has nothing to do with the credit rating of the issue. It simply means that other investors will buy only at terms that will give them the current higher return. If you bought a $1,000 bond paying a rate of 5% at par, and a few months later interest rates go to 6%, another investor will not pay $1,000 for the bond for a 5% return. To match the 6% return on a dollar, the market value of the bond will drop to a level that will return 6% on the money invested, based on its actual 5% return and the period remaining before maturity. Thus, during periods of rising interest rates, the price of bonds issued at lower rates in prior years declines. This can lead to substantial losses. Top-quality bonds are not immune from price declines; the highest credit rating will not protect the market value of a low-interest-paying bond. When this happens there also may be bond bargains, as prices on outstanding bonds decrease.
2. *If interest rates decline below the interest rate of your bond, the value of your bond will increase;* but at the same time, the company, if it has an exercisable call option, may redeem the bond to rid itself of the high interest cost and attempt to raise funds at current lower rates. Thus, an early redemption of the bond could upset your long-range investment plans in that particular issue.

Corporate zero coupon bond. A zero coupon bond is a deep discount obligation issued at considerably less than face value and redeemed at face at a set date. No annual interest is paid. A zero coupon bond allows an investor to lock in a return. He or she knows how much will be received at maturity and so avoids the problem of turning over investments at fluctuating short-term rates. However, zero coupon bonds may be subject to "call" provisions, as previously discussed; an early call would upset your projected return. Brokers have lists of zero coupon bonds; the prices vary with the credit rating of the companies, current market rates, maturity dates, and whether the bond is callable.

Floating rate or variable interest bonds. For investors unwilling to gamble on the future of interest rates, some bonds have been offered with floating interest rates. The rate is updated periodically, but there may be a floor and ceiling limiting the changes. The market price of the bond should remain near par since its interest rate moves with the market. Although this feature is a form of insurance for the investor, it may not be worth its added cost.

30.17 Treasury Bonds, Notes, and U.S. Agency Obligations

The federal government offers the following obligations for investment opportunities. They are guaranteed by the federal government and are exempt from state and local taxes.

Treasury bonds and notes. Treasury bonds have maturity dates in excess of 10 years. The minimum denomination is $1,000. Interest is paid semiannually at a rate that varies with each issue. These bonds may be purchased through a commercial bank or directly from the Federal Reserve Bank.

Treasury notes are similar to Treasury bonds but have shorter maturity dates of from two to 10 years. Minimum investments range from $1,000 to $5,000, depending on the issue. Interest is paid semiannually and interest varies with each issue. Notes are purchased from commercial banks or directly from the Federal Reserve Bank.

Zero coupon Treasury bonds. Certain major brokerage houses have created zero coupon Treasury bonds by stripping the coupons from Treasury bonds and selling the bonds at deep discounts. They have been promoted under such names as TIGRS, LIONS, COUGARS, and CATS as investments suitable for IRAs, retirement plan trusts, and custodian accounts for minors. The U.S. Treasury itself offers its own version of the zero coupon bond under the name STRIPS. The government does not offer STRIPS directly to individual investors, but sells them to banks and brokers who then sell them to the public. Because STRIPS have the direct backing of the U.S. government, they are considered to be the safest zeros and generally yield up to one-tenth of one percent less than brokerage firm or bank created zero coupon bonds, such as TIGRS or CATS. With all zero coupon Treasury obligations, an investor can select a particular maturity date suited to his or her needs, such as the year the investor will start taking IRA distributions or the year a child will start college. For tax reporting rules, *see 30.16* on corporate zero coupon bonds.

Other U.S. obligations, such as savings bonds, are discussed at *30.21* and Treasury bills at *30.14*.

Certain federal agencies, like the Tennessee Valley Authority, offer their own securities. The types of securities offered vary. Such securities must be purchased through brokers or commercial banks.

Caution

Reporting Zero Coupon Bond Discount

Zero coupon bond discount is reported annually as interest over the life of the bond, even though interest is not received. This tax cost tends to make zero coupon bonds unattractive to investors, unless the bonds can be bought for IRA and other retirement plans that defer tax on income until distributions are made.

Zero coupon bonds also may be a means of financing a child's education. A parent buys the bond for the child. The child must report the income, and if the income is not subject to the parent's marginal tax bracket under the "kiddie tax" (Chapter 24), the income subject to tax may be minimal.

The value of zero coupon bonds fluctuates sharply with interest rate changes. This fact should be considered before investing in long-term zero coupon bonds. If you sell zero coupon bonds before the maturity term at a time when interest rates rise, you may lose part of your investment.

Planning Reminder

Electronic Deposit

Treasury notes and bonds are issued in book-entry form only; you do not receive a certificate. Under a direct deposit system, semiannual interest and principal at maturity is electronically deposited in a bank account that you designate.

Federally chartered companies, such as the Government National Mortgage Association ("Ginnie Mae") and the Federal National Mortgage Association ("Fannie Mae"), authorize certain firms and institutions to issue securities based on insured mortgages. While interest on these securities is generally not exempt from state and local taxes, they offer the investor a higher yield than Treasury securities. Some of these obligations carry a U.S. government full faith and credit guarantee; some have only an implied guarantee; and some no backing from the federal government, but risk is generally considered to be negligible.

Ginnie Maes are offered in minimum denominations of $25,000. Monthly payments to security holders include not only interest, but also a return of principal. Rather than buying Ginnie Maes in the open market, you may consider investing in a mutual fund or trust that has a portfolio of such securities. Minimum investment units typically begin at $1,000.

30.18 Investing in Tax-Exempts

Interest on state and local obligations is not subject to federal income tax. It is also exempt from the tax of the state in which the obligations are issued. In comparing the interest return of a tax-exempt with that of a taxable bond, you figure the taxable return that is equivalent to the tax-free yield of the tax-exempt. This amount depends on your tax bracket. For example, a municipal bond of $5,000 yielding 4% is the equivalent of a taxable yield of 5.55% subject to the tax rate of 28%.

You can compare the value of tax-exempt interest to taxable interest for your tax bracket by using this formula:

$$\frac{\text{Tax-exempt return}}{\text{1 minus your tax bracket}}$$

The denominator of the above fraction is:

0.85 if your tax bracket is 15%
0.72 if your tax bracket is 28%
0.69 if your tax bracket is 31%
0.64 if your tax bracket is 36%
0.604 if your tax bracket is 39.6%

EXAMPLE

You are deciding between a tax-exempt bond and a taxable bond. You want to find which will give you more income after taxes. You have a choice between a tax-exempt bond paying 4% and a taxable bond paying 5.25%. Your tax bracket is 28%.

You find that the tax-exempt bond is a better buy in your tax bracket as it is the equivalent of a taxable bond paying 5.55%.

$$T = \frac{0.04}{0.72\,(1.00 - 0.28)}$$

T = .0555, or 5.55%

The following table shows the amount a taxable bond would have to earn to equal the tax-exempt bond, according to the investor's income tax bracket.

A tax-exempt yield of—*

If top income tax rate is—	3%	4%	5%	6%	7%	8%
Is the equivalent of these taxable yields:						
28%	4.2	5.5	6.9	8.3	9.7	11.1
31%	4.3	5.8	7.2	8.7	10.1	11.6
36%	4.7	6.3	7.8	9.4	10.9	12.5
39.6%	5.0	6.6	8.3	9.9	11.6	13.2

Exemption from the tax of the state issuing the bond will increase the yield.

Ratings of tax-exempt bonds. As in the case of commercial bonds, tax-exempt issues are rated by services such as Standard & Poor's and Moody's. In rating a bond, the services will consider the size of the issuer, the amount of its outstanding debt, its past record in paying off prior debts, whether it has competent officials and a balanced budget, its tax assessment and collection record, and whether the community is dominated by a single industry that might be subject to economic change. Generally, an issuer with a good credit rating will offer lower interest rates than one plagued with revenue deficits or similar problems. A basic test is the sufficiency of tax yields or revenues even in times of economic stress.

General obligation bonds will normally be rated higher than revenue bonds because they have the support of the taxing power of the community. Revenue bonds (backed by the revenue of the issuer) may receive high ratings once a capacity to produce earnings is shown.

Purchase and trading of tax-exempts. Tax-exempt municipals are traded over the counter and are generally handled through a firm specializing in this field or having a department for municipals. Prices quoted represent a percentage of par. For example, a par value $5,000 bond quoted at 90 is selling for $4,500 (90% of $5,000); a par value $1,000 bond quoted at 90 is selling for $900 (90% of $1,000). It may not pay to buy tax-exempts unless you intend to hold them to maturity because the additional cost of selling a small order might be as much as a year's interest.

The bid and asked prices of tax-exempt bonds are generally not quoted in the daily newspapers, although some brokerage houses that specialize in them do print such prices. As in the general bond market, an offer of unusually high interest compared with the average bond rates may be an indication that the bonds are riskier than others.

The market for tax-exempts is not as large as the market for stock. This poses a risk if you ever need ready cash and are forced to sell a tax-exempt bond at a discount. If you are concerned with liquidity, restrict your investments to major general obligation bonds of state governments and revenue bonds of major authorities.

You may also invest in tax-free money-market mutual funds. These provide ready liquidity and protect the value of your principal by maintaining a $1 value per share. The tax-exempt yield is generally lower than from a municipal bond fund.

Tax-exempt notes. Although generally bought by banks and large corporations, short-term tax-exempt notes may be available to individuals. The majority of the notes are offered in face amounts of $25,000 and up, but sometimes in denominations of $5,000 and $10,000. They are issued by states and municipalities to tide them over until expected revenues are received or until longer-term money can be raised through an issue of long-term bonds. Where rising interest rates have made the cost of long-term issues high, a government authority may postpone a long-term offering and try to fill the gap with short-term notes. The interest rates on tax-exempt notes may be higher than on tax-exempt bonds if the authority is willing to pay the extra interest for the short term in the expectation that a future long-term offering may be placed at lower rates.

Interest on these short-term notes is exempt from federal tax. Many of the notes are from housing authorities and issued to pay construction costs on projects for which bonds will eventually be issued. Housing notes are guaranteed by the FHA and, because of their safety, their yields are lower than those of more speculative paper.

Tax law restrictions. Most municipal bonds that are issued before July 1, 1983, except for housing issues, are in the form of bearer bonds; the owners are not identified, and interest coupons are cashed as they come due. However, state and municipal bonds issued after June 30, 1983, with a maturity of more than one year, as well as obligations of the federal government and its agencies, are in registered form. Principal and interest are transferable only through an entry on the books of the issuer.

In buying state or local bonds, check the prospectus for the issue date and tax status of the bond. The tax law treats bonds issued after August 7, 1986, as follows:

1. "Public-purpose" bonds. These include bonds issued directly by state or local governments or their agencies to meet essential government functions, such as highway construction and school financing. These bonds are generally tax exempt.
2. "Qualified private activity" bonds. These include bonds issued to finance housing and student loans. There are limits on the amount of qualifying private activity bonds an authority may issue. Interest on qualifying bonds issued after August 7, 1986 (or after August 31, 1986, for certain bonds), is tax free for regular income tax purposes, but is a preference item to be added to taxable income if you are subject to alternative minimum tax. Because of the AMT, a nongovernment-purpose bond may pay slightly more interest than public-purpose bonds. These may be a good investment if you are not subject to AMT tax or if your AMT liability is not substantial. Your broker can help you identify such bonds.

Planning Reminder

Mutual Bond Funds

Instead of purchasing tax-exempts directly, you may consider investing in municipal bond funds. The funds invest in various municipal bonds and, thus, offer the safety of diversity. The value of fund shares will fluctuate with the bond markets. Also, an investment in the fund may be as small as $1,000 compared with the typical $5,000 municipal bond. Check on fees and other restrictions in municipal bond funds.

Filing Instruction

Interest Subject to AMT

Interest on qualified private activity bonds issued after August 7, 1986, is tax free for regular tax purposes but is a tax preference item for alternative minimum tax (AMT) purposes; *see* Chapter 23.

3. "Taxable" municipals. These are bonds issued for nonqualifying private purposes. They are subject to federal income tax, but may be exempt from state and local taxes in the states in which they are issued. Generally, bonds issued after August 15, 1986, are subject to this rule.

30.19 Investing in Unit Investment Trusts

A unit investment trust is a closed-end unmanaged portfolio of bonds marketed by investment houses. Yield is fixed for the life of the trust with interest payable semiannually or more frequently. As bonds in the portfolio mature, a unit holder receives a repayment of principal. Unit trusts provide investors with the possibility of locking into high yields for the long term. However, a trust has this disadvantage: If principal is needed before the end of the trust term, an investor may sacrifice substantial amounts of principal if interest rates rise or if the general investment market is shying away from long-term investments; even where the trust may offer a current return equal to market value, its price may be depressed because there may be few investors willing to take the risk of tying up their funds in long-term investments. Despite these drawbacks, the performance of unit trusts has been rated higher than that of similar mutual funds.

Unit trusts hold varying types of debt instruments. Tax-exempt municipal bond trusts, made up of tax-exempt obligations, are generally favored by investors in the top tax brackets. Taxable unit trusts hold investments such as corporate bonds, bank certificates of deposit, and Treasury obligations. Usually, units are offered in denominations of $1,000. An investor pays a front-end sales charge, but no management fee as there is no need for management once a unit trust is closed.

Maturities of the various trusts range as follows: The short-term, tax-exempt average is three years; intermediate, six to 12 years; and long-term, 18 to 30 years. An average for corporate intermediate is six years, with 25 years for long-term.

30.20 Ordinary Loss for Small Business Stock (Section 1244)

Shareholders of qualifying "small" corporations may claim within limits an ordinary loss, rather than a capital loss, on the sale or worthlessness of Section 1244 stock. An ordinary loss up to $50,000, or $100,000 on a joint return, may be claimed on Form 4797. On a joint return, the $100,000 limit applies even if only one spouse has a Section 1244 loss. Losses in excess of these limits are deductible as capital losses. Any gains on Section 1244 stock are reported as capital gain on Schedule D.

An ordinary loss may be claimed only by the original owner of the stock. If a partnership sells Section 1244 stock at a loss, an ordinary loss deduction may be claimed by individuals who were partners when the stock was issued. If a partnership distributes the Section 1244 stock to the partners, the partners may not claim an ordinary loss on their disposition of the stock.

If an S corporation sells Section 1244 stock at a loss, S corporation shareholders may not claim an ordinary loss deduction. The IRS with Tax Court approval limits shareholders' deductions to capital losses (which are deductible only against capital gains plus $3,000 ($1,500 if married filing separately); *see 5.4*).

To qualify as Section 1244 stock:

1. The corporation's equity may not exceed $1,000,000 at the time the stock is issued, including amounts received for the stock to be issued. Thus, if the corporation already has $600,000 equity from stock previously issued, it may not issue more than $400,000 worth of additional stock.

    If the $1,000,000 equity limit is exceeded, the corporation follows an IRS procedure for designating which shares qualify as Section 1244 stock.

    Preferred stock issued after July 18, 1984, may qualify for Section 1244 loss treatment, as well as common stock.

2. The stock must be issued for money or property (other than stock and securities).

3. The corporation for the five years preceding your loss must generally have derived more than half of its gross receipts from business operations and not from passive income such as rents, royalties, dividends, interest, annuities, or gains from the sales or exchanges of stock or securities. The five-year requirement is waived if the corporation's deductions (other than for dividends received or net operating losses) exceed gross income. If the corporation has not been in existence for the five years before your loss, then generally the period for which the corporation has been in existence is examined for the gross receipts test.

Failure to keep these records will be grounds for disallowing a loss that is claimed on Section 1244 stock.

Planning Reminder

Record-Keeping for Section 1244 Stock

You must keep records that distinguish between Section 1244 stock and other stock interests. Your records must show that the corporation qualified as a small business corporation when the stock was issued, you are the original holder of the Section 1244 stock, and it was issued for money or property. Stock issued for services does not qualify. In addition, the records should also show the amount paid for the stock, information relating to any property transferred for the stock, any tax-free stock dividends issued on the stock, and the corporation's gross receipts data for the most recent five-year period.

30.21 Savings Bond Plans

Savings bond purchases give you an opportunity to defer tax; *see 4.28*. EE bonds can be purchased for one-half the face value (ranging from $50 to a maximum of $10,000).

EE bonds issued on or after May 1, 1997, earn interest at rates tied to Treasury securities immediately from the date of purchase through the next 30 years until the bond matures. Interest earned is 90% of the average market yield on five-year Treasury securities for the preceding six months. Interest is earned monthly, and compounded semiannually. Because the interest rates are dependent upon a variable market rate that changes every six months, there is no way to predict when a bond will reach its face value. While a bond earning an average of 5% would reach face value in 14 ½ years and a bond earning 6% would reach face value in 12 years, in the unlikely event that a bond does not reach face value by the time it is 17 years old, the Treasury will make a one-time adjustment to increase the bond's value to face value at that time.

EE bonds issued on or after May 1, 1997, can be redeemed any time after six months from the date of issue, but bonds cashed in any time before five years are subject to a three-month interest penalty; *see* the Example below.

EXAMPLE

You purchased series EE bonds on May 1, 1998. If you cash them 24 months later, in May 2000, you get your original investment back plus 21 months of interest (instead of 24 months of interest) because of the three-month penalty for redemptions within the first five years of ownership.

EE bonds issued after April 30, 1995, but before May 1, 1997, earn interest at rates tied to Treasury Securities from the date of purchase through original maturity in 17 years. For the first five years they earn a rate (set each May 1 and November 1) that is equal to 85% of the average six-month Treasury bill rate for the preceding three-month period. From five years through 17 years, the rate is 85% of the average yield on five-year Treasury securities during the preceding six-month period.

EE bonds issued before May 1, 1995, earn a guaranteed minimum rate, and if held at least five years, a rate tied to Treasury securities if that is greater than the minimum rate.

Deferring tax on savings bond interest. Unless you report the interest annually, Series E and EE bond interest is deferred *(4.29)* until the year you redeem the bond or it reaches final maturity. When you redeem the bond, the accumulated interest is taxable on your federal return but *not* taxable on your state and local income tax return. If in the year of redemption you use the proceeds to pay for higher education or vocational school costs, the accumulated interest may be tax free for federal tax purposes; *see* Chapter 38.

Interest accrual dates for Series E and Series EE savings bonds. Interest on Series E bonds accrues twice a year. The months of accrual depend on the issue date of the bond, as shown in the chart at the end of this chapter. When you cash a bond, you receive the value of the bond as of the last date that interest was added. If you cash a bond in between accrual months, you will not receive interest for the partial period. For example, if interest accrues in February and August, and you cash a bond in during July, you would earn interest only through February.

A similar twice-a-year accrual rule applies to certain Series EE bonds. *See* the chart at the end of this chapter.

Final maturity for savings bonds. Do not neglect the final maturity date for older bonds. After the final maturity date, no further interest will accrue. For example, Series E savings bonds issued in 1959 matured in 1999 and will not earn further interest. E bonds issued in 1969 also reached final maturity in 1999. E bonds issued in 1960 and in 1970 will reach final maturity in 2000. If you have bonds that are maturing and have deferred the reporting of interest, you may continue the deferral by exchanging the matured bonds for HH bonds. HH bonds are available in multiples of $500 and pay taxable interest semiannually. If the exchange is made, and you choose to continue the deferral, the interest on the E bonds will not be taxed until the HH bonds are cashed or reach maturity. HH bonds mature in 20 years. The exchange may be made within one year after the E bond reaches final maturity.

 Caution

Timing Bond Redemptions

In the year you cash in a savings bond you could lose interest by cashing it in too soon. Interest accrues only twice a year on E bonds. Interest also accrues twice a year on EE bonds issued prior to March 1, 1993, bonds issued from May 1995 through April 1997 and bonds issued from March 1993 through April 1995 that are more than five years old. Bonds issued at different times have different accrual months. If you cash your bonds before the accrual month that applies to your bond, you will lose interest. For a list of interest accrual dates, *see* the chart at the end of this chapter.

Bond	Issue Date	Final Maturity
Series E	May 1941–November 1965	40 years after issue
	December 1965–June 1980	30 years after issue
Series EE	January 1980 or later	30 years after issue
Savings notes (Freedom Shares)	May 1967–October 1970	30 years after issue
H bonds	February 1957–December 1979	30 years after issue

Accrual dates for Series HH bonds. Taxable interest on HH bonds obtained in exchange for savings bonds or savings notes accrues semiannually at a fixed rate. A fixed interest rate applies for the first 10 years you hold an HH bond and the rate is then reset. For HH bonds issued or entering an extended maturity period after February 1993, the rate is 4%. Interest on HH bonds issued before March 1, 1993, will retain their guaranteed minimum rate until they reach original maturity. Interest accrues on HH bonds until final maturity 20 years from the date of issue.

Accrual dates for Series H bonds. These bonds were available before 1980. They were bought at face value and pay semiannual interest that is taxable when received. If you own Series H bonds purchased through the exchange of Series E bonds, *see 4.28* for reporting interest. Final maturity for H bonds is 30 years from original issue.

30.22 Savings Bonds Indexed for Inflation

You may invest in Treasury "I Bonds," which provide a return that rises and falls with inflation. I Bonds are issued at face value in amounts of $50, $75, $100, $200, $500, $1,000, $5,000, and $10,000. You may buy up to $30,000 of I Bonds in any calendar year. I Bonds may be purchased from most banks, credit unions, or savings institutions. They earn interest for 30 years. Interest is added to a bond monthly and paid when the bond is redeemed.

You forfeit three months of interest if an I Bond is redeemed within the first five years. I Bonds are not redeemable within the first six months.

Rates. Interest on an I Bond is determined by two rates. One rate, set by the Treasury Department, remains constant for the life of the bond. The second rate is a variable inflation rate announced each May and November by the Treasury Department to reflect changes reported by the Bureau of Labor Statistics in the Consumer Price Index. If deflation sets in, a decline in the Consumer Price Index does not reduce the redemption value of the bond, even if the deflation rate exceeds the fixed rate.

Income tax reporting. Tax reporting for I Bonds is similar to reporting on EE bonds, as explained in *30.21*. Investors may defer paying federal income taxes on I Bond interest, which is automatically reinvested and added to the principal. Deferral applies to the fixed rate interest as well as the variable inflation rate interest. You may defer federal tax on the interest until you redeem the bond or the bond reaches maturity in thirty years. You may report the interest each year as it accrues instead of deferring the interest. I Bond interest is exempt from state and local income taxes.

If an I Bond is redeemed to pay for college tuition or other college fees, all or part of the interest may be excludable from income under the rules of *38.4*.

 Planning Reminder

Treasury Inflation-Indexed Bonds
The Treasury also offers five-year, 10-year, and 30-year inflation-indexed bonds. They pay interest semiannually. The interest is subject to federal income tax when received, and the inflation adjustment to principal is also taxable in the year the adjustment is made. This contrasts with the new inflation-indexed savings bonds (I Bonds), that allow deferral of federal tax on the interest until the bond is redeemed or maturity is reached in 30 years.

Accrual Dates for Series E and EE Bonds

Issue Date—	Accrual Months—	Example—
February 1957– May 1959 E Bonds	These bonds reached final maturity 40 years after issue and stopped earning interest at that time.*	
June 1959– November 1965 E Bonds	Third month after issue month *and* ninth month after issue month. Bonds reach final maturity 40 years after issue.*	If you have a bond issued in September 1964, interest accrues every December (three months after the September issue month) and every June (nine months after the September issue month).
December 1965– May 1969 E Bonds	These bonds reached final maturity 30 years after issue and stopped earning interest at that time.*	
June 1969– November 1973 E Bonds	Fourth month after issue month *and* tenth month after issue month. Bonds reach final maturity 30 years after issue.*	If you have a bond issued in July 1971, interest accrues every November (four months after the July issue month) and every May (10 months after the July issue month).
December 1973– June 1980 E Bonds	Sixth month after issue month *and* original issue month. Bonds reach final maturity 30 years after issue.*	If you have a bond issued in May 1979, interest accrues every November (six months after the May issue month) and every May (month of original issue).
January 1980– February 1993 EE Bonds	Sixth month after issue month *and* original issue month. Bonds reach final maturity 30 years after issue.*	If you have a bond issued in June 1990, interest accrues every December (six months after the June issue month) and every June (month of original issue).
March 1993– April 1995 EE Bonds	Interest is credited on the first day of every month for the first five years, then semiannually, unless monthly increases are needed to guarantee a 4% return. Bonds reach final maturity 30 years after issue.*	
May 1995– April 1997 EE Bonds	Sixth month after issue month *and* original issue month. Bonds reach final maturity 30 years after issue.*	If you have a bond issued in August 1995, interest accrues every February (six months after the August issue month) and every August (month of original issue).
On or after May 1, 1997 EE Bonds	Interest is credited on the first day of the month. A three-month interest penalty is imposed if the bond is redeemed before five years. Bonds reach final maturity 30 years after issue.*	

Last interest accrual on final maturity date.

Chapter 31

Tax Savings for Investors in Real Estate

Real estate investors may take advantage of the following tax benefits:

- Sale of investment property may be taxed at capital gain rates.
- Depreciation can provide a source of temporary tax-free income; *see 31.1*.
- Rental income can be used to offset passive losses; *see* Chapter 10.
- Tax-free exchanges make it possible to defer tax on exchanges of real estate held for investment; *see 31.3*.

Losses on real estate transactions may be subject to the following disadvantages:

- Rental losses may not be deductible from other income such as salary interest and dividends unless you qualify as a real estate professional or for the special $25,000 rental loss allowance; *see* Chapter 10.
- Compromises of mortgage liability may subject you to tax; *see 31.10*.

Real Estate Investments

Foreclosures and Abandonments of Mortgaged Property

Real Estate Investments

31.1 Investing in Real Estate Ventures

A real estate investment should provide a current income return and an appreciation in the value of the original investment. As an additional incentive, a real estate investment may in the early years of the investment return income subject to little or no tax. That may happen when depreciation and other expense deductions reduce taxable income without reducing the amount of cash available for distribution. This tax savings is temporary and limited by the terms and the amount of the mortgage debt on the property. Payments allocated to amortization of mortgage principal reduce the amount of cash available to investors without an offsetting tax deduction. Thus, the amount of tax-free return depends on the extent to which depreciation deductions exceed the amortization payments.

To provide a higher return of tax-free income, at least during the early years of its operations, a venture must obtain a constant payment mortgage that provides for the payment of fixed annual amounts that are allocated to continually decreasing amounts of interest and increasing amounts of amortization payments. Consequently, in the early years, a tax-free return of income is high while the amortization payments are low, but as the amortization payments increase, nontaxable income decreases. When this tax-free return has been substantially reduced, a partnership must refinance the mortgage to reduce the amortization payments and once again increase the tax-free return; *see* Examples 1 and 2 below.

The tax-free return is based on the assumption that the building does not actually depreciate at as fast a rate as the tax depreciation rate. If the building is depreciating physically at a faster rate, the so-called tax-free return on investment does not exist. Distributions to investors (over and above current income return) that are labeled tax-free distributions are, in fact, a return of the investor's own capital.

 Caution

Management Fees

The promoter may be taking a real estate commission by having a commission paid to a company that he or she controls. A reliable promoter should disclose this fact and be willing to collect the commission only after the investors have recovered their capital. Also check the reasonableness of prepaid management fees and loan fees and whether or not the sale of property to the syndicate is from a corporation in which the syndicator has an interest. If there is such a sale, check its terms, price, interest rates, and whether there is any prepaid interest that may conceal a cash profit payout to the syndicator.

EXAMPLES

1. A limited partnership of 100 investors owns a building that returns an annual income of $100,000 after a deduction of operating expenses, but before a depreciation deduction of $80,000. Thus, taxable income is $20,000 ($100,000 – $80,000). Assuming that there is no mortgage on the building, all of the $100,000 is available for distribution. (Since the depreciation requires no cash outlay, it does not reduce the cash available for distribution.) Each investor receives $1,000. Taxable income being $20,000, only 20% ($20,000 ÷ $100,000) of the distribution is taxable. Thus, each investor reports as income only $200 of his or her $1,000 distribution; $800 is tax free.

2. Same facts as in Example 1, except that the building is mortgaged, and an annual amortization payment of $40,000 is being made. Consequently, only $60,000 is available for distribution, of which $20,000 is taxable. Each investor receives $600, of which $\frac{1}{3}$ ($20,000 ÷ $60,000), or $200, is taxed, and $400 is tax free. In other words, the $60,000 distribution is tax free to the extent that the depreciation deduction of $80,000 exceeds the amortization of $40,000—namely $40,000. If the amortization payment were increased to $50,000, only $30,000 of the distribution would be tax free ($80,000 – $50,000).

Reviewing an investment offering. Consider the following pointers in reviewing an offering:

1. If the venture is constructing a development, discount projected income that may be eroded by increasing construction costs caused by inflation, material shortages, and labor disputes. Escalating costs not accounted for in long-term construction can jeopardize the project or income prospects. Adequate cash reserves should be available for emergencies.
2. Check the market conditions. Has there been overconstruction in the area? Is the area changing socially and economically?
3. Check the fees of managers. See that they are reasonable for your area. A promoter may conceal the amount of money he or she is drawing from the project.
4. Check the experience and reliability of the manager.

Real estate investment trusts (REITs). The tax treatment of real estate investment trusts resembles that of open-end mutual funds. Distributions generally are taxed to the investors in the trust as dividend income. Distributed long-term capital gains are reported by the investors as long-term gains; also *see 4.4.* If the trust operates at a loss, the loss may not be passed on to the investors.

REMICs. A real estate mortgage investment company (REMIC) holds a fixed pool of mortgages. Investors are treated as holding a regular or residual interest. A REMIC is not a taxable entity for federal income tax purposes. It is generally treated as a partnership, with the residual interest holders as partners.

Investors with regular REMIC interests are treated as holding debt obligations. Interest income is reported on Form 1099-INT and original issue discount (OID) on Form 1099-OID.

The net income of the REMIC, after payments to regular interest holders, is passed through to the holders of residual interests. On Schedule E, residual holders report the income or loss reported to them by the REMIC on Schedule Q of Form 1066.

31.2 Sales of Subdivided Land—Dealer or Investor?

An investor faces a degree of uncertainty in determining the tax treatment of sales of subdivided realty. In some situations, investor status may be preferred, and in others, dealer status.

Capital gain on sale. Investor status allows capital gain treatment. Capital losses may offset the gains. For capital gain, an investor generally has to show that his or her activities were not those of a dealer but were steps taken in a liquidation of the investment. To convince an IRS agent or a court of investment activity, this type of evidence may present a favorable argument for capital gain treatment:

- The property was bought as an investment, to build a residence, or received as a gift or inheritance.
- No substantial improvements were added to the tract.
- The property was subdivided to liquidate the investment.
- Sales came through unsolicited offers. There was no advertising or agents.
- Sales were infrequent.
- There were no previous activities as a real estate dealer.
- The seller was in a business unrelated to real estate.
- The property was held for a long period of time.
- Sales proceeds were invested in other investment property.

Section 1237 capital gain opportunity. Section 1237 is a limited tax provision that provides a capital gain opportunity for subdivided lots only if arbitrary holding period rules and restrictions on substantial improvements are complied with. For example, the lots must generally be held at least five years before sale unless they were inherited. If the lots were previously held for sale to customers, or if other lots are so held in the year of sale, Section 1237 does not apply. Furthermore, substantial improvements must not have been made to the lots. According to the IRS, a disqualifying substantial improvement is one that increases the value of the property by more than 10%. The IRS considers buildings, hard surface roads, or utilities, such as sewers, water, gas, or electric lines, as substantial improvements.

Interest expense deductions. The distinction between an investor in land and a dealer is also important in the case of interest expenses. Dealer status is preferable here. Interest expenses incurred by an investor are subject to investment interest deduction limitations; *see* Chapter 15. On the other hand, interest expenses of a dealer in the course of business activities are fully deductible; *see* the Morley Example below.

Planning Reminder

Installment Sales

The distinction between an investor and dealer is significant if land is sold on the installment basis. Investor status is preferable if you want to elect the installment method. Dealers may not elect installment sale treatment; *see 5.21.*

> **EXAMPLE**
>
> Morley was interested in buying farm acreage to resell at a profit. Two and a half million dollars was set as the purchase price. To swing the deal, Morley borrowed $600,000. A short time later, his attempts to resell the property failed, and he allowed the property to be foreclosed. While he held the property he incurred interest costs of over $400,000, which he deducted. The IRS held the interest was not fully deductible. It claimed the interest was investment interest subject to investment interest restrictions. That is, the debt was incurred to purchase and carry investment property. The IRS position was based on the so-called "one-bite" rule, which holds that a taxpayer who engages in only one venture may not under any circumstances be held to be in a business as to that venture. Morley argued that he bought the property not as an investment property but as business property for immediate resale.
>
> The Tax Court sided with Morley, holding that he held the acreage as ordinary business property. The court rejected the "one-bite" rule. The fact that he had not previously sold business property did not mean that he could not prove that he held acreage for resale. Here, he intended promptly to resell it, and the facts supported his intention.

Passive activity. Income from sales of lots is not considered passive activity income. Thus, losses from sales of land may offset salary and other investment income. If you hold rental property and also sell land, make sure that your accounts distinguish between and separate each type of income. This way income and losses from land sales will not be commingled with rent income subject to the passive activity restrictions discussed in Chapter 10. Your activity in real property development counts towards qualifying you as a real estate professional who may deduct rental losses from nonpassive income if material participation tests are met; *see 10.3*.

31.3 Exchanging Real Estate Without Tax

You may trade real estate held for investment for other investment real estate and incur no immediate tax. The potential tax on the gain is postponed to the time you sell the new property for more than your basis. A tax-free exchange may also defer a potential tax due on gain from depreciation recapture and might be considered where the depreciable basis of a building has been substantially written off. Here, the building may be exchanged for other property that will give larger tax deductions.

Fully tax-free exchanges. To transact a fully tax-free exchange, you must satisfy these conditions:

- The property traded must be solely for property of a "like kind." The words *like kind* are liberally interpreted. They refer to the nature or character of the property, not its grade, quality, or use. Some examples of like-kind exchanges are: farm or ranch for city property; unimproved land for improved real estate; rental house for a store building; and fee in business property for 30-year or more leasehold in the same type of property; *see 6.1*. You may not make a tax-free exchange of U.S. real estate for real estate in foreign countries.
- The property exchanged must have been held for productive use in your business or for investment and traded for property to be held for productive use in business or investment. Therefore, trades of property used, or to be used, for personal purposes, such as exchanging a residence for rental property, cannot receive tax-free treatment. Special rules, however, apply when you trade your residence for another home; *see* Chapter 29.
- The trade must generally occur within a 180-day period, and property identification must occur within 45 days of the first transfer; *see 6.4* for further details of this test.

A real estate dealer cannot transact a tax-free exchange of property held for sale to customers. Also, an exchange is not tax free if the property received is held for immediate resale.

Tax-free exchanges between related parties are subject to tax if either party disposes of the exchanged property within a two-year period; *see 6.5*.

Disadvantage of tax-free exchange. Although the postponement of tax from a tax-free exchange is equivalent to an interest-free loan from the government equal to the amount you would have owed in taxes had you sold the property, this tax advantage is offset by a disadvantage in the case of an exchange of depreciable real estate. You must carry over the basis of the old property to the new property; *see* the following Example.

Planning Reminder

Exchanging a Building for Land
A tax-free exchange may be advantageous in the case of land. Land is not depreciable, but it may be exchanged for a depreciable rental building. The exchange is tax free and depreciation may be claimed on the building. However, be aware of a possible tax trap if you exchange rental property for land and the building was subject to depreciation recapture: The recapture provisions override the tax-free exchange rules. The "recapture element" will be taxable as ordinary income.

EXAMPLE

You have property with a basis of $25,000, now valued at $50,000, that you exchange for another property worth $50,000. Your basis for depreciation for the new property is $25,000.

If—instead of making an exchange—you sell the old property and use the proceeds to buy similarly valued property, the tax basis for depreciation would be $50,000, giving you larger deductions than you would get in the exchange transaction. If increased depreciation deductions are desirable, then it may pay to sell the property and purchase new property. Tax may be spread by transacting an installment sale. Project the tax consequences of a sale and an exchange and choose the one giving the greater overall tax benefits. You may find it preferable to sell the property and purchase new property on which MACRS may be claimed.

Partially tax-free exchanges. Not all property exchanges are tax free. To be completely tax-free, the exchange must be solely an exchange of like-kind properties. If you receive "boot," such as cash or property that is not of like kind, gain is taxed up to the amount of the boot.

If you trade mortgaged property, the mortgage released is treated as boot; *see 6.3*. When there are mortgages on both properties, the mortgages are netted. The party giving up the larger mortgage and getting the smaller mortgage treats the excess as boot. *See* the Example below and also the Example in *6.3*, which illustrates how to report an exchange on Form 8824.

If the amount of boot exceeds your actual gain, the entire gain is taxed; taxable boot cannot exceed the amount of your gain.

EXAMPLE

You own a small office building with a fair market value of $170,000, and an adjusted basis of $150,000. There is a $130,000 mortgage on the building. You exchange it for Low's building valued at $155,000, having a $120,000 mortgage, and for $5,000 in cash. You compute your gain in this way:

What you received		
Present value of Low's property		$155,000
Cash		5,000
Mortgage on building traded		130,000
Total received		$290,000
Less:		
Adjusted basis of building traded	$150,000	
Mortgage assumed by you	120,000	270,000
Actual gain on the exchange		$20,000

However, your actual gain of $20,000 is taxed only up to the amount of boot, $15,000.

Figuring boot		
Cash received		$5,000
Mortgage on building traded	$130,000	
Less: Mortgage assumed on Low's property	120,000	10,000
Gain taxed to the extent of boot		$15,000

Planning Reminder

Loss Deduction

A tax-free exchange is not desirable if the transaction will result in a loss, since you may not deduct a loss in a tax-free exchange. To ensure the loss deduction, first sell the property and then buy new property with the proceeds.

31.4 Timing Your Real Property Sales

Generally, a taxable transaction occurs in the year in which title or possession to property passes to the buyer. By controlling the year title and possession pass, you may select the year in which to report profit or loss. For example, you intend to sell property this year, but you estimate that reporting the sale next year will incur less in taxes. You can postpone the transfer of title and possession to next year. Alternatively, you can transact an installment sale, giving title and possession this year but delaying the receipt of all or most of the sale proceeds until next year; *see 5.21*.

31.5 Cancellation of a Lease

Payments received by the tenant on the cancellation of a business lease held long term are treated as proceeds received in a Section 1231 transaction; *see 44.8*. Payments received by the tenant on cancellation of a lease on a personal residence or apartment are treated as proceeds of a capital asset transaction. Gain is long-term capital gain if the lease was held long term; losses are not deductible.

Payments received by a landlord from a tenant for cancelling a lease or modifying lease terms are reported as rental income when received; *see 9.1*.

Cancellation of a distributor's agreement is treated as a sale if you made a substantial capital investment in the distributorship. For example, you own facilities for storage, transporting, processing, or dealing with the physical product covered by the franchise. If you have an office mainly for clerical work, or where you handle just a small part of the goods covered by the franchise, the cancellation is not treated as a sale. Your gain or loss is ordinary income or loss. If the cancellation is treated as a sale, the sale is subject to Section 1231 treatment; *see 44.8*.

31.6 Sale of an Option

The tax treatment of the sale of an option depends on the tax classification of the property to which the option relates.

If the option is for the purchase of property that would be a capital asset in your hands, profit on the sale of the option is treated as capital gain. A loss is treated as a capital loss if the property subject to the option was investment property; if the property was personal property, the loss is not deductible. Whether the gain or loss is long term or short term depends on your holding period.

EXAMPLES
1. You pay $500 for an option to purchase a house. After holding the option for five months, you sell the option for $750. Your profit of $250 is short-term capital gain.
2. The same facts as in Example 1 above, except that you sell the option for $300. The loss is not deductible because the option is related to a sale of a personal residence.

If the option is for a "Section 1231 asset" *(44.8)*, gain or loss on the sale of the option is combined with other Section 1231 asset transactions to determine if there is capital gain or ordinary loss.

If the option relates to an ordinary income asset in your hands, then gain or loss would be ordinary income or loss.

If you fail to exercise an option and allow it to lapse, the option is considered to have been sold on the expiration date. Gain or loss is computed according to the rules just discussed.

The party granting the option realizes ordinary income on its expiration, regardless of the nature of the underlying property. If the option is exercised, the option payment is added to the selling price of the property when figuring gain or loss.

31.7 Granting of an Easement

Granting an easement presents a practical problem of determining whether all or part of the basis of the property is allocable to the easement proceeds. This requires an opinion as to whether the easement affects the entire property or just a part of the property. There is no hard and fast rule to determine whether an easement affects all or part of the property. The issue is factual. For example, an easement for electric lines will generally affect only the area over which the lines are suspended and for which the right of way is granted. In such a case, an allocation may be required; *see* Example 1 below. If the entire property is affected, no allocation is required and the proceeds reduce the basis of the property. If only part of the property is affected, then the proceeds are applied to the cost allocated to the area affected by the easement. If the proceeds exceed the amount allocated to basis, a gain is realized. Capital gain treatment generally applies to grants of easements. The granting of a perpetual easement that requires you to give up all or substantially all of a beneficial use of the area affected by the easement is treated as a sale. The contribution to a government body of a scenic easement in perpetuity is a charitable contribution, not a sale.

Condemnation. If you realize a gain on a grant of an easement under a condemnation or threat of condemnation, you may defer tax by investing in replacement property; *see 18.18.*

 Planning Reminder

Basis Allocation
In reviewing an easement, the IRS will generally try to find grounds for allocating part of a property owner's basis to easement proceeds, especially where the allocation will result in a taxable gain. In opposition, a property owner will generally argue that the easement affects the entire property or that it is impossible to make an allocation because of the nature of the easement or the particular nature of the property. If he or she can sustain an argument, the proceeds for granting the easement reduce the basis of the entire property; *see* Examples 1–3 on this page.

EXAMPLES
1. The owner of a 600-acre farm was paid $5,000 by a power company for the right to put up poles and power lines. The right of way covered 20 acres along one boundary that the owner continued to farm. The cost basis of the farm was $60,000, or $100 an acre. The IRS ruled that he had to allocate the basis. At $100 an acre, the allocated basis for the 20 acres was $2,000. Thus, a gain of $3,000 was realized ($5,000 – $2,000).
2. The owner of a tract of unimproved land gave a state highway department a perpetual easement affecting only part of the land. He wanted to treat the payment as a reduction of the basis of the entire tract and so report no gain. The IRS ruled that he had to allocate basis to the portion affected by the road.
3. The owner of farmland gave a transmission company a 50-foot right of way for an underground pipeline that did not interfere with farming. During construction, the right of way was 150 feet. The owner received payments for damages covering loss of rental income during construction and for the 50-foot permanent right of way. The IRS ruled that the damage payment was taxable as ordinary income; the payment for the right of way was a taxable gain to the extent that it exceeded the basis allocated to the acreage within the 50-foot strip.

Release of a restrictive covenant. A payment received for a release of a restrictive covenant is treated as a capital gain if the release involves property held for investment.

You sell several acres of land held for investment to a construction company subject to a covenant that restricts construction to residential dwellings. Later, the company wants to erect structures other than individual homes and pays you for the release of the restrictive covenant in the deed. You realize capital gain on receipt of the payment. The restrictive covenant is a property interest and a capital asset in your hands.

31.8 Special Tax Credits for Real Estate Investments

To encourage certain real estate investments, the tax law offers the following tax credits:

Low-income housing credit for buildings placed in service after 1986. Qualifying investors are allowed to claim a tax credit in annual installments over 10 years for qualifying newly constructed low-income housing and also to certain existing structures that are substantially rehabilitated. The amount of the credit depends on whether the building is new and whether federal subsidies are received. To claim the credit, you, as the building owner, must receive a certification from an authorized housing credit agency. The agency allocates a credit to you on Form 8609, which you use to claim the credit on Form 8586. You must attach to your return Form 8586, and, in some cases, also Form 8609 and Schedule A, Form 8609.

Rehabilitation credit for pre-1936 buildings or certified historic structures. On Form 3468, you may claim a 10% tax credit for rehabilitating pre-1936 buildings or a 20% credit for rehabilitating certified historic structures. For both types of rehabilitation credits, you must generally incur rehabilitation expenses of $5,000 or your adjusted basis in the building, whichever is greater.

Certified historic structure. A certified historic structure may be used for residential or non-residential purposes. The National Park Service must certify that a planned rehabilitation is in keeping with the building's historic status designation for the credit to be available.

In one case, a developer who rehabilitated a certified historic structure and donated a conservation easement to a historic society in the same year was required to base the credit computation on the rehabilitation expenses minus the charitable deduction claimed. If the donation had been made in a later year, a portion of the original credit claimed would be subject to recapture.

Pre-1936 buildings. The 10% credit for pre-1936 buildings applies only to nonresidential property. A substantial portion of the building's original structure must be retained after the rehabilitation. At least 75% of the external walls must be intact, with at least 50% kept as external walls. At least 75% of the existing internal structural framework must be kept in place.

Tax credit limitations. Tax credits for low-income housing and rehabilitating historic or pre-1936 buildings may be limited by passive activity restrictions on Form 8582-CR (Chapter 10) and by tax liability limits for the general business credit (Chapter 40).

For further details and credit conditions concerning the two types of rehabilitation credits, *see* Form 3468.

Court Decision

Rehabilitating Pre-1936 Building

In one case, the IRS and Tax Court interpreted the 75% external wall test for pre-1936 buildings as requiring that at least 75% of the existing external walls be retained in the same place, thereby denying the credit for a pre-1936 building that was relocated and then renovated. However, a federal appeals court disagreed, holding that there is no relocation restriction; the credit is allowed provided at least 75% of the external walls are retained as such after the renovation.

Foreclosures and Abandonments of Mortgaged Property

31.9 Foreclosures and Voluntary Conveyances to Creditors

If you are unable to meet payments on a debt secured by property, the creditor may foreclose on the property. A foreclosure sale or a voluntary conveyance of the property to the creditor is treated as a sale of the property. If you are personally liable on the debt, and if the value of the property is less than the cancelled debt, you also generally realize ordinary income on the debt cancellation.

Figuring gain or loss. Gain or loss is the difference between your adjusted basis in the property and the amount realized. Determining the amount realized depends on your liability for the debt:

If you are *not* personally liable on the debt, the amount realized includes the full amount of the cancelled debt, regardless of the value of the property.

If you are personally liable, the amount realized includes the portion of the cancelled debt that equals the fair market value of the property. If the fair market value of the property is less than the debt, the foreclosure or voluntary conveyance back to the creditor is treated as two separate transactions:

1. A sale of property. Gain or loss is the difference between adjusted basis and the amount realized, including the cancelled debt up to the fair market value of the property.

2. The receipt of ordinary income upon the cancellation of the debt for less than the face amount of the debt. You generally have cancellation of debt income equal to the excess of the cancelled debt over the fair market value of the property. However, this income may not be taxable, if you come within the exclusion rules discussed at *11.8*, such as being insolvent at the time of the foreclosure. *See also 31.10* for the exclusion on restructurings of business real property debt.

EXAMPLES

1. Jones could not meet the mortgage payments on a condominium that cost him $85,000. He had paid cash of $20,000 and taken a mortgage loan of $65,000 on which he was personally liable. When the remaining balance of the loan was $62,000, he defaulted, and the bank accepted his voluntary conveyance of the unit, cancelling the loan. Similar units at the time were selling for $60,000. On the transaction, Jones incurred a loss of $25,000: the difference between his adjusted basis of $85,000 and the fair market value of the unit of $60,000. The loss is not deductible because the unit was held for personal purposes. Jones also recognizes income on the cancellation of the loan because the amount of the debt exceeded the fair market value of the unit by $2,000. This amount is taxable, unless Jones can show he was insolvent at the time of the transfer to the bank; *see 11.8*.

2. Brown invested in a vacant lot. He put down cash of $10,000 and assumed a mortgage of $20,000. When he could not make payments on the mortgage, the bank foreclosed. The net proceeds from the foreclosure sale were $32,000. Brown received $12,000 and realized a capital gain of $2,000 (the difference between his adjusted basis of $30,000 and the amount realized of $32,000). There is no income from cancellation of indebtedness because the debt was less than the value of the property.

Foreclosure proceeds less than outstanding mortgage. Where a foreclosure sale does not cancel the mortgage debt, there is a conflict of opinion on how to compute the amount realized. Take this case:

In 1982, Aizawa bought rental property for $120,000, paying $30,000 down and giving the seller a $90,000 recourse mortgage note, payable in five years. The Aizawas made timely monthly interest payments but failed to pay off the principal at the end of the fifth year. In 1987, the sellers sued and got a judgment of $133,507 for the original principal due of $90,000, attorneys' fees of $25,000, and extra interest charges. Then, at a foreclosure sale, the sellers bought back the property for $72,700. The judgment and foreclosure sale left a deficiency judgment of $60,807.

The Aizawas deducted a $70,898 loss. They claimed the deficiency judgment of $60,807 should be deducted from the mortgage of $90,000, leaving an amount realized of $29,193. The difference between this amount and the $100,091 undepreciated basis of the property gave them a $70,898 loss. The IRS claimed that the amount realized was $90,000, the amount of the mortgage principal, so that the loss was only $10,091 ($100,091 less $90,000).

The Tax Court disagreed with both sides. The court held that the amount realized was the $72,700 proceeds from the foreclosure sale, so that a loss of $27,391 ($100,091 less $72,700) was incurred. The Aizawas' approach is wrong; they reduced the amount realized by the deficiency award they had not paid. The IRS approach is wrong; it included in the amount realized part of the mortgage debt that the Aizawas still owed.

The court recognized that its approach gave the Aizawas an additional loss of $17,300 ($90,000 less $72,700) based on a debt they might not repay. However, this advantage may be eliminated by later events. If they pay off the remaining debt, they may not deduct any additional loss. If they are discharged from paying the balance of the debt, they may be required to report income on the discharge if they are solvent.

Caution

Form 1099-A Notifies IRS

If your mortgaged property is foreclosed or repossessed, and the bank or other lender reacquires it, or if the lender knows that you have abandoned the property, you should receive from the lender Form 1099-A, which indicates foreclosure proceeds, the amount of your debt, and whether you were personally liable. The IRS may compare its copy of Form 1099-A with your return to check whether you have reported income from the foreclosure or abandonment.

If the lender also cancels your debt of $600 or more, you may instead receive Form 1099-C, on which the information about the foreclosure or repossession will be included.

Filing Tip

Reporting a Foreclosure or Voluntary Conveyance

You report a foreclosure sale or voluntary conveyance to a creditor on Schedule D if the property was held for personal or investment purposes.

Foreclosures and reconveyances of business assets are reported on Form 4797.

If income from cancellation of indebtness is realized and it is not excludable under the rules discussed at *11.8*, you report the taxable amount on Line 21, Form 1040.

31.10 Restructuring Mortgage Debt

Rather than foreclose on a mortgage, a lender (mortgagee) may be willing to restructure the mortgage debt by cancelling either all or part of the debt. As a borrower (mortgagor), do not overlook the tax consequences of the new debt arrangement. A debt cancellation or reduction is taxable unless it fits within specific exceptions, such as insolvency or bankruptcy. As discussed at *11.8*, there is no tax if the debt is restructured by the seller of the property or where a debt is reduced by a third-party lender and you are either insolvent, bankrupt, or are a qualifying farmer. These rules apply also to a restructuring of a nonrecourse debt on which you are not personally liable; *see* the Jones Example below, which shows the IRS approach to figuring insolvency upon a debt cancellation.

In the case of partnership property, tax consequences of the restructuring of a third-party loan are determined at the partner level. This means that if you are a partner and are solvent *(11.8)* you may not avoid tax on the transaction, even if the partnership is insolvent.

EXAMPLE

In 1998, Jones borrowed $1,000,000 from Chester and signed a note payable for $1,000,000. Jones was not personally liable on the note, which was secured by an office building valued at $1,000,000 that he bought from Baker with the proceeds of Chester's loan. In 1999, when the value of the building declined to $800,000, Chester agreed to reduce the principal of the loan to $825,000. At the time, Jones held other assets valued at $100,000 and owed another person $50,000. In 1999, Jones realized income of $175,000 on the reduction of the debt, but he can avoid tax to the extent he is insolvent.

To determine the extent of Jones's insolvency, the IRS compares Jones's assets and liabilities immediately before the discharge. According to the IRS, his assets total $900,000: the building valued at $800,000 plus other assets of $100,000. His liabilities total $1,025,000: the debt of $50,000 plus the liability on the note, which the IRS considers to be $975,000, equal to the $800,000 value of the building and the $175,000 discharged debt. The difference between the assets of $900,000 and liabilities of $1,025,000 is $125,000, the amount by which Jones is insolvent. As Jones is insolvent by $125,000, only $50,000 of the $175,000 discharged debt is treated as taxable income.

Restructuring debt on business real estate. A solvent taxpayer may avoid tax on a restructuring of qualifying business real estate debt *(11.8)* by electing to reduce the basis of depreciable real property by the amount of the tax-free debt discharge. The election to reduce basis is made on Form 982.

EXAMPLE

On July 1, 1999, Grant, who is solvent, owns a building worth $150,000 used in his business. It is subject to a first mortgage of $110,000 and a second mortgage of $90,000. Grant's basis in the building is $120,000. The second mortgagee agrees to reduce the second mortgage to $30,000. This results in debt discharge of $60,000 ($90,000 – $30,000). The $60,000 is considered debt discharge income. But Grant may elect to exclude $50,000. He reports the remaining $10,000 of discharged debt as taxable income. The exclusion limit is calculated as follows:

2nd mortgage before discharge		$90,000
Less: Fair market value of building	$150,000	
Less: First mortgage	110,000	40,000
Excludable amount		$50,000

On Form 982, Grant may elect to exclude $50,000 from tax because the basis of the building is sufficient to absorb a basis reduction of $50,000.

31.11 Abandonments

On an abandonment of business or investment property, you may claim an ordinary loss for the property's adjusted basis (when abandoned) on Form 4797. However, if the abandoned property is later foreclosed or repossessed, you may realize a gain or loss under the rules in *31.9* for foreclosures or voluntary conveyances to creditors. For example, if an abandonment loss for mortgaged property is claimed in 1998 but in 1999 the property is foreclosed upon by the lender, all or part of the cancelled debt will be treated as an amount realized by you on a sale in 1999. The amount realized depends on whether you were personally liable and the value of the property. If personally liable, you may also realize ordinary income from cancellation of the debt; *see 31.9.*

Abandoning a partnership interest. Where real estate values have sharply declined, partnerships may be holding realty subject to mortgage debt that exceeds the current value of the property. Some investors in such partnerships have claimed that they can abandon their partnership interests and claim abandonment losses. In one case, an investor in a partnership holding land in Houston, Texas, argued that he abandoned his partnership interest by making an abandonment declaration at a meeting of partners, and also declaring that he would make no further payments. He offered his interest to the others, who refused his offer. The IRS held that he failed to prove abandonment of his partnership interest or that the partnership abandoned the land. The Tax Court sided with the IRS, emphasizing his failure to show that the partnership abandoned the land. However, the appeals court for the Fifth Circuit reversed and allowed the abandonment loss. It held that the emphasis should be on the partner's actions, not the actions of the partnership. Although neither state law nor the IRS regulations described how a partnership interest is to be abandoned, the appeals court held that the partner's acts and declaration were sufficient to effect an abandonment of his partnership interest. The appeals court also held that the loss on the partnership interest could have been sustained on the basis of the worthlessness of his interest. The partnership was insolvent beyond hope of rehabilitation: (1) the partnership's only asset was land with a fair market value less than the mortgage debt; (2) the partnership had no source of income; and (3) the partners refused to contribute more funds to keep the partnership afloat.

In a subsequent case, the Tax Court held that a doctor had abandoned a movie production partnership interest when he refused to advance any more money or to participate in the venture because he disapproved of the content of the film being produced and feared it might jeopardize his position at a hospital operated by a religious organization. Also, the limited partners had voted to dissolve.

 Planning Reminder

Foreclosure After Abandonment

If, after the year the abandoned loss is claimed, the partnership's mortgaged holdings are foreclosed upon or reconveyed to the lender, each partner's share of the cancelled debt may be treated as an amount realized on a sale, or as ordinary cancellation of debt income; *see 31.9.*

31.12 Seller's Repossession After Buyer's Default on Mortgage

When you, as a seller, repossess realty on the buyer's default of a debt that the realty secures, you may realize gain or loss. (If the realty was a personal residence, the loss is not deductible.) A debt is secured by real property whenever you have the right to take title or possession or both in the event the buyer defaults on his or her obligation under the contract.

Figuring gain on the repossession. Gain on the repossession is the excess of: (1) payments received on the original sales contract prior to and on the repossession, including payments made by the buyer for your benefit to another party, over (2) the amount of taxable gain previously reported prior to the repossession.

Gain computed under these two steps may not be fully taxable. Taxable gain is limited to the amount of original profit less gain on the sale already reported as income for periods prior to the repossession and less your repossession costs.

The limitation on gain does not apply if the selling price cannot be computed at the time of sale as, for example, where the selling price is stated as a percentage of the profits to be realized from the development of the property sold.

These repossession gain rules do not apply if you repurchase the property by paying the buyer a sum in addition to the discharge of the debt, unless the repurchase and payment was provided for in the original sale contract, or the buyer has defaulted on his or her obligation, or default is imminent.

Where the above repossession rules do not apply, gain or loss on the repossession, and basis in the repossessed property, must be determined under the different rules for personal property; *see* IRS Publication 537 for details.

EXAMPLE

Assume you sell land for $25,000. You take a $5,000 down payment plus a $20,000 mortgage, secured by the property, from the buyer, with principal payable at the rate of $4,000 annually. The adjusted basis of the land was $20,000 and you elected to report the transaction on the installment basis. Your gross profit percentage is 20% ($5,000 profit divided by $25,000 selling price). In the year of sale, you include $1,000 in your income on the installment basis (20% of $5,000 down payment). The next year you reported profit of $800 (20% of $4,000 annual installment). In the third year, the buyer defaults, and you repossess the property. The amount of gain on repossession is computed as follows:

1. Compute gain:

Amount of money received	
($5,000 *plus* $4,000)	$9,000
Less: Amount of gain taxed in prior	
years ($1,000 *plus* $800)	1,800
Gain	$7,200

2. Compute limit on taxable gain, assuming cost of repossession is $500:

Original profit		$5,000
Less:		
Gain reported as income	$1,800	
Cost of repossession	500	2,300
Taxable gain on repossession		$2,700

Caution

Character of Gain

The gain limitation rules discussed at *31.12* do not affect the character of the gain. Thus, if you repossess property as a dealer, the gain is subject to ordinary income rates. If you, as an investor, repossess a tract originally held long term whose gain was reported on the installment method, the gain is capital gain.

The basis of repossessed property. This is the adjusted basis of the debt (face value of the debt less the unreported profits) secured by the property, figured as of the date of repossession, increased by (1) the taxable gain on repossession *and* (2) the legal fees and other repossession costs you paid.

EXAMPLE

Same facts as in the previous Example. The basis of the repossessed property is computed as follows:

1. Face value of debt ($20,000 note		
less $4,000 payment)		$16,000
2. *Less:* Unreported profit (20% of the		
$16,000 still due on the note)		3,200
3. Adjusted basis at date of		
repossession		$12,800
4. *Plus:* Gain on repossession	$2,700	
Cost of repossession	500	3,200
5. Basis of repossessed property		$16,000

If you treated the debt as having become worthless or partially worthless before repossession, you are considered to receive, upon the repossession of the property securing the debt, an amount equal to the amount of the debt treated as worthless. You report as income the amount of any prior bad debt deduction and increase the basis of the debt by an amount equal to the amount reported as income.

If your debt is not fully discharged as a result of the repossession, the basis of the undischarged debt is zero. No loss may be claimed if the obligations subsequently become worthless. This rule applies to undischarged debts on the original obligation of the purchaser, a substituted obligation of the purchaser, a deficiency judgment entered in a court of law into which the purchaser's obligation was merged, and any other obligations arising from the transaction.

Personal residence. Special rules apply to repossessions and resales of a personal residence if: (1) under prior law, at least some of the gain on the original sale was not taxed because you made an election to avoid tax under the exclusion for those age 55 or older or you deferred gain on the purchase of a new residence, or you avoided tax on gain under the current law home sale exclusion discussed in Chapter 29; *and* (2) within a year after the repossession you resell the property.

The original sale and resale is treated as one transaction. You refigure the amount realized on the sale. You combine the selling price of the resale with the selling price of the original sale. From this total, you subtract selling expenses for both sales, the part of the original installment obligation that remains unpaid at the time of repossession, and repossession costs. The net is the amount realized on the combined sale-resale. Subtracting basis in the home from the amount realized gives the gain on the combined sale-resale before taking into account the exclusion or deferral rules.

EXAMPLE

At age 60, you sold your house for $250,000. You received $50,000 cash and took back a purchase money mortgage of $200,000. Selling expenses were $3,000; the adjusted basis of the house was $167,000. You realized a profit of $80,000:

Amount realized ($250,000 – $3,000)	$247,000
Less: Adjusted basis	167,000
Gain	$ 80,000

Under prior law, you elected to avoid tax by claiming the exclusion of up to $125,000 for being 55 or older.

In 1999, the buyer defaulted and you repossessed the house and sold it for $300,000, incurring selling expenses of $5,000 and repossession costs of $2,000. The buyer still owed you $200,000 on his installment note. You have a $48,000 taxable gain on the combined sale-resale as follows:

Selling price on resale	$300,000	
Selling price on original sale	250,000	
Total selling price	$550,000	
Less:		
Unpaid buyer's note	$200,000	
Repossession costs	2,000	
Combined selling expenses		
($3,000 + $5,000)	8,000	
	210,000	
Amount realized ($550,000 – $210,000)		$340,000
Less: basis		167,000
Gain on sale-resale		$173,000
Less: $125,000 exclusion		125,000
Taxable gain		$ 48,000

31.13 Foreclosure on Mortgages Other Than Purchase Money

If you, as a mortgagee (lender), bid in on a foreclosure sale to pay off a mortgage that is *not a purchase money mortgage*, your actual financial loss is the difference between the unpaid mortgage debt and the value of the property. For tax purposes, however, you may realize a capital gain or loss and a bad debt loss that are reportable *in the year of the foreclosure sale*.

Your bid is treated as consisting of two distinct transactions:

1. The repayment of your loan. To determine whether this results in a bad debt, the bid price is matched against the face amount of the mortgage.
2. A taxable exchange of your mortgage note for the foreclosed property, which may result in a capital gain or loss. This is determined by matching the bid price against the fair market value of the property.

EXAMPLES

1. *Mortgagee's bid less than market value.* You hold a $40,000 mortgage on property having a fair market value of $30,000. You bid on the property at the foreclosure sale at $28,000. The expenses of the sale are $2,000, reducing the bid price to $26,000. The mortgagor is insolvent, so you have a bad debt loss of $14,000 ($40,000 – $26,000). You also have a $4,000 capital gain (the fair market value of the property of $30,000 – $26,000).
2. *Mortgagee's bid equal to market value.* Suppose your bid was $32,000, and had $2,000 in expenses. The difference between the net bid price of $30,000 and the mortgage of $40,000 is $10,000. As the mortgagor is insolvent, there is a bad debt loss of $10,000. Since the net bid price equals the fair market value, there is neither capital gain nor loss.
3. *Mortgagee's bid greater than market value.* Suppose your bid was $36,000 and you had $2,000 in expenses. Your bad debt deduction is $6,000—the difference between the mortgage debt of $40,000 and the net bid price of $34,000. You also had a capital loss of $4,000 (the difference between the net bid price of $34,000 and the fair market value of $30,000).

 Planning Reminder

Voluntary Conveyance

Instead of forcing you to foreclose, the mortgagor may voluntarily convey the property to you in consideration for your cancelling the mortgage debt. Your loss is the amount by which the mortgage debt plus accrued interest exceeds the fair market value of the property. If, however, the fair market value exceeds the mortgage debt plus accrued interest, the difference is taxable gain. The gain or loss is reportable in the year you receive the property. Your basis in the property is its fair market value when you receive it.

Planning Reminder

Keep Records

Preserve evidence of the property's fair market value. At a later date, the IRS may claim that the property was worth more than your bid and may tax you for the difference. Furthermore, be prepared to prove the worthlessness of the debt in order to support the bad debt deduction.

Where the bid price equals the mortgage debt plus unreported but accrued interest, you report the interest as income. But where the accrued interest has been reported, the unpaid amount is added to the collection expenses.

31.14 Foreclosure Sale to Third Party

When a third party buys the property in a foreclosure, the mortgagee receives the purchase price to apply against the mortgage debt. If it is less than the debt, the mortgagee may proceed against the mortgagor for the difference. Foreclosure expenses are treated as offsets against the foreclosure proceeds and increase the bad debt loss.

You deduct your loss as a bad debt. The law distinguishes between two types of bad debt deductions: business bad debts and nonbusiness bad debts. A business bad debt is fully deductible. A nonbusiness bad debt is a short-term capital loss that can be offset only against capital gains, plus a limited amount of ordinary income *(5.33)*. In addition, you may deduct a partially worthless business bad debt, but you may not deduct a partially worthless nonbusiness bad debt. Remember this distinction if you are thinking of forgiving part of the mortgage debt as a settlement. If the debt is a nonbusiness bad debt, you will not be able to take a deduction until the entire debt proves to be worthless. But whether you are deducting a business or a nonbusiness bad debt, your deduction will be allowed only if you show the debt to be uncollectible—for example, because a deficiency judgment is worthless or because the mortgagor is declared bankrupt.

EXAMPLE

You hold a $30,000 note and mortgage that are in default. You foreclose, and a third party buys the property for $20,000. Foreclosure expenses amount to $2,000. The deficiency is uncollectible. Your $12,000 loss is figured as follows:

Unpaid mortgage debt		$30,000
Foreclosure proceeds	$20,000	
Less: Expenses	2,000	
Net proceeds		18,000
Bad debt loss		$12,000

31.15 Transferring Mortgaged Realty

Mortgaging realty that has appreciated in value is one way of realizing cash on the appreciation without current tax consequences. The receipt of cash by mortgaging the property is not taxed; tax will generally be imposed only when the property is sold. However, there is a possible tax where the mortgage exceeds the adjusted basis of the property and the property is given away or transferred to a controlled corporation. Where the property is transferred to a controlled corporation, the excess is taxable gain. Further, if the IRS successfully charges that the transfer is part of a tax avoidance scheme, the taxable gain may be as high as the amount of the mortgage liability.

Gifts. The IRS holds that a gift of mortgaged property results in taxable income to the donor to the extent that the mortgage liability exceeds the donor's basis.

Tax Pointers for Investors in Mutual Funds

Mutual-fund investments relieve you of the responsibility of making daily investment decisions for securities actively traded or affected by changing market conditions.

Mutual funds are either closed or open end. Open-end funds are more popular than closed-end funds. The value of and number of shares in the portfolio of an open-end fund change daily as investors purchase and redeem shares. A closed-end fund issues a fixed number of shares that trade like shares of publicly held corporations listed on the stock exchange. The daily price of its shares may be below or above the net value of its investment portfolio.

As a mutual-fund shareholder, you may receive several types of distributions, such as ordinary dividends, capital gain distributions, exempt-interest dividends, and return of capital distributions. The rules for reporting the different types of distributions are discussed in this chapter.

Different methods of identifying sold shares and determining the cost basis of those shares are also discussed. The choice of cost-basis methods will affect the computation of gain or loss on a sale of shares.

32.1 Investing in Mutual Funds

A mutual fund is a professionally managed pool of individual investors' contributions invested in a variety of securities. Funds are designed and marketed to meet different investor objectives. Money-market mutual funds allow investors to earn a return based on swings in the short-term money market. Income funds invest in either stocks paying high current dividends or bonds paying interest. Growth funds invest in securities that are expected to appreciate over the long term. Some aggressive growth funds invest in small, developing companies with short track records. Other growth funds invest primarily in established firms. International funds invest in stocks of companies outside the United States. Sector funds specialize in specific industries, such as utilities, gold, or high technology companies. Balanced funds try to promote long-term growth by maintaining a mix of investments in bonds and stocks. Increasingly popular index funds buy the stocks that constitute a broad-based index to replicate the index's performance.

Do some research to find a fund that matches your investment objectives. Check the fund's performance over a substantial period of from five to 10 years. Keep in mind that yields fluctuate and are not guaranteed. In funds other than money markets *(32.2)*, the value per share also fluctuates. Gain or loss may be realized when you redeem shares in growth or income mutual funds. Also consider the rate at which a fund turns over its assets. A fund with a high turnover rate will realize frequent capital gains and losses, increasing the likelihood that capital gain distributions will be short term rather than long term. Short-term capital gain distributions are taxed as ordinary income dividends. Long-term capital gain distributions are subject to the rules for long-term capital gains.

Compare sales charges and redemption fees, if any, before you buy. No-load funds do not have a sales charge. Financial sections of major newspapers list prices of mutual-fund offerings. A no-load fund has the same purchase price and redemption price for fund shares; different prices for purchases and redemptions indicate a sales charge. Funds available through a broker may have a charge for commissions.

32.2 Money-Market Mutual Funds

A money-market mutual-fund portfolio will generally include U.S. government obligations, CDs of major commercial banks, bankers acceptances, and commercial paper of prime-rated firms. Investors should check each fund's charges because they differ.

Yields, which change daily, are not guaranteed. Investments are not federally insured. Some state-chartered banks, however, offer money-market funds insured by a state insurance fund.

Gains and losses are generally not realized in money-market funds; shares are redeemed for exactly what you paid (usually $1 per share) plus accrued dividends if you reinvested your dividends instead of receiving them in cash. Some funds offer limited check-writing privileges.

Tax-free money-market funds. These funds invest in short-term notes of state and local governments issued in anticipation of tax receipts, bond sales, and other revenues, and in "project notes" issued by local entities and backed by the federal government. The dividends paid by these funds is exempt from federal income tax. The yields are lower than those of taxable funds, and are attractive only if they provide greater after-tax returns than similar taxable funds. These funds may offer check-writing privileges.

Investors in certain states may be able to invest in funds that pay dividends that are exempt from state and local, as well as federal, income tax.

A tax-free interest return may also be available through unit investment trusts holding tax-exempt state and municipal bonds. These trusts mature in a specified number of years or as called.

32.3 Timing Your Investment

You may buy a tax liability if you invest in a mutual fund that has already realized significant capital gains during the year. If you invest near the end of the year and the fund shortly thereafter makes a large year-end capital gain distribution, you will in effect have to pay tax on the return of your recently invested money.

On the "record date" for determining which shareholders receive the fund's dividends and capital gain distributions, the value of the fund's shares drops by the amount of the distributions. If you buy just before that, the higher cost for your shares will be offset by the distributions you receive, but you will have to pay tax on the distributions. On the other hand, because you paid the higher pre-distribution price, your higher basis will reduce any capital gain on a later sale, or increase any capital loss.

Caution

Airline Points for Mutual-Fund Investing

If your mutual-fund awards you airline mileage for investing in the fund, you must reduce the basis of your shares by the value of the mileage.

Planning Reminder

Compare Yields

To compare fund yields, check newspaper financial sections that periodically list the yields of both taxable and tax-exempt money-market mutual funds. To increase yields, some funds temporarily waive a portion of fees and absorb expenses. Also check minimum investment and balance requirements.

If you want to limit your current tax and forego the basis increase, postpone your investment until after the record date for distributions. By that time, the value per share that determines the price will have been reduced by the capital gain distribution. Before investing, you may be able to find out from the fund when distributions for the year are expected; investment publications showing the distribution dates for the previous year also may be consulted.

32.4 Reinvestment Plans

Funds allow you to reinvest dividends and capital gain distributions from the fund in new fund shares instead of receiving cash. You report such distributions as if you received them in cash. Form 1099-DIV sent to you by a fund reports the gross amount of taxable distributions that you must report on Schedule B. A key to Form 1099-DIV is on the next page.

Keep track of reinvested distributions. If you reinvest your mutual-fund distributions instead of taking them in cash, keep a record of the distributions and of the shares purchased with the reinvestment. The reinvested distributions are considered your cost basis for the acquired shares. You need a record of reinvestments to figure your cost when you sell your shares; *see 32.9* for calculating gain on the sale of mutual-fund shares.

32.5 Reporting Mutual-Fund Distributions

Mutual-fund distributions are reported to you and the IRS by the fund on Form 1099-DIV or substitute statement. Distributions that you reinvested to acquire additional shares are reported and taxed in the same way as distributions that are actually paid out to you.

The Form 1099-DIV from your fund may include several types of dividend and other distributions. Dividends that you reinvested instead of receiving in cash are included on Form 1099-DIV. A guide to the different distributions, and how you report them, is shown in the "Key to Reporting Mutual-Fund Distributions" on the next page.

32.6 Tax-Exempt Bond Funds

Dividend income from a tax-exempt bond fund is generally tax free, but capital gain distributions are taxable. Exempt-interest dividends are not shown by the fund on 1099-DIV, but are reported separately by the fund. You report tax-exempt interest on Line 8b of Form 1040. The amount on Line 8b is not taxable, but if you receive Social Security benefits, the amount may affect the amount of taxable benefits; *see 34.3*.

Capital gain distributions are shown on Form 1099-DIV and must be reported on your return; *see* the "Key to Reporting Mutual-Fund Distributions" on the next page.

When you redeem your shares in a tax-exempt bond fund or exchange the fund shares for other shares in a different fund, you realize taxable capital gain or deductible loss.

If you received exempt-interest dividends on mutual-fund shares held for six months or less and sold those shares at a loss, the amount of your loss is reduced by the exempt-interest dividend. To reflect this adjustment, you increase the sales price reported on Line 1, column (d) of Schedule D by the loss not allowed. Report the balance as a short-term capital loss.

EXAMPLE

In January 1999, you bought a mutual-fund share for $40. In February 1999, the mutual fund paid a $5 dividend from tax-exempt interest, which is not taxable to you. In March 1999, you sold the share for $34. If it were not for the tax-exempt dividend, your loss would be $6 ($40 – 34). However, you may deduct only $1, the part of the loss that exceeds the exempt-interest dividend ($6 – 5). On Schedule D, column (d), increase the sales price from $34 to $39 (the $5 nondeductible loss). You may deduct $1 as a short-term capital loss.

32.7 Fund Expenses

If you own shares in a *publicly offered* mutual fund, you do not pay tax on your share of the fund expenses. There should be no entry in Box 5 of your Form 1099-DIV. However, expenses of a *non–publicly offered* fund are included in Box 5 of Form 1099-DIV and must be reported as a taxable dividend, even though the amount has not actually been distributed to you. This amount is included as a fully taxable ordinary dividend in Box 1 of Form 1099-DIV. An offsetting deduction may be claimed on Schedule A as a miscellaneous itemized deduction, subject to the 2% adjusted gross income floor; *see 19.24*.

Filing Instruction

Capital Gain Distributions
Your mutual fund will report capital gain distributions to you in Box 2a of Form 1099-DIV. Generally, these must be reported on Line 13 of Schedule D as long-term capital gains. However, if you do not need Schedule D to report other capital gains or losses, and certain other conditions are satisfied, you may enter your capital gain distributions directly on Form 1040 and compute your tax on a worksheet in the IRS instructions. *See* the "Key to Reporting Mutual-Fund Distributions" on the next page.

Filing Instruction

Year-end Dividends
Mutual funds sometimes declare dividends at the end of a calendar year but do not pay them until January of the following year. If the dividend is declared in October, November, or December, and paid in the following January, the fund will report the distribution as taxable in the year it is declared.

For purposes of figuring gain or loss when you redeem or exchange shares, load charges (sales fees) on the purchase of the shares may not be treated as part of your cost if you held the shares for 90 days or less and then reinvested the sales proceeds at a reduced load charge.

Key To Reporting Mutual-Fund Distributions

Type of Distribution	Shown by the Fund in	Where You Report
Ordinary dividends. (This includes your share of fund earnings from dividends, interest, and short-term capital gains.)	Box 1, Form 1099-DIV	If *all* of your mutual-fund distributions from Forms 1099-DIV are ordinary dividends, you may report them on either Form 1040 or Form 1040A. If this total plus your other dividends from all sources is $400 or less, enter them on Line 9 of Form 1040 or Line 9 of Form 1040A. If more than $400, enter the amount on Line 5, Schedule B of Form 1040, or Line 5, Schedule 1 of Form 1040A. **Note:** If you also have capital gain or nontaxable distributions from Form 1099-DIV, you may not use Form 1040A to report the ordinary dividends; your mutual-fund distributions must be reported on Form 1040; *see* below.
Capital gain distributions. (This represents your share of long-term gains realized by a fund on sales made from its portfolio.)	Box 2a, Form 1099-DIV	Schedule D. However, you do not have to file Schedule D if *all three* of the following apply: (1) the only amounts you have to report on Schedule D are capital gain distributions from Box 2a of Forms 1099-DIV or substitute statements; (2) none of the Forms 1099-DIV or substitute statements have an amount in Box 2b (28% rate gain), Box 2c (unrecaptured Section 1250 gain), or Box 2d (Section 1202 gain); *and* (3) if you are filing Form 4952 (relating to investment interest expense deduction), the amount on Line 4e of that form is not more than zero. If all three of the above apply, enter your capital gain distributions on Line 13 of Form 1040 and check the box on that line. Also, be sure you use the capital gain tax worksheet in the IRS instructions to figure your tax.
Return of capital distributions (nontaxable)	Box 3, 1099-DIV	A return of capital distribution is not taxable income. However, if your basis for your shares has been reduced to zero by return of capital gain distributions, report additional nontaxable distributions as capital gain on Schedule D, depending on how long you held the shares.
Exempt-interest dividends	A separate statement; not included on Form 1099-DIV. This will be sent to you within 60 days after the close of the fund's taxable year.	For informational purposes only, report along with other tax-exempt interest on Line 8b of Form 1040 or Form 1040A.
Undistributed capital gains	Undistributed gains shown on Form 2439, Box 1a Tax paid by fund shown on Form 2439, Box 2	Report the undistributed gains on Line 11 of Schedule D. To get a tax credit for the tax paid by the fund, enter the tax on Line 63 of Form 1040. Increase the basis of your mutual-fund shares by the excess of the undistributed gains included on Schedule D over the tax credit claimed on Line 63 of Form 1040.
Fund expenses from non–publicly offered funds	Box 5, Form 1099-DIV	If you itemize, the expenses are itemized deductions, subject to the 2% adjusted gross income floor (19.1).
Foreign taxes	Box 6, Form 1099-DIV. Box 7 shows the country imposing the tax.	The foreign taxes may be claimed as a tax credit on Form 1116 or as an itemized deduction on Schedule A of Form 1040; *see 36.14.*

32.8 Tax Credits From Mutual Funds

Undistributed capital gains. Some mutual funds retain their long-term capital gains and pay capital gains tax on those amounts. Even though not actually received by you, you include as a capital gain distribution on your return the amount of the undistributed capital gain allocated to you by the fund. If the mutual fund paid a tax on the undistributed capital gain, you are entitled to a tax credit.

To claim the credit, check the Form 2439 sent to you by your fund, which lists your share of undistributed capital gain and the amount of tax paid on it by the fund. Enter your share of the tax the fund paid on this gain on Line 63 of Form 1040, and check the box for Form 2439. Attach Copy B of Form 2439 to your return to support your tax credit. Increase the basis of your stock by the excess of the undistributed capital gain over the amount of tax paid by the mutual fund, as reported on Form 2439.

Dividends from foreign investments. The dividends are taxable, but you may be able to claim a foreign tax credit (on Form 1116) or a deduction on Schedule A for your share of the fund's foreign taxes.

In Box 6 of Form 1099-DIV, the fund will report your share of the foreign taxes paid, and in Box 7, the name of the foreign country. The fund should give you instructions for claiming the foreign tax credit or deduction; also *see 36.14*.

32.9 Redemptions and Exchanges of Fund Shares

When you ask the fund to redeem all or part of your shares, you have transacted a sale subject to capital gain or loss rules explained in Chapter 5. Exchanges of shares of one fund for shares of another fund within the same fund "family" are treated as sales. If you owned the shares for more than one year, your gain or loss is long term; if you held them for a year or less, your gain or loss is short term. However, if you received a capital gain distribution before selling shares held six months or less at a loss, your loss must be reported as a long-term capital loss to the extent of the capital gain distribution attributable to the sold shares. Any excess loss is reported as a short-term capital loss. This restriction does not apply to dispositions under periodic redemption plans.

EXAMPLE

In June 1999, you bought mutual-fund shares for $1,000. In August, you received a capital gain distribution of $50, and you sold the shares for $850 in September. Instead of reporting a $150 short-term capital loss ($1,000 cost – $850 proceeds), you must report a long-term capital loss of $50, the amount of the capital gain distribution; the remaining $100 of the loss is a short-term capital loss.

Identifying the shares you sell. Determining which mutual-funds shares are being sold is necessary to figure your gain or loss and whether the gain or loss is short term or long term. *See 32.10* for the identification methods.

Holding period of fund shares. You determine your holding period by using the trade dates. The trade date is the date on which you contract to buy or redeem the mutual-fund shares. Do not confuse the trade date with the settlement date, which is the date by which the mutual-fund shares must be delivered and payment must be made. Most mutual funds will show the trade date on your purchase and redemption confirmation statements.

Your holding period starts on the day after the day you bought the shares. (The day you bought the shares is the trade date.) This same date of each succeeding month is the start of a new month regardless of the number of days in the month before. The day you dispose of the shares (trade date) is also part of your holding period.

32.10 Basis of Redeemed Shares

To figure gain or loss, you need to know the basis per share. Generally, your basis is the purchase price of the shares, including shares acquired by reinvesting distributions back into the fund, plus commission or load charges.

Load charges. Basis does not include load charges (sales fees) on the purchase of mutual-fund shares if you held the shares for 90 days or less and then exchanged them for shares in a different fund in the same family of funds at a reduced load charge.

Caution

Getting Written Confirmation

Make sure your broker sends you a written confirmation of your selling instructions. You should not rely on e-mail or oral affirmations.

Planning Reminder

Keeping Track of Cost Basis

Keep confirmation statements for purchases of shares as well as a record of distributions that are automatically reinvested in your account. These will show the cost basis for your shares. Your basis is increased by amounts reported to you by the fund on Form 2439, representing the difference between your share of undistributed capital gains that you were required to report as income and your share of the tax paid by the fund on undistributed gains. Your basis is reduced by nontaxable dividends that are a return of your investment. Keep copies of Form 2439 and information returns showing nontaxable dividends.

Planning Reminder

Specific Identification Method

When you redeem part of your shares, the specific identification method of identifying the shares sold provides you the most flexibility. However, note the paperwork requirements for this method in Examples 1 and 2 on this page.

Planning Reminder

Shares Received as Gift

To determine your original basis of mutual-fund shares you acquired by gift, you must know the donor's adjusted basis, the date of the gift, the fair market value of the shares at the time of the gift, and whether any gift tax was paid on the shares. *See 5.17.*

EXAMPLE

You pay a $200 load charge on purchasing shares for $10,000 in Fund A. Within 90 days, you exchange the Fund A shares for Fund B shares. Because Fund A and Fund B are in the same family of funds, the $200 load charge that would otherwise be due on the purchase of the Fund B shares is waived. For purposes of figuring your gain or loss on the exchange of Fund A shares, your basis is $10,000, not $10,200. The disallowed $200 is added to the basis of the new Fund B shares, provided those shares are held more than 90 days. If the waived load charge on Fund B shares had been $100, basis for the original Fund A shares would be increased by $100, the excess of the original $200 load charge over the amount waived on the reinvestment.

Identifying the sold shares. If your shares in a mutual fund were acquired at different times, you need to know the basis of the particular shares you are selling in order to determine gain or loss. There are several methods of identifying which shares you are selling:

  • *Specific Identification Method*—allows you to select exactly which shares are being sold (*see* Examples 1 and 2 below).
  • *Average Cost Basis Method*—averages your cost for all shares in the fund (*see* Example 3 below).
  • *First-in, first-out (FIFO) Method*—applies if you do not specifically identify the shares or elect the averaging method (*see* Examples 1 and 2 below).
  See the chart on the following page for details on these identification methods.

EXAMPLES

1. In 1989, you bought 100 shares of a mutual fund for $10 a share. In 1992, you bought another 200 shares for $11 a share, and in 1993, another 500 shares for $15 a share. In 1999, you sell 130 shares at $20 a share, but do not specifically identify the shares being sold. Under the IRS FIFO method, you are treated as having first sold the original 100 shares from 1989, then 30 of the shares bought in 1992. Your basis for the sold shares is $1,330:

100 shares from 1989 costing $10 each	$1,000
30 shares from 1992 costing $11 each	330
	$1,330

   Your taxable gain is $1,270 ($2,600 sales price less $1,330 basis). Had you specifically designated shares from the most recent lot, which cost you more, you would have reduced the taxable gain. For example, if you had given the fund written instructions to sell 130 of the 500 shares that you bought in 1993 at $15 per share, your basis on the sale under the specific identification method would be $1,950 (130 × $15) instead of $1,330. Gain would be reduced from $1,270 to $650 ($2,600 sales price less $1,950 basis).

2. Hall sold by phone part of his holdings in two mutual funds acquired over a number of years without specifying the particular shares being sold. On his return, Hall claimed a net long-term capital loss of about $2,400 using a LIFO method (last-in, first-out). However, using the FIFO method, the IRS held that he had a long-term capital gain of $163,000. In the Tax Court, Hall argued that the specific identification rule applies only to stock certificates, not noncertificate shares left on deposit with a mutual fund. The court disagreed. Without specific identification, the IRS FIFO method is reasonable. If good records are kept, you can select the specific shares being sold at the time of sale. You cannot wait until you file your return to allot specific sales to gain a tax advantage.

   What if you give written instructions to a mutual fund that specific shares should be sold, but the fund does not acknowledge your specification in its written confirmation? Regulations require such a written confirmation within a reasonable time after the sale. However, the Tax Court indicates your written sale identification instructions may be acceptable without a written confirmation.

3. You bought 160 shares of the XYZ Mutual Fund on February 4, 1997, for $4,000. On August 5, 1997, you bought another 240 shares for $4,800. You obtained an additional 10 shares on December 15, 1997, when you reinvested a $300 dividend. On December 16, 1998, you obtained an additional 20 shares when you reinvested a $750 dividend. You sell 200 shares of the fund on September 23, 1999, for $8,000. Using the average basis method, your average basis is $22.91 per share.

   Your total cost basis for all 430 shares is $9,850. Dividing $9,850 by 430 gives you an average basis per share of $22.91. Thus, your basis for the 200 sold shares is $4,582 (200 × $22.91 = $4,582).

Under the average-basis method, the shares you acquired first are the shares deemed to be sold for purposes of determining your capital gain holding period. Thus, you are deemed to have sold the 160 shares bought on February 4, 1997, and 40 of the 240 shares bought on August 5, 1997. The sold shares were held long term on the sale date of September 23, 1999. You have a $3,418 long-term capital gain on the sale: $8,000 proceeds less $4,582 basis figured under the average-basis method.

Key to Identifying Mutual-Fund Shares When You Sell

Method—	Tax Effect—
Specific identification of shares sold	If you sell some of your shares that have been left on deposit with an agent for the fund, and you identify the specific lot of shares being sold in your sell order, you can fix profit or loss on the sale, depending on the cost of the shares selected. *See* Example 1 on page 518. You should give the fund written instructions to sell shares that you bought on a particular date and at a particular price. Ask the fund for a written confirmation that acknowledges your instructions. The IRS requires that written confirmation of your instruction to sell particular shares be received within a reasonable time after the sale.
FIFO (First-in, first-out)	If you do not specifically identify the sold shares as just discussed, and you do not elect to average cost basis as discussed below, the IRS requires you to compute gain or loss as if shares were sold in the order that you acquired them. If the earliest acquired shares are treated as sold, taxable gain on a current sale will generally be higher than if the specific identification method was used, assuming that your least expensive shares were bought first; *see* Example 1 on page 518.
Averaging your basis	You may elect to average the cost of shares acquired at different times and prices. The election applies to mutual-fund shares held by an agent, usually a bank, in an account kept for the periodic acquisition or redemption of shares in the particular fund. You still need records of your total basis, but averaging avoids the difficult task of identifying the exact shares being sold. Some funds ease the record-keeping burden by providing to shareholders who have redeemed shares a statement showing their average cost basis under the single-category method. *See* Example 3 on page 518. The single-category method is easier to apply than the double-category method, as explained below. To elect either averaging method, attach a note to your return specifying the chosen method. Once you have elected a method, you must continue to apply the same method for all sales or exchanges of shares in the same fund. However, you may use the specific identification method or the FIFO method, or the other averaging method for shares of other funds in the same "family" of funds. For example, if you own shares in the XYZ Co. growth fund and also in the XYZ Co. bond fund, you may use an averaging method for the bond fund shares and the specific identification method for the growth fund shares. You can use the average cost basis for sales of shares in one mutual-fund family, and use the specific identification method for sales of shares of other fund families. ***Single-category averaging.*** You figure the average cost per share by dividing your total basis for all shares in the account by the number of shares. For example, if you bought 100 shares of a fund in 1991 at $20 per share and another 100 shares in 1992 at $30 per share, your average basis per share is $25 ($5,000 total cost ÷ 200 shares). If you sell 50 shares in 1999 for $35 a share, your basis for the sold shares is $1,250 (50 × $25 average basis) and your gain on the sale is $500 ($1,750 sales proceeds less $1,250 basis). For holding period purposes, you are treated as having sold shares in the order you acquired them (first-in, first-out). ***Double-category averaging.*** You have to separate your account shares into a long-term category for shares held more than one year and a short-term category for shares held one year or less. You figure the average cost per share in each category by dividing the total basis for all shares in that category by the number of shares in that category. You may specify to the agent handling share transactions the category from which you are selling. If you do not so specify, the long-term shares are deemed to have been sold first. If the number of shares sold exceeds the number in the long-term class, the excess shares are charged to the short-term class.

32.11 Comparison of Basis Methods

As discussed at *32.9*, your choice of basis method can have a significant effect on the computation of capital gains and losses when you sell a portion of your shares in a mutual fund. The following example compares the single averaging method to the specific identification and FIFO methods.

Transaction history. Assume that on February 7, 1992, you made an initial investment of $4,500 for 375 shares in ABC Mutual Fund at $12 per share. Under the dividend reinvestment plan, you reinvested a $400 dividend, received in December 1992, for an additional 40 shares at $10 per share. On June 10, 1993, you bought 350 shares at $15 per share. In December 1993 you reinvested your dividend, this time for 25 shares at $12 per share. On September 16, 1994, you bought 200 shares at $16 per share. You did not reinvest your dividends received in 1994–1999. On October 17, 2000, you ask ABC Mutual Fund to redeem 200 shares and you receive $20 per share. The table below illustrates your transactions.

Date	Action	Share Price	No. of Shares	Shares Owned
2/7/92	Invest $4,500	$12	375	375
12/18/92	Reinvest $400 dividend	$10	40	415
6/10/93	Invest $5,250	$15	350	765
12/14/93	Reinvest $300 dividend	$12	25	790
9/16/94	Invest $3,200	$16	200	990
10/17/2000	Redeem $4,000	$20	200	790

Planning Reminder

Choice of Method

The specific identification method allows you to designate specific shares as the shares sold, allowing you to minimize a gain on the sale or to select shares that, because of their basis, would give you a loss.

The following are three different ways to compute the basis of the shares redeemed on October 17, 2000.

Specific identification method. If you identify the shares you sold, you can use the adjusted basis of those shares to figure your gain or loss. You must specify the particular shares to be redeemed at the time of the sale, as well as receive confirmation of your specification in writing within a reasonable time. Depending on your situation, you may want to either maximize or minimize your gain or loss on the sale. Here, you will have a gain regardless of which shares are treated as being sold. Assuming you want to minimize your gain, then you would specify the 200 shares bought at $16 per share on September 16, 1994, as the shares sold. Since the shares were sold for $20 per share, the gain would be $4 per share, for a total of $800 of long-term capital gain ($4,000 – $3,200).

FIFO (first-in, first-out). If you do not identify which shares you sold or choose the averaging method, you must use the basis of the shares you acquired first as the basis of the shares sold. Therefore, the oldest shares still available, the February 7, 1992, shares, are considered sold first. Thus, the basis of the 200 shares sold would be $12 per share. Your long-term capital gain is $1,600 ($4,000 – $2,400).

Average cost. The ABC Mutual Fund may provide you with your average basis when you make the redemption. If it does not, you may compute the average basis for all shares owned at the time of disposition, regardless of how long you owned them, including shares acquired with reinvested dividends. The basis and gain is computed as follows: You total the number of shares owned prior to the sale, 990, and total your investment in these shares, which is $13,650. You divide $13,650 by 990, which gives an average cost of $13.79 per share and a total cost of $2,758 for the 200 shares. Your gain is $1,242 ($4,000 – $2,758). For holding period purposes, the shares sold are considered to be from the earliest lot in 1992, so your gain is long-term capital gain.

Result: The specific identification method gives you the lowest capital gain under this set of facts.

Family Income Planning

Each additional dollar of ordinary income you receive, such as interest, dividends, and rent, is taxed in your highest bracket. If you can deflect income to a lower tax bracket of a child or other dependent relative, he or she will pay a smaller tax on the income than you would pay. However, the tax advantages of shifting income to children under age 14 are sharply reduced by the "kiddie tax"; *see* Chapter 24.

To split income, you must do more than make gifts of income. You must transfer the actual property from which the income is produced. For example, you do not avoid tax on interest by instructing your savings bank to credit interest to your children's account. Unless you actually transfer the complete ownership of the account to your child, the interest income is earned on money owned by you and must be reported by you. The same holds true with dividends, rents, and other forms of income. Unless you transfer the income-producing property, the income will be taxed to you.

You may not split earned income; income resulting from your services is taxed to you. You may not avoid this result by setting up trusts to receive your earned income.

Gift Planning

33.1 Gift Tax Basics

As family income planning generally requires the transfer of property, you must consider possible gift tax liability. The gift tax rates and credit are the same as those of the estate tax listed in Chapter 39.

Gift tax liability may be avoided by making gifts within an annual exclusion of $10,000 (or $20,000 for joint gifts). To each donee, you may give annually up to $10,000 tax free; furthermore, if your spouse joins in the gift, you may give annually tax free to each donee up to $20,000. The $20,000 exclusion is available even if the entire gift is from your or your spouse's separately owned funds. Thus, if you (with your spouse's consent) make annual gifts to four persons, you could give away without gift tax up to $80,000 (4 × $20,000 exclusion). The $10,000 (or $20,000) annual exclusion is allowed only for cash gifts or gifts of present interests in property; gifts of future interests do not qualify.

Gifts to a spouse who is a U.S. citizen are completely tax free because of the marital deduction. There also is an unlimited gift tax exclusion for paying someone else's tuition or medical expenses, if you directly pay the educational organization or care provider.

If you make an interest-free or low-interest loan to a family member, you may be subject to income tax and gift tax; *see 4.31*.

Filing a gift tax return. A gift tax return generally must be filed on Form 709 for a gift made to an individual other than your spouse if it exceeds $10,000 or is a gift of a future interest (regardless of value). A return does not have to be filed for gifts qualifying for the tuition or medical expense exclusion.

Married couples who consent to "split" gifts of over $10,000 but up to $20,000 must report the gifts to the IRS, although no gift tax is due under the annual exclusion. If your spouse consents to split gifts with you, you may be able to use a short form, Form 709-A, rather than Form 709; *see* the form instructions.

Form 709 or Form 709-A generally must be filed by April 15th of the year following the year of the gift. If you get a filing extension for your income tax return, the extension also applies to the gift tax return. An additional extension may be granted by the IRS for gift tax returns filed on Form 709 if you show good cause; further extensions are not allowed for filing Form 709-A.

Law Alert

Increased Annual Exclusion and Exemption

The $10,000 annual gift tax exclusion is potentially subject to an inflation adjustment for gifts made after 1999, but given the adjustment formula, the $10,000 exclusion may not be raised for several years. In 1999, the applicable credit amount for gift tax and estate tax purposes gives an effective exemption of $650,000. It increases to $675,000 in 2000. Further increases are phased in until the exemption will be fixed at $1,000,000 for 2006 and later years, *see 39.5*.

EXAMPLE

In July 1999 Randall Johnson makes a gift of publicly traded stock to his son, Philip, and his daughter, Ann. He gives each of them 1,000 shares of stock valued at $18,500 ($18.50 per share). His cost basis for the 2,000 shares was $24,000. On Form 709-A, Randall's wife, Claire, consents to split the gifts, thereby doubling the annual exclusion for gifts to each child. Neither Randall nor Claire made any other gifts during 1999. As a result of the gift splitting, no gift tax is due.

If Randall's total gifts for the year to either Philip or Ann exceeded $20,000, the gifts could not be reported on Form 709-A; the longer Form 709 would have to be used.

Even where Form 709 must be filed, gift tax liability computed on the form may be offset by the applicable credit applied to gift taxes as well as estate taxes. For example, in 1999, you and your spouse each have an applicable credit of $211,300 that exempts up to $650,000 of lifetime taxable gifts (exceeding the annual exclusion) from gift tax, *or* transfers of up to $650,000 at death from estate tax. When you report taxable gifts exceeding the annual exclusion, the applicable credit offsets the gift tax liability, so that you do not actually have to pay gift tax to the IRS. The portion of the credit used to offset gift taxes indirectly reduces the credit available for estate tax purposes upon your death; *see* the estate tax computation in Chapter 39.

33.2 Custodian Accounts for Minors

A minor generally lacks the ability to manage property. You could create a formal trust, but this step may be costly. A practical alternative may be a custodian account under the Uniform Gifts to Minors Act (UGMA), or the Uniform Transfers to Minors Act (UTMA), which has replaced the UGMA in many states.

Custodian accounts set up in a bank, mutual fund, or brokerage firm can achieve income splitting; the tax consequences discussed below generally apply to such accounts. Trust accounts that are considered revocable under state law are ineffective in splitting income.

Although custodian accounts may be opened anywhere in the United States, the rules governing the accounts may vary from state to state. The differences between the laws of the states generally do not affect federal tax consequences.

There are limitations placed on the custodian. Proceeds from the sale of an investment or income from an investment may not be used to buy additional securities on margin. While a custodian should prudently seek reasonable income and capital preservation, he or she generally is not liable for losses unless they result from bad faith, intentional wrongdoing, or gross negligence.

When the minor reaches majority age (depending on state law), property in the custodian account is turned over to him or her. No formal accounting is required. The child, now an adult, may sign a simple release freeing the custodian from any liability. But on reaching majority, the child may require a formal accounting if there are any doubts as to the propriety of the custodian's actions while acting as custodian. For this reason, and also for tax record-keeping purposes, a separate bank account should be opened in which proceeds from sales of investments and investment income are deposited pending reinvestment on behalf of the child. Such an account will furnish a convenient record of sales proceeds, investment income, and reinvestment of the same.

Income tax treatment of custodian account. Income from a custodian account is generally taxable to the child. However, taxable income from a custodian account in excess of the annual "kiddie" tax floor ($1,400 in 1999) is taxed at the parent's tax rate if the child is under age 14; computation of the "kiddie tax" is discussed in Chapter 24.

If a parent is the donor of the custodial property or the custodian of the account and income from the account is used to discharge the parent's legal obligation to support the child, the account income is taxed to the parent.

Gift tax treatment of custodian account. When setting up a custodian account, you may have to pay a gift tax. A transfer of cash or securities to a custodian account is a gift. But you are not subject to a gift tax if you properly plan the cash contributions or purchase of securities for your children's accounts. You may make gifts of up to $10,000 per person, which is shielded from gift tax by the annual exclusion. The exclusion applies each year to each person to whom you make a gift. If your spouse consents to join with you in the gift, you may give annually tax free up to $20,000 to each person.

If the custodian account is set up at the end of December, another tax-free transfer of $20,000 may be made in the first days of January of the following year. In this way, a total of $40,000 is shifted within the two-month period.

Even if gifts exceeding the $10,000 (or $20,000) exclusion are made, gift tax liability may be offset by the unified credit applied to gift and estate taxes.

Estate tax treatment of custodian account. The value of a custodian account will be taxed in your estate if you die while acting as custodian of an account before your child reaches his or her majority. However, you may avoid the problem by naming someone other than yourself as custodian. If you should decide to act as custodian, taking the risk that the account will be taxed in your estate, remember that no estate tax is incurred if the tax on your estate is offset by the estate tax credit; *see* Chapter 39.

If you act as custodian and decide to terminate the custodianship, care should be taken to formally close the account. Otherwise, if you die while retaining power over the account, the IRS may try to tax the account in your estate.

 Planning Reminder

Custodian Securities Account
Purchase of securities through custodian accounts provides a practical method for making a gift of securities to a minor child, eliminating the need for a trust. The mechanics of opening a custodian account are simple. An adult opens a stock account for a minor child at a broker's office. He or she registers the securities in the name of a custodian for the benefit of the child. The custodian may be a parent, a child's guardian, grandparent, brother, sister, uncle, or aunt. In some states, the custodian may be any adult or a bank or trust company. The custodian has the right to sell securities in the account and collect sales proceeds and investment income, and use them for the child's benefit or reinvestment. Tax treatment of custodian accounts is discussed on this page.

33.3 Trusts in Family Planning

You establish a trust by transferring legal title to property to a trustee who manages the property for one or more beneficiaries. As the one who sets up the trust, you are called the *grantor* or *settlor* of the trust. The trustee may be one or more individuals or an institution such as a bank or a trust company.

You can create a trust during your lifetime or by your will. A trust created during your lifetime is called an *inter vivos* trust; one established in your will is a testamentary trust. An *inter vivos* trust can be revocable or irrevocable. An irrevocable trust does not allow for changes of heart; it requires a complete surrender of property. By conveying property irrevocably to a trust, you may relieve yourself of tax on the income from the trust principal. Furthermore, the property in trust usually is not subject to estate tax, although it may be subject to gift tax. A trust should be made irrevocable only if you are certain you will not need the trust property in a financial emergency.

Sample Form 709-A

Form **709-A**	**United States Short Form Gift Tax Return**	OMB No. 1545-0021
(Rev. December 1996)	**(For "Privacy Act" notice, see the Form 1040 instructions)**	
Department of the Treasury Internal Revenue Service	Calendar year 19.........	

1 Donor's first name and middle initial Randall M.	**2** Donor's last name Johnson	**3** **Donor's social security number** 1X1 - 01 - X11X
4 Address (number, street, and apartment number) 914 State Street		**5** Legal residence (domicile) State XX
6 City, state, and ZIP code City, State 0X0X0		**7** Citizenship USA

8 Did you file any gift tax returns for prior periods? . . . . ☐ Yes ☒ No

If "Yes," state when and where earlier returns were filed ▶

9 Name of consenting spouse Claire Johnson	**10** **Consenting spouse's social security number** X1Z - 1X - 001X

Note: *Do not use this form to report gifts of closely held stock, partnership interests, fractional interests in real estate, or gifts for which the value has been reduced to reflect a valuation discount. Instead, use Form 709.*

List of Gifts

(a) Donee's name and address and description of gift	(b) Donor's adjusted basis of gift	(c) Date of gift	(d) Value at date of gift

1. Philip S. Johnson, son
    914 State Street, City, State 0X0X0
    Gift of 1,000 Shares of Central Net Corp.
    Common Stock (NYSE) at $18.50 per share
    on 7-12-99
    Cusip No. 001005684
	$ 12,000	7-12-99	$ 18,500

2. Ann C. Johnson, daughter
    10 Lincoln Road, City, State 0X0X0
    Gift of 1,000 Shares of Central Net Corp.
    Common Stock (NYSE) at $18.50 per share
    on 7-12-99
    Cusip No. 001005684
	$ 12,000	7-12-99	$ 18,500

Consent

I consent to have the gifts made by my spouse to third parties during the calendar year considered as made one-half by each of us.

Consenting spouse's signature ▶ *Claire Johnson*   Date ▶ March 13, 2000

Under penalties of perjury, I declare that I have examined this return, and to the best of my knowledge and belief it is true, correct, and complete. Declaration of preparer (other than donor) is based on all information of which preparer has any knowledge.

Donor's signature ▶ *Randall Johnson*   Date ▶ March 13, 2000

Preparer's signature (other than donor's) ▶ *Jonathan K. Carr*   Date ▶ March 13, 2000

Preparer's address (other than donor's) ▶ 200 Adams Lane, City, State 0X0X0

For Paperwork Reduction Act Notice, see the instructions on the reverse side of this form. Cat. No. 10171G Form **709-A** (Rev. 12-96)

Trust income. Where a child is a trust beneficiary, the child reports distributable net trust income as taxable income. If the child is under the age of 14, distributable net income is subject to the "kiddie tax," discussed at *24.3*. Income that is accumulated for the benefit of a minor child is generally not taxable and, thus, not subject to the kiddie tax.

Short-term trusts. Before the tax laws were changed in 1986, 10-year (Clifford) trusts were widely used to shift income to relatives in lower tax brackets. Where a trust met the 10-year exception, trust income was taxed to the beneficiary, usually a minor child. Another type of trust used for income splitting was the spousal remainder trust set up for less than 10 years. It allowed income shifting to a child beneficiary when the trust property went to the grantor's spouse after the end of the trust period.

Under current law, both types of trust may no longer be used to shift income to the income beneficiary. Only 10-year trusts created before March 2, 1986, continue to shift income to the income beneficiary. However, tax savings may be nullified for trust beneficiaries under the age of 14 by the kiddie tax. For example, in 1999 unearned income over $1,400 of a child under age 14 is taxed to the child at the top marginal rate of the parents; *see 24.3*.

Pre–March 2, 1986, 10-year trusts continue to shift income and provide tax savings to trust beneficiaries age 14 or over.

Spousal remainder trusts have been neutralized as tax-saving techniques by current law that treats the grantor as holding a reversionary interest held by his or her spouse. This spousal attribution rule applies to a reversionary interest of a spouse who marries the grantor after the trust is created.

The current tax rules apply to trust transfers made after March 1, 1986. An exception applies to a 10-year trust created pursuant to a binding property settlement entered into before March 2, 1986, that required the taxpayer to establish a grantor trust.

Grantor trusts. The grantor of a grantor trust is taxed on the income of the trust. A trust is treated as a grantor trust where the grantor has a reversionary interest (at the time of the transfer) of more than 5% of the value of the property transferred to the trust. Under an exception, a grantor is not treated as having a reversionary interest if that interest can take effect only upon the death before age 21 of a beneficiary who is a lineal descendant of the grantor. The beneficiary must have the entire present interest in the trust or trust portion for this exception to apply.

Tax rates for trusts and estates. The following rates apply to taxable income of trusts and estates for taxable years beginning in 1999.

If taxable income is over—	The tax is—
$0 but not over $1,750	15% of taxable income
$1,750 but not over $4,050	$262.50 *plus* 28% of excess over $1,750
$4,050 but not over $6,200	$906.50 *plus* 31% of excess over $4,050
$6,200 but not over $8,450	$1,573 *plus* 36% of excess over $6,200
Over $8,450	$2,383 *plus* 39.6% of excess over $8,450

33.4 Gifts of Appreciated Property

Making a gift of appreciated property that will eventually be sold may reduce income tax. To shift the profit and the tax, the gift must be completed before the sale or before the donor has made a binding commitment to sell. By making a gift of interests in the property to several family members, it is possible to spread the profit and the tax among a number of taxpayers in the lowest tax bracket. ***Note:*** The IRS may claim that the gift was never completed if after sale the donor controls the sales proceeds or has the use of them.

Do not make a gift of property that has decreased in value if you want a deduction for the loss. Once you give the property away, the loss deduction is gone forever. Neither you nor your donee can ever take advantage of it. The better way is first to sell the property, get a loss deduction, and then make a gift of the proceeds.

33.5 Splitting Business Income With Your Family

Tax on your business income may be reduced if you can shift it to members of your family. If you keep within the annual gift tax exclusion for each donee, there will be no gift tax consequences. However, the estate tax advantages of "estate freeze" techniques has been limited, making it difficult to avoid estate tax on the appreciation in capital interests transferred to children; *see 39.7*.

Planning Reminder

Revocable Trusts

In a revocable trust, you retain control over the property by reserving the right to revoke the trust. As such, it is considered an incomplete gift and offers no present income tax savings. Furthermore, the trust property will be included as part of your estate. But a revocable trust minimizes delay in passing property to beneficiaries if you die while the trust is in force. When you transfer property to a trust, the property is generally not subject to probate, administration expenses, delays attendant on distributions of estates, or claims of creditors. The interests of trust beneficiaries are generally more secure than those of heirs under a will because a will may be denied probate if found invalid.

Planning Reminder

Transfers of Appreciated Property

Before making a gift of appreciated property, consider the fact that the appreciation on property passed by inheritance escapes income tax; the heir takes a basis equal to estate tax value, which is usually the fair market value at the date of death. Furthermore, appreciated property encumbered by a mortgage may result in income tax to the donor when a gift of the property is made; *see 31.15*.

Business income may be shifted by forming a family partnership or by making your family stockholders in a corporation. An S corporation in which stockholders elect to report income may be used more freely than a partnership to split income.

A minor child will not be recognized as a partner unless he or she is competent to manage his or her own property, or control of the property is exercised by another person as fiduciary for the minor's sole benefit. Here, a trust may be set up to hold the minor's partnership interest. The IRS may review not only the terms of the trust and the partnership agreement but also actual operation of the trust to make certain the grantor-partner has not retained any ownership rights over the interest he or she transferred.

Transfers of stock to a trust for a minor terminate an S election, unless the trust is a qualified trust. For this purpose, a "Subchapter S trust" may be used. Alternatively, stock may be transferred for the minor's benefit to a custodian account for which the parent may act as custodian.

In order to get the income-shifting benefits from setting up a stock custodian account, there must be a *bona fide* transfer of stock entailing a complete surrender by you of any control over the transferred stock.

With a partnership, shifting income may be more difficult, depending on whether capital is a material income-producing factor in the business. If it is, a gift or sale of a partnership interest to a family member is effective. But in a service partnership—real estate or insurance brokers, for example—a mere gift of a partnership interest to a family member will not shift partnership income unless the person actually performs services for the partnership. In one case, the Tax Court held that where substantially all of a family partnership's capital consists of borrowed funds guaranteed by family members, the family partnership interests may be disregarded on the grounds that the borrowed funds are not a material income-producing factor in the business.

In an S corporation, pass-through items must reflect the value of services rendered or capital contributed by family members of the shareholders. If a relative of an S corporation shareholder performs services for or loans money to the corporation without receiving reasonable pay or interest, the IRS may allocate income to reflect the value of the services or capital provided. The "family" of an individual includes only spouse, ancestors, lineal descendants, and any trusts for the primary benefit of such persons.

Payment of wages to your child. Wages paid to your child are not subject to the "kiddie tax" of *24.3*, but investment income earned by the child from investing those wages is subject to the kiddie tax. You may also deduct the wages as a business expense if the payments are reasonable. Set the wages at the scale that you would pay an outsider; keep records of the child's work; withhold tax; and provide the child with a Form W-2. If you are a sole proprietor and your child is age 17 or under, you do not have to withhold FICA taxes (Social Security and Medicare) on wages you pay to your child.

Life Insurance

Court Decision

Policy Owned by Beneficiary

If you are buying a new policy with yourself as the insured, and you want to keep the proceeds out of your gross estate, you must buy the policy in another's name, such as in your spouse's name, or have your beneficiary buy the policy. For example, a daughter applies for a $1 million policy on her father's life and is the policy owner under the terms of the policy. If the father pays the premiums, his payments are treated as gifts, but the proceeds paid at his death are not subject to estate tax because he never had ownership rights in the policy. In the past, the IRS contested this tax-free treatment, but now agrees to follow court decisions that allow it.

33.6 Life Insurance Offers Tax Advantages

Insurance may provide a tax-free accumulation of cash. During the time you pay premiums, the value of your contract increases at compound interest rates. The increase is not subject to income tax. In addition, when your policy is paid at death to your beneficiaries, the proceeds are not subject to income tax; *see 33.7.*

Estate tax planning. To shelter life insurance proceeds from estate tax, you must not have ownership rights in the policy. If you have an existing policy, you must assign your ownership rights, such as the right to change beneficiaries, the right to surrender or cancel the policy, the right to assign it, and the right to borrow against it. An assignment must occur more than three years before death to exclude the proceeds from your estate.

Assigning group-term policies. Group insurance provided by an employer may be assigned. The IRS has agreed to follow a court decision holding that the power to convert a group policy into an individual policy when you leave the company will not subject the group-term insurance proceeds to estate tax. Since the conversion privilege is exercisable only by taking the economically disadvantageous step of quitting, this right is too remote to be considered a retained ownership right in the policy. If other incidents of ownership are transferred, such as the power to name beneficiaries and fix the type of benefit payable, the transfer will remove the policy from your estate.

The substitution of a new group carrier does not jeopardize assignments under a prior carrier.

When you plan to assign a policy, review your gift tax liability on such a transfer. In the case of an assignment of a group policy, the cost of the policy is determined by actuarially apportioning the employer's total premium payment among the covered employees. This is difficult for an individual employee to do, particularly where there are many employees, so the IRS generally allows employees to value the assigned policy using the same tax tables used to determine the amount of the employee's compensation where group coverage exceeds $50,000. *See* the table at *3.3.* Key employees may not use the table to determine gift tax liability.

You may want to readjust your coverage to meet new family conditions. You can exchange your policies without tax; *see 6.11.*

Using a trust to purchase insurance. If you create a trust to carry a policy on your life by transferring income-producing property the income of which is used to pay the premiums, you are taxable on the trust income. Similarly, if your spouse creates the trust to carry the policy on your life, he or she is taxable on the trust income. This tax rule does not apply to the trust funding of life insurance covering the life of a third party other than your spouse. For example, a grandparent transfers income-producing property to a trust to pay the premiums on a policy on the life of his son. His grandchildren are named trust beneficiaries. The grandparent is not taxed on the income earned by the trust on the transferred property because the trust purchased insurance on his son's life, not his own.

Insurance trust to receive proceeds. A trust may be used to receive insurance proceeds where there is concern that the beneficiary may be unable to manage a large insurance settlement. The trustee may be a bank or a person directed to invest the proceeds and pay income to beneficiaries according to standards provided in the trust. The trustee may be given the discretion to pay out more or less as circumstances warrant. He or she may be directed to terminate the trust when the beneficiaries reach a certain age, or when they demonstrate their ability to manage money. There may also be investment advantages in a trust. The trust investments may yield a higher rate of return than that of an insurance company under a settlement option.

Insurance proceeds are not subject to income tax whether paid directly to named beneficiaries or to a trust.

Single-premium policies. Single-premium policies have been touted as tax-sheltered investments. Companies offer competitive current returns and tax-free appreciation on your investment fund. The name of the policy is descriptive: You make a single-premium payment—$5,000, $10,000, $50,000, or more. Part of the premium goes for life insurance coverage and part towards an investment fund.

However, tax benefits of single-premium and other cash value policies have been cut back, as discussed below.

Universal life insurance plans. Universal life insurance offers tax-free buildup of interest income at current market rates and on death, tax-free receipt of insurance proceeds. A universal life insurance policy is made up of (1) life insurance protection and (2) a cash reserve on which interest income accumulates without tax.

The interest rate of universal life is pegged to current bond market rates. Furthermore, a universal life policy lets you withdraw the cash reserve if you want to invest it elsewhere and to allocate how much of your premium payment is to cover insurance protection and how much is to go into the cash reserve.

The tax law sets limits on the amount of premiums that may be earmarked for the cash reserve. If these limits are violated, tax-free treatment for the proceeds may be lost. For these limits, check with the company issuing the policy.

A disadvantage of universal life is that you must incur an upfront commission payment that may be 50% or more of the first premium. There may also be a fee for withdrawing the cash reserve.

See below for restrictions on withdrawals from cash value policies.

Tax on withdrawals from cash value modified endowment contracts. Contracts entered into after June 20, 1988, may be subject to tax penalties if they are considered "modified endowment contracts." Generally, a modified endowment contract is a contract that fails to satisfy a technical "seven-year-pay test." A contract fails the "seven-year-pay test" if the premiums paid during the first seven contract years exceed the sum of the net level premiums that would have been paid by that time had the contract provided for paid-up future benefits after the payment of seven level annual premiums.

Planning Reminder

Insurance Options
Before considering a universal insurance plan, determine the possibility that the purchase of term insurance and an investment in money-market funds or long-term bonds may be a better alternative to a universal life plan.

Amounts received under modified endowment contracts that are not received as an annuity, such as dividends, cash withdrawals, loans, and amounts received upon a partial surrender of the contract, are taxable to the extent the cash surrender value of the contract exceeds the policyholder's investment. Withdrawals that are greater than the excess of cash surrender value over the investment are a tax-free return of capital. Assignments or pledges of a contract to cover burial or prearranged funeral expenses are not considered taxable distributions if the contractual death benefit is $25,000 or less.

To prevent marketing of multiple contracts as a means of avoiding these tax limitations, all modified endowment contracts issued by the same insurer or its affiliates to the same policyholder within the same calendar year are aggregated to determine the amount includible in income.

Penalty for early withdrawals from modified endowment contracts. A 10% premature withdrawal penalty applies to taxable distributions and loans unless the policyholder is over age 59 ½, disabled, or the distribution is one of a series of substantially equal payments over life expectancy or over joint life expectancy with a beneficiary; for further details, *see 7.15*.

33.7 How Life Insurance Proceeds Are Taxed to a Beneficiary

Life insurance proceeds received upon the death of the insured are generally tax free. However, insurance proceeds may be subject to estate tax so that the beneficiary actually receives a reduced amount; *see 39.2*.

Interest paid on proceeds left with the insurer is taxable except in this case: A surviving spouse who elects to receive installments rather than a lump sum does not pay tax on the first $1,000 of interest received each year if the decedent died before October 23, 1986.

Read the following checklist to find how your insurance receipts are taxed—

A lump-sum payment of the full face value of a life insurance policy: The proceeds are generally tax free. The tax-free exclusion also covers death benefit payments made under endowment contracts, workers' compensation insurance contracts, employers' group insurance plans, or accident and health insurance contracts. The exclusion does not apply to a policy combined with a nonrefund life annuity contract where a single premium equal to the face value of the insurance is paid.

Insurance proceeds may be taxable where the policy was transferred for valuable consideration. Exceptions to this rule are made for transfers among partners and corporations and their stockholders and officers.

Installment payments spread over your life under a policy that could have been paid in a lump sum: Part of each installment attributed to interest may be taxed. Divide the face amount of the policy by the number of years the installments are to be paid. The result is the amount that is received tax free each year.

If you are the surviving spouse of an insured who died before October 23, 1986, up to $1,000 of interest paid with the annual installment is also tax free. You are still treated as a spouse if separated from the insured at the date of his or her death, but not if divorced. (If you receive payments under a policy with a "family income rider," *see 33.8*.) The $1,000 interest exclusion is not allowed where the insured died after October 22, 1986.

EXAMPLE

Alice is the wife and beneficiary under her husband John's life insurance policy of $100,000. He died September 30, 1986. She elected to take installment payments for the rest of her life. Alice's life expectancy is 20 years. Thus, $5,000 ($100,000 ÷ 20) is the principal amount spread to each year. The first $6,000 received each year ($5,000 principal plus $1,000 of the spouse's special interest exclusion) is exempt from tax. If Alice lives more than 20 years, she may continue to treat up to $6,000 of annual payments as tax-free receipts.

If the policy guarantees payments to a secondary beneficiary if you should die before receiving a specified number of payments, the tax-free amount is reduced by the present value of the secondary beneficiary's interest in the policy. The insurance company can give you this figure.

Installment payments for a fixed number of years under a policy that could have been paid in a lump sum. Divide the full face amount of the policy by the number of years you are to receive the installments. The result is the amount that is received tax free each year.

Planning Reminder

Accelerated Death Benefits

A person who is terminally ill may withdraw without tax life insurance proceeds to pay medical bills and other living expenses. For policies lacking an accelerated benefits clause, it is possible to sell a life insurance policy without incurring tax to a viatical settlement company; *see 17.16*.

EXAMPLE

Same facts as in the preceding Example, but Alice elects to take installment payments for 10 years. Then $10,000 ($100,000 ÷ 10) is the principal amount received tax free. So up to $11,000 per year may be received tax free by Alice, $10,000 of principal sum plus up to $1,000 of interest, under the surviving spouse's interest exclusion.

Installment payments when there is no lump-sum option in the policy: You must find the discounted value of the policy at the date of the insured's death and use that as the principal amount. The insurance company can give you that figure. After you find the discounted value, you divide it by the number of years you are to receive installments. The result is the amount that is tax free. The remainder is taxed.

EXAMPLE

The insured died in 1999. Under an insurance policy, the surviving wife is entitled to $5,000 a year for life. Her life expectancy is 20 years. There is no lump sum stated in the policy. Say the discounted value of the wife's rights is $60,000. The principal amount spread to each year for the wife is $3,000 ($60,000 ÷ 20). Subtracting $3,000 from each annual $5,000 payment gives her taxable income of $2,000.

Payments to you along with other beneficiaries under the same policy, by lump-sum or varying installments. *See* the following Example for the way multiple beneficiaries may be taxed.

EXAMPLE

Under one life insurance policy of an insured man who died in 1999, a surviving wife, daughter, and nephew are all beneficiaries. The wife is entitled to a lump sum of $60,000. The daughter and nephew are each entitled to a lump sum of $35,000. Under the installment options, the wife chooses to receive $5,000 a year for the rest of her life. (She has a 20-year life expectancy.) The daughter and the nephew each choose a yearly payment of $5,000 for 10 years. This is how each yearly installment is taxed:

Wife: The principal amount spread to each year is $3,000. Subtracting $3,000 from the yearly $5,000 payment gives the wife taxable income of $2,000.

Daughter and Nephew: Both are taxed the same way. The principal amount spread to each of the 10 years is $3,500. Subtracting this $3,500 from the yearly $5,000 installment gives the daughter and the nephew taxable income of $1,500 each.

Interest only option. When proceeds are left on deposit under the "interest only" option, distributions of interest are fully taxed. A surviving spouse of an insured who died before October 23, 1986, may not exclude $1,000 interest under the "interest only" option. However, if the surviving spouse later elects to receive proceeds from the policy in installments, the interest exclusion applies from the time of the election.

33.8 A Policy With a Family Income Rider

Payments received under a family income rider are taxed under a special rule. A family income rider provides additional term insurance coverage for a fixed number of years from the date of the basic policy. Under the terms of a rider, if the insured dies at any time during the term period, the beneficiary receives monthly payments during the balance of the term period, and then at the end of the term period, receives the lump-sum proceeds of the basic policy. If the insured dies after the end of the term period, the beneficiary receives only the lump sum from the basic policy.

When the insured dies during the term period, part of each monthly payment received during the term period includes interest on the lump-sum proceeds of the basic policy (which is held by the company until the end of the term period). That interest is fully taxed. The balance of the monthly payment consists of an installment (principal plus interest) of the proceeds from the term insurance purchased under the family income rider. You may exclude from this balance: (1) a prorated portion of the present value of the lump sum under the basic policy and (2) an additional amount

Caution

Universal Life Policy
A universal life policy allows a policyholder to apply premium payments to cash value instead of to death benefits. Death benefits may be tax free if the policies meet certain technical tests. These tests must be determined by the insurance company. Therefore, you must check with the company paying the proceeds as to whether the payments qualify as tax-free life insurance payments. Other names applied to universal life policies may be "flexible premium" and "adjustable life premium" policies.

Caution

Surrender of Policy for Cash

If the cash received on the surrender of a policy exceeds the premiums paid less dividends received, the excess is taxed as ordinary income (not capital gain). If you take, instead, a paid-up policy, you may avoid tax; *see 6.11*. You get no deduction if there is a loss on the surrender of a policy.

Tax may be avoided by a terminally ill individual on the surrender of a policy under an accelerated death benefit clause or on a sale of the policy to a viatical settlement company; *see 17.16*.

of up to $1,000 attributable to interest if you are a surviving spouse of an insured who died before October 23, 1986. The lump sum under the basic policy is tax free when you eventually receive it.

The rules here also apply to an integrated family income policy and to family maintenance policies, whether integrated or with an attached rider.

In figuring your taxable portions, ask the insurance company for its interest rate and the present value of term payments.

33.9 How Other Insurance Proceeds Are Taxed

Dividends paid by the insurance company as reduction of premiums (taken in cash, left as interest with the company, or used to accelerate the maturity of the policy) are not taxable. They serve to reduce the cost basis of your policy, thus increasing gain sometimes computed upon maturity of some policies. However, interest on such "dividends" is generally taxable, although the interest on GI insurance dividends left on deposit with the VA is tax free.

Matured endowment policies. You generally report as income the difference between the proceeds received and your investment; *see 7.24*. The payment on an endowment contract because of the insured's death is treated as the payment of tax-free life insurance proceeds provided the policy meets certain technical definitions not discussed in this book.

Sale of an endowment contract before maturity. Taxed as ordinary income; *see 7.22*.

Collection of proceeds on policy purchased by or assigned to you on the life of someone else. Where a policy is transferred for valuable consideration, only the amount paid and the premiums paid after the transfer are tax free when collected; the balance is taxed. There is no tax on life insurance proceeds paid under contracts that have been transferred to a partner or to a corporation in which the insured was a shareholder or officer.

Tax Pointers for Senior Citizens

All of your Social Security benefits are tax free if your "provisional income," explained at *34.3*, is $25,000 or less if you are single, or $32,000 or less if you are married and file a joint return. No more than 50% of your benefits are subject to tax if you file a joint return and your provisional income is over $32,000 but no more than $44,000, or if you are single and your provisional income is over $25,000 but no more than $34,000. When provisional income exceeds $34,000 or $44,000 (depending on your filing status), more than 50%, but no more than 85%, of your benefits are subject to tax. If you are married and filing separately, and did not live apart for the whole year, you compute the amount of taxable benefits without considering the base amounts allowed on joint and single returns. If you are married filing separately and you lived apart the entire year, are a head of household, or a qualifying widow(er), use the $25,000 and $34,000 base amounts for single persons.

If you continue to earn wages or self-employed income, you must pay FICA taxes or self-employment tax on that income regardless of your age. Do not confuse this rule with the Social Security benefit rule that allows full benefits for working after you reach age 70; *see 34.5*.

34.1 Special Rules for Senior Citizens

The following special tax rules favor senior citizens:

- *Higher filing thresholds.* If you are single and age 65 or older on or before January 1, 2000, you do not have to file a 1999 return unless your gross income is $8,100 or over. This is $1,050 more than for younger taxpayers. If you are married and you and your spouse are both age 65 or older, a joint return does not have to be filed unless your gross income is $14,400 or over, or $13,550 or over if only one of you is age 65 or older; *see* the chart on page 2 for further details.

- *Higher standard deduction.* If you are age 65 or older on or before January 1, 2000, you receive an additional standard deduction allowance if you do not itemize deductions. If you are single you get an additional $1,050 on your 1999 return, $850 if you are married or a qualifying widow(er); *see* *13.4.* Your 1999 standard deduction is $5,350 if you are single. If married filing jointly, it is $8,050 if one of you is age 65 or over, and $8,900 if both of you are.

- *Tax credit if age 65 or older.* This is a limited tax credit for taxpayers age 65 or older who receive little or no Social Security or Railroad Retirement benefits. The credit may also be available to persons under age 65 who are totally disabled; *see* *34.7.* For example, if you are single, or married but only you are eligible, and receive more than $416 each month from Social Security, you may not claim the credit. If you are married and both you and your spouse are eligible for the credit and file a joint return, you may not claim the credit if you receive more than $625 each month from Social Security.

- *Social Security benefits may be exempt from tax.* If you are married and file jointly, none of your net Social Security benefits are taxable in 1999 if your income is not more than a base amount of $32,000, or $25,000 if your filing status is single, head of household, qualifying widow(er), or you are married filing separately and did not live with your spouse at any time during 1999. Married persons who file separately and live together at any time during the year are not allowed any base amount; *see* *34.3* for computing taxable Social Security benefits.

Social Security Benefits

34.2 Social Security Benefits Subject to Tax

If you received or repaid Social Security benefits in 1999, you should receive Form SSA-1099 by January 31, 2000. The form will show total benefits paid to you and any benefits you repaid to the government in 1999. Amounts withheld for Medicare premiums, workers' compensation offset, or attorneys' fees are itemized and included in Box 3, benefits paid in 1999. Keep Form SSA-1099 for your records; do not attach it to your return.

The *net benefit* shown in Box 5 of Form SSA-1099 (benefits paid less benefits repaid) is the benefit amount used to determine the taxable portion of your benefits (if any) under *34.3.*

Railroad Retirement benefits. The portion of your Tier 1 Railroad Retirement benefits that is equivalent to Social Security retirement benefits is subject to the computation at *34.3* for determining taxable benefits. If any part of your 1999 Tier 1 benefits is equivalent to Social Security benefits, you should receive Form RRB-1099 from the government by January 31, 2000. The *net* Social Security Equivalent Benefit shown on Form RRB-1099 is the amount used to determine taxable benefits under *34.3.* Other Tier 1 Railroad Retirement benefits, as well as Tier 2 benefits, are treated as pension income and not as Social Security benefits for tax purposes.

Benefits paid on behalf of child or incompetent. If a child is entitled to Social Security benefits, such as after the death of a parent, the benefit is considered to be the child's regardless of who actually receives the payment. Whether the child's benefit is subject to tax will depend on the amount of the child's income.

Workers' compensation. If you are receiving Social Security disability payments and workers' compensation for the same disability, your Social Security benefits may be reduced by the workers' compensation. For example, you are entitled to Social Security disability benefits of $5,000 a year. After receiving a $1,000 workers' compensation award, your disability benefits are reduced to $4,000. For purposes of the computation steps of *34.3,* you treat the full $5,000 as Social Security benefits.

Net benefits. The net benefit shown in Box 5 of Form SSA-1099 is the amount used to determine the taxable portion of your benefits. If Box 5 shows a negative amount (a figure in parentheses), none of your benefits are taxable. If the negative amount is related to Social Security benefits included in gross income in a prior year, you may be entitled to a deduction or a credit; *see* IRS Publication 915 for further instructions on how to figure the deduction or credit when your repayments exceed your gross benefits.

Filing Instruction

Repayment of Benefits

If you lose Social Security benefits because of excessive outside income, the forfeited amount reduces your benefits subject to tax. Form SSA-1099 accounts for this reduction. The net benefit amount shown in Box 5 is used to determine if any of your benefits are taxable.

Taxable Social Security benefits are not considered earnings and therefore may not be the basis of an IRA contribution *(8.2)*, earned income credit *(25.12)*, or foreign earned income exclusion *(36.2)*.

Nonresident aliens. Unless provided otherwise by tax treaty, 85% of a nonresident alien's Social Security benefits will be subject to the 30% withholding tax imposed on U.S. source income that is not connected with a U.S. trade or business. *See* IRS Publication 519 for further details.

34.3 Computing Taxable Social Security Benefits

You may use the three worksheets in this section to determine the taxable portion of your Social Security benefits. First fill out Worksheet I for listing your benefits and Worksheet II for determining your *provisional income*. Part of your net Social Security benefits will be subject to tax on Worksheet III if your *provisional income* exceeds a base amount of $25,000 or $32,000.

Note that on Line 1 of Worksheet II *tax-exempt interest* reported on Line 8b of your return is included as part of provisional income for purposes of figuring the taxable part of your Social Security benefits, although this amount is not included when figuring your regular tax liability.

Worksheet I: Personal Benefits Data

Your Social Security benefits:

1. Enter net Social Security benefits from
   Box 5 of SSA-1099 or RRB-1099.   1._____
2. 50% of Line 1.   2._____
3. 85% of Line 1.   3._____

Worksheet II: Figuring Your Provisional Income

1. From *Form 1040*, add Lines 7, 8a, 8b, 9 through 14, 15b,
   16b, 17 through 19, and Line 21. Do not include Line 20a
   (net Social Security benefits). Enter the total here.
   From *Form 1040A*, add Lines 7, 8a, 8b, 9, 10b, 11b, and 12.
   Do not include Line 13a (net Social Security benefits).
   Enter the total here.   1._____
2. *Plus:* Tax-free foreign earned income and foreign
   housing.   _____
   Other exclusions.*   _____ 2._____
3. Add Lines 1 and 2.   3._____
4. Enter adjustments from Line 32 of Form 1040 other than the
   foreign housing deduction, or adjustments from Line 17 of
   Form 1040A. Do not include IRA contributions if you are covered
   by an employer retirement plan; *see* below for alternative
   computation.   4._____
5. Subtract Line 4 from Line 3.   5._____
6. Enter the amount from Line 2, Worksheet I (50% of net
   Social Security benefits).   6._____
7. Add Lines 5 and 6. This is provisional income. Enter this
   amount on Line 1 of Worksheet III.   7._____

Include exclusions for qualifying U.S. Savings Bond interest used for tuition, employer-provided adoption benefits, and income earned as a bona fide resident of Puerto Rico or American Samoa.

IRA contributions. Do *not* use the worksheet below if you are an active participant in an employer retirement plan and you plan to make deductible IRA contributions *(8.4)*. You must use the worksheets printed in IRS Publication 590. With the worksheets, you first determine the amount of Social Security benefits that would be subject to tax, assuming you did not claim any IRA deduction. That amount is then used to figure the allowable IRA deduction, taking into account any limitations under the phase-out rules *(8.4)*, and, finally, the allowable IRA deduction is used to compute the taxable portion of your Social Security benefits.

If you are not covered by an employer retirement plan, you may use the worksheet to figure the taxable portion of your Social Security benefits.

Planning Reminder

Voluntary Withholding on Social Security Benefits

You can use your Social Security benefits to meet your estimated and final tax liability by electing on Form W-4V to have tax withheld from benefits at a 7%, 15%, 28%, or 31% rate.

Caution

Married Filing Separately

If you are married filing separately and during 1999 you lived with your spouse at any time, you must include in your taxable income the lesser of (1) 85% of your net Social Security benefits (Line 3 of Worksheet I) and (2) 85% of the provisional income shown on Line 7 of Worksheet II.

Worksheet III: Figuring Taxable Benefits

Check only one box:
- ❏ A. Single, head of household, or qualifying widow(er) with dependent child.
- ❏ B. Married filing a joint return.
- ❏ C. Married filing separately and LIVED WITH your spouse at ANY TIME during 1999.
- ❏ D. Married filing separately and LIVED APART from your spouse FOR ALL of 1999.

1. Enter Line 7 from Worksheet II (provisional income).   1._____
2. Enter: $25,000 if you checked Box A or D above, or $32,000 if you checked Box B, or 0 if you checked Box C.   2._____
3. Subtract Line 2 from Line 1. If zero or less, enter 0.   3._____
    - If Line 3 is zero, stop. None of your Social Security or Railroad Retirement benefits are taxable.
    - If Line 3 is more than zero, go to Line 4.
4. Enter 50% of Line 3.   4._____
5. Enter the amount from Line 2 of Worksheet I (50% of net Social Security benefits).   5._____
6. Enter: $34,000 if you checked Box A or D above, or $44,000 if you checked Box B, or 0 if you checked Box C.   6._____
7. Subtract Line 6 from Line 1. If zero or less, enter 0 and go to Line 13 now. If Line 7 is more than zero, go to Line 8.   7._____
8. Enter: $4,500 if you checked Box A or D above, or $6,000 if you checked Box B, or 0 if you checked Box C.   8._____
9. Enter the smallest of Line 4, Line 5, and Line 8.   9._____
10. Multiply Line 7 by 85% (.85).   10._____
11. Add Lines 9 and 10.   11._____
12. Enter the amount from Line 3 of Worksheet I (85% of net Social Security benefits).   12._____
13. **Taxable Social Security (or Railroad Retirement) benefits:** If Line 7 is zero, enter on Line 13 the *smaller* of Line 4 and Line 5. If Line 7 is more than zero, enter the *smaller* of Line 11 and Line 12. This is the taxable part of your benefits. Also enter this taxable amount on Line 20b of Form 1040 or Line 13b of Form 1040A. Your net Social Security benefits are reported on Line 20a of Form 1040 or Line 13a of Form 1040A.   13._____

EXAMPLES

1. Frank Adams, who is single, has 1999 earnings of $15,000 from a part-time job, $3,000 of interest income, and $2,000 of dividends. He also receives $8,000 of net Social Security benefits (Box 5 of Form SSA-1099). Completing Worksheet II, Frank's provisional income on Line 7 is $24,000 ($15,000 + 3,000 + 2,000 + 50% of the $8,000 net Social Security benefits). Since $24,000 does not exceed the $25,000 base amount on Line 2 of Worksheet III, none of Frank's Social Security benefits are taxable.

2. Sam and Fran Baker receive in 1999 net Social Security benefits (Box 5 of Form SSA-1099) of $15,000. Their taxable interest, dividends, and capital gains are $20,000, and tax-exempt interest is $10,000. They file a joint return. Their provisional income from Line 7 of Worksheet II is $37,500 ($20,000 + 10,000 + 50% of the $15,000 net Social Security benefits). Since $37,500 exceeds the $32,000 base amount on Line 2 of Worksheet III, part of their Social Security benefits will be taxed. On Worksheet III, Sam and Fran figure that $2,750 of their benefits will be subject to tax:

Worksheet III

1.	Provisional income	$37,500
2.	Base amount for married persons filing jointly	32,000
3.	Line 1 *less* Line 2	5,500
4.	50% of Line 3	2,750
5.	50% of net Social Security benefits	7,500
6.	Adjusted base amount for married persons filing jointly	44,000
7.	Line 1 *less* Line 6	0

Since provisional income does not exceed the adjusted base amount of $44,000, the instructions for Line 13 of Worksheet III state that the taxable portion of Sam and Fran's benefits is $2,750, the lesser of Line 4 ($2,750) and Line 5 ($7,500).

34.4   Election for Lump-Sum Social Security Benefit Payment

If in 1999 you receive a lump-sum payment of benefits covering prior years, you have a choice as to how to determine the taxable portion of the benefits: (1) You may treat the entire payment as a 1999 benefit taxable under the rules of *34.3 or* (2) you may allocate the benefits between 1999 and the earlier years. Choose the method that provides the lowest required increase to income in the current year. For example, if you receive a 1999 lump-sum payment that includes benefits for 1998, you may find that an allocation of benefits is advantageous where your income over the two-year period has fluctuated and benefits allocated to 1998 would be subject to a lower taxable percentage than in 1999.

When you elect to allocate benefits to a prior year, you do not amend the return for that year. You compute the increase in income (if any) that would have resulted if the Social Security benefits had been received in that year. You then add that amount to the income of the current year.

See IRS Publication 915 for instructions on how to allocate and report the allocated income on your return.

34.5   Retiring on Social Security Benefits

Benefits are not paid automatically. You must register at the local Social Security office three months before your 65th birthday to allow time for your application to be processed and to locate all necessary information. Even if you do not plan to retire at age 65, you must register to insure your Medicare coverage.

If you retire before age 65, you may elect reduced Social Security benefits. The reduction formula is based on the number of months before age 65 that you retire. If you retire at the earliest age, 62, the reduction is about 20%.

If you delay retirement beyond age 65, your potential Social Security benefit increases for each year you delay retirement. The increase is 4.5% per year for those born in 1929 or 1930, 5% for those born in 1931 or 1932, 5.5% for those born in 1933 or 1934, 6% for those born in 1935 or 1936, and 6.5% for those born in 1937 or 1938.

Benefits may be reduced because of earnings. If you are under age 70, Social Security benefits are reduced by earned income (wages and self-employment income). If you were age 65 or older but under age 70 in 1999, you could earn $15,500 without losing benefits. If you were under age 65 for the whole year, you could earn $9,600 without losing benefits; this ceiling is subject to annual inflation adjustments. Once you earn more than these ceilings, benefits are reduced. If you are age 65 or over and under age 70, you lose $1 in benefits for each $3 you earn above the earnings ceiling. If you are under age 65, $1 of benefits is lost for every $2 of excess earnings. In the year of retirement, a special monthly earnings ceiling applies.

So long as you continue to work, you pay Social Security taxes on your earnings, regardless of your age.

Regardless of your age, you may receive any amount of income from sources other than work—for example, private pensions or investments—without affecting the amount of Social Security retirement benefits.

Request an estimate of benefits and copy of earnings record. You can get an estimate of retirement benefits by sending for Form SSA-7004. After mailing in a completed Form SSA-7004, you will receive a Personal Earnings and Benefit Estimate Statement, showing your earnings history, Social Security tax payments, and an estimate of your retirement, disability, and survivor's benefits.

Form SSA-7004 is available at your local Social Security office. You can also request the form from the Social Security Administration by calling 1-800-772-1213 or obtain it from the Social Security Administration website at www.ssa.gov.

34.6   How Tax on Social Security Reduces Your Earnings

There is an added tax cost of earning income if the earnings will subject your Social Security benefits to tax. Therefore, if your benefits are not currently exposed to tax, you have to figure *not only* the tax on the extra income *but also* the amount of Social Security benefits subjected to tax by those earnings. If the additional earnings will put you over the base amount *(34.3),* then you will not only have to pay tax on the additional earnings but also on the Social Security benefits that will be subject to tax. As a result, the marginal tax rate on the extra income will be higher than the regular rate that would otherwise apply; *see* Example 2 on the next page.

Planning Reminder

Age 70 or Older

For those age 70 or over, benefits are not reduced by earnings. You can work, earn any amount, and receive full Social Security benefits.

Planning Reminder

Retirement Earnings Test

For individuals age 65–69, here is the amount that may be earned without losing Social Security benefits:

In—	Earnings ceiling—
1999	15,500
2000	17,000
2001	25,000
2002	30,000

1. You are over age 70 and you and your spouse receive net Social Security benefits of $8,000. You file jointly. You have pension income of $25,000 and $3,000 in tax-exempt interest. Your provisional income *(34.3)* is $32,000. No part of your Social Security benefits is taxable because your provisional income of $32,000 does not exceed the $32,000 base amount for married persons filing jointly.
2. Same facts as in Example 1, except that you take a part-time job paying $8,000. This increases your provisional income to $40,000 and subjects $4,000 of Social Security benefits to tax.

Provisional income	$40,000
Less: Base amount	32,000
Excess	$8,000
50% of excess taxable *(34.3)*	$4,000

The $8,000 of additional earnings increased your taxable income by $12,000, which is the $8,000 of earnings plus the $4,000 of Social Security benefits made taxable because of the increase in provisional income. Assuming a 15% tax rate, the tax on the $12,000 is $1,800 ($12,000 × 15%); the effective tax rate on the $8,000 earnings is 22.5% ($1,800 ÷ $8,000), rather than 15%. If you consider employment taxes, the effective tax rate is higher; *see* below.

When earnings result in forfeiture of Social Security benefits. If you are under 70 years of age, it is possible under the current tax structure to earn extra income and yet have only a small gain or even lose money when considering the increased tax on the earnings and on Social Security benefits, and also the forfeiture of benefits when earnings exceed the annual retirement earnings test; *see 34.5.*

Therefore, before taking on work to earn extra income, you should compute the tax cost of the extra earnings and the loss of benefits. As a rule of thumb, you may figure the extra tax cost by multiplying the earnings by your top federal tax bracket and also by the FICA tax rate of 7.65% (Social Security and Medicare withholdings) and by your top rate for state or local taxes. But be aware that this composite rate ignores the effect of the increased tax from crossing the thresholds for taxing up to 50% or 85% of Social Security benefits. Therefore, in such cases, the tax cost will be greater than the estimated composite tax rate. For greater accuracy, figure your tax position as if you were preparing two tax returns: one that does not include the extra income and the other that does include the extra income. The tax difference is the extra income tax cost of earning the extra pay. Add to this cost the FICA tax on the extra earnings and any additional state or local taxes. Then figure the amount of benefits that will be forfeited. This will give you a net gain or in some cases a net loss. If you have a tax consultant, it may be advisable to ask the consultant to make the computations.

Caution

Cost of Losing Benefits

When you work and receive Social Security benefits, do not forget to consider the tax cost of the extra earnings and, if you are under age 70, the possible loss of benefits. There are proposals in Congress to eliminate benefit reductions for working individuals.

Tax Credit for the Elderly and Disabled

34.7 Claiming the Credit for the Elderly and Disabled

You may qualify for a tax credit for 1999 if you meet one of the following conditions:

- Your 65th birthday is on or before January 1, 2000; *or*
- You were under age 65 at the end of 1999, you retired before the end of 1999 because of permanent and total disability and you received taxable disability income in 1999 from your former employer's disability plan. Disability income is taxable wages or payments in lieu of wages paid to you while absent from work because of permanent and total disability. Qualifying disability income does not include payments received after reaching mandatory retirement age.

However, even if you meet one of these tests, you may not be able to claim a credit because your Social Security benefits or adjusted gross income is too high; *see 34.9.*

Disabled. You are considered permanently and totally disabled if you are unable to engage in any substantial gainful activity by reason of any medically determinable physical or mental impairment that can be expected to result in death or that has lasted or can be expected to last for a continuous period of not less than 12 months.

For the first year you claim the credit, you need a physician's certification of your disability. For later years, new certifications are generally not required.

Nonresident aliens. You may not claim the credit if you are a nonresident alien at any time during 1999, unless you are married to a citizen or resident and you have elected to be treated as a resident; *see 1.5.*

Amount of credit. The amount of the credit is 15% times the base amount after reductions. The base amount for the credit is generally $7,500, $5,000, or $3,750, as shown in *34.8.* The base amount is reduced by nontaxable Social Security and other tax-free pensions, as well as by adjusted gross income exceeding specific limits as explained in *34.9.*

How to claim the credit. You claim the credit on Schedule R if you file Form 1040. If you file Form 1040A, claim the credit on Part 3. You may not claim the credit on Form 1040EZ.

The credit is not refundable. That is, it is allowed only up to your tax liability. Follow the tax form instructions.

Married couples. A married couple may claim the credit only if they file a joint return. However, if a husband and wife live apart at all times during the taxable year and file separately, the credit may be claimed on a separate return.

34.8 Base Amount for the Elderly or Disabled Credit

The law fixes an initial base amount for figuring the credit. This base amount is reduced by certain tax-free benefits and excess adjusted gross income; *see 34.9.* The credit is 15% of the base amount after reductions.

The initial base amount is:

- $5,000, if you are single, head of household, or are a qualified widow(er).
- $5,000, if you file a joint return and only one spouse is eligible for the credit.
- $7,500, if you file a joint return and both spouses are eligible for the credit. The credit is figured solely on this base; a separate computation is not made for each spouse.
- $3,750, if you are married and file a separate return. The credit may be claimed on a separate return only if you and your spouse have lived apart at all times during the year.

Base amount if disabled. If you are under age 65 and permanently and totally disabled, the base amount for figuring the credit is the *lower* of your 1999 disability income and the initial base amount for your filing status shown above. For example, if you are single, under age 65, permanently and totally disabled, and received disability income of $4,800, you figure the credit on $4,800, which is less than the base of $5,000 for single persons.

Joint return and both spouses qualify for the credit. If one spouse is age 65 or over and one spouse is under age 65 and receives disability income, the initial base amount is the lesser of (1) $7,500 and (2) $5,000 *plus* the disability income of the spouse under age 65. If both spouses are under age 65 and disabled, the initial base amount is the total of their disability income, not exceeding $7,500.

34.9 Reduction of the Credit Base Amount for the Elderly and Disabled

The $3,750, $5,000, or $7,500 credit base amount *(34.8)* is reduced by nontaxable pensions and Social Security, and also by "excess" adjusted gross income, figured as follows:

Nontaxable Social Security and pensions. The base amount is reduced by:

- Social Security and Railroad Retirement benefits that are *not taxable* under rules of 34.3; *and*
- Tax-free pension, annuity, or disability income paid under a law administered by the Veterans' Administration or under other federal laws.

You do *not* reduce the base amount for: military disability pensions received for active service in the Armed Forces or in the Coast Guard and Geodetic Survey or Public Health Service; certain disability annuities paid under the Foreign Service Act of 1980; and workers' compensation benefits. However, if Social Security benefits are reduced by workers' compensation benefits, the amount of workers' compensation benefits is treated as Social Security benefits that reduce the base.

Excess adjusted gross income. You reduce the base amount by one-half of adjusted gross income (AGI) exceeding: $7,500 if you are single, head of household, or a qualified widow(er); $10,000 if you are married filing a joint return; or $5,000 if you are married, live apart from your

 Caution

Income Limits for Credit

If your adjusted gross income or nontaxable pensions exceed the limits shown at *34.9,* you cannot claim the credit for the elderly or disabled.

spouse for the entire year, and file a separate return. Applying these income floors, the credit is no longer available to a single person when AGI reaches $17,500, $20,000 on a joint return where one spouse is eligible for the credit, $25,000 on a joint return where both spouses are eligible for the credit, and $12,500 where a married person files separately.

EXAMPLES

1. A single person over age 65 has adjusted gross income (AGI) of $9,000 and receives Social Security benefits of $4,200 that are not taxable under *34.3*. His credit is $7.50.

Initial base amount *(34.8)*	$5,000
Less: Nontaxable Social Security	4,200
	$800
Less: 50% of $1,500 ($9,000 AGI *minus* $7,500)	750
Credit base	$50
Credit (15%)	$7.50

2. A married couple, both over age 65, file a joint return showing adjusted gross income of $12,000. They received Social Security benefits of $5,000, which are not subject to tax.

Initial base amount *(34.8)*	$7,500
Less: Nontaxable Social Security	5,000
	$2,500
Less: 50% of AGI over $10,000	1,000
Credit base	$1,500
Credit (15%)	$225

Caution

Low Social Security Benefits Required for Credit

The tax credit for the elderly or disabled is not available to an unmarried individual who receives $5,000 or more of nontaxable Social Security benefits or nontaxable federal pensions such as from the Veterans' Administration. The $5,000 limit also applies if you are married filing jointly and only one spouse qualifies for the credit. The limit is $7,500 if you file a joint return and both spouses qualify for the credit.

Continuing Care Communities

34.10 Tax Effects of Moving to a Continuing Care Facility

Senior citizens who move into "continuing care" or "life-care" facilities pay large upfront entrance fees upon admittance, as well as monthly fees thereafter in return for a residence, meals, and lifetime health care, including long-term skilled nursing care, should that become necessary. The payments raise several tax issues discussed in this section and in *34.11*.

Portion of monthly fees deductible as medical expense. Part of the monthly fees to a life-care community are allocable to health care, which you may deduct as an itemized medical expense subject to the 7.5% floor; *see 17.1*. Continuing care facilities generally send a statement to the residents specifying what portion of their monthly service fees went towards health care.

What about the upfront payments required by life-care communities? Part may be allowable as a medical expense deduction if you can prove what part of the lump sum is allocable to future medical coverage. The IRS recognizes that a deduction may be based on a showing that the life-care facility historically allocates a specified percentage of the fee to future medical care. With such proof there is a current obligation to pay and the allocable medical expenses are deductible when the lump sum is paid. The IRS has allowed deductions in the situations described in the Examples at *17.11*.

Separate sponsorship gift. In one case, an individual was allowed by the Tax Court and an appeals court to claim a charitable contribution deduction for a "sponsorship gift" paid to a life-care retirement facility where she and her husband were residents. The sponsorship gift was entirely separate from her entrance fee; it was not required for admission and did not entitle her to reduced monthly payments. She did not receive any extra benefit from her gift and was not entitled to a refund of any part of it.

34.11 Imputed Interest on Refundable Entrance Fees

You must pay a lump-sum entrance fee when you enter a continuing care community. Depending on the type of plan, a portion of the lump-sum fee may be refundable either to you if you move from the community or to your heirs upon your death. The payment of the fee may also reduce your monthly charges.

These features may result in an unexpected tax liability under the imputed interest rules. Part of the refundable entrance fee is considered a "loan" to the continuing care facility, so that imputed interest income may be charged to you under the rules in *4.31*. According to Congressional committee reports, these loan rules do *not* apply, and thus the imputed interest rules do not apply, to limited refund plans, under which the entrance fee is refundable on a declining pro rata basis over a relatively short number of years.

In applying the imputed interest rules, the tax law distinguishes between qualified and nonqualified continuing care facilities. The tax treatment of nonqualified facilities is currently in a state of limbo. The IRS has delayed ruling on the tax treatment of entrance fees to nonqualified facilities so that the imputed interest rules will not be applied until the IRS releases regulations requiring tax and explaining how to compute the amount of imputed interest. The tax treatment of qualified facilities is specifically covered by law and is explained in the following paragraphs. Generally, qualified care facilities provide long-term nursing care if and when a resident becomes incapacitated. A nonqualified facility provides only limited short-term care, which may be as short as 30 days.

Qualified continuing care facilities. The "loan" portion of an entrance fee of a qualified continuing care facility is not subject to imputed interest unless it exceeds an annual floor. For 1999, refundable loans of up to $137,000 are exempt from the imputed interest rules provided that (1) you or your spouse were at least age 65 during the year and (2) the care facility provides a separate living unit, meals, maintenance, routine medical care, and, if it later becomes necessary, future long-term nursing care for no substantial additional charge. Incoming residents must not initially require long-term nursing care, but such care must be provided when it becomes necessary. A traditional nursing home is not a qualified continuing care facility. The $137,000 exception is subject to increases for inflation.

Since only the refundable portion of the fee is treated as a loan, the larger the payment or refund percentage is, the greater the potential imputed interest liability is. For example, in 1999, you and your spouse paid $170,000 for a two-bedroom apartment. If your guaranteed refund percentage is 75%, the imputed interest rules would not apply in 1999 because the "loan," or $127,500 (75% of $170,000), is below the $137,000 floor. However, if the refund percentage is 85%, the loan is $144,500 (85% of $170,000), and the $7,500 excess over the $137,000 floor is subject to imputed interest.

If imputed interest applies, the care facility should give you a Form 1099 indicating the taxable amount.

 Caution

Charitable Contribution Deductions

Payments made to a tax-exempt organization that operates a life-care community are generally not deductible charitable contributions because you are receiving services in exchange. If you donate amounts over and above your regular monthly fees and do not receive any extra benefit as a result, you may deduct the excess payment as a charitable contribution; *see 14.3.*

Tax Savings for Members of the Armed Forces

Special tax benefits are provided to Armed Forces personnel. A major tax-free benefit is the combat pay exclusion. Under this exclusion, members of the Armed Forces, including active duty reservists, may exclude from gross income all compensation for active service received for any month in which they served in a combat zone or were hospitalized as a result of any wound, injury, or disease incurred while serving in a combat zone. Commissioned officers are allowed an exclusion equal to the highest rate of basic pay at the top pay level for enlisted personnel, plus any hostile fire/imminent danger pay received for the month.

A special law designates Bosnia and Herzegovina, Croatia, and Macedonia as qualified hazardous duty areas.

Another law designated the Federal Republic of Yugoslavia (Serbia/Montenegro), Albania, and nearby waters as a qualified hazardous duty areas after the President had designated these areas as a combat zone. For tax purposes, qualified hazardous duty areas are treated as combat zones.

Other pay benefits may be tax free, and you may be able to get filing extensions and time extensions for home residence replacements. A list of tax-free benefits may be found at *35.2*. Filing extensions are discussed at *35.5*.

35.1 Taxable Armed Forces Pay and Benefits

Armed Forces personnel report as taxable pay the following items:

- Basic pay for active duty, attendance at a designated service school, back wages, drills, reserve training, and training duty
- Special pay for aviation career incentives, diving duty, foreign duty (for serving outside the 48 contiguous states and the District of Columbia), hazardous duty, medical and dental officers, nuclear-qualified officers, and special duty assignments
- Enlistment and reenlistment bonuses
- Payments for accrued leave, and personal money allowances paid to high-ranking officers
- Scholarships, such as the Armed Forces Health Professions Scholarship Program (AFHPSP) and similar programs, granted after August 16, 1986
- Student loan repayment from programs such as the General Educational Loan Repayment Program

State income tax withholding. A state that makes a withholding agreement with the Secretary of the Treasury may subject members of the Armed Forces regularly stationed within that state to its payroll withholding provisions. National Guard members and reservists are not considered to be members of the Armed Forces for purposes of this section.

Where and when to file. Mail your return to the Internal Revenue Service Center for the place you are stationed. For example, you are stationed in Arizona but have a permanent home address in Missouri; you send your return to the Service Center for Arizona. For filing extensions on entering the service, *see 35.7.*

35.2 Tax-Free Armed Forces Benefits

The following benefits are *not* subject to tax:

- Combat pay; *see 35.4*
- Living allowances for BAH (Basic Allowance for Housing). You may deduct mortgage interest and real estate taxes on your home even if you pay these expenses with BAH funds.
- BAS (Basic Allowance for Subsistence) living allowances
- Housing and cost-of-living allowances abroad, whether paid by the U.S. Government or by a foreign government
- VHA (Variable Housing Allowance)
- Family allowances for educational expenses for dependents, emergencies, evacuation to a place of safety, and separation
- Death allowances for burial services, death gratuity payments to eligible survivors (not more than $3,000), and travel of dependents to burial site
- Dislocation allowance, intended to partially reimburse expenses such as lease forfeitures, temporary living charges in hotels, and other expenses incurred in relocating a household
- Temporary lodging expense allowance intended to partially offset the added living expenses of temporary lodging within the United States for up to 10 days and up to 60 days abroad
- A moving-in housing allowance, intended to defray costs, such as for rental agent fees, home-security improvements, and supplemental heating equipment, associated with occupying leased space outside the United States
- Travel allowances for annual round trip for dependent students, leave between consecutive overseas tours, reassignment in a dependent-restricted status, and transportation for you or your dependents during ship overhaul or inactivation
- Defense counseling payments
- ROTC educational and subsistence allowances
- Survivor and retirement protection plan premium payments
- Uniform allowances paid to officers and uniforms furnished to enlisted personnel
- Medical or hospital treatment provided by the United States in government hospitals
- Pay forfeited on order of a court martial
- Education, training, or subsistence allowances paid under any law administered by the Department of Veterans Affairs (VA). However, deductible education costs must be reduced by the VA allowance.
- Adjustments in pay to compensate for losses resulting from inflated foreign currency
- Payments to former prisoners of war from the U.S. Government in compensation for inhumane treatment suffered at the hands of an enemy government
- Benefits under Servicemembers' Group Life Insurance
- Dividends on GI insurance. These are a tax-free return of premiums paid.
- Interest on dividends left on deposit with the Department of Veterans Affairs (VA). The IRS has revoked a prior ruling that subjected such interest to tax.

 Caution

Community Property

If you are married and your domicile (permanent home to which you intend to return) is in one of the following states, your military pay is subject to community property laws of that state: Arizona, California, Idaho, Louisiana, Nevada, New Mexico, Texas, Washington, and Wisconsin. *See 1.6* for community property reporting rules.

Disability retirement pay. Your disability retirement pay may be tax free if you are a former member of the Armed Forces of any country, the Foreign Service, the Coast Guard, the National Oceanic and Atmospheric Administration, or the Public Health Service; *see 2.13*. Tax-free treatment of disability retirement pay is retroactive to the date of the application for benefits.

35.3 Deductions for Armed Forces Personnel

Members of the Armed Forces may deduct the items listed below as miscellaneous itemized deductions subject to the 2% adjusted gross income (AGI) floor; *see 19.1*:

- Board and lodging costs over those paid to you by the government while on temporary duty away from your home base
- Costs of rank insignia, collar devices, gold braids, etc., and the cost of altering rank insignia when promoted or demoted
- Contributions to a "Company" fund made according to Service regulations. But personal contributions made to stimulate interest and morale in a unit are not deductible.
- Court martial legal expenses in successfully defending against the charge of conduct unbecoming an officer
- Dues to professional societies. But you may not deduct dues for officers' and noncommissioned officers' clubs.
- Expense of obtaining increased retirement pay
- Out-of-pocket moving expenses for service-connected moves. The 50-mile test and the 39-week test generally required to deduct moving expenses do not have to be met; *see 12.3*.
- Subscriptions to professional journals
- Transportation, food, and lodging expenses while on official travel status. But you are taxed on mileage and *per diem* subsistence allowance.
- Uniforms. The cost and cleaning of uniforms are deductible if: (1) they must be worn on duty; (2) they cannot under military regulations be worn off duty; and (3) the cost exceeds any tax-free clothing allowance.

35.4 Tax-Free Pay for Service in Combat Zone or Hazardous Duty Area

If your grade is below commissioned officer and you serve in a designated combat zone or hazardous duty area during any part of a month, *all* of your qualifying military pay (*see* below) for that month is excluded from your taxable income. You may also exclude military pay earned during any part of a month that you are hospitalized as a result of wounds, disease, or injury incurred in a combat zone or hazardous duty area. The exclusion for military pay while hospitalized does not apply to any month that begins more than two years after the end of combat activities in that combat zone or hazardous duty area. Your hospitalization does not have to be in the combat zone or hazardous duty area.

Officers. If you are a commissioned officer, you may exclude up to the highest rate of basic pay at the highest pay grade that enlisted personnel receive per month plus any hostile fire/imminent danger pay received for each month during any part of which you served in a combat zone or hazardous duty area.

If you are a commissioned warrant officer, you are considered an enlisted person.

What is included as tax-free pay? The following military pay qualifies for tax-free treatment: (1) active duty pay earned in any month you served in a combat zone or hazardous duty area; (2) a dislocation allowance if the move begins or ends in a month you served in a combat zone or hazardous duty area; (3) a reenlistment bonus if the voluntary extension or reenlistment occurs in a month you served in a combat zone or hazardous duty area; (4) pay for accrued leave earned in any month you served in a combat zone or hazardous duty area (the Department of Defense must determine that the unused leave was earned during that period); (5) pay received for duties as a member of the Armed Forces in clubs, messes, post and station theaters, and other nonappropriated fund activities. The pay must be earned in a month you served in a combat zone or hazardous duty area; and (6) awards for suggestions, inventions, or scientific achievements you are entitled to because of a submission you made in a month you served in a combat zone or hazardous duty area.

Service in the combat zone or hazardous duty area includes any periods you are absent from duty because of sickness, wounds, or leave. If, as a result of serving in a combat zone, you become a prisoner of war or missing in action, you are considered to be serving in the combat zone as long as you keep that status for military pay purposes.

Retirement pay and pensions do not qualify for the combat zone exclusion. According to a recent Fourth Circuit Court of Appeals decision, a Navy severance pay package was taxable although

Filing Tip

Away From Home Base

If your ship or squadron is away from your "home" port or base, you may be able to deduct travel expenses while away. However, you are not considered "away from home" if you are at your *permanent* duty station or you are a naval officer assigned to permanent duty aboard a ship; *see also 20.6*.

Filing Tip

Who Qualifies for Exclusion?

Members of the U.S. Armed Forces qualifying for the exclusion include commissioned officers and enlisted personnel in all regular and reserve units under control of the Secretaries of Defense, Army, Navy, and Air Force, and the Coast Guard. Members of the U.S. Merchant Marines or the American Red Cross are not included.

the recipient became entitled to the payment while on active duty in the Persian Gulf. The court differentiated the package, which was provided in order to entice the man to leave the service, from a reenlistment bonus provided as compensation for active service.

Combat zones and hazardous duty areas. A combat zone is any area the President of the United States designates by Executive Order as an area in which the U.S. Armed Forces are or have engaged in combat. An area becomes and ceases to be a combat zone on the dates designated by the President.

Effective March 24, 1999, the Balkan area was designated a combat zone including: the Federal Republic of Yugoslavia (Serbia/Montenegro), Albania, the Ionian Sea north of the 39th parallel, and the Adriatic Sea. Airspace above these areas is also part of the zone. As of November 21, 1995, a special law designated Bosnia and Herzegovina, Croatia, and Macedonia as a qualified hazardous duty area.

The following locations (including airspace) were designated as combat zones beginning January 17, 1991: the total land areas of Iraq, Kuwait, Saudi Arabia, Oman, Bahrain, Qatar, and the United Arab Emirates; the Persian Gulf; the Red Sea; the Gulf of Oman; the part of the Arabian Sea that is north of 10 degrees north latitude and west of 68 degrees east longitude; and the Gulf of Aden. At the time this book went to press, the Persian Gulf area continued to be a combat zone.

Qualifying service outside combat zone or hazardous duty area. Military service outside a combat zone or hazardous duty area is considered to be performed in a combat zone or hazardous duty area if: (1) the service is in direct support of military operations in the combat zone or hazardous duty area, and (2) the service qualifies you for special military pay for duty subject to hostile fire or imminent danger. Military pay received for this service will qualify for the pay exclusion if the other requirements are met.

Nonqualifying service. The following military service does not qualify as service in a combat zone or hazardous duty area: (1) presence in a combat zone while on leave from a duty station located outside the combat zone; (2) passage over or through a combat zone during a trip between two points that are outside a combat zone; and (3) presence in a combat zone solely for your personal convenience. Such service will not qualify you for the pay exclusion.

Hospitalized while serving in a combat zone or hazardous duty area. If you are hospitalized while serving in a combat zone or hazardous duty area for a wound, disease, or injury, it will be presumed to have been incurred while serving in the combat zone or hazardous duty area unless there is clear evidence to the contrary.

EXAMPLES

1. You are hospitalized for a specific disease after serving in a combat zone for three weeks, and the disease for which you are hospitalized has an incubation period of two to four weeks. The disease is presumed to have been incurred while you were serving in the combat zone. On the other hand, if the incubation period of the disease is one year, the disease would not have been incurred while you were serving in the combat zone.

2. You were hospitalized for a specific disease three weeks after you left the combat zone. The incubation period of the disease is from two to four weeks. The disease is considered to have been incurred while serving in the combat zone.

Form W-2. The wages shown in Box 1 of your Form W-2 should not include combat pay. Retirement pay is not combat pay.

35.5 Tax Deadlines Extended for Combat Zone or Hazardous Duty Area Service

You are allowed an extension of at least 180 days (*see* below) to take care of tax matters if you are a member of the Armed Forces who served in a combat zone or hazardous duty area. The extension applies to filing tax returns, paying taxes, filing a Tax Court petition, filing refund claims, and making an IRA contribution (*see* IRS Publication 3 for details). The time allowed for the IRS to begin an audit or take collection actions is also extended.

Support personnel. The deadline extension also applies if you are serving in a combat zone or hazardous duty area in support of the Armed Forces. This includes Red Cross personnel, accredited correspondents, and civilian personnel acting under the direction of the Armed Forces in support of those forces.

Law Alert

Balkan Combat Zones

As of March 24, 1999, the Federal Republic of Yugoslavia (Serbia/Montenegro), Albania, the Adriatic Sea, and the Northern Ionian Sea were a designated combat zone. Tax relief available to military personnel serving in this area includes a filing extension and eligibility for tax-free combat pay. The extension of filing deadlines also applies to relief workers, accredited journalists, and armed services personnel relocated to support the overall mission. As of November 21, 1995, Bosnia and Herzegovina, Croatia, and Macedonia were classified as qualified hazardous duty areas, entitling those who serve there to the combat pay tax benefits.

Filing Tip

Spouses of Combat Zone Personnel

If your spouse serves in a combat zone or hazardous duty area, you are generally entitled to the same deadline extension as he or she is. However, any extra extension for your spouse's hospitalization within the United States is not available to you. Further, a spouse's extension does not apply to any year beginning more than two years after the end of combat or hazardous duty activities.

Law Alert

Home Sale Exclusion

Generally, to exclude gain on the sale of a principal residence, the residence must be owned and lived in for at least two out of the five years ending on the date of sale. Proposed tax legislation would suspend the five-year period while a member of the uniformed services or the U.S. Foreign Service (or his or her spouse) is on extended duty for over 90 days at a location at least 50 miles away from the individual's principal residence. *See* the Supplement for an update.

Caution

Tax Forgiveness

Tax forgiveness does *not* apply to a U.S. civilian or military employee who dies as a result of an accident or a training exercise. Abatement also does not apply to terroristic action within the United States. However, abatement does apply if the individual dies in the U.S. from a wound or injury incurred in a terroristic or military action outside the United States.

Members of the Armed Forces and civilian employees of the Defense Department who perform services outside the United States on or after March 24,1999 as part of Operation Allied Force qualify for the deadline extensions even if they serve outside the combat zone (Federal Republic of Yugoslavia, Albania, Adriatic Sea, Ionian Sea above the 39th parallel) so long as they are deployed away from their permanent duty station. Civilian employees of defense contractors who produce equipment for Operation Allied Force do not qualify for the deadline extensions unless they are serving in the combat zone in support of the U.S. Armed Forces.

Extension is minimum of 180 days. Your deadline for taking actions with the IRS is extended for at least 180 days after the later of: (1) the last day you are in a combat zone or hazardous duty area (or the last day it qualifies as a combat zone or hazardous duty area), and (2) the last day of any continuous qualified hospitalization for injury from service in the combat zone or hazardous duty area. Hospitalization may be outside the United States, or up to five years of hospitalization in the United States.

Time in a missing status (missing in action or prisoner of war) counts as time in a combat zone or hazardous duty area.

In addition to the 180 days, a filing deadline is also extended by the number of days you had left to file with the IRS when you entered a combat zone or hazardous duty area. If you entered the combat zone or hazardous duty area before the time to file began, the deadline is extended by the entire filing time.

35.6 Tax Forgiveness for Combat Zone or Hazardous Duty Area Deaths

If a member of the Armed Forces is killed in a combat zone or hazardous duty area or dies from wounds or disease incurred while in these zones or areas, any income tax liability for the year of death or any earlier year including service in such zones or areas is waived. In addition, the service member's estate is entitled to a refund for income tax paid while serving there.

If a member of the Armed Forces was a resident of a community property state and his or her spouse reported half of the military pay on a separate return, the spouse may get a refund of taxes paid on his or her share of the combat zone or hazardous duty area pay.

Forgiveness benefits apply to an Armed Forces member serving outside the zone or area if service: (1) was in direct support of military operations there, and (2) qualified the member for special military pay for duty subject to hostile fire or imminent danger.

Missing status. The date of death for a member of the Armed Forces who was in a missing status (missing in action or prisoner of war) is the date his or her name is removed from missing status for military pay purposes. This is true even if death occurred earlier.

How tax forgiveness is claimed. If the individual died in a combat zone or in a terroristic or military action, you file as the individual's representative: (1) Form 1040 if a U.S. individual income tax return (Form 1040, 1040A, or 1040EZ) has not been filed for the tax year. Form W-2, Wage and Tax Statement, must accompany the return. (2) Form 1040X if a U.S. individual income tax return has been filed. A separate Form 1040X must be filed for each year in question.

Check with your local IRS office for the address of the IRS office to which the return is filed.

An attachment should accompany any return or claim and should include a computation of the decedent's tax liability before any amount is forgiven and the amount that is to be forgiven.

The following documents must also accompany all returns and claims for refund: (1) Form 1310, Statement of Person Claiming Refund Due a Deceased Taxpayer; and (2) a certification from the Department of Defense. Department of State certification is required if the decedent was a civilian employee of an agency other than the Department of Defense.

Tax forgiveness for civilian or military personnel killed in terroristic or military action. Tax liability is waived for civilian or military U.S. employees killed in terroristic or military actions outside the U.S., even if the President has not designated the area as a combat zone and it is not a hazardous duty area. Tax liability is waived for the period beginning with the taxable year before the year in which the injuries were incurred and ending with the year of death. Refund claims for prior years must generally be filed on Form 1040X by the later of three years from the time the original return was filed or two years from the time the tax was paid. However, if death occurred in a combat zone, the filing period is extended by the time served in the combat zone, plus the period of continuous hospitalization outside the U.S., plus an additional 180 days. The individual must also be a U.S. employee both on the date of injury and date of death.

Determination of death for Vietnam MIAs. Under prior law, MIAs were generally presumed dead as of December 31, 1982. Under current law, the date of death of service members missing in action in Vietnam is the date determined by the Armed Forces. Thus, under current law, tax abatement may be available for years after 1982. Furthermore, the date of death, as determined by the Armed Forces, also applies for such rules as whether to file as a surviving spouse, and for postponing the due date for filing returns and paying taxes.

35.7 Extension To Pay Your Tax When Entering the Service

If you are unable to pay your tax when you enter the Armed Forces, you may get an extension until six months after your initial period of service ends. Get a form at the IRS office of your District Director or write a letter to the District Director or to the IRS office requesting payment (your spouse or parent may do it for you). An extension, without interest, may be given if your income dropped after entering the military *and* you actually apply for the extension.

The extension does not cover your spouse, who must file a separate return and pay the tax due. But you and your spouse may file a joint return before the postponement period expires even though your spouse filed a separate return for that particular year. No interest is charged on this postponement of your tax.

Automatic extension of time to file your return. If you are on duty outside the U.S. or Puerto Rico on April 17, 2000, you get an automatic two-month extension to file your 1999 return; *see* page 5.

Interest charged on back taxes. If you do not show hardship qualifying you for the above interest-free payment extension, the IRS may reduce its interest rate on the deficiency. The maximum interest rate the IRS may charge for taxes incurred prior to your entry into active service is 6%. This reduced rate applies only to the period of your active duty.

35.8 Tax Information for Reservists

Transportation costs to reservist meetings generally are not deductible. A possible exception is the cost of traveling from your regular job location to a meeting held on a regular workday. The cost would be deductible, subject to the 2% adjusted gross income (AGI) floor for miscellaneous itemized deductions; *see 19.1*.

If you travel overnight away from your tax home *(20.6)* to a meeting or training camp, you may deduct expenses for transportation, lodging, and meals subject to the 50% reduction.

If you are called for active duty away from your tax home, you may deduct travel expenses provided you keep your regular job while on active duty, return to it after you are released, and pay for those expenses at the military post. To the extent they exceed BAH (housing) and BAS (subsistence) allowances, the expenses are deductible only as a miscellaneous itemized deduction subject to the 2% AGI floor.

Deferring tax payments and reduction of IRS interest rate. If you owed a tax deficiency to the IRS before being called to active duty, the IRS may defer payment, without interest, if your ability to pay has been severely impaired by your call-up. If you are not allowed a deferment, the IRS will reduce its interest charge to 6% on the taxes you owed before your call-up.

 Filing Tip

Uniform Costs of Reservists
The cost and upkeep of uniforms is deductible only if you are prohibited from wearing them when off duty; *see 19.6*. A deduction allowed under this test must be reduced by any uniform allowance you receive, and the unreimbursed cost is subject to the 2% adjusted gross income (AGI) floor for miscellaneous itemized deductions.

How To Treat Foreign Earned Income

There is a tax incentive for working abroad—in 1999 up to $74,000 of income earned abroad may escape U.S. income taxes and you may be entitled to an exclusion or deduction for certain housing costs. In measuring the economic value of this tax savings, consider the extra cost of living abroad. In some areas, the high cost of living and currency exchange rates will erode your tax savings.

The exclusion does not apply to investment income or to any other earned income that does not meet the exclusion tests.

To claim a foreign income exclusion you must satisfy a foreign residence or physical presence test *(36.5)*.

Employees of the U.S. Government may not claim an exclusion based on the government pay earned abroad.

36.1 Claiming the Foreign Earned Income Exclusion

In 1999 you may exclude up to $74,000 of foreign earned income. You must file a U.S. return if your gross income *exceeds* the filing threshold for your personal status, even though all or part of your foreign earned income may be tax free. The exclusion is not automatic; you must elect it. You elect the foreign earned income exclusion on Form 2555, which you attach to Form 1040. The housing cost exclusion (36.4) is also elected on Form 2555.

You may file simplified Form 2555-EZ if your 1999 foreign wages are $74,000 or less, you do not have self-employment income, and you do not claim the foreign housing exclusion, housing deduction, business, or moving expenses.

A separate exclusion is allowed for the value of meals and lodging received by employees living in qualified camps; see 36.8.

If you claim the foreign income exclusion of $74,000, you may not:

• Claim business deductions allocable to the excluded income;
• Make a deductible traditional IRA or Roth IRA contribution based on the excluded income; *or*
• Claim foreign taxes, paid on excluded income, as a credit or deduction.

In deciding whether to claim the exclusion, compare the overall tax (1) with the exclusion and (2) without the exclusion but with the full foreign tax credit and allocable deductions. Choose whichever gives you the lower tax; see 36.3 and 36.6.

Once you elect the exclusion, that election remains in effect for all future years unless you revoke it. If you revoke the election, you cannot elect the exclusion again during the next five years without IRS consent. A revocation is made in a statement attached to your return for the year you want it to take effect. The foreign earned income exclusion and the housing cost exclusion must be revoked separately.

36.2 What Is Foreign Earned Income?

Earned income includes salaries, wages, commissions, professional fees, and bonuses. Earned income also includes allowances from your employer for housing or other expenses, as well as the value of housing or a car provided by the employer. It may also include business profits, royalties, and rents, provided this income is tied to the performance of services. Earned income does not include pension or annuity income, payments for nonqualified employee trusts or nonqualified annuities, dividends, interest, capital gains, gambling winnings, alimony, or the value of tax-free meals or lodging under the rules at 3.11. Foreign earned income does not include amounts earned in countries subject to U.S. government travel restrictions.

Foreign earned income eligible for the exclusion must be received no later than the taxable year after the year in which you perform the services. Pay is excludable in the year of receipt if you did not use the full exclusion in the year of the services.

U.S. government pay ineligible. If you are an employee of the U.S. government or its agencies, you may *not* exclude any part of your pay from your government employer. Courts have agreed with the IRS that U.S. government workers were U.S. employees even though they were paid from sources other than Congressionally appropriated funds. If you are not an employee of the U.S. government or any of its agencies, your pay is excludable even if paid by a government source. You are not an employee of the U.S. Government if you work under a contract made between your employer and the government.

Under a special law, tax liability is waived for a civilian or military employee of the U.S. government killed in a military action overseas; see 35.6.

Profits from sole proprietorship or partnership. If your business consists solely of services (no capital investment), 100% of gross income is considered earned income. If services and capital are both income-producing factors, no more than 30% of your net profit may be considered earned income.

If you do not contribute any services to a business (for example, you are a "silent partner"), your share of the net profits is *not* earned income.

EXAMPLES
1. A U.S. citizen resides in England. He invests in an English partnership that sells manufactured goods outside the U.S. He performs no services for the business. His share of net profits does not qualify as earned income.

Caution

Claiming Foreign Tax Credit Revokes Prior Election

If you have been claiming the exclusion and decide that it would be advantageous this year to forego the exclusion and instead claim the foreign tax credit for foreign earned income, be aware that claiming the credit is treated by the IRS as a revocation of the prior exclusion election. You may not claim an exclusion for the next five years unless the IRS allows you to re-elect the exclusion.

Claiming a foreign tax credit also may revoke a prior election to claim the housing cost exclusion. Depending on the foreign earned income in the year the credit is claimed, the credit may be considered a revocation of a prior earned income exclusion election and also a prior housing cost exclusion election, or as a revocation of only one of the elections.

A good faith error in calculating foreign earned income that leads to claiming a foreign credit will not be treated as a revocation of prior elections.

Law Alert

Increased Foreign Earned Income Exclusion

The foreign earned income exclusion is scheduled to increase from $74,000 in 1999 to $76,000 in 2000, $78,000 in 2001, and $80,000 in 2002 and subsequent years. When this book went to press, Congress was considering further increases in the exclusion to $83,000 in 2003 and then an additional $3,000 each year until it reaches $95,000 in 2007. *See* the Supplement for legislative developments.

2. Same facts as in Example 1, except he devotes his full time to the partnership business. Then up to 30% of his share of the net profits may qualify as earned income. Thus, if his share of profits is $50,000, earned income is $15,000 (30% of $50,000), assuming the value of his services is at least $15,000.

3. You and another person are consultants, operating as a partnership in Europe. Since capital is not an income-producing element, the entire gross income of the business is earned income.

The partnership agreement generally determines the tax status of partnership income in a U.S. partnership with a foreign branch. Thus, if the partnership agreement allocates foreign earnings to partners abroad, the allocation will be recognized unless it lacks substantial economic effect.

Fringe benefits. The value of fringe benefits, such as the right to use company property and facilities, is added to your compensation when figuring the amount of your earned income.

Royalties. Royalties from articles or books are earned income if you receive them for transferring all of your rights to your work, or you have contracted to write the articles or book for an amount in cash plus a royalty on sales.

Royalties from the leasing of oil and mineral lands and from patents are not earned income.

Reimbursement of employee expenses. Do not include reimbursement of expenses as earned income to the extent they equal expenses that you adequately accounted for to your employer; *see 20.31*. If your expenses exceed reimbursements, the excess is allocated according to the rules in *36.6*. If reimbursements exceed expenses, the excess is treated as earned income.

Straight commission salespersons or other employees who arrange with their employers, for withholding purposes, to consider a percentage of their commissions as attributable to their expenses treat such amounts as earned income.

Reimbursed moving expenses. Reimbursements of moving expenses are not reported as income if you adequately account to your employer for the expenses; *see 12.8*.

A reimbursement is taxable if received under a non-accountable plan or for moving expenses that are not deductible *(12.3)* or that you deducted in an earlier year. However, for purposes of claiming the earned income exclusion, the reimbursement may be considered to have been earned in a year other than the year of receipt. This is important because an exclusion is allowed only for the year income is earned. If the move is from the U.S. to a foreign country, the reimbursement is considered foreign earned income in the year of the move if you qualify under the foreign residence or physical presence test for at least 120 days during that tax year. Reimbursement of moving expenses from one foreign country to another is considered foreign earned income in the year of the move, if you qualify under the residency or physical presence test at the new location for at least 120 days during the tax year. If you do not meet one of these tests in the year of the move, the reimbursements are earned income that must be allocated between the year of the move and the following tax year.

A taxable reimbursement for a move back to the U.S. is considered income from U.S. sources if you continue to work for the same employer. If you move back to the U.S. and take a job with a new employer *or* if you retire and move back to the U.S. and your old employer reimburses your moving expenses under a prior written agreement or company policy, the reimbursement is considered to be for past services in the foreign country and qualifies as foreign earned income eligible for the exclusion. The reimbursement is considered earned in the year of the move if you qualified under the residency or physical presence test *(36.5)* for at least 120 days during the tax year. Otherwise, the reimbursement is allocated between the year of the move and the year preceding the move. *See* IRS Publication 54 for details.

36.3 Qualifying for the Foreign Earned Income Exclusion

You may elect the exclusion for foreign earned income only if your tax home is in a foreign country *and* you meet either the foreign residence test *or* the foreign physical presence test of 330 days. The tests are discussed at *36.5*. Tax home is discussed at *20.6–20.8*. If your tax home is in the U.S., you may not claim the exclusion but may claim the foreign tax credit and your living expenses while away from home if you meet the rules at *20.9* for temporary assignments that are expected to last, and actually do last, for one year or less. U.S. government employees may not claim either the earned income exclusion or housing exclusion based on government pay.

 Caution

Rental Income

Rental income is generally not earned income. However, if you perform personal services, for example as an owner-manager of a hotel or rooming house in a foreign country, then up to 30% of your net rents may be earned income.

Exclusion prorated on a daily basis. If you qualify under the foreign residence or physical presence test for only part of 1999, the $74,000 exclusion limit is reduced on a daily basis.

EXAMPLES

1. You were a resident of France from February 20, 1997, until June 30, 1999. On July 1 you returned to the U.S. Since your period of foreign residency included all of 1998, thereby satisfying the foreign residence test, you may claim a prorated exclusion for 1999. As you were abroad for 181 of the 365 days in 1999, you exclude earnings up to $36,696, or $^{181}/_{365}$ of the $74,000 maximum exclusion. If you earned more than $36,696 from January through June 1999, the exclusion is limited to $36,696.

2. You worked in France from June 1, 1998, through September 30, 1999. Your only days outside France were a 15-day vacation to the U.S. in December 1998. You do not qualify for an exclusion under the foreign residence test because you were not abroad for a full taxable year; you were not abroad for either the full year of 1998 or 1999. However, you do qualify under the physical presence test; you were physically present abroad for at least 330 full days during a 12-month period. The 12-month period giving you the largest 1999 exclusion is the 12-month period starting October 21, 1998, and ending October 20, 1999. *See 36.5* for figuring the 12-month period. Since you were abroad for at least 330 full days during that 12-month period, you may claim an exclusion. In 1999, you were abroad for 293 days within the 12-month period (January 1 to October 20, 1999, is 293 days). Thus, you exclude earnings up to $^{293}/_{365}$ of the maximum exclusion. If your earnings in France for 1999 were $80,000, your exclusion is limited to $59,403 ($74,000 × $^{293}/_{365}$).

If you are married and you and your spouse each have foreign earned income and meet the foreign residence or physical presence test, you may each claim a separate exclusion. If your permanent home is in a community property state, your earned income is not considered community property for purposes of the exclusion.

Foreign earnings from a prior year. Foreign income earned in a prior year but paid in 1999 does not qualify for the 1999 exclusion. However, if the income was attributable to foreign services performed in 1998, the pay is tax free in 1999 to the extent that you did not use the full 1998 exclusion of $72,000. Under another exception, payments received in 1999 for 1998 services are treated as 1999 income if the payment was within a normal payroll period of 16 days or less that included the last day of 1998. If the services were performed before 1998, no exclusion is available to shelter the pay.

Income for services performed in the U.S. does not qualify for the exclusion, even though it is paid to you while you are abroad.

Foreign tax credit. Foreign taxes paid on tax-free foreign earned income do not qualify for a credit or deduction. But if your foreign pay exceeds $74,000, you may claim a foreign tax credit or deduction for the foreign taxes allocated to taxable income. The instructions to Forms 2555 and 1116 and IRS Publication 514 provide details for making the computation.

36.4 How To Treat Housing Costs

The housing costs of employees and self-employed persons are treated differently by the tax law. Employees get a housing exclusion; self-employed persons get a deduction from *taxable* foreign earned income. If you live in a special camp provided by your employer, all housing costs are excluded; *see 36.8.*

Exclusion for employer-financed housing costs. If you qualify for the exclusion for all of 1999 and your foreign wage or salary income plus the value of employer-financed housing costs in 1999 does not exceed $74,000, both parts of your pay package are tax free. Your housing costs are considered to be employer-financed as long as they are covered by salary, employer reimbursements, a housing allowance, or if they are paid directly by your employer. If wages plus employer-financed housing exceed $74,000, a special housing exclusion elected on Form 2555 will shelter part of your housing costs from tax. The housing exclusion is the difference between the employer's payment of reasonable housing expenses and a "base housing amount." The base housing amount is 16% of the salary for a U.S. Government employee at the GS-14, Step 1, level as of the beginning of the year. If you qualify under the foreign residence or physical presence test for only part of 1999, your base amount is $27.03 for each qualifying day. If you qualify for the entire year, the base amount is $9,865; *see* Line 30 of Form 2555. Employer-financed housing payments exceed-

Caution

Countries Subject to Travel Restrictions
You may not claim the foreign earned income exclusion, or the housing exclusion or deduction, if you work in a country subject to U.S. government travel restrictions. You are not treated as a bona fide resident of, or as present in, a country subject to the travel ban. Libya, Cuba, and Iraq are within this ban. Check Form 2555 for changes to this list.

Filing Tip

Claiming the Housing Exclusion
On Form 2555, you figure the housing exclusion before the foreign income exclusion. The income exclusion is limited to the excess of foreign earned income over the housing exclusion.

ing this housing cost exclusion may also escape tax if your foreign salary is below the maximum foreign earned income exclusion. Your foreign earned income exclusion is limited to your foreign earned income minus your housing cost exclusion; *see* Example 1 below.

EXAMPLES

(Assume qualification for full-year exclusion)

1. In 1999, your salary for work abroad is $57,591 and your employer pays $13,515 for your housing. On Form 2555, you list $71,106 (salary *plus* housing) as your foreign earned income. Assume that the housing cost exclusion is $3,650 (housing costs of $13,515 exceeding a base housing amount of $9,865). Your earned income exclusion is $67,456: $71,106 earned income less $3,650 housing exclusion.

2. In 1999, you earn a salary of $60,108 abroad and your employer pays $13,515 for your housing. Assume the housing exclusion is $3,650 (housing costs of $13,515 exceeding a base housing amount of $9,865). All of your salary plus the full amount of the housing costs avoids tax: the housing cost exclusion of $3,650 and an earned income exclusion of $69,973 ($73,623 foreign earned income less $3,650 housing exclusion).

3. Same as Example 2 above, except that you earn $65,325. Foreign earned income is $78,840 ($65,325 *plus* $13,515), but the total amount of income not subject to tax is $77,650. The total tax-free amount is made up of the housing cost exclusion of $3,650 and the maximum foreign earned income exclusion of $74,000.

Reasonable housing expenses. Include rent, utilities other than telephone costs, insurance, parking, furniture rentals, and repairs for yourself, your spouse, and dependents living with you. The following expenses do not qualify: cost of purchasing a home, furniture, or accessories; home improvements; payments of mortgage principal; domestic labor; and depreciation on a home or on improvements to leased housing. Furthermore, interest and taxes that are otherwise deductible do not qualify for the exclusion.

You may include the costs of a separate household that you maintain outside the U.S. for your spouse and dependents because living conditions at your foreign home are adverse.

Self-employed persons. On Form 2555, self-employed individuals may claim a limited deduction for housing costs exceeding the base housing amount. You may claim this deduction only to the extent it offsets taxable foreign earned income. The deduction is claimed as an "adjustment to income" on Line 32 of Form 1040, even if you do not itemize deductions.

Where you may not deduct expenses because you do not have taxable foreign earned income, expenses may be carried forward one year and deducted in the next year to the extent of taxable foreign earned income.

If you are an employee and self-employed during the same year. Housing expenses above the base amount are partly excludable and partly deductible. For example, if half of your foreign earned income is from services as an employee, half of the excess housing expenses over the base amount are excludable. The remaining excess housing costs are deductible to the extent of taxable foreign earned income. Follow the instructions to Form 2555.

Countries ineligible for tax benefits. Housing expenses incurred in a country subject to a U.S. government travel restriction are not eligible for the tax benefits explained in this section. *See* Form 2555 instructions for a list of countries to which travel restrictions apply.

36.5 Meeting the Foreign Residence or Physical Presence Test

To qualify for the foreign earned income exclusion, you must be either a U.S. citizen (or U.S. resident entitled to tax treaty benefits) meeting the foreign residence test or a U.S. citizen or resident meeting the physical presence test in a foreign country. The following areas are not considered foreign countries: Puerto Rico, Virgin Islands, Guam, Commonwealth of the Northern Mariana Islands, American Samoa, or the Antarctic region.

If war or civil unrest prevented you from meeting the foreign residence or physical presence test, you may claim the exclusion for the period you actually were a resident or physically present abroad. Foreign locations and the time periods that qualify for the waiver of the residency and physical presence tests are listed in the instructions to Form 2555.

If, by the due date of your 1999 return (April 17, 2000), you have not yet satisfied the foreign residence or physical presence test, but you expect to meet either test after the filing date, you may either file on the due date and report your earnings or ask for a filing extension under the rules at *36.7*.

Foreign residence test. You must be a U.S. citizen who is a bona fide resident of a foreign country for an uninterrupted period that includes one full tax year; a full tax year is from January 1 through December 31 for individuals who file on a calendar-year basis. Business or vacation trips to the U.S. or another country will not disqualify you from satisfying the foreign residence test. If you are abroad more than one year but less than two, the entire period qualifies if it includes one full tax year.

EXAMPLE

You are a bona fide foreign resident from September 30, 1998, to March 25, 2000. The period includes your entire 1999 tax year. Therefore, up to $74,000 of your 1999 earnings is excludable. Your overseas earnings in 1998 and 2000 qualify for a proportionate part of the exclusion of $72,000 allowed for 1998 and $76,000 exclusion allowed for 2000.

To prove you are a foreign resident, you must show your intention to be a resident of the foreign country. Evidence tending to confirm your intention to stay in a foreign country is: (1) your family accompanies you; (2) you buy a house or rent an apartment rather than a hotel room; (3) you participate in the foreign community activities; (4) you can speak the foreign language; (5) you have a permanent foreign address; (6) you join clubs there; or (7) you open charge accounts in stores in the foreign country.

You will not qualify if you take inconsistent positions toward your foreign residency. That is, you will *not* be treated as a bona fide resident of a foreign country if you have earned income from sources within that country, filed a statement with the authorities of that country that you are not a resident there, and have been held not subject to the income tax of that country. However, this rule does not prevent you from qualifying under the physical presence test.

If you cannot prove that you are a resident, check to determine if your stay qualifies under the physical presence test.

Physical presence test. To qualify under this test, you must show you were on foreign soil 330 days (about 11 months) during a 12-month period. Whether you were a resident or a transient is of no importance. You have to show you were physically present in a foreign country or countries for 330 full days during any 12-consecutive-month period. The 330 qualifying days do not have to be consecutive. The 12-month period may begin with any day. There is no requirement that it begin with your first full day abroad. It may begin before or after arrival in a foreign country and may end before or after departure from a foreign country. A *full* day is from midnight to midnight (24 consecutive hours). You must spend each of the 330 days on foreign soil. In departing from U.S. soil to go directly to the foreign country, or in returning directly to the U.S. from a foreign country, the time you spend on or over international waters does not count toward the 330-day total.

EXAMPLES

1. On August 9, you fly from New York City to Paris. You arrive there at 10 a.m. August 10. Your first full qualifying day toward the 330-day period is August 11.
    You may count in your 330-day period:
    • Time spent traveling between foreign countries.
    • Time spent on a vacation in foreign countries. There is no requirement that the 330 days must be spent on a job.
    • Time spent in a foreign country while employed by the U.S. government counts towards the 330-day test, even though pay from the government does not qualify for the earned income exclusion.
    • Time in foreign countries, territorial waters, or travel in the air over a foreign country. However, you will lose qualifying days if any part of such travel is on or over international waters and takes 24 hours or more, or any part of such travel is within the U.S. or its possessions.
2. You depart from Naples, Italy, by ship on June 10 at 6:00 p.m. and arrive at Haifa, Israel, at 7:00 a.m. on June 14. The trip exceeded 24 hours and passed through international waters. Therefore, you lose as qualifying days June 10, 11, 12, 13, and 14. Assuming you remain in Haifa, Israel, the next qualifying day is June 15.

Caution

Residence or Domicile?

Residence does not have the same meaning as *domicile*. Your domicile is a permanent place of abode; it is the place to which you eventually plan to return wherever you go. You may have a residence in a place other than your domicile. Thus, you may go, say, to Amsterdam, and take up residence there and still intend to return to your domicile in the U.S. But your leaving your domicile does not, by itself, establish a bona fide residence in a new place. You must intend to make a new place your residence.

Choosing the 12-month period. You qualify under the physical presence test if you were on foreign soil 330 days during any period of 12 consecutive months. Since there may be several 12-month periods during which you meet the 330-day test, you should choose the 12-month period allowing you the largest possible exclusion if you qualify under the physical presence test for only part of 1999.

EXAMPLE

You worked in France from June 1, 1998, through September 30, 1999, and the next day you left the country. During this period, you left France only for a 15-day vacation to the U.S. during December 1998. You earned $80,000 for your work in France during 1999. Your maximum 1999 exclusion is $59,403, figured as follows:

1. Start with your last full day, September 30, 1999, and count back 330 full days during which you were abroad. Not counting the vacation days, the 330th day is October 21, 1998. This is the first day of your 12-month period.

2. From October 21, 1998, count forward 12 months to October 20, 1999, which is the last day of your 12-month period.

3. Count the number of days in 1999 that fall within the 12-month period ending October 20, 1999. Here, the number of qualifying days is 293, from January 1 through October 20, 1999.

4. The maximum 1999 exclusion is $74,000 \times {}^{293}\!/_{365}$, or $59,403. You may exclude $59,403, the lesser of the maximum exclusion and your actual earnings of $80,000.

36.6 Claiming Deductions

You may not deduct expenses that are allocable to the foreign earned income and housing exclusions. If you elect the earned income exclusion, you deduct expenses as follows:

Personal or nonbusiness deductions, such as medical expenses, mortgage interest, and real estate taxes paid on a personal residence, are deductible if you itemize deductions. Business expenses that are attributable to earning excludable income are not deductible. Dependency exemptions are fully deductible; *see* Example 1 below.

If your foreign earnings exceed the exclusion ceiling, you allocate expenses between taxable and excludable income and deduct the amount allocated to taxable earned income; *see* Example 2 below.

EXAMPLES

1. You were a resident of Denmark and elect to exclude your wages of $70,000 from income. You also incurred unreimbursed travel expenses of $2,000. You may not deduct the travel expenses, since the amount is attributable to the earning of tax-free income.

2. You earn wages of $100,000 and satisfy the physical presence test. Your unreimbursed travel expenses for 1999 are $5,000, after reducing meals and entertainment by 50%. If you elect the $74,000 exclusion, 26% of the travel expenses, or $1,300, attributable to the taxable 26% of earnings, may be claimed as a miscellaneous itemized deduction on Schedule A (Form 1040) subject to the 2% AGI floor.

Filing Tip

Overseas Moving Expenses

These expenses are generally treated as related to your foreign earnings. Thus, if you move to a foreign country and exclude your income, you may not deduct your moving expenses. If your earned income exceeds the exclusion limit, you allocate moving expenses between your tax-free and taxable earned income.

If your job expenses are reimbursed and the expenses are adequately accounted for to your employer *(20.30)*, the reimbursements are not reported as income on your Form W-2. If the reimbursement is less than expenses, the excess expenses are allocated as in Example 2 above.

You may have to allocate state income taxes paid on your income.

If either you or your spouse elects the earned income or housing exclusion, you may not claim an IRA deduction based on excluded income.

If you were reimbursed by your employer under a non-accountable plan, or if the reimbursement is for expenses that you deducted in an earlier year, the reimbursement is considered earned income in the year of receipt and is added to other earned income before taking the exclusion and making the allocation. *See 36.2* for allocating reimbursements between the year of the move and the following year for purposes of claiming the exclusion.

If, after working in a foreign country, your employer transfers you back to the U.S. or you move back to the U.S. to take a different job, your moving expenses are deductible under the general rules of *12.3*. If your residence and principal place of work was outside the U.S. and you retire and move back to the U.S., your moving expenses are also deductible, except that you do not have to meet the 39-week test for employees or the 78-week test for the self-employed and partners.

Survivors of workers abroad returning to U.S. If you are the spouse or dependent of a worker who died while his or her principal place of work was outside the U.S., you may deduct your moving expenses back to the U.S. For the costs to be deductible, the move must begin within six months of the worker's death. The requirements for deducting moving expenses apply, except for the 39-week test for employees or the 78-week test for the self-employed and partners.

Compulsory home leave. Foreign service officers stationed abroad must periodically return to the U.S. to reorient themselves to American ways of life. Because the home leave is compulsory, foreign service officers may deduct their travel expenses; travel expenses of the officer's family are not deductible.

36.7 Exclusion Not Established When Your Return Is Due

When your 1999 return is due, you may not have been abroad long enough to qualify for the exclusion. If you expect to qualify under either the residence or physical presence test after the due date for your 1999 return, you may either (1) ask for an extension of time for filing your return on Form 2350 until after you qualify under either rule or (2) file your return on the due date, reporting the foreign income in the return, pay the full tax, and then file for a refund when you qualify.

If you will have tax to pay even after qualifying for the exclusion—for example, your earned income exceeds the exclusion—you may file for an extension to file but you will owe interest on the tax due. To avoid interest charges on the tax, you may take one of the following steps:

1. File a timely return and pay the total tax due without the application of the exclusion. When you do qualify, make sure you file a refund claim within the time limits discussed at Chapter 49; *or*
2. Pay the estimated tax liability when you apply for the extension to file on Form 2350. If the extension is granted, the payment is applied to the tax shown on your return when you file.

36.8 Tax-Free Meals and Lodging for Workers in Camps

If you must live in a camp provided by your employer, you may exclude from income the value of the lodging and meals furnished if the camp is (1) provided because you work in a remote area where satisfactory housing is not available; (2) located as near as is practical to the worksite; and (3) a common area not open to the public normally accommodating at least 10 employees.

You also may qualify for the earned income exclusion.

36.9 Virgin Islands, Samoa, Guam, and Northern Marianas

The Virgin Islands, Guam, American Samoa, and the Commonwealth of the Northern Mariana Islands have their own independent tax departments. Therefore, contact the particular tax authority for the proper treatment of your income and ask the IRS for the 1999 edition of Publication 570, *Tax Guide for Individuals With Income From U.S. Possessions.*

For tax information from Guam, write to Department of Revenue and Taxation, Government of Guam, P.O. Box 23607, GMF, Guam 96921. For information from the Commonwealth of the Northern Mariana Islands, write to the Division of Revenue and Taxation, Commonwealth of the Northern Mariana Islands, P.O. Box 5234, CHRB, Saipan, Northern Mariana Islands 96950. For information from American Samoa, write to the Tax Division, Government of American Samoa, Pago Pago, American Samoa 96799. Also *see* IRS Publication 570.

For information about tax liability in the Virgin Islands, write to Virgin Islands Bureau of Internal Revenue, 9601 Estate Thomas, Charlotte Amalie, St. Thomas, U.S. Virgin Islands 00802. Also *see* IRS Publication 570.

Possession exclusion. A possession exclusion applies to bona fide residents of American Samoa. On Form 4563, such residents may exclude for U.S. tax purposes their income from sources in American Samoa, Guam, and the Commonwealth of the Northern Marianas and income effectively connected with a business in these possessions.

 Filing Tip

Extension of Time To File
If you are living and working abroad on April 17, 2000, you have an automatic extension to June 15, 2000. For an additional two months, file Form 4868 by June 15, 2000, and pay the estimated tax to limit interest and late payment penalties. For a longer extension, in anticipation of owing no tax on your foreign income, you may file Form 2350 either with the Internal Revenue Service, Philadelphia, Pennsylvania 19255, or with a local IRS representative. File Form 2350 before the due date for filing your 1999 return, which is June 15, 2000, if you are abroad and are on a calendar year. If you cannot get Form 2350, apply for the extension on your own stationery. State the facts you rely on to justify the extension and the earliest date you expect to be in a position to determine under which rule you will qualify. You will receive an official letter and copy granting the extension. Generally, you will be granted an extension for a period ending 30 days after the date you expect to qualify for the foreign earned income exclusion.

36.10 Earnings in Puerto Rico

If you are a U.S. citizen who is also a resident of Puerto Rico for the entire year, you generally report all of your income on your Puerto Rico tax return. Where you report income from U.S. sources on the Puerto Rico tax return, a credit against the Puerto Rico tax may be claimed for income taxes paid to the United States.

If you are not a resident of Puerto Rico, you report on a Puerto Rico return only income from Puerto Rican sources. Wages earned for services performed in Puerto Rico for the U.S. government or for private employers are treated as income from Puerto Rican sources.

U.S. tax returns. As a U.S. citizen, you must file a U.S. tax return reporting income from all sources. But if you are a bona fide resident of Puerto Rico for an entire tax year, you do not report on a U.S. tax return any income earned in Puerto Rico during your residence there, except amounts received for services performed in Puerto Rico as an employee of the U.S. government. Similar rules apply if you have been a bona fide resident of Puerto Rico for at least two years before changing your residence from Puerto Rico. On a U.S. tax return, you may not deduct expenses or claim tax credits allocable to the excludable income. Personal exemptions are fully deductible.

If you are not a bona fide resident of Puerto Rico for the entire tax year, or were not a bona fide resident for two years prior to the tax year, you report on your U.S. tax return all income you earned in Puerto Rico, as well as all income from other sources. If you are required to report income earned in Puerto Rico on your U.S. tax return, you may claim a credit for income tax paid to Puerto Rico. You figure the credit on Form 1116.

Planning Reminder

Information for Puerto Rico Filing

Information on Puerto Rico tax returns may be requested from the Bureau of Income Tax, Oficina de Asistencia, Contributiva y Legislacion, Departmento de Hacienda, P.O. Box 2501, San Juan, Puerto Rico 00902-2501.

EXAMPLE

You and your spouse are bona fide residents of Puerto Rico during the entire year of 1999. You receive $25,000 in wages as an employee of the U.S. government working in Puerto Rico, a $100 dividend from a Puerto Rican corporation that does business in Puerto Rico, and a $500 dividend from a U.S. corporation that does business in the U.S. Your spouse earned $18,000 in wages from a Puerto Rican corporation for services performed in Puerto Rico. Your exempt and taxable income for U.S. federal tax purposes is as follows:

	Taxable	Exempt
Your wages	$25,000	
Your spouse's wages		$18,000
Puerto Rican corporation dividend		100
U.S. corporation dividend	500	
Totals	$25,500	$18,100

You file tax returns with both Puerto Rico and the U.S. You have gross income of $25,500 for U.S. tax purposes and $43,600 for Puerto Rican tax purposes. A tax credit may be claimed on the U.S. tax return for income taxes paid to Puerto Rico and on your Puerto Rico return for income taxes paid to the U.S on U.S. source income.

36.11 Tax Treaties With Foreign Countries

Tax treaties between the United States and foreign countries modify some of the rules discussed in this chapter. The purpose of the treaties is to avoid double taxation. Consult your tax advisor about the effect of these treaties on your income. IRS Publication 54 contains a list of tax treaties.

36.12 Exchange Rates and Blocked Currency

Income reported on your federal income tax return must be stated in U.S. dollars. Where you are paid in foreign currency, you report your pay in U.S. dollars on the basis of the exchange rates prevailing at the time the income is actually or constructively received. You use the rate that most closely reflects the value of the foreign currency—the official rate, the open market rate, or any other relevant rate. You may even be required to use the black market rate if that is the most accurate measure of the actual purchasing power of U.S. dollars in the foreign country. Be prepared to justify the rate you use.

Fulbright grants. If 70% of a Fulbright grant is paid in nonconvertible foreign currency, U.S. tax may be paid in the foreign currency. *See* IRS Publication 520 for details.

Blocked currency. A citizen or resident alien may be paid in a foreign currency that cannot be converted into American dollars and removed from the foreign country. If your income is in blocked currency, you may elect to defer the reporting of that income until: (1) The currency becomes convertible into dollars. (2) You actually convert it into dollars. (3) You use it for personal expenses (for example, in the foreign country when you go there). Purchase of a business or investment in the foreign country is not the kind of use that is treated as a conversion. (4) You make a gift of it or leave it in your will. (5) You are a resident alien and you give up your U.S. residence.

If you use this method to defer the income, you may not deduct the expenses of earning it until you report it. You must continue to use this method after you choose it. You may only change with permission of the IRS.

You do not defer the reporting of capital losses incurred in a country having a blocked currency. There may be these disadvantages in deferring income:

- Many years' income may accumulate and all be taxed in one year.
- You have no control over the year in which the blocked income becomes taxable. You usually cannot control the events that cause the income to become unblocked.

You choose to defer income in blocked currency by filing a tentative tax return reporting your blocked taxable income and explain that you are deferring the payment of income tax because your income is not in dollars or in property or currency that is readily convertible into dollars. You must attach to your tentative return a regular return, reporting any unblocked taxable income received during the year or taxable income that became unblocked during the year. When the currency finally becomes unblocked or convertible into a currency or property convertible to dollars, you pay tax on the earnings at the rate prevailing in the year the currency became unblocked or convertible. On the tentative return, note at the top: "Report of Deferrable Foreign Income, pursuant to Revenue Ruling 74-351." File separate returns for each country from which blocked currency is received. The election must be made by the due date for filing a return for the year in which an election is sought.

36.13 Information Returns on Foreign Currency

If you have a financial interest in, signature, or other authority over a foreign bank account, a foreign securities account, or any other foreign financial account, you must report this fact on Form TDF 90-22.1 (Report of Foreign Bank and Financial Accounts) if the aggregate value of the accounts at any time during the year exceeds $10,000. The form does not have to be filed if the accounts were with a U.S. military banking facility operated by a U.S. financial institution. Taxpayers filing Form 1040 must also indicate on Schedule B whether they had an interest in a foreign account during the year. Form TDF 90-22.1 is not filed with your income tax return. The form must be filed by June 30 of the year following the year in which you had this financial interest. Foreign accounts for 1999 must be reported by June 30, 2000.

Treasury regulations impose reporting and record-keeping requirements for currency transfers to and from the U.S. Generally, transactions involving a physical transfer of funds or monetary instruments into or outside the U.S. must be reported if the amount involved exceeds $10,000 on any one occasion; *see* Form 4790.

Financial institutions must file a Form 4789 for each deposit, withdrawal, exchange of currency, or any other currency transaction of more than $10,000.

36.14 Foreign Tax Credit

You may claim an itemized deduction for qualified foreign taxes or you may claim a foreign tax credit. You must file Form 1116 to compute your credit unless the *de minimis* exception discussed in the Filing Tip at the right applies. You may not claim a foreign tax credit or deduction for taxes paid on income not subject to U.S. tax. If all of your foreign earned income is excluded, none of the foreign taxes paid on such income may be taken as a credit or deduction on your U.S. return. If you exclude only part of your foreign pay, you determine which foreign taxes are attributable to excluded income and thus barred as foreign tax credits by applying the fractional computation provided in the instructions to Form 1116 and IRS Publication 514.

In one tax year, you may not elect to deduct some foreign taxes and claim others as a credit. One method must be applied to all taxes paid or accrued during the tax year. If you are a cash-basis taxpayer, you may claim a credit for accrued foreign taxes, but you must consistently follow this method once elected.

The credit is the amount of foreign taxes paid or accrued, not to exceed the effective U.S. tax on foreign income multiplied by a ratio of foreign taxable income over total taxable income.

Filing Tip

Currency Gains and Losses

A special statute, Section 988, governs the treatment of gain or loss on currency transactions. An individual who disposes of foreign currency in a personal transaction is not subject to tax under Section 988 on gain resulting from fluctuating exchange rates if the gain on the transaction is $200 or less.

Filing Tip

***De Minimis* Foreign Tax Credits**

An individual with $300 or less of creditable foreign taxes, $600 for married persons filing jointly, may elect to be exempt from the overall limitation shown at the beginning of *36.15*, provided that the only foreign source income is qualified passive income. If the election is made, a foreign tax credit may be claimed directly on Line 46 of Form 1040 without having to file Form 1116.

Credit disallowed. The credit may *not* be claimed if:

- You are a nonresident alien. However, under certain circumstances, an alien who is a bona fide resident for an entire taxable year in Puerto Rico may claim the credit. Also, a nonresident alien engaged in a U.S. trade or business may claim a credit if he or she receives income *effectively connected* to that business.
- You are a citizen of a U.S. possession (except Puerto Rico) but not a U.S. citizen or resident.

No credit is allowed for taxes imposed by a country designated by the government as engaging in terroristic activities; *see* IRS Publication 514 for a list of these countries.

Taxes qualifying for the credit. The credit is allowed only for foreign income tax, excess profits taxes, and similar taxes in the nature of an income tax. It is not allowed for any taxes paid to foreign countries on sales, gross receipts, production, the privilege to do business, personal property, or export of capital. But it may apply to a:

- Tax similar to a U.S. tax on income.
- Tax paid by a domestic taxpayer in lieu of the tax upon income, which would otherwise be imposed by any foreign country or by any U.S. possession.
- Tax of a foreign country imposing income tax, where for reasons growing out of the administrative difficulties of determining net income or basis within that country, the tax is measured by gross income, sales, and number of units produced.
- Pension, unemployment, or disability funds of a foreign country; certain foreign social security taxes do not qualify.

Reporting foreign income on your return. You report the gross amount of your foreign income in terms of United States currency. You also attach a schedule showing how you figured the foreign income in United States currency.

EXAMPLE

You earn Canadian dividends of $100 (Canadian dollars), from which $15 of Canadian taxes were withheld. When the dividends were declared, a Canadian dollar could be exchanged for $.78 of United States currency. Therefore, the dividend of $100 (in Canadian dollars) is reported on your return as $78 ($100 × .78). The tax withheld that may be taken as a credit is $11.70 ($15 × .78).

36.15 Computing the Foreign Tax Credit

The foreign tax credit is based on the amount of foreign taxes you paid or accrued, subject to this overall limitation, which is figured on Form 1116:

$$\text{U.S. Tax} \times \frac{\text{Taxable income from all foreign sources}}{\text{Taxable income from all sources}}$$

Separate limitation categories. The above fractional limitation must be figured separately for specific categories of foreign income. These categories are (1) passive income (such as dividends, interest, rents, royalties, and gains on certain commodity transactions; (2) foreign interest income subject to withholding at a rate of 5% or more; (3) shipping and aircraft related income; (4) lump-sum retirement distributions from foreign sources subject to special averaging; (5) certain income derived in banking, insurance, or financing businesses. Taxable income for each category must be separately computed and the overall limitation fraction applied. A separate computation also must be made for all other foreign income not within these categories; this "other" income group is called "general limitation income." Follow the instructions to Form 1116 and see IRS Publication 514 for further details.

Recapture of foreign losses. If you sustain an "overall foreign loss" for any taxable year, a recapture provision treats part of foreign income realized in a later year as income from U.S. sources. By treating part of the later year's foreign income as U.S. income, the numerator of the fraction used to compute the overall limitation (*see* above) is reduced and this in turn reduces the maximum foreign tax credit that may be claimed in the later year. More specifically, the portion of foreign income in succeeding years that is treated as U.S. income equals the lower of (1) the amount of the loss and (2) 50% (or a larger percentage, as you may choose) of taxable income from foreign sources. An "overall foreign loss" means the amount by which the gross income for the taxable year from

Filing Tip

Choosing Credit or Deduction

If you qualify for a credit or deduction, you will generally receive a larger tax reduction by claiming a tax credit rather than a deduction. A deduction is only a partial offset against your tax, whereas a credit is deducted in full from your tax. Also, taking a deduction may bar you from carrying back an excess credit from a later year. However, a deduction may give you a larger tax saving if the foreign tax is levied at a high rate and the proportion of foreign income to U.S. income is small. Compute your tax under both methods and choose the one providing the larger tax reduction.

foreign sources for that year is exceeded by the sum of allocated deductions. For this purpose, the following deductions are not subject to recapture: operating loss deductions, any uncompensated foreign expropriation, and casualty loss. Special rules apply to dispositions of property if used predominantly outside the United States in a trade or business. *See* IRS Publication 514 for recapture details.

Taxable income. Income that is tax free under the foreign earned income exclusion is not taken into account when figuring taxable income. Foreign taxable income, for purposes of computing the ratio, is reduced by all expenses directly related to earning the income. Itemized deductions, such as medical expenses, that are not directly related to foreign sources are allocated to foreign income according to relative gross incomes from foreign and U.S. sources. You do not consider personal exemptions when figuring foreign or total taxable income.

The foreign tax credit may not exceed foreign taxes actually paid or accrued. Where a joint return is filed, the limitation is applied to the aggregate taxable income of both spouses.

A limited foreign tax credit may be applied against the alternative minimum tax; *see* Chapter 23.

Capital gains. In figuring the overall limitation, taxable income from foreign countries (the numerator) includes gain from the sale of capital assets only to the extent of foreign source capital gain net income, which is the lower of net capital gain from foreign sources or net capital gain from all sources. If you are entitled to a preferential capital gains rate, you must make an adjustment to account for the rate differential when figuring the credit. Gain on the sale of nondepreciable personal property sold outside the country of your residence may be treated as gain from U.S. sources, unless the gain is subject to a foreign income tax at a rate of 10% or more of the gain. *See* instructions to Form 1116.

36.16 Carryback and Carryover of Excess Foreign Tax Credit

Where the amount allowable as a credit under the overall basis is restricted, the excess may be carried back to the two preceding years and then carried forward to the five succeeding taxable years. The carryback or carryover will not be allowed in a year for which you have no income from foreign sources or the credit limitation already applies to taxes of that year. For further details, *see* IRS Publication 514.

Chapter 37

Planning Alimony and Marital Settlements

Alimony payments that meet tax law tests of this chapter are deductible if you pay them, and taxable if you receive them. Payments are not deductible by the payer unless taxable to the recipient.

You claim a deduction for deductible alimony that you pay on Line 31a of Form 1040. You deduct the payments even if you claim the standard deduction rather than itemizing deductions. You must enter the Social Security number of your ex-spouse. Otherwise, your deduction may be disallowed and you may have to pay a $50 penalty. If you pay deductible alimony to more than one ex-spouse, enter the Social Security number of one of them and provide similar information for the others on a separate statement attached to your return.

If you receive taxable alimony, report the payments on Line 11 of Form 1040. You must give your ex-spouse your Social Security number and could be subject to a $50 penalty if you fail to do so.

Tax Rules for Alimony Payments

Minimum Payments and Recapture of Alimony

Tax Rules for Alimony Payments

37.1 Planning Alimony Agreements

You can arrange beforehand the way in which the costs of a divorce are to be borne. You may specifically state in the decree or agreement that the alimony is neither taxable to the payee-spouse (under IRC Section 71) nor deductible by the payer-spouse (under IRC Section 215). Such a statement effectively disqualifies payments that otherwise would be taxable to the payee-spouse and deductible by the payer-spouse. A copy of the agreement that contains the statement must be attached to the tax return of the payee-spouse for each year the statement is applicable.

The first step in planning the after-tax consequences of alimony is convincing a couple that they may have a common financial interest; the second is projecting future tax consequences.

For example, assume that the husband is to make payments to the wife. If tax planning is approached from the viewpoint of each spouse separately, the tax deduction is an advantage for the husband; tax-free income is an advantage for the wife. However, both advantages cannot be achieved, and the couple must face the reality of the tax law, which allows the husband to deduct payments only if they are taxed as alimony to the wife. The husband and wife must compromise by setting amounts and tax consequences that balance their interests.

One approach is to view both spouses as a single economic tax unit. If this is done and the husband will be in a higher tax bracket during the payout period than the wife, an agreement should generally provide for taxable and deductible alimony. The tax savings provided by the deduction can conserve more of the husband's assets while providing funds required by the wife. The final amount of alimony to be paid depends on the spouses' tax brackets. Where tax brackets do not differ, there may be no advantage in making an agreement for taxable and deductible alimony when viewing the two parties as a unit.

If you agree that one spouse is to pay deductible alimony and the other spouse is to report the alimony as income, these rules must be met:

- The alimony must be paid under the decree of divorce or legal separation agreement or decree of support; *see 37.2.*

- The agreement must provide for cash payments; *see 37.3.* There is no minimum payout period for annual alimony payments of $15,000 or less. One payment of $15,000 can qualify as deductible and taxable alimony. There is also no minimum payout period for annual alimony payments exceeding $15,000. However, recapture of alimony deductions claimed in the first or second year may occur where annual payments of over $15,000 are scheduled and paid, but in the second or third year a reduced payment is made. To avoid recapture of deductions for payments over $15,000, carefully plan schedules of declining payments within the rules discussed at *37.7.*

- In providing for the support of children, a specific allocation to their support or the setting of certain contingencies disqualifies payments as deductible and alimony as taxable; *see 37.5.*

- Divorced and legally separated parties may not live in the same household. If they live in the same household, alimony payments are not deductible or taxable. However, there are these exceptions: A spouse who makes payments while preparing to leave the common residence may deduct payments made within one month before the departure. Also, where you are separated under a written agreement, but not legally separated under a decree of divorce or separate maintenance, you may deduct alimony payments even if you both are members of the same household.

- The payer spouse's liability to pay alimony must end on the death of the payee spouse. The alimony agreement does not have to state expressly that payments end on death if liability ends under state law; *see 37.4.*

37.2 Decree or Agreement Required

Alimony, to be deductible and taxable, must be required by one of the following: (1) a decree of divorce or legal separation; (2) a written separation agreement; or (3) a decree of support. This rule applies to both pre-1985 and post-1984 decrees and agreements. Voluntary payments are not deductible or taxable.

Filing Instruction

Reporting Alimony

If you paid alimony in 1999 meeting the deductible tests, claim your deduction on Line 31a of Form 1040, and enter the recipient's Social Security number. If you receive qualifying alimony payments, report them on Line 11 of Form 1040.

Planning Reminder

Property Transfers

A property transfer to a former spouse that is incident to a divorce is generally treated as a tax-free exchange; *see 6.6* for details.

Divorced or legally separated. The obligation to pay alimony must be imposed by the decree of divorce or separate maintenance or a written agreement incident to the divorce or separation.

Alimony paid under a Mexican divorce decree qualifies. Payments under a Mexican or state decree declared invalid by another jurisdiction do not qualify according to the IRS. Two appeals courts have rejected the IRS position.

Support payments ordered by a court in a wife's home state qualify as alimony, even though not provided for by an ex parte divorce decree obtained by the husband in another state. Similarly, payments qualified when a state court increased support originally ordered before the husband obtained an uncontested Mexican divorce.

Payments made under a separation approved by a Roman Catholic ecclesiastical board do not qualify.

When a decree of divorce or separate maintenance fails to mention alimony, payments qualify as long as they are made under a written agreement considered "incident to" the decree.

Payments made under an agreement amended after a divorce or legal separation may also qualify, if the amendment is considered "incident" to the divorce or separation. For example, the IRS agrees that a written amendment changing the amount of alimony payments is incident to the divorce where the legal obligation to support under the original agreement survived the divorce. However, payments under an amended agreement did not qualify where the original agreement settled all rights between the husband and wife and made no provision for future support. The legal obligation to support the wife did not survive the divorce and could not be revived by the new agreement.

Annulments. Payments made under an annulment decree qualify as deductible (and taxable) alimony.

Separated from spouse. Where a husband and wife are separated and living apart, alimony is deductible by the payer-spouse and taxable to the payee-spouse provided it is paid under either a written separation agreement or decree of support.

A decree of support. Any court decree or order requiring support payments qualifies, including alimony *pendente lite* (temporary alimony while the action is pending) and an interlocutory (not final) divorce decree.

In certain community property states, payments under a decree of alimony pendente lite which do not exceed the wife's interest in community income are neither deductible by the husband nor taxable to the wife; payments exceeding the wife's interest are taxable to her and deductible by the husband.

37.3 Cash Payments Required

Only payments of cash, checks, and money orders payable on demand qualify as taxable and deductible alimony. Your cash payment to a third party for a spouse qualifies if made under the terms of a divorce decree or separation instrument. For example, you pay the rent, mortgage, tax, medical expenses, or tuition liabilities of your former spouse. The payments qualify if made under the terms of the divorce or separation instrument. If taxable as alimony, your former spouse may deduct your payment of real estate taxes, mortgage interest, or medical expenses if he or she claims itemized deductions. You may not deduct payments to maintain property owned by you but used by your spouse. For example, you pay the mortgage expenses, real estate taxes, and insurance premiums for a house that you own and in which your former spouse lives. You may not deduct those payments as alimony even if required by a decree or agreement.

Providing services or transferring or providing property does not qualify. For example, you may not deduct as alimony your note, the assignment of a third party note, or an annuity contract.

Premiums paid for term or whole life insurance on your life made under a divorce or separation instrument qualify as deductible alimony to the extent your former spouse owns the policy.

Planning Reminder

Payments to a Third Party

Cash payments to a third party may be deducted as alimony if they are under the terms of a divorce decree or separation instrument. You may also deduct as alimony payments made to a third party at the written request of the payee spouse. For example, your former wife asks you to make a cash donation to a charitable organization instead of paying alimony installments to her. Her request must be in writing and state that both she and you intend the payment to be treated as alimony. You must receive the written request before you file your return for the taxable year in which the payment was made. Your former wife may deduct the payment as a charitable contribution if she claims itemized deductions.

Key to Alimony and Marital Settlement Issues

Item—	Comments—
Alimony	The same rules determine whether alimony is deductible and taxable. For example, if a husband makes deductible alimony payments to his ex-wife, the payments are taxable to her. He may not deduct payments that are not taxable to her.
	If you are currently planning an alimony agreement, consider the tax consequences to both spouses. As current tax rates may be as high as 39.6% for one spouse and as low as 15% for the other, there may be a substantial tax savings to the couple, when considered as an economic unit, in negotiating an agreement that qualifies the payments as deductible alimony; *see 37.1.*
	Note: Prior tax rules that apply to pre-1985 agreements are not discussed in this chapter. If you have a problem involving a payment of alimony under a pre-1985 agreement, refer to a past issue of *Your Income Tax* or to IRS Publication 504.
Child support agreements	A payment fixed as payable for the support of your child may not qualify as deductible or taxable alimony; *see 37.5.*
Property settlements	Transfers of property between spouses that are incident to a divorce are treated as tax-free exchanges. There is no recognition of gain or loss.
	Future tax consequences should be considered by the spouse receiving appreciated property. When the property is sold, that spouse will be taxed on the appreciation. If this is so, that spouse may want to bargain for larger alimony payments or additional property to compensate for the projected future tax; *see 6.6.*
Alimony to nonresident alien	If you pay alimony payments to a nonresident alien, and you are a U.S. citizen or resident, you must withhold 30% (or a lower rate as set by treaty) on each payment for income tax purposes. *See* IRS Publications 504 and 515 for more information.
Exemptions for children	Exemptions for children of a divorced couple are governed by the rules explained at *21.11.* Further, where a spouse is in the income range requiring the phaseout or disallowance of personal exemptions *(21.15)*, there may be no advantage in providing the exemption to that spouse. The exemption should be given to the spouse who may claim a full deduction for the exemption.
Annuity or endowment policy	Funds for payments of alimony may be provided through the purchase of an annuity or endowment policy. You may not deduct payments made under the policies assigned or purchased for your spouse. For example, to meet an alimony obligation of $500 a month, you buy your spouse a commercial annuity contract. The full $500 a month received by him or her is taxable. You may not deduct these payments.
Trust to pay alimony	To meet your alimony obligations, you may transfer income-producing property to a trust that is to pay the income to your spouse. You may not deduct payments made by the trust. You are not taxable on the income earned by the trust, even though it meets your alimony obligations. This tax treatment is the equivalent of receiving a tax deduction for paying alimony.
	If you receive alimony from a trust, ask the trustee how to report such income. Tax treatment may depend on whether the trust was created before 1985 or after 1984. If the trust was set up after 1984, as a beneficiary you generally report trust income under the general trust reporting rules in Chapter 11. These general trust rules may not apply to certain alimony trusts created before 1985 that were subject to the prior alimony rules. Distributions from such trusts may be treated as taxable alimony regardless of whether the distributions are from income or principal. In any event, the trustee should provide you with the necessary tax information.
Retirement plans	A state court can allocate your interest in a qualified retirement plan to a former spouse in a qualified domestic relations order. The benefits are taxed to your former spouse when they are paid to her or him. Benefits paid to another beneficiary, such as a child, are taxable to you; *see 7.12.*
Remarriage's effect on pre-1985 agreement	The tax deduction allowed for alimony payments made under a pre-1985 decree or agreement hinges on the obligation to support. Once the spouse receiving alimony remarries, the obligation to support generally ends under state law. In these states, any payment after remarriage is not considered alimony and is not deductible. For example, payments to a former wife made after remarriage are considered tax-free gifts if the former husband knows of the remarriage and that he is no longer obligated to pay. If she does not inform him of her remarriage, his payments are taxable to her but are not deductible by him.
Voluntary payments in excess of required alimony	Voluntary payments in excess of required alimony are not deductible or taxable as alimony. Amending the decrees retroactively to cover an increase does not qualify the increase as deductible and taxable alimony. The increase has to be approved by the court before the increased payments are made.

37.4 Payments Must Stop at Death

Payments must stop on the death of the payee-spouse. If not, none of the payments, whether made before or after the payee's death, qualify as taxable or deductible alimony.

The divorce decree or separation agreement does not have to specifically state that payments end at death, if under state law the liability to pay ends on the death of the payee-spouse.

To the extent that one or more payments are to begin, increase in amount, or accelerate after the death of the payee-spouse, such payments may be treated as a substitute for the continuation of payments terminating on the death of the payee-spouse.

EXAMPLES

1. Under the terms of a divorce decree, Smith is obligated to make annual alimony payments of $30,000, terminating on the earlier of the end of six years or the death of Mrs. Smith. She also is to keep custody of their two minor children. The decree also provides that if on her death the children are still minors, Jones is to pay annually $10,000 to a trust each year. The trust income and corpus are to be used for the children until the youngest child reaches the age of majority. Under these facts, Smith's possible liability to make annual $10,000 payments to the trust is treated as a substitute for $10,000 of the $30,000 annual payments. $10,000 of each of the $30,000 annual payments does not qualify as alimony.

2. Same facts as in Example 1, but the alimony is to end on the earlier of the expiration of 15 years and the death of Mrs. Smith. Further, if Mrs. Smith dies before the end of the 15-year period, Smith will pay her estate the difference between the total amount that he would have paid had she survived and the amount actually paid. For example, if she dies at the end of the tenth year, he will pay her estate $150,000 ($450,000 – $300,000). Under these facts, his liability to make a lump-sum payment to the estate is a substitute for the full amount of each of the annual $30,000 payments. Accordingly, none of the annual $30,000 payments qualifies as alimony.

37.5 Child Support Payments Are Not Alimony

A payment is fixed as payable for child support if the divorce or separation instrument specifically fixes an amount payable for support. That amount is not deductible or taxable as alimony.

Even if there is not a specific allocation to child support, a payment will be treated as payable for child support if it is to be reduced on the happening of a contingency relating to the child, such as: the child reaches a specific age or income level, or the child leaves school, marries, leaves the parent's household, or begins to work.

EXAMPLE

On July 1, 1994, a couple is divorced when their children, John (born July 15, 1979) and Jane (born September 23, 1981), are ages 14 and 12. Under the divorce decree, the husband is to make monthly alimony payments of $2,000. The monthly payments are to be reduced to $1,500 on January 1, 2000, and to $1,000 on January 1, 2004. On January 1, 2000, the date of the first reduction, John will be 20 years, 5 months, and 17 days old. On January 1, 2004, the date of the second reduction, Jane will be 22 years, 3 months, and 9 days old. As each reduction is to occur not more than one year before or after each child reaches the age of 21 years and four months, the IRS will presume that the deductions are associated with the happening of a contingency relating to the children. The two reductions total $1,000 per month and are treated as the amount fixed for the support of the children. Thus, $1,000 of the $2,000 monthly payment does not qualify as alimony. To avoid this result, the husband must prove that the reductions were not related to the support of the children.

Caution

Alimony Reductions Tied to Child's Age

If a reduction in your payments is not specifically tied to your child's reaching majority age but the scheduled date for the reduction is within six months before or after your child reaches age 18 or 21 (or other age of majority under local law), the IRS holds that the reduction is tied to the child's age. The reduction amount will be treated as child support unless you can prove that the reduction is for some other purpose. The IRS makes the same presumption if you have more than one child and your alimony payments are to be reduced at least twice and each reduction is within one year of a different child's reaching a particular age between ages 18 and 24; *see* the Example on the right.

If both alimony and child support are specified and a payment is less than the total of the two amounts, then the payment is first allocated to child support.

Tax refund diversion for delinquent child support. The IRS can give your tax refund to a state that is paying support to your child if you fail to make support payments. The IRS will not notify you of the diversion until it is made to the state. The state agency must provide prior notice of the proposed offset and procedures for contesting it.

Minimum Payments and Recapture of Alimony

37.6 No Minimum Payment Period for Alimony

There is no minimum payment period, but a recapture rule applies where payments fall by more than $15,000 within the first three years; *see 37.7.*

37.7 3rd Year Recapture If Alimony Drops $15,000 or More

The recapture rules are designed to prevent the so-called "front loading" of property settlement payments disguised as alimony. However, the rules apply even where no property settlement was intended if you come within their terms. Here are the rules: Deductible payments made in the first year or second year may be recaptured (that is, reported as income) in the third year where payments within the first three years decline by more than $15,000. The three years are called "post-separation years." The first post-separation year is the first calendar year in which you pay alimony under a decree of divorce or separation agreement. The period does not begin with the year of the decree or agreement if no payments are made. Recapture does not apply to temporary support payments made before the final decree or agreement. The second and third post-separation years are the next two calendar years after the first post-separation year whether or not payments are made during those years.

Payments made in the second post-separation year are recaptured if the payments exceed the payments made in the third post-separation year by more than $15,000. Payments made in the first post-separation year are recaptured if they exceed the average payments made in the second post-separation year and the third post-separation year by more than $15,000. The following Examples illustrate how to make these computations.

When recapture does not apply. Recapture is not triggered if payments in both the first and second post-separation years do not exceed $15,000. Recapture also does not apply to:

- Payments made under a continuing liability to pay for at least three years a fixed part of your income from a business or property or from a job or self-employed business or profession, *or*
- Payments that end because of your death or the death of your former spouse or the remarriage of your former spouse at any time before the end of the third post-separation year.

The steps of recapture are:

Step 1. Recapture for the second-year payment is computed first. This is the excess, if any, of the second-year payment over the third-year payment, *minus* $15,000.

Step 2. Recapture for the first-year payment is computed next. There is recapture if the first-year payment exceeds by more than $15,000 the average payment made in the second and third years. In figuring the average payment, reduce the second-year payment by any recapture amount for the second year figured under Step 1.

 Filing Tip

Reporting Recapture on Your Return

The payer-spouse reports the recaptured amount as income in the third year and the payee-spouse claims a deduction for the same amount. The payer reports the recaptured amount on Form 1040, Line 11 (alimony received); cross out "received" and write "recapture" along with the payee-spouse's Social Security number.

The payee-spouse deducts the recaptured amount on Form 1040, Line 31a (alimony paid). He or she crosses out the word "paid" and writes "recapture," and also enters on that line the payer-spouse's Social Security number.

EXAMPLES

1. In 1997, Jones obtains a divorce and pays deductible alimony of $50,000. His wife reports $50,000 as income. In 1998 and 1999, he makes no payments. On his 1999 return, $35,000 of the first year 1997 deduction is recaptured ($50,000 − $15,000) and reported as income by Jones. His ex-spouse deducts $35,000.

2. In 1997, Smith makes his first alimony payment of $50,000; in 1998 he pays $20,000 and, in 1999, he pays nothing. On his 1999 return, $32,500 is recaptured as follows:

Recapture of second-year payment:

Payment in 2nd year		$20,000
Less: 3rd-year payment	$0	
Less: allowance	15,000	15,000
Recapture for second year		$ 5,000

Recapture of first-year payment:

Average calculation:

Payment over the 2nd and 3rd years	$20,000	
Less: recapture in the 2nd year	$ 5,000	
	$15,000	
Average ($15,000 ÷ 2)	$ 7,500	
Payment in first year		$50,000
Less: Average	$ 7,500	
Less: Allowance	15,000	22,500
Recapture for first year		$27,500

Total recaptured in 1999:

For second year	$ 5,000
For first year	$27,500
Total:	$32,500

37.8 Legal Fees of Marital Settlements

If you are receiving taxed alimony, you may deduct part of your legal fees. Ask your attorney to divide his or her fees into charges for arranging: (1) the divorce or separation and (2) details of the alimony payments.

You may deduct the legal fees allocated to (2), but you may not deduct the fee attributed to the divorce or separation negotiation. The deduction is subject to the 2% adjusted gross income (AGI) floor on miscellaneous itemized deductions *(see* Chapter 19). If the alimony is not taxed to you, you may not deduct any part of the fee. However, part of a fee allocated to a property settlement may be added to the basis of the property.

If you are paying deductible alimony, you may not deduct legal fees paid for arranging a divorce or for resisting your spouse's demands for alimony. Furthermore, you may not deduct legal fees incurred in resisting your spouse's claims to income-producing property the loss of which would affect your earnings. However, these rules do not bar you from deducting that part of your legal fee that is identified as being paid for tax advice. The following types of proof may support a deduction:

- The fee is charged by a firm that limits its practice to state and federal matters and is engaged to advise on the consequences of a property settlement involving the transfer of property in exchange for other property and the release of the other spouse's marital rights in the property.

- The fee is charged by a firm engaged in general practice that assigns tax problems, such as the tax consequences of creating an alimony trust, to its special tax department. On the bill, an allocation is made for tax advice based on time, complexity of the case, and the amount of tax involved.

- An attorney handles the divorce for a fixed fee and also gives advice on the right to claim exemptions for the children following the divorce. The bill allocates part of the fee to the tax advice, based on time, and fees customarily charged in the locality for similar services.

 Caution

Spouse's Legal Fees

You may not deduct your payment of your spouse's legal fees as a miscellaneous itemized deduction, even if the fees are only for tax advice. However, the fees may be deductible as alimony under the rules discussed in the sidebar at *37.3* for payments to third parties.

Educational Tax Benefits

The tax law provides several tax benefits for people attending school. If you can take advantage of them, you are in effect receiving a government subsidy that lowers the cost of education.

The following benefit provisions can provide substantial tax savings, but are hedged with restrictions that may bar or limit their availability: Hope and lifetime learning education tax credits, a student loan interest deduction, and a deferral of taxes on interest earned on contributions to state-sponsored college tuition programs and educational IRAs.

Scholarships, Grants, Tuition Plans, and Student Loan Interest

Hope and Lifetime Learning Credits

Education IRAs

Scholarships, Grants, Tuition Plans, and Student Loan Interest

38.1 Scholarships and Grants

Scholarships and fellowships of a degree candidate are tax free to the extent that the grant pays for tuition and course-related fees, books, supplies, and equipment that are required for courses. Amounts for room, board, and incidental expenses are taxable. If you are not a candidate for a degree (*see* the Degree test below), your entire grant is taxable.

You must pay tax on grants or tuition reductions that pay for teaching or other services required as a condition of receiving the grant. This is true even if all degree candidates are required to perform the services. Thus, if you are a graduate student and receive a stipend for teaching, those payments are taxable, subject to withholding, and reported by the school on Form W-2. Similarly, no tax-free exclusion is allowed for federal grants where the recipient agrees to do future work with the federal government.

Degree test. Scholarships given to students attending a primary or secondary school, or to those pursuing a degree at a college or university, meet the degree test. Also qualifying are full-time or part-time scholarships for study at an educational institution that (1) provides an educational program acceptable for full-time credit towards a higher degree or offers a program of training to prepare students for gainful employment in a recognized occupation *and* (2) is authorized under federal or state law to provide such a program and is accredited by a nationally recognized accreditation agency.

38.2 Tuition Reductions for College Employees

Free or partially free tuition for *undergraduate* studies provided to a faculty member or school employee is generally not taxable. The tuition reduction may be for education at his or her own school or at a similar school. Tuition benefits may be taxable to highly compensated employees if the tuition plan discriminates in their favor. Tuition reductions that represent compensation for services are taxable.

Tax-free tuition benefits may also be provided to the employee's spouse, dependent child, a former employee who retired or left on disability, a widow or widower of an individual who died while employed by the school, or a widow or widower of a retired or disabled employee.

A child under the age of 25 qualifies for tuition reduction if both parents have died and one of the parents qualified for tax-free tuition benefits. If the child is age 25 or over, tuition reductions are taxed even if both parents are deceased.

38.3 How Fulbright Awards Are Taxed

Fulbright awards for teaching, lecturing, or research are taxable unless you can claim the foreign earned income exclusion to avoid tax on the grant (Chapter 36). If you do not qualify for the exclusion, your overseas stay is temporary and you intend to return to your regular teaching position in the United States, you may deduct the cost of your travel, meals, and lodgings overseas.

38.4 U.S. Savings Bond Tuition Plans

Consider the use of Series EE bonds *(30.21)* or I bonds *(30.22)* to fund part of a college savings program. You can defer the interest until final maturity (30 years) or report the interest annually. The interest is not subject to state or local tax. For bonds purchased in your child's name, having your child report the interest annually may be advisable where it can be offset by the child's standard deduction or itemized deductions. To the extent interest is offset each year, it escapes tax; *see 4.29*.

Interest exclusion may be available if you redeem EE bonds issued after 1989 or I bonds. If you purchased bonds in your own name or jointly with your spouse after 1989, you may be able to exclude accumulated interest from federal tax in the year you redeem the bonds if you pay tuition and similar education fees in that year. The interest exclusion rule also applies to redemptions of I bonds.

Who qualifies for the exclusion. You must be age 24 or over before the month in which the bonds are purchased, and the bonds must be issued solely in your name or in the joint names of you and your spouse. You may not claim the exclusion for bonds bought in your child's name or owned jointly with your child. In the year the bonds are redeemed you must pay tuition and similar educational fees for yourself, your spouse, or your dependents. Thus, grandparents may not claim the exclusion if they buy savings bonds to fund the college education of grandchildren unless the children are dependents of the grandparents in the year the bonds are cashed. Tuition and fees must be for a college, university, or vocational school that meets federal financial aid standards. Room and board are not eligible expenses.

Caution

Graduate Teaching and Research Assistants

If you must teach, do research, or provide other services to obtain a tuition reduction for graduate studies, a tuition reduction from the school is tax free if it is in addition to regular pay for the services. If the tuition reduction is your compensation, it is taxable.

Excludable amount and phase-out rule. The tax-free amount of interest is figured on Form 8815. The amount of the exclusion varies with the amount of educational expenses you pay and your modified adjusted gross income (MAGI) in the year of redemption. However, no exclusion is allowed to a married person who files separately, regardless of income or amount of tuition paid.

On Form 8815, educational expenses must be reduced by the amount of any nontaxable scholarship or fellowship grant, tax-free distributions from a qualifying state tuition plan *(see 38.5)*, educational expenses taken into account when figuring a Hope or lifetime learning credit *(see 38.7)*, and tax-free distributions from an education IRA *(see 38.12)*. If qualifying savings bonds are redeemed and contributed to a qualifying state tuition plan *(38.5)* or education IRA *(38.11)*, the transfer is treated as an education expense eligible for the exclusion. If the redemption amount exceeds the amount of educational expenses (after any required reduction), the excludable amount is based on the ratio of expenses to redemption amount.

EXAMPLE

In August 1999, you redeem a $10,000 EE bond that was issued in September 1990. You receive $8,268, including $5,000 principal and $3,268 interest. After taking $5,000 of expenses used to figure a lifetime learning credit *(38.9)* into account, you show $7,500 of qualified higher education expenses on Form 8815. The excludable percentage of interest is 90.7% ($7,500 divided by $8,268). Thus, $2,964 (90.7% × $3,268) of the interest is potentially excludable from income, subject to the phase-out rules.

A full interest exclusion is allowed only to persons with MAGI below a phase-out threshold. For 1999, the MAGI phase-out ranges are $79,650 to $109,650 for married persons filing jointly and qualifying widow(er)s, and $53,100 to $68,100 for single persons and heads of households. Married persons filing separately do not qualify. For purposes of applying the phaseout, MAGI is generally your regular adjusted gross income plus the interest on the redeemed EE bonds, student loan interest that you deduct *(38.6)*, and foreign income items and employer-provided adoption assistance which you excluded from income. *See* the Form 8815 instructions.

38.5 Qualified State Tuition Programs

Many states have state-sponsored college savings plans in place or are in the process of approving them. These programs are designed to allow participants to take advantage of federal tax benefits, and some also offer state tax benefits. Each state has its own variation, so it is important to look at the details of the program in the state in which you live. Distributions from the plan can be used to pay the costs of college tuition and fees, books, supplies, and qualified room and board (for students enrolled at least half time).

Types of plans. There are currently two basic types of state-sponsored college savings plans: (1) college tuition prepayment plans and (2) contributory or savings plans.

In a prepayment plan, a parent or other relative pays a child's college tuition at the rate charged by the state's public universities during the year of plan enrollment, even if the child will not start college for 10 or more years. The prepayment will cover state school tuition, regardless of how much it increases in the interim, or the payments and interest earned on them can be transferred to a private or out-of-state school.

In a contributory plan, deposits are made to a state-managed account for the benefit of a specified individual. Earnings build up tax free and are later distributed to pay the beneficiary's qualifying college costs. Plan eligibility is not tied to income of the contributor or beneficiary. The maximum plan amount varies with the state, but potentially can cover the full cost of college attendance.

The same income tax and gift tax rules apply to both types of plans. Earnings are not taxed while the fund accumulates. The student is taxed when plan withdrawals are used to pay college expenses. Part of each withdrawal is treated as a tax-free return of contributions and part is a taxable distribution allocated to earnings on the account. For example, the taxable part of a distribution from a contributory plan is determined by multiplying the distribution by the ratio that the total account earnings bear to the account balance as of the end of the year. The taxable earnings portion of a distribution is reported on Form 1099-G in Box 5.

If the beneficiary of the account does not attend college and a refund is made to the parent or other contributor, the earnings portion of the refund is taxable and the plan will impose a penalty of at least 10% unless the refund was made because of the beneficiary's disability or death or the amount is rolled over within 60 days to the account of another family member.

 Filing Tip

Qualified State Tuition Plans and Education Tax Credits

The student beneficiary of a qualified state tuition plan (or a taxpayer who claims the beneficiary as a dependent) can use withdrawals the state tuition plan to pay for qualified tuition and related expenses that are eligible for the Hope and lifetime learning credits *(38.7)*.

Gift tax consequences. A contribution to a qualified state tuition program is treated as a completed gift of a present interest passed from the contributor to the beneficiary at the time of contribution. Annual contributions are eligible for the gift tax exclusion, which is currently $10,000 for a contribution from an individual (or $20,000 if from a married couple). If your contribution exceeds the regular annual exclusion, you may elect to treat up to $50,000 of the contribution ($100,000 for a married couple who elect gift splitting) as if it was made ratably over a five-year period. If the election is made, you have to report as a taxable gift on Form 709 only 20% of the total contribution (up to the $50,000 or $100,000 limit) in the year of contribution. In each of the next four years an additional 20% is reported. If the contribution exceeds the $50,000 (or $100,000) limit, the excess must be reported on Form 709 in the year of the contribution.

38.6 Student Loan Interest Deduction

If you paid interest on a qualified student loan in 1999, you may be able to claim an above-the-line (directly from gross income) deduction of up to $1,500. Eligibility for the deduction is phased out if you have 1999 modified adjusted gross income (MAGI, *see* below) between $40,000 and $55,000, or between $60,000 and $75,000 if married filing a joint return. If you are married filing separately, you may not claim the deduction regardless of your income. The deduction is claimed on Line 24 of Form 1040 or Line 16 of Form 1040A. A worksheet in the form instructions may be used to figure your student loan interest deduction. The deduction cap will increase to $2,000 in 2000 and to $2,500 in 2001 and thereafter.

Qualified loans and expenses. A qualified student loan is one taken out to pay qualified higher education expenses for you, your spouse, or a person who was your dependent when you took out the loan. The expenses must be paid or incurred within a reasonable time before or after the loan was taken out, and the funds obtained must be used toward education furnished while the student is enrolled at least half-time in a program leading to a degree or other recognized educational credential at an eligible educational institution. Medical and graduate school programs are included. Eligible institutions are colleges, universities, vocational schools, and other post-secondary educational institutions eligible to participate in Department of Education student aid programs.

Qualified higher education expenses include tuition, fees, room and board, books, equipment, and other necessary expenses such as transportation. These costs must be reduced by:

1. Nontaxable employer-provided educational assistance benefits.
2. Nontaxable education IRA distributions.
3. U.S. Savings Bond interest excluded from income because it is used to pay higher education expenses.
4. Qualified tax-free scholarships.
5. Veterans' educational assistance benefits.
6. Tax-free gifts and inheritances received to pay education expenses.

Loan origination fees and capitalized interest (unpaid interest that accrues and is added to the balance of the loan) can be counted as interest paid. In general, a payment, regardless of its label, is treated first as a payment of interest to the extent that accrued interest remains unpaid, second as a payment of any loan origination fees or capitalized interest, until such amounts are reduced to zero, and third as a payment of principal.

60-month rule. The deduction is allowed *only for the first 60 months* in which interest payments are required. The period begins on the date that the loan enters repayment status (as determined by the terms of the loan or, for federally issued or guaranteed loans, under federal regulations), and ends 60 months later, regardless of whether the required interest payments are actually made. You may not deduct interest you pay before the period begins. If the loan entered repayment status on or before December 31, 1997, deductions are allowed only for the interest due and paid during the portion of the 60-month period remaining after that date.

The 60-month period may be suspended only if the borrower meets one of the conditions for deferment or forbearance established by the U.S. Department of Education for federal student loan programs under Title IV of the Higher Education Act of 1965. The period will not be suspended if, under the terms of the loan, interest continues to accrue while the loan is in deferment or forbearance, you have the option to capitalize the interest or pay it immediately, and you choose to pay it immediately.

All refinancings of a loan are treated as a single loan when calculating the 60-month period. Refinancing after the 60-month period will not extend the deductible period.

Caution

Older Loans

If you paid interest on a student loan for more than 60 months before 1999, you may not claim an interest deduction for 1999 or any later year with respect to that loan.

EXAMPLE

You took out a qualified student loan in 1994. Beginning on October 1, 1994, you made a payment on the loan every month. As of the end of 1998, you made 51 monthly interest payments. You may deduct the interest on your first nine payments for 1999. You may not deduct the interest on the next three payments because they were made after the 60-month period (October 1, 1994–September 30, 1999).

Dependents and married persons filing separately are ineligible. You may not claim a student loan interest deduction during any year in which someone claims you as a dependent. However, you may deduct interest payments made in a later year when you are no longer claimed as a dependent.

You may not claim a student loan interest deduction for any year in which you are married and file a separate tax return.

Other restrictions. A revolving line of credit is not a qualified loan unless you agree to use the funds solely to pay education costs.

You may not deduct interest paid on a loan from a relative as educational loan interest; *see 5.6*.

You may not claim a student loan interest deduction for any amount you may deduct under any other tax law provision, for example home mortgage interest. You also cannot use the deduction if you use part of the borrowed money for purposes other than education, for instance to make improvements to your house.

Phaseout. The interest deduction is reduced or eliminated if your modified adjusted gross income (MAGI) exceeds phase-out limits. The reduction applies if MAGI is more than $40,000, or more than $60,000 on a joint return. If MAGI is more than $55,000, or more than $75,000 on a joint return, you may not claim a deduction. MAGI is the same as the adjusted gross income shown on your return (disregarding student loan interest) unless you claimed the exclusion for foreign earned income (Chapter 36) or certain other items of foreign income or expenses were excluded or deducted from your income. Such items generally must be added back to adjusted gross income.

If your MAGI is within the $15,000 phase-out range, figure the reduction to the 1999 deduction by multiplying your deductible interest (up to the $1,500 limit) by a fraction, the numerator of which is your MAGI less $40,000, or $60,000 if married filing jointly, and the denominator of which is $15,000.

The student loan deduction worksheet in the Form 1040 or Form 1040A instructions can be used to figure the phase-out reduction and the amount of your deduction.

EXAMPLE

1. In 1999 you paid $900 interest on a qualified student loan. Your MAGI is $70,000 on a joint return. Your deduction is reduced by $600. You deduct $300 ($900 – $600).

$$\$900 \times {}^{\$70,000 - \$60,000} / {}_{\$15,000} = \$600 \text{ reduction}$$

2. The same facts as in Example 1, except you paid $1,800 interest. The maximum deduction of $1,500 is reduced by $1,000. You deduct $500 ($1,500 – $1,000).

$$\$1,500 \times {}^{\$70,000 - \$60,000} / {}_{\$15,000} = \$1,000 \text{ reduction}$$

Hope and Lifetime Learning Credits

38.7 Education Tax Credits

There are two tax credits for qualifying higher education expenses: The Hope credit and the lifetime learning credit. They are figured on Form 8863. A married couple must file a joint return to claim either education credit. Other rules that apply to both credits are discussed in this section. The Hope credit is discussed further at *38.8* and the lifetime learning credit at *38.9*.

Who may claim a credit. If you pay qualifying higher education expenses for you, your spouse, or a person you claim as a dependent (*see* Chapter 21) on your return, and you are not subject to the credit phaseout because of the amount of your income (*38.10*), you may claim a credit on Form 8863. The credits are subject to a tax liability limit. If your child is claimed by you as your dependent, his or her payment of qualifying expenses is treated as your payment. If you do not claim an exemption for your child on your tax return, your child can claim a credit for qualified expenses he or she paid.

 Caution

Both Education Credits Not Allowed for the Same Student

You may not claim both the Hope credit and the lifetime learning credit for the same student's expenses for the same tax year. For example, if you pay more than $2,000 of qualified tuition expenses for your child, you may not claim the Hope credit for the first $2,000 of expenses and the lifetime learning credit for the balance.

Caution

Effect of Education IRA on Education Credits

If a student receives a tax-free distribution from an education IRA *(38.12)* in a particular tax year, none of the student's expenses can be used as the basis of an education credit for that tax year. However, on Form 8606, the student can waive tax-free treatment for an education IRA distribution. A waiver could allow the student or the student's parents (if the student is their dependent) to claim a credit.

Law Alert

Tax Liability Limitation on Education Credits

The Hope credit and the lifetime learning credit are limited to regular income tax liability. The education credits are subtracted from your tax but are not refundable; if the amount of credit exceeds the tax you owe, the excess is not refunded to you.

What expenses qualify. Qualified tuition and related expenses are tuition and fees required for enrollment or attendance of an eligible student at an eligible educational institution (*see* below). Qualified expenses do *not* include room and board, insurance, medical expenses, transportation, or other personal or family living expenses. The cost of books, supplies, equipment, and student activity fees may be included *only* if it must be paid to the educational institution as a condition of enrollment. Hobby- or sport-related courses and noncredit courses do not qualify for the Hope credit unless they are part of the student's degree program *(38.8)*. Such courses qualify for the lifetime learning credit if they are part of a degree program or are taken to acquire or improve job skills.

Prepaid expenses. If in 1999 you pay qualified tuition and related expenses for an academic period that begins in the first three months of 2000, you can include the prepayment in figuring your 1999 credit. For example, if you pay $1,000 in December 1999 for qualified tuition for the winter 2000 semester that begins in January 2000, you can include that amount in figuring a 1999 credit.

Eligible students and eligible educational institutions. You, your spouse, or an eligible dependent may qualify as an eligible student if enrolled at an eligible educational institution for at least one academic period (semester, trimester, quarter) during the year. An eligible dependent is a person for whom you claim a dependency exemption on your tax return; *see* Chapter 21.

An eligible educational institution generally includes any accredited public, nonprofit, or proprietary *post-secondary* institution eligible to participate in the student aid programs administered by the Department of Education.

If you claim a deduction for higher education expenses on your tax return, for instance, for job-related courses, you may not claim a credit for those same expenses. Similarly, if you pay higher education expenses with a tax-free scholarship, Pell grant, or employer-provided educational assistance, you may not claim a credit for those amounts. You may, however, claim a credit for expenses paid from your (or your dependent's) earnings, loans, gifts, inheritances, and personal savings.

If you pay qualified expenses for more than one eligible student in the same year, you may choose to take credits on a per-student, per-year basis. Thus, you can claim the Hope credit for one child and the lifetime learning credit for another child in the same tax year.

Recapture of credit. If, in a later tax year, you receive a refund of an amount used to figure a higher education credit, you may have to repay all or part of the credit.

Phase-out of credits. Both credits are reduced under a phase-out formula if your modified adjusted gross income (MAGI) comes within the rules of *38.10*.

38.8 Hope Credit

If you pay qualified tuition and related expenses for an eligible student who is enrolled in the first or second year of college or other post-secondary institution, you may figure a Hope credit on Form 8863 of up to $1,500 for the qualified tuition and related expenses paid for the student.

Apart from the general tests at *38.7*, an eligible student must also meet the following requirements: (1) be enrolled in one of the first two years of postsecondary education (generally, the freshman or sophomore years of college), (2) be enrolled in a program that leads to a degree, certificate, or other recognized educational credential, (3) be taking at least one-half of the normal full-time work load for his or her course of study for at least one academic period beginning during the calendar year, and (4) not have any felony conviction for possessing or distributing a controlled substance.

The amount of the Hope credit is 100% of the first $1,000 plus 50% of the next $1,000 paid for each eligible student's qualified tuition and related expenses. This means that you can claim the full $1,500 for each eligible student for whom you pay at least $2,000 for qualified expenses. Your maximum Hope credit in 1999 is $1,500 times the number of eligible students.

If a student is beyond the second year of post-secondary education (is a junior or senior, for example), the lifetime learning credit, but not the Hope credit, may be claimed.

EXAMPLE

Lucy and Ricky are married and file a joint tax return. For 1999, they claim their daughter as a dependent on their tax return and their modified adjusted gross income is $70,000. Their daughter is in her sophomore (second) year of studies at the local university and in 1999 they pay $4,300 of her tuition costs. They can claim a $1,500 Hope credit in 1999, the maximum amount allowed for 1999.

38.9 Lifetime Learning Credit

For academic expenses paid during 1999, you may claim on Form 8863 a lifetime learning credit of up to $1,000 for the total qualified tuition and related expenses paid for yourself, your spouse, or your dependents enrolled in eligible educational institutions *(see 38.7)* during the year.

In contrast to the Hope credit, the lifetime learning credit does not have a degree requirement or a work load requirement. The credit may be claimed for one or more courses at an eligible educational institution that are either part of a post-secondary degree program or part of a nondegree program taken to acquire or improve job skills. The lifetime learning credit is not limited to students in the first two years of postsecondary education, as is the Hope credit, and it covers expenses for graduate-level degree work. There is also no limit on the number of years for which the lifetime learning credit can be claimed for each eligible student.

The lifetime learning credit is 20% of the first $5,000 paid for qualified tuition and related expenses for *all* eligible students in the family. Thus, the maximum lifetime learning credit you may claim for 1999 is $1,000 (20% of $5,000), subject to the income-based phaseout; *see 38.10.*

The $1,000 limit applies regardless of the number of eligible students for whom you pay education expenses. This aspect of the lifetime learning credit differs from the Hope credit, which may be claimed for each eligible student, up to $1,500 each *(see 38.8).*

38.10 Income Phaseout of Education Credits

Both the Hope credit and the lifetime learning credit are phased out on Form 8863 if your modified adjusted gross income is between $40,000 and $50,000, or between $80,000 and $100,000 on a joint return. For most taxpayers, modified adjusted gross income is adjusted gross income (AGI) unless they have tax-free income earned abroad or from certain U.S. territories or possessions. If so, adjusted gross income is increased by such amounts.

EXAMPLES

1. Ron and Jackie are married and file a joint tax return. Their MAGI for 1999 is $85,000. They pay $6,000 of qualifying expenses for their son, Leo, and $7,500 for their daughter, Ally. Both students are claimed as dependents on their parents' return. A Hope credit of $3,000, $1,500 for each child, is allowed prior to taking the phaseout into account. On Form 8863, they figure a $2,250 Hope credit after application of the phase-out rules.

2. John, unmarried, has a MAGI of $42,000. He pays $2,500 in qualified tuition and fees. He figures a lifetime learning credit of $500 (20% of qualified tuition and fees), before taking the phaseout into account. On Form 8863, he figures a $400 lifetime learning credit after application of the phase-out rules.

 Caution

Phaseout

You cannot claim any higher education credits if your modified adjusted gross income exceeds $50,000 ($100,000 on a joint return).

Education IRAs

38.11 Contributing to an Education IRA

An education IRA is a trust or custodial account set up specifically for the purpose of paying the qualified higher education expenses of the designated beneficiary of the account. A designated beneficiary must be a child under age 18.

You may contribute up to $500 each year to an education IRA for a child under age 18. Contributions to an education IRA are not deductible. Any individual (including the child) can contribute to a child's education IRA if the individual's MAGI is not more than $110,000 ($160,000 on a joint return). The $500 maximum contribution for each child is gradually reduced if the contributor's MAGI is between $95,000 and $110,000 (between $150,000 and $160,000 in the case of a joint return). Total contributions per child, per year, may not be more than $500. Amounts deposited in the accounts accumulate tax free until distribution. If the beneficiary dies, any balance in the account must be distributed to the beneficiary's estate, surviving spouse, or family member within 30 days after the date of death.

A 6% excise tax applies to education IRA contributions that exceed $500 for the tax year for any beneficiary. The penalty is imposed on the beneficiary (Form 5329). The penalty also applies to all contributions to the account if any amount is also contributed to a qualified state tuition program on behalf of the same child in the same tax year. The excise tax does not apply if the excess contributions (and any earnings) are withdrawn before the tax return for the year is due, including extensions.

Law Alert

Education IRA Proposals

Congress has considered various proposals expanding the education IRA. These include raising the annual contribution limit to $2,000, expanding the definition of qualified expenses to include elementary and secondary education expenses at both public and private schools, and allowing tax-free education IRA distributions during years when a tuition tax credit is claimed or contributions are made to a qualified state tuition program. However, these proposals had not been enacted at the time this book went to press. *See* the Supplement for an update.

Planning Reminder

Waiver of Tax-Free Treatment

The tax-free treatment of an education IRA distribution may be waived in order to allow a claim for a Hope credit or lifetime learning credit for qualified higher education expenses paid in that tax year. If tax-free treatment for an education IRA distribution is claimed, neither education credit is allowed for that year.

Qualified higher education expenses. Qualified higher education expenses are tuition, fees, books, supplies, and equipment. Expenses of room and board qualify if the designated beneficiary is at least a half-time student at an eligible educational institution. Room and board is limited to the school's posted room and board charge for students living on campus, or $2,500 each year for students living off campus and not at home.

Eligible educational institution. This is any college, university, vocational school, or other postsecondary educational institution eligible to participate in the student aid programs administered by the Department of Education. It includes virtually any accredited public, nonprofit, or proprietary (privately owned profit-making) postsecondary institution.

No contributions can be made to an education IRA on behalf of a child if any amount is contributed during the tax year to a qualified state tuition program on behalf of the same child.

Tax-free rollovers between educational IRAs are allowed within a 60-day period.

38.12 Distributions From Education IRAs

A designated beneficiary of an education IRA is not taxed on withdrawals to pay qualified higher education expenses. Withdrawals are reported on Form 8606. If the total withdrawals for a tax year exceed the qualified higher education expenses, a portion of the amount withdrawn is taxable to the beneficiary. The taxable portion is the amount that represents earnings that have accumulated tax free in the account. On Form 8606, the beneficiary may waive tax-free treatment for distributions used to pay qualifying education expenses. If a waiver is not made and tax-free treatment for any part of the distribution is claimed, *no* Hope credit or lifetime learning credit may be claimed for that year.

Additional tax on taxable distributions. Generally, a taxable distribution is subject to a 10% additional tax. The 10% additional tax does not apply to distributions that are made: (1) to a beneficiary (or to the estate of the designated beneficiary) on or after the death of the designated beneficiary, (2) because the designated beneficiary is disabled, or (3) because the designated beneficiary received a tax-free scholarship or educational assistance allowance that equals or exceeds the distribution.

The 10% additional tax also does not apply to a distribution of an excess contribution (and allocable earnings) made before the tax return due date, including extensions.

A Guide To Estate Taxes and Planning

The federal estate tax is a tax on the transfer of property at death. The tax applies to taxable estates over $650,000 for estates of persons dying in 1999 ($675,000 in 2000), after taking into account allowable deductions, such as deductions for charitable bequests and property passing to a surviving spouse.

By following the guidelines in this chapter, you can estimate your potential estate. If your estate may be subject to tax, you may want to start thinking about property transfers that may reduce or avoid the estate tax. A brief review of estate tax plans is at *39.6*, and gift tax plans are discussed in Chapter 33.

39.1 What Is the Estate Tax?

The estate you built up may not be entirely yours to give away. The federal government and, in most cases, at least one state government stand ready to claim their shares.

Do you know what will remain for your family, your favorite charities, and your other beneficiaries? If you do not, you cannot intelligently estimate what you can give to each. To help you make such an estimate, we offer this general guide to federal estate taxation. It will alert you to the extent of estate tax costs, and help you plan for estate tax savings that you may discuss with an experienced estate tax planning professional.

The federal estate tax is a tax on the act of transferring property at death. It is not a tax on the right of the beneficiary to receive the property; the estate and the estate alone pays the tax, although the property passing to individual beneficiaries may be diminished by the tax.

Understand what the word *estate* means in estate tax law so that you do not underestimate the value of your taxable estate. The estate includes not only your real estate (foreign and domestic), bank deposits, securities, and personal property such as art objects, but can also include insurance, your interest in trusts or jointly held property, and certain interests you have in other estates.

39.2 Take Inventory

The first step in estate tax planning follows a simple business practice of taking inventory of everything you own. Listing your belongings takes thought, time, and a surprising amount of work. On your list you should include records of purchases, fire and theft insurance inventories, bankbooks, brokers' statements, etc. You should also include your cash, real estate (here and abroad), securities, mortgages, rights in property, trust accounts, personal effects, collections, and art works. Life insurance is includible if: (1) payable to your estate; (2) payable to others and you have kept "incidents of ownership" such as the right to change beneficiaries, surrender or assign the policy, or pledge it for a loan; or (3) you assign the policy and die within three years *(33.6)*.

If you own property jointly with your spouse, your estate includes only one-half its value.

If you had appraisals made of specially treasured items or collections, or property of substantial value, file such appraisals with your estate papers and then enter the value on your inventory.

Retirement benefits. The taxable estate generally includes benefits payable at your death from any of the following retirement plans: pension plan, profit-sharing plan, Keogh plan, individual retirement account, or annuity. However, the value of an annuity from an IRA or employer plan that is payable to a beneficiary other than your estate may qualify for a full or partial exclusion if IRA distributions began before 1985 or you separated from service before 1985; no exclusion is allowed to the extent of your own nondeductible contributions to the plan.

A full exclusion is allowed for IRA funds if you began taking distributions from the account before 1983 under a schedule that irrevocably set the form of benefits. If IRA distributions began in 1983 or 1984 and you irrevocably elected the form of benefits before July 18, 1984, a $100,000 exclusion is allowed.

If you began receiving distributions from an employer plan before 1983 under a schedule that irrevocably set the form of benefits, a full estate tax exclusion is allowed. If you separated from service in 1983 or 1984, a $100,000 exclusion is allowed if the form of benefits is not changed before death; this is true even if distributions did not begin until after 1984.

39.3 Finding the Value of Your Estate

When you have completed your inventory, assign to each asset what you consider to be its fair market value. This may be difficult to do for some assets. Resist the tendency to overvalue articles that arouse feelings of pride or sentiment and undervalue some articles of great intrinsic worth. For purposes of your initial estimate, it is better to err on the side of overvaluation. You can list ordinary personal effects at nominal value.

If you have a family business, your idea of its value and that of the IRS may vary greatly. Estate plans have been upset by the higher value placed on such a business by the IRS. You can protect your estate by anticipating and solving this problem with your business associates and counselors.

If your business is owned by a closely held corporation, and there is no ready or open market in which the stock can be valued, get some factual basis for a figure that will be reported on the estate tax return. One of the ways to do this is by arranging a buy-sell agreement with a potential purchaser. This agreement must fix the value of the stock. Generally, an agreement that binds both the estate and the purchaser and restricts lifetime sales of the stock will effectively fix the value of the stock for estate tax purposes. Another way would be to make a gift of some shares to a family member and have value established in gift tax proceedings.

 Caution

Trusts Includible in Estate

There are some assets that you might not ordinarily consider as part of your estate. Nevertheless, include in your inventory any trust arrangements created by you in which you have: (1) a life estate (the income or other use of property for life); (2) income that is to be used to pay your legal obligations (support of a child, for example); (3) the right to change the beneficiary or his or her interest (a power of appointment); (4) the right to revoke a trust transfer or gift; and (5) a reversionary interest (the possibility that the property can come back to you).

If a substantial part of your estate is real estate used in farming or a closely held business, your executor may be able to elect, with the consent of heirs having an interest in the property, to value the property on the basis of its farming or business use, rather than its highest and best use. The special use valuation, however, may not reduce the gross estate by more than $750,000, subject to adjustment for inflation. This savings may be recaptured from your heir if he or she stops using the property in farming or business within 10 years of your death.

 Law Alert

39.4 How the Estate Tax Is Applied

A single unified rate schedule applies to a decedent's estate and all post-1976 lifetime gifts *over* the annual gift tax exclusion. Under the unified gift and estate tax rate, the overall tax on your property holdings is theoretically the same whether or not you make lifetime gifts. In actual cases, however, lifetime gifts may reduce the potential overall tax because of the annual gift tax exclusion *(33.1)*.

You may use IRS Form 706 to estimate what the estate tax would be on your estate. If you make no taxable gifts during your life, estimating estate tax on Form 706 is fairly easy. You start with the total market value of the property in the estate. This is called the *gross estate*. From the gross estate you subtract certain deductions. For example, charitable bequests are deductible. An unlimited marital deduction is allowed for bequests to a surviving spouse who is a U.S. citizen; *see 39.5* for noncitizen surviving spouses. The net amount after deductions is your taxable estate. A unified credit is subtracted from the tax calculated on the taxable estate; *see 39.5*. Other credits, including the state death tax credit, further reduce the federal estate tax on your estate. *See 39.5* for a sample computation of estate tax.

If you make taxable gifts after 1976, estimating your estate tax is more complicated. The estate tax and gift tax are cumulative. That is, the tax rate is applied to the sum of (1) your taxable estate at death, and (2) taxable lifetime gifts made after 1976 (other than gifts included in your estate). The tax you figure on both (1) and (2) is reduced by gift taxes payable on gifts made after 1976. The unified or applicable credit and other credits are then subtracted from the remaining amount.

Generation-skipping transfers. Transfers that "skip" a generation, such as a gift to a grandchild, are subject to a special tax (computed on Schedule R of Form 706) if they exceed a lifetime exemption of $1 million per transferor, subject to inflation adjustments. Because of other exceptions and the complexity of these rules, you should consult an experienced tax practitioner if planning "skip" transfers.

Family-Owned Business

A special estate tax deduction may be allowed for a family business. Up to $675,000 of the adjusted value of the business may be deductible and the deduction, together with the annual exclusion amount, may shield up to $1.3 million of family business assets from estate tax.

The adjusted value of the family-owned business interests generally must exceed 50% of the decedent's adjusted gross estate. A business interest qualifies as family owned if it is at least 50% owned by the decedent's family, or if it is at least 70% owned by two families or 90% by three families and the decedent's family owns at least 30%. For five of the eight years preceding the date of death, the business interests had to be owned by the decedent or family members, and they must have materially participated in the business operations. The business interest must pass to family members or 10-year employees. Such qualified heirs are subject to a recapture tax if they do not meet a material participation test within 10 years of the date of death or if a disposition of the business interest is made to nonqualifying persons.

For details on this complicated deduction, *see* the instructions for Schedule T of Form 706.

39.5 Unified Tax Rates and Credit

Estates of individuals dying after 1997 are entitled to a unified credit that generally shields from estate tax amounts up to the exclusion amount shown below. For estates that qualify for the special family-owned business deduction and that claim less than the maximum $675,000 deduction *(see* the Law Alert on this page), the exclusion amount may vary from the amount shown in the following table.

Individual dying in—	Exclusion amount—	Unified credit—
1998	$625,000	$202,050
1999	650,000	211,300
2000–2001	675,000	220,550
2002–2003	700,000	229,800
2004	850,000	287,300
2005	950,000	326,300
2006 and later years	1,000,000	345,800

Phaseout of graduated rates. The benefit of graduated tax rates *(see* the rate schedule on page 577) is phased out for cumulative transfers (taxable gifts plus estates) above $10 million. For estates of individuals dying before 1999, the tentative estate tax liability figured on Form 706 is increased for estates between $10 million and $17,184,000. The increase is 5% of the excess of the estate over $10 million. Estates over $17,184,000 are taxed at a flat 55%. Taxable gifts after 1976 are added to the estate for purposes of computing the 5% adjustment. The 5% surtax would be repealed for estates of individuals dying after 2000 by the proposed legislation discussed in the Law Alert on page 574.

You Are Now Ready To Estimate the Federal Estate Tax

Gross estate (your estimated inventory) $_____

Less:

1. Administration expenses
   (executor's commissions,
   attorneys' fees, etc.; estimate
   about 5% to 10% of your estate) $_____

2. Debts, mortgages, liens   _____

3. Funeral expenses   _____

4. Marital deduction   _____

5. Charitable deductions   _____

Total of Lines 1–5   _____

Your taxable estate $_____

    Plus: Post-1976 taxable gifts (over the annual exclusion)   _____

Total taxable amount $_____

Tentative tax on total   _____

    Less:

1. Gift tax payable on
   post-1976 gifts $_____

2. Credit   _____

3. State death taxes credit and other credits   _____

Total of line 1–3   _____

Estate tax due $_____

Planning Reminder

Credits Reducing Estate Tax

If there is an estate tax due after applying the unified credit, the tax may be reduced by the credit for state death taxes. There are also credits for foreign death taxes, gift taxes paid on gifts before 1977, and federal estate taxes paid on certain prior transfers.

EXAMPLE

Assume an unmarried person who made no taxable gifts after 1976 leaves a gross estate of $700,000 in 1999. Debts, administration, and funeral expenses total $60,000. The decedent bequeaths $160,000 to charity.

Gross estate		$700,000
Less: Debts, administration, and funeral expenses		60,000
		$640,000
Less: Charitable deduction		160,000
Taxable estate		$480,000
Tentative tax	$149,000	
Less: Unified credit	211,300	
Estate tax due		None

Nonresident alien decedents and surviving spouses. For nonresident aliens, estate tax applies only to the part of the gross estate located in the United States. The estate and gift tax rates applied to U.S. citizens and residents also apply to nonresident aliens. However, the unified credit is limited to $13,000, exempting the first $60,000 of the estate from estate tax. Where required by a tax treaty, a proportionate part of the regular unified credit or applicable credit amount is allowed, based on the percentage of the total gross estate that is situated in the U.S. Estates of certain residents of U.S. possessions are allowed a credit equal to the greater of $13,000, and $46,800 multiplied by the proportion of the gross estate situated in the U.S. to the total gross estate.

Unified Gift and Estate Tax Rates*

If taxable amount is:

Over—	But not over—	The tax is—	Plus%—	Of the amount over—
$0	$10,000	$0	18	$0
10,000	20,000	1,800	20	10,000
20,000	40,000	3,800	22	20,000
40,000	60,000	8,200	24	40,000
60,000	80,000	13,000	26	60,000
80,000	100,000	18,200	28	80,000
100,000	150,000	23,800	30	100,000
150,000	250,000	38,800	32	150,000
250,000	500,000	70,800	34	250,000
500,000	750,000	155,800	37	500,000
750,000	1,000,000	248,300/	39	750,000
1,000,000	1,250,000	345,800	41	1,000,000
1,250,000	1,500,000	448,300	43	1,250,000
1,500,000	2,000,000	555,800	45	1,500,000
2,000,000	2,500,000	780,800	49	2,000,000
2,500,000	3,000,000	1,025,800	53	2,500,000
3,000,000		1,290,800	55	3,000,000

* See *the phaseout of graduated rates on page 575 and the Law Alert on page 574.*

39.6 Reducing or Eliminating a Potential Estate Tax

Here are general approaches to eliminating or reducing a potential estate tax: You can make direct lifetime gifts. Any appreciation on the property transferred will be removed from your estate. Furthermore, each gift, to the extent of the $10,000 per donee annual exclusion, reduces your gross estate; *see 33.1* and *33.2*. Life insurance can be assigned to avoid estate tax, provided the assignment takes place more than three years before death; *see 33.6.* You can provide in your will for bequests that will qualify for the marital and charitable deductions.

Note: These approaches will have to be reevaluated if the proposed reduction and gradual repeal of gift and estate taxes (*see* the Law Alert on page 574) is enacted into law.

The marital deduction. A married person may greatly reduce or eliminate estate tax by using the marital deduction. Property passing to a spouse is generally free from estate or gift tax because of an unlimited marital deduction.

Weigh carefully the tax consequences of leaving your spouse all of your property. For maximum tax savings, you may want to give your spouse only enough property to reduce your taxable estate to the exclusion floor *(see 39.5)*. The unified credit amount will then eliminate tax on that amount at the time of your death. By leaving your spouse less than the maximum deductible amount, you may be able to reduce the estate tax at the time of his or her death.

Life insurance proceeds may qualify as marital deduction property. Name your spouse the unconditional beneficiary of the proceeds with unrestricted control over any unpaid proceeds. If your spouse is not given this control or general power of appointment, and there is no requirement that proceeds remaining on your spouse's death be payable to his or her estate, the insurance proceeds will not qualify for the marital deduction.

What should be done if you believe your spouse cannot manage property? You will not want to give complete and personal control. The law permits you to put the property in certain trust arrangements that are considered equivalent to complete ownership. Your attorney can explain how you can protect your spouse's interest and qualify the trust property for the marital deduction.

Marital deduction restrictions for noncitizen spouses. A marital deduction may not be claimed for property passing outright to a surviving spouse who is not a U.S. citizen. However, the marital deduction is allowed if the surviving spouse's interest is in a qualifying domestic trust (QDOT). At least one trustee must be an individual U.S. citizen or domestic corporation with

 Planning Reminder

Marital Deduction
To qualify for the marital deduction, the property must generally be given to the spouse outright or by other arrangements that are the legal equivalent of outright ownership. There is an exception for income interests in charitable remainder annuity or unitrusts and certain other qualified terminable interest property (QTIP) for which the executor makes an election.

Caution

Get Expert Advice

Estate tax planning is not a do-it-yourself activity. You should contact experienced counsel for help in developing a plan for your future estate that will accomplish your tax and personal objectives.

power to withhold estate tax due from distributions of trust corpus. The trust must maintain sufficient assets as required by IRS regulations. For the marital deduction to apply, the executor must make an irrevocable election on the decedent's estate tax return. On Form 706-QDT, estate tax will apply to certain distributions of trust corpus made prior to the surviving spouse's death, and to the value of the QDOT property remaining at the surviving spouse's death. You should consult an experienced tax practitioner to set up a QDOT trust and plan for distribution provisions.

The estate of a nonresident alien is subject to estate tax only to the extent that the estate is located in the United States. A marital deduction may be claimed by the estate of a nonresident alien for property passing to a surviving spouse who is a U.S. citizen. If the surviving spouse is not a U.S. citizen, then the transferred interest must be in the form of a QDOT.

Periodically review your estate plan. You are now aware of the costs of transferring an estate and of the amount of tax that may be levied. But no estate plan is ever really final. Economic conditions and inflation constantly change values. For this reason, your plan must be reviewed periodically as changes occur in your family and business, as when a birth or death occurs; when you receive a substantial increase or decrease in income; when you enter a new business venture or resign from an old one; or when you sell, retire from, or bring new persons into business. A member of your family may no longer need any part of your estate, while others may need more. Material changes may occur in the health or life expectancy of one of your beneficiaries. Estate or gift tax laws may be revised; *see* the Law Alert on page 574.

39.7 Estate Tax Freeze Advisory

The object of an estate tax freeze is to reduce or eliminate estate tax on the inheritance of property by fixing the value through certain property arrangements. A complicated gift and estate tax law (IRC §§2701–2704) attempts to discourage such plans by applying special valuation rules. The rules cover not only common and preferred stock holdings within the family but also partnership interests, the deferral of dividend payments on preferred stock, life and remainder interests, and buy-sell agreements in family businesses.

The estate freeze rules impose gift tax and estate tax values for property transfers subject to the law. Because of the complexity of these rules and their effect on gift and estate values, we suggest that you seek professional advice in the following situations:

- As an owner of a family business, you plan to give common stock to family members while retaining preferred stock or recapitalize with common and preferred stock.
- You plan to give up a voting interest or liquidating rights attached to preferred stock in a family business.
- You defer payment of dividends in preferred stock in a family business.
- You plan to retain an interest for life in a transfer or purchase of property.
- You plan to give stock to a family member in a company in which you have a buy-sell agreement.

Business Tax Planning

In this part, you will learn how to report your income from a business or profession, and how to reduce your tax liability by claiming expense deductions. Pay special attention to—

- Reporting rules for income and expenses on Schedule C (Chapter 40).
- Restrictions on deducting home office expenses. Your deduction may be limited by a restrictive income test (Chapter 40).
- Keogh, SEP, and SIMPLE retirement plan rules if you are self-employed. These plans offer tax deductions for contributions and tax-free accumulation of income within the plan. In some cases, special averaging for lump-sum distributions from a Keogh plan is allowed (Chapter 41).
- First-year expensing and depreciation write-offs for business assets (Chapter 42).
- The IRS mileage allowance as an alternative to claiming operating expenses and depreciation for your business automobile (Chapter 43).
- Computing and paying self-employment tax on self-employment earnings from a business or profession (Chapter 45).

Income or Loss From Your Business or Profession

As a self-employed person, you report income and expenses from your business or profession separately from your other income, such as income from wages. On Schedule C, you report your business income and itemize your expenses. Any net profit is subject to self-employment tax, as well as regular tax. A net profit can also be the basis of deductible contributions to a SEP or Keogh retirement plan, as discussed in Chapter 41.

If you work out of your home, you may deduct home office expenses.

If you claim a loss on Schedule C, be prepared to show that you regularly and substantially participate in the business. Otherwise, your loss may be considered a passive loss deductible only from passive income, as discussed in Chapter 10.

If you have a 1999 business loss that exceeds your other income, you may carry back the loss and claim a refund; the carryback period is generally two years; *see 40.18.*

If you have no employees and business expenses of $2,500 or less, you may be able to file a simplified schedule called Schedule C-EZ; *see 40.6.*

Organizing Your Business

40.1 Forms of Doing Business

Before doing business, it is important to decide the legal form of your business. This decision will determine the way you report business income and loss, the taxes you pay, the ability of the business to accumulate capital, and the extent of your personal liability. It is beyond the scope of this book to discuss the pros and cons of each form. The decision should be made with the services of a professional experienced in both the legal and tax consequences of doing business in a particular form as it applies to your current and future business prospects.

If you are going into business alone, your choices are: operating as a sole proprietor, incorporating, and forming a limited liability company (LLC). If you are going to operate with associates, you may choose to operate as a partnership, a corporation, or an LLC. If you are concerned with limiting your personal liability, your choice is between a corporation or an LLC. An LLC gives you the advantage of limited liability without having to incorporate.

As a sole proprietor, you report business profit or loss on your personal tax return, as explained in this chapter. If you are a partner, you report your share of partnership profit and loss as explained in Chapter 11. If you incorporate, the corporation pays tax on business income. You are taxable on salaries and dividends paid to you by the corporation. You may avoid this double corporate tax by making an S corporation election, which allows you to report corporate income and loss; *see 11.14.*

If you operate through an LLC as an individual, you report income and loss as a sole proprietor. If you operate an LLC with associates, the LLC reports as a partnership and you report your share of income and loss. However, under the current check-the-box rules, the LLC may elect to report as an association taxable as a corporation on Form 8832.

40.2 Reporting Self-Employed Income

You file a separate Schedule C along with Form 1040 if you are a sole proprietor of a business or a professional in your own practice. If you are an employee with a sideline business, report the self-employment income from that business on Schedule C. Do not file Schedule C if your business is operated through a partnership or corporation. A guide to Schedule C is in *40.6.*

On Schedule C, you deduct your allowable business expenses from your business income. Net business profit (or loss) figured on Schedule C is entered on Line 12, Page 1 of Form 1040. Thus, business profit (or loss) is added to (or subtracted from) nonbusiness income on Form 1040 to compute adjusted gross income. This procedure gives you the chance to deduct your business expenses, whether you claim itemized deductions or nonbusiness deductions on Schedule A, such as charitable contributions, taxes, and medical expenses, or you claim the standard deduction where it exceeds your allowable itemized deductions; *see 13.2.*

You may be able to file a simplified schedule, Schedule C-EZ, if your income and expenses are below certain limits; *see 40.6.*

Passive loss restrictions. Pay special attention to the passive loss restrictions discussed in Chapter 10. Generally, if you do not regularly and substantially participate in your business, losses are considered passive and are deductible only against other passive income.

Filing Tip

Did You Suffer a Loss?

Business persons and professionals with a 1999 net operating loss may get a refund of taxes paid in two prior tax years. If the loss is not fully eliminated by the income of the two prior years, the balance of the loss may be used to reduce your business income for up to 20 of the following years. *See 40.18 for details.*

Accounting for Business Income

40.3 Accounting Methods for Reporting Business Income

Business income is reported on either the accrual or cash basis. If you have more than one business, you may have a different accounting method for each business.

Inventories. If you have inventories, you *must* use the accrual basis.

Cash basis. You report income items in the taxable year in which they are received; you deduct all expenses in the taxable year in which they are paid. Under the cash basis, income is also reported if it is "constructively" received. You have "constructively" received income when an amount is credited to your account, subject to your control, or set apart for you and may be drawn by you at any time. For example, in 1999 you receive a check in payment of services, but you do not cash it until 2000. You have constructively received the income in 1999, and it is taxable in 1999.

Key To Reporting Business and Professional Income and Loss

Item—	Comments—
Tax return to file	If you are self-employed, prepare Schedule C to report business or professional income. If your business expenses are $2,500 or less, and you have no employees, you may be able to file a simplified Schedule C-EZ; *see 40.6*. If you are a farmer, use Schedule F. You attach Schedule C and/or F to Form 1040. If you operate as a partnership, use Form 1065; if you operate as a corporation, use Form 1120S or Form 1120.
Method of reporting income	The cash or accrual accounting rules determine when you report income and expenses. You must use the accrual basis if you sell a product that must be inventoried. The cash-basis and accrual-basis methods are discussed at *40.3*.
Tax reporting year	There are two general tax reporting years: calendar years that end on December 31 and fiscal years that end on the last day of any month other than December. Your taxable year must be the same for both your business and nonbusiness income. Most business income must be reported on a calendar-year basis. If, as a self-employed person, you report your business income on a fiscal-year basis, you must also report your nonbusiness income on a fiscal-year basis. Use of a fiscal year is restricted for partnerships and S corporations.
Office in home	To claim home office expenses as a self-employed person, you must use the home area exclusively and on a regular basis either as a place of business to meet or deal with patients, clients, or customers in the normal course of your business or as your principal place of business. Form 8829 must be used to compute the deduction; *see 40.12*.
Social Security coverage	If you have self-employed income, you may have to pay self-employment tax, which goes to financing Social Security benefits; *see* Chapter 45.
Passive participation in a business	If you do not regularly, continuously, and substantially participate in the business, your business income or loss is subject to passive activity restrictions. A loss is deductible only against other passive activity income. The passive activity restrictions are discussed in detail in Chapter 10.
Self-employed Keogh plan	You may set up a retirement plan based on business or professional income. Individuals who are self-employed may contribute to a self-employed retirement plan, according to the rules of Chapter 41.
Depreciation	Business assets other than real estate placed in service in 1999 are depreciable over three, five, seven, 10, 15, or 20 years. Automobiles and light trucks, computers, and office equipment are in the five-year class. Property in the three-, five-, seven-, and 10-year classes is depreciable using the double declining balance method, switching to the straight-line method so as to maximize the deduction; *see* Chapter 42 for details. Automobiles are subject to special depreciation limits; *see* Chapter 43.

Instead of depreciating equipment, you may claim the first-year expensing deduction. You may generally deduct up to $19,000 in 1999; *see 42.3*. |
| **Health insurance** | In 1999, you may deduct 60% of premium costs of health insurance coverage for yourself, spouse, and dependents. You may also take advantage of a medical savings account plan as explained in *17.17*. |
| **Net operating losses** | A loss incurred in your profession or business is deducted from other income reported on Form 1040. If the 1999 loss (plus any casualty loss) exceeds income, the excess may be first carried back to 1997 and 1998, and then forward 20 years to 2000 through 2019 until it is used up. A loss carried back to a prior year reduces income of that year and entitles you to a refund. A loss applied to a later year reduces income for that year. For certain losses, the carryback is five years or three years rather than two; *see 40.18*.

You may elect to carry forward your 1999 loss for 20 years, foregoing the carryback; *see 40.22*. |
| **Sideline business** | You report business income of a sideline business following the rules that apply to full-time business. For example, if you are self-employed, you report business income on Schedule C or C-EZ. You may also have to pay self-employment tax on this income; *see* Chapter 45. You may also set up a self-employment retirement plan based on such income.

If you incur losses over several years, the hobby loss rules discussed in *40.10* may limit your loss deduction. |

On the cash basis, you deduct expenses in the year of payment. Expenses paid by credit card are deducted in the year they are charged. Expenses paid through a "pay by phone" account with a bank are deducted in the year the bank sends the check. This date is reported by the bank on its monthly statement.

Advance payments. On the cash basis, you may not deduct advance rent payments covering charges of a later tax year. The IRS applies a similar rule to advance payments of insurance premiums; however, an appeals court has allowed an immediate deduction.

Cash method of accounting limited. The following may not use the cash method: a regular C corporation, a partnership with a C corporation as a partner, a tax shelter, or a tax-exempt trust with unrelated business income. Exceptions: The cash method may be used by personal service corporations in the fields of medicine, law, engineering, accounting, architecture, performing arts, actuarial science, or consulting. To qualify, substantially all of the stock must be owned directly or indirectly (through partnerships, S corporations, or personal service corporations) by employees. The cash method may also be used by other businesses with average annual gross receipts of $5 million or less, and farming and timber businesses. Tax shelters may not use the cash method; the $5 million gross receipts exception is not available.

Accrual basis. On the accrual basis, report income that has been earned, whether or not received, unless your right to collect the income is unsure because a substantial contingency may prevent payment; *see* the Example below.

EXAMPLE

You report business income as a calendar-year accrual taxpayer. You sell several products on December 27, 1999, and bill the customer in January 2000. You report the sales income on your 1999 Schedule C, even though payment is not made until 2000. Under the accrual method, you are considered to earn the income when the products are sold and delivered to the customer.

Where you are prepaid for future services that must be completed by the end of the next tax year, you report the income in the year that services are performed; *see* the following Example.

EXAMPLE

In 1999, you receive full payment under a one-year contract requiring you to provide 48 music lessons. In 1999, you give eight lessons, and report one-sixth ($^8/_{48}$) of the payment as income. In 2000, the remaining five-sixths of the payment must be reported, even if you do not actually give the required number of lessons.

Expenses under the accrual method are deductible in the year your liability for payment is fixed, even though payment is made in a later year. To prevent manipulation of expense deductions, there are tax law tests for fixing the timing of accrual method expense deductions. The tests generally require that *economic performance* must occur before a deduction may be claimed, but there are exceptions, such as for "recurring expenses." These rules are discussed in IRS Publication 538, which is available without charge from the IRS. However, the basic application of the accrual expense rule can be understood from the following Examples.

EXAMPLES

1. You report business income as a calendar-year accrual taxpayer. In December 1999, you order and receive supplies with an invoice for payment. You pay the bill in 2000. You deduct the expenses on your 1999 Schedule C. Liability was fixed in 1999, and the supplies were delivered in 1999. What if delivery was not until 2000? The expense is deductible in 1999 if the timing of the order and the delivery follows your normal business practice.

2. In 1999, you pay rent for December 1999 and January 2000. You deduct the rent for December on your 1999 return. You defer the deduction of the January rent to your 2000 return.

Planning Reminder

Advantage of Cash-Basis Accounting

The cash basis has this advantage over other accounting methods: You may defer reporting income by postponing the receipt of income. But make certain that you avoid the constructive receipt rule. For example, if 1999 is a high income year or income tax rates will be lower in 2000, you might delay mailing some of your customers' bills so they do not receive them until 2000. You may also postpone the payment of presently due expenses to a year in which the deduction gives you a greater tax savings.

Planning Reminder

Advantage of Accrual-Basis Accounting

The accrual basis has this advantage over the cash basis: It generally gives a more even and balanced financial report.

Expenses owed to a related cash-basis taxpayer. A business expense owed to your spouse, brother, sister, parent, child, grandparent, or grandchild who reports on the cash basis may not be deducted by you until you make the payment and the relative includes it as income. The same rule applies to amounts owed to a controlled corporation (more than 50% ownership) and other related entities.

Long-term contracts. Section 460 of the Internal Revenue Code has a special percentage of completion method of accounting for long-term construction contractors.

Capitalize costs of business property you produce or buy for resale. A complicated statute (Code Section 263A) requires manufacturers and builders to capitalize certain indirect costs (such as administrative costs, interest expenses, storage fees, and insurance), as well as direct production expenses, by including them in inventory costs.

Retailers and wholesalers who acquire real estate for resale also are subject to the uniform capitalization requirements. Purchasers of personal property (not real estate) for resale are exempt from the capitalization rules, unless average annual gross receipts from all businesses for the three prior tax years exceeded $10 million.

Different capitalization methods apply to resellers and manufacturers. Special exceptions apply for farm products. A special production period rule applies to capitalization of interest expenses. Inventory adjustments may be spread over four years. Authors, artists, and photographers are generally exempt from the capitalization requirements; *see 40.9*. For further details, *see* IRS Publication 538, Form 3115, and the regulations to Code Section 263A.

Deferral of service income. If, on the basis of your experience, a percentage of billings due for your services will not be collected in that year, you do not have to report that "uncollectible" amount until the year you actually receive it.

However, if interest or a penalty is charged for a failure to make a timely payment, income is reported when the amount is billed. Furthermore, if discounts for early payments are offered, the full amount of the bill must be accrued; the discount for early payment is treated as an adjustment to income in the year payment is made.

The amount of income to be deferred is based on a percentage that considers billing and uncollectibles over the current year and the past five most recent years. The percentage is found by dividing the uncollectible amounts by the total billings during the six-year period. That percentage applied to the total billings during the tax year may be deferred. For example, if $200,000 was billed during the six-year period and $20,000 was uncollectible, the percentage is 10% and 10% of the current billings may be deferred. If you do not have a five-year experience, you use the period during which you were in business.

40.4 Tax Reporting Year for Self-Employed

Your taxable year must be the same for both your business and nonbusiness income. If you report your business income on a fiscal-year basis, you must also report your nonbusiness income on a fiscal-year basis.

Generally, you report the tax consequences of transactions that have occurred during a 12-month period. If the period ends on December 31, it is called a *calendar year*. If it ends on the last day of any month other than December, it is called a *fiscal year*. A reporting period, technically called a *taxable year*, can never be longer than 12 months unless you report on a 52-to-53-week fiscal-year basis, details of which can be found in IRS Publication 538. A reporting period may be less than 12 months whenever you start or end your business in the middle of your regular taxable year, or change your taxable year.

To change from a calendar year to fiscal-year reporting for self-employment income, you must ask the IRS for permission by filing Form 1128. Support your request with a business reason such as that the use of the fiscal year coincides with your business cycle. To use a fiscal-year basis, you must keep your books and records following that fiscal-year period.

Fiscal year restrictions. Restrictions on fiscal years for partnerships, personal service corporations, and S corporations are discussed in Chapter 11 and IRS Publication 538.

40.5 Reporting Business Cash Receipts to the IRS

Cash receipts of more than $10,000 in one business transaction or two or more related transactions must be reported on Form 8300. There are penalties for failure to file.

Filing Tip

Changing Your Accounting Method

Generally, you must obtain the consent of the Internal Revenue Service prior to any change in accounting method. Apply for consent by filing Form 3115 as early as possible during the tax year for which you wish to make the change.

File Form 8300 with the IRS within 15 days of each cash transaction of over $10,000. Only cash payments are reported; do not report funds received by bank check or wire transfer where cash was not physically transferred. Foreign currency is considered cash. If multiple payments from a single payer (or a payer's agent) are received within a 24-hour period, the payments are aggregated, and the total must be reported if over $10,000.

The reporting requirement applies to individuals, corporations, partnerships, trusts, and estates, except for certain financial institutions that are already required to report cash transactions to the Treasury. Cash received in transactions occurring entirely outside the U.S. does not have to be reported.

The filing requirement applies to cash received for providing goods or services. Thus, an attorney, doctor, or other professional must report cash payments of over $10,000 from a client. Furthermore, cash received for setting up a trust of more than $10,000 for a client must be reported. The IRS has a program to assess penalties against attorneys who have disregarded the cash reporting rules. Courts have held that an attorney may not refuse to report large cash fees by invoking the attorney-client privilege. However, one appeals court held that disclosure of the name of a client who paid cash exceeding $10,000 was not required where disclosure would implicate the client or would reveal confidential communications made by the client to the attorney. The trial court in a closed hearing heard the attorney's claim and ruled against him, but the appeals court ruled in his favor; the circumstances were not disclosed because of their confidential nature.

On an installment sale of business property, you report each payment exceeding $10,000 within 15 days of receipt. If the initial installment is $10,000 or less, you aggregate it plus all payments received within one year of the initial payment. If the total exceeds $10,000, report the total within 15 days after the receipt of the payment that raised the total to over $10,000. In addition, if—after receiving single or aggregated reportable payments—subsequent payments within one year exceed $10,000 individually or in the aggregate, you must report the payments within 15 days.

EXAMPLE

On February 8, 2000, you receive an initial cash payment of $11,000. For the same transaction, you also receive cash of $4,000 on March 15, 2000; $6,000 on April 19, 2000; and $12,000 on June 13, 2000. You report the February payment by February 23, 2000. You also report the payments totaling $22,000 received from March 15, 2000, through June 13, 2000, by June 28, 2000, that is, within 15 days of the date (June 13) that the later payments, all received within a one-year period, exceeded $10,000.

Cash equivalents of $10,000 or less. Cash equivalents such as money orders, traveler's checks, cashier's checks, and bank drafts with a face value of $10,000 or less are treated as cash in sales of consumer durables, collectibles, and travel or entertainment services costing $10,000 or more. Common examples of consumer durables are autos, boats, and jewelry.

For example, if jewelry costing $12,000 is bought with $2,400 cash and traveler's checks of $9,600, the jeweler must file Form 8300 reporting the transaction. If the $2,400 were paid by personal check, the transaction would not have to be reported because personal checks are not treated as cash. Reporting exceptions are also allowed where the cash equivalent constitutes the proceeds of a bank loan, or where it is used as a down payment or promissory note payment under a payment plan used for all retail sales by the seller.

Form 8300. On Form 8300, you must provide the payer's home address and tax identification number to the IRS. You also must provide the payer with a copy of the form or a similar statement by January 31 of the following year.

A $50 penalty may be imposed for each failure to file a properly completed Form 8300 or provide the payer with a statement, unless reasonable cause is shown. The penalty may be reduced if a timely correction is made. For small businesses meeting a $5 million average gross receipts test, the maximum penalty for failure to file with the IRS is $100,000 per calendar year; otherwise, the maximum is $250,000.

If failure to file is intentional, the penalty for each failure is the *greater* of $25,000 and the cash received in the transaction, but the maximum penalty is $100,000. Criminal penalties apply for willful failure to file Form 8300 or for filing a fraudulent form.

There is an exception to the reporting requirement for persons who act as agents if they receive cash of over $10,000 from their principal and use it within 15 days in a cash transaction, provided they identify the principal to the payee in the cash transaction.

You must keep a copy of each Form 8300 you file with the IRS for five years from the date of filing.

Caution

Splitting Up a Transaction

The cash reporting requirement may not be avoided by splitting up a single transaction into separate transactions. Thus, a sale of property for $36,000 may not be broken down into four separate sales of $9,000 to avoid reporting. Similarly, an attorney who represents a client in a case must aggregate all cash payments by the client, although payments may be spread over several months. If the total exceeds $10,000, it must be reported.

Reporting Income and Expenses on Schedule C

40.6 How To File Schedule C

In this section are explanations of how a sole proprietor reports income and expenses on Schedule C, a sample of which is on page 588.

Schedule C-EZ. This simple form is designed for persons on the cash basis who do not have a net business loss and have:

- Business expenses of $2,500 or less;
- No inventory at any time during the year;
- Only one sole proprietorship;
- No employees;
- No home office expense deduction;
- No prior-year suspended passive activity losses from this business; *and*
- No depreciation to be reported on Form 4562.

Statutory employees. Statutory employees report income and expenses on Schedule C. Thus, expenses may be deducted in full on Schedule C rather than as a miscellaneous itemized deduction *(19.1)*, subject to the 2% adjusted gross income (AGI) floor on Schedule A.

Statutory employees are full-time life insurance salespersons, agent or commission drivers distributing certain foods and beverages, pieceworkers, and full-time traveling or city salespersons who solicit on behalf of and transmit to their principals orders from wholesalers and retailers for merchandise for resale or for supplies.

The term *full time* refers to an exclusive or principal business activity for a single company or person and not to the time spent on the job. If your principal activity is soliciting orders for one company, but you also solicit incidental orders for another company, you are a full-time salesperson for the primary company. Solicitations of orders are considered incidental to a principal business activity if you devote 20% or less of your time to the solicitation activity. A city or traveling salesperson is presumed to meet the principal business activity test in a calendar year in which he or she devotes 80% or more of working time to soliciting orders for one principal.

IRS regulations give this example: A salesman's principal activity is getting orders from retail pharmacies for a wholesale drug company called Que Company. He occasionally takes orders for two other companies. He is a statutory employee only for Que Company.

If you are a statutory employee, your company checks Box 15 on Form W-2, identifying you as a statutory employee. Although a statutory employee may treat job expenses as business expenses, the employer withholds FICA (Social Security and Medicare) taxes on wages and commissions. However, a statutory employee has the option of allowing his or her employer to withhold federal income taxes or to meet the employee's tax liability through the payment of estimated tax.

You must check a box on Line 1 of Schedule C (or C-EZ) to indicate statutory employee status. If you also have self-employment earnings from another business, you must report the self-employment earnings and statutory employee income on separate Schedules C. If both types of income are earned in the same business, allocate the expenses between the two activities on the separate schedules.

Gross receipts or sales on Schedule C (Line 1). If you do not produce or sell goods, but provide only services, you do not determine cost of goods sold, but report only your receipts from services on Line 1. (A sample of Schedule C in the Supplement illustrates the case of a retail business selling merchandise that is required to determine the cost of goods sold using Part III of Schedule C.)

Do not report as receipts on Schedule C the following items:

- Gains or losses on the sale of property used in your business or profession. These transactions are reported on Schedule D and Form 4797.
- Dividends from stock held in the ordinary course of your business. These are reported as dividends from stocks that are held for investment.

Caution

Doctor's Malpractice Insurance
A self-employed doctor may deduct the premium costs of malpractice insurance. However, a doctor who is not self-employed but employed by someone else, say a hospital, may deduct the premium costs only as an itemized deduction. Whether malpractice premiums paid to a physician-owned carrier are deductible depends on how the carrier is organized. If there is a sufficient number of policyholders who are not economically related and none of whom owns a controlling interest in the insuring company, a deduction is allowed provided the premiums are reasonable and are based on sound actuarial principles.

In one case, physicians set up a physician-owned carrier that was required by state insurance authorities to set up a surplus fund. The physicians contributed to the fund and received nontransferable certificates that were redeemable only if they retired, moved out of the state, or died. The IRS and Tax Court held the contributions to the fund were nondeductible capital expenses.

In another case, a professional corporation of anesthesiologists set up a trust to pay malpractice claims, up to specified limits. The IRS and Tax Court disallowed deductions for the trust contributions on the grounds that the PC remained potentially liable. Malpractice claims within the policy limits might exceed trust funds and the PC would be liable for the difference. Since risk of loss was not shifted to the trust, the trust was not a true insurance arrangement.

Sample Schedule C

Part I	**Income**			
1	Gross receipts or sales. **Caution:** *If this income was reported to you on Form W-2 and the "Statutory employee" box on that form was checked, see page C-3 and check here* . . . . . . ▶ ☐		**1**	
2	Returns and allowances		**2**	
3	Subtract line 2 from line 1		**3**	
4	Cost of goods sold (from line 42 on page 2)		**4**	
5	**Gross profit.** Subtract line 4 from line 3		**5**	
6	Other income, including Federal and state gasoline or fuel tax credit or refund (see page C-3) . . .		**6**	
7	**Gross income.** Add lines 5 and 6 . . . . ▶		**7**	

Part II   **Expenses.** Enter expenses for business use of your home **only** on line 30.

8	Advertising	**8**			19	Pension and profit-sharing plans	**19**	
9	Bad debts from sales or services (see page C-3) . .	**9**			20	Rent or lease (see page C-5):		
					a	Vehicles, machinery, and equipment .	**20a**	
10	Car and truck expenses (see page C-3)	**10**			b	Other business property . .	**20b**	
11	Commissions and fees . .	**11**			21	Repairs and maintenance . .	**21**	
12	Depletion	**12**			22	Supplies (not included in Part III) .	**22**	
13	Depreciation and section 179 expense deduction (not included in Part III) (see page C-4) . .	**13**			23	Taxes and licenses	**23**	
					24	Travel, meals, and entertainment:		
					a	Travel	**24a**	
14	Employee benefit programs (other than on line 19) . . .	**14**			b	Meals and entertainment		
15	Insurance (other than health) .	**15**			c	Enter 50% of line 24b subject to limitations (see page C-6) .		
16	Interest:							
a	Mortgage (paid to banks, etc.) .	**16a**			d	Subtract line 24c from line 24b	**24d**	
b	Other	**16b**			25	Utilities	**25**	
17	Legal and professional services	**17**			26	Wages (less employment credits) .	**26**	
18	Office expense	**18**			27	Other expenses (from line 48 on page 2)	**27**	

28	**Total expenses** before expenses for business use of home. Add lines 8 through 27 in columns . ▶		**28**	
29	Tentative profit (loss). Subtract line 28 from line 7		**29**	
30	Expenses for business use of your home. Attach **Form 8829**		**30**	
31	**Net profit or (loss).** Subtract line 30 from line 29.			
	• If a profit, enter on **Form 1040, line 12,** and ALSO on **Schedule SE, line 2** (statutory employees, see page C-6). Estates and trusts, enter on Form 1041, line 3.		**31**	
	• If a loss, you MUST go on to line 32.			
32	If you have a loss, check the box that describes your investment in this activity (see page C-6).			
	• If you checked 32a, enter the loss on **Form 1040, line 12,** and ALSO on **Schedule SE, line 2** (statutory employees, see page C-6). Estates and trusts, enter on Form 1041, line 3.		**32a** ☐ All investment is at risk.	
	• If you checked 32b, you MUST attach **Form 6198.**		**32b** ☐ Some investment is not at risk.	

Deductions on Schedule C. Deductible business expenses are claimed in Part II; the descriptive breakdown of items is generally self-explanatory. However, note these points:

Bad debts (Line 9): Business bad debts that become totally or partially worthless during the year are deductible. *See 5.34* for determining when a debt becomes worthless. However, if you are a cash-basis taxpayer, you may not claim a bad debt deduction for amounts that are not collectible unless you have included those amounts in income. If you are an accrual-basis taxpayer, you may claim a bad debt deduction for an uncollectible receivable if the amount was included in income, either for the year the deduction is claimed or for a prior year.

Generally, you must use the specific charge-off method for deducting business bad debts. For a partially worthless debt, the deduction is limited to the amount you charge off on your books during the taxable year. You may delay the charge-off of a partially worthless bad debt until a later year when more of the debt becomes worthless or until the year in which the debt is totally worthless. In the year that a debt becomes totally worthless, you may deduct the debt to the extent that it was not previously claimed as a partially worthless debt. It is advisable to enter a charge-off on your books for a totally worthless debt. If you do not and the IRS rules that the debt was only partially worthless for that year, you would be unable to claim the deduction since a deduction for a partially worthless bad debt is limited to the amount actually charged off.

If you have not been paid for services you provided and you use the accrual method of accounting, you may use the "nonaccrual-experience" method of accounting for the bad debt instead of the specific charge-off method. If you do not expect to collect an account receivable, that amount may be excluded from income. *See* IRS Publication 535 for details of the nonaccrual-experience method.

Here are some examples of business bad debt transactions:

- You sell merchandise on credit and later the buyer becomes insolvent and does not pay.
- You are in the business of making loans and a loan goes bad.
- You sell your business, but retain some accounts receivable. Later, some of these become worthless.
- You liquidate your business and are unable to collect its outstanding accounts.
- You operate as a promoter of corporations.
- You finance your lessees, customers, or suppliers to help your business.
- You lend money to protect your professional and business reputation.
- You lend money to insure delivery of merchandise from a supplier.

Car and truck expenses (Line 10): In the year you place a car in service, you may choose between the IRS mileage allowance and deducting actual expenses, plus depreciation. You must also attach Form 4562 to support the deduction; *see* Chapter 43.

Depreciation (Line 13): Enter here the amount of your annual depreciation deduction. A complete discussion of depreciation may be found in Chapter 42. You must figure your depreciation deduction on Form 4562 for assets placed in service in 1999, or for cars, computers, or other "listed property," regardless of when the assets were placed in service.

Employee benefit programs (Line 14): Enter your cost for the following programs you provide for your employees: accident or health plans; wage continuation; self-insured medical reimbursement plans; educational assistance programs; supplemental unemployment benefits; and prepaid legal expenses. Retirement plans, such as pension and profit-sharing plans, are reported separately on Line 19.

Insurance other than health insurance (Line 15): Insurance policy premiums for the protection of your business, such as accident, burglary, embezzlement, marine risks, plate glass, public liability, workers' compensation, fire, storm, or theft, and indemnity bonds upon employees, are deductible. State unemployment insurance payments are deducted here or as taxes if they are considered taxes under state law.

Premiums paid on an insurance policy on the life of an employee or one financially interested in a business, for the purpose of protecting you from loss in the event of the death of the insured, are not deductible.

Prepaid insurance premiums are deducted ratably over the term covered by the policy, whether you are on a cash or accrual basis. However, an appeals court allowed a cash-basis taxpayer to take an immediate deduction for premiums paid on a policy covering more than a year.

Premiums for disability insurance to cover loss of earnings when out ill or injured are nondeductible personal expenses. But you may deduct premiums covering business overhead expenses.

Interest (Line 16): Include interest on business debts, but prepaid interest that applies to future years is not deductible.

Deductible interest on an insurance loan is limited if you borrow against a life insurance policy covering yourself as an employee or the life of any other employee, officer, or other person financially interested in your business. Interest on such a loan is deductible only if the loan is no more than $50,000 per employee or other covered person. If you own policies covering the same em-

Filing Tip

Health Insurance Premiums

You do not claim on Schedule C the deduction of 60% of 1999 health insurance costs for yourself, your spouse, and your dependents. You take the deduction on Line 28, Form 1040. *See also 17.17* for the way to claim MSA account contributions on Line 25 of Form 1040.

Law Alert

Coverage of Employee-Spouse Gives 100% Deduction

Congress may enact legislation to allow self-employed persons an above-the-line deduction *(12.2)* for 100% of health insurance costs starting in 2000. If this measure does not become effective in 2000, self-employed persons may still get a 100% deduction for their own coverage by covering a spouse who is an employee of the business. Coverage for the employee-spouse may include the employer-spouse and their dependents as part of the employee-spouse's family unit. The employer-spouse may deduct as a business expense (on Schedule C) the cost of medical coverage, including reimbursements, for both spouses and their dependents.

The spouse must be a bona fide employee and must meet the service requirement spelled out in the plan to be eligible for coverage. The performance of nominal or insignificant services that lack economic substance will be challenged. Further, a spouse who has a financial investment in the business may be treated as self-employed or as a joint owner. If the business is an S corporation and one spouse is a more-than-2% shareholder in the corporation, the other spouse is also treated as a more-than-2% owner and not as an employee for benefit purposes.

Interest on Business Tax Deficiency

Interest on a tax deficiency based on business income reporting is not a deductible business expense according to the IRS; interest on a tax deficiency is always nondeductible personal interest. In limited cases, the Tax Court has allowed a business expense deduction, but it has been overruled by several federal appeals courts that have upheld the IRS position denying a business expense deduction for interest on a tax deficiency.

Filing Tip

Tax Advice and Tax Preparation Costs

On Line 17 of Schedule C, you deduct the portion of tax preparation costs allocable to preparing Schedule C (or C-EZ) and related tax forms. Also deduct on Line 17 fees for tax advice related to the business.

ployees (or other persons) in more than one business, the $50,000 limit applies on an aggregate basis to all the policies. The interest deduction limit applies even if a sole proprietor borrows against a policy on his or her own life and uses the proceeds in a business; interest is not deductible to the extent the loan exceeds $50,000.

Pension and profit-sharing plans (Line 19): Keogh plan or SEP contributions made for your employees are entered here; contributions made for your account are entered directly on Form 1040 as an adjustment to income. In addition, you may have to file an information return by the last day of the seventh month following the end of the plan year; *see 41.8.*

Rent on business property (Line 20): Rent paid for the use of lofts, buildings, trucks, and other equipment is deductible. However, you may not deduct the entire amount of an advance rental in the year of its payment. This is true even if you are on the cash basis. You deduct only that portion of the payment attributed to the use of the property in the taxable year. For example, you sign a 10-year lease calling for yearly rental payments of $2,000. You pay the first year's rent on July 1. In your tax return for the calendar year, you may deduct only $1,000 ($6/_{12}$ of $2,000). However, an appeals court allowed a calendar-year cash-basis lessee to deduct advance rentals where the rental payments covered a period of a year or less. For example, on December 1, 1999, the lessee pays the entire rental due for the lease ending November 30, 2000. While the IRS would allow only $1/_{12}$ of the payment to be deductible in 1999, the appeals court would allow a deduction for the entire payment. The court believes this approach is within the spirit of the cash-basis rule. In the case of a long-term lease where advance rental payments cover no more than a year beyond the year of payment, the IRS proration rule sacrifices the simplicity of the cash-basis method without a meaningful change in the timing of deductions, according to the appeals court.

Taxes on leased property that you pay to the lessor are deductible as additional rent.

Repairs (Line 21): The cost of repairs and maintenance is deductible provided they do not materially add to the value of the property or appreciably prolong its life. Expenses of replacements that arrest deterioration and appreciably increase the value of the property are capitalized and their cost recovered through depreciation.

Taxes (Line 23): Deduct real estate and personal property taxes on business assets here. Also deduct your share of Social Security and Medicare taxes paid on behalf of employees and payments of federal unemployment tax. Federal highway use tax is deductible. Federal import duties and excise and stamp taxes normally not deductible as itemized deductions are deductible as business taxes if incurred by the business. Taxes on business property, such as an *ad valorem* tax, must be deducted here; they are not to be treated as itemized deductions. However, the IRS holds that you may not deduct state income taxes on business income as a business expense. Its reasoning: Income taxes are personal taxes even when paid on business income. As such, you may deduct state income tax only as an itemized deduction on Schedule A. The Tax Court supports the IRS rule on the grounds that it reflects Congressional intent toward the treatment of state income taxes in figuring taxable income.

For purposes of computing a net operating loss, state income tax on business income is treated as a business deduction.

If you pay or accrue sales tax on the purchase of nondepreciable business property, the sales tax is a deductible business expense. If the property is depreciable, add the sales tax to the cost basis for purposes of computing depreciation deductions.

Travel, meals, and entertainment (Line 24): Travel expenses on overnight business trips while "away from home" *(20.6)* and 50% of meals and entertainment for business are deductible. Total meals and entertainment expenses are listed on Line 24b and then reduced by 50% on Line 24c. The total amount after figuring the 50% reduction is reported on Line 24d.

Self-employed persons may use the IRS meal allowance rates discussed at *20.4,* instead of claiming actual expenses. *See also 20.26–20.28* for record-keeping requirements for travel and entertainment expenses.

Utilities (Line 25): Deduct utilities such as gas, electric, and telephone expenses incurred in your business. However, if you have a home office *(40.12),* you may *not* deduct the base rate (including taxes) of the first phone line into your home; *see 19.14.*

Wages (Line 26): You do not deduct wages paid to yourself. You may deduct reasonable wages paid to family members who work for you. If you have an employee who works in your office and also in your home, such as a domestic, you deduct that part of the salary allocated to the work in your office. If you claim a work opportunity, welfare-to-work, empowerment zone or Indian employment tax credit, the wage deduction is reduced by the credit.

Other expenses (Line 27): In Part V of Schedule C, you list deductible expenses not reported in Part II, such as amortizable business start-up costs *(40.11).*

40.7 Deductions for Professionals

The following expenses incurred by self-employed professionals in the course of their work are generally allowed as deductions from income when figuring profit (or loss) from their professional practices on Schedule C:

- Dues to professional societies
- Operating expenses and repairs of car used on professional calls
- Supplies
- Subscriptions to professional journals
- Rent for office space
- Cost of fuel, light, water, and telephone used in the office
- Salaries of assistants
- Malpractice insurance; *see 40.6*
- Cost of books, information services, professional instruments, and equipment with a useful life of one year or less. Professional libraries are depreciable if their value decreases with time. Depreciation rules are discussed at *42.1.*
- Fees paid to a tax preparer for preparing Schedule C and related business forms

Professionals as employees. Professionals who are not in their own practice may not deduct professional expenses on Schedule C. Salaried professionals may deduct professional expenses only as miscellaneous itemized deductions on Schedule A, subject to the 2% adjusted gross income (AGI) floor; *see 19.1.* However, "statutory" employees may use Schedule C; *see 40.6.*

The cost of preparing for a profession. You may not deduct the cost of a professional education; *see 19.16.*

The IRS does not allow a deduction for the cost of a license to practice. However, the Tax Court has allowed attorneys to amortize over their life expectancy bar admission fees paid to state authorities; *see 19.17.*

Payment of clients' expenses. An attorney may follow a practice of paying his or her clients' expenses in pending cases. The IRS will disallow a deduction claimed for these payments on the grounds that the expenses are those of the client, not the attorney. The courts agree with the IRS position where there is a net fee agreement. In a net fee agreement, expenses first reduce the recovery before the attorney takes a fee. However, where the attorney is paid under a gross fee agreement, an appeals court has reversed a Tax Court decision that disallowed the deduction of the attorney's payment of client expenses. Under a gross fee agreement, the attorney's fee is based on the gross award; the prior payment of expenses does not enter into the fee agreement and so is not reimbursed. Because he would not be reimbursed, an attorney claimed his payment of client expenses was deductible. An appeals court accepted this argument and allowed the deduction. The court allowed the deduction although California law disapproved of the practice of paying client expenses without a right of reimbursement. The court believed that there is no ethical difficulty with the practice and other jurisdictions approve of it. It is necessary for and it is the practice of personal injury firms to pay the costs of many of their clients.

If you are not allowed a current deduction for payment of clients' expenses, you may deduct your advance as a bad debt if the claim is worthless in another year; *see 40.6.*

An attorney might deduct a payment to a client reimbursing the client for a bad investment recommended by the attorney. A court upheld the deduction on the grounds that the reimbursement was required to protect the reputation of an established law practice. However, no deduction is allowed when malpractice insurance reimbursement is available but the attorney fails to make a claim.

Daily business lunches with associates have been held to lack business purpose. Courts agree with the IRS that professionals do not need to have lunch together every day to talk shop. The cost of the meals is therefore not deductible.

EXAMPLES

1. A law partnership deducted the meal costs of the staff attorneys who lunched every day at the same restaurant to discuss cases and court assignments. The deductions were disallowed as personal expenses. The Tax Court and an appeals court agreed with the IRS that daily lunches are not necessary. Co-workers generally do not need luncheons to provide social lubrication for business talk, as is true with clients.

2. A physician held luncheon meetings three or four times a week with other physicians. He argued that the purpose of the luncheons was to generate referrals. A court held

Planning Reminder

Continuing Education Courses
The costs of courses taken to keep current with professional developments are usually deductible; *see 19.16.*

that such frequent luncheons became a routine personal event not tied to specific business. The cost of the meals was not deductible.

3. A medical professional corporation (PC) deducted the cost of meals taken by its physician-stockholders at a hospital cafeteria. It argued that the doctors discussed patients and met other doctors who made referrals to them. The Tax Court agreed with the IRS that the meal costs were not deductible; doctors ate in the cafeteria for their personal convenience. Furthermore, the payments were taxed to the doctors as dividends. The court noted that the PC might have been able to claim a deduction had it treated the meal payments as taxable pay; however, the PC refused to take this position, unsuccessfully gambling that it could claim the costs as business deductions.

40.8 Nondeductible Expense Items

Capital expenditures may not be deducted. Generally, the cost of acquiring an asset or of prolonging its life is a capital expenditure that must be amortized over its expected life. If the useful life of an item is less than a year, its cost, including sales tax on the purchase, is deductible. Otherwise, you may recover your cost only through depreciation except to the extent first-year expensing applies; *see 42.3.*

EXAMPLE

A new roof is installed on your office building. If the roof increases the life of the building, its cost is a capital expenditure recovered by depreciation deductions. The cost of repairing a leak in the roof is a deductible operating expense. A deduction was allowed for the cost of a major roof renovation on evidence that the work was not designed to increase the value of the building but to correct the defect.

Expenses while you are not in business. You are not allowed to deduct business expenses incurred during the time you are not engaged in your business or profession.

EXAMPLE

A lawyer continued to maintain his office while he was employed by the government. During that time he did no private law work. He only kept the office to have it ready at such time as he quit the government job and returned to practice. His costs of keeping up his office while he was working for the government were not deductible.

Bribes and kickbacks. Bribes and kickbacks are not deductible if they are illegal under a federal or a generally enforced state law that subjects the payer to a criminal penalty or provides for the loss of license or privilege to engage in business. A kickback, even if not illegal, is not deductible by a physician or other person who has furnished items or services that are payable under the Social Security Act (including state programs). A kickback includes payments for referral of a client, patient, or customer.

In one case, the IRS, with support from the Tax Court and a federal appeals court, disallowed a deduction for legal kickbacks paid by a subcontractor. The courts held that the kickbacks were not a "necessary" business expense because the contractor had obtained nearly all of its other contracts without paying kickbacks, including contracts from the same general contractor bribed here.

40.9 How Authors and Artists May Write Off Expenses

Self-employed authors, artists, photographers, and other qualifying creative professionals may write off business expenses as they are paid. The law (Code Section 263A) that requires expenses to be amortized over the period income is received does not apply to freelancers who personally create literary manuscripts, musical or dance scores, paintings, pictures, sculptures, drawings, cartoons, graphic designs, original print editions, photographs, or photographic negatives or transparencies. Furthermore, expenses of a personal service corporation do not have to be amortized if they directly relate to expenses of a qualifying author, artist, or photographer who owns (or whose relatives own) substantially all of the corporation's stock.

Current deductions are *not* allowed for expenses relating to motion picture films, videotapes, printing, photographic plates, or similar items.

Caution

Penalties and Fines

Penalties or fines paid to a government agency because of a violation of any law are not deductible. You may deduct penalties imposed by a business contract for late performance or nonperformance.

An author or artist with expenses exceeding income may be barred by the IRS from claiming a loss under a profit motive test; in that case, the profit-presumption rule discussed at *40.10* may allow a deduction of the loss.

40.10 Deducting Expenses of a Sideline Business or Hobby

There is a one-way tax rule for hobbies: Income from a hobby is taxable; expenses are deductible only to the extent you have income, and the deduction is limited on Schedule A by the 2% adjusted gross income (AGI) floor for miscellaneous itemized deductions. Hobby losses are considered nondeductible personal losses. A profitable sale of a hobby collection or activity held long term is taxable as capital gain; losses are not deductible.

How to deduct hobby expenses. If the profit presumption discussed later does *not* apply and the activity is held *not* to be engaged in for profit, expenses are deductible only as miscellaneous itemized deductions and only up to the extent of income from the activity; a deduction for expenses exceeding the income is disallowed.

A special sequence is followed in determining which expenses are deductible from income. Deducted first on Schedule A are amounts allowable without regard to whether the activity is a business engaged in for profit, such as mortgage interest and state and local taxes, as well as casualty losses. If any income remains, first deduct "business" operating expenses such as wages, utilities, advertising, repairs, and maintenance. Then deduct depreciation to the extent of remaining income. The "business" expenses and depreciation are allowed only as miscellaneous itemized deductions subject to the 2% AGI floor; *see 19.1*. Thus, even if the expenses offset income from the activity, none of the expenses will be deductible unless your total miscellaneous expenses (including those from the activity) exceed 2% of your adjusted gross income.

Presumption of profit-seeking motive. You are *presumed to be* engaged in an activity for profit if you can show a profit in at least three of the last five years, including the current year. If the activity is horse breeding, training, racing, or showing, the profit presumption applies if you show profits in two of seven consecutive years. The presumption does not necessarily mean that losses will automatically be allowed; the IRS may try to rebut the presumption. You would then have to prove a profit motive by showing these types of facts: You spend considerable time in the activity; you keep businesslike records; you relied on expert advice; you expect the assets to appreciate in value; and losses are common in the start-up phase of your type of business.

Election postpones determination of profit presumption. If you have losses in the first few years of an activity and the IRS tries to disallow them as hobby losses, you have this option: You may make an election on Form 5213 to postpone the determination of whether the above profit presumption applies. The postponement is until after the end of the fourth taxable year (sixth year for a horse breeding, training, showing, or racing activity) following the first year of the activity. For example, if you enter a farming activity in 1999, you can elect to postpone the profit motive determination until after the end of 2003. Then, if you have realized profits in at least three of the five years (1999–2003), the profit presumption applies. When you make the election on Form 5213, you agree to waive the statute of limitations for all activity-related items in the taxable years involved. The waiver generally gives the IRS an additional two years after the filing due date for the last year in the presumption period to issue deficiencies related to the activity.

To make the election, you must file Form 5213 within three years of the due date of the return for the year you started the activity. Thus, if you started your activity during 1999, you have until April 17, 2003, to make the election. If before the end of this three-year period you receive a deficiency notice from the IRS disallowing a loss from the activity and you have not yet made the election, you can still do so within 60 days of receiving the notice. These election rules apply to individuals, partnerships, and S corporations. An election by a partnership or S corporation is binding on all partners or S corporation shareholders holding interests during the presumption period.

40.11 Deducting Expenses of Looking for a New Business

When you are planning to invest in a business, you may incur preliminary expenses for traveling to look at the property and for legal or accounting advice. Expenses incurred during a general search or preliminary investigation of a business are not deductible, including expenses related to the decision whether or not to enter a transaction. However, when you go beyond a general search and focus on acquiring a particular business, you may deduct the start-up expenses. The timing of the deduction depends on whether or not you actually go into the business.

 Planning Reminder

Hobby or Sideline Business

The question of whether an activity, such as dog breeding or collecting and selling coins and stamps, is a hobby or sideline business arises when losses are incurred. As long as you show a profit, you may deduct the expenses of the activity. But when expenses exceed income and your return is examined, an agent may allow expenses only up to the amount of your income and disallow the remaining expenses that make up your loss. At this point, to claim the loss, you may be able to take advantage of a "profit presumption" discussed in *40.10*, or you may have to prove that you are engaged in the activity to make a profit.

 Filing Tip

Start-Up Costs

The election to amortize start-up expenses is made by claiming the deduction on Part VI of Form 4562, and by attaching a statement to the return for the first year you are in business. In the statement, describe the expenses, when they were incurred, the date the business began, and the number of months (not less than 60) in the amortization period.

Amortizable expenses if you go into business. When you go into a business, you may elect to amortize over at least a 60-month period the costs of investigating and setting up the business, such as expenses of surveying potential markets, products, labor supply, and transportation facilities; travel and other expenses incurred in lining up prospective distributors, suppliers, or customers; salaries or fees paid to consultants or attorneys, and fees for similar professional services. The business may be one you acquire from someone else or a new business you create. The amortization period starts when you actually begin or acquire a going business.

Organizational costs for a partnership or corporation. Costs incident to the creation of a partnership or corporation are also amortizable over a period of at least 60 months. For a partnership, qualifying expenses include legal fees for negotiating and preparing a partnership agreement, and management, consulting, or accounting fees in setting up the partnership. Amortization is not allowed for syndication costs of issuing and marketing partnership interests such as brokerage and registration fees, fees of an underwriter, and costs of preparing a prospectus.

For a corporation, amortizable expenses include the cost of organizational meetings, incorporation fees, and accounting and legal fees for drafting corporate documents. Costs of selling stock or securities, such as commissions, do not qualify.

The election to amortize is made on Part VI of Form 4562 for the first year the partnership or corporation is in business. A statement attached to the return must describe the expenses and the amortization period. The election on Form 4562 and the required statement must be filed no later than the return due date, including extensions, for the year in which the business begins.

Nonamortizable expenses. Amortizable expenses are restricted to expenses incurred in investigating the acquisition or creation of an active business, and setting up such an active business. They do not include taxes, interest, research, or experimental costs deductible under Code Section 174. Expenses of looking for investment property may not be amortized. For rental activities to qualify as an active business, there must be significant furnishing of services incident to the rentals. For example, the operation of an apartment complex, an office building, or a shopping center would generally be considered an active business.

You may not claim any deduction for start-up expenses if you do not elect to amortize. For example, if you incur expenses prior to completion of a building to be used in an active rental business, such as rental payments for leasing the land on which the building is to be constructed, you must elect to amortize the expenses or you will lose the deduction. If you do not elect to amortize, you treat the expenses as follows:

- Costs connected with the acquisition of capital assets are capitalized and depreciated; *and*
- Costs related to assets with unlimited or indeterminable useful lives are recovered only on the future sale or liquidation of the business.

If the acquisition fails. Where you have gone beyond a general search and have focused on the acquisition of a particular business, but the acquisition falls through, you may deduct the expenses as a capital loss.

EXAMPLES

1. In search of a business, you place newspaper advertisements and travel to investigate various prospective ventures. You pay for audits to evaluate the potential of some of the ventures. You then decide to purchase a specific business and hire a law firm to draft necessary documents. However, you change your mind and later abandon your plan to acquire the business. According to the IRS, you may not deduct the related expenses for advertisements, travel, and audits. These are considered investigatory. You may deduct the expense of hiring the law firm.

2. Domenie left his job to invest in a business. He advertised and was contacted by a party who wished to sell. He agreed to buy, hired an attorney, transferred funds to finance the business, and worked a month with the company manager to familiarize himself with the business. Discovering misrepresentations, he refused to buy the company and deducted over $5,000 for expenses, including travel and legal fees. The IRS disallowed the deduction as incurred in a business search. The Tax Court disagreed. Domenie thought he had found a business and acted as such in transferring funds and drawing legal papers for a takeover.

Job-hunting costs. For deducting the expenses of looking for a new job, *see 19.7.*

Caution

Nonamortizable Costs

You may *not* amortize the expenses incurred in acquiring or selling securities or partnership interests such as securities registration expenses or underwriters' commissions. You may *not* amortize the costs of acquiring property to be held for sale or property that may be depreciated or amortized, including expenses incident to a lease and leasehold improvements.

40.12 Exclusive and Regular Use of a Home Office

If you operate your business from your home, using a room or other space as an office or area to assemble or prepare items for sale, you may be able to deduct expenses such as utilities, insurance, repairs, and depreciation allocated to your business use of the area. To deduct home office expenses, you must prove that you use the home area *exclusively* and *on a regular basis* either as:

1. ***A place of business to meet or deal with patients, clients, or customers in the normal course of your business (incidental or occasional meetings do not meet this test),*** or
2. ***Your principal place of business.*** Your home office will qualify as your principal place of business if you spend most of your working time there and most of your business income is attributable to your activities there.

Administrative (record-keeping) activity. A home office meets the principal place of business test (Test 2) if: (1) you use it regularly and exclusively for administrative or management activities of your business and (2) you have no other fixed location to do such work. Self-employed persons are the beneficiaries of this administrative/management rule. Employees may not take advantage of the rule because of the application of the convenience-of-the-employer test to an employee's use of a home office; *see* the Example at *19.13*. Examples of administrative and management activities include billing customers, clients, or patients; keeping books and records; ordering supplies; setting up appointments; forwarding orders; and writing reports.

According to the IRS, performance of management or administrative activities under the following conditions do not disqualify a home office as a principal place of business:

- You have a company send out your bills from its place of business (*see* Example 1).
- You do administrative or management activities at times from a hotel or automobile (*see* Example 2).
- You occasionally conduct minimal administrative or management activities at a fixed location outside your home.
- You have suitable space to do administrative or management work outside your home but choose to use your home office for such activities (*see* Example 3).

EXAMPLES

1. A self-employed plumber does all of his repair and installation services outside of his home where he has a small office used to phone customers, order supplies, and keep his books. However, he uses a local bookkeeping service to bill his customers. He has no other fixed location for doing his administrative work. That he uses an outside billing service does not disqualify his home office as a principal place of business.
2. A self-employed sales representative for several products uses a home office to set up appointments and write up orders. When she is out of town, she writes up such orders from a hotel room. The occasional use of a hotel room to write up orders does not disqualify the home office as a principal place of business that otherwise meets the new tests.
3. A self-employed anesthesiologist spends most of his professional time at three local hospitals. One of the hospitals provides him with a small shared office where he could do administrative and management work; however, he does not use this space. He uses his home as an office to: contact patients, surgeons, and hospitals regarding schedules; prepare presentations; keep billing records and patient logs; and read medical journals and books. His choice to use his home office instead of the one provided by one hospital does not disqualify his home office as a principal place of business. He uses that office for accepted administrative activities.

If you work at home and also outside of your home at other locations and you do not meet the administrative/management rule, deductions of home office expenses should be supported by evidence that your activities at home are relatively more important or time consuming than those outside your home.

Exclusive and regular business use of home area required. If you use a room, such as a den, both for business and family purposes, be prepared to show that a specific section of the den is used *exclusively* as office space. For example, a real estate operator was not allowed to deduct the cost of a home office, on evidence that he also used the office area for nonbusiness purposes. A partition or other physical separation of the office area is helpful but not required.

Under the regular basis test, expenses attributable to incidental or occasional trade or business use are not deductible, even if the room is used for no other purpose but business.

 Law Alert

New Deduction Opportunity for Administrative Offices

A home office deduction is now available for 1999 and later years if you regularly and exclusively use part of your home as the only place for conducting the administrative or management activities of your business. The home area qualifies as your principal place of business even if you spend most of your working time providing services at outside locations.

 Caution

Principal Place of Business Test

The tests for deducting office expenses will generally not present problems where the home area is the principal place of business or professional activity. For example, you are a doctor and see most of your patients at an office set aside in your home. A tax dispute may arise where you have a principal place of business elsewhere and use a part of your home for occasional work or administrative paperwork. Occasional use is not sufficient. If your deduction is questioned, you must prove that the area is used regularly and exclusively to meet with customers, clients, or patients or that the home office is the only place where administrative/management activities for the business are conducted. Have evidence that you have actual office facilities. Furnish the room as an office—with a desk, files, and a phone used only for business calls. Also keep a record of work done and business visitors.

Even if you meet these tests, your deduction for allocable office expenses may be substantially limited or barred by a restrictive rule that limits deductions to the income from the office activity. This computation is made on Form 8829 and is illustrated in *40.15*.

Multiple business use of home office. If you use a home office for more than one business, make sure that the home office tests are met for all businesses before you claim deductions. If one business use qualifies and another use does not, the IRS will disallow deductions even for the qualifying use, *see* the following paragraph.

Employee with sideline business. Employees who use a home office for their job and for a sideline business also should be aware of this problem. Most employees are unable to show that their home office is the principal place of their work. Claiming an unallowable deduction for employee home office use will jeopardize the deduction for sideline business use. This happened to Hamacher, who as a self-employed actor earned $24,600 over a two-year period from an Atlanta theater and a few radio and television commercials. He also earned $18,000 each year as the administrator of an acting school at the theater. For his job as administrator, Hamacher shared an office at the theater with other employees. He had access to this office during nonbusiness hours. He also used one of the six rooms in his apartment for an office. Because of interruptions at the theater, he used the home office to work on the school curriculum and select plays for the theater. In connection with his acting business, he used the home office to receive phone calls, to prepare for auditions, and rehearse for acting roles.

The IRS disallowed his deduction for both self-employment and employee purposes because Hamacher's office use as an employee did not qualify. The Tax Court agreed. A single-office space may be used for different business activities, but all of the uses must qualify for a deduction. Here, Hamacher's use of the home office as an employee did not qualify. He had suitable office space at the theater. He was not expected or required to do work at home. As the employee use of the home office did not qualify, the Tax Court did not have to determine if the sideline business use qualified. Even if it had qualified, no allocation of expenses between the two uses would have been made. By requiring that a home office be used "exclusively" as a principal place of business or place for seeing clients, patients, or customers, the law imposes an all-or-nothing test.

Separate structure. If in your business you use a separate structure not attached to your home, such as a studio adjacent but unattached to your home, the expenses are generally deductible if you satisfy the exclusive use and regular basis tests discussed earlier. A separate structure does not have to qualify as your principal place of business or a place for meeting patients, clients, or customers. However, the income limitation discussed at *40.15* applies. In one case, a taxpayer argued that an office located in a separate building in his backyard was not subject to the exclusive and regular business use tests and the gross income limitation. However, the IRS and Tax Court held that it was. The office building was "appurtenant" to the home and thus part of it, based on these facts: The office building was 12 feet away from the house and within the same fenced-in residential area; it did not have a separate address; it was included in the same title and subject to the same mortgage as the house, and all taxes, utilities, and insurance were paid as a unit for both buildings.

Day-care services. The exclusive-use test does not have to be met for business use of a home to provide day-care services for children and handicapped persons, or persons age 65 or older, provided certain state licensing requirements are met. If part of your home is *regularly* but not exclusively used to provide day-care services, you may deduct an allocable part of your expenses. You allocate expenses by multiplying the total costs by two fractions: (1) The total square footage in the home that is available for day-care use throughout each business day and regularly so used, divided by the total square footage for the home. (2) The total hours of operation divided by the total number of hours in a year (8,760, or 365 × 24).

If the area *is* exclusively used for day-care services, only fraction (1) applies.

EXAMPLE

Alice Jones operates a day-care center at home from 7 a.m. to 6 p.m., five days a week, 250 days a year for a total of 2,750 business-use hours during the year. Her family uses the area the rest of the time. Annual home expenses total $10,000 ($5,000 for interest and taxes; $4,000 for electricity, gas, water, trash collection, maintenance, and insurance; and $1,000 for depreciation). The total floor area of the home is 2,000 square feet; 1,500 square feet are used for day-care purposes. Alice multiplies her $10,000 of expenses by 75%, the part of the home used for day-care purposes (1,500 square feet ÷ 2,000 square feet), and also by 31.39%, the percentage of business-use time (2,750 hours ÷ 8,760 hours). Thus, she may deduct $2,354: $10,000 × 75% × 31.39%. The full $2,354 is deductible only if net income generated from the day-care facility is at least that much.

 Filing Instruction

Form 8829

You must report deductible 1999 home office expenses on Form 8829. Part I is used for showing the space allocated to business use *(40.14)*; Part II for reporting deductible expenses allocated to business use *(40.14)*; Part III for figuring depreciation on the business area *(40.13)*; and Part IV for carryover to 2000 of expenses not allowed in 1999 because of income limitations applied in Part II *(40.15)*. A sample copy of Form 8829 is on page 598.

In one case, the Tax Court held that utility rooms, such as a laundry and storage room and garage, may be counted as part of the day-care business area. The IRS had argued that because the children were not allowed in these areas, the space could not be considered as used for business. The Tax Court disagreed. The laundry room was used to wash the children's clothes; the storage room and garage were used to store play items and equipment. Thus, the space was considered as used for child care even though the rooms were off limits to the children.

Storage space and inventory. If your home is the only location of a business selling products, you may deduct expenses allocated to space regularly used for inventory storage, including product samples, if the space is separately identifiable and suitable for storage.

40.13 What Home Office Expenses Are Deductible?

Depending on your income *(40.15)*, a deduction for home business use may include real estate taxes, mortgage interest, operating expenses (such as home insurance premiums and utility costs), and depreciation allocated to the area used for business.

The deduction is figured on Form 8829 and entered on Line 30 of Schedule C.

Household expenses and repairs that do not benefit that space are not deductible. However, a pro rata share of the cost of painting the outside of a house or repairing a roof is deductible. Costs of lawn care and landscaping are not deductible.

If you install a security system for all your home's windows and doors, the portion of your monthly maintenance fee that is allocable to the office area is a deductible operating expense. Furthermore, the business portion of your cost for the system is depreciable. Thus, if the office takes up 20% of your home *(40.14)* you may deduct, subject to the income limitation in *40.15*, 20% of the maintenance fee and a 20% depreciation deduction.

Figuring depreciation. For depreciation purposes, the cost basis of the house is the lower of the fair market value of the house at the time you started to use a part of it for business and its adjusted basis, exclusive of the land. Only that part of the cost basis allocated to the office is depreciable. Form 8829 has a special section, Part III, for making this computation.

 Filing Tip

If You Rent Your Home

If you rent rather than own your home, and you meet the home office tests in *40.12*, enter the rent you paid during the year on Line 20 (Other Expenses) of Form 8829.

EXAMPLE

In April 1999, you start to use one room in your house exclusively and on a regular basis to meet with clients. This room is 10% of the square footage of your home. In 1986, you bought the property for $100,000, of which $90,000 was allocated to the house. The house now has a fair market value of $185,000. You compute depreciation on the cost basis of $90,000, which is lower than the value. You multiply $90,000 by 10% (business-use percentage), which gives you $9,000 as the depreciable basis of the business part of the house. As you started business use in the fourth month of 1999, you multiply the depreciable basis of $9,000 by 1.819%. This percentage is listed for the fourth month in the depreciation rate table for 39-year property shown on page 599. Your depreciation deduction is $163.71 (9,000 × 1.819%).

Nonresidential Real Property (31.5 years—For property placed in service after 1986 and before May 13, 1993)

Use the column for the month of taxable year placed in service.

Year	1	2	3	4	5	6	7	8	9	10	11	12
1	3.042%	2.778%	2.513%	2.249%	1.984%	1.720%	1.455%	1.190%	0.926%	0.661%	0.397%	0.132%
2–7	3.175	3.175	3.175	3.175	3.175	3.175	3.175	3.175	3.175	3.175	3.175	3.175
8	3.175	3.174	3.175	3.174	3.175	3.174	3.175	3.175	3.175	3.175	3.175	3.175
9	3.174	3.175	3.174	3.175	3.174	3.175	3.174	3.175	3.174	3.175	3.174	3.175
10	3.175	3.174	3.175	3.174	3.175	3.174	3.175	3.174	3.175	3.174	3.175	3.174
11	3.174	3.175	3.174	3.175	3.174	3.175	3.174	3.175	3.174	3.175	3.174	3.175
12	3.175	3.174	3.175	3.174	3.175	3.174	3.175	3.174	3.175	3.174	3.175	3.174
13	3.174	3.175	3.174	3.175	3.174	3.175	3.174	3.175	3.174	3.175	3.174	3.175

Sample Form 8829

Name(s) of proprietor(s) **Samuel Brown**					Your social security number **X1X ÷ 01 ÷ 1111**	

Part I   Part of Your Home Used for Business

1	Area used regularly and exclusively for business, regularly for day care, or for storage of inventory or product samples. See instructions	1	500 sq. ft.
2	Total area of home	2	2,500 sq. ft.
3	Divide line 1 by line 2. Enter the result as a percentage	3	20%

• **For day-care facilities not used exclusively for business, also complete lines 4–6.**
• **All others, skip lines 4–6 and enter the amount from line 3 on line 7.**

4	Multiply days used for day care during year by hours used per day	4	hr.
5	Total hours available for use during the year (365 days × 24 hours). See instructions	5	8,760 hr.
6	Divide line 4 by line 5. Enter the result as a decimal amount	6	.
7	Business percentage. For day-care facilities not used exclusively for business, multiply line 6 by line 3 (enter the result as a percentage). All others, enter the amount from line 3 ▶	7	20%

Part II   Figure Your Allowable Deduction

		(a) Direct expenses	(b) Indirect expenses		
8	Enter the amount from Schedule C, line 29, **plus** any net gain or (loss) derived from the business use of your home and shown on Schedule D or Form 4797. If more than one place of business, see instructions			8	3,400

See instructions for columns (a) and (b) before completing lines 9–20.

		(a) Direct expenses	(b) Indirect expenses		
9	Casualty losses. See instructions				
10	Deductible mortgage interest. See instructions		10,000		
11	Real estate taxes. See instructions		4,000		
12	Add lines 9, 10, and 11		14,000		
13	Multiply line 12, column (b) by line 7		2,800		
14	Add line 12, column (a) and line 13			14	2,800
15	Subtract line 14 from line 8. If zero or less, enter -0-			15	600
16	Excess mortgage interest. See instructions				
17	Insurance		1,200		
18	Repairs and maintenance				
19	Utilities		1,800		
20	Other expenses. See instructions				
21	Add lines 16 through 20		3,000		
22	Multiply line 21, column (b) by line 7		600		
23	Carryover of operating expenses from 1998 Form 8829, line 41				
24	Add line 21 in column (a), line 22, and line 23			24	600
25	Allowable operating expenses. Enter the **smaller** of line 15 or line 24			25	600
26	Limit on excess casualty losses and depreciation. Subtract line 25 from line 15			26	- 0 -
27	Excess casualty losses. See instructions				
28	Depreciation of your home from Part III below	1,200			
29	Carryover of excess casualty losses and depreciation from 1998 Form 8829, line 42				
30	Add lines 27 through 29			30	1,200
31	Allowable excess casualty losses and depreciation. Enter the **smaller** of line 26 or line 30			31	- 0 -
32	Add lines 14, 25, and 31			32	3,400
33	Casualty loss portion, if any, from lines 14 and 31. Carry amount to **Form 4684**, Section B			33	- 0 -
34	Allowable expenses for business use of your home. Subtract line 33 from line 32. Enter here and on Schedule C, line 30. If your home was used for more than one business, see instructions ▶			34	3,400

Part III   Depreciation of Your Home

35	Enter the **smaller** of your home's adjusted basis or its fair market value. See instructions	35	238,975
36	Value of land included on line 35	36	50,000
37	Basis of building. Subtract line 36 from line 35	37	188,975
38	Business basis of building. Multiply line 37 by line 7	38	37,795
39	Depreciation percentage. See instructions	39	3.175%
40	Depreciation allowable. Multiply line 38 by line 39. Enter here and on line 28 above. See instructions	40	1,200

Part IV   Carryover of Unallowed Expenses to 2000

41	Operating expenses. Subtract line 25 from line 24. If less than zero, enter -0-	41	- 0 -
42	Excess casualty losses and depreciation. Subtract line 31 from line 30. If less than zero, enter -0-	42	1,200

Nonresidential Real Property (39 years—For property placed in service after May 12, 1993)

Use the column for the month of taxable year placed in service.

	1	2	3	4	5	6	7	8	9	10	11	12
Year												
1	2.461%	2.247%	2.033%	1.819%	1.605%	1.391%	1.177%	0.963%	0.749%	0.535%	0.321%	0.107%
2–39	2.564	2.564	2.564	2.564	2.564	2.564	2.564	2.564	2.564	2.564	2.564	2.564
40	0.107	0.321	0.535	0.749	0.963	1.177	1.391	1.605	1.819	2.033	2.247	2.461

40.14 Allocating Expenses to Business Use

You may allocate to home office use qualifying expenses *(40.13)* as follows: If the rooms are not equal or approximately equal in size, compare the number of square feet of space used for business with the total number of square feet in the home and then apply the resulting percentage to the total deductible expenses.

If all rooms in your home are approximately the same size, you may base the allocation on a comparison of the number of rooms used as an office to the total number of rooms.

EXAMPLE

A doctor rents a apartment using three rooms for his office and seven rooms for his residence. The rooms are not equal in size. The apartment has 2,000 square feet; the office has 600. He allocated 30% ($^{600}/_{2,000}$) of the following expenses to his office:

	Total	Office	Residence
Rent	$7,200	$2,160	$5,040
Light	600	180	420
Heat	1,000	300	700
Wages of domestic	2,000	600	1,400
	$10,800	$3,240	$7,560

Thus, $3,240 is deductible as office expenses, subject to the income limitation of *40.15*.

40.15 Business Income May Limit Home Office Deductions

Even if your home business use satisfies the deduction tests in *40.12*, deductions for the business portion *(40.14)* of utilities, maintenance, and insurance costs, as well as depreciation or rent deductions, may not exceed net income derived from the office use after allocable mortgage interest, real estate taxes, and casualties are subtracted. To make sure that deductible expenses do not exceed income, the IRS requires you to use Form 8829. If you do not realize income during the year, no deduction is allowed. For example, you are a full-time writer and use an office in your home. You do not sell any of your work this year or receive any advances or royalties. Therefore, you may not claim a home office deduction for this year. *See also 40.9* on rules for writers and artists.

Part II of Form 8829 limits the deduction of home office expenses to net income derived from office use. You start with the tentative profit from Schedule C. If you sold your home during the year, increase the tentative profit by any net gain (or decrease tentative profit by any net loss) that is allocable to the office area and reported on Schedule D or Form 4797. The following expenses are listed in Part II of Form 8829 for purposes of applying the income limit: Casualty losses affecting the residence, deductible mortgage interest, real estate taxes, home insurance premiums, repair and maintenance expenses for the residence, utility expenses, rent, and depreciation. Business expenses not related to the home are deducted on the appropriate lines of Schedule C. For example, a salary paid to a secretary is deducted on Line 26 of Schedule C; the cost of depreciable business equipment used in your home is deducted on Line 13 of Schedule C.

The amount of real estate taxes, mortgage interest, or casualty losses not allocated to home office use may be claimed as itemized deductions on Schedule A.

EXAMPLE

Brown does sideline business consulting from a home office that he uses exclusively for business for all of 1999. His income in 1999 from consulting services is $12,400. He paid $3,600 for a photocopy machine and $4,000 for a computer, and had office telephone expenses of $600 and office supply costs of $800.

 Planning Reminder

Carryover Allowed

Expenses disallowed because of the income limitation may be carried forward and treated as home office expenses in a later tax year (Part IV, Form 8829). The carryover as well as the expenses of the later year are subject to the income limitation of that year. For example, tentative net profit for 1999 on Line 29, Schedule C, is $1,000. Rent and other expenses allocated to home office business are $2,000. Only $1,000 of the expenses are deductible; $1,000 is carried over to 2000.

In addition, his home costs are:

Mortgage interest	$10,000
Real estate taxes	4,000
Insurance	1,200
Utilities	1,800

His office space took up 20% of the area of his home, and he figured depreciation allocated to business use of $1,200.

On Schedule C he claims first-year expensing *(42.3)* for the copier and the computer, and deducts the cost of the business phone and supplies on Schedule C. This gives a tentative profit of $3,400 ($12,400 – $9,000) on Line 29, Schedule C.

In Part I of Form 8829, he lists the total area of the home and the area used for business, showing 20% business use.

In Part II, he enters the home costs listed above. We have taken only the relevant lines of the Form 8829 as an illustration. A sample Form 8829 is on page 598.

Form 8829 Line—

8.	Tentative profit from Schedule C, Line 29		$3,400
10b.	Mortgage interest	$10,000	
11b.	Real estate taxes	4,000	
12b.	Total	$14,000	
13 & 14.	Business portion of Line 12		2,800
15.	Remaining tentative profit		600
17b.	Insurance	1,200	
19b.	Utilities	1,800	
21b.	Total	3,000	
22, 24, & 25.	Business portion of Line 21		600
26.	Remaining tentative profit		0

No depreciation is deductible because there is no remaining business income and excess home office expenses may not generate a loss deduction. The depreciation is carried over to 2000. Home office expenses of $3,400 from Lines 14 and 25 are deducted on Line 30, Schedule C.

40.16 Home Office for Sideline Business

You may have an occupation and also run a sideline business from an office in your home. The home office expenses are deductible on Form 8829 if the office is a principal place of operating the sideline business or a place to meet with clients, customers, or patients. *See* the deduction tests at *40.12* and the income limit computation at *40.15*. Managing rental property may qualify as a business.

Planning Reminder

Substantiating the Sideline Business

In claiming home office expenses of a sideline business, it is important to be ready to prove that you are actually in business; *see 40.10*. The Tax Court has held that activities in seeking new tenants, supplying furnishings, and cleaning and preparing six units for tenants are sufficiently systematic and continuous to put a person in the rental real estate business. In some cases, the rental of even a single piece of real property may be a business if additional services are provided such as cleaning or maid service.

EXAMPLE

A doctor is employed full time by a hospital. He also owns six rental properties that he personally manages. He uses one bedroom in his two-bedroom home exclusively as an office to manage the properties. The room is furnished with a desk, bookcase, filing cabinet, calculators, and answering service; furnishings and other materials for preparing rental units for tenants are stored there. He may deduct expenses allocable to the home office.

Managing your own securities portfolio. Investors managing their own securities portfolios may find it difficult to convince a court that investment management is a business activity. According to Congressional committee reports, a home office deduction should be denied to an investor who uses a home office to read financial periodicals and reports, clip bond coupons, and perform similar activities. In one case, the Claims Court allowed a deduction to Moller, who spent about 40 hours a week at a home office managing a substantial stock portfolio. The Claims Court held these activities amounted to a business. However, an appeals court reversed the decision. According to the appeals court, the test is whether or not a person is a trader. A trader is in a business; an investor is not. A trader buys and sells frequently to catch daily market swings. An investor buys securities for capital appreciation and income without regard to daily market developments. Therefore, to be a trader, one's activities must be directed to short-term trading, not the long-term holding of investments. Here, Moller was an investor; he was primarily interested in the long-term growth potential of stock. He did not earn his income from the short-term turnovers of stocks. He had no significant trading profits. His interest and dividend income was 98% of his income.

40.17 Depreciation of Office in Cooperative Apartment

If your home office meets the tests discussed in *40.12*, you may deduct depreciation on your stock interest in the cooperative. The basis for depreciation may be your share of the cooperative corporation's basis for the building or an amount computed from the price you paid for the stock. The method you use depends on whether you are the first or a later owner of the stock.

You are the first owner. In figuring your depreciation, you start with the cooperative's depreciable basis of the building. You then take your share of depreciation according to the percentage of stock interest you own. The cooperative can provide the details needed for the computation.

If space in the building is rented to commercial tenants who do not have stock interests in the corporation, the total allowable depreciation is reduced by the amount allocated to the space used by the commercial tenants.

You are a later owner of the cooperative's stock. When you buy stock from a prior owner, your depreciable basis is determined by the price of your stock and your share of the coop's outstanding mortgage, reduced by amounts allocable to land and to commercial space.

Figuring Net Operating Losses for Refund of Prior Taxes

40.18 Net Operating Losses for Refund of Prior Taxes

A loss incurred in your profession or unincorporated business is deducted from other income reported on Form 1040. If a 1999 loss (plus any casualty loss) exceeds income, the excess may be first carried back to 1997 and 1998, and *then* forward 20 years to 2000 through 2019 until it is used up. However, a five-year carryback period is allowed for farming losses and a three-year carryback period is allowed in the case of individual casualty and theft losses and for certain small businesses suffering disaster losses; *see* the Law Alert on the right. A loss carried back to a prior year reduces income of that year and entitles you to a refund. A loss applied to a later year reduces income for that year. You may elect to carry forward your 1999 loss for 20 years, foregoing the carryback; *see 40.22*.

The rules below apply not only to self-employed individuals, farmers, and professionals, but also to individuals whose casualty losses exceed income, stockholders in S corporations, and partners whose partnerships have suffered losses. Each partner claims his or her share of the partnership loss.

Carryover of loss from prior year to 1999. If you had a net operating loss in an earlier year that is being carried forward to 1999, the loss carryover is reported as a minus figure on Line 21 of Form 1040. You must attach a detailed statement showing how you figured the carryover.

Net operating losses from tax years beginning on or before August 5, 1997, expire after 15 carryforward years.

Change in marital status. If you incur a net operating loss while single but are married filing jointly in a carryback or carryforward year, the loss may be used only to offset your own income on the joint return.

If the net operating loss was claimed on a joint return and in the carryback or carryforward year you are not filing jointly with the same spouse, only your allocable share of the original loss may be claimed; *see* IRS Publication 536.

Passive activity limitation. Losses subject to passive activity rules of Chapter 10 are not deductible as net operating losses. However, losses of rental operations coming within the $25,000 allowance discussed at *10.2* may be treated as a net operating loss if the loss exceeds passive and other income.

Restrictions on loss after accounting method change. You may realize a net operating loss for a short taxable year created by the accounting change. As a condition of allowing the accounting method change, the IRS may require you to forego the right to a loss carryback and agree to a six-year carryforward period.

EXAMPLE

You want to change from a calendar year to a fiscal year ending April 30. Assume further that May through October is your peak selling period. Thus, you may have a net operating loss for the short taxable year January 1–April 30 because of slack business. According to the IRS, if the net operating loss is $10,000 or less, you may apply the regular net operating loss rules that allow you to carry back the loss three years and then forward 15 years. But if the net operating loss exceeds $10,000 and the short period is less than nine months, the operating loss must be deducted ratably over a six-year period starting with the first tax year after the short period.

Law Alert

Carryback and Carryforward Periods

For tax years beginning after August 5, 1997, the carryback period is generally two years; the carryforward period is 20 years. However, the prior law three-year carryback period applies to net operating losses attributable to Presidentially declared disasters incurred by qualifying small businesses. A qualifying small business is a corporation or partnership that has average gross receipts over a three-year period of $5 million or less.

For individual taxpayers, a three-year carryback period applies for net operating losses attributable to casualty and theft losses.

A farming net operating loss arising in a tax year beginning after 1997 may be carried back five years. An election may be made to forego the five-year carryback. If the election to forego the five-year carryback is made, a three-year carryback may be claimed for a farming loss incurred in a Presidentially declared disaster; otherwise, the general two-year carryback period applies. The three-year (disaster loss) or two-year carryback period also applies for a farming business loss incurred in a tax year beginning after August 5, 1997, and before 1998.

40.19 Your Net Operating Loss

A net operating loss is generally the excess of deductible business expenses over business income. The net operating loss may also include the following losses and deductions:

- Casualty and theft losses, even if the property was used for personal purposes; *see* Chapter 18.
- Expenses of moving to a new job location; *see* Chapter 12.
- Deductible job expenses such as travel expenses, work clothes, costs, and union dues; *see 19.3.*
- Your share of a partnership or S corporation operating loss.
- Loss on the sale of Small Business Investment Company stock.
- Loss incurred on Section 1244 stock.

An operating loss may *not* include:

- Net operating loss carryback or carryover from any year.
- Capital losses that exceed capital gain.
- Excess of nonbusiness deductions over nonbusiness income plus nonbusiness net capital gain.
- Deductions for personal exemptions.
- A self-employed person's contribution to a Keogh plan.
- An IRA deduction.

Income from other sources may eliminate or reduce your net operating loss.

EXAMPLE

You are self-employed and incur a business loss of $10,000. Your spouse earns a salary of $10,000. When you file a joint return, your business loss will be eliminated by your spouse's salary. Similarly, if you also had salary from another position, the salary would reduce your business loss.

40.20 Form 1045

You compute your net operating loss deduction on Form 1045. You start with adjusted gross income and personal deductions shown on your tax return. As these figures include items not allowed for net operating loss purposes, you follow the line-by-line steps of Form 1045 to eliminate them. That is, you reduce the loss by the nonallowed items such as deductions for personal exemptions, net capital loss, and nonbusiness deductions exceeding nonbusiness income. On the schedule, the reductions are described as adjustments. The Example at the end of this section illustrates the steps in the schedule.

Adjustment for nonbusiness deductions. Nonbusiness deductions that exceed nonbusiness income may not be included in a net operating loss deduction. Nonbusiness deductions include deductions for IRA and Keogh plans and itemized deductions such as charitable contributions, interest expense, state taxes, and medical expenses. Do not include in this non-allowed group deductible casualty and theft losses, which for net operating loss purposes are treated as business losses. If you do not claim itemized deductions in the year of the loss, you must treat the standard deduction as a nonbusiness deduction.

Nonbusiness income is income that is *not* from a trade or business—such as dividends, interest, and annuity income. The excess of nonbusiness capital gains over nonbusiness capital losses is also treated as part of nonbusiness income that offsets nonbusiness deductions.

EXAMPLE

Income from dividends and interest is $6,000 and nonbusiness deductions are $6,500. The excess deduction of $500 is an adjustment that reduces your loss on Form 1045.

At-risk loss limitations. The loss used to figure your net operating loss deduction is subject to the at-risk rules discussed at *10.17.* If part of your investment is in nonrecourse loans or is otherwise not at risk, you must compute your deductible loss on Form 6198, which you attach to Form 1040. The deductible loss from Form 6198 is reflected in the income and deduction figures you enter on the Form 1045 schedule to compute your net operating loss deduction.

 Filing Instruction

Adjustment for Capital Losses

A net nonbusiness capital loss may not be included in a net operating loss. If nonbusiness capital losses exceed nonbusiness capital gains, the excess is an adjustment that reduces your loss on Form 1045. In figuring your loss, you may take into account business capital losses only up to the total of business capital gains plus any nonbusiness capital gains remaining after the adjustment for nonbusiness deductions.

EXAMPLE

You are single and in 1999 you have a salary of $3,000, interest of $1,200, a net business loss of $10,000 (income of $50,000 and expenses of $60,000), itemized Schedule A deductions of $6,000, and a net nonbusiness capital gain of $1,000. After the required addbacks and adjustments are made, your net operating loss is $6,950. The following computation approximates the steps of the Form 1045 computation schedule starting from the line showing your negative adjusted gross income of $4,800.

Salary		$3,000
Interest		1,200
Capital gain income		1,000
Business loss		($10,000)
Adjusted gross income		($4,800)
Add: Exemption and itemized deductions		(8,700)
		($13,500)
Adjustments:		
Exemption	$2,750	
Excess nonbusiness deduction *	3,800	6,550
Net operating loss		($6,950)

The excess nonbusiness expenses deduction was figured as follows:

Itemized deductions		$6,000
Net capital gain income	$1,000	
Interest income	1,200	2,200
Excess		$3,800

40.21 How To Carry Back Your Net Operating Loss

Tax year 1997 is generally the first year to which you may carry back your 1999 net operating loss; *see 40.18* for exceptions allowing a five-year or three-year carryback. When you carry back the loss to 1997, you recompute your 1997 tax on Form 1045 by deducting the 1999 net operating loss. The net operating loss is deducted from the amount of your original 1997 adjusted gross income. Because of the reduction to adjusted gross income, you have to increase any 1997 medical expense and casualty loss deduction when recomputing 1997 income. You do not have to change the amount of your 1997 charitable deduction. *See* the instructions to Form 1045 and also IRS Publication 536 for details of the recomputation calculation.

After recomputing the 1997 tax on Form 1045, your refund is the difference between the tax originally paid for 1997 and the lower tax figured after deducting the net operating loss deduction.

Use Form 1045 as a "quick refund" claim. The IRS will usually allow or reject your claim within 90 days from the time you file Form 1045. Do not attach Form 1045 to your 1999 Form 1040. File Form 1045 separately, together with a copy of your return. You may file Form 1045 within 12 months after the end of your tax year. Thus, if you are a calendar-year taxpayer, you have until December 31, 2000, to carry back a 1999 loss to 1997 on Form 1045. If the IRS allows the refund, it may still determine later that the refund was excessive and assess additional tax.

Although using Form 1045 is the quickest way to obtain the refund, you may instead file an amended return on Form 1040X to claim the refund. You have three years after the due date (including extensions) of your 1999 tax return to file Form 1040X. Thus, to claim a refund on Form 1040X for 1997, because of a net operating loss carried back from 1999, you have until April 15, 2003, to file. On Form 1040X, you must attach a statement detailing how the loss carryback was figured; the schedule from Form 1045 for computing the loss may be used.

Operating losses from more than one year. If you have more than one year net operating loss to be carried to the same taxable year, you apply the loss from the earliest year first.

40.22 Election To Carry Forward Losses

Instead of carrying back your 1999 net operating loss under the rules of *40.21*, you may elect to forego the carryback. Instead, you just carry forward losses. The carryforward period remains 20 years under the election. The election is irrevocable.

If you are carrying forward a net operating loss from an earlier year to 1999, report the loss carryover as a minus figure on Line 21 of Form 1040 and attach a statement explaining how the carryover was computed.

 Planning Reminder

Advantage of Relinquishing the Carryback

You will generally make the election to relinquish the carryback if you expect greater tax savings by carrying the loss forward. You might also make the election if you are concerned you might be audited for earlier years if you carry back a loss for a refund. You make the election by attaching a statement to this effect to your return for the year of the loss, which must be filed by the due date plus extensions. The IRS refuses to allow a late election and received court approval for its position.

Business Tax Credits

40.23 General Business Credit

The *general business credit* includes the following credits:

- The work opportunity credit on Form 5884;
- The investment credit on Form 3468, consisting of the rehabilitation property credit, the energy credit, and the reforestation credit;
- The alcohol fuels credit on Form 6478;
- The research credit on Form 6765;
- The low-income housing credit on Form 8586;
- The enhanced oil recovery credit on Form 8830;
- The disabled access credit on Form 8826;
- The welfare-to-work credit on Form 8861;
- The renewable electricity production credit on Form 8835;
- The credit for wages paid in an empowerment zone on Form 8844;
- The Indian employment credit on Form 8845;
- The orphan drug credit on Form 8820;
- The credit for employer-paid Social Security and Medicare taxes on certain tips received by employees of food and beverage establishments on Form 8846; *and*
- The credit for contributions to certain community development corporations on Form 8847.

The low-income housing credit and the rehabilitation tax credit are discussed at *31.8.*

Computing the general business credit. You compute each credit separately. If you claim only one credit, that credit is considered your *general business credit* for 1999. The credit is subject to a limitation based on tax liability that is figured on the form used to compute that particular credit. You then enter the allowable credit as your general business credit on Form 1040.

If you claim more than one credit, the credits are combined into one general business credit on Form 3800, except for the empowerment zone wages credit, which is figured on Form 8844 and not carried to Form 3800. Each of the other credits is first computed separately and then listed on Form 3800. The combined credit is subject to a limitation based on tax liability. To figure the limit, you must compute tentative alternative minimum tax (AMT) on Form 6251 even if the complete computation on Form 6251 shows that you do not have an actual AMT liability for the year. Your limit for the general business credit on Form 3800 is your regular tax liability (after tax credits other than the general business credit), *plus* actual AMT liability from Form 6251 (if any), *minus* whichever of the following is larger: either (1) tentative AMT from Form 6251 or (2) 25% of your regular income tax liability (after other credits) over $25,000.

Keep separate records of each of the component credits making up the general business credit. The credits are considered to be used up in a specific order; *see* the instructions to Form 3800.

If your full 1999 general business credit may not be claimed because of the tax liability limitation, you may be able to *carry back* the excess one year, starting with the earliest year. Check the Form 3800 instructions for restrictions on carrying back certain credits. After the carryback, any remaining credit may be *carried forward* 20 years until used up. The carrybacks and carryforwards are listed on Form 3800.

For credits arising in tax years beginning before 1998, the carryback period is three years; the carryforward period is 15 years.

If you have business credits from a passive activity under the rules discussed in Chapter 10, you must figure the credits on Form 8582-CR; generally, the credits are limited to the tax liability from passive activities.

40.24 Other Fuel-Related Credits

For a qualified business use, a refundable credit may be claimed for *gasoline or special fuels.* For example, a credit applies for fuel used in non-highway vehicles (other than motorboats), including generators, compressors, fork-lift trucks, and bulldozers. A credit may also be claimed for aviation fuel used for farming or commercial aviation. Different credit rates apply depending on the type of fuel. You must claim the credit on a timely filed income tax return, including extensions. You compute the credit on Form 4136, which you attach to Form 1040. For further details, *see* IRS Publication 378; farmers should *see* IRS Publication 225.

Law Alert

Carryback and Carryforward

For credits arising in tax years starting after 1997, the carryback period has been reduced to one year from three years, and the carryforward period increased to 20 years from 15 years.

Retirement Plans for Self-Employed

Self-employed persons and partners can take advantage of tax-sheltered Keogh retirement plans or simplified employee pension plans (SEP).

Advantages flow from: (1) tax deductions allowed for contributions to the plan (a form of forced savings); (2) tax-free accumulations of income earned on assets held by the plan; and (3) in some cases, special averaging for lump-sum benefits paid from a Keogh plan on retirement.

If you have employees, you must consider the cost of covering them when setting up your plan.

If you do not have any other retirement plan and have no more than 100 employees, you may set up a salary-reduction SIMPLE IRA plan.

41.1 Who May Set Up a Keogh Plan?

You may set up a self-employed retirement plan called a *Keogh plan* if you earn self-employment income from personal services and have *net earnings* (gross business or professional income less allowable business deductions) from the business for which the plan is established. Income earned abroad and excluded from federal income tax is not considered earned income for purposes of the plan. If you are an inactive owner, such as a limited partner, you do not qualify to set up a Keogh plan—unless you receive guaranteed payments for services that are treated as earnings from self-employment.

Partnership plans. An individual partner or partners, although self-employed, may not set up a Keogh plan. The plan must be established by the partnership. Partnership deductions for contributions to an individual partner's account are reported on the partner's Schedule K-1 (Form 1065) and deducted by the partner as an adjustment to income on Line 29 of Form 1040.

Including employees in your plan. You must include in your plan all employees who have reached age 21 with at least one year of service. An employee may be required to complete two years of service before participating if your plan provides for full and immediate vesting after no more than two years. You generally are not required to cover seasonal or part-time employees who work less than 1,000 hours during a 12-month period.

Your plan may not exclude employees who are over a certain age.

A plan may not discriminate in favor of officers or other highly compensated personnel. Benefits must be for the employees and their beneficiaries, and their plan rights may not be subject to forfeiture. A plan may not allow any of its funds to be diverted for purposes other than pension benefits. Contributions made on your behalf may not exceed the ratio of contributions made on behalf of employees.

41.2 Choosing a Keogh Plan

There are two types of Keogh plans: defined-benefit plans and defined-contribution plans, and different rules apply to each. A defined-benefit plan provides in advance for a specific retirement benefit funded by quarterly contributions based on an IRS formula and actuarial assumptions. A defined-contribution plan does not fix a specific retirement benefit, but rather sets the amount of annual contributions so that the amount of retirement benefits depends on contributions and income earned on those contributions. If contributions are geared to profits, the plan is a profit-sharing plan. A plan that requires fixed contributions regardless of profits is a money-purchase plan.

A defined-benefit plan may prove costly if you have older employees who also must be provided with proportionate defined benefits. Furthermore, a defined-benefit plan requires you to contribute to their accounts even if you do not have profits. The maximum annual retirement benefit for basing 1999 plan year contributions may not exceed the lesser of (a) 100% of the participant's average compensation for the three consecutive years of highest compensation as an active participant, and (b) $130,000. The $130,000 limit may have to be reduced if benefits begin before the Social Security age, which is currently 65. The $130,000 limit might be increased for future years by an inflation adjustment. All plans of a controlled group of businesses are aggregated for purposes of the limitations applied to defined benefits. A defined-benefit plan or defined-contribution plan may take into account Social Security benefits for employees subject to technical nondiscrimination limitations.

A minimum coverage rule requiring that a plan must include at least 40% of all employees (or 50 employees if that is less) applies only to defined benefit plans for years beginning after 1996.

Setting up a trust for investing in Keoghs. If you are interested in following an aggressive investment policy for funds in your Keogh plan, you will set up a trust to receive Keogh contributions. You may name yourself or an independent trustee to oversee the plan.

If you use funds to buy nontransferable annuity contracts from an insurance company, use of a trust is optional. Premium payments may be made directly to the insurance company. The annuity contract may pay a fixed monthly income for life or for a fixed period of years, or may be a variable annuity contract. Life insurance can be included only if it is incidental to retirement benefits.

If you are investing in savings certificates, you need not set up a trust; you may use a custodial account with the bank.

Planning Reminder

Employees Who Are Self-Employed on the Side

If you are an employee-member of a company retirement plan, you may set up a Keogh plan if you carry on a self-employed enterprise or profession on the side. For example, you are employed by a company that has a qualified 401(k) plan to which you make salary deferrals. At the same time, you have a sideline consulting business. You may set up a Keogh plan based on your consultant earnings. Each plan is independent of the other. As an alternative to a Keogh plan, you may contribute to a simplified employee pension plan (SEP), as discussed in *41.4*, or a SIMPLE IRA, discussed in *41.11*.

41.3 Top-Heavy Plan Restrictions

"Top-heavy" plan rules, which apply to corporate plans favoring "key employees," may also apply to a Keogh plan of a self-employed person. The top-heavy rules apply if more than 60% of the account balances or accrued benefits are for key employees; *see* below for the definition of "key employees." Even if your Keogh plan is not currently considered top heavy, your plan may be disqualified, unless it includes provisions that would automatically take effect if the plan becomes top heavy. The major top-heavy restriction requires an accelerated vesting schedule. There is also a lower limit on benefits where a key employee participates in both a defined-contribution plan and defined-benefit plan.

Vesting. A top-heavy plan must provide either 100% vesting after three years of service or graded vesting at the rate of at least 20% after two years of service, 40% after three years of service, 60% after four years of service, 80% after five years of service, and 100% after six years of service. There may be an advantage in electing three-year vesting if you have a high turnover of employees.

The $160,000 pay limit. The first $160,000 of a self-employed person's net earnings in 1999 is considered in determining deductible contributions, whether or not the plan is top heavy. The $160,000 limit may be adjusted for inflation.

Distributions before age 59 $\frac{1}{2}$. The 10% penalty for distributions before age 59 $\frac{1}{2}$ *(7.15)* applies whether or not the plan is top heavy. The penalty does not apply to distributions made because you are disabled. Other exceptions to the penalty are listed at *7.15*.

The IRS has ruled that a tax-free rollover may be made when the Keogh plan is terminated. A timely rollover will avoid the 10% penalty on premature distributions if the recipient is under age 59 $\frac{1}{2}$.

Retirement plan bonds. If you invested Keogh plan funds in Treasury Department Retirement Plan Bonds before May 1, 1982, you may redeem them at any time, even if you are under age 59 $\frac{1}{2}$. To avoid immediate tax, a rollover may be made within 60 days to an IRA or qualified pension or profit-sharing plan.

Who are key employees? The above top-heavy restrictions apply if more than 60% of a defined-contribution plan account balances or more than 60% of the accrued benefits of a defined-benefit plan are for key employees. For the 1999 plan year, key employees are employees who at any time during the plan year own: (1) one of the 10 largest ownership interests and have compensation exceeding $30,000; (2) more than a 5% interest; or (3) more than a 1% interest and also earn compensation of more than $150,000. Officers are considered key employees for 1999 if they have compensation exceeding $65,000. Key employee treatment also applies if the employee was a key employee in any of the four preceding years under the applicable compensation limit for such year. The $30,000 and $65,000 amounts are subject to annual inflation adjustments.

41.4 Choosing a SEP

Under a SEP (simplified employee pension plan), you may contribute to a special type of IRA more than is allowed under the regular IRA rules. Contributions do not have to be made every year. When you do make contributions, they must be based on a written allocation formula and must not discriminate in favor of yourself, other owners with more than a 5% interest, or highly compensated employees. Coverage requirements for employees are at *8.15*. A salary-reduction arrangement for employees may be provided under a qualifying SEP established before 1997 or under a SIMPLE IRA plan established after 1996; *see 8.17*.

Deductible contributions to your personal SEP account for 1999 may not exceed 13.0435% of your net earnings (less 50% of self-employment tax liability) or $24,000, whichever is less; *see 41.5*.

The deadline for both setting up and contributing to a SEP is the due date for your return, *including extensions.* Thus, if you have not set up a Keogh plan by the end of the taxable year *(41.1)*, you may still make a deductible retirement contribution for the year by contributing to a SEP by the due date of your return.

41.5 Deductible Keogh or SEP Contributions

The deductible limit for a Keogh plan depends on whether you have a defined-contribution plan (profit-sharing or money-purchase pension plan) or a defined-benefit plan. A SEP is treated as a profit-sharing plan subject to the defined-contribution plan deduction limits explained below.

If you have a defined-benefit plan, you generally may deduct contributions needed to produce the accrued benefits provided for by the plan. This is a complicated calculation requiring actuarial computations that call for the services of a pension expert.

 Caution

Prohibited Transactions

As an owner-employee (owning more than 10% of the business), your dealings with the Keogh trust are subject to restrictions. You are generally subject to penalties if you borrow funds from the trust *(41.9)*; buy property from or sell property to the trust; or charge any fees for services you render to the trust. These restrictions also apply to any member of your immediate family and any corporation in which you own more than half the voting stock, either directly or indirectly.

Deductible contribution rate for a defined-contribution Keogh Plan or a SEP. Before figuring the deductible contribution you can make for 1999 to a profit-sharing Keogh or SEP account, or to a money-purchase pension plan, you must first figure your self-employment tax liability on Schedule SE and the 50% deduction for self-employment tax to be claimed on Line 27 of Form 1040. In computing your deductible plan contribution, your net profit from Line 31 of Schedule C, Line 3 of Schedule C-EZ, or Line 36 of Schedule F is *reduced* by the deduction for 50% of self-employment tax; *see* the Example on the next page.

As a self-employed person, you are *not* allowed to figure the deductible contribution for yourself by applying the contribution rate stated in your plan. The rate must be reduced, as required by law, to reflect the reduction of net earnings by the deductible contribution itself. If your plan rate is a whole number, the reduced percentage is shown in the table below.

 Caution

Deadline for Setting Up Keogh Plan or SEP

You must formally set up a Keogh plan in writing on or before the end of the taxable year in which you want the plan to be effective. For example, if you want to make a contribution for 1999, your plan must be set up on or before December 31, 1999, if you report on a calendar-year basis. If a profit-sharing Keogh plan is established by the end of 1999, you have up until the due date for filing your return, plus extensions, to make a deductible contribution within the limits of *41.5*.

If you miss the deadline for setting up a Keogh plan, you may contribute to a simplified employee pension plan (SEP) set up by the filing deadline for Form 1040, including extensions. *See 41.4.*

Self-Employed Person's Contribution Rate Table

If plan rate is—	Self-employed person's reduced rate is—
1%	.009901
2	.019608
3	.029126
4	.038462
5	.047619
6	.056604
7	.065421
8	.074074
9	.082569
10	.090909
11	.099099
12	.107143
13	.115044
14	.122807
15*	.130435*
16	.137931
17	.145299
18	.152542
19	.159664
20	.166667
21	.173554
22	.180328
23	.186992
24	.193548
25**	.200000**

*The maximum deduction percentage for contributions to your own profit-sharing Keogh account or to your own SEP account is 13.0435%. For your employees, the maximum rate is 15%.
**The maximum deduction percentage for contributions to your own money-purchase Keogh plan is 20%; for employees it is 25%.

Fractional rates. If the plan rate is fractional and thus not listed in the table above, figure your deductible percentage this way:

1. Write the plan rate as a decimal. For example, if the plan rate is 10.5%, write .105 as the decimal amount.
2. Add 1 to the decimal rate. For example, if the rate is .105, the result is 1.105.
3. Divide Step 1 by Step 2. This gives you the deductible percentage. If the plan rate is .105, the deductible percentage is .095023 (.105 ÷ 1.105).

Figuring your maximum deductible contribution. After figuring your net earnings and reducing that amount by 50% of your self-employment tax liability, you multiply the balance by the adjusted rate from the Self-Employed Person's Rate Table or the fractional rate discussed above.

This is generally your maximum deductible contribution. However, your deduction for 1999 contributions may not exceed the *lesser* of (1) $30,000 and (2) $160,000, multiplied by the stated plan contribution rate shown in the left column of the above Self-Employed Person's Rate Table. The maximum amount of compensation that can be taken into account for 1999 is $160,000.

The following Example illustrates the computation of the maximum deductible contribution.

EXAMPLE

You are a sole proprietor with no employees and have a profit-sharing plan that provides for a 15% contribution rate. Your net self-employment earnings for 1999 from Line 31 of Schedule C are $147,000. On Schedule SE, you figure your self-employment tax liability of $12,939, and you claim a 50% deduction for self-employment taxes of $6,470 ($\frac{1}{2}$ of $12,939 self-employment tax from Schedule SE) on Line 27 of Form 1040. Your maximum deductible profit-sharing contribution is $18,330:

Step 1.	Net earnings reduced by 50% of self-employment tax liability ($147,000 − $6,470)	$140,530
Step 2.	Self-employed person's rate in the right column of the table on the preceding page	.130435
Step 3.	Step 2 rate multiplied by Step 1 reduced net earnings ($140,530 × .130435)	$18,330
Step 4.	Overall contribution limit for 1999: $160,000 multiplied by 15% plan rate, but no more than $30,000	$24,000
Step 5.	Lesser of Step 3 and Step 4. This is your maximum deductible contribution	$18,330

Money-purchase plan may supplement profit-sharing plan. A money-purchase plan requires an employer to make fixed contributions each year, without regard to profit.

As shown in the table on the preceding page, the maximum deduction percentage for a self-employed person's money-purchase plan is 20% (25% for regular employees).

Contributions for your employees. The deduction complications that apply to your own contributions do not apply to contributions for employees. You make contributions for your employees at the rate specified in your plan, based upon their 1999 compensation (but the contribution may not exceed the lesser of $30,000 and $160,000 multiplied by the plan contribution rate). Thus, in the Example above, you would contribute 15% of your employees' pay to the plan. You deduct contributions for employees when figuring your net earnings from self-employment on Schedule C or Schedule F before figuring your own deductible contribution using the steps shown in the Example above.

Contributions allowed after age 70$^1/_2$. You may continue to make contributions for yourself to a Keogh plan or SEP as long as you have self-employment income. However, you must begin to receive required minimum distributions from a SEP by April 1 of the year following the year in which you reach age 70$^1/_2$; *see 8.15.* This age 70$^1/_2$ required distribution beginning date also applies to a Keogh plan if you are a more-than-5% owner of the business; *see 7.13.*

Excess contributions. Contributions to a profit-sharing plan exceeding the 13.0435% deduction ceiling (15% for your employees) may be carried over and deducted in later years subject to the ceiling for those years. However, if contributions exceed the deductible amount, you are generally subject to a 10% penalty on nondeductible contributions that are not returned by the end of

Planning reminder

Money Purchase Plan

To maximize your deductible contributions, you may establish a separate money-purchase plan to supplement a profit-sharing plan. A bank or other plan trustee can help you set up separate plans and stay within your overall contribution limit of 20% of net earnings.

41.6 How To Claim the Keogh or SEP Deduction

Contributions made to your Keogh or SEP account as a self-employed person are deducted as an adjustment to gross income on Line 29 of Form 1040. A deduction for a contribution made for your benefit may not be part of a net operating loss.

Contributions for your employees are entered as deductions on Schedule C (or Schedule F) for purposes of computing profit or loss from your business. Trustees' fees not provided for by contributions are deductible in addition to the maximum contribution deduction.

Deductible Keogh plan contributions may generally be made at any time up to the due date of your return, including any extension of time. However, the plan itself must be set up before the close of the taxable year for which the deduction is sought. If you miss the December 31 deadline for setting up a Keogh plan, you have at least up to April 17, 2000, to set up a SEP for 1999. If you have a filing extension, you have until the extended due date to set up a SEP and make your contribution.

41.7 How To Qualify a Keogh Plan or SEP Plan

You may set up a Keogh plan and contribute to it without advance approval. But since advance approval is advisable, you may, in a determination letter, ask the IRS to review your plan. Approval requirements depend on whether you set up your own administered plan or join a master plan administered by a bank, insurance company, mutual fund, or a prototype plan sponsored by a trade or professional association. If you start your own individually designed plan, you may apply for a determination letter on Form 5300 whether the plan is a defined-benefit plan or defined-contribution plan. You must pay a fee to the IRS when you apply for a determination letter. File Form 8717 showing your fee, together with Form 5300.

If you join a master or prototype plan, the sponsoring organization applies to the IRS for approval of its plan. You should then be given a copy of the approved plan and copies of any subsequent amendments.

To set up a SEP with a bank, broker, or other financial institution, you do not need IRS approval. If you do not maintain any other qualified retirement plan and other tests are met, a model SEP may be adopted using Form 5305-SEP. To adopt a SEP with a qualifying salary-reduction arrangement *(8.16)*, you may be able to use Form 5305A-SEP.

41.8 Annual Keogh Plan Return

Partial relief from one burdensome IRS paperwork requirement may be available if your pension or profit-sharing Keogh plan covers only yourself, or you and your spouse, or you and your business partners and spouses. Such plans are treated as one-participant plans by the IRS.

One-participant plans that hold more than $100,000 at the end of any plan year beginning on or after January 1, 1994, must file a Form 5500-EZ for the first year the assets exceed $100,000 and for each year thereafter, even if total plan assets are reduced to $100,000 or less. For example, if plan assets in a plan that otherwise satisfies the requirements for filing the Form 5500-EZ totaled $110,000 at the end of the 1998 plan year, and a distribution occurred in 1999 so that plan assets totaled $85,000 at the end of the 1999 plan year, a Form 5500-EZ must still be filed for the 1999 plan year.

The Form 5500-EZ due date for a 1999 calendar-year plan is July 31, 2000, unless an extension is obtained from the IRS.

The $100,000 exception applies if you, or you and your spouse, are sole proprietors or sole shareholders of a corporation maintaining the plan. The exception also applies if your business is operated as a partnership and the only plan participants are partners and their spouses.

You must file Form 5500-EZ for the final plan year regardless of the amount of plan assets.

If you cannot use Form 5500-EZ, you must file Form 5500-C/R if there are fewer than 100 plan participants (Form 5500 if there are 100 or more participants). On Form 5500-C/R, you check a box indicating whether the form is being filed as a Form 5500-C or Form 5500-R. Form 5500-R is a shorter form that may be used for a plan year that is not the first plan year or final plan year, provided that you used the longer Form 5500-C for at least one of the two prior plan years. Thus, after the first year, Form 5500-R may be filed in two of every three years. Only some of the Form 5500-C/R pages are filled in by Form 5500-R filers; follow the form instructions. The form must be filed by the end of the seventh month following the end of the plan year. There are penalties for late filing, unless you show reasonable cause or an extension is obtained; follow the Form 5500-C/R instructions for extension rules.

 Caution

Individually Designed Keogh Plans

You can set up an individually designed Keogh plan without advance IRS approval, but it is advisable to get professional assistance and request a determination letter from the IRS.

be filed by the end of the seventh month following the end of the plan year. There are penalties for late filing, unless you show reasonable cause or an extension is obtained; follow the Form 5500-C/R instructions for extension rules.

Electronic filing allowed. Forms 5500-EZ and 5500-C/R may be filed electronically or on magnetic tape by qualifying tax return filers. To file electronically or on magnetic tape, the plan administrator must provide a signed declaration on Form 8453-E.

41.9 Restrictions on Loans

Keogh plan loans to an owner-employee (more than 10% ownership) are subject to prohibited transaction penalties. There are two penalties: (1) a 15% first tier penalty and (2) a 100% penalty.

The 15% penalty applies in the year of the loan and in later years until the loan is repaid with interest. The penalty is figured on a fair market interest factor that is explained in the instructions to Form 5330. You are required to report loans to the IRS on Form 5330 and pay the 15% penalty when you file the form. Form 5330 must be filed within seven months after the end of the taxable year; *see* Form 5330 instructions for filing extension rules.

The 100% penalty is imposed if the loan is not repaid. The penalty may be avoided by repaying the loan within 90 days after the IRS sends a deficiency notice for the 100% tax. The 90-day period may be extended by the IRS to allow you a reasonable time for repayment.

Exception. If you are an owner-employee, you may apply to the Department of Labor for a special exemption from the prohibited transaction penalties.

Keogh plan loans treated as taxable distributions. Self-employed individuals are taxable on certain loans from their Keogh plan under the same rules applied to regular employees, as discussed at *7.16*.

41.10 How Keogh Plan Distributions Are Taxed

Distributions from a Keogh plan generally may not be received without penalty before age 59 ½ unless you are disabled or meet the other exceptions listed at *7.15*. If you are a more-than-5% owner you must begin to receive minimum required distributions by April 1 of the year following the year in which you reach age 70 ½; penalties may apply if an insufficient distribution is received *(see 7.13)*.

A lump-sum distribution may be rolled over tax free to an IRA or other qualified plan and in limited circumstances special averaging is available; *see 7.2* for details. Pension distributions from a Keogh are taxed under the annuity rules discussed in *7.25*, but for purposes of figuring your cost investment, include only nondeductible voluntary contributions; deductible contributions made on your behalf are not part of your investment.

If you receive amounts in excess of the benefits provided for you under the plan formula and you own more than a 5% interest in the employer, the excess benefit is subject to a 10% penalty. The penalty also applies if you were a more-than-5% owner at any time during the five plan years preceding the plan year that ends within the year of an excess distribution.

Other rules discussed at *7.1* to *7.16* apply to Keogh plans as well as qualified corporate plans.

After the death of a Keogh plan owner, distributions to beneficiaries may be spread over the periods discussed at *7.14*.

SEP distributions. Distributions from a SEP are subject to the IRA rules at *8.8*.

41.11 SIMPLE IRA Plans

If you do not maintain any other retirement plan and have 100 or fewer employees, you may set up a salary-reduction type of plan for yourself and your employees. The SIMPLE IRA contribution rules are discussed at *8.18*. A SIMPLE plan may also be made as part of a 401(k) plan; *see 7.17*.

Under a SIMPLE IRA for 1999, you may contribute to your own account $6,000 of net earnings. You may also make a "matching" contribution of up to 3% of your net earnings.

If you have employees, they generally may make elective salary-reduction contributions up to $6,000. You must make a 3% matching contribution unless you choose to make a 2% non-elective contribution.

The $6,000 contribution limit may be increased for 2000 by an inflation adjustment.

See 8.17 and *8.18* for further details on SIMPLE IRAs.

Caution

Loans From SEP Are Prohibited

Borrowing from a SEP is a prohibited transaction under the IRA rules and will result in the loss of the account's tax-exempt status. The account will be treated as if it were distributed to you on the first day of the year; *see 8.8*.

Claiming Depreciation Deductions

There are two methods of claiming expense deductions for your purchases of equipment, fixtures, autos, and trucks used in your business:

- First-year expensing (Section 179 deduction), which allows a deduction of up to $19,000 in 1999 and $20,000 in 2000.

- Regular depreciation, which allows a prorated deduction over a period of years. Most business equipment is depreciable under MACRS over a six-year period. MACRS applies to new and used property. The objective of MACRS is to provide rapid depreciation and to eliminate disputes over useful life, salvage value, and depreciation methods. Useful life and depreciation methods are fixed by law; salvage value is treated as zero. If you do not want to use MACRS accelerated rates, you may elect the straight-line method.

Capital investments in buildings are depreciable using the straight-line method; residential buildings are depreciated over 27.5 years; nonresidential real property placed in service after May 12, 1993, is depreciated over 39 years; *see 42.13*. Specific annual rates for each class of property are provided by IRS tables.

Land is not depreciable.

42.1 What Property May Be Depreciated?

Depreciation deductions may be claimed only for property used in your business or other income-producing activity. If the primary purpose of the property is to produce income but it fails to yield any income, the property may still be depreciated.

Depreciation may not be claimed on property held for personal purposes such as a personal residence or pleasure car. If property, such as a car, is used both for business and pleasure, only the business portion may be depreciated.

EXAMPLES

1. An anesthesiologist suspended his practice indefinitely because of malpractice premium rate increases. He continued to maintain his professional competence by taking courses and keeping up his equipment. The IRS ruled that he could not take depreciation on his equipment. Since he was no longer practicing, the depreciation did not relate to a current trade or business.

2. An electrician spent $1,325 on a trailer to carry his tools and protective clothing. Based on a useful life of three years less salvage value of $25, annual depreciation deductions came to $433. However, the IRS claimed that he could not claim depreciation during the months he was unemployed and the trailer was not used. The Tax Court disagreed. Depreciation is allowed as long as the asset is held for use in a trade or business, even though the asset is idle or its use is temporarily suspended due to business conditions.

Nondepreciable assets. Not all assets used in your business or for the production of income may be depreciable. Land is not depreciable, but the cost of landscaping business property may be depreciated if the landscaping is so closely associated with a building that it would have to be destroyed if the building were replaced. Qualifying trees and bushes are depreciable over 15 years.

Property held primarily for sale to customers or property includible in inventory is not depreciable, regardless of its useful life.

Amortization for business intangibles. The cost of goodwill, going concern value, and other intangibles including covenants not to compete, information bases, customer lists, franchises, licenses, and trademarks is amortizable over a 15-year period.

The amortization rule generally applies to property acquired after August 10, 1993. *See 42.18* for further details.

Residences. For depreciation of rented residences, *see 9.5*.

For depreciation of a sublet cooperative apartment or one used in business, *see 40.17*.

Farm property. Farmland is not depreciable; farm machinery and buildings are. Livestock acquired for work, breeding, or dairy purposes and not included in inventory may also be depreciated. For a detailed explanation of the highly technical rules for depreciating farm property and livestock, *see* IRS Publication 225, Farmer's Tax Guide.

Dispute over importance of useful life. According to the Tax Court, under ACRS (1981–86) and current MACRS law, useful life is irrelevant for claiming depreciation if you can show that an asset is subject to exhaustion, wear and tear, or obsolescence. Thus, in the case of antique musical instruments played by professional musicians, depreciation is allowable because of wear and tear, even though the instruments have an indeterminable useful life. Two federal appeals courts have agreed, allowing professional violinists to deduct ACRS depreciation for their instruments.

In a case involving exotic cars that were not used for transportation but for exhibition, MACRS depreciation was allowed because the owner showed that they were subject to obsolescence. The autos were purchased solely for exhibition. The three state-of-the-art autos were a 1987 Lotus Pantera costing $63,000, a Lotus Espirit costing $48,000, and a Ferrari Testarossa costing $290,453. Over a four-year period, the owner deducted depreciation of over $298,000 while reporting gross income from exhibition fees of $96,630. The IRS disallowed the depreciation because the cars had no determinable useful life. The Tax Court allowed the depreciation because such cars are subject to obsolescence in the car-show business when new models appear with newer designs and high-tech features. One witness testified this could occur in some cases within a year.

The Tax Court warned that such exotic cars should not be confused with museum pieces. If they had been museum pieces, such as antique cars, no depreciation would have been allowed because in the case of art objects and antiques used as business assets, the finding of useful life remains irrelevant because such assets are not subject to exhaustion, wear or tear, or obsolescence.

 Caution

Corrections to Prior Year Returns
If you did not deduct the correct amount of depreciation for a prior year, you may be able to make a correction by filing an amended return. However, if you did not deduct the correct amount of depreciation for two or more consecutive years, you must request an accounting method change; *see* IRS Publication 946 for details. *See also 5.20* for adjustments to basis for unclaimed depreciation taken in prior years.

The IRS has announced that it will continue to dispute and litigate cases in which depreciation is claimed on assets with indeterminable useful lives.

42.2 Claiming Depreciation on Your Tax Return

If you report business or professional self-employed income, use Form 4562 for assets placed in service during 1999 and enter the total deduction on Line 13, Schedule C. For claiming depreciation on "listed property" such as cars, computers, and cellular phones, you use Form 4562, regardless of the year placed in service. Listed property is explained at *42.10*. If your only depreciation deduction is for pre-1999 assets, none of which is listed property, you do not need to use Form 4562; figure the deduction on your own worksheet, and enter it on Line 13, Schedule C.

If you are an employee claiming auto expenses, you must use Form 2106 to claim depreciation on an automobile used for business purposes.

If you report rental income on Schedule E, you must use Form 4562 for claiming depreciation on buildings placed in service in 1999. For buildings placed in service before 1999, enter the depreciation deduction directly on Schedule E. If you have a rental loss on Schedule E, your deduction for depreciation and other expenses may have to be included on Form 8582 to figure net passive activity income or loss; *see* Chapter 10.

See the sample Form 4562 and Schedule E in Part 8 of this book.

42.3 First-Year Expensing Deduction

For qualifying business equipment purchased and placed in service in 1999, you may elect to deduct up to $19,000 of the cost. For equipment placed in service by a business in an "enterprise zone," the deduction may be as high as $39,000. For an automobile, the maximum expensing deduction in 1999 is $3,060; *see 43.4*. The portion of cost not eligible for first-year expensing may be recovered by depreciation under the regular MACRS rules. The first-year expensing deduction is technically called the "Section 179 deduction."

You may *not* elect first-year expensing for property purchased before 1999, even if 1999 is the first year you use it for business.

The election is limited to tangible personal property bought in 1999 for business use, such as machinery, office equipment, a computer, car, or truck acquired from nonrelated parties. The deduction is not allowed for buildings, structural components of buildings, furniture or refrigerators used in operating apartment buildings, property held for the production of income, or equipment previously used for personal purposes, such as an automobile bought for pleasure but later used for business.

When to elect first-year expensing. To claim the first-year expensing deduction on Form 4562, which you attach to your Form 1040, you must make the election on an *original* return for the year the property is placed in service (whether or not the return is timely filed). First-year expensing may *not* be claimed on an amended return unless it is filed within the due date for the original return (including extensions). If you fail to make the election on an original return (or on an amended return filed by the due date including extensions) the election is lost. You may not revoke the expensing election without consent from the IRS.

Partial business use. If you use the equipment for both business and personal use, business use must exceed 50% in the year the equipment is first placed into service to claim a first-year expensing deduction. The expensing deduction may be claimed for the cost allocated to business use up to the $19,000 limit; the 1999 limit for a car is $3,060 *(43.4)*.

To elect first-year expensing for "listed property" such as a computer or car *(42.10)*, business use in the first year you use it must exceed 50%. If it does, you show the amount eligible for expensing in the section for "Listed Property" on Form 4562 and then transfer the amount to the part of Form 4562 where the expensing election is claimed.

Figuring the deduction. The maximum expensing deduction in 1999 is $19,000 of the cost of qualifying property and $3,060 for a car *(43.4)*. For business use of less than 100% (but more than 50%), the expensing deduction is limited to the business portion of the cost. As discussed below, the $19,000 limit may have to be reduced because your taxable income is lower than $19,000, eligible purchases exceed $200,000, or you are married filing separately.

If you qualify for the full $19,000 limit, you do not have to claim the entire amount. If in 1999 you place in service more than one item of property, you may allocate the $19,000 deduction between the items. If you placed in service only one item of qualifying property that cost less than $19,000, your deduction is limited to that cost.

Law Alert

Expensing Limit Increases

The expensing limit is scheduled to increase in 2000 to $20,000; in 2001 and 2002 to $24,000; and after 2002 to $25,000.

Legislation has been proposed to increase the deduction limit to $30,000 beginning in 2000.

If you acquire property in a trade-in, the cost eligible for expensing is limited to the cash you paid. You may not include the adjusted basis of the property traded in, although your basis for the new property includes that amount.

Effect on regular depreciation. If the cost basis of the property exceeds the first-year expensing limit, you compute depreciation on the cost of the property less the amount of the first-year deduction.

EXAMPLE

In 1999, you placed in service a $30,000 machine and a $2,000 lathe. You elect to deduct as a first-year expense $2,000 for the lathe and $17,000 for the machine, a total of $19,000, the maximum first-year deduction. The $2,000 deduction has completely recovered the cost of the lathe. The cost of the machine is reduced by $17,000, giving a depreciable basis of $13,000 ($30,000 − 17,000).

$19,000 limit reduced if taxable income is lower. Your expensing deduction may not exceed net income from all your active businesses; *see* the Caution on this page.

$19,000 limit reduced if qualifying purchases exceed $200,000. If the total cost of qualifying property placed in service during a taxable year is over $200,000, the $19,000 expensing limit is reduced dollar for dollar by the cost of qualifying property exceeding $200,000. For example, if you place in service machinery costing $206,000, the $19,000 limit is reduced by $6,000. The reduced limit of $13,000 is shown on Form 4562 on the line labeled "Dollar limitation for tax year." If the total cost is $219,000 or more, no first-year expensing deduction is allowed.

$19,000 limit reduced if married filing separately. If you and your spouse file separate returns, the expensing limit for both of you is $19,000. Unless you agree to a different allocation, you are each allowed only a $9,500 expensing limit. The $200,000 cost threshold also applies to both of you as a unit. For example, if you place in service qualifying property costing $195,000 and your spouse places $9,000 of property in service, the total cost of $204,000 reduces the $19,000 limit by $4,000 to $15,000. The reduced limit for each of you on separate returns is $7,500.

Partners and S corporation stockholders. For property bought by a partnership or an S corporation, the $19,000 limit and taxable income limit applies to the business, as well as the owners as individual taxpayers. The partnership or S corporation determines its expensing deduction subject to the limits and allocates the deduction, if any, among the partners or shareholders. The allocated deduction may not exceed the net taxable income of the partnership or S corporation from actively conducted businesses.

An individual partner's expensing deduction may not exceed $19,000, regardless of how many partnership interests he or she has. However, the partner must reduce the basis of each partnership interest by the full allocable share of each partnership's expensing deduction, even if that amount is not deductible because of the $19,000 limit.

Disqualified acquisitions from related parties. Property does not qualify for the expense election if:

1. It is acquired from a spouse, ancestor or lineal descendant, or from non–family-related parties subject to the loss disallowance rule, discussed in *5.6*. For purposes of the expensing election, a corporation is controlled by you and thus subject to the loss disallowance rule discussed in *5.6* if 50% or more of the stock is owned by you, your spouse, your ancestors, or your descendants.
2. The property is acquired by a member of the same controlled group (using a 50% control test).
3. The basis of the property is determined in whole or in part (a) by reference to the adjusted basis of the property of the person from whom you acquired it or (b) under the stepped-up basis rules for inherited property.

Recapture of expensing deduction. Recapture of the first-year expensing deduction may occur on a disposition of the asset or if business use falls to 50% or less. If the business use falls to 50% or less after the year the property is placed in service but before the end of the depreciable recovery period *(42.4, 42.10)* you must "recapture" the benefit from the first-year expensing deduction. The amount recaptured is the excess of the expensing deduction over the amount of depreciation that would have been claimed (through the year of recapture) without expensing; *see 42.10*. Recaptured amounts are reported as ordinary income on Form 4797.

When you sell or dispose of the property, the first-year expensing deduction is treated as depreciation for purposes of the recapture rules *(44.1)* that treat gain realized as ordinary income to the extent of depreciation claimed.

 Caution

Losses and Low Income May Limit Deduction

The expensing deduction may not exceed the net taxable income from all businesses that you actively conduct. Net income from active businesses is figured without regard to expensing, the deduction for 50% of self-employment liability, or any net operating loss carryback or carryforward. You may include wage or salary income as active business income and if you are married filing jointly, also include your spouse's net taxable income.

If you have an overall net loss from all actively conducted businesses, you may not claim a 1999 expensing deduction. If net income is less than the cost of qualifying assets, expensing is limited to the income. However, the cost over the income limit is carried forward to 2000 on Form 4562 provided you complete the expensing section of Form 4562 for 1999. You do not get a carryover unless the deduction is claimed on the return for the first year the property is placed in service.

 Planning Reminder

Year-End Purchases

Equipment placed in service on the last day of the taxable year may qualify for the entire $19,000 first-year expensing deduction. You do not have to prorate the $19,000 limit for the amount of time you held the property.

Planning Reminder

Recovery Periods

The depreciation recovery periods for different types of assets are generally fixed by law according to the rules on this page.

Law Alert

Residential Rental Property

The IRS has changed the recovery period for furniture, carpeting, and appliances used in residential rental property from seven years to five years. *See* the Law Alert on page 204.

42.4 MACRS Class Lives

Depreciable assets other than buildings fall within a three-, five-, seven-, 10-, 15-, or 20-year class life under the General Depreciation System (GDS).

Straight-line recovery for buildings is claimed over a period of 27.5 years for residential rental property or 39 years for nonresidential real property, as discussed at *42.13*.

Note: The actual write-off period of depreciation for an asset is one year longer than the class life because of the convention rules explained in *42.5-42.7*.

Three-year property. This class includes property with a class life of four years or less, other than cars and light-duty trucks, which are in the five-year class.

This class includes: special handling devices for the manufacture of food and beverages; special tools and devices for the manufacture of rubber products; special tools for the manufacture of finished plastic products, fabricated metal products, or motor vehicles; and breeding hogs. By law, racehorses more than two years old when placed in service and other horses more than 12 years old when placed in service are also in the three-year class.

Five-year class. This class includes property with a class life of more than four years and less than 10 years such as computers *(42.10)*, typewriters, copiers, duplicating equipment, heavy general-purpose trucks, trailers, cargo containers, and trailer-mounted containers. Also included by law in the five-year class are cars, light-duty trucks (actual unloaded weight less than 13,000 pounds), taxis, buses, computer-based telephone central office switching equipment, computer-related peripheral equipment, semiconductor manufacturing equipment, and property used in research and experimentation.

Seven-year class. This class includes any property with a class life of 10 years or more but less than 16 years. This is also a catch-all category for assets with no class life that have not been assigned by law to another class. Included in the seven-year class are: office furniture and fixtures, such as desks and files; cellular phones; fax machines; refrigerators; dishwashers; and machines used to produce jewelry, musical instruments, toys, and sporting goods. Single-purpose agricultural or horticultural structures are in the 10-year class if placed in service after 1988.

Ten-year property. This includes property with a class life of 16 years or more and less than 20 years, such as vessels, barges, tugs, and water transportation equipment, and assets used in petroleum refining or in the manufacture of tobacco products and certain food products.

The 10-year class includes single-purpose agricultural and horticultural structures, and trees or vines bearing fruit or nuts, if placed in service after 1988. Under a transition rule, the seven-year period will apply to single purpose agricultural or horticultural structures under construction on July 14, 1988, or acquired pursuant to a written contract binding on that date.

Fifteen-year property. This includes land improvements such as fences, sidewalks, docks, shrubbery, roads, and bridges. It also includes other property with a class life of 20 years or more but less than 25 years, such as municipal sewage plants and telephone distribution plants. Gas station convenience stores are in the 15-year class if the property is no more than 1,400 square feet, or at least 50% of the floor space is devoted to selling petroleum products, or at least 50% of revenues are from petroleum sales. The owner of the gas station property does not have to be the operator of businesses on the property.

Twenty-year property. This class includes property with a class life of 25 years or more, such as farm buildings and municipal sewers, except that residential and nonresidential real estate is excluded; *see 42.13.*

42.5 MACRS Rates

The MACRS rate under the General Depreciation System depends on the recovery period *(42.4)* for the property and whether the half-year or mid-quarter convention applies. The 200% declining balance rate for three-year property is 66.67%; for five-year property, 40%; and for seven-year property it is 28.57%. *See 42.8* for the 150% declining balance rate election. These rates are adjusted for the convention rules explained below. When the 200% declining balance rate provides a lower annual deduction than the straight-line rate, the 200% declining balance rate is replaced by the straight-line rate. The rates in the tables at the end of this section reflect the applicable convention and the change to a straight-line recovery.

Conventions. Under the half-year convention, all property acquired during the year, regardless of when acquired during the year, is treated as acquired in the middle of the year. As a result, only one-half of the full first-year depreciation is deductible and in the year after the last class life year, the balance of the depreciation is written off. Furthermore, in the year property is sold, only half of the full depreciation for that year is deductible; *see 42.6.*

The half-year convention applies unless the total cost bases of depreciable assets placed in service during the last three months of the taxable year exceed 40% of the total bases of all property placed in service during the entire year. If this 40% test applies, you must use a mid-quarter convention to figure your annual depreciation deduction, as explained at *42.7*.

Buildings are depreciated using a mid-month convention; *see 42.13*.

Depreciation tables. The following table provides year-by-year rates for property in the three, five-, and seven-year classes. The rates incorporate the adjustment for the half-year or mid-quarter convention and the switch from the 200% declining balance rate to the straight-line method. Use the rate shown in the table under the convention for your asset. The rate is applied to original basis, minus any first-year expensing deduction; *see 42.3*. You claim the deduction from the table in Form 4562, Part II, Section B labeled "General Depreciation System" (GDS).

You use the tables for the entire recovery period unless you claim a deductible casualty loss that reduces your basis in the property. For the year of the casualty loss and later years, depreciation must be based on the adjusted basis of the property at the end of the year. The tables may no longer be used; *see* IRS Publication 946 for further details.

 Caution

Convention Rules

Convention rules affect the depreciation period, as discussed on page 616 and in *42.6* and *42.7*.

MACRS Depreciation Rates

Year	Half-Year Convention	Mid-Quarter Convention			
		1st	2nd	3rd	4th (Quarter)
3-Year Property					
1	33.33%	58.33%	41.67%	25.00%	8.33%
2	44.45	27.78	38.89	50.00	61.11
3	14.81	12.35	14.14	16.67	20.37
4	7.41	1.54	5.30	8.33	10.19
5-Year Property					
1	20.00%	35.00%	25.00%	15.00%	5.00%
2	32.00	26.00	30.00	34.00	38.00
3	19.20	15.60	18.00	20.40	22.80
4	11.52	11.01	11.37	12.24	13.68
5	11.52	11.01	11.37	11.30	10.94
6	5.76	1.38	4.26	7.06	9.58
7-Year Property					
1	14.29%	25.00%	17.85%	10.71%	3.57%
2	24.49	21.43	23.47	25.51	27.55
3	17.49	15.31	16.76	18.22	19.68
4	12.49	10.93	11.97	13.02	14.06
5	8.93	8.75	8.87	9.30	10.04
6	8.92	8.74	8.87	8.85	8.73
7	8.93	8.75	8.87	8.86	8.73
8	4.46	1.09	3.33	5.53	7.64

EXAMPLE

During June 1999, you place in business service a machine costing $20,000. It is your only acquisition in 1999. The machine is in the five-year class and subject to the half-year convention. The depreciation rate for the first year is 20% (*see* the table above for MACRS rates). Your 1999 depreciation deduction is $4,000 ($20,000 × 20%).

Summary of Deductions

Year	Deduction
1	$4,000
2	6,400
3	3,840
4	2,304
5	2,304
6	1,152
Total	$20,000

Planning Reminder

Half-Year Convention

The half-year convention applies unless the total cost basis of depreciable assets placed in service during the last three months of the year exceeds 40% of the total basis of all property placed in service during the year.

Under the half-year convention, all assets placed in service during the year are treated as placed in service at the midpoint of the year.

Planning Reminder

Mid-Quarter Rate

To figure your MACRS deduction for property subject to the mid-quarter convention, use the rate shown in the table in *42.5* for the quarter of the tax year the property is placed in service. In using the table, multiply the original basis, minus any first-year expensing deduction, by the applicable rate.

42.6 Half-Year Convention for MACRS

The half-year convention treats all business equipment placed in service during a tax year as placed in service in the midpoint of that tax year. The same rule applies in the year in which the property is disposed of. The effect of this rule is as follows: A half-year of depreciation is allowed in the first year property is placed in service, regardless of when the property is placed in service during the tax year. For each of the remaining years of the recovery period, a full year of depreciation is claimed. If you hold the property for the entire recovery period, a half-year of depreciation is claimed for the year following the end of the recovery period. If you dispose of the property before the end of the recovery period, a half-year of depreciation is allowable for the year of disposition.

See the Table of MACRS Depreciation Rates in *42.5* for year-by-year rates under the half-year convention. Apply the rate from the table to the original basis, minus any first-year expensing *(42.3)* deduction claimed.

The Example in *42.5* shows the year-by-year deduction computation for five-year property under the half-year convention. If you dispose of the property before the end of the recovery period shown in *42.5*, your deduction for the year of disposition is one-half of the deduction that would be allowed for the full year using the rate shown in the table.

42.7 Last Quarter Placements—Mid-Quarter Convention

A mid-quarter convention applies if the total cost basis of business equipment placed in service during the last three months of the tax year exceeds 40% of the total basis of all the property placed in service during the year. You must use a mid-quarter convention for all property (other than nonresidential real property and residential rental property) placed in service during the year. In applying the 40% rule, you do not count residential rental property, nonresidential realty, and assets that were placed in service and disposed of during the same year.

Under the mid-quarter convention, the first-year depreciation allowance is based on the number of quarters that the asset was in service. Property placed in service at any time during a quarter is treated as having been placed in service in the middle of the quarter. The mid-quarter convention also applies to sales and disposals of property. The disposal is treated as occurring in the midpoint of the quarter.

EXAMPLE

During August 1999, you place in service office furniture costing $1,000, and in October, a computer costing $5,000. You are on the calendar year. The total basis of all property placed in service in 1999 is $6,000. As the $5,000 basis of the computer placed in service in the last quarter exceeds 40% of the total basis of all property placed in service during 1999, you must use the mid-quarter convention for the furniture and the computer. The office furniture, which is seven-year property, and the computer, which is five-year property, are depreciated using MACRS and a mid-quarter convention.

You first multiply the $1,000 basis of the furniture by 10.71%—the seven-year property mid-quarter convention rate for the third quarter (*see* the table in *42.5*). The depreciation deduction is $107. You then multiply the $5,000 basis of the computer by 5%—the five-year property mid-quarter convention rate for the fourth quarter (*see* the table in *42.5*). The deduction is $250. Total depreciation is $357.

42.8 150% Rate Election

Instead of using the 200% declining balance rate for property in the three-, five-, seven-, and 10-year classes, you may elect a 150% rate. You may prefer the 150% rate when you are subject to the alternative minimum tax (AMT). For AMT purposes, you must use the 150% rate and adjust your taxable income if the 200% rate was used for regular tax purposes; *see 23.2*. If for regular tax purposes you elect to apply the 150% rate for property placed in service after December 31, 1998, use the same recovery period (*see 42.4*) you would have used if you had claimed the 200% declining balance rate. Thus, the recovery period is five years for cars and computers and seven years for office furniture and fixtures. If a half-year convention applies, the first-year rate for the five-year class is 15%, and 10.71% for the seven-year class; *see* the table below. Apply the rate from the table to your original basis, minus any first-year expensing deduction claimed. If you are subject to the mid-quarter convention, *see* IRS Publication 946 for the tables showing mid-quarter convention rates.

The election to use the 150% rate must be made for all property within a given class placed in service in the same year. The election is irrevocable.

Half-Year Convention—150% Rate

	Property Class	
Year—	5-Year—	7-Year—
1	15.00%	10.71%
2	25.50	19.13
3	17.85	15.03
4	16.66	12.25
5	16.66	12.25
6	8.33	12.25
7		12.25
8		6.13

42.9 Straight-Line Depreciation

You may not want an accelerated rate and may prefer to write off depreciation at an even pace. There are two straight-line methods. You may make an irrevocable election to use the straight-line method over the regular MACRS recovery period *(42.4)* under the general depreciation system (GDS). Alternatively, you may elect straight-line recovery over the designated recovery period for the class life under the alternative depreciation system (ADS). For some assets, such as cars, the GDS and ADS recovery periods are the same (five years for a car). In some cases, the ADS recovery period is longer than the GDS recovery period. For example, the recovery period for office furniture and fixtures is seven years under GDS and 10 years under ADS.

Half-year and quarter-year conventions apply to both straight-line methods; *see 42.6* and *42.7*. A mid-month convention applies under the straight-line rule for buildings; *see 42.13*.

Straight-line over regular recovery period (GDS). You make this election on Form 4562, Part II, Section B, labeled "General Depreciation System" (GDS). To elect this method for one asset, you must also use it for all other assets in the same class that are placed in service during the year. The straight-line election is irrevocable.

Straight-line under the alternative depreciation system (ADS). Under the alternative depreciation system (ADS), the straight-line recovery period for cars, light trucks, and computers is five years, the same as under GDS. For business office furniture and fixtures, the ADS straight-line recovery period is 10 years. The ADS recovery period for personal property with no class life is 12 years. For nonresidential real and residential rental property, you may elect ADS straight-line recovery over 40 years. *See* IRS Publication 946 for other ADS class lives.

Except for real estate, the ADS election applies to all property within the same class placed in service during the taxable year. For real estate, the election to use the alternative depreciation method may be made on a property-by-property basis. The election is irrevocable. The deduction is claimed on Form 4562, Part II, Section C, labeled "Alternative Depreciation System" (ADS).

Straight-line rate table. The table below shows straight-line rates for five-year, seven-year, and 10-year property under the half-year convention. As discussed earlier, the recovery period depends on whether the GDS or ADS straight-line method is used. If you are subject to the mid-quarter convention *(42.7)*, *see* IRS Publication 946 for tables showing the applicable rates.

 Law Alert

Elective 150% Rate
Effective for property placed in service after December 31, 1998, if you choose to claim the 150% rate instead of the 200% rate for three-, five-, or seven-year property, use the same recovery periods you would have used if you had chosen the 200% declining balance rate.

For property placed in service before 1999, the 150% rate is applied over the ADS *(42.9)* recovery periods.

Half-Year Convention—Straight-Line Rate

	Property Class		
Year—	5-Year—	7-Year—	10-Year—
1	10.00%	7.14%	5.00%
2	20.00	14.29	10.00
3	20.00	14.29	10.00
4	20.00	14.28	10.00
5	20.00	14.29	10.00
6	10.00	14.28	10.00
7		14.29	10.00
8		7.14	10.00
9			10.00
10			10.00
11			5.00

Should You Elect Straight-Line Recovery?

Accelerated rates of MACRS merely give you an opportunity to advance the time of taking your deduction. This may be a decided advantage where the higher deductions in the first few years will provide you with cash for working capital or for investments in other income-producing sources. That is, by accelerating the deductions, you defer the payment of taxes that would be due if you claimed smaller depreciation deductions, using more conservative straight-line rates. The tax deferral lasts until the rapid method provides less depreciation deductions than would the more conservative method. Your ability to receive the benefits of accelerated MACRS generally is more feasible in an ongoing business.

If you are starting a new business in which you expect losses or low income at the start, accelerated MACRS may waste depreciation deductions that could be used in later years when your income increases. Therefore, before deciding to use accelerated MACRS rates, consider your income prospects.

AMT depreciation. For alternative minimum tax (AMT) purposes, depreciation is figured using the 150% declining balance rate if the 200% declining balance rate was used for regular tax purposes; *see 23.2*. If straight-line depreciation was used for regular tax purposes, AMT depreciation is figured using the straight-line alternative depreciation system (ADS) over the class life recovery period. For real estate placed in service after 1986, AMT depreciation is figured using the 40-year ADS straight-line method.

Mandatory straight-line depreciation. You are required to use the alternative depreciation system for automobiles *(43.3)* and certain computers *(42.10)* used 50% or less for business.

Alternative MACRS depreciation must also be used for:

- Figuring earnings and profits;
- Tangible property which, during the taxable year, is used predominantly outside the United States;
- Tax-exempt use property;
- Tax-exempt bond financed property; *and*
- Imported property covered by an executive order.

42.10 Computers and Other Listed Property

"Listed property" is a term applied to certain equipment that may be used for personal and business purposes. For such property, the law allows first-year expensing *(42.3)* or accelerated MACRS *(42.5)* deductions only if business use exceeds 50%. For business use of 50% or less, you must use ADS straight-line depreciation; *see 42.9*. Deductions for listed property are claimed on Form 4562. If the more-than-50% business-use test is met in the first year and first-year expensing or accelerated MACRS is claimed, but business use of listed property falls to 50% or less during the ADS straight-line recovery period *(42.9)*, you must "recapture" first-year expensing and accelerated MACRS deductions; *see* Example 2 below.

What is "listed property"? Listed property includes passenger autos weighing 6,000 pounds or less, trucks (*see 43.3* for exceptions), cellular phones, computers and peripheral equipment, boats, airplanes, and any photographic, sound, or video recording equipment that could be used for entertainment or recreational purposes. However, exceptions remove some items from the listed property class for many businesses. Listed property does not include (1) any computer or peripheral equipment used exclusively at a regular business establishment owned or leased by you, and (2) photographic, phonographic, communications, or video equipment used exclusively and regularly in your business or regular business establishment. A home office that meets the rules in *40.12* is considered a business establishment.

> **EXAMPLES**
>
> 1. You buy a computer in 1999 and use it exclusively in your regular business office. The computer is not listed property. You may claim either first-year expensing *(42.3)* or accelerated MACRS depreciation *(42.5)* for your investment on Form 4562. If business use falls to 50% or less after 1999, the only deduction subject to recapture is the first-year deduction; *see 42.3*.
> 2. You have no regular business establishment and use a computer bought in 1999 as a freelance consultant. The computer is listed property and you may claim MACRS and/or first-year expensing only if you use the computer more than 50% for business. If business use does not exceed 50%, you may only claim ADS straight-line depreciation *(42.9)*. Your deductions are claimed in the section for "Listed Property" on Form 4562.
>
> If business use exceeds 50% in the first year but in a later year drops to 50% or less, MACRS and any first-year expensing deduction are subject to "recapture." In the year in which business use drops to 50% or less, you recapture the excess of (1) the MACRS and first-year expensing deductions claimed in prior years over (2) the deductions that would have been allowed using the straight-line alternative depreciation rates of *42.9*. For the rest of the recovery period, you continue to use the alternative straight-line rate.
>
> Recapture is figured on Form 4797. The recapture computation follows the steps shown in *43.9* for recapture of excess depreciation on an automobile.

Investor's use of computer. For an investor who uses a home computer for managing an investment portfolio, the computer is treated as listed property. Unless the computer is also used for business, and the computer time spent on business work exceeds 50% of the total, only straight-line depreciation may be claimed; neither first-year expensing nor accelerated MACRS is allowed. Although the investment use is disregarded for purposes of the more-than-50% business-use test,

 Caution

Depreciation Restrictions for Computer

A computer must be used more than 50% of the time for business to claim a first-year expensing deduction. If used 50% or less for business, straight-line depreciation is required.

the investment use is combined with the business use for purposes of determining the percentage of depreciable cost. Depreciable investment use must relate to managing investments that produce taxable income. *See* the Examples below.

EXAMPLES

1. In 1999, Jane Adams buys a computer; she uses it 10% of the time for personal purposes, 50% of the time to manage her stock investments and 40% in a part-time research business. The more-than-50% business-use test is not met for claiming first-year expensing or accelerated MACRS deductions. She must use ADS straight-line depreciation over five years *(42.9)*; her depreciable basis is 90% of cost.
2. Assume that Jane used the computer 60% of the time for business and 30% for investment. As business use exceeds 50%, she may claim first-year expensing under the rules discussed in *42.3*. If she instead claims accelerated MACRS, the MACRS rate is applied to 90% of her cost.

Leasing a computer or cellular phone. You may deduct the portion of your lease payments attributable to business use. However, if business use is 50% or less for any year, you must report as income an amount based on the fair market value of the unit, the percentage of business plus investment use, and percentages from two IRS tables shown in Publication 946.

42.11 ACRS Recovery for Assets in Service Before 1987

Assets other than real estate placed in service after 1980 and before 1987 fell within one of the following ACRS classes: three-, five-, or 10-year property.

Three-year property. This class included automobiles, taxis, light-duty trucks (actual unloaded weight of less than 13,000 pounds), equipment used for research and experimentation, hogs used for breeding, racehorses more than two years old, and any other horse more than 12 years old when placed in service.

With the exception of certain automobiles *(43.7)*, three-year property is no longer depreciable.

Five-year property. All tangible personal property had a five-year recovery period, unless specifically included in the three-year or 10-year class. Thus, most equipment and other business assets qualified for a five-year write-off, including office furniture, typewriters, computers, calculators, copiers, and single-purpose agricultural structures. Facilities used for storage of petroleum and its primary products also fell within the five-year class.

Five-year property is no longer depreciable unless you elected straight-line recovery over a period of 25 years; *see 42.12.*

Ten-year property. This is a limited category covering assets in residential mobile homes, theme and amusement parks, railroad tank cars, public utility equipment with an ADR class life of more than 18 but not more than 25 years (except research and experimentation equipment included in the three-year class), and public utility equipment used in coal conversions. If a straight-line recovery over 25 or 35 years was elected, *see 42.12.*

Dispositions. No depreciation deduction is allowed in the year you dispose of three-year, five-year, or 10-year ACRS property.

Real estate. *See 42.16* for ACRS rates.

42.12 Straight-Line Recovery for Equipment in Service Before 1987

You may still be able to claim straight-line deductions for five-year property if a recovery period of 25 years was elected. For 10-year property, an election could have been made to elect straight-line depreciation over 25 or 35 years.

If you made the straight-line election, the straight-line rate to be used on your 1999 return is as follows:

Recovery Period—	Rate—
25 years	4.000%
35 years	2.857%

Planning Reminder

Computer Software

Software purchased "off the shelf" and used for business or investment purposes is depreciable over a three-year period provided it has a useful life exceeding one year. If the useful life does not exceed one year, the cost is immediately deductible. Also *see 42.19.*

Filing Instruction

Pre-ACRS assets

For assets placed in service before 1981, the straight-line and declining balance methods are discussed in IRS Publication 534.

Because of the half-year convention, only 50% of the above percentages was allowed in the year the property was placed in service. If the property is held for the entire elected recovery period, another half-year of depreciation is allowed for the year following the end of the recovery period. If property is disposed of prior to the end of the recovery period, no cost recovery is allowable in the year of disposition. *See* IRS Publication 534 for further details.

42.13 MACRS for Real Estate Placed in Service After 1986

The recovery period for residential rental property placed in service after December 31, 1986, is 27.5 years. The recovery period for nonresidential real property is either 39 years or 31.5 years, depending on when the property was placed in service.

The method of recovery for nonresidential or residential property is the straight-line method using a mid-month convention. See page 623 for rate tables for each class of property.

For nonresidential real property placed in service after December 31, 1986, but before May 13, 1993, the depreciation recovery period is 31.5 years.

For nonresidential real property placed in service after May 12, 1993, the recovery period is 39 years. Under a transition rule, the 31.5-year recovery period rather than the 39-year recovery period applies to a building placed in service before 1994 if before May 13, 1993, you had entered into a binding, written contract to buy or build it, or if, before that date, you had begun construction. The transition rule also applies if you obtained the contract or property from someone else who satisfied the pre–May 13, 1993, contract or construction requirement, provided he or she never put the building in service and you did so before 1994.

Residential rental property is a rental building or structure for which 80% or more of the gross rental income for the tax year is rental income from dwelling units. If you occupy any part of the building, the gross rental income includes the fair rental value of the part you occupy.

A dwelling unit is a house or an apartment used to provide living accommodations in a building or structure, but not a unit in a hotel, motel, inn, or other establishment where more than one-half of the units are used on a transient basis.

Mid-month convention. Under a mid-month convention, all property placed in service or disposed of during any month is treated as placed in service or disposed of on the midpoint of that month. You may determine the first-year deduction for residential rental property by applying the percentage from the table on page 623 to the original depreciable basis. In later years, use the same column of the table to figure your deduction.

EXAMPLE

In February 1999, you buy an apartment building for $100,000 and place it in service. You use the calendar year. The table on the next page gives a first-year depreciation rate of 3.182% for 27.5-year residential rental property placed in service during February. Applying this rate, you get a deduction of $3,182.

For 2000, the rate will be 3.636%, for a deduction of $3,636.

Additions or improvements to property. The depreciation deduction for any additions to, or improvement of, any property is figured in the same way as the deduction for the property would be figured if the property had been placed in service at the same time as the addition or improvement.

Filing Tip

Additions and Improvements

The MACRS class for the addition or improvement is determined by the MACRS class of the property to which the addition or improvement is made. For example, if you put an addition on a rental home that you are depreciating over 27.5 years, the addition is depreciated as 27.5 year residential rental property. The period for figuring depreciation begins on the date that the addition or improvement is placed in service, or, if later, the date that the property to which the addition or improvement was made is placed in service.

Residential Rental Property (27.5 years; *see 42.13*)

USE THE COLUMN FOR THE MONTH OF TAXABLE YEAR PLACED IN SERVICE.

Month	1	2	3	4	5	6	7	8	9	10	11	12
Year												
1	3.485%	3.182%	2.879%	2.576%	2.273%	1.970%	1.667%	1.364%	1.061%	0.758%	0.455%	0.152%
2–9	3.636	3.636	3.636	3.636	3.636	3.636	3.636	3.636	3.636	3.636	3.636	3.636
10	3.637	3.637	3.637	3.637	3.637	3.637	3.636	3.636	3.636	3.636	3.636	3.636
11	3.636	3.636	3.636	3.636	3.636	3.636	3.637	3.637	3.637	3.637	3.637	3.637
12	3.637	3.637	3.637	3.637	3.637	3.637	3.636	3.636	3.636	3.636	3.636	3.636
13	3.636	3.636	3.636	3.636	3.636	3.636	3.637	3.637	3.637	3.637	3.637	3.637
14	3.637	3.637	3.637	3.637	3.637	3.637	3.636	3.636	3.636	3.636	3.636	3.636
15	3.636	3.636	3.636	3.636	3.636	3.636	3.637	3.637	3.637	3.637	3.637	3.637
16	3.637	3.637	3.637	3.637	3.637	3.637	3.636	3.636	3.636	3.636	3.636	3.636
17	3.636	3.636	3.636	3.636	3.636	3.636	3.637	3.637	3.637	3.637	3.637	3.637

Nonresidential Real Property (31.5 years—placed in service before May 13, 1993; *see 42.13*)

USE THE COLUMN FOR THE MONTH OF TAXABLE YEAR PLACED IN SERVICE.

Month	1	2	3	4	5	6	7	8	9	10	11	12
Year												
1	3.042%	2.778%	2.513%	2.249%	1.984%	1.720%	1.455%	1.190%	0.926%	0.661%	0.397%	0.132%
2–7	3.175	3.175	3.175	3.175	3.175	3.175	3.175	3.175	3.175	3.175	3.175	3.175
8	3.175	3.174	3.175	3.174	3.175	3.174	3.175	3.175	3.175	3.175	3.175	3.175
9	3.174	3.175	3.174	3.175	3.174	3.175	3.174	3.175	3.174	3.175	3.174	3.175
10	3.175	3.174	3.175	3.174	3.175	3.174	3.175	3.174	3.175	3.174	3.175	3.174
11	3.174	3.175	3.174	3.175	3.174	3.175	3.174	3.175	3.174	3.175	3.174	3.175
12	3.175	3.174	3.175	3.174	3.175	3.174	3.175	3.174	3.175	3.174	3.175	3.174
13	3.174	3.175	3.174	3.175	3.174	3.175	3.174	3.175	3.174	3.175	3.174	3.175
14	3.175	3.174	3.175	3.174	3.175	3.174	3.175	3.174	3.175	3.174	3.175	3.174
15	3.174	3.175	3.174	3.175	3.174	3.175	3.174	3.175	3.174	3.175	3.174	3.175
16	3.175	3.174	3.175	3.174	3.175	3.174	3.175	3.174	3.175	3.174	3.175	3.174
17	3.174	3.175	3.174	3.175	3.174	3.175	3.174	3.175	3.174	3.175	3.174	3.175

Nonresidential Real Property (39 years—placed in service on or after May 13, 1993; *see 42.13*)

USE THE COLUMN FOR THE MONTH OF TAXABLE YEAR PLACED IN SERVICE.

Month	1	2	3	4	5	6	7	8	9	10	11	12
Year												
1	2.461%	2.247%	2.033%	1.819%	1.605%	1.391%	1.177%	0.963%	0.749%	0.535%	0.321%	0.107%
2–39	2.564	2.564	2.564	2.564	2.564	2.564	2.564	2.564	2.564	2.564	2.564	2.564

42.14 Demolishing a Building

When you buy improved property, the purchase price is allocated between the land and the building; only the building may be depreciated. The land may not; *see 42.2*. If you later demolish the building, you may not deduct the cost of the demolition or the undepreciated basis of the building as a loss in the year of demolition. Expenses or losses in connection with the demolition of any structure, including certified historic structures, are not deductible. They must be capitalized and added to the basis of the land on which the structure is located.

Major rehabilitation. Where you are considering a major rehabilitation of a building that involves some demolition of the building, IRS guidelines may allow you to deduct the costs of demolition and a removal of part of the structure. Under the IRS rules, the costs of structural modification may avoid capitalization if 75% or more of the existing external walls are retained as internal or external walls and 75% or more of the existing internal framework is also retained. For certified historic structures, the modification must also be part of a certified rehabilitation. The 75% tests are effective for work starting after June 5, 1995, and also for open taxable years, if an election is made for those years.

42.15 Leasehold Improvements

Lessee improvements. Leasehold improvements placed in service after 1986 by a lessee are depreciated under MACRS real estate rates listed at *42.13*. You ignore the term of the lease. If the lease term is shorter than the MACRS life and you do not retain the improvements at the end of the term, the remaining undepreciated basis is considered in computing gain or loss at that time.

Pre-1987 improvements. For leasehold improvements placed in service before 1987, the cost of improvements is deductible over the *shorter* of the following periods:

1. The useful life of the improvement if the improvement was before 1981, or the ACRS recovery period if after 1980 but before 1987, *and*
2. The remaining term of the lease.

If (1) is the shorter period, the cost of the improvement is depreciated. If (2) is the shorter period, the cost is amortized ratably.

In determining the shorter period, you must add optional lease renewals to the remaining lease term under (2) if, at the completion of the improvement, the remaining term of the original lease (excluding unexercised renewal options) is less than 60% of the useful life (or ACRS recovery period) of the improvement. Renewals do not have to be taken into account under the 60% test if the lessee can show that it is more probable that the lease would not be renewed than that it would be renewed.

If the lessee and lessor are related, the term of the lease is treated as being equal to the remaining useful life (or recovery period) of the improvement. Related parties include spouses, children, grandchildren, parents, grandparents, brothers, sisters, and certain controlled corporations, partnerships, and trusts.

42.16 Depreciating Real Estate Placed in Service After 1980 and Before 1987

The ACRS recovery period of a building that does not qualify as low-income housing depends on the year in which the building was placed in service:

- For buildings placed in service after May 8, 1985, and before 1987, the recovery period is 19 years.
- For buildings placed in service after March 15, 1984, and before May 9, 1985, the recovery period is 18 years.
- For buildings placed in service before March 16, 1984, and for all low-income housing, the recovery period is 15 years.

Mobile homes and theme parks are in the 10-year class and agricultural, horticultural, and petroleum storage structures are in the five-year class.

Under transitional rules, some 19-year buildings may be depreciated over 18 years, and some 18-year buildings over 15 years if placed in service before 1987. Specifically, recovery over 18 years is allowed for a building placed in service after May 8, 1985, provided that before May 9, 1985, (1) you began construction or had a binding contract to buy the building and (2) you placed the building

Planning Reminder

Abandonment of Leasehold Improvements

Upon the termination of a lease, the adjusted basis of a lessee's leasehold improvements that are abandoned may be claimed as a loss.

For dispositions after June 12, 1996, a lessor may follow the rule applied to lessees if the improvements are irrevocably disposed of or abandoned at the termination of the lease. The lessor may recognize loss for the remaining adjusted basis of the improvements. For dispositions on or before June 12, 1996, the IRS has held that leasehold improvements made by a lessor that are considered structural components of a building must be depreciated in the same manner as the underlying real property, even if such improvements are retired at the end of the lease term.

in service before the end of 1986. The 18-year period also applies if construction was begun, or a contract entered into by a person who transferred the rights to you and you placed the building in service before 1987. Recovery over 15 years is allowed for a building that you (or a prior owner who transferred the right to you) began constructing or contracted for before March 16, 1984, provided you placed it in service before the end of 1986.

Election to use straight-line depreciation. You may have elected to use the straight-line method over the regular recovery period: 19 years for 19-year property, 18 years for 18-year property, and 15 years for 15-year property. Furthermore, for any building, a longer recovery period of either 35 or 45 years was available. An election of the straight-line method for real property had to be made on a property-by-property basis, by the return due date, plus extensions, for the year the property was placed in service.

Rate of recovery. The rate of recovery is listed in Treasury tables that are available in IRS Publication 534. The specific rates are adjusted according to the month in the first year in which a building or improvement is placed in service.

Substantial improvements. Substantial improvements made after 1986 to an ACRS building are depreciable under MACRS *(42.13)*, not ACRS.

Dispositions. If you dispose of 15-year real property, the ACRS deduction for the year of disposition is based on the number of full months in use. However, no deduction is allowed for the month of disposition.

The same full-month convention rule applies to dispositions of 18-year property placed in service before June 23, 1984.

If you dispose of other 18-year or 19-year real property, the ACRS deduction for the year of disposition is based on the number of months in use determined under a mid-month convention. Under the mid-month convention, real property disposed of any time during a month is treated as disposed of in the middle of that month. You count the month of disposition as one-half of a month of use.

See 44.1 for recapture rules on the sale of ACRS property.

 Filing Instruction

Disposition of ACRS Real Estate
In the year you dispose of 15-year ACRS real property, or 18-year property placed in service before June 23, 1984, you may base a deduction on the number of full months the building was used. For other 18-year or 19-year buildings, the deduction for the year of disposition is based on full months of use plus one-half a month for the month of disposition.

42.17 When MACRS Is Not Allowed

If you place in service personal property that you previously used or that was previously owned by a related taxpayer before 1987, you may not be able to apply MACRS rules. This anti-churning restriction is designed to discourage asset transfers between related persons to take advantage of MACRS deductions that exceed the deductions allowed before 1987 under ACRS. The anti-churning restriction does not apply to personal property if, for the first full taxable year of service, the deduction allowable under ACRS would be greater than the deduction allowable under MACRS.

The anti-churning rule also does not bar MACRS rules for real estate acquired after 1986, unless you lease back the real estate to a related party who owned it before 1987.

Special rules also apply to the transfer of property in certain tax-free corporate or partnership transactions where the property was used before 1987. If you receive property in a tax-free exchange, you may have to use the method used by the transferor in computing the ACRS deduction for that part of basis that does not exceed what was the transferor's basis in the property. To the extent that basis exceeds the transferor's, the MACRS rules may apply; for example, when you paid boot in addition to transferring property.

Where property is disposed of and reacquired, the depreciation deduction is computed as if the disposition had not occurred.

42.18 Amortizing Goodwill and Other Intangibles (Section 197)

The costs of intangibles coming within Section 197 are amortized over a 15-year period. The 15-year period applies regardless of the actual useful life of "Section 197 intangibles" acquired after August 10, 1993 (or after July 25, 1991, if elected), and held in connection with a business or income-producing activity.

Generally, the amount subject to amortization is cost. Annual amortization is reported on Form 4562. The 15-year period starts with the month the intangible was acquired.

A "Section 197 intangible" is: (1) goodwill; (2) going-concern value; (3) workforce in place; (4) information base; (5) know-how, but *see* exceptions below; (6) any customer-based intangible; (7) any supplier-based intangible; (8) any license, permit, or other right granted by a governmental unit or agency; (9) any covenant not to compete made in the acquisition of a business; and (10) any franchise, trademark, or trade name.

Goodwill. Goodwill is the value of a business attributable to the expectancy of continued customer patronage, due to the name or reputation of a business or any other factor.

Franchises, trademarks, and trade names. A franchise (excluding sports franchises), trademark, or trade name is a Section 197 intangible. Amounts, whether fixed or contingent, paid on the transfer of a trademark, trade name, or franchise are chargeable to capital account and must be ratably amortized over a 15-year period. The renewal of a franchise, trademark, or trade name is treated as an acquisition of the franchise, trademark, or trade name. Renewal costs are amortized over 15 years beginning in the month of renewal.

Know-how. A patent, copyright, formula, process, design, pattern, format, or similar item may be a Section 197 intangible. However, the following interests are not Section 197 intangibles unless acquired as part of the acquisition of a business: patents, copyrights, and interests in films, sound recordings, videotapes, books, or other similar property.

Customer-based intangibles. Customer-based intangibles include the portion of an acquired trade or business attributable to a customer base, circulation base, undeveloped market or market growth, insurance in force, investment management contracts, or other relationships with customers that involve the future provision of goods or services.

Supplier-based intangibles. The portion of the purchase price of an acquired business attributable to a favorable relationship with persons who provide distribution services, such as favorable shelf or display space at a retail outlet, the existence of a favorable credit rating, or the existence of favorable supply contracts, are Section 197 intangibles.

Going-concern value. This is the additional value that attaches to property because it is an integral part of a going concern. This includes the value attributable to the ability of a trade or business to continue to operate and generate sales without interruption in spite of a change in ownership.

Workforce in place. The portion of the purchase price of an acquired business attributable to a highly skilled workforce is amortizable over 15 years. Similarly, the cost of acquiring an existing employment contract is amortizable over 15 years.

Information base. This includes the cost of acquiring customer lists; subscription lists; insurance expirations; patient or client files; lists of newspaper, magazine, radio, or television advertisers; business books and records; and operating systems. The intangible value of technical manuals, training manuals or programs, data files, and accounting or inventory control systems is also a Section 197 intangible.

Self-created intangibles. A Section 197 intangible created by a taxpayer is generally not amortizable, unless created in connection with a transaction that involves the acquisition of assets of a business. However, this deduction bar for self-created intangibles does not apply to the following: (1) any license, permit, or other right granted by a governmental unit or agency; (2) a covenant not to compete entered into on the acquisition of a business; or (3) any franchise, trademark, or trade name. For example, the 15-year amortization period may apply to the capitalized costs of registering or developing a trademark or trade name.

A person who contracts for or renews a contract for the use of a Section 197 intangible may not be considered to have created that intangible. For example, a licensee who contracts for the use of know-how may amortize capitalized costs over 15 years.

The following intangible assets are not Section 197 intangibles: (1) interests in a corporation, partnership, trust, or estate; (2) interests under certain financial contracts; (3) interests in land; (4) certain computer software; (5) certain separately acquired rights and interests; (6) interests under existing leases of tangible property; (7) interests under existing indebtedness; (8) sports franchises; (9) certain residential mortgage servicing rights; and (10) certain corporate transaction costs.

Planning Reminder

Covenants Not To Compete

A covenant not to compete is a Section 197 intangible if paid for in connection with the acquisition of a business. Excessive compensation or rental paid to a former owner of a business for continuing to perform services or provide the use of property is considered an amount paid for a covenant not to compete if the services or property benefits the trade or business. But an amount paid under a covenant not to compete that actually represents additional consideration for corporate stock is not a Section 197 intangible and must be added to the basis of the acquired stock.

Loss limitations. A person who disposes of an amortizable Section 197 intangible at a loss and at the same time retains other Section 197 intangibles acquired in the same transaction may not deduct the loss. The disallowed loss is added to the basis of the retained Section 197 intangibles. The same rule applies if a Section 197 intangible is abandoned or becomes worthless and other Section 197 intangibles acquired in the same transaction are kept. The basis of the remaining intangibles is increased by the disallowed loss.

You may not treat a covenant not to compete as worthless any earlier than the disposition or worthlessness of the entire interest in a business.

Anti-churning rule. No deduction is allowed for goodwill, going-concern value, or any other Section 197 intangibles acquired by a taxpayer after August 10, 1993, if:

1. The taxpayer or a related person held or used the intangible at any time on or after July 25, 1991, and on or before August 10, 1993;
2. The taxpayer acquired the intangible from a person who held it at any time on or after July 25, 1991, and on or before August 10, 1993, and, as part of the transaction, the user of the intangible does not change; or
3. The taxpayer grants the right to use the intangible to a person or a related person who held or used the intangible at any time on or after July 25, 1991, and on or before August 10, 1993.

Who are related persons? A person may be treated as related to another person if engaged in businesses under common control. A 50% ownership test is used to determine the stock and partnership percentages.

An exception to the "anti-churning" rule may apply if the person from whom the intangible is acquired elects to recognize gain on its disposition and pay a tax on the gain which, when added to other income taxes imposed on the gain, equals the product of the gain and the highest rate of income tax applicable to the person. If the election is made, the anti-churning rules apply to the intangible only to the extent that adjusted basis in the intangible exceeds the recognized gain.

The anti-churning rules do not apply to a Section 197 intangible acquired from a decedent if the basis of the intangible is stepped up to fair market value.

Dispositions. An amortizable Section 197 intangible is not a capital asset. It is treated as depreciable property, and if held for more than one year, it will generally qualify as a Section 1231 asset; *see 44.1*. Amortization claimed on a Section 197 intangible is subject to recapture under Section 1245 and gain on its sale to certain related persons is subject to ordinary income treatment under Section 1239.

42.19 Deducting the Cost of Computer Software

The cost of software installed in a computer that you buy and use in your business is not deducted separately, unless the software cost is separately stated. In most cases, the cost of software bundled with a computer is not separately stated. The cost of the computer including such software is depreciable under the rules in *42.10*.

If you buy software for business use, such as a database or spreadsheet program, the treatment of the cost depends on your use of the program. If you use it for a year or less, such as an annual tax program, you may deduct the cost as a business expense for that year. If the useful life in your business exceeds a year, you may depreciate the cost over 36 months.

See 42.18 for 15-year amortization of certain software acquired in the acquisition of a business.

 Caution

Computer Software Not Subject to Amortization
Computer software is *not* a Section 197 intangible if it: (1) is readily available to the general public; (2) is not subject to an exclusive license; and (3) has not been substantially changed. Furthermore, even computer software falling outside of this exception is considered a Section 197 intangible only if acquired in the acquisition of a business. For software excluded from Section 197 treatment, *see 42.19*.

Deducting Automobile Expenses

The costs of buying and operating a car for business are deductible under rules hedged with restrictions. The maximum depreciation deduction for a car placed in service in 1999 may not exceed $3,060, and this limit is reduced further by the percentage of your personal use. If you do not use your car more than 50% of the time for business, depreciation must be based on the straight-line method.

To avoid accounting for actual auto expenses and depreciation, you may claim an IRS mileage allowance. For the period January 1, 1999, to March 31, 1999, the allowance is 32.5 cents per mile and for the period April 1, 1999, to December 31, 1999, the allowance is 31 cents per mile. Whichever choice you make, keep a record of business trip mileage.

If you are self-employed, you deduct your automobile expenses on Schedule C or Schedule C-EZ if eligible; *see 40.6.* Use Form 4562 to compute depreciation if you claim actual operating costs instead of the IRS mileage allowance. If you are an employee, use Form 2106 to claim unreimbursed automobile expenses, which are deductible only to the extent that together with other miscellaneous itemized deductions they exceed 2% of your adjusted gross income.

43.1 IRS Automobile Allowance

If you start to use your car for business in 1999, you have a choice of either deducting the actual operating costs of your car during business trips or deducting a flat IRS allowance of 32.5/31 cents per mile for business mileage during 1999. For 1999 there are two different mileage allowance rates: the allowance rate for January 1, 1999, to March 31, 1999, is 32.5 cents per mile and the allowance for the period April 1, 1999, to December 31, 1999, is 31 cents per mile.

If you placed a business car in service before 1999 and have always used the IRS mileage allowance, you may apply the 32.5/31 cents-per-mile rate to your 1999 business mileage or deduct your actual operating costs plus straight-line depreciation (assuming the car is not considered fully depreciated).

The mileage rate also applies to business trips in a van or pickup or panel truck as if it were a car.

The rate may not be used to deduct the costs of an automobile used for nonbusiness income-producing activities such as looking after investment property.

First-year election. The choice of the allowance must be made in the first year you place an auto in service for business travel. If you do not use the allowance in the year you first use the car for business, you may not use the allowance for that car in any other year. Thus, if you bought a car for business in 1998 and on your 1998 return you deducted actual operating costs plus depreciation, you may not use the mileage allowance on your 1999 return or in any later year.

The allowance takes the place of fixed operating costs such as gasoline (including state and local taxes), oil, repairs, license tags, insurance, and depreciation. You may not take the allowance and deduct your actual outlays for these expenses. Parking fees and tolls during business trips are allowed in addition to the mileage allowance. The IRS will not disallow a deduction based on the allowance even though it exceeds your actual car costs. If you use more than one automobile in your business travel and elect the allowance, total the business mileage traveled in both cars.

EXAMPLE

1. You buy a car in 1999 and drive it on business trips. You keep a record of your business mileage. You traveled 20,000 miles on business. You traveled 5,000 miles by March 31, 1999, and 15,000 miles between April 1 and December 31, 1999. You may deduct $6,275. This is your allowance for January 1 to March 31 of $1,625 (5,000 x 32.5 cents) plus your allowance of $4,650 (15,000 × 31 cents) for April 1 to December 31. In addition you spend $300 on tolls and parking. You may deduct a total of $6,575.

2. You use one car primarily for business and occasionally your spouse's car for business trips. In 1999, you drove your car on business trips 10,000 miles and your spouse's car 2,000 miles. Total business mileage is 12,000 miles for purposes of the 32.5/31 cents-per-mile allowance.

3. In June 1999, you place in service a new auto costing $20,000 and use it only for business. You travel 20,000 miles on business trips. If you claim the allowance, your deduction is $6,200 (20,000 × 31 cents). All travel took place after March 31, so only the 31 cents-per-mile rate applies. If you claim actual costs, your depreciation deduction is limited to $3,060; see 43.4. To match the IRS allowance, you need actual operating costs (such as gas, oil, and maintenance) of at least $3,140. If these costs exceed $3,140, it is advisable to claim your actual expenses plus depreciation. If you claim actual costs instead of the allowance for 1999, your deduction for 2000 will include depreciation of $5,000 in addition to operating costs. The $5,000 represents the second year depreciation limit on cars placed in service in 1999.

4. Same facts as in Example 2, but you travel only 9,600 business miles. If you elect the allowance, you may deduct only $2,976 (9,600 × 31 cents). If you elect to deduct actual costs, your depreciation deduction of $3,060 by itself exceeds the allowance. Assume your operating costs are $1,500. Your total deduction of $4,560 exceeds the allowance by $1,584.

Records. You may decide to use the allowance if you do not keep accurate records of operating costs. However, you must keep a record of your business trips, dates, customers or clients visited, business purpose of the trips, your total mileage during the year, and the number of miles traveled on business. An IRS agent may attempt to verify mileage by asking for repair bills near the beginning and end of the year if the bills note mileage readings. For your 1999 deduction, your records must distinguish the miles driven before April 1 from the miles driven after March 31 to account for the two 1999 allowance rates.

 Law Alert

Two Mileage Rates for 1999

There are two mileage rates in effect for 1999. From January 1 to March 31, 1999, the rate is 32.5 cents per mile and from April 1 to December 31, 1999, the rate is 31 cents per mile.

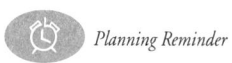 *Planning Reminder*

First-Year Election Affects Later Years

In deciding whether to elect the allowance in the first year, consider not only whether you will get a bigger first-year deduction using the allowance, or deducting actual operating costs plus depreciation, but also project your mileage, operating expenses, and depreciation expenses over the years you expect to use the car. If in the first year you elect to deduct actual costs, including accelerated MACRS or straight-line MACRS depreciation, you may not use the IRS auto allowance for *that car* in a later year. On the other hand, claiming the IRS allowance in the first year you put a car in service forfeits your privilege to use MACRS and first-year expensing. If you switch from the allowance to deducting actual expenses in later years, you may claim straight-line depreciation if the car is not considered fully depreciated.

Mileage allowance for leased cars. The IRS mileage allowance is also available for leased vehicles. If in 1999 you leased a car for business purposes you may claim the 32.5/31 cents-per-mile allowance, but if you claim the allowance for 1999 you will also have to use it for the remainder of the lease period, including renewals.

Interest on a car loan and taxes. *See 43.2* for when a deduction is allowed.

Mileage allowance disallowed. You may not claim the 32.5/31 cents-a-mile allowance if:

- You have depreciated your car using the ACRS or MACRS method, including straight-line MACRS, or you claimed first-year expensing.
- You use in your business two or more cars simultaneously, such as in a fleet operation.
- You use your car for hire—that is, you use it as a taxicab, carrying passengers for a fare.

Key To Deducting Automobile Expenses

Item—	Tax Rule—
IRS mileage allowance	You may avoid the trouble of keeping a record of actual auto expenses and calculating depreciation by electing the IRS mileage allowance. The allowance may give you a larger deduction than your actual outlays plus depreciation. You must elect the allowance in the first year you use the car for business. If you do not, you may not use the allowance for that car in any other year. To claim the allowance, you must be ready to prove business use of the auto and keep a record of your mileage. Of course, if your actual operating costs plus depreciation exceed the allowance, claim your actual operating expenses and depreciation.
Depreciation	If you claim actual operating expenses for a new car, such as gasoline, repairs, and insurance costs, you may also claim depreciation. There is a cap on the annual depreciation deduction. If you placed a car in service in 1999, the maximum deduction is $3,060. This amount is reduced if business use is less than 100%. Furthermore, accelerated MACRS depreciation is allowed only for autos used more than 50% of the time for business driving. Where business driving is 50% or less, straight-line depreciation must be used. MACRS depreciation deductions claimed in prior years may be recaptured if business use declines to 50% or less; *see 43.9*. If the car was placed in service before 1999, *see 43.4* for the maximum depreciation you can take for 1999.
First-year expensing	Whether you choose regular depreciation or first-year expensing, the limit for 1999 is $3,060, assuming 100% business use. If the cost of your car is $15,300 or greater, then you are subject to the $3,060 limit. Regular depreciation under the half-year convention at the 20% first-year MACRS rate *(43.5)* will be at least $3,060 ($15,300 × 20%). Thus, if the cost of your car is more than $15,300, it makes no difference whether you expense or depreciate because the result is the maximum $3,060 either way. If the cost of your car is less than $15,300, you are better off taking first-year expensing up to the $3,060 limit. First-year expensing may also provide a larger deduction if the mid-quarter convention applies; *see 43.5*. The first-year expensing rules are discussed in *42.3*. To claim first-year expensing, the auto must be used more than 50% for business travel. If business use is less than 100% but more than 50%, the $3,060 expensing limit is reduced. For example, if you use the auto 80% for business, the maximum 1999 deduction is $2,448 ($3,060 × 80%). If you elect first-year expensing in 1999, you may not use the IRS mileage allowance in later years for travel in that car. In 2000, you may claim MACRS depreciation, applying the second-year MACRS rate to your original basis reduced by the first-year deduction claimed in 1999; *see 43.5*.
Auto used for business and personal driving	You may deduct only the amount allocated to business mileage. For example, total mileage is 20,000 in 1999 and your business mileage is 15,000. You may claim only 75% of your deductible costs (15,000 ÷ 20,000).
Tax return reporting	If you are an *employee*, you claim actual auto expenses or the IRS allowance on Form 2106. Form 2106 requires you to list mileage for business, commuting, and other personal trips. If your auto costs are not reimbursed by your employer, you must deduct them as miscellaneous deductions subject to the 2% AGI floor on Schedule A. If you are *self-employed*, you deduct business costs on Schedule C and use Form 4562 to compute depreciation if you claim actual operating costs. Costs deducted on Schedule C are not limited by the 2% adjusted gross income (AGI) floor.

Employer reimbursements. If your employer reimburses your auto costs at a rate lower than the IRS allowance, you may use the IRS rate to deduct the excess over your employer's reimbursement; *see* Example 3 at *20.33*.

IRS allowance includes depreciation. When you use the IRS allowance, you may not claim a separate depreciation deduction. The IRS mileage allowance includes an estimate for depreciation. However, for purposes of figuring gain or loss on a disposition, you must reduce the basis of the car according to the following rates: 7 cents per business mile for 1980–1981; 7.5 cents per mile for 1982; 8 cents per mile for 1983, 1984, and 1985; 9 cents per mile for 1986; 10 cents per mile for 1987; 10.5 cents per mile for 1988; 11 cents per mile for 1989, 1990, and 1991; 11.5 cents per mile for 1992 and 1993; and 12 cents per mile for 1994, 1995, 1996, 1997, 1998, and 1999. For years before 1990, the annual cents-per-mile reduction applies only to the first 15,000 miles of business use per year for which the IRS allowance was claimed.

Depreciation when switching from allowance to actual costs. If you use the IRS mileage allowance in the first year, you may switch to the actual-cost method in a later year, but depreciation must be based on the straight-line method over the remaining estimated useful life. However, no depreciation may be claimed if basis has been reduced to zero under the annual cents-per-mile reduction rule just discussed.

43.2 Auto Expense Allocations

If you do not claim the IRS mileage allowance, you may deduct car expenses on business trips such as the cost of gas and oil (including state and local taxes), repairs, parking, and tolls.

If you use your car exclusively for business, all of your operating expenses are deductible. However, if you are an employee, the deduction is limited by the 2% adjusted gross income (AGI) floor; *see 19.1*.

Apportioning car expenses between business and personal use. For a car used for business and personal purposes, deduct only the depreciation and expenses allocated to your business use of the car. Depreciation is discussed at *43.3*, *43.4*, and *43.5*.

The business portion of car expenses is determined by the percentage of mileage driven on business trips during the year.

EXAMPLE

In 1999, you drove your car 15,000 miles. Of this, 12,000 miles was on business trips. The percentage of business use is 80%:

$$\frac{\text{Business Mileage}}{\text{Total Mileage}} \quad = \quad \frac{12,000}{15,000} \quad = \quad 80\%$$

Your actual car expenses (gas, oil, repairs, etc.) for the year were $1,000, of which $800 ($1,000 × 80%) is deductible. If you are an employee, the $800 is deductible as a miscellaneous itemized deduction subject to the 2% AGI floor; *see 19.1*.

Interest on car loan. If you are an *employee*, all of the interest is considered personal interest and is not deductible even if you use the car 100% of the time for your job. If you are *self-employed*, the allocated business percentage of the interest is fully deductible on Schedule C; the personal percentage is not deductible.

Taxes on purchase. Sales tax is not deductible whether you are an employee or self-employed; the tax is added to the basis of the auto for depreciation purposes; *see 43.3*. State and local property taxes are deductible as itemized deductions on Schedule A if you are an employee. If you are self-employed, deduct the business portion of the property taxes on Schedule C and the personal percentage on Schedule A if you itemize.

Leased car. If you lease a car for business use and do not claim the IRS mileage allowance *(43.1)*, you deduct the lease payments plus other costs of operating the car. If the car is also used for personal driving, the lease payments must be allocated between business and personal mileage. *See also 43.11* for rules requiring the reporting of extra income attributable to the lease.

43.3 Auto Depreciation Restrictions

The law contains restrictions that limit and, in some cases, deny depreciation deductions for a business car. Employees may be unable to claim any deduction at all under an employer convenience test. Employees meeting that test and self-employed individuals must determine if they can use accelerated MACRS rates or must use straight-line rates. Finally, regardless of which depreciation method is used, the annual deduction may not exceed a ceiling set by law. For a car placed in service in 1999, the ceiling is $3,060; *see 43.4* for details on the annual ceilings.

 Law Alert

Rural Mail Carriers
U.S. Postal Service employees who use their personal vehicles on rural routes and who receive an equipment maintenance allowance figured under a collective bargaining agreement are treated as being reimbursed for their actual expenses. There is a "wash" for tax purposes. The reimbursement should not be included in the employee's income and the employee has no deduction to report on his or her return.

Employer convenience test. If you are an employee and use your own car for work, you must be ready to prove that you use a car for the *convenience of your employer* who requires you to use it in your job. If you do not meet this employer convenience test, you may not claim depreciation or first-year expensing. A letter from your employer stating you need the car for business will not meet this test.

The facts and circumstances of your use of the car may show that it is a condition of employment. For example, an inspector for a construction company uses his automobile to visit construction sites over a scattered area. The company reimburses him for his expenses. According to the IRS, the inspector's use of the car is for the convenience of the company and is a condition of the job. However, if a company car were available to the inspector, the use of his own car would not meet the condition of employment and convenience of the employer tests.

More-than-50% business-use test for claiming expensing or accelerated MACRS depreciation. An automobile is considered "listed property," as explained in *42.10*, whether you are an employee or are self-employed. As such, you may claim first-year expensing or accelerated MACRS *(43.5)* for a car placed in service during 1999 only if you use it in 1999 more than 50% of the time for business. The same annual ceiling applies to the expensing and MACRS deductions; *see 43.4.*

If business use is *50% or less* in the year the auto is placed in service, first-year expensing and accelerated MACRS are barred; the auto is depreciable over a six-year period under the straight-line method. Technically, the recovery period is five years but the period is extended to six years because, in the first year, a convention rule limits the deductible percentage. *See* the straight-line rate tables at *43.6*. The straight-line method must also be used in future years, even if business use in those years exceeds 50%.

If a car is used for both business and investment purposes, only business use is considered in determining whether you meet the more than 50% business-use test and therefore qualify for MACRS. However, if your business use does exceed 50%, investment use is added to business use in determining your actual deduction.

> ### EXAMPLE
>
> Brown buys an automobile for $30,000 and places it in service in 1999. He uses it 40% for business and 20% for investment activity. Because he does not use his car more than 50% in his business, he may not claim first-year expensing or accelerated MACRS. He figures depreciation using the straight-line method. The business use allocation rate for depreciation is 60% (40% for business use plus 20% investment use).

Trucks and other vehicles. The more-than-50% business-use test generally applies to vehicles other than automobiles such as trucks, vans, boats, motorcycles, airplanes, and buses. However, the test does not apply to taxicabs and other vehicles used substantially all of the time to transport persons or property for hire. The test also does not apply to vehicles that are exempt from record-keeping requirements under *43.10*, such as a school bus, dump truck, farm tractor, or other specialized farm vehicle, delivery truck with seating only for the driver or with a folding jump seat, flat bed truck, garbage truck, passenger bus with capacity of at least 20, refrigerated truck, combine, specialized utility repair truck, unmarked law enforcement vehicle officially authorized for use, and a moving van if personal use is limited by the employer to travel from the employee's home to a move site.

A vehicle not in the exempt list is subject to the more-than-50% test for claiming accelerated MACRS depreciation or first-year expensing. If you do not satisfy the more-than-50% test, you must apply the straight-line recovery rates shown at *43.6*.

Do your employees use the car? In certain cases, an employer who provides a company car to employees as part of their compensation may be unable to count the employee's use as qualified business use, thereby preventing the employer from meeting the more-than-50% business-use test for claiming MACRS. An employer is allowed to treat the employee's use as qualified business use only if: (1) the employee is not a relative and does not own more than 5% of the business and (2) the employer treats the fair market value of the employee's personal use of the car as wage income and withholds tax on that amount. If such income is reported, all of the employee's use, including personal use, may be counted by an employer as qualified business use.

If an employee owning more than a 5% interest is allowed use of a company car as part of his or her compensation, the employer may not count that use as qualified business use, even if the personal use is reported as income. The same strict rule applies if the car is provided to a person who is related to the employer.

Caution

Recapture of MACRS Deductions

If you meet the more-than-50% test in the year the car or other vehicle is placed in service, which entitles you to claim first-year expensing or accelerated MACRS, but business use falls to 50% or less in a later year, the recapture rules discussed at *43.9* apply.

43.4 Annual Ceilings on Depreciation

For cars placed in service after 1986, annual ceilings limit the amount of depreciation you may deduct. The ceilings apply both to self-employed individuals and employees. As a result of the ceilings, the actual write-off period for your car may be several years longer than the minimum recovery period of six years; *see 43.5*. The table below shows the year-by-year ceilings for cars placed in service between 1990 and 1999.

If the ceiling is less than the amount of depreciation figured under the regular MACRS rules, you are limited to the ceiling amount. For example, if in 1999 you bought a car for $20,000 that you used 100% for business, the regular MACRS rules would allow a deduction of $4,000 in 1999 (20% × $20,000), assuming the half-year convention applied; *see 43.5*. However, your 1999 depreciation deduction is limited to $3,060, the ceiling for cars placed in service during 1999. The ceiling is reduced if you use the car for both personal and business driving as discussed below.

You may not exceed the ceiling by claiming first-year expensing *(42.3)*. The $3,060 limit for cars placed in service in 1999 also applies to the first-year expensing deduction. Thus, the first-year expensing deduction in 1999 may not exceed $3,060. If you claim first-year expensing of $3,060, you may not deduct any other depreciation. Claiming first-year expensing on Form 4562 (if self-employed) or Form 2106 (if an employee) may provide a larger deduction than regular MACRS depreciation where your deduction is subject to the mid-quarter convention; *see 43.5*.

Personal driving reduces the annual ceiling. The annual ceilings are reduced if you use a car for both personal and business use. The reduced ceiling is equal to the regular ceiling multiplied by the percentage of business use. For example, in 1999, you buy a car costing $40,000. You use the car 70% for business travel. The MACRS or first-year expensing deduction is limited to $2,142 ($3,060 × 70%). Furthermore, for purposes of figuring whether depreciation is allowed after the end of the recovery period, the basis of the car is reduced by the amount of the depreciation that would have been allowed if you had used the car 100% for business travel; *see 43.7*.

Light trucks and vans subject to the ceilings. The annual depreciation ceilings apply only to "passenger automobiles." For this purpose, a passenger automobile is generally considered to be any four-wheeled vehicle that is manufactured primarily for use on public streets, roads, and highways and that is weight-rated by the manufacturer at 6,000 pounds or less when unloaded (without passengers or cargo). However, a light truck or van that is weight-rated by the manufacturer at 6,000 pounds or less when loaded (gross vehicle weight) is treated as a passenger automobile.

The following are not considered "passenger" automobiles and thus are exempt from the annual ceilings: (1) an ambulance, hearse, or combination ambulance-hearse used directly in a business and (2) a vehicle such as a taxicab used directly in the business of transporting persons or property for compensation or hire.

 Law Alert

Depreciation Limits on Electric Cars

In an effort to encourage the use of electric automobiles, a larger annual depreciation limit is allowed for electric vehicles built by an original manufacturer and placed in service after August 5, 1997. In 1999, the first-year depreciation cap is set at $9,280.

 Filing Tip

Sport Utility Vehicles

Owners of certain sport utility vehicles (SUVs) that are used for business purposes and that have a gross vehicle weight (loaded) of more than 6,000 pounds are not subject to the ceiling on depreciation deductions. This means the owner is entitled to the full depreciation deduction using the MACRS rate shown in *43.5*.

SUV owners should check the manufacturers' specifications for their vehicles to see if the weight exceeds the 6,000 limit.

Annual Depreciation Ceiling

For auto placed in service in—

Ceiling in—	1990	1991	1992	1993	1994	1995	1996	1997	1998	1999
1990	$2,660									
1991	4,200	$2,660								
1992	2,550	4,300	$2,760							
1993	1,475	2,550	4,400	$2,860						
1994	1,475	1,575	2,650	4,600	$2,960					
1995	1,475	1,575	1,575	2,750	4,700	$3,060				
1996	1,475	1,575	1,575	1,675	2,850	4,900	$3,060			
1997	1,475	1,575	1,575	1,675	1,675	2,950	4,900	3,160		
1998	1,475	1,575	1,575	1,675	1,675	1,775	2,950	5,000	3,160	
1999	1,475	1,575	1,575	1,675	1,675	1,775	1,775	3,050	5,000	3,060
2000	1,475	1,575	1,575	1,675	1,675	1,775	1,775	1,775	2,950	5,000
2001	1,475	1,575	1,575	1,675	1,675	1,775	1,775	1,775	1,775	2,950
2002 and later years	1,475	1,575	1,575	1,675	1,675	1,775	1,775	1,775	1,775	1,775

43.5 MACRS Rates for Cars

Business autos placed in service in 1987 and later years are technically in a five-year MACRS class *(42.4)*, but because of the half-year or mid-quarter convention and the annual deduction ceilings, the minimum depreciation period is six years.

MACRS rate. To use accelerated MACRS or first-year expensing, you must meet the more-than-50% business-use test explained at *43.3*. If you do, the MACRS rate is based on the 200% declining balance method with a switchover to straight line. The declining balance rate for a car that is five-year property is 40%. However, the full amount of the deduction is not allowed, because of the convention rules and the annual car limits discussed in this section. Each year the declining balance rate of 40% is applied against the declining balance of the basis of property.

As a shortcut, you may apply the half-year convention rates or the mid-quarter convention rates shown on the following pages, whichever apply in your case. The rates are applied against unadjusted basis, which is your cost minus any first-year expensing deduction. The deduction may not exceed the annual ceiling for auto depreciation, multiplied by the percentage of business use; *see* the Example on the following page.

Straight-line election for car if business use exceeds 50%. If business use of your car exceeds 50%, you may elect to write off your cost under the straight-line method instead of using the regular MACRS 200% declining balance method. The straight-line rates are shown in *43.6*. The straight-line deduction is limited by the annual ceilings shown in *43.4*. By electing straight-line depreciation, you avoid the recapture of excess MACRS deductions if business use drops to 50% or less in a later year; *see 43.9*. If the election is made, you must also use the straight-line method for all other five-year property placed in service during the same year as the car.

Electing 150% rate. The rates shown in this section for the half-year and mid-quarter convention are based on the 200% declining balance method. You may instead elect to apply a 150% declining balance rate. The 150% rate may be advantageous when you are subject to alternative minimum tax (AMT); *see 42.8*.

Half-year or mid-quarter convention. Regardless of the time of year you bought the car in 1999, your deduction is limited by a convention rule. If the only business equipment bought in 1999 was the car, then the half-year convention applies, unless you bought the car in the last quarter of 1999 (October, November, or December). Under the half-year convention, the car is treated as if it were placed in service in the middle of the year and the 40% declining balance rate is reduced to 20%. Use the table below to determine your deduction under the half-year convention.

If the only business equipment bought in 1999 was a car bought in the last quarter (October, November, or December), the mid-quarter convention applies. Under the table for mid-quarter convention rates on page 635, a 5% rate applies for fourth-quarter property, subject to the $3,060 deduction ceiling in 1999.

MACRS Deduction: Half-Year Convention

Year—	Lower of percentage below and annual ceiling*—
1	20.00%
2	32.00
3	19.20
4	11.52
5	11.52
6	5.76

The annual ceiling for the year depends on the year the car was placed in business service. For cars placed in service in 1999, the ceiling on 1999 returns is $3,060. The table on the preceding page shows the ceiling for other years of service. If your car is not used 100% for business in 1999, multiply the business-use percentage by the applicable annual ceiling and compare the result to the deduction figured by multiplying the business-use portion of the unadjusted basis (cost minus first-year expensing) of the car by the rate in the above table. Your deduction is the lower amount; see the following Example.

Filing Tip

Mid-Quarter Rate Limitation

If the application of the mid-quarter convention limits your deduction to less than $3,060 for a car placed in service during 1999, consider an election to claim the first-year expensing deduction at *42.3* if your business-use percentage exceeds 50%. This may allow you to deduct up to $3,060.

If you bought other business equipment in addition to the car, you must consider the total cost basis of property placed in service during the last quarter of 1999. If the total bases of such acquisitions (other than realty) exceed 40% of the total bases of all property placed in service during the year, then a mid-quarter rate applies to all property (other than realty). The mid-quarter rate for each asset then depends on the quarter the asset was placed in service. If the 40% test is not met, then the half-year convention applies to all the property acquisitions. As shown in the mid-quarter convention table below, mid-quarter rates for each year of the recovery period depend on the quarter the property is placed in service.

EXAMPLE

In May 1999, you place in service a car used 100% for business. The car cost $20,000. Here is the depreciation schedule assuming the car is kept for the period shown below and is used 100% for business trips:

1999	3,060
2000	5,000
2001	2,950
2002	1,775
2003	1,775
2004*	1,152
2005	1,775
2006	1,775
2007	738

 Filing Tip

Capital Improvements
A capital improvement to a business auto is depreciable under MACRS in the year the improvement is made. The MACRS deductions for the improvement and the auto are considered as a unit for purposes of applying the limits on the annual MACRS depreciation deduction.

* Note that in year 6 (2004), the depreciation deduction is $1,152 and not $1,775. The $1,152 represents the year 6 MACRS depreciation deduction of 5.76% of $20,000. Since you take the lower of the MACRS percentage and the annual ceiling, the $1,152 is used because it is less than $1,775. In years 7 and 8 (2005 and 2006), the annual ceiling of $1,775 is used as the 6-year MACRS recovery period has run. In year 9 (2007), the balance left to be depreciated, or $738, is deducted.

Assume that in 1999 you use the car only 60% rather than 100% for business. You deduct $1,836 in 1999 (60% of the annual limit of $3,060). Your deduction may not be based on 60% of depreciable basis; this would give a larger deduction of $2,400 ($20,000 × 60% business use × 20% first-year depreciation rate) without considering the first-year deduction limit.

MACRS Deduction: Mid-Quarter Convention*

	Placed in service in—			
Year—	First Quarter	Second Quarter	Third Quarter	Fourth Quarter
1	35.00%	25.00%	15.00%	5.00%
2	26.00	30.00	34.00	38.00
3	15.60	18.00	20.40	22.80
4	11.01	11.37	12.24	13.68
5	11.01	11.37	11.30	10.94
6	1.38	4.26	7.06	9.58

If business use is 100%, you deduct the lower of the annual ceiling (see table on page 633) and the applicable mid-quarter rate multiplied by the unadjusted basis (cost less any first-year expensing deduction). If business use is less than 100%, multiply the lower amount by the business-use percentage to get the allowable deduction.

EXAMPLES

1. In November 1999, you buy a car for $23,000 that you use 100% for business. Applying the 5% rate for the fourth quarter from the table above, your deduction is $1,150 ($23,000 × 5%). This is less than the ceiling of $3,060.

   If the car had been bought in May 1999, the 25% rate for the second quarter would give a deduction of $5,750 ($23,000 × 25%). However, your deduction would be limited to the $3,060 ceiling.

2. In December 1999, you place in service an auto used solely for business. It costs $25,000. Applying the fourth-quarter rate of 5% from the mid-quarter convention table above gives a depreciation deduction of only $1,250. If you elect first-year expensing, the deduction is $3,060.

Caution

Basis Reduced by Depreciation

The basis of a car is reduced by the full amount of depreciation that is allowable, whether or not a full deduction is actually claimed. For example, in 1999 you place in service a car costing $25,000, used 80% for business. Assuming the half-year convention applies, the unadjusted basis of the car is reduced by $3,060, the depreciation that would have been allowed in 1999 for 100% business use, and not by the $2,448 depreciation deduction actually allowed (80% of business use × $3,060 maximum limit for 1999).

Converting a pleasure car to business use. The basis for depreciation is the lower of the market value of the car at the time of conversion and its adjusted basis, which is your original cost plus any substantial improvements and minus any deductible casualty losses or diesel fuel tax credit claimed for the car. In most cases, the value of the car will be lower than adjusted basis, and thus the value will be your depreciable basis. For a car converted to business use in 1999, the MACRS rate is applied to basis allocated to business travel. Unless you have mileage records for the entire year, you should base your business-use percentage on driving after the conversion. For example, in April 1999, you started to use your car for business and in the last nine months of the year you drove 10,000 miles, 8,000 of which were for business. This business percentage of 80% is multiplied by the fraction $^9/_{12}$ (months used for business divided by 12) to give you a business-use percentage for the year of 60% ($^9/_{12}$ of 80%).

43.6 Straight-Line Rate for Business Use of 50% or Less

You may not use accelerated MACRS if your business use of your car is 50% or less. Mandatory straight-line recovery rates for business use of 50% or less using the half-year or mid-quarter convention are shown below. These straight-line rates are also used if you elect straight-line recovery (43.5) instead of the regular MACRS method. Because of the half-year convention, the straight-line recovery period is extended from five to six years.

The annual depreciation ceilings of 43.4 apply.

Straight-line year—	Half-year convention rate—
1	10%
2	20
3	20
4	20
5	20
6	10

EXAMPLE

In April 1999, you place in service an automobile which cost $15,000. You used it 40% for business. The depreciable basis is $6,000 (40% of $15,000). The depreciation deduction in 1999 is $600 (10% of $6,000) if the half-year convention applies.

If the mid-quarter convention applies (43.5), the depreciation deduction depends on the quarter the car was placed in service.

Straight-Line Mid-Quarter Convention*

Placed in service in—

Year	First Quarter	Second Quarter	Third Quarter	Fourth Quarter
1	17.50%	12.50%	7.50%	2.50%
2	20.00	20.00	20.00	20.00
3	20.00	20.00	20.00	20.00
4	20.00	20.00	20.00	20.00
5	20.00	20.00	20.00	20.00
6	2.50	7.50	12.50	17.50

The deduction may not exceed the annual deduction ceiling; see 43.4.

EXAMPLE

In 1999, you place in service a car costing $15,000 used 40% for business. Assume the mid-quarter convention applies. Depending on the applicable quarter, the deduction is listed below, figured on a basis of $6,000 ($15,000 × 40%). The first-year ceiling at 40% business use is $1,224 ($3,060 × 40%). The ceiling does not apply because the mid-quarter rates provide a lower deduction.

Quarter	Deduction
1	$1,050 ($6,000 × 17.5%)
2	750 ($6,000 × 12.5%)
3	450 ($6,000 × 7.5%)
4	150 ($6,000 × 2.5%)

43.7 Depreciation After Recovery Period Ends

If your business use of a car during the recovery period is 100% and your deductions are limited by the annual ceilings (43.4), any remaining basis that was not deducted because of the ceilings may be depreciated in the years after the end of the recovery period.

If the car was used less than 100% for business, any unrecovered basis may be deductible, but to determine unrecovered basis, original basis must be reduced by the depreciation that would have been allowed had the car been used 100% for business.

EXAMPLE

In 1993 you bought a car costing $28,600 that you used 100% for business every year from 1993 through 1998. Your depreciation deductions for the six-year recovery period were limited to a total of $15,235 by the annual ceilings. You deducted the ceiling amounts (see the table on page 633) of $2,860 in 1993, $4,600 in 1994, $2,750 in 1995, and $1,675 in each of 1996, 1997, and 1998 for a total of $15,235.

At the beginning of 1999, your unrecovered basis in the car is $13,365 (the original basis of the $28,600 minus the $15,235 of depreciation deductions allowed from 1993 through 1998). If you continue to use the car 100% for business in 1999 and later years, you can deduct $1,675 in 1999 and also in later years until the $13,365 of unrecovered basis is used up.

If you had not used the car for business 100% of the time in all prior years, your unrecovered basis would still be $13,365. That is because for purposes of figuring unrecovered basis, you must reduce original basis by the depreciation that would have been allowed based on 100% business use. For years after 1998 in which business use is 100%, deductions of $1,675 are allowed until the unrecovered basis is used up. In years of partial business use, the deduction is limited to $1,675 multiplied by the business-use percentage.

43.8 Trade-in of Business Auto

No gain or loss is recognized on a trade-in of a business auto for another business auto. If the old car was used entirely for business, the basis of the new auto is the adjusted basis of the old auto *plus* any additional payment. However, if you trade in an auto acquired after June 18, 1984, and it was not used solely for business, basis for figuring MACRS for the new auto is subject to a reduction. To find the basis of the new car, you start with the basis of the car that was traded in, add any cash paid on the trade-in, and reduce the total by the excess, if any, of (1) the total depreciation that would have been allowable if the old auto had been used solely for business or investment over (2) the total of the depreciation actually allowed.

EXAMPLES

1. You traded in a car with an adjusted basis of $5,000 for a new car and, in addition, paid $8,000 cash for the new car. Both cars are used 100% for business. The unadjusted basis of the new car is $13,000 ($5,000 adjusted basis of the old car plus the $8,000 cash paid).

2. In 1997, you bought a car for $20,000 and used it 80% for business in 1997 and 1998. In January 1999 you traded it in for a new car and paid an additional $11,000. In 1997 you deducted MACRS depreciation of $2,528 (80% x $3,160 ceiling) and in 1998 $4,000 (80% of $5,000 ceiling). Your basis for purposes of figuring 1999 MACRS depreciation is $22,840, figured as follows:

Adjusted basis of old car	
Cost	$20,000
Less: depreciation for 1997 and 1998	6,528
Adjusted basis of old car	$13,472
Basis of new car	
Adjusted basis of old car	$13,472
Cash paid for new car	11,000
	$24,472
Less: depreciation adjustment (*see* below)	1,632
Basis of new car	$22,840
Depreciation adjustment for partial use:	
Depreciation if 100% business use	
1997	$3,160
1998	5,000
Total	$8,160
Less: actual depreciation for 1997 and 1998*	6,528
Adjustment	$1,632

Actual depreciation for 80% business use is $2,528 in 1997 and $4,000 in 1998.

Planning Reminder

Trade-in

When you trade in a car that was used entirely for business, your basis for the new car is the basis of the old car plus any additional payment you make. *See 43.8* for a required basis adjustment where the traded-in car was not used 100% for business.

43.9 Recapture of Deductions on Business Auto

If you use your car more than 50% for business in the year you place it in service, you may use MACRS accelerated rates; *see 43.5*. If business use drops to 50% or less in the second, third, fourth, fifth, or sixth year, earlier MACRS deductions must be recaptured and reported as ordinary income. In the year in which business use drops to 50% or less, you must recapture excess depreciation for all prior years. Excess depreciation is the difference between: (1) the MACRS deductions allowed in previous years, including the first-year expensing deduction, if any, and (2) the amount of depreciation that would have been allowed if you claimed straight-line depreciation based on a six-year recovery period. *See 43.6* for straight-line rates.

The recapture rules do not apply if you elected straight-line recovery instead of applying accelerated MACRS rates.

Recapture is computed on Form 4797, which must be attached to Form 1040. The 50% business-use test and recapture rule apply to trucks and airplanes in addition to cars, but *see* the list of exceptions for taxicabs and other specialty vehicles at *43.3*.

Any recaptured amount increases the basis of the property. To compute depreciation for the year in which business use drops to 50% or less and for later years within the six-year straight-line recovery period, you apply the straight-line rates shown at *43.6*.

EXAMPLE

On June 25, 1996, you bought a car for $11,000 that you used exclusively for business in 1996, 1997, and 1998. The half-year convention applied to your MACRS deductions *(43.5)*. During 1999, you used it 40% for business and 60% for personal purposes. In 1999, as you did not meet the more-than-50% business-use test, excess depreciation of $2,332 is recaptured and reported on Form 4797:

Total MACRS depreciation claimed (1996–1998)		$7,832
Total straight-line depreciation *(43.6)* allowable:		
1996—10% of $11,000	$1,100	
1997—20% of $11,000	2,200	
1998—20% of $11,000	2,200	5,500
Excess depreciation recaptured		$2,332

Your 1999 depreciation deduction is $880 ($11,000 × 20% straight-line rate in fourth year × 40% business use).

The amount of recaptured depreciation increases the adjusted basis for purposes of computing gain or loss on a disposition of the automobile.

43.10 Keeping Records of Business Use

Keep a log or diary or similar record of the business use of a car. Record the purpose of the business trips and mileage covered for business travel. In the record book, also note the odometer reading for the beginning and end of the taxable year. You need this data to prove business use. If you do not keep written records of business mileage and your return is examined, you will have to convince an IRS agent of your business mileage through oral testimony. Without written evidence, you may be unable to convince an IRS agent that you use the car for business travel or that you meet the business use tests for claiming MACRS. You may also be subject to general negligence penalties for claiming deductions that you cannot prove you incurred.

Mileage records are not required for vehicles that are unlikely to be used for personal purposes, such as delivery trucks with seating only for the driver.

Employees using company cars are not required to keep mileage records if (1) a written company policy allows them to use the car for commuting and no other personal driving other than personal errands while commuting home or (2) a written company policy bars all personal driving except for minor stops, such as for lunch, between business travel. Owners, directors, and officers of the company generally do not qualify for exception (1).

43.11 Leased Business Autos: Deductions and Income

If you lease rather than purchase a car for business use, you may deduct the lease charges as a business expense deduction if you use the car exclusively for business. If you also use the car for personal driving, you may deduct only the lease payments allocated to business travel. Also keep a record of business use; *see 43.10.*

Added income. If in 1999 you lease a car for 30 days or more and the fair market value of the car at the beginning of the lease was over $15,500, you may have to report as income an amount based on an IRS table. This income rule applies if you deduct the business portion of your lease payments plus other operating costs; it does not apply if you claim the standard mileage allowance *(43.1).* On Schedule C (if self-employed) or Form 2106 (if an employee), the income inclusion amount reduces your deduction for lease payments so that it equals the amount that would be deductible as depreciation if you had bought the car outright. The income amount is reduced where you leased the car for less than the entire year or business use is less than 100%.

The lease tables, which are in IRS Publication 463, show income amounts for each year of the lease. Publication 463 also has tables showing income amounts for cars leased before 1999.

 Caution

Leased Auto

If in 1999 you leased for at least 30 days a car valued at over $15,500, and you deduct the lease charges as a business expense *(43.11)*, you must reduce the deduction by an "income inclusion amount" based on an IRS table. If you claim the standard mileage allowance *(43.1)*, the income inclusion rule does not apply. *See* IRS Publication 463 for details.

Sales of Business Property

The tax treatment of business assets depends on the type of asset sold.

Inventory items: Profits are taxable as ordinary income; losses are fully deductible. Sales of merchandise are reported on Schedule C if you are self-employed or Schedule F if you are a farmer.

Depreciable property, such as buildings, machinery, and equipment: If you sell at a gain, the gain is taxable as ordinary income to the extent depreciation is recaptured under *44.1 and 44.2.* Any remaining gain may be treated as capital gain or ordinary income, depending on the Section 1231 computation at *44.8.* Losses may be deductible as ordinary losses; *see 44.8.* Sales are reported on Form 4797. Depreciable business equipment subject to recapture is described as a Section 1245 asset. Depreciable livestock is also a Section 1245 asset. Depreciable realty is generally described as Section 1250 assets.

Land: If used in your business, capital gain or ordinary income may be realized under the rules of Section 1231; *see 44.8.* If land owned by your business is held for investment, gain or loss is subject to capital gain treatment. Schedule D is used to report the sale of capital assets.

44.1 Ordinary Income Recapture of Depreciation on Sale of Personal Property

On Form 4797, you report gain or loss on the sale of depreciable property. Gain realized on the sale of depreciable *personal property* (Section 1245 property) is treated as ordinary income to the extent the gain is attributed to depreciation deductions that reduced basis. In other words, the depreciation deductions are "recaptured" as ordinary income. If gain exceeds the amount of depreciation subject to recapture, the excess may be capital gain under Section 1231; *see 44.8.*

Gain on the sale of real estate placed in service before 1987 may be subject to depreciation recapture as discussed in *44.2.*

Gain subject to recapture for Section 1245 property is limited to the lower of (1) the amount realized on the sale less adjusted basis and (2) recomputed basis less the adjusted basis. Recomputed basis is adjusted basis increased by depreciation deductions allowed or allowable. Generally, the depreciation deduction taken into account for each year is the amount allowed or allowable, whichever is greater. However, for purposes of figuring what portion of the gain is treated as ordinary income under the recapture rules (but not for purposes of figuring gain or loss), the depreciation taken into account for any year will be the amount actually "allowed" on your prior returns under a proper depreciation method, rather than the amount "allowable," if the allowed deduction is smaller and you can prove its amount.

The adjusted basis of personal property depreciable under ACRS, such as business equipment and machinery, is fixed as of the beginning of the year of disposition. However, property depreciated under MACRS is subject to the convention rules so that partial depreciation under the applicable convention is allowed in the year of sale; this year of sale depreciation reduces adjusted basis.

Where basis was reduced by an investment credit for property placed in service after 1982, the basis reduction is treated as a depreciation deduction when figuring recapture; *see* Form 4797.

EXAMPLE

In 1997, you placed in service equipment (five-year property) costing $10,000. In 1997 you deducted depreciation of $2,000 and in 1998 you deducted $3,200. In January 1999, you sell it for $6,000. The MACRS deduction allowed for 1999, the year of sale, is $960 (19.20% × $10,000 ÷ 2). The adjusted basis is $3,840 ($10,000 – $6,160 total depreciation). Recomputed basis is $10,000 ($3,840 + $6,160). The amount of recapture is the lower of—
1. $6,160, the recomputed basis of $10,000 less adjusted basis of $3,840; and
2. $2,160, the amount realized of $6,000 less adjusted basis of $3,840.

The lower amount of $2,160 is recaptured as ordinary income on Part III of Form 4797.

44.2 Ordinary Income Recapture on Depreciable Realty

All or part of gain on the sale of depreciable real property may be attributable to depreciation deductions that reduced the basis of the property. For example, you bought an office building for $300,000. You claimed depreciation deductions of $100,000 that reduced the basis of the building to $200,000. If you sell the building for $280,000, you will realize a gain of $80,000 ($280,000 – $200,000). The gain of $80,000 is attributable to the depreciation deductions that reduced basis to $200,000. Under the tax law, all or part of such gain may be treated as recaptured depreciation or unrecaptured Section 1250 gain.

Unrecaptured Section 1250 gain. Gain on the sale of depreciable realty held long term that is attributible to depreciation *not* subject to the ordinary income recapture rules discussed below is unrecaptued Section 1250 gain. Such gain is subject to a 25% capital gain rate in Part IV of Schedule D (rather than the 20% capital gain rate) where your top tax bracket exceeds 15%. Unrecaptured Section 1250 gain may be realized on the sale of depreciable property regardless of when the property was acquired.

Recaptured depreciation. Recaptured depreciation may be realized only on the sale of certain real property acquired before 1987. Gain attributed to recaptured depreciation is taxable as ordinary income. Where only part of gain attributed to depreciation is treated as recaptured depreciation, the balance is treated as unrecaptured Section 1250 gain.

Ordinary income recapture may apply to Section 1250 realty placed in service before 1987. There is no ordinary income recapture on depreciable realty placed in service after 1986 because such realty is subject to straight-line MACRS depreciation *(42.13)*. Section 1250 property includes buildings and structural components, *except* for elevators and escalators or other tangible property used as an integral part of manufacturing, production, or extraction, or of furnishing transportation, electrical energy, water, gas, sewage disposal services, or communications. Property may initially be Section 1250 property and then, on a change of use, become Section 1245 property *(44.1)*. Such property may not be reconverted to Section 1250 property.

Depreciation claimed on realty during the years 1964 through 1969. Depreciation claimed during this period is not recaptured.

 Caution

Dispositions Other than Sales

Exchanges of property *(6.1)* and involuntary conversions *(18.19)* may result in recapture of depreciation. For dispositions that are not sales, exchanges, or involuntary conversions, the amount of recapture is all depreciation claimed, but not in excess of the difference between fair market value at disposition or original cost, whichever is less, and adjusted basis.

Depreciation claimed after 1969 for realty placed in service before 1981. For non-residential realty, 100 percent of the depreciation claimed after 1969 in excess of straight-line recovery is subject to recapture but not in excess of the actual gain.

For residential rental property, there is no recapture of excess depreciation (over straight-line) claimed after 1969 and before 1976. Real property is considered residential rental property if 80% or more of gross income is from dwelling units. One hundred percent of the excess depreciation claimed after 1975 is subject to recapture. Part III of Form 4797 is used to compute the amount of depreciation recapture that is to be reported as ordinary income.

Depreciation claimed on realty placed in service after 1980 and before 1987. For real property placed in service after 1980 and before 1987 that was subject to ACRS, adjusted basis for computing gain or loss is the adjusted basis at the start of the year reduced by the ACRS deduction allowed for the number of months the realty is in service in the year of disposition; *see 42.16.* The recapture rules distinguish between residential and nonresidential property.

If the prescribed accelerated method is used to recover the cost of *nonresidential* property, all gain on the disposition of the realty is recaptured as ordinary income to the extent of recovery allowances previously taken. Thus, nonresidential realty will be treated in the same way as personal property *(44.1)* for purposes of recapture if the accelerated recovery allowance was claimed. If the straight-line method was elected, there is no recapture; all gain is subject to the netting rules of Section 1231 *(44.8).*

If accelerated cost recovery is used for a *nonresidential* building and straight-line depreciation is used for a substantial improvement to that building that you are allowed to depreciate separately *(42.16),* all gain on a disposition of the entire building is treated as ordinary income to the extent of the accelerated cost recovery claimed. Remaining gain is subject to the rules for Section 1231 assets *(44.8).*

For *residential* real estate, there is ordinary income recapture to the extent the depreciation allowed under the prescribed accelerated method exceeds the recovery that would have been allowable if the straight-line method over the ACRS recovery period had been used. If the straight-line method was elected, there is no recapture. All gain is subject to Section 1231 netting *(44.8).*

For *low-income rental housing,* the same rule as for residential realty applies except that recapture is phased out at the rate of one percentage point per month for property held at least 100 months, so that there is no recapture of cost recovery deductions for property held at least 200 months (16 years, 8 months).

44.3 Recapture of First-Year Expensing

On Form 4797, the first-year expensing deduction (Section 179) is treated as depreciation for purposes of recapture. When expensed property is sold or exchanged, gain is ordinary income to the extent of the first-year expense deduction plus ACRS or MACRS deductions, if any; *see 44.1.*

Expensing deductions are also subject to recapture if property placed in service after 1986 is not used more than 50% of the time for business in any year before the end of the recovery period. The amount recaptured is the excess of the first-year *expensing* deduction over the amount of depreciation that would have been claimed in prior years and in the recapture year without expensing.

Automobiles and other "listed property." If the more-than-50% business-use test for a business automobile or other "listed property" such as certain computers *(see 42.10)* is not met in a year after the auto or other "listed property" is placed in service and before the end of the recovery period, any first-year expensing deduction is subject to recapture on Form 4797; *see* the Example at *43.9.*

44.4 Gifts and Inheritances of Depreciable Property

Gifts and charitable donations of depreciable property may be affected by the recapture rules. On the gift of depreciable property, the ordinary income potential of the depreciation carries over into the hands of the donee. When the donee later sells the property at a profit, he or she will realize ordinary income to the extent described in *44.1.* A person receiving a gift of low-income housing property includes in the holding period the period for which the donor held the property for purposes of applying the 200-month phaseout of recapture rule *(44.2).*

On the donation of depreciable property, the amount of the contribution deduction is reduced by the amount that would be taxed as ordinary income had the donor sold the equipment at its fair market value.

On the death of a decedent, the transfer of depreciable property to an heir through inheritance is not a taxable event for recapture purposes. The ordinary income potential does not carry over to the heir because his or her basis is usually fixed as of the date of the decedent's death.

Important: A gift of depreciable property subject to a mortgage may be taxed to the extent that the liability exceeds the basis of the property; *see 14.6* and *31.15.*

Caution

Installment Sale

If you sell property on the installment basis, the first-year expensing deduction claimed for the property in a prior year is recaptured in the year of sale on Form 4797. An installment sale does not defer recapture of the first-year deduction; *see 44.6.*

44.5 Involuntary Conversions and Tax-Free Exchanges

Involuntary conversions. Gain may be taxed as ordinary income in either of the following two cases: (1) you do not buy qualified replacement property or (2) you buy a qualified replacement, but the cost of the replacement is less than the amount realized on the conversion; *see 18.23.* The amount taxable as ordinary income may not exceed the amount of gain that is normally taxed under involuntary conversion rules when the replacement cost is less than the amount realized on the conversion. Also, the amount of ordinary income is increased by the value of any nondepreciable property that is bought as qualified replacement property, such as the purchase of 80% or more of stock in a company that owns property similar to the converted property.

Distributions by a partnership to a partner. A distribution of depreciable property by a partnership to a partner does not result in ordinary income to the distributee at the time of the distribution. But the partner assumes the ordinary income potential of the depreciation deduction taken by the partnership on the property. When he or she later disposes of the property, ordinary income may be realized.

44.6 Installment Sale of Depreciable Property

All depreciation recapture income (including the first-year expensing deduction) is fully taxable in the year of sale, without regard to the time of payment. This rule does not apply to installment sales made after June 6, 1984, under a contract binding on March 22, 1984, and all times thereafter.

If you are reporting on an installment basis a profitable sale of depreciable property made before June 7, 1984, "recaptured" ordinary income is reported before any of the capital gain is reported. You do not allocate the profit element of each installment payment between ordinary income and capital gain. As installments are received, you report all of the ordinary income until that amount is exhausted.

Recapture is figured on Form 4797.

44.7 Sale of a Proprietorship

The sale of a sole proprietorship is not considered as the sale of a business unit but as sales of individual business assets. Each sale is reported separately on your tax return.

A purchase of a business involves the purchase of various individual business assets of the business. To force buyers and sellers to follow the same allocation rules, current law requires both the buyer and the seller to allocate the purchase price of a business among the transferred assets using a residual method formula. Allocations are based on the proportion of sales price to an asset's fair market value and they are made in a specific order set out on Form 8594.

44.8 Property Used in a Business (Section 1231 Assets)

Form 4797 is used to report the sale or exchange of Section 1231 assets. The following properties used in a business are considered "Section 1231 assets":

- Depreciable assets such as buildings, machinery, and other equipment held more than one year. Depreciable rental property fits in this category if held more than one year.
- Land (including growing crops and water rights underlying farmland) held more than one year.
- Timber, coal, or domestic iron ore subject to special capital gain treatment.
- Leaseholds held more than one year.
- An unharvested crop on farmlands, if the crop and land are sold, exchanged, or involuntarily converted at the same time and to the same person and the land has been held more than one year. Such property is not included here if you retain an option to reacquire the land.
- Cattle and horses held for draft, breeding, dairy, or sporting purposes for at least 24 months.
- Livestock (other than cattle and horses) held for draft, breeding, dairy, or sporting purposes for at least 12 months. Poultry is not treated as livestock for purposes of Section 1231.

Section 1231 netting. On Form 4797, you combine all losses and gains, except gains allocated to depreciation recapture, from:

- The sale of Section 1231 assets (from the list at the beginning of this section).
- The involuntary conversion of Section 1231 assets and capital assets held for more than one year for business or investment purposes. You include casualty and theft losses incurred on business or investment property held for more than one year. However, there is an exception if losses exceed gains from casualties or thefts in one taxable year.

Involuntary conversions of capital assets held for personal purposes are not subject to a Section 1231 computation but are subject to a separate computation; *see 18.25.*

Tax–Free Exchanges

Ordinary income generally is not realized on a tax-free exchange or trade-in of the same type of property (unless some gain is taxed because the exchange is accompanied by "boot" *(6.3)* such as money). The ordinary income potential is assumed in the basis of the new property. However, where depreciable realty acquired before 1987 is exchanged for land, the amount of any depreciation recapture is immediately taxable in the year of the exchange.

Capital Gain or Ordinary Loss

Profitable sales and involuntary conversions of Section 1231 assets are generally treated as capital gain, except for profits on equipment *(44.1)* and real estate allocated to recaptured depreciation *(44.2),* and losses are deducted as ordinary loss. However, the exact tax result depends on the net profit and loss realized for all sales of such property made during the tax year. Under the netting rules explained at *44.8,* the net result of these sales determines the tax treatment of each individual sale. In making the computation on Form 4797, you must also consider losses and gains from casualty, theft, and other involuntary conversions involving business and investment property held more than one year. Follow the Form 4797 instructions.

Result of netting.   A net gain on Section 1231 assets from Form 4797 is entered on Schedule D as a long-term capital gain unless the recapture rule (*see* the Caution below) for net ordinary losses applies. A net loss on Section 1231 assets is combined on Form 4797 with ordinary income from depreciation recapture *(44.1)* and with ordinary gains and losses from the sale of business property that does not qualify for Section 1231 netting.

Installment sale.   Gain realized on the installment sale of business or income-producing property held for more than a year may be capital gain one year and ordinary income another year. Actual treatment in each year depends on the net result of all sales, including installment payments received in that year; also *see 44.6.*

Losses exceed gains from casualties or thefts.   On Form 4684, you must compute the net financial result from all involuntary conversions arising from fire, storm, or other casualty or theft of assets used in your business and capital assets held for business or income-producing purposes and held more than one year. The purpose of the computation is to determine whether these involuntary conversions enter into the above Section 1231 computation. If the net result is a gain, all of the assets enter into the Section 1231 computation. If the net result is a loss, then these assets do not enter into the computation; the losses are deducted separately as casualty losses, and the gains reported separately as ordinary income. If you incur only losses, the losses similarly do not enter into the Section 1231 computation.

EXAMPLE

You suffer an uninsured fire loss of $2,000 on business equipment and gain of $1,000 on other insured investment property damaged by a storm. All of the property was held more than one year. Because loss exceeds gain, neither transaction enters into a Section 1231 computation. The gain is reported as ordinary income and the loss is deducted as an ordinary loss. The effect is a net $1,000 loss deduction. If the figures were reversed, that is, if the gain were $2,000 and the loss $1,000, both assets would enter into the Section 1231 computation. If only the fire loss occurred, the loss would be treated as a casualty loss and would not enter into the Section 1231 computation.

44.9 Sale of Property Used for Business and Personal Purposes

One sale will be reported as two separate sales for tax purposes when you sell a car or any other equipment used for business and personal purposes, or in some cases where a sold residence *(see 29.7)* was used partly as a residence and partly as a place of business or to produce rent income.

You allocate the sales price and the basis of the property between the business portion and the personal portion. The allocation is based on use. For example, with a car, the allocation is based on mileage used in business and personal driving.

EXAMPLE

Two partners bought an airplane for about $54,000. They used approximately 75% of its flying time for personal flights and 25% for business flights. After using the plane for eight years, they sold it for about $35,000. Depreciation taken on the business part of the plane amounted to $13,000. The partners figured they incurred a loss of $6,000 on the sale. The IRS, allocating the proceeds and basis between business and personal use, claimed they realized a profit of $8,250 on the business part of the plane and a nondeductible loss of $14,250 on the personal part. The allocation was as follows:

	PARTNERS' CLAIM	IRS POSITION BUSINESS (25%)	PERSONAL (75%)
Original cost	$54,000	$13,500	$40,500
Depreciation	13,000	13,000	
Adjusted basis	41,000	500	40,500
Selling price	35,000	8,750	26,250
Gain (Nondeductible loss)	($6,000)	$8,250	($14,250)

The partners argued that the IRS could not split the sale into two separate sales. They sold only one airplane and therefore there was only one sale. A federal district court and appeals court disagreed and held that the IRS method of allocation is practical and fair.

Caution

Recapture of Net Ordinary Losses

Net Section 1231 gain is not treated as capital gain but as ordinary income to the extent of net Section 1231 losses realized in the five most recent prior taxable years. Losses are recaptured in chronological order on Form 4797. Losses that have already been "recaptured" under this rule in prior years are not taken into account.

44.10 Should You Trade in Business Equipment?

The purchase of new business equipment is often partially financed by trading in old equipment. For tax purposes, a trade-in may not be a good decision. If the market value of the equipment is below its adjusted basis, it may be preferable to sell the equipment to realize an immediate deductible loss. You may not deduct a loss on a trade-in. However, if you do trade, the potential deduction reflected in the cost basis of the old equipment is not forfeited. The undepreciated basis of the old property becomes part of the basis of the new property and may be depreciated. Therefore, in deciding whether to trade or sell where a loss may be realized, determine whether you will get a greater tax reduction by taking an immediate loss on a sale or by claiming larger depreciation deductions.

If the fair market value of the old equipment exceeds its adjusted basis, you have a potential gain. To defer tax on this gain, you may want to trade the equipment in for new equipment. Your decision to sell or trade will generally be based on a comparison between (1) tax imposed on an immediate sale and larger depreciation deductions taken on the cost basis of the new property, and (2) the tax consequences of a trade-in in which the tax is deferred but reduced depreciation deductions are taken on a lower cost basis of the property. In making this comparison, you will have to estimate your future income and tax rates. Also pay attention to the possibility that gain on a sale may be taxed as ordinary income under the depreciation recapture rules; *see 44.1.*

The tax consequences of a trade-in may not be avoided by first selling the used property to the dealer who sells you the new property. The IRS will disregard the sale made to the same dealer from whom you purchase the new equipment. The two transactions will be treated as one trade-in.

44.11 Corporate Liquidation

Liquidation of a corporation and distribution of its assets for your stock is generally subject to capital gain or loss treatment. For example, on a corporate liquidation, you receive property worth $10,000 from the corporation. Assume the basis of your shares, which you have held long term, is $6,000. You have realized a long-term gain of $4,000.

If you incur legal expenses in pressing payment of a claim, you treat the fee as a capital expense, according to the IRS. The Tax Court and an appeals court hold that the fee is deductible as an expense incurred to earn income; the deduction is subject to the 2% adjusted gross income (AGI) floor discussed at *19.1.*

If you recover a judgment against the liquidator of a corporation for misuse of corporate funds, the judgment is considered part of the amount you received on liquidation and gives you capital gain, not ordinary income.

If you paid a corporate debt after liquidation, the payment reduces the gain realized on the corporate liquidation in the earlier year; thus, in effect, it is a capital loss.

If the corporation distributes liquidating payments over a period of years, gain is not reported until the distributions exceed the adjusted basis of your stock.

 Filing Instruction

Trade-in of Car

When you trade in a car used partly for business and partly for pleasure, treat the deal as if you had exchanged and received two different types of assets: a personal asset and a business asset. Allocate part of the costs of the old and new car to your business use and part to your personal use. Figure the results on each part. Trade-in rules for a business auto are discussed at *43.8.*

Figuring Self-Employment Tax

Self-employment tax provides funds for Social Security and Medicare benefits. The self-employment tax is calculated on Schedule SE. You are required to prepare Schedule SE if you have self-employment earnings of $400 or more in 1999, but you will not incur the tax unless your self-employment earnings exceed $433.13. The tax is added to your income tax liability. When preparing your estimated tax liability, you must also include an estimate of self-employment tax; *see* Chapter 27.

On Schedule SE, self-employment income is reduced by a deduction reflected in the decimal of .9235 listed on the form. You also deduct 50% of the self-employment tax on Line 27 of Form 1040.

For 1999, the self-employment tax of 15.3% consists of the following two rates: 12.4% for Social Security and 2.9% for Medicare. After multiplying the net earnings by .9235, the 15.3% rate applies to a taxable earnings base of $72,600 or less; the 2.9% rate applies to all taxable earnings exceeding $72,600. For example, if net earnings are $78,614, the .9235 adjustment reduces them to $72,600. The self-employment tax is $11,107.80 ($72,600 × 15.3%). If the net earnings were $108,284, they would be reduced to $100,000 after the .9235 adjustment. The self-employment tax would be $11,902.40: $11,107.80 on the first $72,600 of taxable self-employment earnings at 15.3% *plus* $794.60 on the excess $27,400 at 2.9%.

You are required to pay self-employment tax on self-employment income even after you retire and receive Social Security benefits.

Filing Tip

Real Estate Investor

The owner of one office building who holds it for investment (rather than for sale in the ordinary course of business) is not a real estate dealer, but a real estate investor. If the only tenant services provided are heat, light, water, and trash collection, report the rental income and expenses on Schedule E. The activity is not a Schedule C business subject to self-employment tax.

45.1 What Is Self-Employment Income?

On Schedule SE, your self-employment income is generally your net profit from your business or profession whether you participate in its activities full or part time. Net profit is generally the amount shown on Line 31 of Schedule C (or Line 3 of Schedule C-EZ) if you are a sole proprietor. If you are a partner, net earnings subject to self-employment tax are taken from Line 15a, Schedule K-1 of Form 1065. If you are a farmer, net farm profit is shown on Line 36, Schedule F.

If you have more than one self-employed operation, your net profit from all the operations is combined. A loss in one self-employed business will reduce the income from another business. You file separate Schedules C for each operation and one Schedule SE showing the combined income (less losses, if any). Contributions to your own Keogh plan or SEP retirement account do not reduce the net earnings subject to self-employment tax.

Married couples. Where you and your spouse *each* have self-employment income, each spouse must figure separate self-employment income on a separate schedule. Each pays the tax on the separate self-employment income. Both schedules are attached to the joint return.

If you live in a community property state, business income is not treated as community property for self-employment tax purposes. The spouse who is actually carrying on the business is subject to self-employment tax on the earnings.

Exceptions. The following types of income or items are *not* included as self-employment income on Schedule SE:

1. Rent from real estate is generally not self-employment income. However, self-employment tax applies to the business income of a real estate dealer or income in a rental business where substantial services are rendered to the occupant, as in the leasing of—

- Rooms in a hotel or in a boarding house.
- Apartments, but only if extra services for the occupants' convenience, such as maid service or changing linens, are provided.
- Cabins or cabanas in tourist camps where you provide maid services, linens, utensils, and swimming, boating, fishing, and other facilities, for which you do not charge separately.
- Farmland in which the landlord materially participates in the actual production of the farm or in the management of production. For purposes of "material participation," the activities of a landlord's agent are not counted, only the landlord's actual participation.

2. Capital gains are not self-employment income. Self-employment income does not include gains from the sale of property unless it is inventory or held for sale to customers in the ordinary course of business. There is an exception for dealers in commodities and options; *see* the chart in *45.6*.

3. Dividends and interest. Generally, dividends and interest are not self-employment income. However, dividends earned by a dealer in securities and interest on accounts receivable are treated as self-employment income if the securities are not being held for investment. A dealer is one who buys stock as inventory to sell to customers.

Net operating loss deduction. A loss carryover from past years does not reduce business income for self-employment tax purposes. Similarly, the personal exemption may not be used to reduce self-employment income.

Statutory employees. Wages of a statutory employee, such as a full-time life insurance salesperson *(40.6)*, are not subject to self-employment tax, as Social Security and Medicare tax have been withheld.

Farmers. Cash or a payment in kind under the "Payment-in-Kind" program is considered earned income subject to self-employment tax.

Business interruption proceeds. The IRS and the Tax Court disagree over whether business interruption insurance proceeds must be reported as earnings subject to self-employment tax. The Tax Court held that insurance payments made to a grocer as compensation for lost earnings due to a fire were not subject to self-employment tax because the payment was not for actual services. The IRS refuses to follow the decision, holding that such payments represented income that would have been earned had business operations not been interrupted.

45.2 Partners Pay Self-Employment Tax

A general partner includes his or her share of partnership income or loss in net earnings from self-employment, including guaranteed payments. If your personal tax year is different from the partnership's tax year, you include your share of partnership income or loss for the partnership tax year ending within 1999.

Law Alert

Former Insurance Salespersons

Termination payments received after 1997 by a former insurance salesperson may be exempt from self-employment tax. They must be received from an insurance company after the termination of a services agreement. No services may be performed for the company after the agreement ends and before the end of the tax year. The payments must be conditioned on the salesperson's entering into a covenant not to compete with the company for at least one year after termination. The amount of the payment must be primarily based on policies sold by (or credited to) the salesperson during the last year of the services agreement or on the period for which such policies remain in force after the termination.

A limited partner is not subject to self-employment tax on his or her share of partnership income except for guaranteed payments for services performed, which are subject to the tax.

If a general partner dies within the partnership's tax year, self-employment income includes his or her distributive share of the income earned by the partnership through the end of the month in which the death occurs. This is true even though his or her heirs or estate succeeds to the partnership rights. For this purpose, partnership income for the year is considered to be earned ratably each month.

Partnership's retirement payments. Retirement payments you receive from your partnership are *not* subject to self-employment tax if the following conditions are met:

1. The payments are made under a qualified written plan providing for periodic payments on retirement of partners with payments to continue until death.
2. You rendered no services in any business conducted by the partnership during the tax year of the partnership ending within or with your tax year.
3. By the end of the partnership's tax year, your share in the partnership's capital has been paid to you in full, and there is no obligation from the other partners to you other than with respect to the retirement payments under the plan.

45.3 Schedule SE

Schedule SE has an introductory "road map" designed to lead you to either the short or long version of Schedule SE. Once you pass through the road map, the preparation of either the short or long schedule is not difficult. In both versions, you multiply your net earnings by a decimal of .9235. Only 92.35% of net earnings is subject to the self-employment tax. The .9235 adjustment is the equivalent of a 7.65% reduction to net earnings, which along with the income tax deduction for 50% of self-employment tax on Line 27 of Form 1040, attempts to place self-employed individuals on the same level as employees subject to FICA taxes.

The .9235 adjustment is made on Line 4 of either the short or long Schedule SE. For example, if your net profit reported on Line 31 of Schedule C is $120,000, the amount subject to self-employment tax after the adjustment is $110,820; *see* the filled-in short Schedule SE worksheet below, and *see* the next page for the long Schedule SE.

Worksheet—Short Schedule SE

Caution

Limited Partners and LLC Members

An IRS attempt in 1997 to impose self-employment tax on active limited partners and LLC members was stymied by a Congressional moratorium that expired July 1,1998. At the time this book went to press, the IRS had not responded to the expiration of the moratorium by either finalizing the 1997 proposed regulations, modifying them, or withdrawing them. The proposed regulations would have subjected all professional services partners (such as in law, medicine, or accounting) to self-employment tax. The proposed regulations also would have subjected limited partners and LLC members to self-employment tax if they participated in the business for more than 500 hours during the year, or had personal liability for partnership or LLC debts, or had authority to contract on behalf of the organization.

Filing Tip

50% Deduction

After you figure your self-employment tax on Schedule SE, deduct one-half of it on Line 27 of Form 1040.

Section A—Short Schedule SE. Caution: *Read above to see if you can use Short Schedule SE.*

1	Net farm profit or (loss) from Schedule F, line 36, and farm partnerships, Schedule K-1 (Form 1065), line 15a	**1**		
2	Net profit or (loss) from Schedule C, line 31; Schedule C-EZ, line 3; Schedule K-1 (Form 1065), line 15a (other than farming); and Schedule K-1 (Form 1065-B), box 9. Ministers and members of religious orders, see page SE-1 for amounts to report on this line. See page SE-2 for other income to report	**2**	120,000	
3	Combine lines 1 and 2	**3**	120,000	
4	**Net earnings from self-employment.** Multiply line 3 by 92.35% (.9235). If less than $400, **do not** file this schedule; you do not owe self-employment tax . . . . ▶	**4**	110,820	
5	**Self-employment tax.** If the amount on line 4 is: • $72,600 or less, multiply line 4 by 15.3% (.153). Enter the result here and on **Form 1040, line 50.** • More than $72,600, multiply line 4 by 2.9% (.029). Then, add $9,002.40 to the result. Enter the total here and on **Form 1040, line 50.**	**5**	12,216	
6	**Deduction for one-half of self-employment tax.** Multiply line 5 by 50% (.5). Enter the result here and on **Form 1040, line 27**	**6**	6108	

45.4 How Wages Affect Self-Employment Tax

If you have both a net profit from self-employment and also wage and/or tip income subject to FICA taxes (Social Security and Medicare), the amount of such FICA earnings will affect the self-employment tax rate applied to your net profit.

If your 1999 FICA wages or tips were $72,600 or over, your net self-employment profit is subject only to the 2.9% Medicare rate.

If your 1999 FICA wages or tips were under the $72,600 limit for the 12.4% Social Security rate, your net self-employment earnings on Line 6 of long Schedule SE (after the .9235 adjustment) are subject to the 12.4% rate to the extent of the excess of $72,600 over your FICA wages or tips. The 2.9% Medicare rate applies to the entire amount of net self-employment earnings. *See* the following Example and the filled-in long Schedule SE worksheet below.

EXAMPLE

You earn a salary of $30,000 in 1999 and have a net profit from self-employment of $35,000. As shown on the long Schedule SE worksheet below, the 12.4% rate applies to the smaller of Line 6 and Line 9. Here, the smaller amount is the Line 6 net earnings (after .9235 adjustment) of $32,322.50. The 2.9% rate applies to the net earnings (after the .9235 adjustment).

12.4% × $32,322.50	$4,007.99
2.9% × $32,322.50	+ 937.35
	4,945.34

Your self-employment tax liability is $4,945. One-half of that, or $2,473 is deductible on Line 27 of Form 1040.

Worksheet—Long Schedule SE

Part I Self-Employment Tax

Note: *If your only income subject to self-employment tax i* **church employee income,** *skip lines 1 through 4b. Enter -0- on line 4c and go to line 5a. Income from se rvices you perfo rmed as a minister or a member of a religious order* **is not** *church employee income. See page SE-1.*

A If you are a minister, member of a religious order, or Christian Science practitioner **and** you filed Form 4361, but you had $400 or more of **other** net earnings from self-employment, check here and continue with Part I. . . . . . ▶ ☐

1	Net farm profit or (loss) from Schedule F, line 36, and farm partnerships, Schedule K-1 (Form 1065), line 15a. **Note:** *Skip this line if you use the farm optional method. See page SE-4* . .	**1**	
2	Net profit or (loss) from Schedule C, line 31; Schedule C-EZ, line 3; Schedule K-1 (Form 1065), line 15a (other than farming); and Schedule K-1 (Form 1065-B), box 9. Ministers and members of religious orders, see page SE-1 for amounts to report on this line. See page SE-2 for other income to report. **Note:** *Skip this line if you use the nonfa rm optional method. See page SE-4*	**2**	35,000
3	Combine lines 1 and 2	**3**	35,000
4a	If line 3 is more than zero, multiply line 3 by 92.35% (.9235). Otherwise, enter amount from line 3	**4a**	32,322 50
b	If you elected one or both of the optional methods, enter the total of lines 15 and 17 here . .	**4b**	
c	Combine lines 4a and 4b. If less than $400, **do not** file this schedule; you do not owe self-employment tax. **Exception.** If less than $400 and you had **church employee income,** enter -0- and continue ▶	**4c**	32,322 50
5a	Enter your **church employee income** from Form W-2. **Caution:** *See page SE-1 for definition of church employee income* . . . . . **5a** [ ]		
b	Multiply line 5a by 92.35% (.9235). If less than $100, enter -0-	**5b**	
6	**Net earnings from self-employment.** Add lines 4c and 5b	**6**	32,322 50
7	Maximum amount of combined wages and self-employment earnings subject to social security tax or the 6.2% portion of the 7.65% railroad retirement (tier 1) tax for 1999	**7**	72,600 00
8a	Total social security wages and tips (total of boxes 3 and 7 on Form(s) W-2) and railroad retirement (tier 1) compensation **8a** 30,000		
b	Unreported tips subject to social security tax (from Form 4137, line 9) **8b**		
c	Add lines 8a and 8b	**8c**	30,000
9	Subtract line 8c from line 7. If zero or less, enter -0- here and on line 10 and go to line 11 . ▶	**9**	42,600
10	Multiply the **smaller** of line 6 or line 9 by 12.4% (.124)	**10**	4,007 99
11	Multiply line 6 by 2.9% (.029)	**11**	937 35
12	**Self-employment tax.** Add lines 10 and 11. Enter here and on **Form 1040, line 50**	**12**	4,945 34
13	**Deduction for one-half of self-employment tax.** Multiply line 12 by 50% (.5). Enter the result here and on **Form 1040, line 27** . . . . **13** 2,472|67		

45.5 Optional Method If 1999 Was a Low-Income or Loss Year

The law provides a small increased tax base for Social Security coverage if you have a low net profit or loss.

The increased tax base is called the optional method. One optional method is for nonfarm self-employment and another for farm income. You may not use the optional method to report an amount less than your actual net earnings from self-employment.

Nonfarm method. You may use the nonfarm optional method for 1999 if you meet all the following tests:

Test 1. Your net earnings (profit) from nonfarm self-employment on Line 31 of Schedule C, Line 3 of Schedule C-EZ, or Line 15a of Schedule K-1 (Form 1065) are less than $1,733 (.9235 × $1,733 = $1,600 maximum income subject to the optional method).

Test 2. Your net earnings from nonfarm self-employment are less than 72.189% of the total gross income you made from nonfarm self-employment.

Test 3. You had net earnings from self-employment of $400 or more in at least two of the following years: 1996, 1997, and 1998.

Test 4. You have not previously used this method for more than four years. There is a five-year lifetime limit for use of the nonfarm optional base. The years do not have to be consecutive.

Income of $2,400 or less. If your gross income from all nonfarm trades or businesses is $2,400 or less and you meet the four tests just discussed, you may report two-thirds of the gross income from your nonfarm business as net earnings from self-employment.

EXAMPLES

1. Brown had net earnings from self-employment of $800 in 1997 and $900 in 1998 and so meets Test 3 above. In 1999, she has gross nonfarm self-employment income of $2,100 and net nonfarm self-employment earnings of $1,200. Net earnings from self-employment of $1,200 are less than $1,733 (Test 1 above) and also less than $1,516 (under Test 2, 72.189% of $2,100 gross income is $1,516). Brown may figure self-employment tax on $1,400 ($^2/_3$ of $2,100).

2. Same facts as in Example 1, but Brown has a net self-employment loss of $700. She may elect to report $1,400 ($^2/_3$ of $2,100) as net earnings under the optional method.

3. Smith had gross nonfarm income of $1,000 and net nonfarm self-employment earnings of $800. He may not use the optional method because net earnings of $800 are not less than $722 (72.189% of gross income of $1,000).

4. Jones has gross nonfarm income of $525 and net nonfarm self-employment earnings of $175. Jones may not use the optional method because two-thirds of his gross income, or $350, is less than the minimum income of $400 required to be subject to the self-employment tax.

Income over $2,400. If your gross income from all nonfarm businesses exceeds $2,400, and you meet the four tests just discussed, you may report $1,600 as your net earnings from nonfarm self-employment.

EXAMPLES

1. White had net earnings from self-employment in 1996 of $8,500; in 1997, $10,500; and in 1998, $9,500. His 1999 gross nonfarm income is $12,000 and net nonfarm earnings are $1,200. Because his net earnings of $1,200 from self-employment are less than $1,733 and also less than 72.189% of his gross income, he may report $1,600 as his net earnings from self-employment.

2. Same facts as in Example 1, but assume net earnings for 1999 are $1,800. White may not use the optional method because his actual net earnings of $1,800 from self-employment are not less than $1,733. He reports $1,800 as net earnings using the regular method.

3. Assume White has a net loss of $700 in 1999. He may use the optional method to report $1,600 of net earnings from self-employment.

 Filing Tip

Optional Method

Electing the optional method to increase the base for Social Security coverage may also increase earned income for dependent care and earned income credit purposes.

Optional farm method. If you have farming income (other than as a limited partner) you may use the farm optional method to figure your net earnings from farm self-employment.

Unlike the nonfarm optional method, the farm optional method does *not* have a two-year self-employment test (Test 3) or a requirement that actual net earnings be less than 72.189% of gross income (Test 2). There is also no limitation on the number of years you may use this method (Test 4).

If your gross income from farming is $2,400 or less, you may report two-thirds of your gross income as your net earnings from farm self-employment. If your gross income from farming exceeds $2,400 and your net earnings from farm self-employment are less than $1,733, you may report $1,600 as your net earnings from farm self-employment. If your gross income from farming exceeds $2,400 and your net earnings from farm self-employment are $1,733 or more, you may not use the optional method.

Farm income includes income from cultivating the soil or harvesting any agricultural commodities. It also includes income from the operation of livestock, dairy, poultry, bee, fish, fruit or truck farm, or plantation, ranch, nursery, range, orchard, or oyster bed, as well as income in the form of crop shares if you materially participate in production or management of production.

45.6 Self-Employment Tax Rules for Certain Positions

If you are—	Tax rule—
Babysitter	Where you perform services in your own home and determine the nature and manner of the services to be performed, you are considered to have self-employment income. However, where services are performed in the parent's home according to instructions by the parents, you are an employee of the parents and do not have self-employment earnings.
Clergy	If you are an ordained minister, priest, or rabbi (other than a member of a religious order who has taken a vow of poverty), you are subject to self-employment tax, unless you elect not to be covered on the grounds of conscientious or religious objection to Social Security benefits. Before 1968, a minister had to elect Social Security coverage.
	An application for exemption from Social Security coverage must be filed on or before the due date of your income tax return for the second taxable year for which you have net earnings from services as a minister of $400 or more (Form 4361).
	An exemption, once granted, is generally irrevocable. However, a law did allow revocation of the exemption for 1977 or 1978. An exemption will not be granted to a minister who elected coverage under prior law.
	Self-employment tax does not apply to the rental value of any parsonage or parsonage allowance provided after retirement. Other retirement benefits from a church plan are also exempted. The exemptions are allowed retroactively for years beginning on, before, or after December 31, 1994, so a refund opportunity is available if self-employment tax was paid on such amounts in a prior year not closed by the statute of limitations.
Consultant	The IRS generally takes the position that income earned by a consultant is subject to self-employment tax. The IRS has also held that a retired executive hired as a consultant by his former firm received self-employment income, even though he was subject to an agreement prohibiting him from giving advice to competing companies. According to the IRS, consulting for one firm is a business; it makes no difference that you act as a consultant only with your former company. The IRS has also imposed self-employment tax on consulting fees, although no services were performed for them. The courts have generally approved the IRS position.
Dealer in commodities and options	Registered options dealers and commodities dealers are subject to self-employment tax on net gains from trading in Section 1256 contracts, which include regulated futures contracts, foreign currency contracts, dealer equity options, and non-equity options. Self-employment tax also applies to net gains from trading property related to such contracts, like stock used to hedge options.
Director	You are taxed as a self-employed person if you are not an employee of the company. Fees for attendance at meetings are self-employment income. If the fees are not received until after the year you provide the services, you treat the fees as self-employment earnings in the year they are received.
Employee of foreign government or international organization	If you are a U.S. citizen and you work in the United States for a foreign government or its wholly owned instrumentality, or an international organization, you pay self-employment tax if Social Security and Medicare taxes are not withheld from your pay.
Executor or guardian	If you are a professional fiduciary, you will always be treated as having self-employment income, regardless of the assets held by the estate. But if you serve as a nonprofessional executor or administrator for the estate of a deceased friend or relative, you will not be treated as having self-employment income unless all of the following tests are met: (1) the estate includes a business; (2) you actively participate in the operation of the business; and (3) all or part of your fee is related to your operation of the business.

The IRS applied similar business tests to deny self-employment treatment for a guardian who was appointed by a court to care for a disabled cousin. The guardian negotiated sales of the cousin's property and invested the proceeds, but these activities were not extensive enough to be considered management of a business.

Lecturer	You are not taxed as a self-employed person if you give only occasional lectures. If, however, you seek lecture engagements and get them with reasonable regularity, your lecture fees are treated as self-employment income.
Nonresident alien	You do not pay Social Security tax on your self-employment income derived from a trade, business, or profession. This is so even though you pay income tax. Your exemption from self-employment tax is not influenced by the fact that your business in the United States is carried on by an agent, employee, or partnership of which you are a member. However, if you live in Puerto Rico, the Virgin Islands, American Samoa, or Guam, you are not considered a nonresident alien and are subject to self-employment tax.
Nurse	If you are a registered nurse or licensed practical nurse who is hired directly by clients for private nursing services, you are considered self-employed. You are an employee if hired directly by a hospital or a private physician and work for a salary following a strict routine during fixed hours, or if you provide primarily domestic services in the home of a client. Where registered or licensed practical nurses are assigned nursing jobs by an agency that pays them, the IRS, in several rulings, has treated such nurses as employees of the agency. Nurses' aides, domestics, and other unlicensed individuals who classify themselves as practical nurses are treated by the IRS as employees, regardless of whether they work for a medical institution, a private physician, or a private household.
Real estate agent or door-to-door salesperson	Licensed real estate agents are considered self-employed if they have a contract specifying that they are not to be treated as employees and if substantially all of their pay is related to sales rather than number of hours worked. The same rule also applies to door-to-door salespeople with similar contracts who work on a commission basis selling products in homes or other non-retail establishments.
Technical service contractor	Consulting engineers and computer technicians who receive assignments from technical service agencies are generally treated as employees and do not pay self-employment tax. The IRS distinguishes between (1) technicians who in three-party arrangements are assigned clients by a technical services agency and (2) those who directly enter into contracts with clients. Employee status covers only technicians in Group 1. Technical specialists who contract directly with clients may be classified as independent contractors by showing that they have been consistently treated as independent contractors by the client, and that other workers in similar positions have also been treated as independent contractors. Thus, they may treat their income as self-employment income. Firms that are treated as employers of technical specialists are responsible for withholding and payroll taxes.
Writer	Royalties from writing books are self-employment income to a writer. Royalties on books by a professor employed by a university may also be self-employment income despite employment as a professor.

Filing Your Return and What Happens After You File

This part is designed to help you —

- Organize your tax data. Whether you plan to prepare your own tax return or have someone else prepare it, you must first gather and organize your tax information.

  In Chapter 46, you will find record-keeping guides for income items and expense deductions.

- Understand how the IRS reviews your return and initiates audit procedures, including information on how the IRS matches your return with reports of distributions to you from banks, corporations, and government agencies.

- Avoid penalties for underpaying your tax. You may avoid penalties for positions taken on your tax return by making certain disclosures, obtaining authoritative support for your position, or showing reasonable cause for a tax underpayment; see 47.5.

- Understand the factors that might lead to an audit. Your chances of being selected for an examination depend on your income, profession, deductions claimed, and even where you live; see 48.1.

- Prepare for an audit. Advance preparations and knowing your rights can help support your position; see 48.3.

- Dispute adverse IRS determinations. You can appeal within the IRS and go to court if you disagree with the IRS audit results. If you win, you may receive attorneys' fees and other expenses; see 48.7 and 48.8.

- File a timely refund claim if you have overpaid your tax; see 49.1.

- File an amended return if you omitted income or claimed excessive deductions on your original return; see 49.8.

Filing Your Return

Whether you prepare your return yourself or retain a professional preparer, you must first collect and organize your tax records. You cannot prepare your return unless you get your personal tax data in order. Good records will help you figure your income and deductions and will serve as a written record to present to the IRS in the event that you are audited.

Review income statements from banks, employers, brokers, and governmental agencies on their respective Form 1099s. Check for miscalculations, additions, and omissions.

Survey Chapters 12–21 of *Your Income Tax 2000* for deductions you can claim directly from gross income and itemized deductions you can claim on Schedule A of Form 1040.

Reviewing your tax return from prior years will help refresh your memory as to how you handled income and expenses in prior years. This review will also remind you of deductions, carryover losses, and other items you might otherwise have overlooked that you might be eligible for.

You may obtain copies of prior year tax returns by filing Form 4506 with the IRS and paying a nominal fee. In this chapter you will find a checklist of steps to take when preparing and checking your return. If you need an extension to file, *see 46.3*.

Preparing Your Return

46.1 Keeping Tax Records

Tax saving requires keeping records. Good record-keeping makes it easier to prepare your return, reduces errors, and provides a defense to any challenge from the IRS.

- Make a habit of jotting down deductible items as they come along.
- Keep a calender or diary of expenses to record deductible items.
- Keep a file of bills. This can be an ordinary folder in which you arrange your bills and receipts alphabetically. This will remind you of deductible items and provide you with supporting evidence to present to the IRS if audited.
- Use your checkbook stubs as a record. If you own a business, you must keep a complete set of account books for it.

IRA records. If you have made nondeductible contributions to a traditional IRA, keep a record of both your nondeductible and deductible contributions. This will help you when you withdraw IRA money to figure the tax-free and taxed parts of the withdrawal. Also keep records of contributions and conversions to Roth IRAs. For these purposes, you should keep copies of Form 8606 and Form 5498; *see 8.8.*

Passive losses. If you have losses that are suspended and carried forward to future years under the passive loss restrictions *(10.13)*, keep the worksheets to Form 8582 as a record of the carry-forward losses.

Home mortgage interest. Keep your bank statements and cancelled checks. If a loan secured by a first or second home is used to make substantial home improvements, keep records of the improvement costs to support your home interest deduction; *see 15.5.*

How long should you keep your records? Your records should be kept for a minimum of three years after the year to which they are applicable, since the IRS generally has three years from the date your return is filed to audit your return. Some authorities advise keeping them for six years, since in some cases where income has not been reported, the IRS may go back as far as six years to question a tax return. In cases of suspected tax fraud, there is no time limitation at all.

Keep records of transactions relating to the *basis* of property for as long as they are important in figuring the basis of the original or replacement property. For example, records of the purchase of rental property or improvements thereto must be held as long as you own the property.

As mentioned above, if you have made any nondeductible IRA contributions, records of IRA contributions and distributions must be kept until all funds have been withdrawn. Similarly, you should save mutual-fund confirmations or other records showing reinvested dividends and cash purchases of shares; these are part of your cost basis and will reduce taxable gain when you sell shares in the fund.

46.2 Getting Ready To File Your Return

You must collect your tax records before you can start the preparation of your return. Even if you employ a tax professional to prepare your return, organizing your tax data is essential. *See* the Tax Record and Return Directories at the end of this chapter for the records you need to report income and expenses and where on your return to report them. If you are using a tax return preparer, *see 46.7.* Once you have compiled all your return information and your records are complete, decide whether to use Form 1040EZ, 1040A, or 1040 with the aid of the checklist at the front of this book on page 6. After you have decided which return to file, review the form to familiarize yourself with its details.

You may use the sample forms in Part 8 to prepare a draft copy of your return. The Supplement will contain forms suitable for filing, or you can obtain forms by phone from the IRS by calling (800) 829-3676. Check the IRS instructions for obtaining forms by fax. If you have a computer with a modem, you may obtain forms from the IRS Internet website at http://www.irs.gov.

Checking for possible errors. After you have completed your return, put it aside and postpone checking your completed return for several hours or even a day so that you can review it in a fresh state of mind. *See* below for common errors that might delay a refund or result in a tax deficiency and interest costs.

 Planning Reminder

Keep Copies

Photocopy your signed return and keep the copy along with copies of Form W-2 and other income statements, receipts, cancelled checks, and other items to substantiate your deductions.

Check your return to ensure the following *before* mailing it to the IRS:

- Your arithmetic is correct.
- Your Social Security number is recorded correctly on each form and schedule.
- You have filled in the proper boxes that state your filing status and exemption claims, and reported the Social Security number of each dependent born before December 1, 1999; *see 21.14.*
- You have claimed the full standard deduction you are entitled to if you are age 65 or older, or blind; *see 13.4.*
- You have claimed the earned income credit if you have one qualifying child and your earned income and your modified adjusted gross income are each less than $26,928, or less than $30,580 if you have more than one qualifying child; *see 25.12.*
- You have used the tax table or schedule applicable to your tax status; *see* Part 8 for the tax tables and the rate schedules. Use the tables if your taxable income is less than $100,000.
- You have put the refund due you or your tax payable on the correct line.
- If you owe any tax, your check should be made out to the "United States Treasury" for the correct amount due and your Social Security number should be on the check. The IRS encourages, but does not require, that you send payment voucher Form 1040-V along with your Form 1040 payment.
- You have signed your return and, if you are filing a joint return, your spouse has also signed; *see 1.3.*
- You have attached the correct copy of your Form W-2 and all appropriate forms and schedules to your return.
- If you have elected to have your refund directly deposited into your personal account, verify that you have provided the IRS with the correct information on Line 66 of Form 1040, Line 41 of Form 1040A, or Line 11 of Form 1040EZ.
- You have correctly addressed the envelope and affixed proper postage; *see 46.4.*

Using a computer to prepare your return. If you have a personal computer, any one of the leading software programs will aid you in preparing your return by facilitating the calculation of sums, percentages, and tax liabilities. However, do not rely entirely on the computer program if you are preparing your return by yourself. You may inadvertently make an error by inputting the wrong information or there might be a quirk in the software itself. A suggestion: prepare a return by hand and then prepare a return using the computer program; each will act as a check for the other.

Form 1040 PC. Some commercially available tax preparation software programs allow you to generate a Form 1040 PC, a condensed tax form that prints only the lines for which you have entries. A paid tax preparer can also produce a Form 1040 PC for you. Form 1040 PC is easier for the IRS to process than a regular return, and allows for a direct deposit of a refund into your personal account.

46.3 Applying for an Extension

If you cannot file your return on time, apply by the due date of the return for an extension of time to file. Send the extension request to the Internal Revenue Service office with which you file your return.

Automatic filing extension. You may get an extension without waiting for the IRS to act on your request. You receive an automatic four-month extension for your 1999 return if you file Form 4868 by April 17, 2000. The extension gives you until August 15, 2000, to file your return. A late *filing* penalty will not be imposed if you fail to submit a payment with Form 4868 provided you make a good faith estimate of your liability based upon available information at the time of filing. However, although the extension will be allowed without a payment, you will be subject to interest charges and possible penalties on 1999 taxes due after April 17, 2000.

You may get an extension by phone (1-888-272-9829) if you use a credit card (American Express, MasterCard, or Discover Card) to make a tax payment; Form 4868 does not have to be filed if you use a credit card.

When you file your return within the extension period, you enter on the appropriate line of the return any tax payment that you sent with your extension request, and include the balance of the unpaid tax, if any.

While the extension is automatically obtained by a proper filing on Form 4868, the IRS may terminate the extension by mailing you a notice at least 10 days prior to the termination date designated in the notice.

Abroad on April 17, 2000. You do not get an automatic extension for filing and paying your tax merely because you are out of the country on the filing due date. If you plan to be traveling abroad on April 17, 2000, and want to get a filing extension, you must submit a claim for the automatic four-month filing extension on Form 4868 or use a credit card (*see* above) to make a payment with an extension request.

 Planning Reminder

Extension for Severe Hardship

If paying the tax due would cause you to suffer a severe hardship you may apply for a special payment extension on Form 1127. This extension is generally limited to six months. Even if the IRS allows the extension, you will still owe interest on the late payment.

The only exception is for U.S. citizens or residents who live and have their main place of business outside the U.S. or Puerto Rico, or military personnel stationed outside the U.S. or Puerto Rico, on April 17, 2000. Such taxpayers qualify for an automatic two-month extension, until June 15, 2000. Such taxpayers may receive an additional two-month extension by filing Form 4868 by June 15 and making a proper estimate of the taxes due; as just discussed, payment of the estimated liability is not required to avoid a late *filing* penalty. However, you will still be subject to interest charges and possible penalties on taxes due after April 17, 2000.

Interest and penalty for underpayment. If, on filing Form 4868, you pay less than the balance of the final tax you owe, you will be charged interest on the unpaid amount. If the tax paid with Form 4868, plus withholdings and estimated tax payments during 1999, is less than 90% of the amount due, you may also be subject to a late-payment penalty (equal to one half of 1% of the unpaid tax per month)—unless you can show reasonable cause.

Installment arrangements. If you cannot pay the tax due for 1999 by the August 15, 2000, extension date, you should file your return and attach Form 9465 to request an installment arrangement. On Form 9465, you may request a monthly payment plan. The IRS will inform you within 30 days if your proposed payment plan is accepted. If it is, you will have to pay a processing fee. Even if the IRS agrees to an installment arrangement, you will have to pay interest and possibly a late-payment penalty (*see* above) on the amount not paid by the due date.

If you owe $10,000 or less and certain conditions are met, the IRS must enter into an installment arrangement if you request one. You must show that full payment cannot be currently made, and that in the previous five years you filed income tax returns and paid the tax and did not enter into an installment arrangement during that period. If the current return is a joint return, your spouse must also meet these tests for the five-year period. You must agree to pay the tax liability in full within three years.

If you are using an installment agreement to pay the tax due on a timely filed return (including extensions), the late payment penalty for months after 1999 is reduced by half from .5% to .25% per month.

Filing extensions beyond August 15, 2000. Filing extensions beyond the automatic four-month period are allowed only if you file Form 2688 and show good cause, such as illness of yourself or a family member, or lack of information returns, such as a Form W-2 or Form 1099, needed to complete your return. Form 2688 must be filed before the end of the original four-month extension period. If the IRS agrees to your request, an additional two-month filing extension will be allowed, until October 16, 2000.

46.4 Where To Send Your Return

If your tax package includes a pre-printed address label and envelope, use them if you have not moved. Make sure you attach sufficient postage, or the envelope will be returned to you by the Post Office. If you moved or do not have a pre-addressed envelope, address the envelope containing your return to the Internal Revenue Service Center for the area where you live. No street address is needed. *See* the chart on the next page for filing addresses. Check the instructions in the IRS booklet for any address changes.

46.5 Electronic Filing

Electronic filing simply involves the transmission of data on your return from the computer of a tax preparer, tax preparation software program, or Internet service to an IRS computer. There is generally a fee for filing electronically. To file electronically, you must use an authorized service. You also fill out and sign Form 8453 (U.S. Individual Income Tax Declaration for Electronic Filing) to authorize the electronic transmission. When filing jointly, both you and your spouse must sign the form. If you report salary income, Forms W-2 are attached to Form 8453, which is mailed to the IRS. If you file electronically through an on-line service provider, use Form 8453-OL.

Electronic filing offers a faster refund—a check mailed within three weeks or a direct deposit to your bank account. You authorize a direct deposit on Form 8453 or Form 8453-OL to a financial institution that was designated in the electronic portion of your return. On the electronic portion of the return, you provide the savings or checking account number and the "routing transit number" of your bank. The routing transit number is the electronic mailing address of your bank that directs the refund to the correct account. The number is on your checks or other account statements. Before naming a bank, first ask if it accepts direct deposits and what its conditions are for receiving a deposit.

Where To File

If you are filing Form 1040 and *not claiming a refund*, or you are filing Form 1040 from outside the U.S., mail your return to the Internal Revenue Service at the following city, state and postal code. If you *are claiming a refund* on Form 1040, use 0102 as the last four digits in the postal code (instead of 0002). The last four digits are 0015 for Form 1040A and 0014 for Form 1040EZ.

ALABAMA—Memphis, TN 37501-0002

ALASKA—Ogden, UT 84201-0002

ARIZONA—Ogden, UT 84201-0002

ARKANSAS—Memphis, TN 37501-0002

CALIFORNIA—File with the IRS Service Center at Ogden, UT 84201-0002, if you live in the counties of Alpine, Amador, Butte, Calaveras, Colusa, Contra Costa, Del Norte, El Dorado, Glenn, Humboldt, Lake, Lassen, Marin, Mendocino, Modoc, Napa, Nevada, Placer, Plumas, Sacramento, San Joaquin, Shasta, Sierra, Siskiyou, Solano, Sonoma, Sutter, Tehama, Trinity, Yolo, and Yuba. All other California residents file at Fresno, CA 93888-0002.

COLORADO—Ogden, UT 84201-0002

CONNECTICUT—Andover, MA 05501-0002

DELAWARE—Philadelphia, PA 19255-0002

DISTRICT OF COLUMBIA—Philadelphia, PA 19255-0002

FLORIDA—Atlanta, GA 39901-0002

GEORGIA—Atlanta, GA 39901-0002

HAWAII—Fresno, CA 93888-0002

IDAHO—Ogden, UT 84201-0002

ILLINOIS—Kansas City, MO 64999-0002

INDIANA—Cincinnati, OH 45999-0002

IOWA—Kansas City, MO 64999-0002

KANSAS—Austin, TX 73301-0002

KENTUCKY—Cincinnati, OH 45999-0002

LOUISIANA—Memphis, TN 37501-0002

MAINE—Andover, MA 05501-0002

MARYLAND—Philadelphia, PA 19255-0002

MASSACHUSETTS—Andover, MA 05501-0002

MICHIGAN—Cincinnati, OH 45999-0002

MINNESOTA—Kansas City, MO 64999-0002

MISSISSIPPI—Memphis, TN 37501-0002

MISSOURI—Kansas City, MO 64999-0002

MONTANA—Ogden, UT 84201-0002

NEBRASKA—Ogden, UT 84201-0002

NEVADA—Ogden, UT 84201-0002

NEW HAMPSHIRE—Andover, MA 05501-0002

NEW JERSEY—Holtsville, NY 00501-0002

NEW MEXICO—Austin, TX 73301-0002

NEW YORK—New York City and counties of Nassau, Rockland, Suffolk, and Westchester—Holtsville, NY 00501-0002

All Other Counties—Andover, MA 05501-0002

NORTH CAROLINA—Memphis, TN 37501-0002

NORTH DAKOTA—Ogden, UT 84201-0002

OHIO—Cincinnati, OH 45999-0002

OKLAHOMA—Austin, TX 73301-0002

OREGON—Ogden, UT 84201-0002

PENNSYLVANIA—Philadelphia, PA 19255-0002

RHODE ISLAND—Andover, MA 05501-0002

SOUTH CAROLINA—Atlanta, GA 39901-0002

SOUTH DAKOTA—Ogden, UT 84201-0002

TENNESSEE—Memphis, TN 37501-0002

TEXAS—Austin, TX 73301-0002

UTAH—Ogden, UT 84201-0002

VERMONT—Andover, MA 05501-0002

VIRGINIA—Philadelphia, PA 19255-0002

WASHINGTON—Ogden, UT 84201-0002

WEST VIRGINIA—Cincinnati, OH 45999-0002

WISCONSIN—Kansas City, MO 64999-0002

WYOMING—Ogden, UT 84201-0002

FOREIGN COUNTRY: U.S. citizens or dual-status aliens and those filing Form 2555, Form 2555-EZ, Form 4563, or if you have an A.P.O. or F.P.O. address—Philadelphia, PA 19255-0215

PUERTO RICO (or if excluding income under Section 933)—Philadelphia, PA 19255-0215

VIRGIN ISLANDS—Nonpermanent residents file with the IRS Service Center in Philadelphia, PA 19255-0215; permanent residents file with the V.I. Bureau of Internal Revenue, 9601 Estate Thomas, Charlotte Amalie, St. Thomas, VI 00802.

GUAM—Nonpermanent residents file with the IRS Service Center in Philadelphia, PA 19255-0215; permanent residents file with the Department of Revenue and Taxation, Government of Guam, P.O. Box 23607, GMF, GU 96921.

AMERICAN SAMOA—Philadelphia, PA 19255-0215

You must decide whether the faster refund is worth the fee charged. Keep in mind that even without electronic filing, you may instruct the IRS to directly deposit your refund to an account that you designate on your return. If you file electronically and owe taxes, you may be able to pay by credit card. If you owe tax and pay by mail, you file Form 1040-V (Payment Voucher) with your payment before April 17, 2000.

Refund anticipation loans. An electronic tax filing service may offer refund anticipation loans. These are loans on expected refunds from lenders affiliated with the electronic filing service. This service is strictly an agreement between you and the preparer; the IRS is not a party to the arrangement. Before agreeing to such a loan, consider the additional cost and whether it is worthwhile in light of the short refund payment period.

46.6 Calling the IRS About Your Refund

You can call the IRS to check on the status of an expected refund. When you call the IRS automated phone service, you must provide the Social Security number shown on the return (or the first Social Security number if you filed jointly), filing status, and the amount of the refund.

The IRS teletax phone number is 1-800-829-4477, but you may also contact the IRS at (800) 829-1040.

46.7 Choosing a Tax Return Preparer

There are two phases in preparing your tax return: (1) collecting your tax data and (2) converting that data into entries on your tax return. You must perform the first step yourself, as discussed at *46.1*. Once this is done, the second step of preparing your return may not be troublesome, especially if your return requires several entries on Form 1040A or Form 1040EZ. If you think tax return preparation is troublesome, or if you do not have the time to prepare your return, ask acquaintances about their knowledge and experience with qualified tax preparers in your area. If they are satisfied, you may want to contact their recommendations. If you cannot get recommendations, visit the offices of established franchised tax preparers.

Fees for tax return preparation depend on the complexity of the return to be filed and the preparer's professional standing. A preparer is not necessarily a trained accountant. Shop around; visit offices of preparers in your locality. This way you will get a firsthand idea of the cost of services.

If you are concerned about a possible IRS audit of your return, consider hiring a preparer who is qualified to represent taxpayers before the IRS. Only CPAs, attorneys, and enrolled agents (EAs) may represent taxpayers before the IRS, at the appeals as well as at the audit level. Attorneys or CPAs automatically qualify to practice before the IRS because of their professional licenses. An enrolled agent qualifies to practice before the IRS after passing an IRS examination or after completing five years of audit-level service as an IRS employee. Enrolled agents are also required by IRS regulations to complete continuing education courses every year. You can find an EA in your area by calling the National Association of Enrolled Agents at (800) 424-4339.

Preparer Responsibilities

Tax preparers are subject to IRS regulations. They may be subject to penalties for understating the tax on a return or failing to keep proper records. Anyone who prepares a return or refund claim for a fee is considered a preparer under the tax law. When more than one person works on the return or claim, each schedule or entry is reviewed separately to determine the preparer of that schedule or item. A practitioner who gives advice directly relevant to a determination of the existence, characterization, or amount of an entry on a return is considered the preparer of that item.

A practitioner who prepares entries on a return that affect entries on the return of another taxpayer may also be considered the preparer of the other return if the entries are directly reflected on the other return and constitute a substantial portion of that return. For example, a practitioner preparing a partnership return may be considered the preparer of a partner's return if the entries that are picked up from the partnership return constitute a substantial portion of the partner's individual tax return. Regulations provide tests for determining whether a part of a return is considered substantial. Under the regulations, an entry is not considered substantial if it is (1) less than $2,000 or (2) less than $100,000 and also less than 20% of adjusted gross income.

You are not a preparer if you merely type or reproduce a return or claim, or prepare a return for your employer or an officer of your employer or a fellow employee.

Caution

Tax Planning Advice

Generally, do not rely on a preparer for tax planning advice. A person who can prepare a return may not have the experience or training to give tax planning advice. Consult a qualified professional, such as an accountant, CPA, tax attorney, or enrolled agent, who will charge more for tax planning services than a person who merely prepares returns during the tax season.

Preparer Penalties

A $250 penalty may be imposed on a preparer for a tax understatement if: (1) the preparer knew (or reasonably should have known) that the understatement was based on a taxpayer position that did not have a realistic possibility of being sustained on its merits and (2) the taxpayer position was frivolous or, if not frivolous, was not adequately disclosed. If the preparer can show good faith and a reasonable cause for the understatement, the $250 penalty will not be imposed. If a tax understatement is willful, or due to reckless disregard of IRS rules, a $1,000 penalty may be imposed; the penalty is $750 if the $250 penalty also applies to the return.

According to the IRS, a taxpayer position has a "realistic possibility" of being sustained on its merits if a person who is knowledgeable in the tax law would conclude, after a well-informed analysis, that there is at least a one-in-three likelihood that the position will be sustained.

For purposes of the $250 or $1,000 penalty, IRS regulations provide that only one person associated with a firm is considered to be the preparer of the return. The practitioner who signs the return is considered to be the preparer. If none of the persons considered to be preparers under IRS rules signs the return, then the person with overall supervisory responsibility is treated as the preparer for tax penalty purposes.

Note: a signing and nonsigning preparer may also be subject to a $1,000 penalty for knowingly aiding and abetting the understatement of tax liability on a return ($10,000 for corporate returns).

Preparers must satisfy the following requirements:

1. Retain a record of the name, Social Security number, and place of work of each preparer whom he or she employs. The records must be kept for three years following the close of the return period and must be made available for inspection upon request of the district director. There is a $50 penalty for each failure to keep and make available a proper record and a $50 penalty for each required item that is missing from the record. The maximum penalty for any return period is $25,000.

2. Furnish a completed copy of the return or refund claim to the taxpayer not later than when it is presented to the taxpayer for signature. There is a $50 penalty for each failure, up to a maximum of $25,000, for documents filed during any one calendar year.

3. Keep for three years and have available for inspection by the IRS a completed copy of each return or claim prepared, or a list of the names and identification numbers of taxpayers for whom returns or claims were prepared. A $50 penalty is imposed for each failure, up to a maximum of $25,000, for any return period. A preparer who sells his or her business is not relieved of the requirement of retaining these records.

4. Sign the return and include his or her identifying number or the identifying number of his or her employer. A $50 penalty is imposed for each failure, up to a maximum of $25,000, for documents filed during any calendar year. Where more than one practitioner has worked on a return, the individual with primary responsibility for overall accuracy must sign the return.

Tax preparers are subject to a $500 penalty if they endorse or negotiate a refund check issued to a taxpayer whose return they have prepared. Business managers for athletes, actors, or other professionals who prepare their clients' tax returns and handle their tax refunds may also be subject to the penalty. To avoid the penalty, the manager must act only as an agent in depositing the client's refund check.

In addition to the penalties imposed, the IRS may also seek to enjoin a preparer from engaging in fraudulent or deceptive practices or from acting as an income tax return preparer. The IRS may also seek an injunction against a preparer for "aiding and abetting" a taxpayer to underpay tax. A list of enjoined preparers is published by the IRS in the Internal Revenue Bulletin.

 Filing Tip

Alternative ID Number for Tax Preparers

On Form W-7P, a paid preparer may apply for a preparer tax identification number (PTIN). A tax preparer can use a PTIN instead of his or her Social Security number when signing returns or refund claims.

 Planning Reminder

Penalty Exception for Preparers

If you can show reasonable cause for failure to meet any of the four preparer requirements on this page, you may avoid the applicable penalty.

Tax Record and Return Directory

The following table lists tax records you need for specific items of income and expense and directs you to the return, schedule, and line on which to report the items. The items are listed in the order in which they appear on Forms 1040, 1040A, and 1040EZ.

Item	Records Needed	Reporting
Exemptions for dependents	Records of support contribution for food, lodging, medical expenses, such as cancelled checks, diary entries. Birth certificates in case age of a child is questioned. School attendance record if student status is questioned. Form 8332 allowing noncustodial parent to claim the exemption. This form must also be attached to return by noncustodial parent claiming exemption; *see 21.11.* Forms 2120 if dependent's support is shared by other persons; *see 21.10.*	Form 1040A, Line 6(c) Form 1040, Line 6(c)
Wages and salaries	Form W-2. Your employer must send your 1999 Form W-2 by February 1, 2000. Attach Copy B to your federal return. Keep Copy C for your records. If you worked for more than one employer during 1999, attach all Copy B forms to your return.	Form 1040EZ, Line 1 Form 1040A, Line 7 Form 1040, Line 7
Tip income	Form 4070 or other record showing your monthly reports of cash tips of $20 or more. Form W-2. Also *see 26.8* for reporting FICA taxes on unreported tips.	Form 1040EZ, Line 1 Form 1040A, Line 7 Form 1040, Line 7
Interest income	Form 1099-INT Form 1099-OID Deposit slips of interest received on money you loaned to others	Form 1040EZ, Line 2 ($400 or less) Form 1040A, Line 8(a); Schedule 1, Part I (over $400) Form 1040, Line 8(a); Schedule B, Part I (over $400)
Dividend income	Form 1099-DIV Company statements of dividend payments, especially if stock dividends have been paid	Form 1040A, Line 9; Schedule 1, Part II (over $400) Form 1040, Line 9; Schedule B, Part II (over $400)
Taxable refund of state and local income tax	Form 1099-G	Form 1040, Line 10
Alimony received	Deposit slips of alimony received and ex-spouse's Social Security number Copy of divorce or separation decree or agreements	Form 1040, Line 11 if taxable
Business income or loss	Business accounting records, deposit slips Business checkbook, deposit slips, invoice receipts, cancelled checks, bank statements Form 1099-MISC	Form 1040, Line 12; Schedule C or C-EZ Form 8582 if passive activity rules apply; *see* Chapter 10
Sale of stocks and bonds	Form 1099-B and broker confirmation statements	Schedule D Form 1040, Line 13
Sale of personal residence	Closing papers, records of purchase, improvements; *see 29.6.*	If taxable gain is realized, Schedule D

Tax Record and Return Directory (continued)

Item	Records Needed	Reporting
Sale of real estate	Closing statement, records of cost and improvements Records of depreciation	Form 4797 Schedule D Form 1040, Line 13
IRA distributions	Form 1099-R	Form 1040A, Line 10 Form 1040, Line 15
Pensions and annuities	Form 1099-R if you receive annuity payments or lump-sum distributions	Form 1040A, Line 11 Form 1040, Line 16
Commercial annuity income	Form 1099-R	Form 1040A, Line 11 Form 1040, Line 16
Rent income	Account records, checkbook, cancelled checks, and receipts	Schedule E Form 1040, Line 17 Form 8582 if passive activity rules apply
Royalty income	Form 1099-MISC	Schedule E Form 1040, Line 17
Partnership income	Schedule K-1, Form 1065	Schedule E Form 1040, Line 17
Beneficiary of trust or estate	Schedule K-1, Form 1041	Schedule E Form 1040, Line 17
S corporation	Schedule K-1, Form 1120S	Schedule E Form 1040, Line 17
Unemployment compensation	Form 1099-G	Form 1040A, Line 12 Form 1040, Line 19
Social Security benefits	Form SSA-1099	Form 1040A, Line 13 Form 1040, Line 20
Gambling income	Form W-2G, diary or other record showing wins and losses, losing tickets	Form 1040, Line 21
Other income	Form 1099-MISC, records of amounts received, date received	Form 1040, Line 21
IRA deductible contribution	Trustee's statements of contribution, copy of plan	Form 1040A, Line 15 Form 1040, Line 23
Student loan interest deduction	Bank statement showing interest paid	Form 1040A, Line 16 Form 1040, Line 24
Medical Savings Account deduction	Trustee's statements and Form 5498-MSA, showing contributions	Form 1040, Line 25 Form 8853
Moving expenses	Cancelled checks or receipts for expenses incurred, diary or log	Form 1040, Line 26 Form 3903
Deduction for self-employment tax	Schedule SE, Form 1040	Form 1040, Line 27
Self-employed health insurance premium	Cancelled check of payment, copy of contract, insurance statement	Form 1040, Line 28
Keogh, SEP, or SIMPLE contribution for yourself	Trustee statement, copy of plan	Form 1040, Line 29
Penalty on early withdrawal of savings	Form 1099-INT	Form 1040, Line 30

Tax Record and Return Directory (continued)

Item	Records Needed	Reporting
Alimony deduction	Cancelled checks, copy of divorce or separation decree, written separation agreement, ex-spouse's Social Security number	Form 1040, Line 31
Employee expenses	Diary logs, receipts, copy of accounting to employer	Form 2106 Schedule A, Line 20
Home office expenses	Records of expenses, business use, and allocation	Form 2106 if an employee; Schedule A, Line 20 Form 8829 if self-employed; Schedule C, Line 30
Medical and dental expenses	Cancelled checks, statements, prescriptions; log of travel expenses and lodging costs	Form 1040 Schedule A, Lines 1–4
Taxes—state and local income, personal property, real estate	Form W-2 for withholding of income tax Cancelled checks Bank statements of property taxes paid by bank (mortgages) Form 1099-DIV for foreign tax Form 1099-INT or tax receipt for foreign tax withheld at source	Form 1040 Schedule A, Lines 5–9
Mortgage interest	Bank statement showing interest paid Form 1098	Form 1040 Schedule A, Line 10
Points	Copy of bank statements, canceled checks	Form 1040 Schedule A, Lines 10 and 12
Cash donations	Cancelled checks, receipt from charity	Form 1040; Schedule A, Line 15
Volunteer expenses for charitable organizations	Log of travel, cancelled checks showing purpose	Form 1040 Schedule A, Line 15
Property donation	Description of property, records of fair market value and cost. Receipt from organization. If at least $250, a written receipt from organization to substantiate donation. Cancelled check is not sufficient. If in excess of $5,000, qualified appraisal report and statement from organization.	Form 1040 Schedule A, Line 16
Casualty and theft losses	See the "Key To Proving a Casualty Loss" on page 342. For thefts, statements from witnesses, police records, or a newspaper account of the crime might help.	Form 1040; Schedule A, Line 19 Form 4684
Gambling losses	Losing tickets or receipts, diary showing daily wagers, wins, and losses	Form 1040 Schedule A, Line 27
Union dues	Wage statements showing withholding for dues or canceled checks	Form 1040 Schedule A, Line 20
Unreimbursed travel and entertainment expenses	Diary log and receipts kept according to the rules of *20.26*	Form 2106 Form 1040; Schedule A, Line 20
Earned income credit	Form W-2 if an employee, Schedule SE if self-employed, to show earnings	Form 1040 EZ, Line 8 Form 1040A, Line 37(a); Schedule EIC Form 1040, Line 59(a); Schedule EIC
Advance payment of earned income credit	Form W-2, Box 9	Form 1040, Line 54 Form 1040A, Line 33

Tax Record and Return Directory (continued)

Item	Records Needed	Reporting
Unreimbursed auto expenses if you are employed	Statement from employer requiring use of car Mileage log Receipts of expenses if actual costs are claimed Cost records of auto if depreciation is claimed	Form 2106 Form 1040 Schedule A, Line 20
Investment expenses	Cancelled checks	Form 1040; Schedule A, Line 22
Safe deposit box fee	Bank statements	Form 1040; Schedule A, Line 22
Tax preparation fees	Cancelled checks	Form 1040; Schedule A, Line 21
"Kiddie" tax	Child's Forms 1099-INT, 1099-DIV, and 1099-OID	Form 1040A, Line 25 Form 1040, Line 40 Form 8615 if income is reported on child's return Form 8814 if parent elects to report child's income on Form 1040
Child and dependent care expenses	Cancelled checks for amounts paid to care for child	Form 1040A, Line 26; Schedule 2 Form 1040, Line 41 Form 2441
Credit for the elderly or the disabled	Physician's statement of condition	Form 1040A, Line 27; Schedule 3 Form 1040, Line 42; Schedule R
Child tax credit and additional child tax credit	Records of support contribution Birth certificates in case age of a child is questioned School attendance record if student status is questioned	Form 1040A, Line 28 and Line 38 Form 1040, Line 43 and Line 60 Form 8812
Education credits	Student's name and taxpayer identification number Cancelled checks and statements of tuition and enrollment fees For dependents, records for support contributions	Form 1040A, Line 29 Form 1040, Line 44 Form 8863
Adoption credit	Adopted child's name, date of birth, and taxpayer identification number. Adoption papers showing the date the adoption became final.	Form 1040A, Line 30 Form 1040, Line 45 Form 8839
Foreign tax credit	Form 1099-DIV; foreign tax returns or statements	Form 1116 Form 1040, Line 46
Prior alternative minimum tax credit	Copy of prior year's Form 6251 Form 8801	Form 1040, Line 47
Advance earned income credit payments	Form W-2	Form 1040A, Line 33 Form 1040, Line 54
Federal taxes withheld	Form 1099 Form W-2 Form W-4V	Form 1040EZ, Line 7 Form 1040A, Line 35 Form 1040, Line 57
Estimated tax payments	Cancelled checks and copy of Form 1040-ES	Form 1040A, Line 36 Form 1040, Line 58

How Tax Data Is Processed by the IRS

Data from filed tax returns and information returns is recorded in computers on magnetic tape that is sent to the National Computer Center in Martinsburg, West Virginia, for posting to the master list of taxpayers arranged by account number. Failure to file returns, duplicate or multiple filings, and other discrepancies can be detected. Data from information returns is matched with the entries on individual returns.

You are required to put your Social Security number on your tax return. Your number also appears on information returns sent to the IRS reporting the wages, interest, dividends, royalties, etc., paid to you. Your number serves as a basis for posting and cross-referencing data to your account in the master IRS file.

You may incur penalties and interest charges if you fail to comply with reporting requirements or fail to pay your taxes on time.

47.1 IRS Preliminary Review

Your return is first checked for arithmetic accuracy by the IRS. If an error is found, you receive either a refund or a bill for additional taxes. Special IRS screening also spots the following types of errors:

- Incorrectly reporting income shown on Forms W-2 or Forms 1099.
- Incorrectly applying the adjusted gross income limitations for medical expenses, casualty and theft losses, and miscellaneous itemized deductions.
- Using an auto mileage rate for business travel exceeding the IRS rate.
- Claiming of the dependent care credit by a married person filing separately; *see 25.1.*
- Using head of household rates without entering on Line 4 of Form 1040 or 1040A the name of a qualifying child who is not your dependent.
- Not supplying the Social Security number of a dependent.

If you make errors of this type, you will probably be advised by mail of the corrections and of additional tax due, or you may be asked to provide additional information to substantiate tax deductions or credits. If you disagree with an IRS assessment of additional tax, you may request an interview or submit additional information. If you file early for 1999 and the correction is made before April 17, 2000, interest is not charged.

If your return is selected for a more thorough review, you are notified by letter. This may not happen for a year or two. How to handle an audit if your return is selected for examination is discussed in Chapter 48.

If you are due a refund on your 1999 return, the IRS follows a practice of expediting refunds to avoid interest costs. Interest is not required to be paid on refunds before June 2, 2000, which is 46 days after April 17, the day the tax was due. If the overpayment is not refunded within 45 days, interest is paid from the date the tax was overpaid up to a date determined by the IRS that can be as much as 30 days before the date of the refund check.

47.2 Information Returns Required by the IRS

The IRS matches tax returns with information returns from employers, payers of interest and dividends, brokers, and others to check whether income has been omitted from an individual's tax return. The IRS processes more than one billion information returns, primarily Forms W-2 and Forms 1099. By matching these information returns against individual tax returns, the IRS assesses billions in additional tax and penalties.

Here is a list of items for which an information return will be sent to the IRS:

Wages. Employers report wage income on Form W-2.

Dividends. Dividend payments of $10 or more during the calendar year are reported to the IRS on Form 1099-DIV. Each payer must furnish you by January 31, 2000, a statement showing the dividend payments made in 1999. Corporations, banks, and other payers, as well as persons or firms who receive such payments for you as nominee, report annually the dividend payments totaling $10 or more per person. Dividends, for reporting purposes, include dividends paid by corporations, and "dividend equivalents" paid to you while your stock is on loan for a short sale. Nontaxable distributions paid to shareholders are reported to the IRS on Form 5452.

Interest. Interest payments of $10 or more during the calendar year are reported to the IRS on Form 1099-INT. Each payer must furnish you by January 31, 2000, a statement showing the interest payments made in 1999. Interest for reporting purposes includes interest on registered corporate bonds, debentures, notes, and certificates, as well as interest on deposits with savings banks, savings and loan associations, stockbrokers, and insurance companies. No returns are required for tax-free interest.

Original issue discount (OID). The discount on time deposits and certificates maturing in more than one year is reported to the IRS on Form 1099-OID if it is at least $10. You should receive a copy of the Form 1099-OID for 1999 by January 31, 2000.

Interest and dividend income information disclosed to Social Security and other agencies. To verify your eligibility for certain government benefits, agencies such as the Social Security Administration, state unemployment compensation agencies, and state welfare agencies may obtain from the IRS information on the interest and dividend income that is shown on your tax return.

Rents or royalties. Royalty payments of $10 or more are reported on intangible property, such as copyrights and interests in oil, gas, and other natural resources, on Form 1099-MISC. Rents collected by a real estate agent on behalf of the property owner of $600 or more also are reported on Form 1099-MISC.

State income tax refunds. States are required to report income tax refunds of $10 or more on Form 1099-G.

 Caution

Failure To Provide a Dependent's Social Security Number

The IRS may give you an opportunity to provide the number. If the IRS disallows the exemption, it may use an immediate assessment procedure. You have 60 days to object to an immediate assessment.

Reporting Sale of Principal Residence

Sales of principal residences with a gross sales price of $250,000 or less ($500,000 or less for married sellers) are exempt from the real estate reporting requirement if the seller provides the person responsible for closing the sale written assurance that the full gain on the sale is excludable from income under the rules discussed at *29.1.*

Unemployment compensation. Unemployment payments of $10 or more during the year are reported to the IRS on Form 1099-G, a copy of which will be furnished to unemployment benefit recipients.

Proceeds from real estate transactions. Real estate sales are generally reported on Form 1099-S to the IRS by the attorney or other party who is responsible for closing the transaction. On the sale of a home, the form must also show the portion of real property taxes imposed on the buyer. However, *see* the Law Alert on the left.

Proceeds from sales of securities. Brokers are required to report to the IRS on Form 1099-B gross proceeds from sales of stocks, bonds, commodities, regulated futures, and forward contracts. Commodity options are not covered by this reporting rule.

Miscellaneous income. Persons who, in the course of business, make payments totaling $600 or more in the calendar year must file Form 1099-MISC with the IRS if the payments are in the form of:

1. Compensation for personal services (including salaries, wages, commissions, and professional fees) from which no tax is withheld. However, no information return is required for payments to a domestic or other household employee.
2. Prizes and awards that are not for services, such as winnings on TV shows (gambling winnings are reported on Form W-2G); *or*
3. Payments of fees to physicians by insurance companies, such as Blue Cross, or by a government agency under Medicare or Medicaid. The physician or other health-care provider must receive a copy of Form 1099-MISC by January 31, 2000, for inclusion of the amount on his or her 1999 return.

Retirement plan distributions. Distributions from pension, profit-sharing and annuity plans, traditional or Roth IRAs, or simplified employee pension plans (SEPs) are reported on Form 1099-R. Contributions to an IRA and the year-end value of an IRA or SEP account are reported on Form 5498.

Mortgage interest. Banks, government agencies, and businesses receiving mortgage interest and points of $600 or more for any calendar year report the payment to the IRS on Form 1098. The reporting requirement applies to interest on all obligations secured by real property. The lender must provide you with a statement of the interest reported to the IRS for 1999 by January 31, 2000.

Foreclosures and abandonments of property. If a business or government agency lends you money and later forecloses on your property or knows that you have abandoned property secured by the loan, the lender must file a report with the IRS on Form 1099-A. The purpose of the reporting requirement is to help the IRS check whether you have realized income from the discharge of indebtedness or gain on foreclosure, or whether you must recapture a previously claimed investment credit. If a report to the IRS has been made, you will be sent a statement by the lender by January 31 following the year of the foreclosure or abandonment.

Tax shelters. A new tax-shelter offering may be required to register with the IRS. If registration is required, the IRS assigns the tax shelter an identification number that must be furnished to investors. As an investor, you must report the registration number on Form 8271. Form 8271 must be attached to your tax return if you report any income or claim any deductions or credits from the shelter. Promoters of registered tax shelters and any other tax-shelter arrangements that the IRS considers potentially abusive must also keep a list of investors for seven years and provide the list to the IRS upon request. Furthermore, an investor who sells his interest in such a tax shelter to another investor must keep records identifying the buyer.

Cooperatives. Cooperatives must file annual information returns for patronage dividends totaling $10 or more during the calendar year. A statement showing the amount reported must be furnished to the patron by the end of January of the following year; *see* Form 1099-PATR.

Partnerships. A partnership does not pay income taxes, but must file an annual information return (Form 1065), stating all items of income and deductions. Also included in the return are the names and addresses of all partners, and the amount of each partner's distributive share. The return is filed at the close of the partnership's tax year, whether or not it coincides with that of its partners. Failure to file the return will result in a penalty assessable against the partnership. If a partner sells or exchanges a partnership interest and payment is partly attributable to the partner's share of unrealized receivables or substantially appreciated inventory, the partnership must be notified of the transaction and the partnership must then file an information return with the IRS, Form 8308. The purpose of the reporting requirement is to enable the IRS to verify the income attributable to the receivables and inventory, which is taxable as ordinary income. Statements to the transferor and transferee of the partnership interest must also be provided.

Barter transactions. The value of the trades by members of a barter club is subject to income tax. If you exchanged services or goods through a barter exchange during 1999, you should receive Form 1099-B from the exchange by January 31, 2000, showing the value received during 1999. The IRS also gets a copy.

Cancelled debts. If a financial institution or federal agency cancels or forgives a debt you owe of $600 or more, the cancellation will be reported to the IRS on Form 1099-C and a copy sent to you. A cancellation of a debt is generally taxable, but see exceptions in *11.8*.

47.3 When the IRS Can Assess Additional Taxes

Three-year statute of limitations. The IRS has three years after the date on which your return is filed to assess additional taxes. When you file a return before the due date, however, the three-year period starts from the due date, generally April 15.

Where the due date of a return falls on a Saturday, Sunday, or legal holiday, the due date is postponed to the next business day.

EXAMPLES

1. You filed your 1999 return on February 4, 2000. The last day on which the IRS can make an assessment on your 1999 return is April 17, 2003.
2. You file your 1998 return on May 27, 1999. The IRS has until May 27, 2002, to assess a deficiency.

Amended returns. If you file an amended return shortly before the three-year limitations period is about to expire and the return shows that you owe additional tax, the IRS has 60 days from the date it receives the return to assess the additional tax, even though the regular limitations period would expire before the 60-day period.

Six-year statute. When you fail to report an item of gross income which is more than 25% of the gross income reported on your return, the IRS has six years after the return is filed to assess additional taxes. An item that is adequately disclosed is not considered an omission.

IRS request for audit extension. If the IRS cannot complete an audit within three years, it may request that you sign Form 872 to extend the time for assessing the tax. However, where an individual was "scared" into signing such an agreement, it was held invalid. *See* the following Example.

EXAMPLE

Robertson, a plumber, won $30,000 in a sweepstakes. An IRS agent asked him to sign an extension agreement. Robertson never had any prior dealings with the IRS, he did not know that his return was under examination, and he was not in touch with the lawyer who prepared the return on which his sweepstakes winnings were averaged.

Robertson wanted to see his lawyer before signing Form 872, but the agent pressed hard for the signature, phoning him and his wife at home and at work 20 times in a week. The agent did not tell him the amount of additional tax that might be involved, or explain that if he refused to sign he would have an opportunity before the IRS and the courts to contest any additional tax. Instead, the agent's comments gave him the impression that his home could be confiscated if he refused to sign. Robertson signed and the IRS later increased his tax.

Robertson argued that the agreement was not valid. He signed under duress. The Tax Court agreed. He convinced the court that he really believed he could lose his house and property if he did not comply. No adequate explanation of the real consequences of refusal to sign was made, although Robertson asked. Since he signed Form 872 under duress, the IRS could not increase his tax after the three-year period.

47.4 Interest on Deficiencies

Interest is charged on a deficiency at rates listed in the following table. The interest rate, which equals the federal short-term rate plus 3%, is determined every quarter. Interest begins to accrue from the due date of the return. Interest is compounded daily except for estimated tax penalties. IRS tables on compound interest may be found in IRS Revenue Procedure 95-17. Where a taxpayer has relied on IRS assistance in preparing a return, and taxes are owed because of a mathematical or clerical error, interest does not begin to accrue until 30 days from a formal demand by the IRS for the payment of additional taxes.

Caution

No Limitation Period for Fraud
Where a false or fraudulent return is filed with intent to evade the tax, or where no return is filed, there is no limitation on when the tax may be assessed.

IRS interest rates on taxes owed are as follows:

From—	To—	Deficiency Rate—
4/1/99	12/31/99	8%
1/1/99	3/31/99	7%
4/1/98	12/31/98	8%
7/1/96	3/31/98	9%
4/1/96	6/30/96	8
7/1/95	3/31/96	9
4/1/95	6/30/95	10
10/1/94	3/31/95	9
7/1/94	9/30/94	8
10/1/92	6/30/94	7
4/1/92	9/30/92	8
1/1/92	3/31/92	9
4/1/91	12/31/91	10

 Law Alert

Interest Rate on Refunds

Since January 1, 1999, individual taxpayers receive the same rate of interest on overpayments as that which is assessed on underpayments.

Refunds. The interest rate on refunds is 1% less than the rate on deficiencies for periods before 1999 but starting January 1, 1999, the interest rates are the same. Generally, no interest is paid on a refund made within 45 days of the due date of the return (disregarding extensions). If you file after the due date, no interest is paid on a refund made within 45 days of the actual filing date. *See 49.5.*

47.5 Tax Penalties

Late payments. If you are late in paying your taxes, a nondeductible monthly penalty of 0.5% ($\frac{1}{2}$ of 1%) is imposed on the net amount of tax due and not paid by the due date. The maximum penalty is 25% of the tax due. The penalty is in addition to the regular interest charge. The penalty does not apply if you can show that the failure to pay is due to reasonable cause and not to willful neglect. The penalty does not apply to the estimated tax.

A similar penalty applies for failure to pay a tax deficiency within 21 calendar days of the date of notice and demand for payment if the tax due is less than $100,000. If the tax is $100,000 or more, the penalty-free payment period is 10 business days.

The monthly penalty may be doubled to 1%, if, after repeated requests to pay and a notice of levy, you do not pay. The increased penalty applies starting in the month that begins after the earlier of the following IRS notices: (1) a notice that the IRS will levy upon your assets within 10 days unless payment is made and (2) a notice demanding immediate payment where the IRS believes collection of the tax is in jeopardy. If the tax is not paid after such a demand for immediate payment, the IRS may levy upon your assets without waiting 10 days.

Late filing. If your return is filed late without reasonable cause, the IRS may impose a penalty of 5% of the net tax due for each month the return is late, with a maximum penalty of 25%. If the return is more than 60 days late, the penalty will not be less than the smaller of $100 and 100% of the tax due. In one case, the IRS tried to impose the $100 minimum penalty on a taxpayer who did not owe any tax because her withholdings exceeded her liability. However, the Tax Court held that the minimum $100 penalty does not apply unless tax is underpaid. The IRS has agreed to follow the decision.

If failure to file is fraudulent, the monthly penalty is 15% of the net tax due, with a maximum penalty of 75%.

If you are subject to penalties for both late payment and late filing, the 0.5% penalty for late payment (but not the 1% penalty) offsets the penalty for late filing during the period that the penalties run concurrently.

Penalties for inaccurate returns. A 20% penalty generally applies to the portion of any tax underpayment attributable to (1) negligence or disregard of IRS rules and regulations; (2) substantial understatement of tax liability; (3) overvaluation of property; or (4) undervaluation of property on a gift tax or estate tax return. These penalties may be avoided by showing good faith and reasonable cause for the underpayment; a stricter version of this exception applies to charitable contribution overvaluations as discussed later in this section.

Negligence or disregard of IRS rules or regulations. The 20% penalty applies to the portion of the underpayment attributable to negligence. Negligence is defined as failing to make a reasonable attempt to comply with the law. Failure to report income shown on an information return, such as interest or dividends, is considered strong evidence of negligence, but negligence is not presumed as it was under prior law. For returns with an original due date before 1990, a 5% negligence penalty is applied to the entire underpayment where any part of it was attributable to negligence.

The 20% penalty may also apply if you take a position on a return which is contrary to IRS revenue rulings, notices, or regulations. This penalty for disregarding IRS rules or regulations may be avoided if you have a reasonable basis for your position and you disclose that position on Form 8275 or on Form 8275-R in the case of a good faith position contrary to a regulation. Thus, disclosure will not avoid a penalty for a position that does not have a reasonable basis.

Substantial understatement of tax. If you understate tax liability on a return by the greater of $5,000 and 10% of the proper tax, you may be subject to a penalty equal to 20% of the underpayment attributable to the understatement.

The penalty may be avoided if you have a reasonable basis for your position and you disclose the position to the IRS on Form 8275, or on Form 8275-R in the case of a position that is contrary to an IRS regulation.

The penalty also may be avoided if you can show that your position was supported by "substantial authority" such as statutes, court decisions, final, temporary, or proposed IRS regulations, IRS revenue rulings and procedures, and press releases or notices published by the IRS in the weekly Internal Revenue Bulletin. You may also rely on IRS private letter rulings and technical advice memoranda issued after October 31, 1976, and IRS actions on decisions and general counsel memoranda issued after March 12, 1981. However, according to the IRS, such rulings and internal IRS memoranda that are more than 10 years old should be accorded very little weight. Congressional committee reports and the tax law explanations prepared by Congress's Joint Committee on Taxation, known as the "Blue Book," may be relied on as authority for your position.

However, if an understatement of tax is due to tax-shelter items, having substantial authority for your position is not enough to avoid the penalty; you must also reasonably believe that your position was "more likely than not" correct. Disclosure does not avoid a penalty for tax-shelter items.

Overvaluing property or basis. The 20% penalty for overvaluing property, such as where inflated charitable contribution deductions are claimed or where the basis of depreciable property is inflated, applies *only* if the claimed value or basis is 200% or more of the correct amount. Furthermore, there is no penalty unless the tax underpayment attributable to the overvaluation exceeds $5,000. The penalty rate is doubled to 40% if the overvaluation is 400% or more of the correct value. To avoid the penalty for donated property on the grounds that you had reasonable cause, the value must be based on a qualified appraisal *(14.12)* and your own good faith investigation of value.

Undervaluation on gift or estate tax return. If property is undervalued on a gift tax return or estate tax return by 50% or more, and if the tax underpayment attributed to the undervaluation exceeds $5,000, a 20% penalty applies. The penalty doubles to 40% if the undervaluation is 75% or more.

Fraud penalty. A 75% penalty applies to the portion of any tax underpayment due to fraud. If the IRS establishes that any part of an underpayment is due to fraud, the entire underpayment will be attributed to fraud, unless you prove otherwise.

Interest on penalties. A higher interest cost is imposed on individuals subject to the following penalties: failure to file a timely return, negligence or fraud, overvaluation of property, undervaluation of gift or estate tax property, *or* substantial understatement of tax liability. Interest starts to run from the due date of the return (including extensions) until the date the penalty is paid. For other penalties, interest is imposed only if the penalty is not paid within 21 calendar days of an IRS demand for payment if the penalty is less than $100,000. The interest-free period is 10 business days after the IRS demand for payment if the penalty is $100,000 or more.

Acting on wrong IRS advice. A penalty will not be imposed if you rely on erroneous advice provided in writing by IRS officials. It is necessary for you to show that you provided accurate information when asking for advice.

47.6 Notify the IRS of Address Changes

If the IRS does not have your current address, payment of a refund due you may be delayed. If you owe taxes, the IRS may enforce a deficiency notice sent to the address on your most recently filed tax return, even if you never receive the IRS notice.

To avoid these problems, file Form 8822 with the IRS to provide notice of an address change. Alternatively, you may send a signed written statement to the IRS Service Center covering your old residence. The statement should state the new and old address, your full name, and your Social Security or employer identification number.

If you and your spouse separate after filing a joint return, you should each notify the IRS of your current address.

If after you move you receive an IRS correspondence that has been forwarded by the Post Office, you may correct the address shown on the letter and mail it back to the IRS. Your correction is considered notice of an address change.

 Caution

Too Good to Be True
If you claim a deduction, credit, or exclusion on your return that would seem to a reasonable person to be "too good to be true" under the circumstances, the IRS is likely to consider you negligent unless you show you made an attempt to verify the correctness of the position.

IRS Tax Audits

Because the IRS is unable to examine every return, it follows a policy of examining returns which, upon preliminary inspection, indicate the largest possible source of potential tax deficiency.

Returns are rated for audit according to a mathematical formula called the discriminant function system (DIF). Various weights are assigned to separate items on each tax return, thus permitting the ranking of returns for the greatest potential error. The method is based on data the IRS compiled from extensive audits of taxpayers under the Taxpayer Compliance Measurement Program (TCMP), which was suspended several years ago. For business taxpayers in specific market segments, the IRS has developed detailed audit guidelines as part of its Market Segment Specialization Program (MSSP).

This chapter discusses what may trigger an audit and how you can handle an audit if your return is selected for examination.

48.1   Odds of Being Audited

The odds are low that your return will be picked for an audit. The IRS does not have the personnel and resources to examine every return, so it selects those returns which upon preliminary inspection have a high audit potential—those that are most likely to result in a substantial tax deficiency.

Audit odds vary depending on your income, profession, type of return, type of transactions reported, and where you live. Individual returns are classified by all income items on the return without regard to losses. Professional or business income reported on Schedule C and farm income reported on Schedule F is classified by total gross receipts, and corporate returns are classified by total assets.

Your return may command special IRS scrutiny because of your profession, the type of transactions reported, or the deductions claimed. The chances of being audited are greater under the following circumstances:

- Your information reported on the tax return does not match information received from third party documentation, such as Forms 1099 and W-2.
- Your itemized deductions exceed IRS targets.
- You claim tax-shelter losses.
- You report complex investment or business transactions without clear explanations.
- You receive cash payments in your work that the IRS thinks are easy to conceal, such as cash fees received by doctors or tips received by cab drivers and waiters.
- Business expenses are large in relation to income.
- Cash contributions to charity are large in relation to income.
- You are a shareholder of a closely held corporation whose return has been examined.
- A prior audit resulted in a tax deficiency.
- An informer gives the IRS grounds to believe that you are omitting income from your return.

Itemized deductions.   If your itemized deductions exceed target ranges set by the IRS, the chances of being audited increase. The IRS does not publicize its audit criteria for excessive deductions, but it does release statistics showing the average amount of deductions claimed according to reported income. Here are IRS figures based on deductions claimed on 1997 returns.

Average Itemized Deductions

AGI (thousands)	Medical	Taxes	Interest	Donations	Total
$ 10–15	$ 3,370	$ 1,635	$ 6,075	$ 1,182	$ 8,778
15–20	7,491	2,119	5,299	1,368	10,735
20–25	4,017	2,250	5,651	1,368	9,920
25–30	4,893	2,249	5,262	1,493	9,985
30–40	3,987	2,772	5,551	1,451	10,392
40–50	4,002	3,285	6,346	1,616	11,756
50–75	6,620	4,236	6,824	1,862	13,385
75–100	8,413	6,200	8,387	2,477	17,471
100 or more	18,463	15,730	12,852	11,501	36,548

48.2   Types of Audits

An examination may be held by correspondence, at a local IRS office, or at the taxpayer's place of business, office, or home. An examination at an IRS office is called a desk or office examination; an examination at a place of business or home is called a field examination. When you are contacted by the IRS, you should receive an explanation of the examination process.

In a correspondence audit, the IRS sends you a letter asking for additional information about an item on your return. For example, the IRS may ask you to document a claimed deduction for charitable contributions or medical expenses. If the IRS is not satisfied with your response, you may be called in for an office audit. The IRS also notifies you by letter of mathematical or clerical errors you have made on your return, or if you have failed to report income, such as interest or dividends, that are shown by payers on information returns and matched to taxpayer returns by IRS computers.

The complexity of the transactions reported on a return generally determines whether a return will be reviewed at an office or field examination.

Most audits of individual returns, except for the self-employed, are conducted at IRS offices. An office audit usually covers only a few specific issues which the IRS specifies in its notice to you. For example, the examining agent may only be interested in seeing proof for travel expense deductions or educational expenses.

Field audits generally involve business returns; they are more extensive and time-consuming than office audits and are handled by more experienced IRS agents. For self-employed individuals, most examinations are field audits at their place of business. It is advisable to have a tax professional go over the potential weak spots in your return and represent you at the examination.

48.3 Preparing for the Audit

After an office audit is scheduled, the first thing to do is look over your return. Refresh your memory. Examine the items the IRS questioned in its notice of audit, and organize your records accordingly. Also check the rest of your return and gather proof for items you are unsure of. At this point, you should take a broad view of your return to anticipate problems you may encounter. Before the actual examination begins, consider possible settlement terms. Assume that the agent will assess additional tax, but establish the range you will consider reasonable. You can always change your mind, but giving some thought beforehand to possible settlement terms will help you later when settlements are actually discussed.

You may authorize an attorney, CPA, enrolled agent, or other individual recognized to practice before the IRS to represent you at the examination without your being there. To do so, give your representative authorization on Form 2848. An attorney or other representative authorized on Form 2848 can perform any acts that you could, including entering into a binding settlement agreement.

If you attend the audit, take only the records related to the items questioned in the IRS notice. Do not volunteer extra records; if the agent sees them, it might suggest new areas for investigation.

If you are concerned that there may be a problem of fraud, see a qualified attorney before you come into contact with an IRS official. The attorney can put your actions in perspective and help protect your legal rights. Besides, what you tell an attorney is privileged information; he or she cannot divulge or be forced to divulge data you have provided, other than data used to prepare your tax return.

A field audit of your business return is likely to involve a comprehensive examination and requires careful preparation. Together with your tax adviser, go over your return for potential areas of weakness. For example, the agent is likely to question deductions you have claimed for business travel. If you are an incorporated professional, the corporation's deductions for expenses of company-owned cars or planes will probably be reviewed. The agent may suspect that a portion of these business deductions are actually nondeductible personal travel costs; be prepared to substantiate the business portion of your total mileage and operating expenses.

Under the Taxpayer Bill of Rights (48.9), the IRS is generally required to hold an office audit at the office located nearest to your home. The IRS generally may not conduct a field audit at the site of a small business if the audit would essentially require the shutting down of the business, unless a direct visit is necessary to determine inventory or verify assets.

48.4 Handling the Audit

If you have authorized someone to represent you at the examination, your representative may appear at the examination without you. If the IRS wants to question you, it must issue you an administrative summons. If you are present and questioned, you may stop the examination to consult with counsel, unless the examination is pursuant to an administrative summons.

Audits conducted at an IRS office may conclude quickly because they usually involve only a few specific issues. In some cases, the audit may take less than an hour. The key to handling the audit is advance preparation. When you arrive at the IRS office, be prepared to produce your records quickly. Records should be organized by topic so that you do not waste time leafing through pages for a receipt or other document.

If the agent decides to question an item not mentioned in the notice of audit, refuse politely but firmly to answer the questions. Tell the agent that you must first review your records. If the agent insists on pursuing the matter, another meeting will have to be scheduled. The agent might decide it is not worth the time and drop the issue.

Common sense rules of courtesy should be your guide in your contacts with the agent. Avoid personality clashes; they can only interfere with a speedy and fair resolution of the examination. However, be firm in your approach and, if the agent appears to be unreasonable in his or her approach, make it clear that—if necessary—you will go all the way to court to win your point. A vacillating approach may weaken your position in reaching a settlement.

If the IRS has scheduled a field audit, ask that the examination be held at your representative's office. If you have not retained professional help and the examination takes place on your business premises, do not allow the agent free run of the area: Provide the agent with a comfortable work

Planning Reminder

Audit Scheduling

Make sure that the examination is scheduled far enough in advance for you to get ready. Do not let the IRS hurry you into an examination until you are prepared. In some localities, particularly rural areas, the IRS may give short notice in scheduling a field audit. An agent may even appear at your home or place of business and try to begin the audit immediately. Resist this pressure and reschedule the meeting at your convenience.

area for examining your records. If possible, the workplace should be isolated so that the agent can concentrate on the examination without being distracted by office operations that might spark questions. Tell your employees not to answer questions about your business or engage in small talk with the agent. As with an office audit, help speed along the field examination by having prepared your records so that requested information can be quickly produced.

Recording the examination. You have the right to make an audio recording of any interview with an IRS official. Video recordings are not permitted. No later than 10 calendar days before the interview, give written notice to the agent conducting the interview that you will make a recording. Later requests are at the discretion of the IRS. You must pay for all recording expenses and supply the equipment. The IRS may also make a recording of the interview, upon giving notice of at least 10 calendar days. However, IRS notice is not necessary if you have already submitted a request to make a recording. You have the right to obtain a transcript, at your own expense, of any recording made by the IRS. Generally, a request for a copy must be received by the IRS agent within 30 calendar days after the recording, although later requests may be honored.

48.5 Agreeing to Audit Changes

After the audit, the agent will discuss proposed changes either with you or your representative.

If you agree with the agent's proposed changes, you will be asked to sign a Form 870, which, when signed, permits an immediate assessment of a deficiency plus penalties and interest, if due. The Form 870 is called "Waiver of Restrictions on Assessment and Collection of Deficiency in Tax and Acceptance of Overassessment."

If you believe that you have done as well or better than expected regarding the proposed deficiency, you can bring the case to a close by signing the Form 870, but the agent's supervisor must also approve the assessment.

By signing the form, you limit the amount of interest charges added to the deficiency. A signed Form 870 does not prevent the IRS from reopening the case to assess an additional deficiency. If on review the deficiency is increased, you will receive a revised Form 870. You can refuse to sign the form. The signed first form has the effect of stopping the interest on the original deficiency. As a matter of practice, however, waivers of acceptances ordinarily result in closing of the case.

It is possible, although unlikely, that upon examining your return, the agent will determine that you are due a refund. In this situation, a signed Form 870 is considered a valid refund claim. You should file a protective refund claim even if you sign the Form 870 acknowledging the overpayment. Generally, the agent will process the refund, but if he or she fails to do so or the review staff puts it aside for some reason and the limitations period expires, the refund will be lost. The refund claim will protect you from such a mishap.

The payment of tax before the deficiency notice (90-day letter) is mailed is, in effect, a waiver of the restrictions on assessment and collection. If the payment satisfies your entire tax liability for that year, you cannot appeal to the Tax Court. You must sue for a refund in either federal district court or the Court of Federal Claims.

48.6 Disputing the Audit Changes

If you disagree with the agent and the examination takes place in an IRS office, you may ask for an immediate meeting with a supervisor to argue your side of the dispute. If an agreement is not reached at this meeting or the audit is at your office or home, the agent prepares a report of the proposed adjustments. You will receive a 30-day letter in which you are given the opportunity to request a conference. You may decide not to ask for a conference and await a formal notice of deficiency (90-day letter).

If your examination was conducted as an office audit or by correspondence, or the disputed amount does not exceed $25,000, you do not have to prepare a written protest for a conference. The written protest is a detailed presentation of your reasons for disagreeing with the agent's report. Even where a formal written protest is not required, you must provide a brief written statement indicating your reasons for disagreeing with the agent when you request an appeals conference. *See* IRS Publication 5, "Appeal Rights and Preparation of Protests for Unagreed Cases."

At the conference you may appear for yourself or be represented by an attorney or other agent, and you may bring witnesses. The conference is held in an informal manner and you are given ample opportunity to present your case.

If you cannot reach a settlement, you will receive a Notice of Deficiency, commonly called a 90-day letter. In it, you are notified that at the end of 90 days from the date it was mailed, the government will assess the additional tax.

Caution

Waiving Your Right To Appeal
Before deciding whether to sign the Form 870, consider that, by signing, you are giving up your right of appeal to both the IRS Office of Appeals and the Tax Court. However, you may still file a refund suit in a federal district court or in the Court of Federal Claims unless you have agreed not to do so on the Form 870.

Caution

Notice of Deficiency
If you do not respond to the 30-day letter, or if you later do not reach an agreement with an appeals officer, the IRS will send you a 90-day letter, also called a "notice of deficiency." This notice will show the 90th day by which you must file your petition with the Tax Court.

Caution

Penalty for Frivolous Tax Court Action

If you bring a frivolous case to the Tax Court or unreasonably fail to pursue IRS administrative remedies, the Tax Court may impose a penalty of up to $25,000. Furthermore, if you appeal a Tax Court decision and the appeals court finds that the appeal was frivolous, you may be penalized.

Planning Reminder

Recovering Attorneys' Fees

Attorneys' fees include the fees paid by a taxpayer for the services of anyone who is authorized to practice before the Tax Court or IRS.

Going to court. When you receive a 90-day letter, if you are still convinced that your position is correct, you may take your case to one of three courts. You may within 90 days file a petition with the Tax Court without having to pay the tax, or you may pay the additional tax, file a refund claim for it, and—after the refund claim is denied—sue for a refund in a federal district court or the U.S. Court of Federal Claims.

Generally, the decision to litigate should be considered by an experienced tax practitioner.

The Tax Court has a small tax case procedure for deficiencies of $50,000 or less. Such cases are handled expeditiously and informally. Cases may be heard by appointed special trial judges. A small claim case may be discontinued at any time before a decision, but the decision when made is final. No appeal may be taken by you or the IRS.

48.7 Recovering Costs of a Tax Dispute

In a tax dispute, you may believe that the IRS has taken an unreasonable position, forcing you to incur legal fees and other expenses to win your case. Here are highlights of the rules for recovering costs from the IRS in a case that commenced after July 30, 1996.

You may recover all or part of—
1. Reasonable administrative costs of proceedings within the IRS, and
2. Reasonable litigation costs in a court proceeding.

A judgment for reasonable litigation costs will not be awarded in any court proceeding if you did not exhaust all IRS administrative remedies. A refusal by the taxpayer to agree to an extension of time for a tax assessment is not a bar to an award, but unreasonably delaying the proceedings is.

To receive an award, you must "substantially prevail" as to the key issues in the case or the amount of tax involved. If you do, you will be entitled to a recovery unless the IRS proves that it was "substantially justified" in maintaining the position that it did. For purposes of recovering costs incurred after January 18, 1999, you are treated as the prevailing party if the IRS obtains a court judgment against you, but the judgment is equal to or less than an amount that you offered in settlement. The offer must be considered a qualified offer made during a period that begins on the date of the first letter of proposed deficiency allowing for an IRS administrative appeal and ends 30 days before the date first set for trial.

The Tax Court and other courts have interpreted "substantially justified" to be a reasonableness standard. The IRS is presumed not to be "substantially justified" if it does not follow its own published regulations, revenue rulings, procedures, notices, announcements, or a private ruling issued to the taxpayer. The IRS may try to rebut the presumption. For costs incurred after January 18, 1999, a court may also consider whether an IRS position has been rejected by federal courts of appeal of other circuits in determining whether the IRS position was substantially justified.

Reasonable administrative costs include IRS fees and expenses of attorney fees, witnesses, and experts. The IRS determines the amount of such an award, which may include costs incurred from the date the IRS sent its first letter of a proposed deficiency allowing you to ask for an administrative appeal. For an award of administrative costs, you must file an application with the IRS before the 91st day after the date on which the IRS mailed you its final decision. To appeal a denial of your application, you must petition the Tax Court within 90 days from the date the IRS mailed the denial.

Reasonable litigation costs include reasonable court costs, fees of witnesses and experts, and attorneys' fees. Fees of witnesses may not exceed the rate paid by the U.S. Attorneys' fees in cases started after July 30, 1996 and incurred before January 1, 1999, are capped at $110 an hour. For attorneys' fees incurred after December 31, 1998, and on or before January 18, 1999, the maximum rate is $120 per hour and for costs incurred after January 18, 1999, the limit is $130 per hour. This amount may be increased for 2000 by an inflation adjustment. The court may also increase the award for attorneys' fees to account for special factors, such as the difficulty of the issues and the availability of local tax expertise.

You may *not* recover attorneys' fees if you represent yourself *(pro se)*. However, you are still entitled to recover fees for witnesses and experts. If you represent a prevailing taxpayer on a *pro bono* basis or for a nominal fee (after January 18, 1999) a court may award you or your employer reasonable attorneys' fees.

You may *not* recover costs if your net worth at the time the action begins exceeds $2 million. For proceedings commenced after August 5, 1997, the $2 million net worth limit applies separately to each spouse in determining whether a married couple filing jointly is entitled to recover legal fees. No recovery is allowed to sole proprietors, partnerships, and corporations if their net worth exceeds $7 million or they have more than 500 employees.

For cases commenced after November 10, 1988 but before July 31, 1996, *see* prior editions of *Your Income Tax*.

48.8 Suing the IRS for Unauthorized Collection

If an IRS employee recklessly, intentionally, or negligently disregards the law or IRS regulations when taking a collection action, you may sue the IRS in federal district court for actual economic damages resulting from the IRS employee's misconduct, plus certain costs of bringing the action. The lawsuit must be filed within two years of the date your right to sue accrued.

For negligent IRS collection activities after July 22, 1998, you may sue for damages of up to $100,000, provided you first exhaust IRS administrative remedies.

For reckless or intentional misconduct, the maximum damage award is $1 million for actions by IRS officers or employees after July 30, 1996. For collection actions before July 23, 1998, an award may be reduced if administrative remedies before the IRS are not exhausted. For IRS actions after July 22, 1998, administrative remedies must be exhausted to obtain an award. If the IRS action was after November 10, 1988, but before July 31, 1996, the maximum award is $100,000, and no amount will be awarded if the court determines that administrative remedies were not exhausted. No suit may be brought for IRS actions prior to November 11, 1988.

According to IRS regulations, actual economic damages that may be recovered are monetary losses you suffer as a direct result of the IRS's action. For example, a business may lose loyal customers and suffer an actual cash loss if the IRS's action damages the business's reputation. Other actual expenses could include the cost of renting a house or a car if the IRS puts a lien on or seizes your property, or loss of income due to the garnishment of your paycheck. Damages from the IRS for loss of reputation, inconvenience, or emotional distress are allowed only to the extent that they result in such actual monetary loss.

The IRS defines "costs of action" that you may recover as (1) fees of the clerk and marshall; (2) fees of the court reporter; (3) fees and disbursements for printing and witnesses; (4) copying fees; (5) docket fees; and (6) compensation for court-appointed experts and interpreters.

Litigation costs and administrative proceeding costs are not treated as "costs of the action." However, if the IRS denies your administrative claim for damages and you successfully sue in federal district court, you are considered a "prevailing party" and may recover attorneys' fees, related litigation expenses, and administrative costs before the IRS as previously discussed.

48.9 Taxpayer Bill of Rights

As a taxpayer, you have the right to be treated fairly, professionally, promptly, and courteously by the IRS and its employees. Because of many complaints of abuse in the past, Congress has passed laws that protect taxpayers from mistreatment by IRS personnel. *See* IRS Publication 1, *Your Rights as a Taxpayer*.

One aim of the Taxpayer Bill of Rights is to have the IRS inform you of the effect of the tax action it is taking and how you can proceed and protect your rights. Thus, when the IRS starts an action against you, you should ask for an explanation of the procedural rules affecting your case, if these are not already included in the documents sent to you. For example, before the IRS may enforce a tax lien by seizing property by levy, the IRS must provide you with a notice of your right to a hearing before an appeals officer, an explanation of the levy procedures, the availability of administrative appeals and the appeals procedures, the alternatives to the proposed levy such as an installment agreement, and the rules for obtaining the release of a lien.

An important section of the Bill of Rights created the Taxpayer Advocate's Office. The purpose of the Taxpayer Advocate is to assist taxpayers in resolving problems with the IRS, identify areas in which taxpayers have problems dealing with the IRS, propose changes in administrative practices of the IRS and identify potential legislative changes that may mitigate the problems. At the Advocate's office, you can receive assistance if you have unsuccessfully tried to resolve your problem with the IRS and have not had your calls or letters returned. You will be assigned a personal advocate who is in the best position to try to resolve your problem. Taxpayer Advocates can be contacted by calling (877) 777-4778, or you may write to the Advocate at the IRS office that last contacted you. You may also order Publication 1546, *The Problem Resolution Program of the Internal Revenue Service*.

 Planning Reminder

IRS Failure To Release Lien

A suit for damages may also be brought in federal district court against the IRS if IRS employees improperly fail to release a lien on your property. Before you sue, you must file an administrative claim for damages. The lawsuit must be filed within two years after your claim arose. You may sue for actual economic damages plus costs of the action; the types of damages that may be recovered are similar to those discussed for suing the IRS for unauthorized collection actions.

Filing Refund Claims, and Amended Returns

File a refund claim on Form 1040X if you want to take advantage of a retroactive change in the law, if you have overpaid your tax because you failed to take allowable deductions or credits, or overstated your income. You may use Form 1040X to correct your return if you underreported your income or improperly claimed deductions.

File a refund claim on time. The time limits discussed at 49.1 must be strictly observed; otherwise, even if you file a valid refund claim, it will be denied because of late filing.

Circumstances in which you do not file a refund claim. You do not have to file a refund claim if you have overpaid your tax due to excessive withholding of taxes on your wages or salary, or if you have overpaid your estimated tax. You get a refund on these overpayments by filing your tax return and requesting a refund for these amounts.

For a refund of an overpayment of FICA taxes, see 26.10 for how to claim a refund on your tax return. If you are not required to file a tax return, you file a refund claim on Form 843.

Earned income credit. If you are entitled to a refund due to the earned income credit for certain low-income working families, you must file your tax return to get your refund, even though your income and filing status would not otherwise require that a return be filed. See Chapter 25.

49.1   Who Should File a Refund Claim

You may file a refund claim on Form 1040X if you have overpaid your tax on your original return because you failed to take allowable deductions or credits, or overstated your income. You may also file for a refund if you wish to take advantage of a retroactive change in the law. You do not have to file a refund claim if you have overpaid your tax due to excessive withholding of taxes on your wages or salary, or if you have overpaid your estimated tax. You will receive a refund on those overpayments by filing your tax return and requesting a refund at that time.

49.2   When To File a Refund Claim

You may file a refund claim on Form 1040X within three years from the time your return was filed, or within two years from the time you paid your tax, whichever is later. A return filed before its due date is treated as having been filed on the due date. The filing deadlines are suspended while you are financially disabled; *see* the Planning Reminder on this page.

A refund claim based on a bad debt or worthless securities may be made within seven years of the due date of the return for the year in which the debt or security became worthless.

The time for filing refund claims based on carrybacks of net operating losses or general business credits is within three years of the due date (including extensions) of the return for the year the loss or credit arose.

A refund claim based on your share of a joint return refund withheld by the IRS to pay your spouse's debts *(49.2)* may be made within six years of the date you received the IRS notice that the refund had been withheld.

If you filed an agreement giving the IRS an extended period of time in which to assess a tax against you, you are allowed an additional period in which to file a claim for refund. The claim, up to certain amounts, may be filed through the extension period and for six months afterwards.

Armed Forces service members and veterans. In determining the time limits within which a refund claim may be filed, you disregard intervening periods of service in a combat zone or hazardous duty area, plus periods of continuous hospitalization outside the United States as a result of combat zone injury, and the next 180 days thereafter.

49.3   Joint Refund Claims

If a joint return was filed for a year in which a refund is due, both spouses are entitled to recover jointly and both must file a joint refund claim. Where separate returns were filed, each spouse is a separate taxpayer and may not file a claim to recover a refund based on the other spouse's return, except if that spouse becomes the fiduciary when one spouse becomes incompetent or dies. To claim a refund on behalf of a deceased spouse, you should complete Form 1310. If you are divorced and incur a net operating loss or credit that may be carried back to a year in which you were married, you may file a refund claim with your signature alone and the refund check will be made out only to you; *see 40.18.*

Refund withheld to pay spouse's debts. If you showed a refund due on a joint return filed with a spouse who owed child support or federal student loans, the IRS may have withheld payment of the refund to cover the obligations. If you are not liable for the past-due payments, and your tax payments (withholdings or estimated tax installments) exceed your income reported on the joint return, you may file Form 8379 to get back your share of the refund.

49.4   Stating the Reasons for Refund Claims

The most important part of a refund claim is a statement of the "reasons" for the refund. A general claim simply noting an overpayment, without supporting facts and grounds, is not sufficient. If a claim is denied by the IRS, it may become the basis of a court suit. If you have not stated all the grounds, you may not be allowed to argue them in court. You must make a claim showing all the:

- Facts that support the claim. Attach all supporting documents and tax forms supporting your claim.
- Grounds for the claim. If you are uncertain about the exact legal grounds, alternate and even inconsistent grounds may be given. For example: "The loss was incurred from an embezzlement; if not, from a bad debt." To protect against understating the amount of the claim, you might preface the claim with this phrase: "The following or such greater amounts, as may be legally refunded."

Caution

Time Limits Must Be Observed

Failure to file a timely refund claim is fatal, regardless of its merits. Even if you expect that your claim will have to be pursued in court, you must still file a timely refund claim. Mailing a return so that it is postmarked by the due date (including extensions) qualifies as a timely filing if you use the U.S. Postal Service. The timely mailing rule also applies to returns that are timely deposited with private delivery services that have been designated by the IRS.

Planning Reminder

Disability Suspends Limitation

In filing a refund claim during any period in which a person is unable to manage his or her financial affairs due to a physical or mental impairment that has lasted or is expected to last for at least one year or to result in death, the law suspends the limitation period. The suspension does not apply during a period in which a guardian is authorized to handle the individual's financial affairs. This law generally took effect on July 22, 1998, but a person who was disabled before that date may take advantage of the suspension period unless a refund claim was already barred as of July 22, 1998.

49.5 Quick Refund Claims

Form 1045 may be used for filing refunds due to carrybacks from net operating losses, and the general business credit. Form 1045 also may be used for a quick refund based on a repayment exceeding $3,000 of income reported in an earlier year. Form 1045 must be filed within 12 months after the loss year. The IRS must act on the claim within 90 days. Payment of quick refund claims is not a final settlement of your return; the IRS may still audit and then disallow the refund claim. Note that the filing of a quick refund, if rejected, may not be the basis of a suit for refund; a regular refund claim must be filed.

Tax-shelter claims. If you file a quick refund claim on Form 1045 and the IRS determines it is likely that you claimed excessive tax-shelter benefits, the IRS will offset the quick refund claim by a deficiency attributable to the tax-shelter items. You will receive the balance and receive a notice of the tax-shelter deficiency.

49.6 Interest Paid on Refunds

If you file a 1999 return on or before April 17, 2000, interest is not paid by the IRS on refunds made within 45 days of the April 17 due date. For example, you file your 1999 return on April 1, 2000, claiming an overpayment due to overwithholding on your wages. Interest does not have to be paid on a refund made before June 2, which is 46 days after April 17, the day the tax was due. A return filed before its due date is treated as having been filed on the due date. If the overpayment is not refunded within 45 days, interest is paid from the date the tax was overpaid up to a date determined by the IRS that can be as much as 30 days before the date of the refund check.

If you get a filing extension or otherwise file after the due date of the return (without regard to extensions of time), no interest is paid if the refund is made within 45 days after the date you filed.

Refund claims. Interest on a refund claim filed within the time limits of 49.1 is paid from the date of overpayment to the date the claim was filed if the IRS pays the refund within 45 days. If the refund is not made within the 45-day period, interest is paid from the date of overpayment to a date set by the IRS that is not more than 30 days before the date of the refund check.

The IRS does not have to pay interest on overpayments resulting from net operating loss carrybacks, or business credit carrybacks if a refund is paid within 45 days of the filing of the refund claim. If a refund claim based on a loss or credit carryback is filed and subsequently a quick refund claim is filed on Form 1045 for the same refund, the 45-day period starts to run on the date Form 1045 is filed.

Interest rates applied to overpayments are as follows:

Amounts outstanding between—	Rate is—
10/1/94 – 3/31/95	8%
4/1/95 – 6/30/95	9
7/1/95 – 3/31/96	8
4/1/96 – 6/30/96	7
7/1/96 – 3/31/98	8
4/1/98 – 3/31/99	7
4/1/99 – 12/31/99	8

49.7 Refunds Withheld by the IRS

The IRS may withhold all or part of your refund if you owe child support or federal debts such as student loans. If you file a joint return with a spouse who owes child support or federal debts, you may be able to obtain your share of a refund due on the joint return; for further details, *see 49.2.*

Tax-shelter claims. The IRS may withhold refunds based on questionable tax-shelter claims. This rule applies to original tax returns showing a refund due as well as to refund claims. In each IRS Service Center, returns of tax-shelter investors are screened to determine if the tax shelter has fraudulently misrepresented tax benefits or grossly overvalued assets or services. If the tax shelter is considered to be abusive and if claimed deductions or tax credits are disallowed, refunds attributable to the tax-shelter items will not be paid. The balance of your refund claim will be paid.

A refund will also be frozen if you file your return after receiving a pre-filing notification letter from the IRS warning you not to claim certain tax-shelter write-offs.

Law Alert

Equalizing Interest Rates
Since the beginning of 1999, the IRS pays the same interest rate on refunds as it charges on tax deficiencies.

49.8 Amended Returns Showing Additional Tax

If, after filing your 1999 return, you find that you did not report some income or claimed excessive deductions, you should file an amended return on Form 1040X to limit interest charges and possible tax penalties. You may also file an amended return to change the status of your return from a separate return to a joint return with your spouse. It is important to note that you may not switch from a joint return to a separate return. An amended return may also be filed if you want to change from itemized deductions to the standard deduction method, or vice versa.

If you filed early and then file an amended return by the filing due date (including any extensions) that shows additional tax due, you will not be charged interest or penalties based on the original return; the amended return is considered a substitute for the original. You must file an amended return within three years from the date of filing your original return, or within two years from the time the tax is paid, whichever is later. This three-year limitation is suspended during any period in which a person is unable to manage his or her financial affairs due to a physical or mental impairment. However, if the person's spouse or guardian is authorized to act on the taxpayer's behalf, this exception will not apply.

You must pay the additional tax due as shown on Form 1040X. Even if you expect a refund on your original return, the IRS will not reduce the refund check to cover the additional tax. You must pay it and you will receive the original refund separately.

Arthur Andersen:
Tax Planning in Perspective

If you're like most people, you think about taxes once a year (or possibly once a quarter) when it's time to file a tax return. But, if that's your approach, you are probably paying more tax than you have to. Taxes that you avoid or postpone can be invested to help meet your financial goals, increase your financial security and provide retirement income. Reducing your tax bill requires planning throughout the year.

It also requires that you determine your goals and adopt strategies designed to meet those goals. Usually, this means thinking about more than your income tax situation. To help you identify opportunities you can use, we have included general strategies that fit many people's needs. These include planning for your child's education, planning for retirement, maximizing the value of charitable contributions, and planning to reduce your estate and gift taxes so that you maximize the value of assets that go to your family and other heirs. Depending on your specific situation, as well as your financial and other goals, other techniques may also be effective. There are no easy answers to the challenges facing taxpayers today. Without careful, multi-year planning, decisions made to help in one tax area may hurt in another.

© Arthur Andersen LLP.

Planning to save taxes before year-end

When it comes to saving taxes, the sooner you start planning the better. Here are several ideas to get you going:

o **Avoid underpayment penalties.** Make sure you have paid enough in federal withholding and/or estimated-tax payments to avoid a penalty. For 2000, you will avoid a penalty for underpayment of estimated tax if your tax payments (including withholdings) are at least equal to (1) 106% of the tax shown on your 1999 tax return or (2) 90% of the tax shown on your 2000 tax return, whichever is less. In addition, there will be no penalty if the amount of the underpayment is less than $1,000.

o **Evaluate opportunities to time the recognition of compensation income.** Depending on your viewpoint, you may be able to time the receipt of commissions, bonuses, or billings. Recognition timing isn't easy, however. You need to consider the time value of money, the impact acceleration might have on various deductions, and other nontax financial factors.

o Given the difference between tax rates on ordinary income and capital gains, try to **shift as much ordinary income to capital gains** as possible, either by expanding your use of incentive stock options or by making "Section 83(b)" elections for restricted stock.

o **Watch your holding period of capital assets.** The short-term capital gains rate is almost twice as much as the rate for long-term capital gains.

o If you decide to defer income, **explore the possibility of using nonqualified vehicles,** such as stock-appreciation rights, nonqualified options and Supplemental Executive Retirement Plans (so-called SERPs, or top-hat plans), to optimize your financial after-tax return.

o **Avoid a potential AMT trap if you have incentive stock options (ISOs).** With reduced capital gains rates, ISOs can be a particularly attractive component of a compensation package. The bargain element — i.e., the excess of the stock's value over the purchase price when the option is exercised — is treated as capital gain when the stock is sold. But careful planning and coordination of the entire compensation package are needed when using these options. An alternative minimum tax (AMT) trap could cause the bargain element to be taxed at an effective rate that well exceeds the 20% capital gains rate.

o Additionally, while capital gains are subject to the same lower rates for AMT purposes, **a large capital gain still could present an AMT burden** for a taxpayer who incurs a significant state and local tax as a result of the gain. This makes it particularly important to plan on a multi-year basis for transactions that trigger the AMT.

o Remember that you may be able to **use disqualifying dispositions of incentive stock options to eliminate deferral preferences** and avoid the AMT.

o Try to **"bunch" your miscellaneous itemized deductions,** such as unreimbursed employee business expenses, costs of business publications, certain legal and accounting fees, certain safe-deposit box rental fees, etc., into alternate years. This planning could allow you to deduct a greater proportion of these expenses as they can only be deducted for regular-tax purposes to the extent they exceed 2% of your AGI. Miscellaneous deductions are not deductible at all for the AMT.

o Try to **bunch unreimbursed medical expenses** as well. Careful timing of discretionary expenses, such as elective (but not cosmetic) surgery, new eyeglasses, hearing aids, etc., can make more of these expenses deductible despite a stiff 7.5%-of-AGI threshold.

o **Consider using appreciated property rather than cash to make charitable contributions.** As the fair market value of appreciated tangible property is deductible for both AMT and regular-tax purposes, the AMT is less of a concern.

o **Consider shifting income-producing investments** to tax-deferred or tax-exempt alternatives, to shelter income from current taxes.

o **Establish a Keogh plan** if you have net self-employment income. As a general rule, these contributions are limited to the lesser of $30,000 or 13.048% of your net self-employment income. In addition, the earnings on your Keogh investments accumulate on a tax-deferred basis.

o **Increase your personal use of a vacation (or other second) home** you rent to others. This could allow you to maximize your home mortgage interest deduction.

o **Increase your participation** in what would otherwise be treated as a "passive activity" or dispose of passive activities with suspended losses or credits. This could allow you to currently use passive activity losses or credits that otherwise would be deferred or lost.

o Alternatively, **decrease your participation** in a profitable business activity so that its income can be sheltered by losses from other passive activities.

o **Decrease debt in a rental activity,** thereby reducing passive activity interest expense.

o If you are a sole proprietor, a partner, or a shareholder in an S corporation, you may wish to **consider changing your form of business organization** — to a limited-liability corporation (LLC) or a regular C corporation — for both tax and nontax financial planning reasons.

Planning Reminder

Timing Deductions May Save Tax

You may want to **explore opportunities to time deductions** for charitable contributions, state and local taxes and other payments whose timing is in your control. If you are accelerating a substantial amount of income into the current year, it may be better to take deductions currently. Likewise, some timing decisions, such as prepaying state income tax, may subject you to the alternative minimum tax (AMT).

o **Recognize capital losses** to offset capital gains and up to $3,000 of other income. This strategy is particularly attractive because capital gains no longer count in raising the limit for deducting investment interest expense. But recall that investment considerations always take precedence over tax considerations in determining when to buy and sell investments.

o **Transfer stock with substantial appreciation** to a relative (for example, a child or parent) whom you want to benefit and let him or her sell the stock and pay the tax at a potentially lower rate.

Planning to save taxes after year-end

Once the year is over, your ability to influence your final tax bill is limited. But a few opportunities are available:

o **Establish or make deductible contributions to an IRA** by the due date of your current-year tax return.

o **Organize your records** to support advantageous tax treatments. Document your deductible expenses, business use of autos and other properties, and participation in activities that could be considered passive.

o **Establish a Simplified Employee Pension (SEP) or Keogh plan** if you are self-employed. Contributions to a SEP must be made by the due date, including extensions, of your current-year tax return. Contributions to a Keogh plan must be made by the due date, including extensions, of your current-year tax return, but the Keogh plan itself must be established by December 31 of the current year.

Planning for a child's education

Planning for a child's college education is one of the most important financial planning tasks most parents undertake. Statistics tell part of the story. Today, the average cost of in-state tuition, room and board for a year at a public university is over $9,500, while at a private university those costs average more than $20,000.

Tax relief opportunities for education expenses

The Taxpayer Relief Act of 1997 created two new tax credits: the Hope credit and the Lifetime Learning credit. For a specific tax year, qualifying taxpayers will be able to elect either the Hope credit, the Lifetime Learning credit, *or* tax-free distributions from an Education Savings Account (discussed later in the text) for each eligible student.

The Hope credit is a nonrefundable tax credit of up to $1,500 per year for the first two years of a post-secondary school degree program. The credit covers qualified tuition payments for the taxpayer, the taxpayer's spouse and dependents. It is available for expenses paid after December 31, 1997, for education beginning after that date. The student(s) must be enrolled on at least a half-time basis, and if a parent can claim the student as a dependent, only that parent can use the credit. Phase-out ranges apply, as depicted in the chart on page 688.

The Lifetime Learning credit is a nonrefundable 20% tax credit that may be applied to the first $5,000 in qualified tuition and related expenses for graduate and undergraduate courses at an eligible institution. Like the Hope credit, it covers tuition payments for the taxpayer, taxpayer's spouse, and dependents. It is available for expenses paid after June 30, 1998, for education beginning after that date. The credit is available if the student is enrolled at least half-time in a degree or certificate program; however, the half-time requirement does not have to be met so long as the classes are to acquire or to improve job skills. The chart on page 688 depicts the applicable phase-out ranges.

Deduction for student-loan interest. Qualified taxpayers may claim an "above-the-line" deduction — meaning the deduction is reflected in AGI — up to $1,000 of interest paid on qualified education loans. The deduction increases $500 annually until it caps at $2,500 in 2001. The deduction applies to the first 60 months of interest payments and is not available if the individual is claimed as a dependent on another person's return. The deduction covers loans used to pay higher-education expenses of the taxpayer, taxpayer's spouse and dependents (as of the time the debt was incurred). The debt must have been used to pay education expenditures when the student was enrolled on at least a half-time basis. Phase-out ranges are shown on page 688.

Employer-provided tuition benefits. Taxpayers may exclude up to $5,250 from income each year for qualified employer-provided educational assistance (tuition, fees, books, supplies, etc.). This exclusion applies to courses of instruction beginning before June 1, 2000. It does not apply to graduate-level courses.

 Caution

Escalating College Costs

The College Board estimates college costs are rising at two to three times the rate of inflation. Without planning, financing a college education will be a significant burden for many families.

Phase-out ranges for new education incentives

	Modified adjusted gross income	
	Full credit/ deduction up to this amount	*No credit/ deduction above this amount*
Hope credit*		
Single	$ 40,000	$ 50,000
Married filing jointly	80,000	100,000
Lifetime Learning credit*		
Single	40,000	50,000
Married filing jointly	80,000	100,000
Deduction for student-loan interest		
Single	40,000	55,000
Married filing jointly	60,000	75,000
Education Savings Account		
Single	95,000	110,000
Married filing jointly	150,000	160,000

* Credits not available for married taxpayers filing separately.

Planning Reminder

Tax Rate Spread Between Children and Parents

Until recently, the promise of higher returns hasn't been enough to outweigh most parents' desire to retain control over their assets. But as the spread between the top tax rate and the rate most children pay on income widens, some strategies may be worth revisiting.

In this section are some alternatives that parents looking to fund a child's education can consider to build a nest egg both within and outside their own net worth.

Saving for future education expenses: control is the issue

For most parents who wish to help pay for a child's higher education, the most important consideration is likely to be *control*. Under current tax law, parents can achieve substantially higher after-tax returns by transferring assets to their children, whose income generally is taxed at a significantly lower level. The trade-off involved in obtaining those tax benefits is just as significant, however. Parents typically must surrender control of the assets they transfer, which become the child's when he or she reaches the age of maturity (between ages 18 and 21, depending upon relevant state law). However, the possibility of the child using the accumulated funds for purposes other than education is often disconcerting to parents.

Shifting income and assets

Outright gifts. The most obvious vehicle for shifting income and assets within the family is an outright gift. With the annual gift tax exclusion, you can transfer up to $10,000 each year to each child ($20,000 if you elect to split the gift with your spouse) without paying gift tax. Such gifts are over and above any support, medical, and educational expenses a parent pays for a dependent child. This amount will be indexed for inflation, effective for gifts made after 1998.

The question is whether an outright gift is the right thing to do, considering your tax and family situation. In answering that question you should consider two issues:

o **Kiddie tax:** Under the "kiddie tax" rules, if the child is under age 14, then any income over $1,400 earned by the assets will be taxed at your rate if that yields higher tax. In other words, until your child is age 14, outright gifts may not reduce your family's overall tax burden. Of course, gifts to a child age 14 or older can reduce the tax burden up to 24 percentage points.

o **Control:** An outright gift leaves your child with complete control over the assets. The tax benefits of a direct transfer are significant, but if you make the gift, there is nothing to prevent the child from squandering the wealth. For some families, the solution to that problem lies in the Uniform Gifts to Minors Act or Uniform Transfers to Minors Act, which is discussed below.

Strategies to avoid the "kiddie tax" on outright gifts. The "kiddie tax" on direct transfers of wealth can be partially or fully avoided by transferring assets that generate little current taxable income such as growth stocks, tax-free bonds, and Series EE savings bonds. For example, you can purchase EE bonds in the child's name and elect to have the child pay the tax on the annual interest buildup to an annual aggregate of $1,400. The first $700 accrues tax free. The second $700 is taxed at the child's rate. If the total interest earned by the assets you transfer exceeds $1,400, you should elect to defer paying income tax on the interest until the savings bonds are redeemed or until the child reaches age 14.

UGMA and UTMA gifts. Parents concerned about making outright gifts to minor children can take some comfort in the Uniform Gifts to Minors Act (UGMA) and Uniform Transfers to Minors Act (UTMA). These acts are uniform state statutes that allow you to make a gift to a child, while placing control of the gift in the hands of a custodian of your choice. The custodian retains control of the assets you transfer until your child reaches the state-designated age of majority, which is generally 18 or 21. At that time, control vests in the child.

How UGMA/UTMA works

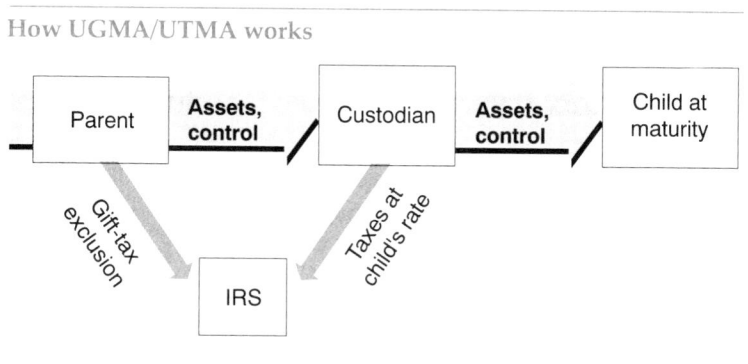

Transfers to children under UGMA or UTMA shift income, income taxes and estate taxes from you to your child. Again, if the child is age 14 or older, tax on the income the assets earn is imposed at the child's rate. Otherwise, under the "kiddie tax" rules, any tax is imposed at your rate if income exceeds $1,400. There is one way to avoid "kiddie tax" considerations: Fund the trust with appreciating assets that generate little current income, such as growth stock that will increase in value.

A word of caution about the custodian of UGMA or UTMA accounts: The custodian should not be the donor. The reason is simple: If the donor dies before the child reaches majority, the assets in the account revert to the donor's estate for estate tax purposes.

Trusts for the benefit of a minor. Another arrangement that makes sense in some cases is a trust for the benefit of a minor. Sometimes this trust is called a "Section 2503(c) trust" because it is named after the section of the tax code that sanctions it. Trust tax rates are very high and make the use of trusts less effective as a way to minimize taxes, in some respects. In some cases, trust income is taxed at higher rates than if the grantor or beneficiary held the assets. However, for parents or grandparents looking to remove assets from their estates, trusts still provide a good means to accumulate funds for a minor child.

How a trust for the benefit of a minor works

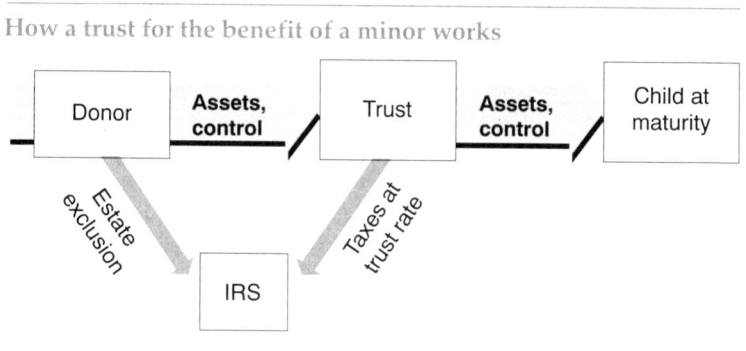

Briefly, the trust for the benefit of a minor works as follows. A parent or grandparent looking to move assets out of his or her estate transfers property (usually money or appreciating securities) to the trust under terms that allow the trustee to accumulate income or pay it out to, or for the benefit of, the child beneficiary. Once the child reaches majority, however, all principal and income accumulated in the trust must be accessible to the child.

Caution

Gift Tax UGMA and UTMA Transfers

Gifts through UGMA or UTMA are subject to gift tax. Through judicious use of the annual gift exclusion and gift splitting, however, parents can achieve sizable buildup in UGMA and UTMA trusts without incurring gift taxes.

Planning Reminder

"Crummey" Trusts

If you're concerned about control issues, a Crummey trust (named after a court case) may be a good alternative. Unlike Section 2503(c) trusts and UGMA/UTMA arrangements, assets do not have to flow to the beneficiary at the age of majority if a Crummey trust is used. Instead, the trust assets are preserved intact, while the beneficiary can withdraw a specified amount from the trust each year. If you are considering a Crummey trust, bear this caveat in mind: If income from the trust is used to pay educational expenses that are considered your parental obligations, the income may be taxed to you.

What are the benefits of this arrangement? Most important, the property transferred to the trust qualifies for the annual gift exclusion, and is removed from the donor's estate. Income also is taxed to the trust or, to the extent it's distributed, to the child beneficiary, but this may or may not be a plus.

What are the downsides? First, the donor irrevocably surrenders control to a trustee who has a fiduciary responsibility to carry out the wishes of the donor as stated in a formal trust document. There are professional fees for preparing the legal trust document, preparing annual income tax returns and fiduciary administration. Also, the income tax savings may be less than anticipated. For 1999, only the first $1,700 of taxable trust income is taxed at the 15% rate, while a 39.6% tax rate applies to taxable trust income over $8,450. Finally, any distributions used to pay expenses that could be characterized as normal obligations of the donor for a minor child (for example, food, clothing, and shelter) may be taxed at the donor's rate. The bottom line: Analyze your situation carefully and consult your financial planner before entering into a trust arrangement.

Retaining control: tax-favored strategies for education expenses

Education Savings Accounts (or EducationIRAs). An Education Savings Account, or education IRA, is a custodial account designed to pay for a beneficiary's higher education costs. Contributions are not deductible, but withdrawals to pay for the beneficiary's college tuition, books, supplies, room, and board may be tax free. Please see page 571 and consult your tax/investment consultant for specific details.

Your 401(k) account. Another option is to fund your 401(k) or other tax-deferred investment vehicle to the fullest extent possible. The funds you set aside grow tax deferred during the accumulation period and may be borrowed tax free to pay higher education expenses.

Of course, some rules apply to education loans from 401(k) plans. Most important:

o Loans must be for less than $50,000 and repaid within five years.
o If one-half of the value of your contributions to the plan plus their earnings (your "nonforfeitable plan benefits") is less than $50,000, only that amount qualifies for treatment as an education loan. Excess withdrawals will be treated as taxable distributions.
o The minimum qualified loan is $10,000.

Despite those restrictions, fully funding a 401(k) or other tax-deferred retirement plan makes sense. Not only do earnings accumulate in the most efficient manner possible — tax free — you pay interest on the loan to a worthy lender: yourself.

Investments to avoid for funding college. What's the best investment option for parents looking to pay for a child's college education? That's tough to say; the right investments depend on your time frame, risk tolerance, and many other factors. It isn't hard, however, to identify investments that don't make sense as college funding vehicles. Here are some investments most people are advised to avoid:

o Most tax-deferred annuities: While there are exceptions, the front-end loads, annual expenses, and applicable surrender charges involved in most annuities make them inefficient college-funding vehicles.
o Long-term bonds that can't be held to maturity or high-yield (junk) bonds: The risk of price fluctuations and loss of principal can be high.
o Life insurance policies that offer slow cash buildup.
o Money market funds: After-tax returns are low relative to historical equity performance.
o Limited partnerships and closely held company stock: Performance is unpredictable at best and liquidity can be an issue.
o Unit trusts: Investors may face early repayment of principal.

IRA withdrawals. Unlike your 401(k) account, you cannot borrow from your IRA. Any loans would be considered distributions subject to ordinary income taxes and a 10% penalty. No 10% penalty is imposed, however, on early withdrawals from an IRA after 1997 when the funds are used to pay qualified higher education expenses for the taxpayer, taxpayer's spouse, child, or grandchild. Qualified expenses include tuition, fees, books, supplies, and certain equipment, as well as room and board, at a post-secondary institution.

Although there is no penalty, these distributions still will be taxed at ordinary income rates. If the distribution is from a nondeductible IRA (i.e., original contributions were not made on a pretax basis), the portion attributed to earnings will be subject to tax at ordinary income rates. As a result, you should assess the impact on your current income tax situation before using IRA funds to pay for education expenses. More significantly, you should assess the longer-term effect this may have on your ability to accumulate sufficient funds for retirement and other goals that you may have for your estate.

 Caution

Drawbacks to 401(k) Plan Loans

There are downsides to borrowing from a 401(k) that you should understand. First, many plans will require you to repay any outstanding loan, in full, if you leave the company. If you cannot, the outstanding balance will be treated as a distribution, subject to taxes at ordinary income rates and a 10% penalty if you have not attained the age of $59^1/_2$. Another risk is the potential opportunity cost of not having your retirement plan assets fully invested.

Prepaid tuition plans. Some states now offer prepaid tuition plans. Although there are some variations from program to program, you generally may pay for tuition in a future year by making a predetermined upfront payment based upon current tuition and when your child is expected to enter college.

If your child chooses not to attend that school or fails to be admitted, you will be entitled to a refund, but may lose some of the investment to administrative fees. Most state prepaid college savings programs do not currently allow the donors to choose their own investments; rather the state program decides how the money will be invested. Therefore, depending upon your timeframe and your asset allocation choices, you may be able to accumulate more funds by investing the money on your own.

Earnings from contributions are taxable to the beneficiary (or contributor) only when distributions (refunds) are received or the value of education provided exceeds the contributions, unless they are excluded under another code section such as a matching grant. Each distribution will be taxed and a penalty of at least 10% is assessed if the donor decides to take the money back.

The law allows tax-free rollovers of account balances to other family members' accounts. In addition, to the extent a distribution is used to pay for qualified tuition or fees, eligible students or parents may be able to claim the Hope or Lifetime Learning credits. This is not true of Education Savings Accounts.

Borrowing for college expenses

As the costs of higher education continue to rise faster than inflation, many people will face a trade-off between saving for college and saving for retirement. After personal savings and financial-aid eligibility are considered, many families still find it necessary to borrow in order to cover at least some of the costs of a college education.

Generally, it is preferable for the student, rather than the parents, to borrow funds for college expenses for several reasons. (1) Typically, tax rates are different. (2) Federally sponsored student-loan programs offer attractive interest rates and repayment terms that typically are not available on conventional loans. (3) In addition, it is not necessary to secure the loan with an asset other than the promise to repay. As noted earlier in this chapter, students may now be able to take a deduction for interest on student loans, depending on their income at the time.

Subsidized and unsubsidized Stafford Loans and other Supplemental Loans for Students (SLS) enable students to borrow up to a certain amount per school year, with maximum limits for undergraduate study and total graduate (including undergraduate) study. Students eligible for subsidized Stafford loans, with specific financial eligibility criteria, can defer interest and principal payments until six months after graduation.

Despite the favorable terms for student loans, many parents still are concerned about burdening their children just out of college with considerable debt. If this is the case, you could consider making annual gifts to your children once they have finished college to help them repay the loans. This would enable you to take advantage of your annual gift tax exclusion, and without putting your retirement savings or your home equity at risk.

"Grandparent" gifts

One last but notable opportunity for meeting educational expenses is the "grandparent" gift. The tax law exempts grandparents and others from gift taxes on unlimited amounts paid for tuition or medical expenses on behalf of another. This applies to tuition payments only, not to living expenses, books or other costs. This rule applies to all levels of schooling, from nursery school to graduate school. The primary stipulation is that the *donor* must write the check *directly to the institution*. This provision is notable because you can use this strategy in addition to taking advantage of the annual gift tax exclusion.

 Planning Reminder

Earnings Grow Tax Deferred in Prepaid Tuition Plan

Prepaid tuition plans for higher education are income-tax deferred if certain requirements are met. This means that, if you are participating in a qualified program, earnings in the trust set up by the state grow free of tax and will not be taxable until distributed to you or the beneficiary or used to pay for tuition.

 Planning Reminder

Tax Decisions Affect Retirement

The tax-related decisions you make today and at various points in your career may have a marked effect on how you save for retirement and how much you will have down the road to support your goals. Many tax decisions you make about retirement are one-time choices that can be very costly to change, so it pays to plan.

Planning for Retirement

Successful retirement planning begins long before retirement. In fact, most of us should be accumulating capital throughout our working careers to sustain us in later years. Sound retirement planning involves reviewing your entire financial life. While taxes are obviously not the only issue, they are central to retirement planning.

To make the right decisions about your retirement plans and taxes, you'll also need to address questions about your cash flow, investments, income taxes, and estate planning strategies.

o **Cash flow.** When can you afford to retire? What impact will Social Security have on your income and income taxes? What will your living expenses be? How will estimated taxes and/or withholding affect your cash flow? Do you expect to have significant nonrecurring expenditures? At what rate do you expect your expenses to increase?

o **Investments.** What are your investment objectives? How should you invest today to meet them? What is your risk tolerance? Should you manage your own money or seek professional advice? How should you coordinate the investments between your retirement plans and your personal accounts?

o **Income taxes.** What should your stock-option exercise strategy be? Will you be subject to the AMT? Will you face investment-interest limitations? How should you fund charitable giving? Do you expect to receive payments from deferred compensation plans and, if so, over what time frame?

o **Estate planning.** Will your estate be liable for substantial taxes at your death? Do trusts make sense in your estate plan? How can you make sure your assets pass to your heirs intact? Should your estate plan be updated? What happens if you're incapacitated? Should you have a living trust? Are your beneficiary designations coordinated with your will or revocable trust?

Individually, these questions might sound straightforward, but together they become much more complicated. In fact, answering them means taking a close look at every aspect of your financial life and often requires professional advice.

How much help will you need in retirement?

People often find the most difficult aspect of retirement planning is simply evaluating their cash flow — determining how much money will be needed in retirement and where it will come from. Most people, too, are surprised to find that the financial issues they face in retirement aren't very different from those they faced in their working years.

One reason for that is that retirees today tend to remain active and to maintain the same quality of life they enjoyed while working. While some business-related expenses naturally drop in retirement — commuting costs, entertainment expenses, and clothing costs, for example — those savings tend to be shifted to other areas, such as travel or increased recreation. Likewise, while some major personal expenses fall with the house paid for and the children out of college, other costs such as medical expenses and insurance premiums may rise substantially. With the future of Medicare under debate, future retirees may need to plan more carefully for medical expenses in retirement.

But another reason is just as important: In retirement we must cope with the unpredictable and corrosive impact of inflation on the purchasing power of our savings and investments.

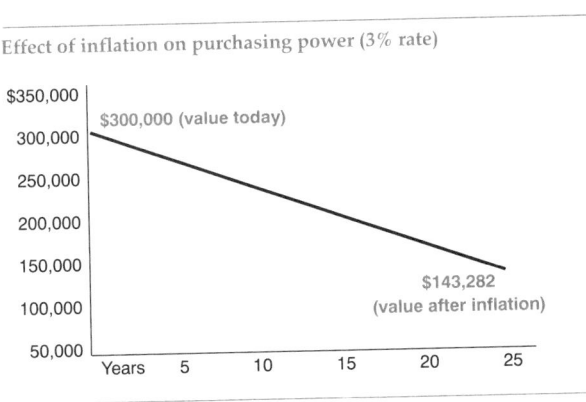

Effect of inflation on purchasing power (3% rate)

$300,000 (value today)

$143,282 (value after inflation)

Where will the money come from in retirement?

As a rule, maintaining the lifestyle you're accustomed to in retirement takes at least two-thirds of your working income. That leads to an important question: Where will the money come from?

If you're like most people, your retirement income will come from five basic sources: Social Security; personal investments including IRAs; the equity in your house and other assets you've accumulated during your working years; nonqualified deferred-compensation plans; and qualified retirement plans such as pension, profit-sharing, or 401(k) plans. Part-time employment could provide a sixth source of income during retirement.

Of course, the tax laws play an important role in the retirement-planning equation. The tax code encourages saving for retirement by allowing, within limits, tax-deferred income to be placed into certain retirement plans, to grow on a tax-deferred basis and to be eligible for special tax treatment upon its distribution. In some cases, you may even be able to reduce your current tax bill with an immediate deduction for the amounts you set aside.

Planning Reminder

Impact of Inflation

The chart shows how serious a toll even a modest 3% level of inflation can take on our savings over the 20+ years most of us can expect to spend in retirement.

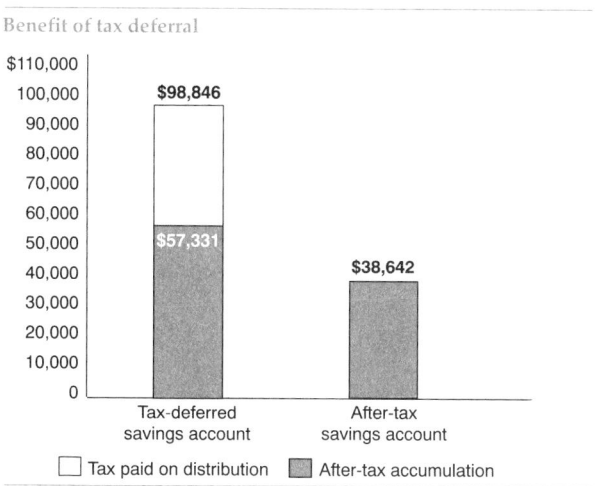

Benefit of tax deferral

$98,846

$57,331

$38,642

Tax-deferred savings account

After-tax savings account

☐ Tax paid on distribution ▨ After-tax accumulation

Planning Reminder

Benefits of Tax-Deferred Growth

As the chart shows, the benefits of tax-deferred growth can be substantial in accumulating wealth over the years. In the example in the chart, $2,000 is contributed annually on a tax-deferred basis into an account earning 8% annually. This amount accumulates to $98,846 at the end of 20 years, $57,331 on an after-tax basis. Assuming an income tax rate of 42%, the after-tax contributions of $1,160, earning 4.64% after tax, accumulate to only $38,642 after 20 years.

There's more to retirement planning than taxes alone. If you have the discipline to save 5% or 6% of your income every year and invest it wisely, you'll wind up with a nice nest egg at retirement, whether you use tax-deferred vehicles or not. Still, planning with tax advantages firmly in mind can help ensure a comfortable retirement.

Social Security. The retirement income over which you have the least control is Social Security. While Social Security benefits provide valuable retirement income for many retirees, you can't start collecting those benefits until you reach age 62 (reduced benefits) or age 65 (full benefits), and the more you make during your working years, the less replacement income Social Security will provide. Beginning in 2000, the age of eligibility for receiving full benefits gradually increases from 65 to 67. If your income exceeds $34,000 (single) or $44,000 (married filing jointly), up to 85% of your Social Security benefits may be taxed. Income for this test includes your adjusted gross income, your tax-exempt income and 50% of your Social Security benefits. As a result, Social Security should be viewed as a supplemental source of retirement income, never as a central part of your retirement finances.

Personal savings and investments. A second source of retirement income is your personal savings and investments, including stocks, bonds and money-market instruments, as well as tax-advantaged investments such as individual retirement accounts. For many people, IRAs have been an important part of a personal retirement savings strategy. IRAs became popular in the early 1980s, when the tax law allowed every wage earner to make a tax-deductible IRA contribution. Since 1987, deductions for IRA contributions have been restricted to individuals who are not covered by a qualified plan or, if they are covered, have AGI below certain levels.

Recent legislation has expanded the availability of deductible IRA contributions to more people. See Chapter 8 for a detailed discussion of the current IRA rules, including nondeductible IRAs, and pay particular attention to the discussion about the new Roth IRA.

Other assets. A third source of retirement income — and one totally under your control — involves cash flows you can tap from assets you acquired during your working years, notably your home.

If you're an empty nester at retirement, you might want to sell your home and trade down to a smaller, more easily maintained condo, townhouse, or other dwelling. If you've owned your home for a number of years, you'll probably reap a handsome profit on the sale. The capital gains exclusion of up to $500,000 for married taxpayers filing jointly and $250,000 for single filers will eliminate, or at least significantly reduce, the tax bite if you choose to follow this strategy.

Nonqualified deferred-compensation plans. Deferred compensation is a fourth source of retirement income, but is not an option that is available to everyone. The decision to defer, while generally still a good one, has become a little more complicated. If deferred compensation is an option for you, you will need to consider the outside rate of return you can earn, the number of years you have until retirement, and your view on future tax rates. The increased spread between ordinary income tax rates and capital gains rates makes it particularly important to analyze various scenarios before settling on a deferral strategy.

All these factors differ from person to person, as do the risks. The wisest course of action is to consult your personal financial adviser on the strategy that's best for you, based on your personal situation, projected liquidity, and current income requirements, and your long-term tax position.

Planning Reminder

Growing Importance of 401(k) Plans

Many factors have contributed to the significant growth in 401(k) plans, but two are most notable: Many employers have reduced their defined-benefit programs in favor of defined-contribution programs such as 401(k)s; and today's employees are more likely to change employers during their careers, thus not accruing the pension benefits of someone who has spent an entire career with one employer.

Qualified retirement plans. The fifth and final source of retirement income, and the foundation of many retirement nest eggs, involves employer-sponsored "qualified" retirement plans such as pension, profit-sharing and/or 401(k) plans. These plans allow the employer to receive a tax deduction for current funding without requiring the employee to report taxable income until funds are received from the plan. Some of these plans permit employees to make limited tax-deductible contributions. The earnings on balances in these plans are not taxed until they are withdrawn.

401(k) plans. Over the last decade, increased attention has been focused on the importance of the 401(k) retirement savings plan, named after the section of the tax code that permits the arrangement. Access Research Inc. of Windsor, Connecticut, projects that by the turn of the century, assets in defined-contribution plans — including 401(k)s — will make up nearly half of all retirement-plan assets, compared to just 27% in 1984.

Under current tax laws, you can ask your employer to place a percentage of your income in a 401(k) plan each year up to a dollar limit adjusted annually for inflation (up to $10,000 in 1999, depending on the plan and the employee), and deduct it from your gross income before taxes are calculated. Neither your contributions nor your investment earnings are taxed until you retire and start to withdraw them. In many cases, employers match participants' contributions with additional contributions of between 25% and 100% of the amount contributed, up to a specified percentage of income. The benefits of a matching contribution are significant. Your investment grows by the amount of the match the moment you make it.

Recent trends in 401(k) plan design have made these plans more attractive to participants. To ensure your plan investments remain aligned with your retirement goals, you need to be aware of these developments.

- **Investment selection.** Most plans today offer increased choice in investments, partially in response to Labor Department regulations specifying that, to be protected from certain fiduciary liabilities, employers must provide participants with the opportunity to control the potential risk and return assumed within their 401(k) accounts. Many plans now offer five or more choices from which participants may construct a portfolio. Other plans are offering "lifestyle" funds consisting of pre-mixed portfolios, and a small but growing number offer self-directed brokerage accounts that enable participants to select from hundreds of mutual funds and even individual stocks and bonds. Along with this increased choice comes a need for careful analysis of retirement goals and risk tolerance, as well as careful determination of your optimal asset allocation.
- **Loans from plans.** Similarly, many plans offer loan features, some of which can be activated automatically through telephonic voice-response systems. 401(k) loans can be a cost-effective means of borrowing for certain needs, and the interest you pay goes directly into your own account. While studies suggest that this feature may lead to greater 401(k) plan participation, you should take time to understand the implications of and rules for taking a loan on your 401(k) account before doing so. For example, if you leave your job with a 401(k) loan outstanding, the entire principal may be due immediately, or you will be subject to the 10% early distribution penalty as well as income taxes on the outstanding balance. Also, while you are paying yourself interest on the borrowed amounts, these amounts will not have the opportunity to earn market returns.
- **Daily valuation and switching.** The automated voice-response systems available in many plans today encourage more active management and the opportunity to change investment allocations or switch assets among funds. Again, be sure to talk with your investment adviser about these decisions to make sure any moves are strategic, rather than merely reactions to market occurrences.

Retirement plans for self-employed or small-business owners

Keogh plans. Keogh plans are retirement plans established by self-employed individuals (or their firms in the case of partnerships) for themselves and their employees. They operate just like employer-sponsored qualified plans and offer the same advantages. Consequently, they play a key role in the development of resources used to fund retirement for most self-employed individuals.

Simplified employee pensions (SEPs). A SEP is an arrangement under which employer contributions are made to IRAs established for individual employees. A SEP established before 1997 also may allow employees of companies with 25 or fewer employees to make limited tax-deductible contributions.

The employer (who may be self-employed) may take a deduction for contributions to the SEP as long as certain qualifications are met. The SEP can be established and funded up until the due date, plus extensions, of the employer's tax return. This means that for a self-employed sole proprietor, a SEP deduction can be available for plans established as late as October 15 of the year following the year for which the deduction is claimed.

SIMPLE retirement plans. Small businesses with 100 or fewer employees can establish a new type of simplified retirement plan called a Savings Incentive Match Plan for Employees, or SIMPLE plan. Under the new rules, a SIMPLE plan covers each employee who received at least $5,000 in compensation during the previous two years and is expected to earn at least the same amount during the plan year.

Employers can choose between a SIMPLE IRA plan for each employee, or a SIMPLE plan as part of a 401(k) plan. A SIMPLE IRA allows eligible employees to make elective, pretax contributions of up to $6,000. Employers are required to either match employee elective contributions, on a dollar-for-dollar basis, up to 3% of the employee's compensation or make a 2%-of-compensation nonelective contribution on behalf of each eligible employee. SIMPLE 401(k) plans are subject to all qualified-plan rules, with safe-harbor provisions that enable them to avoid annual nondiscrimination testing and the top-heavy rules.

Tapping your retirement plans early. Some retirement plans (but not IRAs) allow participants to borrow money from the plan and repay it with interest. Also, some retirement plans (but not IRAs) permit withdrawals in certain hardship circumstances (for example, payments for large, unanticipated medical expenses and long-term or indefinite disabilities). You can contact your plan administrator to determine whether you are eligible for hardship withdrawals. Hardship withdrawals are subject to the regular income tax and, if you are under age $59^1/_2$, the 10% early withdrawal penalty. If you have an IRA, you can ask your IRA custodian to distribute funds to you, and you can use those funds for 60 days without penalty. The funds must be placed back in an IRA within the 60 days or they will be taxed as of the date of distribution. This technique can be used only once during a one-year period ending on the date the funds were paid out of the IRA. Penalty-free withdrawals are allowed for qualifying education expenses and costs associated with the purchase of a first home.

Distributions from retirement plans

Developing a strategy to distribute funds from your retirement plans requires every bit of the careful planning that went into accumulating those funds in the first place, particularly if balances in qualified plans are intended to provide a substantial part of your retirement income. Unfortunately, many people make quick decisions without carefully modeling income under the various available scenarios. One wrong decision can make the difference between meeting your retirement and other goals, or not. It is important to be aware of the rules on distributions from IRAs and employer-sponsored plans and to work with your adviser to determine the strategy that is best for you.

Early withdrawal penalties. Most distributions from a qualified plan, Keogh plan, or IRA prior to age $59^1/_2$ are subject to a 10% penalty tax in addition to regular income tax. There are exceptions for distributions resulting from death, disability, and certain other circumstances.

Minimum-distribution rules. Qualified plans and IRAs carry a required date by which you must begin taking distributions. This generally is April 1 of the calendar year following the year in which you attain the age of $70^1/_2$. There are some limited exceptions, one being distributions from the new Roth IRAs and another being a provision that enables persons still working at age $70^1/_2$ to continue deferring distributions from employer-sponsored plans (but not IRAs). Although the first distribution may be deferred until April 1 of the year following attainment of age $70^1/_2$, all subsequent distributions must be made by December 31 of each year.

In addition, the distribution must be equal to or in excess of the required minimum distribution, an amount determined under complex rules, but generally obtained by dividing the balance of the qualified plan at the beginning of each year by a life expectancy factor. If the minimum amount is not distributed in a timely manner, you will be subject to a penalty equal to 50% of the difference between the amount actually distributed and the required minimum distribution. This is on top of the ordinary income tax due on the distribution. The required minimum distribution is computed separately for each qualified plan of the participant.

Decisions concerning how to calculate the minimum distribution should be made with care, as these decisions are irrevocable. Your adviser can help you analyze the alternatives and develop the most effective strategy for your needs.

Distributions from employer-sponsored plans. Retirement plans typically allow you to choose from a variety of payment options, including:

o A lump-sum payout at or after your retirement or other termination of employment, equal to your entire account balance. If the retirement benefit is computed as an annuity, the lump sum is the present value of that annuity.

Planning Reminder

Periodic Payments From IRA

You also may withdraw money from your retirement plan or IRA in the form of periodic payments without being subject to the early withdrawal penalty tax. The payments must be in substantially equal amounts, not less frequently than annually, over your life expectancy (or the joint expectancies of you and your co-beneficiary, if any). If payments are made from a plan other than an IRA, they must begin following a separation from service. Distributions made to a beneficiary or estate following an individual's death also are not subject to the penalty tax.

Caution

Risks of Taking Lump-sum Distribution

Although lump-sum distributions allow favorable tax treatment, they also involve risk. When you accept a lump sum, you become responsible for managing the money, and you can be left in serious financial straits if your investments perform poorly. There is also the possibility you will exhaust your retirement funds before your death. An annuity can extend for your lifetime (and perhaps that of a spouse or other co-beneficiary) and helps insulate you from investment risks and responsibilities. Thus, a decision between taking a lump sum or an annuity should be based on more than just tax considerations.

o An annuity for the rest of your life.

o An annuity for the joint lives of you and a surviving co-beneficiary. You may have an option to select whether the co-beneficiary receives 50%, 75%, or 100% of your annuity after your death. The higher this percentage, the lower the annuity payments are during your lifetime.

o An annuity that provides a guaranteed minimum payout term (typically 10 years) in the event of your premature death.

o Installment payments over a fixed number of years.

To the extent you have made nondeductible contributions to a retirement plan, you can recover them tax free. They are recovered immediately if you receive a lump-sum distribution or pro rata over your life expectancy if you receive an annuity.

The taxable portion of a lump-sum payout can be subject to tax at regular rates or, in some situations, it can be taxed under special five- or 10-year averaging approaches. Alternatively, it can be rolled over or transferred directly tax free to another qualified plan, a Keogh plan that has been established on the basis of net self-employment income or an IRA. (*See* pages 138 and 139 for more details.)

Some tax strategies to maximize your retirement nest egg

Accelerate contributions to IRAs and Keoghs. To increase the benefits of deferral, it's generally wise to accelerate contributions to IRAs and Keoghs. For example, you can reap nearly $43,000 more over 30 years in a plan returning 10% a year by making a $2,000 contribution on January 1 instead of waiting until April 15 of the following year.

Consider nondeductible IRAs and other tax-deferred investments. For long-term savings, it still makes sense to contribute to nondeductible IRAs, which provide the advantage of tax deferral (not a current tax deduction). Also consider other tax-deferred investments such as Series EE savings bonds, annuities, and securities you can hold for the long-term, recognizing appreciation only at sale. Your adviser can help you determine the best way to take advantage of the greater spread between ordinary income tax rates and the lower capital gains tax rates.

Look into early withdrawals. While the rule of thumb generally is to delay distributions from qualified retirement plans as long as possible to maximize the advantages of deferral, in some cases it makes sense to begin withdrawals earlier than the mandatory date for minimum distributions. If you anticipate being in a high tax bracket for the rest of your life, this strategy might make sense.

Consider reducing holdings of income-producing investments. If you believe you might exceed the threshold for taxable Social Security benefits, you could avoid or reduce the tax in some years by using strategies such as investing in Series EE savings bonds (where recognition of income is deferred), scheduling the maturity of Treasury bills in alternate years, or switching some investments to low-dividend, high-growth stocks that are subject to much lower capital gains taxes. Also, if you are eligible, you could make deductible contributions to an IRA. Each $1,000 you contribute could reduce taxable income by $1,850 (the $1,000 IRA deduction plus a $850 reduction in Social Security benefits that are subject to taxation).

Consider charitable bequests. If you plan to make charitable bequests, it may make sense to name the charity as beneficiary of your IRA or Keogh. That way, the funds avoid income tax, giving the charity up to 16% more in after-tax proceeds than would a cash bequest, while qualifying as a charitable deduction for estate tax purposes.

Maximizing the Value of Charitable Contributions

Obtaining maximum tax benefits from charitable giving is not always easy to achieve. The complex rules determining the tax results of some forms of giving can make the task a difficult one, and because of this complexity some donors tend to make gifts that are more costly than necessary. There are right and wrong ways to give. Doing it right is important, because the spirit of giving should never be diminished by unexpected or adverse tax results.

The basics

Charitable gifts are classified into two broad categories: *present* gifts and *deferred* gifts. In present giving, the donor makes an outright gift. This type of gift requires that the donor immediately transfer possession and use of the gift property to the donee. In deferred giving, the donor also makes a current gift. However, the gift is of the *future* interest, that is, actual possession and use of the gift property by the donee is deferred to some time in the future. The donee's accession to full rights in the gift property occurs upon the expiration of a time period prescribed by the donor. That period is sometimes certain, as when the donor limits it to a term of years, and sometimes uncertain, as when its termination depends on the death of the donor or another person.

Both forms of charitable giving normally yield current tax deductions (income and gift tax or estate tax) to the donor. However, a gift of a present interest yields a relatively greater deduction than a gift of a future interest in the same property because the deductible value of a gift of a future interest is the property's *discounted* present value.

A charitable gift also is distinguished by whether the donor makes the gift during his or her lifetime or delays it until death. The choice between lifetime giving and testamentary giving depends on the personal objectives of the donor. However, a donor should recognize that a lifetime gift may be the most tax-effective form of giving because it provides both an income tax deduction during life and an estate tax deduction at death (through exclusion of the gift property from the estate). Regardless of timing, however, charitable gifts still are classified as either a present gift or a deferred (future interest) gift.

A gift, but no deduction

Almost anything of value — cash, securities, real estate, jewelry, works of art, etc. — can be donated outright to a charitable organization. In more complex transactions, income or remainder (future) interests in property also can be contributed. These gifts usually result in a charitable deduction for tax purposes. That deduction reduces tax otherwise due on an income, gift, or estate tax return.

Some types of gifts, however, do not yield tax deductions at the time of the gift — or sometimes ever. These gifts include:

o *Quid pro quo* gifts (a donor cannot receive full economic benefit in return for a gift).

o Gifts with "strings attached" (a gift must be complete and irrevocable and subsequently beyond the donor's reach).

o Gifts conditioned on the happening or nonhappening of some future event (allowance or disallowance of the deduction turns on whether the happening or nonhappening of the event is "so remote as to be negligible").

o Gifts of personal services (no question about their value; under the law they simply are not deductible).

o Gifts not properly substantiated (some property gifts require appraisals and there are mandatory receipting rules).

o Gifts of future interests in tangible personal property (the gift must be a present interest, or the deduction is deferred).

o Gifts of partial interests not in trust (with a few important exceptions, it must be all or nothing).

o Gifts of the right to use property (under the law, these are partial interests).

o Gifts to individuals (a gift must be made to a qualified charitable organization).

o Involuntary "gifts": (if a "gift" is ordered by a court or government agency, it is not a gift).

o Most gifts to foreign organizations (the donee must be a qualified domestic organization unless a tax treaty provides otherwise).

(These rules apply to the *income tax* charitable deduction; the rules for the gift and estate tax charitable deductions may differ somewhat, depending on the facts.)

A proposed gift sometimes may fit one of the above descriptions. When that happens, the donor should consult a tax adviser before the contribution is consummated (gifts of personal services excepted).

Deduction limits

Contributions to public charities generally are deductible up to 50% of AGI; however, gifts to nonpublic charities (such as private foundations) generally are limited to 30% of AGI. Gifts of property for the use of, but not to, public charities are also limited to 30% of AGI (e.g., a donation of an income interest in property to a public charity through a charitable lead trust, discussed on page 700).

Gifts of qualified long-term capital gain property are limited to 30% of AGI for gifts to public charities and 20% of AGI for gifts to nonpublic charities. Rules governing the interaction of these percentage limitations may further reduce your current-year charitable deduction.

Planning Reminder

Carryover of Contributions Exceeding Deductible Limit

If you itemize, you can carry forward charitable contributions exceeding the percentage limitations for five years. However, current contributions must be considered before carryover contributions, and the carryovers remain subject to their original percentage limitations.

Planning Reminder

Charitable Gifts Reduce Estate Tax

Lifetime charitable gifts are an effective strategy to reduce estate tax. Charitable transfers are exempt from transfer tax regardless of whether they are made during life or after death. Charitable trusts can be structured to achieve more than just charitable benefits. For example, these trusts can be designed to increase cash flow or transfer property to family members at reduced cost. Lifetime charitable gifts are more effective than transfers made after death because they provide the additional benefit of current income tax savings.

Deduction values

The amount of your deduction depends on the nature and circumstances of your gift. Your deduction equals the property's fair market value, rather than your tax basis (usually your cost), if all three of the following conditions are satisfied:

o The property would produce a long-term capital gain if you were to sell it.
o If the gift is of tangible personal property, its use by the charity is related to the charity's exempt purpose.
o The gift is to a public charity.

You generally may deduct your tax basis in other types of gifts. Under limited circumstances, however, a gift of inventory can be deducted at up to twice its cost or its fair market value, whichever is less.

Appreciated property. Many taxpayers who make substantial, continuing gifts to charitable organizations do so with cash and overlook the significant benefits that gifts of appreciated property can bring. As the following example shows, when the fair market value of such property can be deducted — as it now can — for both regular-tax and AMT purposes, it may be poor tax and financial planning to give cash instead of appreciated property, provided the property can be used by the charity in pursuing its tax-exempt purpose.

For example, assume John Smith contributes $5,000 a year to his favorite qualified charity. In the past, he always gave cash. This year, he decides to give $5,000 worth of stock he bought three years ago for $2,000. The result: He still gets a deduction for his charitable contribution of $5,000 but avoids recognizing the $3,000 gain he would have realized had he sold the stock.

If he believes the stock's price will rise further, he can buy back in with the $5,000 in cash he saved this year by making the property contribution, both stepping up his basis in the stock and reducing the gain he must recognize if and when he sells the shares.

Depreciated property. If you own property that has depreciated in value, you should not use it to make a charitable gift. The reason: Your charitable deduction is limited to the fair market value of the property. Accordingly, it generally makes sense to sell the property first, realize the loss and contribute the proceeds to the charity. That way, you realize full tax benefits for the entire amount of your original cost.

When is a contribution deductible?

A charitable contribution is deductible when it is actually paid, and payment generally occurs when the gift property is delivered to the donee. But certain types of gifts have specific rules concerning the timing of their deduction.

Check. A contribution made by check is deductible when the check is unconditionally delivered or mailed, as long as it clears the donor's bank in due course.

Credit card. A contribution charged to a bank credit card is deductible in the year the charge is made, even if payment of the charge is made in a later year.

Stock. A contribution of stock is completed upon the unconditional delivery of a properly endorsed stock certificate to the donee or the donee's agent. If a properly endorsed stock certificate is mailed and is received by the donee or its agent in the ordinary course of the mail, the gift is effective on the date of mailing. If a donor delivers a stock certificate to the issuing corporation or to the donor's broker (who acts as the donor's agent) for transfer to the name of the donee, the contribution is not effective until the stock is actually transferred on the corporation's books.

Real estate. A charitable gift of real estate is generally effective for tax purposes at the time a properly executed deed to the property is delivered by the donor to the donee.

Promissory note. A donor may make a charitable contribution by issuing his or her own note to the donee. In that case, a charitable deduction is not allowed until the donor satisfies the note by payment of cash or other property.

Pledge. A pledge of a gift to a charitable organization, even if legally enforceable, is not deductible by the donor until he or she satisfies the pledge through payment of cash or other property.

Deferred giving

In deferred giving, the donor makes an irrevocable gift of a future interest in property. A future interest occurs where the donee's possession and enjoyment of the property are temporarily deferred. The period of deferment may be definite or indefinite. The donee's interest may mature into full property rights after a specified time period expires. Alternatively, the donee's rights may mature when the donor, or someone named by the donor, dies.

Planning Reminder

Deducting Volunteer Expenses

You can deduct unreimbursed out-of-pocket automobile expenses, such as the cost of gas and oil that are directly related to the use of your car in giving services to a charitable organization. You cannot deduct any part of general repair and maintenance expenses, depreciation, registration fees, or the costs of tires or insurance. If you do not want to deduct your actual expenses, you can use a standard mileage rate of 14 cents a mile to figure your contribution.

The following oversimplified example describes the concept of deferred giving and shows how it differs from the outright-giving transactions previously discussed.

A taxpayer owns valuable income-producing securities and wants to contribute them to a favorite charity. The taxpayer, however, cannot spare the income from the securities during lifetime. This precludes an outright gift. Must the gift be deferred until the taxpayer's death?

The answer, of course, is no. This potential donor need not wait at all to make a gift. The deferred-giving technique allows the donor to make a significant lifetime gift without sacrificing income.

The donor does this by dividing the gift property into two parts. The donor retains the first part — the life income interest. The donor gives the second part — the remainder interest — to the charitable organization. The two parts reunite upon the donor's death. At that time, the donee gains full possession and use of the total property.

From a cash-flow standpoint, such a deferred gift leaves the donor no worse off than before. Indeed, the transaction enhances the donor's immediate cash-flow position because the allowable charitable deduction reduces the income taxes the donor otherwise would owe for the year of the gift.

How does it work?

Deferred giving is not as simple as the above discussion may indicate, however. These gifts require formal legal documents that must include a variety of prescribed provisions. The IRS, however, has provided sample documents that a donor's legal counsel may use to assure that the trust instruments are properly drafted. Thus, a donor can use these standard agreements to simplify deferred giving.

As previously noted, a charitable gift of a partial interest is ordinarily not deductible for income tax purposes. A remainder interest is a partial interest. The allowance of a deduction for such a gift in deferred giving is an exception to the rule.

It is, however, a rather narrow exception. Unless the remainder interest is in a personal residence or farm (discussed later), the donor must contribute the interest through a trust. Further, the trust must be one of the following types:

o Charitable remainder annuity trust.
o Charitable remainder unitrust.
o Pooled income fund.

The deferred giving trusts

Use of charitable remainder trusts (the annuity trust and the unitrust) requires compliance with precise criteria. In both cases, the donor must execute a trust document (governing instrument) containing provisions mandated by income tax law and regulations and provided by the IRS.

Charitable organizations can maintain pooled income funds to receive gifts, from multiple donors. Gifts to these funds also are subject to strict rules.

Failure to follow the technical requirements for charitable remainder trusts and pooled income funds causes disallowance of the charitable deduction for income tax, gift tax and estate tax purposes.

The following discussion highlights the principal characteristics of the three types of deferred-giving trusts.

The annuity trust. Under an annuity-trust arrangement, the donor retains a right to a specified annuity for a definite or indefinite time. If the right extends over a definite time, the term cannot exceed 20 years. If the right to the annuity is for an indefinite period, it must extend over a life expectancy. In both cases, the beneficiary of the annuity is either the donor or another named beneficiary (or beneficiaries). When the term of the annuity extends over a life expectancy, the measuring life must be that of the named beneficiary.

Because the annuity is a fixed amount, it is unaffected by the trust's income. Income in excess of the annuity amount accrues to the charitable beneficiary of the remainder interest. When income is less than the annuity amount, the trust must pay the shortfall from accumulated income or trust principal.

The annuity amount is also unaffected by changes in the fair market value of annuity trust assets.

The unitrust. The unitrust is much like the annuity trust. There is, however, a significant difference in the determination of the annuity amount. Like the annuity trust, the unitrust payout rate cannot be less than 5% or more than 50%. However, the payout rate is applied to the net fair market value of the trust assets, determined annually, to establish the annuity amount each year. This annual computation yields a variable annuity, which changes as the value of trust assets

 Planning Reminder

Fixing Annuity Trust Amount
The donor fixes the annuity payable by an annuity trust at the inception of the trust. The fixed amount cannot be less than 5% or more than 50% of the initial fair market value of the trust assets. The donor may choose the frequency of the annuity payment, but not a frequency less often than annually. Thus, payments may be made monthly, quarterly, semi-annually or annually. The estimated actuarial value of the remainder interest going to charity must be at least 10% of the initial fair market value of the trust's assets.

Planning Reminder

Pooled Income Features

The following features further distinguish a pooled income fund from an annuity trust or unitrust.

o The remainder beneficiaries must be organizations qualified to receive contributions subject to the 50% limitation (thus, public charities).

o A pooled income fund cannot invest in tax-exempt securities.

o The income interests must be payable for the lives of the income beneficiaries. A fund cannot pay an income interest for a term of years.

Planning Reminder

Remainder Interest in Home

The interest contributed need not be in your *principal* residence; it is necessary only that the interest be in one of your *personal* residences. Thus, you can contribute a remainder interest in a vacation home.

Caution

Disadvantage of Charitable Lead Trust

The requirement that the donor treat the trust income as his or her own is ordinarily too high a price to pay for the one-time tax deduction the donor gains in the year of the gift. Therefore, a donor should make such a gift only if unique circumstances warrant it.

A further potential disadvantage of an income gift through a charitable lead trust is the limitation on the charitable deduction. The deduction cannot exceed 30% of the donor's contribution base. This limit applies because the donor makes the gift "for the use of" the donee, rather than directly to it.

Because of the lead trust's basic deficiencies, a donor may tend to summarily reject it as a means of lifetime charitable giving. There are, however, situations in which a charitable lead trust can yield exceptionally good tax results under the right circumstances.

fluctuates from year to year. The donor may impose a ceiling on annual distributions to ensure that they do not exceed trust income in any year. Any shortfalls in required distributions can be recouped in a later year should trust income then exceed the current distribution requirement. In any case, the estimated actuarial value of the remainder interest going to charity must be at least 10% of the fair market value of each contribution to the trust's assets.

The pooled income fund. A pooled income fund is markedly different from both the annuity trust and the unitrust. It is a pooled or common fund made up of many separate contributions of property from numerous donors. These contributions are commingled to minimize investment risks and to maximize investment opportunities. The charitable organization named as the remainder beneficiary of the fund assets maintains the fund, although management of the fund's investments may be delegated to professional investment advisers. The various donors or their designees hold the income interests in the fund.

A pooled income fund's payout to its income beneficiaries is not a fixed percentage as is the payout from a charitable remainder trust. The rate of return that the fund actually earns each year determines the year's payout. Typically, smaller amounts can be transferred to pooled funds than to annuity trusts or unitrusts. Pooled income funds attract multiple donors. Annuity trusts and unitrusts must be "stand alone," so economics dictate larger transfers.

Tax benefits

Any of the deferred gifts discussed above yields a tax deduction (income and gift tax or estate tax) to the donor. The size of the tax benefit realized by the donor depends upon many factors. The most obvious factor is the donor's marginal tax bracket. Will the deduction offset income otherwise taxable at 39.6%, 36%, 31%, 28%, or 15%? Obviously, the higher the donor's marginal tax rate, the lower the real cost of the gift to the donor.

Time is another factor. How long will the charity's possession and use of the property be deferred from the date the donor transfers the property in trust? Is that interim period between transfer and possession measured by a fixed term of years? Or does it depend on the life expectancy of the donor or some other person? If measured by a life expectancy, at what age was the transfer made?

There are other considerations. What is the rate of payout to the income beneficiary? Is that rate applied to the initial value of trust assets (annuity trust)? Or is it applied to the value of trust assets determined annually (unitrust)? Is payout based on the trust's actual rate of return (pooled income fund)? How frequently (monthly, quarterly, semiannually or annually) will payments be made to beneficiaries?

Once the donor considers and resolves these questions, he or she can determine the amount of the charitable deduction. Doing so requires the use of certain tables prescribed by income, gift, and estate tax regulations.

Remainder interest in a personal residence

Many individuals occupy homes their heirs will dispose of outside the family. Some will make charitable bequests of other property. These two facts may suggest use of a form of lifetime charitable giving that produces excellent tax results — a gift of the remainder interest in the residence.

A charitable contribution of the remainder interest in a personal residence (or farm) yields an income-tax deduction equal to the present value of that interest. This type of lifetime deferred gift can provide superior after-tax results because the donor gains the income-tax deduction without an expenditure of cash or a reduction of income. The gift does not increase personal expenses or require a trust. Best of all, the donor continues to use the home as before.

Gifts of income

In deferred giving, a donor gives away "the tree" (the remainder interest) and retains "the fruit" (the income interest). A donor can also give away the fruit and retain the tree. In this form of giving, the donor makes a charitable gift of the income from property.

Charitable lead trust. A donor ordinarily gains less tax benefit from a lifetime charitable gift of an income interest than from a gift of a remainder interest. This is because a charitable gift of income provides no income tax deduction except under narrow conditions. To obtain an income tax deduction, the donor must make the gift to a trust, known as a charitable lead trust. Further, that trust must be one treated by tax law as owned by the donor (a "grantor trust"). Consequently, the donor must include the income received by the trust during its term in his or her own taxable income, even though the income is paid to the charitable donee.

Other gifts

It is impossible to discuss all the many different types of gifts that donors contribute to charitable organizations. Certain gifts, however, deserve specific mention, in addition to those already discussed.

Bargain sales. A bargain sale is a sale of property to a charitable organization for less than the property's fair value. In effect, the seller makes a charitable contribution equal to the difference between the property's fair value and its selling price. The following example illustrates that a bargain sale is part gift and part sale, and both parts must be accounted for separately to determine its tax results.

A taxpayer sells for $20,000 a property that is worth $25,000, thereby making a charitable contribution of $5,000. That contribution is deductible for tax purposes. Because the transaction is also partly a sale, however, the taxpayer must account for any gain realized. If the donor-seller's tax basis in the property is $20,000, the donor-seller must recognize a gain of $4,000 for tax purposes. This gain results because the taxpayer must assign a proportionate part of tax basis in the property to the gift portion of the transaction (in this case, one-fifth). Because the taxpayer cannot offset that part of the tax basis against the sales proceeds, no tax benefit is derived from it. Thus, the sales price ($20,000) less the usable tax basis ($16,000) yields a tax gain of $4,000.

Charitable gift annuities. A charitable gift annuity is a commonly used form of giving. In that transaction, the donor purchases an annuity contract from a charitable organization for more than its fair value. Stated another way, the present value of the future annuity payments is less than the value of the payments the donor could have secured from a commercial insurer for the same consideration.

The difference in values between what the donor could have obtained and what the donor actually obtained represents a charitable contribution that is deductible in the year the donor purchases the annuity. A donor need not pay cash for a charitable gift annuity; donors often make payment with appreciated property. When a donor uses appreciated property, however, the law treats the transaction as a bargain sale. As previously discussed, bargain-sale treatment requires that the donor allocate part of the tax basis to the contribution part of the transaction. Accordingly, the donor cannot use that part of tax basis to reduce the gain realized on the sale part of the transaction.

The contribution portion of a charitable gift annuity transaction is deductible in the year the donor purchases the annuity. The donor usually recognizes the gain element ratably over the term of the annuity.

Life insurance. Life insurance is another important subject of charitable giving. Owners of life insurance policies sometimes realize that a policy purchased years ago for security is no longer needed. Or perhaps a policy was acquired to satisfy estate tax obligations that have been largely mitigated by the present estate tax structure. In such cases, the policy owner may decide that the best use of the policy is to give it to a charitable organization.

Depending on the situation, the gift will provide a tax deduction equal to one of several amounts. The deduction may equal the cash surrender value of the policy, its replacement value, or its "interpolated terminal reserve" value (a value slightly in excess of cash surrender value). In some circumstances, where there has been an adverse change in the health of the insured since the issuance of the policy, it may also be possible to justify a higher fair market value than that determined in the preceding sentence. The deduction, however, cannot exceed the donor's tax basis in the policy.

The insurance laws of some states may prohibit anyone without an insurable interest from directly or indirectly obtaining an insurance policy on the life of another person unless the benefits are to be paid to someone with an insurable interest. A donor should determine the relevance of such statutes to his or her own situation before making a charitable gift of a life insurance policy. It is possible that the effect of such state laws could deny the donor a charitable deduction for such a gift for income, gift, and estate tax purposes.

Much attention has been focused on "wealth replacement trusts," a combination of a charitable remainder trust, the income flow from which is used to fund a companion insurance trust for the benefit of family members. This insurance replaces assets used by the donor to fund the charitable trust. Establishing this arrangement can be complex and requires expert advice on legal and tax technicalities as well as investment input.

Property encumbered by debt. A donor should be wary of making a charitable gift of property encumbered by debt. The reason this is so is that the debt is considered an amount realized by the donor; the result is a bargain sale and the recognition of taxable gain. Debt-encumbered property can also cause tax problems for the donee, for it can result in the realization of unrelated business income.

Planning Reminder

Conservation Gifts

Today, great value is placed on preserving things as they are — farmlands, coastlines, forests, historic structures, etc. A property owner who participates in that preservation effort can obtain a charitable contribution deduction for doing so. To gain the deduction, however, the property owner must forfeit something of value. Accordingly, the owner must place a restriction (granted in perpetuity) on the use that he or she and succeeding owners can make of the property.

Thus, the owner of farmland may restrict it to its present use forever and obtain a contribution deduction. The practical measure of the deduction (though not the technical one) is the decrease in the value of the land caused by the restriction.

Other such gifts may yield comparable tax benefits to the donor. A common one today is a grant of a perpetual easement that precludes alteration of the facade of a certified historic structure.

Caution

Penalties for Exaggerated Charitable Deductions

These penalties have been tightened significantly in recent years. A claimed deduction that exceeds 200% of the actual allowable deduction and that results in a tax underpayment of $5,000 or more can bring a 20% penalty; an overstatement of 400% or more of the correct value can trigger a 40% penalty.

Substantiation requirements and penalties

The IRS allows the charitable deductions you claim only if you are able to substantiate them. Cancelled checks or receipts from the donee charity are not sufficient to substantiate individual contributions of $250 or more. You will need a receipt or letter from the donee acknowledging the contribution and describing any noncash contribution. The receipt must also include a description and good-faith estimate of the value of any goods or services received for the contribution. Documentation also is required for any quid pro quo contribution over $75 — that is, a donation for which you receive a good or service in return. For example, if you pay $1,000 to attend a fundraising dinner and the value of the meal is $150, your receipt must acknowledge your contribution of $1,000 and the $150 value of the meal you received.

Records supporting your contributions should be retained for three years after you file the tax return claiming the deduction.

If you claim a deduction greater than $5,000 for a gift of property (except publicly traded securities), you must obtain an appraisal by a qualified independent appraiser and must attach a summary of the appraisal to your return. Appraisal fees may be claimed as a miscellaneous itemized deduction.

Estate and Gift Planning: Maximizing After-Tax Transfers

Planning Reminder

Estate Planning Is an Ongoing Process

Estate planning is an integral component of any effective financial plan. To meet the full range of personal, family, and financial goals, a regular examination of family objectives, financial status, and available planning options is essential. Individuals who view estate planning as an ongoing process, and not as a discrete event, are generally more successful in meeting their economic and family goals while minimizing transfer tax liabilities.

People who work for a lifetime to build a business or accumulate wealth want their assets to pass intact to their designated heirs. In today's tax environment, that takes careful planning. Federal estate and gift tax rates are currently 53% on transfers between $2.5 million and $3 million and 55% on transfers of $3 million or more, and there is a 5% surtax on transfers between $10 million and $17,184,000. State inheritance taxes can further increase the cost of passing assets on to others. Moreover, "generation-skipping" transfers, such as large gifts to grandchildren, can be subject to an additional 55% tax.

The essentials of estate planning

After determining one's personal, family, and financial goals, the first step in estate planning is to make sure all property is correctly titled, beneficiaries are properly designated, and estate documents are current. In many situations, improper ownership of property will render the will or trust documents ineffective. For most of us, this means getting advice regarding how a new residence, investments, or other major assets should be owned and how to complete beneficiary designation forms for insurance policies and benefit plans. It also means that every three years or so an individual should review and, if necessary, revise a will, a power of attorney for property, a power of attorney for health-care, and possibly a "living will" and one or more trust agreements. Due to the nature of our constantly changing tax law, new legislation can render even the best estate plan obsolete.

A review of existing documents is particularly important given the phased-in annual increase in the unified credit and other 1997 Act changes. Wills or trust documents that refer to specific numbers — such as the $600,000 transfer-tax exemption under prior law — or percentages tied to the prior law may prevent an individual or estate from taking maximum advantage of available opportunities.

Step two is to consider and, if appropriate, implement strategies to reduce transfer (estate and gift) taxes. Most estate-planning techniques seek to move the growth of your wealth out of your estate and into the hands of younger family members or other heirs. If you begin early enough in life, this type of wealth shifting can substantially reduce the transfer-tax burden on your wealth. Of course, you will want to plan carefully to ensure you do not later need the income streams you have transferred to others.

Basic estate planning strategies

The annual exclusion. One of the most powerful estate-planning techniques is also one of the simplest. Every individual is allowed to give away, tax free, each year, $10,000 (indexed) to each donee (recipient). A married couple with three children, therefore, can transfer $60,000 per year to the children free of gift tax. If each child gets married, the potential amount of tax-free gifts from the couple to the children and their spouses rises to $120,000 per year. The amount increases further as grandchildren are born. The $10,000 annual-exclusion amount will be indexed for inflation each year.

A program of annual gifts over many years can shift significant wealth between generations. This is especially true considering that the assets given to children or grandchildren will be reinvested, generating future income that automatically stays out of the parents' estates. Moreover, any appreciation in the assets' values occurring after the date of gift is also excluded from the parents' estates.

If parents do not believe their minor children or grandchildren are ready to manage investments, gifts can be made to a Uniform Gifts (or Transfers) to Minors Act custodian. (*See* the discussion above at page 689.) Transfers can also be made to a trust. Although trusts can be quite flexible, they must be carefully drafted and managed so that gifts to them qualify for the annual exclusion.

Medical and educational gifts. Certain payments made directly to providers of medical and educational services are not treated as taxable gifts to the recipient of these services. For example, a grandmother who wishes to help pay for a granddaughter's education can write tuition checks directly to the school without making a taxable gift. If she writes the check to the granddaughter, however, she will have made a taxable gift of the amount exceeding the $10,000 annual exclusion.

The unified credit. Since 1986, the estate and gift tax laws have provided each U.S. citizen with an automatic credit for the first $192,800 of transfer tax. Because it takes $600,000 of taxable gifts or bequests to generate a tax of $192,800, each U.S. citizen has been able to transfer, tax free, $600,000 in addition to the medical and educational gifts described earlier and gifts protected by the $10,000-per-donee annual exclusion.

Transfers to spouses. Thanks to the marital deduction, gifts or bequests to your spouse are not subject to transfer tax if your spouse is a U.S. citizen. If your spouse is not a U.S. citizen, there are important restrictions on the amount of property that can be transferred and the manner in which you can transfer it without triggering a transfer tax.

Most transfers to spouses only delay rather than avoid transfer tax. In fact, leaving everything to a spouse can actually increase total transfer taxes on the couple's estate. For example, an individual who dies during 1999 with the unified credit available but who leaves everything to his or her spouse wastes an opportunity to transfer $650,000 tax-free to a younger generation. At the spouse's later death (assume it is in 1999), only $650,000 — not the combined $1.3 million — is sheltered from transfer taxes by the unified credit. As the unified credit increases to $1 million by 2006, the detriment after 1999 of leaving everything to the surviving spouse upon the first death also increases.

A basic estate plan often creates two pools of assets. One pool containing assets valued at $650,000 — or an amount equal to the effective transfer-tax exemption as it increases between 2000 and 2006 — passes to children or others, either outright or in a *credit-shelter,* or *bypass, trust.* This type of trust arrangement allows parents to pass assets to their children to reduce estate taxes while giving the surviving spouse access to distributions of income and possibly some principal — with limitations to keep the trust remainder out of the survivor's estate — during his or her lifetime. The credit-shelter, or bypass, trust is so named because it shelters a decedent's property from federal estate tax through the unified credit, and it bypasses the surviving spouse's taxable estate. This type of trust does not qualify for the marital deduction.

The other pool, containing the balance of the assets, passes to the surviving spouse (outright or in trust) and is not immediately taxed due to the marital deduction. Thus, no transfer taxes are created at the first death, and assets that today are worth $650,000 are protected from tax upon the spouse's death.

More-advanced estate planning strategies

A common, but rather advanced transfer strategy is the use of simple taxable gifts during your lifetime. The gift tax is effectively less than the estate tax. Following is a simplified example using a $3 million asset base and a 50% tax rate. During life, the donor could make a $2 million gift and pay $1 million of gift tax (50% × $2 million) with the $3 million asset. However, with a bequest at death, the donor's estate would have to pay a tax of $1.5 million (50% × $3 million) as the entire $3 million is subject to estate tax. This leaves only $1.5 million ($3 million less $1.5 million) to transfer.

Another more-advanced transfer strategy is the use of a trust. Trusts are vehicles for shifting wealth among family members. They used to be for the very rich, but today they are a mainstream financial planning tool for middle-class Americans who want to minimize taxes, avoid costly probate procedures, increase their privacy, and ensure that assets are distributed as intended.

A trust is a legal arrangement in which the grantor transfers legal title of property to a person (the trustee) to hold for the benefit of another person (the beneficiary). A trust agreement tells the trustee how and when to distribute assets.

 Planning Reminder

Taking Advantage of Transfer Tax Exemption

By taking advantage of the exemption through gifts, either outright or in trust, to children, grandchildren or other ultimate beneficiaries, significant transfer taxes can be saved. For many people, it makes sense to use the entire exemption as early in life as possible. The more the gifted property appreciates, the larger the savings. As a result, assets that should grow substantially in value are usually used for this strategy. Generally, the beneficiaries will owe taxes when they sell the appreciated assets, as their tax basis is the cost that the parent or donor paid for the assets. Nevertheless, in many circumstances this tax can be substantially less than the estate taxes that would be due on the same assets had they been left to appreciate within the estate.

 Planning Reminder

Increases in Exemption

For gifts made or individuals dying after 1997, the 1997 Act gradually increases the effective exemption from $600,000 to $1 million in 2006. Therefore, when the increase is fully phased in, a husband and wife will be able to transfer up to $2 million of assets free of estate and gift tax. The effective exemption is $650,000 in 1999 and $675,000 in 2000.

Tax Consequenses of Revocable Living Trust

A revocable living trust, in itself, is not a tax-saving tool. Trust income is taxed to you during your life, and assets owned by the trust at your death are included in your estate. Instead, the primary benefit of a revocable living trust is that it shelters assets passing through the trust from probate proceedings. Thus, use of a revocable trust avoids unnecessary court costs, delay and publicity. Another important benefit of a revocable living trust is that it facilitates administration of assets in the event you become incapacitated. The living trust also lets you escape statutory executors' fees in some states because the assets are not considered probate assets. In addition, it is an ideal vehicle for holding title to real estate outside your home state.

Ensure the Trustee's Accountability

Trustees are usually appointed for life. The best way to ensure that your trustee and any successor trustees continue to act responsibly over the many lifetimes the trust may span is to make your trustee accountable to another authority. You could retain the power to replace the trustee, or you could give your beneficiaries that right. You could empower a third party (a "trust protector") to replace the trustee, or you could name co-trustees or even a board of trustees.

A trust may be created during the grantor's lifetime (living or *inter vivos* trust) or at death by will (testamentary trust). A revocable trust can be cancelled or amended any time during the trust's existence, but an irrevocable trust may not. All revocable trusts become irrevocable upon the death of the grantor. Living trusts may be either revocable or irrevocable, but testamentary trusts are always irrevocable and subject to probate. Revocable trusts typically are created for nontax reasons, such as avoiding probate or controlling the disposition of assets, as the trust's assets usually are treated as the grantor's assets for income tax and estate tax purposes.

Irrevocable trusts frequently are created for tax reasons because they usually are taxed as separate legal entities for income tax purposes and they usually are excluded from the grantor's gross estate for estate tax purposes.

Following are three commonly used trust arrangements.

QTIP trust. One variation of the bypass trust is the qualified terminable interest property trust, or QTIP, which does qualify for the marital deduction. This type of trust can be used when you wish to transfer assets to your spouse but also control who receives them (or their value) after your spouse's death. Under this arrangement, your spouse will have exclusive rights to the trust's income and may also receive trust principal during his or her lifetime. However, the provisions you establish will control who receives the assets remaining in the trust at your spouse's death.

Revocable living trust. This is a trust created by a living person to hold title to his or her assets. In most states, you can serve as both trustee and beneficiary of a living trust, which means that you retain control over your trust assets while you are alive and may dispose of them at any time. When you create the trust, you name a successor trustee who can manage your financial affairs after your death or if you become incapacitated.

Life insurance trust. If you die while you own (or are deemed to own) a life insurance policy on your own life, the proceeds (net of any policy loans) are taxable in your estate unless the beneficiary is your U.S.-citizen spouse or a charity. If you assign all ownership of the policy to an individual or an irrevocable trust at least three years before your death, the death benefit is not included in your estate. Typically, your spouse will receive income (and sometimes distributions of principal) from the irrevocable trust for the rest of his or her life. At your spouse's death, the assets in the trust pass to the next generation tax free.

Many people establish irrevocable life insurance trusts to provide a pool of funds for paying estate taxes, so that existing assets, and particularly business assets, do not have to be liquidated. In deciding whether to set up an irrevocable life insurance trust, it is important to consider these three disadvantages:

o Your spouse can't have direct access to more than a small portion of the funds held in the trust.

o The trust's terms and beneficiaries cannot be changed once they are named.

o The policy proceeds will be taxed in the trust grantor's estate if he or she dies within three years following the date on which an existing policy is transferred to the trust.

Selecting a trustee

Trust documents are only as good as the trustees who carry out their terms. The right trustee can further your hopes for your family's future. The wrong one can undo your tax planning, squander your assets, and alienate your family. Like a good business successor, your trustee should be carefully selected, well trained, and accepted by family members before your death.

The first choice is between an individual and an institution. Many people make this choice based on cost alone. As a result, the "honor" of being trustee is often bestowed on an unsuspecting — and sometimes unqualified — friend or family member. Individuals and institutions have differing capabilities, experience, and personalities. Although a bank trust officer may not be inherently more qualified than a family member when it comes to distribution decisions, he or she may have the advantage of objectivity.

If you want your trust to accomplish your objectives over the long term, consider these suggestions for selecting a trustee:

o **Match the trustee's abilities with responsibilities.** Your trustee need not be a financial wizard, but should be someone who can execute your wishes responsibly. A trustee should possess enough financial acumen to know when professional assistance is needed and to hire competent advisers.

o **Distinguish the trustee's role.** It is not advisable to give family members multiple hats to wear. The best way to avoid confusion and conflicts of interest is to assign different roles to different people and to make sure everyone concerned understands and accepts those roles. You will not need to find a super-human to fill your shoes if you divide these responsibilities among the people and institutions qualified to fill the different roles.

1999 Tax Forms, Tax Tables, and Tax Rate Schedules

In the following pages, you will find IRS tax forms that you can use to file your 1999 tax return. For additional forms, call the IRS at (800) 829-3676. If you have access to the Internet, you can download forms and instructions from the IRS Web Site at **http://www.irs.gov/**. You can use the IRS fax service to obtain forms and instructions by calling (703) 368-9694 from a fax-connected telephone.

Use the tax tables starting on page 781 to look up your tax liability if your taxable income is less than $100,000. If your taxable income is $100,000 or more, use the tax rate schedules on page 793.

If you have long-term capital gains in excess of short-term capital losses, compute your 1999 tax liability on your taxable income, including the capital gains, on Part IV, page 2 of Schedule D. However, if your only long-term capital gains for 1999 are mutual-fund capital gain distributions, you may be able to compute your tax using a worksheet in the instructions to Form 1040 instead of having to make the Schedule D computation; *see* page 516.

Department of the Treasury—Internal Revenue Service

Income Tax Return for Single and
Joint Filers With No Dependents (99) **1999**

OMB No. 1545-0675

Use the IRS label here	Your first name and initial	Last name
	If a joint return, spouse's first name and initial	Last name
	Home address (number and street). If you have a P.O. box, see page 12.	Apt. no.
	City, town or post office, state, and ZIP code. If you have a foreign address, see page 12.	

Your social security number

Spouse's social security number

▲ **IMPORTANT!** ▲
You **must** enter your SSN(s) above.

Presidential Election Campaign
(See page 12.)

Note. *Checking "Yes" will not change your tax or reduce your refund.*

Do you want $3 to go to this fund? ▶ Yes ☐ No ☐

If a joint return, does your spouse want $3 to go to this fund? ▶ Yes ☐ No ☐

Dollars **Cents**

Income

Attach Copy B of Form(s) W-2 here.
Enclose, but do not staple, any payment.

1 Total wages, salaries, and tips. This should be shown in box 1 of your W-2 form(s). Attach your W-2 form(s). **1**

2 Taxable interest. If the total is over $400, you cannot use Form 1040EZ. **2**

3 Unemployment compensation, qualified state tuition program earnings, and Alaska Permanent Fund dividends (see page 14). **3**

4 Add lines 1, 2, and 3. This is your **adjusted gross income.** **4**

Note. You must check Yes or No.

5 Can your parents (or someone else) claim you on their return?

Yes. Enter amount from worksheet on back. ☐

No. If **single,** enter 7,050.00. If **married,** enter 12,700.00. See back for explanation. ☐ **5**

6 Subtract line 5 from line 4. If line 5 is larger than line 4, enter 0. This is your **taxable income.** ▶ **6**

Payments and tax

7 Enter your Federal income tax withheld from box 2 of your W-2 form(s). **7**

8a Earned income credit (see page 15).

b Nontaxable earned income: enter type and amount below.

Type	$	**8a**

9 Add lines 7 and 8a. These are your **total payments.** **9**

10 **Tax.** Use the amount on **line 6 above** to find your tax in the tax table on pages 24–28 of the booklet. Then, enter the tax from the table on this line. **10**

Refund

Have it directly deposited! See page 20 and fill in 11b, 11c, and 11d.

11a If line 9 is larger than line 10, subtract line 10 from line 9. This is your **refund.** **11a**

▶ **b** Routing number

▶ **c** Type: Checking ☐ Savings ☐ **d** Account number

Amount you owe

12 If line 10 is larger than line 9, subtract line 9 from line 10. This is the **amount you owe.** See page 21 for details on how to pay. **12**

I have read this return. Under penalties of perjury, I declare that to the best of my knowledge and belief, the return is true, correct, and accurately lists all amounts and sources of income I received during the tax year.

Sign here ▶
Keep copy for your records.

Your signature	Date	Spouse's signature if joint return. See page 11.	Date
Your occupation		Spouse's occupation	

For Official Use Only

1	2	3	4	5
6	7	8	9	10

For Disclosure, Privacy Act, and Paperwork Reduction Act Notice, see page 23.

Cat. No. 11329W

1999 Form **1040EZ**

Use this form if

- Your filing status is single or married filing jointly.
- You do not claim any dependents.
- You (and your spouse if married) were under 65 on January 1, 2000, and not blind at the end of 1999.
- Your taxable income (line 6) is less than $50,000.
- You do not claim a student loan interest deduction (see page 8) or an education credit.
- You had **only** wages, salaries, tips, taxable scholarship or fellowship grants, unemployment compensation, qualified state tuition program earnings, or Alaska Permanent Fund dividends, and your taxable interest was not over $400. **But** if you earned tips, including allocated tips, that are not included in box 5 and box 7 of your W-2, you may not be able to use Form 1040EZ. See page 13. If you are planning to use Form 1040EZ for a child who received Alaska Permanent Fund dividends, see page 14.
- You did not receive any advance earned income credit payments.

If you are not sure about your filing status, see page 11. If you have questions about dependents, use TeleTax topic 354 (see page 6). If you **cannot use this form,** use TeleTax topic 352 (see page 6).

Filling in your return

For tips on how to avoid common mistakes, see page 29.

Enter your (and your spouse's if married) social security number on the front. Because this form is read by a machine, please print your numbers inside the boxes like this:

9 8 7 6 5 4 3 2 1 0

Do not type your numbers. Do not use dollar signs.

If you received a scholarship or fellowship grant or tax-exempt interest income, such as on municipal bonds, see the booklet before filling in the form. Also, see the booklet if you received a Form 1099-INT showing Federal income tax withheld or if Federal income tax was withheld from your unemployment compensation or Alaska Permanent Fund dividends.

Remember, you must report all wages, salaries, and tips even if you do not get a W-2 form from your employer. You must also report all your taxable interest, including interest from banks, savings and loans, credit unions, etc., even if you do not get a Form 1099-INT.

Worksheet for dependents who checked "Yes" on line 5

(keep a copy for your records)

Use this worksheet to figure the amount to enter on line 5 if someone can claim you (or your spouse if married) as a dependent, even if that person chooses not to do so. To find out if someone can claim you as a dependent, use TeleTax topic 354 (see page 6).

A. Amount, if any, from line 1 on front _____

     +   250.00   Enter total ▶   A. _____

B. Minimum standard deduction . . . . B. _____ 700.00

C. Enter the LARGER of line A or line B here . . . . . C. _____

D. Maximum standard deduction. If **single,** enter 4,300.00; if **married,** enter 7,200.00 . . . . D. _____

E. Enter the SMALLER of line C or line D here. This is your standard deduction . . . . E. _____

F. Exemption amount.
- If single, enter 0.
- If married and—
  —both you and your spouse can be claimed as dependents, enter 0.
  —only one of you can be claimed as a dependent, enter 2,750.00.   F. _____

G. Add lines E and F. Enter the total here and on line 5 on the front . . G. _____

If you checked "No" on line 5 because no one can claim you (or your spouse if married) as a dependent, enter on line 5 the amount shown below that applies to you.

- Single, enter 7,050.00. This is the total of your standard deduction (4,300.00) and your exemption (2,750.00).
- Married, enter 12,700.00. This is the total of your standard deduction (7,200.00), your exemption (2,750.00), and your spouse's exemption (2,750.00).

Mailing return

Mail your return by **April 17, 2000.** Use the envelope that came with your booklet. If you do not have that envelope, see page 32 for the address to use.

Paid preparer's use only

See page 21.

Under penalties of perjury, I declare that I have examined this return, and to the best of my knowledge and belief, it is true, correct, and accurately lists all amounts and sources of income received during the tax year. This declaration is based on all information of which I have any knowledge.

Preparer's signature ▶	Date	Check if self-employed ☐	Preparer's SSN or PTIN
Firm's name (or yours if self-employed) and address ▶		EIN	
		ZIP code	

♻   Form **1040EZ** (1999)

Department of the Treasury—Internal Revenue Service

U.S. Individual Income Tax Return (99) **1999**

IRS Use Only—Do not write or staple in this space.

OMB No. 1545-0085

Label
(See page 19.)

**Use the
IRS label.**

Otherwise,
please print
or type.

L A B E L   H E R E

Your first name and initial | Last name | Your social security number

If a joint return, spouse's first name and initial | Last name | Spouse's social security number

Home address (number and street). If you have a P.O. box, see page 20. | Apt. no.

City, town or post office, state, and ZIP code. If you have a foreign address, see page 20.

▲ IMPORTANT! ▲
You **must** enter your
SSN(s) above.

Presidential Election Campaign Fund (See page 20.)

Do you want $3 to go to this fund? . . . .

If a joint return, does your spouse want $3 to go to this fund?

Yes | No

Note. Checking "Yes" will
not change your tax or
reduce your refund.

Filing status

Check only
one box.

1 ☐ Single

2 ☐ Married filing joint return (even if only one had income)

3 ☐ Married filing separate return. Enter spouse's social security number
above and full name here. ▶ _____

4 ☐ Head of household (with qualifying person). (See page 21.) If the qualifying person is a child
but not your dependent, enter this child's name here. ▶ _____

5 ☐ Qualifying widow(er) with dependent child (year spouse died ▶ 19____). (See page 22.)

Exemptions

If more than
seven
dependents,
see page 22.

6a ☐ **Yourself.** If your parent (or someone else) can claim you as a dependent on his or her tax
return, **do not** check box 6a.

b ☐ **Spouse**

c **Dependents:**

(1) First name Last name	(2) Dependent's social security number	(3) Dependent's relationship to you	(4) ✓ if qualifying child for child tax credit (see page 23)
	:		☐
	:		☐
	:		☐
	:		☐
	:		☐
	:		☐
	:		☐

No. of boxes
checked on
6a and 6b _____

No. of your
children on
6c who:

● **lived with
you**

● **did not live
with you due
to divorce or
separation**
(see page 24)

**Dependents
on 6c not
entered above**

d Total number of exemptions claimed.

Add numbers
entered on
lines above ☐

Income

**Attach
Copy B of
your Form(s)
W-2 here.
Also attach
Form(s)
1099-R if tax
was withheld.**

If you did not
get a W-2, see
page 25.

Enclose, but do
not staple, any
payment.

7 Wages, salaries, tips, etc. Attach Form(s) W-2. | 7

8a **Taxable** interest. Attach Schedule 1 if required. | 8a

b **Tax-exempt** interest. DO NOT include on line 8a. | 8b

9 Ordinary dividends. Attach Schedule 1 if required. | 9

10a Total IRA
distributions. | 10a | **10b** Taxable amount
(see page 25). | 10b

11a Total pensions
and annuities. | 11a | **11b** Taxable amount
(see page 26). | 11b

12 Unemployment compensation, qualified state tuition program earnings,
and Alaska Permanent Fund dividends. | 12

13a Social security
benefits. | 13a | **13b** Taxable amount
(see page 28). | 13b

14 Add lines 7 through 13b (far right column). This is your **total income.** ▶ | 14

Adjusted gross income

15 IRA deduction (see page 30). | 15

16 Student loan interest deduction (see page 30). | 16

17 Add lines 15 and 16. These are your **total adjustments.** | 17

18 Subtract line 17 from line 14. This is your **adjusted gross income.** ▶ | 18

For Disclosure, Privacy Act, and Paperwork Reduction Act Notice, see page 53. | Cat. No. 11327A | Form **1040A** (1999)

Taxable income	**19**	Enter the amount from line 18.	19

20a Check { ☐ **You** were 65 or older   ☐ Blind } **Enter number of**
if: { ☐ **Spouse** was 65 or older ☐ Blind } **boxes checked ▶** 20a [   ]

b If you are married filing separately and your spouse itemizes
deductions, see page 32 and check here . . . . ▶ 20b ☐

21 Enter the **standard deduction** for your filing status. **But** see page 33 if
you checked any box on line 20a or 20b **OR** if someone can claim you
as a dependent.
• Single—$4,300   • Married filing jointly or Qualifying widow(er)—$7,200
• Head of household—$6,350   • Married filing separately—$3,600   21

22 Subtract line 21 from line 19. If line 21 is more than line 19, enter -0-.   22

23 Multiply $2,750 by the total number of exemptions claimed on line 6d.   23

24 Subtract line 23 from line 22. If line 23 is more than line 22, enter -0-.
This is your **taxable income.**   ▶ 24

Tax, credits, and payments

25 Find the tax on the amount on line 24 (see page 34).   25

26 Credit for child and dependent care expenses.
Attach Schedule 2.   26

27 Credit for the elderly or the disabled. Attach
Schedule 3.   27

28 Child tax credit (see page 35).   28

29 Education credits. Attach Form 8863.   29

30 Adoption credit. Attach Form 8839.   30

31 Add lines 26 through 30. These are your **total credits.**   31

32 Subtract line 31 from line 25. If line 31 is more than line 25, enter -0-.   32

33 Advance earned income credit payments from Form(s) W-2.   33

34 Add lines 32 and 33. This is your **total tax.**   ▶ 34

35 Total Federal income tax withheld from
Forms W-2 and 1099.   35

36 1999 estimated tax payments and amount
applied from 1998 return.   36

37a **Earned income credit.** Attach
Schedule EIC if you have a qualifying child.   37a

b Nontaxable earned income:
amount ▶   and type ▶

38 Additional child tax credit. Attach Form 8812.   38

39 Add lines 35, 36, 37a, and 38. These are your **total payments.**   ▶ 39

Refund

Have it directly
deposited! See
page 47 and fill
in 41b, 41c, and
41d.

40 If line 39 is more than line 34, subtract line 34 from line 39.
This is the amount you **overpaid.**   40

41a Amount of line 40 you want **refunded to you.**   41a

▶ **b** Routing
number [   ] ▶ **c** Type: ☐ Checking ☐ Savings

▶ **d** Account
number [   ]

42 Amount of line 40 you want **applied to your
2000 estimated tax.**   42

Amount you owe

43 If line 34 is more than line 39, subtract line 39 from line 34. This is the
amount you owe. For details on how to pay, see page 48.   43

44 Estimated tax penalty (see page 48).   44

Sign here

Joint return?
See page 20.
Keep a copy for
your records.

Under penalties of perjury, I declare that I have examined this return and accompanying schedules and statements, and to the best of my knowledge and belief, they are true, correct, and accurately list all amounts and sources of income I received during the tax year. Declaration of preparer (other than the taxpayer) is based on all information of which the preparer has any knowledge.

Your signature	Date	Your occupation	Daytime telephone number (optional) ( )
Spouse's signature. If joint return, BOTH must sign.	Date	Spouse's occupation	

Paid preparer's use only

Preparer's signature ▶	Date	Check if self-employed ☐	Preparer's SSN or PTIN
Firm's name (or yours if self-employed) and address ▶			EIN
			ZIP code

✪   Form **1040A** (1999)

Schedule 1

(Form 1040A)

Department of the Treasury—Internal Revenue Service

Interest and Ordinary Dividends for Form 1040A Filers (99) **1999**

OMB No. 1545-0085

Name(s) shown on Form 1040A

Your social security number

Part I

Interest

(See page 60 and the instructions for Form 1040A, line 8a.)

Note. If you received a Form 1099-INT, Form 1099-OID, or substitute statement from a brokerage firm, enter the firm's name and the total interest shown on that form.

1 List name of payer. If any interest is from a seller-financed mortgage and the buyer used the property as a personal residence, see page 60 and list this interest first. Also, show that buyer's social security number and address.

Amount

		1	

2 Add the amounts on line 1. **2**

3 Excludable interest on series EE and I U.S. savings bonds issued after 1989 from Form 8815, line 14. You **must** attach Form 8815. **3**

4 Subtract line 3 from line 2. Enter the result here and on Form 1040A, line 8a. **4**

Part II

Ordinary dividends

(See page 60 and the instructions for Form 1040A, line 9.)

Note. If you received a Form 1099-DIV or substitute statement from a brokerage firm, enter the firm's name and the ordinary dividends shown on that form.

5 List name of payer

Amount

		5	

6 Add the amounts on line 5. Enter the total here and on Form 1040A, line 9. **6**

For Paperwork Reduction Act Notice, see Form 1040A instructions.   Cat. No. 12075R   **Schedule 1 (Form 1040A) 1999**

Department of the Treasury—Internal Revenue Service

Child and Dependent Care Expenses for Form 1040A Filers (99) 1999

OMB No. 1545-0085

Name(s) shown on Form 1040A	Your social security number

Before you begin, you need to understand the following terms. See **Definitions** on page 61.

• Dependent Care Benefits • Qualifying Person(s) • Qualified Expenses • Earned Income

Part I

Persons or organizations who provided the care

You MUST complete this part.

1	(a) Care provider's name	(b) Address (number, street, apt. no., city, state, and ZIP code)	(c) Identifying number (SSN or EIN)	(d) Amount paid (see page 62)

(If you need more space, use the bottom of page 2.)

Did you receive **dependent care benefits?**	No ──────▶ Complete only Part II below.
	Yes ──────▶ Complete Part III on the back next.

Caution. If the care was provided in your home, you may owe employment taxes. If you do, you must use Form 1040. See **Schedule H** and its instructions for details.

Part II

Credit for child and dependent care expenses

2 Information about your **qualifying person(s).** If you have more than two qualifying persons, see page 62.

(a) Qualifying person's name		(b) Qualifying person's social security number	(c) Qualified expenses you incurred and paid in 1999 for the person listed in column (a)
First	Last		

3 Add the amounts in column (c) of line 2. DO NOT enter more than $2,400 for one qualifying person or $4,800 for two or more persons. If you completed Part III, enter the amount from line 24. | **3** | |

4 Enter YOUR **earned income.** | **4** | |

5 If married filing a joint return, enter YOUR SPOUSE'S earned income (if your spouse was a student or was disabled, see page 63); **all others,** enter the amount from line 4. | **5** | |

6 Enter the **smallest** of line 3, 4, or 5. | **6** | |

7 Enter the amount from Form 1040A, line 19. **7** | |

8 Enter on line 8 the decimal amount shown below that applies to the amount on line 7.

If line 7 is—		Decimal amount is	If line 7 is—		Decimal amount is
Over	But not over		Over	But not over	
$0—10,000		.30	$20,000—22,000		.24
10,000—12,000		.29	22,000—24,000		.23
12,000—14,000		.28	24,000—26,000		.22
14,000—16,000		.27	26,000—28,000		.21
16,000—18,000		.26	28,000—No limit		.20
18,000—20,000		.25			

8 ✕ .

9 Multiply **line 6** by the decimal amount on line 8. Enter the result here and on Form 1040A, line 26. But if this amount is more than the amount on Form 1040A, line 25, **or** you paid 1998 expenses in 1999, see page 63 for the amount to enter on line 26. | **9** | |

For Paperwork Reduction Act Notice, see Form 1040A instructions.   Cat. No. 10749I   Schedule 2 (Form 1040A) 1999

713

Part III

**Dependent
care benefits**

10 Enter the total amount of **dependent care benefits** you received for 1999. This amount should be shown in box 10 of your W-2 form(s). DO NOT include amounts that were reported to you as wages in box 1 of Form(s) W-2.   **10**

11 Enter the amount forfeited, if any. See page 63.   **11**

12 Subtract line 11 from line 10.   **12**

13 Enter the total amount of **qualified expenses** incurred in 1999 for the care of the qualifying person(s).   **13**

14 Enter the **smaller** of line 12 or 13.   **14**

15 Enter YOUR **earned income.**   **15**

16 If married filing a joint return, enter YOUR SPOUSE'S earned income (if your spouse was a student or was disabled, see the instructions for line 5); if married filing a separate return, see the instructions for the amount to enter; **all others,** enter the amount from line 15.   **16**

17 Enter the **smallest** of line 14, 15, or 16.   **17**

18 **Excluded benefits.** Enter here the **smaller** of the following:
- The amount from line 17, or
- $5,000 ($2,500 if married filing a separate return **and** you were required to enter your spouse's earned income on line 16).   **18**

19 **Taxable benefits.** Subtract line 18 from line 12. Also, include this amount on Form 1040A, line 7. In the space to the left of line 7, enter "DCB."   **19**

To claim the child and dependent care credit, complete lines 20–24 below.

20 Enter $2,400 ($4,800 if two or more qualifying persons).   **20**

21 Enter the amount from line 18.   **21**

22 Subtract line 21 from line 20. If zero or less, **STOP.** You cannot take the credit. **Exception.** If you paid 1998 expenses in 1999, see the instructions for line 9.   **22**

23 Complete line 2 on the front of this schedule. DO NOT include in column (c) any benefits shown on line 18 above. Then, add the amounts in column (c) and enter the total here.   **23**

24 Enter the **smaller** of line 22 or 23 here. Also, enter this amount on line 3 on the front of this schedule and complete lines 4–9.   **24**

Schedule 2 (Form 1040A) 1999

Schedule 3
(Form 1040A)

Department of the Treasury—Internal Revenue Service

Credit for the Elderly or the Disabled
for Form 1040A Filers

(99)   **1999**

OMB No. 1545-0085

Name(s) shown on Form 1040A	Your social security number
	: :

You may be able to take this credit and reduce your tax if by the end of 1999:

- You were age 65 or older,   **OR**   • You were under age 65, you retired on **permanent and total** disability, and you received taxable disability income.

But you must also meet other tests. See the separate instructions for Schedule 3.

(TIP) In most cases, the IRS can figure the credit for you. See the instructions.

Part I	**If your filing status is:**	**And by the end of 1999:**	**Check only one box:**
Check the box for your filing status and age	Single, Head of household, or Qualifying widow(er) with dependent child	**1** You were 65 or older	1 ☐
		2 You were under 65 and you retired on permanent and total disability	2 ☐
	Married filing a joint return	**3** Both spouses were 65 or older	3 ☐
		4 Both spouses were under 65, but only one spouse retired on permanent and total disability	4 ☐
		5 Both spouses were under 65, and both retired on permanent and total disability	5 ☐
		6 One spouse was 65 or older, and the other spouse was under 65 and retired on permanent and total disability	6 ☐
		7 One spouse was 65 or older, and the other spouse was under 65 and **NOT** retired on permanent and total disability	7 ☐
	Married filing a separate return	**8** You were 65 or older and you lived apart from your spouse for all of 1999	8 ☐
		9 You were under 65, you retired on permanent and total disability, and you lived apart from your spouse for all of 1999	9 ☐

Did you check box 1, 3, 7, or 8? —— Yes ——▶ Skip Part II and complete Part III on the back.

—— No ——▶ Complete Parts II and III.

Part II	**IF:**	
Statement of permanent and total disability	**1** You filed a physician's statement for this disability for 1983 or an earlier year, or you filed or got a statement for tax years after 1983 and your physician signed line B on the statement, **AND**	
Complete this part **only** if you checked box 2, 4, 5, 6, or 9 above.	**2** Due to your continued disabled condition, you were unable to engage in any substantial gainful activity in 1999, check this box . . . . ▶ ☐	
	• If you checked this box, you do not have to get another statement for 1999.	
	• If you **did not** check this box, have your physician complete the statement on page 4 of the instructions. You **must** keep the statement for your records.	

For Paperwork Reduction Act Notice, see Form 1040A instructions.   Cat. No. 12064K   **Schedule 3 (Form 1040A) 1999**

Part III	**10**	**If you checked (in Part I):** **Enter:**
Figure your credit		Box 1, 2, 4, or 7 . . . . $5,000
		Box 3, 5, or 6 . . . . $7,500
		Box 8 or 9 . . . . $3,750 **10**

> **Did you check box 2, 4, 5, 6, or 9 in Part I?**
> — Yes ——▶ You **must** complete line 11.
> — No ——▶ Enter the amount from line 10 on line 12 and go to line 13.

11
- If you checked box 6 in Part I, add $5,000 to the taxable disability income of the spouse who was under age 65. Enter the total.
- If you checked box 2, 4, or 9 in Part I, enter your taxable disability income.
- If you checked box 5 in Part I, add your taxable disability income to your spouse's taxable disability income. Enter the total.

TIP For more details on what to include on line 11, see the instructions.   **11**

12 If you completed line 11, enter the **smaller** of line 10 or line 11; **all others,** enter the amount from line 10.   **12**

13 Enter the following pensions, annuities, or disability income that you (and your spouse if filing a joint return) received in 1999.

  a Nontaxable part of social security benefits, and

Nontaxable part of railroad retirement benefits treated as social security. See instructions.   **13a**

  b Nontaxable veterans' pensions and any other pension, annuity, or disability benefit that is excluded from income under any other provision of law. See instructions.   **13b**

  c Add lines 13a and 13b. (Even though these income items are not taxable, they **must** be included here to figure your credit.) If you did not receive any of the types of nontaxable income listed on line 13a or 13b, enter -0- on line 13c.   **13c**

14 Enter the amount from Form 1040A, line 19.   **14**

15 **If you checked (in Part I):**   **Enter:**
Box 1 or 2 . . . . $7,500
Box 3, 4, 5, 6, or 7 . . . . . . $10,000
Box 8 or 9 . . . . $5,000   **15**

16 Subtract line 15 from line 14. If zero or less, enter -0-.   **16**

17 Enter one-half of line 16.   **17**

18 Add lines 13c and 17.   **18**

19 Subtract line 18 from line 12. If zero or less, **stop; you cannot** take the credit. Otherwise, go to line 20.   **19**

20 Multiply line 19 by 15% (.15). Enter the result here and on Form 1040A, line 27. But if this amount is more than the amount on Form 1040A, line 25, **or** you are filing Schedule 2 (Form 1040A), see the instructions for the amount of credit you may take.   **20**

Form **1040**

Department of the Treasury—Internal Revenue Service

U.S. Individual Income Tax Return **1999**

IRS Use Only—Do not write or staple in this space.

For the year Jan. 1–Dec. 31, 1999, or other tax year beginning _____ , 1999, ending _____ , _____   OMB No. 1545-0074

Label

(See instructions on page 18.)

Use the IRS label. Otherwise, please print or type.

LABEL HERE

Your first name and initial | Last name | Your social security number

If a joint return, spouse's first name and initial | Last name | Spouse's social security number

Home address (number and street). If you have a P.O. box, see page 18. | Apt. no.

City, town or post office, state, and ZIP code. If you have a foreign address, see page 18.

▲ **IMPORTANT!** ▲
You **must** enter your SSN(s) above.

Presidential Election Campaign

(See page 18.)

▶ Do you want $3 to go to this fund? . . . .
If a joint return, does your spouse want $3 to go to this fund? . . . .

Yes | No | **Note.** Checking "Yes" will not change your tax or reduce your refund.

Filing Status

Check only one box.

1 ☐ Single
2 ☐ Married filing joint return (even if only one had income)
3 ☐ Married filing separate return. Enter spouse's social security no. above and full name here. ▶ _____
4 ☐ Head of household (with qualifying person). (See page 18.) If the qualifying person is a child but not your dependent, enter this child's name here. ▶ _____
5 ☐ Qualifying widow(er) with dependent child (year spouse died ▶ 19____). (See page 18.)

Exemptions

If more than six dependents, see page 19.

6a ☐ **Yourself.** If your parent (or someone else) can claim you as a dependent on his or her tax return, **do not** check box 6a . . . .
b ☐ **Spouse** . . . .

c **Dependents:**

(1) First name Last name	(2) Dependent's social security number	(3) Dependent's relationship to you	(4)✓ if qualifying child for child tax credit (see page 19)
			☐
			☐
			☐
			☐
			☐
			☐

d Total number of exemptions claimed . . . .

No. of boxes checked on 6a and 6b _____

No. of your children on 6c who:
• lived with you _____
• did not live with you due to divorce or separation (see page 19) _____

Dependents on 6c not entered above _____

Add numbers entered on lines above ▶ ☐

Income

Attach Copy B of your Forms W-2 and W-2G here. Also attach Form(s) 1099-R if tax was withheld.

If you did not get a W-2, see page 20.

Enclose, but do not staple, any payment. Also, please use **Form 1040-V.**

7 Wages, salaries, tips, etc. Attach Form(s) W-2 . . . . . | 7 |
8a **Taxable** interest. Attach Schedule B if required . . . . . | 8a |
b **Tax-exempt** interest. DO NOT include on line 8a . . | 8b | |
9 Ordinary dividends. Attach Schedule B if required . . . . . | 9 |
10 Taxable refunds, credits, or offsets of state and local income taxes (see page 21) . . | 10 |
11 Alimony received . . . . | 11 |
12 Business income or (loss). Attach Schedule C or C-EZ . . . . . . | 12 |
13 Capital gain or (loss). Attach Schedule D if required. If not required, check here ▶ ☐ | 13 |
14 Other gains or (losses). Attach Form 4797 . . . . . | 14 |
15a Total IRA distributions . . | 15a | | b Taxable amount (see page 22) | 15b |
16a Total pensions and annuities | 16a | | b Taxable amount (see page 22) | 16b |
17 Rental real estate, royalties, partnerships, S corporations, trusts, etc. Attach Schedule E | 17 |
18 Farm income or (loss). Attach Schedule F . . . . . | 18 |
19 Unemployment compensation . . . . | 19 |
20a Social security benefits . . | 20a | | b Taxable amount (see page 24) | 20b |
21 Other income. List type and amount (see page 24) ---------- | 21 |
22 Add the amounts in the far right column for lines 7 through 21. This is your **total income** ▶ | 22 |

Adjusted Gross Income

23 IRA deduction (see page 26) . . . . . | 23 |
24 Student loan interest deduction (see page 26) . . . . . | 24 |
25 Medical savings account deduction. Attach Form 8853 . | 25 |
26 Moving expenses. Attach Form 3903 . . . . . | 26 |
27 One-half of self-employment tax. Attach Schedule SE . | 27 |
28 Self-employed health insurance deduction (see page 28) | 28 |
29 Keogh and self-employed SEP and SIMPLE plans . . | 29 |
30 Penalty on early withdrawal of savings . . . . . | 30 |
31a Alimony paid b Recipient's SSN ▶ _____ | 31a |
32 Add lines 23 through 31a . . . . | 32 |
33 Subtract line 32 from line 22. This is your **adjusted gross income** . . . . . ▶ | 33 |

For Disclosure, Privacy Act, and Paperwork Reduction Act Notice, see page 54.   Cat. No. 11320B   Form **1040** (1999)

				34	

Tax and Credits

34 Amount from line 33 (adjusted gross income) . . . . | 34 | |

35a Check if: ☐ **You** were 65 or older, ☐ Blind; ☐ **Spouse** was 65 or older, ☐ Blind.
Add the number of boxes checked above and enter the total here . . . . ▶ **35a** ☐

b If you are married filing separately and your spouse itemizes deductions or
you were a dual-status alien, see page 30 and check here . . . . ▶ **35b** ☐

<table>
<tr><td rowspan="8">Standard Deduction for Most People

Single: $4,300

Head of household: $6,350

Married filing jointly or Qualifying widow(er): $7,200

Married filing separately: $3,600</td><td>36</td><td>Enter your itemized deductions from Schedule A, line 28, OR standard deduction shown on the left. But see page 30 to find your standard deduction if you checked any box on line 35a or 35b or if someone can claim you as a dependent . . . . .</td><td>36</td><td></td></tr>
<tr><td>37</td><td>Subtract line 36 from line 34 . . . .</td><td>37</td><td></td></tr>
<tr><td>38</td><td>If line 34 is $94,975 or less, multiply $2,750 by the total number of exemptions claimed on line 6d. If line 34 is over $94,975, see the worksheet on page 31 for the amount to enter .</td><td>38</td><td></td></tr>
<tr><td>39</td><td>Taxable income. Subtract line 38 from line 37. If line 38 is more than line 37, enter -0-</td><td>39</td><td></td></tr>
<tr><td>40</td><td>Tax (see page 31). Check if any tax is from a ☐ Form(s) 8814 b ☐ Form 4972 . . ▶</td><td>40</td><td></td></tr>
<tr><td>41</td><td>Credit for child and dependent care expenses. Attach Form 2441</td><td colspan="2">41</td></tr>
<tr><td>42</td><td>Credit for the elderly or the disabled. Attach Schedule R . .</td><td colspan="2">42</td></tr>
<tr><td>43</td><td>Child tax credit (see page 33) . . . .</td><td colspan="2">43</td></tr>
</table>

44 Education credits. Attach Form 8863 . . . . . . | **44** |

45 Adoption credit. Attach Form 8839 . . . . | **45** |

46 Foreign tax credit. Attach Form 1116 if required . . . . | **46** |

47 Other. Check if from **a** ☐ Form 3800   **b** ☐ Form 8396
c ☐ Form 8801   **d** ☐ Form (specify) _____ | **47** |

48 Add lines 41 through 47. These are your **total credits** . . . . | **48** | |

49 Subtract line 48 from line 40. If line 48 is more than line 40, enter -0- . . . . . ▶ | **49** | |

Other Taxes

50 Self-employment tax. Attach Schedule SE . . . . | **50** | |

51 Alternative minimum tax. Attach Form 6251 . . . . | **51** | |

52 Social security and Medicare tax on tip income not reported to employer. Attach Form 4137 . | **52** | |

53 Tax on IRAs, other retirement plans, and MSAs. Attach Form 5329 if required . . . . | **53** | |

54 Advance earned income credit payments from Form(s) W-2 . . . . | **54** | |

55 Household employment taxes. Attach Schedule H . . . . | **55** | |

56 Add lines 49 through 55. This is your **total tax** . . . . ▶ | **56** | |

Payments

57 Federal income tax withheld from Forms W-2 and 1099 . . | **57** |

58 1999 estimated tax payments and amount applied from 1998 return . | **58** |

59a **Earned income credit.** Attach Sch. EIC if you have a qualifying child

b Nontaxable earned income: amount . . ▶ _____
and type ▶ ----------------------------- | **59a** |

60 Additional child tax credit. Attach Form 8812 . . . . . | **60** |

61 Amount paid with request for extension to file (see page 48) | **61** |

62 Excess social security and RRTA tax withheld (see page 48) | **62** |

63 Other payments. Check if from **a** ☐ Form 2439 **b** ☐ Form 4136 | **63** |

64 Add lines 57, 58, 59a, and 60 through 63. These are your **total payments** . . . . ▶ | **64** | |

Refund

Have it directly deposited! See page 48 and fill in 66b, 66c, and 66d.

65 If line 64 is more than line 56, subtract line 56 from line 64. This is the amount you **OVERPAID** | **65** | |

66a Amount of line 65 you want **REFUNDED TO YOU** . . . . ▶ | **66a** | |

▶ **b** Routing number ☐☐☐☐☐☐☐☐☐   ▶ **c** Type: ☐ Checking ☐ Savings

▶ **d** Account number ☐☐☐☐☐☐☐☐☐☐☐☐☐☐☐☐☐

67 Amount of line 65 you want **APPLIED TO YOUR 2000 ESTIMATED TAX** ▶ | **67** |

Amount You Owe

68 If line 56 is more than line 64, subtract line 64 from line 56. This is the **AMOUNT YOU OWE**.
For details on how to pay, see page 49 . . . . ▶ | **68** | |

69 Estimated tax penalty. Also include on line 68 . . . . . | **69** |

Sign Here

Under penalties of perjury, I declare that I have examined this return and accompanying schedules and statements, and to the best of my knowledge and belief, they are true, correct, and complete. Declaration of preparer (other than taxpayer) is based on all information of which preparer has any knowledge.

Joint return? See page 18.

Keep a copy for your records.

Your signature	Date	Your occupation	Daytime telephone number (optional) ( )
Spouse's signature. If a joint return, BOTH must sign.	Date	Spouse's occupation	

Paid Preparer's Use Only

Preparer's signature ▶	Date	Check if self-employed ☐	Preparer's SSN or PTIN
Firm's name (or yours if self-employed) and address ▶		EIN	
		ZIP code	

Form **1040** (1999)

⊛ *Printed on recycled paper*

SCHEDULES A&B
(Form 1040)

Department of the Treasury
Internal Revenue Service   (99)

Schedule A—Itemized Deductions

(Schedule B is on back)

► **Attach to Form 1040.** ► **See Instructions for Schedules A and B (Form 1040).**

OMB No. 1545-0074

19**99**

Attachment
Sequence No. **07**

Name(s) shown on Form 1040 | Your social security number

Medical and Dental Expenses

Caution. Do not include expenses reimbursed or paid by others.

1 Medical and dental expenses (see page A-1) . . . . | **1**
2 Enter amount from Form 1040, line 34. | **2**
3 Multiply line 2 above by 7.5% (.075) . . . . | **3**
4 Subtract line 3 from line 1. If line 3 is more than line 1, enter -0- . . . . . . | **4**

Taxes You Paid

(See page A-2.)

5 State and local income taxes . . . . | **5**
6 Real estate taxes (see page A-2) . . . . | **6**
7 Personal property taxes . . . . | **7**
8 Other taxes. List type and amount ► _____ | **8**
9 Add lines 5 through 8 . . . . | **9**

Interest You Paid

(See page A-3.)

Note.
Personal interest is not deductible.

10 Home mortgage interest and points reported to you on Form 1098 | **10**
11 Home mortgage interest not reported to you on Form 1098. If paid to the person from whom you bought the home, see page A-3 and show that person's name, identifying no., and address ►
_____
_____
_____ | **11**
12 Points not reported to you on Form 1098. See page A-3 for special rules . . . . | **12**
13 Investment interest. Attach Form 4952 if required. (See page A-3.) . . . . | **13**
14 Add lines 10 through 13 . . . . | **14**

Gifts to Charity

If you made a gift and got a benefit for it, see page A-4.

15 Gifts by cash or check. If you made any gift of $250 or more, see page A-4 . . . . | **15**
16 Other than by cash or check. If any gift of $250 or more, see page A-4. You **MUST** attach Form 8283 if over $500 | **16**
17 Carryover from prior year . . . . | **17**
18 Add lines 15 through 17 . . . . | **18**

Casualty and Theft Losses

19 Casualty or theft loss(es). Attach Form 4684. (See page A-5.) . . . . | **19**

Job Expenses and Most Other Miscellaneous Deductions

(See page A-5 for expenses to deduct here.)

20 Unreimbursed employee expenses—job travel, union dues, job education, etc. You **MUST** attach Form 2106 or 2106-EZ if required. (See page A-5.) ► _____
_____ | **20**
21 Tax preparation fees . . . . | **21**
22 Other expenses—investment, safe deposit box, etc. List type and amount ► _____
_____ | **22**
23 Add lines 20 through 22 . . . . | **23**
24 Enter amount from Form 1040, line 34. | **24**
25 Multiply line 24 above by 2% (.02) . . . . . . | **25**
26 Subtract line 25 from line 23. If line 25 is more than line 23, enter -0- . . . . | **26**

Other Miscellaneous Deductions

27 Other—from list on page A-6. List type and amount ► _____
_____ | **27**

Total Itemized Deductions

28 Is Form 1040, line 34, over $126,600 (over $63,300 if married filing separately)?

☐ **No.** Your deduction is not limited. Add the amounts in the far right column for lines 4 through 27. Also, enter this amount on Form 1040, line 36. } ► | **28**

☐ **Yes.** Your deduction may be limited. See page A-6 for the amount to enter.

For Paperwork Reduction Act Notice, see Form 1040 instructions.   Cat. No. 11330X   Schedule A (Form 1040) 1999

Name(s) shown on Form 1040. Do not enter name and social security number if shown on other side. | **Your social security number**

Schedule B—Interest and Ordinary Dividends

Attachment
Sequence No. **08**

Note. If you had over $400 in taxable interest, you must also complete Part III.

Part I
Interest

(See page B-1
and the
instructions for
Form 1040,
line 8a.)

Note. If you
received a Form
1099-INT, Form
1099-OID, or
substitute
statement from
a brokerage firm,
list the firm's
name as the
payer and enter
the total interest
shown on that
form.

		Amount
1	List name of payer. If any interest is from a seller-financed mortgage and the buyer used the property as a personal residence, see page B-1 and list this interest first. Also, show that buyer's social security number and address ▶	
2	Add the amounts on line 1	
3	Excludable interest on series EE and I U.S. savings bonds issued after 1989 from Form 8815, line 14. You **MUST** attach Form 8815	
4	Subtract line 3 from line 2. Enter the result here and on Form 1040, line 8a ▶	

Note. If you had over $400 in ordinary dividends, you must also complete Part III.

Part II
Ordinary
Dividends

(See page B-1
and the
instructions for
Form 1040,
line 9.)

Note. If you
received a Form
1099-DIV or
substitute
statement from
a brokerage firm,
list the firm's
name as the
payer and enter
the ordinary
dividends shown
on that form.

		Amount
5	List name of payer. Include only ordinary dividends. If you received any capital gain distributions, see the instructions for Form 1040, line 13 ▶	
6	Add the amounts on line 5. Enter the total here and on Form 1040, line 9 . ▶	

Part III
Foreign
Accounts
and Trusts

(See
page B-2.)

You must complete this part if you **(a)** had over $400 of interest or ordinary dividends; **(b)** had a foreign account; or **(c)** received a distribution from, or were a grantor of, or a transferor to, a foreign trust.

	Yes	No
7a At any time during 1999, did you have an interest in or a signature or other authority over a financial account in a foreign country, such as a bank account, securities account, or other financial account? See page B-2 for exceptions and filing requirements for Form TD F 90-22.1		
b If "Yes," enter the name of the foreign country ▶		
8 During 1999, did you receive a distribution from, or were you the grantor of, or transferor to, a foreign trust? If "Yes," you may have to file Form 3520. See page B-2		

For Paperwork Reduction Act Notice, see Form 1040 instructions.

Schedule B (Form 1040) 1999

SCHEDULE C (Form 1040)	**Profit or Loss From Business** (Sole Proprietorship)	OMB No. 1545-0074
Department of the Treasury Internal Revenue Service (99)	▶ Partnerships, joint ventures, etc., must file Form 1065 or Form 1065-B. ▶ Attach to Form 1040 or Form 1041. ▶ See Instructions for Schedule C (Form 1040).	**19 99** Attachment Sequence No. **09**

Name of proprietor | **Social security number (SSN)**

A Principal business or profession, including product or service (see page C-1)

B Enter code from pages C-8 & 9 ▶

C Business name. If no separate business name, leave blank.

D Employer ID number (EIN), if any

E Business address (including suite or room no.) ▶
City, town or post office, state, and ZIP code

F Accounting method: **(1)** ☐ Cash **(2)** ☐ Accrual **(3)** ☐ Other (specify) ▶

G Did you "materially participate" in the operation of this business during 1999? If "No," see page C-2 for limit on losses . ☐ Yes ☐ No

H If you started or acquired this business during 1999, check here . . . . ▶ ☐

Part I Income

1	Gross receipts or sales. **Caution:** *If this income was reported to you on Form W-2 and the "Statutory employee" box on that form was checked, see page C-2 and check here* . . . . . ▶ ☐	1	
2	Returns and allowances	2	
3	Subtract line 2 from line 1	3	
4	Cost of goods sold (from line 42 on page 2)	4	
5	**Gross profit.** Subtract line 4 from line 3	5	
6	Other income, including Federal and state gasoline or fuel tax credit or refund (see page C-3) . . .	6	
7	**Gross income.** Add lines 5 and 6 . . . . ▶	7	

Part II Expenses. Enter expenses for business use of your home **only** on line 30.

8	Advertising	8		19 Pension and profit-sharing plans	19	
9	Bad debts from sales or services (see page C-3) . .	9		20 Rent or lease (see page C-4):		
10	Car and truck expenses (see page C-3)	10		a Vehicles, machinery, and equipment .	20a	
11	Commissions and fees .	11		b Other business property . .	20b	
12	Depletion	12		21 Repairs and maintenance . .	21	
13	Depreciation and section 179 expense deduction (not included in Part III) (see page C-3) . .	13		22 Supplies (not included in Part III) .	22	
				23 Taxes and licenses	23	
				24 Travel, meals, and entertainment:		
14	Employee benefit programs (other than on line 19) . .	14		a Travel	24a	
15	Insurance (other than health) .	15		b Meals and entertainment		
16	Interest:			c Enter nondeductible amount included on line 24b (see page C-5)		
a	Mortgage (paid to banks, etc.) .	16a				
b	Other	16b		d Subtract line 24c from line 24b	24d	
17	Legal and professional services	17		25 Utilities	25	
				26 Wages (less employment credits) .	26	
18	Office expense	18		27 Other expenses (from line 48 on page 2)	27	

28	**Total expenses** before expenses for business use of home. Add lines 8 through 27 in columns ▶	28	
29	Tentative profit (loss). Subtract line 28 from line 7	29	
30	Expenses for business use of your home. Attach **Form 8829**	30	
31	**Net profit or (loss).** Subtract line 30 from line 29.		
	• If a profit, enter on **Form 1040, line 12,** and ALSO on **Schedule SE, line 2** (statutory employees, see page C-6). Estates and trusts, enter on Form 1041, line 3.	31	
	• If a loss, you MUST go on to line 32.		

32	If you have a loss, check the box that describes your investment in this activity (see page C-6).		
	• If you checked 32a, enter the loss on **Form 1040, line 12,** and ALSO on **Schedule SE, line 2** (statutory employees, see page C-6). Estates and trusts, enter on Form 1041, line 3.	32a ☐	All investment is at risk.
	• If you checked 32b, you MUST attach **Form 6198.**	32b ☐	Some investment is not at risk.

For Paperwork Reduction Act Notice, see Form 1040 instructions.   Cat. No. 11334P   Schedule C (Form 1040) 1999

Part III Cost of Goods Sold (see page C-6)

33 Method(s) used to value closing inventory: **a** ☐ Cost **b** ☐ Lower of cost or market **c** ☐ Other (attach explanation)

34 Was there any change in determining quantities, costs, or valuations between opening and closing inventory? If "Yes," attach explanation . . . . ☐ **Yes** ☐ **No**

35 Inventory at beginning of year. If different from last year's closing inventory, attach explanation	35	
36 Purchases less cost of items withdrawn for personal use	36	
37 Cost of labor. Do not include any amounts paid to yourself	37	
38 Materials and supplies	38	
39 Other costs	39	
40 Add lines 35 through 39	40	
41 Inventory at end of year	41	
42 **Cost of goods sold.** Subtract line 41 from line 40. Enter the result here and on page 1, line 4	42	

Part IV Information on Your Vehicle. Complete this part **ONLY** if you are claiming car or truck expenses on line 10 and are not required to file Form 4562 for this business. See the instructions for line 13 on page C-3 to find out if you must file.

43 When did you place your vehicle in service for business purposes? (month, day, year) ▶ ..../......../........ .

44 Of the total number of miles you drove your vehicle during 1999, enter the number of miles you used your vehicle for:

a Business .... **b** Commuting .... **c** Other ....

45 Do you (or your spouse) have another vehicle available for personal use? . . . . ☐ **Yes** ☐ **No**

46 Was your vehicle available for use during off-duty hours? . . . . ☐ **Yes** ☐ **No**

47a Do you have evidence to support your deduction? . . . . ☐ **Yes** ☐ **No**

  b If "Yes," is the evidence written? . . . . ☐ **Yes** ☐ **No**

Part V Other Expenses. List below business expenses not included on lines 8–26 or line 30.

48 **Total other expenses.** Enter here and on page 1, line 27	48

Net Profit From Business

(Sole Proprietorship)

▶ **Partnerships, joint ventures, etc., must file Form 1065 or 1065-B.**

▶ **Attach to Form 1040 or Form 1041.** ▶ **See instructions on back.**

OMB No. 1545-0074

19**99**

Attachment
Sequence No. **09A**

Name of proprietor | Social security number (SSN)

Part I   General Information

**You May Use
Schedule C-EZ
Instead of
Schedule C
Only If You:**

- Had business expenses of $2,500 or less.
- Use the cash method of accounting.
- Did not have an inventory at any time during the year.
- Did not have a net loss from your business.
- Had only one business as a sole proprietor.

And You:

- Had no employees during the year.
- Are not required to file **Form 4562,** Depreciation and Amortization, for this business. See the instructions for Schedule C, line 13, on page C-3 to find out if you must file.
- Do not deduct expenses for business use of your home.
- Do not have prior year unallowed passive activity losses from this business.

A Principal business or profession, including product or service

B Enter code from pages C-8 & 9
▶

C Business name. If no separate business name, leave blank.

D Employer ID number (EIN), if any

E Business address (including suite or room no.). Address not required if same as on Form 1040, page 1.

City, town or post office, state, and ZIP code

Part II   Figure Your Net Profit

1 **Gross receipts. Caution:** *If this income was reported to you on Form W-2 and the "Statutory employee" box on that form was checked, see **Statutory Employees** in the instructions for Schedule C, line 1, on page C-2 and check here* . . . . ▶ ☐ | **1** |

2 **Total expenses.** If more than $2,500, you **must** use Schedule C. See instructions . . . . . | **2** |

3 **Net profit.** Subtract line 2 from line 1. If less than zero, you **must** use Schedule C. Enter on **Form 1040, line 12,** and ALSO on **Schedule SE, line 2.** (Statutory employees **do not** report this amount on Schedule SE, line 2. Estates and trusts, enter on Form 1041, line 3.) . . . . . | **3** |

Part III   Information on Your Vehicle. Complete this part **ONLY** if you are claiming car or truck expenses on line 2.

4 When did you place your vehicle in service for business purposes? (month, day, year) ▶ ....../....../...... .

5 Of the total number of miles you drove your vehicle during 1999, enter the number of miles you used your vehicle for:

a Business .... **b** Commuting .... **c** Other ....

6 Do you (or your spouse) have another vehicle available for personal use? . . . . ☐ **Yes** ☐ **No**

7 Was your vehicle available for use during off-duty hours? . . . . ☐ **Yes** ☐ **No**

8a Do you have evidence to support your deduction? . . . . ☐ **Yes** ☐ **No**

b If "Yes," is the evidence written? . . . . ☐ **Yes** ☐ **No**

For Paperwork Reduction Act Notice, see Form 1040 instructions.   Cat. No. 14374D   Schedule C-EZ (Form 1040) 1999

723

Instructions

You may use Schedule C-EZ instead of Schedule C if you operated a business or practiced a profession as a sole proprietorship and you have met all the requirements listed in Part I of Schedule C-EZ.

Line A

Describe the business or professional activity that provided your principal source of income reported on line 1. Give the general field or activity and the type of product or service.

Line B

Enter the six-digit code that identifies your principal business or professional activity. See pages C-8 and C-9 for the list of codes.

Line D

You need an employer identification number (EIN) only if you had a Keogh plan or were required to file an employment, excise, estate, trust, or alcohol, tobacco, and firearms tax return. If you need an EIN, file **Form SS-4,** Application for Employer Identification Number. If you do not have an EIN, leave line D blank. **Do not** enter your SSN.

Line E

Enter your business address. Show a street address instead of a box number. Include the suite or room number, if any.

Line 1

Enter gross receipts from your trade or business. Include amounts you received in your trade or business that were properly shown on **Forms 1099-MISC.** If the total amounts that were reported in box 7 of Forms 1099-MISC are more than the total you are reporting on line 1, attach a statement explaining the difference. You must show all items of taxable income actually or constructively received during the year (in cash, property, or services). Income is constructively received when it is credited to your account or set aside for you to use. Do not offset this amount by any losses.

Line 2

Enter the total amount of all deductible business expenses you actually paid during the year. Examples of these expenses include advertising, car and truck expenses, commissions and fees, insurance, interest, legal and professional services, office expense, rent or lease expenses, repairs and maintenance, supplies, taxes, travel, the allowable percentage of business meals and entertainment, and utilities (including telephone). For details, see the instructions for Schedule C, Parts II and V, on pages C-3 through C-7. If you wish, you may use the optional worksheet below to record your expenses.

   If you claim car or truck expenses, be sure to complete Part III of Schedule C-EZ.

Optional Worksheet for Line 2 (keep a copy for your records)

a Business meals and entertainment	a	
b Enter nondeductible amount included on line **a** (see the instructions for lines 24b and 24c on page C-5)	b	
c Deductible business meals and entertainment. Subtract line **b** from line **a**	c	
d	d	
e	e	
f	f	
g	g	
h	h	
i	i	
j **Total.** Add lines **c** through **i.** Enter here and on line 2	j	

SCHEDULE D
(Form 1040)

Department of the Treasury
Internal Revenue Service (99)

Capital Gains and Losses

▶ Attach to Form 1040.   ▶ See Instructions for Schedule D (Form 1040).

▶ Use Schedule D-1 for more space to list transactions for lines 1 and 8.

OMB No. 1545-0074

19**99**

Attachment
Sequence No. **12**

Name(s) shown on Form 1040

Your social security number

Part I   Short-Term Capital Gains and Losses—Assets Held One Year or Less

(a) Description of property (Example: 100 sh. XYZ Co.)	(b) Date acquired (Mo., day, yr.)	(c) Date sold (Mo., day, yr.)	(d) Sales price (see page D-5)	(e) Cost or other basis (see page D-5)	(f) GAIN or (LOSS) Subtract (e) from (d)	
1						

2 Enter your short-term totals, if any, from Schedule D-1, line 2 . . . . **2**

3 **Total short-term sales price amounts.** Add column (d) of lines 1 and 2 . . . . **3**

4 Short-term gain from Form 6252 and short-term gain or (loss) from Forms 4684, 6781, and 8824 . . . . **4**

5 Net short-term gain or (loss) from partnerships, S corporations, estates, and trusts from Schedule(s) K-1 . . . . **5**

6 Short-term capital loss carryover. Enter the amount, if any, from line 8 of your 1998 Capital Loss Carryover Worksheet . . . . **6** ( )

7 **Net short-term capital gain or (loss).** Combine lines 1 through 6 in column (f) ▶ **7**

Part II   Long-Term Capital Gains and Losses—Assets Held More Than One Year

(a) Description of property (Example: 100 sh. XYZ Co.)	(b) Date acquired (Mo., day, yr.)	(c) Date sold (Mo., day, yr.)	(d) Sales price (see page D-5)	(e) Cost or other basis (see page D-5)	(f) GAIN or (LOSS) Subtract (e) from (d)	(g) 28% RATE GAIN or (LOSS) *(see instr. below)
8						

9 Enter your long-term totals, if any, from Schedule D-1, line 9 . . . . **9**

10 **Total long-term sales price amounts.** Add column (d) of lines 8 and 9 . . . . . **10**

11 Gain from Form 4797, Part I; long-term gain from Forms 2439 and 6252; and long-term gain or (loss) from Forms 4684, 6781, and 8824 . . . . **11**

12 Net long-term gain or (loss) from partnerships, S corporations, estates, and trusts from Schedule(s) K-1. . . . . **12**

13 Capital gain distributions. See page D-1 . . . . **13**

14 Long-term capital loss carryover. Enter in both columns (f) and (g) the amount, if any, from line 13 of your 1998 Capital Loss Carryover Worksheet . . . . . . **14** ( ) ( )

15 Combine lines 8 through 14 in column (g) **15**

16 **Net long-term capital gain or (loss).** Combine lines 8 through 14 in column (f) ▶ **16**
     Next: Go to Part III on the back.

*__28% Rate Gain or Loss__ includes **all** "collectibles gains and losses" (as defined on page D-5) and up to 50% of the eligible gain on qualified small business stock (see page D-4).

For Paperwork Reduction Act Notice, see Form 1040 instructions.   Cat. No. 11338H   Schedule D (Form 1040) 1999

Part III	**Summary of Parts I and II**			

17 Combine lines 7 and 16. If a loss, go to line 18. If a gain, enter the gain on Form 1040, line 13 — **17**

   Next: Complete Form 1040 through line 39. Then, go to **Part IV** to figure your tax if:
   - Both lines 16 and 17 are gains, **and**
   - Form 1040, line 39, is more than zero.

18 If line 17 is a loss, enter here and as a (loss) on Form 1040, line 13, the **smaller** of these losses:
   - The loss on line 17, **or**
   - ($3,000) or, if married filing separately, ($1,500) . . . . — **18** ( )

   Next: Skip **Part IV** below. Instead, complete Form 1040 through line 37. Then, complete the **Capital Loss Carryover Worksheet** on page D-6 if:
   - The loss on line 17 exceeds the loss on line 18, **or**
   - Form 1040, line 37, is a loss.

Part IV	**Tax Computation Using Maximum Capital Gains Rates**			

19 Enter your taxable income from Form 1040, line 39 . . . . — **19**

20 Enter the **smaller** of line 16 or line 17 of Schedule D . . . . . — **20**

21 If you are filing Form 4952, enter the amount from Form 4952, line 4e — **21**

22 Subtract line 21 from line 20. If zero or less, enter -0- . . . . . — **22**

23 Combine lines 7 and 15. If zero or less, enter -0- . . . . — **23**

24 Enter the **smaller** of line 15 or line 23, but not less than zero . . . — **24**

25 Enter your unrecaptured section 1250 gain, if any, from line 16 of the worksheet on page D-7 . . . . — **25**

26 Add lines 24 and 25 . . . . — **26**

27 Subtract line 26 from line 22. If zero or less, enter -0- . . . . — **27**

28 Subtract line 27 from line 19. If zero or less, enter -0- . . . . — **28**

29 Enter the **smaller** of:
   - The amount on line 19, **or**
   - $25,750 if single; $43,050 if married filing jointly or qualifying widow(er); } . . . . — **29**
     $21,525 if married filing separately; or $34,550 if head of household

30 Enter the **smaller** of line 28 or line 29 . . . . — **30**

31 Subtract line 22 from line 19. If zero or less, enter -0- . . . . . — **31**

32 Enter the **larger** of line 30 or line 31 . . . . ▶ **32**

33 Figure the tax on the amount on line 32. Use the Tax Table or Tax Rate Schedules, whichever applies — **33**

   Note. If line 29 is less than line 28, go to line 38.

34 Enter the amount from line 29 . . . . — **34**

35 Enter the amount from line 28 . . . . — **35**

36 Subtract line 35 from line 34. If zero or less, enter -0- . . . . . ▶ **36**

37 Multiply line 36 by 10% (.10) . . . . — **37**

   Note. If line 27 is more than zero **and** equal to line 36, go to line 52.

38 Enter the **smaller** of line 19 or line 27 . . . . — **38**

39 Enter the amount from line 36 . . . . — **39**

40 Subtract line 39 from line 38 . . . . ▶ **40**

41 Multiply line 40 by 20% (.20) . . . . — **41**

   Note. If line 25 is zero or blank, skip lines 42 through 47 and read the note above line 48.

42 Enter the **smaller** of line 22 or line 25 . . . . — **42**

43 Add lines 22 and 32 . . . . — **43**

44 Enter the amount from line 19 . . . . — **44**

45 Subtract line 44 from line 43. If zero or less, enter -0- . . . . . — **45**

46 Subtract line 45 from line 42. If zero or less, enter -0- . . . . ▶ **46**

47 Multiply line 46 by 25% (.25) . . . . — **47**

   Note. If line 24 is zero or blank, go to line 52.

48 Enter the amount from line 19 . . . . — **48**

49 Add lines 32, 36, 40, and 46 . . . . — **49**

50 Subtract line 49 from line 48 . . . . — **50**

51 Multiply line 50 by 28% (.28) . . . . — **51**

52 Add lines 33, 37, 41, 47, and 51 . . . . — **52**

53 Figure the tax on the amount on line 19. Use the Tax Table or Tax Rate Schedules, whichever applies — **53**

54 **Tax on all taxable income (including capital gains).** Enter the **smaller** of line 52 or line 53 here and on Form 1040, line 40. . . . . — **54**

Continuation Sheet for Schedule D
(Form 1040)
► See instructions for Schedule D (Form 1040).
► **Attach to Schedule D if you need more space to list transactions for lines 1 and 8.**

Name(s) shown on Form 1040

Your social security number

Part I Short-Term Capital Gains and Losses—Assets Held One Year or Less

(a) Description of property (Example: 100 sh. XYZ Co.)	(b) Date acquired (Mo., day, yr.)	(c) Date sold (Mo., day, yr.)	(d) Sales price (see page D-5)	(e) Cost or other basis (see page D-5)	(f) GAIN or (LOSS). Subtract (e) from (d)	
1						
2 **Totals.** Combine columns (d) and (f). Enter here and on Schedule D, line 2 . . . . ► **2**						

For Paperwork Reduction Act Notice, see Form 1040 instructions.   Cat. No. 10424K   Schedule D-1 (Form 1040) 1999

727

Name(s) shown on Form 1040. Do not enter name and social security number if shown on other side. | **Your social security number**

Part II   Long-Term Capital Gains and Losses—Assets Held More Than One Year

(a) Description of property (Example: 100 sh. XYZ Co.)	(b) Date acquired (Mo., day, yr.)	(c) Date sold (Mo., day, yr.)	(d) Sales price (see page D-5)	(e) Cost or other basis (see page D-5)	(f) GAIN or (LOSS). Subtract (e) from (d)	(g) 28% RATE GAIN or (LOSS) *(see instr. below)
8						
9 **Totals.** Combine columns (d), (f), and (g). Enter here and on Schedule D, line 9 . . . . . ▶ **9**						

* 28% Rate Gain or Loss includes **all** "collectibles gains and losses" (as defined on page D-5) and up to 50% of the eligible gain on qualified small business stock (see page D-4).

Supplemental Income and Loss

(From rental real estate, royalties, partnerships,
S corporations, estates, trusts, REMICs, etc.)

► **Attach to Form 1040 or Form 1041.**   ► **See Instructions for Schedule E (Form 1040).**

OMB No. 1545-0074

1999

Attachment
Sequence No. **13**

Name(s) shown on return

Your social security number

Part I   **Income or Loss From Rental Real Estate and Royalties**   Note: *Report income and expenses from your business of renting personal property on* **Schedule C** *or* **C-EZ** *(see page E-1). Report farm rental income or loss from* **Form 4835** *on page 2, line 39.*

1 Show the kind and location of each **rental real estate property:**

A ....

B ....

C ....

2 For each rental real estate property listed on line 1, did you or your family use it during the tax year for personal purposes for more than the greater of:
- 14 days, **or**
- 10% of the total days rented at fair rental value?

(See page E-1.)

	Yes	No
A		
B		
C		

Income:			Properties			Totals (Add columns A, B, and C.)	
			A	B	C		
3 Rents received	3					3	
4 Royalties received	4					4	
Expenses:							
5 Advertising	5						
6 Auto and travel (see page E-2) .	6						
7 Cleaning and maintenance . . .	7						
8 Commissions	8						
9 Insurance	9						
10 Legal and other professional fees	10						
11 Management fees	11						
12 Mortgage interest paid to banks, etc. (see page E-2)	12					12	
13 Other interest	13						
14 Repairs	14						
15 Supplies	15						
16 Taxes	16						
17 Utilities	17						
18 Other (list) ►	18						
19 Add lines 5 through 18	19					19	
20 Depreciation expense or depletion (see page E-3)	20					20	
21 Total expenses. Add lines 19 and 20	21						
22 Income or (loss) from rental real estate or royalty properties. Subtract line 21 from line 3 (rents) or line 4 (royalties). If the result is a (loss), see page E-3 to find out if you must file **Form 6198** . .	22						
23 Deductible rental real estate loss. **Caution:** *Your rental real estate loss on line 22 may be limited. See page E-3 to find out if you must file* **Form 8582.** *Real estate professionals must complete line 42 on page 2*	23	(	) (	) (	)		
24 **Income.** Add positive amounts shown on line 22. **Do not** include any losses						24	
25 **Losses.** Add royalty losses from line 22 and rental real estate losses from line 23. Enter total losses here						25	( )
26 Total rental real estate and royalty income or (loss). Combine lines 24 and 25. Enter the result here. If Parts II, III, IV, and line 39 on page 2 do not apply to you, also enter this amount on Form 1040, line 17. Otherwise, include this amount in the total on line 40 on page 2						26	

For Paperwork Reduction Act Notice, see Form 1040 instructions.   Cat. No. 11344L   Schedule E (Form 1040) 1999

Name(s) shown on return. Do not enter name and social security number if shown on other side.	**Your social security number**

Note: *If you report amounts from farming or fishing on Schedule E, you must enter your gross income from those activities on line 41 below. Real estate professionals must complete line 42 below.*

Part II   **Income or Loss From Partnerships and S Corporations**   Note: *If you report a loss from an at-risk activity, you MUST check either column (e) or (f) on line 27 to describe your investment in the activity. See page E-5. If you check column (f), you must attach **Form 6198.***

27	(a) Name	(b) Enter P for partnership; S for S corporation	(c) Check if foreign partnership	(d) Employer identification number	**Investment At Risk?**	
					(e) All is at risk	(f) Some is not at risk
A						
B						
C						
D						
E						

	Passive Income and Loss		Nonpassive Income and Loss		
	(g) Passive loss allowed (attach **Form 8582** if required)	(h) Passive income from **Schedule K-1**	(i) Nonpassive loss from **Schedule K-1**	(j) Section 179 expense deduction from **Form 4562**	(k) Nonpassive income from **Schedule K-1**
A					
B					
C					
D					
E					
28a Totals					
b Totals					

29	Add columns (h) and (k) of line 28a	29	
30	Add columns (g), (i), and (j) of line 28b	30	( )
31	Total partnership and S corporation income or (loss). Combine lines 29 and 30. Enter the result here and include in the total on line 40 below	31	

Part III   **Income or Loss From Estates and Trusts**

32	(a) Name	(b) Employer identification number
A		
B		

	Passive Income and Loss		Nonpassive Income and Loss	
	(c) Passive deduction or loss allowed (attach **Form 8582** if required)	(d) Passive income from **Schedule K-1**	(e) Deduction or loss from **Schedule K-1**	(f) Other income from **Schedule K-1**
A				
B				
33a Totals				
b Totals				

34	Add columns (d) and (f) of line 33a	34	
35	Add columns (c) and (e) of line 33b	35	( )
36	Total estate and trust income or (loss). Combine lines 34 and 35. Enter the result here and include in the total on line 40 below	36	

Part IV   **Income or Loss From Real Estate Mortgage Investment Conduits (REMICs)—Residual Holder**

37	(a) Name	(b) Employer identification number	(c) Excess inclusion from **Schedules Q**, line 2c (see page E-6)	(d) Taxable income (net loss) from **Schedules Q**, line 1b	(e) Income from **Schedules Q**, line 3b

38	Combine columns (d) and (e) only. Enter the result here and include in the total on line 40 below	38	

Part V   **Summary**

39	Net farm rental income or (loss) from **Form 4835**. Also, complete line 41 below	39	
40	TOTAL income or (loss). Combine lines 26, 31, 36, 38, and 39. Enter the result here and on Form 1040, line 17 ▶	40	

41	**Reconciliation of Farming and Fishing Income.** Enter your **gross** farming and fishing income reported on Form 4835, line 7; Schedule K-1 (Form 1065), line 15b; Schedule K-1 (Form 1120S), line 23; and Schedule K-1 (Form 1041), line 14 (see page E-6)	41	
42	**Reconciliation for Real Estate Professionals.** If you were a real estate professional (see page E-4), enter the net income or (loss) you reported anywhere on Form 1040 from all rental real estate activities in which you materially participated under the passive activity loss rules . . .	42	

⊛   **Schedule E (Form 1040) 1999**

Earned Income Credit
Qualifying Child Information

*Complete and attach to Form 1040A or 1040
only if you have a qualifying child.*

OMB No. 1545-0074

19**99**

Attachment
Sequence No. **43**

Name(s) shown on return | Your social security number

Before you begin: See the instructions for Form 1040A, lines 37a and 37b, or Form 1040, lines 59a and 59b, to make sure that (1) you can take the EIC and (2) you have a qualifying child.

- If you take the EIC even though you are not eligible, you may not be allowed to take the credit for up to 10 years. See back of schedule for details.
- It will take us longer to process your return and issue your refund if you do not fill in all lines that apply for each qualifying child.
- If you do not enter the child's correct social security number on line 4, at the time we process your return, we may reduce or disallow your EIC.

Qualifying Child Information | Child 1 | Child 2

		Child 1	Child 2
1	**Child's name** If you have more than two qualifying children, you only have to list two to get the maximum credit.	First name ____ Last name ____	First name ____ Last name ____
2	**Child's year of birth**	Year ___ ___ ___ ___ *If born after 1980, skip lines 3a and 3b; go to line 4.*	Year ___ ___ ___ ___ *If born after 1980, skip lines 3a and 3b; go to line 4.*
3	**If the child was born before 1981—**		
a	Was the child under age 24 at the end of 1999 and a student?	☐ **Yes.** *Go to line 4.* ☐ **No.** *Continue*	☐ **Yes.** *Go to line 4.* ☐ **No.** *Continue*
b	Was the child permanently and totally disabled during any part of 1999?	☐ **Yes.** *Continue* ☐ **No.** The child is not a qualifying child.	☐ **Yes.** *Continue* ☐ **No.** The child is not a qualifying child.
4	**Child's social security number (SSN)** The child must have an SSN as defined on page 42 of the Form 1040A instructions or page 41 of the Form 1040 instructions unless the child was born and died in 1999. If your child was born and died in 1999 and did not have an SSN, enter "Died" on this line and attach a copy of the child's birth certificate.		
5	**Child's relationship to you** (for example, son, daughter, grandchild, foster child, etc.)		
6	**Number of months child lived with you in the United States during 1999** • If the child lived with you for more than half of 1999 but less than 7 months, enter "7". • If the child was born or died in 1999 and your home was the child's home for the entire time he or she was alive during 1999, enter "12".	_____ months *Do not enter more than 12 months.*	_____ months *Do not enter more than 12 months.*

Do you want part of the EIC added to your take-home pay in 2000? To see if you qualify, get Form W-5 from your employer or by calling the IRS at 1-800-TAX-FORM (1-800-829-3676).

For Paperwork Reduction Act Notice, see Form 1040A or 1040 instructions.

Cat. No. 13339M

Schedule EIC (Form 1040A or 1040) 1999

Purpose of Schedule

The purpose of this schedule is to give the IRS information about your qualifying child after you have figured your earned income credit.

To figure the amount of your credit, or to have the IRS figure it for you, see the instructions for Form 1040A, lines 37a and 37b, or Form 1040, lines 59a and 59b.

Taking the EIC When Not Eligible. If you take the EIC even though you are not eligible and it is determined that your error is due to reckless or intentional disregard of the EIC rules, you will not be allowed to take the credit for 2 years even if you are otherwise eligible to do so. If you fraudulently take the EIC, you will not be allowed to take the credit for 10 years. You may also have to pay penalties.

Qualifying Child

A qualifying child is a child who is your . . .

Son   Grandchild
Daughter   Stepchild
Adopted child   Foster child*

* A foster child is any child you cared for as your own child.

was at the end of 1999 . . .

Under age 19
OR
Under age 24 and a student
OR
Any age and permanently and totally disabled

who . . .

Lived with you in the United States for more than half of 1999 or, if a foster child, for all of 1999.
If the child did not live with you for the required time, see Exception to "Time Lived With You" Condition on page 42 of the Form 1040A instructions or page 41 of the Form 1040 instructions.

Note. If the child was married or meets the conditions to be a qualifying child of another person (other than your spouse if filing a joint return), special rules apply. For details, see page 42 of the Form 1040A instructions or page 41 of the Form 1040 instructions.

 Printed on recycled paper

Profit or Loss From Farming

► Attach to Form 1040, Form 1041, Form 1065, or Form 1065-B.

► See Instructions for Schedule F (Form 1040).

OMB No. 1545-0074

1999

Attachment
Sequence No. **14**

Name of proprietor

Social security number (SSN)

A Principal product. Describe in one or two words your principal crop or activity for the current tax year.

B Enter code from Part IV ►

D Employer ID number (EIN), if any

C Accounting method:　　(1) ☐ Cash　　(2) ☐ Accrual

E Did you "materially participate" in the operation of this business during 1999? If "No," see page F-2 for limit on passive losses.　☐ Yes　☐ No

Part I　Farm Income—Cash Method. Complete Parts I and II (Accrual method taxpayers complete Parts II and III, and line 11 of Part I.)
　　Do not include sales of livestock held for draft, breeding, sport, or dairy purposes; report these sales on Form 4797.

1	Sales of livestock and other items you bought for resale	1	
2	Cost or other basis of livestock and other items reported on line 1 . . .	2	
3	Subtract line 2 from line 1	3	
4	Sales of livestock, produce, grains, and other products you raised	4	
5a	Total cooperative distributions (Form(s) 1099-PATR)　5a	5b Taxable amount	5b
6a	Agricultural program payments (see page F-2)　6a	6b Taxable amount	6b
7	Commodity Credit Corporation (CCC) loans (see page F-3):		
a	CCC loans reported under election		7a
b	CCC loans forfeited . . . . .　7b	7c Taxable amount	7c
8	Crop insurance proceeds and certain disaster payments (see page F-3):		
a	Amount received in 1999 . . . . . .　8a	8b Taxable amount	8b
c	If election to defer to 2000 is attached, check here ► ☐　8d Amount deferred from 1998 . .		8d
9	Custom hire (machine work) income		9
10	Other income, including Federal and state gasoline or fuel tax credit or refund (see page F-3)		10
11	**Gross income.** Add amounts in the right column for lines 3 through 10. If accrual method taxpayer, enter the amount from page 2, line 51 . . . . ►		11

Part II　Farm Expenses—Cash and Accrual Method. **Do not** include personal or living expenses such as taxes, insurance, repairs, etc., on your home.

12	Car and truck expenses (see page F-4—also attach **Form 4562**) .	12		25	Pension and profit-sharing plans	25	
13	Chemicals	13		26	Rent or lease (see page F-5):		
14	Conservation expenses (see page F-4)	14		a	Vehicles, machinery, and equipment . .	26a	
15	Custom hire (machine work)	15		b	Other (land, animals, etc.) . .	26b	
16	Depreciation and section 179 expense deduction not claimed elsewhere (see page F-4) . .	16		27	Repairs and maintenance . .	27	
				28	Seeds and plants purchased .	28	
				29	Storage and warehousing . .	29	
17	Employee benefit programs other than on line 25 . . .	17		30	Supplies purchased	30	
18	Feed purchased	18		31	Taxes	31	
19	Fertilizers and lime	19		32	Utilities	32	
20	Freight and trucking	20		33	Veterinary, breeding, and medicine .	33	
21	Gasoline, fuel, and oil . . .	21		34	Other expenses (specify):		
22	Insurance (other than health) .	22		a	....	34a	
23	Interest:			b	....	34b	
a	Mortgage (paid to banks, etc.) .	23a		c	....	34c	
b	Other	23b		d	....	34d	
24	Labor hired (less employment credits)	24		e	....	34e	
				f		34f	

35	**Total expenses.** Add lines 12 through 34f . . . . ►	35	
36	**Net farm profit or (loss).** Subtract line 35 from line 11. If a profit, enter on **Form 1040, line 18,** and ALSO on **Schedule SE, line 1.** If a loss, you MUST go on to line 37 (estates, trusts, and partnerships, see page F-6) . .	36	

37	If you have a loss, you MUST check the box that describes your investment in this activity (see page F-6). • If you checked 37a, enter the loss on **Form 1040, line 18,** and ALSO on **Schedule SE, line 1.** • If you checked 37b, you MUST attach **Form 6198.**	37a ☐ All investment is at risk. 37b ☐ Some investment is not at risk.

For Paperwork Reduction Act Notice, see Form 1040 instructions.　　　Cat. No. 11346H　　　Schedule F (Form 1040) 1999

Part III Farm Income—Accrual Method (see page F-6)

Do not include sales of livestock held for draft, breeding, sport, or dairy purposes; report these sales on Form 4797 and do not include this livestock on line 46 below.

38	Sales of livestock, produce, grains, and other products during the year		**38**	
39a	Total cooperative distributions (Form(s) 1099-PATR)	**39a**	**39b** Taxable amount	**39b**
40a	Agricultural program payments	**40a**	**40b** Taxable amount	**40b**
41	Commodity Credit Corporation (CCC) loans:			
a	CCC loans reported under election			**41a**
b	CCC loans forfeited	**41b**	**41c** Taxable amount	**41c**
42	Crop insurance proceeds			**42**
43	Custom hire (machine work) income			**43**
44	Other income, including Federal and state gasoline or fuel tax credit or refund			**44**
45	Add amounts in the right column for lines 38 through 44			**45**
46	Inventory of livestock, produce, grains, and other products at beginning of the year	**46**		
47	Cost of livestock, produce, grains, and other products purchased during the year	**47**		
48	Add lines 46 and 47	**48**		
49	Inventory of livestock, produce, grains, and other products at end of year	**49**		
50	Cost of livestock, produce, grains, and other products sold. Subtract line 49 from line 48*			**50**
51	**Gross income.** Subtract line 50 from line 45. Enter the result here and on page 1, line 11 ▶			**51**

*If you use the unit-livestock-price method or the farm-price method of valuing inventory and the amount on line 49 is larger than the amount on line 48, subtract line 48 from line 49. Enter the result on line 50. Add lines 45 and 50. Enter the total on line 51.

Part IV Principal Agricultural Activity Codes

Caution. File **Schedule C** (Form 1040), Profit or Loss From Business, or **Schedule C-EZ** (Form 1040), Net Profit From Business, instead of Schedule F if:

• Your principal source of income is from providing agricultural services such as soil preparation, veterinary, farm labor, horticultural, or management for a fee or on a contract basis, or

• You are engaged in the business of breeding, raising, and caring for dogs, cats, or other pet animals.

These codes for the Principal Agricultural Activity classify farms by the type of activity they are engaged in to facilitate the administration of the Internal Revenue Code. These six-digit codes are based on the North American Industry Classification System (NAICS).

Select one of the following codes and enter the six-digit number on page 1, line B:

Crop Production

111100	Oilseed and grain farming
111210	Vegetable and melon farming
111300	Fruit and tree nut farming
111400	Greenhouse, nursery, and floriculture production
111900	Other crop farming

Animal Production

112111	Beef cattle ranching and farming
112112	Cattle feedlots
112120	Dairy cattle and milk production
112210	Hog and pig farming
112300	Poultry and egg production
112400	Sheep and goat farming
112510	Animal aquaculture
112900	Other animal production

Forestry and Logging

113000	Forestry and logging (including forest nurseries and timber tracts)

SCHEDULE H (Form 1040)	Household Employment Taxes	OMB No. 1545-0074

SCHEDULE H (Form 1040)

Department of the Treasury
Internal Revenue Service (99)

Household Employment Taxes

(For Social Security, Medicare, Withheld Income, and Federal Unemployment (FUTA) Taxes)

▶ **Attach to Form 1040, 1040NR, 1040NR-EZ, 1040-SS, or 1041.**

▶ **See separate instructions.**

OMB No. 1545-0074

1999

Attachment
Sequence No. **44**

Name of employer

Social security number

Employer identification number

A Did you pay **any one** household employee cash wages of $1,100 or more in 1999? (If any household employee was your spouse, your child under age 21, your parent, or anyone under age 18, see the line A instructions on page 3 before you answer this question.)

☐ **Yes.** Skip lines B and C and go to line 1.
☐ **No.** Go to line B.

B Did you withhold Federal income tax during 1999 for any household employee?

☐ **Yes.** Skip line C and go to line 5.
☐ **No.** Go to line C.

C Did you pay **total** cash wages of $1,000 or more in **any** calendar **quarter** of 1998 or 1999 to household employees? (**Do not** count cash wages paid in 1998 or 1999 to your spouse, your child under age 21, or your parent.)

☐ **No.** **Stop.** Do not file this schedule.
☐ **Yes.** Skip lines 1-9 and go to line 10 on the back.

Part I   Social Security, Medicare, and Income Taxes

1 Total cash wages subject to social security taxes (see page 3) . .	**1**	
2 Social security taxes. Multiply line 1 by 12.4% (.124)	**2**	
3 Total cash wages subject to Medicare taxes (see page 3)	**3**	
4 Medicare taxes. Multiply line 3 by 2.9% (.029)	**4**	
5 Federal income tax withheld, if any	**5**	
6 **Total social security, Medicare, and income taxes** (add lines 2, 4, and 5)	**6**	
7 Advance earned income credit (EIC) payments, if any	**7**	
8 **Net taxes** (subtract line 7 from line 6)	**8**	

9 Did you pay **total** cash wages of $1,000 or more in **any** calendar **quarter** of 1998 or 1999 to household employees? (**Do not** count cash wages paid in 1998 or 1999 to your spouse, your child under age 21, or your parent.)

☐ **No.** **Stop.** Enter the amount from line 8 above on Form 1040, line 55. If you are not required to file Form 1040, see the line 9 instructions on page 4.

☐ **Yes.** Go to line 10 on the back.

For Paperwork Reduction Act Notice, see Form 1040 instructions.   Cat. No. 12187K   **Schedule H (Form 1040) 1999**

Part II   Federal Unemployment (FUTA) Tax

		Yes	No
10	Did you pay unemployment contributions to only one state? **10**		
11	Did you pay all state unemployment contributions for 1999 by April 17, 2000? Fiscal year filers, see page 4 **11**		
12	Were all wages that are taxable for FUTA tax also taxable for your state's unemployment tax? **12**		

Next: If you checked the **"Yes"** box on **all** the lines above, complete Section A.

If you checked the **"No"** box on **any** of the lines above, skip Section A and complete Section B.

Section A

13	Name of the state where you paid unemployment contributions ▶	
14	State reporting number as shown on state unemployment tax return ▶	
15	Contributions paid to your state unemployment fund (see page 4) . **15**	
16	Total cash wages subject to FUTA tax (see page 4) **16**	
17	**FUTA tax.** Multiply line 16 by .008. Enter the result here, skip Section B, and go to line 26 . . **17**	

Section B

18 Complete all columns below that apply (if you need more space, see page 4):

(a) Name of state	(b) State reporting number as shown on state unemployment tax return	(c) Taxable wages (as defined in state act)	(d) State experience rate period		(e) State experience rate	(f) Multiply col. (c) by .054	(g) Multiply col. (c) by col. (e)	(h) Subtract col. (g) from col. (f). If zero or less, enter -0-.	(i) Contributions paid to state unemployment fund
			From	To					

19	Totals **19**		
20	Add columns (h) and (i) of line 19 . . . . **20**		
21	Total cash wages subject to FUTA tax (see the line 16 instructions on page 4) **21**		
22	Multiply line 21 by 6.2% (.062) **22**		
23	Multiply line 21 by 5.4% (.054) **23**		
24	Enter the **smaller** of line 20 or line 23 . . . . **24**		
25	**FUTA tax.** Subtract line 24 from line 22. Enter the result here and go to line 26 . . . . . . **25**		

Part III   Total Household Employment Taxes

26	Enter the amount from line 8 . . . . **26**		
27	Add line 17 (or line 25) and line 26 . . . . **27**		

28   Are you required to file Form 1040?

☐ **Yes.**   **Stop.** Enter the amount from line 27 above on Form 1040, line 55. **Do not** complete Part IV below.

☐ **No.**   You may have to complete Part IV. See page 4 for details.

Part IV   Address and Signature—Complete this part **only** if required. See the line 28 instructions on page 4.

Address (number and street) or P.O. box if mail is not delivered to street address	Apt., room, or suite no.

City, town or post office, state, and ZIP code

Under penalties of perjury, I declare that I have examined this schedule, including accompanying statements, and to the best of my knowledge and belief, it is true, correct, and complete. No part of any payment made to a state unemployment fund claimed as a credit was, or is to be, deducted from the payments to employees.

▶ _____   ▶ _____
   Employer's signature   Date

SCHEDULE J
(Form 1040)

Department of the Treasury
Internal Revenue Service   (99)

Farm Income Averaging

▶ **Attach to Form 1040.**

▶ **See Instructions for Schedule J (Form 1040).**

OMB No. 1545-0074

1999

Attachment
Sequence No. **20**

Name(s) shown on Form 1040

Social security number (SSN)

1	Enter your taxable income from Form 1040, line 39	1
2	Enter your **elected farm income** (see page J-1)	2
3	Subtract line 2 from line 1. If zero or less, enter -0-	3
4	Figure the tax on the amount on line 3. Use the **1999** Tax Table, Tax Rate Schedules, Capital Gain Tax Worksheet, or Schedule D, whichever applies	4

5	If you used Schedule J to figure your tax for 1998, enter the amount from line 11 of that Schedule J. Otherwise, enter the taxable income (but not less than zero) from your **1996** Form 1040, line 37; Form 1040A, line 22; or Form 1040EZ, line 6	5	
6	Divide the amount on **line 2** by 3.0	6	
7	Add lines 5 and 6	7	
8	Figure the tax on the amount on line 7. Use the **1996** Tax Rate Schedules or Capital Gain Tax Worksheet, whichever applies (see page J-2)		8

9	If you used Schedule J to figure your tax for 1998, enter the amount from line 15 of that Schedule J. Otherwise, enter the taxable income (but not less than zero) from your **1997** Form 1040, line 38; Form 1040A, line 22; or Form 1040EZ, line 6	9	
10	Enter the amount from line 6	10	
11	Add lines 9 and 10	11	
12	Figure the tax on the amount on line 11. Use the **1997** Tax Rate Schedules or Schedule D, whichever applies (see page J-3)		12

13	If you used Schedule J to figure your tax for 1998, enter the amount from line 3 of that Schedule J. Otherwise, enter the taxable income (but not less than zero) from your **1998** Form 1040, line 39; Form 1040A, line 24; or Form 1040EZ, line 6	13	
14	Enter the amount from line 6	14	
15	Add lines 13 and 14	15	
16	Figure the tax on the amount on line 15. Use the **1998** Tax Rate Schedules or Schedule D, whichever applies (see page J-4)		16

17	Add lines 4, 8, 12, and 16	17

18	If you used Schedule J to figure your tax for 1998, enter the amount from line 12 of that Schedule J. Otherwise, enter the tax from your **1996** Form 1040, line 38*; Form 1040A, line 23; or Form 1040EZ, line 10	18	
19	If you used Schedule J to figure your tax for 1998, enter the amount from line 16 of that Schedule J. Otherwise, enter the tax from your **1997** Form 1040, line 39*; Form 1040A, line 23; or Form 1040EZ, line 10	19	
20	If you used Schedule J to figure your tax for 1998, enter the amount from line 4 of that Schedule J. Otherwise, enter the tax from your **1998** Form 1040, line 40*; Form 1040A, line 25; or Form 1040EZ, line 10	20	

*Caution. Do not include any amount from Form 4972 or 8814.

21	Add lines 18 through 20	21
22	Subtract line 21 from line 17. Also include this amount on Form 1040, line 40	22
	Caution. Your tax may be less if you figure it using the 1999 Tax Table, Tax Rate Schedules, Capital Gain Tax Worksheet, or Schedule D. Attach Schedule J only if you are using it to figure your tax.	

Self-Employment Tax

▶ See Instructions for Schedule SE (Form 1040).

▶ Attach to Form 1040.

OMB No. 1545-0074

1999

Attachment
Sequence No. **17**

Name of person with **self-employment** income (as shown on Form 1040)	Social security number of person with **self-employment** income ▶

Who Must File Schedule SE

You must file Schedule SE if:

- You had net earnings from self-employment from **other than** church employee income (line 4 of Short Schedule SE or line 4c of Long Schedule SE) of $400 or more, **OR**

- You had church employee income of $108.28 or more. Income from services you performed as a minister or a member of a religious order **is not** church employee income. See page SE-1.

Note: *Even if you had a loss or a small amount of income from self-employment, it may be to your benefit to file Schedule SE and use either "optional method" in Part II of Long Schedule SE. See page SE-3.*

Exception. If your only self-employment income was from earnings as a minister, member of a religious order, or Christian Science practitioner **and** you filed Form 4361 and received IRS approval not to be taxed on those earnings, **do not** file Schedule SE. Instead, write "Exempt–Form 4361" on Form 1040, line 50.

May I Use Short Schedule SE or MUST I Use Long Schedule SE?

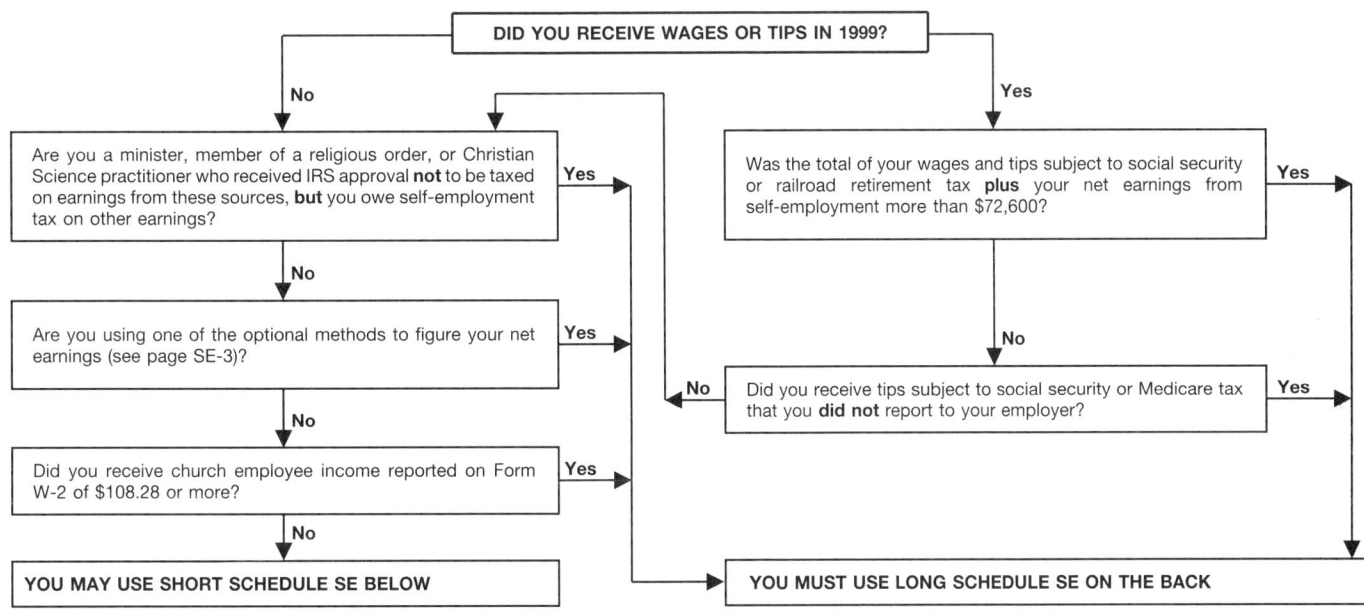

Section A—Short Schedule SE. Caution: *Read above to see if you can use Short Schedule SE.*

1	Net farm profit or (loss) from Schedule F, line 36, and farm partnerships, Schedule K-1 (Form 1065), line 15a	**1**	
2	Net profit or (loss) from Schedule C, line 31; Schedule C-EZ, line 3; Schedule K-1 (Form 1065), line 15a (other than farming); and Schedule K-1 (Form 1065-B), box 9. Ministers and members of religious orders, see page SE-1 for amounts to report on this line. See page SE-2 for other income to report	**2**	
3	Combine lines 1 and 2	**3**	
4	**Net earnings from self-employment.** Multiply line 3 by 92.35% (.9235). If less than $400, **do not** file this schedule; you do not owe self-employment tax . . . . ▶	**4**	
5	**Self-employment tax.** If the amount on line 4 is: • $72,600 or less, multiply line 4 by 15.3% (.153). Enter the result here and on **Form 1040, line 50.** • More than $72,600, multiply line 4 by 2.9% (.029). Then, add $9,002.40 to the result. Enter the total here and on **Form 1040, line 50.**	**5**	
6	**Deduction for one-half of self-employment tax.** Multiply line 5 by 50% (.5). Enter the result here and on **Form 1040, line 27** **6**		

For Paperwork Reduction Act Notice, see Form 1040 instructions.   Cat. No. 11358Z   Schedule SE (Form 1040) 1999

Name of person with **self-employment** income (as shown on Form 1040)	Social security number of person with **self-employment** income ▶		

Section B—Long Schedule SE

Part I   Self-Employment Tax

Note: *If your only income subject to self-employment tax is* **church employee income,** *skip lines 1 through 4b. Enter -0- on line 4c and go to line 5a. Income from services you performed as a minister or a member of a religious order* **is not** *church employee income. See page SE-1.*

A   If you are a minister, member of a religious order, or Christian Science practitioner **and** you filed Form 4361, but you had $400 or more of **other** net earnings from self-employment, check here and continue with Part I . . . . . . ▶ ☐

1	Net farm profit or (loss) from Schedule F, line 36, and farm partnerships, Schedule K-1 (Form 1065), line 15a. **Note:** *Skip this line if you use the farm optional method. See page SE-3* . .	**1**
2	Net profit or (loss) from Schedule C, line 31; Schedule C-EZ, line 3; Schedule K-1 (Form 1065), line 15a (other than farming); and Schedule K-1 (Form 1065-B), box 9. Ministers and members of religious orders, see page SE-1 for amounts to report on this line. See page SE-2 for other income to report. **Note:** *Skip this line if you use the nonfarm optional method. See page SE-3* .	**2**
3	Combine lines 1 and 2	**3**
4a	If line 3 is more than zero, multiply line 3 by 92.35% (.9235). Otherwise, enter amount from line 3	**4a**
b	If you elected one or both of the optional methods, enter the total of lines 15 and 17 here . .	**4b**
c	Combine lines 4a and 4b. If less than $400, **do not** file this schedule; you do not owe self-employment tax. **Exception.** If less than $400 and you had **church employee income,** enter -0- and continue ▶	**4c**
5a	Enter your **church employee income** from Form W-2. **Caution:** *See page SE-1 for definition of church employee income*	**5a**		
b	Multiply line 5a by 92.35% (.9235). If less than $100, enter -0-	**5b**
6	**Net earnings from self-employment.** Add lines 4c and 5b .	**6**
7	Maximum amount of combined wages and self-employment earnings subject to social security tax or the 6.2% portion of the 7.65% railroad retirement (tier 1) tax for 1999	**7**	72,600	00
8a	Total social security wages and tips (total of boxes 3 and 7 on Form(s) W-2) and railroad retirement (tier 1) compensation	**8a**		
b	Unreported tips subject to social security tax (from Form 4137, line 9)	**8b**		
c	Add lines 8a and 8b	**8c**
9	Subtract line 8c from line 7. If zero or less, enter -0- here and on line 10 and go to line 11 . ▶	**9**
10	Multiply the **smaller** of line 6 or line 9 by 12.4% (.124)	**10**
11	Multiply line 6 by 2.9% (.029)	**11**
12	**Self-employment tax.** Add lines 10 and 11. Enter here and on **Form 1040, line 50** . . ▶	**12**
13	**Deduction for one-half of self-employment tax.** Multiply line 12 by 50% (.5). Enter the result here and on **Form 1040, line 27**	**13**		

Part II   Optional Methods To Figure Net Earnings (See page SE-3.)

Farm Optional Method. You may use this method **only** if:
- Your gross farm income[1] was not more than $2,400, **or**
- Your net farm profits[2] were less than $1,733.

14	Maximum income for optional methods	**14**	1,600	00
15	Enter the **smaller** of: two-thirds (⅔) of gross farm income[1] (not less than zero) **or** $1,600. Also include this amount on line 4b above	**15**

Nonfarm Optional Method. You may use this method **only** if:
- Your net nonfarm profits[3] were less than $1,733 and also less than 72.189% of your gross nonfarm income,[4] **and**
- You had net earnings from self-employment of at least $400 in 2 of the prior 3 years.

Caution: *You may use this method no more than five times.*

16	Subtract line 15 from line 14	**16**
17	Enter the **smaller** of: two-thirds (⅔) of gross nonfarm income[4] (not less than zero) **or** the amount on line 16. Also include this amount on line 4b above	**17**

[1]From Sch. F, line 11, and Sch. K-1 (Form 1065), line 15b.
[2]From Sch. F, line 36, and Sch. K-1 (Form 1065), line 15a.
[3]From Sch. C, line 31; Sch. C-EZ, line 3; Sch. K-1 (Form 1065), line 15a; and Sch. K-1 (Form 1065-B), box 9.
[4]From Sch. C, line 7; Sch. C-EZ, line 1; Sch. K-1 (Form 1065), line 15c; and Sch. K-1 (Form 1065-B), box 9.

Schedule SE (Form 1040) 1999

1999 Form 1040-V

What Is Form 1040-V and Do You Have To Use It?

It is a statement you send with your check or money order for any balance due on line 68 of your **1999 Form 1040.** Using Form 1040-V allows us to process your payment more accurately and efficiently. We strongly encourage you to use Form 1040-V, but there is no penalty if you do not do so.

How To Fill In Form 1040-V

Box 1. Enter the amount you are paying by check or money order.

Box 2. Enter the first four letters of your last name. See examples below.

Name	Enter	Name	Enter
John Brown . . .	BROW	Nancy McCarthy . .	MCCA
Juan DeJesus . . .	DEJE	Helen O'Neill . . .	ONEI
Joan A. Lee . . .	LEE	Pedro Torres-Lopez .	TORR

Boxes 3 and 4. Enter your social security number (SSN) in box 3. If you are filing a joint return, enter in box 3 the SSN shown first on your return and in box 4 the SSN shown second.

Box 5. Enter your name(s) and address as shown on your return.

How To Prepare Your Payment

● Make your check or money order payable to the **"United States Treasury." Do not** send cash.

● Make sure your name and address appear on your check or money order.

● Enter "1999 Form 1040," your daytime telephone number, and your SSN on your check or money order. If you are filing a joint return, enter the SSN shown **first** on your return.

● To help us process your payment, enter the amount on the right side of your check like this: $ XXX.XX. **Do not** use dashes or lines (for example, do not enter "$ XXX—" or "$ XXX $\frac{XX}{100}$").

How To Send In Your Return, Payment, and Form 1040-V

● Detach Form 1040-V along the dotted line.

● **Do not** staple or otherwise attach your payment or Form 1040-V to your return or to each other. Instead, just put them loose in the envelope.

● If an envelope came with your tax package, please use it to mail your 1999 tax return, payment, and Form 1040-V.

● If you do not have that envelope or you moved or used a paid preparer, mail your tax return, payment, and Form 1040-V to the Internal Revenue Service at the address shown on the back that applies to you.

Note. If you filed electronically, send your check or money order and Form 1040-V to the applicable address shown on the back.

Paperwork Reduction Act Notice. We ask for the information on Form 1040-V to help us carry out the Internal Revenue laws of the United States. If you use Form 1040-V, you must provide the requested information. Your cooperation will help us ensure that we are collecting the right amount of tax.

You are not required to provide the information requested on a form that is subject to the Paperwork Reduction Act unless the form displays a valid OMB control number. Books or records relating to a form or its instructions must be retained as long as their contents may become material in the administration of any Internal Revenue law. Generally, tax returns and return information are confidential, as required by Internal Revenue Code section 6103.

The time needed to complete and mail Form 1040-V will vary depending on individual circumstances. The estimated average time is 19 minutes. If you have comments about the accuracy of this time estimate or suggestions for making Form 1040-V simpler, we would be happy to hear from you. See the Instructions for Form 1040.

Cat. No. 20975C   ▼ **DETACH HERE AND MAIL WITH YOUR PAYMENT** ▼   Form **1040-V** (1999)

Form 1040-V

Department of the Treasury
Internal Revenue Service (99)

Payment Voucher

► **Do not staple or attach this voucher to your payment.**

OMB No. 1545-0074

1999

1 Enter the amount you are paying by check or money order	2 Enter the first four letters of your last name	3 Enter your social security number
► $.		
4 If a joint return, enter the SSN shown second on that return	5 Enter your name(s)	
	Enter your address	
	Enter your city, state, and ZIP code	

Cat. No. 20975C

IF you live in . . .	THEN use this address if you:		
	Prepared your own return . . .	**Used a paid preparer . . .**	**Filed electronically . . .**
Florida, South Carolina	Atlanta, GA 39901-0002	P.O. Box 105093 Atlanta, GA 30348-5093	P.O. Box 6223 Chicago, IL 60680-6223
Georgia	Atlanta, GA 39901-0002	P.O. Box 105093 Atlanta, GA 30348-5093	P.O. Box 1214 Charlotte, NC 28201-1214
New Jersey, New York *(New York City and counties of Nassau, Rockland, Suffolk, and Westchester)*	Holtsville, NY 00501-0002	P.O. Box 1187 Newark, NJ 07101-1187	P.O. Box 371361 Pittsburgh, PA 15250-7361
New York *(all other counties)*, Connecticut, Maine, Massachusetts, New Hampshire, Rhode Island, Vermont	Andover, MA 05501-0002	P.O. Box 371361 Pittsburgh, PA 15250-7361	P.O. Box 371361 Pittsburgh, PA 15250-7361
Illinois, Iowa, Minnesota, Missouri, Wisconsin	Kansas City, MO 64999-0002	P.O. Box 970011 St. Louis, MO 63197-0011	P.O. Box 970016 St. Louis, MO 63197-0016
Delaware, District of Columbia, Maryland, Pennsylvania, Virginia	Philadelphia, PA 19255-0002	P.O. Box 8530 Philadelphia, PA 19162-8530	P.O. Box 371361 Pittsburgh, PA 15250-7361
Indiana, Kentucky, Michigan, Ohio, West Virginia	Cincinnati, OH 45999-0002	P.O. Box 6223 Chicago, IL 60680-6223	P.O. Box 6223 Chicago, IL 60680-6223
Kansas, New Mexico, Oklahoma, Texas	Austin, TX 73301-0002	P.O. Box 970016 St. Louis, MO 63197-0016	P.O. Box 970016 St. Louis, MO 63197-0016
Alaska, Arizona, California *(counties of Alpine, Amador, Butte, Calaveras, Colusa, Contra Costa, Del Norte, El Dorado, Glenn, Humboldt, Lake, Lassen, Marin, Mendocino, Modoc, Napa, Nevada, Placer, Plumas, Sacramento, San Joaquin, Shasta, Sierra, Siskiyou, Solano, Sonoma, Sutter, Tehama, Trinity, Yolo, and Yuba)*, Colorado, Idaho, Montana, Nebraska, Nevada, North Dakota, Oregon, South Dakota, Utah, Washington, Wyoming	Ogden, UT 84201-0002	P.O. Box 7704 San Francisco, CA 94120-7704	P.O. Box 7704 San Francisco, CA 94120-7704
California *(all other counties)*, Hawaii	Fresno, CA 93888-0002	P.O. Box 60000 Los Angeles, CA 90060-6000	P.O. Box 7704 San Francisco, CA 94120-7704
Alabama, Arkansas, Louisiana, Mississippi, North Carolina, Tennessee	Memphis, TN 37501-0002	P.O. Box 1214 Charlotte, NC 28201-1214	P.O. Box 1214 Charlotte, NC 28201-1214
All APO and FPO addresses, American Samoa, nonpermanent residents of Guam or the Virgin Islands*, Puerto Rico *(or if excluding income under section 933)*, a foreign country *(or if a dual-status alien)*: U.S. citizens or those filing Form 2555, Form 2555-EZ, or Form 4563	Philadelphia, PA 19255-0215	P.O. Box 7328 Philadelphia, PA 19162-7328	P.O. Box 371361 Pittsburgh, PA 15250-7361

* Permanent residents of Guam or the Virgin Islands should not use Form 1040-V.

Form 1040X
(Rev. November 1999)

Department of the Treasury—Internal Revenue Service

Amended U.S. Individual Income Tax Return

▶ See separate instructions.

OMB No. 1545-0091

This return is for calendar year ▶ _____, OR fiscal year ended ▶ _____, _____.

Please print or type	Your first name and initial	Last name	Your social security number
	If a joint return, spouse's first name and initial	Last name	Spouse's social security number
	Home address (no. and street) or P.O. box if mail is not delivered to your home	Apt. no.	Telephone number (optional) ( )
	City, town or post office, state, and ZIP code. If you have a foreign address, see page 2 of the instructions.		For Paperwork Reduction Act Notice, see page 6.

A If the name or address shown above is different from that shown on the original return, check here . . . . ▶ ☐

B Has the original return been changed or audited by the IRS or have you been notified that it will be? . . ☐ Yes ☐ No

C Filing status. Be sure to complete this line. **Note.** You cannot change from joint to separate returns after the due date.

On original return ▶ ☐ Single ☐ Married filing joint return ☐ Married filing separate return ☐ Head of household ☐ Qualifying widow(er)

On this return ▶ ☐ Single ☐ Married filing joint return ☐ Married filing separate return ☐ Head of household* ☐ Qualifying widow(er)

* If the qualifying person is a child but not your dependent, see page 2.

USE PART II ON THE BACK TO EXPLAIN ANY CHANGES		**A. Original amount** or as previously adjusted (see page 2)	**B. Net change—** amount of increase or (decrease)— explain in Part II	**C. Correct amount**
Income and Deductions (see pages 2–5)				
1 Adjusted gross income (see page 3)	**1**			
2 Itemized deductions or standard deduction (see page 3). .	**2**			
3 Subtract line 2 from line 1	**3**			
4 Exemptions. If changing, fill in Parts I and II on the back	**4**			
5 Taxable income. Subtract line 4 from line 3	**5**			
6 Tax (see page 4). Method used in col. C_____	**6**			
7 Credits (see page 4)	**7**			
8 Subtract line 7 from line 6. Enter the result but not less than zero .	**8**			
9 Other taxes (see page 4)	**9**			
10 Total tax. Add lines 8 and 9	**10**			
11 Federal income tax withheld and excess social security and RRTA tax withheld. If changing, see page 4	**11**			
12 Estimated tax payments, including amount applied from prior year's return	**12**			
13 Earned income credit	**13**			
14 Additional child tax credit from Form 8812	**14**			
15 Credits from Form 4136 or Form 2439	**15**			

16 Amount paid with request for extension of time to file (see page 4) **16**

17 Amount of tax paid with original return plus additional tax paid after it was filed **17**

18 Total payments. Add lines 11 through 17 in column C **18**

Refund or Amount You Owe

19 Overpayment, if any, as shown on original return or as previously adjusted by the IRS . . . **19**

20 Subtract line 19 from line 18 (see page 5). **20**

21 **AMOUNT YOU OWE.** If line 10, column C, is more than line 20, enter the difference and see page 5 **21**

22 If line 10, column C, is less than line 20, enter the difference **22**

23 Amount of line 22 you want **REFUNDED TO YOU** **23**

24 Amount of line 22 you want **APPLIED TO YOUR** **ESTIMATED TAX** | **24** |

Sign Here
Joint return? See page 2. Keep a copy for your records.

Under penalties of perjury, I declare that I have filed an original return and that I have examined this amended return, including accompanying schedules and statements, and to the best of my knowledge and belief, this amended return is true, correct, and complete. Declaration of preparer (other than taxpayer) is based on all information of which the preparer has any knowledge.

▶ _____ Your signature _____ Date

▶ _____ Spouse's signature. If a joint return, BOTH must sign. _____ Date

Paid Preparer's Use Only

Preparer's signature ▶	Date	Check if self-employed ☐	Preparer's SSN or PTIN
Firm's name (or yours if self-employed) and address ▶			EIN
			ZIP code

Cat. No. 11360L

Form **1040X** (Rev. 11-99)

Part I　Exemptions. See Form 1040 or 1040A instructions.

If you are **not changing your exemptions,** do not complete this part.
If claiming **more exemptions,** complete lines 25–31.
If claiming **fewer exemptions,** complete lines 25–30.

		A. Original **number** of exemptions reported or as previously adjusted	B. Net change	C. Correct **number** of exemptions
25	Yourself and spouse **25**			
	Caution. If your parents (or someone else) can claim you as a dependent (even if they chose not to), you cannot claim an exemption for yourself.			
26	Your dependent children who lived with you **26**			
27	Your dependent children who did not live with you due to divorce or separation **27**			
28	Other dependents **28**			
29	Total number of exemptions. Add lines 25 through 28 . . . . . **29**			
30	Multiply the number of exemptions claimed on line 29 by the amount listed below for the tax year you are amending. Enter the result here and on line 4.			

Tax year	Exemption amount	But see the instructions for line 4 on page 3 if the amount on line 1 is over:
1999	$2,750	$94,975
1998	2,700	93,400
1997	2,650	90,900
1996	2,550	88,475

30

31 Dependents (children and other) not claimed on original (or adjusted) return:

Note. For tax years after 1997, do not complete column (e) below. For tax years before 1998, do not complete column (d) below.

(a)　First name　　Last name	(b) Dependent's social security number. If born in the tax year you are amending, see page 5.	(c) Dependent's relationship to you	(d) ✔ if qualifying child for child tax credit (see page 5)	(e) No. of months lived in your home
			☐	
			☐	
			☐	
			☐	
			☐	
			☐	

No. of your children on line 31 who:

- lived with you . . ▶ ☐
- **did not** live with you due to divorce or separation (see page 5) . . ▶ ☐

Dependents on line 31 not entered above ▶ ☐

Part II　Explanation of Changes to Income, Deductions, and Credits

Enter the line number from the front of the form for each item you are changing and give the reason for each change. Attach only the supporting forms and schedules for the items changed. If you do not attach the required information, your Form 1040X may be returned. Be sure to include your name and social security number on any attachments.

If the change relates to a net operating loss carryback or a general business credit carryback, attach the schedule or form that shows the year in which the loss or credit occurred. See page 1 of the instructions. Also, check here . . . . . . ▶ ☐

Part III　Presidential Election Campaign Fund. Checking below will not increase your tax or reduce your refund.

If you did not previously want $3 to go to the fund but now want to, check here . . . . ▶ ☐
If a joint return and your spouse did not previously want $3 to go to the fund but now wants to, check here . . . . . ▶ ☐

✹　　　　　　　　　　　　　　　　　　　　　　　　　　Form **1040X** (Rev. 11-99)

Foreign Tax Credit
(Individual, Estate, Trust, or Nonresident Alien Individual)
▶ Attach to Form 1040, 1040NR, 1041, or 990-T.
▶ See separate instructions.

OMB No. 1545-0121

1999

Attachment
Sequence No. **19**

Name	Identifying number as shown on page 1 of your tax return

Use a separate Form 1116 for each category of income listed below. See **Categories of Income** on page 3 of the instructions. Check only one box on each Form 1116. Report all amounts in U.S. dollars except where specified in Part II below.

- **a** ☐ Passive income
- **b** ☐ High withholding tax interest
- **c** ☐ Financial services income
- **d** ☐ Shipping income
- **e** ☐ Dividends from a DISC or former DISC
- **f** ☐ Certain distributions from a foreign sales corporation (FSC) or former FSC
- **g** ☐ Lump-sum distributions
- **h** ☐ Section 901(j) income
- **i** ☐ Income re-sourced by treaty
- **j** ☐ General limitation income

k Resident of (name of country) ▶

Note: *If you paid taxes to only one foreign country or U.S. possession, use column A in Part I and line A in Part II. If you paid taxes to more than one foreign country or U.S. possession, use a separate column and line for each country or possession.*

Part I — Taxable Income or Loss From Sources Outside the United States (for Category Checked Above)

		Foreign Country or U.S. Possession			Total
		A	**B**	**C**	(Add cols. A, B, and C.)
I	**Enter the name of the foreign country or U.S. possession** . . . . ▶				
1	Gross income from sources within country shown above and of the type checked above. See page 7 of the instructions:				**1**
	Deductions and losses (*Caution: See pages 7 through 9 of the instructions*):				
2	Expenses **definitely related** to the income on line 1 (attach statement)				
3	Pro rata share of other deductions **not definitely related:**				
a	Certain itemized deductions or standard deduction. See instructions				
b	Other deductions (attach statement)				
c	Add lines 3a and 3b				
d	Gross foreign source income. See instructions .				
e	Gross income from all sources. See instructions				
f	Divide line 3d by line 3e. See instructions . .				
g	Multiply line 3c by line 3f				
4	Pro rata share of interest expense. See instructions:				
a	Home mortgage interest (use worksheet on page 9 of the instructions)				
b	Other interest expense				
5	Losses from foreign sources				
6	Add lines 2, 3g, 4a, 4b, and 5				**6**
7	Subtract line 6 from line 1. Enter the result here and on line 14, page 2 . . . . ▶			**7**	

Part II — Foreign Taxes Paid or Accrued (See page 9 of the instructions.)

Country	Credit is claimed for taxes (you must check one)	Foreign taxes paid or accrued								
		In foreign currency				In U.S. dollars				
	(m) ☐ Paid **(n)** ☐ Accrued		Taxes withheld at source on:			**(s)** Other foreign taxes paid or accrued		Taxes withheld at source on:		**(w)** Other foreign taxes paid or accrued	**(x)** Total foreign taxes paid or accrued (add cols. (t) through (w))
	(o) Date paid or accrued	**(p)** Dividends	**(q)** Rents and royalties	**(r)** Interest		**(t)** Dividends	**(u)** Rents and royalties	**(v)** Interest		
A										
B										
C										
8	Add lines A through C, column (x). Enter the total here and on line 9, page 2 . . . . ▶									**8**

For Paperwork Reduction Act Notice, see page 12 of the instructions.   Cat. No. 11440U   Form **1116** (1999)

Part III — Figuring the Credit

9 Enter amount from line 8. These are your total foreign taxes paid or accrued for the category of income checked above Part I . . . . | **9**

10 Carryback or carryover (attach detailed computation) . . . . . | **10**

11 Add lines 9 and 10 . . . . | **11**

12 Reduction in foreign taxes. See page 10 of the instructions . . . | **12**

13 Subtract line 12 from line 11. This is the total amount of foreign taxes available for credit . . . . | **13**

14 Enter amount from line 7. This is your taxable income or (loss) from sources outside the United States (before adjustments) for the category of income checked above Part I. See page 10 of the instructions . . | **14**

15 Adjustments to line 14. See page 10 of the instructions. . . . . | **15**

16 Combine the amounts on lines 14 and 15. This is your net foreign source taxable income. (If the result is zero or less, you have no foreign tax credit for the category of income you checked above Part I. Skip lines 17 through 21.) . . . . | **16**

17 **Individuals:** Enter amount from Form 1040, line 37. If you are a nonresident alien, enter amount from Form 1040NR, line 36. **Estates and trusts:** Enter your taxable income without the deduction for your exemption . . . . | **17**

   Caution: *If you figured your tax using the special rates on capital gains, see page 12 of the instructions.*

18 Divide line 16 by line 17. If line 16 is more than line 17, enter "1". . . . . | **18**

19 **Individuals:** Enter amount from Form 1040, line 40, **less** any amounts on Form 1040, lines 41 through 45, and any mortgage interest credit (from Form 8396) and District of Columbia first-time homebuyer credit (from Form 8859) on line 47. If you are a nonresident alien, enter amount from Form 1040NR, line 39, less any amount on Form 1040NR, lines 40, 41, 42, and any mortgage interest credit (from Form 8396) and District of Columbia first-time homebuyer credit (from Form 8859) on line 44.

   Estates and trusts: Enter amount from Form 1041, Schedule G, line 1c, or Form 990-T, lines 36 and 37 . | **19**

20 Multiply line 19 by line 18 (maximum amount of credit) . . . . | **20**

21 Enter the amount from line 13 or line 20, whichever is **smaller.** If this is the only Form 1116 you are completing, skip lines 22 through 29 and enter this amount on line 30. Otherwise, complete the appropriate line in Part IV. See page 12 of the instructions. . . . . ▶ | **21**

Part IV — Summary of Credits From Separate Parts III (See page 12 of the instructions.)

22 Credit for taxes on passive income . . . . | **22**

23 Credit for taxes on high withholding tax interest . . . . | **23**

24 Credit for taxes on financial services income . . . . | **24**

25 Credit for taxes on shipping income . . . . | **25**

26 Credit for taxes on dividends from a DISC or former DISC and certain distributions from a FSC or former FSC . . . . | **26**

27 Credit for taxes on lump-sum distributions . . . . | **27**

28 Credit for taxes on income re-sourced by treaty . . . . | **28**

29 Credit for taxes on general limitation income . . . . | **29**

30 Add lines 22 through 29. . . . . | **30**

31 Reduction of credit for international boycott operations. See instructions for line 12 on page 10 . . | **31**

32 Subtract line 31 from line 30. This is your **foreign tax credit.** Enter here and on Form 1040, line 46; Form 1040NR, line 43; Form 1041, Schedule G, line 2a; or Form 990-T, line 39a. . . . . . ▶ | **32**

✳

Department of the Treasury
Internal Revenue Service (99)

Employee Business Expenses

▶ See separate instructions.

▶ Attach to Form 1040.

OMB No. 1545-0139

1999

Attachment
Sequence No. **54**

Your name	Occupation in which you incurred expenses	Social security number

Part I Employee Business Expenses and Reimbursements

STEP 1 Enter Your Expenses

			Column A Other Than Meals and Entertainment		Column B Meals and Entertainment
1	Vehicle expense from line 22c or line 29. (Rural mail carriers: See instructions.)	1			
2	Parking fees, tolls, and transportation, including train, bus, etc., that **did not** involve overnight travel or commuting to and from work . .	2			
3	Travel expense while away from home overnight, including lodging, airplane, car rental, etc. **Do not** include meals and entertainment	3			
4	Business expenses not included on lines 1 through 3. **Do not** include meals and entertainment	4			
5	Meals and entertainment expenses (see instructions)	5			
6	**Total expenses.** In Column A, add lines 1 through 4 and enter the result. In Column B, enter the amount from line 5	6			

Note: *If you were not reimbursed for any expenses in Step 1, skip line 7 and enter the amount from line 6 on line 8.*

STEP 2 Enter Reimbursements Received From Your Employer for Expenses Listed in STEP 1

7	Enter reimbursements received from your employer that were **not** reported to you in box 1 of Form W-2. Include any reimbursements reported under code "L" in box 13 of your Form W-2 (see instructions)	7			

STEP 3 Figure Expenses To Deduct on Schedule A (Form 1040)

8	Subtract line 7 from line 6. If zero or less, enter -0-. However, if line 7 is greater than line 6 in Column A, report the excess as income on Form 1040, line 7	8			
	Note: *If both columns of line 8 are zero, you cannot deduct employee business expenses. Stop here and attach Form 2106 to your return.*				
9	In Column A, enter the amount from line 8. In Column B, multiply line 8 by 50% (.50). (Employees subject to Department of Transportation (DOT) hours of service limits: Multiply meal expenses by 55% (.55) instead of 50%. For more details, see instructions.)	9			
10	Add the amounts on line 9 of both columns and enter the total here. **Also, enter the total on Schedule A (Form 1040), line 20.** (Fee-basis state or local government officials, qualified performing artists, and individuals with disabilities: See the instructions for special rules on where to enter the total.) . . . . ▶	10			

For Paperwork Reduction Act Notice, see instructions.　　　　Cat. No. 11700N　　　　Form **2106** (1999)

Part II   Vehicle Expenses

Section A—General Information (You must complete this section if you are claiming vehicle expenses.)

		(a) Vehicle 1	(b) Vehicle 2
11	Enter the date the vehicle was placed in service.	11 / /	/ /
12	Total miles the vehicle was driven during 1999	12 miles	miles
13	Business miles included on line 12	13 miles	miles
14	Percent of business use. Divide line 13 by line 12	14 %	%
15	Average daily roundtrip commuting distance	15 miles	miles
16	Commuting miles included on line 12	16 miles	miles
17	Other miles. Add lines 13 and 16 and subtract the total from line 12	17 miles	miles

18   Do you (or your spouse) have another vehicle available for personal use? . . . . ☐ Yes   ☐ No

19   If your employer provided you with a vehicle, is personal use during off-duty hours permitted? ☐ Yes   ☐ No   ☐ Not applicable

20   Do you have evidence to support your deduction? . . . . ☐ Yes   ☐ No

21   If "Yes," is the evidence written? . . . . ☐ Yes   ☐ No

Section B—Standard Mileage Rate (See the instructions for Part II to find out whether to complete this section or Section C.)

22a	Multiply business miles driven **before** April 1, 1999, by 32½¢ (.325)	22a	
b	Multiply business miles driven **after** March 31, 1999, by 31¢ (.31)	22b	
c	Add lines 22a and 22b. Enter the result here and on line 1	22c	

Section C—Actual Expenses

		(a) Vehicle 1		(b) Vehicle 2	
23	Gasoline, oil, repairs, vehicle insurance, etc.	23			
24a	Vehicle rentals	24a			
b	Inclusion amount (see instructions)	24b			
c	Subtract line 24b from line 24a	24c			
25	Value of employer-provided vehicle (applies only if 100% of annual lease value was included on Form W-2—see instructions)	25			
26	Add lines 23, 24c, and 25	26			
27	Multiply line 26 by the percentage on line 14	27			
28	Depreciation. Enter amount from line 38 below	28			
29	Add lines 27 and 28. Enter total here and on line 1	29			

Section D—Depreciation of Vehicles (Use this section only if you owned the vehicle and are completing Section C for the vehicle.)

		(a) Vehicle 1		(b) Vehicle 2	
30	Enter cost or other basis (see instructions)	30			
31	Enter amount of section 179 deduction (see instructions)	31			
32	Multiply line 30 by line 14 (see instructions if you elected the section 179 deduction)	32			
33	Enter depreciation method and percentage (see instructions)	33			
34	Multiply line 32 by the percentage on line 33 (see instructions)	34			
35	Add lines 31 and 34	35			
36	Enter the limit from the table in the line 36 instructions	36			
37	Multiply line 36 by the percentage on line 14	37			
38	Enter the **smaller** of line 35 or line 37. Also enter this amount on line 28 above	38			

Form **2441**

Department of the Treasury
Internal Revenue Service   (99)

Child and Dependent Care Expenses

▶ **Attach to Form 1040.**

▶ **See separate instructions.**

OMB No. 1545-0068

19**99**

Attachment
Sequence No. **21**

Name(s) shown on Form 1040

Your social security number

Before you begin, you need to understand the following terms. See **Definitions** on page 1 of the instructions.

- **Dependent Care Benefits**
- **Qualifying Person(s)**
- **Qualified Expenses**
- **Earned Income**

Part I **Persons or Organizations Who Provided the Care**—You **must** complete this part.
(If you need more space, use the bottom of page 2.)

1	**(a)** Care provider's name	**(b)** Address (number, street, apt. no., city, state, and ZIP code)	**(c)** Identifying number (SSN or EIN)	**(d)** Amount paid (see instructions)

Did you receive **dependent care benefits?**	**No** ⟶ ▶ Complete only Part II below.
	Yes ⟶ ▶ Complete Part III on the back next.

Caution: *If the care was provided in your home, you may owe employment taxes. See the instructions for Form 1040, line 55.*

Part II **Credit for Child and Dependent Care Expenses**

2   Information about your **qualifying person(s).** If you have more than two qualifying persons, see the instructions.

(a) Qualifying person's name		**(b)** Qualifying person's social security number	**(c) Qualified expenses** you incurred and paid in 1999 for the person listed in column (a)
First	Last		

3	Add the amounts in column (c) of line 2. DO NOT enter more than $2,400 for one qualifying person or $4,800 for two or more persons. If you completed Part III, enter the amount from line 24	**3**
4	Enter YOUR **earned income**	**4**
5	If married filing a joint return, enter YOUR SPOUSE'S earned income (if your spouse was a student or was disabled, see the instructions); **all others,** enter the amount from line 4	**5**
6	Enter the **smallest** of line 3, 4, or 5	**6**

7   Enter the amount from Form 1040, line 34 . . . . | **7** |

8   Enter on line 8 the decimal amount shown below that applies to the amount on line 7

If line 7 is—		Decimal amount is	If line 7 is—		Decimal amount is
Over	But not over		Over	But not over	
$0—10,000		.30	$20,000—22,000		.24
10,000—12,000		.29	22,000—24,000		.23
12,000—14,000		.28	24,000—26,000		.22
14,000—16,000		.27	26,000—28,000		.21
16,000—18,000		.26	28,000—No limit		.20
18,000—20,000		.25			

| **8** | × . |

9   Multiply **line 6** by the decimal amount on line 8. Enter the result here and on Form 1040, line 41. But if this amount is more than the amount on Form 1040, line 40, **or** you paid 1998 expenses in 1999, see the instructions for the amount to enter on line 41 . . . | **9** |

For Paperwork Reduction Act Notice, see page 3 of the instructions.   Cat. No. 11862M   Form **2441** (1999)

Part III Dependent Care Benefits

10 Enter the total amount of **dependent care benefits** you received for 1999. This amount should be shown in box 10 of your W-2 form(s). DO NOT include amounts that were reported to you as wages in box 1 of Form(s) W-2 . . . . | **10**

11 Enter the amount forfeited, if any. See the instructions . . . . | **11**

12 Subtract line 11 from line 10 . . . . | **12**

13 Enter the total amount of **qualified expenses** incurred in 1999 for the care of the **qualifying person(s)** . . . | **13**

14 Enter the **smaller** of line 12 or 13 . . . . | **14**

15 Enter YOUR **earned income** . . . . | **15**

16 If married filing a joint return, enter YOUR SPOUSE'S earned income (if your spouse was a student or was disabled, see the instructions for line 5); if married filing a separate return, see the instructions for the amount to enter; **all others,** enter the amount from line 15 . . . | **16**

17 Enter the **smallest** of line 14, 15, or 16 . . . . . | **17**

18 **Excluded benefits.** Enter here the **smaller** of the following:
   - The amount from line 17, or
   - $5,000 ($2,500 if married filing a separate return **and** you were required to enter your spouse's earned income on line 16). | **18**

19 **Taxable benefits.** Subtract line 18 from line 12. Also, include this amount on Form 1040, line 7. On the dotted line next to line 7, enter "DCB" . . . . | **19**

To claim the child and dependent care
credit, complete lines 20–24 below.

20 Enter $2,400 ($4,800 if two or more qualifying persons) . . . . | **20**

21 Enter the amount from line 18 . . . . | **21**

22 Subtract line 21 from line 20. If zero or less, **STOP.** You cannot take the credit. **Exception.** If you paid 1998 expenses in 1999, see the instructions for line 9 . . . . | **22**

23 Complete line 2 on the front of this form. DO NOT include in column (c) any benefits shown on line 18 above. Then, add the amounts in column (c) and enter the total here . | **23**

24 Enter the **smaller** of line 22 or 23. Also, enter this amount on line 3 on the front of this form and complete lines 4–9 . . . . | **24**

Form **2441** (1999)

750

Form 2555

Foreign Earned Income

OMB No. 1545-0067

1999

Department of the Treasury
Internal Revenue Service

▶ See separate instructions.   ▶ Attach to Form 1040.

Attachment Sequence No. **34**

For Use by U.S. Citizens and Resident Aliens Only

Name shown on Form 1040

Your social security number

Part I   General Information

1 Your foreign address (including country)

2 Your occupation

3 Employer's name ▶

4a Employer's U.S. address ▶

b Employer's foreign address ▶

5 Employer is (check any that apply):
- **a** ☐ A foreign entity
- **d** ☐ A foreign affiliate of a U.S. company
- **b** ☐ A U.S. company
- **c** ☐ Self
- **e** ☐ Other (specify) ▶

6a If, after 1981, you filed Form 2555 to claim either of the exclusions or Form 2555-EZ to claim the foreign earned income exclusion, enter the last year you filed the form. ▶

b If you did not file Form 2555 or 2555-EZ after 1981 to claim either of the exclusions, check here ▶ ☐ and go to line 7 now.

c Have you ever revoked either of the exclusions? . . . . ☐ Yes ☐ No

d If you answered "Yes," enter the type of exclusion and the tax year for which the revocation was effective. ▶

7 Of what country are you a citizen/national? ▶

8a Did you maintain a separate foreign residence for your family because of adverse living conditions at your tax home? See **Second foreign household** on page 3 of the instructions . . . . ☐ Yes ☐ No

b If "Yes," enter city and country of the separate foreign residence. Also, enter the number of days during your tax year that you maintained a second household at that address. ▶

9 List your tax home(s) during your tax year and date(s) established. ▶

Next, complete either Part II or Part III. If an item does not apply, enter "NA." If you do not give the information asked for, any exclusion or deduction you claim may be disallowed.

Part II   Taxpayers Qualifying Under Bona Fide Residence Test (See page 2 of the instructions.)

10 Date bona fide residence began ▶   , and ended ▶

11 Kind of living quarters in foreign country ▶ **a** ☐ Purchased house **b** ☐ Rented house or apartment **c** ☐ Rented room
d ☐ Quarters furnished by employer

12a Did any of your family live with you abroad during any part of the tax year? . . . . ☐ Yes ☐ No

b If "Yes," who and for what period? ▶

13a Have you submitted a statement to the authorities of the foreign country where you claim bona fide residence that you are not a resident of that country? (See instructions.) . . . . ☐ Yes ☐ No

b Are you required to pay income tax to the country where you claim bona fide residence? (See instructions.) ☐ Yes ☐ No

If you answered "Yes" to 13a and "No" to 13b, you do not qualify as a bona fide resident. Do not complete the rest of this part.

14 If you were present in the United States or its possessions during the tax year, complete columns **(a)–(d)** below. **Do not** include the income from column **(d)** in Part IV, but report it on Form 1040.

(a) Date arrived in U.S.	(b) Date left U.S.	(c) Number of days in U.S. on business	(d) Income earned in U.S. on business (attach computation)	(a) Date arrived in U.S.	(b) Date left U.S.	(c) Number of days in U.S. on business	(d) Income earned in U.S. on business (attach computation)

15a List any contractual terms or other conditions relating to the length of your employment abroad. ▶

b Enter the type of visa under which you entered the foreign country. ▶

c Did your visa limit the length of your stay or employment in a foreign country? If "Yes," attach explanation ☐ Yes ☐ No

d Did you maintain a home in the United States while living abroad?. . . . . ☐ Yes ☐ No

e If "Yes," enter address of your home, whether it was rented, the names of the occupants, and their relationship to you. ▶

Cat. No. 11900P

Form **2555** (1999)

Part III   Taxpayers Qualifying Under Physical Presence Test (See page 2 of the instructions.)

16   The physical presence test is based on the 12-month period from ▶ .... through ▶ ....

17   Enter your principal country of employment during your tax year. ▶ ....

18   If you traveled abroad during the 12-month period entered on line 16, complete columns **(a)–(f)** below. Exclude travel between foreign countries that did not involve travel on or over international waters, or in or over the United States, for 24 hours or more. If you have no travel to report during the period, enter "Physically present in a foreign country or countries for the entire 12-month period." **Do not** include the income from column **(f)** below in Part IV, but report it on Form 1040.

(a) Name of country (including U.S.)	(b) Date arrived	(c) Date left	(d) Full days present in country	(e) Number of days in U.S. on business	(f) Income earned in U.S. on business (attach computation)	

Part IV   All Taxpayers

Note: *Enter on lines 19 through 23 all income, including noncash income, you earned and actually or constructively received during your 1999 tax year for services you performed in a foreign country. If any of the foreign earned income received this tax year was earned in a prior tax year, or will be earned in a later tax year (such as a bonus), see the instructions.* **Do not** *include income from line 14, column (d), or line 18, column (f). Report amounts in U.S. dollars, using the exchange rates in effect when you actually or constructively received the income.*

If you are a cash basis taxpayer, report on Form 1040 all income you received in 1999, no matter when you performed the service.

1999 Foreign Earned Income		Amount (in U.S. dollars)	
19 Total wages, salaries, bonuses, commissions, etc.	**19**		
20 Allowable share of income for personal services performed (see instructions):			
a In a business (including farming) or profession	**20a**		
b In a partnership. List partnership's name and address and type of income. ▶	**20b**		
21 Noncash income (market value of property or facilities furnished by employer—attach statement showing how it was determined):			
a Home (lodging)	**21a**		
b Meals	**21b**		
c Car	**21c**		
d Other property or facilities. List type and amount. ▶	**21d**		
22 Allowances, reimbursements, or expenses paid on your behalf for services you performed:			
a Cost of living and overseas differential **22a**			
b Family **22b**			
c Education **22c**			
d Home leave **22d**			
e Quarters **22e**			
f For any other purpose. List type and amount. ▶ **22f**			
g Add lines 22a through 22f	**22g**		
23 Other foreign earned income. List type and amount. ▶	**23**		
24 Add lines 19 through 21d, line 22g, and line 23	**24**		
25 Total amount of meals and lodging included on line 24 that is excludable (see instructions)	**25**		
26 Subtract line 25 from line 24. Enter the result here and on line 27 on page 3. This is your **1999 foreign earned income** ▶	**26**		

Part V   **All Taxpayers**

			27		
27	Enter the amount from line 26		27		

Are you claiming the housing exclusion or housing deduction?
☐ **Yes.** Complete Part VI.
☐ **No.** Go to Part VII.

Part VI   **Taxpayers Claiming the Housing Exclusion AND/OR Deduction**

28	Qualified housing expenses for the tax year (see instructions)		28		
29	Number of days in your qualifying period that fall within your 1999 tax year (see instructions) . . . . **29** _____ **days**				
30	Multiply $27.03 by the number of days on line 29. If 365 is entered on line 29, enter $9,865.00 here.		30		
31	Subtract line 30 from line 28. If zero or less, do not complete the rest of this part or any of Part IX		31		
32	Enter employer-provided amounts (see instructions) . . . . . . **32** _____				
33	Divide line 32 by line 27. Enter the result as a decimal (rounded to at least three places), but do not enter more than "1.000"		33	× ●	
34	**Housing exclusion.** Multiply line 31 by line 33. Enter the result but do not enter more than the amount on line 32. Also, complete Part VIII . . . . ▶		34		

Note: *The housing deduction is figured in Part IX. If you choose to claim the foreign earned income exclusion, complete Parts VII and VIII before Part IX.*

Part VII   **Taxpayers Claiming the Foreign Earned Income Exclusion**

35	Maximum foreign earned income exclusion		35	$74,000	00
36	● If you completed Part VI, enter the number from line 29.				
	● All others, enter the number of days in your qualifying period that fall within your 1999 tax year (see the instructions for line 29). } **36** _____ **days**				
37	● If line 36 and the number of days in your 1999 tax year (usually 365) are the same, enter "1.000."				
	● Otherwise, divide line 36 by the number of days in your 1999 tax year and enter the result as a decimal (rounded to at least three places). }		37	× ●	
38	Multiply line 35 by line 37		38		
39	Subtract line 34 from line 27		39		
40	**Foreign earned income exclusion.** Enter the **smaller** of line 38 or line 39. Also, complete Part VIII ▶		40		

Part VIII   **Taxpayers Claiming the Housing Exclusion, Foreign Earned Income Exclusion, or Both**

41	Add lines 34 and 40		41		
42	Deductions allowed in figuring your adjusted gross income (Form 1040, line 33) that are allocable to the excluded income. See instructions and attach computation		42		
43	Subtract line 42 from line 41. Enter the result here and in parentheses on **Form 1040, line 21.** Next to the amount enter "Form 2555." On Form 1040, subtract this amount from your income to arrive at total income on Form 1040, line 22 . . . . ▶		43		

Part IX   **Taxpayers Claiming the Housing Deduction**—Complete this part only if **(a)** line 31 is more than line 34 and **(b)** line 27 is more than line 41.

44	Subtract line 34 from line 31		44		
45	Subtract line 41 from line 27		45		
46	Enter the **smaller** of line 44 or line 45		46		

Note: *If line 45 is **more than** line 46 and you could not deduct all of your 1998 housing deduction because of the 1998 limit, use the worksheet on page 4 of the instructions to figure the amount to enter on line 47. Otherwise, go to line 48.*

47	Housing deduction carryover from 1998 (from worksheet on page 4 of the instructions) . . .		47		
48	**Housing deduction.** Add lines 46 and 47. Enter the total here and on Form 1040 to the left of line 32. Next to the amount on Form 1040, enter "Form 2555." Add it to the total adjustments reported on that line . . . . ▶		48		

✹   Form **2555** (1999)

<table>
<tr><td colspan="2">Form **4562**</td><td colspan="2">**Depreciation and Amortization**</td><td>OMB No. 1545-0172</td></tr>
<tr><td colspan="2">Department of the Treasury
Internal Revenue Service   (99)</td><td colspan="2">(Including Information on Listed Property)
▶ See separate instructions.   ▶ **Attach this form to your return.**</td><td>19**99**
Attachment
Sequence No. **67**</td></tr>
</table>

Name(s) shown on return	Business or activity to which this form relates	Identifying number

Part I   **Election To Expense Certain Tangible Property (Section 179) (Note:** *If you have any "listed property,"* *complete Part V before you complete Part I.***)**

1	Maximum dollar limitation. If an enterprise zone business, see page 2 of the instructions . .	**1**	$19,000
2	Total cost of section 179 property placed in service. See page 2 of the instructions	**2**	
3	Threshold cost of section 179 property before reduction in limitation	**3**	$200,000
4	Reduction in limitation. Subtract line 3 from line 2. If zero or less, enter -0-	**4**	
5	Dollar limitation for tax year. Subtract line 4 from line 1. If zero or less, enter -0-. If married filing separately, see page 2 of the instructions	**5**	

(a) Description of property	(b) Cost (business use only)	(c) Elected cost	
6			

7	Listed property. Enter amount from line 27. . . . . **7**		
8	Total elected cost of section 179 property. Add amounts in column (c), lines 6 and 7 . . .	**8**	
9	Tentative deduction. Enter the smaller of line 5 or line 8	**9**	
10	Carryover of disallowed deduction from 1998. See page 2 of the instructions	**10**	
11	Business income limitation. Enter the smaller of business income (not less than zero) or line 5 (see instructions)	**11**	
12	Section 179 expense deduction. Add lines 9 and 10, but do not enter more than line 11 . .	**12**	
13	Carryover of disallowed deduction to 2000. Add lines 9 and 10, less line 12 ▶ **13**		

Note: *Do not use Part II or Part III below for listed property (automobiles, certain other vehicles, cellular telephones, certain computers, or property used for entertainment, recreation, or amusement). Instead, use Part V for listed property.*

Part II   **MACRS Depreciation for Assets Placed in Service ONLY During Your 1999 Tax Year (Do Not Include Listed Property.)**

Section A—General Asset Account Election

14	If you are making the election under section 168(i)(4) to group any assets placed in service during the tax year into one or more general asset accounts, check this box. See page 3 of the instructions . . . . ▶ ☐

Section B—General Depreciation System (GDS) (See page 3 of the instructions.)

(a) Classification of property	(b) Month and year placed in service	(c) Basis for depreciation (business/investment use only—see instructions)	(d) Recovery period	(e) Convention	(f) Method	(g) Depreciation deduction
15a 3-year property						
b 5-year property						
c 7-year property						
d 10-year property						
e 15-year property						
f 20-year property						
g 25-year property			25 yrs.		S/L	
h Residential rental property			27.5 yrs.	MM	S/L	
			27.5 yrs.	MM	S/L	
i Nonresidential real property			39 yrs.	MM	S/L	
				MM	S/L	

Section C—Alternative Depreciation System (ADS) (See page 5 of the instructions.)

16a Class life					S/L	
b 12-year			12 yrs.		S/L	
c 40-year			40 yrs.	MM	S/L	

Part III   **Other Depreciation (Do Not Include Listed Property.)** (See page 5 of the instructions.)

17	GDS and ADS deductions for assets placed in service in tax years beginning before 1999 .	**17**	
18	Property subject to section 168(f)(1) election	**18**	
19	ACRS and other depreciation	**19**	

Part IV   **Summary** (See page 6 of the instructions.)

20	Listed property. Enter amount from line 26.	**20**	
21	**Total.** Add deductions on line 12, lines 15 and 16 in column (g), and lines 17 through 20. Enter here and on the appropriate lines of your return. Partnerships and S corporations—see instructions . .	**21**	
22	For assets shown above and placed in service during the current year, enter the portion of the basis attributable to section 263A costs . . **22**		

For Paperwork Reduction Act Notice, see page 9 of the instructions.   Cat. No. 12906N   Form **4562** (1999)

Part V **Listed Property—Automobiles, Certain Other Vehicles, Cellular Telephones, Certain Computers, and Property Used for Entertainment, Recreation, or Amusement**

Note: *For any vehicle for which you are using the standard mileage rate or deducting lease expense, complete **only** 23a, 23b, columns (a) through (c) of Section A, all of Section B, and Section C if applicable.*

Section A—Depreciation and Other Information (Caution: *See page 7 of the instructions for limits for passenger automobiles.*)

23a Do you have evidence to support the business/investment use claimed? ☐ **Yes** ☐ **No** **23b** If "Yes," is the evidence written? ☐ **Yes** ☐ **No**

(a) Type of property (list vehicles first)	(b) Date placed in service	(c) Business/ investment use percentage	(d) Cost or other basis	(e) Basis for depreciation (business/investment use only)	(f) Recovery period	(g) Method/ Convention	(h) Depreciation deduction	(i) Elected section 179 cost
24 Property used more than 50% in a qualified business use (See page 6 of the instructions.):								
		%						
		%						
		%						
25 Property used 50% or less in a qualified business use (See page 6 of the instructions.):								
		%				S/L —		
		%				S/L —		
		%				S/L —		

26 Add amounts in column (h). Enter the total here and on line 20, page 1 . . . . . **26**

27 Add amounts in column (i). Enter the total here and on line 7, page 1 . . . . **27**

Section B—Information on Use of Vehicles

Complete this section for vehicles used by a sole proprietor, partner, or other "more than 5% owner," or related person.
If you provided vehicles to your employees, first answer the questions in Section C to see if you meet an exception to completing this section for those vehicles.

	(a) Vehicle 1		(b) Vehicle 2		(c) Vehicle 3		(d) Vehicle 4		(e) Vehicle 5		(f) Vehicle 6	
28 Total business/investment miles driven during the year (DO NOT include commuting miles— see page 1 of the instructions)												
29 Total commuting miles driven during the year												
30 Total other personal (noncommuting) miles driven												
31 Total miles driven during the year. Add lines 28 through 30.												
	Yes	No	Yes	No	Yes	No	Yes	No	Yes	No	Yes	No
32 Was the vehicle available for personal use during off-duty hours?												
33 Was the vehicle used primarily by a more than 5% owner or related person?												
34 Is another vehicle available for personal use?												

Section C—Questions for Employers Who Provide Vehicles for Use by Their Employees

*Answer these questions to determine if you meet an exception to completing Section B for vehicles used by employees who **are not** more than 5% owners or related persons.*

		Yes	No
35	Do you maintain a written policy statement that prohibits all personal use of vehicles, including commuting, by your employees?		
36	Do you maintain a written policy statement that prohibits personal use of vehicles, except commuting, by your employees? See page 8 of the instructions for vehicles used by corporate officers, directors, or 1% or more owners		
37	Do you treat all use of vehicles by employees as personal use?		
38	Do you provide more than five vehicles to your employees, obtain information from your employees about the use of the vehicles, and retain the information received?		
39	Do you meet the requirements concerning qualified automobile demonstration use? See page 8 of the instructions . .		

Note: *If your answer to 35, 36, 37, 38, or 39 is "Yes," you need not complete Section B for the covered vehicles.*

Part VI **Amortization**

(a) Description of costs	(b) Date amortization begins	(c) Amortizable amount	(d) Code section	(e) Amortization period or percentage	(f) Amortization for this year
40 Amortization of costs that begins during your 1999 tax year:					

41 Amortization of costs that began before 1999 . . . . **41**

42 **Total.** Enter here and on "Other Deductions" or "Other Expenses" line of your return . . . **42**

Form **4562** (1999)

Casualties and Thefts

▶ See separate instructions.
▶ Attach to your tax return.
▶ Use a separate Form 4684 for each different casualty or theft.

OMB No. 1545-0177

19**99**

Attachment
Sequence No. **26**

Name(s) shown on tax return

Identifying number

SECTION A—Personal Use Property (Use this section to report casualties and thefts of property **not** used in a trade or business or for income-producing purposes.)

1 Description of properties (show type, location, and date acquired for each):

Property **A** ....
Property **B** ....
Property **C** ....
Property **D** ....

		Properties (Use a separate column for each property lost or damaged from one casualty or theft.)			
		A	**B**	**C**	**D**
2 Cost or other basis of each property	**2**				
3 Insurance or other reimbursement (whether or not you filed a claim). See instructions	**3**				
Note: *If line 2 is **more than** line 3, skip line 4.*					
4 Gain from casualty or theft. If line 3 is **more than** line 2, enter the difference here and skip lines 5 through 9 for that column. See instructions if line 3 includes insurance or other reimbursement you did not claim, or you received payment for your loss in a later tax year	**4**				
5 Fair market value **before** casualty or theft	**5**				
6 Fair market value **after** casualty or theft	**6**				
7 Subtract line 6 from line 5	**7**				
8 Enter the **smaller** of line 2 or line 7	**8**				
9 Subtract line 3 from line 8. If zero or less, enter -0-	**9**				

10 Casualty or theft loss. Add the amounts on line 9. Enter the total	**10**	
11 Enter the amount from line 10 or $100, whichever is **smaller**	**11**	
12 Subtract line 11 from line 10	**12**	
Caution: *Use only one Form 4684 for lines 13 through 18.*		
13 Add the amounts on line 12 of all Forms 4684	**13**	
14 Combine the amounts from line 4 of all Forms 4684	**14**	
15 • If line 14 is **more than** line 13, enter the difference here and on Schedule D. Do not complete the rest of this section (see instructions). • If line 14 is **less than** line 13, enter -0- here and continue with the form. • If line 14 is **equal to** line 13, enter -0- here. Do not complete the rest of this section.	**15**	
16 If line 14 is **less than** line 13, enter the difference	**16**	
17 Enter 10% of your adjusted gross income (Form 1040, line 34). Estates and trusts, see instructions	**17**	
18 Subtract line 17 from line 16. If zero or less, enter -0-. Also enter result on Schedule A (Form 1040), line 19. Estates and trusts, enter on the "Other deductions" line of your tax return	**18**	

For Paperwork Reduction Act Notice, see page 4 of separate instructions.   Cat. No. 12997O   Form **4684** (1999)

Name(s) shown on tax return. Do not enter name and identifying number if shown on other side. | Identifying number

SECTION B—Business and Income-Producing Property

Part I   **Casualty or Theft Gain or Loss** (Use a separate Part I for each casualty or theft.)

19   Description of properties (show type, location, and date acquired for each):

Property **A** ....

Property **B** ....

Property **C** ....

Property **D** ....

Properties (Use a separate column for each property lost or damaged from one casualty or theft.)

		A	B	C	D
20	Cost or adjusted basis of each property	**20**			
21	Insurance or other reimbursement (whether or not you filed a claim). See the instructions for line 3. **Note:** *If line 20 is **more than** line 21, skip line 22.*	**21**			
22	Gain from casualty or theft. If line 21 is **more than** line 20, enter the difference here and on line 29 or line 34, column (c), except as provided in the instructions for line 33. Also, skip lines 23 through 27 for that column. See the instructions for line 4 if line 21 includes insurance or other reimbursement you did not claim, or you received payment for your loss in a later tax year.	**22**			
23	Fair market value **before** casualty or theft	**23**			
24	Fair market value **after** casualty or theft	**24**			
25	Subtract line 24 from line 23	**25**			
26	Enter the **smaller** of line 20 or line 25. **Note:** *If the property was totally destroyed by casualty or lost from theft, enter on line 26 the amount from line 20.*	**26**			
27	Subtract line 21 from line 26. If zero or less, enter -0-	**27**			
28	Casualty or theft loss. Add the amounts on line 27. Enter the total here and on line 29 **or** line 34 (see instructions).		**28**		

Part II   **Summary of Gains and Losses** (from separate Parts I)

(a) Identify casualty or theft	(b) Losses from casualties or thefts		(c) Gains from casualties or thefts includible in income
	(i) Trade, business, rental or royalty property	(ii) Income-producing and employee property	

Casualty or Theft of Property Held One Year or Less

29		( )	( )	
		( )	( )	
30	Totals. Add the amounts on line 29 **30**	( )	( )	

31   Combine line 30, columns (b)(i) and (c). Enter the net gain or (loss) here and on Form 4797, line 14. If Form 4797 is not otherwise required, see instructions   **31**

32   Enter the amount from line 30, column (b)(ii) here. Individuals, enter the amount from income-producing property on Schedule A (Form 1040), line 27, and enter the amount from property used as an employee on Schedule A (Form 1040), line 22. Estates and trusts, partnerships, and S corporations, see instructions   **32**

Casualty or Theft of Property Held More Than One Year

33	Casualty or theft gains from Form 4797, line 32			**33**	
34		( )	( )		
		( )	( )		
35	Total losses. Add amounts on line 34, columns (b)(i) and (b)(ii) **35**	( )	( )		
36	Total gains. Add lines 33 and 34, column (c)			**36**	
37	Add amounts on line 35, columns (b)(i) and (b)(ii)			**37**	

38   If the loss on line 37 is **more than** the gain on line 36:

a   Combine line 35, column (b)(i) and line 36, and enter the net gain or (loss) here. Partnerships (except electing large partnerships) and S corporations, see the note below. All others, enter this amount on Form 4797, line 14. If Form 4797 is not otherwise required, see instructions   **38a**

b   Enter the amount from line 35, column (b)(ii) here. Individuals, enter the amount from income-producing property on Schedule A (Form 1040), line 27, and enter the amount from property used as an employee on Schedule A (Form 1040), line 22. Estates and trusts, enter on the "Other deductions" line of your tax return. Partnerships (except electing large partnerships) and S corporations, see the note below. Electing large partnerships, enter on Form 1065-B, Part II, line 11   **38b**

39   If the loss on line 37 is **less than** or **equal to** the gain on line 36, combine lines 36 and 37 and enter here. Partnerships (except electing large partnerships), see the note below. All others, enter this amount on Form 4797, line 3, column (g)   **39**

Note: *Partnerships, enter the amount from line 38a, 38b, or line 39 on Form 1065, Schedule K, line 7. S corporations, enter the amount from line 38a or 38b on Form 1120S, Schedule K, line 6.*

✪

758

Form **4797**	**Sales of Business Property**	OMB No. 1545-0184
Department of the Treasury Internal Revenue Service (99)	(Also Involuntary Conversions and Recapture Amounts Under Sections 179 and 280F(b)(2)) ▶ Attach to your tax return. ▶ See separate instructions.	**19**99 Attachment Sequence No. **27**

Name(s) shown on return	Identifying number

1 Enter here the gross proceeds from the sale or exchange of real estate reported to you for 1999 on Form(s) 1099-S (or a substitute statement) that you will be including on line 2, 10, or 20 . . . . **1**

Part I Sales or Exchanges of Property Used in a Trade or Business and Involuntary Conversions From Other Than Casualty or Theft—Property Held More Than 1 Year

(a) Description of property	(b) Date acquired (mo., day, yr.)	(c) Date sold (mo., day, yr.)	(d) Gross sales price	(e) Depreciation allowed or allowable since acquisition	(f) Cost or other basis, plus improvements and expense of sale	(g) GAIN or (LOSS) Subtract (f) from the sum of (d) and (e)
2						

3 Gain, if any, from Form 4684, line 39 . . . . **3**

4 Section 1231 gain from installment sales from Form 6252, line 26 or 37 . . . . **4**

5 Section 1231 gain or (loss) from like-kind exchanges from Form 8824 . . . . **5**

6 Gain, if any, from line 32, from other than casualty or theft **6**

7 Combine lines 2 through 6. Enter the gain or (loss) here and on the appropriate line as follows: **7**

Partnerships (except electing large partnerships). Report the gain or (loss) following the instructions for Form 1065, Schedule K, line 6. Skip lines 8, 9, 11, and 12 below.

S corporations. Report the gain or (loss) following the instructions for Form 1120S, Schedule K, lines 5 and 6. Skip lines 8, 9, 11, and 12 below, unless line 7 is a gain and the S corporation is subject to the capital gains tax.

All others. If line 7 is zero or a loss, enter the amount from line 7 on line 11 below and skip lines 8 and 9. If line 7 is a gain and you did not have any prior year section 1231 losses, or they were recaptured in an earlier year, enter the gain from line 7 as a long-term capital gain on Schedule D and skip lines 8, 9, and 12 below.

8 Nonrecaptured net section 1231 losses from prior years (see instructions) **8**

9 Subtract line 8 from line 7. If zero or less, enter -0-. Also enter on the appropriate line as follows (see instructions): **9**

S corporations. Enter any gain from line 9 on Schedule D (Form 1120S), line 14, and skip lines 11 and 12 below.

All others. If line 9 is zero, enter the gain from line 7 on line 12 below. If line 9 is more than zero, enter the amount from line 8 on line 12 below, and enter the gain from line 9 as a long-term capital gain on Schedule D.

Part II Ordinary Gains and Losses

10 Ordinary gains and losses not included on lines 11 through 17 (include property held 1 year or less):

11 Loss, if any, from line 7 . . . . **11** ( )

12 Gain, if any, from line 7 or amount from line 8, if applicable **12**

13 Gain, if any, from line 31 . . . . **13**

14 Net gain or (loss) from Form 4684, lines 31 and 38a **14**

15 Ordinary gain from installment sales from Form 6252, line 25 or 36 . . . . **15**

16 Ordinary gain or (loss) from like-kind exchanges from Form 8824 . . . . **16**

17 Recapture of section 179 expense deduction for partners and S corporation shareholders from property dispositions by partnerships and S corporations (see instructions) **17**

18 Combine lines 10 through 17. Enter the gain or (loss) here, and on the appropriate line as follows: **18**

a For all except individual returns: Enter the gain or (loss) from line 18 on the return being filed.

b For individual returns:

(1) If the loss on line 11 includes a loss from Form 4684, line 35, column (b)(ii), enter that part of the loss here. Enter the part of the loss from income-producing property on Schedule A (Form 1040), line 27, and the part of the loss from property used as an employee on Schedule A (Form 1040), line 22. Identify as from "Form 4797, line 18b(1)." See instructions . . . . **18b(1)**

(2) Redetermine the gain or (loss) on line 18, excluding the loss, if any, on line 18b(1). Enter here and on Form 1040, line 14 . . . . **18b(2)**

For Paperwork Reduction Act Notice, see separate instructions.   Cat. No. 13086I   Form **4797** (1999)

Part III   Gain From Disposition of Property Under Sections 1245, 1250, 1252, 1254, and 1255

19	(a) Description of section 1245, 1250, 1252, 1254, or 1255 property:	(b) Date acquired (mo., day, yr.)	(c) Date sold (mo., day, yr.)
A			
B			
C			
D			

	These columns relate to the properties on lines 19A through 19D. ▶		Property A	Property B	Property C	Property D
20	Gross sales price (**Note:** See line 1 before completing.)	20				
21	Cost or other basis plus expense of sale	21				
22	Depreciation (or depletion) allowed or allowable	22				
23	Adjusted basis. Subtract line 22 from line 21	23				
24	Total gain. Subtract line 23 from line 20	24				
25	**If section 1245 property:**					
a	Depreciation allowed or allowable from line 22	25a				
b	Enter the **smaller** of line 24 or 25a	25b				
26	**If section 1250 property:** If straight line depreciation was used, enter -0- on line 26g, except for a corporation subject to section 291.					
a	Additional depreciation after 1975 (see instructions)	26a				
b	Applicable percentage multiplied by the **smaller** of line 24 or line 26a (see instructions)	26b				
c	Subtract line 26a from line 24. If residential rental property or line 24 is not more than line 26a, skip lines 26d and 26e	26c				
d	Additional depreciation after 1969 and before 1976	26d				
e	Enter the **smaller** of line 26c or 26d	26e				
f	Section 291 amount (corporations only)	26f				
g	Add lines 26b, 26e, and 26f	26g				
27	**If section 1252 property:** Skip this section if you did not dispose of farmland or if this form is being completed for a partnership (other than an electing large partnership).					
a	Soil, water, and land clearing expenses	27a				
b	Line 27a multiplied by applicable percentage (see instructions)	27b				
c	Enter the **smaller** of line 24 or 27b	27c				
28	**If section 1254 property:**					
a	Intangible drilling and development costs, expenditures for development of mines and other natural deposits, and mining exploration costs (see instructions)	28a				
b	Enter the **smaller** of line 24 or 28a	28b				
29	**If section 1255 property:**					
a	Applicable percentage of payments excluded from income under section 126 (see instructions)	29a				
b	Enter the **smaller** of line 24 or 29a (see instructions)	29b				

Summary of Part III Gains. Complete property columns A through D through line 29b before going to line 30.

30	Total gains for all properties. Add property columns A through D, line 24	30	
31	Add property columns A through D, lines 25b, 26g, 27c, 28b, and 29b. Enter here and on line 13	31	
32	Subtract line 31 from line 30. Enter the portion from casualty or theft on Form 4684, line 33. Enter the portion from other than casualty or theft on Form 4797, line 6	32	

Part IV   Recapture Amounts Under Sections 179 and 280F(b)(2) When Business Use Drops to 50% or Less
(See instructions.)

			(a) Section 179	(b) Section 280F(b)(2)
33	Section 179 expense deduction or depreciation allowable in prior years	33		
34	Recomputed depreciation. See instructions	34		
35	Recapture amount. Subtract line 34 from line 33. See the instructions for where to report	35		

Form 4868

Department of the Treasury
Internal Revenue Service (99)

Application for Automatic Extension of Time To File U.S. Individual Income Tax Return

OMB No. 1545-0188

1999

General Instructions

A Change To Note

You may be able to use a credit card to get an extension of time to file without sending in Form 4868. See **Extension of Time To File Using a Credit Card** below for more details.

Purpose of Form

Use Form 4868 to apply for 4 more months to file **Form 1040EZ, Form 1040A, Form 1040, Form 1040NR-EZ,** or **Form 1040NR.**

To get the extra time you **MUST:**

• Properly estimate your 1999 tax liability using the information available to you,

• Enter your tax liability on line 9 of Form 4868, **AND**

• File Form 4868 by the regular due date of your return.

You are not required to make a payment of the tax you estimate as due. But remember, Form 4868 does not extend the time to pay taxes. If you do not pay the amount due by the regular due date, you will owe interest. You may also be charged penalties. For more details, see **Interest** and **Late Payment Penalty** on page 3. Any remittance you make with your application for extension will be treated as a payment of tax.

You do not have to explain why you are asking for the extension. We will contact you only if your request is denied.

Do not file Form 4868 if you want the IRS to figure your tax or you are under a court order to file your return by the regular due date.

If you need an additional extension, see **If You Need Additional Time** on page 3.

Note: Generally, an extension of time to file your 1999 **calendar year** income tax return also extends the time to file a gift or generation-skipping transfer (GST) tax return **(Form 709 or 709-A)** for 1999. Special rules apply if the donor dies during the year in which the gifts were made. See the Instructions for Form 709.

Extension of Time To File Using a Credit Card

You generally can get an extension by phone if you pay part or all of your estimate of income tax due by using a credit card (American Express® Card, MasterCard®, or Discover® Card). To pay by credit card, call **1-888-2PAY-TAX** (1-888-272- 9829) toll free by April 17, 2000, and follow the instructions. Your payment must be at least $1 to use this system. Before you call, fill in Form 4868 as a worksheet. You will be asked to enter certain items from the form during the call. A convenience fee will be charged by the credit card processor based on the amount you are paying. You will be told what the fee is when you call and you will have the option to either continue or cancel the call. You can also find out what the fee will be on the Internet at **www.8882paytax.com.**

You will be given a confirmation number at the end of the call. Keep the confirmation number with your records. Once you receive your confirmation number, you have completed the requirements for requesting an extension of time to file. **Do not** send in Form 4868.

Note: Although an extension of time to file your income tax return also extends the time to file Form 709 or 709-A, you cannot make payments of the gift or GST tax with a credit card. To make a payment of the gift or GST tax, send a check or money order to the service center where the donor's income tax return will be filed. Enter "1999 Form 709" and the donor's name and social security number on the payment. **Do not** send in Form 4868.

Out of the Country

If you already had 2 extra months to file because you were a U.S. citizen or resident and were out of the country, use this form to obtain an additional 2 months to file. Write "Taxpayer Abroad" across the top of Form 4868. "Out of the country" means either **(a)** you live outside the United States and Puerto Rico **and** your main place of work is outside the United States and Puerto Rico, **or (b)** you are in military or naval service outside the United States and Puerto Rico.

For Privacy Act and Paperwork Reduction Act Notice, see page 4.   Cat. No. 13141W   Form **4868** (1999)

▼ DETACH HERE ▼

Form 4868

Department of the Treasury
Internal Revenue Service (99)

Application for Automatic Extension of Time To File U.S. Individual Income Tax Return

For calendar year 1999, or other tax year beginning   ,1999, ending   ,   .

OMB No. 1545-0188

1999

Part I Identification	**Part III** Individual Income Tax

Part I Identification

1 Your name(s) (see instructions)

Address (see instructions)

City, town or post office, state, and ZIP code

2 Your social security number   **3** Spouse's social security number

Part II Complete ONLY If Filing Gift/GST Tax Return

This form also extends the time for filing a gift or generation-skipping transfer (GST) tax return if you file a calendar (not fiscal) year income tax return. Enter your gift or GST tax payment(s) in Part IV and:

Check this box ▶ ☐ if **you** are requesting a **GIFT or GST TAX** return extension.

Check this box ▶ ☐ if **your spouse** is requesting a **GIFT or GST TAX** return extension.

Checking box(es) may result in correspondence if Form 709 or 709-A is not filed.

Part III Individual Income Tax

4 Total tax liability on your income tax return for 1999 $ _____

5 Total 1999 payments . . . . . . _____

6 **Balance.** Subtract 5 from 4 . . . . . _____

Part IV Gift/GST Tax—If you are **not filing** a gift or GST tax return, go to Part V now. See the instructions.

7 Your gift or GST tax payment. . . $ _____

8 **Your spouse's** gift/GST tax payment . _____

Part V Total

9 **Total liability.** Add lines 6, 7, and 8 $ _____

10 Amount you are paying. . . . . ▶ _____

If line 10 is less than line 9, you may be liable for interest and penalties. See page 3.

Form **4868** (1999)

Where To File

If you live in:	And you are making a payment, send Form 4868 with your payment to IRS:	And you are NOT making a payment, send Form 4868 to Internal Revenue Service Center:
Florida, Georgia, South Carolina	P.O. Box 105073 Atlanta, GA 30348-5073	Atlanta, GA 39901
New Jersey, New York (*New York City and counties of Nassau, Rockland, Suffolk, and Westchester*)	P.O. Box 22423 Newark, NJ 07101-2423	Holtsville, NY 00501
New York (*all other counties*), Connecticut, Maine, Massachusetts, New Hampshire, Rhode Island, Vermont	P.O. Box 371410 Pittsburgh, PA 15250-7410	Andover, MA 05501
Illinois, Iowa, Minnesota, Missouri, Wisconsin	P.O. Box 970028 St. Louis, MO 63197-0028	Kansas City, MO 64999
Delaware, District of Columbia, Maryland, Pennsylvania, Virginia	P.O. Box 7990 Philadelphia, PA 19162-7990	Philadelphia, PA 19255
Indiana, Kentucky, Michigan, Ohio, West Virginia	P.O. Box 6252 Chicago, IL 60680-6252	Cincinnati, OH 45999
Kansas, New Mexico, Oklahoma, Texas	P.O. Box 970027 St. Louis, MO 63197-0027	Austin, TX 73301
Alaska, Arizona, California (*counties of Alpine, Amador, Butte, Calaveras, Colusa, Contra Costa, Del Norte, El Dorado, Glenn, Humboldt, Lake, Lassen, Marin, Mendocino, Modoc, Napa, Nevada, Placer, Plumas, Sacramento, San Joaquin, Shasta, Sierra, Siskiyou, Solano, Sonoma, Sutter, Tehama, Trinity, Yolo, and Yuba*), Colorado, Idaho, Montana, Nebraska, Nevada, North Dakota, Oregon, South Dakota, Utah, Washington, Wyoming	P.O. Box 7122 San Francisco, CA 94120-7122	Ogden, UT 84201
California (*all other counties*), Hawaii	P.O. Box 54916 Los Angeles, CA 90054-0916	Fresno, CA 93888
Alabama, Arkansas, Louisiana, Mississippi, North Carolina, Tennessee	P.O. Box 1236 Charlotte, NC 28201-1236	Memphis, TN 37501
American Samoa or Puerto Rico (*or exclude income under section 933*); are a nonpermanent resident of Guam or the Virgin Islands; have an APO, FPO, or foreign address; are a dual-status alien; or file Form 2555, 2555-EZ, or 4563	P.O. Box 7990 Philadelphia, PA 19162-7990	Philadelphia, PA 19255
Guam: Permanent residents	Send Form 4868 and payments to:	Department of Revenue and Taxation Government of Guam P.O. Box 23607 GMF, GU 96921
Virgin Islands: Permanent residents	Send Form 4868 and payments to:	V.I. Bureau of Internal Revenue 9601 Estate Thomas Charlotte Amalie St. Thomas, VI 00802

Form **4952**	**Investment Interest Expense Deduction**	OMB No. 1545-0191
Department of the Treasury Internal Revenue Service (99)	▶ **Attach to your tax return.**	**1999** Attachment Sequence No. **72**

Name(s) shown on return	Identifying number

Part I — Total Investment Interest Expense

1	Investment interest expense paid or accrued in 1999. See instructions	**1**	
2	Disallowed investment interest expense from 1998 Form 4952, line 7	**2**	
3	**Total investment interest expense.** Add lines 1 and 2	**3**	

Part II — Net Investment Income

4a	Gross income from property held for investment (excluding any net gain from the disposition of property held for investment)	**4a**	
b	Net gain from the disposition of property held for investment . . . **4b**		
c	Net capital gain from the disposition of property held for investment **4c**		
d	Subtract line 4c from line 4b. If zero or less, enter -0-	**4d**	
e	Enter all or part of the amount on line 4c, if any, that you elect to include in investment income. Do not enter more than the amount on line 4b. See instructions . . . . ▶	**4e**	
f	Investment income. Add lines 4a, 4d, and 4e. See instructions	**4f**	
5	Investment expenses. See instructions	**5**	
6	**Net investment income.** Subtract line 5 from line 4f. If zero or less, enter -0-	**6**	

Part III — Investment Interest Expense Deduction

7	Disallowed investment interest expense to be carried forward to 2000. Subtract line 6 from line 3. If zero or less, enter -0-	**7**	
8	**Investment interest expense deduction.** Enter the **smaller** of line 3 or 6. See instructions . .	**8**	

Section references are to the Internal Revenue Code unless otherwise noted.

General Instructions

Purpose of Form

Use Form 4952 to figure the amount of investment interest expense you can deduct for 1999 and the amount, if any, you can carry forward to future years. Your investment interest expense deduction is limited to your net investment income.

For more details, see **Pub. 550,** Investment Income and Expenses.

Who Must File

If you are an individual, estate, or a trust and you claim a deduction for investment interest expense, you must complete and attach Form 4952 to your tax return unless **all** of the following apply.

● Your investment interest expense is not more than your investment income from interest and ordinary dividends.

● You have no other deductible expenses connected with the production of interest or dividends.

● You have no disallowed investment interest expense from 1998.

Allocation of Interest Expense Under Temporary Regulations Section 1.163-8T

If you paid or accrued interest on a loan and used the loan proceeds for more than one purpose, you may have to allocate the interest. This is necessary because different rules apply to investment interest, personal interest, trade or business interest, home mortgage interest, and passive activity interest. See **Pub. 535,** Business Expenses.

Specific Instructions

Part I—Total Investment Interest Expense

Line 1

Enter the investment interest paid or accrued during the tax year, regardless of when you incurred the indebtedness. **Investment interest** is interest paid or accrued on a loan (or part of a loan) that is allocable to property held for investment (as defined later).

Include investment interest expense reported to you on Schedule K-1 from a partnership or an S corporation. Include amortization of bond premium on taxable

bonds purchased after October 22, 1986, but before January 1, 1988, unless you elected to offset amortizable bond premium against the interest payments on the bond. A taxable bond is a bond on which the interest is includible in gross income.

Investment interest expense **does not** include any of the following:

● Home mortgage interest.

● Interest expense that is properly allocable to a passive activity. Generally, a passive activity is any business activity in which you **do not** materially participate and any rental activity. See the separate instructions for **Form 8582,** Passive Activity Loss Limitations, for details.

● Any interest expense that is capitalized, such as construction interest subject to section 263A.

● Interest expense related to tax-exempt interest income under section 265.

● Interest expense, disallowed under section 264, on indebtedness with respect to life insurance, endowment, or annuity contracts issued after June 8, 1997, even if the proceeds were used to purchase any property held for investment.

Property held for investment. Property held for investment includes property that produces income (unless derived in the ordinary course of a trade or business) from interest, dividends, annuities, or royalties; and gains from the disposition of property that produces those types of income or is held for investment. However, it does not include an interest in a passive activity.

Property held for investment also includes an interest in an activity of conducting a trade or business in which you did not materially participate and that is not a passive activity. For example, a working interest in an oil or gas property that you held directly or through an entity that did not limit your liability is property held for investment if you did not materially participate in the activity.

Part II—Net Investment Income

Line 4a

Gross income from property held for investment to enter on line 4a includes income (unless derived in the ordinary course of a trade or business) from:

● Interest,

● Ordinary dividends (except Alaska Permanent Fund dividends),

● Annuities, and

● Royalties.

If you are filing **Form 8814,** Parents' Election To Report Child's Interest and Dividends, part or all of your child's income may be included on line 4a. See Form 8814 for details.

Also, include on line 4a net income from the following passive activities:

● Rental of substantially nondepreciable property,

● Equity-financed lending activities, and

● Acquisition of certain interests in a pass-through entity licensing intangible property.

See Regulations section 1.469-2(f)(10) for details.

Also include on line 4a (or 4b, if applicable) net passive income from a passive activity of a publicly traded partnership (as defined in section 469(k)(2)). See Notice 88-75, 1988-2 C.B. 386, for details.

Include investment income reported to you on Schedule K-1 from a partnership or an S corporation. Also include net investment income from an estate or a trust.

Caution: *Do not include on line 4a any net gain from the disposition of property held for investment. Instead, enter it on line 4b.*

Line 4b

Net gain from the disposition of property held for investment is the excess, if any, of total gains over total losses from the disposition of property held for investment. When figuring this amount, include capital gain distributions from mutual funds.

Line 4c

Net capital gain from the disposition of property held for investment is the excess, if any, of net long-term capital gain over net short-term capital loss from the disposition of

property held for investment. Capital gain distributions from mutual funds are treated as long-term capital gains.

Line 4e

Net capital gain from the disposition of property held for investment is excluded from investment income. However, you may elect to include in investment income all or part of the net capital gain from the disposition of property held for investment. If you make the election, you also must reduce the amount of net capital gain eligible for capital gains tax rates by the amount of net capital gain you included in investment income. Therefore, you should consider the effect on your tax using the capital gains tax rates before making this election. Once made, the election may only be revoked with IRS consent.

To make the election, enter on line 4e the amount that you elect to include in investment income. Also enter this amount on line 21 of Schedule D (Form 1040), or on line 20 of Schedule D (Form 1041), if applicable.

You must generally make this election on a timely filed return (including extensions). However, if you timely filed your return without making the election, you can also make the election on an amended return filed within 6 months of the due date of your return (excluding extensions). Write "Filed pursuant to section 301.9100-2" on the amended return and file it at the same place you filed the original return.

Line 5

Investment expenses are your allowed deductions, other than interest expense, directly connected with the production of investment income. For example, depreciation or depletion allowed on assets that produce investment income is an investment expense.

Include investment expenses reported to you on Schedule K-1 from a partnership or an S corporation.

Investment expenses **do not** include any deductions taken into account in determining your income or loss from a passive activity.

If you have investment expenses that are included as a miscellaneous itemized deduction on Schedule A (Form 1040), line 22, you may not have to use the entire amount for purposes of Form 4952, line 5. The 2% adjusted gross income limitation on Schedule A (Form 1040), line 25, may reduce the amount you must include on Form 4952, line 5.

Include on Form 4952, line 5, only the **smaller** of:

● The investment expenses included on Schedule A (Form 1040), line 22, or

● The total on Schedule A (Form 1040), line 26.

Example. Assume Schedule A, line 22, includes investment expenses of $3,000, and line 26 is $1,300 after the 2% adjusted gross income limitation. Investment expenses from Schedule A of $1,300 are used to figure the amount of investment expenses for line 5. If investment expenses of $800 were included on line 22 and line 26 was $1,300, investment expenses from Schedule A of $800 would be used.

Part III—Investment Interest Expense Deduction

Line 8

You may deduct the amount on line 8 as investment interest expense.

Individuals. Generally, enter the amount from line 8 on Schedule A (Form 1040), line 13, even if all or part of it is attributable to a partnership or an S corporation. However, if any portion of this amount is attributable to royalties, enter that part of the interest expense on Schedule E (Form 1040). Also, if any portion is attributable to a trade or business in which you did not materially participate and that is not a passive activity, enter that part of the interest expense on the schedule where you report other expenses for that trade or business.

Estates and trusts. Enter the amount from line 8 on Form 1041, line 10.

Form 6198. If any portion of the deductible investment interest expense is attributable to an activity for which you are not at risk, you must also use **Form 6198,** At-Risk Limitations, to figure your deductible investment interest expense. Enter the portion attributable to the at-risk activity on Form 6198, line 4. Reduce Form 4952, line 8, by the amount entered on Form 6198. See Form 6198 and its instructions for more details, especially the instructions for line 4 of that form.

Alternative minimum tax (AMT). Deductible interest expense may be an adjustment for the AMT. For details, see **Form 6251,** Alternative Minimum Tax—Individuals, or Form 1041, Schedule I, for estates and trusts.

Paperwork Reduction Act Notice. We ask for the information on this form to carry out the Internal Revenue laws of the United States. You are required to give us the information. We need it to ensure that you are complying with these laws and to allow us to figure and collect the right amount of tax.

You are not required to provide the information requested on a form that is subject to the Paperwork Reduction Act unless the form displays a valid OMB control number. Books or records relating to a form or its instructions must be retained as long as their contents may become material in the administration of any Internal Revenue law. Generally, tax returns and return information are confidential, as required by section 6103.

The time needed to complete and file this form will vary depending on individual circumstances. The estimated average time is:

Recordkeeping	13 min.
Learning about the law or the form	16 min.
Preparing the form	21 min.
Copying, assembling, and sending the form to the IRS . .	10 min.

If you have comments concerning the accuracy of these time estimates or suggestions for making this form simpler, we would be happy to hear from you. See the instructions for the tax return with which this form is filed.

Form **4972**	**Tax on Lump-Sum Distributions**	OMB No. 1545-0193
	From Qualified Retirement Plans	19**99**
Department of the Treasury Internal Revenue Service (99)	▶ **Attach to Form 1040 or Form 1041.** ▶ **See separate instructions.**	Attachment Sequence No. **28**

Name of recipient of distribution	Identifying number

Part I Complete this part to see if you qualify to use Form 4972

			Yes	No
1	Was this a distribution of a plan participant's entire balance from all of an employer's qualified plans of one kind (pension, profit-sharing, or stock bonus)? If "No," do not use this form	**1**		
2	Did you roll over any part of the distribution? If "Yes," do not use this form	**2**		
3	Was this distribution paid to you as a beneficiary of a plan participant who died after reaching age 59½ (or who had been born before 1936)?	**3**		
4	Were you a plan participant who received this distribution after reaching age 59½ **and** having been in the plan for at least 5 years before the year of the distribution?	**4**		
	If you answered "No" to both questions 3 **and** 4, do not use this form.			
5a	Did you use Form 4972 after 1986 for a previous distribution from your own plan? If "Yes," do not use this form for a 1999 distribution from your own plan	**5a**		
b	If you are receiving this distribution as a beneficiary of a plan participant who died, did you use Form 4972 for a previous distribution received for that plan participant after 1986? If "Yes," you may not use the form for this distribution	**5b**		

Part II **Complete this part to choose the 20% capital gain election** (See instructions.) Do not complete this part unless the participant was born **before** 1936.

6	Capital gain part from box 3 of Form 1099-R	**6**		
7	Multiply line 6 by 20% (.20)	**7**		
	If you also choose to use Part III, go to line 8. Otherwise, include the amount from line 7 in the total on Form 1040, line 40, or Form 1041, Schedule G, line 1b, whichever applies.			

Part III Complete this part to choose the 5- or 10-year tax option (See instructions.)

8	Ordinary income from Form 1099-R, box 2a minus box 3. If you did not complete Part II, enter the taxable amount from box 2a of Form 1099-R	**8**		
9	Death benefit exclusion for a beneficiary of a plan participant who died before August 21, 1996	**9**		
10	Total taxable amount. Subtract line 9 from line 8	**10**		
11	Current actuarial value of annuity (from Form 1099-R, box 8)	**11**		
12	Adjusted total taxable amount. Add lines 10 and 11. If this amount is $70,000 or more, **skip** lines 13 through 16, and enter this amount on line 17	**12**		
13	Multiply line 12 by 50% (.50), but **do not** enter more than $10,000	**13**		
14	Subtract $20,000 from line 12. If the result is less than zero, enter -0-	**14**		
15	Multiply line 14 by 20% (.20)	**15**		
16	Minimum distribution allowance. Subtract line 15 from line 13	**16**		
17	Subtract line 16 from line 12	**17**		
18	Federal estate tax attributable to lump-sum distribution	**18**		
19	Subtract line 18 from line 17	**19**		
	If line 11 is blank, skip lines 20 through 22 and go to line 23.			
20	Divide line 11 by line 12 and enter the result as a decimal (rounded to at least four places)	**20**	.	
21	Multiply line 16 by the decimal on line 20	**21**		
22	Subtract line 21 from line 11	**22**		

For Paperwork Reduction Act Notice, see separate instructions.   Cat. No. 13187U   Form **4972** (1999)

Part III   5- or 10-year tax option—CONTINUED

5-year tax option

23	Multiply line 19 by 20% (.20)	**23**	
24	Tax on amount on line 23. Use the Tax Rate Schedule for the 5-Year Tax Option in the instructions	**24**	
25	Multiply line 24 by five (5). If line 11 is blank, skip lines 26 through 28, and enter this amount on line 29	**25**	
26	Multiply line 22 by 20% (.20) **26**		
27	Tax on amount on line 26. Use the Tax Rate Schedule for the 5-Year Tax Option in the instructions **27**		
28	Multiply line 27 by five (5)	**28**	
29	Subtract line 28 from line 25. (Multiple recipients, see page 2 of the instructions.) . . .	**29**	

Note: *Complete lines 30 through 36 ONLY if the participant was born before 1936. Otherwise, enter the amount from line 29 on line 37.*

10-year tax option

30	Multiply line 19 by 10% (.10)	**30**	
31	Tax on amount on line 30. Use the Tax Rate Schedule for the 10-Year Tax Option in the instructions	**31**	
32	Multiply line 31 by ten (10). If line 11 is blank, skip lines 33 through 35, and enter this amount on line 36	**32**	
33	Multiply line 22 by 10% (.10) **33**		
34	Tax on amount on line 33. Use the Tax Rate Schedule for the 10-Year Tax Option in the instructions **34**		
35	Multiply line 34 by ten (10)	**35**	
36	Subtract line 35 from line 32. (Multiple recipients, see page 2 of the instructions.) . . .	**36**	
37	Compare lines 29 and 36. Generally, you should enter the **smaller** amount here (see instructions) . . . . ▶	**37**	
38	Tax on lump-sum distribution. Add lines 7 and 37. Also, include this amount in the total on Form 1040, line 40, or Form 1041, Schedule G, line 1b, whichever applies . . . . . . ▶	**38**	

Form **4972** (1999)

Alternative Minimum Tax—Individuals

▶ See separate instructions.

▶ **Attach to Form 1040 or Form 1040NR.**

OMB No. 1545-0227

1999

Attachment
Sequence No. **32**

Name(s) shown on Form 1040

Your social security number

Part I   Adjustments and Preferences

1	If you itemized deductions on Schedule A (Form 1040), go to line 2. Otherwise, enter your standard deduction from Form 1040, line 36, here and go to line 6	**1**
2	Medical and dental. Enter the smaller of Schedule A (Form 1040), line 4 **or** 2½% of Form 1040, line 34	**2**
3	Taxes. Enter the amount from Schedule A (Form 1040), line 9	**3**
4	Certain interest on a home mortgage **not** used to buy, build, or improve your home	**4**
5	Miscellaneous itemized deductions. Enter the amount from Schedule A (Form 1040), line 26 . . .	**5**
6	Refund of taxes. Enter any tax refund from Form 1040, line 10 or line 21	**6** ( )
7	Investment interest. Enter difference between regular tax and AMT deduction	**7**
8	Post-1986 depreciation. Enter difference between regular tax and AMT depreciation	**8**
9	Adjusted gain or loss. Enter difference between AMT and regular tax gain or loss	**9**
10	Incentive stock options. Enter excess of AMT income over regular tax income	**10**
11	Passive activities. Enter difference between AMT and regular tax income or loss	**11**
12	Beneficiaries of estates and trusts. Enter the amount from Schedule K-1 (Form 1041), line 9 . . .	**12**
13	Tax-exempt interest from private activity bonds issued after 8/7/86	**13**

14   Other. Enter the amount, if any, for each item below and enter the total on line 14.

a	Circulation expenditures .	h	Loss limitations . . . . .
b	Depletion	i	Mining costs . . . .
c	Depreciation (pre-1987) .	j	Patron's adjustment . .
d	Installment sales . . .	k	Pollution control facilities .
e	Intangible drilling costs .	l	Research and experimental
f	Large partnerships . . .	m	Section 1202 exclusion . .
g	Long-term contracts . .	n	Tax shelter farm activities .
		o	Related adjustments . .

	14

15	**Total Adjustments and Preferences.** Combine lines 1 through 14 . . . . ▶	**15**

Part II   Alternative Minimum Taxable Income

16	Enter the amount from **Form 1040, line 37.** If less than zero, enter as a (loss) . . . . . . ▶	**16**
17	Net operating loss deduction, if any, from Form 1040, line 21. Enter as a positive amount . . .	**17**
18	If Form 1040, line 34, is over $126,600 (over $63,300 if married filing separately), and you itemized deductions, enter the amount, if any, from line 9 of the worksheet for Schedule A (Form 1040), line 28	**18** ( )
19	Combine lines 15 through 18 . . . . ▶	**19**
20	Alternative tax net operating loss deduction. See page 6 of the instructions	**20**
21	**Alternative Minimum Taxable Income.** Subtract line 20 from line 19. (If married filing separately and line 21 is more than $165,000, see page 7 of the instructions.) . . . . ▶	**21**

Part III   Exemption Amount and Alternative Minimum Tax

22   **Exemption Amount.** (If this form is for a child under age 14, see page 7 of the instructions.)

IF your filing status is . . .	AND line 21 is not over . . .	THEN enter on line 22 . . .	
Single or head of household	$112,500	$33,750	
Married filing jointly or qualifying widow(er) .	150,000	45,000	} . .
Married filing separately.	75,000	22,500	

	22

If line 21 is **over** the amount shown above for your filing status, see page 7 of the instructions.

23	Subtract line 22 from line 21. If zero or less, enter -0- here and on lines 26 and 28 . . . . . ▶	**23**
24	If you reported capital gain distributions directly on Form 1040, line 13, **or** you completed Schedule D (Form 1040) and have an amount on line 25 or line 27 (or would have had an amount on either line if you had completed Part IV) (as refigured for the AMT, if necessary), go to Part IV of Form 6251 to figure line 24. **All others:** If line 23 is $175,000 or less ($87,500 or less if married filing separately), multiply line 23 by 26% (.26). Otherwise, multiply line 23 by 28% (.28) and subtract $3,500 ($1,750 if married filing separately) from the result . . . . ▶	**24**
25	Alternative minimum tax foreign tax credit. See page 7 of the instructions	**25**
26	Tentative minimum tax. Subtract line 25 from line 24 . . . . ▶	**26**
27	Enter your tax from Form 1040, line 40 (minus any tax from Form 4972 and any foreign tax credit from Form 1040, line 46)	**27**
28	**Alternative Minimum Tax.** Subtract line 27 from line 26. If zero or less, enter -0-. Enter here and on Form 1040, line 51 . . . . ▶	**28**

For Paperwork Reduction Act Notice, see page 8 of the instructions.   Cat. No. 13600G   Form **6251** (1999)

Part IV Line 24 Computation Using Maximum Capital Gains Rates

Caution: *If you **did not** complete Part IV of Schedule D (Form 1040), see page 8 of the instructions before you complete this part.*	
29 Enter the amount from Form 6251, line 23	**29**
30 Enter the amount from Schedule D (Form 1040), line 27 (as refigured for the AMT, if necessary). See page 8 of the instructions	**30**
31 Enter the amount from Schedule D (Form 1040), line 25 (as refigured for the AMT, if necessary). See page 8 of the instructions	**31**
32 Add lines 30 and 31	**32**
33 Enter the amount from Schedule D (Form 1040), line 22 (as refigured for the AMT, if necessary). See page 8 of the instructions	**33**
34 Enter the **smaller** of line 32 or line 33	**34**
35 Subtract line 34 from line 29. If zero or less, enter -0- . . . . ▶	**35**
36 If line 35 is $175,000 or less ($87,500 or less if married filing separately), multiply line 35 by 26% (.26). Otherwise, multiply line 35 by 28% (.28) and subtract $3,500 ($1,750 if married filing separately) from the result	**36**
37 Enter the amount from Schedule D (Form 1040), line 36 (as figured for the regular tax). See page 8 of the instructions . . . . ▶	**37**
38 Enter the **smallest** of line 29, line 30, or line 37 . . . . . . ▶	**38**
39 Multiply line 38 by 10% (.10)	**39**
40 Enter the **smaller** of line 29 or line 30	**40**
41 Enter the amount from line 38	**41**
42 Subtract line 41 from line 40 . . . . ▶	**42**
43 Multiply line 42 by 20% (.20)	**43**
Note: *If line 31 is zero or blank, go to line 48.*	
44 Enter the amount from line 29	**44**
45 Add lines 35, 38, and 42	**45**
46 Subtract line 45 from line 44	**46**
47 Multiply line 46 by 25% (.25)	**47**
48 Add lines 36, 39, 43, and 47	**48**
49 If line 29 is $175,000 or less ($87,500 or less if married filing separately), multiply line 29 by 26% (.26). Otherwise, multiply line 29 by 28% (.28) and subtract $3,500 ($1,750 if married filing separately) from the result	**49**
50 Enter the **smaller** of line 48 or line 49 here and on line 24	**50**

Form **6251** (1999)

Department of the Treasury
Internal Revenue Service

www.irs.ustreas.gov

Form 656 (Rev. 2-1999)
Catalog Number 16728N

Form 656

Offer in Compromise

Item 1 — Taxpayer's Name and Home or Business Address

Name

Street Address

| City | State | ZIP Code |

Mailing Address *(if different from above)*

Street Address

| City | State | ZIP Code |

Item 2 — Social Security Numbers

(a) Primary

(b) Secondary

Item 3 — Employer Identification Number *(included in offer)*

Item 4 — Other Employer Identification Numbers *(not included in offer)*

Item 5 — To: Commissioner of Internal Revenue Service

I/We (includes all types of taxpayers) submit this offer to compromise the tax liabilities plus any interest, penalties, additions to tax, and additional amounts required by law (tax liability) for the tax type and period marked below: (Please mark an "X" in the box for the correct description and fill-in the correct tax period(s), adding additional periods if needed).

❑ **1040/1120 Income Tax** — Year(s)

❑ **941 Employer's Quarterly Federal Tax Return** — Quarterly period(s)

❑ **940 Employer's Annual Federal Unemployment (FUTA) Tax Return** — Year(s)

❑ **Trust Fund Recovery Penalty** as a responsible person of (enter corporation name)

for failure to pay withholding and Federal Insurance Contributions Act Taxes (Social Security taxes), for period(s) ending _____ .

❑ **Other Federal Tax(es)** [specify type(s) and period(s)] _____

Note: If you need more space, use another sheet titled "Attachment to Form 656 Dated _____ ." Sign and date the attachment following the listing of the tax periods.

Item 6 — I/we submit this offer for the reason(s) checked below:

❑ **Doubt as to Liability** — "I do not believe I owe this amount." You must include a detailed explanation of the reasons why you believe you do not owe the tax.

❑ **Doubt as to Collectibility** — "I have insufficient assets and income to pay the full amount." You *must* include a complete financial statement, Form 433-A and/or Form 433-B.

Item 7

I/we offer to pay $ _____

❑ Paid in full with this offer.

❑ Deposit of $ _____ is attached to this offer.

❑ No deposit.

Note: Make all checks payable to: The United States Treasury

Check one of the following:

❑ **Cash Offer** (Offered amount will be paid in 90 days or less)

Balance to be paid in: _____ 10, _____ 30, _____ 60, or _____ 90 days from notice of acceptance of the offer. If more than one payment will be made during the time frame checked, provide the amount and date of the payment on the line below.

❑ **Short Term Deferred Payment Offer (offered amount paid in more than 90 days but within 24 months)**

Amount of monthly payment _____

Monthly payment date _____

Balance will be fully paid on _____

Other terms for payment _____

❑ **Deferred Payment Offer (offered amount will be paid over the life of the collection statute)**

Amount of monthly payment _____

Monthly payment date _____

Other terms for payment _____

Note: In addition to the above amounts (for both cash and deferred offers), the Internal Revenue Service (IRS) will add interest from the date we accept the offer until you completely pay the amount offered, as required by section 6621 of the Internal Revenue Code. We compound interest daily, as required by section 6622 of the Internal Revenue Code.

Item 8: By submitting this offer, I/we understand and agree to the following conditions:

(a) I/we voluntarily submit all payments made on this offer.

(b) The IRS will apply payments made under the terms of this offer in the best interest of the government.

(c) If the IRS rejects the offer or I/we withdraw the offer, the IRS will return any amount paid with the offer. If I/we agree in writing, IRS will apply the amount paid with the offer to the amount owed. If I/we agree to apply the payment, the date the IRS received the offer remittance will be considered the date of payment. I/we understand that the IRS will not pay interest on any amount I/we submit with the offer.

(d) **I/we will comply with all provisions of the Internal Revenue Code relating to filing my/our returns and paying my/our required taxes for 5 years or until the offered amount (plus accrued interest) is paid in full, whichever is longer. In the case of a jointly submitted offer to compromise joint tax liabilities, I/we understand that default with respect to the compliance provisions described in this paragraph by one party to this agreement will not result in the default of the entire agreement. The default provisions described in Item 8(o) of this agreement will be applied only to the party failing to comply with the requirements of this paragraph. This provision does not apply to offers based on Doubt as to Liability.**

(e) I/we waive and agree to the suspension of any statutory periods of limitation (time limits provided for by law) for the IRS assessment and collection of the tax liability for the tax periods identified in Item 5. I/we understand that this waiver provision will have no effect after December 31, 2002.

(f) The IRS will keep all payments and credits made, received or applied to the total original tax liability before submission of this offer. The IRS may keep any proceeds from a levy served prior to submission of the offer, but not received at the time the offer is submitted. If I/we have an installment agreement prior to submitting the offer, I/we must continue to make the payments as agreed while this offer is pending. Installment agreement payments will not be applied against the amount offered.

(g) **The IRS will keep any refund, including interest, due to me/us because of overpayment of any tax or other liability, for tax periods extending through the calendar year that the IRS accepts the offer. I/we may not designate an overpayment ordinarily subject to refund, to which the IRS is entitled, to be applied to estimated tax payments for the following year.** This condition does not apply if the offer is based on Doubt as to Liability.

(h) I/we will return to the IRS any refund identified in (g) received after submission of this offer. This condition does not apply to offers based on Doubt as to Liability.

(i) The IRS cannot collect more than the full amount of the tax liability under this offer.

(j) I/we understand that I/we remain responsible for the full amount of the tax liability, unless and until the IRS accepts the offer in writing and I/we have met all the terms and conditions of the offer. The IRS will not remove the original amount of the tax liability from its records until I/we have met all the terms of the offer.

(k) I/we understand that the tax I/we offer to compromise is and will remain a tax liability until I/we meet all the terms and conditions of this offer. If I/we file bankruptcy before the terms and conditions of this offer are completed, any claim the IRS files in the bankruptcy proceedings will be a tax claim.

(l) Once the IRS accepts the offer in writing, I/we have no right to contest, in court or otherwise, the amount of the tax liability.

(m) The offer is pending starting with the date an authorized IRS official signs this form and accepts my/our waiver of the statutory periods of limitation. The offer remains pending until an authorized IRS official accepts, rejects or acknowledges withdrawal of the offer in writing. If I/we appeal the IRS decision on the offer, the IRS will continue to treat the offer as pending until the Appeals Office accepts or rejects the offer in writing. If I/we don't file a protest within 30 days of the date the

IRS notifies me/us of the right to protest the decision, I/we waive the right to a hearing before the Appeals Office about the offer in compromise.

(n) **The waiver and suspension of any statutory periods of limitation for assessment and collection of the amount of the tax liability described in Item 5, continue to apply:**
- **while the offer is pending [see (m) above]**
- **during the time I/we have not paid all of the amount offered**
- **during the time I/we have not completed all terms and conditions of the offer**
- **for one additional year beyond each of the time periods identified in this paragraph**

(o) If I/we fail to meet any of the terms and conditions of the offer and the offer defaults, then the IRS may:
- immediately file suit to collect the entire unpaid balance of the offer
- immediately file suit to collect an amount equal to the original amount of the tax liability as liquidating damages, minus any payment already received under the terms of this offer
- disregard the amount of the offer and apply all amounts already paid under the offer against the original amount of the tax liability
- file suit or levy to collect the original amount of the tax liability, without further notice of any kind.

The IRS will continue to add interest as required by Section 6621 of the Internal Revenue Code, on the amount the IRS determines is due after default. The IRS will add interest from the date the offer is defaulted until I/we completely satisfy the amount owed.

(p) The IRS generally files a Notice of Federal Tax Lien to protect the Government's interest on deferred payment offers. We will release this tax lien when the offered amount plus any accrued interest has been fully paid.

Item 9

If I/we submit this offer on a substitute form, I/we affirm that this form is a verbatim duplicate of the official Form 656, and I/we agree to be bound by all the terms and conditions set forth in the official Form 656.

Under penalties of perjury, I declare that I have examined this offer, including accompanying schedules and statements, and to the best of my knowledge and belief, it is true, correct and complete.

_____
9(a) Signature of Taxpayer — proponent

_____
Date

_____
9(b) Signature of Taxpayer — proponent

_____
Date

For Official Use Only

I accept the waiver of the statutory period of limitations for the Internal Revenue Service.

_____
Signature of Authorized Internal Revenue Service Official

_____
Title

_____
Date

Form **8615**	**Tax for Children Under Age 14** **Who Have Investment Income of More Than $1,400**	OMB No. 1545-0998
Department of the Treasury Internal Revenue Service (99)	▶ Attach ONLY to the child's Form 1040, Form 1040A, or Form 1040NR.	**1999** Attachment Sequence No. **33**

Child's name shown on return	Child's social security number

A Parent's name (first, initial, and last). **Caution:** *See instructions on back before completing.* **B** Parent's social security number

C Parent's filing status (check one):
☐ Single   ☐ Married filing jointly   ☐ Married filing separately   ☐ Head of household   ☐ Qualifying widow(er)

Part I Child's Net Investment Income

1	Enter the child's investment income, such as taxable interest and dividends. See instructions. If this amount is $1,400 or less, **stop;** do not file this form	1	
2	If the child **did not** itemize deductions on **Schedule A** (Form 1040 or Form 1040NR), enter $1,400. If the child **did** itemize deductions, see instructions	2	
3	Subtract line 2 from line 1. If the result is zero or less, **stop;** do not complete the rest of this form but **do** attach it to the child's return	3	
4	Enter the child's **taxable income** from Form 1040, line 39; Form 1040A, line 24; or Form 1040NR, line 38	4	
5	Enter the **smaller** of line 3 or line 4	5	

Part II Tentative Tax Based on the Tax Rate of the Parent Listed on Line A

6	Enter the parent's **taxable income** from Form 1040, line 39; Form 1040A, line 24; Form 1040EZ, line 6; TeleFile Tax Record, line K; Form 1040NR, line 38; or Form 1040NR-EZ, line 14. If less than zero, enter -0-	6	
7	Enter the total net investment income, if any, from Forms 8615, line 5, of **all other** children of the parent identified above. **Do not** include the amount from line 5 above	7	
8	Add lines 5, 6, and 7	8	
9	Enter the tax on line 8 based on the **parent's** filing status. See instructions. If the **Capital Gain Tax Worksheet** or **Schedule D** or **J** (Form 1040) is used to figure the tax, check here ▶ ☐	9	
10	Enter the parent's tax from Form 1040, line 40; Form 1040A, line 25; Form 1040EZ, line 10; TeleFile Tax Record, line K; Form 1040NR, line 39; or Form 1040NR-EZ, line 15. If any tax is from **Form 4972 or 8814,** see instructions. If the **Capital Gain Tax Worksheet** or **Schedule D** or **J** (Form 1040) was used to figure the tax, check here . . . . ▶ ☐	10	
11	Subtract line 10 from line 9 and enter the result. If line 7 is blank, also enter this amount on line 13 and go to **Part III**	11	
12a	Add lines 5 and 7	12a		
b	Divide line 5 by line 12a. Enter the result as a decimal (rounded to at least three places) . .	12b	× .
13	Multiply line 11 by line 12b	13	

Part III Child's Tax—If lines 4 and 5 above are the same, enter -0- on line 15 and go to line 16.

14	Subtract line 5 from line 4	14		
15	Enter the tax on line 14 based on the **child's** filing status. See instructions. If the **Capital Gain Tax Worksheet** or **Schedule D** or **J** (Form 1040) is used to figure the tax, check here ▶ ☐	15	
16	Add lines 13 and 15	16	
17	Enter the tax on line 4 based on the **child's** filing status. See instructions. If the **Capital Gain Tax Worksheet** or **Schedule D** or **J** (Form 1040) is used to figure the tax, check here ▶ ☐	17	
18	Enter the **larger** of line 16 or line 17 here and on Form 1040, line 40; Form 1040A, line 25; or Form 1040NR, line 39	18	

General Instructions

Purpose of Form

For children under age 14, investment income over $1,400 is taxed at the parent's rate if the parent's rate is higher than the child's rate. If the child's investment income is more than $1,400, use this form to figure the child's tax.

See **Pub. 929,** Tax Rules for Children and Dependents, if the child, the parent, or any of the parent's other children under age 14 received capital gain distributions or farm income. It has information on how

to figure the tax using the **Capital Gain Tax Worksheet** or **Schedule D** or **J,** which may result in less tax.

Investment Income

For this form, "investment income" includes all taxable income other than earned income as defined on page 2. It includes taxable interest, dividends, capital gains, rents, royalties, etc. It also includes taxable social security benefits, pension and annuity income, and income (other than earned income) received as the beneficiary of a trust.

Who Must File

Generally, Form 8615 must be filed for any child who was under age 14 on January 1, 2000, had more than $1,400 of investment income, and is required to file a tax return. But if neither parent was alive on December 31, 1999, do not use Form 8615. Instead, figure the child's tax in the normal manner.

Note: *The parent may be able to elect to report the child's interest and dividends (including capital gain distributions) on the parent's return. If the parent makes this election, the child will not have to file a return or Form 8615. However, the Federal*

For Paperwork Reduction Act Notice, see back of form.   Cat. No. 64113U   Form **8615** (1999)

771

income tax on the child's income, including captial gain distributions, may be **higher** if this election is made. For more details, see **Form 8814,** Parents' Election To Report Child's Interest and Dividends.

Additional Information

For more details, see Pub. 929.

Incomplete Information for Parent or Other Children

If the parent's taxable income or filing status or the net investment income of the parent's other children is not known by the due date of the child's return, reasonable estimates may be used. Enter "Estimated" next to the appropriate line(s) of Form 8615. For more details, see Pub. 929.

Amended Return

If after the child's return is filed the parent's taxable income changes or the net investment income of any of the parent's other children changes, the child's tax must be refigured using the adjusted amounts. If the child's tax changes, file **Form 1040X,** Amended U.S. Individual Income Tax Return, to correct the child's tax.

Alternative Minimum Tax

A child whose tax is figured on Form 8615 may owe the alternative minimum tax. For details, see **Form 6251,** Alternative Minimum Tax—Individuals, and its instructions.

Line Instructions

Lines A and B

If the child's parents were married to each other and filed a joint return, enter the name and social security number (SSN) of the parent who is listed first on the joint return.

If the parents were married but filed separate returns, enter the name and SSN of the parent who had the **higher** taxable income. If you do not know which parent had the higher taxable income, see Pub. 929.

If the parents were unmarried, treated as unmarried for Federal income tax purposes, or separated either by a divorce or separate maintenance decree, enter the name and SSN of the parent who had custody of the child for most of the year (the custodial parent).

Exception. If the custodial parent remarried and filed a joint return with his or her new spouse, enter the name and SSN of the person listed first on the joint return, even if that person is not the child's parent. If the custodial parent and his or her new spouse filed separate returns, enter the name and SSN of the person with the **higher** taxable income, even if that person is not the child's parent.

Note: *If the parents were unmarried but lived together during the year with the child, enter the name and SSN of the parent who had the **higher** taxable income.*

Child's Investment Income Worksheet—Line 1 (keep a copy for your records)

1. Enter the amount from the child's Form 1040, line 22; Form 1040A, line 14; or Form 1040NR, line 23, whichever applies . . . . . **1.** _____

2. Enter the child's **earned income** (defined on this page) plus any deduction the child claims on Form 1040, line 30, or Form 1040NR, line 30, whichever applies . . . . **2.** _____

3. Subtract line 2 from line 1. Enter the result here and on Form 8615, line 1 . . . . **3.** _____

Line 1

If the child had no earned income (defined later), enter the child's adjusted gross income from Form 1040, line 34; Form 1040A, line 19; or Form 1040NR, line 34.

If the child had earned income, use the worksheet on this page to figure the amount to enter on line 1. But if the child files **Form 2555** or **2555-EZ** (relating to foreign earned income), has a net loss from self-employment, or claims a net operating loss deduction, you **must** use the worksheet in Pub. 929 instead.

Earned income includes wages, tips, and other payments received for personal services performed. Generally, it is the total of the amounts reported on Form 1040, lines 7, 12, and 18; Form 1040A, line 7; or Form 1040NR, lines 8, 13, and 19.

Line 2

If the child itemized deductions, enter the **greater** of:

- $1,400, **or**

- $700 plus the portion of the amount on **Schedule A** (Form 1040), line 28 (or line 17 of the Form 1040NR Schedule A), that is directly connected with the production of the investment income on Form 8615, line 1.

Line 6

If the parent filed a joint return, enter the taxable income shown on that return even if the parent's spouse is not the child's parent.

Line 9

Figure the tax using the Tax Table, Tax Rate Schedules, the **Capital Gain Tax Worksheet,** or **Schedule D** or **J,** whichever applies. If any net capital gain is included on line 5, 6, or 7, Schedule D must be used to figure the tax unless the Capital Gain Tax Worksheet may be used. See Pub. 929 for details on how to figure the net capital gain included on line 8. If any farm income is included on line 5, 6, or 7, the tax may be less if you use Schedule J.

Line 10

If the parent filed a joint return, enter the tax shown on that return even if the parent's spouse is not the child's parent. If the parent filed **Form 4972, do not** include any tax from that form on line 10. If the parent filed **Form 8814,** enter "Form 8814" and the total tax from line 9 of Form(s) 8814 on the dotted line next to line 10 of Form 8615.

Line 15

Figure the tax using the Tax Table, Tax Rate Schedule X, the Capital Gain Tax Worksheet, or Schedule D or J, whichever applies. If line 14 includes any net capital gain, use Schedule D to figure the tax unless the Capital Gain Tax Worksheet may be used. See Pub. 929 for details on how to figure the net capital gain included on line 14. If any farm income is included on line 14, the tax may be less if you use Schedule J.

Line 17

Figure the tax as if these rules did not apply. For example, if the child has a net capital gain, use Schedule D to figure the child's tax unless the Capital Gain Tax Worksheet may be used.

Paperwork Reduction Act Notice. We ask for the information on this form to carry out the Internal Revenue laws of the United States. You are required to give us the information. We need it to ensure that you are complying with these laws and to allow us to figure and collect the right amount of tax.

You are not required to provide the information requested on a form that is subject to the Paperwork Reduction Act unless the form displays a valid OMB control number. Books or records relating to a form or its instructions must be retained as long as their contents may become material in the administration of any Internal Revenue law. Generally, tax returns and return information are confidential, as required by Internal Revenue Code section 6103.

The time needed to complete and file this form will vary depending on individual circumstances. The estimated average time is: **Recordkeeping,** 13 min.; **Learning about the law or the form,** 13 min.; **Preparing the form,** 45 min.; and **Copying, assembling, and sending the form to the IRS,** 17 min.

If you have comments concerning the accuracy of these time estimates or suggestions for making this form simpler, we would be happy to hear from you. See the instructions for the tax return with which this form is filed.

Form **8814**

Department of the Treasury
Internal Revenue Service (99)

Parents' Election To Report
Child's Interest and Dividends

▶ See instructions below and on back.
▶ Attach to parents' Form 1040 or Form 1040NR.

OMB No. 1545-1128

1999

Attachment
Sequence No. **40**

Name(s) shown on your return

Your social security number

Caution: *The Federal income tax on your child's income, including capital gain distributions, may be less if you file a separate tax return for the child instead of making this election. This is because you cannot take certain tax benefits that your child could take on his or her own return. For details, see* **Tax Benefits You May Not Take** *on the back.*

A Child's name (first, initial, and last)

B Child's social security number

C If more than one Form 8814 is attached, check here . . . . ▶ ☐

Part I Child's Interest and Dividends To Report on Your Return

1a	Enter your child's **taxable** interest. If this amount is different from the amounts shown on the child's Forms 1099-INT and 1099-OID, see the instructions	**1a**	
b	Enter your child's **tax-exempt** interest. **DO NOT** include this amount on line 1a **1b**		
2	Enter your child's ordinary dividends, including any Alaska Permanent Fund dividends. If your child received any ordinary dividends as a nominee, see the instructions	**2**	
3	Enter your child's capital gain distributions. If your child received any capital gain distributions as a nominee, see the instructions	**3**	
4	Add lines 1a, 2, and 3. If the total is $1,400 or less, skip lines 5 and 6 and go to line 7. If the total is $7,000 or more, **do not** file this form. Your child **must** file his or her own return to report the income	**4**	
5	Base amount	**5**	1,400 00
6	Subtract line 5 from line 4. If you checked the box on line C above or if you entered an amount on line 3, see the instructions. Also, include this amount in the total on Form 1040, line 21, or Form 1040NR, line 21. In the space next to line 21, enter "Form 8814" and show the amount. Go to line 7 below . . . . ▶	**6**	

Part II Tax on the First $1,400 of Child's Interest and Dividends

7	Amount not taxed	**7**	700 00
8	Subtract line 7 from line 4. If the result is zero or less, enter -0-	**8**	
9	**Tax.** Is the amount on line 8 less than $700? ☐ **No.** Enter $105 here and see the **Note** below. ☐ **Yes.** Multiply line 8 by 15% (.15). Enter the result here and see the **Note** below.	**9**	

Note: *If you checked the box on line C above, see the instructions. Otherwise, include the amount from line 9 in the tax you enter on Form 1040, line 40, or Form 1040NR, line 39. Be sure to check box* **a** *on Form 1040, line 40, or Form 1040NR, line 39.*

General Instructions

Purpose of Form. Use this form if you elect to report your child's income on your return. If you do, your child will not have to file a return. You can make this election if your child meets **all** of the following conditions.

● Was under age 14 on January 1, 2000.

● Is required to file a 1999 return.

● Had income only from interest and dividends, including Alaska Permanent Fund dividends.

● Had gross income for 1999 that was less than $7,000.

● Had no estimated tax payments for 1999 (including any overpayment of tax from his or her 1998 return applied to 1999 estimated tax).

● Had no Federal income tax withheld from his or her income.

You must also qualify. See **Parents Who Qualify To Make the Election** below.

How To Make the Election. To make the election, complete and attach Form(s) 8814 to your tax return and file your return by the due date (including extensions). A separate Form 8814 must be filed for **each** child whose income you choose to report.

Parents Who Qualify To Make the Election. You qualify to make this election if you file Form 1040 or Form 1040NR and **any** of the following apply.

● You are filing a joint return for 1999 with the child's other parent.

● You and the child's other parent were married to each other but file separate

returns for 1999 AND you had the **higher** taxable income. If you do not know if you had the higher taxable income, see **Pub. 929,** Tax Rules for Children and Dependents.

● You were unmarried, treated as unmarried for Federal income tax purposes, or separated from the child's other parent by a divorce or separate maintenance decree. You must have had custody of your child for most of the year (you were the custodial parent). If you were the custodial parent and you remarried, you may make the election on a joint return with your new spouse. But if you and your new spouse do not file a joint return, you qualify to make the election only if you had **higher** taxable income than your new spouse.

(continued)

For Paperwork Reduction Act Notice, see back of form.

Cat. No. 10750J

Form **8814** (1999)

773

Note: *If you and the child's other parent were not married but lived together during the year with the child, you qualify to make the election only if you are the parent with the **higher** taxable income.*

Tax Benefits You May Not Take. If you elect to report your child's income on your return, you may not take any of the following deductions that your child could take on his or her own return.

- Standard deduction of $1,750 for a blind child.
- Penalty on early withdrawal of child's savings.
- Itemized deductions such as child's investment expenses or charitable contributions.

If your child received **capital gain distributions,** you may pay up to $35 more tax on those distributions if you make this election instead of filing a separate tax return for the child. This is because the tax rate on the child's income between $700 and $1,400 is 15% if you make the election. However, if you file a separate return for the child, the tax rate on those distributions may be 10% because of the preferential capital gains tax rates.

If any of the above apply to your child, first figure the tax on your child's income as if he or she is filing a return. Next, figure the tax as if you are electing to report your child's income on **your** return. Then, compare the methods to determine which results in the lower tax.

Alternative Minimum Tax. If your child received tax-exempt interest (or exempt-interest dividends paid by a regulated investment company) from certain private activity bonds, you must take this into account in determining if you owe the alternative minimum tax. See **Form 6251,** Alternative Minimum Tax—Individuals, and its instructions for details.

Investment Interest Expense. Your child's income (other than Alaska Permanent Fund dividends and capital gain distributions) that you report on your return is considered to be **your** investment income for purposes of figuring your investment interest expense deduction. If your child received Alaska Permanent Fund dividends or capital gain distributions, see **Pub. 550,** Investment Income and Expenses, to figure the amount you may treat as your investment income.

Foreign Accounts and Trusts. Complete Part III of **Schedule B** (Form 1040) for your child if he or she **(1)** had a foreign financial account, or **(2)** received a distribution from, or was the grantor of, or transferor to, a foreign trust. If you answer "Yes" to either question, you must file this Schedule B with **your** return. Enter "Form 8814" next to line 7a or line 8, whichever applies. Also, complete line 7b if applicable.

Change of Address. If your child filed a return for a year before 1999 and the address shown on the last return filed is not your child's current address, be sure to notify the IRS, in writing, of the new address. To do this, you may:

- Use **Form 8822,** Change of Address, or
- Write to the Internal Revenue Service Center where your child's last return was filed, or
- Write to the Chief, Customer Service Division, in your local IRS district office.

Additional Information. See Pub. 929 for more details.

Line Instructions

Name and Social Security Number. If filing a joint return, include your spouse's name but enter the social security number of the person whose name is shown first on the return.

Line 1a. Enter **ALL** taxable interest income received by your child in 1999. If your child received a **Form 1099-INT** for tax-exempt interest, such as from municipal bonds, enter the amount and "Tax-exempt interest" on the dotted line next to line 1a. **Do not** include this interest in the total for line 1a but be sure to include it on line 1b.

If your child received, as a **nominee,** interest that actually belongs to another person, enter the amount and "ND" (for nominee distribution) on the dotted line next to line 1a. **Do not** include amounts received as a nominee in the total for line 1a.

If your child had accrued interest that was paid to the seller of a bond, amortizable bond premium (ABP) allowed as a reduction to interest income, or if any original issue discount (OID) included on line 1a is less than the amount shown on your child's **Form 1099-OID,** follow the instructions above for nominee interest to see how to report the nontaxable amounts. But on the dotted line next to line 1a, enter the nontaxable amount and "Accrued interest," "ABP adjustment," or "OID adjustment," whichever applies. **Do not** include any nontaxable amounts in the total for line 1a.

Line 1b. If your child received any tax-exempt interest income, such as from certain state and municipal bonds, report it on line 1b. Also, include any exempt-interest dividends your child received as a shareholder in a mutual fund or other regulated investment company.

Note: *If line 1b includes tax-exempt interest or exempt-interest dividends paid by a regulated investment company from private activity bonds, see **Alternative Minimum Tax** on this page.*

Line 2. Enter the ordinary dividends received by your child in 1999. Ordinary dividends should be shown in box 1 of **Form 1099-DIV.** Also, include ordinary dividends your child received through a partnership, an S corporation, or an estate or trust.

If your child received, as a **nominee,** ordinary dividends that actually belong to another person, enter the amount and "ND" on the dotted line next to line 2. **Do not** include amounts received as a nominee in the total for line 2.

Line 3. Enter the capital gain distributions received by your child in 1999. Capital gain distributions should be shown in box 2a of Form 1099-DIV. Also, see the instructions for line 6.

If your child received, as a **nominee,** capital gain distributions that actually belong to another person, enter the amount and "ND" on the dotted line next to line 3. **Do not** include amounts received as a nominee in the total for line 3.

Line 6. If you checked the box on line C, add the amounts from line 6 of **all** your Forms 8814. Include the total on line 21 of Form 1040 or Form 1040NR, whichever applies. Be sure to enter "Form 8814" and the total of the line 6 amounts in the space next to line 21.

If your child received capital gain distributions, part or all of those distributions must be reported on your **Schedule D** (Form 1040) or on Form 1040 or on Form 1040NR instead of on Form 8814, line 6. See Pub. 929 for details.

Line 9. If you checked the box on line C, add the amounts from line 9 of **all** your Forms 8814. Include the total on Form 1040, line 40, or Form 1040NR, line 39. Be sure to check box **a** on that line.

Paperwork Reduction Act Notice. We ask for the information on this form to carry out the Internal Revenue laws of the United States. You are required to give us the information. We need it to ensure that you are complying with these laws and to allow us to figure and collect the right amount of tax.

You are not required to provide the information requested on a form that is subject to the Paperwork Reduction Act unless the form displays a valid OMB control number. Books or records relating to a form or its instructions must be retained as long as their contents may become material in the administration of any Internal Revenue law. Generally, tax returns and return information are confidential, as required by Internal Revenue Code section 6103.

The time needed to complete and file this form will vary depending on individual circumstances. The estimated average time is: **Recordkeeping,** 26 min.; **Learning about the law or the form,** 10 min.; **Preparing the form,** 24 min.; and **Copying, assembling, and sending the form to the IRS,** 17 min.

If you have comments concerning the accuracy of these time estimates or suggestions for making this form simpler, we would be happy to hear from you. See the instructions for the tax return with which this form is filed.

Form **8829**	**Expenses for Business Use of Your Home**	OMB No. 1545-1266
Department of the Treasury Internal Revenue Service	▶ **File only with Schedule C (Form 1040). Use a separate Form 8829 for each home you used for business during the year.** ▶ **See separate instructions.**	**1999** Attachment Sequence No. **66**

Name(s) of proprietor(s)	Your social security number

Part I   Part of Your Home Used for Business

1	Area used regularly and exclusively for business, regularly for day care, or for storage of inventory or product samples. See instructions	**1**	
2	Total area of home	**2**	
3	Divide line 1 by line 2. Enter the result as a percentage	**3**	%

- **For day-care facilities not used exclusively for business, also complete lines 4–6.**
- **All others, skip lines 4–6 and enter the amount from line 3 on line 7.**

4	Multiply days used for day care during year by hours used per day .	**4**	hr.
5	Total hours available for use during the year (365 days × 24 hours). See instructions	**5**	8,760 hr.
6	Divide line 4 by line 5. Enter the result as a decimal amount . . .	**6**	.
7	Business percentage. For day-care facilities not used exclusively for business, multiply line 6 by line 3 (enter the result as a percentage). All others, enter the amount from line 3 . . . . . ▶	**7**	%

Part II   Figure Your Allowable Deduction

8	Enter the amount from Schedule C, line 29, **plus** any net gain or (loss) derived from the business use of your home and shown on Schedule D or Form 4797. If more than one place of business, see instructions			**8**	

	See instructions for columns (a) and (b) before completing lines 9–20.	**(a)** Direct expenses	**(b)** Indirect expenses		
9	Casualty losses. See instructions	**9**			
10	Deductible mortgage interest. See instructions .	**10**			
11	Real estate taxes. See instructions	**11**			
12	Add lines 9, 10, and 11.	**12**			
13	Multiply line 12, column (b) by line 7	**13**			
14	Add line 12, column (a) and line 13			**14**	
15	Subtract line 14 from line 8. If zero or less, enter -0- .			**15**	
16	Excess mortgage interest. See instructions . .	**16**			
17	Insurance	**17**			
18	Repairs and maintenance	**18**			
19	Utilities	**19**			
20	Other expenses. See instructions	**20**			
21	Add lines 16 through 20	**21**			
22	Multiply line 21, column (b) by line 7	**22**			
23	Carryover of operating expenses from 1998 Form 8829, line 41 . .	**23**			
24	Add line 21 in column (a), line 22, and line 23			**24**	
25	Allowable operating expenses. Enter the **smaller** of line 15 or line 24			**25**	
26	Limit on excess casualty losses and depreciation. Subtract line 25 from line 15			**26**	
27	Excess casualty losses. See instructions	**27**			
28	Depreciation of your home from Part III below	**28**			
29	Carryover of excess casualty losses and depreciation from 1998 Form 8829, line 42	**29**			
30	Add lines 27 through 29			**30**	
31	Allowable excess casualty losses and depreciation. Enter the **smaller** of line 26 or line 30 . .			**31**	
32	Add lines 14, 25, and 31			**32**	
33	Casualty loss portion, if any, from lines 14 and 31. Carry amount to **Form 4684**, Section B . .			**33**	
34	Allowable expenses for business use of your home. Subtract line 33 from line 32. Enter here and on Schedule C, line 30. If your home was used for more than one business, see instructions ▶			**34**	

Part III   Depreciation of Your Home

35	Enter the **smaller** of your home's adjusted basis or its fair market value. See instructions . .	**35**	
36	Value of land included on line 35	**36**	
37	Basis of building. Subtract line 36 from line 35	**37**	
38	Business basis of building. Multiply line 37 by line 7	**38**	
39	Depreciation percentage. See instructions	**39**	%
40	Depreciation allowable. Multiply line 38 by line 39. Enter here and on line 28 above. See instructions	**40**	

Part IV   Carryover of Unallowed Expenses to 2000

41	Operating expenses. Subtract line 25 from line 24. If less than zero, enter -0-	**41**	
42	Excess casualty losses and depreciation. Subtract line 31 from line 30. If less than zero, enter -0-	**42**	

For Paperwork Reduction Act Notice, see page 4 of separate instructions.   Cat. No. 13232M   Form **8829** (1999)

Form **8839**	**Qualified Adoption Expenses**	OMB No. 1545-1552
Department of the Treasury Internal Revenue Service	▶ **Attach to Form 1040 or 1040A.** ▶ **See separate instructions.**	**19**99 Attachment Sequence No. **38**

Name(s) shown on return	Your social security number

Before you begin, you need to understand the following terms. See **Definitions** on page 1 of the instructions.

- **Eligible Child**   • **Employer-Provided Adoption Benefits**   • **Qualified Adoption Expenses**

Part I Information About Your Eligible Child or Children—You **must** complete this part. See the instructions for details, including what to do if you need more space.

1	(a) Child's name First	(a) Child's name Last	(b) Child's year of birth	(c) born **before 1981** and was disabled	(d) a child with special needs	(e) a foreign child	(f) Child's identifying number
			Check if child was—				
Child 1			**19**	☐	☐	☐	
Child 2			**19**	☐	☐	☐	

Caution: *If the child was a foreign child, see* **Special Rules** *in the instructions for line 1, column (e), before you complete Part II or Part III. If you received* **employer-provided adoption benefits,** *complete Part III on the back next.*

Part II Adoption Credit

			Child 1	Child 2		
2	Enter $5,000 ($6,000 for a child with special needs)	2				
3	Did you file a 1997 or 1998 Form 8839? ☐ **No.** Enter -0-. ☐ **Yes.** See the instructions for the amount to enter.	3				
4	Subtract line 3 from line 2	4				
5	Enter the total **qualified adoption expenses** you paid in: • 1998 if the adoption was not final by the end of 1999. • 1998 and 1999 if the adoption was final in 1999. • 1999 if the adoption was final before 1999.	5				
6	Enter the **smaller** of line 4 or line 5 . .	6				
7	Add the amounts on line 6. If zero, skip lines 8-11 and enter -0- on line 12			7		
8	Enter your modified adjusted gross income (see instructions) . .	8				
9	If line 8 is $75,000 or less, skip lines 9 and 10 and enter -0- on line 11. If line 8 is over $75,000, subtract $75,000 from the amount on line 8	9				
10	Divide line 9 by $40,000. Enter the result as a decimal (rounded to at least three places). Do not enter more than "1.000"			10	✕ .	
11	Multiply line 7 by line 10			11		
12	Subtract line 11 from line 7			12		
13	Enter any credit carryforward from 1997 (line 15 of your 1998 Form 8839)			13		
14	Enter any credit carryforward from 1998 (line 16 of your 1998 Form 8839)			14		
15	Add lines 12, 13, and 14. Then, see the instructions for the amount of credit to enter on Form 1040, line 45, or Form 1040A, line 30			15		
16	**1997 credit carryforward to 2000** (see instructions)	16				
17	**1998 credit carryforward to 2000** (see instructions)	17				
18	**1999 credit carryforward to 2000** (see instructions)	18				

For Paperwork Reduction Act Notice, see page 4 of instructions.   Cat. No. 22843L   Form **8839** (1999)

Part III Employer-Provided Adoption Benefits

		Child 1	Child 2		
19	Enter $5,000 ($6,000 for a child with special needs) **19**				
20	Did you receive **employer-provided adoption benefits** for 1997 or 1998? ☐ **No.** Enter -0-. ☐ **Yes.** See the instructions for the amount to enter. **20**				
21	Subtract line 20 from line 19. If zero or less, enter -0- **21**				
22	Enter the total amount of your employer-provided adoption benefits received in 1999. This amount should be shown in box 13 of your 1999 W-2 form(s) with code **T** **22**				
23	Add the amounts on line 22 . . . . **23**				
24	Enter the **smaller** of line 21 or line 22 **24**				
25	Add the amounts on line 24. If zero, skip lines 26-29, enter -0- on line 30, and go to line 31 . . . . **25**				
26	Enter your modified adjusted gross income (from the worksheet in the instructions) **26**				
27	If line 26 is $75,000 or less, skip lines 27 and 28 and enter -0- on line 29. If line 26 is over $75,000, subtract $75,000 from the amount on line 26 . . . . **27**				
28	Divide line 27 by $40,000. Enter the result as a decimal (rounded to at least three places). Do not enter more than "1.000" . . . **28**	✕ .			
29	Multiply line 25 by line 28 . . . . **29**				
30	**Excluded benefits.** Subtract line 29 from line 25 . . . . **30**				
31	**Taxable benefits.** Subtract line 30 from line 23. Also, include this amount on Form 1040, line 7, or Form 1040A, line 7. On the line next to line 7, enter "AB". **31**				

If the total adoption expenses you paid in 1999 were not fully reimbursed by your employer **AND** the adoption was final in or before 1999, you may be able to claim the adoption credit in Part II on the front of this form.

Form **SS-4**	**Application for Employer Identification Number**		EIN	
(Rev. February 1998)	(For use by employers, corporations, partnerships, trusts, estates, churches, government agencies, certain individuals, and others. See instructions.)			
Department of the Treasury Internal Revenue Service	► **Keep a copy for your records.**		OMB No. 1545-0003	

Please type or print clearly.

1 Name of applicant (legal name) (see instructions)

2 Trade name of business (if different from name on line 1)

3 Executor, trustee, "care of" name

4a Mailing address (street address) (room, apt., or suite no.)

5a Business address (if different from address on lines 4a and 4b)

4b City, state, and ZIP code

5b City, state, and ZIP code

6 County and state where principal business is located

7 Name of principal officer, general partner, grantor, owner, or trustor—SSN or ITIN may be required (see instructions) ► _____

8a Type of entity (Check only one box.) (see instructions)

Caution: *If applicant is a limited liability company, see the instructions for line 8a.*

☐ Sole proprietor (SSN) _____
☐ Partnership   ☐ Personal service corp.
☐ REMIC   ☐ National Guard
☐ State/local government   ☐ Farmers' cooperative
☐ Church or church-controlled organization
☐ Other nonprofit organization (specify) ► _____
☐ Other (specify) ►

☐ Estate (SSN of decedent) _____
☐ Plan administrator (SSN) _____
☐ Other corporation (specify) ► _____
☐ Trust
☐ Federal government/military
(enter GEN if applicable) _____

8b If a corporation, name the state or foreign country (if applicable) where incorporated

State	Foreign country

9 Reason for applying (Check only one box.) (see instructions)
☐ Banking purpose (specify purpose) ► _____
☐ Started new business (specify type) ►_____
_____
☐ Changed type of organization (specify new type) ► _____
☐ Purchased going business
☐ Hired employees (Check the box and see line 12.)
☐ Created a trust (specify type) ► _____
☐ Created a pension plan (specify type) ►
☐ Other (specify) ►

10 Date business started or acquired (month, day, year) (see instructions)

11 Closing month of accounting year (see instructions)

12 First date wages or annuities were paid or will be paid (month, day, year). **Note:** *If applicant is a withholding agent, enter date income will first be paid to nonresident alien. (month, day, year)* . . . . ►

13 Highest number of employees expected in the next 12 months. **Note:** *If the applicant does not expect to have any employees during the period, enter -0-. (see instructions)* . . . . ►

Nonagricultural	Agricultural	Household

14 Principal activity (see instructions) ►

15 Is the principal business activity manufacturing? . . . . ☐ **Yes** ☐ **No**
If "Yes," principal product and raw material used ►

16 To whom are most of the products or services sold? Please check one box. ☐ Business (wholesale)
☐ Public (retail)   ☐ Other (specify) ►   ☐ N/A

17a Has the applicant ever applied for an employer identification number for this or any other business? . . . . ☐ **Yes** ☐ **No**
Note: *If "Yes," please complete lines 17b and 17c.*

17b If you checked "Yes" on line 17a, give applicant's legal name and trade name shown on prior application, if different from line 1 or 2 above.
Legal name ►   Trade name ►

17c Approximate date when and city and state where the application was filed. Enter previous employer identification number if known.

Approximate date when filed (mo., day, year)	City and state where filed	Previous EIN

Under penalties of perjury, I declare that I have examined this application, and to the best of my knowledge and belief, it is true, correct, and complete.	**Business telephone number (include area code)**
	Fax telephone number (include area code)
Name and title (Please type or print clearly.) ►	

Signature ►   Date ►

Note: *Do not write below this line. For official use only.*

Please leave blank ►	Geo.	Ind.	Class	Size	Reason for applying

For Paperwork Reduction Act Notice, see page 4.   Cat. No. 16055N   Form **SS-4** (Rev. 2-98)

779

1999 Tax Table

Use if your taxable income is less than $100,000. If $100,000 or more, use the Tax Rate Schedules.

Example. Mr. and Mrs. Brown are filing a joint return. Their taxable income is $25,300. First, they find the $25,300–25,350 income line. Next, they find the column for married filing jointly and read down the column. The amount shown where the income line and filing status column meet is $3,799. This is the tax amount they should enter on their tax return.

Sample Table

At least	But less than	Single	Married filing jointly *	Married filing separately	Head of a household
			Your tax is—		
25,200	25,250	3,784	3,784	4,265	3,784
25,250	25,300	3,791	3,791	4,279	3,791
25,300	25,350	3,799	3,799	4,293	3,799
25,350	25,400	3,806	3,806	4,307	3,806

If taxable income is— At least	But less than	Single	Married filing jointly *	Married filing separately	Head of a household
			Your tax is—		
0	5	0	0	0	0
5	15	2	2	2	2
15	25	3	3	3	3
25	50	6	6	6	6
50	75	9	9	9	9
75	100	13	13	13	13
100	125	17	17	17	17
125	150	21	21	21	21
150	175	24	24	24	24
175	200	28	28	28	28
200	225	32	32	32	32
225	250	36	36	36	36
250	275	39	39	39	39
275	300	43	43	43	43
300	325	47	47	47	47
325	350	51	51	51	51
350	375	54	54	54	54
375	400	58	58	58	58
400	425	62	62	62	62
425	450	66	66	66	66
450	475	69	69	69	69
475	500	73	73	73	73
500	525	77	77	77	77
525	550	81	81	81	81
550	575	84	84	84	84
575	600	88	88	88	88
600	625	92	92	92	92
625	650	96	96	96	96
650	675	99	99	99	99
675	700	103	103	103	103
700	725	107	107	107	107
725	750	111	111	111	111
750	775	114	114	114	114
775	800	118	118	118	118
800	825	122	122	122	122
825	850	126	126	126	126
850	875	129	129	129	129
875	900	133	133	133	133
900	925	137	137	137	137
925	950	141	141	141	141
950	975	144	144	144	144
975	1,000	148	148	148	148

1,000

At least	But less than	Single	Married filing jointly *	Married filing separately	Head of a household
1,000	1,025	152	152	152	152
1,025	1,050	156	156	156	156
1,050	1,075	159	159	159	159
1,075	1,100	163	163	163	163
1,100	1,125	167	167	167	167
1,125	1,150	171	171	171	171
1,150	1,175	174	174	174	174
1,175	1,200	178	178	178	178
1,200	1,225	182	182	182	182
1,225	1,250	186	186	186	186
1,250	1,275	189	189	189	189
1,275	1,300	193	193	193	193
1,300	1,325	197	197	197	197
1,325	1,350	201	201	201	201
1,350	1,375	204	204	204	204
1,375	1,400	208	208	208	208
1,400	1,425	212	212	212	212
1,425	1,450	216	216	216	216
1,450	1,475	219	219	219	219
1,475	1,500	223	223	223	223
1,500	1,525	227	227	227	227
1,525	1,550	231	231	231	231
1,550	1,575	234	234	234	234
1,575	1,600	238	238	238	238
1,600	1,625	242	242	242	242
1,625	1,650	246	246	246	246
1,650	1,675	249	249	249	249
1,675	1,700	253	253	253	253
1,700	1,725	257	257	257	257
1,725	1,750	261	261	261	261
1,750	1,775	264	264	264	264
1,775	1,800	268	268	268	268
1,800	1,825	272	272	272	272
1,825	1,850	276	276	276	276
1,850	1,875	279	279	279	279
1,875	1,900	283	283	283	283
1,900	1,925	287	287	287	287
1,925	1,950	291	291	291	291
1,950	1,975	294	294	294	294
1,975	2,000	298	298	298	298

2,000

At least	But less than	Single	Married filing jointly *	Married filing separately	Head of a household
2,000	2,025	302	302	302	302
2,025	2,050	306	306	306	306
2,050	2,075	309	309	309	309
2,075	2,100	313	313	313	313
2,100	2,125	317	317	317	317
2,125	2,150	321	321	321	321
2,150	2,175	324	324	324	324
2,175	2,200	328	328	328	328
2,200	2,225	332	332	332	332
2,225	2,250	336	336	336	336
2,250	2,275	339	339	339	339
2,275	2,300	343	343	343	343
2,300	2,325	347	347	347	347
2,325	2,350	351	351	351	351
2,350	2,375	354	354	354	354
2,375	2,400	358	358	358	358
2,400	2,425	362	362	362	362
2,425	2,450	366	366	366	366
2,450	2,475	369	369	369	369
2,475	2,500	373	373	373	373
2,500	2,525	377	377	377	377
2,525	2,550	381	381	381	381
2,550	2,575	384	384	384	384
2,575	2,600	388	388	388	388
2,600	2,625	392	392	392	392
2,625	2,650	396	396	396	396
2,650	2,675	399	399	399	399
2,675	2,700	403	403	403	403
2,700	2,725	407	407	407	407
2,725	2,750	411	411	411	411
2,750	2,775	414	414	414	414
2,775	2,800	418	418	418	418
2,800	2,825	422	422	422	422
2,825	2,850	426	426	426	426
2,850	2,875	429	429	429	429
2,875	2,900	433	433	433	433
2,900	2,925	437	437	437	437
2,925	2,950	441	441	441	441
2,950	2,975	444	444	444	444
2,975	3,000	448	448	448	448

3,000

At least	But less than	Single	Married filing jointly *	Married filing separately	Head of a household
3,000	3,050	454	454	454	454
3,050	3,100	461	461	461	461
3,100	3,150	469	469	469	469
3,150	3,200	476	476	476	476
3,200	3,250	484	484	484	484
3,250	3,300	491	491	491	491
3,300	3,350	499	499	499	499
3,350	3,400	506	506	506	506
3,400	3,450	514	514	514	514
3,450	3,500	521	521	521	521
3,500	3,550	529	529	529	529
3,550	3,600	536	536	536	536
3,600	3,650	544	544	544	544
3,650	3,700	551	551	551	551
3,700	3,750	559	559	559	559
3,750	3,800	566	566	566	566
3,800	3,850	574	574	574	574
3,850	3,900	581	581	581	581
3,900	3,950	589	589	589	589
3,950	4,000	596	596	596	596

4,000

At least	But less than	Single	Married filing jointly *	Married filing separately	Head of a household
4,000	4,050	604	604	604	604
4,050	4,100	611	611	611	611
4,100	4,150	619	619	619	619
4,150	4,200	626	626	626	626
4,200	4,250	634	634	634	634
4,250	4,300	641	641	641	641
4,300	4,350	649	649	649	649
4,350	4,400	656	656	656	656
4,400	4,450	664	664	664	664
4,450	4,500	671	671	671	671
4,500	4,550	679	679	679	679
4,550	4,600	686	686	686	686
4,600	4,650	694	694	694	694
4,650	4,700	701	701	701	701
4,700	4,750	709	709	709	709
4,750	4,800	716	716	716	716
4,800	4,850	724	724	724	724
4,850	4,900	731	731	731	731
4,900	4,950	739	739	739	739
4,950	5,000	746	746	746	746

Continued on next page

* This column must also be used by a qualifying widow(er).

1999 Tax Table—*Continued*

5,000

At least	But less than	Single	Married filing jointly *	Married filing separately	Head of a household
5,000	5,050	754	754	754	754
5,050	5,100	761	761	761	761
5,100	5,150	769	769	769	769
5,150	5,200	776	776	776	776
5,200	5,250	784	784	784	784
5,250	5,300	791	791	791	791
5,300	5,350	799	799	799	799
5,350	5,400	806	806	806	806
5,400	5,450	814	814	814	814
5,450	5,500	821	821	821	821
5,500	5,550	829	829	829	829
5,550	5,600	836	836	836	836
5,600	5,650	844	844	844	844
5,650	5,700	851	851	851	851
5,700	5,750	859	859	859	859
5,750	5,800	866	866	866	866
5,800	5,850	874	874	874	874
5,850	5,900	881	881	881	881
5,900	5,950	889	889	889	889
5,950	6,000	896	896	896	896

6,000

At least	But less than	Single	Married filing jointly *	Married filing separately	Head of a household
6,000	6,050	904	904	904	904
6,050	6,100	911	911	911	911
6,100	6,150	919	919	919	919
6,150	6,200	926	926	926	926
6,200	6,250	934	934	934	934
6,250	6,300	941	941	941	941
6,300	6,350	949	949	949	949
6,350	6,400	956	956	956	956
6,400	6,450	964	964	964	964
6,450	6,500	971	971	971	971
6,500	6,550	979	979	979	979
6,550	6,600	986	986	986	986
6,600	6,650	994	994	994	994
6,650	6,700	1,001	1,001	1,001	1,001
6,700	6,750	1,009	1,009	1,009	1,009
6,750	6,800	1,016	1,016	1,016	1,016
6,800	6,850	1,024	1,024	1,024	1,024
6,850	6,900	1,031	1,031	1,031	1,031
6,900	6,950	1,039	1,039	1,039	1,039
6,950	7,000	1,046	1,046	1,046	1,046

7,000

At least	But less than	Single	Married filing jointly *	Married filing separately	Head of a household
7,000	7,050	1,054	1,054	1,054	1,054
7,050	7,100	1,061	1,061	1,061	1,061
7,100	7,150	1,069	1,069	1,069	1,069
7,150	7,200	1,076	1,076	1,076	1,076
7,200	7,250	1,084	1,084	1,084	1,084
7,250	7,300	1,091	1,091	1,091	1,091
7,300	7,350	1,099	1,099	1,099	1,099
7,350	7,400	1,106	1,106	1,106	1,106
7,400	7,450	1,114	1,114	1,114	1,114
7,450	7,500	1,121	1,121	1,121	1,121
7,500	7,550	1,129	1,129	1,129	1,129
7,550	7,600	1,136	1,136	1,136	1,136
7,600	7,650	1,144	1,144	1,144	1,144
7,650	7,700	1,151	1,151	1,151	1,151
7,700	7,750	1,159	1,159	1,159	1,159
7,750	7,800	1,166	1,166	1,166	1,166
7,800	7,850	1,174	1,174	1,174	1,174
7,850	7,900	1,181	1,181	1,181	1,181
7,900	7,950	1,189	1,189	1,189	1,189
7,950	8,000	1,196	1,196	1,196	1,196

8,000

At least	But less than	Single	Married filing jointly *	Married filing separately	Head of a household
8,000	8,050	1,204	1,204	1,204	1,204
8,050	8,100	1,211	1,211	1,211	1,211
8,100	8,150	1,219	1,219	1,219	1,219
8,150	8,200	1,226	1,226	1,226	1,226
8,200	8,250	1,234	1,234	1,234	1,234
8,250	8,300	1,241	1,241	1,241	1,241
8,300	8,350	1,249	1,249	1,249	1,249
8,350	8,400	1,256	1,256	1,256	1,256
8,400	8,450	1,264	1,264	1,264	1,264
8,450	8,500	1,271	1,271	1,271	1,271
8,500	8,550	1,279	1,279	1,279	1,279
8,550	8,600	1,286	1,286	1,286	1,286
8,600	8,650	1,294	1,294	1,294	1,294
8,650	8,700	1,301	1,301	1,301	1,301
8,700	8,750	1,309	1,309	1,309	1,309
8,750	8,800	1,316	1,316	1,316	1,316
8,800	8,850	1,324	1,324	1,324	1,324
8,850	8,900	1,331	1,331	1,331	1,331
8,900	8,950	1,339	1,339	1,339	1,339
8,950	9,000	1,346	1,346	1,346	1,346

9,000

At least	But less than	Single	Married filing jointly *	Married filing separately	Head of a household
9,000	9,050	1,354	1,354	1,354	1,354
9,050	9,100	1,361	1,361	1,361	1,361
9,100	9,150	1,369	1,369	1,369	1,369
9,150	9,200	1,376	1,376	1,376	1,376
9,200	9,250	1,384	1,384	1,384	1,384
9,250	9,300	1,391	1,391	1,391	1,391
9,300	9,350	1,399	1,399	1,399	1,399
9,350	9,400	1,406	1,406	1,406	1,406
9,400	9,450	1,414	1,414	1,414	1,414
9,450	9,500	1,421	1,421	1,421	1,421
9,500	9,550	1,429	1,429	1,429	1,429
9,550	9,600	1,436	1,436	1,436	1,436
9,600	9,650	1,444	1,444	1,444	1,444
9,650	9,700	1,451	1,451	1,451	1,451
9,700	9,750	1,459	1,459	1,459	1,459
9,750	9,800	1,466	1,466	1,466	1,466
9,800	9,850	1,474	1,474	1,474	1,474
9,850	9,900	1,481	1,481	1,481	1,481
9,900	9,950	1,489	1,489	1,489	1,489
9,950	10,000	1,496	1,496	1,496	1,496

10,000

At least	But less than	Single	Married filing jointly *	Married filing separately	Head of a household
10,000	10,050	1,504	1,504	1,504	1,504
10,050	10,100	1,511	1,511	1,511	1,511
10,100	10,150	1,519	1,519	1,519	1,519
10,150	10,200	1,526	1,526	1,526	1,526
10,200	10,250	1,534	1,534	1,534	1,534
10,250	10,300	1,541	1,541	1,541	1,541
10,300	10,350	1,549	1,549	1,549	1,549
10,350	10,400	1,556	1,556	1,556	1,556
10,400	10,450	1,564	1,564	1,564	1,564
10,450	10,500	1,571	1,571	1,571	1,571
10,500	10,550	1,579	1,579	1,579	1,579
10,550	10,600	1,586	1,586	1,586	1,586
10,600	10,650	1,594	1,594	1,594	1,594
10,650	10,700	1,601	1,601	1,601	1,601
10,700	10,750	1,609	1,609	1,609	1,609
10,750	10,800	1,616	1,616	1,616	1,616
10,800	10,850	1,624	1,624	1,624	1,624
10,850	10,900	1,631	1,631	1,631	1,631
10,900	10,950	1,639	1,639	1,639	1,639
10,950	11,000	1,646	1,646	1,646	1,646

11,000

At least	But less than	Single	Married filing jointly *	Married filing separately	Head of a household
11,000	11,050	1,654	1,654	1,654	1,654
11,050	11,100	1,661	1,661	1,661	1,661
11,100	11,150	1,669	1,669	1,669	1,669
11,150	11,200	1,676	1,676	1,676	1,676
11,200	11,250	1,684	1,684	1,684	1,684
11,250	11,300	1,691	1,691	1,691	1,691
11,300	11,350	1,699	1,699	1,699	1,699
11,350	11,400	1,706	1,706	1,706	1,706
11,400	11,450	1,714	1,714	1,714	1,714
11,450	11,500	1,721	1,721	1,721	1,721
11,500	11,550	1,729	1,729	1,729	1,729
11,550	11,600	1,736	1,736	1,736	1,736
11,600	11,650	1,744	1,744	1,744	1,744
11,650	11,700	1,751	1,751	1,751	1,751
11,700	11,750	1,759	1,759	1,759	1,759
11,750	11,800	1,766	1,766	1,766	1,766
11,800	11,850	1,774	1,774	1,774	1,774
11,850	11,900	1,781	1,781	1,781	1,781
11,900	11,950	1,789	1,789	1,789	1,789
11,950	12,000	1,796	1,796	1,796	1,796

12,000

At least	But less than	Single	Married filing jointly *	Married filing separately	Head of a household
12,000	12,050	1,804	1,804	1,804	1,804
12,050	12,100	1,811	1,811	1,811	1,811
12,100	12,150	1,819	1,819	1,819	1,819
12,150	12,200	1,826	1,826	1,826	1,826
12,200	12,250	1,834	1,834	1,834	1,834
12,250	12,300	1,841	1,841	1,841	1,841
12,300	12,350	1,849	1,849	1,849	1,849
12,350	12,400	1,856	1,856	1,856	1,856
12,400	12,450	1,864	1,864	1,864	1,864
12,450	12,500	1,871	1,871	1,871	1,871
12,500	12,550	1,879	1,879	1,879	1,879
12,550	12,600	1,886	1,886	1,886	1,886
12,600	12,650	1,894	1,894	1,894	1,894
12,650	12,700	1,901	1,901	1,901	1,901
12,700	12,750	1,909	1,909	1,909	1,909
12,750	12,800	1,916	1,916	1,916	1,916
12,800	12,850	1,924	1,924	1,924	1,924
12,850	12,900	1,931	1,931	1,931	1,931
12,900	12,950	1,939	1,939	1,939	1,939
12,950	13,000	1,946	1,946	1,946	1,946

13,000

At least	But less than	Single	Married filing jointly *	Married filing separately	Head of a household
13,000	13,050	1,954	1,954	1,954	1,954
13,050	13,100	1,961	1,961	1,961	1,961
13,100	13,150	1,969	1,969	1,969	1,969
13,150	13,200	1,976	1,976	1,976	1,976
13,200	13,250	1,984	1,984	1,984	1,984
13,250	13,300	1,991	1,991	1,991	1,991
13,300	13,350	1,999	1,999	1,999	1,999
13,350	13,400	2,006	2,006	2,006	2,006
13,400	13,450	2,014	2,014	2,014	2,014
13,450	13,500	2,021	2,021	2,021	2,021
13,500	13,550	2,029	2,029	2,029	2,029
13,550	13,600	2,036	2,036	2,036	2,036
13,600	13,650	2,044	2,044	2,044	2,044
13,650	13,700	2,051	2,051	2,051	2,051
13,700	13,750	2,059	2,059	2,059	2,059
13,750	13,800	2,066	2,066	2,066	2,066
13,800	13,850	2,074	2,074	2,074	2,074
13,850	13,900	2,081	2,081	2,081	2,081
13,900	13,950	2,089	2,089	2,089	2,089
13,950	14,000	2,096	2,096	2,096	2,096

* This column must also be used by a qualifying widow(er).

Continued on next page

1999 Tax Table—*Continued*

If taxable income is—		And you are—			
At least	But less than	Single	Married filing jointly *	Married filing separately	Head of a household
		Your tax is—			
14,000					
14,000	14,050	2,104	2,104	2,104	2,104
14,050	14,100	2,111	2,111	2,111	2,111
14,100	14,150	2,119	2,119	2,119	2,119
14,150	14,200	2,126	2,126	2,126	2,126
14,200	14,250	2,134	2,134	2,134	2,134
14,250	14,300	2,141	2,141	2,141	2,141
14,300	14,350	2,149	2,149	2,149	2,149
14,350	14,400	2,156	2,156	2,156	2,156
14,400	14,450	2,164	2,164	2,164	2,164
14,450	14,500	2,171	2,171	2,171	2,171
14,500	14,550	2,179	2,179	2,179	2,179
14,550	14,600	2,186	2,186	2,186	2,186
14,600	14,650	2,194	2,194	2,194	2,194
14,650	14,700	2,201	2,201	2,201	2,201
14,700	14,750	2,209	2,209	2,209	2,209
14,750	14,800	2,216	2,216	2,216	2,216
14,800	14,850	2,224	2,224	2,224	2,224
14,850	14,900	2,231	2,231	2,231	2,231
14,900	14,950	2,239	2,239	2,239	2,239
14,950	15,000	2,246	2,246	2,246	2,246
15,000					
15,000	15,050	2,254	2,254	2,254	2,254
15,050	15,100	2,261	2,261	2,261	2,261
15,100	15,150	2,269	2,269	2,269	2,269
15,150	15,200	2,276	2,276	2,276	2,276
15,200	15,250	2,284	2,284	2,284	2,284
15,250	15,300	2,291	2,291	2,291	2,291
15,300	15,350	2,299	2,299	2,299	2,299
15,350	15,400	2,306	2,306	2,306	2,306
15,400	15,450	2,314	2,314	2,314	2,314
15,450	15,500	2,321	2,321	2,321	2,321
15,500	15,550	2,329	2,329	2,329	2,329
15,550	15,600	2,336	2,336	2,336	2,336
15,600	15,650	2,344	2,344	2,344	2,344
15,650	15,700	2,351	2,351	2,351	2,351
15,700	15,750	2,359	2,359	2,359	2,359
15,750	15,800	2,366	2,366	2,366	2,366
15,800	15,850	2,374	2,374	2,374	2,374
15,850	15,900	2,381	2,381	2,381	2,381
15,900	15,950	2,389	2,389	2,389	2,389
15,950	16,000	2,396	2,396	2,396	2,396
16,000					
16,000	16,050	2,404	2,404	2,404	2,404
16,050	16,100	2,411	2,411	2,411	2,411
16,100	16,150	2,419	2,419	2,419	2,419
16,150	16,200	2,426	2,426	2,426	2,426
16,200	16,250	2,434	2,434	2,434	2,434
16,250	16,300	2,441	2,441	2,441	2,441
16,300	16,350	2,449	2,449	2,449	2,449
16,350	16,400	2,456	2,456	2,456	2,456
16,400	16,450	2,464	2,464	2,464	2,464
16,450	16,500	2,471	2,471	2,471	2,471
16,500	16,550	2,479	2,479	2,479	2,479
16,550	16,600	2,486	2,486	2,486	2,486
16,600	16,650	2,494	2,494	2,494	2,494
16,650	16,700	2,501	2,501	2,501	2,501
16,700	16,750	2,509	2,509	2,509	2,509
16,750	16,800	2,516	2,516	2,516	2,516
16,800	16,850	2,524	2,524	2,524	2,524
16,850	16,900	2,531	2,531	2,531	2,531
16,900	16,950	2,539	2,539	2,539	2,539
16,950	17,000	2,546	2,546	2,546	2,546

If taxable income is—		And you are—			
At least	But less than	Single	Married filing jointly *	Married filing separately	Head of a household
		Your tax is—			
17,000					
17,000	17,050	2,554	2,554	2,554	2,554
17,050	17,100	2,561	2,561	2,561	2,561
17,100	17,150	2,569	2,569	2,569	2,569
17,150	17,200	2,576	2,576	2,576	2,576
17,200	17,250	2,584	2,584	2,584	2,584
17,250	17,300	2,591	2,591	2,591	2,591
17,300	17,350	2,599	2,599	2,599	2,599
17,350	17,400	2,606	2,606	2,606	2,606
17,400	17,450	2,614	2,614	2,614	2,614
17,450	17,500	2,621	2,621	2,621	2,621
17,500	17,550	2,629	2,629	2,629	2,629
17,550	17,600	2,636	2,636	2,636	2,636
17,600	17,650	2,644	2,644	2,644	2,644
17,650	17,700	2,651	2,651	2,651	2,651
17,700	17,750	2,659	2,659	2,659	2,659
17,750	17,800	2,666	2,666	2,666	2,666
17,800	17,850	2,674	2,674	2,674	2,674
17,850	17,900	2,681	2,681	2,681	2,681
17,900	17,950	2,689	2,689	2,689	2,689
17,950	18,000	2,696	2,696	2,696	2,696
18,000					
18,000	18,050	2,704	2,704	2,704	2,704
18,050	18,100	2,711	2,711	2,711	2,711
18,100	18,150	2,719	2,719	2,719	2,719
18,150	18,200	2,726	2,726	2,726	2,726
18,200	18,250	2,734	2,734	2,734	2,734
18,250	18,300	2,741	2,741	2,741	2,741
18,300	18,350	2,749	2,749	2,749	2,749
18,350	18,400	2,756	2,756	2,756	2,756
18,400	18,450	2,764	2,764	2,764	2,764
18,450	18,500	2,771	2,771	2,771	2,771
18,500	18,550	2,779	2,779	2,779	2,779
18,550	18,600	2,786	2,786	2,786	2,786
18,600	18,650	2,794	2,794	2,794	2,794
18,650	18,700	2,801	2,801	2,801	2,801
18,700	18,750	2,809	2,809	2,809	2,809
18,750	18,800	2,816	2,816	2,816	2,816
18,800	18,850	2,824	2,824	2,824	2,824
18,850	18,900	2,831	2,831	2,831	2,831
18,900	18,950	2,839	2,839	2,839	2,839
18,950	19,000	2,846	2,846	2,846	2,846
19,000					
19,000	19,050	2,854	2,854	2,854	2,854
19,050	19,100	2,861	2,861	2,861	2,861
19,100	19,150	2,869	2,869	2,869	2,869
19,150	19,200	2,876	2,876	2,876	2,876
19,200	19,250	2,884	2,884	2,884	2,884
19,250	19,300	2,891	2,891	2,891	2,891
19,300	19,350	2,899	2,899	2,899	2,899
19,350	19,400	2,906	2,906	2,906	2,906
19,400	19,450	2,914	2,914	2,914	2,914
19,450	19,500	2,921	2,921	2,921	2,921
19,500	19,550	2,929	2,929	2,929	2,929
19,550	19,600	2,936	2,936	2,936	2,936
19,600	19,650	2,944	2,944	2,944	2,944
19,650	19,700	2,951	2,951	2,951	2,951
19,700	19,750	2,959	2,959	2,959	2,959
19,750	19,800	2,966	2,966	2,966	2,966
19,800	19,850	2,974	2,974	2,974	2,974
19,850	19,900	2,981	2,981	2,981	2,981
19,900	19,950	2,989	2,989	2,989	2,989
19,950	20,000	2,996	2,996	2,996	2,996

If taxable income is—		And you are—			
At least	But less than	Single	Married filing jointly *	Married filing separately	Head of a household
		Your tax is—			
20,000					
20,000	20,050	3,004	3,004	3,004	3,004
20,050	20,100	3,011	3,011	3,011	3,011
20,100	20,150	3,019	3,019	3,019	3,019
20,150	20,200	3,026	3,026	3,026	3,026
20,200	20,250	3,034	3,034	3,034	3,034
20,250	20,300	3,041	3,041	3,041	3,041
20,300	20,350	3,049	3,049	3,049	3,049
20,350	20,400	3,056	3,056	3,056	3,056
20,400	20,450	3,064	3,064	3,064	3,064
20,450	20,500	3,071	3,071	3,071	3,071
20,500	20,550	3,079	3,079	3,079	3,079
20,550	20,600	3,086	3,086	3,086	3,086
20,600	20,650	3,094	3,094	3,094	3,094
20,650	20,700	3,101	3,101	3,101	3,101
20,700	20,750	3,109	3,109	3,109	3,109
20,750	20,800	3,116	3,116	3,116	3,116
20,800	20,850	3,124	3,124	3,124	3,124
20,850	20,900	3,131	3,131	3,131	3,131
20,900	20,950	3,139	3,139	3,139	3,139
20,950	21,000	3,146	3,146	3,146	3,146
21,000					
21,000	21,050	3,154	3,154	3,154	3,154
21,050	21,100	3,161	3,161	3,161	3,161
21,100	21,150	3,169	3,169	3,169	3,169
21,150	21,200	3,176	3,176	3,176	3,176
21,200	21,250	3,184	3,184	3,184	3,184
21,250	21,300	3,191	3,191	3,191	3,191
21,300	21,350	3,199	3,199	3,199	3,199
21,350	21,400	3,206	3,206	3,206	3,206
21,400	21,450	3,214	3,214	3,214	3,214
21,450	21,500	3,221	3,221	3,221	3,221
21,500	21,550	3,229	3,229	3,229	3,229
21,550	21,600	3,236	3,236	3,243	3,236
21,600	21,650	3,244	3,244	3,257	3,244
21,650	21,700	3,251	3,251	3,271	3,251
21,700	21,750	3,259	3,259	3,285	3,259
21,750	21,800	3,266	3,266	3,299	3,266
21,800	21,850	3,274	3,274	3,313	3,274
21,850	21,900	3,281	3,281	3,327	3,281
21,900	21,950	3,289	3,289	3,341	3,289
21,950	22,000	3,296	3,296	3,355	3,296
22,000					
22,000	22,050	3,304	3,304	3,369	3,304
22,050	22,100	3,311	3,311	3,383	3,311
22,100	22,150	3,319	3,319	3,397	3,319
22,150	22,200	3,326	3,326	3,411	3,326
22,200	22,250	3,334	3,334	3,425	3,334
22,250	22,300	3,341	3,341	3,439	3,341
22,300	22,350	3,349	3,349	3,453	3,349
22,350	22,400	3,356	3,356	3,467	3,356
22,400	22,450	3,364	3,364	3,481	3,364
22,450	22,500	3,371	3,371	3,495	3,371
22,500	22,550	3,379	3,379	3,509	3,379
22,550	22,600	3,386	3,386	3,523	3,386
22,600	22,650	3,394	3,394	3,537	3,394
22,650	22,700	3,401	3,401	3,551	3,401
22,700	22,750	3,409	3,409	3,565	3,409
22,750	22,800	3,416	3,416	3,579	3,416
22,800	22,850	3,424	3,424	3,593	3,424
22,850	22,900	3,431	3,431	3,607	3,431
22,900	22,950	3,439	3,439	3,621	3,439
22,950	23,000	3,446	3,446	3,635	3,446

* This column must also be used by a qualifying widow(er).

Continued on next page

If taxable income is—		And you are—			
At least	But less than	Single	Married filing jointly *	Married filing separately	Head of a household
		Your tax is—			

23,000

At least	But less than	Single	Married filing jointly	Married filing separately	Head of a household
23,000	23,050	3,454	3,454	3,649	3,454
23,050	23,100	3,461	3,461	3,663	3,461
23,100	23,150	3,469	3,469	3,677	3,469
23,150	23,200	3,476	3,476	3,691	3,476
23,200	23,250	3,484	3,484	3,705	3,484
23,250	23,300	3,491	3,491	3,719	3,491
23,300	23,350	3,499	3,499	3,733	3,499
23,350	23,400	3,506	3,506	3,747	3,506
23,400	23,450	3,514	3,514	3,761	3,514
23,450	23,500	3,521	3,521	3,775	3,521
23,500	23,550	3,529	3,529	3,789	3,529
23,550	23,600	3,536	3,536	3,803	3,536
23,600	23,650	3,544	3,544	3,817	3,544
23,650	23,700	3,551	3,551	3,831	3,551
23,700	23,750	3,559	3,559	3,845	3,559
23,750	23,800	3,566	3,566	3,859	3,566
23,800	23,850	3,574	3,574	3,873	3,574
23,850	23,900	3,581	3,581	3,887	3,581
23,900	23,950	3,589	3,589	3,901	3,589
23,950	24,000	3,596	3,596	3,915	3,596

24,000

At least	But less than	Single	Married filing jointly	Married filing separately	Head of a household
24,000	24,050	3,604	3,604	3,929	3,604
24,050	24,100	3,611	3,611	3,943	3,611
24,100	24,150	3,619	3,619	3,957	3,619
24,150	24,200	3,626	3,626	3,971	3,626
24,200	24,250	3,634	3,634	3,985	3,634
24,250	24,300	3,641	3,641	3,999	3,641
24,300	24,350	3,649	3,649	4,013	3,649
24,350	24,400	3,656	3,656	4,027	3,656
24,400	24,450	3,664	3,664	4,041	3,664
24,450	24,500	3,671	3,671	4,055	3,671
24,500	24,550	3,679	3,679	4,069	3,679
24,550	24,600	3,686	3,686	4,083	3,686
24,600	24,650	3,694	3,694	4,097	3,694
24,650	24,700	3,701	3,701	4,111	3,701
24,700	24,750	3,709	3,709	4,125	3,709
24,750	24,800	3,716	3,716	4,139	3,716
24,800	24,850	3,724	3,724	4,153	3,724
24,850	24,900	3,731	3,731	4,167	3,731
24,900	24,950	3,739	3,739	4,181	3,739
24,950	25,000	3,746	3,746	4,195	3,746

25,000

At least	But less than	Single	Married filing jointly	Married filing separately	Head of a household
25,000	25,050	3,754	3,754	4,209	3,754
25,050	25,100	3,761	3,761	4,223	3,761
25,100	25,150	3,769	3,769	4,237	3,769
25,150	25,200	3,776	3,776	4,251	3,776
25,200	25,250	3,784	3,784	4,265	3,784
25,250	25,300	3,791	3,791	4,279	3,791
25,300	25,350	3,799	3,799	4,293	3,799
25,350	25,400	3,806	3,806	4,307	3,806
25,400	25,450	3,814	3,814	4,321	3,814
25,450	25,500	3,821	3,821	4,335	3,821
25,500	25,550	3,829	3,829	4,349	3,829
25,550	25,600	3,836	3,836	4,363	3,836
25,600	25,650	3,844	3,844	4,377	3,844
25,650	25,700	3,851	3,851	4,391	3,851
25,700	25,750	3,859	3,859	4,405	3,859
25,750	25,800	3,870	3,866	4,419	3,866
25,800	25,850	3,884	3,874	4,433	3,874
25,850	25,900	3,898	3,881	4,447	3,881
25,900	25,950	3,912	3,889	4,461	3,889
25,950	26,000	3,926	3,896	4,475	3,896

26,000

At least	But less than	Single	Married filing jointly	Married filing separately	Head of a household
26,000	26,050	3,940	3,904	4,489	3,904
26,050	26,100	3,954	3,911	4,503	3,911
26,100	26,150	3,968	3,919	4,517	3,919
26,150	26,200	3,982	3,926	4,531	3,926
26,200	26,250	3,996	3,934	4,545	3,934
26,250	26,300	4,010	3,941	4,559	3,941
26,300	26,350	4,024	3,949	4,573	3,949
26,350	26,400	4,038	3,956	4,587	3,956
26,400	26,450	4,052	3,964	4,601	3,964
26,450	26,500	4,066	3,971	4,615	3,971
26,500	26,550	4,080	3,979	4,629	3,979
26,550	26,600	4,094	3,986	4,643	3,986
26,600	26,650	4,108	3,994	4,657	3,994
26,650	26,700	4,122	4,001	4,671	4,001
26,700	26,750	4,136	4,009	4,685	4,009
26,750	26,800	4,150	4,016	4,699	4,016
26,800	26,850	4,164	4,024	4,713	4,024
26,850	26,900	4,178	4,031	4,727	4,031
26,900	26,950	4,192	4,039	4,741	4,039
26,950	27,000	4,206	4,046	4,755	4,046

27,000

At least	But less than	Single	Married filing jointly	Married filing separately	Head of a household
27,000	27,050	4,220	4,054	4,769	4,054
27,050	27,100	4,234	4,061	4,783	4,061
27,100	27,150	4,248	4,069	4,797	4,069
27,150	27,200	4,262	4,076	4,811	4,076
27,200	27,250	4,276	4,084	4,825	4,084
27,250	27,300	4,290	4,091	4,839	4,091
27,300	27,350	4,304	4,099	4,853	4,099
27,350	27,400	4,318	4,106	4,867	4,106
27,400	27,450	4,332	4,114	4,881	4,114
27,450	27,500	4,346	4,121	4,895	4,121
27,500	27,550	4,360	4,129	4,909	4,129
27,550	27,600	4,374	4,136	4,923	4,136
27,600	27,650	4,388	4,144	4,937	4,144
27,650	27,700	4,402	4,151	4,951	4,151
27,700	27,750	4,416	4,159	4,965	4,159
27,750	27,800	4,430	4,166	4,979	4,166
27,800	27,850	4,444	4,174	4,993	4,174
27,850	27,900	4,458	4,181	5,007	4,181
27,900	27,950	4,472	4,189	5,021	4,189
27,950	28,000	4,486	4,196	5,035	4,196

28,000

At least	But less than	Single	Married filing jointly	Married filing separately	Head of a household
28,000	28,050	4,500	4,204	5,049	4,204
28,050	28,100	4,514	4,211	5,063	4,211
28,100	28,150	4,528	4,219	5,077	4,219
28,150	28,200	4,542	4,226	5,091	4,226
28,200	28,250	4,556	4,234	5,105	4,234
28,250	28,300	4,570	4,241	5,119	4,241
28,300	28,350	4,584	4,249	5,133	4,249
28,350	28,400	4,598	4,256	5,147	4,256
28,400	28,450	4,612	4,264	5,161	4,264
28,450	28,500	4,626	4,271	5,175	4,271
28,500	28,550	4,640	4,279	5,189	4,279
28,550	28,600	4,654	4,286	5,203	4,286
28,600	28,650	4,668	4,294	5,217	4,294
28,650	28,700	4,682	4,301	5,231	4,301
28,700	28,750	4,696	4,309	5,245	4,309
28,750	28,800	4,710	4,316	5,259	4,316
28,800	28,850	4,724	4,324	5,273	4,324
28,850	28,900	4,738	4,331	5,287	4,331
28,900	28,950	4,752	4,339	5,301	4,339
28,950	29,000	4,766	4,346	5,315	4,346

29,000

At least	But less than	Single	Married filing jointly	Married filing separately	Head of a household
29,000	29,050	4,780	4,354	5,329	4,354
29,050	29,100	4,794	4,361	5,343	4,361
29,100	29,150	4,808	4,369	5,357	4,369
29,150	29,200	4,822	4,376	5,371	4,376
29,200	29,250	4,836	4,384	5,385	4,384
29,250	29,300	4,850	4,391	5,399	4,391
29,300	29,350	4,864	4,399	5,413	4,399
29,350	29,400	4,878	4,406	5,427	4,406
29,400	29,450	4,892	4,414	5,441	4,414
29,450	29,500	4,906	4,421	5,455	4,421
29,500	29,550	4,920	4,429	5,469	4,429
29,550	29,600	4,934	4,436	5,483	4,436
29,600	29,650	4,948	4,444	5,497	4,444
29,650	29,700	4,962	4,451	5,511	4,451
29,700	29,750	4,976	4,459	5,525	4,459
29,750	29,800	4,990	4,466	5,539	4,466
29,800	29,850	5,004	4,474	5,553	4,474
29,850	29,900	5,018	4,481	5,567	4,481
29,900	29,950	5,032	4,489	5,581	4,489
29,950	30,000	5,046	4,496	5,595	4,496

30,000

At least	But less than	Single	Married filing jointly	Married filing separately	Head of a household
30,000	30,050	5,060	4,504	5,609	4,504
30,050	30,100	5,074	4,511	5,623	4,511
30,100	30,150	5,088	4,519	5,637	4,519
30,150	30,200	5,102	4,526	5,651	4,526
30,200	30,250	5,116	4,534	5,665	4,534
30,250	30,300	5,130	4,541	5,679	4,541
30,300	30,350	5,144	4,549	5,693	4,549
30,350	30,400	5,158	4,556	5,707	4,556
30,400	30,450	5,172	4,564	5,721	4,564
30,450	30,500	5,186	4,571	5,735	4,571
30,500	30,550	5,200	4,579	5,749	4,579
30,550	30,600	5,214	4,586	5,763	4,586
30,600	30,650	5,228	4,594	5,777	4,594
30,650	30,700	5,242	4,601	5,791	4,601
30,700	30,750	5,256	4,609	5,805	4,609
30,750	30,800	5,270	4,616	5,819	4,616
30,800	30,850	5,284	4,624	5,833	4,624
30,850	30,900	5,298	4,631	5,847	4,631
30,900	30,950	5,312	4,639	5,861	4,639
30,950	31,000	5,326	4,646	5,875	4,646

31,000

At least	But less than	Single	Married filing jointly	Married filing separately	Head of a household
31,000	31,050	5,340	4,654	5,889	4,654
31,050	31,100	5,354	4,661	5,903	4,661
31,100	31,150	5,368	4,669	5,917	4,669
31,150	31,200	5,382	4,676	5,931	4,676
31,200	31,250	5,396	4,684	5,945	4,684
31,250	31,300	5,410	4,691	5,959	4,691
31,300	31,350	5,424	4,699	5,973	4,699
31,350	31,400	5,438	4,706	5,987	4,706
31,400	31,450	5,452	4,714	6,001	4,714
31,450	31,500	5,466	4,721	6,015	4,721
31,500	31,550	5,480	4,729	6,029	4,729
31,550	31,600	5,494	4,736	6,043	4,736
31,600	31,650	5,508	4,744	6,057	4,744
31,650	31,700	5,522	4,751	6,071	4,751
31,700	31,750	5,536	4,759	6,085	4,759
31,750	31,800	5,550	4,766	6,099	4,766
31,800	31,850	5,564	4,774	6,113	4,774
31,850	31,900	5,578	4,781	6,127	4,781
31,900	31,950	5,592	4,789	6,141	4,789
31,950	32,000	5,606	4,796	6,155	4,796

* This column must also be used by a qualifying widow(er).

Continued on next page

1999 Tax Table—Continued

32,000 – 34,000

At least	But less than	Single	Married filing jointly *	Married filing separately	Head of a household
32,000					
32,000	32,050	5,620	4,804	6,169	4,804
32,050	32,100	5,634	4,811	6,183	4,811
32,100	32,150	5,648	4,819	6,197	4,819
32,150	32,200	5,662	4,826	6,211	4,826
32,200	32,250	5,676	4,834	6,225	4,834
32,250	32,300	5,690	4,841	6,239	4,841
32,300	32,350	5,704	4,849	6,253	4,849
32,350	32,400	5,718	4,856	6,267	4,856
32,400	32,450	5,732	4,864	6,281	4,864
32,450	32,500	5,746	4,871	6,295	4,871
32,500	32,550	5,760	4,879	6,309	4,879
32,550	32,600	5,774	4,886	6,323	4,886
32,600	32,650	5,788	4,894	6,337	4,894
32,650	32,700	5,802	4,901	6,351	4,901
32,700	32,750	5,816	4,909	6,365	4,909
32,750	32,800	5,830	4,916	6,379	4,916
32,800	32,850	5,844	4,924	6,393	4,924
32,850	32,900	5,858	4,931	6,407	4,931
32,900	32,950	5,872	4,939	6,421	4,939
32,950	33,000	5,886	4,946	6,435	4,946
33,000					
33,000	33,050	5,900	4,954	6,449	4,954
33,050	33,100	5,914	4,961	6,463	4,961
33,100	33,150	5,928	4,969	6,477	4,969
33,150	33,200	5,942	4,976	6,491	4,976
33,200	33,250	5,956	4,984	6,505	4,984
33,250	33,300	5,970	4,991	6,519	4,991
33,300	33,350	5,984	4,999	6,533	4,999
33,350	33,400	5,998	5,006	6,547	5,006
33,400	33,450	6,012	5,014	6,561	5,014
33,450	33,500	6,026	5,021	6,575	5,021
33,500	33,550	6,040	5,029	6,589	5,029
33,550	33,600	6,054	5,036	6,603	5,036
33,600	33,650	6,068	5,044	6,617	5,044
33,650	33,700	6,082	5,051	6,631	5,051
33,700	33,750	6,096	5,059	6,645	5,059
33,750	33,800	6,110	5,066	6,659	5,066
33,800	33,850	6,124	5,074	6,673	5,074
33,850	33,900	6,138	5,081	6,687	5,081
33,900	33,950	6,152	5,089	6,701	5,089
33,950	34,000	6,166	5,096	6,715	5,096
34,000					
34,000	34,050	6,180	5,104	6,729	5,104
34,050	34,100	6,194	5,111	6,743	5,111
34,100	34,150	6,208	5,119	6,757	5,119
34,150	34,200	6,222	5,126	6,771	5,126
34,200	34,250	6,236	5,134	6,785	5,134
34,250	34,300	6,250	5,141	6,799	5,141
34,300	34,350	6,264	5,149	6,813	5,149
34,350	34,400	6,278	5,156	6,827	5,156
34,400	34,450	6,292	5,164	6,841	5,164
34,450	34,500	6,306	5,171	6,855	5,171
34,500	34,550	6,320	5,179	6,869	5,179
34,550	34,600	6,334	5,186	6,883	5,190
34,600	34,650	6,348	5,194	6,897	5,204
34,650	34,700	6,362	5,201	6,911	5,218
34,700	34,750	6,376	5,209	6,925	5,232
34,750	34,800	6,390	5,216	6,939	5,246
34,800	34,850	6,404	5,224	6,953	5,260
34,850	34,900	6,418	5,231	6,967	5,274
34,900	34,950	6,432	5,239	6,981	5,288
34,950	35,000	6,446	5,246	6,995	5,302

35,000 – 37,000

At least	But less than	Single	Married filing jointly *	Married filing separately	Head of a household
35,000					
35,000	35,050	6,460	5,254	7,009	5,316
35,050	35,100	6,474	5,261	7,023	5,330
35,100	35,150	6,488	5,269	7,037	5,344
35,150	35,200	6,502	5,276	7,051	5,358
35,200	35,250	6,516	5,284	7,065	5,372
35,250	35,300	6,530	5,291	7,079	5,386
35,300	35,350	6,544	5,299	7,093	5,400
35,350	35,400	6,558	5,306	7,107	5,414
35,400	35,450	6,572	5,314	7,121	5,428
35,450	35,500	6,586	5,321	7,135	5,442
35,500	35,550	6,600	5,329	7,149	5,456
35,550	35,600	6,614	5,336	7,163	5,470
35,600	35,650	6,628	5,344	7,177	5,484
35,650	35,700	6,642	5,351	7,191	5,498
35,700	35,750	6,656	5,359	7,205	5,512
35,750	35,800	6,670	5,366	7,219	5,526
35,800	35,850	6,684	5,374	7,233	5,540
35,850	35,900	6,698	5,381	7,247	5,554
35,900	35,950	6,712	5,389	7,261	5,568
35,950	36,000	6,726	5,396	7,275	5,582
36,000					
36,000	36,050	6,740	5,404	7,289	5,596
36,050	36,100	6,754	5,411	7,303	5,610
36,100	36,150	6,768	5,419	7,317	5,624
36,150	36,200	6,782	5,426	7,331	5,638
36,200	36,250	6,796	5,434	7,345	5,652
36,250	36,300	6,810	5,441	7,359	5,666
36,300	36,350	6,824	5,449	7,373	5,680
36,350	36,400	6,838	5,456	7,387	5,694
36,400	36,450	6,852	5,464	7,401	5,708
36,450	36,500	6,866	5,471	7,415	5,722
36,500	36,550	6,880	5,479	7,429	5,736
36,550	36,600	6,894	5,486	7,443	5,750
36,600	36,650	6,908	5,494	7,457	5,764
36,650	36,700	6,922	5,501	7,471	5,778
36,700	36,750	6,936	5,509	7,485	5,792
36,750	36,800	6,950	5,516	7,499	5,806
36,800	36,850	6,964	5,524	7,513	5,820
36,850	36,900	6,978	5,531	7,527	5,834
36,900	36,950	6,992	5,539	7,541	5,848
36,950	37,000	7,006	5,546	7,555	5,862
37,000					
37,000	37,050	7,020	5,554	7,569	5,876
37,050	37,100	7,034	5,561	7,583	5,890
37,100	37,150	7,048	5,569	7,597	5,904
37,150	37,200	7,062	5,576	7,611	5,918
37,200	37,250	7,076	5,584	7,625	5,932
37,250	37,300	7,090	5,591	7,639	5,946
37,300	37,350	7,104	5,599	7,653	5,960
37,350	37,400	7,118	5,606	7,667	5,974
37,400	37,450	7,132	5,614	7,681	5,988
37,450	37,500	7,146	5,621	7,695	6,002
37,500	37,550	7,160	5,629	7,709	6,016
37,550	37,600	7,174	5,636	7,723	6,030
37,600	37,650	7,188	5,644	7,737	6,044
37,650	37,700	7,202	5,651	7,751	6,058
37,700	37,750	7,216	5,659	7,765	6,072
37,750	37,800	7,230	5,666	7,779	6,086
37,800	37,850	7,244	5,674	7,793	6,100
37,850	37,900	7,258	5,681	7,807	6,114
37,900	37,950	7,272	5,689	7,821	6,128
37,950	38,000	7,286	5,696	7,835	6,142

38,000 – 40,000

At least	But less than	Single	Married filing jointly *	Married filing separately	Head of a household
38,000					
38,000	38,050	7,300	5,704	7,849	6,156
38,050	38,100	7,314	5,711	7,863	6,170
38,100	38,150	7,328	5,719	7,877	6,184
38,150	38,200	7,342	5,726	7,891	6,198
38,200	38,250	7,356	5,734	7,905	6,212
38,250	38,300	7,370	5,741	7,919	6,226
38,300	38,350	7,384	5,749	7,933	6,240
38,350	38,400	7,398	5,756	7,947	6,254
38,400	38,450	7,412	5,764	7,961	6,268
38,450	38,500	7,426	5,771	7,975	6,282
38,500	38,550	7,440	5,779	7,989	6,296
38,550	38,600	7,454	5,786	8,003	6,310
38,600	38,650	7,468	5,794	8,017	6,324
38,650	38,700	7,482	5,801	8,031	6,338
38,700	38,750	7,496	5,809	8,045	6,352
38,750	38,800	7,510	5,816	8,059	6,366
38,800	38,850	7,524	5,824	8,073	6,380
38,850	38,900	7,538	5,831	8,087	6,394
38,900	38,950	7,552	5,839	8,101	6,408
38,950	39,000	7,566	5,846	8,115	6,422
39,000					
39,000	39,050	7,580	5,854	8,129	6,436
39,050	39,100	7,594	5,861	8,143	6,450
39,100	39,150	7,608	5,869	8,157	6,464
39,150	39,200	7,622	5,876	8,171	6,478
39,200	39,250	7,636	5,884	8,185	6,492
39,250	39,300	7,650	5,891	8,199	6,506
39,300	39,350	7,664	5,899	8,213	6,520
39,350	39,400	7,678	5,906	8,227	6,534
39,400	39,450	7,692	5,914	8,241	6,548
39,450	39,500	7,706	5,921	8,255	6,562
39,500	39,550	7,720	5,929	8,269	6,576
39,550	39,600	7,734	5,936	8,283	6,590
39,600	39,650	7,748	5,944	8,297	6,604
39,650	39,700	7,762	5,951	8,311	6,618
39,700	39,750	7,776	5,959	8,325	6,632
39,750	39,800	7,790	5,966	8,339	6,646
39,800	39,850	7,804	5,974	8,353	6,660
39,850	39,900	7,818	5,981	8,367	6,674
39,900	39,950	7,832	5,989	8,381	6,688
39,950	40,000	7,846	5,996	8,395	6,702
40,000					
40,000	40,050	7,860	6,004	8,409	6,716
40,050	40,100	7,874	6,011	8,423	6,730
40,100	40,150	7,888	6,019	8,437	6,744
40,150	40,200	7,902	6,026	8,451	6,758
40,200	40,250	7,916	6,034	8,465	6,772
40,250	40,300	7,930	6,041	8,479	6,786
40,300	40,350	7,944	6,049	8,493	6,800
40,350	40,400	7,958	6,056	8,507	6,814
40,400	40,450	7,972	6,064	8,521	6,828
40,450	40,500	7,986	6,071	8,535	6,842
40,500	40,550	8,000	6,079	8,549	6,856
40,550	40,600	8,014	6,086	8,563	6,870
40,600	40,650	8,028	6,094	8,577	6,884
40,650	40,700	8,042	6,101	8,591	6,898
40,700	40,750	8,056	6,109	8,605	6,912
40,750	40,800	8,070	6,116	8,619	6,926
40,800	40,850	8,084	6,124	8,633	6,940
40,850	40,900	8,098	6,131	8,647	6,954
40,900	40,950	8,112	6,139	8,661	6,968
40,950	41,000	8,126	6,146	8,675	6,982

* This column must also be used by a qualifying widow(er).

Continued on next page

If taxable income is— At least	But less than	Single	Married filing jointly *	Married filing separately	Head of a household
			Your tax is—		

41,000

At least	But less than	Single	Married filing jointly *	Married filing separately	Head of a household
41,000	41,050	8,140	6,154	8,689	6,996
41,050	41,100	8,154	6,161	8,703	7,010
41,100	41,150	8,168	6,169	8,717	7,024
41,150	41,200	8,182	6,176	8,731	7,038
41,200	41,250	8,196	6,184	8,745	7,052
41,250	41,300	8,210	6,191	8,759	7,066
41,300	41,350	8,224	6,199	8,773	7,080
41,350	41,400	8,238	6,206	8,787	7,094
41,400	41,450	8,252	6,214	8,801	7,108
41,450	41,500	8,266	6,221	8,815	7,122
41,500	41,550	8,280	6,229	8,829	7,136
41,550	41,600	8,294	6,236	8,843	7,150
41,600	41,650	8,308	6,244	8,857	7,164
41,650	41,700	8,322	6,251	8,871	7,178
41,700	41,750	8,336	6,259	8,885	7,192
41,750	41,800	8,350	6,266	8,899	7,206
41,800	41,850	8,364	6,274	8,913	7,220
41,850	41,900	8,378	6,281	8,927	7,234
41,900	41,950	8,392	6,289	8,941	7,248
41,950	42,000	8,406	6,296	8,955	7,262

42,000

At least	But less than	Single	Married filing jointly *	Married filing separately	Head of a household
42,000	42,050	8,420	6,304	8,969	7,276
42,050	42,100	8,434	6,311	8,983	7,290
42,100	42,150	8,448	6,319	8,997	7,304
42,150	42,200	8,462	6,326	9,011	7,318
42,200	42,250	8,476	6,334	9,025	7,332
42,250	42,300	8,490	6,341	9,039	7,346
42,300	42,350	8,504	6,349	9,053	7,360
42,350	42,400	8,518	6,356	9,067	7,374
42,400	42,450	8,532	6,364	9,081	7,388
42,450	42,500	8,546	6,371	9,095	7,402
42,500	42,550	8,560	6,379	9,109	7,416
42,550	42,600	8,574	6,386	9,123	7,430
42,600	42,650	8,588	6,394	9,137	7,444
42,650	42,700	8,602	6,401	9,151	7,458
42,700	42,750	8,616	6,409	9,165	7,472
42,750	42,800	8,630	6,416	9,179	7,486
42,800	42,850	8,644	6,424	9,193	7,500
42,850	42,900	8,658	6,431	9,207	7,514
42,900	42,950	8,672	6,439	9,221	7,528
42,950	43,000	8,686	6,446	9,235	7,542

43,000

At least	But less than	Single	Married filing jointly *	Married filing separately	Head of a household
43,000	43,050	8,700	6,454	9,249	7,556
43,050	43,100	8,714	6,465	9,263	7,570
43,100	43,150	8,728	6,479	9,277	7,584
43,150	43,200	8,742	6,493	9,291	7,598
43,200	43,250	8,756	6,507	9,305	7,612
43,250	43,300	8,770	6,521	9,319	7,626
43,300	43,350	8,784	6,535	9,333	7,640
43,350	43,400	8,798	6,549	9,347	7,654
43,400	43,450	8,812	6,563	9,361	7,668
43,450	43,500	8,826	6,577	9,375	7,682
43,500	43,550	8,840	6,591	9,389	7,696
43,550	43,600	8,854	6,605	9,403	7,710
43,600	43,650	8,868	6,619	9,417	7,724
43,650	43,700	8,882	6,633	9,431	7,738
43,700	43,750	8,896	6,647	9,445	7,752
43,750	43,800	8,910	6,661	9,459	7,766
43,800	43,850	8,924	6,675	9,473	7,780
43,850	43,900	8,938	6,689	9,487	7,794
43,900	43,950	8,952	6,703	9,501	7,808
43,950	44,000	8,966	6,717	9,515	7,822

44,000

At least	But less than	Single	Married filing jointly *	Married filing separately	Head of a household
44,000	44,050	8,980	6,731	9,529	7,836
44,050	44,100	8,994	6,745	9,543	7,850
44,100	44,150	9,008	6,759	9,557	7,864
44,150	44,200	9,022	6,773	9,571	7,878
44,200	44,250	9,036	6,787	9,585	7,892
44,250	44,300	9,050	6,801	9,599	7,906
44,300	44,350	9,064	6,815	9,613	7,920
44,350	44,400	9,078	6,829	9,627	7,934
44,400	44,450	9,092	6,843	9,641	7,948
44,450	44,500	9,106	6,857	9,655	7,962
44,500	44,550	9,120	6,871	9,669	7,976
44,550	44,600	9,134	6,885	9,683	7,990
44,600	44,650	9,148	6,899	9,697	8,004
44,650	44,700	9,162	6,913	9,711	8,018
44,700	44,750	9,176	6,927	9,725	8,032
44,750	44,800	9,190	6,941	9,739	8,046
44,800	44,850	9,204	6,955	9,753	8,060
44,850	44,900	9,218	6,969	9,767	8,074
44,900	44,950	9,232	6,983	9,781	8,088
44,950	45,000	9,246	6,997	9,795	8,102

45,000

At least	But less than	Single	Married filing jointly *	Married filing separately	Head of a household
45,000	45,050	9,260	7,011	9,809	8,116
45,050	45,100	9,274	7,025	9,823	8,130
45,100	45,150	9,288	7,039	9,837	8,144
45,150	45,200	9,302	7,053	9,851	8,158
45,200	45,250	9,316	7,067	9,865	8,172
45,250	45,300	9,330	7,081	9,879	8,186
45,300	45,350	9,344	7,095	9,893	8,200
45,350	45,400	9,358	7,109	9,907	8,214
45,400	45,450	9,372	7,123	9,921	8,228
45,450	45,500	9,386	7,137	9,935	8,242
45,500	45,550	9,400	7,151	9,949	8,256
45,550	45,600	9,414	7,165	9,963	8,270
45,600	45,650	9,428	7,179	9,977	8,284
45,650	45,700	9,442	7,193	9,991	8,298
45,700	45,750	9,456	7,207	10,005	8,312
45,750	45,800	9,470	7,221	10,019	8,326
45,800	45,850	9,484	7,235	10,033	8,340
45,850	45,900	9,498	7,249	10,047	8,354
45,900	45,950	9,512	7,263	10,061	8,368
45,950	46,000	9,526	7,277	10,075	8,382

46,000

At least	But less than	Single	Married filing jointly *	Married filing separately	Head of a household
46,000	46,050	9,540	7,291	10,089	8,396
46,050	46,100	9,554	7,305	10,103	8,410
46,100	46,150	9,568	7,319	10,117	8,424
46,150	46,200	9,582	7,333	10,131	8,438
46,200	46,250	9,596	7,347	10,145	8,452
46,250	46,300	9,610	7,361	10,159	8,466
46,300	46,350	9,624	7,375	10,173	8,480
46,350	46,400	9,638	7,389	10,187	8,494
46,400	46,450	9,652	7,403	10,201	8,508
46,450	46,500	9,666	7,417	10,215	8,522
46,500	46,550	9,680	7,431	10,229	8,536
46,550	46,600	9,694	7,445	10,243	8,550
46,600	46,650	9,708	7,459	10,257	8,564
46,650	46,700	9,722	7,473	10,271	8,578
46,700	46,750	9,736	7,487	10,285	8,592
46,750	46,800	9,750	7,501	10,299	8,606
46,800	46,850	9,764	7,515	10,313	8,620
46,850	46,900	9,778	7,529	10,327	8,634
46,900	46,950	9,792	7,543	10,341	8,648
46,950	47,000	9,806	7,557	10,355	8,662

47,000

At least	But less than	Single	Married filing jointly *	Married filing separately	Head of a household
47,000	47,050	9,820	7,571	10,369	8,676
47,050	47,100	9,834	7,585	10,383	8,690
47,100	47,150	9,848	7,599	10,397	8,704
47,150	47,200	9,862	7,613	10,411	8,718
47,200	47,250	9,876	7,627	10,425	8,732
47,250	47,300	9,890	7,641	10,439	8,746
47,300	47,350	9,904	7,655	10,453	8,760
47,350	47,400	9,918	7,669	10,467	8,774
47,400	47,450	9,932	7,683	10,481	8,788
47,450	47,500	9,946	7,697	10,495	8,802
47,500	47,550	9,960	7,711	10,509	8,816
47,550	47,600	9,974	7,725	10,523	8,830
47,600	47,650	9,988	7,739	10,537	8,844
47,650	47,700	10,002	7,753	10,551	8,858
47,700	47,750	10,016	7,767	10,565	8,872
47,750	47,800	10,030	7,781	10,579	8,886
47,800	47,850	10,044	7,795	10,593	8,900
47,850	47,900	10,058	7,809	10,607	8,914
47,900	47,950	10,072	7,823	10,621	8,928
47,950	48,000	10,086	7,837	10,635	8,942

48,000

At least	But less than	Single	Married filing jointly *	Married filing separately	Head of a household
48,000	48,050	10,100	7,851	10,649	8,956
48,050	48,100	10,114	7,865	10,663	8,970
48,100	48,150	10,128	7,879	10,677	8,984
48,150	48,200	10,142	7,893	10,691	8,998
48,200	48,250	10,156	7,907	10,705	9,012
48,250	48,300	10,170	7,921	10,719	9,026
48,300	48,350	10,184	7,935	10,733	9,040
48,350	48,400	10,198	7,949	10,747	9,054
48,400	48,450	10,212	7,963	10,761	9,068
48,450	48,500	10,226	7,977	10,775	9,082
48,500	48,550	10,240	7,991	10,789	9,096
48,550	48,600	10,254	8,005	10,803	9,110
48,600	48,650	10,268	8,019	10,817	9,124
48,650	48,700	10,282	8,033	10,831	9,138
48,700	48,750	10,296	8,047	10,845	9,152
48,750	48,800	10,310	8,061	10,859	9,166
48,800	48,850	10,324	8,075	10,873	9,180
48,850	48,900	10,338	8,089	10,887	9,194
48,900	48,950	10,352	8,103	10,901	9,208
48,950	49,000	10,366	8,117	10,915	9,222

49,000

At least	But less than	Single	Married filing jointly *	Married filing separately	Head of a household
49,000	49,050	10,380	8,131	10,929	9,236
49,050	49,100	10,394	8,145	10,943	9,250
49,100	49,150	10,408	8,159	10,957	9,264
49,150	49,200	10,422	8,173	10,971	9,278
49,200	49,250	10,436	8,187	10,985	9,292
49,250	49,300	10,450	8,201	10,999	9,306
49,300	49,350	10,464	8,215	11,013	9,320
49,350	49,400	10,478	8,229	11,027	9,334
49,400	49,450	10,492	8,243	11,041	9,348
49,450	49,500	10,506	8,257	11,055	9,362
49,500	49,550	10,520	8,271	11,069	9,376
49,550	49,600	10,534	8,285	11,083	9,390
49,600	49,650	10,548	8,299	11,097	9,404
49,650	49,700	10,562	8,313	11,111	9,418
49,700	49,750	10,576	8,327	11,125	9,432
49,750	49,800	10,590	8,341	11,139	9,446
49,800	49,850	10,604	8,355	11,153	9,460
49,850	49,900	10,618	8,369	11,167	9,474
49,900	49,950	10,632	8,383	11,181	9,488
49,950	50,000	10,646	8,397	11,195	9,502

* This column must also be used by a qualifying widow(er).

Continued on next page

50,000

At least	But less than	Single	Married filing jointly *	Married filing separately	Head of a household
50,000	50,050	10,660	8,411	11,209	9,516
50,050	50,100	10,674	8,425	11,223	9,530
50,100	50,150	10,688	8,439	11,237	9,544
50,150	50,200	10,702	8,453	11,251	9,558
50,200	50,250	10,716	8,467	11,265	9,572
50,250	50,300	10,730	8,481	11,279	9,586
50,300	50,350	10,744	8,495	11,293	9,600
50,350	50,400	10,758	8,509	11,307	9,614
50,400	50,450	10,772	8,523	11,321	9,628
50,450	50,500	10,786	8,537	11,335	9,642
50,500	50,550	10,800	8,551	11,349	9,656
50,550	50,600	10,814	8,565	11,363	9,670
50,600	50,650	10,828	8,579	11,377	9,684
50,650	50,700	10,842	8,593	11,391	9,698
50,700	50,750	10,856	8,607	11,405	9,712
50,750	50,800	10,870	8,621	11,419	9,726
50,800	50,850	10,884	8,635	11,433	9,740
50,850	50,900	10,898	8,649	11,447	9,754
50,900	50,950	10,912	8,663	11,461	9,768
50,950	51,000	10,926	8,677	11,475	9,782

51,000

At least	But less than	Single	Married filing jointly *	Married filing separately	Head of a household
51,000	51,050	10,940	8,691	11,489	9,796
51,050	51,100	10,954	8,705	11,503	9,810
51,100	51,150	10,968	8,719	11,517	9,824
51,150	51,200	10,982	8,733	11,531	9,838
51,200	51,250	10,996	8,747	11,545	9,852
51,250	51,300	11,010	8,761	11,559	9,866
51,300	51,350	11,024	8,775	11,573	9,880
51,350	51,400	11,038	8,789	11,587	9,894
51,400	51,450	11,052	8,803	11,601	9,908
51,450	51,500	11,066	8,817	11,615	9,922
51,500	51,550	11,080	8,831	11,629	9,936
51,550	51,600	11,094	8,845	11,643	9,950
51,600	51,650	11,108	8,859	11,657	9,964
51,650	51,700	11,122	8,873	11,671	9,978
51,700	51,750	11,136	8,887	11,685	9,992
51,750	51,800	11,150	8,901	11,699	10,006
51,800	51,850	11,164	8,915	11,713	10,020
51,850	51,900	11,178	8,929	11,727	10,034
51,900	51,950	11,192	8,943	11,741	10,048
51,950	52,000	11,206	8,957	11,755	10,062

52,000

At least	But less than	Single	Married filing jointly *	Married filing separately	Head of a household
52,000	52,050	11,220	8,971	11,769	10,076
52,050	52,100	11,234	8,985	11,784	10,090
52,100	52,150	11,248	8,999	11,800	10,104
52,150	52,200	11,262	9,013	11,815	10,118
52,200	52,250	11,276	9,027	11,831	10,132
52,250	52,300	11,290	9,041	11,846	10,146
52,300	52,350	11,304	9,055	11,862	10,160
52,350	52,400	11,318	9,069	11,877	10,174
52,400	52,450	11,332	9,083	11,893	10,188
52,450	52,500	11,346	9,097	11,908	10,202
52,500	52,550	11,360	9,111	11,924	10,216
52,550	52,600	11,374	9,125	11,939	10,230
52,600	52,650	11,388	9,139	11,955	10,244
52,650	52,700	11,402	9,153	11,970	10,258
52,700	52,750	11,416	9,167	11,986	10,272
52,750	52,800	11,430	9,181	12,001	10,286
52,800	52,850	11,444	9,195	12,017	10,300
52,850	52,900	11,458	9,209	12,032	10,314
52,900	52,950	11,472	9,223	12,048	10,328
52,950	53,000	11,486	9,237	12,063	10,342

53,000

At least	But less than	Single	Married filing jointly *	Married filing separately	Head of a household
53,000	53,050	11,500	9,251	12,079	10,356
53,050	53,100	11,514	9,265	12,094	10,370
53,100	53,150	11,528	9,279	12,110	10,384
53,150	53,200	11,542	9,293	12,125	10,398
53,200	53,250	11,556	9,307	12,141	10,412
53,250	53,300	11,570	9,321	12,156	10,426
53,300	53,350	11,584	9,335	12,172	10,440
53,350	53,400	11,598	9,349	12,187	10,454
53,400	53,450	11,612	9,363	12,203	10,468
53,450	53,500	11,626	9,377	12,218	10,482
53,500	53,550	11,640	9,391	12,234	10,496
53,550	53,600	11,654	9,405	12,249	10,510
53,600	53,650	11,668	9,419	12,265	10,524
53,650	53,700	11,682	9,433	12,280	10,538
53,700	53,750	11,696	9,447	12,296	10,552
53,750	53,800	11,710	9,461	12,311	10,566
53,800	53,850	11,724	9,475	12,327	10,580
53,850	53,900	11,738	9,489	12,342	10,594
53,900	53,950	11,752	9,503	12,358	10,608
53,950	54,000	11,766	9,517	12,373	10,622

54,000

At least	But less than	Single	Married filing jointly *	Married filing separately	Head of a household
54,000	54,050	11,780	9,531	12,389	10,636
54,050	54,100	11,794	9,545	12,404	10,650
54,100	54,150	11,808	9,559	12,420	10,664
54,150	54,200	11,822	9,573	12,435	10,678
54,200	54,250	11,836	9,587	12,451	10,692
54,250	54,300	11,850	9,601	12,466	10,706
54,300	54,350	11,864	9,615	12,482	10,720
54,350	54,400	11,878	9,629	12,497	10,734
54,400	54,450	11,892	9,643	12,513	10,748
54,450	54,500	11,906	9,657	12,528	10,762
54,500	54,550	11,920	9,671	12,544	10,776
54,550	54,600	11,934	9,685	12,559	10,790
54,600	54,650	11,948	9,699	12,575	10,804
54,650	54,700	11,962	9,713	12,590	10,818
54,700	54,750	11,976	9,727	12,606	10,832
54,750	54,800	11,990	9,741	12,621	10,846
54,800	54,850	12,004	9,755	12,637	10,860
54,850	54,900	12,018	9,769	12,652	10,874
54,900	54,950	12,032	9,783	12,668	10,888
54,950	55,000	12,046	9,797	12,683	10,902

55,000

At least	But less than	Single	Married filing jointly *	Married filing separately	Head of a household
55,000	55,050	12,060	9,811	12,699	10,916
55,050	55,100	12,074	9,825	12,714	10,930
55,100	55,150	12,088	9,839	12,730	10,944
55,150	55,200	12,102	9,853	12,745	10,958
55,200	55,250	12,116	9,867	12,761	10,972
55,250	55,300	12,130	9,881	12,776	10,986
55,300	55,350	12,144	9,895	12,792	11,000
55,350	55,400	12,158	9,909	12,807	11,014
55,400	55,450	12,172	9,923	12,823	11,028
55,450	55,500	12,186	9,937	12,838	11,042
55,500	55,550	12,200	9,951	12,854	11,056
55,550	55,600	12,214	9,965	12,869	11,070
55,600	55,650	12,228	9,979	12,885	11,084
55,650	55,700	12,242	9,993	12,900	11,098
55,700	55,750	12,256	10,007	12,916	11,112
55,750	55,800	12,270	10,021	12,931	11,126
55,800	55,850	12,284	10,035	12,947	11,140
55,850	55,900	12,298	10,049	12,962	11,154
55,900	55,950	12,312	10,063	12,978	11,168
55,950	56,000	12,326	10,077	12,993	11,182

56,000

At least	But less than	Single	Married filing jointly *	Married filing separately	Head of a household
56,000	56,050	12,340	10,091	13,009	11,196
56,050	56,100	12,354	10,105	13,024	11,210
56,100	56,150	12,368	10,119	13,040	11,224
56,150	56,200	12,382	10,133	13,055	11,238
56,200	56,250	12,396	10,147	13,071	11,252
56,250	56,300	12,410	10,161	13,086	11,266
56,300	56,350	12,424	10,175	13,102	11,280
56,350	56,400	12,438	10,189	13,117	11,294
56,400	56,450	12,452	10,203	13,133	11,308
56,450	56,500	12,466	10,217	13,148	11,322
56,500	56,550	12,480	10,231	13,164	11,336
56,550	56,600	12,494	10,245	13,179	11,350
56,600	56,650	12,508	10,259	13,195	11,364
56,650	56,700	12,522	10,273	13,210	11,378
56,700	56,750	12,536	10,287	13,226	11,392
56,750	56,800	12,550	10,301	13,241	11,406
56,800	56,850	12,564	10,315	13,257	11,420
56,850	56,900	12,578	10,329	13,272	11,434
56,900	56,950	12,592	10,343	13,288	11,448
56,950	57,000	12,606	10,357	13,303	11,462

57,000

At least	But less than	Single	Married filing jointly *	Married filing separately	Head of a household
57,000	57,050	12,620	10,371	13,319	11,476
57,050	57,100	12,634	10,385	13,334	11,490
57,100	57,150	12,648	10,399	13,350	11,504
57,150	57,200	12,662	10,413	13,365	11,518
57,200	57,250	12,676	10,427	13,381	11,532
57,250	57,300	12,690	10,441	13,396	11,546
57,300	57,350	12,704	10,455	13,412	11,560
57,350	57,400	12,718	10,469	13,427	11,574
57,400	57,450	12,732	10,483	13,443	11,588
57,450	57,500	12,746	10,497	13,458	11,602
57,500	57,550	12,760	10,511	13,474	11,616
57,550	57,600	12,774	10,525	13,489	11,630
57,600	57,650	12,788	10,539	13,505	11,644
57,650	57,700	12,802	10,553	13,520	11,658
57,700	57,750	12,816	10,567	13,536	11,672
57,750	57,800	12,830	10,581	13,551	11,686
57,800	57,850	12,844	10,595	13,567	11,700
57,850	57,900	12,858	10,609	13,582	11,714
57,900	57,950	12,872	10,623	13,598	11,728
57,950	58,000	12,886	10,637	13,613	11,742

58,000

At least	But less than	Single	Married filing jointly *	Married filing separately	Head of a household
58,000	58,050	12,900	10,651	13,629	11,756
58,050	58,100	12,914	10,665	13,644	11,770
58,100	58,150	12,928	10,679	13,660	11,784
58,150	58,200	12,942	10,693	13,675	11,798
58,200	58,250	12,956	10,707	13,691	11,812
58,250	58,300	12,970	10,721	13,706	11,826
58,300	58,350	12,984	10,735	13,722	11,840
58,350	58,400	12,998	10,749	13,737	11,854
58,400	58,450	13,012	10,763	13,753	11,868
58,450	58,500	13,026	10,777	13,768	11,882
58,500	58,550	13,040	10,791	13,784	11,896
58,550	58,600	13,054	10,805	13,799	11,910
58,600	58,650	13,068	10,819	13,815	11,924
58,650	58,700	13,082	10,833	13,830	11,938
58,700	58,750	13,096	10,847	13,846	11,952
58,750	58,800	13,110	10,861	13,861	11,966
58,800	58,850	13,124	10,875	13,877	11,980
58,850	58,900	13,138	10,889	13,892	11,994
58,900	58,950	13,152	10,903	13,908	12,008
58,950	59,000	13,166	10,917	13,923	12,022

* This column must also be used by a qualifying widow(er).

Continued on next page

If taxable income is—		Single	Married filing jointly *	Married filing separately	Head of a household
At least	But less than				
		Your tax is—			

59,000

At least	But less than	Single	Married filing jointly *	Married filing separately	Head of a household
59,000	59,050	13,180	10,931	13,939	12,036
59,050	59,100	13,194	10,945	13,954	12,050
59,100	59,150	13,208	10,959	13,970	12,064
59,150	59,200	13,222	10,973	13,985	12,078
59,200	59,250	13,236	10,987	14,001	12,092
59,250	59,300	13,250	11,001	14,016	12,106
59,300	59,350	13,264	11,015	14,032	12,120
59,350	59,400	13,278	11,029	14,047	12,134
59,400	59,450	13,292	11,043	14,063	12,148
59,450	59,500	13,306	11,057	14,078	12,162
59,500	59,550	13,320	11,071	14,094	12,176
59,550	59,600	13,334	11,085	14,109	12,190
59,600	59,650	13,348	11,099	14,125	12,204
59,650	59,700	13,362	11,113	14,140	12,218
59,700	59,750	13,376	11,127	14,156	12,232
59,750	59,800	13,390	11,141	14,171	12,246
59,800	59,850	13,404	11,155	14,187	12,260
59,850	59,900	13,418	11,169	14,202	12,274
59,900	59,950	13,432	11,183	14,218	12,288
59,950	60,000	13,446	11,197	14,233	12,302

60,000

At least	But less than	Single	Married filing jointly *	Married filing separately	Head of a household
60,000	60,050	13,460	11,211	14,249	12,316
60,050	60,100	13,474	11,225	14,264	12,330
60,100	60,150	13,488	11,239	14,280	12,344
60,150	60,200	13,502	11,253	14,295	12,358
60,200	60,250	13,516	11,267	14,311	12,372
60,250	60,300	13,530	11,281	14,326	12,386
60,300	60,350	13,544	11,295	14,342	12,400
60,350	60,400	13,558	11,309	14,357	12,414
60,400	60,450	13,572	11,323	14,373	12,428
60,450	60,500	13,586	11,337	14,388	12,442
60,500	60,550	13,600	11,351	14,404	12,456
60,550	60,600	13,614	11,365	14,419	12,470
60,600	60,650	13,628	11,379	14,435	12,484
60,650	60,700	13,642	11,393	14,450	12,498
60,700	60,750	13,656	11,407	14,466	12,512
60,750	60,800	13,670	11,421	14,481	12,526
60,800	60,850	13,684	11,435	14,497	12,540
60,850	60,900	13,698	11,449	14,512	12,554
60,900	60,950	13,712	11,463	14,528	12,568
60,950	61,000	13,726	11,477	14,543	12,582

61,000

At least	But less than	Single	Married filing jointly *	Married filing separately	Head of a household
61,000	61,050	13,740	11,491	14,559	12,596
61,050	61,100	13,754	11,505	14,574	12,610
61,100	61,150	13,768	11,519	14,590	12,624
61,150	61,200	13,782	11,533	14,605	12,638
61,200	61,250	13,796	11,547	14,621	12,652
61,250	61,300	13,810	11,561	14,636	12,666
61,300	61,350	13,824	11,575	14,652	12,680
61,350	61,400	13,838	11,589	14,667	12,694
61,400	61,450	13,852	11,603	14,683	12,708
61,450	61,500	13,866	11,617	14,698	12,722
61,500	61,550	13,880	11,631	14,714	12,736
61,550	61,600	13,894	11,645	14,729	12,750
61,600	61,650	13,908	11,659	14,745	12,764
61,650	61,700	13,922	11,673	14,760	12,778
61,700	61,750	13,936	11,687	14,776	12,792
61,750	61,800	13,950	11,701	14,791	12,806
61,800	61,850	13,964	11,715	14,807	12,820
61,850	61,900	13,978	11,729	14,822	12,834
61,900	61,950	13,992	11,743	14,838	12,848
61,950	62,000	14,006	11,757	14,853	12,862

62,000

At least	But less than	Single	Married filing jointly *	Married filing separately	Head of a household
62,000	62,050	14,020	11,771	14,869	12,876
62,050	62,100	14,034	11,785	14,884	12,890
62,100	62,150	14,048	11,799	14,900	12,904
62,150	62,200	14,062	11,813	14,915	12,918
62,200	62,250	14,076	11,827	14,931	12,932
62,250	62,300	14,090	11,841	14,946	12,946
62,300	62,350	14,104	11,855	14,962	12,960
62,350	62,400	14,118	11,869	14,977	12,974
62,400	62,450	14,132	11,883	14,993	12,988
62,450	62,500	14,146	11,897	15,008	13,002
62,500	62,550	14,162	11,911	15,024	13,016
62,550	62,600	14,177	11,925	15,039	13,030
62,600	62,650	14,193	11,939	15,055	13,044
62,650	62,700	14,208	11,953	15,070	13,058
62,700	62,750	14,224	11,967	15,086	13,072
62,750	62,800	14,239	11,981	15,101	13,086
62,800	62,850	14,255	11,995	15,117	13,100
62,850	62,900	14,270	12,009	15,132	13,114
62,900	62,950	14,286	12,023	15,148	13,128
62,950	63,000	14,301	12,037	15,163	13,142

63,000

At least	But less than	Single	Married filing jointly *	Married filing separately	Head of a household
63,000	63,050	14,317	12,051	15,179	13,156
63,050	63,100	14,332	12,065	15,194	13,170
63,100	63,150	14,348	12,079	15,210	13,184
63,150	63,200	14,363	12,093	15,225	13,198
63,200	63,250	14,379	12,107	15,241	13,212
63,250	63,300	14,394	12,121	15,256	13,226
63,300	63,350	14,410	12,135	15,272	13,240
63,350	63,400	14,425	12,149	15,287	13,254
63,400	63,450	14,441	12,163	15,303	13,268
63,450	63,500	14,456	12,177	15,318	13,282
63,500	63,550	14,472	12,191	15,334	13,296
63,550	63,600	14,487	12,205	15,349	13,310
63,600	63,650	14,503	12,219	15,365	13,324
63,650	63,700	14,518	12,233	15,380	13,338
63,700	63,750	14,534	12,247	15,396	13,352
63,750	63,800	14,549	12,261	15,411	13,366
63,800	63,850	14,565	12,275	15,427	13,380
63,850	63,900	14,580	12,289	15,442	13,394
63,900	63,950	14,596	12,303	15,458	13,408
63,950	64,000	14,611	12,317	15,473	13,422

64,000

At least	But less than	Single	Married filing jointly *	Married filing separately	Head of a household
64,000	64,050	14,627	12,331	15,489	13,436
64,050	64,100	14,642	12,345	15,504	13,450
64,100	64,150	14,658	12,359	15,520	13,464
64,150	64,200	14,673	12,373	15,535	13,478
64,200	64,250	14,689	12,387	15,551	13,492
64,250	64,300	14,704	12,401	15,566	13,506
64,300	64,350	14,720	12,415	15,582	13,520
64,350	64,400	14,735	12,429	15,597	13,534
64,400	64,450	14,751	12,443	15,613	13,548
64,450	64,500	14,766	12,457	15,628	13,562
64,500	64,550	14,782	12,471	15,644	13,576
64,550	64,600	14,797	12,485	15,659	13,590
64,600	64,650	14,813	12,499	15,675	13,604
64,650	64,700	14,828	12,513	15,690	13,618
64,700	64,750	14,844	12,527	15,706	13,632
64,750	64,800	14,859	12,541	15,721	13,646
64,800	64,850	14,875	12,555	15,737	13,660
64,850	64,900	14,890	12,569	15,752	13,674
64,900	64,950	14,906	12,583	15,768	13,688
64,950	65,000	14,921	12,597	15,783	13,702

65,000

At least	But less than	Single	Married filing jointly *	Married filing separately	Head of a household
65,000	65,050	14,937	12,611	15,799	13,716
65,050	65,100	14,952	12,625	15,814	13,730
65,100	65,150	14,968	12,639	15,830	13,744
65,150	65,200	14,983	12,653	15,845	13,758
65,200	65,250	14,999	12,667	15,861	13,772
65,250	65,300	15,014	12,681	15,876	13,786
65,300	65,350	15,030	12,695	15,892	13,800
65,350	65,400	15,045	12,709	15,907	13,814
65,400	65,450	15,061	12,723	15,923	13,828
65,450	65,500	15,076	12,737	15,938	13,842
65,500	65,550	15,092	12,751	15,954	13,856
65,550	65,600	15,107	12,765	15,969	13,870
65,600	65,650	15,123	12,779	15,985	13,884
65,650	65,700	15,138	12,793	16,000	13,898
65,700	65,750	15,154	12,807	16,016	13,912
65,750	65,800	15,169	12,821	16,031	13,926
65,800	65,850	15,185	12,835	16,047	13,940
65,850	65,900	15,200	12,849	16,062	13,954
65,900	65,950	15,216	12,863	16,078	13,968
65,950	66,000	15,231	12,877	16,093	13,982

66,000

At least	But less than	Single	Married filing jointly *	Married filing separately	Head of a household
66,000	66,050	15,247	12,891	16,109	13,996
66,050	66,100	15,262	12,905	16,124	14,010
66,100	66,150	15,278	12,919	16,140	14,024
66,150	66,200	15,293	12,933	16,155	14,038
66,200	66,250	15,309	12,947	16,171	14,052
66,250	66,300	15,324	12,961	16,186	14,066
66,300	66,350	15,340	12,975	16,202	14,080
66,350	66,400	15,355	12,989	16,217	14,094
66,400	66,450	15,371	13,003	16,233	14,108
66,450	66,500	15,386	13,017	16,248	14,122
66,500	66,550	15,402	13,031	16,264	14,136
66,550	66,600	15,417	13,045	16,279	14,150
66,600	66,650	15,433	13,059	16,295	14,164
66,650	66,700	15,448	13,073	16,310	14,178
66,700	66,750	15,464	13,087	16,326	14,192
66,750	66,800	15,479	13,101	16,341	14,206
66,800	66,850	15,495	13,115	16,357	14,220
66,850	66,900	15,510	13,129	16,372	14,234
66,900	66,950	15,526	13,143	16,388	14,248
66,950	67,000	15,541	13,157	16,403	14,262

67,000

At least	But less than	Single	Married filing jointly *	Married filing separately	Head of a household
67,000	67,050	15,557	13,171	16,419	14,276
67,050	67,100	15,572	13,185	16,434	14,290
67,100	67,150	15,588	13,199	16,450	14,304
67,150	67,200	15,603	13,213	16,465	14,318
67,200	67,250	15,619	13,227	16,481	14,332
67,250	67,300	15,634	13,241	16,496	14,346
67,300	67,350	15,650	13,255	16,512	14,360
67,350	67,400	15,665	13,269	16,527	14,374
67,400	67,450	15,681	13,283	16,543	14,388
67,450	67,500	15,696	13,297	16,558	14,402
67,500	67,550	15,712	13,311	16,574	14,416
67,550	67,600	15,727	13,325	16,589	14,430
67,600	67,650	15,743	13,339	16,605	14,444
67,650	67,700	15,758	13,353	16,620	14,458
67,700	67,750	15,774	13,367	16,636	14,472
67,750	67,800	15,789	13,381	16,651	14,486
67,800	67,850	15,805	13,395	16,667	14,500
67,850	67,900	15,820	13,409	16,682	14,514
67,900	67,950	15,836	13,423	16,698	14,528
67,950	68,000	15,851	13,437	16,713	14,542

* This column must also be used by a qualifying widow(er).

Continued on next page

68,000

At least	But less than	Single	Married filing jointly *	Married filing separately	Head of a household
68,000	68,050	15,867	13,451	16,729	14,556
68,050	68,100	15,882	13,465	16,744	14,570
68,100	68,150	15,898	13,479	16,760	14,584
68,150	68,200	15,913	13,493	16,775	14,598
68,200	68,250	15,929	13,507	16,791	14,612
68,250	68,300	15,944	13,521	16,806	14,626
68,300	68,350	15,960	13,535	16,822	14,640
68,350	68,400	15,975	13,549	16,837	14,654
68,400	68,450	15,991	13,563	16,853	14,668
68,450	68,500	16,006	13,577	16,868	14,682
68,500	68,550	16,022	13,591	16,884	14,696
68,550	68,600	16,037	13,605	16,899	14,710
68,600	68,650	16,053	13,619	16,915	14,724
68,650	68,700	16,068	13,633	16,930	14,738
68,700	68,750	16,084	13,647	16,946	14,752
68,750	68,800	16,099	13,661	16,961	14,766
68,800	68,850	16,115	13,675	16,977	14,780
68,850	68,900	16,130	13,689	16,992	14,794
68,900	68,950	16,146	13,703	17,008	14,808
68,950	69,000	16,161	13,717	17,023	14,822

69,000

At least	But less than	Single	Married filing jointly *	Married filing separately	Head of a household
69,000	69,050	16,177	13,731	17,039	14,836
69,050	69,100	16,192	13,745	17,054	14,850
69,100	69,150	16,208	13,759	17,070	14,864
69,150	69,200	16,223	13,773	17,085	14,878
69,200	69,250	16,239	13,787	17,101	14,892
69,250	69,300	16,254	13,801	17,116	14,906
69,300	69,350	16,270	13,815	17,132	14,920
69,350	69,400	16,285	13,829	17,147	14,934
69,400	69,450	16,301	13,843	17,163	14,948
69,450	69,500	16,316	13,857	17,178	14,962
69,500	69,550	16,332	13,871	17,194	14,976
69,550	69,600	16,347	13,885	17,209	14,990
69,600	69,650	16,363	13,899	17,225	15,004
69,650	69,700	16,378	13,913	17,240	15,018
69,700	69,750	16,394	13,927	17,256	15,032
69,750	69,800	16,409	13,941	17,271	15,046
69,800	69,850	16,425	13,955	17,287	15,060
69,850	69,900	16,440	13,969	17,302	15,074
69,900	69,950	16,456	13,983	17,318	15,088
69,950	70,000	16,471	13,997	17,333	15,102

70,000

At least	But less than	Single	Married filing jointly *	Married filing separately	Head of a household
70,000	70,050	16,487	14,011	17,349	15,116
70,050	70,100	16,502	14,025	17,364	15,130
70,100	70,150	16,518	14,039	17,380	15,144
70,150	70,200	16,533	14,053	17,395	15,158
70,200	70,250	16,549	14,067	17,411	15,172
70,250	70,300	16,564	14,081	17,426	15,186
70,300	70,350	16,580	14,095	17,442	15,200
70,350	70,400	16,595	14,109	17,457	15,214
70,400	70,450	16,611	14,123	17,473	15,228
70,450	70,500	16,626	14,137	17,488	15,242
70,500	70,550	16,642	14,151	17,504	15,256
70,550	70,600	16,657	14,165	17,519	15,270
70,600	70,650	16,673	14,179	17,535	15,284
70,650	70,700	16,688	14,193	17,550	15,298
70,700	70,750	16,704	14,207	17,566	15,312
70,750	70,800	16,719	14,221	17,581	15,326
70,800	70,850	16,735	14,235	17,597	15,340
70,850	70,900	16,750	14,249	17,612	15,354
70,900	70,950	16,766	14,263	17,628	15,368
70,950	71,000	16,781	14,277	17,643	15,382

71,000

At least	But less than	Single	Married filing jointly *	Married filing separately	Head of a household
71,000	71,050	16,797	14,291	17,659	15,396
71,050	71,100	16,812	14,305	17,674	15,410
71,100	71,150	16,828	14,319	17,690	15,424
71,150	71,200	16,843	14,333	17,705	15,438
71,200	71,250	16,859	14,347	17,721	15,452
71,250	71,300	16,874	14,361	17,736	15,466
71,300	71,350	16,890	14,375	17,752	15,480
71,350	71,400	16,905	14,389	17,767	15,494
71,400	71,450	16,921	14,403	17,783	15,508
71,450	71,500	16,936	14,417	17,798	15,522
71,500	71,550	16,952	14,431	17,814	15,536
71,550	71,600	16,967	14,445	17,829	15,550
71,600	71,650	16,983	14,459	17,845	15,564
71,650	71,700	16,998	14,473	17,860	15,578
71,700	71,750	17,014	14,487	17,876	15,592
71,750	71,800	17,029	14,501	17,891	15,606
71,800	71,850	17,045	14,515	17,907	15,620
71,850	71,900	17,060	14,529	17,922	15,634
71,900	71,950	17,076	14,543	17,938	15,648
71,950	72,000	17,091	14,557	17,953	15,662

72,000

At least	But less than	Single	Married filing jointly *	Married filing separately	Head of a household
72,000	72,050	17,107	14,571	17,969	15,676
72,050	72,100	17,122	14,585	17,984	15,690
72,100	72,150	17,138	14,599	18,000	15,704
72,150	72,200	17,153	14,613	18,015	15,718
72,200	72,250	17,169	14,627	18,031	15,732
72,250	72,300	17,184	14,641	18,046	15,746
72,300	72,350	17,200	14,655	18,062	15,760
72,350	72,400	17,215	14,669	18,077	15,774
72,400	72,450	17,231	14,683	18,093	15,788
72,450	72,500	17,246	14,697	18,108	15,802
72,500	72,550	17,262	14,711	18,124	15,816
72,550	72,600	17,277	14,725	18,139	15,830
72,600	72,650	17,293	14,739	18,155	15,844
72,650	72,700	17,308	14,753	18,170	15,858
72,700	72,750	17,324	14,767	18,186	15,872
72,750	72,800	17,339	14,781	18,201	15,886
72,800	72,850	17,355	14,795	18,217	15,900
72,850	72,900	17,370	14,809	18,232	15,914
72,900	72,950	17,386	14,823	18,248	15,928
72,950	73,000	17,401	14,837	18,263	15,942

73,000

At least	But less than	Single	Married filing jointly *	Married filing separately	Head of a household
73,000	73,050	17,417	14,851	18,279	15,956
73,050	73,100	17,432	14,865	18,294	15,970
73,100	73,150	17,448	14,879	18,310	15,984
73,150	73,200	17,463	14,893	18,325	15,998
73,200	73,250	17,479	14,907	18,341	16,012
73,250	73,300	17,494	14,921	18,356	16,026
73,300	73,350	17,510	14,935	18,372	16,040
73,350	73,400	17,525	14,949	18,387	16,054
73,400	73,450	17,541	14,963	18,403	16,068
73,450	73,500	17,556	14,977	18,418	16,082
73,500	73,550	17,572	14,991	18,434	16,096
73,550	73,600	17,587	15,005	18,449	16,110
73,600	73,650	17,603	15,019	18,465	16,124
73,650	73,700	17,618	15,033	18,480	16,138
73,700	73,750	17,634	15,047	18,496	16,152
73,750	73,800	17,649	15,061	18,511	16,166
73,800	73,850	17,665	15,075	18,527	16,180
73,850	73,900	17,680	15,089	18,542	16,194
73,900	73,950	17,696	15,103	18,558	16,208
73,950	74,000	17,711	15,117	18,573	16,222

74,000

At least	But less than	Single	Married filing jointly *	Married filing separately	Head of a household
74,000	74,050	17,727	15,131	18,589	16,236
74,050	74,100	17,742	15,145	18,604	16,250
74,100	74,150	17,758	15,159	18,620	16,264
74,150	74,200	17,773	15,173	18,635	16,278
74,200	74,250	17,789	15,187	18,651	16,292
74,250	74,300	17,804	15,201	18,666	16,306
74,300	74,350	17,820	15,215	18,682	16,320
74,350	74,400	17,835	15,229	18,697	16,334
74,400	74,450	17,851	15,243	18,713	16,348
74,450	74,500	17,866	15,257	18,728	16,362
74,500	74,550	17,882	15,271	18,744	16,376
74,550	74,600	17,897	15,285	18,759	16,390
74,600	74,650	17,913	15,299	18,775	16,404
74,650	74,700	17,928	15,313	18,790	16,418
74,700	74,750	17,944	15,327	18,806	16,432
74,750	74,800	17,959	15,341	18,821	16,446
74,800	74,850	17,975	15,355	18,837	16,460
74,850	74,900	17,990	15,369	18,852	16,474
74,900	74,950	18,006	15,383	18,868	16,488
74,950	75,000	18,021	15,397	18,883	16,502

75,000

At least	But less than	Single	Married filing jointly *	Married filing separately	Head of a household
75,000	75,050	18,037	15,411	18,899	16,516
75,050	75,100	18,052	15,425	18,914	16,530
75,100	75,150	18,068	15,439	18,930	16,544
75,150	75,200	18,083	15,453	18,945	16,558
75,200	75,250	18,099	15,467	18,961	16,572
75,250	75,300	18,114	15,481	18,976	16,586
75,300	75,350	18,130	15,495	18,992	16,600
75,350	75,400	18,145	15,509	19,007	16,614
75,400	75,450	18,161	15,523	19,023	16,628
75,450	75,500	18,176	15,537	19,038	16,642
75,500	75,550	18,192	15,551	19,054	16,656
75,550	75,600	18,207	15,565	19,069	16,670
75,600	75,650	18,223	15,579	19,085	16,684
75,650	75,700	18,238	15,593	19,100	16,698
75,700	75,750	18,254	15,607	19,116	16,712
75,750	75,800	18,269	15,621	19,131	16,726
75,800	75,850	18,285	15,635	19,147	16,740
75,850	75,900	18,300	15,649	19,162	16,754
75,900	75,950	18,316	15,663	19,178	16,768
75,950	76,000	18,331	15,677	19,193	16,782

76,000

At least	But less than	Single	Married filing jointly *	Married filing separately	Head of a household
76,000	76,050	18,347	15,691	19,209	16,796
76,050	76,100	18,362	15,705	19,224	16,810
76,100	76,150	18,378	15,719	19,240	16,824
76,150	76,200	18,393	15,733	19,255	16,838
76,200	76,250	18,409	15,747	19,271	16,852
76,250	76,300	18,424	15,761	19,286	16,866
76,300	76,350	18,440	15,775	19,302	16,880
76,350	76,400	18,455	15,789	19,317	16,894
76,400	76,450	18,471	15,803	19,333	16,908
76,450	76,500	18,486	15,817	19,348	16,922
76,500	76,550	18,502	15,831	19,364	16,936
76,550	76,600	18,517	15,845	19,379	16,950
76,600	76,650	18,533	15,859	19,395	16,964
76,650	76,700	18,548	15,873	19,410	16,978
76,700	76,750	18,564	15,887	19,426	16,992
76,750	76,800	18,579	15,901	19,441	17,006
76,800	76,850	18,595	15,915	19,457	17,020
76,850	76,900	18,610	15,929	19,472	17,034
76,900	76,950	18,626	15,943	19,488	17,048
76,950	77,000	18,641	15,957	19,503	17,062

* This column must also be used by a qualifying widow(er).

Continued on next page

77,000

At least	But less than	Single	Married filing jointly*	Married filing separately	Head of a household
77,000	77,050	18,657	15,971	19,519	17,076
77,050	77,100	18,672	15,985	19,534	17,090
77,100	77,150	18,688	15,999	19,550	17,104
77,150	77,200	18,703	16,013	19,565	17,118
77,200	77,250	18,719	16,027	19,581	17,132
77,250	77,300	18,734	16,041	19,596	17,146
77,300	77,350	18,750	16,055	19,612	17,160
77,350	77,400	18,765	16,069	19,627	17,174
77,400	77,450	18,781	16,083	19,643	17,188
77,450	77,500	18,796	16,097	19,658	17,202
77,500	77,550	18,812	16,111	19,674	17,216
77,550	77,600	18,827	16,125	19,689	17,230
77,600	77,650	18,843	16,139	19,705	17,244
77,650	77,700	18,858	16,153	19,720	17,258
77,700	77,750	18,874	16,167	19,736	17,272
77,750	77,800	18,889	16,181	19,751	17,286
77,800	77,850	18,905	16,195	19,767	17,300
77,850	77,900	18,920	16,209	19,782	17,314
77,900	77,950	18,936	16,223	19,798	17,328
77,950	78,000	18,951	16,237	19,813	17,342

78,000

At least	But less than	Single	Married filing jointly*	Married filing separately	Head of a household
78,000	78,050	18,967	16,251	19,829	17,356
78,050	78,100	18,982	16,265	19,844	17,370
78,100	78,150	18,998	16,279	19,860	17,384
78,150	78,200	19,013	16,293	19,875	17,398
78,200	78,250	19,029	16,307	19,891	17,412
78,250	78,300	19,044	16,321	19,906	17,426
78,300	78,350	19,060	16,335	19,922	17,440
78,350	78,400	19,075	16,349	19,937	17,454
78,400	78,450	19,091	16,363	19,953	17,468
78,450	78,500	19,106	16,377	19,968	17,482
78,500	78,550	19,122	16,391	19,984	17,496
78,550	78,600	19,137	16,405	19,999	17,510
78,600	78,650	19,153	16,419	20,015	17,524
78,650	78,700	19,168	16,433	20,030	17,538
78,700	78,750	19,184	16,447	20,046	17,552
78,750	78,800	19,199	16,461	20,061	17,566
78,800	78,850	19,215	16,475	20,077	17,580
78,850	78,900	19,230	16,489	20,092	17,594
78,900	78,950	19,246	16,503	20,108	17,608
78,950	79,000	19,261	16,517	20,123	17,622

79,000

At least	But less than	Single	Married filing jointly*	Married filing separately	Head of a household
79,000	79,050	19,277	16,531	20,139	17,636
79,050	79,100	19,292	16,545	20,154	17,650
79,100	79,150	19,308	16,559	20,170	17,664
79,150	79,200	19,323	16,573	20,185	17,678
79,200	79,250	19,339	16,587	20,201	17,692
79,250	79,300	19,354	16,601	20,216	17,706
79,300	79,350	19,370	16,615	20,234	17,720
79,350	79,400	19,385	16,629	20,252	17,734
79,400	79,450	19,401	16,643	20,270	17,748
79,450	79,500	19,416	16,657	20,288	17,762
79,500	79,550	19,432	16,671	20,306	17,776
79,550	79,600	19,447	16,685	20,324	17,790
79,600	79,650	19,463	16,699	20,342	17,804
79,650	79,700	19,478	16,713	20,360	17,818
79,700	79,750	19,494	16,727	20,378	17,832
79,750	79,800	19,509	16,741	20,396	17,846
79,800	79,850	19,525	16,755	20,414	17,860
79,850	79,900	19,540	16,769	20,432	17,874
79,900	79,950	19,556	16,783	20,450	17,888
79,950	80,000	19,571	16,797	20,468	17,902

80,000

At least	But less than	Single	Married filing jointly*	Married filing separately	Head of a household
80,000	80,050	19,587	16,811	20,486	17,916
80,050	80,100	19,602	16,825	20,504	17,930
80,100	80,150	19,618	16,839	20,522	17,944
80,150	80,200	19,633	16,853	20,540	17,958
80,200	80,250	19,649	16,867	20,558	17,972
80,250	80,300	19,664	16,881	20,576	17,986
80,300	80,350	19,680	16,895	20,594	18,000
80,350	80,400	19,695	16,909	20,612	18,014
80,400	80,450	19,711	16,923	20,630	18,028
80,450	80,500	19,726	16,937	20,648	18,042
80,500	80,550	19,742	16,951	20,666	18,056
80,550	80,600	19,757	16,965	20,684	18,070
80,600	80,650	19,773	16,979	20,702	18,084
80,650	80,700	19,788	16,993	20,720	18,098
80,700	80,750	19,804	17,007	20,738	18,112
80,750	80,800	19,819	17,021	20,756	18,126
80,800	80,850	19,835	17,035	20,774	18,140
80,850	80,900	19,850	17,049	20,792	18,154
80,900	80,950	19,866	17,063	20,810	18,168
80,950	81,000	19,881	17,077	20,828	18,182

81,000

At least	But less than	Single	Married filing jointly*	Married filing separately	Head of a household
81,000	81,050	19,897	17,091	20,846	18,196
81,050	81,100	19,912	17,105	20,864	18,210
81,100	81,150	19,928	17,119	20,882	18,224
81,150	81,200	19,943	17,133	20,900	18,238
81,200	81,250	19,959	17,147	20,918	18,252
81,250	81,300	19,974	17,161	20,936	18,266
81,300	81,350	19,990	17,175	20,954	18,280
81,350	81,400	20,005	17,189	20,972	18,294
81,400	81,450	20,021	17,203	20,990	18,308
81,450	81,500	20,036	17,217	21,008	18,322
81,500	81,550	20,052	17,231	21,026	18,336
81,550	81,600	20,067	17,245	21,044	18,350
81,600	81,650	20,083	17,259	21,062	18,364
81,650	81,700	20,098	17,273	21,080	18,378
81,700	81,750	20,114	17,287	21,098	18,392
81,750	81,800	20,129	17,301	21,116	18,406
81,800	81,850	20,145	17,315	21,134	18,420
81,850	81,900	20,160	17,329	21,152	18,434
81,900	81,950	20,176	17,343	21,170	18,448
81,950	82,000	20,191	17,357	21,188	18,462

82,000

At least	But less than	Single	Married filing jointly*	Married filing separately	Head of a household
82,000	82,050	20,207	17,371	21,206	18,476
82,050	82,100	20,222	17,385	21,224	18,490
82,100	82,150	20,238	17,399	21,242	18,504
82,150	82,200	20,253	17,413	21,260	18,518
82,200	82,250	20,269	17,427	21,278	18,532
82,250	82,300	20,284	17,441	21,296	18,546
82,300	82,350	20,300	17,455	21,314	18,560
82,350	82,400	20,315	17,469	21,332	18,574
82,400	82,450	20,331	17,483	21,350	18,588
82,450	82,500	20,346	17,497	21,368	18,602
82,500	82,550	20,362	17,511	21,386	18,616
82,550	82,600	20,377	17,525	21,404	18,630
82,600	82,650	20,393	17,539	21,422	18,644
82,650	82,700	20,408	17,553	21,440	18,658
82,700	82,750	20,424	17,567	21,458	18,672
82,750	82,800	20,439	17,581	21,476	18,686
82,800	82,850	20,455	17,595	21,494	18,700
82,850	82,900	20,470	17,609	21,512	18,714
82,900	82,950	20,486	17,623	21,530	18,728
82,950	83,000	20,501	17,637	21,548	18,742

83,000

At least	But less than	Single	Married filing jointly*	Married filing separately	Head of a household
83,000	83,050	20,517	17,651	21,566	18,756
83,050	83,100	20,532	17,665	21,584	18,770
83,100	83,150	20,548	17,679	21,602	18,784
83,150	83,200	20,563	17,693	21,620	18,798
83,200	83,250	20,579	17,707	21,638	18,812
83,250	83,300	20,594	17,721	21,656	18,826
83,300	83,350	20,610	17,735	21,674	18,840
83,350	83,400	20,625	17,749	21,692	18,854
83,400	83,450	20,641	17,763	21,710	18,868
83,450	83,500	20,656	17,777	21,728	18,882
83,500	83,550	20,672	17,791	21,746	18,896
83,550	83,600	20,687	17,805	21,764	18,910
83,600	83,650	20,703	17,819	21,782	18,924
83,650	83,700	20,718	17,833	21,800	18,938
83,700	83,750	20,734	17,847	21,818	18,952
83,750	83,800	20,749	17,861	21,836	18,966
83,800	83,850	20,765	17,875	21,854	18,980
83,850	83,900	20,780	17,889	21,872	18,994
83,900	83,950	20,796	17,903	21,890	19,008
83,950	84,000	20,811	17,917	21,908	19,022

84,000

At least	But less than	Single	Married filing jointly*	Married filing separately	Head of a household
84,000	84,050	20,827	17,931	21,926	19,036
84,050	84,100	20,842	17,945	21,944	19,050
84,100	84,150	20,858	17,959	21,962	19,064
84,150	84,200	20,873	17,973	21,980	19,078
84,200	84,250	20,889	17,987	21,998	19,092
84,250	84,300	20,904	18,001	22,016	19,106
84,300	84,350	20,920	18,015	22,034	19,120
84,350	84,400	20,935	18,029	22,052	19,134
84,400	84,450	20,951	18,043	22,070	19,148
84,450	84,500	20,966	18,057	22,088	19,162
84,500	84,550	20,982	18,071	22,106	19,176
84,550	84,600	20,997	18,085	22,124	19,190
84,600	84,650	21,013	18,099	22,142	19,204
84,650	84,700	21,028	18,113	22,160	19,218
84,700	84,750	21,044	18,127	22,178	19,232
84,750	84,800	21,059	18,141	22,196	19,246
84,800	84,850	21,075	18,155	22,214	19,260
84,850	84,900	21,090	18,169	22,232	19,274
84,900	84,950	21,106	18,183	22,250	19,288
84,950	85,000	21,121	18,197	22,268	19,302

85,000

At least	But less than	Single	Married filing jointly*	Married filing separately	Head of a household
85,000	85,050	21,137	18,211	22,286	19,316
85,050	85,100	21,152	18,225	22,304	19,330
85,100	85,150	21,168	18,239	22,322	19,344
85,150	85,200	21,183	18,253	22,340	19,358
85,200	85,250	21,199	18,267	22,358	19,372
85,250	85,300	21,214	18,281	22,376	19,386
85,300	85,350	21,230	18,295	22,394	19,400
85,350	85,400	21,245	18,309	22,412	19,414
85,400	85,450	21,261	18,323	22,430	19,428
85,450	85,500	21,276	18,337	22,448	19,442
85,500	85,550	21,292	18,351	22,466	19,456
85,550	85,600	21,307	18,365	22,484	19,470
85,600	85,650	21,323	18,379	22,502	19,484
85,650	85,700	21,338	18,393	22,520	19,498
85,700	85,750	21,354	18,407	22,538	19,512
85,750	85,800	21,369	18,421	22,556	19,526
85,800	85,850	21,385	18,435	22,574	19,540
85,850	85,900	21,400	18,449	22,592	19,554
85,900	85,950	21,416	18,463	22,610	19,568
85,950	86,000	21,431	18,477	22,628	19,582

* This column must also be used by a qualifying widow(er).

Continued on next page

86,000

At least	But less than	Single	Married filing jointly *	Married filing separately	Head of a household
86,000	86,050	21,447	18,491	22,646	19,596
86,050	86,100	21,462	18,505	22,664	19,610
86,100	86,150	21,478	18,519	22,682	19,624
86,150	86,200	21,493	18,533	22,700	19,638
86,200	86,250	21,509	18,547	22,718	19,652
86,250	86,300	21,524	18,561	22,736	19,666
86,300	86,350	21,540	18,575	22,754	19,680
86,350	86,400	21,555	18,589	22,772	19,694
86,400	86,450	21,571	18,603	22,790	19,708
86,450	86,500	21,586	18,617	22,808	19,722
86,500	86,550	21,602	18,631	22,826	19,736
86,550	86,600	21,617	18,645	22,844	19,750
86,600	86,650	21,633	18,659	22,862	19,764
86,650	86,700	21,648	18,673	22,880	19,778
86,700	86,750	21,664	18,687	22,898	19,792
86,750	86,800	21,679	18,701	22,916	19,806
86,800	86,850	21,695	18,715	22,934	19,820
86,850	86,900	21,710	18,729	22,952	19,834
86,900	86,950	21,726	18,743	22,970	19,848
86,950	87,000	21,741	18,757	22,988	19,862

87,000

At least	But less than	Single	Married filing jointly *	Married filing separately	Head of a household
87,000	87,050	21,757	18,771	23,006	19,876
87,050	87,100	21,772	18,785	23,024	19,890
87,100	87,150	21,788	18,799	23,042	19,904
87,150	87,200	21,803	18,813	23,060	19,918
87,200	87,250	21,819	18,827	23,078	19,932
87,250	87,300	21,834	18,841	23,096	19,946
87,300	87,350	21,850	18,855	23,114	19,960
87,350	87,400	21,865	18,869	23,132	19,974
87,400	87,450	21,881	18,883	23,150	19,988
87,450	87,500	21,896	18,897	23,168	20,002
87,500	87,550	21,912	18,911	23,186	20,016
87,550	87,600	21,927	18,925	23,204	20,030
87,600	87,650	21,943	18,939	23,222	20,044
87,650	87,700	21,958	18,953	23,240	20,058
87,700	87,750	21,974	18,967	23,258	20,072
87,750	87,800	21,989	18,981	23,276	20,086
87,800	87,850	22,005	18,995	23,294	20,100
87,850	87,900	22,020	19,009	23,312	20,114
87,900	87,950	22,036	19,023	23,330	20,128
87,950	88,000	22,051	19,037	23,348	20,142

88,000

At least	But less than	Single	Married filing jointly *	Married filing separately	Head of a household
88,000	88,050	22,067	19,051	23,366	20,156
88,050	88,100	22,082	19,065	23,384	20,170
88,100	88,150	22,098	19,079	23,402	20,184
88,150	88,200	22,113	19,093	23,420	20,198
88,200	88,250	22,129	19,107	23,438	20,212
88,250	88,300	22,144	19,121	23,456	20,226
88,300	88,350	22,160	19,135	23,474	20,240
88,350	88,400	22,175	19,149	23,492	20,254
88,400	88,450	22,191	19,163	23,510	20,268
88,450	88,500	22,206	19,177	23,528	20,282
88,500	88,550	22,222	19,191	23,546	20,296
88,550	88,600	22,237	19,205	23,564	20,310
88,600	88,650	22,253	19,219	23,582	20,324
88,650	88,700	22,268	19,233	23,600	20,338
88,700	88,750	22,284	19,247	23,618	20,352
88,750	88,800	22,299	19,261	23,636	20,366
88,800	88,850	22,315	19,275	23,654	20,380
88,850	88,900	22,330	19,289	23,672	20,394
88,900	88,950	22,346	19,303	23,690	20,408
88,950	89,000	22,361	19,317	23,708	20,422

89,000

At least	But less than	Single	Married filing jointly *	Married filing separately	Head of a household
89,000	89,050	22,377	19,331	23,726	20,436
89,050	89,100	22,392	19,345	23,744	20,450
89,100	89,150	22,408	19,359	23,762	20,464
89,150	89,200	22,423	19,373	23,780	20,478
89,200	89,250	22,439	19,387	23,798	20,494
89,250	89,300	22,454	19,401	23,816	20,509
89,300	89,350	22,470	19,415	23,834	20,525
89,350	89,400	22,485	19,429	23,852	20,540
89,400	89,450	22,501	19,443	23,870	20,556
89,450	89,500	22,516	19,457	23,888	20,571
89,500	89,550	22,532	19,471	23,906	20,587
89,550	89,600	22,547	19,485	23,924	20,602
89,600	89,650	22,563	19,499	23,942	20,618
89,650	89,700	22,578	19,513	23,960	20,633
89,700	89,750	22,594	19,527	23,978	20,649
89,750	89,800	22,609	19,541	23,996	20,664
89,800	89,850	22,625	19,555	24,014	20,680
89,850	89,900	22,640	19,569	24,032	20,695
89,900	89,950	22,656	19,583	24,050	20,711
89,950	90,000	22,671	19,597	24,068	20,726

90,000

At least	But less than	Single	Married filing jointly *	Married filing separately	Head of a household
90,000	90,050	22,687	19,611	24,086	20,742
90,050	90,100	22,702	19,625	24,104	20,757
90,100	90,150	22,718	19,639	24,122	20,773
90,150	90,200	22,733	19,653	24,140	20,788
90,200	90,250	22,749	19,667	24,158	20,804
90,250	90,300	22,764	19,681	24,176	20,819
90,300	90,350	22,780	19,695	24,194	20,835
90,350	90,400	22,795	19,709	24,212	20,850
90,400	90,450	22,811	19,723	24,230	20,866
90,450	90,500	22,826	19,737	24,248	20,881
90,500	90,550	22,842	19,751	24,266	20,897
90,550	90,600	22,857	19,765	24,284	20,912
90,600	90,650	22,873	19,779	24,302	20,928
90,650	90,700	22,888	19,793	24,320	20,943
90,700	90,750	22,904	19,807	24,338	20,959
90,750	90,800	22,919	19,821	24,356	20,974
90,800	90,850	22,935	19,835	24,374	20,990
90,850	90,900	22,950	19,849	24,392	21,005
90,900	90,950	22,966	19,863	24,410	21,021
90,950	91,000	22,981	19,877	24,428	21,036

91,000

At least	But less than	Single	Married filing jointly *	Married filing separately	Head of a household
91,000	91,050	22,997	19,891	24,446	21,052
91,050	91,100	23,012	19,905	24,464	21,067
91,100	91,150	23,028	19,919	24,482	21,083
91,150	91,200	23,043	19,933	24,500	21,098
91,200	91,250	23,059	19,947	24,518	21,114
91,250	91,300	23,074	19,961	24,536	21,129
91,300	91,350	23,090	19,975	24,554	21,145
91,350	91,400	23,105	19,989	24,572	21,160
91,400	91,450	23,121	20,003	24,590	21,176
91,450	91,500	23,136	20,017	24,608	21,191
91,500	91,550	23,152	20,031	24,626	21,207
91,550	91,600	23,167	20,045	24,644	21,222
91,600	91,650	23,183	20,059	24,662	21,238
91,650	91,700	23,198	20,073	24,680	21,253
91,700	91,750	23,214	20,087	24,698	21,269
91,750	91,800	23,229	20,101	24,716	21,284
91,800	91,850	23,245	20,115	24,734	21,300
91,850	91,900	23,260	20,129	24,752	21,315
91,900	91,950	23,276	20,143	24,770	21,331
91,950	92,000	23,291	20,157	24,788	21,346

92,000

At least	But less than	Single	Married filing jointly *	Married filing separately	Head of a household
92,000	92,050	23,307	20,171	24,806	21,362
92,050	92,100	23,322	20,185	24,824	21,377
92,100	92,150	23,338	20,199	24,842	21,393
92,150	92,200	23,353	20,213	24,860	21,408
92,200	92,250	23,369	20,227	24,878	21,424
92,250	92,300	23,384	20,241	24,896	21,439
92,300	92,350	23,400	20,255	24,914	21,455
92,350	92,400	23,415	20,269	24,932	21,470
92,400	92,450	23,431	20,283	24,950	21,486
92,450	92,500	23,446	20,297	24,968	21,501
92,500	92,550	23,462	20,311	24,986	21,517
92,550	92,600	23,477	20,325	25,004	21,532
92,600	92,650	23,493	20,339	25,022	21,548
92,650	92,700	23,508	20,353	25,040	21,563
92,700	92,750	23,524	20,367	25,058	21,579
92,750	92,800	23,539	20,381	25,076	21,594
92,800	92,850	23,555	20,395	25,094	21,610
92,850	92,900	23,570	20,409	25,112	21,625
92,900	92,950	23,586	20,423	25,130	21,641
92,950	93,000	23,601	20,437	25,148	21,656

93,000

At least	But less than	Single	Married filing jointly *	Married filing separately	Head of a household
93,000	93,050	23,617	20,451	25,166	21,672
93,050	93,100	23,632	20,465	25,184	21,687
93,100	93,150	23,648	20,479	25,202	21,703
93,150	93,200	23,663	20,493	25,220	21,718
93,200	93,250	23,679	20,507	25,238	21,734
93,250	93,300	23,694	20,521	25,256	21,749
93,300	93,350	23,710	20,535	25,274	21,765
93,350	93,400	23,725	20,549	25,292	21,780
93,400	93,450	23,741	20,563	25,310	21,796
93,450	93,500	23,756	20,577	25,328	21,811
93,500	93,550	23,772	20,591	25,346	21,827
93,550	93,600	23,787	20,605	25,364	21,842
93,600	93,650	23,803	20,619	25,382	21,858
93,650	93,700	23,818	20,633	25,400	21,873
93,700	93,750	23,834	20,647	25,418	21,889
93,750	93,800	23,849	20,661	25,436	21,904
93,800	93,850	23,865	20,675	25,454	21,920
93,850	93,900	23,880	20,689	25,472	21,935
93,900	93,950	23,896	20,703	25,490	21,951
93,950	94,000	23,911	20,717	25,508	21,966

94,000

At least	But less than	Single	Married filing jointly *	Married filing separately	Head of a household
94,000	94,050	23,927	20,731	25,526	21,982
94,050	94,100	23,942	20,745	25,544	21,997
94,100	94,150	23,958	20,759	25,562	22,013
94,150	94,200	23,973	20,773	25,580	22,028
94,200	94,250	23,989	20,787	25,598	22,044
94,250	94,300	24,004	20,801	25,616	22,059
94,300	94,350	24,020	20,815	25,634	22,075
94,350	94,400	24,035	20,829	25,652	22,090
94,400	94,450	24,051	20,843	25,670	22,106
94,450	94,500	24,066	20,857	25,688	22,121
94,500	94,550	24,082	20,871	25,706	22,137
94,550	94,600	24,097	20,885	25,724	22,152
94,600	94,650	24,113	20,899	25,742	22,168
94,650	94,700	24,128	20,913	25,760	22,183
94,700	94,750	24,144	20,927	25,778	22,199
94,750	94,800	24,159	20,941	25,796	22,214
94,800	94,850	24,175	20,955	25,814	22,230
94,850	94,900	24,190	20,969	25,832	22,245
94,900	94,950	24,206	20,983	25,850	22,261
94,950	95,000	24,221	20,997	25,868	22,276

* This column must also be used by a qualifying widow(er).

Continued on next page

1999 Tax Table—*Continued*

If taxable income is—		And you are—				If taxable income is—		And you are—			
At least	But less than	Single	Married filing jointly *	Married filing separately	Head of a house-hold	At least	But less than	Single	Married filing jointly *	Married filing separately	Head of a house-hold
		Your tax is—						Your tax is—			

95,000

95,000	95,050	24,237	21,011	25,886	22,292	98,000	98,050	25,167	21,851	26,966	23,222
95,050	95,100	24,252	21,025	25,904	22,307	98,050	98,100	25,182	21,865	26,984	23,237
95,100	95,150	24,268	21,039	25,922	22,323	98,100	98,150	25,198	21,879	27,002	23,253
95,150	95,200	24,283	21,053	25,940	22,338	98,150	98,200	25,213	21,893	27,020	23,268
95,200	95,250	24,299	21,067	25,958	22,354	98,200	98,250	25,229	21,907	27,038	23,284
95,250	95,300	24,314	21,081	25,976	22,369	98,250	98,300	25,244	21,921	27,056	23,299
95,300	95,350	24,330	21,095	25,994	22,385	98,300	98,350	25,260	21,935	27,074	23,315
95,350	95,400	24,345	21,109	26,012	22,400	98,350	98,400	25,275	21,949	27,092	23,330
95,400	95,450	24,361	21,123	26,030	22,416	98,400	98,450	25,291	21,963	27,110	23,346
95,450	95,500	24,376	21,137	26,048	22,431	98,450	98,500	25,306	21,977	27,128	23,361
95,500	95,550	24,392	21,151	26,066	22,447	98,500	98,550	25,322	21,991	27,146	23,377
95,550	95,600	24,407	21,165	26,084	22,462	98,550	98,600	25,337	22,005	27,164	23,392
95,600	95,650	24,423	21,179	26,102	22,478	98,600	98,650	25,353	22,019	27,182	23,408
95,650	95,700	24,438	21,193	26,120	22,493	98,650	98,700	25,368	22,033	27,200	23,423
95,700	95,750	24,454	21,207	26,138	22,509	98,700	98,750	25,384	22,047	27,218	23,439
95,750	95,800	24,469	21,221	26,156	22,524	98,750	98,800	25,399	22,061	27,236	23,454
95,800	95,850	24,485	21,235	26,174	22,540	98,800	98,850	25,415	22,075	27,254	23,470
95,850	95,900	24,500	21,249	26,192	22,555	98,850	98,900	25,430	22,089	27,272	23,485
95,900	95,950	24,516	21,263	26,210	22,571	98,900	98,950	25,446	22,103	27,290	23,501
95,950	96,000	24,531	21,277	26,228	22,586	98,950	99,000	25,461	22,117	27,308	23,516

96,000

96,000	96,050	24,547	21,291	26,246	22,602	99,000	99,050	25,477	22,131	27,326	23,532
96,050	96,100	24,562	21,305	26,264	22,617	99,050	99,100	25,492	22,145	27,344	23,547
96,100	96,150	24,578	21,319	26,282	22,633	99,100	99,150	25,508	22,159	27,362	23,563
96,150	96,200	24,593	21,333	26,300	22,648	99,150	99,200	25,523	22,173	27,380	23,578
96,200	96,250	24,609	21,347	26,318	22,664	99,200	99,250	25,539	22,187	27,398	23,594
96,250	96,300	24,624	21,361	26,336	22,679	99,250	99,300	25,554	22,201	27,416	23,609
96,300	96,350	24,640	21,375	26,354	22,695	99,300	99,350	25,570	22,215	27,434	23,625
96,350	96,400	24,655	21,389	26,372	22,710	99,350	99,400	25,585	22,229	27,452	23,640
96,400	96,450	24,671	21,403	26,390	22,726	99,400	99,450	25,601	22,243	27,470	23,656
96,450	96,500	24,686	21,417	26,408	22,741	99,450	99,500	25,616	22,257	27,488	23,671
96,500	96,550	24,702	21,431	26,426	22,757	99,500	99,550	25,632	22,271	27,506	23,687
96,550	96,600	24,717	21,445	26,444	22,772	99,550	99,600	25,647	22,285	27,524	23,702
96,600	96,650	24,733	21,459	26,462	22,788	99,600	99,650	25,663	22,299	27,542	23,718
96,650	96,700	24,748	21,473	26,480	22,803	99,650	99,700	25,678	22,313	27,560	23,733
96,700	96,750	24,764	21,487	26,498	22,819	99,700	99,750	25,694	22,327	27,578	23,749
96,750	96,800	24,779	21,501	26,516	22,834	99,750	99,800	25,709	22,341	27,596	23,764
96,800	96,850	24,795	21,515	26,534	22,850	99,800	99,850	25,725	22,355	27,614	23,780
96,850	96,900	24,810	21,529	26,552	22,865	99,850	99,900	25,740	22,369	27,632	23,795
96,900	96,950	24,826	21,543	26,570	22,881	99,900	99,950	25,756	22,383	27,650	23,811
96,950	97,000	24,841	21,557	26,588	22,896	99,950	100,000	25,771	22,397	27,668	23,826

97,000

97,000	97,050	24,857	21,571	26,606	22,912
97,050	97,100	24,872	21,585	26,624	22,927
97,100	97,150	24,888	21,599	26,642	22,943
97,150	97,200	24,903	21,613	26,660	22,958
97,200	97,250	24,919	21,627	26,678	22,974
97,250	97,300	24,934	21,641	26,696	22,989
97,300	97,350	24,950	21,655	26,714	23,005
97,350	97,400	24,965	21,669	26,732	23,020
97,400	97,450	24,981	21,683	26,750	23,036
97,450	97,500	24,996	21,697	26,768	23,051
97,500	97,550	25,012	21,711	26,786	23,067
97,550	97,600	25,027	21,725	26,804	23,082
97,600	97,650	25,043	21,739	26,822	23,098
97,650	97,700	25,058	21,753	26,840	23,113
97,700	97,750	25,074	21,767	26,858	23,129
97,750	97,800	25,089	21,781	26,876	23,144
97,800	97,850	25,105	21,795	26,894	23,160
97,850	97,900	25,120	21,809	26,912	23,175
97,900	97,950	25,136	21,823	26,930	23,191
97,950	98,000	25,151	21,837	26,948	23,206

$100,000 or over — use the Tax Rate Schedules

* This column must also be used by a qualifying widow(er).

1999
Tax Rate
Schedules

Use **only** if your taxable income (Form 1040, line 39) is $100,000 or more. If less, use the **Tax Table.** Even though you cannot use the Tax Rate Schedules below if your taxable income is less than $100,000, all levels of taxable income are shown so taxpayers can see the tax rate that applies to each level.

Schedule X—Use if your filing status is **Single**

If the amount on Form 1040, line 39, is: Over—	But not over—	Enter on Form 1040, line 40	of the amount over—
$0	$25,750	15%	$0
25,750	62,450	$3,862.50 + 28%	25,750
62,450	130,250	14,138.50 + 31%	62,450
130,250	283,150	35,156.50 + 36%	130,250
283,150	....	90,200.50 + 39.6%	283,150

Schedule Y-1—Use if your filing status is **Married filing jointly** or **Qualifying widow(er)**

If the amount on Form 1040, line 39, is: Over—	But not over—	Enter on Form 1040, line 40	of the amount over—
$0	$43,050	15%	$0
43,050	104,050	$6,457.50 + 28%	43,050
104,050	158,550	23,537.50 + 31%	104,050
158,550	283,150	40,432.50 + 36%	158,550
283,150	....	85,288.50 + 39.6%	283,150

Schedule Y-2—Use if your filing status is **Married filing separately**

If the amount on Form 1040, line 39, is: Over—	But not over—	Enter on Form 1040, line 40	of the amount over—
$0	$21,525	15%	$0
21,525	52,025	$3,228.75 + 28%	21,525
52,025	79,275	11,768.75 + 31%	52,025
79,275	141,575	20,216.25 + 36%	79,275
141,575	....	42,644.25 + 39.6%	141,575

Schedule Z—Use if your filing status is **Head of household**

If the amount on Form 1040, line 39, is: Over—	But not over—	Enter on Form 1040, line 40	of the amount over—
$0	$34,550	15%	$0
34,550	89,150	$5,182.50 + 28%	34,550
89,150	144,400	20,470.50 + 31%	89,150
144,400	283,150	37,598.00 + 36%	144,400
283,150	....	87,548.00 + 39.6%	283,150

1999 Earned Income Credit (EIC) Table

 This is **not** a tax table.

	And you have—		
If the amount you are looking up from the worksheet is—	No children	One child	Two children
At least — But less than	Your credit is—		
4,800 — 4,850	347	1,641	1,930
4,850 — 4,900	347	1,658	1,950
4,900 — 4,950	347	1,675	1,970
4,950 — 5,000	347	1,692	1,990

1. To find your credit, read down the "At least – But less than" columns and find the line that includes the amount you were told to look up from your EIC Worksheet.

2. Then, read across to the column that includes the number of qualifying children you have. Enter the credit from that column on your EIC Worksheet.

Example. If you have one qualifying child and the amount you are looking up from your EIC Worksheet is $4,875, you would enter $1,658.

If the amount you are looking up from the worksheet is—		And you have— No children	One child	Two children	If the amount you are looking up from the worksheet is—		And you have— No children	One child	Two children	If the amount you are looking up from the worksheet is—		And you have— No children	One child	Two children	If the amount you are looking up from the worksheet is—		And you have— No children	One child	Two children
At least	But less than	Your credit is—			At least	But less than	Your credit is—			At least	But less than	Your credit is—			At least	But less than	Your credit is—		
$1	$50	$2	$9	$10	2,200	2,250	170	757	890	4,400	4,450	339	1,505	1,770	6,600	6,650	273	2,253	2,650
50	100	6	26	30	2,250	2,300	174	774	910	4,450	4,500	342	1,522	1,790	6,650	6,700	270	2,270	2,670
100	150	10	43	50	2,300	2,350	178	791	930	4,500	4,550	347	1,539	1,810	6,700	6,750	266	2,287	2,690
150	200	13	60	70	2,350	2,400	182	808	950	4,550	4,600	347	1,556	1,830	6,750	6,800	262	2,304	2,710
200	250	17	77	90	2,400	2,450	186	825	970	4,600	4,650	347	1,573	1,850	6,800	6,850	258	2,312	2,730
250	300	21	94	110	2,450	2,500	189	842	990	4,650	4,700	347	1,590	1,870	6,850	6,900	254	2,312	2,750
300	350	25	111	130	2,500	2,550	193	859	1,010	4,700	4,750	347	1,607	1,890	6,900	6,950	251	2,312	2,770
350	400	29	128	150	2,550	2,600	197	876	1,030	4,750	4,800	347	1,624	1,910	6,950	7,000	247	2,312	2,790
400	450	33	145	170	2,600	2,650	201	893	1,050	4,800	4,850	347	1,641	1,930	7,000	7,050	243	2,312	2,810
450	500	36	162	190	2,650	2,700	205	910	1,070	4,850	4,900	347	1,658	1,950	7,050	7,100	239	2,312	2,830
500	550	40	179	210	2,700	2,750	208	927	1,090	4,900	4,950	347	1,675	1,970	7,100	7,150	235	2,312	2,850
550	600	44	196	230	2,750	2,800	212	944	1,110	4,950	5,000	347	1,692	1,990	7,150	7,200	231	2,312	2,870
600	650	48	213	250	2,800	2,850	216	961	1,130	5,000	5,050	347	1,709	2,010	7,200	7,250	228	2,312	2,890
650	700	52	230	270	2,850	2,900	220	978	1,150	5,050	5,100	347	1,726	2,030	7,250	7,300	224	2,312	2,910
700	750	55	247	290	2,900	2,950	224	995	1,170	5,100	5,150	347	1,743	2,050	7,300	7,350	220	2,312	2,930
750	800	59	264	310	2,950	3,000	228	1,012	1,190	5,150	5,200	347	1,760	2,070	7,350	7,400	216	2,312	2,950
800	850	63	281	330	3,000	3,050	231	1,029	1,210	5,200	5,250	347	1,777	2,090	7,400	7,450	212	2,312	2,970
850	900	67	298	350	3,050	3,100	235	1,046	1,230	5,250	5,300	347	1,794	2,110	7,450	7,500	208	2,312	2,990
900	950	71	315	370	3,100	3,150	239	1,063	1,250	5,300	5,350	347	1,811	2,130	7,500	7,550	205	2,312	3,010
950	1,000	75	332	390	3,150	3,200	243	1,080	1,270	5,350	5,400	347	1,828	2,150	7,550	7,600	201	2,312	3,030
1,000	1,050	78	349	410	3,200	3,250	247	1,097	1,290	5,400	5,450	347	1,845	2,170	7,600	7,650	197	2,312	3,050
1,050	1,100	82	366	430	3,250	3,300	251	1,114	1,310	5,450	5,500	347	1,862	2,190	7,650	7,700	193	2,312	3,070
1,100	1,150	86	383	450	3,300	3,350	254	1,131	1,330	5,500	5,550	347	1,879	2,210	7,700	7,750	189	2,312	3,090
1,150	1,200	90	400	470	3,350	3,400	258	1,148	1,350	5,550	5,600	347	1,896	2,230	7,750	7,800	186	2,312	3,110
1,200	1,250	94	417	490	3,400	3,450	262	1,165	1,370	5,600	5,650	347	1,913	2,250	7,800	7,850	182	2,312	3,130
1,250	1,300	98	434	510	3,450	3,500	266	1,182	1,390	5,650	5,700	347	1,930	2,270	7,850	7,900	178	2,312	3,150
1,300	1,350	101	451	530	3,500	3,550	270	1,199	1,410	5,700	5,750	342	1,947	2,290	7,900	7,950	174	2,312	3,170
1,350	1,400	105	468	550	3,550	3,600	273	1,216	1,430	5,750	5,800	339	1,964	2,310	7,950	8,000	170	2,312	3,190
1,400	1,450	109	485	570	3,600	3,650	277	1,233	1,450	5,800	5,850	335	1,981	2,330	8,000	8,050	166	2,312	3,210
1,450	1,500	113	502	590	3,650	3,700	281	1,250	1,470	5,850	5,900	331	1,998	2,350	8,050	8,100	163	2,312	3,230
1,500	1,550	117	519	610	3,700	3,750	285	1,267	1,490	5,900	5,950	327	2,015	2,370	8,100	8,150	159	2,312	3,250
1,550	1,600	120	536	630	3,750	3,800	289	1,284	1,510	5,950	6,000	323	2,032	2,390	8,150	8,200	155	2,312	3,270
1,600	1,650	124	553	650	3,800	3,850	293	1,301	1,530	6,000	6,050	319	2,049	2,410	8,200	8,250	151	2,312	3,290
1,650	1,700	128	570	670	3,850	3,900	296	1,318	1,550	6,050	6,100	316	2,066	2,430	8,250	8,300	147	2,312	3,310
1,700	1,750	132	587	690	3,900	3,950	300	1,335	1,570	6,100	6,150	312	2,083	2,450	8,300	8,350	143	2,312	3,330
1,750	1,800	136	604	710	3,950	4,000	304	1,352	1,590	6,150	6,200	308	2,100	2,470	8,350	8,400	140	2,312	3,350
1,800	1,850	140	621	730	4,000	4,050	308	1,369	1,610	6,200	6,250	304	2,117	2,490	8,400	8,450	136	2,312	3,370
1,850	1,900	143	638	750	4,050	4,100	312	1,386	1,630	6,250	6,300	300	2,134	2,510	8,450	8,500	132	2,312	3,390
1,900	1,950	147	655	770	4,100	4,150	316	1,403	1,650	6,300	6,350	296	2,151	2,530	8,500	8,550	128	2,312	3,410
1,950	2,000	151	672	790	4,150	4,200	319	1,420	1,670	6,350	6,400	293	2,168	2,550	8,550	8,600	124	2,312	3,430
2,000	2,050	155	689	810	4,200	4,250	323	1,437	1,690	6,400	6,450	289	2,185	2,570	8,600	8,650	120	2,312	3,450
2,050	2,100	159	706	830	4,250	4,300	327	1,454	1,710	6,450	6,500	285	2,202	2,590	8,650	8,700	117	2,312	3,470
2,100	2,150	163	723	850	4,300	4,350	331	1,471	1,730	6,500	6,550	281	2,219	2,610	8,700	8,750	113	2,312	3,490
2,150	2,200	166	740	870	4,350	4,400	335	1,488	1,750	6,550	6,600	277	2,236	2,630	8,750	8,800	109	2,312	3,510

(Continued)

1999 Earned Income Credit (EIC) Table Continued   (Caution: This is **not** a tax table.)

At least	But less than	No children	One child	Two children	At least	But less than	No children	One child	Two children	At least	But less than	No children	One child	Two children	At least	But less than	No children	One child	Two children
8,800	8,850	105	2,312	3,530	13,850	13,900	0	2,086	3,518	16,650	16,700	0	1,638	2,928	19,450	19,500	0	1,191	2,339
8,850	8,900	101	2,312	3,550	13,900	13,950	0	2,078	3,507	16,700	16,750	0	1,630	2,918	19,500	19,550	0	1,183	2,328
8,900	8,950	98	2,312	3,570	13,950	14,000	0	2,070	3,497	16,750	16,800	0	1,622	2,907	19,550	19,600	0	1,175	2,318
8,950	9,000	94	2,312	3,590	14,000	14,050	0	2,062	3,486	16,800	16,850	0	1,614	2,897	19,600	19,650	0	1,167	2,307
9,000	9,050	90	2,312	3,610	14,050	14,100	0	2,054	3,476	16,850	16,900	0	1,606	2,886	19,650	19,700	0	1,159	2,297
9,050	9,100	86	2,312	3,630	14,100	14,150	0	2,046	3,465	16,900	16,950	0	1,598	2,876	19,700	19,750	0	1,151	2,286
9,100	9,150	82	2,312	3,650	14,150	14,200	0	2,038	3,455	16,950	17,000	0	1,591	2,865	19,750	19,800	0	1,143	2,275
9,150	9,200	78	2,312	3,670	14,200	14,250	0	2,030	3,444	17,000	17,050	0	1,583	2,855	19,800	19,850	0	1,135	2,265
9,200	9,250	75	2,312	3,690	14,250	14,300	0	2,022	3,434	17,050	17,100	0	1,575	2,844	19,850	19,900	0	1,127	2,254
9,250	9,300	71	2,312	3,710	14,300	14,350	0	2,014	3,423	17,100	17,150	0	1,567	2,834	19,900	19,950	0	1,119	2,244
9,300	9,350	67	2,312	3,730	14,350	14,400	0	2,006	3,413	17,150	17,200	0	1,559	2,823	19,950	20,000	0	1,111	2,233
9,350	9,400	63	2,312	3,750	14,400	14,450	0	1,998	3,402	17,200	17,250	0	1,551	2,812	20,000	20,050	0	1,103	2,223
9,400	9,450	59	2,312	3,770	14,450	14,500	0	1,990	3,392	17,250	17,300	0	1,543	2,802	20,050	20,100	0	1,095	2,212
9,450	9,500	55	2,312	3,790	14,500	14,550	0	1,982	3,381	17,300	17,350	0	1,535	2,791	20,100	20,150	0	1,087	2,202
9,500	9,550	52	2,312	3,816	14,550	14,600	0	1,974	3,371	17,350	17,400	0	1,527	2,781	20,150	20,200	0	1,079	2,191
9,550	9,600	48	2,312	3,816	14,600	14,650	0	1,966	3,360	17,400	17,450	0	1,519	2,770	20,200	20,250	0	1,071	2,181
9,600	9,650	44	2,312	3,816	14,650	14,700	0	1,958	3,350	17,450	17,500	0	1,511	2,760	20,250	20,300	0	1,063	2,170
9,650	9,700	40	2,312	3,816	14,700	14,750	0	1,950	3,339	17,500	17,550	0	1,503	2,749	20,300	20,350	0	1,055	2,160
9,700	9,750	36	2,312	3,816	14,750	14,800	0	1,942	3,328	17,550	17,600	0	1,495	2,739	20,350	20,400	0	1,047	2,149
9,750	9,800	33	2,312	3,816	14,800	14,850	0	1,934	3,318	17,600	17,650	0	1,487	2,728	20,400	20,450	0	1,039	2,139
9,800	9,850	29	2,312	3,816	14,850	14,900	0	1,926	3,307	17,650	17,700	0	1,479	2,718	20,450	20,500	0	1,031	2,128
9,850	9,900	25	2,312	3,816	14,900	14,950	0	1,918	3,297	17,700	17,750	0	1,471	2,707	20,500	20,550	0	1,023	2,118
9,900	9,950	21	2,312	3,816	14,950	15,000	0	1,910	3,286	17,750	17,800	0	1,463	2,697	20,550	20,600	0	1,015	2,107
9,950	10,000	17	2,312	3,816	15,000	15,050	0	1,902	3,276	17,800	17,850	0	1,455	2,686	20,600	20,650	0	1,007	2,096
10,000	10,050	13	2,312	3,816	15,050	15,100	0	1,894	3,265	17,850	17,900	0	1,447	2,676	20,650	20,700	0	999	2,086
10,050	10,100	10	2,312	3,816	15,100	15,150	0	1,886	3,255	17,900	17,950	0	1,439	2,665	20,700	20,750	0	991	2,075
10,100	10,150	6	2,312	3,816	15,150	15,200	0	1,878	3,244	17,950	18,000	0	1,431	2,655	20,750	20,800	0	983	2,065
10,150	10,200	2	2,312	3,816	15,200	15,250	0	1,870	3,234	18,000	18,050	0	1,423	2,644	20,800	20,850	0	975	2,054
10,200	12,500	0	2,312	3,816	15,250	15,300	0	1,862	3,223	18,050	18,100	0	1,415	2,633	20,850	20,900	0	967	2,044
12,500	12,550	0	2,302	3,802	15,300	15,350	0	1,854	3,213	18,100	18,150	0	1,407	2,623	20,900	20,950	0	959	2,033
12,550	12,600	0	2,294	3,792	15,350	15,400	0	1,846	3,202	18,150	18,200	0	1,399	2,612	20,950	21,000	0	951	2,023
12,600	12,650	0	2,286	3,781	15,400	15,450	0	1,838	3,192	18,200	18,250	0	1,391	2,602	21,000	21,050	0	943	2,012
12,650	12,700	0	2,278	3,771	15,450	15,500	0	1,830	3,181	18,250	18,300	0	1,383	2,591	21,050	21,100	0	935	2,002
12,700	12,750	0	2,270	3,760	15,500	15,550	0	1,822	3,171	18,300	18,350	0	1,375	2,581	21,100	21,150	0	927	1,991
12,750	12,800	0	2,262	3,750	15,550	15,600	0	1,814	3,160	18,350	18,400	0	1,367	2,570	21,150	21,200	0	919	1,981
12,800	12,850	0	2,254	3,739	15,600	15,650	0	1,806	3,149	18,400	18,450	0	1,359	2,560	21,200	21,250	0	911	1,970
12,850	12,900	0	2,246	3,729	15,650	15,700	0	1,798	3,139	18,450	18,500	0	1,351	2,549	21,250	21,300	0	903	1,960
12,900	12,950	0	2,238	3,718	15,700	15,750	0	1,790	3,128	18,500	18,550	0	1,343	2,539	21,300	21,350	0	895	1,949
12,950	13,000	0	2,230	3,708	15,750	15,800	0	1,782	3,118	18,550	18,600	0	1,335	2,528	21,350	21,400	0	887	1,939
13,000	13,050	0	2,222	3,697	15,800	15,850	0	1,774	3,107	18,600	18,650	0	1,327	2,518	21,400	21,450	0	879	1,928
13,050	13,100	0	2,214	3,686	15,850	15,900	0	1,766	3,097	18,650	18,700	0	1,319	2,507	21,450	21,500	0	871	1,917
13,100	13,150	0	2,206	3,676	15,900	15,950	0	1,758	3,086	18,700	18,750	0	1,311	2,497	21,500	21,550	0	863	1,907
13,150	13,200	0	2,198	3,665	15,950	16,000	0	1,750	3,076	18,750	18,800	0	1,303	2,486	21,550	21,600	0	855	1,896
13,200	13,250	0	2,190	3,655	16,000	16,050	0	1,742	3,065	18,800	18,850	0	1,295	2,476	21,600	21,650	0	847	1,886
13,250	13,300	0	2,182	3,644	16,050	16,100	0	1,734	3,055	18,850	18,900	0	1,287	2,465	21,650	21,700	0	839	1,875
13,300	13,350	0	2,174	3,634	16,100	16,150	0	1,726	3,044	18,900	18,950	0	1,279	2,454	21,700	21,750	0	831	1,865
13,350	13,400	0	2,166	3,623	16,150	16,200	0	1,718	3,034	18,950	19,000	0	1,271	2,444	21,750	21,800	0	823	1,854
13,400	13,450	0	2,158	3,613	16,200	16,250	0	1,710	3,023	19,000	19,050	0	1,263	2,433	21,800	21,850	0	815	1,844
13,450	13,500	0	2,150	3,602	16,250	16,300	0	1,702	3,013	19,050	19,100	0	1,255	2,423	21,850	21,900	0	807	1,833
13,500	13,550	0	2,142	3,592	16,300	16,350	0	1,694	3,002	19,100	19,150	0	1,247	2,412	21,900	21,950	0	799	1,823
13,550	13,600	0	2,134	3,581	16,350	16,400	0	1,686	2,992	19,150	19,200	0	1,239	2,402	21,950	22,000	0	792	1,812
13,600	13,650	0	2,126	3,571	16,400	16,450	0	1,678	2,981	19,200	19,250	0	1,231	2,391	22,000	22,050	0	784	1,802
13,650	13,700	0	2,118	3,560	16,450	16,500	0	1,670	2,970	19,250	19,300	0	1,223	2,381	22,050	22,100	0	776	1,791
13,700	13,750	0	2,110	3,550	16,500	16,550	0	1,662	2,960	19,300	19,350	0	1,215	2,370	22,100	22,150	0	768	1,781
13,750	13,800	0	2,102	3,539	16,550	16,600	0	1,654	2,949	19,350	19,400	0	1,207	2,360	22,150	22,200	0	760	1,770
13,800	13,850	0	2,094	3,529	16,600	16,650	0	1,646	2,939	19,400	19,450	0	1,199	2,349	22,200	22,250	0	752	1,759

(Continued)

1999 Earned Income Credit (EIC) Table Continued   (Caution: *This is **not** a tax table.*)

At least	But less than	No children	One child	Two children
22,250	22,300	0	744	1,749
22,300	22,350	0	736	1,738
22,350	22,400	0	728	1,728
22,400	22,450	0	720	1,717
22,450	22,500	0	712	1,707
22,500	22,550	0	704	1,696
22,550	22,600	0	696	1,686
22,600	22,650	0	688	1,675
22,650	22,700	0	680	1,665
22,700	22,750	0	672	1,654
22,750	22,800	0	664	1,644
22,800	22,850	0	656	1,633
22,850	22,900	0	648	1,623
22,900	22,950	0	640	1,612
22,950	23,000	0	632	1,602
23,000	23,050	0	624	1,591
23,050	23,100	0	616	1,580
23,100	23,150	0	608	1,570
23,150	23,200	0	600	1,559
23,200	23,250	0	592	1,549
23,250	23,300	0	584	1,538
23,300	23,350	0	576	1,528
23,350	23,400	0	568	1,517
23,400	23,450	0	560	1,507
23,450	23,500	0	552	1,496
23,500	23,550	0	544	1,486
23,550	23,600	0	536	1,475
23,600	23,650	0	528	1,465
23,650	23,700	0	520	1,454
23,700	23,750	0	512	1,444
23,750	23,800	0	504	1,433
23,800	23,850	0	496	1,423
23,850	23,900	0	488	1,412
23,900	23,950	0	480	1,401
23,950	24,000	0	472	1,391
24,000	24,050	0	464	1,380
24,050	24,100	0	456	1,370
24,100	24,150	0	448	1,359
24,150	24,200	0	440	1,349
24,200	24,250	0	432	1,338
24,250	24,300	0	424	1,328
24,300	24,350	0	416	1,317
24,350	24,400	0	408	1,307
24,400	24,450	0	400	1,296

At least	But less than	No children	One child	Two children
24,450	24,500	0	392	1,286
24,500	24,550	0	384	1,275
24,550	24,600	0	376	1,265
24,600	24,650	0	368	1,254
24,650	24,700	0	360	1,244
24,700	24,750	0	352	1,233
24,750	24,800	0	344	1,222
24,800	24,850	0	336	1,212
24,850	24,900	0	328	1,201
24,900	24,950	0	320	1,191
24,950	25,000	0	312	1,180
25,000	25,050	0	304	1,170
25,050	25,100	0	296	1,159
25,100	25,150	0	288	1,149
25,150	25,200	0	280	1,138
25,200	25,250	0	272	1,128
25,250	25,300	0	264	1,117
25,300	25,350	0	256	1,107
25,350	25,400	0	248	1,096
25,400	25,450	0	240	1,086
25,450	25,500	0	232	1,075
25,500	25,550	0	224	1,065
25,550	25,600	0	216	1,054
25,600	25,650	0	208	1,043
25,650	25,700	0	200	1,033
25,700	25,750	0	192	1,022
25,750	25,800	0	184	1,012
25,800	25,850	0	176	1,001
25,850	25,900	0	168	991
25,900	25,950	0	160	980
25,950	26,000	0	152	970
26,000	26,050	0	144	959
26,050	26,100	0	136	949
26,100	26,150	0	128	938
26,150	26,200	0	120	928
26,200	26,250	0	112	917
26,250	26,300	0	104	907
26,300	26,350	0	96	896
26,350	26,400	0	88	886
26,400	26,450	0	80	875
26,450	26,500	0	72	864
26,500	26,550	0	64	854
26,550	26,600	0	56	843
26,600	26,650	0	48	833

At least	But less than	No children	One child	Two children
26,650	26,700	0	40	822
26,700	26,750	0	32	812
26,750	26,800	0	24	801
26,800	26,850	0	16	791
26,850	26,900	0	8	780
26,900	26,950	0	*	770
26,950	27,000	0	0	759
27,000	27,050	0	0	749
27,050	27,100	0	0	738
27,100	27,150	0	0	728
27,150	27,200	0	0	717
27,200	27,250	0	0	706
27,250	27,300	0	0	696
27,300	27,350	0	0	685
27,350	27,400	0	0	675
27,400	27,450	0	0	664
27,450	27,500	0	0	654
27,500	27,550	0	0	643
27,550	27,600	0	0	633
27,600	27,650	0	0	622
27,650	27,700	0	0	612
27,700	27,750	0	0	601
27,750	27,800	0	0	591
27,800	27,850	0	0	580
27,850	27,900	0	0	570
27,900	27,950	0	0	559
27,950	28,000	0	0	549
28,000	28,050	0	0	538
28,050	28,100	0	0	527
28,100	28,150	0	0	517
28,150	28,200	0	0	506
28,200	28,250	0	0	496
28,250	28,300	0	0	485
28,300	28,350	0	0	475
28,350	28,400	0	0	464
28,400	28,450	0	0	454
28,450	28,500	0	0	443
28,500	28,550	0	0	433
28,550	28,600	0	0	422
28,600	28,650	0	0	412
28,650	28,700	0	0	401
28,700	28,750	0	0	391
28,750	28,800	0	0	380
28,800	28,850	0	0	370

At least	But less than	No children	One child	Two children
28,850	28,900	0	0	359
28,900	28,950	0	0	348
28,950	29,000	0	0	338
29,000	29,050	0	0	327
29,050	29,100	0	0	317
29,100	29,150	0	0	306
29,150	29,200	0	0	296
29,200	29,250	0	0	285
29,250	29,300	0	0	275
29,300	29,350	0	0	264
29,350	29,400	0	0	254
29,400	29,450	0	0	243
29,450	29,500	0	0	233
29,500	29,550	0	0	222
29,550	29,600	0	0	212
29,600	29,650	0	0	201
29,650	29,700	0	0	191
29,700	29,750	0	0	180
29,750	29,800	0	0	169
29,800	29,850	0	0	159
29,850	29,900	0	0	148
29,900	29,950	0	0	138
29,950	30,000	0	0	127
30,000	30,050	0	0	117
30,050	30,100	0	0	106
30,100	30,150	0	0	96
30,150	30,200	0	0	85
30,200	30,250	0	0	75
30,250	30,300	0	0	64
30,300	30,350	0	0	54
30,350	30,400	0	0	43
30,400	30,450	0	0	33
30,450	30,500	0	0	22
30,500	30,550	0	0	12
30,550	30,580	0	0	3
30,580 or more		0	0	0

*If the amount you are looking up from the worksheet is at least $26,900 but less than $26,928, your credit is $2. Otherwise, you cannot take the credit.

Professional Tax Practice

Tax Law Sources

The federal income tax law is based on statutes passed by Congress. The statutes are organized into a Code, which is currently cited as the Internal Revenue Code of 1986.

Ideally, there should be no need for legal sources other than the Code, and this is true where a statute as passed by Congress is so clear and specific that no one doubts its application. However, where the wording of a statute in the Code is general and may be interpreted in several ways, you must seek interpretations which may help you resolve a tax question or support your point of view in a tax dispute. Authoritative interpretations are made by the Treasury and the Internal Revenue Service in regulations and rulings and by federal courts in specific decisions. The relative authoritativeness of these sources is discussed in this part.

LEGISLATIVE SOURCES

Internal Revenue Code

The 1986 Tax Act redesignated the Internal Revenue Code as the Internal Revenue Code of 1986. The prior designation date was 1954.

The title of the Code remains fixed with the date 1986, although sections of the Code may be amended every year. Structurally, the Code is divided into:

Subtitles (for example, Subtitle A: Income Taxes; Subtitle B: Estate and Gift Taxes, etc.);

Chapters (for example, Chapter I of Subtitle A: Normal Taxes and Surtaxes);

Subchapters (for example, Subchapter A of Chapter 1: Determination of Tax Liability);

Parts (for example, Part I of Subchapter A: Tax on Individuals); and Sections (for example, Section I of Part 1: Tax Imposed).

Sections run consecutively in the Code from Section 1 up to Section 9833. However, in the sequence, many numbers are missing to allow for further expansion. Each section itself is then broken down as follows:

Lettered subsections: (a), (b), (c), etc.

Numbered paragraphs: (1), (2), (3), etc.

Capital-lettered subparagraphs: (A), (B), (C), etc.

Roman-numbered sub-subparagraphs: (i), (ii), (iii), etc.

Congressional Committee Reports

The legislative history of a section may be found in the reports of the Congressional committee that wrote the section. Under the Constitution, tax bills originate in the House of Representatives, although in practice, the Senate has sometimes considered tax legislation before the House. In the typical case, the Ways and Means Committee of the House of Representatives holds public hearings and then prepares a tax bill accompanied by a written report explaining its provisions. The House then considers the bill and after it passes the bill, sends it to the Senate. At this point, the Senate Finance Committee holds hearings and prepares its version of the bill, which is also accompanied by a report. The Senate version may differ from the House bill. If the Senate passes the bill, the House and Senate Committee will then meet in a Joint Conference to settle differences between the two bills. The Conference Committee will also issue a report. The compromised bill then goes back to each House, where it is usually accepted and sent to the President for approval. The bill becomes law after the President signs it. Thus, the legislative history of a section can be found in:

1. The Report of the Ways and Means Committee (cited as H.R. Rep.).
2. The Report of the Senate Finance Committee (cited as S. Rep.).
3. The Conference Report of the Joint Conference Committee (cited as Conf. Rep.).

These reports are published by the Government Printing Office and in recent years have been included in the IRS Cumulative Bulletin (see the next column under Revenue Rulings). Committee reports are helpful authority, particularly if Treasury regulations (see below) have not been issued covering the section.

Further, the Joint Committee on Taxation may prepare a general explanation of the law commonly called the "Blue Book," which is also considered part of the legislative history.

ADMINISTRATIVE SOURCES

Treasury Regulations

Regulations authorized by the Internal Revenue Code have the force and effect of law and may be relied upon as authority. Failure to comply with such a regulation can result in a negligence penalty.

The validity of a regulation can be questioned. Courts are not bound by regulations and can overrule them if they are unreasonable and plainly inconsistent with the Code.

Once a regulation has interpreted a Code provision, passage of a similar law with the exact wording is regarded by the courts as evidence that Congress is satisfied with the regulation and, thus, the regulation generally will not be overruled. If a regulation is disapproved by a court, the IRS can continue to enforce the regulation unless the regulation is reversed by the Supreme Court.

New regulations are generally first announced as proposed regulations. During a stated time limit, tax professionals and taxpayers are allowed to suggest changes or additions. Often, the IRS will hold special hearings to discuss the proposals, and then, after reviewing the suggestions, will issue final regulations as Treasury Decisions (TDs), which include a general explanation of the regulations and are published in the Federal Register. Tax services for professionals provide the text of proposed and final regulations to their subscribers.

Each section of the regulations is preceded by the section, subsection, or paragraph of the Internal Revenue Code which it interprets. The sections of the regulations are distinguished from sections of the Code by the Arabic numeral 1, followed by a decimal point (1.) before the corresponding provision of the Internal Revenue Code. This designation is then followed by a dash (-) and a number further identifying a section of the regulation. With these numbers you can find regulations interpreting a Code provision. Thus, the regulation explaining IRC Section 301 is designated 1.301, and a section of that regulation is identified as 1.301-1.

Revenue Rulings

Revenue Rulings make up a large body of IRS interpretations of the tax law. They are generally official replies by the IRS National Office to specific problems raised by taxpayers. They are published to provide guidance in cases having similar facts to those presented in the rulings.

Revenue Rulings are published weekly in the Internal Revenue Bulletin. Every half-year, these rulings are republished in a book, called the Cumulative Bulletin, which is available to the public from the Government Printing Office.

See below for references to Revenue Rulings appearing in the Internal Revenue Bulletin and the Cumulative Bulletin.

In the Weekly Internal Revenue Bulletin

Rev. Rul. 99-29, 1999-27 IRB 3, means that the particular ruling in 1999 is numbered as 29, appears in the 27th weekly bulletin of that year, and, in that bulletin, can be found on page 3.

In the Cumulative Bulletin

Rev. Rul. 94-43, 1994-2 CB 198—means that the ruling appears in the second semiannual Cumulative Bulletin for 1994 and, in that book, can be found on page 198.

Other IRS Rulings and Releases

After Revenue Rulings, there are several other IRS releases and rulings that are helpful in determining IRS policy.

Revenue procedures. These describe internal practices and procedures within the IRS and filing procedures for taxpayers. They are published in the Internal Revenue Bulletin. References to them are prefixed by the abbreviation "Rev. Proc."

Notices and announcements. These describe current IRS policy toward a specific issue. They are primarily intended to provide IRS guidance on new tax law developments. They may contain the advance text of Revenue Rulings. Announcements and Notices are published in the Internal Revenue Bulletin.

Letter rulings. These include private rulings, determination letters, and technical advice memoranda. Such rulings resemble Revenue Rulings except that they are not officially published and may not be cited as a precedent by any other taxpayer. However, they may be helpful, as they reflect the IRS's policy and inter-pretation of the law. In one case, the Supreme Court noted that private letter rulings are evidence of an IRS position, although they have no authoritative force. Virtually all letter rulings are open to public inspection after all information that could identify the taxpayer involved has been deleted. Letter rulings are referred to by a seven-number citation—the first two numbers indicating the year, the next two numbers the week of the year the ruling is issued, and the last three numbers are the letter ruling numbers in sequence for that week. For example, Letter Ruling 9409001 was issued in the 9th week of 1994. It was the 1st letter ruling of that week.

General counsel memoranda, actions on decisions, technical memoranda. These are internal IRS documents which provide reasons for rulings, regulations, and acquiescences or nonacquiescences to court decisions. In response to a lawsuit, the IRS has agreed to make available to the public all of these documents, including those dating back to July 1967. The documents are released by the IRS after deletions are made to remove identifying information. General Counsel Memoranda (GCMs) are legal opinions on proposed revenue rulings, private rulings, and technical advice memoranda. Actions on Decisions (AODs) recommend whether or not to appeal adverse court decisions. Technical Memoranda (TMs) indicate the legal and policy basis for proposed Treasury regulations.

JUDICIAL SOURCES

A taxpayer who receives a notice of deficiency can appeal to the Tax Court without actually paying the deficiency. Alternatively, the deficiency can be paid and a claim for a refund filed with the IRS; if the refund claim is denied, a refund suit can be brought in Federal District Court. A refund suit may also be brought in the U.S. Court of Federal Claims. Appeals from these courts are heard by a Federal Court of Appeals.

Court Decisions

The authority of court decisions varies. When using court decisions, keep these points in mind:

- The IRS is not bound to follow a court decision in any other case apart from the case in which the decision has been handed down. The only exception to this rule is a decision of the Supreme Court.

- Courts are not bound to follow the decision of another court. The only exception again is for Supreme Court decisions.

- Court decisions are not of equal weight. A decision of the Tax Court has substantially greater significance than a decision rendered by a Federal District Court and often by a Federal Court of Appeals, primarily because the Tax Court hears cases all over the nation and will apply its decisions on a nationwide basis.

- Federal District Courts are local federal courts and a Court of Appeals hears appeals only on a regional basis. So whereas one decision of the Tax Court will generally be applied throughout the United States, there may be several conflicting interpretations between district courts in various localities and Courts of Appeals in the various geographical regions. For example, a district court in California is not bound to follow a decision handed down by a district court in New York. And a Court of Appeals for one region is not bound to follow a decision of a Court of Appeals for another region. On the other hand, the precedent of a Tax Court decision rendered in New York is generally controlling authority in a Tax Court hearing held anywhere else in the United States. However, the Tax Court generally will follow a decision of the Court of Appeals to which the current case is appealable if that prior decision is squarely on point.

U.S. Tax Court

The Tax Court is a special court for taxpayers who appeal tax deficiencies imposed by the IRS for income, estate, or gift taxes. It is independent of the IRS and the Treasury department; its members are judges, and its decisions are subject to the same judicial review as that of any other federal court. They can be appealed at a Court of Appeals and then to the Supreme Court.

The Tax Court has a small tax case procedure for deficiencies of $50,000 or less (IRC §7463). Such cases are handled expeditiously and informally. It is available at the option of the taxpayer if the Court concurs. Cases may be heard by appointed special trial judges. A small claim case can be discontinued at any time before a decision, but the decision, when made, is final. No appeal can be taken. A decision does not have precedential value.

Between the years 1924 and 1942, the Court was known as the Board of Tax Appeals. In 1942, it received the present name of Tax Court. Cases decided by the Court before 1942 are referred to, for example, as 20 BTA 45 and cases afterwards as 30 TC 43. (The first number of the citation designates the volume of the particular series of court decisions; the second number designates the page within the volume in which the case can be found.)

The IRS is not bound by a Tax Court decision except in the particular case in which the decision has been rendered. It can continue to litigate the same issue in other cases before the Tax Court and in other courts. However, in a tax dispute with a taxpayer involving the same issue which the Court decided against the government, the IRS may be more inclined to negotiate a settlement than have the taxpayer bring a case before the Tax Court for another unfavorable decision against its position.

There are two types of Tax Court decisions:

Regular decisions. These are officially reported by the Tax Court and can be found in officially bound reports. They are recognized by the abbreviation TC between the number representing the number of the official volume and the page within the volume, followed by the year of the decision. Private tax services such as Commerce Clearing House print regular decisions, and decisions may also be obtained from online services.

Memorandum decisions. These are not collected in any official volumes but are released only in mimeographed form, copies of which go to the litigants. Private tax services print memorandum decisions. For example, Commerce Clearing House publishes these decisions in volumes called *Tax Court Memorandum Decisions,* abbreviation TCM. In this book, memorandum decisions are referred to in their place within the Commerce Clearing House service.

What is the court test for reporting a case as either a regular decision or as a memorandum decision? The Court says a memorandum decision involves no question of law, but merely facts that the Court believes are limited to a number of cases. If a memorandum decision does involve a question of law, the question is usually one which has been decided previously by the Tax Court and followed by the Court of Appeals. However, taxpayers can and do appeal memorandum decisions to the Court of Appeals as they can regular decisions.

Although these are considered by the Court as minor decisions, they are further examples of Tax Court policy toward a particular tax issue. Furthermore, memorandum decisions are often appealed and the decision of the appeals court in these cases may become important authority.

Current Tax Court policy in issues disputed by two or more Courts of Appeals is to follow the opinion of the Court to which the appeal may be taken, if that Court has ruled on the issue.

IRS response to decision. The IRS follows a policy of announcing its acceptance of or disagreement with a Tax Court holding against a position held by the IRS in an officially reported decision. No policy statements are made for memorandum decisions. These announcements are made in the weekly Internal Revenue Bulletin, as acquiescences or nonacquiescences. The IRS cautions that an acquiescence of a particular decision merely signifies its acceptance of the Court's conclusion. It does not necessarily mean that it has accepted or approved of the Court's reasons for the conclusion, and it advises its officials to apply the rule of acquiesced cases only to cases that have substantially the same facts and circumstances as the acquiesced case. An acquiescence or nonacquiescence of a reported case can be recognized by the abbreviation (*Acq.*) or (*Nonacq.*) at the end of the case citation. However, if you are going to rely on an acquiesced case, try to find the exact terms of the IRS approval from the weekly Internal Revenue Bulletin or Cumulative Bulletin. Sometimes an acquiescence is limited only to one particular issue of a case. Finally, the IRS is free to withdraw an acquiescence or non-acquiescence.

Federal District Court

There is at least one Federal District Court for each state, with the more populous states having two or more district courts. A Federal District Court can hear only tax cases in which a taxpayer sues for a refund after his or her claim has been denied by the IRS.

Not all district court decisions are rendered in written form. But where they are in writing, they may be handed down as an Opinion, Findings of Fact and Conclusions of Law, or both. Generally, a district court opinion is not strong authority, primarily because of the local nature of a district court. However, a well-reasoned district court decision may be accepted by other courts and even the IRS, and in the absence of any other authority on a particular issue, a decision of a district court may prove helpful as presenting at least one published view of the problem.

District court decisions are referred in this book to their place in the Federal Supplement Series published by the West Publishing Company. For example, take the case *Seymour Gale,* 768 F. Supp. 1305

(N.D. IL. (1991)). *Seymour Gale* is the name of the case; 768 refers to the volume of the Federal Supplement Series, 1305 to the page within that volume, N.D. IL. to the Northern District of Illinois, and 1991 to the year of decision. District court decisions not cited to the Federal Supplement Series are cited to the U.S. Tax Cases published by Commerce Clearing House. These citations are explained in the section on Court of Appeals decisions below.

U.S. Court of Federal Claims

The only tax cases heard by the U.S. Court of Federal Claims (formerly called the U.S. Claims Court) are those involving refunds of taxes. Decisions by the U.S. Court of Federal Claims on income tax questions have not had an important effect on the development of the income tax law. However, a favorable decision of the Court of Federal Claims on a particular issue which you may be disputing with the IRS may encourage you to choose that court to hear your case. And a well-reasoned decision rendered by the Court of Federal Claims may be followed by the other courts. Appeals from the Court of Federal Claims decisions are heard by the Court of Appeals for the Federal Circuit.

Court of Federal Claims decisions are referred in this book to their place in the Federal Supplement Series published by West Publishing Company. If citations to the Federal Supplement Series are not available, Court of Federal Claims decisions are cited to the U.S. Tax Cases published by Commerce Clearing House.

Court of Appeals Decisions

There are 12 Courts of Appeals that hear appeals taken either by taxpayers or the government from decisions rendered by the Tax Court or Federal District Court. Eleven of these are regional courts that hear cases arising within their regions, which are technically called circuits; the twelfth hears cases arising within the District of Columbia. The circuits and the states within each circuit are listed in the table on page 804.

Appeals of tax refund decisions from the U.S. Court of Federal Claims are heard by a separate appeals court, the U.S. Court of Appeals for the Federal Circuit.

Court of Appeals decisions make up an important part of federal tax law. But the effectiveness of a particular decision may vary because of these factors:

- The IRS is not bound to follow any precedent set by an appeals court decision. The IRS will sometimes announce its decision to follow or not to follow a Court of Appeals decision.
- The Tax Court does not consider itself bound to follow any precedent set by an appeals court decision. The Tax Court view is that its nationwide jurisdiction cannot be restricted by the rules of the 12 different appeals courts. However, it will generally follow an appeals court decision in the circuit to which the case before it may be appealed.
- A Court of Appeals of one region is not bound to follow the precedent of a Court of Appeals in another region. Consequently, a decision of a particular appeals court is far stronger for taxpayers who can bring their appeals before that court than for taxpayers who must appeal to other appeals courts. A court will generally follow its own precedents unless it is overruled or later decides its original position was wrong.

Court of Appeals decisions are referred in this book to their place in the Federal Series reports published by the West Publishing Company. The first series is cited as "F.," the second series as "F.2d," and the third as "F.3d." For example, take the citation Albertson's, Inc.,

12 F.3d 1529 (9th Cir. (1994)). Albertson's, Inc., is the name of the taxpayer, 12 refers to the volume of the third series of the Federal Series reports, 1529 to the page within that volume, 9th Cir. refers to the circuit appeals court, and 1994 is the year of the decision.

In some instances, citations are not available for the Federal Series. For example, *James L. Robertson,* 99-2 USTC ¶50,875 (5th Cir. 1999), may be found in *U.S. Tax Cases* published by Commerce Clearing House. These reports contain tax decisions from all levels of federal courts except the Tax Court. Except for years prior to 1934, two Commerce Clearing House volumes appear for each year. 99-2 refers to the second volume of 1999; ¶50,875 is the paragraph at which the case is located.

Tax case decisions may also be obtained from online services, such as Westlaw and Lexis.

Supreme Court Decisions

Supreme Court decisions are the only decisions that the Internal Revenue Service and lower courts are required to follow. They have the same force as the Code and remain in force until Congress specifically changes the Court's interpretation or unless the Supreme Court in a later decision reverses its own position. Tax cases come before the Supreme Court when either a taxpayer or the government files a petition for a Writ of Certiorari, asking the Court to review the decision of a U.S. Court of Appeals. However, the Supreme Court limits its review of tax disputes generally to cases where there is a conflict of decisions among several U.S. Courts of Appeals on a specific interpretation of a tax law.

An example of a reference to a Supreme Court decision is: *Harold Davis,* 495 U.S. 472 (1990).

Harold Davis is the name of the taxpayer involved in the case; 495 refers to the official volume in which the case can be found; U.S. designates the official Supreme Court volumes; 472 refers to the page within the volume; and 1990 refers to the year of the decision. The case can also be found in volumes published by private publishers which are released before the official Supreme Court volumes. For example, unofficial Supreme Court decisions may be found in the Supreme Court Reporter, put out by West Publishing Company. An example of a West citation is: *Robert F. Lundy,* 116 S. Ct. 647 (1996).

States Within Court of Appeals Regions

FIRST CIRCUIT

Maine
Massachusetts
New Hampshire
Rhode Island
Puerto Rico

SECOND CIRCUIT

Connecticut
New York
Vermont

THIRD CIRUIT

Delaware
New Jersey
Pennsylvania
Virgin Islands

FOURTH CIRCUIT

Maryland
North Carolina
South Carolina
Virginia
West Virginia

FIFTH CIRCUIT

Canal Zone
Louisiana
Mississippi
Texas

SIXTH CIRCUIT

Kentucky
Michigan
Ohio
Tennessee

SEVENTH CIRCUIT

Illinois
Indiana
Wisconsin

EIGHTH CIRCUIT

Arkansas
Iowa
Minnesota
Missouri
Nebraska
North Dakota
South Dakota

NINTH CIRCUIT

Alaska
Arizona
California
Hawaii
Idaho
Montana
Nevada
Oregon
Washington
Guam

TENTH CIRCUIT

Colorado
Kansas
New Mexico
Oklahoma
Utah
Wyoming

ELEVENTH CIRCUIT

Alabama
Florida
Georgia

CIRCUIT FOR THE DISTRICT OF COLUMBIA

Washington, D.C.

Citations of Authority

Part 11 contains the citations of authority for the text and material in Parts 1–7. You may use the Chapter Contents starting on page vii or the Indexes starting on page 949 to locate the tax topic you are interested in researching. After locating the topic, authority for the discussion can be found by locating the same number in this part. Regardless of where you find the number of your topic—from the text, the index, or the checklists—you will find the citation of authority under that number in this part. The tax information in the text of Parts 1–7 is identified further by the use of italics under the identical number in this Part 11. For example, if you are interested in the tax law authorities for the discussion of tax-free employer accident and health plans at *3.1* on page 48, these may be found under *3.1* in Part 11 on page 812.

The references to law reviews, tax journal articles, and private letter rulings in this section are not cited as authority for any position taken in *Your Income Tax*. They are provided as a reference for your further study of the topics under which they are cited.

KEY TO CITATIONS

Authority	*Example*	*Page*
Internal Revenue Code of 1986	IRC § 305(b)(2)	801
Treasury Regulation	Reg. § 1.305-1	801
U.S. Tax Court		
Regular decision, in bound volume	DeWayne Bond, 100 TC 32 (1993)	802
Regular decision, not in bound volume	Robert L. Whitmire, 109 TC No. 13 (1997)	
Memorandum opinion, in bound volume	Douglas Kemmerer, 66 TCM 550 (1993)	
Memorandum opinion, not in bound volume	James D. Schlicher, TC Memo 1997-37	
Reversed or affirmed	George S. Nalle, III, 997 F.2d 1134 (5th Cir. 1993), rev'g 99 TC 187 (1992)	
Board of Tax Appeals (predecessor to U.S. Tax Court)		
Regular opinion	Steven Smith, 30 BTA 49	802
Memorandum opinion	A.F.C. Oil Co., BTA Memo. Dec. 10, 958-F (1939)	
Treasury Acquiescence	Jones, 12 TC 49 (Acq.)	803
Treasury Nonacquiescence	Smith, 13 TC 62 (Nonacq.)	803
Federal District Court		
Decision in Federal Supplement	Chester J. Maleszewski, 827 F. Supp. 1553 (D.C. Fla. 1993)	803
Decision not in Federal Supplement	Orval P. Russell, 97-2 USTC ¶50494 (W.D. Mich. 1997)	
U.S. Claims Court (renamed U.S. Court of Federal Claims, October 29, 1992)	Anthony Stack, 25 Ct. Cl. 634 (1992)	803
U.S. Court of Federal Claims		
Opinion, in bound volume	Robert P. Kliethermes, 27 Fed. Cl. 111 (1992)	803
Recent opinion, not in bound volume	George S. Davis, Fed. Cl. 97-2 USTC ¶50497	
U.S. Court of Appeals		
Opinion, in bound volume	Mickey L. Worden, 2 F.3d 359 (10th Cir. 1993)	803
Recent opinion, not in bound volume	Rosser B. Melton, Jr., 97-2 USTC ¶50492 (5th Cir. 1997)	
U.S. Supreme Court		
Opinion, in bound volume	Harvey F. Euge, 444 U.S. 707 (1980)	804
Recent opinion, not in bound volume	Marian Brockamp, 117 S. Ct. 849 (1997)	
Treasury Acquiescence	Jones, 12 TC 49 (Acq.)	804
Treasury Nonacquiescence	Smith, 13 TC 62 (Nonacq.)	804

Revenue Rulings, Treasury Decisions, Releases, and Abbreviations

Revenue Ruling found in Cumulative Bulletin	Rev. Rul. 94-44,1994-2 CB 190	801
Revenue Ruling found in Internal Revenue Bulletin	Rev. Rul. 97-1, 1997-2 IRB 10	
Announcement	Announcement 96-5, 1996-4 IRB 47	
Internal Revenue News Release	News Release IR 95-29, 3/29/95	
Notice found in the Cumulative Bulletin	Notice 93-12, 1993-1 CB 298	
Notice found in the Internal Revenue Bulletin	Notice 94-28, 1994-14 IRB 13	
Private Letter Ruling (the asterisk indicates that it may not be cited as authority)	* Letter Ruling 9530005 (pre-1999), 199929043 (post-1998)	
Revenue Procedure found in Internal Revenue Bulletin	Rev. Proc. 97-48, 1997-43 IRB 19	
Revenue Procedure found in Cumulative Bulletin	Rev. Proc. 93-26, 1993-1 CB 504	
Treasury Decision	T.D. 8494, 1993-35 IRB 6	

Law Reviews and Periodicals

Articles are cited according to their title, author, and periodical title. The number before the periodical title is the volume number, and the number following is the page number, which is then followed by the year of publication.

FILING YOUR RETURN

FILING TESTS

Income limits
IRC § 6012
IRC § 6017 (self-employed)

Filing for dependents
IRC § 6012(a)(1)(c)

Joint returns
IRC § 6013

File jointly even though spouse had no earnings
IRC § 6013(a)
Reg. § 1.6013-1(a)(1)

Determination of marital status
IRC § 7703

Qualifying widow(er)
IRC § 2(a)
Reg. 1.2-2

Spouse missing in combat
IRC § 2(a)(3)

Head of household
IRC § 2(b)

Self-employment income
IRC § 6017

Married, living apart
IRC § 2(c)
IRC § 7703(b)

Different tax years bar joint return
IRC § 6013(a)(2)
Reg. § 1.6013-1(c)

Different tax years before marriage
Frank E. Bertucci, 146 F. Supp. 949 (Ct. Cl. 1957)

Dependent
IRC § 6012(a)(1)(C)(iv)

Nonresident alien
IRC § 6012(a)(2)(C)(i)(ii)

Tax year of less than 12 months because of accounting period change
IRC § 6012(a)(2)(C)(ii)
IRC § 63(c)(6)(c)(1)

Gross income
IRC § 61

WHERE TO FILE

IRC § 6091
Reg. §1.6091-2

Armed Forces
IRS Publication 3

FILING DEADLINES

IRC § 6072
Reg. § 1.6072-1

Due date falls on weekend or holiday
IRC § 7503

Timely mailing is timely filing
IRC § 7502
Reg. § 301.7502-1

Postage meter date ignored
Irving Fishman, 51 TC 869 (1969), aff'd per curiam, 420 F.2d 491 (2d Cir. 1970)

Combat zone
IRC § 7508
IRC § 112

Spouse traveling outside U.S.
Rev. Rul. 82-161, 1982-2 CB 379

1 FILING STATUS

1.1 WHICH FILING STATUS SHOULD YOU USE?

* "Why the Marriage Penalty in Federal Income Tax Continues to Increase," Wallace Hoffman and Rachel Price, 77 Taxes 43 (July 1999)

Joint Returns
IRC § 6013

Qualifying widow(er)
IRC § 2(a)
Reg. § 1.2-2

Head of household
IRC § 2(b)

Unmarried individuals
IRC § 1(c)

1.2 TAX RATES BASED ON FILING STATUS

IRC § 1

1.3 FILING SEPARATELY INSTEAD OF JOINTLY

IRC § 1(d)
* "Filing Separately Can Provide Tax Savings for Many Couples," Brett J. Long and Randy Gardner, 54 Taxation for Accountants 219 (April 1995)

Non-community property states; joint accounts
Rev. Rul. 59-66, 1959-1 CB 60

Three years to elect joint return after separate returns
Reg. § 1.6013-2

Alternative minimum tax exemption
IRC § 55(d)

Standard deduction restriction
IRC § 63(c)(6)(A)

3% reduction of itemized deductions
IRC § 68

Phaseout of exemptions on separate return
IRC § 151(d)(3)(B)
IRC § 151(d)(3)(C)(iv)

1.4 FILING A JOINT RETURN

Joint return with new spouse denied when state law invalidates prior Mexican divorce
A. Gersten, 267 F.2d 195 (9th Cir. 1957), aff'g in part 28 TC 756 (1957)
H.K. Lee, 64 TC 552, aff'd, 550 F.2d 1201 (9th Cir. 1977)

Interlocutory divorce decree
William F. Holcomb, 237 F.2d 502 (9th Cir. 1956)
J. R. Calhoun, Jr., 27 TC 115 (1956) (Acq.)
Joyce P. Lane, 26 TC 405 (1956) (Acq.)
Rev. Rul. 57-368, 1957-2 CB 896

Joint return with new spouse allowed although prior divorce decree declared invalid by state law
Harold E. Wondsel, 350 F.2d 339 (2d Cir. 1965), cert. denied, 383 U.S. 935
Herman Borax Est., 349 F.2d 666 (2d Cir. 1965), rev'g 40 TC 1001 (1963), cert. denied, 383 U.S. 935

Rev. Rul. 67-442, 1967-2 CB 65 (IRS will not follow Wondsel or Borax decisions)

Each spouse liable for tax
IRC § 6013(d)(3)
Reg. § 1.6013-4(b)
Vaughn C. Payne, 247 F.2d 481 (8th Cir. 1957), cert. denied, 355 U.S. 923
W. L. Kann, 210 F.2d 247 (3d Cir. 1954), cert. denied, 347 U.S. 967
Myrna S. Howell, 175 F.2d 240 (6th Cir. 1949)
Alma Helfrich, 25 TC 404 (1955) (Acq.)
Virginia M. Wilkins, 19 TC 752 (1953) (Acq.)
Eva M. Manton, 11 TC 831 (1948) (Acq.)
William W. Kellet, 5 TC 608 (1945) (Acq.)

Spouse relieved of joint return liability
IRC § 6015
Notice 98-61, 1998-51 IRB 13

Divorce or legal separation
IRC § 143(a)(2)
IRC § 6013(d)
Reg. § 1.6013-4(a)
Kenneth T. Sullivan, 256 F.2d 664 (4th Cir. 1958), aff'g 29 TC 71 (1957)

Executor disaffirms
IRC § 6013(a)(3)
Reg. § 1.6013-1(d)(5)

Dependent's joint return used as refund claim
Rev. Rul. 54-567, 1954-2 CB 108, affirmed by Rev. Rul. 65-34, 1965-1 CB 86

Sign as spouse's agent
Reg. § 1.6013-1(a)(2)
Reg. § 1.6012-1(a)(5)

Note: Paragraph numbers refer to Volume One. Items marked * are research aids, not citations of authority; see "Key to Citations" on page 806.

Sick spouse
Rev. Rul. 70-216, 1970-1 CB 265

Intended joint return
Walter M. Ferguson, Jr., 14 TC 846 (1950) (Acq.)
Alfred E. Whitehouse Est., 14 TCM 501 (1955)
John Young, 11 TCM 239 (1952)
Jeremy H. Peirce, 43 TCM 400 (1982)
Frank Boyle, 67 TCM 294 (1994)

One spouse agreed to have other spouse handle tax matters
Muriel Heim, 251 F.2d 44 (8th Cir. 1958)
Myrna S. Howell, 10 TC 859 (1948), aff'd, 175 F.2d 240 (6th Cir. 1949)

Answers indicate intent
W. L. Kann, 210 F.2d 247 (3d Cir. 1954), cert. denied, 347 U.S. 967

Explain spouse's failure
Joyce P. Lane, 26 TC 405 (1956) (Acq.)

May elect joint return after separate return was filed
IRC § 6013(b)(2)

After joint return filed may not elect separate returns after due date
Reg. § 1.6013-1(a)(1)
Matthew L. Ladden, 38 TC 530 (1962) (Acq.)
Thomas J. Leger, 29 TCM 101 (170)

IRS settlement with bankrupt husband does not protect wife
Carolyn S. Kroh, 98 TC 29 (1992)

1.5 NONRESIDENT ALIEN SPOUSE

Nonresident alien spouse generally bars joint return
IRC § 6013(a)(1)
Reg. § 1.6013-1(b)

Claim nonresident alien spouse as exemption
IRC § 151
Reg. § 1.151-1

Joint return under election
IRC § 6013(g)

Special election where nonresident alien spouse becomes a resident during the year
IRC § 6013(h)

1.6 COMMUNITY PROPERTY RULES
*IRS Publication No. 555

Community property rules do not apply where couple does not elect joint return
IRC § 879

One-half vested interest
Aimee D. Bagur, 66 TC 817 (1976), rem'd, 603 F.2d 491 (5th Cir. 1979)

Community rules inapplicable to certain separated couples
IRC § 66(a)

Community property rules for earned income disregarded—spouse not notified of income
IRC § 66(b)

Community property rules disregarded—innocent spouse

IRC § 66(c)

Spouse receiving temporary alimony
Charlotte J. Kimes, 55 TC 774 (1971)

Renunciation of interest
Anne G. Mitchell, 403 U.S. 190 (1971)

Self-employment tax for spouses
Rev. Rul. 82-39, 1982-1 CB 119

Intention to move to a community property state
George D. Hampton, Jr., 38 TC 131 (1962)

Dependency exemption on joint return
Thomas R. Jones, 38 TCM 599 (1977)

1.7 INNOCENT SPOUSE RULES
*IRS Publication 971
*"IRS Restructuring and Reform Act of 1998 Gives Innocent Spouses a Much Needed Break," Gary M. Fleischman and Jingzhi Shen, 77 Taxes 25 (August 1999)
*"The New Spouse Provision: Reason and Law Walking Hand in Hand?" Toni Robinson and Mary Ferrari, 80 Tax Notes 835 (August 17, 1998)

Innocent spouse election — 1998 Act
IRC § 6015(b)

Partial relief — 1998 Act
IRC § 6015(b)(2)

Tax Court appeal — 1998 Act
IRC § 6015(e)

Equitable relief — 1998 Act
IRC § 6015(f)

Lack of knowledge standard — Pre-1998 Act
Bokum II, 94 TC 126 (1990), aff'd, 922 F.2d 1132 (1993)
Gwen Erdahl, 58 TCM 1532 (1990), rev'd and rem'd, 930 F.2d 585 (8th Cir. 1991)
Patricia A. Price, 887 F.2d 959 (9th Cir. 1989)
Janet Bliss, 59 F. 3d 374 (2d Cir., 1995), aff'g 66 TCM 522 (1993) (attorney's knowledge imputed to spouse)
Lucille E. Kistner, 18 F.3d 1521 (11th Cir. 1994)

1.8 SEPARATE LIABILITY ELECTION FOR FORMER SPOUSES

Separate liability election
IRC § 6015(c)

Tax Court appeal
IRC § 6015(e)

1.9 DEATH OF YOUR SPOUSE IN 1999

Joint return for decedent and survivor
IRC § 6013(a)(3)
Reg. § 1.6013-1(d),-3,-4

Remarriage
Reg. § 1.6013-1(d)(2)

Change in accounting period
IRC § 6013(a)(2)
IRC § 443(a)(1)
Reg. § 1.6013-1(d)(2)

Nonresident alien
IRC § 6013(a)(1) and (g)(4)(B)
Reg. § 1.6013-1(b)

Disaffirmance by executor
Reg. § 1.6013-1(d)(5) and (6)

Co-executrix could not disaffirm
Frank J. Floyd Est., 51-2 USTC ¶9415 (Orphans' Ct., Del. County, Pa. 1951)

Treat as late return
Reg. § 1.6013-1(d)(5) and (6)

Signing
IRC § 6061
Reg. § 1.6061-1
Reg. § 1.6012-2(b)(1)
Reg. § 1.6013-1(a)(2)

Privilege of treating survivor's return as joint return
IRC § 2
Reg. § 1.2-2
Reg. § 1.6013-1(e)

Survivor bound to joint return liability
Maxine Ruzich, 47 TC 380 (1967)

1.10 QUALIFYING WIDOW(ER) STATUS IF YOUR SPOUSE DIED IN 1998 OR 1997

Qualifying Widows or Widowers
IRC § 2(a)

1.11 QUALIFYING AS HEAD OF HOUSEHOLD
IRC § 1(b)
IRC § 2(b)
Reg. § 1.2-2(b), (c), and (d)

Special rule for parents
IRC § 2(b)(1)(B)
Reg. § 1.2-2(c)(2)

Status denied when children change residence after separation agreement
Fred J. Stanback, Jr., 77-1 USTC ¶9181 (D.N.C. 1977)

Parent in rest home
Rev. Rul. 70-279, 1970-1 CB 1

Foster child, adopted child
IRC § 2(b)(1)
IRC § 152(b)(2)
Reg. § 1.151-3

Foster child must be dependent
Rev. Rul. 84-89, 1984-1 CB 5

Taxpayer must reside in same home as dependent for substantial period
John C. Muse, 434 F.2d 349 (4th Cir. 1970)
Levon P. Biolchin, 433 F.2d 301 (7th Cir. 1970)

Relative resides in your household
IRC § 2(b)(1)
Reg. § 1.2-2(b)

Same residence for taxpayer and dependent
Reg. § 1.2-2(c)
Rev. Rul. 72-43, 1972-1 CB 4
Sharon Stanford, 69 TCM 78 (1995)

Note: *Paragraph numbers refer to Volume One. Items marked ˙ are research aids, not citations of authority; see "Key to Citations" on page 806.*

808

Mother is head of household for child living in different states
Clair Smith, 332 F.2d 671 (9th Cir. 1964)
Rev. Rul. 72-43, 1972-1 CB 4 (IRS nonacq. to Smith)

Husband living in separate residence not head of household
W. E. Grace, 51 TC 685 (1969), aff'd per curiam, 421 F.2d 165 (5th Cir. 170)
James A. Petrie, IV, 70 TCM 1566 (1995)

Interlocutory decree
Carole F. Brown, 31 TCM 194 (1972)

Support order pendente lite as interlocutory decree
Walter G. Brusey, 41 TCM 1223 (1981)

Old-age home
Rev. Rul. 57-307, 1957-2 CB 12
John Robinson, 51 TC 520 (1968) (Acq.), vacated and rem'd, 442 F.2d 873 (9th Cir. 1970)

Nonresident alien not a dependent
Rev. Rul. 55-711, 1955-2 CB 13, amplified by Rev. Rul. 74-370, 1974-2 CB 7

Two-family house
Jean F. Fleming Est., 33 TMC 619 (1974)

Can still get dependency credit
Katherine Atchison, 17 TCM 718 (1958)

Same person can qualify only once
Reg. § 1.2-2(b)(2)

Illegitimate child
Rev. Rul. 54-498, 1954-2 CB 107

Can move household
Reg. § 1.2-2(c)

Dependent confined in hospital
Reg. § 1.2-2(c)
Abbie D. Reardon, 158 F. Supp. 745 (D.S. Dak. 1958)

Father's absence because of marital dispute
Walter Petlow, 34 TCM 51 (1975)

Probably never return
Harold K. Brehmer, 191 F. Supp. 421 (D. Minn. 1961)
Walter J. Hein, 28 TC 826 (1957) (Acq.)
Rev. Rul. 66-28, 1966-1 CB 31

Pay more than one-half of household costs
IRC § 2(b)
Reg. § 1.2-2(d)

Figuring household costs
Donald G. Teeling, 42 TC 671 (1964) (Acq.)

Need not be head of family
Rev. Rul. 57-415, 1957-2 CB 13

Custody decree has no effect where son in boarding school
Allan L. Blair, 63 TC 214 (1974) (Acq.), aff'd, 538 F.2d 155 (7th Cir. 1976)

Separated spouse must live apart for last six months
Laurel Hopkins, 63 TCM 3113 (1992)

Mother keeps separate house for mentally ill son
Lillie B. McDonald, 61 TCM 2764 (1991)

1.12 FILING FOR YOUR CHILD

Minor's earnings and deductions
IRC § 73
Reg. § 1.73-1

Filing requirement for dependent child
IRC § 6012(a)(1)(C)
IRC § 63(c)(5)
Reg. § 1.73-1
Reg. § 1.6012-1(a)(4)

Signing return
Rev. Rul. 82-206, 1982-2 CB 356

Exemptions for dependent children
IRC § 151(e)
Reg. § 1.151-1
Reg. § 1.151-2
Reg. § 1.151-3

Deduction for pay to minor
Zeno J. Pucci, 10 TCM 529 (1951)
Samuel Rottenberg, 20 BTA 589 (Acq.)
Rev. Rul. 73-393, 1973-2 CB 33

Salary to young children
Nathaniel A. Denman, 48 TC 439 (1967)

Filing for Social Security self-employment tax
IRC § 1401
IRC § 1402
IRC § 6017

Parental responsibility
IRC § 6201(c)

Minors under age 14
IRC § 1(g)

Social Security number of dependent
IRC § 6109(e)
IRC § 6724(d)(3)(D)
IRC § 6723 ($50 penalty)

Child must pay penalties for parents' failure to file
Skye Bassett, 100 TC 41 (1993)

1.13 RETURN FOR DECEASED
* IRS Publication 559

Responsibility for filing
IRC § 6012(b)
Reg. § 1.6012-3(b)(1)
Reg. § 1.6012-1(a)(2)(ii)

How reported
IRC § 443
Reg. § 1.443-1(a)(2)
IRC § 451(b)

U.S. Savings Bonds—jointly owned
Rev. Rul. 58-435, 1958-2 CB 370, distinguished by Rev. Rul. 68-145, 1968-1 CB 203

Community property
R. D. Merrill, 211 F.2d 297 (9th Cir. 1954)
Hunt Henderson Est., 155 F.2d 310 (5th Cir. 1946)
Stella W. Bishop, 152 F.2d 389 (9th Cir. 1946)
Rev. Rul. 55-726, 1955-2 CB 24

Income received after death
IRC § 691
Reg. § 1.691(a)-1

Income accrued

IRC § 451(b)
Reg. § 1.451-1(b)

Returns
IRC § 6012(b)(1) and (4)
Reg. § 1.6012-3

Deduction for estate tax
IRC § 691(b)
Reg. § 1.691(a)-4
Reg. § 1.691(c)-1

Marital status
IRC § 143
Reg. § 1.143-1

Exemptions
IRC § 153
Reg. § 1.153-1

No estimated tax for years ending before 2 years after decedent's death
IRC § 6654(1)(2)

Due date
IRC § 6072
Reg. § 1.6071-1(b)
Reg. § 1.6072-1(b)

Refund
Reg. § 301.6402-2

Death before return filed for previous year
Reg. § 1.6013-1(d)(3)

Request for prompt assessment
IRC § 6501(d)

1.14 RETURN FOR AN INCOMPETENT PERSON
* "Guidelines for Preparing the Fiduciary Income Tax Return," G. Philip Morehead, 21 Prac. Accountant 17 (Jan. 1988)

Guardian files
IRC § 6012(b)(2)
Reg. § 1.6012-3(b)(3)
Rev. Rul. 55-387, 1955-1 CB 131

Incompetency bars joint return
David Herman, 38 TCM 119, aff'd in unpublished opinion (3d Cir. Dec. 13, 1979)

Spouse may file
Rev. Rul. 55-387, 1955-1 CB 131 (joint return for missing spouse)
Rev. Rul. 56-22, 1956-1 CB 558, modified by Rev. Rul. 58-267, 1958-1 CB 327 (return for incompetent spouse)

1.15 HOW A NONRESIDENT ALIEN IS TAXED
IRC § 871
* IRS Publication 519
* "U.S. Tax Residency Rules Broadened in Final Regulations," Alan S. Lederman and Robbe Hirsh, 77 Journal of Taxation 152 (September 1992)

Resident taxed as U.S. citizen
Reg. § 1.871-1
Prop. Reg. § 1.871-1(a)

Nonresident subject to 30% tax
IRC § 871(a)

Capital gains

Note: Paragraph numbers refer to Volume One. Items marked * *are research aids, not citations of authority; see "Key to Citations" on page 806.*

Note: Paragraph numbers refer to Volume One. Items marked ˚ are research aids, not citations of authority; see "Key to Citations" on page 806.

Salary advances
Anson Beaver, 55 TC 85 (1970)

Deferred pay in trust fixed
Candido Jacuzzi, 61 TC 262 (1973)

State or local government deferred pay plan
IRC § 457

Model Rabbi trust
Rev. Proc. 92-64, 1992-2 CB 214

Qualified cash or deferred arrangement
IRC § 401
IRC § 401(k)

Nonqualified plans
IRC § 403(c)
IRC § 404(a)
Rev. Rul. 60-31, 1960-1 CB 174
IRC § 457(f)

2.9 DID YOU RETURN WAGES RECEIVED IN A PRIOR YEAR?

IRC § 1341
Reg. § 1.1341-1
* "The Claim of Right Doctrine and Section 1341," Robert R. Wootton, 34 Tax Lawyer 297 (1981)

Return of embezzled funds—no claim of right computation
Rev. Rul. 65-254, 1965-2 CB 50

Return of unreasonable salary under agreement deductible
Rev. Rul. 69-115, 1969-1 CB 50

Author lacked unrestricted right to advanced royalties
Stewart H. Holbrook, 194 F. Supp. 252 (U.S.Dist. Ct. Ore. 1961)

No deduction where repayment not required
John G. Pahl, 67 TC 286 (1976)

Repayment of supplemental unemployment benefits—above-the-line deduction
IRC § 62(a)(12)

Restitution payments may be deductible
Jess Kraft, et ux., 114 S. Ct. 467 cert. denied, 991 F.2d 292 (6th Cir. 1993)

Hedge agreement allows Section 1341 recalculation
Eugene Van Cleave, 718 F.2d 193 (6th Cir. 1983)

Escrow payment for contested liability deductible
Warnock Davies, 101 TC 282 (1993)

2.10 WAIVER OF EXECUTOR'S AND TRUSTEE'S COMMISSIONS

* "Tax Consequences Resulting From the Waiver of Executor's Commissions," E. Everett, E. Chester, M. Loening, 24 NYU Inst. 295 (1966)
George M. Breidert, 50 TC 844 (1968) (Acq.)
Rev. Rul. 66-167, 1966-1 CB 20
Rev. Rul. 64-225, 1964-2 CB 15
Rev. Rul. 56-472, 1956-2 CB 21

2.11 SICK PAY IS TAXABLE

IRC § 61

Tax-free benefits from private insurance

IRC § 104(a)(3)

2.12 WORKERS' COMPENSATION IS TAX FREE

Workers' compensation
IRC § 104(a)(1)
Reg. § 1.104-1(b)

Given to employer
Rev. Rul. 56-83, 1956-1 CB 79

N.Y.C. teacher under Board of Ed. regulations
Madeline G. Dyer, 71 TC 560 (1979) (Acq. in result only)

N.Y.C. retirees may exclude job-related disability pay
Rev. Rul. 83-91, 1983-1 CB 38

Civil Service Retirement Act payments not worker's compensation
Daniel S. Haar, 78 TC 864 (1982), aff'd per curiam, 709 F.2d 1207 (8th Cir. 1983)

Policeman's sick leave under labor contract not worker's compensation
William Rutter, 48 TCM 1269 (1984), aff'd per curiam, 760 F.2d 466 (2d Cir. 1985)

Sheriff's sick leave elected under worker's compensation statute is tax free
Donald Givens, 90 TC 1145 (1988) (Nonacq.; 89-1 CB 1)

Policeman's disability amounts under state law not affected by PBA contract
James Fotis, 57 TCM 697 (1989)

Disability is not workers' compensation
Peter Benjamin, 66 TCM 575 (1993)

New York City law change allows tax-free sick leave for police and firefighters
Local Law 87, 12/29/88
Local Law 78, 10/25/89

2.13 EMPLOYER AND FEDERAL GOVERNMENT DISABILITY PENSIONS

Federal government services
IRC § 104(a)(4)
IRC § 104(b)

Injuries from terrorist attacks
IRC § 104(a)(5)

2.14 DEFERRED PAY PLANS

* "Nonqualified Plans Can Avoid Limits on Deferred Comp.," Lucia Jones and Randy Gardner, 54 Taxation for Accountants 266 (May 1995)
* "Golden Parachutes Remain Popular Despite Strict Rules," Charles F. Feldman, 49 Taxation for Accountants 204 (October 1992)
* "Maximizing the Benefits of Deferred Compensation Plans Funded Through Secular Trusts," Deborah Walker and Sallie Olson, 77 Journal of Taxation 90 (August 1992)
* "Rewarding Executives With Stock and Stock-Value Arrangements," Alan J. Hawksley and Michael S. Melbinger, 48 Taxation for Accountants 292 (May 1992)
* "Deferred Comp. Package Affected by Estate

Plans," Robert S. McCarty, 19 Estate Planning 158 (May/June 1992)

2.15 INSURANCE PLANS MAY BE TAX FREE

* "Split-Dollar Life Insurance," Lee Slavutin, 77 Taxes 47 (January 1999)
* "Opportunities abound for making life insurance an executive perk," Robert E. Madden, 61 Taxation for Accountants 85 (August 1998)

Assignment of group policy
Rev. Rul. 76-490, 1976-2 CB 300
Rev. Rul. 68-334, 1968-1 CB 403

Split-dollar
Rev. Rul. 78-420, 1978-2 CB 67
Rev. Rul. 64-328, 1964-2 CB 11, amplified by Rev. Rul. 66-110, 1966-1 CB 112
* Letter Ruling 9604001

Taxability of disability insurance
Hines, 72 TC 715 (1979)
John L. Stolte, TC Memo 1999-271

Permanent and paid-up insurance—taxed to employee
Reg. § 1.61-2(d)(2)
* Letter Ruling 9604001
Frank D. Yuengling, 69 F.2d 971 (3d Cir. 1934)
W. F. Parker, 38 BTA 989
Rev. Rul. 56-400, 1956-2 CB 116
Rev. Rul. 78-420, 1978-2 CB 67
Rev. Rul. 64-328, 1964-2 CB 11, amplified by Rev. Rul. 66-110, 1966-1 CB 112

Qualified group legal services plan
IRC § 120

2.16 STOCK APPRECIATION RIGHTS (SARs)

No tax on receipt of SARs
Rev. Rul. 80-300, 1980-2 CB 165

Tax on expiration of SARs
* Letter Ruling 8120103

No constructive receipt on SAR tied to stock option
Rev. Rul. 82-121, 1982-1 CB 79

2.17 STOCK OPTIONS AND RESTRICTED STOCK

* "Stock Option Planning," Barbara J. Raash and Judith L. Rowland, 77 Taxes 39 (January 1999)
* "Living and Dying with the Complex Rules of Incentive Stock Options," Carol Cantrell, 87 Journal of Taxation 76 (Aug. 1997)
* "Ninth Circuit's Section 83 Decision May Reopen Planning Opportunities for Stock Compensation," Paul J. Sax and Gary A. Herrmann, 85 Taxation 87 (August 1996)
* "Stock Compensation Plans Get a Boost from RRA '93," Michael S. Melbinger, 51 Taxation for Accountants 289 (November 1993)
* "Using Discount Stock Options As Executive Compensation," Harry J.J. O'Neill and David A. Schenck, 72 Journal of Taxation 348 (June 1990)

Qualified statutory stock options
IRC § 421

Note: Paragraph numbers refer to Volume One. Items marked ˚ are research aids, not citations of authority; see "Key to Citations" on page 806.

Incentive stock options
IRC § 422
Temp. Reg. § 14a.422A-1

Employee stock purchase plans
IRC § 423

Nonqualified stock options
IRC § 83
Reg. § 1.83-7
Pagel, Inc., 91 TC 200 (1988) (upholding Reg. § 1.83-7)

Restricted stock
IRC § 83(c)

Executive cannot deduct loss on sale of restricted stock to key employees
Henry C. Tilford, Jr., 75 TC 134 (1980), rev'd, 705 F.2d 828 (6th Cir. 1983)

Electing tax on unrestricted value within 30 days
IRC § 83(b)

Attorney taxed on income remitted to firm
* Letter Ruling 9514008

Finder's fee
Pasquale N. Cassetta, 39 TCM 188 (1979)

Sale treated as option
Reg. § 1.83-3(a)(2)

Not given in option exercise
John H. Rolfe, 488 F.2d 1092 (9th Cir. 1974), aff'g 58 TC 361 (1972)

Restricted stock options (pre-1964)
IRC § 424

Lapsed restrictions disregarded
IRC § 422A(e)(10)

2.18 EDUCATIONAL BENEFITS FOR EMPLOYEES' CHILDREN

Grants by private foundations
Rev. Proc. 76-47, 1976-2 CB 670, amplified by Rev. Proc. 77-32, 1977-2 CB 541
* Letter Ruling 9018068 (scholarship plan approved)

Educational benefits trusts
Rev. Rul. 75-448, 1975-2 CB 55
Richard T. Armantrout, 67 TC 996 (1977), aff'd per curiam, 570 F.2d 210 (7th Cir. 1978)
Grant-Jacoby, Inc., 73 TC 700 (1980)
John C. Saunders, 720 F.2d 871 (5th Cir. 1983), aff'g 45 TCM 82 (1982)
Reg. § 1.677(b)-1(f)

3 FRINGE BENEFITS

3.1 TAX-FREE HEALTH AND ACCIDENT COVERAGE UNDER EMPLOYER PLANS
* "Final Regs Under COBRA — Long-Overdue Clarifications on Group Health Plan Coverage," Paul J. Schneider, Part I, 91 Journal of Taxation 102 (August 1999); Part II, 91 Journal of Taxation 172 (September 1999)

Employer-paid premiums not taxable
IRC § 106(a)
Rev. Rul. 82-196, 1982-2 CB 53 (retired employee not taxed and deceased employee's survivors not taxed)
Rev. Rul. 85-121, 1985-2 CB 57 (laid-off employee not taxed)
* Letter Ruling 9409006
Rugby Productions, 100 TC 35 (1993)
Notice 94-103, 1994-51 IRB 10

Employee taxed on coverage for domestic partner
* Letter Ruling 9717018
* Letter Ruling 9603011

MSA deductions
IRC § 220
"New MSA and Health Insurance Rules Create Opportunities," Benjamin C. Avers and Elizabeth Plummer, 58 Taxation for Accountants 260 (May 1997)

Employer contributions
IRC § 106

Access and portability rules for group health plans
IRC § 9811, as added by 1997 Act
IRC § 9812, as added by 1997 Act

Continuing coverage required
IRC § 4980B
Rev. Rul. 96-8, 1996-1 CB 286

3.2 TAX-FREE PAYMENTS FROM EMPLOYER HEALTH AND ACCIDENT PLANS

Specific reimbursements of medical expenses
IRC § 105(b)
Reg. § 1.105-2
Rev. Rul. 63-181, 1963-2 CB 74

Self-insured medical reimbursement plans
IRC § 105(h)
Reg. § 1.105-11

Highly compensated under medical self-insured plans
IRC § 105(h)(5)
IRC § 401(k)(12)

Employee-spouse of self-employed
ISP Coordinated Issue Paper, 3/29/99 (UIL-162.35-02)

Domestic partners eligible for health benefits
* Letter Ruling 9231062

Physicals may be given to executives only
Reg. § 1.105-11(g)(1)

Permanent loss of use of part of body
IRC § 105(c)
Reg. § 1.105-3

Benefit must be based on injury
Randall Beisler, 814 F.2d 1304 (9th Cir. 1987)
Kenneth Rosen, 829 F.2d 506 (4th Cir. 1987)

Hypertension not loss of body function
Frank S. Watts, 82-1 USTC ¶9226 (D. Cal. 1982), aff'd, 83-1 USTC ¶9286 (9th Cir. 1983)

Taxable benefits under employer-paid coverage

IRC § 105(a)
Reg. § 1.105-1

Tax-free benefits under private policy
IRC § 104(a)(3)
Reg. § 1.104-1(d)

Disability payments from profit-sharing plan taxed
George H. Gordon, 88 TC 630 (1987)
Michael J. Berman, 58 TCM 919 (1989)

Close corporations
Alan B. Larkin, 48 TC 629 (1967), aff'd, 394 F.2d 494 (1st Cir. 1968)
Arthur R. Seidel, 30 TCM 1021 (1971)
Sanders & Sons, Inc., 26 TCM 671 (1967)

3.3 GROUP-TERM LIFE INSURANCE PREMIUMS
IRC § 79
Reg. § 1.79-0 through 3
Temp. Reg. § 1.79-4T

IRS rate table
Temp. Reg. § 1.79-3(d)(2)

Assignment of policy
Rev. Rul. 73-174, 1973-1 CB 43

Combination policies
Reg. § 1.79-1(b)

Former employees
IRC § 79(e)

Key employees taxed under discriminatory plans
IRC § 79(d)
Temp. Reg. § 1.79-4T, question 6

Key employees defined
IRC § 416(i)
IRC § 79(d)(6) (includes retirees)

Separate discriminatory testing of active and retired employees
Reg. § 1.79-4T, questions 7 and 8

Retire on disability
IRC § 79(b)(1)

Group-term insurance for dependents
Notice 89-110, 1989-49 IRB 17

3.4 DEPENDENT CARE ASSISTANCE

Child-care services
IRC § 129

Identify employer provider of child care on return
IRC § 129(e)(9)

3.5 ADOPTION BENEFITS
IRC § 23
*IRS Publication 968
* "Tax Implications of New Legislation Designed to Provide Adoption Incentives," Julia K. Brazelton, 75 Taxes 426 (Aug. 1997)

3.6 EDUCATION ASSISTANCE PLANS

Education assistance exclusion

Note: Paragraph numbers refer to Volume One. Items marked ˙ are research aids, not citations of authority; see "Key to Citations" on page 806.

IRC § 127

IRC § 127(d), extended for courses beginning before January 1, 2002 by the 1997 Act

"Employer Paid Educational Assistance Exclusion Reinstated," Jeffrey L. Hamm, 58 Taxation for Accountants 91 (Feb. 1997)

Working condition benefit
IRC § 132(h)(9)

Tuition reductions
IRC § 117(d)
* Letter Ruling 9040045 (faculty and staff)
Daniel Wolpaw, 47 F.3d 787 (6th Cir. 1995)

3.7 COMPANY CARS, PARKING, AND TRANSIT PASSES
IRC § 132(a)(3)
Temp. Reg. § 1.132-5T
* "Maximize Mileage From Transportation Fringe Benefits," Scott N. Cairns, Diane A. Riordan and Michael P. Riordan, 58 Taxation for Accountants 25 (Jan. 1997)

Valuation of benefits
Temp. Reg. § 1.61-2T (for 1985 through 1988)
Reg. § 1.61-21 (for 1989 and future years)

Excludable non-personal use vehicles
Temp. Reg. § 1.274-5T(k)

100% inclusion rule for cars
Reg. § 1.274-6T(c)

Chauffeur bodyguard
Reg. § 1.132-5(m)

Transit passes and parking benefits
IRC § 132(f)
Notice 94-3, 1994-3 IRB 14

Parking Benefits After 1997
IRC § 132 (f)(4), as amended by '97 Act

3.8 WORKING CONDITION FRINGE BENEFITS
IRC § 132(d)
Reg. § 1.132-5
* "IRS Draws Map for Exclusion of Outplacement Services as Working Condition Fringe," Robert J. Werner, 77 Journal of Taxation 350 (December 1992)

Job-placement assistance
Rev. Rul. 92-69, 1992-2 CB 51

Frequent flyer cash rebate
* Letter Ruling 9340007

Financial counseling
* Letter Ruling 199929043

3.9 DE MINIMIS FRINGE BENEFITS
IRC § 132(e)
Reg. § 1.132-6

3.10 EMPLOYEE ACHIEVEMENT AWARDS
IRC § 74(c)

Taxable amount
Prop. Reg. § 1.74-2

3.11 EMPLOYER-FURNISHED MEALS OR LODGING
* "A legislative reversal of Boyd Gaming? 1998 Act revises employee meal facilities rules," John B. Truskowski, 89 Journal of Taxation 150 (Sept. 1998)

Meals and lodging
IRC § 119
Reg. § 1.119-1
Maschmeyer's Nursery, Inc., 71 TMC 2188 (1996)
Boyd Gaming Corp., 117 F3d 1096 (9th Cir. 1999)

Liberalized meal exclusion — 1998 Act
IRC § 119 (b) (4)

Casino employees
Boyd Gaming Corp., 117 F.3d 1096 (9th Cir. 1999)

Utilities
Charles R. Considine, 68 TC 52 (1977)
Rev. Rul. 68-579, 1968-2 CB 61

Lodging off premises
Charles Anderson, 371 F.2d 59 (6th Cir. 1967), rev'g 42 TC 410 (1964), cert. denied, 387 U.S. 906
Gordon S. Dole, 351 F.2d 308 (1st Cir. 1965), aff'g per curiam 43 TC 697 (1964) (Acq.)
Harold T. Giesinger, 66 TC 6 (1976) (Acq.)
Jack B. Lindeman, 60 TC 609 (1973) (Acq.)

School superintendent one block away
Virgil L. Erdelt, 715 F. Supp. 278 (D.C. N. Dak. 1989), aff'd, 909 F.2d 510 (8th Cir. 1990), IRS Action on Decision 1992-001

Lodging for dorm parents and evening house is tax free
* Letter Ruling 9404005

College president taxed on lodging four miles away
Richard D. Winchell, 564 F. Supp. 131 (D. C. Neb. 1983), aff'd without opinion, 725 F.2d 689 (8th Cir. 1983)
* Letter Ruling 9404005

Executive luncheon
Carlton R. Mabley, 24 TCM 1794 (1965)

Restaurant employees
Reg. § 1.119-1(d)

Waitress's day off
Reg. § 1.119-1(d)

Company cafeteria
Reg. § 1.119-1(d)

Short meal period
Reg. § 1.119-1(a)(2)(ii)(A) and (d)
* Letter Ruling 9602001

Emergency
Reg. § 1.119-1(a)(2)(ii)(a)
Reg. § 1.119-1(d)

Bank teller
Reg. § 1.119-1(f)

Faculty housing
IRC § 119(d)

Hospital lodging not a condition of employment where others live in apartments
* Letter Ruling 8938014

Employer deducts fixed amount from pay
IRC § 119(b)
Reg. § 1.119-1(a)(3)(ii)
Melvin J. Boykin, 260 F.2d 249 (8th Cir. 1958)
Rev. Rul. 59-307, 1959-2 CB 48

Unprepared food
Walter Jacob, 493 F.2d 1294 (3d Cir. 1974)
Michael A. Tougher, Jr., 441 F.2d 1148 (9th Cir. 1971), cert. denied, 404 U.S. 856

Employer gives cash allowance
Reg. § 1.119-1

Hotel manager or executive
Charles N. Anderson, 371 F.2d 59 (6th Cir. 1967), cert. denied, 387 U.S. 906
Jack B. Lindeman, 60 TC 609 (1973) (Acq.)
Atlanta Biltmore Hotel Corp., 22 TCM 1266 (1963), mod'd and aff'd, 349 F.2d 677 (5th Cir. 1965)
Adolph Coors Co., 27 TCM 1351 (1968)

State civil service employee
Reg. § 1.119-1(d)

No exclusion for purchases at commissary
Michael A. Tougher, Jr., 51 TC 737 (1969), aff'd per curiam, 441 F.2d 1148 (9th Cir. 1971), cert. denied, 404 U.S. 856

Farm supervision
M. Caratan, 442 F.2d 606 (9th Cir. 1971)

Other employees
Lloyd N. Farnham, 6 TCM 1049 (1947)
Special Ruling, December 3, 1950

Workers in remote area
Reg. § 1.119-1(d)
William L. Olkjer, 32 TC 464 (1959) (Acq.)

Park employee
Robert L. Coyner, 344 F.2d 736 (3d Cir. 1965)

Insufficient eating facilities
Reg. § 1.119-1(a)(2)(ii)(c)

Peace Corps volunteer
IRC § 912

Partnerships
C.C. Wilson 376 F.2d 280 (Court of Claims 1967) (reimbursed food taxed)
Ann L. Armstrong 394 F.2d 661 (5th Cir. 1968) (meals and lodging excludable)

Hotel partnership deductions
George A. Papineau, 16 TC 130 (1952) (Nonacq.)

VISTA volunteer
Carol Goldstein, 73 TC 164 (1979)

3.12 MINISTER'S RENTAL ALLOWANCE
* "Who Is a 'Minister of the Gospel' for Purposes of the Parsonage Exclusion?" J. Block, 51 Taxes 47 (1973)

Tax free
IRC § 107
Reg. § 1.107-1

Note: Paragraph numbers refer to Volume One. Items marked * *are research aids, not citations of authority; see "Key to Citations" on page 806.*

Services performed by minister
Reg. § 1.1402(c)-5

Exclusion limited to amount spent
Fred B. Marine, 47 TC 609 (1967)

Minister's professional expenses not deductible to extent of tax-free income
David E. Deason, 41 TC 465 (1964) (Acq.)

Exclusion allowed for ordained executive directors of parochial schools
Rev. Rul. 62-171, 1962-2 CB 39

No deduction for ordained minister working for a nonreligious organization
Rev. Rul. 68-68, 1968-1 CB 51

Not allowed for unordained ministers
Rev. Rul. 59-270, 1959-2 CB 44

Unordained educational director
Robert D. Lawrence, 50 TC 494 (1968)

Cantors
Abraham A. Salkov, 46 TC 190 (1966) (Nonacq.)
Max Silverman, 253 F.2d 849 (8th Cir. 1958)
Rev. Rul. 78-301, 1978-2 CB 103

Traveling evangelist
Rev. Rul. 64-326, 1964-2 CB 37

Retired minister
Rev. Rul. 63-156, 1963-2 CB 79

Widow not entitled to exclusion
Rev. Rul. 72-249, 1972-1 CB 36

Anti-Communist crusade
James D. Colbert, 61 TC 449 (1974)

Priest living as layman
Francis E. Kelley, 62 TC 131 (1974)

Not allowed for unordained executive of tax-exempt nonreligious organization
W. Astor Kirk, 425 F.2d 492 (D.C. Cir. 1970), cert. denied, 400 U.S. 853

Civilian chaplain at VA hospital
Rev. Rul. 72-462, 1972-2 CB 76

Administrator of nonreligious old-age home
Jesse A. Toavs, 67 TC 897 (1977)
Rev. Rul. 72-606, 1972-2 CB 78

No exclusion for rabbi as director of interreligious affairs
Marc H. Tanenbaum, 58 TC 1 (1972)

Exclusion for rabbi as UJA director
Melvin Libman, 44 TCM 371 (1982)

Minister teaching at church-related college
* Letter Ruling 9144047

3.13 CAFETERIA PLANS PROVIDE CHOICE OF BENEFITS

IRC § 125
Prop. Reg. § 1.125-2
Prop. Reg. § 1.125-3
* Letter Ruling 9104050
* "Complying With the Cafeteria Plan Proposed Regulations," R. Stephen Lee, 73 Journal of Taxation 362 (Dec. 1990)
* "Cafeteria Plans: New Law Removes Proposed IRS Restrictions and Adds Certain Operations," Peter L. Knox, 33 Taxation for Accountants 168

(Sept. 1984) and 13 Taxation for Lawyers 102 (Sept. 10, 1984)

Key employees
IRC § 125(b)(2)

3.14 FLEXIBLE SPENDING ARRANGEMENTS

IRC § 125
Prop. Reg. § 1.125-2
Prop. Reg. § 1.125-3
* "Choosing Between the Child Care Credit and Flexible Accounts," Sidney J. Basendale, Richard E. Coppage, and Alan Attaway, 50 Taxation for Accountants 278 (May 1993)

Health plan flexible spending arrangements
Prop. Reg. § 1.125-2
Prop. Reg. § 1.125-3

3.15 COMPANY SERVICES PROVIDED AT NO ADDITIONAL COST

IRC § 132(b)
Reg. § 1.132-2

Highly compensated employees
IRC § 132(h)

Line of business limitation
Reg. § 1.132-4
Temp. Reg. § 54.4977-1T (1985 election)

3.16 DISCOUNTS ON COMPANY PRODUCTS OR SERVICES

IRC § 132(c)
Reg. § 1.132-3
* Letter Ruling 9328016

4 DIVIDEND AND INTEREST INCOME

4.1 REPORTING CORPORATE DIVIDENDS

IRC § 301
IRC § 305
* "From the Thoughtful Tax Advisor—Stock Dividends: Pitfalls and Opportunities," Robert Willens, 68 Taxes 237 (March 1990)

4.2 DIVIDENDS FROM A PARTNERSHIP, S CORPORATION, ESTATE, OR TRUST

Partners
IRC § 702(a)(5)
IRC § 702(b)

S Corporations
IRC § 1368(c)(2)

Trusts
IRC § 652(b)

4.3 HOW MUTUAL-FUND DISTRIBUTIONS ARE TAXED

* IRS Publication 564

Ordinary dividend portion
IRC § 854(b)(2)
Reg. § 1.854-2
Rev. Rul. 77-149, 1977-1 CB 82

Long-term capital gain
IRC § 852(b)(3)(B)

Exempt-interest dividend
IRC § 852(b)(5)(B)

Undistributed capital gain
IRC § 852(b)(3)(D)

Deferred annuities
Rev. Rul. 81-220, 1981-2 CB 175
Rev. Rul. 82-54, 1982-1 CB 11

Dividend declared in October, November, or December paid by following February
IRC § 852(b)(7)

4.4 REAL ESTATE INVESTMENT TRUST (REIT) DIVIDENDS

IRC § 857

Shares held six months or less
IRC § 857(b)(7)

Dividend declared in October, November, or December
IRC § 857(b)(8)

4.5 TAXABLE DIVIDENDS OF EARNINGS AND PROFITS

IRC § 301

Definition of dividend
IRC § 316

4.6 STOCK DIVIDENDS ON COMMON STOCK

* "Keeping Corporate Distributions of Stock and Stock Rights Nontaxable," Dennis A. Diersen, 40 Taxation for Accountants 202 (Apr. 1988)

Stock dividends and rights
IRC § 305
Reg. § 1.305-1
Reg. § 1.61-9(b)

Cash in lieu of fractional share
Reg. § 1.305-3(c)

Shareholder approved sale plan
Rev. Rul. 69-15, 1969-1 CB 95
Rev. Rul. 69-202, 1967-1 CB 576

Elective dividend taxable
IRC § 305(b)(1)
Reg. § 1.305-2

4.7 DIVIDENDS PAID IN PROPERTY

Dividend in kind
Reg. § 1.61-9(b)
IRC § 301
Reg. § 1.301-1
IRC § 317(a)
Reg. § 1.317-1

Corporate benefits
James B. Munson, 40 TCM 173 (1980)
B. Morgan Heglin Inc., 38 TCM 255 (1979)
Richard F. Tyson, 38 TCM 557 (1979)

4.8 TAXABLE STOCK DIVIDENDS

IRC § 305
House Report No. 91-413 (Part I), p. 113; (Part II), p. 88 (1969)

Note: Paragraph numbers refer to Volume One. Items marked ` are research aids, not citations of authority; see "Key to Citations" on page 806.

Senate Report No. 91-782, p. 152, 153 (1969)
* "Keeping Corporate Distributions of Stock and Stock Rights Nontaxable," Dennis A. Diersen, 40 Taxation for Accountants 202 (Apr. 1988)

Option to redeem stock dividend
Rev. Rul. 76-258, 1976-2 CB 95

Constructive dividends
Roy J. Champayne, 26 TC 634 (1956) (Acq.)
Charles Dreifus Co., 140 F. Supp. 499 (E.D. Pa. 1956)

Dividend reinvestment plan
Rev. Rul. 79-42, 179-1 CB 130
Rev. Rul. 78-375, 1978-2 CB 130
Rev. Rul. 77-749, 1977-1 CB 82
Rev. Rul. 76-33, 1976-1 CB 87

4.9 WHO REPORTS THE DIVIDEND

Dividends on stock sold
Reg. § 1.61-9(c)

4.10 YEAR DIVIDENDS ARE REPORTED

IRC § 451(a)
Reg. § 1.451-1
Reg. § 1.301-1(b)

Dividend payable 12/31
Sewell Lee Avery, 292 U.S. 210 (1934)
George E. Rex, 3 TCM 1260 (1944)
Harkness, 31 BTA 1100 (Acq.)
A. S. Eldridge, 30 BTA 1322, aff'd, 79 F.2d 629 (9th Cir. 1935)

Dividend checks mailed by savings and loan association
Maurice Fox, 218 F.2d 347 (3d Cir. 1955), aff'g 20 TC 1094 (1953) (Acq.)

Reasonable action could get dividend
Frank W. Kunze, 203 F.2d 957 (2d Cir. 1953), aff'g 19 TC 29 (1952)

Dividends received year after year declared
F. H. Mason, 275 U.S. 175 (1927)

Dividend taxed to seller retaining life income rights to stock
Willard S. Heminway, 44 TC 96 (1965) (Acq.)

4.11 DISTRIBUTION NOT OUT OF EARNINGS: RETURN OF CAPITAL

IRC § 301(c)(2) and (3)
IRC § 316(a)

"Dividends" on paid-up life insurance
Reg. § 1.72-11(b)

4.12 REPORTING INTEREST ON YOUR TAX RETURN

*IRS Publication 550

Summary of interest income rules
IRC § 61(a)(4)
Reg. § 1.61-7(a)

Year received
Reg. § 1.446-1(c)(1)(i)

U.S. obligations
IRC § 103

Interest available
Reg. § 1.451-2

Tax sale certificates
Charles H. Wiltsie, 3 F. Supp. 743 (Ct. Cl. 1933), cert. denied, 291 U.S. 664

Open accounts without specific agreement
Kurtz Bros., 42 BTA 561

Usurious interest
Reg. § 1.61-7(a)

Discount on notes
Reg. § 1.61-7(a)
Reg. § 1.61-7(c)

Interest received in form of property
Reg. § 1.61-1

Autos, boats received for long-term deposits
I.R. News Release 1032, April 14, 1970

Coupons from tax-exempt bonds
H. Gates Lloyd, 154 F.2d 643 (3d Cir. 1946), cert. denied, 329 U.S. 717
Rev. Rul. 55-73, 1955-1 CB 236

Note with accrued interest
Missouri State Life Insurance Co., 78 F.2d 778 (8th Cir. 1935)
Pontiac Commercial and Savings Bank, 41 F.2d 602 (6th Cir. 1930)

Wrap-around annuities
Rev. Rul. 80-274, 1980-2 CB 27

Saving certificates, deferred interest plans
Reg. § 1.232
Rev. Rul. 73-220, 1973-1 CB 297

Deferred interest as original issue discount
I.R. News Release 1215, March 13, 1972

Six-month certificates
Prop. Reg. § 1.451-2(a)(2)
Prop. Reg. § 1.232-3(b)
Rev. Rul. 80-157, 1980-1 CB 186

Interest penalty bars constructive receipt on CD of one year or less
Reg. § 1.451-2

Serviceman's interest
Rev. Rul. 67-450, 1967-2 CB 174

Interest on loan arrangement
Rev. Rul. 81-148, 1981-1 CB 207

4.13 INTEREST ON FROZEN ACCOUNTS NOT TAXED

IRC § 451(g)
IRC § 165(1)

4.14 INTEREST INCOME ON DEBTS OWED TO YOU

* "Income Can Be Deferred Without Running the Risk of Constructive Receipt Being Applied," Judith H. Pizzica O'Dell, 39 Taxation for Accountants 398 (Dec. 1987)
* "Lending or Renting to Offspring May Benefit Tax-payers," Ralph Switzer and Kathleen Holloway, 54 Taxation for Accountants 355 (June 1995)

Interest uncollectible
Corn Exchange Bank, 37 F.2d 34 (2d Cir. 1930)
Atlantic Coast Line RR Co., 31 BTA 730 (Acq.), aff'd, 81 F.2d 309 (4th Cir. 1936), cert. denied,

298 U.S. 656

Four restrictions on withdrawal of interest not considered substantial; bonus interest; closing agreements
Reg. § 1.451-2(a)
Rev. Proc. 64-24, 1964-1 CB 693

Agreement with debtor
Annie B. Smith, 12 TCM 131 (1953)
W. H. Hughes, 11 TCM 797 (1952)
Rev. Rul. 63-57, 1963-1 CB 103

Debtor gives new note
George J. Mellinger, 21 F. Supp. 964 (Ct. Cl. 1938)

Interest in advance
Reg. § 1.61-7(a)

Obligations given away
Ida S. Austin, 161 F.2d 666 (6th Cir. 1947), cert. denied, 332 U.S. 767

4.15 REPORTING INTEREST ON BONDS BOUGHT OR SOLD

Redemption
Special Ruling, February 7, 1949

Included in sales price
Reg. § 1.61-7(d)

Included in purchase price
Reg. § 1.61-7(c)

Tax-free covenant bond
IRC § 32(2)

Guarantor pays interest
Rev. Rul. 54-563, 1954-2 CB 50

Accrued interest in reorganization exchange
IRC § 354(a)(2)(B)

Flat price
Reg. § 1.61-7(c)

4.16 FORFEITURE OF INTEREST ON PREMATURE WITHDRAWALS

IRC § 62(a)(9)

Deductible amount on Form 1099-INT
Rev. Rul. 75-20, 1975-1 CB 29
Rev. Rul. 73-511, 1973-2 CB 402, clarified by Rev. Rul. 75-21, 1975-1 CB 367

Forfeited principal
Rev. Rul. 82-27, 1982-1 CB 32

4.17 AMORTIZATION OF BOND PREMIUM

Election
IRC § 171
Reg. § 1.171-1
Reg. § 1.171-3

Premium treated as offset to interest
IRC § 171(e)

Computing amortization
IRC § 171(b)(3)
Rev. Rul. 82-10, 1982-1 CB 46

Elect on return
IRC § 171(c)(2)

---

*Note: Paragraph numbers refer to Volume One. Items marked * are research aids, not citations of authority; see "Key to Citations" on page 806.*

Reg. § 1.171-3(a)

Effect on other bonds
Reg. § 1.171-3(a)

Sale and purchase of similar bonds
Rev. Rul. 55-353, 1955-1 CB 381

Premium amortization reduces OID
IRC § 1272(a)(7)

Straight-line method
Reg. § 1.171-2(f)

Yield-to-maturity method
171(b)(3)

Allocate premium for conversions
Reg. § 1.171-2(c)

4.18 DISCOUNT ON BONDS

IRC § 1271 (retirement or sale of debt instruments)
IRC § 1272 (current income treatment of OID)
IRC § 1273 (what is OID)
IRC § 1281 (short-term debt)

4.19 HOW TO REPORT ORIGINAL ISSUE DISCOUNT (OID) ON YOUR RETURN

*IRS Publication 1212

4.20 REPORTING INCOME ON MARKET DISCOUNT BONDS

IRC § 1276

Partial principal payments
IRC § 1276(a)(3)

Exceptions repealed for short-term bonds and tax-exempt obligations
IRC § 1278(a)(1), repealed by Revenue Reconciliation Act of 1993 §1278(c)

Deferral of interest deduction
IRC § 1277

Deferral of interest does not apply to tax-exempt obligations
IRC §1278(a)(1)(C)

Election to currently report discount
IRC § 1278(b)

4.21 DISCOUNT ON SHORT-TERM OBLIGATIONS

Current inclusion required
IRC § 1281

Tax-exempts excluded from inclusion rule
IRC § 1283(a)(1)(B)

Deferred interest deduction
IRC § 1282

4.22 STRIPPED COUPON BONDS AND STOCK

IRC § 1286
* "Where Has All the Income Gone? The Mysterious Relocation of Interest and Principal in Coupon Stripping and Related Transactions," Bruce Kayle, 7 Va. L. Rev. 303 (Fall 1987)

OID treatment for stripped preferred stock

IRC § 305(e), added by the Revenue Reconciliation Act of 1993
*IRS Publication 1212

4.23 SALE OR RETIREMENT OF BONDS AND NOTES

IRC § 1271
IRC § 1272
*IRS Publication 550

Registered form
IRC § 1287

Retirement defined
Donald S. McClain, 311 U.S. 527 (1941)

Unearned original issue discount is capital gain
Ted Bolnick, 44 TC 245 (1965) (Acq.)

4.24 STATE AND CITY INTEREST GENERALLY TAX EXEMPT

State, city obligations
IRC § 103(a)
Reg. § 1.103-1
Rhode Island Hospital Trust Co., 8 BTA 555, vacated and remanded, 29 F.2d 339 (1st Cir. 1929)

Agreement of purchase and sale
Newlin Machinery Corp., 28 TC 837 (1957) (Acq.)

Sale of municipal certificates of indebtedness to municipality
Palm Beach Trust Co., 9 TC 1060 (1947), aff'd per curiam, 174 F.2d 527 (D.C. Cir. 1949), cert. denied, 338 U.S. 825

Qualified private activity bonds not taxed
IRC § 141(e)

4.25 TAXABLE STATE AND CITY INTEREST

IRC § 103(e)

Qualified private activity bonds not taxed
IRC § 141(e)

Community open account purchases
Kurtz Bros., 42 BTA 561

Volunteer fire companies
Seagrave Corp., 38 TC 247 (1962)

Tax sale certificates
Charles H. Wiltsie, 3 F. Supp. 743 (Ct. Cl. 1933), cert. denied, 291 U.S. 664

Municipal bond in open market
Rev. Rul. 57-49, 1957-1 CB 62
Rev. Rul. 60-210, 1960-1 CB 38, modified by Rev. Rul. 60-376, 1960-2 CB 38

4.26 TAX-EXEMPT BONDS BOUGHT AT A DISCOUNT

IRC § 1288

Bond bought at discount
Rev. Rul. 73-112, 1973-1 CB 47
Rev. Rul. 57-49, 1957-1 CB 62
Rev. Rul. 60-210, 1960-1 CB 38

Redeemed old bond at premium
Rev. Rul. 72-587, 1972-2 CB 74

District Bond Co., 1 TC 837 (1943)

Redemption of bonds issued after June 8, 1980
Rev. Rul. 80-143, 1980-1 CB 89, modifying Rev. Rul. 72-587, 1972-2 CB 74

Market discount rules do not apply to tax-exempt bonds
IRC § 1278

Stripped tax-exempt obligations
IRC § 1286(d)

4.27 TREASURY BILLS, NOTES, AND BONDS

Taxable interest
Reg. § 1.61-7

Taxed at maturity
IRC § 454(b)

Acquisition discount currently taxed to accrual-basis taxpayers and dealers
IRC § 1281

Gain on sale of short-term obligations
IRC § 1271(a)(3)
Prop. Reg. § 1.1271-3

Interest deductions limitation
IRC § 1281
IRC § 1282

4.28 INTEREST ON U.S. SAVINGS BONDS

Annual increase in value
IRC § 454
Reg. § 1.454-1
Rev. Rul. 48-25, 1948-2 CB 12

Election to report interest annually on timely return
Rev. Rul. 55-655, 1955-2 CB 253

Change in taxpayer's reporting method
Rev. Proc. 89-46, 1989-2 CB 597

H bond exchange
Announcement, November 19, 1959

4.29 DEFERRING U.S. SAVINGS BOND INTEREST

Changing from annual reporting to deferral
Rev. Proc. 89-46, 1989-2 CB 597

Postpone tax during extended maturity period
IRC § 454(c)
Reg. § 1.454-1

Change form of registration of E Bond
IRC § 454(c)
Reg. § 1.454-1
Rev. Rul. 55-278, 1955-1 CB 471
Rev. Rul. 54-327, 1954-2 CB 50

Correction of error in registration
Rev. Rul. 70-428, 1970-2 CB 5

Co-owners
Rev. Rul. 54-143, 1954-1 CB 12
Rev. Rul. 55-278, 1955-1 CB 471
Rev. Rul. 58-435, 1958-2 CB 370, distinguished by Rev. Rul. 68-145, 1968-1 CB 203

---

*Note: Paragraph numbers refer to Volume One. Items marked * are research aids, not citations of authority; see "Key to Citations" on page 806.*

Death of owner
Rev. Rul. 64-104, 1964-1 CB 223, distinguished by Rev. Rul. 68-145, 1968-1 CB 203

Transfer to charity
* Letter Ruling 8010082

Bonds transferred by gift without reissue
Edward G. Chandler, 410 U.S. 257 (1973), rev'g 460 F.2d 1281 (9th Cir. 1972)
Mae Elliott Est., 57 TC 152 (1971), aff'd per curiam, 474 F.2d 1008 (5th Cir. 1973)
Lyla C. Curry Est., 409 F.2d 671 (6th Cir. 1969)
Alice H. Silverman, 259 F.2d 731 (3d Cir. 1958)
Helen K. Chambless, 1970 WL 319 (DCSC) (1970)

Election on decedent's return
Rev. Rul. 68-145, 1968-1 CB 203

4.30 MINIMUM INTEREST RULES
IRC § 7872 (loans)
IRC § 1274 and § 483 (seller financing)

4.31 INTEREST-FREE OR BELOW-MARKET-INTEREST LOANS
IRC § 7872
Prop. Reg. § 1.7872-1 through § 1.7872-14
* "Interest-Free Loans Can Still Be Used for Tax Planning," David S. Rhine, The Practical Accountant, March 1987

$10,000 gift loan exception
IRC § 7872 (c)(2)
Prop. Reg. § 1.7872-8(b)

$100,000 gift loan exception
IRC § 7872(d)
Prop. Reg. § 1.7872-8(c)

Loan to Continuing Care Facility
IRC § 7872(g)
Rev. Rul. 98-59, 1998-52 IRB

4.32 MINIMUM INTEREST ON SELLER-FINANCED SALES
IRC § 1274
IRC § 1275
IRC § 483
Prop. Reg. § 1.1274-1 through § 1.1274.7
Prop. Reg. § 1.483-1 through § 1.483-5
* IRS Publication 537
* "Taxpayer Bill of Rights 2 Offers Added Protection," Gerald A. Kafda, 57 Taxation for Accountants 196 (Oct. 1996)
* "Taxpayer Bill of Rights 2," Patricia Nodoushani and Aurelle S. Locke, 74 Taxes 535 (Sept. 1996)
* "Using the Imputed Interest Safe Harbor for Intrafamily Installment Sales," Andrew R. Henderson, 74 Journal of Taxation 100 (Feb. 1991)
* "Planning Real Estate Transactions Under the OID Rules," James W. Banks and Joseph F. Tyrell, The Practical Accountant (March 1987)

General rate required
IRC § 1274A

Definitions and special rules
IRC § 1275

Minimum interest not applicable to buyer of personal-use property
IRC § 1275(b)

6% rate for land sales between related parties
IRC § 483(e)

9% safe harbor
IRC § 1274A(b)
Prop. Reg. § 1.274A-1

Inflation adjustment to seller-financed amount for safe harbor
IRC § 1274A(d)(2)
Rev. Rul. 98-59, 1998-52 IRB

Which AFR rate applies to sales
Prop. Reg. § 1.1274-6(e)
Prop. Reg. § 1.483-4(d)

Timing of reporting under § 483
Reg. § 1.483-2(a)(ii)

Cash method election
IRC § 1274A(C)
Rev. Rul. 98+58, 1998-52 IRB (inflation adjustment for 1999 sales)

5 REPORTING PROPERTY SALES

5.1 TAX PATTERN OF PROPERTY SALES
*IRS Publication 544

5.2 HOW PROPERTY SALES ARE CLASSIFIED AND TAXED
IRC § 1(h) as amended by 1998 Act
IRC § 1221
IRC § 1222
*IRS Publication 544

5.3 CAPITAL GAIN RATES AND HOLDING PERIODS
IRC § 1(h) as amended by 1998 Act
IRC § 1222 (long-term, short-term defined)
IRC § 1223 (holding period)

5.4 CAPITAL LOSSES AND CARRYOVERS
IRC § 1211
IRC § 1212
IRC § 1222(10)
Reg. § 1.1222-1

Carryover loss if taxable income is negative
IRC §1212(b)(2)(B)

Loss must be considered even if no tax benefit is realized
Rev. Rul. 76-177, 1976-1 CB 224

Not deductible as a business expense
Frank Lester, 70 TMC 77 (1995)

5.5 CAPITAL LOSSES OF MARRIED COUPLES

One capital loss deduction on joint return
John E. Ross, 37 TC 445 (1961)
Reg. § 1.1211-1(d)
Reg. § 1.1211-1(c)

Surviving spouse may not use deceased spouse's loss carryover
* Letter Ruling 8510053

5.6 LOSSES MAY BE DISALLOWED ON SALES TO RELATED PERSONS
* "Related-Party Sales Can Produce Unexpected Tax Results," Monica Brown Gianni, 59 Taxation for Accountants 23 (July 1997)

Nondeductible losses
IRC § 267
Reg. § 1.267(a)-1(a)

Bona fide
Reg. § 1.267(a)-1(c)
Nathan Blum, 5 TC 702 (1945)

Stock exchange
John P. McWilliams, 331 U.S. 694 (1947)
John B. Shethar, 28 TC 1222 (1957)

Foreclose mortgage
Thomas Zacek, 8 TC 1056 (1947)

Pledgee's sale
Charles E. Cooney, 1 TCM 55 (1942)

Members of family
IRC § 267(b)(1) and (c)(4)
Reg. § 1.267(c)-1(a)(4)

Nominee
Charles J. Stamler, 45 BTA 37
O. Phil Nordling, 166 F.2d 703 (9th Cir. 1948), cert. denied, 337 U.S. 938

Wife's relative
J. Henry DeBoer, 194 F.2d 989 (2d Cir. 1952), (Nonacq.)

Son-in-law
Fervel Topek, 9 TC 763 (1947)
* Letter Ruling 9017008

Family hostility may not be considered
David L. Miller, 75 TC 182 (1980)

Withdrawal from joint ventures and partnerships
T. N. Mauritz, 205 F.2d 135 (5th Cir. 1953)
Fritz Busche, 229 F.2d 437 (5th Cir. 1956)
Henry V. B. Smith, 5 TC 323 (1945)

Controlled corporation
IRC § 267
Reg. § 1.267(b)-1
Reg. § 1.267(c)-1

Other losses disallowed
IRC § 267
Reg. § 1.267(b)-1

Partnership and controlling persons
IRC § 707(b)(1)(A)

Related party's profitable resale
IRC § 267(d)

5.7 DEFERRING OR EXCLUDING GAIN ON SMALL BUSINESS STOCK INVESTMENT
IRC § 1045 (rollover of gain from small business stock, added by 1997 Act)
IRC § 1202 (exclusion of gain)

*Note: Paragraph numbers refer to Volume One. Items marked * are research aids, not citations of authority; see "Key to Citations" on page 806.*

5.8 SAMPLE ENTRIES OF CAPITAL ASSET SALES

*IRS Publication 544

Reporting capital gains and losses
IRC § 1(h)
IRC § 1222
* IRS Publication 544

Short-term and long-term transactions
IRC § 1222

Capital losses
IRC § 1211(b) and 1212(b)
IRC § 62(a)(3)

5.9 COUNTING THE MONTHS IN YOUR HOLDING PERIOD

Long- and short-term capital gain or loss
IRC § 1222
IRC § 1223
Reg. § 1.1222-1
Reg. § 1.1223-1(a)

Exclude day asset acquired
Lewis Caspe, 694 F.2d 1116 (8th Cir. 1982), aff'g 80-1 USTC ¶9201 (D.C. IA. 1980)

Holding period rules
IRC § 1222

Futures transactions
IRC § 1222

5.10 HOLDING PERIOD FOR SECURITIES

Stock exchange transactions
Rev. Rul. 72-381, 1972-2 CB 233
Rev. Rul. 70-598, 1970-2 CB 168

Installment sale not allowed for publicly traded stock
IRC § 453(k)(2)

Stock subscriptions
Mayme C. Sommers, Admtrx., 63 F.2d 551 (10th Cir. 1933)
William J. Wineberg, 20 TCM 1715 (1961), aff'd, 326 F.2d 157 (9th Cir. 1964)

Stock dividends, exercise of rights
IRC § 1223(5)(6)
Reg. § 1.1223-1(f)
Rev. Rul. 56-572, 1956-2, CB 182

Different lots
Reg. § 1.1223-1(i)

Employee option stock
John H. Rolfe, 58 TC 361 (1972), aff'd per curiam, 488 F.2d 1092 (9th Cir. 1974)

Commodity satisfaction of futures contract
IRC § 1223(8)
Reg. § 1.1223-1(h)

"When issued" transactions
I.T. 3721, 1945 CB 164, as modified by Rev. Rul. 57-29, 1957-1 CB 519

"Wash sales"
IRC § 1223(4)
Reg. § 1.1223-1(d)

5.11 HOLDING PERIOD FOR REAL ESTATE

Rev. Rul. 54-607, 1954-2 CB 177

New construction
M. A. Paul, 206 F.2d 763 (3d Cir. 1953)
Fred Draper, 32 TC 545 (1959) (Acq.)

Portion of building constructed within long-term holding period
Rev. Rul. 75-524, 1975-2 CB 342

5.12 HOLDING PERIOD FOR GIFTS, INHERITANCES, AND OTHER PROPERTY

Gift after 1920
IRC § 1223(2)
Reg. § 1.1223-1(b)

Donee's sale at loss
Rev. Rul. 59-86, 1959-1 CB 209

Property acquired from decedent sold within one year
IRC § 1223(11)

Bequest created by will
E. Franklin Brewster, 280 U.S. 327 (1930)

Property purchased by executors
Marjorie K. Campbell, 313 U.S. 15 (1941)
Richard Van Nest Gambrill, 313 U.S. 11 (1941)

Contribution to partnership
Gordon S. Hogg, 214 F.2d 640 (5th Cir. 1954)
Rev. Rul. 55-39, 1955-1 CB 403

Distribution in kind from partnership
IRC § 735(b)
Reg. § 1.735-1

Involuntary conversion
IRC § 1223(1)(A)
Reg. § 1.1223-1(a)

5.13 CALCULATING GAIN OR LOSS

Gain or loss
IRC § 1001
Reg. § 1.1001-1 (amount realized)

5.14 AMOUNT REALIZED IS THE TOTAL SELLING PRICE

* "'Money' and 'Property' (Other Than Money): An Exploration of 'Amount Realized' Under Section 1001(b)," George W. Craven, 70 Taxes 912 (December 1992)

Selling price
Reg. § 1.1001
IRC § 1001

Mortgage included in price
Beulah B. Crane, 331 U.S. 1 (1947)

Property valued at less than mortgage
John F. Tufts, 456 U.S. 960 (1983)

Reduce price by expenses
Seleths O. Thompson, 9 BTA 1342 (Acq.)
Samuel C. Chapin, 12 TC 235 (1949), aff'd, 180 F.2d 140 (8th Cir. 1950)

Legal fee—cost of sale

Fred W. Gunn, 49 TC 38 (1967)

5.15 FINDING YOUR COST

Unadjusted basis
IRC § 1012
Reg. § 1.1012-1

Improvements
IRC § 1016
Reg. § 1.016-2

Adjusted basis
IRC § 1011
Reg. § 1.1011-1

Improvements not covered by note
Glenda P. McCormick, 99-1 USTC ¶50,380

5.16 UNADJUSTED BASIS OF YOUR PROPERTY

* IRS Publication 551

Basis is cash cost
IRC § 1012
Reg. § 1.1012-1

Adjusted cost after depreciation allowed
IRC § 1016
Reg. § 1.1016-3

Rendering services
Reg. § 1.61-2
W. H. Weaver, 25 TC 1067 (1956)
Lawrence S. Vadner, 14 TCM 866 (1955)

Taxable exchange of property
Philadelphia Park Amusement Co., 126 F. Supp. 184 (Ct. Cl. 1954)
Rev. Rul. 56-100, 1956-1 CB 624

Tax-free exchange of property
IRC § 1031
Reg. § 1.1031(d)-1

Basis of new residence after home sale deferral
IRC § 1034(e)
Reg. § 1.1034-1

Life estate or remainder interest
Reg. § 1.1014-5

Sale of life estate—zero basis
IRC § 1001(e)

Property subject to lease
Harriet M. Bryant Trust, 11 TC 374 (1948) (Acq.)

Property subject to mortgage
Beulah B. Crane, 331 U.S. 1 (1947)

Distribution to settle claim
Rev. Rul. 55-117, 1955-1 CB 233

Compulsory or involuntary conversion
IRC § 1033(b)

Prenuptial agreement
Doris Farid-es-Sultaneh, 160 F.2d 812 (2d Cir. 1947), rev'g 6 TC 652 (1946)

Property purchased prior to March 1, 1913
IRC § 1053
Reg. § 1.1053-1

Distribution on orders of SEC
IRC § 1081

---

*Note: Paragraph numbers refer to Volume One. Items marked * are research aids, not citations of authority; see "Key to Citations" on page 806.*

Reg. § 1.1081

Dividends in property
IRC § 301
Reg. § 1.301-1

5.17 BASIS OF PROPERTY YOU INHERITED OR RECEIVED AS A GIFT

* "Basis of Inherited Property Is Not Always Date of Death Value," William M. Dougherty, 48 Taxation for Accountants 17 (January 1992)
* "Can Nonrecourse Debt in Excess of FMV Be Included in the Basis of Inherited Realty?" Sally M. Jones, 82 The Journal of Taxation 220 (April 1995)

Foreign property
Rev. Rul. 84-139, 1984-2 CB 168

Gift after December 31, 1920
IRC § 1015
Reg. § 1.1015-1

Gift tax paid increases basis
IRC § 1015(d)(6)

Gift in trust before January 1, 1921
IRC § 1015(c)
Reg. § 1.1015-3

Inheritance from decedent
IRC § 1014
Reg. § 1.1014-1
Reg. § 1.1014-2

Inheritance of property transferred to decedent within one year of death
IRC § 1014(e)

Estate tax value questioned
Sam F. McIntosh, 26 TCM 1164 (1967)

Right to buy deceased's property
J. Gordon Mack, 3 TC 390 (1944), aff'd 148 F.2d 62 (3d Cir. 1945), cert. denied, 326 U.S. 719

Distributions from trust
IRC § 1015
Reg. § 1.1015-2
IRC § 643(e)

Distribution from trust before June 2, 1984
Reg. § 1.661(a)-2(f)

5.18 JOINT TENANCY BASIS RULES FOR SURVIVING TENANTS

IRC § 1014
Reg. § 1.1014-2
IRC § 2040(b)
* IRS Publication 551
* "Allocating Basis for Jointly-Owned Property Still Presents Unresolved Questions," P. Harris, 58 Journal of Taxation 234 (1983)

Spousal joint tenancies created before 1977
M. Lee Gallenstein, 975 F.2d 286 (6th Cir. 1992)
Joy B. Patten, 116 F.3d 1029 (4th Cir. 1997)
Therese Hahn, 110 TC No. 14 (1998)

5.19 ALLOCATING COSTS AMONG SEVERAL ASSETS

Apportionment of cost
Frederick Leake, 140 F.2d 451 (6th Cir. 1944), cert. denied, 323 U.S. 722
Nathan Blum, 5 TC 702 (1945)
Johnson Lumber Corp., 12 TC 348 (1949) (Acq.)
Fairfield Plaza, Inc., 39 TC 706 (1963) (Acq.)

Apportion land
McDonald, BTA Memo, P-H 41,409
Harlan E. McGregor, 14 TCM 897 (1955)

Sale of stock first bought
Reg. § 1.1012-1(c)
A. F. Mack, 31 BTA 1149

5.20 HOW TO FIND ADJUSTED BASIS

Improvements and betterments to property
IRC § 1016
Reg. § 1.1016-2
Edgar S. Appleby Est., 123 F.2d 700 (2d Cir. 1941)

Commissions on security sales
Adolph B. Spreckles, 315 U.S. 626 (1942)

Carrying charges
IRC § 1016
Reg. § 1.1016-2

Personal residence
Isaiah Megibow, 218 F.2d 687 (3d Cir. 1955)

Purchaser's share of real estate tax
IRC § 164(d)
Reg. § 1.164-6

Unharvested crops
IRC § 1016(a)(11)
Reg. § 1.1016-5(g)

Demolition cost
Reg. § 1.165-3
Edgar S. Appleby Est., 123 F.2d 700 (2d Cir. 1941)

Deduction from basis
IRC § 1016
Reg. § 1.1016-1 through 8

Return of capital
IRC § 1010(a)(4)
Reg. § 1.1016-5(a)(1-2)

Casualty loss
IRC § 1016(a)(1)
Pasquale Colabella, 17 TCM 704 (1958)

Depletion allowances
IRC § 1016(a)(2)
Reg. § 1.1016-3 and 4

Depreciation, amortization, obsolescence
IRC § 1016(a)(2)
Reg. § 1.1016-3 and 4
Rev. Proc. 97-37, 1997-33 IRB 18 (adjustment for unclaimed depreciation in a closed year)

5.21 TAX ADVANTAGE OF INSTALLMENT SALES

IRC § 453
* IRS Publication 537

Not applicable to year-end sale of securities

IRC § 453(k)(2)

Timeshares and residential lots
IRC § 453(1)(2) and (1)(3)

Not applicable to sale of inventory
Andrew A. Monaghan, 40 TC 680 (1963) (Acq.)
IRC § 453(6)(2)(B)
Crispo Gallery Inc., 2nd Cir. (6/13/96)

Not applicable to building contractor
Rev. Rul. 73-438, 1973-2 CB 156

Farmer who does not inventory
Temp. Reg. § 15A.453-1(b)(4)

Depreciation recapture
IRC § 453(i)

Dealers
IRC § 453(b)(2)

5.22 FIGURING THE TAXABLE PART OF INSTALLMENT PAYMENTS

Selling price
Temp. Reg. § 15A.453-1(b)(2)(ii)

Contract price
Temp. Reg. § 15A.453-1(b)(2)(iii)

Payments received
Temp. Reg. § 15A.453-1(b)(3)

Gross profit
Temp. Reg. § 15A.453-1(b)(2)(v)

Wrap-around mortgages
Temp. Reg. § 15A.453-1(b)(3)(ii)

Tax Court rejects IRS wrap-around regs.
Professional Equities, Inc., 89 TC 165 (1987) (Acq.)

Pledges of installment obligations
IRC § 453A(d)

5.23 ELECTING NOT TO REPORT ON THE INSTALLMENT METHOD

IRC § 453(d)
Reg. § 15A.453-1(d)

Late election out barred for change in capital gain law
Rev. Rul. 90-46, 90-1 CB 107

Switch to installment method denied after n.o.l. reduced
* Letter ruling 8338004

Inadvertent election out not revocable
* Letter Ruling 8501014

Switch to installment method allowed after accountant's mistake
* Letter Ruling 8943039
* Letter Ruling 9141013

5.24 RESTRICTION ON INSTALLMENT SALES TO RELATIVES

IRC § 453(e) and (g)

Two-year cutoff for property other than marketable securities
IRC § 453

Note: Paragraph numbers refer to Volume One. Items marked * *are research aids, not citations of authority; see "Key to Citations" on page 806.*

Note: Paragraph numbers refer to Volume One. Items marked ` are research aids, not citations of authority; see "Key to Citations" on page 806.

438 (2d Cir. 1954)

Usurious loan
William K. Harriman, 26 TCM 941 (1967)

Usurious loan as a business loss
Herbert E. Tharp, 31 TCM 22 (1972)

Debtor-creditor relationship
Kentucky Rock Asphalt Co., 108 F.2d 779 (6th Cir. 1940)
W. M. Robertson, 7 TCM 62 (1948)

Loan included in income
IRC § 166
Reg. § 1.166-1

Consulting engineer
Jack Shapiro, 20 TCM 579 (1961)

Worthless during year
IRC § 166
Reg. § 1.166-1

Bankruptcy by court order
Reg. § 1.166-2(c)

Final liquidation dividend
Leedom & Worrall Co., 10 BTA 825
First National Bank of Los Angeles, 6 BTA 850 (Acq.)

Corporation liquidation resolution
Pantex Oil Corp., 8 TCM 1079 (1949)

Disappearance of debtor
Fridolin Pabst, 36 F.2d 614 (D.C. Cir. 1930)

Debtor's refusal to pay
Philip C. Hughes, 10 TCM 204 (1951)

Revocation of corporate charter
Leila S. Kirby, 35 BTA 578 (Acq. and nonacq.), aff'd in part, rev'd in part, 102 F.2d 115 (5th Cir. 1939)

Cancelled debt
Nathan Fink, 29 TC 1119 (1958) (Acq.)

No hope of later value
American Trust Co., 31 F.2d 47 (9th Cir. 1939), aff'g 10 BTA 490
Alemite Die Casting & Manufacturing Co., 1 BTA 548

Debt worthless before due
Clarence Bonynge, 117 F.2d 157 (2d Cir. 1941)

Statute of limitations has run
Ralph H. Cross, 54 F.2d 781 (9th Cir. 1932)
Leo Stein, 4 BTA 1016

Statute ran before death
Clara Burdette, 69 F.2d 410 (9th Cir. 1934)

Debt guaranteed by collateral
John Hubble, 42 TCM 1537 (1981)

Release an endorser
Reg. § 1.166-8
Eleanor A. Bradford, 22 TC 1057 (1954), rev'd, 233 F.2d 935 (6th Cir. 1956)

Breach of contract
Zelma T. Kyle, 242 F.2d 825 (2d Cir. 1957)

Less than full payment

Edgar H. Gleason, Jr., 62 TCM 600 (1991)

Embezzled funds
Reg. § 1.165-8

5.35 LOANS BY STOCKHOLDERS

Business motive must dominate
E. Generes, 405 U.S. 93 (1972)

Loan by shareholder-employees to protect job
Edna Generes, 405 U.S. 93 (1972), rev'g 427 F.2d 279 (5th Cir. 1970)
Harry Litwin, 983 F.2d 997 (10th Cir. 1993)
Donald C. Niblock, Jr., 417 F.2d 1185 (7th Cir. 1969)
James O. Gould, 64 TC 132 (1975)
Odee Smith, 55 TC 260 (1970), vacated and rem'd per curiam, 457 F.2d 797 (5th Cir. 1972), on rem'd 60 TC 316 (1973) (Acq.)
Lawrence J. Doerfler, 36 TCM 789 (1977)
William G. Young, 33 TCM 397 (1974)

Loans to corporations
Kadlec, 71 TCM 2399 (1996) (closely held corporation)
Donald C. Van Pelt, 191 F.2d 861 (6th Cir. 1951)
Janet McBride, 23 TC 926 (1955) (Acq.)
Weldon D. Smith, 17 TC 135 (1951), rev'd, 203 F.2d 310 (2d Cir. 1953), cert. denied, 346 U.S. 816
Sam Schaltzer, 13 TC 43 (1949) (Acq.), aff'd per curiam, 183 F.2d 70 (9th Cir. 1950), cert. denied, 340 U.S. 911
Rev. Rul. 60-48, 1960-1 CB 112

Unpaid stockholder loans to corporation
A. J. Whipple, 373 U.S. 193 (1963)

Stockholder loan to key employee deductible
Charles W. Carter, 39 TCM 456 (1979)

5.36 FAMILY BAD DEBTS

Reg. § 1.166-1
Griffin Andrew, 54 TC 239 (1970) (Acq.)
Ben Perlmutter, 373 F.2d 45 (10th Cir. 1967)

Debt due from friend
Robert H. Montgomery, 23 F. Supp. 130 (Ct. Cl. 1938), cert. denied, 307 U.S. 632
Charles J. Matthews, 8 TC 1313 (1947)

Defaulted support payment
Carolyn Perry, 92 TC 470 (1989) (reaffirms Swenson)
Dale Swenson, 43 TC 897 (1965)
Shirley S. Imeson, 487 F.2d 319 (9th Cir. 1973), aff'g per curiam 28 TCM 899 (1969), cert. denied, 418 U.S. 917
Rev. Rul. 93-27, 1993 CB 32 (IRS rejects Ninth Circuit's possible deduction arguments)
M. J. Williford, 34 TCM 354 (1975)

Loans to family
Loy Bowman, 69 TCM 286 (1995)
Myer B. Barr, 77 TCM 1370 (1999)

6 TAX-FREE EXCHANGES OF PROPERTY

6.1 TRADES OF LIKE-KIND PROPERTY

IRC § 1031
* "The 'State of the Art' in Like-Kind Exchanges," Richard M. Lipton, 91 Journal of Taxation 78 (August 1999)
* "Effect of the Taxpayer Relief Act of 1997 on Code Sec. 1031 Tax-Deferred Exchanges," Michael J. Novogradac, 76 Taxes 23 (June 1998)
* "Deferred Like-Kind Exchanges in 20 Easy Steps," Michael J. Nathanson, 57 Taxation for Accountants 31 (July 1996)

Exchange solely for like-kind property
IRC § 1031(a)
Reg. § 1.1031(a)-1
Wittig, 70 TCM 824 (withdrawn 11/9/95)

Farms exchanged
Rev. Rul. 59-229, 1959-2 CB 180

Farm for city property
L. M. Dyke, 1 BTA Memo 32-157
E. R. Braley, 14 BTA 1153 (Acq.)

Land for water rights
Rev. Rul. 55-749, 1955-2 CB 295, distinguished by Rev. Rul. 67-255, 1967-2 CB 270

Exchange of partnership interests
IRC § 1031(a)(2)(D)
Rollin E. Meyers, Sr., Est., 503 F.2d 556 (9th Cir. 1974), aff'g per curiam, 58 TC 311 (1972) (Nonacq.)
Reg. § 1.1031(a)-1(a) and (e)

U.S. and foreign real estate not "like kind"
IRC § 1031(h)

Tax-free oil lease for ranch
Rev. Rul. 68-331, 1968-1 CB 352

Exchange of ownership interest in realty for 30 year leasehold
Reg. § 1.1031(a)-1(c)
Rev. Rul. 78-72, 1978-1 CB 258

Taxable oil lease for ranch
William Fleming, 356 U.S. 260 (1958), rev'g 241 F.2d 78 (5th Cir. 1957)

Timber rights
Oregon Lumber Co., 20 TC 192 (1953) (Acq.)

Exchange of cattle of different sexes
IRC § 1031(e)

Must be used in trade or business or for investment
IRC § 1031(a)
Reg. § 1.1031(a)-1

Depreciable equipment on which there is potential gain
IRC § 1245(b)(3)

Exception—residence for other residence
IRC § 1034
Reg. § 1.1034-1
Ethel Black, 35 TC 90 (1960)

Personal property used predominately in the U.S.
IRC § 1031 (h)(i), as amended by the 1997 Act

Joint tenancy and tenancy in common
Rev. Rul. 46-437, 1956-2 CB 507

---

*Note: Paragraph numbers refer to Volume One. Items marked * are research aids, not citations of authority; see "Key to Citations" on page 806.*

Citations of Authority

Other exchanges
IRC § 1002
Reg. § 1.1002-1

6.2 PERSONAL PROPERTY HELD FOR BUSINESS OR INVESTMENT

*"Like-Kind Exchanges of Personal Property — A Practical Tour Through Uncharted Territory," Jeffrey K. Eisen, Burton A. Mitchell, and Stephen D. Katzman, 72 Taxes 72 (February 1994)
*"New Personal Property and Multi-Asset Exchange Regulations," Howard J. Levine, 73 Journal of Taxation 16 (July 1990)

Like-class test for depreciable personal business property
Reg. § 1.1031(a)-2
Rev. Proc. 87-56, 1987-2 CB 674

Multiple property exchanges
Reg. § 1.1031(j)-1

6.3 RECEIPT OF CASH AND OTHER PROPERTY—"BOOT"

* "Many Transaction Costs Can Reduce Boot in Like-Kind Exchanges," Craig W. Murel and Richard L. Panich, 74 Journal of Taxation 320 (May 1991)

Boot is taxed
IRC § 1031(b)
Reg. § 1.1031(b)-1

No loss recognized if boot given
IRC § 1031(c) and (d)
Reg. § 1.1031(c)-1 and (d)-1

Mortgage release is boot
Reg. § 1031(d)-2
Beulah B. Crane, 331 U.S. 1 (1947)
Wittig, 70 TCM 824 (withdrawn 11/9/95)

Basis of property received
Reg. § 1.1031(d)-2

6.4 TIME LIMITS FOR DEFERRED EXCHANGES

* "Deferred Swaps Can Be a Problem for Client and Advisor," Kneave Riggall, 52 Taxation for Accountants 268 (May 1994)
* "Deferred Exchanges Easier to Set Up Under Final Regs.," Richard M. Lipton, 47 Taxation for Accountants 76 (Aug. 1991)
* "Deferred Exchange Regulations," Terence Floyd Cuff, 69 Taxes 451 (August 1991)

Time limits
IRC § 1031(a)(3)
Reg. § 1.1031(k)-1(b)

Identifying replacement property
Reg. § 1.1031(k)-1(c) and (d)

Safe harbors for security arrangements
Reg. § 1.1031(k)-1(g)

Direct deed transfer
Rev. Rul. 90-34, 1990-1 CB 154

6.5 EXCHANGES BETWEEN RELATED PARTIES

IRC § 1031(f)

* "Like-Kind Exchanges and Related Parties Under New Section 1031(f)," James A. Fellows and Michael A. Yuhas, 68 Taxes 352 (May 1990)

Two-year freeze on exchange with related party
IRC § 1031(f)

Prearranged plans
IRC § 1031(f)(4)

6.6 PROPERTY TRANSFERS BETWEEN SPOUSES AND EX-SPOUSES

IRC § 1041
Temp. Reg. § 1.041-IT
"Interest paid to an ex-spouse incident to divorce — yes, it can be deductible," Richard P. Algeo, 89 Journal of Taxation 310 (November 1998)
* "Form, Substance, and Section 1041," Deborah A. Geier, 60 Tax Notes 519 (July 26, 1993)
* "Not All Transfers of Marital Property in a Divorce Are Tax-Free," Robert S. Mintz, 51 Taxation for Accountants 4 (July 1993)
* "Marital Dissolution Can Significantly Affect Tax Situation of the Parties," Brian R. Greenstein and Linda Johnson, 48 Taxation for Accountants 286 (May 1992)
* "Internal Revenue Code Section 1041 Is Anything But Model Tax Reform Legislation," Katherine D. Podris and Gary J. Podris, 69 Taxes 438 (July 1991)

Nonresident spouses
IRC § 1041(a)

Divorce-related stock redemption is tax free
Joann C. Arnes, 981 F.2d 456 (9th Cir. 1993)
John A. Arnes, 102 TC 20 (1994)

Divorce-related stock redemption is taxable
Gloria T. Blatt, 102 TC 5 (1994)
* Letter Ruling 9427009

Divorced wife taxed on sale of business
Vincent Yonadi, 21 F.3d 1292 (1994)

Tax-free transfer for relinquishment of community property right to retirement pay
Hazel E. Balding, 98 TC 368 (1992)

Transfer of Savings Bonds
Rev. Rul. 87-112, 1987-2 CB 207

Gain realized on transfer in trust
IRC § 1041(e)
Temp. Reg. § 1.1041-1T

Cash paid for house transfer in property settlement
Michael J. Godlewski, 90 TC 200 (1988)

6.7 TAX-FREE EXCHANGES OF STOCK

Tax-free exchange of stock for stock in same company
IRC § 1036
Reg. § 1.1036-1

Recapitalization is a type of reorganization
IRC § 368(a)(1)(E)
Reg. § 1.368-2(e)

Stock dividends and stock rights
IRC § 305(a)

6.8 JOINT OWNERSHIP INTERESTS

Exchange of tenants in common
Rev. Rul. 73-476, 1973-2 CB 300

Joint tenancy and tenancy in common
Rev. Rul. 56-437, 1956-2 CB 507
Boot not offset by assumption of liability
Rev. Rul. 79-44, 1979-1 CB 265

6.9 SETTING UP CLOSELY HELD CORPORATIONS

IRC § 351

Securities as boot
IRC § 351(a) as amended by 1989 Revenue Reconciliation Act

6.10 EXCHANGES OF COINS AND BULLION

IRC § 1031

Mexican pesos for Austrian coronas
Rev. Rul. 76-214, 1976-1 CB 218

Silver bullion for gold bullion not tax free
Rev. Rul. 82-166, 1982-2 CB 190

U.S. gold coins for S. African Krugerrands
Rev. Rul. 79-413, 1979-2 CB 309

Swiss francs for U.S. double eagle coins not like-kind exchange
California Fed. Life Ins. Co., 76 TC 107 (1981), aff'd, 680 F.2d 85 (9th Cir. 1982)

6.11 TAX-FREE EXCHANGES OF INSURANCE POLICIES

* "Un-Needed Endowment, Annuity, or Life Insurance Policies May Be Exchanged Tax Free," Paul J. Streer, 8 Taxation for Lawyers 222 (1980)

Tax-free exchanges
IRC § 1035
Reg. § 1.1035-1

Tax-free exchange of key executive policy
Rev. Rul. 90-109, 1990-2 CB 191

Tax-free exchange of policy from financially troubled insurer
Rev. Proc. 92-44,1992-1 CB 875, amplified by Rev. Proc. 92-44A

Partial tax-free exchange of annuity contracts
Dona Conway, 111 TC No. 20 (1998)

7 RETIREMENT AND ANNUITY INCOME

7.1 RETIREMENT DISTRIBUTIONS ON FORM 1099-R

*IRS Publication 575
*"Planning for Qualified Plan and IRA Distributions," Seymour Goldberg, 74 Taxes 111 (February 1996)
*"Retirees' Pensions Insulated from State Income Tax," Terry L. Lantry, 57 Taxation for Accountants 132 (September 1996)
*"Tax Planning for Optimum Benefits in Choosing the Form of Pension Income," Dennis R. Lassila and Bob G. Kilpatrick, 80 Journal of

Note: Paragraph numbers refer to Volume One. Items marked ˙ are research aids, not citations of authority; see "Key to Citations" on page 806.

822

Taxation 220 (April 1994)
*"Best Plan Payout Depends on the Taxpayer,"
Richard Banham and Robert D. Hayes, 54 Taxa-
tion for Accountants 68 (February 1995)

**Companies may not limit ex-employees'
investments**
Rev. Rul. 96-47, 1996-2 CB 35

State's ability to tax pension income limited
P.L. 104-95 (1/10/96)

Waiver of pension benefits taxable
Alfred Gallade, 106 TC 20 (1996)

7.2   LUMP-SUM DISTRIBUTIONS
*IRS Publication 575

Qualified plans
IRC § 401

Definition of lump sum
IRC § 402(e)(4)
Prop. Reg. § 1.402(e)-2(d)

Averaging for QDRO lump sum
IRC § 402(e)(4)

One-time election for lump-sum treatment
Prop. Reg. § 1.402(e)(4)(B)

IRS lump-sum restriction for pension plans
T.I.R. 1403, Question M-15, 9/17/75

Lump-sum treatment at normal retirement age
* Letter Ruling 7748053

**Five-year participation test for 10-year
averaging**
IRC § 402(e)(4)(H)
Prop. Reg. § 1.402(e)-2(e)(3)

**Lump sum from Section 457 not eligible for
averaging**
Roy Rheal, 58 TCM 229 (1989)

**Early retirement package not eligible for
averaging**
Fredric Gruder, 68 TCM 923 (1994)

7.3   LUMP-SUM OPTIONS IF YOU WERE BORN BEFORE 1936

20% withholding rate
IRC § 3405(c)

Irrevocability of rollover election
Temp. Reg. § 1.402(a)(5)-1T (Q&A-4)

**Lump-sum treatment denied on retroactive
revocation of plan qualification**
John V. Fazi, 102 TC 31 (1994) (Tax Court will
no longer follow its Baetens decision and will
follow appeals courts)
Curtis B. Woodson, 73 TC 779 (1980), rev'd, 651
F.2d 1094 (5th Cir. 1981)
Theodore L. Baetens, 82 TC 152 (1984), rev'd,
777 F.2d 1160 (6th Cir. 1985)
Donald L. Benbow, 82 TC 941 (1984), rev'd, 774
F.2d 740 (7th Cir. 1985)

**Partial lump-sum treatment on retroactive
plan disqualification**
Harold D. Greenwald, 366 F.2d 538 (2d Cir.
1982)

Making a partial rollover bars averaging
Sanford O. Barnes, Jr., 67 TCM 2341 (1994)

7.4   AVERAGING ON FORM 4972

**Five-year averaging after age 59¹/₂ for those
born before 1936**
IRC § 402(d)

**Five-year averaging after age 59¹/₂ for those
born after 1936**
IRC § 402(d)(repealed starting in the year 2000)

**Averaging election must apply to all eligible
lump sums received in same year**
Robert O. Fowler, 98 TC 503 (1992)

**10-year or five-year averaging if born before
1936**
P.L. 99-514 (1986 Tax Reform Act), Act Section
1122(h)(3) and (h)(5)

One lifetime election for averaging
IRC § 402(e)(4)(B)

Taxable portion
IRC § 402(a)(1)
Prop. Reg. § 1.402(a)-1(a)(9)(b)
IRC § 402(e)(4)(D)
Prop. Reg. § 1.402(c)-2(d)(2)

Community property
Prop. Reg. § 1.402(e)-2(e)(2)

"Look-back" rule for pre-1992 distributions
IRC § 402(e)(2)
Reg. § 1.402(e)-2(c)(2)

Tax on distribution including annuity contract
Reg. § 1.402(e)-2(c)(1)

7.5   CAPITAL GAIN TREATMENT FOR PRE-1974 PARTICIPATION

**Electing 20% capital gain treatment if age 50
before 1986**
P.L. 99-415 (1986 Tax Reform Act), Act Section
1122(h)(3)(B)

7.6   LUMP-SUM DISTRIBUTION UPON SEPARATION FROM SERVICE
IRC § 402(e)(4)
Reg. § 1.402(e)-2(d)

**Lump-sum treatment denied on merger or
reorganization**
Rev. Rul. 79-336, 1979-2 CB 187
Steven Gegax, 73 TC 329 (1979)
Jack E. Schlegel, 46 TC 706 (1986)
William Haggart, 410 F.2d 449 (8th Cir. 1969),
rev'g 274 F. Supp. (D. N. Dak. 1967)

**Lump-sum treatment allowed on merger or
reorganization**
Joseph J. Enright, Jr., 35 TCM 1770 (1976)
Patty Smith, 460 F.2d 1005 (6th Cir. 1972)
* Letter Ruling 8327033

**Change in form of business ownership may/
may not be separation from service**
Francis C. Burton, Jr., 99 TC 32 (1992)
Lear Eye Clinic, Ltd., 106 TC 23 (1996)

Civil Service retirement system with trust fund
Rev. Rul. 70-150, 1970-2 CB 106

**Pensions after 59¹/₂ but before normal
retirement age**
*Technical Information Release 1403, 9-17-75
*Special Ruling 10-29-76
* Letter Ruling 7748053
* Letter Ruling 8137048

Employee who became partner
Rev. Rul. 73-414, 1973-2 CB 144
Rev. Rul. 81-26, 1981-1 CB 200
Harry P. Ridenour, Jr., 83-2 USTC ¶9491 (Cl. Ct.
1983)

Work after retirement
William S. Bolden, 39 TC 829 (1963)

Must be retired
Edward I. Rieben Est., 32 TC 1205 (1959)

**Full-time independent contractor not separated
from service**
Jules Reinhardt, 85 TC 511 (1985)

**Retiree working as part-time consultant with
same company is separated from service**
* Letter Ruling 8931054

7.7   LUMP-SUM PAYMENTS RECEIVED BY BENEFICIARY
IRC § 402(e)(4)(A)(i)
Richard Gunnison, 461 F.2d 496 (7th Cir. 1972),
aff'g 54 TC 1766 (1970)
Robert A. Stefanowski Est., 63 TC 386 (1974)

**Five-year participation of employee not
required**
Prop. Reg. § 1.402(e)-2(e)(3)

**Beneficiary does not have to meet age test but
deceased employee does**
Mary E. Cebula, 101 TC 5 (1993)

Capital gain treatment
Prop. Reg. § 1.403(a)-2(b)
Prop. Reg. § 1.402(e)-2(d)

**Lump-sum distribution to more than one
beneficiary**
T.I.R. 1426, 12/15/75

Distribution to trust or estate
Reg. § 1.402(c)-3
Reg. § 1.402(e)-2(e)(6)

$5,000 death benefit exclusion
IRC § 101(b)

7.8   TAX-FREE ROLLOVERS
* "Rollover Opportunities and withholding on
Distributions Both Expanded by New Law,"
Nicholas P. Damico, 78 Journal of Taxation 4
(January 1993)
* "Qualified Plans Face New Rollover and With-
holding Rules," Kenneth S. Greenberg and
Andrew L. Oringer, 50 Taxation for Accountants
4 (January 1993)
* "Spousal Rollovers Require Selective Use and
Careful Planning," Bruce E. Bell, 69 Taxes 513
(Aug. 1991)

Rollover of distributions
IRC § 402(c)

**20% withholding if plan does not make direct
rollover**
IRC § 3405(c)
Notice 93-3,1993-3 IRB 4

*Note: Paragraph numbers refer to Volume One. Items marked * are research aids, not citations of authority; see "Key to Citations" on page 806.*

Employer required to explain options
IRC § 402(f)
Reg. § 1.402(f)-1

Hardship distributions from 401(k) or 403(b) plan cannot be rolled over
IRC § 402(c)(4)(c)
IRC § 403(b)(8)(B)
Notice 99-5, 1999-3 IRB

Extension of 60-day period for frozen assets
IRC § 402(c)(7)

Employee contributions cannot be rolled over
Rev. Rul. 89-50, 1989-1 CB 112

Rollover treatment disallowed for minimum required distributions
IRC § 402(c)(4)(B)
IRC § 408(d)(3)(E)

Rollover by surviving spouse
IRC § 402(c)(9)
IRC § 408(d)(3)

Conduit IRAs
IRC § 408(d)(3)(A)(ii)

Commingled IRA funds prevent conduit rollover treatment
* Letter Ruling 9604028

Distribution of life insurance
Rev. Rul. 81-275, 1981-2 CB 75

Tax-sheltered annuity rollover
IRC § 403(b)(8)
IRC § 408(d)(3)(A)(iii)

Diversification of rollover permitted
Rev. Rul. 79-265, 1979-2 CB 186

Distribution under qualified domestic relations order (QDRO) to spouse or ex-spouse may be rolled over
IRC § 402(e)(1)

7.9 ROLLOVER OF PROCEEDS FROM SALE OF PROPERTY

Rollover of sales proceeds
IRC § 402(a)(6)(D)

Designation of cash
IRC § 402(a)(6)(D)(iii)(II)

Designation of employee contributions
IRC § 402(a)(6)(D)(iii)(I)

Allocation methods
IR-2086, February 6, 1979

7.10 DISTRIBUTION OF EMPLOYER SECURITIES

* "Basis Issues Complicate Qualified Plan Distributions of Employer Securities," 77 Journal of Taxation 334 (December 1992)

Unrealized appreciation due to employee's contributions
IRC § 402(e)(4)
Reg. § 1.402(a)-1(b)
Reg. § 1.402(a)-1(a)(9)(B)

Unrealized appreciation due to employer's contributions

IRC § 402(e)(4)
Reg. § 1.402(a)-1(b)
Reg. § 1.402(a)-1(a)(9)(B)
Reg. § 1.401(e)-2(d)(2)

Waiving tax-free treatment
IRC § 402(e)(4)(B)

Shares valued below your cost
Rev. Rul. 71-251, 1971-1 CB 129, amplified by Rev. Rul. 72-15, 1972-1 CB 114

Worthless shares
Rev. Rul. 72-328, 1972-8 CB 224

Holding period
Reg. § 1.402(a)-1(b)

Holding period for post-distribution appreciation
Rev. Rul. 81-122, 1981-1 CB 202

Distribution other than lump sum
Reg. § 1.402(a)-1(b)(3)
Reg. § 1.402(a)-1(a)(9)(b)

Unrealized appreciation affects pro rata recovery for non-lump sum
Notice 89-25, 1989-1 CB 662

NUA attributable to employee contributions immediately taxed on rollover of partial distributions
IRC § 402(a)(5)(D)(iv)

Electing to include NUA in income
Notice 89-25, 1989-1 CB 662

7.11 SURVIVOR ANNUITY FOR SPOUSE
IRC § 401(a)(1)

Survivor annuity requirements
IRC § 417
Reg. § 1.417(e)-1
Reg. § 1.401(a)-1(a) and § 1.401(a)-

20 questions and answers
Notice 94-23, 1994-1 CB 340

Involuntary cash outs
IRC § 417(e)

7.12 COURT DISTRIBUTIONS TO FORMER SPOUSE

* "A Crack in the Antenuptial Shield: Antenuptial Agreements and Survivor Benefits from Qualified Retirement Plans," Robyn M Cotrona, 67 New York State Bar Journal 40 (February 1995)
* "Taxing Retirement Distributions at Divorce in the Absence of a Qualified Domestic Relations Order," John C. Zimmerman, 73 Taxes 326 (June 1995)

QDRO defined
IRC § 414(p)

QDRO drafting requirements
IRC §1457 (Small Business Job Protection Act of 1996)

Averaging
IRC § 402(d)(4)(J)

Spouse treated as payee
IRC § 402(e)(1)

Marcia Fraser, 56 F.3d 722 (6th Cir. 1995)

Rollover
IRC § 402(e)(1)(B)

Husband taxed on QDRO distribution
Robert L Karem, 100 TC 34 (1993)

7.13 WHEN RETIREMENT BENEFITS MUST BEGIN

Premature distributions
IRC § 72(t)

Age 70¹/₂ or when you retire requirement
IRC § 401(a)(9)(C)

Age 70¹/₂ rule for 403(b) annuities
IRC 403(b)(10)

Distribution methods
IRC § 401(a)(9)(A) and (B)
Prop. Reg. § 1.401(a)(9)-1

Penalty for not receiving minimum distributions
IRC § 4974(a)

Governmental and church plans
IRC § 401(a)(9)(C)

7.14 PAYOUTS TO BENEFICIARIES
*IRS Publication 575
*"Who Should Be the Beneficiary of Your Qualified Retirement Plan Benefits?" Karen J. Folb, 76 Taxes 47 (January 1998)

Plan may specify payout for beneficiaries
Prop. Reg. § 1.401(a)(9)-1

Revocable trust can be beneficiary of qualified plan
Prop. Reg. § 1.401(a)(9)-1

7.15 PENALTY FOR DISTRIBUTIONS BEFORE AGE 59¹/₂
IRC § 72(t)

Penalty exceptions
IRC § 72(t)(2)

7.16 RESTRICTIONS ON LOANS FROM COMPANY PLANS
IRC § 72(p)
Prop. Reg. § 1.72(p)-1
* "Loan Programs Enhance the Appeal of Qualified Plans," John M. Wolff, 46 Taxation for Accountants 150 (Mar. 1991)

Interest deduction on loans after 1986
IRC § 72(p)(3)

50% security cap
Labor Dept. Reg. 2550.408(b)-1

Residence used as loan collateral
* Letter Ruling 8933018

Loan repayment plan
Thomas Gray Estate, 70 TCM 556 (1995)

Unpaid loan at separation from service
Notice 93-3, 1993-3 IRB 11

Outstanding loan on annuity is taxable
Harry D. Dean, 65 TCM 2757 (1993)

Note: Paragraph numbers refer to Volume One. Items marked ˙ are research aids, not citations of authority; see "Key to Citations" on page 806.

Note: Paragraph numbers refer to Volume One. Items marked * are research aids, not citations of authority; see "Key to Citations" on page 806.

7.25 REPORTING EMPLOYEE ANNUITIES

IRC § 72(d)
* IRS Publications 575 and 721

7.26 SIMPLIFIED RULE FOR CALCULATING TAXABLE EMPLOYEE ANNUITY

IRC § 72(d)(1)(B)
*IRS Publications 575 and 721

Applying the simplified rule: annuity starting date after July 1, 1986, and before November 19, 1996
Notice 88-118,1988-2 CB 450

7.27 EMPLOYEE'S COST IN ANNUITY

Amounts paid
IRC § 72(b) and (e)
IRC § 403
Reg. § 1.403(a)
Reg. § 1.72-8

Employer's payments
Reg. § 1.72-8

7.28 WITHDRAWALS BEFORE ANNUITY STARTING DATE

IRC § 72(e)(8)
Notice 87-13, 1987-1 CB 432
* "Planning for Nonannuity Distributions from Contribution Plans," Labh S. Hira, 65 Taxes 514 (1987)

Employee contributions (and interest allocable) treated as separate contract
IRC § 72(d)
IRC § 414(k) (defined benefit plans)
Notice 87-13, 1987-1 CB 432 (Q & A 14)

Plans existing on May 5, 1986
IRC § 72(e)(8)(D)

7.29 CIVIL SERVICE RETIREMENT

*IRS Publication No. 721

Survivor's civil service annuity
Rev. Rul. 71-18, 1971-1 CB 33

Lump-sum from federal civil service plan is taxed
Robert E. Montgomery, 18 F.3d 500 (7th Cir. 1994), rev'g 829 F. Supp 1061 (S.D. IN 1993)

7.30 RETIRED MILITARY PERSONNEL ALLOWED ANNUITY ELECTION

IRC § 122
Reg. § 1.122-1

Reductions previously taxed
IRC § 122(b)

Cost of contract to survivor
IRC § 72(n)

Death benefit exclusion
IRC § 101(b)(2)(D)

8   IRAs

8.1 STARTING A TRADITIONAL IRA

Individual retirement account
IRC § 408(a)
Reg. § 1.408-2

Prototype IRAs and SEPs
Rev. Proc. 87-50, 1987-2 CB 647, modified and amplified by Rev. Proc. 90-17, 1990-1 CB 479, modified by Rev. Proc. 92-38, 1992-1 CB 859, and Rev. Proc. 91-44, 1991-2 CB 733

Individual retirement annuity
IRC § 408(b)
Reg. § 1.408-3

Loss on surrender of IRA annuity nondeductible
Rev. Rul. 80-268, 1980-2 CB 141

Flexible premiums
IRC § 408(b)(2)
Prop. Reg. § 1.408-3(b)(6)

Endowment contract issued after November 6, 1978
Reg. § 1.408-3(e)

Broker restrictions
Special Ruling, August 24, 1983

Retirement bonds
IRC § 409
Reg. § 1.409-1

Retirement bonds not issued after April 30, 1982
TD News Release April 27, 1982

Time for making contributions
IRC § 219(f)(3)

Tax treatment of distribution
IRC § 408(d)
Reg. § 1.408-4

Diversification of investment permitted
Rev. Rul. 79-265, 1979-2 CB 186

Federal and state coins allowed in IRA
IRC § 408(m)(3)

8.2 CONTRIBUTIONS MUST BE BASED ON EARNINGS

IRC § 219(b)

Time for making contribution
IRC § 219(f)(3)

Compensation defined
Reg. § 1.219-1(c)(1)

Unemployment benefits
Donald G. Russell, 71 TCM 3184 (1996)

Earned income
IRC § 219
IRC § 401(c)(2)
IRC § 1402(a)

Self-employment losses do not offset wages
Rev. Rul. 79-286, 1979-2 CB 121

Aggregating businesses
IRC § 1402(a)
Reg. § 1.1402(a)-2(c)

Trader activities not earned income
Robert Miller, 77 TC 97 (1981)

Endowment contract
IRC § 219(d)(3)
Reg. § 1.408-3(e)

Payment of fees
Rev. Rul. 84-146, 1984-2 CB 61

8.3 CONTRIBUTIONS TO A TRADITIONAL IRA IF YOU ARE MARRIED

Deduction limitations for married couples filing jointly
IRC § 219(g)
IRC § 219(c)

Married couples filing separately and living together
IRC § 219(g)(1)
Announcement 89-20, 1989-6 IRB 37

Married couples filing separately and living apart
IRC § 219(g)(4)

Higher spousal IRA Contributions
IRC § 219, as amended by 1997 Act

Deductions for nonworking spouse
IRC § 219(c)

Working for spouse without receiving payment of wages
* Letter Ruling 8707004

8.4 DEDUCTION RESTRICTIONS FOR ACTIVE PARTICIPANTS IN EMPLOYER PLAN

*IRS Publication 590

Deduction limitations
IRC § 219(c)
IRC § 219(g)
Notice 87-16, 1987-1 CB 446

New spousal participation rule
IRC § 219(g)(7), as amended by 1998 Act

No IRA deduction in year of joining or leaving plan
Sara Wartes, 65 TCM 2058 (1993)

8.5 ACTIVE PARTICIPATION IN EMPLOYER PLAN

IRC § 219(g)(5)
Notice 87-16, 1987-1 CB 446

Active participation rule for 401(k)
Jeffrey W. Baumann, 70 TCM 61 (1995)
* Letter Ruling 8919064

Note: Paragraph numbers refer to Volume One. Items marked ˚ are research aids, not citations of authority; see "Key to Citations" on page 806.

8.6   NONDEDUCTIBLE IRA CONTRIBUTIONS

IRC § 408(o)

Penalties relating to nondeductible contributions
IRC § 6693(b)

8.7   PENALTY FOR EXCESS CONTRIBUTIONS TO TRADITIONAL IRAs

Excess contributions
IRC § 4973
Prop. Reg. § 54.4973-1
IRC § 408(d)(4): contributions returned before due date
IRC § 408(d)(5): contributions withdrawn after due date
Reg. § 1.408-1(c)(1)

Excess contributions treated as made in subsequent years
IRC § 219(f)(6)

8.8   TAXABLE DISTRIBUTIONS FROM TRADITIONAL IRAs

IRC § 408(d)(1)
* "Distribution Options for IRAs Offer Tax-Saving Opportunities," Michael F. Lynch and David J. Beausejour, 58 Taxation for Accountants 213 (April 1997)
* "Trusts as Beneficiaries May Prolong IRA Distributions and Save Taxes," Leonard J. Witman and Laura Weyant Kearney, 84 The Journal of Taxation 86 (February 1996)
* "Estate Planning for IRA and Qualified Plan Distributions," Kenneth A. Hansen, 56 Taxation for Accountants 289 (May 1996)
* "Planning for Qualified Plan and IRA Distributions," Seymour Goldberg, 74 Taxes 111 (February 1996)

Pre-59$^{1}/_{2}$ penalty
IRC § 72(t)
Robert Dwyer, 106 TC 18 (1996)

Excess distributions
IRC § 4980A (15% penalty suspended for years 1997, 1998, 1999)

IRA protected under state bankruptcy law
Neil Solomon, 67 F. 3D 1128 (4th Cir. 10/23/95)

Penalty on garnished IRA
Vorwald, TC Memo 1997-15

8.9   PARTIALLY TAX-FREE TRADITIONAL IRA DISTRIBUTIONS ALLOCABLE TO NONDEDUCTIBLE CONTRIBUTIONS

Figuring tax if nondeductible contributions have been made
IRC § 408(d)(2)
Notice 87-16, 1987-1 CB 446

Excess contributions treated as made in subsequent years
IRC § 219(f)(6)

8.10   TAX-FREE ROLLOVERS AND DIRECT TRANSFERS TO TRADITIONAL IRAs

Rollover within 60 days not taxed
IRC § 408(d)(3)

Rollover treatment disallowed for minimum required distribution
IRC § 408(d)(3)(E)

60-day period extended for frozen deposits
IRC § 408(d)(3)(F)
Letter Ruling 199933038

Rollover after age 70$^{1}/_{2}$
Rev. Rul. 82-153, 1982-2 CB 56

Direct transfer of account between trustees is not rollover
Rev. Rul. 78-406, 1978-2 CB 157

Beneficiary can authorize trustee-to-trustee transfer
* Letter Ruling 8716058

60-day loan
* Letter Ruling 901007

Taxpayer not at fault for failure to meet 60-day deadline
William Wood, 93 TC 114 (1989)
* Letter Ruling 9211035

IRA funded by husband's pension
Mario Rodoni, 105 TC 3 (1996)

Withdrawals following bank failure
Alan Aronson, 98 TC 283 (1992)

Stock bought with IRA funds — no rollover
Albert Lemishaw, 110 TC 26 (1998)

8.11   TRANSFER OF TRADITIONAL IRA TO SPOUSE AT DIVORCE OR DEATH

Transfer because of divorce
IRC § 408(d)(6)

QDRO
IRC § 402(e)(1)(B)
IRC § 402(d)(4)(J)

Surviving spouse
IRC § 408(d)(3)(C)
IRC § 408(a)(6)
* Letter Ruling 9524020

8.12   PENALTY FOR IRA WITHDRAWALS BEFORE AGE 59$^{1}/_{2}$

IRC § 72(t)
*IRS Publication 590
* "Planning for Qualified Plan and IRA Distributions," Seymour Goldberg, 74 Taxes 111 (February 1996)
* "Level Payments Avoid Penalty on Pre-59$^{1}/_{2}$ IRA Distributions," Gerald E. Wittenburg and Martha Altus-Buller, 53 Taxation for Accountants 333 (December 1994)
* "Structuring Substantially Equal Payments to Avoid the Premature Withdrawal Penalty," Richard B. Toolson, 73 Journal of Taxation 276 (November 1990)

* "IRS Provides Ample Flexibility for Tapping Retirement Accounts," Labh S. Hira, 68 Taxes 454 (June 1990)

Distribution used for home down payment penalized
Gerald M. Harris, 67 TCM 1983 (1994)

New IRA penalty exceptions for higher education and first-time homebuyer expenses
IRC § 72(2)(t)(E) and (F), as added by the 1997 Act

Disability exception
Robert Dwyer, 106 TC 18 (1996)
IRC § 72(t)(2)(A)(iii)

Interest charges added to penalty
* Letter Ruling 9401040

Pre-59$^{1}/_{2}$ distributions under annuitized formula
Notice 89-25, 1989-1 CB 662
* Letter Ruling 9217048
* Letter Ruling 9241063
* Letter Ruling 8911069
* Letter Ruling 8911071

Pre-59$^{1}/_{2}$ withdrawals allowed for medical expenses after 1996
IRC § 72(t)(2)

No exceptions to 60-day rollover period
Letter Ruling 199933038

COLA triggers 59$^{1}/_{2}$ IRA penalty
Letter Ruling 199943050

8.13   MANDATORY DISTRIBUTIONS FROM A TRADITIONAL IRA AFTER AGE 70$^{1}/_{2}$

* "Trusts as Beneficiaries May Prolong IRA Distributions and Save Taxes," Leonard J. Witman and Laura Weyant Kearney, 84 The Journal of Taxation 86 (February 1996)
* "Estate Planning for IRA and Qualified Plan Distributions," Kenneth A. Hansen, 56 Taxation for Accountants 289 (May 1996)
* "Planning for Qualified Plan and IRA Distributions," Seymour Goldberg, 74 Taxes 111 (February 1996)

Insufficient distribution penalty
IRC § 4974(b)

IRS rules for figuring minimum required distribution
Prop. Reg. § 1.408-8
* IRS Publication 590

Distributions don't have to be from each account
Notice 88-38 1988-15 IRB 9

Reasons for insufficiency
IR-2086, February 6, 1979

Life expectancy refigured annually
IRC § 408(a)(6) and 401(a)(9)(D)

Recalculation method forces immediate payout to estate or beneficiary
* Letter Ruling 9604027

Note: Paragraph numbers refer to Volume One. Items marked * *are research aids, not citations of authority; see "Key to Citations" on page 806.*

Waiver of penalty if reasonable mistake
Prop. Reg. § 54.4974-2 (Q-8)

8.14 INHERITED IRAS

* "How the Death of a Qualified Plan Beneficiary Affects Long-Term Deferral of Income," Jay A. Soled, Bruce E. Mantell, and Leonard Witman, 91 Journal of Taxation 165 (September 1999)
* "Recent Developments Highlight Plan and IRA Beneficiary Designations," Karl W. Schettenhelm, Jr., 24 Estate Planning 274 (July 1997)
* "Benefits: QTiping Qualified Plan and IRA Distributions," Kathleen M. Franklin and Edward Falk, New York State Bar Journal 53 (January 1995)
IRC § 408(a)(6)
IRC § 401(a)(9)
Prop. Reg. § 1.401(a)(9)-1
*IRS Publication 590
* Letter Ruling 9305025
* Letter Ruling 9371037

Multiple beneficiaries
Letter Ruling 199931048

8.15 SEP BASICS

IRC § 219(b)(2)
IRC § 404(h)
IRC § 408(j), (k), and (l)
Reg. § 1.219-1(d)(4) and -3
Reg. § 1.404(h)-1
Reg. § 1.408-7 through 9
* Letter Ruling 9302022

Overall tax-free SEP contribution limit after 1986
IRC § 402(h)

Salary-reduction SEP
IRC § 408(k)(6)

Elective salary-reduction limit
IRC § 402(g)(1)

8.16 SALARY REDUCTION SEP SET UP BEFORE 1997

*"Retirement Plan Reform: The Aftermath of the Small Business Job Protection Act of 1996," Natasha M. Mulleneaux, 75 Taxes 438 (Aug. 1997)

SEP
IRC § 408(k)(6)

SIMPLE
IRC § 408(p)

8.17 WHO IS ELIGIBLE FOR A SIMPLE IRA?

IRC § 408(p)

8.18 SIMPLE IRA CONTRIBUTIONS AND DISTRIBUTIONS

IRC § 408(p)

8.19 ROTH IRA ADVANTAGES

IRC § 408A
*IRS Publication 590
* "Final Regs. Provide Roadmap for Taxpayers on

the Roth IRA Bandwagon," Matthew A. Melone, 63 Tax Strategies 33 (July 1999)
* "Why the Roth IRA is a 'Tax Break' to Avoid," Rolf Auster, 62 Tax Strategies 359 (June 1999)
* "Roth IRAs after the '98 Act — Congress Improves the Product," Stanley D. Baum, 89 Journal of Taxation 144 (Sept. 1998)
* "Roth IRA or Regular IRA: How to Decide Which One is Preferable," Martin Silfen, 25 Estate Planning 108 (March/April 1998)

IRS guidelines for Roth IRAs
Prop. Reg. § 1.408A-1 through A-9

8.20 ANNUAL CONTRIBUTIONS TO A ROTH IRA

*IRS Publication 590

Annual contributions to Roth IRA
IRC § 408A(c)
Prop. Reg. § 1.408A-3

Excess contributions to Roth IRA
IRC § 4973(f)

8.21 CONVERTING A TRADITIONAL IRA TO A ROTH IRA

Conversion to Roth IRA
IRC § 408A(c)(3)(B)
IRC § 408(d)(3) (tax on conversion including four-year spread for 1998 conversions)
Final Reg. § 1.408A-4

12/31/99 recharacterization deadline
Announcement 99-104; News Release IR-1999-78 (modifying IRS Announcement 99-57, 199924 IRB 50)

Undoing a conversion
Final Reg. § 1.408A-5

Limits on reconversions
IRS Notice 98-50, 1998-44 IRB
Final Regs. § 1.408A1-A9

8.22 DISTRIBUTIONS FROM A ROTH IRA

IRC § 408A(d)
Final Reg. § 1.408A-6

---

9 INCOME FROM RENTS AND ROYALTIES

9.1 REPORTING RENTAL INCOME AND EXPENSES

IRC § 61(a)(5) and (6)
IRC § 469
Reg. § 1.61-8
*IRS Publications 527 and 925

Rents received
Reg. § 1.61-8

Cash basis
Morris-Poston Coal Co., 42 F.2d 620 (6th Cir. 1930)
Andrew J. Pembroke, 23 BTA 1176, aff'd 70 F.2d 850 (D.C. Cir. 1935)
Jas. M. Butler, 18 BTA 718 (Acq.)

Accrual basis
Suffolk & Berks, 40 BTA 1121 (Acq.)
American Fork & Hoe Co., 33 BTA 1139
Oregon Terminals Co., 29 BTA 1332 (Nonacq.)

Advance rentals or bonuses
Reg. § 1.61-8(b)
Hyde Park Realty, Inc., 211 F.2d 462 (2d Cir. 1954), aff'g 20 TC 43 (1953)
Chateau Frontenac, 147 F.2d 856 (6th Cir. 1945)
Clinton Hotel Realty Corp., 128 F.2d 968 (5th Cir. 1945)
Beach D. Lyon, 97 F.2d 70 (9th Cir. 1938)
Edward A. Renwick, 87 F.2d 123 (7th Cir. 1937)
R. L. Harcum, 164 F. Supp. 650 (E.D. Vir. 1958)
John Mantell, 17 TC 1143 (1952) (Acq.)

Advances transferred to new landlord
Hyde Park Realty, Inc., 211 F.2d 462 (2d Cir. 1954), aff'g 20 TC 43 (1953)

Security for performance
Astor Holding Co., 135 F.2d 47 (5th Cir. 1943)
Clinton Hotel Realty Corp., 128 F.2d 968 (5th Cir. 1942)
R. L. Harcum, 164 F. Supp. 650 (E.D. Vir. 1958)
Andrew J. Pembroke, 70 F.2d 850 (D.C. Cir. 1935)
John Mantell, 17 TC 1143 (1952) (Acq.)

Taxes, interest, etc. as rent
Reg. § 1.61-8(c)

Insurance proceeds
John S. Mellinger, 228 F.2d 688 (5th Cir. 1956)
Oppenheim's Inc., 90 F. Supp. 107 (D. Mich. 1960)

Cancelled lease
Reg. § 1.61-8(b)
Walter M. Hort, 313 U.S. 28 (1941)

Amortizing lease cancellation cost over term of old lease
Handlery Hotels, Inc., 663 F.2d 892 (9th Cir. 1981)

Expenses deductible
E. M. Godson, 5 TCM 648 (1946)
Louis F. Tucker, Sr., 9 TCM 956 (1950)

Improvement by tenant
IRC § 109
Reg. § 1.109-1

9.2 CHECKLIST OF RENTAL DEDUCTIONS

Management expenses
IRC § 212
Reg. § 1.212-1

Maintenance expenses
IRC § 212
Reg. § 1.212-1

Salaries and wages
IRC § 212
Reg. § 1.212-1

Travel expenses
E. M. Goodson, 5 TCM 648 (1946)

Legal expenses
Arthur T. Galt, 19 TC 892 (1953), aff'd in part,

Note: Paragraph numbers refer to Volume One. Items marked ˙ are research aids, not citations of authority; see "Key to Citations" on page 806.

828

rev'd in part, 216 F.2d 41 (7th Cir. 1954), cert. denied, 348 U.S. 951
Louis F. Tucker, Sr., 9 TCM 956 (1950)
E. M. Godson, 5 TCM 648 (1946)

Interest on mortgages
IRC § 163(c)
Reg. § 1.163-1

Commissions to secure rental
Mary C. Young, 59 F.2d 691 (9th Cir. 1953), cert. denied, 287 U.S. 652, on remand, 14 TCM 869 (1955)
John Griffiths, 70 F.2d 946 (8th Cir. 1934)
Louis A. Meyran, 63 F.2d 986 (3d Cir. 1933)
Central Bank Block Assn., 57 F.2d 5 (5th Cir. 1932)

Commissions to acquire property
IRC § 263
Reg. § 1.263(a)-1 and 2

Abandonment loss
Reg. § 1.167(a)-8
Belridge Oil Co., 11 BTA 127
I. G. Zumwalt, 25 BTA 566
Rev. Rul. 54-581, 1954-2 CB 112

Insurance premiums
Reg. § 1.162-1

Year deductible
Reg. § 1.461-1(a)(1)
Rev. Rul. 70-413, 1970-2 CB 103

Inherited lease
Mary Y. Moore, 207 F.2d 265 (9th Cir. 1953), cert. denied, 347 U.S. 942, on remand, 14 TCM 869 (1955)

Release from mortgage
Rev. Rul. 57-198, 1957-1 CB 94

Tenant in common
Elmer B. Boyd Est., 28 TC 564 (1957)

Payment of full tax by co-tenant deductible
Lulu Lung Powell, 26 TCM 161 (1967)

No deduction for co-tenant without proof of payment
Donald Peters, 29 TCM 1441 (1970)

Rent for less than fair value
Nicath Realty (Hummel), 25 TCM 1260 (1966)

Cost of cancelling a lease
Handlery Hotels, Inc., 663 F.2d 892 (9th Cir. 1981)

9.3 DISTINGUISHING BETWEEN A REPAIR AND AN IMPROVEMENT

Capital improvements
IRC § 263
Reg. § 1.263(a)-1 and -2

Painting
Michael Markovits, 11 TCM 823 (1952)
Charles H. Cohen, 7 TCM 681 (1948)
Jones Hollow Ware Co., 12 BTA 48 (Acq.)
Leedom & Worrall Co., 10 BTA 825

Replacement of roof
George W. Ritter, 163 F.2d 1019 (6th Cir. 1947)

Thomas J. Locke, 8 BTA 534 (Acq.)
Georgia Car & Locomotive Co., 2 BTA 986 (Nonacq.)

Heating system
Republican Co., BTA Memo. (Feb. 20, 1934)

General improvement program
Home News Publishing Co., 18 BTA 1008
Cowell, 18 BTA 997

Repairs and improvements unconnected
W. A. Stoeltzing, 266 F.2d 374 (3d Cir. 1959), aff'g 17 TCM 567 (1958)

Major hotel allowed deduction for maintenance during improvement plan
Jerome Moss, 831 F.2d 833 (9th Cir. 1987)

9.4 REPORTING RENTS FROM A MULTI-UNIT RESIDENCE
* IRS Publication 527

Three-way allocation
Rev. Rul. 76-287, 1976-2 CB 80

Rental of condo during slack market
Edward W. Andrews, 931 F.2d 132 (1st Cir., 1991)

9.5 DEPRECIATION ON CONVERTING A HOME TO RENTAL PROPERTY
* IRS Publication 527

Take depreciation
IRC § 167(a)
Reg. § 1.212-1(h)

Recapture of pre-MACRS depreciation
IRC § 1250(d)(7)
Reg. § 1.1250-3(g)

27$1/_2$-year recovery
IRC § 168(c)(1)

Lower of adjusted basis and value at conversion
Reg. § 1.167(g)-1
J. Russell Parsons, 227 F.2d 437 (3d Cir. 1956)
Louise Biesek, 22 TCM 464 (1963)

Basis when you sell
Reg. § 1.165-9(b)
Tindle and Union Trust Co., 276 U.S. 582 (1928)
Mary Louise Bok, 46 BTA 678 (Acq.), aff'd, 132 F.2d 365 (3d Cir. 1942)
Bert P. Newron, 11 TC 512 (1948) (Acq.)
Alan H. Colcord, 9 TCM 729 (1950)

Need of appraisal
Sam Perry Robinson, 19 TCM 1374 (1960)

Depreciation on vacant residence
Hulet P. Smith, 26 TCM 149 (1967), aff'd, 397 F.2d 804 (9th Cir. 1968)
George W. Mitchell, 47 TC 120 (1966) (Nonacq.)
Frank A. Newcombe, 54 TC 1298 (1970)
James J. Sherlock, 31 TCM 383 (1972)
Edward G. Lowry, Jr., 384 F. Supp. 257 (D. N.H. 1974)

9.6 RENTING TO A RELATIVE
IRC § 280A(d)(2)(A)

IRC § 280A(d)(3)

Renting vacation home to a close relative
Cedric R. Kotowicz, 62 TCM 1229 (1991)

Renting inherited home to relatives
Ronald P. Barranti, 76 TCM 957 (1998)

9.7 PERSONAL USE AND RENTAL OF A RESIDENTIAL UNIT DURING THE YEAR
IRC § 280A(d)

"Mini motorhome" as vacation home
Ronald L. Haberkorn, 75 TC 259 (1980)

Time spent on repairs not personal use
Robert J. Twohey, 66 TCM 1394 (1993)

Renting vacation home to close relative
Cedric R. Kotowicz, 62 TCM 1229 (1991)

No deductions for rental of home space to employer
IRC § 280A(c)(6)

Rental for less than 15 days
IRC § 280A(g)

9.8 COUNTING PERSONAL-USE AND RENTAL DAYS
IRC § 280A(d)

Personally used (14-day/10%) residence exempt from passive activity rules
IRC § 469(j)(10)

14-day or 10% personal-use tests
IRC § 280A(d)(1)

Personal-use day defined
IRC § 280A(d)(2)

Income limitation on deductions
IRC § 280A(c)(5)

Shared equity financing agreement
IRC § 280A(d)(3)(C)
Prop. Reg. § 1.280A-1(e)(3)

Rental of personal residence
IRC § 280A(d)(4)
Stephen Bolaris, 776 F.2d 1428 (9th Cir. 1985), rev'g 81 TC 840 (1983)

Rental pool arrangements
Prop. Reg. § 1.280A-3(e)
Richard S. Fine, 493 F. Supp. 540 (D. Ill. 1980), aff'd, 647 F.2d 763 (7th Cir. 1981)
Kenneth G. Byers, Jr., 82 TC 919

9.9 ALLOCATING EXPENSES TO RENTAL DAYS
* "Interest and Property Tax Deductions on a Vacation Home: The Allocation Controversy," Scott N. Cairns and Diane A. Riordan, 71 Taxes 433 (July 1993)

IRS allocation method
Prop. Reg. § 1.280A-3(d)(3)

Allocation method
Dorance D. Bolton, 77 TC 104 (1981), aff'd, 694 F.2d 556 (9th Cir. 1982)
Edith McKinney, 732 F.2d 414 (10th Cir. 1983),

*Note: Paragraph numbers refer to Volume One. Items marked * are research aids, not citations of authority; see "Key to Citations" on page 806.*

cert. denied (1984)

Interest expense
IRC § 163(h)
IRC §469(j)(7)

9.10 RENTALS LACKING PROFIT MOTIVE
IRC § 280A
IRC §183

Profit motive
IRC § 183
Terence D. Clancy, 37 TCM 400 (1978)
Marvin Eisenstein, 37 TCM 441 (1978)
Truett E. Allen, 72 TC 28 (1979) (Acq.)
Lester W. Lindow, 37 TCM 1257 (1978)
Richard H. Nelson, 37 TCM 1204 (1978)
Mark M. Vandeyacht, 62 TCM 2606 (1994)

Failure to charge fair rental value
Lawrence E. Colbert, 63 TCM 1818 (1992)

Mobile home not rented for profit
James E. Wittstruck, 645 F.2d 618 (8th Cir. 1981), aff'g per curiam 39 TCM 1168 (1980)

Temporary rental preceding sale
Stephen Bolaris, 776 F.2d 1428 (9th Cir. 1985), rev'g 81 TC 840 (1983)

9.11 REPORTING ROYALTY INCOME

License fees for use of patented article
Reg. § 1.61-8(a)

Renting fees
Reg. § 1.61-8(a)

Author's royalties
Reg. § 1.61-8(a)
Rev. Rul. 60-31, 1960-1 CB 174, modified by Rev. Rul. 64-279, 1964-2 CB 121 and Rev. Rul. 70-435, 1970-2 CB 100

Works of art, etc.
Reg. § 1.61-8(a)

Partial sale of rights
Reg. § 1.61-8(a)

Lessee's payment of taxes
Wallin Coal Corp., 71 F.2d 521 (4th Cir. 1934)
Rev. Rul. 64-91, 1964-1 CB (Part 1) 219

Amortization of production costs of motion pictures, etc.
IRC § 280

Royalty taxed as ordinary income
IRC § 61(a)(6)
Reg. § 1.61-8(a)

Depletion allowed
IRC § 611
Reg. § 1.611

Bonus payment
Reg. § 1.612-3(a)(3)
Reg. § 1.613-2(c)(5)
H. H. Weinert Est., 294 F.2d 740 (5th Cir. 1961)
Ann. 76-34, 1976-12 IRB 28
Rev. Rul. 73-537, 1973-2 CB 197

Percentage depletion allowed on advanced

royalty
Fred Engle, 677 F.2d 564 (7th Cir. 1982), aff'd, 464 U.S. 206 (1984)
Ann. 84-59 1984-23 IRB 58

Local law
Henry Harmel, 287 U.S. 103 (1932)

Delay rental
Reg. § 1.612-3(c)

Overriding royalty
Reg. § 1.613-2 and 3(b)
E. G. Palmer v. Bender, 287 U.S. 551 (1933)
West Prod. Co., 121 F.2d 9 (5th Cir. 1941), cert. denied, 314 U.S. 682
H. R. Cullen, 118 F.2d 651 (5th Cir. 1941)

Production payments treated as loans
IRC § 636

Oil payments
J. Steve Anderson, 310 U.S. 404 (1940)
Caldwell Oil Corp., 141 F.2d 559 (5th Cir. 1944)
Mamie S. Hammonds, 106 F.2d 420 (10th Cir. 1939)
Roy H. Laird, 97 F.2d 730 (5th Cir. 1938)
William Fleming, 82 F.2d 328 (5th Cir. 1936)
Chester Addison Jones, 82 F.2d 329 (5th Cir. 1936)
Elliott Petroleum Corp., 82 F.2d 193 (9th Cir. 1936)

Proof of oil payment
J. A. Morgan, 321 F.2d 781 (5th Cir. 1963), on remand, 245 F. Supp. 388 (D. Miss. 1965)

Both oil payment and overriding royalty
J. Steve Anderson, 310 U.S. 404 (1940)
E. G. Palmer v. Bender, 287 U.S. 551 (1933)
H. R. Cullen, 118 F.2d 651 (5th Cir. 1941), rev'g 41 BTA 1042
Marrs McLean, 120 F.2d 942 (5th Cir. 1941), cert. denied, 314 U.S. 670
Fred T. Hogan, 1 TCM 208 (1942), aff'd, 141 F.2d 92 (5th Cir. 1944), cert. denied, 323 U.S. 710

Net profits
Kirby Petroleum Co., 326 U.S. 599 (1946)
Thomas A. O'Donnell, 303 U.S. 370 (1938)

Carried interest
Abercrombie Co., 162 F.2d 338 (5th Cir. 1947), aff'g 7 TC 120 (1946) (Nonacq.)
Donald McMurray, 60 F.2d 843 (10th Cir. 1935), cert. denied, 287 U.S. 664

Carved-out oil payments
P. G. Lake, Inc., 356 U.S. 260 (1958)
Murphy J. Foster, 324 F.2d 702 (5th Cir. 1963)

9.12 PRODUCTION COSTS OF BOOKS AND CREATIVE PROPERTIES
IRC § 263A

Exemption for freelance authors, artists, and playwrights
Code § 263A(h)

9.13 DEDUCTING THE COST OF PATENTS OR COPYRIGHTS

Patent and copyright
Reg. § 1.167(a)-6(a)

Depreciation deduction
Associated Partners, Inc., 4 TC 979 (1945)
Rev. Rul. 67-136, 1967-1 CB 58

Inherited
IRC § 1014
John L. Whitehurst, 12 BTA 1416 (Nonacq.)

Worthless interest
Robert S. Davis, 241 F.2d 701 (7th Cir. 1958)
James Petroleum Corp., 238 F.2d 678 (2d Cir. 1956), cert. denied, 353 U.S. 910

9.14 INTANGIBLE DRILLING COSTS
IRC § 263(c)

Recapture of intangible drilling costs
IRC § 1254
Prop. Reg. § 1.1254

Prepaid expenses, Pre–March 31, 1984
Stephen A. Keller, 725 F.2d 1173 (8th Cir. 1984)

Tax-shelter prepayments after March 31, 1984
IRC § 461(i)(2)(D)

9.15 DEPLETION DEDUCTION
*IRS Publication 535
IRC § 611 through § 613
Reg. § 1.611-1
Reg. § 1.612-1
Reg. § 1.613-1 and 2

9.16 OIL AND GAS PERCENTAGE DEPLETION
*IRS Publication 535
* "New Domestic Energy Exploration Tax Incentives Under RRA '90," J. Ray Jones and Ted E. McElroy, 74 Journal of Taxation 178 (Mar. 1991)

Percentage depletion for gas and oil wells
IRC § 613A

Retail sales less than $5 million
IRC § 613A(d)(2)

Repeal of transfer rule
Section 1152(a) of the Revenue Reconciliation Act of 1990 (PL. 101-508), repealing IRC § 613A(c)(9) and IRC § 613A(c)(10)
Prop. Reg. § 1.613A-3(h)(2)

Exceptions to anti-transfer rule
IRC § 613A(c)(9)(B)

Depletable gas quantity
Reg. § 1.613A-5

Limit of 100% of taxable income from the property
IRC § 613(a)
IRC § 613A(c)(6) (suspension of limitation through 2001

Limit of 65% of taxable income from all sources
IRC § 613A(d)

No depletion for lease bonuses
IRC § 613A(d)(5)
Prop. Reg. § 1.613A-3(j)

Note: Paragraph numbers refer to Volume One. Items marked ˙ are research aids, not citations of authority; see "Key to Citations" on page 806.

Note: Paragraph numbers refer to Volume One. Items marked * *are research aids, not citations of authority; see "Key to Citations" on page 806.*

Taxation 20 (Jan. 1988)

Closely held corporations
IRC § 469 (j)(1)

Personal service corporations
IRC § 469(j)(2)

Material participation tests
IRC § 469(h)(4)

Full-time manager or employees
IRC § 465(c)(7)(C)

Passive losses offset net active income
IRC § 469(e)(2)

10.16 SALES OF PROPERTY AND OF PASSIVE ACTIVITY INTERESTS
IRC § 469(g)
Temp. Reg. § 1.469-2T(c)

Installment sale
IRC § 469(g)(3)

Appreciated property formerly used in nonpassive activity
Temp. Reg. § 1.469-2T(c)(2)(iii)

Property used in more than one activity in a 12-month period preceding disposition
Temp. Reg. § 1.469-2T(c)(2)(ii)

Partnership and S corporation interests
Temp. Reg. § 1.469-2T(e)(3)

10.17 AT-RISK LIMITS
IRC § 465
Prop. Reg. § 1.465-1 through § 95

Activities subject to at-risk rules
IRC § 465(c)
Arnold Berger, 67 TCM 3144 (1994)

Active corporation
IRC § 465(c)(7)(B)

Aggregation of partnership or S corporation activities until further notice
Notice 89-39, 1989-1 CB 681

10.18 WHAT IS AT RISK?
IRC § 465(b)
* "Borrowed Funds Do Not Always Increase Amounts At Risk," Joseph R. Oliver, 48 Taxation for Accountants 348 (June 1992)

Special at-risk rule for real estate
IRC § 465(b)(6)

Personal liability note to general partner not at risk
Rev. Rul. 80-327, 1980-2 CB 23

Recourse financing may not increase risk capital
Prop. Reg. § 1.465-8

Nonrecourse financing arrangements
Prop. Reg. § 1.465-6

Activities begun before 1976
Conference Committee Rep. No. 94-1236, 94th Cong., 2d Sess. 412 (1976)

10.19 AMOUNTS NOT AT RISK

Borrowing from relatives
IRC § 465(b)(3)(A)

Dispositions of interest in property used in at-risk activity
Prop. Reg. § 1.465-68

Recourse not convertible to nonrecourse
Rev. Rul. 81-283, 1981-2 CB 115

T.V. film investment
Rev. Rul. 78-413, 1978-2 CB 167

Gold mine venture
Rev. Rul. 80-72, 1980-I CB 109
Prop. Reg. § 1.465-41
Ernest J. Saviano, 80 TC 955 (1983)

Potential cash call
John Callahan, 98 TC 22 (1992)
Jerry Pritchett, et al., 85 TC 580 (1985), rev'd, 527 F.2d 644 (9th Cir. 1987)

10.20 AT-RISK INVESTMENT IN SEVERAL ACTIVITIES

Aggregation allowed for partnership or S corporation leasing of Section 1245 property
IRC § 465(c)(2)(B)

Aggregation for actively managed businesses
IRC § 465(c)(2)(B)(ii)
IRC § 465(c)(3)(B)

10.21 CARRYOVER OF DISALLOWED LOSSES
IRC § 465(a)(2)
"Emerging Audit Issues in the Application of the Passive Loss Provisions to Real Estate," Patricia Eason, Tim Krumweide and Raymond A. Zimmerman, 75 Taxes 575 (Oct. 1997)

10.22 RECAPTURE OF LOSSES WHERE AT RISK IS LESS THAN ZERO
IRC § 465(e)
IRC § 61

---

11 OTHER INCOME

11.1 PRIZES AND AWARDS
IRC § 74(a)
* "The Taxation of Prizes and Awards — Tax Policy Winners and Losers," Bruce I. Kogan, 63 Wash. L. Rev. 257 (Apr. 1988)

Prizes and awards
IRC § 74
Reg. § 1.74-1

Civic achievement award
Rev. Rul. 65-161, 1965-1 CB 38

Pulitzer prize
Reg. § 1.74-1
Rev. Rul. 54-110, 1954-1 CB 28

Government award
Francis M. Rogallo, 474 F.2d 1 (4th Cir. 1974), rev'g 341 F. Supp. 998 (D. Va. 1972)

Door prize
Reg. § 1.74-1

Essay contest
Arsham Amirkian, 197 F.2d 442 (4th Cir. 1952)
Herbert Stein, 14 TC 494 (1950)
Frederick V. Waugh, 9 TCM 309 (1950)

Lottery ticket
* Letter Ruling 9217004

Award under Incentive Awards Act
Hobart M. Griggs, 314 F. Supp. 515 (Ct. Cl. 1963)

Prize from employer
Reg. § 1.74-1

NASA award taxable
Robert Jones, 79 TC 1008 (1982)

Manufacturer's trip prize to dealer
Bell Electric Co., 45 TC 158 (1965) (Acq.)

Prize of car to football player
Paul Hornung, 47 TC 428 (1967) (Acq.)

Radio or TV contest
Reg. § 1.74-1(b)

Prize of merchandise
Reg. § 1.74-1(a)(2)

Vacation trip
Nathan L. Wade, 55 TCM 413 (1988)

Steamship ticket
Reginald Turner, 13 TCM 462 (1954)

Car prize
Lawrence W. McCoy, 38 TC 841 (1962) (Acq. 1963-1 CB 4)

Script award
Rev. Rul. 70-331, 1970-1 CB 14

Taxable scholarship to Miss America
Rev. Rul. 68-20, 1968-1 CB 55

Treasure you find
Rev. Rul. 53-61, 1953-1 CB 17

Transfer to charity or governmental unit
IRC § 74(b)
Rev. Proc. 87-54, 1987-2 CB 669

Employee achievement
IRC § 74(c)

11.2 LOTTERY AND SWEEPSTAKE WINNINGS

Lump-sum option ignored if installments received
IRC § 451(h)

Prize taxed when received not won
Roy V. Thomas, 99-1 USTC ¶50,451

Raffle winnings
Diane M. Solomon, 25 TC 936 (1956)
H. Collings Downes, 30 TC 396 (1958)

Sweepstake winnings divided among family members
Henry Braunstein, 21 TCM 1132 (1962)

Couple's joint ownership agreement
* Letter Ruling 9217004

Note: Paragraph numbers refer to Volume One. Items marked ˙ are research aids, not citations of authority; see "Key to Citations" on page 806.

Ticket bought for foreign uncle
Alfonso Diaz, 58 TC 560 (1972) (Acq.)

Sweepstake winnings held by court
Rev. Rul. 67-203, 1967-1 CB 105

Lottery prize held by parents as custodians
Joseph Anastasio, 67 TC 814 (1977)

Agreement to share winnings
Samuel L. Huntington, 35 BTA 835 (Acq.)

Agreement to pool winnings
Christian H. Droge, 35 BTA 829 (Acq.)

11.3 GAMBLING WINNINGS AND LOSSES
IRC § 165(d)
Reg. § 1.165-10
*"Wagering War With the Service: Winning Gambling Deductions," Nancy B. Nichols and Diane A. Riordan, 60 Taxation for Accountants 279 (May 1998)

Diary supported loss deduction
Leon Faulkner, 40 TCM 1 (1980)

Tickets with sequential numbers supported loss deduction
Theodore L. Wolkomir, 40 TCM 1078 (1980)

Professional gambler may deduct loss as business expense
Anthony J. Ditunno, 80 TC 362 (1983)

Full-time gambler is in business
Robert P. Groetzinger, 107 S. Ct. 980 (1987)

Game show contestant is not in business
Stanley Whitten, 70 TCM 1064 (1995)

"Comps" offset by gambling losses
Robert Libutti, 71 TCM 2343 (1996)

Casino debt
David Zarin, 90-2 USTC ¶50,530 (3rd Cir. 1990)

11.4 GIFTS AND INHERITANCES

Gifts and inheritances exempt
IRC § 102
Reg. § 1.102-1

Incompetent's gift taxable
Carl Elmer Henry Bader, 23 TC 813 (1973)

No fixed rule to determine taxability of gifts
Mose Duberstein, 363 U.S. 278 (1960)

Will compromise
Munro L. Lyeth v. Hoey, 305 U.S. 188 (1938)

Sale of expected inheritance
Rev. Rul. 70-60, 1970-1 CB 11

Bequest to executor
Frederick L. Merriam, 263 U.S. 179

Bequest to attorney
Lee S. Jones, 23 TCM 235 (1964)
Victor R. Wolder, 493 F.2d 608 (2d Cir. 1974), aff'g 58 TC 974 (1972) (Nonacq.), cert. denied, 419 U.S. 828

Campaign contributions—when taxable
Rev. Rul. 68-19, 1968-1 CB 42

When beneficiary is taxed
IRC § 652

When grantor is taxed
IRC § 671

11.5 REFUNDS OF STATE AND LOCAL INCOME TAX DEDUCTIONS
IRC § 111
*IRS Publication 525

Prior law recovery exclusion
Reg. § 1.111-1

11.6 OTHER RECOVERED DEDUCTIONS
IRC § 111

Refund of adjustable rate mortgage interest
Rev. Rul. 92-91, 1992-2 CB 49

Donated property returned
Sidney W. Rosen, 611 F.2d 942 (1st Cir. 1979)

Reimbursement of loss absorbed by $100 floor not taxable
Rev. Rul. 80-65, 1980-1 CB 183

Debt forgiveness of accrual-basis debtor with carryover
IRC § 111(c), as added by § 2(c) of Pub. L. No. 96-589

11.7 HOW LEGAL DAMAGES ARE TAXED
IRC § 104(a)(2)
* "New Tax Planning Needed For Employment-Related Damages," John H. Skarbnik, 58 Taxation for Accountants 343 (June 1997)
* "What Damage Awards Are Excludable From Gross Income?" Charles E. Price and Leonard G. Weld, 57 Taxation for Accountants 136 (September 1996)

Compensatory damages received on account of physical injury or sickness after August 20, 1996
IRC § 104(a)(2) as amended by The Small Business Job Protection Act of 1996

Punitive damages received after August 20, 1996
IRC § 104(a)(2) as amended by the Small Business Job Protection Act of 1996
IRC § 104(c)

Personal injuries: pre-1996 Small Business Job Protection Act
IRC § 104(a)(2)
Erich E. Schleier, 115 S. Ct. 2159 (1995)
Rev. Rul. 74-77, 1974-1 CB 33

Loss of profit
Phoenix Coal Co., 231 F.2d 420 (2d Cir. 1956)
D. T. Longino Est., 32 TC 904 (1959)

Loss of wages
Bill McKay, 5th Cir. (4/10/96)

Punitive damages for personal injuries: pre-1996 Small Business Job Protection Act
Ernest Horton, 33 F.3d 625 (6th Cir. 1994), aff'd, 100 TC 8 (1993)
Kelly M. O'Gilvie, 92-2 USTC ¶50, 567 (Dist. Ct., Ks. 1992)
Elizabeth A. Reese, Fed. Cl., 8/29/93
Bonnie Miller, 914 F.2d 586 (4th Cir. 1990), rev'g

93 TC 29 (1989)
Maurie Starrels, 304 F.2d 574 (9th Cir. 1962)
Rev. Rul. 84-108, 1984-2 CB 32, revoking Rev. Rul. 75-45, 1975-1 CB 47
A. P. Burford, 642 F. Supp. 635 (D.C. Ala. 1986), rejecting Rev. Rul. 84-108, 1984-2 CB 32
Glenshaw Glass Co., 348 U.S. 426 (1955)
Ray Wesson, 48 F.3d 894 (5th Cir. 1995)
Estate of Chester Moore, 53 F.2d 712 (5th Cir. 1995)

Unstated pre-judgment interest
Joseph Rozpad, 154 F.3d 1 (1998)

Slander or libel—state law governs
James E. Threlkeld, 87 TC 1294 (1986), aff'd 848 F.2d 81 (6th Cir. 1988)
Paul F. Roemer, Jr., 79 TC 398 (1982), rev'd 716 F.2d 693 (9th Cir. 1983) (Nonacq.) Rev. Rul. 85-143, 1985-2 CB 55

Defamation legal costs nondeductible to extent of tax-free damages
Wade E. Church, 80 TC 1104 (1983)

Breach of promise to marry
Lyde McDonald, 9 BTA 1340 (Acq.)

Alienation of affection
C. A. Hawkins, 6 BTA 1023 (Acq.)
Rev. Rul. 74-77, 1974-1 CB 33

Support of children
IRC § 71(b)
Reg. § 1.71-1

Breach of duty of fair representation
Banks, 81 F.3d 874 (9th Cir., 1996)

Business reputation
Mason Knuckles, 23 TCM 182 (1964), aff'd 349 F.2d 610 (10th Cir. 1965)
Paul Draper, 26 TC 201 (1956) (Acq.)

Prejudgement interest
John Brabson, 73 F.3d 1040 (10th Cir., 1996)

Goodwill
Farmers and Merchants Bank of Catlettsburg, Kentucky, 59 F.2d 912 (6th Cir. 1932)
William Basle, 16 TCM 745 (1957), aff'd per curiam, 256 F.2d 381 (3d Cir. 1958)

Embezzlement forgiven
Rev. Rul. 61-185, 1961-2 CB 9

Extortion
James Rutkin, 343 U.S. 130 (1952), aff'g 189 F.2d 431 (3d Cir. 1951)
James J. Moran, 236 F.2d 361 (2d Cir. 1956), cert. denied, 352 U.S. 909

Swindlers
James A. Akers, 167 F.2d 718 (5th Cir. 1948), cert. denied, 335 U.S. 823

Attorney receives payment
Thomas H. Hannaford, 19 TCM 409 (1960)

Effect of contingent legal fee
Ethel Cotnam, 263 F.2d 119 (5th Cir. 1959)
Willie M. Davis, TC Memo 1998-248

11.8 CANCELLATION OF DEBTS YOU OWE
* "IRS Adopts Inconsistent Positions on Nonrecourse Debt in Loan Workouts," Richard N.

---

*Note: Paragraph numbers refer to Volume One. Items marked * are research aids, not citations of authority; see "Key to Citations" on page 806.*

Lipton, 77 Journal of Taxation 196 (October 1992)
* "Planning for Noncorporate Debt Workouts Outside of Bankruptcy," Richard M. Lipton, 70 Taxes 275 (May 1992)
* "Determining If a Taxpayer Is Insolvent for Purposes of the COD Income Exclusion," Robert C. Livsey, 76 Journal of Taxation 224 (April 1992)
* "Avoiding Cancellation of Debt Income Where the Liability Is Disputed," William R. Culp, Jr. and Richard E. Marsh, Jr., 74 Journal of Taxation 288 (May 1991)
* "Avoiding Gain When Mortgage Payments Cannot Be Met," Richard M. Plutzer, 46 Taxation for Accountants 220 (Apr. 1991)

Cancelled debts
Reg. § 1.61-12

Exclusion for certain discharged debt
IRC § 108

Reduction of tax attributes
IRC § 108(b)

Reduce basis of depreciable property
IRC § 108(b)(5)
IRC § 108(c)
IRC § 1017

Appreciated asset transferred to pay off debt taxable
James Gehl, 102 TC 37 (1994)

Loan cancelled by foundations
IRC § 108(f)

Price adjustment not taxed
IRC § 108(e)(5)

Student loan cancelled
IRC § 108(f)

Farm indebtedness
IRC § 108(g)

Debtor taxed on reduction of nonrecourse mortgage debt
Rev. Rul. 91-31, 1991-1 CB19
Rev. Rul. 92-53,1992-2 CB 48 (effect of debt reduction on solvency)

Prepayment of mortgage at discount
Rev. Rul. 82-202, 1982-2 CB 35

Insolvency of debtor
IRC § 108(a)(1)(B)
George Aberl, 78 F.3d 241 (6th Cir., 1996)

Insolvency determined at partnership level
IRC § 108(d)(6)
Pre-1980 cases: Estate of Michael Newman, 934 F.2d 426 (2d Cir. 1991), rev'g 59 TCM 543 (1990)
D.B. Merkel, 99-2 USTC ¶50,848

Proceedings under Bankruptcy Act
Reg. § 1.61-12
Reg. § 1.1016-7
In re: James Bruner, 55 F.3d 195 (5th Cir. 1995)
In re: Bernice Haas, 48 F.2d 1153 (11th Cir. 1995)

Business real estate debt
IRC § 108(8)(1)(D)
IRC § 108(c)

Financial institution reporting of discharged debt
Reg. §1.6050P-1

Voluntary forgiveness by creditor
American Dental Co., 318 U.S. 322 (1943)

Creditor intended a gift
New York Creditmen's Adjustment Bureau, Inc., 110 F. Supp. 214 (S.D.N.Y. 1953)

Identify debt cancelled
Lewis F. Jacobson, 336 U.S. 28 (1949)

Adjust purchase price
Des Moines Improvement Co., 7 BTA 279 (Nonacq.)
Sobel, Inc., 40 BTA 1263 (Nonacq.)

Decline in value of property
Kalman Hirsch, 115 F.2d 656 (7th Cir. 1940)

Borrow money
Manual A. Frank, 44 F. Supp. 729 (D. Pa. 1942), aff'd, 131 F.2d 864 (3d Cir.)

No legal obligation
Kern Co., 1 TC 249 (1942) (Acq.)
Hotel Astoria, Inc., 42 BTA 759 (Acq.)
Fulton Gold Corp., 31 BTA 519

Partial cancellation of indebtedness
Gehring Publishing Co., Inc., 1 TC 345 (1942) (Acq.)

Unauthorized sale of pledged stock is discharge of indebtedness
Regina A. Poczatek, 71 TC 371 (1978)

Inventory
Rev. Rul. 76-86, 1976-1 CB 37

11.9 SCHEDULE K-1
*IRS Publications 541 (partnership), 559 (estate), 589 (S corporation)

11.10 HOW PARTNERS REPORT PARTNERSHIP PROFIT AND LOSS
*IRS Publication 541
* "Partnership Regs. Attach Gain to Some Distributions," Deborah H. Zabava and Murray E. Ascher, 56 Taxation for Accountants 265 (May 1996)
* "How 15-Year Amortization and Other RRA '93 Changes Affect Planning for Retiring Partners," Robert A. Snyder, Jr. and Christopher C. Adler, 82 The Journal of Taxation 12 (January 1995)
* "Anti-Abuse Reg. Confuses and Clarifies," Avi O. Liveson, 54 Taxation for Accountants 260 (May 1995)
* "Tax Consequences of the Departure of a Partner or an S Corporation Shareholder," Don W. Llewellyn, 71 Taxes 648 (October 1993)
* "Alternative Methods for Measuring a Partnership Interest," James R. Hamill and Richard L. Allitzer, 51 Taxation for Accountants 10 (July 1993)
* "Partner Transactions Under the Final 707 Regs. and New Law," Robert D. Howard and John Delaney, 78 Journal of Taxation 46 (January 1993)
* "Dissecting the Regulations on Partnership Disguised Sales," Terence Floyd Cuff, 71 Taxes 451 (August 1993)
* "Final Rules on Allocation of Partnership Liabilities Still Leave Unanswered Questions," M. Celeste Pickron, 76 Journal of Taxation 272

(May 1992)
* "How to Make Sure That Payments to Partners Qualify for Treatments as Guaranteed Payments," Rudolph Rameli, Taxation for Accountants, June 1987

Final check-the-box regulations
Reg. § 301.7701-1 through 301.7701-3

Partnership not taxed
IRC § 701
Reg. § 1.701-1

What is a partnership?
IRC § 761
Reg. § 1.761-1

Health insurance premiums
IRC § 162(l)

Salary from partnership guaranteed
IRC § 707(c)
Reg. § 1.707-1(c)

Special allocations
IRC § 704(b)

Substantial economic effect
Reg. § 1.704-1(b)(2)
Mary Ogden, 84 TC 871 (1985)

Allocations to partners upon property contributions made after December 20, 1993
Reg. § 1.704-3

No advance ruling of partnership provisions re substantial economic effect
Rev. Proc. 79-14, 1979-1 CB 496

Change of partnership interest during the year
IRC § 706(d)

Passive loss limitations
IRC § 469

IRS may allow unincorporated businesses to choose partnership of corporate taxation
Notice 95-14, 1995-14 IRB 7 (check-the-box initiative)

Failure to file information return
IRC § 6698

Sales to controlled partnership
IRC § 1239(b) and (c)

Partner reports
IRC § 702
Reg. § 1.702-1

Transferring partnership interests
IRC § 6050K
Reg. § 1.6050K-1

Composite 25 transfer rule
Reg. § 1.6050K-1(a)(3)

Substantially appreciated inventory
IRC § 751(d)(1), as amended by the Revenue Reconciliation Act of 1993

Assignment of outside referral fees to partnership
Stephen B. Schneer, 97 TC 643 (1991)

Retroactive allocations
IRC § 706(d)

Note: Paragraph numbers refer to Volume One. Items marked ˙ are research aids, not citations of authority; see "Key to Citations" on page 806.

Net operating loss
Reg. § 1.702-2

Credits deductible
IRC § 702(b)
Reg. § 1.702-2

Partner's distributive share
Temp. Reg. § 1.704-IT
P.L. 103-465 12/8/94

Partnership distribution of contributed property within two years
IRC § 707(a)(2)(B)
Reg. § 1.707-3 through § 1.707-9

Recognition of gain by partner on distribution of contributed property
IRC § 732

11.11 WHEN A PARTNER REPORTS INCOME OR LOSS

When a partnership reports income or loss
IRC § 706
Reg. § 1.706-1
Harry W. Lehman, 19 TC 659 (1953)

Fiscal year limitations
IRC § 706(b)(1)

Fiscal year election
IRC § 444
Temp. Reg. § 1.444-1T

Limitations on electable fiscal years
Temp. Reg. § 1.444-1T(b)(3)

Required payment
IRC § 7519

Refund of required payments
IRC § 7519(c)
Announcement 90-112, 1990-40 IRB 37

11.12 PARTNERSHIP LOSS LIMITATIONS
IRC § 704
Reg. § 1.704-1
F. A. Falconer, 40 TC 1011 (1963) (Acq.)

Limitation on losses
IRC § 704(d)
IRC § 465

Partners may not increase basis by accrued partnership liabilities
Rev. Rul. 88-77, 1988-2 CB 128

11.13 UNIFIED TAX AUDITS OF PARTNERSHIPS
IRC §§ 6221-6231
* "Tax Matters Partners: Scope of Authority and Factors in Making an Effective Choice," Carla A. Green, 45 Taxation for Accountants 114 (August 1990)

11.14 STOCKHOLDER REPORTING OF S CORPORATION INCOME AND LOSS
IRC § 1361 through 1379 as amended by the Small Business Job Protection Act of 1996

Pass-through of income and losses
IRC § 1366

Distributions

IRC § 1368
IRC § 1366(d)(1)(A)

Income must be included in return
IRC § 1367(b)

Allocation for new and old shareholder
IRC § 1377(a)

Family allocation
IRC § 1366(e)

Health insurance premiums
IRC § 162(l), as amended by the Small Business Job Protection Act of 1996
IRC § 1362(d)(3)
IRC § 1366(f)(3)
IRC § 1375

Appreciated property distribution
IRC § 1363(d)
IRC § 1362(a)
IRC § 1362(b)

Effect of election on corporation
IRC § 1363(e)

Invalid elections may be corrected
IRC § 1362(b)(5) and 1362(f), added by the Small Business Job Protection Act of 1996

Built-in gains tax
IRC § 1374
Rev. Rul. 86-141, 1986-2 CB 151
IRC § 1362(d)

Inadvertent terminations
IRC § 1362(f) as amended by the Small Business Job Protection Act of 1996

Treatment of termination year
IRC § 1362(e)

Re-election following termination
IRC § 1362(g) as amended by Section 1317(b) of the Small Business Job Protection Act of 1996
IRC § 1372

Waiver of tax
IRC § 1375(d)
IRC § 1374

IRS may approve invalid elections
IRC § 1362(b)(5)
IRC § 1362(f)

Agreement to terminate year
IRC § 1377

Audit rules
IRC §§ 6241-6245 repealed (corporate level audit procedures)
IRC § 6037(c) (shareholder must report consistently with S Corporation return)

Retroactive re-election
IRC § 1362(g)

Adjustments before the loss limitation
IRC § 1366(d)(1)(A)
IRC § 1368(d)

Income in respect of a decedent
IRC § 1367(b)(4)

11.15 HOW BENEFICIARIES REPORT ESTATE OR TRUST INCOME
IRC § 652

Reg. § 1.652(a) and (b)
*IRS Publication 559
* "Estates and Trusts File the Same Return, But Use Different Rules," Louis S. Harrison, 47 Taxation for Accountants 172 (Sept. 1991)
* "Guidelines for Preparing the Fiduciary Income Tax Return," G. Philip Morehead, 21 Prac. Accountant 17 (Jan. 1988)
* "Income Taxation of Trusts and Estates Under TRA '86," Lisa Brown Petkun and Deborah Lerner, 38 Journal of Taxation 66 (1987)

Depreciation and depletion
IRC § 167(g)
IRC § 611(b)(3)

Net operating losses
IRC § 642(d)
Reg. § 1.642(h)-1
George W. Balkwill, 25 BTA 1147, aff'd, 77 F.2d 569 (6th Cir. 1935), cert. denied, 296 U.S. 609
George C. Reeves, 15 TCM 394 (1956)

When to report
IRC § 652
Reg. § 1.652(a)-1

Multiple trusts
IRC § 643(f)

Consistent reporting by beneficiaries
IRC § 6034A(c), as amended by the 1997 Act
IRC § 6048(d), as amended by the 1997 Act

11.16 REPEAL OF THROWBACK RULE FOR DISTRIBUTIONS OF ACCUMULATED TRUST INCOME
IRC § 665(c), as amended by the 1997 Act

Accumulations (pre-8/5/97)
IRC § 662
IRC § 663
IRC § 665
IRC § 666

Trust for spouse (pre-8/5/97)
IRC § 677

Method of calculating tax (Form 4970) (pre-8/5/97)
IRC § 667

No throwback for years before beneficiary attains age 21 (pre-8/5/97)
IRC § 665(b)

Denial of refund (pre-8/5/97)
IRC § 666(e)

Special rule for exchanges within two years of transfer (pre-8/5/97)
IRC § 644

Two-year rule inapplicable if guarantor dies within two years (pre-8/5/97)
IRC § 644(e)(4)

Trust sale of capital gain property within two years of transfer (pre-8/5/97)
IRC § 644, repealed by the 1997 Act

11.17 DEDUCTIONS FOR INCOME SUBJECT TO ESTATE TAX
* "Income and Estate Tax Impact of Income in Respect of a Decedent," David M. Maloney, 23

Note: Paragraph numbers refer to Volume One. Items marked ˚ *are research aids, not citations of authority; see "Key to Citations" on page 806.*

Note: Paragraph numbers refer to Volume One. Items marked ˙ are research aids, not citations of authority; see "Key to Citations" on page 806.

836

Note: Paragraph numbers refer to Volume One. Items marked * *are research aids, not citations of authority; see "Key to Citations" on page 806.*

IRC § 501(c)(3)
Emanuel Kolkey, 27 TC 37 (1956) (Acq.), aff'd, 254 F.2d 51 (7th Cir. 1958)
Saint Germain Foundation, 26 TC 648 (1956) (Acq.)
Mark B. Lloyd, 29 TCM 453 (1970)

Purchase of church building bond
Rev. Rul. 75-112, 1975-1 CB 274
Rev. Rul. 58-262, 1958-1 CB 143

Foreign governments
R. Hess, 30 TCM 1043 (1971) (State of Israel)

Value in return for contribution
Katherine Channing, 67 F.2d 98 (1st Cir.), cert. denied, 291 U.S. 686
Morris N. Scharf, 32 TCM 124 (1973)
Albin J. Strandquist, 29 TCM 38 (1970)
Rev. Rul. 67-246, 1967-2 CB 104 distinguished by Rev. Rul. 74-348
1974-2 CB 80
Rev. Rul. 58-303, 1958-1 CB 61

Tuition
Harold De Jong, 309 F.2d 373 (9th Cir. 1962), aff'g 36 TC 896 (1961)
Rev. Rul. 71-112, 1971-1 CB 93
Jacob Oppewal, 30 TCM 1177 (1971), aff'd, 468 F.2d 1000 (1st Cir. 1972)

Rest home
O. J. Wardwell Est., 35 TC 443 (1960), rev'd, 301 F.2d 632 (8th Cir. 1962)

Deduction allowed for retirement community sponsorship gift
Ruth Dowell, 553 F.2d 1233 (10th Cir. 1977)

Son's payment for mother's apartment
Ernest S. & Janet M. Klapperbach, 52 TCM 437 (1986)

Donation of services
Reg. § 1.170A-1(g)
Rev. Rul. 67-236, 1967-2 CB 103
Rev. Rul. 57-462, 1957-2 CB 157
William W. Grant, 84 TC 809 (1985)

Blood donations
Rev. Rul. 162, 1953-2 CB 127

Directory of churches
Rev. Rul. 57-525, 1957-2 CB 159

Value of use of property
IRC § 170(f)(3)(A)
Reg. § 1.170A-7(d)

No deduction for donated vacation home time
Rev. Rul. 89-51, 1989-1 CB 89

No deduction for payments to support Mormon missionary
Harold Davis, 110 S. Ct. 2014 (1990)

No deduction for Church of Scientology trainings
Robert L. Hernandez, 490 U.S. 680 (1989)

14.3 CONTRIBUTIONS THAT PROVIDE YOU WITH BENEFITS

Token benefits
Rev. Proc. 90-12, 1990-1 CB 471, amplified by Rev. Proc. 92-49, 1992-1 CB 987

Membership benefits
Prop. Reg. §1.170 A-13 (f)(8)(i)(B)

Deductible dues
Eunice A. Horne, 16 TCM 953 (1957)
Rev. Rul. 54-565, 1954-2 CB 95, modified by Rev. Rul. 68-432, 1968-2 CB 104
Rev. Rul. 55-192, 1955-1 CB 294, amplified by Rev. Rul. 86-25, 1986-1 CB 202

Dues may be allocable
Rev. Rul. 68-432, 1968-2 CB 104

Benefit tickets
Rev. Rul. 74-348, 1974-2 CB 80

No deduction for regular price tickets even if not used
Charles F. Urbauer, 63 TCM 2492 (1992)

Athletic stadium tickets
IRC § 170(m)

14.4 UNREIMBURSED EXPENSES OF VOLUNTEER WORKERS

Out-of-pocket costs deductible
Reg. § 1.170 A-1 (g)

Written acknowledgment of services required for expenses of $250 or more
Prop. Reg. § 1.170 A-13 (f)(10)

No deduction for travel unless elements of personal pleasure absent
IRC § 170(j)
Notice 87-23, 1987-1 CB 467, modified by Rev. Proc. 90-15, 1990-1 CB 476

Travel expenses
Francois Louis, 25 TCM 1047 (1966)
Rev. Rul. 59-160, 1959-1 CB 59
Rev. Rul. 58-279, 1958-1 CB 145
Rev. Rul. 58-240, 1958-1 CB 141, clarified by Rev. Rul. 71-135, 1971-1 CB 94
Rev. Rul. 57-327, 1957-2 CB 155
Rev. Rul. 55-4, 1955-1 CB 291

No deduction for value of donated services
Reg. § 1.170A-1(g)
William W. Grant, 84 TC 809 (1985)

Per diem allowances
Rev. Rul. 74-433, 1974-2 CB 92
Rev. Rul. 67-30, 1967-1 CB 9

Uniform costs
Rev. Rul. 56-508, 1956-2 CB 126

Delegate
Harris W. Seed, 57 TC 265 (1971)
John R. Wood, 57 TC 220 (1971), aff'd per curiam, 462 F.2d 691 (5th Cir. 1972)
Rev. Rul. 58-240, 1958-1 CB 141, clarified by Rev. Rul. 71-135, 1971-1 CB 94
* Letter Ruling 8242042

Services authorized
Russell Doty, Jr., 62 TC 587 (1974)
Travis Smith, 60 TC 988 (1973) (Acq.)

Replacing engine while doing volunteer work
Rev. Rul. 59-239, 1959-2 CB 100

Volunteer's auto allowance after 1997

IRC § 170(i), as amended by the 1997 Act

Noncompensated minister deducts car expenses
Rev. Rul. 69-645, 1969-2 CB 37

CAP volunteer
Larry A. Miller, 34 TCM 1207 (1975)

Repairs attributable to charitable services deductible
John Orr, 343 F.2d 553 (5th Cir. 1965)
Rev. Rul. 58-279, 1958-1 CB 145

Babysitting costs
Rev. Rul. 73-597, 1973-2 CB 69

Foster care costs
Rev. Rul. 77-280, 1977-2 CB 14
Kingman Babcock, 71 TCM 2257 (1996)

14.5 SUPPORT OF A STUDENT IN YOUR HOME
IRC § 170(g)
Reg. § 1.170A-2

14.6 WHAT KIND OF PROPERTY ARE YOU DONATING?

Gift of property
IRC § 170
Rev. Rul. 55-410, 1955-1 CB 297
Magnolia Development Corp., 19 TCM 934 (1960)

Stock donation to private foundation
IRC § 170(e)(5)(D)(ii), as amended by the 1997 Act

No deduction if voting rights retained
Rev. Rul. 81-282, 1981-2 CB 78

Fair market value of property
Philip Kaplan, 43 TC 663 (1965) (Acq.)
Daniel S. McGuire, 44 TC 801 (1965) (Acq.)
Morris Schapiro, 27 TCM 205 (1968)
Alexia DuPont O. De Bie Est., 56 TC 876 (1971) (Acq.)
Lucky Stores, Inc., 105 TC 28 (1996)

Ordinary income property
IRC § 170(e)(1)(A)
Reg. § 1.170A-4(b)(1)
Leonard Greene, 13 F.3d 577 (2nd Cir. 1994)

Partnership property
Rev. Rul. 96-11, 1996-4 IRB 28

Deduction limits for tangible personal property
IRC § 170(e)(1)(B)

Bargain sale
IRC § 170(e)(2)
IRC § 1011(b)
Reg. § 1.170A-4(c)(2)
Leonard Greene, 13 F.3d 577 (2nd Cir. 1994)

Donated property sold by charity
Stuart A. Rogers, 38 TC 785 (1962) (Nonacq.)

Guidelines for valuations
Rev. Rul. 66-49, 1966-1 CB 36, amplified by Rev. Rul. 72-366, 1972-2 CB 91

Partial interests
IRC § 170(f)(3)(A) and (B)

Note: Paragraph numbers refer to Volume One. Items marked ` are research aids, not citations of authority; see "Key to Citations" on page 806.

Reg. § 1.170A-7

Future interests in tangible personal property
IRC § 170(a)(3)

Election to reduce appreciation
IRC § 170(b)(1)(C)(iii)
Reg. § 1.170A-8(d)(2)
Rev. Rul. 74-53, 1974-1 CB 60

Congressman's papers
James H. Morrison, 71 TC 683 (1979), aff'd per
curiam, 611 F.2d 98 (5th Cir. 1980)

Capital gain property donated to private foundation
IRC § 170(b)(1)(D)
IRC § 170(e)

Fair market value deduction for gift of publicly traded stock to private foundation
IRC § 170(e)(5)

Trust interests
IRC § 170(f)(2)

Prepaid interest
IRC § 170(f)(5)
Reg. § 1.170A-3

Donation of remainder interests
IRC § 664
Reg. § 1.664-4

Gift of mortgaged property
Rev. Rul. 81-163, 1981-1 CB 433
Winston Guest, 77 TC 9 (1981) (Acq.)
Leo Ebben et al.,783 F.2d 906 (9th Cir. 1986)

Gift of depreciable mortgaged property
Aaron Levine Est., 634 F.2d 12 (2d Cir. 1980)
Teofilo Evangelista, 629 F.2d 1218 (7th Cir. 1980)

Delivery of stock gift
Jack W. Londen, 45 TC 106 (1965)

14.7 PROPERTY THAT HAS DECLINED BELOW COST

Deduction limited to cost
LaVar Withers, 69 TC 900 (1978)

14.8 BARGAIN SALES OF APPRECIATED PROPERTY

IRC § 170(e)(2)
IRC § 1011(b)
Reg. § 1.170A-4(c)(2)
Reg. § 1.1011-2

Appreciation reduction for contributed portion only
Estate of Pauline Bullard, 87 TC 261 (1986)

Basis allocation applies even if annual ceiling bars deduction
Warner W. Hodgdon, 98 TC 31 (1992)

14.9 ART OBJECTS

Art not used for tax-exempt purposes
IRC § 170(e)(1)(B)(i)

IRS statement of value
Rev. Proc. 96-15, 1996-3 IRB 41

Appraising contributions of art works
Adolph Posner, 35 TCM 943 (1976)
Edwin F. Gordon, 35 TCM 1227 (1976)

Appraisal fee an itemized expense
Rev. Rul. 67-461, 1967-1 CB 125

Family's allocation of portion of collection
Gifford M. Mast, 56 TCM 1523 (1989)

Deduction allowed despite lack of possession
James Winokur, 90 TC 733 (1988) (Acq.)

14.10 INTERESTS IN REAL ESTATE

Fractional transfers
IRC § 170(f)(3)(B)(ii)
Rev. Rul. 58-261, 1958-1 CB 143

Remainder interests
IRC § 170(f)(4)
Prop. Reg. § 1.170A-12

Option on realty
Rev. Rul. 82-197, 1982-2 CB 72

Farms or residences
IRC § 170(f)(3)(B)(i)
Rev. Rul. 76-357, 1976-2 CB 285

Vacation use retained
Rev. Rul. 75-420, 1975-2 CB 78

Right to use of property
IRC § 170(f)(3)(A)
Reg. § 1.170A-7(d)
Charles M. Petgers, 35 TCM 770 (1976)

Certain partial interests donated for conservation purposes
IRC § 170(h)

Donating use of vacation home
Rev. Rul. 89-51, 1989-1 CB 89

14.11 LIFE INSURANCE

* "Life Insurance and Charitable Giving: Important Tax Rules," Lee Slavatin, 75 Taxes 29 (Jan. 1997)

Deductible if irrevocably assigned
Eppa Hunton, IV, 1 TC 821 (1943) (Acq.)

Premiums deductible if beneficiary a charity
Mortimer C. Adler, 5 BTA 1063
Rev. Rul. 58-372, 1958-2 CB 99

Charity's insurable interest
* Letter Ruling 9147040, revoking Letter Ruling 9110016

Contribution of cash surrender value not deductible
Rev. Rul. 76-143, 1976-1 CB 63
Rev. Rul. 76-1, 1976-1 CB 57

Split-dollar insurance
IRS Notice 99-36, 1999-26 IRB

14.12 FORM 8283 AND WRITTEN APPRAISAL REQUIREMENTS

1984 Tax Act (P.L. 98-369) Section 155

IRS warns about need to file Forms 8283 and 8282
Announcement 90-25, 1990-8 IRB 25

Qualified appraisals
Reg. § 1.170A-13(c)
Notice 95-1, 1995-1 CB 288

20% penalty for overvaluation
IRC § 6662(e)

14.13 BUSINESS INVENTORY

Corporate inventory
Reg. § 1.170A-4(e)

Gifts at fair market value
IRC § 170(e)
Charles N. Prothro, 209 F.2d 331 (5th Cir. 1954)
David C. Whitge, 104 F. Supp. 213 (D. Kan. 1952)
Rev. Rul. 55-138, 1955-1 CB 223

Crops
Clyde G. Tatum, 46 TC 736 (1966), aff'd, 400 F.2d 242 (5th Cir. 1968)

Certain corporate contributions for care of ill, needy, or infants
IRC § 170(e)(3)

14.14 DONATIONS THROUGH TRUSTS

* "Revise Tax Planning for Charitable Remainder Trusts," Gregory Herman-Giddens, 60 Taxation for Accountants 260 (May 1998)
* "Charitable Remainder Trusts Offer Noncharitable Benefits," Michael K. Moyers, Alan D. Spiegel and E. Richard Baum, 58 Taxation for Accountants 285 (May 1997)

Income interests
IRC § 170(f)(2)(B)
IRC § 671

Charitable remainder trusts
IRC § 170(f)(2)(A)
IRC § 170(f)(3)(B)
IRC § 170(f)(4)
IRC § 170(f)(7)
IRC § 664

Life income plans
IRC § 170(f)(2)(A)
IRC § 642(c)(5)
IRC § 664

IRS valuation tables
Notice 89-60, 1989-1 CB 700

14.15 RECORDS NEEDED TO SUBSTANTIATE YOUR CONTRIBUTIONS

* "Reporting and Substantiation Requirements for Charitable Contributions," Tim Krumwiede, David Beausejour and Raymond Zimmerman, 72 Taxes 14 (January 1994)
* "New Substantiation and Disclosure Rules Increase Burden on Charities and Donors," Eugene Gorrin and Marc J. Honigfeld, 81 The Journal of Taxation 310 (November 1994)

Substantiation requirement for charitable contributions of $250 or more
IRC § 170(f)(8)
Prop. Reg. §§ 1.170A-13(f)(10) and (14)
Notice 95-15, 1995-1 CB 299

Charity disclosure statement for donations

Note: Paragraph numbers refer to Volume One. Items marked `*` *are research aids, not citations of authority; see "Key to Citations" on page 806.*

exceeding $75
IRC § 6115

Contribution by check
Reg. § 1.170A-1(b)
Elie B. Witt Est., 160 F. Supp. 521 (D. Fla. 1956)
Estelle Broussard, 16 TC 23 (1951)
Modie J. Spiegel Est., 12 TC 524 (1949) (Acq.)
Rev. Rul. 54-465, 1954-2 CB 93

14.16 PENALTY FOR SUBSTANTIAL OVERVALUATION OF PROPERTY

20% penalty
IRC § 6662 (e)(1)(A)

40% penalty
IRC § 6662 (h)

Reasonable cause reliance on appraisal
Reg. § 1.6664.4 (g)

Professional appraiser subject to penalty
IRC § 6701

Auto donations
AICPA Not-For-Profit Industry Conference, 6/14/99

14.17 CEILING ON CHARITABLE DEDUCTIONS

Organizations qualifying for 50% ceiling
IRC § 170(b)(1)(A)
Reg. § 1.170A-9

30% limit for capital gain property
IRC § 170(b)(1)(C)

30% limit for non-operating foundations
IRC 170(b)(1)(B)

20% limit for certain capital gain property
IRC § 170(b)(1)(D)

Donations by corporations
IRC § 170(b)(2)

Order of taking deductions
IRC § 170(b)(1)(C) and (D)
Reg. § 1.170A-8(f)

14.18 FIVE-YEAR CARRYOVER FOR EXCESS DONATIONS

Individuals
IRC § 170(d)(1)
Sidney Rimmer, 69 TCM 2620 (1995)

Corporations
IRC § 170(d)(2)

Donations to foundations
IRC § 170(b)(1)(B)
IRC § 170(b)(1)(D)

14.19 ELECTION TO REDUCE PROPERTY GIFT APPRECIATION

Reduction for appreciation
IRC § 170(e)(1)

Electing 50% ceiling
IRC § 170(b)(1)(C)(iii)
Reg. § 1.170A-8(d)(2)

Election is irreversible

Orin Woodbury, 900 F.2d 1457 (10th Cir. 1990)

---

15 ITEMIZED DEDUCTION FOR INTEREST EXPENSES

15.1 HOME MORTGAGE INTEREST

Residential mortgage interest
IRC § 163(h)(2)(D)
IRC § 163(h)(3)
Temp. Reg. § 1.163-10T

Two-residence test
IRC § 163(h)(4)(A)

Home mortgage certificates
IRC § 25
Temp. Reg. § 1.25-1T through 8T

Qualified residence
H. Roger Lawler, 69 TCM 1699 (1995)

Beneficial owner
Paul Trans Dang, TC Memo 1999-233

15.2 HOME ACQUISITION LOANS

Acquisition indebtedness limits
IRC § 163(h)(3)(B)

Seller's debt
Wendell Belden, 70 TCM 274 (1995)

Refinancing
IRC § 163(h)(3)(B)(i)
IRC § 163(h)(3)(D)(iii) and (iv)

Passive activity interest
IRC § 469

Married—separate returns
IRC § 163(h)(4)(A)(ii)

Cooperatives
IRC § 163(h)(4)(B)

Destroyed house rebuilt
Rev. Rul 96-32, 1996-25 IRB 4

15.3 HOME EQUITY LOANS

Home equity indebtedness limits
IRC § 163(h)(3)(C)

15.4 HOME CONSTRUCTION LOANS

Residence under construction
Temp. Reg. § 1.163-10T(p)(5)
Notice 88-74, 1988-2 CB 385

15.5 HOME IMPROVEMENT LOANS

Residence under improvement
IRC § 163(h)(3)(B)(i)(I)

15.6 MORTGAGE PAYMENT RULES

Joint owners
Barbara S. Finney, 35 TCM 1504 (1976)

Penalty for prepaying mortgage
Rev. Rul. 57-198, 1957-1 CB 94

Delinquency charges not deductible

Robert G. West, 61 TCM 1694 (1991)

Graduated payment mortgages
* Letter Ruling 8031087

Reverse mortgage loan
Rev. Rul. 80-248, 1980-2 CB 164

Zero interest mortgages
Rev. Rul. 82-124, 1982-1 CB 89

Shared appreciation mortgage
Rev. Rul. 83-51, 1983-1 CB 48

Mortgage assistance payments under § 235 of the National Housing Act not deductible
Reg. § 1.163-1(d)
Rev. Rul. 75-271, 1975-2 CB 23

H.U.D. interest reduction payments
Rev. Rul. 76-75, 1976-1 CB 14
Alvin V. Graff, 74 TC 743 (1980)

15.7 INTEREST ON REFINANCED LOANS
* "Refinancing a Home Mortgage May Have Adverse Tax Costs," Norman L. Eule and Michael B. Richman, 49 Taxation for Accountants 102 (August 1992)

Refinancing
IRC § 163(h)(3)(B)(i)
IRC § 163(h)(3)(D)(iii) and (iv)
James R. Huntsman, 91 TC (1988), rev'd by 905 F.2d 1182 (8th Cir. 1990)
Rev. Rul. 87-22, 1987-1 CB 146
Rev. Proc. 87-15, 1987-1 CB 624
David A. Kelly, 62 TCM 401 (1991)
(Huntsman exception inapplicable)

15.8 "POINTS"
* "Points in Refinancing Some Home Mortgages May Now Be Currently Deductible," Mark Higgins, 45 Taxation for Accountants 140 (September 1990)

"Points" treated as prepaid interest
IRC § 461(g)

IRS position on deducting points
Rev. Proc. 94-27, 1994-1 CB 613

Seller-paid points
Rev. Proc. 94-27, 1994-1 CB 613

Amortize points starting in second year
Letter Ruling 199905033

VA and FHA loan origination fees deductible as points
Rev. Proc. 92-12A, 1992-1 CB 664

Loan fees amortized
Karl Von Muff, 46 TCM 1185 (1983)
Richard Goodwin, 75 TC 424 (1981)
Rev. Rul. 81-161, 1981-1 CB 313
Rev. Rul. 81-160, 1981-1 CB 312

Loan fees: prior law
Robert E. Stewart, 41 TCM 318 (1980)

Refinancing
James R. Huntsman, 91 TC (1988), rev'd by 905 F.2d 1182 (8th Cir. 1990)
Rev. Rul. 87-22, 1987-1 CB 146
Rev. Proc. 87-15, 1987-1 CB 624
David A. Kelly, 62 TCM 401 (1991)

Note: Paragraph numbers refer to Volume One. Items marked *are research aids, not citations of authority; see "Key to Citations" on page 806.*

(Huntsman exception inapplicable)

Points withheld from principal not deductible
Roger A. Schubel, 77 TC 701 (1981)

15.9 COOPERATIVE AND CONDOMINIUM APARTMENTS

* "Calculating Allowable Depreciation for Tenant-Stockholders of Cooperatives," Albert Feuer, 60 Journal of Taxation 268 (1984)
* "How to Insure Maximum Benefits for Co-ops and Condominiums As Well As Their Owners," Douglas R. Holm, 10 Taxation for Lawyers, 158 and 27 Taxation for Accountants 252 (1981)
* "Depreciating the Cooperative Apartment," Joel E. Miller, 11 J. Real Estate Tax 307 (Summer 1984)
* "Commercial Condominiums: Tax Considerations for Unit Purchasers and the Association," D. S. Shapiro, 41 Journal of Taxation 204 (1974)

Cooperative apartments
IRC § 163(h)(4)(B)
IRC § 216
Reg. § 1.216-1(c) and (d)
Rev. Rul. 59-257, 1959-2 CB 101
Rev. Rul. 53-120, 1953-2 CB 130
Rev. Rul. 73-15, 1973-1 CB 141

Holdover tenants do not jeopardize deductions to co-op owners
Rev. Rul. 80-299, 1980-2 CB 82

Condominiums
Rev. Rul. 64-31, 1964-1 (Pt. 1) CB 300
Raymond J. Wachter, 75-1 USTC ¶9172 (D. Wash. 1975)

15.10 INVESTMENT INTEREST LIMITATIONS

* "Deducting Deficiency Interest as a Business Expense: Recent Developments Since IRA '86," Linda M. Johnson and Giles B. Sutton, 74 Taxes 318 (May 1996)

Investment interest
IRC § 163(d)(3)
IRC § 163(h)(2)(B)
Rev. Rul. 95-16, 1995-1 CB 9
Warren Halle, 83 F.3d 649 (4th Cir. 1996)

Net capital gain excluded from investment income after 1992
IRC § 163 (d)(4)(B)

Carryforward
IRC § 163(d)(2)

Passive activity interest
IRC § 469

15.11 DEBTS TO CARRY TAX-EXEMPT OBLIGATIONS

Frank Batten, 322 F. Supp. 629 (E. D. Vir. 1971)
Amedeo Louis Marionenzi, 32 TCM 681 (1973), aff'd per curiam, 490 F.2d 92 (1st Cir. 1974)

Interest on borrowings to carry tax-exempt obligations
IRC § 265
Reg. § 1.265-2
Constance M. Bishop, 41 TC 154 (1963), aff'd, 342 F.2d 757 (6th Cir. 1965)

Rev. Proc. 72-18, 1972-1 CB 740, clarified by Rev. Proc. 74-8, 1974-1 CB 419

Interest on joint venture mortgage
Max R. Israelson, 367 F. Supp. 1104 (D. Md. 1974), aff'd per curiam, 75-1 USTC (4th Cir. 1975)

Interest on loan to carry mutual fund shares paying exempt-interest dividends
IRC § 265(a)(4)

Short sales
IRC § 265(a)(5)

15.12 EARMARKING USE OF LOAN PROCEEDS

Prop. Reg. § 1.163-8T

Expenses within 30 days of depositing loan in account
Notice 89-35, 1989-1 CB 675

Pre-existing debt
Warren Halle, 83 F.3d 649 (4th Cir. 1996)

15.13 YEAR TO CLAIM AN INTEREST DEDUCTION

Promissory note is not payment of interest
Francis R. Hart, 54 F.2d 848 (1st Cir. 1932)

Increasing of loan
Julius I. Peyser, 1 TCM 807 (1943)
Fred W. Leadbetter, 39 BTA 629 (Nonacq.)

Life insurance loan
L. B. Hirsch, 42 BTA 566 (Acq.), aff'd, 124 F.2d 24 (9th Cir. 1941)
Arthur A. Beaudry, 1 TCM 838 (1943), modified and rem'd, 150 F.2d 20 (2d Cir. 1945), on remand, 5 TCM 61 (1946)
J. Simpson Dean, 35 TC 1083 (1961) (Nonacq.)

Margin account with broker
Rev. Rul. 70-221, 1970-1 CB 33

Contested note or obligation
Allegheny Steel Co., 18 F. Supp. 398 (Ct. Cl. 1937)
Shellabarger Grain Products Co., 2 TC 75 (1943) (Acq.), aff'd in part, rev'd in part, 146 F.2d 177 (7th Cir. 1944)

Partial payment of loan
McConway & Torley Corp., 2 TC 593 (1943)
Theodore R. Plunkett, 41 BTA 700 (Acq.), aff'd on other grounds, 118 F.2d 644 (1st Cir. 1941)
Paul N. Bowen Est., 2 TC 783 (1973)
George R. Newhouse, 59 TC 783 (1973)
John B. Ferenc, 33 TCM 136 (1974)

Full settlement of debt
William J. Petit, 8 TC 228 (1947) (Acq.)
Warner Co., 11 TC 419 (1948), aff'd per curiam, 181 F.2d 599 (3d Cir. 1950)

Using borrowed funds to pay interest
News Release IR-83-93, July 6, 1983
Barry L. Battelstein, 631 F.2d 1182 (5th Cir. 1980), cert. denied
Donald L. Wilkerson, 655 F.2d 980 (9th Cir. 1981)

Note that is renewed
S. E. Thomason, 33 BTA 576

David J. Secunda, 36 TCM 763 (1977)

Interest paid with a loan from lender
Charles Davison, 107 TC 4 (1996)

15.14 PREPAID INTEREST

IRC § 461(g)

---

16 DEDUCTIONS FOR TAXES

16.1 DEDUCTIBLE TAXES

IRC § 164

16.2 NONDEDUCTIBLE TAXES

IRC § 164
Reg. § 1.164-1

Sales tax deduction repealed
1986 Tax Act § 134(a)(1), repealing prior law Code § 164 (a)(4), § 164(b)(2) and (5)

Sales tax added to basis of business or investment property
IRC § 164(a)

Transfer taxes on securities sale reduces amount realized
Announcement 88-54, 1988-13 IRB 35
IRC § 164(a)

Nondeductible taxes
IRC § 275

Federal minimum tax not deductible
Rev. Rul. 77-396, 1977-2 CB 86

Cash basis
IRC § 461
IRC § 1.461-1(a)(1)
Joseph Shalleck, 1 TCM 292 (1942)

Borrowed funds
In re Barry L. Battelstein, 77-2 USTC ¶9516 (S.D. Tex. 1977)

Payment by bank
Frank J. Hradesky, 65 TC 87 (1975), aff'd per curiam, 540 F.2d 821 (5th Cir. 1976)
Rev. Rul. 78-103, 1978-1 CB 58

Water bills
Benjamin Mahler, 119 F.2d 869 (2d Cir. 1941), aff'g on the point BTA Memo., P-H 39,468, cert. denied, 314 U.S. 660
Rufus K. Steel, 7 TCM 558 (1948)

Assessments not deductible as taxes
Rev. Rul. 77-29, 1977-2 CB 538
Rev. Rul. 76-495, 1976-2 CB 43

Parking meter charges
Rev. Rul. 73-91, 1973-1 CB 71

Sewer fees
Louis M. Roth, 17 TC 1450 (1952) (Acq.)

Postage
Reg. § 1.164-2

Transfer taxes
Rev. Rul. 65-313, 1965-2 CB 47

Turnpike or thruway tolls
Donald L. Cox, 41 TC 161 (1963)

Note: Paragraph numbers refer to Volume One. Items marked * *are research aids, not citations of authority; see "Key to Citations" on page 806.*

16.3 Deducting State Income Taxes

Taxes withheld from pay
Special Ruling, October 15, 1959
Davis, 160 Mich. App. 98 rev'd and rem'd 489 US 803 (1989)

State tax paid before end of year
Lillian B. Glassell, 12 TC 232 (1949)
Aaron Lowenstein Est., 12 TC 694 (1949) (Acq.), aff'd on other grounds, 183 F.2d 172 (5th Cir. 1950), cert. denied, 340 U.S. 911
Special Ruling, February 13, 1946
Rev. Rul. 74-140, 1974-1 CB 50
Rev. Rul. 82-208, 1982-2 CB 58

Alabama unemployment tax deductible
Rev. Rul. 75-156, 1975-1 CB 66

Rhode Island disability deductible
James R. McGowan, 67 TC 599 (1976)
News Release IR-1742 (1/28/77)

California disability deductible
Anthony Trujillo, 68 TC 56 (1977)
IR-1967, March 10, 1978

New York and New Jersey disability deductible
News Release IR-1967, March 10, 1978

Accrual taxpayer contested liability
IRC § 461(f)

16.4 When Taxes and Interest Are Capitalized

IRC § 263A
IRC § 266
Reg. § 1.263A-IT(b)(2)
Reg. § 1.266-1
Notice 88-99, 1988-2 CB 422

Developer required to capitalize taxes on raw land
Von Lusk, 104 TC 8 (1995)
Reg § 1.263A-6 (a)
Reg § 1.263A-8
* "Broad View of 'Production' Led to Capitalization," 82 The Journal of Taxation 224 (April 1995)

Election to capitalize irrevocable
George Stamos Est., 55 TC 468 (1970)

Prior deduction for interest
Rev. Rul. 72-594, 1972-2 CB 199

16.5 Assessments

Charges for local benefits
IRC § 164(c)(1)
Reg. § 1.164-4

Home owner's association fees not deductible
Rev. Rul. 76-495, 1976-2 CB 43

16.6 Deducting Real Estate Taxes

Payments to bank escrow account deductible when disbursed to tax authorities
Rev. Rul. 78-103, 1978-1 CB 58

Buyer of foreclosed property
* Letter Ruling 8207030

Beneficial owner
Paul Trans Dang, TC Memo 1999-233

16.7 Tenants' Payment of Taxes

Deductible
Hawaii real property tax law:
Rev. Rul. 64-327, 1964-2 CB 56
California real property tax law:
Rev. Rul. 68-84, 1968-1 CB 71

Not deductible
Tax surcharge
Rev. Rul. 75-301, 1975-2 CB 66
U.K. rates tax:
Maynard Waxenberg, 62 TC 594 (1974); Rev. Rul. 73-600, 1973-2 CB 47
Maryland-Prince George's County renters: Rev. Rul. 75-558, 1975-2 CB 67
New York: Rev. Rul. 79-180, 1979-1 CB 95

16.8 Allocating Taxes When You Sell or Buy Realty

IRC § 164(d)
Reg. § 1.164-6

Form 1099-S
IRC § 6045(e)

Accrual-basis deduction
IRC § 164(d)(2)(B)
Reg. § 1.164-6(d)(6)
IRC § 461(c) (ratable election)

Seller on cash basis
Reg. § 1.164-6(d)(1)

Buyer's payment of seller's back taxes capitalized
Al S. Reinhardt, 75 TC 47 (1980)

16.9 Who May Deduct Real Property Taxes

Husband for his wife
William A. Colston, 59 F.2d 867 (D.C. Cir. 1932), aff'g 21 BTA 396, cert. denied, 287 U.S. 640
Charles F. Dean Est., 1 BTA 27

Mortgage required husband to pay
Eugene W. Small, 27 BTA 1219

Condominium apartment owner
Rev. Rul. 64-31, 1964-1 (Pt. 1) CB 300

Life tenant
Cornelia C. F. Horsford, 2 TC 826 (1943) (Acq.)

Tenant
Reg. § 1.162-11
Denholm & McKay Co., 39 BTA 767
Caroline T. Kissel, 15 BTA 1270 (Acq. and Nonacq.)

Foreclosed for failure to pay taxes
Charles H. McGlue, 54 BTA 761 (Acq.)

Cooperative apartment owner
IRC § 216

Jointly and severally liable for tax
Rev. Rul. 72-79, 1972-1 CB 51

Tenancy by the entirety
Thomas D. Conroy, 17 TCM 21 (1958)

F. C. Nicodemus, Jr., 26 BTA 125 (Acq.)
Rev. Rul. 71-268, 1971-1 CB 58

Tenant in common
Lulu Lung Powell, 26 TCM 161 (1967)
Joseph James, 70 TCM 1420 (1995)

Mortgagee
John Hancock Mutual Life Ins. Co., 10 BTA 736 (Acq.)
Lucy S. Schiffelin Est., 44 BTA 137 (Acq.)

Tax on others' property
Albion D. T. Libby, 133 F.2d 203 (3d Cir. 1943), aff'g BTA Memo. P-H 42,252
J. Raymond Batcheller, 5 TCM 746 (1946)
Solomon N. Scale, 9 TCM 48 (1950)
Gordon W. Bonnette Est., 9 TCM 158 (1950)
Eugene W. Small, 27 BTA 1219 (1971)
Virginia N. Cramer, 55 TC 1125 (1971) (Acq.)
Gregory E. Macdonald, 35 TCM 346 (1976)

Have interest in property
Alfred J. Grosso, BTA Memo. P-H 41,581
A. J. Gilbert, 11 TCM 457 (1952)

Protection of beneficial interest
Rev. Rul. 67-21, 1967-1 CB 45

Trust for life of another
Herman A. Harper, 4 TCM 1097 (1945)
Robert C. Ligget, 4 TCM 598 (1945)
John H. Hord, 95 F.2d 179 (6th Cir. 1944), rev'g 33 BTA 342

Realty owned by parent
J. Raymond Batcheller, 5 TCM 746 (1946)

Stockholder property interest
Fred N. Acker, 258 F.2d 568 (6th Cir. 1958), aff'd, 361 U.S. 87 (1959)

16.10 Automobile License Fees

Reg. § 1.164-3(c)
Rev. Rul. 74-454, 1974-2 CB 57

16.11 Taxes Deductible as Business Expenses

IRC § 162
IRC § 212
Reg § 1.263A-2(a)

16.12 Foreign Taxes

IRC § 164(a)(3)

17 Medical and Dental Expense Deductions

17.1 Medical Expenses Must Exceed 7.5% of AGI

IRC § 213(a)
* "Maximizing Tax Benefits of Medical Expenses," Shirley H. Olsen, 45 Taxation for Accountants 269 (Nov. 1990)

Loan as payment
William J. Granan, 55 TC 753 (1971)
Rev. Rul. 78-173, 1978-1 CB 73

Credit card charge
Rev. Rul. 78-39, 1978-1 CB 73

Note: Paragraph numbers refer to Volume One. Items marked ˙ are research aids, not citations of authority; see "Key to Citations" on page 806.

17.2 ALLOWABLE MEDICAL CARE COSTS

* "Diagnose Payments for Bigger Medical Expense Deductions," Ron West, 62 Tax Strategies 289 (May 1999)
* "Medical Deduction Now Covers Home Health Care Costs," Jay A. Soled and Gary A. Prince, 59 Taxation for Accountants 41 (July 1997)

IRC § 213
Reg. § 1.213-1
*IRS Publication 502

Prescribed drugs
IRC § 213(b)
IRC § 213(d)(3)

IRS position on special foods
Rev. Rul. 55-261, 1955-1 CB 307

Extra cost of health food
Theron G. Randolph, 67 TC 481 (1976)
Leona VonKalb, 37 TMC 1511 (1978)
Warren L. Becher, 53 TCM 683 (1987) (taxpayer appeal pending)

Childbirth classes
* Letter Ruling 8919009

Chiropractor (lic.)
Rev. Rul. 55-261, 1955-1 CB 307

Christian Science practitioners
Rev. Rul. 55-261, 1955-1 CB 307

Dermatologist
Rev. Rul. 55-261, 1955-1 CB 307

Obstetrical services
Reg. § 1.213-1(e)(1)(ii)

Osteopath (lic.)
Rev. Rul. 55-261, 1955-1 CB 307

Nurses
Reg. § 1.213-1(e)(1)(ii)
Jacob Hentz, Jr., Est., 12 TCM 368 (1953)
George B. Wendell, 12 TC 161 (1949)
Rev. Rul. 58-339, 1958-2 CB 106
Rev. Rul. 55-261, 1955-1 CB 307

Psychiatrists
Rev. Rul. 53-143, 1953-2 CB 129, modified by Rev. Rul. 63-91, 1963-1 CB 54
Rev. Rul. 55-261, 1955-1 CB 307
Rev. Rul. 56-263, 1956-1 CB 135

Payments to unlicensed practitioners
Rev. Rul. 63-91, 1963-1 CB 54

Dental services
Reg. § 1.213-1(e)(1)(ii)

Equipment and supplies
Reg. § 1.213-1(e)(1)(ii)
Rev. Rul. 55-261, 1955-1 CB 307

Auto devices for handicapped
Rev. Rul. 66-80, 1966-1 CB 57

Elevator
Edna G. Hollander, 219 F.2d 934 (3d Cir. 1955), rev'g 22 TC 646 (1954)
James E. Berry, 174 F. Supp. 748 (D. Okla. 1958)
W. A. Post, 150 F. Supp. 299 (D. Ala. 1956)
W. E. Snellings, 149 F. Supp. 825 (E.D. Vir. 1956)
Rev. Rul. 59-411, 1959-2 CB 100

Elastic hosiery
Bessie Cohen, 10 TCM 29 (1951)

Fluoridation unit
Rev. Rul. 64-267, 1964-2 CB 69

Invalid chair
Rev. Rul. 58-155, 1958-1 CB 156
Rev. Rul. 66-80, 1966-1 CB 57
Rev. Rul. 67-76, 1967-1 CB 70

Wig
Rev. Rul. 62-189, 1962-2 CB 88

Medical treatments
Reg. § 1.213-1(e)(1)(ii)
Rev. Rul. 55-261, 1955-1 CB 307

Lodging
* Letter Ruling 8516025

Hospital services
Reg. § 1.213-1(e)(1)(ii)
Rev. Rul. 55-261, 1955-1 CB 307

Premiums
Reg. § 1.213-1(e)(1)(i)

Premiums allocable to lost wages, loss of life or limbs
Reg. § 1.213-1(e)(4)

Medicare by persons not automatically covered
Rev. Rul. 79-175, 1979-1 CB 117

Alcoholic's inpatient care
Rev. Rul. 72-325, 1973-1 CB 75

Birth control pills
Rev. Rul. 73-200, 1973-1 CB 140

Clarinet lessons
Rev. Rul. 62-210, 1962-2 CB 89

Navajo sings
Raymond H. Tso, 40 TCM 1277 (1980)

Health institute
Rev. Rul. 55-261, 1955-1 CB 307

Smoking cessation costs
Rev. Rul. 99-28, 1999-25 IRB

Drug center costs
Rev. Rul. 72-226, 1972-1 CB 96

Legal fees
Carl A. Gerstacker, 414 F.2d 448 (6th Cir. 1969)
Rev. Rul. 71-281, 1971-1 CB 121

Nurses' board and wages
Reg. § 1.213-1(e)(1)(ii)

Federal Insurance Contributions Act
Rev. Rul. 57-489, 1957-2 CB 207

Remedial reading
Rev. Rul. 69-607, 1969-2 CB 40

Seeing-eye dog
Rev. Rul. 55-261, 1955-1 CB 307

Sterilization
Rev. Rul. 73-603, 1973-2 CB 76

Tuition fee
Rev. Rul. 54-457, 1954-2 CB 100

Wages of guide
Rev. Rul. 64-173, 1964-1 (Pt. 1) CB 121

Organ transplant costs
Rev. Rul. 68-452, 1968-2 CB 111

Telephone-teletype
Rev. Rul. 71-48, 1971-1 CB 99, amplified by Rev. Rul. 73-53, 1973-1 CB 139

Television adapter for closed caption service
Rev. Rul. 80-340, 1980-2 CB 81

Braille book
Rev. Rul. 75-318, 1975-2 CB 88

Weight loss program for specific ailment deductible
Rev. Rul. 79-151, 1979-1 CB 116
* Letter Ruling 8004111

Laetrile
Rev. Rul. 78-325, 1978-2 CB 124

Contact lens replacement insurance protection
Rev. Rul. 74-429, 1974-2 CB 83

Radial keratotomy
* Letter Ruling 9625049

17.3 NONDEDUCTIBLE MEDICAL EXPENSES
Reg. § 1.213-1

Cosmetic surgery
IRC § 213(d)(9)

Payroll withholding to cover Medicare A not deductible
Rev. Rul. 66-216, 1966-2 CB 100

Car insurance premiums not deductible
Rev. Rul. 73-483, 1973-2 CB 75

Toothpaste
Reg. § 1.213-1(e)(2)

Antiseptic diaper service and maternity clothes
Rev. Rul. 55-261, 1955-1 CB 307

Monument
Carolyn W. Libby Est., 14 TCM 699 (1955)

No deduction for advance payment of services to be performed next year
R.M. Rose, 435 F.2d 149 (5th Cir. 1970)

Anticipated expenses not deductible
W.B. Andrews, 37 TCM 744 (1978)

Illegal operations, etc.
Reg. § 1.213-1(e)(1)(ii)

Divorced wife
IRC § 213(a)

Cost of oil furnace
Reg. § 1.213-1(e)(1)(ii)

Special hospital room
Reg. § 1.213-1(e)(i)(iv)

Specially designed car
Rev. Rul. 55-261, 1955-1 CB 307
Rev. Rul. 58-8, 1958-1 CB 154, amplified by Rev. Rul. 67-76, 1967-1 CB 70

Special food or beverages
Rev. Rul. 55-261, 1955-1 CB 307
Leo R. Cohn, 38 TC 387 (1962) (Nonacq.)
John R. Newman, 902 F.2d 159 (2nd Cir. 1990)
T. G. Randolph, 67 TC 481 (1976)

Note: Paragraph numbers refer to Volume One. Items marked * are research aids, not citations of authority; see "Key to Citations" on page 806.

843

Organically grown food
Warren Becher, 53 TCM 683 (1987)

Bottled water
Rev. Rul. 56-19, 1956-1 CB 135

Health programs
Rev. Rul. 57-130, 1957-1 CB 108

Domestic help
Rev. Rul. 58-339, 1958-2 CB 106

Athletic club
Rev. Rul. 55-261, 1955-1 CB 307

Health spa
Jill Ford Murray, 43 TCM 1377 (1982)

Healthy child to boarding school
Samuel Ochs, 17 TC 130 (1951), aff'd, 195 F.2d
692 (2d Cir. 1952), cert. denied, 344 U.S. 827

Tuition for problem child
Gordon Pascal, 15 TCM 434 (1956)

Transportation costs
James Donnelly, 28 TC 1278 (1957), aff'd, 262
F.2d 411 (2d Cir. 1959)
Rev. Rul. 55-261, 1955-1 CB 307

Toiletries and sundries
Reg. § 1.213-1(e)(2)
O. G. Russell, 12 TCM 1276 (1953)

Hotel costs
Reg. § 1.213-1(e)(1)(iv)
Loren Wilks, 27 TCM 1086 (1968)

Living costs of outpatient
Harlin H. Lucas, 25 TCM 1312 (1966)

Look for new place to live
Gunnar E. Erickson, 13 TCM 1045 (1954)

Change of environment trip
Rev. Rul. 56-474, 1956-2 CB 157

Dance lessons
John J. Thoene, 33 TC 62 (1959)
Irving A. Adler, 22 TCM 965 (1963), aff'd, 330
F.2d 91 (9th Cir. 1964)
Rose France, 49 TCM 508 (1980), aff'd, 82-1
USTC 9225 (6th Cir. 1982)

Fallout shelter
Fred H. Daniels, 41 TC 324 (1963)

Travel to golf course
Leon S. Altman, 53 TC 487 (1969)

Scientology fees
Donald H. Brown, 62 TC 551 (1974), aff'd per
curiam, 523 F.2d 365 (8th Cir. 1975)
Rev. Rul. 78-190, 1978-1 CB 74

Divorce costs
Joel H. Jacobs, 62 TC 813 (1974)

Marriage counseling fee
Rev. Rul. 75-319, 1975-2 CB 88

Hotel room for sex therapy
Rev. Rul. 75-187, 1975-1 CB 92

Veterinary fees
L. J. Schoen, 34 TCM 736 (1975)

Babysitter expenses

Rev. Rul. 78-266, 1978-2 CB 123

Tattooing and ear piercing
Rev. Rul. 82-111, 1982-1 CB 48

Moving from airport noise
Luke W. Findlay, Jr., 44 TCM 123 (1982)

17.4 REIMBURSEMENTS REDUCE DEDUCTIBLE EXPENSES

Reimbursements reduce deduction
IRC § 213(a)
Reg. § 1.213-1(g)

Failure to make claim
* Letter Ruling 8102010

Loss of earnings, etc.
Reg. § 1.213-1(e)(4)(i)

Excess reimbursements
Rev. Rul. 69-154, 1969-1 CB 46

Injury awards treated as medical cost reimbursements
Benjamin D. Morgan, 55 TC 376 (1970)
Daniel T. Cooney, 30 TCM 845 (1971)

17.5 PREMIUMS OF MEDICAL CARE POLICIES

IRC § 213(d)(1)(C)

Policy for loss of life, limb, or sight—premium not deductible
Reg. § 1.213-1(e)(4)

No deduction for policy guaranteeing specific amount for hospitalization
Rev. Rul. 68-451, 1968-2 CB 111

Self-employed health insurance deduction
IRC §162(l)(1)
* Letter Ruling 9409006

17.6 EXPENSES OF YOUR SPOUSE

Deduction allowed
IRC § 213(a)
Reg. § 1.213-1(a)(3)

Status at the time medical expense is incurred or paid
Reg. § 1.213-1(e)(3)

17.7 EXPENSES OF YOUR DEPENDENTS

Dependents
William A. Jewell, 69 TC 791 (1978) (Acq.)

Must contribute half of support
IRC § 152
Reg. § 1.152-1 and 2

Not related at time of bill
Rev. Rul. 57-310, 1957-2 CB 206

Parent's welfare payments used to pay medical bills
Robert W. Hodge, 44 TC 186 (1965)

Adopted children
Benny L. Kilpatrick, 68 TC 469 (1977)
Rev. Rul. 60-255, 1960-2 CB 105

Deduction allowed for nondependent children
IRC § 213(d)(5)

Multiple support
IRC § 152(c)
Reg. § 1.152-3
Loring P. Litchfield, 330 F.2d 509 (1st Cir. 1964)

17.8 DECEDENT'S MEDICAL EXPENSES

IRC § 213(d)
Reg. § 1.213-1(d)
Rev. Rul. 77-357, 1977-2 CB 328

17.9 TRAVEL COSTS MAY BE MEDICAL DEDUCTIONS

Medical deduction for traveling expenses
IRC § 213(d)(1)(B)
Reg. § 1.213-1(e)(1)(iv)

Relieve specific chronic ailments
Rev. Rul. 58-110, 1958-1 CB 155
Rev. Rul. 55-261, 1955-1 CB 307
Sally L. Bilder, 369 U.S. 499 (1963), rev'g 289
F.2d 291 (3d Cir. 1961)

Taxi fare
Rev. Rul. 98-63, 1998-52 IRB

10 cents per mile
Rev. Proc. 97-58, 1997-52 IRB24

Out-of-pocket auto expenses
Maurice S. Gordon, 37 TC 986 (1962)

Lodging $50 daily allowance
IRC § 213(d)(2)
Letter Ruling 8516025

Transportation to Florida deductible but not $50 lodging allowance
Earlene Polyak, 94 TC 20 (1990)

Extra cost of salt-free food
Leo Cohn, 38 TC 387 (1962) (Nonacq.)
Leo Cohn, 240 F. Supp. 786 (D. Ind. 1965)

Hotel costs for convalescent
Daniel S. W. Kelly, 440 F.2d 307 (7th Cir. 1971),
rev'g 28 TCM 1208 (1969)

Nurse's fare
Rev. Rul. 58-110, 1958-1 CB 155

Parent's trip prescribed
Martin J. Lichterman, 37 TC 586 (1961) (Acq.)
(to take child to school — deductible)
Rev. Rul. 58-533, 1958-2 CB 108 (to visit child—
deductible)
Robert Rose, 52 TC 21 (1969) (taking child on
trip for health reason — deductible)
* Letter Ruling 7813004 (picking up mentally
disturbed son—transportation plus overnight
food and lodging — deductible)

Visit specialist
Bertha M. Rodgers, 25 TC 254 (1955) (Acq.),
aff'd, 241 F.2d 552 (8th Cir. 1957)

Escape bad climate
Reg. § 1.213-1(e)(1)(iv)
L. Keever Stringham, 12 TC 580 (1949) (Acq.),
aff'd, 183 F.2d 579 (6th Cir. 1950)
Rev. Rul. 53-261, 1955-1 CB 307

Note: Paragraph numbers refer to Volume One. Items marked ˚ are research aids, not citations of authority; see "Key to Citations" on page 806.

Alcoholics Anonymous
Rev. Rul. 63-273, 1963-2 CB 112

Disabled veteran's commuting
Sanford H. Weinzimer, 17 TCM 712 (1958)

Wife's trip to provide nursing care deductible
Daniel S. W. Kelly, 28 TCM 1208 (1969), rev'd on other grounds, 440 F.2d 307 (7th Cir. 1971)

Travel costs of kidney transplant donor or prospective donor
Rev. Rul. 73-189, 1973-1 CB 139

General improvement
Reg. § 1.213-1(e)(1)(iv)
Margherita Diamond Est., 22 TCM 1073 (1963)

Driving as therapy
Michael R. Bordas, 29 TCM 458 (1970)

Annual trips south are personal expenses
Bertha M. Rodgers, 241 F.2d 552 (8th Cir. 1957), aff'g 25 TC 254 (1955) (Acq.)

Meals en route
Morris C. Montgomery, 428 F.2d 243 (6th Cir. 1970), aff'g 51 TC 410 (1968)

Treatment in distant city
Reg. § 1.213-1(e)(1)(iv), contra:
Stanley D. Winderman, 32 TC 1197 (1959) (Acq.)

Meals and lodging (pre-1984 decisions)
Reg. § 1.213-1(e)(1)(iv)
Max Carasso, 34 TC 1139 (1960), aff'd, 292 F.2d 367 (2d Cir. 1961), cert. denied, 369 U.S. 874
Sally L. Bilder, 369 U.S. 499 (1963), rev'g 289 F.2d 291 (3d Cir. 1961)

Meals and lodging in transit deductible
Morris C. Montgomery, 428 F.2d 243 (6th Cir. 1970), aff'g 51 TC 410 (1968)

Spiritual aid
Vincent P. Ring, 23 TC 950 (1955)

Climate more suitable to ill wife's condition
Lawrence Prem, 21 TCM 873 (1962)

Moving household furnishings
C. Earle Phares, 21 TCM 1446 (1962)

Auto for leg condition
Benjamin Ginsberg, 237 F. Supp. 968 (S.D.N.Y. 1965)

Special vehicle
Rev. Rul. 55-261, 1955-1 CB 307
Rev. Rul. 66-80, 1966-1 CB 57
Rev. Rul. 70-606, 1970-2 CB 66

Convalescence cruise
Margherita Diamond Est., 22 TCM 1073 (1963)

Transporting invalid child to public school
Rev. Rul. 65-255, 1965-2 CB 76

Loss on sale of car
Robert K. Weary, 510 F.2d 435 (10th Cir. 1975), cert. denied, 423 U.S. 838

Patient on medical seminar cruise
Rev. Rul. 76-79, 1976-1 CB 70

17.10 SCHOOLING FOR THE MENTALLY OR PHYSICALLY HANDICAPPED

Reg. § 1.213-1(e)(1)(v)
Rev. Rul. 55-261, 1955-1 CB 307
"Deductibility of Private School Costs for Disabled Children," Claudia L. Kelley, John P. Geary and DeAnna Leeper Maxwell, 76 Taxes 39 (July 1998)

Private school with psychologists
C. Fink Fischer, 50 TC 164 (1968) (Acq.)
Hobart J. Hendrick, 35 TC 1223 (1960) (Acq.)

Boarding school recommended by therapist
John A. Dreifus, 36 TCM 368 (1977)

Hyperactive child in regular boarding school
Ernest M. Newkirk, 611 F.2d 373 (6th Cir. 1979)

Deduction for child's behavior therapy at school
Charles F. Urbauer, 63 TCM 2492 (1992)

Private military academy
H. Grant Atkinson, Jr., 44 TC 39 (1965) (Acq.)
Edward S. Enck, 26 TCM 314 (1967)
Rolland T. Olson, 23 TCM 2008 (1964)
Everett F. Glaze, 20 TCM 1276 (1961)

School in Arizona
Martin J. Lichterman, 37 TC 586 (1961) (Acq.)

Cost of college for deaf child (deductible)
Reuben A. Baer Est., 26 TCM 170 (1967)

Blind student at regular school
Arnold P. Grunwald, 51 TC 108 (F.2d 1968)

Halfway house
* Letter Ruling 7714016

Special public school class for retarded: cost of tuition and travel
Rev. Rul. 70-285, 1970-1 CB 52

Cost of remedial reading school
Paul H. Ripple, 54 TC 1442 (1970)

Cost of private school for epileptic
DeVora R. Shidler, 30 TCM 529 (1971)

17.11 SENIOR CITIZEN CARE FACILITIES

Reg. § 1.213-1(e)(1)(v)
James J. Matles, 23 TCM 1489 (1964)
W. D. Counts, 42 TC 755 (1964) (Acq.)
Rev. Rul. 67-185, 1967-1 CB 70

Apartment rent
Sidney J. Ungar, 22 TCM 766 (1963)

Lump-sum payment to retirement home
Rev. Rul. 76-481, 1976-2 CB 82
Rev. Rul. 68-525, 1968-2 CB 112

Payment for future lifetime care
<BRev. Rul. 75-302, 1975-2 CB 86
Rev. Rul. 75-303, 1975-2 CB 87
Rev. Rul. 76-481, 1976-2 CB 82
Rev. Rul. 93-72, 1993-2 CB 77

Entrance fee to retirement community
Est. of Helen Smith, 79 TC 313 (1982)

17.12 NURSES' WAGES

Daughter acting as nurse
Myrtle P. Dodge Est., 20 TCM 811 (1961)

Working parents
Maurice Levy, Jr., 20 TCM 1534 (1961)

Domestic
John Frier, 30 TCM 345 (1971)
Rev. Rul. 58-339, 1958-2 CB 106

Allocation of medical and household services
Rev. Rul. 76-106, 1976-1 CB 71

Clerk's salary
Sidney J. Ungar, 22 TCM 766 (1963)

Nonprofessional therapy
Rev. Rul. 70-170, 1970-1 CB 51

Relative providing care
Walter D. Bye, 31 TCM 238 (1972)

17.13 HOME IMPROVEMENTS AS MEDICAL EXPENSES

Reg. § 1.213-1(e)(1)(iii)
John Riach, 302 F.2d 374 (9th Cir. 1962)
Raymon Gerard, 37 TC 826 (1962) (Acq.)
Karlis A. Pols, 24 TCM 1140 (1965)

Air conditioning device
Rev. Rul. 55-261, 1955 CB 307

Removal of lead-based paint
Rev. Rul. 79-66, 1979-1 CB 114

Special bathroom in rented house
Rev. Rul. 70-395, 1970-2 CB 65

Operating costs
Reg. § 1.213(e)(iii)

Swimming pool of osteoarthritis patient
Rev. Rul. 83-33, 1983-1 CB 70

Least expensive construction
Collins H. Ferris, 36 TCM 765 (1977), rev'd, 582 F.2d 1112 (7th Cir. 1978)

Buying house with pool
Paul A. Lerew, 44 TCM 918 (1982)

Pool of emphysema patient
Herbert Cherry, 46 TCM 1033 (1983)

Pool as personal convenience
C. W. Haines, 71 TC 257 (1979)

Handicap exception for ramps, etc.
Conference Committee Report to P.L. 99-514, Act Sec. 133, 1986-3 (vol. 4) CB 22
Rev. Rul. 87-106, 1987-2 CB 67

17.14 COSTS DEDUCTIBLE AS BUSINESS EXPENSES

Medical checkup for job
Rev. Rul. 58-382, 1958-2 CB 59

Throat specialist fee
Rev. Rul. 71-45, 1971-1 CB 51

Services for physically handicapped
Rev. Rul. 75-317, 1975-2 CB 57

Note: Paragraph numbers refer to Volume One. Items marked * are research aids, not citations of authority; see "Key to Citations" on page 806.

Psychoanalysis for social worker
Harry H. Voigt, 74 TC 82 (1980) (Nonacq.)

Therapy for psychiatrist
Kenneth Porter, 52 TCM 615 (1986)

17.15 LONG-TERM CARE COSTS OF CHRONICALLY ILL

* "How to Compare Long-Term Care Insurance Policies," Sam E. Deller, 26 Estate Planning 296 (August/September 1999)
* "New Law Provides Ways to Reduce Tax Burdens Relating to Long-term Care Expenses," A. Mark Christopher, 86 Journal of Taxation 20 (Jan. 1997)

Long-term care premiums
IRC § 213(d)(1)(D)
IRC § 213(d)(10)

Long-term care services
IRC § 213(d)(1)(C)
IRC § 7702B(c)

17.16 LIFE INSURANCE USED TO PAY MEDICAL COSTS OF TERMINALLY ILL

* "Accelerated Death Benefits Finally Afford Exclusion," Julia K. Brazelton and Rebecca Kaenzig, 75 Taxes 57 (Jan. 1997)
* "Changes Affecting Life Insurance Enacted By New Laws," Kevin D. Millard, 24 Estate Planning 3 (Jan. 1997)

Terminally ill: tax- free accelerated benefits after 1996
IRC § 101(g)(1)(A)
IRC § 101(g)(4)(A)

Chronically ill: tax-free accelerated benefits after 1996
IRC §101(g)(1)(B)
IRC §101(g)(3)
IRC §101(g)(4)(B)

Viatical settlements
IRC §101(g)(2)

Pre-1997 IRS position
Prop. Reg. §1.7702-2(d)

17.17 MEDICAL SAVINGS ACCOUNTS (MSAs)

*IRS Publication 569
* "The Federal Income Taxation of Medical Savings Accounts," Dennis Van Mieghem and Craig L. Pichette, 75 Taxes 243 (May 1997)
* "New MSA and Health Insurance Rules Create Opportunities," Benjamin C. Avers and Elizabeth Plummer, 58 Taxation for Accountants 260 (May 1997)

MSA deductions
IRC § 220

Employer contributions
IRC § 106

IRS guidelines on MSAs
Notice 96-53, 1996-51 IRB 5

18 CASUALTY AND THEFT LOSSES AND INVOLUNTARY CONVERSIONS

18.1 WHEN TO DEDUCT A CASUALTY OR THEFT LOSS

Reimbursement expected
Reg. § 1.165-1(d)
Arthur T. Davidson, 34 TCM 1010 (1975)

Year in which insurance company denies liability is not controlling
Louis Gale, 41 TC 269 (1963)

Flood loss deducted year claim settled
Earl Callan, 235 F.2d 190 (9th Cir. 1956)

Unseasonable blizzard
Emory M. Nourse, 73 F. Supp. 70 (D. Iowa 1947)

Hurricane damage
Willard T. Burkett, 10 TM 948 (1951)

Loss allowed in year of drought not later year of discovery
Alfred M. Cox, 24 TCM 23 (1965), aff'd per curiam, 354 F.2d 659 (3d Cir. 1966)

Swimming pool damages not deductible in later year
Donald H. Kunsman, 49 TC 62 (1967)

Subsequent recovery of insurance taxable
John E. Montgomery, 65 TC 511 (1975)

18.2 DISASTER LOSSES
IRC § 165(h)
Reg. § 1.165-11
* "Casualty Gains—An Oxymoron, or Just a Trap for Unwary Taxpayers?" Steven C. Thompson and Nell Adkins, 73 Taxes 318 (June 1995)

Insurance reimbursements for unscheduled personal property are tax free
IRC §1033 (h)(1)(A), added by the Revenue Reconciliation Act of 1993

Early election may be revoked up to filing due date
Chester Matheson, 74 TC 834 (1980) (Acq. in results only)

Relocation or demolition of house
IRC § 165(k)

Sale of land after disaster
Rev. Rul. 96-32, 1996-25 IRB 5

IRS interest abatement
IRC § 6404(h)

18.3 WHO MAY CLAIM THE LOSS DEDUCTION

Separate return
Robert M. Loewenstein, 27 TCM 1112 (1968)
Rev. Rul. 75-347, 1975-2 CB 70

No deduction for cost of repairing rented car
J. Gill, 34 TCM 10 (1975)

Corporate shareholder

Drew Jensen, 39 TCM 163 (1979)

18.4 BANK DEPOSIT LOSSES
* "Deduction Choice for Uninsured Bank Deposit Loss," Bruce M. Bird and Gene Poindexter, 84 Taxation for Accountants 147 (March 1996)

Bad debt deduction
IRC § 166

Casualty and ordinary loss elections
IRC § 165(1)
Clyde Fincher, 105 TC 11 (1995)

Election of ordinary loss or casualty loss
Notice 89-28, 1989-1 CB 667

Foreign bank — no loss deduction
Joyce Aston, 109 TC 109 (1998)
IRC § 166

18.5 SUDDEN EVENT TEST FOR PERSONAL PROPERTY LOSSES
IRC § 165(c)(3)

Great Lakes high water level
Rev. Rul. 76-134, 1976-1 CB 54

Water damage to wallpaper
Rupert Stuart, 20 TCM 938 (1961)

Termites
E. G. Kilroe, 32 TC 1304 (1959) (Nonacq.)
Alan M. Winsor, 18 TCM 383 (1959), aff'd, 278 F.2d 634 (1st Cir. 1960)
Rev. Rul. 63-232, 1963-2 CB 97

Southern pine beetle
Paul W. Black, 36 TCM 1347 (1977)
Herbert Nelson, 27 TCM 158 (1968)
Rev. Rul. 79-174, 1979-1 CB 99

Foreseeable damage
Jack R. Farber, 57 TC 714 (1972) (Acq.)
Harry Heyn, 46 TC 714 (1966) (Acq.)

Car towed away and destroyed
Abraham Hananel, 62 TCM 439 (1991)

Ring destroyed by disposal unit
William H. Carpenter, 25 TCM 965 (1966)

Ring destroyed by closing of door
John P. White, 48 TC 430 (1967) (Acq.)

Diamond unexplainedly lost
Theodore R. Kielts, 42 TCM 238 (1981)

Sinking ship from failure of pump
William D. Shields, 54 TCM 711 (1987)

Fire loss, damage, destruction
IRC § 165
Reg. § 1.165-7

Judgment paid by tenant
Rev. Rul. 73-41, 1973-1 CB 74

Automobile
Tracy V. Buckwalter, 20 BTA 1005, aff'd, 61 F.2d 571 (6th Cir. 1932)

Furniture and home
E. C. O'Rear, 80 F.2d 473 (6th Cir. 1935)
W. B. Brooks, 12 BTA 31, aff'd, 35 F.2d 178 (4th Cir. 1929)

Note: Paragraph numbers refer to Volume One. Items marked ˙ are research aids, not citations of authority; see "Key to Citations" on page 806.

Hurricane
Alfred M. Hickman, 207 F.2d 460 (4th Cir. 1953)
Willard T. Burkett, 10 TCM 948 (1951)

Tornado
Richard E. Stein, 14 TCM 191 (1955)

Heavy rains
Clarence E. Stewart, 12 TCM 921 (1953)

Lightning
S. F. Horn, 18 TCM 177 (1959)

Floods
W. M. Ferguson, 59 F.2d 893 (10th Cir. 1933)
E. T. Hutchings, 41-2 USTC ¶9673 (D. Ky. 1941)

Storms
Webb, 1 BTA 759
Robert B. Honeyman, Jr., BTA Memo. P-H 39,021

Landslides
W. K. Stowers, 169 F. Supp. 246 (D. Mass. 1959)

Smog
Rev. Rul. 71-560, 1971-2 CB 126

Drought
Jack M. Short, 55 TCM 54 (1988) (deduction claimed too late)
Frank Buttram, 87 F. Supp. 322 (D. Okl. 1943)
Rev. Rul. 66-303, 1966-2 CB 55
Rev. Rul. 54-85 1954-1 CB 58
Norman H. Ruecker, 41 TCM 1587 (1981)

Dust storms
R. F. Barry, 175 F. Supp. 308 (D. Okl. 1959)

Poor construction
Irving J. Hayutin, 31 TCM 509 (1972), aff'd, 508 F.2d 462 (10th Cir. 1975)

Shipwreck
IRC § 165(c)(3)
Edward H. R. Green, 19 BTA 904

Sinking of land
Harry Johnston Grant, 30 BTA 1028 (Acq.)

Tidal wave
M. A. Ferst, 129 F. Supp. 606 (D. Ga. 1955)
Rev. Rul. 76-134, 1976-1 CB 54

Disturbances below earth's surface
Harry Johnston Grant, 30 BTA 1028 (Acq.)

Ice pressure
Paul E. Jackson, 13 TCM 1175 (1954)
Seward City Mills, 44 BTA 173

Underground water
Delbert P. Hesler, 13 TCM 972 (1954)

Car falling through ice
Rev. Rul. 69-88, 1969-1 CB 58

Ice damage
Sherman L. Whipple, 25 F.2d 520 (D. Mass. 1928)
Richard R. Hollington, 15 TCM 668 (1956)
Frederick H. Nash, 22 BTA 482 (Acq.)

Cave-ins
W. K. Stowers, 169 F. Supp. 246 (D. Miss. 1959)
Harry Johnston Grant, 30 BTA 1028 (Acq.)

Quarry blast

Ray Durden, 3 TC 1 (1944) (Acq.)

Severe winter blizzard
Emory M. Nourse, 73 F. Supp. 70 (D. Iowa 1947)

Vandals
Burrell E. Davis, 34 TC 586 (1960) (Acq.)

Rentals for temporary living quarters
Rev. Rul. 59-398, 1959-2 CB 76

Potential buyer's resistance
Harvey Pulvers, 48 TC 245 (1967), aff'd per curiam, 407 F.2d 838 (9th Cir. 1969)
Lewis F. Ford, 33 TCM 496 (1974)
Charles W. P. Kamanski, 29 TCM 1702 (1970), aff'd, 477 F.2d 452 (9th Cir. 1973)

Jointly owned property
J. H. Anderson, 7 TCM 811 (1948)

Life estate holder may deduct damage for wind storm
Katherine Bliss, 27 TC 770 (1957) (Acq.), rev'd, 256 F.2d 533 (2d Cir. 1958)

Latent effects not considered
Leonard J. Jenard, 20 TCM 346 (1961)

Decrease in value of land
Bessie Knapp, 23 TC 716 (1955) (Acq.)

Cost less depreciation
Edmund W. Cornelius, 56 TC 976 (1971) (Acq.)
Myron E. Cherry, 26 TCM 556 (1967)

Market value based on inventory
Loy L. Stone, 31 TCM 1042 (1972)

Damage to trees, shrubs, etc.
John M. Winters, Jr., 58-1 USTC ¶9205 (D. Okl. 1958), rev'd on other grounds, 261 F.2d 675 (10th Cir. 1959), cert. denied, 359 U.S. 943
Bessie Knapp, 23 TC 716 (1955) (Acq.)

Subsoil shrinkage during drought
Rev. Rul. 54-85, 1954-1 CB 58

Wreck caused by icy road
George L. Shearer, 16 F.2d 995 (2d Cir. 1927)

Collision caused by faulty driving
Reg. 1.165-7(a)(3)
Elwood J. Clark, 5 TCM 236 (1946), aff'd, 158 F.2d 851 (6th Cir. 1947)

Lawn damage caused by careless use of weed killer
Jack R. Farber, 57 TC 714 (1972) (Acq.)

Defending suit for damages
L. Oransky, 1 BTA 1239

Sonic boom
Rev. Rul. 60-329, 1960-2 CB 67

Property used by dependent
Thomas J. Draper, 15 TC 135 (1950)
Howard Scharf, 32 TCM 1281 (1973), rem'd per curiam, 535 F.2d 1250 (4th Cir. 1976)

High water levels
Rev. Rul. 75-134, 1975-1 CB 33

Preventative measures nondeductible
Cade L. Austin, 74 TCM 1334 (1980)

Buyer resistance

George W. Finkbohner, Jr.,788 F.2d 723 (11th Cir. 1986)

18.6 DAMAGE TO TREES AND SHRUBS

Shrubbery
Reg. § 1.165-7(b)(2)

Tree loss
David W. Murray, Jr., 20 TCM 7 (1962)

Casualty losses for property
Reg. § 1.165-7

Cost of replacing trees
Rev. Rul. 68-29, 1968-1 CB 74

Cost of removing infested trees
Anthony B. Cristo, 44 TCM 1057 (1982)

Winter freeze in Florida
Ben R. Thebaut, Jr., 47 TCM 401 (1983)

Dutch elm disease
Howard F. Burns, 285 F.2d 436 (6th Cir. 1961)
John Alan Appleman, 338 F.2d 729 (7th Cir. 1964), cert. denied, 380 U.S. 956
Arthur Coleman, 76 TC 580 (1981)

Lethal yellowing disease
John A. Maher, 76 TC 593 (1981), aff'd, 680 F.2d 91 (11th Cir. 1982)

Horse eats tree bark
Rev. Rul. 73-123, 1973-1 CB 76

18.7 DEDUCTING DAMAGE TO YOUR CAR

Damage to car deductible
Reg. §1.165-7(a)(3)

No deduction for litigation and settlement expenses
Alexandre R. Tarsey, 56 TC 44 (1971)

Using car on business
Forest Anderson, 81 F.2d 457 (10th Cir. 1936), rev'g 30 BTA 597

Accident between two locations of same business deductible as business expense
Harold Dancer, 73 TC 1103 (1980)

Accident occurring during trip between different jobs nondeductible as business expense
Julian D. Freedman, 35 TC 1179 (1961), aff'd, 301 F.2d 359 (5th Cir. 1962)

Accident costs while commuting nondeductible business expense
Eldon Hall, 41 TCM 282 (1981), aff'd in unpublished opinion (1st Cir. 1981)

Race car
* Letter Ruling 8227010

Deduction allowed only for uninsured losses
Emanuel Hollman, 38 TC 251 (1962)

Damage to engine—not deductible
Emil Wold, 22 TCM 732 (1963)
Lyle W. Mader, 25 TCM 917 (1966)

Towing costs are not deductible
Virginia M. Cramer, 55 TC 1125 (1971) (Acq.)

Note: Paragraph numbers refer to Volume One. Items marked * are research aids, not citations of authority; see "Key to Citations" on page 806.

Citations of Authority

Car in child's name
Frank W. Oman, 30 TCM 767 (1971)

Failure to winterize car
Mohiuddin, TC Memo 1996-422

Damage to rented car
Robert M. Miller, 34 TCM 528 (1975)

18.8 THEFT LOSSES
Reg. § 1.165-8

Necessity of proving cost
Jane V. Elliott, 40 TC 304 (1963) (Acq.)
Stanley J. Prescott, 28 TCM 435 (1969)

Must prove property was stolen
Paul Bakewell, Jr., 23 TC 803 (1955)
Mary F. Allen, 16 TC 163 (1951)
John L. Seymour, 14 TC 1111 (1950)
Edna M. Oatis, 6 TCM 569 (1947)

State law determines if theft committed
Arthur C. Bromberg, Exr., 232 F.2d 107 (5th Cir. 1956)

Locked valuable pin in compartment
Warner L. Jones, 24 TC 525 (1955) (Acq.)

Report to police
James W. Thomas, 12 TCM 41 (1953)
Henrietta Sava-Goiu, 9 TCM 128 (1950)

Allowed even though not reported
Robert W. Jorg, 52 TC 288 (1969) (Acq.)
Frederick C. Moser, 18 TCM 116 (1959)

Year reported
Reg. § 1.165-1(d)(3)
Reg. § 1.165-8
Virginia M. Cramer, 55 TC 1125 (1971) (Acq.)

Cannot recover property
Henry Kraft Mercantile Co., 14 TCM 833 (1955)

Legal fee
Katherine Ander, 47 TC 592 (1967)
Appraisal value on stamp collection
Max P. Engel, 31 TCM 1223 (1972)

Building contractor absconded
Thomas Miller, 19 TC 1046 (1953) (Acq.)
Allen Hartley, 26 TCM 1281 (1977)

Contractor runs out of money
Otis B. Kent, 12 TCM 1491 (1953)

Additional money to correct defects
IRC § 1016(a)(1)
Reg. § 1.1016-2

Payments to subcontractor
Evelyn Nell Norton, 40 TC 500 (1963) (Acq.), aff'd, 333 F.2d 1005 (9th Cir. 1964)

Theft of trees
Ella Gene Raberge, 20 TCM 1490 (1961)

Embezzlement losses
Mary O. Alsop, 34 TC 606 (1960), aff'd, 290 F.2d 726 (2d Cir. 1961)

Embezzlement not cause of bank depositor's loss
Rev. Rul. 77-383, 1977-2 CB 66

Worthless stock
Paul C. Vietzke, 37 TC 504 (1961) (Acq.)

Illegal sale of unregistered stock not a theft loss
Carroll J. Beilis, 61 TC 453 (1973), aff'd, 540 F.2d 448 (9th Cir. 1976)

No deduction for confiscation by foreign government
William J. Powers, 36 TC 1191 (1961)
L.B.G. Farcasanu, 70-2 USTC ¶ 9753 (D.C. Cir. 1970)
H.W. Mongold, 43 TCM 117 (1981)

Loss from tax avoidance scheme based on fraudulent statements of advisor
Perry A. Nichols et al., 43 TC 842 (1965) (Nonacq.)

Extortion and ransom payment
Rev. Rul. 72-112, 1972-1 CB 60

Expenses of recovering abducted child nondeductible
Ebrahim Otmishi, 41 TCM 237 (1980)

Swindled by friend
Nanette Holt Price, 94-1 USTC ¶50,160 (N.D. OK. 1994)

Fortune tellers
George John Kreiner, 60 TCM 1251 (1990)

Seizure of car by creditors
Robert V. Rafter, 489 F.2d 752 (2d Cir. 1974), cert. denied, 419 U.S. 826

Payment for forged divorce decree deductible
* Letter Ruling 8146030

Vandalism
Ann E. Lattimore, 353 F.2d 379 (9th Cir. 1966)
Charles Gutwirth, 40 TC 666 (1963) (Acq.)
Burrell E. Davis, 34 TC 586 (1960) (Acq.)

Riot damage
IRC § 165(c)(3) and (e)

Perishable food discarded after civil disturbance
Rev. Rul. 69-354, 1969-1 CB 58

18.9 NONDEDUCTIBLE LOSSES

Termite damage
Umit Sahkul, 29 TCM 260 (170)
Rev. Rul. 63-232, 1963-2 CB 97

Carpet beetles
J. Peter Meersman, 370 F.2d 109 (6th Cir. 1967)

Dry rot
Rudolph Lewis Hoppe, 42 TC 820 (1964), aff'd, 354 F.2d 988 (9th Cir. 1966)
Worth Rowley, 38 TCM 1297 (1979), aff'd in unpublished opinion (D.C. Cir. 1981)

Personal injuries
Karl Stern, 199 F. Supp. 488 (D. Ohio 1954)

Legal expenses in defending suit
L. Oransky, 1 BTA 1239

Personal property wrongfully seized
Fred J. Hughes, 1 BTA 944

Temporary quarters
Rev. Rul. 59-398, 1959-2 CB 76

Personal property lost in storage or transit
W. W. Bercaw, 6 TCM 27 (1947), aff'd, 165 F.2d 521 (4th Cir. 1948)

Passenger's luggage lost
Mildred Bauman, 10 TCM 31 (1951)

Accidental loss of ring
Edgar F. Stevens, 6 TCM 805 (1947)

Joint property taken by wife
Grover Tyler, 13 TC 186 (1949) (Acq.)

Loss of dog
Waddell F. Smith, 10 TC 701 (1948)

Damage to crop by insects
Rev. Rul. 57-599, 1957-2 CB 142

Excavation on adjoining property
Daniel F. Ebbert, 9 BTA 1402

Rust of understructure of house
Hugh M. Matheson Exr., 54 F.2d 537 (2d Cir. 1931), aff'g 18 BTA 674

Moth damage
Rev. Rul. 55-327, 1955-1 CB 25

Dry well
James I. Goski, 24 TCM 828 (1965)
Charles E. Springer, 16 TCM 1075 (1957)

Natural phenomena
Texas & Pacific Railway Co., 1 TCM 863 (1943)

Damage to library book
Luther Ely Smith, 3 TC 695 (1944) (Acq. in part, nonacq. in part)

Damage to watch
Williard Thompson, 15 TC 609 (1950), rev'd and rem'd on other grounds, 193 F.2d 586 (10th Cir. 1952)
Jack Ward, 11 TCM 340 (1952)

Drop in securities
Reg. § 1.165-1(d)
Adams, 1 BTA 985
Chicago Railway Equipment Co., 4 BTA 452 (Acq.), aff'd and rev'd in part, 39 F.2d 378 (7th Cir. 1930), rev'd, 282 U.S. 295 (1931)
E. O. Walgren, 4 BTA 1066
W. P. Davis, 6 BTA 1267

Loss due to illness
Jones, BTA Memo. P-H 42,324

Loss of contingent interest
Lillian S. Procter, 19 TC 387 (1952)

Improper police seizure
Fred J. Hughes, 1 BTA 944

Chinaware upset by pet
Robert M. Diggs, 18 TCM 443 (1959), aff'd, 281 F.2d 326 (2d Cir. 1960), cert. denied, 364 U.S. 908
J. Raymond Dyer, 35 TCM 456 (1961) (Acq.)

Temporary fluctuation
Clarence A. Peterson, 30 TC 660 (1958)

Fire deliberately set by owner
Biltmore Blackman, 88 TC 677 (1987)

18.10 PROVING A CASUALTY LOSS

Appraisal upheld
Doyle E. Collup, 21 TCM 128 (1962)

Auto bluebook
Gus S. Caras, 23 TCM 1103 (1964)

*Note: Paragraph numbers refer to Volume One. Items marked * are research aids, not citations of authority; see "Key to Citations" on page 806.*

848

Cleanup expenses
Ralph Walton, 20 TCM 653 (1961)

Dealer's estimate of trade-in not evidence
Gus S. Caras, 23 TCM 1103 (1964)

Fire damage
John Pfalzgraf, 67 TC 784 (1977) (Acq.)

Inventories of property destroyed by fire sustained loss
Loy L. Stone, 31 TCM 1042 (1972)

18.11 FLOORS FOR PERSONAL-USE PROPERTY LOSSES

$100 floor
IRC § 165(h)(1)
Reg. § 1.165-7(b)(4)

10% AGI floor
IRC § 165(h)(2)

18.12 FIGURING YOUR LOSS ON FORM 4684

IRC § 165
Reg. § 1.165-7

10% adjusted gross income limit
Reg. § 165(h)

$100 floor
IRC § 165(h)(1)
Reg. § 1.165-7(b)(4)

Cost less depreciation method
E.W. Cornelius, 56 TC 976 (Acq. 1977-2 CBI)

Proof of cost
Donald Owens, 305 U.S. 468
Hal Millsap, Jr., 46 TC 751 (1966) (Acq.), aff'd 387 F.2d 420 (8th Cir. 1968)
Jay Beams, 67 TCM 3152 (1994)
Vitale, TC Memo 1999-272

Separate computation for each item
Rev. Rul. 66-50, 1966-1 CB 40

Community property damaged before divorce settlement
Armore L. Kamins, 54 TC 977 (1970)

Loss of records in fire no bar
John Pfalzgraf, Jr., 67 TC 784 (1977) (Acq.)

Appraisals for disaster relief
IRC § 165(i)(4), as amended by the 1997 Act

18.13 PERSONAL AND BUSINESS USE OF PROPERTY

IRC § 165
Reg. § 1.165-7(b)(4)(iv)
*IRS Publication 547

18.14 REPAIRS MAY BE A "MEASURE OF LOSS"

Cost of repairs
Reg. § 1.165-7(a)(2)(ii)
S. P. Keith, Jr., 52 TC 41 (1969) (Acq.)

Estimated repairs not measure of loss
Claire E. Lamphere, 70 TC 391 (1978) (Acq.)
Venancio A. Bagnol, 37 TCM 1038 (1978)

Repairs, though not made, may affect post-

casualty value
Paul Abrams, 41 TCM 1459 (1981)

Loss of value exceeds repair costs
George E. Conner, 439 F.2d 974 (5th Cir. 1971)
Anne Marie Hagerty, 34 TCM 356 (1975)

18.15 INSURANCE REIMBURSEMENTS

Reimbursements reduce loss
IRC § 165(a)
Reg. § 1.165-1(c)(4)

Disaster relief
Rev. Rul. 76-144, 1976-1 CB 17

Relocation Act payments
Paul J. Smith, 76 TC 459 (1981) (Acq.)

Adjuster's fee
Ben R. Stein, 31 TCM 663 (1971), aff'd and remanded in unpublished opinion (7th Cir. March 4, 1974)

Voluntary payments from employer
Rev. Rul. 55-131 1953-2 CB 112, distinguished by Rev. Rul. 57-1, 1957-1 CB 15 and Rev. Rul. 64-329, 1964-2 CB 463

Gifts from friends do not reduce loss
Rev. Rul. 64-329, 1964-2 CB 58

Insurance claim must be filed: 1986 Tax Act
IRC § 165(h)(4)(E)

Failure to make insurance claim pre-1986 Tax Act
David Axelrod, 56 TC 248 (1971)
F. T. Morgan, 37 TCM 524 (1978)
IRS Publication No. 17, 1980 ed.

Pre-1987 deduction allowed despite failure to make claim
Henry L. Hill, 76 TC 484 (1981), aff'd 691 F.2d 997 (1st Cir. 1982)

Red Cross
Special Ruling, 5-11-52

18.16 EXCESS LIVING COSTS PAID BY INSURANCE ARE NOT TAXABLE

IRC § 123
Reg. § 1.123-1

Taxable income determined at end of dislocation period
Rev. Rul. 93-43, 1993-2 CB 69

18.17 DO YOUR CASUALTY LOSSES EXCEED YOUR INCOME?

Carryback of losses
IRC § 172
Reg. § 1.172-1
Reg. § 1.172-3(b)

18.18 DEFER GAIN BY REPLACING PROPERTY

IRC § 1033
*IRS Publication 549
* "Planning for Real Estate Condemnation Awards in Light of Recent Favorable Rulings," Charles E. Falbe and William E. Singer, 59 Journal of Taxation 400 (December 1983)

18.19 INVOLUNTARY CONVERSIONS QUALIFYING FOR TAX DEFERRAL

What is an involuntary conversion?
IRC § 1033
Reg. § 1.1033(a)-1
IRS Publication 549

Threat of condemnation by government employee
Frank O. Maixner, 33 TC 191 (1959) (Acq.)
Carson Estate Co., 22 TCM 425 (1963)

Voluntary sale
Harry G. Masser, 30 TC 741 (1958) (Acq.)
Rev. Rul. 59-361, 1959-2 CB 183
Rev. Rul. 63-221, 1963-2 CB 332

Condemnation as unfit for habitation
Rev. Rul. 57-314, 1957-2 CB 523

Threat of building code violation not sufficient
Thorpe Glass Mfg. Corp., 51 TC 300 (1968)

Farmers—irrigation project
Reg. § 1.1033(d)-1

Cattle diseased
IRC § 1033(d)
Reg. § 1.1033(e)-1

Livestock sales due to drought
IRC § 1033(e)
Reg. § 1.1033(f)-1

Sale to private party after governmental threat of conversion
Creative Solutions, Inc., 320 F.2d 809 (5th Cir. 1963)

Identity of threatening authority not disclosed
Rev. Rul. 74-8, 1974-2 CB 200

Tax sale
Rev. Rul. 77-370, 1977-2 CB 306

Gain on involuntary conversion
IRC § 1033
Reg. § 1.1033(a)-1 and 2
Russel C. Smith, 59 TC 107 (1972)

Pesticide crop damage
* Letter Ruling 9615041

House destroyed by a tornado
Rev. Rul. 96-32, 1996-1 CB 177

Contested award
Conlorez Corp., 51 TC 467 (1968) (Acq.)
Harry D. Aldridge, 51 TC 475 (1968)
Casalina Co., 60 TC 694 (1973) (Acq.), aff'd per curiam, 511 F.2d 1162 (4th Cir. 1975)

18.20 HOW TO ELECT TO DEFER TAX

Dissolution of partnership not termination
Morton Fuchs, 80 TC 506 (1983)

18.21 TIME PERIOD FOR BUYING REPLACEMENT PROPERTY

* "Rollover Rules for Disaster Insurance Proceeds Clarified," 82 The Journal of Taxation 294 (May 1995)

Three-year replacement for condemned realty
IRC § 1033(g)(4)

---

*Note: Paragraph numbers refer to Volume One. Items marked * are research aids, not citations of authority; see "Key to Citations" on page 806.*

Four-year replacement period for principal residence involuntarily converted by disaster
IRC § 1033 (h)(1)(B)

Election irrevocable
John McShain, 65 TC 686 (1976)

No substitution of replacement property
Rev. Rul. 83-39, 1983-1 CB 190

Advance payment of award starts replacement period
Stewart & Co., 57 TC 122 (1971)

Estate makes replacement
John E. Morris Est., 55 TC 636 (1971), aff'd per curiam, 454 F.2d 208 (4th Cir. 1972)
Isaac Goodman Est., 199 F.2d 895 (3d Cir. 1952)
Rev. Rul. 64-161, 1964-1 (Pt. 1) CB 298

Environmental Protection Agency order
Rev. Rul. 89-2, 1989-1 CB 259

Investment by widow
George W. Jayne Est., 61 TC 744 (1974)

Must report details of replacement
Reg. § 1.1033(a)-2(c)(2)

File for refund
Reg. § 1.1033(a)-2(c)(2)

18.22 Types of Qualifying Replacement Property

Business or investment property damaged in disaster area
IRC § 1033(h)(2)

Like-kind test
IRC § 1033(g)
Reg. § 1.1031(a)-1(b)

Related use
Liant Record Inc., 303 F.2d 326 (2d Cir. 1963), on rem'd, 22 TCM 203 (1963)
Clifton Investment Co., 312 F.2d 719 (6th Cir. 1963), cert. denied, 373 U.S. 921
Loco Realty Co., 306 F.2d 207 (8th Cir. 1962)
Thomas McCaffrey Jr., 275 F.2d 27 (2d Cir. 1960), cert. denied
Arnold L. Santucci, 32 TCM 840 (1973)
Rev. Rul. 64-237, 1964-2 CB 319

Replacement of rental house by residence does not qualify
Rev. Rul. 76-84, 1976-1 CB 219

Contract to buy does not qualify
Herrick L. Johnston Est., 51 TC 290 (1968), aff'd, 430 F.2d 1019 (6th Cir. 1970)

Purchase of leasehold of at least 30 years
Rev. Rul. 68-392, 1968-2 CB 338

Improvements to retained land
Rev. Rul. 67-255, 1967-2 CB 270
Rev. Rul. 67-255, 1967-2 CB 270
* Letter Ruling 9117030
* Letter Ruling 9118007
A.S. Davis, 589 F.2d 446 (9th Cir. 1979)

18.23 Cost of Replacement Property Determines Postponed Gain

Replacement
IRC § 1033(a)(2)
Reg. § 1.1033(a)-2(b) and (c)
Rev. Rul. 70-466, 1970-2 CB 165, amplified by Rev. Rul. 76-84, 1976-1 CB 219
John E. Morris Est., 55 TC 636 (1971), aff'd per curiam, 454 F.2d 208 (4th Cir. 1972)

Replacement of livestock—environmental contamination
IRC § 1033(f)

Buying a replacement from a relative
IRC § 1033(i), as amended by the 1997 Act

Payments to mortgagee
Reg. § 1.1033(a)-2(c)(1)
Frank W. Babcock, 28 TC 781 (1957) (Nonacq.), aff'd, 259 F.2d 689 (9th Cir. 1958)
Fortee Properties, Inc., 211 F.2d 915 (2nd Cir. 1954), cert. denied, 348 U.S. 826

Real property condemned
IRC § 1033(g)

Insurance proceeds allocated
Rev. Rul. 70-501, 1970-2 CB 163

18.24 Special Assessments and Severance Damages

IRS computation method
*IRS Publication 549

Must allocate or entire award is payment for condemnation
Seaside Improvement Co., 105 F.2d 990 (2d Cir. 1938), cert. denied, 308 U.S. 618
Marshall C. Allaben, 35 BTA 327

Allocation allowed although not fixed in award
L. A. Beeghly, 36 TC 111 (1961) (Acq. in result only)
Rev. Rul. 64-183, 1964-1 (Pt. 1) CB 297

Special assessment
Rev. Rul. 68-37, 1967-1 CB 359

Allocation to purchase of nonadjacent property
Rev. Rul. 72-433, 1972-2 CB 470
John L. McKitrick, 373 F. Supp. 471 (D. Ohio 1974)

Severance damage gain deferred by like-kind investment
Rev. Rul. 83-49 1983-1 CB 191

18.25 Reporting Gains From Casualties

Casualty gains exceed casualty losses
IRC § 165(h)(2)(B)

Involuntary conversion netting
IRC § 1231(a)(3)(A)
IRC § 1231(a)(4)(C)

19 Deducting Job Costs and Other Miscellaneous Expenses

19.1 2% AGI Floor Reduces Miscellaneous Deductions
IRC § 67(a)
Temp. Reg. § 1.67-1T
IRC § 62(a)(2)(A)
*IRS Publication 529

19.2 Effect of 2% AGI Floor on Deductions
IRC § 67

19.3 Checklist of Job Expenses Subject to the 2% AGI Floor
IRC § 67
*IRS Publication 529
* "Cases Illustrate Nature and Level of Investment Activities Needed to Attain Trader Status," Avi D. Liveson, 82 The Journal of Taxation 290 (May 1995)

19.4 Job Expenses Not Subject to the 2% AGI Floor
*IRS Publication 529

Impairment-related work expense
IRC § 67(d)

Performing artists
IRC § 62(a)(2)(B)
IRC § 62(b)

19.5 Dues and Subscriptions

Professional society
Henry P. Keith, 1 TCM 184 (1942), aff'd, 139 F.2d 596 (2d Cir. 1944)
Kenneth Blanchard, 12 TCM 550 (1953)

Trade association
Robert S. LeSage, 6 TCM 1263 (1947), aff'd in part and rev'd in part on other issues, 173 F.2d 826 (5th Cir. 1949)

Stock exchange
Charles E. Robertson, 1 BTA 501 (Acq.)

Community "booster" club
Security-First National Bank of Los Angeles, BTA Memo., February 27, 1934

Chamber of Commerce
Smith-Bridgman & Co., 16 TC 287 (1951) (Acq.)
Jeff Rubin, 13 TCM 1094 (1954)

Union membership
George A. Tatum, Jr., 10 TCM 602 (1951)
Rev. Rul. 54-190, 1954-1 CB 46

Union building fund nondeductible
Carl Briggs, 75 TC 465 (1980), aff'd, 694 F.2d 614 (9th Cir. 1983)
Kenneth M. Ridder, 76 TC 867 (1981)

Note: Paragraph numbers refer to Volume One. Items marked ˙ are research aids, not citations of authority; see "Key to Citations" on page 806.

Union election costs
James P. Carey, 56 TC 477 (1971) (Acq.), aff'd per curiam, 460 F.2d 1259 (4th Cir. 1972), cert. denied, 409 U.S. 990

Union assessments for old-age fund
Rev. Rul. 54-190, 1954-1 CB 46

Service charge to non-union members
Rev. Rul. 68-82, 1968-1 CB 68

Union dues
Rev. Rul. 72-463, 1972-2 CB 93

19.6 Uniforms and Work Clothes

Protective clothing
Oron R. Morgan, 80 F. Supp. 537 (D. Tex. 1948)
Louis M. Roth, 17 TC 1450 (1952) (Acq.)
Lewis F. Cooper, 12 TCM 471 (1953)
T. G. Frazier, Jr., 12 TCM 1129 (1953)

Overalls
Louis M. Roth, 17 TC 1450 (1952) (Acq.)
O. G. Russell, 12 TCM 1276 (1953)

Harder use than customary garments
Louis Drill, 8 TC 902 (1947)

Soiled after day's work
Louis M. Roth, 17 TC 1450 (1952) (Acq.)

Plumber
Vern W. Pratt, 11 TCM 335 (1952)

Sanitation inspector
C. W. Strickler, 11 TCM 252 (1952)

Machinist's helper
Carl E. Noe, 11 TCM 431 (1952)

Carpenter
E. M. Taylor, 11 TCM 651 (1952)
Roy J. Coffman, 16 TCM 353 (1957)

Telephone repairman
John Young, 11 TCM 239 (1952)

Painter
Rev. Rul. 57-143, 1957-1 CB 89

Airline pilots' uniforms
Dean L. Phillips, 9 TCM 51 (1950)

Nurse
Helen K. Harsaghy, 2 TC 484 (1943) (Acq.)

State highway patrol officer
Marcus O. Benson, 146 F.2d 191 (9th Cir. 1945)

Bakery salesman
Bennie Blatt, 6 TCM 94 (1947)
Marshall J. Hammons, 12 TCM 1318 (1953)

Cement finisher
Williard Thompson, 15 TC 609 (1950) (Acq. in part, nonacq. in part), rev'd and rem'd on other grounds, 193 F.2d 586 (10th Cir. 1952)

Commercial fisherman
Rev. Rul. 55-235, 1955-1 CB 274

Dairy worker
Ben A. Puente, 10 TCM 735 (1951), aff'd without discussion, 199 F.2d 940 (9th Cir. 1952)

Factory foreman's white coat and safety shoes

Oron R. Morgan, 80 F. Supp. 537 (D. Tex. 1948)

Hospital attendant
Oliver W. Bryant, 11 TCM 430 (1952)

Musician's formal wear
Wilson J. Fisher, 23 TC 218 (1954) (Acq. in part), aff'd on other issue, 230 F.2d 79 (7th Cir. 1956)

Paint machine operator
T. G. Frazier, Jr., 12 TCM 1129 (1953)

Plumber's special shoes and gloves
Lewis F. Cooper, 12 TCM 471 (1953)

Railroad firefighter
O. G. Russell, 11 TCM 334 (1952)
O. G. Russell, 12 TCM 1276 (1953)

Fashion expert's clothing deductible
Betsy L. Yeomans, 30 TC 757 (1958) (Acq.)

Boutique manager's clothes nondeductible
Barry Pevsner, 38 TCM 121 (1979), rev'd, 628 F.2d 467 (5th Cir. 1980)

Tennis clothing nondeductible
Cecil Mella, 52 TCM 1216 (1986)

Women's slacks
Oron R. Morgan, 80 F. Supp. 537 (D. Tex. 1948)

Dirty clothes a hazard
Elwood J. Clark, 158 F.2d 851 (6th Cir. 1947), aff'g per curiam 5 TCM 236 (1946)

Clothes worn at work only
Oliver W. Bryant, 11 TCM 430 (1952)

Allowance is taxable
Rev. Rul. 72-110, 1972-1 CB 24

19.7 Expenses of Looking for a New Job

Job search while temporarily unemployed
Rev. Rul. 75-120, 1975-1 CB 55, clarified by Rev. Rul. 77-16, 1977-1 CB 37

Driving costs of unemployed secretary
Herman Campana, 60 TCM 289 (1990)

CPA forms partnership
Howard L. Cormutt, 45 TCM 515 (1983)

Remained at same position
Kenneth R. Kenfield, 54 TC 1197 (1970)

Reimbursement of fees
Rev. Rul. 66-41, 1966-1 CB 233, distinguished by Rev. Rul. 73-351, 1973-2 CB 323

Payment of fee by employer
Rev. Rul. 73-351, 1973-2 CB 323

Company interested in your services
Rev. Rul. 63-77, 1963-1 CB 177

Former customers entertained
Harold Haft, 40 TC 2 (1963) (Acq.)

19.8 Unusual Job Expenses

Shoeshine costs
Robert C. Fryer, 33 TCM 122 (1974)

Lobbying
James M. Jordan, 60 TC 770 (1973) (Acq.)

Depreciation on furnishings
LeRoy Gillis, 32 TCM 429 (1973)

Cost of meal assessments
Robert E. Cooper, 67 TC 870 (1977) (Nonacq.)

Executive's purchase of blazers
Norman L. Jetty, 44 TCM 373 (1982)

Repayment of lay-off benefits
Rev. Rul. 82-178, 1982-2 CB 59

Salesman's private plane
William F. Sherman, Jr., 44 TCM 1324 (1982)

Job dismissal insurance
* Letter Ruling 8321074

Public officials
Rev. Rul. 84-110, 1984-2 CB 35

Musician's depreciation deduction
Richard L. Simon, 103 TC 15 (1994) (violin bow)
Brian P. Liddle, 103 TC 16 (1994) (Ruggeri bass viol)

Exotic dancer
Cynthia Hess, TC Memo 1994-79

19.9 Computers and Cellular Phones

Writing off cost of computer
IRC § 280F(b)
IRC § 280F(d)(4)

Employee deductions barred
Robert L. Bryant, 66 TCM 1594 (1993), aff'd by unreported 3d Circuit decision (September 15, 1994)
Rev. Rul. 86-129, 1986-2 CB 48 (aerospace engineer)
* Letter Ruling 8710009 (insurance agent)
* Letter Ruling 8615024 (nursing professor)
* Letter Ruling 8615071 (engineers)

Telemarketing sales manager allowed deduction
Sherri Mulne, 72 TCM 111 (1996)

Husband and wife allowed deduction
Thomas Cadwallader, 57 TCM 1030 (1989)

19.10 Calculators, Copiers, Fax Machines, and Typewriters

IRC § 280F(b)
IRC § 280F(d)(4)
Temp. Reg. § 1.280F-6T(b)

Hand-held calculator deductible
Robert G. Galazin, 38 TCM 851 (1979)

19.11 Small Tools

Substantiation of tool costs
Donald F. McGraw, 35 TCM 1016 (1976)
Ion Z. Josan, 33 TCM 645 (1974)
Harlan White, 33 TCM 652 (1974)

Reimbursements
Rev. Rul. 75-497, 1975-2 CB 29

19.12 Automobile Used for Work

*IRS Publication 463

Note: Paragraph numbers refer to Volume One. Items marked ˙ are research aids, not citations of authority; see "Key to Citations" on page 806.

19.13 EMPLOYEE HOME OFFICE DEDUCTIONS

IRC § 280A
* "Home Office Marches On (In Spite of Soliman)," Pamela K. Revak, 75 Taxes 549 (Oct. 1997)
* "Home Office Deductions Alive and Well After Soliman," Ann Burstein Cohen, 58 Taxation for Accountants 275 (May 1997)

Administrative office deductions allowed starting in 1999
IRC § 280A(c)(1), as amended by the 1997 Act, overturning result of Supreme Court's Soliman decision

Supreme Court sets principal place of business tests
Nader Soliman, 113 S. Ct. 701 (1993)
Rev. Rul. 94-24, 1994-1 CB 87 (IRS examples applying Soliman tests)
Notice 93-12, 1993-1 CB 298 (IRS response to Supreme Court's Soliman decision)

Violinist's studio not principal place of business
Ernest Drucker, 715 F.2d (2d Cir. 1983), rev'g 79 TC 605 (1982)

Professor's home office
David J. Weissman, 751 F.2d 512 (2d Cir. 1985)

Anesthetist employed by hospital
Byron K. Anderson, 44 TCM 1305 (1982)

Phone calls as dealing with clients
John W. Green, 78 TC 428 (1982), rev'd, 707 F.2d 404 (9th Cir. 1983)
Max Frankel, 82 TC 318 (1984)

Teachers not allowed to deduct home office costs
* Letter Ruling 7734023

Professors with sideline writing/consulting business not allowed deduction
* Letter Rulings 8030024, 8030025

Separate structure appurtenant to house
Charles A. Scott, 84 TC 683 (1985)

No deduction for renting space to employer
IRC § 280A(c)(6)

19.14 TELEPHONE COSTS

No deduction for main phone line
IRC § 262(b)

Telephone calls and telegrams for business
Reg. § 1.162-6
Leo R. Marshall, 8 TCM 508 (1949)

Installation of home phone for business
Charles J. Voigt, 8 TCM 662 (1949)
Robert A. Phillips, 8 TCM 587 (1949)
C. W. Strickler, 11 TCM 252 (1952)
O. G. Russell, 11 TCM 334 (1952)
Robert H. Lee, 19 TCM 317 (1960)

Taxpayer deducted all toll charges
Paul E. Jackson, 14 TCM 1175 (1955)

Businessman confined to home
Dan R. Hanna, Jr., 10 TCM 566 (1951)

Deduction allowed for telephone but not for home office
Charles E. Shepherd, 35 TCM 219 (1976), aff'd in unpublished opinion (7th Cir. April 22, 1977)

Allocation of business phone
Robert G. Galazin, 38 TCM 851 (1979)

19.15 TYPES OF DEDUCTIBLE EDUCATION COSTS

Reg. § 1.162-5
*IRS Publication 508

2% floor
IRC § 67(a)

19.16 WORK-RELATED TESTS FOR EDUCATION COSTS

* "The Tax Consequences of Graduate Educational Expenses and Reimbursements," Michael J. Delaney, Richard T. Helleloid, and Scott M. Kudialis, 68 Taxes 286 (April 1990)

Minimum job requirements
Eduardo Antuna, 36 TCM 1778 (1977)
David Cooper, 37 TCM 529 (1978)

Maintain or improve skills
1.162-5(c)(1)
Clark S. Marlor, 251 F.2d 615 (2d Cir. 1958)

MBA expenses deductible
Robert C. Beatty, 40 TCM 438 (1980)
Frank S. Blair, 41 TCM 289 (1980)

MBA expenses not deductible
Ross L. Link, 90 TC 460 (1988)
Ronald T. Smith, 41 TCM 1186 (1981)
Eduardo Antuna, 36 TCM 1778 (1977)

Undergraduate courses not deductible by accountant
Diane Zimmer, 64 TCM 1388 (1992)

Undergraduate courses not deductible by financial planner
Judith Meredith, 65 TCM 2876 (1993)

Undergraduate courses not deductible by office manager
Theresa M. Malek, 50 TCM 792 (1985)

Undergraduate college costs not deductible by policeman
James A. Carroll, 51 TC 213 (1968), aff'd, 418 F.2d 91 (7th Cir. 1969)

Industrial psychologist
Cosimo A. Carlucci, 37 TC 695 (1962) (Acq.)

Engineering aide to maintain skills
Ralph A. Fattore, 22 TCM 1093 (1963)

Attorney attending graduate courses
Albert C. Ruehmann, 30 TCM 675 (1971)
Charles B. Johnson, 332 F. Supp. 906 (D. La. 1971)
Larry R. Adamson, 32 TCM 484 (1973)

Unemployed teacher
Edward J. P. Zimmerman, 71 TC 367 (1978), aff'd, 79-2 USTC ¶9617 (2nd Cir. 1979)

Teacher did not abandon profession

John C. Ford, 56 TC 1300 (1971), aff'd per curiam, 487 F.2d 1025 (9th Cir. 1973)

Engineer not established in his profession
Barry Reisine, 29 TCM 1429 (1970)
Thomas W. Gallery, 57 TC 257 (1971)

Orthodontic course
Rev. Rul. 74-78, 1974-1 CB 44

CPA review course not deductible
Rev. Rul. 69-282, 1969-1 CB 55
William D. Glenn, 62 TC 270 (1974)

Private tutoring in management
Walter G. Lage, 52 TC 119 (1969) (Acq.)

Bar admission fee not deductible
Arthur E. Ryman, Jr., 51 TC 799 (1969)
William J. Brennan, 22 TCM 1222 (1963)

Broker license cost not deductible
Robert Kersey, 50 F.3d 15 (9th Cir. 1995)

Music therapy courses not deductible
Herbert Hewett, 71 TCM 2350 (1996)

Flying lessons of freelance news photographer
Alan Aaronson, 29 TCM 786 (1970)

Prerequisites not deductible
Neal F. Krauss, 39 TCM 725 (1979)

19.17 LAW SCHOOL COSTS

Law school
Reg. § 1.162-5(b)(2) and (3)
Jeffrey S. Augen, 33 TCM 1022 (1974)
Robert J. Connelly, 72-1 USTC ¶9188 (1st Cir. 1972)
Charles M. Watkins, 59 TCM 467 (1990)

Tax law courses taken by lawyer
Joseph T. Booth, III, 35 TC 1144 (1961)

CPA
Patrick L. O'Donnell, 62 TC 781 (1974), aff'd in unpublished decision (7th Cir. 1975)

Business law teacher
Juanita Ardavany, 38 TCM 569 (1979)

Bar admission fee not deductible
Arthur E. Ryman, Jr., 51 TC 799 (1969)
William J. Brennan, 22 TCM 1222 (1963)

Bar review
Larry R. Adamson, 32 TCM 484 (1973)
Arthur E. Ryman, Jr., 51 TC 799 (1969)

Amortization of fees to state bar admission authorities
Joel Sharon, 591 F.2d 1273 (9th Cir. 1978), aff'g 66 TC 515 (1976)

Costs to practice in second state
Joseph J. Vetrick, 37 TCM 392 (1978), aff'd, 628 F.2d 885 (5th Cir. 1980)

Lawyer must practice profession
Albert C. Ruehmann, III, 30 TCM 675 (1971)
Richard M. Randick, 35 TCM 195 (1976)
Paul R. Wassenaar, 72 TC 1195 (1979)
David M. Kohen, 44 TCM 1518 (1982)
* Letter Ruling 9112003

Not qualified to take bar exam
Rev. Rul. 76-62, 1976-1 CB 12, distinguished by

Note: Paragraph numbers refer to Volume One. Items marked ˚ are research aids, not citations of authority; see "Key to Citations" on page 806.

Rev. Rul. 76-352, 1976-2 CB 37

Foreign attorney
Yaroslaw Horodysky, 54 TC 490 (1970)

Pre-law courses
Ben H. Kim, 28 TCM 671 (1969)

19.18 COURSES TAKEN BY DOCTORS AND NURSES
Reg. § 1.162-5(b)(3)

Cost of physician's assistant course
Matthew J. Reisinger, 71 TC 568 (1979)

Psychiatry courses
John S. Watson, 31 TC 1014 (1959) (Nonacq.)

Psychoanalytic courses
Ramon M. Greenberg, 367 F.2d 663 (1st Cir. 1966)

Psychiatrist's therapy by phone and cassette
Kenneth Porter, 51 TCM 481 (1986)

Prior law: doctor's law school costs
Joseph E. Campbell, 250 F. Supp. 941 (D. Pa. 1966)

19.19 COURSES TAKEN BY TEACHERS
Reg. § 1.162-5(b)(2)

Effect on tenure
Harold H. Davis, 38 TC 175 (1962), rev'd in unpublished opinion (9th Cir. 1964)
Evelyn Devereaux, 292 F.2d 637 (3d Cir. 1961)

Change from professor to president
Rev. Rul. 68-580, 1968-2 CB 72

Qualifying in second state
Rev. Rul. 71-58, 1971-1 CB 55

Social worker denied deduction for education necessary for faculty position
Kenneth C. Davis, 65 TC 1014 (1976)

Professional license
Howard K. Michaelson, 313 F.2d 668 (9th Cir. 1963)
Elmer R. Johnson, 313 F.2d 668 (9th Cir. 1963)
Woodard W. Hartrick, 22 TCM 145 (1963)
Lonnie R. Lenderman, 22 TCM 511 (1963)
Sandra M. Hering, 33 TCM 1329 (1974)

Teaching assistant denied deduction of graduate study costs
Arthur M. Jungreis, 55 TC 581 (1970)

Teaching assistant denied deduction for bachelor degree
George Baisr, 56 TCM 781 (1988)

Paraprofessional
Leonarda Diaz, 70 TC 1067 (1978), aff'd, 607 F.2d 995 (2d Cir. 1979)

Discussion leader
Gerald Schwerm, 51 TCM 271 (1986)

19.20 PROFESSOR'S RESEARCH EXPENSES
Rev. Rul. 63-275, 1963-2 CB 85
Robert E. Drury, 36 TCM 35 (1977)
Rev. Rul. 63-275, 1963-2 CB 85
Robert E. Drury, 36 TCM 35 (1977)

* "Professors' Taxable Income and Deductions," G. Gibbs, 39 Accounting Review 1004 (1964)

19.21 LEAVE OF ABSENCE TO TAKE COURSES

IRS one-year test
Rev. Rul. 68-591, 1968-2 CB 73
* Letter Ruling 8538068

High school teacher's graduate course deductible
Mary O. Furner, 47 TC 165 (1966), rev'd, 393 F.2d 292 (7th Cir. 1968)

Unemployed student's college degree not deductible
Don Cornish, 29 TCM 235 (1970)

Resigned principal—three-year course
Robert Picknally, 36 TCM 1292 (1977)

Manager quits for two-year MBA
Stephen G. Sherman, 36 TCM 1191 (1977)

Texas professor—two-year leave of absence
Junius J. Johnson, 55 TCM 700 (1988)

IRS does not object to teacher's two-year absence
M. V. Damm, 41 TCM 1359 (1981)
Mary O. Furner, 47 TC 165 (1966), rev'd, 393 F.2d 292 (7th Cir. 1968)
Don Cornish, 29 TCM 235 (1970)
Rev. Rul. 68-591, 1968-2 CB 73

19.22 LOCAL TRANSPORTATION AND TRAVEL AWAY FROM HOME TO TAKE COURSES
IRC § 274(m)(2)

Professor's nondeductible educational travel
Theodore Keller, TC Memo 1996-300

19.23 HOW TO DEDUCT EDUCATION COSTS ON YOUR RETURN
Reg. § 1.162-5
*IRS Publication 508

Costs of typing
Rev. Rul. 67-421, 1967-2 CB 84

Sightseeing
Reg. § 1.162-5(d) and (e)

Trip between work and school
Gerhard F. B. Boerner, 30 TCM 240 (1971)
Robert J. Burton, 30 TCM 243 (1971)

Employer reimbursement or direct payment of tuition
Rev. Rul. 76-71 1976-1 CB 308, distinguished by Rev. Rul. 76-352, 1976-2 CB 37

Stipend paid by employer is taxable
Rev. Rul. 76-65, 1976-1 CB 46, distinguished by Rev. Rul. 76-352, 1976-2 CB 37

Payment for substitute teacher fund
Rev. Rul. 76-286, 1976-2 CB 41

Payments from VA
Rev. Rul. 83-3 1983-1 CB 72

19.24 CHECKLIST OF DEDUCTIBLE INVESTMENT EXPENSES
IRC § 212
Reg. § 1.212-1(b)
* "Accounting and Legal Fees Can Be Structured to Increase Portion That Is Deductible," Thomas H. Gooding, Jr., 12 Tax for Law 218 (Jan./Feb. 1984)

2% floor
IRC § 67(a)

Fees to bank in dividend reinvestment plan
Rev. Rul. 75-548, 1975-2 CB 331

Expense of collecting tax-exempt income nondeductible
IRC § 265(a)(1)
Reg. § 1.265-1

Office of investor
Joseph J. Imhoff, 29 TCM 966 (1970)

Safe-deposit box for securities
Albina E. Bodell, 1 TCM 395 (1943)
W. N. Fry, 5 TC 1058 (1945)
Daniel S. W. Kelly, 23 TC 682 (1955) (Acq.), aff'd on other issue, 228 F.2d 512 (7th Cir. 1956)

Home safe
* Letter Ruling 8218077

Traveling to check investments deductible
E. M. Godson, 5 TCM 648 (1946)
Martha E. Henderson, 27 TCM 109 (1968)

Investor may not deduct travel to business sites
William R. Kinney, 66 TC 122 (1976)

Proxy fight expenses
R. Walter Graham, 326 F.2d 878 (4th Cir. 1964)
J. Raymond Dyer, 23 TCM 1208 (1964), aff'd, 352 F.2d 948 (8th Cir. 1965)
Rev. Rul. 64-236, 1964-2 CB 64

Trip to broker not deductible
Stanley S. Walters, 28 TCM 22 (1969)

Trip to investigate prospective investments not deductible
Doran S. Weinstein, 420 F.2d 700 (Ct. Cl. 1970)

Mutual-fund fees
Rev. Rul. 55-23, 1955-1 CB 275

Business advice to produce income
Reg. § 1.212-1(g)
Andrew Jergens, 2 TCM 385 (1943)
Edward E. Bishop, 4 TC 862 (1945) (Acq.)
Amelia E. Collins, 3 TCM 223 (1944)
Elma M. Williams, 3 TC 200 (1944) (Acq.)
Raymond Fitzgerald, 15 TCM 1450 (1956)

Building improvements on replacement property
* Letter Ruling 9421001

Expenses of fiduciary
Reg. § 1.212-1(j)

Incompetency fees
Elsie Weil Est., 13 TCM 653 (1954)

Reduce income-producing ability
Ann F. Day, 57-1 USTC ¶9270 (D. Ariz. 1957)
Gertrude Lytton-Smith, 57-1 USTC ¶9271 (D.

Note: Paragraph numbers refer to Volume One. Items marked ˙ are research aids, not citations of authority; see "Key to Citations" on page 806.

853

Citations of Authority

Ariz. 1957)
Robert S. Howard, 32 TC 1284 (1959) (Acq.)

Capital expenditures
IRC § 263
Reg. § 1.263(a)-1 and 2
Reg. § 1.212-1(n)

No deduction for investor while on trip for company
J. D. O'Connor, 13 TCM 623 (1959)

Director's deduction for investment club convention
Walter Gustin, 46 TCM 1505 (1983)

Deduction barred for general investment seminar
IRC § 274(h)(7)

Trip to investigate rental property not deductible
Patrick L. O'Donnell, 62 TC 781 (1974), aff'd in unpublished decision (7th Cir. 1975)

Travel cost to stockholders' meetings nondeductible
Rev. Rul. 56-511, 1956-2 CB 170

Trip to present stockholder resolution deductible
* Letter Ruling 8220084

No deduction for investor's home office expenses
IRC § 280A
Joseph Moller, 721 F.2d 810 (Fed. Cir. 1983)

19.25 COSTS OF TAX RETURN PREPARATION AND AUDITS
IRC § 212(3)
Reg. § 1.212-1(1)

2% floor
IRC § 67(a)

Fees allocable to Schedule C, E, or F
Rev. Rul. 92-29, 1992-1 CB 20
David Burleson, 68 TCM 288 (1994) ($55 fee allowed on Schedule C despite non-business income)

Foreign tax
Philip T. Sharples, 533 F.2d 550 (Ct. Cl. 1976)

Legal fees deductible although underlying transaction is capital
Philip T. Sharples, 533 F.2d 550 (Ct. Cl. 1976)

Tax advice on real estate deal
James A. Collins, 54 TC 1656 (1970) (Acq.)

Tax deficiency imposed on business income
Clarence Wood, 37 TC 70 (1961) (Acq.)
Clyde E. Thomas, Sr., 41 TC 614 (1964)

Interest on business-related deficiency
James Redlark, 106 TC 2 (1996)

Criminal tax fraud charge
Michael Shapiro, 278 F.2d 556 (7th Cir. 1960)

Tax advice on future deals
Basil L. Kaufman, 227 F. Supp. 807 (D. Mo. 1964)

Tax books deductible

Donald W. Fausner, 30 TCM 1170 (1971), aff'd on other issue, 413 U.S. 838 (1973)

Personal checking account fees nondeductible
Florence E. Callander, 75 TC 334 (1980)

NOW account fees nondeductible
Rev. Rul. 82-59, 1982-1 CB 47

Money-market account fee
* Letter Ruling 8345067

19.26 DEDUCTING LEGAL COSTS
IRC § 162
IRC § 212
Reg. § 1.212-1(1)
* "Deducting Legal Costs of Defending Against Claims of Sexual Harassment In the Workplace," David R. Brennan and Susan L. Meguard, 84 Journal of Taxation 94 (February 1996)

Suspension of license arose from personal activity
Kenneth A. Cameron, 79-2 USTC ¶9477 (9th Cir. 1979)

Employment-related legal costs
Walter F. Tellier, 383 U.S. 687 (1966)
Don Gilmore, 372 U.S. 39 (1963)
Stanley Waldheim, 25 TC 839 (1956) (Acq.), aff'd on other issue, 244 F.2d 1 (7th Cir. 1957)
M. S. Kaufman, 12 TC 1114 (1949) (Acq.)
Jean Nidetch, 37 TCM 1307 (1978)
Steve Sikey, 37 TCM 548 (1978)
Milton Margoles, 27 TCM 319 (1968)
Rev. Rul. 64-277, 1964-2 CB 55

Libel suits
James E. Threlkeld, 87 TC 1294 (1986), aff'd, 848 F.2d 81 (6th Cir. 1988)
Paul F. Roemer, Jr., 716 F.2d 693 (9th Cir. 1983), rev'g 79 TC 398
J. Raymond Dyer, 36 TC 456 (1961) (Acq.)
Paul Draper, 26 TC 201 (1956) (Acq.)
Rev. Rul. 58-418, 1958-2 CB 18, distinguished by Rev. Rul. 75-230, 1975-1 CB 93

Allocation of fees where compensatory and punitive damages received
Rev. Rul. 85-98, 1985-2 CB 51

Libel suit of public official
* Letter Ruling 8018077

Will contest
Reg. § 1.212-1(k)
Charles E. Parker, 573 F.2d 42 (Ct. Cl. 1978)

Wrongful death actions
Lawrence E. DeWeese, 276 F. Supp. 901 (D. Ore. 1967)

Injury during a business trip remains personal
Thomas Stricker, 70 TCM 1192 (1995)

Title issues or disputes
Reg. § 1.212-1(k)
Fred W. Woodward, 397 U.S. 572 (1970)
Hilton Hotels Corp., 397 U.S. 580 (1970)
Walter W. Cruttenden, 70 TC 191 (1978), aff'd, 644 F.2d 1368 (9th Cir. 1981) (deduction allowed)

Allocation of legal fees where dispute involves

title and income
Reg. § 1.212-1(k)
Daniel S. W. Kelly, 228 F.2d 512 (7th Cir. 1956), aff'g 23 TC 682 (1955) (Acq.)
Andrew J. Stormfeltz, 142 F.2d 982 (8th Cir. 1944)
Birdie Kimbrell, 80 F. Supp. 695 (D. Ill. 1948)
Joseph P. Morgan Est., 37 TC 31 (1961) (Acq.), aff'd in part, rev'd in part, 332 F.2d 144 (6th Cir. 1964)
E. W. Brown, Jr., 19 TC 87 (1952), aff'd in part, rev'd in part and rem'd, 215 F.2d 697 (5th Cir. 1954)
Agnes P. Coke, 17 TC 403 (1951) (Acq.), aff'd per curiam, 201 F.2d 742 (5th Cir. 1953)
William A. Falls, 7 TC 66 (1946) (Acq.)

Legal fees for tax advice and tax return preparation
IRC § 212(3)
Reg. § 1.212-1(1)

Fees of defending criminal tax fraud charge deductible
Michael Shapiro, 278 F.2d 556 (7th Cir. 1960)
Rev. Rul. 68-662, 1968-2 CB 69

Defense of illegal business
John DiFronzo, 75 TCM 1693 (1998)
Ellis L. McDonald, U.S. Dist. Ct. Al., 12/23/98

Fee to reduce assessment
Rev. Rul. 70-62, 1970-1 CB 30

Estate planning fee
Sidney Merians, 60 TC 187 (1973) (Acq.)

20 TRAVEL AND ENTERTAINMENT EXPENSE DEDUCTIONS

20.1 DEDUCTION GUIDE FOR TRAVEL AND TRANSPORTATION EXPENSES
Reg. § 1.162-2

Temporary assignments of one year or less
IRC § 162 (a)
Rev. Rul. 93-86, 1993-2 CB 71 (IRS's realistic expectation test)

IRS temporary assignment guidelines (pre-1993 expenses)
Rev. Rul. 83-82, 1983-1 CB 45

20.2 COMMUTING EXPENSES
* "Travel and Moving Expenses for Multistate Workers," Theodore E. Degnan and A. George Petrie, 5 Taxation for Accountants 24 (January 1996)
* "Transportation Expense Deduction Limited for Home-Officed Taxpayers," Wiliam V. Vetler 73 Taxes 107 (March 1995)
* "Should Deductible Commuting Be Contingent on Principal-Place-of-Business Criteria?" Ronald S. Ross, 83 Journal of Taxation 88 (August 1995)

Commutation not deductible
Reg. § 1.162-2(e)
Reg. § 1.262-1(b)(5)
Oran R. Morgan, 80 F. Supp. 537 (N.D. Tex. 1948)
Leo M. Verner, 39 TC 749 (1963) (Acq.)

Note: Paragraph numbers refer to Volume One. Items marked ` are research aids, not citations of authority; see "Key to Citations" on page 806.

Joseph M. Winn, 32 TC 220 (1959)
Clarence H. O'Donnell, 21 TCM 609 (1962)

Commuting to a temporary location
Rev. Rul. 99-7, 1999-5 IRB

Commuting to temporary job — pre-1999 IRS policy
Rev. Rul. 94-47, 1994-2 CB 18, amplifying Rev. Rul. 90-23, 1990-1 CB 28
Robert Burleson, 68 TCM 288 (1994)

Lumberjack's commuting costs
Charles W. Walker, 101 TC 537 (1993)
Rev. Rul. 94-47, 1994-2 CB 18 (IRS will not follow Walker)
Robert M. Burleson, 68 TCM 288 (1994) (Tax Court holds that IRS may not apply Rev. Rul. 94-47 retroactively)

Police officers' commuting expenses deductible
John R. Pollei, 877 F.2d 838 (10th Cir. 1989)

Doctor's emergency calls to hospital
Margaret G. Sheldon, 50 TC 24 (1968)

Carrying tools to work
Rev. Rul. 75-380, 1975-2 CB 59

Commute to nuclear power plant
John C. Banekatis, 56 TCM 376 (1988)

Electrician's commute to power plant
Philip D. Williams, 60 TCM 627 (1990)

Deductible travel from office in home
Thomas C. St. John, 29 TCM 1045 (1970)
Joe J. Adams, 43 TCM 1203 (1982) (repairman)
Thomas L. Wicker, 51 TCM 225 (1986)
Robert Leitch, 58 TCM 343 (1989)
Julio Mazzotta, 57 TC 427 (1971)

Musician driving from home office to restaurant
Leroy Kahuku, 58 TCM 1247 (1990)

Travel from union hall to job
Russell Anderson, 60 TC 834 (1973)

20.3 OVERNIGHT-SLEEP TEST LIMITS DEDUCTION OF MEAL COSTS

Sleep or rest rule
Homer O. Correll, 389 U.S. 299 (1968), rev'g 369 F.2d 87 (6th Cir. 1966)

Nap in parked car
Frederick J. Barry, 54 TC 1210 (1970), and per curiam, 435 F.2d 91 1290 (1st Cir. 1971)

Railroad personnel
Rev. Rul. 75-170, 1975-1 CB 60

Truck drivers
Rev. Rul. 75-168, 1975-1 CB 58

Meal costs during overtime not deductible
D. S. Courtney, 32 TC 334 (1959)
W. K. Liang, 34 TCM 1298 (1975)

20.4 IRS MEAL ALLOWANCE
Rev. Proc. 96-28, 1996-1 CB 685 (meal expenses after 1996)
*IRS Publications 17 and 1542

20.5 BUSINESS TRIP DEDUCTIONS
Reg. § 1.162-2(a)

Laundry, cab fare
Rev. Rul. 63-145, 1963-2 CB 86

Lavish or extravagant
Rev. Rul. 63-144, 1963-2 CB 129

Limit on cruise ship costs
IRC § 274(m)(1)

Saturday-night stayover
* Letter Ruling 9237014

20.6 WHEN ARE YOU AWAY FROM HOME?

Place of business as tax home
Raymond K. Yeates, 55 TCM 1077 (1988)
J. N. Flowers, 326 U.S. 465 (1946)
Lee E. Daly, 72 TC 190 (1979), rev'd 631 F.2d 351 (4th Cir. 1980), aff'g Tax Court and rev'g after hearing en banc, 662 F.2d 253 (4th Cir. 1981)

Ethel Merman case
Robert F. Six, 450 F.2d 66 (2d Cir. 1971)
Robert Rosenspan, 438 F.2d 905 (2d Cir. 1971), cert. denied, 404 U.S. 864

Residence is tax home
Charles W. Rambo, 69 TC 920 (1978) (Acq. in result only)
Edward M. McKarzel, 30 TCM 366 (1971)
Eli F. McOimsey, 30 TCM 521 (1971)
Rev. Rul. 71-247, 1971-1 CB 54

Army officer at permanent duty port
H. A. Stidger, 386 U.S. 287 (1967)

Unmarried person
Robert Rosenspan, 438 F.2d 905 (2d Cir. 1971), cert. denied, 404 U.S. 864
Irving M. Sapson, 49 TC 636 (1968) (Acq.)
Max W. Tugel, 20 TCM 693 (1961)
Curtis L. Ralston, 27 TCM 1312 (1968)
Rev. Rul. 773-529, 1973-2 CB 37
Arthur Crossland, 33 TCM 1278 (1974), aff'd, 535 F.2d 1240 (2nd Cir. 1976)

Multiple short job at same locale
Thomas J. Mitchell, TC Memo 1999-283

20.7 FIXING A TAX HOME IF YOU WORK IN DIFFERENT LOCATIONS
Edward W. Andrews, 60 TCM 277 (1990), rev'd, 931 F.2d 132 (1st Cir. 1991)
Francis Markey, 491 F.2d 1249 (6th Cir. 1974), rev'g 31 TCM 766 (1972)
Joseph Sherman, 16 TC 332 (1951) (Acq.)
Chong, TC Memo 1996-232
S. M. R. O'Hara, 6 TC 841 (1946)
Richard E. Benson, 27 TCM 1555 (1968)
John H. Webster, 9 TCM 550 (1950)
W. Edward Winterhalter, 10 TCM 268 (1951)
Vincent Treanor, 10 TCM 336 (1951)
Rev. Rul. 55-604, 1955-2 CB 49
Rev. Rul. 63-82, 1963-1 CB 33
Thomas J. Mitchell, TC Memo 1999-283

Baseball players, coaches, pilots, etc. might have other business
Rev. Rul. 54-147, 1954-1 CB 51
Tracy Stright, 66 TCM 1490 (1993)

Special Ruling, December 29, 1953
Maury Wills, 411 F.2d 537 (9th Cir. 1969)

20.8 TAX HOME OF MARRIED COUPLE WORKING IN DIFFERENT CITIES
Robert A. Coerver, 297 F.2d 837 (3d Cir. 1962), aff'g 36 TC 252 (1951)
Arthur B. Hammond, 213 F.2d 43 (5th Cir. 1954)
Virginia Foote, 67 TC 1 (1976)
George P. Leyland, 34 TCM 1502 (1975)
Charles J. Hundt, 20 TCM 369 (1961)

20.9 DEDUCTING LIVING COSTS ON TEMPORARY ASSIGNMENT
* "A House Is Not Necessarily a Tax Home, An Examination of the Deductibility of Away-From-Home Expenses," Richard Weber and Edmund Outslay, 65 Taxes 275 (May 1987)

Temporary assignments—one year or less (costs paid or incurred after December 31, 1992)
IRC § 162 (a)
Rev. Rul. 93-86, 1993-2 CB 71 (IRS's realistic expectation test)
Notice 93-29, 1993-29 CB 311

IRS "temporary assignment" guidelines (costs incurred before 1993)
Rev. Rul. 83-82, 1983-1 CB 45

IRS "temporary assignment" guidelines
Rev. Rul. 83-82, 1983-1 CB 45

Family at temporary post
Emil J. Michaels, 53 TC 269 (1969) (Acq.)

Federal crime investigations
IRC § 162(a), as amended by the 1997 Act

Engineer on 20-month job
Philip Rolbin, 29 TCM 848 (1970)

Retired Florida stenographer
Virginia C. Avery, 29 TCM 1187 (1970)

Student's summer job
Saterios Hantzis, 38 TCM 1169 (1979), rev'd, 638 F.2d 248 (1st Cir. 1981), cert. denied, 101 S. Ct. 3112

Court rejection of one-year test
David L. Cowger, 25 TCM 513 (1966)
Ronald Brown, 30 TCM 41 (1971)
Louis R. Frederick, 457 F. Supp. 1274 (D.N. Dak. 1978), aff'd, 603 F.2d 1292 (8th Cir. 1979)

Recurrent summer job
Franklin C. Dilley, 58 TC 276 (1972)

State judge traveling to other circuits
Frank Fisher, 24 TC 269 (1955) (Acq.)

State judge who must live in district
James A. Emmert, 146 F. Supp. 322 (S.D. Ind. 1955)

Employed for test period
Richard C. Lipps, 21 TCM 358 (1962)
Rev. Rul. 60-314, 1960-2 CB 48

Employment for part of a year
James R. Whitaker, 24 TC 750 (1955)
George R. Lanning, 34 TCM 1366 (1975)
F. J. McGinley, Jr., 15 TCM 641 (1956)

*Note: Paragraph numbers refer to Volume One. Items marked * are research aids, not citations of authority; see "Key to Citations" on page 806.*

855

Linesman working out of Oakland, California
Max W. Tugel, 20 TCM 693 (1961)

Baseball player's expenses
Rev. Rul. 54-147, 1954-1 CB 51

Professional football player
Ronald C. Gardin, 64 TC 1079 (1975)

Temporary assignment
James E. Peurifoy, 358 U.S. 59 (1958)
Michael Kuris, 15 TCM 854 (1956)
Robert K. Denning, 14 TCM 838 (1955)
Rev. Rul. 60-189, 1960-1 CB 60

Temporary becomes permanent
Hansel H. Johnson, Jr., 77 TCM 1966 (1999)

Itinerant worker
George H. James, 308 F.2d 204 (9th Cir. 1962),
aff'g 176 F. Supp. 270 (D. Nev. 1959)

One-year test disregarded
Michael L. Hanna, 63 TCM 2917 (1992)
Ronald Brown, 30 TCM 41 (1971)

20.10 BUSINESS-VACATION TRIPS WITHIN THE UNITED STATES
Reg. § 1.274-4(e)(2)
IRC § 274(c)(3)

Saturday night stayover deductible
* Letter Ruling 9237014

20.11 BUSINESS-VACATION TRIPS OUTSIDE THE UNITED STATES
IRC § 274(c)

Control over trip, managing executive, related to employer
Reg. § 1.274-4(f)(5)

Counting days outside U.S.
Reg. § 1.274-4(c)

Allocation formula
Reg. § 1.274-4(f)

No allocation necessary if not managing executive or self-employed
Reg. § 1.274-4(f)(5)

20.12 DEDUCTING EXPENSES OF BUSINESS CONVENTIONS
* "Company Conventions: Business Discussions Do Not Necessarily Avoid Tax Problems," Malcolm Osborn, 12 Taxation for Lawyers 268 (March/April 1984)

Business or pleasure trip
Reg. § 1.162-2(b)

Convention expenses
Reg. § 1.162-2(d)
Rev. Rul. 63-266, 1963-2 CB 88

Connection with business
Rev. Rul. 59-316, 1959-2 CB 57, clarified by Rev. Rul. 63-266, 1963-2 CB 88

No deduction for investment seminars after 1986
IRC § 274(h), as amended by 1986 Tax Reform Act

Lawyer's convention expenses
Wade H. Ellis, 50 F.2d 343 (D.C. Cir. 1931)

Legal secretary's convention expenses
Rita M. Callinan, 12 TCM 170 (1953)

Insurance agent
C. J. D. Rudolph, 291 F.2d 841 (5th Cir. 1961), aff'g 189 F. Supp. 2 (N.D. Tex. 1960), cert. dismissed, 370 U.S. 269 (1962)

Business convention in coastal resort
Rev. Rul. 56-168, 1956-1 CB 93
Reg. § 1.162-2(b)(1)

Cruises
DeWitt N. Burnham, 17 TCM 240 (1958)
Reuben B. Hoover, 35 TC 566 (1961) (Acq.)

No deduction for Super Bowl weekend meetings
Danville Plywood Corp., 16 Cl. Ct. 584 (1989), aff'd, 899 F.2d 3 (Fed. Cir. 1990)

Fraternal organizations' conventions
Reg. § 1.162-2(d)

20.13 TRAVEL EXPENSES OF A SPOUSE OR DEPENDENTS

Deduction restrictions for costs incurred after 1993
IRC § 274 (m)(3), as amended by the Revenue Reconciliation Act of 1993

Spouse as employee
Madyo A. Poletti, 330 F.2d 818 (8th Cir. 1965)
IRS policy (pre-1993 travel costs)
Rev. Rul. 63-144, 1963-2 CB 129

Spouse's expenses on convention or business trip (pre-1993 travel)
Reg. § 1.162-2(c)
William N. Clement, Sr., 331 F. Supp. 877 (E.D.N.C. 1971)
Donald W. Scarborough, 30 TCM 613 (1971)

Company convention policy
J. C. Thomas, 289 F.2d 108 (5th Cir. 1961), cert. denied, 368 U.S. 837

Spouse acting as nurse
Allenberg Cotton Co., 61-1 USTC ¶9131 (W. D. Tenn. 1961)
William E. Reisner, 34 TC 1122 (1960) (Acq.)
Preston R. Riely, 23 TCM 449 (1964)

Spouse acting as host or hostess
Pierre C. Warwick, 236 F. Supp. 761 (E.D. Va. 1964)
Ron Merritt, 21 TCM 1011 (1962)
Roy O. Disney, 267 F. Supp. 1 (C.D. Cal. 1967), aff'd, 413 F.2d 783 (9th Cir. 1969)
Bank of Stockton, 36 TCM 114 (1977)

Spouse of controlling stockholder
Bywater Sales and Service Co., 24 TCM 849 (1965)

Spouse of foreign service employee
Fraser Wilkins, 348 F. Supp. 1282 (D. Neb. 1972)

20.14 RESTRICTIONS ON FOREIGN CONVENTIONS AND CRUISES

Reasonableness of foreign location
IRC § 274(h)

Reporting rule
274(h)(5)

Costa Rica
Treasury Dept. Announcement, 1991

Saint Lucia
Treasury Dept. Announcement, 1991

Jamaica not foreign
Treaty, 12/16/81

U.S. Virgin Islands, Samoa, Guam in North American Area
Rev. Rul. 82-151, 1982-2 CB 75

Trinidad & Tobago
Treasury Dept. News Release NB-684, 1990

Honduras
Treasury Dept. Announcement, 1990

Cruise ship rules
274(h)(2)

20.15 50% DEDUCTION LIMIT

Allowable entertainment costs
IRC § 274(a)

50% deduction limit
IRC § 274(n)(1)
Reg. § 1.274(a)(3)
Reg. § 1.274(m)(3)
* "Vulnerability of Entertainment and Meal Deductions Under the Sutter Rule," Timothy J. McNally, 62 Taxes 184 (March 1984)
* "Substantiation Is the Key to Preventing the Disallowance of Business Entertainment Expenses," Cary R. Miteles, 32 Taxation for Accountants 342 (June 1984)

20.16 THE RESTRICTIVE TESTS FOR MEALS AND ENTERTAINMENT
IRC § 274(a)
Senate Comm. Report on Pub. L. No. 87-834
Reg. §1.274(a)(3)
Reg. § 1.274(m)(3)

Lavish and extravagant entertainment
IRC § 274(k)
Reg. § 1.274-1
Rev. Rul. 63-144, 1963-2 CB 129
Donald G. Harper, 23 TCM 461 (1964)

Entertainment defined
Reg. § 1.274-2(b)(1)(ii)

Business associates
Reg. § 1.274-2(b)(2)(iii)

Prospective investors
* Letter Ruling 9414040

Note: Paragraph numbers refer to Volume One. Items marked ˙ are research aids, not citations of authority; see "Key to Citations" on page 806.

20.17 DIRECTLY RELATED DINING AND ENTERTAINMENT

IRC § 274(a)(1)
Reg. § 1.274-2(a)

Directly related entertainment
Reg. § 1.274-2(c)
Rev. Rul. 63-144, 1963-2 CB 129

Annual party for associates deductible
Robert Moore, 96-2 USTC ¶50413 (Dist. Ct. Va. 1996)

Doctor's entertainment
Karl Wolf, 64-1 USTC (W.D. Mo. 1964)
Richard A. Sutter, 21 TC 170 (1953)
C. W. Lokey, 16 TCM 18 (1957)
Kenneth Branchard, 12 TCM 550 (1953)

Hunting trips for clients not deductible
* Letter Ruling 9608004

20.18 GOODWILL ENTERTAINMENT

IRC § 274(a)(1)(A)
Reg. § 1.274-2(a)(1)(ii)
Reg. § 1.274-2(d)
Rev. Rul. 63-144, 1963-2 CB 129

No deduction for entertaining co-workers
Donald Scalley, 63 TCM 2238 (1992)

20.19 HOME ENTERTAINING

Reg. § 1.274-2(f)(2)(i)(b)
Rev. Rul. 63-144, 1963-2 CB 129

20.20 YOUR PERSONAL SHARE

* "Vulnerability of Entertainment and Meal Deductions Under the Sutter Rule," Timothy J. McNally, 62 Taxes 184 (March 1984)
John D. Moss, Jr., 80 TC 1073 (1983), aff'd, 758 F.2d 211 (7th Cir. 1985)
Ray A. Smith, 33 TC 1059 (1960)
Richard A. Sutter, 21 TC 170 (1953)
James P. Fenstermaker, 37 TCM 898 (1978)
Rev. Rul. 63-144, 1963-2 CB 129

20.21 ENTERTAINMENT COSTS OF SPOUSES

Directly related test
Reg. § 1.274-2(d)(4)

Goodwill entertainment
Rev. Rul. 63-144, 1963-2 CB 129

Entertainment of out-of-town customer's spouse
Rev. Rul. 63-144, 1963-2 CB 129

20.22 ENTERTAINMENT FACILITIES AND CLUB DUES

IRC § 274(a)(1)(B)

Luncheon club not facility
Reg. § 1.274-2(e)(3)(ii)

Deduction for club dues barred after 1993
IRC § 274 (a)(3)
Reg. § 1.274-2 (a)(2)(iii) (IRS exception for civic or public service organizations and professional associations)

20.23 RESTRICTIVE TEST EXCEPTION FOR REIMBURSEMENTS

IRC § 274(e)
Reg. § 1.274-2(f)
Proposed Regulation 1.274-2(a)(2)(111)

20.24 50% COST LIMITATION ON MEALS AND ENTERTAINMENT

IRC § 274 (n)(1)

Restaurants and nightclubs
IRC 274(e)(8)

Limited to face value of ticket
IRC § 274(1)

Charitable sporting events
IRC § 274(1)(B)

De minimis rule for employee meals
IRC § 274(n)(2)(B)
IRC § 119(b)(4)

Employee reimbursement
IRC § 62(a)(2)(A)

Transportation industry workers
IRC § 274(n)(3)

Sky boxes
IRC § 274(1)(2)

Free employee meals
Boyd Gaming Corp., 117 F.3d 1096 (9th Cir. 1999)

20.25 BUSINESS GIFT DEDUCTIONS ARE LIMITED

IRC § 274(b)
Reg. § 1.274-3
Rev. Rul. 63-144, 1963-2 CB 129

Gift to secretary
Richard Steel, 28 TCM 1301 (1969), aff'd per curiam, 437 F.2d 71 (2d Cir. 1971)

Gifts to employees
IRC § 102(c)

Employee achievement awards
IRC § 274(j)
Prop. Reg. § 1.274-8

20.26 RECORD-KEEPING REQUIREMENTS

IRC § 274(d)
Reg. § 1.274-5(a)
Rev. Proc. 63-4, 1963-1 CB 474
* "Careful Recordkeeping of T&E Even More Vital Now Because of New Restrictions," Stephen C. Fox, 16 Taxation for Lawyers 274 (Mar./Apr. 1988)
* "Deductions Can Be Substantiated in Many Different Ways Depending on Expense Involved," Mark A. Pridgeon, 40 Taxation for Accountants 180 (Mar. 1988)

What your records must show
Reg. § 1.274-5(b)
Reg. § 1.274-5(c)

Business purpose
Reg. § 1.274-5(c)(2)(ii)(b)

Need of receipt with diary
William F. Sanford, 50 TC 823 (1968), aff'd per curiam, 412 F.2d 201 (2d Cir. 1969), cert. denied, 396 U.S. 841

Inadequate travel and entertainment records not a basis for negligence penalties
John Robinson, 51 TC 520 (1968) (Acq.), aff'd, 422 F.2d 873 (9th Cir. 1969)

Oral testimony accepted
Harry G. La Forge, 434 F.2d 370 (2d Cir. 1970)

Oral testimony ignored
Arthur Hughes, 451 F.2d 975 (2d Cir. 1972)
Norman E. Kennelly, 56 TC 936 (1971), aff'd, 456 F.2d 1335 (2nd Cir. 1972)

Lost records
Raymond W. Jackson, 34 TCM 1315 (1975)
Joe F. Gizzi, 65 TC 342 (1975)

Credit card statements
John Shea, 112 TC 183 (1999)

20.27 SUBSTANTIATING DEDUCTIONS FOR TRAVEL AND ENTERTAINMENT

Travel receipt threshold raised to $75
Notice 95-50, 1995-2 CB 333

Diary
Reg. § 1.274-5(c)(2)
Joseph L. Weinfeld, 20 TCM 70 (1961)
Warren Cummings, 20 TCM 1699 (1961)

Hotel bill not needed if per diem allowance received
Rev. Proc. 63-4, 1963-1 CB 494

Receipts
Reg. § 1.274-5(c)(2)(iii)
Notice 95-50, 1992-2 CB 333

Noting expense items
Reg. § 1.274-5(c)
Reg. § 1.274-5(c)(6)

Failure to show business purpose
Norman E. Kennelly, 56 TC 936 (1971), aff'd, 456 F.2d 1335 (2nd Cir. 1972)

Time limit for keeping records
Reg. § 1.274-5(c)(2)(iv)

Credit cards
Reg. § 1.274-5(e)(2)
Rev. Rul. 59-410 1959-2 CB 64

Excuses for inadequate records
Reg. § 1.274-5(c)

Attorney required to keep travel and entertainment records
William Andress, Jr., 51 TC 863 (1969), aff'd per curiam, 423 F.2d 679 (5th Cir. 1970)

Loss of records
Lewis M. Bryan, 33 TCM 1188 (1974)

Bills but no other proof
Cam F. Dowell, Jr., 522 F.2d 708 (5th Cir. 1975), cert. denied, 26 U.S. 920

Loss due to eviction
Irvin A. Murray, 41 TCM 337 (1980)

Note: Paragraph numbers refer to Volume One. Items marked * *are research aids, not citations of authority; see "Key to Citations" on page 806.*

Loss due to destruction by estranged wife
Matthew J. Canfield, 41 TCM 461 (1980)

Loss of records due to fire
Robert Inazo, 76 TCM 231

20.28 REPORTING T&E EXPENSES AS SELF-EMPLOYED PERSON

Diary and receipts
Rev. § 1.274-5(c)

20.29 REPORTING UNREIMBURSED T&E EXPENSES

2% floor
IRC § 67

50% limit on meals and entertainment for 1997
IRC § 274(n)(1)

20.30 TAX TREATMENT OF REIMBURSEMENTS
* IRS Publication 463

Accountable plan requirements
Reg. § 1.62-2

Per diem arrangements
Rev. Proc. 93-21, 1993-1 CB 529

Reimbursements of club dues or spousal travel costs
Reg. §§ 1.132-5(s) and (t)
* "How to Avoid Income on Employee Reimbursements," Ray A. Knight and Lee G. Knight, 49 Taxation for Accountants 278 (November 1992)
IRC § 62(c)

20.31 WHAT IS AN ACCOUNTABLE PLAN?
IRC § 62(c)
Reg. § 1.62-2(c)(2) and (c)(4)

Reimbursement given to avoid FICA
* Letter Ruling 9504002

Failure to get reimbursed
Earl M. Coplon, 18 TCM 166 (1959), aff'd, 277 F.2d 534 (6th Cir. 1960)
Marvin A. Heidt, 18 TCM 149 (1959), aff'd, 274 F.2d 25 (7th Cir. 1960)
Eugene J. Rogers, 18 TCM 866 (1959)
Jack C. Morgan, 24 TCM 644 (1965)

Frequent flyer allowance under accountable plans
* Letter Ruling 9547001

20.32 PER DIEM TRAVEL ALLOWANCE UNDER ACCOUNTABLE PLANS
* IRS Publication 1542
Rev. Proc. 98-63, 1998-52 IRB (high-cost *per diem* areas for 1999)

20.33 AUTOMOBILE MILEAGE ALLOWANCE
Announcement 99-7, 1999-2 IRB, modifying Rev. Proc. 98-63, 1998-52 IRB

20.34 REIMBURSEMENTS UNDER NON-ACCOUNTABLE PLANS
Reg. § 1.62-2(c)(3) and (c)(5)
* Letter Ruling 9443025

21 PERSONAL EXEMPTIONS

21.1 HOW MANY EXEMPTIONS MAY YOU CLAIM?
IRC § 151

No exemption for dependent on own return
IRC § 151(d)(2)
IRC § 152

21.2 YOUR SPOUSE AS AN EXEMPTION

Taxpayer's and spouse's exemption
IRC § 151(b)
Reg. § 1.151-1(b)

Spouse not dependent
IRC § 152(a)(9)
Reg. § 1.151-1(b)
Joel Dewsbury, 146 F. Supp. 467 (Ct. Cl. 1954)
Charles W. Jamieson, 23 TCM 2091 (1964), aff'd 353 F.2d 1 (7th Cir. 1965)

Determination of marital status
IRC § 7703

Divorce or separation
IRC § 143(a)

Interlocutory decree
Reg. § 1.6013-4(a)
William G. Ostler, 237 F.2d 501 (9th Cir. 1956)
Alice H. Evans, 19 TC 1102 (1953) (Acq.), aff'd, 211 F.2d 378 (10th Cir. 1954)
Rev. Rul. 75-536, 1975-2 CB 462
Rev. Rul. 57-368, 1957-2 CB 896, revoking I.T. 3942, 1949-1 CB 69

Filing separate return
IRC § 151(c)
Reg. § 1.151-1(b)

Spouse died during year
IRC § 153(1)
Reg. § 1.153-1
Asa C. Epps, 26 TC 843 (1956)
Rev. Rul. 71-158, 1971-1 CB 50

Remarried before end of year
Rev. Rul. 71-158, 1971-1 CB 50

Widow remarrying can be exemption
Rev. Rul. 71-159, 1971-1 CB 50

21.3 TEST 1. RELATIONSHIP TEST

Qualifying relatives
IRC § 152
*IRS Publication 501

Infants
Reg. § 1.152-1(b)

Unborn child does not qualify
Andrea L. Cassman, 31 Fed Cl. 121 (1994)

Unborn child is not a dependent
Michael Cassman, 31 Fed. Cl. 121 (1994)

Adopted or placed for adoption
IRC § 152(b)(2)
Rev. Rul. 54-70, 1954-1 CB 69

Foster child
IRC § 152(b)(2)

Nephew, niece, uncle, aunt
IRC § 152(a)(7) and (10)
Reg. § 1.152-1(a)(1)
Reg. § 1.152-2(d)

Contributions to a relative
Lena Hahn, 22 TC 212 (1954)

In-laws
IRC § 152(a)(8)
Reg. § 1.152-1(a)(1)

Cannot claim spouse's brother's wife
Rev. Rul. 1971-72, 1971-1 CB 49

Stepchild's husband, wife, child
IRC § 152
Reg. § 1.152-1(a)(1)

Close relationship not necessary on joint return
Reg. § 1.152-2(d)

Close relative not living with you
IRC § 152(a)(9)
Reg. § 1.151-2(a)
Reg. § 1.152-1(a)(1)

Cousin not allowed
Rebecca Pettigrew, 24 TCM 745 (1965)

21.4 UNRELATED OR DISTANTLY RELATED DEPENDENTS LIVING WITH YOU

Friends
IRC § 152(a)(9)
Reg. § 1.152-1(b)
Robert W. Trowbridge, 30 TC 879 (1958), aff'd per curiam, 268 F.2d 208 (9th Cir. 1959)

Foster children
IRC § 152(b)

Living in another's house
Zelta Bombarger, 31 TC 473 (1958)

Housekeeper does not qualify as dependent
William Thomas Hamilton, 34 TC 927 (1960)

Spouse not dependent
IRC § 152(a)(9)
Reg. § 1.152-1(b)
Joe A. Dewsbury, 146 F. Supp. 467 (Ct. Cl. 1957)
Rev. Rul. 55-325, 1955-1 CB 18

Divorce void
Daniel Buckley Est., 37 TC 664 (1962) (Acq.)

Illegal relationship
IRC § 152(b)(5)
Leon Turnipseed, 27 TC 758 (1957)
Leonard J. Eichbauer, 30 TCM 581 (1970)

Unmarried couple: state law controls
Nevett F. Ensminger, 610 F.2d 189 (4th Cir. 1979) (violates N.C. law)
L. J. Eichbauer, 30 TCM 581 (1970) (violates

Note: Paragraph numbers refer to Volume One. Items marked ˚ are research aids, not citations of authority; see "Key to Citations" on page 806.

Washington law)

S. J. Martin, 32 TCM 656 (1972) (violates Alabama law)

In re Mary M. Shackelford, 3 Bankr. 42 (W. Dist. of MO, Bankruptcy Ct. 1980) (does not violate Missouri law)

21.5 TEST 2. GROSS INCOME LIMIT FOR DEPENDENTS

Gross income test
IRC § 151(c)
Reg. § 1.151-2(a)

Gross receipts from business
Rayburn E. Hahn, 271 F.2d 739 (5th Cir. 1959), aff'g 30 TC 195 (1958)

Gifts not gross income
IRC § 102
Reg. § 1.102-1(a)

Share of partnership gross income
Doris V. Clark, 29 TC 196 (1957) (Acq.)

Social Security not gross income
Rev. Rul. 70-217, 1970-1 CB 12

Dividends excluded by dividend exclusion of gross income
IRC § 116
Reg. § 1.116-1

Certain military pay
IRC § 112
Reg. § 113
Reg. § 1.112-1
Reg. § 1.113-1

Insurance proceeds not gross income
IRC § 101
Reg. § 1.101-1

Disability benefit
Reg. § 1.152-1(a)(2)(ii)

Disabled person's workshop income not gross income
IRC § 151(c)(5)

21.6 CHILDREN UNDER AGE 19 OR FULL-TIME STUDENTS UNDER AGE 24

No gross income test
IRC § 151(c)(1)(B)
Reg. § 1.151-2

Rule applies to child, stepchild
IRC § 151(c)(3)
Reg. § 1.151-3(a)

Adopted child
IRC § 152(b)(2)

Foster child
IRC § 152(b)(2)

Brother does not meet rule
John E. Young, 19 TCM 1519 (1960)

Full-time course
Reg. § 1.151-3(b)
Rev. Rul. 72-449, 1972-2 CB 83

"Co-op" job
IRC § 151(c)(4)
Reg. § 1.151-3(c)
Rev. Rul. 57-561, 1957-2 CB 114

Education institution
Reg. § 1.151-3(c)

Intern not a student
John F. Bayley, 35 TC 288 (1960) (Acq.)

21.7 TEST 3. 50% SUPPORT TEST

* "Establishing Support Is the Crucial Part of the Test for Qualifications as a Dependent," Nicholas J. Crocetti, 14 Taxation for Lawyers 232 (Jan./Feb. 1986), 35 Taxation for Accountants 364 (Dec. 85)

Dollar amount
IRC § 152(a)
Reg. § 1.152-3

Promise to pay is not sufficient
Rev. Rul. 67-61, 1967-1 CB 27

Obligation to pay in later year
Rose De. Seraydar, 50 TC 756 (1968) (Acq.)
Rev. Rul. 58-404, 1958-2 CB 56, clarified by Rev. Rul. 67-61, 1967-1 CB 27

Support includes board, lodging, etc.
Reg. § 1.152-1(a)(2)(i)

Educational expenses
Ernest W. Herne, 52 TC 572 (1969)

Payment by insurance company
Rev. Rul. 64-223, 1964-2 CB 50

Parent uses Social Security benefits
Reg. § 1.152-1(a)(2)(ii)

Social Security to children
Rev. Rul. 74-543, 1974-2 CB 39
Rev. Rul. 74-115, 1974-1 CB 100
Rev. Rul. 57-344, 1957-2 CB 112

Medical care premiums
Rev. Rul. 64-223, 1964-2 CB 50

Medicare benefits not counted as support
Alfred H. Turecamo, 64 TC 720 (1975), aff'd, 554 F.2d 564 (2nd Cir. 1977) (Acq.)
Rev. Rul. 79-173, 1979-1 CB 86

Medicaid benefits not counted as support
Mary Archer, 73 TC 963 (1980)

Use of welfare payments
Rev. Rul. 71-468, 1971-2 CB 115
Norman Williams, 71 TCM 2423 (1996)
Eddie Carter, 55 TC 109 (1970) (Acq.)

Foster care payments
Rev. Rul. 77-280, 1977-2 CB 14
Pavel Dobra, TC No. 19

State payments for adopted child's care
Rev. Rul. 74-153, 1974-1 CB 20

Summer camp
Betty A. Shapiro, 54 TC 347 (1970) (Acq.)

Singing and drama lessons
Raymond McKay, 34 TC 1080 (1960)

Child-care payments
Paul Lustig, 30 TC 926 (1958) (Acq.), aff'd, 274

F.2d 448 (9th Cir. 1960), cert. denied, 364 U.S. 840
Dorothy H. Limpert, 37 TC 447 (1961) (Acq.)

Confinement in public hospital
Hazel Newman, 28 TC 550 (1957)

Veteran's tuition, subsistence allowances
Reg. § 1.152-1(c)
Florence L. Long, 30 TCM 588 (1971)

War orphans payments
Mary Keegstra, 48 TC 897 (1967) (Acq.)
Rev. Rul. 68-415, 1968-2 CB 65

West Point
Rev. Rul. 55-347, 1955-1 CB 21

Navy scholarship
Rev. Rul. 58-403, 1958-2 CB 49

Naval ROTC
Charles P. Ide, 40 TC 72 (1963), aff'd, 335 F.2d 852 (3d Cir. 1964)

Father in religious home
Rev. Rul. 58-303, 1958-1 CB 61

Dependent inducted into Armed Forces
Helena Thompson, 12 TCM 348 (1953)
Louis Lindauer, 15 TCM 896 (1956)
Bennet H. Darmer, 20 TC 822 (1953)
Ralph A. Romine, 25 TC 859 (1956) (Acq.)

Allotment for member of Armed Forces
Rev. Rul. 70-87, 1970-1 CB 29

Cost of car and T.V. may be support items
Rev. Rul. 77-282, 1977-2 CB 52

Surviving spouse receives life insurance
Rev. Rul. 58-419, 1958-2 CB 57, modified by Rev. Rul. 64-222, 1964-2 CB 47

Does not include life insurance premiums
Miriam G. Sauer, 12 TCM 1377 (1953)
John C. Robertshaw, 38 TCM 935 (1979)

Funeral expenses not support
Special Ruling, September 17, 1959

Student loan
John L. Ketterl, 29 TCM 1694 (1970)
Philip J. McCauley, 56 TC 48 (1971)

Value of personal care
Mildred Bartsch, 41 TC 883 (1964)
Frank Markarian, 352 F.2d 870 (7th Cir. 1965), aff'g 42 TC 640 (1964), cert. denied, 384 U.S. 988
Lolita M. Mosher, 29 TCM 251 (1970)

Child attends school on scholarship
IRC § 152(d)
Reg. § 1.152-1(c)
Charles P. Ide, 335 F.2d 852 (3d Cir. 1964), aff'g 40 TC 72 (1963), cert. denied, 384 U.S. 988
Norman Manning, 29 TCM 1707 (1970)

Student nurse's board and lodging
Rev. Rul. 58-338, 1958-2 CB 54

State aid to handicapped
Rev. Rul. 59-379, 1959-2 CB 51, clarified by Rev. Rul. 60-190, 1960-1 CB 51

State aid to educate retarded child is a scholarship

Note: Paragraph numbers refer to Volume One. Items marked * *are research aids, not citations of authority; see "Key to Citations" on page 806.*

Note: Paragraph numbers refer to Volume One. Items marked ` are research aids, not citations of authority; see "Key to Citations" on page 806.

860

Note: Paragraph numbers refer to Volume One. Items marked * *are research aids, not citations of authority; see "Key to Citations" on page 806.*

861

Edith W. Zoltan, 79 TC 490 (1982)

Airplane transportation of children to grandparents ineligible
Caroline Perry, 92 TC 470 (1989)

Employer dependent care reduces credit base
IRC § 21(c)

Dependent care provider must be identified on return
IRC § 21(e)(9)

25.8 DEPENDENT CARE CREDIT RULES FOR SEPARATED COUPLES

Marital status
IRC § 21(e)(3)

Spouse is not member of your household
IRC § 21(e)(4)

Special rule if you are divorced or separated
IRC § 21(e)(5)
Reg. § 1.44A-1(b)(2)

25.9 PAYING AND WITHHOLDING TAXES FOR HOUSEHOLD EMPLOYEES

* IRS Publication 926
P.L. 103-842 (10/11/94)
* "The Nanny Tax: Lessons Unlearned," Mark A. Luscombe, 74 Taxes 332 (May 1996)

25.10 SOCIAL SECURITY AND MEDICARE TAXES (FICA) FOR HOUSEHOLD EMPLOYEES

Notice 95-18, 1995-17 IRB 13

FICA withholding under Social Security Domestic Employment Reform Act of 1994
IRC § 3121(A)(7)
IRC § 3121(x)
IRC § 3510

FICA exemption for parent, child, spouse
IRC § 3121(b)(3)

25.11 FEDERAL UNEMPLOYMENT TAXES (FUTA) FOR HOUSEHOLD EMPLOYEES

Notice 95-18, 1995-17 IRB 13

FUTA on household wages over $1,000
IRC § 3306(a)(3)
Notice 95-18, 1995-17 IRB 13
IRS Release 1997-9 IRB 17

25.12 QUALIFYING TESTS FOR EIC

Qualifying child
IRC § 32(c)(3)

Eligible individual after 1993
IRC § 32(c)(1)
P.L. 103-465 (12/8/94)

After 1993, childless workers may qualify for the credit
IRC § 32(b)(1)(A)

Employer identification number required
Announcement 95-71, 1995-35 IRB 22

Social Security number of eligible taxpayer and spouse required
IRC § 32(c)(1)(F)

Married must file jointly
IRC § 32(d)
IRC § 7703

25.13 INCOME TESTS FOR EIC

IRC § 32(b)
* IRS Publication 596

Amount of credit for 1999
Rev. Proc. 99-42, 1996-2 CB 392

Earned income eligible for credit
IRC § 32(c)(2)

Denial of credit if excessive investment income
IRC § 32(i), as amended by the Personal Responsibility and Work Opportunity Act of 1996

Phaseout of credit based on modified adjusted gross income
IRC § 32(a)(2)
IRC § 32 (c)(5)

Credit determined by tables
IRC § 32(f)

Inflation adjustments
IRC § 32(j)
Rev. Proc. 95-53, 1995-2 CB 445 (1996 limits)

Union paid strike benefits
Rev. Rul. 78-191, 1978-1 CB 8

Military housing allowance
Michael C. Neff, Ct. Cl., 5/25/99

25.14 LOOK UP EIC IN GOVERNMENT TABLES

*IRS Publication 596

25.15 ADVANCE PAYMENT OF EARNED INCOME CREDIT

IRC § 32(g)
IRC § 3507

25.16 QUALIFYING FOR THE ADOPTION CREDIT

IRC § 23, as amended by the 1997 Act

Qualifying employer adoption assistance program
Announcement 97-64, IRB 1997-26
* "Tax Implications of New Legislation Designed to Provide Adoption Incentives," Julia K. Brazelton, 75 Taxes 426 (August 1997)

25.17 CLAIMING THE ADOPTION CREDIT ON FORM 8839

* IRS Publication 968, Notice 97-9 IRB 1997-2

---

26 TAX WITHHOLDINGS

26.1 WITHHOLDINGS SHOULD COVER ESTIMATED TAX

* IRS Publication 505

Form W-2

IRC § 6051

Social Security maximum
IRC § 31(b)(1)
Reg. § 1.31-2

Graduated withholding rates
IRC § 3402

Voluntary Social Security withholding
IRC § 3402(p)

Indicate marital status on exemption certificate
IRC § 3402(f)(1)

Allowable exemption on Form W-4
Reg. § 31.3402(f)(1)-1

26.2 WHEN INCOME TAXES ARE WITHHELD ON WAGES

* "Employee or Independent Contractor: Revitalizing Ideas Through New Definitions," Loren Callan Rosenzweig, 74 Taxes 242 (April 1996)

Wages
IRC § 3401(a)
Reg. § 31.3401(a)-1

Fringe benefits
Temp. Reg. § 31.3401(a)

Bonuses and supplemental wages—28% rate
Section 13273 of the Revenue Reconciliation Act of 1993

Payments other than wages (annuities, supplemental unemployment benefits)
IRC § 3402(o)
Reg. § 31.3402(o)-1

Domestics
Reg. § 31.3401(a)-3(b)

Agricultural workers
IRC § 3401(a)(2)

Computer operators
* Letter Ruling 9534002

Ministers
Reg. § 31.3401(A)(9)-1

Nonresident aliens
Reg. § 31.3401(a)(6)-1

Public officials
Reg. § 31.3401(a)-2(b)

Traveling advances
Reg. § 31.3401(a)-1(b)(2)

Board, lodging, health benefits, etc.
Reg. § 31.3401(a)(11)-1
Reg. § 31.3401(a)-1(b)(9) and (10)

Foreign government pay
Reg. § 31.3401(a)(5)-1

Foreign residents
Reg. § 31.3401(a)(8)(A)-1

U.S. possessions
Reg. § 31.3401(a)(8)(B)-1

No withholding on cancellation of employment contract
Rev. Rul. 58-301, 1958-1 CB 23, distinguished by Rev. Rul. 74-252, 1974-1 (withholding re-

---

Note: Paragraph numbers refer to Volume One. Items marked ˙ are research aids, not citations of authority; see "Key to Citations" on page 806.

quired on dismissal payments) CB 287 and Rev. Rul. 75-44, 1975-1 CB 15 (withholding on payment for relinquishment of seniority rights)

Terminated employee
IRC § 6051(a)

Refund of employer overwithholding
Rev. Rul. 82-84, 1982-1 CB 208

26.3 INCREASING WITHHOLDING
* "Tax Pointer: When and How to Change Withholding on Wages," 74 Taxes 330 (May 1996)
IRC § 3402(i) and (p)
Temp. Reg. § 32.1(a) to (g)

Electronic filing of W-4
Reg. § 31.3402 (f)(5)-1(c)

Voluntary Social Security withholding
IRC § 3402(p)

26.4 AVOIDING WITHHOLDING
IRC § 3402(n)

26.5 WITHHOLDING ALLOWANCES
IRC § 3402(m)
Reg. § 31.3402(m)-1

IRS instructions for credits not shown on Form W-4
Notice 88-42, 1988-1 CB 527

26.6 WHEN TO FILE A NEW FORM W-4
IRC § 3402(f)(2)

Change in number of exemptions
Reg. § 31.3402(f)(2)-1(b) and (c)

When new withholding exemption takes effect
IRC § 3402(f)(3)
Reg. § 31.3402(f)(3)-1

26.7 VOLUNTARY WITHHOLDING ON CERTAIN GOVERNMENT PAYMENTS
IRC § 3402(p)

26.8 WHEN TIPS ARE SUBJECT TO WITHHOLDING

Tax withheld on tips
IRC § 3402(k)
Reg. § 31.3402(k)

Written report
IRC § 6053

FICA tax
IRC § 3101
IRC § 3102
Rev. Rul. 95-7, 1995-1 CB 185

Tip allocation rules
IRC § 6053(c)
Reg. § 31.6053-3

26.9 WITHHOLDING ON GAMBLING WINNINGS
IRC § 3402(q)

26.10 FICA WITHHOLDINGS
IRC § 3121

Rate of tax
IRC § 3101 (employee)
IRC § 3111 (employer)

"Wages" same as for income tax
Rowan Companies, Inc., 81-1 USTC ¶9479 (S. Ct. 1981)

Responsible person for withholding
Edward Finley, 82 F.3d 966 (10th Cir., 1996)
Mary Phillips,73 F.3d 939 (9th Cir., 1996)

Responsible person must be given written IRS notice before penalty
IRC § 6672(b) as amended by 1996 Taxpayer Bill of Rights 2

Deferred pay plans
Rev. Rul. 78-263, 1978-2 CB 253
Prop. Reg. §31.3121(v)(2)-1,2
Prop. Reg. § 31.3306(r)(2)-1

Sick pay
IRC § 3121(a)(2)
IRC § 3231(e)

Spouse and children as employees
IRC § 3121(b)(3)(A) and (B)

26.11 WITHHOLDING ON RETIREMENT DISTRIBUTIONS
IRC § 3405

20% withholding from employer plans
IRC § 3405(c)
Notice 93-3, 1993-1 CB 293

Withholding on payments outside U.S.
IRC § 3405(e)(13)

26.12 BACKUP WITHHOLDING
IRC § 3406

$50 penalty
IRC § 6723 and §6724(d)(3)

---

27 ESTIMATED TAX PAYMENTS

27.1 ESTIMATING YOUR TAX
* IRS Publication 505
IRC § 6654

$1,000 threshold
IRC § 6654(e)(1)

90% or prior year safe harbor
IRC § 6654(d)

Safe harbor percentage if adjusted gross income exceeds $150,000
IRC § 6654(d)(1)(C)

No liability in prior tax year
IRC § 6654(e)(2)
Rev. Rul. 57-185, 1957-1 CB 454
Rev. Rul. 58-369, 1958-2 CB 894
John A. Guglielmetti, 35 TC 668 (1961) (Acq.)

Penalty waiver for hardship, retirement, or disability
IRC § 6654(e)(3)

Farmers and fishermen
IRC § 6654(i)

Amending your estimate
IRC § 6654(c)

Pay estimated taxes with credit cards
News Release IR 1999-87; Form 1040 instructions

27.2 DATES FOR PAYING ESTIMATED TAXES
*IRS Publication 505

Due dates for required installments
IRC § 6654(c)

Return filed by January 31
IRC § 6654(h)

Partners
Reg. § 1.6654-2(d)(2)

Farmers and fishermen
IRC § 6654(i)

27.3 ESTIMATES BY HUSBAND AND WIFE
*IRS Publication 505
Reg. § 1.6654-2

27.4 FINAL PAYMENT FOR 1999

Must file final return
IRC § 6012
Reg. § 1.6012-1
IRC § 6072(a)
Reg. § 1.6072-1

Get refund or credit
IRC § 6402(b)

Interest on overpayment
IRC § 6611
IRC § 6513(d)
Reg. § 301.6513-1(d)

Interest if mathematics wrong
IRC § 6601
Rev. Rul. 55-448, 1955-2 CB 595

27.5 PENALTY FOR UNDERESTIMATING YOUR 1999 TAX

Penalty for underpayments
IRC § 6654(a)
Reg. § 1.6654-1

Reasonable cause no bar to penalty
Barney Ruben Est., 33 TC 1071 (1960)

Underpayment
IRC § 6654(b)

Required amounts
IRC § 6654(d)

Withholding
IRC 6654(g)

---

28 TAX PLANNING

28.1 WHEN TO DEFER INCOME AND ACCELERATE DEDUCTIONS
* "Shifting Income Back to the Present Year Can Be Beneficial," Douglas R. Holm, 54 Taxation for Accountants 164 (March 1995)

---

*Note: Paragraph numbers refer to Volume One. Items marked * are research aids, not citations of authority; see "Key to Citations" on page 806.*

Note: Paragraph numbers refer to Volume One. Items marked `\` are research aids, not citations of authority; see "Key to Citations" on page 806.

864

Isolated rental
Charles A. Foehl, Jr., 20 TCM 418 (1961)

Intent to sell at profit, loss allowed
Lucille H. Gaunt, 69 F. Supp. 747 (W.D. Ky.)
Albert W. Bassett, 35 TCM 40 (1976)

Vandalism
Elbert S. Tillotson, 12 TCM 171 (1953)

Architect
Leonard Hyatt, 20 TCM 1635 (1961), supplemented by 20 TCM 1712 (1961), aff'd, 325 F.2d 715 (5th Cir. 1964), cert. denied, 379 U.S. 832

Listing for sale or rent
George D. Morgan, 76 F.2d 390 (5th Cir. 1935), cert. denied, 296 U.S. 601
Walden E. Sweet, 68-2 USTC ¶9656 (N.D. Cal. 1968)
James J. Sherlock, 31 TCM 383 (1972)

Rental to buyer
Henry B. Dawson, Jr., 31 TCM 5 (1972)

Expenses of rental attempt
Paul F. Stutz, 24 TCM 888 (1965)

Deducting expense of vacant building put up for sale
George W. Mitchell, 47 TC 120 (1966) (Nonacq.)

Limit on expense deductions where house used for personal purposes during the year
IRC § 280a

Widow allowed capital loss not rental loss
Victoria Balsamo, 54 TCM 608 (1987)

Stock in co-op apartment
Rev. Rul. 60-76, 1960-1 CB 296
Cecil P. Stewart, 5 TCM 229 (1946)
William M. Calder, Jr., 16 TC 144 (1951) (Acq.)

29.10 LOSS ON RESIDENCE ACQUIRED BY GIFT OR INHERITANCE

Residence acquired by gift or inheritance
IRC § 165(c)(2)
N. Stuart Campbell, 5 TC 272 (1945) (Acq.)
Maria Assmann Est., 16 TC 632 (1951)
Reed A. Watkins, 32 TCM 1260 (1973)
George W. Carnrick, 9 TC 756 (1947) (Acq.)
Pauline Miller Est., 26 TCM 229 (1967)

30 TAX SAVINGS FOR INVESTORS IN SECURITIES

30.1 PLANNING YEAR-END SECURITIES TRANSACTIONS

Capital gain holding period
IRC § 1222

Capital loss deduction against ordinary income
IRC § 1211(b)

Gain and loss recognized on trade date for year-end sale of publicly traded securities
IRC § 453 (k)(2)

30.2 EARMARKING STOCK LOTS

Registered in own name
Reg. § 1.1012-1(c)(5)
James E. Davidson, 305 U.S. 44 (1938)

Margin account registered in "street" name
James L. Rankin, Exr., 295 U.S. 123 (1936)
Laura M. Curtis, 101 F.2d 40 (2d Cir. 1939)
James L. Rankin, Exr. 84 F.2d 551 (3d Cir. 1936)

Recapitalization
Robert E. Ford, 33 BTA 1229 (Acq.)

Reorganization—identified
Amelia D. Bloch, 148 F.2d 452 (9th Cir. 1945)

Failure to show certificate numbers
Kluger Associates, 69 TC 925 (1978), aff'd, 617 F.2d 323 (2d Cir. 1980)

Reorganization—average cost
Christian W. Von Gunten, 76 F.2d 670 (6th Cir. 1935)
Harry M. Runkle, 39 BTA 458
Pio Crespi, 126 F.2d 699 (5th Cir. 1942)
Big Wolf Corp., 2 TC 751 (1943) (Acq.)

Split-up
Robert E. Ford, 33 BTA 1229 (Acq.)
Herbert H. Franklin, 37 BTA 471 (Acq.)
Solomon B. Kraus, 88 F.2d 616 (2d Cir. 1937)

Stock dividends
George Vawter, 83 F.2d 11 (10th Cir. 1936), cert. denied, 299 U.S. 578

Stock rights
Williams R. Perkins, 12 F. Supp. 481 (Ct. Cl. 1935), cert. denied, 297 U.S. 710

30.3 SALE OF STOCK DIVIDENDS

Holding period
IRC § 1223
Reg. § 1.1223-1

Public utility stock dividend
IRC § 305(e)

30.4 STOCK RIGHTS

Stockholder rights expire
IRC § 1223
IRC § 307
Reg. § 1.1223-1(e)
Reg. § 1.307-1 and 2
Sidney Z. Mitchell, 18 BTA 994, aff'd, 48 F.2d 697 (2d Cir. 1931), cert. denied, 284 U.S. 646

Stock rights sold
IRC § 1223(5)
Reg. § 1.1223-1(e)

Stock rights exercised
IRC § 1223(6)
Reg. § 1.1223-1(f)

Rights purchased
IRC § 1223
Reg. § 1.1223-1

Figuring basis of stock rights
IRC § 307

IRC § 307(b)(1)(B) ("less than 15%" exception)
Reg. § 1.307-1

Election
Reg. § 1.307-2

30.5 SHORT SALES

Appreciated financial position at year-end
IRC § 1259
* "Tax Planning for Short-Sale Transactions," Rolf Auster, 60 Taxation for Accountants 90 (Feb. 1998)

Special short-sale rules
IRC § 1233(b)
Reg. § 1.1233-1(c)(2)

Special rule on short-sale losses
IRC § 1233(d)
Reg. § 1.1233-1(c)(4)

Payment in lieu of dividends: 46-day rule
IRC § 263(b)

Extraordinary dividends
IRC § 263(h)(2)
IRC § 263(h)(3)

Husband and wife
Reg. § 1.1233-1(d)(3)

Short sale closing
H. S. Richardson, 121 F.2d 1 (2d Cir. 1941), cert. denied, 314 U.S. 684
William P. Doyle, 286 F.2d 654 (7th Cir. 1961), rev'g 19 TCM 677 (1960)
* Letter Ruling 9436017

Puts (options to sell)
IRC § 1233(c)
Reg. § 1.1233-1(c)(3)

Expenses of short sales; stock dividends
Rev. Rul. 72-521, 1972-2 CB 178

Cash dividends paid on stock sold short
IRC § 263(h)
1955 Production Exposition, Inc., 41 TC 85 (1963)
Main Line Distributors, Inc., 37 TC 1090 (1962), aff'd, 321 F.2d 562 (6th Cir. 1963)

Compensation for use of collateral
IRC § 263(h)(5)

Time of loss
Walter Hendricks, 29 TCM 36 (1970), aff'd, 423 F.2d 485 (4th Cir. 1970)

Arbitrage transactions
IRC § 1233(f)
Reg. § 1.1233-1(f)

Death before sale is closed
Rev. Rul. 73-524, 1973-2 CB 307

Wash sales
IRC § 1091(e)

30.6 WASH SALES

Wash sales
IRC § 1091
Reg. § 1.1091-1 and 2
Rev. Rul. 74-218, 1974-1 CB 202

Note: Paragraph numbers refer to Volume One. Items marked * *are research aids, not citations of authority; see "Key to Citations" on page 806.*

Note: Paragraph numbers refer to Volume One. Items marked * are research aids, not citations of authority; see "Key to Citations" on page 806.

* "Real Estate Investment Trusts Are Now a More Attractive Investment Vehicle for Tax Savings," Martin M. Shenkman, 40 Taxation for Accountants 208 (April 1988) and 16 Taxation for Lawyers 334 (May/June 1988)

Syndicates
Reg. § 301.7701-1

Limited partnership not taxable as corporation
Phillip G. Larson, 66 TC 159 (1976) (Acq.)
Rev. Rul. 79-106, 1979-1 CB 448

IRS to study minimum capitalization requirement
Ann. 83-4, 1983-2 IRB 31

Publicly traded partnerships
IRC § 7704
IRC § 469

Real estate investment trusts
IRC § 856
IRC § 857
IRC § 858
Reg. § 1.856
Reg. § 1.857
Reg. § 1.858

REMICs
IRC § 860A-860G

31.2 SALES OF SUBDIVIDED LAND— DEALER OR INVESTOR?
IRC § 1237
Reg. § 1.1237-1
* "When Capital Gains Can Be Obtained Upon the Sale of Subdivided Real Estate," Tony A. Flesher and William Wallace, 31 Taxation for Accountants 98 (Aug. 1983)

Liquidation of business property—no capital gain
John W. Kelley, 18 TCM 329 (1959), aff'd, 281 F.2d 527 (9th Cir. 1959)

No sales effort
Robert E. Austin, 263 F.2d 460 (9th Cir. 1959)
William T. Minor, Jr., 18 TCM 14 (1959)
James G. Hoover, 32 TC 618 (1959) (Acq.)
Allen Moore, 30 TC 1306 (1958) (Acq.)
Sam E. Broadhead Est., 32 TCM 1047 (1973)
Robert L. Adams, 60 TC 996 (1973) (Acq.)

Substantial improvements bar Section 1237 treatment
Jesse W. English, 65 TCM 2160 (1993)

Dealers may not use installment method
IRC § 453(b)(2)(A)
IRC § 453(l)

Sale to controlled corporation
Ralph E. Gordy, 36 TC 855 (1961) (Acq.)

Real estate dealer
Richard H. Pritchett, 63 TC 149 (1974) (Acq.)

Effect of condemnation
Thomas K. McManus, 65 TC 197 (1975)
Tri S. Corp., 400 F.2d 862 (10th Cir. 1968) (capital gains allowed)
Theodore H. Case, 633 F.2d 1240 (6th Cir. 1980) (capital gains denied)

Developer allowed capital gains on sale to city
Est. of Eileen Knudsen, 40 TCM 510 (1980)
Oscar Fraley, 66 TCM 100 (1993)

Developer not allowed capital gain on land sale
Robert P. Walsh, 67 TCM 3134 (1994)

31.3 EXCHANGING REAL ESTATE WITHOUT TAX
IRC § 1031
* "The 'State of the Art' in Like-Kind Exchanges," Richard M. Lipton, 91 Journal of Taxation 78 (August 1999)
* "Effect of the Taxpayer Relief Act of 1997 on Code Sec. 1031 Tax-Deferred Exchanges," Michael J. Novogradac, 76 Taxes 23 (June 1998)
* "Deferred Exchange Easier to Set Up Under Final Regs," Richard M. Lipton, 47 Taxation for Accountants 76 (Aug. 1991)
* "Deferred Exchange Regulations," Terence Floyd Cuff, 69 Taxes 451 (August 1991)
* "Many Transaction Costs Can Reduce Boot in Like-Kind Exchanges," Craig W. Murrel and Richard L. Panich, 74 Journal of Taxation 320 (May 1991)

"Like kind"
Reg. § 1.1031(a)-1(b) and (c)
Rev. Rul. 59-229, 1959-2 CB 180
P. G. Lake, Inc., 356 U.S. 260 (1958)

Productive use in trade or business
IRC § 1031
Reg. § 1.1031(a)-1(a)

Time limits
IRC § 1031(a)(3)
Prop. Reg. 1.1031(a)-3

Direct deed transfer
Rev. Rul. 90-34, 1990-1 CB 154

Two-year freeze on exchange with related party
IRC § 1031(f)

Basis
IRC § 1031(d)
Reg. § 1.1031(d)-1 and -2

Dealer
IRC § 1031
Reg. § 1.1031(a)-1(a)
Luther A. Harr, 15 F. Supp. 1004 (D.D. Pa. 1936)

Resale
Ethel Black, 35 TC 90 (1960)

Exchanges of remainder and life interests
Rev. Rul. 72-601, 1972-2 CB 467

Boot
Reg. § 1.1031(b)-1

Partially tax-free exchanges
IRC § 1031(b)
Reg. § 1.1031(b)-1

Receipt of cash contractually obligated to be applied against liabilities not boot
Earlene T. Barker, 74 TC 555 (1980)

Loss not recognized
IRC § 1031(a)
Reg. § 1.1031(a)-1

Planning tax-free exchange
Rev. Rul. 77-297, 1977-2 CB 304

99-year lease exchanged for fee interest is like-kind
Carl E. Koch, 71 TC 54 (1978) (Acq.)

Optional renewal periods added to initial lease terms
Century Electric, 192 F.2d 155 (8th Cir. 1951), cert. denied, 342 U.S. 954

31.4 TIMING YOUR REAL PROPERTY SALES

Installment sales
IRC § 453

Tax in year of sale
Milton S. Yunker, 26 TC 161 (1956), rev'd on other issue, 256 F.2d 130 (6th Cir. 1958)

Title passes
Alfred M. Bedell, 30 F.2d 622 (2d Cir. 1929)

Completion of terms of contingent sale
E. F. Baertschi, 412 F.2d 494 (6th Cir. 1969), rev'g 49 TC 289 (1967)

Deliver deed and possession
William C. King, 10 BTA 308 (Acq.)
Big Western Oil & Gas Co., 9 BTA 427 (Acq.)

Possession this year, deed next year
J. T. Pittard, 5 BTA 929 (Acq.)
Standard Lumber Co., 28 BTA 352

Buyer in possession
Ted F. Merrill, 40 TC 66 (1963), and per curiam, 366 F.2d 771 (9th Cir. 1964)
Marshall E. Boykin, 344 F.2d 889 (5th Cir. 1965)

Property held in escrow
Arthur Long, 1 BTA 796
Harry C. Moir, 14 BTA 23 (Nonacq.), aff'd, 45 F.2d 356 (7th Cir. 1930)

Deed delivered
William F. Scruggs, 281 F.2d 900 (10th Cir. 1960)

Option to sell exercised next year
Samuel C. Chapin, 180 F.2d 140 (8th Cir. 1950)

Contract to sell
Rev. Rul. 69-93, 1969-1 CB 139

No fair market value
A. M. Nichols, 44 F.2d 157 (3d Cir. 1930)
Nina Ennis, 17 TC 465 (1951)

Purchase price held
George I. Bumbaugh, 10 BTA 672
R. M. Waggoner, 9 BTA 629 (Nonacq.)
Preston R. Bassett, 33 BTA 182, aff'd per curiam, 90 F.2d 1004 (2d Cir. 1950)
K. E. Merren, 18 BTA 156 (Acq.), aff'd, 51 F.2d 44 (5th Cir. 1931)

31.5 CANCELLATION OF A LEASE
IRC § 1241
Reg. § 1.1241-1

31.6 SALE OF AN OPTION
IRC § 1234
Reg. § 1.1234-1

Note: Paragraph numbers refer to Volume One. Items marked *are research aids, not citations of authority; see "Key to Citations" on page 806.*

31.7 Granting of an Easement

David Fasten, 71 TC 650 (1979) (Acq.)
Inaja Land Co. Ltd., 9 TC 727 (1947) (Acq.)
Rev. Rul. 59-121, 1959-1 CB 212, clarified by
Rev. Rul. 68-291, 1968-1 CB 351
Rev. Rul. 72-433, 1972-2 CB 470
Rev. Rul. 73-161, 1973-1 CB 366
Rev. Rul. 72-255, 1972-1 CB 221

Restrictive covenant released
Rev. Rul. 70-203, 1970-1 CB 171

31.8 Special Tax Credits for Real Estate Investments

* "A Practical Guide To The Low-Income Housing Credit," Linda M. Johnson and Kathleen F. Schober, 72 Taxes 331 (June 1994)
* "Rehabilitation Tax Credit Not Always Advantageous," John O. Everett, 71 Journal of Taxation, 96 (Aug. 1989)

Low-income housing credit permanently extended
IRC § 42

Rehabilitating old and historic buildings
IRC § 47

Substantial rehabilitation test applies to entire building
Karl R. Alexander III, 97 TC 244 (1991)

Credit allowed for relocated building
George Nalle, 997 F.2d 1134 (5th Cir., 1993)

Effect of charitable deduction on credit
Rome I, Ltd, 96 TC 697 (1991)

31.9 Foreclosures and Voluntary Conveyances to Creditors

* "IRS Adopts Inconsistent Positions on Nonrecourse Debt in Loan-Workouts," Richard M. Lipton, 77 Journal of Taxation 196 (October 1992)
* "Even Insolvent Taxpayers May Have Income When Property Is Abandoned," Timothy M. Larsson, 45 Taxation for Accountants 88 (August 1990)

Sale or exchange requirement
IRC § 1222

Capital asset treatment for lapse, cancellation, abandonment, etc., of commodity options
IRC § 1234A

Property pledged as collateral
Morgan W. Jopling, 46 BTA 262

Voluntary conveyance of mortgaged property
Rev. Rul. 78-164, 1978-1 CB 264
Eugene L. Freeland, 74 TC 970 (1980)

Transfer by insolvent taxpayer
Rev. Rul. 90-16, 1990-1 CB 12

Foreclosure proceeds less than outstanding mortgage
Joseph Aizawa, 99 TC 197 (1992), aff'd. without published opinion, 29 F. 3d 630 (9th Cir. 1994)

Foreclosure bid price more than fair market value
Richard Frazier, 111 TC No. 11 (1998)

Business lease as 1231 asset

Rev. Rul. 72-85, 1972-1 CB 234

31.10 Restructuring Mortgage Debt

IRC § 61(a)(12)

Tax-free debt reductions
IRC § 108(a)

Restructuring nonrecourse debt
Rev. Rul. 91-31, 1991-1 CB 19

IRS computation of insolvency
Rev. Rul. 92-53, 1992-2 CB 48

Relief for discharge of business real estate debt
IRC § 108(a)(1)(D)
IRC § 108(c)

31.11 Abandonments

Abandonment treated as sale
Milledge L. Middleton, 77 TC 310 (1981), aff'd, 693 F.2d 124 (11th Cir., 1982)
James W. Yarbro, 45 TCM 170 (1982), aff'd, 737 F.2d 479 (5th Cir. 1984)

Abandonment of partnership interest
John C. Echols, 93 TC 553 (1989), rev'd by 950 F.2d 209 (5th Cir. 1991)
Philip Citron, 97 TC 200 (1991)

31.12 Seller's Repossession After Buyer's Default on Mortgage

IRC § 1038
Reg. § 1.1038-1 through 3
* "Gain on Repossession Will Depend on Whether Property Was Real or Personal and Its Use," Ollie S. Towers and Caroline D. Strobel, 26 Taxation for Accountants 36 (1981)

End of holding period for depreciation recapture purposes where property foreclosed
IRC § 1250(D)(10)

Personal residence
IRC § 1038(e)

31.13 Foreclosure on Mortgages Other than Purchase Money

You bid on property at foreclosure sale
Reg. § 1.166-6(a)(1) and (b)(1)
Hadley Falls Trust Co., 110 F.2d 887 (1st Cir. 1940)

Unreported but accrued interest as income in foreclosure
Midland Mutual Life Ins. Co., 300 U.S. 216 (1937)

Bid price as fair market value
West Production Co., 121 F.2d 9 (5th Cir. 1941), cert. denied, 314 U.S. 682
Harold S. Weil, 111 F. Supp. 390 (D. La. 1953)

Must prove worthlessness of debt
Reg. § 1.166-2

Property voluntarily conveyed in satisfaction of debt
Achilles H. Kohn, 197 F.2d 480 (2d Cir. 1952)

Nonrecourse debt is not protected by insolvency

Rev. Rul. 91-31, 1991-1 CB 19
Rev. Rul. 92-53, 1992-2 CB 48
James J. Gehl, 102 TC 37 (1994)
* Letter Ruling 9302001

Unreported but accrued interest as income in voluntary conveyance
Reserve Loan Life Ins. Co., 18 BTA 359 (Acq. and nonacq.)
Prudential Ins. Co. of America, 33 BTA 332 (Nonacq.)

Year deductible
Hadley Falls Trust Co., 110 F.2d 887 (1st Cir. 1940)
William C. Heinemann & Co., 40 BTA 1090

31.14 Foreclosure Sale to Third Party

* "Gain on Foreclosure Sales of Realty Need Not Be Recognized," Edward J. Schnee, 54 Taxation for Accountants 292 (May 1995)

Foreclosure expenses
Coeur d'Alene Hotel Inc., BTA Memo., Dec. 12,097-A
Bowles Lunch, Inc., 33 F. Supp. 235 (Ct. Cl. 1940)

Foreclosure sale at less than your mortgage
Reg. § 1.166-6(a)(1)

Business bad debt is fully deductible
IRC § 166(a)

Nonbusiness bad debt is a limited capital loss
IRC § 166(d)

Partially worthless debts
IRC § 166(a)(2) and (d)(1)(A)

Business and nonbusiness bad debt must be uncollectible
IRC § 166(a)(1) and (d)

31.15 Transferring Mortgaged Realty

Corporation
IRC § 351
IRC § 357
F. W. Drybrough, 376 F.2d 350 (6th Cir. 1967)

Gifts
Est. of Aaron Levine, 634 F.2d 12 (2d Cir. 1980)
Teofilo Evangelista, 629 F. 2d 1218 (7th Cir. 1980)

---

32 Tax Pointers for Investors in Mutual Funds

32.1 Investing in Mutual Funds
* IRS Publication 564

Airline miles
Letter Ruling 199920031

32.2 Money-Market Mutual Funds
IRC § 61(a)(7)
IRC § 852

Note: Paragraph numbers refer to Volume One. Items marked ˙ are research aids, not citations of authority; see "Key to Citations" on page 806.

32.3 TIMING YOUR INVESTMENT
* IRS Publication 564
* "Tax Considerations for Mutual Fund Investors," Tim Krumwiede, 72 Taxes 248 (May 1994)

Capital gain
IRC § 852(b)(3)
IRC § 854(a)

Deferred annuities
Rev. Rul. 81-220, 1981-2 CB 175
Rev. Rul. 82-54, 1982-1 CB 11

Dividend declared in October, November or December paid by following February
IRC § 852(b)(7)

32.4 REINVESTMENT PLANS
*IRS Publication 564

32.5 REPORTING MUTUAL-FUND DISTRIBUTIONS
*IRS Publication 564

Ordinary dividend portion
IRC § 854(b)(2)
Reg. § 1.854-2
Rev. Rul. 77-149, 1977-1 CB 82

Long-term capital gain
IRC § 852(b)(3)(B)

32.6 TAX-EXEMPT BOND FUNDS

Exempt-interest dividend
IRC § 852(b)(5)(B)

32.7 FUND EXPENSES
IRC §67(c)(2)

32.8 TAX CREDITS FROM MUTUAL FUNDS

Undistributed capital gains
IRC §852(b)(3)(D)

Foreign dividends
* IRS Publication 514

32.9 REDEMPTIONS AND EXCHANGES OF FUND SHARES

Mutual-fund loss when stock held six months or less
IRC § 852(b)(4)
Reg. § 1.852-4(d)

Sales charges incurred after 10/3/89
IRC § 852(f)

32.10 BASIS OF REDEEMED SHARES

Interfund transfers
Rev. Rul. 56-246, 1956-1 CB 316

Specific identification of sold shares
Joseph Hall, 92 TC 64 (1989)

Averaging cost on sale of shares
Reg. § 1.1012-1(e)(i)

FIFO method if no specific identification
Reg. § 1.1012-1(c)

32.11 COMPARISON OF BASIS METHODS
* IRS Publication 564

Specific identification of sold shares
Joseph Hall, 92 TC 64 (1989)

FIFO method if no specific identification
Reg. § 1.1012-1(c)

Averaging cost on sale of shares
Reg. § 1.1012-1(e)(i)

33 FAMILY INCOME PLANNING

33.1 GIFT TAX BASICS
IRC § 2502 (gift tax rates)
IRC § 2503 (taxable gifts)
IRC § 2505 (unified credit)
IRC § 2522 (charitable deduction)
* "Annual Exclusion Gift Checks and the Relation-Back Doctrine," Albert Kalter and Lawrence Newman, 25 Estate Planning 402 (Nov. 1998)
* "Taxpayer Relief Act of 1997 Offers Significant Estate Planning Opportunities," James G. Blasé, and John M. Jennings, 75 Taxes 531 (October 1997)
* "Intrafamily Transfers May Lessen Estate and Gift Tax Liability," Bart Basi, 50 Taxation for Accountants 215 (April 1993)
* "Using Crummey Powers in Trusts for Annual Giving," Jonathan D. Reiff, 58 Taxation for Accountants 150 (March 1997)
* "When Should the Option to Split Gifts Be Chosen," Robert W. Benjamin, 22 Estate Planning 24 (January/February 1995)

Marital deduction
IRC § 2523
* Letter Ruling 9606008

Gifting employee stock options
* Letter Ruling 9514017

Exclusion for educational or medical expenses
IRC § 2503(e)

$10,000 gift tax exclusion
IRC § 2503(b)
John A. Metzger, et al.
* Letter Ruling 9532001

Gift tax exclusion for contingent trust beneficiaries
Est. of Maria Cristofani, 97 TC 74 (1991)
IRS Action on Decision 1992-09 (IRS does not concede Cristofani issue)
* Letter Ruling 9141008 (IRS denies exclusion for contingent trust interests)

Loans to relatives taxable
IRC § 7872
Esther C. Dickman, 465 U.S. 330 (1984)
Elizabeth Miller, 71 TCM 1674 (1996)

Cannot assign income
Paul R. G. Horst, 311 U.S. 112 (1940)
Guy C. Earl, 281 U.S. 11 (1930)
Edward T. Blair, 300 U.S. 5 (1937)

Donees liable for gift tax
Kirkman O'Neal, II, 102 TC 28 (1994)

Art donations valued by IRS
Rev. Proc. 96-15, 1996-1 CB 627

Assignment of licensing agreement by inventor
Lewis R. Heim, 262 F.2d 887 (2d Cir. 1959)

Pre-paid tuition
Letter Ruling 199941013

33.2 CUSTODIAN ACCOUNTS FOR MINORS
*"Gifts to Minors Can Be Tied Up with More Than Pretty Ribbons," Ron West, 60 Taxation for Accountants 353 (June 1998)
* "Gifts to Minors Can Reduce Estate, But Require Choices," Barbara B. Ferguson and William R. Mureiko, 50 Taxation for Accountants 38 (January 1993)

Investment income of children under age 14
IRC § 1(g)

Income taxed to child
Rev. Rul. 55-469, 1955-2 CB 519
Rev. Rul. 56-484, 1956-2 CB 23
Rev. Rul. 59-357, 1959-2 CB 212

Trust accounts ineffective to split interest income
Roy K. Heintz, 41 TCM 429 (1980)

Child remains dependent and exemption allowed
IRC § 151(e)
Reg. § 1.151-2

Gift tax
IRC § 2501
IRC § 2503
Reg. 25.2503-3
Reg. 25.2503-4
IRC § 2505
IRC § 2513
Rev. Rul. 56-86, 1956-1 CB 449

Trust for child under 21
IRC § 2503(c)

Invalid custodian account
John Dubisky, 1994 USTC ¶13745 (N. Dist. of Ill.), rehearing denied (7th Cir. 1995)

Estate tax
IRC § 2001
IRC § 2010
Rev. Rul. 57-366, 1957-2 CB 618

No estate tax where securities purchased with jointly owned funds in which deceased custodian had no interest
Estate of Jack F. Chrysler, 361 F.2d 508 (2d Cir. 1966)

No estate tax on estate of deceased spouse who was custodian and agreed to gift splitting
Rev. Rul. 74-556, 1974-2 CB 300

No estate tax where custodian made gift of custodial securities before death
Antonia B. Vogel Est., 36 TCM 875 (1977)

33.3 TRUSTS IN FAMILY PLANNING
* "Shifting Assets to Trusts for Minors After RRA '93 Requires Change in Focus," William V.A. Zorn and Christine S. Anderson, 79 Journal of Taxation 352 (December 1993)
* "Defective Grantor Trusts Offer Many Tax Advantages," Michael D. Mulligan, 19 Estate Plan-

*Note: Paragraph numbers refer to Volume One. Items marked * are research aids, not citations of authority; see "Key to Citations" on page 806.*

ning 131 (May/June 1992)

Repeal of 10-year trust rule
1986 Tax Reform Act Section 1402, amending IRC 673

Kiddie tax
IRC § 1(g)

5% grantor trust rule
IRC § 673(a)

Minor lineal descendants
IRC § 673(b)

Grantor trusts: spouse's interest
IRC § 672(e)

Tax rates for trusts and estates
IRC § 1(e)
Rev. Proc. 96-59, 1996-2 CB 392 (1997 rates)

Division of income
T. N. Mauritz, 206 F.2d 135 (5th Cir. 1953)
Estelle Morris Trusts, 51 TC 20 (1968), aff'd per curiam, 427 F.2d 1361 (9th Cir. 1970)

Trust for spouse may be taxed to creator
IRC § 677(a)

"Apocalypse" family trust
Rev. Rul. 75-257, 1975-2 CB 251
Rev. Rul. 75-258, 1975-2 CB 503
Rev. Rul. 75-259, 1975-2 CB 361
Rev. Rul. 75-260, 1975-2 CB 376

Family trust for earned income is tax avoidance scheme
Richard L. Wesenberg, 69 TC 1005 (1978) (Nonacq.)

Family trust materials not deductible
Louis P. Contini, 76 TC 447 (1981) (Acq.)
Rev. Rul. 79-324, 1979-2 CB 119

Trust sale of appreciated property within two years
IRC § 644

Escape estate tax
IRC § 2038
Green Estate, 68 F.3d 151 (6th Cir. 1995) (identical trusts)

Gift tax
IRC § 2511
Reg. § 1.2511-1

Revocable trust—no tax savings
IRC § 676
IRC § 2038

Testamentary trust—estate tax
IRC § 2037

Accumulation trust
IRC § 665 through 667

Foreign trusts with U.S. beneficiaries
IRC § 643
IRC § 668
IRC § 679

Generation-skipping transfers
IRC §§ 2601 through 2622

33.4 GIFTS OF APPRECIATED PROPERTY

Give appreciated property
W. G. Farrier Est., 15 TC 277 (1950) (Acq.)
Charles N. Prothro, 209 F.2d 331 (5th Cir. 1954)
Elsie Sorelle, 22 TC 459 (1954) (Acq.)
Marvin Berry, 11 TCM 301 (1952)
Emily J. Haley, 381 F. Supp. 3431 (M.D. Ga. 1974)
Rev. Rul. 55-531, 1955-2 CB 520, distinguished by Rev. Rul. 63-66, 1963-1 CB 13, as modified by Rev. Rul. 75-11, 1975-1 CB 27

Avoid claim that gift not completed
William R. Tracy, 70 F.2d 93 (6th Cir. 1934)
Rev. Rul. 58-337, 1958-2 CB 13
Richard G. Shafto, 246 F.2d 338 (4th Cir. 1957)
Jeannette W. FitzGibbon, 19 TC 78 (1952)

Get loss deduction by selling first
Reg. § 1.165-1(b)

Private annuities—gain reported ratably over life expectancy
Rev. Rul. 69-74, 1969-1 CB 43

Gain immediately taxed on secured private annuity
Bell Est., 60 TC 469 (1973)
212 Corp., 70 TC 788 (1978)

Recovery of basis defers gain in private annuity
Esther LaFargue, 689 F.2d 845 (9th Cir. 1982)

No interest deduction for annuity payments
Rebecca Bell, 76 TC 233 (1981), aff'd per curiam, 668 F.2d 448 (8th Cir. 1982)

33.5 SPLITTING BUSINESS INCOME WITH YOUR FAMILY

* "Compensation Planning in the Family Corporation," K. J. Caraway and J. R. Hamill, 46 Taxation for Accountants 168 (Mar. 1991)
* "Valuation of Family Limited Partnership Interests," D. John Thornton and Gregory A. Byron, Fall Valuation Strategies II (1997)

Estate freeze plans
IRC § 2701-2704

IRS allows minority discount when valuing block of stock in family corporation
Rev. Rul. 93-12, 1993-12 CB 479, revoking Rev. Rul. 81-253, 1981-1 CB 187, and acquiescing to Estate of Elizabeth M. Lee, 69 TC 860 (1978)

Wage deduction disallowed
Thai Pham and Khuy Bui, 70 TCM 814 (1995)

S corporation allocation
IRC § 1366(e)

Trust can be partner
Frank Trust, 44 BTA 934

Trust ignored
Max J. Kuney, 448 F.2d 22 (9th Cir. 1971)

S transfer disregarded
Gino A. Speca, 38 TCM 544 (1979), aff'd, 630 F.2d 554 (7th Cir. 1980)

Control kept by parent
Henry D. Duarte, 44 TC 193 (1965)

Transfer to children recognized where mother was active custodian
Donald O. Kirkpatrick, 36 TCM 1122 (1977)

Court reporter still taxed on his corporation's income
Elvin V. Jones, 64 TC 1066 (1975)

Corporation to split commission income
Frederick H. Foglesong, 621 F.2d 865 (7th Cir. 1982), rev'g 35 TCM 1309 (1976)

Family partnership interests disregarded where capital comes from borrowed funds
Carriage Square, Inc., 69 TC 10 (1977)

Family partnership in CPA firm disregarded
Melvin P. Ketter, 70 TC 637 (1978)

33.6 LIFE INSURANCE OFFERS TAX ADVANTAGES

* "Tax Traps To Avoid In The Ownership And Transfer Of Life Insurance Policies," Lee Slavutin, 74 Taxes 26 (January 1996)
* "New Life Insurance Forms Enhance Its Use as an Effective Estate Planning Tool," George H. Rogers, III, 45 Taxation for Accountants 102 (August 1990)

Estate tax on life insurance
IRC § 2042
Reg. § 20.2042-1(c)

Policy transferred within three years of death included in taxable estate
IRC § 2035
* Letter Ruling 9533001

IRS concedes policy is excluded from estate where insured held no incidents of ownership
IRS Action on Decision 1991-012
Estate of Eddie L. Headrick, 918 F.2d 1263 (6th Cir. 1990), aff'g 93 TC 171 (1989)
Estate of Joseph Leder, 893 F.2d 237 (10th Cir. 1989), aff'g 89 TC 235 (1987)
Estate of Frank Martin Perry, 927 F.2d 209 (5th Cir. 1991), aff'g 59 TCM 67 (1990)
Estate of Samuel Ard, Jr., 59 TCM 869 (1990)

Assignment of group-term policy
Rev. Rul. 84-147, 1984-2 CB 201

Substitution of group carrier does not jeopardize prior assignments
Rev. Rul. 80-289, 1980-2 CB 270

Assigned policy used by husband as collateral for loan
Hilton W. Goodwyn Est., 32 TCM 1026 (1973)
Max Krischer Est., 32 TCM 821 (1973)

Son paid premiums
Morris R. Silverman Est., 61 TC 338 (1974) (Acq.), aff'd, 521 F.2d 574 (2d Cir. 1975)

Right to select type of payment defeats assignment
Est. of James H. Lumpkin, Jr., 474 F.2d 1092 (5th Cir. 1973)

Assigned flight insurance subject to estate tax
Fay L. Berman Exrx, 487 F.2d 70 (5th Cir. 1973)

Note: Paragraph numbers refer to Volume One. Items marked `*` *are research aids, not citations of authority; see "Key to Citations" on page 806.*

Veto power subjects assigned policy to tax
Rev. Rul. 75-70, 1975-1 CB 301

Gift tax
Reg. § 25.2512-6
Reg. § 25.2503-2

Marital deduction
IRC § 2056

Funding buy-and-sell contracts
Rev. Rul. 59-184, 1959-1 CB 65

Modified endowment contracts
IRC § 7702A
IRC § 72(e)(10)
IRC § 72(v) (premature withdrawal penalty)

33.7 HOW LIFE INSURANCE PROCEEDS ARE TAXED TO A BENEFICIARY

IRC § 101
Reg. § 1.101-1 to § 1.101-4

Spouse's exclusion for interest: deaths before 12/23/86
IRC § 101(d)(1)(B)
Reg. § 1.101-4(a)

Taxable interest on installment payments
IRC § 101(c)
Reg. § 1.101-3

No exclusion for combined insurance-annuity pre-1986 Tax Act
Rev. Rul. 65-57, 1965-1 CB 56

Remarriage does not affect interest exclusion pre-1986 Tax Act
Rev. Rul. 72-164, 1972-1 CB 28

Universal life policy issued before 1985
IRC § 101(f)

Universal life policy issued after 1984
IRC § 7702

33.8 A POLICY WITH A FAMILY INCOME RIDER

Reg. § 1.101-4(h)

33.9 HOW OTHER INSURANCE PROCEEDS ARE TAXED

* "Tax Traps to Avoid in the Ownership and Transfer of Life Insurance Policies," Lee Slavotin, 74 Taxes 26 (January 1996)

Dividends as reduction of premium
Special Ruling, December 13, 1940
Special Ruling, September 22, 1941
Veterans Administration Release, February 14, 1957

Endowment policies paid because of death
Reg. § 1.101-1(a)

Gain on surrender of policy
Reg. § 1.72-11(d)
William W. Bodine, 103 F.2d 982 (3d Cir. 1939), cert. denied, 308 U.S. 576
Frank Hawkins, 3 TCM 1135 (1944), rev'd on other issue, 152 F.2d 221 (5th Cir. 1946)

Surrender of policy for cash—loss
Standard Brewing Co., 6 BTA 980
London Shoe Co., Inc., 80 F.2d 230 (2d Cir. 1935), cert. denied, 298 U.S. 663

Policy transferred for valuable consideration
IRC § 101(b)
Reg. § 1.101-1(b)

Sale of policy to viatical company is income
* Letter Ruling 9443020

---

34 TAX POINTERS FOR SENIOR CITIZENS

34.1 SPECIAL RULES FOR SENIOR CITIZENS

Higher filing threshold
IRC § 6012(a)(1)(B)

Higher standard deduction
IRC § 63(f)

Credit for elderly
IRC § 22

Threshold for Social Security benefits tax
IRC § 86

34.2 SOCIAL SECURITY BENEFITS SUBJECT TO TAX

*IRS Publication 915
IRC § 86

Benefits to child
House Ways and Means Committee Report to P.L. 98-21

Workers' compensation
IRC § 86(d)(3)

Repayments
IRC § 86(d)(2)

Nonresident alien
IRC § 871(a)(3)

34.3 COMPUTING TAXABLE SOCIAL SECURITY BENEFITS

Base amount and adjusted base amount
IRC § 86(c)

Effect of IRA deductions
Announcement 88-38, 1988-10 IRB 60

34.4 ELECTION FOR LUMP-SUM SOCIAL SECURITY BENEFIT PAYMENT

IRC § 86(e)

34.5 RETIRING ON SOCIAL SECURITY BENEFITS

Public Law 104-121 (3/29/96) (Social Security earnings limit increased for those 65 or older)
42 USCA § 1382
* "The Impact of Retirement Plans on Medicaid Eligibility," William J. Browning, 19 Estate Planning 362 (November 1992)

34.6 HOW TAX ON SOCIAL SECURITY REDUCES YOUR EARNINGS

IRC § 86

34.7 CLAIMING THE CREDIT FOR THE ELDERLY AND DISABLED

IRC § 22
*IRS Publication 524

Age 65 or retired on disability
IRC § 22(b)

Married couples
IRC § 22(e)(1)

Nonresident alien ineligible
IRC § 22(f)

34.8 BASE AMOUNT FOR THE ELDERLY OR DISABLED CREDIT

Initial base amount
IRC § 22(c)

Disability income limit
IRC § 22(c)(2)(B)

Disability income defined
IRC § 22(c)(2)(B)(iii)

Permanent disability defined
IRC § 22(e)(3)

34.9 REDUCTION OF THE CREDIT BASE AMOUNT FOR THE ELDERLY AND DISABLED

IRC § 22(c)(3)(A) (Social Security and pensions)
IRC § 22(d) (adjusted gross income)

34.10 TAX EFFECTS OF MOVING TO A CONTINUING CARE FACILITY

* "Long-Term Care Insurance Helps Preserve An Estate," Walter Feldesman and JoAnn Canning, 20 Estate Planning 76 (Mar-Apr 1993)

Portion of fees allocable to medical expenses
Rev. Rul. 75-302, 1975-2 CB 86

Charitable deduction for sponsorship gift
Ruth Dowell, 553 F.2d 1233 (10th Cir. 1977)

No charitable deduction for donation that represents cost of apportionment
Ernest Klappenbach, 52 TCM 437 (1986)

Investment in community equivalent to home purchase
* Letter Ruling 8837022
Highland Farms, Inc., 106 TC 12

34.11 IMPUTED INTEREST ON REFUNDABLE ENTRANCE FEES

Imputed interest exception for continuing care facilities
IRC § 7872(g)(1)
* Letter Ruling 9521001

Inflation-adjusted loan limit
Rev. Rul. 98-59, 1998-52 IRB

Note: Paragraph numbers refer to Volume One. Items marked * *are research aids, not citations of authority; see "Key to Citations" on page 806.*

35 TAX SAVINGS FOR MEMBERS OF THE ARMED FORCES

35.1 TAXABLE ARMED FORCES PAY AND BENEFITS
* IRS Publication 3

Regular pay, leave pay, enlistment bonuses taxable
Rev. Rul. 55-249, 1955-1 CB 21

35.2 TAX-FREE ARMED FORCES BENEFITS
* IRS Publication 3
* IRS Publication 945

Tax-free combat pay
IRC § 112

Exclusion for qualified military benefits
IRC § 134
Adjustments for inflated foreign currency
IT 3725, 1945 CB 60

Allotments for dependents
Special Ruling, Jan. 10, 1946
Rev. Rul. 70-87, 1970-1 CB 29

Former prisoners of war
Rev. Rul. 55-132, 1955-1 CB 213
Rev. Rul. 56-462, 1956-2 CB 20

Bonuses
Rev. Rul. 56-610, 1956-2 CB 25

State bonus
Rev. Rul. 68-158, 1968-1 CB 47

Gratuity
Rev. Rul. 55-330, 1955-1 CB 236

Dividends on GI insurance
Special Ruling, February 3, 1947

Interest on VA life insurance dividends
Rev. Rul. 91-14, 1991-1 CB 18 revoking
Rev. Rul. 57-441, 1957-2 CB 45

Serviceman's Readjustment Act
Veterans Administration Release, February 14, 1957
Ephraim Banks, 17 TC 1386 (1952)

Family separation allowance
Clifford Jones, 60 Ct. Cl. 552
Rev. Rul. 70-281, 1970-1 CB 16

Pay forfeited on court martial order
Armed Forces Fed. Income Tax, '77 ed.

Subsistence allowance
Rev. Rul. 55-572, 1955-2 CB 45, distinguished by Rev. Rul. 63-64, 1963-1 CB 30

Moving and storage
IRC § 217(g), as amended by the Revenue Reconciliation Act of 1993

Mustering out pay
IRC § 113
Reg. § 1.113-1

Naval attaché expense money
Rev. Rul. 77-351, 1977-2 CB 23

Retirement pay reduction to provide survivor

annuity
IRC § 122

Injuries or sickness
Career Compensation Act of 1949, Sec. 402

Return to active duty
Special Ruling, January 24, 1945

Medical and pension benefit from Veteran's Administration
Rev. Rul. 72-605, 1972-2 CB 35

Subsistence payments
Veterans Administration Release, February 14, 1957

Travel expenses—permanent duty station
W. W. Bercaw, 165 F.2d 521 (4th Cir. 1948)
Rev. Rul. 55-571, 1955-2 CB 44

Uniforms, uniform allowances
Reg. § 1.61-2(b)

VA death benefits
Veterans Administration Release, February 14, 1957

Disability retirement pay
IRC § 104(a)(4)
IRC § 104(b)
Career Compensation Act of 1949, Sec. 402
Zebulon L. Strickland, Jr., 540 F.2d 1196 (4th Cir. 1976)
Rev. Rul. 78-161, 1978-1 CB 31

35.3 DEDUCTIONS FOR ARMED FORCES PERSONNEL

Board and lodging costs
Rev. Rul. 55-571, 1955-2 CB 44, modified by Rev. Rul. 67-438, 1967-2 CB 82

Cost of insignia
Charles A. Harris, 12 TCM 42 (1953)

Fatigues
Rev. Rul. 67-1 15, 1967-1 CB 30

Contributions to "Company" fund
Rev. Rul. 73-296, 1973-2 CB 67
Rev. Rul. 55-201, 1955-1 CB 269
B. O. Mahaffey, 1 TC 176 (1942), rev'd, 140 F.2d 879 (8th Cir. 1944)
Morris Investment Corp., 156 F.2d 748 (3d Cir. 1946), cert. denied, 329 U.S. 788
Jacob Kaplan, 21 TC 134 (1953) (Acq.)
William F. Krahl, 9 TC 862 (1947)

Court martial expenses
Lindsay C. Howard, 202 F.2d 28 (9th Cir. 1953), aff'g 16 TC 157 (1951) (Acq.)

Professional societies
Rev. Rul. 55-250, 1955-1 CB 270

Increased retirement pay
IRC § 212

Professional journals
Charles A. Harris, 12 TCM 42 (1953)

No away from home expenses for those at permanent duty station
Howe Stidger, 386 U.S. 287 (1967)

Travel status and duty expenses
Rev. Rul. 67-438, 1967-2 CB 82, modifying Rev.

Rul. 55-571, 1955-2 CB 44
Charles A. Harris, 12 TCM 42 (1953)

Temporary lodging allowance
Rev. Rul. 76-2, 1976-1 CB 82

35.4 TAX-FREE PAY FOR SERVICE IN COMBAT ZONE OR HAZARDOUS DUTY AREA

Combat pay exclusion
IRC § 112
Prop. Reg. § 1.112-1

Officers
IRC § 112(b), as amended by Public Law 104-117 (3/20/96) (pay excluded from income is raised, effective date 11/21/95)

Bosnia and Herzegovina, Croatia, Macedonia
Public Law 104-117 (3/20/96) designates qualified hazardous duty area
IRS Notice 96-34, 1996-24 IRS 15 (question and answer guidance on hazardous duty area rules)

Hospitalized serviceman
IRC § 112(a)(2)

"Missing" status
IRC § 112(d)

Joint return election by spouse of person MIA
IRC § 6013(f)(1)

Waiver of tax
Rev. Rul. 68-393, 1968-2 CB 292
Rev. Rul. 72-169, 1972-1 CB 43

Severance pay not included
Ralph P. Waterman, 110 T.C. 103 (1998)

35.5 TAX DEADLINES EXTENDED FOR COMBAT ZONE OR HAZARDOUS DUTY AREA SERVICE
* IRS Publication 945
IRC § 7508(a)

Bosnia and Herzegovina, Croatia, Macedonia
Public Law 104-117 (3/20/96) designates qualified hazardous duty area
IRS Notice 96-34, 1996-24 IRS 15 (question and answer guidance on hazardous duty area rules)

Desert Shield personnel qualify for extension
IRC § 7508(f)

Extension for Persian Gulf service runs consecutively with tax season
News release IR-91-46, 3/26/91
Notice 91-17, 1991-1 CB 319, corrected by Announcement 91-102, 1991-28 IRB 54 (IRA contribution extension)

Extensions available to spouse
IRC § 7508(c)

35.6 TAX FORGIVENESS FOR COMBAT ZONE OR HAZARDOUS DUTY AREA DEATHS

Combat zone
IRC § 692

Bosnia and Herzegovina, Croatia, Macedonia
Public Law 104-117 (3/20/96) designates quali-

Note: Paragraph numbers refer to Volume One. Items marked `*` are research aids, not citations of authority; see "Key to Citations" on page 806.

fied hazardous duty area
IRS Notice 96-34, 1996-24 IRS 15 (question and answer guidance on hazardous duty area rules)

Terroristic or military actions
IRC § 692(c)

MIAs
IRA § 692(b)

Filing extension for refund claims if combat zone death
IRC § 7508(b)

35.7 EXTENSION TO PAY YOUR TAX WHEN ENTERING THE SERVICE
Rev. Proc. 57-25, 1957-2 CB 1092
Soldiers' and Sailors' Civil Relief Act of 1940, Sec. 513
T.D. 5279, 1943 CB 952, amended by T.D.'s 5293, 5429, 5444, 5959

35.8 TAX INFORMATION FOR RESERVISTS

Travel costs to meeting no longer allowed
Rev. Rul. 90-23, 1990-1 CB 28

Readjustment payments
Rev. Rul. 67-350, 1967-2 CB 58

36 HOW TO TREAT FOREIGN EARNED INCOME

36.1 CLAIMING THE FOREIGN EARNED INCOME EXCLUSION
* IRS Publication 54

Foreign earned income exclusion
IRC § 911

Exclusion amount
IRC § 911(b)(2)(D)

Must file return even if exclusion is available
Reg. § 1.911-6
IRC § 6012
Reg. § 1.6012-1(a)(3)
William Faltesek, 92 TC 78 (1989)

Panama Canal Commission employees
1986 Tax Act Section 1232

36.2 WHAT IS FOREIGN EARNED INCOME?
IRC § 911(b)

Reimbursed moving expenses
Rev. Rul. 75-84, 1975-1 CB 236, amplified by Rev. Rul. 76-162, 1976-1 CB 197
Clifford Dammers, 76 TC 835 (1981)

36.3 QUALIFYING FOR THE FOREIGN EARNED INCOME EXCLUSION
* "Employment Overseas and the Tax Home Issue: Exclusion versus Deduction," L. Stillabower and L. Phillips, 61 Taxes 202 (1983)

Taxation of expatriates
IRC § 877

Foreign residence and foreign physical presence test

IRC § 911(d)(1)

Foreign tax home
IRC § 911(d)(1)
IRC § 911(d)(3)

Exclusion allowed in year services performed
IRC § 911(b)(2)(B)

Prorating exclusion on daily basis
IRC § 911(b)(2)

Exclusion must be elected
IRC § 911(a)

No foreign tax credit on excluded income
IRC § 911(d)(6)

No exclusion for countries under U.S. travel ban
IRC § 911(d)(8)
Rev. Rul. 87-35, 1987-1 CB 182, revoked in part by Rev. Rul. 92-63, 1992-2 CB 195, corrected by Rev. Rul. 92-63A, 1992-2 CB 196

Workers paid with nonappropriated funds
David Matthews, 907 F.2d 1173 (DC Cir. 1990), aff'g 92 TC 351 (1989)

Professor on sabbatical does not have foreign tax home
Lynn W. Gelhar, 63 TCM 2466

36.4 HOW TO TREAT HOUSING COSTS

Exclusion for employer-financed housing
IRC § 911(c)

Qualifying housing expense
IRC § 911(c)(2)

Deduction for housing costs not paid for by employer
IRC § 911(c)(3)

36.5 MEETING THE FOREIGN RESIDENCE OR PHYSICAL PRESENCE TEST

Bona fide residence test
IRC § 911(d)(1)(A)
IRC § 911(d)(5)

Physical presence test—330-day/12-month requirement
IRC § 911(d)(1)(B)

Waiver of time tests due to war or civil unrest
IRC § 911(d)(4)

36.6 CLAIMING DEDUCTIONS

No deduction for expenses attributable to excluded income
IRC § 911(d)(6)

Deducting expenses of moving overseas
IRC § 217(h), as amended by the Revenue Reconciliation Act of 1993

Retirees and survivors of workers abroad returning to U.S.
IRC § 217(i)

Deduction for compulsory home leave expenses
Rev. Rul. 82-2, 1982-1 CB 367
Bruce C. Stratton, 448 F.2d 1030 (9th Cir. 1971)

36.7 EXCLUSION NOT ESTABLISHED WHEN YOUR RETURN IS DUE
IRS Form 2350

36.8 TAX-FREE MEALS AND LODGING FOR WORKERS IN CAMPS
IRC § 119(c)

36.9 VIRGIN ISLANDS, SAMOA, GUAM, AND NORTHERN MARIANAS
*IRS Publication 570

Guam, Samoa, N. Mariana Islands
IRC § 931

Virgin Islands
IRC § 932
IRC § 934

U.S. or agencies
IRC § 931(d)
Rev. Rul. 54-612, 1954-2 CB 169

36.10 EARNINGS IN PUERTO RICO
IRC § 933
Reg. § 1.933-1
Rev. Rul. 56-585, 1956-2 CB 166

Moving expenses allocable to tax-exempt income from Puerto Rico not deductible
Alberto Roque, 65 TC 920 (1976)

36.11 TAX TREATIES WITH FOREIGN COUNTRIES
IRC § 894
IRC § 877 (taxation of expatriates)
Reg. § 1.894-1
IRC § 7852(d)
Notice 95-31, 1995-22 IRB 5

36.12 EXCHANGE RATES AND BLOCKED CURRENCY
*IRS Publication 54

Foreign currency gains and losses
IRC § 988

Euro conversion
TD 8776; Reg. Sec. § 1.985-8T

36.13 INFORMATION RETURNS ON FOREIGN CURRENCY
IRS Forms 4789 and 4790

36.14 FOREIGN TAX CREDIT
*IRS Publication 514

Foreign tax credit
IRC § 901(a)
Reg. § 1.901-1 and 2

Deduction in lieu of credit
IRC § 164(a)

36.15 COMPUTING THE FOREIGN TAX CREDIT
* "New Tax Law Makes Major Changes to the Foreign Tax Credit Limitation," Gerald T. Ball, Donald Carter, and Tom B. Wight, 66 Journal of Taxation 140 (March 1987)

Overall limitation

*Note: Paragraph numbers refer to Volume One. Items marked * are research aids, not citations of authority; see "Key to Citations" on page 806.*

IRC § 904(a)

Separate credit limitation categories
IRC § 904(d)

Recapture of overall foreign loss
IRC § 904(f)

Capital gains
IRC § 904(b)(2)

36.16 CARRYBACK AND CARRYOVER OF EXCESS FOREIGN TAX CREDIT
IRC § 904(c)

---

37 PLANNING ALIMONY AND MARITAL SETTLEMENTS

37.1 PLANNING ALIMONY AGREEMENTS
*"Divorcing Business Owners Need Tax Planning," Edward Schnee, 60 Taxation for Accountants 76 (Feb. 1998)
* "Tax Consequences of Divorce Can Be Avoided," Stephen C. Robinson, 53 Taxation for Accountants 132 (September 1994)

Alimony paid deductible from gross income
IRC § 62(a)(10)
IRC § 215
IRC § 1.215-1

Alimony received included in gross income
IRC § 71
Reg. § 1.71

Same household rule
IRC § 71(b)(1)(c)
Temp. Reg. § 71-1T (Q-8)
Bertram Coltman, Jr., 980 F.2d 1134 (7th Cir. 1992)

Designate nonqualifying payments
IRC § 71(b)(1)(B)
Temp. Reg. § 1.71-1T (Q-9)

Husband not taxed on payments from transferred property
IRC § 71(d)

Alimony payments to nonresident alien
* IRS Publication 504

Wife not taxed on tax-exempt interest from alimony trust
Mary C. Ellis, 416 F.2d 894 (6th Cir. 1969)

Alimony trusts
IRC § 682

Voluntary payment
Natalia D. Murray, 174 F.2d 816 (2d Cir. 1949)
Benjamin B. Cox, 176 F.2d 226 (3d Cir. 1949), aff'g 10 TC 955 (1948)

Permanent alimony after remarriage
Allen Hoffman, 54 TC 1607 (1971), aff'd, 455 F.2d 161 (7th Cir. 1972)
Alfredo Mass, 81 TC 112 (1983)

Voluntary payments after court order denies temporary alimony
Sylvia E. Taylor, 55 TC 1134 (1971)

Payments from oil lease
Ronald Prater, 55 F.3d 527 (10th Cir. 1995)

Payments recommended by state domestic relations master are not deductible
Eugene E. Deyette, 36 TCM 1343 (1977)

Wife taxable on voluntary alimony
Rev. Rul. 81-8, 1981-1 CB 42

Excess payments are voluntary
George H. Moore, 449 F. Supp. 163 (D.D. Tex. 1978)

Gift tax on voluntary payments
Rev. Rul. 79-118, 1979-1 CB 315

Post-remarriage payments not alimony
Martha K. Brown, 415 F.2d 310 (4th Cir. 1969)
Allen Hoffman, 54 TC 1607 (1970) (Acq.), aff'd per curiam, 455 F.2d 161 (7th Cir. 1972)

Deductible in year paid
Reg. § 1.71-2
Lily R. Reighley, 17 TC 344 (1951)

No deduction if paid by another
Reg. § 1.215-1(b)

Deduction for estate
Homer Laughlin Est., 167 F.2d 828 (9th Cir. 1948)
Daniel G. Reid Est., 15 TC 573 (1950), aff'd, 193 F.2d 625 (2d Cir. 1952)

Prior notice to offset
Elinor Nelson, 731 F.2d 105 (2nd Cir. 1984), cert. denied, 105 S. Ct. 175 (1984)

37.2 DECREE OR AGREEMENT REQUIRED
*IRS Publication 504

Decree required—Pre-1985 law
IRC § 71(a)(1)
Reg. § 1.71-1(b)(1)

Decree or separation agreement required—Post-1984 law
IRC § 71(b)(1)(A)
IRC § 71(b)(2)

State decree declared invalid by another state: IRS view disallowing alimony deduction
Rev. Rul. 67-442, 1967-2 CB 65
Harold K. Lee, 550 F.2d 1201 (9th Cir. 1977)

State decree declared invalid by another state
Harold E. Wondsel, 350 F.2d 339 (2d Cir. 1965), cert. denied, 383 U.S. 935
Est. of Herman Borax, 349 F.2d 666 (2d Cir. 1965)
George J. Feinberg, 198 F.2d 260 (3d Cir. 1952)

Local support order after out-of-state divorce
Rev. Rul. 70-61, 1970-1 CB 18

Local support order before Mexican decree
Rev. Rul. 71-390, 1971-2 CB 82

Roman Catholic ecclesiastical board
Harold L. Clark, 40 TC 57 (1965)

Sample clauses for alimony agreements
Rev. Proc. 82-53, 1982-2 CB 842

Amendment of written agreement after divorce or legal separation
Rev. Rul. 60-140, 1960-1 CB 31
Rev. Rul. 60-141, 1960-1 CB 33
Rev. Rul. 58-152, 1958-1 CB 32

Agreement not incident
Rev. Rul. 60-142, 1960-1 CB 34

Annulment
Andrew M. Newburger, 61 TC 457 (1974) (Acq.)
George F. Reisman, 49 TC 570 (1968) (Acq.)
Anne S. Laster, 48 TC 178 (1967) (Acq.)

Written separation agreement
Howard Bogard, 59 TC 97 (1972) (Acq.)

Oral modification not valid
Eugene H. Bishop, 46 TCM 15

Reference to agreement not sufficient
Welford E. Garner, Jr., 32 TCM 353 (1973)

Support decree
Rev. Rul. 59-248, 1959-2 CB 31

Support decree valid after divorce
Joanne S. Knobler, 59 TC 261 (1972)

Support decree not valid after divorce
Benjamin Wolman, 64 TC 883 (1975)

37.3 CASH PAYMENTS REQUIRED
IRC § 71(b)(1)

Payments to third party
Temp. Reg. § 1.71-1T (Q-6 to 7)

37.4 PAYMENTS MUST STOP AT DEATH
IRC § 71(b)(1)(D)
McNeill Stokes, 68 TCM 705 (1994)
Richard E. Hoover, 102 F. 3d 846 (6th Cir. 1996)

37.5 CHILD SUPPORT PAYMENTS ARE NOT ALIMONY
IRC § 71(c)
Reg. § 301.6402-5
Temp. Reg. § 1.71-1T (Q-15, 16, 17, 18)

Refund diversion for delinquent child support
IRC § 6402(c)
Reg. § 301.3402-5(b)

Federal Court must provide notice
Elinor Nelson, 731 F.2d 105 (2nd Cir. 1984)
Kenneth Marcello, 574 F. Supp. 586 (D.C., RI. 1984).

37.6 NO MINIMUM PAYMENT PERIOD FOR ALIMONY

Pre-1987 agreements
IRC § 71(f)(1)
Notice 87-9, 1987-1 CB 421

37.7 3RD YEAR RECAPTURE IF ALIMONY DROPS $15,000 OR MORE
IRC § 71(f)
Notice 87-9, 1987-1 CB 421

Exceptions
IRC § 71(f)(5)

37.8 LEGAL FEES OF MARITAL SETTLEMENTS

Deduction allowed for legal fees for arranging details of alimony
Reg. § 1.262-1(7)

---

*Note: Paragraph numbers refer to Volume One. Items marked * are research aids, not citations of authority; see "Key to Citations" on page 806.*

*Note: Paragraph numbers refer to Volume One. Items marked * are research aids, not citations of authority; see "Key to Citations" on page 806.*

Note: Paragraph numbers refer to Volume One. Items marked ` are research aids, not citations of authority; see "Key to Citations" on page 806.

Constructive receipt
Reg. § 1.451-2

Deductions—generally
IRC § 461
Reg. § 1.461-1(a)

All events test—economic performance test
IRC § 461(h)
Reg. § 1.461-4

3¹/₂ month test for services or goods
Reg. § 1.461-4(d)(6)

Taxes
Reg. § 1.461-4(g)(6)

Economic performance—recurring item exception
IRC § 461(h)(3)
Prop. Reg. § 1.461-5

8¹/₂ month test
Reg. § 1.461-5(b)(ii)

Cash-basis tax shelters
IRC § 461(i)

Payment through "pay by phone" account
Rev. Rul. 80-335, 1980-2 CB 170

Accrued bonus payable within 2¹/₂ months after tax year
Truck and Equipment Co. of Harrisonburg, 98 TC 141 (1992)
Temp. Reg. § 1.404(b)-IT

Deferred payments for use of property or services
IRC § 467

Deeded retirement home
Highland Farms, Inc., 106 TC 12 (1996)
Richard A. Childs, 103 TC 36 (1995)

Income not deferred by agent
Rev. Rul. 70-294, 1970-1 CB 13

Income deferred on wheat sale
Rev. Rul. 58-162, 1958-1 CB 234, distinguished by Rev. Rul. 70-294, 1970-1 CB 13

Capitalization rule: $10 million exception
Rev. Rul. 89-26, 1989-1 CB 87

Advance payments deductible
R. D. Cravens, 272 F.2d 895 (10th Cir. 1960), rev'g 30 TC 903 (1958)
John Ernst, 32 TC 181 (1959) (Acq.)

Payment to related cash-basis taxpayer of salary and interest
IRC § 267(a)(2)

Long-term contracts
IRC § 460

Advance interest payments ("paid or accrued")
IRC § 163

Advance tax payments ("paid or accrued")
IRC § 164

Interest on tax deficiency
James Redlark, 106 TC 2 (1996) (disagrees with 8th Cir. Miller, 65 F.3d 687 (1995))

Prepaid insurance—proration
Boylston Market Ass'n, 131 F.2d 966 (1st Cir. 1942)

Prepaid insurance—immediate deduction
Waldheim Realty and Investment, 245 F.2d 823 (8th Cir. 1957)

Accrual-effect of contingency
Safety Car Heating Co., 297 U.S. 88 (1936)
Continental Tie & Lumber Co., 286 U.S. 290 (1932)
American Code Co., 280 U.S. 445 (1930)

Uncollectable amounts for services
IRC § 1.448-2T(b)

Responsible person for withholding taxes
IRC § 6672

40.4 TAX REPORTING YEAR FOR SELF-EMPLOYED

* "Fiscal Years Are Resurrected by RA '87, But Required Payments Put a Price on Deferral," Robert A. Rombro, 40 Taxation for Accountants 302 (May 1988)
* "How Can a Client Retain Its Fiscal Year After TRA '86," D. Alden Newland, 67 Journal of Taxation 382 (Dec. 1987)

Taxable year
IRC § 441(b)
Reg. § 1.441-1(b)
*IRS Publication 538

Calendar year
IRC § 441(d)

Fiscal year
IRC § 441(e)

Personal service corporation year
IRC § 441(i)

Partnership year
IRC § 706(b)

S corporation year
IRC § 1378(b)

52–53 weeks
IRC § 441(f)
Reg. § 1.441-2

Period of less than 12 months
IRC § 443
Reg. § 1.443-1

Sole proprietor's tax year
Rev. Rul. 58-389, 1957-2 CB 298, modified by Rev. Rul. 77-293, 1977-2 CB 91

Change of accounting period
IRC § 442
Reg. § 1.442-1(b)

40.5 REPORTING BUSINESS CASH RECEIPTS TO THE IRS

IRC § 6050 I
Reg. § 1.6050 I-1
Reg. § 1.6050 I-2

Attorneys must identify clients paying over $10,000
News Release IR-93-113 (intentional disregard penalties may be imposed)
Goldberger and Dubin, 935 F.2d 501 (2nd Cir. 1991)
Richard H. Sindel, 53 F.3d 874 (8th Cir. 1995) (disclosure of client identity not required if it would reveal confidential communications)

Attorney not required to identify client paying over $10,000 where IRS does not follow summons procedure
Gertner, 65 F.3d 963 (1st Cir.,1995)

Failure to report business car over $10,000
Announcement 90-142, 1990-53 IRB 63

Cash equivalents under $10,000
Reg. § 1.6050I-1(c)(1)(ii)

$3,000 cash log requirement dropped
Treasury Regulations Bank Secretary Act § 103.29
News Release IR 95-37

Cash bail over $10,000
Reg. § 1.6050 I-2

Penalty for not providing statement
IRC § 6721
Annnouncement 94-113, 1994-37 IRB 37

40.6 HOW TO FILE SCHEDULE C

*IRS Publication 535

Statutory employees
IRC § 3121(d)(3)
Reg. 31.3121(d)-1(d)(3)(IV)

Business expenses—adjusted gross income
IRC § 62

Business expenses—in general
IRC § 162
Reg. § 1.162-1

Unreasonable business expense
Palo Alto Town & Country Village, Inc., 32 TCM 1048 (1973), aff'd in part, rev'd in part and rem'd, 565 F.2d 1388 (9th Cir. 1978)

Inventory losses
Reg. § 1.165-7(a)(4)
Reg. § 1.471-2(c)
National Home Products, 71 TC 501 (1979)

Bad debts
IRC § 166

Reserve for bad debts repealed
IRC § 166(c), repealed by 1986 Tax Reform Act Section 805(a)

Workers' compensation
Harvey R. Otten, 68 TCM 1342 (1994)

Insurance premiums
Reg. § 1.162-1

Disability insurance
Marvin J. Blaess, 28 TC 710 (1957)
Rev. Rul. 58-480, 1958-2 CB 62

Termination payments
Robert E. Milligan, 38 F.3d 1094 (9th Cir. 1994)

Prepaid premiums
Waldheim Realty & Investment, 245 F.2d 823 (8th Cir. 1957)
Boylston Market Ass'n, 131 F.2d 966 (1st Cir. 1942)

Premiums for disability insurance
Rev. Rul. 55-331, 1955-1 CB 271, modified by Rev. Rul. 68-212, 1968-1 CB 91

Health insurance for self-employed
IRC § 162(1)

---

*Note: Paragraph numbers refer to Volume One. Items marked * are research aids, not citations of authority; see "Key to Citations" on page 806.*

Rev. Rul. 71-588, 1971-2 CB 91

Premium for malpractice insurance
Rev. Rul. 60-365, 1960-2 CB 49

Non-practicing malpractice insurance
Merlin A. Steger, 113 TC No. 18

Malpractice premiums to physician-owned carrier
Rev. Rul. 80-120, 1980-1 CB 41

Physicians may not deduct cost of setting up insurance carrier
Carl Herman, et al., 84 TC 120 (1985)

Policies for business overhead expenses
Rev. Rul. 55-264, 1955-1 CB 11

Interest
IRC § 163
Reg. § 1.163-1

Interest deduction limited to $50,000 on employee life insurance
IRC § 264(a)(4)

Interest on deferred pay accounts
Albertson's, Inc., 12 F.3d 1539 (9th Cir. 1994)

Interest owed on business tax deficiency
James Redlark, 98-1 USTC § 50, 322 (9th Cir. 1998), rev'g 106 TC 2 (1996)
David Miller, 65 F.3d 687 (8th Cir. 1995), aff'g 841 F. Supp. 305 (N.D. 1993) (interest never deductible)
*"Redlark reversed but interest deductions for business tax deficiencies is still an open issue," Richard M. Lipton, 89 Journal of Taxation 24 (July 1998)
Richard R. Allen, Sr., 99-1 USTC ¶50,470 (4th Cir. 1999)
Nick Kikalos, 99-2 USTC ¶50,823 (7th Cir. 1999)

Interest on funds used in personal affairs
Ebb. J. Ford, Jr., 29 TC 499 (1957)

Payments before title passes treated as interest
Warren Halle, 83 F.3d 649 (4th Cir. 1996)

Losses
IRC § 165
Reg. § 1.165-1

Rents
Reg. § 1.162-1
Reg. § 1.162-11
Rev. Rul. 74-209 1974-1 CB 46

Advance rents
Martin J. Zaninovich, 616 F.2d 429 (9th Cir. 1980)

Repairs
Reg. § 1.162-4
Louise Kingsley, 11 BTA 296 (Acq.)

Incidental repairs deductible
Indopco, Inc., 112 S. Ct. 1039 (1992), aff'g 918 F. 2d 426 (2nd Cir. 1991)
Rev. Rul. 94-12, 1994-1 CB 36

Taxes
IRC § 164
Reg. § 1.164

State income taxes not a business deduction
D.H. Tanner, 363 F.2d 36 (4th Cir. 1966)

Salaries and wages
IRC § 162(a)(1)
Reg. § 1.162-7(a)

Legal fees
Rev. Rul. 74-392, 1974-2 CB 10
Rev. Rul. 71-470, 1971-2 CB 12

Deduction for legal fee of unsuccessful defense of criminal charge arising out of business
Walter F. Tellier, 383 U.S. 687 (1966)

Litigation expense of retired officer's rank
Rev. Rul. 72-169, 1972-1 CB 43

Expenses of discontinued business
Rev. Rul. 67-12, 1967-1 CB 29

Wages to your children deductible
Walt E. Eller, 77 TC 934 (1981)
James A. Moriarty, 48 TCM 59 (1984)

40.7 Deductions for Professionals

IRS list of deductible professional expenses
Reg. § 1.162-6

Cost of establishing professional reputation
Miron Kroyt, 20 TCM 1665 (1961)

Amortization of bar admission costs
Joel A. Sharon, 66 TC 515 (1976), aff'd, 591 F.2d 1273 (9th Cir. 1978), cert. denied

Doctor may amortize patient's records
Los Angeles Central Animal Hospital, Inc., 58 TC 269 (Acq.)

Doctor
Richard M. Boe, 35 TC 720 (1961), aff'd, 307 F.2d 339 (9th Cir. 1962)
Chester R. Johnson, Jr., 61-1 USTC 9278 (W.D. Tex. 1961)
William Wells-Lee, 360 F.2d 665 (8th Cir. 1966), rev'g and rem'g 23 TCM 1931 (1964)

Payment for hospital rights
S. M. Howard, 39 TC 833 (1963)
E. Vance Walters, 383 F.2d 922 (6th Cir. 1967)

Amortizing cost of right to practice in a hospital
Rev. Rul. 70-171, 1970-1 CB 55

Payment of client's expenses
Reginald G. Hearn, 36 TC 672 (1961), aff'd, 309 F.2d 431 (9th Cir. 1962), cert. denied, 373 U.S. 909
C. Doris Pepper, 36 TC 886 (1961) (Acq.)

Advances to client deductible/not deductible
Warren Burnett, 356 F.2d 755 (5th Cir. 1966), cert. denied, 385 U.S. 832
James Boccard, 95-1 USTC § 50,284 (9th Cir. 1995)

Professionals not in own practice
Wesley J. Rogers, 20 TCM 1515 (1961)

No deduction if failed to make malpractice claim
Rev. Rul. 78-141, 1978-1 CB 380

Extracurricular teaching costs
Samuel F. Patterson, 30 TCM 1003 (1971), on remand from 436 F.2d 359 (9th Cir.), rev'g and rem'g 27 TCM 640 (1968)
Seymour Feinstein, 29 TCM 1338 (1970)
Earl T. Jefferson, 74-1 USTC ¶9205 (N.D. Ga.

1974)

Luncheon discussion
John D. Moss, Jr., 758 F.2d 211 (7th Cir. 1985), cert. denied, 474 U.S. 979 (1985)
Richard R. Hankenson, 47 TCM 1567 (1984)
Myron W. Mizell, et al., 55 TCM 169 (1988)

40.8 Nondeductible Expense Items

Capital expenditures
IRC § 263
Reg. § 1.263(a)

Uniform capitalization rules under 1986 Tax Reform Act
IRC § 263A
Temp. Reg. Sec. 1.263A-1T

New roof on building
George W. Ritter, 163 F.2d 1019 (6th Cir. 1947)
Oberman Mfg., 47 TC 471 (1967) (Acq.)
Thomas J. Locke, 8 BTA 534 (Acq.)
Georgia Car and Locomotive Co., 2 BTA 986 (Nonacq.)

State income taxes not deductible from gross income
Reg. § 1.62-1(d)
Douglas H. Tanner, 45 TC 145 (1965), aff'd per curiam, 363 F.2d 36 (4th Cir. 1966)

State income taxes for net operating loss
Rev. Rul. 70-40, 1970-1 CB 50

Business property tax
E. W. Brown, Jr., 439 F.2d 1065 (5th Cir. 1954)

Personal expenses paid with business funds
IRC § 262
Reg. § 1.262-1

Expenses while not in business
Henry G. Owen, 23 TC 377 (1955)

Payment of fines
IRC § 162(f)
Hoover Motor Express Co., Inc., 356 U.S. 38 (1958)
Tank Truck Rentals, Inc., 356 U.S. 30 (1958)
Herbert Davis, 26 TC 49 (1956) (Acq.)
Harry Wiedetz, 2 TC 1262 (1943)

Kickback
IRC § 162(c)
Reg. § 1.162-1(c)

Subcontractor's legal kickback not deductible
Car-Ron Asphalt Paving Co., Inc., 758 F.2d 1132 (6th Cir. 1985), aff'g 46 TCM 1314 (1983)

Contributions to campaigns
IRC § 162(e)

40.9 How Authors and Artists May Write Off Expenses

IRC § 263A(h)
Notice 89-67, 1988-1 CB 55
*IRS Publication 538

Pre-1987 expenses
IRC § 280, repealed by 1986 Tax Reform Act Section 803(b)(2)(A)
Arthur T. Hadley, 819 F.2d 359 (2d Cir. 1987), reversing 51 TCM 948 (1986)

Note: Paragraph numbers refer to Volume One. Items marked ˙ are research aids, not citations of authority; see "Key to Citations" on page 806.

40.10 Deducting Expenses of a Sideline Business or Hobby

IRC § 183
* IRS Publication 535
* "Hobby Activities Can Increase Tax Liability," Alan D. Campbell, 53 Taxation for Accountants 78 (August 1994)
* "Supreme Court Narrows Home Office Deductions in Soliman," Michael M. Megaard and Susan L. Megaard, 78 Journal of Taxation 132 (March 1993)
"When Is a 'Hobby' a Business for Tax Purposes?" Gary L. Maydew, 59 Taxation for Accountants 90 (Aug. 1997)

Order of claiming hobby deductions
Reg. § 1.183-1(b)

Election to postpone determination of profit presumption
Temp. Reg. § 12.9

Waiver of statute of limitations—items affected
IRC § 183(e)(4)

Determining presumption period
Rev. Rul. 78-22, 1978-1 CB 72

Presumption period ends with death
Rev. Rul. 79-204, 1979-2 CB 111

Manner business conducted
James Jasienski, 64 TCM 1369 (1992)
Robert Matlock, 63 TCM 3108 (1992)
Leonard F. Barcus, 32 TCM 660 (1973), aff'd, 492 F.2d 1237 (2d Cir. 1974)
C. West Churchman, 68 TC 696 (1977)
Lester R. Westphal, 68 TCM 1038 (1994)
Danny Eldridge, 70 TCM 380 (1995)
Holowinski, TC Memo 1997-168

History of income/losses from activity
Warren T. Brown, 280 F. Supp. 854 (D.N. Mex., 1968)
Henry P. White, 23 TC 90 (1954), aff'd per curiam, 227 F.2d 779 (6th Cir. 1956), cert. denied, 351 U.S. 939
Leonard P. Sasso, 20 TCM 1068 (1961)
Charles D. Eggert, 16 TCM 1010 (1957)
Lawrence Hoyle, 68 TCM 1321 (1994)
Anthony Ranciato, 52 F.3d 23 (2nd Cir. 1995)

Sideline charter boat
John R. Zwicky, 48 TCM 1025 (1984)
Douglas C. Heppe, 70 TCM 63 (1995)

Elements of personal pleasure/recreation
Valentine Howell, 41 TC 13 (1963), aff'd per curiam, 332 F.2d 428 (3d Cir. 1964)
Charles H. Carter, 37 TCM 859 (1978)
Peter Hurd, 37 TCM 499 (1978)
Norman D. Demler, 25 TCM 620 (1966)
Tolbert Wilkinson, 71 TCM 1959 (1996)

Aspiring authors
Paul Snyder, 674 F.2d 1359 (10th Cir. 1982) (allowed)
Maurice Dreicer, 78 TC 642 (1982) (disallowed), aff'd in unpublished opinion (D.C. Cir. 2/22/83)
Partnerships subject to IRC § 183
Rev. Rul. 77-320, 1977-2 CB 78

40.11 Deducting Expenses of Looking for a New Business

* "Speed Up the Deduction of Business Expansion Costs," Edward J. Schnee, 63 Tax Strategies 4 (July 1999)
* "Organization Costs May Be Amortized If Election is Made," John C. Zimmerman and Jim Swayze, 57 Taxation for Accountants 150 (September 1996)
* "Search and Start-Up Expenses for a New Business: When Are They Deductible?" Donald R. Quinn, 17 Practical Accountant 77 (1984)
*IRS Publication 334

Amortization of business start-up costs
IRC § 195

Amortizable organization costs of corporation
IRC § 248

Amortizable organization costs of partnership
IRC § 709

Partnership syndication costs not amortizable
Rev. Rul. 89-11, 1989-1 CB 179

Expenses of getting a savings and loan charter; loss deduction is allowed
Harris W. Seed, 52 TC 880 (1969) (Acq.)

Funds advanced for mining
Charles T. Parker, 1 TC 709 (1943) (Acq.)

Investigating new business which is not entered into
Frank B. Polachek, 22 TC 858 (1954)
Morton Frank, 20 TC 511 (1953)
Johan Domenie, 34 TCM 469 (1975)
Rev. Rul. 77-254, 1977-2 CB 63

Search for car agency not deductible
William E. Day, 15 TCM 1303 (1956)

40.12 Exclusive and Regular Use of a Home Office

IRC § 280A
Prop. Reg. § 1.280A-1 through 3
*IRS Publication 587

Favorable law change for administrative offices effective after 1998
IRC § 280A (c)(1), as amended by the Taxpayer Relief Act of 1997; effectively overruling Supreme Court's Soliman decision
*"Home Office Deduction Rules Eased — Next Year," Gary M. Fleischman, 60 Taxation for Accountants 103 (Feb. 1998)

Supreme Court sets principal place of business tests
Nader Soliman, 113 S. Ct. 701 (1993)
Rev. Rul. 94-24, 1994-1 CB 87 (IRS examples applying Soliman tests)

Principal place of business (before Supreme Court's Soliman decision)
Rudolph Baie, 74 TC 105 (1980) (road stand)
Ernest Drucker, 79 TC 605 (1982) (musician), rev'd 715 F.2d 67 (2d Cir. 1983)
David J. Weissman, 751 F.2d 512 (2d Cir. 1985) (college professor)
Stanley Pomerantz, 860 F.2d 960 (9th Cir. 1988) (emergency room physician)

Multiple use of home office
Alfred Hamacher, 94 TC 348 (1990)

Day-care in home
IRC § 280A(c)(4)
Brian Uphus, 67 TCM 2229 (1994)
Rev. Rul. 92-3, 1992-1 CB 141

Inventory storage and product samples
IRC § 280A(c)(2)

Portion of room as office
George H. Weightman, 42 TCM 104 (1981) (allowed); 45 TCM 167 (1982) (disallowed for following year on other grounds)
Reg. § 1.280A-2(g)(1) (no partition required—follows Weightman case)
Sharon L. Gomez, 41 TCM 585 (1980) (failed to prove business use)

Practicing medicine at home—no deduction
Joon Chong, 71 TCM 3035 (1996)

Backyard office is "appurtenant"
Charles A. Scott, 84 TC 683 (1985)

Art gallery in home
Joseph Cunningham, 71 TCM 2527 (1996)

40.13 What Home Office Expenses Are Deductible?

Depreciable basis
*IRS Publication 587

Recovery period
IRC § 168(c), as amended by the Revenue Reconciliation Act of 1993

Lawn care not deductible
Tom E. Butz, 35 TCM 532 (1976)

Home security system
Rev. Rul. 86-148, 1986-2 CB 43

40.14 Allocating Expenses to Business Use

Any reasonable method accepted
Rev. Rul. 62-180, 1962-2 CB 52
Joseph Cunningham, 71 TCM 2527 (1996)

40.15 Business Income May Limit Home Office Deductions

IRC § 280A(c)(5)
Prop. Reg. § 1.280A-2(i) and 2(iii)
Letter Ruling 8347012

40.16 Home Office for Sideline Business

Doctor with rental properties
Edwin R. Curphey, 73 TC 766 (1980)

Investors carrying on business
Joseph Moller, 553 F.2d 1071 (CA-Fed. Cir., 83-2 USTC ¶ 9698)

40.17 Depreciation of Office in Cooperative Apartment

IRC § 216(c)
Reg. § 1.216-2

Note: Paragraph numbers refer to Volume One. Items marked `*` *are research aids, not citations of authority; see "Key to Citations" on page 806.*

40.18 NET OPERATING LOSSES FOR REFUND OF PRIOR TAXES

IRC § 172
Reg. § 1.172
*IRS Publication 536

Five-year averaging for farmers
IRC § 172 (b)(1)(G)

Accounting change
Rev. Rul. 85-16, 1985-1 CB 180

40.19 YOUR NET OPERATING LOSS

IRC § 172
*IRS Publication 536

40.20 FORM 1045

IRC § 172
*IRS Publication 536

40.21 HOW TO CARRY BACK YOUR NET OPERATING LOSS

IRC § 172 (b)(1)
*IRS Publication 536

Quick refund
IRC § 6411(a)(1)

Effect of spouse's death on carryback
Rev. Rul. 65-140, 1965-1 CB 127

Widow active in business allowed late husband's carryover
Vivian Rose, 32 TCM 965 (1973)

40.22 ELECTION TO CARRY FORWARD LOSSES

IRC § 172(b)(3)(C)

Fifteen-year carryforward
IRC § 172(b)(1)(B)

Timely filed return
John H. Young, 83 TC 831 (1984)

Election to forego carryback avoided
M. Lane Powers, 51 F.3d 34 (5th Cir. 1995)

40.23 GENERAL BUSINESS CREDIT

* "Empowerment Zones and Other Business Incentives May Provide Only Limited Benefits," Adam M. Handler, 79 Journal of Taxation 274 (November 1993)

General business credit
IRC § 38

Work opportunity credit replaces targeted jobs credit
IRC § 51

Welfare-to-work credit
IRC § 51A

Disability access credit
IRC § 44

Alcohol fuels credit
IRC § 40

Research credit
IRC § 41

Low-income housing credit
IRC § 42

Empowerment zone employment credit
IRC § 1396(a)

Indian employment credit
IRC § 45A

Employer Social Security credit on tips
IRC § 45B(a)

Rehabilitation investment credit
IRC § 48(g)
IRC § 46(b)(4)

Business energy credit
IRC § 46(b)

Community development corporations credit
Section 13311 of the 1993 Revenue Reconciliation Act

Investment credit
IRC § 46 through 48

Investment credit transition property
IRC § 49(e)
Rev. Rul. 87-113, 1987-2 CB 33

Investment credit carryovers
IRC § 49(c) (35% reduction)
IRC § 39(d)

Recapture of investment credit
IRC § 47(a)(1)
Reg. § 1.47-1

Investment credit recapture for automobiles and other listed property
Temp. Reg. § 1.280F-3T

When recapture does not apply
IRC § 47(b)

No disposition under Bankruptcy Act
IRC § 1017(c)(2), as amended by § 2(b) of the Bankruptcy Tax Act

Transfer from private practice to professional corporation requires recapture
Rev. Rul. 76-514, 1976-2 CB 11

40.24 OTHER FUEL-RELATED CREDITS

Diesel vehicles
IRC § 6427(g)

Federal gasoline and oil tax credit
*IRS Publication 510
IRC § 34

Alternative fuel production credit
IRC § 29

Enhanced oil recovery credit
IRC § 43

Renewable electricity production credit
IRC § 45

---

41 RETIREMENT PLANS FOR SELF-EMPLOYED

41.1 WHO MAY SET UP A KEOGH PLAN?

IRC § 401(d)
IRC § 401(c)
Reg. § 1.401-11
*IRS Publication 560

Earnings from more than one trade or business
IRC § 401(d)(1), repealed by the Small Business Job Protection Act of 1996
Reg. § 1.401-10(b)(2)
Reg. § 1.401-10(c)

Controlled businesses
Reg. § 1.401-12(1), (2), and (3)

S corporation shareholder may not set up a Keogh plan
Antonio Durando, 70 F.3d 584 (9th Cir. 1995)

Including employees in the plan
IRC § 410

Contributions based on compensation
IRC § 1.401-10
IRC § 1.401-11

41.2 CHOOSING A KEOGH PLAN

IRC § 401
Reg. § 401(e)

Integration with Social Security
IRC § 401(1)

Minimum participation requirement
IRC § 401(a)(26), as amended by the Small Business Job Protection Act of 1996

41.3 TOP-HEAVY PLAN RESTRICTIONS

IRC § 416

Vesting
IRC § 416(b)

Minimum benefits
IRC § 416(c)

Prior law premature distribution penalty
IRC § 72(m)(5)

Rollover of retirement bonds
IRC § 402(e)(5)

Key employees
IRC § 416

41.4 CHOOSING A SEP

SEP defined
IRC § 408(k)

Overall limit on employer SEP contributions
IRC § 402(h)

Deductions for SEP contributions
IRC § 404(h)

Deductible SEP contributions up to filing date plus extensions
IRC § 404(h)(1)(B)
Prop. Reg. § 1.408-7(b)

41.5 DEDUCTIBLE KEOGH OR SEP CONTRIBUTIONS

*IRS Publication 560

Contribution limits

---

*Note: Paragraph numbers refer to Volume One. Items marked * are research aids, not citations of authority; see "Key to Citations" on page 806.*

IRC § 415(b) and (c)

10% penalty for nondeductible contributions
IRC § 4972

Earned income reduced by deductible contributions
IRC § 401(c)(2)(A)(v)
IRC § (a)(8)(D)

Compensation limit
IRC § 401(a)(17)
News Release, IR-1999-80 ($170,000 compensation limit for 2000)
IRC § 401(a)(17), as amended by the Revenue Reconciliation Act of 1993

Deductions
IRC § 404
Reg. § 1.404(a)-1

Deductible Keogh contributions up to due date of return
IRC § 404(a)(6)

Deduction limit for profit-sharing plans
IRC § 404(a)(3)

41.6 How To Claim the Keogh or SEP Deduction

IRC § 404
Reg. § 1.404(a)-I

Time for making contributions
Temp. Reg. § 11.40(a)(6)-I

Keogh contributions do not reduce self-employment income
Seymour L. Gale, 91-2 USTC ¶ 50,356 (Dist. Ct., Ill. 1991)

41.7 How To Qualify a Keogh or SEP Plan

IRC § 401
IRC § 404
IRC § 405

Failure to set up written plan
Nelson H. Jones, 51 TC 651 (1969)

Correction of defects made more affordable
Rev. Proc. 94-16, 1994-1 CB 576

41.8 Annual Keogh Plan Return

Short form 5500EZ
Announcement 90-22, 1990-7 IRB 28

41.9 Restrictions on Loans

Prohibited transaction penalties
IRC § 4975(a) as amended by the Small Business Job Protection Act of 1996
IRC § 4975(b)
IRC § 4962

90-day correction period
IRC § 4963(e)(1)

Labor Department exemption
1986 Tax Reform Act Section 1898(i)

41.10 How Keogh Plan Distributions Are Taxed

Lump-sum averaging
IRC § 402(d), as amended by the Small Business Job Protection Act of 1996
Sections 1122(h)(3)-(6) of 1986 Tax Reform Act (P.L. 99-514)

10% penalty for excess benefits under plan formula
IRC § 72(m)(5)(A)

Disqualification of plan completely bars tax-free rollover
Reg. § 1.402(a)-1(a)(i)
John U. Fazi, 102 TC 31 (1994)

41.11 Simple Retirement Plans

IRC § 408(p)
Notice 97-6, 1997-2 IRB 26
* "Retirement Plan Reform: The Aftermath of the Small Business Job Protection Act of 1996," Natasha M. Mulleneaux, 75 Taxes 438 (Aug. 1997)
* "Small Businesses Have Simple Retirement Option," Susan Anderson, 59 Taxation for Accountants 135 (Sept. 1997)
* IRS Publication 560

---

42 Claiming Depreciation Deductions

42.1 What Property May Be Depreciated?

IRC § 168
* IRS Publication 534
* "Accelerated Cost Recovery Deduction for Fine Art," Steven L. Zisser, 66 Taxes 171 (Mar. 1988)

Depreciation allowed on violin
Richard Simon, 68 F.3d 41 (2nd Cir., 1995), aff'g, 103 TC 15 (1994)
Brian P. Liddle, 65 F.3d 329 (3rd Cir. 1995), aff'g 103 TC 285 (1994)

Depreciation allowed on exotic cars
Bruce Selig, TC Memo 1995-519

Depreciation not allowed on equipment in suspended medical practice
Rev. Rul. 77-32, 1977-1 CB 38

Depreciation allowed on equipment while owner unemployed
Charles D. Gallagher, 39 TCM 291 (1979)

Ownership interest
Rev. Rul. 78-411, 1978-2 CB 112

Land
Reg. § 1.167(a)-2
Clarence D. Hawkins, 14 TCM 382 (1955), rev'd on another issue, 234 F.2d 359 (6th Cir. 1956)

Cost of education not depreciable
Nathaniel A. Denman, 48 TC 439 (1967) (Acq.)

Goodwill, customer lists, agreements not to compete, and other intangibles
IRC § 197, as enacted by the Revenue Reconciliation Act of 1993

Election to apply amortization of intangibles retroactively

Revenue Reconciliation Act of 1993, Act Sec. 13261(g)(2)-(3)

One year or less
W. H. Tompkins Co., 47 BTA 292
International Shoe Co., 38 BTA 81 (Acq.)
Rev. Rul. 59-249, 1959-2 CB 55

Car partly for business
IRC § 280F
J. R. James, 2 BTA 1071 (Acq.)
Kenneth Branchard, 12 TCM 550 (1953)
Paul McWilliams, 9 TCM (1950)
W. H. Wilson, 5 TCM 592 (1946), aff'd, 161 F.2d 556 (4th Cir. 1947), cert. denied, 332 U.S. 769

Offered for sale
Marjorie May, 299 F.2d 725 (4th Cir. 1962)

Depreciation not allowed on idle ranch residence held by business
John T. Steen, 61 TC 298 (1973), aff'd per curiam, 508 F.2d 268 (5th Cir. 1975)

Depreciation on residence put up for sale
Hulet P. Smith, 26 TCM 149 (1967), aff'd per curiam, 397 F.2d 804 (9th Cir. 1968)

Nonproducing property
Reg. § 1.212-1(b)
George W. Mitchell, 47 TC 120 (1966) (Nonacq.)
Maurice H. Connell, 11 TCM 771 (1952)
Charles D. Gallagher, 39 TCM 291 (1979)

Improvements for tenants
Henry F. Grinalds, 65 TCM 1971 (1993)

Work of art not depreciable
Rev. Rul. 68-232, 1968-1 CB 79

Depreciating paintings in office
D. Joseph Judge, 35 TCM 1264 (1976)

Cannot accumulate depreciation
Fort Orange Paper Co., 1 BTA 1230 (Acq.)
First National Bank of Thompson, Iowa, 2 BTA 735
Morris & Bailey Steel Co., 9 BTA 205 (Acq.)

Depreciation on building bought with intention to demolish
Rev. Rul. 67-445, 1967-2 CB 94

Farm property
Reg. § 1-167(a)(6)

When depreciation is claimed
Reg. § 1.167(a)-10

42.2 Claiming Depreciation on Your Tax Return

IRC § 168
*IRS Publication 534

42.3 First-Year Expensing Deduction

IRC § 179
* IRS Publication 534
* IRS Publication 946
* "RRA '93 Increases Benefits of Asset Expense Election," Larry R. Garrison, 51 Taxation for Accountants 363 (December 1993)
* "Final Regulations Offer Guidance for Expensing Depreciable Assets," 71 Taxes 309 (May 1993)

Note: Paragraph numbers refer to Volume One. Items marked * *are research aids, not citations of authority; see "Key to Citations" on page 806.*

Note: Paragraph numbers refer to Volume One. Items marked ˙ are research aids, not citations of authority; see "Key to Citations" on page 806.

IRC § 163(h)(2)(A)
IRC § 163(d)(6)

Diary record of business mileage
John E. Frankel, 27 TCM 817 (1968)

Two cars used at one time
Carroll H. West, 63 TC 252 (1974)

Married couple's separately owned cars
* Letter Ruling 8343005

Useful life: prior law
Rev. Proc. 75-3, 1975-1 CB 643

60,000 miles as useful life: prior law
Rev. Proc. 81-54, 1981-2 CB 649

Investment credit and IRS rate: prior law
Rev. Rul. 67-348, 1967-2 CB 7

43.2 AUTO EXPENSE ALLOCATIONS

Allocation based on mileage
Temp. Reg. Sec. 1.280F-6T(e)
* IRS Publication 463

Some car expenses capitalized
Doris Jones, 11 TCM 529 (1952)

Apportioning car expense between business and personal use
IRC 163(h)(2)(A)
Lawrence Au, 40 TC 264 (1963), aff'd per curiam, 330 F.2d 1008 (9th Cir. 1964), cert. denied, 379 U.S. 960
Clarence J. Sapp, 309 F.2d 143 (5th Cir. 1962), aff'g 36 TC 852 91 (1961) (Acq.)

43.3 AUTO DEPRECIATION RESTRICTIONS

IRC § 280F
* "Auto Depreciation Is Now Limited After the Tax Reform Act, But Advantages Still Exist," Robert E. Nelson, 39 Taxation for Accountants 322 (Nov. 1987)

More than 50% business-use test
Temp. Reg. § 280F(b)
Temp. Reg. § 1.280F-6T(d)(4)

Business-investment percentage
Temp. Reg. § 1.280F-6T(d)(3)
Temp. Reg. § 1.280F-2T(i)

Employer convenience test
IRC § 280F(d)(3)

Employee use of company car
IRC § 280F(d)(6)
Temp. Reg. § 1.280F-6T(d)(2)

Vehicles other than cars
IRC § 280F(d)(4)
Temp. Reg. § 1.280F-6T(b)

Vehicles exempted from more-than-50%-business-use test
Temp. Reg. § 1.280F-6T(b)
Temp. Reg. § 1.274-5T(k)

Transportation for hire
IRC § 280F(d)(4)(C)

Diesel vehicle credit reduces basis
IRC § 6427(g)(7) (credit repealed for vehicles bought after 3/20/96 by the Small Business Job

Protection Act of 1996)

43.4 ANNUAL CEILINGS ON DEPRECIATION

Annual limit on depreciation
IRC § 280F(a)
Rev. Proc. 99-14, 1999-5 IRB

First-year expensing limitation
IRC § 280F(d)(1)

Personal-use percentage reduces ceiling
IRC § 280F(a)(2)
Temp. Reg. § 1.280F-2T(i)

Luxury auto excise tax phased down after 1995
IRC § 4001(f), as amended by the Small Business Job Protection Act of 1996

Passenger automobile defined
IRC § 280F(d)(5)

43.5 MACRS RATES FOR CARS

*IRS Publication 917
IRC § 168(e)(3)(B)(i)
IRC § 168(b)
IRC § 168(c)

Annual deduction limits
IRC § 280F(a)

Conventions
IRC § 168(d)

Basis reduction for personal use
Temp. Reg. § 1.280F-2T(g)

43.6 STRAIGHT-LINE RATE FOR BUSINESS USE OF 50% OR LESS

Mandatory straight-line recovery
IRC § 280F(b)(2) and (b)(4)
Temp. Reg. § 1.280F-3T(c) and (e)

Optional straight-line recovery if business use exceeds 50%
IRC § 168(f)(2)(c)
Prop. Reg. 1.168-2(c)

43.7 DEPRECIATION AFTER RECOVERY PERIOD ENDS

*IRS Publication 463

Converting a pleasure car to business use
Prop. Reg. § 1.168-2(j)(1)

Increase in business use after recovery period
Prop. Reg. § 1.168-2(j)(2) (Pre-6/18/84 cars)

43.8 TRADE-IN OF BUSINESS AUTO

IRC § 1.031(d)
Reg. § 1.1031(d)-1
W. Schmidt, 28 TCM 481 (1969)

43.9 RECAPTURE OF DEDUCTIONS ON BUSINESS AUTO

Business use drops to 50% or less
IRC § 280F(b)(2)
IRC § 280F(b)(3)
Temp. Reg. § 1.280F-3T(c)(2)

43.10 KEEPING RECORDS OF BUSINESS USE

* "Substantiation of Automobile Business Use Under the New Regulations," Donna M. Pawlikowski and Claireen Herting, 64 Taxes: The Tax Magazine 382 (June 1986)

Record-keeping requirements after 1985
IRC § 274(d)
Temp. Reg. § 1.274-5T

Vehicles exempted from record-keeping requirements
IRC § 274(d)(4)
Temp. Reg. § 1.274-5T(k)

Written company policy restricting personal use
Temp. Reg. § 1.274-6T

Control employees, owners and highly compensated
Reg. § 1.274-6T(a)(3)(i)(E)
Reg. § 1.61-2T(f)(5) and (f)(6)

43.11 LEASED BUSINESS AUTOS: DEDUCTIONS AND INCOME

IRS § 280F(c)
*IRS Publication 463

---

44 SALES OF BUSINESS PROPERTY

44.1 ORDINARY INCOME RECAPTURE OF DEPRECIATION ON SALE OF PERSONAL PROPERTY

* IRS Publication 544
IRC § 1245(a)
IRC § 1250

44.2 ORDINARY INCOME RECAPTURE ON DEPRECIABLE REALTY

IRC § 1250

25% tax rate for unrecaptured Section 1250 gain
IRC § 1(h)(1)(D)

Computing excess over straight line
Reg. § 1.1250 (b)(1)

Holding period where property is foreclosed
IRC § 1250 (d)(10)
Reg. § 1.1250-1 through 5

44.3 RECAPTURE OF FIRST-YEAR EXPENSING

* IRS Publication 544
IRC § 179(d)(10)

44.4 GIFTS AND INHERITANCES OF DEPRECIABLE PROPERTY

IRC § 1245(a)

Tax not imposed at time of gift or inheritance
IRC § 1245(b)(1), (2), and (3)
Reg. § 1.1245-4

44.5 INVOLUNTARY CONVERSIONS AND TAX-FREE EXCHANGES

* IRS Publication 544

---

*Note: Paragraph numbers refer to Volume One. Items marked * are research aids, not citations of authority; see "Key to Citations" on page 806.*

IRC § 1245(b)(4)
IRC § 1250(d)(4)
Reg. § 1.704-4
Reg. § 1.737-1-5 (gain/loss recognition on partnership distributions of contributed property)

44.6 INSTALLMENT SALE OF DEPRECIABLE PROPERTY
Reg. § 1.1245-6(d)

Sales after June 6, 1984
IRC § 453(i)

44.7 SALE OF A PROPRIETORSHIP
* "Covenants Not to Compete Are Still Useful After RRA '93," Michael Schlesinger, 51 Taxation for Accountants 204 (October 1993)

Amortization of goodwill, customer lists, agreements not to compete, and other intangibles
IRC § 197

Individual proprietorship
IRC § 1231
Reg. § 1.1231-1
Aaron F. Williams, 152 F.2d 570 (2d Cir. 1946)
IRC § 1060
Rev. Rul. 55-79, 1955-1 CB 370

44.8 PROPERTY USED IN A BUSINESS (SECTION 1231 ASSETS)
IRC § 1231
Reg. § 1.1231-1 and 2
* "Capital and Section 1231 Asset Transactions, Status and Planning Opportunities Under the New Law," Philip J. Harmelink and Phyllis V. Copeland, 65 Taxes 176 (March 1987)

12 months for livestock
IRC § 1231(b)(3)

Recapture of ordinary loss
IRC § 1231(c)

44.9 SALE OF PROPERTY USED FOR BUSINESS AND PERSONAL PURPOSES

Sale of airplane
Hugh Sharp, Jr., 199 F. Supp. 743 (D. Del. 1961), aff'd, 303 F.2d 783 (3d Cir. 1962)

44.10 SHOULD YOU TRADE IN BUSINESS EQUIPMENT?

Loss on trade-in
National Outdoor Advertising Bureau, Inc., 89 F.2d 878 (2d Cir. 1937), on remand, BTA Dec. 10,072-C, 6/24/38

Sale to dealer
Rev. Rul. 61-119, 1961-1 CB 395

Trade-ins of personal property
IRC § 1031(d)
Reg. § 1.1031(d)-1
Rev. Rul. 72-111, 1972-1 CB 56

44.11 CORPORATE LIQUIDATION
IRC § 331
* "General Utilities Repeal: A Transactional Analysis," George Brodie, Jr., 66 Journal of Taxation

322 (June 1987)
* "How Liquidations and S Elections May Avoid the Impact of TRA '86," John W. Schmehl, 67 Journal of Taxation 30 (July 1987)
* "Spin-offs, Split-offs and Split-ups Remain Tax Favored Despite the Tax Reform Act of 1986," Ross S. Friedman, Taxation for Accountants (March 1987)
Louis Greenspan, 229 F.2d 947 (8th Cir. 1956)
Susan J. Carter, 170 F.2d 911 (2d Cir. 1948)
L. M. Graves, 11 TCM 467 (1952)
Rev. Rul. 59-228, 1959-2 CB 89

Legal expenses of collecting claim
Otto C. Doering, Jr., 335 F.2d 738 (2d Cir. 1964)

---

45 FIGURING SELF-EMPLOYMENT TAX

45.1 WHAT IS SELF-EMPLOYMENT INCOME?
IRC § 1402
IRC § 6017
Reg. § 1.6017-1(b)
Reg. § 1.1402(a)-1
Reg. § 1.1402(b)-1
*IRS Publication 533

Rents
Reg. § 1.1402(a)-4

Dividends and interest
Reg. § 1.1402(a)-5

Capital gains and losses
Reg. § 1.1402(a)-6

Net operating loss carryover
IRC § 1402(a)(4) and (5)

Husband and wife
IRC § 6017

Business interruption insurance proceeds not self-employment income
Max G. Newberry, 76 TC 441 (1981)

Illegal employment
Rev. Rul. 60-77, 1960-1 CB 386

Employee can be independent contractor for Keogh purposes
James S. Reece, 63 TCM 3129 (1992)

Insurance agent subject to SE tax
Bruce Isom, 70 TCM 376 (1996)

Extended earnings
Herbert Gump, Federal Cir. (6/12/96)
Robert Schelbe, 71 TCM 3166 (1996)

45.2 PARTNERS PAY SELF-EMPLOYMENT TAX
IRC § 701
Reg. § 1.701-1
Reg. § 1.702-1

Limited partner not subject to self-employment tax
IRC § 1402(a)(13)

IRS proposed definition of limited partner blocked by 1997 law
Prop. Reg. § 1.1402 (a)-2 (January 1997)

Section 935 of Taxpayer Relief Act of 1997 bars regulations before 7/1/98

Partner dying during taxable year
Reg. § 1.1402(f)-1

Retirement payments for partnerships
IRC § 1402(a)(10)
Rev. Rul. 79-34, 1979-1 CB 285

Restricting partnership status of foreign consultant does not avoid self-employment tax
Atef A. Gamal-Eldin, 55 TCM 582 (1988) (taxpayer appeal pending)

45.3 SCHEDULE SE
*IRS Publication 533

Income tax deduction for 50% of self-employment tax
IRC § 164(f)

7.65% deduction for self-employment tax computation
IRC § 1402(a)(12)

45.4 HOW WAGES AFFECT SELF-EMPLOYMENT TAX

Effect of wages on self-employment tax rates
IRC § 1402(b)
* Letter Ruling 9530005

All wages subject to Medicare tax after 1993
IRC § 1402(b), as amended by the Revenue Reconciliation Act of 1993

45.5 OPTIONAL METHOD IF 1997 WAS A LOW-INCOME OR LOSS YEAR
*IRS Publication 533
IRC § 1402(a)(15)

45.6 SELF-EMPLOYMENT TAX RULES FOR CERTAIN POSITIONS
* IRS Publication 533
* "IRS's Worker Classification Program—An Inside Look At New Ways To Resolve The Problems," Phil Brand, 85 Journal of Taxation 17 (July 1996)
* "Employee or Independent Contractor: Revitalizing Ideas Through New Definitions," Loren Callan Rosenzweig, 74 Taxes 242 (April 1996)
* "Self-employment Tax Rules May Exclude Some LLC Members," William E. Sider, 54 Taxation for Accountants 132 (March 1995)

Self-employed
IRC § 1401
IRC § 1402
IRC § 1403
Reg. § 1.1401-1
Reg. § 1.1402(a)-1
Reg. § 1.1402(b)-1
Reg. § 1.1402(c)-1

Safe-haven employee rule
1996 Act: § 1122 of the Small Business Job Protection Act of 1996

Babysitter
Rev. Rul. 77-279, 1977-2 CB 12

Clergy

Note: Paragraph numbers refer to Volume One. Items marked ˙ are research aids, not citations of authority; see "Key to Citations" on page 806.

IRC § 1402(e)
Temp. Reg. § 1.1402(e)-5T
James B. Hall, 30 F.3d 1304 (10th Cir. 1994)

Consulting
Rev. Rul. 82-210, 1982-2 CB 203
Grosswald v. Schweicker, 653 F.2d 58 (2d Cir. 1981)
Steffens v. United States, 707 F.2d 478 (11th Cir. 1983)
James M. Hornaday, 81 TC 830 (1983) (fees received without services)

Independent contractor
Dan P. Butts, 49 F.3d 713 (11th Cir. 1995)

LLC members
Prop. Regs. §§ 1.1402 (a)-18
Rev. Proc. 95-10, 1995-1 CB 501

Insurance agent treated as independent contractor
Dan P. Butts, 49 F. 3d 713 (11th Cir. 1995)

Director's fees
IRC § 1402(a)
Rev. Rul. 68-595, 1968-2 CB 378

Drivers
Boles Trucking, Inc., 8th Cir. (2/12/96)

Adult entertainers
303 West 42nd Street Enterprises, Inc., NY District Court (2/28/96)

Used car salesmen
Martin Springfield, 9th Cir. (7/3/96)

Employees of foreign government or international organization
Reg. § 1.1402(c)-3(d)
Jessica M. Smart, 222 F. Supp. 65 (S.D.N.Y. 1963)

Technical specialists
Section 1706 of 1986 Tax Reform Act
Rev. Rul. 87-41, 1987-1 CB 296

Fees as executor
Cresence E. Clarke, 27 TC 861 (1957)
Rev. Rul. 58-5, 1958-1 CB 322, distinguished by Rev. Rul. 72-86, 1972-1 CB 273

Nonprofessional executor or administrator
Rev. Rul. 58-5, 1958-1 CB 322, distinguished by Rev. Rul. 72-86, 1972-1 CB 273
Special Ruling, August 19, 1952
Special Ruling, March 5, 1952
Special Ruling, January 10, 1952
Special Ruling, March 20, 1957

Guardian for disabled cousin
* Letter Ruling 8845025

Trust beneficiaries not self-employed
Reg. § 1.1402(a)-2(b)

Fee for occasional speech
Rev. Rul. 55-431, 1955-2 CB 312

PIK payments to farmers
Pub. L. No. 98-4
Announcement 83-43, 1983-10 IRB 29

Nurses: IRS traditional tests
Rev. Rul. 75-101, 1975-1 CB 318
Rev. Rul. 61-96, 1961-2 CB 155
* Letter Ruling 8845049

Nurses obtaining job through agency

Rev. Rul. 75-41, 1975-1 CB 323
Rev. Rul. 75-101, 1975-1 CB 318
* Letter Ruling 8913002
* Letter Ruling 8839073
* Letter Ruling 8904033
Hospital Resource Personnel, Inc., 68 F.3d 421 (11th Cir. 1995)

Payroll taxes withheld from practical nurse's wages
* Letter Ruling 9123005

Gambling income not subject to self-employment tax
Alfred A. Gentile, 6 TC 1 (1946)

Nonresident alien
IRC § 1402(b)

Public official
IRC § 1402(c)
Reg. § 1.402(c)-2

Writer
Rev. Rul. 68-498, 1968-2 CB 377
Rev. Rul. 79-390, 1972-2 CB 308
Rev. Rul. 55-385, 1955-1 CB 100 (professor's writing as self-employment income)

Dealers in commodities and options
IRC § 1402(i)

Real estate salesman and door-to-door salesman
IRC § 3508(a)
Rev. Rul. 85-63, 1985-1 CB 292

---

46 FILING YOUR RETURN

46.1 KEEPING TAX RECORDS
* IRS Publications 552

46.2 GETTING READY TO FILE YOUR RETURN
* IRS instructions to Forms 1040, 1040A, and 1040EZ

46.3 APPLYING FOR AN EXTENSION
IRC § 6081
Reg. § 1.6081-4
Reg. § 1.6081-1
Reg. § 1.6073-4

Timely mailing treated as timely filing
IRC § 7502(a)
* "To Be Safe in Sixth Circuit, Taxpayers Must Use Certified or Registered Mail to IRS," 84 Journal of Taxation 309 (May 1996)
* "Tax Filings Fall Through Cracks in the Mailbox Rule," G.E. Wittenburg, N.A. Oestreich, and J.E. Williamson, 56 Taxation for Accountants, 283 (May 1996)

Foreign postmarks
Paul J. Pekar, 113 TC No. 12

IRS-designated private delivery services
IRC § 7502(f), as amended by the 1996 Taxpayer Bill of Rights 2
Notice 99-41, 1999-35 IRB 325

Automatic four-month filing extension
IRC § 6081
Rev. Rul. 83-27, 83-1 CB 337
Temp. Reg. § 1.6081-4T (payment not required

but proper estimate must be made)

Extension for being out of the country
Notice 88-40, 1988-1 CB 526
International News Release 93-7, 4/12/93

IRS may terminate on 10 days' notice
Reg. § 1.6081-4(c)

Penalty for late payment—90% exception
IRC § 6651(a)(2)
Reg. § 301.6651-1(c)(3)

Extension of time to pay tax
IRC § 6161
Reg. § 1.616101

Still must pay interest
IRC § 6601(b)(1)

46.4 WHERE TO SEND YOUR RETURN
* IRS Publication 17
* IRS Instructions to Forms 1040, 1040A, or 1040EZ

46.5 ELECTRONIC FILING
IRS News Release IR-98-19, 3/12/98
IRS News Release IR-98-10, 2/19/98

46.6 CALLING THE IRS ABOUT YOUR REFUND
*IRS Publication 17
*IRS Instructions to Forms 1040, 1040A, or 1040EZ

46.7 CHOOSING A TAX RETURN PREPARER
* "Prudent Practitioners Guard Against Return Preparer Penalties," Susan A. Berson, 61 Taxation for Accountants 144 (Sept. 1998)
* "New Reasonable Basis Standard for Return Disclosure Likely to Be Troublesome," Paul M. Predmore, 80 Journal of Taxation 22 (January 1994)
* "Furnishing Advice May Subject Practitioners to Preparer Penalties," Sandra K. Miller, 50 Taxation for Accountants 102 (February 1993)
* "Conduct Required of Taxpayers and Preparers Is Not Well-Coordinated by Final Regs.," Chad Muller and Karen Hawkins, 72 Journal of Taxation 196 (April 1992)
* "Final Regulations on Return Preparers' Penalties: IRS Refused to Deal, Preparers' Fears Prove to Be Real/Penalty Roulette—Roll the Wheel/Who Knows How the Courts Will Feel?" Sheldon I. Banoff and Harvey L. Coustan, 70 Taxes 137 (March 1992)

$250 penalty for tax understatement due to unrealistic position
IRC § 6694(a)
Reg. § 1.6694-2 (a)

Disclosure avoids $250 penalty if position is not frivolous
IRC § 6694(a)(3)

$1,000 penalty for willful understatement of liability
IRC § 6694(b)
Reg. § 1.6694-3

Penalty for knowingly aiding in understatement of tax

Note: Paragraph numbers refer to Volume One. Items marked * *are research aids, not citations of authority; see "Key to Citations" on page 806.*

IRC § 6701

No penalty for failure to report estimated tax additions
Reg. § 1.6694-1(c)

Unable to sign
Rev. Proc. 79-7, 1979-2 CB 403

Failure to keep copy of return or list
IRC § 6107(b) (copy required)
IRC § 6695(d) (penalty)

Signing the return
IRC § 6695(b)

Furnish identification number
IRC § 6695(c)

Substantial entries on partner's return
Randall Goulding, 957 F.2d 1420 (7th Cir. 1992)

Keep record of employed preparers
IRC § 6060 (record requried)
Reg. § 1.6060-1
IRC § 6695(e) (penalty)

Negotiating client's refund check
IRC § 6695(f)
* Letter Ruling 8720021

Sale of business: retention of records required
Rev. Rul. 79-400, 1979-2 CB 403

Penalty for failure to list interest from Form 1099
Rev. Rul. 80-262, 1980-2 CB 375

Penalty for using wrong table
Rev. Rul. 80-263, 1980-2 CB 376

Penalty for not asking about entertainment records
Rev. Rul. 80-266, 1980-2 CB 378

Penalty for depositing refund checks
Rev. Rul. 80-35, 1980-2 CB 305

Software seller treated as preparer
Rev. Rul. 85-189, 1985-2 CB 341
IR-86-62 (5-5-86)

Computerized tax preparer service
Rev. Rul. 85-187, 1985-2 CB 338

---

47 How Tax Data Is Processed by the IRS

47.1 IRS Preliminary Review
* IRS Publication 1
* IRS Publication 594
* IRS Fact Sheet FS-97-21, September 1997 (methods of selecting returns for examination)

Mathematical or clerical error
IRC § 6213(b)(1) and (b)(2)
IRC § 6213(f)

Streamlined IRS collection and notice procedure
News Release IR 95-4 (1/18/95)

47.2 Information Returns Required by the IRS
IRC § 6041-6050N
Reg. § 1.6041-1 through 6

Tax-exempt interest must be reported on return
IRC § 6012(d)

Mortgage interest
IRC § 6050H

Real estate sales
IRC § 6045(e)
Announcement 87-39, 1987-18 IRB 49

Real estate sales exception
IRC § 6045(e), as amended by the Taxpayer Relief Act of 1997

Points
IRC § 6050H(b)(2)(c)

Abandonment and foreclosures
IRC § 6050J
Temp. Reg. § 1.6050J-1T

Partnerships
IRC § 6031

Tax-shelter registration number
IRC § 6111

List of investors
IRC § 6112

47.3 When the IRS Can Assess Additional Taxes
IRC § 6501(a) through (e)
Reg. § 301.6501(a)-1 through (h)-1
Leslie Robertson, 32 TCM 955 (1973)
* "Can the Three-Year Statute of Limitations Period Apply to Assessable Penalties?" John W. Schmehl, 68 J. Taxation 108 (Feb. 1988)

Unidentified check is a deposit, not a tax payment
Robert B. Risman, 100 TC 13 (1993)

Amended return following fraudulent return does not start limitations period
Ernest Bodaracco, 464 U.S. 386 (1984)

IRS has 60 days to assess tax on amended return
IRC § 6501(c)(7)

Seizure of state tax refunds
R.A. Ketcham, 99-2 USTC ¶50,796

Six-year limitations period for omitting 25% of gross income
IRC § 6501(e)(1)(A)
Stephen G. Colestock, 102 TC 12 (1994) (six-year statute applies to all items on return)

Streamlined IRS collection and notice procedure
News Release IR 95-4 (1/18/95)

47.4 Interest on Deficiencies
IRC § 6601
IRC § 6621

Same interest rate for deficiencies and refunds after 1998
IRC § 6621(a)(1)(B)

Quarterly rates after 1986
IRC § 6621(b)

Table of interest rates on overpayments and underpayments through 1999
Rev. Rul. 99-36, 1999-35 IRB

Quarterly interest rates based on short-term federal rate
Notice 88-59, 1988-1 CB 546

Interest runs from due date without extensions to date paid
IRC § 6601(a)
IRC § 6601(b)(1)

Deposit stops interest accrual
Rev. Proc. 82-51, 1982-2 CB 841

Interest and dividend information disclosed to government agencies
IRC § 6103(1)(7)

47.5 Tax Penalties
* "The Substantial Understatement, Negligence and Tax-Return Preparers' Penalties—An Overview," Kip Dellinger, 77 Taxes 41 (November 1999)
* "Reasonable Cause Can Be A Defense To Civil Penalties," Michael W. Dong, 58 Taxation for Accountants 139 (March 1997)
* "New Reasonable Basis Standard for Return Disclosure Likely to be Troublesome," Paul M. Predmore, 80 Journal of Taxation 22 (January 1994)
* "Will a Phobia of Tax Forms Exempt a Taxpayer from the Failure-to-File Penalty?" Terri Gutierrez, 72 Taxes 570 (September 1994)
* "Final Regulations on Accuracy-Related Penalties: Taxpayers Beware, the Feds Are Out There/ There's Danger in the Air—Be Aggressive If You Dare!" Sheldon I. Banoff, 70 Taxes 178 (March 1992)

Monthly penalty for late filing
IRC § 6651(a)(1)

No tax due, no late filing penalty
Christine Patronik-Holder, 100 TC 374 (1993) (acq. 1993-38 IRB 4)

Reasonable/not reasonable cause for failure to file
Elizabeth Gravett, 67 TCM 2651 (1994)
Douglas D. Kemmerer, 66 TCM 550 (1993)

Monthly penalty for late payment
IRC § 6651(a)(2)

Accuracy-related penalties for returns due after 1989
IRC § 6662, as amended by the Revenue Reconciliation Act of 1993
Reg. §1.662 (TD 8617 9/1/95)
Reg. § 1.664 (TD 8617 9/1/95)

To avoid negligence penalties, reasonable reliance
Herbert T. Cobey, Jr., 67 TCM 24 (1994)
Henery, 99-1 USTC ¶50,636

Negligence or disregard of rules or regulations
IRC § 6662(b)(1) and (c)
Reg. § 1.6662-3

Substantial understatement of tax
IRC § 6662(d)
Anthony J. Pasqualini, et al., 68 TCM 89 (1994)

Automatic filing extension invalid
Patrick Healey, 71 TCM 3148 (1996)

Reasonable basis required for disclosed position on return due after 1993
IRC § 6662(d)(2)(B)(ii)

Note: Paragraph numbers refer to Volume One. Items marked ˙ are research aids, not citations of authority; see "Key to Citations" on page 806.

Temp. Reg. § 1.6662-7T
Reg. § 1.6662-4
Proposed Regulation § 1.6664-4

Substantial valuation misstatement
IRC § 6662(e)
Reg. § 1.6662-5

Reasonable cause exception for accuracy-related penalties
IRC § 6664(c)
Reg. § 1.6664-4

Fraud penalty
IRC § 6663

Negligence penalty applies to entire underpayment: prior law
Asphalt Products Co. Inc., 482 U.S. 117 (1987)

Bad check
IRC § 6657
Reg. § 301.6657-1

Disclosure prevents penalties
Emmanuel Fellouzis, 95-1 USTC § 50,287

Criminal penalty for willful failure to pay or file
IRC § 7203

Criminal fraud and false statements
IRC § 7206

Criminal willful evasion
IRC § 7201

Information returns
IRC § 6721-6724

Failure to report Social Security number of dependents
IRC § 6724(d)(3)(D)

Failure to file partnership return
IRC § 6698

Substantial understatement
William Woods II, 91 TC 11 (1988)

Interest on penalties
IRC § 6601(e)(2)(A)

Higher interest on certain penalties
IRC § 6601(e)(2)(B)

Frivolous return penalty
IRC § 6702
Martin Bradley, 817 F.2d 1400 (9th Cir. 1987)

47.6 NOTIFY THE IRS OF ADDRESS CHANGES

Last known address rule for deficiency notices
Rev. Proc. 90-18, 1990-1 CB 491
Barbara Abeles, 91 TC 1019 (1988) (acq. 1989-31 IRB 4)
Nancy J. Bayer, 98 TC 19 (1991)

48 IRS TAX AUDITS

48.1 ODDS OF BEING AUDITED

Average itemized deductions
IRS Statistics of Income Bulletin, Volume 17, number 4 (Spring 1998)

48.2 TYPES OF AUDITS

*IRS Publication556
* "Successful Preparation and Negotiation May Reduce the Time and Breadth of an IRS Audit," Thomas C. Pearson and Dennis R. Schmidt, 40 Taxation for Accountants 234 (April 1988)
* "When Should Taxpayers Agree to Extend the Time That the Service Has to Examine a Return?" Martin A. Schainbaum, 16 Taxation for Lawyers 172 (Nov./Dec. 1987)

Time and place for audits
Temp. Reg. § 301.7605-1T

48.3 PREPARING FOR THE AUDIT

*IRS Publication 1
*"Forewarned is Forearmed at IRS Audits," Richard A. Carpenter, 60 Taxation for Accountants 154 (March 1998)

Notice of deficiency
IRC § 6212

Extension of confidentiality privilege to authorized practitioner
IRC § 7525, added by 1998 IRS Restructuring and Reform Act

Work product
Monroe Adlman, 68 F.3d 1495 (2d Cir. 1995)

Time and place for audits
Temp. Reg. § 301.7605-1T

Explanation of audit process
IRC § 7521(b)

Valuation dispute leads to a battle for supporting documents
Bradford C. Bernardo, 104 TC 677 (1995)

Lawyer-accountant privilege
Fredericks, 99-1 USTC ¶50,465, 4/16/99, amended on 5/18/99

48.4 HANDLING THE AUDIT

*IRS Publication 1

Representative handling your case
IRC § 7521(b)(2) and (c)

Transfer of records privileged
Street, Dist. Ct. VA 5/27/99

Time and place for audits
Temp. Reg. § 301.7605-1T

Recording IRS examination
IRC 7521(a)
Notice 89-51, 1989-1 CB 691

Tips for handling the audit
Gene Erekson, 70 F.3d 1153 (10th Cir., 1995)

48.5 AGREEING TO AUDIT CHANGES

* "Taxpayers' Rights to Refund Claims After Administrative Settlements With IRS," Herman Spence, III, 72 Journal of Taxation 290 (May 1990)

Waiver of restrictions on assessment
IRC § 6213(d)

48.6 DISPUTING THE AUDIT CHANGES

*IRS Publication 5
* "Amended Tax Court Rules Reflect New Juris-

diction and Goal of Increased Efficiency," F. Brook Voght, 73 Journal of Taxation 404 (Dec. 1990)

Petition to Tax Court
IRC § 6213
IRC § 741-7465

Small tax cases
IRC § 7422

Civil action for refund
IRC § 7422

Lien on commissions
Jefferson-Pilot Life Insurance Co., 37 F.3d 1495 (4th Cir., 1994)

Penalty for frivolous Tax Court action
IRC § 6673(a)(1)

Penalty on attorney for Tax Court delay
IRC § 6673(a)(2)

Appeals court penalty
IRC § 7482(c)(4)

IRS liberalizes offers-in-compromise policy
Internal Revenue Manual § 57(10)
News Release IR 93-45, (1993)

Refund suit allowed in Court of Federal Claims although interest and penalties were not paid
Sig Shore, 93-2 USTC ¶50,623

IRS can reopen an estate audit despite closing letter
Estate of Bommer, 69 TCM 2541 (1995)

IRS may abate interest charges
Reg. § 301.6404-2

48.7 RECOVERING COST OF A TAX DISPUTE

IRC § 7430, as amended by the 1998 IRS Restructuring and Reform Act for costs incurred after January 18, 1999

Exhausting administrative remedies
Reg. Sec. 301.7430-1

Substantially justified same as reasonableness test
Ronald Sokol, 92 TC 760 (1989)

Tax expertise does not support increased award
Walter J. Levy, 63 TCM 2927 (1992)
Robert T. Cozean, 109 TC 227 (1997)

Winning the dispute does not guarantee legal fees
Benjamin Harrison, 69 TCM 1969 (1995)

Legal fees disallowed
Walker B. Fite, 67 TCM 2794 (1994) (IRS position held justified)
Laura E. Austin, TC Memo 1997-157

Legal fee award for excessive IRS penalties
David Heasley, 967 F.2d 116 (5th Cir. 1992), rev'g 61 TCM 2503 (1991)

Penalty for bringing frivolous suit against the IRS
IRC 6673(b)(1)

IRS concession no guarantee of award
Ronald Sokol, 92 TC 760 (1989)

---

*Note: Paragraph numbers refer to Volume One. Items marked * are research aids, not citations of authority; see "Key to Citations" on page 806.*

Pre-1986 cases: IRS pre-litigation position considered
Comer Family Trust, 856 F.2d 775 (6th Cir. 1988)
Sylvia Sliva, 839 F.2d 602 (9th Cir. 1988)
David Kaufman, 758 F.2d 1 (1st Cir. 1985)
David Powell, 791 F.2d 385 (5th Cir. 1986)
Pre-1986 cases: Only IRS litigating position considered
Robert Baker, 83 TC 822 (1984), aff'd 787 F.2d 637 (D.C. Cir. 1986)
Eva Wickert, 842 F.2d 1005 (8th Cir. 1988)
Ewing and Thomas, P.A., 803 F.2d 613 (11th Cir. 1986)
Balanced Financial Management Inc., 769 F.2d 1440 (10th Cir. 1985)

Refund of third party's tax payment allowed
Lori Williams, 115 S. Ct. 1611 aff'g 24 F.3d 1143 (9th Cir. 1995)
Net worth limitation in recovery of legal fees
IRC § 7430(c)(4)(D)
Cases begun after Nov. 10, 1988 but before July 31, 1996
IRC 7430, as amended by Section 6239(a) of the 1988 Tax Act
Expenses of administrative proceedings after Nov. 10, 1988
IRC 7430(c)(2) and (c)(7)

48.8 SUING THE IRS FOR UNAUTHORIZED COLLECTION

IRC 7433, as amended by the 1998 IRS Restructuring and Reform Act
Prop. Reg. § 301.7433-1
Suing the IRS for improper nonrelease of lien
IRC 7432
Unauthorized IRS sales
Carole Marshall, 921 F. Supp. 641 (Dist. Ct. Minn. 1996)
Commissions paid to independent contractor subject to continuous wage levy
Jefferson-Pilot Life Insurance Co., 49 F.3d 1020 (4th Cir. 1995), aff'g 95-1 USTC § 50,263 (1994)

48.9 TAXPAYER BILL OF RIGHTS

IRS Restructuring and Reform Act of 1998
* "Taxpayers Remain Burdened Despite Shifted Burden of Proof," Lisa M. Ivancic and Richard E. Coppage, 62 Tax Strategies 284 (May 1999)
* "Restructuring and Reforming the IRS and the Code — Congress Takes a Quantum Leap," Gerald A. Kafka, 89 Journal of Taxation 133 (Sept. 1998)
* "Reformation of the Tax Collection Process — Cumulatively, a Giant Step," Gerald A. Kafka, 89 Journal of Taxation 207 (Oct. 1998)
Attorneys' fees
IRS § 7430(c), as amended by the 1998 IRS Restructuring and Reform Act
Taxpayer advocate
IRC § 7802(c)
New offer-in-compromise program
News Release IR-1999-30, 3/29/99
News Release IR-1999-64, 7/19/99
News Release IR-1999-76, 10/4/99
Installment agreement
IRC § 6159
IRC § 6159(c) (IRS must agree to installment arrangement in certain cases)
Representative handling your case
IRC § 7521(b)(2) and (c)
Recording IRS examination
IRC § 7521(a)

Notice 89-51, 1989-1 CB 691
Hardship relief order
IRC § 7811
Interest abatement
IRC § 6404(e)
Relying on erroneous IRS advice
IRC § 6404(f)
Reg. § 301.6404-3
Property exempt from levy
IRC § 6334, as amended by 1998 IRS Restructuring and Reform Act
Appealing erroneous lien
IRC § 6326
Reg. § 301.6326-1
Validity and priority of IRS lien
IRC § 6323
IRC § 6323(j) (IRS may withdraw public notice of lien and must advise creditors at request of taxpayer or National Taxpayer Advocate)
Bank holds account for 21 days
IRC § 6332(c)
Summonses
IRC § 7609(a)(13)
Qualified private carriers
IRC § 7502(f)
Disputed information returns
IRS Announcement 96-5, 1996-4 IRB 99
Interest-free period after notice and demand for payment
IRC § 6601(e)(3)
Annual reminder of delinquent account
IRC § 7524

49 FILING REFUND CLAIMS, AND AMENDED RETURNS

49.1 WHO SHOULD FILE A REFUND CLAIM

Filing for disabled persons
Rev. Proc. 99-21, 1997-17 IRB

49.2 WHEN TO FILE A REFUND CLAIM

Refund for overpayment
IRC § 6401
IRC § 6402
Reg. § 301.6401-1
Reg. § 301.6402-2(c) and -3
Three-year and two-year rule for filing refund claim
IRC 6511(a)
Tax Court refunds for delinquent filers
IRC § 6512 (b)(3), as amended by the Taxpayer Relief Act of 1997 (allowing three-year lookback period barred under 1996 Supreme Court Lundy decision, effective for refunds for tax years ending after 8/5/97)
Robert Lundy, 116 S. Ct. 647 (1996)
Suspension of limitations period during period of disability
IRC § 6511 (h)(1), added by 1998 IRS Restructuring and Reform Act (reverses effect of supreme court's Brockamp decision in certain cases)
Marian Brockamp, 117 S. Ct. 849 (1997)
Overpayment of estimated tax
Rev. Rul. 54-149, 1954-1 CB 159
Bad debt and worthless securities
IRC § 6511(d)(1)
Divorce and net operating loss carryback

Rev. Rul. 75-368, 1975-2 CB 480
Net operating loss carryback
IRC § 6511(d)(2)
Credit against future estimated tax liability
IRC § 6402(b)
Refund diversion for overdue child support
IRC § 6402(c)
Refund withheld if debt owed federal agency
IRC § 6402(d)
Extension for Armed Forces combat zone service
IRC § 7508
Payment with request for extension of time to file
Troy W. Ott, 98-1 USTC ¶50,331 (9th Cir. 1998)

49.3 JOINT REFUND CLAIMS

*IRS Publication 504

Carryback of net operating loss after divorce
Rev. Rul. 75-368, 1975-2 CB 480, modified by Rev. Rul. 80-6, 1980-1 CB 296

Refund withheld to pay spouse's past-due debts
IRC § 6402(c)
IRC § 6402(d)
Reg. § 301.6402-5
Temp. Reg. § 301.6402-6T

49.4 STATING THE REASONS FOR REFUND CLAIMS

Reg. § 301.6402-2(b)
Form 1040X

49.5 QUICK REFUND CLAIMS

IRC § 6411
Reg. § 1.6411-1(a)

Tax-shelter refunds
Rev. Proc. 84-84, 1984-2 CB 782

49.6 INTEREST PAID ON REFUNDS

IRC § 6611

Rate of interest on refund
IRC § 662(a)(1)(B), as amended by the 1998 IRS Restructuring and Reform Act

Interest from date of overpayment
Reg. § 301.6611-1(a)

Interest to 30 days before date of refund check
IRC § 6611(b)(2)

Interest on net operating loss carryback
IRC § 6611(f)
Reg. § 301.6611-1(e)

45-day rule for original returns
IRC § 6611(e)(1)

45-day rule for refund claims after 1994
IRC § 6611(e)(2), as amended by the Revenue Reconciliation Act of 1993

49.7 REFUNDS WITHHELD BY IRS

Rev. Proc. 84-84, 1984-2 CB 782

49.8 AMENDED RETURNS SHOWING ADDITIONAL TAX

Reg. § 301.6402-3(a)

Note: Paragraph numbers refer to Volume One. Items marked are research aids, not citations of authority; see "Key to Citations" on page 806.*

Practice Before the IRS

Because the IRS is unable to examine every return, it follows a policy of examining returns which, upon preliminary inspection, indicate the largest possible source of potential tax deficiency.

Returns are rated for audit according to a mathematical formula called the *discriminant function system* (DIF). Various weights are assigned to separate items on each tax return, thus permitting the ranking of returns for the greatest potential error. The specific factors entering into the DIF formula are not disclosed by the IRS.

The IRS releases manuals and other data explaining its internal operations. Knowledge of operating procedures and positions may provide you with a perspective on the overall techniques and strategies suggested to agents in dealing with taxpayers.

Some taxpayers have tried to force the IRS to disclose the statistical data used to establish audit criteria. After federal courts ordered the IRS to disclose this data, Congress passed a law allowing the IRS to refuse disclosure of the standards used to select returns for audit or the data used for determining such standards.

The IRS must clearly inform a taxpayer in IRS Publication 1, *Your Rights as a Taxpayer*, of the right to be represented by an accountant, attorney, or other tax professional. Once the taxpayer has chosen a representative, the IRS may not interview the taxpayer alone, unless consent is given. Together with the first letter of proposed tax deficiency, the IRS must give the taxpayer a clear and complete explanation of the administrative process from examination and appeals to the collection of taxes.

HOW RETURNS ARE EXAMINED
Preliminary Examination

Correspondence notices are used to correct the following types of obvious errors spotted at IRS Service Centers: medical expenses under the 7.5% adjusted gross income limitation; personal casualty and theft losses under the 10% adjusted gross income limitation; auto mileage rates for business transportation in excess of the IRS mileage allowance; and income on Form W-2 or Form 1099 incorrectly reported on a tax return. Taxpayers are advised by mail of the corrections and of additional tax due. The taxpayer may request an interview or submit additional information if he or she disagrees. Where the correction is made and additional tax is paid before the due date for filing the return, the taxpayer may avoid interest charges.

Where an underpayment of tax results from a mathematical or clerical error, the IRS may use a summary assessment procedure. However, the IRS must give the taxpayer an explanation of the error, and time to file a request for the abatement of the assessment. The IRS must honor that request (IRC §6213(b)(2)). It must then follow the normal deficiency procedures. These procedures are followed for the following types of mathematical and clerical errors: (1) arithmetic errors (addition, subtraction, multiplication, or division); (2) errors in transferring amounts on the tax forms; (3) missing schedules or forms; (4) incorrect use of any Treasury table; and (5) entries that exceed statutory limitations. Summary procedures also apply to the omission of a correct Social Security number by a taxpayer claiming personal exemptions, the dependent care tax credit, child tax credit, higher education credits, or the earned income credit (IRC §6213 (g) (2) (F), and (H) (I), and (J)).

Where an arithmetic error is made by an IRS representative who is helping a taxpayer prepare a return, the IRS may abate any interest due on the underpayment of tax for any period ending on or before the 30th day following the date of notice and demand for payment of the deficiency (IRC §6404(d)).

The IRS may abate interest charges attributable to IRS procedural or mechanical errors that unreasonably delay processing of a deficiency, such as delays resulting from the loss of records, IRS personnel transfers, or extended training, illness, or leave of IRS personnel (IRC §6404(e)(1)(A)). Interest is not eligible for abatement if delay is related to general administrative decisions including IRS work priorities, discretionary judgments, or decisions concerning the application of the tax laws. An abatement request is made on Form 843.

The Tax Court may review whether the IRS has abused its discretion in failing to abate interest if the taxpayer meets the net worth and size requirements for recovering attorneys' fees (IRC §6404(i)). An eligible taxpayer must file a petition and pay a $60 filing fee (unless hardship is shown); *see* Tax Court rule 281 for petition details.

Types of Personal Examinations

A specific examination of a tax return may be by correspondence, at a local IRS office, or at the taxpayer's place of business, office, or home. An examination at an IRS office or by correspondence is called a desk or office examination; an examination at a place of business or home is called a field examination. The complexity of the transactions reported on a return generally determines whether a return will be subject to an office or field examination.

An office examination is initiated by a letter of notification listing the items to be examined. The agent will ordinarily not go beyond these items. However, the agent may, in his or her discretion, extend an office examination to other items. A field examination may involve a review of the entire return.

A correspondence examination is used to question simple individual returns; it is a type of office examination handled entirely through correspondence. The taxpayer is asked to explain a particular item or to send supporting evidence. A correspondence examination may end up as an interview type of office examination or a field examination. Whether it does or not will depend on how satisfactory the answers to correspondence are and whether or not the answers indicate problems not appearing on the face of the return. If you feel that it is impractical to handle the examination through correspondence or that it places you at a disadvantage, request an office examination conference. Practitioners generally feel that the absence of personal contact and discussion is a disadvantage. The use of this type of examination is decreasing since the IRS has found that many taxpayers, especially those who do not use professional advisors, have been unable to adequately handle the questionnaires.

You may request a transfer of a case from an office examination to a field examination. Requests for transfers have been granted in cases of voluminous records or physical incapacity. A request will be denied if it is clear that you have no legitimate reason for the transfer.

A field examination may be shifted to the office of the taxpayer's representative if he or she has the client's records and it is more convenient to hold the examination there.

An individual taxpayer may appear at an examination in his or her own behalf, and a corporation may be represented by an officer. The preparer of a tax return may, if authorized, represent the client before an agent in connection with the return although the preparer is not enrolled to practice before the IRS. An attorney or CPA may also represent a taxpayer before the IRS.

If you represent a taxpayer, file a power of attorney, IRS Form 2848. Ask the IRS to send you all correspondence involving the examination. In your correspondence with the IRS, always reference the IRS code symbols found on the IRS's letter to you. Before the examination, review not only the return in question but also the records of prior examinations of the client's return. The agent has reviewed these records and will use them as a starting point for the present examination.

Restrictions on IRS Examinations of Books

The IRS may not make more than one examination of a taxpayer's books of accounts for any taxable period unless the taxpayer requests otherwise, or the IRS, after investigation, notifies the taxpayer in writing that an additional inspection is necessary (IRC §7605(b)). However, this restriction does not bar the IRS from examining public records or bank accounts. Nor does it bar examination of the books of a third party, such as the taxpayer's corporation, unless the identities of the taxpayer and his corporation are so inextricably that the examination of the books of one constitutes an examination of the books of the other.

A taxpayer may protest a second examination by refusing to give the agent access to his books. The IRS may then issue a summons. If the taxpayer still refuses access, the IRS may seek enforcement of the summons in district court. The taxpayer then has the opportunity at a hearing in the district court to show that a second examination is unnecessary.

The IRS tries to avoid examining the same items appearing on a taxpayer's returns for more than one year, such as the treatment of installment sale payments. Thus, where the taxpayer's return was examined in either of the two years prior to the current examination for the same items, and that examination resulted in no change in tax liability, the IRS will suspend the current examination, upon the taxpayer's notifying the appointment clerk or the examiner, pending a review of its files to determine whether the examination should proceed. If the IRS decides to proceed with the examination, the taxpayer has no recourse.

The IRS may not conduct audits based on financial status or "economic reality" unless there is a reasonable likelihood that income has not been reported (IRC§7602(e)).

Handwriting samples. The Supreme Court has ruled that the IRS can compel a taxpayer to furnish handwriting samples in the same manner as it can demand other physical evidence (*Harvey F. Euge*, 444 U.S. 707 (1980)).

Administrative Appeal Procedures Applicable to an Examined Return

It is important to follow IRS administrative appeal procedures to lay a basis for recovering from the IRS litigation costs and for shifting the burden of proof in a later noncriminal court case. If the IRS takes an unreasonable position at an audit and the dispute goes to court, you may not recover an award for litigation costs unless you have exhausted administrative remedies within the IRS (IRC § 7430(b)(1)).

Similarly you may not shift the burden of proof to the IRS, if you did not exhaust all adminstrative appeals. In tax litigation, there is a presumption in favor of the IRS's determination of tax liability. This requires a taxpayer to come forward with evidence to disprove the IRS's determinations by a "preponderance of the evidence." A taxpayer may in a court action shift the burden of proof to the IRS with respect to factual issues relevant in determining tax liability. However, before the burden is shifted, the taxpayer must show: (1) compliance with substantiation and record-keeping requirements imposed by the Code or IRS regulations; (2) cooperation with reasonable requests by the IRS for meetings, information, and access to witnesses, as well as exhaustion of all IRS adminstrative appeals (IRC § 7491).

How To Handle the Examination

Common sense rules of courtesy should be your guide in your contacts with the agent. Avoid personality clashes; they can only interfere with a speedy and fair resolution of the examination. However, be firm in your approach and, if the agent appears to be unreasonable, make it clear that, if necessary, you will go all the way to court to win your point. A vacillating approach may weaken your position in reaching a settlement.

Where a practitioner is handling the audit, the taxpayer should not be present during discussions with the agent. The taxpayer can add nothing to the discussion that the practitioner does not already know after becoming thoroughly acquainted with the return. The taxpayer's presence may damage the case by volunteering information harmful to his or her position.

In a field audit, the agent will want to review original books and records. If the agent also wants supporting secondary records, ask him or her to give you a list of needs, which you can then present as a unit.

Original records should not be taken out of your client's office; give *copies* of relevant records to the agent. Do not volunteer data. The agent will ask for any needed information. Try to provide an adequate area to work in.

After the review and before the report is prepared, the agent will discuss his or her findings and recommendations. At this stage, disputes generally involve questions of fact. The agent will readily use discretion in compromising issues of fact where, for example, there are inadequate primary records but there is other convincing evidence that the taxpayer has made a valid claim. As for conflicting interpretations of law, the agent will abide by well-defined IRS policy. The agent will not lean to an interpretation conflicting with or not covered by IRS policy. Compromises

involving open issues or conflicts between IRS and court positions are possible at a higher level conference in the Appeals office. Occasionally, a disputed point in an examination may be resolved by asking the IRS for technical advice.

In some instances, you may be asked by the agent to submit a legal memorandum. This may be a signal that the agent is not sure of the legal issues involved in your case and wants your help. You are not required to do this and may refuse where the memo might reveal more of your case than you would care to divulge. However, where the facts are not in dispute and you feel a clarification of the law might expedite the case, a memo may be advisable. Keep in mind that anything submitted to the agent becomes part of the record which will pass through the levels of IRS review.

Also be alert to the possibility that the agent may be developing a fraud issue, which may be evidenced by the appearance of another agent. If you suspect such a possibility, consider whether you should allow the agent to see further records that may be incriminating. Also consider contacting a practitioner experienced in tax fraud issues.

Your readiness to compromise will depend on the extent of the agent's examination and the amount of the proposed deficiency or refund. Sometimes an agent will pick up one point but fail to develop another that could lead to a substantial deficiency. Here, it may be tactically advisable to accept the proposal. Carrying the case beyond this point might lead to an opening of other items on the return.

If You Agree With the Examiner

When you agree to the agent's proposed changes, your client will be asked to sign a Form 870, "Waiver of Restrictions on Assessment and Collection of Deficiency in Tax and Acceptance of Overassessment," or other appropriate agreement form. When signed, it permits an immediate assessment of a deficiency. It is used in the District Director's office at any stage when an agreement is reached.

The only advantage in signing is to stop the running of interest on the tax deficiency within 30 days after the date the waiver is filed. In an overassessment, that is, where a refund is due, a signed waiver is merely an acknowledgment of the overassessment.

A signed Form 870 does not prevent the IRS from reopening the case to assess an additional deficiency. If on review the deficiency is increased, you will receive a revised Form 870. Your client can refuse to sign the form. The signed first form has the effect of stopping the interest on the original deficiency. As a matter of practice, however, waivers or acceptances ordinarily result in a closing of the case.

If your client signs a Form 870 after a formal deficiency notice (90-day letter) has been mailed, his or her right to appeal to the Tax Court is retained. But if Form 870 is signed before a deficiency notice has been mailed, your client loses the right to appeal to the Tax Court. Although an appeal to the Tax Court may not be made, a suit for a refund may still be filed unless your client agrees on the form not to seek a refund.

The payment of a tax before the deficiency notice is mailed is, in effect, a waiver of the restrictions on assessment and collection. If the payment satisfies your client's entire tax liability for that year, an appeal cannot be made to the Tax Court. The taxpayer's only recourse is to sue for a refund in either the District Court or U.S. Court of Federal Claims.

If a refund is due and a Form 870 is signed, you may file a protective refund claim. Generally, an agent will process the refund, but if he or she fails to do so or the review staff puts it aside for some reason and the limitation period expires, the refund will be lost. The refund claim will protect your client from such a mishap.

An Agreed Case Is Always Reviewed

Once a Form 870 is signed, the agent prepares the report, which is sent to a review group in the Examination Division of the District Director's office. While the agent's report is approved in most cases, do not assume that this review is a mere formality. Agreed cases receive closer review than unagreed cases. Once approved, an agreed case has, except for isolated cases, "reached the end of the line." A reviewer thus realizes that he or she has a greater responsibility in checking the agreed case than in an unagreed case where the facts and law may be reviewed several times as the case proceeds through administrative channels. The reviewer will check the following points:

Facts appearing in the agent's report and in the return filed by the taxpayer. The reviewer may find facts that the agent overlooked or emphasize facts that did not appear important to the agent.

Agent's interpretation and application of the Code's provisions to the facts in the case.

Agent's judgment. The taxpayer might not have substantiated all of the deductions claimed with primary evidence. But the agent allowed a portion of the deduction based on secondary evidence. The reviewer may question the judgment of the agent or believe that the agent was too lenient. The agent may try to justify his or her position, but if the reviewer and agent cannot agree, the chief reviewer will resolve the problem.

Other tax returns. Where an individual's return shows income from an estate, trust, or partnership, the reviewer will usually ask the agent to check the estate, trust, or partnership return, or to transfer the case to an agent who may be examining one of these returns.

Tax returns of prior tax years. The agent may be required to examine the facts on the prior returns. The inquiry may result in the development of new facts which may widen the scope of the audit. The number of ways in which a reviewer may develop new facts depends only on his or her ingenuity, experience, and zeal. Therefore, remember that even after an agreement is signed (Form 870), the agent may ask for additional facts, and confront you with new interpretations.

You will not be allowed to argue your case directly with the reviewer. But you may be sure that the agent will present your case in the best light if for no other reason than to justify his or her own judgment.

What To Do If You Disagree With the Agent

If you disagree with the agent at an office examination, the agent is required to explain the adjustments and available appeal rights. If you desire an immediate conference with the agent's supervisor, it will be granted if practicable. Otherwise, you will receive a report of the examination from the District Director and a 30-day letter providing the following alternatives: (1) You can agree to the proposed adjustments and sign an enclosed Form 870; (2) you can request an Appeals office conference by written protest or small case request; or (3) you may ignore the letter, in which case you will eventually receive a statutory notice of deficiency (90-day letter).

If you disagree with the agent at the field examination, he or she will prepare a complete examination report fully explaining the proposed adjustments. The agent will then send it to the district examination review staff for a technical and procedural review. If the review staff agrees with the agent, you will receive a 30-day letter, as in the case of the office examination. The 30-day letter is accompanied by a copy of the examination report and a detailed explanation of the available appeal procedures, with a request that you inform the District Director of your choice of action. You have the following alternatives:

1. Sign a Form 870 (which precludes appeal to the Tax Court);
2. Request an Appeals office conference by written protest or small case request;
3. Ignore the 30-day letter and wait for the statutory notice of deficiency (90-day letter); or
4. Pay the tax and file a claim for refund.

A 30-day letter is not required by the Code and, if the IRS wants to, it may dispense with it and send you the 90-day letter. The 30-day letter is merely an additional attempt by the IRS to settle the case without going to trial. If necessary, you may get additional time to file your protest or a small case request. However, if the limitation period for the assessment of tax is running out on the tax year in question, you will get neither a 30-day letter nor an extension unless you sign a waiver extending the limitation period.

Should You Ask for a Conference?

The answer lies in the nature of your disagreement with the auditing agent. You may feel his or her authority to accept proposals for settlement is too limited. You may believe the agent has overemphasized certain facts, or disregarded or failed to give proper weight to other facts. Perhaps he or she has misinterpreted applicable tax law or misapplied it to your case. The agent may even have ignored law that supports your claim.

The very existence of the conference procedure is in itself a recognition that your objection to the agent's decision may be right. If the IRS were convinced that the auditing agent was always correct, there would be no purpose to the conferences.

It is usually advisable to take your case to the Appeals Office. The chances of a settlement are favorable. Most cases are settled in conference. But before going ahead, consider these points:

1. When the IRS has an established policy regarding the disputed issue, taking a case further in the IRS usually gains nothing. All IRS personnel are bound by the same rules.
2. Interest continues to run. It does not stop unless you deposit money with the District Director.
3. The IRS will find out your position on all issues. If the case comes to trial, there can be no element of surprise.
4. The IRS can always find additional issues.

Appealing Your Case

You start an appeal by filing either a written protest or a small tax request.

A small tax request is generally limited to tax disputes of $25,000 or less. A small tax request is simply a letter asking for a review of the tax dispute and noting the changes to which you object and your reasons. However, *no* small case requests are allowed for tax disputes, of any amount involving partnerships, S Corporations, employee plans and exempt organizations.

A written protest requires much more detail and preparation than a small tax request.

There is no special form for the protest. The important thing is to include information and arguments that will present your case in the best light to the appeals officer.

Seven specific points must be included in the protest:

1. Taxpayer's name, address, and daytime telephone number.

2. Date and symbols on the 30-day letter transmitting the proposed adjustments.

3. Years covered and the amounts of tax liability in dispute for each year. List here only the amount of the proposed deficiency with which you disagree. This is often less than the entire proposed deficiency.

4. An itemized schedule of the agent's findings with which you disagree. Make sure you cover every item contested. Where more than one finding is involved, list each separately and number it.

5. State the facts supporting your position for each of the items named in (4). Use separate numbered paragraphs for each issue; make sure the number of each paragraph corresponds with the number of the item in (4) which it covers.

6. State the law on which you rely for each of the items listed in (4); use separate paragraphs, numbered to correspond with the items in (4).

7. A request for a hearing with the Appeals office. You must make such request in the protest. Otherwise, you will get no hearing and the case will be decided on the basis of what you submit as your protest.

The most important part of the protest is the presentation of your arguments. These you divide into three parts: (1) Give the arguments in summary form, numbered. (2) Provide a statement of facts covering the disputed items. (3) Develop each argument and support it by citations of authority.

Separate protests do not have to be filed if more than one tax year is involved. All the tax years covered in the 30-day letter may be covered in one protest.

An original and a copy of the protest must be filed.

Stress the equities of your case. A case that shows that a decision against you would be unfair may be stronger than one where you have the technicalities on your side.

Write the facts so that they can be understood. They should be clear and accurate. List them in the order in which they happened.

Do not omit the facts that seem to be against you. When explained, they may not be as detrimental to your case as they first appear.

Substantiate the facts with exhibits, affidavits, or any other proof.

Try to avoid unimportant facts which are not relevant to the issue. Make sure you understand the principles of law affecting any fact you state. Otherwise, the argument you will later make may be weak.

Discuss the issues in the order of their importance. Leave the least important for last. Say what and who is involved.

Write short descriptive headings before each issue. Repeat important facts if they help your argument.

Summarize your point and show how it applies to your case.

Sometimes a short quotation from a leading case is effective if you can relate the case to your facts.

Be sure that every case you cite stands for what you say it does.

Try to put yourself in the place of the conferee who is going to read the protest. Ask yourself what you would want to know in order to answer the questions, and then try to supply the information.

Take the time to write a well-organized, succinct, and interesting protest.

Consider the appearance of the letter. Give it eye appeal. Use side heads to break up solid pages of type. Sometimes graphs, photographs, charts, and other illustrations help make your point in an attractive manner.

How the protest is signed. Your client must certify, under penalty of perjury, that the statements of facts in the protest are true. Add the following signed statement to the protest: "Under penalties of perjury, I declare that I have examined the statement of facts presented in this protest and in any accompanying schedules and, to the best of my knowledge and belief, it is true, correct, and complete." If the taxpayer's representative submits the protest, a substitute declaration may be used, stating that the representative prepared the protest and indicating whether he or she personally knows that the statements of facts are true and correct. A power of attorney should be attached to the protest, if not previously filed.

You file the original and one duplicate copy of the protest with the District Director, who sends the protest along with your case to the Appeals office. No filing fee is necessary.

District Directors may have screening groups to review protests before they are sent to the Appeals office. If, after reading a protest, a reviewer believes that there is a basis for settlement, he or she will refer the case back to the Examination Division for settlement. For this reason, make sure that your protest presents your case well so that a reviewer can have a basis for such a decision.

How Your Disagreed Case Is Processed

Step 1 AGENT'S EXAMINATION	Step 2 REVIEW STAFF Examination Division	Step 3 APPEAL OFFICE CONFERENCE
If you do not agree to the adjustments, the agent will prepare his or her report and send it to the District Review Staff.	You receive a 30-day letter from the District Director. You may ask for an Appeals office conference or wait for a 90-day letter.	You appear before an appeals officer.

Step 4 REVIEW	Step 5 IN THE TAX COURT
You receive a 90-day letter from which you move for appeal as outlined in Step 5.	Before trial, you may have a chance to settle your case at a hearing with the Appeals office or District Counsel.

How the Appeals Office Operates

In the Appeals office, your case is assigned to an appeals officer. After he or she becomes acquainted with your case, the officer sets the time of the conference. If it is inconvenient, you may ask for another date or time. An immediate hearing may be granted if you have some unusual reason for it. The hearing may be held in a Regional Commissioner's office, a District Director's office, a local branch of the Service, or "on circuit" (appeals officers sometimes travel to outlying districts to save taxpayers the expense and time involved in a trip to a metropolitan area).

The Appeals office is separated functionally from the District Director's office. The major purpose of the separation is to provide an appellate procedure which, organizationally at least, will tend to produce free and unbiased opinions. An officer in the Appeals office is not responsible to the District Director who controls the Revenue Agent and his or her supervisor. Thus, the officer is less likely to be unduly influenced by the conclusions reached in that office and more likely to reach decisions objectively. The officer does not need, and does not seek, the approval of the Revenue Agent, Supervisor, or District Director for any decisions made.

When you protest the conclusions reached in the District Director's office, the entire case file is sent to the Appeals office, and the District Director's control over the case ceases.

A primary concern of the Appeals office is the status of the statute of limitations. If not much time is available, a District Director's office may not transmit a case to a regional Appeals office unless at least 120 days remain before the limitations period expires. As a condition to appellate review, a taxpayer may be asked to sign either a Form 872 (Consent to Extend the Time to Assess Tax) or a Form 872-A (Special Consent to Extend the Time to Assess Tax).

In the majority of cases, neither the agent nor any other representative of the District Director will attend your conference with the appeals officer. If, in a few situations, the agent does attend a conference, it will be at the invitation of the Appeals office and only for the purpose of establishing the facts. Since you are appealing from the recommendations of the agent, do not reargue the case with him or her. Your sole problem will be to convince the appeals officer. In all cases, however, you should remember that the officer has a copy of the agent's recommendations and confidential report, which you never see.

Cases which reach the Appeals office after the 90-day letter has been issued are known as "90-day cases." Conferences at this stage are not easily granted. You must generally show that you have not had a previous conference for reasons beyond your control, and there is a reasonable expectation that a settlement will be reached.

The settlement authority in the Appeals office is broader than in the Examination Division. The Appeals office may trade or split issues where substantial uncertainties exist either in law or in fact, or in both, as to the correct application of the law. They may also settle issues based on their judgment as to the hazards of litigation. The agents have no authority to consider litigation hazards. One explanation for the reluctance of district office personnel to close a case is that they realize there is another administrative step following theirs. If they have any doubts about the acceptability of a settlement proposal, they can resolve their doubts by recommending that the case be considered by the Appeals office. The appeals officer thinks in terms of the cost and possible result of extended litigation. Cases are generally settled on the "merit approach." That is, the merits of each issue are considered, regardless of the amount of tax involved. A second, less preferred method of settlement is on the basis of a flat sum or percentage of the dollars involved. This second method is limited in use and may not be used, for example, where an issue will recur in subsequent years or where the issue is present in other similar cases, unless they are all to be disposed of together upon the same basis.

Settlement authority of appeals officers may also depend on whether or not the issue is on an IRS appeals coordinated issue list. If the issue is on the list, the officer does not have independent settlement authority; he or she must submit the proposed settlement to a person within the regional office who is in charge of reviewing issues placed on the coordination list. If this person does not agree to the settlement, the appeals officer may present the dispute to an appeals director in the region for a decision. You will not be given the chance to argue your position at this stage because the appeal coordination list procedure is an internal administration measure through which the IRS attempts to provide a consistent national settlement policy on certain issues which involve large numbers of taxpayers.

How To Handle the Conference

The conference is held in an informal manner. No stenographic record is made. Testimony under oath is not taken. Your approach to the conference will vary, depending on whether your client wishes to settle, whether the issues in dispute are factual or legal, and how strong you feel your case is on a specific issue.

You can assume the conferee:

- **Has the agent's** recitation of the facts, opinions, and recommendations—all of which appear in a transmittal memo which you do not receive. He or she also has a record of the informal conference and copies of reports covering examinations of prior years.

- **Has read your protest** with your version of the facts and your arguments. He or she will read the cases you cite. When you cite a case, make sure that it is on point. If you cite it for the dicta incorporated in the opinion, indicate that fact. There is nothing more discouraging than wading through a case only to find that it is not on point. The appeals officer may well conclude that you do not understand the issue, that you think the conferee does not understand the issue, or that you believe the conferee is careless enough to accept citations without reading the cases. Such conclusions will affect you adversely.

- **Knows the strengths and weaknesses of your position** and what you would settle for. If your case is the type that should be settled, the appeals officer has thought of possible settlements. As a general proposition, an officer would rather settle cases than send them to the Tax Court. But rarely is he or she more anxious to settle than you are.

You may bring witnesses. However, do not plan on using witnesses unless they are absolutely necessary and you are sure they will not testify beyond your objectives. Instead, you may want to present their statements in affidavit form. Facts brought up for the first time will be referred back to the District Director's office for reconsideration.

Sufficient time is given to present your side of the case. Additional hearings are granted as needed.

An attorney may become aware that his or her client has no hope of winning but is stalling the date of actual payment of the deficiency by going through the various appellate procedures. This tactic violates IRS rules of practice and professional canons of ethics.

Does It Pay To Settle Your Tax Dispute with the IRS?

Here are some approaches followed by practitioners:

If you want rapid settlement of the dispute and cannot convince the IRS of your position, consider paying the deficiency—then suing for refund in the District Court or Court of Federal Claims. But first check the docket of the District Court where you will sue. Some District Courts are as overloaded as the Tax Court.

In a dispute involving a difference of opinion over the facts, accept a fair offer from the IRS. You may not do any better before the Tax Court. Where the IRS refuses to accept any settlement offer, you may take your case to court. You will have to wait for a hearing, but you stand a good chance of getting a better break.

In a complicated case or one involving a difficult point of law, the Tax Court is favored over the District Court. There is less risk of judicial misinterpretation of the tax law since the Tax Court judges are more familiar with the intricacies of the Code.

Where you have a question of fact and your position is appealing to the average person, pay the deficiency and then sue for a refund in the District Court where a jury will determine the facts. In the Tax Court, the facts are determined by judges who may be less sympathetic. You are not entitled to a jury trial in Tax Court. Your case is also decided by a judge if you pay the deficiency and sue for a refund in the Court of Federal Claims.

What Happens When You Propose a Settlement

Settlement proposals are generally made orally but more complicated proposals may be in writing. If your proposal is accepted, you are asked to sign either a Form 870 or 870-AD. Form 870 is signed for a settlement based on a complete agreement with the changes originally recommended by the agent. Where the IRS makes concessions in reaching a settlement in the Appeals office, a conditional consent, Form 870-AD, is signed. Form 870-AD contains pledges against reopening; the Form 870 does not. This means that once a Form 870-AD is executed, the IRS may not make an additional assessment. If Form 870 is executed, it acts as a waiver of restriction on assessment when received whereas Form 870-AD is not effective until it is signed by the Commissioner of Internal Revenue or her delegate.

Form 870-AD has been called an informal closing agreement. It is an agreement not to file a claim for refund, except for overassessments shown on the agreement form and amounts attributed to a net operating loss carry-back deduction. Similarly, the IRS agrees not to assert further deficiencies for the year in question, except where there is fraud, malfeasance, concealment, or misrepresentation of a material fact, an important mathematical error, an excessive tentative allowance of a net operating loss carryback or investment credit carryback, or deficiencies determined at a partnership-level audit or S corporation level audit.

The effect of an 870-AD is one-sided. The taxpayer agrees to an immediate assessment of the deficiency, whereas the IRS does not agree to pay an immediate refund as, for example, where the agreement covers two years, and one year involves an overassessment. It may, therefore, be advisable to file a protective claim for refund at the same time as the Form 870-AD is signed, or at least before the expiration of the refund period for the year in question. The refund claim should be accompanied by a letter explaining that the purpose of the claim is to protect the taxpayer against an unfavorable disposition of the waiver issue, and that the claim will be withdrawn upon the IRS' favorable action on the waiver.

Whether or not Form 870-AD is binding on the IRS and the taxpayer as a closing agreement has been litigated. The decisions present conflicting opinions on the issue.

Filing a Form 870-AD does not automatically stop the running of interest. Interest stops 30 days after the date the IRS accepts the form. In any event, the accumulation of interest can be avoided by prepaying the deficiency.

After Form 870-AD is signed, the appeals officer presents the report to a reviewing officer, such as an Associate Chief. If the official approves the proposed settlement, he or she will accept the agreement and the case is then ready for closing.

What if the settlement on review is rejected by the Associate Chief or other official? He or she will then discuss the case with the appeals officer. If the case remains unapproved, you may ask for a hearing before the reviewer who turned down the settlement.

What if you do not submit a settlement or the appeals officer rejects your proposal? The officer then prepares the report together with a proposed statutory notice of deficiency. This is sent to an Associate Chief or other official for review. If the official approves the report, the case is then reviewed by the Chief Appeals Officer. The statutory notice of deficiency is checked by the Regional Counsel. After final approval by both offices, a 90-day letter is then mailed to your client.

Cash Deposit Stops Interest Accrual on Deficiency While Retaining Appeal Rights

An individual who faces a potentially large interest charge on a tax deficiency may cut off the accrual of interest by making a cash deposit against an estimated deficiency. Before a deficiency notice is mailed, this may be done by identifying a payment as a "deposit in the nature of a cash bond." Interest stops running on the deposit as of the date it is received by the IRS. However, interest continues to accrue on accrued interest unless the deposit is large enough to cover the interest. If an agreement is not reached, and the deposit does not cover the proposed deficiency, the IRS will send a deficiency notice which may be appealed to the Tax Court. If you agree to the proposed deficiency, no deficiency notice is mailed and the deposit is applied to the deficiency. By paying the deficiency, you also lose the right to petition the Tax Court.

Details of making a cash bond deposit are in Rev. Proc. 84-58, 1984-2 CB 501.

The IRS claimed that under Rev. Proc. 84-58, a taxpayer could not designate a payment as interest and claim an interest deduction if the underlying tax had not been paid. However, the Tax Court disagreed and allowed an interest deduction to a taxpayer who, in response to a 1983 deficiency notice, calculated the accrued interest, mailed a check to the IRS for that amount, and requested that it be credited towards interest due (*Perkins*, 92 TC 749 (1989)). The IRS acquiesced in Perkins (IRB 1990-23, 4), but only because the IRS did not follow the procedures of Rev. Proc. 84-58. Under current law, claiming an interest deduction is no longer possible given the phaseout of the deduction for personal interest.

What To Do After Receiving a 90-Day Letter

Before the IRS can assess a deficiency, it must send by registered or certified mail a statutory notice of deficiency (IRC §6212(a)). This notice is called a "90-day letter." It gives your client the chance, within 90 days from the date of its mailing, to file a petition to the Tax Court of the United States. If the notice is mailed to an address outside of the United States, you are allowed 150 days. In the event the 90th or 150th day falls on a Saturday or Sunday, or on a legal holiday in the District of Columbia, you have until the next business day to file a petition with the Tax Court (IRC § 6213(a)).

The IRS must specifically note on deficiency notices when the 90-day period ends (IRC § 6213(a)).

Your client receives a 90-day letter at the end of the period allowed in the 30-day letter if he or she has not signed a Form 870 or filed a formal protest, or after an Appeals office conference. At the end of the 90 (or 150) days, the deficiency is assessed.

On receipt of the 90-day letter, you can do one of the following:

File a petition with the Tax Court. No assessment can be made until its decision (which includes all appeals) becomes final. For a timely Tax Court petition, the Tax Court must receive the petition no later than the 90th day after the IRS's mailing of the deficiency notice. A petition postmarked by the U.S. Post Office by the 90th day is considered timely even if received by the Tax Court after the 90th day.

A dated receipt from an IRS-approved private delivery service also qualifies under the "timely-mailing-is-timely-filing" rule. Specific services from the following companies have been approved: DHL Worldwide Express, Airborne Express, Federal Express, and United Parcel Service.

Do nothing and wait for the assessment of the deficiency. Sign the Form 870. This limits the interest on the deficiency. Your client can still take his or her case to the Tax Court, or pay the disputed deficiency and file a refund claim. When it is rejected, your client can sue for a refund in a Federal District Court or the U.S. Court of Federal Claims.

An assessment may only be made if a notice of deficiency is sent to the taxpayer's last known address. Generally, a taxpayer's address is the address shown on his most recently filed return.

For a deficiency involving a joint return, the 90-day letter is mailed as a single joint notice. So, where a husband and wife have separated, notify the IRS of their separate addresses to insure receipt of the notice. The IRS will then send a duplicate original of the joint notice to both the husband and wife.

The IRS may issue more than one 90-day letter for the same year before the earliest of the following events: (1) expiration of the assessment period; (2) execution of a final closing agreement or compromise; or (3) filing of a timely petition to the Tax Court.

When a 90-Day Letter Is Not Necessary

The 90-day letter is the only notice of deficiency which the law requires the IRS to send. Without it, you cannot petition the Tax Court to litigate your matter. However, there are situations in which the 90-day letter is not required and you have no recourse to the Tax Court.

1. A 90-day letter is not sent where a mathematical error has been made in your return. Taking an excessive credit on your tax liability for taxes withheld or for estimated taxes paid is considered a mathematical error.
2. A voluntary payment "paid as a tax or in respect of a tax" eliminates any deficiency, allowing the IRS to assess without the issuance of a 90-day letter.
3. An immediate assessment may be made without issuance of a 90-day letter whenever the IRS believes that assessment or collection will be jeopardized by delay. For example, if the IRS finds out that a taxpayer is leaving the country with all assets before paying his or her tax liability, it is not necessary to send a 90-day letter and then wait 90 days before assessment.
4. In the case of bankruptcy or receivership, an assessment may be made before a 90-day letter is sent.
5. If you sign a Form 870 before a 90-day letter is sent, you are not thereafter entitled to a 90-day letter.

Getting a Settlement After Filing a Petition with the Tax Court

You may still be able to get a settlement even after you have filed a petition in the Tax Court. If you have brought your case to the Tax Court without first appealing to the Appeals office for a conference to settle the dispute, you will be asked to discuss a settlement with the Appeals office. The District Counsel's office may refer your case to the Appeals office for settlement for up to six months if the deficiency is $10,000 or less, with a possible extension where a settlement is considered likely.

Even if you have filed a Tax Court petition after an unsuccessful conference in the Appeals office, your case will still be referred back to the Appeals office for settlement unless the Counsel determines that there is little likelihood of a settlement. The Appeals office may enter into a binding settlement. If the case is returned to the Counsel's office, it determines whether to settle or proceed to trial.

Post-Review Checkup

Each Regional Commissioner is charged with the responsibility of arranging the post-review check-up for his or her region. The reviews are general and determine:

- Quality and technical accuracy of examinations.
- Extent and degree of uniformity in the application of tax law and policy questions.
- Categories in which the most frequent procedural and technical errors are made in closed cases. (Closed cases are not reopened unless there is a substantial error or evidence of fraud or collusion.)

After the review, exception and advisory letters are sent to the District Director's offices advising them of cases that are to be reconsidered and of the types of error that will cause a reopening of cases.

To provide for nationwide uniformity, the National Office at Washington receives reports from each review office on those cases for which advisory and exception letters were issued. From these reports, a study is published and sent to the review offices in each region. In this way, a regional office gets the chance to compare its policies with the policies of other regions. If it finds that its policies differ from those applied throughout the country, it changes them to conform with policies of the other regions.

AUDIT RULES FOR PARTNERSHIPS

The IRS determines the tax treatment of partnership items at the partnership level in a unified administrative proceeding rather than in separate proceedings with the individual partners. All partnerships with more than 10 partners are subject to the rules. Partnerships with 10 or fewer partners, all of whom are individuals, C corporations, or estates of deceased partners are exempt, but may elect to have the rules apply (IRC § 6231(a)(1)(B)).

S corporations. For tax years beginning after 1996, S corporation shareholders are audited on a shareholder-by-shareholder basis. Shareholders must report S corporation items consistent with the treatment on the corporation's Form 1120S unless the shareholder identifies the inconsistency in a statement to the IRS (IRC § 6037(c)). Before 1997, a unified audit procedure similar to that of a partnership applied.

Partnership Audit Procedures and Judicial Review

The IRS generally may not audit individual partners but must bring proceedings at the partnership level. The IRS must conduct an administrative proceeding to challenge the partnership's treatment of income, deductions, or credit items (IRC § 6223). Notice of the proceeding is first given to a so-called "tax matters partner" (TMP). The TMP is a specially designated general partner or, in the absence of a designation, the general partner having the largest interest in partnership profits at the end of the taxable year involved (IRC §6231(a)(7)). Notice of the proceeding is given to the other partners (except for certain indirect partners) by the IRS and the TMP (IRC §6223). In partnerships with more than 100 partners, the IRS does not have to give separate notice to partners with less than a 1% interest, but a group of partners with an aggregate interest of at least 5% may designate one of such partners to receive notice from the IRS (IRC §6223(b)). All partners are entitled to participate in the partnership proceeding.

If the IRS enters into a settlement with some partners, similar settlement terms must be offered to all other partners (IRC §6224).

Within 90 days of the IRS final partnership administrative adjustment (FPAA), the TMP may petition the Tax Court for review. Other notice partners are given an additional 60 days to file a court petition if the TMP does not do so. An appeal from the FPAA may also be filed in a Federal District Court or the U.S. Court of Federal Claims if the petitioning partner first deposits with the IRS an amount equal to the tax that would be owed if the FPAA determination were sustained. A petition filed in the Tax Court takes precedence over petitions filed in other courts. The first Tax Court petition filed is heard; if other partners have also filed petitions, their cases will be dismissed. If no Tax Court petitions are filed, the first petition filed in a Federal District Court or the U.S. Court of Federal Claims takes precedence. Regardless of which petition takes precedence, all partners who hold an interest during the taxable year involved will be bound by the decision unless the statute of limitations with respect to that partner has run (IRC §6226).

Statute of Limitations Against Partners

To assess tax against a partner, the IRS must do so within three years following the later of the actual filing date or the due date for the partnership return (IRC §6229(a)). If the IRS and the TMP so agree, the limitations period may be extended for all partners. Extension agreements may also be made with each partner. If the partnership understates gross income by more than 25%, the limitations period increases to six years. If the partnership return is fraudulent, there is an unlimited limitations period for partners participating in the fraud and a six-year period for other partners. If the IRS mails notice of an FPAA to the TMP, the statute of limitations stops running until one year after a final court decision is made, or, if the FPAA is not appealed, the limitations period is extended until one year after the period for filing a petition for court review expires (IRC §6229(d)).

Refund Requests by Partners

Partners must make refund claims by filing a "request for administrative adjustment," or RAA (IRC §6227), on Form 8082. The RAA request must be filed within three years of the actual filing date of the partnership return or the due date for the return (without extensions), whichever is later. The IRS may decide to conduct a partnership proceeding in response to the refund request.

If an RAA on behalf of all the partners is filed by the TMP and the IRS has not allowed any part of it within six months of filing, the TMP may petition the Tax Court, a Federal District Court, or the U.S. Court of Federal Claims to uphold the claim. A court petition must be filed between six months and two years after the RAA was filed. It must also be filed before the IRS has notified the partners that it plans to conduct a partnership proceeding. If the IRS conducts a partnership proceeding and notice of an FPAA determination is given to the TMP, a subsequent court petition on the RAA is barred; the TMP must seek review of the FPAA. All partners may participate in a court proceeding related to an RAA (IRC §6228).

If an RAA is filed by a partner other than the TMP and the IRS does not allow any part of the request within six months, that partner may sue for a refund in a Federal District Court or the U.S. Court of Federal Claims; the suit must generally commence within two years of the filing of the RAA. Once a refund action is filed, the partner will not be bound by a subsequent FPAA or judicial review of an FPAA. If the partner is notified that the items in question are to be treated as nonpartnership items, the partner may sue for a refund within two years of the IRS notice (IRC §6228).

THE TIME LIMITS WITHIN WHICH THE IRS MUST ACT FOR ADDITIONAL TAXES

The Three-Year Rule

Generally, the IRS has three years after the date on which your tax return is filed to proceed against you (IRC §6501(a)). However, when you file a return before the due date, the period does not start from the filing date but from the day after the due date. To illustrate, instead of filing your last quarterly estimated tax payment on January 15, you file a final return on January 31. The limitation period on the final return begins the day after April 15, the date the final return is due, not on January 31, the date the return is filed.

To start the running of the statute of limitations, the District Director or your regional Service Center must receive your return. In any controversy concerning the statute, you must prove that you filed a return. If you fail to do this, there is no limit on the time during which the government may make an assessment against you. Similarly, filing a return containing insufficient information of your tax liability does not start the running of the statute.

What Is the Starting Date for the Limitation Period?

Amended return. The statute starts running when the original return was filed. For amended returns, the IRS has 60 days from the date of receipt to assess additional tax, even though the regular limitations period would expire before the end of the 60-day period (IRC §6501(c)(7)).

Incorrect return form. The statute starts running when you file (or from the due date), if the return has all of the information on which the correct tax liability can be figured.

Tax information on a form other than a return. The statute starts running when you file the information (or from the due date), if it contains the information on which your tax liability can be figured. If you claim you do not have to pay a tax, notify the IRS of your claim and the basis for it. A tentative return does not start the period running since it does not specifically state the items of gross income and deductions.

Improperly executed return. The statute starts running when the return is properly executed. Example: A corporate return must be signed by one of the corporation's officers. A return signed by an unauthorized person is not good, and the filing of such a return does not start the running of the statute.

Sometimes, a taxpayer or a group of taxpayers may operate as a trust or as a partnership without knowing that the organization under the tax law is really a corporation, and so must file a corporate return rather than a trust or partnership return. Even though a partnership or trust return is filed, this filing can be treated as the filing of a corporate return for purposes of starting the statute. To obtain this result, the taxpayer or taxpayers must prove that the determination of the trust or partnership status was made in good faith.

A similar rule covers a situation where a taxpayer, in good faith, determines that it is an exempt organization. In such cases, the filing of a return for an exempt organization starts the statute—even though it is later held to be a taxable corporation for that tax year.

There are several exceptions to the general rule that the filing of a return starts the running of the statutory period:

- Where a false or fraudulent return is filed with intent to evade tax, tax may be assessed at any time (IRC §6501(c)(1)). The Supreme Court has held (*Badaracco*, 464 U.S. 386 (1984)) that a later filing of an amended nonfraudulent return does not start the running of the three-year period of limitations.
- Where a willful attempt in any manner is made to defeat or evade the tax, tax may be assessed at any time (IRC §6501(c)(2)).
- Where a return is executed by the IRS (IRC §6501(b)(3)), the statute does not run with the making of the return.
- Where no return is filed (IRC §6501(c)(3)), the tax may be assessed at any time, but the subsequent filing of a nonfraudulent return starts the running of the three-year limitation period.

If More Than 25% of Gross Income Is Omitted

If you omit an amount which is more than 25% of the gross income shown on your return, the IRS may make an assessment within six years after the return is filed rather than three years (IRC §6501(e)(1)(A)). For example, on a 1999 return (filed on April 17, 2000), gross income of $50,000 is reported. But a $20,000 gain from the sale of a home has been omitted. In this case, the IRS has until April 17, 2006, to assess a deficiency on the 1999 return. The reason: The omitted $20,000 gain is more than 25% of the gross income reported on the return (25% of $50,000, or $12,500). However, if gross income is $100,000, the three-year statute applies rather than the six-year statute because the omission is not more than 25% of the reported gross income (25% of $100,000, or $25,000).

To apply the six-year statute, the IRS has the burden of proving that there is an omission and that it exceeds 25% of the reported gross income. If it fails to sustain its claim, the three-year statute applies. To be successful against such a claim, you must then show that the items were not omitted, for example, that the item was tax free or not taxable in the particular year, or that the IRS's valuation is incorrect. You cannot base your defense on a plea of an honest mistake or the use of an incorrect method of accounting, or that the omission was reduced to less than 25% by an amended return. The statute runs from the filing of the original return. It is not affected by the filing of an amended return.

In figuring gross income, *do not confuse the way income is reported on a tax return with the concept of gross income.* The tax return does not provide for the term *gross income*. For example, when reporting capi-

tal gains and losses, the net gain or loss is reported on a return. But this amount is not gross income. For purposes of computing the gross income omission, gross income would include the capital gains before they are reduced by either capital losses or by any capital gain deduction, or by both. Where you are in business, gross income means gross receipts, that is, the total amount received from the sale of goods or services unreduced by the cost of such goods or services. Gross income of a partner's share of partnership income means the partner's share of the partnership gross income, not partnership net income.

If you omit a questionable item from gross income, you may prevent an extension of the statute by adequately disclosing the facts of the omission. If the disclosure *adequately* tells the IRS of the nature and amount of the item omitted, that item will not be counted in determining whether there has been an omission of more than 25% of gross income.

The following are examples of adequate disclosure: (1) sales receipts were fully stated, but claimed deductions were excessive; (2) opening inventory was overstated, resulting in understated profits; (3) total income was revealed by a schedule attached to the return; and (4) total income was disclosed on the return, but was erroneously claimed as exempt.

There was not an adequate disclosure where the taxpayer liquidated his real estate corporation, attaching a statement of depreciation on the liquidation property, but failed to report gain realized on the liquidation.

When the Limitation Period May Be Reduced

To expedite the closings of income tax cases of estates and of liquidated corporations, the statutory period may be reduced to 18 months (IRC §6501(d)). After you have filed a return reporting income received by a decedent in his or her lifetime, an estate during administration, or a corporation being liquidated, send the Commissioner a letter specifically asking for a prompt assessment on the return in the following 18 months. Make this request after the return is filed, or it will not be effective. Send your letter in a separate envelope. Do not mail it with the return.

When the request is made for a corporation, you must notify the Commissioner that liquidation is contemplated within 18 months, begin the liquidation in good faith within that time, and complete the liquidation.

When you request a prompt assessment for an estate, also send evidence of your authority to act for the estate.

The receipt of the filing of the request for prompt assessment starts the 18-month period. The shortened limitation period will not apply if more than 25% of gross income is omitted from the return or if there is fraudulent or a willful attempt to evade tax.

Limitation Rules for Carryback

Net operating loss or capital loss carryback. A deficiency resulting from an erroneous carryback may be assessed within the statutory period of the loss year in which the carryback originated (IRC §6501(h)). For example, a net operating loss in 1999 carried back to 1997 results in a refund of $5,000; in an audit of the 1999 return, the carryback is reduced and it is determined that the refund should have been $1,000. The IRS has until April 17, 2003, to recover $4,000 of the refund attributed to the carryback to 1997.

Foreign tax credit carryback. A deficiency resulting from an improper carryback of the foreign tax credit may be assessed within one year after the period for assessment for the year producing the excess foreign tax credit (IRC §6501(i)).

Investment credit or other general business credit carryback. A deficiency resulting from an erroneous carryback may be assessed within the statutory period of the year producing the credit (IRC §6501(j)).

Where a quick refund was elected, the IRS has an extended time to audit the year to which the carryback was made (except in the case of foreign tax credit). The IRS may assess within the statutory period for the year which produced the carryback a tax deficiency not to exceed the amount of the refund or credit arising from the carryback (IRC §6501(k)).

EXAMPLES

1. A calendar year corporation files a quick refund claim for 1995 based on an unused investment credit of $50,000 arising in 1998 and receives a refund of $50,000. In 1999, the IRS reduces the unused investment credit from $50,000 to $30,000. As the corporation filed its 1998 return on March 15, 1999, the period for assessing the excess $20,000 does not expire until March 15, 2002.
2. Same facts as in Example 1, but the IRS also finds that the corporation owes $40,000 of additional tax for 1995 because of its failure to report certain income for that year. The IRS may assess on or before March 15, 2002, a deficiency not in excess of $30,000.

Other Limitation Rules for Married Couples

Where separate returns were originally filed and later a joint return is filed, the period of limitations must extend to at least one year after the time the joint return was actually filed. The regular limitation periods are figured from the following filing dates, but if those periods would expire before one year after the joint return was filed, then the period is extended until the end of that one year (IRC §6013(b)(3) and (b)(4)).

Where both spouses previously filed separate returns, the regular limitation period begins on the last date that either spouse could have filed a separate return.

Where only one spouse filed a return because the other had gross income under the requirement for filing a return, the regular limitation period begins on the last date the spouse who filed could have filed his or her return.

Where only one spouse filed a return, even though the other had gross income requiring the filing of a return, the regular limitation period begins when they file the joint return.

Limitation Periods Where Recognition of Gain Is Deferred

Where an involuntary conversion has occurred, tax on the gain may be deferred by investing the proceeds in similar property. When tax is deferred, the three-year period starts when the District Director is notified that the property has been replaced or that no replacement has been or will be made (IRC §1033(a)(2)(C)).

If a replacement is made before the beginning of the last year in which any part of the gain is received on the conversion, then the limitation period for any year before that year (during which the election to replace was in effect) ends when the limitation period for the last year ends (IRC §1033(a)(2)(D)).

Warning: Failure to notify the District Director prevents the statute from closing.

Where a principal residence was sold before May 7, 1997 and a new one is bought within two years before or after the sale, part or all of the gain may not be taxed. But the three-year period of limitations on assessments does not begin until the District Director is notified that a new residence has been bought, giving its cost, or that no residence has been bought within the time limit, or that there is no intention to buy a new residence within the time limit (IRC §1034(j)).

Waiving the Limitation Period

If a return is being examined during a time close to the expiration of the statutory period for assessing deficiencies, the IRS may ask for a waiver of the statute of limitations on a Form 872.

Should a Waiver Extending the Statute Be Signed?

A return is subject to a possible deficiency assessment for at least three years. An extension of the statute of limitations may be an advantage because the time to file refund claims is extended by the extension period plus six months. However, taxpayers generally regard an extension as a disadvantage. They assume the IRS, in making the request, has become suspicious of the return after a preliminary examination and a more thorough examination is likely to lead to a deficiency assessment.

It is advisable to agree to the consent if it is anticipated that disputed items may be amicably compromised.

If consent is refused, the statute of limitations binds both the taxpayer and the Commissioner. Neither party is obliged to agree to an extension.

What is the practical result of a refusal to consent? If the refusal comes:

- **Before the agent has had the opportunity to make an examination,** he or she can recommend the disallowance of every claimed deduction. A statutory notice of deficiency (90-day letter) can be sent on that basis. Since the refusal to an extension prevented any reasonable determination, the agent is forced to do this to protect the government's interest. The agent can, in appropriate cases, also recommend a jeopardy assessment. If a 90-day letter is issued without an audit, the IRS's action may be attacked as arbitrary.
- **Before the agent has completed the examination,** or before he or she has time to consider the merits of your position, the agent's recommendations will be based on the assumption that there is no merit to your position.
- **Before the Group Chief or in the Appeals office** and before either has an opportunity to consider the merits of your position, the agent's recommendations might be sustained.

In all of these situations, the case may have to go to court. There will be delay and expense. Give all these facts thought before you object to signing a Form 872.

You may stipulate on the Form 872 how long the statute of limitations is to be extended.

Form 872-A permits flexibility by extending the statute of limitations until 90 days after you are mailed a deficiency notice, or 90 days after you terminate or the IRS terminates the agreement (by filing Form 872-T).

An IRS request after 1999 that you agree to an extension of the limitations period for tax assessments must include a notice that you have the right to refuse an extension or limit an extension (IRC § 6501(c)(4)(B)).

When the Running of the Statute Is Suspended

The limitation period is automatically suspended in the following cases:

When a 90-day letter is sent, the period of limitations is automatically suspended for 150 days. (Technically, this includes the 90-day period during which the IRS cannot assess a deficiency, plus an additional 60 days.) However, if the period would have expired during the suspended period, the IRS cannot assess an additional deficiency after that time, though it can still assess the original deficiency (IRC §6503(a)(1)).

Note: Where a deficiency notice is sent to a corporation, the suspension covers not only the corporation but any other corporation with which it filed a consolidated return for the year covered by the notice (IRC §6503(a)(2)).

If you file a timely petition in the Tax Court, the limitation period is extended until the Tax Court decision (including all appeals) becomes final and for 60 days afterwards (IRC §6503(a)(1)).

Where a Title 11 bankruptcy case has commenced, a notice of deficiency may be mailed but assessment by the IRS is barred until 60 days after the termination of the case, or, if earlier, 60 days after the stay on assessment is lifted by the bankruptcy court (IRC §6503(h)).

Where there is a receivership, the period of limitation is suspended for the period beginning with the date of the institution of receivership proceedings until 30 days after the Commissioner in Washington is notified of the receivership. But the period cannot be extended for more than two years because of bankruptcy or receivership (IRC §6872).

Where assets are in the custody or control of a court, the period of limitation for collection after assesment is suspended for the period in which the assets are in the hands of the court and for six months thereafter (IRC §6503(b)).

When a taxpayer is out of the country for a continuous period of six months or more, the limitation period is suspended during the absence. The period of limitation does not expire until six months after he or she returns to the United States (IRC §6503(c)).

Where property of a third party is wrongfully seized by the government, the limitation period for collection after assesment is suspended. The suspension begins when the property is wrongfully seized or received and ends 30 days after the IRS determines the levy was wrongful and returns the property. If the third party goes to court, the suspension ends 30 days after entry of a final judgment that the levy was wrongful (IRC §6503(f)).

If the IRS is attempting to obtain records from a third party and a dispute over the records is not solved within six months after the IRS issues an administrative summons, the period is suspended until the issue is resolved. Further, if you intervene in a dispute between the IRS and the third-party record keeper, the limitation period is suspended from that date until the entire dispute is resolved (IRC §7609(e)).

Mitigating the Effect of the Limitation Period to Avoid Double Tax

Suppose income which should have been reported on a 1994 return is reported on a 1993 return. In 1998, after the limitation period for filing a refund claim for 1993 has expired, the IRS asserts a deficiency on this item for 1994. You take the case to the Tax Court, but it upholds the government's position.

Can you get a refund for the tax paid on this item in 1993 even though the statute has run out on that year?

The answer is yes. In this and in certain other cases, the limitation period is lifted, not only to prevent double taxation of the taxpayer, but also to protect the government in cases where an item of income might otherwise escape taxation (IRC §1311).

EXAMPLES

1. For the year 1994, a trustee, directed to accumulate trust income, made no distribution to the income beneficiary. So the entire trust income was taxed to the trust; the return was filed in 1995. In 1996, a state court held invalid the trust clause directing the accumulation. The trustee then filed a refund claim for the tax paid in 1995. In 1999, a federal court sustained the claim. Even though the limitation period for assessing a deficiency against the beneficiary for the year 1994 has expired, the government may assess a deficiency against him or her.

2. Jones and his son were partners. Each was entitled to one-half of partnership profits. On his 1994 return, Jones Sr. included the entire partnership profits. In 1998, he filed a refund claim for that portion of tax he paid on his son's share for the year 1994. In 1999, a Federal District Court approved the claim. The IRS then could assess a deficiency against the son for that portion of the 1994 profits on which he did not pay tax.

3. Howe assigned his salary in 1993 to his wife. She reported it on her return for the year. In 1996, the IRS assessed a deficiency against Howe for the omission of the salary in 1993. In 1998, the Tax Court upheld the IRS's position. Mrs. Howe was then entitled to a refund on the tax paid on his salary for 1993, even though the statute had expired for that year.

When a Closed Year May Be Reopened

Before the limitation period can be lifted, the taxpayer or the IRS must show there has been a final determination that requires an adjustment specifically covered by the relief statute. A final determination (IRC §1313(a)) may be a:

Closing agreement.   It is considered final when the agreement is approved.

Decision of the Tax Court or other competent court.   It is considered final at the end of the time allowed for taking an appeal if no appeal has been taken.

Final disposition of a refund claim.   It is considered final as to:

- *Allowed items* either on the date of the allowance of the refund or the credit or on the date of mailing a notice of disallowance. The last situation arises when the allowed items are offset by other items.
- *Disallowed items* when time for filing a refund suit expires (unless a suit is started before that time). This rule covers items disallowed in whole or in part, or items which have reduced a refund.
- *Informal agreement signed by the taxpayer and the IRS (Form 2259).*

As pointed out above, a closed year may be reopened for an adjustment only in limited cases (IRC §1312). The law allows for a reopening in the following seven situations (an eighth situation involving affiliated companies is not discussed here). In the first five situations, there must have been an inconsistent position.

1. The determination includes in gross income an item which was erroneously included in the taxpayer's gross income or in the gross income of a related taxpayer in a tax year that is now closed (IRC §1312(1)).

Example: Smith, who keeps his books on the cash basis, included in his 1994 return an item of accrued rent. In 1999, after the limitation period for 1994 has expired, the IRS claims that the rent was received in 1995, and asserts a deficiency. It is upheld by the Tax Court. Smith can get a refund for tax paid on the rent on his 1994 return.

2. The determination allows a deduction or a credit which was erroneously allowed to the taxpayer or to a related taxpayer in a tax year now closed (IRC §1312(2)).

Example: Green, on his 1997 return, claimed and was allowed a deduction for the destruction of his house by a fire. The fire actually occurred in 1998. After the end of the period of limitations for the assessment of a deficiency in 1997, Green files a refund claim for 1998 based upon a deduction for the casualty loss in that year. The refund claim is allowed for 1998, and the IRS may make an assessment for the deduction taken in 1997.

3. The determination excludes from gross income an item on which the taxpayer paid a tax or which was included in a filed return (whether or not he paid a tax on it). However, in a closed year, the item was erroneously excluded or omitted from the taxpayer's gross income or from the gross income of a related taxpayer (IRC §1312(3)(A)).

Example: Brown, in 1995, received under a contract payments which were included in his 1995 return. Thereafter, he filed a refund claim for 1995, asserting he was on the accrual basis, and since the payments had accrued in 1994, they should have been taxed then. The claim is allowed in 1999. An assessment may be made for 1994, even though the statute has run out on that year.

4. The determination involves the correction of a deduction or income item of an estate or a trust, or beneficiaries of either. An adjustment to the closed year is allowed where a determination requires the disallowance of an estate or trust deduction of an amount erroneously included in the income of a beneficiary or heir, or where a determination allows an estate or trust deduction for an amount that was erroneously omitted from income of a beneficiary or heir (IRC §1312(5)).

Example: A trustee claimed in a trust's return for 1994 a deduction for income distributed to the beneficiary. The beneficiary was taxed. In 1998, the IRS asserted a deficiency against the trust on the ground that the amount given to the beneficiary was corpus, not income. In 1999, the deficiency is sustained by the Tax Court. Even though the period for filing claims for a refund by the beneficiary for 1994 has expired, there still may be a refund.

5. The determination fixes the basis of property for any purpose, and the adjustment affects either an error made in the treatment of a transaction which the basis depends on or an error made in treating the transaction as one involving the basis in the first place (IRC §1312(7)). In applying this rule, the following two tests have to be met:

a. This error has to be either an erroneous:

- Inclusion in or omission from gross income;
- Recognition or nonrecognition of gain or loss;
- Deduction of an item that should have been charged to a capital account; or
- Charge to a capital account that should have been deducted from income.

b. Before any one of the above mistakes may be corrected in a closed year the taxpayer or the IRS must show that a determination was made in:

The taxpayer's case; or

A tax case of a party who received title to the property from the taxpayer after it was acquired in a transaction in which he or she treated improperly the basis of the property; or

A tax case of a party who received title from the taxpayer by gift after erroneously treating a transaction which affected the basis of the donated property. Note that the improperly treated transaction does not have to be the one in which the taxpayer acquired the property. Compare this with the above rule in which the transaction is required to be the one in which the party acquired title.

Example: In 1993, Stone transferred property which had cost him $5,000 to A Co. in exchange for an original issue of stock worth $10,000. On his 1993 return, he treated the exchange as tax free.

In 1999, A Co. claims that gain should have been recognized and so the property should have a $10,000 basis. If its argument is sustained, there can be no adjustment in the 1993 tax of A Co. There was no erroneous inclusion in or omission from its gross income or an erroneous recognition or nonrecognition of gain or loss. Nor was there an erroneous deduction of an item which should have been charged to a capital account or a charge to a capital account which should have been deducted from income. As for Stone, the determination did not affect his tax. Nor does the determination relate to a transaction in which he acquired the property. It applies to the property A Co. acquired.

In 1999, Stone sells stock and claims that since gain should have been recognized on the exchange in 1993, the basis for figuring gain or loss should be $10,000. If his claim is allowed, an adjustment will be made to his 1993 tax. The basis for computing gain on the sale depends on the 1993 transactions. Here there was an erroneous non-recognition of gain to Stone. He was the taxpayer for whom the determination was made.

Assume Stone does not sell the stock but gives it to his son, who later sells it and claims the $10,000 basis. A closing agreement sustains his claim. Stone's 1993 tax will be adjusted. The basis for computing gain or loss on the sale by his son depends on the 1993 transaction where there was an erroneous nonrecognition of gain. Stone is deemed the person who acquired title in the transaction and from whom his son derived title subsequent to the transaction.

6. The determination disallows a deduction or a credit which should have been allowed to, but was not allowed to, the taxpayer or to a related taxpayer in a tax year now closed (IRC §1312(4)).

Important: Here, a refund or a credit is allowed only if the deduction was not barred at the time the taxpayer first claimed it in writing, that is, where he or she files a return, a refund claim, or a petition to the Tax Court.

Example: Burns reports on the accrual basis. In 1995, he deducted an expense item which he paid in that year. (At the time he filed his 1995 return, the statute had not expired for 1994.) Later, the IRS claimed that the item should have been accrued in 1994. In 1999, the Tax Court disallows the deduction for 1995. But Burns can get an adjustment for 1994 even though it is now a closed year. The reason: When he took the 1995 deduction, 1994 was still an open year. (**Note:** Suppose the liability should have been accrued in 1990 instead of 1994—Burns could not get an adjustment if a refund or credit for the year 1990 was already barred when he took the deduction by error in 1995.)

7. The determination rejects an IRS deficiency for an item of income that the taxpayer did not report or pay tax for, *but* holds that the income should have been reported in the taxpayer's gross income or in the gross income of a related taxpayer in a different tax year now closed (IRC §1312(3)(B)).

Important: Here, an adjustment is allowed only if a deficiency assessment was not barred at the time the IRS first claimed, either in a deficiency notice or before the Tax Court, that the item should be reported for the tax year to which the determination relates.

Example: Jones reports on the accrual basis. In 1994, he did some work for A Co. He got paid in 1994 and 1995. He did not report the 1995 payment in either year. In 1996, the IRS sent him a deficiency notice for 1994, claiming he should have reported all the payments then. Jones contested the deficiency notice on the basis that in 1994 he had no accruable right to the payments received in 1995. In 1999, the Tax Court agrees with him. But the IRS can assess a deficiency for 1995, even though it is now a closed year. The reason: A deficiency assessment for 1995 was not barred at the time the deficiency notice for 1995 was sent.

Inconsistent Positions Requirement

In the first five situations previously discussed which allow the lifting of the statute of limitations, the taxpayer or the IRS must have maintained an inconsistent position in the determination (IRC §1311(b)(1)). This means that either party would benefit unfairly if the closed year was not reopened for an adjustment (either for a refund or an assessment of a deficiency). Here is how the rule works:

For an additional assessment: The taxpayer—not the IRS—must have maintained an inconsistent position.

Example: Adam, on his 1993 return, claimed and was allowed a deduction for a fire loss. In 1998, he filed a refund claim for the year 1994, claiming that the fire loss took place in 1994. The claim finally was allowed. Adam maintained a position inconsistent with the allowance of the deduction for 1993 by filing a refund claim for 1994 based on the same deduction. So the Commissioner may assert an additional assessment for 1993.

For a refund or credit: The Commissioner—not the taxpayer—must have maintained an inconsistent position.

Example: Evans, in his 1994 return, erroneously included an item of income which should have been reported on his 1995 return. After the limitation period for 1994 has expired, the Commissioner asserts a deficiency for the year 1995 on this item. The Tax Court sustains the deficiency. Here, the Commissioner has maintained an inconsistent position. She got Evans's tax for both 1994 and 1995. Evans may get a refund for the year 1994.

Related taxpayers. Where a taxpayer maintained an inconsistent position, a deficiency adjustment may not affect a related taxpayer unless his or her relationship to the taxpayer was maintained when the inconsistent position was taken in a return, in a refund claim, or in a Tax Court petition (IRC §1311(b)(3)). If a taxpayer does not hold an inconsistent position, then the relationship must be fixed at the time of the final determination. These rules do not apply to situation No. 7 above, which is not subject to the inconsistent position rule.

Only the following are considered "related taxpayers (IRC §1313(c))":

Husband and wife
Grantor and fiduciary
Grantor and beneficiary
Decedent and decedent's estate
Partners
Fiduciary and legatee, heir, or beneficiary
Members of an affiliated group of corporations

If the Statute Is Lifted

If there is an additional assessment for any of the adjustments described in the preceding pages, you will receive a statutory notice of deficiency (90-day letter). You can pay the deficiency and sue for a refund, or appeal to the Tax Court. The IRS must send a deficiency notice within one year from the date of the determination (IRC §1314(b)).

If entitled to a refund or credit, you must file a refund claim within one year from the date of the determination, unless the IRS makes the refund without a claim (IRC §1314(b)). If the claim is turned down, you can sue for a refund.

An informal agreement involving a closed year can be revoked or altered. When this happens, a later readjustment is treated in the same way as the original adjustment was treated.

Where the adjustment results in an additional assessment by the IRS, you will be charged with interest and penalties. Where the adjustment results in a refund to you, the IRS will pay interest. However, the adjustment which is made by lifting the statute of limitations is not affected by any item other than the one that is the subject of the adjustment.

FILING REFUND CLAIMS

The technical rules outlined in this chapter should be strictly observed. Often, refunds are denied because of a taxpayer's failure to comply with a technical rule. Moreover, the filing of a refund claim is the first step that must be taken before suing the government. Unless a proper claim has been filed, a suit will be dismissed.

But before you decide to file a refund claim, carefully review the return involved for accuracy. A refund claim opens the return to a thorough investigation in which the IRS may find errors that reduce or completely eliminate the refund claim, and may even lead to the assessment of a deficiency.

Some practitioners wait until the end of the limitation period to file refund claims. If the IRS, after the limitation period, finds a deficiency, it can use the deficiency only to offset the claimed refund.

If, in good faith, you accept an erroneous refund and the IRS later discovers its mistake, repay the refund promptly. Otherwise, you will be liable for interest.

File Timely Refund Claims

A refund claim for income taxes must meet a time limitation and a dollar limitation.

Time limitation. The claim must be filed within three years from the time the return was filed or two years from the time the tax was paid, whichever period ends later (IRC §6511(a)). For purposes of determining the three-year period, a return which is filed before the original due date is deemed to have been filed on the due date. For example, a return due on April 15 but filed April 1 is deemed filed on April 15, the due date. However, where an extension for filing is obtained, a return filed before the extended due date is deemed to have been filed on the actual date of filing and not on the extended due date. For example, if your due date for filing is April 15 but you get an extension to August 15 and actually file the return on August 1, your return is deemed to have been filed on August 1.

You may file a protective refund claim when a particular issue is being litigated by other taxpayers and you want to await the outcome. This type of claim is generally accompanied by a cover letter to the IRS explaining its nature. Filing the protective refund claim preserves your right to sue for a refund. A suit must be brought before the expiration of two years from the date that the District Director's notice of disallowance of your claim was mailed.

With agreement of the IRS, Form 907 may be used to extend the two-year period for filing suit. The two-year period may not be extended once it has run out.

File your refund claim with the IRS Service Center serving the district in which the tax was paid. Where circumstances have forced you to wait until the last minute to file a refund claim, make sure that you meet the filing deadline. This does not mean that the claim must be received on or before the last day of the statutory period. You can make a timely filing if you mail a claim so that the enclosing envelope is postmarked by the U.S. Postal Service on the last day of the statutory period. Where the claim is sent by registered mail, the registration date takes the place of the postmark date. To ensure a timely mailing, deliver the claim's mailing package to the Post Office for a postmark cancellation. Also, make certain that it is properly addressed and that the postage is prepaid. Failure to do this will invalidate the timely mailing. Another safe method of getting a timely filing is to deliver the claim at the District Director's office. Here, a receiving clerk will stamp the duplicate copy of the claim with the date of the filing.

IRS-designated private delivery services have the same status as the U.S. Postal Service under the "timely-mailing-is-timely-filing" rule.

Where the last day for filing falls on a Saturday, Sunday, or legal holiday, a timely filing is made if the return is filed or postmarked on the next work day. A legal holiday includes a legal holiday in the District of Columbia, as well as a legal holiday in the state in which you have to file the claim.

Example: The last day for filing a refund claim falls on a Saturday. You can make a timely filing by delivering the claim at the District Director's office on Monday, or by mailing the claim to the Service Center so that it is postmarked on or before Monday.

You may file a protective claim when the statutory period is about to expire. It may omit facts or grounds, but it must be amended with the complete data and grounds before it is rejected by the IRS.

Disability suspends limitations period for refund claims. The statute of limitations is suspended for refund claims made during any period in which a person is unable to manage financial affairs because of a physical or mental impairment that may be expected to result in death or to last for a period of not less than 12 months (IRC § 6511(h)). This rule does not apply, however, if a party is authorized to act on the disabled person's behalf in financial matters. The suspension applies to disabilities existing before as well as on or after July 22, 1998, but only if the regular three-year statute of limitations period for filing a refund claim had not expired as of July 22, 1998.

Dollar limitation. The amount of the refund is limited to the amount of tax paid within the three-year period (plus any extension of time for filing) preceding the filing of the claim, or, if the claim is not filed within the three-year period, to the amount of tax paid within the two-year period preceding the filing of the claim (IRC §6511(b)(2)). A taxpayer has no absolute right to the refund of an overpayment. The Commissioner may credit the amount of an overpayment against any tax liability of the taxpayer.

Example: Smith's 1996 return is due on April 15, 1997. He obtains an extension for filing until August 15, 1997. His return is actually filed on August 4, 1997, and he remits a check with his return for a tax liability of $2,000. On July 15, 1999, Smith files a claim for a refund for $1,000 on his 1996 return. The claim is timely filed since he meets the time limitation (within three years of the actual date of filing, August 4, 1997) and the amount limitation (tax paid within three years of filing of the return).

All estimated taxes and taxes withheld by an employer are deemed to have been paid on the original due date of the return. For example, your return was due on April 15, 1997, but because of an extension you filed the return on August 3, 1997. Any estimated tax or withholding tax paid before April 15, 1997, is deemed paid on April 15, not August 3. Now suppose you file a claim for a refund of a portion of the estimated or withholding tax on July 13, 2000. The claim is timely, even though the estimated or withholding tax is deemed paid on April 15, 1997, or more than three years prior to the claim for refund. You meet the time limitation since the claim is filed within three years of the date the return was filed, August 3, 1997. Also, the dollar limitation is met since the claim is filed within three years, *plus any extensions of time for filing the return,* of the date of payment of estimated or withholding tax, April 15, 1997.

If no return was filed, the refund claim must be made within two years from the time the tax was paid, and the amount of refund cannot be more than the tax paid during the two years immediately preceding the filing of the claim.

When you agree with the IRS to extend the time during which it can assess your tax, you may file a refund claim during this extended period plus an additional six months afterwards (IRC §6511(c)). A refund made during this time includes the refund you would have received if you had filed a claim at the time the extension was signed, plus the tax paid after the agreement was signed, but before you filed your claim (IRC §6511(c)(2)). These extension period rules do not apply to refunds of estate taxes. Where your claim is filed more than six months after the end of the extended period, the refunded amount cannot be more than the tax paid during the two years before the filing of the claim (IRC §6511 (c)(3)(B)).

Example: A 1995 return, filed on April 15, 1996, is under audit. In January 1999, an agreement is made to extend the statutory period of assessment to July 7, 2000. But for this extension, the period during which a refund claim may be filed would have closed on April 15, 1999. With the extension, you now have until January 7, 2001, to file a refund claim on your 1995 return.

Other limitation periods for filing a claim for refund are: (1) You have three years for claiming a refund of estate and gift taxes paid by the regular due date. (2) If you file a claim for a failure to take a bad debt deduction or worthless security deduction, you have seven years from the due date of your return. Here, all you get back is the tax related to the bad debt or worthless security deduction.

Refund lookback period for nonfilers. If no return is filed, a refund claim must be made within two years from when the tax was paid, and the amount of the refund cannot exceed the tax paid during the two years immediately preceding the filing of the claim (Reg. §301.6511(b)-1(b)(1)(iii)).

Under pre-1997 law, the Supreme Court held that if a refund claim was not filed as of the date of the deficiency notice, the Tax Court could only award a refund for taxes paid in the two years preceding the deficiency notice; the rule allowing a refund for taxes paid in the prior three-year period did not apply. Thus, if the IRS deficiency notice was mailed more than two years after the due date of the return, no refund at all could be obtained in the Tax Court for overwithheld taxes, which are deemed to have been paid on the return due date (*Lundy*, 116 S.Ct. 647 (1996)). Under current law, if a nonfiler receives an IRS deficiency notice in the third year after the return due date, a refund may be obtained in the Tax Court for a tax year ending after August 5, 1997, for taxes paid within the three years preceding the date of the deficiency notice (IRC § 6512(b)(3)).

What Refund Form to Use

Refund claims should be filed on Form 1040X (for an individual who originally filed on Form 1040, Form 1040A, or Form 1040EZ) or on Form 1120X (for a corporation which filed Form 1120). Where an income tax form other than Form 1040, Form 1040A, Form 1040EZ, or Form 1120 was filed, a refund claim is generally made on an amended return. However, a partner must use Form 8082 to make a refund claim in the form of a request for administrative adjustment (RAA) of partnership items. Form 843 may be used for claiming refunds for estate, gift, and employment taxes or certain excise taxes.

To correct an error on a return filed before its due date, you can file a corrected return on or before its due date. This return is not considered an amended return. However, a corrected return filed after the due date is an amended return and acts as a refund claim.

Letters to the IRS are usually held by the courts as not satisfying the requirements for an adequate refund claim.

Overwithheld taxes. You need not file a formal claim for overpayment of personal income tax resulting from excessive withholding of taxes on wages or excessive estimated tax payments. In these two cases, a tax return requesting a refund of the overpayment acts as a claim for refund. But there is one exception. On the death of an individual who has overpaid tax, the administrator or executor of the estate files a refund claim on Form 1310.

Generally, refunds for excessive withholding or estimating of tax are made soon after a tax return is filed. However, a return may be subject to a "pre-refund" audit, especially where the income shown on the return is less than $10,000 or there are large deductions or many exemptions that require substantiation.

Preparing Your Refund Claim

The most important part of a refund claim is stating the "reasons" for the refund. A general claim where you just note an overpayment, without supporting facts and grounds, is not sufficient. If a claim is denied by the IRS, it may become the basis of a court suit. If you have not stated all the grounds, you may not be allowed to show them in court. The courts have limited taxpayers to the exact claim shown on the form. Make a full claim and show:

- All the facts that support the claim. You may attach to the form as much evidence as is helpful. Be sure your facts are simply and fully stated.
- All the grounds for the claim. You may hedge if you are uncertain about the exact grounds; alternate and even inconsistent grounds may be given. For example:

   The loss was incurred from an embezzlement; if not, it was incurred from a bad debt.

   The gain from the sale is entitled to capital gain treatment as the property sold was a capital asset; if not, it was depreciable property used in business.

   The loss was due to a loss on the acquisition of real estate and from a partial bad debt (where the claim arose from the extinguishing of a mortgage by a deed in lieu of a foreclosure).

While it is necessary to be complete and precise in specifying the facts and reasons for your claim, you are not required to present your evidence; you must merely inform the IRS of the basis for your claim.

To protect against your understating the amount of your claim, it may be advisable to preface the claim with this phrase: *"The following or such greater amounts as may be legally refunded."* However, neither this nor any other "protective clause" will allow you to support your refund claim on grounds other than those mentioned in the original claim or in amendments made before the period of limitations has expired.

A separate claim must be made for each year in which a refund is claimed. It must be made in duplicate and signed under oath by the taxpayer or the duly authorized agent. If an agent signs, he or she must attach to the claim evidence of authority. If the claim is based on a joint return, it must be signed by both spouses.

A refund claim filed before there is an overpayment is invalid, unless the IRS waives the defect.

When you file a petition to the Tax Court, thus giving that court jurisdiction over your case, you may no longer file a refund claim for any part of the tax for the taxable year in question.

Amending the Refund Claim

You may generally amend your refund claim before the occurrence of either of the following events: (1) expiration of the period for filing the original claim (generally two years after paying the tax or three years after filing the return, whichever is later), and (2) final action taken by the IRS on the refund claim. After the expiration of the time limitation, you may not raise new issues or grounds in an amended refund claim, even though the original claim was timely.

Regardless of the time limitations above, file your amended claim immediately upon discovering the need for the amendment. Make certain that your amended claim meets all the technical standards discussed in the previous paragraphs.

Filing an Informal Claim

There is no advantage in filing an informal claim for refund. An informal claim must meet the same requirements as a formal claim made on the official IRS form (Form 1040X, Form 1120X, or Form 843). Although some informal claims have been allowed, many more have been denied and have not been permitted to be the basis of refund suits. For example, you may not base a refund suit on an informal claim that is limited to a:

- Letter suggesting a change in tax computation;
- Request for a ruling stating the facts and grounds for a refund; or
- Sworn statement which states the facts and grounds for a refund but does not include a demand for one.

Refunds based on informal claims have been allowed where an informal claim was accompanied by a brief that gave the basis of the claim or where, as a result of a conference, letters and memoranda stating the taxpayer's position were filed and a general claim referring to these papers was later filed.

Getting a Partial Refund in a Contested Case

The IRS, in three situations, may allow partial refunds in cases where contested issues still remain to be settled.

1. Two or more refund issues where some issues are settled and others are still contested. Here, a refund may be allowed on the settled issues.

   Example: You file a refund claim based on two issues. The first one, which would result in a $1,000 refund, is settled. The second one, which would result in a $500 refund, is contested. The IRS may give you a partial refund of $1,000.

2. Two or more issues where some issues will result in a refund and the others in a deficiency, but the overall netting results in a refund.

Example: A case involves a refund issue which is not contested and a deficiency issue which is contested. The allowance of the refund issue would result in a net overassessment of $5,000 after offsetting the deficiency issue. A $5,000 refund may be allowed, even though the contested issue is still pending.

3. Two or more years are under examination. In one year, there is a contested proposed deficiency. In the other year, there is an agreement on an overassessment which is greater than the proposed deficiency.

Example: For year 1999, the IRS proposes a deficiency of $4,000 which you contest. But for 2000, the IRS agrees that it owes you a refund of $7,000. A partial refund of not more than $3,000 may be made.

Note: The IRS will not give partial refunds in cases where there may be an overall deficiency, even though there is no dispute on the tax refunding issue.

If the refund differs from the amount you sought, you usually get a notice of adjustment explaining the difference before receiving the refund. But sometimes the refund is received without prior explanation. In that case, the IRS recommends this action: If the refund is smaller than you claimed, cash the check and write to your IRS Service Center asking why the refund was less than the amount claimed. If the refund exceeds your claim, return the check to the Service Center with a request for an explanation.

After a Refund Claim Is Filed

No matter how small a refund claim is, it is thoroughly scrutinized by the Examination Division of the District Director's office.

The examination procedure is like the one used in examining your return. It provides for an agent's examination in a desk examination or in the field, and if the agent disputes your claim you may ask for a conference at a higher level. If you cannot settle your case at a conference, you may sue for a refund in a Federal District Court or in the U.S. Court of Federal Claims.

If your claim is finally turned down, you are notified by registered mail. A disallowed claim may not be amended. Sometimes the IRS will reconsider a denied claim. But this reopening cannot extend the time in which you can sue for a refund. Of course, you may file a new claim so long as the limitation period within which a claim may be filed has not expired, but it must be on new grounds.

If a claim is allowed, you receive a Certificate of Overassessment. Check it for accuracy. The IRS does not have to pay interest for the period *after* the filing of the claim if the refund is paid by the 45th day after the claim is filed. If the refund is not paid within the 45-day period, interest is calculated from the date of overpayment to a date preceding the date of the check by no more than 30 days (IRC §6611 (e)(2)).

Before the check is mailed, the District Director's office investigates to see that no taxes are owed by the taxpayer for other years. If the taxpayer's record is clear, the check is mailed. If not, the check is held up until payment of the taxes, or it is credited against the outstanding balance.

Refunds in Excess of One Million Dollars Checked by Congress

A tax refund or credit over $1,000,000 may not be made until 30 days after a report is made to Congress's Joint Committee on Taxation (IRC §6405). This provision of the law does not apply to refunds or credits resulting from tentative carryback adjustments. Where the refund claim is for the prior taxable year under the special disaster area loss election (IRC §165(i)), the IRS has discretion to allow the refund without regard to the 30-day rule, and to make a later report to the

Joint Committee. These cases do not require greater documentation and are not subject to closer examination than regular cases. The right to appeal within the IRS is the same as in other cases. If a protest is not made and no Tax Court petition is filed, the report to the Joint Committee will be prepared by regional specialists in the Examination Division, called Joint Committee Coordinators. If a protest is made, the report is prepared either by an appeals officer or counsel attorney. The report contains:

The name of the person to whom the refund or credit is to be made;
The amount of the refund or credit;
A summary of the facts of the case; and
The decision of the Commissioner.

Quick Refund for Carryback of Loss or Unused Credit

You may file an application for a tentative carryback adjustment of prior years' taxes due to a carryback of net operating loss, unused general business credit, corporate capital loss, or a previously reported income item under claim of right. If accepted, you may receive a quick refund without extensive audit procedures (IRC §6411).

The application, on Form 1045 (Form 1139 for corporations), must be filed within 12 months from the end of the taxable year in which the loss or unused credit occurs. The IRS must act on your application within 90 days of filing or 90 days from the last day of the month in which your return is due, whichever is later. In the case of a quick refund based on a claim of right under IRC §1341(b)(1), the IRS must act within 90 days from the date on which the application is filed or the date of overpayment (the last day for the payment of tax for the year in which a deduction is allowed for the restoration of income held under a claim of right), whichever is later.

The IRS may refuse your application if there are computational errors or material omissions which cannot be corrected within the 90-day period. Further, quick refund claims attributable to questionable tax-shelter losses may be withheld by the IRS. If the IRS determines that a carried back net operating loss is "highly likely" the result of a gross misvaluation or false or fraudulent tax-shelter promotion (under IRC §6700), the IRS may reduce the refund to take into account the improper loss (see Revenue Ruling 84-175, 1984-2 CB 296).

The application does not act as a claim for refund. You may file a separate claim for refund before, at the same time, or after you file your application.

Even though the IRS allows the carryback adjustments according to your application and refunds prior taxes to you, it is not barred from later assessing a deficiency. The purpose of the quick refund procedure is to give you cash immediately when you most likely need it.

HOW TO ARRANGE CLOSING AGREEMENTS AND COMPROMISES

A closing agreement may be used to fix the final tax liability of a taxable period or to determine the tax consequences of specific items without settling the final tax liability of that period (IRC §7121).

A closing agreement is the only statutorily authorized method for entering into an agreement binding on both the service and a taxpayer. Section 7121 permits but does not require the IRS to enter into a closing agreement. As a result, the IRS has the discretion to decide whether and under what conditions a closing agreement is executed.

You may want a closing agreement, even though no tax is due for the period to which the agreement relates. You may enter into a series of agreements relating to the tax liability of a single period. To cover these and other situations, the IRS provides the following closing agreement forms:

Form 866, which covers liability for any past period.

Form 906, which closes specific items of tax liability for either past, current, or future periods.

Procedures for entering into closing agreements are also detailed in IRS Revenue Procedure 68-16, 1968-1 CB 770.

Before entering into a closing agreement, make sure that you understand all of its consequences. After both you and the IRS sign, you cannot change your position. A closing agreement is final on the matter expressly stated in the agreement, unless there is a showing of fraud, malfeasance, or misrepresentation of a material fact. It cannot be modified, set aside, or disregarded in a later suit, action, or proceeding.

Why Use a Closing Agreement?

The main object of a closing agreement is to protect the individual against the reopening of an agreed matter at some later date by the IRS. It also stops an individual from suing or filing other claims for refund. A closing agreement also may be used to fix tax liability for a year barred or arguably barred by the statute of limitations.

You may want a closing agreement for recurring transactions. Cost, fair market value, or adjusted basis as of a given date in the past may be established.

Establishing tax liability may facilitate a transaction such as the sale of stock.

A corporation in the process of liquidation or dissolution may want an agreement to wind up its affairs.

In estate tax proceedings, a closing agreement can assure the fiduciary that the estate is closed for federal tax purposes.

When Is Form 866 Used?

Form 866, called Agreement as to Final Determination of Tax Liability, is used for tax periods ending before the agreement. It closes the total liability of the individual for those periods. It is used where the tax period for which the agreement is asked has ended, and tax liability for the period has been determined.

The total tax liability determined has to be separated into tax periods and types of taxes. Also, the exact section of the law under which each tax covered was imposed must be noted.

Whenever Form 866 is used, the tax liability stated for each period shown in the agreement has to be the total tax liability determined for each period, without any penalty or interest. But the government may want the closing agreement to include ad valorem penalties which have been incurred. Then the tax and penalty are described in the agreement. Three copies of Form 866 must be completed.

When Is Form 906 Used?

Closing agreements on specific items are made on Form 906. This is so whether they are related to past, current, or future periods. A closing agreement of a year ending after the agreement is always made on Form 906. It relates only to a specific item or items affecting tax liability. It cannot attempt to conclude total tax liability for any period. Specific items on past periods which it may cover are items such as:

Amount of gross income, deductions for losses, depreciation, or depletion;

Year for which an item of income is to be included in gross income;

Year for which an item of loss is to be deducted; and

Value of property on a specified date.

Example: You own 500 shares of stock acquired by gift from someone who purchased them before March 1, 1913, and you plan to sell 200 shares. Either before or after the sale, a closing agreement on Form 906 may be used to fix the basis for the 500 shares.

Combined Agreements

Neither Form 866 nor Form 906 is designed to determine both tax liability and tax consequences of specific items. Instead, a combined agreement may be used. The format is shown in Revenue Procedure 68-16, 1968-1 CB 770. The main reason for a combined agreement is that a determination of liability does not fix the amount of income or deductions taken into account in reaching liability. Later, you may be able to prove a net operating loss for the year liability was determined, even though the tax was based on facts showing taxable income. In such a case, while the tax liability has been fixed, the effect of transactions of that year on other years has not. If agreed, the problem may be avoided by a combined agreement determining taxable income for such year and any carryovers from the year.

How To Apply for Closing Agreements

To apply for a closing agreement, send your request to the District Director with audit jurisdiction over the returns, or to the Appeals office if your request relates to a case pending before it.

A request is only an offer. It may be withdrawn any time before it is accepted. The closing agreement may be prepared by the taxpayer or the examining agent, but in most cases collaboration is preferable. The taxpayer executes the agreement first, but may withdraw prior to the signing on behalf of the Commissioner.

If it covers a joint return, both spouses have to sign. When an attorney or agent signs, he or she has to include papers proving the authority to sign. Specific instructions for the preparation of closing agreements are contained in Revenue Procedure 68-16, 1968-1 CB 770.

When preparing a closing agreement:

- Fill in the required number of forms. All copies have to be exactly the same. Avoid erasures or corrections; do not switch type-writers.
- Include a statement of how you want the liability fixed and your reasons.
- Use words describing the kind of tax liability involved, such as "Federal income tax."
- Mention all statutes, regulations, and decisions supporting your case, and show how they apply to your facts.
- Describe the taxes involved.
- Include anything else that will help the IRS decide the case.

When a closing agreement is submitted either on Form 866 or Form 906, the taxpayer is asked to sign a Form 870. This permits the immediate assessment and collection of the agreed deficiency. But it may be conditioned on the approval of the final closing agreement. The IRS will insert a paragraph stating this.

IRS Policy on Closing Agreements

The policy is to enter into a closing agreement in any case in which you can show:

- An advantage in having the case permanently closed, as, for example, where, in the settlement of disputed issues, you and the government have made mutual concessions.
- Good and sufficient reasons for desiring a closing agreement, and that the government will suffer no disadvantage if the agreement is entered into.
- The purpose is to mitigate the effect of the statute of limitations or to allow a deficiency dividend.
- Properly executed amended returns have been filed, after the expiration of the period in which assessments might have been made, and no fraud was involved.

A request for a closing agreement is reviewed much more closely than a request for a ruling. The very fact that the IRS is being asked to enter into a binding agreement often makes it suspicious of your motives. Because of the involved nature of the procedure connected with a closing agreement, the IRS is not anxious to use this form. It prefers the much simpler rulings procedure.

There is no assurance in the case of a closing agreement that the Commissioner will agree to it. But no application for a closing agreement can or will be rejected solely because it gives no apparent advantage to the IRS.

Offers in Compromise

The IRS may compromise any civil or criminal case (IRC §7122) unless the case has already been referred to the Department of Justice for prosecution or defense. Once the referral takes place, the Attorney General has the final authority to compromise.

An offer in compromise is a proposal by the taxpayer to pay a sum in full satisfaction of the unpaid tax liability, including interest, penalties, and other additions. When an offer has been accepted and the taxpayer has been notified by letter of the acceptance, the compromise is a legally enforceable contract between the IRS and the taxpayer. All questions of tax liability for the years in question are conclusively and finally settled. Neither the taxpayer nor the IRS may reopen the case except for the showing of falsification, concealment, or mutual mistake of a material fact.

The compromise of a tax liability may rest upon: (1) doubtful liability, (2) doubtful collectibility, or (3) economic hardship. An offer in compromise will be accepted by the IRS if the amount offered reasonably reflects collection potential.

The offer in compromise is filed on Form 656 with the local IRS district office. A sample Form 656 is in Part 9. Form 656 must be accompanied by either Form 433-A (individuals) or Form 433-B (businesses), which are statements of financial condition.

Under the terms of Form 656, the taxpayer agrees that any refunds or overpayments due will be retained by the IRS, that the statute of limitations applicable to the assessment and collection of the compromised liability is suspended for one year after the offered amount is paid, and, if the offer is accepted, the amount of the compromised liability will not be contested.

Economic hardship. This is a new category for requesting a compromise of tax liability. It is based on ability to pay and follows Congressional criticism of prior IRS restrictive policies limiting acceptances of compromise offers. Under this category, it is possible to compromise a tax liability even if you have assets to pay the tax. What you must generally show is that full collection of tax would create economic hardship. You state your basis of economic hardship on Form 656-A that is filed with Form 656, the standard form for an offer-in-compromise. To qualify for an offer-in-compromise for economic hardship, you may not be in bankruptcy and must have a record of filing and paying taxes on time.

Form 656-A provides a page on which to explain why payment of the full tax would cause economic hardship.

IRS examples of economic hardship include situations where long-term illness of a dependent requires a larger living allowance than normally allowed and where liquidation of assets to pay an outstanding tax liability would prevent you from meeting basic living expenses.

To help determine economic hardship, the IRS will provide national and local living allowance schedules.

Before rejecting a proposed offer, the IRS must provide for independent administrative review and if an offer is rejected, you must be notified of the right to appeal to the IRS Office of Appeals.

HOW TO GET THE IRS's OPINION ON A TAX PROBLEM

The IRS provides an invaluable service in giving, through letter rulings and determination letters, opinions on tax questions asked by taxpayers. Any taxpayer may ask for an opinion, and requesting one is often a necessary step in making business decisions. Not every tax problem may be satisfactorily resolved, and where an adverse tax holding might disrupt a planned transaction, requesting an IRS opinion before undertaking the proposed move is advisable. A fee must be paid to the IRS with your ruling request as discussed below.

An IRS opinion may also be requested for a closed transaction to determine how to report it on a tax return.

The IRS's discretion to rule on taxpayers' problems is broad. But as a matter of policy, it does not give opinions in certain areas and also distinguishes between the type of opinions that can be given by IRS personnel. Here, an important distinction is made between letter rulings and determination letters. A letter ruling is issued by the National Office in Washington and is in response to questions involving prospective transactions or completed transactions before a return is filed. A determination letter is issued by a District Director in response to questions involving completed transactions. As for prospective transactions, determination letters are issued for determining the qualification of proposed pension or profit-sharing plans, or the exempt status of certain organizations.

Revenue rulings are generally modifications of letter rulings that have been selected because of their importance or interest for publication in the Internal Revenue Bulletin.

Procedures for requesting rulings and determination letters are detailed in Revenue Procedure 99-1, 1999-1 IRB 6.

Should You Ask for an IRS Ruling?

Before requesting a ruling, it is advisable to carefully research the tax law applying to your problem. If your review shows that IRS policy is against your position, do not ask for a ruling. If you proceed without a ruling, there is always the chance that, if the transaction is examined, a settlement might be reached at that time.

Ask for a ruling if you have a fair chance of receiving a favorable ruling or have an alternative plan if you receive an unfavorable reply. Even if the request is turned down, at least you know that you will encounter possible litigation if you proceed with the transaction. This knowledge may also be important in planning and executing the transaction.

User Fee for Ruling

You must pay the IRS a fee for handling a ruling request. The amount of the fee depends on the specific type of ruling involved.

The user fee schedule can be found in Appendix A of Revenue Procedure 99-1, 1999-1 IRB 6.

Getting Advice for Future Transactions

If your question involves a prospective transaction, then only the National Office in Washington has the authority to answer in a letter ruling. Unless the law or regulations specifically provide otherwise, the issuance of an answer is a matter that rests within the discretion of the National Office.

If the question is about the qualification of proposed pension, profit-sharing, or stock bonus plans, then a District Director has the authority to issue a determination letter (*see* Revenue Procedure 99-6, 1999-1 IRB 187).

Only certain District Directors are authorized to issue determination letters involving exempt status under IRC §501. The 10 key districts, the areas covered, and the application procedures are detailed in Revenue Procedure 90-27, 1990-1 CB 514 (modified by Revenue Procedure 99-8, 1999-1 IRB 229 for user fee details).

Getting Advice on Closed Transactions

A problem concerning a completed transaction may be answered by the National Office in a ruling if no return has been filed, and the answer requires the establishment of principles and policies in the interpretation of the law.

If the answer to the question requires simply the routine application of established principles and policies, a District Director may answer in a determination letter. For a District Director to answer, the return to be affected must be filed in his or her district.

In a particular case, it may be difficult to draw the line between a novel or routine problem. If you are not sure of your position, you can send your question to the National Office in Washington. The final decision on whether a question is routine or novel, simple or complex, rests with the IRS. If you send a question to a District Director on the theory that the matter is routine, he or she may decide that it is novel and refer the question to the National Office. You will be notified of the change.

If the closed transaction has been reported in a filed return but has not been examined as yet, you may let well enough alone and wait out the limitation period. However, if future transactions are affected, you may need a present opinion. If you do decide to ask for an opin-

ion, send your request to the District Director. If answered before an examination by a Revenue Agent, the response is considered a tentative finding and not a determination letter. If the question is novel or complex, rather than routine and simple, the National office will take the question and its decision will be forwarded to the District Director. Normally, however, the request results in an examination by a Revenue Agent. The transaction will be considered by that agent in the usual way.

You Cannot Get a Ruling for . . .

- Hypothetical transactions.
- Questions of fact involving: market value of property; reasonableness of compensation; accumulated earnings penalty.
- Matters involving a court decision adverse to IRS policy and the IRS has not decided whether to follow or litigate the issue.
- An issue that is identical to an issue involved in a return filed by the taxpayer for an earlier year and that issue is under examination or has been examined by a District Director or has been considered by an Appeals office, and the statute of limitations has not yet expired.
- Questions involved in pending tax cases—if the government's position would be hurt by giving you a ruling.
- Tax avoidance schemes (you must have a legitimate business purpose in carrying out your transaction).
- Questions that the IRS thinks it cannot properly settle by rulings.
- An issue that is expected to be covered by imminent legislation.
- Questions on replacing involuntarily converted property, even though replacement has not been made, if a return has been filed for the year in which the property was converted. The District Director can give a determination letter on this issue.

A listing of the areas for which the IRS will not issue rulings or determination letters is published from time to time in the Internal Revenue Bulletin. (*See* Revenue Procedure 99-1, 1999-1 IRB 6 for a general discussion of no-ruling areas, and for a detailed list *see* Revenue Procedure 99-3, 1999-1 IRB 103.) The list is not all-inclusive since the IRS may decline to issue rulings or determination letters on other questions whenever warranted by the facts or circumstances of a particular case. Finally, when there has been new legislation, the IRS hesitates to rule on issues involving Code sections for which regulations have not been made final.

You cannot, by court action, force the IRS to give you a ruling or to apply a ruling in your favor.

Generally, rulings are not issued to business, trade, or industrial associations or to other similar groups relating to the application of the tax laws to members of the groups. However, rulings may be issued to such groups or associations relating to their own tax status or liability.

How To Request a Ruling

Your request must be in writing. The IRS does not issue rulings or determination letters upon oral requests. IRS employees ordinarily will not discuss a substantive tax issue prior to the receipt of a written request for a ruling. If they do, their oral opinions are not binding upon the IRS. This should not discourage an inquiry on whether the IRS will rule on a particular question or a discussion on the procedure for submitting a request for a ruling.

Conference before making a request. Sometimes, it is advisable to ask for a conference before you make your request for a ruling. There are advantages in having a conference before submitting your request. If you are uncertain whether you will get the ruling, the conference allows you to sound out the IRS without exposing the essential facts of the proposed transaction. In making a formal request for a ruling, you are required to supply the National Office with abundant materials and data, such as financial statements, minutes, and balance sheets. These are not returned if the ruling request is denied but are transmitted to the District Director where they become part of your file.

If a conference is held, understand that what is said during the meeting is merely an aid. It does not bind the IRS. Before going to the conference, prepare your case well. Take with you the draft of your request for a ruling and any proposed contracts or other documents.

Making a request.   Your request for a determination or ruling will be processed quickly if you follow these rules detailed in Revenue Procedure 99-1, 1999-1 IRB 6:

1. Submit the request in duplicate if:

    More than one issue is presented in the request.
    A closing agreement is requested on the issue presented.

    It is not necessary to present requests in duplicate under other circumstances.

    A declaration under penalties of perjury that the facts presented are true, correct, and complete must be signed by the person on whose behalf the request is made.

2. Send your letter ruling request to the appropriate Associate Chief Counsel (Domestic, Employee Benefits and Exempt Organizations, Enforcement Litigation, or International), at the following address:

    Internal Revenue Service, Attention: CC: DOM: CORP: TSS, P.O. Box 7604, Ben Franklin Station, Washington D.C. 20044. If a private delivery service is used, the package should be sent to Room 6561, 1111 Constitution Avenue, N.W., Washington, D.C. 20224.

    For determination letters, send the request to the District Director of Internal Revenue whose office has or will have audit jurisdiction.

3. Do not submit alternative plans in requests for a ruling.
4. Be sure to include:

    Complete facts.
    Names, addresses, and taxpayer account numbers of all interested parties.
    The district office which has audit jurisdiction.
    Copies, not originals, of all pertinent documents. The copies should be attested to be the same as the originals. Do not send originals, as they become part of the IRS file and are not returned.
    The balance sheet nearest the date of the transaction, if a corporate reorganization, distribution, or similar transaction is involved.
    If documents are submitted, they must be accompanied by an analysis of their relevancy to the issue.

5. Give the business reason for the transaction (favorable rulings often depend upon the existence of a bona fide business reason for the transaction).
6. Give the grounds for your stand and your supporting authority and specify what ruling or rulings you want. If you want a particular determination, explain the basis for your contentions, together with a statement of relevant authorities. Even if you do not urge a particular determination, you must give your view of the tax result, supported by a statement of relevant authorities such as statutes and regulations. All requests must include a statement of whether the applicable law is uncertain and whether the issue is adequately addressed by relevant authorities.

7. The IRS encourages the disclosure of any legislation, regulations, revenue rulings, or revenue procedures contrary to the taxpayer's position. The IRS believes that disclosure will lead to more rapid action. Technically, the IRS encourages but does not require the statement of contrary authorities. However, if contrary authorities are not provided, the IRS wants the ruling request to include a statement that there are *no* contrary authorities. If the taxpayer does not take either action and refuses a subsequent request of the IRS to do so, the IRS may refuse to issue a ruling. (Section 8.01(7) of Revenue Procedure 99-1, 1999-1 IRB 6) The IRS specifically requires that any relevant *pending* legislation be identified in the ruling request. The IRS must also be notified if legislation is introduced after the request is filed but before a ruling is issued (Section 8.01(8) of Revenue Procedure 99-1, 1999-1 IRB 6).

8. If a conference on the issues is desired, ask for one in the ruling request or soon afterwards in writing.

9. Sign the request. If you are representing a taxpayer, include your power of attorney and if you are an enrolled agent, show evidence of enrollment. The ruling request is signed by the taxpayer or by an authorized representative who is (1) an attorney who has filed a written declaration that he or she is currently qualified as an attorney and is authorized to represent the taxpayer; (2) a certified public accountant who files with the IRS written declaration that he or she is currently qualified as a certified public accountant and is authorized to represent the taxpayer; (3) a person, other than an attorney or certified public accountant, enrolled to practice before the Service; or (4) any other person who has received a Letter of Authorization from the IRS Director of Practice to represent the taxpayer in this particular matter.

10. Submit payment. Each ruling request must be accompanied by a check or money order, payable to the Internal Revenue Service, in the appropriate amount. For specific payment instructions, *see* Section 15 of Revenue Procedure 99-1, 1999-1 IRB 6; user fees for employee plans and exempt organizations are in Section 6 of Revenue Procedure 99-8, 1999-1 IRB 229.

Requests that do not comply with the above requirements will be acknowledged, and the requirements which have not been met will be pointed out. If the missing information is not supplied within 21 days, and an extension is not granted, the IRS will notify you in writing that the ruling request has been closed. If you supply the missing information after the closing letter is mailed, your request will be reopened and treated as a new request as of the date of the receipt of the information, but a new user fee must be paid.

The IRS has an alternate two-part procedure to expedite the processing of ruling requests for proposed transactions. Under the procedure, you may submit, together with the detailed statement of facts, documents and other required information, a summary statement of the controlling facts which support your request. If the National Office finds your summary satisfactory, the ruling will be based on these facts. This procedure has the advantage of eliminating many of the facts which the reviewer must assess. In addition, it removes some of the subjectivity exercised by the reviewer in determining whether the transaction was carried out substantially as proposed and whether minor deviations are material. On the other hand, this procedure poses the problem of what is a sufficient statement of the facts.

Withdrawing your request.   You may withdraw your request for a ruling or a determination letter at any time prior to the signing of the letter of reply. However, this may prove futile. The National Office may give its views on your request to the District Director. The information you submitted with your request will be considered by the

District Director in a later audit or examination of your return. Even though you withdraw your request, all correspondence and exhibits are retained by the IRS and are not returned to you.

Your Ruling Will Be Open to Public Inspection

Code §6110 requires the IRS to open to public inspection virtually all letter rulings, determination letters, and technical advice memoranda (called "written determinations") and related background files. Before your ruling is made public, it must be "sanitized" by deleting the following information:

1. Identifying details, such as names, addresses, social security numbers, and any other information which would identify any person (other than certain third parties who communicate with the IRS regarding the determination). Identifying details include information that would permit a person in the appropriate community (such as an industry or geographic location) to identify any person.
2. Information specifically authorized to be kept secret in the interest of national defense or foreign policy.
3. Information exempt from disclosure under other laws.
4. Trade secrets and privileged or confidential commercial or financial information.
5. Information the disclosure of which would constitute a clearly unwarranted invasion of personal privacy. This would include, for example, details not yet made public of a pending divorce or of medical treatment.
6. Information concerning the agency regulation of financial institutions.
7. Geological and geophysical information and data, including maps concerning wells.

Requesting deletions from written determination. When you request a determination letter, ruling, or technical advice memorandum, you must also submit a separate statement of proposed deletions (Section 8.01(9) of Revenue Procedure 99-1, 1999-1 IRB 6). At the same time the letter ruling or determination letter on your case is issued, you will receive a notice that it will be disclosed to the public. You will also receive a copy of the text the IRS proposes to disclose on which is indicated the material the IRS proposes to delete, any substitutions, and any third-party communications. (In the case of a background file or written determination that is disclosed only on written request for disclosure, the disclosure notice will be mailed to you within a reasonable time after the IRS received its first request for disclosure.) You then have 20 days after the notice is mailed to submit a written statement identifying those items which you believe should be deleted but were not. You must also submit a copy of the proposed IRS text and indicate by brackets further deletions that you want the IRS to make. Generally, the IRS will not delete any material which you had not earlier proposed be deleted. The IRS will mail to you its final administrative conclusions regarding deletions within 20 days of receiving your response. The IRS will attempt to resolve the differences, but will not grant a conference specifically for that purpose. However, you may discuss issues involving deletions at any conference that has been otherwise scheduled with respect to the requested ruling or determination letter.

Court remedies when you and the IRS do not agree on deletions. If you are still not satisfied with the deletions proposed by the IRS, you may file a petition in the Tax Court (anonymously, if appropriate) within 60 days after the date on which the IRS mailed the disclosure notice (IRC §6110(f)(3)). You must have exhausted your remedies within the IRS prior to petitioning the Tax Court. If your request for deletions has not been responded to by the IRS within 50 days of the mailing of the disclosure notice, this is considered an exhaustion of administrative remedies allowing a filing of a petition in the Tax Court (Reg. §301.6110-5(b)(3)).

Within 15 days, the IRS will notify by registered or certified mail any other person identified by name and address in the written determination or background file that a petition has been filed in the Tax Court. Such person may intervene in the Tax Court action (anonymously, if appropriate) (IRC §6110(f)(4)(B)).

The Tax Court will make a decision as soon as possible on the extent of deletions and may close its proceedings on the issue to the public (IRC §6110(f)(5)).

When Written Determinations Are Open to Public Inspection

Generally, written determinations and background files will be open to public inspection not less than 75 days and not more than 90 days after the IRS mailed you the disclosure notice. If you sued in the Tax Court regarding deletions, the written determination or background file will be open to the public within 30 days after the court order becomes final, although the court may extend the 30-day period to give the IRS time to comply with its order (IRC §6110(g)).

Request for Delay of Disclosure

Where the transaction which is the subject of the written determination is not complete when the determination is issued, you may request that the IRS postpone disclosure until 15 days after the transaction is completed. However, disclosure generally must occur within 180 days after the IRS mailed you the disclosure notice (IRC §6110 (g)(3)). If the transaction is still not completed within the 180-day period, and disclosure would interfere with the transaction, you may again request a postponement until 15 days after the transaction. Overall, postponement may not exceed 360 days after the IRS mailing of the disclosure notice (IRC §6110 (g)(4); Reg. §301.6110-5(c)(2)(ii)(B)).

Your request for postponement must be in writing and state the date on which you expect to complete the transaction. To get the first postponement, send your request so that the IRS receives it within 60 days after the disclosure notice. To get the second postponement, send your request so that the IRS receives it within 15 days before the date you stated you expected to complete the transaction (Reg. §301.6110-5(c)(2)(ii)(C)).

You must notify the IRS when you complete the transaction if that happens earlier than you expected. The written determination will be open to public inspection 30 days after notice of completion or on the date originally scheduled for disclosure, whichever date is earlier (Reg. §301.6110-5(c)(2)(ii)(D)).

What To Do When the IRS Fails to Meet the Time Limitations or Fails to Make Deletions

Where the IRS fails to meet the time limitations, such as disclosing before 75 days after the disclosure notice was mailed to you or failing to postpone disclosure pursuant to your request, you may sue the government in the U.S. Court of Federal Claims. You or any other person identified in the determination may sue the government in the U.S. Court of Federal Claims if the IRS fails to make deletions as required by its own agreement or by court order. Where the court determines that any employee of the IRS intentionally or willfully failed to make a deletion or failed to act within the time limits, you may recover your actual damages (but not less than $1,000) plus costs and reasonable attorneys' fees for bringing the action (IRC §6110(j)).

How Soon May You Receive an Answer?

Letter rulings and determination letters are issued on a first-come-first-served basis. You may get a preference by showing a clear need for a faster consideration. But the IRS will not assure you that your request will be processed within the time set by you. You may request that the IRS fax you or your representative a copy of the letter ruling, but the ruling is not considered "issued" until it is mailed (Section 8.02(5) of Revenue Procedure 99-1, 1999-1 IRB 6).

To learn the status of a tax ruling, contact the Branch representative indicated on the IRS acknowledgment of your request.

You May Get an Information Letter

Even though you request a ruling or a determination letter, you may receive an information letter. This is a statement issued either by the National Office or by a District Director. It does no more than call attention to a well-established interpretation or principle of tax law without applying it to a specific set of facts. You may receive an information letter if your request seeks general information or does not meet all the requirements for a ruling or determination letter (Section 2.04 of Revenue Procedure 99-1, 1999-1 IRB 6).

Can You Rely on a Letter Ruling?

You can usually rely on a letter ruling sent to you, although the IRS has the power to revoke the ruling retroactively. However, the IRS only under rare circumstances exercises this power. If the ruling is changed or revoked, the effect is almost always prospective. Be sure, in applying a ruling to the actual transaction, that the facts of the transaction are as you had stated them in your request and that the law has not changed in the meantime (Section 12.05 of Revenue Procedure 99-1, 1999-1 IRB 6).

When preparing the return for the year in which the transaction involved takes place, attach a copy of the ruling or letter to the return. IRS personnel compare the facts reported on the return with the representations upon which the ruling was based. They do this to determine whether there has been a misstatement or omission of a material fact, or if the transaction upon which the ruling was based was actually carried out in a manner materially different from that represented.

When you receive a ruling, the IRS will generally audit the return reporting the transaction that is the subject of the ruling.

You are not justified in relying on a written determination issued to another taxpayer. The law specifically states that written determinations may not be used as precedent by either the IRS or taxpayers (IRC §6110(k)(3)). The Supreme Court has stated that although the law bars the use of private rulings as precedents, they are nonetheless "evidence" of IRS views. The IRS may designate in a widely circulated official government publication (such as the Internal Revenue Bulletin) that a determination will be used as precedent.

You may not rely on a letter ruling issued to another taxpayer although the ruling may be helpful in discerning the IRS position on a particular issue.

You may rely on Revenue Rulings published in the Internal Revenue Bulletin in determining the rule applicable to your own case if the facts and circumstances of your transaction are substantially the same as in the published ruling.

Review and Revocation of Determination Letters

Determination letters involving income taxes are not generally reviewed by the National Office, as they merely repeat a position previously established in a regulation, ruling, or court decision published in the Internal Revenue Bulletin. If you believe a determination letter to be in error, you may ask the District Director to reconsider the matter. You may also ask the District Director to request technical advice from the National Office (Section 6.08 of Revenue Procedure 99-1, 1999-1 IRB 6).

A District Director may revoke a determination letter on re-examination of the issue or on an audit of the taxpayer's return. The revocation is automatically retroactive because the letter was issued for a completed transaction. Therefore, you did not rely upon the letter when entering into the transaction. The revocation of a determination letter on the status of pension and profit-sharing plans and exempt organizations, however, is generally prospective in effect.

How Letter Rulings Become Revenue Rulings

Revenue Rulings are generally revised letter rulings that the IRS believes have value as precedents or guides for taxpayers and IRS personnel. Although it is on the same subject matter, a Revenue Ruling differs from a letter ruling. When a letter ruling is edited for publication as a Revenue Ruling, the taxpayers' names and identifying facts are deleted. However, the ruling retains relevant facts with modifications to fit within the IRS's intention to propound a general rule. Finally, Revenue Rulings are subject to higher review, whereas many letter rulings are issued with no review above the branch level.

Requesting Technical Advice from the National Office

During an audit or conference, you may request that an issue on a closed transaction be referred to the National Office for technical advice. You may do this on the grounds that the issue has not been handled by the IRS in a uniform manner, or the issue, because of its complexity or unusualness, warrants consideration by the National Office. Request for technical advice should be made as early as possible. If you wait until the case is in the Appeals office, the request for technical advice may be made before the Appeals office conference.

The IRS official handling your case may agree that technical advice should be given. However, if your statement of facts and points at issue are not wholly acceptable, you will be advised in writing and will have 10 days to reply. If agreement cannot be reached, your statements and those of the district official will be forwarded to the National Office. Similarly, if the IRS initiated the request for technical advice, you may challenge its statement of facts and points at issue within 10 days after receipt of the proposed questions. Your statement explaining your position on the issues and citing precedents will be forwarded to the National Office with the request for advice (Section 9 of Revenue Procedure 99-5, 1999-1 IRB 158).

Whether the request for technical advice is initiated by you or by the IRS, you must also submit, within the 10-day period, a statement of proposed deletions. If the IRS does not receive your statement of proposed deletions within 10 days, it may decline to request technical advice.

The list of information that may be deleted and the procedure to follow when you and the IRS do not agree on deletions are outlined on page 910. Technical advice memoranda and related background files are subject to the same rules on disclosure as letter rulings and determination letters.

You will be informed of your right to a conference in the National Office in the event an adverse decision is indicated. If you ask for a conference, it will be arranged by telephone, if possible, and must be held within 21 days after contact has been made. Extensions of time are granted only if justified in writing and approved by the appropriate branch chief. Generally, you are entitled to only one conference, but, under special circumstances, the National Office may invite you back for another conference (Section 14 of Revenue Procedure 99-5, 1999-1 IRB 158).

Within 21 days after the conference, you may furnish the National Office with any additional data, lines of reasoning, and precedents proposed by you and discussed at the conference but not previously or adequately presented in writing. The National Office will forward a copy to the IRS office handling your case. It may verify the additional facts and data presented and comment on them.

You or your representative may obtain information as to the status of the technical advice request by contacting the District or Appeals office that requested the advice.

IRS officials may turn down your request for technical advice. You will be informed and have 10 days to appeal to the office handling your case. Your appeal must include a statement of the facts, law, and arguments with respect to the issue, and the reason why you believe the matter should be referred to the National Office for advice.

The examining officer or conferee will submit your statement to the chief of the office handling your case. If the official determines that technical advice should not be requested, you will be informed in writing of his or her intention to deny the request, and, generally, the reasons for the proposed denial. You may not appeal the official's decision to reject your request for technical advice, but you have 10 days to notify the office chief if you do not agree. The data will be submitted to the National Office, which will notify the office whether the request is appropriate. The decision is made solely on the basis of the written record, and no conference will be held in the National Office (Section 11.04 of Revenue Procedure 99-5, 1999-1 IRB 158).

The reply by the National Office to the requests for technical advice is called the Technical Advice Memorandum. It contains: (1) a recitation of the pertinent facts; (2) a discussion of the facts, precedents, and reasoning of the National Office; and (3) the conclusions of the National Office. Accompanying the technical advice memorandum is a notice of intention to disclose the memorandum and a copy of the version proposed to be open to public inspection.

The conclusions of the National Office in the memorandum give direct answers, whenever possible, to the specific questions of the IRS officials handling your case. Generally, the IRS will give you a copy of the technical advice memorandum, including the notice of intention to disclose and the version proposed to be disclosed, after it has been adopted. However, you will not receive a copy where the case involved criminal or civil fraud investigation, jeopardy, or termination assessment until all proceedings with respect to the investigation or assessment are completed. The National Office may advise the office handling your case not to give you a copy of the memorandum, and you will be so advised when you request a copy.

You have no right of appeal from an action of the National Office.

Effect of technical advice. A technical advice memorandum represents the IRS's views of the law, applied to the facts of a specific case. Generally, a technical advice memorandum has the same effect as a ruling on a closed and completed transaction. It usually disposes of the matter in which it was requested and usually applies retroactively. But note: (1) Technical advice is not binding in a subsequent year, even though it is not revoked. (2) The IRS office handling your case may raise an issue in any taxable period, even though it has received technical advice concerning the same issue in another taxable period.

Technical advice memoranda often form the basis for revenue rulings.

Note: Other details on the furnishing of technical advice are in Revenue Procedure 99-5, 1999-1 IRB 158.

How To Get Written Determinations Issued to Other Taxpayers

While you may not use letter rulings, determination letters, or technical advice memoranda issued to other taxpayers as precedent, they may be helpful as they reflect IRS policy and interpretation of the law. Written determinations are available in government reading rooms; background files are open to inspection only on written request.

Disclosure is not required of any technical advice memorandum (and its related background file) where the case involves civil fraud, criminal investigation, jeopardy, or termination assessment, until any action relating to the investigation or assessment is completed. Furthermore, a determination relating to IRS approval of the adoption or change in accounting method or period, qualified retirement plan funding method or plan year, or taxable year of a partner or partnership need not be open to public inspection, although the IRS must honor a written request for inspection.

Where You May Inspect Written Determinations

Rulings and technical advice memoranda are located in the National Office Reading Room. Determination letters are available in the Reading Room of the Regional Office in which is located the District Office that issued the determination letter. Written determinations available only on written request are available only from the National Office Reading Room. Background files must be requested from the reading room where the related determination is available for inspection (301.6110-1(c)). The following are the mailing addresses of the IRS regional reading rooms (Reg § 601.702(b)(3))

NATIONAL OFFICE

Freedom of Information Reading Room, Internal Revenue Service, 1111 Constitution Avenue, N.W., Washington, D.C. 20224.

NORTH-ATLANTIC REGION

Freedom of Information Reading Room, Internal Revenue Service; 11th Floor, 120 Church Street, New York, New York 10007.

MID-ATLANTIC REGION

Freedom of Information Reading Room, Internal Revenue Service, 600 Arch Street, Philadelphia, Pennsylvania 19105.

SOUTHEAST REGION

Freedom of Information Reading Room, Internal Revenue Service, 275 Peachtree St., N.E., Room 342, Atlanta, Georgia 30043.

MIDWEST REGION

Freedom of Information Reading Room, Internal Revenue Service, 230 S. Dearborn Street, Room 1980, Chicago, Illinois 60604.

CENTRAL REGION

Freedom of Information Reading Room, Internal Revenue Service, 201 W. Fourth Street, Covington, KY 41019.

SOUTHWEST REGION

Freedom of Information Reading Room, Internal Revenue Service 1100 Commerce Street, Room 11B15, Dallas, Texas 75242.

WESTERN REGION

Freedom of Information Reading Room, Internal Revenue Service, 450 Golden Gate Avenue, Room 2307, San Francisco, California 94102.

You may request copies of documents. Copies may be free up to a specified limit. For specific copying charges, contact the Regional Office Reading Room.

Some private publishing firms, such as Tax Analysts, Research Institute of America, and Commerce Clearing House, regularly publish such written determinations.

Actions To Obtain Additional Disclosure

You may seek disclosure of additional information on any written determination or background file open to public inspection. You must request the additional disclosure from the Internal Revenue Office which issued the written determination, specifying the deleted information which you believe should be disclosed and why. The IRS says it will not disclose names, addresses, or identifying numbers.

The IRS will notify all people identified by name and address in the determination or background file that additional disclosure is sought. If all agree to the additional disclosure within 20 days, the determination or background file will be revised to reflect the additional disclosure. If anyone objects, the IRS will deny your request (Reg. §301.6110-5(d)).

You may then file a petition in Tax Court or the District Court for the District of Columbia for the additional disclosure. The IRS will notify anyone identified by name and address in the determination or background file of the suit within 15 days by registered or certified mail, and such person may intervene in the suit (anonymously, if appropriate).

WHO MAY PRACTICE BEFORE THE IRS

Anybody may fill out a tax return for anyone else. But if the return is questioned, only a qualified practitioner may represent a taxpayer before the IRS.

To represent anyone at conferences above the Examination Division level, you have to meet certain requirements. If you are not an attorney or a certified public accountant, you must, in most cases, be enrolled to practice before the IRS.

The requirements, privileges, and duties of persons qualified to practice before the IRS are described in Treasury Department Circular No. 230, which is available from the Director of Practice, Internal Revenue Service. The following discussion summarizes parts of Circular No. 230.

Attorneys, CPAs, and Enrolled Actuaries File a Declaration

Any attorney or certified public accountant may practice before the IRS by filing a written declaration that he or she is currently qualified as an attorney or certified public accountant and is authorized to represent the particular party on whose behalf he or she acts (Reg. §10.3, Circular 230).

What the declaration should contain. If you are an attorney, the declaration should show the state bar of which you are a member, your name, address, telephone number, and a statement that you are authorized to represent the particular taxpayer, giving the taxpayer's name and address.

If you are a certified public accountant, the declaration should show the state in which you are qualified to practice, your name, address, telephone number, and a statement that you are authorized to represent the particular taxpayer, giving the taxpayer's name and address.

The declaration may be filed with a power of attorney (IRS Form 2848).

Enrolled actuary. If you are enrolled as an actuary by the Joint Board for the Enrollment of Actuaries, you may practice before the IRS with respect to issues involving specified statutory provisions (such as those related to qualified employee plans), provided you file a writtten declaration with the IRS that you are currently qualified as an enrolled actuary and have authorization from the party on whose behalf you are acting (Reg § 10.3, Circular 230).

Enrollment Requirements for Practice Before the IRS

Individuals other than attorneys and certified public accountants must demonstrate technical competence in tax matters before an application for enrollment to practice before the IRS may be filed. A special enrollment examination must be taken, except for certain former IRS employees who may apply for enrollment without examination, as discussed below. The examination is given annually. The application form for the examination, Form 2587, must be filed with a nonrefundable fee by the end of July. There are four parts to the examination, which generally must be completed within four years. The instructions to Form 2587 allow applicants to obtain IRS study materials and sample questions and answers from a prior examination free of charge.

Former IRS employees. You may be admitted to practice before the IRS even without taking the examination if you apply for enrollment within three years from the date you separated from service with the IRS. You must have had at least five years of continuous service with the IRS, and, during those five years, you must have been engaged in applying and interpreting the provisions of the Internal Revenue Code and regulations. The permission to practice may, at the discretion of the IRS, be limited to certain areas (Reg. §10.4, Circular 230).

Application for enrollment. Individuals who have passed the special enrollment examination and former Internal Revenue Service employees who qualify without examination may apply for enrollment on Form 23.

Mail Form 23, with a check or money order for the fee noted on the form payable to Internal Revenue Service, U.S. Treasury/IRS Enrollment, P.O. Box 845854, Dallas, TX 75284-5854. The fee is not refundable if your application is rejected.

Upon receipt of a properly executed application, the Commissioner may grant you temporary recognition to practice pending a determination as to whether permanent enrollment should be granted.

If your application is denied, you will be informed of the reasons for the denial. You may then, within 30 days after receipt of the notice of denial, file a written notice of appeal, together with supporting reasons, to the Director of Practice. If the denial of enrollment is sustained by the Director of Practice, you have 30 days after its receipt to appeal to the Secretary of the Treasury (Reg. § 10.5, Circular 230).

Upon enrollment, you will be issued a permanent enrollment card. The card remains valid so long as you remain in good standing.

You should carry your enrollment card whenever you appear before the IRS. Revenue agents generally ask to see it.

No Enrollment Required in Special Cases

No enrollment is required if you represent yourself or a member of your immediate family. In addition, enrollment is not required in the following cases: (1) You represent your regular full-time employer or a partnership in which you are a partner or full-time employee. (2) You are an officer or regular full-time employee representing a corporation, trust, estate, association, or organized group. (3) You are a fiduciary or full-time employee, representing your trust, receivership, guardianship, or estate. (4) You are an officer or regular employee in the course of your official business, representing a governmental unit, agency, or authority. (5) You are serving as representative outside of the United States before personnel of the IRS. (6) You prepared and signed a tax return for a taxpayer, or prepared a return that you were not required to sign under IRS rules, and you present proper authorization from the taxpayer; representation, here, is limited to appearances before revenue agents and examining officers of the Examination Division in the offices of District Directors, and to questions regarding the tax liability of the year, or period covered by that return. You may not represent the taxpayer at conferences (Reg. §10.7, Circular 230).

The Commissioner may also authorize any person to represent another without enrollment for the purpose of a particular matter.

Continuing Education Required To Renew Enrollment

IRS rules require enrolled agents to renew enrollment status and to complete educational courses as a requirement for renewal. Within the three-year period starting February 1, 1999 and ending January 31, 2002 all enrolled agents generally have to complete 72 hours of qualifying courses, with at least 16 hours per year, to qualify for another renewal (Reg. §10.6 (e), Circular 230). Qualifying courses include tax or tax-related courses such as accounting, financial management, or business computer science. Similar rules apply for each later three-year period. Individuals who receive initial enrollment during a three-year cycle have to complete two hours of courses for each month (or part of month) enrolled during the initial enrollment cycle (Reg. §10.6 (e)(2)(iii)). Writing articles or teaching courses are given partial credit towards the minimum education requirement (Reg. §10.6 (f), Circular 230).

What Attorneys, Certified Public Accountants, and Enrolled Agents Can Do

You may appear for hearings, conferences, and discussions. But in doing so, you also agree to: (1) advise your client promptly when you know anything indicating that he or she has not complied with the law, or has made an error in or omission from any return or document; (2) exercise due diligence in preparing, approving, and filing returns, documents, affidavits, and other papers relating to tax matters or in any representations you make to your client or to the IRS; (3) produce records or evidence upon proper demand; and (4) disclose upon request from the Director of Practice violations of the enrollment regulations, unless you believe in good faith that the information is privileged.

What Attorneys, Certified Public Accountants, Enrolled Agents, and Enrolled Actuaries Must Not Do

You must not unreasonably delay the prompt disposition of any matter before the IRS. Thus, an IRS request for or attempt to obtain records or information should be refused only if you believe in good faith and on reasonable grounds that the information sought is privileged or that the effort to obtain it is of doubtful legality (Reg. §10.20, Circular 220).

You must not, as notary public, with respect to any matter administered by the IRS take acknowledgments, administer oaths, certify papers, or perform any official act in connection with matters in which you are employed as counsel, attorney, or agent or in which you are in any way interested before the IRS.

You must not employ or accept assistance from any person who has been suspended or disbarred from practice before the IRS. Nor may you share fees with such a person.

You must not charge an unconscionable fee for representation of a client in any matter before the IRS. You must not charge a contingent fee for preparing an original return. For an amended return or refund claim (other than refund claim on original return) you may charge a contingent fee if at the time of the fee arrangement you reasonably anticipate that the IRS will substantively review the return (Reg. §10.28, circular 230).

You must not represent conflicting interests in your practice before the IRS except by express consent of all directly interested parties after full disclosure has been made.

If you also are an income tax return preparer, you may not endorse or otherwise negotiate any check made to a taxpayer other than yourself.

Any attorney, certified public accountant, enrolled agent or enrolled actuary may be disbarred or suspended from practice before the IRS for willfully violating any of the practice regulations or engaging in "disreputable" conduct such as giving false or misleading information to the IRS, or by permitting a client to do so. The penalty of disbarment or suspension from practice is not limited solely to the forms of disreputable conduct specifically enumerated in Reg. § 10.51 of Circular 230.

Further, a $1,000 penalty ($10,000 with respect to corporate returns) may be imposed on a representative who presents a return or other document (such as an affidavit) at an IRS examination knowing that it understates tax (IRC §6701).

Advertising and solicitation. Solicitation of employment in matters related to the IRS is generally prohibited. However, advertising of professional services, including fee information and the statement that you are enrolled to practice before the IRS, is permitted in professional lists, telephone directories, print media, radio and television, and certain mailings. Details on solicitation and advertising restrictions are in Regulation §10.30 of Circular 230.

Advising clients on tax return positions. An income tax return preparer eligible to practice before the IRS may not advise a client to take a position on a tax return, or prepare that portion of the return, unless (1) there is a "realistic possibility" that the position will be sustained on the merits, or (2) the position is not frivolous and the practitioner advises the client to adequately disclose the position. The realistic possibility standard requires that after a reasonable, well-informed analysis, a person knowledgeable in the tax law would conclude that the position has at least a one-in-three likelihood of being sustained on the merits. This is the same "reasonable possibility" test adopted by the Treasury in the preparer penalty regulations (Reg. §1.6694-2(b)). A practitioner may not sign a return as a preparer if the return contains a position that does not meet the 'realistic possibility' test unless the position is not frivolous and it is adequately disclosed to the IRS. A practitioner is subject to suspension or disbarment from practice before the IRS only if failure to comply was willful, reckless or the result of gross incompetence (Reg. §10.34, Circular 230).

Practice by Former Government Employees

As a former government employee, you may not represent a client in a matter on which you previously worked as a government employee. The matter may have involved a decision, a finding, a letter ruling, technical advice, or approval or disapproval of a contract. You are considered to have participated in a matter if you were substantially involved in making decisions. You also are disqualified if you prepared or reviewed documents (with or without the right to exercise a judgment of approval or disapproval), participated in conferences or investigations, or gave substantial advice.

You may also be disqualified where you had official responsibilities for a transaction within a period of one year before you left government service. In such a case, you may not represent or assist in that transaction any person who is or was a specific party to that transaction, within one year after your government employment ended. You are considered to have had official responsibility if you had direct administrative or operating authority, whether intermediate or final, exercisable alone or with others, to approve, disapprove, or otherwise direct government action.

Within one year after leaving government service, you may not appear before the IRS in a matter involving the publication, withdrawal, amendment, modification, or interpretation of a rule if you participated in its development or, within a period of one year prior to the termination of your government employment, you had official responsibility for developing the rule. However, you may appear on your own behalf or represent a client in a transaction involving the application or interpretation of the rule provided you do not use or disclose any confidential information you acquired in the development of the rule and do not argue that the rule is invalid or illegal. A rule includes Treasury Regulations, whether issued or under preparation for issuance as Notices of Proposed Rule Making or as Treasury Decisions, and revenue rulings and revenue procedures published in the Internal Revenue Bulletin (Reg. §10.26, Circular 230).

Firm representation. A firm of which you are a member may not represent or knowingly assist a person who was or is a specific party in any transaction in which you participated as a government employee, *unless:*

1. No member of the firm who knew of your participation in the transaction initiated discussions with you concerning your becoming a member of the firm until your government employment ended or six months after the termination of your participation in the transaction, whichever is earlier;
2. You did not initiate any discussions concerning becoming a member of the firm while participating in the transaction or, if such discussions were initiated, they conformed with 18 U.S.C. 208 (b); and
3. The firm isolated you in such a way that you do not assist in the representation.

If you had official responsibility for a transaction, no member of your firm may represent or knowingly assist a person who was or is a specific party in that transaction, unless you are isolated in such a way that you do not assist in the representation. You and another member of your firm must sign a statement under oath that you will be isolated from participating in the transaction, and the statement must be filed with the IRS Director of Practice (Reg. §10.26 (c), Circular 230).

When Unenrolled Tax Return Preparers May Represent Taxpayers at Audits

Any unenrolled person who signs an income tax return as having prepared it may appear as the taxpayer's representative at an audit in the Examination Division office of a District Director. A preparer also may appear where no space is provided on a return for a preparer's signature or where the regulations do not require his or her signature. However, the preparer of the return must show authorization by the taxpayer to represent him or her. The preparer may use Form 2848 or any other written authorization which the taxpayer signs before a notary public or two disinterested witnesses.

An unenrolled preparer is strictly limited to an audit on the return prepared. He or she cannot represent a taxpayer at conferences after an examination. Where net operating losses are involved, the preparer cannot deal with prior or later returns he or she has not prepared and signed. This individual cannot execute claims for refunds, receive checks in payment of any refund, or execute waivers, consents or closing agreements or a "30-day letter." If the taxpayer wants to have an informal conference or file a protest to the regional Appeals Office, the taxpayer must do it him- or herself or engage an enrolled representative (Reg. §10.7, Circular 230).

Who Must File a Power of Attorney

You must file a power of attorney to receive a check from the Treasury in payment of a client's refund and to execute a client's Form 870, a waiver of notice of disallowance of a claim for credit or refund, a Form 872, or a closing agreement.

A power of attorney may be filed on IRS Form 2848.

The power of attorney must be signed according to the following rules (Reg. §601.503):

1. For an individual taxpayer, by the taxpayer.
2. For a joint return, by both spouses if the representative is representing both of them.
3. For a partnership, by all the partners, or by one in the name of the partnership, if duly authorized to sign by the others.
4. For a corporation or association, by an officer authorized in writing to bind the corporation or association.
5. For a guardian or other court-appointed fiduciary, by the fiduciary. In addition, there must accompany the power of attorney an official court document as proof of the appointment and that the appointment has not terminated.

The power must specify the matters for which representation is authorized and the years involved. The power must include a declaration by the representative that he or she is currently eligible to practice before the IRS, is aware of the practice regulations included in Circular 230, and is authorized to represent the taxpayer(s) indentified in the power of attorney (Reg. §601.502 (c)).

When Must a Tax Information Authorization Be Filed?

If you do not file a power of attorney, you have to file a tax information authorization in order to receive certain confidential tax information of your client, such as the tax return, and to receive certain information, such as the IRS's position towards his or her liability. The tax information authorization is signed by the taxpayer and specifies the particular authorization given. IRS Form 8821 may be used.

No tax information authorization is required where: (1) a power of attorney has already been filed for the same matter, or (2) the taxpayer is present, such as at a conference, when the information is divulged, or (3) the receipt of notices and other matters are not of a confidential nature.

Attorney-Client Privilege Extended to Tax Practitioners Who Are Not Attorneys

The attorney-client privilege generally protects an attorney from being forced to divulge information provided by a client in the course of obtaining legal advice. The IRS Restructuring and Reform Act of 1998 extends this confidentiality privilege to all non-attorney tax practitioners authorized to practice before the IRS, such as certified public accountants, enrolled agents, and enrolled actuaries. The privilege applies to authorized practitioners to the extent client information would be considered privileged information if it were between a taxpayer and his attorney (IRC § 7525) . The privilege is limited to any noncriminal tax matter before the IRS, and noncriminal tax proceedings in federal court brought by or against the United States. The privilege does not apply to any written communication between a federally authorized tax practitioner and corporate client in connection with the promotion of the direct or indirect participation of such corporation in any tax shelter (IRC § 7525(b)). The Code defines "tax shelter" as a partnership or other entity, or any plan or arrangement, a significant purpose of which is the avoidance or evasion of federal income tax(IRC § 6662 (d)(2)(C)(iii))).

INCOME TAX RETURN PREPARERS

Preparers are subject to penalties for negligent or fraudulent preparation of returns and for violation of specific disclosure and record requirements. Thus, the rules discussed in this chapter deserve careful consideration by all tax practitioners.

Who Is a Preparer?

Anyone who prepares or employs another to prepare a substantial part of any income tax return or refund claim for compensation is considered an income tax return preparer (IRC §7701(a)(36)(A)). You need not physically make the entries on the return to be a preparer. You may be considered a preparer where you:

- Provide advice or information that reduces the filling out of the return to a clerical matter; or
- Provide advice on matters of tax law or IRS policy concerning a particular deduction or income item. You are considered a preparer in relation to those items if the advice is given in connection with the preparation of a return and is directly related to a specific entry on the return or refund claim. The advice must be for events that have already occurred rather than for the consequences of contemplated actions (Reg. §301.7701-15(a)(2)).

A person may be considered a preparer regardless of educational qualifications or professional status (Reg. §301.7701-15(a)(3)). But an IRS employee performing his or her official duties is not considered an income tax preparer (Reg. §301.7701-15(a)(6)).

You are not a preparer if you perform only the following services (Reg. §301.7701-15(d)):

- Merely type or reproduce returns; or
- Prepare a return or refund claim for your employer, an officer of your

employer, a fellow employee, or a general partner in a partnership in which you are a general partner or an employee. An employee of a subsidiary corporation is also considered an employee of the parent corporation; or
- Prepare a return as fiduciary; or
- Prepare a claim for refund in response to a notice of deficiency issued to the taxpayer or a waiver of restriction after initiation of an audit of the taxpayer or another taxpayer, or a determination if the audit of that other taxpayer affects the liability of the taxpayer for tax.
- Prepare a return for a friend, a relative, or neighbor with no implicit or explicit agreement for compensation, even though you receive a gift or return service or favor (Reg. §301.7701-15(a)(4)).

Even though entries on a return you prepare affect entries on the return of another taxpayer, you are not the preparer of the other return, unless the entries on the return you prepared are directly reflected on that other return and constitute a substantial portion of that return. For example, if you prepare a partnership return, you are not the preparer of a partner's return, unless the entries on the partnership return reportable on the partner's return constitute a *substantial portion* (discussed below) of the return (Reg. §301.7701-15(b)(3)).

Consultants.   The IRS has listed four situations in which a tax "consultant" is considered the preparer: (1) The "consultant" fills out a return, (2) prepares a statement which the taxpayer may mechanically follow to fill out the return, (3) recommends substantial changes to a taxpayer's draft of a return which the taxpayer follows in completing the return, or (4) reviews the taxpayer's return and after concluding that no changes are necessary, mails it to the IRS under the taxpayer's instructions. In any of these circumstances, the consultant must sign the return as a preparer or be subject to the $50 penalty for failure to sign, unless there is reasonable cause for not signing (Revenue Ruling 84-3, 1984-1 CB 264).

Sellers of tax software.   A company or individual that prepares and sells software programs to customers is considered a "tax preparer" by the IRS because the software program is used to calculate tax return items based on information punched into the computer by the customer.

The software seller is potentially subject to a negligence penalty if the program is incomplete or inadequate and results in an underpayment of tax by the taxpayer using the program. The penalty for willfully attempting to underestimate the liability could also be imposed in extreme cases. Before imposing a penalty, the IRS will consider the nature, frequency, and materiality of the errors. If the software seller's normal office procedures indicate that a particular error would rarely occur, the IRS may consider this a mitigating factor in deciding whether to apply penalties.

Computerized tax return preparer services.   Firms that provide tax practitioners with worksheets and then feed the information from the practitioners into computers to prepare completed tax returns are potentially subject to penalties if the program used contains errors or is incomplete, leading to an understatement of tax liability. Penalties for negligence or willful understatement of tax liability may be imposed after the IRS takes into account the nature, frequency, and materiality of the errors, as well as the preparer's normal office practice. The $500 penalty for endorsing or negotiating a client's refund check may also be imposed (IRC§6695(f)).

Substantial preparation.   Where more than one person worked on the preparation of a return or claim for refund, a determination of who is the "preparer" will be made according to Treasury rules on substantial preparation.

Under Treasury regulations, each schedule, entry, or other portion of the return or refund claim is reviewed separately to determine who is the preparer (Reg. §301.7701-15(b)(1)). You are considered the preparer of an entry if you rendered advice that is directly relevant to a determination of the existence, characterization, or amount of an entry, return, or refund claim; further, regulations provide a mechanical test for determining whether a part of a return and refund claim is considered substantial. An item is not considered substantial if it involves an amount which is: (1) less than $2,000, or (2) less than $100,000 and also less than 20 percent of the taxpayer's adjusted gross income. Where more than one schedule, entry, or other portion is involved, the items are aggregated (Reg. §301.7701-15(b)(2)).

Example: You prepare a schedule on a taxpayer's return for dividend income which totals $1,500 and also give advice on a schedule of medical expenses which results in a medical expense deduction of $1,500. You are not a preparer of the return if the taxpayer's adjusted gross income on the return exceeds $15,000, as $3,000 is 20% of $15,000.

What Forms Are "Income Tax Returns"?

The penalties for income tax return preparers stem from the preparation of only certain forms specified in the regulations (Reg. §301.7701-15(c)). These are:

- Individual or corporation income tax return;
- Fiduciary income tax return for trust or estate;
- Regulated investment company undistributed capital gains tax return;
- Charitable remainder trust return;
- Return of a transferor of stock or securities to a foreign corporation, trust, or partnership;
- S corporation return;
- Partnership's return;
- DISC return;
- Small business corporation income tax return;
- Refund claim for a credit against any income tax; and
- Information return by or on behalf of a person or entity that is not a taxable entity and reports information which is or may be reported on the return of a taxpayer under the income tax provisions.

The income tax preparer penalties do not apply to an estate or gift tax return, any other return of excise taxes or income taxes collected at source on wages, an individual or corporate declaration of estimated tax, an application for an extension of time to file an individual or corporation income tax return, or an informational statement on Form 990, any Form 1099, or similar form.

Penalties

A $250 penalty applies to you as a preparer if all of the following apply: (1) tax is understated on the return; (2) you knew or reasonably should have known that the understatement was due to a taxpayer position that did not have a "realistic possibility" (discussed below) of being sustained on its merits; and (3) the taxpayer position was either frivolous, or, if not frivolous, was not adequately disclosed on the return or in a separate statement (IRC §6694(a)). The penalty will not be imposed if there is reasonable cause for the understatement of tax and the preparer acted in good faith. In deciding whether this exception applies, the IRS will consider the nature, materiality and frequency of the errors, the normal office practice of the preparer, and whether the advice of other preparers was relied upon (Reg. § 1.6694-2 (d)).

Generally, you may rely in good faith without verification upon information supplied by a taxpayer (Reg. §1.6694-1(e)). You are not required to ferret out documents or other evidence supporting the taxpayer's information. However, you may not ignore the implications of furnished information or information known to you. Where the taxpayer's information appears incorrect or incomplete, you must make reasonable inquiries.

If a tax understatement is either willful or due to reckless disregard of IRS rules, a $1,000 penalty applies. The penalty is reduced to $750 if the $250 penalty also applies to the return (IRC §6694(b)).

For purposes of the $250 or $1,000 penalty, Treasury regulations provide that only one person associated with a firm is treated as the preparer of the return. The practitioner who signs the return is considered the preparer. If more than one person is considered a preparer of the return under IRS rules but none of them signs the return, the person with overall supervisory responsibility is treated as the preparer for penalty purposes (Reg. §1.6694-1(b)).

In addition to the preparer, the preparer's employer may *also* be subject to the $250 or $1,000 penalty if (1) one or more of the principal managers or officers of the firm or branch office participated in or knew of the conduct that subjects the individual preparer to a penalty, or (2) the employer failed to provide reasonable and appropriate review procedures for the position or conduct giving rise to the penalty, or (3) existing review procedures were disregarded. A partnership is treated as an employer when the preparer is a member of the partnership (Reg.§1.6694-2(a)(2) and Reg. §1.6694-3(a)(2)).

Realistic possibility test. According to the IRS, a taxpayer position has a "realistic possibility" of being sustained on its merits if a person knowledgeable in the tax law would conclude, after a well-informed analysis, that there is at least a one-in-three likelihood that the position will be sustained (Reg. §1.6694-2(b)(1)). Treasury regulations include examples of how the analysis of relevant authorities such as statutes, Congressional Committee reports, and regulations affect the determination of whether the realistic possibility standard is satisfied (Reg. §1.6694-2(b)(3)).

Disclosure of nonfrivolous positions. Even where a position taken does not satisfy the realistic possibility standard, the $250 penalty is not imposed if the position is not frivolous and it is adequately disclosed (IRC §6694(a)(3)). Treasury Regulations provide different disclosure rules for "signing preparers" than for "nonsigning preparers." For signing preparers, an item-specific disclosure is generally required on Form 8275, or on Form 8275-R where a position is taken contrary to a Treasury regulation. However, disclosure on the return itself may be permitted if authorized by the IRS in an annual revenue procedure or other announcement (Reg. §1.6694-2(c)(3)). A "nonsigning" preparer may disclose in the same way, but the IRS also allows disclosure in the form of a statement to the taxpayer or to another preparer to whom advice was given. Where advice was given to a taxpayer, a warning to the taxpayer that the taxpayer must disclose a position which lacks substantial authority to avoid a 20% penalty (IRC §6662(d)) for substantial understatement of tax is generally considered adequate disclosure by the nonsigning preparer (Reg. §1.6694-2(c)(3)(ii)(A)). Where a nonsigning preparer has advised another preparer, the nonsigning preparer's statement that disclosure of the position is required under the preparer penalty rule of IRC §6694 is considered adequate disclosure (Reg. §1.6694-2(c)(3)(ii)(B)).

A signing preparer may avoid the $1,000 penalty for willful tax understatements or reckless disregard of IRS rules by making an adequate disclosure of a nonfrivolous position on Form 8275, or on 8275-

R where the position is contrary to a regulation (Reg. §1.6694-3(e)(1)). A nonsigning preparer may also make a disclosure on Form 8275 or 8275-R. Where advice was provided by a nonsigning preparer to a taxpayer or to another preparer, a warning that positions contrary to IRS rules or regulations must be disclosed is considered adequate disclosure (Reg. §1.6694-3(e)(2)).

Aiding and abetting understatements.   A preparer may be subject to a separate $1,000 penalty ($10,000 for corporate returns) for aiding and abetting the willful understatement of tax liability on a tax return or other document (IRC §6701).

The $1,000/$10,000 penalty for aiding and abetting the understatement of tax liability (IRC §6701) is an alternative to the $250 or $1,000 preparer penalties (IRC §6694). The $1,000/$10,000 penalty may be imposed on a person who knows *or* has "reason to believe" that a return or document which he or she has helped prepare will be used in connection with tax matters. A supervisor who does not actually prepare a return or document is subject to the penalty if he or she orders or causes a subordinate to take actions subject to the penalty, or if the supervisor knows of such an act by a subordinate but does not attempt to prevent it.

Disclosure and Record-Keeping Requirements

Apart from the penalties just discussed for understating tax liability, you, as a preparer, must keep records of returns and meet certain notation requirements in preparing returns.

Retention of records on preparers.   Self-employed preparers and preparers who employ other preparers must retain a record of the name, social security number, and place of work of each employed preparer. The records must be retained for a three-year period following the close of the return period (defined as a 12-month period beginning on July 1 of each year), and the records must be made available for inspection upon request by the District Director (Reg. §1.6060-1(a)). There is a $50 penalty for each failure to retain and make available a proper record and $50 for each required item that is missing from the record. The maximum penalty for any return period is $25,000 (IRC §6695(e)). Showing reasonable cause may avoid the penalty.

Return or refund claim requirements.   A preparer has four responsibilities towards each return or refund claim he or she prepares.

- Each return must be signed;
- Each return must contain the preparer's address and identification number;
- A copy of the return must be furnished to the client; and
- A copy of the return must be retained by the preparer or a list containing the names of clients for whom returns were prepared.

Signing.   A preparer must sign a return or refund claim in the space provided and include his or her address and identification number. Preparers must physically sign the return or refund claim after it is completed but before it is presented to the client. A stamped signature or signature label may not be used unless one of the exceptions to the manual signature rule applies, as discussed below (Reg. §1.6695-1(b)(1)). Initialing a return does not satisfy the signature requirement. If physically unable to manually sign due to a disability, the words "unable to sign" must be printed, typed, or stamped on the preparer's signature line, followed by the preparer's name which is printed, typed, or stamped (Rev. Proc. 79-7, 1979-1 CB 486).

The penalty for failing to sign is $50 for each return unless reasonable cause is shown; the maximum penalty is $25,000 for returns filed during any calendar year (IRC §6695(b)). If more than one person

worked on the return, the person with the primary responsibility for the return's overall accuracy is considered the preparer who must sign (Reg. §1.6695-1(b)(2)). If the preparer is unavailable to sign the return, another preparer must so advise the client, review the entire preparation of the return or claim, and then sign it (Reg. §1.6695-1(b)(1)).

The manual signature requirement may be satisfied by a photocopy of a manually signed copy of a return or refund claim (Reg. §1.6695-1(b)(4)(i)). Before it is photocopied, no one but the preparer may alter entries on the manually signed copy except to correct arithmetical errors. The individual preparer or the employer-preparer must retain the manually signed copy, as well as a record of any corrected arithmetical errors. If the return or refund claim is prepared by a computer not under the individual preparer's control, and no other person has altered the information in the return or refund claim except for corrections of arithmetical errors, the preparer may satisfy the manual signature requirement by attaching a manually signed attestation that the information in the return or refund claim was obtained from the taxpayer and is correct to the best of his or her knowledge. The data submitted to the computer must be retained by the individual preparer or the employer-preparer along with a record of any arithmetical corrections (Reg. §1.6694-1(b)(4)(ii)). A facsimile signature may be used for the return of a nonresident alien taxpayer if the preparer submits a manually signed letter that identifies each document bearing the facsimile signature and states that the facsimile signature is the signature used to sign the documents (Reg. §1.6694-1 (b)(4)(iii)).

Address.   A return or claim for refund prepared by a preparer must also list the street address, city, state, and postal zip code of the place of business where the return or claim for refund was prepared. If the place of business is not maintained on a year-round basis, the return or claim for refund must bear the street address, city, state, and postal zip code of his or her principal office or business location, or if none, his or her residence (Reg. §1.6109-2(b)(1)). Preparers, after written notice to the IRS, may satisfy the address requirement by disclosing only the postal zip code of the applicable place of business (Reg. §1.6109-2(b)(2)).

No penalties are imposed for failure to furnish the required address.

Identification number.   A $50 penalty is charged a preparer who without reasonable cause does not include an identification number on each return or refund claim (IRC §6695(c)). There is a $25,000 maximum penalty for returns filed in a calendar year. Individual preparers with no employees use social security numbers as identification numbers (Reg. §1.6109-2(a)(1)). A preparer with one or more employees uses the employer identification number, and an individual employed by another should use the employer identification number of the employer, as well as his social security number (Reg. §1.6109-2(a)). For this purpose, a partner in a partnership is considered an employee and should use the partnership's identification number in addition to the social security number.

In the signature section of Form 1040, a self-employed preparer must check a box next to his or her social security number.

The penalty is not imposed on a preparer who is an employee of another preparer of the return or refund claim, nor is it imposed on a partner of a partnership which also is a preparer of the return or refund claim (Reg. §1.6695-1(c)(2)). Neither is the penalty imposed on one who merely gives advice on specific issues of law or who prepares another return which affects amounts on the return (Reg. §1.6695-1(c)(1)).

Alternative preparer ID numbers. If you do not want to disclose your Social Security number on returns you prepare, you may get an alternative identification number, the Preparer Tax Identification Number (PTIN). This number can be used on returns and refunds filed after December 31, 1999. To receive a PTIN, file W7-P, application for Preparer Tax Identification Number.

Furnishing client with copy of return or refund claim. Before the return or refund claim is presented to the client for signature, a copy of the return or claim must be furnished (IRC §6107(a)). Where two or more persons are considered preparers with respect to the same return, and there is an employment relationship between them, the employer is responsible for furnishing the copy; where there is a partnership relationship, the partnership must furnish the copy (Reg. §1.6107-1(c)).

Failure to furnish a copy results in a penalty of $50 for each failure, unless it can be shown that failure was due to reasonable cause and not due to willful neglect (IRC §6695(a)). There is a $25,000 maximum penalty per calendar year.

The preparer may request a receipt as proof of having satisfied this requirement (Reg. §1.6107-1(a)).

Records. A preparer must keep for three years copies of all returns and refund claims he or she prepares or a list of the taxpayers for whom returns were prepared, including each name, taxpayer identification number, taxable year of the taxpayer for whom the return or refund claim was prepared, and the type of return or refund claim prepared (IRC §6107(b)). A $50 penalty may be imposed for each failure, with a maximum penalty of $25,000 for each return period (IRC §6695(d)).

A tax preparer who sells his or her business is not relieved of the obligation to keep the returns prepared (Rev. Rul. 79-400, 1979-2 CB 403).

If the preparer is a corporation or partnership which goes out of business before the end of the three-year period, the person who is responsible for winding up the affairs of the corporation or partnership under state law must retain the records until the three-year period ends. If state law does not specify who is responsible for winding up, the directors or general partners are subject to the record-retention rules. These individuals will be jointly and severally liable for the $50 penalty for each failure to retain records, up to the maximum penalty of $25,000 per return period (Reg. §1.6107-1(b)).

Where there is an employment relationship or a partnership relationship, *see* "Furnishing client with copy of return or refund claim," discussed above.

Negotiation of refund checks prohibited. A preparer is subject to a $500 penalty for each endorsement or negotiation of a refund check resulting from a return which he or she prepared (IRC §6695(f)). However, the penalty does not apply to a preparer-bank where the full amount of the refund check is deposited to the taxpayer's account (IRC §6695(f)). A preparer who endorses a client's refund check is subject to the penalty even if he or she has a power of attorney from the client authorizing negotiation of the refund check (Letter Ruling 8720021).

A preparer who operates a check-cashing business and who occasionally cashes refund checks of clients is not exempted from the penalty when the client endorses the check prior to negotiation or endorsement by the preparer (Rev. Rul. 78-220, 1978-1 CB 447, revoking Rev. Rul. 77-184, 1977-1 CB 407).

A business manager for athletes, actors, or other professionals who prepares the client's tax returns and handles their tax refunds may avoid penalty where he or she acts only as an agent in depositing a client's endorsed refund check. Thus, the manager who receives the refund check pursuant to a power of attorney and deposits the check in a client's checking account is not liable for the penalty since he or she is not "negotiating" the check, but merely acting in the capacity as agent (Rev. Rul. 80-35, 1980-1 CB 305).

Preparer Penalty Assessment Procedures

Penalties under IRC §6694(a) for understatements of tax due to unrealistic positions, or the penalties under IRC §6695 for failure to meet the disclosure and record-keeping requirements, must be assessed within three years after a return or refund claim is filed; no court proceeding for collection of the penalty without assessment may be begun after the three-year period (IRC §6696(d)(1)). Penalties for willful or reckless understatements of tax liability under IRC §6694(b) may be assessed, or court proceedings for collection without assessment may begin, at any time.

The IRS will issue a preparer a 30-day letter notifying a preparer of a proposed penalty and offering an opportunity to pursue administrative remedies prior to assessment of the penalty (Reg. §1.6694-4(a)(1)). The preparer has the burden of proving for purposes of the unrealistic positions penalty (IRC 6694 (a)) that he or she did not know (or reasonably could have known) that the questioned position was taken on the return, that there was reasonable cause and good faith, and that adequate disclosure was made (Reg. §1.6694-2 (e)). The preparer also has the burden of proving for purposes of the penalty under IRC §6694 (b) that he or she did not recklessly or intentionally disregard an IRS rule or regulation, that the position is a good faith challenge to a regulation, and that adequate disclosure was made (Reg. §1.6694-3(h)). However, the IRS bears the burden of proof on the issue of whether the preparer willfully attempted to understate a taxpayer's tax liability (IRC §7427; Reg. §1.6694-3(h)). If the preparer appeals an IRS penalty determination, the IRS cannot assess the penalties until after a final determination is made (Reg. §1.6694-4(a)(1)).

If a penalty for understatement of tax is assessed and the preparer does not pursue an administrative remedy or pursues such a remedy but receives an adverse final administrative determination from the IRS, the preparer has two alternatives:

1. Pay the entire amount assessed and file a claim for refund of the amount paid not later than three years from the date the penalty is paid (Reg. §1.6694-4(a)(3)(i)), which if denied may be appealed in court; or
2. Pay 15% or more of the penalty within 30 days of the IRS' statement of notice and demand for payment and file a claim for refund of the amount paid within the same 30-day period (Reg. §6694-4(a)(3)(ii)). Form 6118 is used to claim the refund.

If under alternative (2) a preparer timely pays at least 15% of the penalty and files a refund claim, the IRS has six months to act on the claim. During that period, the IRS may not seek collection of the remaining 85% of the penalty (Reg. §1.6694-4(a)(4)). If the IRS denies the refund claim, the preparer may bring an action for refund in a federal district court within 30 days of the date of denial. The action must be brought within the 30-day period to postpone or avoid collection measures by the IRS as to the remaining 85% of the penalty under the second alternative above. If the IRS does not deny a claim for refund by the end of six months after the claim is made, the preparer may bring an action in federal district court within 30 days after the expiration of the six-month period. If such an action is not brought, the IRS may pursue collection of the remaining 85% of the penalty (Reg. §1.6694-4(b)). If such an action is brought, the IRS may counterclaim for the balance of the penalty (Reg. §1.6694-4(a)(4)).

IRS May Seek Injunction Against Preparer

The IRS may seek an injunction in a federal district court to prohibit improper conduct by an income tax return preparer (IRC §7407). An injunction may be sought regardless of whether penalties have been or may be assessed against the preparer. An injunction may be issued where the court finds that the preparer has:

- Engaged in conduct subject to the disclosure requirement penalties or the understatement of taxpayer liability penalties;
- Engaged in conduct subject to criminal penalties under the Internal Revenue Code;

- Misrepresented his or her eligibility to practice before the IRS or his or her experience or education as a tax return preparer;
- Guaranteed payment of any tax refund or the allowance of any tax credit; or
- Engaged in other fraudulent or deceptive conduct that interferes with administration of the tax laws.

A court may also enjoin the person from acting as a preparer if it finds that the person has repeatedly engaged in the above practices (IRC §7407(b)).

Preparing a Federal Estate Tax Return

The estate tax return, Form 706, is due nine months after death. For the estate of an individual dying in 1999, Form 706 generally must be filed if the gross estate plus adjusted taxable gifts after 1976 exceeds $650,000. This threshold increases to $675,000 for estates of individuals dying in 2000 and 2001.

THE ESTATE TAX RETURN—GENERAL REQUIREMENTS

The estate tax return, Form 706, must be filed within nine months after the date of the decedent's death unless an extension of time to file is allowed. Form 4768, Application for Extension of Time To File a Return and/or Pay U.S. Estate (and Generation-Skipping Transfer) Taxes, is used to apply for an extension of time. A copy of the extension is attached to Form 706.

The value of the gross estate on the date of death determines the necessity of filing an estate tax return, even if the executor or administrator elects the alternate valuation date and value at that date is less. Post-1976 taxable gifts that are *not* treated as part of the gross estate are added to the gross estate. Generally, these are gifts made after December 31, 1976, exceeding the annual gift tax exclusion.

The return must be verified and filed in the district in which the decedent was domiciled at death or at the IRS Service Center in Pennsylvania if the decedent was a nonresident U.S. citizen. If the return is filed in the wrong district, it generally will be transferred to the proper district. In exceptional cases, the IRS, upon application, may permit the return to be filed in another district.

The executor or administrator is required to file the return. If there is no qualified executor or administrator, the responsibility falls on any person in actual or constructive possession of property belonging to the decedent.

Where there is more than one executor or administrator, the return must be made jointly by all. If the executor is unable to make a return reporting the complete gross estate, he should give all the information concerning the property, including a full description and the name of every person holding a legal or beneficial interest in the property. The District Director can require that every such person make a return reporting that part of the gross estate that he or she holds.

Tax practitioners generally advise delaying the filing of the return until after the alternate valuation date, which is six months after the date of death. Until this time, it generally is not possible to determine whether values will be lower at the date of death or the alternate valuation date.

Collecting Information for the Return

Immediately after the death of the decedent, the executor or administrator and his attorney should begin to collect information for filing the estate tax return. They should save the stock market pages of the newspaper for the date of death, the alternate valuation date, and date on which any security is sold. The decedent's files and records should also be reviewed. Recent income tax returns will provide valuable data. The size and nature of a decedent's income usually indicate the make-up of the estate. Schedules of dividends furnish a list of decedent's stocks. These may also be obtained from the broker's statement of recent sales, purchases, and holdings. Deductions for real estate taxes and expenses disclose the existence and, frequently, the location of land and buildings. Deductions for interest paid indicate the existence of debts.

If appraisals of estate property are to be submitted with the return, the closer to the date of death they are made, the more accurate and valuable they will be. Select an experienced appraiser soon after the decedent's death. An appraisal by an expert is usually desirable to establish the value of both personal and real property. A combination of factors, such as sales of comparable property, rentals, mortgages, and local market conditions, is important in arriving at a conclusion as to the value of the property in question. Assessed valuation usually is not a reliable indication of the fair market value of real estate.

All gift tax returns for gifts made after September 8, 1976, should be collected. Gifts of certain interests, such as life insurance, made within three years of death are included in the gross estate. Furthermore, gift tax paid on gifts made within three years of death also is included in the estate. Taxable gifts after 1976 that are not included in the gross estate affect the computation of the estate tax.

Checklist of Property Subject to Estate Tax

Although the gross estate includes all property to the extent of decedent's interest at the time of death, this checklist may prevent the omission of includible property:

Real estate wherever located

Stocks

Dividends payable to decedent as stockholder of record on date prior to date of death, even though not paid at date of death

Bonds

Accrued interest to date of death

Mortgages and notes

Joint and survivor annuity

Refund annuity

Insurance proceeds payable to estate or to others where decedent owned the policy

Tax-exempt bonds, even though exempt from income tax

Accrued income to date of death, including salaries, commissions, and annuity payments

Value of dower, curtesy, or similar interests

Community property to the extent of decedent's interest

Interest in land contracts

Jointly held property (one-half if co-owner is spouse; otherwise subtract the proportion of other joint tenant's contribution)

Vested remainders

Cash on hand and in bank accounts

Partnership interests

Household and personal belongings such as furniture, jewelry, automobiles, and art objects

Gift tax paid on gifts made within three years of death

Gifts made within three years of death of an interest which if retained would have been included in the gross estate under Internal Revenue Code Section 2036 (retained life estate), 2037 (transfer taking effect at death), 2038 (revocable transfers), or 2042 (proceeds of life insurance)

Gifts within three years of death of life insurance on decedent's life

Transfers in which decedent retained some legal or beneficial interest in property

Refund claims

Vested death benefits

General powers of appointment

Patent and copyright rights

Flight insurance

Lump-sum distributions from pension plans, Keogh plans, and IRAs

Retirement annuities. The value of an annuity from an IRA or employer plan that is payable to a beneficiary other than the estate may qualify for a full or partial exclusion if IRA distributions began before 1985 or the decedent separated from employer service before 1985; no exclusion is allowed to the extent of the decedent's own nondeductible contributions to the plan.

A full exclusion is allowed for IRA funds if the decedent began taking distributions from the account before 1983 under a schedule that irrevocably set the form of benefits. If IRA distributions began in 1983 or 1984 and the decedent irrevocably elected the form of benefits before July 18, 1984, a $100,000 exclusion is allowed.

If the decedent began receiving distributions from an employer plan before 1983 under a schedule that irrevocably set the form of benefits, a full estate tax exclusion is allowed. If the decedent separated from service in 1983 or 1984, a $100,000 exclusion is allowed if the form of benefits is not changed before death; this is true even if distributions did not begin until after 1984.

Also included in the gross estate are the following items:

Tax refund claims.   Report the value of decedent's interest in a claim for refund of income taxes, even if it is being contested by the government. If a tax refund is made, report the amount actually received.

Wrongful death claims.   The proceeds of a wrongful death action are not generally includible in the decedent's estate. However, if the decedent became entitled during his or her lifetime for damages such as pain and suffering and medical expenses, the IRS will include the proceeds in the decedent's estate.

Compensation for services.   Include compensation and commissions earned by decedent prior to death to which he or she had a contractual or other legal claim. This would include severance pay which his or her employer agreed to pay in installments to his or her widow(er). Do not include a gratuitous payment made by an employer. Contingent fee claims of an attorney-decedent are also includible in the estate.

Contingent claims.   Any contingent claim is includible unless defeated by the decedent's death.

Nonresident aliens.   Only that part of the gross estate that is located in the United States is includible.

Property Not Subject to Estate Tax

The following items are exempt from estate tax:

- Federal survivors insurance benefits paid under the Social Security Act to widow(er), children, or parents
- Dividends declared but not payable to decedent as stockholder of record at time of death
- Life estate held by decedent created by another
- Insurance payable to beneficiaries other than estate where incidents of ownership are not held by decedent
- Death benefits in which decedent did not hold any vested rights
- Contingent remainders defeated by decedent's death
- Profits or income earned after decedent's death
- Unenforceable claims
- Retired U.S. service member's survivor annuity
- Claims of the decedent which were barred by a statute of limitations at date of decedent's death. The estate has the burden of proving that the claim was barred.

As discussed in the checklist of taxable property, an exclusion for retirement annuity benefits may be available for estates of certain individuals under pre-1985 transitional rules.

PREPARING FORM 706

A sample filled-in Form 706 may be found starting on page 934. Generally, the instructions accompanying each schedule of the form adequately explain the treatment of common items held by an estate. As a supplement to the instructions, a discussion of selected points is presented in the following pages. A complete discussion of estate tax problems is beyond the scope of this chapter. Where the official instructions and the following material do not cover a particular item, an estate tax service should be consulted.

Alternate Valuation Date

An executor may elect to value assets as of the date of death or six months later. The election may not be made if the value of the gross estate was below the filing threshold on the date of death. An election applies to all the assets of the estate. It may not be made for some assets and not for others.

The principal purpose of the election is to protect the estate from the effects of a falling market. Assets of the estate are generally not distributed until several months after the decedent's death. If, in the interim, the assets depreciated substantially and the executors were forced to use the date of death value, there might not be sufficient cash to meet the estate tax liability.

Alternate valuation may be elected only if the election decreases both the value of the gross estate and the estate tax liability. This rule prevents an estate with appreciated assets from electing alternate valuation in order to provide a surviving spouse with a stepped-up basis although the assets are not subject to estate tax because of the unlimited marital deduction.

If the election is made, values are fixed according to these rules: (1) For property distributed, sold, exchanged, or otherwise disposed of within six months after death, the value on the date of distribution, sale, or exchange. (2) If the property is not distributed, sold, or exchanged within six months, the value six months after the date of death. Changes in value due to mere lapse of time are disregarded. Valuation adjustments which are not due to the mere lapse of time must be accounted for. Examples of property interests which steadily decrease in value ("limited life" property) with the passage of time are patents and life estates. However, changes in the value of limited life property attributable to causes other than mere lapse of time may be reflected in the alternate valuation.

When the alternate valuation date is elected and the property is distributed or otherwise disposed of during the six-month period, the value on the date of disposition fixes the value for estate tax purposes. Later dispositions or sales by transferees of the estate are disregarded. Thus, if four months after the death of a decedent, the executor distributes stock valued at $10,000 to a beneficiary who sells it for $12,000 one month later, $10,000 is the value used on the estate tax return if the executor elects the alternate valuation date.

Filing the election.   An alternate valuation election for the estate must be made on an original estate tax return filed no later than one year after the filing date, including extensions. An election is irrevocable once made, even though adjustments on audit might make it disadvantageous.

EXAMPLE—

Albert Reddington died on February 4, 1999. His estate consisted of the following assets at date-of-death values: 1,000 shares of oil stock, $64,000; cash, $30,000; investment in a joint venture, $100,000; the family home, $425,000; and miscellaneous items such as the family car, paintings, jewelry, etc., $20,000.

On June 4, 1999, four months later, the executor distributed to the beneficiaries 500 shares of oil stock when their value was $30,000. Value on August 4, 1999, six months after decedent's death, was $25,000. The remaining 500 shares were distributed October 4, 1999. The joint venture suffered substantial reverses immediately after decedent's death, and the executor, on July 1, 1999, accepted a $50,000 payment for the decedent's interest in the venture. A painting was sold on June 4, 1999, at a loss of $2,000, although by August 4, 1999, the painting (now in the hands of the purchaser) had risen to its former value.

The table at the bottom of this page illustrates how each of the items is treated. If the alternate valuation date were elected by the executor, the gross estate would be $578,000; if no election were made, the gross estate would be $639,000.

Valuing Stocks and Bonds

Publicly traded stocks. If there were sales on the valuation date, report the mean between the highest and lowest quoted selling price on that date. If only the closing selling prices are available, then the fair market value is the mean between the quoted closing selling price on the valuation date and on the trading day before the valuation date. If there were no sales on the valuation date, the value is the weighted average of the means between the highest and lowest sales on the nearest dates before and after the valuation date. In computing this average, note: (1) you ignore nontrading days, such as holidays and weekends, and (2) you apply the number of trading days to the stock values as illustrated in the following examples (Reg. §20.2031-2).

EXAMPLES—

1. The valuation date is Friday, May 15. The mean sales prices per share on the nearest sales dates were $10 on Wednesday, May 13, two trading days before, and $15 on Wednesday, May 20, three trading days after the valuation date (Saturday, May 16 and Sunday, May 17 were not trading days). The value of the stock is fixed at $12 per share, arrived at as follows:

$$\frac{(3 \times 10) + (2 \times 15)}{5} = \frac{60}{5} = \$12$$

2. Same facts as in Example 1 except that the mean sale prices per share were $15 on May 13 and $10 on May 20. The value is fixed at $13 per share as follows:

$$\frac{(3 \times 15) + (2 \times 10)}{5} = \frac{65}{5} = \$13$$

3. The decedent died on Sunday. The mean prices per share were $20 on Friday and $23 on Monday. (Saturday and Sunday were not trading days.) Each share of stock is valued at $21.50.

$$\frac{(1 \times 23) + (1 \times 20)}{2} = \frac{43}{2} = \$21.50$$

If there were no actual sales within a reasonable period before and after the valuation date, value is fixed by use of bona fide bid and asked prices (Reg. § 20.2031-2 (c)). Take the mean between the bid and asked prices, if any, on the valuation date, or use the nearest trading dates before and after the valuation date and prorate according to the weighted average method described above.

If actual sales prices or bid and asked prices are not available either before or after the valuation date, then take as the value the mean between the highest and lowest available sales or bid and asked prices.

If a security is listed on more than one exchange, use the records of the exchange where the security is principally traded or the composite listing of combined exchanges, if available, in a publication of general circulation.

If price quotations of unlisted securities are obtained from brokers, attach letters furnishing such quotations to the return. Evidence of the sale of securities obtained from officers of the issuing companies should also be attached.

Blockage. If the quantity of stock to be valued is relatively large, the "blockage" method of valuation may be used. Under the blockage method, value is based on an estimate of the prices at which the quantity could be sold during a reasonable time.

Valuing unlisted or closely held stocks. The methods of valuing stocks and bonds described above may not be used if there are no sales or other market activity. This would be the case where a company's shares are closely held by one or a relatively limited number of stockholders. In fixing the value of inactive securities, all available financial data and all relevant factors are considered. In valuing stock of closely held corporations or the stock of corporations where marked quotations are either lacking or too scarce to be recognized, the IRS requires that certain factors be given careful analysis. *See* Revenue Ruling 59-60, 1959-1 CB 237, as modified by Revenue Ruling 65-193, 1965-2 CB 370, and amplified by Revenue Ruling 77-287, 1977-2 CB 319, Revenue Ruling 80-213, 1980-2 CB 101, and Revenue Ruling 83-120, 1983-2 CB 170. Treasury regulations also include a list of these factors. Buy-sell agreements may serve to fix valuation where the decedent is bound during life and his or her estate is bound after death to sell or offer for sale his or her share at a fixed or determinable price.

Valuing mutual-fund shares (open end). Open-end mutual-fund shares are valued at the redemption (bid) price and not at the higher "asked" price.

Reporting U.S. Savings Bonds

Include U.S. Savings Bonds owned by decedent at their redemption value. Redemption values for savings bonds are determined as follows: For Series E and EE Bonds, consult the Supplement to this book, obtain the values on the Internet at www.savingsbonds.gov/, or send for the book of redemption values which may be obtained for a small charge from the Superintendent of Documents, Government Printing Office, Washington, D.C. 20402. Specify the date of the decedent's death in your request. For Series H bonds, report par value plus accrued interest to date of death.

If a savings bond is registered in the name of the decedent and another as co-owners, it is included in the decedent's estate according to the joint ownership rules explained on the next page.

Assets (Example, page 854)	Value at Date of Death—	Value on Date of Distribution or Sale—	Value Six Months After Death—	Alternate Valuation—
500 shares of oil stock	$ 32,000	$ 30,000	$ 25,000	$ 30,000
500 shares of oil stock	32,000	—	25,000	25,000
Cash	30,000	—	—	30,000
Joint venture	100,000	50,000	—	50,000
Family home	425,000	—	425,000	425,000
Miscellaneous, including paintings	20,000	18,000	20,000	18,000
Total value	$639,000	—	—	$578,000

Most savings bonds records are maintained alphabetically by name and address of the registered owner or first-named co-owner. To obtain information from the Treasury Department on lost or misplaced bonds, or on cashing bonds where no co-owner or beneficiary is named, send the request to the Claims Department, Bureau of Public Debt, P.O. Box 1328, Parkersburg, West Virginia 26106-1328, together with proof of your appointment as legal representative, certified under the court seal.

Reporting Household Goods and Personal Effects

All household effects owned by a decedent at the time of death are included in the gross estate, including articles owned by the decedent but used by other members of his or her family.

The IRS requires an itemized list of all personal and household tangible property, with descriptions and specific valuations. For articles valued in excess of $3,000 (jewelry, furs, paintings, etc.) or a collection of similar articles valued in excess of $10,000, an appraisal should be submitted by an expert under oath, with a statement by the executor describing the expert's qualifications, as required by Treasury regulations.

The closer to the death date the appraisal is made, the more accurate it is, and the more acceptable it will be for estate tax purposes. Where an executor has an appraisal made, he will be able to dispose of the decedent's property before filing the return or waiting for an audit.

In the case of an item of property generally obtained by the public in the retail market, its fair market value is the price at which the item or a comparable item would be sold at retail. Thus, the fair market value of an automobile is the price for which an automobile of the same or approximately the same description, make, model, age, and condition could be purchased by a member of the general public, and not the price for which the particular automobile of the decedent would be purchased by a dealer in used automobiles.

Valuing Farm and Closely Held Business Real Property

The executor may elect, with the consent of the heirs, to value real property used in farming or a closely held business on the basis of its farming or business use, rather than its highest and best use, which is the fair market value. The special valuation, however, may not reduce the gross estate by more than $750,000 and applies only to the extent of the property passing to a qualified heir (explained below). You may make the election on a late filed return so long as it is the first return filed. The law provides standards for calculating the special use valuation and a method which may be used for valuing farm property (IRC §2032A(a)).

For estates of individuals dying after 1998, the $750,000 limit on the decrease in value that can result from special-use valuation will be adjusted for inflation.

To qualify for special use valuation: (1) the decedent must have been a citizen or resident of the United States at death; (2) the value of the farm or closely held business assets in the decedent's estate, including both real and personal property (but reduced by debts attributable to the real and personal property), must be at least 50 percent of the decedent's gross estate (reduced by debts and ex-penses) without regard to its special use value; (3) at least 25 percent of the adjusted value of the gross estate without regard to the special use value must be qualified farm or closely held business real property; (4) the real property qualifying for special use valuation must pass to a member of the decedent's family (a "qualified heir"); (5) such real property

must have been owned by the decedent or a member of his or her family and used or held for use as a farm or closely-held business for five of the last eight years prior to the decedent's death; and (6) there must have been material participation in the operation of the farm or closely held business by the decedent or a member of his or her family in five years out of the eight years immediately preceding the decedent's death.

If, within 10 years after the decedent's death (unless the heir dies sooner), the heir stops using the property as a farm or closely held business or sells or otherwise disposes of the property to nonfamily members, the tax savings from the special valuation are subject to recapture. The amount potentially subject to recapture is the excess of the estate tax liability which would have been incurred had the special use valuation provision not been utilized over the actual estate tax liability. The qualified heir remains personally liable for additional tax but may furnish a bond for the maximum additional tax that could be imposed should recapture result. No recapture occurs where involuntary conversion proceeds are invested in similar property.

An estate tax deduction for qualifying family-owned businesses is discussed on page 930.

Lifetime Transfers Includible in the Gross Estate

Retention of voting rights to stock in controlled cor-poration. Where a decedent gives away the stock but retains voting rights, the stock is included in the estate. The corporation is considered to be controlled if at any time after the transfer and within three years of death, the decedent owned (through the attribution rules), or had the right (either alone or in conjunction with any person) to vote, stock possessing at least 20 percent of the total combined voting power of all classes of stock. This rule applies for gifts after June 22, 1976 (IRC §2036(b)(2)).

Gifts within three years of death. Only certain gifts within three years of death are included in the estate (IRC §2035(d)). These are transfers of life insurance policies (IRC §2042), transfers of a retained life estate (IRC §2036), transfers of a retained reversionary interest (IRC §2037), and transfers of a revocable power (IRC §2038).

Gift tax paid within three years of death. All gift tax paid within three years of death is included in the estate (IRC 2035(c)). However, where the deceased and his or her spouse consented to "split" gifts made within the three-year period, and the deceased was the consenting spouse rather than the donor spouse, gift tax paid by the surviving spouse on the split gift is not included in the deceased spouse's estate.

Restrictions on estate freeze techniques for business holdings. Technical rules (IRC §§2701–2704) fix for gift tax and estate tax purposes the value of business interests transferred to family members. The valuation rules apply not only to typical "freeze" transactions involving the transfer of common stock and retention of preferred stock by a business owner but also to the release of voting or liquidation rights, the deferral of dividends on retained preferred stock holdings, the creation of life and remainder interests, and buy-sell agreements. For example, the law generally increases the gift tax value of transferred interests by assuming that nonmandatory retained rights, such as liquidation or conversion rights, or retained put or call rights, will not be exercised. The retained rights are generally treated as having a zero value but there are exceptions for rights that must be exercised at a specific time and at a specific amount, such as a right to a fixed-rate preferred stock cumulative dividend.

Obtaining IRS Valuation Statement

An executor or a donor may request in writing a statement from the IRS of its basis for valuing an item of property subject to estate or gift tax. The IRS must supply the information within 45 days of the request or the date it determined the value, whichever is later. The statement must explain the basis on which the value was determined, any computation used in arriving at the value, and a copy of any expert appraisal made by or for the IRS. The IRS, however, is not bound by its determination of value. By obtaining the IRS's statement, the executor or donor may be in a better position to decide whether to accept the IRS valuation or to litigate.

Penalty For Undervaluing Property

A 20% penalty may be imposed on estate tax or gift tax returns if the value claimed for any property is 50% or less of the correct value. There is no penalty unless the undervaluation results in a tax deficiency exceeding $5,000 (IRC §6662(g)). If the value claimed is 25% or less of the correct value, the penalty will be 40% of the underpayment, rather than 20% (IRC §6662(h)(2)(C)). The penalty may be avoided by showing reasonable cause for the claimed valuation.

Reporting Jointly Held Property

Different rules apply to joint tenancies between husbands and wives than apply to joint tenancies between persons who are not married (IRC 2040).

Joint tenant is surviving spouse. One-half the value of jointly owned property is included in the estate of the first spouse to die, regardless of who paid for the property. The one-half included in the estate is offset by the marital deduction. This rule also has income tax consequences to the surviving spouse. The half included in the estate at fair market value is part of the survivor's income tax basis. However, a 1992 Sixth Circuit decision held that where the joint interest was created before 1977, and the first spouse to die contributed the entire purchase price, 100% of the value is includible in his or her estate, and a stepped-up basis for 100% of the date-of-death value is allowed to the surviving spouse (*Gallenstein*, 975 F.2d 286 (6th Cir. 1992)). *See* Example 3 on page 107 for a summary of the Sixth Circuit's decision, which the Tax Court and Fourth Circuit have followed.

EXAMPLES—

1. Jones and his wife jointly own a vacation house which cost them $50,000 in 1983. In 1999 Jones dies when the house is worth $200,000. $100,000 is included in his estate. For income tax purposes, Mrs. Jones's basis for the house is $125,000.

Her original basis	$ 25,000
Basis for inherited portion	100,000
	$125,000

   On a sale of the home in 1999 for $200,000, Mrs. Jones would realize a $75,000 long-term capital gain ($200,000 – $125,000).

2. If Jones had owned the house in his own name and left it to Mrs. Jones, the house would have been included in his estate at $200,000. However, it would be offset by the marital deduction and Mrs. Jones's income tax basis would be $200,000. Thus, if she sold the house in 1999 for $200,000, there would be no taxable gain.

Joint tenant is someone other than surviving spouse. The full value of jointly held property is included in the gross estate. However, the value of the property is excludable from the estate to the extent that the estate can prove that a part of the property originally belonged to the surviving owner and was never received from the decedent for less than its value, or part of the property was acquired with funds originally belonging to the surviving owner. With the return, file an affidavit setting forth the circumstances.

If the property was acquired by the decedent and other owners by gift or inheritance, only the decedent's fractional interest is taxed. To figure the value of decedent's interest, divide the full value of the property by the number of joint tenants.

EXAMPLES—

1. Decedent and his brother acquired the property by gift as joint tenants. Include one-half of the value of the property in decedent's gross estate.
2. Decedent and his two surviving brothers had acquired the property as joint tenants under their uncle's will. Include one-third of the value of the property in decedent's gross estate.

Where the decedent furnished only part of the consideration, that proportionate part of the entire value is included in his estate.

EXAMPLE—

The fair market value of the jointly held property at the date of decedent's death is $60,000. The property originally cost $30,000, $25,000 of which was paid by the decedent. The amount included in decedent's estate is $50,000, that is, the value of the property at the date of death, $60,000, multiplied by the fraction $25,000/$30,000.

If the decedent, before acquiring the property, gave the surviving owner money or other property which was later used to help purchase the property, the value of the entire property is included in the decedent's estate, even though the property received as a gift may have appreciated in value between the time of the gift and the time of the purchase of the jointly held property. However, if the decedent made a gift of property during his or her life and income from that property was used to purchase jointly held property, the value attributable to that income is not includible.

The estate tax rules applicable to joint tenancies apply as well to funds on deposit in the joint names of the decedent and another. In the common forms of joint bank accounts, the survivor is entitled to the entire balance at his or her co-owner's death. However, not every bank account in the names of two or more persons is a joint tenancy. The owners might hold the account as tenants in common. State law should be consulted to determine the property rights created by the language of the account. If the funds on deposit in a joint account are payable to the surviving owner, they are includible in the decedent's estate unless the executor can prove that part of the funds originally belonged to the survivor. Proof of this nature is particularly difficult since it involves proving not only deposits but also withdrawals.

Where the decedent created joint property out of corporate stock, stock dividends issued are included in the decedent's gross estate unless the executor can show that the dividends were capitalized out of corporate profits earned after the date of the gift.

Where joint tenants assume a purchase money mortgage on the joint property, each is considered as having made an original contribution of one-half the amount of the mortgage.

Where the decedent registered U.S. Savings Bonds in co-ownership form, full redemption value of the bonds is included in decedent's gross estate, even if the decedent tried to give his or her interest to the other co-owner. The decedent can only make such a gift and so avoid estate tax by having the bonds re-issued in the name of the donee.

Deductions From the Gross Estate

Funeral expenses. The reasonable cost of a tombstone, monument, mausoleum, or burial plot, including the cost of future care, is deductible.

Executor's or administrator's commissions. Commissions that have actually been paid or, at the time of filing the estate tax return, may reasonably be expected to be paid, are deductible. If the commissions have not been fixed by court decree, the deduction will be allowed when the return is finally audited if the following three conditions are satisfied: (1) the District Director is reasonably satisfied that the commissions claimed will be paid, (2) the amount claimed is within the legally allowable limits of the law of the state in which the estate is being administered, and (3) it is usually accepted practice in the state to allow such an amount in estates of similar size and character. If the fees claimed have not been paid by the time the final audit of the return is made, the executor must submit an affidavit, stating that the amount claimed as a deduction has been agreed upon and will be paid.

The executor is under a continuing obligation to inform the District Director of any change in the status of his or her commissions. Thus, if the executor waives them after they have been allowed on the final audit, the additional tax must be paid with interest: A bequest or devise to the executor in lieu of commissions is not deductible. If the decedent fixed in the will the amount of commissions to be paid, this amount is deductible, provided it is not in excess of state law or practice.

Deduction for attorneys' fees. The rules applicable to the deduction of the executor's commissions are equally applicable to the deduction of attorneys' fees. A deduction for attorneys' fees incurred in contesting an asserted deficiency or in prosecuting a claim for refund should be claimed when the deficiency is contested or when the refund claim is prosecuted. The additional fees actually paid in contesting the deficiency or prosecuting the refund claim will be allowed whether or not the fees were claimed as a deduction on the estate tax return or refund claim.

Attorneys' fees incurred by beneficiaries incident to litigation as to their respective interests are not deductions of the estate.

Miscellaneous administration expenses. These expenses include court costs, surrogates' fees, accountants' fees, and appraisers' fees. Expenses necessarily incurred in marshalling assets and preserving and distributing the estate, including the cost of storing, insuring, or maintaining property of the estate, are deductible where immediate distribution to the beneficiaries is not feasible. Expenses of selling property of the estate are deductible if the sale is necessary to pay the decedent's debts, administration expenses, or taxes, to preserve the estate, or to effect distribution. These expenses include brokerage fees, auctioneers' fees, etc., if they are reasonably necessary. The IRS disallows expenses incurred in a sale made for the benefit or convenience of heirs. Courts conflict on this issue.

Where an item included in gross estate is disposed of in a bona fide sale to a dealer in such items at a price below its fair market value, the expense of selling the item is the lesser of the following amounts: (a) the amount by which the fair market value of the property on the applicable valuation date (date of death or alternate valuation date) exceeds the proceeds of the sale; or (b) the amount by which the fair market value of the property on the date of the sale exceeds the proceeds of the sale.

The handling of the deductions from the gross estate is also affected by the community property laws. The deduction for administrative and funeral expenses depends on whether the expenses are deemed to be an expense of the community estate or of the decedent's separate estate. If they are expenses of the community estate, only one-half the amount expended is deductible. If such expenses are allowable against the separate estate of the decedent, they are deductible to the extent so allowable. Similarly, if losses have been incurred with property which had been held in community, only one-half the loss is deductible. Also, if debts or mortgages are community obligations, only one-half the amounts should be listed as obligations of the estate.

Charitable bequests. A deduction is allowable for bequests to most charitable and nonprofit organizations. Unlike the charitable deduction for income tax purposes, there is no percentage limitation on the amount of the deduction. Furthermore, an outright bequest to a foreign charity is also deductible. Local law should be consulted in cases where close relatives are disinherited in favor of a charity. Some states may preclude all or a portion of such a bequest.

These considerations should also be noted:

If administration expenses or estate or inheritance taxes are payable out of a charitable bequest, the deduction is limited to the amount the charity actually receives.

Where, as a result of a qualified disclaimer executed by a legatee, a charity receives part of a decedent's estate, a charitable deduction may be allowed. The disclaimer must be irrevocable, timely (*see* page 931), voluntary, and made without consideration paid to the disclaiming legatee.

Subscriptions or pledges made by a decedent during his or her life are generally deductible if legally enforceable against the estate.

Where the will creates a trust for both private and charitable purposes, a deduction may be allowable for the charitable interest. The deduction is for the value of the charitable interest at the date of the decedent's death, computed actuarially according to Treasury tables. Bequests of both income interests and remainder interests will qualify for the charitable deduction only if the trust is either in an annuity trust or unitrust form. An annuity trust is one which fixes the noncharitable interest as a specific dollar amount payable each year. A unitrust fixes the noncharitable interest at a fixed percentage of the trust assets, as valued annually and payable each year.

Deductions are allowable for remainder bequests that are not in trust form where the property is a personal residence or a farm.

The Marital Deduction

Almost all property passing to the surviving spouse who is a U.S. citizen qualifies for the marital deduction on Schedule M of Form 706. There are no percentage or dollar limitations. Furthermore, certain terminable income interests may qualify for the marital deduction. The surviving spouse's income interest in a charitable remainder annuity trust or unitrust qualifies for the marital deduction as long as the decedent and spouse possess the only non-charitable interests.

A marital deduction is allowed for a terminable interest where the surviving spouse receives a general power of appointment over a specific portion of property. However, for estates of individuals dying after October 24, 1992, a qualifying "specific portion" must be determined on a fractional or percentage basis; interests that are expressed as a fixed dollar amount do not qualify (IRC §2056 (b)(10)).

The marital deduction also may be claimed for Qualified Terminable Interest Property, or QTIP (IRC 2056 (b) (7)). To qualify, the surviving spouse must be entitled for life to all the income from the property, payable at least annually. No person may have the power to appoint any part of the property to anyone other than the surviving spouse. The executor must elect to have the income propety treated as QTIP on the estate return. For example, a will may leave the surviving spouse income from trust property for life and direct that he or she receive the property after his or her death. If the executor makes the QTIP election, the decedent's estate may claim the marital deduction for the value of the entire property, not just for the surviving spouse's life income interest.

The QTIP election may also be made for part of a qualified terminable property interest. Relating to a fractional or percentile share of the property. The fraction or percentage share may be defined by a formula.

The executor makes the QTIP election on Schedule M of Form 706 simply by listing the qualified terminable interest property on Schedule M and deducting its value. The QTIP election is *presumed* to have been made if this is done. The election is *irrevocable*.

The election postpones tax until the earlier of two events: a sale or other disposition of the interest by the surviving spouse or the death of the surviving spouse. If the property is held to death, it is included in the surviving spouse's estate. The estate of the spouse is entitled to recover the tax imposed on the life income interest from the person or persons receiving the property unless the surviving spouse's will provides otherwise.

The QTIP election does not apply to an income interest fixed for a term of years or which ends on the happening of an event, such as remarriage. Furthermore, the QTIP election does not qualify for a marital deduction where an accumulation clause allows the trustee to accumulate income above the amount thought necessary for the surviving spouse's needs (*Estate of Ellington*, 96 TC 760 (1991)).

During the surviving spouse's life, principal may be withdrawn only for the surviving spouse's benefit. The decedent may give the surviving spouse or other person the power to appoint the principal remaining at the surviving spouse's death; this power is exercisable only at or after the surviving spouse's death.

A marital deduction is allowed under the QTIP rules for a transfer to a spouse of an interest in a joint and survivor annuity in which only the surviving spouse can have the right to receive any payments before his or her death. However, the executor may irrevocably elect out of the QTIP treatment on Schedule M of Form 706.

The rules for providing a life QTIP interest in trust are similar to the rules applied to power of appointment trusts under prior law. The basic difference is that a QTIP income interest qualifies for the marital deduction even though the surviving spouse does not have a power of appointment. The power to choose the final beneficiaries remains with the spouse who owns the property. Thus, the QTIP rules provide an important planning technique for a spouse who wants to provide for his survivor but at the same time wants to control who takes the property on the death of the survivor.

Marital deduction for noncitizen surviving spouse. A marital deduction may not be claimed for property passing to a surviving spouse who is not a United States citizen unless: (1) the surviving spouse becomes a citizen before the estate return is filed, and was a resident of the U.S. at all times after the decedent's death and before becoming a citizen, or (2) the surviving spouse's interest is in a qualified domestic trust (QDOT) (IRC §2056A). Generally, in a QDOT, the trust instrument must provide that at least one trustee be an individual U.S. citizen or a domestic corporation with the right to withhold estate tax due on distributions of trust corpus. The IRS may waive the requirement of a U.S. trustee and recognize certain nontrust arrangements as QDOT trusts.

If the value of the QDOT assets as of the date of death exceeds $2 million, Treasury regulations require that at least one trustee be a U.S. bank or a U.S. branch of a foreign bank if there is also a U.S. co-trustee

at all times. Alternatively, the trustee may furnish security in the form of a bond or letter of credit. If the value of the QDOT assets is $2 million or less, the bank or security requirement does not have to be met if the trust instrument provides that no more than 35% of the value of the assets may be invested in real property located outside of the U.S. (Reg. § 20.2056A-2(d)).

For the marital deduction to apply, the executor must make an irrevocable election on the decedent's estate tax return for the entire value of the trust property; *see* Schedule M of Form 706. Estate tax applies to any distribution from a QDOT before the death of the surviving spouse except for distributions of income to the surviving spouse, distributions of corpus made to the surviving spouse on account of hardship or reimbursements to the surviving spouse for income tax paid on a lump-sum distribution from a qualified plan, or on certain nonassignable annuities (Reg. Sec. §20.2056A-5). Estate tax also applies upon the death of the surviving spouse, or if the trust ceases to qualify as a QDOT. The estate tax due on these "taxable events" is reported on Form 706-QDT. Form 706-QDT must also be filed for years in which a hardship distribution is made although no tax is due on such distributions.

Marital deduction planning. The unlimited marital deduction may lure an individual into leaving everything to a spouse in an effort to save taxes. While it is true that this will save taxes for the first estate, such a complete bequest may be unnecessary and unwise. This is because each estate has a credit which protects a sizable portion of it from tax. Moreover, what is saved by the first estate from leaving everything to a spouse may be at the expense of the surviving spouse's estate.

You may want to take advantage of the unlimited marital deduction if the major asset of the estate is a substantial income-producing asset. The marital deduction permits the asset to pass free of taxes which, if incurred, might have required a sale of the asset. On the other hand, in some situations, it may be advisable to leave only up to 50% of an estate to a spouse. If both estates are subject to tax, they will be subject to lower graduated estate tax rates.

Expenses, debts, and state death taxes may limit the deduction. In planning for the marital deduction, a planner should be aware that even when the unlimited marital deduction is used and all property is left to a spouse, an estate tax may be incurred in these situations: (1) administration expenses of the estate are taken as an income tax deduction, (2) debts against the estate are charged against marital deduction property, and (3) state death taxes are incurred and charged against marital deduction property.

EXAMPLE—
> An estate of $1,200,000 is left entirely to a surviving spouse. The estate has administration expenses of $300,000. The marital deduction is $900,000. There is no estate tax if the expenses are claimed as an estate tax deduction. But if the expenses are claimed as an income tax deduction, there may be an estate tax based on a taxable estate of $300,000 unless credits eliminate the tax.

If the couple has a large estate and also lives in a state which has a substantial estate tax, especially one which does not permit an unlimited marital deduction, federal estate tax may be incurred on the first estate. The large state death tax which exceeds the federal credit allowed for state death taxes may reduce the amount of the marital deduction and thus subject the estate to federal estate tax.

To utilize the marital deduction most effectively, estimate the estate taxes that will be due on both estates under alternative dispositions of property. After deducting the value of marital deduction property passing to the surviving spouse, estimate the tax liability on the estate of the spouse who is assumed, for purposes of the estimate, to be the first to die. Then calculate the potential estate tax liability of the surviving spouse's estate, which includes the property inherited from the first estate. Compare the combined tax liability after distributions for the marital deduction with the combined tax liability without these distributions. Vary the amounts qualifying for the deduction and figure the tax costs. By doing this, you can determine how much each estate should hold so that the "combined estate tax" will be in the range that will best achieve tax saving while providing for your surviving spouse. You may find that you can shelter property from tax through the unified credit rather than leave marital deduction property which may be subject to tax in the estate of the surviving spouse. If the estate is not greater than the amount that would be offset by the unified credit, you need not be concerned with the amount of the marital deduction as an estate tax reducing item. The minimum amount to be left the spouse is determined by state law and the maximum amount by personal desires.

Property which does not qualify for the marital deduction and which is sheltered by the unified credit may still benefit a spouse by being placed in a nonmarital deduction or bypass trust.

Formula clauses. Between the time an estate plan is drawn and the time of death, property values may change, and new assets may be acquired and others disposed of. These changes will affect the amount of the marital deduction. Property going to the spouse may be worth more or less than the amount projected as the deduction. This projected tax saving may be lost. Periodic reviews which may lead to revisions of the will or other property dispositions are the most direct way to meet changes in property holdings. But this is not always practical, and you may prefer to solve the difficulty by using a formula clause. With the increase in the exemption equivalent, a formula clause may be based on an amount directed to an heir other than the spouse or to a nonmarital deduction or by-pass trust with the balance of your estate passing directly to a surviving spouse or to a marital deduction trust.

The "estate" on which the percentage will be computed should be defined carefully. The clause should select the date on which the property will be valued; whether or not administrative expenses will be deducted before computing the value of the estate; and whether or not assets which pass outside of the will will be considered.

Rather than use a formula clause, a couple may rely on the surviving spouse to decide how much of the marital deduction property should be taken through the exercise of a disclaimer.

You may consider combining a disclaimer with an unlimited marital deduction disposition. If there is no need for the unlimited provision, the survivor can disclaim part of the bequest. The disclaimer must be made within nine months after death of the first spouse. A QTIP election may also serve a similar purpose.

Wills in existence prior to September 12, 1981, in which formula clauses were defined in terms of the old marital deduction limitation, should be reviewed. Unless the clause is amended, the formula clause in the will may apply to limit property passing to the surviving spouse and will limit the amount of the marital deduction.

A "survivorship presumption" clause. Where a couple dies at the same time and the order of death is unknown, state laws generally presume that the person whose estate is being distributed survived the person who was to inherit from the estate. For example, a married couple perish together in an air accident; the order of their deaths is not known. Under state law, neither would inherit from the other, and no marital deduction could be claimed by the estate of either spouse. To prevent this result, a will may state that the spouse shall be presumed to have survived the testator if the order of their deaths cannot be established. If the couple do, in fact, die simultaneously, two estates will automatically come into being. The estate of the spouse considered first to die may claim the marital deduction. A survivorship-presumption clause will have

no effect if the order of death from a common disaster is known, as where, for a short time after the accident, one spouse survives.

Bequests to spouse subject to a condition. If the spouse's right to property is subject to a condition, the marital deduction may not be allowed. For example, a spouse is given life income in a trust, with the remainder to her estate. But the trust is subject to this condition: "If my wife should remarry, then her interest will terminate." No part of the trust qualifies for the marital deduction.

By law, the following condition will not disqualify a bequest from the marital deduction: That a surviving spouse outlive the decedent by at least six months or not die as a result of a common disaster in which the decedent died. A will may combine the six-month condition with the common disaster condition and qualify property for the marital deduction.

Life insurance qualifying for the marital deduction. Insurance proceeds qualify for the marital deduction if the proceeds are payable to the surviving spouse in a lump sum.

If the proceeds are payable in installments to the surviving spouse, a marital deduction is allowed provided: Installments, including interest, are payable annually or more frequently, starting not later than 13 months after the decedent's death. The surviving spouse alone must have the power to have the proceeds paid to him- or herself or the estate. This power is usually expressed in terms of a "right of withdrawal" or "right to direct payment." If a policy provides for the proceeds to go to secondary beneficiaries in the event of the spouse's death, the proceeds will not qualify unless there is an overriding provision that, notwithstanding any other provision contained in the policy, the spouse may exercise a power of appointment over all or a specific portion of the proceeds.

Life insurance policies generally allow for an election of a settlement payment plan under which the insured may designate the manner in which the proceeds will be paid out to the beneficiary. These options vary, and it is possible that a particular settlement plan in a policy may fail to meet one or more of the above tests. Following are examples of terms frequently found in settlement payment plans and their estate tax consequences:

1. The policy provides that the spouse receives the entire interest in the policy and either the installments are to continue for his or her life, or the installment or interest payments generally extend for a definite time (for example, 10 years in annual payments), with the remainder to his or her estate. The proceeds qualify for the marital deduction, because the spouse is entitled to all of the proceeds.

2. The policy provides that payments are to be made to the spouse for a guaranteed period. This does not satisfy the requirement that the spouse is to receive all of the proceeds because he or she is not entitled to the entire proceeds or a specific portion of the proceeds. Therefore, no part of the proceeds qualify for the marital deduction.

3. The policy provides that a specific percentage of the proceeds are earmarked for the spouse, for example, one-half, payable in installments for the spouse's life, with the remainder to the spouse's estate. Only one-half the proceeds qualify for the marital deduction.

The insurance company may require that the right of withdrawal be exercised on a particular form or that it receive reasonable notice. The company's requirement would not disqualify the proceeds for the marital deduction.

Effect of a disclaimer by spouse. A surviving spouse may want to disclaim an interest in property bequeathed to him or her. For example, the surviving spouse may disclaim an interest in property to allow the disclaimed interest to pass directly to the children. When the surviving spouse's present wealth is sufficient to meet his or her own desires for life, might be advisable to disclaim property. A disclaimer is often used to reduce taxes on the estate and/or avoid a later gift tax if the surviving spouse plans to give away the property during his or her life. A disclaimer by a surviving spouse will not be disqualified where the interest disclaimed passes to such a spouse as, for example, where the disclaimed property passes to a trust in which the spouse is income beneficiary, but the spouse's power to direct enjoyment of the disclaimed property must be limited; see Reg.§ 25.2518-2(e)(2)).

Where a surviving spouse is entitled to receive a property interest in decedent's estate as a result of a disclaimer made by another person, such interest will be treated as property passing from the decedent to the spouse if such person made a qualified disclaimer.

Valuation of the interest passing to the surviving spouse. It is the value of the property less claims against the property or claims of the spouse against the decedent, which the property was intended to satisfy (Reg. § 20.2056 (b)-4).

EXAMPLES—

1. Jones devised a residence valued at $125,000 to his wife, with a direction that she pay $5,000 to his sister. For the purpose of the marital deduction, the value of the property interest passing to his wife is $120,000.

2. Smith devised real property to his wife in satisfaction of a debt owing to her. The debt is a deductible claim on Schedule K of Form 706. If the wife is obligated to relinquish the claim as a condition to acceptance of the devise, the value of the devise is, for the purpose of the marital deduction, reduced by the amount of the claim.

3. Brown bequeathed securities to his wife in lieu of her interest in property held by them as community property under state law. The wife elected to relinquish the community property interest and take the bequest. For the purposes of the marital deduction, the value of the bequest is reduced by the value of the community property interest relinquished by her. If the bequest had been in lieu of the wife's dower interest (or statutory estate created in lieu of dower or courtesy), the value of the bequest is not reduced by the value of the dower interest relinquished by her.

If, under the terms of the decedent's will or under local law, the executor is required to discharge a mortgage or other encumbrance on property passing from the decedent to his or her spouse out of other assets of the estate or is required to reimburse the spouse for the amount of the mortgage, the payment or reimbursement constitutes an additional interest passing to the surviving spouse.

Deduction Options for Estate Losses and Administrative Expenses

Administrative expenses and losses of an estate generally may not be claimed on both the estate tax return and the estate's income tax return. The executor must decide on which return the deduction will provide the larger tax reduction.

To claim the deduction on the income tax return, he or she must file in duplicate a statement that the item has not already been allowed as a deduction for estate tax purposes, and waive the right to have it allowed.

When the executor claims the deduction on the estate tax return, he or she may do so without filing a statement and waiver. Thus, if it later develops that the deduction will benefit the estate more by taking it on the income tax return, the executor may do so if: (1) the statute of limitations for the year in which the income tax deduction is sought has not expired, and (2) the estate tax return on which the

deduction has already been claimed is not closed.

Where it is not known immediately on which return to claim the deduction, the best procedure is to claim the deduction on the estate tax return and make the election when all the facts necessary for a proper determination become known.

EXAMPLE—

Jim Anderson died January 1, 1995. The executor retained an attorney for the estate whose fee is an allowable deduction from the gross estate and also from the estate's gross income for that year. The estate tax return is filed in September 1995. On it, the attorney's fee is taken as a deduction. The estate's income tax return is filed April 15, 1997, without having claimed the fee as a deduction. The executor has until April 15, 2000 (or earlier, if the estate tax deduction is finally allowed before that date), to make the election on the estate's income tax return.

A deduction for estate tax purposes is "allowed" (at which time the election may no longer be made) either at the expiration of the statute of limitations for assessment of a deficiency or when the estate has entered into a closing agreement.

Deductible items may be split between the estate and income tax returns. For example, the executor may claim part of the item for income tax purposes by filing the waiver and claim the balance for estate tax purposes.

Certain expenses may be claimed on both returns where the expenses relate to "income in respect of a decedent," such as interest, taxes, and business expenses which accrued at the date of death. These items are deductible, not only as claims against the estate, but also as income tax deductions. For example, real property tax or interest accrued but unpaid at the time of the decedent's death may be deducted on both returns.

Selling expenses. A double deduction is not allowed for expenses incurred by an estate in selling securities to pay taxes and other expenses. For example, with securities, commissions and other selling expenses are deductible as administration expenses on the decedent's estate tax return or as an offset against the selling price in computing gain on the estate's income tax return. An expense item may not be used to offset the sales price for income tax purposes if the same expense item is deducted for estate tax purposes.

Deduction for Qualified Family-Owned Business Interest (QFOBI)

For estates of individuals dying after 1997, a deduction of up to $675,000 may be elected for an estate with a qualifying interest in a family business (Code Section 2057). The deduction is subject to qualification tests and possible recapture. The deduction is coordinated with the unified credit. The deduction and the credit together may shield a maximum of $1.3 million of assets from estate tax. If the maximum $675,000 deduction for qualified family owned business interests is claimed, the applicable exclusion amount is limited to $625,000. If the deduction is less than $675,000, the applicable exclusion amount is $625,000 plus the excess of $675,000 over the allowable deduction, but no more than the applicable exclusion amount available to estates not claiming the family-owned business interest deduction. For example, the estate of an individual dying in 1999 claimed a QFOBI deduction of $665,000; the applicable exclusion amount for the estate is $635,000 ($675,000 – 665,000 + 625,000). This is the equivalent of a unified credit of $205,750. If the QFOBI deduction were $575,000, the applicable exclusion would be $650,000, the maximum 1999 exclusion, which gives a unified credit of $211,300.

To qualify for the deduction, the adjusted value of the family-owned business interests generally must exceed 50% of the decedent's adjusted gross estate. A business interest qualifies as family owned if it is at least 50% owned by the decedent's family, or if it is at least 70% owned by two families or 90% by three families and the decedent's family owns at least 30%. For five of the eight years preceding the date of death, the business interests had to be owned by the decedent or family members, and they must have materially participated in the business operations. The business interest must pass to family members or 10-year employees. Such qualified heirs are subject to a recapture tax if they do not meet a material participation test within 10 years of the date of death or if a disposition of the business interest is made to non-qualifying persons. A qualified heir will not be treated as having disposed of a business interest by ceasing to engage in that busness if any member of a qualified heir's family continues in the business.

For further technical details, see instructions to Schedule T of Form 706.

Disclaimers

A qualified disclaimer not to accept property will be recognized for federal tax purposes, even if local law does not technically characterize the refusal as a "disclaimer," or if the person refusing the property was considered to have been the owner of the legal title to the property before disclaiming it.

A "qualified disclaimer" is an irrevocable and unqualified refusal to accept an interest in property that meets four tests: (1) It is in writing. (2) It is received by the transferor of the interest, the legal representative, or the holder of the legal title to the property not later than nine months after the day on which the transfer creating the interest is made (IRC §2518). Persons under age 21 have until nine months after their 21st birthday to deliver the disclaimer (Reg. §25.2518-2(d)(3)). (3) The person must not have accepted the interest or any of its benefits before making the disclaimer. (4) As a result of the disclaimer the interest must pass without any direction on the part of the person making the disclaimer to the surviving spouse or a person other than the person making the disclaimer (IRC § 2518 (b)(4)). However, the rule that the disclaimed interest must pass to a person other than the person making the disclaimer does not apply where the disclaimant is the surviving spouse, but the spouse's power to direct the enjoyment of the disclaimed property must be limited (Reg. § 25.2518-2 (e)(2)).

The person making a qualified disclaimer will not be treated as having made a gift to the person to whom the interest passes by reason of the disclaimer.

Computing the Estate Tax

If the decedent did not make taxable gifts, the estate tax rates (*see* page 933) are applied to the amount of the taxable estate (IRC §2001). The resulting tax is then reduced by the applicable credits. The separate generation-skipping transfer tax, if any, is computed on Schedule R of Form 706.

If the decedent made taxable gifts after 1976, the tax rates are applied to the sum of the: (1) taxable estate, and (2) adjusted taxable gifts, *less* (3) the amount of gift tax paid on gifts made after 1976. Adjusted taxable gifts are gifts made after 1976 which exceed the $10,000 annual exclusion ($3,000 exclusion before 1982) and which are not otherwise included in the taxable estate as a gift within three years of death or because rights were retained by the decedent until death. In computing adjusted taxable gifts, the IRS may not revalue gifts that were reported on a timely filed gift tax return if the gift tax statute of limitations has expired. The value of the prior gifts is the value as finally determined on a gift tax return that is not challenged by the IRS, or determined by the IRS or a court, or by a settlement agreement between the taxpayer and the IRS, even if no gift tax was paid or assessed (IRC § 2001(f)).

A credit for gift taxes paid on pre-1977 gifts is available where such gifts are included in the estate. Pre-1977 gifts may be included because of rights retained by the decedent until death. For post-1976 gifts, an indirect "credit" for gift taxes is built into the estate tax computation as discussed in the preceding paragraph. That is, gift tax paid on post-1976 gifts is subtracted from the tentative tax computed on the taxable estate plus adjusted taxable gifts.

EXAMPLE—

An individual dying in 1999 leaves a taxable estate of $665,000. He did not make any gifts subject to gift tax.

Taxable estate		$665,000
Tax on $500,000	$155,800	
Tax on excess of $165,000 at 37%	61,050	
Tentative tax		216,850
Less: Unified credit*		211,300
Tax		$ 5,550

The unified credit is explained below.

Credits

The following credits reduce estate tax if they apply:

Unified credit (or applicable credit amount). The tax credit is the same for gift tax and estate tax purposes. The benefits of the graduated rates are phased out once cumulative transfers exceed $10,000,000. For the estate of an individual dying in 1999, the credit is $211,300 (IRC §2010). The credit gradually increases until it reaches $1 million in 2006.

Individual dying in—	Exclusion amount—	Unified Credit—
1999	$650,000	$211,300
2000–2001	$675,000	$220,550
2002–2003	$700,000	$229,800
2004	$850,000	$287,300
2005	$950,000	$326,300
2006	$1,000,000	$345,800

The unified tax credit replaced the $60,000 estate tax exemption and $30,000 lifetime gift tax exemption allowed prior to 1977. Where part or all of the $30,000 lifetime gift tax exemption was used against gifts made after September 8, 1976, and before January 1, 1977, the unified credit is reduced by 20% of the amount allowed as an exemption on those gifts (IRC §2010(b)). Thus, if the entire $30,000 exemption was used on a gift made after September 8, 1976, the unified credit is permanently reduced by $6,000 (20% of $30,000).

Phaseout of graduated rates. The benefit of graduated tax rates is phased out if the taxable estate plus adjusted taxable gifts made after 1976 exceeds $10 million. Tax liability is increased by 5% of the excess over $10 million until the benefits are completely phased out. The 5% additional tax applies to transfers in excess of $10,000,000 but not over $17,184,000 (IRC §2001(c)(2)). Estates exceeding $17,184,000 are taxed at a flat 55%.

State death tax credit. State death taxes are credited against the federal estate tax. Most states impose death taxes that are at least equal to the maximum credit allowed. The credit is computed on the taxable estate reduced by $60,000 (IRC §2011 (b)). Note that the unified tax credit is deducted from the tentative estate tax before applying the state death tax credit.

Credit for federal estate tax on prior transfers. It sometimes happens that part of the property in an estate was taxed in another estate. A federal estate tax credit is provided to save the second estate from paying full tax again on such property. To get the benefit of this credit, the property must have been included in a taxable estate within 10 years before or two years after the death of the person in question. The amount of the credit is in proportion to the time lapse between the date the property was previously taxed and the date of death of the person whose estate is claiming the credit (IRC §2013). The credit is computed on Schedule Q of Form 706.

Foreign death credit. Sometimes when a person dies, part of his or her property is in a foreign country to which death taxes must be paid. The IRS allows a credit to the estate for such taxes paid (IRC §2014). This credit is fixed by law or tax treaty.

Extension of Time To File Form 706

If a reasonably complete return cannot be filed within nine months from the date of death, the District Director, upon a showing of reasonable cause, may extend the time to file up to six months from the due date (IRC §6081). The application for an extension, Form 4768, must be made within the nine-month period after death. A full explanation of the cause for delay must be furnished with the application.

An extension of time for filing a return does not postpone the time for payment of the estate tax, or the running of interest, which starts after the due date of the return.

Even where all the data or assets of the estate cannot be determined by the filing date, a return should be filed on time with an attached statement, explaining and specifying which information or assets have not been included and the reasons for their exclusion. When the information is obtained, the District Director should be notified, or, at the time of the examination of the return, the information can be given to the examining officer.

Extensions of Time for Payment of Tax

An application may be made on Form 4768 for an extension of time to pay estate tax. The extension period is generally up to 12 months, but the IRS has discretion to allow extensions of up to ten years (IRC §6161(a)(2)). By law, reasonable cause must be shown for extensions of up to 10 years, but IRS regulations also require reasonable cause for the 12-month extension.

The regulations give the following examples to illustrate reasonable cause (Reg. §20.6161-1(a)):

1. A gross estate has sufficient liquid assets to pay the estate tax, but the assets are located in several jurisdictions and not under the executor's immediate control. Although the executor has used due diligence, he cannot readily marshal the liquid assets.
2. A substantial part of the estate consists of payments to be made in the future (royalties and accounts receivable). These assets do not provide present cash for payment of the tax, and the only terms upon which the estate could borrow against such assets would inflict a loss upon the estate.
3. The estate includes a substantial claim which cannot be collected without litigation. The actual size of the taxable estate is unascertainable when the tax is due.
4. Without borrowing at a rate of interest higher than usually available, the estate does not have sufficient funds with which to pay the entire estate tax and, at the same time, satisfy claims due against it and make a reasonable allowance for the widow(er) and children during the administration period.

IRS regulations also provide the following examples of "undue hardship," which before the 1976 Tax Reform Act was the standard

for obtaining an extension of up to 10 years (Reg. §20.6161-1(a)(2)). These situations should qualify under the more liberal "reasonable cause" test that applies under current law for up-to-10-year extensions as well as up-to-12-month extensions.

1. A farm or a closely held business makes up a significant portion of an estate. It does not meet the percentage requirements for an election to postpone payment without approval of the District Director (under IRC §6166; *see* below), but sufficient funds for payment of estate tax are not available. Although the business could be sold to an unrelated person for fair market value, the executor needs time to raise cash from other sources to pay the tax.
2. The assets of the estate, which must be liquidated to provide cash for the tax, must be sold at a sacrifice price or in a depressed market.

In the above cases, the amount of the tax subject to the extension would be limited to the amount of cash which the estate cannot raise to pay the tax.

The granting of an extension of time to pay the estate tax does not relieve the executor from the duty of filing the return on or before the date it is due or prevent the running of interest.

Election to extend payment if estate has large interest in a closely held business (IRC § 6166). In some cases the executor may elect to extend over a 14-year period the payment of the tax attributable to an interest in a closely held business without permission from the District Director. The first installment may be postponed until the end of the fifth year after the regular due date. The entire tax is due in at least two but no more than 10 equal installments. After the first payment, installments are made annually. Interest on the tax for the five-year deferral period accrues at the rate of two percent according to a formula which may be found on pages 8–9 of the instructions to Form 706. Interest paid on installment payments is not deductible as an administrative expense of the estate.

To qualify for the 14-year extension, the value of the interest in a closely held business must exceed 35% of the adjusted gross estate. Qualifying ownership percentages for corporations and partnerships may be found on page 8 of the instructions to From 706.

When the election is made. The executor may make the election at any time up to the due date of the return (IRC §6166(d)). Where an election is made, the executor may elect a special lien provision and be discharged from personal liability for the estate tax if all parties with an interest in the property consent (IRC §6324A).

Redeeming Stock To Pay Death Taxes

Generally, the redemption of stock runs the risk of being treated as a dividend and taxed at ordinary income rates. However, where stock is included in an estate, the redemption proceeds may be taxable as capital gain under special rules. Capital gain treatment is allowed where the value of stock of the redeeming corporation included in the estate of a decedent exceeds 35% of the excess of the gross estate over the deductions for expenses, debts, taxes, and losses. If the stock is included in the estate, capital gain treatment extends to a redemption from the estate, a beneficiary, or a third party (such as a donee who received it as a gift within three years of decedent's death), but only if the owner's interest is reduced either directly or through a binding obligation to contribute toward the payment of debts, expenses, or taxes (IRC §303).

Estate Tax Return for Nonresident Aliens

For estate tax purposes, a nonresident alien is a decedent who is neither a U.S. citizen nor U.S. resident at the time of death (IRC §2101 (a)). An estate tax return for a nonresident alien must be filed on Form 706-NA if the gross estate subject to U.S. estate tax is greater than $60,000, reduced by taxable gifts made after 1976 that are not includible in the gross estate and by the specific gift tax exemption allowed for gifts made after September 8, 1976, and before 1977.

Form 706-NA for nonresident aliens is filed with the Internal Revenue Service Center, Philadelphia, Pennsylvania 19255.

For nonresident aliens, only that part of the gross estate that is located in the United States is subject to estate tax (IRC §2103). For estates of decedents dying after November 10, 1988, the estate and gift tax rates that apply to U.S. citizens and residents also apply to estates of nonresident aliens. However, instead of a credit that applies to gift taxes and estates of U.S. citizens and residents, the estate of a nonresident alien is allowed an estate tax credit (no credit for gift tax is allowed) of only $13,000, which exempts the first $60,000 of the estate from estate tax (IRC §2102(c)(1)). Where permitted by treaty, the estate of a nonresident alien may use the credit allowed to a U.S. citizen multiplied by a percentage. This percentage is figured by dividing the value of the decedent's gross estate located in the United States by the value of the entire estate wherever it is located (IRC §2102 (c)(3)).

A marital deduction is allowed for U.S. property passing from a nonresident alien decedent to a spouse who is a U.S. citizen under the same rules that apply to estates of decedents who are U.S. citizens or residents. If the surviving spouse is not a U.S. citizen, property transferred from the estate of a nonresident alien decedent qualifies for a marital deduction only if it is in a qualified domestic trust (QDOT), as discussed on page 928.

For estates of certain residents of possessions of the United States, dying after November 10, 1988, the unified credit is equal to the greater of $13,000 and $46,800 multiplied by a percentage. This percentage is figured by dividing the value of the decedent's gross estate located in the United States by the value of the entire estate wherever located (IRC §2102(c)(2)). This unified credit rule only applies to individuals who obtained U.S. citizenship solely by being citizens of a U.S. possession, or by birth or residence within a U.S. possession (IRC §2209)).

U.S. CITIZEN OR RESIDENT DECEDENTS—RATE SCHEDULES AND CREDITS

Table A—Unified Rate Schedule

Column A Taxable amount over	Column B Taxable amount not over	Column C Tax on amount in Column A	Column D Rate of tax on excess over amount in Column A
			(Percent)
0	$10,000	0	18
$10,000	20,000	$1,800	20
20,000	40,000	3,800	22
40,000	60,000	8,200	24
60,000	80,000	13,000	26
80,000	100,000	18,200	28
100,000	150,000	23,800	30
150,000	250,000	38,800	32
250,000	500,000	70,800	34
500,000	750,000	155,800	37
750,000	1,000,000	248,300	39
1,000,000	1,250,000	345,800	41
1,250,000	1,500,000	448,300	43
1,500,000	2,000,000	555,800	45
2,000,000	2,500,000	780,800	49
2,500,000	3,000,000	1,025,800	53
3,000,000	—	1,290,800	55*

For cumulative transfers over $10 million, see page 931 for phase-out rule.

Table B—Computation of Maximum Credit for State Death Taxes

(Based on federal adjusted taxable estate which is the federal taxable estate reduced by $60,000)

Adjusted taxable estate equal to or more than— (1)	Adjusted taxable estate less than— (2)	Credit on amount on in Column (1) (3)	Rate of credit excess over amount in Column (1) (4)	Adjusted taxable estate equal to or more than— (1)	Adjusted taxable estate less than— (2)	Credit on amount in Column (1) (3)	Rate of credit on excess over amount in Column (1) (4)
			(Percent)				
0	$40,000	0	None	2,040,000	2,540,000	106,800	8.0
$40,000	90,000	0	0.8	2,540,000	3,040,000	146,800	8.8
90,000	140,000	$400	1.6	3,040,000	3,540,000	190,800	9.6
140,000	240,000	1,200	2.4	3,540,000	4,040,000	238,800	10.4
240,000	440,000	3,600	3.2	4,040,000	5,040,000	290,800	11.2
440,000	640,000	10,000	4.0	5,040,000	6,040,000	402,800	12.0
640,000	840,000	18,000	4.8	6,040,000	7,040,000	522,800	12.8
840,000	1,040,000	27,600	5.6	7,040,000	8,040,000	650,800	13.6
1,040,000	1,540,000	38,800	6.4	8,040,000	9,040,000	786,800	14.4
1,540,000	2,040,000	70,800	7.2	9,040,000	10,040,000	930,800	15.2
				10,040,000	—	1,082,800	16.0

Form **706** (Rev. July 1999) Department of the Treasury Internal Revenue Service	**United States Estate (and Generation-Skipping Transfer) Tax Return** Estate of a citizen or resident of the United States (see separate instructions). To be filed for decedents dying after December 31, 1998 For Paperwork Reduction Act Notice, see page 1 of the separate instructions.	OMB No. 1545-0015

Part 1.—Decedent and Executor

1a Decedent's first name and middle initial (and maiden name, if any) William B.	**1b** Decedent's last name Jones	**2** Decedent's Social Security No. X10 XX 00X0

3a Legal residence (domicile) at time of death (county, state, and ZIP code, or foreign country) 20 Jane Lane, Yonkers, New York 1X0X0	**3b** Year domicile established 1955	**4** Date of birth 6/12/1919	**5** Date of death March 17, 1999

6a Name of executor (see page 4 of the instructions) Elizabeth Jones	**6b** Executor's address (number and street including apartment or suite no. or rural route; city, town, or post office; state; and ZIP code)
6c Executor's social security number (see page 4 of the instructions) XXX XX XXX	20 Jane Lane, Yonkers, New York 1X0X0

7a Name and location of court where will was probated or estate administered Surrogate's Court, White Plains, New York	**7b** Case number 0000-1999

8 If decedent died testate, check here ▶ [X] and attach a certified copy of the will. **9** If Form 4768 is attached, check here ▶ ☐

10 If Schedule R-1 is attached, check here ▶ ☐

Part 2.—Tax Computation

1	Total gross estate less exclusion (from Part 5, Recapitulation, page 3, item 12)	**1**	934,272
2	Total allowable deductions (from Part 5, Recapitulation, page 3, item 23)	**2**	763,980
3	Taxable estate (subtract line 2 from line 1)	**3**	170,292
4	Adjusted taxable gifts (total taxable gifts (within the meaning of section 2503) made by the decedent after December 31, 1976, other than gifts that are includible in decedent's gross estate (section 2001(b)))	**4**	- 0 -
5	Add lines 3 and 4	**5**	170,292
6	Tentative tax on the amount on line 5 from Table A on page 12 of the instructions	**6**	45,293
7a	If line 5 exceeds $10,000,000, enter the lesser of line 5 or $17,184,000. If line 5 is $10,000,000 or less, skip lines 7a and 7b and enter -0- on line 7c. **7a**		
b	Subtract $10,000,000 from line 7a **7b**		
c	Enter 5% (.05) of line 7b	**7c**	- 0 -
8	Total tentative tax (add lines 6 and 7c)	**8**	45,293
9	Total gift tax payable with respect to gifts made by the decedent after December 31, 1976. Include gift taxes by the decedent's spouse for such spouse's share of split gifts (section 2513) only if the decedent was the donor of these gifts and they are includible in the decedent's gross estate (see instructions)	**9**	- 0 -
10	Gross estate tax (subtract line 9 from line 8)	**10**	45,293
11	Maximum unified credit (applicable credit amount) against estate tax . **11** 211,300		
12	Adjustment to unified credit (applicable credit amount). (This adjustment may not exceed $6,000. See page 4 of the instructions.) **12**		
13	Allowable unified credit (applicable credit amount) (subtract line 12 from line 11)	**13**	211,300
14	Subtract line 13 from line 10 (but do not enter less than zero)	**14**	- 0 -
15	Credit for state death taxes. Do not enter more than line 14. Figure the credit by using the amount on line 3 less $60,000. See Table B in the instructions and **attach credit evidence** (see instructions) .	**15**	- 0 -
16	Subtract line 15 from line 14	**16**	- 0 -
17	Credit for Federal gift taxes on pre-1977 gifts (section 2012) (attach computation) **17**		
18	Credit for foreign death taxes (from Schedule(s) P). (Attach Form(s) 706-CE.) **18**		
19	Credit for tax on prior transfers (from Schedule Q) **19**		
20	Total (add lines 17, 18, and 19)	**20**	- 0 -
21	Net estate tax (subtract line 20 from line 16)	**21**	- 0 -
22	Generation-skipping transfer taxes (from Schedule R, Part 2, line 10)	**22**	- 0 -
23	Total transfer taxes (add lines 21 and 22)	**23**	- 0 -
24	Prior payments. Explain in an attached statement **24**		
25	United States Treasury bonds redeemed in payment of estate tax . **25**		
26	Total (add lines 24 and 25)	**26**	
27	Balance due (or overpayment) (subtract line 26 from line 23)	**27**	- 0 -

Under penalties of perjury, I declare that I have examined this return, including accompanying schedules and statements, and to the best of my knowledge and belief, it is true, correct, and complete. Declaration of preparer other than the executor is based on all information of which preparer has any knowledge.

Signature(s) of executor(s) _____   Date _____

Signature of preparer other than executor _____   Address (and ZIP code) _____   Date _____

Cat. No. 20548R

934

Form 706 (Rev. 7-99)

Estate of: William B. Jones

Part 3—Elections by the Executor

Please check the "Yes" or "No" box for each question. (See instructions beginning on page 5.)		Yes	No
1 Do you elect alternate valuation?	**1**		X
2 Do you elect special use valuation? If "Yes," you must complete and attach Schedule A–1.	**2**		X
3 Do you elect to pay the taxes in installments as described in section 6166? . . . . If "Yes," you must attach the additional information described on page 8 of the instructions.	**3**		X
4 Do you elect to postpone the part of the taxes attributable to a reversionary or remainder interest as described in section 6163?	**4**		X

Part 4—General Information (Note: *Please attach the necessary supplemental documents.* **You must attach the death certificate.)** *(See instructions on page 9.)*

Authorization to receive confidential tax information under Regs. sec. 601.504(b)(2)(i); to act as the estate's representative before the IRS; and to make written or oral presentations on behalf of the estate if return prepared by an attorney, accountant, or enrolled agent for the executor:

Name of representative (print or type) Karen Smith	State NY	Address (number, street, and room or suite no., city, state, and ZIP code) 8 Main Street, White Plains, New York X10XX

I declare that I am the ☒ attorney/ ☐ certified public accountant/ ☐ enrolled agent (you must check the applicable box) for the executor and prepared this return for the executor. I am not under suspension or disbarment from practice before the Internal Revenue Service and am qualified to practice in the state shown above.

Signature	CAF number	Date 11/4/99	Telephone number 914-999-9999

1 Death certificate number and issuing authority (attach a copy of the death certificate to this return).
X0X1X-0X1

2 Decedent's business or occupation. If retired, check here ▶ ☒ and state decedent's former business or occupation.
   Attorney

3 Marital status of the decedent at time of death:

☒ Married

☐ Widow or widower—Name, SSN, and date of death of deceased spouse ▶ ....

....

☐ Single
☐ Legally separated
☐ Divorced—Date divorce decree became final ▶

4a Surviving spouse's name Elizabeth Jones	**4b** Social security number XXX XX XXX	**4c** Amount received (see page 9 of the instructions) $597,983.00

5 Individuals (other than the surviving spouse), trusts, or other estates who receive benefits from the estate (do not include charitable beneficiaries shown in Schedule O) (see instructions). For Privacy Act Notice (applicable to individual beneficiaries only), see the Instructions for Form 1040.

Name of individual, trust, or estate receiving $5,000 or more	Identifying number	Relationship to decedent	Amount (see instructions)
Michael Jones	X0X-1X-X1X1	Son	$105,326
Lisa Jones	XXX-00-XXXX	Niece	30,000
All unascertainable beneficiaries and those who receive less than $5,000 . . . . ▶			45,000
Total			180,326

Please check the "Yes" or "No" box for each question.	Yes	No
6 Does the gross estate contain any section 2044 property (qualified terminable interest property (QTIP) from a prior gift or estate) (see page 9 of the instructions)?		X

(continued on next page)   **Page 2**

Form 706 (Rev. 7-99)

Part 4—General Information (continued)

Please check the "Yes" or "No" box for each question.

		Yes	No
7a	Have Federal gift tax returns ever been filed?		X
	If "Yes," please attach copies of the returns, if available, and furnish the following information:		

7b Period(s) covered	7c Internal Revenue office(s) where filed

If you answer "Yes" to any of questions 8–16, you must attach additional information as described in the instructions.

		Yes	No
8a	Was there any insurance on the decedent's life that is not included on the return as part of the gross estate?		X
b	Did the decedent own any insurance on the life of another that is not included in the gross estate?		X
9	Did the decedent at the time of death own any property as a joint tenant with right of survivorship in which **(a)** one or more of the other joint tenants was someone other than the decedent's spouse, and **(b)** less than the full value of the property is included on the return as part of the gross estate? If "Yes," you must complete and attach Schedule E		X
10	Did the decedent, at the time of death, own any interest in a partnership or unincorporated business or any stock in an inactive or closely held corporation?		X
11	Did the decedent make any transfer described in section 2035, 2036, 2037, or 2038 (see the instructions for Schedule G beginning on page 11 of the separate instructions)? If "Yes," you must complete and attach Schedule G		X
12	Were there in existence at the time of the decedent's death:		
a	Any trusts created by the decedent during his or her lifetime?		X
b	Any trusts not created by the decedent under which the decedent possessed any power, beneficial interest, or trusteeship?		X
13	Did the decedent ever possess, exercise, or release any general power of appointment? If "Yes," you must complete and attach Schedule H		X
14	Was the marital deduction computed under the transitional rule of Public Law 97-34, section 403(e)(3) (Economic Recovery Tax Act of 1981)?		X
	If "Yes," attach a separate computation of the marital deduction, enter the amount on item 20 of the Recapitulation, and note on item 20 "computation attached."		
15	Was the decedent, immediately before death, receiving an annuity described in the "General" paragraph of the instructions for Schedule I? If "Yes," you must complete and attach Schedule I		X
16	Was the decedent ever the beneficiary of a trust for which a deduction was claimed by the estate of a pre-deceased spouse under section 2056(b)(7) and which is not reported on this return? If "Yes," attach an explanation.		X

Part 5—Recapitulation

Item number	Gross estate		Alternate value	Value at date of death
1	Schedule A—Real Estate	1		$ 320,000
2	Schedule B—Stocks and Bonds. . . .	2		382,994
3	Schedule C—Mortgages, Notes, and Cash . .	3		24,876
4	Schedule D—Insurance on the Decedent's Life (attach Form(s) 712) . . .	4		105,326
5	Schedule E—Jointly Owned Property (attach Form(s) 712 for life insurance) .	5		22,490
6	Schedule F—Other Miscellaneous Property (attach Form(s) 712 for life insurance)	6		78,586
7	Schedule G—Transfers During Decedent's Life (att. Form(s) 712 for life insurance)	7		none
8	Schedule H—Powers of Appointment	8		none
9	Schedule I—Annuities	9		none
10	Total gross estate (add items 1 through 9).	10		$ 934,272
11	Schedule U—Qualified Conservation Easement Exclusion	11		none
12	Total gross estate less exclusion (subtract item 11 from item 10). Enter here and on line 1 of Part 2—Tax Computation	12		$934,272

Item number	Deductions		Amount
13	Schedule J—Funeral Expenses and Expenses Incurred in Administering Property Subject to Claims . . .	13	$ 34,525
14	Schedule K—Debts of the Decedent	14	8,149
15	Schedule K—Mortgages and Liens	15	105,550
16	Total of items 13 through 15	16	148,224
17	Allowable amount of deductions from item 16 (see the instructions for item 17 of the Recapitulation) .	17	148,224
18	Schedule L—Net Losses During Administration	18	none
19	Schedule L—Expenses Incurred in Administering Property Not Subject to Claims	19	none
20	Schedule M—Bequests, etc., to Surviving Spouse	20	597,983
21	Schedule O—Charitable, Public, and Similar Gifts and Bequests	21	17,773
22	Schedule T—Qualified Family-Owned Business Interest Deduction	22	none
23	Total allowable deductions (add items 17 through 22). Enter here and on line 2 of the Tax Computation	23	$ 763,980

Page 3

Form 706 (Rev. 7-99)

Estate of: William B. Jones

SCHEDULE A—Real Estate

- *For jointly owned property that must be disclosed on Schedule E, see the instructions on the reverse side of Schedule E.*
- *Real estate that is part of a sole proprietorship should be shown on Schedule F.*
- *Real estate that is included in the gross estate under section 2035, 2036, 2037, or 2038 should be shown on Schedule G.*
- *Real estate that is included in the gross estate under section 2041 should be shown on Schedule H.*
- *If you elect section 2032A valuation, you must complete Schedule A and Schedule A-1.*

Item number	Description	Alternate valuation date	Alternate value	Value at date of death
1	House and lot, 20 Jane Lane, Yonkers, County of Westchester, State of New York (Lot No. 5 Block 1) Value based on attached appraisal of W. Klien 37 B .y Court, Yonkers, New York			$ 320,000
	Total from continuation schedules or additional sheets attached to this schedule . . .			
	TOTAL. (Also enter on Part 5, Recapitulation, page 3, at item 1.)			$320,000

(If more space is needed, attach the continuation schedule from the end of this package or additional sheets of the same size.)
(See the instructions on the reverse side.)

Schedule A—Page 4

Estate of: William B. Jones

SCHEDULE B—Stocks and Bonds

(For jointly owned property that must be disclosed on Schedule E, see the instructions for Schedule E.)

Item number	Description including face amount of bonds or number of shares and par value where needed for identification. Give 9-digit CUSIP number.	CUSIP number	Unit value	Alternate valuation date	Alternate value	Value at date of death
1	680 shares - Telephone & Telegraph Co., (New York Stock Exchange)		61			$41,480
	Dividend on item 1 of $2.35 per share payable on March 1, 1999 to holders of record on January 31, 1999					1,598
	120 shares of Tabacco Co.,common (New York Stock Exchange)		66			7,920
	300 shares Motor Corp., common (New York Stock Exchange)		51			15,300
	Dividend on item 4 of $1.00 per share payable on March 1, 1999 to shareholder of record on January 31, 1999					300
	1468 shares of Business Machine		78			114,504
	200 shares Textile Co., common (New York Stock Exchange)		28.67			5,734
	437 shares Steel Co., common (New York Stock Exchange)		42			19,866
	$20,000 State of New York 6% due		101			20,200
	Interest payable 1/1 and 7/1 Accrued interest on item 9 from 1/1/99 to 1/17/99 (value obtained from Jones Brothers, Inc.)					200
	200,000 shares Hartco, Inc. (unlisted closed corporation)		.55			110,000
	18,560 shares Gold Inc., common		.40			7,424
	2,400 shares Speculative stock fund		16.02			38,448
	Total from continuation schedules (or additional sheets) attached to this schedule . . .					
	TOTAL. (Also enter on Part 5, Recapitulation, page 3, at item 2.)					$ 382,994

(If more space is needed, attach the continuation schedule from the end of this package or additional sheets of the same size.)
(The instructions to Schedule B are in the separate instructions.)

Schedule B—Page 12

Form 706 (Rev. 7-99)

Estate of: William B. Jones

SCHEDULE C—Mortgages, Notes, and Cash

(For jointly owned property that must be disclosed on Schedule E, see the instructions for Schedule E.)

Item number	Description	Alternate valuation date	Alternate value	Value at date of death
1	Cash on hand			$ 640
2.	County Trust Co. Checking account no. 00931567			2,503
3.	County Savings and Loan Co., Savings account no. 85710256			4,857
4.	Federal National Bank, savings account no. 25867			4,808
5.	12,068 shares Ready Cash Fund			12,068
	Total from continuation schedules (or additional sheets) attached to this schedule . .			
	TOTAL. (Also enter on Part 5, Recapitulation, page 3, at item 3.)			$24,876

(If more space is needed, attach the continuation schedule from the end of this package or additional sheets of the same size.)
(See the instructions on the reverse side.)

Schedule C— Page 13

Estate of: William B. Jones

SCHEDULE D—Insurance on the Decedent's Life

You must list **all** policies on the life of the decedent and attach a Form 712 for each policy.

Item number	Description	Alternate valuation date	Alternate value	Value at date of death
1	$ 105, 326.10 policy no. 56925, Mutual Insurance Co. of New York, payable to decedent's estate in one lump sum (owner: William Jones; Beneficiary: estate of William Jones)			$ 105,326
	$ 250,000 policy no. 817625, Manhatten Life Insurance Co., Payable to the decedent's widow, Elizabeth Jones, who has owned all incedents of ownership and paid the premiums on the policy			
	See Form 712 attached			
	Total from continuation schedules (or additional sheets) attached to this schedule . .			
	TOTAL. (Also enter on Part 5, Recapitulation, page 3, at item 4.).			$ 105,326

(If more space is needed, attach the continuation schedule from the end of this package or additional sheets of the same size.)

(See the instructions on the reverse side.)

Schedule D— Page 15

Form 706 (Rev. 7-99)

Estate of: William B. Jones

SCHEDULE E—Jointly Owned Property
(If you elect section 2032A valuation, you must complete Schedule E and Schedule A-1.)

PART 1.—Qualified Joint Interests—Interests Held by the Decedent and His or Her Spouse as the Only Joint Tenants (Section 2040(b)(2))

Item number	Description For securities, give CUSIP number.	Alternate valuation date	Alternate value	Value at date of death
1	Checking account no. 87-10863 White Plains Commercial Bank 1001 White Plains Road, White Plains, New York X1111			$ 2,752
2	Savings account no. 85712, County Savings & Loan Company 7044 Front Street Yonkers, New York 100XX			2,250

	Total from continuation schedules (or additional sheets) attached to this schedule			
1a	Totals			$ 5,002
1b	Amounts included in gross estate (one-half of line 1a)			$ 2,501

PART 2.—All Other Joint Interests

2a State the name and address of each surviving co-tenant. If there are more than three surviving co-tenants, list the additional co-tenants on an attached sheet.

	Name	Address (number and street, city, state, and ZIP code)
A.	Michael Jones	1717 Mockingbird Lane, Rye, New York XX011
B.		
C.		

Item number	Enter letter for co-tenant	Description (including alternate valuation date if any) For securities, give CUSIP number.	Percentage includible	Includible alternate value	Includible value at date of death
1	A	Savings account no. 88801 National Savings Bank 100 Bank Drive Rye, New York 1001X			$ 12,600
2	A	Savings account no. 91120 New York Savings Bank 123 Main Street White Plains, New York 1XX10			7,389

	Total from continuation schedules (or additional sheets) attached to this schedule			
2b	Total other joint interests			$ 19,989
3	**Total includible joint interests** (add lines 1b and 2b). Also enter on Part 5, Recapitulation, page 3, at item 5			$ 22,490

(If more space is needed, attach the continuation schedule from the end of this package or additional sheets of the same size.)
(See the instructions on the reverse side.)   **Schedule E— Page 17**

Form 706 (Rev. 7-99)

Estate of: William B. Jones

SCHEDULE F—Other Miscellaneous Property Not Reportable Under Any Other Schedule
(For jointly owned property that must be disclosed on Schedule E, see the instructions for Schedule E.)
(If you elect section 2032A valuation, you must complete Schedule F and Schedule A-1.)

		Yes	No
1	Did the decedent at the time of death own any articles of artistic or collectible value in excess of $3,000 or any collections whose artistic or collectible value combined at date of death exceeded $10,000? . . . . If "Yes," submit full details on this schedule and attach appraisals.	X	
2	Has the decedent's estate, spouse, or any other person, received (or will receive) any bonus or award as a result of the decedent's employment or death? . . . . If "Yes," submit full details on this schedule.		X
3	Did the decedent at the time of death have, or have access to, a safe deposit box? . . . . If "Yes," state location, and if held in joint names of decedent and another, state name and relationship of joint depositor. If any of the contents of the safe deposit box are omitted from the schedules in this return, explain fully why omitted.		X

Item number	Description For securities, give CUSIP number.	Alternate valuation date	Alternate value	Value at date of death
1	Household possessions located at 20 Jane Lane, Yonkers, New York Value based on appraisal by Smith Co. 756 County Place, White Plains, New York See attachment			$ 14,480
	One 1994 Cadillac Deville			6,950
	One 1989 Camry			1,850
	One U.S. Gold coin			256
	One mobile by Alexander Calder value based on appraisal by Arnold Co., 600 Madison Avenue, New York, New York			55,050

Total from continuation schedules (or additional sheets) attached to this schedule . .		
TOTAL. (Also enter on Part 5, Recapitulation, page 3, at item 6.)		$ 78,586

(If more space is needed, attach the continuation schedule from the end of this package or additional sheets of the same size.)
(See the instructions on the reverse side.)

Schedule F— Page 19

Estate of:

SCHEDULE J—Funeral Expenses and Expenses Incurred in Administering Property Subject to Claims

Note: *Do not list on this schedule expenses of administering property not subject to claims. For those expenses, see the instructions for Schedule L.*

If executors' commissions, attorney fees, etc., are claimed and allowed as a deduction for estate tax purposes, they are not allowable as a deduction in computing the taxable income of the estate for Federal income tax purposes. They are allowable as an income tax deduction on Form 1041 if a waiver is filed to waive the deduction on Form 706 (see the Form 1041 instructions).

Item number	Description	Expense amount	Total amount
1	**A. Funeral expenses:**		
	Edwards Funeral Home, Yonkers, New York	$ 1,500	
	Yonkers Florist (funeral flowers)	600	
	Kensico Cemetery (for perpetual care)	9,500	
	Tombstone	6,000	
	Total funeral expenses . . . . ▶		$ 17,600
	B. Administration expenses:		
1	Executors' commissions—amount estimated/agreed upon/paid. (Strike out the words that do not apply.) . .		6,650
2	Attorney fees—amount estimated/agreed upon/paid. (Strike out the words that do not apply.) . .		8,500
3	Accountant fees—amount estimated/agreed upon/paid. (Strike out the words that do not apply.) . .		
4	Miscellaneous expenses:	Expense amount	
	W. Klein, 37 Bay Court, Yonkers, New York - appraisals	$ 200	
	Smith Co., 756 County Place, White Plains, New York	250	
	Arnold Co., 600 Madison Avenue, New York, New York - appraisals	325	
	Surrogate's Court, White Plains, New York - surrogate's fees	625	
	J. Cuoller Co., Certified Public Accountants	375	
	Total miscellaneous expenses from continuation schedules (or additional sheets) attached to this schedule		
	Total miscellaneous expenses . . . . ▶		$ 1,775
	TOTAL. (Also enter on Part 5, Recapitulation, page 3, at item 13.) . . . . ▶		$34,525

(If more space is needed, attach the continuation schedule from the end of this package or additional sheets of the same size.)
(See the instructions on the reverse side.)

Schedule J—Page 23

Form 706 (Rev. 7-99)

Estate of: William B. Jones

SCHEDULE K—Debts of the Decedent, and Mortgages and Liens

Item number	Debts of the Decedent—Creditor and nature of claim, and allowable death taxes	Amount unpaid to date	Amount in contest	Amount claimed as a deduction
1	Dr. S. Miller, Medical			$ 400
2	White Plains Hospital			300
3	Dist. Dir. IRS, 1999 income tax			4,897
4	State Tax Commissioner - 1999 state income tax			1,260
5	Socony Mobil Oil Co. - auto			300
6	Zone Pharmacy - medicine			124
7	Senate Ambulance Co. - medicine			65
8	CitiBank Master Charge - personal			803

Total from continuation schedules (or additional sheets) attached to this schedule . . . .

TOTAL. (Also enter on Part 5, Recapitulation, page 3, at item 14.) . . . .   **$ 8,149**

Item number	Mortgages and Liens—Description	Amount
1	Mortgage on decedent's residence, 20 Jane Lane, Yonkers, New York (Schedule A, Item 1). Decedent was personally liable. Mortgage is County Savings and Loan Co., Yonkers, New York This is a 25-year mortgage level payments dated February 1, 1983. Face amount $ 160,000. Interest rate of 7% per annum. unpaid principal	$ 105,550

Total from continuation schedules (or additional sheets) attached to this schedule . . . .

TOTAL. (Also enter on Part 5, Recapitulation, page 3, at item 15.) . . . .   **$ 105,550**

(If more space is needed, attach the continuation schedule from the end of this package or additional sheets of the same size.)
(The instructions to Schedule K are in the separate instructions.)   **Schedule K— Page 25**

Form 706 (Rev. 7-99)

Estate of: William B. Jones

SCHEDULE M—Bequests, etc., to Surviving Spouse

Election To Deduct Qualified Terminable Interest Property Under Section 2056(b)(7).—If a trust (or other property) meets the requirements of qualified terminable interest property under section 2056(b)(7), and

a. The trust or other property is listed on Schedule M, and

b. The value of the trust (or other property) is entered in whole or in part as a deduction on Schedule M,

then unless the executor specifically identifies the trust (all or a fractional portion or percentage) or other property to be excluded from the election, the executor shall be deemed to have made an election to have such trust (or other property) treated as qualified terminable interest property under section 2056(b)(7).

If less than the entire value of the trust (or other property) that the executor has included in the gross estate is entered as a deduction on Schedule M, the executor shall be considered to have made an election only as to a fraction of the trust (or other property). The numerator of this fraction is equal to the amount of the trust (or other property) deducted on Schedule M. The denominator is equal to the total value of the trust (or other property).

Election To Deduct Qualified Domestic Trust Property Under Section 2056A.—If a trust meets the requirements of a qualified domestic trust under section 2056A(a) and this return is filed no later than 1 year after the time prescribed by law (including extensions) for filing the return, and

a. The entire value of a trust or trust property is listed on Schedule M, and

b. The entire value of the trust or trust property is entered as a deduction on Schedule M,

then unless the executor specifically identifies the trust to be excluded from the election, the executor shall be deemed to have made an election to have the entire trust treated as qualified domestic trust property.

		Yes	No
1	Did any property pass to the surviving spouse as a result of a qualified disclaimer?		X
	If "Yes," attach a copy of the written disclaimer required by section 2518(b).		
2a	In what country was the surviving spouse born? ___U.S.A.___		
b	What is the surviving spouse's date of birth? ___9/5/24___		
c	Is the surviving spouse a U.S. citizen?	X	
d	If the surviving spouse is a naturalized citizen, when did the surviving spouse acquire citizenship? _____		
e	If the surviving spouse is not a U.S. citizen, of what country is the surviving spouse a citizen? _____		
3	**Election Out of QTIP Treatment of Annuities.**—Do you elect under section 2056(b)(7)(C)(ii) **not** to treat as qualified terminable interest property any joint and survivor annuities that are included in the gross estate and would otherwise be treated as qualified terminable interest property under section 2056(b)(7)(C)? (see instructions)		X

Item number	Description of property interests passing to surviving spouse	Amount
1	Checking account, White Plains Commercial Bank, jointly with Elizabeth Jones (widow of decedent). (Schedule E, Part 1, Item 1)	$ 1,376
2	Savings account #85712, County Savings and Loan Co., jointly with Elizabeth Jones (widow of decedent). (Schedule E, Part 1, Item 2)	1,125
3	Specific bequests listed in paragraphs three and ten of decedent's will	595, 482

	Total from continuation schedules (or additional sheets) attached to this schedule		
4	**Total** amount of property interests listed on Schedule M	**4**	$ 597,983

5a	Federal estate taxes payable out of property interests listed on Schedule M . .	**5a**	0	
b	Other death taxes payable out of property interests listed on Schedule M	**5b**	0	
c	Federal and state GST taxes payable out of property interests listed on Schedule M	**5c**	0	
d	Add items a, b, and c		**5d**	0
6	Net amount of property interests listed on Schedule M (subtract 5d from 4). Also enter on Part 5, Recapitulation, page 3, at item 20		**6**	$ 597,983

(If more space is needed, attach the continuation schedule from the end of this package or additional sheets of the same size.)
(See the instructions on the reverse side.)

Schedule M— Page 27

Form 706 (Rev. 7-99)

Estate of: William B. Jones

SCHEDULE O—Charitable, Public, and Similar Gifts and Bequests

		Yes	No
1a If the transfer was made by will, has any action been instituted to have interpreted or to contest the will or any of its provisions affecting the charitable deductions claimed in this schedule? . . . . If "Yes," full details must be submitted with this schedule.			X
b According to the information and belief of the person or persons filing this return, is any such action planned? If "Yes," full details must be submitted with this schedule.			X
2 Did any property pass to charity as the result of a qualified disclaimer? . . . . If "Yes," attach a copy of the written disclaimer required by section 2518(b).			X

Item number	Name and address of beneficiary	Character of institution	Amount
1	New York University, New York, NY Cash gift under paragraph fifteen of decedent's will	Educational Institution	$ 17,773

Total from continuation schedules (or additional sheets) attached to this schedule		
3 Total	**3**	$ 17,773
4a Federal estate tax payable out of property interests listed above	**4a** none	
b Other death taxes payable out of property interests listed above	**4b** none	
c Federal and state GST taxes payable out of property interests listed above	**4c** none	
d Add items a, b, and c	**4d**	
5 Net value of property interests listed above (subtract 4d from 3). Also enter on Part 5, Recapitulation, page 3, at item 21	**5**	$ 17,773

(If more space is needed, attach the continuation schedule from the end of this package or additional sheets of the same size.)
(The instructions to Schedule O are in the separate instructions.)

Form 706

You may find the following blank copy of Form 706 and selected schedules useful as a draft worksheet.

Form 706

928

Sample Form 706

Form 706
(Rev. July 1999)

Department of the Treasury
Internal Revenue Service

United States Estate (and Generation-Skipping Transfer) Tax Return

Estate of a citizen or resident of the United States (see separate instructions).
To be filed for decedents dying after December 31, 1998
For Paperwork Reduction Act Notice, see page 1 of the separate instructions.

OMB No. 1545-0015

Part 1.—Decedent and Executor

1a Decedent's first name and middle initial (and maiden name, if any)	1b Decedent's last name	2 Decedent's Social Security No.

3a Legal residence (domicile) at time of death (county, state, and ZIP code, or foreign country)	3b Year domicile established	4 Date of birth	5 Date of death

6a Name of executor (see page 4 of the instructions)	6b Executor's address (number and street including apartment or suite no. or rural route; city, town, or post office; state; and ZIP code)

6c Executor's social security number (see page 4 of the instructions)

7a Name and location of court where will was probated or estate administered	7b Case number

8 If decedent died testate, check here ▶ ☐ and attach a certified copy of the will.   9 If Form 4768 is attached, check here ▶ ☐

10 If Schedule R-1 is attached, check here ▶ ☐

Part 2.—Tax Computation

1	Total gross estate less exclusion (from Part 5, Recapitulation, page 3, item 12)	**1**
2	Total allowable deductions (from Part 5, Recapitulation, page 3, item 23)	**2**
3	Taxable estate (subtract line 2 from line 1)	**3**
4	Adjusted taxable gifts (total taxable gifts (within the meaning of section 2503) made by the decedent after December 31, 1976, other than gifts that are includible in decedent's gross estate (section 2001(b)))	**4**
5	Add lines 3 and 4	**5**
6	Tentative tax on the amount on line 5 from Table A on page 12 of the instructions	**6**
7a	If line 5 exceeds $10,000,000, enter the lesser of line 5 or $17,184,000. If line 5 is $10,000,000 or less, skip lines 7a and 7b and enter -0- on line 7c . **7a**	
b	Subtract $10,000,000 from line 7a **7b**	
c	Enter 5% (.05) of line 7b	**7c**
8	Total tentative tax (add lines 6 and 7c)	**8**
9	Total gift tax payable with respect to gifts made by the decedent after December 31, 1976. Include gift taxes by the decedent's spouse for such spouse's share of split gifts (section 2513) only if the decedent was the donor of these gifts and they are includible in the decedent's gross estate (see instructions)	**9**
10	Gross estate tax (subtract line 9 from line 8)	**10**
11	Maximum unified credit (applicable credit amount) against estate tax . **11**	
12	Adjustment to unified credit (applicable credit amount). (This adjustment may not exceed $6,000. See page 4 of the instructions.) **12**	
13	Allowable unified credit (applicable credit amount) (subtract line 12 from line 11)	**13**
14	Subtract line 13 from line 10 (but do not enter less than zero)	**14**
15	Credit for state death taxes. Do not enter more than line 14. Figure the credit by using the amount on line 3 less $60,000. See Table B in the instructions and **attach credit evidence** (see instructions) .	**15**
16	Subtract line 15 from line 14	**16**
17	Credit for Federal gift taxes on pre-1977 gifts (section 2012) (attach computation) **17**	
18	Credit for foreign death taxes (from Schedule(s) P). (Attach Form(s) 706-CE.) **18**	
19	Credit for tax on prior transfers (from Schedule Q) **19**	
20	Total (add lines 17, 18, and 19)	**20**
21	Net estate tax (subtract line 20 from line 16)	**21**
22	Generation-skipping transfer taxes (from Schedule R, Part 2, line 10) . . .	**22**
23	Total transfer taxes (add lines 21 and 22)	**23**
24	Prior payments. Explain in an attached statement **24**	
25	United States Treasury bonds redeemed in payment of estate tax . **25**	
26	Total (add lines 24 and 25)	**26**
27	Balance due (or overpayment) (subtract line 26 from line 23)	**27**

Under penalties of perjury, I declare that I have examined this return, including accompanying schedules and statements, and to the best of my knowledge and belief, it is true, correct, and complete. Declaration of preparer other than the executor is based on all information of which preparer has any knowledge.

Signature(s) of executor(s) _____   Date _____

_____

Signature of preparer other than executor _____   Address (and ZIP code) _____   Date _____

Cat. No. 20548R

Form 706 (Rev. 7-99)

Estate of:

Part 3—Elections by the Executor

Please check the "Yes" or "No" box for each question. (See instructions beginning on page 5.)

			Yes	No
1	Do you elect alternate valuation?	1		
2	Do you elect special use valuation? If "Yes," you must complete and attach Schedule A–1.	2		
3	Do you elect to pay the taxes in installments as described in section 6166? . . . . . If "Yes," you must attach the additional information described on page 8 of the instructions.	3		
4	Do you elect to postpone the part of the taxes attributable to a reversionary or remainder interest as described in section 6163?	4		

Part 4—General Information (Note: *Please attach the necessary supplemental documents.* **You must attach the death certificate.**)
(See instructions on page 9.)

Authorization to receive confidential tax information under Regs. sec. 601.504(b)(2)(i); to act as the estate's representative before the IRS; and to make written or oral presentations on behalf of the estate if return prepared by an attorney, accountant, or enrolled agent for the executor:

Name of representative (print or type)	State	Address (number, street, and room or suite no., city, state, and ZIP code)

I declare that I am the ☐ attorney/ ☐ certified public accountant/ ☐ enrolled agent (you must check the applicable box) for the executor and prepared this return for the executor. I am not under suspension or disbarment from practice before the Internal Revenue Service and am qualified to practice in the state shown above.

Signature	CAF number	Date	Telephone number

1   Death certificate number and issuing authority (attach a copy of the death certificate to this return).

2   Decedent's business or occupation. If retired, check here ▶ ☐ and state decedent's former business or occupation.

3   Marital status of the decedent at time of death:
☐ Married
☐ Widow or widower—Name, SSN, and date of death of deceased spouse ▶ -
- -
☐ Single
☐ Legally separated
☐ Divorced—Date divorce decree became final ▶

4a Surviving spouse's name	4b Social security number	4c Amount received (see page 9 of the instructions)

5   Individuals (other than the surviving spouse), trusts, or other estates who receive benefits from the estate (do not include charitable beneficiaries shown in Schedule O) (see instructions). For Privacy Act Notice (applicable to individual beneficiaries only), see the Instructions for Form 1040.

Name of individual, trust, or estate receiving $5,000 or more	Identifying number	Relationship to decedent	Amount (see instructions)
All unascertainable beneficiaries and those who receive less than $5,000 . . . . ▶			

Total   . . . .

Please check the "Yes" or "No" box for each question.

		Yes	No
6	Does the gross estate contain any section 2044 property (qualified terminable interest property (QTIP) from a prior gift or estate) (see page 9 of the instructions)?		

(continued on next page)

Form 706 (Rev. 7-99)

Part 4—General Information (continued)

Please check the "Yes" or "No" box for each question.	Yes	No
7a Have Federal gift tax returns ever been filed?		
If "Yes," please attach copies of the returns, if available, and furnish the following information:		

7b Period(s) covered	**7c** Internal Revenue office(s) where filed

If you answer "Yes" to any of questions 8–16, you must attach additional information as described in the instructions.

	Yes	No
8a Was there any insurance on the decedent's life that is not included on the return as part of the gross estate?		
b Did the decedent own any insurance on the life of another that is not included in the gross estate?		
9 Did the decedent at the time of death own any property as a joint tenant with right of survivorship in which **(a)** one or more of the other joint tenants was someone other than the decedent's spouse, and **(b)** less than the full value of the property is included on the return as part of the gross estate? If "Yes," you must complete and attach Schedule E		
10 Did the decedent, at the time of death, own any interest in a partnership or unincorporated business or any stock in an inactive or closely held corporation?		
11 Did the decedent make any transfer described in section 2035, 2036, 2037, or 2038 (see the instructions for Schedule G beginning on page 11 of the separate instructions)? If "Yes," you must complete and attach Schedule G		
12 Were there in existence at the time of the decedent's death:		
a Any trusts created by the decedent during his or her lifetime?		
b Any trusts not created by the decedent under which the decedent possessed any power, beneficial interest, or trusteeship?		
13 Did the decedent ever possess, exercise, or release any general power of appointment? If "Yes," you must complete and attach Schedule H		
14 Was the marital deduction computed under the transitional rule of Public Law 97-34, section 403(e)(3) (Economic Recovery Tax Act of 1981)?		
If "Yes," attach a separate computation of the marital deduction, enter the amount on item 20 of the Recapitulation, and note on item 20 "computation attached."		
15 Was the decedent, immediately before death, receiving an annuity described in the "General" paragraph of the instructions for Schedule I? If "Yes," you must complete and attach Schedule I		
16 Was the decedent ever the beneficiary of a trust for which a deduction was claimed by the estate of a pre-deceased spouse under section 2056(b)(7) and which is not reported on this return? If "Yes," attach an explanation		

Part 5—Recapitulation

Item number	Gross estate		Alternate value	Value at date of death
1	Schedule A—Real Estate	**1**		
2	Schedule B—Stocks and Bonds	**2**		
3	Schedule C—Mortgages, Notes, and Cash	**3**		
4	Schedule D—Insurance on the Decedent's Life (attach Form(s) 712) . . .	**4**		
5	Schedule E—Jointly Owned Property (attach Form(s) 712 for life insurance) .	**5**		
6	Schedule F—Other Miscellaneous Property (attach Form(s) 712 for life insurance)	**6**		
7	Schedule G—Transfers During Decedent's Life (att. Form(s) 712 for life insurance)	**7**		
8	Schedule H—Powers of Appointment	**8**		
9	Schedule I—Annuities	**9**		
10	Total gross estate (add items 1 through 9)	**10**		
11	Schedule U—Qualified Conservation Easement Exclusion	**11**		
12	Total gross estate less exclusion (subtract item 11 from item 10). Enter here and on line 1 of Part 2—Tax Computation	**12**		

Item number	Deductions		Amount
13	Schedule J—Funeral Expenses and Expenses Incurred in Administering Property Subject to Claims . . .	**13**	
14	Schedule K—Debts of the Decedent	**14**	
15	Schedule K—Mortgages and Liens	**15**	
16	Total of items 13 through 15	**16**	
17	Allowable amount of deductions from item 16 (see the instructions for item 17 of the Recapitulation) .	**17**	
18	Schedule L—Net Losses During Administration	**18**	
19	Schedule L—Expenses Incurred in Administering Property Not Subject to Claims	**19**	
20	Schedule M—Bequests, etc., to Surviving Spouse	**20**	
21	Schedule O—Charitable, Public, and Similar Gifts and Bequests	**21**	
22	Schedule T—Qualified Family-Owned Business Interest Deduction	**22**	
23	Total allowable deductions (add items 17 through 22). Enter here and on line 2 of the Tax Computation	**23**	

Form 706 (Rev. 7-99)

Estate of:

SCHEDULE A—Real Estate

- *For jointly owned property that must be disclosed on Schedule E, see the instructions on the reverse side of Schedule E.*
- *Real estate that is part of a sole proprietorship should be shown on Schedule F.*
- *Real estate that is included in the gross estate under section 2035, 2036, 2037, or 2038 should be shown on Schedule G.*
- *Real estate that is included in the gross estate under section 2041 should be shown on Schedule H.*
- *If you elect section 2032A valuation, you must complete Schedule A and Schedule A-1.*

Item number	Description	Alternate valuation date	Alternate value	Value at date of death
1				

Total from continuation schedules or additional sheets attached to this schedule . . .

TOTAL. (Also enter on Part 5, Recapitulation, page 3, at item 1.) . . . .

(If more space is needed, attach the continuation schedule from the end of this package or additional sheets of the same size.)

(See the instructions on the reverse side.)

Schedule A—Page 4

Estate of:

SCHEDULE B—Stocks and Bonds

(For jointly owned property that must be disclosed on Schedule E, see the instructions for Schedule E.)

Item number	Description including face amount of bonds or number of shares and par value where needed for identification. Give 9-digit CUSIP number.		Unit value	Alternate valuation date	Alternate value	Value at date of death
		CUSIP number				
1						
	Total from continuation schedules (or additional sheets) attached to this schedule . . .					
	TOTAL. (Also enter on Part 5, Recapitulation, page 3, at item 2.)					

(If more space is needed, attach the continuation schedule from the end of this package or additional sheets of the same size.)

(The instructions to Schedule B are in the separate instructions.)

Form 706 (Rev. 7-99)

Estate of:

SCHEDULE C—Mortgages, Notes, and Cash

(For jointly owned property that must be disclosed on Schedule E, see the instructions for Schedule E.)

Item number	Description	Alternate valuation date	Alternate value	Value at date of death
1				

Total from continuation schedules (or additional sheets) attached to this schedule . .			
TOTAL. (Also enter on Part 5, Recapitulation, page 3, at item 3.)			

(If more space is needed, attach the continuation schedule from the end of this package or additional sheets of the same size.)
(See the instructions on the reverse side.)

Schedule C—Page 13

Estate of:

SCHEDULE D—Insurance on the Decedent's Life

You must list **all** policies on the life of the decedent and attach a Form 712 for each policy.

Item number	Description	Alternate valuation date	Alternate value	Value at date of death
1				
	Total from continuation schedules (or additional sheets) attached to this schedule . .			
	TOTAL. (Also enter on Part 5, Recapitulation, page 3, at item 4.)			

(If more space is needed, attach the continuation schedule from the end of this package or additional sheets of the same size.)

(See the instructions on the reverse side.)

Form 706 (Rev. 7-99)

Estate of:

SCHEDULE E—Jointly Owned Property

(If you elect section 2032A valuation, you must complete Schedule E and Schedule A-1.)

PART 1.—Qualified Joint Interests—Interests Held by the Decedent and His or Her Spouse as the Only Joint Tenants (Section 2040(b)(2))

Item number	Description For securities, give CUSIP number.	Alternate valuation date	Alternate value	Value at date of death
Total from continuation schedules (or additional sheets) attached to this schedule				
1a Totals **1a**				
1b Amounts included in gross estate (one-half of line **1a**) **1b**				

PART 2.—All Other Joint Interests

2a State the name and address of each surviving co-tenant. If there are more than three surviving co-tenants, list the additional co-tenants on an attached sheet.

Name	Address (number and street, city, state, and ZIP code)
A.	
B.	
C.	

Item number	Enter letter for co-tenant	Description (including alternate valuation date if any) For securities, give CUSIP number.	Percentage includible	Includible alternate value	Includible value at date of death
		Total from continuation schedules (or additional sheets) attached to this schedule			
2b	Total other joint interests			
3	**Total includible joint interests** (add lines 1b and 2b). Also enter on Part 5, Recapitulation, page 3, at item 5			

(If more space is needed, attach the continuation schedule from the end of this package or additional sheets of the same size.)
(See the instructions on the reverse side.)

Schedule E—Page 17

Form 706 (Rev. 7-99)

Estate of:

SCHEDULE F—Other Miscellaneous Property Not Reportable Under Any Other Schedule

(For jointly owned property that must be disclosed on Schedule E, see the instructions for Schedule E.)
(If you elect section 2032A valuation, you must complete Schedule F and Schedule A-1.)

		Yes	No
1	Did the decedent at the time of death own any articles of artistic or collectible value in excess of $3,000 or any collections whose artistic or collectible value combined at date of death exceeded $10,000? . . . . If "Yes," submit full details on this schedule and attach appraisals.		
2	Has the decedent's estate, spouse, or any other person, received (or will receive) any bonus or award as a result of the decedent's employment or death? . . . . If "Yes," submit full details on this schedule.		
3	Did the decedent at the time of death have, or have access to, a safe deposit box? . . . . If "Yes," state location, and if held in joint names of decedent and another, state name and relationship of joint depositor.		

If any of the contents of the safe deposit box are omitted from the schedules in this return, explain fully why omitted.

Item number	Description For securities, give CUSIP number.	Alternate valuation date	Alternate value	Value at date of death
1				
	Total from continuation schedules (or additional sheets) attached to this schedule . .			
	TOTAL. (Also enter on Part 5, Recapitulation, page 3, at item 6.)			

(If more space is needed, attach the continuation schedule from the end of this package or additional sheets of the same size.)
(See the instructions on the reverse side.)

Schedule F—Page 19

Form 706 (Rev. 7-99)

Estate of:

SCHEDULE J—Funeral Expenses and Expenses Incurred in Administering Property Subject to Claims

Note: *Do not list on this schedule expenses of administering property not subject to claims. For those expenses, see the instructions for Schedule L.*

If executors' commissions, attorney fees, etc., are claimed and allowed as a deduction for estate tax purposes, they are not allowable as a deduction in computing the taxable income of the estate for Federal income tax purposes. They are allowable as an income tax deduction on Form 1041 if a waiver is filed to waive the deduction on Form 706 (see the Form 1041 instructions).

Item number	Description	Expense amount	Total amount
1	**A. Funeral expenses:**		
	Total funeral expenses . . . . ▶		. . . .
	B. Administration expenses:		
1	Executors' commissions—amount estimated/agreed upon/paid. (Strike out the words that do not apply.)		. . . .
2	Attorney fees—amount estimated/agreed upon/paid. (Strike out the words that do not apply.). .		. . . .
3	Accountant fees—amount estimated/agreed upon/paid. (Strike out the words that do not apply.).		. . . .
4	Miscellaneous expenses:	Expense amount	
	Total miscellaneous expenses from continuation schedules (or additional sheets) attached to this schedule		
	Total miscellaneous expenses . . . . ▶		
	TOTAL. (Also enter on Part 5, Recapitulation, page 3, at item 13.) . . . . ▶		

(If more space is needed, attach the continuation schedule from the end of this package or additional sheets of the same size.)
(See the instructions on the reverse side.)

Schedule J—Page 23

Estate of:

SCHEDULE K—Debts of the Decedent, and Mortgages and Liens

Item number	Debts of the Decedent—Creditor and nature of claim, and allowable death taxes	Amount unpaid to date	Amount in contest	Amount claimed as a deduction
1				
	Total from continuation schedules (or additional sheets) attached to this schedule			
	TOTAL. (Also enter on Part 5, Recapitulation, page 3, at item 14.)			

Item number	Mortgages and Liens—Description	Amount
1		
	Total from continuation schedules (or additional sheets) attached to this schedule	
	TOTAL. (Also enter on Part 5, Recapitulation, page 3, at item 15.)	

(If more space is needed, attach the continuation schedule from the end of this package or additional sheets of the same size.)
(The instructions to Schedule K are in the separate instructions.)

Schedule K—Page 25

Form 706 (Rev. 7-99)

Estate of:

SCHEDULE M—Bequests, etc., to Surviving Spouse

Election To Deduct Qualified Terminable Interest Property Under Section 2056(b)(7). If a trust (or other property) meets the requirements of qualified terminable interest property under section 2056(b)(7), and

a. The trust or other property is listed on Schedule M, and

b. The value of the trust (or other property) is entered in whole or in part as a deduction on Schedule M,

then unless the executor specifically identifies the trust (all or a fractional portion or percentage) or other property to be excluded from the election, the executor shall be deemed to have made an election to have such trust (or other property) treated as qualified terminable interest property under section 2056(b)(7).

If less than the entire value of the trust (or other property) that the executor has included in the gross estate is entered as a deduction on Schedule M, the executor shall be considered to have made an election only as to a fraction of the trust (or other property). The numerator of this fraction is equal to the amount of the trust (or other property) deducted on Schedule M. The denominator is equal to the total value of the trust (or other property).

Election To Deduct Qualified Domestic Trust Property Under Section 2056A. If a trust meets the requirements of a qualified domestic trust under section 2056A(a) and this return is filed no later than 1 year after the time prescribed by law (including extensions) for filing the return, and

a. The entire value of a trust or trust property is listed on Schedule M, and

b. The entire value of the trust or trust property is entered as a deduction on Schedule M,

then unless the executor specifically identifies the trust to be excluded from the election, the executor shall be deemed to have made an election to have the entire trust treated as qualified domestic trust property.

		Yes	No
1	Did any property pass to the surviving spouse as a result of a qualified disclaimer? **1**		
	If "Yes," attach a copy of the written disclaimer required by section 2518(b).		
2a	In what country was the surviving spouse born? _____		
b	What is the surviving spouse's date of birth? _____		
c	Is the surviving spouse a U.S. citizen? **2c**		
d	If the surviving spouse is a naturalized citizen, when did the surviving spouse acquire citizenship?_____		
e	If the surviving spouse is not a U.S. citizen, of what country is the surviving spouse a citizen? _____		
3	**Election Out of QTIP Treatment of Annuities**—Do you elect under section 2056(b)(7)(C)(ii) **not** to treat as qualified terminable interest property any joint and survivor annuities that are included in the gross estate and would otherwise be treated as qualified terminable interest property under section 2056(b)(7)(C)? (see instructions) **3**		

Item number	Description of property interests passing to surviving spouse	Amount
1		
	Total from continuation schedules (or additional sheets) attached to this schedule	
4	**Total** amount of property interests listed on Schedule M **4**	
5a	Federal estate taxes payable out of property interests listed on Schedule M . . **5a**	
b	Other death taxes payable out of property interests listed on Schedule M . . . **5b**	
c	Federal and state GST taxes payable out of property interests listed on Schedule M **5c**	
d	Add items 5a, b, and c **5d**	
6	Net amount of property interests listed on Schedule M (subtract 5d from 4). Also enter on Part 5, Recapitulation, page 3, at item 20 . . . . **6**	

(If more space is needed, attach the continuation schedule from the end of this package or additional sheets of the same size.)
(See the instructions on the reverse side.)

Form 706 (Rev. 7-99)

Estate of:

SCHEDULE O—Charitable, Public, and Similar Gifts and Bequests

		Yes	No
1a If the transfer was made by will, has any action been instituted to have interpreted or to contest the will or any of its provisions affecting the charitable deductions claimed in this schedule? . . . . If "Yes," full details must be submitted with this schedule.			
b According to the information and belief of the person or persons filing this return, is any such action planned? If "Yes," full details must be submitted with this schedule.			
2 Did any property pass to charity as the result of a qualified disclaimer? . . . . If "Yes," attach a copy of the written disclaimer required by section 2518(b).			

Item number	Name and address of beneficiary	Character of institution	Amount
1			

Total from continuation schedules (or additional sheets) attached to this schedule . . . .

3	Total		**3**	
4a	Federal estate tax payable out of property interests listed above	**4a**		
b	Other death taxes payable out of property interests listed above	**4b**		
c	Federal and state GST taxes payable out of property interests listed above	**4c**		
d	Add items 4a, b, and c		**4d**	
5	Net value of property interests listed above (subtract 4d from 3). Also enter on Part 5, Recapitulation, page 3, at item 21		**5**	

(If more space is needed, attach the continuation schedule from the end of this package or additional sheets of the same size.)
(The instructions to Schedule O are in the separate instructions.)

Glossary & Index

The following glossary and index will help you quickly find answers to your specific tax questions.

Glossary: The useful glossary explains technical tax terms in plain, easy-to-understand language.

Index: The index directs you to the exact page and section where an item you are interested in is discussed.

Glossary of Tax Terms

A

Accelerated Cost Recovery System (ACRS). A statutory method of depreciation allowing accelerated rates for most types of property used in business and income-producing activities during the years 1981 through 1986. It has been superseded by the Modified Accelerated Cost Recovery System (MACRS) for assets placed in service after 1986; *see 42.4* and *42.11.*

Accelerated depreciation. Depreciation methods that allow faster write-offs than straight-line rates in the earlier periods of the useful life of an asset. For example, in the first few years of recovery, MACRS allows a 200% double declining balance write-off, twice the straight-line rate; *see 42.5–42.8.*

Accountable reimbursement plan. An employer reimbursement or allowance arrangement that requires you to adequately substantiate business expenses to your employer, and to return any excess reimbursement; *see 20.31.*

Accrual method of accounting. A business method of accounting requiring income to be reported when earned and expenses to be deducted when incurred. However, deductions generally may not be claimed until economic performance has occurred; *see 40.3.*

Acquisition debt. Debt used to buy, build, or construct a principal residence or second home and that generally qualifies for a full interest expense deduction; *see 15.2.*

Active participation. Test for determining deductibility of IRA deductions. Active participants in employer retirement plans are subject to IRA deduction phase-out rules if adjusted gross income exceeds certain thresholds; *see 8.4.*

Adjusted basis. A statutory term describing the cost used to determine your profit or loss from a sale or exchange of property. It is generally your original cost, increased by capital improvements, and decreased by depreciation, depletion, and other capital write-offs; *see 5.20.*

Adjusted Gross Income (AGI). Important tax term representing gross income less allowable adjustments, such as IRA, alimony, and Keogh deductions. AGI determines whether various tax benefits are phased out, such as personal exemptions, itemized deductions, and the rental loss allowance; *see 12.1* and modified adjusted gross income (MAGI).

Alimony. Payments made to a separated or divorced spouse as required by a decree or agreement. Qualifying payments are deductible by the payor and taxable to the payee; *see 37.1–37.8.*

Alternative minimum tax (AMT). A tax triggered if certain tax benefits reduce your regular income tax below the tax computed on Form 6251 for AMT purposes; *see* Chapter 23.

Amended return. On Form 1040X, you may file an amended return within a three-year period to correct a mistake made on an original or previously amended return; *see* Chapter 49.

Amortizable bond premium. The additional amount paid over the face amount of an obligation taht may be deducted under the rules of *4.17.*

Amortization. Writing off an investment in intangible assets over the projected life of the assets; *see 42.18.*

Amount realized. A statutory term used to figure your profit or loss on a sale or exchange. Generally, it is sales proceeds plus mortgages assumed or taken subject to, less transaction expenses, such as commissions and legal costs; *see 5.14.*

Amount recognized. The amount of gain reportable and subject to tax. On certain tax-free exchanges of property, gain is not recognized in the year it is realized; *see 6.1.*

Annualized rate. A rate for a period of less than a year computed as though for a full year.

Annuity. An annual payment of money by a company or individual to a person called the *annuitant.* Payment is for a fixed period or the life of the annuitant. Tax consequences depend on the type of contract and funding; *see 7.22–7.30.*

Applicable federal rate. Interest rate fixed by the Treasury for determining imputed interest; *see 4.31* and *4.32.*

Appreciation in value. Increase in value of property due to market conditions. When you sell appreciated property, you pay tax on the appreciation since the date of purchase. When you donate appreciated property held long term, you may generally deduct the appreciated value; *see 14.6.*

Assessment. The IRS action of fixing tax liability that sets in motion collection procedures, such as charging interest, imposing penalties, and, if necessary, seizing property; *see 47.3.*

Asset. Anything owned that has cash or exchange value.

Assignment. The legal transfer of property, rights, or interest to another person called an *assignee.* You cannot avoid tax on income by assigning the income to another person.

At-risk rules. Limits loss deductions to cash investments and personal liability notes. An exception for real estate treats certain nonrecourse commercial loans as amounts "at risk"; *see 10.17.*

Attorneys' fee awards. Taxpayers who prevail in the Tax Court or other federal court may recover up to a certain amount for attorneys' fees, plus other litigation expenses, by showing that the IRS position was unreasonable; *see 48.7.*

Audit. An IRS examination of your tax return, generally limited to a three-year period after you file; *see* Chapter 48.

Averaging. Some retirees may use favorable averaging methods to compute tax on a lump-sum distribution if they participated in the plan for at least five years; *see 7.2–7.7.*

Away from home. A tax requirement for deducting travel expenses on a business trip. Sleeping arrangements are required for at least one night before returning home; *see 20.3* and *20.5–20.6..*

B

Balloon. A final payment on a loan in one lump sum.

Basis. Generally, the amount paid for property. You need to know your basis to figure gain or loss on a sale; *see 5.16.*

Boot. Generally, the receipt of cash or its equivalent accompanying an exchange of property. In a tax-free exchange, boot is subject to immediate tax; *see 6.3.*

C

Calendar year. A year that ends on December 31.

Cancellation of debt. Release of a debt without consideration by a creditor. Cancellations of debt are generally taxable; *see 11.8.*

Capital. The excess of assets over liabilities.

Capital asset. Property subject to capital gain or loss treatment. Almost all assets you own are considered capital assets except for certain business assets or works you created; *see 5.2.*

Capital expenses. Costs that are not currently deductible and that are added to the basis of property. A capital expense generally increases the value of property. When added to depreciable property, the cost is deductible over the life of the asset.

Capital gain or loss. The difference between amount realized and adjusted basis on the sale or exchange of capital assets. Long-term capital gains are taxed favorably, as explained in Chapter 5. Capital losses are deducted first against capital gains, and then again up to $3,000 of other income; *see 5.2* and *5.3.*

Capital gain distribution. A mutual-fund distribution allocated to gains realized on the sale of fund portfolio assets. You report the distribution as long-term capital gain even if you held the fund shares short term; *see 32.5.*

Capital loss carryover. A capital loss that is not deductible because it exceeds the annual $3,000 capital loss ceiling. A carryover loss may be deducted from capital gains of later years plus up to $3,000 of ordinary income; *see 5.4.*

Capitalization. Adding a cost or expense to the basis of the property.

Carryback. A tax technique for receiving a refund of back taxes by applying a deduction or credit from a current tax year to a prior tax year. For example, a business net operating loss incurred in 1999 may be carried back for two years.

Carryforward. A tax technique of applying a loss or credit from a current year to a later year. For example, a business net operating loss may be carried forward 20 years instead of being carried back for two years.

Cash method of accounting. Reporting income when actually or constructively received and deducting expenses when paid. Certain businesses may not use the cash method; *see 40.3.*

Casualty loss. Loss from an unforeseen and sudden event that is deductible, subject to a 10% income floor and $100 reduction for personal losses; *see 18.11.*

Charitable contributions. An itemized deduction is allowed for donations to qualifying charities. For property donations, the deductible amount depends on the type of property and donee organization, your holding period, and in some cases how the property is used; *see* Chapter 14.

Check the box. A term describing a classification rule that provides automatic partnership pass-through treatment for most businesses with two or more members unless the members elect on Form 8832 to be taxed as a corporation.

Child and dependent care credit. A credit of up to 30% based on certain care expenses incurred to allow you to work; *see 25.3.*

Child support. Payments to support a minor child generally to a custodial parent under a divorce or separation decree or agreement. The payments are not deductible; *see 37.5.*

Clifford trust. A short-term trust in which the principal is reserved by the grantor and current income is paid to the beneficiary. The tax-saving features of such trusts have been blocked by current tax rules; *see 33.3.*

Community income. Income earned by persons domiciled in community property states and treated as belonging equally to husband and wife; *see 1.6.*

Condemnation. The seizure of property by a public authority for a public purpose. Tax on gain realized on many conversions may be deferred; *see 18.18–18.19* and *18.25.*

Constructive receipt. A tax rule that taxes income that is not received by you but that

you may draw upon; *see 2.2.*

Consumer interest. Interest incurred on personal debt and consumer credit. Consumer interest is not deductible.

Convention. Rule for determining MACRS depreciation in the year property is placed in service. Either a half-year convention or mid-quarter convention applies; *see 42.5–42.7.*

Corporation. An entity organized under state law and generally treated as a separate taxpayer unless an S election is made.

Credit. A tax credit directly reduces tax liability, as opposed to a deduction that reduces income subject to tax.

D

Declining balance method. A rapid depreciation method determined by a constant percentage based on useful life and applied to the adjusted basis of the property; *see 42.5* and *42.8.*

Deductions. Items directly reducing income. Personal deductions such as for mortgage interest, state and local taxes, and charitable contributions are allowed only if deductions are itemized on Schedule A, but deductions such as for alimony, capital losses, moving expenses to a new job location, business losses, student loan interest, and IRA and Keogh deductions are deducted from gross income even if itemized deductions are not claimed; *see* Chapter 12.

Deferred compensation. A portion of earnings withheld by an employer or put into a retirement plan for distribution to the employee at a later date. If certain legal requirements are met, the deferred amount is not taxable until actually paid, for example, after retirement; *see 2.8.*

Deficiency. The excess of the tax assessed by the IRS over the amount reported on your return; *see 47.1.*

Defined benefit plan. A retirement plan that pays fixed benefits based on actuarial projections; *see 41.2.*

Defined contribution plan. A retirement plan that pays benefits based on contributions to individual accounts, plus accumulated earnings. Contributions are generally based on a percentage of salary or earned income; *see 41.2.*

Dependency exemption. A fixed deduction allowed to every taxpayer, except those who may be claimed as a dependent by another person. Extra exemption deductions are allowed for a spouse on a joint return and for each qualifying dependent. A deduction of $2,750 is allowed for each exemption claimed on 1999 returns, but the deduction is phased out for certain high income individuals; *see 21.15.*

Dependent. A person supported by another person. If certain tests are met, a dependency exemption may be claimed for the

dependent; *see* Chapter 21.

Depletion. Deduction claimed for the use of mineral resources; *see 9.15.*

Depreciable property. A business or income-producing asset with a useful life exceeding one year; *see 42.1.*

Depreciation. Writing off the cost of depreciable property over a period of years, usually its class life or recovery period specified in the tax law; *see 42.4.*

Depreciation recapture. An amount of gain on the sale of certain depreciable property that is treated as ordinary income in case of personal property. Recapture is computed on Form 4797; *see 44.1.* Recapture on sale of realty; *see 44.2.*

Disaster losses. Casualty losses such as from a storm, in areas declared by the President to warrant federal assistance. An election may be made to deduct the loss in the year before the loss or the year of the loss; *see 18.2.*

Dividend. A distribution made by a corporation to its shareholders generally of company earnings or surplus. Most dividends are taxable but exceptions are explained in Chapter 4.

E

Earned income. Compensation for performing personal services. You must have earned income for a deductible IRA; *see 8.2,* or to claim the earned income credit, *see 25.13.*

Earned income credit. A credit allowed to taxpayers with earned income or adjusted gross income (AGI) below certain thresholds; *see 25.12.*

Education credits. There are two education credits: the Hope credit and the lifetime learning credit; *see 38.7.*

Education IRA. A special IRA account set up to fund education expenses of a student; *see 38.11–38.12.*

Estate tax. Imposed on the value of a decedent's taxable estate, after deductions and credits; *see 39.4.*

Estimated tax. Advance payment of current tax liability based either on wage withholdings or installment payments of your estimated tax liability. To avoid penalties, you generally must pay to the IRS either 90% of your final tax liability, or either 100% or 106% of the prior year's tax liability, depending on your adjusted gross income; *see 27.2* and *27.5.*

Exemption. *See* **Dependency exemption.**

F

Fair market value. What a willing buyer would pay to a willing seller when neither is under any compulsion to buy or sell.

Fiduciary. A person or corporation such as a trustee, executor, or guardian who manages property for another person.

First-year expensing. In 1999, a deduction of up to $19,000 (or $39,000 for qualifying businesses in an enterprise zone) of the cost of business equipment in the year placed in service; *see 42.3.*

Fiscal year. A 12-month period ending on the last day of any month other than December. Partnerships, S corporations, and personal service corporations are limited in their choice of fiscal years and face special restrictions.

Flexible spending arrangements. A salary reduction plan that allows employees to pay for enhanced medical coverage or dependent care expenses on a tax-free basis; *see 3.14.*

Foreign earned income exclusion. In 1999, up to $74,000 of foreign earned income is exempt from tax if a foreign residence or physical presence test is met; *see 36.1–36.2.*

Foreign tax credit. A credit for income taxes paid to a foreign country or U.S. possession; *see 36.14.*

401(k) plan. A deferred pay plan, authorized by Section 401(k) of the Internal Revenue Code, under which a percentage of an employee's salary is withheld and placed in a savings account or the company's profit-sharing plan. Income accumulates on the deferred amount until withdrawn by the employee at age 59 ½ or when the employee retires or leaves the company; *see 7.17.*

G

Gift tax. Gifts in excess of a $10,000 per donee annual exclusion are subject to gift tax, but the tax may be offset by a unified gift and estate tax credit; *see 33.1.*

Grantor trust rules. Tax rules that tax the grantor of a trust on the trust income; *see 33.3.*

Gross income. The total amount of income received from all sources before exclusions and deductions.

Gross receipts. Total business receipts reported on Schedule C or Schedule C-EZ before deducting adjustments for returns and allowances and cost of goods sold; *see 40.6.*

Group-term life insurance. Employees are not taxed on up to $50,000 of group-term coverage; *see 3.3.*

H

Head of household. Generally, an unmarried person who maintains a household for dependents and is allowed to compute his or her tax based on head of household rates, which are more favorable than single person rates; *see 1.11.*

Hobby loss. Hobby expenses are deductible only up to income from the activity; loss deductions are not allowed; *see 40.10.*

Holding period. The length of time that an asset is owned and that generally determines long- or short-term capital gain treatment; *see 5.1 and 5.9.*

Home equity debt. Debt secured by a principal residence or second home to the extent of the excess of fair market value over acquisition debt. An interest deduction is generally allowed for home equity debt up to $100,000 ($50,000 if married filing separately); *see 15.3.*

I

Imputed interest. Interest deemed earned on seller-financed sales or low-interest loans, where the parties' stated interest rate is below the applicable IRS federal rate; *see 4.31 and 4.32.*

Incentive stock option. Options meeting tax law tests that defer tax on the option transaction until the obtained stock is sold; *see 2.17.*

Income in respect of a decedent. Income earned by a person before death but taxable to an estate or heir who receives it; *see 1.13 and 11.4.*

Independent contractor. One who controls his or her own work and reports as a self-employed person; *see* Chapters 40 and 45.

Individual retirement account (IRA). A retirement account to which up to $2,000 may be contributed annually, but deductions for the contribution are restricted if you are covered by a company retirement plan. Earnings accumulate tax free on IRA contributions. Restrictions and limits are discussed in Chapter 8.

Innocent spouse. A spouse who claims that he or she should not be liable on a joint return; *see 1.7.*

Installment sale. A sale of property that allows for tax deferment if at least one payment is received after the end of the tax year in which the sale occurs. The installment method does not apply to year-end sales of publicly traded securities. Dealers may not use the installment method. Investors with very large installment balances could face a special tax; *see 5.21.*

Intangible assets. Intangible assets that come within Section 197, such as goodwill, are amortizable over a 15-year period; *see 42.18.*

***Inter vivos* or lifetime trust.** A trust created during the lifetime of the person who created the trust. If irrevocable, income on the trust principal is generally shifted to the trust beneficiaries; *see 33.3.*

Investment in the contract. The total cost investment in an annuity. When annuity payments are made, the portion allocable to the cost investment is tax free; *see 7.22 and 7.27.*

Investment interest. Interest on debt used to carry investments, but not including interest expense from a passive activity. Deductions are limited to net investment income; *see 15.10.*

Involuntary conversion. Forced disposition of property due to condemnation, theft, or casualty. Tax on gain from involuntary conversions may be deferred if replacement property is purchased; *see 18.19.*

Itemized deductions. Items, such as interest, state and local taxes, charitable contributions, and medical deductions, claimed on Schedule A of Form 1040. Itemized deductions are subtracted from adjusted gross income to arrive at taxable income; *see* Chapter 13. The amount of itemized deductions is also subject to a reduction when adjusted gross income exceeds certain limits; *see 13.7.*

J

Joint return. A return filed by a married couple reporting their combined income and deductions. Joint return status provides tax savings to many couples; *see 1.4.*

Joint tenants. Ownership of property by two persons. When one dies, the decedent's interest passes to the survivor; *see 5.18.*

K

Keogh plan. Retirement plan set up by a self-employed person, providing tax-deductible contributions, tax-free income accumulations until withdrawal, and favorable averaging for qualifying lump-sum distributions; *see* Chapter 41.

Kiddie tax. The tax on the investment income of a dependent child under age 14 in excess of $1,400, based on the parents' marginal tax rate and computed on Form 8615; *see 24.3.*

L

Legally separated. A husband and wife who are required to live apart from each other by the terms of a decree of separate maintenance. Payments under the decree are deductible by the payor and taxable to the payee as alimony; *see 37.2.*

Like-kind exchange. An exchange of similar assets used in a business or held for investment on which gain may be deferred; *see 6.1.*

Lump-sum distribution. Payments within one tax year of the entire amount due to a participant in a qualified retirement plan because of retirement, separation from service, reaching age 59 ½, death, or, in the case of a self-employed person, disability or reaching age 59 ½. Qualifying lump sums may be directly rolled over tax free, or, in some cases, are eligible for current tax under a favorable averaging method; *see 7.2.*

Luxury automobile limits. Ceiling placed on annual depreciation deductions for autos used for business; *see 43.3 and 43.4.*

M

Marital deduction. An estate tax and gift tax deduction for assets passing to a spouse. It allows estate and gift transfers completely free of tax; *see 39.6.*

Market discount. The difference between face value of bond and lower market price, attributable to rising interest rates. On a sale, gain on the bond is generally taxed as ordinary income to the extent of the discount; *see 4.20.*

Material participation tests. Rules for determining whether a person is active in a business activity for passive activity rule purposes. Unless the tests are met, passive loss limits apply; *see 10.6.*

Medical Savings Account (MSA). A type of medical plan combining high deductible medical insurance protection with an IRA-type savings account fund to pay unreimbursed medical expenses; *see 17.17.*

Miscellaneous itemized deductions. Generally, itemized deductions for job and investment expenses subject to a 2% of adjusted gross income floor; *see* Chapter 19.

Modified ACRS (MACRS). Depreciation methods applied to assets placed in service after 1986.

Modified Adjusted Gross Income (MAGI). This is generally adjusted gross income increased by certain items such as tax-free foreign earned income. MAGI usually is used to determine phaseouts of certain deductions and credits.

Mortgage interest. Fully deductible interest on up to two residences if acquisition debt secured by home is $1 million or less, and home equity debt is $100,000 or less; *see 15.1.*

Moving Expenses. Certain expenses of moving to a new job location are deductible if distance and time tests are met; *see* Chapter 12.

N

Net operating loss. A business loss that exceeds current income may be carried back against income of prior years and carried forward as a deduction from future income until eliminated. The carryback and carryforward periods are discussed in *40.18* and *40.21.*

Nonperiodic distributions. A 20% withholding rule applies to nonperiodic distributions, such as lump-sum distributions, paid directly to employees from an employer plan; *see 7.8* and *26.11.*

Nonrecourse financing. Debt on which a person is not personally liable. In case of nonpayment, the creditor must foreclose on property securing the debt. At-risk rules generally bar losses where there is nonrecourse financing, but an exception applies to certain nonrecourse financing for real estate; *see 10.17.*

Nonresident alien. A person who is not a United States citizen or a permanent resident. Tax is generally limited to income from U.S. sources; *see 1.15.*

O

Ordinary and necessary. A statutory requirement for the deductibility of a business expense; *see 40.6.*

Ordinary income. Income other than capital gains.

Ordinary loss. A loss other than a capital loss.

Original issue discount (OID). The difference between the face value of a bond and its original issue price. OID is reported on an annual basis as interest income; *see 4.19.*

P

Partnership. An unincorporated business or income-producing entity organized by two or more persons. A partnership is not subject to tax but passes through to the partners all income, deductions, and credits, according to the terms of the partnership agreement; *see* Chapter 11.

Passive activity loss rules. Rules that limit the deduction of losses from passive activities to income from other passive activities. Passive activities include investment rental operations or businesses in which you do not materially participate; *see 10.1.*

Patronage dividend. A taxable distribution made by a cooperative to its members or patrons.

Pension. Payments to employees from an employer-funded retirement plan for past services; *see 7.25.*

Percentage depletion. A deduction method that applies a fixed percentage to the gross income generated by mineral property; *see 9.15.*

Personal exemption. An automatic exemption given to a taxpayer unless he or she may be claimed as a dependent by another taxpayer. For 1999, the exemption amount is $2,750. Exemptions are phased out for certain high income taxpayers; *see 21.15.*

Personal interest. Tax term for interest on personal loans and consumer purchases. Such interest is not deductible.

Placed in service. The time when a depreciable asset is ready to be used. The date fixes the beginning of the depreciation period; *see 42.5.*

Points. Charges to the homeowner at the time of the loan. A point is equal to 1 percent. Depending on the type of loan, points may be currently deductible or amortized over the life of the loan; *see 15.8.*

Premature distributions. Withdrawals before age 59 ½ from qualified retirement plans are subject to penalties unless specific exceptions are met; *see 7.15* and *8.12.*

Principal residence. On a sale of a principal residence, you may avoid tax under the rules explained in Chapter 29.

Probate estate. Property held in a decedent's name passing by will; *see 39.1.*

Profit-sharing plan. A defined contribution plan under which the amount contributed to the employees' accounts is based on a percentage of the employer's profits; *see 8.5* and *41.2.*

Provisional income. If your provisional income exceeds a base amount, part of your Social Security benefits may be subject to tax. To figure provisional income, *see 34.3.*

Q

Qualified charitable organization. A nonprofit philanthropic organization that is approved by the U.S. Treasury to receive charitable contribution deductions; *see 14.1.*

Qualified plan. A retirement plan that meets tax law tests and allows for tax deferment and tax-free accumulation of income until benefits are withdrawn. Pension, profit-sharing, stock bonus, employee stock ownership, and Keogh plans and IRAs may be qualified plans; *see* Chapters 7, 8, and 41.

Qualifying widow or widower. A filing status entitling the taxpayer with dependents to use joint tax rates for up to two tax years after the death of a spouse; *see 1.9.*

R

Real estate investment trust (REIT). An entity that invests primarily in real estate and mortgages and passes through income to investors; *see 31.1.*

Real estate professional. An individual who, because of his or her real estate activity, qualifies to deduct rental losses from nonpassive income; *see 10.3.*

Real property. Land and the buildings on land. Buildings are depreciable; *see 42.13* and *42.16.*

Recognized gain or loss. The amount of gain or loss to be reported on a tax return. Gain may not be recognized on certain exchanges of property; *see 6.1.*

Recovery property. Tangible depreciable property placed in service after 1980 and before 1987 and depreciable under ACRS; *see 42.11* and *42.16.*

Refundable tax credit. A credit that entitles you to a refund even if you owe no tax for the year.

Residence interest. Term for deductible mortgage interest on a principal residence and a second home; *see 15.1–15.2.*

Residential rental property. Real property in which 80% or more of the gross income is from dwelling units. Under MACRS, depreciation is claimed over 27.5 years under the straight-line method; *see 42.13.*

Return of capital. A distribution of your investment that is not subject to tax unless the distribution exceeds your investment; *see 4.11.*

Revocable trust. A trust that may be changed or terminated by its creator or another person. Such trusts do not provide an income tax savings to the creator; *see 33.6.*

Rollover. A tax-free reinvestment of a distribution from a qualified retirement plan into an IRA or other qualified plan within 60 days; *see 7.3, 7.8,* and *8.10.*

Roth IRA. A nondeductible contributory IRA that allows for tax-free accumulation of income; *see 8.19.*

Glossary

Royalty income. Amounts received for the use of property such as mineral property, a book, a movie, or a patent; *see 9.11.*

S

Salvage value. The estimated value of an asset at the end of its useful life. Salvage value is ignored by ACRS and MACRS rules.

S corporation. A corporation that elects S status in order to receive tax treatment similar to a partnership; *see* Chapter 11.

Scholarships. Grants to degree candidates receive tax-free treatment if awarded after August 16, 1986, and used for tuition and course-related expenses, but not room and board; *see 38.1.*

Section 179 deduction. Expensing deduction, in 1999 up to $19,000, allowed for investments in depreciable business equipment in the year the property is placed in service. The deduction may be as high as $39,000 for qualifying businesses in an enterprise zone; *see 42.3.*

Section 457 plan. Deferred compensation plan set up by state or local government, or tax-exempt organization, that allows tax-free deferrals of salary, generally up to the lesser of $7,500 and one-third of pay; *see 7.21.*

Section 1231 property. Depreciable property used in a trade or business and held for more than a year. All Section 1231 gains and losses are netted; a net gain is treated as capital gain, a net loss as an ordinary loss; *see 44.8.*

Self-employed person. An individual who operates a business or profession as a proprietor or independent contractor and reports self-employment income on Schedule C; *see* Chapters 40 and 45.

Self-employment tax. Tax paid by self-employed persons to finance Social Security coverage. In 1999, there are two rates. A 12.4% rate applies to a taxable earnings base of $72,600 or less and a 2.9% rate on all net earnings; *see* Chapter 45.

Separate return. Return filed by married person who does not file a joint return. Filing separately may save taxes where each spouse has separate deductions, but certain tax benefits require a joint return; *see 1.3.*

Short sale. Sale of borrowed securities made to freeze a paper profit or to gain from a declining market; *see 30.5.*

Short tax year. A tax year of less than 12 months. May occur with the startup of a business or change in accounting method.

Short-term capital gain or loss. Gain or loss on the sale or exchange of a capital asset held one year or less; *see 5.1, 5.2,* and *5.10.*

Simplified employee plan (SEP). IRA-type plan set up by an employer, rather than the employee. Salary-reduction contributions may be allowed to plans of small employers; *see 8.15.*

Single. The filing status of an individual who is not married on December 31 of the year for which the return is filed; *see 1.1.*

Standard deduction. A fixed deduction allowed to taxpayers who do not itemize deductions. The amount depends on filing status, age, and blindness; *see 13.1.*

Standard mileage rate. A fixed rate allowed by the IRS for business auto expenses in place of deducting actual expenses; *see 43.1.*

Statutory employees. Certain employees, such as full-time life insurance salespersons, who may report income and deductions on Schedule C rather than on Schedule A, as a miscellaneous itemized deduction; *see 40.6.*

Stock dividend. A distribution of additional shares of a corporation's stock to its shareholders; *see 4.6.*

Stock option. A right to buy stock at a fixed price.

Straddle. Taking an offsetting investment position to reduce the risk of loss in a similar investment; *see 30.9.*

Straight-line method. A method of depreciating the cost of a depreciable asset on a pro rata basis over its cost recovery period; *see 42.9, 42.12.*

T

Tangible personal property. Movable property, such as desks, computers, machinery, and autos, depreciable over a five-year or seven-year period; *see 42.4.*

Taxable income. Net income after claiming all deductions from gross income and adjusted gross income, such as IRA deductions, itemized deductions, or the standard deduction, and personal exemptions; *see 22.1.*

Tax deferral. Shifting income to a later year, such as where you defer taxable interest to the following year by purchasing a T-bill or savings certificate maturing after the end of the current year; *see* Chapter 4. Investments in qualified retirement plans provide tax deferral (*see* Chapters 7, 8, and 41).

Tax home. The area of your principal place of business or employment. You must be away from your tax home on a business trip to deduct travel expenses; *see 20.6–20.9.*

Tax identification number. For an individual, his or her Social Security number; for businesses, fiduciaries, and other nonindividual taxpayers, the employer identification number.

Tax preference items. Items that may subject a taxpayer to the alternative minimum tax (AMT); *see 23.3.*

Tax rate schedules. Used by taxpayers with taxable incomes of $100,000 or more; *see* Part 8.

Tax-sheltered annuity. A type of retirement annuity offered to employees of charitable organizations and educational systems, generally funded by employee salary-reduction contributions; *see 7.20.*

Tax tables. Used by taxpayers with taxable incomes of less than $100,000 to look up their tax; *see* Part 8.

Tax year. A period (generally 12 months) for reporting income and expenses; *see 40.4.*

Tenancy by the entireties. A joint tenancy in real property in the name of both husband and wife. On the death of one tenant, the survivor receives entire interest.

Tenants in common. Two or more persons who have undivided ownership rights in property. Upon death of a tenant, his or her share passes to his or her estate, rather than to the surviving tenants.

Testamentary trust. A trust established under a will.

Trust. An arrangement under which one person transfers legal ownership of assets to another person or corporation (the trustee) for the benefit of one or more third persons (beneficiaries).

U

Unrecaptured Section 1250 gain. Long-term gain realized on the sale of depreciable realty attributed to depreciation deductions and subject to a 25% capital gain rate; *see 5.3* and *44.2.*

Useful life. For property not depreciated under ACRS or MACRS, the estimate of time in which a depreciable asset will be used.

V

Vacation homes. The tax law limits deductions for vacation homes, broadly defined as any dwelling unit used by the owner or the owner's relatives for more than a specified period; *see 9.7.*

W

Wash sales. Sales on which losses are disallowed because you recover your market position within a 61-day period; *see 30.6.*

Withholding. An amount taken from income as a pre-payment of an individual's tax liability for the year. In the case of wages, the employer withholds part of every wage payment. Backup withholding from dividend or interest income is required if you do not provide the payer with a correct taxpayer identification number. Withholding on pensions and IRAs is automatic unless you elect to waive withholding; *see* Chapter 26.

Index

Index

Index

Index

Index

Index

N

O

Index

Index

Real estate taxes
  allocating, when you sell or buy realty, 16.8:311–13
  co-tenant's deduction for, 9.2:204
  deducting, 16.6:311
  foreign, 16.12:314
  who may deduct, 16.9:313
Real estate taxes, 9.2:203
Real property
  depreciable, ordinary income recapture on, 44.2:641–42
  timing sales of, 31.4:504
Rebates of insurance agent's commission, 2.5:37
Recapture
  of depreciation on business property, 44.1:641, 44.2:641–42
  of expensing deduction, 42.3:615
  of first-year expensing, 44.3:642
Receipts, as record of expense, 20.27:394–95
Recharacterization rule to Roth IRA, 8.21:197
Record-keeping
  adminstrative activity in home office, 40.12:596
  against audits, 48.1:675
  of automobile expenses, 43.1:629–30, 43.10:639
  of convention business travel, 20.12:388
  excuses for inadequate, 20.27:395
  for home improvements, 29.6:472
  keeping for at least 3 years, 20.27:394–95
  to substantiate contributions, 14.15:288–89
  for tax records, 664–67
  for travel and entertainment, 20.26:394
Recovered deductions and tax credits, 11.6:245–46
Recreation expenses, as support item, 21.7:406
Redemptions
  before maturity of a savings certificate, loss on, 4.16:76
  interest on bonds and, 4.15:75
Refinanced mortgage loans, points paid on, 15.7:299–301, 15.8:301–2
Reforestation amortization, 12.1:260, 12.2:261
Refund of taxes paid or withheld, 47.4:671–72
  amended to show additional tax, 49.7:682
  Armed Forces service members and, 49.2:681
  calling IRS about, 46.6:662
  credited to state estimated tax, 16.3:310
  decedent's, 1.13:23
  interest income rules for, 4.15:74
  quick claims, 49.5:682
  state and local taxes deducted in prior year, 11.5:243–45
  stating reasons for claim, 49.4:681
  when to file, 49.2:681
  who should file, 49.1:681
  withheld by IRS, 49.7:682
Rehabilitation credit for pre-1936 buildings or certified historic structures, 31.8:506
Reimbursements
  of club dues, 20.30:396–97
  from employer, 20.30:396–99
  of employee expenses, restrictive test exception, 20.23:391
Reimbursement plans for travel and entertainment expenses
  accountable plans, 20.30:396–97, 20.31:397
  accounting requirements, 20.31:397
  automobile mileage allowances, 20.33:399

as de minimis fringe benefit, 3.9:58
nonaccountable plans, 20.30:396–97, 20.34:399, 20.34:399
per diem travel allowance under accountable plans, 20.32:398
Reinvestment
  in company stock, 4.8:69
  in mutual funds, 32.4:515
Related parties
  acquisitions from, 42.3:615
  disallowed loss on sales to, 5.6:95–96
  exchanges between, 6.5:130
  gain from sale of remainder interest to, 29.1:467
Related persons, definition of, 42.18:627
Relationship or member of household test for dependents, 21.3:402–3
Relatives. See also Children; Spouse
  dependent care credit and payments to, 25.7:441–43
  dependent, head of household status, 1.11:19–21
  installment sales to, 5.24:113–15
  renting residential unit to, 9.6:208
  tax-free exchanges between, 6.5:130
Relocation due to disaster loss, 18.2:335
Remainder interest in a home or farm, charitable donation of, 14.10:285
Remainder trusts, charitable, 14.14:288
Remarriage, exemption for spouse and, 21.2:402
REMICS, original issue discount (OID) reporting, 4.19:78
Rental activities, passive activity restrictions on, 10.1:219–20
Rental allowance, minister's, 3.12:61
Rental days, counting personal use days and, 9.8:209–10
Rental income, Ch. 9. See also Leases
  advance rentals as, 9.1:203
  deducting tax preparation fee for reporting on Schedule E, 19.25:370
  deductions from, 19.24:369
    checklist of, 9.2:203–5
    insurance premiums, 9.2:204
    repairs and improvements, distinctions between, 9.3:205
  depreciation on converting home to, 9.5:207
  home, allocation of expenses to rental days, 9.9:210–12
  improvements by tenants not considered, 9.1:203
  information returns required by IRS, 47.2:669
  insurance proceeds as, 9.1:203
  lacking profit motive, 9.10:212–13
  losses, 9.1:203
  from multi-unit residences, 9.4:206
  nondeductible as property tax, 16.7:311
  redeemable ground rents, 15.6:299
  reporting, 9.1:203
    personal use and, 9.7:208–9
  security deposits not considered, 9.1:203
  self-employment income and, 45.1:648
  support test for dependents and, 21.8:407
Rental loss allowance
  phaseout, 10.2:222
  of up to $25,000, passive activities, 10.2:220–22
Rental pool arrangements, 9.8:210
Rental property
  before sale, barring loss on, 29.9:474

conversion of residence to, 29.9:473–74
gain on sale of, 29.9:474
improvements, records for, 5.13:102
MACRS for, 42.13:622–23
profit-making purposes, 29.9:473–74
residence converted to, loss on, 29.9:473–74
residential, recovery period for, 42.4:616
self-employment income and, 45.1:648
trips to investigate prospective, 19.24:370
use of personal residence as, 29.7:472–73
Rentals to employer, 19.13:363
Rented residences, depreciation of, 9.5:206–7, 42.1:613
Reorganizations
  exchanging market discount bonds in, 4.20:80
  interest on bonds and, 4.15:75
Repair costs, as evidence of loss of value, 18.14:347
Repairs to home
  not adding to cost of basis of property, 29.6:471
  rental income and, 9.3:205
Repayment
  of disallowed T & E expenses, 2.9:39
  exceeding $3,000, 2.9:39
  of income received in prior year, 2.9:39
  of supplemental unemployment benefits, 2.9:39
Replacement property
  extension of time to replace, 18.22:352
  to fully deter tax on, 18.23:352–53
  time period for buying, 18.21:350–51
  types or qualifying, 18.22:352
Reporting on return, employer benefits, 3.4:54; 3.5:54
Repossessed home, 29.5:470. See also Ch. 31
  of personal real property sold on installment, 5.29:118
  of property, 31.12:509–11
Repurchase agreements (repos), 30.14:490
Requisitioned property, as involuntary conversion qualifying for tax deferral, 18.19:349
Research assistants, tuition reductions for, 3.6:55
Research expenses
  AMT and, 23.2:426
  professor's, 19.20:367
Reservists, tax information for, 35.8:545
Residence, multiple use of, 29.1:467
Residency termination date, resident aliens, 1.17:26
Resident alien
  defining as, 1.15:23; 1.17:24–26
  dual status, in first year of residency, 1.17:25–26
  exemption for dependents who are, 21.12:411
  first-year election, 1.17:25
  green cards, 1.17:24
  income subject to taxation, 1.16:24
  individual taxpayer I.D. number for, 21.3:402
  last year of residence, 1.17:26
  lawful permanent test of residence, 1.17:24–25
  residency termination date, 1.17:26
  sailing permit (certificate of compliance), 1.18:26
  substantial presence of residence, 1.17:24–26
  tax treaty definitions of residence and, 1.17:25
Residential lots, installment sales of, 5.31:119
Residential units, rental, personal use and, 9.7:208–9

Index

Index

Index

Index